NY MILES UNDERGROUND IN POROUS ROCKS ■ THERE ARE OVE

Y SPORT ■ ROD LAVER WAS THE FIRST MAN TO ACHIEVE THE GRAND SLAM TWICE ■

VER 100,000 TIMES A DAY ■ THE HUMAN BODY CONTAINS 30,000 BILLION RED BLOOD

AT THE STAATSOPER IN VIENNA IN 1991 – 1 HR 20 MIN ■ THE LONGEST RUNNING

E MAKE UP ABOUT 45% OF EVERYTHING WE WRITE ■ 'O' IS THE OLDEST LETTER STILL

■ WHEN ALL THE HYDROGEN IS USED UP THE UNIVERSE WILL DIE ■ FORMATION OF

THE WORLD POPULATION AT THE TURN OF THE MILLENNIUM WILL BE 6.158 BILLION ■

EOPLE DIED FROM STARVATION IN THE POTATO FAMINE IN IRELAND IN 1846, FOLLOWED

MOST COMMON BUG IS *E.COLI* FOUND IN THE GUT ■ SMALLPOX IS THE ONLY DISEASE

88 ■ IN 1995, A SUPERCOMPUTER CALCULATED π TO 6.4 BILLION PLACES IN UNDER

OF INFORMATION ■ WALT DISNEY HAS WON THE MOST OSCARS – 20 STATUETES AND

IE OF *GANDHI* ■ MORE THAN TWO MILLION CHEMICAL COMPOUNDS HAVE BEEN MADE

OM TEMPERATURE ■ ONE BILLION SECONDS ADDS UP TO APPROXIMATELY 31 YEARS 8

LF A DAY PER MILLENNIUM ■ THE EARTH IS OVER 4.6 BILLION YEARS OLD ■ NEARLY

000,000,000,000,000,000 KG ■ THE VICTORIA FALLS ARE 1708 M WIDE ■ ANGEL

CASPIAN SEA IS 1.5 TIMES THAT OF THE UK ■ OVER 80% OF BANGLADESH COULD BE

IOMIC GROWTH RATES OF ANY COUNTRY IN THE 1990S ■ LONDON HEATHROW DEALS

IRPORTS TOGETHER HANDLE OVER 40 PEOPLE PER SECOND ■ AS WELL AS PAINTING,

ED ABOUT 13,500 PAINTINGS AND DESIGNS IN HIS 78-YEAR CAREER ■ ONE SQUARE

NOT SWEAT UNTIL THE TEMPERATURE REACHES 40°C AND THEY CAN SURVIVE A WATER

ER HORSE' ■ PYTHAGORAS'S THEOREM IS THE MOST PROVED OF ALL, WITH OVER 370

ALWAYS MEET ON A SPHERE ■ THE US POSTAL SERVICE, WITH 870,160 STAFF, IS THE

THAT IS US$1380 FOR EVERY PERSON ALIVE ■ IGNEOUS ROCKS GET THEIR NAME FROM

D'S OCEANS ■ THE WEIGHT OF THE OCEANS' WATER IS 1.39 QUINTILLION TONNES ■

PEAK A WORD UNTIL THE AGE OF THREE ■ THERE ARE NO THUNDERSTORMS IN POLAR

VOLCANIC ERUPTION EVER RECORDED WAS SANTORÍNI IN GREECE IN 1550 BC ■ BILL

MS ■ HELMUT KOHL IS THE LONGEST-SERVING GERMAN RULER SINCE BISMARCK ■

GUINNESS BOOK OF KNOWLEDGE

Published in the USA by Guinness Media Inc.,
Six Landmark Square, Stamford, CT 06901-2701

British Library Cataloguing in Publication Data
A catalogue record for this book is available from the British Library
ISBN 0-85112-046-6

Managing Editor
Anne Marshall

Consultant Editor
Clive Carpenter

Editor
Sally McFall

Writer/Researcher
Sandip Shah

Editorial Assistants
John Mapps
Naomi Peck

Picture Research
Kate Duffy

Designer
Jo Brewer

Design Assistant/Artwork
Adam Kelsey

Design Assistant
Keith Jackson

Artwork
Peter Harper
Yahya El-Droubie

Production Director
Chris Lingard

Colour Origination
Dot Gradations Ltd

Printing and Binding
Printer Industria Grafica SA
Barcelona

Paper
Printed on wood-free, chlorine-free and acid-free paper

Cover
Ron Callow
at Design 23

Joint Publishing Directors
Ian Castello-Cortes Michael Feldman

GUINNESS BOOK OF KNOWLEDGE

CONTENTS

SPACE AND TIME ▷

'Space isn't remote at all. It's only an hour's drive away if your car could go straight upwards'
– Fred Hoyle

THE UNIVERSE

▶ **The total mass-energy of the Universe was apparently formed out of nothing, something which cannot yet be explained by anyone on this planet.**

▶ **The solar system will probably last for another 5000 million years before the Sun starts to become unstable and enters its 'red giant' stage.**

▶ **The Earth is travelling around the Sun at an average speed of 30 km/s.**

THE NATURE OF THE UNIVERSE

▶ **The Universe is the sum total of all that exists in space and time.**
▶ **Although we have a good idea as to when the Universe began and how it grew to its present complexity and size, we do not know when it will end or precisely what that ending will be.**

The study of the Universe is known as 'cosmology', which has its roots at the beginning of the 20th century with the introduction of Albert Einstein's theories of relativity (see p. 119), which joined space and time into a single continuum.

THE BIG BANG THEORY

It has been proven that the stars are not fixed but moving. As a result, it is known that the Universe is expanding. One consequence of this discovery was the realization that reversing time led to a contraction of the Universe to a point-like source or singularity. The origin of the Universe was therefore a cataclysmic event known popularly as the 'Big Bang'. Since space and time also began at this point, there is no 'time' before the Big Bang – an explanation for the apparent formation out of nothing of the total mass-energy of the Universe may have to wait for a quantum theory of gravity.

The original Big Bang theory, developed in the 1920s by Aleksandr Friedmann (Russia) and Georges Le Maitre (Belgium), was improved upon by the 'inflationary models' conceived by Alan Guth (USA) in 1979, which explain both the large-scale smoothness of the Universe and the small-scale non-uniformities (that is, the clumping of matter into galaxies). This was done by suggesting that all parts of the Universe were in contact with each other during the critical period before 10^{-35} seconds, but that after this there was a 10^{50} expansion, possibly due to the separation of the strong force from the electroweak forces.

Events in the Universe's early history occurred very rapidly. All the light elements were initially formed within the first 15 minutes. Quarks, and leptons such as electrons and neutrinos, as well as an equal number of anti-particles, were formed after only 10^{-35} seconds but, by 10^{-32} seconds, all of the anti-particles had been destroyed: only one particle in a billion of those present at the beginning remained.

Between a thousand-millionth and one-tenth of a second, when the temperature fell from 100 trillion to 10 billion °C (10^{14}–10^{10} °C), protons and neutrons began to form from quarks. In the next 900 seconds, neutrons combined with protons to form nuclei of the light elements deuterium (heavy hydrogen), helium and lithium. After that, any remaining neutrons decayed to protons, electrons and neutrinos.

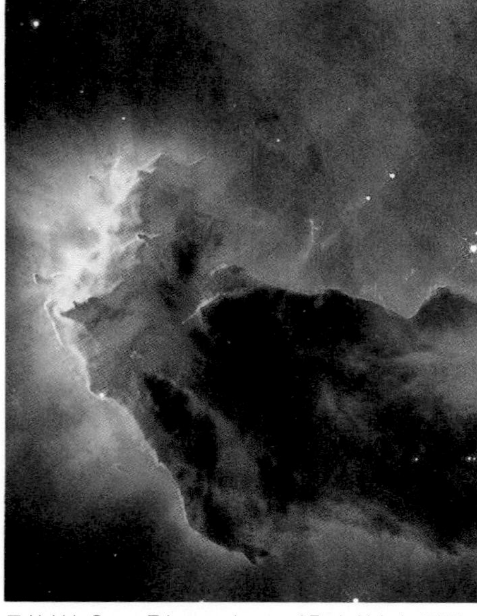

■ *Hubble Space Telescope image of Eagle Nebula, 7000 light years from the Earth, showing the dense hydrogen and dust cloud from which new stars are emerging*

After 100,000 years, when the temperature had fallen to 3700°C (6700°F), ions and electrons joined together to form atoms of these light elements. Proto-galaxies began to form when the temperature had reached 100°C (212°F) and the formation of coherent galaxies is calculated to have begun one billion (10^9) years after the Big Bang.

Proof of the Big Bang is considered to be the detection of the cosmic background radiation by Arno Penzias and Robert W. Wilson (both USA) in 1965. The Universe was filled with a 'sea' of cosmic radiation during its formation, and this has since cooled. According to the Big Bang theory, the temperature in the microwave region should now be 2.73 K and this is exactly the temperature observed.

The end of the Universe will be dire. Either it will expand for ever or reach an equilibrium size. In both cases all of the hydrogen will be used up and the Universe will die, or gravity will overcome the amount of mass in the Universe and it will collapse back to a point-like source.

? WHAT MAKES UP THE UNIVERSE

▷ A galaxy is a huge aggregate of stars, gas and dust held together by gravitational attraction, usually in the form of a flattened disc, and generally with the matter being contained in spiral arms radiating away from the central nucleus of the disc.

▷ The Milky Way is our own galaxy, one of 100 billion to a trillion known galaxies.

▷ Stars are globes of gas in which nuclear fusion reactions at the centre create vast quantities of energy which become radiated into space mainly in the form of light, heat and ultraviolet radiation.

▷ The Sun is the nearest star, the star at the centre of our solar system.

▷ Planets are major-sized bodies directly orbiting a star. In the case of our own solar system, including Pluto, there are nine planets. Smaller bodies orbiting the Sun are given special names such as 'asteroids'.

▷ A satellite is any body which orbits an object which is directly orbiting a star, i.e. a planet or smaller body.

? HOW DO WE KNOW THE UNIVERSE IS EXPANDING

▶ **In 1842, Christian Doppler (Austria) suggested that the reason the pitch of the noise of a vehicle rises as the vehicle is approaching, then diminishes as it moves away, is a change in the frequency of sound waves.**
▶ **The Doppler effect indicates that stars are not fixed but moving.**

The Doppler effect is valid for all waves and was extended to light by Armand Fizeau (France) in 1848. In 1868, Sir William Huggins (UK) found that the spectra of certain stars were displaced towards the red end of the spectrum (red-shifted), whilst others were shifted towards the violet end (blue-shifted). This was then interpreted as a Doppler effect, indicating that the stars were not fixed but were moving relative to the Sun, with red-shifted stars moving away and vice-versa.

Red-shifts were extended to the cosmological scale by Vesto Melvin Slipher (USA) in 1912, who noted that nearly all of the nebulae were red-shifted and only a few, such as the Andromeda Nebula, were blue-shifted. In 1924 Edwin Powell Hubble (USA) was able to show that the nebulae were in fact galaxies in their own right. Subsequent measurements of red-shifts and magnitudes, as well as an estimate of distances, led Hubble to propose in 1929 that the speed of recession of a galaxy (v) was related to its distance (r) and red-shift (z) by the relationship $v = z.c = H.r$, where c is the velocity of light and H is a constant now known as the Hubble Constant. Current estimates of the Hubble Constant are between 55 and 85 km/s/Mpc (kilometres per second per megaparsec), with a gradual convergence towards the median value of 70 km/s/Mpc.

The Hubble relationship states that the distance of a galaxy is directly proportional to its recession velocity. This suggests a uniformly expanding Universe. Therefore, the age of the Universe can be related to the Hubble Constant. A value of this constant of 70 km/s/Mpc leads to a 'Hubble age' of 14 billion years, which coincides with 14 ± 3 billion years for the age of the Universe, obtained from cosmochronology (a measure of the relative abundances of radioactive nuclei used to determine the timescale).

GALAXIES

▶ **Galaxies result from the accumulation of gas on to the proto-galaxies, which were formed by density fluctuations and gravity instabilities in the expanding primordial fireball.**
▶ **The proto-galaxies appear to have formed on the 'surfaces' of 'bubbles', each about 100 million light years in diameter, and in the process the centres of the bubbles became virtually devoid of matter.**

The subsequent formation of huge stars, eventually destroyed in supernova explosions, led to the formation of heavy elements and the accumulation of cosmic dust, which accounts for about 2% of all matter. There are estimated to be between 100 billion and a trillion (10^{11} to 10^{12}) galaxies, each containing about 100 billion stars, so the number of stars is between 10^{22} and 10^{23}.

Hubble classified galaxies into three types: elliptical, spiral and irregular. Elliptical galaxies (E) appear as luminous elliptical discs with a smooth distribution of

BRIGHTEST STARS

Name	Bayer designations	Visual magnitude apparent	absolute	Brightness on scale Sun = 1	Distance in light years
Sirius	α Canis Majoris	**–1.46	+1.4	22	8.5
Canopus*	α Carinae	–0.72	–8.5	220,000	1,200
Rigel Kentaurus*	α Centauri	†–0.27	†+4.1	A 1.5 B 0.44	4.3
Arcturus	α Bootis	–0.04	–0.3	110	37
Vega	α Lyrae	+0.03	+0.6	49	25
Capella	α Aurigae	†+0.08	†–0.5	A 79 B 62	43
Rigel	β Orionis	+0.12	–7.1	58,000	900
Procyon	α Canis Minoris	+0.38	+2.7	7.3	11
Achernar*	α Eridani	+0.46	–1.6	370	85
Betelgeuse	α Orionis	v+0.50	v,s–5.6	15,000	310

A and B indicates a double star
* Not visible from the British Isles
** The apparent visual magnitude of Sirius will reach a maximum of –1.67 in AD 61,000
† Combined magnitude for a double star system
v Average value for a very variable star
s Distance based on spectroscopic data only

NEAREST STARS

The closest approach by a star to the Sun in the near future will be to within 0.94 light years (59,000 astronomical units) by the binary Wolf 424 in AD 9570 (its present distance is 14.0 light years).

Name	Distance in light years	Visual magnitude apparent	absolute	Brightness on scale Sun = 1
Proxima Centauri	4.24	11.10	15.53	0.000052
Alpha Centauri	4.35	A –0.01 B 1.33	A 4.37 B 5.71	A 1.5 B 0.44
Barnard's Star	5.98	9.54	13.22	0.00043
Wolf 359	7.78	13.46	16.57	0.000020
Lalande 21185	8.26	7.48	10.46	0.0055
Sirius	8.55	A –1.46 B 8.44	A 1.45 B 11.35	A 22 B 0.0024
Luyten 726-8*	8.73	A 12.54 B 13.00	A 15.40 B 15.86	A 0.000058 B 0.000038
Ross 154	9.45	10.45	13.31	0.00040
Ross 248	10.32	12.27	14.77	0.00010
Epsilon Eridani	10.70	3.73	6.15	0.29

A and B indicates a double star
* The B star is known as UV Ceti

light and are sub-classified as being between types E0 (face on) and E7 (edge on). Spiral galaxies are either normal (S), in which spiral-shaped arms emerge from the nucleus, or barred (SB), in which the arms originate through a 'bar' that appears through the centre of the galaxy. Lenticular (lens-shaped) galaxies are intermediate between the elliptical and spiral galaxies. Irregular-shaped galaxies are divided into type Irr I, which appear to be an extension of the spiral type Sc, and type Irr II, which include all other irregular-shaped galaxies.

The centres of regular-shaped galaxies are believed to contain massive black holes with masses millions to billions times that of the Sun. These black holes may be quiescent (inactive), as in the case of our own galaxy, or extremely active, emitting large amounts of radiation. Quasars (quasi-stellar sources) represent the detection of these active galactic nuclei and currently over 7200 are known.

THE MILKY WAY GALAXY

Although only seen edge on, our own galaxy is considered to be a typical spiral galaxy about 75,000 light years in diameter. It is a member of the so-called 'Local Group' of about 20 galaxies, which is about 6 million light years in extent and which is dominated at one end by our own galaxy and at the other by the much larger Andromeda galaxy. The latter is currently 2,930,000 light years distant, but these two galaxies are approaching each other and may collide several billion years in the future.

STARS

▶ Stars are accretions of gas that radiate energy through nuclear fusion reactions.
▶ Below about 0.08 solar masses, nuclear fusion either cannot occur or, if it does so, then only sporadically: such failed stars are known as brown dwarfs and the first one, Gliese 224B, was only discovered in 1995.

Stars form from the gravitational contraction of a cloud of gas and dust with a central core forming rapidly and the remainder of the surrounding cloud falling onto the core to form the star (see p. 8). The gravitational collapse continues until the core is both hot and dense enough to initiate the nuclear fusion of hydrogen to helium. The vast amount of energy produced counteracts the gravitational collapse and the star achieves a state of equilibrium which can last up to 10,000 million years in the case of a star the size of the Sun, but only about one million years for a very massive star. Eventually a critical amount of hydrogen will have been used up, nuclear fusion will cease, and the core will again start to contract. This releases gravitational energy, resulting in fusion reactions in the hydrogen envelope which surrounds the core. This 'shell' swells up and, because of the reduced temperature, glows red rather than white and the star becomes a 'red giant'.

WHITE DWARFS

For stars about the size of our Sun, core collapse continues until the electron fields surrounding the nuclei of the atom become compressed and the core density reaches about 100,000 times the density of the Earth. Such a core may then be the size of the Earth, but a mass equal to that of the Sun. These cores are known as 'white dwarf' stars, which may continue to shine for several thousand million years by using up the thermal energy that was stored in the core collapse. However, eventually they cool completely.

NEUTRON STARS AND PULSARS

For stars between 8 and 50 solar masses, the contraction of the core leads to temperatures over 1000 million °C (1800 million °F). This first leads to the fusion of helium in the core to carbon, and then to the formation of elements up to iron. The outer envelope also collapses onto the core, resulting in the formation of very heavy elements. The energy created in this process is so great that these outer layers are blown back into space, emitting such intense radiation that the expanding sphere, known as a 'supernova', can briefly outshine a whole galaxy. The core also rapidly collapses during this explosion to a final diameter of only 10–30 km (6–20 mi). Yet, since it still has a mass of about one to three times that of the Sun, it has a density 10^{14} times that of the Earth. This is due to the collapse of the electrons in the atoms onto the nuclei, so that the protons react with the electrons to form neutrons, hence 'neutron' stars. Some neutron stars rapidly rotate: this can be detected as a pulse caused by an interaction between the stars' emission of radiation and its magnetic field. Such stars are 'pulsars': the first was detected in 1967.

UNITS OF ASTRONOMY

Astronomical Unit (AU): the mean distance of the Earth from the Sun as defined in 1938. The current value is 149,597,871 km (92,955,907 mi).

Light Year (ly): the distance travelled by light in vacuum in one tropical year of 365.24219878 mean solar days, that is 9,460,528,405,000 km (5,878,499,814,000 mi).

Parsec (pc): The distance at which an angle of one second of arc will represent the distance from the Earth to the Sun, that is 206,264.806 astronomical units or 3.2616 light years or 30,856,776,000,000 km (19,173,511,000,000 mi).

BLACK HOLES

For stars in excess of 50 solar masses, the core collapse is so extreme that the whole mass may collapse into a single point. The intense concentration of mass causes a distortion of local space-time to such an extent that even radiation (i.e. light) cannot escape from the 'sphere of influence', which theoretically extends to a radius of 29.5 km (18.3 mi) for a ten solar mass core, and would therefore appear as a 'black hole' with a diameter of 59 km (37 mi).

THE SOLAR SYSTEM

▶ The solar system is located 26,100 light years from the centre of the Milky Way and was formed about 4540 million years ago from a globe of gas and dust.
▶ Most of the mass became concentrated in the central core to form the Sun, but part of the surrounding matter formed a flattened disc, which evolved into the nine planets and other objects of the solar system.

The boundary between the inner and outer solar system is taken to be the orbit of Jupiter. The inner solar system consists of the four terrestrial planets, Mercury, Venus, Earth and Mars, as well as the asteroid belt. The outer solar system comprises the four next planets – Jupiter, Saturn, Uranus and Neptune. These outer planets are all giant 'gas' planets; although they are all expected to have

THE MAGNITUDE SCALE

The scale is such that a first magnitude star is exactly 100 times brighter than a sixth magnitude star, so that a star has a magnitude of $(100)^{(1/5)}$ or 2.51186 to that of the next magnitude. The magnitude of a star as viewed from Earth is the 'apparent' magnitude (m_V) but, for purposes of comparison, the intrinsic brightness or 'absolute' magnitude (M_V) must be known and this is defined as the magnitude which a star would have if viewed at a distance of 10 parsecs (32.6 light years). On this basis, the Sun's apparent magnitude of –26.75 (negative because of the intense brightness of the Sun as viewed from Earth) would be reduced to an absolute magnitude of +4.82 or a four trillionfold (4×10^{12}) reduction in observed brightness.

THE SUN

▶ At the centre of the solar system is the Sun, a mass composed of 73% hydrogen, 25% helium and 2% other elements, and with a temperature of 15,400,000°C (27,700,000°F).
▶ The Sun has a diameter of 1,391,950 km (864,940 mi) and a mass of 1.9889 x 10^{27} tonnes – 332,946.05 times the Earth's mass.

The internal structure of the Sun consists of a helium-rich core, in which hydrogen undergoes fusion to helium. The core is surrounded by a radiative layer several hundred thousand kilometres in thickness and an outer convective layer several tens of thousands of kilometres in thickness, in which heat is transported by convection in the form of cells. The surface or 'photosphere' is about 300 km (200 mi) thick and has an overall temperature of 5504°C (9939°F).

The Sun's surface is transparent and gives the maximum depth of visibility into the interior, revealing the top of the convective layer as a patchwork of granules. The rotation of the photosphere at a rate of 25.38 days is worked out from 'sunspots' which occur in the outer layer and are due to magnetic anomalies. The darkness of the spots is merely a contrast effect, since they are at a temperature about 2000°C (3600°F) lower than the photosphere temperature.

The atmosphere of the Sun consists of a 'chromosphere', which extends to about 10,000 km (6000 mi) above the photosphere. It has a sufficiently high temperature, so that all of the elements present are ionized; its pinkish hue is due to ionized hydrogen. The chromosphere only becomes visible during total eclipses, when the photosphere is blocked out. The outer atmosphere or 'corona' is an extremely thin gas at a high temperature which appears as a white halo. It allows the continuous dispersal into space of the Sun's matter in the form of a plasma of charged particles. This 'solar wind' permeates the whole of the solar system. Solar flares are huge jets of gas flung many thousands of kilometres from the top of the chromosphere, which then loop back in to the chromosphere due to the effect of intense magnetic fields.

■ *Computer image of the solar system, showing a portion of the Sun (bottom left), followed by the nine planets (from bottom to top) Mercury, Venus, Earth, Mars, Jupiter, Saturn, Uranus, Neptune and Pluto*

rock-iron cores, it is the composition and behaviour of the outer gas layers which gives each its unique characteristics. Pluto is still classed as the outermost planet, but this small solid body is much smaller than many of the satellites and may better be regarded as the largest member of the newly discovered Kuiper-Edgeworth Belt of objects.

MERCURY

Mercury's surface looks similar to that of the Moon, but lacks the frozen lava 'seas' ('maria') seen on the nearside of the Moon. Mercury's surface is dominated by large basins representing different epochs in the formation of the crust. The largest of these, Caloris, has a major diameter of 1340 km (830 mi). There are a large number of impact craters, the largest of which is Boccaccio, with a diameter of 160 km (100 mi). The deepest crater is Ictinus, which is 4800 m (15,750 ft) from floor to rim. The high density of the planet is due to its iron-rich core, which is 3600 km (2200 mi) in diameter and accounts for 65% of Mercury's mass.

The atmospheric pressure is only one-trillionth (10^{-12}) that of Earth and, without the protection of an atmosphere, there is a wide variation in surface temperature, from up to 420°C (790°F) in the day down to –180°C (–290°F) at night. Because Mercury's rotation period is exactly two-thirds of the orbital period, this peculiar relationship means that a 'day' on the planet (sunrise to sunrise) is equal to two Mercurian years, or 176 Earth days.

VENUS

Although similar in size to Earth, Venus is an extremely hostile planet with an atmosphere rich in carbon dioxide. It has a surface pressure 94 times that of the Earth at an overall temperature of 464°C (867°F), the high temperature being maintained by a runaway 'greenhouse' effect in which radiation received from the Sun is trapped in the atmosphere. A thick planet-wide cloud cover, 50–75 km (30–45 mi) above the surface, contains a high concentration of droplets of sulphuric acid, which may be due to emissions from active volcanoes.

Although the surface cannot be seen from Earth, extensive radar mapping by the Pioneer, Venus and Magellan orbitors have revealed that it is essentially flat (with 80% being within 1 km (0.6 mi) of the planet's average radius). However, there are a number of notable highlands (similar to the continents on Earth), including Aphrodite Terra, close to the Equator, which is 3000 km (1900 mi) wide and 9700 km (6000 mi) in length, and Ishtar Terra in the north, which is 2900 km (1800 mi) in diameter. Here, the Maxwell Montes mountain chain rises up to 8 km (5 mi) above the surrounding plateau. Venus does not have the same type of tectonic geological structure as the Earth, but appears to periodically undergo extensive resurfacing, so that the current surface is relatively young – only 500 million years old. Although the rotation period is longer than its year, a Venusian 'day' (sunrise to sunrise) is equivalent to 116 Earth days.

EARTH

Because the astronomical unit is a defined quantity, then the true distance of the Earth from the Sun is 1.00000102 astronomical units, or 149,598,023 km (92,955,902 mi). The Earth (see pp. 26–27) is the largest and densest of the inner planets, with an atmosphere consisting mainly of 78% nitrogen and 21% oxygen at an average temperature of 15°C (59°F). Two-thirds of the surface is covered by oceans and the mean (average) sea level can be used as reference from which the maximum deviations are a depth of 11,022 m (36,160 ft) for the Mariana Trench in the Pacific ocean and a maximum height of 8863 m (29,078 ft) for Mount

Everest in the Himalaya, a difference of 19.9 km (12.4 mi) – only 0.3% of the Earth's radius.

THE MOON

With an equatorial diameter of 3476.3 km (2160.1 mi), a polar diameter of 3471.9 km (2157.4 mi) and a mass of 7.348 x 10^{19} tonnes or 0.0123 Earth masses, the Moon is the fifth largest and fifth most massive satellite in our solar system. It is in synchronous (captured) rotation, always turning the same face to the Earth, but there is a certain amount of movement within the orbit, so that 59% of the surface is visible.

Extensive space probe photography has now recorded the whole of the lunar surface showing the presence of craters, mountain ranges and broad plains of frozen lava known as 'seas' or 'maria'. It now appears that the surfaces of the maria are at a constant level and were therefore unable to fill the gravitationally higher craters on the far side of the Moon. Most of the craters formed are believed to be due to multiple impacts by planetesimals (small bodies that formed early in the history of the solar system). In fact, the largest impact basin on the Moon, called South Pole–Aitkin, has a diameter of 2250 km (1400 mi) and an average depth of 12 km (7 mi) – the largest such crater in the solar system. Because the Moon has no atmosphere, there is a wide variation in surface temperature, from 117°C (243°F) at the Equator at mid-day to –163°C (–261°F) after nightfall.

Since certain rock and soil samples brought back from the Moon are 4500 million years old, this indicates that the satellite was formed early on in the solar system and this must be taken in to account in any theory of the Moon's origin. The current theory of the Moon's formation is the 'giant impact' theory, suggesting that in the violent early history of the solar system, the newly formed Earth was struck by at least one and possibly several very large planetesimals. These disrupted the surface layers of the Earth, and the planetesimal(s), with such force that debris was flung into space by gas pressure and collected just beyond the limit of stability (the 'Roche' limit) at 18,500 km (11,500 mi). Here, it coalesced into the Moon, which then began to recede from the Earth into its present orbit.

MARS

Like Venus, the atmosphere of Mars is mainly carbon dioxide, but only at a surface pressure about 116th that of Earth at an average temperature of –53°C (–63°F), which is 68°C (122°F) lower than that of Earth. The surface is highly complex, consisting of flat plains, craters, dormant volcanoes and pole caps. A number of the volcanoes are of immense size, such as Olympus Mons in the Tharsis region, which is 600 km (370 mi) in diameter and rises 26 km (16 mi) above the surrounding plain. There are also a number of large channels such as 'Valles Marineris', which is at least 4000 km (2500 mi) long, up to 600 km (370 mi) wide and 7 km (5 mi) deep. Ash from ancient volcanoes has formed dark areas such as Syrtis Major and periodic sweeping of the ash on these plains changes the surface features. These changes, visible telescopically from Earth, were originally interpreted as the growth and receding of vegetation. It now appears that life on Mars could only have developed to a micro-biological level. Although there is evidence that many channels must have been fashioned by large quantities of water in the past, there is now no evidence of water in the outermost surface layers or in the atmosphere, although water ice is still present under the frozen carbon dioxide polar caps. The two small moons of Mars were discovered by Asaph Hall (USA) in 1877.

ASTEROIDS OR MINOR PLANETS

The theory of Titius of Wittenberg, Germany, in 1766, which was promoted by Johan Bode and henceforth known as the Titius-Bode Rule, suggested that the six known planets occurred at predictable intervals. According to their formula, however, there was a gap at 2.8 astronomical units. The discovery of the planet Ceres by the Italian Giuseppe Piazzi in 1801 appeared to fill this gap, but the discovery of a second planet, Pallas, in a similar orbit a year later, and three further such planets by 1845, only appeared to confuse the issue. The introduction of astronomical photography led to the detection of thousands of such minor planets or 'asteroids' and the total number is estimated to be about 50,000, of which the orbits of about 8000 have been accurately computed.

Most asteroids orbit between Mars and Jupiter (the 'Main Belt'), confined to distances 300 million–500 million km (200 million–300 million mi) from the Sun, but there are two groups which could directly intervene in the future of the Earth if impacts should occur: the 'Atens', which have an average orbital distance less than that of the Earth, but large eccentricities may mean that they cross the Earth's path; and the 'Apollos', which are Earth-crossers and which may number in hundreds.

The total mass of the asteroids is only about $^{1}/_{25}$ of our Moon's mass, and the three largest asteroids, Ceres, Pallas and Vesta, account for over half of this mass. It is likely that the nearby massive Jupiter prevented the planetesimals in this area from forming a planet and instead dispersed much of the mass into the inner solar system. (For more information on asteroids, see the table on p. 13.)

JUPITER

A model of Jupiter suggests that it may have a central rock-iron core about 15,000 km (9000 mi) in diameter, weigh about 15 Earth masses, and is surrounded by a shell of metallic hydrogen extending to a radius of 55,000 km (34,000 mi) from its centre. An outer envelope, which consists mainly of liquid molecular hydrogen, diffuses into the gaseous atmosphere, which is mainly hydrogen but with about 18% of helium and small amounts of ices of water and ammonia and other compounds. These impart the characteristic light and dark bands seen in the planet's atmosphere when viewed through a telescope from Earth. The 'Great Red Spot', which was first seen in 1664, is a long-lived swirling storm which rises up to 8 km (5 mi) above the surrounding cloud deck. The planet has a very strong magnetic field, about five to ten times stronger than that of the Earth. This results in the formation of extremely lethal radiation belts about 10,000 times more powerful than those of Earth.

The ring system on Jupiter was discovered in 1979 and has three components. The first is the inner halo – a faint ring 20,000 km (12,400 mi) thick, which may extend down to the cloud tops. The second component is the main ring – a bright central ring 7000 km (4300 mi) wide and only 30 km (20 mi) thick, with an abrupt edge at 129,130 km (80,240 mi), which is controlled by the satellite Adrastea. And the third component is the gossamer ring – a very tenuous ring extending out to 214,000 km (133,000 mi).

THE SATELLITES OF JUPITER

Of the sixteen satellites, the four large Galilean satellites, named after Galileo Galilei, are worlds in their own right. The first three – Io, Europa and Ganymede – all possess large iron-rich cores surrounded by rocky mantles, but it is in the outer surface layers that they differ. Io is subject to gravitational interactions with Jupiter and the large amount of energy produced leads to the surface continuously being subject to volcanic eruptions. Europa is also subject to gravitational interactions with Jupiter and it is believed that the outer layer may consist of a warm ocean of water under a relatively thin ice shell, which raises the serious possibility that life may have formed in these oceans. Ganymede has an outer ice shell 800 km (500 mi) thick, whilst the outermost Galilean satellite, Callisto, does not have an iron-rich core, but is a complete mixture of iron, rock and ice.

PLANETARY INFORMATION

Planet		Diameter km	Diameter mi	Mass* kg	Density g/cm³	Mean distance from Sun km	Mean distance from Sun mi	Sidereal period days
MERCURY		4,880	3,032	3.302 x 10^{23}	5.428	57,909,100	35,983,000	87.9693
VENUS		12,104	7,521	4.869 x 10^{24}	5.244	108,208,600	67,237,700	224.7008
EARTH	Equ.	12,756	7,926	5.974 x 10^{24}	5.515	149,598,000	92,955,900	365.2564
	Polar	12,714	7,900					
MARS	Equ.	6,794	4,221	6.419 x 10^{23}	3.934	227,939,200	141,634,800	686.9799
	Polar	6,752	4,196					
JUPITER	Equ.	142,984	88,846	1.899 x 10^{27}	1.325	778,298,400	483,612,200	4,332.59
	Polar	133,708	83,082					
SATURN	Equ.	120,536	74,898	5.685 x 10^{26}	0.685	1,429,394,000	888,184,000	10,759.2
	Polar	108,718	67,560					
URANUS	Equ.	51,118	31,763	8.683 x 10^{25}	1.271	2,875,039,000	1,786,466,000	30,688.5
	Polar	49,946	31,035					
NEPTUNE	Equ.	49,532	30,778	1.024 x 10^{26}	1.638	4,504,450,000	2,798,935,000	60,182.3
	Polar	48,684	30,251					
PLUTO		2,320	1,442	1.31 x 10^{22}	2.01	5,913,514,000	3,674,490,000	90,777.6

* Excluding satellites.

WAS THE FIRST EXTRA-SOLAR PLANET DISCOVERED ORBITING AROUND A NORMAL STAR IN 1995

SATURN

Saturn's internal structure is generally considered to be similar to that of Jupiter, but with a much smaller metallic hydrogen layer extending to only 26,000 km (16,000 mi) from the centre of the planet. Also, the molecular hydrogen layer is much richer in helium, which leads to a depletion in the outer atmosphere. Occasional white spots may be observed on the cloud tops, but these are less long-lived than the Great Red Spot of Jupiter.

The true nature of Saturn's rings, initially vaguely observed by Galileo in 1610, was deduced by Christiaan Huygens (Netherlands) in 1659. Composed mainly of water ice, the main ring system is 273,550 km (169,980 mi) in diameter, but only about 10 m (33 ft) thick.

THE SATELLITES OF SATURN

Although officially Saturn has eighteen satellites, many more candidates have been observed from re-examination of photographs from the Voyager 2 encounter and from Hubble Space Telescope observations during the 1995 ring-plane crossings when the rings were seen edge-on. Confirmation of any of these satellites will have to wait until the detailed study of the Saturn system by the Cassini spacecraft in 2004.

The largest of the moons, Titan, is the only satellite in the solar system with an extensive atmosphere. It has a surface pressure one and a half times greater than that of Earth's. The atmosphere consists mainly of nitrogen, but methane present is affected by sunlight, and forms complex molecules in the upper atmosphere, which form an orange haze and obscure the surface from view. Of the other satellites, Iapetus has an extraordinary appearance, with 40% of an otherwise bright surface being covered with a coal black deposit. This may have occurred when a large comet struck the nearby proto-Hyperion and flung dust into the path of Iapetus. Hyperion is unique in that it has chaotic rotation, that is it takes on different rotation rates depending on the relative positions of Saturn, the Sun and Titan.

URANUS

Uranus can just be seen with the naked eye, but it was actually discovered by William Herschel in March 1781. Although originally thought to be a comet, its orbit was subsequently shown to agree quite closely to the one predicted for the next planet using the Titius-Bode Rule. This much smaller gas planet is believed to have a rock-iron core surrounded by a 'sea' of water, methane and ammonia. The outer atmosphere is composed mainly of hydrogen, but with about 26% of helium and a small amount of methane, which is responsible for the greenish colour of the atmosphere. Unlike the other giant planets, Uranus does not radiate back into space more heat than it receives from the Sun, and this might explain why the cloud cover is virtually featureless.

The large tilt of Uranus's axis (98°) means that day and night on some parts of the planet may last up to 21 years, but the present sunlit 'south' pole and dark 'north' pole differ very little in temperature. This suggests that there is a strong temperature equilibrium within the atmosphere. The magnetic axis of Uranus is offset 7000 km (4300 mi) from the centre and is also inclined at an angle of 59° to the axis of rotation – this difference has been used to suggest that the large tilt of the Equator may have been due to a catastrophic collision between Uranus and a large planetesimal.

Uranus's rings were initially discovered mainly from stellar occultations (temporary disappearances of a celestial body as it moves out of sight behind another body) in 1977–78. The Diffuse ring 1986 U2R and the Lambda ring were discovered during the Voyager 2 encounter. The rings are very dark and probably rich in carbon. The outermost ring, Epsilon, is being controlled by the satellites Cordelia and Ophelia.

THE SATELLITES OF URANUS

The five major satellites (see p. 13) were identified telescopically from Earth, but the ten others were discovered during the Voyager 2 encounter from 1985–86. These ten small inner satellites may have been formed by the fragmentation of a larger satellite about 3500 million years ago, whilst it is possible that the satellites Miranda and Ariel may have been disrupted and reformed at least once and possibly several times.

NEPTUNE

The planet Neptune is invisible to the naked eye. It was discovered in September 1846 by the German astronomers Johann Galle and Heinrich d'Arrest, based on the mathematical predictions of Urbain Le Verrier in France and John Couch Adams in the UK, who independently deduced that the orbit of Uranus was being affected by the gravity of another planet.

Neptune is an extremely dynamic world with many discernible cloud features and extremely high wind speeds. Atmospheric features may be more transient than for Jupiter. For example, a 'Great Dark Spot', observed during the Voyager 2 encounter in 1989, had disappeared by the Hubble Space Telescope observations in 1994. The planet radiates 161% more heat back into space than it receives from the Sun, but the reason for Neptune's dynamic nature is unknown, since it is expected to have an internal structure similar to the docile Uranus. It may be related to its more remote distance from the Sun. The bluish colour of the planet is due to the presence of methane in the atmosphere.

The Voyager 2 encounter proved that there were three distinct rings and a diffuse ring of material between 38,000–59,000 km (23,600–36,700 mi) from Neptune's centre. The Galle ring is a broad dusty ring, 1700 km (1060 mi) wide, centred at 41,900 km (26,000 mi). The Leverrier ring is a narrow dusty ring, only 30 km (19 mi) wide, centred at 53,200 km (33,060 mi). The Adams ring is a narrow ring, 15 km (9 mi) wide, containing four dusty arcs named Courage, Liberté, Egalité and Fraternité.

SATELLITES OF NEPTUNE

In 1989, the Voyager imaging team discovered six new satellites in addition to the two already known, although almost certainly one of these – Larissa – was fortuitously detected during a stellar occultation in 1981.

The largest of the satellites, Triton, has a large orbital inclination (157°) and a retrograde orbit (opposite to the direction of Neptune's rotation), suggesting that it may have been captured, possibly from the nearby Kuiper-Edgeworth Belt (see right). It is believed that the satellite has an outer shell of ice, 150–200 km (90–120 mi) thick, overlaid with a highly reflective coating of nitrogen and methane ices. The slightly dark red colour of the surface is due to the formation of organic polymer materials – a product of the effect of sunlight on the methane. Although the average surface temperature of –235°C (–391°F) is the coldest measured surface in the solar system, it is possible that there are local hot spots which cause sub-surface nitrogen to heat up and escape, together with dust, through vents as geysers, which reach up to 8 km (5 mi) into the very thin Triton atmosphere.

PLUTO

The discovery of Pluto was announced by the American Clyde Tombaugh in March 1930, but little was known about this object until the discovery of its moon, Charon, in June 1978. Although long given the status as a planet, the small size and mass of Pluto – its diameter is only two-thirds of that of our Moon and its mass one-sixth – together with the discovery of the Kuiper-Edgeworth Belt of objects (see below), now suggests that Pluto should more properly be treated as being simply the largest of these objects, especially since 30–40% of those discovered so far are in similar orbits to Pluto's.

Pluto appears to be a twin of Neptune's moon Triton, with a similar density and a similar covering of a nitrogen and methane layer overlaying a water ice shell. Again its surface is reddened – possibly from the forming of organic polymers. The surface temperature is expected to be similar to that of Triton at –235°C (–391°F), but with hot spots about 20°C (36°F) warmer.

THE SATELLITE OF PLUTO

With a mass one-eighth that of Pluto, the Pluto-Charon system should more properly be described as being a binary (a double planet). The moon is in synchronous (captured) rotation and the two objects always have the same faces opposite each other. The surface of Charon is water ice and has a bluish appearance, in contrast to Pluto's reddish appearance.

KUIPER-EDGEWORTH BELT OBJECTS AND CENTAURS

Both Kenneth Edgeworth (UK), in 1949, and Gerard Kuiper (USA), in 1951, predicted that the source of short-period comets was a belt of objects orbiting just beyond Neptune. The first of more than 40 of these objects, 1992 QB1, was discovered in 1992, and it is predicted that there may be up to 70,000 with diameters in excess of 100 km (62 mi) and a billion of smaller size. There appear to be two distinct orbital types: 'Plutinos', those orbiting between 5400 million–6000 million km (3400 million–3700 million mi) from the Sun in the same highly eccentric, inclined orbit as Pluto, in stable resonance with Neptune's orbit so that they do not collide with that planet, and a second more general orbital type found between 6100 million–7100 million km (3800 million–4400 million mi). However, one object, 1996 TL66, has a very eccentric orbit, taking it 19.7 billion km (12.2 billion mi) from the Sun at aphelion (the point in a body's orbit when it is at its greatest distance from the Sun) and this may represent a new class of objects.

Occasionally the gravity field of one of the large planets will dislodge a Kuiper-Edgeworth Belt object into a highly eccentric, unstable orbit, between Jupiter and Neptune. Such objects are known as 'Centaurs' and seven are known, although it is predicted that there may be 300 with diameters in excess of 100 km (62 mi). The first discovered, 2060 Chiron, was found by the American Charles Kowal in 1977 and shows periodic outgassing from the surface and the formation of a large coma (a luminous cloud surrounding the frozen solid nucleus in the head of a comet, formed by vaporization of part of the nucleus when a body is close to the Sun). This is cometary behaviour and Chiron is often classed as being the largest comet, although it never gets closer than 1265 million km (786 million mi) to the Sun.

In general, both Kuiper-Edgeworth Belt objects and Centaurs are very dark red. This is due to the formation of organic deposits on the surface by the bombardment of surface methane ice with cosmic rays since the beginning of the solar system.

■ THE KUIPER-EDGEWORTH BELT AND OORT CLOUD MAY CONTAIN OVER A TRILLION OBJECTS

■ *Composite Voyager 2 image of Uranus (the blue planet) and five of its moons (clockwise from bottom left): Ariel, Umbriel, Oberon, Titania (the largest) and Miranda*

10 LARGEST ASTEROIDS

	Number/name	Year of discovery	Average diameter km	mi	Rotation period hours
1	1 Ceres	1801	941	585	9.075
2	2 Pallas	1802	530	329	7.814
3	4 Vesta	1807	512	318	5.342
4	10 Hygeia	1849	457	284	27.623
5	511 Davida	1903	344	214	5.129
6	704 Interamnia	1910	317	197	8.727
7	52 Europa	1858	303	188	5.632
8	87 Sylvia	1866	277	172	5.184
9	15 Eunomia	1851	272	169	6.083
10	65 Cybele	1861	269	167	4.041

COMETS

▶ **Comets were once heralded as apparitions in the sky which appeared to be portents of triumph or disaster.**
▶ **Their actual structure is more mundane, consisting of a central nucleus which is a conglomeration of rock and ice.**

On approaching the Sun, the ice starts to evaporate, producing a cloud or 'coma' around the nucleus. There are generally two tails streaming away from the nucleus, one of which is an ion tail repelled by sunlight and the other a dust tail repelled by the solar wind. Therefore, even when moving away from the Sun, the tails of the comet lead.

The most famous comet is Halley's Comet, named after Edmund Halley (UK) who correctly predicted its return in 1758, sixteen years after his death. Several bright comets appear most centuries, the most recent being the spectacular Hale-Bopp which was seen during 1997. However, these comets tend to have very long orbital periods and it is impossible to predict when the next bright comet will appear. The source of short-period comets may be the Kuiper-Edgeworth belt (see p. 12), but longer-period comets, or those on parabolic orbits which are simply swept out of the solar system, may originate in the 'Oort Cloud', the remnant of the original globe of gas and dust from which the solar system was formed.

In spite of their immensely long tails, the actual nuclei of comets tend to be very small in astronomical terms, with Halley's Comet having an average diameter of only about 10 km (6 mi) and Hale-Bopp of 35 km (22 mi). These diameters are probably typical of comets which penetrate into the inner solar system, but the Centaur 2060 Chiron (see p. 12), which shows cometary behaviour, has a diameter of 182 km (113 mi).

SATELLITES OF THE SOLAR SYSTEM

A total of 61 satellites are officially accepted. Whilst most lie in nearly circular orbits lying close to the equatorial plane of the planet, the more remote satellites tend to be in highly inclined, very eccentric orbits. The remote satellites have individual rotation periods, whereas most of the inner satellites are in synchronous (captured) rotation, always turning the same face to the planet so that their rotation period is equal to their orbital period.

No.	Name	Average diameter km	mi	Orbital period in days	Distance from centre of planet km	mi	Year of discovery
EARTH							
I	Moon	3,474	2,159	27.321662	384,399	238,855	–
MARS							
I	Phobos	22	14	0.318910	9,379	5,828	1877
II	Deimos	12	8	1.262441	23,461	14,578	1877
JUPITER							
XVI	Metis	40	25	0.294779	127,979	79,522	1979
XV	Adrastea	20	12	0.298260	128,980	80,144	1979
V	Amalthea	172	107	0.498179	181,366	112,695	1892
XIV	Thebe	100	62	0.674536	221,889	137,875	1979
I	Io	3,643	2,263	1.769138	421,767	262,074	1610
II	Europa	3,130	1,945	3.551181	671,049	416,971	1610
III	Ganymede	5,268	3,273	7.154553	1,070,400	665,116	1610
IV	Callisto	4,806	2,986	16.689018	1,882,630	1,169,810	1610
XIII	Leda	18	11	238.72	11,094,000	6,890,000	1974
VI	Himalia	157	98	250.5662	11,480,000	7,130,000	1904
X	Lysithea	34	21	259.22	11,720,000	7,280,000	1938
VII	Elara	70	43	259.6528	11,737,000	7,290,000	1905
XII	Ananke	25	16	631 R	21,200,000	13,200,000	1951
XI	Carme	41	25	692 R	22,600,000	14,000,000	1938
VIII	Pasiphae	57	35	735 R	23,500,000	14,600,000	1908
IX	Sinope	34	21	758 R	23,700,000	14,700,000	1914
SATURN							
XVIII	Pan	20	12	0.575038	133,583	83,004	1990
XV	Atlas	32	20	0.601692	137,665	85,541	1980
XVI	Prometheus	95	59	0.612986	139,377	86,605	1980
XVII	Pandora	84	52	0.628504	141,713	88,056	1980
XI	Epimetheus	117	73	*0.694323	*151,413	*94,084	†1980
X	Janus	178	111	*0.694664	*151,462	*94,114	†1980
I	Mimas	398	247	0.942422	185,536	115,287	1789
II	Enceladus	499	310	1.370218	238,036	147,909	1789
III	Tethys	1,060	659	1.887803	294,674	183,102	1684
XIII	Telesto	22	14	**1.887803	**294,674	**183,102	1980
XIV	Calypso	19	12	**1.887803	**294,674	**183,102	1980
IV	Dione	1,120	696	2.736916	377,416	234,515	1684
XII	Helene	32	20	**2.736916	**377,416	**234,515	1980
V	Rhea	1,528	949	4.517503	527,069	327,506	1672
VI	Titan	5,150	3,200	15.945448	1,221,870	759,230	1655
VII	Hyperion	266	165	21.276668	1,481,090	920,310	1848
VIII	Iapetus	1,436	892	79.330947	3,561,690	2,213,130	1671
IX	Phoebe	220	137	550.48 R	12,952,000	8,048,000	1898
URANUS							
VI	Cordelia	26	16	0.335033	49,752	30,914	1986
VII	Ophelia	32	20	0.376409	53,764	33,407	1986
VIII	Bianca	44	27	0.434577	59,165	36,763	1986
IX	Cressida	66	41	0.463570	61,767	38,380	1986
X	Desdemona	58	36	0.473651	62,659	38,934	1986
XI	Juliet	84	52	0.493066	64,358	39,990	1986
XII	Portia	110	68	0.513196	66,097	41,071	1986
XIII	Rosalind	58	36	0.558459	69,927	43,451	1986
XIV	Belinda	68	42	0.623525	75,255	46,761	1986
XV	Puck	154	96	0.761832	86,004	53,440	1985
V	Miranda	472	293	1.413479	129,848	80,684	1948
I	Ariel	1,158	719	2.520379	190,390	118,638	1851
II	Umbriel	1,169	727	4.144176	265,980	165,272	1851
III	Titania	1,578	980	8.705865	436,278	271,091	1787
IV	Oberon	1,523	946	13.463232	583,427	362,525	1787
NEPTUNE							
III	Naiad	58	36	0.294396	48,227	29,967	1989
IV	Thelassa	80	50	0.311485	50,075	31,115	1989
V	Despina	148	92	0.334655	52,526	32,638	1989
VI	Galatea	158	98	0.428745	61,953	38,496	1989
VII	Larissa	192	119	0.554654	73,548	45,701	†1989
VIII	Proteus	403	250	1.122316	117,647	73,102	1989
I	Triton	2,705	1,681	5.876854 R	354,759	220,437	1846
II	Nereid	340	211	360.13538	5,513,410	3,425,880	1949
PLUTO							
I	Charon	1,230	764	6.387242	19,636	12,201	1978

R Retrograde motion (opposite to the rotation direction of the planet).
* Epimetheus and Janus periodically exchange orbits – the average orbital period is 0.694590 days and the average distance 151,452 km (94,108 mi).
** It is assumed that the long-term orbits of Telesto and Calypso are identical to that of Tethys and that of Helene is identical to Dione.
† Tentative evidence of Epimetheus and Janus was obtained in 1966, whilst Larissa was detected in 1981.

BETWEEN THEM ■ 19 PARTS OF THE COMET SHOEMAKER-LEVY 9 CRASHED ON TO JUPITER IN 1994 ■

SPACE TRAVEL

- The shortest manned spaceflight was made by Alan Shepard on board *Mercury-Redstone 3*, lasting 15 min 28 sec.
- The longest manned spaceflight lasted 437 days 17 hr 58 min 16 sec, when Valeri Poliakov was launched to the *Mir* space station on board *Soyuz TM18* and returned on board *Soyuz TM20*.
- The most powerful manned booster had a thrust of 3,402,000 kg, the least 35,381 kg.
- America has undertaken the greatest number of flights (113), spending 1413 days 1 hour in space.
- The Soviets/Russians have undertaken 83 flights and spent the greatest amount of time in space – 5623 days 10 hours.

■ *The Space Shuttle* Columbia *lifts off on 22 February 1996 with seven crew on board*

MANNED SPACEFLIGHTS

1961
1 Vostok 1 (USSR 1): 12 Apr, Yuri Gagarin, 1 hr 58 min – landed separately from craft after ejecting at 1 hr 48 min.
2 Freedom 7 (USA 1): 5 May, Alan Shepard, 15 min 28 sec – suborbital.
3 Liberty Bell 7 (USA 2): 21 Jul, Gus Grissom, 15 min 37 sec – spacecraft sank.
4 Vostok 2 (USSR 2): 6 Aug, Gherman Titov, 1 day 1 hr 18 min – at 25, youngest person in space.

1962
5 Friendship 7 (USA 3): 20 Feb, John Glenn, 4 hr 55 min 23 sec – first American to orbit.
6 Aurora 7 (USA 4): 24 May, Scott Carpenter, 4 hr 56 min 5 sec – landing overshoot of 402.3 km (250 mi).
7 Vostok 3 (USSR 3): 11 Aug, Andrian Nikolyev, 3 day 22 hr 25 min.
8 Vostok 4 (USSR 4): 12 Aug, Pavel Popovich, 2 day 22 hr 59 min – came to within 6.4 km (4 mi) of *Vostok 3*.
9 Sigma 7 (USA 5): 3 Oct, Wally Schirra, 9 hr 13 min 11 sec – Pacific splashdown.

1963
10 Faith 7 (USA 6): 15 May, Gordon Cooper, 1 day 10 hr 19 min 49 sec – final US one-man flight.
11 Vostok 5 (USSR 5): 14 Jun, Valeri Bykovsky, 4 day 23 hr 7 min 2 sec – solo flight record-holder.
12 Vostok 6 (USSR 6): 16 Jun, Valentina Tereshkova, 2 day 22 hr 50 min 8 sec – first woman in space.

1964
13 Voskhod 1 (USSR 7): 12 Oct, Vladimir Komarov, Konstantin Feoktistov, Boris Yegerov, 1 day 0 hr 17 min 3 sec – riskiest flight, no spacesuits.

1965
14 Voskhod 2 (USSR 8): 18 Mar, Pavel Belyayev, Alexei Leonov, 1 day 2 hr 2 min 17 sec – Leonov made first walk in space.
15 Gemini 3 (USA 7): 25 Mar, Gus Grissom, John Young, 4 hr 52 min 51 sec – Grissom first man in space twice.
16 Gemini 4 (USA 8): 3 Jun, James McDivitt, Edward White, 4 day 1 hr 56 min 12 sec – Edward White makes first US spacewalk.
17 Gemini 5 (USA 9): 21 Aug, Gordon Cooper, Charles Conrad, 7 day 22 hr 55 min 14 sec – new record.
18 Gemini 7 (USA 10): 4 Dec, Frank Borman, James Lovell, 13 day 18 hr 35 min 1 sec – broke endurance record.
19 Gemini 6 (USA 11): 15 Dec, Wally Schirra, Tom Stafford, 1 day 1 hr 51 min 54 sec – rendezvous with *Gemini 7*.

1966
20 Gemini 8 (USA 12): 16 Mar, Neil Armstrong, David Scott, 10 hr 41 min 26 sec – emergency landing after first space docking.
21 Gemini 9 (USA 13): 3 Jun, Tom Stafford, Eugene Cernan, 3 day 20 min 50 sec – rendezvous, spacewalk.
22 Gemini 10 (USA 14): 18 Jul, John Young, Michael Collins, 2 day 22 hr 46 min 39 sec – docking, spacewalk.
23 Gemini 11 (USA 15): 12 Sep, Charles Conrad, Richard Gordon, 2 day 23 hr 17 min 8 sec – reached altitude of 1368 km (850 mi) using the docked *Agena* rocket stage.
24 Gemini 12 (USA 16): 11 Nov, James Lovell, Edwin Aldrin, 3 day 22 hr 34 min 31 sec – docking, 2 hr spacewalk.

1967
25 Soyuz 1 (USSR 9): 23 Apr, Vladimir Komarov, 1 day 2 hr 47 min 52 sec – Komarov killed, parachute fails.

1968
26 Apollo 7 (USA 17): 11 Oct, Wally Schirra, Donn Eisele, Walt Cunningham, 10 day 20 hr 9 min 3 sec – Earth orbit test.
27 Soyuz 3 (USSR 10): 26 Oct, Georgi Beregovoi, 3 day 22 hr 50 min 45 sec – failed to dock with *Soyuz 2*.
28 Apollo 8 (USA 18): 21 Dec, Frank Borman, James Lovell, William Anders, 6 day 3 hr 42 sec – lunar orbit.

1969
29 Soyuz 4 (USSR 11): 14 Jan, Vladimir Shatalov, 2 day 23 hr 20 min 47 sec – returned with two cosmonauts from *Soyuz 5*.
30 Soyuz 5 (USSR 12): 15 Jan, Boris Volynov, Alexei Yeleseyev, Yevgeny Khrunov, 3 day 0 hr 54 min 15 sec – spacewalk to *Soyuz 4* after docking.
31 Apollo 9 (USA 19): 3 Mar, James McDivitt, David Scott, Russell Schweickart, 10 day 1 hr 54 sec – test of lunar module in Earth orbit.
32 Apollo 10 (USA 20): 18 May, Tom Stafford, John Young, Eugene Cernan, 8 day 3 min 23 sec – lunar module tested in lunar orbit.
33 Apollo 11 (USA 21): 17 Jul, Neil Armstrong, Michael Collins, Edwin Aldrin, 8 day 3 hr 18 min 35 sec – Armstrong and Aldrin walk on Moon.
34 Soyuz 6 (USSR 13): 11 Oct, Georgi Shonin, Valeri Kubasov, 4 day 22 hr 42 min 47 sec – welding tests.
35 Soyuz 7 (USSR 14): 12 Oct, Anatoli Filipchenko, Vladislav Volkov, Viktor Gorbatko, 4 day 22 hr 40 min 23 sec – to within 488 m (1600 ft) of *Soyuz 8*.
36 Soyuz 8 (USSR 15): 13 Oct, Vladimir Shatalov, Alexei Yeliseyev, 4 day 22 hr 51 min 49 sec – observation.
37 Apollo 12 (USA 22): 14 Nov, Charles Conrad, Richard Gordon, Alan Bean, 10 day 4 hr 36 min 25 sec – pinpoint landing near *Surveyor 3*.

1970
38 Apollo 13 (USA 23): 11 Apr, James Lovell, Jack Swigert, Fred Haise, 5 day 22 hr 54 min 41 sec – service module exploded 55 hours into mission, crew limped home using lunar module.
39 Soyuz 9 (USSR 16): 1 Jun, Andiran

■ 9000 PIECES OF DEBRIS, RANGING IN SIZE FROM A MOBILE PHONE TO A SPACE STATION, ARE

Nikolyev, Vitali Sevastyanov, 17 day 16 hr 58 min 50 sec – set endurance record.

1971

40 Apollo 14 (USA 24): 31 Jan, Alan Shepard, Stuart Roosa, Edgar Mitchell, 9 day 2 min 57 sec – Shepard only *Mercury* project astronaut to walk on Moon.
41 Soyuz 10 (USSR 17): 23 Apr, Vladimir Shatalov, Alexei Yeliseyev, Nikolai Ruckavishnikov, 1 day 23 hr 45 min 54 sec – failed to enter *Salyut 1* space station.
42 Soyuz 11 (USSR 18): 6 Jun, Georgi Dobrovolsky, Vladislav Volkov, Viktor Patsayev, 23 day 18 hr 21 min 43 sec – crew died as craft depressurized.
43 Apollo 15 (USA 25): 26 Jul, David Scott, Alfred Worden, James Irwin, 12 day 7 hr 11 min 53 sec – first lunar rover.

1972

44 Apollo 16 (USA 26): 16 Apr, John Young, Ken Mattingly, Charles Duke, 11 day 1 hr 51 min 5 sec – lunar rover.
45 Apollo 17 (USA 27): 7 Dec, Eugene Cernan, Ron Evans, Jack Schmitt, 12 day 13 hr 51 min 59 sec – last manned expedition to Moon.

1973

46 Skylab 2 (USA 28): 25 May, Charles Conrad, Joe Kerwin, Paul Weitz, 28 day 49 min 49 sec – Skylab 1 space station habitation.
47 Skylab 3 (USA 29): 28 Jul, Alan Bean, Owen Garriott, Jack Lousma, 59 day 11 hr 9 min 4 sec – crew for *Skylab 1* space station.
48 Soyuz 12 (USSR 19), 27 Sep, Vasili Lazarev, Oleg Makarov, 1 day 23 hr 15 min 32 sec – test of space ferry.
49 Skylab 4 (USA 30): 16 Nov, Gerry Carr, Edward Gibson, Bill Pogue, 84 day 1 hr 15 min 31 sec – crew for *Skylab 1* space station.
50 Soyuz 13 (USSR 20): 18 Dec, Pyotr Klimuk, Valetin Lebedev, 7 day 20 hr 55 min 35 sec – science mission.

1974

51 Soyuz 14 (USSR 21): 3 Jul, Pavel Popovich, Yuri Artyukhin, 15 day 17 hr 30 min 28 sec – first space spies.
52 Soyuz 15 (USSR 22): 26 Aug, Gennadi Serafanov, Lev Demin, 2 day 0 hr 12 min 11 sec – failed to dock with *Salyut 3*.
53 Soyuz 16 (USSR 23): 2 Dec, Anatoli Filipchenko, Nikolai Ruckavishnikov, 5 day 22 hr 23 min 35 sec – rehearsal for US-USSR joint flight.

1975

54 Soyuz 17 (USSR 24): 11 Jan, Alexei Gubarev, Georgi Grechko, 29 day 13 hr 19 min 45 sec – aboard *Salyut 4*.
55 Soyuz 18-1 (USSR 25): 5 Apr, Vasili Lazarev, Oleg Makarov, 21 min 27 sec – second stage failed, flight aborted.
56 Soyuz 18 (USSR 26): 24 May, Pyotr Klimuk, Vitali Sevastyanov, 62 day 23 hr 20 min 8 sec – aboard *Salyut 4*.
57 Soyuz 19 (USSR 27): 15 Jul, Alexei Leonov, Valeri Kubasov, 5 day 22 hr 30 min 51 sec – docked with *Apollo 18*.
58 Apollo 18 (USA 31): 15 Jul, Tom Stafford, Vance Brand, Deke Slayton, 9 day 1 hr 28 min 24 sec – docked with *Soyuz 19*.

1976

59 Soyuz 21 (USSR 28): 6 Jul, Boris Volynov, Vitali Zholobov, 49 day 6 hr 23 min 32 sec – crew for *Salyut 5* space station.
60 Soyuz 22 (USSR 29): 22 Sep, Valeri Bykovsky, Vladimir Aksyonov, 7 day 21 hr 52 min 17 sec – Earth survey.
61 Soyuz 23 (USSR 30): 14 Oct, Vyacheslav Zudov, Valeri Rozhdestvensky, 2 day 0 hr 6 min 35 sec – failed to dock with *Salyut 5*.

1977

62 Soyuz 24 (USSR 31), 7 Feb, Viktor Gorbatko, Yuri Glazkov, 17 day 17 hr 25 min 50 sec – crew for *Salyut 5* space station.
63 Soyuz 25 (USSR 32): 9 Oct, Vladimir Kovalyonok, Valeri Ryumin, 2 day 0 hr 44 min 45 sec – failed to dock with *Salyut 6*.
64 Soyuz 26 (USSR 33): 10 Dec, Yuri Romanenko, Georgi Grechko, 96 day 10 hr 0 min 7 sec – crew for *Salyut 6* space station, broke endurance record.

1978

65 Soyuz 27 (USSR 34): 10 Jan, Vladimir Dzhanibekov, Oleg Makarov, 5 day 22 hr 58 min 58 sec – crew for *Salyut 6*.
66 Soyuz 28 (USSR 35): 2 Mar, Alexei Gubarev, Vladimir Remek, 7 day 22 hr 16 min – Remek from Czechoslovakia, first non-American and non-Soviet in space.
67 Soyuz 29 (USSR 36): 15 Jun, Vladimir Kovalyonok, Alexander Ivanchenkov, 139 day 14 hr 47 min 32 sec – crew for *Salyut 6* space station.
68 Soyuz 30 (USSR 37): 27 Jun, Pyotr Klimuk, Miroslaw Hermaszewski, 7 day 22 hr 2 min 59 sec – Hermaszewski from Poland.
69 Soyuz 31 (USSR 38): 26 Aug, Valeri Bykovsky, Sigmund Jahn, 7 day 29 hr 49 min 4 sec – Jahn from East Germany.

1979

70 Soyuz 32 (USSR 39): 25 Feb, Vladimir Lyakhov, Valeri Ryumin, 175 day 0 hr 35 min 37 sec – visit to *Salyut 6*.
71 Soyuz 33 (USSR 40): 10 Apr, Nikolai Ruckavishnikov, Georgi Ivanov; 1 day 23 hr 1 min 6 sec – failed to dock with *Salyut 6*, Ivanov from Bulgaria.

1980

72 Soyuz 35 (USSR 41): 9 Apr, Leonid Popov, Valeri Ryumin, 184 day 20 hr 11 min 35 sec – *Salyut 6* mission.
73 Soyuz 36 (USSR 42): 26 May, Valeri Kubasov, Bertalan Farkas, 7 day 20 hr 45 min 44 sec – visit to *Salyut 6*, Farkas from Hungary.
74 Soyuz T2 (USSR 43): 5 Jun, Yuri Malyshev, Vladimir Aksyonov, 3 day 22 hr 19 min 30 sec – test of new *Soyuz* model.
75 Soyuz 37 (USSR 44): 23 Jul, Viktor Gorbatko, Pham Tuan, 7 day 20 hr 42 min – visit to *Salyut 6*, Tuan from Vietnam.
76 Soyuz 38 (USSR 45): 18 Sep, Yuri Romanenko, Arnaldo Mendez, 7 day 20 hr 43 min 24 sec – Mendez from Cuba.
77 Soyuz T3 (USSR 46): 27 Nov, Leonid Kizim, Oleg Makarov, Gennadi Strekalov, 12 day 19 hr 7 min 42 sec – maintenance crew for *Salyut 6*.

1981

78 Soyuz T4 (USSR 47): 12 Mar, Vladimir Kovalyonok, Viktor Savinykh, 74 day 17 hr 37 min 23 sec – *Salyut 6* space station crew.
79 Soyuz 39 (USSR 48): 22 Mar, Vladimir Dzhanibvekov, Jugderdemidyin Gurragcha, 7 day 20 hr 42 min 3 sec – *Salyut 6* visit, Gurragcha from Mongolia.
80 Columbia STS 1 (USA 32): 12 Apr, John Young, Bob Crippen, 2 day 6 hr 20 min 52 sec – maiden flight of Space Shuttle.
81 Soyuz 40 (USSR 49): 15 May, Leonid Popov, Dumitru Prunariu, 7 day 20 hr 41 min 52 sec – crew for *Salyut 6* space station, Prunariu from Romania.
82 Columbia STS 2 (USA 33): 12 Nov, Joe Engle, Dick Truly, 2 day 6 hr 13 min 11 sec – second test flight.

1982

83 Columbia STS 3 (USA 34): 22 Mar, Jack Lousma, Gordon Fullerton, 8 day 0 hr 4 min 46 sec – third test flight.
84 Soyuz T5 (USSR 50): 13 May, Anatoli Berezevoi, Valentin Lebedev, 211 day 9 hr 4 min 32 sec – first visit to *Salyut 7*.
85 Soyuz T6 (USSR 51): 24 Jun, Vladimir Dzhanibekov, Alexander Ivanchenkov, Jean-Loup Chrétien, 7 day 21 hr 50 min 52 sec – visit to *Salyut 7*, Chrétien from France.
86 Columbia STS 4 (USA 35): 27 Jun, Ken Mattingly, Hank Hartsfield, 7 day 1 hr 9 min 31 sec – military flight.
87 Soyuz T7 (USSR 52): 19 Aug, Leonid Popov, Alexander Serebrov, Svetlana Savitskaya, 7 day 21 hr 52 min 24 sec – Savitskaya second woman in space.
88 Columbia STS 5 (USA 36): 11 Nov, Vance Brand, Robert Overmyer, Joe Allen, William Lenoir, 5 day 2 hr 14 min 26 sec –first commercial mission of Shuttle.

1983

89 Challenger STS 6 (USA 37): 4 Apr, Paul Weitz, Karol Bobko, Don Peterson, Story Musgrave, 5 day 0 hr 23 min 42 sec – deployed Tracking and Data Relay satellite 1.
90 Soyuz T8 (USSR 53): 20 Apr, Vladimir Titov, Gennadi Strekalov, Alexander Serebrov, 2 day 0 hr 17 min 48 sec – failed to dock with *Salyut 7*.
91 Challenger STS 7 (USA 38): 18 Jun, Bob Crippen, Rick Hauck, John Fabian, Sally Ride, Norman Thagard, 6 day 2 hr 24 min 10 sec – satellite deployment mission, first US woman in space.
92 Soyuz T9 (USSR 54): 27 Jun, Vladimir Lyakhov, Alexander Alexandrov, 149 day 10 hr 46 min – *Salyut 7* mission.
93 Challenger STS 8 (USA 39): 30 Aug, Richard Truly, Dan Brandenstein, Guoin Bluford, Dale Gardner, William Thornton, 6 day 1 hr 8 min 40 sec – night launch and landing.
Soyuz T10-1 (USSR): 27 Sep, Vladimir Titov, Gennadi Strekalov, 5 min 30 sec – launcher exploded on pad, crew saved by launch escape system.
94 Columbia STS 9 (USA 40): 28 Nov, John Young, Brewster Shaw, Owen Garriott, Robert Parker, Byron Lichtenberg, Ulf Merbold, 10 day 7 hr 47 min 23 sec – *Spacelab 1*, Merbold from Germany.

1984

95 Challenger STS 41B (USA 41): 3 Feb, Vance Brand, Robert Gibson, Bruce McCandless, Robert Stewart, Ronald McNair, 7 day 23 hr 15 min 54 sec – first independent spacewalk using Manned Manoeuvring Unit by McCandless.
96 Soyuz T10 (USSR 55): 8 Feb, Leonid Kizim, Vladimir Solovyov, Oleg Atkov, 236 day 22 hr 49 min 4 sec – longest manned space mission.
97 Soyuz T11 (USSR 56): 3 Apr, Yuri Malyshev, Gennadi Strekalov, Rakesh Sharma, 7 day 21 hr 40 min – visit to *Salyut 7*, Sharma from India.
98 Challenger STS 41C (USA 42): 6 Apr, Bob Crippen, Dick Scobee, George Nelson, Terry Hart, James van Hoften, 6 day 23 hr 40 min 5 sec – repaired Solar Max satellite
99 Soyuz T12 (USSR 57): 17 Jul, Vladimir Dhzanibekov, Svetlana Savitskaya, Oleg Volk, 11 day 19 hr 14 min 36 sec – Savitskaya became first woman spacewalker (outside *Salyut 7*).
100 Discovery STS 41D (USA 43): 30 Aug, Hank Hartsfield, Michael Coats, Judy Resnik, Steven Hawley, Michael Mullane, Charlie Walker, 6 day 0 hr 56 min 4 sec – three satellites deployed.
101 Challenger STS 41G (USA 44): 5 Oct, Bob Crippen, Jon McBride, Sally Ride, Kathy Sullivan, David Leestma, Marc Garneau, Paul Scully Power, 8 day 5 hr 23 min 33 sec – Sullivan first US woman to spacewalk, Garneau from Canada.
102 Discovery STS 51A (USA 45): 8 Nov, Rick Hauck, Dave Walker, Joe Allen, Dale Gardner, Anna Fisher, 7 day 23 hr 45 min 54 sec – two spacewalks to retrieve lost communications satellites.

FIRSTS IN MANNED SPACEFLIGHT

In space: Yuri Gagarin (USSR) 12 Apr 1961
American in orbit: John Glenn 20 Feb 1962
Woman in space: Valentina Tereshkova (USSR) 16 Jun 1963
Walk in space: Alexei Leonov (USSR) 18 Mar 1965
Person to make two flights: Gus Grissom (USA) 25 Mar 1965
Spacecraft manoeuvres: *Gemini 3* (USA) 25 Mar 1965
Rendezvous in space: *Gemini 6* and *7* (USA) 16 Dec 1965
Docking: *Gemini 8* (USA) 16 Mar 1966
Night launch: *Soyuz 1* (USSR) 23 Apr 1967
Flight to the Moon: *Apollo 8* (USA) 21 Dec 1968
Solo lunar orbit flight: John Young (USA) 18 May 1969
Landing on the Moon: *Apollo 11* (USA) 16 Jul 1969
Men on the Moon: Neil Armstrong and Buzz Aldrin (USA) 16 Jul 1969
Night landing: *Soyuz 10* (USSR) 23 Apr 1971
Military mission: *Soyuz 14* (USSR) 3 Jul 1974
Non-US, non-Soviet spaceman: Vladimir Remek (Cze) 2 Mar 1978
Independent spacewalk: Bruce McCandless (USA) 3 Feb 1984
Woman spacewalker: Svetlana Savitskaya (USSR) 17 Jul 1984
Mother in space: *Anna Fisher* (USA) 8 Nov 1984
Passenger-observer: Jake Garn (USA) 12 Apr 1985
Person to be launched on both Russian and US rockets: Sergei Krikalev (Rus) who flew *Soyuz TM7* (1988), *TM12* (1991) and *STS 60* (1994)
Briton in space: Helen Sharman 18 May 1991

■ *The* Apollo 17 *mission in 1972 was the last manned expedition to the Moon. The rocket landed east of the Sea of Serenity and astronauts brought back 110 kg of Moon rocks*

1985

103 Discovery STS 51C (USA 46): 24 Jan, Ken Mattingly, Loren Shriver, Ellison Onizuka, James Buchli, Gary Payton, 3 day 1 hr 33 min 13 sec – military mission.
104 Discovery STS 51D (USA 47): 12 Apr, Karol Bobko, Don Williams, Rhea Seddon, Jeff Hoffman, David Griggs, Charlie Walker, Jake Garn, 6 day 23 hr 55 min 23 sec – deployed three communications satellites, Senator Jake Garn first passenger observer in space.
105 Challenger STS 51B (USA 48): 29 Apr, Bob Overmyer, Fred Gregory, Don Lind, William Thornton, Norman Thagard, Lodewijk van den Berg, Taylor Wang, 7 day 8 min 50 sec – *Spacelab 3* research mission.
106 Soyuz T13 (USSR 58): 6 Jun, Vladimir Dzhanibekov, Viktor Savinykh, 112 day 3 hr 12 min – complete overhaul of *Salyut 7* after systems failures.
107 Discovery STS 51G (USA 49): 17 Jun, Dan Brandenstein, John Creighton, Shannon Lucid, Steve Nagel, John Fabian, Patrick Baudry, Abdul Aziz Al-Saud, 7 day 1 hr 38 min 58 sec – satellite deployment and research mission, Prince Abdul Aziz Al-Saud from Saudi Arabia.
108 Challenger STS 51F (USA 50): 20 Jul, Gordon Fullerton, Roy Bridges, Karl Henize, Anthony England, Story Musgrave, John-David Bartoe, Loren Acton, 7 day 22 hr 45 min 27 sec – *Spacelab 2* research mission.
109 Discovery STS 51I (USA 51): 27 Aug, Joe Engle, Dick Covey, William Fisher, James van Hoften, Mike Lounge, 7 day 2 hr 14 min 42 sec – three satellites deployed, *Leasat 3* captured, repaired and redeployed, spacewalks.
110 Soyuz T14 (USSR 59): 17 Sep, Vladimir Vasyutin, Georgi Grechko, Alexander Volkov, 64 day 21 hr 52 min – mission cut short after Vasyutin became ill.
111 Atlantis STS 51J (USA 52): 3 Oct, Karol Bobko, Ron Grabe, Dale Hilmers, Bob Stewart, William Pailes, 4 day 1 hr 45 min 30 sec – military mission.
112 Challenger STS 61A (USA 53): 30 Oct, Hank Hartsfield, Steve Nagel, Bonnie Dunbar, Guion Gluford, James Buchli, Ernst Messerschmitt, Reinhard Furrer, Wubbo Ockels, 7 day 44 min 51 sec – West German-funded *Spacelab D1* mission, Ockels from Netherlands, record eight-up mission.
113 Atlantis STS 61B (USA 54): 27 Nov, Brewster Shaw, Bryan O'Connor, Mary Cleave, Jerry Ross, Sherwood Spring, Rudolpho Neri Vela, Charlie Walker, 6 day 21 hr 4 min 50 sec – Neri Vela from Mexico, assembled structures during spacewalks.

1986

114 Columbia STS 61C (USA 55): 12 Jan, Robert Gibson, Charles Bolden, Franklin Chang-Diaz, George Nelson, Steve Hawley, Robert Cenker, Bill Nelson, 6 day 2 hr 4 min 9 sec – most-delayed mission.
Challenger STS 51L (USA): 28 Jan, Dick Scobee, Mike Smith, Judith Resnik, Ronald McNair, Ellison Onizuka, Christa McAuliffe, Gregory Jarvis, 73 sec – disintegrated at 14,330 m (47,000 ft), crew killed, first flight to take off but not to reach space, first US in-flight fatalities.
115 Soyuz T15 (USSR 60): 13 Mar, Leonid Kizim, Vladimir Solovyov, 125 day 0 hr 1 min – first mission to new space station *Mir*, also docked with *Salyut 7*.

1987

116 Soyuz TM2 (USSR 61): 5 Feb, Yuri Romanenko, Alexander Laveikin, 326 day 11 hr 38 min –record duration mission by Romanenko aboard *Mir.*
117 Soyuz TM3 (USSR 62): 22 Jul, Alexander Viktorenko, Alexander Alexandrov, Muhammed Faris, 7 day 23 hr 4 min 5 sec – Faris from Syria.
118 Soyuz TM4 (USSR 63): 21 Dec, Vladimir Titov, Musa Manarov, Anatoli Levchenko, 365 day 22 hr 39 min – Titov and Manarov make year-long flight.

1988

119 Soyuz TM5 (USSR 64): 7 Jun, Anatoli Solovyov, Viktor Savinykh, Alexander Alexandrov, 9 day 20 hr 10 min – *Mir* mission.
120 Soyuz TM6 (USSR 65): 31 Aug, Vladimir Lyakhov, Valeri Polyakov, Abdol Mohmand, 8 day 20 hr 27 min – Mohmand from Afghanistan.
121 Discovery STS 26 (USA 56): 29 Sep, Rick Hauck, Dick Covey, Mike Lounge, David Hilmers, George Nelson, 4 day 1 hr 0 min 11 sec – America's return to space 32 months after *Challenger* disaster.
122 Soyuz TM7 (USSR 66): 26 Nov, Alexander Volkov, Sergei Krikalev, Jean-Loup Chrétien. 151 day 11 hr 10 min – visit to *Mir*, Chrétien (French) first non-American, non-Soviet to make a spacewalk.
123 Atlantis STS 27 (USA 57): 2 Dec, Robert Gibson, Guy Gardner, Jerry Ross, Mike Mullane, William Shepherd, 4 day 9 hr 5 min 35 sec – military mission.

1989

124 Discovery STS 29 (USA 58): 13 Mar, Michael Coats, John Blaha, James Buchli, James Bagian, Robert Springer, 4 day 23 hr 38 min 52 sec – deployed Tracking and Data Relay satellite.
125 Atlantis STS 30 (USA 59): 4 May, David Walker, Ron Grabe, Norman Thagard, Mary Cleave, Mark Lee, 4 day 0 hr 57 min 31 sec – deployed *Magellan* Venus orbiter.
126 Columbia STS 28 (USA 60): 8 Aug, Brewster Shaw, Richard Richards, David Leestma, James Adamson, Mark Brown, 5 day 1 hr 0 min 9 sec – military mission to deploy KH-12 spy satellite.
127 Soyuz TM8 (USSR 67): 6 Sep, Alexander Viktorenko, Alexander Serebrov, 166 day 6 hr 58 min – occupied *Mir* space station. First Soviet test of tethered Manned Manoeuvring Unit.
128 Atlantis STS 34 (USA 61): 18 Oct, Donald Williams, Michael McCulley, Shannon Lucid, Franklin Chang-Diaz, Ellen Baker, 4 day 23 hr 39 min 24 sec – deployed Jupiter orbiter *Galileo.*
129 Discovery STS 33 (USA 62): 22 Nov, Frederick Gregory, John Blaha, Story Musgrave, Manley Carter, Kathryn Thornton, 5 day 0 hr 6 min 46 sec – military mission.

1990

130 Columbia STS 32 (USA 63): 9 Jan, Dan Brandenstein, James Wetherbee, Bonnie Dunbar, Marsha Ivins, David Low, 10 day 21 hr 0 min 37 sec – retrieved Long Exposure Duration Facility satellite from orbit.
131 Soyuz TM9 (USSR 68): 11 Feb, Anatoli Solovyov, Alexander Balandin, 179 day 2 hr 19 min – occupation of *Mir* space station, executed 7 hr spacewalk, a Soviet record .
132 Atlantis STS 36 (USA 64): 28 Feb, John Creighton, John Caspar, Mike Mullane, David Hilmers, Pierre Thuot, 4 day 10 hr 18 min 22 sec – military mission.
133 Discovery STS 31 (USA 65): 24 Apr, Loren Shriver, Charles Bolden, Steven Hawley, Bruce McCandless, Kathryn Sullivan, 5 day 1 hr 16 min 6 sec – deployed Hubble Space Telescope.
134 Soyuz TM10 (USSR 69): 1 Aug, Gennadi Manakov, Gennadi Strekalov, 130 day 19 hr 36 min –occupation of *Mir* space station.
135 Discovery STS 41 (USA 66): 6 Oct, Richard Richards, Robert Canbana, Thomas Akers, Bruce Melnick, William Shepherd, 4 day 2 hr 10 min 12 sec – deployed *Ulysses* solar polar orbiter.
136 Atlantis STS 38 (USA 67): 15 Nov, Richard Covey, Frank Culbertson, Robert Springer, Carl Meade, Sam Gemar, 4 day 21 hr 54 min 27 sec – military mission.
137 Columbia STS 35 (USA 68): 2 Dec, Vance Brand, Guy Gardner, Jeff Hoffman, Mike Lounge, Robert Parker, Ronald Parise, Samuel Durrance, 8 day 23 hr 5 min 7 sec – Astro-1 observatory.
138 Soyuz TM11 (USSR 70): 2 Dec, Viktor Afanasyef, Musa Manarov, Toyohiro Akiyama, 175 day 1 hr 51 min 18 sec – *Mir* mission, Akiyama a Japanese journalist.

1991

139 Atlantis STS 37 (USA 69): 5 Apr, Steven Nagel, Ken Cameron, Jay Apt, Linda Godwin, Jerry Ross, 5 day 23 hr 33 min 44 sec – development of Gamma Ray Observatory.
140 Discovery STS 39 (USA 70): 28 Apr, Michael Coats, Blaine Hammond, Guion Bluford, Gregory Harbaugh, Richard Heib, Donald McMonagle, Charles Veach, 8 day 7 hr 22 min 2 sec – Star Wars research mission.
141 Soyuz TM12 (USSR 71): 18 May, Anatoli Artsebarski, Sergei Krikalyov, Helen Sharman, 144 day 15 hr 22 min – Sharman first Briton in space, returned in *TM11*.
142 Columbia STS 40 (USA 71): 5 Jun, Bryan O'Connor, Sidney Gutierrez, James Bagian, Tamara Jernigan, Rhea Seddon, Drew Gaffney, Millie Hughes-Fulford, 9 day 2 hr 14 min 20 sec – Spacelab Life Sciences 1 mission.
143 Atlantis STS43 (USA 72): 2 Aug, John Blaha, Michael Baker, James Adamson, David Low, Shannon Lucid, 8 day 21 hr 21 min 25 sec – deployed Tracking and Data Relay satellite.
144 Discovery STS 48 (USA 73): 12 Sep, John Creighton, Kenneth Reightler, Mark Brown, James Buchli, Sam Gemar, 5 day 8 hr 27 min 34 sec – deployment of Upper Atmosphere Research satellite (UARS).
145 Soyuz TM13 (USSR 72): 2 Oct, Alexander Volkov, Taktar Aubakirov, Franz Viebock, 175 day 2 hr 52 min – Aubakirov first Kazakh and Viebock first Austrian in space.
146 Atlantis STS 44 (USA 74): 24 Nov, Frederick Gregory, Terence Henricks, Story Musgrave, Mario Runco, James Voss, Thomas Hennen, 6 day 22 hr 50 min 42 sec – deployed DSP early warning satellite and conducted reconnaissance mission, with first US 'space spy' Hennen.

1992

147 Discovery STS 42 (USA 75): 22 Jan, Ronald Grabe, Stephen Oswald, Norman Thagard, David Hilmers, William Readdy, Roberta Bondar, Ulf Merbold, 8 day 1 hr 14 min 45 sec – International Microgravity Laboratory mission.
148 Soyuz TM14 (Russia 1): 17 Mar, Alexander Viktorenko, Alexander Kaleri, Klaus Dietrich Flade, 145 day 14 hr 10 min – new residents for *Mir.*
149 Atlantis STS 45 (USA 76): 24 Mar, Charles Bolden, Brian Duffy, Kathryn Sullivan, Michael Foale, David Leestma, Byron Lichtenberg, Dirk Frimout, 8 day 22 hr 9 min 25 sec – Atlas science mission, Frimout first Belgian in space.
150 Endeavour STS 49 (USA 77): 7 May, Dan Brandenstein, Kevin Chilton, Rick Hieb, Bruce Melnick, Pierre Thuot, Kathryn Thornton, Tom Akers, 8 day 21 hr 17 min 38 sec – retrieved *Intelsat 6* and re-boosted it into geo-stationary orbit. Record-breaking 8 hr 29 min spacewalk by Thuot, Hieb and Akers.
151 Columbia STS 50 (USA 78): 25 Jun, Richard Richards, Kenneth Bowersox, Bonnie Dunbar, Ellen Baker, Carl Meade, Lawrence De Lucas, Eugene Trinh, 13 day 19 hr 30 min 4 sec – US Microgravity Laboratory mission 1.
152 Soyuz TM15 (Russia 2): 27 Jul, Anatoli Solovyov, Sergei Avdeyev, Michel Tognini, 188 day 21 hr 40 min – new occupation of *Mir.*
153 Atlantis STS 46 (USA 79): 31 Jul 1992, Loren Shriver, Andrew Allen, Claude Nicollier, Marsha Ivins, Jeff Hoffman, Franklin-Chang Diaz, Franco Malerba, 7 day 23 hr 15 min 5 sec – deployed Eureca and Tethered satellites, Nicollier first Swiss astronaut, Malerba first Italian in space.

■ THERE HAVE BEEN A TOTAL OF 146 SPACEWALKS, OF WHICH 14 WERE ON THE MOON ■

5 MOST EXPERIENCED PERSONS IN SPACE

	NO. OF FLIGHTS	TIME day	hr
1 **Valeri Poliakov** (Rus)	2	678	16
2 **Musa Manarov** (USSR/Rus)	2	541	0
3 **Alexander Viktorenko** (USSR/Rus)	4	489	1
4 **Sergei Krikalev** (USSR/Rus)*	3	471	14
5 **Anatoli Solovyov** (USSR/Rus)*	4	457	7

* includes time on US Space Shuttle

Note: The most experienced woman in space is Shannon Lucid (USA) who has made five flights and spent a total of 223 days 5 hours (including time on Russian *Mir* space station) in space

154 Endeavour STS 47 (USA 80): 12 Sep, Robert Gibson, Curtis Brown, Mark Lee, Jay Apt, Jan Davis, Mae Jemison, Mamoru Mohri, 7 day 22 hr 31 min 11 sec – Japan's Spacelab J mission, Lee and Davis first married couple.
155 Columbia STS 52 (USA 81): 22 Oct, James Wetherbee, Michael Baker, Charles Veach, William Shepherd, Tamara Jernigan, Steven MacLean, 9 day 20 hr 56 min 13 sec – science research mission.
156 Discovery STS 53 (USA 82): 2 Dec, David Walker, Robert Cabana, Guion Bluford, James Voss, Michael Clifford, 7 day 7 hr 19 min 17 sec – final US Dept. of Defense Shuttle mission.

1993
157 Endeavour STS 54 (USA 83): 13 Jan, John Casper, Donald McMonagle, Gregory Harbaugh, Mario Runco, Susan Helms, 5 day 23 hr 38 min 17 sec – satellite deployment, science spacewalk mission.
158 Soyuz TM16 (Russia 3): 24 Jan, Gennadi Manakov, Alexander Polishchuk, 19 day 0 hr 44 min – crew rotation flight to *Mir* space station.
159 Discovery STS 56 (USA 84): 8 Apr, Kenneth Cameron, Stephen Oswald, Michael Foale, Kenneth Cockrell, Ellen Ochoa, 9 day 6 hr 8 min 19 sec – Atlas 2 laboratory mission.
160 Columbia STS 55 (USA 85): 26 Apr, Steven Nagel, Tom Henricks, Jerry Ross, Charles Precourt, Bernard Harris, Ulrich Walter, Hans W. Schlegel, 9 day 23 hr 39 min 59 sec – German-funded Spacelab D2 mission.
161 Endeavour STS 57 (USA 86): 21 Jun, Ronald Grabe, Brian Duffy, David Low, Nancy Sherlock, Jeff Wisoff, Janice Voss, 9 day 23 hr 46 min 1 sec – *Eureca* retrieval.
162 Soyuz TM17 (Russia 4): 1 Jul, Vasili Tsiblyev, Alexander Serebrov, Jean-Pierre Haignere, 196 days 17 hr 45 min – crew rotation to *Mir,* Serebrov made five mission spacewalks, bringing his total to ten, a record.
163 Discovery STS 51 (USA 87): 12 Sep, Frank Culbertson, William Readdy, James Newman, Daniel Bursch, Carl Walz, 9 day 20 hr 11 min 7 sec – deployed ACTS communications satellite.
164 Columbia STS 58 (USA 88): 18 Oct, John Blaha, Richard Searfoss, Rhea Seddon, William McArthur, David Wolf, Shannon Lucid, Martin Fettmann, 14 day 0 hr 13 min 32 sec – Spacelab Life Sciences 2 mission.
165 Endeavour STS 61 (USA 89): 2 Dec, Richard Covey, Ken Bowersox, Claude Nicollier, Story Musgrave, Jeff Hoffman, Tom Akers, Kathryn Thornton, 10 day 19 hr 58 min 33 sec – Hubble space telescope servicing and repair mission.

1994
166 Soyuz TM18 (Russia 5): 8 Jan, Viktor Afanasyev, Yuri Usachev, Valeri Poliakov, 182 day 0 hr 27 min – new residency aboard *Mir* space station, Poliakov remained on *Mir* for record 437-day stay.
167 Discovery STS 60 (USA 90): 3 Feb, Charles Bolden, Kenneth Reightler, Franklin-Chang Diaz, Jan Davis, Ron Sega, Sergei Krikalev, 8 day 7 hr 9 min 22 sec – Krikalev first Russian on a US mission.
168 Columbia STS 62 (USA 91): 4 Mar, John Casper, Andrew Allen, Pierre Thuot, Sam Gemar, Marsha Ivins, 13 day 23 hr 16 min 33 sec – third Extended Duration Orbiter mission.
169 Endeavour STS 59 (USA 92): 9 Apr, Sidney Gutierrez, Kevin Chilton, Linda Godwin, Jay Apt, Michael Clifford, Thomas Johns, 11 day 5 hr 49 min 30 sec – Space Radar Laboratory mission.
170 Soyuz TM19 (Russia 6): 1 Jul, Yuri Malenchencko, Talgat Musabayev, 125 day 22 hr 53 min – new *Mir* crew.
171 Columbia STS 65 (USA 93): 8 Jul, Robert Cabana, James Halsell, Richard Hieb, Carl Walz, Leroy Chiao, Donald Thomas, Chiaki Naito-Mukai, 14 day 17 hr 55 min 1 sec – International Microgravity Laboratory 2 mission.
172 Discovery STS 64 (USA 94): 9 Sep, Dick Richards, Blaine Hammond, Carl Meade, Mark Lee, Susan Helms, Jerry Linenger, 10 day 22 hr 49 min 57 sec – Earth observation, science and spacewalk mission.
173 Endeavour STS 68 (USA 95): 30 Sep, Mike Baker, Terry Wilcutt, Tom Jones, Steve Smith, Jeff Wisoff, Dan Bursch, 11 day 5 hr 46 min 9 sec – Space Radar Laboratory 2 mission for Earth observation.
174 Soyuz TM20 (Russia 7): 3 Oct, Alexander Viktorenko, Yelena Kondakova, Ulf Merbold, 169 day 5 hr 21 min 20 sec – Kondakova first woman to make a long duration space flight.
175 Atlantis STS 66 (USA 96): 3 Nov, Donald McMonagle, Curtis Brown, Ellen Ochoa, Scott Parazynsky, Joseph Tanner, Jean-Francois Clervoy, 10 day 22 hr 34 min 2 sec – Atlas 3 Earth atmosphere research mission.

1995
176 Discovery STS 63 (USA 97): 3 Feb, James Wetherbee, Eileen Collins, Michael Foale, Bernard Harris, Janice Ford, Vladimir Titov, 8 day 6 hr 28 min 15 sec – rendezvous with *Mir* space station.
177 Endeavour STS 67 (USA 98): 2 Mar, Stephen Oswald, Bill Gregory, Wendy Lawrence, Tamara Jernigan, John Grunsfield, Sam Durrance, Ron Parise, 16 day 15 hr 8 min 47 sec – Astro 2 astronomy mission.
178 Soyuz TM21 (Russia 8): 14 Mar, Vladimir Dezhurov, Gennadi Strekalov, Norman Thagard: 115 day 8 hr 44 min – mission to *Mir* with first US astronaut.
179 Atlantis STS 71 (USA 99): 27 Jun, Robert Gibson, Charles Precourt, Ellen Baker, Bonnie Dunbar, Gregory Harbaugh, Anatoli Solovyov, Nikolai Budarin, 9 day 19 hr 23 min 7 sec – first Shuttle/*Mir* docking mission.
180 Discovery STS 70 (USA 100): 13 Jul, Tom Henricks, Kevin Kregal, Don Thomas, Nancy Sherlock, Mary Ellen Weber, 8 day 23 hr 20 min 5 sec – deployed Tracking and Data Relay satellite.
181 Soyuz TM22 (Russia 9): 3 Sep, Yuri Gidzenko, Sergei Avdeyev, Thomas Reiter, 179 day 1 hr 42 min – new shift for *Mir.*
182 Endeavour STS 69 (USA 101): 7 Sep, David Walker, Ken Cockrell, James Voss, James Newman, Mike Gernhardt, 10 day 20 hr 29 min 52 sec – deployments, retrievals, spacewalk.
183 Columbia STS 73 (USA 102): 20 Oct, Ken Bowersox, Kent Rominger, Kathryn Thornton, Michael Lopez-Algeria, Catherine Coleman, Fred Leslie, Albert Sacco, 15 day 21 hr 52 min – US Microgravity Laboratory 2.
184 Atlantis STS 74 (USA 103): 12 Nov, Ken Cameron, James Halsall, Jerry Ross, Bill McArthur, Chris Hadfield, 8 day 4 hr 30 min 44 sec – second Shuttle/Mir docking mission.

1996
185 Endeavour STS 72 (USA 104): 11 Jan, Brian Duffy, Brent Jett, Leroy Chiao, Daniel Barry, Winston Scott, Kiochi Wakata, 8 day 22 hr 0 min 41 sec – deployment, retrieval, spacewalk mission.
186 Soyuz TM23 (Russia 10): 21 Feb, Yuri Onufrienko, Yuri Usachev, 172 day 1 hr 30 min – new crew for *Mir.*
187 Columbia STS 75 (USA 105): 22 Feb, Andrew Allen, Scott Horowitz, Maurizio Cheli, Claude Nicollier, Jeff Hoffman, Franklin Chang-Diaz, Umberto Guidoni, 15 day 17 hr 40 min 22 sec – tethered satellite System reflight, tether breaks.
188 Atlantis STS 76 (USA 106): 22 Mar, Kevin Chilton, Richard Searfoss, Ronald Sega, Rich Clifford, Linda Godwin, Shannon Lucid, 9 day 5 hr 15 min 53 sec – delivered Shannon Lucid to *Mir*.
189 Endeavour STS 77 (USA 107): 19 May, John Casper, Curtis Brown, Dan Bursch, Mario Runco, Andrew Thomas, Marc Garneau, 10 day 0 hr 39 min 18 sec – deployments, retrievals.
190 Columbia STS 78 (USA 108): 20 Jun, Tom Henricks, Kevin Kregal, Susan Helms, Charles Brady, Richard Linnehan, Jean-Jacques Favier, Robert Thirsk, 16 day 21 hr 47 min 45 sec – life and microgravity mission.
191 Soyuz TM24 (Russia 11): 17 Aug, Valeri Korzun, Alexander Kaleri, Claudie Andre-Deshays, 196 day 16 hr 26 min – new *Mir* crew, French visitor.
192 Atlantis STS 79 (USA 109): 16 Sep, William Readdy, Terrence Wilcutt, Tom Akers, Jerome Apt, Carl Walz, John Blaha, 10 day 13 hr 18 min 26 sec – delivered Blaha to *Mir* and returned Lucid.
193 Columbia STS 80 (USA 110): 19 Nov, Ken Cockrell, Kent Rominger, Tamara Jernigan, Thomas Jones, Story Musgrave, 17 day 15 hr 53 min 26 sec – deployments, retrievals, Musgrave oldest space traveller at 61.

1997
194 Atlantis STS 81 (USA 111): 12 Jan, Michael Baker, Brent Jett, John Grunsfield, Jeff Wisoff, Marsha Ivins, Jerry Linenger, 10 day 4 hr 55 min 22 sec – delivered Linenger to *Mir* and returned Blaha.
195 Soyuz TM25 (Russia 12): 10 Feb, Vasili Tsiblyev, Alexander Lazutkin, Reinhold Ewald, still in orbit – new *Mir* crew, German visitor.
196 Discovery STS 82 (USA 112): 11 Feb, Ken Bowersox, Scott Horowitz, Steven Haweley, Mark Lee, Gregory Harbaugh, Steve Smith, Joe Tanner, 9 day 23 hr 37 min 9 sec – spacewalk servicing Hubble.
197 Columbia STS 83 (USA 113): 4 Apr, Jim Halsell, Susan Still, Janice Voss, Donald Thomas, Mike Gernhardt, Roger Crouch, Gregory Linteris, 3 day 23 hr 12 min 39 sec – aborted microgravity flight.

■ *Astronaut Leroy Chiao spacewalks outside the Shuttle* Endeavour *as it passes over Australia on 17 January 1996*

Religious Festivals

- **The Jewish festival of 'Passover' gets its name from the eve of the Jewish flight from Egypt when the last of the ten plagues 'passed over' the homes of the Israelites, killing only the firstborn sons of the Egyptians.**
- **In England, Shrove Tuesday is also known as Pancake Day, when pancakes are prepared from eggs and fats (foods which are discouraged during the time of Lent), and eaten as part of a celebratory feast.**
- **In Pre-Islamic western Arabia, Ramadan was the month during which all tribal warfare was suspended.**

CHRISTIAN FESTIVALS

In some Roman Catholic countries, the celebration of Catholic festivals that fall during the week are being transferred to the nearest Sunday.

Epiphany – 6 January
The Festival of the Epiphany commemorates the manifestation of the infant Christ to the Magi or 'wise men'. It is a public holiday in several European countries.

Shrove Tuesday – Any Tuesday between 3 February and 9 March
This last day before the start of Lent was originally set aside for the confession of sins ('shrove' is the past tense of 'shrive', meaning 'to hear confession'). Later, it came to be marked by festivities before the rigours of Lent and is celebrated by carnivals in such countries as Portugal, Brazil and parts of Germany.

Ash Wednesday – Any Wednesday between 4 February and 10 March
The first day of Lent takes its name from the custom of scattering ashes on the heads of penitents (nowadays shown by Christians marking their foreheads with ashes in the sign of the Cross).

Lent – February to March or March to April
Lent is a period of 40 days beginning on Ash Wednesday and ending at midnight on Holy Saturday, the day before Easter. Lent is observed as a period of reflection, repentance and preparation for Easter – a reminder of Christ's time spent in the wilderness.

■ *This Corpus Christi procession in Seville, Spain, is honouring the body* (corpus) *of Christ in the Eucharist*

Palm Sunday – Any Sunday between 15 March and 18 April
The last Sunday of Lent marks Christ's entry into Jerusalem when His way was lined by palm branches.

Maundy Thursday – Any Thursday between 19 March and 22 April
Observed on the last Thursday of Lent, it takes its name from the Latin *dies mandati*, meaning 'the day of the mandate', referring to the mandate given by Christ to His disciples to love one another. In the Roman Catholic Church it is marked by the symbolic washing of feet by the priest, in commemoration of Christ washing the feet of the disciples.

Good Friday – Any Friday between 20 March and 23 April
This commemoration of the Crucifixion is a public holiday in most Christian countries.

Holy Saturday (or Easter Eve) – Any Saturday between 21 March and 24 April
Often wrongly called 'Easter Saturday', Holy Saturday is the last day of Lent.

Easter Day – Any Sunday between 22 March and 25 April
The celebration of the Resurrection of Christ falls on the first Sunday after the Full Moon that happens on or following 21 March. If the Full Moon falls upon a Sunday, Easter is celebrated upon the following Sunday. A hypothetical 'calendar Moon' whose cycles alternate in periods of 30 and 29 days is used in these calculations. Festivities in Orthodox Churches take place later because they still use the Julian calendar. The day following Easter Sunday is a public holiday in most Christian countries.

Ascension Day – Any Thursday between 30 April and 3 June
The Ascension of Christ into Heaven, celebrated 40 days after Easter Day, is a public holiday in many Christian countries.

Pentecost (Whit Sunday) – Any Sunday between 10 May and 13 June
Pentecost, falling seven weeks after Easter Day, commemorates the descent of the Holy Spirit upon the apostles. Its English name 'Whit' Sunday is said to come from 'White' Sunday in a reference to the white robes worn by the newly baptized. Whit Monday is also a public holiday in some Christian countries.

Trinity Sunday – Any Sunday between 17 May and 20 June
This is a celebration of the Holy Trinity.

Corpus Christi – Any Thursday between 21 May and 24 June
Held in devotion to the Eucharist (Holy Communion), this festival is celebrated on the Thursday following Trinity Sunday and is a public holiday in many Catholic countries.

The Assumption – 15 August
This Roman Catholic and (Eastern) Orthodox festival commemorates the doctrine of the assumption of Mary – in both body and soul – into Heaven at the end of her earthly life. It is a public holiday in most Roman Catholic countries and in Greece.

All Saints' Day – 1 November
A celebration of the lives of all the saints of the Church, this is a public holiday in some Christian (mainly Roman Catholic) countries.

All Souls' Day – 2 November
This Catholic festival is a day of prayer for the souls of the departed now in Purgatory and is a public holiday in some Latin American countries.

Advent Sunday – The Sunday nearest to 30 November (any Sunday between 27 November and 3 December)
This day marks the start of the preparation for Christmas and is named after the Latin *adventus* meaning 'coming'.

Immaculate Conception – 8 December
Commemorating the (Roman Catholic) doctrine that Mary was conceived free from the effects of original sin, this festival is a public holiday in some Catholic countries.

Christmas Eve – 24 December
The day before the celebration of Christmas is a public holiday in a few Christian countries.

Christmas Day – 25 December
This celebration of the birth of Christ to Mary at Bethlehem in *c.* 4 BC has been celebrated by Christians from the earliest times. However, there is no proof that this historical event took place on 25 December. Although Orthodox Churches celebrate Christmas on 25 December, their festivities take place in January.

St Stephen's Day – 26 December
The day following Christmas Day is traditionally when Christmas 'boxes' or presents are exchanged. St Stephen's Day (known as Boxing Day in some English-speaking countries) is a public holiday in some countries.

JEWISH FESTIVALS

Jewish festivals commence on the evening of the dates shown and last until sunset on the following day. Other festivals are celebrated according to the Jewish calendar (see p. 21). The equivalent date in the Gregorian calendar varies from one year to another.

Rosh Hodesh: A monthly festival celebrating the new Moon.

15 Shebat – Tu B'shevat (Festival for New Trees): In modern times, this festival commemorates the planting of trees in Israel.

13 Adar – Taanit Ester (Fast of Ester)

14 Adar – Purim (Festival of Lots): Celebrates the deliverance of Persian Jews from persecution in the 5th century BCE (see Jewish calendar).

14 Nisan – Taanit Behorim (Fast of the First-born)

15 Nisan – Pesah (Passover): Commemorates the Israelites' servitude in Egypt and their subsequent exodus from Egypt.

27 Nisan – Yom Ha-Shoah (Holocaust Day): Commemoration of the victims of the Holocaust (but not marked by a public holiday).

MOVABLE CHRISTIAN HOLIDAYS

Ash Wednesday	Easter Day	Ascension Day	Pentecost (Whit Sunday)	Advent Sunday
1998 25 Feb	1998 12 Apr	1998 21 May	1998 31 May	1998 29 Nov
1999 17 Feb	1999 4 Apr	1999 13 May	1999 23 May	1999 28 Nov
2000 8 Mar	2000 23 Apr	2000 1 Jun	2000 11 Jun	2000 3 Dec
2001 28 Feb	2001 15 Apr	2001 24 May	2001 3 Jun	2001 28 Nov
2002 13 Feb	2002 13 Mar	2002 9 May	2002 19 May	2002 28 Nov

Easter festivals in the Orthodox Church:

Holy Friday (Good Friday)	Orthodox Easter
1998 17 Apr	1998 19 Apr
1999 9 Apr	1999 11 Apr
2000 28 Apr	2000 30 Apr

■ **CURRENT EVIDENCE POINTS TO CHRIST'S BIRTHDAY BEING IN SEPTEMBER, NOT DECEMBER** ■

4 Iyar – Yom H'zikharon (Remembrance Day): Modern commemoration not marked by a public holiday.

18 Iyar – the 33rd Day of 'Counting the Omer'

28 Iyar – Yom Yerushalayim (Jerusalem Day)

6–7 Sivan – Shavuot (the Festival of Weeks, or Pentecost): Festival commemorating the revelation of the Torah (Law) at Sinai.

20 Sivan – the Fast of 20 Sivan

17 Tammuz – the Fast of 17 Tammuz

9 Ab – Tisha B'Av (the Fast of 9 Ab)

15 Ab – Tu B'Av (the Festival of 15 Ab)

1 Elul – Festival of 1 Elul

1–2 Tishri – Rosh Hashanah (New Year): Festival celebrating the New Year of the Jewish calendar which also begins the Ten Days of Penitence ending on Yom Kippur (see below). These ten days are considered the Days of Judgement for all mankind and many rabbinic laws govern behaviour during this time – including the strict prohibition of work as well as the enjoyment of celebrations.

3 Tishri – Tsom Gedaliah (the Fast of Gedaliah)

10 Tishri – Yom Kippur (the Day of Atonement): This most solemn and holy day in the Jewish calendar is spent in prayer and fasting, and sins are confessed in acts of reconciliation.

15 or 16–22 or 23 Tishri – Sukkot (the Festival of Tabernacles): A remembrance of the Israelites' wanderings after the Exodus, Sukkot is named after the booths (*sukkot* means 'booth') that the Israelites lived in during this time and commemorated in Israel by a series of half-day public holidays.

22 or 23 Tishri – Shemini Atzeret (the Eighth Day of Conclusion): Final day of Festival of Tabernacles, celebrated independently.

23 Tishri – Simhat Torah (Rejoicing in the Torah): Festival celebrating the completion of the cycle of readings from the Torah.

25 Kislev – 2 Tebet – Hanukah (the Festival of the Dedication of the Temple, otherwise known as the Festival of Lights): Celebrating the revolt against the Seleucid Empire and the rededication of the Temple in 164 BCE (see Jewish calendar, p. 21), this eight-day festival is characterized by songs, candles, feasting and giving gifts to children.

10 Tebet – the Feast of 10 Tebet

ISLAMIC FESTIVALS

Many of the following festivals are public holidays in Islamic countries. As these holidays are celebrated according to the Islamic lunar calendar (see p. 21), the equivalent date in the Gregorian calendar varies from one year to another.

Day of Assembly – a weekly festival on Friday

1 Muharram – New Year's Day

1–10 Muharram – Muharram (New Year Festival)

12 Rabîa – I Eid Milad-un-Nabi (Festival of the Prophet's Birthday)

26 Rajab – Shab-i-Maraj (Festival of the Prophet's Night Journey and Ascension)

15 Shaabân – Night of Forgiveness

1–29/30 Ramadan – Ramadan: Annual fast lasting a month and demanding abstention from most physical nourishment, dawn to dusk.

1 Shawwâl – Eid-ul-Fitr (Festival of Fast Breaking): Celebrated at the end of Ramadan by feasting and visiting graves.

9 Dhû'l Hijja – Day of Arafat

Dhû'l Hijja – Haj (Pilgrimage to Mecca)

10 Dhû'l Hijja – Eid-ul-Adha (Festival of Sacrifice): Marks the end of the Pilgrimage to Mecca.

WEEKLY DAYS OF REST

The Jewish Sabbath (or *Shabbat*), from sunset on Friday to sunset on Saturday, is the one true day of rest in all religions. God rested from creative work on the seventh day of the week and gave the Jewish people the blessing of a day when they should undertake no mundane work, such as cooking or farming, but devote themselves to spiritual recreation. Humane acts are, of course, encouraged. Jews respond to the Sabbath in various ways, even in Israel. There is a saying, 'Tel Aviv plays, Jerusalem prays'!

Sunday, the first day of the week, is the Christian holy day, celebrating the resurrection of Jesus. Work is forbidden on the holy day, in accordance with the Fourth Commandment. Some Christians follow a strict regime of worship, prayer and Bible study and refuse to participate in sporting events. Others take part in secular enjoyments.

■ *A Muslim says his noon prayers inside the Zamboanga Mosque in the Philippines*

Friday is the Muslim weekly holy day. Even in a country like Saudi Arabia, work stops only during the period of the noon prayer. However, the Western fashion of closing businesses on the Christian and Jewish weekly holy days has caused a number of public offices to be closed for the whole day in some Muslim countries. The day is often spent (by those Muslims who can afford it) in preparing extra food for the poor.

Other religions tend not to have special weekly days. New Moon and Full Moon days are popular in the Islamic, Hindu and Buddhist religions, but believers have to combine observance with the mundane activities of life.

■ *Children celebrate the life of Krishna during the Hindu festival of Kumbha Mela, held once every 12 years*

HINDU FESTIVALS

January
Makar Sankranti: Winter solstice festival.
Pongal: Harvest festival in southern India.
Kumbha Mela: Festival held every 12 years when worshippers bathe in the waters at the confluence of the Ganges and Jumna rivers.

January–February
Vasanta Panchami: Held in honour of the goddess Saraswati.
Mahashivratri ('Great Night of Shiva'): Celebrated by vigils, vows, fasting and worship of the god Shiva.

February–March
Ramakrishna utsav (20 Feb): Festival for the Hindu saint Ramakrishna.
Holi: Boisterous festival characterized by bonfires and the throwing of red powder.
Shivrati: Main festival in honour of Shiva which is spent in meditation.

March–April
Ramanavami: Celebration of the birth of Shi Rama which is observed in sanctity and fasting.
Hanuman Jayanti: Celebration in honour of the god Hanuman.

April–May
Baisakhi: New Year festival celebrated by gift-giving, feasting, praying and bathing in sacred waters.

May–June
Ganga Dussehra: In honour of the goddess Ganga, devotees bathe in the sacred waters of the River Ganges.

June–July
Jagannatha (Ratha-yatra): Celebration of Krishna as the Lord of the Universe.

July–August
Naga Panchami: Festival celebrating the birth of serpents when worshippers empty pots of milk over snakes from the temple of Shiva.
Raksha Bandhan: Old festival in which sisters give wrist decorations to their brothers to ward off evil spirits.

August–September
Ganesh Chaturthi: Festival in honour of the elephant-headed god, Ganesh.
Janmashtani: Festival celebrating the birth of Krishna.

September–October
Dussehra (Durja Puja): Celebration of the goddess Durga during the period of Navratri ('Nine Nights').
Gandhi Jayanti (2 Oct): Celebration of the birth of Mahatma Gandhi.
Diwali (Oct/Nov): Major festival honouring Laksmi, the goddess of wealth, during which time merchants open fresh accounts and festivities include visiting, exchanging gifts, decorating houses, feasting and wearing new clothes.

■ FOOD, DRINK, AND SEXUAL INTERCOURSE ARE FORBIDDEN ALL DAY DURING RAMADAN ■

Measurement of Time

- When Britain adopted the Gregorian calendar in 1752, mobs rioted on the streets demanding their 11 days back.
- Computers record years by using two digits, not four. This may cause them to crash at the end of 1999 – the 'Millennium Timebomb'.
- Subjective time is the perception that time speeds up when you are having fun, but slows down when you are not.
- According to Einstein, the faster you travel, the slower time flows.

TIME

▶ Time, according to one definition, is the continuous passage of existence.
▶ The rate at which time passes depends upon the speed of the observer.

Like distance, time separates events and objects, and so is considered to be one of the four dimensions of reality. In fact, modern physics does not distinguish between space and time, and sees them as one entity, space-time. But, unlike length, breadth and depth, time is not gauged directly, but is measured by observing the way in which the passage of time affects things. Only recently has time been measured with great accuracy.

THE SECOND

The fundamental unit of time is the second. It was originally defined as one 86,400th of a mean day, but the Earth is not a reliable timekeeper, and so an accurate alternative was sought.

Scientists settled on the atom, where regular and precise events in time exist, and the second was redefined in relation to the natural vibration of the atoms of the element caesium. To a scientist, one second is the time taken for an atom of caesium-133 to oscillate 9,192,631,770 times.

DAYS AND YEARS

The cycles of nature provided early humans with reference points against which time could be measured. Perhaps the most obvious marker of the passage of time is the day, the time taken for the Earth to revolve once on its axis. A solar day lasts 24 hours, and is measured against the mean Sun (an imaginary Sun moving at a constant speed, in contrast to the real Sun's varying speed).

A sidereal day is calculated with regard to the relatively fixed reference points of the stars, and is the time taken between successive passes of the observer's meridian by the same star. (The meridian is an imaginary line from due north to due south running through a point directly above the observer.) One sidereal day lasts 23 hours 56 minutes and 4 seconds.

A year is the time taken for the Earth to complete one orbit of the Sun. The Earth's true revolution period is 365 days 6 hours 9 minutes and 10 seconds, known as a sidereal year. This is measured against the mean Sun (see above). However, to complicate things, the direction of the Earth's axis is not fixed but wobbles, an effect known as precession. The result is that the Sun's apparent path across the sky is changing with respect to the stars. A tropical year compensates for this, and is calculated to be 365 days 5 hours 48 minutes and 45 seconds long. The tropical year is used as the basis for our calendar.

TIMEPIECES AND CLOCKS

The earliest device for measuring time was the sundial, which has its origins in *c.* 3500 BC in the Middle East. A sundial comprises a rod or plate called a gnomon that casts a shadow on a disc; the direction in which the shadow points indicates the position of the Sun and hence the time of day.

Mechanical clocks, driven by falling weights, appeared in the 14th century in Europe, although they had been known in China for several centuries. The first mechanical watches, driven by a coiled mainspring, were made during the 16th century. The increasing accuracy of such devices led to the application of the hour-and-minute time divisions, which came into common use in about 1600.

The first clock driven by a pendulum was invented by Christiaan Huygens (1629–95), a Dutch physicist, in 1656. Accurate clocks could now be produced relatively cheaply, and over the next century or so the grandfather clock became a common sight in people's homes.

However, pendulum clocks could not be used aboard ships due to the ship's motion and this led to the British Longitude Board offering a prize for the invention of a marine chronometer. John Harrison (1693–1776) produced the first chronometer in 1735, after seven years' work. This invention allowed European navigators to voyage further afield and draw up accurate maps.

Other breakthroughs in clockmaking include the first electric-battery clocks, which were first developed in 1840 but not perfected until 1906. Wristwatches were introduced in about 1900.

QUARTZ AND ATOMIC CLOCKS

As technology has become more advanced, so timekeeping has become more accurate. The first quartz clocks appeared in 1929. These operate through the vibrations of a quartz crystal through which an electrical voltage is applied. Such oscillations are accurate to within one second in ten years; the cost-effective quartz crystal is now at the heart of most everyday timepieces.

The atomic clock was developed in the USA in 1948. Based on the oscillations of the element caesium, it measures the resonance frequencies of its atoms and molecules. Atomic clocks are accurate to one second in 1.6 million years.

A worldwide system of atomic clocks working together provides what is known as Coordinated Universal Time (UTC). Scientists are able to attain even greater precision by taking an average of these clocks. Nonetheless, due to minute fluctuations on the Earth's surface and in its rotation, even these atomic clocks are not absolutely perfect. To adjust for these inaccuracies, occasional 'leap seconds' are inserted into a year, usually at the end of June or December.

A recent development in the measurement of time has seen an atomic clock, based at Greenwich in the UK, receive time signals from five orbiting satellites, which are free from surface distortion. Such techniques provide as accurate a measurement of time as is currently available.

■ *Sundials, like this German one, were one of the early means of measuring the passing of time*

■ *Detail of the chime-control mechanism in an early weight-driven pendulum clock designed by Dutch physicist Christiaan Huygens (1629–95)*

■ *This chronometer, built by John Harrison (1693–1776) in 1759, was used for measuring time and longitude at sea*

■ ONE BILLION SECONDS ADDS UP TO APPROXIMATELY 31 YEARS 8 MONTHS 1 WEEK AND

CALENDARS

▶ The year the Julian calendar was introduced became known as 'the year of confusion' because so few people fully understood the change.
▶ The French republican calendar had descriptive names for each month, translated into English as: Vintage, Mist, Frost, Snow, Rain, Wind, Seedtime, Blossom, Meadow, Harvest, Heat and Fruits.

THE JULIAN AND GREGORIAN CALENDARS

The most widespread calendar is the Gregorian, which is based on the Julian calendar. The Julian calendar was established by Julius Caesar in 46 BC to reform the confusing Roman calendar which had become out of sync with the solar year. On the advice of the Egyptian astronomer Sosigenes, the year 46 BC was lengthened to 445 days to realign it with the solar year, and a period of three years, each lasting 365 days, was followed by a leap year with 366 days. Each year was divided into 12 months, each of 30 or 31 days except February, which had 28 days (except in a leap year, when it was given an extra day, making 29 in all).

The Julian system assumed that the average length of a year was 365.25 days, but this is actually slightly too long (by 11 minutes 14 seconds) when compared to the astronomical year. Over time this discrepancy became even more obvious, and by 1582 the calendar was ten days ahead of the astronomical year. Consequently, Pope Gregory XIII solved the problem by making 5 October 1582 into 15 October 1582. This new system was known as the Gregorian calendar, and most Roman Catholic countries adopted it immediately. Several Protestant nations did not instigate the change until 1700. Britain aligned itself in 1752, and Russia adhered to the Julian system until 1918.

To ensure that the slight error in the Julian calendar would not be repeated, it was decided that century years would be leap years only if they were divisible by 400. Thus 1600 was a leap year, and 2000 will be a leap year, but 1700, 1800 and 1900 were not. The Gregorian system has an error of 0.0005 days per year, and it will not need to be revised for many hundreds of years. The next calendar adjustment will probably not need to be made until AD 4000, which may lose its leap year status, although minute variations in the Earth–Sun relationship have not made this a certainty.

New Year

In early medieval times, the Christian countries of Europe regarded 25 March (Annunciation Day) as New Year's Day. Anglo-Saxon England used 25 December to mark the year's beginning until William I decreed that 1 January should be used instead. However, England later fell in line with the rest of Europe by choosing 25 March. During the 16th century, several European states adopted 1 January as New Year's Day, and the introduction of the Gregorian calendar in 1582 confirmed this day as the year's beginning. By the time Britain adopted it again in 1751, it was being used in most Christian countries.

Months

All the months of the year are derived from their equivalents in the Roman republican calendar. Since the Roman year began in March, September was considered the seventh month, and it was named accordingly (Latin *septem* means 'seven'). October, November and December derive their names similarly.

January: 31 days; named after Janus, god of doorways and of beginnings.
February: 28 days (29 in a leap year); named after Februa, the Roman festival of purification.
March: 31 days; named after the god Mars.
April: 30 days; possibly named after Aphrodite, the Greek equivalent to the Roman goddess Venus. It may also have been derived from the Latin *aperire*, 'to open', which refers to the blossoming of spring.
May: 31 days; named after the god Maia.
June: 30 days; named after the god Juno.
July: 31 days; named after Julius Caesar in 44 BC.
August: 31 days; named after the emperor Augustus in 8 BC.
September: 30 days; from Latin *septem* ('seven').
October: 31 days; from Latin *octo* ('eight').
November: 30 days; from Latin *novem* ('nine').
December: 31 days; from Latin *decem* ('ten').

Days of the week

The names of the days in English generally have their roots in Norse mythology, with only Saturday deriving from Latin.

Sunday: named after the Sun.
Monday: named after the Moon.
Tuesday: named after Tiw, the Anglo-Saxon counterpart of the Nordic god Tyr, son of Odin.
Wednesday: named after Woden, the Anglo-Saxon counterpart of the Nordic god Odin, the god of war.
Thursday: named after Thor, the Nordic god of thunder, eldest son of Odin.
Friday: named after Frigg, the Nordic goddess of love, wife of Odin.
Saturday: named after Saturn, Roman god of agriculture and vegetation.

Seasons

The solstices, from the Latin *sol* (Sun) and *sistere* (to stand still), are the two times in the year when the Sun is farthest from the Equator and appears to be standing still. The equinoxes, from the Latin *aequalis* (equal) and *nox* (night), are the two times of the year when day and night are of equal length, and is when the Sun crosses the Equator. The

ISLAMIC CALENDAR

The Islamic calendar is based on lunar years, beginning with the year of the Hejirah (AD 622 in the Julian calendar), when Muhammad travelled from Mecca to Medina.

The calendar runs in cycles of 30 years. There are leap years in the 2nd, 5th, 7th, 10th, 13th, 16th, 18th, 21st, 24th, 26th and 29th years of the 30-year cycle. The Hejirah system of years is used principally in Iran, Turkey, Saudi Arabia and other Arabian peninsula states, Egypt, Malaysia and certain parts of India.

The Islamic year consists of 12 months of alternately 30 days and 29 days. In a leap year, one day is inserted at the end of the 12th month, Dhû'l Hijja. This means that common years have 355 days, while leap years have 356. The extra day is inserted into the calendar on leap years in order to reconcile the date of the first day of the month with the date of the actual New Moon. Some Muslims register the first of the month on the evening that the crescent becomes visible. The Moon is particularly important in Ramadan, the month of fasting. According to the *Qur'an*, Moslems must see the New Moon with the naked eye before they can both begin and end their fast.

	No. of days	Islamic year 1418 (AD 1997–98)	Islamic year 1419 (AD 1998–99)
Muharram	30	9 May–7 Jun	28 Apr–27 May
Safar	29	8 Jun–6 Jul	28 May–25 Jun
Rabîa I	30	7 Jul–5 Aug	26 Jun–25 Jul
Rabîa II	29	6 Aug–3 Sep	26 Jul–23 Aug
Jumâda I	30	4 Sep–3 Oct	24 Aug–22 Sep
Jumâda II	29	4 Oct–1 Nov	23 Sep–21 Oct
Rajab	30	2 Nov–1 Dec	22 Oct–20 Nov
Shaabân	29	2 Dec–30 Dec	21 Nov–19 Dec
Ramadan	30	31 Dec–29 Jan 1998	20 Dec–18 Jan 1999
Shawwâl	29	30 Jan–27 Feb	19 Jan–16 Feb
Dhû'l-Qa'da	30	28 Feb–29 Mar	17 Feb–18 Mar
Dhû'l Hijja	29*	30 Mar–27 Apr	19 Mar–16 Apr

* 30 days in a leap year

JEWISH CALENDAR

It is thought that the Jewish calendar has been in popular use since the 9th century BC. It is based on biblical calculations that place the creation as 3761 BC.

The complicated rules of festivals and fasts in the Jewish calendar have resulted in a calendar scheme in which a year can be one of six types:

Minimal Common (353 days); Regular Common (354 days); Full Common (355 days); Minimal Leap (383 days); Regular Leap (384 days); and Full Leap (385 days).

The Jewish calendar is split into 12 months, of either 29 or 30 days. A 13th month is inserted into the calendar every 3rd, 6th, 8th, 11th, 14th, 17th and 19th year of a 19-year cycle. This month, Ve-Adar, contains all the religious observances that usually occur in Adar. The Jewish New Year begins with the month of Tishri.

	No. of days	Jewish year 5758 (AD 1997–98)	Jewish year 5759 (AD 1998–99)
Tishri	30	Oct 2–31 Oct	21 Sep–20 Oct
Cheshvan (Marcheshvan)	29/30[1]	1 Nov–29 Nov	21 Oct–19 Nov
Kislev	29/30[1]	30 Nov–29 Dec	20 Nov–19 Dec
Tebet	29	30 Dec–27 Jan 1998	20 Dec–17 Jan 1999
Shebat	30	28 Jan–26 Feb	18 Jan–16 Feb
Adar	29[2]	27 Feb–27 Mar	17 Feb–17 Mar
Ve-Adar[3]	29		
Nisan	30	28 Mar–26 Apr	18 Mar–16 Apr
Iyar	29	27 Apr–25 May	17 Apr–15 May
Sivan	30	26 May–24 Jun	16 May–14 Jun
Tammuz	29	25 Jun–23 Jul	15 Jun–13 Jul
Ab	30	24 Jul–22 Aug	14 Jul–12 Aug
Elul	29	23 Aug–20 Sep	13 Aug–10 Sep

[1] Can have either 29 or 30 days depending on the year
[2] 30 in a leap year
[3] Intercalated month

longest day has the longest interval between sunrise and sunset, and falls on the summer solstice. The solstices and equinoxes provide the basis for the astronomical division of the seasons. In the northern hemisphere, the four seasons are:

Spring: from the vernal equinox (about 21 March) to the summer solstice (21 or 22 June).
Summer: from the summer solstice (21 or 22 June) to the autumnal equinox (about 21 September).
Autumn: (or Fall in the USA) from the autumnal equinox (about 21 September) to the winter solstice (21 or 22 December).
Winter: from the winter solstice (21 or 22 December) to the vernal equinox (about 21 March).

In the southern hemisphere, this is reversed, with the northern hemisphere autumn corresponding to spring in the southern hemisphere, winter to summer, spring to autumn, and summer to winter.

CHINESE CALENDAR

The Chinese calendar has been in existence for perhaps 2500 years. It is based on a lunar year, and consists of 12 months of alternately 29 and 30 days, making 354 days in total, which is about 12 full lunar cycles.

To keep the calendar aligned with the solar year, intercalary months are inserted. The months are numbered, and sometimes given one of the 12 animal names that are usually attached to years and hours in the Chinese calendar. The Chinese New Year begins at the first New Moon after the Sun enters Aquarius, and thus falls between 21 January and 19 February in the Gregorian reckoning.

The ancient calendar was in continual use until the overthrow of the last Manchu emperor and the establishment of the republic in 1911, after which the Gregorian system was introduced. Although the old system was formally banned in China in 1930, the New Year remains a national holiday. The ancient system still has widespread unofficial use in China, Singapore, Malaysia and Chinese communities elsewhere.

Each year is associated with one of 12 animals, so every 12th year belongs to the same animal. For the 20th century, the animal years are:

Rat	1900, 1912, 1924, 1936, 1948, 1960, 1972, 1984, 1996, 2008
Ox	1901, 1913, 1925, 1937, 1949, 1961, 1973, 1985, 1997, 2009
Tiger	1902, 1914, 1926, 1938, 1950, 1962, 1974, 1986, 1998, 2010
Rabbit[1]	1903, 1915, 1927, 1939, 1951, 1963, 1975, 1987, 1999, 2011
Dragon	1904, 1916, 1928, 1940, 1952, 1964, 1976, 1988, 2000, 2012
Snake	1905, 1917, 1929, 1941, 1953, 1965, 1977, 1989, 2001, 2013
Horse	1906, 1918, 1930, 1942, 1954, 1966, 1978, 1990, 2002, 2014
Sheep[2]	1907, 1919, 1931, 1943, 1955, 1967, 1979, 1991, 2003, 2015
Monkey	1908, 1920, 1932, 1944, 1956, 1968, 1980, 1992, 2004, 2016
Chicken[3]	1909, 1921, 1933, 1945, 1957, 1969, 1981, 1993, 2005, 2017
Dog	1910, 1922, 1934, 1946, 1958, 1970, 1982, 1994, 2006, 2018
Pig	1911, 1923, 1935, 1947, 1959, 1971, 1983, 1995, 2007, 2019

[1] Sometimes known as the Year of the Hare
[2] Sometimes known as the Year of the Goat
[3] Sometimes known as the Year of the Cockerel

JAPANESE CALENDAR

The Japanese calendar has the same structure as the Gregorian system in terms of years, months and weeks, but differs in how the years are numbered. Whereas the Gregorian calendar bases its numeration upon one religious event, the birth of Christ, the Japanese system is based upon a series of imperial epochs, with each one calculated from the accession of an emperor.

Epochs of the Japanese calendar

The four most recent epochs are based on the reigns of the last four emperors, who are referred to by their epoch names – their personal names are never used.

Epoch Meiji: 13 Oct 1868–31 Jul 1912 (Emperor Mutsuhito)
Epoch Taisho: 1 Aug 1912–25 Dec 1926 (Emperor Yoshihito)
Epoch Showa: 26 Dec 1926–7 Jan 1989 (Emperor Hirohito)
Epoch Heisei: began 8 Jan 1989 (Emperor Akihito)

Months and days of the Japanese calendar

Months are unnamed, and are simply numbered. The days of the week have individual names as follows:

Nichiyobi	Sun-day	(Sunday)
Getsuyobi	Moon-day	(Monday)
Kayobi	Fire-day	(Tuesday)
Suiyobi	Water-day	(Wednesday)
Mokuyobi	Wood-day	(Thursday)
Kinyobi	Metal-day	(Friday)
Doyobi	Earth-day	(Saturday)

INDIAN CALENDARS

The main Indian calendars reckon their epochs from historical events such as the accession or death of a ruler or religious founder.

Vikrama era

The Vikrama era originated in northern India and is still used in western India. It dates from 23 February 57 BC in the Gregorian calendar.

Saka era

The Saka era dates from 3 March AD 78 in the Gregorian calendar. It is based on the solar year, beginning with the spring equinox. There are 365 days in a year (366 in a leap year), divided into 12 months. The first five months are of 31 days and the remaining seven are of 30 days. In a leap year, the first six months have 31 days.

The Saka era was declared the national calendar of India in 1957, and was to run concurrently with the Gregorian calendar.

Buddhist era

The believed date of Buddha's death in 543 BC marks the point of origin of the Buddhist era, although many Buddhist sects adopt different dates for his death. The actual date was 487 BC.

Jain era

The Jain era dates from the death of the founder of the Jainist religion, Vardhamana, in 527 BC.

Parsee (Zoroastrian) era

The Parsee era dates from 16 June AD 632 in the Gregorian calendar.

COPTIC CALENDAR

The Coptic calendar dates from 29 August AD 284 of the Gregorian calendar. It is still used in areas of Egypt, Ethiopia and Eritrea for religious purposes. There are 12 months of 30 days followed by five complementary days. In a leap year, there is an additional complementary day.

FRENCH REPUBLICAN CALENDAR

The French republican calendar was adopted in 1793 in the wake of the French Revolution. The calendar marked a significant departure from the Gregorian system, and it took some of its structure from Coptic elements.

The year was divided into 12 months of 30 days, with five complementary days (six in a leap year) at the end of the year. Seven-day weeks were replaced by decades of ten days, and there were three decades per month. The system, which was more secular and regular than the Gregorian calendar, was dated from 22 September 1795. It was abolished by Napoleon I on 1 January 1806.

The months of the calendar, together with their Gregorian equivalents, were: Vendémaire (23 September to 22 October); Brumaire (23 October to 21 November); Frimaire (22 November to 21 December); Nivôse (22 December to 20 January); Pluviôse (21 January to 19 February); Ventôse (20 February to 21 March); Germinal (22 March to 20 April); Floréal (21 April to 20 May); Plairial (21 May to 19 June); Messidor (20 June to 19 July); Thermidor (20 July to 18 August); and Fructidor (19 August to 22 September).

ASTROLOGICAL CALENDAR

Astrology is the interpretation of the supposed influence of planets and stars upon human lives. Astrologers believe that if an event occurred when the planets were in a particular configuration, then similar events are likely to happen when those planetary circumstances are repeated. Astrology also builds up character profiles based on detailed planetary information about the time and place of a person's birth. Conceived in Mesopotamia about 5000 years ago and developed in ancient Greece, astrology was absorbed into Indian, Islamic and western European cultures. In the same way that alchemy gave rise to the science of chemistry, astrology was an ancestor of astronomy.

The zodiac is an imaginary belt that extends 8° on either side of the annual path of the Sun. It is divided into 12 equal areas (the signs of the zodiac) each of 30°. The orbits of the Moon and of all the major planets except Pluto lie within the zodiac. Although the original periods during which the Sun appears to be in each of the constellations of the zodiac no longer apply, astrologists nevertheless adhere to the original dates.

Sign	Symbol	Conventional dates for the Sun's passage through sign
Aries	Ram	21 Mar–20 Apr
Taurus	Bull	21 Apr–21 May
Gemini	Twins	22 May–21 Jun
Cancer	Crab	22 Jun–22 Jul
Leo	Lion	23 Jul–23 Aug
Virgo	Virgin	24 Aug–22 Sep
Libra	Scales	23 Sep–22 Oct
Scorpio*	Scorpion	23 Oct–21 Nov
Sagittarius	Archer	22 Nov–21 Dec
Capricorn	Goat	22 Dec–20 Jan
Aquarius	Water Bearer	21 Jan–19 Feb
Pisces	Fish	20 Feb–20 Mar

* The second half of Scorpio is sometimes referred to as Ophiuchus (symbol: the Serpent Bearer) by some European astrologers

ASTROLOGY WAS TAUGHT AT SOME EUROPEAN UNIVERSITIES DURING THE MIDDLE AGES

WHAT DAY WAS IT

Here is a way to work out the day of the week for any date in the 20th century. Using 8 November 1973 as an example, follow the steps set out below:

Step		
1	Write down the date	8
2	Write down the value of the month (November) from the table below, left	3
3	Write down the year	73
4	Divide the previous line by 4 and ignore the remainder: 73 divided by 4	18
5	Add these figures together	102
6	Divide this figure by 7	14 remainder 4
7	Compare the remainder with the second table below: 4 = Thursday. Thus 8 November 1973 was a Thursday.	

Month	Value
January	0 (leap year 6)
February	3 (leap year 2)
March	3
April	6
May	1
June	4
July	6
August	2
September	5
October	0
November	3
December	5

Day	Value
Monday	1
Tuesday	1
Wednesday	3
Thursday	4
Friday	5
Saturday	6
Sunday	7

DIVISION OF TIME

Several time divisions are in everyday use, although only the second is accepted as part of the International System of Units (SI).

UNIT	DURATION
second	–
minute	60 seconds
hour	60 minutes
day	24 hours
week	7 days
fortnight	2 weeks
month	30 days (in general)
year	12 months
decade	10 years
century	100 years
millennium	1000 years

DAYLIGHT SAVING TIME

Daylight saving takes advantage of summer's extra daylight hours. Clocks are put forward one hour (usually in spring), thus gaining an hour's sunlight during conventional waking hours.

The practice was first suggested, half-seriously, in 1784 in an essay by the American statesman and scientist Benjamin Franklin. It was not until World War I that several countries, including Australia, Britain, Germany and the United States, adopted daylight saving as a means of conserving fuel resources.

Apart from increasing leisure time, benefits of daylight saving include energy conservation (by using less electricity in the evenings) and providing safe homeward journeys for schoolchildren. The clocks go back one hour again in autumn. Not all countries – or states within countries – practise daylight saving.

TIME ZONES

▶ The Sun rises earlier in eastern countries than in western ones because of the Earth's rotation. In other words, the time of day varies, depending on where you are.

▶ Moving west over the International Date Line at midnight Saturday will take you into Monday without ever experiencing Sunday.

Before the middle of the 19th century, hundreds of different time systems were in use throughout the world based on the rising of the Sun. Because of increased global trading and faster transport and communications it became necessary to devise a simpler system, which could be standardized around the world.

GREENWICH MEAN TIME

Greenwich Mean Time (GMT) was introduced at the International Meridian Conference in Washington, DC, in 1884. The foundation for GMT is the Greenwich (or prime) meridian, the zero longitude, that passes through the Royal Greenwich Observatory in south-east London.

The world was divided up into 24 time zones, each of 15° longitude. The 12 zones to the east of the Greenwich meridian were designated to be ahead of the time at Greenwich by one hour per zone. Similarly, the 12 zones to the west of Greenwich are behind. Each time zone extends 7½° on either side of its central meridian.

The other important time meridian is the International Date Line, which is also known simply as the Date Line. This is the 180° meridian, an imaginary line running between the South Pole and the North Pole, and marks each calendar day from the next. Along this line, the time zone 12 hours ahead of GMT is alongside the time zone 12 hours behind GMT. By crossing the International Date Line from east to west, Sunday becomes Monday, while travelling eastwards, Sunday becomes Saturday.

The Date Line is not perfectly straight, but zigzags for geopolitical reasons – to ensure, for example, that all of Alaska remains in the US time zone and that Siberia is in the Asian zone. The Date Line also varies to accommodate certain Pacific islands in the one time zone.

A very few countries, or regions within countries, do not adhere to the Greenwich system at all, while some islands in the Pacific and Atlantic are an hour ahead or behind the time zone they lie in for geopolitical reasons.

Some other countries have elected not to divide themselves into different zones and have kept the same time for the entire nation. China, for example, is eight hours ahead of GMT, although it lies in five different time zones. Yet other countries, including Suriname, Iran, Afghanistan and India, use differences of half an hour.

Certain countries, such as Iran, while having an official national time, have local differences because of religious rituals based on the exact moment of sunrise and sunset. Israel also adheres to time zones in accordance with religious practices, and so is about two hours behind the rest of its time zone.

The GMT time system, also known as Universal Time (UT), is now of vital importance in our increasingly global culture. Without a regulated and universally coordinated system of time, chaos would ensue for international defence systems, airline pilots, financial markets and worldwide computer networks.

TIME ZONE MAP ▶

EUROPEAN TIME ZONES

Time zone	Hours ahead of GMT	
GMT	0	Iceland, Ireland, Portugal, UK
Mid-European	1	Albania, Andorra, Austria, Belgium, Bosnia-Herzegovina, Croatia, Czech Republic, Denmark, France, Germany, Gibraltar, Hungary, Italy, Liechtenstein, Luxembourg, Macedonia, Monaco, Netherlands, Norway, Poland, San Marino, Slovakia, Slovenia, Spain, Sweden, Switzerland, the Vatican, Yugoslavia
East European	2	Belarus, Bulgaria, Cyprus, Estonia, Finland, Greece, Latvia, Lithuania, Moldova, Romania, Ukraine

UNITED STATES TIME ZONES

Time zone	Hours ahead of GMT	
Eastern	5	Connecticut, Florida (except far west), Georgia, Indiana, Kentucky (eastern), Maine, Maryland, Massachusetts, Michigan, New Hampshire, New Jersey, New York State, North Carolina, Ohio, Pennsylvania, Rhode Island, South Carolina, Tennessee (eastern), Vermont, Virginia, Washington DC, West Virginia
Central	6	Alabama, Arkansas, Florida (far west), Illinois, Iowa, Kansas (except far west), Kentucky (western), Louisiana, Minnesota, Mississippi, Missouri, Nebraska (except far west), North Dakota (eastern), Oklahoma, South Dakota (eastern), Tennessee (western), Texas (except far western), Wisconsin
Mountain	7	Arizona, Colorado, Idaho (except far northern), Kansas (far west), Montana, Nebraska (far west), New Mexico, North Dakota (western), Oregon (far eastern), South Dakota (western), Texas (far western), Utah and Wyoming
Pacific	8	California, Idaho (far northern), Nevada, Oregon (except far eastern), Washington
Alaska	9	Alaska
Hawaii/Aleutian	10	Hawaii, Aleutian Islands

THE WORD 'ZODIAC' COMES FROM THE GREEK *ZOIDIAKOS*, WHICH MEANS 'CIRCLE OF ANIMALS' ■

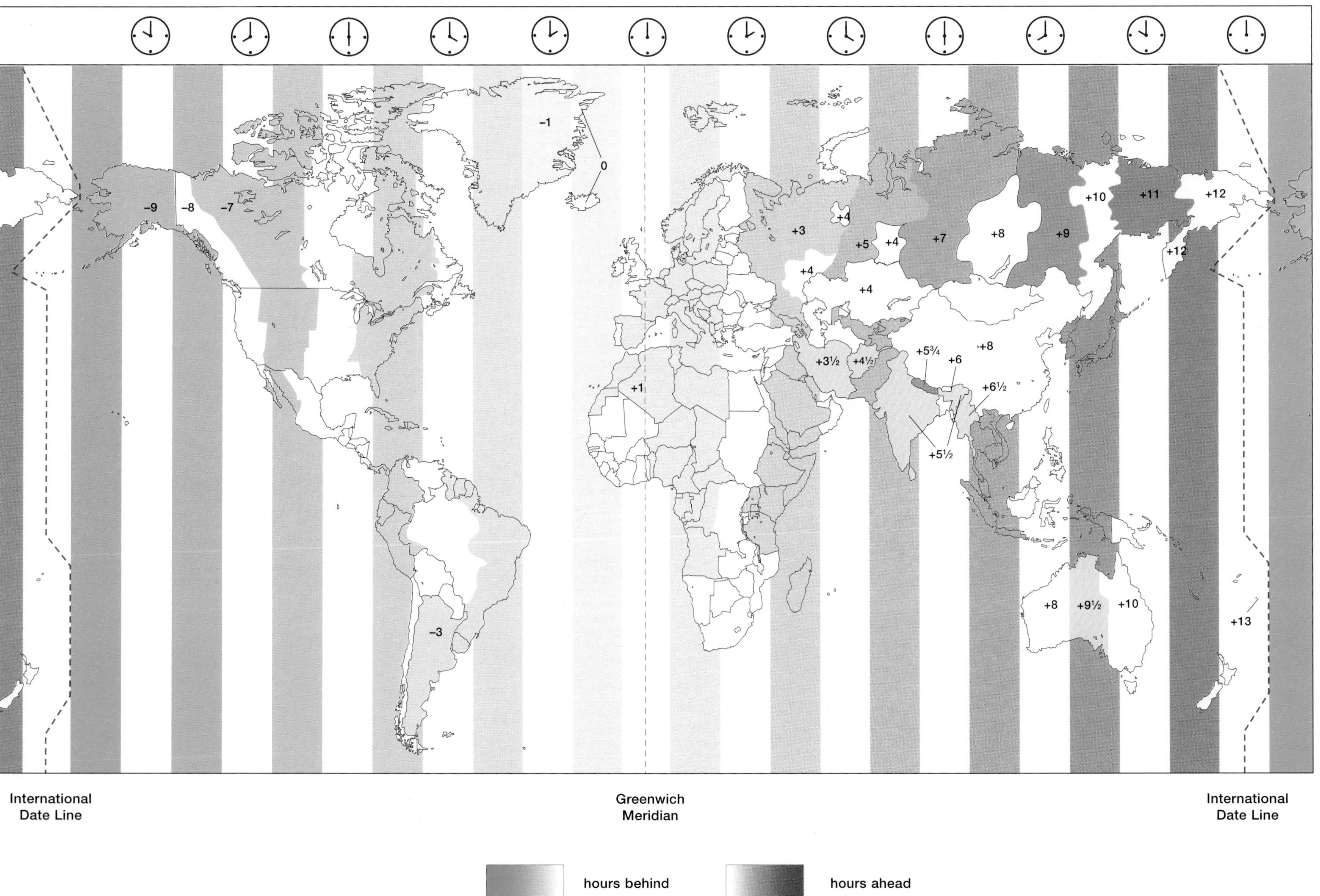
–1
0
–9
–8
–7
+3
+4
+5
+4
+7
+8
+9
+10
+11
+12
+12
+4
+4
+3½
+4½
+5¾
+6
+8
+6½
+5½
+1
–3
+8
+9½
+10
+13
International Date Line
Greenwich Meridian
International Date Line
hours behind
hours ahead

THE EARTH ▷

'The world is nothing
but an endless seesaw'
– Montaigne

THE EARTH'S STRUCTURE

- The density at the centre of the Earth is up to 12 times greater than the density at the surface and the average density of the Earth is 5.517 times the density of water.
- The Precambrian era, which accounts for 80% of the Earth's time scale, saw the beginnings of life on Earth.
- Rocks – the study of which is called petrology – are made up of chemical compounds and divided into three main groups: igneous, sedimentary and metamorphic, according to the processes that resulted in their formation.
- The Earth can be divided into three main layers: the crust, the mantle and the core.

THE CRUST

▶ The Earth's thin outermost layer – the crust – has an average thickness of 24 km (15 mi).
▶ The crust accounts for only 1.14% of the Earth's volume and 0.53% of its weight (mass).

The Earth's crust varies greatly in thickness. Three main crustal types – continental, oceanic and transitional (a combination of continental and oceanic) – have been identified. The continental crust averages between 30–50 km (19–31 mi) in thickness, although beneath the central valley of California, for example, the crust is only about 20 km (12 mi) thick, and beneath major mountain ranges, such as the Himalaya, it can exceed 80 km (50 mi). In contrast, the oceanic crust is only 5–15 km (3–9 mi) thick and can be as little as 3 km (2 mi) under ocean fracture zones. The thickness of the transitional crust at islands, island arcs and continental margins averages 15–30 km (9–19 mi).

The elements oxygen, silicon and aluminium dominate the crust's composition. The main mineral type – the feldspars – are alumino-silicates of the alkali and alkaline-earth metals. The second most common group – quartz – is silicon dioxide. The major continental crust rock types reflect this basic composition, with differences mainly due to small amounts of other minerals. In contrast, the oceanic crust is mainly basalt, which contains both feldspars and quartz, but also has notable amounts of olivine and pyroxene, which are magnesium iron silicates.

The lower crust is often considered differently from the upper crust because of its composition. This is known because seismic waves pass through it at a higher velocity. It is thought the predominant rock in the lower crust is gabbro (a rock with the same composition as basalt but coarser grained).

THE MANTLE

▶ The sharp boundary between the crust and the mantle is called the Mohorovicic discontinuity (or Moho for short) after the Croatian seismologist Andrija Mohorovicic (1857–1936) who discovered it in 1909.
▶ The mantle extends from the base of the crust to the core, is 2865 km (1780 mi) thick, and occupies 82.54% of the Earth's volume and 66% of its mass.

The rocks of the Earth's upper mantle are rich in the minerals olivine and pyroxenes. Discontinuities revealed by seismic data show several distinct layers in the mantle. The outermost – the lithosphere – is generally 50–100 km (31–62 mi) thick under the oceans and 100–200 km (62–124 mi) thick under the continents. The strong rigid lithosphere overlays a weak thick layer known as the asthenosphere. The asthenosphere – which is 320 km (199 mi) thick – has an average temperature of about 1300°C (2372°F), which approaches the melting points of its constituent rocks. It is probable that magma – molten or semi-molten rock – is formed in this region.

A major discontinuity at a depth of 670 km (416 mi) from the surface separates the upper and lower mantles. Below this discontinuity there appears to be a change in mineral types brought about by the increasing pressure. There is also a 10% jump in density and a rise in temperature from about 1560°C (2840°F) to 1710°C (3110°F). The major mineral type in the lower mantle appears to be pyroxenes, especially magnesium silicate. In the D layer – the lowest 200 km (124 mi) of the mantle – temperatures reach up to 2660°C (4820°F). It is thought that the D layer is richer in aluminium and calcium than the higher layers of the mantle.

THE CORE

▶ The Earth's core extends from the base of the mantle to the centre of the Earth, is 6964 km (4327 mi) in diameter, and accounts for 16.32% of the Earth's volume, but 33.4% of its mass.
▶ The discontinuity between the mantle and core is called the core–mantle boundary or, sometimes, the Gutenberg discontinuity, after its discoverer the German-American seismologist Beno Gutenberg.

The Earth's core comprises two distinct parts – a liquid outer core, which is 2260 km (1404 mi) thick, and a solid inner core, which has a radius of 1222 km (759 mi). The core is chemically distinct from the mantle and comprises about 89% iron and 6% nickel. The remaining 5% comprises a lighter element, which is possibly sulphur but may be oxygen and silicon. There is a 78% increase in density at the mantle–core boundary and a 700°C (1290°F) jump in temperature to about 3360°C (6080°F). There is a smooth increase in temperature to a maximum of about 4530°C (8190°F) at the very centre of the core. Scientists believe that the intense heat generated by the inner core causes the liquid outer core and the mantle to move in currents, called convection currents, which are believed to emit the Earth's magnetic field.

THE MAGNETIC FIELD

▶ By measuring the orientation of the magnetic field within a rock it is possible to tell the position of the North Pole at the time the rock was formed.
▶ The Earth's magnetic field has reversed on a number of occasions. For example, 30,000 years ago Magnetic North was at the South Pole.

The Earth has a magnetic field, which is why a compass needle points approximately north at most places on the Earth's surface. The magnetic field has two parts. Most of it is a simple dipole; it is as if a giant bar magnet were placed at the centre of the Earth sloping at 11° to the Earth's axis of rotation. However, a small proportion of it is much more complicated and changes very rapidly. This is why a compass needle points in a slightly different direction each year (see p.30).

The rapid changing suggests that the magnetic field must be produced in a part of the Earth that is fluid, most probably the outer core, for no solid region could reorganize itself rapidly enough without shaking the planet to pieces. The only conceivable way in which a magnetic field could be generated within the Earth is by the flow of very large electric currents, and electric currents need a conductor. The Earth's core is the most conductive zone in the whole planet, because it consists largely of iron. The silicates of the mantle simply would not conduct well enough.

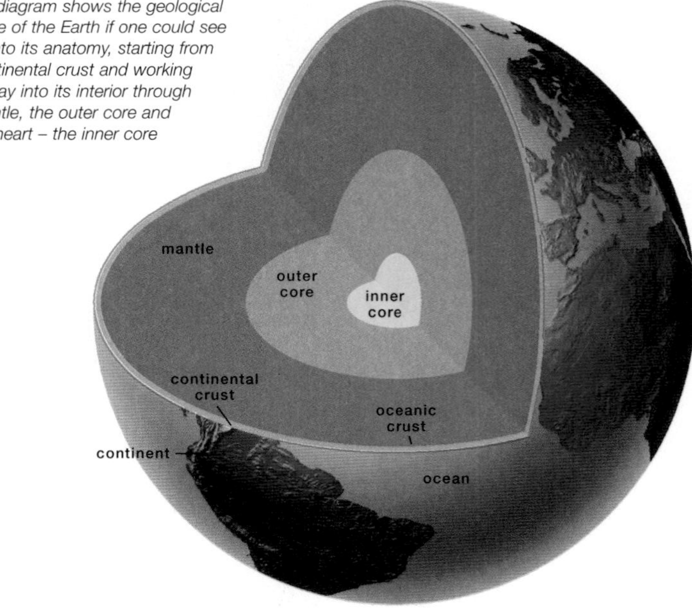

■ *This diagram shows the geological structure of the Earth if one could see inside into its anatomy, starting from the continental crust and working one's way into its interior through the mantle, the outer core and into its heart – the inner core*

■ THE EARTH IS OVER 4.6 BILLION YEARS OLD ■ NEARLY 30% OF THE EARTH IS MADE UP

■ *The continents of North and South America with Antarctica to the south*

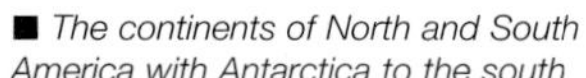

■ *North and South America on the left with Europe and Africa appearing to the right*

■ *The continents of Europe, Asia and Africa with the Middle East at centre right*

■ *Oceania (Australasia) and Asia, with a central view of the Indonesian archipelago*

STUDYING THE EARTH'S STRUCTURE

▶ The temperature at the centre of the Earth is estimated to be 4530°C (8190°F).
▶ The oldest fragment of the Earth's crust is zircon crystals, which were discovered in the Jack Hills, 700 km (430 mi) north of Perth, Australia, in August 1984, and found to be 4276 million years old.

It is difficult for scientists to fully understand the structure of the Earth as there has been little penetration through the crust into its interior. The deepest mine, located in South Africa, is only 3.8 km (2.4 mi) deep, and the deepest drilling, in Russia, is only 12.3 km (7.6 mi) deep – or 0.19% of the Earth's radius, which has an average value of 6371 km (3959 mi). The only other direct access to the internal nature of Earth is the study of lava flows from volcanic eruptions.

As we are unable to visit the Earth's deep interior or place instruments very far within it, we must explore the Earth's interior in more subtle ways. One method is to measure natural phenomena, in particular the magnetic and gravitational fields, which are measured at the Earth's surface and from satellites. These observations can be interpreted to tell us about the planet's internal properties. A second approach is to study the Earth through the use of seismic waves emitted by earthquakes. As seismic waves pass through the Earth, they undergo changes in direction and velocity at certain depths. These depths mark the major boundaries, or discontinuities, that divide the Earth into crust, mantle and core.

KEY

- Iron (Fe) 35.9%
- Oxygen (O) 28.5%
- Silicon (Si) 14.3%
- Magnesium (Mg) 13.2%
- Nickel (Ni) 2.0%
- Calcium (C) 1.9%
- Sulphur (S) 1.8%
- Aluminium (Al) 1.8%
- Other 0.5%

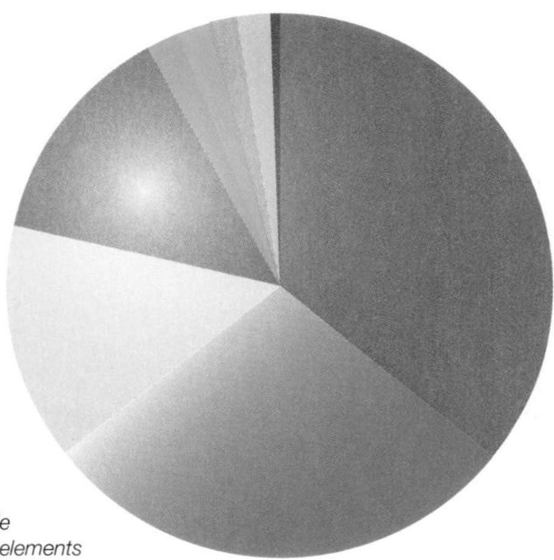

■ *The overall composition of the Earth, including crust, mantle and core, in terms of the major elements*

MASS, DENSITY AND VOLUME

▶ The average density of the Earth is 5.517 g/cm³.
▶ The Earth, including its atmosphere, has a mass of 5.976 x 10^{21} tonnes.

The atmosphere of the Earth weighs 5.24 x 10^{15} tonnes or 0.000088% of the total mass. The mass of the Earth is being added to as the planet picks up about 40,000 tonnes of cosmic dust each year. The volume of the Earth is 1,083,207,000 km³ (259,875,300,000 cu mi), calculated using an average Earth radius of 6371 km (3957 mi).

The density in g/cm³, the percentage of mass (in terms of the total Earth mass), the thickness, and percentage of volume (in terms of the total Earth volume) of each layer of the Earth are given in the table below.

MODERN DATING METHODS

▶ Geological time now extends back about 4600 million years ago to the beginning of the Precambrian era.
▶ The greatest age of any scientifically dated rock is 3962 million years, which was discovered about 320 km (200 mi) north of Yellowknife, Northwest Territories, Canada, by Dr Samuel Bowring of the USA in May 1984.

In the early 20th century, radioactive decay was used as a geochronological measurement. In 1907, US chemist and physicist B.B. Boltwood showed, using the uranium-lead method of radioactive decay dating, that a sample of Precambrian rock dated from 1640 million years BP (before the present).

Modern developments, using accelerator equipment, allow carbon-14 dating to extend back beyond 100,000 years. Other dating methods include thermoluminescence (used since 1968) and amino acid racemization (used since 1972): the latter method is dependent upon the rate of change of amino acids from optically active to inactive forms over a long period of time.

THE EARTH'S LAYERS

	DENSITY g/cm³	% OF MASS	THICKNESS km	THICKNESS mi	% OF VOLUME
OCEAN	1.020	0.03	3	2	0.14
UPPER CRUST	2.600	0.27	21	13	1.00
LOWER CRUST	2.900	0.23			
MANTLE	variable	*65.99	2,865	1,780	82.54
OUTER CORE	11.238	31.82	2,260	1,404	15.62
INNER CORE	12.980	1.66	1,222	759	0.70

* Mantle: the percentage of the mass is calculated as a remainder

DIMENSIONS OF THE EARTH

▶ The equatorial diameter is 12,756.2726 km (7926.5966 mi) or 2,237,942 Rolls Royce lengths.
▶ The polar diameter is 12,713.5032 km (7900.0205 mi) or 2,230,439 Rolls Royce lengths.
▶ The equatorial circumference is 40,075.012 km (24,902.138 mi) or 7,030,704 Rolls Royce lengths.
▶ The polar meridianal circumference is 40,007.858 km (24,860.41 mi) or 7,018,922 Rolls Royce lengths.

The Earth has a pear-shaped asymmetry with the north polar radius being 44 m (144 ft) longer than the south polar radius, and there is also a slight ellipticity of the Equator since its long axis (about latitude 14.95°W) is 139 m (456 ft) greater than the short axis.

FORMATION OF ROCK

The Earth is perpetually recycling its rocks. Material brought to the surface is eroded, transported and ultimately returned to the Earth's interior, where it becomes available to begin the cycle all over again. This series of processes is known as the rock cycle or geological cycle. The energy to maintain it comes partly from the Sun (to fuel the erosion processes) and partly from the Earth's interior (to generate volcanic activity and uplift).

IGNEOUS

Igneous rocks originated deep in the Earth as molten magma. This magma was then forced up through the crust to cool and solidify through processes of volcanic activity. Magma is a mixture of oxides (compounds with oxygen) and silicates (compounds with silica and oxygen). When it cools and solidifies, the oxides and silicates form a complex mixture of mineral crystals.

The nature and properties of the crystals in any specific igneous rock depend partly on the composition of the original magma and partly upon the physical conditions under which the magma crystallized. Igneous rocks that form on the Earth's surface are known as extrusive rocks. Those that form within the crust from magma that never reached the surface are known as intrusive. Intrusive rocks cool more slowly because, being surrounded by other rock rather than being open to the air, the heat cannot escape so readily. As a result, the crystals have longer to grow, and the mineral grains are larger (coarser). Despite the many varieties of igneous rock, just six account for most of the igneous components of the Earth's crust – granite, diorite and gabbro, which are coarse-grained intrusive rocks, and rhyolite, andesite and basalt, which are fine-grained extrusive rocks.

SEDIMENTARY

Sedimentary rock is mostly formed when rock of any type is weathered down into fine particles that are then eroded and redeposited elsewhere, and later compressed.

At least 75% of all sedimentary rock is known as clastic sedimentary rock, which means that it is derived from the erosion products of other rocks. All rocks, even those in the most massive mountain ranges, are ultimately broken down into small fragments. When the particles become small enough they are then transported by water, wind or ice to a depositional basin, most commonly an ocean. There they fall as sediment to the ocean floor where, under the pressure of subsequent deposits, they are compacted into hard rock. The most common clastic sedimentary rock is sandstone.

The remaining 25% of sediment is either chemical or organic. Water dissolves minerals out of the rocks through which it passes, and these mineral solutions end up in oceans or inland basins. When these waters reach their saturation limit for a particular mineral, the excess is precipitated out as solid particles, which fall to the ocean or basin floor. The most common chemical sedimentary rock is limestone (calcium carbonate). Not all limestone is precipitated chemically, however. Many ocean organisms extract calcium carbonate from water to build their shells, which sink to the ocean floor to again form sediment when they die. Limestone is also the most common organic sedimentary rock. Other organisms generate silica sediments in similar ways.

Most sedimentary rocks are a mixture of clastic, chemical and organic, although one type usually predominates. Sedimentary rocks cover 75% of the Earth's surface, but are less than 5% of the total volume of the Earth's crust.

METAMORPHIC

When igneous or sedimentary rocks are subjected to high temperatures and pressures, especially in the presence of percolating fluids, their internal structures and sometimes even their mineralogical compositions may be changed. The processes involved are collectively known as metamorphism. The sort of temperatures and pressures required are, respectively, 300°C (572°F) and 100 megapascals (equivalent to almost 100 atmospheres).

The most extreme conditions in the Earth's crust occur at plate boundaries where continents collide. Most metamorphic rocks are thus generated in the roots of mountains. Depending upon temperature and pressure, there are various grades of metamorphism; but in the most intense (high-grade) metamorphism, rock structures, holes and even fossils are so completely obliterated that the original rock type can no longer be identified.

As a result of minerals realigning under pressure, many metamorphic rocks are layered, or banded. Sometimes the layering is visible; but when it is not, it can often be detected by the way the rock breaks. A good example is slate, which easily breaks into thin sheets along the layering. However, not all metamorphic rock is layered: non-layered varieties include marble, formed by the metamorphism of limestone, and quartzite, derived from sandstone.

■ *This granite arch is one of the many spectacular features in the Sierra Nevada mountain system, which runs along the eastern edge of the State of California in the western USA. Most granite comes from magma which has come to the surface, cooled and then solidified, but it can also be the product of granitic fluids emerging from deep within the Earth. Granite is a coarse-grained igneous rock, made up of the minerals feldspar (its main ingredient), quartz (at least 20%) and mica. It is the most common igneous rock found in the Earth's crust. Its strength and resilience has made it one of humankind's most popular building materials, used in highways, large buildings and tombstones*

■ *These jagged mounds in western Australia's Bungle Bungle National Park are made of delicate sandstone covered in a skin of silica. Sandstone is a clastic sedimentary rock, meaning it is made up of the eroded material from other rocks. Rivers and streams flowing from nearby mountains c. 350 million years ago washed sand and pebbles into the area and the sediment gradually compacted to form a sandstone massif 200 m high. Over time, heavy rains carved deep gorges into the rock, causing many of the dome-like towers to stand on their own. Due to the fragility of sandstone, the whole structure would have eroded completely without its protective layering of silica (orange) and lichen (black)*

■ *This metamorphic rock is gneiss, a medium- to coarse-grained rock with a distinct, uneven parallel banding. However, unlike schist, it does not have a tendency to split along the bands. Gneiss may contain large amounts of quartz and feldspar, alternating with areas of micas and amphiboles (minerals consisting of the silicates of calcium, iron, magnesium, sodium and aluminium). This may be what gives it its visible banding, between the dark mica and the pale feldspar minerals within it. Gneiss is the main rock found in large areas of metamorphic terrain. Like all the metamorphic rocks, gneiss is formed under high pressure and temperature, and represents the last stage of metamorphism in rock before it melts*

■ IGNEOUS ROCKS GET THEIR NAME FROM THE LATIN *IGNEUS*, MEANING 'FIRE' ■ THE WORD

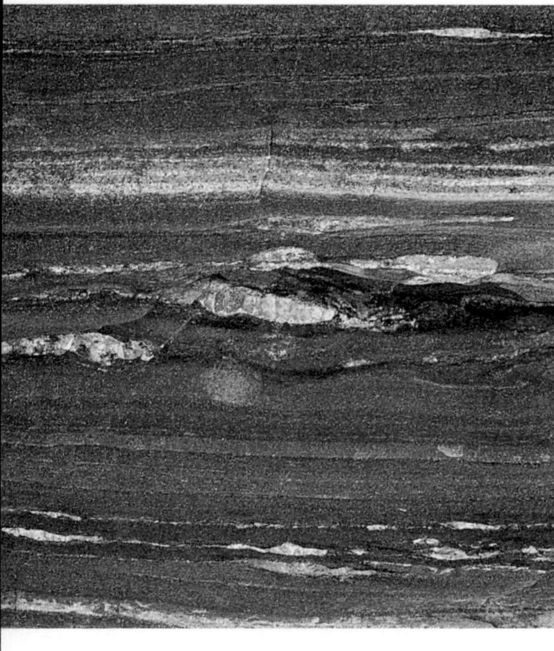

GEOLOGICAL TIMECHART

ERA	PERIOD	EPOCH	BEGAN (millions of years ago)	GEOGRAPHY
CENOZOIC	QUATERNARY	Holocene	0.01	Retreat of glaciers leaves continents, seas and landscapes in more or less their present forms.
		Pleistocene	1.6	The thickest continental glaciers depressed the Earth's crust to such an extent that large areas of north-western Europe and North America are still rising at a considerable rate today (30 mm a year around Hudson Bay).
	TERTIARY	Pliocene	5.3	Time of marked, often rapid change. Uplift of the isthmus of Panama results in the connection of North and South America.
		Miocene	23	Africa moves northwards into Eurasia. The Himalaya are raised as the Indian plate collides with Eurasia. The Red Sea opens and the Mediterranean has its origin.
		Oligocene	34	The main phase of Alpine mountain-building begins, followed soon afterwards by East African and Red Sea rifting. South America separates from Antarctica.
		Eocene	53	The Indian plate begins to collide with Eurasia (leading to the formation of the Himalaya in the Miocene). The Eurasian Basin opens as the final fragmentation of the Eurasian continent occurs. Pyrenean mountains form in the late Eocene. Australia separates from South America and Antarctica.
		Palaeocene	65	Iberia converges on Europe. The Atlantic and Pacific Oceans are linked through the straits of Panama.
MESOZOIC	CRETACEOUS		135	India separates from Antarctica, while Atlantic rifting brings about the separation of South America from Africa. Further opening of Atlantic and the separation of Greenland.
	JURASSIC		205	At the start of the Jurassic, rifting occurs between Gondwanaland and Laurasia, initially separating southern Europe from Africa and eventually tearing Pangaea in two. Central Atlantic opens.
	TRIASSIC		250	The start of the Mesozoic era sees all the major continents joined together. Consequently almost all of the Earth's land surface is concentrated on one side of the globe, with the result that large areas lie far from the oceans and become very arid.
PALAEOZOIC	PERMIAN		300	Pangaea is formed and, in the late Permian, Siberia collides with northern Pangaea to form the Ural Mountains.
	CARBONIFEROUS Divided in USA into Mississippian (early part) and Pennsylvanian (later part)		355	The major continents move closer and closer together until, early in the next period, Laurasia collides with Gondwanaland to form the supercontinent Pangaea.
	DEVONIAN		410	The gap between Laurasia and Gondwanaland has narrowed, but ocean levels remain high.
	SILURIAN		438	Laurasia forms as Laurentia and Baltica become welded together. Ocean levels are high, probably from melting of the ice cap.
	ORDOVICIAN		510	Baltica moves from South Polar region towards the Equator and closer to Laurentia. Meanwhile Gondwanaland moves towards the South Pole, and increased glaciation causes lowering of the sea level.
	CAMBRIAN		570	Near the end of the Precambrian era most landmasses fused into a giant supercontinent but, by the late Cambrian, Gondwanaland, Siberia and Laurentia are separate continents and more or less sit astride the Equator.
PRECAMBRIAN			4600	North America, Greenland and Scotland united as Laurentia, equatorial in position. Gondwanaland in the southern hemisphere.

'METAMORPHIC' COMES FROM THE GREEK WORDS *META* (CHANGE) AND *MORPHE* (FORM)

The Continents

▶ The Earth's land surface comprises seven continents, each with attendant islands, and is divided into 15 tectonic plates of various sizes.

▶ Europe, Africa and Asia, though politically distinct, physically form one land mass known as Afro-Eurasia, covering 57.2% of the Earth's land area.

▶ The Earth's land was once one enormous land mass called Pangaea.

CONTINENTAL DRIFT

▶ There is ever-increasing evidence that the Earth's land surface once comprised a single primeval land mass, now called Pangaea.
▶ This land mass split during the Upper Cretaceous period (100 to 65 million years ago) into two super-continents: Laurasia in the north and Gondwanaland in the south.

Throughout most of human history, people thought the continents were fixed in their present positions and the ocean floors were the oldest, most primitive parts of the planet. However, both assumptions were suddenly overthrown during the 1960s, as it became possible to prove that the continents are drifting across the Earth's surface, that the ocean floors are spreading, and that none of the oceanic crust is more than about 200 million years old, less than 5% of the Earth's age.

HOW IT WAS PROVED

Many rocks contain tiny magnetic particles, usually oxides of iron and titanium. When a rock forms, these particles become magnetized in the direction of the Earth's magnetic field at the particular site. Using highly sensitive instruments, it is possible to measure this weak magnetism and determine from it the position of the North Pole at the time the rock was formed.

Scientists were surprised to discover that for rocks older than a few million years, the North Poles determined in this way did not lie at the present North Pole, and that the older the rocks were, the greater the discrepancy. They were even more surprised to find that rocks of the same age from different continents gave ancient North Poles in quite different positions. However, there can be only one North Pole at any given time, and that must lie close to the north end of the Earth's rotational axis. Therefore, the only way of explaining the rock magnetic data was to assume that the continents had drifted with respect to both the present North Pole and each other.

TECTONIC PLATES

▶ Tectonic plates are either oceanic, continental, or a combination of both.
▶ The boundaries of tectonic plates are where mountains form and where most earthquakes and volcanoes occur.

The lithosphere – the rigid layer of Earth comprising the crust and the uppermost mantle – is divided into 15 tectonic plates. The plates 'float' on a partially molten layer called the asthenosphere, which is located below. Because they are floating, they have the freedom to move horizontally.

There are three types of tectonic plates – oceanic, continental, or a mixture of both. The Pacific Ocean is almost entirely an oceanic plate, but most plates include both oceanic and continental lithosphere.

PLATE MOVEMENT

▶ The Alps were formed by the plates of Africa and Eurasia colliding.
▶ The Red Sea was formed by two plates moving apart.

When two plates collide, one plate overrides the other and the lower plate is aborbed back into the Earth's mantle. If both plates are oceanic, these result in ocean trenches, seismic activity or volcanic islands. When one plate is continental, mountains may form. If both plates are continental, extremely high mountain ranges form, such as the Himalayas.

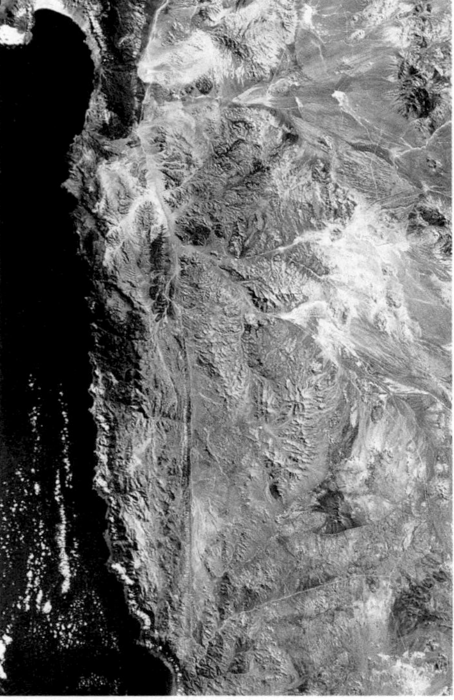

■ *The line running vertically, left of centre, in this satellite view is the Atacama Fault, Atacama Desert, Chile – one of many faults located on the Pacific coast*

When two plates move apart, there are rifts in the Earth's crust. If both plates are oceanic, ocean ridges and sea-floor spreading occur. If one of the plates is continental, rift valleys may form, such as the Great Rift Valley in Africa, which stretches from Mozambique to Syria.

When plates slide past each other, their grinding activity releases tiny earthquakes or tremors. However, certain areas of the plates lock together for long periods of time, sometimes hundreds of years, until the block is overcome. When the plates unlock, the released energy causes a major earthquake. The San Andreas Fault in California is an example where two plates are slowing sliding past each other, causing constant tremors and earthquake activity.

■ *This aerial view from a space shuttle, shows the Red Sea Rift formed by two tectonic plates moving apart, separating the Sinai Peninsula from the continent of Africa*

TECTONIC PLATES AND THEIR BOUNDARIES

Convergent boundary
Divergent boundary
Transform boundary

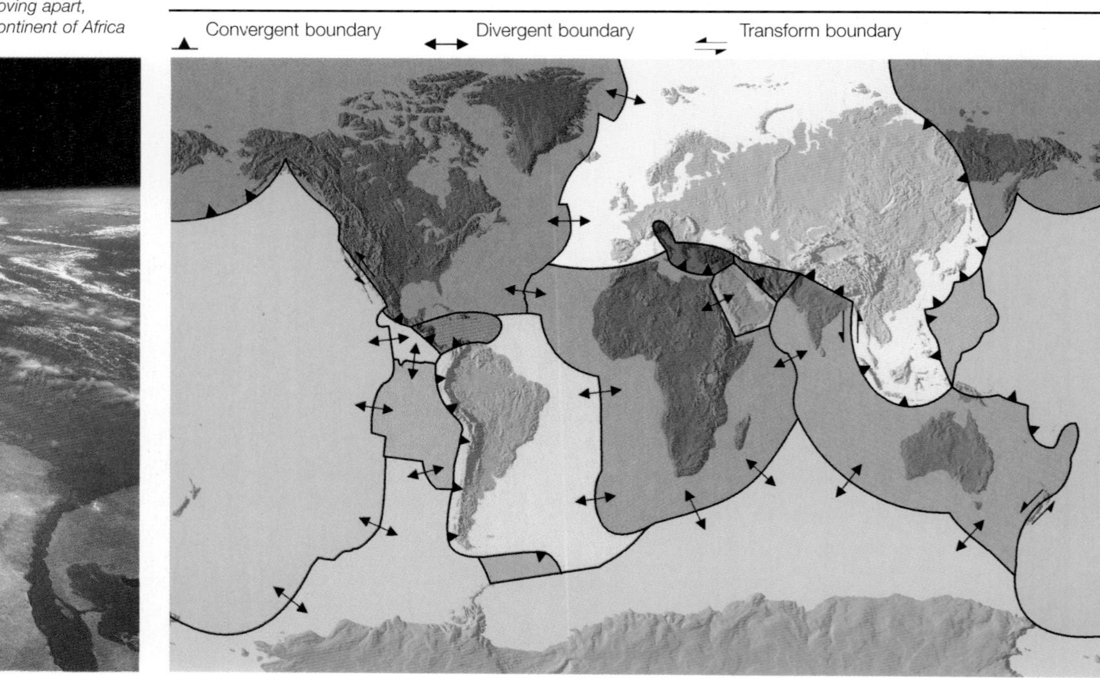

CONTINENTAL BOUNDARIES

ASIA

▷ Russia, which straddles the divide between Asia and Europe, does not recognize a dividing line between the continents. However, a political boundary running along the eastern foot of the Ural Mountains and then following the boundary of Kazakhstan to the Caspian Sea is generally recognized internationally.

▷ The boundary between Asia and Europe in the Caucasus is disputed. Some authorities recognize the crest of the Caucasus Mountains between the Black Sea and the Caspian as the dividing line, while others prefer a boundary following the valley of the River Manych to the estuary of the River Don.

AFRICA

▷ The boundary between Africa and Asia is usually regarded as the Suez Canal rather than the political boundary between Egypt and Israel/Gaza.

▷ The islands of Madeira, the Azores and the Canaries, which are all strictly attendant islands to Africa, are almost always included within Europe as they are integral parts of either Portugal or Spain.

▷ The island of Socotra, which is politically part of Yemen, is almost always included in Asia although it is strictly an attendant island to Africa.

NORTH AMERICA

▷ Central America (which includes Mexico) is often included in North America (Canada, the USA and Greenland), with South America being regarded as a separate continent.

▷ Hawaii, although physically part of Oceania, is often included in North America because it is politically part of the USA.

SOUTH AMERICA

▷ The northern boundary of South America is usually taken as the Panama–Colombia boundary rather than the Panama Canal. (Until the 20th century, what is now Panama was considered to be part of South America.)

▷ South America includes the Caribbean islands of Trinidad and Tobago, Aruba, Bonaire, Curaçao, and the Venezuelan Antilles.

EUROPE

▷ Physically, Europe excludes Asiatic Turkey, thus dividing the city of Istanbul between two continents. However, for economic and political purposes Turkey is usually regarded as being part of Europe.

▷ The islands of Madeira, the Azores and the Canaries, although strictly attendant islands to Africa, are almost always included in Europe.

▷ The island of Cyprus, an attendant island to Asia, is almost always included in Europe.

▷ The former Soviet republics of Armenia and Georgia, which are south of the crest of the Caucasus Mountains, regard themselves as being European. Together with Azerbaijan, which straddles the crest of the Caucasus Mountains, all three Transcaucasian states are often included within Europe.

OCEANIA/AUSTRALASIA

▷ In the east, the boundary between Asia and Oceania is disputed. Western New Guinea (Irian Jaya) is politically part of Indonesia but is generally regarded as part of Oceania rather than part of Asia. The rest of Indonesia is regarded as Asian.

■ *The Caucasus Mountains in the Tusheti Region of Georgia are at the disputed continental boundary of Europe and Asia*

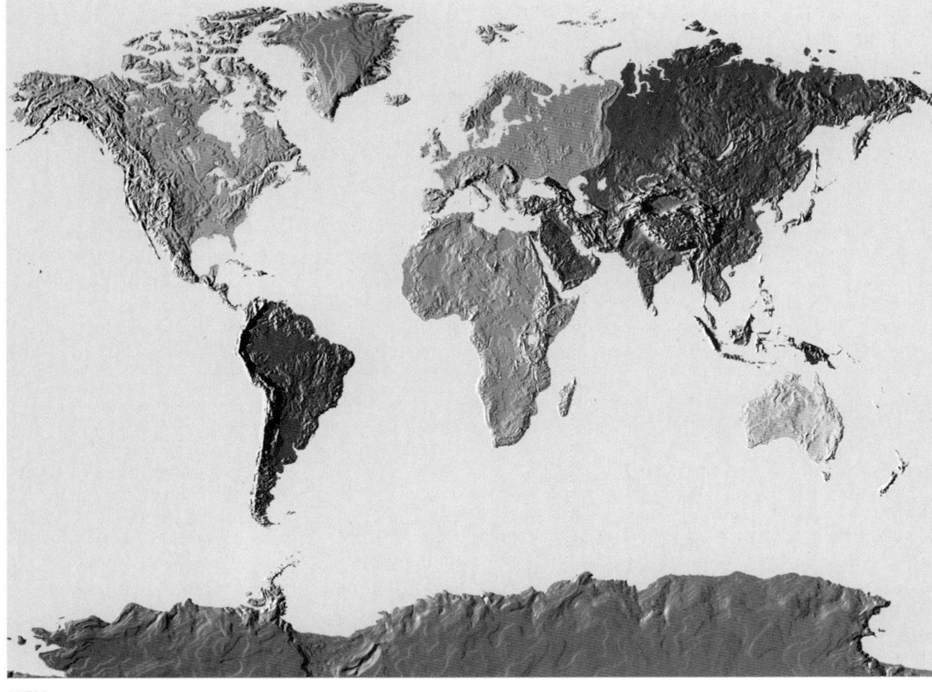

KEY

■ North America ■ South America ■ Europe ■ Africa
■ Asia ■ Oceania/Australasia ■ Antarctica
■ Disputed boundaries (located between Africa and Asia, Europe and Asia, and Oceania/Australasia and Asia)

FACT FINDER

CONTINENT	AREA km²	AREA sq mi	GREATEST EXTREMITY km	mi	
ASIA	44,614,000	17,226,000	6,435	4,000	north to south
			7,560	4,700	east to west
AFRICA	30,216,000	11,667,000	7,080	4,400	north to south
			6,035	3,750	east to west
NORTH AMERICA	24,230,000	9,355,000	7,885	5,000	north to south
			6,035	3,750	east to west
SOUTH AMERICA	17,814,000	6,878,000	7,240	4,500	north to south
			5,150	3,200	east to west
ANTARCTICA	14,245,000	5,500,000	4,340	2,700	north to north
EUROPE	10,505,000	4,056,000	2,900	1,800	north to south
			4,000	2,500	east to west
OCEANIA/AUSTRALASIA	8,503,000	3,283,000	3,000	1,870	north to south
			3,700	2,300	east to west

Seas and Oceans

- Nearly 71% or three-quarters of the Earth's surface is covered by oceans.
- The Pacific, Atlantic, Indian and Arctic oceans are the world's four oceans.
- World ocean water levels have increased 10–15 cm over the last 100 years.
- Most areas of the world have two high and two low tides daily.
- The depth of the oceans is very small compared with their area.

SEA WATER

▶ About 94% of the Earth's water is in the oceans.
▶ An average of about 3.5% of the volume of sea water consists of dissolved substances – mainly salt.

The saltiness, or salinity, of sea water depends on the amount of substances dissolved in it. Sodium and chlorine (which together in their solid form make up sodium chloride – common salt) are the most abundant of these, and together with magnesium, calcium and potassium make up over 90% of the elements dissolved in sea water. Other elements are present only in very small amounts.

High evaporation removes more of the pure water, leaving behind the dissolved substances. Therefore, the salinity is higher where evaporation is high, particularly if the sea water is also enclosed and cannot mix easily with the sea water in a larger ocean. This occurs, for example, in the Mediterranean and Red seas.

Low values of salinity occur in polar regions, particularly in the summer months when melting ice dilutes the sea water. Low salinity also occurs in seas such as the Baltic, which is fed by a large number of freshwater rivers and linked to the Atlantic Ocean by only a narrow channel.

More pure water is evaporated from the oceans than is returned as precipitation, e.g. in the form of rain or snow. However, the volume of water in the oceans remains the same because water also returns to the oceans from the land by rivers.

WAVES

▶ Most waves are caused by wind blowing across the surface of the ocean.
▶ Tidal waves (or tsunamis), which are not caused by wind, travel at very high speeds – around 750 km/h (470 mph).

Sea water is rarely still: it is usually moving in waves, tides or currents. The height of a wave is determined by the wind speed, the time the wind has been blowing, and the distance the wave has travelled over the ocean (known as its fetch). Waves play an important role in the shaping of coastlines.

Water does not move along with waves. Instead the water changes shape as a wave passes, moving in a roughly circular motion, rising towards a wave crest as it arrives and falling as it passes. This motion can be seen by watching a boat: the boat bobs up and down as the waves move past it but does not move along with the waves.

Tsunamis, although popularly called tidal waves, are not caused by tides. They are due to earthquakes or the eruption of undersea volcanoes, which move a large amount of water rapidly, disturbing the sea surface and creating waves that travel away from the area of the earthquake or volcano.

In the open ocean, tidal waves cause little damage as their wave height is usually less than 1 m (3 ft). However, in shallow water they slow down and their height can increase to 10 m (33 ft) or more, often causing extensive damage when they hit the shore.

TIDES

▶ Tides are caused by the gravitational pull of the Moon and the Sun on the Earth, causing the level of the oceans to change.
▶ The tidal range varies from less than 1 m (3 ft) in the Mediterranean Sea to 14.5 m (47 ft) in Canada's Bay of Fundy.

High tides occur when a point on the Earth's surface faces the Moon, and there is a stronger gravitational pull. They also occur when the Earth is on the other side of the Moon, which causes the sea water to rise away from the Moon.

As the Sun is much further away than the Moon, its effect on tides is less than half that of the Moon, despite its greater size. However, when both the Moon and Sun are on the same or opposite sides of the Earth, the pull is at its strongest, producing very high tides called spring tides. Weaker tides, called neap tides, occur when the Moon and the Sun form a right angle with the Earth, pulling in different directions. Spring tides occur every 14 days and neap tides halfway between each spring tide.

CURRENTS

▶ Currents are drifts of water moving in a given direction.
▶ Surface currents move much more slowly than the wind, with speeds of less than 8 km/h (5 mph).

Surface currents flow in circular or spiral movements influenced by the wind and the Earth's rotation. They move clockwise in the northern hemisphere and counterclockwise in the southern hemisphere. This is known as the Coriolis force. The water in currents is warmed at the Equator, driven by the wind, then rotated partly by the deflection of the coastline and partly by the Coriolis force. Deep (or density) currents also exist in oceans and are caused by variations in temperature and salinity.

■ *As waves travel into shallower water, they tend to slow down, causing them to grow in height before breaking*

THE SEA BED

The sea bed is made up of two sections: the continental margin (which includes the continental shelf, slope and rise) and the deep-ocean floor, with its ridges, seamounts, abyssal plains and trenches.

CONTINENTAL MARGIN

▶ Some 25% of the world's oil and gas comes from the continental shelf.
▶ The sea over continental shelves usually has abundant marine life and most fishing is done here.

The continental shelf is the shallowest part of the sea bed. It is around 130 m (430 ft) deep, relatively flat, and about 100 km (60 mi) wide. The continental slope is the area that slopes steeply from the continental shelf to the deep-ocean floor. A continental rise is a fan of sediment at the bottom of a continental slope.

DEEP-OCEAN FLOOR

▶ The deepest part of the ocean floor is 11,022 m (36,160 ft) – over 2000 m (6000 ft) greater than the height of Mount Everest.
▶ Fish or crustaceans living in the abyssal plains on the deep-ocean floor are often blind or have their own light sources.

OCEANIC RIDGES

Oceanic ridges are vast, rugged, undersea mountain chains, often at the centre of oceans. On average, they are some 1000 km (620 mi) wide and stand up to 3000 m (10,000 ft) above the adjacent ocean basins. The ridges form a more or less linked system about 80,000 km (50,000 mi) long and can be found in all the major oceans.

On average, ridge crests lie 2500 m (8200 ft) below the ocean surface. However, there are a few places, such as Iceland, where they rise above the ocean's surface and form an island.

ABYSSAL PLAINS

Between the ocean ridges and the continental margins there are abyssal plains. These are very flat and featureless parts of the sea floor, around 4000 m (13,000 ft) deep.

Abyssal plains contain very little marine life as light cannot penetrate to these depths and the temperature never rises above 4°C.

SEAMOUNTS

Abyssal plains are broken in some places by seamounts – underwater volcanoes that have erupted from the sea floor.

Hawaii is a seamount which has risen above the sea surface to form an island. The highest known seamount is located near the Tonga Trench between Samoa and New Zealand and rises 8700 m (28,500 ft) from the sea bed.

OCEAN TRENCHES

The deepest parts of the oceans are the ocean trenches – on average about 100 km (62 mi) wide, 7000–8000 m (23,000–26,000 ft) deep, and up to thousands of kilometres long. Ocean trenches are formed by one oceanic tectonic plate sliding underneath the other, causing the ocean floor to be dragged down.

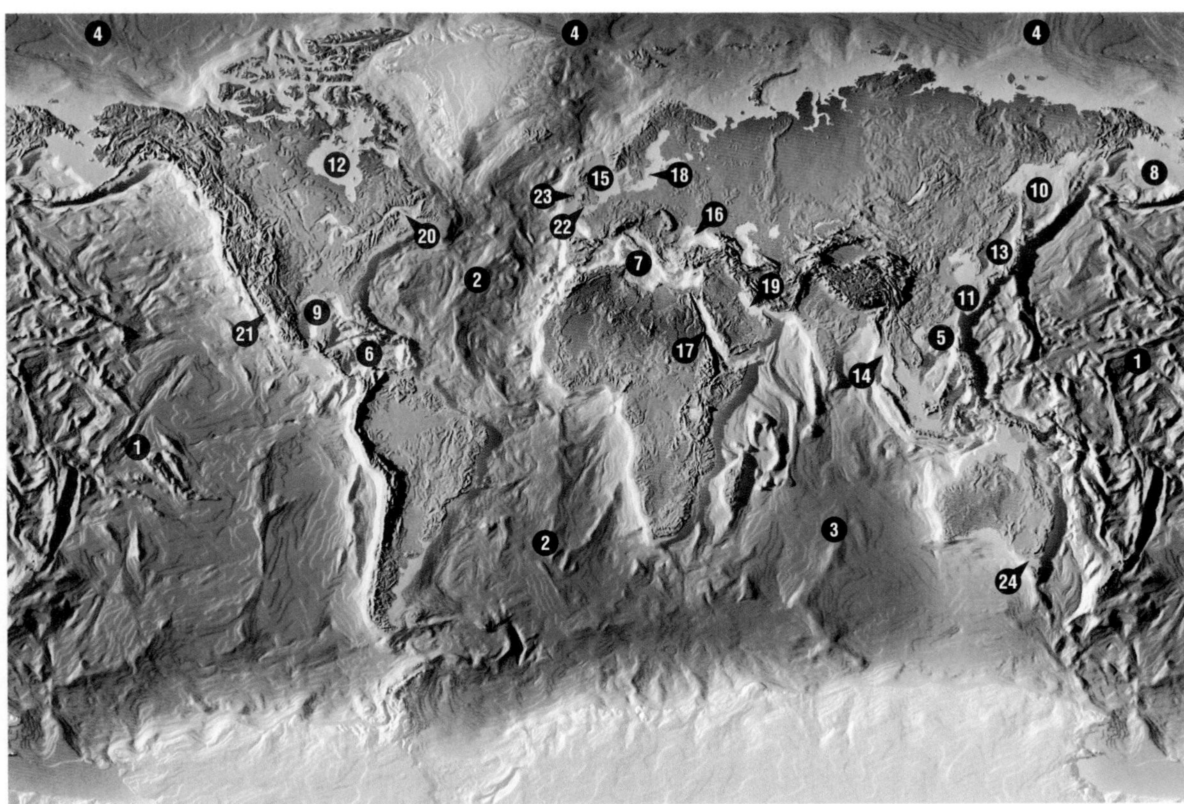

① The Pacific is the world's largest and deepest ocean, covering over one-third of the Earth's surface

② The Atlantic is the youngest ocean, formed when surrounding continents split apart about 200 million years ago

③ The Indian Ocean is rich in minerals, such as petroleum, gas, iron ore, copper, manganese and chrome

④ Most of the Arctic Ocean, centred on the North Pole, is covered by up to 4 m (14 ft) of ice all year round

⑦ The Suez Canal, built in 1869, linked the Mediterranean Sea to the Indian Ocean via the Red Sea

⑧ The Bering Sea (named after the Danish explorer Vitus Bering) is usually frozen from October to June

⑲ The highest sea temperature recorded – 36.5°C (96°F) on the surface – was in the Persian (Arabian) Gulf

㉒ In 1994 the UK and France were connected by the Channel Tunnel, built 40 m (131 ft) under the English Channel sea bed

5 SHORTEST COASTLINES

	km	mi
① MONACO	5.6	3.5
② NAURU	19	12
③ BOSNIA	20	13
④ JORDAN	25	16
⑤ SLOVENIA	30	19

▶ The country with the longest coastline is Canada, including its islands, with a length of 244,800 km (152,100 mi).

10 DEEPEST SEA TRENCHES

	m	ft
① MARIANA TRENCH (western Pacific)	11,022	36,160
② TONGA-KERMADEC TRENCH (southern Pacific)	10,882	35,702
③ KURIL-KAMCHATKA TRENCH (western Pacific)	10,542	34,587
④ PHILIPPINE TRENCH (western Pacific)	10,497	34,439
⑤ IDZU-BONIN TRENCH (western Pacific)	9,810	32,185
⑥ PUERTO RICO TRENCH (western Atlantic)	9,220	30,249
⑦ NEW HEBRIDES TRENCH (southern Pacific)	9,165	30,069
⑧ NEW BRITAIN TRENCH* (southern Pacific)	9,140	29,988
⑨ YAP TRENCH (western Pacific)	8,527	27,976
⑩ JAPAN TRENCH (western Pacific)	8,412	27,599

* Also known as the Solomon Trench

FACT FINDER

	AREA km²	AREA sq mi	AVERAGE DEPTH m	AVERAGE DEPTH ft
OCEANS				
① PACIFIC	166,240,000	64,190,000	4,188	13,740
② ATLANTIC	86,560,000	33,420,000	3,736	12,260
③ INDIAN	73,430,000	28,350,000	3,872	12,700
④ ARCTIC	13,230,000	5,110,000	1,205	3,950
SEAS				
⑤ SOUTH CHINA SEA	2,974,600	1,148,500	1,200	4,000
⑥ CARIBBEAN SEA	2,753,000	1,063,000	2,400	8,000
⑦ MEDITERRANEAN SEA	2,503,000	966,500	1,485	4,875
⑧ BERING SEA	2,268,180	875,750	1,400	4,600
⑨ GULF OF MEXICO	1,542,985	595,750	1,500	5,000
⑩ SEA OF OKHOTSK	1,527,570	589,800	840	2,750
⑪ EAST CHINA SEA	1,249,150	482,300	180	600
⑫ HUDSON BAY	1,232,300	475,800	120	400
⑬ SEA OF JAPAN	1,007,500	389,000	1,370	4,500
⑭ ANDAMAN SEA	797,700	308,000	865	2,850
⑮ NORTH SEA	575,300	222,140	90	300
⑯ BLACK SEA	461,980	178,380	1,100	3,600
⑰ RED SEA	437,700	169,000	490	1,610
⑱ BALTIC SEA	422,160	163,000	55	180
⑲ PERSIAN GULF*	238,790	92,200	24	80
⑳ GULF OF ST LAWRENCE	237,760	91,800	120	400
㉑ GULF OF CALIFORNIA	162,000	62,550	810	2,660
㉒ ENGLISH CHANNEL	89,900	34,700	54	180
㉓ IRISH SEA	88,550	34,200	60	200
㉔ BASS STRAIT	75,000	28,950	70	230

* Also referred to as the Arabian Gulf or, popularly, the Gulf

Note: Seas listed are those recognized by the International Hydrographic Bureau. Other so-called seas are actually parts of larger seas or oceans. For instance, the Tyrrhenian, Ligurian, Adriatic, Ionian and Aegean seas are part of the Mediterranean Sea, and the Timor, Banda, Arafura, Seram and Flores seas are part of the Indian Ocean.

ISLANDS

- An island is a body of land, smaller than a continent, that is completely surrounded by water.
- Islands range in size from very small mud and sand islands of only a few square metres, to Greenland, which has an area of 2,175,600 km^2.
- The newest island, still unnamed, appeared in Tonga's Ha'apai group in the south-west Pacific on 6 June 1995.
- Australia is normally considered to be a continent rather than an island.

Islands have a large range of origins, especially those found in seas and oceans. Islands can develop through constructional processes, such as build-ups of sediment or volcanic activity, or they can be formed by erosional, or destructive, processes that cause an area of land to become separated from the mainland. Rising sea levels can also lead to the development of islands, by drowning low-lying areas of land and separating higher areas from the main land mass. Islands are classified as two types: continental (unsubmerged parts of the continental shelf which are surrounded by water) or oceanic (those which rise to the surface from the ocean floor).

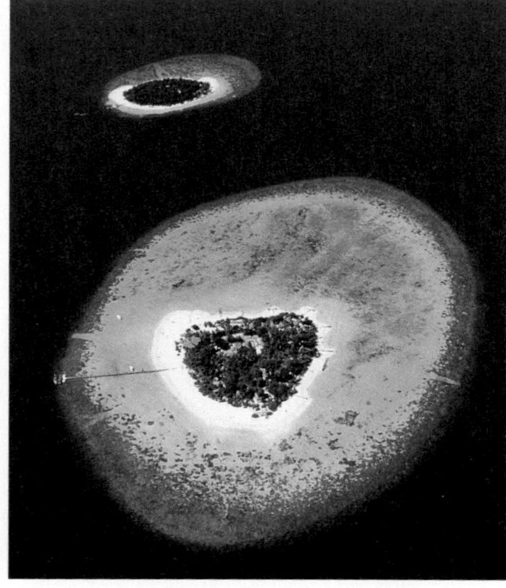

This view of Vabbinfaru, Muratti Island, Maldives, shows the coral reef and lagoon characteristic of coral islands

VOLCANIC ISLANDS

▶ When volcanic activity occurs beneath the oceans, it can lead to the growth of islands.
▶ The explosion of Krakatoa in 1883 reduced two-thirds of this volcanic island to dust and created many small islets. In 1952 a new island, known as Anak Krakatau (The Son of Krakatoa), surfaced.

Volcanic islands are the result of movement of the Earth's crustal plates. Islands occur both at constructive plate margins, such as mid-oceanic spreading sites (e.g. Iceland) and at destructive margins where tectonic plates are moving together (e.g. the Japanese islands). Volcanic islands can also form far from any plate boundary, such as the Hawaiian Islands, which are located above a volcanic 'hot spot' in the middle of the Pacific plate.

Iceland, situated on the Mid-Atlantic Ridge, is the largest example of a volcanic island formed at a constructive plate margin. It started forming about 20 million years ago (the age of the oldest rocks on the island) and is still growing in size today, as new material is periodically added to the land along a line of volcanic activity running south-west to north-east.

Much of the volcanic activity responsible for Iceland's growth has not been in the form of spectacular eruptions. Instead, quiet extrusive fissure eruptions, involving the outpouring of large quantities of lava from cracks in the Earth's surface, have repeatedly given rise to basaltic rock. Spectacular eruptions have, however, also played their part. For example, in 1963, eruptions occurred off the south coast of Iceland. In the space of a few weeks, ash and lava built up on the sea floor and a new, small island named Surtsey, 35 km (22 mi) off the coast of Iceland, was born.

ARCHIPELAGOS

▶ An archipelago is a group of islands or an area of sea containing a group of islands.
▶ The world's largest archipelago is the 5600-km (3500-mi) crescent of more than 17,000 islands that make up Indonesia.

The collision of crustal plates at destructive margins can trigger volcanic activity. If this occurs at the edge of a land mass it can cause mountain building, but when the collision occurs beneath an ocean, island development can result. Islands which are born in this way do not occur singly, but in chains or archipelagos ('arcs') that form parallel to the plate boundary.

This is well illustrated on the western side of the Pacific Ocean. Here thousands of islands – most of them volcanic but some formed by the folding up of the ocean floor – mark the western edge of the Pacific plate. These islands start in the south at New Zealand, run north to the Tongan chain before heading west to New Guinea, and north again through the Philippines, Japan, the Kurile island chain and finally the Aleutian Islands, which continue to the mainland of North America.

CORAL ISLANDS

▶ Coral islands and reefs occur in warm tropical and subtropical oceans and seas.
▶ They are formed from the skeletons of the group of primitive marine organisms known as corals.

Coral islands develop where coral grows up towards the ocean surface from shallow submarine platforms – often from volcanic cones. If the cone is totally submerged, then a coral atoll will develop – a circular or horseshoe-shaped coral ring which encloses a body of sea water called a lagoon. Upward growth of the coral ceases once sea level has been reached. Coral islands are therefore flat and low, unless a change in sea level has caused their elevation to change.

SEA LEVEL AND ISLANDS

▶ Changes in sea level can cause new islands to appear or existing ones to disappear.
▶ Some scientists believe that island groups, such as The Maldives, are in danger of vanishing due to global warming and the resulting rise in sea levels.

During the last Ice Age (10,000–72,000 years ago), eastern Britain was joined to mainland Europe, because sea levels were lower as much of the world's water was frozen in the ice caps and glaciers. As the ice melted, and the sea level rose, the North Sea and the Straits of Dover were re-established. By about 8500 years ago, Britain was again an island.

FRESHWATER ISLANDS

▶ The island of Marajó, in the mouth of the River Amazon, is larger in area than Switzerland.
▶ Bananal, Brazil, is the world's largest inland island (i.e. land surrounded by rivers).

Islands also occur in freshwater lakes and in the freshwater estuarine mouths of rivers. Such islands are often the result of depositions of eroded material, although they may also owe their origin to a number of other causes, including glaciation.

(1) GREENLAND

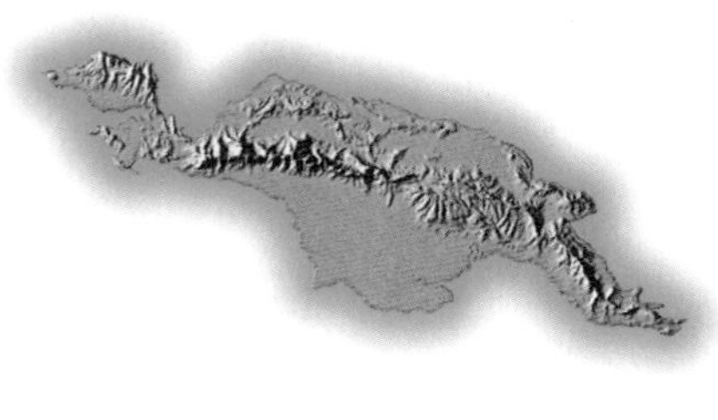

(2) NEW GUINEA

(3) BORNEO

(4) MADAGASCAR

■ The volcanic island of Surtsey was formed in 1963 after an eruption on Iceland, when lava spewed into the sea and came to rest on the ocean floor, eventually forming this small island

25 LARGEST ISLANDS

	AREA km²	AREA sq mi	LOCATION	STATUS
1 GREENLAND	2,175,600	840,070	Arctic Ocean	an internally self-governing part of the kingdom of Denmark
2 NEW GUINEA	808,510	312,190	western Pacific	divided between Indonesia and Papua New Guinea
3 BORNEO	757,050	292,320	Indian Ocean	divided between Indonesia, Malaysia and Brunei
4 MADAGASCAR	594,180	229,430	Indian Ocean	republic
5 SUMATRA (SUMATERA)	524,100	202,370	Indian Ocean	part of Indonesia
6 BAFFIN ISLAND	476,070	183,830	Arctic Ocean	part of Nunavut Territory, Canada
7 HONSHU	230,460	88,990	NW Pacific	part of Japan
8 GREAT BRITAIN	229,870	88,760	N Atlantic	part of United Kingdom
9 ELLESMERE ISLAND	212,690	82,130	Arctic Ocean	part of Northwest Territories, Canada
10 VICTORIA ISLAND	212,200	81,940	Arctic Ocean	part of Northwest Territories, Canada
11 CELEBES (SULAWESI)	189,040	73,000	Indian Ocean	part of Indonesia
12 SOUTH ISLAND, NZ	150,460	58,100	SW Pacific	part of New Zealand
13 JAVA (JAWA)	134,050	51,760	Indian Ocean	part of Indonesia
14 NORTH ISLAND, NZ	114,690	44,290	SW Pacific	part of New Zealand
15 CUBA	114,530	44,230	Caribbean Sea	republic
16 LUZON	104,690	40,430	western Pacific	part of the Philippines
17 ICELAND	102,820	39,700	N Atlantic	republic
18 NEWFOUNDLAND	95,830	37,000	NW Atlantic	part of Canada
19 MINDANAO	94,630	36,540	western Pacific	part of the Philippines
20 IRELAND	83,050	32,070	N Atlantic	divided between Republic of Ireland and Northern Ireland
21 HOKKAIDO	78,460	30,300	NW Pacific	part of Japan
22 HISPANIOLA	78,460	30,300	Caribbean Sea	divided between the Dominican Republic and Haiti
23 SAKHALIN	76,400	29,500	NW Pacific	part of Russia
24 TASMANIA	68,330	26,390	SW Pacific	a state of Australia
25 SRI LANKA	65,610	25,340	Indian Ocean	republic

4 The island of Madagascar has 90% unique wildlife species due to an ancient continental shift away from Africa

7 Honshu, with over 100 million inhabitants, is larger than all the other 3921 Japanese islands put together

13 The island of Java is only 7% of the area of Indonesia, but is the home of 60% of the country's population

23 Although the Pacific island of Sakhalin is at the same latitude as France, it has a cold near-Arctic climate

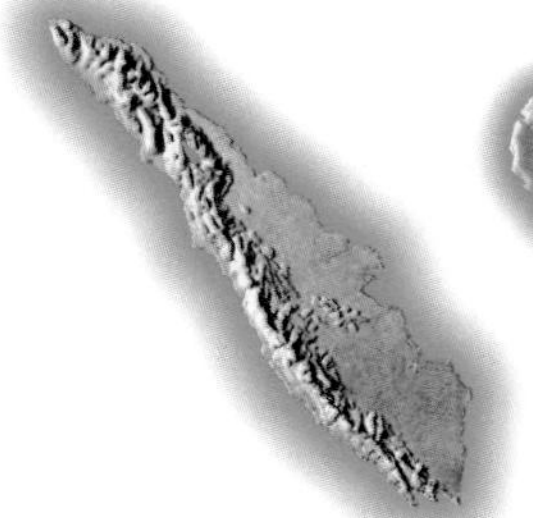

5 SUMATRA

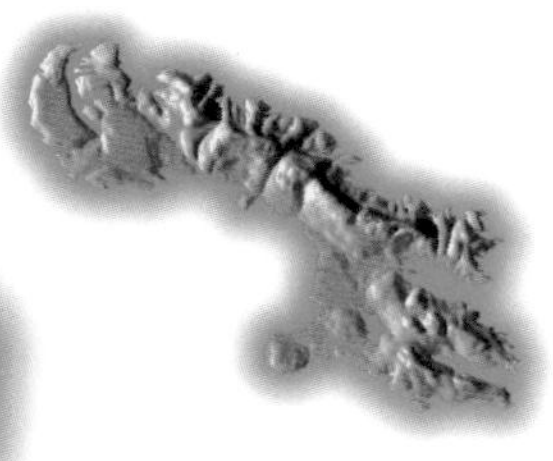

6 BAFFIN ISLAND

7 HONSHU

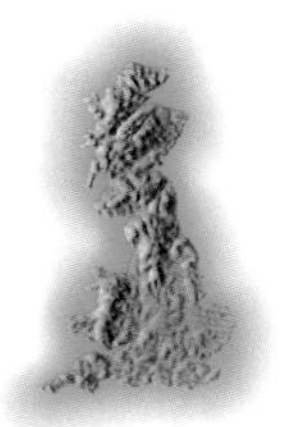

8 GREAT BRITAIN

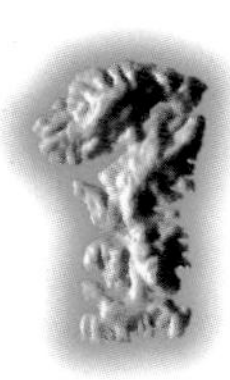

9 ELLESMERE ISLAND

10 VICTORIA ISLAND

MOUNTAINS

- A commonly used definition of a mountain is an upward projection of the Earth's surface, often having a rocky summit, and with an altitude over 600 m.
- Mauna Kea in the Hawaiian Islands is 10,203 m high from its base on the Pacific Ocean floor to its peak, making it the world's highest mountain overall (although only 4208 m of the mountain is above sea level).
- Mountain ranges can have major impacts on regional climates, for example by creating rain shadow zones behind them, which can cause deserts.
- The lowest-lying countries in the world are the Maldives (highest point – 4 m), the Marshall Islands (6 m), Tuvalu (6 m) and The Gambia (43 m).
- Submerged mountains with heights of over 1000 m from the ocean floor are called seamounts.

WHERE DO MOUNTAINS OCCUR?

▶ The majority of the world's largest mountains occur along the boundaries between the Earth's tectonic plates.
▶ Mountains also occur near the centre of tectonic plates associated with volcanic hot spots.

Individual mountains and mountain ranges are one of the most prominent features of the Earth's surface, with mountain chains such as the Himalaya in central Asia reaching heights of over 8.8 km (5.5 mi) and ranges like the Andes in South America stretching for over 7200 km (4480 mi). Mountains are not only prominent landscape features but also exert a major influence upon regional climates by causing air masses to rise over them or divert around them. They may also have a major impact on human activity, traditionally acting as obstructions to communication routes such as roads and railways.

The distribution of the world's largest mountain ranges closely follows the zones on the Earth's land surface where earthquakes and volcanoes are common – in other words, the boundaries between the Earth's tectonic plates. The biggest mountain ranges occur where tectonic plates are in collision with one another. Most of the large ranges, including the Alps, Himalaya, Andes and Rockies, are relatively young in geological terms, resulting from the collision of tectonic plates within the last 25 million years or so.

Not all mountain ranges, however, are at currently active tectonic plate boundaries. For example, the Scottish Highlands, Scandinavian mountains and Appalachians, which are hundreds of miles away from any plate margin, formed between 300–400 million years ago in locations where ancient tectonic plates collided and fused together. Other mountains, such as many Australian ranges, are deeply eroded remnants in the centre of tectonic plates and may be up to 3000 million years old.

HOW DO MOUNTAINS FORM?

▶ Mountains can be formed by earth movements caused by the collision of tectonic plates or by volcanic activity.
▶ Many mountain ranges, including the Alps, Andes, Rockies and Himalaya, are still being formed and are rising at the present day.

Mountains and mountain ranges form in three very different ways: as a result of tectonic movement, fault-block movement or volcanic activity. The height of a mountain represents the balance between the mountain-building processes (often termed orogenic processes) which are forming it (or, in the case of ancient ranges, which led to its formation in the past) and the various erosive processes which are trying to wear it away.

FOLDED MOUNTAINS

The largest and most complex mountain ranges, generally found on continental land masses, are the result of tectonic plates colliding at convergent plate margins. In simple terms, when two relatively rigid lithospheric or tectonic plates collide, the margin of one of the plates is forced upwards, forming an upland mountainous area. These upland areas are usually referred to as fold mountains, because the rocks at the collision zone are folded, faulted and deformed due to interaction of the tectonic plates. In addition to the uplift caused by plates colliding, considerable heat may be generated, leading to volcanic activity and expansion of the crust. For example, much of the Andean mountain range is formed by a combination of volcanic activity and uplift at a colliding plate margin.

Fold mountains can occur at any convergent plate boundary, and mountain building is still occurring today. For example, the Andes were formed and are still forming as a result of the oceanic Pacific plate colliding with the continental American plate. However, the largest mountains are formed where two continental tectonic plates collide, as was the case when the Indian plate collided with the Eurasian plate to form the Himalaya, causing the uplift of the Tibetan Plateau. This uplift is still occurring today as the plates continue to converge. Many older fold mountain ranges are the product of plate collisions which ceased long ago, such as the Scottish Highlands, which were at a convergent plate margin millions of years ago.

FAULT-BLOCK AND UPWARPED MOUNTAINS

Other types of mountain exist that have been indirectly influenced by tectonic plate activity occurring elsewhere. The most common examples of these types of mountains are fault-block mountains and upwarped mountains.

In fault-block mountains, a block of the Earth's crust, bounded by fault zones, has sunk, while surrounding parts of the crust have been uplifted. This usually occurs by the crust compressing, causing some parts to be forced downwards and other parts to rise. Fault-block mountains, for example, exist in the Basin and Range Province of Utah, New Mexico and Arizona, and the Sierra Nevada of California, USA. Here the crust has been subjected to considerable pressure from interactions between the Pacific and American tectonic plates.

In upwarped mountains, the opposite situation occurs, with a central fault-bounded crustal block being forced upwards relative to the surrounding crust, again as a result of compression. Examples of upwarped mountains include the Black Hills of Dakota and the Adirondacks of New York, USA.

VOLCANIC MOUNTAINS

Spectacular mountains and mountain chains are also created as a result of volcanic activity. These occur in three distinctly different locations. Some of the most impressive volcanic mountains are found at tectonic collision sites where continental and oceanic plates are moving together. These processes have led to the formation of major volcanic mountain masses, such as those of Guatemala in Central America. Volcanic mountain chains also form along tectonic spreading sites, such as the Mid-Atlantic Ridge. Many volcanic mountains are submerged beneath the sea but, where volcanic activity is sufficiently great, they may emerge to form mountainous islands. Volcanic mountain chains also form at locations such as along the Great African Rift, where volcanic activity occurs from a rift zone within the African tectonic plate. Isolated mountains also occur at the centre of tectonic plates, such as Mauna Kea and Mauna Loa in the Hawaiian Islands, which were formed by volcanic activity associated with volcanic hot spots.

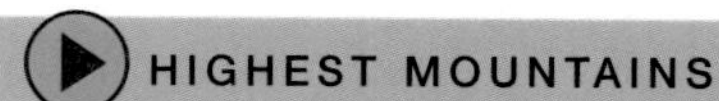

Subsidiary peaks or tops within the same range are listed after the main mountain.
Key to ranges: H = Himalaya; K = Karakoram.

	HEIGHT m	ft	RANGE
Mt Everest*	8,863	29,078	H
Everest South Summit	8,750	28,707	H
K2 (Chogori)	8,610	28,250	K
Kangchenjunga	8,598	28,208	H
Yalung Kang (Kangchenjunga West)	8,502	27,894	H
Kangchenjunga South Peak	8,488	27,848	H
Kangchenjunga Middle Peak	8,475	27,806	H
Lhotse	8,511	27,923	H
Subsidiary Peak	8,410	27,592	H
Lhotse Shar	8,383	27,503	H
Makalu I	8,481	27,825	H
Makalu South-East	8,010	26,280	H
Dhaulagiri I	8,167	26,795	H
Manaslu I (Kutang I)	8,156	26,760	H
Cho Oyu	8,153	26,750	H
Nanga Parbat (Diamir)	8,124	26,660	H
Annapurna I	8,091	26,546	H
Annapurna East	8,010	26,280	H
Gasherbrum I (Hidden Peak)	8,068	26,470	K
Broad Peak I	8,047	26,400	K
Broad Peak Middle	8,016	26,300	K
Broad Peak Central	8,000	26,247	K
Shisham Pangma (Gosainthan)	8,046	26,398	H
Gasherbrum II	8,034	26,360	K

* Known in Chinese as Qomolangma, in Nepalese as Sagarmatha and in Tibetan as Mi-ti gu-ti cha-pu long-na

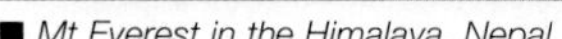
■ Mt Everest in the Himalaya, Nepal

■ Kilimanjaro volcano in Tanzania

■ Mt McKinley in Alaska, USA

■ Aconcagua in the Andes, Argentina

GREATEST MOUNTAIN RANGES

	LOCATION	LENGTH km	mi	CULMINATING PEAK	HEIGHT m	ft
Andes	western South America	7,200	4,500	Cerro Aconcagua	6,960	22,834
Rocky Mountains	western North America	4,800	3,000	Mt Elbert	4,400	14,436
Himalaya–Karakorum–Hindu Kush	southern central Asia	3,800	2,360	Mt Everest	8,863	29,078
Great Dividing Range	eastern Australia	3,600	2,240	Mt Kosciusko	2,230	7,316
Trans Antarctic Range	Antarctica	3,500	2,180	Mt Vinson	5,140	16,864
Brazilian Atlantic Coast Range	eastern Brazil	3,000	1,870	Pico de Bandeira	2,890	9,482
West Sumatran–Java Range	west Sumatra and Java	2,900	1,800	Mt Kerintji	3,805	12,484
Aleutian Range	Alaska and NW Pacific*	2,650	1,650	Shishaldin	2,861	9,386
Tien Shan	Kyrgyzstan/China	2,250	1,400	Pik Pobedy	7,439	24,406
Central New Guinea Range	Irian Jaya/Papua New Guinea	2,000	1,250	Ngga Pulu	5,030	16,503
Altai Mountains	Russia/Mongolia	2,000	1,250	Gora Belukha	4,505	14,780
Ural Mountains	Russia	2,000	1,250	Gora Narodnaya	1,894	6,214
Kamchatka Mountains	eastern Russia	1,930	1,200	Klyuchevskaya Sopka	4,850	15,912
Atlas Mountains	north-west Africa	1,930	1,200	Jebel Toubkal	4,165	13,665
Verkhoyanskiy Mountains	Russia	1,610	1,000	Gora Mas Khaya	2,959	9,708
Western Ghats	India	1,610	1,000	Anai Madi	2,694	8,839
Sierra Madre Oriental	Mexico	1,530	950	Volcan Citlaltépetl (Pico de Orizaba)	5,610	18,406
Zagros Mountains	Iran	1,530	950	Mt Zard Kuh	4,547	14,918
Scandinavian Range	Norway/Sweden	1,530	950	Mt Galdhöpiggen	2,469	8,098
Ethiopian Highlands	Ethiopia	1,450	900	Ras Dashan	4,620	15,157
Sierra Madre Occidental	Mexico	1,450	900	Nevado de Colima	4,265	13,993
Malagasy Range	Madagascar	1,370	850	Tsaratanana peak	2,876	9,436
Drakensberg	southern Africa	1,290	800	Mt Thabana Ntlenyana	3,482	11,425
Chersky Range	Russia	1,290	800	Gora Pobeda	3,147	10,325
Caucasus	Georgia/Russia/Azerbaijan	1,200	750	Mt Elbrus	5,642	18,510
Alaska Range	Alaska, USA	1,130	700	Mt McKinley	6,194	20,320
Assam Burma Range	Assam (India)–W Burma	1,130	700	Hkakado Razi	5,881	19,296
Cascade Range	NW USA/Canada	1,130	700	Mt Rainier	4,392	14,409
Central Borneo Range	Borneo (Indonesia)/Malaysia	1,130	700	Mt Klnabalu	4,101	13,455
Apennines	Italy	1,130	700	Corno Grande	2,931	9,616
Appalachians	eastern USA	1,130	700	Mt Mitchell	2,037	6,683
Alps	central Europe	1,050	650	Mont Blanc	4,807	15,771

* Continuous mainland length (excluding islands) 720 km (450 mi)

■ Mt Vinson in Ellesworth Land, Antarctica

■ Mt Elbrus in the Caucasus, Russia

■ Mont Blanc in the Alps, France and Italy

HIGHEST MOUNTAIN PEAKS IN EACH CONTINENT

	PEAK	HEIGHT m	ft	LOCATION
ASIA	Mt Everest	8,863	29,078	Nepal/China
AFRICA	Mt Kilimanjaro	5,894	19,340	Tanzania
NORTH AMERICA	Mt McKinley	6,194	20,320	USA
SOUTH AMERICA	Cerro Aconcagua	6,960	22,834	Argentina
ANTARCTICA	Mt Vinson	5,140	16,863	Ellesworth Land
EUROPE*	Mt Elbrus	5,642	18,510	Russia
	Mont Blanc	4,807	15,771	France/Italy
OCEANIA/AUSTRALASIA**	Ngga Pulu (Jayakusuma)	5,030	16,503	Indonesia

* Under some definitions of Europe, the Caucasus region is included in the Continent and, therefore, the highest mountain would be Elbrus at 5642 m (18,510 ft)

** Some definitions of Oceania exclude New Guinea, in which case the highest mountain would be Mt Cook in New Zealand at 3754 m (12,315 ft)

■ Ngga Pulu (Jayakusuma) in Indonesia

VOLCANOES

- The highest volcano in Europe that has been active in historical times is Pico de Teide, which rises 3716 m on the island of Tenerife in the Canary Islands off the north-west coast of Africa and south of Spain.
- The eruption of Mount Pinatubo in 1991 in Luzon, the Philippines, was the most violent this century.
- Even now, hundreds of volcanoes are erupting unseen on the sea bed beneath the world's oceans.
- Ash clouds from massive volcanic eruptions can block out the Sun's rays and cause lowering of global temperatures (one of the more popular theories for the extinction of the dinosaurs).
- Volcanoes are also known to exist on the planets Venus and Mars and on Io, one of Jupiter's moons.

■ *Mauna Ulu Crater in Hawaii's Kilauea (meaning 'much spreading') volcano, the world's largest active volcano mass*

■ *Eruption of Mt Etna, May 1983 – one of many eruptions this century, the most recent being in 1996*

■ *Volcanic rock covers Keanae Peninsula on Maui on Hawaii, USA – an island created by two volcanoes*

WHAT IS A VOLCANO?

▶ Over 800 volcanoes have been active during historical times.
▶ Volcanic eruptions can create new land masses, such as the island of Surtsey to the south of Iceland.

A volcano is a mountain, often conical in shape, which has been built up above an opening, or vent, in the Earth's crust during violent and spectacular eruptions. When eruptions occur, molten rock, or magma, wells up from deep below the ground and is either thrown out with great force or flows out through the opening, or crater, frequently along with other rock debris and gases. Volcanoes can exist both on land or beneath the oceans.

Few spectacles in nature are more awesome or more terrifying than volcanic eruptions. In the most violent ones, tremendous explosions inside the volcano hurl large rocks, cinders and great clouds of ash, steam and gas high into the sky from the crater, at the top. Streams of molten rock known as lava, and sometimes boiling mud, pour down the surrounding slopes, destroying everything in their path. Fast moving clouds of steam and gas, termed *nuée ardentes*, may also move down the slope of the volcano.

In prehistoric times, 500–350 million years ago, there were very violent periods of volcanic activity when thousands of volcanoes erupted constantly. Many mountain ranges in existence today consist of the remains of long dead volcanoes.

MAJOR RECENTLY ACTIVE VOLCANOES

	RANGE/LOCATION	HEIGHT m	ft	LAST NOTIFIED ERUPTION
OJOS DEL SALADO	Andes, Argentina/Chile	6,895	22,622	1981 (steams)
LLULLAILLACO	Andes, Argentina/Chile	6,723	22,058	1877
SAN PEDRO	Andes, Chile	6,199	20,339	1960
GUALLATIRI	Andes, Chile	6,060	19,882	1993
SAN JOSÉ	Andes, Chile	5,919	19,425	1931
COTOPAXI	Andes, Ecuador	5,897	19,348	1975
EL MISTI	Andes, Ecuador	5,862	19,233	1878
TUTUPACA	Andes, Ecuador	5,844	19,174	1902
ANTISANA	Andes, Ecuador	5,793	19,006	1801 (subglacial)
UBINAS	Andes, Peru	5,710	18,739	1969
LASCAR	Andes, Chile	5,641	18,508	1991
TUPUNGATITO	Andes, Chile	5,640	18,504	1986
VOLCÁN CITLALTEPETL (Pico de Orizaba)	Altiplano de Mexico, Mexico	5,610	18,406	1687
ISLUGA	Andes, Chile	5,566	18,262	1960
POPOCATÉPETL	Altiplano de Mexico, Mexico	5,451	17,884	1997
RUIZ	Andes, Colombia	5,435	17,829	1992
TOLIMA	Andes, Colombia	5,249	17,222	1943
SANGAY	Andes, Ecuador	5,230	17,159	1989 (rumbles)
TUNGURAHUA	Andes, Ecuador	5,048	16,562	1944
GUAGUA PICHINCHA	Andes, Ecuador	4,880	16,011	1988 (rumbles)
KLYUCHEVSKAYA SOPKA (Kamchatka Peninsula)	Khrebet Mountains, Russia	4,850	15,912	1997
CUMBAL	Andes, Colombia	4,795	15,732	1926
PURACE	Andes, Colombia	4,590	15,059	1988 (steams)
CERRO NEGRO DE MAYASQUER	Andes, Colombia	4,499	14,761	1936
MT RAINIER	Cascade Range, USA	4,392	14,410	1882
MT SHASTA	Cascade Range, USA	4,317	14,169	1855
EL GALERAS	Andes, Colombia	4,294	14,088	1993
DOÑA JUANA	Andes, Colombia	4,277	14,032	1906
TAJUMULCO	Sierra Madre, Guatemala	4,220	13,845	rumbles (ongoing)
MAUNA LOA	Hawaii, USA	4,170	13,681	1988 (rumbles)
TACANÁA	Sierra Madre, Guatemala	4,078	13,380	rumbles (ongoing)
MT CAMEROON	isolated mountain, Cameroon	4,069	13,380	1986
EREBUS	Ross Island, Antarctica	3,795	12,451	1997
FUJIYAMA	Kanto, Japan	3,776	12,389	steams (ongoing)
RINDJANI	Lombok, Indonesia	3,726	12,225	1966
PICO DE TEIDE	Tenerife, Canary Islands, Spain	3,718	12,198	1909
SEMERU	Java, Indonesia	3,676	12,060	1996
NYIRAGONGO	Virunga, Congo (ex-Zaïre)	3,470	11,385	1994
KORYAKSKAYA	Kamchatka Peninsula, Russia	3,456	11,339	1957

■ ACTIVE VOLCANOES IN EUROPE TODAY INCLUDE HEKLA IN ICELAND AND ETNA IN ITALY ■

Many volcanoes soar to great heights amid the Earth's major mountain ranges. The highest volcano is Cerro Aconcagua, a snow-clad peak 6960 m (22,834 ft) high in the Andes of Argentina. Because Cerro Aconcagua no longer erupts, it is said to be extinct. Other volcanoes that have not erupted for a very long time, but may erupt again, are described as dormant. Volcanoes that are known to have erupted in historic times are referred to as active, and these are always dangerous. The highest volcano regarded as active is Ojos del Salado, which rises to a height of 6895 m (22,588 ft) on the frontier between Chile and Argentina. The mountain has recently produced vents, known as fumaroles, which emit hot gases and steam.

In modern times, scientists have been able to observe and record the dramatic birth and growth of new volcanoes. A famous example is Paricutín, Mexico, which began as a plume of smoke emerging from a small fissure in the ground in a farmer's field in 1943 and, by 1952, had grown more than 430 m (1400 ft). Another appeared 20 years later, when the volcanic island of Surtsey (see p. 35) emerged from the sea off southern Iceland amid loud explosions and billowing clouds of ash and steam. The new island now occupies 2.5 km^2 (1 sq mi).

■ *Voluminous clouds of volcanic ash and rock blasted from the side of Mt St Helens in south-western Washington State, USA, on 22 July 1980. The volcano had been dormant since 1857, but was set off by a severe nearby earthquake*

WHAT CAUSES VOLCANIC ERUPTIONS?

▶ Volcanic eruptions are not always violent and explosive.
▶ The eruption of Mount St Helens in 1980 sent a plume of dust and ash up to 20 km (12.5 mi) high into the atmosphere.

Volcanoes are like gigantic safety valves that release the tremendous pressures that build up inside the Earth. These pressures are affected by the constant movement of the plates that make up the surface crust. As a result of this movement, molten magma in the mantle is sometimes forced upward under pressure through any breaks it can find in the surface rocks. As it rises, gases dissolved in it are released by the fall in pressure, and the magma shoots out of the volcano in explosive eruptions.

Volcanic eruptions can be either extremely explosive or relatively quiet, depending upon the type of molten magma being extruded from deep below the Earth's crust. Magma composed of mostly iron- and silica-rich minerals tends to be very viscous (thick and gummy) and resists flow, leading to violent eruptions such as that of Mount St Helens in 1980. These types of volcanoes, often referred to as central volcanoes, produce central cones from a build-up of lava, as well as ignimbrites and welded tuffs (both types of rock formed from the cooling of *nuée ardentes*). In contrast, magnesium- and iron-rich basaltic magmas are much more fluid and cause more subdued lava eruptions, such as those occurring on Mauna Loa in the Hawaiian Islands. These types of volcanoes, referred to as fissure volcanoes, extend for many kilometres and are usually found along fractures in the Earth's crust.

THE EARTH'S VOLCANIC ZONES

▶ Most volcanoes occur along the margins of the Earth's crustal tectonic plates.
▶ They also occur in the middle of tectonic plates, in areas called volcanic hot spots.

Volcanoes are found where the Earth's crust is weakest, especially along crustal plate edges, and most notably in the 'Ring of Fire' around the Pacific Ocean plate. Many volcanoes, known as abyssal volcanoes, are also scattered over the ocean floors away from plate margins. Here the crust is only about 5 km (3 mi) thick and easily breached by molten magma rising from the mantle below. Localized hot spots in the mantle, found on land away from the plate margins (such as those in the Hawaiian Islands), also cause volcanoes to form.

MAJOR VOLCANIC ERUPTIONS

	LOCATION	HEIGHT m	HEIGHT ft	DATE	NOTES
SANTORÍNI (Thira)	Cyclades, Greece	584	1,960	*c.* 1550 BC	A massive explosion virtually destroyed the island, and is thought by some to have contributed to the demise of Minoan civilization on nearby Crete. The disaster may also have given rise to the legend of the lost city of Atlantis
MT VESUVIUS	Bay of Naples, Italy	1,280	4,198	AD 79	The towns of Pompeii, Herculaneum and Stabiae were completely buried, and thousands died. In 1631, 3000 people were killed, since when there have been around 20 major eruptions, the last in 1944
UNNAMED	North Island, NZ	unknown		*c.* AD 130	Around 30 million tonnes of pumice were ejected, creating the vast caldera now filled by Lake Taupo. An area of *c.* 16,000 km^2 (6180 sq mi) was devastated – the most violent of all documented volcanic events
KELUD	Java, Indonesia	1,731	5,679	1586	10,000 people killed. Another eruption in 1919 killed 5000 people
MT ETNA	Sicily, Italy	3,311	10,855	1669	20,000 people were killed, and lava overran the west part of the city of Catania, 28 km (17 mi) from the summit
TAMBORA	Jumbawa, Indonesia	2,850	9,350	1815	An estimated 150–180 km^3 of rock and molten material (36–43 cu mi) was blasted from the cone, which dropped in height from 4100 m (13,450 ft) to 2850 m (9350 ft) in minutes. About 90,000 people were killed in the explosion and subsequent giant wave, or died later of famine
KRAKATOA	Krakatoa, Indonesia	813	2,667	1883	163 villages were wiped out and 36,417 people killed by the giant wave caused by this, the greatest volcanic explosion recorded – although possibly only one-fifth of the Santoríni explosion. Rocks were thrown 55 km (34 mi) into the air, and dust fell 5330 km (3313 mi) away 10 days later. The explosion was heard over one-thirteenth of the Earth's surface
MONT PELÉE	Martinique, West Indies	1,397	4,582	1902	Within three minutes a *nuée ardente* destroyed the town of St Pierre, killing all 26,000 inhabitants – except for one, a prisoner who survived in the thick-walled prison
MT ST HELENS	Washington State, USA	2,549	8,360	1980	66 people were presumed dead and 260 km^2 (100 sq mi) of forest destroyed. Smoke and ash rose to a height of 6000 m (20,000 ft), depositing ash 800 km (500 mi) away
MT PINÁTUBO	Luzon, Philippines	1,745	5,723	1991	847 people were killed and over one million displaced as a result of the most violent volcanic eruption of the 20th century. Volcanic ash was ejected up to 30 km (19 mi) into the atmosphere, lowering average global temperatures by around 1°C (34°F)

■ THE LARGEST VOLCANIC ERUPTION EVER RECORDED WAS SANTORÍNI IN GREECE IN 1550 BC ■

EARTHQUAKES

- In the past 800 years there have been 17 earthquakes known to have caused 50,000 or more deaths.
- A 1960 earthquake in Chile, originally measured at 8.3 on the Richter Scale, was later updated to 9.5, making it the largest recorded earthquake.
- Over 1.1 million people died following an earthquake which shook the eastern Mediterranean in July 1201.
- After flooding, earthquakes represent the greatest hazard to human life.

■ *This satellite view shows ground displacement after an earthquake registering 7.3 on the Richter Scale took place at Landers, California, on 28 June 1992. Each colour fringe (from purple to red to yellow to blue) represents the degree of horizontal ground displacement. The black lines on the right are the earthquake's fault lines*

■ *This computer graphic of the globe shows epicentres of earthquakes recorded since 1980. Epicentres with Richter Scale magnitudes greater than or equal to 5 are marked in red, with plate boundaries shown as yellow lines. Land elevation and ocean depth is colour-coded using the metre scale on the right*

WHAT IS AN EARTHQUAKE?

▶ Seismology is the science of the study of seismic activity, or earthquakes.
▶ Earthquake shock waves may travel at speeds of up to 6 km/h (3.7 mph) in the upper part of the Earth's crust.

An earthquake is a sudden release of energy in the Earth's crust or upper mantle. As the planet's tectonic plates jostle against each other, becoming distorted, tremendous strain builds up – and from time to time the energy from the strain is discharged in zones where the rocks are weakest. The result is a sudden, violent shock that can have highly destructive effects on the Earth's surface nearby.

The damaging effects of an earthquake are due to the vibrations (seismic waves) emitted by the shock. For a brief moment, the waves shake the ground close to the earthquake, producing often permanent effects. Few people are killed or injured directly by an earthquake; death and injury usually result from the collapse of buildings caused by the earthquake.

Whether or not people or buildings are present, earthquakes can cause fissures to appear in the ground, produce changes in the level and tilt of the ground surface, divert rivers and streams, trigger landslides and avalanches, and cause seemingly solid ground to turn into a quicksand-like mass. For example, the 180,000 people who died in the 1920 earthquake in Gansu Province, China, were killed by a massive landslide set off by the earthquake. Undersea earthquakes may also give rise to tidal waves (tsunamis) – huge amounts of sea water that can travel across the oceans for thousands of kilometres, causing devastation when they hit land.

WHERE DO EARTHQUAKES OCCUR?

▶ The Earth's crust has been displaced by over 1000 km (622 mi) in the San Andreas Fault zone, located in the western USA, in the last 25 million years alone.
▶ Earthquakes can be predicted by knowledge of locations and cycles of past earthquake activity, by identification of foreshocks, by minor tremors immediately prior to a major event, or even by abnormal animal behaviour.

Most earthquakes take place along tectonic plate boundaries – along transform faults, oceanic ridges (see p. 32) and subduction zones (where a tectonic plate is sliding under the other) – because this is where the plates interact most intensely, and where the build-up of distortion and strain are greatest.

However, not all earthquakes occur along plate margins. In North America, for example, the most damaging earthquakes of historic times have taken place not in California, through which runs a transform fault (the San Andreas Fault), but in South Carolina and Missouri, both of which are far from plate margins. The reasons for this are unclear, but earthquakes within the interiors of plates may be due to deep, still active faults remaining from a much earlier phase of plate tectonics. However, California is still America's greatest seismic area, because earthquakes occur there most frequently.

The point at which an earthquake occurs is called the focus, or hypocentre. The point on the Earth's surface directly above the focus is called the epicentre. It is at this point that the intensity of the earthquake is at its greatest. A world map of epicentres is largely a map of the Earth's plate boundaries (see the epicentre map above).

All earthquake foci lie within about the upper 700 km (435 mi) of the Earth. Within this range, earthquakes are classified as shallow (focal depths of 0–70 km/0–43 mi), intermediate (70–300 km/43–186 mi) or deep (below 300 km/186 mi). There are about three times as many intermediate earthquakes as there are deep ones, and about ten times as many shallow ones.

It is the shallow shocks that cause most damage at the Earth's surface, for the obvious reason that they are closer to it. Collectively, shallow earthquakes also release the most energy – about 75% of the total, compared to 3% for deep earthquakes.

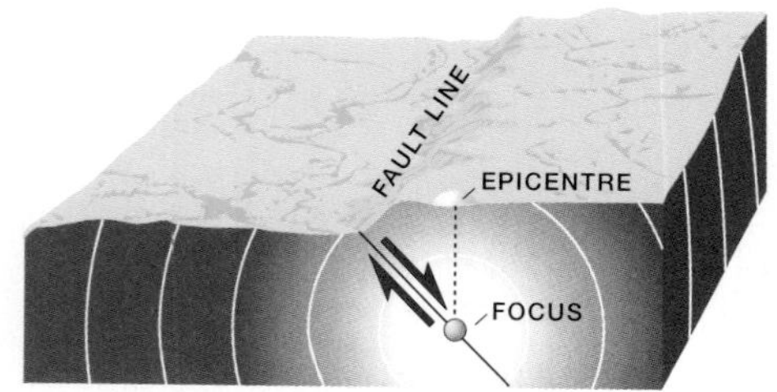

■ *The focus of an earthquake is the site of movement on a geological fault line and the centre of energy release. The epicentre is the point on the Earth's surface directly above the focus. The red arrows indicate the movement of the two tectonic plates rubbing and jostling against each other*

MEASURING EARTHQUAKES

▶ Earthquakes are monitored by the World-Wide Standard Seismological Network, comprising a global network of over 125 monitoring stations, originally set up to monitor nuclear weapons testing.
▶ The energy released by the Hiroshima atomic bomb would be equivalent to 5.7 on the Richter Scale.

The size of an earthquake is specified by its magnitude, sometimes called the Richter magnitude, after the American seismologist Charles Richter, who devised the scale in 1935.

Magnitude is actually a measure of the size (amplitude) of the waves emitted by the earthquake. However, the magnitude scale is logarithmic. This means that each step up the scale represents a ten-fold increase in the amplitude of the emitted waves. Thus, the waves from a magnitude-7 earthquake are 10 times bigger than those from a magnitude-6 shock, 100 times bigger than those from a magnitude-5 event, and so on.

Magnitude can also be regarded as a measure of the energy released by an earthquake, because energy is related to wave size. The relationship is such that each division on the magnitude scale represents an approximately thirty-fold difference in energy. Thus a magnitude-7 earthquake releases about 30 times more energy than a magnitude-6 shock and about 30 x 30 (i.e. 900) times more than a magnitude-5 event. This explains why most of the energy released by earthquakes comes from the very few big shocks that occur each year, rather than from the million or so smaller earthquakes.

To specify the size of an earthquake in terms of its effects, an intensity scale, the Richter Scale, is used. In Japan and Russia, a slightly different system, the Modified Mercalli Scale, devised by

■ A MAGNITUDE-6 EARTHQUAKE IS TEN TIMES AS STRONG AS A MAGNITUDE-5 SHOCK ■

RICHTER SCALE

The Richter Scale is the earthquake measurement scale that is most widely used. It is a measurement of an earthquake's magnitude and, as such, would mean little to the layperson. It is, however, possible to convert these readings to a scale of intensity:

Magnitude 1	Detectable only by instruments
Magnitude 2	Barely detectable, even near the epicentre
Magnitude 3	Detectable near epicentre, but causes minimal damage
Magnitude 4–5	Detectable within 32 km (20 mi) of the epicentre; possible slight damage within a small area
Magnitude 6	Moderately destructive
Magnitude 7	A major earthquake
Magnitude 8	A great earthquake

MODIFIED MERCALLI SCALE

This scale is mostly used in Japan and the former Soviet republics, and is in increasing use globally. However, as Japan (and Georgia and Armenia) are among the areas of the world that are most prone to earthquakes, the Modified Mercalli Scale is often quoted with regard to earthquakes in those countries. The readings on this scale have been converted into a scale of intensity that may be summarized as follows:

I	Not felt except by a few
II	Felt by a few people at rest. Delicately suspended objects swing
III	Felt noticeably indoors. Standing cars may rock
IV	Felt generally indoors. Sleeping people are woken
V	Felt generally. Some plaster falls and dishes and windows are broken. Pendulum clocks stop
VI	Felt by all. Many are frightened. Chimneys and plaster are damaged. Furniture is moved and objects are displaced
VII	Everyone runs outdoors. Felt in moving cars. Moderate structural damage
VIII	General alarm. Weak structures are badly damaged. Walls and furniture fall over. Water level changes in wells
IX	Panic. Weak structures are totally destroyed. Extensive damage to well-built structures, foundations and underground pipes. Ground is fissured and cracked
X	Panic. Only the strongest buildings survive. Ground badly cracked. Rails bent. Water slopped over river banks
XI	Panic. Few buildings survive. Broad fissures open up in the ground. Fault scarps are formed. Underground pipes are put out of service
XII	Total destruction. Waves are seen on the ground, and lines of sight and level are distorted. Objects are thrown up into the air

Father Giuseppi Mercalli, is used. This is based on the amount of vibration people feel during low-magnitude tremors and the extent of damage to buildings during high-magnitude events.

The destructive effect of an earthquake depends not only on its size but also on the area's population, the type of buildings and the natural events that may be triggered. Timing is also an important factor – this century's worst earthquake, in terms of the number of people killed, occurred at 3:42 a.m., levelling the city of Tangshan, China, while most people were asleep, and killing 242,000.

MAJOR 20TH-CENTURY EARTHQUAKES

		RICHTER SCALE	FATALITIES
Colombian coast	31 Jan 1906	8.6	unknown
San Francisco, USA	18 Apr 1906	8.3	452
Messina, Italy	28 Dec 1908	7.5	80,000
Avezzano, Italy	13 Jan 1915	unknown	29,970
Gansu, China	16 Dec 1920	8.2	242,000
Kanto Plain, Japan	1 Sep 1923	8.3	142,807
Gansu Province, China	26 Dec 1932	7.6	70,000
Quetta (now Pakistan)	31 May 1935	7.5	25,000
Erzincan, Turkey	27 Dec 1939	7.9	30,000
Assam, India	15 Aug 1950	8.6	1500
Kamchatka, Russia	4 Nov 1952	8.5	unknown
Aleutian Islands, Alaska, USA	9 Mar 1957	8.3	unknown
Agadir, Morocco	29 Feb 1960	5.8	12,000
Lebu, Chile	22 May 1960	8.3	unknown
Anchorage, Alaska, USA	28 Mar 1964	8.5	131
northern Peru	31 May 1970	7.7	66,800
Los Angeles, USA	9 Feb 1971	6.5	64
Nicaragua	23 Dec 1972	6.2	5000
Guatemala	4 Feb 1976	7.5	22,700
Tangshan, China	27 Jul 1976	8.2	242,000
Bucharest, Romania	4 Mar 1977	7.5	1541
Tabas, NE Iran	16 Sep 1978	7.7	25,000
El Asnam, Algeria	10 Oct 1980	7.5	2327
Potenza, Italy	23 Nov 1980	6.8	*c.* 3000
Yemen	13 Dec 1982	6.0	2800
Papayan, Colombia	31 Mar 1983	5.5	264 (150,000 homeless)
north Honshu, Japan	26 May 1983	7.7	58 (mostly due to the effects of a tidal wave)
Eastern Turkey	30 Oct 1983	7.1	1233
Algarroba, Chile	3 Mar 1985	7.8	177 (150,000 homeless)
Mexico City, Mexico	19–20 Sep 1985	8.1	20,000 (31,000 homeless, 40,000 injured)
NE Ecuador	5 Mar 1987	7.0	2000 (75,000 injured)
SW China	6 Nov 1988	7.6	over 1000 (500,000 homeless)
Armenia	7 Dec 1988	6.9	25,000 (500,000 homeless)
Tajikistan	22 Jan 1989	5.3	574 (all owing to a mud slide on the village of Sharora)
San Francisco Bay, USA	17 Oct 1989	7.1	67
Algiers, Algeria	29 Oct 1989	6.0	24 (746 injured)
Newcastle, NSW, Australia	27 Dec 1989	5.5	40 (120 injured)
Qinghai Province, China	27 Apr 1990	6.9	115 (160 injured, many homeless)
Roudhon, NW Iran	21 Jun 1990	7.3	at least 36,000
Luzon, Philippines	17 Jul 1990	7.7	over 1000 (in area north of Manila)
southern Iran	6 Nov 1990	6.8	22 (over 12,000 homeless)
Sicily, Italy	13 Dec 1990	4.7	12
NW frontier, Pakistan	1 Feb 1991	6.7	over 1000 (many more homeless)
Costa Rica/Panama	22 Apr 1991	7.5	over 80 (800 injured)
Georgia	29 Apr 1991	7.2	100
eastern Turkey	14 Mar 1992	6.2	over 1000
Cairo, Egypt	12 Oct 1992	5.9	at least 540 (largely caused by collapse of poorly built tenements; 4000 injured)
Hokkaido, Japan	12 Jul 1993	7.8	192 (most on island of Okushiri)
Latur, India	30 Sep 1993	6.5	9748
Papua New Guinea	13 and 16 Oct 1993	max. of 6.8	60 (in four earthquakes)
Los Angeles	17 Jan 1994	6.6	57 (25,000 homeless)
Sumatra, Indonesia	16 Feb 1994	6.5	131 (2700 injured, mainly in town of Liwa)
SW Colombia	7 Jun 1994	–	401 (in avalanches following a minor quake)
Mascara, Algeria	18 Aug 1994	5.6	149
Japan	4 Oct 1994	8.2	16 (killed in Russian Kuril Islands as a result of submarine earthquake off Hokkaido)
northern Japan	28 Dec 1994	7.5	3 (267 injured)
Kobe, Japan	17 Jan 1995	7.2	over 5,000 (275,000 homeless)
Neftegorsk, Sakhalin Island, Russia	28 May 1995	7.5	*c.* 2,000
Aiyion region, Greece	15 Jun 1995	6.1	17
Dinar, W Turkey	2 Oct 1995	6.1	57
Jalisco State, western Mexico	9 Oct 1995	7.6	56
Yunnan Province, China	24 Oct 1995	6.5	29
Yunnan Province, China	3 Feb 1996	7.0	240
Irian Jaya Province, Indonesia	17 Feb 1996	7.5	32 (mainly arising from a tidal wave)
Baluchistan Province, western Pakistan	28 Feb 1997	7.3	over 110
Ardabil region, NW Iran	28 Feb 1997	5.5	over 1000 (2600 injured)
Qayen, NE Iran	10 May 1997	7.1	4000

■ RICHTER ONCE SAID 'ONLY FOOLS, CHARLATANS AND LIARS PREDICT EARTHQUAKES' ■

Waterfalls and Lakes

- Victoria Falls, on the Zambia–Zimbabwe border, is known to locals as Mosi-oa-Tunya – 'the smoke that thunders'.
- The completion of the Owen Falls Dam on the River Nile in Uganda in 1954 marginally raised the level of the natural Lake Victoria, technically turning it into a reservoir with a capacity of 2,700,000 m^3.
- The world's fresh- and salt-water lakes contain about 180,000 km^3 of water, or 0.01% of the Earth's water resources.
- Waterfalls can represent a major problem to navigation where they occur on major rivers.

WHY DO WATERFALLS OCCUR?

▶ Waterfalls most commonly form where rivers cross from resistant to less resistant rocks.
▶ Waterfalls may also occur where rivers cross geological faults or where rivers adjust their gradient (slope) following a change in base level (the lowest level to which a land surface can be eroded by rivers or streams).

The term waterfall is usually applied to any section of a river or stream system where there is a vertical fall of water. Where a number of waterfalls occur in succession, this is referred to as a cataract. Rapids are less pronounced irregularities within a river system and consist of short, steep sections of channel which may be completely submerged by water when river levels are high. Although small, high waterfalls are common features of upland or mountainous rivers and streams, they are relatively unusual on large rivers of a global scale and are generally restricted to bedrock channels.

WATER RESISTANCE OF ROCKS

Waterfalls may form for a variety of reasons. The great majority of falls occur where a river system erodes weaker rock from beneath a more resistant cap rock. This is most commonly found where one part of the river is underlain by a resistant rock, but then crosses onto a softer rock type. The classic example of this type of waterfall is Niagara Falls. The Niagara River flows over resistant limestone above the Falls and then passes onto less resistant shale. The river has been able to cut down rapidly into the shale, but is less able to carve through the limestone. The force of water and sediment going over the Falls and into the plunge pool at its base actively undermines the limestone by cutting into the weaker underlying shales. This causes the Falls to progressively erode back in an upstream direction.

GEOLOGICAL FAULTS

Faulting and dislocation of the Earth's crustal blocks due to earthquake activity has been responsible for the creation of many spectacular falls, especially in Africa. The Victoria Falls, on the Zambia–Zimbabwe border, for example, are controlled by fault zones that have been eroded into by the River Zambezi.

■ *The Victoria Falls astounded Dr David Livingstone when he came across them on his African travels in 1855, and still strike awe in the many people who visit them*

10 HIGHEST WATERFALLS

	HEIGHT m	ft	RIVER	LOCATION	NOTES
1 **Angel**	979	3,212	Carrao, an upper tributary of the Caroni	Venezuela	highest fall 807 m (2648 ft)
2 **Tugela**	947	3,107	Tugela	Kwazulu Natal, South Africa	5 falls (highest 410 m/ 1345 ft)
3 **Utigård**	800	2,625	Jostedal Glacier	Nesdale, Norway	highest fall 600 m (1969 ft)
4 **Mongefossen**	774	2,540	Monge	Mongebekk, Norway	
5 **Yosemite**	739	2,425	Yosemite Creek, a tributary of the Merced	Yosemite Valley, Yosemite National Park, California, USA	Upper Yosemite 435 m (1447 ft), Cascades in middle section 205 m (675 ft), Lower Yosemite 97 m (320 ft)
6 **Ostre Mardola Foss**	656	2,152	Mardals	Eikisdal, W. Norway	highest fall 296 m (971 ft)
7 **Tyssestrengane**	646	2,120	Tysso	Hardanger, Norway	highest fall 289 m (948 ft)
8 **Kukenaam** (or Cuquenán)	610	2,001	Arabopó, upper tributary of Caroni	Venezuela	
9 **Sutherland**	580	1,903	Arthur	nr. Milford Sound, Otago, New Zealand	highest fall 248 m (814 ft)
10 **Kile** (or Kjellfossen)	561	1,841	Naerö Fjord feeder	nr. Gudvangen, Norway	highest fall 149 m (489 ft) – Main Fall only, omitting Leaping Water and Rainbow Falls

GREATEST WATERFALLS

	MAX. HEIGHT m	ft	MEAN ANNUAL FLOW m^3/s	ft^3/s	LOCATION
Buyoma (formerly Stanley)	60	197	17,000	600,000	R. Congo, nr. Kisangani (The Congo/ ex-Zaïre)
Khône	21	70	11,500	410,000	R. Mekong, Laos
Niagara					
Horseshoe/Canadian	48	157	5,640	199,300	Niagara R., Lake Erie to Lake Ontario (Canada/USA)
American	50	164	360	12,700	
Paolo Afonso	58	190	2,800	100,000	R. São Francisco, Brazil
Iguazú	93	308	1,700	61,660	R. Iguazú, Brazil/Argentina
Patos–Moribondo	35	115	1,500	53,000	Rio Grande, Brazil
Victoria (Mosi-oa-tunya)	108	355	*1,100	38,430	R. Zambezi, Zambia/Zimbabwe

* This figure applies to the main fall only, omitting Leaping Water and Rainbow Falls

LOST WATERFALLS

Two of the world's greatest waterfalls – in terms of the volume of water passing over them – are being, or have been, inundated by the rising water behind the Itaipu Dam (Paraguay/Brazil). These falls were, respectively, the second and sixth greatest in the world by volume. They were:

Guaíra (or Salto dos Sete Quedras)	114	374	**13,000	470,000	Alto Paraná, Paraguay/Brazil
Urubu-punga	12	40	2,700	97,000	Alto Paraná, Paraguay/Brazil

** The flow of water over Guaíra peaked at 50,000 m^3/s.

KNICKPOINTS

Vertical drops in river channels may also be associated with knickpoints. A knickpoint is a discontinuity or kink in the slope of a river channel, usually formed due to a drop in the altitude of the base level to which the river is eroding. Changes in base level may occur due to a drop in relative sea level (either due to a real fall in sea level or a rise in the elevation of the land due to a tectonic plate uplift), or river capture (when one river captures another river through a tributary, changing the waterflow of both rivers). A lowering of base level will cause a river to erode more rapidly along the lower parts of its course, which can lead to the channel slope steepening downstream. If this process coincides with the river channel crossing different types of rock, as in the case of Niagara Falls, then a waterfall may develop as the river tries to erode its bed to re-create a smooth slope and remove the knickpoint or kink in its profile.

■ THE VICTORIA FALLS ARE 1708 M WIDE ■ ANGEL FALLS ARE 3.25 TIMES AS HIGH AS THE

WHAT IS A LAKE?

▶ A lake is generally defined as a body of water, entirely surrounded by land, which has an upper surface exposed to the atmosphere, no surface gradient and is unconnected to the sea except by rivers or streams.
▶ Lakes are important resources for water, food, energy, recreation and tourism.

Lakes form an important component of the hydrological cycle in almost all of the Earth's major climatic zones. A commonly used definition of a lake is that it is a body of water occupying a hollow in the Earth's surface which has an upper surface exposed to the atmosphere and has no appreciable gradient (slope). The latter part of this definition is important as it distinguishes lakes from other water bodies such as rivers and streams which have sloping water surfaces. The term 'lake' embraces a wide range of water bodies, including ponds (which are small, shallow lakes), reservoirs (which are artificial or semi-artificial lakes), and marshes and swamps (which contain standing water). Where lakes do not naturally occur in the bottoms of valleys in drainage systems, they may be created by the construction of a dam across a stream channel.

LAKE SOURCES

Lakes can receive water from a variety of sources, including rainfall, streams, rivers, water flowing over the land surface, and inputs from soil water and ground water. Not all lakes have clearly identifiable inputs, such as a stream. Many small lakes and ponds are fed predominantly by rainfall or soil water. In addition to receiving water, lakes also lose water. This loss most commonly occurs at an outlet, where water drains over a natural or artificial dam, but may also be due to evaporation, seepage to ground water, or as a result of water extraction for human consumption.

HUMAN BENEFITS

Lakes are important from the viewpoint of human activity. Firstly, they are frequently used as a source of fresh water and food. Where lakes have been artificially dammed to a higher level than their natural outlet they may also be used to provide hydroelectric power. Many areas with lakes are also recognized as regions of outstanding natural beauty and may act as important locations for recreation and tourism.

▶ LARGEST RESERVOIRS

Artificial lakes, or reservoirs, are either constructed as sources of water supply for an area and/or as sources to generate electricity by water power.

BY CAPACITY

	LOCATION	CAPACITY (million m³)
Kakhovskaya	R. Dnepr, Russia	182,000
Kariba	R. Zambezi, Zimbabwe/Zambia	180,600
Bratskoye	R. Angara, Russia	169,270
Lake Nasser	R. Nile, Egypt	168,900
Lake Volta	R. Volta, Ghana	153,000

BY AREA

	LOCATION	AREA km²	sq mi
Lake Volta	R. Volta, Ghana	8,482	3,275
Kuybyshev Reservoir	R. Volga, Russia	2,490	961
Rybin Reservoir	R. Volga, Russia	1,768	683

WHAT CONTROLS A LAKE'S SIZE?

▶ The main factors controlling the size of a lake are the shape of the lake basin and the balance between water inputs and outputs.
▶ Lakes can be severely affected by human activity – the Aral Sea has lost more than two-thirds of its volume since 1960 due to water extraction.

Lakes are relatively short-lived features on the geological time scale. They often disappear gradually as their outlet streams erode to lower levels, or as they fill up with sediments that have been transported into the lake by the inlet stream. The time that this takes depends upon the quantity and rate of sediment erosion in the stream catchment above the lake basin.

Lakes may also disappear more catastrophically, such as when glacially dammed lakes disappear due to glacier advance, or where a landslide across a stream causes a temporary lake to form but is subsequently overtopped by the river.

WATER INPUT AND OUTPUT

The principal factor controlling the size of a lake is the relative balance between the amount of water entering the lake and the amount being removed.

In the majority of natural lakes in humid temperate environments, the volume of water entering the lake is balanced by the amount lost. The water level within these lakes roughly coincides with the water table (loosely, the level of the surrounding ground area) and tends to remain fairly stable throughout the year as stream inputs, ground water and soil water seepage replace any water lost by outflow or evaporation. In areas where water is extracted for human consumption, there is often a seasonal drop in lake level due to summer water use.

The situation is different in many arid-region lakes, which commonly have no surface outlet. In these lakes, the water level (and therefore the lake's area) is largely determined by the balance between inflows and loss by evaporation. If the rate of inflow increases, then the lake level will rise. In lakes where climatic conditions constantly favour evaporation over input, water may be absent from the basin for much of the year, and the lake bed may be covered with salt deposits. These lakes are referred to as salt lakes or playas.

Lake levels may also change in size in response to climatic variations, both on short and longer time scales. For example, if temperatures in a region increase and precipitation levels drop, then a lake is likely to dry up. Conversely, if temperatures decrease and precipitation increases, then a natural lake will increase its water level up to the point where the water overspills any natural outlet.

BASIN SHAPE

Whilst lake levels basically reflect the balance between water inputs and outputs, the maximum possible level of any lake and the rate at which the level changes is determined by the characteristics of the lake basin.

A lake is controlled by the height of outlets from the lake system – it is only able to fill up to the level of the lowest outflow point. Therefore, the rate of lake level change is controlled by the shape of the basin. Deep, steep-sided basins in mountainous areas may increase their depth relatively rapidly in response to increased water inputs, while their surface area increases only slowly. Conversely, shallow basins will increase rapidly in surface area but relatively slowly in depth if water input increases.

10 LARGEST LAKES

① **CASPIAN SEA**
Location: Russia, Kazakhstan, Turkmenistan, Azerbaijan and Iran
Area: 371,800 km² (143,552 sq mi)

② **SUPERIOR**
Location: Canada and USA
Area: 82,350 km² (31,795 sq mi)

③ **VICTORIA NYANZA**
Location: Uganda, Tanzania and Kenya
Area: 69,500 km² (26,834 sq mi)

④ **HURON**
Location: Canada and USA
Area: 59,600 km² (23,011 sq mi)

⑤ **MICHIGAN**
Location: USA
Area: 58,000 km² (22,394 sq mi)

⑥ **ARAL SEA (ARAL'SKOYE MORE)**
Location: Uzbekistan and Kazakhstan
Area: 40,000 km² (15,444 sq mi)

⑦ **TANGANYIKA**
Location: The Congo (ex-Zaïre), Tanzania, Malawi and Mozambique
Area: 32,900 km² (12,703 sq mi)

⑧ **GREAT BEAR**
Location: Canada
Area: 31,800 km² (12,279 sq mi)

⑨ **BAIKAL (OZERO BAYKAL)**
Location: Russia
Area: 30,500 km² (11,776 sq mi)

⑩ **MALAWI**
Location: Malawi, Tanzania and Mozambique
Area: 29,600 km² (11,429 sq mi)

RIVERS

- A river is a freshwater body confined in a channel which flows down a slope into another river, a lake or the sea, or sometimes into an inland desert.
- One-tenth of the entire continent of Africa is drained by the River Nile, the second-longest river in the world.
- The River Nile was prone to severe seasonal flooding until the Aswan Dam was built in 1971, creating Lake Nasser.
- The shortest river in the world is the North Fork Roe River, located near the Great Falls of Montana, USA – it is only 17.7 m long.
- There are three types of rivers in the world – perennial, seasonal and ephemeral.

■ *This river, near Driggs, Idaho, is an example of a river meandering and braiding (linking back up), and forming oxbow lakes. This is caused by the river eroding through its neck, which changes its course, and cuts off a body of water that becomes an oxbow lake*

PERENNIAL RIVERS

▶ A river is perennial when it is cut deeply enough to be fed by ground water or when it is fed by an unlimited source (such as the St Lawrence River, flowing from the Great Lakes).
▶ Perennial rivers usually exist in temperate areas, such as western Europe, the north-eastern USA and New Zealand, and in the wet tropics.

When enough precipitation falls evenly throughout the year, it replenishes ground water constantly, allowing rivers to flow all year round. These types of rivers are called perennial rivers. They can, however, experience seasonal and day-to-day variations in the volume of water they carry (the flow regime), owing to seasonal fluctuations in precipitation and additional inputs from individual storms.

Surprisingly, perennial rivers can exist even in desert areas. The Nile, for example, despite experiencing a distinctly seasonal flow regime, flows all year round through the Egyptian Desert; likewise, the Colorado River passes through desert areas of the south-western USA. The reason that these and other rivers can successfully exist in deserts is that their catchments (source areas) lie in areas with wetter climates.

SEASONAL RIVERS

▶ A river is seasonal, or intermittent, when its flow is severely affected by seasonal changes.
▶ The River Finke, located almost midway between Alice Springs and Uluru (also known as Ayer's Rock) in Australia, is a substantial river, despite being only seasonal.

Some rivers may only flow seasonally, particularly in environments with Mediterranean-type climates, which have a very distinct wet, winter season and a dry summer. Rivers in glaciated areas may also have very seasonal flow regimes. Glacial meltwater streams, which receive their water directly from glaciers, usually only flow during the few months in the summer when the ice melts.

EPHEMERAL RIVERS

▶ Ephemeral rivers are often caused by uncommon rainstorms with high precipitation.
▶ During a storm in Tamanrasset in the central Sahara, 36 mm (1⅖ in) of rain was recorded to have fallen in 40 minutes.

In dry desert climates, rivers may not flow for years on end, because of the infrequency of desert storms, and then only for a few days, or even hours. However, when storms do occur these ephemeral rivers may flow at great rates, because desert rainfall is often very heavy. This gives them considerable power and the ability to erode and transport large quantities of sediment.

RIVER BASINS

▶ The Amazon is the largest river basin in the world and, of its countless tributaries, the Madeira is the world's largest tributary.
▶ The whole of the Earth's land surface can be divided up into river drainage basins.

Only some very short rivers are able to flow from a source to the sea without either being joined by others or becoming a tributary of a large river. Most rivers, therefore, form part of a drainage network, occupying a drainage basin. These basins are separated by areas of relatively high ground called watersheds. Some drainage basins occupy only a few square kilometres, while others – like the Amazon river basin, which has an area of 7,050,000 km^2 (2,722,00 sq mi) – are enormous.

? WHERE DO RIVERS GET THEIR WATER FROM

▶ Rivers may receive their water from several sources, but all of these are directly or indirectly related to precipitation.
▶ Precipitation is the fall of moisture on to the Earth's surface from the atmosphere.

RAINWATER

Rain falling on the ground may immediately run down slopes as overland flow, becoming concentrated and eventually forming a stream. This tends to happen when the ground surface is impermeable, that is when water cannot pass through it, as is the case with certain kinds of rock. It can also occur when the ground is already saturated with water, or when rainfall is very heavy.

SPRING WATER

Rivers can also receive their water from springs. This is because rainfall will often soak into the ground, to accumulate in the soil or to pass into permeable and porous rocks, and become ground water. In permeable rock, water can pass right through the rock itself, whereas in porous rock there are holes and fissures through which water can pass. Springs occur where the top of the aquifer – a layer of rock containing water – intersects with the ground surface. Ground water is important as a source for rivers because it can supply water even when precipitation is not occurring, thereby constantly maintaining river flow.

MELTWATER

A third source of water for rivers is the melting of solid precipitation in the form of snow, or snow which has been turned to ice to form a glacier or ice sheet. This is particularly important in high-latitude and mountainous areas.

Meltwater from major mountain systems gives rise to some of the world's greatest rivers. The Himalayas are the source of 19 major rivers. Two of Europe's most important rivers – the Rhine and the Rhône – originate in the Alps. The Rockies are the birthplace of four of North America's greatest rivers – the Missouri, Rio Grande, Columbia and Colorado.

■ *The Colorado River runs through Marble Canyon, Cape Solitude, Grand Canyon National Park, Arizona, USA, draining the most arid area of the North American continent. No other river in the world has cut so many deep trenches – more than 1610 km (1000 mi) of its course – of which the Grand Canyon is the largest and most spectacular*

15 LONGEST RIVERS IN EUROPE

	LENGTH km	LENGTH mi	LOCATION	COURSE
① VOLGA	3,530	2,193	Russia	After (nameless) headwaters of 160 km (99 mi), the Volga flows into the Rybinskoye reservoir in the Valdai Hills north of Moscow and becomes known as the Volga. It then flows south and east to the Caspian Sea
② DANUBE	2,850	1,770	Germany, Austria, Slovakia, Hungary, Yugoslavia (Serbia), Romania, Bulgaria and Ukraine	Rises as the rivers Breg and Brisach in the Black Forest in Germany and flows east through central and south-east Europe into the Black Sea
③ URAL	2,540	1,578	Russia and Kazakhstan	The Ural is sometimes quoted as the third longest river in Europe, but much of its path to the Caspian Sea is through Asiatic Kazakhstan
④ DNEPR	2,285	1,420	Russia, Belarus and Ukraine	Rises west of Moscow and flows south through Russia, Belarus and Ukraine to the Black Sea
⑤ DON	1,969	1,224	Russia	Rises in south-west Russia and flows south to the Sea of Azov
⑥ PECHORA	1,809	1,124	Russia	Rises in the Ural Mountains and flows north to the Barents Sea
⑦ KAMA	1,805	1,122	Russia	Rises north of Perm and flows south through Russia to join the Volga through the Kuybyshevskoye reservoir
⑧ OKA	1,500	930	Russia	Rises south-west of Moscow and flows east through Russia to join the Volga near Nizhny Novgorod
⑨ BELAYA	1,430	889	Russia	Rises in the south of the Ural Mountains and flows north to join the River Kama
⑩ DNESTR	1,352	840	Ukraine and Moldova	Rises near the Polish border in western Ukraine and flows east through Ukraine and Moldova to reach the Black Sea in Ukraine
⑪ RHINE	1,320	820	Switzerland, Liechtenstein, Austria, Germany, France and the Netherlands	Rises in the Swiss Alps and flows east, then north, across northern Europe, to the North Sea
⑫ NORTHERN DVINA	1,302	809	Russia	Rises in northern Russia as the Sukhona and flows north to the White Sea
⑬ ELBE	1,165	724	Czech Republic and Germany	Rises in Bohemia and flows north to the North Sea
⑭ VISTULA	1,069	664	Poland	Rises near the Polish–Czech border and flows north to the Baltic Sea
⑮ LOIRE	1,020	634	France	Rises in the Massif Central of France and flows north and then west to the Atlantic Ocean

① The Volga is fed mostly by snow (60%), with ground water (30%) and rain water (10%) also contributing

② The Danube flows through eight countries and four capitals: Vienna, Belgrade, Budapest and Bratislava

③ In the 1970s, a canal was begun by the Russians to divert water from the Volga to the Ural, just south of Uralsk

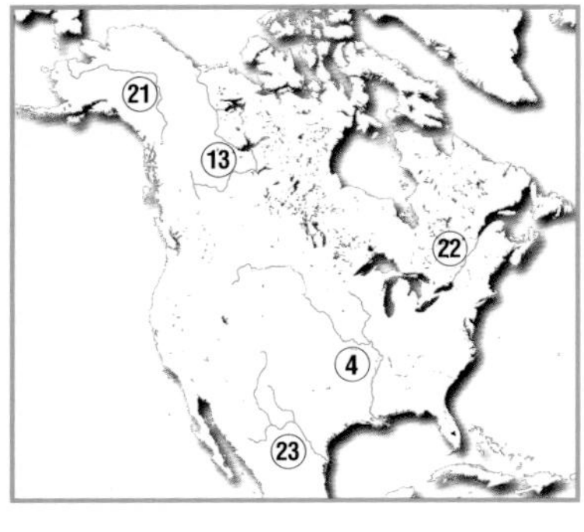

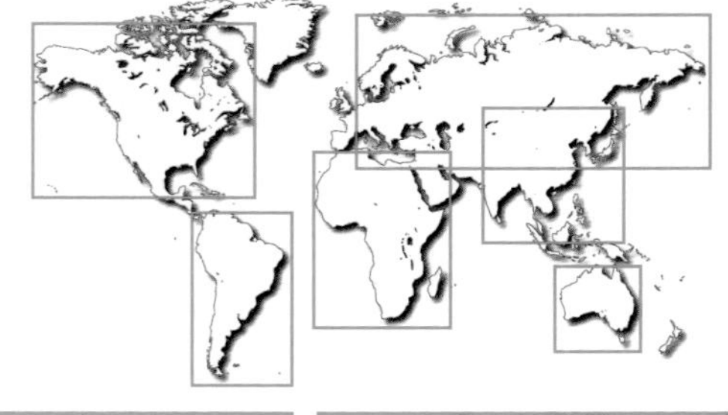

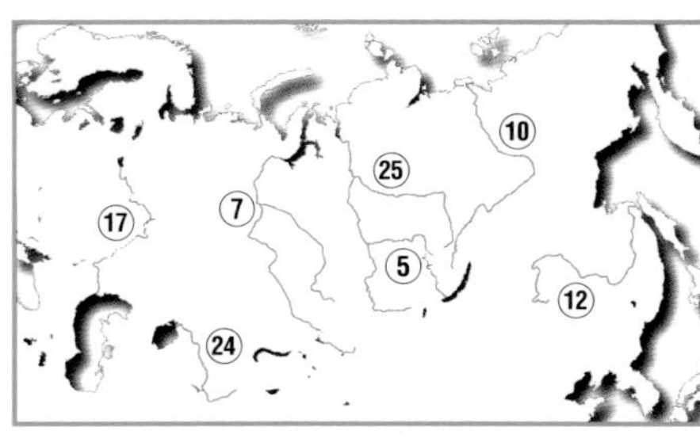

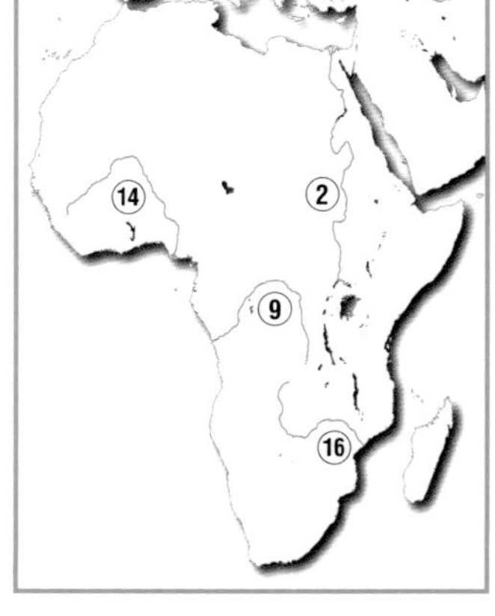

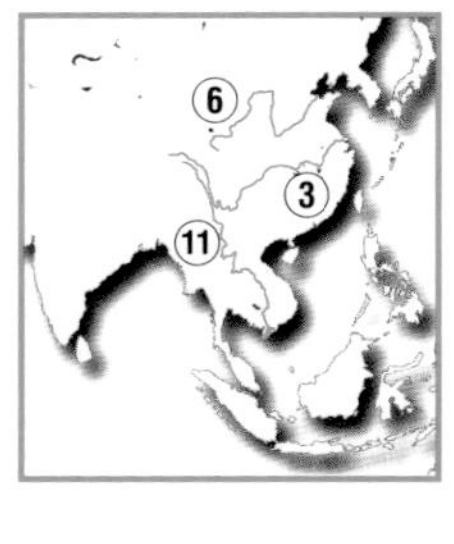

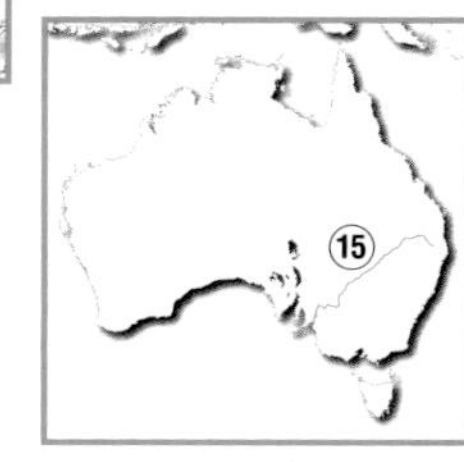

25 LONGEST RIVERS

	LENGTH km	mi	SOURCE	COURSE	NOTES
1 **AMAZON** (Amazonas)	6,750	4,194	Peru: Lago Villafro, head of the Apurimac branch of the Ucayali, which joins the Maranon to form the Amazon	Through Colombia to equatorial Brazil (Solimoes) to South Atlantic (Canal do Sul)	Total of 15,000 tributaries, ten over 1600 km (1000 mi). Navigable 3700 km (2300 mi) upstream. Delta extends 400 km (250 mi) inland
2 **NILE** (Bahr-el-Nil)–White Nile (Bahr el-Jabel)–Albert Nile–Victoria Nile–Victoria Nyanza–Kagera–Luvironza	6,670	4,145	Burundi: Luvironza branch of the Kagera, a feeder of the Victoria Nyanza	Through Tanzania (Kagera), Uganda (Victoria Nile and Albert Nile), Sudan (White Nile), Egypt to the eastern Mediterranean	Navigable length to first cataract (Aswan 1545 km/960 mi). Egyptian Irrigation Dept. states a length of 6700 km (4164 mi)
3 **YANGTZE** (Chang Jiang)	6,300	3,915	Western China: Kunlun Shan Mountains (as Tuotuo and Tongtian)	Begins west of Tuotuohe in Qinghai, through Yunnan, Sichuan, Hubei, Anhui, Jiangsu to Yellow Sea	Estuary: 190 km (120 mi) long
4 **MISSISSIPPI–** Missouri–Jefferson–Beaverhead–Red Rock	6,020	3,741	Beaverhead County, southern Montana, USA	Through N. and S. Dakota, Nebraska, Iowa, Missouri, Kansas, Illinois, Kentucky, Tennessee, Arkansas, Mississippi, Louisiana, South West Pass into Gulf of Mexico	Missouri is 3725 km (2315 mi) long; the Jefferson–Beaverhead–Red Rock is 349 km (217 mi) long; total Mississippi from Lake Itasca (Minn) is 3778 km (2348 mi)
5 **YENISEY–** Angara–Selenge	5,540	3,442	Mongolia: Ideriin branch of Selenge (Selenga)	Through Buryatia (Russia): Selenge branch into Lake Baikal, then via Angara to Yenisey	Estuary: 386 km (240 mi) long. Yenisey is 3540 km (2200 mi) long; the Angara is 1850 km (1150 mi)
6 **HWANG HE** (Yellow River)	5,464	3,395	China: West of Bayan, Qinghai Province	Through Gansu, Inner Mongolia, Henan, Shandong to Gulf of China, Yellow Sea	Changed mouths by 400 km (250 mi) in 1852. Only last 40 km (25 mi) is navigable
7 **OB–** Irtysh	5,409	3,361	Mongolia: Kara (Black) Irtysh via northern China (Xinjiang) feeder	Through Kazakhstan into Russia to Ob confluence at Khanty Mansiysk, then as the Ob to Kara Sea	Estuary is 725 km (450 mi) long. Ob is 3679 km (2286 mi) long; Irtysh is 2960 km (1840 mi) long
8 **PARANÁ–** Rio de la Plata	4,880	3,032	Brazil: as Paranáiba. Flows south to east Paraguay border and into eastern Argentina	Emerges into confluence with R. Uruguay to form Rio de la Plata	After the 120-km (75-mi) long delta estuary, the river shares the 340-km (210-mi) long estuary of the Uruguay called the Rio de la Plata
9 **CONGO**	4,700	2,920	Zambia–The Congo (ex-Zaïre) border as Lualaba	Through The Congo (ex-Zäire) and along Zäire/Congo-Brazzaville border to Angola	Navigable for 1730 km (1075 mi) from Kisangani to Kinshasa. Estuary: 96 km (60 mi)
10 **LENA–** Kirenga	4,400	2,734	Russia: hinterland of west central shores of Lake Baikal as Kirenga	Northwards through eastern Russia to Leptev Sea, Arctic Ocean	Lena delta extends 177 km (110 mi) inland. Estuary frozen Oct to Jul
11 **MEKONG** (Me Nam Kong)	4,350	2,702	Central Tibet: as Lants'ang on slopes of Dza-Nag-Lung-Mong	Flows into China, then south to form Burmese–Laotian, and most of Thai–Laotian borders, then via Cambodia and Vietnam to South China Sea	Source discovered 1995
12 **AMUR–** Argun (Heilongjiang)	4,345	2,700	Northern China in Khingan Ranges as Heilongjiang	North along Inner Mongolian–Russian and Chinese–Russian border for 3743 km (2326 mi) to Tatar Strait, Sea of Okhotsk	Amur is 2824 km (1755 mi) long. *China Handbook* claims total length of 4670 km (2903 mi)

■ The Amazon and its tributaries contain two-thirds of the Earth's river water

■ The Nile Valley and delta support most of Egypt's agriculture and 99% of its population

■ Three Gorges, Yangtze River, China – the site of the world's greatest engineering project

■ The Mississippi basin contains 31 US states and two Canadian provinces

	LENGTH km	mi	SOURCE	COURSE	NOTES
(13) **MACKENZIE–** Peace River–Slave	4,241	2,635	Tatlatui Lake, Skeena Mts, Rockies, British Columbia, Canada	Flows as Finlay for 400 km (250 mi) to confluence with Peace, then 1690 km (1050 mi) to join Slave (415 km/258 mi), which feeds Great Slave Lake, from which Mackenzie flows to Beaufort Sea	Peace River is 1923 km (1195 mi) long; Mackenzie is 1733 km (1077 mi) long
(14) **NIGER**	4,181	2,600	Guinea: Loma Mts near Sierra Leone border	Flows through Mali, Niger and along Benin border into Nigeria and the Atlantic	Delta extends 128 km (80 mi) inland and 200 km (124 mi) in coastal length
(15) **MURRAY–** Darling–Condamine	3,750	2,330	Queensland (Australia): as the Condamine, a tributary of the Culgoa, which is a tributary of the Balonne branch of the Darling	Balonne (intermittent flow) crosses into New South Wales to join Darling, which itself joins the Murray on the NSW–Victoria border, and flows west into Lake Alexandrine (South Australia)	Darling is *c.* 2740 km (1700 mi) long; Murray 2590 km (1609 mi), or 1870 km (1160 mi) if only permanent streams are considered
(16) **ZAMBEZI** (Zambeze)	3,540	2,200	Zambia; north-west extremity as Zambezi	Flows after 72 km (45 mi) across E. Angola for 354 km (220 mi) and back into Zimbabwe, later forming border with Namibia. After Victoria Falls, it forms the Zambia–Zimbabwe border before entering Mozambique and reaching the Indian Ocean	Navigable 610 km (380 mi) up to Quebrabasa Rapids
(17) **VOLGA**	3,530	2,193	Russia: in Valdai Hills, north-west of Moscow	Flows south and east in great curve and empties in a delta into the north of the Caspian Sea	Delta exceeds 280 km (175 mi) inland and arguably 450 km (280 mi) inland
(18) **MADEIRA–** Mamoré–Guapay	3,380	2,100	Bolivia: rises on the Beni near Illimani	Flows north and east into Brazil to join the Amazon at the Ilha Tupinambaram	World's longest tributary. Navigable for 1070 km (663 mi)
(19) **JURUA**	3,283	2,040	Peru: south of Puerto Portillo	Flows east and north into Brazil to join Amazon below Fonte Boa	Navigable for 965 km (600 mi). Most pronounced meanders in Amazon Basin
(20) **PURUS**	3,211	1,995	Peru: as Alto Purus	Flows north and east into Brazil to join Amazon below Beruri	Navigable for 2575 km (1600 mi). Purus was formerly called the Coxiuara
(21) **YUKON** –Teslin	3,185	1,979	North-west British Columbia	Flows north into Yukon Territory and into west Alaska (USA) and then to Bering Sea	Delta 136 km (85 mi) inland. Navigable for shallow draft boats for 2855 km (1775 mi)
(22) **ST LAWRENCE**	3,130	1,945	Head of St Louis River, MN (USA)	Flows into Lake Superior, then lakes Huron, Erie, Ontario, to Gulf of St Lawrence and N. Atlantic	Estuary: 407 km (253 mi) long or 616 km (383 mi) to Anticosti Island
(23) **RIO GRANDE** –Rio Bravo	3,035	1,886	South-west Colorado (USA): in San Juan Mts	Flows south through New Mexico and along Texas–Mexico border to Gulf of Mexico	
(24) **SYRDARYA** –Naryn	3,019	1,876	Kyrgyzstan: in Tien Shan Mts	Flows west through Kyrgyzstan and Tajikistan, then north and west through Kazakhstan to the Aral Sea	Known to the Ancient Greeks as the Jaxartes
(25) **NIZHNAYA TUNGUSKA**	2,989	1,857	In central Siberia, Russia	Flows east then west and north to the Yenisey	

Deserts of Sand and Ice

▶ **Deserts are defined as large, extremely dry areas with sparse vegetation.**

▶ **Wind is an important factor in the making of deserts, as it causes erosion which can lead to desert conditions.**

▶ **Glaciers and ice caps are sometimes referred to as ice deserts.**

▶ **The oldest desert in the world is thought to be the Namib sand desert.**

DESERTS OF SAND

▶ **Desert areas are defined in terms of aridity or the availability of water.**
▶ **The largest sand desert in the world is the Sahara Desert, located in North Africa.**

Deserts of sand are categorized as semi-arid, arid or hyper-arid, according to the amount of precipitation they receive. In general, semi-arid areas receive on average 200–500 mm (8–20 in) of precipitation per annum and arid areas 25–200 mm (1–8 in). Hyper-arid areas are those in which a continuous period of 12 months can go by without any rainfall. However, these definitions are very approximate because a desert may contain areas experiencing each of these conditions and rainfall levels may vary greatly between years. Also, deserts are advancing on many fronts and, in some places, being reclaimed. Globally, 13.3% of the world's land area is semi-arid, 13.7% is arid and 5.8% is hyper-arid.

■ *Sand dunes, such as these in the Libyan portion of the Sahara, cover about 15% of the Sahara Desert's area*

WHAT CAUSES DESERTS?

Deserts of sand are caused by a variety of reasons, ranging from atmospheric high pressure belts to obstructive landscape features, and are often a result of a combination of factors. However, all of these factors interfere with the level of precipitation received by desert areas. The following are some of the main components that can cause decreased precipitation and lead to desert conditions.

High pressure belts

Many of the world's deserts coincide with areas of stable atmospheric high pressure, conditions unfavourable to rainfall. Air heated at the Equator rises and cools, causing moisture to condense and fall over the tropics. The remaining dry air drifts and falls near latitudes 30°N and 30°S. High pressure belts are responsible for the Sahara and Kalahari in Africa and the deserts of Arabia and Australia.

Continentality

Some deserts, such as the Gobi Desert in Central Asia, exist because of their continentality, that is their distance from the sea. This prevents them being reached by moisture-bearing winds from the oceans and decreases the chances of precipitation. In contrast, islands such as Great Britain, New Zealand, New Guinea and Japan have a relatively high level of rainfall, as few areas of these countries are far from the coasts.

Landscape

Lack of precipitation may also be caused by the shape of the landscape. For example, moist air coming in from the sea will precipitate on mountains as rain or snow, and by the time the air has reached the far side of the mountains it will be dry, so forming a rain-shadow desert. Such deserts occur, for example, to the north of the Himalayas.

■ *Most sand is of a yellow, brown or red colour, indicating the presence of iron as one of its mineral components*

Ocean currents

The deserts of the west coast of southern Africa and South America (the Namib and Atacama deserts) are affected by the presence of cold ocean currents running along the coast. These cool the air that they come into contact with, so preventing the evaporation of moisture from the ocean surface and the formation of rain. At some places in the Atacama Desert, no rain was recorded for 400 years prior to 1971. The cold ocean water does, however, cause a high frequency of fog, which is the major source of moisture in these extremely dry, or hyper-arid, deserts.

DESERTIFICATION

▶ **The word 'desert' comes from the Latin word *desertus*, meaning 'abandoned'.**
▶ **Most deserts are natural features and not the result of human intervention.**

In 1949, the French explorer André Aubreville discovered in the Sahel of Africa that the savannah grasslands and tropical rain forest were being damaged by farming. The land was deteriorating, the trees were being cleared and the desert appeared to be advancing. He coined the word 'desertification' to describe what was happening.

There is an assumption in the very word 'desert' that it was once a better environment. The Latin *desertus* means 'abandoned', which implies that it was formerly inhabited and adequately watered for agriculture. This, in turn, implies that deserts are the result of human activity and can be reclaimed by planting vegetation around the fringes of wadis (rocky watercourses that collect precipitation during the rainy season). Underlying such theories is a misconception about the very nature of the desert and the climate that created it. Most deserts are natural features. The desert landscape, its soils and what little flora there is are a perfect adaptation to that climate. By assuming that deserts are human-induced rather than being a response to climate, we are in danger of assuming that it is possible to reclaim deserts on a large scale.

LARGEST DESERTS

	AREA km²	AREA sq mi	LOCATION
THE SAHARA	8,400,000	3,250,000	North Africa. Includes Libyan and Nubian deserts
AUSTRALIAN DESERT	1,550,000	600,000	Australia. Embraces the Great Sandy (or Warburton), Great Victoria, Simpson (Arunta), Gibson, and Sturt deserts
ARABIAN DESERT	1,300,000	500,000	Arabian peninsula. Includes the Rub' al Khali or 'Empty Quarter', Syrian and An Nafud deserts
THE GOBI	1,040,000	400,000	Mongolia and China (Inner Mongolia)
KALAHARI DESERT	520,000	200,000	Botswana, South Africa, Namibia
TAKLA MAKAN	320,000	125,000	Xinjiang, China
NAMIB DESERT	310,000	120,000	Namibia
SONORAN DESERT	310,000	120,000	Arizona and California, USA and Mexico
KARA KUM	270,000	105,000	Turkmenistan (with Kyzyl Kum, known as the Turkestan Desert)
SOMALI DESERT	260,000	100,000	Somalia
THAR DESERT	260,000	100,000	North-western India and Pakistan
ATACAMA DESERT	180,000	70,000	Northern Chile
KYZYL KUM	180,000	70,000	Uzbekistan, Kazakhstan

DESERTS OF ICE

▶ It is estimated that over one-tenth of the Earth's land surface – about 15,600,000 km^2 (6,020,000 sq mi) – is permanently covered with ice.
▶ The world's largest glacier is the Lambert-Fisher Ice Passage in Antarctica, which is 515 km (320 mi) long.

Ice is, in fact, the world's biggest reservoir of fresh water. Over three-quarters of the Earth's water is contained in ice sheets, ice caps and glaciers. These range in size from the huge Antarctic and Greenland ice sheets, to the small glaciers found in high-latitude and high-altitude mountain ranges.

HOW DESERTS OF ICE ARE FORMED

Ice bodies develop where winter snowfall is able to accumulate and endure throughout the summer. Over time this snow is compressed into an ice body, which may then grow to blanket the landscape as an ice sheet or ice cap. Alternatively, the ice body may grow to form a mass that flows down a slope – a glacier. The glacier will often cut a valley as it moves, eroding rock material that is eventually deposited at a lower altitude as the ice melts.

Ice bodies

Ice bodies may be formed by rain freezing as it hits an ice surface, but usually develop from a build-up of snow. Obviously, not all the snow that falls is turned into ice.

During winter in the northern hemisphere, over one-half of the world's land surface and up to one-third of the surfaces of the oceans may be blanketed by snow and ice. However, most of this snow and ice is only temporary, as the Sun's warmth and energy are able to melt the cover during warm winter days or as winter passes into spring and summer.

In other places, however, the summer warmth is unable to melt all the snowfall of the previous winter. This may be because summer temperatures are rather low, or summer is very short, or because winter snowfall is very high. Where this occurs, snow lies all year round (this snow is sometimes called firn or névé) and becomes covered by the snow of the next winter. As this process continues from year to year, the snow that is buried becomes compressed and transformed into glacier ice.

Latitude and altitude both determine where permanent snow can accumulate. The level that separates permanent snow cover from places where the snow melts in the summer is called the snowline or firnline. The snowline increases in altitude towards the Equator: in polar regions it lies at sea level, in Norway at 1200–1500 m (4000–5000 ft) above sea level, and in the Alps at about 2700 m (9000 ft). Permanent snow and ice can even occur close to the Equator. In East Africa, for example, the snowline lies at approximately 4900 m (16,000 ft), so that glaciers are found on Mount Kenya, Kilimanjaro, and the Ruwenzori Mountains.

Ice sheets and ice caps

Ice sheets and ice caps are ice bodies that have grown into domes that blanket an area of land, submerging valleys, hills and mountains. Ice sheets are defined as having an area over 50,000 km^2 (19,000 sq mi), whereas ice caps are smaller. Occasionally, 'islands' of land, called nunataks, protrude through the 'sea' of ice. Greenland is an example of a nunatak.

Sea ice

There is no ice sheet over the North Pole because there is no land there. However, the Arctic Ocean is always frozen and, during the winter, Arctic sea ice covers about 12 million km^2 (4.6 million sq mi).

An area of sea ice that is joined to a coast is an ice shelf. In the Arctic, ice shelves are joined to the coasts of northern Canada and Greenland. Ice shelves can be very large – the Ross Ice Shelf in the Antarctic covers an area greater than France. Ocean currents and seasonal melting can cause ice sheets to break up, creating pack ice or ice floes.

Glaciers

Glaciers move and flow under the influence of gravity. Frozen water, obviously, moves much slower than water in its liquid form. Most glaciers flow at a velocity of 3–300 m (10–1000 ft) per year. Glaciers on steep slopes may move much faster. Quarayaq Glacier, supplied with ice from the Greenland Ice Sheet, averages 20–24 m (65–80 ft) per day.

Although glacier movement is often steady and gradual, many glaciers experience surges. These may last only a few days or several years. During these times the glacier's flow is extremely rapid, reaching rates of up to 10 km (6 mi) a year.

A glacier erodes the landscape by plucking blocks of rock from its bed and by abrading rock surfaces – breaking off small particles and rock fragments – as it moves. The rock that is eroded is transported by the ice and deposited as the glacier travels down slope and melts. Fjords, such as those found along the coasts of Norway and Alaska, are formed by the movement of rocks at the base of a glacier carving out a U-shaped valley which becomes submerged by the sea after the ice from the glacier melts.

ICE AGES

▶ At its height, the most recent glacial period saw Canada and Scandinavia covered by great ice sheets.
▶ In Europe during the last ice age, ice caps were centred on Highland Scotland, Snowdonia, the English Lake District and the Alps, with outlet and valley glaciers extending out over the lowlands.

Ice ages, more correctly called glacial periods, have been a major phenomenon of the last two million years. Geological evidence, however, demonstrates that glacial periods have affected the Earth periodically over 2300 million years.

It is not known why the Earth's atmosphere and surface change substantially, allowing the build-up of ice, although it is generally thought that the causes of major ice ages relate to cyclic changes in the pattern and character of the Earth's orbit around the Sun.

Evidence for glacial periods comes from a range of sources. Much can be learned from studies of sediments which have accumulated in deep oceans and lake basins. Ocean sediments in particular can show long, undisturbed sequences that are dated using modern radiometric and palaeomagnetic methods. Also, investigations of long cores of ice extracted from Antarctic and Greenland ice sheets indicate that there have been between 15 and 22 glacial periods during the last two million years. Glacial periods previous to these have been too difficult to determine.

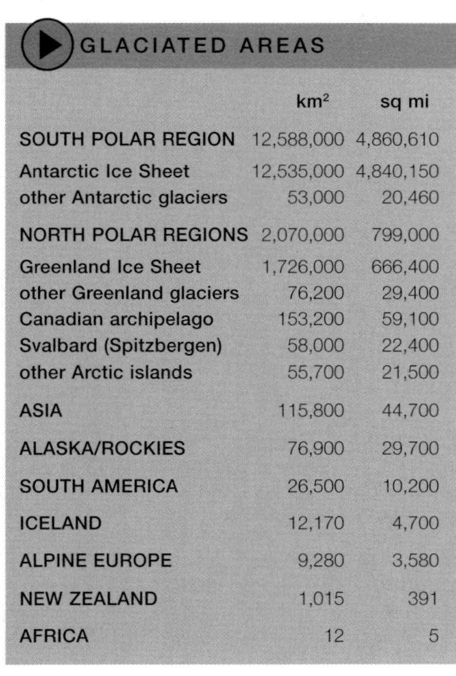

GLACIATED AREAS

	km^2	sq mi
SOUTH POLAR REGION	12,588,000	4,860,610
Antarctic Ice Sheet	12,535,000	4,840,150
other Antarctic glaciers	53,000	20,460
NORTH POLAR REGIONS	2,070,000	799,000
Greenland Ice Sheet	1,726,000	666,400
other Greenland glaciers	76,200	29,400
Canadian archipelago	153,200	59,100
Svalbard (Spitzbergen)	58,000	22,400
other Arctic islands	55,700	21,500
ASIA	115,800	44,700
ALASKA/ROCKIES	76,900	29,700
SOUTH AMERICA	26,500	10,200
ICELAND	12,170	4,700
ALPINE EUROPE	9,280	3,580
NEW ZEALAND	1,015	391
AFRICA	12	5

■ *Ruth Glacier Region in Denali National Park, Alaska*

WEATHER AND CLIMATE

- The extreme minimum temperature of –89.2°C was recorded on 21 July 1983. This reading was taken at the Soviet base of Vostok, Antarctica, at an altitude of 3420 m.
- The annual average sunshine at Yuma, Arizona, USA, is 4055 out of a possible 4456 hours of sun.
- The strongest wind recorded on the Earth's surface was 371 km/h on 12 April 1934 on Mt Washington, New Hampshire, USA; in general, wind speeds increase with height above 600 m.
- The wettest place on Earth has an average of over 11 m of rain each year; the driest area has none.
- Areas of coastal urbanization could be inundated through sea-level rise due to global warming. It is thought that 13 million people in Bangladesh and 20 million people in China could be put at risk.
- The highest recorded air temperature at an official reporting station was 58°C at Al'azizyah, Libya.

■ *Forked lightning illuminates Chicago's city skyline during an intense summer storm*

WEATHER

▶ Weather is the condition of the atmosphere at any one place and time, as described by air temperature and humidity, wind speed and direction, cloud cover, atmospheric pressure, precipitation, sunshine and visibility.
▶ Heat from the Sun drives the Earth's weather systems.

Climate is the normal or average weather for an area for a period of time, usually a month, a season or a year. The climate of an area is described using an average of the statistics of the various weather factors over a period of time, usually 30 years. At any one time the weather may be quite different from the expected climate. Average values of weather may change from one 30-year period to another though usually the differences are not large.

ATMOSPHERIC TEMPERATURE

The Sun is the Earth's main source of energy. The planet revolves around the Sun in an elliptical orbit, spinning at an angle of 23° to the vertical. Most solar energy is received when the Sun is high in the sky – easily recognized by the difference in its intensity at midday and in the evening. Due to these astronomic controls on the input of energy, the tropics are warmer than the polar regions, summer is warmer than winter, and day is usually warmer than night. Temperatures over the oceans show a steady poleward temperature gradient apart from areas of warmer and colder ocean currents like the Gulf Stream. Over land, the pattern is more varied – coastal areas are affected by the influence of the sea and have less extreme temperatures than those in the continental interiors. Mountain ranges and cloudiness also affect global temperature patterns.

THE ATMOSPHERE

▶ The Earth's atmosphere is composed of a mixture of gases which surround the planet, and which are prevented from escaping by the pull of the Earth's gravity. The atmosphere can be divided, by temperature, into four separate layers: the troposphere (closest to the Earth), the stratosphere, the mesosphere, and the thermosphere which gradually merges with space.
▶ The Earth is 12,000 km (7457 mi) in diameter, and the atmosphere lies within 30 km (18.6 mi) of the Earth's surface.

We need to know about meteorology, the science of the atmosphere, to understand how weather works. The atmosphere comprises a mixture of gases. Some, such as oxygen and nitrogen, have a constant proportion (21 and 78% respectively), others, such as water vapour, carbon dioxide (CO_2) and ozone (O_3), may vary. CO_2 is released into the atmosphere by burning wood and fossil fuels such as coal and oil (see p. 56) – when forests are cut down and converted to other uses, CO_2 is added to the atmosphere. Ozone in the high atmosphere provides a shield from ultraviolet radiation from the Sun (see p. 55). Near the Earth's surface it is a toxic pollutant formed as a by-product of sunlight and hydrocarbons (see p. 56).

All three variable gases have a very important function; they allow sunlight to pass through the atmosphere but absorb the radiation given off by the Earth. This has been called the natural Greenhouse Effect which helps to keep the Earth warmer than it would be without the atmosphere. As amounts of CO_2 are increasing it is thought that the Earth is becoming warmer.

WATER IN THE ATMOSPHERE

Water vapour comprises 1–4% of the atmosphere. The recycling of water is a continuous process – water evaporates from the oceans and moist land, vapour condenses as dew, fog or cloud, and precipitation falls from clouds and soaks into the soil before making its way into rivers and back to the oceans. Plants may extract some of this moisture from the soil and release it as water vapour through transpiration (see p. 62).

The warmer the air, the more vapour it can hold, though there is a maximum amount for any given temperature. The moisture content of the atmosphere is measured by its relative humidity (RH). This is the actual vapour content of air expressed as a percentage of the maximum that can be held by air at that temperature. Saturated air has an RH of 100% – this is called the dew point. If the air is not saturated, for instance it has an RH of only 80%, then if it is cooled to its dew point, some vapour will be released as visible water droplets. These droplets can be seen during night-time cooling as mist forms, or when air rises, cools sufficiently and clouds start to develop.

TOPOGRAPHY

Mountains have a marked effect on weather and climate. It is generally colder at the top of mountains, wetter on their windward side (the side from which the wind blows), and drier on the leeward side (the side to which the wind blows). Winds usually increase in strength with altitude to give more severe weather at higher altitudes.

WIND

The prevailing (predominant) wind systems and the storms which control the weather in temperate latitudes are produced by the differential heating across the globe together with the Earth's rotation and variable surface of mountains, land and sea. In tropical areas, the prevailing winds are from the east, in the northern hemisphere they are the north-east trade winds, and in the southern hemisphere, the south-east trade winds, getting their name from the Saxon word *trada*, meaning track. Their flow changes over the larger continents such as Africa and Asia to produce a major seasonal reversal of winds; during summer the winds become south-westerly in the northern hemisphere and bring the wet season to West Africa, India and China which is known as the monsoon.

Further towards the poles, the winds are mainly from the west. Within these westerlies are rotating eddies called depressions or low-pressure systems. As the surface air converges into these lows, the air is forced to rise giving cloud and precipitation.

PRECIPITATION

Precipitation is the result of air cooling to below its dew point. Air may cool by contact with a cold ground surface, in which case dew, frost or fog will occur. Air also cools through expansion when lifted into areas of lower atmospheric pressure. The lifting may be caused by mountains, by thermal currents above hotter ground surfaces or by air of different densities converging within a low pressure system or depression. Cloud forms once air has cooled to dew point or below. If thick enough and containing enough water droplets, clouds may give precipitation which reaches the ground – but not all produce rain.

BEAUFORT SCALE

A scale of numbers, designated Force 0 to Force 12, was originally devised by Commander Francis Beaufort in 1805. Force 13 to 17 were added in 1955 by the US Weather Bureau, but are not in international use.

Force	Description	Wind speed km/h	mph	knots
0	Calm	0–1	0–1	0–1
1	Light air	1–5	1–3	1–3
2	Light breeze	6–11	4–7	4–6
3	Gentle breeze	12–19	8–12	7–10
4	Moderate breeze	20–28	13–18	11–16
5	Fresh breeze	29–38	19–24	17–21
6	Strong breeze	39–50	25–31	22–27
7	Near gale	51–61	32–38	28–33
8	Gale	62–74	39–46	34–40
9	Strong gale	75–87	47–54	41–47
10	Storm	88–101	55–63	48–55
11	Violent storm	102–117	64–73	56–63
12	Hurricane	over 118	over 74	over 64

■ *Hurricanes form in intense low pressure; dense clouds driven by high winds swirl around the hurricane's 'eye'*

■ *A thunderstorm releases heavy rain over the Reese River Valley in the Shoshone mountains, Nevada, USA*

■ *High winds speed the passage of a violent thunderstorm across the plains near Decorah, Iowa, USA*

AVERAGE PRECIPITATION (MM)

	Zone	Jan	Feb	Mar	Apr	May	Jun	Jul	Aug	Sep	Oct	Nov	Dec	Yearly total
Singapore	A	285	164	154	160	131	177	163	200	122	184	236	306	2,282
Bombay, India	A	0	0	0	0	2	591	771	440	245	49	1	0	2,099
Lagos, Nigeria	A	40	57	100	115	215	336	151	59	214	222	77	41	1,625
Sydney, Australia	C	104	125	129	101	115	140	94	83	72	80	77	86	1,208
Rio de Janeiro, Brazil	C	137	137	143	116	73	43	43	43	53	74	97	127	1,086
Buenos Aires, Argentina	C	135	101	107	75	73	69	72	69	62	94	87	83	1,027
New York, USA	C	83	86	97	87	88	107	109	94	90	86	90	89	1,106
Montreal, Canada	D	75	63	76	78	68	86	93	90	89	77	85	91	971
Geneva, Switzerland	C	60	63	58	54	66	88	62	106	87	61	88	58	852
Rome, Italy	C	83	73	52	50	48	18	9	18	70	110	113	105	749
Beijing, China	D	4	5	8	17	35	79	245	143	58	16	10	3	623
London, UK	C	54	40	37	38	46	45	56	59	50	57	64	48	594
Paris, France	C	50	45	41	33	56	58	52	56	46	44	55	49	585
Bucharest, Romania	C	42	36	31	49	74	81	56	43	38	42	44	42	578
Moscow, Russia	D	31	28	33	35	52	67	74	74	58	51	36	36	575
Berlin, Germany	C	41	37	30	39	44	60	67	65	45	45	44	39	556
Stockholm, Sweden	D	43	30	26	31	34	45	61	76	60	48	53	48	555
Cape Town, South Africa	C	11	15	14	53	89	84	83	73	45	31	17	11	526
Madrid, Spain	C	38	34	45	44	44	27	11	14	31	53	47	48	436
Athens, Greece	C	62	36	38	23	23	14	6	7	15	51	56	71	402
Tehran, Iran	B	33	29	32	35	15	2	0	0	0	8	24	30	208
Jeddah, Saudi Arabia	B	5	0	0	0	0	0	0	0	0	0	25	31	61

■ *Cirrus uncinus: delicate white filaments ending in a tuft*

■ *Cirrostratus: thin white veils often of smooth appearance*

■ *Nimbostratus: flat layers of rain-bearing cloud*

CLOUDS

▶ Clouds comprise water drops or ice crystals suspended in air.
▶ They are classified according to the height of their base above the ground and whether they are rounded (cumulus) or flat (stratus).

Clouds consist of water droplets or ice crystals. Their appearance depends upon the processes which produce them and the state of the atmosphere in terms of temperature, humidity and wind speed. Water droplets do not freeze automatically at 0°C (32°F), but because of their size can remain liquid when supercooled to temperatures of –30°C (–22°). Below this temperature an increasing number of water drops freeze to ice crystals. At temperatures below –40°C (–40°F), clouds consist of ice crystals alone. Clouds are usually classified on the basis of their shape and the height of formation.

The modern method of cloud classification was created by the English meteorologist Luke Howard in 1803. His system originally established three classes – cirrus, cumulus and stratus. The World Meteorological Organization (WMO) currently uses the following system of cloud types divided into three stages – high (base above 5000 m/16,500 ft), middle (base 2000–7000 m/6500–23,000 ft) and low (base at or below 2000 m/6500 ft).

HIGH CLOUD

cirrus: (Latin 'lock of hair'): contain ice crystals in air colder than –30°C (–22°F), and usually higher than about 5000 m (16,500 ft); detached clouds forming delicate white filaments, or white, or mostly white, patches or narrow bands; a fibrous (hair-like) appearance or a silky sheen, or both; the highest of the standard cloud forms.
cirrocumulus: rounded small clouds, rather than feathery or hair-like; appear in the form of grains or ripples; often more or less regularly arranged.
cirrostratus: appear like a white veil of smooth fibrous ice crystal; often seen making a halo around the Sun or Moon.

MIDDLE CLOUD

altocumulus: grey or white clouds having rounded shapes, sometimes touching.
altostratus: flat, thick sheet cloud, often obscuring the Sun and totally hiding it when about to rain or snow; all shades of grey.
nimbostratus: flat, relatively shapeless clouds; the main source of rain in temperate latitudes.

LOW CLOUD

cumulus: detached clouds with sharp billowing upper contours, which develop upwards in thermals; vary in appearance from small fleeces to giant cauliflower shapes.
cumulonimbus: tallest of the cumulus clouds; sometimes have an ice-crystal anvil-shaped top at the limit of convection; give showers of rain, snow or hail, often with thunder and lightning.
stratus: patches or sheets of shapeless low grey cloud; often thin enough to see the Sun through, especially when about to disperse; often start as fog and later lifted by strengthening wind; give drizzle and (in winter) snow grains.
stratocumulus: patches of cloud, or whole sheets, with discernible rounded shapes; often formed by cumulus clouds spreading out under an inversion of temperature.

AVERAGE TEMPERATURES (°C)

	Zone	Jan	Feb	Mar	Apr	May	Jun	Jul	Aug	Sep	Oct	Nov	Dec	Yearly average
Jeddah, Saudi Arabia	B	24.1	23.7	24.5	27.4	28.6	30.3	31.6	32.1	30.5	29.4	27.6	24.8	27.9
Bombay, India	A	24.8	25.3	27.3	29.6	30.4	29.6	28.7	27.6	28.4	29.7	28.2	26.4	27.6
Singapore	A	26.1	26.7	27.2	27.6	27.8	28.0	27.4	27.3	27.3	27.2	26.7	26.3	27.1
Lagos, Nigeria	A	26.7	27.5	27.7	27.4	26.7	25.6	24.4	24.3	25.0	25.6	26.8	26.8	26.2
Rio de Janeiro, Brazil	C	25.9	26.1	25.5	23.9	22.3	21.3	20.8	21.1	21.5	22.3	23.1	24.4	23.2
Athens, Greece	C	9.3	9.9	11.3	15.3	20.0	24.6	27.6	27.4	23.5	19.0	14.7	11.0	17.8
Sydney, Australia	C	21.9	21.9	21.2	18.3	15.7	13.1	12.3	13.4	15.3	17.6	19.4	21.0	17.0
Tehran, Iran	B	3.6	5.8	10.3	16.9	22.4	27.0	30.2	29.4	25.5	18.0	11.6	5.3	17.5
Buenos Aires, Argentina	C	24.3	23.2	21.0	17.6	14.5	11.4	11.2	12.8	14.9	17.5	20.0	23.1	17.3
Cape Town, South Africa	C	20.3	20.0	18.8	16.1	14.0	12.6	11.6	12.3	13.7	15.0	17.6	19.3	15.0
Rome, Italy	C	8.0	9.0	10.9	13.7	17.5	21.6	24.4	24.2	21.5	17.2	12.7	9.5	15.9
Madrid, Spain	C	4.9	6.5	10.0	12.7	15.7	20.6	24.2	23.7	19.8	14.0	8.9	5.6	13.9
New York, USA	C	0.2	1.8	5.9	11.3	17.4	22.5	25.0	24.7	20.3	14.3	8.7	2.0	13.6
Beijing, China	D	–4.7	–1.9	4.8	13.7	20.1	24.7	26.1	24.9	19.9	12.8	3.8	–2.7	11.8
Bucharest, Romania	C	–2.3	1.4	5.6	12.7	17.3	21.0	23.4	23.3	18.6	12.7	6.5	1.0	11.4
Paris, France	C	3.1	3.8	7.2	10.3	14.0	17.1	19.0	18.5	15.9	11.1	6.8	4.1	10.9
London, UK	C	4.2	4.4	6.6	9.3	12.4	15.8	17.6	17.2	14.8	10.8	7.2	5.2	10.5
Geneva, Switzerland	C	1.8	2.6	6.4	10.8	14.7	18.6	20.9	19.3	16.5	11.0	6.3	2.7	10.3
Berlin, Germany	C	–0.5	0.2	3.9	9.0	14.3	17.7	19.4	18.8	15.0	9.6	4.7	1.2	9.5
Stockholm, Sweden	D	–2.9	–3.1	–0.7	4.4	10.1	14.9	17.8	16.6	12.2	7.1	2.8	0.1	6.6
Montreal, Canada	D	–10.6	–9.6	–3.9	6.2	13.7	18.2	21.5	20.8	15.4	9.6	2.3	–7.6	6.0
Moscow, Russia	D	–9.9	–9.5	–4.2	4.7	11.9	16.8	19.0	17.1	11.2	4.5	–1.9	–6.8	4.4

■ *Cumulus: these clouds disperse when the Sun sets*

■ *Cumulonimbus: distinctive storm clouds with anvil heads*

■ *Lenticular clouds: formed by undulating air streams*

FORECASTING THE WEATHER

▶ Weather maps or charts are compiled by information gathered from all around the world. The World Meteorological Organization (WMO) has 170 member countries.

▶ James Glaisher made some of the first daily weather charts and in 1848 started the first newspaper weather report in Europe for the London *Daily News*.

Before the 19th century people could only try to predict the weather by using indicators such as the Moon, cloud shapes and sky colour, without instruments and any knowledge of the causes of weather. Some sayings of weather 'lore' such as 'clear sky, frost nigh' remain today, but scientific advances have turned predictions into more accurate forecasts.

Weather forecasting is based upon data obtained by satellites, weather balloons and ocean buoys together with land surface and ship weather observations taken at sites all over the world. The material is collected and retransmitted after processing on an international telecommunications network organized by the WMO. Each observation can be plotted in symbol form on a map at the position it was made; this is done by computer. Some current weather information can be obtained from the Internet together with satellite images.

One of the main items plotted is atmospheric pressure. Computers draw in lines of equal pressure, called isobars. These isobars form a variety of patterns. Some form roughly concentric patterns (sharing the same centre) around low and high pressure centres. They indicate approximate wind direction at about 600 m (1970 ft) above ground, where it is considered to be unaffected by the surface drag created by land. The wind blows parallel to the isobars, so that if you stand with your back to the wind, low pressure is on the left-hand side in the northern hemisphere, and on the right-hand side in the southern hemisphere. Winds blow anticlockwise around low pressure areas in the northern hemisphere (cyclones) and clockwise around high pressure areas (anticyclones); the directions are reversed in the southern hemisphere. Wind speed is inversely proportional to the distance between the isobars, which means the stronger the wind, the closer the isobars on the map.

From the other plotted data, forecasters can detect the boundaries between air masses which have different temperatures and levels of humidity. A warm front is the surface boundary between approaching warm air and existing cool air. The warm air may be forced over the cooler air by upper atmospheric divergence to form sheets of cloud several hundred kilometres ahead of the surface warm front, giving rain (or snow in winter).

A cold front is the surface boundary between approaching cold air and existing warm air. It often forms a narrow band of cloud, sometimes giving a line of heavy showers. A cold front usually travels faster than a warm front, eventually catching up with it so that no warm air remains at the surface. The fronts are then said to be occluded. Satellite pictures show how variable frontal cloud formations can be – those around a low pressure system are often most impressive, showing as a large comma-shaped mass sweeping away from the low pressure centre along the line of the cold front.

EL NIÑO

In recent years, research has been carried out on the dynamic interactions that occur between the atmosphere and the Earth's surface. One such correlation is the El Niño effect, which is a not-entirely-understood example of sea-surface temperature and climactic weather patterns influencing each other. El Niño is a weather phenomenon of the Pacific Ocean; an abnormal heating of water on the surface of the ocean reverses the direction of the usual easterly trade winds. This results in a current which flows in the Pacific Ocean between Papua New Guinea and Micronesia, westwards across the Pacific towards Peru. El Niño has the power to influence global weather patterns, as it brings drought to South-East Asia and Australia, significantly higher rain than is usual in South America, and coastal storms throughout the Americas.

The El Niño current was first noticed by fishermen in Spanish ports in the Pacific in the 17th century. It gets its name (Spanish for 'boy child') because its visible effects occur near Christmas time. The effects can be catastrophic. Storm damage can amount to billions of US dollars, and crops can fail. The human cost is also high: the 1982 El Niño caused 1500 deaths, whilst the 1939–41 cycle caused drought in Bengal that killed hundreds of thousands of people. Sea-life is also adversely affected – small fish such as anchovies are driven away from warm ocean surfaces, and the birds and larger fish dependent on these die *en masse*. It is said that the gas of decaying sealife brought by El Niño blackens ships that pass through the Pacific Ocean. And for those regions of the world which are not affected by El Niño directly, there are several knock-on effects, which include shortages of certain foodstuffs and consequently higher prices for those crops and livestock.

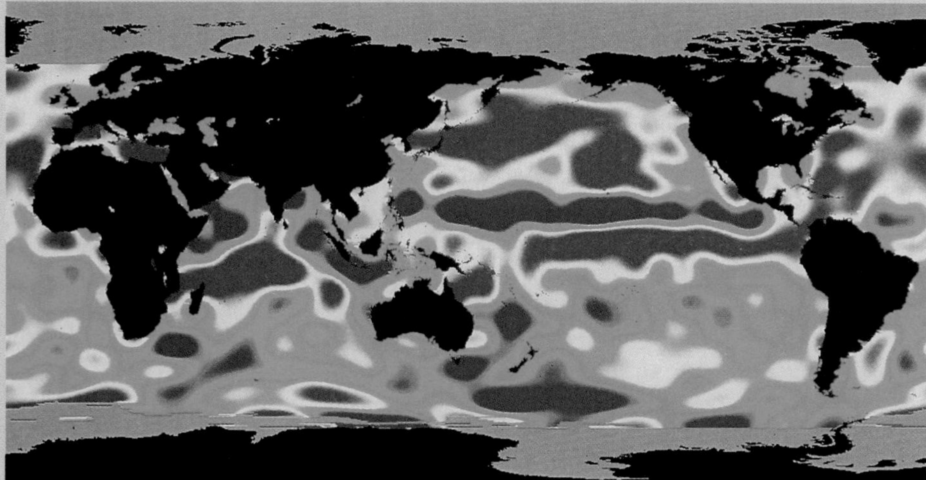

■ *The El Niño effect is clearly visible in the centre-right of this satellite image. It shows the difference between average sea levels and those during an El Niño event. The colours run from purple (10 cm below normal level) through to blue and green (normal level) to yellow and finally red (10 cm above normal level). The El Niño counter current is the red band (centre right) found running across the Pacific Ocean at the Equator*

ZONE A
Tropical rainy climate:
The average monthly temperatures always exceed 18°C (64°F). There is no cool season. Annual rainfall is large, exceeding annual evaporation to give a water surplus.

ZONE B
Dry climate:
On average, precipitation is low. Most moisture is quickly evaporated to give persistent lack of moisture. Dry climates can be hot as in tropical areas or cool as in continental Asia.

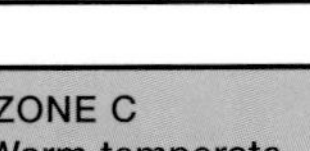

ZONE C
Warm temperate climate:
The mean (average) temperature of the coldest month lies between 18°C (64°F) and −3°C (27°F). At least one month has a mean temperature above 10°C (50°F). Seasonal differences from winter to summer are clear.

ZONE D
Cold, boreal forest climate:
The mean temperature of the coldest month is below −3°C (27°F), but that of the warmest month is above 10°C (50°F). This isotherm (a line on a map linking all places with the same temperature at a given time) is used as it coincides approximately with the limit of forest growth near the poles.

ZONE E
Polar climate:
Mean temperature of the warmest month is below 10°C (50°F), so even summers are cool. Winters are cold.

ZONE H
Highland climate:
Variable climates displaying marked differences from the climatic zone in which they occur. Temperatures decline with height. Precipitation is variable.

■ *Zone A: Monsoon rains can cause severe flooding throughout south and South-East Asia*

■ *Zone B: Eroded rock formations loom over the barren desert outback at Coober Pedy, Australia*

■ *Zone C: Vineyards are found only in the world's warmer temperate climatic zones*

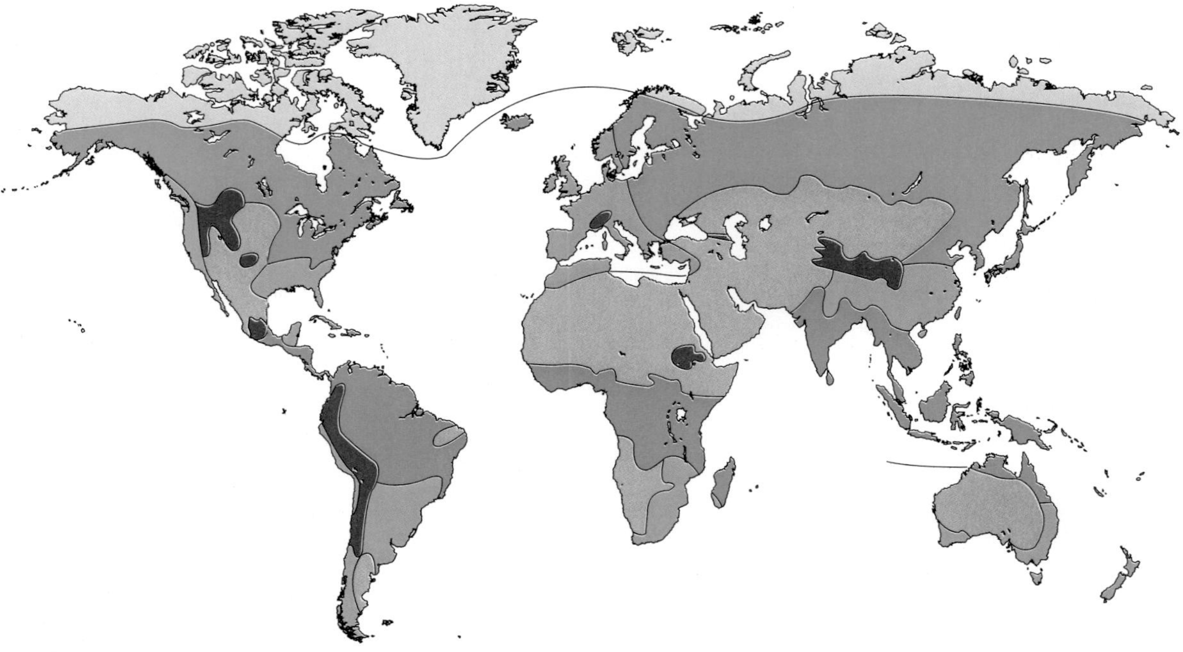

■ *Zone D: Bordered by steppe to the south and tundra to the north are the taiga forests of Siberia*

■ *Zone E: The snowy landscape of Antarctica is one of the Earth's last wildernesses*

■ *Zone H: The dramatic scenery of mountainous Banff National Park, Alberta, Canada*

THE WORLD'S CLIMATIC REGIONS

▶ A climatic region possesses a particular set of similar characteristics relating to seasonal temperature, precipitation and wind.
▶ Climates have changed over geological time: tropical parts of India contain rocks originally deposited by ice sheets.

Climate is often described as average weather and is the result of several factors. Some are astronomic, such as the shape and size of the Earth and its distance from the Sun, which determines how much solar energy reaches the Earth's surface. Others are geographical, such as the relative positions of the continents and oceans and the location of mountain ranges, which affect climate through their effects on air movement and altitude. Temperatures decrease with height, and precipitation (rain, hail and snow) often increases with altitude, as do wind speeds. Because natural vegetation is controlled by climate, many similarities are found between world climatic zones and vegetation.

TEMPERATURE

Globally, temperatures can vary from tropical heat of about 30–35°C (86–95°F) to polar cold below –40°C (–40°F). Over the oceans the rate at which temperature declines roughly follows the bands of latitude except over particularly warm or cold ocean currents, such as the Gulf Stream. Over continental areas, wherever the prevailing winds blow from sea to land they make the climate less extreme. This effect is caused by the fact that water is able to store heat more efficiently than land.

PRECIPITATION

Rain falls where air is able to rise and cool. Rainfall is abundant in low pressure areas near the Equator, and sparse in the high-pressure dominated areas of the sub-tropics, where many of the world's deserts are found. Strong seasonal rainfall in India, southern China, northern Australia and parts of west and eastern Africa, is caused by a reversal of the winds, which is called the monsoon. From 40° to about 70° latitude, low pressure gives frequent but irregular rainfall, mixed with spells of high pressure; in the lower latitudes, the rain falls mainly in winter to give the Mediterranean zones their precipitation. Further polewards, rain can fall from low pressure systems throughout the year, as in the UK.

WIND

Alternating bands of high and low pressure determine the prevailing winds. In the northern hemisphere these are the north-east trade winds, and in the southern hemisphere the south-east trade winds. Both blow toward the equatorial low-pressure area called the doldrums where wind movement is weak. High pressure areas produce light and variable winds, but intense heating of desert surfaces in this zone can cause locally strong winds. In temperate latitudes (40°–60°), alternating low and high pressure give a variable wind direction; the winds strengthen as low pressure deepens. The strongest winds usually occur in autumn and winter when the intensity of the lows is greatest. In the southern hemisphere there are few land masses to modify the main force of the westerly winds. This zone is popularly known as the 'Roaring Forties'.

GLOBAL WARMING

▶ The average atmospheric temperature of the Earth has risen by 0.5°C (33°F) since records began in 1860.
▶ This may seem a very small increase in real terms, but the rate of temperature change is now faster than at any time in the past.

As incoming short-wave solar energy passes through the atmosphere, about 50% of the energy is absorbed, scattered or reflected, leaving the remainder to heat the oceans and the land. Under normal conditions, all the incoming energy leaves the Earth's atmosphere and is reflected back into space as long-wave outgoing energy. If this process did not take place, the planet would overheat. As a result of long-wave radiation, the average temperature of the Earth has remained at about 14°C (57°F) over the last 10,000 years.

To appreciate how global warming occurs, the atmosphere's vertical structure must be understood. The lower layer (up to 17 km (11 mi) thick) is known as the troposphere (see p. 50). It is here that the Earth's daily weather is formed and most air pollution accumulates. The stratosphere exists above the troposphere, 17–48 km (11–30 mi) above the surface of the Earth, and this is where the atmospheric ozone layer is found.

THE OZONE LAYER

Ozone (O_3) is a form of oxygen and a highly reactive and unstable gas which occurs naturally in the atmosphere. Although very poisonous, in the stratosphere the ozone layer acts as a shield against the Sun's harmful ultraviolet (UV) radiation. In 1985, a thinning of the ozone layer was noticed over the South Pole. By 1991 measurements dropped almost 50% from the 1977 levels; since then further fluctuations have occurred. By 1993 the ozone layer over the Arctic had also been depleted by 25% of the amount recorded in 1969.

This depletion is caused by gases produced by the petrochemical industry, including chlorofluorocarbons (CFCs) – used in aerosol spray cans, refrigerators, solvent cleaners and in the manufacture of some plastics. The gases rise into the atmosphere and decompose into methyl chloroform and carbon tetrachloride. They concentrate in the stratosphere above the North and South poles and destroy the ozone molecules, allowing more of the dangerous ultraviolet light to reach the Earth's surface.

Exposure to UV light damages crops, kills plankton and fish larvae, and causes sunburn in humans, which can cause skin cancers and cataracts in the long term. In recent years, the incidence of skin cancers has doubled in northern Europe.

GREENHOUSE GASES

Chlorofluorocarbons (CFCs) are the most harmful of the greenhouse gases; one molecule destroys the same amount of atmospheric ozone as 10,000 molecules of carbon dioxide (CO_2). There are about 30 greenhouse gases in the stratosphere, which include CO_2, methane (CH_4), nitrogen oxides (NO_x), CFCs and benzine. The main reason for global warming is the large increase of so-called greenhouse gases in the lower atmosphere.

The most abundant of the greenhouse gases is CO_2 with a concentration of about 358 parts per million (ppm) in the atmosphere. The amount has risen by 35% on the pre-industrial level recorded in 1850, and is predicted to reach 600 ppm by the year 2050. CO_2 is currently responsible for 58% of the increase in the Earth's temperature and 80% of the gas originates from the burning of wood and fossil fuels, especially coal and oil. Even if ozone-depleting substances were totally banned it would take about 50 years for the hole in the Antarctic ozone layer to return to 1985 levels.

SOURCES OF GREENHOUSE GASES

Agriculture contributes large amounts of methane gas. Rice (paddy) fields contribute 115 million tonnes of methane each year from decomposition of organic matter. Domesticated farm animals (mainly the world's 1.2 billion cattle) release 73 million tonnes from their digestive system. The quantity of methane gas in the atmosphere has increased by more than 200% this century, a faster increase than that of CO_2.

Transport is a major source of greenhouse gases. In 1990, it accounted for 24% of all such emissions, of which 30% was contributed by industrial and commercial vehicles. Road traffic is the greatest single source of nitrogen oxides (NO_x), especially in the UK where it makes up 51% of the total. In order to reduce levels of NO_x, most new vehicles must be fitted with exhaust gas control, such as catalytic converters. It is estimated that in the USA, one-tenth of poorly maintained old vehicles emit up to 60% of all vehicle pollutants.

Industry produces greenhouse gases in vast quantities. In the UK, industry and commerce (excluding transport) accounted for 43% of all CO_2 emissions in 1990.

CONTROLLING GREENHOUSE GASES

Until recently, countries tried to deal with pollutants by building higher chimneys or adding more cleansing devices. However, the governments of most industrial nations have now toughened-up their approach and have introduced a 'polluter pays' policy in which an industry is charged for the amount of pollution it discharges.

In 1987, world leaders undertook to cut back the production of greenhouse gases. Under the terms of the Montreal Protocol, the major industrialized nations agreed to halve the use of CFCs by 1998. However, in July 1990, evidence showed that even more stringent targets were required and a total ban on their use in the developed world by 2000 was agreed. Today, world consumption of certain CFCs is already 50% lower as a result of more environmentally friendly alternatives being used.

To encourage developing countries to use ozone-friendly products, which are usually more expensive and require new technological skills, a fund of $240 million has been provided by the developed countries of the northern hemisphere to help the economies of developing countries.

THE IMPACT OF GLOBAL WARMING

Most of the world's oceans and seas are found in the southern hemisphere. As water can absorb more heat than land, the southern hemisphere will not get as hot as a result of global warming as the northern hemisphere, which is covered by large land masses. The Arctic region may become about 8°C (46°F) warmer than at present by the year 2100, causing a global rise in sea levels of 60–100 cm (24–40 in). In 1996, giant cracks in the Antarctic Ice Sheet were reported; it has been estimated that a rise of 10°C (50°F) would cause it to break up, which would take 200 years of continued global warming at the present rate.

THE DEBATE ON GLOBAL WARMING

Controversy surrounds predictions of the nature and extent of future global warming. Some experts claim that the rise in the Earth's temperature is a natural fluctuation in the long-term history of our planet, and that the existence of the Ice Age about one million years ago is evidence of a natural 'cooling-down' of the world's temperature. The current increase, therefore, is just a reverse of this trend. However, it was decided in 1996 that the current phase of global warming was due to human activities, a conclusion accepted by many governments including all those in Europe.

■ IT IS THOUGHT THAT AVERAGE GLOBAL TEMPERATURES WILL BE 3°C HOTTER BY 2100 ■

POLLUTION

- One person dies every six seconds from drinking water contaminated with water-borne diseases.
- The *Exxon Valdez* ran aground in Alaska in March 1989, spilling 45 million litres of crude (unrefined) oil into the sea. Over 100,000 sea birds died, and $2.2 billion was spent cleaning up the effects of the disaster.
- Each household in the UK produces about 1 tonne of rubbish each year; some 20 million tonnes in total.
- Air pollution levels in Mexico City exceed World Health Organization standards on 310 days each year.

Pollution has become a worldwide problem. The rise of industry in the northern hemisphere has brought with it material wealth at the expense of the local environment. Cities and factories have spread, and the smoke from their chimneys, together with cars and other forms of transport, has released harmful chemicals into the air. The widespread use of disposable convenience goods that are 'energy inefficient' has contributed to the waste of scarce resources, for example the batteries that power personal stereos take 50 times more energy to manufacture than they produce. A developing Third World which follows the environmentally damaging practices of the developed nations could propel the Earth into an ecological disaster within decades.

AIR POLLUTION

▶ An air pollutant is any gas or particulate material which accumulates in the atmosphere to such proportions that it causes harm.
▶ One in four people worldwide is breathing air which is damaging their health.

Air pollution can affect humans, animals or vegetation. It prevents the normal operation of natural processes and can cause damage to the built environment. Nowadays, most air pollution is a result of human activity. Man-made pollutants are notorious for their chemical complexity, their reactivity once released into the atmosphere and their interaction with the living components of the biosphere (the area of the Earth which supports life).

However, natural sources of air pollution can sometimes exceed the quantity of human-produced pollutants. In June 1991, Mount Pinatubo in the Philippines released 18 million tonnes of sulphur dioxide (SO_2), equivalent to all the SO_2 produced in the USA in just one year. Radon gas, which emanates naturally from rocks such as granite, can accumulate in the cavities of buildings and become an environmental hazard for humans, resulting in an increased risk of lung cancer.

GASES

Gaseous pollution presents a major problem for modern industrial societies, affecting both health and the environment. Gases are usually invisible and once released can be transported hundreds of kilometres and react with other elements in the atmosphere to produce secondary pollutants. It is far easier to trap and clean the primary gases at the point of release than to cleanse the atmosphere of the secondary pollutants.

■ *Downtown Los Angeles, California, USA, is shrouded by smog, which regularly exceeds safety levels in summer*

All combustion (the process of burning) releases gases into the atmosphere. In the 1950s and 1960s, sulphur dioxide (SO_2) derived from the burning of coal, was the major gaseous pollution problem. The shift to oil and natural gas in the 1970s has reduced this, but its place has been taken by the various gaseous products released by the combustion of fuel; mostly from motor vehicles.

PHOTOCHEMICAL SMOG

The modern internal combustion engine used in vehicles produces a cocktail of potentially dangerous gases such as carbon monoxide, hydrocarbons and oxides of nitrogen (NO_x). Combined with sunlight, the latter two gases form low atmosphere ozone, a major irritant and pollutant and the main ingredient in photochemical smog. First recorded in the 1940s in Los Angeles, California, photochemical smog now occurs in industrial cities worldwide. The problem becomes most serious in summer time when there is more sunlight and stationary air allows the build-up of high concentrations of these gases. The World Health Organization (WHO) has set a safety limit of 120 parts per billion (ppb), though this figure is often exceeded and has reached a peak of 600 ppb in California. Concentrations of 300 ppb are enough to irritate the eyes, nose and throat, while even lower concentrations can severely damage citrus fruits.

PARTICULATE MATTER

Particulates are produced when coal, oil and wood are not completely burned up during combustion. In the 1940s and 1950s they were responsible for the choking 'pea soup' smogs of northern British industrial cities. Unlike gases, particulates have a physical presence and weight, and will gradually fall out of the atmosphere to form the dust, grit and grime common in large cities. Large particles, over 10 micrometres (1 micrometre = 0.001 mm) in size, normally fall out of the atmosphere within five or six hours of their release. The finest particles, smaller than 1 micrometre, can remain in the air for several months, or even years. Particles less than 10 micrometres make up the so-called PM10 group, the most damaging of the particulates, as they can enter the lungs and seriously affect health, and are thought to be a contributing cause of asthma.

Soot, rubber and tarmac particles are known to be carcinogenic and are associated with lung cancer. Lead, which used to be commonly added to petrol to improve the smooth running of engines, can lead to damage of the brain and central nervous system, especially in children. Although this is a particulate pollutant, because the particles are less than 5 micrometers in size, they function in the same way as gaseous pollutants and once released, are extremely hard to control.

ACID PRECIPITATION

▶ Acid precipitation is rain (or snow), which contains various acids as a result of industrial processes and exhaust gases from vehicles.
▶ A total of 67% of Britain's trees have been damaged by acid rain – the highest percentage in Europe.

Many of the chemicals released into the air during the combustion of fossil fuels can lead to the phenomenon known as acid precipitation or rain, a major form of air pollution. The most important gases in this process are sulphur and nitrogen; both elements are major components of proteins in living plants and animals, and of their fossil remains, so that when organic matter (such as oil or coal) is burned they are released as their oxides. Sulphur dioxide (SO_2) is one of the most abundant of these pollutants and when it combines with atmospheric moisture, it forms sulphurous acid, which in turn oxidizes in air to give dilute sulphuric acid. Similarly, NO_x can lead to the formation of nitric acid. Fossil-fuel power stations are probably responsible for almost two-thirds of atmospheric SO_2 and vehicles produce one-half of the NO_x. Acid rain (or snow) is the main atmospheric fallout of industrial pollutants, although these may also occur as dry deposits such as ash.

EFFECTS OF ACID RAIN

Temperate forests have been seriously damaged by acid rain; the Black Forest in Germany has been steadily losing its trees through Waldsterben ('tree death'), and the problem is also very acute in the north of Bohemia (Czech Republic).

Acid rain upsets the fine chemical balance in lakes. Even a slight dip in pH levels causes heavy metals such as aluminium, mercury, and lead to become more concentrated, decreasing the amount of oxygen that fish can absorb and eventually causing their death, and that of other water-bound life. This destabilizes the ecosystem and the effects are felt throughout the food chain. In southern Norway, 80% of the lakes are devoid of fish life, and Sweden has around 20,000 acidified lakes.

Acid rain can contaminate ground water, and damage the soil. High levels cause heavy metals to become concentrated and disturb the life-cycle of bacteria and fungi, responsible for breaking down organic matter into nutrients. Soil can thus lose its ability to support forests or agriculture.

Not only ecosystems are damaged by acid rain: metal corrosion and the weathering of building materials has become a serious problem for the older buildings of Europe. There is also evidence to suggest that acidic water vapour may enter the human respiratory system, increasing illnesses such as bronchitis and asthma.

Currently, acid rain is causing serious problems in southern Scandinavia, northern and Eastern Europe, southern China, the USA's eastern seaboard, south-east Brazil and Colombia.

■ THE USA GENERATES MORE THAN 420 TONNES OF HAZARDOUS WASTE EVERY MINUTE

CONTROLLING AIR POLLUTION

So severe is the damage to the environment caused by air pollution that stringent legislation has been introduced by most governments, particularly in the developed world. Urban air quality has improved during the 1980s and 1990s, however the WHO claims that 625 million people still breathe air which fails to meet the safety standards for SO_2 levels.

There are various methods of reducing the amount of pollutants reaching the atmosphere, such as using lead-free petrol and fitting catalytic converters to car exhausts. Modern techniques for dealing with particulates include fitting filter systems to reduce dangerous emissions from power stations and industrial plants, and electrostatic precipitators – a series of electrically charged plates that hold back the tiny particles of ash, so preventing their release into the atmosphere. However, some measures may control one type of pollution but create other environmental hazards; lead-free petrol, for example, reduces airborne lead by up to 50%, but increases the level of benzine in the atmosphere. Benzine is extremely aggressive and will probably have an effect that far exceeds that of chlorofluorocarbons (CFCs) on the ozone layer.

WATER POLLUTION

▶ Water pollution occurs whenever substances are intentionally or accidentally added, making the quality of the water unfit for its intended use.
▶ Polluted drinking water is regularly consumed by almost one-fifth of the world's population – 1.2 billion people.

Rivers and seas have been used for the dumping of wastes since earliest times. The flow of rivers and the tidal movements of seas have been used as a means of natural disposal for all forms of wastes.

RIVERS

Rivers can normally dilute small amounts of pollution quickly and safely. However, when overloaded with pollutants, or when the volume of water is reduced during summer drought, this becomes impossible and pollution occurs.

Nitrates, phosphates and pesticides not only cause pollution during their manufacture, but also much contamination occurs accidentally from the leaching (washing out) of these elements through the soil and into rivers, streams and lakes. Nitrates can cause eutrophication, when water becomes enriched so that plants, especially aquatic algae, grow too fast, reducing light and oxygen and ultimately killing all aquatic life. Pesticides can also cause serious harm, for example mercury can enter the food chain and cause severe poisoning in animals and humans. Leaks in underground storage tanks for petrol and oil are another source of water contamination.

In less developed countries and in eastern Europe most rivers are severely polluted. Over 66% of India's rivers are polluted and 90% of child deaths there are attributable to waterborne disease. In Poland, almost 50% of the nation's untreated water is unfit even for industrial use and it is thought that by the year 2000, all naturally occurring water in Poland will be unfit for human consumption.

SEAS

The oceans receive not only river-borne pollution, but also direct inputs of sewage, oil spills from tankers and offshore drilling platforms, and industrial waste dumped at sea. Ocean dumping around the world currently exceeds 175 million tonnes of solid waste each year, of which about 80% comprises dredged materials taken from rivers to maintain shipping channels. Another 10% comes from

■ *Polluted water, turned orange by chemicals and other mining waste, is pumped into a riverbed in Mexico*

industrial wastes, and the remainder from sewage sludge. EC legislation banned the dumping of dredged materials into European waters in 1995 and dumping sewage sludge will be prohibited by the end of 1998.

Sewage sludge has been shown to be especially poisonous to marine life. Beaches have become seriously contaminated from sewage sludge and also from the indiscriminate dumping of hospital wastes. Tough EC 'guide' values were met by only 33.7% of British beaches, comparing poorly with 91% for Greece, 89% for Ireland and 81% for Italy. Some 2 million sea birds and over 100,000 marine mammals worldwide die each year by poisoning or by becoming entangled in plastic netting.

CONTROLLING WATER POLLUTION

Prevention of water pollution as well as cleaning up past pollution has proved expensive. Britain spent £13.7 billion between 1989 and 1992 on new sewage plants, and since 1983 the US has spent more than $700 million on cleaning the Chesapeake Bay area of domestic sewage effluent produced by the 17 million people living around it. In the USA, a greater use of technology is seen as the way to reduce water pollution. This method is called MACT (Maximum Available Control Technology). Many ecologists believe that reliance on this approach, the so-called 'technological fix', will become too expensive and has no guarantee of success.

As an alternative, low-cost treatment methods need to be developed, for example 'bio-digestion' in which untreated sewage is filtered through reed beds which oxidize and reduce pollution to harmless levels. In Calcutta, settled sewage is used as a feedstock for fish (mainly carp), which can be used as a source of food. Because of the health risk, most developed countries have comprehensive laws and regulations concerning water quality, and around 54 countries in the developed world have set legal safewater standards.

■ *A bulldozer ploughing rubbish at a landfill site in Japan*

LAND POLLUTION

▶ Land pollution is the contamination of, and physical damage to, the surface of the Earth.
▶ Dumping toxic waste is cheaper than treating it.

Throughout history, humans have been polluting the Earth; as the levels of population and industrialization grew, so did the amount and complexity of pollution. Abandoned land that has been physically despoiled or disfigured as a result of past activity, is called derelict land. In the past, pollution control tended to be less stringent, and many old industrial areas bear the scars of extractive industries (coal mining, brick works, china clay quarries). Formal land-use planning, which resulted in the zoning of land use, was largely unknown in Europe and North America before 1945 and as a result, industrial land was intermingled with residential and agricultural landscapes.

WASTE DISPOSAL

A major problem facing developed countries is the disposal of domestic and industrial rubbish. This comprises solids and liquids originating from domestic, commercial, construction, industrial, medical, transport and agricultural sources, and can be classified into three types: inert (such as building waste and domestic refuse), toxic (such as medical and industrial effluent) and inflammable materials (such as chemicals, rubber and timber).

The amount of waste produced grows each year. Modern waste contains a high proportion of non-degradable products – metals, chemicals and some plastics. Unless properly disposed of, these items can cause long-term contamination. Packaging presents a special problem. In the EC some 50 million tonnes of packaging were generated in 1991, of which only 19% was recycled. By 2002, EU regulations will require 60% of packaging to be made from recycled materials and 90% of all packaging waste must be recycled.

CONTROLLING LAND POLLUTION

Traditionally, rubbish has been burned or dumped into disused quarries or at sea. None of these methods is acceptable today; burning can generate highly toxic gases, old quarries have all been filled in and dumping at sea creates major water pollution. Incineration at high temperatures effectively destroys many forms of refuse and produces ash with a volume of only 10% of the original waste. This has proved to be an economic means of refuse disposal and it is widely used in Europe.

The USA produces about 5.5 billion tonnes of waste each year, of which two-thirds is buried in landfill sites. This includes 8 million television sets a year and 2.5 million non-returnable bottles per hour. As part of a major attempt to avoid further land pollution, the US Environmental Protection Agency recommends the following hierarchy of disposal methods: reuse, waste reduction, recycling resource recovery incineration, and finally landfill.

Governments of the developed world now recognize that the rehabilitation of polluted land areas requires an integrated approach. It involves preventing further pollution at source, minimizing the risk to human health, applying the most appropriate and technologically advanced solutions to restoring degraded areas and managing them by means of sustainable land-use policies. The principle of integrated control in which air, water and land pollution become the total responsibility of one environmental management body has been adopted by many European countries. In addition, exceeding the safe levels of pollution discharge can result in fines or even imprisonment.

DEFORESTATION

- **Only one tree is planted for every ten that are cut down. At this rate, all remaining tropical forests will be destroyed by the year 2035.**
- **An estimated two million species of plants and animals exist in tropical forests – deforestation causes species to become extinct.**
- **Tropical rainforests once covered over 30 million km², that is over 20% of the Earth's land surface.**
- **Today, tropical rainforests cover 12% of the Earth's land surface.**

THE LOSS OF OUR FORESTS

▶ Deforestation is the process whereby extensive areas of trees are cut down. This is usually followed by a change in land use.
▶ For every commercially useful tree that is cut down, it is thought that up to 100 'non-useful' trees are also destroyed.

It is difficult to assess figures for deforestation because forests tend to be located in remote areas. From satellite images, it has been estimated that 170,000 km² (65,642 sq mi) of forest is cleared worldwide each year.

Forests have undergone almost continuous destruction from felling, burning, firewood collection and grazing by domesticated animals. At their maximum extent 2000 years ago, forests covered 47% of the Earth's land surface. Today, about 33% of the land is covered by forest, mainly in low-latitude tropical forest. The mid-latitudes of Europe were gradually cleared over 2000 years while North America was deforested in only 200 years. Nowadays, most northern hemisphere countries practise reafforestation policies, replanting soon after mature forest areas have been harvested. Germany currently has about 30% of its land area forested, France 27%, the UK 10% and Ireland 5%.

Use of Landsat satellite images, during the late 1980s, to calculate deforestation in the Amazon Basin, the last great area of virgin (untouched) rainforest, showed a far more serious loss of forest than earlier ground surveys had calculated. At least 30,000 km² (11,584 sq mi) of forest was cleared each year during the late 1980s, equivalent to 0.8% of the total area of tropical rainforest in Brazil (or 12,000 football pitches each day).

Forests are 'sustainable' resources – that is they are capable of providing a continuous harvest not only of timber but also of food, industrial extracts (gums, resins and dyes) and also valuable components for the medical, pharmaceutical and cosmetic industries. Organizations such as the World Wide Fund for Nature (WWF) and the Food and Agriculture Organization (FAO) are monitoring the rate of deforestation around the world, and the International Tropical Timber Association (ITTA) is trying to prevent clear felling of forests and the illegal 'poaching' of valuable trees such as the Brazilian mahogany. The International Council for Bird Preservation is also working to ensure sustainable forest management in order to enhance the survival of tropical forest bird species.

RATES OF DEFORESTATION

	%
Jamaica	7.2
Haiti	4.8
Bangladesh	3.9
Pakistan	3.5
Philippines	3.3
Thailand	3.3
Costa Rica	3.0
Dominican Republic	2.75
Paraguay	2.75
El Salvador	2.25

Note: These figures show the average annual tropical deforestation rates, 1981–90.

THE DESTRUCTION OF THE TROPICAL RAINFOREST

▶ Tropical rainforests are those which lie between the tropic of Capricorn and the tropic of Cancer, and which contain evergreen broadleaved trees.
▶ The amount of the world's tropical rainforest equals the total of all other types of forest (coniferous, deciduous, and mixed) added together.

The indiscriminate removal of forests is generally most destructive in tropical and equatorial latitudes; nowadays, the term deforestation tends to be associated with the removal of tropical rainforest. Thick forest once covered virtually all of the Amazon basin of South America, the West African coasts, the drainage basin of the River Congo and its tributaries, the islands of Indonesia and most of Malaysia and Papua New Guinea in South-East Asia. Today, figures produced by the Food and Agriculture Organization in 1990 showed that deforestation in tropical Africa is just under 0.7% per year, compared with 1.77% per year for tropical America and 1.62% per year for tropical Asia.

THE CONSEQUENCES

Deforestation in the tropics has several extremely important consequences, which are all interrelated. The effects can be environmental, ecological and social; not only will they be felt locally, but some will have worldwide repercussions.

Environmental

The high rainfall totals cause major soil erosion. Equatorial soils are especially infertile and while a forest protects the soil, once cleared the earth is exposed to severe erosion and leaching (washing away) of nutrients. Farmland established on such newly exposed soils may remain agriculturally productive for as little as five years before the soil becomes completely exhausted. The term 'green desert' has been applied to some of the exhausted areas. In Madagascar, where 0.8% of forest cover was removed on average each year between 1981 and 1990, severe gullying of the landscape has formed within two or three years of deforestation.

An immense amount of water is held within a tropical rainforest ecosystem. Deforestation causes a major disruption to the flow of this water from the land to rivers because of reduced evapo-transpiration from the leaves which also results in a lowering of atmospheric humidity. After deforestation has occurred, the soil's ability to hold water is

■ *Large tracts of rainforest in Brazil have been stripped of vegetation, often for commercial logging or mining projects*

reduced and the flow of water, which normally catches and holds the rainwater on the leaves, branches and roots, is speeded up, and soil erosion is also increased.

The rainforests are the 'lungs' of the planet. The plants and trees absorb vast amounts of CO_2 from the atmosphere during photosynthesis, using the carbon to create leaves and wood. This helps to regulate the type of gases in the atmosphere, minimizing the possibility of atmospheric warming. Widespread deforestation through logging or burning results instead in most of the carbon being released into the atmosphere as CO_2, increasing the rate of global warming (see p. 55). Deforestation is thought to be responsible for releasing about 2 million tonnes of CO_2 into the atmosphere each year, and since 1860, the average world temperature has risen by about 0.5°C (32.9°C).

Ecological

Deforestation also causes a major loss in habitats for species which are dependent on trees. Scientists have established that one rainforest tree in the Amazon provides a home for 2000 species. Work in Papua New Guinea has shown that 74% of mammals (20 species), 61% of birds (102 species), 44% of reptiles (15 species) and 65% of frogs (15 species) would probably become extinct if the forest was replaced by grassland or agriculture. In Madagascar, where 84% of the original tropical forest has been cleared, it is estimated that around 25% of the surviving animal species will become extinct within the next 50 years.

Social

Deforestation also destroys the habitats of indigenous tribes. An estimated 250 million people – about one person in 20 – still live in the rainforest regions. Once displaced, these people drift to the large cities, swelling the numbers of landless peasants who already live there. Another important consequence is that many modern drugs, for example aspirin and quinine (which fights malaria), have their origins in the flora (plants and trees) of the rainforest. About 25% of modern medicines contain at least one component from tropical forests. There are also unknown genetic resources contained within the forest species. So far, only about 1% of all tropical rainforest plants have been assessed for their medical potential.

■ ONE SQUARE KILOMETRE OF TROPICAL RAINFOREST IS DESTROYED EVERY TWO MINUTES ■

LIFE SCIENCES ▷

'...whilst this planet
has gone cycling on
according to the fixed
law of gravity, from so
simple a beginning
endless forms most
beautiful and most
wonderful have been,
and are being, evolved'
– Charles Darwin

THE BEGINNING OF LIFE

▶ Each human body cell contains one metre of DNA made up of 5 billion base pairs.

▶ Bacterial cell walls are stronger than reinforced concrete, yet even Bacteria are infected by viruses, which are called bacteriophages (phages).

▶ Truffles are highly prized edible fungi that live symbiotically with the roots of oaks, hazelnuts and lindens.

▶ The Bacteria which cause tetanus produce a toxin which can kill with a dose of only 0.00023 g.

LIVING THINGS

- Single-cell or filamentous organisms lacking a nucleus (formerly called Super Kingdom Prokaryota)
  - Archaea* – minute, simple-celled organisms (one of three domains) see p. 61
  - Bacteria* (one of three domains)
    - Bacteria see p. 61
    - Cyanobacteria see p. 61
- Organisms whose cells contain a nucleus (formerly called Super Kingdom Eucaryota)
  - Eucaryotes (Domain Eukarya, one of three domains)
    - Protoctists (Kingdom Protista or Protoctista) see p. 61
    - Fungi (Kingdom Fungi) see p. 61
    - Plants (Kingdom Plantae) see pp. 62–65
    - Animals (Kingdom Animalia) see pp. 66–91

* The most recent classifications have replaced the Kingdom Monera with these two domains

ORIGINS OF LIFE ON EARTH

▶ The Earth was formed 4500 million years ago.
▶ One thousand million years later (3500 million years ago), fossil evidence suggests that living cells were present.

The early evolutionary history of life on Earth is dominated by unicellular organisms (multicellular organisms did not evolve until 1000 million years ago). Whether these living cells evolved on Earth from inanimate matter or arrived here from another planet is unknown. As single-celled organisms rarely leave fossils and, because much of the early sedimentary rock has been 'recycled' by volcanic activity or erosion, fossils of this period are rare. Therefore, to understand the early evolutionary history of the Earth, comparisons with extant (living) organisms must be made.

COMMON ANCESTRY

A comparison of the biochemistry of many living cells has established that all life on Earth is derived from a common ancestor. The hallmark of common ancestry is present in the core biological machinery that drives all cells. The hereditary and genetic material of all cellular life is DNA. A transient copy of the DNA is made from RNA. RNA is translated from amino acids into proteins by ribosomes using the same three-letter code found in humans, cellular slime mould, oak trees and typhoid bacteria. These fundamental biochemical processes of the cell exist in all living things because they were present in the common ancestor and are the most compelling evidence that all life on Earth had a single origin.

APPEARANCE OF ORGANISMS

million years ago (approx.)	
1100	coral, jellyfish, worms
560	trilobites, molluscs
450	sporebearing land plants
400	trees, sharks, amphibians, insects
290	first seed plants (cone-bearing trees)
250	turtles, crocodiles, dinosaurs
210	birds, small primitive mammals
135	flowering plants
60	primitive bats, camels, cats, horses, monkeys, rhinoceroses, whales
40	apes, dogs, elephants, rodents
25	flowering plants and trees recognizably modern
5	recognizable human beings appear
2	modern human beings

THE THREE MAJOR LINEAGES

▶ Living things are divided into three major lineages: Bacteria, Archaea and Eukarya.
▶ The Archaea have only recently been recognized as a distinct group of organisms.

The techniques of molecular biology allow us to determine the nucleotide sequence of genes and these sequences can be used to determine evolutionary relationships. The sequence of the gene coding for the ribosomal RNA has been obtained from many different living organisms. These sequences clearly show that all living things can be placed in one of three major lineages and implies that all three have diverged from the common ancestor. Two of these lineages or domains, the Bacteria and the Archaea, are exclusively unicellular, whereas the lineage that includes humans, the Eukarya, contains a mixture of unicellular and multicellular organisms. The Archaea are, perhaps, the least known of the major extant lineages of life, as they generally avoid oxygen and tend to live in environments that the other lineages would consider inhospitable (such as the hot springs in Yellowstone National Park, soda lakes, or hydrothermal vents in the ocean depths).

THEIR DIVERGENCE

A rough guide can now be given to the evolution of life on Earth – from the single-celled ancestor to the three major lineages now recognized. The divergence of the Bacteria, Eukarya and the Archaea probably occurred by 2500 million years ago. At this time all three lineages were still unicellular and the Earth was without free oxygen. Soon after the divergence from the other two groups, the ancestor to the eucaryote lineage evolved the nucleus, a compartmentalization of the genetic material that is characteristic of all Eukarya. The nucleus and its apparatus released the eucaryotes from the need for the rigid cell wall used by other organisms to distribute genetic material between daughter cells at cell division. Freed of the constraint of a rigid cell wall, unicellular eucaryotes were able to engulf and eat other organisms, just as amoeba do today.

PHOTOSYNTHESIS

▶ Photosynthesis generates food (sugar) from carbon dioxide, water and sunlight.
▶ The evolution of photosynthesis represents one of the major revolutions in energy production in the history of the Earth.

The primary source of energy for early organisms was complex chemical reactions of the sort that are still used by some Archaea living at hydrothermal vents in the ocean depths. Photosynthesis appeared in the bacterial lineage about 2500 million years ago. A waste product of photosynthesis is oxygen. Between 2500–1800 million years ago the photosynthetic Bacteria were responsible for one of the greatest acts of environmental pollution in the world's history. Vast quantities of oxygen derived from photosynthesis entered an environment that had never seen this highly reactive element before. At first, geological chemical reactions absorbed much of the oxygen and enormous quantities of iron rust were released by the oceans (these deposits are our major source of iron ore today). However, eventually the oxygen accumulated in the atmosphere and the Earth became aerobic.

The Archaeal lineage never really coped with this new environment and these organisms still occupy anaerobic (non-oxygenated) environments. However, the single-celled eucaryotes of the time were successful at dealing with the oxygenated atmosphere, probably because their cell walls could more easily form a barrier to this gas.

■ MOST LIVING CELLS RANGE IN SIZE FROM 0.01–0.1 MM ■ BACTERIA CAN LIVE MANY MILES

RESPIRATION TO ENDOSYMBIOSIS

▶ Respiration is the process of taking in oxygen and giving out carbon dioxide.
▶ Endosymbiosis is the symbiotic (dependent) relationship between Bacteria and Eukarya.

The next major step in the evolution of all life on Earth occurred when a member of the Bacteria evolved the ability to 'burn' sugar in the now freely available oxygen. This process is called respiration and generates far more energy than the anaerobic fermentative process all cells can carry out.

Our single-celled ancestors, members of the eucaryotic lineage, were able to benefit from the evolution of respiration by exploiting a bacterial cell in an extraordinary process called endosymbiosis. Endosymbiosis began when a eucaryotic cell engulfed a bacterial cell and, instead of digesting it, formed a mutually beneficial partnership in which the bacterial cell lived within the eucaryotic cell and carried out respiration using sugar and oxygen supplied by the Eukarya. Over time, the Bacteria became increasingly dependent on the eucaryotic cell and eventually lost the ability to be a free-living organism. Today, the relic of this once free-living bacteria, although barely discernible, can be identified in every human cell as the cellular organelle the mitochondria (containing enzymes responsible for energy production). Within it are the remains of the original bacterial genetic material and the nucleotide sequence of this DNA points plainly to the mitochondria's bacterial origin.

MULTICELLULARITY

▶ Mitochondria helped the next advance of the eucaryotes – the evolution of multicellularity.
▶ Multicellular eucaryotes, such as seaweeds (the ancestors of all modern plants), are present in fossils of 1000 million years ago.

Once again, a eucaryote formed a mutually beneficial association with a bacterium, now barely recognizable as the photosynthetic organelle in all plants – the chloroplast (see p. 62) – a descendant of the first endosymbiotic photosynthesis called cyanosynthesis (a primitive, less efficient form of photosynthesis). Plant cells contain genetic material from three sources: the chromosomal DNA representing the eucaryotic lineage, the mitochondria, and the chloroplast (representing the two bacterial cells that became endosymbionts).

THE RISE OF THE EUCARYOTES

Armed with a nucleus, photosynthesis, respiration, and multicellularity, the eucaryotes have come to dominate the Earth. Most major animal lineages had evolved in the oceans by 550 million years ago. By 400 million years ago, the plants began to leave the sea and explore the land, followed by the arthropods; it was millions of years before the vertebrates ventured onto land, where there has been an explosion in diversity of eucaryote forms, resulting in the many species alive today, through the evolution of the primates to present-day humans.

VIRUSES

▶ Viruses are so small (0.000018–0.0006 mm) that they can only be visualized by an electron microscope magnified about x30,000.
▶ An infectious virus particle consists of genetic material (either DNA or RNA) covered in a protein coat.

Viruses are considered as the borderline between living cells and inert matter. Like living cells, they contain genetic material, reproduce and evolve. Yet they are unable to perform any functions without a host cell. They are parasites that hijack the biochemical machinery of their host cell to produce more virus particles.

The host cell for a bacteriophage is a bacterial cell; the host cell of the AIDS virus is the human immune system cell. The relationship between host cell and virus is often specific – the AIDS virus will not infect other human cells nor will it infect chimpanzee immune-system cells. Often the host cell dies as the virus replicates, but some viruses can integrate into the genetic material of the host cell. Integrated viruses are replicated passively as the host cell replicates, but occasionally the virus may activate in response to a specific trigger. For example, a dormant cold-sore virus (the herpes virus) may be triggered to replicate by exposure to sunlight. Because they need a living cell to replicate, viruses can be extremely difficult to grow and study.

■ *Electron micrograph of an Ebola virus, which causes Ebola fever, accompanied by skin rash, haemorrhage and often rapid death*

SIMPLE LIFE FORMS

▶ Water is the prime requisite for all known forms of life.
▶ Recent evidence suggests there may once have been life on Mars, as the conditions for life have been proved to have existed there.

Around every star in the universe – of which the Sun is but one – there is a zone, the ecosphere, where water could potentially exist as a liquid. If there is a body of sufficient mass in this zone, such as a planet, with sufficient gravitational force to hold onto water and a gaseous atmosphere, then the conditions for life may be present. The earliest simple life forms include the following.

PROKARYOTES

▶ The term prokaryote (without nucleus) applies to two groups of organisms: the Bacteria and the recently identified Archaea.
▶ These two groups (or domains) of organisms are as evolutionarily distant from each other as Bacteria and humans.

Of the five kingdoms of living organisms, the prokaryotes are structurally the simplest, consisting of single-celled organisms that do not require a nucleus or subcellular organelles. Yet, in terms of diversity of habitat, biochemical abilities, and in sheer numbers, prokaryotes reign supreme.

ARCHAEA

Some Archaea live in extreme habitats, such as hot springs at temperatures close to boiling water (these organisms will not grow at room temperature) and in soda lakes of saturated salt solution. However, Archaea have also been recovered from the surface layers of the Atlantic and from soil samples, where they are apparently quite common. They produce methane (marsh-gas) as a waste product – a process unique to certain Archaea – and they have evolved a simple form of photosynthesis in salt-loving (halophilic) species. Members of this very diverse group of unicellular organisms only infrequently interact with humans (they do not cause disease), which may explain why so little is known about them.

BACTERIA

Known for causing disease to humans and their domesticated animals (as in cholera, tuberculosis and syphilis), Bacteria are remarkable for the different ways they 'make a living'. Photosynthesis first evolved among the Bacteria, and free-living photosynthetic bacteria (Cyanobacteria) can cause algal blooms on lakes polluted with nitrates and phosphates. Most Bacteria are harmless passengers on humans (commensals) or free-living in the environment, where they recycle biological material. The diversity of biochemical pathways that Bacteria have available is amazing; some, for example, consider phenol, coal tar, or even oil as suitable food materials. Bacteria can also exchange genes between extremely dissimilar species, causing major problems for the treatment of bacterial disease, as genes for resistance to specific antibiotics have appeared in important human pathogens (agents that cause disease) such as tuberculosis.

KINGDOM PROTOCTISTA

▶ About 1500 million years ago, microscopic single-celled organisms became much larger than the Bacteria which had preceded them, marking the beginning of the protists.
▶ The protists and all later, more advanced forms of life – fungi, plants and animals – are known as eucaryotes (meaning 'true kernel').

The protoctists (or protists) are a large and diverse group of single-celled organisms with cell nuclei, such as algae, the malaria parasite, amoeba, slime moulds and potato blight. All have a nucleus and some have mitochondria. Others have chloroplasts and can make their own food by photosynthesis. Amoeba digest solid particles such as living or dead Bacteria. The slime moulds live on decayed leaves and rotting logs. Algae are photosynthetic organisms living mostly in aquatic environments.

KINGDOM FUNGI

▶ The important antibiotic drug Penicillin was obtained in 1928 by Alexander Fleming from a mould – it kills Bacteria by weakening the cell wall so that the bacterium explodes.
▶ The *Saccharomyces cerevisiae* species of yeast is used both for brewing and making bread – it acts upon sugars to make alcohol (ethanol) and generates carbon dioxide gas which inflates bread and gives fizz to beer.

Fungi are not photosynthetic; they obtain their food by decomposing dead organisms or by acting parasitically upon living organisms, particularly plants, where they cause diseases. Many fungi are not made up of cells but of long, microscopically thin, branching tubes (hyphae) which form a network (mycelium) over or throughout the food. Enzymes are secreted from the hyphae to digest the food and the soluble products are absorbed. The umbrella-shaped growth known as a mushroom produces spores to disperse the organism.

Fungi reproduce asexually by means of fine spores containing cytoplasm and nuclei. However, there is a sexual process in reproduction which may come before the asexual production of spores.

Yeasts are fungi but most do not form true hyphae. They feed on sugars from flower nectar or from sweet fruits such as grapes. Yeasts are single-celled organisms that contain both a nucleus and mitochondria. They reproduce by budding.

THE PLANT KINGDOM

- The coco-de-mer palm (*Lodoicea maldivica*) produces the largest seeds, which weigh 23 kg and are called double coconuts.
- Some flower petals have ultraviolet absorbing patterns which are visible to insects but not humans.
- Around 40 million tonnes of bananas are eaten each year, making it the world's most popular fruit.
- There are over 275,000 flowering plants and trees presently known to science.

■ *The thistle, a relation of the daisy, is a member of the angiosperm plant group (flowering plants)*

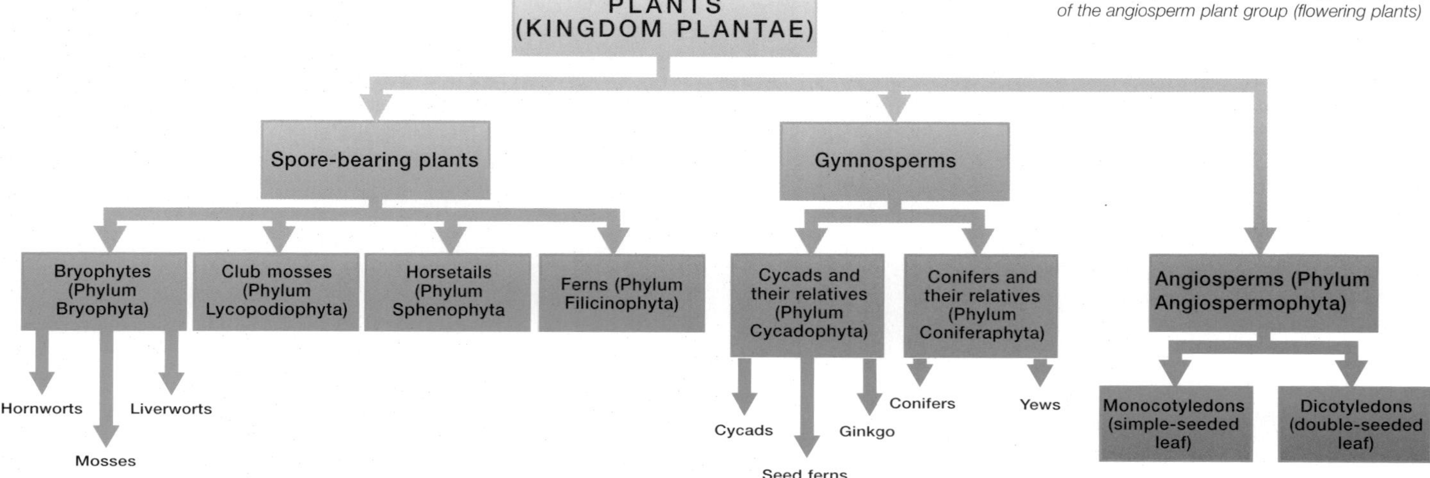

EVOLUTION OF PLANTS

▶ Over millions of years, plants have evolved into three main groups: spore-bearing plants; gymnosperms (plants producing seeds outside an ovary); and angiosperms (plants producing seeds encased in an ovary).
▶ Plants range in size from tiny algae with no true stems, roots and leaves (which are visible only under a microscope), to giant trees which can grow to over 100 m (328 ft).

The first algae to venture out of the sea to colonize moist soil may be indicated by fossils 1200 million years old. It was not until 460 million years ago that more complex organisms evolved.

The ferns and horsetails diverged from the bryophytes (mosses and liverworts) about 400 million years ago. They are all spore-bearing plants.

The first seed plants which had naked seeds (gymnosperms), such as conifers and cycads, diverged about 380 million years ago, followed about 150 million years ago by the flowering plants, which have their seeds in an ovary (angiosperms). Seeds advanced the colonization of the land by protecting plant embryos from drying out and other hazards. A seed consists of an embryo packaged along with a food store within a protective covering.

SPORE-BEARING PLANTS

▶ Spore-bearing plants are amongst the most primitive types of plants that exist today, and reproduce by means of tiny cells called spores, rather than by seeds.
▶ Sphagnum moss, found in bogs, can soak up 25 times its own dry weight.

Spore-producing plants were dominant in the Carboniferous period (about 300–350 million years ago), living in shallow tropical swamps. The dead plants did not completely decay in the stagnant conditions and peat accumulated, later to be overlaid by sediments. Following heat and pressure, the peat was deoxygenated and dehydrated to leave coal, which is largely composed of carbon.

? WHAT IS A PLANT

▷ A plant is characterized by the ability to photosynthesize (see p. 64) – meaning that it can produce food from water, minerals and carbon dioxide using energy from the sun, and the green pigment chlorophyl, which is absent from animals. Oxygen is given off and glucose, the energy-rich substance, is retained and used to make the plants' cell components.

▷ Plants have clearly defined cell walls made of cellulose, a polymer of glucose, and contain a nucleus.

▷ It is believed that the ancestor of all plants was a single-celled non-photosynthetic organism that engulfed a photosynthetic bacterium. The pair of organisms formed a mutually beneficial relationship: the photosynthetic bacterium lived inside the plant cell (this is known as endosymbiosis). Eventually the bacterium degenerated to become the chloroplast, an organelle found in all plants and incapable of an independent existence.

▷ Plants organisms are generally immobile as they have no need to search for food.

▷ The great majority of the organisms considered to be plants are members of the Angiospermophyta, the flowering plants, and this group also includes many trees.

MOSSES, LIVERWORTS AND HORNWORTS

This group of primitive plants are called the bryophytes and are small, often inconspicuous plants that grow in dense mats in shaded, damp places. Their smallness of size is due to the lack of strengthening tissues in their stems.

Compared to water-living algae, the mosses (and their inconspicuous leaf-shaped relatives – the liverworts and hornworts) are adapted to life on land by the possession of a waxy cuticle which reduces water loss, and moist organs for the production and protection of the sex cells – the gametes.

These plants first appeared during the Silurian period (425 million years ago). They quickly achieved world dominance, and during the Devonian and Carboniferous periods (300–410 million years ago) they formed vast forests that eventually rotted down and were compressed to form the Carboniferous coal measures. Today, few of these plants remain, yet one example is sphagnum moss, which is common in boggy areas and contributes to the formation of peat. Mosses can also be found in cold regions, as well as in deserts next to hot springs; other mosses are epiphytic (meaning they live on other plants, but not as parasites) and are abundant in tropical rain forests. Some liverworts are flat and have no leaves; most, however, have leaves like mosses.

Mosses and their relatives differ from flowering plants in that they are simpler, having no true roots, stems or leaves, although they sometimes have a rudimentary vascular system of tube structures to convey water. They require moist conditions, as their sexual reproduction requires sperms, produced by a male organ (male gametophyte), to be able to swim to the female gametophyte.

Once fertilization has taken place, a dispersal phase or sporophyte generation is formed, which is usually parasitic on the gametophyte generation. The

The spores are produced by division (a process known as meiosis) in which the normally duplicated chromosomes are reduced to a single copy. Cells with a single copy of each chromosome are called haploid (sex cells such as sperm or ovum). Cells with a double complement of each chromosome are called diploid. The spore germinates to produce a small haploid plant which produces both sperm and eggs. However, these come from different regions and are produced at different times to ensure cross-fertilization (i.e. a sperm from one fern and an egg from another). When a sperm and egg fuse, the resulting fertilized egg (zygote) is a diploid plant. The egg grows into the fern plant proper (which is itself diploid since the DNA in the fertilized egg is faithfully copied at each stage of cell division).

■ *Ferns produce spores on the undersides of their leaves, which fall to the ground where they can germinate*

■ *Horsetails are amongst the world's most ancient plants*

spores are usually produced in a capsule which dries out and then ejects the spores. If it falls in a favourable environment, the spore germinates to form a threaded mesh (protonema) which eventually turns into a bud, giving rise to a male or female gametophyte plant.

Plants like the mosses are important ecologically because they can colonize barren areas, frequently invading after lichens have gained a hold. Mosses can also inhibit soil erosion. In the Carboniferous era (355–410 million years ago), the ancestors of these plants were more dominant than now, reaching heights of 40 m (131 ft).

CLUB MOSSES

Now modest inhabitants of the forest floor, club mosses, or lycopodophytes, had huge ancestors in the Devonian (410–438 million years ago) and Carboniferous eras. Their spore capsules, often arranged in conelike structures (strobili), are located on the bottom of special leaves called sporophylls.

HORSETAILS

These ancient plants, also known as sphenophytes, date back to Devonian times when they reached heights of 15 m (49 ft). Now only about 15 plant-like species remain, inhabiting damp places. Spores are formed from the terminal conelike structures.

FERNS

Ferns belong to the phylum Pteridophyta. They originated in the Devonian era and there are now more than 12,000 species. They flourish in forests, needing damp and shade to maintain a moist environment so that their sperms can swim towards the source of a chemical released from the cells surrounding the female sex cells. Their spores, released from many spore-producing organs called sporangia on the under-surface of the leaves, are literally given a flying start by being catapulted up to several metres.

■ *The unusual welwitschia plant, a native of Namibia, lives on dew and has leaves that can grow up to 18 m long*

■ *Pine trees bear cones which are either male or female*

GYMNOSPERMS

▶ Gymnosperms are plants whose seeds are not enclosed in an ovary.
▶ The species *Weltwitschia mirabilis*, which belongs to the Gymnospermae phylum Gnetophyta, can live for up to 2000 years.

Ancestors of these naked-seeded plants grew alongside the spore-producing plants in the Carboniferous period, evolving before the presently dominant angiosperms. Today, there are four phyla of gymnosperms, which include three rare examples of ancient gymnosperms and the common conifers: Cycadophyta, palm-like cycads (true palms are flowering plants); Ginkgophyta, which have fanlike leaves and are deciduous (lose their leaves in autumn – in this respect, ginkgos are unusual for gymnosperms); Gnetophyta, including the strange Weltwitschia genus; and Coniferaphyta, or conifers.

CONIFERS

This group of about 550 cone-carriers includes pines, firs, spruce, larches, yews, junipers, cedars, cypresses and redwoods. Most are large evergreen trees, which dominate many northern areas where the growing season is short. They can photosynthesize even in winter and can take advantage of sunny spring days when deciduous trees are still bare. The needle-shaped leaves are adapted to dry conditions as the small surface area minimizes water loss. Redwood trees can reach a height of 110 m (360 ft).

The life cycle of a conifer, such as a pine, involves the production of pollen, which is transferred by the wind. This is a truly terrestrial adaptation, in contrast with the watery conditions necessary for the transfer of freely swimming sperms produced by mosses and ferns.

The pine tree is diploid (has double sets of chromosomes) and it bears both pollen cones and ovulate cones, which produce the male and female haploid gametes (reproductive cells). It takes more than one year before fertilization is achieved following pollination because the pollen tube has to digest its way through a structure called the nucellus to reach the female gametophyte, which itself is in the process of formation during the year. The pine embryo, whilst still in the cone, already has a rudimentary root and the beginnings of leaves, a food supply from the female haploid gametophyte and a surrounding seed coat derived from the parent tree.

■ *Hummingbirds and other nectar-feeding birds brush past pollen-bearing anthers to reach the nutritious sweetened water*

PHOTOSYNTHESIS

▶ Photosynthesis is the process by which plants, algae and various bacteria convert simple inorganic molecules into complex compounds necessary for life.
▶ Oxygen is given off as a by-product of photosynthesis – oxygen is essential to virtually all life forms, so that without plants, life on Earth would cease to exist.

Life is based upon the element carbon. Green plants obtain this from the air in the form of carbon dioxide, which they change into carbohydrates (such as sugars) and starch through photosynthesis.

Photosynthesis is powered by the energy from sunlight absorbed by chlorophyll (the chemical in plants that gives them their green colour). Chloroplasts (miniature organs within plant cells) acquire carbon dioxide after it has entered the leaf through the stomata (see p. 65). In photosynthesis, the carbon dioxide is then transformed into carbohydrates; initially the sugar glucose, and eventually sucrose and starch. The energy from sunlight also splits water molecules into hydrogen and oxygen. In this way, the plant not only obtains the materials of which it is composed, but also produces oxygen.

Vegetation is the primary food of all animal food chains, so it is by photosynthesis that almost all of the carbon enters the living world. Similarly, the oxygen ultimately released by plants is the source of all oxygen in the atmosphere of this planet. Because in photosynthesis carbon dioxide is used up and oxygen is given out as a waste product – the reverse of plant and animal respiration – the overall effect of plants and animals living together is to keep the atmospheric levels of these gases more or less constant.

Plants also give off water vapour through the open stomata. As this water loss is potentially a problem in arid climates, many plants living in such environments have evolved physiological adaptations to overcome the danger. Many succulent plants, for example, keep their stomata closed during the day but open them at night. The carbon dioxide is assimilated (or 'fixed') at night, not into sugars but into certain organic acids, which later, during daylight hours, release the carbon dioxide within the leaf when the stomata are closed. The carbon dioxide then participates in photosynthesis in the normal way.

FLOWERING PLANTS AND TREES

▶ Angiosperms are characterized by the presence of a flower – a specialized part of the plant that develops into a fruit and which contains one or more seeds contained in ovaries or seed cases.
▶ The largest flower is the giant rafflesia (*Rafflesia arnoldii*), which can grow up to 105 cm (3 ft 6 in) in diameter and weigh up to 7 kg (15 lb 5 oz).

This group had become common by the end of the Cretaceous era (65 million years ago). The earliest fossil angiosperm dates from 120 million years ago (early Cretaceous era), but 200-million-year-old Triassic rocks have been found to contain evidence of angiosperm pollen.

Flowering plants are the most diverse, widespread and abundant group of multicellular plants. They grow in a very wide range of habitats and, to cope with this, they have evolved an enormous variety of adaptations in form and in life cycle.

LIFE CYCLE OF FLOWERING PLANTS

Pollination occurs when a pollen grain (originating either from the stamens within the plant or transported by wind, birds or insects from an adjacent flower of the same type) is deposited on the stigma and forces a channel (the pollen tube) down to the ovary. The fusion of egg and pollen nucleus causes fertilization and the ovary swells to form a fruit, within which is the seed that contains an embryo. For example, peas are seeds enclosed in an ovary, which is the pod.

Fruits protect dormant seeds and aid their dispersal. When ripe, the brightly coloured berries also contain sugar, which tempts animals and birds to eat them. The indigestible seeds are thus later deposited with a supply of fertilizer in droppings at a location possibly well distant from the parent plant. Some seeds, such as those of the dandelion and sycamore tree, are designed to be airborne and are equipped with parachutes and propellers. Other seeds are carried as they stick to the fur of passing animals by means of hooks called burrs.

FLOWERING PLANT CLASSIFICATION

Despite such an amazing variety of species, the flowering plants can be divided into two main groups, based upon the structure of the embryo. These are the monocots (monocotyledons – 40,000 species) and the dicots (dicotyledons – 250,000 species). The monocots can be recognized by the single leaf (cotyledon) produced from the germinating embryo, hence the term monocotyledon, which is applied to a group of plants that have many other things in common. They are considered to be more simple than the second group, the dicots, which produce two seed leaves.

Monocots

These plants, which include grasses, sedges, lilies, orchids, daffodils and date palms, have fibrous root systems (which enable grasses in particular to guard against soil erosion by binding the soil together). The fibrous roots in a large bamboo plant can be as thick as rope. The stem of a monocot, such as a yucca, is generally spongy or fibrous, in contrast to the true thickening in the stems of dicots such as oak trees. Many monocots produce a horizontal underground stem called a rhizome. The leaves of monocots frequently sheath the stem of the plant and are usually sword-shaped with parallel veins.

Monocotyledons include cereals (wheat, rye, barley, oats, millet, corn, rice and sorghum), vegetables

■ *The barbed leaves of the pineapple plant protect flowers on the central stem. These eventually fuse to form the fruit*

■ *Wild bananas are monocots and are mostly pollinated at night by bats, as these mammals hunt for nectar*

■ RED-FLOWERED PLANTS ARE OFTEN POLLINATED BY BIRDS ■ WATER CAN FLOW THROUGH A

(onion, leek, garlic, shallots, root tubers of yams) and fruits (coconut, date, banana). They can be used as fibre (coconut matting), sisal rope, and are also used in construction (bamboo, grass stems).

Dicots

The leaves of dicots, which includes the majority of flowering plants, generally show a midrib and a netlike arrangement of veins. The stems have xylem and phloem (see right) arranged around the perimeter of the stem and between them an active growing region called the cambium. As the plant grows, the stem thickens and becomes woody. Dicots frequently have a large tap root which is able to secure the plant or tree firmly in the ground. Shrubs have many branches and grow low to the ground (up to 5 m (16 ft) tall), whereas trees grow a long trunk and tend to suppress such branching. Examples include oak trees, roses and dandelions.

Dicotyledons include vegetables (cabbage, potato, tomato, lettuce, marrows, cucumbers, beans, peas), and fruits (apple, pear, plum, peach, orange, lemon, strawberry, blackcurrant, melon). Some are used as a source of timber (all hardwoods, such as beech, oak, cedar).

Herbaceous plants are non-woody and some have culinary uses. For example, coriander leaves and seeds and horseradish roots are used to flavour food.

■ *Cabbages, and their close relatives the brussels sprout, broccoli, cauliflower and kale are all dicotyledons*

FRUIT OR VEGETABLE

▶ **To a botanist a fruit is a mature ovary containing seeds, which can be produced by 'woody' plants such as apple, orange and pear trees, or herbaceous plants, such as melons and strawberries. Usually, vegetables are herbaceous plants having parts that can be used as food.**

▶ **Tomatoes are actually many-seeded fruits, but are commonly consumed and known as a vegetable. They are actually the most popular 'vegetable', with 57.5 million tonnes being consumed around the world each year.**

FRUIT

As a fruit ripens, it often changes colour from green to yellow or red, to advertise the fact that the plant is ready to dispense its bounty. There would be no point in immature non-viable seed being wasted by being distributed too early.

Fruits from temperate zones contain up to 15% sugar when ripe. In the tropics, extra sunshine means that the ripe fruit's sugar content is generally between 20% and 60%. Emission of attractive aromas also indicate ripeness.

Some seeds, such as peach and avocado, are too large to be swallowed, while others may be distasteful or even poisonous (apple and citrus seeds contain cyanide). These seeds tend to be carried only short distances before being discarded. However, some seeds, such as tomato, are numerous and small and are frequently swallowed by animals. These seeds pass through the animals' gastrointestinal tracts and will germinate afterwards. They are frequently, therefore, carried much further distances.

Botanists define a nut as a one-seed fruit surrounded by a hard shell that is unable to open on its own. In everyday speech the term 'nut' is used to cover many kinds of dry edible seed or fruit that grow in a woody shell. The whole fruit or just the kernel are commonly referred to by the same name.

Most nuts are a good source of dietary protein and oil, however chestnuts contain more starch than protein. Almonds, coconuts and peanuts are in fact not true nuts. Almonds are the seed of a plumlike fruit and the coconut is anatomically similar. Peanuts are more like peas than nuts. They grow on a leguminous bush which pushes its woody fruit capsules below ground as they mature. Useful culinary nuts include almonds, walnuts, pecans, hazelnuts (filberts), pistachios, cashews and brazils.

VEGETABLES

Vegetables are generally savoury rather than sweet and may be derived from the roots (carrot, turnip, radish, beet), the young leaves (lettuce, cabbage), the stem (celery, asparagus) and the flower (artichoke, broccoli). Potatoes are starch and protein storage organs – the swollen tips of the underground stem.

Some savoury foods which appear as if they should be classified as vegetables, for example peas, green beans, aubergines (egg plant), avocado pear, tomato, cucumber and corn kernels, are, botanically, fruits.

■ *Strawberries are actually false fruits, as the fleshy part is formed from the flower receptacle rather than the female parts. The 'seeds' are the true fruits. Traditionally, straw was placed under a strawberry plant (classified as a perennial herb) to prevent the 'fruit' from rotting on the soil and to keep insects from eating the berries*

FLOWERING PLANT STRUCTURE

▶ **Flowers protect the immature seeds of a plant until they become mature and help to attract birds and insects, thus ensuring that the plant will be pollinated.**

▶ **Most plants have both male and female reproductive organs (stamens and ovaries) in each flower.**

The roots of a plant anchor it in the soil and collect moisture, which contains all the dissolved nutrients needed for growth. From the roots arise either a single, vertical cylindrical stem, or a multiple, branched stem.

The stem is made rigid by pumping water into each cell, or by the presence of a strengthening material (lignin) in woody plants which allows them to grow taller than herbaceous and other plant types, so avoiding the attention of some browsing animals and increasing the rate of photosynthesis. Flowers grow from the nodes (junctions) between the leaves and the stem.

On the outside of the plant are the leaf-like sepals which protect the flower at its bud stage. Inside are the petals, which are either brightly coloured, as in pollinators, helping to attract insects, or drab, as in grasses which are wind-pollinated. At the centre of the flower is the carpel, consisting of the sticky stigma, the style, and the ovary, which protects the fertilized egg. Immediately surrounding the stigma are the stamens – thick stalks with pollen sacs at their ends. Each pollen sac ripens to produce large numbers of tiny pollen grains (the male sperm).

The plant absorbs carbon dioxide through small holes called stomata, which occur mostly on the undersides of leaves. Light energy is absorbed by the green pigment chlorophyll contained in chloroplasts, which enable carbohydrate and protein synthesis to take place.

Vascular tissue (xylem) carries water and mineral salts from the roots to the rest of the plant, whilst phloem convey food substances such as sucrose (sugar) and amino acids to the non-photosynthesizing roots and stem cells.

■ Psychoda *flies are attracted by the Arum lily's odour. On the flower's stem are ovaries (bottom), pollen-bearing anthers (middle) and a trap (top), which keeps the flies inside the plant until the trap dies. Then, the flies escape, so pollinating the next lily that they visit*

The Animal Kingdom

- The word zoology – the science which studies the animal kingdom (Kingdom Animalia) – comes from the Greek word *zoion*, which means 'animal'.
- The first authenticated system for classifying the animal kingdom is attributed to Aristotle.
- Vertebrates include mammals, birds, reptiles, amphibians and fishes – yet they are only a tiny proportion of the world's animals.
- Over 1,500,000 animals have been classified, of which some 1,000,000 are insects.

What is the animal kingdom

▶ The animal kingdom (Kingdom Animalia) is unsurpassed in size and diversity.
▶ The animal kingdom is divided into two types: invertebrates and vertebrates.

Invertebrates are simply defined as those animals which do not have a backbone. They range from simple sponges and corals through a host of more complex animals, such as insects and squid. There are approximately one million invertebrates in the animal kingdom.

Vertebrates are those animals in which a backbone, spinal column and brain case are present (they also never have more than two pairs of limbs). They include the most complex animals of all – the birds and mammals. Vertebrates appear in the fossil record in the following order: lancelets; jawless fish; placoderms (extinct jawed fish); sharks and rays and bony fishes; amphibia; reptiles and birds; and mammals. There are approximately 50,000 vertebrates in the animal kingdom.

What is an animal

▷ Animals lack the cell walls that are characteristic of plants.

▷ Animals are multicellular and have cells with nuclei.

▷ Animals obtain their food from ready-made sources, that is they are dependent on plants or the body tissues of other animals.

▷ Although some aquatic animals, such as sea anemones and corals, are more or less immobile and can rely upon their food coming to them, the majority of animals must actively find it or seize it. Unlike plants, therefore, animals generally require some degree of mobility.

▷ Movement in multicellular animals requires coordination between different body parts. In all but the simplest animals, such as jellyfish, this entails a moderately sophisticated nervous system.

▷ An animal needs to move in a particular direction, thus requiring some form of sensory apparatus connected with its nervous system. Although plants can detect various environmental stimuli and react accordingly, animals have evolved an amazing range of systems by which they can perceive what is going on around them.

▷ Most animals have a digestive tract or cavity.

▷ Most animals have a central coordinating point of the nervous system – the brain.

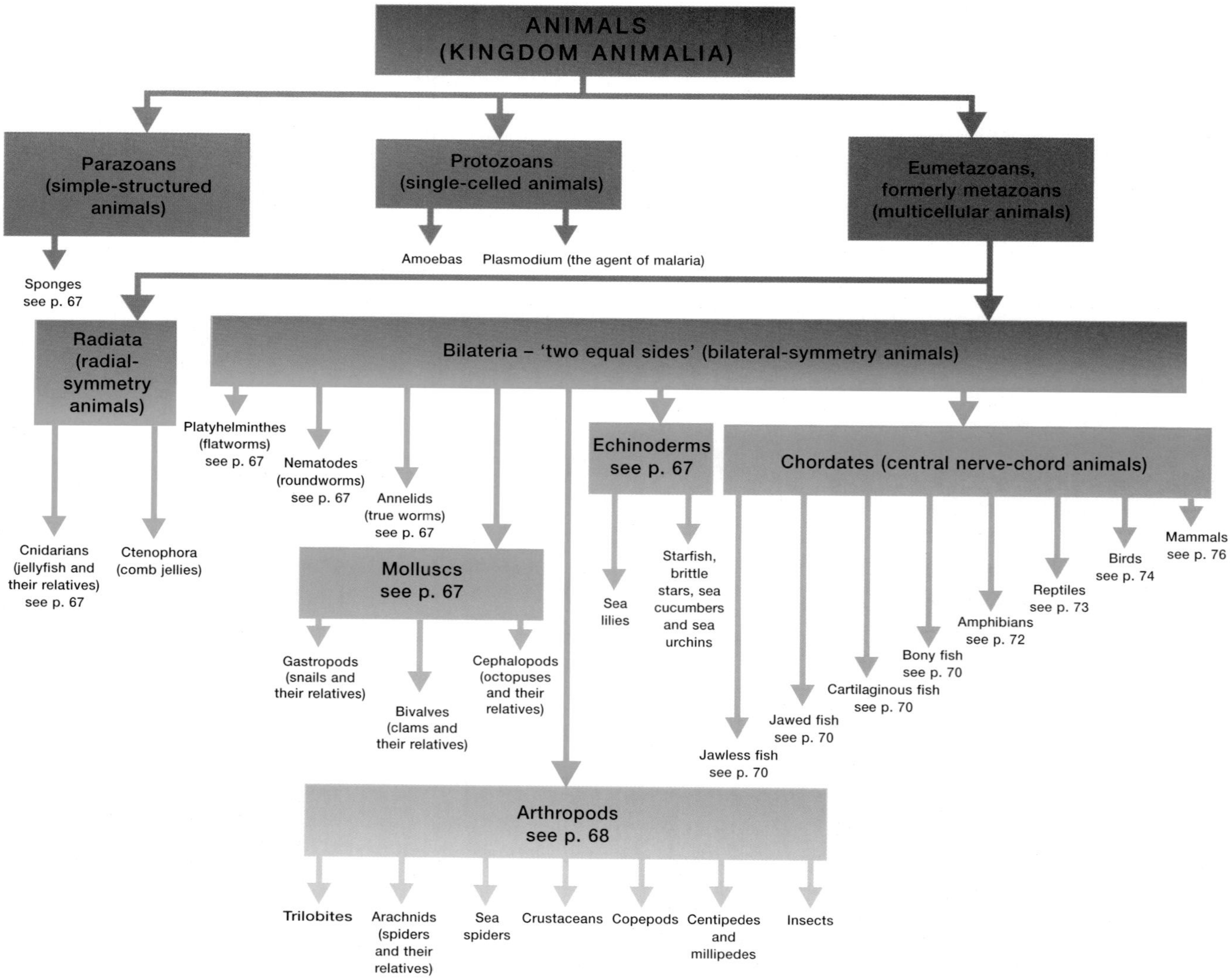

ANIMALS (KINGDOM ANIMALIA)

- **Parazoans (simple-structured animals)**
  - Sponges see p. 67
- **Protozoans (single-celled animals)**
  - Amoebas
  - Plasmodium (the agent of malaria)
- **Eumetazoans, formerly metazoans (multicellular animals)**
  - **Radiata (radial-symmetry animals)**
    - Cnidarians (jellyfish and their relatives) see p. 67
    - Ctenophora (comb jellies)
  - **Bilateria – 'two equal sides' (bilateral-symmetry animals)**
    - Platyhelminthes (flatworms) see p. 67
    - Nematodes (roundworms) see p. 67
    - Annelids (true worms) see p. 67
    - **Molluscs see p. 67**
      - Gastropods (snails and their relatives)
      - Bivalves (clams and their relatives)
      - Cephalopods (octopuses and their relatives)
    - **Arthropods see p. 68**
      - Trilobites
      - Arachnids (spiders and their relatives)
      - Sea spiders
      - Crustaceans
      - Copepods
      - Centipedes and millipedes
      - Insects
    - **Echinoderms see p. 67**
      - Sea lilies
      - Starfish, brittle stars, sea cucumbers and sea urchins
    - **Chordates (central nerve-chord animals)**
      - Jawless fish see p. 70
      - Jawed fish see p. 70
      - Cartilaginous fish see p. 70
      - Bony fish see p. 70
      - Amphibians see p. 72
      - Reptiles see p. 73
      - Birds see p. 74
      - Mammals see p. 76

PRIMITIVE ANIMALS

Sponges, cnidarians, worms, molluscs and echinoderms are all invertebrates.

SPONGES

▶ Sponges are among the simplest and most primitive of multicellular animals.
▶ With over 9000 species, sponges form an overwhelming 99% of marine species.

Sponges have all the properties associated with animals, despite their appearance. They feed on other organic matter and reproduce sexually by means of an ovum (egg) and a spermatozoon. Movement in mature sponges is limited to slight contraction of muscle-like cells. There is some coordination of activity, even though there is no real nervous system. Sponges live in marine habitats, ranging from the intertidal zone to the greatest depths, and also exist in freshwater. Some sponges are only 1 cm long, but others can reach more than 1 m (39 in) in height and breadth.

To feed, sponges beat flagella (whip-like projections) which draw water (containing food particles) in through pore cells. Hermaphroditic, sperm and eggs are produced from the same individual and eggs are retained while the sperm is released into the surrounding water. Both self- and cross-fertilization occur. The zygote (fertilized egg) develops into a free-swimming larva which, if it survives, turns inside out and settles on a suitable surface. Sponges have no tissues, but are rather a colony of cells with some degree of specialization.

CNIDARIANS

▶ There are about 10,000 species of cnidarians, most of which are marine.
▶ Cnidarians form the largest living structure on Earth – Australia's Great Barrier Reef.

Cnidarians have a simple two-layered contractible body wall surrounding a central gut with a single opening. Tentacles bearing stinging cells surround the mouth in corals and sea anemones, and form a fringe to the bell of jellyfish. Jellyfish are given strength by the jelly between the two cell layers, whereas corals lay down a rigid basal skeleton. Cnidarians possess a simple nerve net but not a brain – they react but do not learn.

There are cylindrical forms of cnidarians called polyps which attach themselves to a rock and extend tentacles above their mouth, waiting for prey. A medusa is a flattened mouth-down version of a polyp, drifting through water, which propels itself by contractions of its bell-shaped body, as in a jellyfish. Some cnidarians pass from one form to the other as part of their life-cycles or in alternations of generations. For example, a medusa stage, at which the animal is free-swimming and reproduces sexually, leads to a sedentary stage (polyp) from which medusae are produced asexually. Sea anemones, corals and hydroids spend most of their lives as polyps, singly or in colonies, whereas jellyfish spend almost all their lives as medusae.

WORMS

▶ True worms, represented by 15,000 species, range in size from 1 mm (1/25 in) to 3 m (9 ft 8 in) – as in the giant Australian earthworm.
▶ About 80,000 species of roundworms are known, yet this is thought to be only 10% of the roundworm species yet to be discovered.

Worms are divided into three groups: flatworms (flukes and tapeworms); roundworms (eelworms, threadworms and hookworms); and segmented true worms (earthworms and leeches).

FLATWORMS

Flatworms are characterized by a gut which acts as both a digestive and excretory system. There are some 20,000 species of flatworms, living in marine, freshwater and damp terrestrial habitats, both free and as parasites. They can reproduce asexually by splitting in two and regrowing the missing part, or sexually as hermaphrodites by passing sperms to the eggs of a partner.

ROUNDWORMS

Roundworms, also known as nematodes, are found in soil, freshwater and saltwater, in decomposing organic matter, and range in size from 1 mm (1/25 in) to 1 m (39 in). Their smooth, tough, unsegmented, transparent bodies have longitudinal muscles that produce a thrashing movement. During growth they moult four times. They reproduce sexually from separate males and females. The female fertilizes the eggs internally – up to 100,000 eggs can be produced in one day.

TRUE WORMS

True worms (Annelida or segmented worms) have long thin bodies with distinct head and tail ends. Made up of a series of separate segments, the body usually has external hair-like protrusions (chaetae). An extensive internal body cavity separates the gut from the body wall, distinguishing them from other worms. A simple circulatory system pumps blood containing oxygen-carrying haemaglobin molecules around the body. They move by coordinated contractions of their ringlike muscles in sequence. Earthworms are hermaphrodites (each has both male and female reproductive organs) and they cross-fertilize each other. Found in saltwater, freshwater and moist soil. they burrow through earth, feed on decaying vegetation and pass soil through the digestive tract, extracting nutrients.

Leeches (Hirudinea) are the most advanced annelid worms. They are either predatory or externally parasitic bloodsuckers with suckers at each end of the body. They do not crawl like other worms, but have adopted a looping method of movement.

MOLLUSCS

▶ There are over 100,000 mollusc species.
▶ Most molluscs are marine animals, but some live in freshwater and some are terrestrial.

Molluscs are a highly varied group of unsegmented animals that includes snails and octopuses. Classic mollusc characteristics include a broad locomotory foot, a protective shell, a rasp-like feeding organ (radula), and a special respiratory gill (ctenidium). Most are protected by a shell of calcium carbonate, though some (such as cuttlefish) have internalized their shells in the course of evolution.

GASTROPODS

Gastropods are monovalves (single shell) and include the land snails and slugs, and the sea snails. They form the largest group of molluscs and are the most diverse in their feeding habits. All gastropods have a muscular foot for walking or swimming, enabling them to move by means of a rippling motion, and a radula – a tongue-like feeding organ. Most have one coiled shell, as in the whelk and snail, but in slugs the shell is only present in a larval stage. Some gastropods retract into their shell and close off the entrance with an operculum (a bony plate) until danger has passed and some have two eyes on the end of tentacles.

Gastropods use a radula, or rasp, to tear apart the food – vegetation in the case of a limpet; other molluscs in the case of the whelk which, using the radula and a shell-softening chemical, can drill its way into an oyster shell. Marine gastropods have separate sexes and either shed sperm over eggs in the water or introduce it into the female with a penis. The zygotes grow into larvae, some of which have shells. Slugs and snails are hermaphrodites.

BIVALVES

The bivalves (molluscs whose shell is made of two parts connected by an elastic hinge) include clams, oysters, cockles and mussels. Inside the two-valved shell are massive mucus-covered gills that act as a filter pump, sieving particles from the water and covered with whip-like projections (cilia), which sort and sweep particles of food towards the mouth. The two shells are usually open but, when alarmed, strong muscles pull them closed and hold them shut. Bivalves have a strong muscular foot which they can extend, swell, then retract to pull them along and down into the sand or mud for food and safety. Streamlined razor-shell clams can burrow very rapidly. Clams swim by flapping their shells. Some scallops have numerous eyes near the edge of their shells.

CEPHALOPODS

Cephalopods (octopus (see left), cuttlefish, nautilus and squid) are carnivorous. Their tentacles have developed from the modified foot, and in the mouth behind the beak is a classic mollusc radula. With powerful muscular contractions, they can dart through the water at great speed by ejecting water. They have excellent sensory faculties and can change colour instantly (to hide, intimidate others or in sexual display). Their complex brains possess powers of learning and memory. They inject poison into their prey after biting them with a beaklike mouth. Giant squids, living in deep water and rarely seen, are the largest invertebrates known – over 5 m (16 ft) long.

ECHINODERMS

▶ Echinoderms consist of some 7000 marine species, including sea lilies, sea urchins, starfish, brittle stars and sea cucumbers.
▶ The spines of sea urchins can be poisonous.

Echinoderms have bony internal skeletons consisting of plates, and hydraulically operated tube feet used for movement, feeding and, in some species, gas exchange (oxygen is absorbed and carbon dioxide released into the water). Starfish (see opposite page) can attach themselves to clam shells and, by brute force, open them against the clam's efforts to resist. The starfish then inverts its stomach through its mouth and secretes digestive juices onto the clam's soft body. Male and female individuals release their sperm and eggs into the water, where fertilization occurs.

ARTHROPODS

- Insects' colour-range perception is different from that of humans, in that they see ultraviolet light – plants that seem dull to us may appear bright and colourful to an insect.
- There are more insect species (well over one million) than all other animal and plant species put together.
- Mayflies may spend 2–3 years as nymphs on the bed of a lake or stream, then live for one hour as winged adults.
- A large decline in the whale population has led to a huge build-up of shrimplike crustaceans called krill, the whale's main food source, which humans beings have begun to harvest as domestic animal food and fertilizer.
- Tarantula spiders can measure 3 cm across their body and their legspan can be 18 cm.

WHAT IS AN ARTHROPOD?

▶ Arthropods (Arthropoda) are characterized by having external skeletons and pairs of jointed limbs.
▶ The word Arthropoda means, literally, 'jointed feet', but it is the legs rather than the feet which are jointed.

In terms of numbers of individuals, the arthropods are the most successful phylum of animals ever to exist. Their success can be attributed to their segmented structure, their hard exoskeleton made of a long-chain polysaccharide called chitin, and their jointed appendages.

The origins of the Arthropoda are still mysterious, but following their emergence they seem to have diverged into four subphyla: trilobites (now extinct), arachnids (spiders, scorpions, ticks and mites), insects and their relatives, and crustaceans (crabs, lobsters, shrimps, barnacles and woodlice).

TRILOBITES

▶ Fossils of trilobites are particularly abundant in fossils found from the Cambrian and Silurian periods.
▶ Trilobites were able to roll themselves up like woodlice due to the flexibility of their thorax (the area between the head and the abdomen).

Once very numerous and successful arthropods, trilobites lived as bottom-dwelling scavengers in the sea during the Palaeozoic Era, 590–250 million years ago. They became extinct by the end of the Permian period, 245 million years ago, when the fossil record shows a decrease in the diversity of all marine organisms; primarily corals, but also bivalves and fish. This sudden loss of diversity is one of many that can be identified in the fossil record and is known as the Permian extinction.

Trilobites were small creatures, 1–7 cm (⅓–3 in) long, and were segmented, although the attached appendages showed little variation from one segment to the next. As arthropods continued to evolve, the segments tended to fuse together and the appendages became more specialized.

ARACHNIDS

▶ The arachnids (Arachnida) are the largest group of arthropods after the insects, with over 60,000 species.
▶ The arachnid group includes scorpions, spiders, ticks and mites.

An arachnid's body is divided into two parts: a combined head and thorax (called a cephalothorax) and an abdomen. Arachnids have six pairs of appendages, four of which are used for walking and the purpose of the other two varies. The majority of arachnids are carniverous (eating other arachnids, insects and even birds) and lay eggs. Many secrete poison to kill or paralyse their victims.

SCORPIONS

These were among the earliest terrestrial animals, appearing on land in the Carboniferous period (350–285 million years ago). They can grow to 20 cm (8 in) long and seem to have evolved very little over the last 450 million years. Nocturnal and secretive, they hide under stones or logs by day and are found in most warm habitats, including deserts. They detect prey with highly sensitive vibration and odour receptors. Waiting for their prey to move into range, they grip it with their massive claws and inject a paralysing venom with the sting in their tail. The venom of some species may cause death in humans. Scorpions undertake intricate courtship rituals culminating in fertilization of the female, who then broods the young.

■ *Young garden spiders cluster together on leaves*

SPIDERS

The spider has a large abdomen and a combined head and thorax. The front section bears four pairs of walking legs and two other pairs of appendages – one is a pair of hollow fangs used to inject venom into prey; the other is leg-like in females, and a complicated reproductive structure in males. At the tip of the abdomen there are a number of glands (developed only in females) that are used to produce silks. Fluids secreted by these glands dry into threads as they are forced out through three pairs of nozzles called spinnerets. The silk is used by many spiders to construct a variety of webs to catch different insects: orb webs, slung across gaps, catch flying insects, while sheet and hammock webs trap insects that crawl or hop on to them.

Spiders feed mainly on insects and have evolved an amazing variety of techniques for capturing prey. Camouflaged crab spiders, for instance, sit in flowers and ambush visiting insects, while trapdoor spiders leave radiating silken trip lines and rush out from their burrow when an insect stumbles over one. Spiders are often not particular about their prey, and as the female is usually larger, the male must go through elaborate rituals (such as offering her food wrapped in silk) to mate successfully and avoid being eaten. Eggs are only laid when mature and the sperm from the male spider is then released over them. The fertilized eggs are then wrapped in silk threads to protect them when being carried around or are hidden until ready to hatch.

TICKS AND MITES

Most ticks and mites are tiny – adult mites are often less than 1 mm ($\frac{1}{25}$ in) in length, although some ticks are larger. Characteristically they have an oval body with four pairs of limbs, and a mouthpart adapted for biting, sucking or sawing. They function as plant and animal parasites, as carriers of disease in both animals and humans, and as food pests.

■ *Praying mantis hunts its insect prey on a passion flower*

INSECTS AND THEIR RELATIVES

▶ Insects form by far the largest class of animals, accounting for over 80% of all animal species on Earth.
▶ Insects are the only invertebrates that have the ability to fly.

Insects appeared in the Devonian period some 400 million years ago (see p. 29) and flight evolved in the Carboniferous and Permian periods (350–250 million years ago). As well as the usual arthropod characteristics of exoskeleton and jointed limbs, the body is clearly divided into three parts. The head houses a large brain; within the thorax there is a mass of muscles and associated respiratory structures; and the abdomen contains the organ systems responsible for much of their digestion, excretion and reproduction.

The primary task of the adult insect is to mate and reproduce. Many insects mate only once in a lifetime and sperm are deposited either directly in the female's body or as a packet which the female can pick up and store for later use in fertilizing eggs.

Often colour (butterflies, see inset right), sounds (grasshoppers) or odours (moths) are used so that males and females can recognize each other.

Development of insects to adulthood can involve incomplete metamorphosis (as in locusts where the young resemble adults but are smaller) or complete metamorphosis, where the egg hatches out to form a larval stage such as a grub, maggot or caterpillar which then transforms. Eggs are laid on an appropriate food source and the primary task of the larvae is to eat and grow, moulting as appropriate.

CENTIPEDES

Secretive and predatory animals, centipedes are usually found in damp terrestrial places (beneath bark, logs, stones, etc.). They are confined to such habitats by their vulnerability to water loss in dry air. The head has large jaws concealed beneath the modified first pair of legs, which form poison fangs. The thorax consists of 15 or so similar segments with strong walking legs. Nocturnal in habit, they are able to move very quickly, sensing their prey by means of chemical detectors (chemoreceptors) on the head, and killing with their poison fangs.

MILLIPEDES

These herbivorous scavengers are found in similar habitats to centipedes. Millipedes appear to have two pairs of legs on each segment, but in reality these are two fused segments, which may number as many as 100. They move slowly over the ground, but their legs and movement pattern are suitable for burrowing. As millipedes cannot escape rapidly from predators, they are heavily armoured and have developed chemical defences in the form of poisons.

■ *A young squat lobster clings to the rocks, along with its barnacle relatives, in the sea near St Abbs, Scotland*

CRUSTACEANS

▶ **The first crustaceans were discovered in fossils from the Cambrian period, which began *c.* 570 million years ago.**

▶ **The largest crustacean is the Japanese giant spider crab (*taka-ashi-gani*), which can reach 18 kg (40 lb) in weight, with a claw span of around 2.5 m (8 ft).**

Crustaceans, the 'insects of the sea', include fairy shrimps; copepods (plankton); barnacles; decapods (crabs, lobsters, shrimps and prawns); sand hoppers; and woodlice. The subphylum Crustacea contains some 42,000 species, divided into ten classes. This varied group is abundant throughout the sea, and a few – woodlice and the land crabs – have successfully adapted to life on land.

The bodies of crustaceans have many segments, each with a pair of limbs, and are divided into a tail or abdomen and a head/thorax region. The head/thorax is often covered by a protective shell plate – a carapace. Many shed their carapaces, forming or finding new ones as they grow.

In simple crustaceans the head segments, bearing the antennae and mouthparts, are followed by a series of similar limbs, often fringed with hairs for food sifting. In more complex forms the various limbs differ in function and structure – thorax limbs are used for walking and swimming, abdominal limbs usually for respiratory purposes and in reproduction. The front limbs of some crustaceans are adapted as claws for food capture and defence.

In lobsters, females seek out males, secreting pheromones to subdue his aggressive tendencies. The male fertilizes the female by passing a packet of sperm into the female's reproductive pore using a specialized appendage designed for the process. Crustacea have one or two swimming larval stages.

FAIRY SHRIMPS

The fairy (or brine) shrimps live in temporary pools where they escape predation. They are classic primitive crustaceans, with rows of similar limbs used for movement and feeding, and they feed by sieving particles from the water.

COPEPODS

These are small crustaceans of immense importance in the economy of the sea. They are the principal grazers of marine phytoplankton (tiny planktonic plants) and are themselves the food of commercially important fish such as herring.

BARNACLES

Barnacles are highly modified for feeding on marine phytoplankton. As larvae, they resemble other crustaceans, but they later settle on a carefully chosen surface, usually close to other members of the same species, and attach themselves by means of head glands. The animal then secretes a protective shell, complete with closing lid, from which the thorax limbs, fringed with hairs, are protruded to catch plankton.

DECAPODS

This group, known as the decapods (meaning ten legs), includes most of the many commercially important crustaceans. Most are scavengers or predators. The lobster has 21 segments, those of the head and thorax being fused. On each of the six successive segments of the head are found compound eyes, sensory antennae (two pairs), toothed jaws and two pairs of maxillae to convey food to the mouth. The thorax has eight segments, bearing maxillipeds (which macerate food and pass it to the mouth), feathery gills, pinching claws and four pairs of walking legs. The seven segments of the abdomen bear appendages specialized for sexual reproduction and swimming.

? HOW DO THEY FLY

▶ **The rate of an insect's wing-beat varies from 300 per minute in some butterflies to an amazing 50,000 beats per minute in certain tiny midges.**

▶ **Except for flies, all flying insects have two pairs of wings, but do not necessarily use both for flight.**

Insect flight is diverse and complex. Insects are thought to have developed the ability to fly when projections from the thorax, giving hopping insects a gliding ability, became more and more mobile, eventually evolving into effective wings – thin layers of chitin, stiffened by tubular veins.

For some insects, such as dragonflies, flight is achieved by raising and lowering the two pairs of wings by means of muscles attached to the wings. The wings beat out of phase in such a way as to give maximum efficiency.

In more complex insects, the wings are either linked together and beat as one or, as in the case of beetles, one pair is stiff, held out as an aerofoil, while the other provides the propulsive force. In flies, one pair of wings is reduced to a pair of fast-vibrating knobs that function as gyro-stabilizers. The flight muscles are not attached to the wings but to the thorax wall.

Flight muscles operate best in warm conditions and flight is impossible in cold conditions for small insects. Some insects undertake 'pre-flight' exercises to warm up their muscles. The most proficient fliers, such as hover flies, can fly forwards, backwards and hover by subtly altering the way the wings thrust on the air.

Flying is very energy-consuming and insects in flight have a very high metabolic rate, using large amounts of energy stored in the thorax.

■ *A cicada emerges from a nymph into adulthood, where it can test its wings for the first time. Some cicadas spend up to 17 years underground as nymphs*

FISH

- **Bristlemouths are the most abundant fish – billions of them inhabit the oceans, outnumbering all other fish.**
- **The black swallower can extend its jaw and stomach to eat fish twice its own size.**
- **Filefish and pufferfish have poisonous flesh which, if eaten, can produce sickness or death.**
- **The world's smallest fish is the marine dwarf goby, which has an average length of 8.6 mm.**
- **The largest fish is the whale shark, with specimens recorded at 12.65 m.**

■ *These blue chromis, swimming amidst coral in the Red Sea, belong to the family Pomacentridae, relatives of the damselfish, and are also known for their beautiful colours*

WHAT IS A FISH?

▶ Fish inhabit the largest ecosystem on Earth – the water – and have the longest ancestry of any vertebrate.
▶ Unlike aquatic mammals such as whales and dolphins, fish are cold-blooded and (with a few exceptions) can only use oxygen if it is dissolved in water.

Modern fish are extremely diverse in structure and, although they can be grouped under a single heading 'aquatic cold-blooded vertebrates', they have not attained their present form by following a single evolutionary path. The 22,000 living species of fish are classified in four (sometimes five) classes, containing a total of more than 40 orders. This division at the class level implies a degree of difference among the various fish groups equivalent to that between, for example, reptiles and mammals.

The most primitive class, the jawless fish (Agnatha), comprises around 60 species of lamprey and hagfish – soft-bodied fishes that lack jaws and are barely vertebrate. All other fishes have jaws and are therefore sometimes grouped together in the superclass Gnathostomata: within this group, two classes are of pre-eminent importance – the cartilaginous fish and the bony fish.

The cartilaginous fishes (class Chondrichthyes – nearly 600 species) include sharks (see opposite page), skates and rays. The bony fishes (class Osteichthyes – over 21,000 species) include modern fishes, such as herring and tuna. This class is again divided into two unequal subclasses: the small subclass Sarcopterygii (fleshy-finned fishes), which contain the coelacanth and the lungfishes; and the much larger subclass Actinopterygii (ray-finned fishes), which is made up almost entirely of the group known as the teleosts. The teleosts are the dominant fishes of the world today, accounting for over 95% of all living species. They are the most successful of all vertebrate groups in terms of diversification, with more species than all other vertebrates put together. They are widely distributed in freshwater and saltwater from Arctic to Antarctic regions.

ANATOMY

▶ Almost all fish take in water through the mouth and expel it to the exterior across their gills (internal blood-rich organs that extract oxygen from the water).
▶ Fish skin is impermeable to water, and often amply supplied with mucus cells, spines or bony plates for further protection.

The characteristic adaptations of fishes are related to propulsion through water and extraction of oxygen from water. Typically, fishes have well-muscled paddles called fins, and the tail is well developed, to provide power and aid steering.

In cartilaginous fishes, the skeleton is formed from gristly, partially calcified cartilage, and the body is solidly muscled. Like most other fishes, their body fluids have a lower salt content than that of their environment, and because they lack the swim bladder or lungs possessed by bony fishes they must keep moving to maintain their position. Generally their skins are rough and leathery, with many minute toothed scales, and their fins are fleshy. The bodies of rays and skates are flattened, with the mouth and gill slits on the underside, and the eyes and two gill spiracles (modified gill slits) on the upper surface.

Bony fishes have internal skeletons made of true bone. The head and shoulder regions are covered by large bony plates, while the rest of the body is typically covered in iridescent bony scales. There is flexibility in both body and tail, and the fins are supported by bony rays, often bearing sharp spines. Their pelvic fins are generally well developed. In some species, such as eels, the knife fish and the lungfishes, the dorsal or anal fins provide propulsion.

A few bony fishes have stiffly rayed pectoral fins that can be used as props or stilts. The climbing perch of India and the Asian and African mudskippers are able to move on land, while the bizarre shortnose batfish of the Caribbean, a poor swimmer, crawls over the sea bed on arm-like fins. The coelacanth, found only off the Comoros near Madagascar, has remained physically unchanged for 90 million years. It was once thought that its fleshy bone-supported fins were used to walk on the sea bed. In fact these fins are used primarily for balance and for putting on the occasional burst of speed. However, the coelacanth and the related lungfishes move their fins alternately, just like salamanders walking on land, and it is thought that these fins are the precursors of land-vertebrate limbs.

Lampreys and hagfishes lack jaws, but they have rasping horny teeth. Many species attach themselves to other fishes by means of their sucker-like mouths, and feed on their blood and tissues.

■ *The discus-shaped masked butterfly fish, related to the angelfish, is a favourite in seawater aquarium displays*

GILLS AND LUNGS

Jawless fishes and some cartilaginous fishes have visible gill slits on each side of the neck region, while bony fishes have a pair of hard bony flaps (the opercula) covering their gill exits. Rays and some sharks that also have spiracles may take in water chiefly through these openings, rather than through the mouth.

Lungs are found in the most primitive bony fishes, but in teleosts they have been transformed into the swim bladder, a gas-filled buoyancy aid. Some fishes, typically mud, estuary and swamp dwellers, use the swim bladder in addition to the gills for gas exchange, gulping in air when at the surface. Lungfishes have one or two lungs, which they use when drought forces dormancy periods in their dried-up burrows.

THE SENSES

Most fish have large well-developed eyes, with a reflective layer (the kzpeturn) inside the eye and more cells in the retina sensitive to low light than land animals. This allows fish to make maximum use of light filtering through water or generated by other fish. The sense of smell is very important for migratory fish, allowing them to find their beach or river of origin.

■ THE ELECTRIC EEL CAN DISCHARGE 1 AMP AT 400 VOLTS ■ THE STONEFISH'S POISON

Fish can detect magnetic and electrical fields, as well as vibration and sound. Changes in their environment can be sensed by means of specialized organs, located on the head and within the lateral lines. Skates, rays, the South American knife fish and the Nile elephant snout fish all use their sensitivity to electrical fields to help them hunt in muddy waters and at night.

DIET

▶ Although most sharks are voracious carniverous predators, 90% of shark species present no real threat to humans because they are either too small, their teeth are inadequate or they live at too great a depth.
▶ The archerfish of Australasia and South-East Asia shoots jets of water from its mouth to knock insects off vegetation and eat them.

Some fishes are vegetation-eaters, feeding on fallen fruit, plants or bottom detritus. Most, however, are predatory carnivores, eating crustaceans such as copepods, krill and other shrimps, invertebrates such as jellyfish, and any vertebrates they can catch, including mammals, birds and other fishes.

Some fishes are specialized for dealing with their food. Parrotfishes have strong beaked teeth at the front of the mouth and crushing teeth at the back, to scrape algae and coral off the reefs they inhabit. The pacu, related to the carnivorous piranhas, also has crushing teeth, and eats fruit and seeds.

The basking shark is one of the largest fishes, and the whale shark is the biggest of all, sometimes growing to around 18 m (60 ft). Despite their great size, however, they resemble baleen whales in their method of feeding, living on plankton and small fishes sieved from sea water as it passes across their gills. Their passive feeding behaviour contrasts sharply with the aggression shown by other sharks and the active hunting of smaller fishes such as barracuda, tuna, swordfish and sailfish.

REPRODUCTION

▶ Males and females of most fishes differ in appearance, if only in size and sometimes in brightness of colour.
▶ The Nile mouthbrooder carries its newly hatched young inside its mouth.

The eggs of most bony fish are fertilized externally – the male sprays the eggs with sperm after they have been laid by the female. Eggs are provided with a supply of yolk and a protective coat.

Spawning fishes can gather in huge numbers. At high spring tides, millions of grunion are carried up on to the beaches of the south-western USA, where eggs and sperm are shed and the fertilized eggs are buried in the sand. The eggs hatch only at the next high tide – an example of moon-phase spawning.

Where eggs are internally fertilized, as in the coelacanth, the young usually develop inside the female, hatching at or soon before expulsion. Internal fertilization is normal in cartilaginous fishes, the males of which have the pelvic fins adapted as claspers, to help maintain contact during copulation and to assist in funnelling in sperm. The common dogfish and skates produce their eggs in hard black capsules with corner tendrils, sometimes called 'mermaids' purses'.

Adult fish generally desert their eggs, but there are examples of guarding and nursing behaviour. The discus of South America carries its young on its sides, where they feed on the mucus covering its scales. Male Siamese fighting fish make a nest of bubbles for the young. The European sticklebacks use plant material, and the male guards the eggs until they hatch. Some African cichlid species retain their young in their mouths, even after hatching.

Most hatched young are miniatures of their parents, but there are exceptions. The larvae of the North American and European eel undergoes an extraordinary multi-stage development (metamorphosis) before reaching the adult state. The young of flatfishes, such as flounders and plaice, are round-bodied, but as they mature, the body twists to the left or right (depending on the species), so that both eyes end up on one side, with the mouth at the edge.

ADAPTATION TO HABITATS

▶ Up to 80% of fish species carry 'lights' of some kind, often as lures to trap prey or to aid sight at great depths.
▶ The three remaining species of lungfish, based in Australia, Africa and South America, are possible relics of a transitional stage between fish and amphibians and use their lungs during dry seasons in order to survive.

Fishes are ectotherms – their metabolic system is generally adapted to the temperature of their habitat, so they are effectively cold-blooded. Fast swimmers such as tuna maintain their body temperatures slightly higher than the surrounding water by eating almost constantly. Antarctic cod survive water temperatures of –2°C (28°F) using a protein-based antifreeze in their blood. In the twilight zone at depths of 200–1000 m (660–3300 ft), the commonest fish in the oceans, the luminous cyclothone, is found in great shoals. In this region, luminescence becomes commoner as location of mates, prey or predators by sight is impossible.

In the deepest parts of the oceans, below 2000 m (7000 ft), fishes have evolved bizarre adaptations to their habitat. Many anglerfishes have a luminous 'fishing rod', formed from a ray of the dorsal fin, which extends above the mouth and attracts prey with its fleshy 'bait'. Others, such as the gulper eels, trawl for food with their huge mouths gaping open.

Perhaps the richest habitats for colourful fishes are the tropical coral reefs. Many of these fishes have beaks as well as teeth, which they use to graze on coral and seaweed. The clownfish lives in a symbiotic relationship with stinging sea anemones, thereby gaining protection from predators.

DO FISH DRINK

Marine fish drink a lot to overcome loss of water from their bodies by osmosis (water naturally passes from where it is at high concentration in the fish across its membranes into the salty water where it is at a lower concentration). At the same time, marine fish excrete salt from their gills and in a small amount of urine.

Freshwater fish have the opposite problem in that osmosis causes water to enter their bodies, which are relatively high in salts and other solutes, so that they do not need to drink, but their kidneys need to excrete high volumes of watery urine and their gills absorb salts from the water.

DEFENCE BEHAVIOUR

▶ Fishes may use their teeth or their speed to avoid predators.
▶ The stingray lashes out with its tail and injects poison through a sharp spine, sometimes causing death in humans.

Some fishes, such as stonefishes and the weever fish, can inject poison through their spines. The weever fish rests hidden in the sandy shallow waters of the eastern Atlantic and Mediterranean, and can give the unwary bather a very painful sting if trodden on. Many fishes have spiny scales or fin supports which are capable of inflicting severe damage. Trigger-fishes have three stout spines on their dorsal fin, which help lock them into crevices, while boxfishes are protected by a bony shell.

The members of the pufferfish family have an astonishing array of defences. Pufferfishes swallow water or air until they are spherical, turning into balls of spines; many species also contain a powerful nerve poison. Despite this, a Pacific species of pufferfish is considered a great delicacy in the Far East, where several deaths a year result from incorrectly prepared servings of this fish.

Some fishes make use of the natural electrical activity of muscles. By storing huge numbers of tiny voltages, the Atlantic torpedo (a ray) can produce over 200 volts, and the electric eel of the Amazon up to 500 volts. The African electric catfish may reach 1.2 m (4 ft) in length, and can easily stun a human being. Such electric charges may also be used aggressively and in courtship.

Amphibians and Reptiles

- Tree frogs – such as the red-bellied tree frog (opposite page) of Suriname – have suckers on their toes that can cling to bark and leaves and some can jump from tree to tree and glide for up to 12 m.
- The largest living amphibian is the Japanese giant salamander, which can grow up to 1.5 m long and weigh up to 100 kg.
- The oldest recorded tortoise is one which was presented by Captain Cook to the royal family of Tonga in 1773 or 1774. It stayed with the family until it died in 1965, making it at least 188 years old.
- The longest snake ever recorded is a reticulated python, which measured an amazing 10 m in length.

■ *These blue poison-arrow frogs secrete poison from their skin glands. Their bright colouring is a warning to predators*

AMPHIBIANS

▶ Amphibians, the majority of which are frogs and toads, have never achieved a total separation from water, and usually spend at least one stage of their life in water.
▶ Sharing a common ancestry with fish, amphibians often possess gills as well as lungs, and most have a moist skin, to allow air to pass through it.

The class Amphibia contains over 4000 species and is subdivided into three orders: frogs and toads (Anura), newts and salamanders (Urodela), and caecilians (Apoda).

ANATOMY

The structure of amphibian skin allows oxygen dissolved in water to pass through it and to be absorbed directly into the bloodstream. On land the skin is kept moist by glands that secrete mucus. Most frogs and salamanders are highly efficient at 'skin breathing', but toads are more reliant on their lungs, and will drown if unable to get out of water.

Amphibians – like fish, reptiles and birds – have a single passage – the cloaca – for release of eggs and sperm and expulsion of body wastes. Their eggs are generally covered in gel, and lack shells and complicated membranes.

The teeth of amphibians are often undeveloped or absent, and they rely on adhesive tongues or gripping jaws to capture and subdue their prey. Large amphibians can eat nestling birds, snakes, mice, other amphibians and even bats, while smaller amphibians rely for their diet on insects, fish, tadpoles, slugs and snails.

FROGS AND TOADS

Frogs and toads have well-developed forelegs and fingers, adapted for digging or holding, while the hind limbs are elongated for leaping or running. Tree frogs have adhesive discs on their toes, making landing more secure. All frogs and toads have large eyes and eyelids, which they blink when they swallow. Many also have a third eyelid – the nictitating membrane – which lubricates and cleans their eyes, and colour vision with a special sensitivity for blue light, which helps them to identify water quickly. A special feature of many frogs and toads is a highly extendable tongue, which is flicked out, tipped with sticky saliva, to trap unwary prey.

Frog and toad skeletons are highly modified for their hopping style of locomotion: a single neck vertebra, a short trunk and very short fused ribs. The lower spine and pelvis are fused to form the urostyle – the double-arched, saddleshaped structure that gives adult anurans their squat, humped shape and acts as a shock absorber for leaping. The tail is absent, thus the name Anura (meaning 'tailless' in Greek) for the order of frogs and toads.

NEWTS AND SALAMANDERS

By contrast, newts and salamanders have well-developed necks and tails, up to 100 vertebrae, and lack the urostyle found in frogs and toads. In general, they spend more of their lives in water than frogs and toads, keep internal gills into adulthood, and can 'breathe' through their skins. Fully aquatic species are often neotenous, meaning they retain juvenile features even when sexually mature.

CAECILIANS

The eyes and limbs of burrowing amphibians (caecilians) are small or vestigial, their main sense organs being tentacles on their cheeks. They have up to 250 vertebrae and lack tails. Unlike other amphibians, they often have scales buried in their skin, which is ringed like an earthworm's. These are all adaptations to a burrowing life.

REPRODUCTION

The gel-covered eggs of frogs and toads are fertilized outside of the mother's body, as also happens in fish. The smell of water and algae attracts both sexes to ponds, streams and damp places. Closeness of male and female is vital and is ensured by a clasping reflex (the amplexus). Females may carry males on their backs for weeks before laying eggs, at which point sperm is immediately shed by the male through the cloaca.

Successful fertilization results in the familiar masses of eggs or spawn. Frog spawn lays in clumps that float at the surface. Toad spawn forms into strings, and is found in deeper water. Once the eggs are laid, the adults generally take no further interest in them, leaving them to develop on their own.

In most other amphibians, fertilization happens inside the female's body and takes place underwater (in the case of newts and salamanders) or underground (in the case of most burrowing amphibians). Male newts and salamanders have glands on their cheeks or in the cloaca that release chemical signals called pheromones, which attract females and make them relax during mating. This allows the transfer of a gel-covered sperm package, the spermatophore, which is picked up by the female using her cloaca.

The eggs are usually kept inside the female until hatching. With the European salamander and some burrowing amphibians, the young develop inside the mother's body, nurtured by internal secretions. The immature forms of newts and salamanders resemble adults more closely than do frog tadpoles, except that they have external gills and tail fins.

DISTRIBUTION AND HABITATS

Amphibians are cold-blooded (ectotherms) and rely on external heat to maintain normal activity. Their body temperature is similar to the surrounding temperature, affecting their habitats and behaviour.

Frogs and toads are found in all continents except Antarctica, with a greater concentration of species in warmer parts. They have exploited water, land and trees equally well. The Javan flying frog glides between trees, using highly developed footwebs. Some have adapted to dry conditions, such as the Arizona spadefoot toad, which spends the dry months in underground burrows, only emerging after the seasonal rains, and can survive for up to nine months buried in sand.

Most newts and salamanders live in the northern hemisphere and are well represented in more temperate regions. They can breathe through the skin as well as the lungs, allowing some salamanders to live in mud and swamps. The olm lives in the underground cave pools of Yugoslavia, and has lost both its sight and pigmentation. Salamanders can also withstand the cold – some species are even found in the Himalaya and Siberian Arctic.

Caecilians are the most specialized amphibians, living in water and earth burrows exclusively in the Equatorial belt.

■ SNAKES HAVE UP TO 450 VERTEBRAE, EACH WITH A PAIR OF RIBS ■ THE CHAMELEON'S

DEFENCE BEHAVIOUR

Most amphibians are relatively defenceless. Frogs scream or squeak, and toads puff themselves up with air and stand on their tiptoes, appearing to grow to three or four times their normal size.

Toads, some salamanders and the great crested newt have another line of defence. Salivary glands in the head and glands in the body skin secrete poisons – bufotoxins – that affect blood pressure, nerves and muscles in predators. These poisons are extremely potent, hence the use of frog poison by Amazonian Indians to tip their arrows.

REPTILES

▶ Reptiles succeeded in making a complete break from water by developing two features lacking in amphibians – scaled waterproof skins and shelled yolk-bearing eggs.
▶ It is particularly due to these developments that reptiles have succeeded in adapting to a far wider range of habitats than amphibians.

The class Reptilia is divided into four orders: crocodilians – crocodiles, alligators and the gavial, or gharial (Archosauria); turtles and tortoises (Chelonia); lizards and snakes (Squamata); and a single species of a lizard-like, mainly extinct order, the tuatara (Rhynchocephalia). Of the 6250 or so species of reptile, over 95% are lizards or snakes.

ANATOMY

Reptilian scales are modifications of skin and made of keratin (a protein also found in hair, nails, hooves, etc.). Scales are small and granular in many lizards, smooth and iridescent in snakes, and large, thick and shield-like in tortoises and alligators. Scales may be periodically shed in flakes, or (in the case of snakes) cast off in a slough of the whole skin.

The vertebral column of reptiles is well developed, with snakes having up to 450 vertebrae, each with a pair of ribs. Like fish, birds and amphibians, reptiles have a single passage (the cloaca) through which eggs and sperm are released, and body wastes expelled. Almost all reptiles have tails.

Most lizards and all crocodilians have four well-developed limbs, with up to five toes on each. Chelonians have powerful limbs, often heavily clawed for digging, or beautifully adapted as paddles for life in the ocean. The limbs of snakes and burrowing lizards are absent or vestigial (reduced in size and function).

The distinguishing feature of turtles and tortoises is their box-like shell, which protects the soft inner organs. It is composed of an upper section, the carapace, and a lower plate, the plastron. In many species the head, tail and limbs can be withdrawn into the shell for safety.

An obvious feature of snakes and some lizards is the forked tongue. This is flicked rapidly in and out of the mouth, carrying odour molecules to a special sense gland in the roof of the mouth.

DIET

Most reptiles are carnivorous, eating invertebrate and vertebrate prey. However, some are herbivores, including many land tortoises and the marine iguana of the Galapagos Islands. Snakes can open their mouths very wide, owing to elastic ligaments between the lower jaw and the skull, enabling them to swallow large prey whole. Anacondas and pythons can even swallow prey the size of young deer and goats.

Pit vipers and boas locate their prey at night using a pair of sense organs in pits on their snouts, and are able to detect temperature differences of as little as 0.2°C (0.4°F). They can pinpoint the position of prey at distances of around 0.5 m (20 in) by comparing signals from their left and right pits.

Saltwater reptiles such as sea snakes, marine turtles and the marine iguana need to excrete the excess salt they consume. Snakes and lizards achieve this through a nasal gland (similar to that of birds), and turtles by weeping highly salty tears.

REPRODUCTION

Fertilization in reptiles is internal, and follows a courtship ritual in which female chemical signals (pheromones) and tactile stimulation are important. Clutches of eggs are laid, usually in holes in the earth or in mud.

Reptilian eggs are well protected by chalky or leathery shells. Within the shell, the embryo is surrounded by the amnion, a membrane that assists gas exchange. Waste material is collected in another membranous sac, the allantois. These membranes are characteristic of the amniote vertebrates, which also include birds and mammals. Unlike amphibians, reptiles do not pass through an aquatic larval stage, and the hatchlings are miniatures of the parents.

Many species of lizard and snake are ovoviviparous, meaning that they retain their eggs in the oviduct during the development of the young, which hatch as the eggs are laid. A few species of skink (burrowing lizards) are viviparous – they have placenta-like arrangements in the oviduct, similar to those of mammals supplying nutrition to the developing young. Most species of sea snake hatch their young within the body, so they do not have to leave the water to breed.

Most reptiles abandon their eggs, but there are exceptions. All crocodiles provide nests for their eggs and protect them until they are ready to hatch. A female may also respond to the call of her young at hatching time, and help them to emerge from the eggs. Some species of crocodile also provide parental care after hatching. Cobras and the Indian python coil themselves around their eggs and warm them by rapid muscle tremors.

DISTRIBUTION AND HABITAT

Reptiles are ectotherms (dependent on their surroundings to maintain their normal body temperature) and are therefore generally cold-blooded. If the body temperature of most reptiles falls below 25–30°C (75–85°F), metabolic functions are reduced in most reptiles, and they become sluggish. Reptilian kidneys are highly efficient at water conservation, however, so reptiles can survive colder, hotter and drier conditions than amphibians. Many reptiles, including certain turtles, tortoises, snakes and lizards, hibernate during colder months, slowing down their metabolism dramatically.

MOVEMENT

Snakes move on the ground, in trees, or in water by using their ribs, side muscles and body scales in various ways. The sidewinder of the southern USA and Mexico moves across loose sand by sideways wriggling and throwing its body forwards. Some snakes, such as the black mamba of Africa, can exceed 16 km/h (10 mph) for short bursts by lifting the front of their bodies off the ground and 'running' on their ribs. Sea snakes have bodies flattened from side to side and wriggle through the water.

Lizards are generally agile when warm. The South American basilisk can even run on its hind legs on water – hence its local name, the Jesu Cristo lizard. With their streamlined shape, marine turtles make graceful and powerful swimmers. Using their strong forelimbs as synchronized paddles, they travel many thousands of kilometres a year.

DEFENCE BEHAVIOUR

Many lizards have sharp teeth, but most rely on their agility to escape predators. Some chameleons resemble dead leaves to avoid predators, while others alter their skin colour in response to their surroundings. The frilled lizard of Australia stands on its hind legs, opens its brightly coloured mouth and expands its neck ruff to scare away predators or rivals. The Australian hooded scaly-foot resembles a snake and closely mimics the threat display of a poisonous cobra. Snakes of the viper family, such as the South American fer-de-lance or the North American rattlesnake, can inject their prey with poison (venom) from one bite. The North American bull snake (see opposite page) hisses and vibrates its tail, causing it to be mistaken for a rattlesnake, but its bite is not poisonous.Only two lizard species (the Gila monster and the beaded lizard of the southern USA and Mexico) have poisonous bites, with venom glands located in the lower jaw.

A defensive mechanism called autotomy allows some lizards to cast off a length of tail, which breaks off at a fracture plane running through the tail vertebrae. The discarded tail continues to wriggle as the lizard escapes. The soft part of the tail regrows, although never to the original length, but the vertebrae are not replaced.

■ *The dramatic forest dragon of Papua New Guinea*

BIRDS

- The bee hummingbird is only 5 cm long and weighs 3 g; its nest is the size of a half walnut shell.
- The incubation of eggs can take only ten days in small songbirds but 80 days in the albatross.
- Except when nesting, swifts spend all their life in the air, and feed entirely on insects, which they catch in flight.
- The Arctic tern migrates between the North and South poles each year – a distance of *c.* 38,000 km.

WHAT IS A BIRD?

▶ Birds are four-legged vertebrates, with the forelimbs adapted as wings.
▶ The three features that most conspicuously distinguish them from other animals are a beak, a pair of wings, and feathers.

Birds share a common ancestry with reptiles. The first bird, the *Archaeopteryx* (see p. 102), had many characteristics in common with certain dinosaurs. Also, like reptiles, birds lay eggs in which the developing embryo is protected by a fluid-filled bag. Unlike reptiles, however, birds are warm-blooded, generating their body heat from the breakdown of their food – a feature they share with mammals.

Birds who live in close contact with land and freshwater often show clear differences between the sexes – in size, colour and feather patterns. Their diversity of habitat and diet, in comparison to sea birds, has led to a larger range of territorial and mating behaviour, as well as more variations in size, shape and aerodynamics. Most land birds belong to a single order (the perching birds).

ANATOMY

▶ The most characteristic feature of birds is their feathers, which is also a unique feature.
▶ The modern bird has lost the teeth that were a feature of its ancestors, which has reduced the weight of its head, making it easier to fly.

A bird's feathers help it to keep dry and warm and also help it to fly. The feathers are made of keratin, the same material as that found in a mammal's hair and nails. Each feather has a central shaft (the quill) and its own blood and nerve supply. Many soft hair-like projections called barbs are set out in two rows, one on each side of the quill; the barbs interlock to provide insulation and minimal air resistance. Closer to the skin is a layer of soft short feathers (down), which give added insulation. Feathers (like hair) can become erect in order to regulate temperature.

The flight feathers on the wings and the tail feathers have the strongest quills, in order to withstand the tremendous stresses of flight and steering (see box right). In addition, the flight feathers on the wings are embedded in the armbones. To maximize insulation and water-repellence, the feathers of penguins are particularly soft and filamentous, and are closely packed on the skin.

The vertebrae in the backbone near the pelvic girdle (see below) are fused together to form the synsacrum, which gives firm support for the legs and helps absorb the shock of landing after flight. The neck has many more vertebrae than a mammal (up to 28 rather than seven) to give flexibility on landing. Birds have efficient hearts, with four chambers, and lungs. They have evolved to be endothermic – that is, they maintain a steady temperature under most conditions.

Next to a bird's tail is the preen (uropygeal) gland, which secretes skin oil. This oil is particularly important in sea and water birds, because it waterproofs the surface feathers as a bird preens itself. The secretions from this gland may give birds their characteristic smell, such as the muskiness of storm petrels. Several ocean-going birds, such as gannets and albatrosses, excrete excess salt (from sea water taken in with food) not through the kidneys, but through modified tear glands, ejecting the salt-rich fluid from their nostrils or mouth.

GROUND AND PERCHING BIRDS

In ground and perching birds, the forelimbs are modified into wings, while the hind, or pelvic, limbs (the legs) are often covered in scales and armed with curving nails, the claws. Ground birds use their claws to dig and gather food, while perching birds use them to grip branches. Three digits face forward for propulsion and one backwards as a support.

In owls and tree-living birds, such as woodpeckers, the third toe also faces backwards, increasing the strength of their grip. In owls, all toes are equally well developed, with very sharp talons for grappling with prey. Parrots use their beaks for climbing, using the upper part to lever themselves up.

■ *The front and side view of the skeleton of a tawny owl (species* Strix aluco*) clearly showing the armbones of the wings*

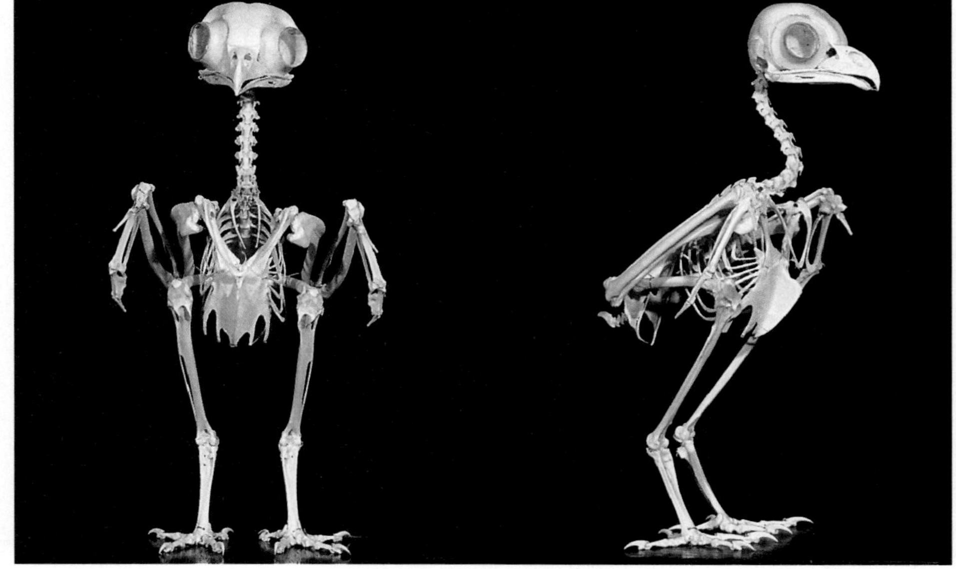

VISION

▶ For most birds, vision is the most important sense.
▶ The barn owl's sight is up to 100 times better than a human's.

Sea and air birds have large eyes and good vision. Those that sight their prey while flying are able to detect movement and detail at much greater distances than humans. Hunting birds such as hawks, eagles and owls have eyes set towards the front of the head, providing good forward and binocular vision. Hawks have a double fovea (part of the retina) in which there are only cones – nerve cells sensitive to fine detail in bright light – allowing them to pinpoint their prey. Vultures have a higher magnification in the centre of their field of view, enabling them to recognize prey even if it is not moving. Penguins, on the other hand, have flat corneas (the transparent part at the front of the eye) – ideal for underwater vision but making them very short-sighted on land. Nocturnal birds, such as owls, have large eyes with a high proportion of rods – retinal cells sensitive to movement in dim light. Dippers and divers have flexible lenses in their eyes, allowing good sight underwater as well as in the air.

DIET

▶ Instead of teeth, modern birds have beaks or bills (horny coverings to their jaws), the shape of which often reflects their diet.
▶ Many birds, including owls, gulls and starlings, cough up food they are unable to digest, such as fur and bones, in a condensed form called a pellet.

Most ocean birds are fish-eaters, and their bills are sharp and strong, with serrated edges and often hooked tips to hold slippery fish. Pelicans dive into the sea and catch fish with their long bills, storing them in a pouch under the bill. Storm petrels of the southern hemisphere skip at the surface of the sea, collecting small fish, plankton and crustaceans. Groups of gannets dive from heights of up to 30 m (100 ft) to take shoaling fish. Ocean birds follow their food wherever it is most abundant, often to the extremes of the Arctic and Antarctic seas.

Coastal birds, such as fulmars and auks, live on rocky cliffs, whereas terns, waders and some gulls prefer flatter ground. Puffins live in burrows. All either catch fish by diving and swimming, or gather crustaceans, shellfish or insects on mud flats or shores using their long beaks.

Some birds are scavengers, such as the snowy sheathbill of the south Atlantic and Antarctica, which eats seaweed, carrion and sometimes young seals. Although feeding on fish at other times, its counterpart in the North Atlantic, the great skua, harries nesting and feeding birds during its own nesting season to steal their eggs, chicks and food. The frigate bird of the Galapagos Islands has a long hooked beak with which it scoops up fish, squid and jellyfish. It also terrorizes other birds into regurgitating their food, which it then steals. Many

■ RUPPELL'S GRIFFON VULTURE, THE HIGHEST FLYING BIRD, CAN REACH AN ALTITUDE OF

BIRDSONG AND CALLS

▶ All birds use calls to communicate with each other and birdsong is part of territorial and mating behaviour.
▶ Many birds sing regularly from the same locations, called song posts, and may repeat their song over 1000 times each day.

In most species it is only the male that sings. In songbirds, the syrinx (an organ at the base of the windpipe with its own muscles and nerve supply) is especially well developed. As air vibrates the syrinx membranes, the muscles alter their tension, allowing tones of different pitch and timbre to be produced.

The young chicks inherit basic sound patterns, but more complex patterns are learned from older birds. Canaries are well known for their varied repertoire. At the end of each breeding season, brain cells die and songs are lost; at the beginning of the next season new cells grow and new songs enter the repertoire.

Some birds are less selective about songs they copy. Starlings will imitate a ringing telephone, and the Asian mynas are excellent mimics. Parrots and crows (considered the two most intelligent bird groups) can learn and repeat human-language phrases. African grey parrots are particularly skilled at this and may have vocabularies of around 1000 words. Yet, this ability is pure mimicry – it does not indicate an understanding of human speech.

HOW DO THEY FLY

■ *Snow geese in flight over Quebec, Canada*

▶ Most of the 8600 or so species of bird alive today are able to fly.
▶ The wings of flying birds create lift in exactly the same way as the wings of an aircraft (see pp. 160–161) – by causing air to move faster over the convex upper surface than the concave lower surface.

A bird's wings are attached to the body at mobile shoulder joints by the wishbone (or furcula), which increases the spring of the wing beat, helping to damp the unequal and jarring stresses imposed when a bird wheels in the air or changes speed suddenly. The power needed for flight comes from two pairs of massive pectoral muscles anchored to the large sternum or breastbone (see bird skeleton, p. 75). Greatly lengthened and fused digits form the outer third of the wing, supporting the main flight feathers. Manoeuvrability is assisted by rotation of the wings at the shoulders, angulation of the tail, and alteration of the position of the tail and flight feathers.

Although this wing profile is shared by all flying birds, there is a great variety in flight style. Most large flying birds rely mainly on gliding or soaring. Large land birds such as vultures, buzzards and eagles have broad wings with splayed feathers, allowing them to 'float' on columns of warm rising air. Albatrosses and other large sea birds use long, thin wings to glide on strong ocean winds, typically accelerating rapidly downwind and then turning and climbing steeply against the wind.

In contrast, the majority of smaller birds flap their wings to fly. Lift and forward thrust are created simultaneously on the downstroke by twisting the wing as it cleaves through the air. On the upstroke the wing is twisted the other way to reduce drag. Hummingbirds hover by means of a unique figure-of-eight 'stirring' motion of the wings, at a rate of 50 or more beats a second. By rotating their wings, first one way, then the other, they produce lift on both the up and the downstroke.

gulls have adapted to feeding on human refuse and are steadily moving inland in some areas.

The diet of birds of prey is almost entirely carniverous and includes birds, reptiles, mammals and sometimes fish. The birds of prey have strong hooked beaks, and their toes, arranged three forward and one back, are armed with long sharp curving claws (talons).

The osprey is widely distributed throughout the world and eats fish, diving at them feet-first and gripping them with its claws and spiked soles. The American bald eagle is also a fish-eater, and often follows salmon on their spawning runs to catch exhausted fish. Most hawks and eagles perch or soar until they sight prey on the ground, then drop from a height to stun and kill it. Others, such as the peregrine falcon, hobby and goshawk of the northern hemisphere, are aggressive and acrobatic hunters, chasing and catching birds on the wing.

Hummingbirds are nectar-sippers, helping to pollinate the long-tubed flowers that they feed at. They also eat insects, catching them in flight or on flowers.

REPRODUCTION

▶ Pair-bonding is the norm for birds and the same pair may reproduce from year to year in species such as swans and grebes.
▶ Over 70 bird species, including cuckoos and some cowbirds, deposit their eggs in the nests of other birds.

Most birds exhibit patterns of behaviour or body characteristics that attract females to males that are superior in some way. Males do not necessarily have to fight for a female: European pheasant females, for instance, prefer to mate with males that have longer leg spurs, a feature that appears to be genetically associated with greater offspring viability, and therefore males with this characteristic are chosen by the female. In the case of the European swallow, it is the length of the male's outer tail feathers that determines attractiveness.

Fertilization in all birds is internal. Sperm is passed by cloacal contact, apart from birds such as ducks and geese (known as Anseriformes) and the ratites (flightless birds), which have a protrusible cloaca that serves as a penis. In general, the male climbs upon the female's back and she twists her tail so that the vents of their cloacas come into contact. As the fertilized ovum passes down the female's oviduct to the exterior, it is coated in various layers. First, it is provided with a food supply (the yolk), and then robed in albumen (the egg white), which acts as a cushion and supplies water. The albumen is then coated in membranes (to offer protection against bacteria), and finally covered in several shell layers. Shells are protective and waterproof, but have pores and allow gas transfer. The eggs are incubated in a nest, mostly by the female.

Many sea and coast birds, such as auks, gannets and penguins, nest in huge colonies. The passage from egg to independence may take as little as seven weeks (as in the North Atlantic razorbill), or as long as 10 months (as in the albatross) for incubation, rearing and learning how to fly. The young albatross then sets off to ride the trade winds around the globe for years before it reaches sexual maturity and begins to seek a nesting site.

Emperor penguins do not make nests: the single egg is transferred as soon as it is laid to a pouch between the male bird's belly and feet. Thousands of males then huddle together, so that the eggs are protected from the cold of the Antarctic ice.

A few species of swifts glue their nests together with saliva. Those of cave swiftlets – used to make Chinese bird's-nest soup – are entirely made up of hardened saliva. Most birds of prey make their nests in or on trees, or on rocky ledges. Sparrowhawks and peregrines have even been known to nest on the window ledges of high city buildings.

FLIGHTLESS BIRDS

▶ The ratites are a group of ten flightless bird species, the remnants of a group that was once far more common and found worldwide.
▶ Ratites have flat breastbones, often large legbones and diminished wings (it is now thought that such birds were never able to fly).

Apart from the New Zealand kiwi (50 cm (20 in) tall), flightless birds range in size from 1.5 m (5 ft) to the ostrich of Africa, up to 2.75 m (9 ft) tall – the largest living bird. Their feathers are hair- or plume-like. Several females often lay their eggs in the same nest, which are then incubated by the male. An ostrich egg is equal in volume to 25–40 chicken eggs, while the huge extinct elephant birds of Madagascar laid eggs weighing up to 10 kg (22 lb). Some flying birds, such as the New Zealand rails and the kakapo (a nocturnal parrot), have become flightless, usually in island habitats in the absence of predators. Such birds are now in danger both from humans and from introduced predators.

■ *Masked booby chick, in his youthful grey coat feathers, waits to be fed by a parent on Galapagos Islands, Ecuador*

MAMMALS

- The largest land mammal known was a long-necked hornless early type of rhinoceros that roamed western Asia and Europe *c.* 35 million years ago, measuring 5.41 m to the top of the shoulder, with a total length of 11.27 m.
- Savi's white-toothed, or pygmy, shrew – weighing only 2 g – is the world's smallest non-flying mammal.
- The duck-billed platypus and the two species of echidna are the only mammals to lay eggs.
- The koala is the fussiest eater of the mammals – it will eat the leaves of only six of the 500 kinds of Australian eucalyptus trees and sift through 9 kg of leaves a day to find the 0.5 kg that it consumes.
- The smallest flying mammal, Kitti's hog-nosed bat, is about the size of a large bee.

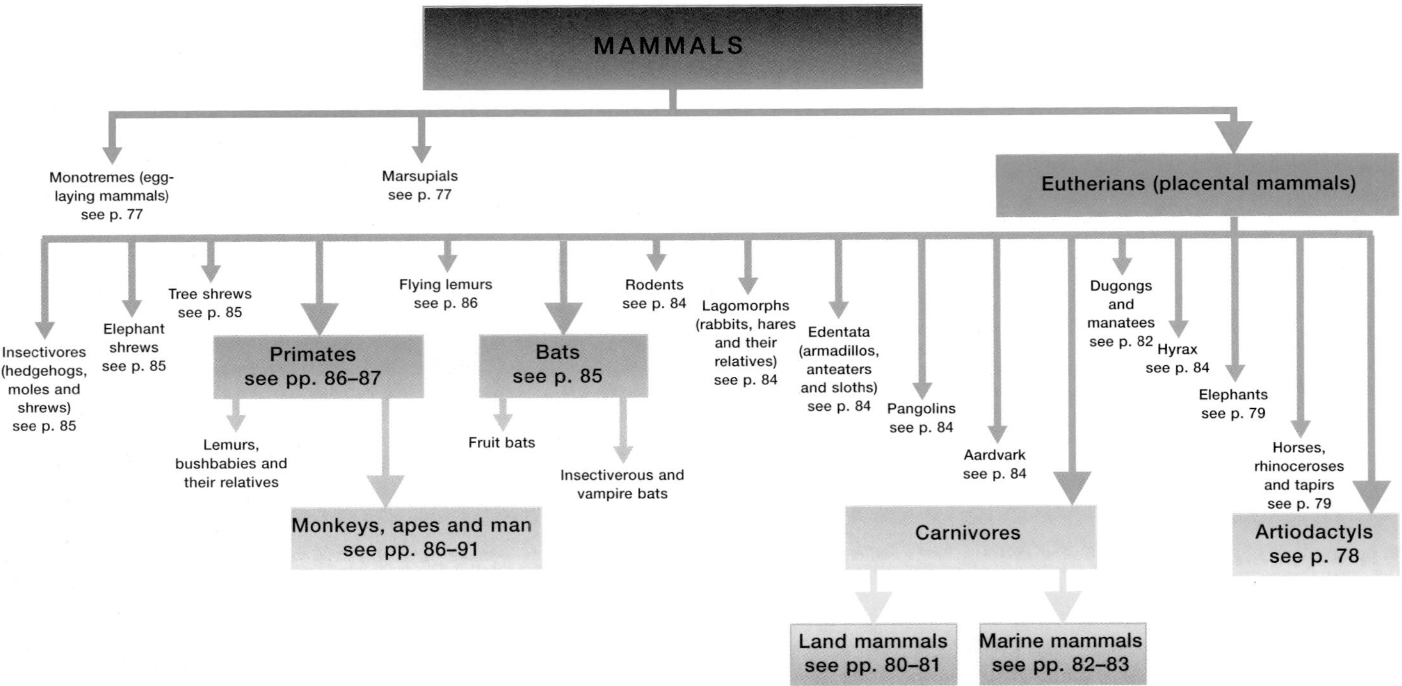

THE FIRST MAMMALS

▶ It was during the later Triassic, about 220 million years ago, that the first true mammals appeared.
▶ By the end of the Cretaceus period, 65 million years ago, the first primate, *Purgatorius*, had made its appearance, bearing a striking resemblance to a present-day group of mammals, the tree shrews.

Throughout the age of the dinosaurs, the mammals remained small, and were shrew-like or rat-like in appearance and life style. Because of their fur and warm-bloodedness, they could adapt to nocturnal activity, unlike the cold-blooded dinosaurs. When the dinosaurs became extinct, the mammals began to extend their range and to adapt themselves to a wide range of habitats. They were by no means dominant at first: for a time giant flightless flesh-eating birds – about 2 m (6 ft 6 in) tall and with skulls as large as horses' heads – were the dominant carnivores. In spite of this, the mammals were able to establish themselves.

Because the land was divided into different continents, similar-looking mammals evolved independently on the different continents. However, although not directly related, these animals would have shared a common ancestor. For example, on the grasslands of South America there were animals resembling modern camels, horses, rhinoceroses and elephants, and even a large marsupial cat.

A major event in the history of the mammals occurred during the Miocene epoch, 23 million years ago, when Africa collided with Eurasia at either end of what is now the Mediterranean. This new land connection allowed the mammals of Europe and Asia to invade Africa while elephants and apes, migrated north to conquer Eurasia.

THE GRASSLANDS

▶ Fundamental changes in mammalian life came about with the gradual replacement of forests and woodlands by grasslands (18–28 million years ago).
▶ The present-day game reserves of East Africa, with their great variety of specialized mammals, represent the type of ecosystem that first arose in the Miocene grasslands.

With the proliferation of the grasslands, horse species that had been browsers were replaced by long-legged, fast-running grazers. The same basic changes occurred among the cattle and antelopes. The favoured species, as well as being able to run fast, were able to observe the approach of predators over large distances on the open grasslands. Many of the main groups of carnivores became extinct as their prey evolved. In this new environment, modern cats and dogs evolved in the Miocene epoch (5.3–23 million years ago). Neither cats nor dogs can catch their prey by simply chasing it – they do not have the speed or stamina. Instead they use complex stratagems: dogs hunt in packs and cats, although solitary, use cunning and stealth to pounce on their victims.

Another consequence of the great reduction of forests was that the tree-dwelling primates found themselves on open grasslands. But because of their intelligence and ability to work together in teams, the savannah-living apes of the Miocene epoch in Africa and Eurasia were able not only to survive, but to spread over vast areas. This diversity was severely reduced in most parts of the world with the ice ages of the Pleistocene epoch, 1.6 million to 10,000 years ago.

THE ICE AGES

▶ During the ice ages the environment changed so rapidly that the ability to adapt was crucial.
▶ The extinction of many ice-age mammals is believed to be due to the disappearance of the plant-rich tundra at the end of the last ice age (10,000 years ago) and to early man's hunting skills.

During the ice ages, cattle (in the form of bison in North America), sheep and pigs were the key herbivores everywhere, and the most adaptable of the carnivores – the cats and dogs – held their own by virtue of their intelligence. But it was the rats and mice that became the most numerous and successful of all the mammals. One other highly adaptable mammal, with an ability to use tools and harness fire, also began to emerge – man. When the ice caps spread from the polar regions into central Europe, the permafrost and tundra reached as far south as the Alps and Himalaya. The great plains of Eurasia and North America were inhabited by woolly mammoths and woolly rhinoceroses, which grazed on the tundra. The tundra at this period supported a much richer plant-life than it does today. These large mammals were preyed upon by carnivores such as the sabre-toothed cat, with its long stabbing canine teeth.

WHAT IS A MAMMAL

Mammals are distinguished from other animal groups by a collection of characteristic features, although not all of them are found in all mammals.

▷ The word mammal is derived from the Latin *mamma* ('the breast') and refers to the fundamental feature of the group: the production of milk from the mother.

▷ In virtually all mammals the foetus develops inside the uterus (womb) of the mother. The exceptions are the monotremes and marsupials (see below). In the placental mammals, which comprise the vast majority of modern species, including man, nutrients and oxygen are passed to the foetus via an organ within the uterus called the placenta.

▷ In order that the young can suckle and breathe at the same time, the food and air passages of mammals are separated by a bony secondary palate. This also allows food to be processed in the mouth.

▷ Mammals have developed different types of teeth for accomplishing different tasks: incisors are used for biting, canines for stabbing, and cusped teeth (premolars and molars) for chewing and grinding.

▷ Mammals are warm-blooded, maintaining a constant internal temperature (homeothermic) by means of a high metabolic rate in conjunction with an insulating covering of either hair or fur.

▷ All mammals possess three sound-conducting bones (ossicles) in the middle ear – the stapes, incus and malleus. Two of these are thought to be derived from part of the jaw hinge in reptiles.

▷ The way in which the head articulates with the rest of the body separates mammals from all other animals. The joint system of the neck, involving a pivotal joint between the first and second vertebrae (the atlas and the axis), allows the head to be turned from side to side.

▷ One of the most significant characteristics of mammals is their intelligence. The cerebral cortex (the part of the brain concerned with intelligent behaviour) is better developed in higher mammals than in any other group of vertebrates.

MONOTREMES AND MARSUPIALS

▶ The monotremes and marsupials are the least complex of living mammals.
▶ Unlike other mammals, monotremes or marsupials do not retain their young in the womb until well developed.

Monotremes are unique among mammals in that they lay eggs and do not have nipples, whereas marsupials give birth to tiny, near-embryonic young.

MONOTREMES

▶ There are just three living species of living monotreme (Monotrema): the single species of the platypus family, and the two species of echidna, or spiny anteater.
▶ Monotremes are found only in Australia and New Guinea.

Despite laying eggs and sharing certain anatomical similarities with reptiles, the monotremes have two distinct mammalian features – mammary glands (although they do not have nipples) and body hair.

The distinctive characteristics of the duck-billed platypus – leathery duck-like bill, flattened tail and webbed feet and dense water-repellent fur – are suited to its semi-aquatic lifestyle. It is a strong swimmer and eats freshwater shrimps and insect larvae. The feet are clawed and used for burrowing in riverbanks where it makes its home. Males are larger than females (up to 60 cm (24 in) long) with horny spurs, which can inject venom, projecting from the back of the ankle of each hind foot.

The echidnas, or spiny anteaters, of Australia and New Guinea are burrowers. Superficially like hedgehogs in appearance, they have powerful claws for digging, and long snouts and sticky tongues with which to trap their insect prey. Like the platypus, echidnas possess ankle spurs, but these do not contain a venom gland.

MARSUPIALS

▶ There are some 250 species of marsupial mammal, divided into 15 families, the majority of which are found only in Australasia.
▶ Marsupials range in size from insectivorous dasyurids of 2 g (1/14 oz) to large grazing kangaroos weighing up to 90 kg (200 lb).

Australia separated from other land masses before placental mammals were able to establish themselves, allowing marsupials (Marsupialia) to realize their full potential. Found in Australasia, particularly New Guinea, they are represented in the Americas by the opossums. All marsupials give birth to undeveloped young, which then clamber up the mother's hair to her nipples, usually situated within a pouch (the marsupium) on the abdomen, where the young then complete their development.

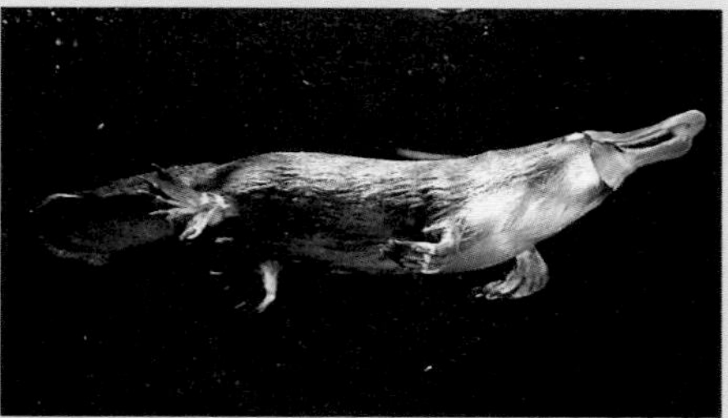

■ *The platypus is adapted to a semi-aquatic life*

■ *Female eastern grey kangaroo suckling her offspring*

■ *Koala sleeping in a eucalyptus tree, his source of food*

KANGAROOS

There are over 50 species of the kangaroo family (Macropodidae), the biggest of which – the red kangaroo of the arid plains of central Australia – can grow to a height of 1.5 m (5 ft) or more. Kangaroos are the only mammals, with the exception of man, to move mainly or solely on two legs. The small forelimbs are generally held clear of the ground while the enlarged well-muscled hind limbs provide the propulsive force for their bounding movement. Larger kangaroos attain high speeds as they move forward in huge leaps of 6 m (20 ft) or more. The kangaroo's long powerful tail acts as a counterweight, providing stability on landing. The tail also serves as a balance for the few species – the tree kangaroos – that live in the tropical forests of New Guinea and Queensland.

DASYURID MARSUPIALS

The main group of carnivorous and insectivorous marsupials, the dasyurids (family Dasyuridae), contains nearly 50 mostly nocturnal species. They range in size from tiny marsupial 'mice' (dunnarts), around 9.5 cm (3¾ in) long, to native 'cats' such as the quoll, nearly 1 m (39 in) long. The smaller species are voracious predators, often killing prey almost as big as themselves.

THE KOALA

The koala of eastern Australia superficially resembles a small thick-set bear. It is a highly specialized tree-climbing species, lacks a tail, and feeds almost exclusively on eucalyptus trees. The single offspring remains in the mother's pouch for up to six months, and then rides around on her back until it is about one year old.

NEW WORLD MARSUPIALS

Three families of marsupial, of around 83 species, are found in the Americas. Some 70 species belong to the opossum family (Didelphidae) and most of the others resemble opossums. Most opossums are rat-like in appearance, having similar scaly hairless tails, but some look more like shrews. Most are forest-dwellers, but the water opossum, or yapok, has adapted to an aquatic life.

OF UP TO 60 KM/H ■ THE SPINY ANTEATER CAN ROLL UP INTO A BALL WHEN THREATENED ■

UNGULATES

- After a prolonged period without water, camels have been known to drink over 100 litres in a matter of minutes.
- The tallest mammal is the adult male giraffe, which has an average height of between 4.7–5.3 m.
- The smallest pig is the pygmy hog from the foothills of the Himalaya, which is only around 50 cm long.
- Artiodactyls, the most diverse large mammal group, use scent glands to communicate with their social groups.

■ *Giraffes at a watering hole in Etosha National Park, Namibia. They are social animals, living in loosely associated groups*

■ *The lesser mouse deer, a chevrotain, is only 48 cm long*

WHAT IS AN UNGULATE?

▶ Over 200 species of mammal – collectively known as ungulates – are distinguished from all others by their possession of hooves.
▶ Except for pigs and peccaries, almost all ungulates are strictly herbivorous, whether as grazers (feeding on grasses) or as browsers (feeding on foliage).

Ungulates walk on their toes, with the heel raised off the ground. These toes have evolved into hooves, formed by the broadening of the bone at the tip of the toe. A structure equivalent to claws and nails has become modified to surround this bone, while a soft pad in the centre of the underpart absorbs shock as the foot strikes the ground. Ungulates are divided into two orders, according to the number of toes: the larger order (Artiodactyla) comprises even-toed ungulates, or artiodactyls; the smaller order (Perissodactyla) is made up of odd-toed ungulates.

RUMINATION

▶ All artiodactyls are ruminants (apart from pigs, peccaries and hippopotamuses) – they ruminate, or 'chew the cud', as part of their digestive process.
▶ Camels have a three-chambered stomach; other ruminants have a specialized stomach with four chambers.

Rumination is necessary because of the indigestible nature of grass. Ruminants prepare grass for a complex mixture of bacteria that live in the organ known as the reticulum, which can digest grass. The ruminants then digest the excess bacteria. While grazing, a ruminant crops plant matter as fast as possible, masticating it with its large and mobile tongue. When swallowed, the food passes into the rumen (the large storage chamber) and the reticulum, where the cellulose of plant cell walls (which cannot be digested by gastric juices), is broken down by symbiotic micro-organisms. Later, the animal lies down to ruminate: the partially digested plant material, known as 'cud', is regurgitated, chewed further, and reswallowed. The food now passes into the omasun, where most of the water is absorbed, and then into the abomasum – the 'true' stomach, corresponding to the stomach of other mammals – where it is acted upon by ordinary digestive juices.

ARTIODACTYLS

▶ Artiodactyls include about 200 species in nine families: pigs, peccaries, hippos, camels, deer, chevrotains, giraffes, bovids and pronghorn.
▶ Artiodactyls are native to all the larger land masses except Australasia.

The foot of most artiodactyls has four toes, but only the middle two are usually hooved and bear the weight of the animal. The other two (the dew claws) are small, and do not touch the ground. All artiodactyl (except pigs and peccaries) are herbivorous, and have teeth specialized for cutting and grinding plant material, and most are ruminants.

PIGS

The eight species of pig form a single family (Suidae). Pigs have short legs, heavy bodies, long pointed head ends and large flexible snouts. The body of most wild pigs is covered in coarse bristly hair, which in males (boars) may form a crest along the spine. The snout, sensitive but resilient, is strengthened at the end with a cartilaginous disc and further reinforced by a bone not found in most other mammals. The upper incisors and canines can form sharp tusks which, in males, grow continuously and can be dangerous weapons.

Pigs are largely nocturnal, living primarily in forest and woodland. They eat much vegetable matter, but will eat anything edible, including carrion. In addition to grazing and browsing, they grub in forest litter using their snouts and tusks in search of insect larvae, worms and other invertebrates. Most pigs live in small family groups (sounders) of four to six members, but some, such as the wart hog and wild boar, inhabit much larger sounders. The wild boar is still widespread in mainland Europe, and the wart hog is a familiar sight in East Africa's national parks.

PECCARIES

The three species of peccary (Tayassuidae family) are found in Central and South America. They are similar to pigs in appearance and habits, yet slightly smaller. Further distinguishing features are the tusks, curving downwards instead of up, and the prominent scent gland located on their backs. Their sounders (see above) are larger and can number up to 100.

HIPPOPOTAMUSES

The hippopotamus family (Hippopotamidae) has two species: the common and the pygmy hippopotamus. The common hippopotamus is one of the largest land mammals, only surpassed in weight by elephants. Hippos can weigh up to 4.5 tonnes, and stand 1.5 m (5 ft) at the shoulder. They live only in Africa and are amphibious, spending most of the day sleeping and resting in water, and emerging at night to graze, mostly on grasses, which they crop with the front teeth and lips. When lying in water, hippos can submerge almost the entire body, with only their nostrils, eyes and ears (all set on top of the huge, bulbous head) appearing above the surface. The pygmy hippopotamus is confined to the forests of West Africa. Similar in appearance to its larger relative, it stands about 85 cm (33 in) at the shoulder and weighs around 225 kg (500 lb). It is less aquatic than the common hippo, not gregarious, and has probably always been rare.

CAMELS

The camel family (Camelidae) has six species. The Old World camels are among the largest of the artiodactyls. The two-humped Bactrian camel grows to over 2 m (7 ft) at the shoulder; the one-humped dromedary is usually slightly taller, at 2.4 m (8 ft).

Camels are well-adapted to desert life. Their feet (like those of other camelids) have two toes joined by a web of skin that can be splayed, to keep from sinking into soft sand. The eyes are protected from sand by heavy lashes; the nostrils can be closed to exclude sand. Fat in the hump can be biochemically metabolized to give water as well as energy. The camel's ability to go for long periods without drinking (over a week while travelling long distances) is due to adaptations to conserve water. The number of sweat glands is heavily reduced, and heat accumulated in the body during the day is dissipated in the cool of the night.

Four species of camelid live in South America: vicuna, guanaco, and the guanaco's domesticated relatives – the llama and alpaca. All four grow to a length of around 1.5 m (5 ft). Slender-legged, grass-eating animals, they have a long neck supporting a head that resembles that of the camels, except that the ears are larger. Their hair is soft and woolly.

DEER

The 38 species of deer (Cervidae) are widespread in the northern hemisphere and South America. They have adapted to a broad range of habitat, from tropical forest to arctic tundra. Typically, deer are delicately built, with long legs terminating in cloven (split) hooves, and all are swift and elegant runners. Their senses are also acute – vital in species so vulnerable to predators. Most deer are fairly uniform in size, growing to a body length of 1–1.5 m (40–60 in) – but the largest species, the elk (or moose in North America), can exceed 2.5 m (8 ft) in length. Deer are mainly browsers (feeding on leaves), but have adapted to grazing on grass and other vegetable matter where forests have been cleared.

The characteristic branching antlers are unique to deer. In most deer, antlers are carried by males alone; only in the reindeer (caribou) do both sexes have them. The musk deer of Asia and the Chinese water deer lack antlers, but the males of both species have short tusks formed from elongated upper canines. Antlers consist of bone and grow yearly from knobs on the skull. While growing, they are covered in soft velvety fur, but once fully grown, the blood supply is cut off, and the fur peels off, leaving only the hard bony core. Each successive set of antlers (they are shed after the breeding season) is larger and more branched, until a deer reaches maturity. Although the sexes typically live in separate herds for the rest of the year, during the breeding season, or rut, the males of many species become territorial and defend harems of females. Most deer have only one or two young, which are well developed and often able to follow their mother within hours of birth. Unlike adults, which tend to be drab brown, young are frequently heavily spotted.

CHEVROTAINS

The four species of chevrotain (mouse deer; Tragulidae) are closely related to deer. Like tiny deer in appearance, they grow to 20–35 cm (8–14 in) at the shoulder. Generally found near water in the tropical forests and swamps of Africa and Asia, chevrotains graze and browse at night on the forest undergrowth. They lack horns or antlers, but in males the upper canines have developed into tusks.

THE GIRAFFE FAMILY

The giraffe family (Giraffidae) has two living species: the elusive okapi of the tropical forests of The Congo (ex-Zaïre) and the giraffe. Male okapis and giraffes of both sexes have two or three skin-covered horns, formed from bony outgrowths and never shed. Now restricted to sub-Saharan Africa, the giraffe is relatively abundant in eastern and southern Africa. With its long slender legs and enormously elongated neck, it is the tallest land animal; male giraffes grow to about 5.5 m (18 ft), a metre taller than females. A giraffe's neck has only seven vertebrae, the same as most other mammals, but the bones are greatly elongated and the joints are of the ball-and-socket kind, giving extra flexibility. To allow blood to ascend to the head and to prevent a sudden surge of blood when the animal bends down to drink, there is a series of valves within the neck to regulate blood supply. When giraffes walk or run, the neck moves rhythmically backwards and forwards, shifting the centre of gravity to maintain balance. The giraffe's tongue is nearly 45 cm (18 in) long, enabling it to browse on the tops of trees. Giraffes usually remain standing even while sleeping.

BOVIDS

Bovids (Bovidae) are a highly diverse group with 128 species of antelope, cattle, sheep and related species, and include some important domestic animals. Most numerous and diverse in Africa, they also live in much of Eurasia and North America. Bovids have adapted to a wide range of other habitats, but most favour open grassland, scrub or desert. They range in size from the tiny royal (or pygmy) antelope of West Africa (only 25 cm (10 in) at the shoulder), to the massive bisons of North America and Europe, growing to a shoulder height of 2.2 m (7 ft 3 in). Bovids have certain common features: all are ruminants (see p. 78) and almost exclusively herbivorous. Their teeth are modified for browsing and grazing: grass or foliage is cropped with the upper lip and lower incisors (upper incisors are missing), and then ground down by large cheek teeth. All male bovids and the females of most species carry horns, which are bony cores covered in a sheath of horny material constantly renewed from within; they are unbranched and never shed.

The term 'antelope' is used loosely to describe a number of bovids that have followed different lines of development. Long-legged and fast-running (often their long horns may be laid along their backs when in full flight), they live mainly in grassland, but some have adapted to marshes.

The subfamily Caprinae includes sheep and goats. Most are woolly or have long hair. Many, such as wild goats, chamois and ibex, are agile cliff- and mountain-dwellers. Caprinae can tolerate extreme conditions: barbary and bighorn sheep have adapted to arid deserts, Rocky Mountain sheep to high mountains, and musk ox to arctic tundra.

THE PRONGHORN

The North American pronghorn is the sole survivor of a family of herbivorous ruminants (Antilocapridae), similar in habits and appearance to the Old World antelopes. Males and most females carry horns that consist of a bony core covered with a horny sheath, which is shed after each breeding season.

PERISSODACTYLS

▶ Perissodactyls are 17 species of odd-toed ungulates (horses, rhinoceroses and tapirs).
▶ They reached their zenith around 40 million years ago.

In perissodactyls, the weight of the body is borne on the central toes, with the main axis of the limb passing through the central (third) and longest toe. In horses, only the single central toe on each foot is functional. In rhinoceroses, there are three hoofed toes on all feet, while in the tapirs four functional toes have been retained on the fore feet and three on the hind feet. All other toes have been lost or reduced to mere vestiges. All Perissodactyla are herbivorous and (except the forest-dwelling tapirs) are adapted for fast running on open plains, where they feed mostly on grasses. Unlike ariodactyls, they never ruminate and have smaller, simpler stomachs.

HORSES AND THEIR RELATIVES

The eight species of horse, ass (donkey) and zebra (the equids) are closely related in a single family (Equidae). Fast, elegant runners, they are naturally gregarious, living in herds. Feeding mostly on grasses, their elongated jaw houses teeth adapted for their diet – incisors for cropping grass and large cheek teeth for grinding. The wild horse is extinct in the wild. The Asian wild ass, once abundant in open, arid habitats, is now found only in isolated populations. The African wild ass, once widespread in North Africa, is now near extinction. However, descendants of the wild horse and wild ass have been widely domesticated. Four species of zebra were once widespread south of the Sahara: the southernmost (quagga) is extinct; the mountain zebra is reduced to a few isolated populations in south-western Africa; the common zebra (Burchell's zebra) is relatively widespread in east and south Africa; and Grevy's zebra, slightly larger and with narrower, more numerous stripes than the common zebra, is still found in northern Kenya and Ethiopia.

RHINOCEROSES

Five species of rhinoceros remain in Africa and three in Asia. Massively built, with short stocky legs ending in three hooved toes, their large heads have one or two fibrous horns composed of compressed hair (keratin) on top of the snout. All are herbivorous, whether as browsers or as grazers. Rhinos rarely form even semi-permanent pairings. The white rhinoceros (generally greyish in colour) is the largest living land mammal after the elephant, standing up to 2 m (6 ft 6 in) at the shoulder and weighing over 3.5 tonnes. In common with the black rhino (the other African species) and the Sumatran rhino, the white rhino has two horns. It is primarily a grazer, with distinctive square lips for cropping grass. The black rhino, which is usually grey, is principally a browser. Both African species were widespread in open grasslands and woodlands south of the Sahara, but indiscriminate hunting has reduced them to scattered populations. The Sumatran rhinoceros, the smallest rhino, grows to a shoulder height of up to 1.5 m (5 ft). It is now reduced to scattered and isolated populations. The Indian rhinoceros is much the same height as the white rhino, but far less massively built, weighing around 2 tonnes. It has a single horn, and its thick skin is heavily folded at the joints, giving the appearance of armour-plating. The Javan rhinoceros is like a small version of the Indian rhino in appearance, with similar folded skin and a single horn.

TAPIRS

One species of tapir is found in South-East Asia, the other three in Central and South America. They are shy, browsing animals that live close to water. The head tapers into a flexible proboscis, or trunk, overhanging the upper lip, and is used to scoop leaves and other vegetable matter into the mouth. Adults of different species vary greatly in colour.

ELEPHANTS

▶ Mastodons and mammoths – close relatives of the elephants – occurred in the New World and across northern Eurasia.
▶ Elephants (order Proboscidea) are not classified as ungulates; despite sharing many ungulate characteristics, their feet are not hooved, but are large, flattened pads.

An elephant's long, flexible, muscular trunk is formed by an enormous elongation of the nose and upper lip. The nostrils are at the tip, and the sensitive grasping lip is used to pluck foliage or to pick up objects as small as a nut. As well as providing an efficient means of gathering food, the trunk is also used for drinking and smelling, and for producing the loud trumpeting used in communication and courtship. An elephant's tusks are highly modified teeth, continuously growing upper incisors. The largest tusks measure around 3.5 m (11 ft 6 in) and pairs can weigh over 110 kg (240 lb), with record pairs weighing nearly twice this. However, because of relentless hunting, huge 'tuskers' are now rare; it is unusual to see an elephant with tusks weighing much more than 30 kg (66 lb).

The African elephant is the largest living land animal: males may stand over 3.5 m (11 ft 6 in) at the shoulder, and weigh 7 tonnes. The Asian elephant is smaller, with a shoulder height of 3 m (10 ft) and weighing up to 6 tonnes. The African elephant is also distinguished by its larger ears, sparser hair and less domed head. The female Asian elephant usually lacks tusks, and the male's tusks are generally much smaller than those of the African species. Both species are gregarious, living in herds in habitats from forest to savannah. They are vegetarian and, despite their massive bulk, are surprisingly graceful and swift on their feet. Their gestation period is very long – between 20 and 22 months, after which usually a single calf is born.

Land Mammals

- Lions, tigers, leopards and jaguars can roar because they have a special ligament in the throat which can vibrate.
- Australian dingoes are descendants of domesticated dogs introduced by the Aboriginal settlers.
- The cheetah, the fastest land mammal, has been known to achieve a speed of 100 km/h.

WHAT IS A CARNIVORE?

▶ Although the name 'carnivore' is applied generally to any carnivorous, or flesh-eating, animal, the term is used specifically to describe the group of mammals belonging to the order Carnivora.
▶ Most carnivores are land mammals, but a few have adapted to an air or marine life.

Some members of the order Carnivora are active hunters, while others are mainly scavengers. However, despite their name, many carnivores eat plant matter and insects as well as flesh, and a few species are even vegetarian. Carnivora contain some 245 species in seven families. There are believed to have been two lines of evolutionary development within the order, allowing these families to be divided into two groups. The suborder Aeluroidea contains three families: cats, civets and their relatives, and hyenas; the suborder Arctoidea contains four families: dogs and their relatives, bears, raccoons and their relatives, and weasels and their relatives.

■ *A female cheetah preying on a gazelle in Kenya*

CATS

▶ Despite differences in size and colour, the 37 living species of cat (family Felidae) are remarkably uniform in shape and structure, and all resemble the familiar domestic cat.
▶ Cats usually hunt at night and can see about six times better than humans can in the dark.

All cats are predatory and their characteristics are perfectly suited to the life of a hunter. As well as specialized teeth, all species (except the cheetah) have claws that can be withdrawn into sheaths, thus keeping the claws razor-sharp and allowing the animal to stalk noiselessly on its pads.

The tiger, the biggest cat, has a head-and-body length sometimes in excess of 2.5 m (8 ft). Although its colour varies, all its subspecies are striped, giving excellent camouflage in forest habitat. Nocturnal and usually solitary, tigers tend to hunt large prey, and can eat 23 kg (50 lb) of meat in a single meal.

Generally only slightly smaller than the tiger, male lions are larger than females and are further distinguished by the heavy mane around the neck and shoulders. Unlike most other cats, lions live together in groups (prides), which usually contain about nine individuals. They inhabit open savannah and are usually active during the day. Lionesses do most of the hunting, preying mainly on mammals such as zebra, wildebeest and other antelope.

The leopard typically grows to around 1.5 m (5 ft), excluding the tail. Most leopards are marked with characteristic rosette-shaped spots, but they can be entirely black (and then known as panthers). Like most other cats, the leopard is solitary and generally nocturnal. However, in Sri Lanka, where lions and tigers are absent, it is active by day. Several other cats are similar to the leopard. The jaguar, the largest New World cat, resembles the leopard in proportions and colour, but is of slightly heavier build and not quite so agile. The snow leopard also has spotted markings, but its fur is thicker and softer. It has a long tail, almost as long as its body.

The cheetah, or hunting leopard, is the fastest land animal. Superbly adapted for speed, it has long legs and a slender supple body. The cheetah hunts in open plains, and relies on bursts of speed that may exceed 80 km/h (50 mph) to run down its prey, mostly gazelles.

Among the smaller cats, the wildcat is one of the most widely distributed, occurring in a wide range of habitats. Similar to an oversized domestic cat in appearance, the wildcat is largely solitary and nocturnal. Although an agile climber, it mainly stalks small mammals and birds on the ground.

MONGOOSES, CIVETS AND THEIR RELATIVES

▶ The viverrids – civets, genets, mongooses, fossas and linsangs – belong to some 75 species making up the civet family (Viverridae).
▶ Nearly all viverrids have scent glands in the anus, the secretion from which is used both in perfumery and medicine.

Although variable in habit and appearance, viverrids tend to have long lithe bodies, short legs, pointed snouts and very long tails, sometimes even longer than the animal's body. Many civets, genets and linsangs are boldly spotted or striped, with banded tails. Viverrids have adapted to many habitats, from tropical forest to savannah. Some have adapted to spending much of their life in water. Viverrids have acute senses of sight, smell and hearing, usually catching their prey by stalking and pouncing. Most are solitary in behaviour, but some species are notably gregarious. Their diet consists of a large range of food, including small mammals, birds and their eggs, reptiles, insects and fruit.

HYENAS

▶ Despite a superficial resemblance to dogs, the four species of hyenas (Hyaenidae) are more closely related to cats and civets.
▶ Hyenas live in socially complex groups and their organized cooperation in hunting allows them to tackle large prey such as wildebeest which would be impossible for one hyena.

Although noted as scavengers, the hyenas are also effective predators. On the plains of the Serengeti, one-quarter of all carcasses on which lions feed are animals killed by hyenas. When available, they also eat considerable quantities of fruit such as melons. The aardwolf, of the drier habitats of sub-Saharan Africa, is lighter than the other hyenas, and has weak jaws and minute teeth. It feeds almost exclusively on termites and other insects. The other three species – the spotted, brown and striped hyenas – look very dog-like. Their distinctive sloping gait is due to their hind legs being shorter than their forelegs. All have massive heads and powerful jaws capable of crushing bones. The spotted hyena is particularly noted for its laughing cry.

DOGS AND THEIR RELATIVES

▶ The 37 species of dogs and their relatives (family Canidae) occur in almost all habitats and in virtually all parts of the world.
▶ Dogs are the most vocal of the carnivores, uttering whines, howls and barks which help them to communicate when hunting in packs for large prey.

Canids are typically long-legged with a muscular torso and bushy tail. The muzzle is usually elongated, and the teeth are long and sharp. Senses are acute, particularly that of smell and hearing. Unlike cats, canids have blunt non-retractable claws. Dogs are principally meat-eaters. Some species are strictly carnivorous, such as the Africa hunting dog, while others, including the foxes, feed on both animal and vegetable matter.

■ *Polar bear in his white coat – a camouflage in the snow*

The ancestor of the domestic dog is the wolf. It has been ruthlessly persecuted and, once widespread, is now extinct over much of its former range. Wolves are gregarious animals, living and hunting in family groups, or packs. Within the pack a strict social hierarchy is reinforced by ritual gestures and posturing. The North American coyote resembles a small wolf. It has been more successful at surviving persecution, moving into the prairies, where it has forced out wolves. It has even managed to colonize city suburbs. The maned wolf of South America lives mainly in savannah, where its exceptionally long legs enable it to see above tall grass.

Hunting in packs is particularly important for the more carnivorous species, especially for those relying on larger prey, since success may depend on organized attack. Several fox species, on the other hand, including the red fox, are opportunistic in their feeding and have less need to move in groups. The red fox is usually solitary, and although it may take poultry and sick lambs, it mostly feeds on small animals such as voles or even insects.

■ DOGS HAVE BEEN DOMESTICATED FOR AT LEAST 12,000 YEARS ■ THE POLAR BEAR IS THE

It is as adaptable as the coyote, with a wide distribution throughout the northern hemisphere.

The Arctic fox, which is confined to the Arctic of North America and Eurasia, exists in two colours: the white form, which turns brown in summer, and the less widespread blue form, which remains bluey-grey all year. Although living in large dens, Arctic foxes hunt alone, with lemmings as their chief prey. Extremely hardy animals, they can survive temperatures as low as –80°C (–112°F), and travel long distances, covering around 1500 km (940 mi) in one journey. The fennec fox, the smallest fox, has adapted to harsh arid desert conditions. Its huge ears both enhance hearing and help it to lose heat.

The raccoon dog of eastern Asia is similar in appearance to the New World raccoons, with squat body, short legs and a black facial mask. It feeds mainly on fish, amphibians and other small mammals. Unlike all other dogs, it enters a state of semi-hibernation for over four months of the year, although it does emerge at intervals to feed.

BEARS

▶ The eight living species of bears (Ursidae) once ranged throughout the northern hemisphere, but their presence is now reduced.
▶ The bear's large head is dog-like, pointing to the common ancestry of bears and dogs.

■ *Red pandas, related to raccoons, live in bamboo trees*

Despite variations, bears are characteristically large and heavily built, with stocky bodies, flat feet with long curved claws, and a short tail, or no tail. Among the bears are the largest living carnivores: the brown bear and the polar bear of the Arctic regions. An adult male polar bear weighs on average about 403 kg (888 lb), growing to a length of 2.5 m (over 8 ft). Most bears are omnivorous and opportunistic in their feeding, eating a wide range of food including roots, leaves, berries, nuts, insects and small mammals. The exception is the largely carnivorous polar bear, which feeds mostly on seals.

The smallest bear, the sun bear (or honey bear) of South-East Asia, grows to a length of about 1 m (39 in), but is powerfully built and a good tree-climber. It spends most of the day sleeping or sunbathing in trees, only becoming active in the cool of the night. It eats mainly plants, but may also strip off bark with its sharp claws in search of honey or insects. The sloth bear of India and Sri Lanka lacks upper incisors, and has lips and tongue modified for its specialized diet of ants and termites. After it has dug open an ant or termite nest with its claws, it purses its mobile lips, closes its nostrils and sucks up insects like a vacuum cleaner.

The giant panda shows so many specialized anatomical modifications that it has often been classified quite separately from the bears. However, recent studies of the sequence of genes indicate that bears and the panda are indeed closely related. Once widespread, the panda is now confined to three small areas of mountainous bamboo forest in western China, where it feeds almost exclusively on bamboo shoots. The front paw has a special pad – the so-called sixth finger that enables pandas to hold bamboo stems. The nutritional value of the panda's bamboo diet is relatively poor, so pandas need to spend 10–12 hours a day eating.

RACCOONS AND THEIR RELATIVES

▶ The raccoon family (Procyonidae) has 19 species of small to medium-sized mammals.
▶ The six species of raccoon proper all grow to a body length of around 50 cm (20 in).

One of the most widespread mammals in North America is the common raccoon. Like other procyonids, the raccoon is an active and inquisitive animal, and a good climber. It can use its forepaws with extraordinary dexterity, and is very adept at fishing – flicking crayfish, small salmon and other fish from the water. The raccoon has proved highly adaptable to urban and suburban life, and it is often seen – conspicuous by its black face mask and ringed tail – rummaging among garbage cans.

The kinkajou of the tropical forests of Central America and northern South America spends almost its entire life in trees, where it is active at night and feeds mainly on fruit. It is also fond of honey and, like the sun bear, is sometimes called the honey bear. It is similar in body size to the raccoon, but is not so stockily built and has a longer tail. Its tail is prehensile, adding to its great agility in climbing from branch to branch.

The olingo, similar in appearance and distribution to the kinkajou, is also an adept climber. However, its tail is bushier, not prehensile, and more raccoon-like. The South American coatis are notable for their long, banded tails and their pointed flexible snouts, with which they probe for insects and other invertebrates. Unlike most other procyonids, which tend to be solitary, female coatis live in groups of a dozen or more members, although males are solitary outside the breeding season.

The red, or lesser, panda is found from the Himalaya to southern China. It is like the raccoon in size and built with a bushy, banded tail, but its coat is a lustrous rusty red. It is also known as the cat bear, from its habit of sleeping during the day curled up on a branch with its tail over its head. It generally feeds on the ground at night, eating mainly bamboo shoots and other plant matter.

WEASELS AND THEIR RELATIVES

▶ The weasel family (Mustelidae) contains nearly 70 species and includes weasels, skunks, badgers and otters.
▶ Mustelids occur on nearly all land masses except Australasia, and have adapted to a wide variety of habitats.

Mustelids tend to have long supple bodies, often arched near the hindquarters. At the front, the body typically tapers into a long neck supporting a relatively small pointed head. The tail is usually long, and sometimes bushy. Mustelids are generally highly carnivorous with well-developed cheek teeth that interlock in a scissor-like action to cut through tough flesh and sinew. Most species are skilled hunters. The wolverine of the subarctic regions of America and Eurasia, although only around 1 m (39 in) from nose to tail, is a fearsome predator. It often preys on animals larger than itself, and has been known to drive bears and pumas off their kills. The ratel (or honey badger), a polecat of sub-Saharan Africa and southern Asia, is another tenacious predator. Its favourite food, however, is honey.

Weasels can kill animals larger than themselves and eat mice, squirrels, frogs, earthworms, lizards, snakes, small birds and even chickens. They quickly kill their prey by severing the spinal column just below the skull. The smallest living carnivore, the least weasel, is found in most temperate parts of the northern hemisphere, growing to a total length (including tail) of about 20 cm (8 in). In the northern parts of its range, its fur turns white in winter. A similar colour change is undergone by the slightly larger but closely related stoat, whose white winter coat provides ermine. Another close relative, the mink, has been farmed for its luxuriant fur, while the martens (which include the sable) are also prized for their dense, soft pelts.

All mustelids have well-developed anal scent glands, which are generally used for marking the boundaries of their territory. In some species – most notably the polecats, such as the African zorilla and the ratel, and the skunks of North and Central America – the scent glands are also used as a very effective deterrent to would-be intruders. A foul-smelling liquid is ejected with remarkable accuracy in the form of an aerosol vapour from two glands

■ *The north Pacific sea otter breeds its young in the water*

located just inside the anus. The skunks and other mustelids that use this defensive strategy often have conspicuous coloration, usually black and white, intended to warn potential attackers to steer clear.

Badgers live throughout Eurasia and North America. Most species are similar in size and appearance, being stockily built and with distinctive black-and-white facial markings. All badgers are efficient burrowers, typically active by night, emerging from their burrows to feed on a wide diet of animal and plant material. The American badger is mostly solitary; the Eurasian badger is social, living in family groups in extensive underground burrows (setts). The oriental stink badgers and ferret badgers use defensive strategies similar to that of the skunks.

All otter species, although mustelids, are adapted for aquatic life, having streamlined bodies and webbed feet, as well as broad tails to propel them when swimming. Most specialized of all are the sea otters, the largest of the mustelids, which are capable of living their entire life without ever coming on shore. Unlike most aquatic mammals, such as whales and seals, otters lack a thick layer of blubber, and are insulated from the cold water by a layer of air trapped in the fibres of their dense fur. Sea otters can close their nostrils when diving, and can dive for several minutes without surfacing.

LARGEST LAND CARNIVORE – ONE WAS FOUND THAT WEIGHED 1000 KG AND WAS 3.4 M LONG ■

MARINE MAMMALS

- The killer whale is the largest predator of warm-blooded prey, feeding on seals, penguins and other species of whale.
- Dugongs may be what sailors once referred to as mermaids, as mariners thought the females resembled naked women with tails when they suckle their single young while partly raised out of the water.
- The blue whale can grow to 30 m in length and weigh 120 tonnes – it is the largest animal in existence.
- The Weddell seal can dive to a depth of 600 m and stay underwater for a period of up to 70 minutes.

WHAT IS A MARINE MAMMAL?

▶ Some mammals, in the course of evolution, returned to the sea, where millions of years previously their fish ancestors had lived.
▶ Some marine mammals, such as seals, have to return to land to breed, but whales, manatees and others are entirely aquatic – they eat, sleep and give birth in water.

There are three groups of mammals that took to the sea at a late stage of evolution. First, the carnivorous seals and the walruses (pinnipeds), who are related to the land carnivores. Second, the manatees and the dugongs (sirenians), who share a common ancestry with elephants and, like elephants, are herbivorous. And third, the whales and dolphins (cetaceans) who form a completely separate group, related neither to the seals nor to the sirenians.

Internally, the bones and organs of marine mammals all closely resemble those of land mammals and, although superficially fish-like, their paddles are in fact modified limbs. Like all other mammals, marine mammals breathe by taking in oxygen from the air, and so have to return to the surface at intervals to breathe. In some species, the respiratory system is similar to that of land mammals, but in the whales, the nose or blowhole is set high up on the head, and the nostrils can be closed by valves to prevent water from entering the lungs during dives.

■ *A manatee, living off the coast of Florida, USA. Manatees suffer danger from water traffic, as they tend to get caught in the propellers of motor boats – their slow, cumbersome bodies can make it difficult for them to get out of the way quickly*

SEALS AND WALRUSES

▶ Although pinnipeds are more at home in water, all are capable of moving on land and return to the shore to breed and to moult.
▶ The largest of the 34 known species of pinniped is the southern elephant seal – bulls typically grow to a length of 5.8 m (19 ft).

Seals and walruses (pinnipeds) are superbly adapted to their aquatic environment. Their hands and feet are flattened into flippers, and the body is streamlined. They have a thick layer of fat (blubber) to insulate against the cold and to act as an energy store, and most species have a covering of coarse hair to protect the skin when on shore. Walruses and the eared seals are able to bring their hind limbs forward to facilitate movement on land – an ability lacking in the true seals.

Most pinnipeds are highly gregarious. During the breeding season, they gather in large numbers at traditional breeding grounds called rookeries. Males (much larger than females in most species) typically become highly territorial, with dominant males seeking to defend female harems. All sea lions and many other seal species give birth to young conceived during the previous breeding season, so allowing birth and mating to be synchronized in the short period when adults are together on land.

Although less mobile than other pinnipeds on land, earless seals are superb swimmers and divers. The Weddell seal of the Antarctic, for instance, regularly dives to depths of over 300 m (985 ft), and one was recorded at 600 m (1970 ft). To facilitate prolonged dives, seals are able to shut off the blood supply to all the organs except the brain (the muscles operate on their own stored oxygen), and the blood itself has a higher oxygen-storage capacity than that of other mammals.

Walruses are usually found in the shallow coastal waters of the Arctic. Male walruses can grow to around 3.5 m (11 ft 6 in) and weigh around 1.5 tonnes. Tusks formed from the upper canine teeth are present in both sexes, but are larger in males. They grow continually for up to 30 years, reaching lengths of over 1 m (39 in). The walrus uses its tusks to heave itself on to ice floes and to keep open breathing holes in the ice. They are also used to plough up the sea bed in search of molluscs and for sparring with rival males in the breeding season.

■ *A group of walruses in Walrus Islands Game Sanctuary, Bristol Bay, Alaska, USA*

MANATEES AND DUGONGS

▶ The sirenians (manatees and dugongs) are also known as sea cows, as they are the only herbivorous marine mammals, feeding mainly on seaweed and other marine plants.
▶ The Stellar's sea cow, confined to the Bering Sea, was the only species adapted to cold water – it had been hunted to extinction within three decades of its discovery in 1741.

Manatees are found in the tropical and subtropical coastal waters of the Atlantic and adjacent river systems, while the dugong is found at similar latitudes in the Indian Ocean, the Red Sea and the western Pacific. They grow to about 4 m (13 ft) in length. All have heavy but streamlined bodies, tapering to the rear. The forelimbs are modified into paddles, and the hind limbs are absent. The tail is horizontally flattened – the dugong's into a crescent-shaped fluke, the manatee's into an oval fluke. Although the body is virtually hairless, the muzzle is covered in thick stiff whiskers.

The dugong has a flexible overhanging upper lip, which it uses to uproot clumps of seaweed and other plants, and males have tusks formed from the incisor teeth. Manatees have a deeply split upper lip, allowing each half to be moved independently, which helps them in grazing for food. The dugong is mainly solitary, while manatees are more gregarious, sometimes gathering in large herds.

■ MOST DOLPHINS CAN SWIM AT 24–32 KM/H FOR LONG PERIODS OF TIME ■ WHALES CAN

■ *A humpback whale breaches the ocean's surface near Cabo San Lucas, Baja California, on its way from its summer home in Alaska to its winter home in Hawaii*

WHALES, PORPOISES AND DOLPHINS

▶ Unlike all other marine mammals, the cetaceans (whales, dolphins and porpoises) spend their entire life in water.
▶ In order to detect prey, most cetaceans use a form of ultrasonic sonar (echolocation), similar to that used by bats, emitting rapid high-pitched squeaks and clicks to gauge the position of surrounding objects.

The order Cetacea is divided into two groups: toothed whales (dolphins, porpoises and most smaller whales); and baleen whales, including most of the giants of the sea, such as the blue whale. They occur in all oceans, as well as a few of the larger river systems and lakes connected to them. Their adaptations to marine life are similar to those of seals: the body is streamlined, the limbs are modified into paddles and there is an insulating layer of blubber. In cetaceans, however, like sirenians, the hind limbs are absent. Instead there is a horizontally flattened tail fluke, which provides the principal means of propulsion. To varying degrees, all whales are gregarious, forming groups known as schools. All species have teeth, ranging from a single pair in some of the beaked whales to as many as 260 in some dolphin species – a record for any mammal. Toothed whales eat mainly fish, octopus and squid.

TOOTHED WHALES

Most dolphins are characterized by their streamlined form and beaked snouts. They are extremely gregarious, forming schools of sometimes over 100 individuals (not necessarily of a single species), in which a well-developed social hierarchy is established. Of the toothed whales, dolphins generally grow to between 2.5–4 m (8–13 ft), and the largest, the killer whale, can grow to over 9 m (30 ft). Dolphins produce a single offspring which, like all marine mammals, is well developed at birth. The calf is usually born tail-first and is helped to the surface by its mother to take its first breath of air.

River dolphins are found in the major river systems of India, South America and China (see lower right). They have long slender beaks and foreheads. Because their native rivers are muddy and murky, they are dependent on echolocation to avoid obstacles and detect prey, and some, such as the Ganges dolphin, are blind.

The porpoises are the smallest of the whales. They are very similar to dolphins, but are shorter and stockier, and do not have a beaked snout. They are generally found in coastal waters, often venturing up rivers for several kilometres.

The largest of the toothed whales is the sperm whale. Males formerly grew to about 24 m (79 ft), roughly twice the size of females, but two centuries of intensive hunting has led to a considerable decrease in size. The most striking feature of the sperm whale is its huge squarish head, which contains the largest brain of any animal – weighing around 9.2 kg (over 20 lb). The majority of the head, however, is filled with spermaceti wax, nearly 2000 litres (440 gallons) of it – which gives the whale its name. The precise function of this wax is not known, but it may be involved in sound transmission, or help to regulate buoyancy during dives. Sperm whales can dive to around 1000 m (3280 ft) and remain submerged for up to 75 minutes. They feed mainly on deepwater squid.

The two species of white whale are restricted to Arctic coastal waters. One of them, the narwhal, has an extraordinary spiral tusk, which may grow to over 2.5 m (8 ft 3 in) – sometimes as long as the whale's body. It is in fact a hugely elongated upper incisor, but its precise function is unclear.

BALEEN WHALES

There are three families of baleen whales: the single species of the grey whale family (Eschrichtidae) of the coastal waters of the northern Pacific; three species of right whale (Balaenidae); and six species of rorqual whale (Balaenopteridae). Despite their great size, all baleen species feed by filtering food from sea water. In the southern oceans, krill (tiny planktonic crustaceans) form the principal part of their diet, but other planktonic animal life and even small fish may also be eaten.

In order to accommodate this specialized diet, the teeth are replaced by hundreds of sheets of horny brush-like material known as baleen (or whalebone), which hang from the upper jaw. The inner edges of these sheets are fringed with long fibres, which mat together to form a sieve. When feeding, a baleen whale takes a huge mouthful of water, half shuts the mouth, and then presses the tongue forward. The water is forced out, while the krill (or other food) remains behind and is swallowed.

This diet sustains the vast blue whale which can grow up to 30 m (100 ft) long. It feeds only during the summer, consuming over 2 tonnes of krill daily during this time.

Among the rorqual whales the humpback is more gregarious than the blue whale, and is usually seen in family groups of three or four members. As is the case with other rorquals, these whales are great migrants. They move from their summer feeding grounds off Alaska to spend the winter in the tropical waters off Hawaii, where they give birth to the calves conceived during the previous breeding season, mate, and indulge in their famous singing. Their complex songs usually last about 10 minutes, and may be repeated for hours on end. Their purpose is not clear, but they seem to be mainly confined to the breeding season and are specific to different populations. They may aid identification and help to coordinate movement during migration.

Right whales are so called because they were regarded by whalers as the 'right' whales to kill: they are stockier and less streamlined than other baleen whales, and so more easily overtaken. They have enormous heads, which can accommodate up to 700 baleen plates.

? HOW DO THEY DIVE

▶ Marine mammals are not only able to stay submerged for long periods of time, but also to dive to great depths.
▶ Bottlenose whales occasionally remain underwater for up to two hours, while sperm whales can descend to depths of 1000 m (3300 ft).

Dives are typically long and shallow, or short and steep. For humans, maximum submergence time is only a few minutes and return to the surface from deep dives brings with it the risk of 'the bends' – sickness caused by bubbles of nitrogen forming in the blood vessels and blocking the flow of blood to vital organs.

At the beginning of a dive, marine mammals do not take a lungful of air, but exhale and collapse the lungs. The diaphragm lies at an oblique angle across the body, and as the animal dives and the external water pressure increases, the flexible chest wall collapses inwards and the diaphragm flattens, pushing the little remaining air from the lungs into rigid-walled respiratory passages. Thus at the bottom of the dive, when the water pressure is at its greatest, all air has been excluded from the lungs and excess nitrogen cannot dissolve in the blood. Expelling air prior to a dive also has the added advantage of reducing buoyancy.

Marine mammals limit their oxygen requirements by reducing the flow of blood to all but the most vital organs, such as the brain and heart. 'Surplus' blood is stored in special sinuses. In seals, the heart rate slows from 86 to 16 beats a minute, and metabolism is reduced. The blood of marine mammals can carry more oxygen than that of land mammals, and the swimming muscles store oxygen in a special pigment called myoglobin. The muscles can also work without oxygen for long periods and repay the 'oxygen debt' when the animal surfaces.

■ *The Yangtze river dolphin is found only in Lake Dongting, China, and is now considered an endangered species*

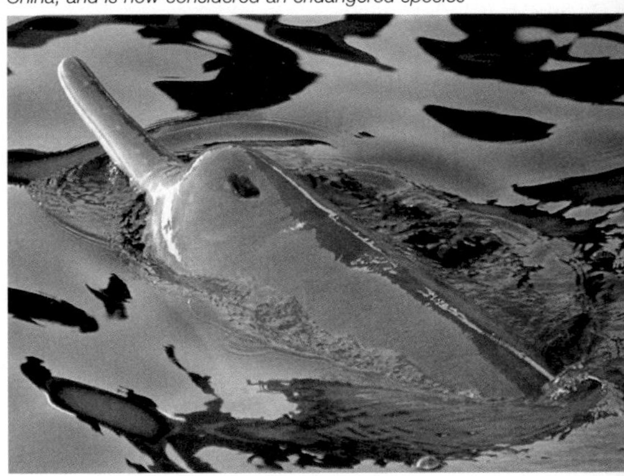

Small Mammals

- Asian and African porcupines have stiff, protective spines on their backs that can grow up to 35 cm in length.
- The three-toed sloth is the slowest mammal, moving at an average speed of 0.1–0.16 km/h.
- The capybara is the world's largest rodent – the size of a small pig – and can weigh up to 50 kg.

RODENTS

▶ The order Rodentia is by far the largest order of mammals, containing around 1650 species in 28 families; they account for about 40% of all known mammal species and occur on all continents except Antarctica.
▶ Many desert-dwelling species (the Australian mice, for example) can live their entire lives without ever drinking – they manage to derive all the water they need from the seeds and grains upon which they feed.

Rodents are remarkably uniform in structure. All have a similar arrangement of the teeth, with two pairs of incisors, one above and one below, then a gap before the cheek teeth – the canines and the anterior premolars are missing. In all species, the characteristic incisors grow continuously. They are coated with enamel on the outside surface only, and thus wear down faster on the inside; and because the upper pair grow over the lower pair and constantly work against them, the incisors are self-sharpening. Many species have cheek pouches, used for carrying food. Rodents are mainly vegetarian, feeding on seeds, leaves, roots and other plant matter. Some species are specialized, rodents in general eat a remarkable variety of foods. Most rodents are relatively small. The largest – the capybara – grows to 50 kg (110 lb) or more, but the majority are less than 1 kg (2.2 lb) and there are many species weighing less than 10 g (⅓ oz).

SQUIRRELS AND SIMILAR RODENTS
Squirrels are found in most countries, except Australia, but are particularly diverse in Asia, where most are tree-dwelling and often very agile. Most are keen-sighted and are active by day. Many are extremely brightly coloured. Some species (the flying squirrels) can glide on a membrane stretched between the front and hind feet.

Ground squirrels are widespread in North America, and some species (prairie dogs) are often highly gregarious. Prairie dogs live in huge colonies ('towns'), which sometimes have populations running into millions and in which a complex system of social organization operates. Marmots, the largest squirrels, can grow to 7.5 kg (16 lb). Unlike the majority of rodents, marmots hibernate.

The two species of beaver, among the larger rodents, are well adapted to their semi-aquatic life style: the ears and nostrils can be closed when the animal is submerged, while the webbed hind feet and paddle-shaped tail provide excellent propulsion and control when swimming.

RATS, MICE AND THEIR RELATIVES
Rats and mice are found almost worldwide. They have long snouts and naked scaly tails, and are among the most successful and adaptable of all mammals. Their powers of reproduction are remarkable: female house mice can breed at the age of six weeks, producing five litters a year. The naked mole rat family (which are not naked, moles nor rats) live entirely in underground burrows and feed on plant roots and bulbs. Virtually blind, they are superb diggers, gnawing their way through soil. Working in teams, they have an extraordinary social organization similar to that found in beehives, with a single dominant reproductively active female. Males are divided into castes of workers and fighters.

PORCUPINES, CAVIES AND THEIR RELATIVES
Most porcupines are active by night, feeding on a variety of plant matter. They are characterized by the long spines (formed from modified hair) that grow thickly on the back and sides. New and Old World species are similar in appearance, but most American porcupines are tree-dwelling. Cavies, or guinea pigs, are ground-dwelling rodents found in South America: most are social, and have the 'plump' character of the pet guinea pig. Although in a separate family, the capybara of South America, the largest rodent, looks like a giant guinea pig. It is semi-aquatic and has partially webbed feet. It too is a social animal, always living in family groups.

■ *The semi-aquatic capybaras live only in South America*

■ *Mole rats live in narrow tunnels in sub-Saharan Africa*

■ *New World porcupine with her young in Montana, USA*

HYRAXES
Hyraxes (dassies) are not rodents, but 11 species of small rodent-like herbivores (family Procaviidae). Living in North Africa and west Asia, they have robust bodies, short tails and short snouts.

RABBITS, HARES AND PIKAS

▶ The order Lagomorpha has just two families: some 40 species of rabbit and hare (Leporidae) and 14 species of pika (Ochotonidae).
▶ Lagomorphs have two pairs of incisors in the upper jaw; only one is functional, the other being tiny and undeveloped.

Lagomorphs are herbivorous, and have the curious habit of eating their own fecal pellets, to gain extra nutritional value from their food. They live in a wide variety of habitats, but generally favour open grassy habitats. The hind limbs are strong and disproportionately large, giving rabbits and hares their swift bounding movement. Although the names are often used loosely, 'rabbit' is usually used to describe those species that live in burrows and give birth to small undeveloped young; hares live in shallow surface depressions (forms), and their young are well developed at birth, with eyes already open and a full coat of hair. As well as enhancing hearing, the large ears typical of rabbits and hares help species that live in dry, hot areas to disperse excess heat. Pikas, or conies, have short rounded ears, a rounded body and a stubby tail. They collect green plants in summer, which they dry and store away for use in winter, but they do not hibernate. The Tibetan pika occupies one of the highest habitats of any mammal – up to 6000 m (20,000 ft) in the Himalaya.

EDENTATES, PANGOLINS AND THE AARDVARK

▶ Pangolins, the aardvark and edentates – armadillos, anteaters and sloths – have a superficial similarity in that they lack some or all of their teeth.
▶ This reduction or loss of teeth is associated with their specialized diet: with the exception of plant-eating sloths, they feed mainly or solely on insects, especially ants and termites.

The order Edentata have small brains with a large olfactory region (scent is important for catching their prey). The feet have efficient claws, which they use to burrow or hang. The Manidae family (the pangolins and scaly anteaters) is nocturnal and tree-dwelling: their overlapping external scales function as armour. The aardvark, which is isolated from all other families, can search out food underground with its snout and swallow it – and still breathe.

ARMADILLOS
The 21 species of armadillo are found in Central and South America, with one species (the nine-banded armadillo) also occurring in the southern USA. They range in size from the endangered giant armadillo, at around 1.5 m (5 ft) long, to the tiny pichiciegos, or fairy armadillos, some 15 cm (6 in) long. Their armour-like plates, made of bone and covered in horny scales, are set in bands and cover most or all of the exposed upper part of the body, including the head and tail. The plates are interspersed with flexible skin, and most armadillos can roll up into a ball for protection. They have powerful claws, are efficient burrowers and feed mostly on insects, worms and other invertebrates, although some species also eat plant matter.

ANTEATERS
The anteater species occur in tropical forests and savannah between Mexico and Argentina. All species are toothless, and have long tapering snouts and sticky tongues to trap ants or termites. The forelimbs have powerful claws for ripping open

insect nests. The giant anteater, the largest species, is ground-dwelling and grows to over 2 m (7 ft) long. Lesser anteaters and the silky (or pygmy) anteater are tree-dwelling, and have prehensile tails.

SLOTHS

The three species of three-toed sloth and two species of two-toed sloth live in tropical forests of Central and South America. They are slow-moving, tree-dwelling vegetarians that spend almost all their life upside down. Their hands and feet have hook-like claws with which they hang from branches: they eat, sleep, mate and give birth upside down.

PANGOLINS

Pangolins (scaly anteaters) resemble armadillos, but their armour is in scales not bands of bony plates. Four species live in Africa, three in Asia. Nocturnal, they eat ants and termites, tearing open nests with their five strong claws on each front foot. Pangolins have a tapering body, a small pointed head, and a long broad tail. Covered in large overlapping horny scales, they can roll into a ball if alarmed. They have no teeth, but their stomachs have muscular walls embedded with tiny stones, enabling them to grind insects. The roots of their tongue muscles are anchored to the pelvis; the tongue can be extended nearly half the length of its body.

THE AARDVARK

The aardvark grows to a length of 1.4 m (4 ft 6 in), and lives in Africa south of the Sahara. It spends the day sheltered in excavated burrows, emerging at night to find ants and termites; it opens nests with its large powerful claws and extracts insects with its long sticky tongue – up to 30 cm (12 in) long.

BATS

▶ **Well over 900 bat species have been described and new ones regularly discovered.**
▶ **Bats are the only mammals that are capable of true flight.**

The flying membrane of bats consists of skin stretched between the four extremely elongated fingers of each hand; only the thumb remains free, and is used for grooming. The elastic membrane is attached to the bat's ankles, and in many species it is connected to the tail. Many species have light, fluttery flight; others are powerful fliers capable of covering great distances: migratory species regularly fly 400 km (250 mi) or more. Bats occur almost worldwide, except the colder regions. Because they fly at night, bats are mostly drab-coloured, usually brown. They vary in size from Kitti's hog-nosed bat of Thailand (about the size of a bumblebee) to fruit bats, with wingspans in excess of 1.5 m (5 ft). Most bats are insectivores, consuming huge numbers of tiny insects, such as midges and mosquitoes, in one night. In the tropics, many species feed on nectar and pollen. The three species of vampire bat feed entirely on the blood of warm-blooded vertebrates. Their front teeth are modified into two triangular razors, which they use to make a small incision. They then lap up the blood. The bat's saliva contains anticoagulants to prevent the blood from clotting. A few species are carnivorous.

Fruit bats (flying foxes), of the tropical and subtropical regions of Australia and the Old World, mostly eat fruit, but some also eat nectar. Most have dog-like faces; many are the rusty colour of the red fox. Most fruit bats have large eyes and rely mainly on sight; they are most active at dusk or dawn, flying up to 70 km (44 mi) in search of fruit.

Fruit bats often live in treetops in communal roosts, often in huge numbers. Smaller fruit bats roost in the roofs of caves, in colonies of up to nine million members. They often move in flocks of a thousand or more to suitable feeding sites. Except most fruit bat species, the majority of bats depend for navigation on echolocation, a sophisticated form of sonar. Echolocation involves emitting high-pitched squeaks (mostly above the range of human hearing) and instinctively measuring how long it takes for the noise to bounce back from intervening objects. By this means bats are able to fly in total darkness.

INSECTIVORES

▶ **The seven families of insectivores (shrews, moles and hedgehogs) comprise 375 species of mammal, the order Insectivora.**
▶ **Some simpler forms appear to be similar to primitive, unspecialized ancestral mammals.**

■ *Pikas, related to rabbits, live in Asia and North America*

■ *Scaly anteater in Mausadona National Park, Zimbabwe*

■ *Three-toed sloth and young, native to tropical rainforests*

Insectivores are small, have long narrow snouts, and simple peg-like teeth. They have five-clawed digits on each limb, and usually have minute eyes and flat feet. Most species live on or under the ground, and generally eat insects, but some are carnivorous.

SHREWS

The most numerous family of insectivores is the shrews, with around 265 species worldwide. Small mouse-like animals, with dense fur and pointed snouts, they are mostly ground-dwelling. A few species have adapted to aquatic life: some species of water shrew have fringes of stiff hairs on their feet to aid swimming. The pygmy white-toothed shrew is one of the world's smallest mammals, weighing about 2 g (1/14 oz). The hero (or armoured) shrew of Central Africa is one of the most resilient: it has a reinforced vertebral column of such extraordinary strength that it can sustain the weight of an adult human, apparently without suffering damage.

Some shrews have poisons in their saliva, which although only mildly toxic to larger animals can incapacitate invertebrates such as earthworms. Shrews are very active, feeding in short bursts. To meet its energy requirements, the common shrew may eat well over its own weight in food in a day. Shrews never hibernate – it would be impossible for them to build up sufficient reserves of food.

MOLES

The 27 or so species of mole (family Talpidae) are confined to the northern hemisphere. They are adapted to life underground and to digging, and are restricted to habitats with soft soil. Their shovel-like forepaws are permanently turned outwards, and they have short thick arms with powerful muscles. The fur is short and velvety, and can brush in any direction, allowing the mole to move backwards and forwards through its tunnels with equal ease. They have very small eyes and are virtually blind, but have long sensitive snouts. Moles mainly eat earthworms, which are trapped as they fall into the mole's system of burrows. Surplus worms are stored, immobilized by having their front segments bitten off.

GOLDEN MOLES

The 18 species of golden mole (family Chrysochloridae) are confined to central and southern Africa. Although structurally similar to true moles, they are only distantly related. Their thick woolly fur has a lustre, often giving them a golden or bronze appearance. Some species, despite being blind, hunt on the surface, but usually only after rain, or at night. Most species feed on invertebrates.

TENRECS

All but three of the 34 species of tenrec (family Tenrecidae) are confined to Madagascar and the Comoros. The common (or tailless) tenrec has rather spiny fur, while the hedgehog tenrecs are so spiny as to be superficially very similar to the true hedgehogs. The three other species of tenrec – the otter shrews – are found in western Africa, and are indeed rather otter-like in appearance.

HEDGEHOGS

The hedgehog family (Erinacidae) has two main groups, the moon rats (gymnures) of South-East Asia, and the true hedgehogs. Moon rats lack spines, but have long blunt-nosed snouts like true hedgehogs, and are among the largest insectivores, weighing up to 2 kg (4.5 lb). True hedgehogs, native to Africa and Eurasia, are covered in spines, and when alarmed can curl into a defensive ball. They feed on a wide range of small invertebrates, such as slugs, snails, insects and their larvae, as well as young mice, birds' eggs and other small animals. The European and Romanian hedgehogs hibernate; more southerly species may aestivate (become torpid) in the summer heat.

SOLENODONS

The two living species of solenodon (family Solenodontidae) are confined to the Caribbean islands of Cuba and Hispaniola. They resemble large robust shrews, and can weigh up to 1 kg (2.2 lb). Although they mostly eat insects and fruit, they also feed on reptiles and poultry. Both species are protected, but are in imminent danger of extinction.

ELEPHANT SHREWS

All species of elephant shrew are found only in Africa. They take their name from their long flexible snout, which can be moved around as the animal searches for food. The largest – growing to around 50 cm (20 in), of which just under half is tail – is the chequered elephant shrew of central Africa, which feeds mainly on ants, termites and beetle larvae.

■ THE FEMALE NORWAY LEMMING HAS THE ABILITY TO REPRODUCE FROM THE AGE OF 14 DAYS ■

PRIMATES

- Orang-utans (which means 'people of the forest') can swing from tree to tree, reaching branches over 2 m apart.
- Lemurs live in essentially matriarchal societies – they form small groups of about 20 members, which are led by the females, within territories marked by the male's scent.
- The largest primate is the male eastern lowland gorilla, which stands up to 1.8 m high and weighs up to 175 kg.
- Human and chimpanzee proteins show a 99% similarity in their amino acid sequences.

WHAT IS A PRIMATE?

▶ The order Primates consists of around 180 species, ranging in size from the tiny mouse lemur to the powerful gorilla.
▶ Apart from man, primates are largely confined to the tropical regions of the world.

Within the Primates order, two suborders are recognized: the prosimians (lower primates), which include lemurs, the aye-aye, lorises and tarsiers; and the anthropoids (higher primates), which include marmosets, monkeys, apes and man.

Although highly varied in form, primates are distinguished as a group by certain common characteristics, including a flexibility of behaviour that is linked to their relatively large brains. Many of their distinguishing characteristics are related to their essentially arboreal (tree-dwelling) nature. While smell is the most important sense for most ground-living mammals, the primates – particularly the anthropoids – have a well-developed visual system, with forward-facing eyes and binocular (i.e. stereoscopic) vision, and a highly refined sense of touch, with sensitive tactile pads on fingers and toes and flat nails rather than claws. It is possible that it was this development of sight and touch that has allowed primates – particularly man – to become so highly versatile in their behaviour. The large brains of primates, notable for the complexity and elaboration of the cerebral cortex, resulted in the development of intelligence, particularly in the higher primates such as man.

■ *A common langur in Kanha National Park, central India*

Other characteristic primate features are prehensile (grasping) hands and feet, vital for moving around safely in trees, and the opposable thumb and big toe, which are capable of being moved freely and rotated. Although less well developed in the prosimians – who were the very first primates to appear (during the Eocene epoch) – this ability gives primates both power and precision in their grip.

Most primates usually have single births or twins, and all have a long life-cycle and gestation period relative to their size. But the most notable feature of primates is not in the gestation period itself, but in the length of time the young remain psychologically dependent on their parents – two to four years in lemurs, three to four years in monkeys, three and a half to five years in apes, and 12–14 years or more in man. These periods of dependence seem to be correlated with brain size and the complexity of the social system.

Although the similarity between man and the ape has long been recognized, the likeness was regarded by many as purely coincidental and no particular significance was placed on the fact. Indeed, when Linnaeus (see p. 108) classified man as a primate in 1758, it was generally regarded as a great blow to human dignity, and subsequent classifications persisted in placing man in a separate order. Only after the discoveries of Darwin (see p. 108) was it generally accepted that man does indeed belong with the primates.

■ *A pygmy marmoset from the upper Amazon basin*

LEMURS

▶ Most of the 22 species of lemur are confined to the forests of Madagascar, although some are found in the nearby Comoro Islands, where they may have been introduced by man.
▶ The smallest lemurs are the seven species of mouse lemur (family Cheirogaleidae), with a head-and-body length of 12–15 cm (5–6 in).

Lemurs are primarily arboreal (tree-dwelling) but may come down to the ground to look for food. Their diet includes insects, small vertebrates, fruit buds, shoots, leaves and bark. Many species are nocturnal. All (except the indri family) have long tails, often longer than the head and body combined. The young are usually produced annually and suckled for six months. Both sexes have special scent glands to mark their territorial boundaries.

Most lemurs (16 species) grow to around 45 cm (18 in). The ring-tailed lemur has a conspicuous bushy tail banded in black and white. It is active by day and spends much time on the ground. The indri (family Indriidae) is the largest lemur, growing up to 90 cm (3 ft) long, and is almost tailless. The closely related sifakas are around half their size and can leap considerable distances from tree to tree – up to 10 m (33 ft).

LORISES, POTTOS AND GALAGOS

▶ Eleven species of the family Lorisidae – the lorises, pottos and galagos (or bushbabies) – are found in Africa and southern Asia.
▶ Lorisidae, mostly nocturnal and arboreal, closely resemble lemurs, except that their large, round eyes are directed more forward.

■ *A spider monkey, found in forests from Brazil to Mexico*

Lorises and pottos are small (less than 40 cm (16 in) long) and have no tails. Although slow-moving and not known to leap or jump, they are skilled climbers. Feeding largely on insects, they approach their prey stealthily and then seize it with their hands.

The galagos, by contrast, are agile leapers and have long furry tails. The largest species, the greater galago, grows to 37 cm (14 ft 6 in) plus a tail of 47 cm (18 ft 6 in) and the smallest, Demidoff's galago, to around 10 cm (4 in) with a tail of 15 cm (6 in). Galagos eat a wide variety of insects and other small animals, as well as gums and nectar.

TARSIERS

▶ The three closely related species of tarsier (family Tarsiidae) are found in the forests and other thickly vegetated habitats of the Philippines and Indonesia.
▶ The tarsier's most obvious features are its huge eyes, which are 16 mm (⅔ in) in diameter.

Tarsiers are at the most 16 cm (6 ft 4 in) long, with a naked tail up to 27 cm (11 in). They have short arms

■ PRIMATES ARE THE ONLY GROUP THAT CAN PRESS THEIR THUMBS AGAINST THEIR FINGERS and long legs, and the fingers and toes are all tipped with soft round pads enabling them to grip almost any surface. They are proficient jumpers: on the ground they can leap distances of 1.7 m (5 ft 6 in) and to a height of 0.6 m (2 ft), and can make even greater leaps from tree to tree.

MARMOSETS AND TAMARINS

▶ The family Callitrichidae (marmosets and tamarins) is the smallest of the anthropoids – they have body lengths of 13–37 cm (5¼–15 in) and long tails.
▶ Marmosets and tamarins live primarily in tropical forest, especially in the Amazon basin.

Marmosets and tamarins, along with the monkeys of the Cebidae family (see below), are the only non-human primates found in the New World. Both families have flat noses with widely spaced nostrils, in contrast to the Old World monkeys (see right). Many have tufts or ruffs of fur round their heads, and all have claws on hands and feet, with a flat nail only on the big toe. Like all the anthropoids, except the night monkey, they are active by day. They are mainly arboreal, bounding swiftly through the trees rather like squirrels. They have a varied diet including nuts, insects, bark and sap, and are sociable animals living in small family groups.

THE OLD WORLD MONKEYS

▶ The 85 species of Old World monkey (family Cercopithecidae) include the macaques, mandrills, mangabeys and others.
▶ They are found in Africa and Asia, in a much greater range of habitats than the South American monkeys.

Old World monkeys walk on all fours and have thin noses with forward-pointing nostrils. None has a prehensile tail. Some species, such as baboons, are found in arid, open, often rocky areas, and spend most of their time on the ground, although they usually sleep in trees. The Japanese macaque is the only primate other than man that lives in latitudes where winter temperatures drop below freezing.

The Old World monkeys are generally larger than the South American primates, and often have heavy manes and bare buttock pads, sometimes brightly coloured. The male proboscis monkey of Borneo has a huge pendulous nose up to 18 cm (7 in) long that straightens out when it makes its loud honking call. The females are generally smaller – sometimes only half the size – and less brightly coloured, with lighter manes or none at all. Old World monkeys are primarily vegetarian, but some may supplement their diet with insects and small animals.

THE GREAT APES

▶ The four types of great ape – the orang-utan, chimpanzee, bonobo and gorilla – are man's closest living relatives.
▶ Despite their ferocious reputations, gorillas rarely fight – instead, they try to scare their enemies by staring at them, roaring, thumping their chests and tearing up plants.

The arboreal orang-utan, confined to the rainforests of Borneo and Sumatra, is the second largest primate, weighing up to 90 kg (198 lb). Males are much larger and heavier than females, and as they grow old they develop distinctive cheek flaps. Orang-utans live alone or in small family groups. Fruit is their staple diet.

The chimpanzee is found in Africa, having a relatively wide range in woodland and forest south of the Sahara and north and east of the River Congo, while the pygmy chimpanzee, or bonobo, is found only in The Congo (ex-Zaïre). Like gorillas and man, chimpanzees are largely terrestrial, and both chimpanzees and gorillas walk on the knuckles of their hands. Chimpanzees are intelligent and social animals, using a wide range of gestures and sound for communication. They live in groups of varying composition, sometimes having as many as 50 members. Basically vegetarian, they eat a wide range of food, which can also include insects, birds' eggs and small birds and mammals. They use sticks as tools to winkle termites or ants from their mounds, hurl stones at intruders, and use leaves as sponges to soak up water. They build nests to sleep in, constructing a fresh one each night. The young live with their mothers for about three years.

The largest of the primates is the gorilla, found in the forests of the Congo basin, with isolated populations of mountain gorillas on the slopes of the mountains between Rwanda and The Congo (ex-Zaïre). When standing they are not much taller than large chimpanzees, but they are much more heavily and powerfully built. A male gorilla may measure up to 175 cm (70 in) around the chest and weigh up to 275 kg (606 lb). Although females and young gorillas climb trees, males rarely do so because of their size. Gorillas live in close-knit family groups of 12–14 with a 'silverback' (a mature male, so-called because his hair has begun to turn grey) at the head. Gorillas are almost exclusively vegetarian in their diet; like chimpanzees, they build a nest each night to sleep in.

■ *A male mandrill, showing his multicoloured markings*

■ *An elder and younger chimpanzee in northern Zambia*

■ *The tree-dwelling orang-utan in Camp Leakey, Borneo*

THE NEW WORLD MONKEYS

▶ There are 31 species of cebidaens (New World monkeys), including capuchins, howlers, spider monkeys and woolly monkeys.
▶ They are mostly confined to the tropical forests of South America and are largely arboreal (tree-dwelling).

Apart from the uakari, the New World monkeys all have long, often strongly prehensile, tails, which serve as a fifth limb when swinging through the forest. Often the tail has other special features which help it to grip, such as the rubbery skin on the underside of the spider monkey's tail. They range in size from the squirrel monkeys, which are around the size of marmosets, to the massive howler monkeys, with body lengths of 80–90 cm (31–35 in). Howlers are noted for their powerful voices, which can be heard up to 3 km (2 mi) away. The male howler calls loudly for periods of up to half an hour to signal possession of a territory. All New World monkeys are gregarious, living in family-based groups with much visual and vocal communication. Their diet is largely vegetarian.

THE GIBBONS (LESSER APES)

▶ The nine species of gibbon are all found in the forests of South-East Asia and Indonesia.
▶ The largest gibbon is the siamang, with a body length of 90 cm (3 ft) and a spread of 1.5 m (5 ft) from hand to hand.

All members of the ape family (Pongidae) have protruding jaws and lack tails, but the slender, agile gibbons are otherwise very different from the sturdy, powerful great apes. Smaller in size, they are perhaps the best adapted of all mammals for moving swiftly through the forest canopy, using their extremely long arms and hooked hands to swing from branch to branch. Their deeply cleft thumbs and big toes can be strongly opposed to the other digits, giving them enormous dexterity.

Most male gibbons have an inflatable throat sac used to amplify their voice. The loud calls are important both for communicating within the family group (usually of two to six members), and for defining their territory. Primarily fruit eaters, they also eat plants, eggs, insects and other small animals.

The Human Body

- The longest bone in the body is the femur, or thigh bone, which is likely to be 50 cm long in a man 1.8 m tall.
- The largest artery is the aorta, which has a diameter of 3 cm at the point where it leaves the heart.
- The stomach, when empty, has a capacity of 0.5 litre but can expand to 5 litres in order to hold a large meal.
- Each day, 7 litres of digestive fluid are secreted into the human digestive tract.
- In the course of a year, the average human male would produce enough sperm to populate the world five times over.

THE SKELETON

▶ The skeleton supports the soft tissues of the body, giving it shape and form.
▶ Children have about 300 bones, but some of these fuse together so that the adult human body contains only 206 bones.

Apart from giving the body shape, the skeleton has several other functions. It protects the internal organs, such as the brain, lungs and heart, from injury and enables the body, along with the attached muscles, to undertake movement. Bones also store minerals such as calcium and phosphorus. Some bones contain a substance called bone marrow, which is responsible for manufacturing the millions of red blood cells which are essential to life.

Bones are living organs and the bone cells are supplied with oxygen and nutrient molecules, such as glucose, via blood vessels, which are enclosed in tunnels in the bone. The outside of a bone is hard and compact, but within lies spongy bone which contains spaces in the red bone marrow where red blood cells are synthesized. The red marrow cells produce red blood cells in the ribs, pelvis and sternum (the breast bone). In the centre of the larger bones of the body is yellow marrow which is fatty; it functions as an energy store.

Bones are connected together by flexible joints called ligaments, and muscles are connected to bones by means of tendons. Both ligaments and tendons are made of cartilage, the material which meat-eaters recognize as gristle.

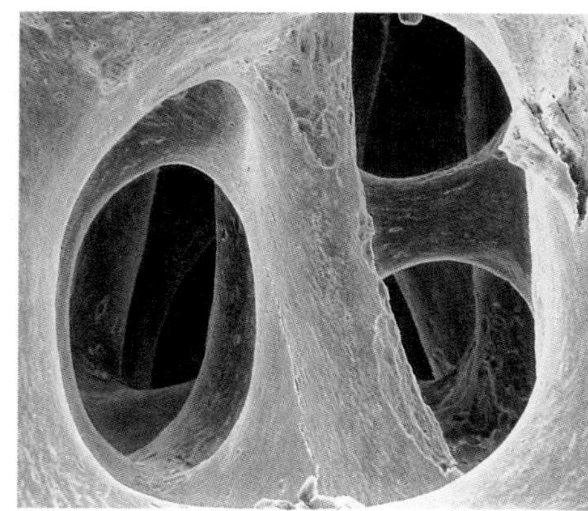

■ *Long bones, such as the femur, consist of two types of bones: exterior compact bone and interior cancellous (spongy) bone, shown on the right. This cancellous bone, arranged like an open honeycomb, is made up of trabeculae – sculptured pillars of bone that form cavities which, in living tissue, contain bone marrow*

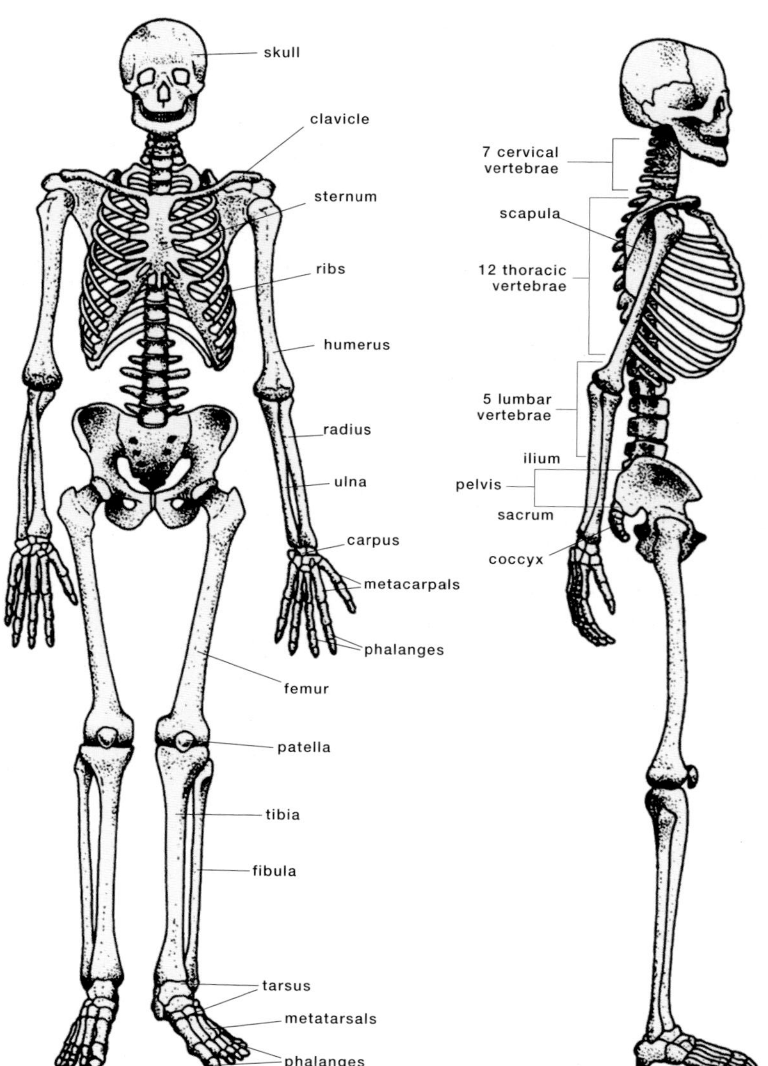

■ *Front and side view of the human skeleton with the main bones labelled. There are c. 206 bones in the human skeleton, containing about 2/3 of the body's calcium and phosphorus, which account for about one-sixth of a human's body weight*

TYPES OF JOINT

Bones meet one another to form joints, of which there are six main types. The degree of movement possible at a joint is determined by the surface of the bone ends and the joint space and fluid between them.

Ball and socket
The hip joint is an example of a ball-and-socket joint, where a long bone, ending in a ball, fits into a socket. The large smooth-surfaced ball, covered in cartilage, is lubricated by synovial fluid and movement is possible in any direction.

Saddle
The joint between the thumb and hand is a saddle joint, allowing movement in many directions, giving the hand its incredible dexterity.

Hinge
The knee and elbow are hinge joints, with movement mostly in one plane.

Condyloid
These joints, between the bones of the hand and the fingers and between the foot and toes, are round or ellipsoid in shape. They allow both rotation and backward and forward movement.

Pivotal
A pivotal joint is mainly restricted to rotational movement. Where the first vertebra – the atlas (so named because it holds the weight of the head) – joins the next vertebra, the axis, a pivotal joint is formed. Movement occurs between the ring of the atlas and the toothlike peg of the axis, allowing rotation or turning of the head to look over the shoulder.

Plane
A plane joint, such as that between the pelvis and the base of the spine (known as the sacro-iliac joint), allows only very limited movement, except in pregnancy when the pelvis expands to accommodate the growing foetus.

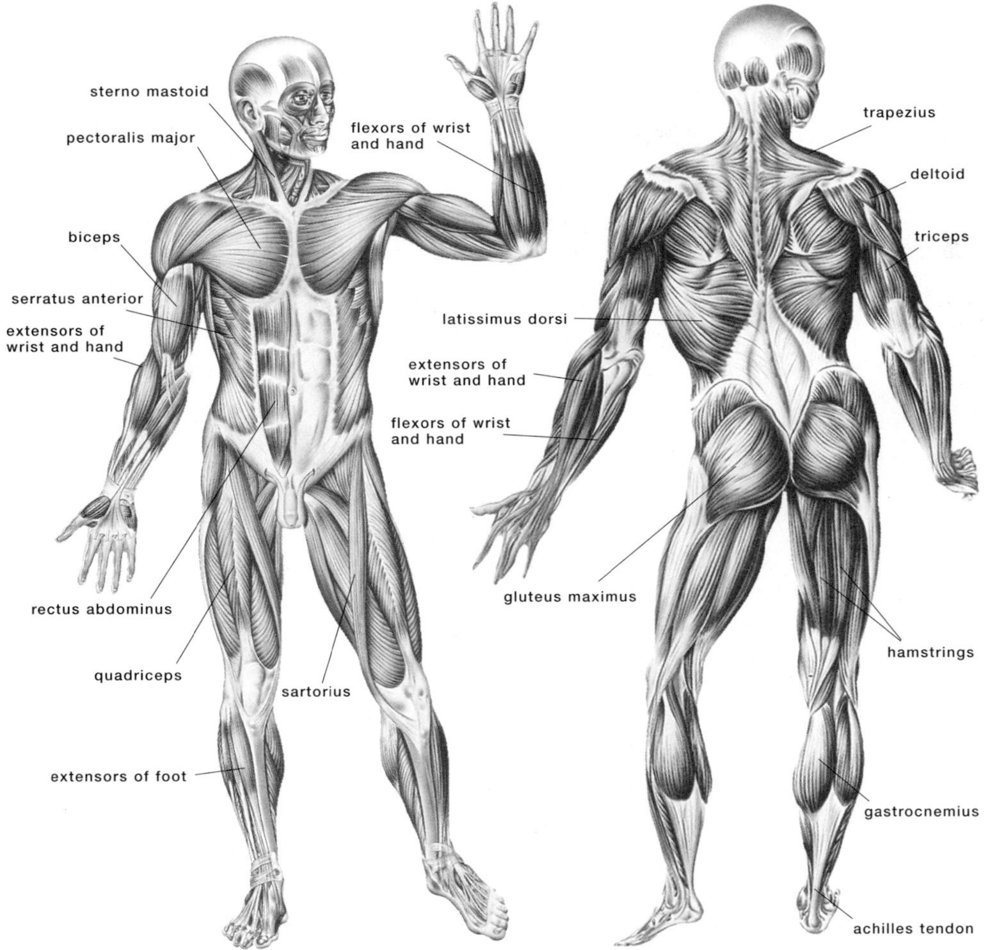

■ *The front and back view of the human skeletal muscles with the main muscles of the body labelled. The white areas are tendons, which attach the (red) muscles, known as the voluntary muscles, to the bones of the skeleton. Skeletal muscle accounts for up to 45% of a human being's body weight*

MUSCLES

▶ Muscles make up 30% of the human body.
▶ There are 600 individual muscles which are under voluntary control, and if they could all pull together they would be able to lift a load of 25 tonnes.

Muscle is basically of two types: that which can be controlled by the owner, known as voluntary, striped or skeletal muscle, and that which cannot be controlled, otherwise known as smooth, autonomic or involuntary muscle. Although the heart muscle is not under the owner's direct control it is usually classed separately as cardiac muscle.

VOLUNTARY MUSCLE

Voluntary muscle is composed of long thin cells or fibres enclosed in an outer coat. Under a microscope, the muscle fibres show alternate light and dark bands, which is why they are sometimes referred to as striped. When a message to move is sent by the brain to a muscle via the nerves, its contraction is triggered by the receipt of a chemical messenger molecule called acetyl choline, which is released by the motor neurone (nerve) cell. The muscle fibres contain two protein molecules, actin and myosin, which telescope together causing contraction. When fully contracted, a muscle such as the biceps can contract up to 50% in length to produce a powerful movement of the arm. These movements are fuelled by the molecule ATP (adenosine triphosphate). Thus, every movement one makes is accomplished by the co-operation of thousands of muscle fibres which contain millions of molecules working together.

Although human beings can directly cause voluntary muscles to contract, they rarely do so. The usual course is to direct a movement, like walking upstairs. Such a command initiates action in whole groups of muscles that act in harmony to perform a coordinated manoeuvre.

INVOLUNTARY MUSCLE

Involuntary or smooth muscle is found in the walls of the digestive tract, in the respiratory system, and in the urinary and reproductive tracts. It is the main tissue in the middle coat of the smaller arteries and determines the diameter of these vessels. By regulating the resistance of the vessels, it controls the distribution of blood to the various tissues and organs and helps control blood pressure.

In the eye, involuntary muscle controls the amount of light entering by adjusting the size of the pupil, and in the skin it causes the hair to stand erect when we are cold or frightened.

This type of muscle has the simplest construction, but it is capable of very strong contractions. During birth the smooth muscle of the uterus contracts powerfully to expel the foetus, and the act of defecating or vomiting brings smooth muscle in the digestive tract into play with considerable force.

CARDIAC MUSCLE

The heart muscle is unique in construction. Certain special fibres make up the conducting system by which electrical impulses spread to the other fibres and bring about the rhythmical sequence of contraction and relaxation that allows the heart to empty itself of blood and then refill.

THE CIRCULATORY SYSTEM

▶ The heart and blood vessels form a closed system, with the blood circulating continuously around within it.
▶ The heart is a very powerful muscle, contracting between 60 and 200 times a minute depending on the level of activity.

The heart is a double pump – a right and a left pump – each consisting of two chambers, an atrium and a ventricle. The right atrium receives blood from parts of the body and passes it into the right ventricle, which pumps it to the lungs (pulmonary circulation). The oxygenated blood then returns to the left atrium and into the left ventricle, which pumps it to all parts of the body (systemic circulation).

Blood is pumped around the body by the heart in order to carry oxygen and nutrients (including glucose) to the cells and to receive the waste products of the cells, such as water and carbon dioxide. To ensure that the blood moves in only one direction through the heart, the openings between the atria and ventricles and between the ventricles and blood vessels are guarded by valves.

The blood vessels leaving the heart are called arteries. The pulmonary artery goes to the lungs and the aorta to all the organs and tissues of the body. As they get further from the heart, they branch into smaller and smaller arteries. Arteries appear circular in cross-section, with thick muscular walls. The smaller arteries eventually become capillaries – thin-walled vessels through which oxygen and other substances are transferred between the blood and interstitial fluid (fluid which comes from tiny openings between the vessels). At the same time, carbon dioxide and other waste products leave the interstitial fluid and enter the blood. The capillaries then converge, forming larger and larger vessels known as veins, which are thin-walled and of indefinite shape. Veins contain valves which aid the movement of blood from the lower parts of the body, against gravity. Eventually they merge into two large veins – the superior vena cava and inferior vena cava – which return blood to the right atrium.

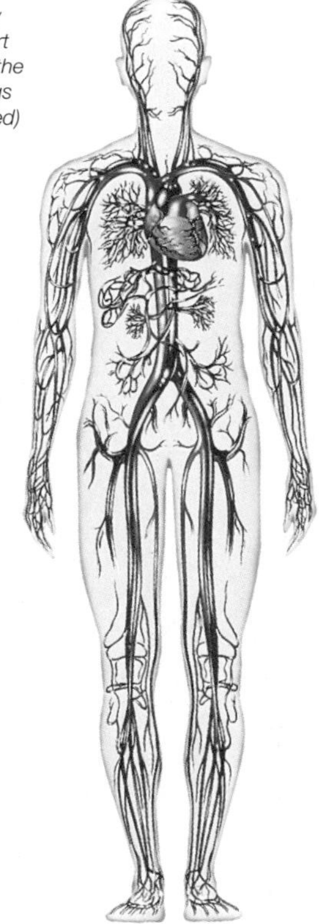

■ *The human circulatory system showing the heart in the upper centre and the blood vessels of the lungs on each side. Arteries (red) carry the oxygenated blood to the body and veins (blue) return the deoxygenated blood to the heart. The body of an average adult contains about 5 litres of blood*

HUMAN REPRODUCTION

▶ A baby develops from the union of one of its mother's eggs and one sperm cell from its father.
▶ Sperm carries 23 chromosomes (threadlike structures that bear genes containing DNA) and every cell that grows from the fused egg and sperm will contain 46 chromosomes.

Even before birth, a female baby possesses her full quota of ova, or eggs, stored in the ovaries – two glands that, in adults, are about the size of pigeons' eggs. Only a few ova will ever ripen and have the potential to be fertilized by sperm.

The human male is also born with cells that will produce sperm in adult life. Sperm are produced in the testes at the rate of 1000 per second.

Each sperm starts with 46 chromosomes but sheds half of these as it matures (a process that takes 74 days). If it loses its Y chromosome and goes on to fertilize an egg, the resulting baby will be a girl; if the X chromosome has been shed the child will be a boy. A mature sperm is still less than 0.05 mm (1/500 in) long.

OVULATION

Each month one ovum ripens, breaks free from its protective follicle and is swept up by the fringe-like endings (fimbriae) of one of the fallopian tubes. Its journey down the fallopian tube to the uterus (womb) lasts four days. For a few hours only it is in a state of readiness to be fertilized by a sperm. If it is unfertilized, it will pass on and out of the woman's body. The enriched blood supply lining the uterus in preparation for receiving a fertilized ovum is shed soon after.

COITUS AND FERTILIZATION

During sexual intercourse, or coitus, the erect penis is inserted into the vagina and rhythmical movements lead to orgasm and the ejaculation of semen – sperm in a nutrient fluid. A sperm swims by using rapid movements of its long, threadlike tail, and the head of the sperm contains stores of glucose to provide energy for its long swim to the ovum. The sperm swim from the neck of the womb at 3 mm (1/8 in) per hour towards the top of the womb where the two fallopian tubes open out. If there is an egg in one of the fallopian tubes, a few hundred sperm may reach it, having journeyed for about six hours. Only one sperm is able to penetrate the egg. Having shed its tail, the sperm merges with the egg to produce a single cell called the zygote.

■ *Illustration of the process of fertilization showing penetration of an ovum by a single spermatozoon*

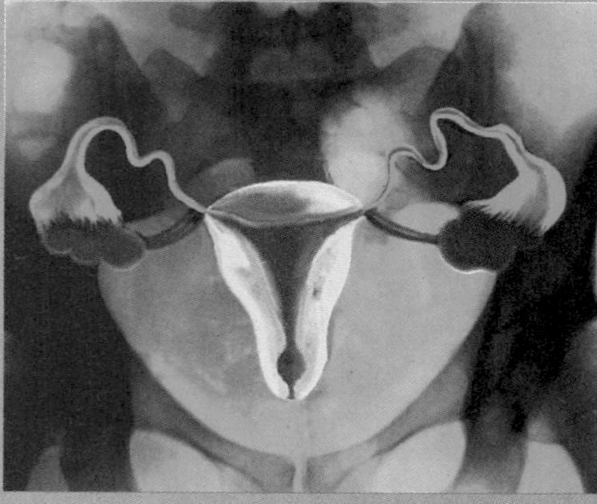

■ *Coloured X-ray of the female reproductive organs, showing the ovaries (pink), where the egg is released, and the fallopian tube (blue), which carries the egg to the uterus (red and yellow) where the egg may implant and grow into a foetus*

CELL DIVISION AND IMPLANTATION

Within hours of conception the fertilized egg (zygote) begins to divide. Three days after fertilization, the zygote has divided three times producing eight cells. Four days later, containing 16 cells, the zygote reaches the uterus.

Three days after that, the zygote implants itself into the uterine wall. Now called a blastocyst and 0.1 mm (1/250 in) in size, its cells change into two types – embryoblast cells that will eventually become the baby, and trophoblast cells that will form the placenta. The placenta is the developing baby's life-support system, bringing oxygen and nutrients for its growth and taking away carbon dioxide and other wastes via the umbilical cord.

At five weeks, the embryo is only 1 cm (2/5 in) long but it shows eyes, heart, liver and the rudiments of all other organs. Throughout, the developing child is contained in a water-filled sac called the amnion, filled with amniotic fluid. At seven weeks the first bone cells appear in cartilage and it is then classified as a foetus. By 14 weeks the foetus is 6 cm (2⅓ in) long and at 24 weeks it is about 30 cm (12 in) in length.

BIRTH

The baby is born when a series of strong contractions of the womb is initiated by an interplay of hormonal signals from the mother and from the baby. There are three clearly defined stages of labour.

In the first stage, the muscular wall of the uterus gradually builds up the force and frequency of its contractions until the cervix (neck of the womb) is fully dilated. This stage is the longest, taking an average of 8–10 hours for a first baby.

The second stage is shorter (½–2 hours). The baby moves down the birth canal (the cervix and vagina) and is born. The uterus contracts swiftly and forcefully during this stage and the mother experiences an overwhelming desire to 'bear down' or push with her abdominal muscles to help the baby to be born.

The third stage is the delivery of the placenta or 'afterbirth'.

Changing hormone levels trigger the production of milk in the mother's mammary glands soon after the baby's birth.

THE IMMUNE SYSTEM

▶ White blood cells known as lymphocytes form one of the immune system's most important components.
▶ If an infection is present, lymphocytes multiply, causing the swelling of glands, for example, in the armpits and under the jaw.

The cells destined to become lymphocytes originate in the bone marrow. Some of them travel in the blood to the thymus gland in the neck, where they mature into T-lymphocytes. The thymus gland seems to have a role in ensuring that only those T cells that recognize foreign proteins (as opposed to the body's own proteins) are released into the circulatory system. However, some of the immature cells remain in the bone marrow for the rest of their development and become B-lymphocytes. Once mature, the T and B cells migrate in the blood to the spleen, the lymph nodes and other components of the lymphoid tissue, such as the tonsils.

The spleen is an organ found on the left side of the body, below the diaphragm. One of its functions is to filter circulating micro-organisms from the blood. The lymph nodes, present throughout the body, filter the lymph – a clear fluid that drains from the body tissues. The lymph collects in the vessels of the lymphatic system and eventually returns to the blood, first passing through the lymph nodes where any micro-organisms or cancer cells are filtered out.

The body defends itself from attack by invaders using white blood cells of two main types. One type, called a phagocyte, acts like an amoeba. It can squeeze out between the gaps between cells of capillaries and ingest bacteria. The other type produces protein molecules called antibodies, which stick foreign cells and viruses together into clumps which are then ingested by the amoeboid white cells.

THE RESPIRATORY SYSTEM

▶ Respiration is the process whereby blood is oxygenated in the lungs – oxygen and carbon dioxide are produced by the body's tissues and carbon dioxide is removed from the blood in the lungs.
▶ If you spread out the human lungs, the surface area would be 100 m² (1076 sq ft).

Air enters the respiratory system through the nose or mouth and passes down the trachea, which

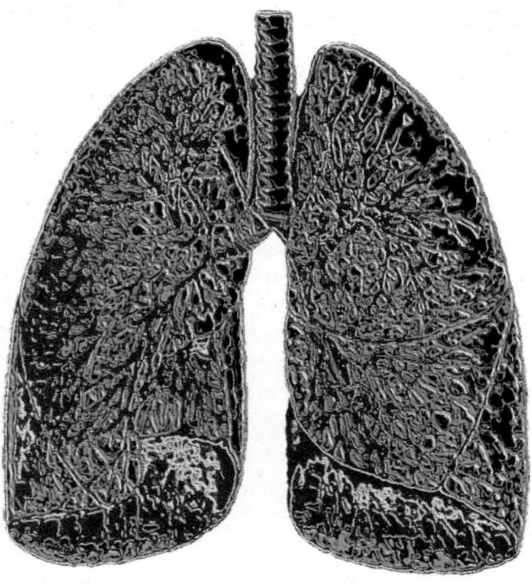

■ *The human lungs with the trachea, or windpipe (upper centre), which introduces air into the respiratory system. The trachea branches into two bronchi which divide, within each lung, into a network of smaller, finer bronchioles that finally end in tiny air sac alveoli (too small to be seen here)*

■ THE HUMAN INTESTINES ARE APPROXIMATELY 9 M IN LENGTH ■ HUMAN DNA IS 90%

branches in the lungs into smaller and smaller tubes or bronchioles, and finally into alveoli. Here oxygen passes into fine capillaries and carbon dioxide from the blood is released and discharged to be exhaled.

This occurs as a result of muscle contraction. Breathing in (inspiration) occurs when two sets of muscle contract – the diaphragm, which separates the chest from the abdomen, and the intercostals, which lie between each rib. Contraction of these muscles increases the volume within the thoracic cavity (chest). This causes the lungs to expand and air to rush in. When the muscles stop contracting, they relax passively and the lungs deflate again, forcing the air out (expiration).

THE DIGESTIVE SYSTEM

▶ The gastrointestinal tract is a long tube about 9 m (30 ft) long, which passes through the body from the mouth to the anus.
▶ Food and drink are broken down here by the digestive system to release small molecules (water, amino acids, sugars, fats, mineral salts and vitamins) which pass into the bloodstream, from where any cell can draw its requirements.

After cutting and crushing by the teeth, food is mixed with saliva which contains the enzymes which start the breakdown of starch into sugars. The food then passes down the oesophagus into the acidic environment of the stomach, which acts as a temporary storage area and mixes the food until it is in a semi-fluid state called chume. This is then released slowly into the duodenum.

Most digestion takes place in the duodenum. Enzymes, secreted by the pancreas into the duodenum, split proteins into amino acids, fats into fatty acids, and glycerol and polysaccharides into glucose and fructose. These are absorbed through the walls of the ileum (part of the small intestine). The small intestine is 7 m (23 ft) long and lined with countless fingerlike projections (villi) which increase the surface area up to the size of a tennis court. From here, glucose, fructose and amino acids are absorbed into the bloodstream and carried to the liver. Fatty acids and glycerol are absorbed into the lymphatic system and enter the bloodstream later.

Substances that cannot be digested pass into the colon (the large intestine) which is about 1.5 m (5 ft) long. The colon functions to remove most of the remaining water. Some compounds are fermented by the bacteria there and others are excreted as waste products in the faeces via the rectum.

THE NERVOUS SYSTEM

▶ The nervous system is a vast, complex network regulating every aspect of human life.
▶ The central nervous system, consisting of the brain and spinal cord, governs the body's network – its role is largely to do with sensations and voluntary movement.

The central nervous system communicates with the peripheral nervous system through 12 pairs of cranial nerves and 31 pairs of spinal nerves, which leave the brain and spinal cord. These nerve fibres eventually make their way to the body extremities.

The body also has an autonomic nervous system which has been called the 'involuntary nervous system' because of its role in controlling physiological events in which normally there is no conscious input. These include routine matters of body maintenance, such as breathing, heart rate, blood flow, temperature control, digestion, glandular secretion and excretion.

NERVE CELLS

The basic functional unit of the nervous system is the nerve cell, or neurone. There are billions of neurones in the central nervous system, varying greatly in shape and size, but all communicate with their neighbours electrochemically, forming an intricate network with a circuitry far more complex than that of the most advanced electronic computer.

Neurones consist of a cell body, with its nucleus, and projecting filaments – the axon and the dendrites. The axon is the cell's longest process – its 'main cable' – and it carries outgoing signals. An axon may extend all the way from the central nervous system to a finger or toe to connect with the muscle on which it acts. Axons are like telephone cables in that they have a central electrical conductor surrounded by an insulating layer. Smaller axons conduct impulses smoothly and slowly – about 1 m (39 in) per second. Larger fibres conduct much faster – up to 100 m (328 ft) per second. The dendrites, which vary in number, are the short, branched, threadlike extensions of nerve cells which pick up messages from other cells.

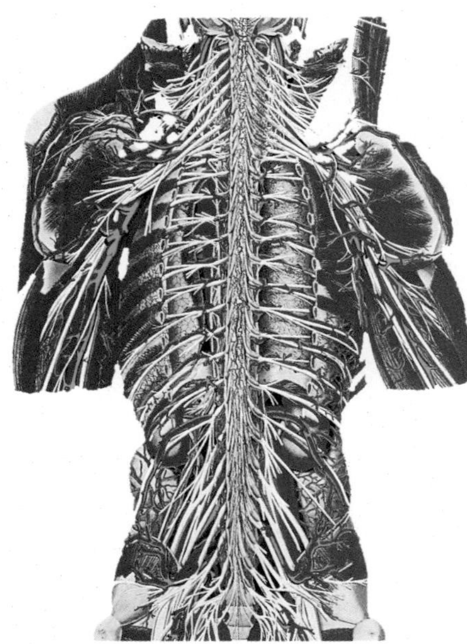

■ *Illustration showing the human spinal cord and nerves, the red and blue blood vessels and the red muscles of the back and upper arms. The spinal cord is a mass of (yellow) nerve fibres running vertically. The lowest nine nerves supply the legs, forming a spray known as the* cauda equina

THE ENDOCRINE SYSTEM

▶ The endocrine system, together with the nervous system, allows cells to communicate with one another.
▶ Endocrine glands are groups of cells which produce a messenger molecule, or hormone, which is released directly into the blood stream.

The endocrine system consists of endocrine glands, scattered throughout the body, which produce chemicals (hormones) that are transported in the blood to distant tissues whose activity they modify. Hormones exert their effects in four basic biological areas: growth and development, energy production regulation, internal environment control, reproduction.

Examples of hormones are insulin, which regulates glucose levels, and adrenaline, which mediates the flight/fight response. There are about ten main glands from head to groin which manufacture and release hormones, including the pituitary at the base of the brain (which secretes at least nine different hormones), the thyroid in the neck, and the ovaries in women or the testes in men. Some glands respond to chemical levels in the blood and others to nerve signals from the brain.

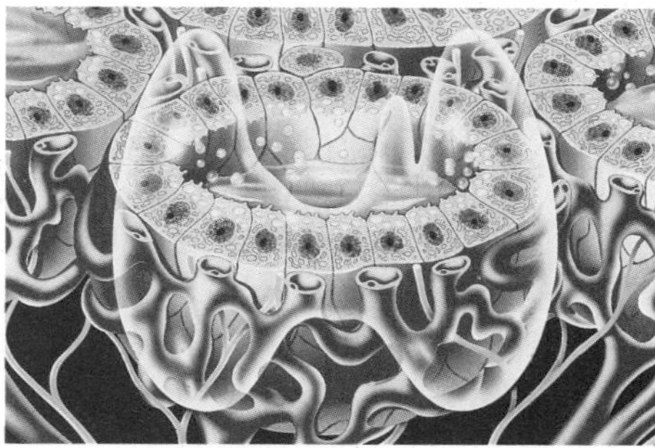

■ *Illustration of cell structure of thyroid gland (outlined at centre) which controls metabolism and growth. The round follicles (purple), surrounded by capillaries (red), secrete hormones (light blue) into a central storage chamber*

THE URINARY SYSTEM

▶ The kidneys receive 25% of the blood flow from the heart and, although 1000 litres (260 gallons) of blood is filtered each day, only about 1 litre (1/5 gallon) of fluid is excreted as urine – the other 999 litres of fluid is reabsorbed.
▶ The kidneys dispose of excess water from the body and also filter the blood 300 times a day.

Many chemical reactions that take place in the body produce compounds that would be toxic if allowed to accumulate. Blood must therefore be purified and toxic waste products excreted – the role of the kidneys. Each kidney contains one million tiny filtration units (nephrons), each dealing with a droplet of blood at a time. The high pressure in the small capillaries in the kidney forces the fluid part of the blood through the capillary walls. Blood cells and proteins are too large to squeeze through the gaps in the capillary wall and remain. Much of the filtrate, such as water and useful solutes such as glucose and salts, is reabsorbed into the capillaries.

The residue from this process – urine – contains excess salts and urea. Urine from the kidneys is stored in the bladder. The bladder feels full when in fact it is only 25% full. If urination is delayed, the muscles and nerves of the bladder wall temporarily stop sending signals to the brain, so that humans can choose the moment of urination, rather than having to empty the bladder automatically when full.

■ *X-ray of the human kidneys (the branched green structures at top), with the long (green) ureters which lead to the bladder, where there is a pool of urine (also green)*

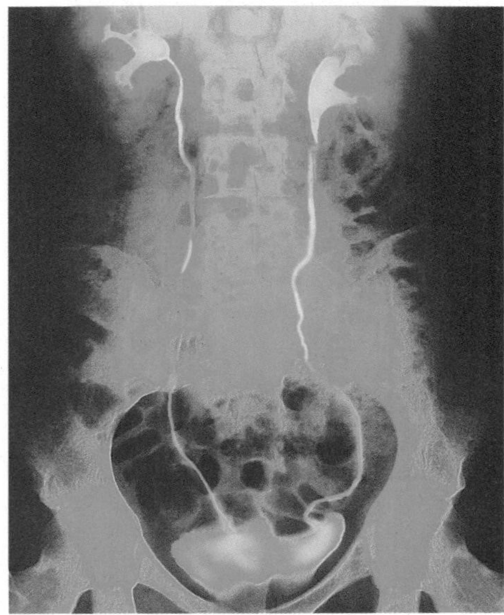

Infectious Diseases

▷ **The oldest known infection is leprosy, a disease characterized by skin lesions and destruction of the peripheral nerves leading to loss of sensation, which was first described in ancient Egypt in 1350 BC.**

▷ **The Great Plague in London (1664–65) killed one in six of the population. Plague is a rodent-borne disease that can be transmitted to man by flea bites or by airborne infection.**

▷ **Incurable infections include Creutzfeldt-Jakob disease (CJD), AIDS, Lassa fever, diphtheria and poliomyelitis.**

▷ **AIDS is now the most extensively researched infectious disease in the world. It was first identified in Los Angeles, California, USA, in 1981.**

▷ **Evidence of tuberculosis (TB) has been found in an Egyptian mummy from the 10th century BC.**

An infectious disease is one in which an organism inhabits and multiplies on or within another, harming it in the process. It does this either by producing toxic substances or by damaging, digesting or destroying part or all of the other organism's cellular structure. Such harmful organisms are mostly microscopic – viruses, bacteria and protozoans – but some are much larger, for example fungi, worms and insects. For many years it was thought that infections were receding. In recent years, however, resistance to modern antibiotics and the appearance of new diseases, such as AIDS and Creutzfeldt-Jakob disease, has shown that these organisms are still a major threat to health. Infections can be transmitted in the following ways:

Airborne transmission infection through infected droplets in the air from the nose, throat/lungs or saliva, or from dust particles from fallen skin.
Contamination infection through food or water supplies containing infected material such as faeces or urine.
Direct contact (contagion) infection from close contact with an infected person.
Sexual transmission infection through vaginal or anal intercourse, or oral sex. The use of condoms may reduce the risk of infection.
Blood-borne transmission infection through the injection of contaminated blood or blood products, or by improperly sterilized instruments. Blood-borne transmission is most common among haemophiliacs and intravenous drug users, and is occasionally the result of tattooing or acupuncture.
Animal-borne transmission infection through the injection of contaminated saliva; for example malaria (carried by the mosquito) and bubonic plague (transmitted by flea bites).

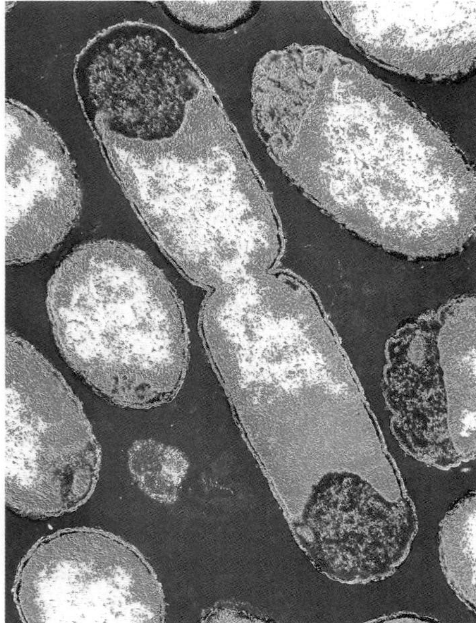

■ *Colour-enhanced magnification of the bacterium* Escherichia coli, *commonly known as* E. coli, *an organism often used in genetic engineering experiments. The pair in the centre are in the act of separating following binary fission, the process by which a bacterium divides in two.* E. coli *usually inhabits the human intestine but, under certain conditions, can become harmful, causing infection*

AIDS
AIDS – acquired immune deficiency syndrome – was first identified in Los Angeles, USA, in 1981. The virus responsible for causing AIDS was isolated in 1983 and has become known as HIV (human immunodeficiency virus). The disease is spreading rapidly throughout the western world, and has reached epidemic proportions in Africa and parts of South-East Asia.

The virus attacks one particular type of white blood cell in the body (the helper/inducer lymphocytes) and this eventually causes immunosuppression (reduced ability to combat infection). It may also attack the nervous system and cause dementia. Those infected with HIV do not go on to develop AIDS immediately, but once it does occur, the course of the disease usually involves increasingly serious episodes of infection, and it is often fatal within two years.

Advances in treatment now offer real hope to those who are infected by the virus but have not yet gone on to develop full-blown AIDS. Regular therapy with combinations of new drugs seems to reduce the number of viruses circulating in the blood and thus prevents them damaging the body's immune system.

ANTHRAX
Anthrax is a form of blood poisoning in cattle, sheep and horses that is normally fatal. It can upon rare occasions be passed to vets or butchers disposing of infected carcases or to people handling infected animal hides, wool or bone meal.

CHOLERA
Cholera is an acute infection of the intestine that causes profuse watery diarrhoea, vomiting and dehydration. It is caused by drinking water or eating food contaminated by the bacterium *Vibrio comma*, which is found in faeces.

Vaccination is effective for six to nine months, after which booster doses are needed.

COMMON COLD (CORYZAL)
At least 40 different viruses – either airborne or transmitted by direct contact – can cause sneezing, coughing, sore throat, running eyes and nose, headache and mild fever.

CREUTZFELDT-JAKOB DISEASE (CJD)
CJD causes dementia that can appear before old age. The infecting organisms are called prions, and seem to be smaller and simpler than viruses.

Recently, a new form of CJD has been discovered. Many scientists believe there is a direct link between this form of CJD and so-called Mad Cow Disease, once prevalent in Britain. The disease is caught by eating infected beef.

FOOD POISONING
Most short-lasting cases of food poisoning (gastroenteritis) are due to viral gastroenteritis. The most common cause is human rotavirus, to which children under the age of three are particularly susceptible. Bacterial gastroenteritis may be caused by a number of bacteria, including *Salmonella*, *Listeria* and more rarely, *Clostridium botulinum* (which causes the often fatal disease called botulism). Raw meat, poultry or eggs can be contaminated by the *Salmonella* bacterium, which is able to survive deep freezing. If thawing is not complete, or if the cooking time or temperature is inadequate, the cooked food remains infected. Symptoms of diarrhoea, fever and vomiting usually begin 12 to 48 hours after the food has been consumed. Other forms of food poisoning are due to the release of a toxic chemical from the contaminating organism, rather than infection by the organism itself. Such infection usually begins within one to six hours of eating. Examples include *staphyloccal* toxin (often from infected cream, sometimes from meat or poultry) and the toxin of *Bacillus cereus* (from fried rice). All forms of gastroenteritis may be prevented by high standards of hygiene in food preparation and by the provision of a clean water supply.

GLANDULAR FEVER
Glandular fever – or infectious mononucleosis – is caused by the Epstein-Barr virus. Transmission is by direct contact and, because it mainly affects young adults (aged 15 to 25), a popular theory was that it was contracted by kissing. The initial symptom is a particularly sore throat, often producing a thick white coating over the area of the tonsils. Other characteristics include fever and enlargement of the lymph glands of the neck and sometimes also of the liver and spleen. This enlargement can last ten or more days and is often followed by a period of severe fatigue and mild depression before complete recovery.

HEPATITIS
Hepatitis is inflammation of the liver, usually caused by a virus. It can also be caused by excessive alcohol or drug consumption. Viral hepatitis is classified as A, B, and Non A, Non B.

■ THE MOST COMMON BUG IS *E.COLI* FOUND IN THE GUT ■ SMALLPOX IS THE ONLY DISEASE

Preventive hepatitis vaccination is very effective, but once infection occurs (with the exception of the milder form, hepatitis A) death may result.

HERPES SIMPLEX

There are two common types of herpes simplex, a viral infection transmitted by direct contact.

The most common lesion produced by Type I of this virus is the 'cold sore' – a small crop of painful blisters that usually develop around the lips or nose and last for several days before fading. The virus may then be latent and flare up again in response to such events as another infection, trauma, emotional upset or exposure to sunlight. Other infections include blisters of the fingers (whitlow), ulceration of the cornea of the eye, and, rarely, a serious encephalitis (brain infection) to which infants are vulnerable. Those suffering from cold sores should therefore avoid close contact with infants.

A variety of Type II of this virus causes genital herpes, a painful recurrent blistering eruption of the genitalia similar in appearance to a cold sore but transmitted through sexual contact.

INFLUENZA

Influenza is an airborne viral infection. Symptoms include fever, muscle pain, sore throat, coughing, loss of appetite and general weakness. A major complication is viral pneumonia, which can lead to a rapidly progressive pneumonia owing to further bacterial infection. Influenza may be fatal in elderly people.

LEPROSY

Leprosy is a chronic inflammatory disease caused by the bacterium *Mycobacterium leprae*, and transmitted by prolonged or close contact. The infection attacks nerves and skin, but characteristics are very variable. Doctors treat the disease with sulphone drugs. Plastic surgery may be used to restore damaged skin.

MALARIA

Malaria is caused by a protozoan and is transmitted to the bloodstream of humans by the female *Anopheles* mosquito. Infection results in the destruction of red blood cells, causing intermittent fever and anaemia. The most dangerous infection – malignant tertian malaria, in which the brain can be affected – can lead to fits or coma and even sudden death.

Every year in the tropics more than a million people die of malaria and two million new cases appear, despite worldwide efforts to control the disease. In some regions, malaria has become resistant to commonly used drugs, which means that drugs to prevent the disease are becoming more complex.

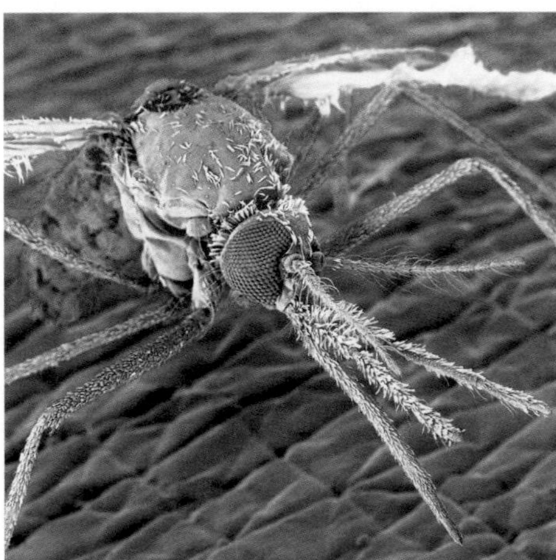

■ *Close-up of a mosquito,* Anopheles sp., *one of several species that transmit malaria. The parasite that causes malaria is present in the saliva of female mosquitos. Emerging from the head (lower right) is the proboscis which is used to draw blood. Malaria is a major health problem in many countries and is potentially fatal*

MENINGITIS

Meningitis is a viral or bacterial infection, causing inflammation of membranes surrounding the brain.

Symptoms include fever, severe headache, neck stiffness, intolerance of bright lights and vomiting.

The speed of onset depends on the infecting organism – viral (tubercular) meningitis has a gradual onset. Viral meningitis can be caused by a great number of viruses. It is usually not as serious as the bacterial form, and often clears up without specific treatment.

Bacterial meningitis can be caused by a number of organisms – the most common are meningococcal meningitis, pneumococcal meningitis and haemophilus meningitis. Meningococcal type is particularly rapid and can cause sudden collapse and the rapid appearance of a rash looking like small bruises or blood blisters. Antibiotic therapy must be started urgently.

PLAGUE

Plague is a disease of rodents that can be transmitted to humans by flea bites or by airborne infection. It is caused by the bacterium *Yersinia pestis*. Symptoms include fever, weakness and delirium, as well as painful buboes (swelling of lymph nodes), hence the name 'bubonic' plague.

The condition is often fatal. During the 14th century, one-quarter of the population of Europe died because of plague, known as the Black Death.

RABIES

Rabies is an acute viral infection that ordinarily leads to death in humans. The virus is endemic in warm-blooded animals in Africa and in Eurasia as far west as central Europe. (Rabies reached central France in the 1980s, but it is thought that France, the Low Countries and most of Germany no longer have infected wild animals.)

The disease is transmitted in the saliva of warm-blooded animals through broken skin as a result of a bite (for example from dogs or foxes). Symptoms include spasm of the throat muscles when swallowing is attempted, aversion to water (hence the alternative name 'hydrophobia'), maniacal behaviour, and finally involvement of other muscles to cause paralysis and death. A vaccine is available for those in high-risk occupations.

SCHISTOSOMIASIS (BILHARZIA)

Schistosomiasis is a tropical disease caused by infestation of the body with larvae of the parasitic flatworm *Schistosoma*. Symptoms include diarrhoea, and enlargement of the spleen and liver. The condition can be fatal.

Flatworm eggs excreted in the faeces or urine of infected people enter freshwater snails and grow inside them. Larvae released by the snails penetrate the skin of people bathing in infected water and colonize blood vessels in the intestine, causing the disease.

TETANUS (LOCKJAW)

The bacterium *Clostridium tetani* is widespread in nature, commonly occurring in topsoil. Tetanus spores enter the body through cuts, resulting in intense muscle spasm ('lockjaw').

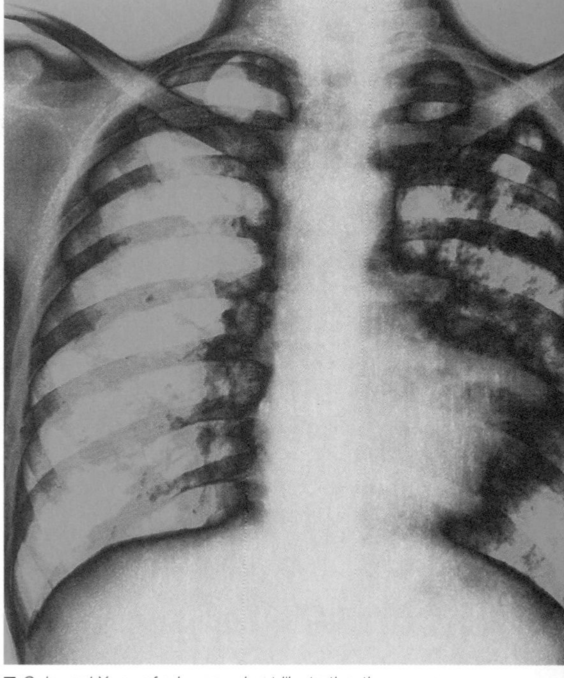

■ *Coloured X-ray of a human chest illustrating the presence of pulmonary tuberculosis in the patient's left lung (shown by the fluffy red areas). The disease is caused by the bacterium* Mycobacterium tuberculosis, *which is inhaled into the lungs and forms lesions*

Prevention is by immunization, given as three doses in infancy with booster doses at school age and then every five years. If immunity has waned, the initial three doses are repeated.

TUBERCULOSIS (TB)

Tuberculosis is caused by the bacterium *Mycobacterium tuberculosis*, first discovered in 1882 by the German scientist Robert Koch (1843–1910). TB has been a scourge for thousands of years – evidence of the disease has been found in an Egyptian mummy from the 10th century BC. More recently, the mortality rate in England and Wales in the 1850s was 60,000 per year, both adults and children dying of what was known as 'consumption'.

There are two strains – human and bovine (cattle). The main source of bovine tuberculosis was infected milk, but this has been eliminated in the developed world by pasteurization. The source of the human strain is the respiratory tract of an 'open' case of pulmonary tuberculosis – the organism is coughed up or breathed out by the sufferer.

The initial infection is in the lungs and the lymph glands in the middle of the chest cavity. In most cases there are no symptoms and the infection heals without treatment, but may leave a scar on the lung. During this primary infection the body develops an immunity, which can be detected by a test. In this test a tiny amount of dead tubercle is injected just under the skin surface and if immunity is present, a raised red lump develops. In a minority of primary infections, insufficient immunity develops and the infection spreads either all through the lungs (consumption or miliary pulmonary tuberculosis) or to other organs leading to meningitis or kidney or bone infection.

Modern drug treatment is very effective for all forms of the disease, but 'open' cases are kept in isolation until their sputum becomes free of the infecting organism. People are immunized by a vaccine called BCG (Bacille Calmette-Guérin), a very mild form of TB, first used in 1906.

Non-infectious Diseases

- Infectious diseases such as smallpox, tuberculosis and diphtheria have been ousted from their positions as major killers by cancer, heart disease and strokes.
- Almost one-third of all deaths from cancer could be avoided if people stopped smoking tobacco.
- Coronary heart disease is the most common form of heart disease in developed countries and the most common cause of sudden death.
- Alzheimer's disease is the commonest reason for dementia in people over the age of about 60 years.

Medicine is the science of treating and preventing disease. There are more than 20,000 non-infectious diseases which are known to occur in humans. Many, such as hay fever and other such allergies, lead to no long-term harm while others remain and often get worse over a period of months or years. These are the so-called chronic diseases such as arthritis. A further third type of non-infectious disease may progress to death if it is not treated quickly and effectively.

ALLERGIES

An allergy is a hypersensitivity or an abnormal response in the body to contact with a particular substance.

Hay fever (allergic rhinitis)

A seasonal allergy characterized by sneezing, nasal congestion and itching of the eyes. It is caused by sensitivity to pollen from grass or trees in the spring and summer months.

Hives (urticaria)

An intensely itchy skin reaction characterized by raised smooth red or pale weals. In severe cases there may be swelling of the lips or the skin around the eyes. Someone with hives may be allergic to food (for example fish, eggs or berries), to drugs, such as penicillin, or to contact with chemicals, feathers or fur. Allergy to drugs may also take the form of a red blotchy rash rather like measles.

Asthma

A respiratory disorder characterized by wheezing owing to narrowing of the airways (bronchi), partly because of spasm in the muscle of the bronchi, and partly because of swelling and congestion of the lining (mucosa) of the bronchi. Childhood asthma, unlike asthma in later life, often occurs in those who are prone to allergy, and allergy to such things as house dust, feathers, pollen, and animal fur or hair can trigger asthma attacks. There is often a family history of allergy; boys are more often affected than girls, and childhood asthma may disappear at puberty. Attacks can also be triggered by infections, by irritants such as cold air or cigarette smoke, or by stress. A number of drug treatments are now available, many in the form of inhalers.

ARTHRITIS

Arthritis is a term applied to a variety of conditions which cause pain in the joints. There are two main forms, osteoarthritis and inflammatory arthritis.

Osteoarthritis

This is the most common form of arthritis. It is a degeneration caused by 'wear and tear'. The cartilage covering the bone ends becomes eroded and this eventually leads to roughening and swelling of the bone itself, especially at the edges of the joint. Surgery to replace hip and knee joints which have been badly affected by osteoarthritis is now commonly performed.

Inflammatory arthritis

This type of arthritis takes many different forms but is in general due to inflammation of the tissues lining the joints (synovium). The milder forms are popularly known as rheumatism; more severe forms can be due to rheumatoid arthritis, gout, or bacterial infection. In rheumatoid arthritis, the body's immune system starts to react against its own synovial tissue, damaging it, and in the process causing pain, stiffness and swelling of the joints. Any joint may be affected, but the fingers are often an obvious site. In its severe forms, joints gradually become deformed.

CANCER

Cancer occurs when cells grow out of control. A single cell can accumulate changes in its genes that allow it to replicate in an uncontrolled way. Such a cell can give rise to a tumour, which may show itself as a palpable lump or mass. Once cells become cancerous they lose the function that they once had; they simply reproduce themselves indefinitely.

A tumour is said to be benign if it remains localized in the place where it originated. Nevertheless, benign tumours can be life-threatening if they jeopardize normal structures, for example benign tumours of the brain.

Malignant tumours have the capacity to spread around the body. Individual cells, or groups of cells, can detach themselves from the primary tumour, migrate via the blood or the lymph and become deposited on other organs. There they form secondary tumours.

In many cases the cause of the cancer is unknown. Treatment for cancer varies according to the type of tumour, the site of the primary tumour, and the extent of the spread of cancerous cells. Drug therapy (chemotherapy) can in some forms of cancer produce long remissions, but side effects occur as normal cells are damaged and white blood cells become depleted. Radiation therapy uses ionizing radiation – including X-rays and gamma rays – to destroy cancer cells. Surgery is used to remove malignancies but is only effective if cancer cells have not migrated into other parts of the body.

■ *This colour-enhanced scan shows the surface of the trachea (windpipe) with inhaled pollen (orange) and dust (brown). These airborne particles can cause asthma or hay fever. The surface of the trachea is made up of cells with hair-like cilia (green) which, together with mucus, trap airborne particles*

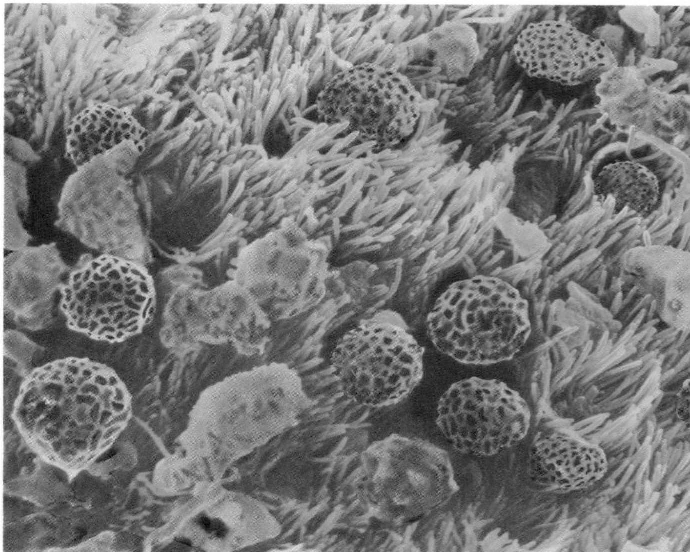

■ *Computer-enhanced X-ray showing a patient suffering from severe rheumatoid arthritis. The affected swollen joints (orange) cause the fingers and hands to become deformed. It typically affects the joints of the fingers, wrist, feet and hips. Treatment for pain and inflammation is given and physiotherapy may help to preserve joint movement*

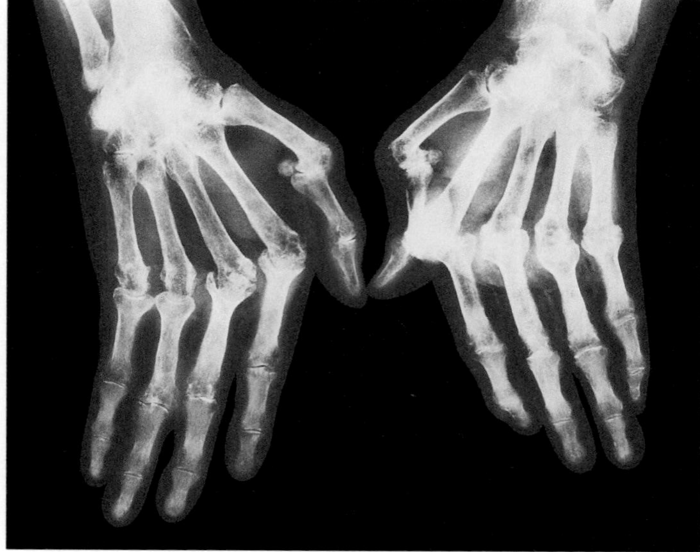

■ SKIN CANCER IS THE MOST COMMON MALIGNANCY WORLDWIDE ■ POLLEN IS THE MOST

GENETIC DISEASES AND DISORDERS

Cystic fibrosis

A hereditary disease caused by a genetic mutation, resulting in abnormally thick mucous secretions in the lungs and intestine. This disorder affects about one person in 1500. Treatment for digestive problems and lung infections can help to prolong the lives of people with this condition, many of whom survive into their mid-20s.

Down's syndrome

A chromosomal abnormality in which the affected child has an extra copy of chromosome number 21. Those born with Down's syndrome have a flat face and nose, a vertical fold of skin at the inner edge of the eye, short fingers, and mental retardation. Formerly known as mongolism, the syndrome is named after the English physician John Langdon-Down (1828–96).

Haemophilia

A single-gene disorder causing a life-long tendency to excessive bleeding owing to a deficiency of factor VIII, a substance necessary for blood clotting. Haemophilia varies in severity and often features severe spontaneous external bleeding from the slightest wound and painful internal bleeding, particularly in the joints, without any apparent cause. Damaged joints may become deformed. The transmission of the condition is sex-linked – it is suffered almost exclusively by males.

Huntington's chorea

A particularly distressing hereditary disease, affecting one person in 20,000. Symptoms become apparent in middle age, and sufferers experience dementia (a disorder of the mental processes) and uncontrolled movements. By this time, he or she has often had children who risk suffering the same fate.

Retinitis pigmentosa

This disease affects about one person in 4000. There is a progressive degeneration of the retinas, leading to poor night vision and sometimes eventual blindness.

Sickle-cell disease

A hereditary blood disease that mainly affects those with malarial immunity, usually people from Africa and their descendants. Large numbers of red blood cells in sufferers become sickle-shaped and can cause obstructions in the blood vessels, with possible damage to organs such as the kidneys and brain. No satisfactory treatment has yet been developed.

HEART DISEASES

The coronary arteries supply blood to the heart muscle. If the lining of these arteries becomes gradually thickened by fatty tissue (atheroma), the blood supply decreases. This causes episodes of chest pain (angina) often brought on by exercise. If a blood clot then develops at one such thickened area (coronary thrombosis), the artery becomes completely blocked causing a heart attack (myocardial infarction) or even sudden death. The main factors which put an individual at risk of coronary disease are cigarette smoking, high blood pressure and high levels of cholesterol in the blood. Other risk factors include obesity, lack of exercise, diabetes, stress and genetic factors such as a family history of coronary disease. Many drug treatments are now available and surgery can bypass a narrowed artery or artificially widen it.

High blood pressure (hypertension)

The high pressure within the arteries forces the heart to pump against a greater resistance. This strain initially causes an increase in the thickness of the heart muscle, and then an enlargement of the heart itself. If this condition is left untreated, the heart becomes unable to cope and heart failure results.

MAJOR ENVIRONMENTAL DISEASES

Environmental hazards such as radiation and pollutants are responsible for some types of disease. People normally encounter only small doses of radiation, from diagnostic X-rays, or perhaps as a treatment for cancer. In addition, everyone is exposed to low background levels of natural radiation from the Sun and from some types of rock.

However, excessive doses of radiation may follow accidents, for example those that take place at nuclear reactors. Chemical hazards are probably more often encountered in the workplace than at home. The list of industrial diseases is long and includes poisoning by lead, mercury and other heavy metals.

MEDICAL MEASUREMENTS

Blood pressure is measured using a *sphygmomanometer* fitted around the upper arm. Two readings are taken: one represents the pressure of blood as it leaves the heart (systolic pressure), the other is the pressure returning to the heart (diastolic pressure). Normal readings are: 120 mm of mercury (systolic) and 80 mm of mercury (diastolic). Blood pressure is high if the systolic reading is greater than 160 mm of mercury, and diastolic is greater than 90 mm. There is no agreed lower level, but if no reading is detectable, the patient is said to be in shock.

Temperature is measured using a thermometer placed in the mouth. A normal temperature is 37°C (98.6°F); a fever is anything greater than 38°C (100.4°F). The human body's upper temperature limit is 41°C (106°F); the lower limit is 29°C (85°F). Either of these extremes is likely to lead rapidly to death.

Asbestosis

This is an industrial disease caused by inhaling fibres of asbestos. The lungs become fibrous and the affected person not only experiences increasing breathlessness, with failure of the heart and lungs, but also has an increased risk of developing lung cancer.

Lead poisoning

A debilitating condition resulting from an accumulation of lead in the body, usually from water pipes or lead-based paint. Symptoms are variable and include digestive problems, irritability, severe abdominal pain, constipation, anaemia and paralysis. The illness can be acute in children, and may result in brain damage, blindness, deafness and death.

Radiation sickness

A disease caused by high exposures of radiation. It is characterized by loss of cells from the bone marrow and the lining of the stomach. The affected person loses appetite and suffers diarrhcea, sickness, chills, fever and extreme tiredness. Death may follow because of the damage to the bowel and bone marrow.

■ *Cancer occurs when cells grow out of control. This colour-enhanced micrograph shows a small lung tumour (red) filling an alveolus. The alveoli are the blind-ended air sacs of which the lungs are composed. The individual cancer cells are coated with microscopic hair-like structures known as microvilli*

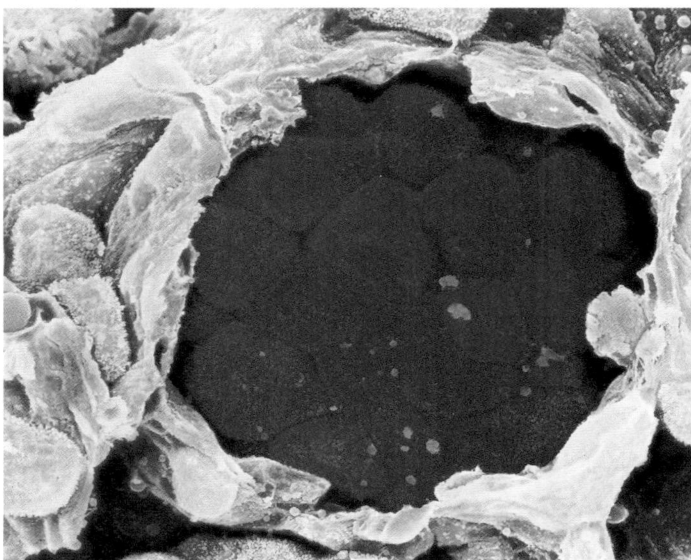

■ *Coloured X-ray of the chest of a patient showing a pacemaker fitted. The battery-run device supplies electrical impulses to the heart to maintain a regular rate heartbeat. The yellow lead connects the pacemaker to the heart. The device can be worn externally or implanted in the chest as seen here*

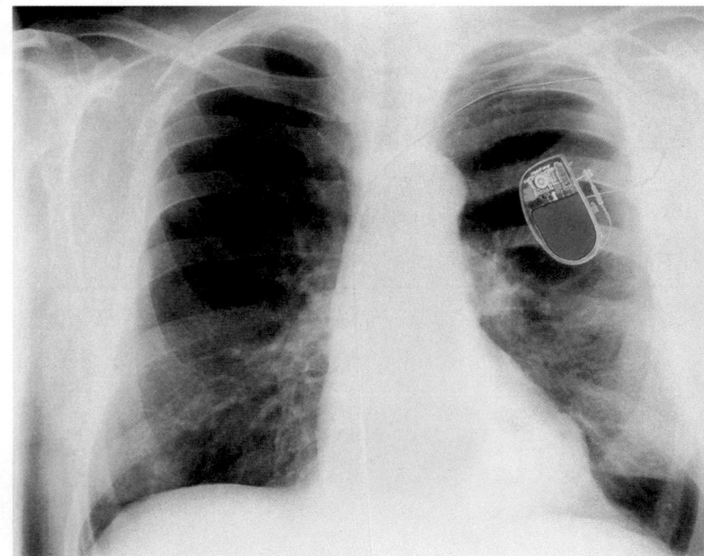

Psychology

- Perception – how sensory information is gathered by the brain to enable us to view the world.
- Learning and memory – the processes that enable us to understand, store and recall information.
- Motivation – the driving force behind all our actions.
- Personality – the set of characteristics that makes us unique.

Psychology is literally translated to mean 'study of the mind', but more broadly it refers to the scientific study of the mind and the brain and their interactions with behaviour. It is a common misconception that psychologists have a mystical ability to read the minds of others, and that psychology is only concerned with understanding the mentally abnormal or insane. In fact, much of psychology is interested in understanding the normal functioning of both humans and other animals. The rapid growth in the knowledge of brain structure and function has placed psychology in a new and ever-widening perspective calling for more sophisticated techniques of research. Throughout the development of psychology, a number of different approaches have been utilized, mostly with the goal of understanding the fundamental processes of perception and attention, learning and memory, language, motivation and individual differences.

PERCEPTION

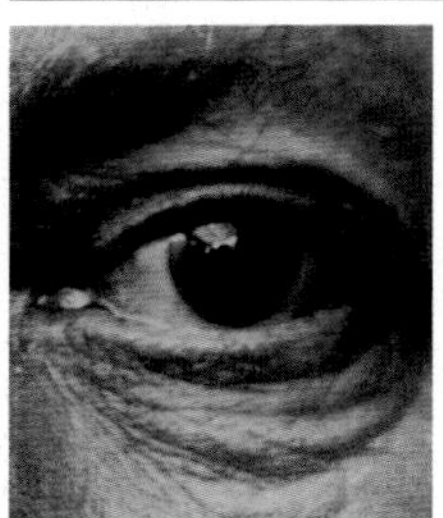

▶ Perception is the collection of mental processes that allows us to organize input from the senses so that we can view the world as we do.

Perception begins with physical energy such as light in the case of vision, or sound in the case of hearing which reaches the sense organs. This energy is transduced (changed) by the sensory systems into a form that the brain can understand. Perception is a selective process in that the brain has a limited capacity and cannot process everything that reaches the sense organs. Therefore the perceptual system makes inferences about missing information to fill in the gaps. This is why under certain conditions, for example visual illusions, we make errors in judgement.

LEARNING AND MEMORY

▶ The cognitive processes of acquiring, retaining and retrieving knowledge about stimuli, events, ideas and images.

Psychologists are typically interested in knowing how an organism learns and remembers something. Learning and memory cannot be directly observed and can only be inferred from observable behaviour. Learning and memory consist of three related processes; registration, storage and retrieval. Many questions remain about the processes of learning and memory. Psychologists have learnt a lot by performing controlled experiments on normal people, and also from the observation of brain damaged patients where head injury or illness has caused a lesion to parts of the brain thought to be involved in these functions.

MOTIVATION

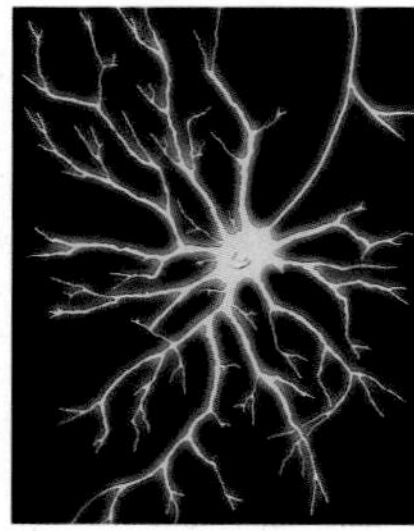

▶ The force that drives an animal or human to interact with its environment.

Motivated behaviours include activities such as feeding, drinking, social interaction and sexual behaviour that enable an organism to survive and reproduce. In psychological terms, motivated behaviour is based on a desire to seek pleasure but avoid pain. Freudian psychologists are interested in unconscious motivations, believing these to reveal deep-rooted conflicts. We can observe cases when motivational processes have 'gone wrong' in individuals suffering from eating disorders (anorexia nervosa, bulimia nervosa), or drug abuse.

PERSONALITY

▶ The set of characteristics which differentiate one person from another.

Personality attributes are a product of both genetics and environmental experience. A continuing debate for psychologists has been whether we are all truly unique (an idiopathic approach) or can be categorized along certain traits or types. Abnormalities of personality have been identified. These include the antisocial personality (a disorder resulting in abnormally aggressive or irresponsible behaviour), schizoid personality (one who lives in isolation from others in a fantasy world, and may be more susceptible to the development of schizophrenia), obsessional personality (rigid, inflexible behaviours) and paranoid personality (overly suspicious with inflated self-opinion).

SCHOOLS OF PSYCHOLOGY

Adlerian psychology: see Individual psychology.

analytic psychology: a branch of psychology developed by Carl Jung.

applied psychology: any form of psychology motivated by the aim of practical application.

behaviourism: a psychological approach arguing that psychological investigation should only be concerned with observable behaviour. Developed by J.B. Watson and, later, B.F. Skinner. The central tenet is that human behaviour can be modified by reinforcement.

clinical psychology: a practically based area of psychology in which research findings are applied to both normal and abnormal human behaviour.

developmental psychobiology: the study of biological processes that affect the development of behaviour.

educational psychology: concerned with the practical problems of teaching and learning, and directed both to the production of improved teaching methods and to the assistance of people with learning disabilities.

existential therapy: a form of therapy focusing on the free will of the patient and the necessity for individual choice and action.

humanistic psychology: a branch of psychology developed by Carl Rogers in which the self-image of the patient (client) is paramount. The therapist is honest with the patient, but does not seek to change the patient by any approval or disapproval.

individual psychology: a branch of psychoanalysis founded by Alfred Adler, who regarded the individual as responsible for his own actions and able to work towards his own goals.

introspectionism: early idea that the mind could be studied by analysing one's own mental processes.

Jungian theory: a branch of psychology contained within the ideas of Carl Jung and covering a wide spectrum of psychology.

learning theory: a group of psychological theories that aim to explain individual behaviour and personality as arising from learned reactions and responses to the environment.

neo-Freudian theory: any psychoanalytic approach departing from the original Freudian position with a greater emphasis on social, cultural and interpersonal factors.

neurolinguistics: a combination of psychology, linguistics and neurology that looks at the acquisition, production and processing of language.

neuropsychiatry: the study of organic brain disorders and the effects they have on behaviour.

occupational psychology: the application of psychology to the problems of industry, management, business and the workplace.

psychiatry: the medical treatment of mental, emotional, behavioural and personality disorders.

psychoanalysis: a method of treating mental illness originated by Sigmund Freud aiming to uncover unconscious fears and conflicts.

psychometrics: concerned with assessing intelligence, aptitude and personality through testing.

psychopathology: the study of abnormal behaviour.

psychobiology: an approach aiming to integrate psychology with biological processes.

radical therapy: therapeutic movement whereby the patient's behaviour is not seen as abnormal, but rather as a normal reaction to social problems.

social psychiatry: the examination of mental disorder as a part of society with the aim of developing social methods of prevention.

PHOBIAS

▶ A phobia is an intense or irrational or inappropriate fear of an object, person, organism or situation, of a degree that interferes with normal living.
▶ Phobias are most effectively treated by behaviour therapy.

HEALTH AND ANATOMY

beards pogonophobia
blood haematophobia
cancer cancerophobia, carcinophobia
childbirth tocophobia
cholera choleraphobia
death, corpses necrophobia, thanatophobia
deformity dysmorphophobia
disease nosophobia, pathophobia
drugs pharmacophobia
eyes ommatophobia
faeces coprophobia
germs spermophobia
hair chaetophobia
heart conditions cardiophobia
heredity patroiophobia
illness nosemaphobia
infection mysophobia
inoculations, injections trypanophobia
insanity lyssophobia, maniaphobia

knees genuphobia
leprosy leprophobia
mind psychophobia
physical love erotophobia
poison toxiphobia
pregnancy maieusiophobia
semen spermatophobia
sex genophobia
sexual intercourse coitophobia
skin dermatophobia
skin disease dermatosiophobia
soiling rypophobia
surgical operations ergasiophobia
syphilis syphilophobia
teeth odontophobia
tuberculosis phthisiophobia
venereal disease cypridophobia
vomiting emetophobia
wounds, injury traumatophobia

ANIMALS AND PLANTS

animals zoophobia
bacteria bacteriophobia, microphobia
bees apiphobia, melissophobia
birds ornithophobia
cats ailurophobia, gatophobia
chickens alektorophobia
dogs cynophobia
feathers pteronophobia
fish ichthyophobia
flowers anthophobia
fur doraphobia
horses hippophobia
insects entomophobia
leaves phyllophobia
lice pediculophobia
mice musophobia
microbes bacilliphobia
parasites parasitophobia
reptiles batrachophobia
snakes ophidiophobia, ophiophobia
spiders arachnophobia
trees dendrophobia
wasps spheksophobia
worms helminthophobia

SENSES

being cold frigophobia
being dirty automysophobia
being scratched amychophobia
being touched haphephobia
blushing ereuthophobia, eyrythrophobia
cold cheimatophobia
colour chromatophobia, chromophobia, psychrophobia
fatigue kopophobia, ponophobia
heat thermophobia
itching acarophobia, scabiophobia
noise phonophobia
odours osmophobia
odours (body) osphresiophobia
pain algophobia, odynophobia
pleasure hedonophobia
sleep hypnophobia
smell olfactophobia
smothering, choking pnigerophobia

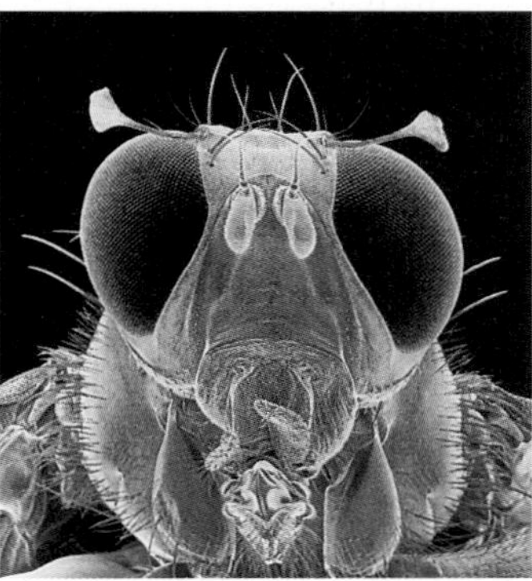

sound akousticophobia
speaking halophobia
speaking aloud phonophobia
speech alophobia
sourness acerophobia
stings cnidophobia
stooping kyphophobia
taste geumatophobia
thinking phronemophobia
touch haptophobia
touching haphephobia, thixophobia
trembling tremophobia

GROUPS

children paediphobia
human beings anthropophobia
men androphobia
robbers harpaxophobia
women gynophobia
young girls parthenophobia

RELIGION

churches ecclesiaphobia
demons demonophobia
God theophobia
heaven ouranophobia
hell hadephobia, stygiophobia
sacred things hierophobia
Satan Satanophobia
sinning peccatophobia

ENVIRONMENT

auroral lights auroraphobia
clouds nephophobia
dampness, moisture hygrophobia
flood antlophobia
fog homichlophobia
ice, frost cryophobia
lakes imnophobia
lightning astraphobia
meteors meteorophobia
precipices cremnophobia
rain ombrophobia
rivers potamophobia
sea thalassophobia
snow chionophobia
stars siderophobia
sun heliophobia
thunder brontophobia, keraunophobia
water hydrophobia
wind ancraophobia

TRAVEL

crossing a bridge gephyrophobia
crossing streets dromophobia
flying, the air aerophobia
motion kinesophobia, kinetophobia
sea swell cymophobia
speed tachophobia
travel hodophobia
travelling by train siderodromophobia
vehicles amaxophobia, ochophobia
walking basiphobia

FOOD AND DRINK

drink, alcohol potophobia

drinking dipsophobia
eating phagophobia
food sitophobia
meat carnophobia

INANIMATE OBJECTS

books bibliophobia
crystals, glass crystallophobia
glass nelophobia
machinery mechanophobia
metals metallophobia
mirrors eisoptrophobia
missiles ballistophobia
money chrometophobia
needles belonophobia
pins enetephobia
points aichurophobia
slime blennophobia, myxophobia
string linonophobia

SITUATIONS

being alone monophobia, autophobia
being beaten rhabdophobia
being bound merinthophobia
being buried alive taphophobia
being looked at scopophobia
crowds demophobia, ochlophobia
enclosed spaces claustrophobia
going to bed clinophobia
heights acrophobia, altophobia
high places hypsophobia
home domatophobia, oikophobia
home surroundings ecophobia
infinity apeirophobia
passing high objects batophobia
places topophobia
public places agoraphobia
school scholionophobia
shadows sciophobia
sitting idle thaasophobia
solitude eremitophobia, eremophobia
standing stasophobia
standing upright stasiphobia

MISCELLANEOUS

certain names onomatophobia
darkness nyctophobia
dawn eosophobia
daylight phengophobia
depth bathophobia
dirt mysophobia
disorder ataxiophobia
draughts anemophobia
dreams oneirophobia
dust amathophobia, koniphobia
electricity electrophobia
everything pantophobia
failure kakorraphiaphobia
fall of man-made satellites keraunothnetophobia
fears phobophobia
fire pyrophobia
flashes selaphobia
flogging mastigophobia
freedom eleutherophobia
ghosts phasmophobia

graves taphophobia
gravity barophobia
ideas ideophobia
imperfection atelophobia
jealousy zelophobia
justice dikephobia
marriage gamophobia
monsters, monstrosities teratophobia
music musicophobia
names nomatophobia
narrowness anginaphobia
neglect of duty paralipophobia
new things neophobia
night, darkness achluophobia
novelty cainophobia
nudity gymnophobia
number 13 triskaidekaphobia, terdekaphobia
one thing monophobia
poverty peniaphobia
punishment poinephobia
responsibility hypegiaphobia
ridicule katagelophobia
ruin atephobia
rust iophobia
shock hormephobia
stealing kleptophobia
stillness eremophobia
strong light photophobia
void kenophobia
weakness asthenophobia
words logophobia
work ergophobia
writing graphophobia

Complementary Medicine

- Acupuncture marks were discovered on the 'ice man', the 5300-year-old mummified corpse of a man found in the Tyrolean Alps in 1991.
- Osteopathy is the only complementary therapy that is fully recognized by Western medicine.
- A large number of modern drugs are, like herbal remedies, derived from plants – the heart drug digoxin is produced from the foxglove, and the group of painkillers known as opiates are derived from the opium poppy.
- Acupuncture and osteopathy are the most commonly used complementary therapies.

Complementary, or alternative, medicine encompasses all the forms of healing that lie outside the sort of medicine people normally receive from a local doctor or hospital. It includes a wide variety of different therapies used by millions of people worldwide. How they work, however, is still to a large extent a mystery. The common feature that seems to run through every one of these alternative treatments is the importance placed on the whole person, not just on specific symptoms – this is known as the holistic approach.

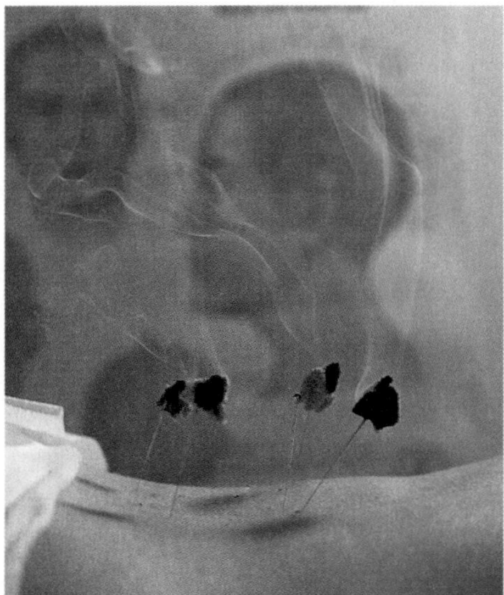

■ *'Moxibustion' is used in the art of acupuncture. A small cone of moxa (dried mugwort) is placed around the head of each needle and ignited. This clears the channels and reinforces the energy flow*

ACUPUNCTURE

Acupuncture originated in China thousands of years ago. The technique uses fine needles inserted at specific points on the body in order to restore the balance of an inner 'life force' known as chi energy and believed to flow along a number of meridians or channels in the body. Each of the 12 main meridians is believed to have its own pulse – six in each wrist – and the acupuncturist checks these in order to decide which points to stimulate.

The technique has been shown to be remarkably successful at stopping pain, and scientists have discovered that the needles appear to make the body produce its own natural painkillers, endorphins.

Acupuncture is also claimed to be effective in treating a very wide range of diseases, including respiratory, digestive, bone and muscle disorders.

ALEXANDER TECHNIQUE

The Alexander technique is a method of producing postural changes, which are claimed to relieve a number of physical disorders. The technique was developed in the 19th century by an Australian actor, Matthias Alexander (1869–1955). He realized that the way he positioned his head and neck were the cause of his frequent loss of voice during performances, and found that by altering his posture he could cure himself.

During a series of lessons – 12 or more – the patient 'relearns' how to use the body, breaking harmful postural habits. The technique is claimed to be beneficial for everyone, but in particular for those who have suffered long spells of general ill-health – lethargy and poor sleeping, for example.

AROMATHERAPY

Aromatherapy is principally a massage technique in which essential oils derived from herbs, flowers and spices are rubbed into the skin and eventually inhaled. The natural fragrances these oils produce are said to be particularly effective for psychological complaints such as anxiety or depression, but are also used to treat a range of conditions including skin disorders and burns.

CHIROPRACTIC

Chiropractic was founded by the Canadian osteopath D.D. Palmer (1845–1913). The central philosophy of chiropractic is that malalignments or 'subluxations' of the bones in the spine cause disturbances of the nervous and vascular systems, leading to diseases not only in the bones and muscles themselves, but in any organ of the body.

Chiropractitioners work with the help of X-rays to discover where the malalignments are and to identify 'intersegmental dysrelationships'. They then manipulate the bones using short, but very forceful, thrusts to the 'subfluxed' joint, thus relieving the root cause of the problem. Unlike osteopathy, often regarded as complementary to orthodox medicine, chiropractors regard their philosophy as a completely alternative system of medicine.

Chiropractic should never be used in any case of bone malignancy or where the spinal chord is compressed.

HERBALISM

Herbalism is an ancient form of medicine. From the dawn of humanity, people have been using plants to cure their illnesses.

From the Middle Ages, herbals – manuals listing the names of plants and what they could be used for – were widely used. In the 17th century, Nicholas Culpeper (1616–54) combined herbalism with astrology in his *Complete Herbal* (1653).

Herbalists today use the roots, leaves, stems, flowers and seeds of plants to produce medicines. Once a diagnosis is made, the herbalist will dilute a concentrated extract of a certain herb in water or mix it into a paste to form a cream or ointment.

■ *The herb chamomile is used as a pain-reliever, a general tonic and also helps to stimulate the appetite*

Conditions such as arthritis, colds and coughs, skin problems, digestive disorders and minor injuries are regarded as the most likely to benefit from herbalism.

HOMEOPATHY

Homeopathy was invented by a German doctor, Samuel Hahnemann (1755–1843). He reasoned that since many of the symptoms people suffer during illness – fever or pain, for example – are actually visible signs of the body's own defences working against the disease, it would make sense to try to boost these defences.

He based his therapy on the principle that 'like cures like', giving patients tiny quantities of substances known to produce exactly these symptoms in healthy people. One homeopathic remedy for fever, for instance, is sulphur, which produces a feeling of heat and promotes sweating if taken orally in larger doses.

Homeopathy offers remedies for virtually every medical complaint, but it is less frequently used in acute or life-threatening illness. Homeopathic remedies are prescribed by some doctors as well as by homeopaths.

In order to produce the tiny quantities that are needed for homeopathic remedies, the active substance must be diluted. This process is known as potentizing. The active substance is diluted in proportions of 1 to 10, usually in distilled water, and this dilution is carried out six or more times in succession – the homoeopathic 'potency 6' is one million times diluted.

Theoretically, with sufficient dilution, there can be none of the active substance left. So how is it that these remedies can still work? The secret is claimed to lie in the rapid shaking, or 'succussion', that must be performed after each dilution. If the succussion is not carried out, the remedy is

ineffective. The explanation for this phenomenon is best given by comparing each molecule of the homeopathic remedy, suspended in the dilution, to a person walking across a snowfield. Once the person has passed by, nothing physical remains, and only the footprints are left in the snow. Although there are few, if any, molecules of the active ingredient left, its 'footprints', thought to be produced by succussion, remain to do their work in the body.

IRIDOLOGY

Iridology is the study of examining the iris of the eye as a tool for diagnosing illness. It is used by a range of alternative therapists including acupuncturists, osteopaths, herbalists and homeopaths.

The left side of the body is reflected in the left eye, and vice versa. The head is revealed at the top, the feet at the bottom of the eye. There are three zones: the inner zone represents the functions of digestion and absorption; the middle zone transport, utilization and elimination by the kidneys; and the outer zone, structure, skeleton and skin.

OSTEOPATHY

Osteopathy is a manipulative technique founded by the American doctor Andrew Taylor Still (1828–1917). Joints are pushed and occasionally pulled so as to restore them to their natural positions, thus relieving tensions on surrounding muscles, tendons and ligaments.

Osteopaths tend to concentrate their work on the spine because this contains the spinal chord and all the nerves that control the body. Back pain is the disorder most commonly treated.

REFLEXOLOGY

Like acupuncture, reflexology is based on the idea that the body contains channels of 'life force'. Reflexologists believe that this force exists in ten 'zones' of energy, each beginning in the toes and ending in the fingers. By touching and feeling the toes and feet, reflexologists claim to be able to feel blocks in these channels of energy (they say these feel like crystals below the skin surface). They can then attempt to move the blockage, and so cure the illness, by manipulating and massaging the foot in a specific way. Like acupuncture, reflexology is used to treat most conditions.

OTHER ALTERNATIVE THERAPIES

Bach flower remedies

Dr Edward Bach (1880–1936) used plants to impregnate spring water and dew to produce 38 flower herbal remedies. These are used by practitioners in the treatment of conditions such as anxiety and depression.

Hydrotherapy

Water is used in a number of therapies, for example to stimulate circulation or in colonic irrigation. Various elimination treatments – including sweating and the drinking of mineral waters – are also employed.

Rolfing

This is a system of deep massage developed by Dr Ida Rolf (1896–1979) in the 1920s and 1930s to break down connective tissues that have become thickened.

Shiatsu

This Japanese system of deep massage is used to stimulate acupuncture points (see above). Claimed to be preventive as well as a cure, Shiatsu is widely practised within Japanese families. When a practitioner treats him- or herself, the therapy is referred to as Do-in.

MIND-BODY THERAPIES

Whilst many forms of conventional medicine focus upon either the psychological or the physical symptoms of the patient in isolation, several activities akin to alternative medicine seek to harmonize the mind and the body holistically. For these techniques, the basic belief is that a healthy mind promotes a healthy body and vice versa. Several of these techniques are not strictly therapies, but they strive to maintain good health in the person practising them, and so may be regarded as forms of complementary medicine.

YOGA

Yoga, which comes from the Sanskrit word for union, seeks to unify the human and the divine, and in doing so brings about a yoking of mind and body. This harmonization will result in good health. Yoga has three basic aspects: posture, breathing and meditation. The various, often difficult, postures that yoga practitioners have to master aim to discipline the body and the mind, and also to keep the body supple. Breathing exercises also regulate the body and mind, and help alleviate tension. The posturing and breathing aspects are physical disciplines which help promote the internal aspect of meditation. By concentrated effort of meditation upon an object, one hopes to achieve contemplative union with that object, and ultimately achieve *samadhi*, or escape from the cycle of life and death. There are many forms of yoga, which has its origins in Hindu philosophy. Some are more meditation-based, whilst others focus on the physical aspects of yoga. Yoga has become increasingly popular in the West.

■ *The secret of T'ai Chi is tranquillity. The movements are performed with the mind and body totally relaxed*

T'AI CHI

T'ai Chi is a form of meditation in motion. Akin in some ways to martial arts techniques, it is practised as a series of ritual flowing circular movements. It seeks to tune in the body to the *chi*, the Chinese metaphysical life-force, and allow this energy to express itself through movement. As well as balancing the body and focusing the mind, T'ai Chi helps develop muscle control.

DANCE THERAPY

Whilst some mind-body therapies have a religious or metaphysical background, dance therapy is a secular (non-religious) technique which has similar benefits. Dancing, which has always been a popular pastime of children and adults alike, can develop muscular and postural control. It has also been used throughout history as a means of emotional and artistic expression, by translating inner feelings into bodily movement. As well as ritual dance therapy, such as that practised in tribal and shamanistic cultures to achieve trance states, many Western societies have seen dance therapy flourish as a means of self-expression in recent years. It has been used particularly to help mentally and emotionally challenged people find a bodily voice for their feelings.

SENSE THERAPIES

Some complementary medicinal techniques focus upon certain senses as a channel for healing, especially as regards the psychological aspects of health. Colour therapy seeks to explore the effects of different colours and other visual stimuli on the patient's nervous system. Similarly, music therapy explores the therapeutic properties of sound, noise and music on the mind and body. Another sense-based therapy is art therapy, which allows people to creatively express themselves through illustration and sculpture. Art therapy has been used in cases of drug and alcohol addiction, in the treatment of anorexia nervosa, and in psychotherapy. Other forms of sense therapy include controlled sensory deprivation: the isolation tank and floatation tank both carefully remove sensory stimuli to allow relaxation and meditative contemplation.

MEDITATION

Whilst the previous mind-body techniques have been primarily body-based, meditation has its basis in focusing and controlling the mind. Meditation has many schools, each with their own goals and approaches. Meditation is a combination of correct breathing and body-control, and controlled mental focus. It has been used for a variety of holistic health purposes, from relieving tension in times of stress, to helping concentration and intellectual prowess, to helping come to terms with (and even curing) serious diseases. Meditation forms the core of many other therapies, such as yoga, and although it is, in itself, irreligious, it has widespread use in many Eastern religions.

HYPNOTHERAPY

Hypnotherapy is a form of psychotherapy using hypnosis. Hypnosis is an induced altered state of consciousness, between asleep and awake, where many mental functions are quietened, allowing deeply buried aspects of the Unconscious to rise to the surface. Hypnosis should always be carried out by a trained hypnotist, who will induce a trance state in their patient. While in this trance state, the hypnotized person is open to suggestion and the hypnotist can suggest that psychological, physical or emotional ailments disappear. For example, many people have lost their addiction to nicotine through hypnotic suggestion. Hypnotherapy has also been used as a means of exploring the Unconscious, to help overcome past traumas, and even, some people believe, to relive 'past lives'. Hypnotherapy has parallels with other forms of therapy, such as autosuggestion and dream therapy. Autosuggestion is a form of self-hypnosis, whereby one may suggest positive health while in a self-induced trance. Dream therapy is similar to hypnosis in that it explores the Unconscious, but it does so through the interpretation and exploration of dreams.

CHINESE DOCTORS HAVE OPERATED ON PATIENTS USING ONLY ACUPUNCTURE TO RELIEVE PAIN

DINOSAURS

▶ **The fastest dinosaurs were ornithomimosaurs, some of which were thought to have run at speeds over 60 km/h.**

▶ **The largest known dinosaur eggs are those of *Hypselosaurus priscus* – 30 cm long and 25.5 cm in diameter.**

▶ **New dinosaur species are being discovered at the rate of one every seven weeks.**

THE REIGN OF DINOSAURS

▶ Dinosaurs, the most advanced reptiles of all time, dominated the Earth for 140 million years, compared with the 2 million years that Man has been on the planet.
▶ Unlike reptiles alive today – which propel themselves with their limbs extended out to their sides – dinosaurs walked with their limbs directly under their bodies, just like modern mammals and birds.

The dinosaurs thrived during the 'Age of Reptiles', the Mesozoic era (235 to 65 million years ago), before they became extinct. It is generally believed that most dinosaurs were cold-blooded, although recent theories suggest that they may have actually been warm-blooded. Many dinosaurs were of gigantic size, some weighing up to 100 tonnes.

There were two groups of dinosaur: the *Saurischia* ('lizard-hipped') and the *Ornithischia* ('bird-hipped'). Saurischians – with pelvic girdles like that of modern lizards – exclusively included two-legged carnivores such as *Tyrannosaurus* and huge four-legged, semi-aquatic, mostly plant-eating sauropods such as *Diplodocus*. Ornithischians – whose pelvic girdle was like that of a bird – included ankylosaurs, stegosaurs, ceratopsids, hadrosaurs and iguanodontids.

EXTINCTION OF THE DINOSAURS

▶ The asteroid impact theory imagines a scenario in which the Earth's atmosphere was choked with dust for up to 5000 years.
▶ One of the more bizarre theories of dinosaur extinction is mass exhaustion brought on by over-exertive sexual activity.

The greatest mystery surrounding the dinosaurs is their ultimate extinction from the planet at the boundary of the Cretaceous and Tertiary eras (see p. 29), known as the K-T boundary. Although dinosaur species were constantly becoming extinct over this period (the average duration of a dinosaur species was 2–3 million years), the K-T boundary marked their total demise. Many other large reptilian creatures, such as pterosaurs and plesiosaurs, became extinct at the same time. This suggests that a cataclysmic event occurred to cause massive upheaval among dominant life forms on the planet. Numerous theories have been put forward to explain this upheaval. As yet, no theory fits all the data and new hypotheses are constantly being proposed. Extinction theories include:

PSYCHOLOGICAL
Behavioural changes in dinosaur activity may have upset the natural balance of power, resulting in the disastrous collapse of the dinosaur ecosystem. Alternatively, some theories suggest that, due to decreasing species diversity, the dinosaurs simply lost the will to live. Other psychological theories imply a lack of intelligence, some form of senility or even mass suicide caused by deep melancholia.

BIOLOGICAL
These include the notion that dinosaurs fell victim to some form of poisoning, possibly from plants which heightened their secondary defence mechanisms by increasing their alkaloid toxicity; fatal disease or an epidemic; an imbalance in the sex ratios of the dinosaurs or widespread loss of sex drive; nutritional difficulties resulting in annihilation through digestive problems such as constipation or diarrhoea; sterility and/or eggshell thinning caused by climatic change.

ECOLOGICAL
The rise of the mammal has been blamed for the fall of the dinosaur, claiming that increased predatory behaviour by the mammals, perhaps focusing on dinosaur eggs in particular, resulted in these quicker, newer and smaller creatures overriding the dinosaur. Alternatively, the domination of angiosperms (flowering plants) over gymnosperms (conifers) and resulting shifts in dominance within the hierarchy of animal life may have caused the dinosaur's decline.

■ *A skeleton of a Chasmosaurus. This horned ceratopsid had a spectacular frill which was probably used as a display structure. The inset shows another horned ceratopsid – Triceratops – as it may have looked when alive*

ENVIRONMENTAL
One plausible recent theory suggests dinosaurs may have died out through suffocation due to falling oxygen levels. Evidence from amber (fossilized tree sap) suggests a possible decline in atmospheric oxygen content in the run-up to the K-T boundary. Whilst animals such as crocodiles and lizards would have survived due to their low metabolic requirements, the resultant lack of oxygen would have proved catastrophic for the dinosaur.

GEOPHYSICAL
Many theories fall into this category. They include huge volcanic activity over a sustained period of time, climatic cooling or global warming, continental drift, changing sea levels, a reversal in the Earth's magnetic field or a combination of these factors.

EXTRA-TERRESTRIAL
These theories postulate some form of contact with alien life, such as alien viruses, or a Martian attack.

IMPACT
Some of the most plausible scenarios involve a massive collision between the Earth and a wayward celestial body – possibly an asteroid, spanning 10–20 km (6.3–12.5 mi) across, which hit the Earth somewhere near the Yucatan Peninsula, Mexico. The impact would have sent a dust cloud into the sky, blocking out light and heat from the Sun and causing ecological havoc on the planet, perhaps forcing a radical restructuring of the hierarchies of life. Evidence for this comes from the Iridium Anomaly – an unusually high level of the element iridium in the Earth's rock dating from 65 million years ago. Since iridium is usually found in great quantity in extra-terrestrial sources, this suggests that a major impact did occur at the K-T extinction boundary. Other impact theories suggest that comets from the Oort Cloud of space debris were disturbed from their orbit by either an unseen solar companion (Nemesis theory) or a tenth planet (Planet X theory).

COSMIC
These focus on a range of possibilities which might explain the decline of the dinosaur; a supernova, radiation from colliding stars, the solar system crossing the galactic plane, orbital eccentricity or even toxic gases from passing celestial bodies.

RELIGIOUS
Many creationists take a strongly anti-evolutionary stance, and believe dinosaurs were killed by the wrath of God, or died because there was no room for them in Noah's Ark.

The sheer diversity of these theories has caused much speculation and debate about the dinosaur's disappearance, although currently some form of impact theory holds the most favour with scientists. The discovery in 1997 of traces of 'asteroid dust' in 65-million-year-old sedimentary layers of the Earth's rocks would seem to provide conclusive evidence for this. The extinction of the dinosaurs has thrown up many questions: was it gradual or sudden? Was it part of a recurring 26-million-year cycle of mass extinction? What are the implications for the future survival of the human race? Whatever the reason for their disappearance, dinosaurs live on in the human imagination, their extinction having become one of the most enduring mysteries about life on Earth.

■ **THERE ARE REPUTED TO BE OVER 90 DIFFERENT DINOSAUR EXTINCTION THEORIES CIRCULATING** ■

MAJOR DINOSAUR ORDERS

Dinosaurs are split into two groups: the *Saurischia* and the *Ornithischia*.

SAURISCHIA

The *Saurischia* are further subdivided into sauropodomorphs and theropods.

SAUROPODOMORPHS

Sauropodomorphs were large herbivores and included:

prosauropods: large bipedal (two-legged) and quadruped (four-legged) dinosaurs whose herbivorous eating habits were illustrated by ridged beechleaf-shaped teeth. Prosauropods were the earliest known sauropodomorphs.

sauropods: extremely large, heavy, generally quadruped and herbivorous, sauropods had small skulls and brains, long necks and tails, and sturdy upright limbs as seen, for example, in *Diplodocus*.

THEROPODS

Theropods consisted of a wide number of meat-eating, bipedal dinosaurs, and included such ferocious predators as *Tyrannosaurus rex.* Theropod groups included:

carnosaurs: a diverse range of large carnivores with large heads, small necks, short arms, long and powerful legs and long tails. These were the largest carnivores to roam the Earth and included species such as *Tyrannosaurus rex* and other tyrannosaurids.

coelurosaurs: small meat-eating theropods which are characteristically agile and slender.

dromeosaurs: bipedal carnivores with raptorial talons for slashing and highly mobile hand-wrist complexes; fast-moving and agile, they include the *Velociraptor* and other efficient hunter-killers.

elmisaurids: small, quick and agile predators with raptorial claws.

ornithomimosaurs: medium to large-sized toothless theropods, lightly built, with long fore limbs, slender hind limbs and beak-like jaws.

oviraptorosaurs: similar to ornithomimosaurs, but had a toothless skull with curious large lumps and were probably egg-scavengers.

troodontids: small-sized dinosaurs with long, slender hindlimbs and the largest relative brain size of any dinosaur.

ORNITHISCHIA

ankylosaurs: the widest dinosaurs; heavily armoured quadrupeds with broad flattened skulls and long tails.

ceratopsids: medium to large rhinoceros-like quadrupeds with developed horns and frills.

hadrosaurs: so-called 'duck-billed' dinosaurs, they were large bipedal herbivores similar to iguanodontids, but with a broad beak.

iguanodontids: large bipedal herbivores with large back legs, long muscular tails and smaller front limbs, named after the *Iguanodon* dinosaur.

pachycephalosaurs: very thick-headed dinosaurs, often with a dome-shaped head.

psittacosaurs: dinosaur group characterized by a narrow parrot-like beak in front of the mouth.

stegosaurs: medium to large quadruped herbivores with massive short forelimbs and heavy plating along the spine.

MAJOR DINOSAUR GENERA

Ankylosaurus ('fused lizard'): a dinosaur whose body was covered in a thick armour of fused bony plates.

Apatosaurus: originally known as Brontosaurus, it weighed 30 tonnes, lived for up to120 years and was equally at home swimming in lakes or walking on land.

Baryonyx ('heavy claw'): named 'claws' after the massive claw on its hand, which was thought to have been used for disembowelling other dinosaurs or catching fish.

Brachiosaurus ('arm lizard'): 12 m (39 ft) tall and 23 m (75 ft) long, this dinosaur weighed 80 tonnes and had long front legs.

Compsognathus ('pretty jaw'): a chicken-sized dinosaur, related to birds, that fed on lizards.

Deinonychus ('terrible claw'): 3 m (10 ft) long, this leaping dinosaur had a sickle-like claw on each hind foot for killing prey.

Diplodocus ('double beam'): with a total length of 23 m (75 ft), this sauropod has the longest known tail of all dinosaurs – 11 m (36 ft) long.

Gallimimus ('chicken-mimic'): an ostrich-like dinosaur, 4 m (13 ft) long, with a large, toothless beak.

Iguanodon ('iguana tooth'): a plant-eating dinosaur with a pronounced bony spike on its 'thumb'.

Kentrosaurus ('centre lizard'): a dinosaur with long sharp spikes running along its back and tail.

Maiasaurus ('mother lizard'): a duck-billed dinosaur which built nests and cared for its young in 'dinosaur nurseries'.

Mamenchisaurus: with a total length of 23 m (75 ft), this sauropod had the longest known neck of any dinosaur – 11 m (36 ft).

Megalosaurus ('giant lizard'): this flesh-eater, 9 m (30 ft) long, was the first dinosaur ever discovered.

Mussaurus ('mouse lizard'): 200 mm (8 in) long and the smallest known relative of the sauropods.

Pachycephalosaurus ('thick-head lizard'): a bone-headed dinosaur with a distinctive massive bony thickening on the top of its head forming a 'battering ram'.

Parasaurolophus ('near ridged lizard'): a duckbilled dinosaur with a hollow crest 2 m (7 ft) long – containing nasal passages – projecting behind its head.

Plateosaurus ('flat lizard'): 6 m (20 ft) long, this plant-eating ancestor of the sauropods had a strong claw on each hand and small serrated teeth.

Polacanthus ('many spines'): 4 m (13 ft) long, this dinosaur had a large square bony 'blanket' over its hips and triangular plates along its back and tail.

Protoceratops ('first horned'): 2 m (7 ft) long, this ancestor of *Triceratops* possessed a similar bony frill over the neck but had no horns.

Saltasaurus ('lizard from Salta, Argentina'): a sauropod with bony plates – each 12 cm (5 in) in diameter – embedded in the skin.

Seismosaurus ('earthquake lizard'): at 33 m (108 ft) long, this is one of the largest land animals that ever lived.

Shantungosaurus ('Shantung lizard'): at 12 m (39 ft) long, this was the largest of the duck-billed dinosaurs.

Stegosaurus ('roof lizard'): at 9 m (30 ft) long, this dinosaur had two pairs of spikes on its tail and a row of large triangular plates – 1 m (3 ft) high – running along its back.

Supersaurus: 15 m (49 ft) tall and 30 m (98 ft) long, this large dinosaur may have weighed up to 100 tonnes.

Torosaurus ('bull lizard'): a dinosaur with a bony frill, extending over its shoulders, and a skull – 2.6 m (8.5 ft) long – which was the largest known of any land animal.

Triceratops ('three horned'): a dinosaur 9 m (30 ft) long with a bony frill over its neck and three long horns on its forehead.

Tyrannosaurus ('tyrant lizard'): 12 m (39 ft) long, this slow-moving flesh-eating scavenger had relatively small two-fingered hands.

Velociraptor ('speedy predator'): 1.8 m (6 ft) long (about the size of a coyote), this dromaeosaurid was a highly adapted hunter-killer with a sharp sickle-claw on each hind foot.

■ *This artist's impression is of a group of* Velociraptors *of the* Saurischia *order. These bipedal predators possessed sharp, sectorial teeth, long raptorial hands and weighed between 30–80 kg. One of the most important finds of the 1970s was a complete* Velociraptor *skeleton with its arms wrapped around the skeleton head of a* Protoceratops *– the first discovery of a predator and prey in action*

Prehistoric Animals

- **The first bird – *Archaeopteryx* – was, in many respects, indistinguishable from a small carnivorous dinosaur, but it was warm-blooded, covered in perfect feathers and could fly.**
- **The 'Eve hypothesis', although controversial, suggests that humankind descended from one particular female who lived in Africa about 200,000 years ago.**
- **During the Mesozoic era, the seas and oceans were inhabited by a host of marine reptiles which, like the airborne pterosaurs (called 'flying dinosaurs'), cannot be classified as dinosaurs.**
- **Many marine reptiles lived alongside dinosaurs and also became extinct at the end of the Cretaceous period.**

■ *Fossil of an* Ichthyosaurus *mother with an infant behind her and five more waiting to be born. The* Ichthyosaurus *survived two great extinctions, only to perish before the dinosaurs 65 million years ago*

BIRDS, FLYING REPTILES AND MARINE REPTILES

▶ The pterosaurs included the *Pterodactyl* and the *Pteranodon,* which were amongst the largest creatures ever to fly above the Earth, with wingspans up to three times greater than any bird alive today.
▶ Some people believe that the Loch Ness monster is a surviving example of a plesiosaur.

Although certain insects developed the ability to fly over 220 million years ago, it was a further 50 million years before the first flying reptiles entered the fossil record. One of the major groups – the pterosaurs – were large flying reptiles with vast wingspans. Often confused with dinosaurs, it is incorrect to call pterosaurs 'flying dinosaurs', despite co-existing with them. Pterosaurs died out during the Cretaceous period (see p. 29), and have left no surviving descendants.

Whilst pterosaurs ruled the skies, other landborne reptiles were evolving towards flight. The first bird was *Archaeopteryx,* the remains of which were discovered in 1861 in Germany. Studies of its weak breastbone structure suggest that its power of flight was somewhat limited. Whilst *Archaeopteryx* resembled its dinosaur relatives in many ways, further fossilized remains of birds dating from 30 million years after the first birds had much more avian (birdlike) characteristics. By the time of the K–T boundary, 65 million years ago, when dinosaurs became extinct, the reptilian aspects of birds had virtually disappeared, and several newer groups, including penguins and ducks, came into existence. However, there were also several groups of birds that lived during the Tertiary period (see p. 29) which did not survive into modern times, such as *Aepyornis* – the 'elephant bird' of Madagascar – and the giant *Diatryma* of North America.

Whilst dinosaurs dominated the land, and bird and flying reptiles ruled the realm of the sky, prehistoric seas and oceans were also swarming with animals. As well as fish, many marine reptiles co-existed with the dinosaurs. This fact has led to some confusion, with animals such as plesiosaurs being referred to as 'marine dinosaurs'. Although related, dinosaurs and marine reptiles were not one and the same.

PREHISTORIC BIRDS, FLYING REPTILES AND MARINE REPTILES

Aepyornis: a giant ostrich-like bird, 3 m (10 ft) high – the largest bird known to have existed – whose remains were found in abundance on Madagascar and whose fossilized eggs were used by sailors to hold their rum. This bird gave rise to the legendary 'Roc' of Sinbad.
Archaeopteryx ('ancient wing'): the first bird known to have existed, crow-sized and with many characteristics in common with dinosaurs – such as a long bony tail and teeth in its jaws – which lived *c.* 175 million years ago.
Archelon: a large marine turtle, 3–5 m (10–16 ft) long, broadly equivalent in size to a car.
Diatryma: a 2-m (7-ft) tall flightless flesh-eating bird which lived at the beginning of the age of mammals, 60 million years ago.
Gigantornis: a bird with an 8-m (26-ft) wingspan which lived *c.* 50 million years ago.
Hesperornis ('western bird'): a flightless diving bird with teeth.
Ichthyornis ('fish bird'): a tern-like bird the size of a domestic pigeon that was once believed to have had teeth in its jaws.
Ichthyosaurus ('fish lizard'): highly-adapted marine reptile about 3 m (10 ft) long, with dorsal fins and vertical tail fins.
Mosasaurus: a giant 9-m (30-ft) marine lizard and close relative of the monitor lizard family.
Plesiosaurus: large marine reptiles with paddle-like tails, stiff torsos and short or long necks.
Pteranodon: large highly-developed gliding reptile with a wingspan of about 7.5 m (25 ft) and a characteristic crest at the back of its skull.
Pterodactyl: a flying reptile, 4–5 m (13–16 ft) long, whose membranous wings spanned up to 11–12 m (36–39 ft).

PREHISTORIC MAMMALS

▶ From detailed study of skulls of prehistoric reptiles that conquered the land about 295 million years ago, it is now presumed that they were the ancestors of the first mammals.
▶ Modern mammal species can differ greatly in size from their prehistoric ancestors – some ancient armadillos were up to 3 m (10 ft) long, compared to some modern ones measuring as little as 16 cm ($6\frac{1}{3}$ in), and the earliest horse was the size of a small dog, compared to horses today which can be as tall as 2 m (7 ft).

The origins of mammals can be traced back to the Carboniferous period, 345–280 million years ago. At this time there existed one of the first reptile groups – the synapsids – often referred to as mammal-like reptiles. From these evolved the therapsids – small and active reptiles which lived in the shadow of their more impressive cousins, the dinosaurs.

The two distinguishing characteristics that linked therapsids to the modern mammal were their specialized teeth and the positioning of their legs directly under their bodies – like modern birds and mammals.

From these small, carnivorous 'paramammals' evolved the first true mammals of the Triassic period (about 200 million years ago), although from the fossil record it is impossible to pinpoint the exact moment that mammals evolved into a separate class of animals. The ability of mammals to adapt allowed them to survive the dinosaurs and, from the end of the Cretaceous period, 65 million years ago, they became more dominant and more diverse.

The last 65 million years has seen a huge growth in the variety of mammals both on land and in water, although many species of mammal became extinct even before the rise of humankind. The sabre-tooth cat, often depicted in cinema and literature as co-existing with dinosaurs, actually lived many millions of years after the Great Extinction.

Possibly, in the not-too-distant future, once extinct mammals will roam the Earth again. Already, genetic scientists are trying to bring a version of the woolly mammoth back to life by extracting mammoth sperm from frozen remains to fertilize elephant eggs, and using a living elephant as an incubator.

PREHISTORIC MAMMALS

Arsinoitherium: a rhinoceros-like animal with horns side by side on its snout; *c.* 35 million years old.
Basilosaurus: a small-headed whale, 20 m (66 ft) long, with the appearance of a 'sea serpent', which lived *c.* 50 million years ago.
Brontotherium: a large rhinoceros-like animal, 2.5 m (8 ft) at the shoulder, which had double-curved horns at the tip of the snout and lived *c.* 30 million years ago.
Coelodonta: a thick-haired woolly rhinoceros which lived during the last Ice Age.
Diprotodon: a giant rhinoceros-sized wombat, 4 m (13 ft) long.
Enteledon: a giant, pig-like animal, 2 m (7 ft) long, with bony projections on its lower jaws and sides of its skull – it has been called the ugliest mammal ever.
Glyptodon: a heavily armoured relative of the armadillo – 3.3 m (11 ft) long and 1.5 m (5 ft) high.
Icaronycteris: the first known insect-eating bat which lived *c.* 50 million years ago.
Indricotherium: a giant hornless rhinoceros, weighing 30 tonnes and standing 5.5 m (18 ft) at the shoulder, which lived *c.* 30 million years ago.
Kuehneotherium: the first true mammal, about the size of a shrew, dating from 220 million years ago.
Mammuthus: the woolly mammoth – a thick-haired large elephant with spirally curved tusks inhabiting the tundra during the last Ice Age (2.5 million to 10,000 years ago). It is thought to have been hunted by early man.
Megaloceros: a giant deer, weighing 45 kg (99 lb), whose antlers had a 3.7-m (12-ft) span and which lived during the last Ice Age.
Megatherium: a giant ground sloth – 5.5 m (18 ft) tall – with huge clawed feet.
Pakicetus: the first toothed whale, which had four paddle-like legs and lived *c.* 53 million years ago.
Procoptodon: a giant, short-faced kangaroo standing 3 m (10 ft) tall.
Propalaeotherium: a four-toed horse, 40 cm (16 in) high, which lived *c.* 50 million years ago.
Purgatorius: named after Purgatory Hill, Montana, USA, where remains of this first primate were found alongside dinosaur remains.
Smilodon: a sabre-tooth cat, larger than the modern lion, with long, stabbing canine teeth up to 20 cm (8 in) long.
Thoatherium: a one-toed horse-like litoptern, not related to true horses.
Thylacoleo: a marsupial lion with incisor 'stabbing' teeth at the front of its jaws.
Thylacosmilus: a pouched (marsupial) sabre-tooth cat as large as a modern jaguar (unrelated to true sabre-tooths) which lived *c.* 15 million years ago.

PREHISTORIC MAN

▶ A piece of evidence indicating the common ancestry of humans and monkeys is the coccyx bone, found at the base of the spine in humans, which is thought to be the remains of a tail and which has now become a vestigial structure (one that no longer functions).
▶ *Ramapithecus,* an early hominoid of the Miocene epoch, was once thought to be the ancestor of man, but is now believed to be a relative of the orang-utan.

The origins of humankind lie in the earliest primitive primates of the early Tertiary period, about 65 million years ago. During the Oligocene epoch (38–26 million years ago) these developed into, amongst other species, primitive monkeys and very primitive anthropoid apes. Primates evolved further during the Miocene epoch (26–19 million years ago) when the first hominids appeared.

The evolution of a larger brain and more developed limb structure in primates resulted in the genus *Australopithecus,* the man-apes, or woodland apes. This genus appeared with perfect erect posture in southern and eastern Africa about 6–4 million years ago, at the boundary of the Miocene and Pliocene epochs (see p. 29). Australopithecines, the earliest known hominids (the primate family that includes modern man), were adapted to walking on two legs. The two main strands of this genus were gracile (the earlier, smaller species) and robust, developing later. The gracile strand gave rise to the genus *Homo*, co-existing with robust Australopithecines until the latter died out about one million years ago.

DEVELOPMENT OF THE GENUS *HOMO*

c. 2.4 million years ago	Probable appearance of *Homo habilis*, the earliest generally recognized species of *Homo*. First tools in Africa
c. 1.7 million years ago	*Homo habilis* builds first structured habitats in southern and eastern Africa
c. 1.6 million years ago	Emergence of *Homo erectus* in eastern Africa
c. 1.5 to 1.2 million years ago	Sophisticated stone tools used in Africa. *Homo erectus* probably controls fire during this period
c. 500,000 years ago	Emergence of *Homo sapiens*
c. 100,000 years ago	*Homo sapiens* splits into two lines: *Homo sapiens neanderthalensis* ('Neanderthal Man') and *Homo sapiens sapiens* (modern man)
c. 80,000 to *c.* 35,000 years ago	*Homo sapiens sapiens* spread into western Asia, Australia and Europe
c. 34,000 to *c.* 30,000 years ago	Neanderthals become extinct or are genetically absorbed by newer sapients. Rise of Cro-Magnon Man (an early type of modern man)

■ *Stages in human evolution. The first,* proconsul *(23–15 million years ago), is a hypothetical drawing of an African ape with both primitive and advanced characteristics. The second,* Australopithecus afarensis *(4–2.5 million years ago), was fully bipedal (walking on two legs). The third,* Homo habilis *(2.4 million years ago), was the first truly human species and used stone tools. The fourth,* Homo erectus, *appeared first in Africa, used fire and wooden tools, and migrated into Eurasia. The fifth,* Homo neanderthalensis *(100,000 years ago), lived in Europe and the Middle East and was closely related to modern man (the sixth stage)*

ENDANGERED ANIMALS

- The blue whale population that lives in the southern hemisphere is only 0.2% of its original size.
- CITES (Convention on International Trade in Endangered Species of Wild Fauna and Flora), is a global treaty aimed at protecting endangered wildlife by monitoring and regulating its trade.
- The price of 1 kg of ivory increased from $63 to $260 in the ten years from 1976, when its sale became illegal.
- Three species of tiger (Caspian, Javan and Bali) became extinct in the 19th century.
- More than 90% of the entire world's rhinoceros population has disappeared since 1970.

Endangered species are those that are in grave danger of extinction, and which can only survive if the threats which menace their existence are removed through the implementation of conservation measures. Endangered and vulnerable species (ones which may become endangered if their numbers continue to drop) are collectively known as threatened species.

Extinction is a natural process of life, and there have been several mass extinctions of which the best known is the one that wiped out the dinosaurs 65 million years ago. However, the actions of humans have greatly accelerated natural extinction rates. By 1996, the International Union for Conservation of Nature and Natural Resources (IUCN) had compiled a 'Red List' of 5205 species threatened with extinction.

There are several key factors that contribute to the threat of extinction. Most important are the destruction of the natural habitat, competition from introduced species, and human exploitation by hunting or fishing a species to exhaustion, and by poaching. Some species can adapt to environmental changes, but in so doing often evolve into a distinctly new species.

SPECIES AT RISK

	Mammals and birds
Indonesia	232
Brazil	174
China	165
India	148
Philippines	135
Peru	110
Australia	103
Mexico	100
Papua New Guinea	88
USA	85
Vietnam	85
Thailand	79
Malaysia	76
Myanmar (Burma)	75
Madagascar	74
Russia	69
Kenya	67
Congo (ex-Zaïre)	64
Tanzania	63
Japan	62

ELEPHANTS

African elephant
(*Loxodonta africana*) Whilst its population has more than halved from 1.3 million in 1979 to 586,000 in 1995, the African elephant has managed to survive in several big reserves. However, their number has, in some cases, exceeded the capacity of the land to support them, prompting several countries to ask for a resumption in a controlled ivory trade.

Asian elephant
(*Elephas maximus*) The Asian elephant (above), which once roamed across Asia, is now confined to areas between India and Vietnam. They live in areas of rapid human population expansion, and the human need for space has resulted in the disruption of the natural elephant migration routes.

PRIMATES

Gorilla
(*Gorilla gorilla*) The largest of the primates (right), it is under threat from poachers. Its natural habitat in Rwanda and The Congo (ex-Zaïre) has been encroached upon in recent years by civil war, disorder and the pressure of increasing human population.

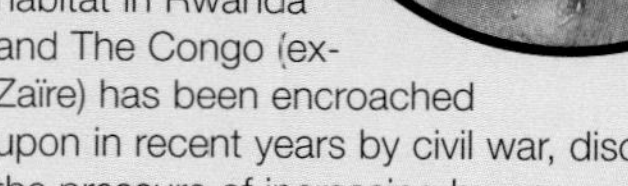

Lemur family
(*Lemuridae*) Some 14 species of these very small-to-medium primates existed 50 years ago in Madagascar. Some are already extinct, the remainder are under threat because of drought and deforestation (see p. 58).

Madagascan aye-aye
(*Daubentonia madagascariensis*) These lemur-like animals, of which very few remain, are the subject of a captive breeding programme at Jersey Zoo.

Orang-utan
(*Pongo pygmaeus*) This primate's natural habitat in Indonesia and Malaysia is threatened by destruction of the rainforest.

Golden lion tamarin
(*Leontopitthecus rosalia*) One of the most threatened of all mammals, this critically endangered primate is found only in several fragmented groups in Brazil.

RHINOCEROS

Black rhino
(*Diceros bicornis*) This species (right) has seen a drastic decline in population. In 1970 there were about 65,000 black rhinos, whereas less than 2000 are estimated to be alive today. This represents a decline of 97% in just 27 years.

Indian rhino
(*Rhinoceros unicornis*) Less than 2000 wild rhinos are left.

Javan rhino
(*Rhinoceros sondaicus*) Under 100 animals remain in isolated populations on Java and in Vietnam.

Sumatran rhino
(*Dicerorhinus sumatrensis*) There are 400–500 Sumatran rhinos left in the wild.

White rhino
(*Ceratotherium simum*) There used to be two significant populations of the white rhino, in northern and southern Africa. The northern population has been almost entirely decimated. The southern population, based in South Africa, has experienced a rise in numbers – at the turn of the century they were nearly extinct, but now number about 6000.

WILD CATS

Asiatic lion
(*Panthera leo persica*) Under 200 Asiatic lions (right) remain, principally in the Gir National Park in India.

Iriomote cat
(*Felis iriomotensis*) The 100 specimens or so that remain are confined to Iriomote Island in the Ryukyu chain of islands, near Okinawa, Japan, and a few Japanese zoos.

Tigers
All the existing subspecies are at risk: Siberian tiger (*Panthera tigris altaica*) less than 200; South China tiger (*Panthera tigris amoyensis*) less than 80; Indo-Chinese tiger (*Panthera tigris corbetti*) under 1800; Bengal tiger (*Panthera tigris tigris*) less than 4000; Sumatran tiger (*Panthera tigris sumatrae*) under 500. Only about 6000 wild tigers exist in Asia and eastern Russia. This figure compares with 100,000 at the beginning of the 20th century.

GIANT PANDA

(*Ailuropoda melanoleuca*) Only around 700 specimens exist in the wild, and there is a real chance that they may become extinct by the end of the century. They are confined to the Sichuan mountains in China. The main causes of population decline are the loss of natural habitat coupled with poaching, a crime punishable by death in China. A problem in the past has been the removal of pandas from the wild to zoos, but this is now carefully monitored. The giant panda has become a focus for the international conservation movement; its plight has attracted help for its own cause, and engendered interest in the state of endangered wildlife. It is the symbol of the World Wild Fund for Nature (WWF), an international organization dedicated to the preservation of wildlife.

BEARS

Asiatic black bear
(*Ursus thibetanus*) This species (right) from Tibet and the Himalayas is one of the most threatened of the six endangered bear species. Its inner organs are prized in oriental medicine.

Sloth bear
(*Melursus ursinus*) Locally known as *bhalu*, this Asian species is adapted for life in trees, having long claws which allow it to hang from branches in a sloth-like manner. Like other threatened bear species, hunting and loss of habitat mean that it is in urgent need of protection.

Sun bear
(*Helarctos malayanus*) Also known as the Malay bear, this is the smallest of the bear species.

INSECTS

Queen Alexandra's birdwing
(*Ornithoptera alexandrae*) The world's largest butterfly (right), found in Papua New Guinea, is one of many endangered butterfly species.

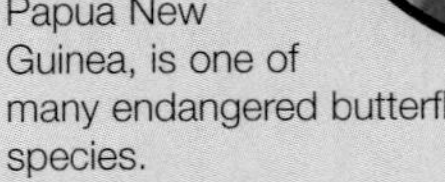

Saint Francis' satyr butterfly
(*Neonnympha mitchellii francisci*) Thought extinct, the species was rediscovered in 1992. It is found only in a small area of the USA.

St Helena giant earwig
(*Labidura herculeana*) This species is already believed to be extinct – the last recorded sighting was in 1965.

OTHER MAMMALS

Arabian oryx
(*Oryx leucoryx*) Found in Jordan, Oman and Saudi Arabia, this species (right) was hunted almost to extinction by 1972. Numbers are now increasing as animals bred in captivity (mainly at Marwell Zoo, Hampshire, UK) are released.

Black-footed ferret
(*Mustela nigripes*) This North American species has only recently been rediscovered in the wild. Its decline was the result of the destruction of its main source of food, the prairie dog. It is now the focus of a captive breeding and reintroduction programme.

European bison
(*Bison bonasus*) Less than 2000 individuals remain in Bialowieza Forest (on the borders of Poland and Belarus) and the Caucasus.

Père David's deer
(*Elaphurus davidianus*) Originally from China, this species of deer became extinct in the wild in about 1920, although some specimens were kept in zoos and other collections (principally at Woburn Abbey and Whipsnade Zoo, Bedfordshire UK). Individuals reared in captivity are now being reintroduced back into the wild in parts of China.

Tibetan antelope
(*Pantholops hodgsoni*) This rare antelope species has been hunted for its fine wool (shahtoosh), which fetches high prices.

REPTILES

Abingdon Island giant tortoise
(*Geochelone abingdoni*) This species of Galápagos giant tortoise is represented by one single living specimen, an old male called Lonesome George. There is little chance of finding another specimen and so when this individual dies the species will become extinct.

Day geckos
(*Phelsuma* species) These reptiles are found in the wild in only a few islands in the Indian Ocean. One of the main causes for their rapid decline is the exportation of specimens to the Western world to cater for the huge demand in exotic pets.

Komodo dragon
(*Varanus komodoensis*) Only a few hundred of this large monitor lizard (above) exist on the island of Komodo and a few on the neighbouring Lesser Sunda islands of Indonesia.

Round Island keel-scaled boa
(*Casarea dussumieri*) This species, from a small island off the coast of Mauritius, is currently being bred in captivity at Jersey Zoo, Channel Islands.

BIRDS

California condor
(*Gymnogyps californianus*) Close to extinction in the wild, where only a handful of captive-bred specimens live, there are about 70 condors in captivity.

Japanese crested ibis
(*Nipponia nippon*) The destruction of the natural habitat has resulted in very few surviving specimens. Most of the captive individuals (above) are too old to breed.

Nene
(*Branta sandvicensis*) Once extinct in the wild, the nene, or Hawaiian goose, has been successfully reintroduced from captivity at Slimbridge, UK, back into Hawaii, where some 500 individuals now live.

New Zealand kakapo
(*Strigops habroptilus*) Hunted almost to extinction. The few specimens that still exist are predominantly male.

Spix's macaw
(*Cyanopsitta spixii*) About 30 of these macaws exist in captivity, but there is only one known wild specimen in Brazil.

WATER LIFE

Blue whale
(*Balaenoptera musculus*) The largest ever mammal (right), there are only 500 individuals today in the southern hemisphere, down from an estimated 250,000.

Caribbean monk seal
(*Monachus tropicalis*) This seal is so rare it may have already become extinct.

Devil's hole pupfish
(*Cyprinodon diabolis*) There are about 200–500 individuals, but they are restricted to a small pool in Nevada. Recent pumping of underground water has affected their habitat.

Fin whale
(*Balaenoptera physalus*) Hunted and exploited in the wild. Over the past three generations, its population has more than halved.

Mediterranean monk seal
(*Monachus monachus*) Between 420 and 560 individuals remain. Its natural habitat is accessible to scuba divers and motor boats, and these seals may get tangled in nets. The animals are of a very nervous disposition and disturbances can result in pregnant females spontaneously aborting their unborn young.

White-toothed cowry
(*Cypraea leucodon*) Only two specimens are known – the second was discovered in 1960.

Yangtze river dolphin
(*Lipotes vexillifer*) Also known as baiji, there are less than 150 individuals of this species in China.

NATIONAL PARKS

- Death Valley National Park is the lowest point in the Western Hemisphere at 85 m below sea level.
- In the Galápagos Islands, now a national park, Charles Darwin found much of the evidence for his theory of evolution.
- Great Barrier Reef National Park is the world's largest marine park.

National parks are regions set apart by governments for the preservation of the natural world. Many areas of the world are disappearing, and flora, fauna and vivid landscapes are being destroyed. Thus these parks are vital realms of the wild where endangered species such as the Asiatic lion, the bald eagle and the giant panda can flourish and survive. National parks vary in size, and while some concentrate on the preservation of animals, others seek to preserve the landscape from erosion. Many parks survive through controlled tourism – thus enabling these last wildernesses to be enjoyed today and in the future.

■ *A pride of lions resting in Gir National Park, Gujarat, India*

MAJOR NATIONAL PARKS AND NATURE RESERVES

PARK, COUNTRY	LOCATION	km²	sq mi	FAUNA
ABRUZZI, Italy	Part of the Apennine mountains	392	151	brown bear, chamois, golden eagle, lynx, polecat, wolf
AMAZONIA, Brazil	Area of tropical rain forest along the Amazon river basin	10,000	4,000	armadillo, capybara, tapir, great anteater, manatee, many species of monkey, birds (hummingbirds, toucans, parrots, macaws)
ANGKOR, Cambodia	Tropical forest surrounding Angkor temple ruins	107	41	primarily designated to preserve the historic site
ARUSHA, Tanzania	Region of mountains, swamps, forest and lakes	137	53	hippopotamus, elephants, various species of antelope, flamingos
BANFF, Alberta, Canada	Mountainous terrain in central Canadian Rockies	6,641	2,564	mule deer, caribou, elk, golden eagle, bear (grizzly, black)
BIALOWIESKI, Poland and BELOVEZHSKAYA, Belarus	Best-preserved primeval lowland forest in Europe	928	358	European bison, tarpan, lynx, brown bear
CANAIMA, Venezuela	The large mountainous La Gran Sabana basin	30,000	11,583	jaguar, tiger cat, tapir, peccary, armadillo, agouti, capybara, opossums, spider monkeys, jacamars, harpy eagle, puffbirds
CARLSBAD CAVERNS, New Mexico, USA	System of 35 limestone caverns in the Guadelupe Mountains	189	73	bats, surface mammals
CÉVENNES, France	South of the Massif Central	844	326	genet, golden eagle, mountain sheep, wild boar
CORBETT, Uttar Pradesh, India	Foothills of the Himalayas on the banks of the River Ramganga	520	201	elephant, tiger, leopard, sloth bear, spotted deer
DAISETSUZAN, Japan	Part of the Ishikari volcanic mountain range in Hokkaido	2,309	892	Asiatic black bear, Japanese macaque, northern pika, chipmunk, black woodpecker, three-toed woodpecker
DARTMOOR, England, UK	Moorland in central Devon	945	365	fallow, red and roe deer; wild pony
DEATH VALLEY, – California, Nevada, USA	Large low-lying desert surrounded by mountains	8,368	3,231	desert bighorn sheep, cougar, fishes descended from fish of the Pleistocene Age
DENALI, Alaska, USA	Mountainous area on northern flank of the Alaska Range, including North America's highest mountain, Mt McKinley	24,419	9,428	moose, grizzly bear, Arctic ground squirrel, golden eagle
ETOSHA, Namibia	Semi-arid plains around the Etosha Pan	22,270	8,598	elephants, rhinoceros, lion, leopard, lynx, Burchell's zebra, various species of antelope
EVERGLADES, Florida, USA	Large flat area of swamps and islands, plus Florida Bay	5,661	2,186	manatee, saltwater crocodile, matamata and other turtles, cougar, ibis, bald eagle, kites
FIORDLAND, New Zealand	Rugged area on south-western coast of South Island	12,116	4,678	seals, many birds (mountain parrot, bush hawk, kiwi – a refuge for the takahe and kakapo) and mammals introduced by man
FUJI-HAKONE–IZU, Japan	Comprises Mount Fuji, Izu peninsula and the seven active volcanic islands of Izu	1,232	476	skia deer, wild boar, Japanese macaque monkeys, Japanese dormouse, Japanese auk, many other birds
GALÁPAGOS, Ecuador	Santa Cruz Island on Galápagos archipelago	6,790	2,621	giant tortoise, giant iguana, flamingo, pelican, Darwin's finches
GEMSBOK, Botswana	Region of desert, plains and grasslands in south-east Botswana	24,305	9,384	eland, gemsbok, hartebeest, springbok, wildebeest, kuku
GIR LION, Gujarat, India	Hilly region on Kathiawar Peninsula	1,412	545	lion, leopard, hyena, antelope, deer, wild pig, sloth bear, monkey
GRAND CANYON, Arizona, USA	Gorge of the Colorado River (the gorge's rocks represent a vast stretch of geological time)	4,931	1,904	100 species of mammals, 100 varieties of birds, 25 kinds of reptiles and amphibians
GRAN PARADISO, Italy	In the Alps on the Piedmont–Valle d'Aosta border	700	270	chamois, golden eagle, otter, ibex, marten, ptarmigan, white grouse
GREAT BARRIER REEF, Australia	2900 individual reefs and hundreds of islands and coral cays stretching for 2000 km (1250 mi)	207,000	80,000	humpback whale, whale shark, sea turtle, dugong, about 1500 fish species, 350 coral species (it has the world's largest structure of living corals)
HOHE TAUERN, Austria	Eastern Alps (includes the Grossglockner)	2,589	1,000	chamois, marmot
HORTOBÁGYI, Hungary	Steppe and marshes in central Hungary	520	201	many species of geese
HWANGE, Zimbabwe	Expanse of the Kalahari Desert, including Nyamandhlovu Pan	14,651	5,657	black rhinoceros (for which it is a refuge), buffalo, brindled gnu, roan antelope, impala, sassaby
JASPER, Alberta, Canada	Part of the eastern Canadian Rockies	10,878	4,200	elk, moose, mountain caribou, cougar, osprey, golden eagle, blue grouse
KAFUE, Zambia	Plateau area including some of the Kalahari Desert in the south, bordered by the River Kafue	22,400	8,650	hippopotamus, black rhinoceros (for which the park is a refuge), crocodile, many species of antelope, numerous birds
KATMAI, Alaska, USA	Area of dying volcanoes in the Aleutian Range	16,550	6,390	Alaskan brown bear (the largest land carnivore), caribou, moose, many small mammals, birds, fish

■ YOSEMITE NATIONAL PARK, CALIFORNIA, HAS THE HIGHEST WATERFALL IN AMERICA AT 739 M ■

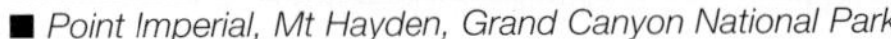

■ Point Imperial, Mt Hayden, Grand Canyon National Park

■ Serengeti National Park in Tanzania, Africa, is one of the most popular national parks for filming TV wildlife programmes

PARK, COUNTRY	LOCATION	km²	sq mi	FAUNA
KHAO YAI, Thailand	Area of mountains and plateaus in south-west Thailand	2,168	837	elephant, tiger, wild boar, mongoose, civet, langur, gibbon, numerous birds (silver pheasant, red-billed blue magpie)
KOSCIUSZKO, New South Wales, Australia	Area of alpine peaks and plateaus in the Great Dividing Range	6,297	2,431	grey forester kangaroos, brush-tailed rock wallaby, wombats, marsupial and pouched mice, koala, duck-billed platypuses, many birds (emu, currawongs)
KRUGER, South Africa	Area of hills and plains	19,485	7,523	white rhinoceros (for which the park is a refuge), African buffalo, red jackal
LAKE DISTRICT, England, UK	Mountains of Cumbria	2,243	866	fell ponies, mountain sheep, red deer
LAKE MEAD, Arizona–Nevada, USA	Area of canyons of the Colorado River (canyons contain fossils of prehistoric animals)	6,057	2,338	desert bighorn sheep, wild burro, cougar, bobcat, many small animals
MANOVO–GOUNDA–SAINT FLORIS, Central African Republic	Part of the upper basin of the River Chari	17,400	6,718	buffalo, large antelope, many species of birds including egret
MANU, Peru	Comprises a rugged Andean area, part of the Amazon River system and tropical forest	15,328	5,918	various birds and small mammals
MOUNT ASPIRING, New Zealand	Mountainous region including slopes of the Southern Alps on South Island	2,873	1,109	many varieties of birds (parakeets, owl parrot), red deer, possum
NAMIB DESERT/ NAUKLUFT, Namibia	Stretches from the Atlantic coast to the Namib Desert and the Naukluft Mountains	23,400	9,035	elephant shrew, desert golden mole, black-backed jackal, bat-eared fox, sand grouse, egret, lark
NGORONGORO, Tanzania	Several extinct volcanic craters, some including lakes	8,292	3,202	cross-section of wildlife typical of African savannah
PALLAS–OUNASTUNTURI, Finland	Plateau in Lapland	500	193	brown bear, crane, elk, lemming, reindeer, whooper swan
PEMBROKESHIRE COAST, Wales, UK	Coastal region of Pembrokeshire	583	225	many varieties of bird (including buzzard, chough, merlin and sea birds), grey seal, otter, polecat
PFÄLZERWALD, Germany	The Palatinate plateau	1,793	692	European bison, mountain sheep, mountain goat
REDWOOD, California, USA	Pacific coast	442	171	Roosevelt elk, fox, squirrel, rabbit, salmon, trout, numerous birds
ROCKY MOUNTAIN, Colorado, USA	Region in Front Range of the Rocky Mountains	1,068	412	bighorn sheep, elk, beaver, deer, cougar, golden eagle, hawks
RONDANE, Norway	Mountainous region on the borders of Hedmark and Oppland	572	221	brown bear, elk, golden eagle, lemming, lynx, reindeer, wolf
SAREK, Sweden	Mountainous area in Lapland	1,940	749	similar species to those found in Rondane (above)
SERENGETI, Tanzania	Large plain with hilly ranges and rocky kopjes	14,763	5,700	elephant, black rhinoceros (for which the park is a refuge), lion, leopard, cheetah, hyena, buffalo, zebra, giraffe, various species of antelope
SKAFTAFELL, Iceland	In the south of Iceland	500	193	bear, grey seal, many species of sea bird
SNOWDONIA, Wales, UK	Mountainous area around Snowdon	2,171	838	otter, polecat, pine marten
TSAVO, Kenya	Stretching from the semi-arid plains in the SE to the Chyulu Hills and foothills of Mt Kilimanjaro in the W	20,821	8,039	black rhinoceros, various species of antelope (lesser kudu, fringe-eared oryx, gerenuk, hartebeest), numerous birds
ULURU, Northern Territory, Australia	Area of rocky terrain, including Ayers Rock, the monolith cluster of Mt Olga and aboriginal rock paintings	1,261	487	kangaroo, wallaby, euro, dingo, bandicoot rat, emu, various snakes and lizards
VALLE DE ORDESA, Spain	Deep ravines and glacial moraines of the Río Ara	20	8	brown bear, Spanish ibex, alpine chough, lammergeiers
VANOISE, France	Along the Italian border in Savoy	528	204	chamois, golden eagle, otter, ibex, marten, ptarmigan, white grouse
WOOD BUFFALO, Alberta–Northwest Territories, Canada	Area of open plains between Lake Athabasca and Great Slave Lake	44,800	17,300	bison (wood buffalo, plains buffalo), elk, moose, woodland caribou, bear (black, grizzly), lynx, whooping crane, grouse (the park is a refuge for bison and whooping cranes)
YELLOWSTONE, Wyoming–Montana–Idaho, USA	Part of Rocky Mountains (largest thermal area in the park contains sulphur pools and geysers, including the famous 'Old Faithful')	8,984	3,469	wapiti, bison, over 200 species of birds (trumpeter swan, tanager, Canada goose)
YOSEMITE, California, USA	Region of canyons, gorges and peaks in the Sierra Nevada	3,079	1,189	bear, deer, ground squirrel, chipmunk, Steller's jay, Clark's nutcracker, mountain quail

■ THE WORLD'S OLDEST NATIONAL PARK (1872) IS YELLOWSTONE IN WYOMING, USA ■

Life Scientists

- Ronald Ross, who discovered that mosquitoes spread malaria, campaigned for the destruction of the mosquito as the only way to eradicate the disease.
- In the 19th century, before the important discoveries of Robert Koch and Selman Waksman, one-seventh of the world's population died from tuberculosis.
- Pliny (the Elder) died through volcanic gas poisoning during the eruption of Mt Vesuvius.

Adrian, Lord (Edgar Douglas Adrian; 1889–1977), English physiologist who – with Sherrington – studied the nerve cell, discovering the mechanism by which nerves carry messages to and from the brain.

Agassiz, Jean Louis (1807–73), Swiss-born US naturalist who made important contributions to glaciation research, proving ice ages existed.

Alcmaeon (*c.* 520 BC), Greek physician who is the first recorded practitioner of anatomical dissection.

Aristotle (see p. 120)

Avery, Oswald Theodore (1877–1955), Canadian-born US bacteriologist whose studies of pneumococci (bacterium found in the respiratory tracts) had important implications for later DNA research.

Avicenna (Abu-Ali al-Husayn ibn-Sina; 980–1037), Uzbek-born Persian philosopher and pioneer physician who was an outstanding compiler of an encyclopedia covering medicine, mathematics and natural sciences.

Barr, Murray Llewellyn (1908–95), Canadian geneticist who discovered the now-called Barr bodies – densely staining nuclear bodies present in the somatic cells of female mammals.

Bartholin, Thomas (1616–80), Danish physician and mathematician who described the human lymphatic system.

Bateson, William (1861–1926), English biologist who named the science 'genetics'. His experiments concerning plant inheritance provided evidence that was fundamental to modern studies of heredity.

Beadle, George Wells (1903–89), US biochemist who proposed that specific genes control the production of specific enzymes.

Berg, Paul (1926–), US molecular biologist who identified the first adaptor (1956) and devised a way of inserting 'foreign' genes into bacteria.

Bernard, Claude (1813–78), French physiologist who made important discoveries concerning the part played by the pancreas in digestion, the glycogenic role of the liver and the way in which vasomotor nerves regulate the blood supply.

Borelli, Giovanni (1608–79), Italian physicist and physiologist who first explained muscular movement.

Brown, Robert (see p. 120)

Candolle, Augustin Pyrame de (1778–1841), Swiss botanist who was the first to use the word taxonomy for the classification of plants by morphology (forms) rather than by their physiology (functions).

Cohn, Ferdinand Julius (1828–98), German botanist who laid the foundations of modern bacteriology.

Crick, Francis (1916–), English biophysicist who – with Watson and Wilkins – determined the molecular structure of DNA.

Cuvier, Baron Georges (1769–1832), French naturalist who classified animals according to principles of comparative anatomy.

Darwin, Charles Robert (1809–82), English naturalist who proposed the modern theory of evolution. In his *On the Origin of Species by Means of Natural Selection* (1859), based upon observations made on a five-year expedition in South America and the Pacific region, he surmised that species evolve by means of a process of natural selection involving the survival of the fittest and a gradual adaptation of animals to survive in changed circumstances or habitats. In *The Descent of Man* (1871), Darwin rationalized the evolution of man from a primitive animal he believed was also an ancestor of the apes. His theories were highly controversial and had a profound effect upon both scientific and religious opinion.

Dawkins, Richard (1941–), English ethologist who – in *The Selfish Gene* (1976) – identified the apparently altruistic behaviour of some animals as the 'selfish gene' ensuring the survival of the species.

Delbrück, Max (1907–81), German-born US pioneer in molecular genetics.

de Vries, Hugo (1848–1935), Dutch geneticist and plant physiologist who studied heredity in plants.

d'Herelle, Felix (1873–1949), Canadian bacteriologist who discovered bacteriophage – a virus parasitic in bacterium which multiplies within its host and is destroyed when new viruses are released.

Dobzhansky, Theodosius (1900–75), Ukrainian-born US geneticist whose studies of the fruit fly demonstrated that genetic variations within populations are far greater than had previously been imagined.

Dulbecco, Renato (1914–), Italian-born US molecular biologist and physician who introduced the concept of cell transformation in biology.

Ehrlich, Paul (1854–1915), German bacteriologist who pioneered developments in haematology and immunology, and who founded the science of chemotherapy.

Engler, Adolf (1844–1930), German botanist who – in his monumental *The Natural Plant Families* – developed a system of plant classification.

Erlanger, Joseph (1874–1965), US neurophysicist who studied the differentiated functions of nerve fibres.

Fleming, Sir Alexander (1881–1955), Scottish bacteriologist who accidentally discovered that the fungus *Penicillium notatum* was able to kill bacteria (1928).

Franklin, Rosalind (1920–58), English crystallographer who played an important part in discovering DNA structure with her X-ray photograph of hydrated DNA (see p. 109).

Galen (*c.* 131–200), Greek physician whose writing on anatomy was the standard text for 1500 years.

Gallo, Robert (1937–), US physician who was one of the first to identify HIV, the virus responsible for AIDS.

Golgi, Camillo (1843–1926), Italian cytologist who discovered the organelles Golgi bodies.

Haeckel, Ernst (1834–1919), German biologist who was an important supporter of Darwinism.

Haldane, J(ohn) B(urdon) S(anderson) (1892–1964), Scottish biologist who explored new fields of research in genetics and evolution.

Hall, Marshall (1790–1857), English physiologist who proposed a scientific theory to explain reflex action.

Haller, Albrecht von (1708–77), Swiss physiologist, botanist, anatomist and poet regarded as the founder of experimental physiology.

Harvey, William (1578–1657), English physician who discovered the nature of blood circulation in the body and the heart's function as a pump.

Hershey, Alfred Day (1908–), US biologist who is best known for an experiment in 1952 which appears to show that DNA is more involved than protein in the replication of genes.

Hopkins, Sir Frederick Gowland (1861–1947), English biochemist who discovered growth-stimulating vitamins.

Huxley, Hugh Esmor (1924–), English biologist who – with Hanson – proposed the sliding filament theory of muscle contraction.

Huxley, Sir Julian (1887–1975), English biologist and educator whose studies included projects in embryology, behaviour and evolution.

Huxley, T(homas) H(enry) (1825–95), English biologist who advanced Darwin's theory of evolution but suggested that change could be 'step-like' rather than gradual.

Jenner, Edward (1749–1823), English physician who developed the vaccination against smallpox.

Khorana, Har Gobind (1922–), Indian-born US biochemist who has studied the genetic composition of the cell nucleus.

Koch, Robert (1857–1932), German biochemist who is one of the founders of bacteriology and contributed much work on life-threatening diseases.

Krebs, Sir Hans Adolf (1900–81), German-born British biochemist who is remembered for his discovery of the Krebs cycle.

Lamarck, Jean-Baptiste (1744–1829), French naturalist who defined vertebrates and invertebrates.

Landsteiner, Karl (1868–1943), Austrian pathologist who identified the blood types A, AB, B and O.

Lederberg, Joshua (1925–), US geneticist who demonstrated genetic and behaviour systems in bacteria.

Leeuwenhoek, Anton van (1632–1723), Dutch biologist whose observations with a microscope were cited as the first steps in microbiology.

Leonardo da Vinci (1452–1519), Italian Renaissance polymath whose contributions to art, architecture and science were prodigious. His work in science was not recognized until the 19th century, when his notebooks were finally published.

Levene, Phoebus Aaron Theodor (1869–1940), Russian-born US biochemist who established that nucleic acids are genuine molecules independent of proteins.

Linnaeus, Carolus (Carl Linné; 1707–78), Swedish botanist who systematically arranged an animal, plant and mineral kingdom. He defined classes of plants on the basis of the number and arrangement of their stamens. Despite being overtaken by dramatic advances in biology, his binomial nomenclature of plants remains the basic pattern for the naming of all living systems with a generic name and a specific name.

Lucretius (*c.* 95–55 BC), Roman philosopher whose recognition of the struggle for existence anticipated Darwin by nearly 2000 years.

McClintock, Barbara (1902–93), US geneticist who, working on *Drosophila* (fruit fly), showed that gene action was connected with chromosomes.

Malpighi, Marcello (1628–94), Italian physiologist who showed how blood reaches tissues through tiny tubes called capillaries. Malpighi is thought to be the first to use microscopy to study animal and plant tissues.

Maynard Smith, John (1920–), English biologist who is known for his influential *Theory of Evolution* (1958).

Mendel, Gregor (1822–84), Austrian monk and botanist who discovered the basic principles of heredity by plant and garden pea experiments, leading him to lay the mathematical foundations of the science of genetics. Mendel's two basic laws were the law of segregation and the law of independent assortment.

Meselson, Matthew Stanley (1930–), US molecular biologist who demonstrated the semiconservative nature of DNA replication.

Metchnikoff, Elie (Ilya Mechnikov; 1845–1916), Russian microbiologist and zoologist who discovered in animals amoeba-like cells that engulf bacteria.

Miescher, Johann Friedrich (1844–95), Swiss physiologist who discovered nucleic acids (1869).

Monod, Jacques (1910–76), French biochemist who postulated the existence of messenger-RNA.

Morgan, Thomas Hunt (1866–1945), US geneticist who established the chromosome theory of heredity.

Müller, Johannes (1801–58), German physiologist who described the nature of sensory nerves.

Nägeli, Karl Wilhelm von (1817–91), Swiss botanist who did pioneering work on plant cells.

Paracelsus (see p. 133)

Pasteur, Louis (1822–95), French chemist and microbiologist who proved that living microorganisms cause disease and fermentation. He also laid the foundations of modern vaccine theory. While studying anthrax in the 1870s, he inoculated chickens with chicken cholera culture; the birds survived and proved immune to subsequent inoculations of the same virus. Unwittingly, Pasteur had attenuated the virus, meaning he had weakened it so that the body's own natural defences could defeat it.

Pavlov, Ivan (1849–1936), Russian physiologist who is best known for developing the concept of the conditioned reflex (Pavlov's dogs).

Plato (see p. 123)

Pliny (the Elder) (AD 23–79), Roman philosopher who recognized that the Earth is round. His *Natural History* increased interest in the natural world.

Réamur, René-Antoine de (1683–1757), French physicist and entomologist who devised the Réamur temperature scale, isolated gastric juice and made a major contribution to the study of insects.

Roberts, Richard (1943–), English molecular biologist who – with Sharp – discovered split genes.

Ross, Ronald (1857–1932), British physician who discovered that the mosquito was the carrying agent for human malaria.

Sabin, Albert (1906–94), Polish-born US microbiologist who developed an oral polio vaccine.

Sachs, Julius von (1832–97), German botanist whose transpiration and photosynthesis research added to the knowledge of plant physiology.

Salk, Jonas Edward (1914–95), US physician who developed a vaccine for polio.

Schwann, Theodor (1810–82), German physiologist who was one of the first to propose the cell theory in biology.

Sharp, Phillip (1944–), US molecular biologist who – with Roberts – discovered split genes.

Sherrington, Sir Charles (1861–1952), English neurologist who – with Adrian – researched the integrated nervous system (the motor-nerve system) of higher animals.

Spallanzani, Lazzaro (1729–99), Italian biologist who studied animal reproduction, mammalian bodily functions and microscopic life in nutrient cultures.

Starling, Ernest Henry (1866–1927), English physiologist who researched the mechanical controls on heart functions. He also studied digestion and coined the word 'hormone'.

Swammerdam, Jan (1637–80), Dutch entomologist whose pioneering studies of insects under the microscope resulted in the first detailed descriptions of many species.

Tatum, Edward L(awrie) (1909–75), US biochemist who pioneered work in molecular genetics.

Varmus, Harold (1939–), US microbiologist who has done major research into oncogenes (genes with a cancer-causing capacity).

Vesalius, Andrea (Andreas van Wesel; 1514–64), Flemish physician who was one of the first to dissect human corpses.

Waksman, Selman (1888–1973), Ukrainian-born US microbiologist who isolated antibiotics – a word that he coined – from micro-organisms.

Wallace, Alfred Russell (1823–1913), Welsh naturalist known for developing a theory of evolution of 'survival of the fittest' independently of Darwin.

Watson, James (1928–), US geneticist who, with Crick, discovered the molecular structure of DNA.

Weismann, August (1834–1914), German biologist who created the 'germ plasm' theory in genetics.

White, Gilbert (1720–93), English cleric and naturalist whose *Natural History of Selborne* (1789) was a landmark in nature study.

Wilkins, Maurice (1916–), New Zealand-born British biophysicist who researched the molecular model of DNA with Crick and Watson.

NOBEL PRIZEWINNERS

Nobel Prizes are awarded under the terms of the will of Alfred Nobel by the Royal Caroline Medico-Chirurgical Institute in Stockholm (Sweden).

1901 Emil von Behring, German: for his work in serum therapy.

1902 Sir Ronald Ross, English: for his discovery of how malaria enters an organism.

1903 Niels R. Finsen, Danish: for his work on light radiation treatment of skin diseases.

1904 Ivan Pavlov, Russian: for work on the physiology of digestion.

1905 Robert Koch, German: for tuberculosis research.

1906 Camillo Golgi, Italian, and S. Ramón y Cajal, Spanish: for studies of the structure of the nervous system.

1907 Alphonse Laveran, French: for his discovery of the role of protozoa in diseases.

1908 Paul Ehrlich, German, and Ilya Mechnikov (Elie Metchnikoff), Russian: for immunity systems research.

1909 Emil Kocher, Swiss: for work on the physiology, pathology and surgery of the thyroid gland.

1910 Albrecht Kossel, German: for cellular chemistry research.

1911 Allvar Gullstrand, Swedish: for his work on the dioptics of the eye.

1912 Alexis Carrel, French: for studies of vascular suture and transplantation of organs.

1913 Charles Richet, French: for anaphylaxis research.

1914 Robert Bárány, Austrian: for studies on the vestibular apparatus of the inner ear.

1915–18 No awards

1919 Jules Bordet, Belgian: for his studies of the immunity system.

1920 August Krogh, Danish: for the discovery of the capillary motor-regulating mechanism.

1921 No award

1922 Archibald Hill, English: for studies of heat production in muscles; and Otto Meyerhof, German: for work on lactic acid metabolism in muscles.

1923 Sir Frederick Banting, Canadian, and John James R. Macleod,

ALMOST MADE IT...

UNLOCKING THE KEY TO DNA

One of the most important discoveries of the 20th century, the unlocking of the structure of DNA, is normally accredited to the famous trio of Crick, Watson and Wilkins. Not many people remember the contributions made by Rosalind Franklin (1920–58), a British X-ray crystallographer. Her work on DNA's structure provided direct scientific evidence that the others used for their double-helix model. She was working on a paper of her own which outlined a similar model when Crick and Watson published their famous paper in the spring of 1953. Indeed, evidence suggests that she had deduced the sugar-phosphate backbone of the helix before Crick and Watson's publication. Despite her important contribution, she did not get the recognition she deserved. To add to her neglect, she was denied the possibility of a Nobel Prize, which is only given to living people, and Crick, Watson and Wilkins won it in 1962, four years after Franklin died of cancer.

THE ORIGINS OF THE EVOLUTION THEORY

Most people today would attribute evolution theory to Charles Darwin. However, Alfred Wallace, produced a strikingly similar theory independently of Darwin. Wallace (pictured left) was a very unassuming man, who met misfortune in his work when much of his naturalist studies were lost in a ship fire. This may have delayed his work but, in 1855, he still managed to develop a pre-Darwinian theory of evolution through natural selection. Unfortunately, it attracted little public attention. It was only when he sent a further essay to Darwin in 1858 that Darwin realized that his work echoed his own, and they offered joint papers to the Linnean Society in 1858. Wallace's role became subordinate to Darwin's, due to the latter's greater efforts at publicizing his ideas. An innately modest and diffident man, he coined the term 'survival of the fittest', although he himself did not survive long in the public's memory.

Scottish: for the discovery and production of insulin.

1924 Willem Einthoven, Dutch: for the discovery of electrocardiogram mechanism.

1925 No award

1926 Johannes Fibiger, Danish: for cancer research.

1927 Julius Wagner-Jauregg, Austrian: for malaria inoculation in dementia paralytica.

1928 Charles Nicolle, French: for typhus research.

1929 Christiaan Eijkman, Dutch: for his discovery of antineuritic vitamin; and Sir Frederick Hopkins, English: for his discovery of growth-stimulating vitamins.

1930 Karl Landsteiner, Austrian-born US citizen: for his work in the grouping of human blood.

1931 Otto Warburg, German: for the discovery of the nature and action of a respiratory enzyme.

1932 Edgar D. Adrian (Lord Adrian) and Sir Charles Sherrington, English: for their studies on the function of neurons.

1933 Thomas Hunt Morgan, US: for his work on the role of chromosomes in transmission of heredity.

1934 George R. Minot, William P. Murphy and George H. Whipple, all US: for work on liver therapy to treat anaemia.

1935 Hans Spemann, German: for work on organization in embryos.

1936 Sir Henry Dale, English, and Otto Loewi, German-born US citizen: for work on the chemical transmission of nerve impulses.

1937 Albert Szent-Györgyi, Hungarian-born US citizen: for his studies on biological combustion.

1938 Corneille Heymans, Belgian: for research on the role of sinus and aortic mechanisms in respiration regulation.

1939 Gerhard Domagk, German (who declined the award as Hitler refused to allow Germans to accept Nobel Prizes): for work on the antibacterial effect of prontosil.

1940–42 No awards

1943 Henrik Dam, Danish: for the discovery of vitamin K; and Edward A. Doisy, US: for the discovery of the chemical nature of vitamin K.

1944 Joseph Erlanger and Herbert S. Gasser, both US: for studies of the differentiated functions of nerve fibres.

1945 Sir Alexander Fleming, Scottish, Ernst Boris Chain, German-born British citizen, and Howard Florey (Lord Florey), Australian: for the discovery of penicillin and its curative value.

1946 Hermann J. Muller, US: for the production of mutations by X-ray irradiation.

1947 Carl F. Cori and Gerty Cori, both Czech-born US citizens: for their discovery of the catalytic conversion of glycogen (the form in which carbohydrate is stored in the liver and muscles of man and animals); and Bernardo Houssay, Argentinian: for research on pituitary hormone function in sugar metabolism.

1948 Paul Müller, Swiss: for work on the properties of DDT.

1949 Walter Rudolf Hess, Swiss: for the discovery of the function of the midbrain; and António Egas Moniz, Portuguese: for work on the therapeutic value of leucotomy psychoses.

1950 Philip S. Hench and Edward Kendall, both US, and Tadeusz Reichstein, Polish-born Swiss citizen: for adrenal cortex hormones research.

1951 Max Theiler, South African-born US citizen: for his research on yellow fever.

1952 Selman A. Waksman, Ukrainian-born US citizen: for the discovery of streptomycin.

1953 Fritz A. Lipmann, German-born US citizen, and Sir Hans Krebs, German-born British citizen: for the discovery of coenzyme, a citric acid cycle in the metabolism of carbohydrates.

1954 John F. Enders, Thomas H. Weller and Frederick Robbins, all US: for their work on the tissue culture of poliomyelitis viruses.

1955 Axel Hugo Theorell, Swedish: for his work on the nature and mode of action of oxidation enzymes.

1956 Werner Forssmann, German, Dickinson Richards, US, and André F. Cournand, French-born US citizen: for their work on heart catheterization and circulatory changes.

1957 Daniel Bovet, Swiss-born Italian citizen: for the production of synthetic curare.

1958 George W. Beadle and Edward L. Tatum, both US: for their work on genetic regulation of chemical processes; and Joshua Lederberg, US: for work on genetic recombination.

1959 Severo Ochoa, Spanish-born US citizen, and Arthur Kornberg, US: for the production of artificial nucleic acids.

1960 Sir MacFarlane Burnet, Australian, and Sir Peter B. Medawar, English: for research into acquired immunity in tissue transplants.

1961 Georg von Békésy, Hungarian-born US citizen: for research on functions of the inner ear.

1962 Francis Crick, English, James D. Watson, US, and Maurice Wilkins, New Zealand-born British citizen: for the discovery of the molecular structure of DNA.

1963 Sir John Eccles, Australian, Sir Alan Lloyd Hodgkin, English, and Sir Andrew Huxley, English: for work on transmission of nerve impulses along a nerve fibre.

1964 Konrad Bloch, German-born US citizen, and Feodor Lynen, German: for research into cholesterol and fatty acid metabolism.

1965 François Jacob, Jacques Monod and André Lwoff, all French: for research into regulatory activities of body cells.

1966 Charles B. Huggins, Canadian-born US citizen, and Francis Peyton Rous, US: for cancer research.

1967 Haldan Keffer Hartline and George Wald, both US, and Ragner A. Granit, Finnish-born Swedish citizen: for research on the chemical and physiological visual processes in the eye.

1968 Robert W. Holley, US, H. Gobind Khorana, Indian-born US citizen, and Marshall W. Nirenberg, US: for research into deciphering the genetic code.

1969 Max Delbrück, German-born US citizen, Alfred D. Hershey, US, and Salvador E. Luria, Italian-born US citizen: for research into viruses and viral diseases.

1970 Julius Axelrod, US, Sir Bernard Katz, German-born British citizen, and Ulf von Euler, Swedish: for work on the chemistry of nerve transmission.

1971 Earl W. Sutherland, US: for studies of the action of hormones.

1972 Gerald M. Edelman, US, and Rodney Porter, English: for research into the chemical structure of antibodies.

1973 Karl von Frisch and Konrad Lorenz, both Austrian, and Nikolaas Tinbergen, Dutch: for research on animal behaviour patterns.

1974 Albert Claude, Belgian-born US citizen, Christian R. de Duve, Belgian, and George E. Palade, Romanian-born US citizen: for work on the structural and functional organization of cells.

1975 Renato Dulbecco, Italian-born US citizen, Howard M. Temin and David Baltimore, both US: for work on interactions between tumour viruses and the genetic material of the cell.

1976 Baruch S. Blumberg and Daniel Carleton Gajdusek, both US: for studies on the origin and spread of infectious diseases.

1977 Rosalyn S. Yalow, US, Roger Guillemin, French-born US citizen, and Andrew Schally, Polish-born US citizen: for the development of radio-immuno-assay (to detect and quantify important biological substances) and research on pituitary hormones.

1978 Werner Arber, Swiss, Daniel Nathans and Hamilton O. Smith, both US: for the discovery and application of enzymes that fragment DNA.

1979 Allan M. Cormack, South African-born US citizen, and Sir Godfrey N. Hounsfield, English: for the development of computerized axial tomography scanning.

1980 Baruj Benacerraf, Venezuelan-born US citizen, George D. Snell, US, and Jean Dausset, French: for work on genetic control of the immune response to foreign substances.

1981 Roger W. Sperry, US: for studies of the functions of the cerebral hemispheres; and Torsten N. Wiesel, Swedish, and David H. Hubel, Canadian-born US citizen: for work on visual information processing by the brain.

1982 Sune K. Bergström and Bengt I. Samuelsson, both Swedish, and Sir John R. Vane, English: for work on the biochemistry and physiology of prostaglandins.

1983 Barbara McClintock, US: for the discovery of mobile plant genes which affect heredity.

1984 Niels K. Jerne, British-born, Georges J. F. Köhler, German, and César Milstein, Argentinian-born British citizen: for the technique for producing monoclonal antibodies.

1985 Michael S. Brown and Joseph L. Goldstein, both US: for the discovery of cell receptors involved in cholesterol metabolism.

1986 Stanley Cohen, US, and Rita Levi-Montalcini, Italian: for the discovery of chemical agents that help regulate cell growth.

1987 Tonegawa Susumu, Japanese: for research into genetic aspects of antibodies.

1988 Sir James W. Black, Scottish, Gertrude B. Ellison and George H. Hitchings, both US: for the development of new classes of drugs.

1989 Harold Varmus and Michael Bishop, both US: for cancer research.

1990 Joseph Murray and E. Donnall Thomas, both US: for transplant surgery.

1991 Erwin Neher and Bert Sakmann, both German: for research in cell biology, particularly the understanding of disease mechanisms.

1992 Edmond Fischer and Edwin Krebs, both US: for discovering the cellular regulatory mechanism used to control various metabolic processes.

1993 Richard Roberts, English, and Phillip Sharp, US: for their discovery of split genes.

1994 Martin Rodbell and Alfred G. Gilman, both US: for the discovery of G-proteins, and their role, in cells.

1995 Edward B. Lewis, US, Eric F. Wieschaus, US, and Christiane Nüsslein-Volhard, German: for discoveries concerning the generic control of early embryonic development.

1996 Peter C. Doherty, Australian, and Rolf M. Zinkernagel, Swiss: for discoveries concerning the specificity of the cell mediated immune defence.

PHYSICAL SCIENCES ▷

'The whole of science is nothing more than a refinement of everyday thinking'
– Albert Einstein

WEIGHTS AND MEASURES

▶ The Egyptian cubit was based on the length of the arm, measured from the elbow to the tips of the outstretched fingers.

▶ A billion used to be defined in two different ways: in British usage it meant a million million, whereas in the United States it meant a thousand million. The American definition has now replaced the British.

▶ The league was an ancient Gaulish measurement that the Romans estimated to be equivalent to 1500 paces.

MEASUREMENT

▶ Metrology is the science of measurement.
▶ An acre was originally defined as the area of land that a pair of oxen could plough in a day.

The first units of weight and length were based on the proportions of the human body – the length of the thumb was the precursor of the inch, for example. The average pace of a man was a common unit in many ancient civilizations, as were the lengths of ploughs and the area of fields in common use. As civilization and trade developed, the need for standardization grew. Units were fixed by local tradition or by national rulers, and many different systems developed.

Measurement is a matter of comparison. An item of unknown length, weight or capacity is compared to an item with a known length, weight or capacity. The result is expressed in terms of units that the people using the system all agree on.

In theory, it is possible to measure any quantity in terms of any other comparable quantity. To avoid unmanageably large or small numbers, it is important to use an appropriate unit of measurement. For example, it is possible to measure the distance between stars using the width of a hair as the base unit, but since this would produce incredibly large numbers, a more suitable unit is normally used – in this case, light years.

THE METRIC SYSTEM

▶ International standards of the metric units are kept at the Bureau International des Poids et Mésures (BIPM) near Paris.
▶ A forerunner of the metric system was first proposed in France in 1670.

The metric system was adopted in Revolutionary France in 1799 to replace the existing traditional, illogical units. It was based upon a natural physical unit to ensure that it should be unchanging. The unit selected was one ten-millionth of a quadrant of a great circle of the Earth, measured around the poles of the meridian that pass through Paris. This unit – equivalent to 39.37003 inches in the British Imperial system – was called the metre.

Several other metric units are derived from the metre. The gram – the unit of weight – is 1 cubic centimetre of water at its maximum density, while the litre – the unit of capacity – is 1 cubic decimetre. Prefixes – from Danish, Latin and Greek – are used for multiples of ten from atto (x 10^{-18}) to exa (x 10^{18}).

BASE UNITS

The metric system is centred on a small number of base units. These relate to the fundamental standards of length, mass and time, together with a few others to extend the system to a wider range of physical measurements, for example to electrical and optical quantities. Base units are defined by fixed physical standards, which in theory are the same anywhere. For example, the metre is defined as the length travelled by light waves in a vacuum in 1/299,792,458 of a second. This length is the same in all parts of the world, and thus a standard is maintained. Only the kilogram is now defined in terms of an actual physical object (a piece of the metal platinum).

These few base units can be combined to form a large number of other units. There are also two geometrical units that are sometimes referred to as supplementary units.

SI UNITS

A number of systems of units based upon the metric system have been in use. Initially the cgs system – based upon the centimetre for length, the gram for mass and the second for time – was widespread. It has, however, largely been replaced by the mks system in which the fundamental units are the metre for length, the kilogram for mass and the second for time.

Scientists and engineers need a global standard for measurement. The system employed is the SI system, based on the mks system. SI refers to the Système International d'Unités, which was adopted by the 11th General Conference on Weights and Measures in 1960. The SI units are now employed for all scientific and most technical purposes, and are in general use for most other purposes in the majority of countries. The seven SI base units are:

metre: the unit of length
kilogram: the unit of mass
second: the unit of time
ampere: the unit of electric current
kelvin: degree of temperature measured on the Kelvin scale
candela: the unit of luminous intensity
mole: the unit of substance.

OTHER SYSTEMS

▶ In 12th-century England, a royal ordinance subdivided the inch into three barley corns.
▶ Some units of the Imperial system have fallen into disuse in North America. The yard, for example, is only used in sport.

Apart from the metric system, the most widely used systems of units are the related (British) Imperial System and the US Customary Units. Although the names of most of the units of both systems are the same, the sizes of some of the units differ.

IMPERIAL SYSTEM

The two basic units are the yard (the unit of length) and the pound (mass). Subdivisions and multiples of these units are traditional in origin and do not follow the metric system's logical multiples of ten.

The Imperial system is complicated by the existence of three different systems of measurement of weight. The avoirdupois system is the most widely used. The troy system is used to measure precious metals, while the apothecaries' system uses the same units as the troy system but with certain differences of name.

The use of the metric system was legalized in the United Kingdom in 1897. The intention to switch to the metric system 'within ten years' was declared in May 1965 by the President of the Board of Trade, although in March 1976 the government decided not to proceed with the second reading of the Weights and Measures (Metrication) Act. However, since 1965 the metric system has replaced the Imperial system for many purposes

US CUSTOMARY UNITS

The differences between English and American units make conversion difficult; for example, a ton in Britain is a unit of mass equivalent to 2240 lb (or 1016.046909 kg), while a ton in the United States and Canada is equivalent to 2000 lb (or 907.184 kg). There are also considerable differences between the English and American gallon, and the English and American bushel.

IMPERIAL UNITS

Imperial units are defined by the (British) Weights and Measures Act, 1963:
yard (yd) is equal to 0.9144 m.
pound (lb) is equal to 0.45359237 kg.
gallon (gal) is the space occupied by 10 pounds weight of distilled water of density 0.998859 gram per millilitre weighed in air of density 0.001217 g per millilitre against weights of density 8.136 g per millilitre.

UNITS OF LENGTH
12 inches = 1 foot
3 feet = 1 yard
5½ yards = 1 rod, pole or perch
4 rods = 1 chain
10 chains = 1 furlong
5280 feet = 1 mile
1760 yards = 1 mile
8 furlongs = 1 mile

NAUTICAL LENGTH
6 feet = 1 fathom
100 fathoms = 1 cable length
6080 feet = 1 nautical mile

UNITS OF AREA
144 square inches = 1 square foot
9 square feet = 1 square yard
304¼ square yards = 1 square rod, pole or perch
40 square rods = 1 rood
4 roods = 1 acre
4840 square yards = 1 acre
640 acres = 1 square mile

UNITS OF WEIGHT (AVOIRDUPOIS)
437½ grains = 1 ounce
16 drams = 1 ounce
16 ounces = 1 pound
14 pounds = 1 stone
28 pounds = 1 quarter
4 quarters = 1 hundredweight
20 hundredweights = 1 ton

UNITS OF VOLUME
1728 cubic inches = 1 cubic foot
27 cubic feet = 1 cubic yard
5.8 cubic feet = 1 bulk barrel

UNITS OF CAPACITY
8 fluid drams = 1 fluid ounce
5 fluid ounces = 1 gill
4 gills = 1 pint
2 pints = 1 quart
4 quarts = 1 gallon
2 gallons = 1 peck
4 pecks = 1 bushel
8 bushels = 1 quarter
36 gallons = 1 bulk barrel

SPEED
1 knot = 1 nautical mph

■ THE TERM 'METRE' COMES FROM THE ANCIENT GREEK WORD *METRON*, MEANING 'MEASURE'

METRIC AND IMPERIAL CONVERSIONS

Column 1 Imperial	Column 2 Metric	To convert Col. 2 to Col. 1 multiply by	To convert Col. 1 to Col. 2 multiply by
LENGTH			
inch (in)	centimetre (cm)	0.39370078	2.54*
foot (ft)	metre	3.280840	0.3048*
yard (yd)	metre	1.09361	0.9144*
mile	kilometre (km)	0.6213711	1.609344*
fathom	metre	0.54680	1.8288*
chain	metre	0.04970	20.1168*
UK nautical mile	kilometre	0.5396118	1.853184*
International nautical mile	kilometre	0.5399568	1.852*
ångström unit (Å)	nanometre	10	10^{-1}
AREA			
square inch	square centimetre	0.15500	6.4516*
square foot	square metre	10.7639	0.092903*
square yard	square metre	1.19599	0.836127*
acre	hectare (ha) (10^4 m^2)	2.47105	0.404686*
square mile	square kilometre	0.38610	2.589988*
VOLUME			
cubic inch	cubic centimetre	0.061024	16.3871*
cubic foot	cubic metre	35.31467	0.028317*
cubic yard	cubic metre	1.30795	0.764555*
CAPACITY			
litre	cubic centimetre or millilitre	0.001*	1000*
pint	litre	1.759753	0.568261
UK gallon	litre	0.219969	4.546092
barrel (for beer)	hectolitre	0.611026	1.63659
US gallon	litre or dm^3	0.264172	3.785412
US barrel (for petroleum)	hectolitre	0.628998	1.58983
fluid ounce	millilitre	0.035195	28.413074
VELOCITY			
feet per second (ft/s)	metres per second	3.280840	0.3048
miles per hour (mph)	kilometres per hour	0.621371	1.609344
UK knot (1.00064 Int knots)	kilometres per hour	0.5396118	1.853184
ACCELERATION			
feet per second per second (ft/s^2)	metres per second per second (m/s^2)	3.280840	0.3048*
MASS			
grain (gr)	milligram (mg)	0.0154324	64.79891
dram (dr)	gram	0.564383	1.77185
ounce (avoirdupois)	gram	0.0352740	28.349523125
pound (avoirdupois)	kilogram	2.20462*	0.45359237*
stone	kilogram	0.15747304	6.35029318*
quarter	kilogram	0.0787375	12.70058636*
hundredweight (cwt)	kilogram	0.0196841	50.80234544*
ton (long)	tonne (= 1000 kg)	0.9842065	1.0160469088
DENSITY			
pounds per cubic inch	grams per cubic centimetre	0.0361272	27.6799
pounds per cubic foot	kilograms per cubic metre	0.06234280	16.0185
FORCE			
dyne (dyn)	newton	10^5	10^{-5}
poundal (pdl)	newton	7.23301	0.138255
pound-force (lbf)	newton	0.224809	4.44822
tons-force	kilonewton (kN)	0.100361	9.96402
kilogram-force (kgf or kilopond)	newton	0.101972	9.80665
ENERGY (WORK, HEAT)			
erg	joule	10^7	10^{-7}
horse-power (hp) (550 ft/lbf/s)	kilowatt (kW)	1.34102	0.745700
therm	mega joule (MJ)	0.00947817	105.506
kilowatt hour (kWh)	mega joule (MJ)	0.277778	3.6
calorie (international)	joule	0.238846*	4.1868*
British thermal unit (Btu)	kilo-joule (kJ)	0.947817	1.05506
PRESSURE, STRESS			
millibar (mbar or mb)	Pa	0.01*	100*
standard atmosphere (atm)	kPa	0.0098692	101.325
pounds per square inch (psi)	Pa	0.000145038	6894.76
pounds per square inch (psi)	kilogram-force per cm^2	14.2233	0.0703070

*Exact figure

THE SI UNITS

QUANTITY	UNIT	SYMBOL	DEFINITIONS
BASE UNITS			
length	metre	m	The length of a path travelled by light in a vacuum during a time interval of 1/299,792,458 of a second.
mass	kilogram	kg	The mass of the international prototype of the kilogram, which is kept by the Bureau International des Poids et Mésures (BIPM) at Sèvres near Paris, France.
time	second	s	The duration of 9,192,631,770 periods of the radiation corresponding to the transition between the two hyperfine levels of the ground state of the caesium-133 atom.
electric current	ampere	A	That constant current which, if maintained in two straight parallel conductors of infinite length of negligible circular cross-section, and placed 1 metre apart in a vacuum, would produce between these conductors a force equal to 2 x 10^{-7} newtons per metre of length.
thermodynamic temperature	kelvin	K	The fraction 1/273.16 of the thermodynamic temperature of the triple point of water. The triple point of water is the point where water, ice and water vapour are in equilibrium.
luminous intensity	candela	cd	The luminous intensity, in a given direction, of a source that emits monochromatic radiation of frequency 540 x 10^{12} Hz and has a radiant intensity in that direction of (1/683) Watts per steradian.
amount of substance	mole	mol	The amount of substance of a system that contains as many elementary entities as there are atoms in 0.012 kg of carbon-12. When the mole is used, the elementary entities must be specified, and may be atoms, molecules, ions, electrons, other particles or specified groups of particles.
SUPPLEMENTARY UNITS*			
plane angle	radian	rad	The plane angle between two radii of a circle that cut off on the circumference an arc equal in length to the radius.
solid angle	steradian	sr	The solid angle that, having its vertex in the centre of a sphere, cuts off an area of the surface of the sphere equal to that of a square having sides of length equal to the radius of the sphere.

* Dimensionless units

MULTIPLES AND SUBMULTIPLES

In the metric system the following decimal multiples and submultiples are used:

PREFIX	SYMBOL	VALUE	FACTOR
yocto-	y	septillionth	x 10^{-24}
zepto-	z	sextillionth	x 10^{-21}
atto-	a	squintillionth	x 10^{-18}
femto-	f	quadrillionth	x 10^{-15}
pico-	p	trillionth	x 10^{-12}
nano-	n	thousand millionth part or billionth	x 10^{-9}
micro-	m	millionth part	x 10^{-6}
milli-	m	thousandth part	x 10^{-3}
centi-	c	hundredth part	x 10^{-2}
deci-	d	tenth part	x 10^{-1}
deka-	da	tenfold	x 10
hecto-	h	hundredfold	x 10^2
kilo-	k	thousandfold	x 10^3
mega-	M	millionfold	x 10^6
giga-	G	thousand millionfold or billionfold	x 10^9
tera-	T	trillion	x 10^{12}
peta-	P	quadrillion	x 10^{15}
exa-	E	quintillion	x 10^{18}
zetta-	Z	sextillion	x 10^{21}
yotta-	Y	septillion	x 10^{24}

PHYSICS

▶ The highest manmade temperature ever achieved, at the Princeton Plasma Physics Laboratory in the USA, is 510 million°C, which is 30 times hotter than the centre of the Sun.

▶ Relativity Theory describes the large-scale universe, whereas Quantum Theory looks at events on a very small scale.

▶ During a lightning strike, an instantaneous current of 10,000,000 amps can flow at a speed of 50,000 km/s, heating the air to 30,000°C.

▶ Light takes 1.25 seconds to travel from the Moon to the Earth and some eight minutes to travel here from the Sun.

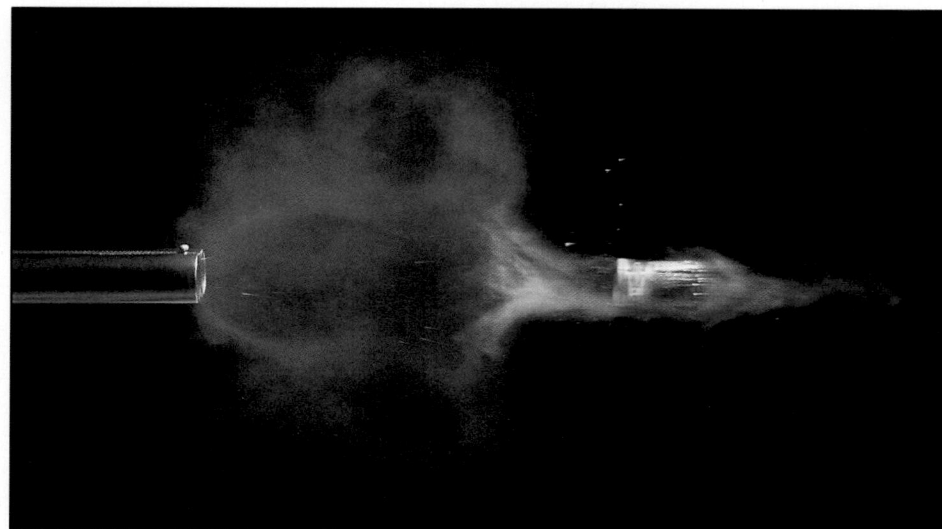

■ *A 12-bore shotgun and its discharged cartridge, 4.5 milliseconds after detonation. The recoil of the gun is a result of Newton's third law of motion – 'To every action there is an equal and opposite reaction'*

INTRODUCTION TO PHYSICS

▶ Physics is the study of the basic laws that govern matter.
▶ Galileo and Descartes were the first to insist that science should use only precise mathematical concepts in its theories.

The work of physicists is broad, and includes the study of bodies in motion, forces, heat and energy, waves, electricity, magnetism and atomic physics. Physics covers the science of the very large – for example, the large-scale structure of the universe – to the very small, such as quantum physics, which describes matter billions of times smaller than the thickness of a human hair. The laws of physics are based upon mathematical calculations and thus mathematics plays a central role in physics.

MOTION AND MECHANICS

▶ When a body is in motion, it can be thought of as moving in space and time.
▶ Mechanics is the branch of physics that describes the movement or motion of objects, ranging in scale from a planet to the smallest particle within an atom.

Sir Isaac Newton (see p. 122) developed a theory of mechanics that proved successful in describing most types of motion. His work has been described as one of the greatest advances in the history of science.

KINEMATICS

Kinematics is the study of bodies in motion. It covers a broad range of topics, from bodies falling to earth, to the description of bodies moving in a straight line, to circular motion. There are general laws that can be stated about bodies in motion, stemming from the work of Sir Isaac Newton, which are true for most situations. However, if studying speeds approaching the speed of light, or motion on a very small scale, Newton's laws break down.

KINEMATIC EQUATIONS

The set of equations known as kinematic equations describe the relationship between displacement, velocity and acceleration. For a body moving in a straight line with uniform acceleration, the following equations hold true:

1 $v = u + at$

2 $s = \frac{1}{2}at^2$

3 $v^2 = u^2 + 2as$

4 $s = \frac{1}{2}t(u + v)$

where s = displacement, t = time, u = initial or starting velocity, v = acceleration after time (t), and a = acceleration.

If one element of the equation is unknown, and the others are known, then it is possible to complete the equation. To use kinematic equations to solve a problem, it is necessary to identify the information given, then identify which of the four equations can be manipulated to give the answer required.

Speed is the ratio of a distance covered by a body in a given amount of time, to that time. The distance moved is called the displacement. Physicists usually measure speed in metres per second: (average) speed = distance moved over time taken.

Speed is not considered to be in any particular direction. However, velocity is speed measured in a particular direction. Any quantity, such as speed, where the direction is not specified or applicable, is called a scalar quantity. Velocity, however, is a vector quantity, which is one in which both the magnitude and direction are stated.

When the velocity of a car increases, one says that the car is accelerating (getting faster). When the velocity of the car is decreasing, one says that the car is decelerating. Acceleration is the rate of change of velocity. Since velocity is a vector quantity, a body is said to be accelerating if it changes direction even though it maintains its same speed. Acceleration may be defined as the change in velocity over a given time interval. At its simplest, acceleration = change in velocity over time taken for this change. Acceleration is measured in m/s^2 (or ms^{-2}). It is usual to speak of decelerating bodies as

NEWTON'S LAWS OF MOTION

Newton's three laws of motion state the fundamental relationships between the acceleration of a body and the forces acting on it. These laws have made it possible to calculate accurate trajectories for any number of moving bodies, from balls thrown in the air to spacecraft travelling to the outer planets.

1 A body will remain stationary or travelling at a constant velocity unless it is acted upon by an external force.
The tendency of a body to remain at rest or move with constant velocity is called the inertia of the body. The inertia is related to the mass, which is the amount of substance in the body. Newton imagined matter to be made of small particles, each of which possessed a definite mass, which is measured in kilograms. The mass of an object is the sum of the masses of all its atoms. Newton's first law explains why we lurch forward in a car when it suddenly breaks, and why we are pushed back into our seats when a car suddenly accelerates.

2 The resultant force exerted on a body is directly proportional to the acceleration produced by the force.
The second law of motion can be expressed in an equation: force = mass x acceleration, or $F = ma$. A force is something that causes a change in an object's velocity. A body will only accelerate (or decelerate) if there is a force acting upon it, otherwise it will travel at the same speed. Forces are measured in newtons. A force of 1 newton will accelerate a mass of 1 kg by 1 m/s^2. Since force is directly proportional to mass, doubling the mass requires double the force to produce the same acceleration.

3 To every action there is an equal and opposite reaction.
Newton's third law of motion states that a single isolated force cannot exist on its own; there is also a resulting 'mirror-image' force. When a bullet is fired, the gun recoils backwards. This is caused by a reaction force on the gun from the bullet. Similarly, this law explains how when a rocket flies through a vacuum of space, the exhaust gases push the rocket on its way, whilst the rocket pushes the exhaust gases in the opposite direction. From this law can be derived the principle of the conservation of momentum. Momentum, which Newton called the 'quantity of motion', is the product of mass and velocity. The conservation of momentum principle states that when two bodies interact, the total momentum before impact is the same as the total momentum after impact.

those with a negative acceleration. Thus a ball which is travelling at 20 m/s, and which decelerates in one second to 15 m/s, is accelerating at –5 m/s^2.

NEWTON'S LAW OF GRAVITATION

In addition to his laws of motion, Newton formulated the concept of gravity, which he defined as a mutual force of attraction between two masses. Thus every particle in the universe attracts every other particle in the universe. Newton realized that two masses (m_1 and m_2) are attracted to each other by a force which is proportional to both masses. But the force (*F*) decreases as the distance (*r*) between the masses increases. If the separation (*r*) is doubled, the force (*F*) decreases to one-quarter of its former value. This is called an inverse square relationship. Newton's Law of Gravitation is thus: $F = Gm_1m_2/r^2$, where *G* is the 'universal gravitational constant'. Further experiments on gravity proved that: $G = 6.67206 \times 10^{-11}$ Nm^{-2}kg^{-2}. This small number is the force of attraction in newtons between two masses each of 1 kg separated by 1 m.

Newton's second law of motion made it possible to work out the gravitational acceleration near the Earth's surface. All bodies falling to Earth have the same acceleration (disregarding air resistance). Near the surface of Earth, this acceleration is 9.81 m/s^2, but latitude and elevation cause small variations. From this figure, it follows that the gravitational intensity on Earth is 9.81 N/kg. Gravity exists on other planets and their satellites (moons) also, but because gravity depends upon the mass of these bodies and their diameters, the strength of the gravitational force is different than it is on Earth.

The force of attraction of the Earth (or any planet) for an object is called its weight. Thus a woman 'weighing' 60 kg should strictly be said to have a mass of 60 kg; her weight is 60 x 9.81 = 589 newtons. On the Moon, which has a gravitational intensity one-sixth that of the Earth, her mass would still be 60 kg, but her weight would only be 98 N.

HEAT AND WORK

▶ Heat was once thought to be a substance, caloric, which flowed from a hot body to a cold body, but caloric turned out to be weightless.
▶ Modern physics sees heat as energy collectively possessed by the particles making up a gas, liquid or solid.

A body which possesses energy has the ability to do work. Work is done when a force (*F*) moves through a distance (*d*): $W = F \times d$. If *F* is measured in newtons and *d* in metres, then *W* is measured in Nm, otherwise called joules. All forms of energy are now measured in joules.

A red hot piece of iron could be made to do work by using it to boil water to drive a steam engine; the steam engine could then lift a load, thus doing work. The thermal energy of the red hot iron is in the fiercely vibrating atoms within the metal.

Each body has kinetic and potential energy. Kinetic energy is the energy a body has because it is moving, and is dependent upon velocity, i.e. $\frac{1}{2}mv^2$, where *m* is its mass and *v* its instantaneous velocity. In contrast, potential energy is dependent upon position, i.e. the gravitational potential energy of a body of mass (*m*) at a height (*h*) above the ground is *mgh*, where *g* is the acceleration due to gravity.

THERMODYNAMICS

Thermodynamics is the study of the behaviour and properties of heat, energy and temperature within systems. There are some general statements that can be made about heat and energy that are true in all circumstances. Perhaps the most simple and obvious principle is that of thermal equilibrium. If the energy entering a body from its environment is matched by the energy leaving the body to its environment, then the body is said to be in thermal equilibrium with its surroundings, i.e. there is zero net energy flow from body to environment. This principle can also be expressed as: If body *x* is in thermal equilibrium with body *y*, and body *y* is in thermal equilibrium with body *z*, then body *x* is also in equilibrium with body *z*. All three bodies, *x*, *y* and *z*, will be at the same temperature.

Another fundamental principle is that of the conservation of energy. The total magnitude, or quantity, of a certain physical property of a system, such as its mass, charge or energy, will remain unchanged, even though that particular property might be exchanged between various components of that system. This means that energy (or mass, or charge) cannot be created or destroyed. This law is fundamental not only to thermodyamics, but to physics and the laws of nature in general.

The conservation of energy principle holds true even when observation seems to suggest otherwise. For example, imagine a box that is slid across a floor. After a while, it will slow down and come to a rest, and the kinetic energy it had due to its motion will appear to have been 'lost'. However, much of that seemingly 'lost' energy is converted into internal energy; in this case, kinetic energy is converted into thermal energy. Processes that turn kinetic energy into thermal energy include viscosity and friction.

The first law of thermodynamics

The first law of thermodynamics states that the total amount of energy in any closed system always remains the same. In other words, energy is always conserved as it is transferred from one form to another. Heat is a form of energy and, therefore, if heat is produced, exactly the same amount of some other form of energy must have been supplied. For example, in an ideal situation, the heat produced by an electric fire is equal to the electrical energy supplied to it. Another statement of this law is that it is possible to convert work totally into heat.

The second law of thermodynamics

The second law of thermodynamics states that heat will always flow from a hotter object to a colder one, and not the other way round. Thus this law shows that certain processes only operate in one direction, and are irreversible. It implies that heat cannot entirely be converted into work.

One interesting way of expressing the second law of thermodynamics involves the term entropy. Entropy is a measure of the disorder of a system. The second law states that the entropy (disorder) of a system can only remain the same or increase as time passes – it can never spontaneously decrease. One conclusion that can be drawn from the fact that we live in an entropic universe is that it provides a basic distinction between the past and the future. Physical processes, according to the law of increasing entropy, work in one temporal direction only, namely forward in time.

The third law of thermodynamics

The third law states that on approaching absolute zero, extracting energy from a system becomes increasingly harder. All bodies have thermal energy, or heat. Absolute zero is the theoretical point at which a body ceases to have any heat. This value is –273.15°C (–459.67°F) or 0 K (Kelvin). At this temperature, which is impossible to physically attain, the molecules in a body will cease to vibrate, and thus the body will have no internal energy.

HEAT TRANSFER

▶ Heat is a form of energy and heat flow is a transfer of energy resulting from differences in temperature.
▶ When a red hot piece of iron cools down, it transfers energy to its surroundings in three possible ways: conduction, convection or radiation.

Conduction: Heat conduction occurs when kinetic and molecular energy pass from one molecule to another. As a red hot iron cools, it transfers energy to the surface on which the iron is resting by transfer of vibrational energy from the iron atoms to the atoms of the surface. Metals are good heat conductors because of electrons that transport energy through the material. Air is a poor conductor in comparison. Thus, a string vest keeps its wearer warm by trapping air, preventing the conduction of heat outwards from the body.

Convection: Heat convection results from the motion of the heated substance. As a red hot iron cools, the air in contact with the iron becomes heated by conduction, whereupon it expands, becoming less dense than the surrounding cold air and, according to Archimedes's principle, becomes buoyant and rises. To continue this process, cooler air is drawn in. Convection is the main mechanism for mixing the atmosphere and diluting pollutants emitted into the air.

Radiation: All bodies radiate energy in the form of electromagnetic waves. The cooling iron rod transfers energy through infrared radiation and the loss of visible light. Radiation may pass across a vacuum, and thus the Earth receives energy radiated from the Sun. A body remains at a constant temperature when it both radiates and receives energy at the same rate.

THE KINETIC THEORY OF MATTER

The kinetic theory of matter explains gases, liquids and solids in terms of the movement of their particles:

Gases

Gases are readily compressible by a factor up to one thousand, showing that there must be large spaces between the molecules. The molecules in a gas are able to translate (move freely), rotate and vibrate. Each type of movement is associated with the energy storage in the gas. The temperature of a gas is a measure of the average kinetic energy of its molecules. Since temperature is based on average measurements, it is unrelated to the actual quantity of gas involved, whereas the heat energy content of the gas does depend on the quantity of gas.

Liquids

Liquids are not easily compressible (making them useful in hydraulic systems which transfer and amplify forces). Liquids are much more dense than the corresponding gases from which they are condensed. For example, 1 m^3 of oxygen at room temperature and pressure, weighing 1.33 kg on cooling to –183°C, shrinks to only 1160 cm^3 of liquid. In a liquid the molecules are in contact with each other, yet able to move around as the molecules vibrate and disturb each other.

Solids

Solids are not at all easily compressible. Their particles are arranged in a very orderly pattern if the substance is crystalline, slightly less so in glassy materials and plastics. In a solid the particles vibrate ever more vigorously as the temperature is raised.

ON JUPITER'S SURFACE ONE WOULD WEIGH 2.4 TIMES AS MUCH AS ONE DOES ON EARTH

WAVES

▶ A wave is a phenomenon whereby energy is moved without the transference of any material.
▶ X-rays, ultraviolet rays, light and radio waves all travel at the same speed through a vacuum.

Waves can consist of oscillating particles or oscillating fields. Examples of waves include water waves, sound waves, light and X-rays. Although waves can be diverse, they have a shared set of properties which may be described and mathematically explained.

There are two main types of waves: transverse and longitudinal. In transverse waves the vibrations are perpendicular to the direction of travel, whereas in longitudinal waves the vibrations are parallel to the direction of travel. Examples of transverse waves include waver waves, where the water particles oscillate up and down at right angles to the wave's direction of propagation. Light is also a transverse wave, in which it is electric and magnetic fields that oscillate. In contrast, sound waves are longitudinal waves, in which the air molecules oscillate backwards and forwards in the same direction as the direction of propagation of the wave. As a sound passes a point, compression (squeezing) and rarefaction (stretching) of the air occur.

WAVELENGTH AND FREQUENCY

The distance between successive wave crests is called the wavelength, λ (lamda). Light waves have a very short wavelength, λ, from 4×10^{-7} m (purple light) to 7×10^{-7} m (red light). The frequency (*f*) of a wave is defined as the number of complete oscillations per second. Frequency is measured in hertz (Hz). By combining the values of wavelength and frequency, one gets the distance travelled by a wave in one second – the velocity (*v*) of the wave:

$$v = f\lambda$$

Audible sound frequencies range from 20 Hz (a low rumble) to about 20,000 Hz (a shrill whistle).

The frequency of visible light ranges from 8×10^{14} Hz (red light) to 4×10^{15} Hz (violet light). Thus, as red light enters the eye, during one second 8×10^{14} waves enter the eye travelling at 3×10^{8} m/s.

If one listens to middle C on the piano, 256 sound waves per second enter the ear, travelling at 344 m/s:

$$\lambda = v/f = 344/256 = 1.34 \text{ m}$$

In other words, the wavelength is 1.34 m.

The speed of a sound wave in air at 20°C (68°F) is 344 m/s, but in water sound travels at 1461 m/s and in steel its speed is 5000 m/s. Light waves travel at about 300,000 km/s in a vacuum but slow down slightly in air and more so in water or glass.

PROPERTIES OF WAVES

Waves have several properties, including reflection, refraction, diffraction and interference.

Reflection

Reflection is the process whereby part or all of a wave is returned when it encounters the boundary between two different materials or media. Perhaps the most obvious example of reflection is when one looks in a mirror – the light waves are bounced back off the mirror's silvered surface. Another example of a wave reflection is an echo, when sound waves bounce off a far-away surface.

The angle between the direction of the wavefront and the normal (perpendicular angle) at which the wave strikes the surface is known as the angle of incidence (*i*). The angle at which the wave is bounced from the surface is known as the angle of reflection (*r*). These angles, *i* and *r*, are equal.

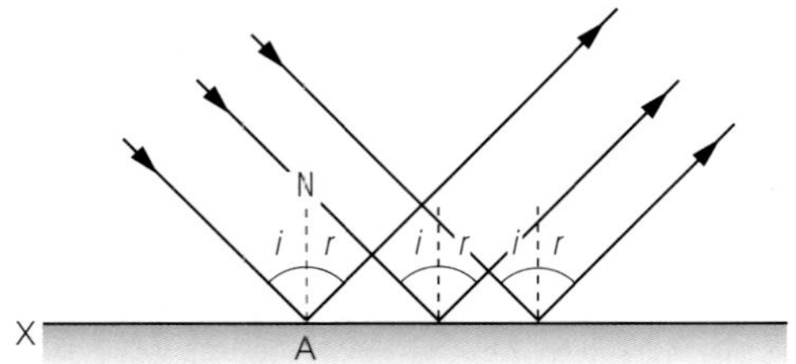

■ *Reflection of plane waves at a plane surface. The waves are parallel as they approach XY and after they are reflected. AN is the normal (perpendicular angle) to XY at A*

Refraction

Refraction is the change of direction of a wavefront as it passes obliquely (at any angle which is not perpendicular or parallel) from one medium to another in which its speed is altered. An example is when light enters a lens or prism – the light is bent. It is the principle of refraction that makes the lenses in spectacles work.

The refraction or bending of waves, including light, was investigated by Willebrord Snell (see p. 123) and is described in Snell's Law:

$$n_1 \sin i = n_2 \sin r$$

where n_1 is the refractive index of the first medium in which $n = v/c$, where *v* is the velocity of light in the first medium and *c* is the velocity of light in a vacuum; *i* is the angle that the incident ray makes with the normal; and *r* is the angle that the reflected ray makes with the normal.

The refractive index varies slightly with wavelength. Thus white light, which contains all colours, can be dispersed into a rainbow by passing through a prism made of glass.

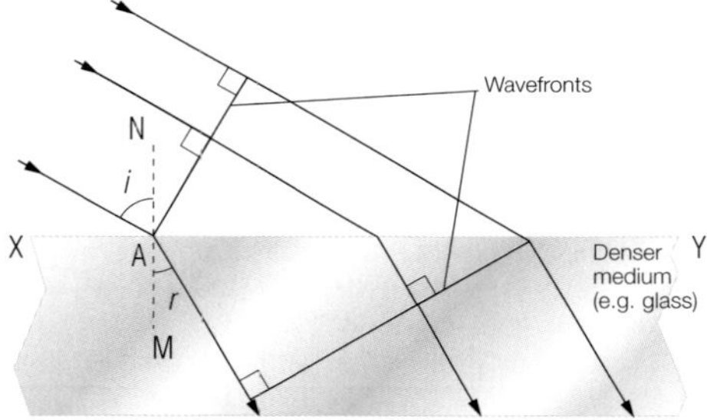

■ *Refraction of a plane wavefront. MAN is the normal (perpendicular angle) to XY; i is the angle of incidence; r is refraction. The waves are parallel after refraction*

Diffraction

Diffraction occurs when waves passing through a slit which is narrow compared to the wavelength are spread out and depart from the expected straight line direction. This explains how we can hear the words of someone who is facing away from us. The sound waves issuing from the mouth of the person speaking are diffracted right round to the back of the person's head.

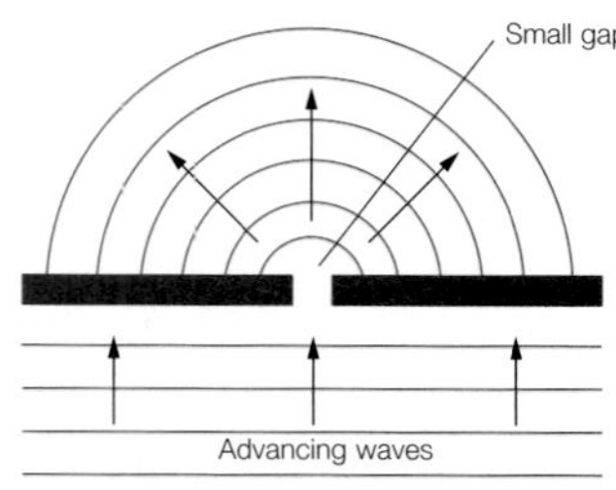

■ *Diffraction of waves passing through a small gap*

Interference

Interference is the phenomenon that occurs when two or more waves combine together as dictated by the principle of superposition. The superposition principle states that when two waves are in the same place at the same time, their amplitudes (heights) are combined. If the resultant wave amplitude is greater than that of the individual waves then constructive interference is taking place. If the resultant wave is smaller, then destructive interference is taking place.

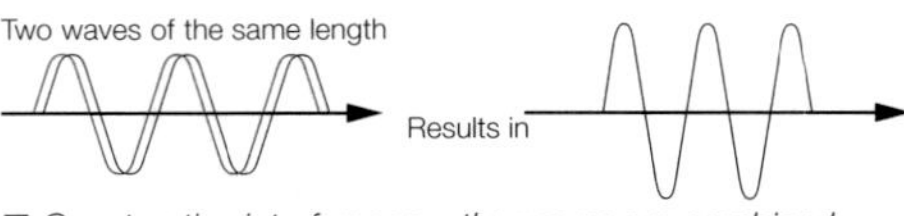

■ *Constructive interference – the waves are combined*

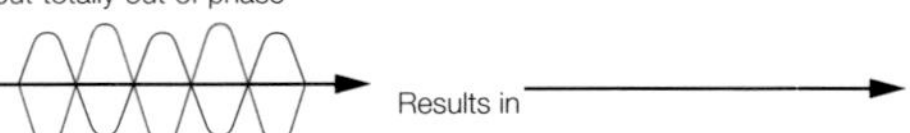

■ *Destructive interference – the waves cancel each other out*

ELECTROMAGNETIC WAVES

Electromagnetic waves are caused by a mutual fluctuation in electric and magnetic fields. These fields are perpendicular to each other, and perpendicular to the direction of wave propagation.

All the properties of sound and water waves, such as refraction and diffraction, exist in electromagnetic waves, but they differ in that they are able to transmit energy in a vacuum. They travel extremely fast: at 299,792,458 m/s in a vacuum. This is the equivalent of 27 return trips from London to New York in a second. However, they slow down in a medium, causing an element of diffraction.

Electromagnetic waves include light, microwaves, infrared radiation and X-rays. The different types of waves depend on varying wavelengths and frequencies. Since, in a vacuum, the speed of an electromagnetic wave is unchanging, it follows that the higher its frequency, the smaller its wavelength.

The electromagnetic spectrum is the collective set of waves over a broad range of wavelengths, from gamma waves (wavelength 10^{-16} m) to radio waves (wavelength 10^{3} m). Light is the small portion of the electromagnetic spectrum that is detectable to the human eye. Ultraviolet light and infrared radiation fall either side of visible light.

ELECTROMAGNETISM

▶ Electricity and magnetism were originally observed separately, but in the 19th century scientists found that they were both manifestations of a single force – the electromagnetic force.
▶ Electromagnetism is the study of the effects caused by stationary and moving electric charges.

The electromagnetic force is one of the fundamental forces of nature, the others being gravitational force and the strong and weak nuclear forces. Magnetism has been known about since ancient times, but it was not until the late 18th century that the electric force was identified – by the French physicist Charles Augustin de Coulomb (see p. 120).

MAGNETISM

Pieces of some metallic ores, such as lodestone, are magnetic – when suspended freely from a thread they point north–south. Lodestone attracts iron but not other substances. Such magnetic compasses have been used since 500 BC.

THE ELECTROMAGNETIC SPECTRUM

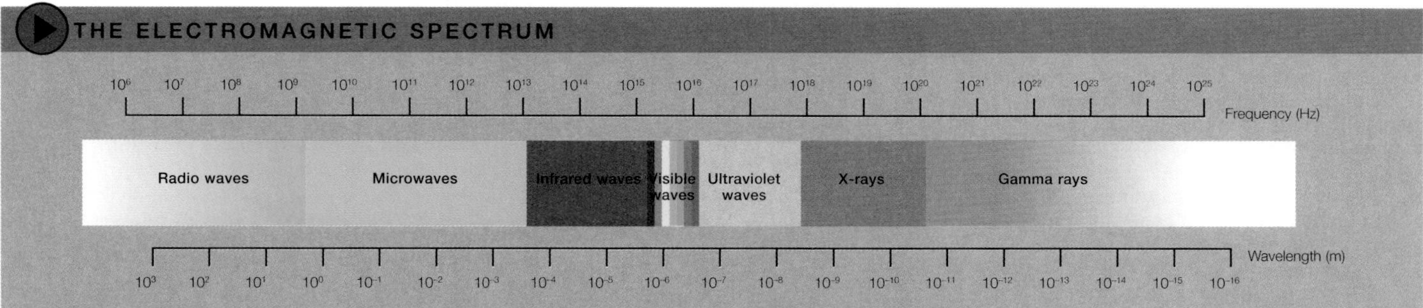

Prior to Maxwell's discoveries, it had been known that light was a wave motion, although the type of wave motion had not been identified. Maxwell was the first to show that the oscillations were of the electric and magnetic field. Hertz later proved the existence of electromagnetic waves, producing them in his laboratory with a a wavelength of 60 cm – much longer than light waves. At present, science recognizes a spectrum of electromagnetic radiation that extends from about 10^{-15} m to 10^9 m. It is subdivided into smaller, sometimes overlapping, ranges. The extension of astronomical observations from visible to other electromagnetic wavelengths has revolutionized humankind's knowledge of the universe.

Radio waves have a large range of wavelengths, from a few millimetres up to several kilometres.

Microwaves are radio waves with shorter wavelengths, between 1 mm and 30 cm, and are used in radar and microwave ovens.

Infrared waves of different wavelengths are radiated by bodies at different temperatures. (Bodies at higher temperatures radiate either visible or ultraviolet waves.) The Earth and its atmosphere, at a mean temperature of 250 K (–23°C or –9.4°F) radiates infrared waves with wavelengths centred at about 10 micrometres (µm) or 1^{-5} m (1 µm = 10^{-6} m).

Visible waves have wavelengths of 400–700 nanometres (nm; 1 nm = 10^{-9} m). The peak of the solar radiation (temperature of about 6000 K/6270°C/11,323°F) is at a wavelength of about 550 nm, where the human eye is at its most sensitive.

Ultraviolet waves have wavelengths from about 380 nm down to 60 nm. The radiation from hotter stars, above 25,000°C (45,000°F), shifts towards the violet and ultraviolet parts of the spectrum.

X-rays have wavelengths from about 10 nm down to 10^{-4} nm.

Gamma rays have wavelengths less than 10^{-11} m. They are emitted by certain radioactive nuclei and in the course of nuclear reactions.

It is now known that the Earth itself has magnetic properties (see p. 26). Investigation of the properties of magnetic materials gave birth to the concept of magnetic fields, showing the force one magnet exerts upon another. These lines of force can be demonstrated by means of small plotting compasses or iron filings. An important feature of a magnet is that it has two poles, one of which is attracted to the Earth's magnetic North Pole, while the other is attracted to the South Pole. Magnets are identified by the fact that unlike or opposite poles (north and south) attract each other, while like poles (north and north, or south and south) repel each other.

STATIC ELECTRIC CHARGES

Static electricity involves electric charges at rest. Thales, a Greek philosopher who lived around 500 BC (see p. 185) noted that when amber (*elektron* in Greek) was rubbed with a cloth, it attracted small pieces of straw. In 1600, William Gilbert (1544–1603) found that diamond, glass, sulfur and wax could be similarly 'charged by friction'. In 1646 the word 'electricity' was coined by Sir Thomas Browne (1605–82).

In the early 18th century the idea of positive and negative electric fluids arose: it was realized that when the following solids had been charged by friction, glass repelled glass and amber repelled amber, but glass and amber attracted. Like charged objects were seen to repel, whereas oppositely charged objects were seen to attract.

In 1746, Benjamin Franklin (see p. 121) proposed that only one electric fluid was needed. Positively charged objects had an excess of it and negatively charged objects had a deficiency. In 1785, Franklin conducted electricity from a thunder cloud, using a kite.

Also in 1785, Coulomb formulated the Law of Attraction and Repulsion between electrically charged bodies:

$$F = k\,Q_1Q_2/r^2$$

where F is the force, k is a constant, Q_1 and Q_2 are the sizes of the charges (+ or –), and r is the distance between the charges. This is an inverse square law, similar to Newton's Law of Gravitation (see p. 115) between masses.

In 1786, Luigi Galvani (1737–98) inadvertently made an electric cell by hanging a copper hook on an iron railing and observed a freshly killed frog's legs twitch as he did so.

ELECTRIC CURRENT

In the late 1790s, Count Alessandro Volta (see p. 123) was the first to realize that when two different metals are in contact with moisture, an electrical effect (later called a voltage) is produced. Volta made the first battery, called a voltaic pile, using alternating discs of zinc and silver separated from each other by discs of cloth moistened with salt solution. Voltaic piles thus made a steady source of electric current available.

The first practical primary cell (non-rechargeable) was produced by John Frederic Daniell (1790–1845) in 1836, using zinc and copper electrodes. This was followed by the first secondary (rechargeable) cell invented by Gaston Planté (1834–89) in 1859. This cell, based upon the use of lead and sulfuric acid, is still employed as the car battery. The Leclanche 'Dry' Cell of the 1860s was developed into the modern ordinary torch battery. It has a zinc case and a carbon electrode down its centre.

In 1820, Hans Christiaan Oersted (see p. 122) noticed that an electric current flowing in a wire could move the needle of a compass held near the wire. André Ampère (see p. 120), later in 1820, showed that parallel wires with current flowing in them attracted each other if the currents were opposed. He also showed that a helical coil of wire acted like a bar magnet when a current flowed in it.

In 1827, Georg Simon Ohm (see p. 122) introduced the concept of resistance (to the flow of an electric current) and stated Ohm's Law:

$$I = V/R$$

which translates as: I, the current in amperes (amps) in the conductor, to V, the potential difference in volts across the ends of the conductor and R, the resistance of the conductor.

In 1831, Michael Faraday (see p. 121) confirmed his hypothesis that magnetism could produce electricity when he found that a magnet moving in a coil of wire induced a current in the wire when the wire was present in an electric circuit. These discoveries soon led to the electric motor and to the dynamo, a device for generating electricity by spinning a coil of wire between the poles of a suitably shaped magnet.

James Clerk Maxwell (see p. 122) predicted in 1873 that by using oscillating electric currents it should be possible to generate electromagnetic waves which travel at the speed of light. In the late 1880s, Heinrich Hertz (see p. 122) produced such waves, which were soon used for wireless transmissions.

In 1891, George Johnstone Stoney (see p. 123) suggested electric currents consisted of moving particles which he called electrons. In 1897, Sir J.J. Thomson (see p. 123) first measured the charge to mass ratio, e/m of the electron. Then, in 1913, Robert Andrews Millikan (see p. 122) measured the electronic charge, enabling the mass of the electron to be calculated. It is a very light particle with a mass of 9 x 10^{-30} kg, or approximately 1/2000 the mass of the lightest atom (hydrogen).

Measuring current

The names of many of the scientists who were involved in discoveries based on electric charge and current have been ascribed to certain aspects and measurements in the field of electromagnetics. This can be seen in many of the equations stated below.

A Faraday of electric charge is equivalent to 1 mole (6.02 x 10^{23}) of electrons, which is equivalent to 96,500 coulombs of electric charge. A current of one ampere (amp) consists of 1 coulomb of electric charge flowing past a given point every second. Thus a 1 amp current has 6 x 10^{23}/96,500 or approximately 6 x 10^{18} electrons passing a given point in the circuit every second. A one-volt battery supplies one joule of energy to each coulomb of electric charge that it produces.

Mechanical power is measured in watts (joules per second). If a 6v battery is supplying 5 amps (5 coulombs per second), it is thus producing 6 joules per coulomb and a total of 5 x 6 = 30 joules per second. The general formula for power supplied is:

$$P = V \times I$$

where P is the power in watts, V is the voltage (also known as Potential Difference) and I is the current in amps.

ATOMIC THEORIES

▶ **Nuclear energy can be released from fission or fusion, which are both forms of nuclear reaction.**
▶ **Some thermonuclear bombs were made which were only the size of a dustbin, yet had an explosive yield equivalent to that of 20 million tonnes of the high explosive TNT.**

John Dalton (see p. 121) revolutionized science in 1803 when he hypothesized that atoms of different chemical elements, such as hydrogen and oxygen, had different characteristic masses. J.J. Thomson (see p. 123) discovered the first subatomic particle – the electron – in 1897. Ernest Rutherford (see p. 123) revealed the presence of a dense central nucleus in atoms in 1911. In 1913, Niels Bohr (see p. 120) proposed that electrons in atoms are confined to certain allowed (restricted) orbits. Light is emitted from an atom when the electron jumps from one allowed orbit further from the nucleus to another allowed orbit nearer to the nucleus.

In 1924, Prince Louis Victor de Broglie (see p. 121) produced a better description of atoms, which included the wavelike property of the quickly orbiting electrons. By 1928, Edwin Schrödinger (see p. 123), Wolfgang Pauli (see p. 123) and Max Born (see p. 120) had described the atom using quantum mechanical principles.

RADIOACTIVITY

Radioactivity was gradually understood in terms of the disintegration of atomic nuclei, but it was not until 1932 that the discovery of the neutron by Sir James Chadwick (see p. 120) made the existence of isotopes (atoms of the same chemical element with different masses) understandable. The three types of radiation are alpha decay, beta decay and gamma decay.

Alpha radiation occurs when an unstable nucleus breaks down so as to eject a fast-moving nucleus of helium, which consists of two protons and two neutrons. Beta radiation occurs when an unstable nucleus breaks down so that a neutron in the nucleus splits into a proton, which stays in the nucleus, and an electron (or positron, which is identical to an electron but with a positive charge) is ejected from the nucleus at very high velocity. After alpha or beta decay, the remaining nucleus is very often left in an 'excited' state from which it 'relaxes' with the emission of a gamma (or X-ray) photon. This is the origin of gamma radiation.

NUCLEAR FISSION AND FUSION

Otto Hahn (see p. 121) and Fritz Strassman (1902–80) discovered nuclear fission in 1938. When an isotope of uranium-235 was bombarded with neutrons, it split into two lighter nuclei (which varied from fission to fission) along with, on average, three neutrons. These neutrons were capable of bombarding and splitting other nuclei, causing more fission to take place. If the mass of uranium-235 was above a certain level (the critical mass) this produced a chain reaction. It was the production of this chain reaction which, in turn, led to the development of the first nuclear bomb. Fission is used in both nuclear reactors and atomic weapons.

Nuclear fusion occurs when two small nuclei collide and combine, breaking the weak nuclear force and releasing energy. This type of reaction releases considerably more energy than a fission process for a given mass of material. However, unlike nuclear fission, humankind has not yet found a way to properly contain or control the process. Many scientists today are searching for the key to controlled room-temperature fusion reactions, referred to as 'cold fusion'.

An example of uncontrolled fusion reaction is the hydrogen (thermonuclear) bomb, which relies on the fusion of light atoms (the same type of reaction which produces the energy in the core of the Sun) to give heavier atoms, with the destruction of matter releasing the observed energy.

NUCLEAR PARTICLES

The proton and neutron, which were once thought to be the basic blocks of matter, are now known to be made up of over 200 elementary particles. Elementary particles can be divided into two types: hadrons (meaning 'bulky' in Greek), which are heavy particles subject to the strong force, and leptons (meaning 'small' in Greek), which are small particles not subject to the strong force. Elementary particles have a further distinction between fermions, which are permanently existing particles, and bosons, which can be produced and destroyed freely (providing the laws of conservation are maintained).

Every type of particle is thought to have a companion antiparticle, which is opposite to it in some characteristic way. For instance, the positron, with positive charge, is the antiparticle of the electron, with a negative charge. Some particles, such as the photon, serve as their own antiparticles.

Protons and neutrons are composed of simpler particles named quarks. The six types ('flavours') of quark are: up, down, charmed, strange, top and bottom. The proton is considered to consist of two up quarks and a down quark, whilst the neutron consists of two down quarks and an up quark.

Mesons are short-lived subatomic particles composed of two quarks each. Mesons jump between protons and neutrons, thus holding them together. Neutrinos are particles which can carry much energy away from nuclear reactions, such as those involved in radioactivity, but they are difficult to detect, as they only interact very weakly with ordinary matter. They are capable of passing right through the Earth undetected.

▶ THE FOUR FUNDAMENTAL FORCES

The interactions between matter can be explained by four forces:

Gravitational: the weakest of the four forces, the gravitational force is the mutual attraction between masses. Although its effect is small in the realm of subatomic particles, it has great cosmic power, and is the force that holds solar systems and galaxies together.

Electromagnetic: this force explains the magnetic field and the electron-nucleus structure of an atom.

Strong: some 100 times stronger than the electromagnetic force, the strong force holds together the protons and neutrons within an atomic nucleus. It explains why protons, which have a positive charge and thus repel each other, are found in such close proximity in the densely packed atomic nucleus.

Weak: this force is associated with the radioactive beta-decay of some nuclei. The electromagnetic and weak forces have recently been shown to be part of an electro-weak force.

■ *The 100-Trillion-Watt Particle Beam Fusion Accelerator II in Sandia National Laboratories, Albuquerque, New Mexico, USA, was the first machine able to ignite a controlled thermonuclear fusion reaction in a laboratory setting. On its first firing, on 11 December 1985, it was considered to be the most powerful particle beam accelerator in the world*

SPECIAL AND GENERAL THEORIES OF RELATIVITY

▶ Special relativity equates space with time and matter with energy.
▶ General relativity shows an interdependence between space-time, mass and gravity.

An experiment by A.A. Michelson (see p. 122) and E.W. Morley (1838–1923) in 1887 showed that the velocity of light is unaffected by the motion of the source relative to the observer. The implications of this unexpected fact (which is not true for sound) were explored by Einstein. His startling conclusions, later fully verified by various experiments, led to the formulation of the special theory of relativity (1905).

SPECIAL RELATIVITY

The special theory of relativity states that nothing can exceed the speed of light, which is the same in all inertial (non-accelerating) time frames and that all inertial time frames are equally good for carrying out experiments.

The classical view of time is that if two events take place simultaneously with reference to one frame, then they must also occur simultaneously within another frame. In terms of special relativity, however, two events that occur simultaneously in one frame may not be seen as simultaneous in another frame moving relative to the first. The sequence of cause and effect is not, however, affected.

In special relativity each observer has an individual timescale. Time and space have to be considered as unified and not as two separate things; this merged entity is known as space-time. This means that time is related to the frame of reference in which it is being measured. Special relativity theory leads to the simple prediction that the length of a moving body in the direction of its motion measured in another frame is reduced by a factor dependent on its velocity with respect to the observer.

In other words, when two spaceships, A and B, travel with very high uniform velocity relative to each other, each perceives the other to be contracted (decreased in size) in the direction of its motion. In addition, if the spaceship increases its speed towards *c* (the speed of light), its mass tends to infinity. Einstein then postulated that this additional mass came from energy, and thus the energy and mass of a body are equivalent. Matter and energy are aspects of the same phenomenon, matter-energy, and are linked in the famous equation:

$$E = mc^2$$

where E is the energy released when mass (m) is destroyed, as in a nuclear reaction, and c is the velocity of light. It indicates that when 1 kg is destroyed, 9×10^{16} joules of energy are released.

Einstein foresaw the possibility of making a nuclear bomb based on his theories and warned against it. Yet, in 1945, the first such bomb used in warfare was detonated over Hiroshima. This same process of nuclear fission, in which uranium atoms split into smaller fragment atoms with the annihilation of some mass, is used in nuclear power plants.

GENERAL RELATIVITY

In his general theory of relativity, Einstein considered systems accelerating with respect to each other. He concluded that the effects of acceleration and gravity were equivalent. Using the theory, he was able to explain a discrepancy in the slow rotation of the planet Mercury's elongated orbit, which Newtonian mechanics had been unable to explain. Einstein explained the effect of a large concentrated mass, in this case the Sun, by saying it 'warped' the space around it. Thus space, or rather space-time, is curved. The degree of curvature depends upon the magnitude of the mass, and so matter-energy determines the curvature of space-time.

White dwarf stars are 25,000 times more dense than the Sun and the emissions from their atoms show a 'time dilation' as predicted by general relativity – the gravitational field slows down the vibration of the atoms by just the expected amount.

QUANTUM THEORY

▶ Quantum theory describes the behaviour of particles within atoms and the absorption and emission of electromagnetic radiation by matter in its various states.
▶ Quantum theory was established in the early 1900s in response to the failure of Newton's mechanics to describe the absorption and emission of light by atoms and molecules.

A quantum is the minimum quantity of energy which can be gained or lost from a 'system' (such as an atom, molecule, ion, etc.). Thus the energy of an atom is not able to take any chosen value, but there are only certain 'allowed' energy values. For example, a hydrogen atom can only 'jump' between certain energy states. When an atom gives up energy, the energy is given out in the form of a 'packet' of energy called a quantum, or photon, whose frequency (f) is given by Planck's Equation:

$$E = hf$$

where h is Planck's constant ($= 6.626 \times 10^{-34}$ Js). Thus a quantum of X-radiation ($f = 3 \times 10^{12}$ MHz) has 10,000 times the energy of a visible light quantum ($f = 3 \times 10^{8}$ MHz), which itself has a million times as much energy as radio wave's quantum used in television transmission ($f = 3 \times 10^{2}$ MHz). This explains why X-rays are feared for their ability to cause genetic damage, but radio waves are harmless in this respect.

When light is directed at a clean metal surface in a vacuum chamber there is a critical frequency (colour) above which electrons start to be emitted into the vacuum from the metal. This photoelectric effect was first explained by Einstein. Only if the quantum has adequate energy ($hf_{critical}$) will it be capable of ejecting an electron from the metal surface. If the frequency (f) is greater than the critical frequency, the excess energy of the quantum appears as kinetic energy of the ejected electron.

HEISENBERG UNCERTAINTY PRINCIPLE

The Heisenberg Uncertainty Principle (1927) concerns the accuracy with which the position and momentum of a particle (such as an electron) can be determined. It is usually stated in the form:

$$\Delta x \Delta p \geq h/4\pi$$

Where Δx is the uncertainty in the position of the particle, Δp is the uncertainty in the momentum of the particle and h is the Planck Constant (momentum = mass x velocity).

If Δx is small, then Δp will be large. Thus an accurate determination (measurement) of one quantity leads to the impossibility of measuring the other accurately. As both quantities cannot be known precisely, it follows that limits are set on the accuracy of any predictions made using these measurements. Therefore, the classical relationship between cause and effect of Newtonian Mechanics is blurred because to calculate the new position of a particle and its momentum accurately, one needs to know its previous values for these quantities.

The uncertainty principle arises because to observe a particle such as an electron, photons would have to be bounced off it. If the photon has a short wavelength (high frequency) its energy will be high and it will change the position of the particle in an unpredictable way. Long wavelength photons are inherently less able to locate a particle even if they would displace the particle to a lesser degree.

CONCEPTS IN MODERN PHYSICS

SCHRODINGER'S CAT

Quantum theory has many strange quirks. One of these, the indeterminacy of the wave function, has given rise to the Schrödinger's Cat scenario.

In the experiment (which is imaginary, and never actually conducted), a cat is placed inside a box for one hour with a radioactive atom whose probability of decay is 50% per hour. If the atom decays, a Geiger counter triggers, a mechanism breaks a capsule of lethal cyanide gas and the cat quietly dies. If the atom does not decay, the cat remains alive. According to quantum mechanics, the state of the system is uncertain until it is observed, so that until the box is opened by the observer, the cat remains in a simultaneously alive and dead state. Scientifically speaking, the cat can be described by a wave function which is the sum of a live cat and a dead cat. Only when the box is opened is the outcome determined. In this paradoxical thought experiment, the very small world of the quantum is expanded to the everyday scale, giving bizarre results.

One of the more interesting ways out of the paradox of the cat which is alive and dead at the same time is multi-universe theory, known as the Everett-Wheeler-Graham model. This posits the scenario that all possible universes exist. For every quantum event which has a number of outcomes, the universe splits into various universes, each with a different outcome. Thus the solution to the Schrödinger Cat paradox is simple: the cat is alive in one universe and dead in another. The Everett-Wheeler-Graham model (also known as the many-worlds theory) has interesting philosophical implications. For example, it assumes that a parallel universe exists for every decision one makes in one's life. In some universes, life never evolved, whilst in others, history is totally different to what it is in this universe.

STRING THEORY

One of the problems with current models of physics is that relativity and quantum theory are, to some extent, inconsistent with each other. So far, no physicist has been able to provide a quantum theory of gravity which would combine the two fields. This search for a Grand Unified Theory (GUT) has occupied many scientists for much of this century.

A recent possible theoretical model is (super)string theory. String theory suggests that the universe is made up of very small vibrating strings. These strings are about 100 billion billion times smaller than a proton, which itself is less than a billionth of a metre in size. In addition, these strings are vibrating in ten dimensions. The different resonances at which these strings vibrate produce the varied fundamental particles, such as quarks, leptons and electrons, that are known to exist.

String theory also predicts the relativistic equations of Einstein. Thus the theory has managed to unify several separate aspects of modern physics. However, it too is not yet complete: there are many millions of mathematical solutions to the field theory of strings, and the correct solution is still beyond the grasp of contemporary physics.

BY MURRAY GELL-MANN IN 1964 FROM A WORD IN JAMES JOYCE'S NOVEL *FINNEGANS WAKE* ■

Physicists

- Donald Glaser, who won the Nobel Prize in 1960 for his bubble chamber, got his inspiration from watching the bubbles in a glass of beer.
- Wilhelm Röntgen, discoverer of X-rays, never sought a patent or any kind of financial reward for his discovery and gave his Nobel Prize money to the University of Würzburg for scientific research.
- Marie Curie is the only person to have won Nobel Prizes in two separate science fields: she won one for physics in 1903 and one for chemistry in 1911.
- As well as framing the US constitution, Benjamin Franklin invented the lightning rod.

Albert the Great, St (*c.* 1200–80), German bishop and philosopher who undertook 'to make intelligible' Aristotle's *Physica*.

Alvarez, Luis (1911–88), US physicist who discovered resonance particles.

Amontons, Guillaume (1663–1705), French physicist who discovered that the temperature and pressure of gases are related.

Ampère, André Marie (1775–1836), French physicist who founded the branch of physics that he named electrodynamics and which is now known as electromagnetism. Ampère established a mathematical and physical description of the magnetic force between two electric currents. He formed a law of electromagnetism – Ampère's law – and pioneered techniques in measuring electricity.

Anderson, Carl David (1905–91), US physicist who discovered the positron, the first known particle of antimatter. He also discovered the first meson (1935).

Angström, Anders Jonas (1814–74), Swedish physicist who pioneered the science of spectroscopy. He undertook major research in heat conduction.

Aristotle (*c.* 384–322 BC), Greek philosopher and scientist who reviewed the entire field of human knowledge known in his time. His theory of causality stated that every event has four causes: material cause (the matter involved), formal cause (the way it is placed), efficient cause (which triggers the action or change), and final cause (what the event leads to). Aristotle travelled the Hellenic world founding academies and tutored Alexander the Great before settling in Athens in 335 BC.

Avogadro, Amadeo (1776–1856), Italian physicist. Avogadro's law states that under the same conditions of pressure and temperature, equal volumes of different gases contain an equal number of molecules.

Babinet, Jacques (1794–1872), French physicist who standardized light measurement.

Bacon, Roger (*c.* 1214–92), English Franciscan, philosopher and scientist who pioneered important work on the magnifying glass and advocated the primacy of mathematical proof in science.

Balmer, Johann Jakob (1825–98), Swiss physicist who discovered the first mathematical formula to describe the wavelengths of spectral lines. This formula is basic to the development of atomic theory.

Becquerel, Antoine Henri (1852–1908), French physicist who is the father of radioactivity. He found a previously unknown type of radiation being emitted from uranium atoms within fluorescent uranium salts. His colleague Marie Curie later named this phenomenon radioactivity.

Bernoulli, Daniel (1700–82), Swiss physician and mathematician who described the theory of statics and the motion of fluids in his *Hydrodynamica* (1738).

Black, Joseph (1728–99), Scottish physicist who rediscovered 'fixed air' (carbon dioxide) and developed the concepts of latent and specific heat.

Blackett, Patrick (Baron Blackett; 1897–1974), English physicist who discovered the positron – an elementary particle having the same magnitude of mass and charge as an electron, but with a positive charge.

Bloch, Felix (1905–83), Swiss-born US physicist who developed Bloch bands – sets of discrete, closely adjacent energy levels that arise from quantum states when a non-degenerate gas condenses to a solid.

Bohm, David Joseph (1917–), US physicist whose *Quantum Theory* (1951) was a landmark in that field.

Bohr, Niels (1885–1962), Danish physicist who played a major role in the development of nuclear physics. In his classic paper *On the Constitution of Atoms and Molecules* (1913), the Bohr theory of the atom – combining Rutherford's model with Planck's quantum theory of radiation – accounted for the known patterns of atomic radiation seen in spectra and had an important impact on the development of quantum mechanics.

Boltzmann, Ludwig (1844–1906), Austrian theoretical physicist who made important advances in the theory of radiation and in statistical treatment of the behaviour of molecules in gases.

Born, Max (1882–1970), German physicist whose work on crystals led to the development of the Born-Haber cycle, a theoretical cycle of reactions and changes by which the lattice energy of ionic crystals may be calculated. Born is, however, best known for his work on quantum physics.

Bose, Sir Jagadis Chandra (1858–1937), Indian physicist and botanist who is best known for his studies of electric waves.

Bose, Salyendranath (1894–1974), Indian physicist, chemist and mathematician who developed Bose statistics, the forerunner of modern quantum theory.

Bothe, Walther (1891–1957), German atomic physicist who devised the coincidence method of detecting the emission of electrons by X-rays.

Boyle, Robert (1627–91), Anglo-Irish physicist and chemist who formulated the law – now called Boyle's law – stating that, at a given temperature, the pressure of a gas is proportional to its volume. He pioneered the concept of elements in his suggestion of a corpuscular view of matter. He also distinguished between elements and compounds.

Boys, Sir Charles Vernon (1855–1944), English physicist who determined the value of the gravitational constant.

Bragg, Sir William (1862–1942), English physicist who pioneered work in solid-state physics.

Brewster, Sir David (1781–1868), Scottish physicist who is known for his research on polarization of light.

Brown, Robert (1773–1858), Scottish physician and botanist who discovered the nucleus in cells and observed, under the microscope, what came to be known as Brownian Motion – the agitation of small suspended particles.

Carnot, Nicholas Léonard Sadi (1796–1832), French physicist who virtually founded the science of thermodynamics by proposing an early form of the second law of thermodynamics.

Cavendish, Henry (1731–1810), English chemist and physicist whose discoveries included the properties of hydrogen, the composition of air, the composition of water and various properties of electricity.

Celsius, Anders (1701–44), Swedish astronomer who suggested the scale for measuring temperature that now bears his name.

Chadwick, Sir James (1891–1974), English physicist who discovered the neutron.

Chapman, Sydney (1888–1970), English mathematician and physicist who developed the theory of thermal diffusion.

Charles, Jacques (1746–1823), French physicist who developed Charles's law, which relates the expansion of gas with a rise in temperature.

Chladni, Ernst (1756–1827), German physicist who is regarded as one of the founders of the science of acoustics.

Clausius, Rudolph (1822–88), German physicist who formulated the second law of thermodynamics.

Cockcroft, Sir John Douglas (1897–1967), English physicist who – with Walton – split the atom (1932).

Copernicus, Nicolaus (Mikolaj Kopernik; 1473–1543), Polish astronomer who proposed that the Earth was in daily motion around its axis and in yearly motion around a stationary Sun.

Coulomb, Charles-Augustin de (1736–1806), French physicist who developed Coulomb's law stating that the force between two electrical charges is proportional to the product of the charges and inversely proportional to the square of the distance between them.

Curie, Marie Sklodowska (1867–1934), Polish-born French chemist who – with her husband Pierre – pioneered research into radioactivity. Following Becquerel's discovery of radioactivity, which Marie Curie named, she and Pierre studied pitchblende (uranium ore) to establish whether it owed much of its radioactivity to tiny quantities of highly active impurities. The Curies discovered the elements polonium and radium. The great radioactivity of the latter confirmed the immense possibilities of the energy that could be gained from atomic processes.

Curie, Pierre (1859–1906), French physicist who researched the relationship between magnetism and heat, discovering that, above a certain critical point (now known as the Curie point), ferromagnetic substances lose their magnetism. He formulated Curie's law which related how easy it is to magnetize a substance to its temperature. He also studied radioactivity with his wife, Marie.

d'Alembert, Jean Le Rond (1717–83), French philosopher and mathematician who formulated the d'Alembert principle – a generalization of Newton's third law of motion.

1969'S PHYSICS NOBEL PRIZEWINNER MURRAY GELL-MANN ENTERED YALE UNIVERSITY

Dalton, John (1766–1844), English chemist and physicist who developed the atomic theory of matter, defining the atom as the smallest particle of substance that can take part in a chemical reaction. His early studies on gases led to the formulation of Dalton's law which states that the total pressure of a mixture of gases is equal to the sum of the partial pressures of the individual component gases.

de Broglie, Prince Louis Victor (1892–1987), French physicist who is best known for his theory that – just as waves can behave like particles – particles can have wave-like properties. He stated that an electron can behave as if it were a wave motion – now known as a de Broglie wave.

Dehmelt, Hans Georg (1922–), German-born US physicist who isolated a single electron (1973).

de Sitter, Willem (1872–1934), Dutch mathematician and astronomer who proposed what came to be known as the de Sitter universe.

Dirac, Paul (1902–84), English mathematician and physicist who developed a general formulism for quantum mechanics (1926). His relativistic theory describes the properties of the electron.

Doppler, Christian Johann (1803–53), Austrian physicist and mathematician who discovered the wave effect that now bears his name.

Einstein, Albert (1879–1955), German-born US physicist who revolutionized physics by developing the special and general theories of relativity. His international impact upon physics began in 1905 when he published four research papers, each one containing a major discovery in the subject: the special theory of relativity (which he proposed to account for the constant speed of light); the theory of Brownian movement; the photon theory of light; and the equation relating mass and energy. His general theory of relativity was presented in 1916 and verified in 1919. Einstein spent much of his life applying the general theory to cosmological problems, as well as trying to formulate a single theory that would cover both gravitation and electrodynamics.

Eötvös, Baron Roland von (1848–1919), Hungarian physicist who introduced the Eötvös law, an equation that relates surface tension, temperature, density, and the relative molecular mass of a liquid.

Esaki, Leo (1925–), Japanese physicist who has discovered a mechanical effect he named 'tunnelling'.

Everett, Hugo (1930–82), US physicist whose Relative State Formulation of Quantum Mechanics (1957) was one of the most influential works in quantum mechanics.

Fahrenheit, Gabriel Daniel (1686–1736), German-born physicist of Dutch ancestry who was the first person to use mercury in a thermometer. He also devised a scale for his thermometer which now bears his name.

Fairbank, William (1917–89), US physicist who announced in 1979 that he had isolated the quark – no one has managed to reproduce his experiments.

Faraday, Michael (1791–1867), English physicist and chemist who made important advances in electromagnetism. Becoming an assistant to Davy, who recognized his potential and taught him, Faraday discovered electromagnetic induction in 1821, and built a primitive model which demonstrated the continuous production of current from a conductor moving in a field – in effect, a primitive dynamo. Faraday also liquefied chlorine and isolated benzene. In 1833 he formulated quantitative laws to express magnitudes of electrolytic effects, now known as Faraday's laws of electrolysis. In 1831 he made observations that led to the formulation of the law of induction which now bears his name.

Fermi, Enrico (1901–54), Italian-born US physicist who established the theory of beta decay in the 1930s. He discovered statistical laws obeyed by particles such as the electron and researched means of producing controlled and self-sustaining nuclear fission reaction. The result – the first nuclear reactor – was built and tested in Chicago in 1942. In 1943 Fermi helped to test the first atomic bomb.

Ferraris, Galileo (1847–97), Italian physicist and electrical engineer who discovered the principle of rotary magnetic field which led to the development of the self-starting electric motor still in use today.

Feynman, Richard Phillips (1918–88), US physicist who developed the quantum approach to electromagnetic theory.

Fizeau, Armand-Hippolyte-Louis (1819–96), French physicist who achieved fame for his experiments determining the speed of light.

Flerov, Georgii (1913–), Russian physicist who synthesized elements 102, 103, 104, 105, 106 and 107.

Foucault, Jean-Bernard-Léon (1819–68), French physicist who devised a way of measuring absolute velocity of light to within 1% of its true value.

Fourier, Jean-Baptiste (1768–1830), French mathematician and physicist who showed how the conduction of heat in solid bodies could be analysed in terms of infinite mathematical series, now known as the Fourier Series.

Franklin, Benjamin (1706–90), US inventor, diplomat, printer and publisher. As a scientist his most important work was in studying electricity.

■ *Physicists Enrico Fermi and Julius Robert Oppenheimer both worked on the first atom bomb, which was tested in Alamogordo, New Mexico, USA, on 16 July 1945*

Fresnel, Augustine Jean (1788–1827), French physicist who worked on the theory that light is a transverse wave motion.

Frisch, Otto Robert (1904–79), Austrian-born British physicist who worked with his aunt, Lise Meitner, on the discovery of nuclear fission.

Gabor, Dennis (1900–79), Hungarian-born British physicist who pioneered holography – the means by which a three-dimensional photographic image is created without the use of a lens.

Galileo, Galilei (1564–1642), Italian astronomer, physicist and mathematician who was a pioneer in developing scientific methods of testing by systematic experimentation. The popular story concerning dropping weights from the famous Leaning Tower of Pisa is unsupported by evidence. Most of his work was concerned with the study of mechanics and he was the first to apply mathematics in this field. Galileo was convicted of heresy for his support of Copernicus and was obliged to recant.

Geiger, Hans (1882–1945), German physicist who assisted Rutherford. In 1913 he developed the Geiger counter for detecting atomic particles.

Gell-Mann, Murray (1929–), US physicist who developed the theory of quantum particles. He postulated the existence of quarks in protons and neutrons, choosing the name for the particles from a novel by James Joyce.

Glaser, Donald (1926–), US physicist who developed the bubble chamber for tracking and detecting sub-atomic particles.

Glashow, Sheldon Lee (1932–), US physicist who is best known for an explanation of the forces that hold together elementary particles of matter.

Hahn, Otto (1879–1968), German chemist who – with Strassmann – discovered nuclear fission. He worked with Meitner, mainly studying the application of radioactive methods to solve chemical problems and, during this period, they discovered the element protactinium. After Meitner fled from Germany (1938), Hahn continued his studies with Strassmann. They proved that when uranium was bombarded with neutrons, one of the products formed was a much lighter radioactive form of barium. This indicated that the uranium atom had divided into two lighter atoms. Hahn sent his results abroad to Meitner who developed an explanation for what had happened and named the process nuclear fission.

Halley, Edmund (1656–1742), English astronomer and physicist who formulated the mathematical law relating pressure and height. Halley is, however, best known for his work in astronomy.

Hawking, Stephen (1942–), English physicist who is best known for his theory of exploding black holes which draws upon both quantum mechanics and relativity theory. Hawking's *Brief History of Time* was a hugely popular exploration of space-time problems.

Heisenberg, Werner (1901–76), German physicist who formulated quantum mechanics in terms of matrices, and is best known for the famous Heisenberg uncertainty principle.

Helmholtz, Hermann von (1821–94), German scientist, mathematician and philosopher who made important discoveries in acoustics, optics, physiology and meteorology. He is best known for his statement of the law of conservation of energy, the first law of thermodynamics.

Henry, Joseph (1797–1878), US scientist who discovered a number of important electrical properties, including self-induction.

Henry, William (1775–1836), English chemist and physician who formulated the gas law which now bears his name.

Hertz, Gustav (1887–1975), German physicist who – with Franck – proved that energy can be absorbed by an atom only in definite amounts.

Hertz, Heinrich (1857–94), German physicist who discovered radio waves. Hertz established that heat and light are electromagnetic radiations.

Hittorf, Johann Wilhelm (1824–1914), German physicist and chemist who showed how the relative speeds of ions can be calculated.

Hooke, Robert (1635–1703), English physicist and chemist who discovered the law of elasticity that is now known by his name. Hooke worked as an assistant to Boyle and put forward the first rational theory of combustion.

Huygens, Christiaan (1629–95), Dutch mathematician, physicist and astronomer who formulated the wave theory of light.

Jeans, Sir James (1877–1946), English astronomer, mathematician and physicist who was the first person to suggest that matter is continuously created throughout the universe.

Joliot-Curie, Frédéric (Frédéric Joliot; 1900–58), French physicist who – with his wife Irène (q.v.) – discovered artificial radioactivity.

Joliot-Curie, Irène (Irène Curie; 1896–1956), French physicist who was the daughter of Pierre and Marie Curie and the wife of Frédéric Joliot. Irène and Frédéric discovered radioactive elements that had been created artificially.

Joule, James Prescott (1818–89), English physicist who determined the relationship between heat and mechanical energy. He established that the different forms of energy – heat, mechanical energy and electrical energy – are basically the same.

Kamerlingh-Onnes, Helke (1853–1926), Dutch physicist who worked in low-temperature physics and discovered superconductivity.

Kant, Immanuel (1724–1804), German philosopher who addressed the challenge of Newtonian mechanics. He proposed two basic forces: the attractive or gravitational force and the repulsive or elastic force.

Kelvin of Largs, Baron (William Thomson; 1824–1907), Scottish engineer, physicist and mathematician who was a major influence on scientific developments in his day. He played an important role in the development of the conservation law of energy, the mathematical analysis of electricity and magnetism, and research in hydrodynamics. He is best known for his work on the absolute scale of temperature, which is now given in degrees Kelvin.

■ *Dr Lise Meitner made a major contribution to the study of nuclear fission, but because she was Jewish she had to leave Nazi Germany and continue her work in Sweden*

Kepler, Johannes (1571–1630), German astronomer who was the first to prove that the Earth orbits the Sun rather than the other way round.

Kirchhoff, Gustav Robert (1824–87), German physicist who is remembered for Kirchhoff's laws which describe the currents and electric forces in electrical networks.

Kurchatov, Igor (1903–60), Russian physicist who led the team that exploded the first Soviet atomic bomb.

Lagrange, Count Joseph Louis (1736–1813), Italian-born French physicist and mathematician who summarized research in mechanics after Newton and whose work laid the foundations of the metric system.

Landau, Lev (1908–68), Azeri physicist who was the first to describe ferromagnetism – the phenomenon in which certain electrically uncharged materials strongly attract others.

Langevin, Paul (1872–1946), French physicist who developed what is now known as sonar.

Lawrence, Ernest Orlando (1901–58), US physicist who invented the cyclotron (a particle accelerator) in the early 1930s.

Lenz, H(einrich) F(riedrich) E(mil) (1804–65), Russian physicist whose research on induced electric current led him to formulate what is now known as Lenz's law.

Leonardo da Vinci (1452–1519), Italian Renaissance polymath whose contributions to art, architecture and science were prodigious. In science his ideas were not recognized until the 19th century when his notebooks were finally published.

Lorentz, Hendrik Antoon (1853–1928), Dutch physicist who developed the theory of electromagnetic radiation.

Mach, Ernst (1838–1916), Austrian physicist who did important work in wave theory, optics and mechanics.

Maiman, Theodore Harold (1927–), US physicist who is best known for his pioneering work with laser beams.

Maxwell, James Clerk (1831–79), Scottish physicist whose formulation of the electromagnetic theory of light revolutionized physics. He suggested that light is an electromagnetic vibration, which was later proved by Hertz. Maxwell also researched colour sensation and the kinetic theory of gases.

Mayer, Maria Goeppert (1906–72), German-born US physicist who independently developed a theory of the structure of atomic nuclei.

Meitner, Lise (1878–1968), Austrian-born Swedish physicist whose research, with Hahn and Strassmann, led to the discovery of nuclear fission. Meitner worked with Hahn for 30 years and together they discovered protactium, as well as studying beta decay and the results of the nuclear bombardment of uranium. Being Jewish, Meitner left Nazi Germany for Sweden in 1938 and Hahn and Strassmann continued to involve her in their research at a distance. She correctly described – and named – the nuclear fission achieved by Hahn and Strassmann in 1938–39.

Michelson, A(lbert) A(braham) (1852–1931), German-born US physicist who established the speed of light as a fundamental constant.

Millikan, Robert Andrews (1868–1953), US physicist who determined the charge on the electron (1912) and studied the photoelectric effect.

Mössbauer, Rudolph Ludwig (1929–), German physicist who discovered the effect that now bears his name and which is also known as recoil-free gamma-ray resonance.

Musschenbroek, Pieter van (1692–1761), Dutch physicist who developed a device capable of storing and (under control) releasing electricity.

Nambu, Yoichipo (1921–), Japanese physicist who has made important discoveries concerning the nature of quarks.

Newton, Sir Isaac (1642–1727), English mathematician and physicist who could be regarded as the founder of modern physics. By 1666, at the age of 24, he had made important discoveries in mathematics (the binomial theorem and differential calculus, which he called fluxions), optics (the theory of colours) and medicine. In 1687 he published his *Philosophiae Naturalis Principia Mathematica,* generally known as the *Principia.* Through careful analysis of the available experimental data and the application of his theory he was able to explain many previously inexplicable phenomena, such as the tides and the precession of equinoxes. Using a prism, he split sunlight into the spectrum. He is chiefly remembered for his laws of motion and gravity.

Oersted, Hans Christiaan (1777–1851), Danish physicist who, in 1819, discovered the magnetic effect produced by an electric current after noticing that the needle of a compass, which was close to a wire that was carrying a current, swung erratically and then came to rest at a right-angle to the wire. This made Oersted realize that there was a magnetic field around the wire.

Ohm, Georg Simon (1787–1854), German physicist who discovered the law that is now named after him. Ohm's law states that the current flow through a conductor is directly proportional to the potential difference (voltage) and inversely proportional to the resistance.

Oppenheimer, J(ulius) Robert (1904–67), US physicist who directed

■ THE STORY OF ISAAC NEWTON BEING STRUCK ON THE HEAD WITH AN APPLE WHILE SITTING

the Los Alamos laboratory during the development of the atomic bomb (1943–45).

Pascal, Blaise (1623–62), French mathematician and physicist who discovered what became known as Pascal's theorem at the age of 16, when he was writing a book on conic sections. At the age of 19, he invented the first calculating machines, which performed addition and subtraction. He also investigated what became known as Pascal's triangle, and helped to develop the theory of probability before abandoning mathematics in favour of theology. In physics, Pascal is remembered for the principle (or law) which bears his name and which states that in a fluid at rest in a closed container a pressure change in one part is transmitted without loss to every portion of the fluid and to the walls of the container.

Pauli, Wolfgang (1900–58), Austrian-born US-Swiss physicist who discovered the exclusion principle, which states that in an atom no two electrons can have the same set of quantum numbers.

Peltier, Jean-Charles (1785–1845), French physicist who discovered what is now known as Peltier's effect whereby, at the junction of two different metals, an electric current will produce either heat or cold.

Penrose, Roger (1931–), English mathematician who is also an influential theoretical physicist (in particular in the field of black holes). Penrose has developed a new cosmology based on complex geometry.

Penzias, Arno Allan (1933–), German-born US astrophysicist who – with Wilson – discovered cosmic microwave background radiation.

Perrin, Jean (1870–1942), French physicist whose studies of the Brownian motion of suspended minute particles confirmed the atomic nature of matter.

Planck, Max (1858–1949), German physicist who discovered the quantum theory of radiation, which states that energy from an oscillating particle is emitted not continuously but rather in discrete packets of energy called quanta. Planck is generally regarded, with Einstein, as the co-founder of 20th-century physics. He expressed the relationship between energy emitted or absorbed by a body and the frequency of radiation mathematically as $E = nhv$, where E is the energy, n is the number, v is the frequency and h is the constant of proportionality, now known as the Planck constant.

Plato (*c.* 428–347 BC), Greek philosopher whose influence on religion, education, politics, ethics and philosophy was profound. Plato also made important contributions to science – he questioned what accounted for the 'uniform and orderly motions' of the planets and he established the principle of the mathematical analysis of nature.

Poincaré, Henri (1854–1912), French mathematician, philosopher and astronomer who was a major influence in cosmology, relativity and topology.

Poynting, John Henry (1852–1914), English physicist who is best known for Poynting's vector, showing that the flow of energy at a point can be expressed by a simple formula in terms of electric and magnetic forces.

Rabi, Isidor Isaac (1899–1988), Austrian-born US physicist who pioneered atomic exploration.

Raman, Chandrasekhara Venkata (1888–1970), Indian physicist who discovered that when light traverses a material, some of that light changes in wavelength. This is now known as the Raman effect.

Rayleigh, Lord (John William Strutt; 1843–1919), English physicist whose discoveries in acoustics and optics are fundamental to the theory of wave propagation in fluids.

Richter, Burton (1931–), US physicist who, with his colleagues, created and detected a heavy elementary particle they called the psi.

Romer, Ole (1644–1710), Danish astronomer who demonstrated conclusively – from his observations of Jupiter's moons – that light travels at finite speed.

Röntgen, Wilhelm Conrad (1845–1923), German physicist who discovered X-rays (although the true nature of X-rays was not established until 1912).

Rumford, Count (Sir Benjamin Thompson; 1753–1814), US-born British physicist who was the first to suggest that heat is a form of energy.

Rutherford, Ernest (Baron Rutherford; 1871–1937), New Zealand physicist who founded modern atomic theory and was the first to split the atom. His theory of the scattering of alpha particles (1910) led him to suggest that the atom consists of a positively charged nucleus which is surrounded by orbiting planetary electrons. This model is known as the Rutherford electron.

Rydberg, Johannes Robert (1854–1919), Swedish physicist who explained the atomic spectrum of hydrogen by means of a simple formula, which includes the Rydberg constant and two variables whose values are positive integers.

Sakharov, Andrei (1921–89), Russian physicist who made a major contribution to the development of Soviet nuclear weapons and offered evidence for the existence of quarks. He is best known, however, as a campaigner for civil rights in the former Soviet Union.

Schrödinger, Edwin (1887–1961), Austrian theoretical physicist who – with Dirac – contributed significantly to the wave theory of matter.

Wilhelm Conrad Röntgen won the first Nobel Prize for physics in 1901 for his discovery of X-rays, which transformed the field of medicine and ushered in a new era of physics

Schuster, Sir Arthur (1851–1934), German-born British physicist who was the first to show that an electric current is conducted by ions.

Snell, Willebrord (1591–1626), Dutch mathematician and physicist who created Snell's law in optics, formulating the relationship between the path taken by a ray of light in crossing the boundary of separation between two contacting surfaces and the refractive index of each.

Stern, Otto (1888–1969), German-born US physicist who developed the molecular beam as a tool for studying the characteristics of molecules.

Stokes, Sir George Gabriel (1819–1903), Anglo-Irish physicist and mathematician who is best known for Stokes's law, giving the force-resisting motion of a spherical body through a viscous fluid.

Stoney, George Johnstone (1826–1911), Irish physicist who introduced the term 'electron'.

Sturgeon, William (1783–1850), English physicist who devised the first electromagnet.

Szilard, Leo (1898–1964), Hungarian-born US physicist who was one of the first people to realize the significance of nuclear fission.

Teller, Edward (1908–), Hungarian-born US physicist who was the main scientific force behind the US development of the hydrogen bomb.

Thomson, Sir George Paget (1892–1975), English physicist who demonstrated that electrons undergo diffraction.

Thomson, Sir Joseph John (1856–1940), English physicist whose discovery of the electron resulted in revolutionizing the understanding of atomic structure.

Tomonaga, Shin'ichiro (1906–79), Japanese physicist who developed changes that made the quantum theory of mechanics fully consistent with the quantum theory of relativity.

Torricelli, Evangelista (1608–47), Italian mathematician and physicist who invented the barometer.

Tyndall, John (1820–93), Anglo-Irish physicist who described the Tyndall effect, the scattering of light by particles of matter in its path.

Van de Graaff, Robert Jemison (1901–67), US physicist who developed both the Van de Graaff generator and accelerator.

van der Waals, Johannes Diderik (1837–1923), Dutch physicist who formulated the van der Waals equation, describing the behaviour of real gases.

Volta, Count Alessandro (1745–1827), Italian physicist who invented the battery cell – the 'voltaic pile' made from copper and zinc discs which were separated by cardboard soaked in salt solution. He also discovered methane gas.

von Karman, Theodore (1881–1963), Hungarian-born US aerodynamicist who discovered Karman vortices, the alternating vortices found behind obstacles placed in moving fluids.

Watson-Watt, Sir Robert Alexander (1892–1973), Scottish physicist who played a major role in the development of radar.

Weber, Wilhelm Eduard (1804–91), German physicist who investigated magnetism and, in 1833, devised the electromagnetic telegraph.

Wilson, Kenneth (1936–), US physicist who developed a theory that explains the behaviour of different substances under pressure and temperature.

Witten, Edward (1951–), US physicist who developed string theory, which attempts to unify general relativity with quantum mechanics, and helps to explain nuclear events.

Young, Thomas (1773–1829), English physicist who established the principle of interference of light, thus confirming the wave theory of light.

Yukawa, Hideki (1907–81), Japanese physicist who predicted the existence of the meson – an unstable subatomic particle made up of two indivisible elementary particles called quarks.

Zernike, Frits (1888–1966), Dutch physicist who invented the phase-contrast microscope in 1935 which allowed specimens to be examined without having to stain cells first.

NOBEL PRIZEWINNERS

1901 Wilhelm Röntgen, German: for the discovery of X-rays.

1902 Hendrik Antoon Lorentz and Pieter Zeeman, Dutch: for the investigation of influences of magnetism on radiation.

1903 Antoine Henri Becquerel, French: for the discovery of spontaneous radioactivity; Pierre Curie, French, and Marie Curie, Polish-born French citizen: for investigating radiation phenomena.

1904 Lord Rayleigh (John William Strutt), English: for discovering argon.

1905 Philipp von Lenard, Hungarian-born German: for research on cathode rays.

1906 Sir Joseph J. Thomson, English: for investigation of electrical conductivity of gases.

1907 A.A. Michelson, German-born US: for establishing the speed of light as a constant and for his other metrological and spectroscopic investigations.

1908 Gabriel Lippmann, Luxembourg-born French: for photographic reproduction of colours.

1909 Guglielmo Marconi, Italian, and Karl Braun, German: for the development of wireless telegraphy.

1910 Johannes van der Waals, Dutch: for investigating relationships between states of gases and liquids.

1911 Wilhelm Wien, German: for investigating the laws governing heat radiation.

1912 Nils Gustav Dalén, Swedish: for the invention of automatic regulators for lighting buoys and beacons.

1913 Helke Kamerlingh-Onnes, Dutch: for studies into the properties of matter at low temperatures and producing liquid helium.

1914 Max von Laue, German: for diffraction of X-rays using crystals.

1915 Sir William Bragg and Sir Lawrence Bragg, both English: for the analysis of crystal structure using X-rays.

1916 No award

1917 Charles Barkla, English: for the discovery of characteristics of X-radiation of elements.

1918 Max Planck, German: for formulating the first quantum theory.

■ *Einstein stands before a blackboard during one of his lectures at Princeton University, where he worked from 1933, after fleeing from Germany because he was a Jew*

1919 Johannes Stark, German: for discovering the Doppler effect in positive ion rays and the division of spectral lines when the source of light is subjected to strong electric force fields.

1920 Charles Guillaume, Swiss: for discovering anomalies in alloys.

1921 Albert Einstein, German-born US: for elucidating theories fundamental to theoretical physics.

1922 Niels Bohr, Danish: for investigations into atomic structure and radiation.

1923 Robert Millikan, US: for work on elementary electric charge and the photoelectric effect.

1924 Karl Siegbahn, Swedish: for work on X-ray spectroscopy.

1925 James Franck and Gustav Hertz, German: for defining the laws governing the impact of an electron upon an atom.

1926 Jean-Baptiste Perrin, French: for work on the discontinuous structure of matter.

1927 Arthur Holly Compton, US: for the discovery of wavelength change in diffused X-rays; Charles Wilson, Scottish: for the invention of cloud chamber.

1928 Sir Owen Richardson, English: for the discovery of Richardson's law, concerning the electron emissions by hot metals.

1929 Prince Louis de Broglie, French: for the discovery of the wave nature of electrons.

1930 Sir Chandrasekhara Raman, Indian: for work on light diffusion and discovery of the Raman effect.

1931 No award

1932 Werner Heisenberg, German: for formulating the indeterminacy principle of quantum mechanics.

1933 Paul Dirac, English, and Erwin Schrödinger, Austrian: for the introduction of wave-equations in quantum mechanics.

1934 No award

1935 Sir James Chadwick, English: for the discovery of the neutron.

1936 Victor Hess, Austrian: for the discovery of cosmic radiation.

1937 Clinton Davisson, US, and Sir George Thomson, English: for demonstrating interference phenomenon in crystals irradiated by electrons.

1938 Enrico Fermi, Italian-born US: for the discovery of radioactive elements produced by neutron irradiation.

1939 Ernest Lawrence, US: invention of the cyclotron.

1940–42 No awards

1943 Otto Stern, German-born US: for the discovery of the magnetic moment of the proton.

1944 Isidor Isaac Rabi, Austrian-born US: for discovering the resonance method for observing the magnetic properties of atomic nuclei.

1945 Wolfgang Pauli, Austrian-born US-Swiss: for the discovery of the exclusion principle.

1946 Percy Bridgman, US: for discoveries in high-pressure physics.

1947 Sir Edward Appleton, English: for the discovery of the Appleton Layer in the upper atmosphere.

1948 Patrick Blackett, English: for discoveries in nuclear physics and cosmic radiation.

1949 Hideki Yukawa, Japanese: for predicting the existence of mesons.

1950 Cecil Powell, English: for developing the photographic method of studying nuclear processes and for discoveries about mesons.

1951 Sir John Cockcroft, English, and Ernest Walton, Irish: for pioneering the use of accelerated particles to study atomic nuclei.

1952 Felix Bloch, Swiss-born US, and Edward Purcell, US: for discovering nuclear magnetic resonance in solids.

1953 Frits Zernike, Dutch: for discovering the phase-contrast microscopy method.

1954 Max Born, German-born British: for statistical studies on wave functions; Walther Bothe, German: for inventing the coincidence method of detecting the emission of electrons.

1955 Willis Lamb, Jr, US: for discoveries in the hydrogen spectrum; Polykarp Kusch, German-born US: for measuring the magnetic moment of the electron.

1956 William Shockley, English-born US, John Bardeen, US, and Walther Brattain, US: for investigating semi-conductors and discovering the transistor effect.

1957 Tsung-Dao Lee and Chen Ning Yang, Chinese-born US: for the discovery of violations of principle of parity.

1958 Pavel A. Cherenkov, Ilya M. Frank, and Igor Y. Tamm, Russian: for investigating the effects produced by high-energy particles (the Cherenkov effect).

1959 Emilio Segrè, Italian-born US, and Owen Chamberlain, US: for confirming the existence of the antiproton.

1960 Donald Glaser, US: for the development of the bubble chamber.

1961 Robert Hofstadter, US: for determining the shape and size of atomic nucleons; Rudolf Mössbauer, German: for the discovery of the Mössbauer effect (the emission of gamma rays from certain crystal substances).

1962 Lev D. Landau, Azeri: for contributions to the understanding of condensed states of matter.

■ NOBEL PRIZEWINNER GUGLIELMO MARCONI BECAME A HERO WHEN A SHIP HEARD A CRY FOR HELP

■ *A display at the Museum of La Villette in Paris features circular holograms, an invention by Dennis Gabor which won him a Nobel Prize for physics in 1971*

1963 Johannes H.D. Jensen, German, and Maria Goeppert-Mayer, Polish-German-born US: for the shell model theory of the structure of atomic nuclei; Eugene Paul Wigner, Hungarian-born US: for work on principles governing interaction of protons and neutrons in the nucleus.

1964 Charles H. Townes, US, Nikolay G. Basov, Russian, and Aleksandr M. Prokhorov, Russian: for studies in quantum electronics leading to construction of instruments based on maser-laser principles.

1965 Julian S. Schwinger, US, Richard P. Feynman, US, Shin'ichiro Tomonaga, Japanese: for work on basic principles of quantum electrodynamics.

1966 Alfred Kastler, French: for work on optical methods for studying Hertzian resonances in atoms.

1967 Hans A. Bethe, German-born US: for discoveries concerning the energy production of stars.

1968 Luis W. Alvarez, US: for the discovery of resonance states as part of work with elementary particles.

1969 Murray Gell-Mann, US: for the classification of elementary particles and their interactions.

1970 Hannes Alfvén, Swedish, and Louis Néel, French: for work on magneto-hydrodynamics and antiferromagnetism and ferrimagnetism.

1971 Dennis Gabor, Hungarian-born British: for the invention of holography.

1972 John Bardeen, Leon N. Cooper and John R. Schrieffer, US: for developing the theory of superconductivity.

1973 Leo Esaki, Japanese, Ivar Giaever, Norwegian-born US, and Brian Josephson, Welsh: for tunnelling in semiconductors and superconductors.

1974 Sir Martin Ryle and Antony Hewish, English: for work in radio astronomy.

1975 Aage Bohr, Danish, Ben R. Mottelson, US-born Danish, and L. James Rainwater, US: for contributions to the understanding of the atomic nucleus.

1976 Burton Richter and Samuel C.C. Ting, US: for discovering a new class of elementary particles (psi).

1977 Philip W. Anderson, US, Sir Neville Mott, English, and John H. Van Vleck, US: for contributions to understanding the behaviour of electrons in magnetic, non-crystalline solids.

1978 Pyotr L. Kapitsa, Russian: for inventing helium liquefier, and its applications; Arno A. Penzias, German-born US, and Robert W. Wilson, US: for discovering cosmic microwave background radiation.

1979 Sheldon Glashow, US, Abdus Salam, Pakistani, and Steven Weinberg, US: for establishing an analogy between electromagnetism and the 'weak' interactions of subatomic particles.

1980 James W. Cronin and Val L. Fitch, US: for research on the simultaneous violation of both charge-conjugation and parity-inversion.

1981 Kai M. Siegbahn, Swedish, and Nicolaas Bloembergen, Dutch-born US: for research on electron spectroscopy for chemical analysis; Arthur L. Schawlow, US: for the development and use of lasers in spectroscopy.

1982 Kenneth G. Wilson, US: for the analysis of continuous phase transitions.

1983 Subrahmanyan Chandrasekhar, Indian-born US, and William A. Fowler, US: for contributions to understanding the evolution and devolution of stars.

1984 Carlo Rubbia, Italian, and Simon van der Meer, Dutch: for the discovery of the short-lived subatomic particles (W and Z), carriers of the so-called weak force, which supported the Weinberg-Salam electro-weak theory.

1985 Klaus von Klitzing, German: for the discovery of the Hall effect, permitting exact measurements of electrical resistance.

1986 Ernst Ruska, German, Gerd Binnig, German, and Heinrich Rohrer, Swiss: for the development of special electron microscopes.

1987 J. Georg Bednorz, German, and K. Alex Müller, Swiss: for discovering new superconducting materials.

1988 Lwon Lederman, Melvin Schwartz, and Jack Steinberger, US: for research into subatomic particles.

1989 Norman Harvey, US: for the development of the separated field method; Hans Dehmelt, German-born US, and Wolfgang Paul, German: for developing and exploiting the ion trap.

1990 Richard E. Taylor, Canadian, Jerome Friedman, US, and Henry Kendall, US: for proving the existence of the quark.

1991 Pierre-Gilles de Gennes, French: for studies in changes in liquid crystals.

1992 George Charpak, Polish-born French: for devising an electronic detector that reads trajectories of subatomic particles.

1993 Russell A. Hulse and Joseph H. Taylor, US: for the discovery of a new type of quasar.

1994 Clifford Shull, US, and Bertram Brockhouse, Canadian: for neutron-scattering techniques.

1995 Martin L. Perl, US, and Fredrick Reines, US: for pioneering experimental contributions to lepto physics.

1996 David M. Lee, Douglas D. Osheroff and Robert C. Richardson, all US: for the discovery of superfluidity in helium-3.

ALMOST MADE IT...

POLITICS INTERFERING WITH SCIENCE

Continual frustration in the world of science can have alarming consequences. Philipp Lenard (1862–1947), a Slovak physicist who later became a German citizen, was thwarted in several scientific fields, and became a bitter and twisted figure of Fascism. His early career was illustrious and, during this time, he almost discovered X-rays. He blamed his failure on a move to Aachen in 1895. Nevertheless, he did help the actual discoverer of X-rays, Wilhelm Röntgen, with equipment and made essential theoretical and experimental contributions. However, he was never acknowledged for this, nor (he claimed) for work he produced that J.J. Thomson used without due recognition. He also presaged a nuclear model of the atom a decade before Rutherford, and discovered properties of the photoelectric effect that Einstein later explained correctly. These frustrations, combined with disenchantment after World War I, led to him becoming a rabid supporter of Hitler. He argued for a racially-pure practice of science, was vehemently anti-Semitic and launched pathological attacks on Einstein's character. Lenard may well be remembered, but not for his scientific work.

THE HELIOCENTRIC THEORY OF THE SOLAR SYSTEM

Most people today would attribute Copernicus with the discovery of the heliocentric (meaning that the Earth orbits around the Sun) view of cosmology. However, nearly two millennia before the Copernican theory sent shockwaves throughout Renaissance society, it had been suggested by a Greek astronomer and philosopher. Aristarchus of Samos (*c.* 320 to *c.* 250 BC), about whom little is known, postulated the idea that the Earth was not motionless, but revolved on its axis, causing the apparent rotation of the sphere of stars. According to Archimedes, he also considered the Sun to be at rest, with the Earth and other planets orbiting it. He even anticipated Copernicus by explaining the lack of parallax movement by the stars as being due to their extreme distance from the Earth. This theory resulted in claims that he ought to be indicted for impiety by Cleanthes the Stoic. His idea did not catch on, however, and for the next 1800 years the Ptolemic geocentric model of the universe was adhered to. Aristarchus is not entirely forgotten – a lunar crater is named after him, and a peak at its centre is the Moon's brightest formation.

CHEMISTRY

▶ **Alchemy, from which modern chemistry derives its name, probably originated 4000 years ago in the Khimi region of the Nile Delta, where it was discovered that the action of heat on minerals could isolate metals and glasses.**

▶ **The art of distilling alcohol from fermented juices is one of the first examples of a chemical separation technique.**

▶ **The two lightest elements – hydrogen and helium – together account for *c.* 99% of all the atoms in the universe. These two elements were also the first to be formed just after the Big Bang.**

▶ **As there is no limit to the number of possible compounds, chemists will always be able to make new substances.**

INTRODUCTION TO CHEMISTRY

▶ **Chemistry is the scientific study of substances.**
▶ **Chemical matter is either an element, a compound or a mixture.**

Modern chemistry is the study of the building blocks of matter. The fundamental units of chemistry are elements. There are about 90 naturally occurring elements. Gold, for instance, is an element because no one has ever found a simpler substance within it. Elements can combine to form compounds. For example, glucose is a compound because it is made up of the elements carbon, hydrogen and oxygen. Similarly, water is a compound of the elements hydrogen and oxygen. Millions of different compounds exist naturally, and chemists have synthesized hundreds of thousands more in the laboratory. Yet most materials and objects encountered in everyday life, such as soil, milk or seawater, are mixtures – they contain many different compounds mixed in variable proportions.

STATES OF MATTER

Matter can exist in three states – solid, liquid or gas (vapour). The state in which a particular substance exists depends on the temperature and upon the pressure being exerted on it. Virtually all substances are able to exist in more than one of these three states. Water is a liquid at room temperature, for example, but can become a solid (ice) or vapour (steam), depending upon temperature and pressure.

ATOMIC STRUCTURE

▶ **The word atom is derived from the Ancient Greek word *atomos,* meaning 'indivisible'.**
▶ **The fundamental belief in the importance of understanding the physical laws that govern the behaviour and structure of atoms and molecules is the core of modern chemistry.**

Atoms are the smallest particle of an element that can exist, and can be regarded as the building blocks of everything. Atoms can combine to form molecules. Molecules are the smallest particle of either an element or a compound that can exist independently. Thus the smallest possible unit of water is the water molecule, which is made up of two atoms of hydrogen and one atom of oxygen. This can be written scientifically as H_2O.

SUBATOMIC PARTICLES

The chemical properties of elements depend on the structure of their atoms. The atom is made up of sub-atomic particles: the proton, the neutron and the electron. The protons and neutrons are concentrated together in a tiny, enormously dense structure in the centre of the atom, called the nucleus. The electrons orbit this nucleus at a very high speed. The various elements differ from each other in the number of protons and electrons they have. For example, gold has 79 protons in its nucleus, whilst carbon has six. The subatomic particles carry an electrical charge: the proton is positively charged, the electron is negatively charged, whilst the neutron is neutral. Atoms are electrically neutral because they contain equal numbers of protons and electrons.

It is the arrangements of the electrons around the nucleus that give elements their particular chemical properties. Electrons are arranged in 'shells', and it is the state of the outermost shell which is crucial. A stable atom has a complete outer shell – only the elements known as the noble gases (such as helium) have this structure, and so they are stable as single atoms. Other elements have incomplete outer shells, so they bond with other atoms to form stable molecules. For example, two oxygen atoms bond in such a way as to create a stable outer shell of one oxygen molecule, O_2. The electron configuration can tell us much about how certain elements behave. Chemists can also classify elements into groups which have the same number of electrons in their outer shell.

ATOMIC MASS

▶ **The nucleus contains over 99.9% of the mass of the atom.**
▶ **Helium is such a light element that its atoms can escape into space.**

It was discovered that pure substances reacted together in a definite ratio by weight. For example, 3 g of magnesium always combine with 2 g of oxygen to give 5 g of magnesium oxide and 1 g of hydrogen combines with 8 g of oxygen to form 9 g of water. In seeking to explain such apparently fixed whole-number ratios, John Dalton, in 1808, revived the atomic theory first put forward by the Ancient Greeks. Dalton proposed that one element differed from another in the weight of its atoms. It took a further 60 years or so before many of his contemporaries accepted the idea of atoms, let alone the idea of atomic weight (now more correctly called atomic mass).

It is possible to calculate the mass of an atom by considering the number of the subatomic particles: the proton, neutron and electron. When considering approximate atomic masses, the mass of the proton can be used as the unit of measurement. The mass of the neutron is almost exactly the same as that of the proton, and so can also be said to weigh one unit. The electron is 1/2000 the mass of the proton, and can be considered negligible when calculating approximate atomic mass. Thus, for sodium, which contains 11 protons and 12 neutrons (and 11 electrons), the relative atomic mass is 23.

ISOTOPES

The number of neutrons in the nucleus of an atom is not easily predictable from the number of protons. Certain ratios are stable and others are not. For example, all sodium atoms contain 11 protons and for this number of protons it happens that only 12 neutrons can keep the protons together to form a stable nucleus. If 11 or 13 neutrons are present, the nucleus is unstable, making it a radioactive isotope of sodium which will change into another element with the release of much energy. However, some atoms do have variable numbers of neutrons in their nucleus; they are known as isotopes.

Isotopes are atoms of an element with the same number of protons and electrons but with a different number of neutrons and therefore differing atomic masses. Isotopes are either stable or radioactive. For most elements there are several stable isotopes, which occur in almost fixed ratio, no matter the geographical or chemical source of the element. For instance, chlorine always contains about 75% of the isotope chlorine-35 and 25% of the isotope chlorine-37. Since there are three atoms of chlorine-35 for each atom of chlorine-37, these four atoms weigh in total 35 + 35 + 35 + 37 = 142 units and the average mass of the four atoms is 142 ÷ 4 = 35.5 units. Therefore, the average mass of chlorine atoms all over the world is 35.5 and this is known as the (approximate) chemical atomic mass of chlorine. The existence and distribution of isotopes of the elements was first shown by the mass spectrometer (see diagram below), an instrument which is now used to measure the relative masses of whole molecules.

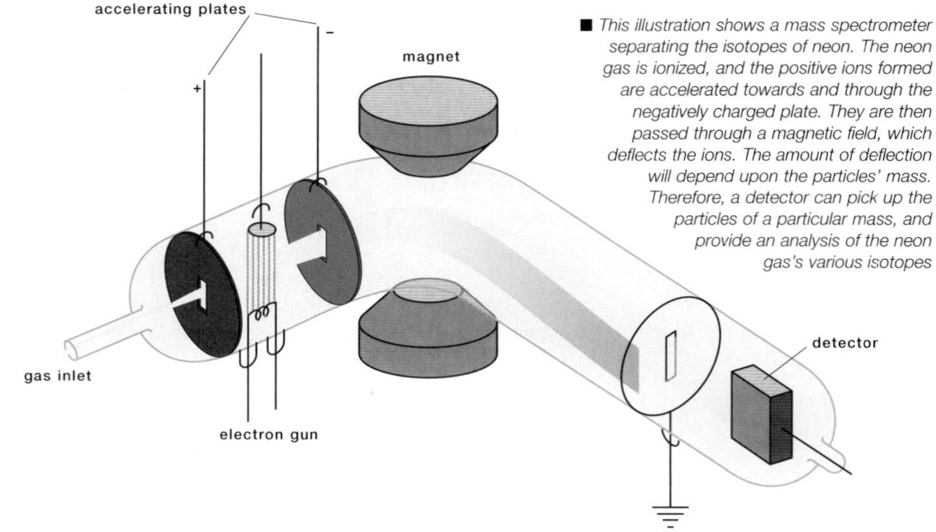

■ *This illustration shows a mass spectrometer separating the isotopes of neon. The neon gas is ionized, and the positive ions formed are accelerated towards and through the negatively charged plate. They are then passed through a magnetic field, which deflects the ions. The amount of deflection will depend upon the particles' mass. Therefore, a detector can pick up the particles of a particular mass, and provide an analysis of the neon gas's various isotopes*

■ A HUMAN BEING CONTAINS ABOUT 100 000 TIMES MORE ATOMS THAN THERE ARE STARS IN THE

METHODS OF CHEMISTRY

▶ Chemists have developed many methods for separating pure substances.
▶ The melting point of a substance can reveal a great deal about its physical properties, and can vary greatly – for example, helium melts at –272°C (–458°F) whereas carbon, in the form of diamond, melts at 3500°C (6332°F).

One of chemistry's main roles is to separate pure samples of various compounds from their natural sources, such as rocks, plants and animals. The difficulty is to extract quantities that are large enough to be chemically analysed, so that the specific amount of each element present can be established. In order that other chemists can recognize the compound when they make it or come across it in the future, it is necessary to find out the substance's physical properties, including its density, its melting point, and its ability to absorb electromagnetic radiation such as natural, infrared and ultraviolet light.

CRYSTALLIZATION
Solids are usually obtained in a pure form by the process of crystallization. The impure solid is dissolved in a (warm) liquid called a solvent and filtered to remove any insoluble impurities. The filtrate obtained in this manner can be concentrated, if necessary, by evaporating the solvent until crystals start to form. Slow cooling should produce a crop of crystals which can then be filtered off. Repeated crystallization may be required to give pure material. After each stage, impurities are left behind in the solvent so that the material gradually becomes purer and purer. Impurities always lower the melting point of a solid, so crystallization is repeated until there is no further increase in the measured melting point.

SUBLIMATION
Some solids, such as iodine, are volatile (meaning they are readily vaporized), in which case they can be obtained in a pure form by gently heating the mixture so that the vapour comes off and leaves any involatile impurities behind. The vapour condenses directly back to crystals of the solid when it meets a cold surface. This process is called sublimation, as shown in the diagram below.

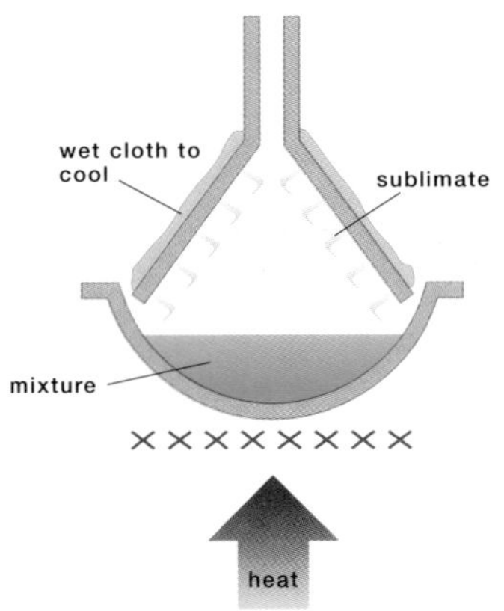

ZONE REFINING
Some solids, such as silicon, are not readily soluble in any solvent. In this case, a large rod of the impure silicon is melted by a slowly moving electric furnace so as to melt a zone of the silicon. Impurities tend to remain in the molten zone and, after the furnace has passed, the silicon recrystallizes. When the molten zone reaches the end of the rod, it is cut off and discarded and the furnace is applied to the opposite end of the rod for another pass down the rod. In this way hyper-pure silicon is made for use in silicon chip manufacture.

GAS–LIQUID CHROMATOGRAPHY
Mixtures of gases and readily vaporized liquids, such as those found in crude oil, may be separated from each other on a very small scale by the method of gas–liquid chromatography.

The sample to be analysed is heated to vaporize it, then swept through a long column by means of a carrier gas such as nitrogen or hydrogen. In the column is an involatile (non-vaporizing) liquid which is absorbed into a porous (able to absorb water, air or other fluids) solid. The solid retains the various vapours to different degrees so that they come out of the column one after another. A detector senses the different components and records them on a chart showing how much there is of each one.

DISTILLATION
Many liquids can be separated by distillation. The mixture is boiled and the vapours pass up a tall tower in which there are baffles (which restrain or regulate the flow of fluid) or trays designed to present a large internal surface area to the vapours. Vapours with high boiling points condense at a lower point in the tower, whereas vapours with lower boiling points condense higher up. The condensed liquid fractions are then extracted at different levels from the tower. Distillation is used to separate petrol from crude oil and to separate alcohol from water in the manufacture of spirits such as whisky.

Mixtures of gases are difficult to separate, so the trick is to first cool the mixture down until it is liquid and then distil it. Air cooled down to –200°C turns into liquid air, which can then be distilled at low temperature to give pure liquid constituents such as nitrogen (boiling point –196°C) and oxygen (boiling point –183°C) for industrial and medical uses.

GAS DIFFUSION
Where two gases have almost identical boiling points, separation may be achieved by gas diffusion. This method is used to separate the isotopes of uranium by allowing the vapours of uranium hexafluoride to diffuse through a series of porous membranes. The molecules of UF_6 contain the lighter isotope, uranium-235, and diffuse slightly faster than the molecules containing uranium-238. This enables uranium to be enriched in the lighter isotope which is needed for nuclear fuel in nuclear power reactors.

CHEMICAL GROUPS

▶ Metals can be defined chemically as elements that dissolve (or whose oxides dissolve) in acids, usually to form positively charged ions called cations.
▶ Non-metallic elements, such as carbon, hydrogen and oxygen, are few in number but vital in the make-up of living organisms.

It is possible to make broad classifications in describing the elements. Perhaps the most useful division is between metals and non-metals. Each of these groups can then be further divided and categorized. For example, alkali metals are a subgroup of metals, whilst halogens and noble gases are subgroups of non-metals.

METALS
There are some 90 metallic elements with a wide range of reactivities. Many pure metals and their mixtures with other metals (alloys) are crystalline when examined under the microscope. As the molten metal solidifies, crystals grow and interlock.

Metals are found on the left of the Periodic Table (see p. 130) and most have one, two or three electrons in the outermost electron shell. It is these electrons which bond the solid metal together by wandering freely throughout the array of atoms in a metal crystal. These mobile electrons are responsible for the beautiful shiny surface of clean metals and for their ability to conduct electricity.

Metals form the majority of the elements and their chemical reactivity ranges from gold, which is found 'native' (uncombined), to metals such as potassium and sodium. Metal oxides are basic. A basic oxide is able to react with an acid to produce a salt and water only, for example:

$$MgO + H_2SO_4 \rightarrow MgSO_4 + H_2O$$

magnesium oxide + sulphuric acid → magnesium sulphate + water

The alkali metals are the most reactive metals in the Periodic Table. These elements – lithium, sodium, potassium, rubidium, caesium and francium – (located in group 1 of the Periodic Table) are soft metals. Their softness and low melting point are the result of the weakness of their metallic bonding. The elements of group 1 are called alkali metals because alkalis are formed when they react with either air or water. The pure metals themselves are not alkalis.

The alkaline earth metals are the elements of group 2 – beryllium, magnesium, calcium, strontium, barium and radium. Of these elements, calcium and magnesium are the most common. The alkaline earth metals are not as reactive as the alkali metals.

NON-METALS
Non-metals' atoms generally have four, five, six or seven electrons in their outermost shells. By sharing electrons with other non-metal atoms, so as to create 'bonding-pairs' of electrons, non-metal atoms can manage to resemble their aristocratic cousins, the noble gases. Non-metal oxides are either acidic or neutral.

Noble gases
The noble gases, a family of elements found on the far right of the Periodic Table, are extremely unreactive. This seems to be associated with the fact that they have an especially stable arrangement of electrons in their outermost shells. Helium has two electrons in its outer shell, but the others (neon, argon, krypton, xenon) have eight.

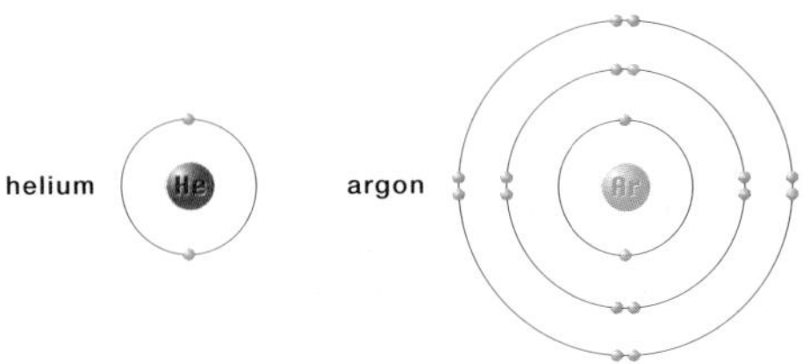

When other atoms react they very often end up resembling the noble gases in that they manage to attain a noble gas electron configuration.

Halogens
Halogens, consisting of fluorine, chlorine, bromine and iodine (plus astatine), are reactive non-metals. As a group they share certain characteristics: they all have two atoms for each molecule; they are coloured (chlorine and fluorine are green gases, bromine is a brown liquid, and iodine is grey as a solid and purple as a vapour); and reactivity decreases down the group, so fluorine is more reactive than iodine. Halogen atoms have one electron less in their outer shells than noble gases, and must gain an electron to gain a stable structure, making them reactive. Halogens react vigorously with metals and hydrogen to form halides (organic compounds with halogen atoms in their molecules).

THE ELEMENTS

▶ In an element, all the atoms are of the same kind.
▶ 98% of the Earth's crust is made up of just eight elements – oxygen, silicon, aluminium, iron, calcium, sodium, magnesium and potassium.

The elements have been identified from the rocks, oceans and atmosphere throughout history by a long series of experiments. These investigations were carried out with a variety of motives. Gold has always been highly prized and, for centuries, alchemists tried to make it from other substances – always without success. However, the alchemists made many important discoveries along the way. Even the distinguished scientist Isaac Newton (see p. 122) tried his hand at alchemy, but his contemporary Robert Boyle (see p. 132) began the process of realization that certain substances, such as gold and carbon, cannot be broken down to simpler substances.

DISCOVERING THE ELEMENTS

The Ancient Greeks believed that all matter was composed of just four elements: earth, fire, air and water. However, the elements of carbon, sulfur, gold and lead were discovered in prehistoric times. Other elements which were found in ancient times include copper (*c.* 8000 BC), iron and silver (*c.* 4000 BC), tin (*c.* 3500 BC), mercury (*c.* 1600 BC) and antimony (*c.* 1000 BC). Other than arsenic, which was discovered in the Middle Ages (*c.* 1220), and phosphorous, (1669), all the other elements were discovered from the 18th century onwards.

It was Lavoisier (see p. 133) who produced the first fairly reliable list of elements. However, it contained substances which had not, up to that time, yielded up their true elements, such as magnesia. Only with the discovery of the electric battery by Volta did the means become available to split magnesia (actually magnesium oxide). The metal magnesium was obtained for the first time by Humphry Davy (see p. 132), using electrolysis. Davy also became famous for releasing the elements potassium, sodium, calcium, strontium and barium from their compounds, none of which had ever been seen before. All of these metals react vigorously or violently with water to produce alkaline solutions. They are much more reactive than metals such as copper, lead, tin and iron, which humans had learnt to extract from the rocks by the process of smelting, in which the rock was heated strongly with charcoal or coke. However, the vast majority of elements are stable. Bismuth, which has the atomic number of 83, is the last element in the list with a stable nucleus. Beyond 83, all elements are unstable (radioactive). The atomic number of an element is the number of protons in the nucleus.

THE NEWEST ELEMENTS

Elements 107 to 112 were produced at the Gessellschaft für Schwerionenforschung Nuclear Research Laboratory in Darmstadt, Germany, from 1981–96. These elements were produced by bombarding lead or bismuth targets with heavy ions, chronologically, of chromium, iron, nickel and zinc and were identified virtually on an atom-to-atom basis. Accurate measurements of the properties of the decay chains allowed identification with already known nuclides and this was considered to confirm the discoveries. None of the new element nuclides has half-lives (the time taken for half the atoms in a radiactive material to undergo decay) over 0.2 second, but it is hoped, eventually, to discover nuclides around element 114 which are predicted to form an 'island of stability' with much longer half-lives than those currently being observed.

THE 112 ELEMENTS

Atomic number	Symbol [Note 1]	Element name [Notes 2 & 3]	Atomic weight [Note 4]	Density at 20°C (unless otherwise stated) g/cm³ [Note 5]	Melting point °C	Boiling point °C	No. of nuclides
1	H	Hydrogen	1.00794	0.0871 (solid at mp) 0.00008989 (gas at 0°C)	–259.198	–252.762	3
2	He	Helium	4.002602	0.1908 (solid at mp) 0.0001785 (gas at 0°C)	–272.375 24.985 atm* [Note 6]	–268.928	8
3	Li	Lithium	6.941	0.5334	180.54	1,640	8
4	Be	Beryllium	9.012182	1.846	1,290	2,456	9
5	B	Boron	10.811	2.333 (Beta Rhombahedral)	2,130	3,910	13
6	C	Carbon	12.0107	2.266 (Graphite) 3.515 (Diamond)	4,730 at 100 atm	3,704 sublimes	15
7	N	Nitrogen	14.00674	0.9426 (solid at mp) 0.001250 (gas at 0°C)	–209.999	–195.798	14
8	O	Oxygen	15.9994	1.359 (solid at mp) 0.001429 (gas at 0°C)	–218.792	–182.953	15
9	F	Fluorine	18.9984032	1.780 (solid at mp) 0.001696 (gas at 0°C)	–219.763	–188.191	14
10	Ne	Neon	20.1797	1.434 (solid at mp) 0.0008999 (gas at 0°C)	–248.594	–246.053	17
11	Na	Sodium	22.989770	0.9688	97.794	882.940	17
12	Mg	Magnesium	24.3050	1.737	650	1,095	18
13	Al	Aluminium	26.981538	2.699	660.323	2,523	18
14	Si	Silicon	28.0855	2.329	1,414	3,190	21
15	P	Phosphorus	30.973761	1.825 (white) 2.361 (violet)	44.13 597 at 45 atm	277 431 sublimes	21
16	S	Sulfur	32.066	2.070 (rhombic)	115.18	444.614	22
17	Cl	Chlorine	35.4527	2.038 (solid at mp) 0.003214 (gas at 0°C)	–100.97	–33.97	20
18	Ar	Argon	39.948	1.622 (solid at mp) 0.001784 (gas at 0°C)	–189.344	–185.848	20
19	K	Potassium	39.0983	0.8591	63.58	758	20
20	Ca	Calcium	40.078	1.526	842	1,495	19
21	Sc	Scandium	44.955910	2.989	1,541	2,830	17
22	Ti	Titanium	47.867	4.504	1,670	3,360	21
23	V	Vanadium	50.9415	6.099	1,928	3,410	24
24	Cr	Chromium	51.9961	7.193	1,860	2,680	25
25	Mn	Manganese	54.938049	7.472	1,246	2,051	26
26	Fe	Iron	55.845	7.874	1,537	2,840	28
27	Co	Cobalt	58.933200	7.874	1,495	2,940	27
28	Ni	Nickel	58.6934	8.905	1,455	2,890	30
29	Cu	Copper	63.546	8.934	1,084.62	2,570	27
30	Zn	Zinc	65.39	7.140	419.527	908	27
31	Ga	Gallium	69.723	5.912	29.765	2,211	27
32	Ge	Germanium	72.61	5.327	938.2	2,770	29
33	As	Arsenic	74.92160	5.781	817 at 38 atm	603 sublimes	29
34	Se	Selenium	78.96	4.810 (Trigonal)	221.14	685	30
35	Br	Bromine	79.904	3.937 (solid at mp) 3.119 (liquid at 20°C)	–7.25	59.74	29
36	Kr	Krypton	83.80	2.801 (solid at mp) 0.003749 (gas at 0°C)	–157.375	–153.340	31
37	Rb	Rubidium	85.4678	1.534	39.29	687	29
38	Sr	Strontium	87.62	2.582	768	1,388	32
39	Y	Yttrium	88.90585	4.468	1,522	3,300	31
40	Zr	Zirconium	91.224	6.506	1,854	4,360	30
41	Nb	Niobium	92.90638	8.595	2,472	4,860	32
42	Mo	Molybdenum	95.94	10.22	2,622	4,710	32
43	Tc	Technetium	(97.9702)	11.40	2,180	4,860	33
44	Ru	Ruthenium	101.07	12.37	2,333	4,320	34
45	Rh	Rhodium	102.90550	12.42	1,963	3,840	33
46	Pd	Palladium	106.42	12.01	1,554.8	2,990	33
47	Ag	Silver	107.8682	10.50	961.78	2,167	33
48	Cd	Cadmium	112.411	8.648	321.069	768	33
49	In	Indium	114.818	7.289	156.599	2,022	34
50	Sn	Tin	118.710	7.288	231.928	2,590	38
51	Sb	Antimony	121.760	6.693	630.628	1,635	37
52	Te	Tellurium	127.60	6.237	449.81	989	37

■ MORE THAN TWO MILLION CHEMICAL COMPOUNDS HAVE BEEN MADE DURING THE LAST

Atomic number	Symbol [Note 1]	Element name [Notes 2 & 3]	Atomic weight [Note 4]	Density at 20°C (unless otherwise stated) g/cm³ [Note 5]	Melting point °C	Boiling point °C	No. of nuclides
53	I	Iodine	126.90447	4.947	113.6	185.1	36
54	Xe	Xenon	131.29	3.410 (solid at mp) 0.005897 (gas at 0°C)	–111.745	–108.083	37
55	Cs	Caesium	132.90545	1.886	28.46	669	37
56	Ba	Barium	137.327	3.595	727	1,740	38
57	La	Lanthanum	138.9055	6.145	921	3,410	34
58	Ce	Cerium	140.116	6.688 (Beta) 6.770 (Gamma)	799	3,470	33
59	Pr	Praseodymium	140.90765	6.772	934	3,480	33
60	Nd	Neodymium	144.24	7.006	1,021	3,020	32
61	Pm	Promethium	(144.9127)	7.141	1,042	3,000	28
62	Sm	Samarium	150.36	7.517	1,077	1,794	30
63	Eu	Europium	151.964	5.243	822	1,556	29
64	Gd	Gadolinium	157.25	7.899	1,313	3,270	28
65	Tb	Terbium	158.92534	8.228	1,356	3,230	27
66	Dy	Dysprosium	162.50	8.549	1,412	2,570	29
67	Ho	Holmium	164.93032	8.794	1,474	2,700	29
68	Er	Erbium	167.26	9.064	1,529	2,810	30
69	Tm	Thulium	168.93421	9.319	1,545	1,950	32
70	Yb	Ytterbium	173.04	6.967	817	1,227	30
71	Lu	Lutetium	174.967	9.839	1,665	3,400	35
72	Hf	Hafnium	178.49	13.28	2,230	4,700	32
73	Ta	Tantalum	180.9479	16.67	3,020	5,490	31
74	W	Tungsten	183.84	19.26	3,414	5,850	33
75	Re	Rhenium	186.207	21.01	3,185	5,550	33
76	Os	Osmium	190.23	22.59	3,127	5,300	35
77	Ir	Iridium	192.217	22.56	2,446	4,625	35
78	Pt	Platinum	195.078	21.45	1,768.2	3,850	37
79	Au	Gold	196.96655	19.29	1,064.18	2,870	35
80	Hg	Mercury	200.59	14.17 (solid at mp) 13.55 (liquid at 20°C)	–38.829	356.661	34
81	Tl	Thallium	204.3833	11.87	303	1,470	32
82	Pb	Lead	207.2	11.35	327.462	1,748	35
83	Bi	Bismuth	208.98038	9.807	271.402	1,566	32
84	Po	Polonium	(208.9824)	9.155	254	948	29
85	At	Astatine	(209.9871)	7.0	302	377	31
86	Rn	Radon	(222.0176)	4.7 (solid at mp) 0.01004 (gas at 0°C)	–64.9	–61.2	33
87	Fr	Francium	(223.0197)	2.8	23	650	33
88	Ra	Radium	(226.0254)	5.50	707	1,530	33
89	Ac	Actinium	(227.0277)	10.04	1,230	3,600	28
90	Th	Thorium	232.0381	11.72	1,760	4,660	29
91	Pa	Protactinium	231.03588	15.41	1,570	4,490	28
92	U	Uranium	238.0289	19.05	1,134	4,160	22
93	Np	Neptunium	(237.0482)	20.47	637	4,090	20
94	Pu	Plutonium	(244.0642)	20.26	940	3,270	19
95	Am	Americium	(243.0614)	13.76	1,176	2,023	14
96	Cm	Curium	(247.0703)	13.68	1,340	3,180	14
97	Bk	Berkelium	(247.0703)	14.65	1,050	2,710	12
98	Cf	Californium	(251.0796)	15.20	900	1,612	20
99	Es	Einsteinium	(252.0830)	9.05	860	996	17
100	Fm	Fermium	(257.0951)	9.42	852	1,077	18
101	Md	Mendelevium	(258.0984)	–	–	–	16
102	No	Nobelium	(259.1010)	–	–	–	11
103	Lr	Lawrencium	(262.1097)	–	–	–	10
104	Rf	Rutherfordium	(261.1088)	–	–	–	10
105	Db	Dubnium	(262.1141)	–	–	–	8
106	Sg	Seaborgium	(266.1219)	–	–	–	6
107	Bh	Bohrium	(264.1247)	–	–	–	3
108	Hs	Hassium	(267.1318)	–	–	–	3
109	Mt	Meitnerium	(268.1388)	–	–	–	2
110	Uun	Ununnilium	(271.1461)	–	–	–	3
111	Uuu	Unununium	(272.1535)	–	–	–	1
112	Uub	Ununbium	(277.1641)	–	–	–	1

* atm means atmospheres

■ *Liquid nitrogen being poured into a flask. Nitrogen turns liquid below 77.4 Kelvin (–198°C) and is used in this state as a refrigerant in cryogenics (low temperature physics)*

NOTES TO TABLE

1 The modern element symbols were introduced by J.J. Berzelius (Sweden) in 1811. Where European names for the elements were completely different, he based the symbols on the Latin names of the elements or their compounds (in particular note element 80 where the name literally means 'liquid silver'). The exception was element 74 where the symbol is based on the German name 'Wolfram' named directly after one of the main ores 'wolframite'. Alternative names for the following elements are listed below:

Atomic number	Symbol	Name
11	Na	Natrium
19	K	Kalium
26	Fe	Ferrum
29	Cu	Cuprum
47	Ag	Argentum
50	Sn	Stannum
51	Sb	Stibium
74	W	Wolfram
79	Au	Aurum
80	Hg	Hydrargyrum
82	Pb	Plumbum

2 The element names given in the table are those recommended by the International Union of Pure and Applied Chemistry (IUPAC). For element 16, the obsolete spelling 'sulphur' is still widely used in the UK, whilst in the USA element 13 is spelt 'aluminum' and element 55 'cesium'.

3 The names of elements 104–109 are those recommended by IUPAC in February 1997. They now differ from those recommended by the American Chemical Society in that, for element 105, the latter selected 'Hahnium', symbol Ha, after Otto Hahn (1879–1968) (Germany), and for element 107 they prefer the longer spelling to include the Christian name of Bohr as 'Nielsbohrium',symbol Ns. The names for elements 110–112 are those provisionally assigned by IUPAC pending the adoption of official names.

4 For the highly radioactive elements, the atomic weight in brackets is the relative atomic mass of the isotope with the longest known half-life.

5 For the highly radioactive isotopes, the density value has been calculated for the longest living isotope.

6 As far as is known helium does not solidify under atmospheric pressure. The value quoted is the minimum in the melting-point curve.

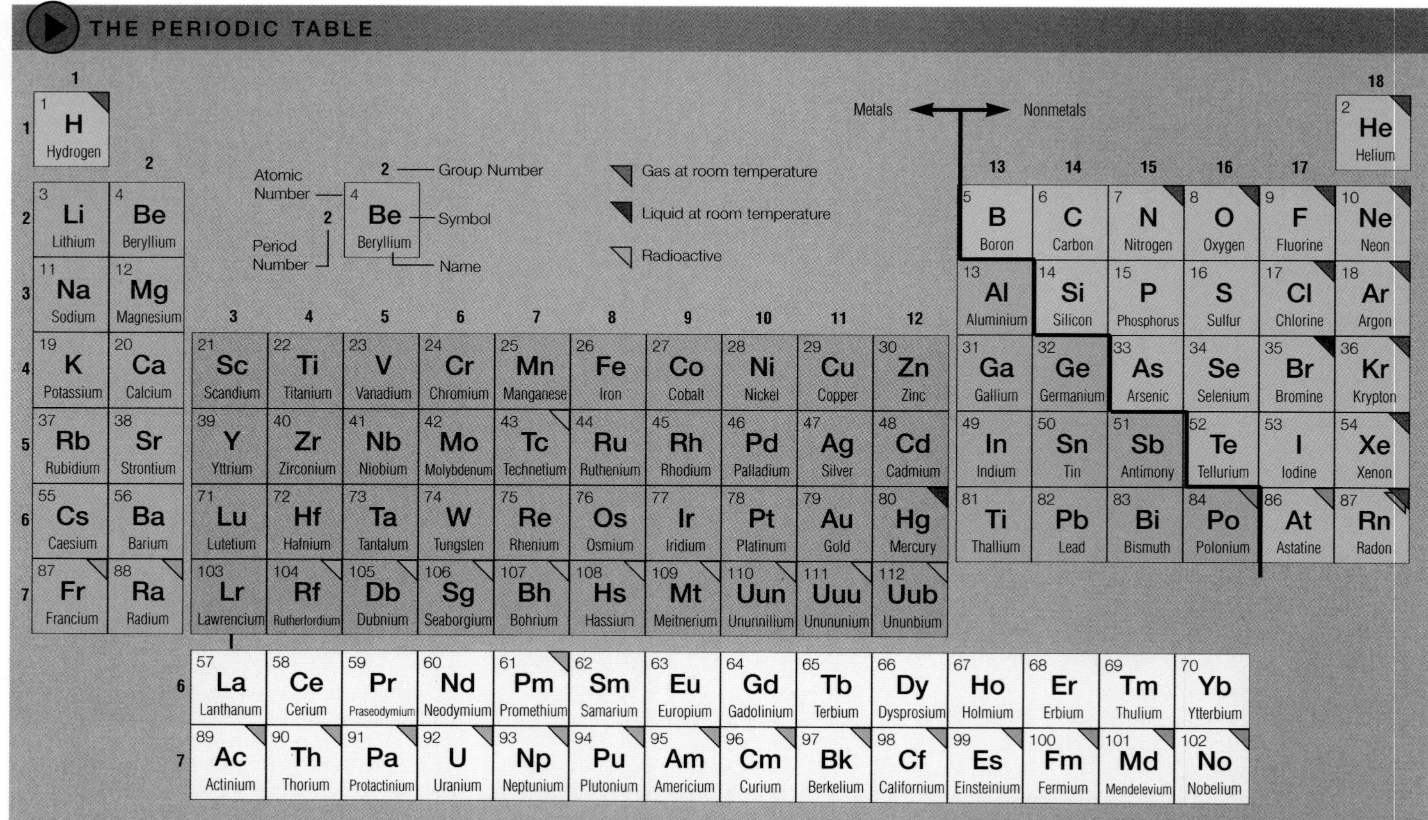

The Periodic Table lists the elements, according to their atomic number. In it, the elements appear in increasing atomic number as one reads from left to right across the table and from top to bottom. The Periodic Table also shows the elements categorized into periods and groups – the former being rows in the table, the latter being columns. This classification enables one to group together elements with similar structures and chemical properties.

Atomic mass was the key concept which allowed Dimitri Mendeleyev (see p. 133) to arrange the 63 then-known elements in order of their atomic masses, thus discovering the Periodic Table. Using his chemical knowledge, he was bold enough to adjust the atomic masses of some elements to fit his pattern, which were later found to be fully justified. He also left gaps for undiscovered elements, such as germanium, gallium and scandium, whose properties he accurately predicted and led to the general acceptance of his Periodic Law – that the chemical nature of an element is a periodic (repeating) function of its atomic mass. Mendeleyev's genius lay in the fact that he recognized the underlying order of the elements – he did not design the Periodic Table, he discovered it. Since he published his table in 1869, over 40 elements have been found or produced by nuclear reactions and the table has been amended to include them.

CHEMICAL BONDS

▶ A molecule is either made up of two or more atoms of the same element, or of atoms of two or more different elements held together by a chemical bond.
▶ The two main types of chemical bond are ionic and covalent.

Although there are only 112 known elements, there are millions of chemical substances found in nature or made artificially. These substances are not simply mixtures of two or more elements, but chemical compounds, formed by combining two or more elements together in a chemical reaction. The chemical 'glue' that holds compounds together is called chemical bonding. Chemical bonding also holds together atoms in the molecules of an element.

There are two main types of chemical bond: covalent and ionic. Both work by bringing two atoms together in such a way as to make them appear stable. This is achieved by interaction in the atoms' outermost shell of electrons (valence shell). By either sharing or donating electrons, both atoms can fill up their valence shell with electrons and achieve a stability similar to the noble gases.

COVALENT

Covalent bonding occurs when two atoms share electrons in their outer shell. Fluorine atoms, for example, each have seven outer electrons, but to gain a stability they need eight outer electrons. Thus two fluorine atoms can share an electron each, forming a covalent bond. If one pair of electrons is shared, a single bond is formed; if two pairs of electrons are shared, as in the oxygen molecule, a double bond is formed; if three pairs of electrons are shared, a triple bond is formed.

IONIC

Ionic bonding (or electrovalent bonding) occurs when one atom 'donates' an electron to another atom. For example, sodium (Na) has one electron in its outer shell, whilst fluorine has seven. If the sodium atom transfers an electron to fluorine, both atoms attain a stability in their outer shell. When this transfer happens, both atoms become ions. The sodium atom, having lost a negatively charged electron, has a net positive charge, and is known as a cation: Na^+. The fluorine atom, having gained an electron, has a net negative charge and is called a fluoride anion: F^-.

CHEMICAL REACTIONS

▶ Chemical reactions are the means by which new substances are formed from old ones.
▶ So much heat is released during the reaction of potassium and water that the highly inflammable hydrogen gas frequently ignites above the molten metal.

Chemical reactions occur all the time – when fuels are burnt, in the industrial extraction of metals from their ores, and in many natural life processes. The study of reactions is important to chemistry, as it is the means by which substances change.

CHEMICAL EQUATIONS

Information about reactions can be recorded using balanced chemical equations. Conventionally, the substances that react together, the reactants, are placed on the left-hand side, and the substances that result from the reaction, the products, are placed on the right-hand side. The equation will describe, in quantitative terms, how much of a product will be formed from a given mass of reactants. An example of a chemical reaction is when coal is burnt in air:

$$C + O_2 \rightarrow CO_2$$

Here, coal (which is a form of carbon) reacts with oxygen molecules to give carbon dioxide (and heat). In chemical equations, (g) = gas, (l) = liquid, (s) = solid and (aq) = aqueous solution are sometimes used. Since carbon in the form of coal is a solid which reacts with the gas oxygen to produce carbon dioxide gas, the equation above can be rewritten:

$$C(s) + O_2(g) \rightarrow CO_2(g)$$

ENERGY IN CHEMICAL REACTIONS

An important aspect of all chemical reactions is the exchange of energy between the reacting system and the surroundings. This exchange can be one of two types – exothermic or endothermic. In exothermic reactions, heat is given to the surroundings from the reacting system. In endothermic reactions, heat is taken from the surroundings into the reacting system.

Most of the chemical reactions which go well are exothermic – they give out heat, as in the burning of fuels in oxygen. When methane, CH_4, is burned, very hot carbon dioxide and steam is released:

$$CH_4 + 2O_2 \rightarrow CO_2 + 2H_2O$$

What is happening in this reaction is that the reactants have a certain amount of energy stored in their bonds. The energy stored in the bonds of the products is less than that of the reactants, and so the excess energy is given off as light and heat.

Endothermic reactions are those which require a continuous input of heat to make them happen. An example is the reaction used to make calcium oxide by heating calcium carbonate to 900°C.

$$CaCO_3 \rightarrow CaO + CO_2$$

In this case, the energy in the bonds of the products is more than that of the reactants, so energy is required to maintain the reaction.

RATES OF REACTION

Reactions can occur at different speeds. A match, when struck, will combust almost immediately, whilst iron nails can take a while to rust. The rate of reaction depends mostly on the reactants concerned – some naturally react faster than others. However, certain factors can help speed up reactions. By increasing the heat of the reactants, the molecules will move faster, thus increasing the chances of a reaction-inducing collision. Similarly, by increasing the concentration of the reactants, more molecules will be present to react, increasing the chances of a successful collision. A third method of speeding up reactions is to use a catalyst. Catalysts increase the rate of reaction by temporarily holding reactants together, enabling them to react. Catalysts remain unchanged at the end of a reaction, and do not affect the nature of the products, only the rate at which they are formed.

NEUTRALIZATION

Since there is so much water on our planet, water is regarded as 'neutral'. It is relatively harmless. On the other hand, acids and alkalis are anything but harmless when they are pure or present as strong solutions in water. Both can damage living tissue rapidly by destroying important components which make up living cells. However, if an acid is mixed with an alkali in the correct proportions, the acid and alkali react exothermically to be replaced by a salty substance and a neutral liquid – water. For example, the alkali sodium hydroxide reacts exothermically with hydrochloric acid to give sodium chloride (common table salt) and water:

$$NaOH + HCl \rightarrow NaCl + H_2O$$

REDOX REACTIONS

Redox reactions involve a transfer of electrons from one type of chemical entity to another. The chemical entity may be an atom, a molecule or an ion. When magnesium burns in oxygen, two electrons are transferred from each of the magnesium's atoms to each of the oxygen's atoms, forming the ionic compound MgO. This compound contains the ions Mg^{2+} and O^{2-}. The magnesium atom is oxidized (loses electrons), whilst the oxygen atom is reduced (gains electrons). The terms reduction and oxidation are confusing, as they have obscure historical origins. Therefore, reduction can be called electronation and oxidation can be called de-electronation.

In living cells, the processes of storing energy and later using this stored energy occur by the intervention of many sequential redox reactions. In photosynthesis, using the energy of sunlight, electrons originally contained in the hydrogen atoms of water are eventually transferred to carbon atoms obtained from carbon dioxide in the air. The overall result is the production of the energy-rich molecule glucose and oxygen gas:

$$6CO_2 + 6H_2O \rightarrow C_6H_{12}O_6 + 6O_2$$

The whole process is reversed during aerobic respiration when cells take in oxygen and release the energy from the glucose.

ORGANIC CHEMISTRY

▶ Organic chemistry derives its name from the once-held belief that organic compounds could only be produced through living (organic) sources.

▶ The chemistry of carbon is very special in that it is the atomic building block from which all naturally occurring compounds in living systems are constructed.

The element carbon readily forms covalent bonds with other elements to form compounds. In particular, carbon can bond with hydrogen, oxygen, chlorine and nitrogen. Carbon's sheer versatility is shown not only in the different ways it can occur as an element (such as diamond, graphite or buckminsterfullerine), but also in the way it can create millions of different compounds. The study of such carbon compounds (excluding carbon oxides) is known as organic chemistry.

It used to be thought that compounds such as alcohol could only be made by living organisms – hence the name organic chemistry. However, in 1828, Friedrich Wöhler made urea (a substance found in urine) from inorganic (i.e. mineral) precursors without the intervention of any living organism. It is now possible for chemists to make synthetically almost any chemical compound that nature produces.

Many useful things involve organic compounds, some made naturally, such as food and drink, cotton, wood, wool and leather. Synthetic (manmade) organic compounds are becoming increasingly available, such as artificial fibres, plastics, explosives, dyestuffs and medicines.

ORGANIC COMPOUNDS

Coal, the fossilized remains of land-living plants, was once the source of many organic chemical starting materials. However, today most organic chemicals are manufactured starting from petroleum (crude oil). Petroleum is the fossilized remains of sea creatures such as plankton that settled to the bottom of ancient oceans where they were overlaid with sediments and converted under conditions of heat and pressure into hydrocarbons (compounds of carbon and hydrogen). One of the main groups of hydrocarbons in petroleum is the alkanes.

Alkanes have the general formula C_nH_{2n+2}. Methane, CH_4, an important natural gas, is the alkane formed when n = 1. When there are four carbon atoms, the alkane is butane, C_4H_{10}, another important fuel.

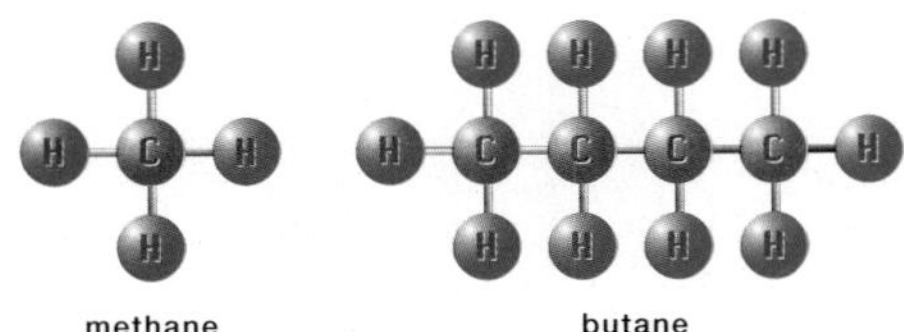

methane butane

Other organic compounds in everyday life include ethanol, which is the intoxicant of alcoholic drinks, and ethanoic acid, the active ingredient of vinegar.

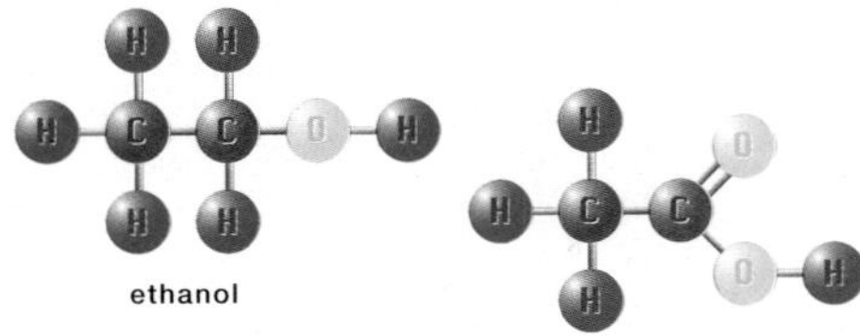

ethanol ethanoic acid

POLYMERS

▶ The word 'polymer' comes from the Greek words *polys* (meaning 'many') and *meros* (meaning 'parts').

▶ Most polymers are made from organic compounds, although some are based on the element silicon.

Polymers are chemicals composed of large molecules in which a group of atoms is repeated. Nature makes many of these long-chain molecules, which structurally resemble a string of beads. The molecules that constitute the beads are called monomers, of which there can be hundreds or even millions linked together in a chain. The way in which these chains interact with one another depends upon the monomers used, and can differ greatly. This accounts for the wide range of properties that polymers possess, including flexibility, strength and heat resistance.

NATURAL

Some polymers are naturally occurring, such as cellulose, starches, proteins, fats and DNA. Starch and cellulose are both polymers of glucose, but their structures are subtly different – starch is digestible, but cellulose is not. Proteins are polymers of amino acids. There are 20 different common types of amino acid which can be linked in countless different sequences, enabling proteins to be just about the most versatile of biological molecules. Proteins make up enzymes and much of the structure of muscle, hair, nails, bones and tendons.

ARTIFICIAL

There are also many artificial polymers, more commonly called plastics. Polythene (or polyethene) is a polymer made from the monomer ethene, a gas which can be made to link up to itself by heating it in the presence of a catalyst.

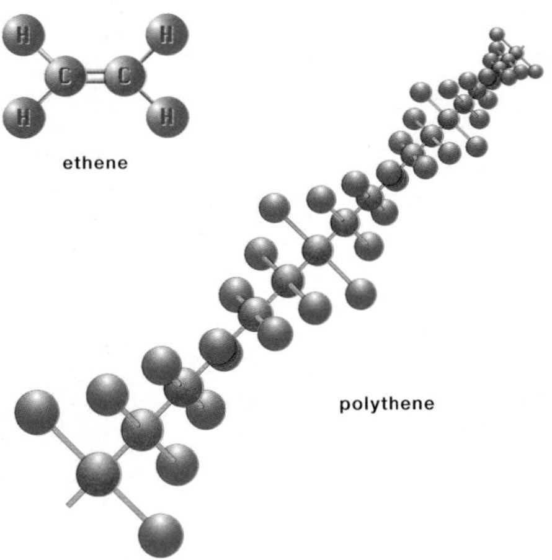

ethene polythene

Other artificial polymers include polystyrene, nylon and polyvinyl chloride (PVC).

Artificial polymers are either thermoplastic or thermosetting. Thermoplastic polymers such as polythene, PVC, nylon and polystyrene can be melted and remelted for fabrication and restyling. Thermosetting polymers, such as bakelite and formica, are made by reaction of the monomers in a mould of the required shape. They are generally rigid and hard and attempts to melt them only cause decomposition because their structures have a giant three-dimensional nature which can only break up at high temperatures. However, the thermoplastic polymer molecules can wriggle and writhe around each other as the temperature rises, causing the plastic to soften and eventually melt.

Chemists

- Marie Curie's daughter, Irène Joliot-Curie, received a Nobel Prize in chemistry, like her mother and, also like her mother, died of leukaemia brought about by radiation poisoning.
- Willard Libby, winner of the 1960 Nobel Prize for radio-carbon dating, recalculated the time of the last ice age to be 10,000 years ago, rather than 25,000 as previously believed.
- Frederick Sangar's discoveries with insulin led to the ability to produce synthetic insulin, which enhanced the lives of many people suffering from diabetes.
- The findings of Paul Sabatier were used in developing pharmaceuticals, perfumes, detergents and margarine.

Abegg, Richard (1869–1910), German chemist whose 'rule of eight', concerning the electric basis of linkages between atoms, was a major contribution to the development of the modern valency theory.

Andrews, Thomas (1813–85), Irish chemist who discovered the critical temperature of gases.

Arrhenius, Svante August (1859–1927), Swedish chemist who developed the ionic theory of electrodes.

Astbury, William Thomas (1889–1961), English chemist who pioneered research on protein fibres.

Baeyer, Adolf von (1835–1917), German organic chemist who devised practical methods for creating dyes.

Beckmann, Ernst Otto (1853–1923), German chemist who devised apparatus for determining freezing and boiling points, and the sensitive thermometer that is named after him.

Beilstein, Friedrich Konrad (1838–1906), Russian-born German chemist whose *Handbook of Organic Chemistry* (1881) was a landmark.

Bernal, John Desmond (1901–71), Irish crystallographer and pioneer of molecular biology.

Berthelot, Marcellin (1827–1907), French chemist who discovered the detonation wave.

Berthollet, Count Claude Louis (1748–1822), French chemist who was the first to discover that the completeness of chemical reactions depends, in part, upon the masses of the reacting substances.

Berzelius, Jöns (1779–1848), Swedish chemist who prepared the first accurate list of atomic weights.

Bessemer, Sir Henry (1813–98), English metallurgist who decarbonized iron (1856), thus allowing the large-scale manufacture of steel.

Bosch, Carl (1874–1940), German chemist who devised the Bosch process, by which hydrogen is obtained from water gas and superheated steam.

Boyle, Robert (1627–91), Anglo-Irish physicist and chemist who formulated the law concerning the behaviour of gases – Boyle's law states that, at a given temperature, the pressure of a gas is proportional to its volume. He pioneered the concept of elements, suggesting a corpuscular view of matter, and distinguished between elements and compounds.

Bronsted, Johannes Nicolaus (1879–1947), Danish physical chemist who devised the Bronsted–Lowry definition, which defines an acid as a substance with a tendency to lose a proton and a base as a substance that tends to gain a proton.

Bunsen, Robert (1811–99), German chemist who developed the Bunsen burner and laid the foundations for the field of spectrum analysis.

Cannizzaro, Stanislao (1826–1910), Italian chemist who is best known for his studies of atomic weights.

Cavendish, Henry (1731–1810), English chemist and physicist whose discoveries included the properties of hydrogen, the composition of air, the composition of water and various properties of electricity.

Chain, Ernst (1906–79), German-born British chemist who isolated and purified penicillin.

Claisen, Ludwig (1851–1930), German chemist who developed the Claisen-Schmidt condensation reactions.

Claude, Georges (1870–1960), French chemist and engineer who developed a process of separating the constituent gases of air by distillation of liquefied air.

Corey, Elias James (1928–), US synthetic chemist who is responsible for over 100 first syntheses.

Curie, Marie Sklodowska (1867–1934), Polish-born French chemist who – with her husband Pierre – pioneered research into radioactivity. Following Becquerel's discovery of radioactivity – which Marie Curie named – she and Pierre studied pitchblende (uranium ore) to establish whether it owed much of its radioactivity to tiny quantities of highly active impurities. The Curies discovered the elements polonium and radium. The great radioactivity of the latter confirmed the immense possibilities of the energy that could be gained from atomic processes.

■ *Michael Faraday discovered electrolysis in 1832 when he produced the first electrical transformer – and went on to work out the laws that control it which are named after him*

Dalton, John (1766–1844), English chemist and physicist who developed the atomic theory of matter, defining the atom as the smallest particle of substance that can take part in a chemical reaction. His early studies on gases led to the formulation of Dalton's law which states that the total pressure of a mixture of gases is equal to the sum of the partial pressures of the individual component gases.

Dam, Carl Peter Henrik (1895–1976), Danish biochemist who isolated vitamin K.

Davy, Sir Humphry (1778–1829), English chemist who investigated the electrolysis of molten salts, discovering the metallic elements sodium, potassium, calcium, barium and magnesium and isolating strontium. He later found boron. As well as discovering more elements than any other individual, Davy became well known for his invention of the miner's safety lamp.

Debye, Peter (1884–1966), Dutch-born US physicist and chemist who is best known for the Debye-Hückel theory of electrolytes.

Draper, John William (1811–82), Anglo-US chemist who founded the science of photo-chemistry.

Dumas, Jean-Baptiste André (1800–84), French chemist who produced the substitution theory in chemistry.

Edeleman, Gerald Maurice (1929–), US biochemist whose work elucidates the chemical structure of antibodies.

Faraday, Michael (1791–1867), English physicist and chemist who made important advances in electromagnetism. Becoming an assistant to Davy, who recognized his potential and taught him, Faraday discovered electromagnetic induction in 1821 and built a primitive model which demonstrated the continuous production of current from a conductor moving in a field – in effect, a primitive dynamo. Faraday also liquefied chlorine and isolated benzene. In 1833 he formulated quantitative laws to express magnitudes of electrolytic effects, now known as Faraday's laws of electrolysis. In 1831 he made observations that led to the formulation of the law of induction which now bears his name.

Fischer, Emil (1852–1919), German chemist and biochemist whose work on sugars and peptides did much to establish biochemistry as a separate science.

Fleischmann, Martin (1927–), Czech-born British chemist who announced in 1989 that he and Stanley Pons had achieved nuclear fusion by an electrolytic method under laboratory conditions.

Flory, Paul John (1910–85), US chemist whose major work was on nonlinear polymers.

Frankland, Sir Edward (1825–99), English chemist who was a pioneer in structural chemistry.

Fresenius, Carl (1818–97), German analytical chemist who wrote works on qualitative and quantitative analysis that became standards.

Gay-Lussac, Joseph (1778–1850), French chemist and physicist who pioneered investigations into the behaviour of gases and formulated the law of combining volumes.

Gerhardt, Charles (1816–56), French chemist who formulated a theory of types to classify organic chemical compounds.

Gibbs, Josiah Willard (1839–1903), US founder of the science of chemical thermodynamics.

Graham, Thomas (1805–69), Scottish chemist who defined diffusion and is held to be the founder of colloid chemistry.

Haber, Fritz (1868–1934), German chemist who is known for discovering an industrial process for synthesizing ammonia from nitrogen and hydrogen.

Haworth, Sir Walter (1883–1950), English chemist who was the first person to synthesize a vitamin.

Hittorf, Johann Wilhelm (1824–1914), German chemist and physicist who showed how relative speeds of ions can be calculated.

Hodgkin, Dorothy (1910–94), English chemist who is best known for her work on the structures of penicillin and vitamins.

Ipatieff, Vladimir (1867–1952), Russian-born US chemist who pioneered research in high-pressure catalytic reactions of hydrocarbons.

Jabir, ibn Hayyan (or Haijan; *c.* 721–815), Arabian (now Iran) alchemist and writer who is regarded as one of the founders of chemistry.

Lavoisier, Antoine-Laurent (1743–94), French chemist whose work and discoveries laid the basis for much of modern chemistry. His researches concerned the gain or loss of weight of substances that are burned or reduced using charcoal and ascribed these differences to the absorption or loss of a substance he later called oxygen. He described the composition of water, combustion and the chemistry of many compounds.

Le Bel, Joseph Achille (1847–1930), French chemist who devised the graphic conventions for drawing chemical formulae.

Le Châtelier, Henry-Louis (1850–1936), French chemist who developed what is now known as the Le Châtelier principle, by which it is possible to predict the effect a change of conditions, such as temperature or pressure, will have on a chemical reaction.

Libby, Willard (1908–80), US chemist who, after discovering the radioactive isotope carbon-14, pioneered carbon-dating technique.

Liebig, Baron Justus von (1803–73), German chemist whose application of chemistry to biology pioneered biochemistry.

Lowry, Thomas (1874–1936), English chemist who confirmed that optical activity depends upon the wavelength of light.

Martin, A(rcher) J(ohn) P(orter) (1910–), English biochemist who, with Synge, pioneered a versatile method of separating complex chemical substances: partition chromatography.

Mendeleyev, Dmitri (1834–1907), Russian chemist who discovered that, by arranging the chemical elements in order of increasing atomic weight, a notable repetition of chemical properties at regular intervals was revealed. Recognizing the underlying order this implied, Mendeleyev discovered the Periodic Table.

Meyer, Lothar (1830–95), German chemist who is best known for Meyer's curves, which show the periodicity of chemical elements.

Meyer, Viktor (1848–97), German chemist who devised a way of measuring the density of gases and vapours.

Miller, Stanley (1930–73), US biochemist who synthesized amino acids.

Müller, Paul (1899–1965), Swiss chemist who developed DDT (dichlorodiphenyltrichloroethane).

Mulliken, Robert Sanderson (1896–1986), US physicist and chemist who, with Hund, developed the molecular-orbital theory of chemical bonding.

Nernst, Walther Hermann (1864–1941), German chemist who is regarded as one of the founders of modern physical chemistry, creating the third law of thermodynamics.

Newlands, John (1838–98), English chemist who – before Mendeleyev – noticed that by arranging the chemical elements in order of increasing atomic weight a curious repetition of physical properties emerged.

Ostwald, Wilhelm Friedrich (1853–1932), Latvian-born German chemist who pioneered the development of physical chemistry as a separate branch of chemistry.

ALMOST MADE IT...

THE DISCOVERY OF OXYGEN

Traditionally, Joseph Priestley isolated oxygen on 1 August 1774. However, Karl Scheele – a Swedish chemist from a poor background with little schooling – discovered it at least two years beforehand. Scheele, working in a remote laboratory, isolated oxygen, or 'fire air' as he called it, in 1772 and wrote a treatise outlining his find, *A Chemical Treatise on Air and Fire,* which was ready for the printers in 1775. Yet it was not published then, as Scheele was waiting for a Preface for the work from Torbern Bergman, who took two years to deliver it. By this time, Priestley had already announced his discovery. Scheele, a dedicated scientist interested in the search for truth over financial reward, discovered many elements, but publishing delays lost him due credit. Nonetheless, Scheele shunned offers of money and fame and has never taken his place as one of the great 18th-century scientists.

THE CLASSIFICATION OF ELEMENTS

One of the most familiar representations in chemistry is the periodic table. Mendeleyev produced this famous scheme in 1869, but a British chemist, John Newlands, almost discovered it years before. In various papers in 1864 and 1865, Newlands stated his law of octaves. He noticed that if elements were listed down in order of their atomic weights, a pattern of repeating properties emerged after every group of seven elements, drawing an analogy with the musical scale. However, his ideas were met with scorn and ridicule, as other scientists stated that his system was as arbitrary as an alphabetical listing. Only after Mendeleyev's periodic table had been accepted by the scientific community did Newlands' discovery gain the respect it deserved. He eventually published his findings in *On the Discovery of the Periodic Law* in 1884 but, of course, the glory had already gone to another.

Paracelsus (Philippus Bombast von Hohenheim; 1493–1541), Swiss doctor and alchemist sometimes called the Father of Chemistry.

Pardee, Arthur Beck (1921–), US biochemist who – with François Jacob and Jacques Monod – formulated the concept of a repressor molecule.

Pauling, Linus (1901–94), US chemist who applied the principles of quantum mechanics to his studies of chemical bonding. In 1939 he collected his work together in a book called *The Nature of the Chemical Bond* which was possibly the most influential chemical text of this century. In 1951 he announced that he had solved an important general structure of proteins, now known as the alpha-helix, which inspired Crick and Watson in their successful attempt to find the structure of DNA.

Priestley, Joseph (1733–1804), English cleric, political theorist and scientist who was one of the discoverers of oxygen.

Proust, Joseph Louis (1754–1826), French chemist who created a law stating that all compounds contain elements in definite proportions.

Ramsay, Sir William (1852–1916), Scottish chemist who discovered the noble gases neon, argon, krypton and xenon.

Sabatier, Paul (1854–1941), French chemist who worked on the hydrogenation of organic compounds.

Sangar, Frederick (1918–), English biochemist who pioneered developments with insulin and conducted work on DNA sequencing.

Scheele, Karl Wilhelm (1742–86), Swedish chemist who discovered oxygen (1771) and chlorine (1774). As he did not publish his results until 1777, Priestley was credited with the discovery.

Seaborg, Glenn Theodore (1912–), US nuclear chemist who is associated with the discovery or first isolation of elements 93–98, 101 and 102.

Smith, Michael (1932–), English-born Canadian biochemist who introduced the concept of site specific mutagenesis (changing the genetic contents of a cell by altering the structure of the DNA by means of a special agent, such as electromagnetic radiation) into molecular biology.

Svedberg, Theodor (1884–1971), Swedish chemist who introduced the ultracentrifuge to investigate the molecular weights of very large molecules.

Urey, Harold Clayton (1893–1981), US chemist who discovered deuterium (heavy hydrogen).

Van't Hoff, Jacobus Henricus (1852–1911), Dutch chemist who created stereochemistry, the study of the three-dimensional structure of organic compounds.

Werner, Alfred (1866–1919), Swiss chemist who is known for his influential *New Ideas on Inorganic Chemistry.*

Wöhler, Friedrich (1800–82), German chemist who, in 1828, was the first person to synthesize an organic chemical compound (urea) from an inorganic chemical compound.

Woodward, R(obert) B(urns) (1917–79), US chemist who synthesized complex organic substances including quinine, cholesterol and vitamin B.

ALFRED NOBEL AND HIS LEGACY

Alfred Nobel (1833–96) was a Swedish chemist, inventor and engineer whose life in an age of industrial expansion led him to become one of the most powerful industrialists of his time. The name Nobel conjures up a sense of international human achievement, yet, paradoxically, the man who gave his name to the most highly regarded Peace award also invented dynamite and was considered by many to be the archetype of a 'mad scientist'.

Born in Stockholm, Alfred was well-educated, with a passion for literature and poetry. But his father sought a more pragmatic career for his son, sending him abroad to study chemical engineering. Nobel became fascinated with the workings of nitroglycerine, a highly explosive liquid that was, at that time, too unstable to be useful. Returning to St Petersburg, he continued to work with explosives, aiding and supplying the Russian army via the family business.

During the 1860s, having returned to Sweden, Nobel began developing this volatile compound – a dangerous activity fraught with tragedy and travail. An explosion in 1864 at a factory he built killed several people, including his own brother Emil. Following this, the Swedish authorities decided nitroglycerine production was too dangerous to be conducted within Stockholm city limits and Nobel was forced to work from a barge on Lake Mälaren. Nevertheless, he persevered, and in 1867 he patented dynamite, a paste mixture of nitroglycerine and silica. He also developed a blasting cap to aid detonation, and a smokeless gunpowder, ballistite, in 1889. These inventions, which greatly assisted the expanding construction industries and brought Nobel massive wealth, were swiftly used as weapons of mass destruction.

Alfred Nobel was a private, hardworking man who spent much of his time travelling throughout the Western world. Towards the end of his life, he had amassed a vast fortune. Nobel bitterly rued the fact that dynamite was being used as an instrument of death and, as a gesture of atonement, his will dedicated his entire fortune to those who had 'conferred the greatest benefit on mankind'. He bequeathed around $9 million to be administered as annual prizes in physics, chemistry, physiology and medicine, peace and literature, reflecting the fields of interest that concerned him most. Although the will was contested by surprised relatives, Nobel's final wish was realized in the birth of the Nobel Foundation in 1901,with the first five prizes awarded on the fifth anniversary of his death. A sixth category for economics was instituted in 1969. Given annually except during war years, the Nobel Prize is considered to be the most prestigious honour attainable in human achievement.

NOBEL PRIZEWINNERS

1901 Jacobus van't Hoff, Dutch: for laws of chemical dynamics and osmotic pressure.

1902 Emil Fischer, German: for work on sugar and purine syntheses.

1903 Svante Arrhenius, Swedish: for his theory of electrolytic dissociation.

1904 Sir William Ramsay, Scottish: for discovery and periodic system classification of inert gas elements.

1905 Adolf von Baeyer, German: for work on organic dyes and hydroaromatic compounds.

1906 Henri Moissan, French: for the Moissan furnace, and isolation of fluorine.

1907 Eduard Buchner, German: for discovering non-cellular fermentation.

1908 Ernest Rutherford, New Zealand: for his description of atomic structure and the chemistry of radioactive substance.

1909 Wilhelm Ostwald, Latvian-born German: for pioneering catalysis, chemical equilibrium and reaction velocity work.

1910 Otto Wallach, German: for pioneering work on alicyclic combinations.

1911 Marie Curie, Polish-born French: for the discovery of radium and polonium, and isolation of radium.

1912 Victor Grignard, French: for Grignard reagents; and Paul Sabatier, French: for his method of hydrogenating compounds.

1913 Alfred Werner, French-born Swiss: for work on the linkage of atoms in molecules.

1914 Theodore Richards, US: for the precise determination of atomic weights of many elements.

1915 Richard Willstätter, German: for pioneering research on plant pigments, especially chlorophyll.

1916–17 No awards

1918 Fritz Haber, German: for synthesis of ammonia.

1919 No award

1920 Walther Nernst, German: for work in thermo-chemistry.

1921 Frederick Soddy, English: for study of radioactive materials, and the occurrence and nature of isotopes.

1922 Francis Aston, English: for work on mass spectrography, and on whole number rule.

1923 Fritz Pregl, Austrian: for his method of micro-analysis of organic substances.

1924 No award

1925 Richard Zsigmondy, German: for the elucidation of the heterogeneous nature of colloidal solutions.

1926 Theodor Svedberg, Swedish: for work on disperse systems.

1927 Heinrich Wieland, German: for research into bile acids' constitution.

1928 Adolf Windaus, German: for work on the constitution of sterols and their connection with vitamins.

1929 Sir Arthur Harden, English, and Hans von Euler-Chelpin, German-born Swedish: for studies of sugar fermentation and enzymes involved.

1930 Hans Fischer, German: for chlorophyll research, and discovering haemoglobin in the blood.

1931 Carl Bosch, German, and Friedrich Bergius, German: for the invention and development of high-pressure methods.

1932 Irving Langmuir, US: for furthering understanding of surface chemistry.

1933 No award

1934 Harold Urey, US: for the discovery of heavy hydrogen.

1935 Frédéric Joliot-Curie, French, and Irène Joliot-Curie, French: for the synthesis of new radioactive elements.

1936 Peter Debye, Dutch: for work on dipole moments and the diffraction of X-rays and electrons in gases.

1937 Sir Walter Haworth, English: for vitamin C and carbohydrate research; and Paul Karrer, Swiss: for research into carotenoid, flavin, and vitamins.

1938 Richard Kuhn, German: for carotenoid and vitamin research (award declined as Hitler forbade Germans to accept Nobel prizes).

1939 Adolf Butenandt, German: for work on sex hormones (award declined as Hitler forbade Germans to accept Nobel prizes); and Leopold Ruzicka, Croat-born Swiss: for research on steroid hormones.

1940–42 No awards

1943 George von Hevesy, Hungarian: for the use of isotopes as tracers in research.

1944 Otto Hahn, German: for discovering the fusion of heavy nuclei.

1945 Arturri Virtanen, Finnish: for his method of fodder preservation.

1946 James Sumner, US: for the discovery of enzyme crystallization; and John Northrop, US, and Wendell Stanley, US: for the preparation of pure enzymes and virus proteins.

1947 Sir Robert Robinson, English: for alkaloid and plant biology research.

1948 Arne Tiselius, Swedish: for research on electrophoretic and absorption analysis, and serum proteins.

1949 William Giauque, Canadian-born US: for work on the behaviour of substances at very low temperatures.

1950 Otto Diels, German, and Kurt Alder, German: for the discovery and development of diene synthesis.

1951 Edwin McMillan, US, and Glenn Seaborg, US: for the discovery of and research on trans-uranium elements.

1952 Archer Martin and Richard Synge, both English: for developing partition chromatography.

1953 Hermann Staudinger, German: for work on macromolecules.

1954 Linus Pauling, US: for studies on the nature of the chemical bond.

1955 Vincent Du Vigneaud, US: for pioneer work on the synthesis of a polypeptide hormone.

1956 Nikolay Semyonov, Russian, and Cyril Hinshelwood, English: for work on the kinetics of chemical reactions.

1957 Alexander Todd, Scottish: for work on nucleotides and nucleotide coenzymes.

1958 Frederick Sanger, English: for determining the structure of the insulin molecule.

1959 Jaroslav Heyrovsky, Czech: for the discovery and development of polarography.

1960 Willard Libby, US: for the development of radio-carbon dating.

1961 Melvin Calvin, US: for studies of the chemical stages that occur in photosynthesis.

1962 John C. Kendrew, English, and Max F. Perutz, Austrian-born British: for determining the structure of haemoproteins.

1963 Giulio Natta, Italian, and Karl Ziegler, German: for research into the structure and synthesis of plastics polymers.

1964 Dorothy Hodgkin, English: for determining the structure of compounds essential in combating pernicious anaemia.

1965 Robert B. Woodward, US: for synthesizing sterols, chlorophyll, etc. (previously produced only by living things).

1966 Robert S. Mulliken, US: for investigations into chemical bonds and electronic structure of molecules.

1967 Manfred Eigen, German, Ronald G.W. Norrish, English, and George Porter, English: for studies of extremely fast chemical reactions.

1968 Lars Onsager, Norwegian-born US: for his theory of the thermo-dynamics of irreversible processes.

1969 Derek H.R. Barton, English, and Odd Hasell, Norwegian: for determining the actual 3-dimensional shape of certain organic compounds.

1970 Luis F. Leloir, French-born Argentinian: for his discovery of sugar nucleotides and their role in carbohydrate biosynthesis.

1971 Gerhard Herzberg, German-born Canadian: for research on the structure of molecules.

1972 Christian B. Anfinsen, Stanford Moore, and William H. Stein, all US: for contributions to the fundamentals of enzyme chemistry.

1973 Ernst Fischer, German, and Geoffrey Wilkinson, English: for work in organometallic chemistry.

1974 Paul J. Flory, US: for studies of long-chain molecules.

1975 John Cornforth, Australian-born British, and Vladimir Prelog, Bosnian-born Swiss: for work on stereochemistry.

1976 William N. Lipscomb, US: for work on the structure of boranes (compounds of boron and hydrogen).

1977 Ilya Prigogine, Russian-born Belgian: for work in advanced thermodynamics.

1978 Peter D. Mitchell, English: for his theory of energy transfer processes in biological systems.

1979 Herbert C. Brown, English-born US, and Georg Wittig, German: for introducing boron and phosphorus compounds in the synthesis of organic compounds.

1980 Paul Berg, US: for the first preparation of a hybrid DNA; and Walter Gilbert, US, and Frederick Sanger, English: for chemical and biological analysis of the structure of DNA.

1981 Fukui Kenichi, Japanese, and Roald Hoffmann, Polish-born US: for orbital symmetry interpretation of chemical reactions.

1982 Aaron Klug, Lithuanian-born South African (a British naturalized citizen): for determining the structure of some biologically active substances.

1983 Henry Taube, Canadian: for studies into electron transfer reactions.

1984 Bruce Merrifield, US: for formulating a method of polypeptide synthesis.

1985 Herbert A. Hauptman and Jerome Karle, both US: for developing a means of mapping the chemical structure of small molecules.

1986 Dudley R. Herschbach, US, Yuan T. Lee, Taiwanese-born US, and John C. Polanyi, Canadian: for introducing methods for analysing basic chemical reactions.

1987 Donald J. Cram, US, Charles J. Pedersen, Korean-born US, and Jean-Marie Lehn, French: for developing molecules that could link with other molecules.

1988 Johann Deisenhofer, Robert Huber, and Hartmut Michel, all German: for studies into the structure of the proteins needed in photosynthesis.

1989 Tom Cech, US, and Sidney Altman, Canadian-born US: for establishing that RNA catalyses biochemical reactions.

1990 Elias Corey, US: for work on synthesizing chemical compounds based on natural substances.

1991 Richard R. Ernst, Swiss: for refining the technology of nuclear magnetic resonance imaging (NMR and MRI).

1992 Rudolph A. Marcus, US: for mathematical analysis of the cause and effect of electrons jumping from one molecule to another.

1993 Kary B. Mullis, US: for the invention of his PCR method; and Michael Smith, English-born Canadian: for contributions to oligonucleotide-based, site-directed mutagenesis.

1994 George Olah, US: for pioneering work in controlling hydrocarbon reactions.

1995 Paul Crutzen, Dutch, Mario Molina, Mexican, and F. Sherwood Rowland, US: for work in atmospheric chemistry, particularly concerning the formation and decomposition of ozone.

1996 Robert F. Curl, Jr, US, Sir Harold W. Kroto, English, and Richard E. Smalley, US: for the discovery of fullerenes.

■ *This computer graphics representation is of a segment of a beta-deoxyribonucleic acid (B-DNA) molecule – a structure containing the inherited instructions necessary for the development of life. The atoms shown within the DNA molecule are phosphate (yellow), oxygen (red), nitrogen (blue) and carbon (pink), which are twisted into a helical shape called a helix, two of which form the double helix of DNA*

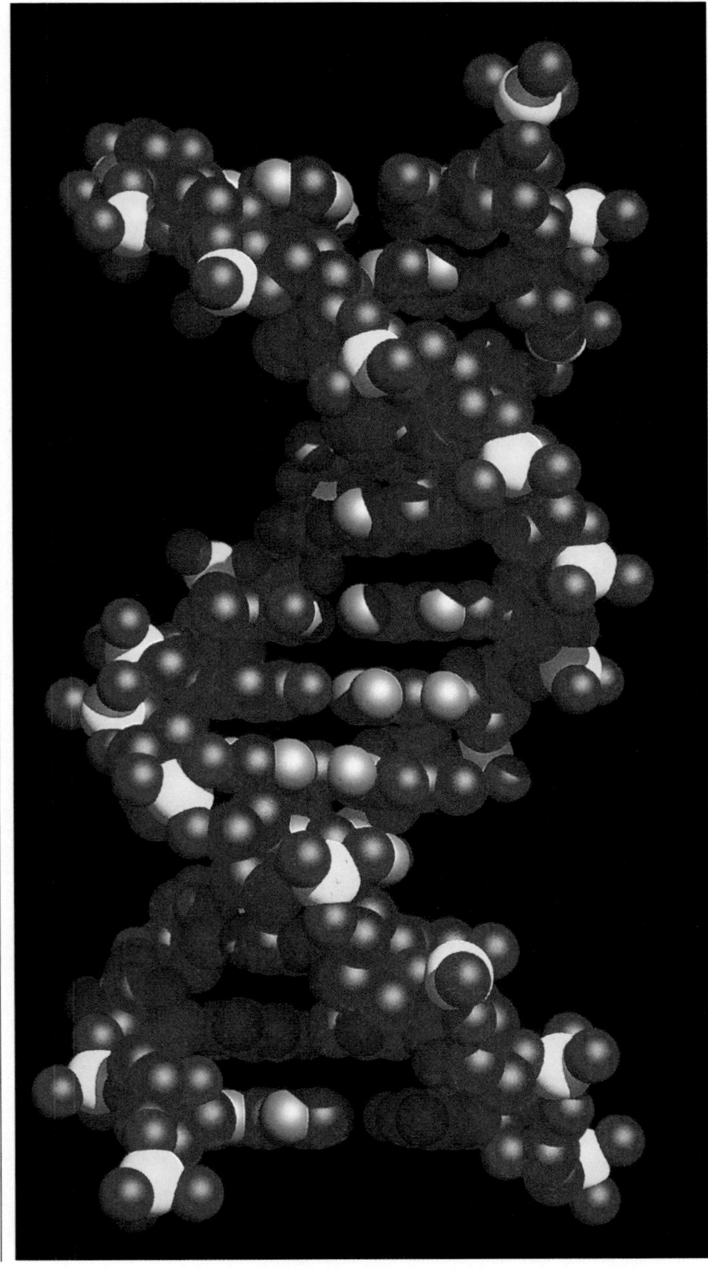

MATHEMATICS

▶ Thousands of years ago, Babylonian astronomers measured circles and angles the same way people still do today, dividing a circle into 360 degrees.

▶ One suggestion why the symbol V is the Roman numeral for 5 is that it resembles an outstretched palm.

▶ The word plus is short for surplus: originally the symbol + was scrawled on boxes or sacks that were overweight and the symbol – on those which were underweight.

▶ The Mayans of Mexico used a base-20 number system 1500 years ago to create highly accurate calendars.

NUMBERS

▶ Natural numbers, or whole numbers, are those that we use in counting.
▶ They are represented by a combination of numeric symbols – 1, 2, 3, 4, 5, 6, 7, 8, 9 and 0.

Whole numbers can be positive or negative. If they are positive, they can be denoted with a positive sign (+), although this is usually omitted. If they are negative, the minus symbol (–) is placed in front of the numeral. Thus –9 represents 'minus nine'. An integer is any positive or negative whole number. Zero, 0, is an integer, but is neither positive nor negative.

Numbers can be operated on in several ways. The four most basic operations are addition, subtraction, multiplication and division. It is important to note that addition is the inverse operation to subtraction, whilst multiplication is the inverse of division. It is also important that in addition and multiplication, the ordering of the sequence of numbers does not affect the result, but in subtraction and division it does.

TYPES OF NUMBERS

Even numbers: any integers that will divide by 2 exactly, that is, without leaving a remainder. For example: 2, 4, 6, 8, 10, 12, 14, 16, 18 and 20.

Odd numbers: any integers which will not divide by 2 exactly. For example: 1, 3, 5, 7, 9, 11, 13, 15, 17 and 19.

Prime numbers: any natural numbers which can only be divided by themselves and 1. The number 1 is not considered to be a prime number. The first ten prime numbers are: 2, 3, 5, 7, 11, 13, 17, 19, 23, 29.

Perfect numbers: any numbers that are equal to the sum of their factors (see Division on this page), excluding the number itself. The first perfect number is 6 whose factors (excluding 6 itself) are 1, 2 and 3. As 1 + 2 + 3 = 6, 6 is a perfect number. The next perfect number is 28. The factors of 28 are 1, 2, 4, 7 and 14, and 1 + 2 + 4 + 7 + 14 = 28. Only about 30 perfect numbers have been discovered.

ADDITION

Addition is the mathematical operation by which the sum of two numbers is calculated. The operation is normally indicated by the symbol +. For example: 3 + 4 = 7.

SUBTRACTION

Subtraction is the mathematical operation in which one number is taken from another. The operation is normally indicated by the symbol –. For example: 7 – 3 = 4.

The difference is the result when the smaller of two numbers is subtracted from the larger. Thus 4 is the difference of 7 and 3. It should be noted that the addition of a negative number is equivalent to subtraction. For example: 7 + (–3) = 4.

MULTIPLICATION

Multiplication is the mathematical operation by which one number is added to itself by the number of times specified by a second number. The final answer is called the product of the two numbers. The symbol usually used to denote multiplication is ×. For example: 5 × 7 means seven lots of 5 added to each other, or (5 + 5 + 5 + 5 + 5 + 5 + 5), which is equal to 35. Therefore, 5 x 7 = 35.

A multiple is any number which is the product of a given number and any other whole number. For example: 35 is a multiple of 5, and a multiple of 7.

DIVISION

Division is the mathematical operation by which one number is repeatedly subtracted from another until 0, or as close to it as possible, is reached. The quotient is the result of dividing one number by another. The symbol for division is ÷. For example, 12 ÷ 3 = 4, because there are 4 lots of 3 in 12, and 4 is the quotient.

Some numbers divide into other numbers exactly, whilst others do not. When one number does not exactly go into another number a certain number of times, then the remainder is the amount left over at the end of the operation. For example: 14 ÷ 3 gives 4 remainder 2.

Any number which divides exactly into another number is called a factor. For example, 3 is a factor of 12, but 3 is not a factor of 14.

The reciprocal of a number is 1 divided by that number. Thus the reciprocal of 8 is $\frac{1}{8}$. Conversely, it should be noted that the reciprocal of $\frac{1}{8}$ is 8.

POWERS AND INDICES

▶ An index, or exponent, is a number placed above the line after another number to show how many times the number is to be multiplied by itself.
▶ The number of times that the number occurs in the operation is called the power. Thus, 7 × 7 × 7 × 7 × 7 is the fifth power of 7. In index form, this may be written as 7^5.

A square number is any number that has been formed by multiplying a whole number by itself. For example, 4 × 4 = 16, thus 16 is a square number. In index form, this may be written as 4^2, that is to say, 'four squared'.

The inverse of a square is a square root. For example, 5 × 5 = 25, thus 5 is the square root of 25. A square root is any number which, when multiplied by itself, gives a specified number. The symbol for square root is √. Thus $\sqrt{36} = 6$ and $\sqrt{81} = 9$.

A cubic number is any number that has been formed by multiplying a whole number by itself and then multiplying the result by the whole number. Thus 4 x 4 x 4 = 64, which makes 64 a cubic number, and 4 x 4 x 4 may be written as 4^3, that is to say, 'four cubed'.

A negative index is the reciprocal of its positive index. Consider eight squared, 8^2. The reciprocal of 8^2 is $\frac{1}{8^2}$ which can be written as 8^{-2}. Similarly, 10^{-6} is the reciprocal of 10^6, or $\frac{1}{1{,}000{,}000}$.

Using exponents can be useful for expressing very large or very small numbers. For example, the number 8 million, which in numerals is 8,000,000, can now be broken down as: 8 x 1,000,000. Now 1,000,000 is ten multiplied by itself six times, so:

$$8 \times (10 \times 10 \times 10 \times 10 \times 10 \times 10) = 8 \times 10^6.$$

In the same way, the very small number $\frac{1}{4{,}000{,}000{,}000}$ can be written as 4×10^{-9}.

FRACTIONS AND DECIMALS

▶ Fractions and decimals are two ways of showing the same information – parts of whole numbers.
▶ A fraction is any quantity that is defined in terms of a numerator and a denominator.

Fractions and decimals are used in mathematics to express values which are not integers, that is, not whole numbers. Fractions can be used as pure numbers, or to demonstrate a proportion of some other quantity.

FRACTIONS

A fraction has two parts, the numerator and the denominator. The numerator is the term above the line in a fraction which indicates how many parts of a specified number of parts of a unit are being taken. A denominator is the term below the line in a fraction which indicates the number of equal parts into which the whole is divided. Examples include $\frac{1}{2}$ (one-half), $\frac{1}{4}$ (one-quarter) and $\frac{3}{5}$ (three-fifths).

A vulgar fraction (or proper fraction) is a fraction in which the numerator is smaller than the denominator, for example in $\frac{3}{7}$, $\frac{6}{12}$ and $\frac{5}{14}$.

An improper fraction is a fraction in which the numerator is larger than the denominator, for example $\frac{3}{2}$, $\frac{7}{5}$ and $\frac{18}{11}$.

Two fractions which express the same relationship of quantities are known as equivalent fractions, for example: $\frac{3}{4}$, $\frac{6}{8}$, $\frac{9}{12}$ and $\frac{12}{16}$ are equivalent fractions. Of these, $\frac{3}{4}$ is the fraction with the lowest terms – the numerator and the denominator cannot be further divided by the whole numbers.

A mixed number is a number that comprises an integer and a fraction, for example $3\frac{3}{4}$ (in other words 3 + $\frac{3}{4}$).

It is useful when comparing fractions to use the same denominator. For example, the three fractions $\frac{1}{2}$, $\frac{3}{5}$ and $\frac{7}{10}$, can be expressed in terms of the same denominator: $\frac{1}{2} = \frac{5}{10}$, $\frac{3}{5} = \frac{6}{10}$, and $\frac{7}{10} = \frac{7}{10}$. The denominator 10 is called the lowest common denominator (LCM) – the smallest integer into which all three denominators can be divided exactly.

BINARY SYSTEM

▶ The standard number system is base ten – it uses ten different basic numerals or combinations of them. Binary uses two symbols: 0 and 1.
▶ This base-two number system is used extensively in modern computing.

Binary works in the same way as decimal in that once all the symbols have been used in one column, another column is added to the left. In binary:

zero = 0
one = 1

When all the symbols have been used in the first column, a column is added to the left, thus:

two = 10
three = 11

Again, another column is added:

four = 100
five = 101
six = 110
seven = 111
eight = 1000
nine = 1001
ten = 1010 . . . and so on.

Whereas in the decimal system each column represents an additional power of ten, in binary each column represents an additional power of two. For example, in decimals 3056 is:

$(3 \times 10^3) + (0 \times 10^2) + (5 \times 10^1) + (6 \times 10^0)$
$= 3,000 + 0 + 50 + 6$
$= 3056$

and, in binary 10110110 is:

$(1 \times 2^7) + (0 \times 2^6) + (1 \times 2^5) + (1 \times 2^4) +$
$(0 \times 2^3) + (1 \times 2^2) + (1 \times 2^1) + (0 \times 2^0)$
$= 128 + 0 + 32 + 16 + 0 + 4 + 2 + 0$
$= 182$

DECIMALS

A decimal is a fraction with an unwritten denominator of some power of ten. This is shown by the decimal point which is placed before the numerator. For example: 5.25 represents 5 whole units, 2 tenths and 5 hundredths, that is 0.25 is another way of saying $^2/_{10} + ^5/_{100}$, or $^{25}/_{100}$. Similarly,

123.456 is $100 + 20 + 3 + ^4/_{10} + ^5/_{100} + ^6/_{1000}$

Some fractions, when converted into decimal notation, produce recurring sequences of digits which never end, for example:

$^1/_3$ = 0.333333333333333333 . . .

and this can be shown by 0.333' where the symbol ' denotes that the pattern continues indefinitely. Similarly,

$^1/_7$ = 0.142857142857142857 . . . = 0.142857'

PERCENTAGES

A percentage, shown by the symbol %, can also be regarded as a fraction. It shows a quantity as part of 100. Thus $^3/_5$ of 50 is the same as $^{60}/_{100}$ of 50. This can be written as 60% of 50, which is 30.

To express a number, *a*, as a percentage of another number, *b*, divide *a* by *b* and multiply by 100. For example, to express 70 as a percentage of 500, calculate 70 ÷ 500 = 0.14 and multiply by 100, to get 14. Thus 70 is 14% of 500.

RATIONAL AND IRRATIONAL NUMBERS

A rational number is any number which can be expressed as a fraction (or 'ratio'). Some numbers cannot be expressed as fractions. These are known as irrational numbers, for example π, $\sqrt{2}$ and $\sqrt{3}$.

ROMAN NUMERALS

▶ This system uses seven of the Roman letters of the alphabet, used in isolation or in various combinations, to represent numbers.
▶ The Romans incorporated a subtractive system in which a lesser symbol appearing before a greater one altered the value of the latter. Thus LX represents 60 while XL represents 40.

The following is a list of Arabic numerals, the most commonly used today, and their equivalents in Roman numerals.

Arabic	Roman	Arabic	Roman	Arabic	Roman
1	I	11	XI	30	XXX
2	II	12	XII	40	XL
3	III	13	XIII	50	X
4	IV	14	XIV	60	LX
5	V	15	XV	70	LXX
6	VI	16	XVI	80	LXXX
7	VII	17	XVII	90	XC
8	VIII	18	XVIII	100	C
9	IX	19	XIX	200	CC
10	X	20	XX	500	D
		25	XXV	1000	M

Thus the number 1998 would be MCMXCVIII.

RATIO AND PROPORTION

A ratio is the relation between quantities – two or more – of the same kind. Ratios are another way of expressing the same relationship that can be seen in a fraction. Since ratio is a comparison of sizes (such as masses, prices of item, lengths or heights), no units are needed in this comparison. For example, the ratio of a journey of 5 km to a journey of 25 km is 5 km:25 km, or (since the units are the same) 5:25. This ratio cancels down to 1:5 in its simplest form as both 5 and 25 can be divided by 5.

Ratios and fractions are linked. For example, the ratio 2:10 may also be expressed as the fraction $^2/_{10}$; the ratio 3:15 may also be expressed as the fraction $^3/_{15}$; likewise, the ratio 7:35 may also be expressed as the fraction $^7/_{35}$. All of these fractions cancel down to $^1/_5$; therefore the ratios 2:10, 3:15 and 7:35 may be expressed in the simplest form as 1:5.

Ratios can be used to solve problems. For example, 120 tonnes may be divided in the ratio 1:5. The ratio 1:5 means that altogether 6 parts (1 plus 5) are involved in the division of the 120 tonnes. Each share is therefore worth 20 tonnes (that is, 120 divided by six); one share is 20 tonnes and five shares is 100 tonnes. Therefore 120 tonnes divided in the ratio of 1:5 is 20 tonnes:100 tonnes.

Proportion is the comparative relation between things, such as their price, size or amount. There are two principal proportion relationships – direct and inverse.

Direct proportion is the relationship between two quantities whereby an increase in one quantity is matched by a proportionate increase in a second quantity. So that if a doubling of a quantity *a* is matched by a doubling in quantity *b*, then *a* and *b* are directly proportional to each other.

Two quantities are also in direct proportion if a decrease in one quantity is matched by a proportionate decrease in the second quantity.

Inverse proportion is the relationship whereby an increase in one quantity produces a decrease in a second quantity in the same ratio. So that if a doubling of a quantity *a* is matched by a halving of quantity *b*, then *a* and *b* are inversely proportional to each other.

STATISTICS

▶ Statistics is that which is concerned with the collection, study and analysis of numerical data.
▶ It is sometimes treated as a branch of mathematics, but can also be regarded as a separate science.

Statistical data can be presented in various forms. The most common devices used are the bar chart, the pictogram, the pie chart and the histogram.

Bar graph

This is a popular method of displaying statistical data. A bar graph (or bar chart) consists of columns that are arranged either vertically or horizontally. Each bar is the same width and, where there are spaces between them, those spaces are uniform. The length (in a horizontal bar chart, below left) or the height (in a vertical bar chart, below right) depends upon the size of the section of the data that it represents.

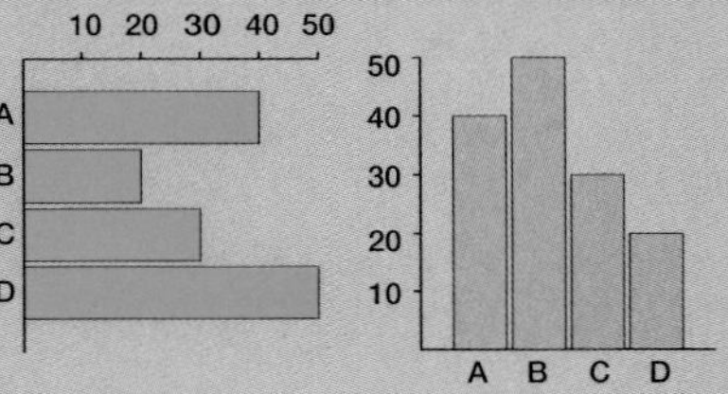

Pictogram

This is similar to a bar chart but a small symbol is piled up vertically (or stretched out horizontally) instead of the bar. For example, to represent the consumption of chocolate per head of population in different countries, the symbol for a chocolate bar could be repeated.

Pie chart

This is useful for showing the proportions of the total as slices of a pie. The total angle at the centre of the pie is 360°. So to represent, for example, 19% in a pie chart format, an angle at the centre equal to ($^{19}/_{100}$) x 360°, i.e. 68.4°, should be used.

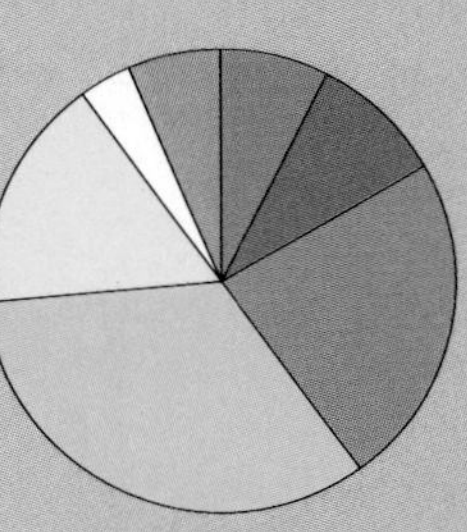

Histogram

This method represents data as areas. It resembles a bar chart but there are no gaps between the bars. An example is the record of data from an experiment, say, if two dice are thrown and the total score is recorded. If this procedure is repeated 1000 times and the number of times each score (from 2 to 12) is obtained, it can be shown in the histogram.

MEAN, MEDIAN AND MODE

For data such as the above, with a 'central tendency' such that the data cluster around a particular value, it is useful to have a measure of the 'spread' of the data. Using just nine numbers, we can see how the mean, median and mode differ from each other:

1, 3, 3, 3, 4, 8, 8, 9, 11 (total = 50)

The average value, called the mean, is found by totalling the numbers and dividing by the number of sample numbers involved: mean = $^{50}/_9$ = 5.55' (a recurring decimal). The middle value is called the median. Since there are nine numbers, the middle value is the fifth one, so the median value is 4. The mode is the value that occurs most often, so here the mode is 3.

ALGEBRA

▶ Algebra is a form of generalized arithmetic using variables or letters to represent numbers.
▶ In 1632, Descartes was already writing algebraic equations in the modern form – for example: $3x^2 - 5x + 6 = 0$.

In modern usage, letters from the beginning of the alphabet are used to represent numbers in general. Thus, $a + b = b + a$ applies, whatever a and b might be. For example, $6 + 2 = 2 + 6$, where $a = 6$ and $b = 2$.

Letters from the end of the alphabet are used to represent specific unknown numbers. Thus, the equation $x + 5 = 6$ is only true if $x = 1$.

Algebra can be used to solve mathematical problems in which there are unknown quantities. For example: A farmer has 42 chickens and goes to market and purchases an unknown number of chickens. When these additional chickens are added to the flock the farmer has a total of 53 chickens. This may be expressed as $42 + x = 53$, where x is the unknown number of additional chickens. In this case, $x = 11$.

The operations of addition, subtraction, multiplication and division that are used in basic arithmetic can also be used in algebra, with certain basic restrictions. In algebraic addition and subtraction, it is only possible to collect 'like' terms (that is, terms that are expressed as parts or multiples of the same unknown quantity). For example:

$3b + 2b + b + 7b = 13b$
$3x + 2y + 5x + y + 2y + 6x = 14x + 5y$

Multiplication and division in algebra also follow certain simple rules – the multiplication and division signs may be omitted and the numbers placed in juxtaposition to indicate multiplication. For example:

$7 \times a = 7a$
$-b \times c = -bc$
$12y \div 4 = 3y$

Thus, in algebraic shorthand, $a.b$ or just ab stands for 'a times b'. Note that $a.b = b.a$ (for example, $2 \times 6 = 6 \times 2$).

BRACKETS
Brackets are used to enclose a classified grouping within specified limits. For example, $(-2) + (-3)$ and $(4x + 5)^2$. In the removal of brackets in an expression, each term inside the bracket has to be multiplied by the number or term outside the bracket. For example, $7(z + 2)$ is 7 multiplied by z, plus 7 multiplied by 2, or $7z + 14$.

The opposite of removing brackets from an equation is called factorization. Thus, to factorize $4x + 4y$, the common term 4 can be pulled out to leave $4(x + y)$. Similarly, $6a - 3b$ becomes $3(2a - b)$. Note that in this example 3 is the common factor.

EQUATIONS
An equation is a statement of equality between two quantities (expressed as numbers and/or letters). The equality of the two parts of the equation is shown by the equal sign (=).

Working out the answer to an equation is said to be 'solving' it. In solving a simple equation, the aim is to group the letters on one side of the equation and the numbers on the other. $9x - 3 = 7x + 3$, for example, becomes $9x - 7x = 6$, giving $x = 3$. Note that when terms are moved from one side of an equation to the other, the addition and subtraction signs change. Thus, for example, $9x - 3 = 7x + 3$ becomes $9x - 7x = 3 + 3$, which gives $2x = 6$.

Inequalities and inequations can be expressed using symbols in the same way that equality (=) can. The most simple symbol is $\neq$, which means 'does not equal'. Thus $4 \neq 6$. If $x \neq y$, then it follows that the terms x and y are different.

The symbols $<$ and $>$ are used to express a certain comparative relationship between terms. The statement $x < y$ means that x is less than y (also expressed as y is greater than x); the statement $x > y$ means that x is greater than y (y is less than x). The symbols $\leq$ and $\geq$ are also used in mathematical statements. The symbol $\leq$ means less than or equal to; the symbol $\geq$ means greater than or equal to.

POWERS OF THE SAME NUMBER
In equations and expressions, the powers of the same number are added together in multiplication and subtracted in division. For example, in multiplication:

$b^2 \times b^3 = b.b \times b.b.b = b.b.b.b.b = b^5$

In general, $x^n \times x^q = x^{(n+q)}$

For example, in division:

$b^3/b^2 = b.b.b/b.b = b^1 = b$

In general, $p^x \div p^y = p^{(x-y)}$

Using these two rules, several basic facts about indices can be demonstrated: $x^1 = x$ multiplied by itself once, therefore $x^1 = x$ for all real values of x; and $x^0 = x^{(1-1)} = x^1 \div x^1 = x \div x = 1$ and so, therefore: $x^0 = 1$ for all real values of x.

FORMULAE
A formula is a set of symbols that express a mathematical rule. An example of a formula is:

$v = s/t$

where v is speed, s is distance travelled and t is the time taken. If a body travels 50 km in 2 hours then its speed = 50 km/2 hr = 25 km/h. (Note that when inserting values into a formula it is best to include the appropriate unit with the associated numbers.)

TRANSFORMING FORMULAE
A transformation of a formula (or change of subject) is a simple rearrangement of a formula.

Using $v = s/t$, t can be made the subject of the formula by multiplying both sides of the equation by t/v. Thus:

$v.t/v = s.t/vt$
$t = s/v$
or time = distance/speed

For example: How long will it take to travel 50 km at 25 km/h?

Time needed = s/v = (50 km)/(25 km/h) = 2 hr

The method for handling division by fraction is shown by the following scenario. For example: What is the speed of a car in km/h which travels 10 km in 5 minutes. Using $v = s/t$:

$t = (5/60)$ hr $= (1/12)$ hr

$v = 10$ km$/(1/12)$ hr

To divide by a fraction, multiply the top and bottom of the expression by the reciprocal of the fraction so that the denominator becomes equal to 1.

$v = 10 \times 12$ km$/(1/12)(12)$ hr $= 120$ km/h

PROBABILITY

▶ At its most basic, probability may be described as the study of chance and choice.
▶ Probability theory describes with mathematical rigour the chance of an action or happening having a particular outcome. It may not, even then, be possible to make the right choice, but at least a choice will have been made which can be justified.

SETS

▶ A set is a collection of objects or ideas, such as flock of geese, a collection of numbers, or the rules of chess.
▶ A set can be specified by stipulating some property for an object as a condition of membership of a set, or by listing the members of a set in any order. Conventionally, this is written within braces, i.e. curly sets of brackets { }.

In mathematics, capital letters are used to name sets. Thus a family may be designated F and its members may be Adam, Becky, Charlotte and Dave. In set notation, this may be abbreviated to F = {A, B, C, D}. A set may also be defined in terms of its properties. Thus, the set N = {2, 4, 6, 8} consists of all even numbers from 2 to 8.

Finite sets
These contain a definite number of members. For example, W = {1, 2, 3, 4} contains just four members.

Infinite sets
These contain an endless number of members as shown by the three dots. For example, X = {1, 2, 3, 4, . . .}.

Equivalent sets
These have the same number of members, so that they can be matched to each other. For example, B = {Alexander, Edward, Henry} and G = {Alexandra, Edwina, Henrietta}. This equivalence is shown as B↔G, which is read as 'set B is equivalent to set G'.

Overlapping sets
These have one or more members in common. For example, from the two sets M = {bat, fox, elephant, whale} and S = {octopus, herring, whale, coral}, the whale is common to both. We write: M ∩ S = {whale}, which is read as 'the intersection of sets M and S is whale or 'M intersect S equals whale'; only whale belongs to both set M and set S.

Union of sets (∪)
This includes all members of both sets without repeating any members. Thus, using the sets M and S above, M ∪ S = {bat, fox, elephant, whale, octopus, herring, coral}.

Universal sets (ξ)
These contain all members being considered in a particular circumstance. For example, if all integers up to 10 are being considered:
ξ = {1, 2, 3, 4, 5, 6, 7, 8, 9, 10}

Subsets
These are sets contained within other sets. Thus A = {1, 3, 5, 7, 9 } and B = {2, 4, 6, 8, 10 } are both subsets of ξ = {1, 2, 3, 4, 5, 6, 7, 8, 9, 10}. This is shown symbolically as A ⊂ ξ and B ⊂ ξ where ⊂ means 'is included in'.

Disjoint sets
These have no common members so that A and B above are disjoint.

Not all actions have completely predictable results. Often, there is only a limited range of possible outcomes, but it is impossible to know with certainty which of these to expect. By use of numbers the relative likelihood of two events, A and B, occurring can be compared.

When a coin is tossed, there is an equal chance that it will fall heads (*h*) or tails (*t*). The probability of the coin coming down heads is ½ (0.5) and the probability of the coin coming down tails is also ½. If two coins are tossed, they may fall *hh*, *ht*, *th* or *tt* with equal probability. Therefore, the probability of them both falling heads (*hh*) is ¼ (0.25). The probability of the coins falling with non-identical faces is 2/4 or ½ , that is 0.5, since there are two ways (*ht* and *th*) out of the four that this can happen.

When two dice are thrown, there are six ways in which each die can fall so that each number on the first can be paired with six numbers on the second die. There are thus 36 possible outcomes:

1,1; 1,2; 1,3; . . . 1,6

2,1; 2,2; 2,3; . . . 2,6

3,1; 3,2; 3,3; . . . 3,6

6,1; 6,2; 6,3; . . . 6,6

Thus the probability of two twos being thrown is 1/36. , but the probability of a two and a one being thrown is 2/36 = 1/18, since this combination occurs twice (as 1,2 and as 2,1).

COORDINATES AND GRAPHS

▶ A graph (short for graphic formula) is a diagram that shows the relationship between sets of numbers. It may be thought of as a picture that shows the values taken by a function.
▶ A function is a relationship between two quantities or 'variables', whereby the values of one (the dependent variable) are uniquely determined by values of the other (the independent variable).

On a graph, a function can be represented by a curve, or by a straight line, giving a picture of how a process changes and develops. Graphs have axes. An axis is a straight line of reference, and a typical graph will have two axes, the horizontal (*x*-axis) and vertical (*y*-axis). Real numbers can be represented geometrically by a line (axis) marked off from the origin (0), using some numerical scale.

Any point in a plane can be similarly represented by the pair of numbers that correspond to its respective distances from two such axes; these numbers are the coordinates of the point. A coordinate can be defined as any of two or more magnitudes used to define the position of a point on a graph. Coordinates are known as an ordered pair of numbers, as they are always given in the same form (*x*,*y*). The *x* value is always given first, followed by the *y* value. For example, the curve representing the function $y = x^2$ is the set of the pairs (*x*,*y*) of real numbers for which *y* is the square of *x*; thus, for example, (2,4), (–1,1), (–2,4), (√2,2) are all in the graph of the function.

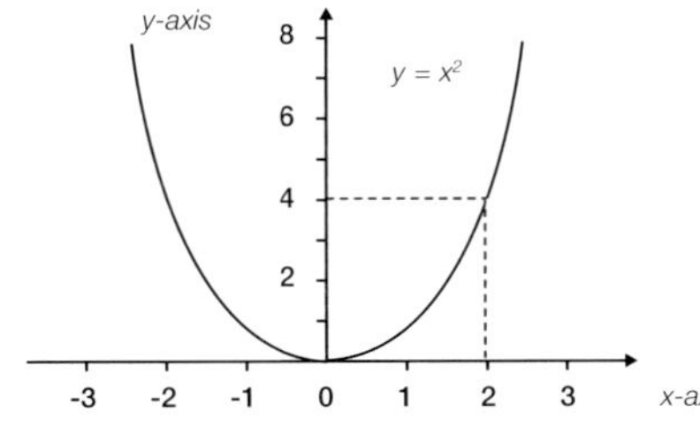

This system of coordinates is named after the French philosopher and mathematician René Descartes (or des Cartes, hence the adjective Cartesian to refer to this system of coordinates).

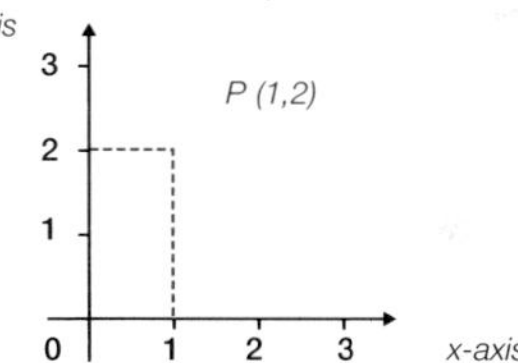

The origin of a graph is the point at which the axes cross. The origin has often, but by no means always, the coordinates (0,0). The gradient is the rate of ascent or descent of a line on a graph. Gradients may be either positive or negative, depending on which direction the line slopes. A positive gradient is a gradient in which the line slopes upwards from left to right; a negative gradient is one in which the line slopes downwards from left to right. The gradient of a straight line can be worked out by dividing the change in the vertical distance by the change in the distance to the right horizontally. The intercept is the point at which a line or curve intersects an axis. Thus the *x*-intercept is the coordinate at which a graphical function crosses the *x*-axis.

It is possible to combine the features of gradient and intercept in a straight-line equation. The generic straight-line equation can be expressed as:

$y = mx + c$

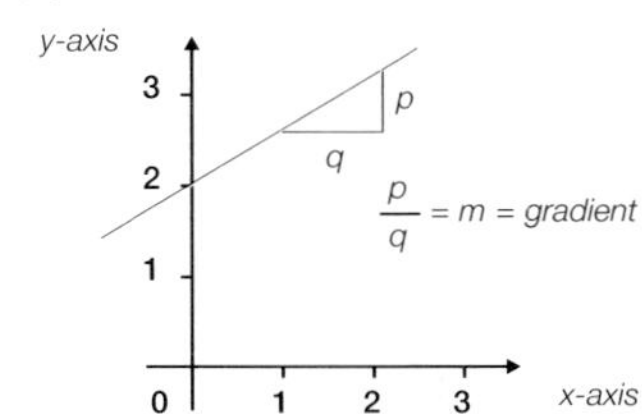

This equation represents a straight line on a graph, for which *m* is the value of the gradient and *c* is the *y*-intercept. For example, $y = 4x + 5$ represents a straight line of gradient 4, which passes through the *y*-axis through the point (0,5).

GEOMETRY

▶ Geometry is the branch of mathematics which deals with properties of lines, points, surfaces and solids.
▶ The rules of geometry – which have been discovered and not invented – are used to derive angles, areas and distances which may not otherwise be measured directly.

PLANE GEOMETRY

The simplest branch of geometry considers problems in two dimensions, that is with figures on a plane or flat surface. In geometry, a point has a position in space, but no size. A line has length but no width. In this sense, geometry deals with abstract ideas which can only be approximated in practice.

If two lines in a plane never meet no matter how long the lines are made, then it can be said that the lines are parallel. Otherwise they will intersect at an angle.

POLYGONS

Polygons are closed plane figures with three or more straight sides. The sum of the interior angles of a polygon with *n* sides is 90° x (2*n* – 4) divided by *n*. Any polygon with three sides is called a triangle, and any polygon with four sides is called a quadrilateral. Other polygons include: pentagon (5 sides), hexagon (6), heptagon (7), octagon (8), nonagon (9), decagon (10) and dodecagon (12).

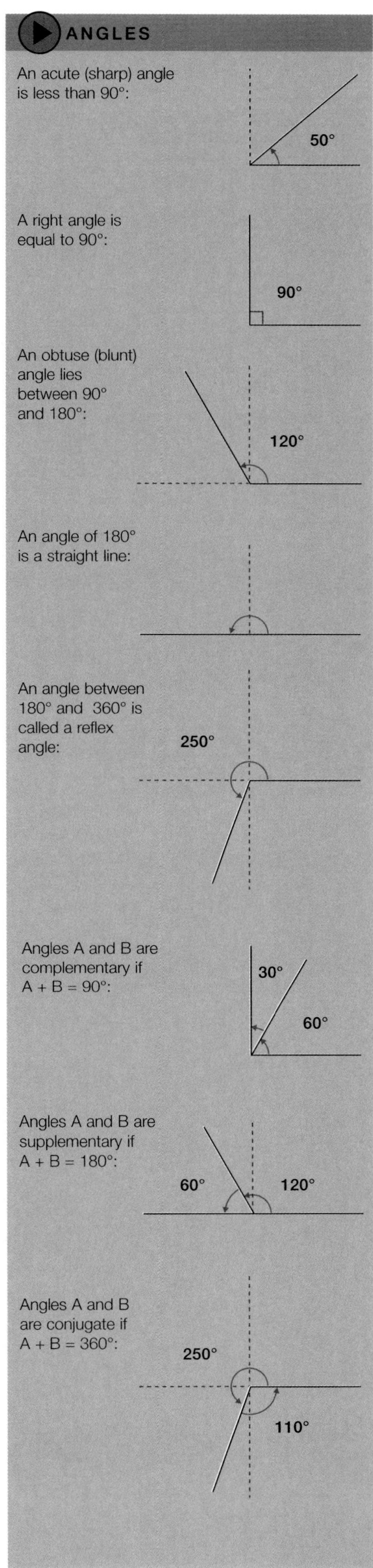

TRIANGLES

Three non-parallel lines in a plane will intersect with each other to form a triangle. The 'points' of a triangle are called the vertices (singular vertex). If the lengths of a triangle are *a*, *b* and *c*, various names can be given to the types of triangle which are possible. The angle opposite to side *a* is usually written *A*; angle *B* is opposite *b*, etc.

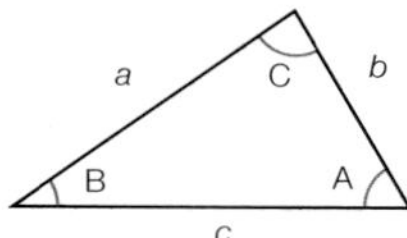

The sum of the internal angles of all triangles is 180°. This is readily shown by tearing the corners from a paper triangle and placing them together to form a straight line.

Scalene triangles have all three sides of different length, that is $a \neq b \neq c$, and $A \neq B \neq C$:

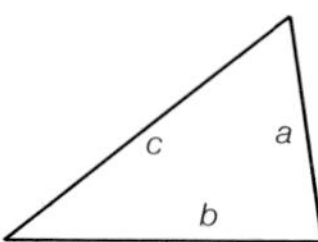

Equilateral triangles have all sides equal, that is $a = b = c$ and the internal angles are all 60°:

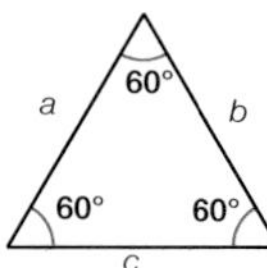

Isosceles triangles have two sides equal, that is $a = b$ and $A = B$:

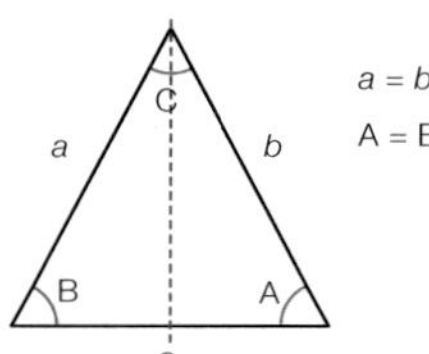

Right-angled triangles have one angle of 90°. If *a* is the longest side (the one opposite the right angle, also called the hypotenuse) then $a^2 = b^2 + c^2$, which is an expression of Pythagoras's theorem. This theorem can be stated as: the area of the square drawn on the hypotenuse of a right-angled triangle is equal to the sum of the squares drawn on the other two sides. Thus if the length of two of the sides of a right-angled triangle are known, the third may be calculated by using the theorem.

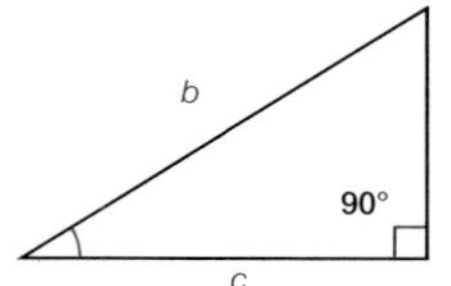

Similar triangles have the same three internal angles, but their corresponding sides are not the same length. If the sides of the two similar triangles are *a*, *b*, *c* and *a*', *b*', *c*', then $a = ra'$, $b = rb'$ and $c = rc'$, where *r* is the scale factor. (If, say, $r = 2$, then the sides of the second triangle are twice the length of the sides of the first triangle.)

Congruent triangles have corresponding sides and angles that are the same. Triangles can be shown to be congruent if $A = A'$ and $B = B'$ and $C = C'$; or if one side and two angles are the same; or if two sides and the enclosed angle are the same.

The area of a triangle is equal to half the base times the perpendicular height.

The word means literally triangle measurement. By measuring accessible angles and distances some inaccessible distances can be obtained, such as the heights of mountains or the distances to planets and nearby stars.

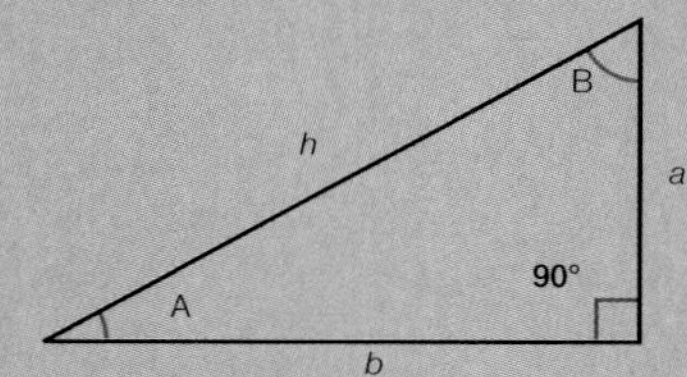

In the above right-angled triangle of sides *a*, *b*, *h*, where *h* is the hypotenuse, if angle *A* is opposite *a*, and angle *B* is opposite *b*, then the ratios of the various sides to each other are given names as follows:

$a/b = \tan A$ which is read 'tangent of *A*'
$a/h = \sin A$ which is read 'sine of *A*'
$b/h = \cos A$ which is read 'cosine of *A*'

QUADRILATERALS

A quadrilateral has four sides and may be a rectangle, a square, a parallelogram, a rhombus, a trapezium or none of these.

A rectangle is a quadrilateral in which all the angles are right angles, thus the opposite sides are parallel in pairs.

A square is a certain type of rectangle whose sides are equal. It has four lines of symmetry – both diagonals and the two lines joining the middle points of pairs of opposite sides. A rectangle that is not a square has two lines of symmetry.

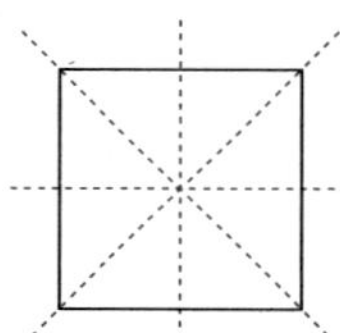

A parallelogram is a quadrilateral whose opposite sides are equal in length and parallel. It has no lines of symmetry, unless it is also a rectangle, but it does have rotational symmetry about its centre, the point where the diagonals meet. If one angle of a parallelogram is a right angle, then all the angles are right angles, and it is a rectangle. Any parallelogram can be dissected into a rectangle by cutting a right-angled triangle off one end, and sliding it to the opposite end. The dissection changes neither the area of the parallelogram nor the length of the sides – the area of any parallelogram is equal to the area of a rectangle with the same base and the same length:

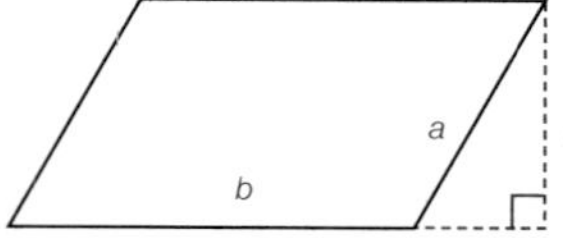

A rhombus is a parallelogram whose sides are all equal in length. Its diagonals are both lines of symmetry, and therefore bisect each other at right angles:

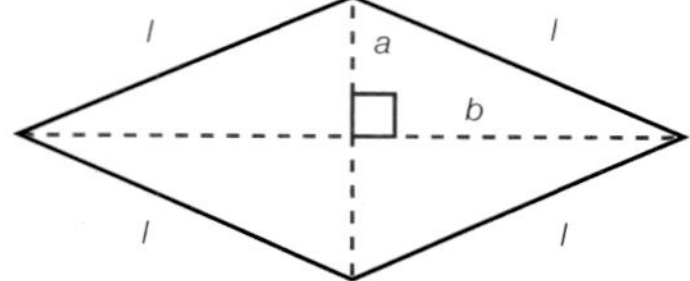

A trapezium (also known as a trapezoid in North America) is a quadrilateral with two parallel sides of unequal length. (In North America, a trapezium is a quadrilateral with no parallel sides.) To find the area of a trapezium, three measurements have to be taken – the height between the pair of parallel sides and the lengths of both of the parallel sides. The area of a trapezium is equal to the height multiplied by the average length of the parallel sides: that is, ½ (the sum of the parallel sides) × the perpendicular distance between them.

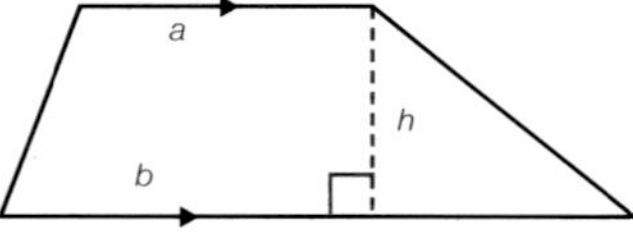

CIRCLES AND OTHER CONIC SECTIONS

A circle is the path of a point that moves at a constant distance, the radius, from a fixed point (the centre of a circle). The circle is a special case of an ellipse (see below). The perimeter of a circle is called its circumference. If the radius of the circle is *r*, then the circumference of the circle is $2\pi r$, where π is the irrational number equivalent to 3.141592654 (to 10 decimal places). A line from one point on the circumference to another is called a chord. If a chord passes through the centre of the circle, then it is known as the diameter, which is twice the length of the radius. An arc is any part of the circumference. A segment is the area bounded by an arc and a chord. A sector is the area bounded by two radii and an arc

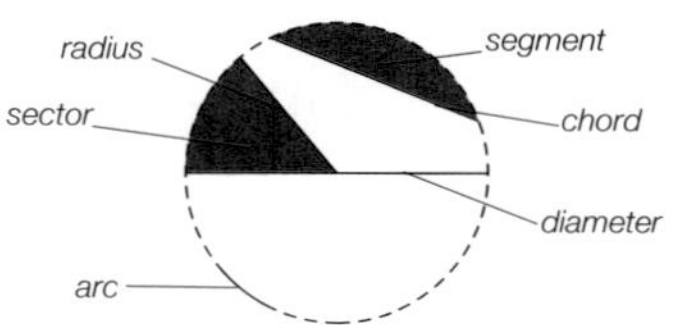

The area of a circle of radius *r* is πr^2. The general equation of a circle, the centre of which is at $-g$, $-f$, is: $x^2 + y^2 + 2gx + 2fy + c = 0$. The basic equation of a circle with the centre at the origin is $x^2 + y^2 = r^2$.

An ellipse is a closed conic section with the appearance of a flattened circle. It is formed by an inclined plane that does not intersect at the base of the cone. An ellipse can also be thought of as a circle that has been stretched in one direction. The orbital path of each of the planets round the Sun is approximately an ellipse.

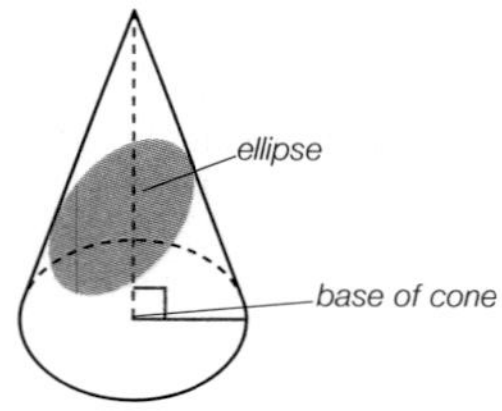

There are many ways to draw an ellipse. One of the simplest is to stretch a loop of thread round two pins, and hold it taut with a pencil. The path of the pencil will form an ellipse. The area of an ellipse = πab.

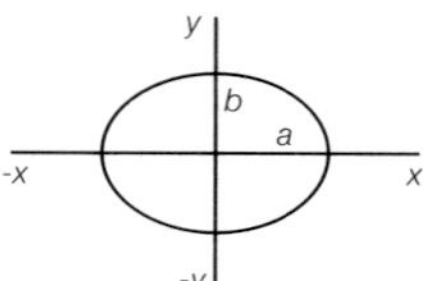

The basic equation of an ellipse with the centre at the origin is:

$$\left(\frac{x_2}{a_2} + \frac{y_2}{b_2}\right) = 1$$

PYTHAGORAS'S THEOREM IS THE MOST PROVED OF ALL, WITH OVER 370 DIFFERENT PROOFS

A parabola is a conic section that is formed by the intersection of a cone by a plane parallel to its sides. If a ball is thrown up in the air then the path of the ball will be approximately a parabola, with its axis vertical:

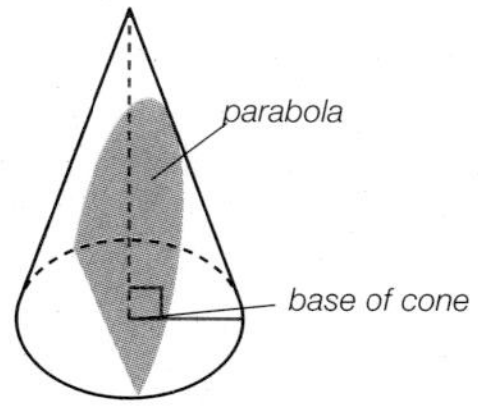

The basic equation for a parabola which is symmetrical about the *x*-axis with the focus at a,0 is $y^2 = 4ax$:

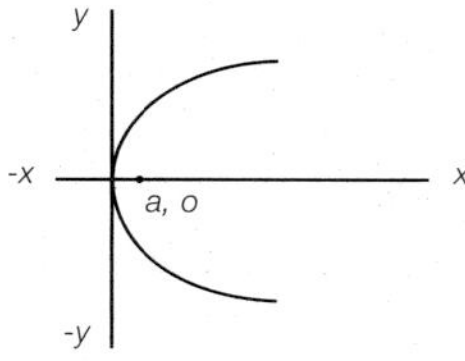

A hyperbola is a conic section that is formed by a plane that cuts a cone making a larger angle with the base than the angle made by the side of the cone. The basic equation of a hyperbola with the centre at the origin is:

$$\left(\frac{x^2}{a^2} - \frac{y^2}{b^2}\right) = 1$$

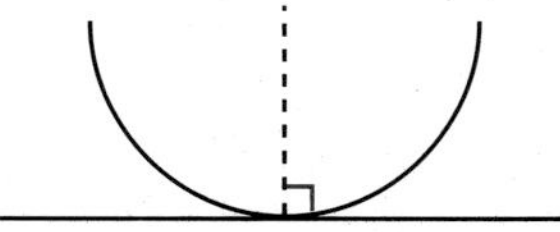

A tangent is a line touching, but not intersecting, a curve or surface at one point only. A tangent to a circle is always at right angles to the radius at point of contact:

SOLID GEOMETRY

Solids are three-dimensional figures – they have length, breadth and depth. Solids include rectangular blocks, prisms, pyramids, tetrahedrons, cylinders, cones and spheres.

A rectangular block, also called a cuboid, is a solid figure, all the faces of which are rectangles. The surface area of a cuboid of length *l*, breadth *b* and height *h* is $2(lb + bh + hl)$, and the volume is lbh. A cuboid of which all the faces are squares (that is, $l = b = h$) is more commonly known as a cube.

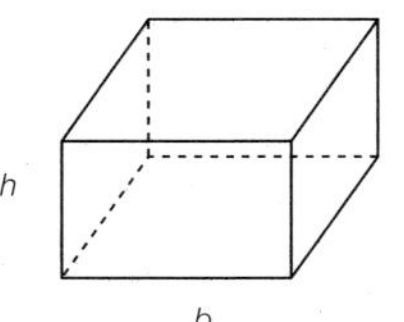

A prism is defined as a solid body whose ends are identical polygons and whose sides are parallelograms, which may be rectangles. Thus, a cube is the most symmetrical of possible prisms; if the length of its side is *a*, then its volume is a^3.

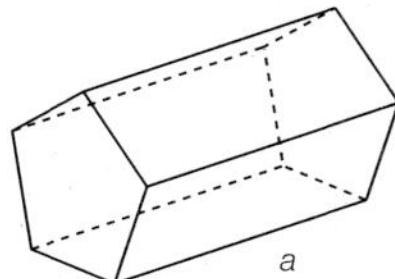

In general, the volume of a prism equals the area of either of the ends, multiplied by the perpendicular distance between the ends.

A pyramid is mathematically a solid figure whose base is a polygon and whose special vertex (the apex) is joined to each vertex of the base. Thus all its faces, except the base, are triangles. The volume of a pyramid is given by ⅓ of the area of the base × the perpendicular height. Any pyramid can be fitted inside a prism so that the base of the pyramid is one end of the prism, and the apex of the pyramid is on the other end of the prism.

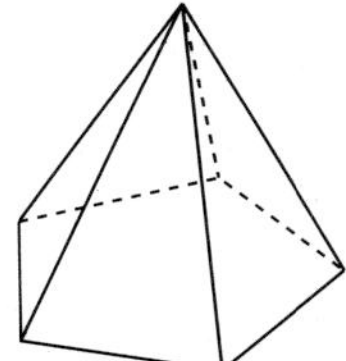

A tetrahedron is a pyramid whose base is a triangle. The regular tetrahedron has four faces which are equilateral triangles, and thus any of the faces may be considered as the base. The volume of a tetrahedron is ¹/₃ the area of the triangular base × the height (see box right).

A cylinder is a solid figure with straight sides and a circular section. The area of the curved surface of a cylinder is $2\pi rh$. If the circles at both ends are included, then the total surface area is $2\pi rh + 2\pi r^2$. The volume of a cylinder can be found by considering it as a special case of a prism. The volume equals the area of the base multiplied by the height. The volume of a cylinder = $\pi r^2 h$.

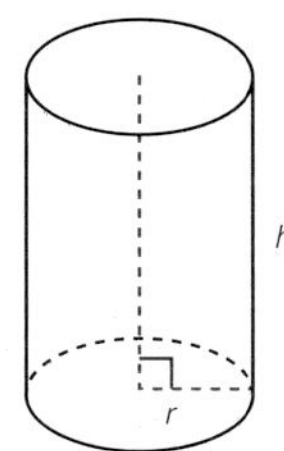

A cone is a solid figure with a circular plane base, narrowing to a point or apex. If the slant height of the cone is *l*, the area of the curved surface of the cone = πrl. The volume of the cone can be found by considering it as a special case of a pyramid. The volume is one-third the volume of a cylinder with the same base and height, that is $1/3\ \pi r^2 h$.

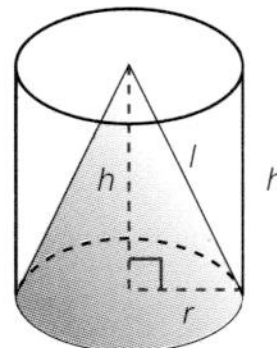

A sphere is a solid figure, every point of whose surface is equidistant from its centre. The surface area of a sphere of radius *r* is $4\pi r^2$, and its volume is $4/3\ \pi r^3$.

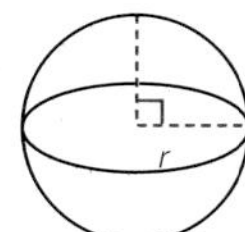

POLYHEDRA

A polyhedron is a solid shape bounded by plane faces. The cube and the regular tetrahedron are examples of regular polyhedra (or Platonic solids), which have identical faces. The regular versions of the octahedron, dodecahedron and icosahedron are the only other regular polyhedrons.

There are many more irregular polyhedra. The simplest to visualize have faces that are mixtures of two kinds of regular polygons. For example, the faces of the cuboctahedron are equilateral triangles and squares.

The tetrahedron has four faces, all of which are equilateral triangles, with four vertices and six edges.

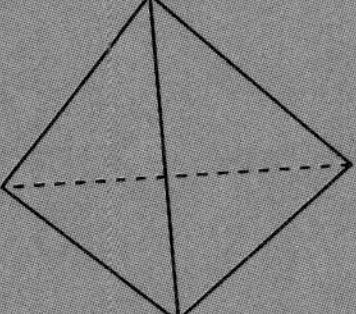

A cube has six faces, all of which are squares, with eight vertices and 12 edges:

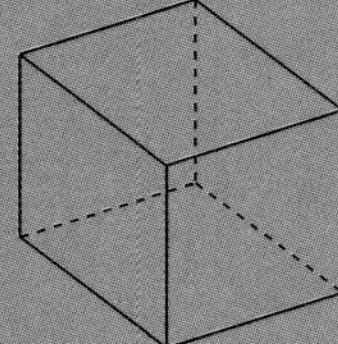

An octahedron has eight faces, all of which are equilateral triangles, with six vertices and 12 edges:

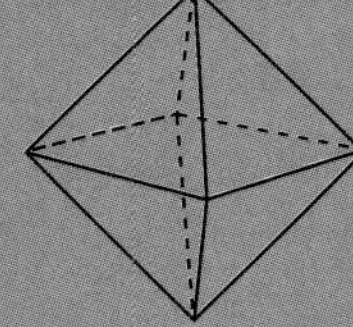

A dodecahedron has 12 faces, all of which are regular pentagons, with 20 vertices and 30 edges:

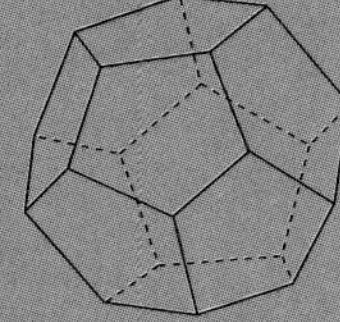

An icosahedron has 20 faces, all of which are equilateral triangles, with 12 vertices and 30 edges:

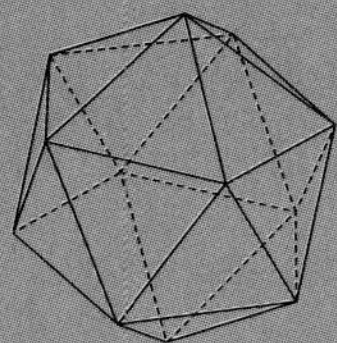

The mathematician Leonhard Euler (see p. 142) made an interesting discovery about the relationship between the number of faces (*F*), vertices (*V*) and edges (*E*) of polyhedra: $F + V - E = 2$. This equation is true for all polyhedra. The same relationship is true for an area divided into any number of regions (*R*) by boundaries or arcs (*A*) that join at nodes (*N*). Thus, $R + N - A = 2$.

MATHEMATICIANS

▶ **Archimedes, the mathematician who cried 'Eureka', was so engrossed in a mathematical problem that he failed to rise to the challenge of a Roman soldier, who killed him.**

▶ **Fermat's last theorum, one of mathematics' great unsolved mysteries, was finally proved in 1995 by an English mathematician, Andrew Wiles.**

▶ **Fibonacci introduced Arabic numerals to Europe and earned the title *Stupor Mundi* (wonder of the world).**

Apollonius (3rd century BC), Greek mathematician remembered for his treatise on conic sections describing geometrical concepts of the cone.

Archimedes (*c.* 287–212 BC), Greek mathematician and philosopher. His extensions of the work of Euclid concerned the surface and volume of the sphere and the study of other solid shapes. His methods anticipated the fundamentals of integral calculus. He gave the first systematic account of determining centres of gravity.

Argand, Jean Robert (1768–1822), Swiss mathematician who revived a geometrical method of representing complex numbers.

Aristotle (see p.120)

Avicenna (Abu-Ali al-Husayn ibn-Sina; 980–1037), Uzbek-born Persian philosopher. A pioneer physician, he compiled an encyclopaedia covering mathematics, medicine and the natural sciences.

Bernoulli, Daniel (see p.120)

Bernoulli, Jakob (1654–1705), Swiss mathematician who laid down the foundations of calculus of variations.

Bessel, Friedrich Wilhelm (1784–1846), German astronomer and mathematician whose solutions of certain differential equations are now known as Bessel Functions.

Boole, George (see p. 182)

Bose, Salyendranath (see p.120)

Cantor, George (1845–1918), Russian-born mathematician whose most important work was on finite and infinite sets, founding set theory.

Cardano, Geronimo (1501–76), Italian physician and mathematician whose *Ars Magna* played a major role in the foundation of modern algebra.

Cartan, Elie (1869–1951), French mathematician who contributed to the development of differential geometry and differential calculus.

Cauchy, Baron Augustin-Louis (1789–1857), French mathematician and physicist who developed the modern treatment of calculus and also the theory of functions.

Conway, John Horton (1938–), English mathematician who is famous for his serious studies of mathematical recreations.

d'Alembert, Jean Le Rond (see p.120)

Desargues, Girard (1591–1661), French engineer, architect and geometrician who invented modern projective geometry.

Descartes, René (1596–1650), French philosopher, mathematician and military scientist who created analytical geometry.

Diophantus of Alexandria (3rd century AD), Greek mathematician and pioneer in algebra.

Euclid (*c.* 3rd century BC), Greek mathematician who devised the first axiomatic treatment of geometry, studied irrational numbers and wrote the great book *The Elements*.

Eudoxus (408–347 BC), Greek mathematician who is known for his theory of proportion.

Euler, Leonhard (1707–83), Swiss-born mathematician who made particular contributions to analytical geometry, trigonometry and calculus, and was responsible for much of modern mathematical notation.

Fermat, Pierre de (1601–65), French lawyer and mathematician who contributed to developments in analytic geometry, calculus and probability theory. A founder of the modern theory of numbers, he is most famous for his last theorem, which he claimed to have solved, without recording his proof.

Fibonacci, Leonardo (also known as Leonardo Pisano) (*c.* 1170–1230), Italian mathematician who popularized the Hindu system of counting in Europe.

Fourier, Jean-Baptiste (1768–1830), French mathematician and physicist who showed how the conduction of heat in solid bodies could be analyzed in terms of the infinite mathematical series now known as Fourier Series.

Frege, Gottlob (1848–1925), German philosopher who gave a formal definition of a cardinal number.

Galileo, Galilei (see p.121)

Gauss, Friedrich Carl (1777–1855), German mathematician who developed the theory of complex numbers.

Gödel, Kurt (1906–78), Austrian-born US mathematician who stunned the world of mathematics in the 1930s by showing that Hilbert's dream of a general method of proving any mathematical theorem could not be realized.

Grassman, Hermann (1809–77), German mathematician who discovered the calculus of extension, which may be regarded as an 'algebra' of geometry.

Hero of Alexandria (7th century AD), Greek mathematician known for his formula for the area of a triangle and his method of finding a square root.

Hilbert, David (1862–1943), German mathematician who, in 1901, listed 23 major unsolved maths problems – many of which still remain unsolved.

Hipparchus (2nd century BC), Greek astronomer who was a pioneer in trigonometry.

al Khwarizmi (Muhammad ibn Musa al Khwarizmi; *c.* 825), Arabian mathematician whose book on algebra (from the word *al-jabr*) was influential in Europe when translated into Latin in the 12th century.

Klein, Felix (1849–1925), German mathematician who introduced a programme for the classification of geometry in terms of group theory.

Lagrange, Count Joseph Louis (see p.122)

Lambert, Johann Heinrich (1728–77), German mathematician who was the first to show that pi (π) is not a rational number.

Laplace, Marquis Pierre-Simon de (1749–1827), French mathematician, astronomer, physicist and politician who established probability theory on a rigorous basis.

Leibniz, Gottfried Wilhelm (1646–1716), German mathematician, philosopher, logician, linguist, lawyer and diplomat who invented calculus independently of Newton. Leibniz's notation was, however, superior. He was the first, in 1671, to build a calculating machine that could multiply.

Levi-Civita, Tullio (1873–1941), Italian mathematician who, with Ricci, developed absolute differential calculus.

Mandelbrot, Benoit (1924–), Polish-Lithuanian-born US mathematician who is best known for the Mandelbrot set, which is constructed from simple mapping by marking dots on a complex plane.

Maupertius, Pierre-Louis de (1698–1759), French mathematician and astronomer who formulated the principle of least action.

Minkowski, Hermann (1864–1909), Lithuanian-born German mathematician who contributed to geometry and to the theories of numbers and of relativity.

Monge, Gaspard (1746–1818), French mathematician who invented descriptive geometry.

Napier, John (see p.182)

Newton, Sir Isaac (see p. 122)

Noether, (Amalie) Emmy (1882–1935), German mathematician, described as the 'most creative abstract algebraist of modern times'. Initially, she had difficulty obtaining a lectureship because she was a woman.

Pappus of Alexandria (4th century AD), Greek mathematician whose *Synagoge* is a systematic study of ancient Greek mathematics. He is best known as a geometer.

Pascal, Blaise (see p. 123)

Peano, Giuseppe (1858–1932), Italian mathematician who is best known for his work on the mathematical development of logic.

Pearson, Karl (1857–1936), English biometrician who introduced many concepts to mathematics, including standard deviation and chi-square.

Poincaré, Henri (1854–1912), French mathematician, philosopher and astronomer – a major influence in cosmology, relativity and topology.

Pythagoras (*c.* 582–500 BC), Greek philosopher and mathematician best known for Pythagoras' theorem – there is no evidence that he was the originator of it.

Ramanujan, Srinivasa Aaiyangar (1887–1920), Indian mathematician who, without prior knowledge, managed to re-derive over 100 years of Western mathematics in isolation. He had an astonishing intuition for correct results, although many were not proved until after his death.

Regiomontanus (Johann Müller; 1436–76), German mathematician who was the leading practitioner of trigonometry in medieval Europe.

Ricci-Curbastro, Gregorio (1853–1925), Italian mathematician, played a leading role in the discovery of the absolute differential calculus.

Seki, Kowa (1642–1708), Japanese mathematician who invented a form of calculus, and used determinants before Liebniz.

Stevin, Simon (1548–1620), Flemish mathematician, helped establish the use of decimal fractions.

Sylvester, James Joseph (1814–97), English mathematician who developed the theory of algebraic invariants.

Weierstrass, Karl (1815–97), German mathematician who was a pioneer in the modern theory of functions.

Whitehead, Alfred (1861–1947), English mathematician who collaborated with Russell on *Principia Mathematica* (1910–14).

Wiener, Norbert (1894–1964), US mathematician who founded the science of cybernetics.

■ RAMANUJAN SAID THAT A HINDU GODDESS INSPIRED HIM WITH HIS FORMULAE IN DREAMS ■

TECHNOLOGY ▷

'Any sufficiently advanced technology is indistinguishable from magic'
– Arthur C. Clarke

HYDROELECTRIC POWER

To generate hydroelectricity, a reliable supply of water is needed, a substantial drop in height, and a turbine. This sounds simple but it usually requires a large dam and robust engineering.

The dam holds back the water, creating a reservoir that can be called upon whenever power is needed. At the top of the dam are channels, called penstocks, that can be opened to let the water flow through.

The water falls down the penstocks and, near the bottom of the dam, passes through turbines, making them spin. At the other end of the turbines, away from the water, are generators. When the wire coils of the generators spin inside magnetic fields, an electric current is created and fed into the national energy network.

Once the water has passed through the turbines, it escapes from the dam down the tailrace. As the dam is usually built across the course of a river, the water flows away along the river bed.

The dam can be the easiest element of a hydroelectric scheme to build. Tunnelling can be the costliest. The Majes dam project in Peru involves 98 km of tunnels for hydroelectric and water-supply purposes.

An exception to the common plan of hydroelectric schemes is the pumped storage system. It comes into its own when the national energy network is generating too much electricity. Coal, gas, oil and nuclear power stations cannot be adjusted constantly to match supply with demand. Therefore, some of the surplus electricity is diverted and used to power the turbines in reverse and pump water from a reservoir at the bottom, up the penstocks to the top of the system.

When the demand for electricity surges, it is allowed to fall through the turbines again, generating enough power within seconds to meet the network's demands. Electricity producers often have to activate them during the TV adverts of popular television programmes – when millions of electric kettles are switched on.

NUCLEAR POWER

Extracting useful amounts of electricity from atomic particles is a process that needs four steps to change energy from one form to another.

The process starts with a rare variety, or isotope, of the element uranium. Uranium 235 is used because it can be mined from the ground and its atoms can be 'split' more easily than most elements. The splitting, or fission, is the first energy change.

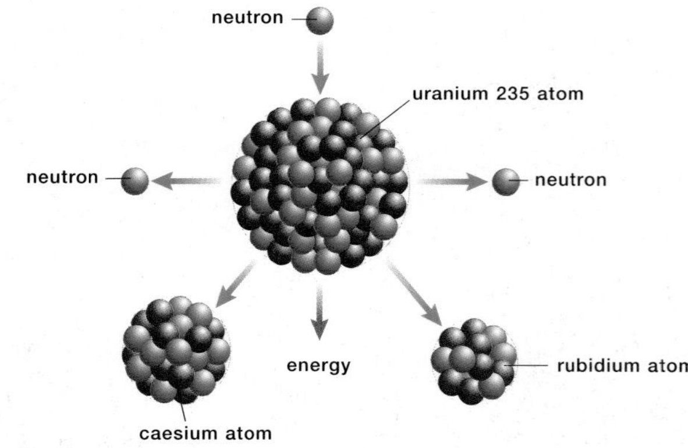

Fission happens when a slow-moving atomic particle, called a neutron, crashes into a nucleus of uranium 235. The nucleus becomes unstable and two more neutrons break free. The uranium divides into smaller nuclei of two different elements – caesium and rubidium. At the same time a lot of energy is released. The two free neutrons collide with other uranium 235 nuclei and the fission is repeated, again and again, in a nuclear reaction.

In the 55 years since the first nuclear reaction, engineers have invented better methods of control. When a power station is built, engineers improve the chances of the neutron collisions by using enriched uranium 235, and they slow the neutrons down by surrounding the isotope with water or graphite. To control the rate of the reaction, minute by minute rods of boron or cadmium are lowered into the core. They absorb neutrons.

The energy that is released by fission is heat. This is carried away from the core by pressurized water in a closed circuit of pipes. In turn, the pipes pass through a tank of water which absorbs the heat and boils.

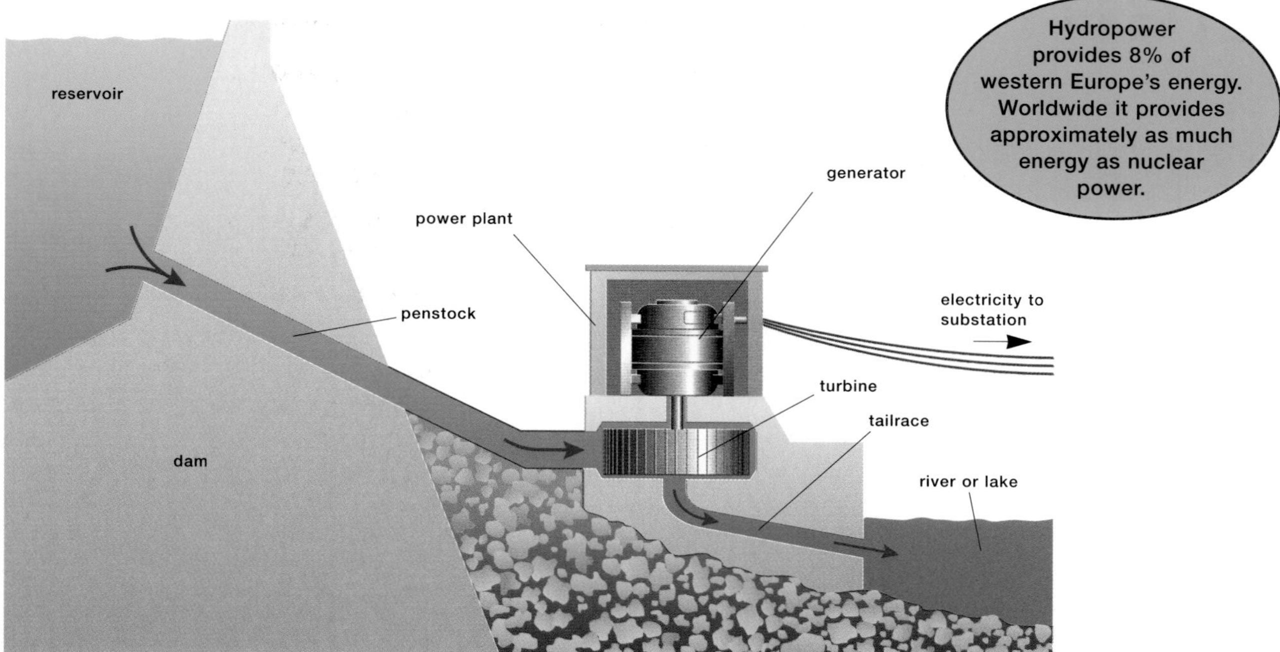

Hydropower provides 8% of western Europe's energy. Worldwide it provides approximately as much energy as nuclear power.

The success of hydroelectric schemes depends a lot on local geography and economics. It can be cheapest to build a dam at the head of a deep narrow river valley, near an industrialized centre of population that needs the electricity. Norway, Brazil and The Congo (ex-Zaïre) generate virtually all of their electricity using hydro plants. Britain, which has few deep river valleys or major rivers, only generates 2% of its electricity from water.

New large-scale hydroelectric plants are becoming less popular because of general concerns that people have about the impact they have on the environment.

The steam from the boiling water makes a turbine spin. The heat has now been converted into motion.

The turbine spins a coil of wire inside a magnet and this generates an electric current. This is the fourth and final change in energy. The electricity is fed into the national energy supply network. Meanwhile, the steam comes into contact with pipes containing cold water drawn from a river or the sea. The steam condenses and is ready to be converted back to steam once more.

The major drawback of nuclear fission is that it irradiates material which is toxic to living cells. Therefore, the nuclear reactor has to be totally isolated from the environment and all its waste material must be sealed and kept secure.

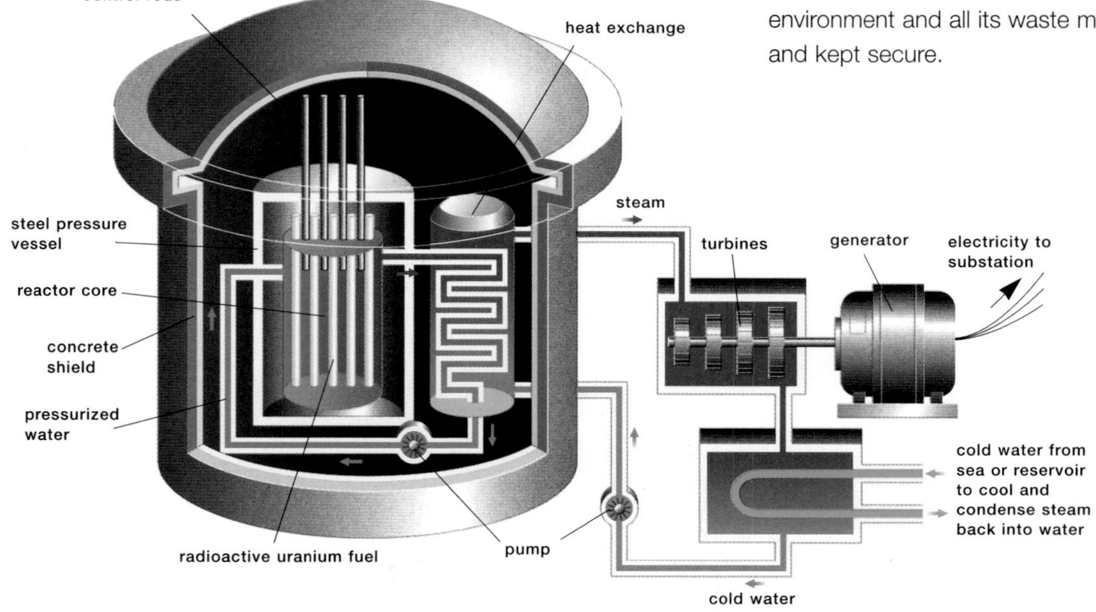

The largest nuclear power station is the six-reactor Zaporizhzhya power station in the Ukraine which has a gross output of 6000 MW.

LIGHT BULB

The light bulb is the most familiar, useful and widespread electrical invention on Earth.

This everyday brainwave is based on the simple fact that very thin wires get hot when an electric current is passed through them, and some even glow. The trick is to find the best material that will glow the brightest, for longest. Today, the metal tungsten is used in nearly all bulbs – it does not melt until it reaches 3382°C and as it approaches this temperature little of the metal evaporates.

However, the tungsten filament is only half the story. The light bulb pioneers at the turn of the century, Sir Joseph Wilson Swan in England and Thomas Alva Edison in America, first had to work out how to make something glow enough to give off light but not get so hot that it disintegrated.

A bulb has been manufactured that will work for one million hours – more than 100 years – but it hardly glows at all and gives off no useful amount of light.

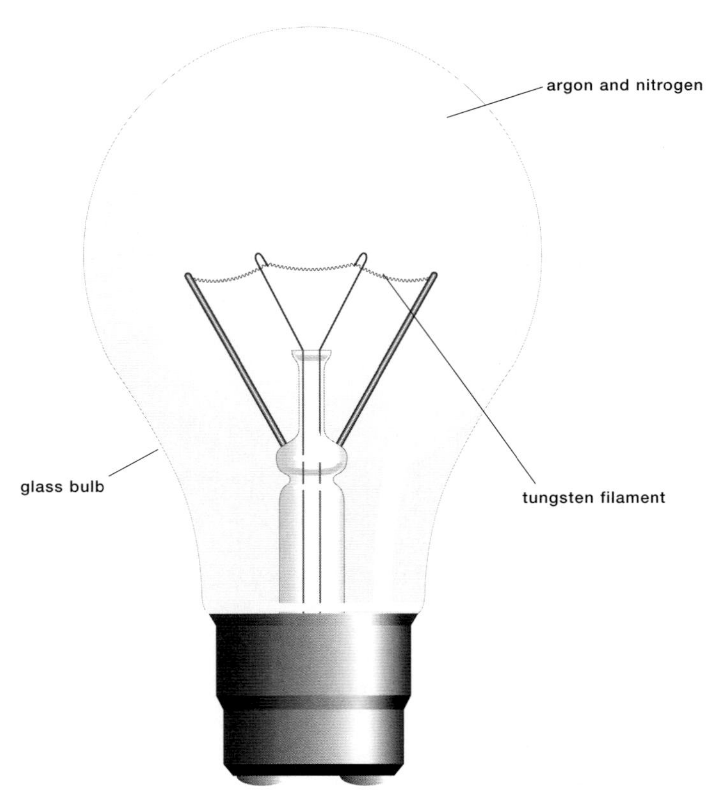

FLUORESCENT TUBE

The strip lights that illuminate supermarkets, airports, offices, schools and homes barely get warm at all. This is because they are extremely efficient at converting electricity into light. The energy is not wasted as heat.

The glass tube contains mercury vapour and a small quantity of argon gas. At both ends of the tube are metal electrodes. These have been specially coated so that when an electric current is applied to them they give off electrons very easily.

Some fluorescent lights flicker when first switched on. This is because the mercury in the tube has to become electrically charged, or ionized. This is achieved by a small starter device at each end of the tube which blasts out electrons at up to four times the usual voltage through the gas. As soon as the mercury vapour becomes ionized by this jolt the starter device automatically shuts down and the light operates normally. It might take two or three jolts to get things started, although the small amount of argon gas speeds up the process.

As soon as the vapour is ionized, electrons crash into the mercury atoms which then emit ultraviolet light that is invisible to the human eye. If the tube was made of plain glass it would not cast any useful light at all. Therefore, it is coated on the inside, usually with zinc silicate or magnesium tungstate.

These chemicals come into their own when ultraviolet light shines on them. They are fluorescent and they glow, converting ultraviolet light into white light. So it is the coating of the fluorescent tube that gives the shadow-free, diffused illumination.

A fluorescent tube can run for 20,000 hours before the electrodes fail.

The QL Induction Lamp is guaranteed to work continuously for five years. It uses electromagnetic radiation to excite a phosphorous coating into emitting light.

The solution was to put the filament in a glass bulb, pump out as much of the air as possible so that there is nearly a complete vacuum inside, then seal the end. With almost no air around it the hot filament cannot burn and break up. To allow the filament to glow even hotter, and so give off even whiter, brighter light, the bulb today is filled with special gases, such as argon and nitrogen, which slow down the evaporation of the tungsten.

Since the basic bulb was first used commercially in 1880 to light up the steamship *Columbia*, the design has been improved. The inside of the bulb is frosted with acid to diffuse the light and stop it glaring. The filament is twisted into coils to give off even brighter light. Today's white and coloured bulbs are lined with a ceramic coating.

However, a light bulb is not very efficient. Only about 5% of the electrical energy that goes into it is converted into visible light. A little is turned into ultraviolet light but most is turned into heat. In fact, the temperature of the glass of a standard 100 W ceiling bulb is about 230°C.

Table lamp bulbs are a lot cooler at about 108°C because the heat is carried away more quickly.

An average 100 W bulb will give light for approximately 1000 hours. By then so much of the filament has evaporated that it gets too thin and snaps.

Long-life light bulbs for home use have no filament. They are compact fluorescent tubes with a special phosphor coating so that the light they emit closely matches that produced by ordinary filament lamps. They will give light for approximately 10,000 hours.

When the world's largest lighting manufacturer, Philips, celebrated its centenary in 1991 it calculated that it had made enough fluorescent tubes to stretch to the Moon and back seven times.

Britain uses the longest fluorescent tubes in the world, 2.44 m (8 ft) long. The rest of the world makes do with tubes 1.82 m (6 ft) long.

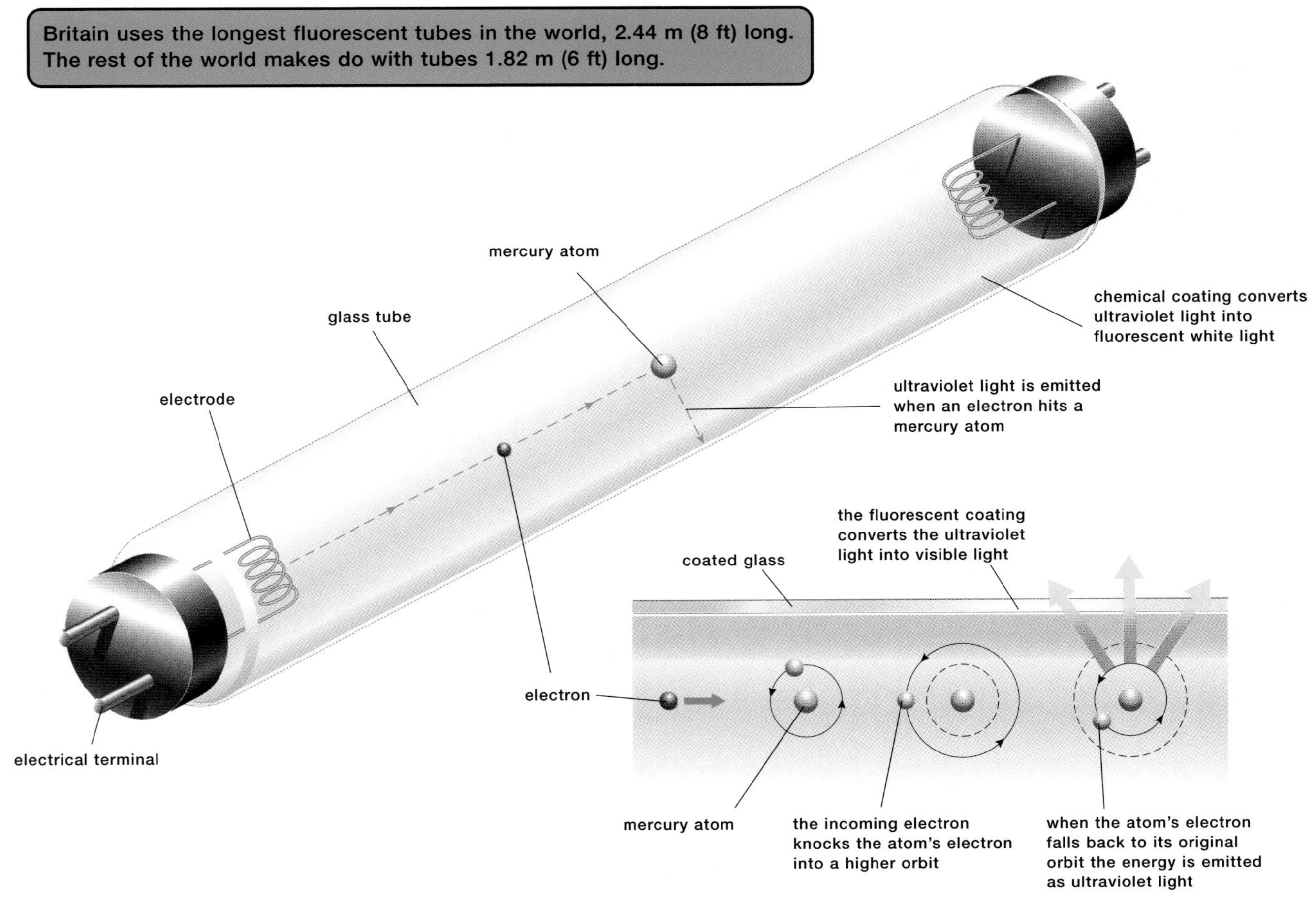

TELEVISION

Television has changed the way people see the world. It entertains and informs in a way that no other communication system has ever done before. Sound and moving vision are broadcast around the globe in a fraction of a second.

This is made possible by the use of cheap, reliable receivers – TV sets. In many homes they are the most complex electrical devices – some contain more digital circuitry and software than spacecraft did 20 years ago.

The television receives electromagnetic waves collected by the aerial from broadcast transmissions. The waves contain several signals all of which the television has to filter, amplify, separate, interpret and act upon.

The signals carry information about the programme being broadcast – the moving colours, their brightness and the sound. There are also signals that keep all the information co-ordinated and synchronized so that, for example, people's voices are heard as their lips move. When the signals have been cleaned up, boosted and divided they pass to the heart of the television – the cathode ray tube.

Despite research costing millions of pounds, televisions still rely on the bulky cathode ray tube, the first of which was invented by William Crookes in England in 1878. He was investigating the properties of invisible beams emitted from a negatively charged terminal (or cathode). He placed the cathode in a glass tube, pumped out most of the air so it would not absorb the beam, applied a high voltage and saw that one end of the tube glowed.

What he was observing was a beam of electrons striking the glass. The modern TV set works in the same way, except that the electron beams are precisely controlled by the television signals to create an illusion of coloured moving images on the glass.

First the beam sweeps from side to side, laying down 625 horizontal lines of electrons across the inside of the screen. The cathode itself does not move but the beam is deflected rapidly by electromagnetic coils. A series of positively charged terminals (anodes) accelerate and focus the beam on its short journey to the screen.

The inside surface of the screen is covered with phosphor which glows when hit by electrons. In fact, it is a mosaic of a million phosphor dots arranged in threes – one red, one green and one blue. The beam moves extremely quickly, refreshing the screen 25 times every second. It traces every other line, then it returns to fill in the blanks. This is called 'interlacing' and makes movement on the screen appear smoother.

This process is so rapid that it appears to create a constantly moving image. We are also fooled into seeing it as full colour when, in fact, our brain is unable to detect that just the three colours are used – red, blue and green.

Colour televisions have three electron beams, one for each primary colour. A system of filters, mirrors and masks ensures that the beam carrying the red signal illuminates only red phosphorescent dots, and likewise for green and blue. All the other hues are created by varying the intensity of the beams as they hit adjacent dots. Yellow, for example, is created by combining equal amounts of red and green, and black by momentarily switching the beams off.

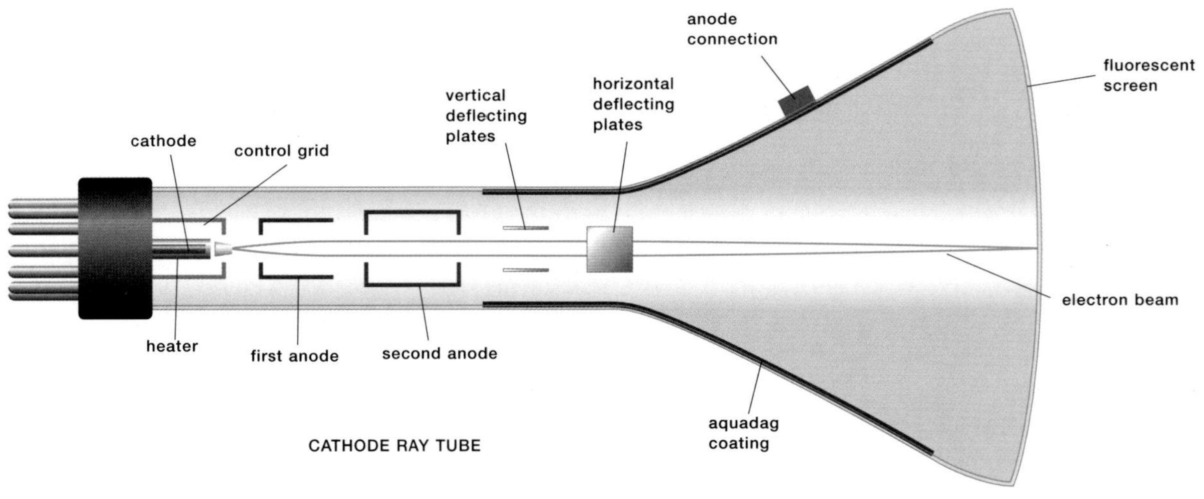

CATHODE RAY TUBE

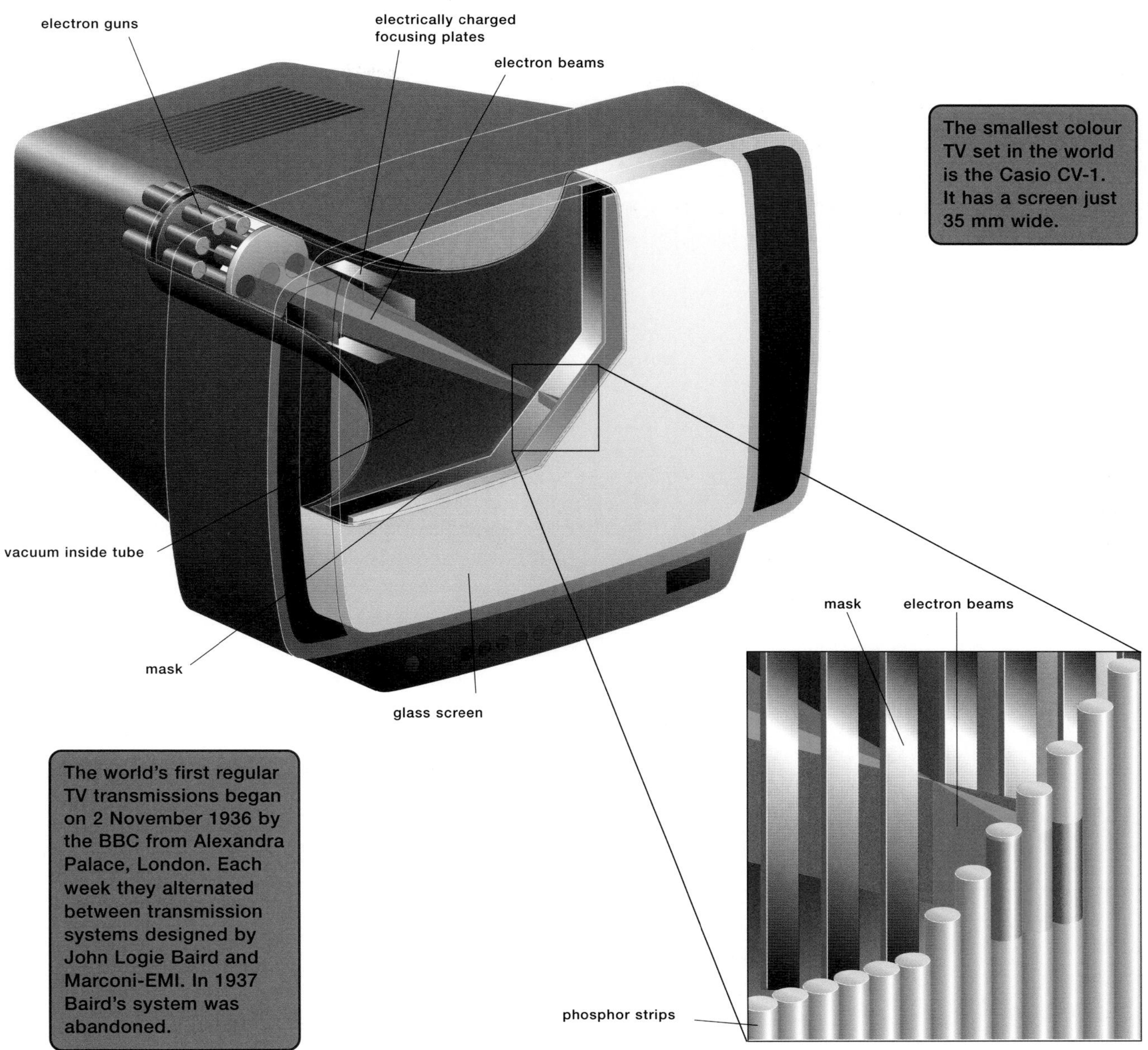

The smallest colour TV set in the world is the Casio CV-1. It has a screen just 35 mm wide.

The world's first regular TV transmissions began on 2 November 1936 by the BBC from Alexandra Palace, London. Each week they alternated between transmission systems designed by John Logie Baird and Marconi-EMI. In 1937 Baird's system was abandoned.

The Sony Jumbo Tron colour TV screen at the Tsukuba International Exposition in 1985 is the world's largest, measuring 24.3 x 45.7 m.

TELETEXT

The world's first teletext system was introduced in Britain in 1973. It works on the principle that not all of the 625 lines show up on the set – some are above or below the screen. So the signals that would usually carry information for the part of the picture that won't be seen are used instead to carry teletext data. There is not room for much data in these signals so teletext pages look relatively crude, carrying only 24 lines with just 40 characters on each. The teletext signal is separated inside the set and translated by a decoder. When teletext is required, the decoded signals then instruct the electron guns.

DIGITAL TV

With conventional television the signals that are transmitted to sets vary continuously. In the forthcoming digital broadcasts the signals will consist of a stream of discrete packets, each with a value. The receiver will collect these packets in sequence and feed them to software that will control the electron beams. Digital transmission is a more precise way of delivering broadcasts which improves the quality of both pictures and sound. The techniques of data compression also mean that the transmitted signals are not as bulky, so that more than one channel will be broadcast along the same frequency.

VIDEO RECORDER

Videotape recorders have revolutionized the television and film industry. The first commercial machine was launched in 1956, and from the late 1970s models were available for home use. Programmes can now be recorded for future viewing or commercial films can be rented or bought.

The video cassette contains a plastic tape coated with iron oxide particles. These can be magnetized when they come into contact with an electromagnetic recording head. The strength of the magnetic field created by the head changes according to the strength of the signal transmitted by the broadcaster. As the tape moves past the recording head the tape stores the fluctuations in the signal. When it is played back, the magnetized particles move past another head, inducing an electrical current identical to the one created by the original broadcast signal.

The fastest production of a pre-recorded video cassette was by Thames Video Collection on 23 July 1986 of Prince Andrew's wedding to Sarah Ferguson. The tape was on sale 5 hr 41 min after the couple left for their honeymoon.

All of this is very similar to the way an audio tape recorder works – with one vital difference. A television signal carries up to 300 times as much information as an audio signal and the video tape must somehow store it all without becoming too long. Two different solutions are implemented to avoid this.

The first is to mount the heads on a cylinder that revolves 30 times a second. There are at least two recording heads on the cylinder so the signal is captured 60 times a second. The second is to tilt the cylinder so that, as the tape moves past horizontally, a diagonal track is recorded on it by the first head. Just as the first head comes to the end of its diagonal sweep at the edge of the tape, the second head starts recording next to and below the first track. By laying thin diagonal stripes across almost the entire width of the tape a reasonable amount of vision data can be stored. The sound signal from the transmission is stored horizontally at one edge of the tape by another head not attached to the cylinder.

MICROWAVE OVEN

Microwaves are electromagnetic radiation with wavelengths that lie between the infrared range and that used for broadcasting ultra-high frequency television signals. The wavelengths are from 1 mm to 30 cm.

As they fall between light and ordinary radio waves, they share some of the characteristics of both. Like light they travel in straight lines and can be blocked by solid objects. They can also be focused, beamed and reflected. Microwaves made their first major impact on the modern world when it was discovered that they were ideal for radar.

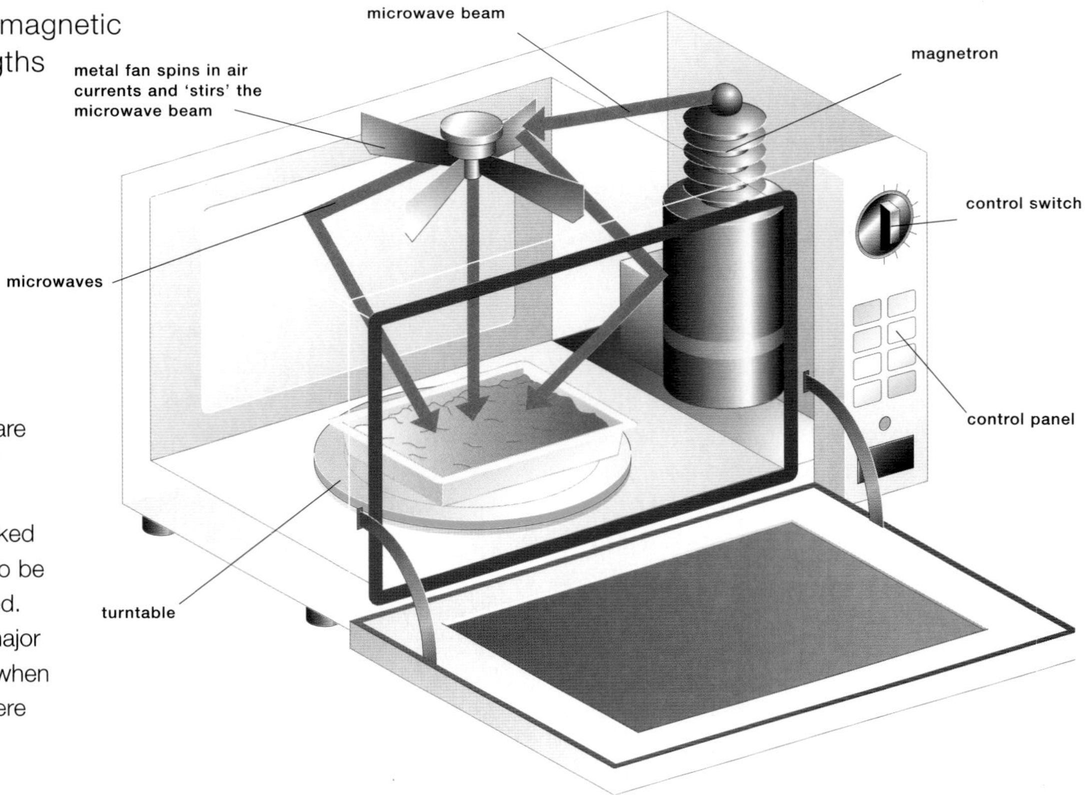

Hollywood now makes more money out of video cassette sales than from cinema tickets.

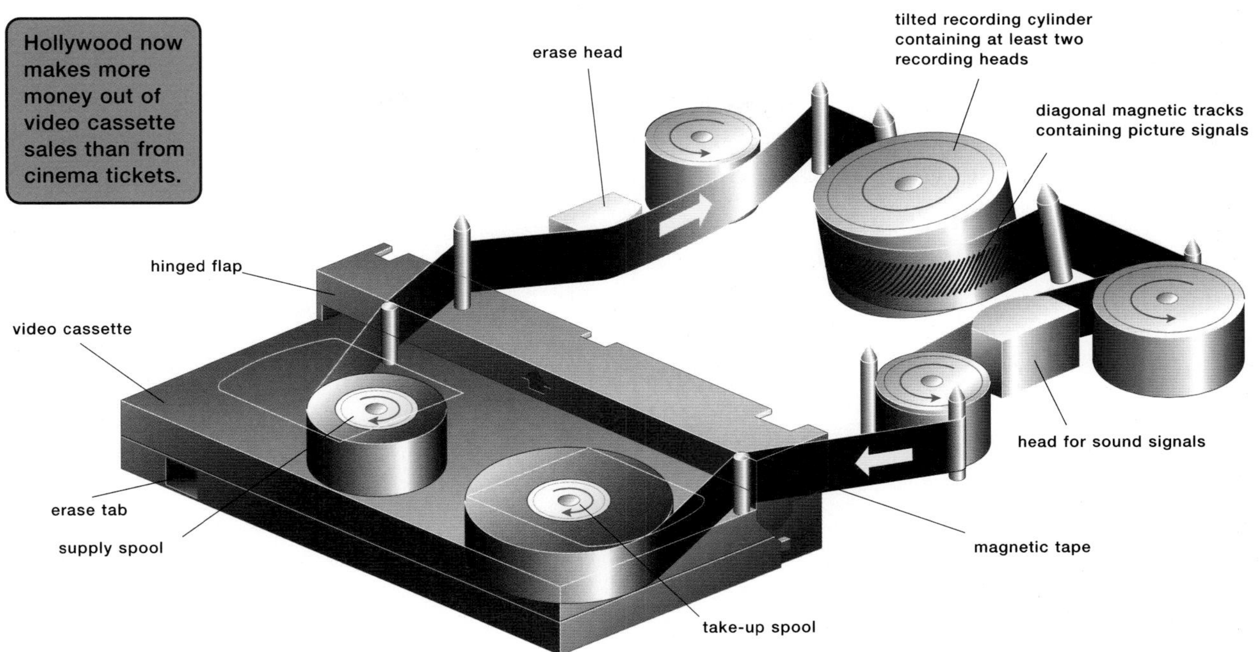

When a video cassette is placed in the recorder it triggers a mechanical sequence. The hinged flap on the cassette is lifted, two capstans draw out a length of tape and wrap it around the cylinder, ready for recording or playback.

When new recordings are being made there is an erase head within the machine that wipes the tape clean just before it reaches the cylinder – but this only operates if the plastic tab on the cassette is intact.

In fact, the origin of the microwave oven owes its existence to radar. A physicist named Percy Le Baron Spencer was working at the American radar manufacturer Raytheon in the early 1940s. Allegedly, he left his sandwiches beside the radar equipment, only to find they became warm. Then he put some maize in a paper bag next to the radar device and it exploded into popcorn. He then went on to melt chocolate.

Raytheon patented a refined system in 1945 and made the first cooker, the 'Radarange' for hospital and military kitchens. It wasn't until 1967 that it made the first domestic microwave ovens.

The microwaves, pulsing 2450 million times a second, can penetrate food and the electromagnetic energy excites some of the molecules, particularly water, fats and sugars. They vibrate and heat up. Conventional ovens have to heat the air surrounding the food but microwaves do not heat the air at all. By heating just the food, the cooking time is reduced dramatically.

The microwaves used in ovens oscillate between one and 30 billion times a second.

Percy Spencer, a physics engineer, invented microwave ovens and patented his idea in 1953. His first experiment involved cooking a bag of popcorn.

The microwaves are made by a vacuum-tube generator called a magnetron. They have to be 'stirred' by a fan, or the food has to be placed on a rotating platform, so that all of the dish heats through equally. Even so, a dish that contains layers with different moisture contents may cook unevenly. The waves can penetrate glass, paper and polyethylene plastics, but are blocked by metal.

Microwaves can damage human tissue so there is a fail-safe device on the door locks of ovens to switch off the magnetron when the door is opened. However, some engineers have explored the possibilities of heating rooms using microwaves. They experimented on themselves and found they were warmed by low energy microwaves. The furniture and the air, however, remained cold.

TELEPHONE

Capturing speech and sending it halfway round the world in a fraction of a second is a modern wonder. The telephone is the beginning and end of a worldwide communications network. It has four basic parts – a microphone, an earpiece, a dial and a ringer.

When the handset is picked up a switch is connected and the telephone exchange immediately sends a specific current to the phone that triggers a dial tone in the earpiece. This is turned off as soon as the exchange detects the first digit of a number has been dialled.

The exchange recognizes the tones created by the phone pad. When the last digit has been dialled, the local exchange determines whether it is a local call or needs to be routed to other exchanges.

The telephone lines can be made of copper or optical fibres (see below). Microwaves are also used to carry telephone conversations between the phone companies' transmitters on the land and radio waves bounce them between satellites that are in stationary orbit.

Eventually, the exchange nearest the person being called is alerted and it sends a specific current to their phone to make it ring. When they pick up the phone their local telephone exchange stops the ringing current.

The world's largest telephone ever made was 2.47 m high. The 7.14 m long handset had to be lifted by crane.

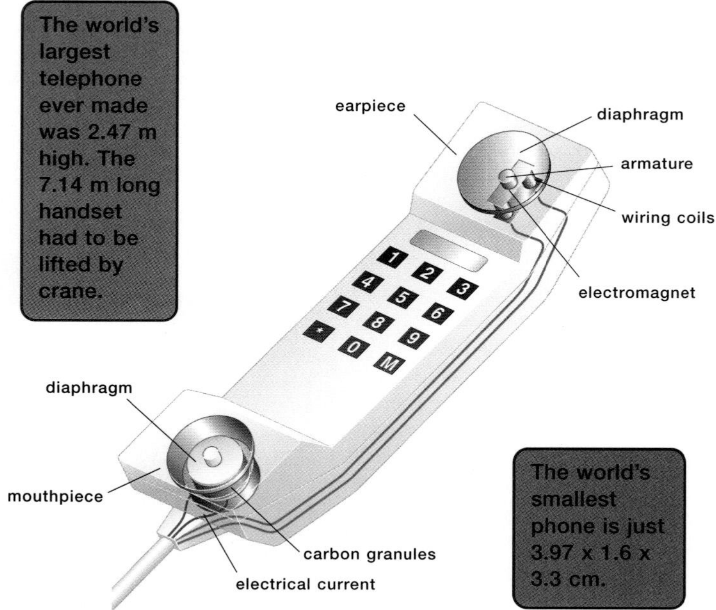

The world's smallest phone is just 3.97 x 1.6 x 3.3 cm.

For many years the microphone in the handset converted speech into fluctuating electric currents by using a thin diaphragm on top of carbon granules which are trapped between electrodes. Sound makes the diaphragm vibrate, squeezing the granules and altering their resistance to current flowing between the electrodes. In today's more compact, lighter phones the carbon granules have been replaced by an electrode. It vibrates in an electric field, again making the current vary.

FIBRE OPTIC CABLE

Optical fibres are sometimes called 'light pipes' because that is how they behave – any light that enters one end is trapped in the pipe until it falls out of the other end. However, there is no hole down the middle. An optical fibre is a thin strand of transparent material (glass or plastic), coated with a thin sheath of a different transparent material. It is usually less than one millimetre in diameter and can be as fine as 0.0004 mm. The glass or plastic is so pure that light is not impeded by it – but the boundary between the core and the sheath, from the light's point of view, is like the wall of a pipe.

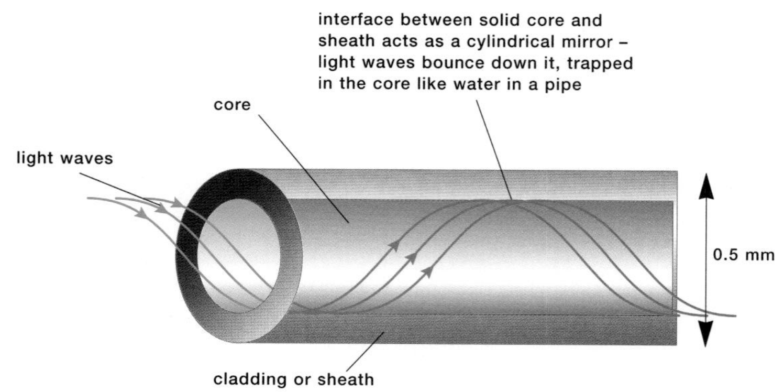

The longest underwater optical fibre telephone cable runs for 43,450 km, from Japan to Britain. It links 11 countries and can carry 600,000 simultaneous calls.

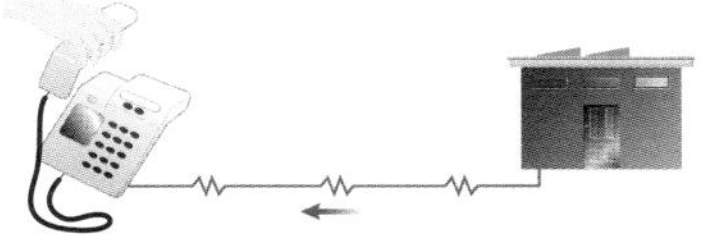

pick up receiver, switch is closed inside receiver, exchange sends dial tone to earpiece

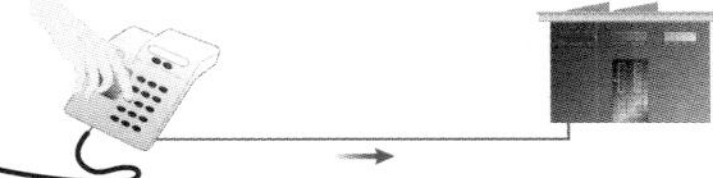

dialling first digit stops dial tone, exchange waits until it receives final digit before choosing how to route the call

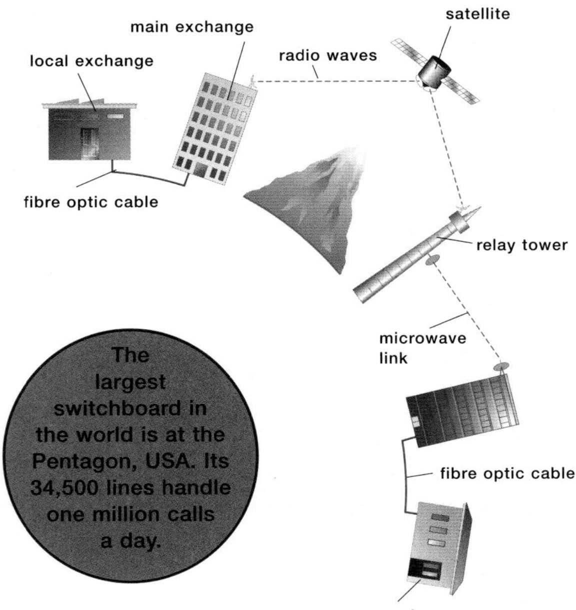

It is this changing pattern of current that is sent down the line electronically, being amplified and cleaned up as it travels to the other end. It enters the receiver's earpiece, which contains a magnet wound by wire. The varying current goes through the wire, making the magnetic field vary which, in turn, makes a small piece of iron move. The iron is attached to an aluminium diaphragm which then vibrates according to the current fluctuations, recreating the words spoken into the microphone by the caller.

The largest switchboard in the world is at the Pentagon, USA. Its 34,500 lines handle one million calls a day.

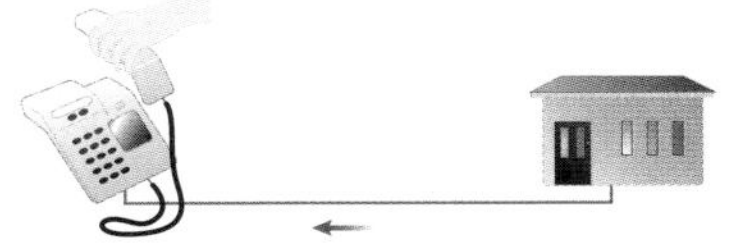

when recipient picks up handset ringing current is switched off and connection is made

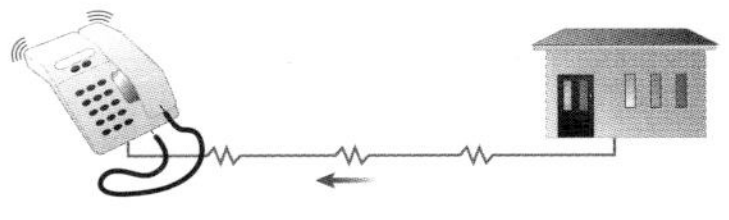

remote exchange sends current to recipient's phone to make it ring

The light waves continually bounce off this wall as they progress down the fibre. The surface where the core and sheath meet acts like a cylindrical mirror for the length of the fibre, reflecting light repeatedly. The phenomenon is called total internal reflection and it works as long as the sheath material has a lower refractive index than the core.

The principle was first demonstrated in 1870 by a Victorian physicist, John Tyndall. He had no strand of glass but did show that light was conducted along the curved path of a stream of water. Alexander Graham Bell, inventor of the telephone, patented a device to carry voices on light waves but never tried to combine his technology with Tyndall's.

It was not until the 1950s that physicists made coated fibres with glass that was pure enough to reduce light losses to practical levels. They knew how useful it would be to conduct light waves along curving paths. Light is electromagnetic radiation and, if it is made to fluctuate, the changes in its signal can be used to convey information, just like electricity.

However, light travels much faster than electricity and is far less susceptible to interference from other electromagnetic sources. Light waves have a very high frequency so they can carry much more information. The signals can travel up to 100 km (62 mi) before they need to be boosted by repeater stations. Traditional electrical signals have to be boosted every 1.5 km (0.9 mi).

In the last 20 years optical fibres have been carrying telephone and television signals. The signals are made by shining solid state laser diodes into the ends of the fibre, varying their intensity according to the information they are carrying.

The most expensive carpet tile in the world was made by artist Alan Titterington for the 50th birthday celebrations of HM Sultan Qaboos bin Said of Oman. The 1 m^2 rug contained 10,000 individual optical fibres.

PERSONAL COMPUTER

The personal computer carries out a wide variety of tasks and is composed of four basic parts: an input device, a central processing unit, memory and an output device. The input device is usually a keyboard and a mouse, but joysticks, lightpens, optical scanners, touch-screens and even microphones are also used.

Through the input device, instructions can be given to the machine. Data that is already stored internally or accessible from memory devices such as floppy disks, hard disks or CD-ROMs can be manipulated. New software or data can also be added.

These instructions are passed to the heart of the machine, the central processing unit, sometimes known as the 'chip'. The computer uses binary digital technology – all its messages are transferred, stored and manipulated as strings of electronic pulses representing zeros and ones (see pp. 136–37). The central processing unit retrieves the relevant data and carries out the arithmetic and logic operations. It also synchronizes the traffic of digits so nothing is lost. All this is done by miniature electrical circuits etched on to a tiny sliver of silicon.

The solid, manufactured components of a computer are called hardware. The programmes of electronic instructions that run on the computer are called software.

An operating system, such as MS-DOS, Windows or Macintosh, is installed on to a computer in order to make it easy to use. The operating system is software which makes sure that all of the hardware and software work together and it is usually stored on a secure memory chip called ROM (read-only memory). RAM (random access memory) chips temporarily store elements of other software programmes and the data as they are being used. All data and the software can be stored to more permanent memories, such as the rapidly rotating 'hard disk', which stores the signals from the digital electronic pulses as magnetized particles.

When the central processing unit has completed the instructions from the input device it sends the results to the appropriate output device – usually the monitor, the speakers, the printer or the modem. It may also save the results to one of its memory devices.

The average memory of a home computer in the early 1980s was 64 K – it is now in the region of 32 MB – a 512-fold increase.

PHOTOCOPIER

Photocopiers use electrical charges to persuade millions of tiny ink particles, called toner powder, to stick to paper in the right patterns, thus creating the document copy.

When a printed sheet is illuminated, the white parts reflect light on to a metal drum that has previously been given a negative charge. As the light hits it the charge disappears. Positively charged ink particles are then brushed on to the drum and they stick to the parts where the negative charge has survived, creating on the drum a mirror image of the original. This powder pattern is then transferred on to a piece of paper the right way round. It is fixed in place with heat before emerging from the machine.

Photocopying was invented in 1903 by the American office clerk G.C. Beidler. He developed a machine and patented it in 1906.

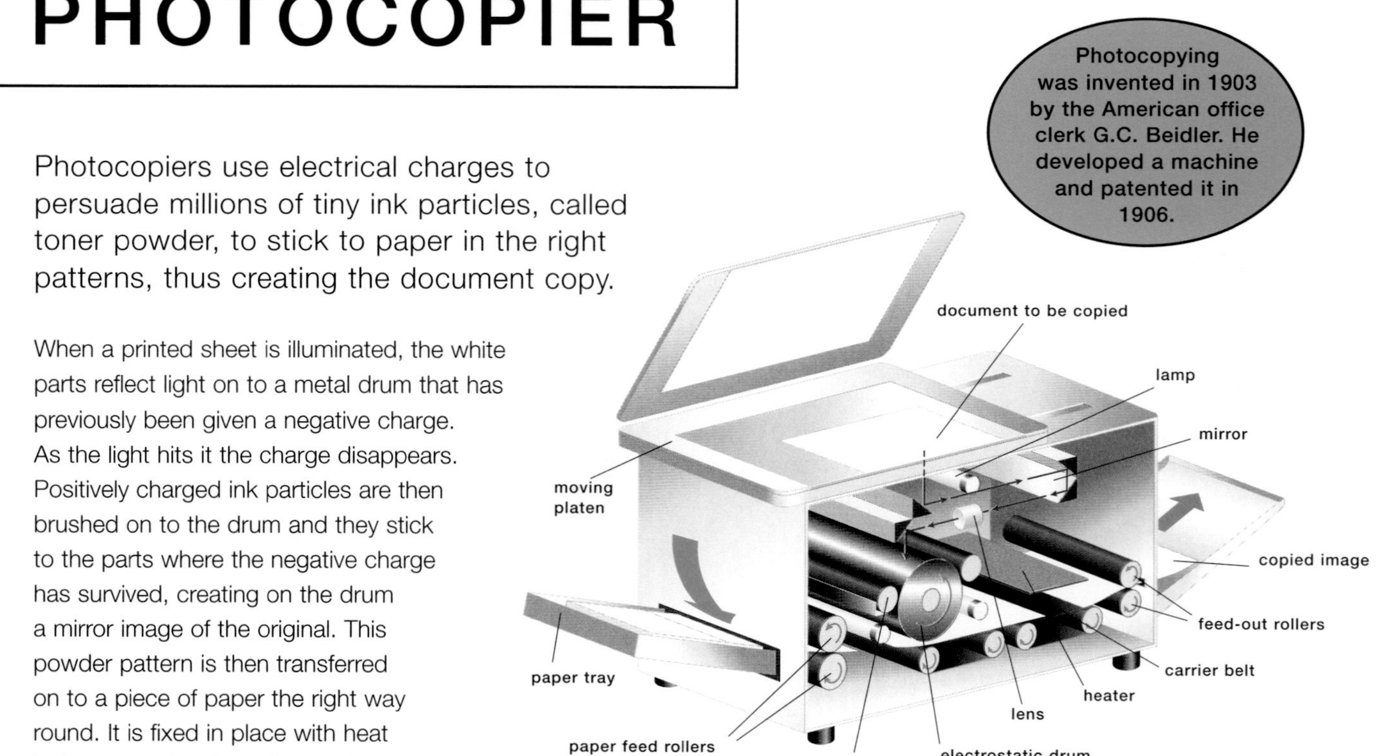

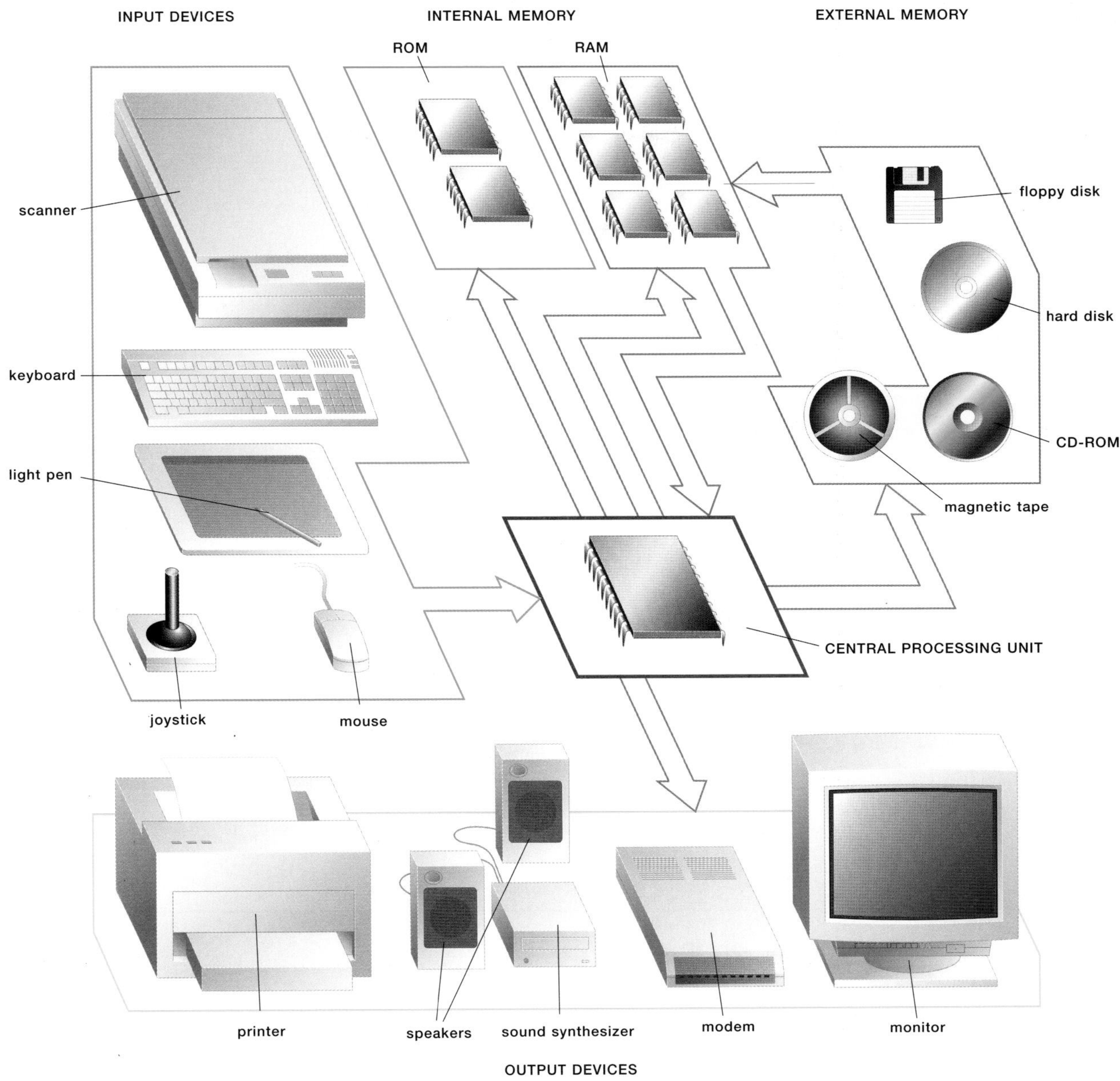

CD-ROM

The CD-ROM is a robust and convenient way to store large amounts of digital data. It contains up to 630 megabytes of information which is 400 times the capacity of a floppy disk.

Unlike a floppy disk, you cannot save data to a CD-ROM inside your computer. The initials stand for Compact Disc Read-Only Memory – once it has been manufactured the data cannot be overwritten or altered. It can only be read.

The CD-ROM is made in the same way as the audio CD. Electronic circuits digitize signals from sound and video sources. Those from computers are already digitized. A blank master disc is coated with light-sensitive material and spins at hundreds of revolutions a minute in front of a laser. When the electronic digital pulses are fed to the laser it switches on and off. When it is lit, the laser burns small pits in the surface of the disc. When it is unlit, ridges, known as 'lands', remain. The track of the laser spirals out from the centre of the disc. This process creates the master disc.

This master is used to stamp many copies of transparent plastic discs. A reflective aluminium layer is stuck to one side of the copy disc and sealed with more plastic. When the disc is put into the CD-ROM drive of a computer it is spun quickly and a low-intensity laser shines on to the spiral track. When the beam hits a land it is reflected back to a light sensor to generate a digital pulse. When the beam hits a pit the light is dispersed so that the sensor does not detect anything and no pulse is created.

LASERS

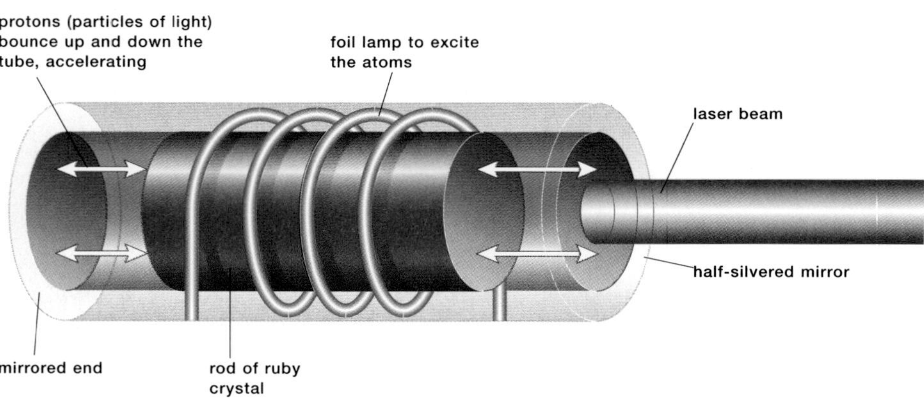

Laser light is light that has been very well organized. The beam from an ordinary torch can be compared to people streaming out of a stadium – moving at different speeds and in different directions. But with lasers, all the photons, or light particles, have the same wavelength. They march in step with each other and do not disperse.

The shortest pulses of light ever made lasted 11 femtoseconds. A femtosecond is a million billionth of one second. The laser pulse was made at Washington State University.

To make a laser, physicists use a tube of material whose atoms have electrons that can be easily excited, such as ruby crystal or neon-helium gas. Liquids and even semi-conducting materials are also used.

Pulses of energy excite the electrons into a higher energy orbit around their atoms. When they fall back into their normal, lower energy orbit, they shed their excess energy in the form of photons.

The photons meet more atoms and cause them to give off yet more photons which are identical. The energy is amplified as the photons bounce back and forth through the material, reflected by mirrors at the ends of the tube. Some of this light is allowed to escape through a half-silvered mirror at one end. This is the laser beam. Laser is an acronym for 'light amplification by stimulated emission of radiation'.

HOLOGRAMS

Credit cards, video cassettes and even bank notes carry holographic stickers as security devices. Capturing a three-dimensional image is simply a trick of the light.

Technically speaking, a hologram is not the eerie floating image seen trapped behind or in front of a glossy panel. A hologram is the film itself and it is composed of a record of all the information contained in the light which is reflected from an object.

A photograph records only the colour and intensity of the reflected lightwaves but a hologram also stores the shape of the reflected wave front. Imagine dropping a stone into the middle of a pond. A jetty is jutting out into the water. As the ripples radiate out from the stone, the leading edge of the first wave will reach the end of the jetty first. Other points of the same wave will lap up against the jetty's edge in succeeding moments.

This is what a hologram manages to capture. It records not only the colour and brightness but also the time it takes for light waves to envelop an object. This element of time is stored as an 'interference pattern' that can be rebuilt into an image of the object when the hologram is illuminated.

Making the hologram depends on having organized, laser light. The laser beam is split in two. Half illuminates an object and is then reflected on to the photographic plate. The other half travels directly to the plate, via a mirror, arriving at an acute angle and interfering with the light reflected by the object. To reconstruct the image of the object a similar light source illuminates the hologram.

In fact, two images are usually generated. One is on the same side of the hologram as the illuminating light and is called 'virtual'. It is impossible to photograph because the light producing the image does not pass through it. The other image is in front of the plate and is called 'real'.

The fact that a laser emits regular light with guaranteed attributes makes it very useful for scientists. It can be used almost like a ruler, to measure materials and substances that reflect, scatter or absorb it. Sensors collect the reflected light and, by comparing it with the original laser beam, some characteristics of the material can be deduced.

A laser beam is also very intense and powerful. It can be focused so that its energy heats metals to be welded or burns holes in diamonds. By using extremely quick bursts of laser light, surgeons can cut and cauterize human tissue without damaging surrounding tissues.

Scientists are trying to harness the power of laser light to create a new kind of power station, called nuclear fusion. Lasers will squeeze a fuel pellet so hard that its particles will fuse together and liberate huge amounts of energy.

Lasers can also be used to carry large amounts of digital information. In outer space the beam barely disperses so that it can easily relay data to a target receiver. A laser beam can do the same task through optical fibres.

The first working laser was invented less than 40 years ago, and yet its use is now widespread – for example, in scanning goods at supermarket check-outs.

The most powerful laser is the Petawatt at the Lawrence Livermore National Laboratory, California, USA. In one fleeting moment it can produce power 1300 times greater than the combined output of all the electrical generating plants in the USA.

A 20-second black-and-white holographic movie has been made in Japan, but it is not a practical system. Even when the special film is cooled to –261.15°C it decays within hours.

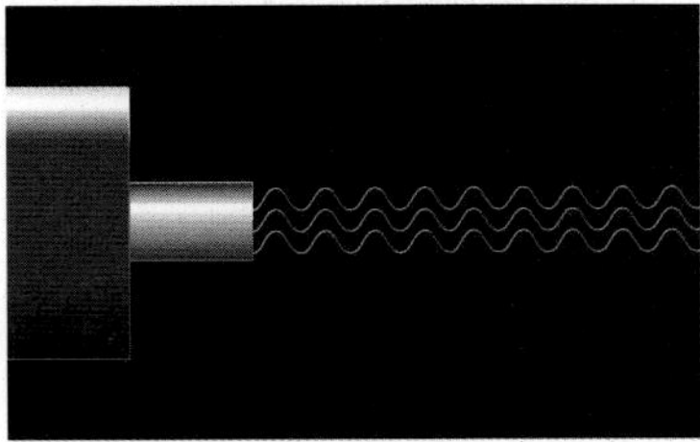

■ *Organized, 'coherent' laser light*

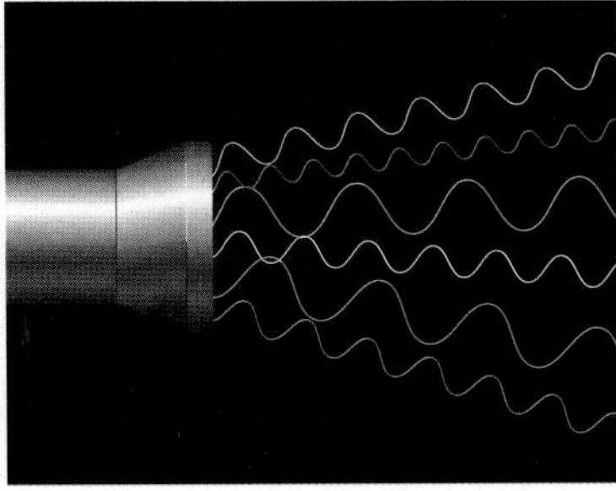

■ *Light of different wavelengths emitted by a torch*

The first hologram was made in 1962 at the University of Michigan by Emmett N. Leith and Juris Upatnieks.

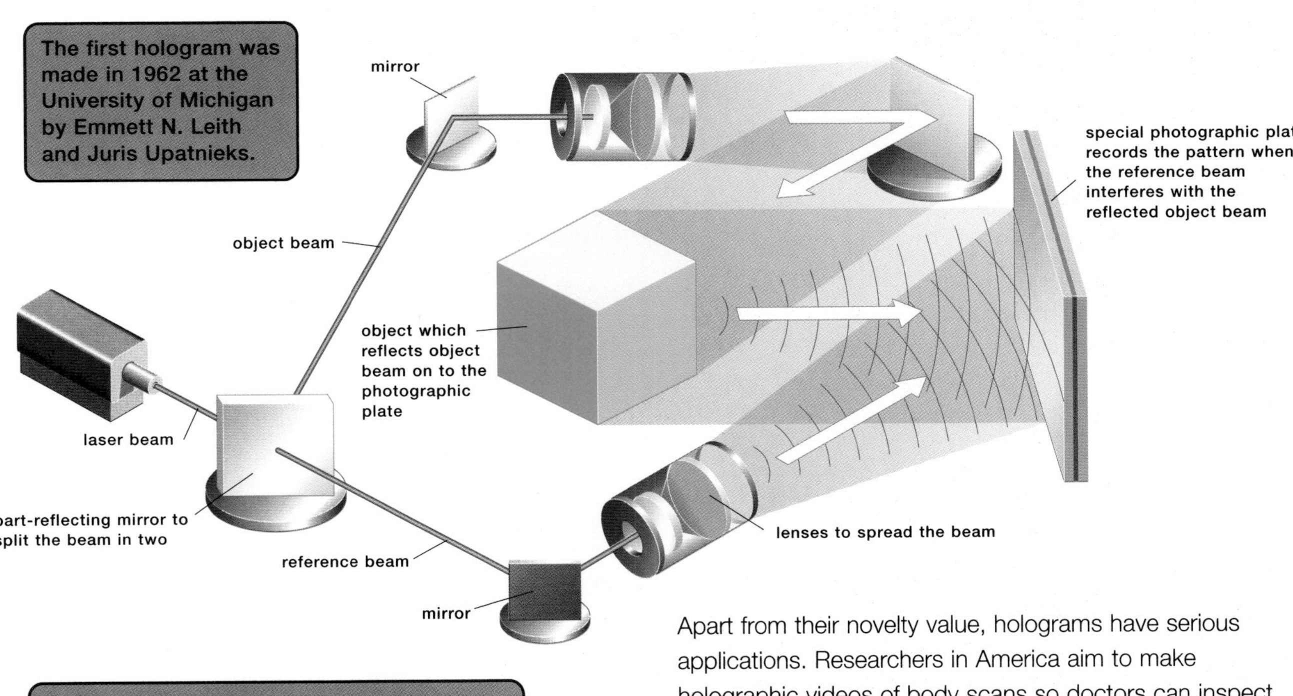

Dennis Gabor first conceived the idea of holograms in the 1940s. However, nobody was able to build them until lasers were invented in the early 1960s. Gabor received the Nobel Prize for Physics in 1971.

Apart from their novelty value, holograms have serious applications. Researchers in America aim to make holographic videos of body scans so doctors can inspect the inside of a patient from all angles without surgery. Engineers at Rover use holograms to analyse the vibration of engine components. Holographic lenses make bar-code readers work at supermarket check-outs.

CAR ENGINE

There are thousands of explosions every minute beneath the bonnet of a car. The task of the engine is to control these explosions and harness the energy they release to effect movement.

Enormous amounts of money and time have been spent worldwide on the design and advancement of the petrol engine since its invention. Engineers have perfected many ways of refining the design so that it uses fuel economically, is easier to control, and cheaper to build. However, petrol engines still work on the same basic principles invented by Nikolaus August Otto in 1861.

A car engine is a solid block of cast iron or aluminium alloy out of which has been drilled an even number of hollow cylinders, usually four. Each cylinder (see right) has a close-fitting piston inside it. The cylinders have valves that let in a mix of petrol and air. When the piston squeezes the mixture to the right pressure it is ignited by a spark from a spark-plug. The explosion drives the piston back down the cylinder. When it moves up the cylinder again, the piston pushes the burnt gases out through a second valve. Finally, it moves down, drawing in more of the petrol-air mixture, ready for another compression and ignition (see below right).

All the pistons are attached to a shaft called a crankshaft. When they are forced back down the cylinders by internal combustion, their motion is transferred to the shaft in a circular movement. This movement, through the means of a gearbox, enables the wheels to turn, and thus the car to travel forwards or backwards.

If all four cylinders fired at the same time the engine would not move smoothly. There would be a massive release of energy followed by a period of calm. To rectify this, the pistons are attached to the crankshaft out of step with each other. They are lined up so that each is at a different phase in the sequence. The explosive force in one cylinder drives the piston down, turning the crankshaft which, in turn, pushes another piston up, ready for combustion in its cylinder.

The biggest production car engine ever built has a capacity of 13.5 litres. It was manufactured 80 years ago for the US Pierce-Arrow 6-66 Raceabout.

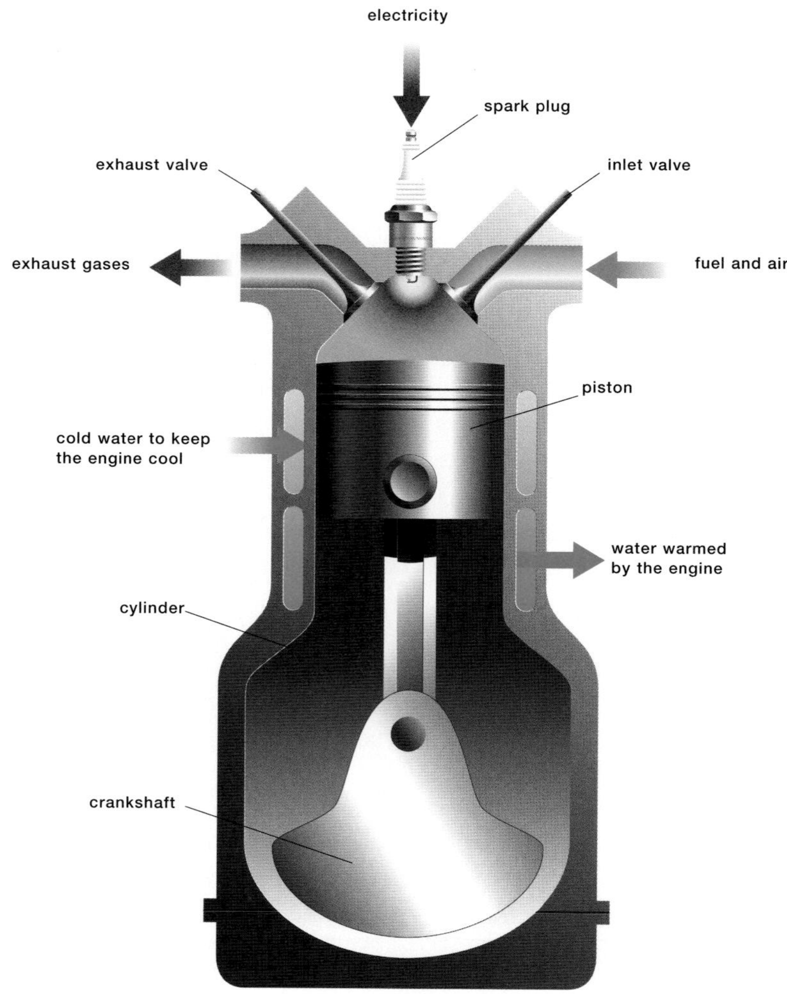

1 The piston moves down and the petrol/air mix is drawn into the cylinder through the inlet valve

2 The piston moves up, compressing the mixture in the cylinder

The first supercharged engine was built for racing purposes in 1907.

Recent developments in engine technology have seen cars running on alcohol, gas, manure, orange juice and solar power.

Every minute, approximately 100 car engines are fitted into new vehicles.

As the sequence, or cycle, is repeated quickly and involves burning gases, a lot of heat is generated. This has to be removed before the cylinders get so hot that the metal melts. Water is usually used to effect this cooling process. It surrounds the engine and transfers the heat to the radiator at the front of the car. As the car moves forward, the passage of cool air lowers the temperature of the water, thus cooling the engine. Other energy is lost as heat in the exhaust gases. In total, 60% of the energy generated by an internal combustion engine is lost as heat.

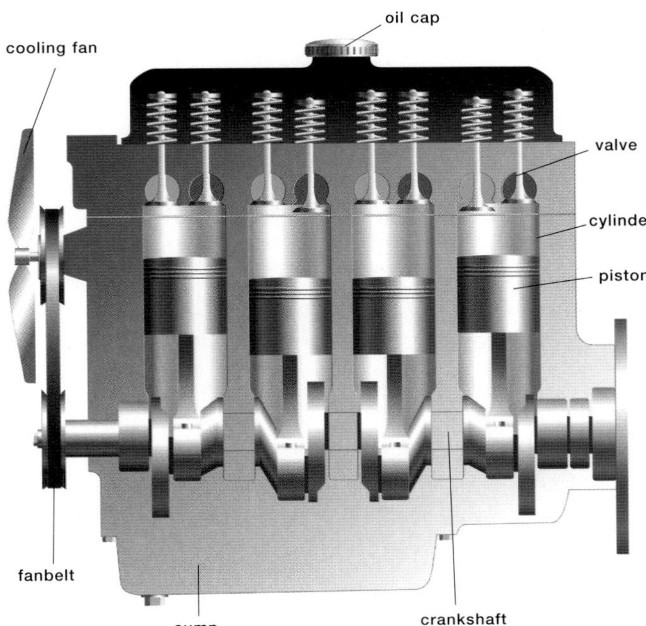

To increase its efficiency, engine manufacturers have replaced some mechanical parts with electronically controlled systems. To do this, they have built sensors into the engine to monitor engine temperature, throttle position, ignition timing and the composition of the exhaust gases. All the data are processed by on-board computers which, in turn, send out instructions to the systems that make up the engine.

For example, in a standard car engine the petrol and the air are mixed together in the carburettor. Electronically managed engines now use fuel injection instead. A pump passes fuel to a distributor which delivers measured amounts, precisely timed, to injectors that spray it into the cylinders. With better timing and quantities, the combustion can be made more efficient. Less fuel is used to create the same amount of motion.

3 A spark ignites the mixture and the explosion drives the piston down, turning the crankshaft

4 The piston moves up, expelling the burnt gases through the exhaust valve

The spark-plugs that trigger the explosion in the cylinders have traditionally been controlled by a spinning arm, called the rotor arm, that sends a high voltage current to each plug in turn. However, this mechanical device is now being replaced by an electronic system which manages the distribution of the current. Electronic systems do not have moving parts that wear out and are therefore more reliable. Most car engines have cylinders that have a capacity of 1.5 litres or less, producing the same amount of energy as those twice their size built 30 years ago.

There have been tremendous advances made in engine design and control in the last 25 years, as petrol has become increasingly expensive. Today, engineers are concentrating on other parts of the car in order to improve performance. Aerodynamics, overall weight and the transmission of energy to the wheels are all being studied. The petrol engine also now faces new rivals in electrically powered cars that are much more environmentally friendly in that they do not create exhaust gases which cause pollution.

AIRCRAFT

Flying is now so commonplace it is easy to forget that human beings had never flown in a craft heavier than air until 1903. Now the variety of aircraft is huge but most rely on the same principles.

Aircraft designers think of the air like we think of water – it is fluid and it has mass. So, just as a lake will support a water skier, air will support a flying machine – as long as it keeps moving fast enough.

The main thing that keeps an aircraft aloft is the angle of attack of its wings. If a skier lets the tip of her ski dip into the water then the whole ski follows and she sinks. But, by leaning back, the tip rises just above the surface and the skier carries on. This lean by an aircraft wing is called the angle of attack.

When an angled wing moves forwards, its bottom surface pushes the air beneath it downwards. According to Isaac Newton's third law of motion, every action has an equal and opposite reaction. In this case the reaction is for the air to push the wing up.

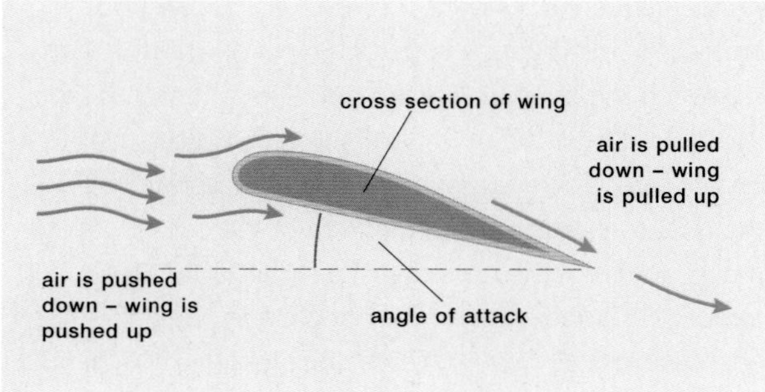

Air flowing over the top of the wing helps the process. The airstream follows the downward slope of the top surface and leaves the rear, trailing edge of the wing at the same downward angle. Once again, Newton's third law says that if the air has been displaced downwards then there must be an opposite force shifting the aircraft up. That is why wings slope.

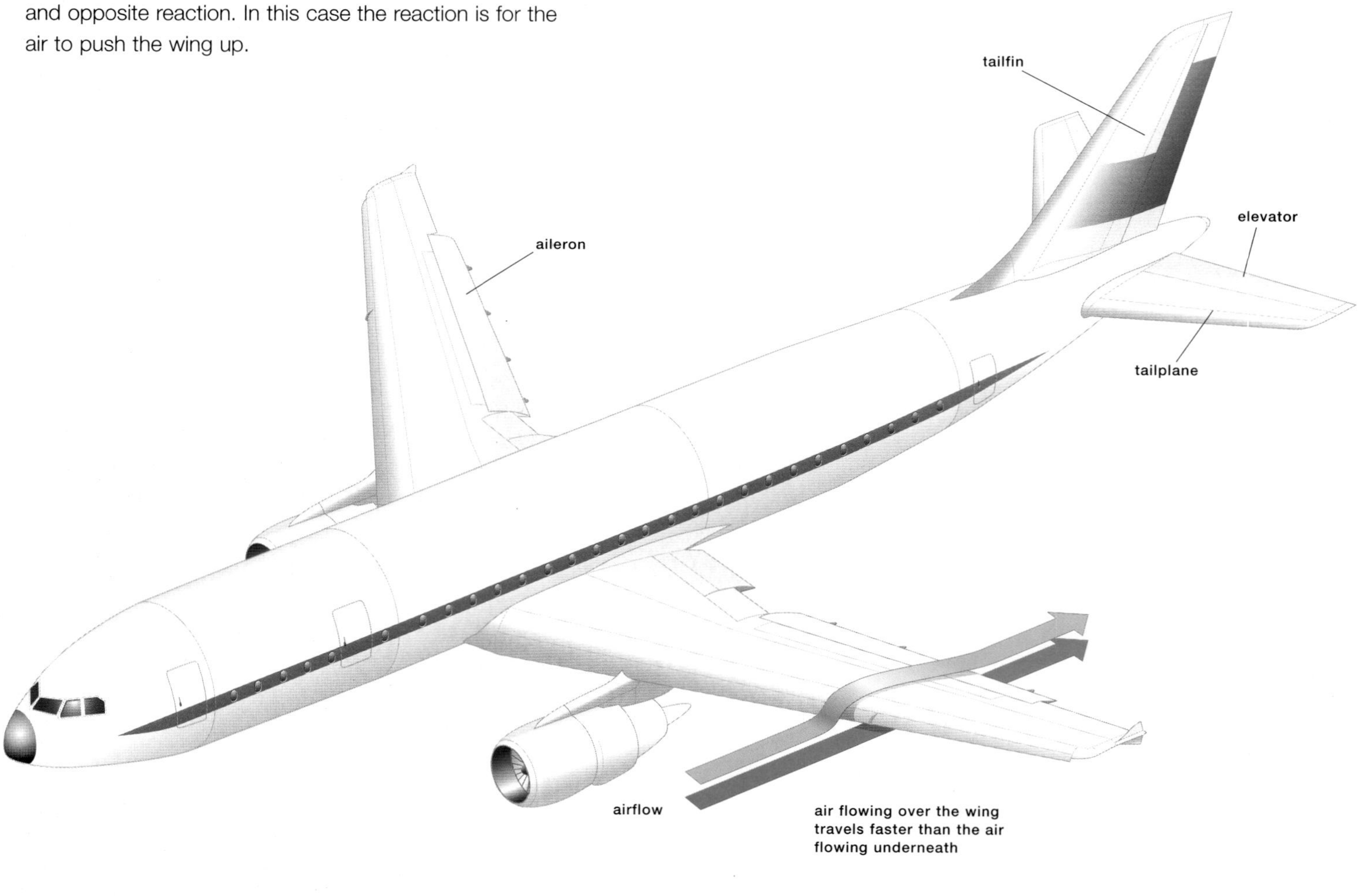

tailfin
aileron
elevator
tailplane
airflow
air flowing over the wing travels faster than the air flowing underneath

The first aircraft flight around the world without refuelling lasted 9 days 3 min 44 sec (14–23 December 1986). Dick Rutan and Jeana Yeager flew 40,212 km in the *Voyager*.

The Spruce Goose flying boat had the largest wingspan in the world, 97.51 m, and was 66.65 m long. Its only flight was on 2 November 1947.

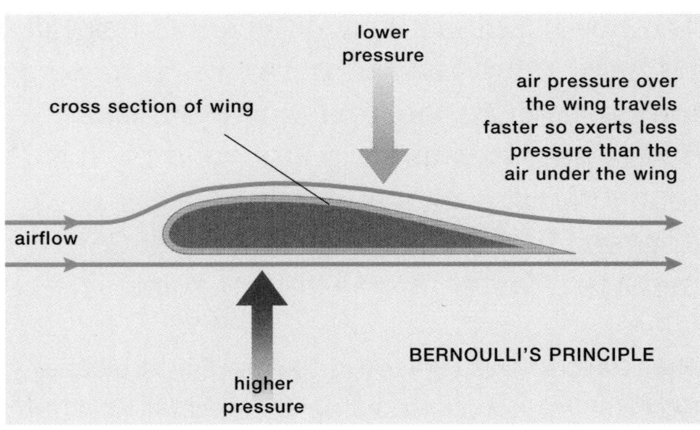

Aerodynamicists then went on to discover that the whole design could generate more upwards lift if the wing was built with a bulge in the top surface, at its front, leading edge. This shape, called an aerofoil, forces the air that crosses the top surface to travel faster than the air passing underneath the wing. By flowing faster it becomes less dense than the air flowing underneath. If it is less dense it must also be at a lesser pressure than the air underneath. As a result, the wing will rise upwards, lifted by the relatively high pressure below the wing into the lower pressure air above.

Even with this clever trick, called Bernoulli's Principle, an ordinary aircraft with just a pair of wings is not going to fly far without crashing. A water skier can hold onto a rope to stay upright but an aircraft needs something else to give it stability – a tail. The vertical tailfin stops it from rolling over and the horizontal tailplane helps keep it at the right angle to the oncoming airstream.

The tailplane is also crucial for getting the plane to climb, descend and turn. The pilot can control hinged flaps, called elevators, at the rear, trailing edge of the tailplane. When the pilot makes them stick up, the tail is pressed down by the air and the nose rises. With the wings now at a greater angle of attack the plane meets more resistance from the airstream, a force called drag, and the pilot must speed up the engine. The aircraft climbs.

The US Air Force reconnaissance jet Lockheed SR-71A is the fastest plane in the world. A speed of 3529.56 km/h was achieved in July 1976.

If the elevators are pointed down, the tail is pushed up by the air and the nose falls. Drag also falls, and as a consequence the plane accelerates and the pilot slows down the engines to compensate.

The vertical tailfin also has a hinged flap. When it's moved to the right, the tail goes left and the nose of the plane steers right. Move the flap left and the plane goes left. Sharper turns are made by banking the aircraft. Flaps at the trailing edge of the wings, called ailerons, are connected so that they move in opposite directions and make the aircraft bank.

Of course, a water skier is pulled across the water by a motor boat. Without the forward motion the skier would sink, no matter how much she leans back. In the same way, the aeroplane needs something to move it forwards through the air for the aerodynamic properties of the wing and tailplane to take effect.

Propellers and jet engines are the commonest devices. Their positioning can change the way the air flows around the wings. Aircraft engineers make sure the flows are improved so that the aircraft flies efficiently. Other control surfaces on the plane – flaps and slats – let the pilot alter the airflow so that the plane flies well at all speeds and for all manoeuvres.

When landing the plane, the pilot simply increases the angle of attack of the wings, by raising the nose, until the smooth airflow around them disintegrates and all the lifting force dissipates.

The smallest biplane ever flown was Bumble Bee Two, capable of carrying one person. It had a wingspan of 1.68 m. On 8 May 1988 it flew to 120 m, crashed and was totally destroyed.

HOVERCRAFT

The hovercraft is barely 40 years old and is probably more familiar to travellers crossing the English Channel than anywhere else. The largest hovercraft in the world ply this route, carrying cars and passengers between France and England in just 35 minutes – faster than rival ferry ships.

The hovercraft was invented in 1959 by Sir Christopher Cockerell. He recognized the fact that vehicles which are in contact with the ground are impeded by bumps and are largely restricted to even surfaces such as roads and rails. In the sea, boats are slowed down because they have to push their way through the water.

His solution to these problems was to raise the hovercraft above the surface of the land and water by creating a cushion of air underneath the vehicle. This is done with large fans, powered on the largest craft by gas-turbine engines, that draw in air through ducts on the top of the craft and expel it underneath the hull.

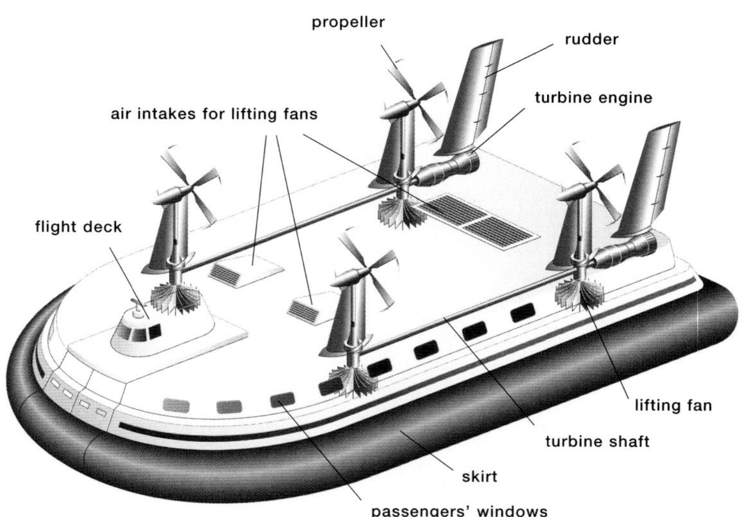

The bottom of the hull is flat with a flexible skirt surrounding it. Air from the fans is expelled through vents in the skirt towards the centre of the hull. The skirt and the air currents trap the air and keep it beneath the craft for as long as possible. As the pressure of air underneath rises, it gradually lifts the hovercraft off the surface, by as much as 3 m (10 ft).

MAGLEV TRAIN

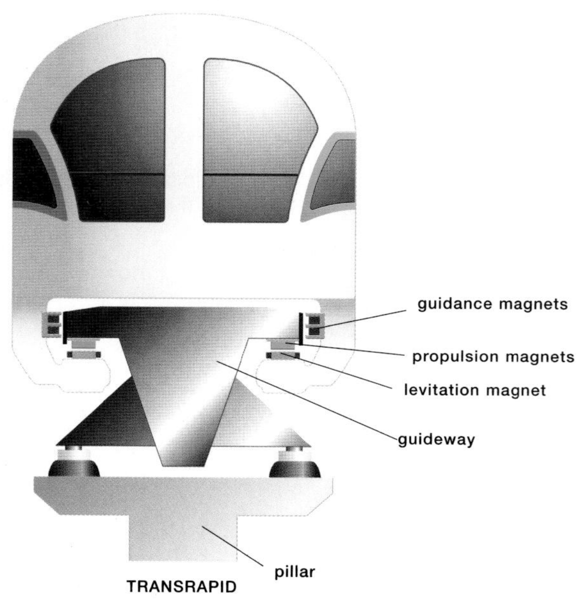

Maglev technology is used to hurl a carriage containing 20 people from 0–88 km/h in under four seconds on the Outer Limits Flight of Fear roller-coaster at Richmond, Cincinnati, USA.

The fastest trains of the next millennium will float above the tracks on magnetic fields, reaching speeds of up to 550 km/h.

These high-speed magnetically levitating (maglev) trains are being built in Germany and Japan and a cut-down version already connects Birmingham airport to its traditional railway station. As they do not make contact with the rails, there is no friction to slow maglevs down and no moving parts to wear out. However, their sophisticated electrical systems are not easy to build.

The German Transrapid train, running between Berlin and Hamburg, will open in 2005. It will cruise on a continuous T-shaped concrete guideway. Running along the underside of the arms of the T are metal rails. The base of the train itself wraps around and under the arms. Electric magnets in the bottom section of the train are attracted upwards towards the metal rails. When fed enough electricity the magnets create an attraction force strong enough to lift the train. Another magnetic field, from components attached to the rails, pulls the train along.

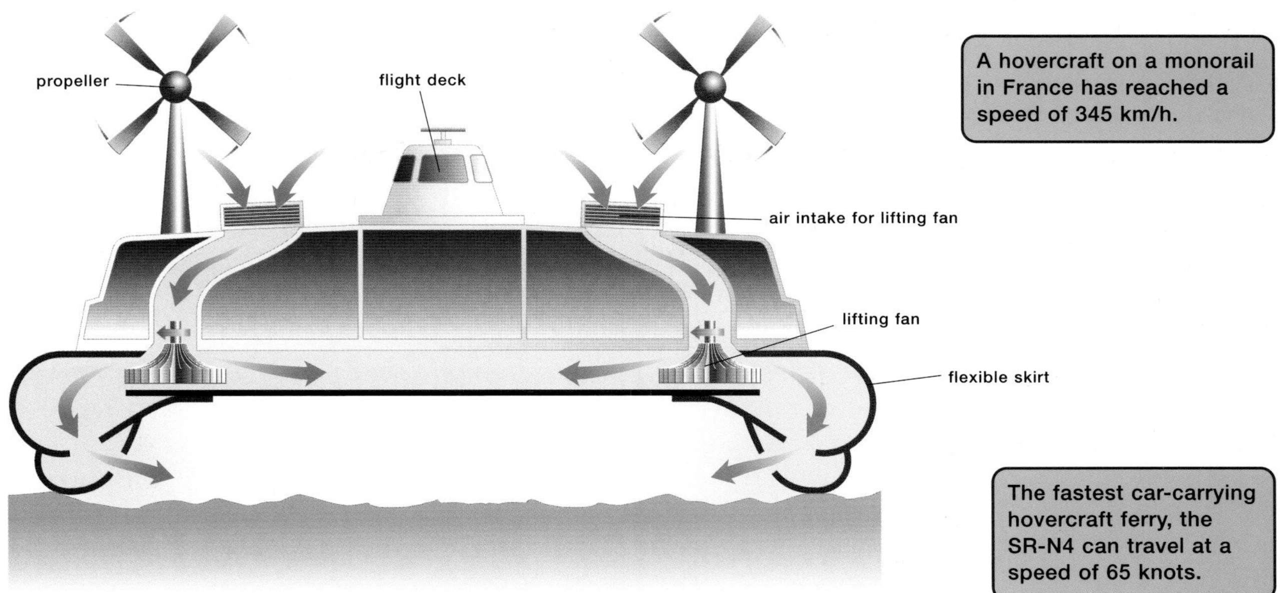

A hovercraft on a monorail in France has reached a speed of 345 km/h.

The fastest car-carrying hovercraft ferry, the SR-N4 can travel at a speed of 65 knots.

On a level surface the hovercraft will not move in any direction so propellers are fitted to direct its motion. The propellers of commercial ferry hovercraft are usually placed above the lifting fans and are driven by the same gas-turbine engines. To slow the hovercraft down, the pitch of the propellers is changed or the direction of airflow through the skirt vents is altered.

During the first ten years of their existence, hovercraft were hailed as the next fast boat system. However, their inability to operate in heavy seas means they are now used primarily as true amphibious vehicles. They can cross surfaces which no other vehicles can traverse. For example, medical teams use small hovercraft to travel along rainforest rivers to reach patients in remote villages.

Suitcases are to be transported by maglev technology when the new automated baggage-handling system is installed at Heathrow, London.

American senators travel on maglev trains every day. They have an underground maglev railway that carries them from their office block in Washington to the Senate House.

The problem with this design is making sure that the train's magnets do not get so close to the rails that they touch and stick. A series of sensors monitor the gap between train and rail and continually adjust the amount of electricity being supplied to the magnets.

In addition to this system, there is another rival design in existence that does not have a problem in measuring the gap – the Japanese maglev train. Instead of using the magnetic force of attraction, this train uses the same force but in an opposite way. It harnesses magnetic repulsion to lift the train off the ground. Superconducting magnets on board push up and away from other magnets fixed to the flat track. In the same way, magnetic forces also propel the train forwards.

The Japanese system only works well once the train is moving at speed so it has to run on small wheels until it reaches 100 km/h (62 mph), when it rises into the air. For Japan, where earth tremors and minor quakes can easily shake the track, the design proves to be the most robust and successful.

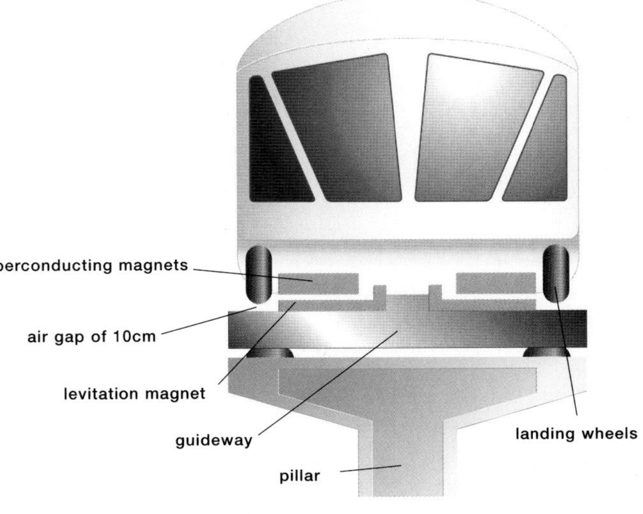

JAPANESE MAGLEV TRAIN

INVENTIONS

- Patents are documents granted to inventors giving them control and rights over their creations.
- The can opener was invented in 1855, 45 years after the tin can.
- Edison was granted over 1000 patents over 55 years.
- The first margarine was made using, amongst other things, chopped cow's udder.
- Coca-Cola was initially launched as a 'brain tonic' in 1884.

Scottish teacher and audiologist Alexander Graham Bell speaks into his recent invention, the Centennial telephone. This was developed with the help of Thomas Watson, and it was to him that he spoke the first words on the telephone: 'Mr Watson, come here, I want you'. Bell patented the first device in 1876, just hours before another telephone inventor, Elisha Gray

WHAT, WHO, WHEN, WHERE

What	Who	When	Where
abacus	unknown	*c.* 3000 BC	Middle East
adding machine	Wilhelm Schickard	1623	Germany
aeolipile (an early steam engine)	Hero of Alexandria	60	Egypt
aircraft (controlled)	Orville and Wilbur Wright	1903	USA
aircraft (practical)	Clément Ader	1890	France
aircraft (theory)	Emmanuel Swedenborg	1717	Sweden
airship (non-rigid)	Henri Giffard	1852	France
airship (rigid)	Count Ferdinand von Zeppelin	1900	Germany
anaesthetic (ether)	Dr C.W. Long	1842	USA
anaesthetic (nitrous oxide)	Horace Wells	1846	USA
artificial heart	Robert Jarvik	1970	USA
autogyro	Juan de la Cierva	1923	Spain
bakelite	Leo Baekeland	1909	USA
ball-point pen	John J. Loud	1888	USA
ball-point pen (low-cost)	László and Georg Biro	1938	Hungary
barbed wire	Lucien B. Smith	1867	USA
barometer	Evangelista Torricelli	1644	Italy
battery (electric)	Alessandro Volta	1800	Italy
bicycle	Kirkpatrick Macmillan	1839	Scotland
bicycle tyres	John Boyd Dunlop	1888	Scotland
bifocal lens	Benjamin Franklin	1784	USA
binary system	Gottfried Wilhelm Leibniz	1679	Germany
boats (rowing)	unknown	7th millennium BC	Egypt
boats (sailing)	unknown	3rd millennium BC	Egypt
Braille	Louis Braille	1829	France
bridge (metal)	Abraham Darby	1779	England
bronze	unknown	*c.* 3700 BC	Egypt
Bunsen burner	Robert Wilhelm von Bunsen	1855	Germany
burglar alarm	Edwin T. Holmes	1858	USA
calculator (advanced): difference engine	Charles Babbage	1823	England
calculator (mechanical)	Blaise Pascal	1642	France
cannon	unknown	*c.* 1280	China
car (petrol-driven)	Karl Benz	1885	Germany
car tyres (pneumatic)	André and Edouard Michelin	1895	France
carburettor	Gottlieb Daimler	1876	Germany
carpet sweeper	Melville R. Bissell	1876	USA
cash register	James Ritty	1879	USA
cassette (compact)	Philips	1963	Netherlands
cat's eyes	Percy Shaw	1934	England
cathode ray tube	Sir J.J. Thomson	1897	England
cellophane	Dr Jacques Brandenberger	1908	Switzerland
celluloid	J.W. Hyatt	1870	USA
cement (Portland)	Joseph Aspdin	1824	England
chronometer	John Harrison	1761	England
clock (mechanical)	I-Hsing, Liang-Tsan	725	China
clock (pendulum)	Christiaan Huygens	1656	Netherlands
clockwork	unknown	80 BC	Greece
colour printing	Jakob Le Bon	1719	Germany
communication satellite (theory)	Arthur C. Clarke	1945	England
compact disc	Philips, Sony	1978	Netherlands, Japan
computer (programmable electronic)	Prof. Max Newman, T.H. Flowers	1943	England
computer language (logical)	Gottfried Wilhelm Leibniz	1666	Germany
diesel engine	Rudolph Diesel	1895	Germany
disc brake	Dr F. Lanchester	1902	England
dynamo	Hyppolite Pixii	1832	France
electric flat iron	H.W. Seeley	1882	USA
electric lamp	Thomas Alva Edison	1879	USA
electric motor (AC)	Nikola Tesla	1888	USA
electric motor (DC)	Zénobe Gramme	1873	Belgium
electroencephalograph	Hans Berger	1929	Germany
electromagnet	William Sturgeon	1824	England
electron microscope	Ernst Ruska, Max Knoll	1931	Germany
endoscope	Hermann von Helmholtz	1851	Germany
escalator	Jesse W. Reno, George A. Wheeler	1892	USA
Esperanto	Dr Ludwig L. Zamenhof	1887	Poland
food can (tin)	Peter Durand	1810	England
fountain pen	Lewis E. Waterman	1884	USA
galvanometer	André-Marie Ampère	1834	France
gas lighting	William Murdock	1792	England
glass (blowing)	unknown	1st century BC	Syria
glassware	unknown	*c.* 2600 BC	Iraq
glider	Sir George Cayley	1853	England
gold leaf electroscope	Abraham Bennet	1787	England
gramophone	Thomas Alva Edison	1878	USA
Greek fire	Kallinikos	673	Byzantium
gunpowder	unknown	*c.* 850	China
gyroscope	Jean-Bernard-Léon Foucault	1852	France
helicopter (operational)	Igor Sikorsky	1936	Germany
helicopter (theory)	Leonardo da Vinci	*c.* 1500	Italy
hologram	Dennis Gabor	1947	Germany
hot-air balloon (full-size)	Jacques and Joseph Montgolfier	1783	France
hot-air balloon (model)	Father Bartolomeu	1709	Portugal
hovercraft	Sir Christopher Cockerell	1959	England
ink	unknown	2nd century AD	China
integrated circuit	Geoffrey Dummer	1952	England
internal-combustion-powered vehicle	Isaac de Rivaz	1805	Switzerland
jet engine	Frank Whittle	1930	England
laser	Theodore Maiman	1960	USA
lift	Elisha G. Otis	1852	USA
lightning conductor	Benjamin Franklin	1752	USA
linoleum	Frederick Walton	1860	England
lithography	Aloys Senefelder	1796	Germany
logarithms	John Napier	1614	Scotland
loudspeaker	Horace Short	1900	England
machine gun (Gatling gun)	Richard Gatling	1862	USA
mackintosh	Charles Mackintosh	1823	Scotland
maps	unknown	*c.* 2300 BC	Mesopotamia
margarine	Hippolyte Mège-Mouriès	1869	France
maser	C.H. Townes	1958	USA
match (safety)	Anton von Schrötter	1845	Austria
measure (length): the megalithic yard	unknown	*c.* 3500 BC	NW Europe
measure (weight): the beqaa	unknown	*c.* 3800 BC	Egypt

■ *Orville Wright struggles to land the Wright Flyer I at Kill Devil Hill, Kitty Hawk, North Carolina, USA, on 17 December 1903. The plane made two flights that day, one of 12 seconds and one of almost one minute. Orville, who developed and built the plane with his brother Wilbur, was the lucky pilot on this fateful day, marking the first ever powered flights of any aircraft*

■ *A Graf Zeppelin, the first rigid aluminium framework airship. Covered by treated cotton, these giant engine-driven flying machines by Daimler were used initially for pleasure trips, but were subsequently used to drop bombs on London in WWI. Over 50,000 people used the Zeppelin in its 40-year history. It lost its appeal after the Hindenburg ship burst into flames in New York on 6 May 1937*

mezzotint process	Ludwig van Siegen	1642	Germany
microcomputer (single chip)	Gilbert Hyatt	1968–71	USA
microphone	Alexander Graham Bell	1876	USA
microprocessor	Marcian E. Hoff, Jr	1971	USA
microscope	Zacharias Janssen	1590	Netherlands
microwave oven	Percy LeBaron Spencer	1945	USA
motorcycle	Gottlieb Daimler	1885	Germany
moveable type	Pi Sheng	1040–50	China
neon lamp	Georges Claude	1910	France
nuclear reactor	Enrico Fermi	1942	USA
nylon	Walter Carothers	1935	USA
paper	Ts'ai Lun	105	China
papyrus paper	unknown	3000 BC	Egypt
parachute	Louis-Sébastien Lenormand	1783	France
parking meter	Carlton C. Magee	1935	USA
pasteurization	Louis Pasteur	1860s	France
pencil	J.N. Conté	1792	France
photocopier	Chester Carlson	1937	USA
photography	Joseph Nicéphore Niepce	1826	France
pocket calculator	Jack St Clair Kilby, James van Tassell, Jerry D. Merryman	1971	USA
polythene (polyethene)	R.O. Gibson, E.W. Fawcett	1933	England
porcelain	unknown	800	China
potter's wheel	unknown	*c.* 6500 BC	Asia Minor
pressure cooker	Denis Papin	1679	France
printing press	Johannes Gensfleisch (Johannes Gutenberg)	c. 1450	Germany
printing (blocks)	unknown	2nd century AD	China
printing (linotype)	Otto Mergenthaler	1884	USA
printing (monotype)	Tolbert Lanston	1887	USA
programmable device (card-fed loom)	J.M. Jacquard	1804	France
pyramid	Imhotop	2856 BC	Egypt
radar	Dr Albert H. Taylor, Leo C. Young	1922	USA
rail transport	unknown	1550	France
railway (electric)	Werner von Siemens	1879	Germany
railway (steam locomotive)	Richard Trevithick	1803	England
rayon	Sir Joseph Swan	1883	England
razor (electric)	Col. Jacob Schick	1928	USA
record (gramophone)	Emile Berliner	1901	USA
record (long-playing)	Dr Peter Goldmark	1948	USA
refrigerator	James Harrison, Alexander Catlin Twining	1850	Australia, USA
robot	George C. Devol, Joseph F. Engelberger	1961	USA
rocket (war)	unknown	1042	China
rubber (latex foam)	Dunlop Rubber Co.	1928	England
rubber (vulcanized)	Charles Goodyear	1841	USA
safety pin	Walter Hunt	1849	USA
Scotch tape	Richard Drew	1930	USA
screw propeller	Sir Francis Pettit Smith	1836	England
self-starter	Charles F. Kettering	1911	USA
sewing machine	Barthélemy Thimonnier	1830	France
ship (power-driven)	William Symington	1801–02	Scotland
shorthand	Sir Isaac Pitman	1839	England
silicon chip	Jack Kilby	1958	USA
silk manufacture	unknown	*c.* 50 BC	China
skyscraper	William Le Baron Jenny	1882	USA
slide rule	William Oughtred	1621	England
spectacles (concave)	Nicholas of Cusa	*c.* 1450	Italy
spectacles (convex)	unknown	*c.* 1286	Italy
sphygmomanometer	Dr Scipione Riva-Rocci	1896	Italy
spinning jenny	James Hargreaves	1764	England
steam engine	Thomas Savery	1698	England
steam engine (piston)	Thomas Newcomen	1712	England
steel production	Henry Bessemer	1855	England
stereophonic sound	EMI	1933	England
stethoscope	René Laënnec	1816	France
submarine	David Bushnell	1776	USA
submersible	Cornelius Drebbel	1624	Netherlands
supercomputer	Seymour Cray	1976	USA
tank	Sir Ernest Swinton	1914	England
tape recorder	AEG Telefunken, IG Farben (companies)	1935	Germany
telegraph (mechanical)	M. Lammond	1787	France
telegraph code	Samuel B.P. Morse	1837	USA
telephone (practical)	Alexander Graham Bell	1876	USA
telephone (theory)	Antonio Meucci	1849	Italy
telephone automatic exchange	Alfred Strowger	1889	USA
telescope (reflecting)	Isaac Newton	1668–69	England
telescope (refractor)	Hans Lippershey	1608	Netherlands
television	John Logie Baird	1925	Scotland
television camera	Vladimir Zworykin	1931	USA
terylene	J.R. Whinfield	1941	England
thermometer	Galileo Galilei	1593	Italy
transistor	John Bardeen, William Shockley, Walter Brattain	1948	USA
transistor radio	Sony	1952	Japan
turbine (ship)	Hon. Sir Charles Parsons	1894	England
turbojet engine	Dr Hans Pabst von Ohain	1937	Germany
typewriter	Christopher Sholes	1868	USA
tyres (rubber)	Thomas Hancock	1846	England
vaccination	Edward Jenner	1796	England
vacuum cleaner	Hubert Cecil Booth	1901	England
vacuum pump	Otto von Guericke	1654	Germany
vehicle (gas-powered)	Samuel Brown	1826	England
video recorder	A.M. Poniatoff	1958	USA
Walkman	Sony	1980	Japan
washing machine	Hurley Machine Co., A.J. Fisher	1907	USA
watch	unknown	before 1462	Italy
watch (wrist)	Jacquet-Droz, Leschot	1790	Switzerland
water closet	Sir John Harington	1589	England
weaving (flying shuttle)	John Kay	1733	England
welder (electric)	Elisha Thomson	1877	USA
wheel	unknown	*c.* 3580 BC	Sumeria
windmill	unknown	*c.* 600	Iran
writing	unknown	*c.* 3600 BC	Sumeria
zip fastener	Whitcomb L. Judson	1893	USA

(EQUIVALENT TO £1 MILLION IN TODAY'S MONEY) FOR INVENTING THE MARINE CHRONOMETER ■

ENERGY

▷ **The greatest recorded gas flare burnt at Gassi Touil in the Algerian Sahara from 13 November 1961 to 28 April 1962 – the flames rose to a height of 137 m.**

▷ **The Nurek hydroelectric dam on the River Vakhsh, Tajikistan, is the world's highest at 300 m.**

▷ **The USA has an estimated 22,457 million barrels of oil in reserve, which is estimated to be exhausted in nine years at the current rates of extraction. The UK has 4293 million barrels, which will be exhausted in four years.**

▷ **The USA has the most nuclear reactors (109) which generate 29.5% of the world's total nuclear power.**

Energy is vital to every nation. In the developed and developing worlds, energy is provided by means of electricity – the most convenient and flexible method of transferring energy from its source to where it is needed. However, there are problems in deciding which available method to use in generating electricity. There is the gradual but inevitable damage to the environment caused by burning fossil fuels such as coal and oil, and the unlikely but potentially catastrophic risks associated with nuclear power. The environmentally friendly and safe sources of energy – wind, solar and geothermal – still account for very little of the world's energy.

COAL

▶ **Coal is a carbon-based mineral that formed over many millions of years as a result of the gradual compacting of partially decomposed plant matter.**
▶ **In 1942, at Honkeiko (Benxihu) Colliery in China, 1549 people were killed by a coal dust explosion – the world's most devastating mining disaster.**

Three basic types of coal are found – lignite, bituminous coal (soft coal) and anthracite (hard coal). Lignite (brown coal) has the lowest heat value, since it was formed more recently and contains less carbon and more water than other varieties. Anthracite contains the most carbon and produces the most heat. About one-half of coal mined is used for generating electricity, one-quarter is used by the steel industry as coking coal, and the remainder is used in other industries or for domestic heating.

The burning of fossil fuels such as coal in power stations leads to the emission of several byproducts that are potentially damaging to the environment. Fly ash, which results from burning pulverized coal, is effectively removed by passing the flue (or waste) gases from the furnace through an electrostatic precipitator (see p. 57).

Other byproducts pass straight out of the chimney and into the atmosphere, including sulphur dioxide (SO_2) and nitrogen oxides (No_x) – the major causes of acid rain (see p. 56) – and carbon dioxide (CO_2), which contributes to the greenhouse effect (see p. 55). Major coal-fired stations are likely to include desulphurization equipment.

OIL AND NATURAL GAS

▶ **Both oil and natural gas are hydrocarbons: organic compounds built from two elements – hydrogen and carbon.**
▶ **The Interprovincial Pipe Line Inc. in North America is the longest crude-oil pipeline, stretching over 3787 km (2354 mi).**

Crude oil and natural gas are often found in close proximity to each other, because they are formed in the same way and collect in the same kind of geological conditions. Three types of rock are needed to form an oil reserve: a layer of sedimentary rock in which the hydrocarbons form; porous rock that can store the oil and gas like a sponge; and an impervious layer of rock over the top, ideally in the form of a dome, to form a trap. When a likely area of oil has been identified, exploratory drilling begins. If economic amounts of oil are found, production wells are drilled. From a single derrick, many holes can be bored, fanning outwards to reach all corners of the reserve. A large field may be drilled from several different platforms. Once drilled, an arrangement of pipework and valves – called a 'Christmas tree' because of its shape – is installed at the surface to control the flow. The pressure of the oil may be enough to drive it to the surface, but pumps can also be used. As pressure falls, it may be increased by pumping water down other holes. Even with such techniques, no more than 30–40% of the oil can be recovered.

The development of long-distance pipelines and ships that carry liquefied natural gas has greatly increased the market for gas, which is both an excellent fuel and a useful raw material for the chemical industry. Gas flows more readily than crude oil, so as much as 80% of the gas in place may be recovered. The processing of gas involves separating it from any liquids and 'sweetening' it by removing gases such as hydrogen sulphide and CO_2. The end product consists mostly of methane (more than 80%), combined with smaller amounts of ethane, propane and butane.

■ *The emissions of the Drax coal-fired power station mingle with the colours of dusk in Selby, Yorkshire, England*

COAL

CONSUMERS	tonnes per year (millions)	PRODUCERS	tonnes per year (millions)
China	1,232	China	1,240
USA	844	USA	938
India	285	Russia	275
Russia	279	India	274
Germany	276	Germany	265
Poland	171	Australia	226
South Africa	141	Poland	201
Japan	123	South Africa	184
Australia	103	Kazakhstan	109
North Korea	100	North Korea	98

Note: The UK consumes 81 million tonnes and produces 48 million tonnes annually.

CRUDE OIL

CONSUMERS	barrels per year (millions)*	PRODUCERS	barrels per year (millions)*
USA	5,024	Saudi Arabia	2,976
Russia	1,689	USA	2,505
Japan	1,637	Russia	2,254
China	1,024	Iran	1,353
Germany	784	China	1,090
UK	629	Mexico	994
Saudi Arabia	589	Norway	988
France	563	UK	914
South Korea	562	Venezuela	913
Italy	545	United Arab Emirates	804

* one barrel averages 159 litres (42 gal)

NATURAL GAS

CONSUMERS	m^3 per year (millions)	PRODUCERS	m^3 per year (millions)
USA	591,754	Russia	582,988
Russia	327,275	USA	559,261
Germany	92,770	Canada	175,897
UK	79,391	Netherlands	78,778
Canada	78,223	UK	71,144
Ukraine	75,467	Indonesia	61,864
Japan	58,029	Algeria	51,817
Italy	49,513	Uzbekistan	45,300
Netherlands	48,841	Mexico	38,454
Iran	40,056	Saudi Arabia	37,718

ENERGY PRODUCERS

	kW-hr per year (millions)
ELECTRICITY	
USA	3,268,250
Japan	964,328
China	928,083
Russia	875,914
Canada	554,186
Germany	528,221
France	475,622
India	384,422
UK	325,383
Brazil	260,682
NUCLEAR POWER	
USA	663,455
France	360,046
Japan	271,940
Germany	152,128
Canada	108,066
Russia	98,102
UK	88,504
Ukraine	81,131
Sweden	73,302
South Korea	58,588
HYDROELECTRIC POWER	
Canada	328,078
USA	281,070
Brazil	242,956
Russia	176,935
China	167,983
Norway	112,822
France	80,856
Japan	75,216
India	71,118
Sweden	59,299

Note: The UK produces 6508 million kW-hr annually.

NUCLEAR POWER

▶ Controlled nuclear energy is released when uranium-packed fuel rods are bombarded by neutrons in a nuclear reactor – a process known as nuclear fission.

▶ During fission, a single tonne of uranium generates energy equivalent to 25,000 tonnes of coal.

In terms of electricity generation, the only difference between nuclear power stations (see p. 145) and conventional stations is the means of raising steam to drive the turbines: the coal- or oil-burning furnace is simply replaced by a nuclear reactor.

Uranium-235 (U-235) is the form (or isotope) of the element uranium which is the fuel used in most nuclear reactors. However, it is only present in tiny quantities – less than 1% – in mined uranium. The rest is made up of uranium-238. For many reactors, the proportion of U-235 has to be increased by a complex and very costly process known as enrichment. The fuel – enriched or natural uranium as required – is packed into fuel rods, which are placed in the core of a nuclear reactor. The nuclei of U-235 atoms sometimes break apart when struck by neutrons, in a process known as nuclear fission (see pp. 144–145).

TYPES OF NUCLEAR REACTORS

The first commercial nuclear power station, opened in 1956 at Calder Hall in Cumbria, England, was a magnox reactor. Magnox reactors are so called because their fuel – unenriched uranium – is clad in an alloy of magnesium and aluminium called magnox. They are cooled by CO_2. In the 1970s a new generation of much bigger gas-cooled reactors was developed in Britain – the advanced gas-cooled reactors or AGRs. In an AGR, the heat exchangers are located within the pressure vessel itself. The carbon-dioxide coolant is pressurized and heated up to 600°C (1112°F) or more as it is pumped through the core, which is made up of fuel rods filled with enriched uranium dioxide.

Today, the most widespread nuclear power plants are light-water reactors (LWRs). The coolant and moderator – ordinary 'light' water – is readily available and cheap, but the uranium fuel has to be highly enriched. In the case of boiling-water reactors (BWRs), the water is allowed to boil to make steam, which is less efficient at cooling and moderating the reactor, and so must be prevented from building up in the reactor core.

In pressurized-water reactors or PWRs, the water must remain at even higher pressure than is required in a BWR, so that it can reach useful temperatures without boiling.

The world's reserves of uranium will not last for ever, but one type of reactor could help to extend this time – the fast-breeder reactor or FBR. The drawback of fast reactors is that they require the reprocessing of spent nuclear fuel both to extract plutonium (its main fuel) in the first place and to recover it from the uranium blanket. Reprocessing is a highly complex and expensive operation – as well as being unpopular with environmentalists. Reservations about fast reactors have led to some countries halting FBR programmes and research.

HYDROELECTRIC POWER

▶ Electricity that is generated by harnessing the energy of water is called hydroelectric power (HEP) or hydropower.

▶ In some countries, hydroelectric power is the most important energy source; it provides 8% of western Europe's energy, and worldwide it provides roughly the same amount of energy as nuclear power.

In a typical hydroelectric power plant (see pp. 144–145), a river is dammed to create a reservoir that can provide a steady and controllable supply of running water. Major projects can be controversial as they may involve flooding environmentally sensitive areas. However, the latest design of low-head water turbines has reduced the necessary height difference (the 'head') between the turbine and the surface of the reservoir, making it possible to build smaller barrages or to place turbines directly into river beds.

The world's largest HEP plant is the Itaipu Dam on the Paraná River on the border of Brazil and Paraguay. It has a capacity of 12,600 MW and a planned capacity of 13,320 MW. The Turukhansk (Lower Tunguska) plant, which is under construction in Russia, will have a capacity of 20,000 MW.

SUSTAINABLE ENERGY

▶ Wind, solar and geothermal power are all types of 'clean' energy sources, meaning they are more environmentally friendly than fossil fuels or nuclear power and are considered to be sustainable forms of energy, that is ones which are not finite.

▶ There is enough heat in the top 10 km (6 mi) of the Earth's crust to supply all our energy needs for hundreds of years.

Traditional windmills have used the power of the wind to generate energy for many centuries. Their

■ *Wind farms, such as this one in California, USA, harness only a fraction of the potential power of the wind*

modern counterpart is far more sophisticated. The largest have blades resembling giant aircraft propellers up to 60 m (200 ft) across, generating up to 3 MW of electricity. Two such machines provide a significant proportion of the electricity of the Orkney Islands, Scotland, and several large 'wind farms' have been built at coastal sites both in Europe and in the USA. Another approach, pioneered in Britain, is a wind turbine with blades like a giant letter H, which rotate around a vertical axis. The mechanism of this tilts the blade tips inwards in high winds, thus regulating the supply.

Direct solar energy is one of the simplest sources of power. Building designs, old and new, take advantage of the Sun for heating and lighting. Today, more active designs are becoming widespread. Each square metre (12 sq ft) of a solar collector in northern Europe receives roughly 1000 kW-hrs of solar energy in the course of a year, and can use about one-half of this energy to heat water. A similar collector in California receives twice as much energy.

Just 30 km (19 mi) beneath our feet, the rock's temperature is around 900°C (1650°F). This heat primarily comes from the gradual radioactive decay of elements within the Earth. This source of power is not strictly renewable, but it is immense. In some parts of the world – for example, Iceland – the amount of geothermal heat reaching the surface is considerably greater than elsewhere, and can be used directly as a means of domestic heating. In other countries, blocks of flats are heated by hot water from wells 2–3 km (1.3–1.8 mi) deep.

The largest reserves of geothermal heat, however, are to be found deeper still, at approximately 6 km (3.7 mi). As the rocks at this depth are dry, it is harder and more costly to extract the heat, because it is necessary to pump down water in order to allow the heat to reach the surface.

■ *A run-off pond at the Svartsengi geothermal power plant in Iceland stays warm through the winter*

AIR TRANSPORT

- A plane takes off or lands every 35 seconds at Chicago O'Hare International Airport.
- Memphis, USA, handles more freight than any other airport because it is the main hub for Federal Express, the international air-freight company.
- Boeing's main assembly plant in Everett, Washington state, USA, has a capacity of 13.4 million m^3, equivalent to 11 Wembley Stadiums.
- British Airways had a 1995 operating profit of $1.1 billion.

Air transport began in 1903, when Orville and Wilbur Wright took to the air near Kitty Hawk, North Carolina, USA, to make the world's first controlled powered flight, lasting for 59 seconds. Until 1939 virtually all aircraft were powered by piston engines driving a propeller. During and after World War II, the propeller gave way to the turbojet for most purposes. Transport by air has now become firmly entrenched as the fastest and most efficient means of travelling between continents and, to a lesser extent, within countries. Major domestic and international airports are seeing aircraft movements approaching one million per year, most of them passenger planes; air-cargo movements are also increasing. The formation of large cooperatives of the top airlines, together with competition from small airlines and charter-flight companies, has kept prices relatively low, opening up air travel to those who at one time could not have afforded it. In the long term, we can look forward to even faster means of air travel, such as high-altitude aircraft that move in a low orbit around the planet.

A young elephant from Kruger National Park, South Africa, awaiting transportation to an overseas game park

Hong Kong is one of the most densely populated areas in the world. This is evident from the airport, which has tower blocks in close proximity to the runway

Reported to be the world's most expensive building project ever, Kansai International Airport in Japan cost £10 billion. Built on an artificial island at a distance of 5 km from the shore in Osaka Bay, it was stabilized with one million sand piles

15 MAJOR AIRPORTS

The world's major airports as measured by aircraft movements per year (aircraft movements include all take-offs and landings).

	Airport	Movements
1	Chicago	900,275
2	Dallas/Fort Worth	879,371
3	Atlanta	761,618
4	Los Angeles	732,639
5	Miami	576,936
6	St Louis	519,156
7	Oakland	515,955
8	Detroit	508,037
9	Las Vegas	503,698
10	Boston	477,334
11	Long Beach	476,716
12	Santa Ana	473,059
13	Minneapolis–St Paul	465,518
14	Denver	465,407
15	Pittsburgh	448,235

MOST AIRPORTS

Country	Airports
USA	834
Australia	400
Canada	301
Brazil	139
Papua New Guinea	129
China	113
Mexico	83
Indonesia	81
Japan	73
France	66
India	66
Colombia	63
Russia	58
Norway	50
UK	50

30 BUSIEST AIRPORTS

The world's busiest airports as measured by the total number of passengers handled each year.

	Airport	millions
1	Chicago	67.26
2	Atlanta	57.74
3	London Heathrow	54.45
4	Dallas/Fort Worth	54.30
5	Los Angeles	53.91
6	Tokyo Haneda	45.82
7	Frankfurt	38.18
8	San Francisco	36.26
9	Miami	33.24
10	Denver	31.03
11	Seoul	30.94
12	New York JFK	30.33
13	Detroit	29.01
14	Paris Charles de Gaulle	29.01
15	Hong Kong	28.08
16	Las Vegas	28.00
17	Phoenix	27.82
18	Minneapolis–St Paul	26.78
19	Paris Orly	26.65
20	Newark	26.57
21	St Louis	25.72
22	Amsterdam	25.36
23	Boston	24.74
24	Houston	24.73
25	Tokyo Narita	24.22
26	Honolulu	23.58
27	Singapore	23.20
28	Bangkok	22.93
29	Seattle–Tacoma	22.79
30	London Gatwick	22.55

LONDON HEATHROW DEALS WITH MORE INTERNATIONAL PASSENGERS THAN ANY OTHER

■ Aircraft at Hartsfield International Airport, Atlanta, Georgia, USA, awaiting take-off. Hartsfield has the world's largest terminal. Opened in 1980, it has a floor area of 131 acres and is still expanding. It has the capacity to handle 70 million passengers a year

THE WORLD'S LEADING AIRCRAFT

	NATIONALITY	WINGSPAN			LENGTH			MAX. CRUISING SPEED		RANGE WITH MAX. PAYLOAD		MAX. TAKEOFF WEIGHT		MAX. SEATING CAPACITY
		m	ft	in	m	ft	in	km/h	knots	km	naut mi	kg	lb	
Airbus A300	International	44.84	147	1	54.08	177	5	897	484	9,450	5,100	171,700	378,535	375
Airbus A320	International	34.09	111	9	37.57	123	3	903	487	5,430	2,930	73,500	162,040	179
BAC Aérospatiale Concorde	International	25.56	83	10	62.10	203	9	2,179	1,176	6,230	3,360	185,065	408,000	128
BAC One-eleven	UK	28.50	93	6	32.61	107	0	871	470	2,744	1,480	47,400	104,500	119
Boeing 707	USA	44.42	145	9	46.61	152	11	973	525	9,265	5,000	151,315	333,600	219
Boeing 727	USA	32.92	108	0	46.69	153	2	964	520	3,966	2,140	92,025	202,900	189
Boeing 737 300	USA	28.88	94	9	33.40	109	7	908	491	4,973	2,685	62,824	138,500	128
Boeing 747 300 and 400	USA	64.31	211	0	70.66	231	10	985	532	13,528	7,300	394,625	870,000	660
Boeing 757	USA	38.05	124	10	47.32	155	3	914	493	5,150	2,780	115,670	255,000	239
Boeing 767 300	USA	47.55	156	1	54.94	180	3	900	486	7,415	4,000	159,210	351,000	290
Boeing 777 300	USA	60.93	199	11	73.86	242	1	1,077	581	8,926	4,820	299,370	660,000	440
De Havilland DHC-8 300	Canada	27.43	90	0	25.68	84	3	528	285	1,482	800	19,505	43,000	56
Fokker F27 Friendship	Netherlands	29.00	95	2	23.56	77	3	480	259	2,070	1,117	20,410	45,000	44
McDonnell Douglas DC-8	USA	45.23	148	5	57.12	187	5	887	479	8,950	4,830	161,025	355,000	269
McDonnell Douglas DC-9 (Series 40 and 50)	USA	28.47	93	5	36.37	119	3	929	501	3,326	1,796	54,885	121,000	239
McDonnell Douglas DC-10	USA	50.40	165	4	55.50	182	1	908	490	7,413	4,000	259,450	572,000	380
McDonnell Douglas MD-80	USA	32.87	107	10	45.06	147	10	855	478	2,896	1,563	63,500	140,000	172

20 TOP CARGO HANDLERS

		Billions of tonne-km
1	**USA**	17.11
2	**Germany**	15.93
3	**France**	9.75
4	**Russia**	7.83
5	**Japan**	5.99
6	**Canada**	5.82
7	**South Korea**	4.83
8	**Spain**	4.15
9	**Singapore**	3.67
10	**Slovenia**	3.55
11	**Taiwan**	3.41
12	**The Netherlands**	3.27
13	**UK**	2.95
14	**Mexico**	2.45
15	**China**	2.40
16	**Australia**	1.67
17	**Brazil**	1.56
18	**Switzerland**	1.51
19	**Chile**	1.43
20	**Argentina**	1.29

20 TOP PASSENGER AIRLINES

		Passengers carried (millions)	Passenger -km (billions)	Aircraft
1	**Delta Air Lines**	88.89	138.97	543
2	**American Airlines**	79.80	165.63	635
3	**United Airlines**	79.00	179.94	558
4	**USAir**	56.70	60.94	510
5	**Northwest Airlines**	49.30	100.61	380
6	**Southwest Airlines**	44.79	37.54	224
7	**Lufthansa**	40.70	79.09	314
8	**All Nippon Airways**	37.60	43.81	125
9	**Continental Airlines**	37.58	64.41	309
10	**British Airways**	32.33	95.95	293
11	**Japan Airlines**	28.81	72.42	127
12	**Trans World Airlines**	21.64	40.08	188
13	**Korean Air**	21.42	34.28	107
14	**Alitalia**	20.90	31.75	162
15	**SAS**	18.84	18.51	152
16	**Japan Air System**	16.91	13.74	77
17	**America West Airlines**	16.85	21.42	93
18	**Qantas**	16.05	51.20	135
19	**Air Inter Group**	15.70	37.54	55
20	**Air France**	15.00	51.71	141

PASSENGER JOURNEYS

The greatest number of air passenger-kilometres on scheduled flights per year (in billions). This measurement is obtained by multiplying the number of passengers by the number of kilometres travelled.

USA	835.60
Japan	114.60
Germany	107.83
UK	97.50
Russia	76.68
China	65.20
France	59.46
Australia	48.41
Singapore	48.40
Canada	46.58
The Netherlands	41.77
Spain	39.75
South Korea	39.26
Taiwan	38.25
Brazil	32.63
Italy	29.66
Thailand	27.13
Mexico	25.83
Malaysia	22.56
Switzerland	19.73
Saudi Arabia	18.50
New Zealand	17.72
India	17.51
Philippines	14.40
Indonesia	14.33

ROAD TRANSPORT

- Between 1955 and 1995, road building in the United Kingdom increased the total length of roads by 21%; at the same time, the number of cars increased by 660%.
- The M25 London Orbital Motorway is the world's longest ring road. Constructed between 1972 and 1986, it is 195.5 km long and cost an estimated £909 million to build.
- Interstate 405 (the San Diego Freeway) in Orange County, California, USA, has a peak-hour traffic volume of 25,500 vehicles on a 1.5-km stretch between Garden Grove Freeway and Seal Beach Boulevard.
- South Korea was the only major car-producing nation in the world not to suffer a slump in manufacturing during the late 1980s and early 1990s.
- On average, there is one motor vehicle for every 30 m of road in the United States of America.

Road transport by car and truck now has a history spanning 100 years. In that time, cars have come to be the dominant mode of short- to mid-range transport. All countries, no matter how small, have a road system, although only the developed world can afford to build motorways and similar multi-lane highways. Cars may have given people unprecedented mobility, but they have also created a number of serious problems, most notably traffic congestion, air pollution and the destruction of the countryside as more and more roads are built. Governments have responded in various ways, for example by encouraging the use of catalytic converters to filter out some of the harmful substances in car exhausts, but only time will tell if such measures are sufficient. On the positive side, the future will probably see cars becoming cleaner and possibly – one of the cleanest options of all – cars which will be powered by electricity or the sun. Despite the problems they bring, cars seem to be here to stay, and car ownership levels are growing, particularly in many developing countries. The use of road transport to carry goods and freight is continually increasing. In western Europe and North America, road transport has gradually taken the place of the railways in road haulage. Many railway branch lines solely dedicated to freight have been axed, even though the resulting increase in large lorries, such as juggernauts, is widely regarded as an environmental disaster.

■ *Highways intersect in Atlanta, Georgia – the USA has the longest road network in the world*

25 LONGEST ROAD NETWORKS

		km	mi
1	USA	6,283,868	3,904,721
2	India	2,160,000	1,342,198
3	Brazil	1,660,352	1,031,723
4	Japan	1,130,892	702,722
5	China	1,083,476	673,259
6	Russia	942,000	585,347
7	Canada	849,404	527,810
8	France	811,200	504,070
9	Australia	810,264	503,488
10	Germany	636,282	395,378
11	Turkey	386,704	240,293
12	UK	386,631	240,248
13	Poland	363,116	225,636
14	Spain	331,961	206,277
15	Indonesia	315,458	196,021
16	Italy	303,518	188,602
17	Ukraine	273,700	170,074
18	Mexico	252,725	157,040
19	Argentina	215,578	133,958
20	Pakistan	194,922	121,122
21	Bangladesh	193,283	120,104
22	South Africa	188,309	117,013
23	Kazakhstan	164,900	102,467
24	Philippines	160,709	99,863
25	Romania	153,014	95,081

▶ The country with the smallest road network is the Vatican City, with less than 2 km (1.2 mi).

 WHO DRIVES ON THE LEFT

Most people drive on the right-hand side of the road; those in left-hand driving countries are decidedly in the minority. Driving on the left may be a legacy from the times in Britain when it was thought better to pass an approaching horseman or carriage right side to right side so that in case of sudden attack, swords could be drawn (with the right hand). On the Continent, carriages had riders (postilions) mounted on the horse positioned on the rear, left-hand side in a team; therefore the driver's vision of the road ahead was better if coaches kept to the right, passing each other left side to left side.

People in the following countries all drive on the left-hand side: Antigua and Barbuda, Australia, Bahamas, Bangladesh, Barbados, Bhutan, Botswana, Brunei, Cyprus, Dominica, Fiji, Grenada, Guyana, India, Indonesia, Ireland, Jamaica, Japan, Kenya, Kiribati, Lesotho, Malaysia, Malawi, Malta, Mauritius, Mozambique, Namibia, Nepal, New Zealand, Pakistan, Papua New Guinea, St Christopher Nevis, St Lucia, St Vincent and the Grenadines, Seychelles, Singapore, Solomon Islands, Somalia, South Africa, Sri Lanka, Suriname, Swaziland, Tanzania, Thailand, Tonga, Trinidad and Tobago, Tuvalu, Uganda, United Kingdom, Zambia and Zimbabwe.

Left-hand driving is also practised in the following UK dependent territories: Anguilla, Bermuda, Cook Islands, Falkland Islands, Guernsey and its dependencies, Jersey, Isle of Man, Montserrat, Norfolk Island, Turks and Caicos Islands and the Virgin Islands (British). The Hong Kong region of China also drives on the left-hand side.

10 TOP CAR PRODUCERS

		VEHICLES (millions)
1	General Motors	4.37
2	Ford	3.45
3	Toyota	3.17
4	Peugeot	1.82
5	Volkswagen	1.77
6	Chrysler	1.72
7	Nissan	1.71
8	Renault	1.67
9	Fiat	1.55
10	Mitsubishi	1.33

Note: these car producers exclude overseas subsidiaries.

ACCESS TO CARS

Countries whose populations have, on average, the greatest or least access to cars, indicated by a low or high number of people per car.

NUMBER OF PEOPLE PER CAR

GREATEST		LEAST	
San Marino	0.9	Nepal	2,259
USA	1.3	Ethiopia	856
Andorra	1.5	Rwanda	697
Liechtenstein	1.5	Bangladesh	655
Monaco	1.5	Myanmar/Burma	619
Australia	1.7	Burkina Faso	402
Canada	1.7	Uganda	402
Luxembourg	1.7	Chad	361
Italy	1.8	Bhutan	348
New Zealand	1.8	Malawi	315
Austria	1.9	Afghanistan	295
Germany	1.9	Mali	294
Brunei	2.0	Somalia	287
France	2.0	Tanzania	262
Iceland	2.0	Cambodia	240
Japan	2.0	Congo	229
Switzerland	2.0	Mozambique	224

Note: The UK has 2.5 people per vehicle.

■ *Traffic congestion along Hollywood Freeway, Los Angeles, California, USA*

■ *Heat haze on Highway 25 which leads across the Atacama Desert in northern Chile*

ROAD HAULAGE

Road haulage in terms of tonne-kilometres, the amount of road cargo (in tonnes) multiplied by the kilometres travelled.

	Billions of tonne-km
USA	1,189.90
China	407.05
Japan	281.60
Brazil	260.40
India	210.00
Germany	202.90
Italy	182.75
Spain	154.50
France	146.00
Mexico	140.23
UK	126.50
Turkey	97.84
Australia	88.21
Iran	68.25
Poland	57.10

30 MOST CARS

1	USA	146,314,000
2	Japan	40,772,407
3	Germany	39,086,000
4	Italy	29,600,000
5	France	24,385,000
6	UK	20,479,000
7	Canada	13,477,896
8	Spain	13,440,694
9	Brazil	12,974,991
10	Russia	10,499,000
11	Australia	8,280,211
12	Mexico	8,014,143
13	Poland	6,771,000
14	The Netherlands	5,755,000
15	Argentina	4,856,000
16	South Korea	4,271,253
17	Belgium	4,109,601
18	Taiwan	3,798,800
19	Sweden	3,566,040
20	South Africa	3,488,570
21	Austria	3,367,626
22	India	3,330,000
23	Switzerland	3,137,619
24	Ukraine	2,920,000
25	Turkey	2,862,000
26	China	2,859,800
27	Greece	2,807,447
28	Saudi Arabia	2,762,132
29	Czech Republic	2,693,905
30	Portugal	2,210,000

▶ **The country with the fewest cars is Kiribati with a total of 307.**

INTERNATIONAL VEHICLE REGISTRATION LETTERS

A Austria
AND Yemen
AFG Afghanistan
AL Albania
AND Andorra
AUS Australia

B Belgium
BD Bangladesh
BDS Barbados
BG Bulgaria
BH Belize
BIH Bosnia and Herzegovina
BR Brazil
BRN Bahrain
BRU Brunei
BS Bahamas
BUR Myanmar (Burma)

C Cuba
CDN Canada
CH Switzerland
CI Côte d'Ivoire (Ivory Coast)
CL Sri Lanka
CO Colombia
CR Costa Rica
CZ Czech Republic
CY Cyprus

D Germany
DK Denmark
DOM Dominican Republic
DY Benin
DZ Algeria

E Spain
EAK Kenya
EAT Tanzania
EAU Uganda
EC Ecuador
ES El Salvador
EST Estonia
ET Egypt
ETH Ethiopia

F France and territories
FIN Finland
FJI Fiji
FL Liechtenstein
FO Faeroe Islands

GB United Kingdom
GBA Alderney
GBG Guernsey
GBJ Jersey
GBM Isle of Man
GBZ Gibraltar
GCA Guatemala
GE Georgia

GH Ghana
GR Greece
GUY Guyana

H Hungary
HK Hong Kong
HKJ Jordan
HR Croatia

I Italy
IL Israel
IND India
IR Iran
IRL Republic of Ireland
IRQ Iraq
IS Iceland

J Japan
JA Jamaica

K Cambodia
KS Kyrgyzstan
KWT Kuwait
KZ Kazakhstan

L Luxembourg
LAO Laos
LAR Libya
LB Liberia
LS Lesotho
LT Lithuania
LV Latvia

M Malta
MA Morocco
MAL Malaysia
MC Monaco
MEX Mexico
MK Macedonia
MS Mauritius
MW Malawi

N Norway
NA Netherlands Antilles
NAM Namibia
NIC Nicaragua
NL Netherlands
NZ New Zealand

P Portugal
PA Panama
PK Pakistan
PE Peru
PL Poland
PNG Papua New Guinea
PY Paraguay

RA Argentina
RB Botswana
RC Taiwan
RCA Central African Republic
RCB Congo(-Brazzaville)
RCH Chile

RH Haiti
RI Indonesia
RIM Mauritania
RL Lebanon
RM Madagascar
RMM Mali
RN Niger
RO Romania
ROK Korea
ROU Uruguay
RP Philippines
RSM San Marino
RU Burundi
RUS Russia
RWA Rwanda

S Sweden
SD Swaziland
SGP Singapore
SK Slovakia
SLO Slovenia
SME Suriname
SN Senegal
SU Belarus
SY Seychelles
SYR Syria

T Thailand
TG Togo
TJ Tajikistan
TM Turkmenistan

TN Tunisia
TR Turkey
TT Trinidad and Tobago

UA Ukraine
USA United States of America
UZ Uzbekistan

V Vatican City
VN Vietnam

WAG Gambia
WAL Sierra Leone
WAN Nigeria
WD Dominica
WG Grenada
WL St Lucia
WS Samoa
WV St Vincent

YU Yugoslavia
YV Venezuela

Z Zambia
ZA South Africa
ZRE Congo (ex-Zaïre)
ZW Zimbabwe

Rail Transport

- What was probably the world's first steam locomotive operated in Merthyr Tydfil, Wales, in 1804. Built by William Trevithick, the engine could pull 70 men and a 10-tonne load of iron.
- The highest railway summit in the world is near Ticlio, in Peru. Here, high in the Andes Mountains, the Central Railway reaches a height of 4758 m above sea level.
- London has the world's largest metro system. Just under 430 km long, it consists of 408 km of Underground and 21.7 km of Docklands Light Rail.
- A shortage of horses in the 1790s was one reason for early interest in the potential of steam horsepower.

Rail transport has a history dating back nearly 200 years. From humble beginnings, with George Stephenson (1781–1848) building his first locomotive in 1814, it has grown to become one of the most important and efficient ways of transporting goods and passengers from one place to another, despite competition from the speed of air travel and the personal convenience of the motor car. This is particularly so in large cities, where traffic congestion has meant that speedy underground and rapid-transport rail systems have the edge over the car. Rail transport also has environmental advantages – the electrified two-track, high-speed railway takes up less space than multilane highways, and is cost-effective, efficient and relatively low-polluting. A recent development is the increasing worldwide tendency for private investors to take over the ownership and management of railways, for example, in Japan, New Zealand, Brazil and the UK.

■ *Tongi train station, Bangladesh – an overcrowded train transports pilgrims to the Bisho Estema Muslim festival*

Passenger Journeys

The highest number of train journeys in terms of passenger-kilometres, obtained by multiplying the number of passengers by the distance travelled.

	millions
China	363,281
India	319,365
Japan	244,375
Russia	227,102
Ukraine	70,882
Germany	60,514
France	58,675
Italy	48,900
Egypt	46,338
South Korea	28,859
UK	28,656
Pakistan	16,385

Rail Freight

The top 12 rail-freight countries, in terms of tonne-kilometres, obtained by multiplying the tonnes of freight carried by the distance travelled.

	millions
USA	1,911,023
China	1,242,602
Russia	1,195,473
Canada	283,833
India	252,411
Ukraine	200,423
Kazakhstan	143,250
South Africa	93,487
Germany	69,483
Poland	64,719
France	47,953
Mexico	37,613

■ *Japan's Shinkansen (or bullet) high-speed trains entered service in 1964. The fastest trains can achieve speeds of up to 160 km/h and seat more than 1000 passengers*

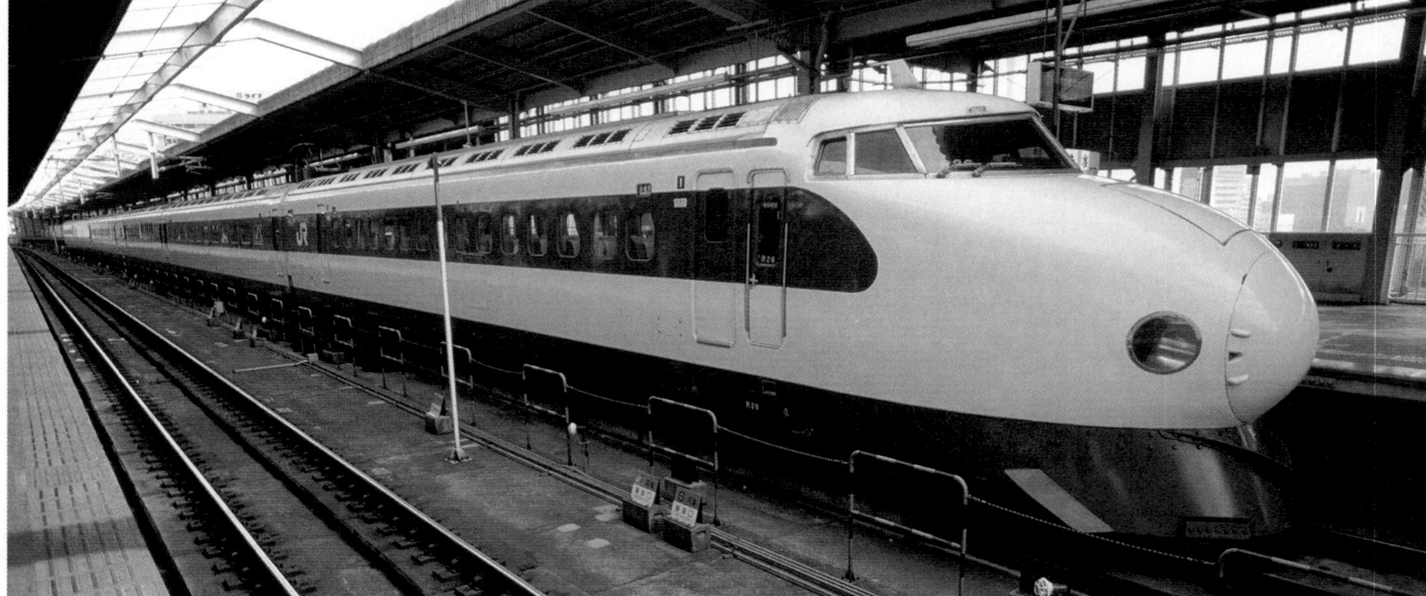

■ YOU CAN TRAVEL FROM MOSCOW TO VLADIVOSTOK (9297 KM) WITHOUT CHANGING TRAINS

20 LARGEST RAILWAY SYSTEMS

The huge land masses of North America and Asia put the USA, Canada, Russia, China and India at the top of the league for length of rail system, although passenger travel by train in the USA has all but been eclipsed by the plane.

	YEAR OPEN	GAUGE mm	GAUGE ft in	LENGTH km	LENGTH mi	OWNERSHIP
1 USA	1830	1,435	4 8½	223,155	138,666	private, except Alaska RR 846 km (526 mi), state-owned
2 Canada	1836	1,435	4 8½	89,599	55,676	National 31,339 km (19,474 mi); Pacific 44,770 km (27,820 mi); Viarail 13,490 km (8383 mi)
3 Russia	1837	1,524	5 0	67,469	41,924	state-owned
4 India	1853			62,461	38,813	state-owned
		1,676	*5 6*	*37,824*	*23,500*	
		1,000	*3 3⅜*	*20,653*	*12,832*	
		610 / *762*	*2 0* / *2 6*	*3,985*	*2,476*	
5 China	1880	1,435	4 8½	53,992	33,550	state-owned
6 Germany	1835			41,718	25,923	state-owned
		1,435	*4 8½*	*41,443*	*25,752*	
		narrow		*275*	*171*	
7 Australia	1854			37,143	23,077	National Rail Corporation owned by separate states; Australian National, 6151 km (3822 mi) of three gauges sold to private business in 1997
		1,600	*5 3*	*5,982*	*3,717*	
		1,435	*4 8½*	*15,600*	*9,694*	
		1,067	*3 6*	*15,561*	*9,669*	
8 Argentina	1857			33,821	21,016	state-owned but privately operated by concessionaries
		1,676	*5 6*	*19,196*	*11,928*	
		1,435	*4 8½*	*3,707*	*2,304*	
		1,000	*3 3⅜*	*10,918*	*6,783*	
9 France	1832	1,435	4 8½	32,275	20,055	state-owned
10 Poland	1845			25,166	15,638	state-owned
		1,435	*4 8½*	*22,655*	*14,078*	
		narrow gauges		*1,855*	*1,153*	
		1,524	*5 0*	*656*	*408*	
11 South Africa	1860			24,047	14,943	state-owned
		1,065	*3 5⅞*	*23,611*	*14,672*	
		610	*2 0*	*436*	*271*	
12 Brazil	1854			23,311	14,485	being privatized
		1,600	*5 3*	*1,739*	*1,081*	
		1,440	*4 8½*	*194*	*121*	
		1,000	*3 3⅜*	*21,559*	*13,397*	
		760	*2 6*	*13*	*8*	
13 Ukraine	1866	1,524	5 0	22,631	14,063	state-owned
14 Mexico	1850			20,477	12,724	state-owned
		1,435	*4 8½*	*20,387*	*12,668*	
		914	*3 0*	*90*	*56*	
15 Japan	1872			20,141	12,515	all privatized
		1,067	*3 6*	*18,104*	*11,250*	
		1,435	*4 8½*	*2,037*	*1,266*	
16 UK	1825			16,889	10,495	now privately owned and operated
Railtrack		*1,435*	*4 8½*	*16,532*	*10,273*	
N. Ireland Railways Co. Ltd		*1,600*	*5 3*	*357*	*222*	
17 Italy	1839	1,435	4 8½	16,118	10,016	state-owned
also in Sardinia and Sicily		*950*	*3 1½*	*867*	*539*	
18 Kazakhstan	1897	1,524	5 0	13,841	8,600	state-owned
19 Spain	1848	1,668	5 5⅝	12,570	7,810	state-owned
also high speed line		*1,435*	*4 8½*	*471*	*293*	
20 Romania	1868	1,435	4 8½	11,374	7,067	state-owned

25 LONGEST METRO SYSTEMS

	YEAR OPEN	ROUTE km	ROUTE mi	NO. OF LINES	NO. OF STATIONS
1 London, UK	1863	430	267	15	298
2 New York, USA	1868	392	244	25	469
3 Paris, France	1900	332	206	17	438
4 Moscow, Russia	1935	244	152	9	150
5 Tokyo, Japan	1927	244	152	12	216
6 Mexico City, Mexico	1969	178	111	10	154
7 Chicago, USA	1892	173	107 ½	7	144
8 Copenhagen, Denmark	1934	170	106	7	61
9 Washington DC, USA	1976	144	89 ½	5	74
10 Berlin, Germany	1902	141	88	11	166
11 Seoul, South Korea	1974	132	82	4	114
12 Boston, USA	1897	127	79	3	53
13 Madrid, Spain	1919	121	75	10	164
14 San Francisco, USA	1972	115	71 ½	4	34
15 Stockholm, Sweden	1950	110	68	3	100
16 Osaka, Japan	1933	106	66	7	85
17 Hamburg, Germany	1912	98	61	3	87
18 St Petersburg, Russia	1955	92	57	4	54
19 Nagoya, Japan	1957	76	47	5	74
20 Barcelona, Spain	1924	72	45	4	99
21 Milan, Italy	1964	72	45	3	83
22 Singapore	1987	67	42	3	42
23 Atlanta, USA	1979	65	40	6	33
24 Montreal, Canada	1966	64	40	4	65
25 Toronto, Canada	1954	61	38	3	65

■ *Waterloo International Railway Station – Britain's largest railway station, covering 30.5 acres. In 1993, five new platforms were added for the Channel Tunnel trains*

■ IN MAY 1990 A FRENCH TGV ATLANTIQUE TRAIN SET A WORLD SPEED RECORD OF 515.3 KM/H ■

WATER TRANSPORT

- The first commercial nuclear-powered merchant ship was the *Savannah*, which was launched in 1959.
- The largest-ever collision was in 1977 when two oil tankers each with a deadweight tonnage of over 330,000 struck each other.
- The total current weight of the worldwide merchant fleet exceeds the combined mass of every human who has ever lived.
- Ultra Large Crude Carrier oil tankers can weigh more than 400,000 tonnes.

Water transport was, for thousands of years, the only practicable way to move goods and people long distances. Propulsion was by oars at first, then sails, until steam was introduced in the 19th century. Change has been rapid since. Economic pressures and advances in technology have led to radical changes in ship design, in both commercial and naval vessels. The rise of air travel has been the most serious recent challenge to water transport, and most long-distance passenger vessels have now disappeared, although ferries and cruise ships still flourish. Shipping's real advantage is in carrying bulk cargoes – today's merchant fleet (ships that carry cargo) is bigger than ever before, with a total gross tonnage in excess of half a billion.

MAJOR PORTS

	TONNAGE SHIPPED PER YEAR (millions)
Singapore	305.48
Rotterdam, Netherlands	291.23
New Orleans, Louisiana, USA	207.04
Chiba, Japan	176.20
Shanghai, China	166.00
Nagoya, Japan	142.62
Yokohama, Japan	131.48
Ulsan, South Korea	127.29
Hong Kong, China	127.18
Kwangyang, South Korea	108.41
Antwerp, Belgium	108.07
Inchon, South Korea	105.18
Kitakyushu, Japan	97.10
Long Beach, USA	95.52
Pusan, South Korea	93.44
Kobe, Japan	91.70

LEADING CARGO CARRIERS

A large proportion of the world's merchant shipping flies flags of convenience. Ships are registered by their owners in other countries that offer financial, legal or other incentives to fly their flag. The first countries to offer such advantages were Liberia and Panama, which now have two of the world's biggest registered merchant fleets (by number of vessels), although almost all of the vessels are owned by European and North American companies. Merchant fleet sizes ranked by the number of registered vessels with gross tonnages greater than 300.

	VESSELS	GROSS TONNAGE (millions)
Panama	4,335	70.67
Japan	3,571	18.36
China	1,968	15.74
Russia	1,958	10.01
Liberia	1,579	58.87
Cyprus	1,571	24.00
Greece	1,408	29.07
Norway	1,119	20.61
Malta	1,060	17.04
Bahamas	1,019	22.93

■ *The port of Kobe was Japan's biggest in terms of goods handled. However, on 17 January 1995, a disastrous earthquake caused massive destruction – over 5000 people were killed and 275,000 were made homeless*

LONGEST INLAND WATERWAYS

BY COUNTRY	LENGTH km	mi
China	138,600	86,124
Russia	100,000	62,139
Brazil	50,000	31,069
USA	41,009	25,482
Indonesia	21,579	13,409
Vietnam	17,702	11,000
India	16,180	10,054
Congo (ex-Zaïre)	15,000	9,320
France	14,932	9,278
Colombia	14,300	8,886

■ *Tanjong Pagar Container Terminal, Singapore – the world's largest container port – is one of six which provides for vessels ranging from oceangoing liners to lighters (flat-bottomed cargo barges). It covers a total area of 93 km²*

LONGEST SHIP CANALS

	ROUTE	YEAR OPENED	LENGTH km	LENGTH mi
St Lawrence Seaway[1] (Canada–USA)	Montreal to Lake Ontario	1959	304	189
Main–Danube Canal (Germany)	Main River (Bamberg) to Danube River (Kelheim)	1992	171	106
Suez Canal (Egypt)	Mediterranean Sea to Red Sea	1869	162	101
Albert Canal (Belgium)	River Meuse (Maes) to River Scheld	1939	129	80
Kiel Canal (Germany)	North Sea to Baltic Sea	1895	99	62
Alfonso XIII Canal (Spain)	Seville to Gulf of Cadiz	1926	85	53
Panama Canal (Panama)	Pacific Ocean to Caribbean Sea	1914	81	50
Sabine–Neches Waterway (USA)[2]	Beaumont to Gulf of Mexico	1916	72	45
Houston Ship Canal (USA)[2]	Houston to Gulf of Mexico	1914	69	43
Manchester Ship Canal (UK)	Manchester to the Mersey estuary	1894	58	36
Welland Canal (Canada)	Lake Ontario to Lake Erie	1933	44	28
North Sea Canal (Noordzeekanaal) (Netherlands)	Amsterdam to Ijmuiden, North Sea	1876	27	17
Chesapeake and Delaware Canal (USA)[3]	Chesapeake Bay to Delaware River	1829	22	14

[1] The canalized section of the St Lawrence Seaway that enables shipping to sail 3769 km (2342 mi) from the North Atlantic up the St Lawrence estuary and through the Great Lakes to Duluth, Minnesota

[2] Part of a series of artificial and natural channels providing a discontinuous navigation, linking the Texan Gulf coast ports with the Mississippi Delta and Florida. Total length: 1770 km (1100 mi)

[3] Part of the Atlantic Intracoastal Waterway, a series of artificial and natural channels providing a discontinuous navigation of 3057 km (1900 mi) between Massachusetts and Florida

WHAT ARE SHIPPING TONNAGES

Tonnage is a measure of the capacity of a ship. It may be one of four types:

Gross tonnage: used for merchant shipping. It represents the volume of all enclosed space on a vessel, including cargo space, crew space, engine rooms and so on. It is expressed as a figure, for example 'a gross tonnage of 200,000', not '200,000 tonnes'.

Net tonnage: also used for merchant shipping. It represents the volume of all cargo spaces, and is expressed as a figure, in the same way as gross tonnage.

Deadweight tonnage (DWT): used mainly for oil tankers to give an indication of the weight of oil carried. It is measured in tonnes.

Displacement tonnage: used for warships. It is the number of tonnes of sea water displaced by a vessel charged to its load-water line.

LONGEST BARGE CANALS

	ROUTE	YEAR OPENED	LENGTH km	LENGTH mi
Volga–Baltic Waterway (Russia)	Astrakhan to St Petersburg	1965	2,977	1,850
Grand Canal (China)	Beijing to Harchon	540 BC – AD 1327	1,781	1,107
Karakumsky Canal (Turkmenistan)	Amu-Dar'ya (Oxus) to Khrebet Kopet Dag	1980	1,069	664
New York State Barge Canal (USA)	Hudson River to Lake Erie	1918	837	520
Rajasthan Canal (India)	Bamgarh to western Haryana	1955	649	403
Irtysh–Karaganda Canal (Kazakhstan)	Karaganda to River Irtysh	1971	451	280
Trent Canal (Canada)	Lake Huron to Lake Ontario	1833–1918	443	275

■ *The nuclear-powered aircraft carrier USS* Dwight D. Eisenhower *transits the Suez Canal en route to the Mediterranean Sea*

GIANTS OF THE SEA

LARGEST SHIP

The world's largest ship of any kind is the oil tanker *Jahre Viking* (formerly the *Happy Giant* and *Seawise Giant*), at 564,763 tonnes deadweight. The tanker is 458.45 m (1504 ft) long overall, has a beam of 68.80 m (226 ft) and a draught (the depth of a loaded vessel in the water, taken from the level of the waterline to the lowest point of the hull) of 24.61 m (80 ft 9 in). Declared a total loss after being disabled by severe bombardment in 1987–88 during the Iran-Iraq war, the tanker underwent $60 million-worth of renovations in Singapore and Dubai, United Arab Emirates, and was relaunched under its new name in November 1991.

LARGEST BATTLESHIPS

The largest battleships ever commissioned were the Japanese *Yamato* and *Musashi* (both completed and sunk during World War II). Both had a full load displacement of 69,988 tonnes, an overall length of 263 m (863 ft), a beam of 38.7 m (127 ft) and a full load draught of 10.8 m (35 ft 5 in).

LARGEST PASSENGER VESSEL

The largest passenger vessel ever built is Carnival Cruise Line's *Carnival Destiny* (see below), which has a displacement tonnage of 101,353. She has an overall length of 272 m (893 ft) and is 38 m (125 ft) in breadth.

THE WORLD'S LARGEST PORT, COVERS 238 KM^2 AND HAS A 1215 KM NAVIGABLE WATERFRONT ■

WONDERS OF CONSTRUCTION

- **The total length of the Great Wall of China spans one-tenth of the circumference of the Earth.**
- **The Universal Financial Centre in Shanghai, China, when completed in 2001, will be the world's tallest building, standing at 454 m high – it will be one and a half times taller than the Eiffel Tower.**
- **Constructing ground-breaking structures can be very dangerous – 66 people died building Japan's Seikan rail tunnel.**
- **The CN Tower in Toronto, Canada, was built to resist extreme winds – it sways only 25 cm in 210 km/h winds.**

THE SEVEN WONDERS OF THE ANCIENT WORLD

▶ In the 2nd century BC, the writer Antipater of Sidon described seven structures as the pre-eminent sights of the ancient world.

▶ Today, of all the wonders, only the pyramids of Giza retain most of their original structure.

The Pyramids of Giza (Egypt)
Built between 2575 and 2465 BC, the pyramids at Giza are the oldest of the Seven Wonders. The Great Pyramid of Cheops is 137.5 m (451 ft 1 in) high, although it used to be 9 m (29 ft 6 in) higher. About 100,000 workers took 20 years to position the 2.5 million blocks (each weighing 2.5 tonnes).

The Hanging Gardens of Babylon
A series of landscaped terraces, the hanging gardens were built by Nebuchadnezzar II (*c.* 630–562 BC) for his Persian wife, Amytis, who missed the mountains when she moved to the flat plains of Babylon. The gardens were irrigated by water from the River Euphrates and carried up by slaves.

The Statue of Zeus at Olympia
Made from ivory and gold around 430 BC by Phidias of Athens, this huge statue depicted the Greek god Zeus enthroned. It truly was a wonder of epic scale, with the statue's head alone being built 13 m (43 ft) high.

The Temple of Artemis at Ephesus
A structure famed for its great size, the marble Temple was originally constructed *c.* 550 BC, but was burnt down and rebuilt. It originally consisted of 127 Ionic columns and included a gold statue of Artemis, which was destroyed. Only one of the columns now remains.

The Mausoleum of Halicarnassus
This massive marble tomb was dedicated to the Anatolian king, Mausolus. Built *c.* 350 BC by his widow Artemisia, only the foundations remain, although some of its statues can be found in the British Museum, London.

The Colossus of Rhodes
A vast bronze statue that took its sculptor, Chares, 12 years to complete. Commemorating the siege of Rhodes (305–304 BC), this bronze statue was 35 m (115 ft) high and placed at the entrance to the harbour of Rhodes. The statue, depicting the Sun god Helios, was destroyed in an earthquake.

The Pharos of Alexandria
Built *c.* 280 BC, this wonder was a huge lighthouse on the island of Pharos near Alexandria. It was built for Ptolemy II of Egypt, and had three bronze mirrors to magnify the light of a lantern. It was destroyed by a series of earthquakes in 1326.

BRIDGES

Akashi-Kaikyo Bridge
Planned for completion in spring 1998, the Akashi-Kaikyo road bridge is one of three bridges linking Honshu and Shikoku in Japan. The main span of this bridge will be 1990.8 m (6531 ft 6 in) and in total, including the side spans, it will measure 3911.1 m (12,831 ft 8 in) – making it 75% longer than the Humber Bridge, UK. The towers that will support the cable will be 297 m high (974 ft 3 in), making the bridge not only the longest in the world, but also the tallest.

Confederation Bridge
The Confederation Bridge, which joins Prince Edward Island to New Brunswick on the Canadian mainland, is 12.9 km (8 mi) long. The two-laned bridge, which took 33 months to build, was opened in 1997 and is the longest bridge running continuously over the sea.

Second Lake Pontchartrain Causeway
The longest bridge in the world is the Second Lake Pontchartrain Causeway, which connects Mandeville and Metairie, Louisiana, USA. Completed in 1969, it is 38.4 km (23.9 mi) long.

BUILDINGS

Empire State Building
The Empire State Building was the world's tallest building from 1930–71. Built in only 18 months, it transformed the New York skyline and has come to symbolize the city. At a height of 381 m (1250 ft), it includes over 60,000 tonnes of steel beams, which contribute to the building's total weight of 365,000 tonnes. The building has gradually recessed walls, a feature common to many New York skyscapers due to the city's building code, which prohibits a straight unbroken rise of more than 38.1 m (125 ft).

Imperial Palace, Beijing
The largest palace in the world is the Imperial Palace in Beijing, China, which covers 720,000 m² (861,141 sq yd). The outline dates from its initial construction under the third Ming Emperor, Yongle (1402–24), but most of the intramural buildings (five halls and 17 palaces) date from the 18th century. The palace, with 9000 rooms, was the seat of imperial power for 500 years.

■ *The five-sided Pentagon in Arlington, Virginia, houses the offices of the US Department of Defense*

Las Vegas MGM
The impressive MGM Grand Hotel/Casino in Las Vegas, Nevada, USA, is the world's largest hotel, consisting of four 30-storey towers on a site covering a total area of 45.3 ha (113 acres). It boasts 5005 rooms with suites of up to 560 m² (6000 sq ft) in size, a 15,200 seat arena, and a 13.3-ha (33-acre) theme park. The hotel entrance is 26.8 m (88 ft) tall and takes the form of the MGM lion. Other features include themed rooms, such as 'The Wizard of Oz', 'Hollywood' and 'Casablanca'.

The Leaning Tower of Pisa
Started in 1174, the Leaning Tower of Pisa, Italy, is famous for its tilted form. Designed by Bonanno Pisano as part of an architectural plan including the impressive cathedral and baptistry, the circular tower (campanile) never achieved perfect verticality because of inadequate foundations. It is 55 m (179 ft) high, but is in serious danger of collapsing.

Notre Dame de la Paix
The largest church in the world is the Basilica of Our Lady of Peace (Notre Dame de la Paix) at Yamoussoukro, Ivory Coast. Completed in 1989, it covers 30,000 m² (323,000 sq ft), has seating for 7000 people, and was modelled on St Peter's in Rome. Including its golden cross, it is 158 m (518 ft) high. One interesting feature is the 29 million holes that pierce the dome lining; this was done to minimize sound distortion. The gigantic church has over 7400 m² (8850 sq yd) of stained glass.

The Pentagon
The largest administrative building in the world is the Pentagon in Arlington, Virginia, USA. It covers a larger ground area than any other office building and 23,000 military and civilian staff work there. Built to house the US Defense Department's offices, it was completed in 1943 at an estimated cost of US$83 million. Each of the outermost sides is 281 m (921 ft) long, and the perimeter of the building is about 1405 m (4610 ft). Its five storeys enclose a floor area of 604,000 m² (149 acres), and the total length of the corridors is 28 km (17 mi).

Petronas Towers
Designed by Argentinian-born US architect Cesar Pelli, and completed in 1997, the Petronas Towers in Kuala Lumpur, Malaysia, is the tallest building in the world. The 88-storey twin towers and decorative spires reach a height of 451.9 m (1482 ft 8 in) – just under one-and-a-half times the height of the Eiffel Tower. The stainless-steel clad towers have a circular plan, with set-backs producing a tapering look as the building rises. A skybridge halfway up the structure connects double-height 'skylobbies' in each tower, whilst at the base there is a six-storey shopping centre, an underground car park for 5000 vehicles and a tunnel to serve it.

Sydney Opera House
The Sydney Opera House is perhaps Australia's most recognizable building. Amongst the 1000 rooms are five separate concert halls, an exhibition hall, bars, restaurants, over 60 dressing-rooms and a library. Its roof is covered with one million tiles, and the shell-like structure is faced with over 6000 m^2 (64,586 sq ft) of glass. The relatively little known architect, Jorn Utzon, left the project in 1966 over differences of opinion and never set foot inside. After his departure, significant changes were made to the design, and the Sydney Opera House was finally opened in 1973 at a cost of A$102 million.

Taj Mahal
Regarded by many as the most beautiful building in the world, the Taj Mahal near Agra, India, is a symbol of love and mourning. The Emperor Shah had it built in memory of his wife Mumtaz. Designed by an unknown architect and built by over 20,000 labourers, work started in 1631 and continued for 20 years. The mausoleum cost 40 million rupees to build and has a dome 67 m (220 ft) high.

■ *Grand Coulee Dam on the Columbia River, Washington, USA, helps to control floods and provides hydroelectric power*

DAMS
Cornelia Tailings Dam
The largest dam in the world by volume is the earth-fill Cornelia Tailings on Ten Mile Wash in Arizona, USA. It has a volume of 209,000,000 m^3 (273,000,000 cu yd).

Grand Coulee Dam
Built between 1933 and 1942, the Grand Coulee on the Columbia River, Washington State, USA, is the world's longest concrete dam. It is 168 m (550 ft) high and has a crest length of 1272 m (4173 ft). It contains 8,092,000 m^3 (10,585,000 cu yd) of concrete, at a weight of 19,600,000 tonnes.

Grande Dixence Dam
The world's highest concrete dam is the Grande Dixence on the River Dixence, Switzerland. Its height is 285 m (935 ft), and it has a crest length of 700 m (2297 ft). The dam used 5,960,000 m^3 (7,800,000 cu yd) of concrete in its construction.

Itaipu Dam
Completed in 1984, the Itaipu Dam, on the River Paraná near the Brazil–Paraguay border, is part of the world's most powerful hydroelectric power plant. It used 12.3 million tonnes of concrete, equivalent to all the buildings in a city of 4 million inhabitants.

DEFENCE BARRIERS
Great Wall of China
The Great Wall of China is the longest wall in the world, with a mainline length of 3460 km (2150 mi) and branches and spurs totalling 3530 km (2195 mi). The wall, which was built to repel Mongol invaders, took nearly 2000 years and the sweat of millions of labourers and political prisoners to construct. It has an average height of 6–9 m (20–30 ft) and is 6–7.5 m (20–25 ft) thick. There are an estimated 25,000 watchtowers dotted along its length.

Oosterscheldedam
The Oosterscheldedam (Eastern Scheldt), a storm-surge barrier in the southern Netherlands, is the largest flood prevention structure, 9 km (5.5 mi) long. Built to secure the south-east Netherlands against potentially catastrophic floods, it opened in 1986. Made of 65 concrete piers (each weighing 18,000 tonnes) and 62 gates (each more than 5 m (16 ft) thick, 39 m (128 ft) wide and 500 tonnes), it used 450,325 m^3 (589,000 cu yd) of concrete.

MONUMENTS
Angkor Wat
Cambodia's Angkor Wat ('City Temple') is the largest religious structure in the world. Built 1113–50 by Khmer King Suryavarman II to the Hindu god Vishnu, it covers 162.6 ha (402 acres). Its curtain (non-load-bearing) wall is 1.64 km^2 (0.63 sq mi) and its population, before it was abandoned in 1432, was 80,000. The whole complex of 72 major monuments extends over 192 km^2 (74 sq mi).

Mount Rushmore
One of the world's largest sculptures is the Mount Rushmore carving in South Dakota, USA, which depicts four US presidents: George Washington, Thomas Jefferson, Theodore Roosevelt and Abraham Lincoln. The sculpture involved the removal of 450,000 tonnes of rock, and each head measures about 18 m (59 ft) high. The entire structure took over 15 years to complete.

Quetzalcóatl Pyramid
The biggest pyramid in the world, and the largest monument constructed to date, is the Quetzalcóatl pyramid at Cholula de Rivadabia, 101 km (63 mi) south-east of Mexico City. The edifice is 54 m (177 ft) tall and its base covers an area of almost 18.2 ha (45 acres).

Statue of Liberty
A familiar feature of the New York skyline, the Statue of Liberty was a gift from France to the USA to cement their friendship and mark the centenary of the American Revolution. Sculpted by Frédéric-Auguste Bartholdi, it was dedicated in 1886. At 93 m (305 ft) high, it was the tallest monument in the world at the time, and stands on a pedestal 27 m (89 ft) high.

TOWERS
CN Tower
The tallest free-standing structure in the world is the CN Tower in Toronto, Canada. The $63-million (£28-million) tower rises to a height of 553.34 m (1815 ft 5 in). The tower was completed in 1975, and the 416-seat restaurant in the Sky Pod, which revolves at a height of 351 m (1151 ft) can offer views of hills 120 km (75 mi) away. The tower, which weighs 130,000 tonnes, was built by Canadian National Railways to help increase the clarity of television signals. It demonstrates almost perfect verticality, as the structure, as it stands, is no more than 3 cm (1⅕ in) off the true perpendicular.

Eiffel Tower
Designed in 1889 by Gustave Eiffel, the Eiffel Tower was intended to be the temporary centrepiece of the Exposition Universelle, an exhibition which marked the centenary of the French Revolution. However, it was not dismantled and for over 40 years after its construction remained the tallest building in the world at 301.8 m (990 ft 2 in). The tower is comprised of 18,000 components held together by 2 million rivets, and has become one of Paris's best-known symbols.

KTHI-TV Tower
The world's tallest tower – the television transmitting tower located between Fargo and Blanchard, North Dakota, USA – is 629 m (2063 ft) tall. It was built by 11 men in 30 days in 1963. However, the tallest structure ever built was the Warsaw radio mast at Konstantynow, Poland. Prior to its fall during renovation work in 1991, it measured 646.38 m (2120 ft 8 in), more than double the height of the Eiffel Tower. This guyed (supported by rope, chain or wire) structure was felled by high winds and storm damage.

TUNNELS
Channel Tunnel
The first historic breakthrough under the Channel occurred on 1 December 1990, 15.6 km (9.7 mi) from France and 22.3 km (13.9 mi) from the United Kingdom. The Channel Tunnel was officially opened on 6 May 1994 by Queen Elizabeth II and President Mitterrand. There are three tunnels, each 50 km (31 mi) long, with about 38 km (23.6 mi) running under the Channel. These tunnels produced 8,000,000 m^3 (10,481,481 cu yd) of spoil when dug. They have 720,000 lining segments, 268 cross-passages, 500 doors, 450 km (279.6 mi) of pipework and 2500 km (1553 mi) of electric cabling.

Seikan Tunnel
The Seikan Tunnel, which connects the Japanese islands of Honshu and Hokkaido, is the world's longest rail tunnel. It has an overall length of 53.85 km (33.46 mi) and was bored to a depth of 240 m (787 ft) beneath sea level and 100 m (328 ft) below the sea bed of the Tsugaru Strait. Tests on the 23.3-km (14.5-mi) underwater section began in 1964, construction started in 1972, and the first test run took place in March 1988.

STATUE OF LIBERTY'S CROWN SYMBOLIZE THE SEVEN CONTINENTS AND THE SEVEN SEAS ■

COMPUTERS

- **Computers worth £500 today have the same computational power as those costing over £1 million 20 years ago.**
- **If a human could communicate with a device without seeing it and never know that the device was a computer, then the device would have passed the Turing Test for true intelligence – a test no computer has yet passed.**
- **The use of the word 'bug' comes from when a moth clogged up a mechanical computer in 1946.**
- **A mobile phone today carries more computing power than the Apollo missions to the Moon.**

■ *Women work on Colossus, the computer built by Alan Turing that helped to save many British lives during WWII*

HOW COMPUTERS WORK

▶ The heart of a computer is the CPU – the Central Processing Unit.
▶ Personal computer microchips can contain up to five million transistors.

Computers are machines that carry out actions on coded information (data) controlled by a program of instructions. The familiar digital computer uses number codes to represent letters of the alphabet, numbers, images, sounds, commands and other information. All this has been made possible by the ability to construct electronic circuits in incredibly small crystals, called chips, of the element silicon.

Digital computers use binary numbers (see pp. 136–37) as units of information. Consisting of only the digits 0 and 1 (referred to as bits, from 'binary digit'), they are easy to represent electrically – a 1 by current flowing or a voltage present, 0 by no-current or no-voltage. Bits are usually grouped into eight, forming a byte. As computers deal with large amounts of data, larger units need to be used, such as the kilobyte (1 Kb = 1024 bytes), megabyte (1 Mb = 1024 Kb) and gigabyte (1 Gb = 1024 Mb).

HARDWARE AND SOFTWARE

Hardware consists of all electronic and mechanical components of a computer (see pp. 154–55). The electronic heart, or central processor, carries out arithmetic and comparison actions on pairs of binary digits. These bytes are stored electronically in the memory that is connected to the processor, so that bytes can be read, processed and written as quickly as possible. The unit of time used to measure memory speed is the nanosecond (1 ns = 10^{-9} seconds, a billionth of a second). The timing of actions is determined by the clock rate, the rate of applying electrical pulses to the processor. This is measured in MHz (millions of pulses per second). Circuits called ports deal with the input of new data and the output of processed data to the screen, printer or disk. All computing actions are carried out under the control of a program, which is another set of bytes in code. The program and the data are the system's software. Hardware can be compared to a record player and software to the records played on it – the hardware is useless without the software.

PROGRAMS

Programming development has aimed to make team programming easier and reduce the inevitable errors in large programs. No language is perfect, and no program is ever totally free of defects (bugs).

The operating system is an important aid. This is a program that attends to the needs of the system, such as controlling the memory, keyboard, disk system, screen and other outputs. The operating system also provides the environment, meaning, for example, the use of images (icons) with on-screen pointers moved by the mouse. The other main aid is the use of modern programming languages.

STORAGE AND PROCESSING

Data is stored inside the computer in memory. The memory is a set of electrically charged units of information, organized into bytes and with each set accessible by using an address number applied to the memory chips. The two fundamental types of memory are ROM and RAM (see glossary).

Backing stores are used for long-term retention. At the present time, the usual backing is a hard drive, a set of magnetic disks that can store upwards of 850 Mb of data. Removable 3.5-in floppy (magnetic) disks can store 1.4 Mb on a disk, and the CD-ROM stores data in read-only form using an optical disk (identical to an audio compact disc). Modern CD drives can both read and write data.

SPEED AND PERFORMANCE

The 'power' of a computer is measured by its processing speed, memory capacity, and backing store size. Microcomputers can be connected together into networks to share a common backing store and printer(s), and mainframe machines can also be included in such a network.

Modern microcomputers currently operate with four-byte units, with the internal timing system regulated by a crystal clock oscillating at many millions of times per second. The timing clock is synchronized with the operating speed of the processor, and taken together they provide a general value for the speed of a computer. The clock speed is measured in megahertz (millions of cycles per second), with typical values for personal home computers in excess of 150 MHz. These computers operate with anything up to 64 Mb of memory and with a hard drive of between 500 Mb to 5 Gb. The speed can be improved by using memory caches – small pieces of fast-acting memory. Since the same data is often needed several times, it can be reached more quickly from fast memory than from main memory or backing stores.

DEVELOPMENT OF COMPUTERS

▶ The first programmable electronic computer was the 1500-valve Colossus, first run in 1943 to break coding machines used by the Germans in World War II.
▶ The first personal computer was the MITS Altair 8800, which went on the market in 1975.

Digital computers started life as huge machines, using rooms full of radio valves, and programmed using sets of switches. This machine-code programming, or first-generation language, is feasible only for very short programs, and was soon replaced by assembly-language programming, a second-generation language. Assembly languages use brief instruction words like ADD to act as mnemonics (memory aids) for machine code. A program called an assembler then reads the words and associated numbers and converts them into machine code, but such programming demands that the programmer should have a very detailed knowledge of how the hardware works.

As computer hardware developed, firstly using transistors and later using chips in place of valves, software also developed, with third-generation programming languages that use commands that look like instructions in English and which need no detailed knowledge of the machine.

Most computers nowadays are microcomputers, small enough to be placed on a desktop. There is still a need for large computers, such as mainframes or supercomputers, that deal with vast amounts of information very rapidly, and at the other end of the scale, miniature computers, consisting of one plug-in unit, that are used for industrial controllers. Laptop machines can now match the performance of desktop machines, though at much higher prices, and subject to the limitations of batteries. Palm-top computers, which can be held in the palm of the hand, are a recent development on the market.

COMPUTING NOW AND IN THE FUTURE

▶ In the future, computers may be controlled by alpha-wave thought processes alone.
▶ Computers are being developed that use biological enzymes operating on DNA code.

Small computers, along with new software, now permit a range of activities that would have been impossible even on the largest machines of a few years ago. The use of multimedia (see glossary) is now commonplace. Using the Internet, one can write to or talk with any other user in the world for the price of a local telephone call, and even videophone (see and talk) facilities are now possible.

Developments under way include computers that can pick up data based on the movement of an arm or even the blink of an eye. Users will soon be able to dictate letters without the need to type, to send such letters electronically, and to hear them read out, offering enormous benefits to the physically challenged. The actions of the telephone, fax, TV, video recorder and computer will also start to be combined, allowing people to view and hear what they want, anytime they choose.

The ways in which we interact and interface with computers may also change. Today, the most common methods used for telling the computer what to do are the keyboard, the mouse and, increasingly, speech. However, constant innovations in biotechnology and nanotechnology may result in humans becoming directly interfaced to computers: a direct link between the central nervous system and the central processing unit. Computers are also becoming increasingly small and, through nanotechnology, we may one day see computers so tiny they are able to exist in our bloodstream and regulate disease. One thing is certain – computers have considerably changed the way we live, and will continue to shape our lives for a long while to come.

CYBERSPACE AND VIRTUAL REALITY

▶ Virtual-reality visionaries envisage a future where humans will be directly wired in to the digital realm of cyberspace.
▶ Cyberspace junkies refer to the human body as 'meat'.

Cyberspace and virtual reality are buzzwords of our new digital culture. Developments in the way we interact with computers has resulted in a new horizon of possibilities for the user.

The word 'Cyberspace' was coined by cyberpunk science-fiction writer William Gibson in 1984 in his novel *Neuromancer,* where he defined it as 'a consensual hallucination', the sum total of all the data in the global network of computers. Cyberspace can be thought of as the realm of data, and the interconnecting structures that support it. Thus cyberspace covers a broad range of networks, from telephone interchanges to the sprawling global network of the World Wide Web.

Cyberspace can be presented to the human user in a variety of ways, from simple VDU screens through to multimedia presentations to complete simulated realities. Virtual reality (VR) is one such interface between the electronic and human worlds. The term 'virtual reality' was coined by Jaron Lanier, computer scientist and author, in the 1980s, and the concept of VR offers us telepresence – reality at a distance. VR seeks to represent data in the form of realistic imitation of environment through technological body-enhancements, and offers the user an artificial world of sight, touch and sound. The ultimate aim is to totally immerse the human senses in a constructed reality through eye-phones, datagloves and datasuits, all connected to a computer that provides continual stimulation.

■ *This is a still from the film* The Lawnmower Man *(1992), one of the films made in the last 16 years, along with* Johnny Mnemonic *(1995) and* Tron *(1982), that have been inspired by developments in virtual reality*

The person is then able to experience a projected reality and interact with it.

There are many uses for virtual reality, from remote surgery to bomb disposal, from virtual shopping malls to re-enactments of historical events. Scientists will be able to walk around molecular structures, architects could walk their clients around buildings that only exist on the drawing board, and school trips could involve walks on alien landscapes without ever leaving planet Earth. Although the technology is relatively crude at present, continual developments in computing means that VR will, in the future, allow virtual landscapes, virtual cities and virtual societies.

Some critics suggest that cyberspace, VR and Internet communications will result in a generation of autistic, socially challenged people. However, others believe that the opposite will be true and that there will be no prejudice in cyberspace.

GLOSSARY OF COMPUTER TERMS

application: a program that operates on data, such as a word processor, database or spreadsheet.
archive: data stored in a form intended for long-term retention.
ASCII (American Standard Code for Information Interchange): a binary 7-bit standard code for text characters, digits and punctuation marks.
bug: a fault in a program.
CD-ROM: a form of compact disc that contains digitally coded text, sounds and pictures. This is used for program distribution and for multimedia.
character: any symbol (including numbers, letters, punctuation marks, mathematical symbols, etc.) that can be stored and processed by a computer.
clock: an electronic circuit that provides electrical pulses for timing processor actions. Clock rates in excess of 200 MHz (200 million pulses per second) are now common.
clone: a close copy of a machine that will run the same software.
crash: a total program failure.
cursor: a small block or pointer arrow on the computer screen that can be moved by the mouse.
data: characters or symbols stored in a computer for processing.
database: a collection of data that can be analysed and interrogated on computer to retrieve items (or combinations of items) that match selected criteria.
desktop publishing (DTP): a program for typesetting with graphics and illustrations to provide leaflets and book or magazine pages.
dot-matrix: the use of a set of dots to produce characters on the VDU screen or on paper.
fibre optics: the use of thin glass fibres to carry light signals, replacing the use of copper cable carrying electrical signals.
GUI (Graphical User Interface): an operating system which uses images (icons) arranged in windows to represent data files and programs. The icons can be selected or moved using a pointing device (mouse).
hacker: a person who gains illegal access to other computers either mischievously or for criminal intent.
icon: see GUI.
ink-jet: a form of printer mechanism in which ink is squirted from a matrix of tiny jets on to the paper.
interface: an electronic circuit that converts electronic signals from one form to another. An interface is needed to allow the computer to be connected to another piece of equipment, such as the disk system and the screen.
Internet: a set of connected (mainframe) computers. By linking one's computer into this set, using a modem, one has access to a vast amount of information and can both send and receive words, sounds and pictures.
microprocessor: the basic unit of a microcomputer which can be programmed to perform simple actions on bytes of data.
monitor (VDU): the display device on a computer. Desktop machines use a TV-style unit with a cathode-ray tube; laptops use the LCD type of flat screen.
mouse: a hand-held device that rolls across a table or board and moves the cursor on the screen.
multimedia: software that uses a CD to provide text, pictures (still or moving) and sounds, making this a vitally important aid to education and for information storage.
network: a system of computers connected to each other to share data.
OCR (Optical Character Recognition): software for converting scanned text into data for a word processor.
program: a set of instructions that a system follows to carry out tasks.
RAM (Random-Access Memory): memory which can be read or written and is volatile – its contents are lost when power is cut off.
ROM (Read-Only Memory): memory which can be read but not changed or erased.
scanner: a device that transforms an image on paper into digitally coded signals that can be stored on computer and redisplayed. Scanned text can be converted into a word-processor file (see OCR).
SCSI (Small Computer System Interface, pronounced 'scuzzy'): a general purpose link between a computer and one or more external devices.
spreadsheet: a form of data-analysing program that can be used for a very wide range of applications ranging from word tables to the analysis of complex mathematical relationships.
terminal: device linked to a computer, including a keyboard, screen, or both.
voice recognition: a computer's ability to respond to spoken words.
window: a portion of a screen used as if it were an independent screen, whose size and position can be changed.
word processor: a program for composing text and producing printed pages to a specified design.
workstation: the equipment used by a computer operator and, increasingly, the associated furniture, lighting and working environment.

THE NET

▶ The Internet Worm, a self-replicating program released online in 1988, brought areas of the Internet to a standstill.

▶ Intranets are local computer networks modelled on the principle of the Internet.

▶ A corporate 'firewall' is a virtual security cordon around sensitive data to deter would-be hackers.

▶ Some experts believe that 21st-century terrorist activities will involve attacks on the infrastructure of the Internet.

▶ To use capital letters on the Internet can be the virtual equivalent of shouting in a small room.

NETWORKING

▶ The speed of everyday data transmission via a modem has increased 2100% in the last 15 years.
▶ The fastest network links are provided by using fibre-optic cables which carry coded light beams.

A network is a set of computers connected together. If the network is within one building with connections by cable, this is a local area network, or LAN. LANs can be connected to each other using a device called a router to form a wide area network or WAN. The WAN links can be provided in many ways: by telephone, by special cables (ISDN), by radio link or by satellite.

Telephone lines are convenient but, although the links between telephone exchanges use digital signalling, the links between the home or office and the exchange are of the older voice type. A device called a *modem* can be used at each end of such a line to convert the signals. If a more modern type of link (ISDN) is used, no modems are needed, and communication can be much faster.

THE INTERNET

▶ The Internet, or Net, consists of a vast number of private, public, corporate and academic networks linked worldwide.
▶ Current estimates claim that over 50 million users are linked to the Net.

The origin of the Internet, in 1969, came from the fear that a nuclear blast could cripple US defences by destroying computers. Therefore, a network was designed that would continue to work even if some of the cables connecting it were broken. This resulted in the development of software which enabled each computer to be connected to a few of its neighbours and for information to go by the shortest possible route and not follow a prescribed fixed path – the basis of the modern Internet. The most important part of the software implements the standardized methods of working, which are called protocols. These allow the various networks and computers to talk to each other without difficulty. In particular, the Transmission Control Protocol/Internet Protocol (TCP/IP) is still used.

In 1990 the Internet lost its military connections. As it is now unregulated, in that no one owns or runs it, the number of links and users can only be guessed.

CONNECTING TO THE NET

A home user will normally connect to the Internet by way of the telephone, using a modem. Office or other business users might set up an ISDN link. Once connected, one can open an account with a firm which runs a large network and will act as an information provider (IP), also known as Internet Access Providers (IAPs), or Internet Service Providers (ISPs). The user will either pay a set monthly fee for unlimited Net access, or pay according to the use of the Net. On top of this, the user will also, of course, pay for telephone use. Only time is charged, not distance. The IP will often provide users with software when they join, making the task of linking up much easier. When a user connects, the main uses of the IP will be to provide e-mail, news, and full Net access. Some IPs can provide e-mail alone at a reduced rate, since this is often all that a business user needs.

E-MAIL

Using e-mail, one can send and receive messages (which can contain sounds and pictures) by using the IP's host computer as a form of electronic mailbox. A message that one person sends will be stored until the recipient switches on and uses the software that allows e-mail to be received and sent. Once a message has been read, it can be deleted, replied to, saved locally or forwarded to another contact. A message may be sent or copied simultaneously to more than one user. All of this is controlled by the e-mail software, which is often a part of the main Net software, such as Microsoft Internet Explorer or Netscape Navigator.

Each user of e-mail must have a unique address, which takes the general form of name@provider. The name portion consists of one's own name (or whatever one would like to be called), using lower-case letters and with no spaces (though full-stops and hyphens can be used). The provider part is set by the IP. If the provider is mailhost.com and the user name is Jim Dandy, the e-mail address may be jim.dandy@mailhost.com, for example.

NEWS GROUPS

News groups are discussion groups classified by any of a vast number of topics. Each news site is locally run and is organized by a news administrator. Some sites are moderated, meaning that the messages are checked to remove offensive or irrelevant material, and a few sites require a password and charge a fee for use. The network of news groups is collectively known as USENET.

Users do not need to contribute to a group and might learn all they want to know by 'lurking', that is, reading messages but not sending (posting) any. Messages often form a thread, meaning an original query or statement which spawns a long trail of answers and arguments. The user can save, copy, print, or reply to, messages using news software, usually incorporated in Net software (browsers).

In any group, once discussion has started, a list of frequently asked questions (FAQ) is assembled, and new subscribers should always read this list to avoid wasting time in repeating answers to queries.

THE WEB

The Web (World Wide Web, WWW or W3) is the largest section of the Net. Web documents are in hypertext, meaning that the text of a document contains icons or coloured text. Selecting an icon will call up a further relevant document, menu, sound or picture which may contain further links. The program that is used to scan (or surf) the Web is known as a browser, of which the best known are Microsoft Internet Explorer and Netscape Navigator (which also contain news and mail actions). Such programs also allow files (programs, pictures or sounds) to be downloaded.

Typically, Web addresses start with http//:www, followed by a specific site address whose sections are separated by a full-stop. These site addresses reveal the country of origin (otherwise the country is the USA) and also reveal whether the source is academic (ac), a commercial firm (co or com), government organization (gov), or other.

DIGITAL COMMUNICATIONS

▶ The speed, quality and efficiency of modern digital communications can allow the entire contents of a library to be transmitted in under a minute.
▶ By the year 2000, a mesh of satellite networks may provide digital communications for 90% of the globe.

Until recently, communications using telephone or radio relied on analogue methods, meaning the sound wave into a microphone was converted to an electrical wave and then transmitted, converting back to a sound wave at the other end of the link. Television relies on the scene viewed by a TV camera being sampled at several thousand points to produce an electrical wave, which is transmitted. Distortion and interference plague these methods and, since each link needs to use radio waves, the world is running out of available radio frequencies.

Digital communications rely heavily on sampling and conversion. Sampling involves taking an analogue signal and measuring it a set number of times per second. The higher the sampling rate, the more accurate the conversion. A sound wave, for example, can be sampled at around 40,000 times per second, and the size (amplitude) of each sample is converted to a number using 16 bits of binary code. When compact discs first appeared (see pp. 154–55),sampling at this rate was only just possible, but now it is possible to sample at the higher rates needed for television, using methods that involve less sampling less often and use a smaller number of digits without much loss of quality.

Once the waves are converted to a stream of numbers, there are a number of advantages: errors, distortion and interference can be reduced to negligible proportions; gross errors can be kept to a minimum and corrected; and streams of numbers can be interleaved, so that several transmissions can be sent at the same time to reduce the range of radio frequencies that are needed.

Digital methods are, therefore, used in a range of media: for the most recent cellular telephones; for digital TV, which has recently reached various parts of the world with an abundant choice of channels; and for digital radio, which is likely to replace existing systems before the end of the 20th century. Links between telephone exchanges have been entirely digital for some time, and it may not be long before the link between the exchange and the home is also digital, permitting a much wider range of data to be transmitted along telephone lines.

NETIQUETTE

The Internet has developed in recent years to become a formidable and dynamic means of communicating with people all over the world. Just as everyday talking has certain rules and protocols, electronic methods of communication have evolved several guides for conducting oneself while on the Internet. These rules are collectively known as netiquette.

Netiquette is not a rigid system and hardly ever enforced. Rather, people on the Net are expected to observe netiquette in the same way that people in everyday conversation are normally polite. But of course, not everyone in cyberspace is polite; indeed, the lack of physical presence often influences people to be ruder, cruder and more abusive. To be rude and hurl verbal abuse on the Net is known as flaming, and there are even areas of the Net designated for people to flame each other in. Whilst being flamed can be quite daunting, the art of good flaming can be the height of verbal and mental dexterity.

Other people break netiquette conduct by sending unsolicited e-mail (generally, advertisements of a junk-mail type) to millions of addresses, or by blanket posting a news-group article to areas not relevant to its content. This latter activity is known as spamming. Another generally frowned-upon activity in cyberspace is trolling, or posting a deliberately provocative article onto a news group or website with the intention of creating a reaction and hopefully starting a flamewar – a prolonged series of flames.

EMOTICONS

When communicating in cyberspace, whether through e-mail, Internet Relay Chat or in news-group articles, it can be quite difficult to convey emotions simply through text. Since people reading someone's text do not yet have visual or audio cues as to the person's mood, a system of using various text symbols to represent emotions has evolved. Called 'emoticons', these crude pictures often mimic smiles or frowns (especially when viewed from the side). Thus a colon followed by a close bracket imitates a smiling face, and this emoticon :) is used to convey happiness, or a general good mood. Some emoticons can be extremely elaborate, and often need no further explanation to be understood. Emoticons include:

:)	smile
:-)	smile (with a nose)
:o)	another smile
:D	laugh or big smile
:-I	grim face
<g>	grin
<vbg>	very big grin
<eg>	evil grin
<wg>	wicked grin
:*	kiss
;)	wink (suggests cheekiness or sarcasm)
:X	my lips are sealed
:P	tongue poking out
:o#)	man with a moustache
{}	a hug
:(	frown (conveys sadness)
:'(	crying
O:)	angel
}:>	devil
<3	a heart
@--->	a rose
<------	referring to yourself
c[]]	a pint of beer
(_)?	coffee
[_]?	tea
>^,,^<	a cat
<><	a small fish

Using the Internet to communicate with others can become an expensive activity, and so several acronyms have evolved as a convenient keyboard shorthand to save time (and money). These are especially used in Internet Relay Chat forums, where the ability to convey emotion and sense quickly is most important. Some of these acronyms include:

afk	away from keyboard
atk	at the keyboard
bak	back at keyboard
bbl	be back later
bfn or b4n	bye for now
brb	be right back
btw	by the way
fwiw	for what it's worth
gmta	great minds think alike
imho	in my humble (or honest) opinion
lol	laughing out loud
ltns	long time no see
ttyl	talk to you later
rofl	rolling on the floor laughing
rotf	rolling on the floor
wb	welcome back
wtg	way to go!

GLOSSARY OF INTERNET TERMS

attachment: a binary file sent along with e-mail text.

BBS (Bulletin Board System): a mail system which is not part of the Internet.

binary data: data which is not text (ASCII), such as a file which stores a picture.

browsing: looking at Web pages and clicking hyperlinks to follow an item of interest, or just scanning to find anything of interest. Also called surfing.

client: a program that requests services on a network, frequently from a computer running a server program in a client-server arrangement.

domain: the location of a host computer, usually part of its Internet address.

download: to receive text or other files through the Internet link.

electronic mail (e-mail): a method of transmitting typed text through a network of computers to any other user. Each user has a unique identification 'address'.

FAQ (Frequently Asked Questions): a list of questions that should not have to be asked again, and their answers.

flame: an abusive reply to a question or comment to a news group, often because of a user's failure to read the FAQ.

FTP (File Transfer Protocol): a standard system for transmitting files (usually programs) over the Internet. Anonymous FTP means that you do not need to sign an agreement to download such material.

gateway: a computer used to link one network to another of a different kind, especially where different protocols are used.

home page: the first Internet page that a browser program downloads, often containing links to other useful pages.

host: an individual computer on the Internet, usually a large mainframe computer.

IP (Internet protocol) address: the number-code for the domain name of the main provider computer.

ISDN (Integrated Services Digital Network): a digital link provided by telecommunications companies to subscribers whose local exchange is digital. ISDN provides a complete, dial-up digital connection, operating at speeds many times that of a standard modem.

JPEG (Joint Photographic Experts Group): a compressed form of file for images used to save transmission time on the Net.

MIME (Multipurpose Internet Mail Extension): a protocol which permits files containing binary data to be sent by e-mail.

MPEG (Motion Picture Experts Group): a compressed file format for video images.

modem (abbreviation of modulate demodulate): a device for converting a digital signal into a continuous (analogue) tone signal for transmission along a telephone line or radio link and which reverses the process at the other end (demodulation), so restoring the original digital signal. The speed at which a modem operates is measured in bits per second.

node: a single computer or device attached to a network which can transmit or receive data, frequently both, and which is identified by a node ID number.

packet: a collection of binary digital data, together with network information such as the address of the particular packet and its sequence in a transmission.

POP (Points of Presence): the range of telephone numbers that a provider can use. Ideally, the provider would have a POP on a local exchange.

PPP (Point-to-Point Protocol): set of programs which enable a computer to link to the Internet conforming to the TCP/IP protocols and supplanting SLIP.

protocol: a standard system that allows two computers or two networks to communicate.

router: a computer specifically designed to link one network to another.

server: a program that provides services on a network; used also to refer to the fileserver machine.

SLIP (Serial Line Internet Protocol): a set of older programs, now replaced by PPP, which enable a computer to link to the Internet conforming to the TCP/IP protocols.

SMTP (Simple Mail Transfer Protocol): part of the TCP/IP family of protocols governing the transmission of mail messages.

spamming: sending multiple messages, particularly commercial advertising.

surfing: see browsing.

TCP/IP (Transmission Control Protocol/Internet Protocol): the essential protocols upon which the Internet is founded and which have their roots in the Unix operating system. Essentially, TCP organizes the data into addressed packets and adds a sequence number to them with information for error detection; then IP is responsible for routing the packets through the system, from computer to computer.

text file: as distinct from a binary file – one which contains alphabet characters, numbers and punctuation, commonly represented by the ASCII code.

Unix: a computer operating system developed in 1969 and used by many large computers, such as the main computers on the Internet.

upload: to send files (text or binary) to other Internet users.

URL (Uniform Resource Locator): the method of addressing WWW sites.

WWW (World Wide Web): the extended Internet, covering the globe, can present text, graphics, movies and sound together in a multimedia format. The WWW, also known simply as the Web, is linked together, allowing users to browse for information.

Leading Figures in Computing

- **Bill Gates paid $30.8 million in 1994 for a Leonardo da Vinci manuscript which predicted the invention of the steam engine and the submarine.**
- **John von Neumann, along with his significant contributions to computer science, meteorology and the study of logic, was instrumental in the development of the hydrogen bomb and intercontinental ballistic missiles.**
- **Alan Turing committed suicide through taking a bite out of an apple soaked in potassium cyanide.**

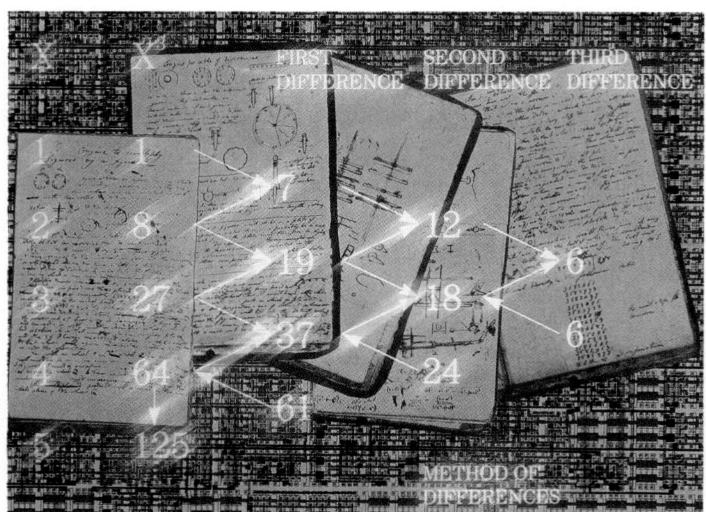

■ *Pages showing a representation of the Method of Differences (which Babbage used to design his difference engine) from his notebooks, which were discovered in 1937*

Aiken, Howard (1900–73), US mathematician working at Harvard University who, in the 1940s, created a very early digital computer. The machine was adapted from adding machines and the program was fed into the machine from a roll of punched paper tape.

Atanasoff, John V. (1903–), US physicist and inventor who worked with thermionic valves for a calculator at Iowa State College in the 1930s. He had demonstrated this device to several people, including John Mauchly, the co-designer of the ENIAC machine, and, on this basis, claimed successfully that the ENIAC patent was invalid.

Babbage, Charles (1792–1871), British mathematician and inventor. He had worked on calculating values of logarithms and ways of mechanizing calculations before designing and building an analytical engine – a mechanical form of computer. Plagued by problems of mechanical tolerances, it led him to design a more powerful machine – the difference engine – which for the first time used programming for a calculating machine. This work was financed by a grant from the Admiralty, who wanted to use the machine to calculate times of tides, but the work was never completed at the time.

Boole, George (1815–64), British mathematician and logician who, following the ideas of Leibnitz, developed the system called Boolean algebra, in which symbols are used for logical actions such as AND and OR. Boole showed that his algebra could allow logical propositions to be tested mathematically, using his algebraic rules which are now applied to the design of modern computers.

Byron, Augusta Ada (Lady Lovelace) (1815–52), the daughter of the English poet Lord Byron, who designed programs for the Babbage 'Difference Engine'.

Eckert, John Presper, Jr (1919–), US engineer and co-inventor, along with John Mauchly, of the ENIAC computer at the University of Pennsylvania in 1946. The name means Electronic Numerical Integrator And Computer, and the machine used 18,000 thermionic valves, giving a speed of several hundred multiplications per minute. Like Turing's Colossus (of which Eckert was not aware because of wartime secrecy), the program was wired into the processor and had to be manually altered.

Hollerith, Herman (1860–1929), American statistician who, in the 1880s, used perforated cards, similar to Jacquard's boards, for storing data. This data could then be read at high speed by passing the punched cards over electrical contacts. The Hollerith corporation later developed into IBM.

Jacquard, Joseph Marie (1752–1834), French inventor who designed an automatic loom that used thin, wooden boards to control the weaving of complicated designs. This was the first example of a programmed device.

Jobs, Steve (1955–), US entrepreneur who, together with Steve Wozniak, designed and built the first Apple personal computer. This machine, thanks to the development of the first spreadsheet program called Visicalc, became the most sought-after small computer in the late 1970s, and made Apple Computer Corporation a billion-dollar enterprise. Later Apple machines – the Lisa and the Macintosh – became the first to use the form of window and icon operating system that is virtually universal today.

Leibniz, Gottfried Wilhelm von (1646–1716), German philosopher and mathematician who, in the 1670s, improved on Pascal's calculator by devising a method for multiplying numbers mechanically.

Napier, John (1550–1617), Scottish mathematician who invented logarithms in 1614 as a way of coping with astronomical problems. In 1617 he described a method of multiplication using rods (Napier's bones) with number scales. This developed into the slide-rule which was used for calculations until the development of the electronic pocket calculator.

Neumann, John von (1903–57), Hungarian-American who devised the principle of storing a program into a computer which he built in 1945. This allowed, for the first time, a computer to work faster than the paper-tape reader which supplied information, and also permitted reprogramming without the need to rewire the computer. Von Neumann is remembered particularly for the principle of a computer working on one instruction at a time in sequence, and this, which became known as von Neumann architecture, is the basis of all but the most advanced computers working today.

Pascal, Blaise (1623–62), French mathematician, physicist and religious philosopher who discovered the modern theory of probability. In 1642, he devised a calculator which used a series of wheels, each with ten teeth and with each tooth representing a digit from 0 to 9. The wheels were geared so that numbers could be added to each other by moving the wheels.

Poulsen, Valdemar (1869–1942), Danish telephone engineer who invented magnetic recording in 1898, making possible later developments for storing data on magnetic discs.

Turing, Alan Mathison (1912–54), British mathematician whose pioneering work on computer logic was applied to code-breaking in World War II, and who became known for his achievements only much later. In 1936 he published a paper *On Computable Numbers,* which outlined the principles of a computing machine. In 1943, working at the Bletchley Park decoding station, he built the Colossus computer, which used thermionic valves for high-speed operation, and was programmed to crack German wartime codes.

Wozniak, Steve (1951–), US electronics engineer, largely self-taught, who, along with Steve Jobs, constructed the prototype of what became the first Apple computer in 1976. Until 1981 Wozniak specialized in technical developments, leaving Jobs to work on marketing. Wozniak finally resigned in 1985, and thereafter pursued his interest in music.

Zuse, Konrad (1910–), German mathematician who developed a mechanical computer for ballistics problems in 1941. This used relays to store binary data in on-off form, but had no memory for storing programs – reprogramming was carried out by rewiring.

Bill Gates – Head of Microsoft

William (Bill) H. Gates III (1955–) is a pioneer of computer software – the code that tells a computer what to do. He began computer programming at the age of 13 and entered Harvard in 1973, where he developed the home computer language BASIC for the MITS Altair – the first personal computer. BASIC has since become one of the most popular home programming languages. Gates dropped out of Harvard to pioneer Microsoft, a software company he set up in 1975 with Paul Allen. While many in computing were focusing their energies on hardware, Bill Gates, guided by a prophetic belief that the PC would become a powerful global tool, began to develop software for the personal computer. Microsoft developed into the world's largest software provider, with two-thirds of all computers using its software. A symbol of the entrepreneurial spirit governing computer development, Bill Gates has been called the Thomas Edison of the Information Age. A billionaire by the age of 31, with ownership of over 280 million shares in Microsoft, he is reputed to be worth $36.4 billion, making him the world's richest private individual. Gates also has professional interests in cellular phones, biotechnology and visual archives (he founded Corbis Corporation, which is developing a large database of art and photography from global sources).

■ BLAISE PASCAL DEVISED HIS CALCULATING MACHINE TO HELP HIS FATHER IN HIS ACCOUNTS ■

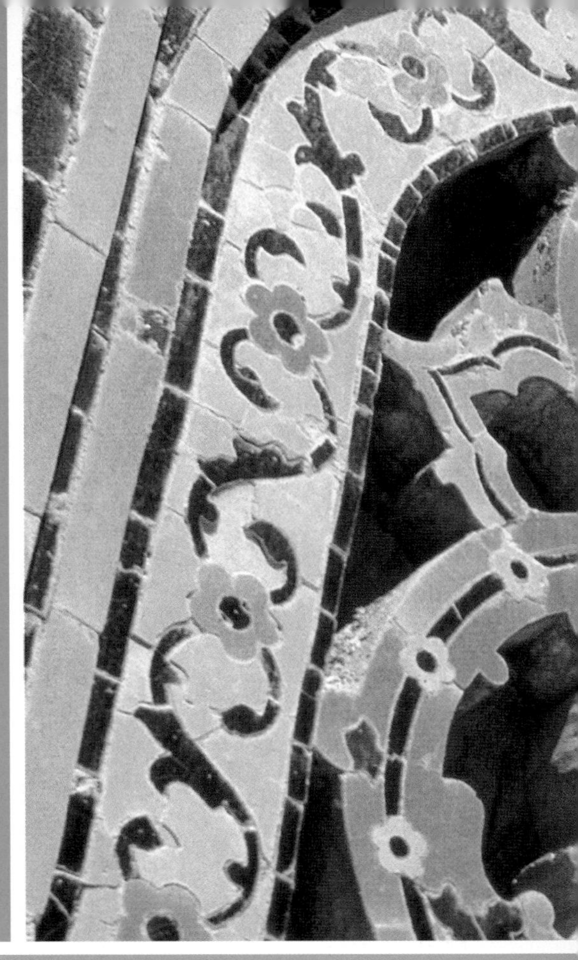

BELIEFS AND IDEAS ▷

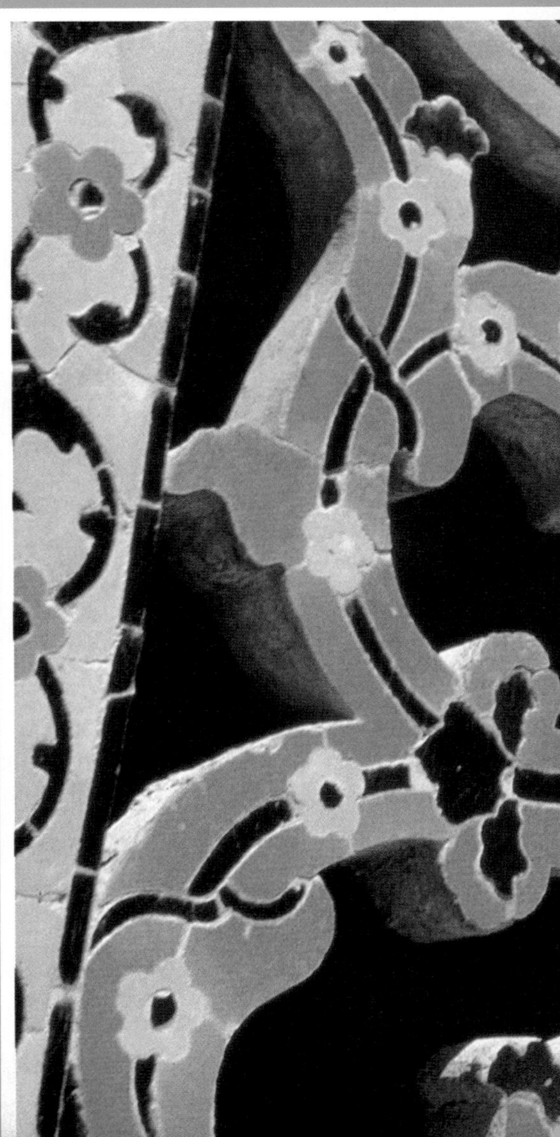

'What was once
thought can never
be unthought'
– Friedrich Dürrematt

PHILOSOPHY

- If time travel were possible, what would happen if you went back in time and killed your ancestors before you were born?
- Are there any experiences which cannot be described by language? If so, how may we tell others about them?
- How do I know that the colour I see and call blue is the same colour that you see and call blue?

Philosophy is the investigation of the general principles that are the basis for all our knowledge and activity. It differs from religion because it seeks to avoid dogma and faith; and it differs from science because it is willing to go beyond conclusively established facts. The founders of Western philosophy were the great thinkers of Ancient Greece – Socrates, Plato and Aristotle. They regarded philosophy as the highest expression of human virtue, but in the modern world philosophy includes any attempt to question or reinterpret the things in our thinking that we take for granted. Philosophers have always had conflicting opinions and theories, and are divided into different schools of thought. Modern philosophy has three main movements: Hegelianism, analytic philosophy and phenomenology. This contrasts with classical philosophy's three fields – metaphysics, ethics and epistemology.

Adorno, Theodor (1903–69), German philosopher who combined Marxism with avant-garde aesthetics.

Anselm (1033–1109), Italian Augustinian and realist. Anselm is famous for his examination of the proof of God's existence.

Aquinas, St Thomas (1225–74), Italian scholastic philosopher. Aquinas sought to unite Christianity with Aristotelianism. His philosophical system is known as Thomism.

Aristotle (384–322 BC), Greek philosopher and scientist, whose works have influenced the whole of Western philosophy. He taught that there are four factors in causation: form; matter; motive cause, which produces change; and the end, for which a process of change occurs. Aristotle was a pupil of Plato. He thought of the good as divine, but his ethics had a more 'practical' bent. He equated happiness with the good and was responsible for the doctrine of the golden mean. This stated that every virtue is a middle-point between the extremes of self-indulgence and self-renunciation.

Augustine of Hippo (AD 354–430), African philosopher who was an exponent of optimism. One of the greatest influences on medieval Christian thought, Augustine believed that God transcends human comprehension.

Averroës (1126–98), great philosopher of Muslim Spain, and a leading commentator on Aristotle. Averroës regarded religion as allegory for the common man and philosophy as the path to truth.

Avicenna (980–1037), Arabic follower of Aristotle and Neo-Platonism. Avicenna's works revived interest in Aristotle in 13th-century Europe.

Ayer, Alfred J. (1910–89), English philosopher. Ayer was the principal British advocate of logical positivism, developed from Russell.

Bacon, Francis (1561–1626), English statesman and philosopher of science who sought to promote empirical methods in the study of nature.

Beauvoir, Simone de (1908–86), French existentialist and founder of modern feminist philosophy.

Bentham, Jeremy (1748–1832), English utilitarian who regarded pleasure and pain rather than basic principle as the motivation for right action.

Berkeley, George (1685–1753), Anglo-Irish idealist and theist who taught that things exist only in being perceived and that the very idea of matter is contradictory.

Comte, Auguste (1798–1857), French philosopher. Comte was the founder of positivism, which stated that the Divinity and man were one, and that scientific principles explain all phenomena.

Croce, Benedetto (1866–1952), Italian philosopher noted for his role in the revival of historical realism.

Davidson, Donald (1917–), US philosopher of language, and follower of Quine.

Derrida, Jacques (1930–), French philosopher. The founder of deconstruction, a development of Heidegger's technique of interpreting traditional philosophers with great care in order to reveal their constant incoherence.

Descartes, René (1596–1650), French philosopher and scientist who regarded sensory knowledge as an inadequate foundation for science. His ideal of certainty was the statement 'I think therefore I am': for however deep my doubt, I must exist in order to doubt.

Dewey, John (1859–1952), US pragmatist who saw humans as continuous with, but distinct from, nature.

Erasmus, Desiderius (1466–1536), Dutch philosopher. The greatest of the humanists, Erasmus helped spread the ideas of the Renaissance throughout northern Europe.

Feuerbach, Ludwig (1804–72), German philosopher who argued that religion was no more than a projection of human nature. He was an important influence on Marx.

Fichte, Johann Gottlieb (1762–1814), German philosopher who formulated a philosophy of absolute idealism based on Kant's ethical concepts.

Frege, Gottlob (1848–1925), German mathematician who revolutionized formal logic and thus paved the way for analytic philosophy.

Habermas, Jurgen (1929–), German liberal Marxist philosopher who has affinities with Kant.

Hegel, Georg Wilhelm Friedrich (1770–1831). German philosopher who regarded all previous conceptions of philosophy as lifeless, one-sided and unhistorical. He argued that philosophy must always be rooted in history, but that it strives for a conception of reality as a single developing whole, every part of which is animated by all the others.

Heidegger, Martin (1889–1976), German student of Husserl who furthered the development of phenomenology and greatly influenced atheistic existentialists.

Heraclitus of Ephesus (533–475 BC), Greek philosopher who opposed the concept of a single ultimate reality and held that the only permanent thing is change.

Hobbes, Thomas (1588–1679), English materialist who believed the natural state of humanity is war.

Hume, David (1711–76), Scottish empiricist, philosopher and historian. Hume developed the ideas of Locke into a system of scepticism.

Husserl, Edmund (1859–1938), German philosopher who developed a system called phenomenology, which sought to ground knowledge in pure experience without presuppositions.

James, William (1842–1910), US psychologist and pragmatist who held that reality is always in the making.

Kant, Immanuel (1724–1804), German founder of critical philosophy. At first influenced by Leibniz, then by Hume, Kant sought to find an alternative approach to the rationalism of the former and the scepticism of the latter. In ethics, he formulated the Categorical Imperative, which states that what applies to oneself must apply to everyone else unconditionally.

Kierkegaard, Søren (1813–55), Danish religious existentialist, who taught that only existence has reality, and the individual has a unique value.

Leibniz, Gottfried Wilhelm von (1646–1716), German idealist and absolutist. Leibniz's optimistic view was ridiculed by Voltaire in *Candide*.

Lévi-Strauss, Claude (1908–), French anthropologist and proponent of structuralism. His writings investigate the relationship between culture (exclusively an attribute of humanity) and nature, based on the distinguishing characteristics of humans – the ability to communicate in a language.

Locke, John (1632–1704), English empiricist who sought to refute the rationalist view that knowledge derives from first principles.

Maimonides (1135–1204), Jewish student of Aristotle. Maimonides sought to combine Aristotelian teaching with that of the Bible.

Marcuse, Herbert (1898–1979), German-born US philosopher who attempted to combine existentialism and psychoanalysis with a libertarian Marxism which was critical of communism.

Marx, Karl (1818–83), German revolutionary thinker and follower of Hegel who was claimed as the founder of 20th-century communism.

Merleau-Ponty, Maurice (1907–61), French phenomenologist who insisted on the role of the human body in our experience of the world.

Mill, John Stuart (1806–73), English utilitarian who differed from Bentham by recognizing differences in quality as well as quantity in pleasure.

Nietzsche, Friedrich Wilhelm (1844–1900), German philosopher who held that the 'will to power' is basic in life and that the spontaneous is to be preferred to the orderly.

Parmenides of Elea (*c.* 495 BC), Greek philosopher. A member of the Eleatic school, Parmenides formulated the basic doctrine of idealism.

Pascal, Blaise (1623–62), French theist who held that sense and reason are mutually deceptive, that truth lies between dogmatism and scepticism.

Peirce, Charles S. (1839–1914), US logician and founder of pragmatism. Peirce regarded logic as the basis of philosophy and taught that the test of an idea is whether it works.

Plato (*c.* 428–347 BC), Greek philosopher. The founder of the Academy at Athens, Plato developed the idealism of his teacher Socrates and was the teacher of Aristotle. The idealist school began with Plato, who developed his system of ethics in a series of dialogues involving Socrates discussing the problems of philosophy. Socrates draws out wisdom from those he talks to, and argues that the good comes from the realm of 'ideas' or 'forms'. This is a perfect world of which the world of ordinary experience is only a pale replica.

Popper, Karl (1902–94), Austrian-born British critical rationalist. He held that scientific laws can never be proved and that the most that can be claimed is that they have survived attempts to disprove them.

Quine, Willard van Orman (1908–), US analytic philosopher and pragmatist who destroyed many of the dogmas of logical positivism.

Rousseau, Jean-Jacques (1712–78), French social and political philosopher who sought to counteract the inequality among men brought about by civilized society through a 'return to nature'.

Russell, Bertrand (1872–1970), English philosopher who built on Frege's revolution in logic and combined it with empiricism.

Sartre, Jean-Paul (1905–80), French philosopher who developed the existentialist thought of Heidegger. An atheistic supporter of a subjective, irrational human existence, he was opposed to an orderly overall reality. His slogan was 'existence before essence'.

Schopenhauer, Arthur (1788–1860), German idealist and pessimist who gave the will a leading place in his metaphysics.

Socrates (*c.* 470–399 BC), Greek philosopher and teacher of Plato, through whose writings his idealistic philosophy and dialectical method were brought to a larger audience. Socrates taught that virtue was based on knowledge. Accused of impiety and corruption of youth, Socrates was condemned to death, and died by drinking hemlock.

Spinoza, Benedict de (1632–77), Dutch rationalist metaphysician who developed the ideas of Descartes in the direction of pantheism.

Thales of Miletus (624–550 BC), Greek philosopher. Thales – an exponent of monism – is regarded as the first Western philosopher.

Whitehead, Alfred North (1861–1947), English evolutionist and mathematician who held that reality must not be interpreted in atomistic terms, but in terms of events. He held that God is intimately present in the universe, yet distinct from it – a view called pantheism.

Wittgenstein, Ludwig (1889–1951), Austrian philosopher whose work was highly influential in Britain, and focused on the complex relations between language and the world.

Zeno of Elea (*c.* 495–430 BC), Greek philosopher who argued that plurality and change are appearances, not realities.

PHILOSOPHICAL TERMS AND THEORIES

a posteriori knowledge: knowledge that comes from experience.

a priori knowledge: knowledge that can be derived from pure reasoning, without reference to experience (as in mathematics and logic).

aesthetics: study of the nature of beauty and taste, especially in art.

altruism: the principle of living and acting in the interest of others rather than for oneself.

analytic philosophy: a movement founded at the beginning of the 20th century by the English philosopher Bertrand Russell, building on the work of the German mathematician Gottlob Frege. It is based on the idea that philosophy is essentially the study of formal patterns of reasoning abstracted from their metaphysical, ethical, epistemological or historical contexts.

analytic truths: truths that can be proved purely by analysing the concepts they involve.

atomism: the belief that the entire universe is ultimately composed of interchangeable, indivisible units.

axiom: a necessary and self-evident proposition requiring no proof.

causality: the relationship between a cause and its effect.

critical theory: a philosophical version of Marxism associated with the Frankfurt school (founded 1921).

criticism: the theory that the path to knowledge lies midway between dogmatism and scepticism.

deduction: reaching a conclusion by purely a priori means.

determinism: the belief that the universe and everything in it (including individual lives) follows a fixed or pre-determined pattern. This belief has often been used to deny free will.

dialectic: literally, debate; by extension, the technique of proceeding from a thesis, through its negation or antithesis, to a synthesis in which both are reconciled on a higher level.

dialectical materialism: the theory – often attributed to Marx – that reality is strictly material but essentially conflictual, and is based on an economic struggle between opposing forces, with occasional interludes of harmony.

dogmatism: the assertion of a belief without arguments in its support.

dualism: the belief that the world consists of two radically independent and absolute elements, e.g. good and evil, or (especially) spirit and matter.

empirical knowledge: knowledge derived from experience rather than reason.

empiricism: the doctrine that there is no knowledge except what is derived from experience. Empiricism holds that, at birth, the mind is a passive blank sheet on which knowledge is then imprinted. The classic representative of Empiricism was John Locke, a 17th-century English philosopher.

Epicurean: often used to describe one who indulges in excessive pleasure, but the usage is not just. The Greek philosopher Epicurus did not condone excesses. On the contrary, he said that pleasure was only good when moderate and calm.

epistemology: the study of the nature, grounds and validity of human knowledge – how we come to know; how far we can rely on different kinds of belief; how science can be separated from superstition; and how conflicts between rival scientific theories can be resolved. The epistemologists who are usually called rationalists assert that knowledge is born in the individual and has only to be drawn forth. The other point of view – empiricism – is that at birth the mind is a passive blank sheet on which knowledge is then imprinted.

ethics: the study of how we decide how people ought to live and act. Philosophers' opinions about ethics tend to resolve into an opposition between two main schools: the idealists and the utilitarians. The idealists consider that the goodness or badness of a course of action must be judged by standards derived from outside the everyday world – from God or heaven, or perhaps from a human higher self. The utilitarians hold that the effects that a course of action produces in this world are all that is relevant to its ethical value. The utilitarians are more directly concerned than the idealists with earthly welfare. The earliest Western philosopher of this tradition was the Greek philosopher Epicurus.

existentialism: the doctrine that the human self and human values are fictions, but inevitable ones, and that it is bad faith to deny one's own free will, even in a deterministic universe.

fatalism: the doctrine that what will happen will happen and nothing we do will make any difference.

hedonism: the doctrine that pleasure is the highest good.

humanism: any system that regards human interests as paramount.

idealism: any system that regards thought or the idea as the basis either of knowledge or existence. Idealists consider that the goodness or badness of a course of action must be judged by standards derived from outside the everyday world – from God or heaven, or perhaps from a human higher self. The idealist school began with the Greek philosopher Plato.

induction: the process of drawing general conclusions from particular instances.

interactionism: the theory that physical events can cause mental events, and vice versa.

logic: the study of the structure or form of valid arguments, disregarding their content.

materialism: the doctrine that asserts the existence of only one substance – matter.

metaphysics: originally the title of one of Aristotle's treatises. It probably meant only that he wrote it after his treatise *Physics*, but the term is usually employed to describe speculation as to the ultimate nature of reality.

monism: a belief in only one ultimate reality, whatever its nature.

naturalism: the attempt to explain all phenomena by means of strictly natural (as opposed to supernatural) categories.

nominalism: the doctrine that general terms are nothing more than words.

operationalism: the doctrine that scientific concepts are tools for prediction rather than descriptions of hidden realities.

pantheism: the belief that God is identical with the universe.

paradox: a statement whose truth implies its falsehood, for example the Cretan philosopher Epimenides said, 'All Cretans are liars'. As he was Cretan himself, is his statement true or false?

phenomenology: a movement founded by the German philosopher Edmund Husserl which has dominated 20th-century European philosophy. It claims that the fundamental question is: Why should our experience be framed in terms of a distinction between an objective world and our subjective experience of it?

pluralism: the belief that there are more than two kinds of reality.

positivism: the doctrine that there is no knowledge outside science.

pragmatism: a philosophical method that makes practical consequences the test of truth.

predestination: the doctrine that the events of a human's life are determined beforehand.

rationalism: the theory that reason alone, without the aid of experience, can provide us with knowledge.

realism: the doctrine that general terms have a real existence.

relativism: the rejection of the concept of absolute and invariable truths.

scepticism: the doctrine that nothing can be known with certainty.

scholasticism: Christian philosophy of the Middle Ages, particularly that of St Thomas Aquinas.

sensationalism: the theory that sensations are the ultimate and real components of the world.

sophistry: a fallacious argument.

stoicism: the philosophical doctrine that happiness depends on inner peace, not outward circumstance.

structuralism: the doctrine that language is essentially a system of rules; or the extension of this idea to culture as a whole.

synthesis: the outcome of the confrontation of two arguments by which a truth is discovered.

teleology: explaining processes in terms of what they achieve rather than what preceded them.

theism: the belief in a God.

transcendentalism: the belief in an ultimate reality that transcends human experience.

utilitarianism: the belief that the effects that a course of action has on human happiness are all that is relevant to its ethical value.

voluntarism: the theory that will is a determining factor in the universe.

Ancient Religions

▶ The earliest evidence of religion was among *Homo sapiens neanderthalensis*, as seen in human burials in a cave in northern Iraq *c.* 60,000 BC.

▶ The practice of using religion to consolidate political power existed as far back as the Inca and Ancient Egyptian civilizations.

▶ Most ancient religions were polytheistic (believing in more than one god).

■ *Ancient Greek influence spread far, as shown by these ruins of the Temple of Jupiter in Baalbek, Lebanon*

ANCIENT GREEK AND ROMAN RELIGION

▶ The Greeks regarded the gods as the immortal controllers of natural forces.
▶ Roman sacrifices were always accompanied by the words *macte esto* ('be you increased') because worshippers believed that the product sacrificed would revitalize the divinity and enable it to fulfil requests.

The earliest written evidence about religion in Europe is found in the Linear B texts of the Mycenaean civilization in Greece (*c.* 1450 BC). These show the importance of Poseidon the sea god and of 'the Lady', who is presumed to be a mother goddess. Some other divine names occur in the texts, such as Zeus and Hera, who later appear in the epic poetry of Homer.

Homer's gods lived ageless and immortal on Mount Olympus, but acted like humans – and not particularly well-behaved ones at that. Although they could change shape, intervene in human life, and might respond to gifts and prayers to change human destiny, they seemed incapable of changing human nature.

By the 6th century BC, the Olympian gods were part of the official worship of the Greek city-states. As Ancient Greek religion had little to do with morality, the moral, metaphysical and scientific concerns of the Athenian philosophers of the 5th and 4th centuries BC led to ideas of God which challenged popular religion. In 399 BC the philosopher Socrates was condemned to death, accused of atheism and corrupting youth by undermining the gods of the state.

In Ancient Rome, two forms of religious expression developed: domestic piety, which recognized household gods (*lares* and *penates*); and the state cult, which ensured corporate well-being. As Rome encountered Greek culture, the state deities were identified with Olympian equivalents.

Also, as the Roman Empire expanded, its armies brought back foreign cults and a variety of religious ideas. The most important of these cults – until Christianity became the state religion in the 4th century AD – was Mithraism, a male-only mystery cult based on the worship of Mithras – Persian god of light, truth and justice.

■ *This Roman temple at Segesta, Sicily, shows a similarity to Ancient Greek architecture, seen in the right-hand photo*

ANCIENT GREEK AND ROMAN GODS

THE TWELVE OLYMPIAN GODS

Zeus (Roman – Jupiter): the overlord of the Olympian gods; the god of the sky and its properties.
Hera (Roman – Juno): wife of Zeus and goddess of the sky; the protector of women and marriage.
Poseidon (Roman – Neptune): the god of the sea, earthquakes and horses.
Demeter (Roman – Ceres): the goddess of the harvest.
Apollo (no direct Roman equivalent): the god of prophecy, herdsmen, music and medicine.
Artemis (Roman – Diana): the goddess of chastity, childbirth and the young.
Ares (Roman – Mars): the god of war.
Aphrodite (Roman – Venus): the goddess of love and beauty.
Hermes (Roman – Mercury): the messenger god of trade and travellers.
Athene, or Athena (Roman – Minerva): the protectress of Athens; the goddess of courage, prudence and wise council.
Hephaestus (Roman – Vulcan): the god of fire and metalcraft.
Hestia (Roman – Vesta): the goddess of fire.

OTHER IMPORTANT DEITIES

Adonis: the god of vegetation and rebirth.
Aeolus: the god of the winds.
Alphito: the barley goddess of Argos.
Arethusa: the goddess of springs and of fountains.
Asclepius: the god of healing.
Atlas: a Titan who carries the Earth.
Attis: the god of vegetation.
Boreas: the god of the northern wind.
Cronus: the father of the god Zeus.
Cybele: the goddess of the Earth.
Dionysus (Roman – Bacchus): the god of wine and the 'good life'.
Eos (Roman – Aurora): the goddess of the dawn.
Erebus: the god of darkness.
Eros (Roman – Cupid): the god of love.
Gaia, or Gaea: the goddess of the Earth.
Ganymede: the beautiful youth who became cupbearer to Zeus.
Hades: see Pluto.
Hebe: the goddess of youth.
Hecate: the goddess of witchcraft, magic and the Moon.
Helios (Roman – Sol): the god of the Sun.
Hygiea (Roman – Salus): the goddess of health.
Hypnos (Roman – Somnus): the god of sleep.
Irene (Roman – Pax): the goddess of peace.
Iris: the goddess of the rainbow.
Morpheus: the god of sleep and of dreams.
Nemesis: the god of retribution.
Nereus: the god of the sea.
Nike (Roman – Victoria): the goddess of victory.
Oceanus: the Titan with divinity of the rivers and the seas.
Pan (Roman – Sylvanus): the god of flocks and of herds; also associated with fertility.
Persephone (Roman – Proserpina): the goddess of the underworld and of corn.
Pluto (or Hades): the god of the underworld.
Prometheus: the Titan who was the god of fire and of the creation of man.
Rhea: wife of Cronus; a Titaness and the mother of many gods.
Selene (Roman – Luna): the goddess of the moon.
Thanatos (Roman – Mors): goddess of night and death.
Triton: a merman; the sea god.
Uranus: the sky god who was responsible for the sun and rain.

■ ONE OF THE FIRST GREEK GODS MENTIONED IN WRITING WAS POSEIDON, GOD OF THE SEA ■

ANCIENT EGYPTIAN RELIGION

▶ Many Ancient Egyptian tombs were supplied with objects from the person's daily life (food, drink, household goods and even servants), as they believed they would also need them in the afterlife.
▶ Userkaf, first king of the 5th dynasty, built a Sun temple in honour of the god Re at Abu Gurab *c.* 2494 BC – the next five kings felt obliged to follow his example.

In Ancient Egypt, the kings (known as pharaohs) were regarded as divine and referred to as 'Horus' or 'Son of Re'. Re was the Sun god and ruler of the gods and the people believed the pharaoh embodied the life-giving power of the Sun. Horus was the son of Isis, the Divine Mother, and of Osiris, the god of inundation, vegetation and the dead. As Horus, the pharaoh embodied the periodic renewal of life and fertility borne on the annual flooding of the land by the River Nile. In this way, Egyptian mythology was instrumental in legitimizing the autocratic rule of the pharaohs.

Local deities were often linked with national ones. The most significant was Amun, the god of invisibility, one of the characteristic elements of chaos out of which the Earth emerged. From *c.* 2000 BC he was combined with Amun to become Amun-Re, whose temple at Thebes was to become the most powerful and wealthiest in Egypt.

Ancient Egyptian religion is noted for its optimism, with the belief that the afterlife could be very pleasant, as long as you were provided for.

GODS AND GODDESSES OF ANCIENT EGYPT

■ *This relief, found in the mortuary temple of Ramses II in Abydos, Egypt, depicts him being given the breath of life by the falcon-headed god Horus*

Amun: the god of Thebes; often represented as a man, often with an erect penis.
Anubis: the jackal-headed god of the necropolis; patron of the embalmers.
Aten: the creator god manifest in the Sun disc.
Atum: the original Sun god of Heliopolis.
Bastet: the cat goddess.
Bes: the domestic god, usually depicted as a dwarf.
Edjo: the cobra goddess who appears as the pharaoh's protector on the royal diadem.
Geb: the god of the Earth; the physical support of the world.
Hathor: often represented as a cow, a cow-headed woman, or a woman with a cow's headdress; recognized as the suckler of the pharaoh.
Horus: the falcon god identified with the pharaoh during his reign; the son of Osiris and Isis; grew up to avenge his father's murder by Seth.
Imhotep: the architect of the Step Pyramid, and the chief minister of Djoser (*c.* 2700 BC); later venerated as the god of learning and of medicine.
Isis: the wife of Osiris and mother of Horus.
Khepri: the scarab-beetle god who was identified with the Sun god Re as the creator god.
Maat: usually depicted as a woman with an ostrich feather on her head; the goddess of truth, justice and order.
Min: the god of fertility and of the harvest; the protector of desert travellers and the god of the road.
Mut: the vulture goddess of Thebes; a mighty divine mother.
Nekhbet: the vulture goddess; sometimes appears beside Edjo on the royal diadem.
Nephthys: the sister of Isis.
Nut: the goddess of the sky.
Osiris: the god of the dead; also god of the Nile and vegetation; identified with the dead king and depicted as a mummified king.
Ptah: the creator god of Memphis and the patron of craftsmen; represented as a mummified man.
Ptah-Soker-Osiris: the god combining the principal gods of creation, death and the afterlife; depicted as a mummified king.
Re or Ra: the Sun god of Heliopolis and the supreme judge (other gods aspiring to universal recognition would link their name to his, for example Amun-Re).
Re-Harakhti: the falcon god; incorporating the characteristics of Re and Horus.
Sebek: a protector of reptiles and patron of kings.
Sekhmet: the lion-headed goddess; wife of Ptah; regarded as the bringer of sickness and destruction to the enemies of Re.
Seth: the god of violence and storms; brother and murderer of Osiris; represented as an animal of unidentified type.
Shu: the god of light and air.
Sobek: the crocodile god.
Thoth: the ibis-headed god of Hermopolis; the scribe to the gods and inventor of writing.
Thoueris: the hippopotamus goddess; patron of women in childbirth.

AZTEC AND INCA RELIGION

▶ Aztecs believed they had a mission to prevent what they thought to be the fifth destruction of the Earth, as all previous ones had been caused by the death of the Sun, which could only be sustained by the sacrifice of human hearts and blood.
▶ The Inca religion relied on priests and 'Chosen Women' – girls who were picked out at an early age for their beauty and skills, housed in temples, sworn to a life of chastity weaving textiles and sometimes sacrificed.

Aztec religion was a combination of the beliefs of other Central American peoples. The Aztec religion and calendar were closely linked with important dates marked by elaborate rituals performed by priests. The gods were appeased by constant sacrifices, sometimes human, and blood letting.

CELTIC GODS

Belenus: the god of war.
The Brigits: three Irish mother goddesses who presided over poetry, metalwork and healing (Celtic goddesses frequently manifested themselves in 'trinities').
Cernunnos: the stag-horned Lord of the Animals; a shamanistic figure who appeared on many surviving artifacts.
Lug: the Sun god; also the patron of music and the master of crafts.
Macha: known in Britain as Rhiannon (and as Epona in Gaul), Macha was the mare goddess; a symbol of fertility and one of the most powerful Celtic deities.
Manannan: the god of the oceans.
Morrigan: the powerful crow goddess, known as the 'Great Queen' personified both death and rebirth; associated with death and battle.

Inca religion combined animism with nature worship and fetishism (a belief in objects having magical powers). Several constellations of stars had religious importance for the Inca. The constellation of Lyra (which was said to be shaped like a llama) was invoked for protection. The Pleiades were called 'the Little Mothers' and festivals were held to mark their reappearances. The cult of Viracocha was highly organized and, as the state religion of the Inca Empire, was compulsory. However, the cults of conquered peoples were also tolerated. Religious practice was elaborate and was characterized by divination and by both human and animal sacrifice.

CELTIC RELIGION

▶ Little is known about Celtic deities owing to a lack of written material.
▶ The druids – the priest-poets of the Celts – took their name from an ancient Indo-European word meaning 'knowing the oak'.

Celtic religious beliefs were centred around the relationship between the divine spirit world with the land and the waters. Hills, rocks, springs, rivers and many other features were thought to be the homes of guardian spirits. Trees were also inhabited by spirits and certain species had a ritualistic role. Two seasonal festivals were held in May and November.

GERMANIC (NORSE) RELIGION

▶ The first lucid account of the customs and religious practices of Germanic tribes was written in AD 98 by Tacitus in his book *Germanica.*
▶ Germanic religions believed in an impending disaster called *Ragnarök* ('Twilight of the Gods') in which the Sun would turn black, the stars would vanish and the Earth would sink into the sea.

The religions of the Germanic peoples survived into the Middle Ages: Denmark, Norway and Iceland did not become Christian until the 10th and 11th centuries, and Sweden not until the 12th century. Many Germanic peoples converted to Christianity because of its promise of a better afterlife.

Germanic religion had many deities. In early times, Odin, Tyr and Thor in particular were worshipped: Odin was the god of battle, poetry and death; Tyr a war god; and Thor the god of thunder. It was best to die a warrior, with sword in hand, as they had the best chance of entering Valhalla – Odin's great hall for slain warriors and the Norse version of heaven. There was no supreme deity, only a chaos of divine energy. Worshippers chose the individual divinity they thought would be most likely to serve them.

■ THE INCA PRIESTS ACTED AS SORCERERS, CONFESSORS, CURERS AND DIVINERS OF LUNGS ■

Modern Religions

- In most religions, the devotees attempt to honour and/or influence their god or gods – commonly through such practices as prayer, sacrifice or right behaviour.
- The human desire to find an ultimate meaning and purpose in life is the main impetus behind religion.
- Religion is practised across virtually all cultures, from the very earliest times to the present day, and is one of the most universal activities known to humankind.
- During the 20th century, Christianity has decreased in Europe, although it has increased in Africa.

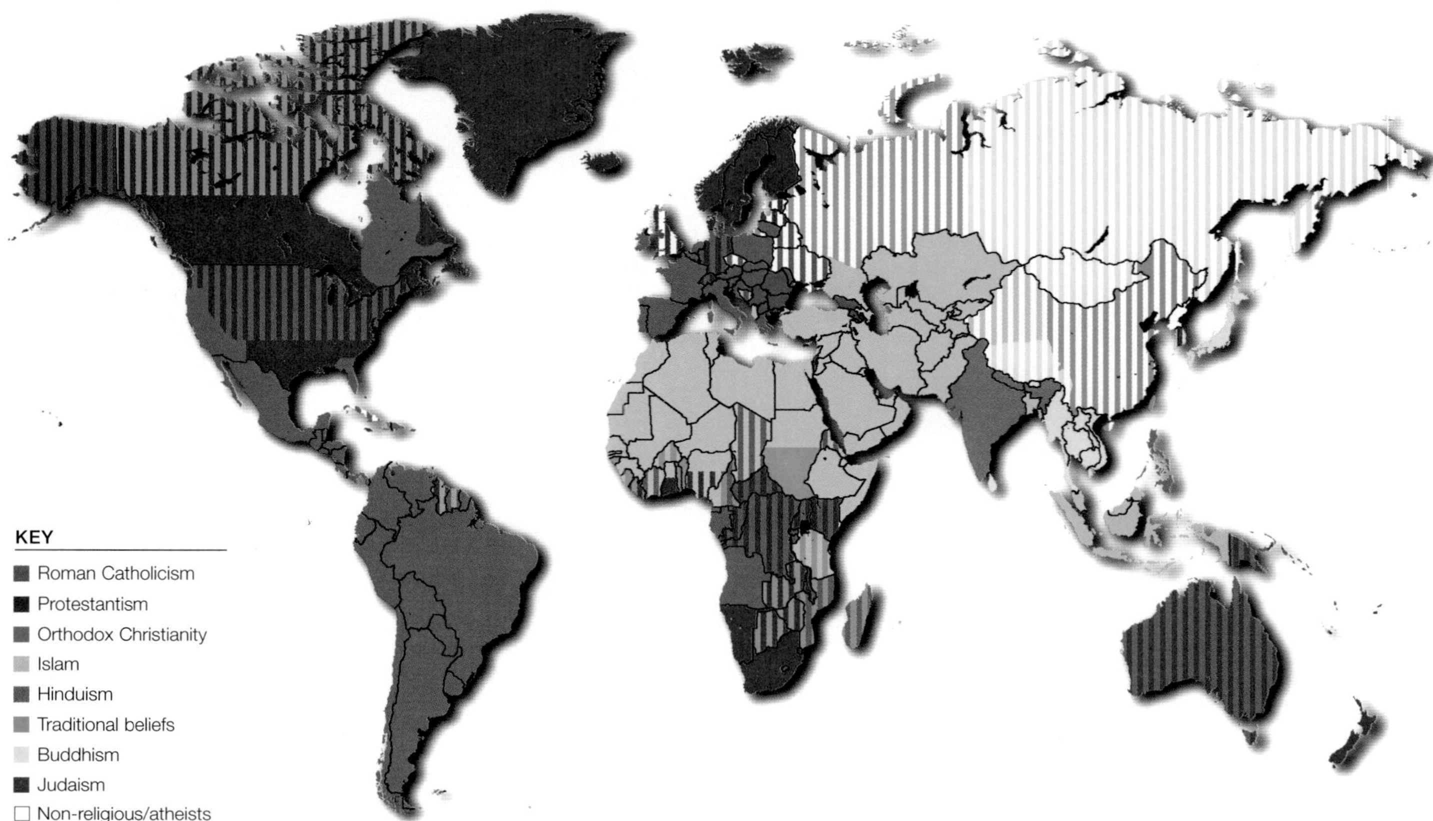

■ *White-robed worshippers and brightly attired priests kneel in prayer during a ceremony in the Cao Dai Great Temple at Tay Ninh, near Ho Chi Minh City, Vietnam – the religion's headquarters. Colourful dragons adorn the building's interior columns and the exterior facades are decorated with one of the Cao Dai symbols for God – an eye in a triangle*

Modern Distribution of Religions

During the 20th century the number of practising Christians has decreased in Europe. However, Christianity has increased greatly in Africa, where Islam has also made many converts. In Europe and North America the number of practising Christians belonging to long-established denominations has, in general, fallen, and vocations to the ministry and religious life have decreased.

Religious practice has also diminished sharply in the Far East. In China, traditional beliefs are now followed by only a minority and most Chinese are non-religious. In Japan, the practice of Shintoism and Buddhism (often by the same individuals) has, for the overwhelming majority, become more of a social custom than a religious belief.

However, the spread of Islam has been notable. The religion has increased its numbers in Europe through both migrant and local populations. Religious practice rather than mere affiliation has also been on the increase, as witnessed by the spectacular growth of fundamentalism in countries such as Iran, Egypt and Turkey. There has also been a resurgence of Islam in Central Asia following the collapse of the Soviet Union, where the practice of Islam was restricted.

Another remarkable feature of religious life this century has been the growth of 'new' religions, particularly in North America.

It is difficult to obtain figures for the number of adherents, either practising or nominal, of the world's major religions. The estimates given here relate to 1995 and refer to religious 'affiliation', that is some formal or nominal connection with a religion. In some cases the numbers of people practising a religion on a regular basis are much lower.

WORLD DISTRIBUTION

The following is a list of religions existing in the world today, with the number of adherents to these religions estimated in millions and the estimated percentage of the world's population affiliated to these religions. Note that the percentages do not add up to 100, as adherents of some religions may follow a second religion.

	millions	%
CHRISTIANITY	**1,930**	**33.7**
Roman Catholic Church	970	17
Protestant Churches (excluding Anglicanism)	395	6.9
Pentecostalist Churches*	100	1.7
Reformed and Calvinist Churches	70	1.2
Lutheran Churches	60	1
Methodist Churches	60	1
Baptist Churches	35	0.6
Orthodox Churches	220	3.8
Anglican Churches	70	1.2
Other Christian Churches	275	4.8
Coptic Churches (including Ethiopian Orthodox)	27	0.5
Seventh-day Adventists	20	0.3
Mormons	10	0.2
Kimbanguist Church	6	0.1
Jehovah's Witnesses	5	<0.1
ISLAM	**1,100**	**19.2**
Sunni Islam	915	16
Shia Islam	175	3.1
HINDUISM	**780**	**13.7**
BUDDHISM	**325**	**5.7**
CHINESE FOLK RELIGIONS (including Daoism)	**225**	**3.9**
SHINTOISM**	**120**	**2.1**
NEW RELIGIONS	**120**	**2.1**
Candomblé	15	0.25
Scientologists	11	0.2
Spiritists	10	0.2
Krishna Consciousness	8	0.2
Baha'ism	6	0.1
Transcendental Meditation	4	<0.1
Chondogyo	4	<0.1
Cao Dai	3	<0.1
Wicca	3	<0.1
PRIMAL RELIGIONS	**115**	**2**
African primal religions	75	1.3
Asian primal religions (including Shamanism)	40	0.7
SIKHISM	**19**	**0.3**
JUDAISM	**14**	**0.2**
JAINISM	**5**	**0.1**
CONFUCIANISM	**5**	**0.1**
NON-RELIGIOUS AND ATHEISTS	**1,060**	**18.5**
Non-religious	840	14.7
Atheists	220	3.8

* Estimates of the number of Pentecostalists vary between 60 million and 130 million.
** Shintoism and Buddhism in Japan overlap, with many people following both religions (see pp. 197 and 199).

NEW RELIGIONS

The following is a description of some of the major 'new' religions that have recently emerged and have influenced a significant number of devotees.

CANDOMBLÉ

In Brazil, African and Amerindian influences interwove with spiritism and Roman Catholicism to produce Candomblé. Complex rituals express devotion to African deities, Jesus Christ and the Christian saints. Divination and a quest for spiritual and physical healing is an important part of religious practice. Candomblé has been strongly condemned by the Roman Catholic Church but many of the millions of participants in these practices still consider themselves to be Catholics.

SCIENTOLOGISTS

The Church of Scientology, founded in 1955 by the American science-fiction writer L. Ron Hubbard, derives from dianetics, a type of psychotherapy he developed. Followers aim to 'clear' or free the mind from past painful experiences or 'engrams'. Scientologists believe in a highly structured spiritual world, the 'thetan' (soul) and reincarnation. Scientology has attracted criticism concerning its claims and the cost of its courses. With its principal bases in Florida and California, Scientology is strongest in the USA.

SPIRITISTS

Spiritism, or modern spiritualism, dates from the work of American Andrew Jackson Davis between 1844 and 1910. Central to spiritism is a belief that the spirit leaves the body at death and, sooner or later, can manifest itself to the living in a number of forms, often through the intervention of mediums. There is also a belief in successive reincarnations. Spiritism is strongest in Europe and the USA.

KRISHNA CONSCIOUSNESS

Started in 1966 in the USA, the International Society for Krishna Consciousness was begun by the activities of an Indian monk, or sannyasi, Bhaktivedanta Swami, known to his Western and Indian followers as Prabhupada. A neo-Hindu movement based on a philosophy from northern India, it focuses on love of the god Krishna. Service to Krishna and humanity involves temple worship, chanting and singing the deity's name.

BAHA'ISM

Baha'ism emphasizes the importance of all religion and the spiritual unity of all humanity. It emerged from the teachings of two 19th-century Iranian visionaries, Mirza Ali Muhammad, the Bab ('gateway'), and Mirza Husain Ali, Baha'ullah ('Glory of God'). In 1863 Baha'ullah announced that he was the manifestation of God sent to redeem the world, as earlier prophesied by the Bab. Imprisoned and exiled many times, he developed his teachings into a religion based on a new scripture, the Kitab Akdas. Baha'ism is present in over 70 countries but predominantly in south-west Asia. The faith has been persecuted in Iran since 1979 and all Baha'i institutions have been banned there since 1983.

TRANSCENDENTAL MEDITATION

Transcendental meditation (TM) was founded in India in 1958 by the Indian Maharishi Mahesh Yogi, whose teachings became very popular among young people in the West in the 1960s. The Maharishi developed a system of meditation using a mantra (a word or phrase in Sanskrit) which is repeated mentally to bring an individual into a deeper, quieter sense of consciousness. Followers are trained and receive a personal mantra. The majority of practitioners are in India and the USA.

CHONDOGYO

Chondogyo (meaning 'the religion of the Heavenly Way') is confined to Korea and to communities of Koreans living abroad. Its founder, Ch'oe Suun (1824–64), called the new religion Tonghak, literally 'Eastern learning', in contrast to Western Christian learning. The faith teaches the existence of one God, combining Confucian and Daoist motifs with aspects of Christian practice. Its main tenets are that God pervades the entire world and is present in individuals. Followers, called on to treat others as God, believe oneness with God can be achieved through honest practice of the faith. The writings of Ch'oe Suun, and of his two successors as the movement's leaders, form the scripture of Chondogyo. Religious practice includes prayer, scripture reading and silent meditation. The egalitarian nature of the religion has meant that it has been tolerated in Communist North Korea.

CAO DAI

Cao Dai, founded in Vietnam by Ngo Van Chieu (1879–1932) in 1926, means 'high tower', the Daoist symbol for the Supreme Being. Elements of Confucianism, traditional beliefs, Buddhism, Islam and Christianity are interwoven. Its founder sought the unity of all faiths but Cao Dai developed as a religion on its own. Christianity, for example, is represented by a copy of the Roman Catholic hierarchy: the head of Cao Dai is a Pope, under whom are cardinals, archbishops, bishops and priests. Religious practice owes much to Daoism and Confucianism as well as Roman Catholicism. Although a Supreme Being is recognized, reverence is also shown to other spirits including Jesus Christ, Muhammad, Confucius, the Buddha, Chinese nationalist leader Sun Yat-sen, Joan of Arc and Victor Hugo. Cao Dai is largely confined to former South Vietnam and Vietnamese communities in exile.

WICCA

This faith is not so much a 'new' religion as a reinterpretation of ancient beliefs. Wicca, popularly known as witchcraft (and sometimes wrongly confused with Satanism), incorporates beliefs that are thought to have their origin in Neolithic times as well as some Celtic mythology and practices. In its most common form, Wicca (which means 'wisdom') recognizes a god and a goddess and emphasizes humanity's close relationship with nature. Fertility and the passage of the seasons have an important place in ritual. Wicca is largely confined to North America and western Europe.

RASTAFARIANISM

The Rastafari movement has its origins in the United Negro Improvement Association, founded in 1914 by the Jamaican leader Marcus Garvey (1887–1940). The 1930s saw deep unrest and poverty among Black West Indians. This coincided with the publicity attracted by the coronation in 1930 of the Ethiopian emperor Haile Selassie (originally called Ras Tafari), who became a symbol to Garvey. Rastafarians, largely Black Jamaicans, saw their residence in the West Indies as a form of punishment. They regarded Haile Selassie as a living god and Ethiopia as a paradise to which exiled Blacks would return. These beliefs have modified with time and the role ascribed to Haile Selassie has diminished after his deposition (1974) and murder (1975).

Christianity

- The Western calendar, shaped and determined by Christianity, sees the birth of Jesus of Nazareth, known as the Christ, as the turning point of history.
- The Bible, including both the Old and the New Testaments, is the sacred writing of Christianity and is probably the most influential book in history.
- For Christians, the Jewish child born in Bethlehem was no ordinary human. He was and is both human and divine, the Son of God.
- While it is possible to say that a historical person named Jesus lived between *c.* 4 BC and *c.* AD 29, it is only faith that can claim that he was the Christ, the anointed one of God, the long-awaited Messiah of the Jews.
- New Christian denominations are still forming throughout the world, especially in Africa and Latin America.

ROMAN CATHOLICISM

▶ Rome was the only Western Church founded by an apostle (St Peter).
▶ Roman Catholics recognize the Pope as the lawful successor of St Peter, who was appointed head of the Church by Christ.

In the 16th century most of northern Europe broke with Rome to create reformed Protestant Churches. Catholic Christianity was extended to the Americas and parts of Asia and Africa. Since the Second Vatican Council (1962–66), Latin has largely given way to local languages for worship. The Roman Catholic Church claims catholicity inasmuch as it was charged (*de jure*) by Christ to 'teach all nations' and *de facto* as it is the largest Christian Church. It claims to be infallible in interpreting both the written and unwritten word of God. The Pope has delegated certain administrative powers to the Curia, the work of which is done by 11 permanent departments or congregations.

ROMAN CATHOLIC CHURCH STRUCTURE

The Pope, the bishop of Rome, is considered by Catholics to be the Vicar of Christ on Earth and the successor of St Peter, the first bishop of Rome. He is elected by the College of Cardinals, meeting in secret conclave. At the end of 1994 there were 166 cardinals, 120 of whom were under the age of 80 and therefore qualified as electors. There have been over 30 antipopes – rivals to the papacy elected in opposition to the one chosen canonically.

The Church is served by about 1.5 million full-time professional staff (bishops, priests, nuns, monks, other religious and lay people). Roman Catholics represent almost 17% of humankind (see p. 189).

CHRISTIAN TEACHING

▶ Jesus taught that God is like a father who cares for every person on Earth.
▶ Jesus referred to himself as 'the Son of Man', perhaps in reference to his suffering for mankind – it was his disciples who gave him the title 'the Son of God'.

The life and teaching of Christ are recorded in the four Gospels and in several quotations and stories found in other books of the New Testament of the Bible. These were all written by Christians who believed Jesus to be in some way both human and divine. Our knowledge of Jesus therefore comes from the pens of believers. Jesus taught that through repentance and forgiveness, God calls all humanity to him in love and seeks every individual to do his will on Earth. He taught that through living as God wishes, the Kingdom of God – justice, love, mercy and peace – could come upon Earth, either in individual lives or possibly to the world as a whole.

Local authority is exercised by bishops and archbishops in some 2360 dioceses throughout the world. Bishops gather in local, national or regional conferences to discuss local policies and visit Rome every five years to report direct to the Pope.

UNIAT CHURCHES

Some smaller non-Latin Churches also owe allegiance to the Pope. These eight organizations are called the Uniat Churches. Although in full communion with the Roman Catholic Church, these Churches retain their own organization and liturgies. Most Uniat rites are headed by a patriarch.

By far the largest Uniat Church is the Ukrainian Uniat Church, which was founded in 1596 to enable Orthodox clergy who transferred their allegiance to the Pope to retain their Eastern rite. The Soviet authorities forcibly incorporated the Uniats into the Russian Orthodox Church, but clergy owing allegiance to the Pope continued to function as an 'underground' Church. The Church is now one of the three major Christian bodies of independent Ukraine. Its head is the Archbishop of Lvov. There are about 8 million Ukrainian Uniat Catholics worldwide with about 60% in Ukraine.

Other Uniat Churches include the Jacobite Church (the Malankara Orthodox Syrian Church) in southern India and the Maronite Church, the Melkiterite Church, the Armenian Church, the Chaldean Church and the Syrian Church, most of which are based in the Middle East.

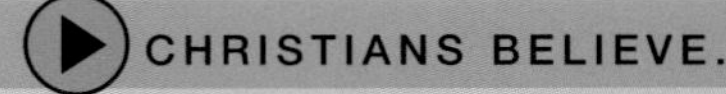

CHRISTIANS BELIEVE...

▶ In the doctrine of the Trinity – that God is one but has three co-equal 'persons' – God the Father, God the Son (Jesus Christ) and the Holy Spirit.

▶ God is the creator of the universe and all life.

▶ Jesus Christ is the only Son of God, who has existed with God the Father from before time began.

▶ Jesus was incarnated (given human form) when, by the power of the Holy Spirit, his human mother, Mary, gave birth to him.

▶ The purpose of Christ's incarnation, according to Christianity, was to reconcile humanity with God, as human sinfulness had broken the relationship with God.

▶ Through the death of Jesus upon the Cross at Calvary, God broke the power of sin and evil.

▶ Through the Resurrection (the rising) of Jesus from the dead on the third day, God showed the triumph of life over death, and gave the promise of everlasting life to those who believe in Jesus.

▶ Through the Holy Spirit God gives life and direction to his people.

■ Pope John Paul II was born at Wadowice, near Krakow, Poland, on 20 May 1920. The Archbishop of Krakow from 1964–78, he was created a Cardinal in 1967 and elected Pope on 16 October 1978. Known for his extensive travels to reach Christians all over the world, he is shown here giving Communion to the people in Kisangani, The Congo (ex-Zaïre)

■ JESUS' FIRST FOUR DISCIPLES WERE FISHERMEN ■ JESUS MEANS 'THE SAVIOUR', TAKEN

THE SUCCESSION OF POPES

St Peter *c.* 33–67
St Linus 67–76
St Cletus (also called Anacletus) 76–88
St Clement I 88–97
St Evaristus 97–105
St Alexander I 105–15
St Sixtus I 115–25
St Telesphorus 125–36
St Hyginus 136–40
St Pius I 140–55
St Anicetus 155–66
St Soterus 166–75
St Eleutherius 175–89
St Victor I 189–99
St Zephyrinus 199–217
St Callistus I 217–22
St Urban I 222–30
St Pontian 230–35
St Anterus 235–36
St Fabian I 236–50
St Cornelius 251–53
St Lucius I 253–54
St Stephen I 254–57
St Sixtus II 257–58
St Dionysius 259–68
St Felix I 269–74
St Eutychianus 275–83
St Caius 283–96
St Marcellinus 296–304
St Marcellus I 308–09
St Eusebius 309–10
St Miltiades 311–14
St Silvester I 314–35
St Mark 336–37
St Julius I 337–52
Liberius 352–66
St Damasus 366–84
St Siricius 384–99
St Anastasius I 399–401
St Innocent I 401–17
St Zosimus 417–18
St Boniface I 418–22
St Celestine I 422–432
St Sixtus III 432–40
St Leo I 440–61
St Hilary 461–68
St Simplicius 468–83
St Felix II 483–92
St Gelasius I 492–96
St Anastasius II 496–98
St Symmachus 498–514
St Hormisdas 514–23
St John I 523–26
St Felix III 526–30
Boniface II 530–32
John II (Mercurius) 533–35
St Agapetus I 535–36
St Silverius 536–37
Vigilius 537–55
Pelagius I 556–61
John III 561–74
Benedict I 575–79
Pelagius II 579–90
St Gregory I 590–604
Sabinianus 604–06
Boniface III 607
St Boniface IV 608–15
St Deusdedit I 615–18
Boniface V 619–25
Honorius I 625–38
Severinus 638–40
John IV 640–42
Theodore I 642–49
St Martin I 649–55
St Eugenius I 654–57
St Vitalian 657–72
Deusdedit II 672–76
Donus 676–78
St Agatho 678–81
St Leo II 681–83
St Benedict II 683–85
John V 685–86
Conon 686–87
St Sergius I 687–701
John VI 701–05
John VII 705–07
Sisinnius 707
Constantine 708–15
St Gregory II 715–31
St Gregory III 731–41
Saint Zacharias 741–52
Stephen 'II' 752 (died before he could be enthroned)
Stephen II or III 752–57
St Paul I 757–67
Stephen III or IV 768–72
Adrian I 772–95
St Leo III 795–816
Stephen IV or V 816–17
St Paschal I 817–24
Eugenius II 824–27
Valentine 827
Gregory IV 827–44
Sergius II 844–47
St Leo IV 847–55
Benedict III 855–58
St Nicholas I 858–67
Adrian II 867–72
John VIII 872–82
Marinus I 882–84
Adrian III 884–85
Stephen V or VI 885–91
Formosus 891–96
Boniface VI 896
Stephen VI or VII 896–97
Romanus 897
Theodore II 897
John IX 898–900
Benedict IV 900–03
Leo V 903
Sergius III 904–11
Anastasius III 911–13
Lando 913–14
John X 914–28
Leo VI 928
Stephen VII or VIII 928–31
John XI 931–35
Leo VII 936–39
Stephen VIII or IX 939–42
Marinus II 942–46
Agapetus II 946–55
John XII 955–64
Leo VIII 963–65
Benedict V 964–65
John XIII 965–72
Benedict VI 973–74
Benedict VII 974–83
John XIV (Pietro Canepanova) 983–84
John XV 985–96
Gregory V (Bruno of Carinthia) 996–99
Silvester II (Gerbert) 999–1003
John XVII (Sicco) 1003
John XVIII (Fasino) 1003–09
Sergius IV (Pietro Buccaporci) 1009–12
Benedict VIII 1012–24
John XIX 1024–32
Benedict IX 1032–44
Silvester III 1045
Benedict IX (restored) 1045
Gregory VI 1045–46
Clement II 1046–47
Benedict IX (restored) 1047–48
Damasus II (Poppo) 1048
St Leo IX 1048–54
Victor II 1055–57
Stephen IX or X 1057–58
Nicholas II 1058–61
Alexander II 1061–73
St Gregory VII (Hildebrand de Soana) 1064–85
Victor III (Desiderius, Prince of Benevento) 1086–87
Urban II (Odon de Lagery) 1088–99
Paschal II (Ranieri) 1099–1118
Gelasius II (Giovanni Gaetani) 1118–19
Callistus II (Gui de Bourgogne) 1119–24
Honorius II (Lamberto Scannabecchi) 1124–30
Innocent II (Gregorio Papareschi) 1130–43
Celestine II (Guido di Castello) 1143–44
Lucius II (Gerardo Caccianemici) 1144–45
Eugenius III (Bernardo Paganelli) 1145–53
Anastasius IV (Corrado) 1153–54
Adrian IV (Nicholas Breakspeare) 1154–59
Alexander III (Rolando Bandinelli) 1159–81
Lucius III (Ubaldo Allucingoli) 1181–85
Urban III (Uberto Crivelli) 1185–87
Gregory VIII (Alberto di Morra) 1187
Clement III (Paolo Scolari) 1187–91
Celestine III (Giacinto Buboni) 1191–98
Innocent III (Lothario, Count of Segni) 1198–1216
Honorius III (Cencio Savelli) 1216–27
Gregory IX (Ugolino, Count of Segni) 1227–41
Celestine IV (Goffredo Castiglioni) 1241
Innocent IV (Sinibaldo Fieschi) 1243–54
Alexander IV (Rainaldo, Count of Segni) 1254–61
Urban IV (Jacques Pantaléon) 1261–64
Clement IV (Gui Faucois) 1265–68
Gregory X (Theobaldo Visconti) 1271–76
Innocent V (Pierre de Tarentaise) 1276
Adrian V (Ottobono dei Fieschi) 1276
John XXI (Pedro Juliani) 1276–77
Nicholas III (Giovanni Gaetano Orsini) 1277–80
Martin IV (Simon de Brion) 1281–85
Honorius IV (Giacomo Savelli) 1285–87
Nicholas IV (Girolamo Moschi) 1288–92
St Celestine V (Pietro del Morrone) 1294
Boniface VIII (Benedetto Gaetani) 1294–1303
Benedict XI (Nicola Boccasini) 1303–04
Clement V (Bertrand de Got) 1305–14
John XXII (Jacques Duèse) 1316–34
Benedict XII (Jacques Fournier) 1334–42
Clement VI (Pierre Roger) 1342–52
Innocent VI (Etienne Aubert) 1352–62
Urban V (Guillaume Grimoard) 1362–70
Gregory XI (Pierre Roger de Beaufort) 1370–78
Urban VI (Bartolommeo Prignano) 1378–89
Boniface IX (Pietro Tomacelli) 1389–1404
Innocent VII (Cosimo dei Migliorati) 1404–06
Gregory XII (Angelo Corrari) 1406–15
Martin V (Odo Colonna) 1417–31
Eugenius IV (Gabriele Condolmieri) 1431–47
Nicholas V (Tommaso Parentucelli) 1447–55
Callistus III (Alonso Borgia) 1455–58
Pius II (Aeneas Piccolomini) 1458–64
Paul II (Pietro Barbo) 1464–71
Sixtus IV (Francesco della Rovere) 1471–84
Innocent VIII (Giovanni Battista) 1484–92
Alexander VI (Roderigo Borgia) 1492–1503
Pius III (Francesco Todeschini) 1503
Julius II (Giuliano della Rovere) 1503–13
Leo X (Giovanni de Medici) 1513–21
Adrian VI (Adrian Florensz Boeyens) 1522–23
Clement VII (Giulio de Medici) 1523–34
Paul III (Alessandro Farnese) 1534–49
Julius III (Giovanni Maria Ciocchi del Monte) 1550–55
Marcellus II (Marcello Cervini) 1555
Paul IV (Giovanni Pietro Carafa) 1555–59
Pius IV (Gianangelo de Medici) 1559–65
St Pius V (Antonio Michele Ghislieri) 1566–72
Gregory XIII (Ugo Buoncompagni) 1572–85
Sixtus V (Felice Perretti) 1585–90
Urban VII (Giovanni Battista Castagna) 1590
Gregory XIV (Niccolo Sfondrati) 1590–91
Innocent IX (Giovanni Antonio Facchinetti) 1591
Clement VIII (Ipollito Aldobrandini) 1592–1605
Leo XI (Alessandro Ottaviano de Medici) 1605
Paul V (Camillo Borghese) 1605–21
Gregory XV (Alessandro Ludovisi) 1621–23
Urban VIII (Maffeo Barberini) 1623–44
Innocent X (Giovanni Battista Pamfili) 1644–55
Alexander VII (Fabio Chigi) 1655–67
Clement IX (Giulio Rospigliosi) 1667–69
Clement X (Emilio Altieri) 1670–76
Innocent XI (Benedetto Odescalchi) 1676–89
Alexander VIII (Pietro Ottoboni) 1689–91
Innocent XII (Antonio Pignatelli) 1691–1700
Clement XI (Gianfrancesco Albani) 1700–21
Innocent XIII (Michelangelo de Conti) 1721–24
Benedict XIII (Pietro Francesco Orsini) 1724–30
Clement XII (Lorenzo Corsini) 1730–40
Benedict XIV (Prospero Lambertini) 1740–58
Clement XIII (Carlo della Torre Rezzonico) 1758–69
Clement XIV (Giovanni Ganganelli) 1769–74
Pius VI (Giovanni Angelo Braschi) 1775–99
Pius VII (Barnabo Chiaramonti) 1800–23
Leo XII (Annibale della Genga) 1823–29
Pius VIII (Francesco Xaverio Castiglioni) 1829–30
Gregory XVI (Bartolomeo Cappellari) 1831–46
Pius IX (Giovanni Maria Mastai-Ferretti) 1846–78
Leo XIII (Vincenzo Gioacchino Pecci) 1878–1903
St Pius X (Giuseppe Sarto) 1903–14
Benedict XV (Giacomo della Chiesa) 1914–22
Pius XI (Achille Ratti) 1922–39
Pius XII (Eugenio Pacelli) 1939–58
John XXIII (Angelo Giuseppe Roncalli) 1958–63
Paul VI (Giovanni Battista Montini) 1963–78
John Paul I (Albino Luciani) 1978
John Paul II (Karol Wojtyla) 1978–

THE ORTHODOX CHURCH

▶ Most Orthodox Churches derive from the Greek-speaking Christianity of the eastern Mediterranean.
▶ The head of the Orthodox Church (the Ecumenical Patriarch) is not like the Roman Pope – he is merely first in honour among equals in jurisdiction and cannot speak and act for the entire Church by himself.

The Orthodox Church maintains that it is the 'one true Church of Christ which is not and has not been divided' and it regards the Roman Catholic Church as schismatic. Its traditions are linked to Churches founded by apostles and those of the Christian Roman Empire (the Byzantine Empire) that lasted until 1453. The Ecumenical Patriarch of Constantinople (Istanbul) is the senior figure, but each autonomous Church has its own patriarch and is self-governing. The current Ecumenical Patriarch of Constantinople is Patriarch Bartholomew I.

The largest Orthodox Churches are the Russian, the Ukrainian (which still owes its allegiance to the Moscow Patriarchate), the Ukrainian Autocephalous (also known as the Ukrainian Orthodox Church-Kiev patriarchate, which has seceded from the Russian Orthodox Church), the Romanian, the Greek, the Belarusian, the Bulgarian, the Serbian (including the Serbian Church in Bosnia), the US (Eastern Orthodox), the Georgian, the Armenian, the Russian (Moldovan), the Macedonian, the Polish, the Cypriot and the Australian. Other Orthodox Churches include the Orthodox Church of Finland, and of the Czech Republic and Slovakia. There are Russian Orthodox minorities in the Baltic States (Estonia, Latvia and Lithuania), Kazakhstan, Uzbekistan and other former Soviet republics and in the West (mostly France and the USA), and Greek Orthodox minorities in many countries in North America, Australasia and western Europe (such as in the UK).

The collapse of Communism in the former Soviet Union and in eastern Europe has resulted in a remarkable revitalization of the Churches in those countries. In some cases, for example in Russia itself, the Orthodox Church has been the principal beneficiary of this growth. However, other Christian Churches, particularly Baptists and various new movements, have also seen a dramatic expansion in numbers in this area of the world.

■ *An Orthodox priest wears traditional robes in the Church of the Holy Sepulchre, Jerusalem, Israel. Israel's Orthodox Churches have many Arab followers – the liturgy is recited in Greek in monasteries and in Arabic in parish churches*

PROTESTANTISM

▶ Protestant Churches all reject the Pope as the supreme worldly authority and mediator of truth on Earth.
▶ Some Protestant Churches, such as the Anglican Communion, have much in common with Roman Catholic and Orthodox Churches.

In 16th-century Europe, movements to reform the Church accompanied fresh interpretations of the Bible and the use of everyday language in worship in place of Latin. These movements rejected Roman authority and established reformed national structures of Christianity in the various states of northern Europe, such as Lutheranism in Sweden and parts of Germany, Calvinism in Switzerland and Scotland, and Anglicanism in England. This process is known as the Reformation. The majority Protestant movement aimed to reform the Church within each state while maintaining the idea that the Church embraced the whole community. The Radical (or Anabaptist) movement insisted that the Church consisted only of those who made a commitment to Christ, and broke the link with the state. Although a minority religion in Europe, this movement was of great significance in America.

In the 18th century, movements for spiritual reform in Protestant countries brought the majority and radical streams closer together and European emigration brought all the Protestant traditions to America, Canada and Australia. In the USA they took on new life and new shapes in a huge community – largely Christian, but multi-ethnic and with no national Church. Some completely new forms of Christianity also arose, such as Pentecostalism.

PENTECOSTALS

Pentecostalism grew out of the revivalist movement in some Protestant Churches in the USA during the later part of the 19th century. Its origins as a Church are often traced to the work of Charles Parham in Kansas and Illinois in 1900. Pentecostals emphasize 'baptism by the Holy Spirit', a post-conversion religious experience which may be accompanied by divine healing and 'speaking in tongues'. In 1996 there were about 100 million members of various Pentecostalist Churches worldwide.

REFORMED CHRISTIANS AND PRESBYTERIANS

The Reformed Churches are Calvinistic rather than Lutheran in doctrine. They trace their origins to the teaching of the French Protestant John Calvin (1509–64), a leader of the Reformation in France and Switzerland. While believing that faith is dependent upon Scripture alone, Calvinists insist that, as man lacks free will, only the elect are predestined to be saved. The Reformed Churches include the Presbyterians, whose name is derived from their form of government by lay leaders – known as presbyters or elders – and by pastors.

The established Church of Scotland is Presbyterian in constitution. It is presided over by a Moderator who is chosen annually by the elected General Assembly, at which the British sovereign (as head of the Church) is represented by a Lord High Commissioner. Scotland is divided into 12 synods for administrative purposes.

The principal Reformed and Presbyterian Churches are the Presbyterian Church in the USA with about 3.8 million members, followed by the Federation of Swiss Protestant Churches (comprising 18 reformed Churches) with about 2.8 million members, and the Netherlands Reformed Church with about 2.3 million members.

■ CHRIST MEANS 'THE ANOINTED ONE', FROM THE GREEK VERB *CHRIO*, 'TO ANOINT' ■

THE ANGLICAN COMMUNION

Henry VIII renounced the supremacy of the Pope in 1534, founding the Church of England with the monarch as its head. Protestant reforms were instituted during the reign of Edward VI (1547–53). After the reign of Catholic Mary I, the independent Church of England was re-established in 1558.

The Church of England retains the episcopal form of government and has preserved many of the Catholic traditions of liturgy. However, it holds most of the basic tenets of the reformed faith of Protestantism. Its doctrine is based upon the Thirty-Nine Articles; its liturgy is based upon *The Book of Common Prayer* (1549 and 1662) and its successors. The 18th-century Evangelical Movement emphasized the Protestant tradition, while the 19th-century Oxford Movement emphasized the Catholic tradition. These two movements continue in the Church of England as the Low Church and the High Church. Each of the Churches of the Anglican Communion is self-governing. The Archbishop of Canterbury is recognized as first among equals by the leaders of the provinces of the Anglican Communion.

The largest Anglican Churches are the Church of England plus the Church in Wales and the Scottish Episcopal Church with about 33.4 million nominal members (about 1.5 million practising members), followed by the Church of the Province of Nigeria with about 10 million members and the Church of the Province of Uganda with about 4.9 million.

LUTHERANS

The beliefs of the Lutheran Churches are derived from the teaching of the German Martin Luther (1483–1546) and were formulated in the Augsburg Confession of 1530. Luther taught that redemption could only be achieved through faith in Christ (justification by faith), and that Scripture is the sole rule of faith. About 60 million people belong to Lutheran Churches, whose greatest influence is in Germany and in Scandinavia. The United Evangelical Lutheran Church in Germany is the largest, with about 11.2 million members.

METHODISM

Methodism developed out of the religious revival within the Church of England led by John Wesley (1703–91) and his brother Charles (1707–88). The differences between the early Methodists and contemporary Anglicans were largely of emphasis rather than doctrine. All Methodist Churches have a strong central authority, and those of the American tradition are episcopal. About 60 million people belong to Methodist Churches, mostly in the USA and southern and western Africa.

The principal Methodist Churches are the United Methodist Church in the USA with about 8.6 million members, and the African Methodist Episcopal Church in the USA with about 3.5 million members.

BAPTISTS

Baptist Churches, which take their name from the practice of baptism by immersion of adult believers, developed within the English and American Puritan movements in the 17th century. Each Baptist Church is self-governing. There are about 35 million Baptists, the majority of whom live in the USA.

The principal Baptist Churches, based in the USA, are the Southern Baptist Convention with about 15.4 million members, followed by the National Baptist Convention with about 8.2 million members.

COPTIC

The Coptic Churches are monophysite, that is they believe that Christ is primarily divine but with human attributes, rather than being made man. The largest Coptic denomination, the Ethiopian Orthodox Church, is headed by a patriarch, or *abuna,* but recognizes the honorary primacy of the patriarch of Alexandria as the head of the Coptic Church in Egypt. The Ethiopian Church is characterized by lay officials trained in theology who play a leading role in the Church; the clergy, by contrast, is generally not trained. Coptic Christians in Egypt, Sudan, Ethiopia and Eritrea number about 27 million.

SEVENTH-DAY ADVENTISTS

Adventist Churches emphasize the imminence of the Second Coming. The Seventh-day Adventist Church was established in the 19th century in the USA where the Church has 749,000 members with an extra 44,000 in Canada.

INDEPENDENT AFRICAN CHURCHES

Dissatisfaction with forms of worship from the West has encouraged the emergence of a number of African Churches. The Kimbanguist Church of The Congo (ex-Zaïre) began in the 1920s when followers were attracted by the preaching and miraculous healings of Simon Kimbangui, a Baptist catechist.

Various Zion Churches in South Africa emphasize adult baptism by immersion, divine healing and preparation for a Second Coming. Aladura ('Owners of Prayer') Churches in West Africa emphasize prophets and divine healing. The incorporation of traditional African beliefs and values is a feature of a number of these Churches.

The largest African Churches are the Church of Jesus Christ on Earth through the Prophet Simon Kimbangui, in The Congo (ex-Zaïre), with 5 million members, followed by the Zion Christian Church, in South Africa, with 4 million members, the Church of the Lord – Aladura, in Nigeria, with 1.1 million members, and the African Israel Nineveh Church, in Kenya, with 350,000 members.

OTHER PROTESTANT CHURCHES

Congregationalists

The liberal Protestant Congregationalist churches developed from the Independents in England in the 16th and 17th centuries. Each congregation is independent in organizing its own affairs. In Canada, the USA, England, Australia and India the majority of Congregationalist churches have joined United Churches (see below).

Christian Scientists

The Church of Christ, Scientist, is a liberal Protestant denomination founded in the USA by Mary Baker Eddy in 1879. Christian Scientists – who deny the deity but not the divinity of Jesus – emphasize the practice of spiritual healing. They use their own sources of knowledge supplementary to the Scriptures. The Church claims about 2500 congregations worldwide, mostly in North America.

The Disciples of Christ

The Disciples of Christ were founded during a period of religious revival on the American frontier in the first half of the 19th century. They attempted to unite the divisions of Protestantism through a return to New Testament practice. The Principal Church of the Disciples is the Christian Church (Disciples of Christ; USA) with 1 million disciples.

Society of Friends (Quakers)

The Society of Friends was founded in the 17th century by English Puritan George Fox. Emphasizing the immediate application of Christ's teaching to everyday life, it rejects the need for formalized services, creeds or clergy. Friends' meetings wait in silence for the 'inward light'. Quakers are pacifists. In the UK there are 18,000 members.

Unitarians

Unitarians deny the doctrine of the Trinity. The belief that God is one person was held by some in the early Church (Arianism), but modern Unitarianism dates in Europe from the 16th century, and in the English-speaking world from 1774, when Theophilus Lindsey founded a Unitarian chapel in London.

United Churches

The ecumenical movement among Christian Churches has resulted in the union of a number of Protestant Churches. The pressure for unity has been particularly strong in countries without a Christian tradition where the historic differences between denominations appear meaningless. The principal United Churches are the Church of South India with about 2.2 million members, followed by the United Church of Christ, in the USA, with about 1.5 million members and the Uniting Church in Australia with 1.4 million members.

MARGINAL GROUPS

JEHOVAH'S WITNESSES

The Jehovah's Witnesses – or the Watchtower Movement as they are officially known – grew out of the International Bible Studies Association, founded in Pittsburgh, Pennsylvania, USA, by Charles Taze Russell in 1872.

Known for their literal interpretation of the Bible and their concern with Armageddon (the imminent final battle in which Witnesses will be saved), Jehovah's Witnesses deny Christ's divinity, but recognize Jesus as God's agent. They believe that the Theocracy (God's Kingdom) will be established on Earth after Armageddon and the Second Coming.

The Witnesses have faced persecution in a number of countries because of their refusal to comply with certain institutional regulations. For instance, they are renowned for not accepting blood transfusions and for their refusal to vote.

MORMONS

The Mormons – or the Church of Jesus Christ of Latter-Day Saints as they are officially known – are active missionaries. They were founded in the USA in 1830 by Joseph Smith. He claimed to have received the Book of Mormon – accepted by the Latter-Day Saints as an addition to the Scripture – from an angel.

Mormons believe that God evolved from man and that man himself has the potential to attain deity. Mormonism denies the Trinity in favour of a polytheistic belief in three independent persons. It teaches that after death there is a full resurrection of the body and a reuniting of families. Dead relatives can be baptized or married in the faith to ensure their salvation.

The Mormons were led to their current centre in Salt Lake City, Utah, by Brigham Young. There are over 6 million Mormons, the majority (4.7 million) in North America.

UNIFICATION CHURCH

Sometimes known as 'the Moonies', the Unification Church was founded in the 1950s by a Korean, Sun Myung Moon. It is thought to have over 2 million members, the majority in South Korea and Japan.

The Church teaches the 'Divine Principle', which holds that, following humanity's fall from grace, a restoration to perfection is achievable through the first messiah, Jesus, and the second, the Reverend Moon. Love of creation and family life are of central importance to members.

ISLAM

- The Arabic term 'islam' means 'the act of resignation' to God. It is derived from the root letters 'slm', from which come the noun *salam* (which means 'peace') and the verb *aslama* (which means 'he submitted').
- Muslims believe that Islam is the religion that brings peace to humankind when people commit themselves to God and submit themselves to His will.
- Muslims believe that God's will was made known through the *Qur'an* (Koran), the book revealed to His messenger, the Prophet Muhammad.
- Islam emphasizes an uncompromising monotheism and a strict adherence to religious practices.

THE PROPHET MUHAMMAD

▶ Muslims begin their calendar from July 622 – the date of Muhammad's flight from Mecca to Medina, referred to as the Hegira (*hijrah*).
▶ Muhammad's political power was strengthened by his battle victories against his Meccan opponents, especially at the siege of Medina in 627.

Muhammad (*c.* 570–632) was a member of the Quraysh tribe, which guarded the sacred shrine known as the Kaaba in the Arab trading city of Mecca (*Makkah*). In 610 Muhammad received his first revelations, which commissioned him to preach against the idolatry and polytheism of the Arab tribes. In 622, he led his followers to Medina (*al-Madina*), where political power was added to his spiritual authority. Before Muhammad died in 632, the whole of Arabia had embraced Islam or entered into a peace treaty with the Prophet.

Muslims believe that – over a period of 20 years – Muhammad received revelations from God (*Allah*) via the Archangel Gabriel. These revelations form the Qur'an (literally 'The Recitation'), Islam's scripture. Muhammad was informed that God had given Scriptures to Moses (*Musa*), i.e. the *Pentateuch,* David (*Dawud*), i.e. the *Psalter,* and Jesus (*Isa*), i.e. the *New Testament.* Belief in these scriptures is an element of Muslim Faith. The collections of Muhammad's sayings and doings – the *Hadith* – are next in importance, for the Prophet is regarded as the best model of obedience to God's will. Muslims teach that Islam was the religion of Adam and all prophets sent by God to call man back to his path. Muslims revere Abraham, Moses and Jesus amongst other prophets, but Muhammad is the final prophet, because the *Qur'an* completed and superseded earlier revelations.

LARGEST ISLAMIC POPULATIONS

	Adherents (millions)		
	Sunni	Shia	Total
Indonesia	172.84	–	172.84
Pakistan	100.13	26.7	126.83
Bangladesh	108.67	–	108.67
India	79.0	26.0	105.0
Turkey	62.53	–	62.53
Iran	3.52	58.22	61.74
Egypt	54.81	–	54.81
Nigeria	51.96	–	51.96
Algeria	28.43	–	28.43
Morocco	26.66	–	26.66
Sudan	22.68	–	22.68
Afghanistan	19.04	3.40	22.44
Iraq	7.39	13.39	20.78
Uzbekistan	20.42	–	20.42
Saudi Arabia	17.59	0.62	18.21

LARGEST ISLAMIC MINORITIES

	Adherents (millions)
China	18.0
Ethiopia	17.06
Russia	6.0
USA	3.8
Philippines	3.28
France	3.21
Cameroon	2.97
Ghana	2.43
Thailand	2.42
Mozambique	2.32

■ *Pilgrims flock to Mecca to pray during the annual* Hajj. *Muslims are expected to attend the pilgrimage once in their lives unless prevented by health or financial difficulties*

SHARI'AH – ISLAMIC LAW

▶ Islamic Law is known as the *Shari'ah*, meaning 'the path leading to the watering place'.
▶ The scope of Islamic Law is wider than that of secular law, as it covers not only the relationship of humankind to the State and to his neighbour, as in secular law, but also humankind's relationship to God.

The *Shari'ah* – the Islamic legal system and courts which regulate the lives of those who profess Islam – is in force in many countries of the Islamic world. Beginning with the Five Pillars of Faith, religious duties are specified in detail for pilgrimage and prayer and there are specific laws concerning such family matters as marriage, the custody of children and inheritance. Punishments are laid down for certain offences, such as the amputation of a hand for theft, or 30 lashes for drinking alcohol. Conduct is divided into acts that are considered praiseworthy (*mandub*), or blameworthy (*makruh*). The following indicates the role of Islamic Law in countries containing a large number of adherents of Islam:

Countries in which only Islamic Law is in force: Afghanistan, Djibouti, Jordan, Iran, Kuwait, Libya, the Maldives, Mauritania, Oman, Pakistan, Saudi Arabia, Sudan, the United Arab Emirates, and Yemen. (Gambling and alcohol are forbidden in Afghanistan, Algeria, Bangladesh, Brunei, Djibouti, Iran, Kuwait, Libya, Mauritania, Oman, Pakistan, Qatar, Saudi Arabia, the United Arab Emirates, and Yemen.)

Countries in which a combination of Islamic and secular law is in force: Algeria, Bangladesh, the Comoros, Egypt, Iraq, Mali, Morocco, Qatar, Somalia, and Syria. In Brunei secular law and Islamic law exist side by side.

Countries of the Islamic world in which only secular law is in force: Albania, Azerbaijan, Bahrain, Bosnia-Herzegovina, Chad, Gambia, Guinea, Indonesia, Kazakhstan, Kyrgyzstan, Malaysia, Niger, Senegal, Tajikistan, Turkey, Turkmenistan, and Uzbekistan.

Countries in which Islam is the state religion established by law: Algeria, Bahrain, Bangladesh, Brunei, Comoros, Egypt, Iran, Iraq, Jordan, Kuwait, Libya, Malaysia, Maldives, Mauritania, Morocco, Oman, Pakistan, Qatar, Saudi Arabia, Tunisia, and United Arab Emirates. (In Lebanon, Islam is one of two recognized state religions. In Indonesia Islam is recognized as a state religion alongside five other faiths.)

Countries of the Islamic world which limit the freedom of other religions: Afghanistan, Iran, Iraq, Libya, Malaysia, Pakistan, Saudi Arabia, Sudan, Turkey and Yemen.

■ A mosque in Qurum, Oman. The tall minaret on the right has a balcony at the top where the muezzin stands, a man whose job it is to call Muslims to prayer five times a day

THE PILLARS OF FAITH

▶ There are five essential religious duties of Islam, described as the 'Five Pillars'.
▶ The Five Pillars are intended to develop the spirit of submission to God.

The Five Pillars of Islam were compiled soon after the death of Muhammad to summarize the fundamental religious duties of the Muslim community. A sixth Pillar, the *jihad,* was added by the Khawarij sect, but this was not accepted by the general Muslim community. The Pillars are:

PROFESSION OF THE FAITH

The basic belief of Islam is expressed in the *Shahada,* the Muslim confession of faith: 'There is no God but Allah and Muhammad is his Prophet!' From this fundamental belief are derived beliefs in angels (particularly Gabriel), the revealed Books (of the Jewish and Christian faiths in addition to the *Qur'an*), a series of prophets, and the Last Day, the Day of Judgement.

PRAYER

The act of worship is performed five times a day – at dawn, midday, mid-afternoon, sunset and before going to bed. After washing themselves, Muslims face in the direction of Mecca and pray communally at the mosque or individually in any place that is ritually clean, often using a prayer rug. Each prayer consists of a set number of 'bowings', for example two at dawn, four at midday. The 'bowing' procedure is composed of a prescribed succession of movements, in which the worshipper stands, bows, kneels with forehead to the ground, and sits back on the haunches. Recitations in Arabic of verses from the *Qur'an* accompany each movement. Attendance at the mosque is not compulsory, but men are required to go to the special congregational prayers held every Friday at noon. (The mosque also has an educational role and teaching ranges from advanced theology to religious instruction for children.)

ALMSGIVING

An offering, known as *zakat* (purification), is given by Muslims with sufficient means as an annual charitable donation. This offering is meant to purify the giver and make the rest of his wealth legal and 'pure'. The *zakat* is collected by the government to be used for the benefit of the poor.

FASTING

Muslims fast from shortly before sunrise until sunset every day during the Islamic month of Ramadan, the month in which they believe the Qur'an was first revealed. The person fasting may not eat, drink or smoke. However, the sick, the elderly and children are exempt from fasting.

PILGRIMAGE

Pilgrimage to Mecca (the *hajj*) is to be undertaken at least once in a lifetime by every Muslim who can afford it. The pilgrimage takes place during the Islamic month of Dhu'l-Hijja.

Jihad is another religious duty. It means striving against a visible enemy and one's own passions. If Muslims or Islam are endangered, defence by Muslims is required.

ISLAMIC DENOMINATIONS

▶ Sunnism and Shiism (or Shia Islam) are the two main denominations of Islam.
▶ Although the majority of Muslims are Sunnis, the Shiites are dominant in Iran, which is about 93% Shiite.

The main difference between Sunni and Shia Islam lies in the latter's belief that the charisma of the Prophet was inherited by his descendants, in whom they invest supreme spiritual and political authority. The Sunnis believe that orthodoxy is determined by the consensus of the community. Sunni caliphs exercised political but not spiritual authority – the historic caliphate ceased to exist in 1924 in Turkey.

Shiism has produced a variety of denominations, including the Ismailis and Zaidis, although the majority are known as 'Twelvers' (Ithna 'Ashariyya). They believe that the 12th Imam, or successor to Muhammad in linear descent, disappeared and is now the Hidden Imam, who will return as the Mahdi before the end of the world. Senior religious lawyers, known as *mujtahids,* interpret the Hidden Imam and share his authority. The Ayatollah (literally 'sign of God') Khomeini was regarded, in Iran, as such a *mujtahid.* Other Shiites revere living Imams, such as the Aga Khan Khojas, whose leader (the Aga Khan) claims to be a descendant of the Prophet Muhammad through Ismail, the 7th Imam.

Shiite branches include Ithna 'Ashariyya, which is dominant in Azerbaijan, Bahrain, Iran and Iraq, and Zaidi, which is dominant in Yemen. The Ibadi sect is often regarded as belonging to neither the Sunni nor Shiite traditions and is dominant in Oman.

Islam's mystical or Sufi tradition has both Sunni and Shiite adherents. Many of its orders or circles have appointed or hereditary shaikh or *pirs* (spiritual guides) and venerate their predecessors as saints. Sufi missionaries played an important role in Islam's expansion into Africa and Asia.

The small exclusive Druze sect, in Syria and Lebanon, has an eclectic system of doctrines.

THE MUSLIM COMMUNITY

▶ Islam as a total way of life is a missionary religion committed to bringing all men into the Household of Faith (*Dar-al-Islam*).
▶ Islam affords special status to followers of its sister faiths, Judaism and Christianity, which have existed as protected minority communities in many Muslim lands.

Although the sheer variety of races and cultures embraced by Islam has produced differences, all segments of Muslim society are bound by a common faith and a sense of belonging to a single community. With the loss of political power during the period of Western colonialism in the 19th and early 20th centuries, the concept of the Islamic community, instead of weakening, became stronger.

This, in harness with the discovery of immense oil reserves, helped various Muslim peoples in their struggle to gain political freedom and sovereignty in the mid-20th century.

■ The Kaaba stone, built into the Great Mosque in Mecca, is deeply revered by Muslims. An irregular cube, 12 m high, contains the sacred stone, which is c. 2 m wide and thought to be of meteoric origins. Muhammad believed the stone had been given to Abraham by the Archangel Gabriel

THE SUNNI FOUR SCHOOLS OF LAW

Hanafi: Dominant in Afghanistan, Bangladesh, Djibouti, Jordan, Kazakhstan, Kyrgyzstan, Lebanon, Pakistan, Palestine, Syria, Tajikistan, Turkey, Turkmenistan and Uzbekistan. In Egypt, Hanafi, Maliki and Shafi Islam are all significant.

Hanbali: Confined to Qatar and Saudi Arabia.

Malik: Algeria, Chad, Egypt (see also Hanafi, above), Gambia, Guinea, Kuwait, Libya, Mali, Mauritania, Morocco, Niger, Senegal, Sudan and Tunisia.

Shaf: Brunei, Comoros, Egypt (see above), Indonesia, Malaysia, the Maldives, Somalia and the United Arab Emirates.

RELIGIONS OF INDIA

▷ **The largest religious structure in the world is the Hindu temple of Angkor Wat in Cambodia, which covers 162.6 ha.**

▷ **The largest Buddhist temple, built in the 8th century near Jogjakarta in Indonesia, is Borobudur, measuring 123 m^2 and 31.4 m in height.**

▷ **The most important Sikh temple is the 16th-century Golden Temple at Amritsar.**

HINDUISM

▶ **The ancient Aryans, the fathers of Hinduism, worshipped nature-deities, including *Agni* (fire) and *Surya* (Sun).**
▶ **The three High Gods of Hinduism (Brahma, Vishnu and Shiva) form the Hindu Trinity or *Trimurti* ('the One or Whole with Three Forms').**

The word Hindu was first used by Arab invaders in the 8th century AD to describe those living beyond the Sind or Indus Valley. It was only later that the term Hinduism was coined by 19th-century English writers to describe the religion and social institutions of the great majority of the people of India. The origins of Hinduism (or *Sanatan-Dharma*, meaning 'ancient way of life') lie in the *Arya-Dharma* (Aryan way of life) of the Indo-Europeans who invaded the Indus Valley from Asia Minor and Iran *c.* 1500 BC. They wrote the *Vedas (Rig-Veda, Yajur-Veda, Sama-Veda, Atharva-Veda)*, which are collections of prayers, hymns and formulas for worship.

The Aryans absorbed some of the traditions of the indigenous inhabitants. This process of assimilation resulted in the great epic poems composed between 200 BC and AD 200, the *Ramayana* and the *Mahabharata*, which includes the famous *Bhagavadgita*. Three deities dominate these epics: Brahma, Vishnu and Shiva, representing, in turn, creation, preservation and destruction. There are other gods and demi-gods, and also important *avatars* (incarnations), such as Krishna (a form of Vishnu). Some gods, such as the goddess of smallpox, are renowned for certain activities; others are local deities worshipped only in a particular area.

PHILOSOPHICAL HINDUISM

Philosophical Hinduism developed in the 5th century BC with a core of 18 *Upanishads* (philosophical scriptures). The laws of Manu were written during the first two centuries AD and contain the concept that God created distinct orders of men: priests (*Brahmans*); soldiers and rulers (*Kshatriyas*); farmers and traders (*Vaisyas*); and artisans and labourers (*Sudras*). This belief planted the seed which later developed into the so-called caste system.

Hinduism tolerates a great variety of beliefs and practices and there is total freedom regarding the choice and mode of one's philosophy. Brahmans recognize six schools as orthodox. The three best-known are yoga, sankhya and vedanta. Yoga teaches the mystical union of the self with the Supreme Being through a state of total tranquillity and awareness brought about by exercises, postures and controlled breathing. Sankhya teaches the eternal interaction of spirit and matter. Vedanta teaches that only *Brahma* (creation) has reality, while the whole phenomenal world is the outcome of illusion *(maya)*. The great philosopher Shankara (Sankara, AD 788–820) was an exponent of Vedanta.

The Brahmans regard Buddhism and Jainism as heterodox, meaning that they are in conflict with accepted Hindu beliefs. The aim of Hinduism is to be reunited with the absolute, thus escaping the wheel of existence (*Samsara*), which is determined by *Karma* (literally 'deeds' or 'actions'). *Moksa* (release) may be gained through yoga, *Jnana* (knowledge) or *Bhakti* (devotion to one's God).

Hinduism traditionally divides life into four ideal periods: *Brahmacharya* (celibate period), *Grihastha* (householder), *Vanaprastha* (retired stage), and *Sannyasa* (renunciation). The Hindu religion embraces many local as well as national traditions and has numerous pilgrim centres, temples, ashrams (religious retreats) and orders of monks.

A Hindu temple (*mandir*) may be a huge, ornate building dedicated to the worship of a major deity – visited particularly during festivals and pilgrimages – or a small roadside shrine at which offerings to a local spirit are made. The concept of the spiritual teacher, or guru, is important; many contemporary gurus attract European as well as Indian devotees.

■ *A man meditates as he sits by the Ganges (the Hindus' holiest river) in the classical position: legs interlocked and hand in the 'Om' position, the three fingers symbolizing the gods Brahma (creation), Vishnu (preservation) and Shiva (destruction)*

HINDU CHRONOLOGY

The Hindu timescale is vast. It is based around the *yuga* or world age, of which there are four: *Krta, Treta, Dvapara* and *Kali*. The first, *Krtayuga*, lasts 1,728,000 years. The *Tretayuga* lasts 1,296,000 years, *Dvaparayuga* 864,000 years and *Kaliyuga* (the present world-age) 432,000 years.

The shortening length of each *yuga* corresponds to an increasing reduction in the world's physical and moral standards. The four *yugas*, taken together, form a *mahayuga*, which thus lasts 4,320,000 years. A *kalpa*, or aeon, lasts 1000 *mahayugas*, or 8640 million human years. An aeon is only one day in the life of the god Brahma, whose lifespan of 100 days and 100 nights (each equal to a *kalpa*) is a *para*. We are currently halfway through the current *para*. Thus there are approximately 1.7 trillion years until the Hindu universe comes to its end and, like the Hindu soul, is again reborn.

HINDU GODS

GODS OF THE VEDAS
Indra: Thunder god, god of battle.
Varuna: Guardian of order; divine overseer.
Agni: God of fire.
Surya: God associated with the Sun.

MAJOR GODS OF HINDUISM
Brahma: The creator; linked with the goddess Saraswati.
Vishnu: The preserver; with Shiva, one of Hinduism's greatest gods. Vishnu has ten incarnations or avatars, and is married to Lakshmi.
Shiva: A great god, associated with destruction. In Hindu mythology, Shiva is married to Parvati and is the father of Ganesh.
Ganesh: The elephant-headed god, worshipped as the remover of obstacles and god of good luck.
Hanuman: The monkey warrior-god, associated with the god Rana.

VISHNU'S TEN AVATARS (INCARNATIONS)
Hindus believe that whenever universal law is threatened, Vishnu will take on earthly form to restore balance, through his ten incarnations. These forms ascend from animal to fully human.
Matsya: The fish.
Kurma: The tortoise.
Varaha: The boar.
Narasimha: The man-lion.
Vamana: The dwarf.
Parasurama: Rama bearing an axe.
Ramachandra or Rama: The god of the Ramayana epic, identified by his bow and quiver of arrows.
Krishna: The important god featured in the Bhagavadgita. He is worshipped particularly as a baby and as a flute-playing cowherd.
The Buddha: The great teacher from the 6th–5th centuries BC and founder of Buddhism.
Kalki: 'The one to come'; a future avatar.

MAJOR GODDESSES OF HINDUISM
The goddesses are manifestations of the great creative spirit or Shakti. The most popular are:
Parvati: Wife of Shiva; also known as Uma.
Durga: All-powerful warrior goddess, also known as Amba, and linked with Shiva.
Kali: Goddess associated with destruction.
Lakshmi: Goddess of beauty, wealth and good fortune; wife of Vishnu.
Sarawat: Goddess of learning, arts and music; wife of Brahma.

BUDDHISM

▶ Siddhartha Gautama was later named 'Buddha' by his followers, meaning 'Enlightened One'.
▶ Buddha's teaching made no provision for either God or the soul.

Buddhism is based on the teachings of Siddhartha Gautama (*c.* 563–483 BC) of the Gautama clan of the Sakyas, a royal family belonging to the Ksatriya, or warrier, caste in north-east India. After an early life of pleasure, Gautama became deeply dissatisfied. He then experimented with asceticism and yoga before experiencing *bodhi* or 'awakening' during a long period of meditation under a tree. For the rest of his long life, Gautama taught about the impermanence and suffering of human life and the way to escape such suffering.

The Buddha taught the four noble truths which culminate in a 'Way' to end suffering. The 'Way' differs according to the school of Buddhism. Zen Buddhists rely upon meditation; Therevada Buddhists believe that craving ceases by means of the *Eightfold Path* of right view, right thought, right speech, right action, right livelihood, right effort, right mindfulness and right concentration. This is represented in the Wheel of Law (*dharma chakra*), which has eight spokes for the eight steps towards enlightenment (*nirvana*).

Since impermanence (*anicca*) is an unalterable fact of life, the Buddha taught that we can be truly happy only by becoming detached from the delusive notions of 'me' and 'mine'. This detachment is called the not-self (*anatta*). He taught the law (*dharma*) of cause and effect, and encouraged his disciples to take refuge in the *sangha*, the monastic way of celibacy, non-violence, poverty and vegetarianism.

SCHOOLS OF BUDDHISM

THEREVADA BUDDHISM ('THE SCHOOL OF THE ELDERS')

Said to have been the original Buddhism of India, this school remains non-theistic and emphasizes the importance of the celibate life to gain nirvana. In 1956, over 4 million of India's untouchables converted to Therevada Buddhism. Therevada Buddhism is practised in Sri Lanka, Myanmar (Burma) and Thailand.

MAHAYANA BUDDHISM ('GREATER VEHICLE')

In Mahayana, the concept of the Bodhisattva ('one bound for enlightenment who delays entry into nirvana in order to help others') developed to include many such heavenly beings alongside, but subordinate to, the Buddha. Buddha was regarded as having three bodies *(kaya)* – the historical body, the bliss body and the absolute body. Its subdivisions include Zen and Pure Land Buddhism. Mahayana Buddhism is practised in Vietnam, Cambodia, Laos, China and Japan.

TANTRAYAMA BUDDHISM

Developed in Tibet, this school makes much use of mantras (sacred chants) and of images, which depict the Bodhisattvas as very active in the world, opposing evil. The male quality of compassion is often united with the female quality of wisdom.

THE FRIENDS OF THE WESTERN BUDDHIST ORDER

The Friends of the Western Buddhist Order was formed in 1969 and seeks to find forms of expression amenable to the West, which some call *Navayana* (a 'New Vehicle').

SIKHISM

▶ Sikhism originated in the Punjab in India, where it is still the majority religion.
▶ The founder of Sikhism was Guru Nanak (1479–1539), who taught how to lead a good life and seek final union with God.

Sikhism is based on the concept of the guru: God is the true Guru; Sikh spiritual teachers are called gurus; and the scriptures, the *Granth,* are said to be the guru. Sikhs believe in the existence of only one true God and that, through worship and meditation, the most devoted Sikhs can experience and know Him. They believe that each person is trapped in his own failings and weaknesses, and that the only hope is found in the mercy of the true Guru.

WORSHIP AND SOCIETY

The holy scripture, the *Guru Granth*, is the central document for all Sikh rituals and ceremonies. It contains the teachings of the first five gurus. There are ten orthodox Sikh gurus, with Nanak (1469–1539) as the first guru and Gobind Singh (1666–1708) as the last; each successive guru was chosen by his predecessor on the basis of his spiritual enlightenment.

The Sikhs worship in temples known as *gurdwara* (the guru's door). There are no priests to conduct the services: anyone can lead the worship, although some are specially trained to read the *Granth*.

Sikhism has spread outside the Punjab during the 20th century to the United Kingdom, the USA, Canada and also to parts of southern and eastern Africa. It is an ethnic religion in that it attempts to keep the community intact and does not aim to convert members from outside. It does not deny the existence of other faiths but strives for its members to be devoted to God.

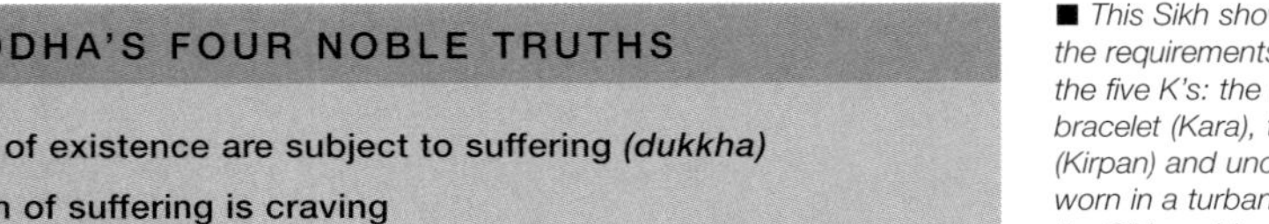

BUDDHA'S FOUR NOBLE TRUTHS

- **All forms of existence are subject to suffering *(dukkha)***
- **The origin of suffering is craving**
- **The cure for suffering is the cessation of craving**
- **There is a 'Way' to end suffering**

■ Buddhism in all its forms has recently spread to the West, attracting significant followings. These Tibetan Buddhist monks, holding cymbals and chanting in religious costumes, are part of a ceremony taking place in the town of Washington in New Jersey, USA

■ This Sikh shows three of the requirements listed in the five K's: the metal bracelet (Kara), the dagger (Kirpan) and uncut hair worn in a turban, on which the Sikh emblem is fixed, and uncut beard (Kesh)

THE FIVE K'S

The first five gurus of Sikhism developed the majority of the Sikh doctrines. The final guru, Gobind Singh, established the Sikh community by giving the names *Singh* and *Kaur* to men and women respectively, and creating the shared symbols which initiates must possess, referred to as the five K's:
Kesh: uncut hair worn in a turban and uncut beard
Kangha: a comb, to keep the hair clean
Kara: a metal bracelet
Kaccha: knee-length undershorts
Kirpan: a dagger

Religions of Asia and Africa

- The spirits of the dead are important in many primal religions – in Madagascar some people still dig up their ancestors once a year on the Day of the Dead and dance with them.
- After World War II, Shintoism was no longer recognized as Japan's state religion.
- The Shaman's narrations of his trips to the netherworld (spirit world) are the content of most popular epic poetry among Shamanistic societies.
- Confucius believed that people should attain nobility through character rather than inheritance.

CHINESE FOLK RELIGIONS AND DAOISM (TAOISM)

▶ In Chinese folk religions, the family unit is perceived as including both the living and the dead members of the family.
▶ Daoists emphasize spontaneity and naturalness. Practitioners are encouraged to abandon themselves to the current of the *Dao*.

Chinese folk religions are now mainly practised by members of the 64 officially recognized minority peoples in the People's Republic of China. These traditional beliefs are most commonly encountered in remote areas, but remnants of folk religion survive elsewhere in China and are widely practised along with Daoism both in rural areas and in the cities.

DEMONS AND DIVINATIONS

Ancient traditional Chinese religions focus on demons and divination and there is a constant interplay between the spirit world and the present physical world. Demons – the *kuei-shen* – are manifested in all aspects of the natural world but, in particular, in mountains, rivers and rocks. There are also other spirits, such as ghosts, fairies and other supernatural beings, with whom humankind must contend. As all these spirits shun the light, firecrackers, bonfires and torches – as well as various charms – are used to scare the *kuei* away.

ANCESTOR WORSHIP

The centre of Chinese folk religion is, however, ancestor worship. Respect for the elderly and concern for the family have always been emphasized in Chinese society. This ancestor cult includes outward displays of family clan groups, as well as expressions of reverence in the home and at the graves of family members. Funeral rites and pilgrimages to family graves are important aspects of Chinese folk religions.

DAOISM

The practice of Daoism is almost inseparable from these traditional folk religions. Daoism, the Chinese teachings of 'the Way' or *Dao*, is grounded in the works of Lao-tzu (6th–5th century BC) and Chuang-tzu (4th century BC). The *Dao-te Ching* (meaning 'Classic of the Way of Power'), written by Lao-tzu, is the seminal sacred text of Daoism. It teaches that the *Dao* is the source of all things, the Absolute, or 'Uncarved Block', experienced only in mystical ecstasy. The *Dao* works within the world, bringing about harmonious development. It also acts as a model for rulers and for leaders, who should allow their people to live spontaneously according to their own conditions and needs.

Unlike Confucianism, Daoism advocates spontaneity and naturalness instead of formality. Everything, good or bad, is the sublime operation of the *Dao* and should not be interfered with. The *Dao* is symbolized by water and by female imagery rather than male imagery.

The goal of 'the Way' is immortality, which can only be achieved by the return to a properly balanced body composed of *yin* (the quiescent, feminine side) and *yang* (the active, male side). Daoists naturally tend to solitude, meditation and simple living. Their techniques of quiet contemplation are similar to Buddhist meditation.

Despite having its origins in the 6th century BC, Daoism did not develop as a movement of organized religious communities until the 2nd century AD. It continued to developed many schools and texts until the 16th century. After that time, it still had some impact on popular religion in synthesis with other philosophical ideas and religious practices. The aspects of Daoism that are the most well known in the West are *yin* and *yang*, and a meditative form of exercise called *T'ai Chi*.

CONFUCIANISM

▶ Confucianism is better described as a philosophy or code of social behaviour than a religion – it has no church or clergy and is not a formal institution.
▶ Kongfuzi (Confucius) was said to have attracted more than 3000 students during his lifetime, of whom 72 were close disciples.

Confucianism is an approach to life and way of thinking based on the teachings of Kongfuzi (Confucius; 551–479 BC). Kongfuzi was not the sole founder of Confucianism, but was rather a member of the founding group of *Ju* or 'meek ones'. He was a scholar-official and keeper of accounts from the province of Lu in China.

THE TEACHINGS OF KONGFUZI

Kongfuzi taught that the main ethic is *jen* (benevolence), and that truth involves the knowledge of one's own faults. He believed in altruism and restraint, and insisted on family piety. He believed that people could be led by example, and encouraged the rulers of his own time to imitate those in former periods whose leadership had brought about prosperity. He stressed *li*, the rules of proper conduct in ritual, etiquette and social behaviour. His teachings were transmitted to later generations through the *Lun yü* (meaning Analects or 'Conversations').

Kongfuzi himself is considered to represent the Confucian 'Ideal Person', a model of sincerity, modesty and rightmindedness. Gradually, through diligent training and study ('self-cultivation'), he was able to remould his own character to conform to the Will of Heaven.

THE TEACHINGS OF MENGZI

The teachings of Kongfuzi were developed by Mengzi (Mencius; 372–289 BC) and became the basis of Chinese ethics and behaviour, in which there is an emphasis on the preservation of the family and the state, and the performance of proper rites for the ancestors. As Kongfuzi had hoped for a true king (*wang*) who would rule by moral example rather than constraint, Mencius actively encouraged people to rebel against rulers intent on personal power and profit, sharply contrasting governments established on the basis of moral virtue (*jen*) and those established on tyrannical authority.

THE IMPACT OF CONFUCIANISM

As its object was to emphasize the development of human nature and the person, Confucianism had a great hold over Chinese education for many years. During the early 19th century a good deal of Confucian teaching remained alongside other aspects of Chinese philosophy and practice. Confucianism has even survived the onslaught of Communist ideology.

SHAMANISM

▶ Shamanism consists of a wide range of traditional beliefs and folk religions that are usually closely related to the land.
▶ Shamanistic religions have survived mainly in remote areas.

Shamanism is characterized by a whole range of religious specialists, including the medicine men of North America and the shamans of Siberia and the Arctic. The religion is generally found in hunting and gathering societies and among peoples living in scattered, often migratory, groups. It is the dominant religious element among the Inuit (Eskimo) from Greenland to Alaska, and among the reindeer herders and fishers of north-eastern Asia.

THE SHAMAN'S ROLE

The shaman is a medicine man (or woman), priest, and death escort. The role of the shaman is to cure sicknesses, direct communal services and, in times of trouble, mediate with the spirit world on behalf of the people, often escorting the souls of the dead to the other world. The shaman's power lies in his ability to enter an ecstatic trance. During ecstasy the shaman sends out his (or her) soul to communicate with the spirit world, to ensure a favourable result for the hunt or to diagnose or cure disease. Sickness is considered as a loss of the soul, which has either strayed from the body or been stolen by demons, and the shaman uses spirits to find the soul of a sick person.

■ *This shaman in northern China went through initiation trials and instructions. Shamans are mostly chosen from hereditary lines or from 'election' by supernatural forces*

DAOISM AND CONFUCIANISM HAVE SHAPED CHINESE LIFE FOR MORE THAN 2000 YEARS

■ *Shinto priests pray in the religious gardens of a shrine in Nara, Japan. The harmony of nature and architecture is important in Shinto shrines, and greenery plays a vital role*

SHINTOISM

▶ Shinto ('the way of the gods') is the native religion of Japan.
▶ The earliest surviving Shinto texts include semi-mythological genealogies of the emperors, tracing their divine descent from *Amaterasu,* the Sun-goddess.

The Shinto religion gained its name during the 6th century AD in order to distinguish it from Buddhism, which was then reaching Japan from mainland China. Early Shinto was based on ritual practices to do with agriculture, not on philosophical or moral beliefs. People sought help from the sacred power (*kami*) for their physical and spiritual needs, and great stress was laid upon offerings, prayer and purification by Shinto priests. *Kami* is usually translated as 'god' or 'divinity' and the truthfulness of the *kami* can be recognized in every being at every moment.

Worship at shrines is important in Shintoism. The more important national shrines were dedicated to well-known national figures, but other shrines were set up for worshipping mountain and forest deities.

Unlike the other traditional religions that arose thousands of years ago, Shintoism is distinguished by its possession of a written, rather than an oral, sacred literature.

SHINTO DENOMINATIONS

Throughout its history Shintoism has been affected by outside influences, especially Buddhism, Daoism and Confucianism. In the 19th century, the Shinto religion was divided into Shrine Shinto (*jinja*) and Sect Shinto (*kyoha*). A number of denominations were formed and these were dependent on private support for their teaching and organization. Different denominations had very little in common and varied widely in belief and practice. Some adhered to the traditional Shinto deities while others did not. Of the 13 denominations, *Tenrikyo* is the best known.

STATE SHINTO

In 1871, Shinto became the Japanese national religion. State Shinto taught that a citizen's religious duty was obedience to the divine emperor. Shinto's perceived close links with extreme nationalism damaged its standing in postwar Japan. In 1946 Emperor Hirohito renounced all claims to divinity, and the new postwar constitution safeguards religious freedom and prohibits any association between religion and state.

SHINTO TODAY

Estimates of the number of practising adherents of Shinto range between 2.8 million and 120 million. Because the practice of Shinto and its traditions became the traditions of the Japanese nation, the majority of Japanese may be said to belong to the 'Shinto culture'. Therefore, about 120 million people have some allegiance to Shintoism. They take part in some Shinto ceremonies, if only at a social level as 'rites of passage' during life. Shinto ceremonies and festivals (*matsuri*) have became inseparable from general government affairs. *Matsuri* usually involve ritual purification, the reciting of prayers, offerings of nourishment to the *kami,* religious music and dance, serious worship and jubilant celebration.

Many Japanese, however, also practise some form of Buddhism. There are 36 million who practise Shinto as their principal religion, but also practise Buddhism. Only a small proportion practise Shinto to the exclusion of all other faiths.

At present, there are 2.8 million active and regular participants who regard Shinto as a religion and not a culture. However, interest in Shinto is increasing and in 1990 Emperor Akihito was enthroned according to Shinto rites. Shintoism has neither sought nor attracted non-Japanese followers.

■ Ema – *small wooden prayer boards given by Shinto worshippers – hang on the wall of a shrine in Kyoto, Japan*

PRIMAL RELIGIONS

▶ Common themes in African primal religions include divination, cults of affliction and possession, ancestor veneration and secret societies.
▶ The word 'primal' is used to convey that these religions came first in human history, not to indicate that they are 'savage' or 'primitive'.

Primal religions underlie all the major religions of the world. It is wrong to think of these religions as primitive, as they often contain beliefs and ideas about the world that achieve high levels of sophistication. The primal religions that survive today are the religions of non-literate, usually tribal societies.

Unlike the universal religions such as Christianity, Islam, Hinduism and Buddhism – which have a wealth of written records and scriptures – the primal religions have no written sources. This does not mean, however, that primal religions are without history or are in some way 'fossilized' remnants of a past age. Like the universal religions, they have long and complex histories.

Although Christianity and Islam are popular in Africa, many traditional religions are practised there by various tribal groups, such as the Nuer, Dinka, Dogon, Yoruba, Zande and Shona. These religions developed in pre-literate communities and environments that were often independent of one another and far apart. In African traditional religions – as in most primal religions – there is a conception of a supreme being, sometimes prominent in religious life, sometimes remote and uninterested in human affairs.

DEITIES AND DIVINITIES

The Ashanti of Ghana call their god Nyame, and other West African peoples have similar names for their deity. The supreme god of the Yoruba people of Nigeria is known as Olorun, 'Owner of the Sky'. He is the creator of all things, the giver of life and breath, and the final judge of all people. In many parts of Africa the supreme being is considered so great and so remote that he is not worshipped. Divinities and ancestors, who act as intermediaries between people and the supreme god, are worshipped instead. Only in times of extreme distress is the god directly approached by the people.

Divinities are powerful, named spirits, each with their own specific characteristics. Most African peoples believe in a multitude of divinities other than the supreme god. In the Americas, Asia and Oceania, there is widespread belief in many deities. As well as powerful divinities and ancestor spirits, most primal peoples believe in numerous minor spirits, who may be good, bad or unpredictable. They may be the souls of the forgotten dead, who haunt the living, or the spirits of places such as rivers, mountains, bridges, rocks or trees.

MANA

In Oceania and in some other societies mana is a spiritual power or life force that is believed to permeate the universe. Originally a Melanesian word, it is now applied by anthropologists to spiritual power in other primal religions. Mana is not a spirit, and it has no will or purpose – it is impersonal and flows from one thing to another, and can be manipulated to achieve certain ends. Charms, amulets and medicines contain this power for the benefit of the wearer and user.

JUDAISM

▶ **Every Jew in the world is said to be descended from one of the 12 sons of Jacob, each of whom began a tribe, referred to as the 12 tribes of Israel.**

▶ **The first Zionist Congress, to discuss the creation of a separate Jewish State, was held in Basel, Switzerland, in August 1897.**

▶ **Jews do not use the term BC ('Before Christ') to indicate that time period; instead they use BCE, meaning 'Before the Common Era'.**

▶ **Judaism is the world's oldest monotheistic (worship of one God) religion.**

■ *Women and children crowd together to pray at the Western Wall, a holy site for Jews which qualifies as a synagogue, with separate areas for men and women*

ORIGINS AND BELIEFS

▶ **The esoteric name of the Jewish God, given to Moses on the mountain, is *YHWH,* meaning 'I am, shall be what I am, shall be'.**
▶ **Although Judaism expects non-Jews to observe certain basic ethical laws, it does not regard Jewish ritual as obligatory and does not seek converts.**

The biblical account of the origin of the Jewish religion begins in *c.* 2000 BCE with Abraham's revolt against the idol-worship of his native Mesopotamia (now Iraq), when he smashed his father's idols and fled to Canaan (present-day Israel). The word Jew is derived from the Latin *Judaeus*, which in turn comes from the Hebrew *Yehudhi*, signifying a descendant of Jacob, Abraham's grandson.

The observance of the Passover (*Pesach*) from Egypt makes every believing Jew a participant in the event that delivered their ancestors from bondage and established a special relationship between themselves and God. This special relationship consists of an undertaking by the Jewish people to keep God's laws faithfully. However, God promises the righteous of all peoples (Jews and non-Jews alike) a place in the world to come in the eventual re-establishment of the royal house of David. The *Messiah* (meaning the 'anointed') will then inaugurate an age of universal peace and security.

SCRIPTURES

▶ **Judaism's most sacred text is the *Torah.***
▶ **The *Talmud* includes subjects as diverse as agriculture, astrology, dream interpretation, geography, mathematics and architecture.**

Jewish scripture includes the same books as the Christian Old Testament. The *Torah* is the Hebrew name for the Law of Moses (the *Pentateuch*) which was divinely revealed to Moses on Mount Sinai, soon after the Exodus. The Hebrew scriptures also contain the books of the prophets, the wisdom literature (such as Solomon) and the historical writings (such as Kings). The *Talmud* contains civic and religious laws and is a collection of originally oral traditions. The Mishnah is the oral law dating from the 1st century BCE to the 3rd century AD.

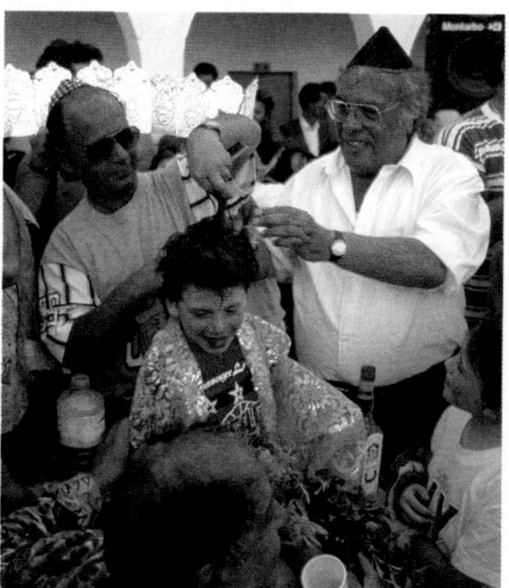

■ *A child gets a haircut during Lag Be Omer, the 33rd day of Passover, at the El Ghriba Synagogue (a chief pilgrimage site for North African Jews) near Er Riadh, Djerba, Tunisia*

THE DIASPORA

▶ **The word 'Diaspora' is used to describe the dispersion of Jews after the Babylonian and Roman conquests of Palestine. It also refers to all Jewish communities outside Israel.**
▶ **The largest and most important Jewish settlement in the early Diaspora was in Egypt.**

The fall of Jerusalem in AD 70 resulted in the Diaspora, which led to Jews settling throughout Europe, Africa and Asia Minor, often under severe discrimination and disabilities. Jewish emancipation began in 1791 in France with Jews being granted citizenship. The new climate stimulated the growth of the Reform movement, giving Judaism the status of a religious sect within the European nations, loyal to their countries of adoption, and led to variations in the practice of Judaism. Orthodox Judaism regards all religious authority as deriving from the *Torah,* and Orthodox Jewish beliefs were codified as the Thirteen Principles of Faith by Rabbi Moses Maimonides (1135–1204). Conservative Judaism, strongest in the USA, stands midway between Orthodox and Reformed Judaism, teaching that the faith must find its place in the contemporary world. There are also Liberal and Progressive Jews who reject the divinity of the *Torah* and rabbinic authority, believing, to varying degrees, that Jewish practice must adapt to changing circumstances. They have introduced changes such as holding services partly in the vernacular (rather than in Hebrew).

The majority of Jews still live in the Diaspora, but the State of Israel, established in 1948, is important to most Jews as a symbol of the hope and pride that sustained their faith during centuries of persecution. Different groups from the Diaspora preserve their distinctive traditions – including the Sephardim (from Portugal, Spain and North Africa), the Ashkenazim (from central Europe) and, most recently, the Falasha (from Ethiopia).

RITUALS

▶ **During the *Shabbat* – the Jewish Day of Rest – carrying, writing, cooking and travelling (except short distances by foot) are prohibited.**
▶ **Orthodox Jews recite blessings from the *Talmud* for the most common everyday activities, from opening one's eyes in the morning to tying one's shoes.**

Judaism lays down a complex set of laws of *kashrut*, which distinguishes permitted (*kosher*) from prohibited (*treifa*) foods. Only cloven-hoofed mammals that chew the cud, such as cows and sheep, are permitted as food, which must be killed by a skilled *shochet* in a way that minimizes pain to the animal and drains as much blood as possible. Fish must have scales and fins (eels, sturgeon and shellfish are forbidden). Birds of prey are also prohibited. Milk and meat and their derivatives must be strictly separated and must not be cooked or prepared together, nor eaten at the same meal.

Judaism as a total way of life revolves around the family. Jews cannot surrender their religion. You are a Jew if your mother was Jewish. A boy becomes a man for religious purposes at his *bar mitzvah* at the age of 13, but is circumcised eight days after birth.

WORSHIP

▶ **Synagogues used to be built with galleries for the women but, later, side rooms were built to serve this purpose.**
▶ **Israel has two chief rabbis – one for the Ashkenazic (European) community and one for the Sephardic (Oriental) community.**

Synagogues were first built to serve as temporary places of worship after the destruction of the Temple in Jerusalem by the Babylonians (586 BCE). Although the Jews rebuilt the Temple, the use of local houses of prayer continued. The second Temple was also destroyed, but never rebuilt. Today the synagogue service is modelled upon, and refers to, the Temple service. Many synagogues use ancient Jewish symbols in their decoration such as the Star of David, the *Menorah* (the seven-branched Temple candlestick) and the two tablets containing the Ten Commandments. The congregation usually faces the Ark – a cupboard containing the *Torah* scrolls handwritten on parchment. Above the Ark (usually in the wall facing Jerusalem) a light is kept burning as a sign of God's eternal presence.

Synagogue services – held evening, morning and afternoon – centre on a period of silent prayer. For a formal service to take place, a quorum of ten men (a *minyan*) must be present, otherwise the *Torah* cannot be read. Any of the *minyan* can read the *Torah* or lead prayers. The rabbi is a teacher and interpreter of the Law.

■ **THE FIRST TEMPLE OF THE JEWS WAS BUILT BY KING DAVID'S SON, SOLOMON, *c.* 922 BCE** ■

THE ARTS ▷

'The object of art is to give life a shape'
– Jean Anouilh

Stage and Screen

- The first feature-length talking film, *The Jazz Singer* (US 27), opened with Al Jolson uttering the immortal words, 'Wait a minute! Wait a minute! You ain't heard nothin' yet!'
- Actors are still sometimes called 'thespians' after Thespis, the Greek founder of theatre.
- The most successful director is Steven Spielberg, whose films have grossed more than $2.1 billion to date.
- The Indian cinema industry, affectionately called 'Bollywood' (a combination of Bombay and Hollywood), has the highest output of films per year, with a record 948 in 1990.
- The film *Trainspotting* (GB 96) took 25 times more at the box office than the figure it cost to make.

ORIGINS OF THEATRE

▶ Theatre has its roots in magic rituals and religious ceremonies.
▶ Early tribesmen acted out the hunt in the hope of improving their success and placating the spirits of their prey. Farmers re-enacted fertility rites, such as that of the death and rebirth of the god Osiris in Egypt.

Western drama developed in Ancient Greece at formal religious ceremonies. A priest called Thespis added a solo performer to a ritual song and dance who engaged in a dialogue with the chorus leader. Two more male solo actors were then added who wore masks, allowing them to appear and reappear as different characters in the same play. Thespis is said to have toured with a group of actors around the countryside performing in market places.

In the 6th and 5th centuries BC, the great plays of Aeschylus, Sophocles and Euripides were staged as part of religious festivals in open-air theatres constructed on hillsides with seating curving around a circular dance floor, known as the orchestra. Greek plays related powerful tragic stories from mythology and history, often followed by bawdy comedies which mocked well-known figures.

The Romans developed the Greek theatre, but the plays became increasingly rude and bawdy which met with disapproval from Christian churchmen and led to theatres being closed and plays being banned in the 6th century AD by Emperor Justinian. However, it was within the Christian Church that theatre was reborn in medieval Europe, again from the dramatization of part of religious services. However, this again brought fresh disapproval and theatre moved outside the Church.

■ *The well-preserved theatre at Epidaurus, Greece, is still used today for productions, seating about 12,000 people*

THE GOLDEN AGE OF DRAMA

In the late 16th century, travelling players often performed in the galleried yards of inns which became the model for the first permanent theatres in England and Spain in which the work of Shakespeare and Lope de Vega were performed. Open to the sky, with a platform jutting out into a standing audience, and surrounded by tiered galleries, they gave actors close contact with large audiences – perhaps 3000 in the case of the Globe Theatre in London. Plays were also given indoors in palaces and public halls.

This age of drama produced some of the greatest theatre works, with plays written by Marlowe, Jonson and Shakespeare. Progress in set design also continued, and the early 17th century saw the work of Inigo Jones, perhaps the greatest stage decorator of all time. However, the Puritans thought that theatre-going led to poor church attendance and in 1642 English theatres were closed.

THEATRE RISES AGAIN

The theatres reopened in 1660, and western drama developed throughout the 18th and 19th centuries. In Britain, France and Germany drama tended to be sentimental, but performances were popular. This sentimental drama laid the groundwork for the great actor-managers such as David Garrick. This strand of social drama developed through the 19th century in a variety of forms, including pantomime, music-hall and melodrama.

Towards the end of the 18th century, the Romantic movement began to be explored on stage. Germany led the way with its *Sturm und Drang* ('Storm and Stress') movement, whose most prominent dramatists were Goethe and Schiller.

In the 19th century drama began to be more realistic, with greater attention being paid to natural gestures and actors working together in an ensemble. The audience was now usually ranged around a horseshoe-shaped stage with the actors performing behind a curtained arch. Gas, and later electricity, helped control the lighting in the auditorium and on stage.

As the 19th century drew to a close, several important theatres had emerged in Europe. These included the Théâtre-Libre in Paris, the Freie Bühne in Berlin, and the Moscow Art Theatre – all produced avant garde productions.

Much drama was still relatively superficial light entertainment, although dramatists such as Henrik Ibsen and George Bernard Shaw were already writing plays that discussed political ideas and social problems – a movement which developed in the 20th century and which placed a greater emphasis on stimulating the audience to think as well as providing wit and entertainment.

THE 20TH CENTURY AND BEYOND

Dramatists and directors began to experiment in the 20th century, relying less on realistic stage designs, situations and dialogue, and asking more of the actors to create the performance. The audience has become increasingly involved and seating is often grouped more around the actors. A diverse range of experimental concepts have developed, shown in the work of, for example, Brecht, Lorca and Beckett – all playwrights who have helped develop and push forward new ideas and concepts.

Today, theatre continues to develop – stage technology has enabled spectacular productions, thrilling because they are pieces of theatre, evoking rather than reproducing time and place.

LIGHTS, CAMERA, ACTION...

▶ Cinema's beginnings go back to the start of the 19th century.
▶ The first public film shown to a paying audience was given by Auguste and Louis Lumière in Paris on 28 December 1895.

In the early 19th century, scientists became aware that the brain retains an image for a moment longer than the eye sees it. This phenomenon, known as the 'persistence of vision', led to the invention of visual toys, including the zöetrope ('wheel of life'). This was a cylinder with slits through which a sequence of drawings was viewed. When the cylinder was rotated, the images seemed to move.

The persistence of vision gave rise to the idea of taking a sequence of photographs and projecting them on to a screen to give the appearance of movement. Techniques for doing this were developed in the late 19th century.

The subjects of early films were not exactly spectacular – the Lumière film showed workers leaving through a factory gate, and the first American film showed a laboratory assistant sneezing. However, films evolved quickly to show short scenes of real life or brief staged incidents such as the execution of Mary Queen of Scots, complete with trick photography. The first narrative films were made soon after the turn of the century, including the 12-minute *The Great Train Robbery* (US 03), *Rescued by Rover* (GB 05), and the hour-long *The Story of the Kelly Gang* (Aus 06).

THE RISE OF HOLLYWOOD

Technical and artistic progress was rapid. Within ten years, spectacular films were being made using sophisticated editing techniques. They drew huge audiences and, in California, Hollywood became the home of big film studios catering for an international market. Thriving film companies also developed in Europe and then in Asia.

Films had no sound, and were usually accompanied by live music, ranging from a single pianist to full orchestras for major films at some big cinemas. Silent films had a big advantage over later 'talkies' – they had no language problems and were easily adapted for export to any country.

■ The Jazz Singer *(US 27) – the first talking feature film*

■ THE WORD 'THEATRE' COMES FROM THE GREEK *THEATRON*, WHICH MEANS 'A PLACE

Film-makers made various experiments in adding sound, but the first successful commercial release was *Don Juan* (US 26), made by Warner Bros, which had synchronized sound that was played separately alongside the film. This was soon followed by the first true talkie, *The Jazz Singer* (US 27), which included singing and dialogue.

Another major development was the introduction of colour. Some films had been tinted by hand as early as 1905, and a system called Kinemacolor was invented in 1906 by Englishman George Albert Smith. His first colour film was made outside his house in Brighton and showed his children playing on the lawn. The first Technicolor film, *The Gulf Between* (US 17), was premiered in New York in 1917, and the first three-colour Technicolor film was a Walt Disney cartoon, *Flowers and Trees* (US 32).

THE SMALL-SCREEN CHALLENGE

During the 1950s, Hollywood and the cinema industry faced competition from a new medium, namely television. It quickly made news and current affairs its own. Newsreels shown in cinemas were no match for the instant response of television, which reacted to events more quickly than a film could be produced and distributed. Film-going audiences began to drop, and film-makers were forced to cut costs or to offer something new to win people back.

At this period in time, television still appeared in only black and white, so that film-makers increasingly began to produce films in colour. Other innovations, such as stereophonic sound, 3-D and ultra-wide screen formats such as Cinerama and CinemaScope, were introduced.

■ *B-movies from the 1950s have today gained cult status*

Since then, the film industry and television have increasingly worked together. With the development of video recorders, films are sold or rented on tape for home viewing, and fees for television transmission add to the income from cinema exhibition. Television companies now also invest in film production.

THE ALLURE OF THE SILVER SCREEN

Cinema still retains its original magic and excitement. The presence of a big screen, accompanied by high-quality sound and the feeling of being part of a large audience all add up to an experience that cannot be matched by watching a film at home on television.

Cinema is now a multibillion-dollar global industry. Hollywood still dominates the blockbuster-entertainment market, but independent producers and directors of more thoughtful movies also flourish, and there are dynamic industries in Europe, India, Australasia and the Far East.

Film-makers continue to innovate. Special effects and computer-enhanced imagery have created totally believable visual delights. Giant IMAX cinema screens and digital sound also enhance the cinema experience. Interactive films, in which the audience gets to choose the plot, are still at the experimental stage, but may one day become commonplace.

MOVIE MAGIC – SPECIAL EFFECTS

Ever since the birth of cinema, film-makers have been employing visual trickery. Special effects (or FX) is the art of bringing the wildest imaginings of the storyteller or director to the screen.

Early special effects may seem crude by modern standards, but they impressed the audiences of the time. Perhaps the first-ever special effect was used in *The Execution of Mary Queen of Scots* (US 1895). An actress playing the queen walked up to the block, then a cut was made during which the actress was replaced by a dummy. The dummy lost its head, and the resulting piece of cinema seemed convincing since it smoothed over the cut. Of course, this technique had more to do with clever editing and cutting than 'special effects' in the modern sense, but it showed that cinema was from the very start a medium for making the unpresentable presentable.

Some special effects were a boon to the film-maker. For example, at the beginning of the silent era, a motor-driven carousel with panoramic scenery painted on it would be rotated, and live action shot in front of it. Thus a scene of cowboys riding through the Wild West could be done in a studio without the cost of a location shoot. Such tricks continued to develop, and in the 1910s and 1920s this technique evolved into the travelling matte, in which a moving foreground element was combined with pre-shot backdrops. This effect would later develop into the blue-screen shot which is a staple trick in the cinema effects repertoire.

USING MODELS

Models were used to present grand ideas without having to build grand sets. By using mirrors, models could be projected into the action. A variation on this involved shooting through glass on which models had been drawn. Models could be used to depict vast landscapes, such as in Fritz Lang's *Metropolis* (Ger 26). This vision of the future used the Schüfftan process, which enabled live action and models to be combined effectively. Another innovation was stop-animation. A scene would be shot frame by frame, the models being moved between the frames to give the illusion of movement, as in *King Kong* (US 33).

■ *Effects used in* King Kong *(US 33), crude by today's standards, caused a stir when the film was first shown*

Stanley Kubrick's *2001: A Space Odyssey* (GB 68) broke new ground in visual effects while grounding the film in a believable setting. Less than ten years later, another breakthrough film showed the way of the future: *Star Wars* (US 77). George Lucas's work placed cinema special effects on the same footing as live-action. His visual effects company, Industrial Light and Magic, employed a clever technique to produce the stunning space dogfights that are scattered throughout the film. Although models were still used, an electronically controlled camera took the same sequence of shots over and over. While the camera repeated its manoeuvres, it would film a different element each time, be it X-wing Fighter or Millennium Falcon. These various elements would then be combined to give a convincing sense of total illusion that had not been seen before.

Special effect involves more than just camera illusion. Effects make-up has been vital in convincing audiences. From bloody gunshot wounds in Westerns to graphic depictions of monsters in horror films, good make-up always makes an impact. When combined with models and animatronics, make-up effects can be stunning; John Carpenter's remake of *The Thing* (US 82) and *An American Werewolf in London* (GB 81) are two examples that work chillingly well.

THE COMPUTER AGE

The 1980s and 1990s have seen great leaps in visual effects through the use of the computer. One of the earliest films to make use of this new technology was *Tron* (US 82). The film, in which the main character enters a computer system, combined a live action foreground with a background that was computer-generated.

Computer ray-tracing techniques generate realistic images allowing directors to produce fantastic effects. For example, Industrial Light and Magic created an organically real alien in *The Abyss* (US 89). Such films as *Jurassic Park* (US 93) and *Independence Day* (US 96) used computer modelling of wireframe images to produce objects that could be blended with live action. In some films, such as *The Lawnmower Man* (GB/US 92), there are entire sequences generated by computer with no live action at all.

A newer development is to use a computer to digitally manipulate live images. One such technique is morphing, in which one image or form is smoothly transformed into another. In this process, certain key features, such as the eyes and nose, are used as fixed reference points. The end result is a highly convincing metamorphosis that seems to be almost magical. *Terminator 2: Judgment Day* (US 91) was the first commercially successful film to employ this technique of morphing, and it has been used many times since. Other image-manipulation techniques have also become popular, especially in short films such as pop videos.

Special effects teams strive ever harder to meet audience demands for increasingly spectacular visuals. As they do, the dividing line between live action and special effect becomes harder to detect. Some say that special effects are overused and that they stifle creativity in other areas, that much of the time they are used simply for their own sake. Nonetheless, there is no doubt that the future of special effects is linked to the computer, and that films in years to come may make our current blockbusters seem as primitive as the silent films at the dawn of cinema.

20TH-CENTURY ACTORS AND DIRECTORS

* *Denotes Academy Award*

Adjani, Isabelle (1955–), French actress: *The Story of Adèle H.* (Fr 75), *Camille Claudel* (Fr 87).

Aimée, Anouk (1932–), French actress: *Un Homme et une Femme* (Fr 66).

Allen, Woody (Allen Stewart Konigsberg; 1935–), US actor and director: *What's New Pussycat* (US 65), *Annie Hall* (US 77*), *Hannah and Her Sisters* (US 86), *Crimes and Misdemeanours* (US 90).

Altman, Robert (1925–), US director: *M*A*S*H* (US 70), *The Player* (US 92), *Short Cuts* (US 94).

Anderson, Judith (1898–1992), Australian-born actress.

Anderson, Lindsay (1923–94), English film director: *This Sporting Life* (GB 63).

Andrews, Julie (Julia Wells; 1934–), English actress: *Mary Poppins* (US 64*), *The Sound of Music* (US 65).

Antoine, André (1858–1943), French actor, director, critic and film producer.

Artaud, Antonin (1896–1949), French actor and director.

Ashcroft, Peggy (Edith Margaret Ashcroft; 1907–91), English stage and film actress. She was an outstanding Juliet in Gielgud's *Romeo and Juliet* in 1935.

Astaire, Fred (1899–1987), US actor and dancer: *Top Hat* (US 35), *Funny Face* (US 57).

Attenborough, Richard (1923–), English actor, producer and director: *Gandhi* (GB 82) (director); *The Sand Pebbles* (US 66), *Jurassic Park* (US 93).

Aumont, Jean-Pierre (1909–), French actor and playwright: *Hôtel du Nord* (Fra 38).

Babenco, Hector (1946–), Brazilian director: *Kiss of the Spider Woman* (US/Bra 85).

Bacall, Lauren (Betty Jean Perske; 1924–), US actress: *To Have and Have Not* (US 44), *The Big Sleep* (US 46), *Key Largo* (US 48).

Bancroft, Anne (Anna Maria Italiano; 1931–), US film and stage actress: *The Miracle Worker* (US 62*).

Bardot, Brigitte (Camille Javal; 1933–), French film actress: *And God Created Woman* (Fra 56), *En Cas de Malheur* (Fra/Ita 57), *Babette Goes to War* (Fra 59), *Vie Privée* (Fra 61), *Viva Maria* (Fra 65).

Barker, Harley Granville (1877–1946), English-born director and producer who worked mainly in France.

Barrymore, Ethel (Ethel Blythe; 1878–1959), US stage and film actress.

Barrymore, John (1882–1942), US actor who played romantic leading men and Shakespearean roles.

Barrymore, Lionel (1878–1954), US character actor and director.

Bates, Alan (1934–), English stage and film actor: *The Fixer* (US 68).

Baylis, Lillian (1874–1937), English theatre manager who founded the Old Vic, Bristol.

Beatty, Warren (1937–), US film actor: *Splendour in the Grass* (US 61), *Bonnie and Clyde* (US 67), *Shampoo* (US 75), *Reds* (US 81), *Dick Tracy* (US 90).

Beck, Julian (1925–85), US producer, director and actor.

Bene, Carmelo (1937–), Italian actor, director and dramatist.

Bergman, Ingmar (1918–), Swedish film writer, producer and director: *The Seventh Seal* (Swe 57), *Through a Glass Darkly* (Swe 61), *Cries and Whispers* (Swe 72).

Bergman, Ingrid (1915–82), Swedish film actress: *Intermezzo* (US 36), *Casablanca* (US 43), *For Whom the Bell Tolls* (US 43), *Gaslight* (US 44*), *Spellbound* (US 45), *Joan of Arc* (US 48), *Anastasia* (US 56*), *The Inn of the Sixth Happiness* (US 58).

Berkeley, Busby (William Berkeley Enos; 1895–1976), US film director whose films were characterized by spectacular dancing sequences: *Gold Diggers of 1933* (US 33).

Berkoff, Steven (1937–), English stage and film actor.

Bernhardt, Sarah (1844–1923), French actress who gained international acclaim for her tragic roles in *Phèdre, La Dame aux camélias* and *L'Aiglon.*

Berri, Claude (1954–), French film director: *Jean de Florette* (Fra 86), *Manon des Sources* (Fra 86).

Bertolucci, Bernardo (1940–), Italian film director: *Last Tango in Paris* (Fra/Ita/US 72), *The Last Emperor* (Ita/HK/GB 88).

Bigelow, Kathryn (1951–), US director: *Point Break* (US 91).

Binoche, Juliette (1964–), French actress: *The Unbearable Lightness of Being* (US 87), *The English Patient* (US 96*).

Blin, Roger (1907–84), French actor.

Bogarde, Dirk (Derek Van Den Bogaerd; 1921–), English film actor: *Doctor in the House* (GB 53), *A Tale of Two Cities* (GB 58), *The Servant* (GB 63), *The Damned* (GB 69), *Death in Venice* (Ita 70).

Bogart, Humphrey (1899–1957), US film actor: *A Devil with Women* (US 30), *The Maltese Falcon* (US 41), *Casablanca* (US 42), *To Have and Have Not* (US 43), *The Big Sleep* (US 46), *Key Largo* (US 48), *The African Queen* (US 51*), *The Caine Mutiny* (US 54).

Bondarchuk, Sergei (1920–94), Russian film director: *Boris Godunov* (USSR 86).

Borgnine, Ernest (1917–), US film actor: *Marty* (US 55*).

Bow, Clara (1905–65), US film actress: *Mantrap* (US 26), *It* (US 27), *Wings* (US 27).

Branagh, Kenneth (1961–), Irish-born British actor-director: *Henry V* (GB 89), *Dead Again* (US 91), *Hamlet* (US 96).

Brando, Marlon (1924–), US film actor: *A Streetcar Named Desire* (US 51), *The Wild One* (US 53), *On the Waterfront* (US 54*), *The Teahouse of the August Moon* (US 56), *The Young Lions* (US 58), *The Godfather* (US 72*), *Last Tango in Paris* (Fra/Ita/US 72).

Bresson, Robert (1907–), French film director: *Les Anges du péché* (Fra 43), *Un condamné à mort s'est echappé* (Fra 56).

Brook, Peter (1925–), English stage director, noted for innovative productions of international theatre.

Brynner, Yul (Youl Bryner; 1915–85), Russian-born film and stage actor: *The King and I* (US 56*), *The Brothers Karamazov* (US 58), *The Magnificent Seven* (US 60), *Invitation to a Gunfighter* (US 64).

Buñuel, Luis (1900–83), Spanish film director who collaborated with Salvador Dali in the first surreal films: *Un Chien Andalou* (Fra 28), and notable later films including *Belle de Jour* (Fra/Ita 66) and *The Discreet Charm of the Bourgeoisie* (Fra/Spa/Ita 72).

Burton, Richard (Richard Jenkins; 1925–84), Welsh film and stage actor: *Look Back in Anger* (GB 59), *Cleopatra* (US 62), *The VIPs* (GB 63), *Becket* (GB 64), *The Night of the Iguana* (US 64), *Who's Afraid of Virginia Woolf?* (US 66), *Anne of the Thousand Days* (GB 70).

Burton, Tim (1960–), US director: *Beetlejuice* (US 88), *Batman* (US 89).

Cacoyannis, Michael (1922–), Greek film director: *Stella* (Gre 55), *Electra* (Gre 61).

Cagney, James (1899–1986), US film actor: *The Public Enemy* (US 31), *Angels with Dirty Faces* (US 38), *Yankee Doodle Dandy* (US 42*).

Caine, Michael (Maurice Micklewhite; 1933–), English film actor: *Zulu* (GB 63), *The Ipcress File* (GB 65), *Educating Rita* (GB 83), *Hannah and Her Sisters* (US 85).

Cameron, James (1954–), Canadian director: *The Terminator* (US 84), *The Abyss* (US 89).

Campbell, Mrs Patrick (Beatrice Stella Tanner; 1865–1940), English actress.

Campion, Jane (1954–), New Zealand director: *An Angel at My Table* (NZ/Aus 90), *The Piano* (Aus 93).

Capra, Frank (1897–1991), US film director of gently satirical comedy films: *It Happened One Night* (US 34), *Mr Deeds Goes to Town* (US 36), *You Can't Take It with You* (US 38), *It's a Wonderful Life* (US 46).

Carné, Marcel (1909–96), French film director: *Le Jour se Lève* (Fra 39), *Les Enfants du Paradis* (Fra 45).

Cassavetes, John (1929–89), US actor and director: *The Dirty Dozen* (US 67).

Chabrol, Claude (1930–), French film director: *Le Boucher* (Fra 69).

Chaney, Lon (Alonzo Chaney; 1883–1930), US film actor: *The Hunchback of Notre Dame* (US 23), *The Phantom of the Opera* (US 25).

Chaplin, Charles (1889–1977), English-born US film actor and director: *The Tramp* (US 15), *The Kid* (US 20), *The Gold Rush* (US 24), *The Circus* (US 28), *City Lights* (US 31), *Modern Times* (US 36), *The Great Dictator* (US 40), *Limelight* (US 52).

Chen Kaige (1952–), Chinese director: *Yellow Earth* (Chi 84), *Farewell My Concubine* (Chi 93).

Chevalier, Maurice (1888–1972), French actor and singer: *Love Me Tonight* (US 32), *Gigi* (US 58), *Fanny* (US 61).

Christie, Julie (1940–), English film actress: *Darling* (GB 65*), *Doctor Zhivago* (US 65), *The Go-Between* (GB 71), *Heat and Dust* (GB 83).

Chukrai, Grigori (1921–), Russian film director: *The Forty-First* (USSR 56).

Cimino, Michael (1943–), US director: *The Deer Hunter* (US 78), *Heaven's Gate* (US 80).

Clair, René (1898–1981), French film director: early comedies, including *An Italian Straw Hat* (Fra 27), films experimenting with sound, including *Sous les toits de Paris* (Fra 30) and notable later films, including *Les Belles de Nuit* (Fra 52).

Clift, Montgomery (1920–66), US film actor: *Red River* (US 48), *A Place in the Sun* (US 51), *From Here to Eternity* (US 53), *The Misfits* (US 60), *Freud* (US 63).

Close, Glenn (1947–), US stage and film actress: *Jagged Edge* (US 85), *Dangerous Liaisons* (US 88).

Cocteau, Jean (1889–1963), French writer, critic and film director who experimented with film as a serious art form: *Blood of a Poet* (Fra 30).

Coen, Joel (1955–), US film director: *Raising Arizona* (US 87), *Fargo* (US 96).

Colbert, Claudette (Lily Claudette Chauchoin; 1905–96), French film actress: *It Happened One Night* (US 34*), *I Met Him in Paris* (US 37), *Three Came Home* (US 50).

Colman, Ronald (1891–1958), English film actor: *Raffles* (US 30), *A Tale of Two Cities* (US 35),

The Prisoner of Zenda (US 37), *Random Harvest* (US 42), *A Double Life* (US 48*).

Connery, Sean (Thomas Connery; 1929–), Scottish film actor: *Doctor No* (GB 62), *From Russia With Love* (GB 63), *Goldfinger* (GB 64), *The Untouchables* (US 87*).

Cooper, Gary (Frank J. Cooper; 1901–61), US film actor: *Mr Deeds Goes to Town* (US 36), *Sergeant York* (US 41*), *For Whom the Bell Tolls* (US 43), *High Noon* (US 52*), *Vera Cruz* (US 54).

Coppola, Francis Ford (1939–), US film director: *The Godfather* (US 72), *Apocalypse Now* (US 79), *Bram Stoker's Dracula* (US 92).

Costner, Kevin (1955–), US film actor and director: *The Untouchables* (US 87), *Dances with Wolves* (US 90*).

Coward, Sir Noel (1899–1973), English actor, writer and director: *In Which We Serve* (GB 41), *Our Man in Havana* (GB 59).

Crawford, Joan (Lucille le Sueur; 1906–77), US film actress: *Grand Hotel* (US 32), *The Women* (US 39), *Mildred Pierce* (US 45*), *Whatever Happened to Baby Jane?* (US 62).

Cronenberg, David (1943–), Canadian film director associated with bodily graphic and disturbing films: *Videodrome* (Can 82), *The Fly* (US 86).

Cronyn, Hume (1911–), US actor.

Crosby, Bing (Harry Lillis Crosby; 1901–77), US film actor and singer: *Road to Singapore* (US 40), *Going My Way* (US 44*), *The Bells of St Mary's* (US 45), *White Christmas* (US 54).

Cruise, Tom (1962–), US film actor: *Top Gun* (US 85), *Rain Man* (US 88), *Born on the Fourth of July* (US 89), *Interview With the Vampire* (US 94), *Mission Impossible* (US 96), *Jerry Maguire* (US 96).

Cukor, George (1899–1983), US film director: *Little Women* (US 33), *A Star Is Born* (US 54), *My Fair Lady* (US 64).

Curtis, Tony (Bernard Schwarz; 1925–), US film actor: *Some Like It Hot* (US 59), *Spartacus* (US 60).

Curtiz, Michael (1888–1962), Hungarian-born director: *Casablanca* (US 42).

Cusack, Cyril (1910–94), Irish actor, dramatist and director: *Odd Man Out* (GB 47).

Cushing, Peter (1913–94), English actor best known for roles in horror films: *The Curse of Frankenstein* (GB 57).

Darrieux, Danielle (1917–), French actress: *Mayerling* (Fra 35).

Dassin, Jules (1911–), US film director: *Never on Sunday* (Gre 59).

Davis, Bette (Ruth Elizabeth Davis; 1908–89), US film actress: *Dangerous* (US 35*), *The Private Lives of Elizabeth and Essex* (US 39), *The Little Foxes* (US 41), *All About Eve* (US 50), *Whatever Happened to Baby Jane?* (US 62).

Davis, Sammy Jr (1925–90), US singer and actor: *Robin and the Seven Hoods* (US 64).

Day, Doris (Doris Kappelhoff; 1924–), US film actress and singer: *Calamity Jane* (US 53), *The Pajama Game* (US 57), *Pillow Talk* (US 59).

Day-Lewis, Daniel (1958–), English actor: *My Beautiful Laundrette* (GB 85), *The Unbearable Lightness of Being* (US 88), *My Left Foot* (GB 89).

De Mille, Cecil B. (1881–1959), US film producer and director: *The Ten Commandments* (US 23), *King of Kings* (US 27), *The Greatest Show on Earth* (US 52).

De Niro, Robert (1943–), US film actor: *The Godfather Part II* (US 74*), *The Deer Hunter* (US 78), *Raging Bull* (US 80*), *The Mission* (GB 86), *Goodfellas* (US 90), *Casino* (US 95), *Heat* (US 95).

De Palma, Brian (1940–), US director: *Carrie* (US 76), *The Untouchables* (US 87).

De Sica, Vittorio (1902–74), Italian director: *Bicycle Thieves* (Ita 48).

Dean, James (1931–55), US film actor: *East of Eden* (US 55), *Rebel Without a Cause* (US 55).

Dench, Judi (Judith Dench; 1935–), English stage actress and director.

Deneuve, Catherine (Catherine Dorleac; 1943–), French film actress: *Les Parapluies de Cherbourg* (Fra 64), *Belle de Jour* (Fra 67), *Mayerling* (Fra 68).

Depardieu, Gerard (1948–), French film actor and director: *Le Dernier Metro* (Fra 80), *Jean de Florette* (Fra 85), *Trop Belle Pour Toi* (Fra 89), *Cyrano de Bergerac* (Fra 91).

Depp, Johnny (1963–), US actor: *Edward Scissorhands* (US 90), *Benny & Joon* (US 92), *Don Juan DeMarco* (US 95), *Donnie Brasco* (US 96).

Dietrich, Marlene (Maria Magdalena von Losch; 1901–92), German film actress: *The Blue Angel* (US 30), *Shanghai Express* (US 32), *Destry Rides Again* (US 39), *A Foreign Affair* (US 48).

Disney, Walt (1901–66), US film producer and director who created the cartoon characters Mickey Mouse and Donald Duck.

Dmytryk, Edward (1908–), US film director: *Crossfire* (US 47).

Donat, Robert (1905–58), English actor: *The Thirty-Nine Steps* (GB 35), *The Citadel* (GB 38), *Goodbye Mr Chips* (GB 39*), *The Winslow Boy* (GB 48).

Douglas, Kirk (Issur Danielovitch Demsky; 1916–), US film actor: *Gunfight at the OK Corral* (US 57), *Paths of Glory* (US 57), *Spartacus* (US 60), *Lonely Are the Brave* (US 62).

Douglas, Michael (1944–), son of Kirk, US film actor and producer: *Wall Street* (US 87*), *Basic Instinct* (US 92), *Falling Down* (US 92).

Dunaway, Faye (1941–), US film actress: *Bonnie and Clyde* (US 67), *Network* (US 76*).

Eastwood, Clint (1930–), US film actor and director: *A Fistful of Dollars* (Ita/Ger/Spa 64), *For a Few Dollars More* (Ita/Spa/Ger 65), *The Good, The Bad and The Ugly* (Ita 66), *Dirty Harry* (US 71), *Every Which Way But Loose* (US 78), *Unforgiven* (US 93*).

Eisenstein, Sergei (1898–1948), Russian director who used symbols to reinforce ideas and edited shots to make a 'collision' of images: *Battleship Potemkin* (USSR 25).

Eldridge, Florence (1901–88), US stage actress.

Espert, Nuria (1936–), Spanish actress.

Evans, Edith (1888–1976), English actress: *The Importance of Being Earnest* (GB 52).

Fairbanks, Douglas (Douglas Ullman; 1883–1939), US film actor: *The Mark of Zorro* (US 20), *The Three Musketeers* (US 21), *Robin Hood* (US 21), *The Thief of Baghdad* (US 23), *Don Q Son of Zorro* (US 25).

Fassbinder, Rainer Werner (1946–82), German film director: *Despair* (Ger/Fra 77).

Fellini, Federico (1920–93), Italian film director: *La Strada* (Ita 54), *La Dolce Vita* (Ita 59).

Fields, W.C. (Claude Dukinfield; 1879–1946), US film actor: *David Copperfield* (US 34), *My Little Chickadee* (US 40), *The Bank Dick* (US 40).

Fiennes, Ralph (1962–), English stage and film actor: *Schindler's List* (US 93), *The English Patient* (US 96).

Finch, Peter (William Mitchell; 1916–77), English actor: *A Town like Alice* (GB 56), *The Trials of Oscar Wilde* (GB 60), *Sunday Bloody Sunday* (GB 71), *Network* (US 76*).

Finney, Albert (1936–), English stage and film actor: *The Dresser* (GB 83).

Flynn, Errol (1909–59), Australian-born US actor: *Captain Blood* (US 35), *The Adventures of Robin Hood* (US 38), *The Sea Hawk* (US 40), *They Died with Their Boots On* (US 41), *Too Much Too Soon* (US 58).

Fo, Dario (1926–), Italian actor, writer and director of popular political theatre.

Fonda, Henry (1905–82), US actor: *Young Mr Lincoln* (US 39), *The Grapes of Wrath* (US 40), *Twelve Angry Men* (US 57), *On Golden Pond* (US 81*).

Fonda, Jane (1937–), daughter of Henry, US film actress: *They Shoot Horses Don't They?* (US 69), *Klute* (US 71*), *Coming Home* (US 78*), *On Golden Pond* (US 81).

Marlon Brando, *A Streetcar Named Desire* (US 51)

Charlie Chaplin, *Modern Times* (US 36)

Julie Christie with Alan Bates, *Far from the Madding Crowd* (GB 67)

Francis Ford Coppola directing *Bram Stoker's Dracula* (US 92)

James Dean

Ralph Fiennes with Kristin Scott Thomas, *The English Patient* (US 96)

Fontanne, Lyn (Lillie Louise Fontanne; 1887–1983), English-born US actress who usually played opposite her husband Alfred Lunt.

Ford, Harrison (1942–), US film actor: *American Graffiti* (US 73), *Star Wars* (US 77), *Raiders of the Lost Ark* (US 81), *Blade Runner* (US 82), *Witness* (US 85), *Patriot Games* (US 92), *The Fugitive* (US 93).

Ford, John (Sean O'Feeney; 1895–1973), US film director: *The Grapes of Wrath* (US 40), *How Green Was My Valley* (US 41), *The Quiet Man* (US 52), and Western films, including *Stagecoach* (US 39).

Forman, Milos (1932–), Czech film director: *The Fireman's Ball* (Cze/Ita 67). *One Flew Over the Cuckoo's Nest* (US 75*), *Amadeus* (US 84*).

Forsyth, Bill (1947–), Scottish film director: *Gregory's Girl* (GB 80), *Local Hero* (GB 83).

Fosse, Bob (1925–88), US film director: *All That Jazz* (US 79).

Gabin, Jean (Alexis Moncourge; 1904–76), French stage and film actor: *Pepe le Moko* (Fra 37), *La Grande Illusion* (Fra 37), *La Bete Humaine* (Fra 38), *Le Jour se Leve* (Fra 39), *Le Chat* (Fra 72).

Gable, Clark (1901–60), US film actor: *It Happened One Night* (US 34*), *Mutiny On the Bounty* (US 35), *Gone With the Wind* (US 39), *The Misfits* (US 61).

Gambon, Michael (1940–), English stage and film actor: *The Cook, the Thief, His Wife and Her Lover* (GB 89).

Gance, Abel (1899–1981), French film director: the epic *Napoléon* (Fra 27), which used a wide screen with three overlapping images.

Garbo, Greta (Greta Gustafson; 1905–90), Swedish film actress: *Grand Hotel* (US 32), *Queen Christina* (US 33), *Anna Karenina* (US 35), *Camille* (US 36), *Ninotchka* (US 39).

Gardner, Ava (1922–90), US film actress: *Show Boat* (US 51), *The Barefoot Contessa* (US 54), *The Night of the Iguana* (US 64).

Garland, Judy (Frances Gumm; 1922–69), US film actress and singer: *The Wizard of Oz* (US 39), *Meet Me in St Louis* (US 44), *A Star is Born* (US 54).

Gassman, Vittorio (1922–), Italian actor-director: *A Wedding* (US 78).

Gere, Richard (1949–), US film actor: *Yanks* (US 79), *An Officer and a Gentleman* (US 82), *Pretty Woman* (US 90).

Gibson, Mel (1956–), US-born Australian actor and director: *Mad Max: Beyond the Thunderdome* (Aus 85), *Lethal Weapon* (US 87), *Braveheart* (US 95*).

Gielgud, John (1904–), English stage and film actor known for classical and modern roles. He played Hamlet more than 500 times.

Gish, Lillian (Lillian de Guiche; 1896–1993), US film actress: *Birth of a Nation* (US 15), *Intolerance* (US 16), *The Wind* (US 28), *A Wedding* (US 78), *The Whales of August* (US 87).

Godard, Jean-Luc (1930–), French film director: *A Bout de Souffle* (Fra 60).

Goddard, Paulette (Marion Levee; 1905–90), US film actress: *Modern Times* (US 36), *The Great Dictator* (US 40).

Gordon, Ruth (1896–1985), US actress: *Harold and Maude* (US 71), *Rosemary's Baby* (US 68).

Grant, Cary (Archibald Leach; 1904–86), English-born US actor: *She Done Him Wrong* (US 33), *Bringing Up Baby* (US 38), *The Philadelphia Story* (US 40), *Arsenic and Old Lace* (US 44), *North by Northwest* (US 59).

Greenaway, Peter (1942–), English director: *The Draughtsman's Contract* (GB 82), *Drowning by Numbers* (GB 88), *The Cook, the Thief, His Wife and Her Lover* (GB 89).

Griffith, D.W. (1875–1948), US director: *The Birth of a Nation* (US 15), *Intolerance* (US 16).

Grotowski, Jerzy (1933–), Polish director of the innovative Lab Theatre.

Guinness, Sir Alec (1914–), English stage and film actor: *Oliver Twist* (GB 48), *Kind Hearts and Coronets* (GB 49), *The Lavender Hill Mob* (GB 51), *The Bridge on the River Kwai* (GB 57*), *Tunes of Glory* (GB 60), *Lawrence of Arabia* (GB 62), *Star Wars* (US 77).

Güney, Yilmaz (1937–84), Turkish film director: *Yol* (Swi 81).

Guthrie, Tyrone (1900–71), Anglo-Irish stage director.

Hackman, Gene (1930–), US film actor: *Bonnie and Clyde* (US 67), *The French Connection* (US 71*), *Mississippi Burning* (US 89).

Hall, Peter (1930–), English director: founder of the Royal Shakespeare Company.

Hanks, Tom (1956–), US actor: *Big* (US 88), *Philadelphia* (US 93*), *Forrest Gump* (US 94*), *Apollo 13* (US 95).

Hardy, Oliver (1892–1957), US comedy film actor, and **Laurel, Stan** (Arthur Stanley Jefferson; 1890–1965), English-born US comedy film actor: *The Music Box* (US 32), *Sons of the Desert* (US 33), *Way Out West* (US 36), *Blockheads* (US 38), *A Chump at Oxford* (US 40).

Harlow, Jean (Harlean Carpentier; 1911–37), US film actress: *Hell's Angels* (US 30).

Harrison, Rex (Reginald Carey; 1908–90), English stage and film actor: *Blithe Spirit* (GB 45), *My Fair Lady* (GB 64*), *The Yellow Rolls-Royce* (GB 64), *Doctor Dolittle* (US 67).

Havilland, Olivia de (1916–), US film actress: *Gone with the Wind* (US 39), *To Each His Own* (US 46*), *The Heiress* (US 49*).

Hawks, Howard (1896–1977), US director: *Bringing Up Baby* (US 38), *Only Angels Have Wings* (US 39).

Hayes, Helen (Helen Brown; 1900–93), US stage and film actress: *Sin of Madelon Claudet* (US 32*), *Airport* (US 70*).

Hayworth, Rita (Margarita Carmen Cansino; 1918–87), US film actress: *The Strawberry Blonde* (US 41), *Cover Girl* (US 44), *Gilda* (US 46), *Miss Sadie Thompson* (US 53), *Pal Joey* (US 57).

Hepburn, Audrey (Audrey Hepburn-Ruston; 1929–93), Belgian-born US film actress: *Roman Holiday* (US 53*), *The Nun's Story* (US 59), *Breakfast at Tiffany's* (US 61), *Charade* (US 63).

Hepburn, Katharine (1907–), US film actress: *Morning Glory* (US 33*), *Little Women* (US 33), *The Philadelphia Story* (US 40), *The African Queen* (US 51), *Guess Who's Coming to Dinner?* (US 67*), *The Lion in Winter* (US 68*), *On Golden Pond* (US 81*).

Hepworth, Cecil (1874–1956), English film-maker: *Rescued by Rover* (GB 05), an early film shot on outside location.

Herzog, Werner (1942–), German film director: *Aguirre, Wrath of God* (Ger 73), *Fitzcarraldo* (Ger 82).

Heston, Charlton (John Charlton Carter; 1924–), US film actor: *The Ten Commandments* (US 56), *Ben Hur* (US 59*), *El Cid* (US 61), *55 Days at Peking* (US/Spa 63), *The Agony and the Ecstasy* (US 65), *Khartoum* (GB 66).

Hitchcock, Alfred (1899–1980), English film director who worked in Hollywood from 1939: *Rebecca* (US 40), *To Catch a Thief* (US 55), *Vertigo* (US 58), *Psycho* (US 60), *The Birds* (US 63).

Hoffman, Dustin (1937–), US film actor: *The Graduate* (US 67), *Midnight Cowboy* (US 69), *All the President's Men* (US 76), *Kramer vs Kramer* (US 79*), *Tootsie* (US 83), *Rain Man* (US 88*).

Holden, William (1918–81), US film actor: *Sunset Boulevard* (US 50), *Stalag 17* (US 53*), *The Bridge on the River Kwai* (GB 57), *The Wild Bunch* (US 69).

Holm, Ian (1931–), English stage and film actor.

Hope, Bob (Leslie Townes Hope; 1903–), English-born US film actor: *Thanks For the Memory* (US 38), *Road to Singapore* (US 40), *Road to Morocco* (US 42).

Hopkins, Anthony (1937–), Welsh stage and film actor: *The Elephant Man* (US 80), *The Silence of the Lambs* (US 91*), *The Remains of the Day* (US 93).

Hopper, Dennis (1936–), US actor: *Easy Rider* (US 69); actor and director, *The American Friend* (US 75), *Blue Velvet* (US 86).

Horniman, Annie (1860–1937), English theatre manager who started the repertory theatre movement in Britain.

Howard, Alan (1937–), English stage actor.

Howard, Leslie (Leslie Stainer; 1890–1943), English actor: *The Scarlet Pimpernel* (GB 35), *Pygmalion* (GB 38), *Gone with the Wind* (GB 39).

Howard, Ron (1954–), US television actor who later became successful as a director: *Apollo 13* (US 95).

Howard, Trevor (1916–88), English actor: *Brief Encounter* (GB 46), *The Third Man* (GB 49), *Mutiny on the Bounty* (US 62), *The Charge of the Light Brigade* (GB 68).

Hudson, Rock (1925–85), US film actor: *Magnificent Obsession* (US 54), *Pillow Talk* (US 59).

Huston, John (1906–87), US film director: *The Maltese Falcon* (US 41), *The African Queen* (US 51), *The Night of the Iguana* (US 64).

Jackson, Glenda (1937–), English stage and film actress and politician: *Women in Love* (US 70*), *Sunday Bloody Sunday* (GB 71), *A Touch of Class* (GB 73*).

Jacobi, Derek (1938–), English stage and film actor: *Henry V* (GB 89).

Jancsó, Miklós (1921–), Hungarian director: *The Round-Up* (Hun 66), *The Confrontation* (Hun 69).

Jarman, Derek (1942–94), English director: *Sebastiane* (GB 76), *Caravaggio* (GB 86).

Jolson, Al (Asa Yoelson; 1886–1950), Lithuanian-born US film actor: *The Jazz Singer* (US 27), *The Singing Fool* (US 28), *Sonny Boy* (US 29).

Jouvet, Louis (1887–1951), French actor, director and designer who had a great influence on 20th-century French theatre.

Karloff, Boris (William Henry Pratt; 1887–1969), English-born US actor: *Frankenstein* (US 31), *The Mask of Fu Manchu* (US 32).

Kaye, Danny (David Daniel Kaminsky; 1913–87), US film actor: *The Secret Life of Walter Mitty* (US 47), *Hans Christian Andersen* (US 52).

Kazan, Elia (Elia Kazanjoglou; 1909–), Greek-born US film director: *A Streetcar Named Desire* (US 51), *On the Waterfront* (GB 54).

Keaton, Buster (1895–1966), US comedy film actor: *The Butcher Boy* (US 17), *The Paleface* (US 22).

Kelly, Gene (Eugene Curran Kelly; 1912–96), US film actor and dancer: *For Me and My Gal* (US 42), *An American in Paris* (US 51), *Singin' in the Rain* (US 52), *Invitation to the Dance* (US 56).

Kelly, Grace (1928–82), US film actress: *The Country Girl* (US 54*), *Rear Window* (US 54), *High Society* (US 56).

Kerr, Deborah (Deborah Kerr-Trimmer; 1921–), Scottish actress: *Love on the Dole* (GB 41), *From Here to Eternity* (US 53), *The King and I* (US 56), *The Sundowners* (GB/Aus 60).

Kline, Kevin (1947–), US stage and film actor: *A Fish Called Wanda* (US 88*).

Knipper, Olga (1868–1959), Russian actress who gained great acclaim in leading roles in the plays of her husband, Chekhov.

Kobayashi, Masaki (1916–), Japanese film director: *The Human Condition* (Jap 59–61).

Korda, Alexander (1893–1956), Hungarian-born director: *The Private Life of Henry VIII* (GB 33).

Kozintsev, Grigori (1905–73), Soviet film director: *Hamlet* (USSR 64).

Kramer, Stanley (1913–), US director: *The Defiant Ones* (US 58), *Guess Who's Coming to Dinner?* (US 67).

Kubrick, Stanley (1928–), US film director and writer: *Paths of Glory* (US 57), *Lolita* (GB 62), *2001: A Space Odyssey* (GB 68), *A Clockwork Orange* (GB 71).

Kurosawa, Akira (1910–), Japanese film director: *Seven Samurai* (Jap 54), *Ran* (Jap 86).

Ladd, Alan (1913–64), US film actor: *This Gun For Hire* (US 42), *The Great Gatsby* (US 49), *Shane* (US 53).

Lamour, Dorothy (Dorothy Kaumeyer; 1914–96), US film actress: *Road to Singapore* (US 40), *Road to Morocco* (US 42).

Lancaster, Burt (1913–94), US film actor: *From Here to Eternity* (US 53), *Elmer Gantry* (US 60*), *Birdman of Alcatraz* (US 62).

Lang, Fritz (1890–1976), Austrian film director: *Metropolis* (Ger 31).

Laughton, Charles (1899–1962), English film and stage actor: *The Private Life of Henry VIII* (GB 33*), *Mutiny on the Bounty* (US 35), *The Hunchback of Notre Dame* (US 39), *Hobson's Choice* (GB 54).

Laurel, Stan, *see* Hardy, Oliver.

Leachman, Cloris (1926–), US film actress: *The Last Picture Show* (US 71*).

Lean, David (1908–91), English film director: *Oliver Twist* (GB 48), *The Bridge on the River Kwai* (GB 57), *Lawrence of Arabia* (GB 62).

Lee, Bruce (1940–73), US film actor and martial arts expert: *Enter the Dragon* (US 73), *Fist of Fury* (US 76).

Lee, Spike (1956–), US director: *Do The Right Thing* (US 89), *Malcolm X* (US 92).

Leigh, Mike (1943–), English director: *Life Is Sweet* (GB 90), *Secrets and Lies* (GB 95).

Leigh, Vivien (Vivien Hartley; 1913–67), English film and stage actress: *Gone With the Wind* (US 39*), *Lady Hamilton* (US 41), *A Streetcar Named Desire* (US 51*).

Lemmon, Jack (1925–), US film actor: *Mister Roberts* (US 55*), *Some Like It Hot* (US 59), *Irma La Douce* (US 63), *The Odd Couple* (US 68), *Save the Tiger* (US 73*).

Leone, Sergio (1921–89), Italian-American director of spaghetti Westerns: *A Fistful of Dollars* (Ita/Ger/Spa 64), *The Good, The Bad and the Ugly* (Ita 66).

Linder, Max (1883–1925): French comic actor, writer and director: *A Cinematographic Show* (Fra 07), *Be My Wife* (Fra 21).

Littlewood, Joan (1914–), innovative English stage director.

Loach, Ken (1936–), English film director: *Kes* (GB 70), *Riff-Raff* (GB 90).

Lollobrigida, Gina (1927–), Italian film actress: *Belles de Nuit* (Fra/Ita 52), *Solomon and Sheba* (US 59).

Loren, Sophia (Sophia Scicoloni; 1934–), Italian film actress: *Boy on a Dolphin* (US 57), *Two Women* (Ita/Fra 61*), *The Millionairess* (GB 61).

Lorre, Peter (1904–64), Hungarian-born actor of German and US films: *M* (Ger 31).

Losey, Joseph (1909–84), US film director who worked mainly in Britain: *The Servant* (GB 63), *The Go-Between* (GB 71).

Loy, Myrna (Myrna Williams; 1905–93), US film actress: *The Jazz Singer* (US 27), *The Mask of Fu Manchu* (US 32), *The Rains Came* (US 39), *The Best Years of Our Lives* (US 46).

Lubitsch, Ernst (1892–1947), German-born US director of comedies: *Heaven Can Wait* (US 43).

Lucas, George (1944–), US director: *American Graffiti* (US 73), *Star Wars* (US 77).

Lunt, Alfred (1892–1977), US actor-director who was particularly associated with the plays of Noel Coward – see also Fontanne, Lyn.

Lynch, David (1946–), US director: *The Elephant Man* (US 80), *Dune* (US 84), *Blue Velvet* (US 86), *Wild at Heart* (US 90).

MacDonald, Jeanette (1901–65), US operetta singer and actress: *The Merry Widow* (US 34).

McKellen, Ian (1939–), English stage and film actor.

MacLaine, Shirley (Shirley MacLean Beaty; 1934–), US stage and film actress: *Irma La Douce* (US 63), *Sweet Charity* (US 68), *Terms of Endearment* (US 83*).

MacLiammóir, Michaél (1898–1978), Irish stage actor-director.

McQueen, Steve (1930–80), US film actor: *The Magnificent Seven* (US 56), *The Great Escape* (US 63), *The Cincinnati Kid* (US 65), *Bullitt* (US 68).

Magnani, Anna (1908–73), Italian stage actress.

Malina, Judith (1926–), German-born US stage producer and director.

Malkovich, John (1953–), US stage and film actor: *Dangerous Liaisons* (US 88).

Malle, Louis (1932–95), French film director: *Les Amants* (Fra 58), *Au Revoir les Enfants* (Fra 87).

Mankiewicz, Joseph L. (1909–93), US director: *A Letter to Three Wives* (US 49*), *All About Eve* (US 50*).

Mann, Michael (1943–), US director: *Manhunter* (US 86), *Heat* (US 96).

March, Fredric (1897–1975), US stage and film actor: *The Best Years of Our Lives* (US 96*).

Marvin, Lee (1924–87), US film actor: *Cat Ballou* (US 65*).

Martin, Steve (1945–), US comedy film actor: *The Jerk* (US 79), *The Man with Two Brains* (US 83), *Planes, Trains and Automobiles* (US 87), *Father of the Bride* (US 91).

Marx Brothers, The: **Chico** (1886–1961), **Harpo** (1888–1964), **Groucho** (1890–1977), **Zeppo** (1901–79), Family of US slapstick comedy actors. A fifth brother, **Gummo** (1893–1977), left the brothers before they moved to Hollywood: *Horse Feathers* (US 32), *Duck Soup* (US 33).

Mason, James (1909–84), English film and stage actor: *The Wicked Lady* (GB 46), *The Desert Fox* (US 51), *A Star Is Born* (US 54), *The Shooting Party* (GB 84).

Mastroianni, Marcello (1923–96), Italian film actor: *La Dolce Vita* (Ita/Fra 59), *Divorce Italian Style* (Ita 62).

Matthau, Walter (Walther Matasschanskayasky; 1920–), US film actor: *The Fortune Cookie* (US 66*), *The Odd Couple* (US 68), *Hello Dolly* (US 69), *The Sunshine Boys* (US 75).

Méliès, Georges (1861–1938), French impresario who turned his theatre into a cinema and developed trick photography, using stop action and double exposure: the fantasy film *Voyage to the Moon* (Fra 02).

Meyerhold, Vsevolod Emilievich (1874–1940), Russian actor, director and producer who experimented in 'non-realistic' theatre.

Milland, Ray (Reginald Truscott-Jones; 1905–86), US film actor: *The Lost Weekend* (US 45*).

Miller, Jonathan (1934–), English director of plays for stage and television, and of opera.

Mills, Sir John (1908–), English stage and film actor: *Waterloo Road* (GB 44), *Great Expectations* (GB 46), *Hobson's Choice* (GB 54), *Tunes of Glory* (GB 60), *Oh! What a Lovely War* (GB 69), *Ryan's Daughter* (GB 71*).

Minnelli, Liza (1946–), US film actress: *Cabaret* (US 72*).

Harrison Ford, *Star Wars* (US 77)

Greta Garbo, *Queen Christina* (US 33)

Judy Garland with Jack Haley, Ray Bolger and Bert Lahr, *The Wizard of Oz* (US 39)

Sir Alec Guinness, *Star Wars* (US 77)

Stan Laurel and Oliver Hardy, *Hollywood Party* (US 34)

CABARET (US 72) WON EIGHT OSCARS IN 1972, YET FAILED TO WIN BEST PICTURE

Mirren, Helen (1946–), English stage and film actress: *The Madness of King George* (GB 94).

Mitchum, Robert (1917–97), US film actor: *Night of the Hunter* (US 55), *The Sundowners* (GB/Aus 60), *Ryan's Daughter* (GB 71).

Monroe, Marilyn (Norma Jean Baker; 1926–62), US film actress: *All About Eve* (US 50), *Gentlemen Prefer Blondes* (US 53), *The Seven Year Itch* (US 55), *Some Like It Hot* (US 59), *The Misfits* (US 61).

Montand, Yves (1921–91), Italian-born singer and actor in French films: *The Wages of Fear* (Fra/Ita 53).

Moreau, Jeanne (1928–), French actress: *The Lovers* (Fra 59), *Jules et Jim* (Fra 61), *Diary of a Chambermaid* (Fra/Ita 64).

Moskvin, Ivan Mikhailovich (1874–1946), Russian actor.

Murnau, F.W. (1888–1931), German film-maker: *Nosferatu* (Ger 21), an early Dracula film.

Neagle, Anna (Marjorie Robertson; 1904–86), English stage and film actress: *Nell Gwyn* (GB 34), *Victoria the Great* (GB 37), *Nurse Edith Cavell* (GB 39).

Nemirovich-Danchenko, Vladimir (1858–1943), Russian director, drama teacher and co-founder of the Moscow Art Theatre.

Nero, Franco (1941–), Italian actor: *Camelot* (US 67).

Neville, John (1925–), English actor and director, who has been particularly associated with the Stratford Festival in Ontario, Canada.

Newman, Paul (1925–), US film actor: *The Hustler* (US 61), *Butch Cassidy and the Sundance Kid* (US 69), *The Color of Money* (US 86).

Nichols, Mike (1931–), US director: *Who's Afraid of Virginia Woolf?* (US 66), *The Graduate* (US 67).

Nicholson, Jack (1937–), US film actor: *Easy Rider* (US 69), *Five Easy Pieces* (US 70), *One Flew Over the Cuckoo's Nest* (US 75*), *The Shining* (GB 80), *Terms of Endearment* (US 83*), *Prizzi's Honor* (US 85), *Batman* (US 90).

Niven, David (1909–83), Scottish actor: *Raffles* (US 40), *Around the World in Eighty Days* (US 56), *Separate Tables* (US 58*).

Nunn, Trevor (1940–), English director – particularly associated with the Royal Shakespeare Company.

O'Neill, James (1846–1920), Irish-born US actor.

O'Toole, Peter (1932–), Irish film actor: *Lawrence of Arabia* (GB 62), *Becket* (GB 64), *The Lion in Winter* (GB 68), *Goodbye Mr Chips* (GB 69).

Oberon, Merle (Estelle O'Brien Merle Thompson; 1911–79), English film actress: *The Scarlet Pimpernel* (GB 34), *Wuthering Heights* (US 39).

Olivier, Laurence (1907–89), English stage and film actor and director: *Wuthering Heights* (US 39), *Pride and Prejudice* (US 40), *Henry V* (GB 44*), *Hamlet* (GB 48*), *Richard III* (GB 56), *The Entertainer* (GB 60).

Pabst, Georg (1887–1967), German film director: *Pandora's Box* (Ger 28).

Pacino, Al (Alfredo Pacino; 1939–), US film actor: *The Godfather* (US 72), *Scent of a Woman* (US 93*).

Page, Geraldine (1924–87), US stage actress.

Pasolini, Pier Paolo (1922–75), Italian film director: *Gospel According to St Matthew* (Ita/Fra 63).

Paxinou, Katina (1900–74), Greek stage and film actress.

Peck, Gregory (1916–), US film actor: *The Gunfighter* (US 50), *The Big Country* (US 58), *Beloved Infidel* (US 59), *To Kill a Mockingbird* (US 62*).

Peckinpah, Sam (1926–84), US director of Western films: *The Wild Bunch* (US 69).

Pickford, Mary (Gladys Smith; 1893–1979), Canadian film actress: *Pollyanna* (US 60), *Little Lord Fauntleroy* (US 21), *Coquette* (US 29*).

Pidgeon, Walter (1897–1984), Canadian film actor: *How Green Was My Valley* (US 41), *Mrs Miniver* (US 42).

Piscator, Erwin (1893–1966), German producer and director, who, with Brecht, developed 'epic theatre'.

Pitt, Brad (1963–), US film actor: *Thelma and Louise* (US 91), *Kalifornia* (US 93), *Seven* (US 95), *12 Monkeys* (US 95).

Planchon, Roger (1931–), French director of the Theatre National Populaire since 1972.

Poitier, Sidney (1924–), US film actor: *The Blackboard Jungle* (US 55), *Porgy and Bess* (US 59), *Lilies of the Field* (US 63*), *In the Heat of the Night* (US 67), *Guess Who's Coming to Dinner?* (US 67).

Polanski, Roman (1933–) Polish film director: *Rosemary's Baby* (US 68), *Chinatown* (US 74).

Porter, Edwin (1869–1941), pioneer US film-maker: the 12-minute *The Great Train Robbery* (US 03), which was shot on outside location.

Porter, Eric (1928–95), English stage actor.

Powell, Michael (1905–90), English film director who worked in collaboration with Emeric Pressburger: *Black Narcissus* (GB 47), *The Red Shoes* (GB 48), *Peeping Tom* (GB 60).

Preminger, Otto (1906–86), Austrian-born US film director: *Anatomy of a Murder* (US 59), *Exodus* (US 61).

Presle, Micheline (1922–), French actress: *Paradise Lost* (Fra 39), *Devil in the Flesh* (Fra 47).

Pressburger, Emeric (1902–88), Hungarian film director who worked in collaboration with Michael Powell: *Black Narcissus* (GB 47), *The Red Shoes* (GB 48).

Quinn, Anthony (1915–), US film actor: *Viva Zapata* (US 52*), *Lust for Life* (US 56*), *Zorba the Greek* (GB 64).

Raimu (1883–1946), French actor: *César* (Fra 37).

Ray, Satyajit (1921–92), Indian film director: *Pather Panchali* (Ind 55).

Redford, Robert (1936–), US film actor and director: *Butch Cassidy and the Sundance Kid* (US 69), *The Candidate* (US 72), *The Sting* (US 73), *All the President's Men* (US 76), *Sneakers* (US 92).

Redgrave, Michael (1908–85), English stage actor.

Redgrave, Vanessa (1937–), English film and stage actress; daughter of Michael: *Camelot* (US 67), *Isadora* (GB 68), *Julia* (US 77*), *The Ballad of the Sad Cafe* (US/GB 91).

Reed, Carol (1906–76), English film director: *The Third Man* (GB 49), *Oliver!* (GB 68*).

Reed, Oliver (1937–), English film actor: *Women in Love* (GB 69), *The Three Musketeers (The Queen's Diamond)* (Pan 73).

Reinhardt, Max (Max Goldman; 1873–1943), Austrian director who was instrumental in the foundation of the Salzburg Festival.

Reisz, Karel (1926–), Czech-born British film director: *Saturday Night and Sunday Morning* (GB 60), *The French Lieutenant's Woman* (GB 84).

Réjane (Gabrielle Réju; 1856–1920), French actress.

Renoir, Jean (1894–1979), French film director: *Le Crime de Monsieur Lange* (Fra 35), *La Grande Illusion* (Fra 37), *La Règle du Jeu* (Fra 39).

Resnais, Alain (1922–), French film director: *Hiroshima Mon Amour* (Fra/Jap 59).

Richardson, Ralph (1902–83), English stage actor, known for his classical and modern roles.

Riefenstahl, Leni (1902–94), German film director: the propagandist films *Triumph of the Will* (Ger 34), *Olympia* (Ger 38).

Robeson, Paul (1898–1976), US actor and singer.

Robinson, Edward G. (Emanuel Goldenberg; 1893–1973), Romanian-born US film actor: *Little Caesar* (US 30), *Double Indemnity* (US 44), *Key Largo* (US 48), *The Cincinnati Kid* (US 65).

Robson, Flora (1902–84), English stage and film actress: *Saratoga Trunk* (US 45).

Roeg, Nicolas (1928–), English director: *Performance* (GB 70), *Bad Timing* (GB 80).

Rogers, Ginger (Virginia McMath; 1911–95), US film actress and dancer: *Flying Down to Rio* (US 33), *Top Hat* (US 35), *Follow the Fleet* (US 36), *Kitty Foyle* (US 40*).

Rohmer, Eric (1920–), French director: *Ma Nuit Chez Maud* (Fra 69).

Rooney, Mickey (Joe Yule, Jnr; 1920–), US film actor: *Boys' Town* (US 38*), *Babes in Arms* (US 39), *The Bold and the Brave* (US 56).

Rossellini, Roberto (1906–77), Italian film director: *Rome, Open City* (Ita 45).

Russell, Jane (1921–), US film actress: *The Paleface* (US 48), *Gentlemen Prefer Blondes* (US 53).

Russell, Ken (1927–), English film director: *Women in Love* (GB 69), *Tommy* (GB 75).

Rutherford, Margaret (1892–1972), English stage and film actress: *The VIPs* (GB 63).

Sanders, George (1906–72), US film actor: *The Moon and Sixpence* (US 42), *The Picture of Dorian Gray* (US 44), *All About Eve* (US 50*).

Schlesinger, John (1926–), English film director: *Midnight Cowboy* (US 69).

Schwarzenegger, Arnold (1947–), US film actor: *Conan the Barbarian* (US 82), *The Terminator* (US 84), *Total Recall* (US 90), *Terminator 2: Judgment Day* (US 91), *True Lies* (US 94).

Scofield, Paul (1922–), English Shakespearean actor.

Scorsese, Martin (1942–), US director: *Mean Streets* (US 73), *Taxi Driver* (US 76), *Raging Bull* (US 80), *Goodfellas* (US 90).

Scott, George C. (1927–), US stage and film actor and director: *Patton* (US 70).

Scott, Ridley (1937–), English film director: *Blade Runner* (US 82), *Thelma and Louise* (US 91).

Segal, George (1934–), US film actor: *The Owl and the Pussycat* (US 70), *A Touch of Class* (GB 73).

Sellers, Peter (1925–80), English film actor: *I'm All Right Jack* (GB 59), *Only Two Can Play* (GB 62), *The Pink Panther* (US 63), *Dr Strangelove* (GB 63), *Being There* (US 79).

Sennett, Mack (1884–1960), US director of slapstick comedy films: the cleverly edited and speeded-up antics of the Keystone Cops, and films featuring such actors as Roscoe 'Fatty' Arbuckle, Charlie Chaplin and Buster Keaton.

Sher, Anthony (1949–), South African-born British stage actor.

Signoret, Simone (1921–85), French actress: *Room at the Top* (GB 59*).

Simmons, Jean (1929–), English actress: *Great Expectations* (GB 46), *Black Narcissus* (GB 46), *Elmer Gantry* (US 60).

JACK NICHOLSON'S ART COLLECTION IS WORTH ABOUT $150 MILLION ■ MAE WEST NEVER

Sinatra, Frank (1915–), US singer and film actor: *From Here to Eternity* (US 53*), *The Man With the Golden Arm* (US 56), *High Society* (US 56), *Pal Joey* (US 57), *The Manchurian Candidate* (US 62).

Smith, Maggie (1934–), English stage and film actress: *The VIPs* (GB 63), *The Prime of Miss Jean Brodie* (GB 69*), *California Suite* (US 78*).

Spielberg, Steven (1947–), US film director and producer: *E.T.* (US 82), *The Color Purple* (US 86), *Jurassic Park* (US 93), *Schindler's List* (US 93*).

Stallone, Sylvester (1946–), US film actor: *Rocky* (US 76), *Rambo* (US 85).

Stanislavsky, Constantin (1863–1938), Russian actor and director who developed the Stanislavsky method of acting, better known as 'the method'.

Stanwyck, Barbara (1907–90), US film actress: *Stella Dallas* (US 37), *The Lady Eve* (US 41), *Double Indemnity* (US 44).

Steiger, Rod (1925–), US film actor: *On the Waterfront* (US 54), *Al Capone* (US 58), *In the Heat of the Night* (US 67*).

Sternberg, Josef von (1894–1969), Austrian-born US film director: *Blue Angel* (Ger 30).

Stewart, James (1908–97), US film actor: *Mr Smith Goes to Washington* (US 39), *Destry Rides Again* (US 39), *The Philadelphia Story* (US 40*), *It's a Wonderful Life* (US 46), *Harvey* (US 50).

Stone, Oliver (1946–), US director: *Platoon* (US 86), *Born on the Fourth of July* (US 89).

Streep, Meryl (Mary Louise Streep; 1951–), US film and stage actress: *The Deer Hunter* (US 78), *Kramer vs Kramer* (US 79*), *The French Lieutenant's Woman* (GB 81), *Sophie's Choice* (US 82*), *Silkwood* (US 83), *Out of Africa* (US/GB 86).

Streisand, Barbra (1942–), US singer and actress: *Funny Girl* (US 68), *Hello Dolly* (US 69), *Funny Lady* (US 75), *A Star Is Born* (US 76), *The Mirror has Two Faces* (US 96).

Sturges, Preston (1898–1959), US comedy director: *Sullivan's Travels* (US 41), *The Palm Beach Story* (US 42).

Sutherland, Donald (1935–), Canadian film actor: *M*A*S*H* (US 70), *Kelly's Heroes* (US 70), *Klute* (US 71).

Swanson, Gloria (G. Svensson; 1897–1983), US film actress: *Sadie Thompson* (US 28), *Queen Kelly* (US 28), *Sunset Boulevard* (US 50).

Szabó, István (1938–), Hungarian film director: *Mephisto* (Hun 81).

Tarantino, Quentin (1963–), US film director and scriptwriter: *Reservoir Dogs* (US 93), *Pulp Fiction* (US 94).

Tarkovsky, Andrei (1932–88), Russian film director: *Andrei Rublev* (USSR 66), *Solaris* (USSR 71).

Tati, Jacques (1908–82), French actor and director of comedy films: *Monsieur Hulot's Holiday* (Fra 51).

Taylor, Elizabeth (1932–), British-born US film actress: *National Velvet* (US 44), *Cat on a Hot Tin Roof* (US 58), *Butterfield 8* (US 60*), *Cleopatra* (US 62), *Who's Afraid of Virginia Woolf?* (US 66*).

Temple, Shirley (1928–), US child film actress: *Bright Eyes* (US 34*).

Terry, Ellen (1847–1928), English actress – leading lady in many of Henry Irving's productions. Both Ibsen and Shaw created roles for her.

Thompson, Emma (1959–), English stage and film actress and screenwriter: *Howards End* (GB 93*), *Sense and Sensibility* (GB/US 95*).

Thorndyke, Sybil (1882–1976), English Shakespearean actress who created the title role in George Bernard Shaw's *Saint Joan*.

Thurman, Uma (1970–), US film actress: *Dangerous Liaisons* (US 88), *Pulp Fiction* (US 94).

Tracy, Spencer (1900–67), US film actor: *The Power and the Glory* (US 33), *Captains Courageous* (US 37*), *Northwest Passage* (US 40), *Pat and Mike* (US 52), *Guess Who's Coming to Dinner?* (US 67).

Travolta, John (1954–), US film actor: *Saturday Night Fever* (US 77), *Grease* (US 78), *Pulp Fiction* (US 94).

Tree, Herbert Beerbohm (1853–1917), English actor-manager.

Truffaut, François (1932–84), French film director: *Les Quatre-cent Coups* (Fra 59), *Day for Night* (Fra/Ita 73).

Tutin, Dorothy (1931–), English stage and film actress.

Ustinov, Peter (1921–), English film and stage actor and dramatist: *Topkapi* (US 64).

Valentino, Rudolph (Rodolpho d'Antonguolla; 1895–1926), Italian-born US film actor: *The Four Horsemen of the Apocalypse* (US 21), *The Sheik* (US 21), *Blood and Sand* (US 22), *Son of the Sheik* (US 26).

Vidor, King (1894–1982), American film director and producer: *The Big Parade* (US 25), *Hallelujah!* (US 29), *The Citadel* (GB 38).

Visconti, Luchino (1906–76), Italian film director: *Ossessione* (Ita 42), *Death in Venice* (Ita 70).

Von Sydow, Max (1929–), Swedish actor, often cast in Ingmar Bergman films: *The Seventh Seal* (Swe 57), *Hawaii* (US 66), *Pelle the Conqueror* (Den/Swe 87).

Wajda, Andrzej (1926–), Polish film director: *Ashes and Diamonds* (Pol 58).

Walsh, Raoul (1892–1981), US actor and film director: *The Birth of a Nation* (US 14), *The Thief of Bagdad* (US 24).

Warner, Jack (1882–1978), US film producer who founded – with his brothers Harry (1881–1958), Albert (1884–1967) and Samuel (1888–1927) – the Warner Brothers film studios.

Washington, Denzel (1954–), US film actor: *Cry Freedom* (GB 87), *Malcolm X* (US 92).

Wayne, John (Marion Morrison; 1907–79), US film actor: *The Big Trail* (US 30), *Stagecoach* (US 39), *The Searchers* (US 56).

Weigel, Helen (1900–72), German stage actress.

Weine, Robert (1881–1938), German film director: *Cabinet of Dr Cagliari* (Ger 19), a film using expressionist settings.

Weir, Peter (1944–), Australian film director: *Picnic at Hanging Rock* (Aus 75), *Dead Poets Society* (US 89).

Welles, Orson (1915–85), US film director and stage and film actor: *Citizen Kane* (US 40), *The Third Man* (GB 49), *The Trial* (Fra/Ita/Ger 62).

Wenders, Wim (1945–), German director: *Paris, Texas* (Ger/Ita 84), *Wings of Desire* (Fra/Ger 87).

West, Mae (1892–1980), US actress who wrote much of her own material: *She Done Him Wrong* (US 33).

Wilder, Billy (Samuel Wilder; 1906–), Austrian-born US film director: *Double Indemnity* (US 44), *Sunset Boulevard* (US 50).

Williams, Emlyn (1905–87), Welsh actor-dramatist.

Williamson, Nicol (1938–), Scottish stage actor.

Wolfit, Donald (1902–68), English actor-manager.

Woo, John (Wu Yusen; 1946–), Chinese film-maker and director: *The Killer* (HK 89), *Broken Arrow* (US 96).

Wood, Natalie (Natasha Gurdin; 1938–81), US film actress: *Rebel Without a Cause* (US 55), *West Side Story* (US 61), *Bob and Carol and Ted and Alice* (US 69).

Worth, Irene (1916–), American actress.

Wyler, William (1902–81), US film director: *The Best Years of Our Lives* (US 46).

Zeffirelli, Franco (Franco Zeffirelli Corsi; 1923–), Italian stage and film director and designer: *Romeo and Juliet* (GB 68).

Zhang Yimou (1950–), Chinese director: *Ju Dou* (Chn 89), *Raise the Red Lantern* (Chn 91).

Zinnemann, Fred (1907–97), Austrian-born US film director: *High Noon* (US 52), *A Man For All Seasons* (GB 66), *The Day of the Jackal* (GB/Fra 73).

Zukor, Adolphe (1873–1976), Hungarian-born US film-maker and founder of the Famous Players-Paramount studios: *The Count of Monte Cristo* (US 08) and *The Prisoner of Zenda* (US 12).

Martin Scorsese directing Paul Newman, *The Color of Money* (US 86)

Jack Nicholson, *One Flew Over the Cuckoo's Nest* (US 75)

Arnold Schwarzenegger, *The Terminator* (US 84)

Martin Scorsese with Robert De Niro, *Casino* (US 95)

John Travolta with Samuel L. Jackson, *Pulp Fiction* (US 94)

Mae West in *The Love Goddesses* (US 65)

ACADEMY AWARDS

The Academy of Motion Picture Arts and Sciences annually award the Oscars for outstanding achievements in cinema in the previous calendar year. The Academy was set up in 1927 by 36 leading film industry figures, and Douglas Fairbanks was elected the first president. Soon after the Academy formed, the film producer Louis B. Mayer suggested that it should sponsor awards to the film industry, and thus the Oscars were born. The first award ceremony was held in 1928. The Oscars are now considered to be among the highest accolades in the entertainment world, and the annual award ceremony is always an extravagant and glitzy affair. The awards are also financially important, and a Best Picture Oscar can earn a film an extra $20 million at the box office.

There are 24 main categories for awards: Best Picture, Director, Actor, Actress, Supporting Actor, Supporting Actress, Art Direction, Costume Design, Sound Effects Editing, Makeup, Live Action Short Film, Animated Short Film, Documentary Short Subjects, Documentary Feature, Visual Effects, Sound, Film Editing, Music (original score), Music (dramatic score), Music (original song), Cinematography, Foreign Language Film, Original Screenplay, and Adapted Screenplay. There are also honorary awards and the Gordon E. Sayer Award. Of the major awards, the Big Five are considered to be Best Film, Director, Actor, Actress and Screenplay (original or adapted). Only three films have taken all five big Oscars – *It Happened One Night* (US 34), *One Flew Over the Cuckoo's Nest* (US 75) and *The Silence of the Lambs* (US 91).

Listed below are all of the winners in these categories (note that Oscars for Best Supporting Actor and Actress were not awarded until 1936 and 1937 respectively). All films are American, except where specified otherwise.

YEAR	FILM	DIRECTOR	ACTOR	ACTRESS	SUPPORTING ACTOR	SUPPORTING ACTRESS	SCREENPLAY*	
1927–28	*Wings*	Frank Borzage *Seventh Heaven* Lewis Milestone *Two Knights*	Emil Jannings *The Way of All Flesh*	Janet Gaynor *Seventh Heaven*			**Original story** Ben Hecht *Underworld*	**Adaptation** Benjamin Glazer *Seventh Heaven*
1928–29	*Broadway Melody*	Frank Lloyd *The Divine Lady*	Warner Baxter *In Old Arizona*	Mary Pickford *Coquette*			**Achievement** Hans Kraly *The Patriot*	
1929–30	*All Quiet on the Western Front*	Lewis Milestone *All Quiet on the Western Front*	George Arliss *Disraeli*	Norma Shearer *The Divorcee*			Frances Marion *The Big House*	
1930–31	*Cimarron*	Norman Taurog *Skippy*	Lionel Barrymore *Free Soul*	Marie Dressler *Min and Bill*			**Original story** John Monk Saunders *The Dawn Patrol*	**Adaptation** Howard Estabrook *Cimarron*
1931–32	*Grand Hotel*	Frank Borzage *Bad Girl*	Fredric March *Dr Jekyll and Mr Hyde* Wallace Beery *The Champ*	Helen Hayes *The Sin of Madelon Claudet*			Frances Marion *The Champ*	Edwin Burke *Bad Girl*
1932–33	*Cavalcade*	Frank Lloyd *Cavalcade*	Charles Laughton *Private Life of Henry VIII* (GB)	Katharine Hepburn *Morning Glory*			Robert Lord *One Way Passage*	Victor Heermna & Sarah Y. Mason *Little Women*
1934	*It Happened One Night*	Frank Capra *It Happened One Night*	Clark Gable *It Happened One Night*	Claudette Colbert *It Happened One Night*			Arthur Caesar *Manhattan Melodrama*	Robert Riskin *It Happened One Night*
1935	*Mutiny on the Bounty*	John Ford *The Informer*	Victor McLaglen *The Informer*	Bette Davis *Dangerous*			**Original story** Ben Hecht & Charles MacArthur *The Scoundrel*	**Screenplay** Dudley Nichols *The Informer*
1936	*The Great Ziegfield*	Frank Capra *Mr Deeds Goes to Town*	Paul Muni *The Story of Louis Pasteur*	Luise Rainer *The Great Ziegfeld*	Walter Brennan *Come and Get It*	Gale Sondergaard *Anthony Adverse*	Pierre Collings & Sheridan Gibney *The Story of Louis Pasteur*	Pierre Collings & Sheridan Gibney *The Story of Louis Pasteur*
1937	*The Life of Emile Zola*	Leo McCarey *The Awful Truth*	Spencer Tracy *Captains Courageous*	Luise Rayner *The Good Earth*	Joseph Schildkraut *The Life of Emile Zola*	Alice Brady *In Old Chicago*	William A. Wellman & Robert Carson *A Star is Born*	Heinz Herald, Geza Herczeg & Norman Reilly Raine *The Life of Emile Zola*
1938	*You Can't Take It With You*	Frank Capra *You Can't Take It With You*	Spencer Tracy *Boys' Town*	Bette Davis *Jezebel*	Walter Brennan *Kentucky*	Fay Bainter *Jezebel*	**Original story** Eleanore Griffin & Dore Schary *Boys' Town*	**Adaptation** Ian Dalrymple, Cecil Lewis & W.P. Lipscomb *Pygmalion* (GB) (by George Bernard Shaw)
1939	*Gone With the Wind*	Victor Fleming *Gone With the Wind*	Robert Donat *Goodbye Mr Chips* (GB)	Vivien Leigh *Gone With the Wind*	Thomas Mitchell *Stagecoach*	Hattie McDaniel *Gone With the Wind*	**Original story** Lewis R. Foster *Mr Smith Goes to Washington*	**Screenplay** Sidney Howard *Gone With the Wind*
1940	*Rebecca*	John Ford *The Grapes of Wrath*	James Stewart *The Philadelphia Story*	Ginger Rogers *Kitty Foyle*	Walter Brennan *The Westerner*	Jane Darwell *The Grapes of Wrath*	Benjamin Glazer & John S. Toldy *Arise, My Love*	Donald Ogden Stewart *The Philadelphia Story*
1941	*How Green Was My Valley*	John Ford *How Green Was My Valley*	Gary Cooper *Sergeant York*	Joan Fontaine *Suspicion*	Donald Crisp *How Green Was My Valley*	Mary Astor *The Great Lie*	Harry Segall *Here Comes Mr Jordan*	Sidney Buchman & Seton I. Miller *Here Comes Mr Jordan*

YEAR	FILM	DIRECTOR	ACTOR	ACTRESS	SUPPORTING ACTOR	SUPPORTING ACTRESS	SCREENPLAY*	
							Original story	**Adaptation**
1942	*Mrs Miniver*	William Wyler *Mrs Miniver*	James Cagney *Yankee Doodle Dandy*	Greer Garson *Mrs Miniver*	Van Heflin *Johnny Eager*	Teresa Wright *Mrs Miniver*	Emeric Pressburger *The Invaders* (GB)	George Froeschel, James Hilton, Claudine & Arthur Wimperis *Mrs Miniver*
1943	*Casablanca*	Michael Curtiz *Casablanca*	Paul Lukas *Watch on the Rhine*	Jennifer Jones *The Song of Bernadette*	Charles Coburn *The More the Merrier*	Katina Paxinou *For Whom the Bell Tolls*	William Saroyan *The Human Comedy*	Julius J. Epstein, Philip G. Epstein & Howard Koch *Casablanca*
1944	*Going My Way*	Leo McCarey *Going My Way*	Bing Crosby *Going My Way*	Ingrid Bergman *Gaslight*	Barry Fitzgerald *Going My Way*	Ethel Barrymore *None but the Lonely Heart*	Leo McCarey *Going My Way*	Frank Butler & Frank Cavett *Going My Way*
1945	*The Lost Weekend*	Billy Wilder *The Lost Weekend*	Ray Milland *The Lost Weekend*	Joan Crawford *Mildred Pierce*	James Dunn *A Tree Grows in Brooklyn*	Anne Revere *National Velvet*	Charles G. Booth *The House on 92nd Street*	Charles Brackett & Billy Wilder *The Lost Weekend*
1946	*The Best Years of Our Lives*	William Wyler *The Best Years of Our Lives*	Fredric March *The Best Years of Our Lives*	Olivia de Havilland *To Each His Own*	Harold Russell *The Best Years of Our Lives*	Anne Baxter *The Razor's Edge*	Clemence Dane *Vacation from Marriage* (GB)	Robert E. Sherwood *The Best Years of Our Lives*
1947	*Gentleman's Agreement*	Elia Kazan *Gentleman's Agreement*	Ronald Colman *A Double Life*	Loretta Young *The Farmer's Daughter*	Edmund Gwenn *Miracle on 34th Street*	Celeste Holm *Gentleman's Agreement*	Valentine Davies *Miracle on 34th Street*	George Seaton *Miracle on 34th Street*
							Motion picture story	**Screenplay**
1948	*Hamlet* (GB)	John Huston *The Treasure of the Sierra Madre*	Laurence Olivier *Hamlet* (GB)	Jane Wyman *Johnny Belinda*	Walter Huston *The Treasure of the Sierra Madre*	Claire Trevor *Key Largo*	Richard Sweizer & David Wechsler *The Search* (US/Swi)	John Huston *The Treasure of the Sierra Madre*
1949	*All the King's Men*	Joseph L. Mankiewicz *A Letter to Three Wives*	Broderick Crawford *All the King's Men*	Olivia de Havilland *The Heiress*	Dean Jagger *Twelve O'Clock High*	Mercedes McCambridge *All the King's Men*	Douglas Morrow *The Stratton Story*	Joseph L. Mankiewicz *A Letter to Three Wives*
1950	*All About Eve*	Joseph L. Mankiewicz *All About Eve*	José Ferrer *Cyrano de Bergerac*	Judy Holliday *Born Yesterday*	George Sanders *All About Eve*	Josephine Hull *Harvey*	Edna & Edward Anhalt *Panic in the Streets*	Joseph L. Mankiewicz *All About Eve*
1951	*An American in Paris*	George Stevens *A Place in the Sun*	Humphrey Bogart *The African Queen* (GB)	Vivien Leigh *A Streetcar Named Desire*	Karl Malden *A Streetcar Named Desire*	Kim Hunter *A Streetcar Named Desire*	Paul Dehn & James Bernard *Seven Days to Noon* (GB)	Michael Wilson & Harry Brown *A Place in the Sun*
1952	*The Greatest Show on Earth*	John Ford *The Quiet Man*	Gary Cooper *High Noon*	Shirley Booth *Come Back, Little Sheba*	Anthony Quinn *Viva Zapata!*	Gloria Grahame *The Bad and the Beautiful*	Frederick M. Frank, Theodore St John & Frank Cavett *The Greatest Show on Earth*	Charles Schnee *The Bad and the Beautiful*
1953	*From Here to Eternity*	Fred Zinnemann *From Here to Eternity*	William Holden *Stalag 17*	Audrey Hepburn *Roman Holiday*	Frank Sinatra *From Here to Eternity*	Donna Reed *From Here to Eternity*	Ian McLellan Hunter *Roman Holiday*	Daniel Taradash *From Here to Eternity*
1954	*On the Waterfront*	Elia Kazan *On the Waterfront*	Marlon Brando *On the Waterfront*	Grace Kelly *The Country Girl*	Edmond O'Brien *The Barefoot Contessa*	Eva Marie Saint *On the Waterfront*	Philip Yordan *Broken Lance*	George Seaton *The Country Girl*
1955	*Marty*	Delbert Mann *Marty*	Ernest Borgnine *Marty*	Anna Magnani *The Rose Tattoo*	Jack Lemmon *Mister Roberts*	Jo Van Fleet *East of Eden*	Daniel Fuchs *Love Me or Leave Me*	Paddy Chayefsky *Marty*
							Original screenplay	**Adapted screenplay**
1956	*Around the World in 80 Days*	George Stevens *Giant*	Yul Brynner *The King and I*	Ingrid Bergman *Anastasia* (GB)	Anthony Quinn *Lust for Life*	Dorothy Malone *Written on the Wind*	Albert Lamorisse *The Red Balloon* (Fra)	James Poe, John Farrow & S.J. Perelman *Around the World in 80 Days*
1957	*The Bridge on the River Kwai* (GB)	David Lean *The Bridge on the River Kwai* (GB)	Alec Guinness *The Bridge on the River Kwai* (GB)	Joanne Woodward *The Three Faces of Eve*	Red Buttons *Sayonara*	Miyoshi Umeki *Sayonara*	George Wells *Designing Woman*	Pierre Boulle, Michael Wilson & Carl Foreman *The Bridge on the River Kwai* (GB)
1958	*Gigi*	Vincente Minnelli *Gigi*	David Niven *Separate Tables*	Susan Hayward *I Want to Live*	Burl Ives *The Big Country*	Wendy Hiller *Separate Tables*	Nathan E. Douglas & Harold Jacob Smith *The Defiant Ones*	Alan Jay Lerner *Gigi*

ACADEMY AWARDS

YEAR	FILM	DIRECTOR	ACTOR	ACTRESS	SUPPORTING ACTOR	SUPPORTING ACTRESS	SCREENPLAY*	
1959	*Ben-Hur*	William Wyler *Ben-Hur*	Charlton Heston *Ben-Hur*	Simone Signoret *Room at the Top* (GB)	Hugh Griffith *Ben-Hur*	Shelley Winters *The Diary of Anne Frank*	Russell Rouse & Clarence Greene (story), Stanley Shapiro & Maurice Richlin (screenplay) *Pillow Talk*	Neil Paterson *Room at the Top* (GB)
1960	*The Apartment*	Billy Wilder *The Apartment*	Burt Lancaster *Elmer Gantry*	Elizabeth Taylor *Butterfield Eight*	Peter Ustinov *Spartacus*	Shirley Jones *Elmer Gantry*	Billy Wilder & I.A.L. Diamond *The Apartment*	Richard Brooks *Elmer Gantry*
1961	*West Side Story*	Jerome Robbins and Robert Wise *West Side Story*	Maximilian Schell *Judgment at Nuremberg*	Sophia Loren *Two Women* (Ita/Fra)	George Chakiris *West Side Story*	Rita Moreno *West Side Story*	William Inge *Splendor in the Grass*	Abby Mann *Judgment at Nuremberg*
1962	*Lawrence of Arabia* (GB)	David Lean *Lawrence of Arabia* (GB)	Gregory Peck *To Kill a Mockingbird*	Anne Bancroft *The Miracle Worker*	Ed Begley *Sweet Bird of Youth*	Patty Duke *The Miracle Worker*	Ennio de Concini, Alfredo Giannetti & Pietro Germi *Divorce – Italian Style*	Horton Foote *To Kill a Mockingbird*
1963	*Tom Jones* (GB)	Tony Richardson *Tom Jones* (GB)	Sidney Poitier *Lilies of the Field*	Patricia Neal *Hud*	Melvyn Douglas *Hud*	Margaret Rutherford *The VIPs*	James R. Webb *How the West was Won*	John Osborne *Tom Jones* (GB)
1964	*My Fair Lady*	George Cukor *My Fair Lady*	Rex Harrison *My Fair Lady*	Julie Andrews *Mary Poppins*	Peter Ustinov *Topkapi*	Lila Kedrova *Zorba the Greek*	S.H. Barnett (story), Peter Stone & Frank Tarloff (screenplay) *Father Goose*	Edward Anhalt *Becket* (GB)
1965	*The Sound of Music*	Robert Wise *The Sound of Music*	Lee Marvin *Cat Ballou*	Julie Christie *Darling* (GB)	Martin Balsam *A Thousand Clowns*	Shelley Winters *A Patch of Blue*	Frederic Raphael *Darling* (GB)	Robert Bolt *Dr Zhivago*
1966	*A Man for All Seasons* (GB)	Fred Zinnemann *A Man for All Seasons* (GB)	Paul Scofield *A Man for All Seasons* (GB)	Elizabeth Taylor *Who's Afraid of Virginia Woolf*	Walter Matthau *The Fortune Cookie*	Sandy Dennis *Who's Afraid of Virginia Woolf*	Claude Lelouch (story), Peter Uytterhoeven & Claude Lelouch (screenplay) *A Man and a Woman* (Fra)	Robert Bolt *A Man for All Seasons* (GB)
1967	*In the Heat of the Night*	Mike Nichols *The Graduate*	Rod Steiger *In the Heat of the Night*	Katharine Hepburn *Guess Who's Coming to Dinner*	George Kennedy *Cool Hand Luke*	Estelle Parsons *Bonnie and Clyde*	William Rose *Guess Who's Coming to Dinner*	Stirling Silliphant *In the Heat of the Night*
1968	*Oliver!* (GB)	Sir Carol Reed *Oliver!* (GB)	Cliff Robertson *Charly*	Katharine Hepburn *The Lion in Winter* (GB)	Jack Albertson *The Subject Was Roses*	Ruth Gordon *Rosemary's Baby*	Mel Brooks *The Producers*	James Goldman *The Lion in Winter* (GB)
1969	*Midnight Cowboy*	John Schlesinger *Midnight Cowboy*	John Wayne *True Grit*	Maggie Smith *The Prime of Miss Jean Brodie* (GB)	Gig Young *They Shoot Horses, Don't They?*	Goldie Hawn *Cactus Flower*	William Goldman *Butch Cassidy and the Sundance Kid*	Waldo Salt *Midnight Cowboy*
1970	*Patton*	Franklin Schaffner *Patton*	George C. Scott *Patton* (refused)	Glenda Jackson *Women in Love* (GB)	John Mills *Ryan's Daughter* (GB)	Helen Hayes *Airport*	Francis Ford Coppola & Edmund H. North *Patton*	Ring Lardner Jr *M*A*S*H*
1971	*The French Connection*	William Friedkin *The French Connection*	Gene Hackman *The French Connection*	Jane Fonda *Klute*	Ben Johnson *The Last Picture Show*	Cloris Leachman *The Last Picture Show*	Paddy Chayefsky *The Hospital*	Ernest Tidyman *The French Connection*
1972	*The Godfather*	Bob Fosse *Cabaret*	Marlon Brando *The Godfather* (refused)	Liza Minnelli *Cabaret*	Joel Grey *Cabaret*	Eileen Heckart *Butterflies Are Free*	Jeremy Larner *The Candidate*	Mario Puzo & Francis Ford Coppola *The Godfather*
1973	*The Sting*	George Roy Hill *The Sting*	Jack Lemmon *Save the Tiger*	Glenda Jackson *A Touch of Class* (GB)	John Houseman *The Paper Chase*	Tatum O'Neal *Paper Moon*	David S. Ward *The Sting*	William Peter Blatty *The Exorcist*
1974	*The Godfather, Part II*	Francis Ford Coppola *The Godfather, Part II*	Art Carney *Harry and Tonto*	Ellen Burstyn *Alice Doesn't Live Here Any More*	Robert de Niro *The Godfather, Part II*	Ingrid Bergman *Murder on the Orient Express*	Robert Towne *Chinatown*	Francis Ford Coppola & Mario Puzo *The Godfather, Part II*
1975	*One Flew Over the Cuckoo's Nest*	Milos Forman *One Flew Over the Cuckoo's Nest*	Jack Nicholson *One Flew Over the Cuckoo's Nest*	Louise Fletcher *One Flew Over the Cuckoo's Nest*	George Burns *The Sunshine Boys*	Lee Grant *Shampoo*	Frank Pierson *Dog Day Afternoon*	Lawrence Hauben & Bo Goldman *One Flew Over the Cuckoo's Nest*
1976	*Rocky*	John G. Avildsen *Rocky*	Peter Finch *Network*	Faye Dunaway *Network*	Jason Robards *All the President's Men*	Beatrice Straight *Network*	Paddy Chayefsky *Network*	William Goldman *All the President's Men*

YEAR	FILM	DIRECTOR	ACTOR	ACTRESS	SUPPORTING ACTOR	SUPPORTING ACTRESS	SCREENPLAY*	
1977	*Annie Hall*	Woody Allen *Annie Hall*	Richard Dreyfuss *The Goodbye Girl*	Diane Keaton *Annie Hall*	Jason Robards *Julia*	Vanessa Redgrave *Julia*	Woody Allen & Marshall Brickman *Annie Hall*	Alvin Sargent *Julia*
1978	*The Deer Hunter*	Michael Cimino *The Deer Hunter*	Jon Voight *Coming Home*	Jane Fonda *Coming Home*	Christopher Walken *The Deer Hunter*	Maggie Smith *California Suite*	Nancy Dowd (story), Waldo Salt & Robert C. Jones (screenplay) *Coming Home*	Oliver Stone *Midnight Express* (GB)
1979	*Kramer vs Kramer*	Robert Benton *Kramer vs Kramer*	Dustin Hoffman *Kramer vs Kramer*	Sally Field *Norma Rae*	Melvyn Douglas *Being There*	Meryl Streep *Kramer vs Kramer*	Steve Tesich *Breaking Away*	Robert Benton *Kramer vs Kramer*
1980	*Ordinary People*	Robert Redford *Ordinary People*	Robert de Niro *Raging Bull*	Sissy Spacek *Coal Miner's Daughter*	Timothy Hutton *Ordinary People*	Mary Steenburgen *Melvin and Howard*	Bo Goldman *Melvin and Howard*	Alvin Sargent *Ordinary People*
1981	*Chariots of Fire* (GB)	Warren Beatty *Reds*	Henry Fonda *On Golden Pond*	Katharine Hepburn *On Golden Pond*	John Gielgud *Arthur*	Maureen Stapleton *Reds*	Colin Welland *Chariots of Fire* (GB)	Ernest Thompson *On Golden Pond*
1982	*Gandhi* (GB)	Richard Attenborough *Gandhi* (GB)	Ben Kingsley *Gandhi* (GB)	Meryl Streep *Sophie's Choice*	Louis Gossett Jnr *An Officer and a Gentleman*	Jessica Lange *Tootsie*	John Briley *Gandhi* (GB)	Costa-Gavras and Donald Stewart *Missing*
1983	*Terms of Endearment*	James L. Brooks *Terms of Endearment*	Robert Duvall *Tender Mercies*	Shirley Maclaine *Terms of Endearment*	Jack Nicholson *Terms of Endearment*	Linda Hunt *The Year of Living Dangerously*	Horton Foote *Tender Mercies*	James L. Brooks *Terms of Endearment*
1984	*Amadeus*	Milos Forman *Amadeus*	F. Murray Abraham *Amadeus*	Sally Field *Places in the Heart*	Haing S. Ngor *The Killing Fields*	Peggy Ashcroft *A Passage to India*	Robert Benton *Places in the Heart*	Peter Shaffer *Amadeus*
1985	*Out of Africa* (US/GB)	Sydney Pollack *Out of Africa* (US/GB)	William Hurt *Kiss of the Spider Woman* (US/Bra)	Geraldine Page *The Trip to Bountiful*	Don Ameche *Cocoon*	Anjelica Huston *Prizzi's Honor*	William Kelley, Pamela Wallace & Earl W. Wallace *Witness*	Kurt Luedtke *Out of Africa* (US/GB)
1986	*Platoon*	Oliver Stone *Platoon*	Paul Newman *The Color of Money*	Marlee Matlin *Children of a Lesser God*	Michael Caine *Hannah and Her Sisters*	Dianne Wiest *Hannah and Her Sisters*	Woody Allen *Hannah and Her Sisters*	Ruth Prawer Jhabvala *A Room with a View* (GB)
1987	*The Last Emperor* (Ita/HK/GB)	Bernardo Bertolucci *The Last Emperor* (Ita/HK/GB)	Michael Douglas *Wall Street*	Cher *Moonstruck*	Sean Connery *The Untouchables*	Olympia Dukakis *Moonstruck*	John Patrick Shanley *Moonstruck*	Mark Peploe & Bernardo Bertolucci *The Last Emperor* (Ita/HK/GB)
1988	*Rain Man*	Barry Levinson *Rain Man*	Dustin Hoffman *Rain Man*	Jodie Foster *The Accused*	Kevin Kline *A Fish Called Wanda*	Geena Davis *The Accidental Tourist*	Ronald Bass & Barry Morrow *Rain Man*	Christopher Hampton *Dangerous Liaisons*
1989	*Driving Miss Daisy*	Oliver Stone *Born on the Fourth of July*	Daniel Day-Lewis *My Left Foot* (GB)	Jessica Tandy *Driving Miss Daisy*	Denzel Washington *Glory*	Brenda Fricker *My Left Foot* (GB)	Tom Schulman *Dead Poet's Society*	Alfred Uhry *Driving Miss Daisy*
1990	*Dances With Wolves*	Kevin Costner *Dances With Wolves*	Jeremy Irons *Reversal of Fortune*	Kathy Bates *Misery*	Joe Pesci *Goodfellas*	Whoopi Goldberg *Ghost*	Bruce Joel Rubin *Ghost*	Michael Blake *Dances With Wolves*
1991	*The Silence of the Lambs*	Jonathan Demme *The Silence of the Lambs*	Anthony Hopkins *The Silence of the Lambs*	Jodie Foster *The Silence of the Lambs*	Jack Palance *City Slickers*	Mercedes Ruehl *The Fisher King*	Callie Khouri *Thelma and Louise*	Ted Tally *The Silence of the Lambs*
1992	*Unforgiven*	Clint Eastwood *Unforgiven*	Al Pacino *Scent of a Woman*	Emma Thompson *Howards End* (GB)	Gene Hackman *Unforgiven*	Marisa Tomei *My Cousin Vinny*	Neil Jordan *The Crying Game* (GB)	Ruth Prawer Jhabvala *Howards End* (GB)
1993	*Schindler's List*	Steven Spielberg *Schindler's List*	Tom Hanks *Philadelphia*	Holly Hunter *The Piano* (Aus)	Tommy Lee Jones *The Fugitive*	Anna Paquin *The Piano* (Aus)	Jane Campion *The Piano* (Aus)	Steven Zaillian *Schindler's List*
1994	*Forrest Gump*	Robert Zemeckis *Forrest Gump*	Tom Hanks *Forrest Gump*	Jessica Lange *Blue Sky*	Martin Landau *Ed Wood*	Dianne Wiest *Bullets over Broadway*	Quentin Tarantino & Roger Avary *Pulp Fiction*	Eric Roth *Forrest Gump*
1995	*Braveheart*	Mel Gibson *Braveheart*	Nicolas Cage *Leaving Las Vegas*	Susan Sarandon *Dead Man Walking*	Kevin Spacey *The Usual Suspects*	Mira Sorvino *Mighty Aphrodite*	Christopher McQuarrie *The Usual Suspects*	Emma Thompson *Sense & Sensibility*
1996	*The English Patient*	Anthony Minghella *The English Patient*	Geoffrey Rush *Shine* (Aus)	Frances McDormand *Fargo*	Cuba Gooding Jr *Jerry Maguire*	Juliette Binoche *The English Patient*	Ethan Coen and Joel Coen *Fargo*	Billy Bob Thornton *Sling Blade*

* The names of the screenplay awards have been changed several times. Significant changes have been added in the columns in the relevant years

MEL GIBSON HAVE ALL WON OSCARS FOR BEST DIRECTOR BUT FAILED TO WIN BEST ACTOR

CANNES FILM FESTIVAL

The Cannes Film Festival was established by the French government in 1939, but was not held until 1946 due to World War II. A number of awards are presented annually, with the most prestigious being the Palme d'Or for the Best Film. The Palme d'Or is considered by many in the film world as the most coveted award after the Oscars.

1946 *La Bataille du Rail* (Fra)
1947 *Antoine et Antoinette* (Fra)
1948 No festival
1949 *The Third Man* (GB)
1950 No festival
1951 *Miracle in Milan* (Ita)
Miss Julie (Swe)
1952 *Othello* (Mor)
Two Cents Worth of Hope (Ita)
1953 *Wages of Fear* (Fra)
1954 *Gate of Hell* (Jap)
1955 *Marty* (US)
1956 *World of Silence* (Fra)
1957 *Friendly Persuasion* (US)
1958 *The Cranes Are Flying* (USSR)
1959 *Black Orpheus* (Fra)
1960 *La Dolce Vita* (Ita)
1961 *Viridiana* (Spa)
Une Aussie Longue Absence (Fra)
1962 *The Given Word* (Bra)
1963 *The Leopard* (Ita)
1964 *The Umbrellas of Cherbourg* (Fra)
1965 *The Knack* (GB)
1966 *A Man and a Woman* (Fra)
Signore e Signori (Ita)
1967 *Blow-Up* (GB)
1968 Festival disrupted – no awards
1969 *If* (GB)
1970 *M*A*S*H* (US)
1971 *The Go-Between* (GB)
1972 *The Working Class Goes to Paradise* (Ita)
The Mattei Affair (Ita)
1973 *Scarecrow* (US)
The Hireling (GB)
1974 *The Conversation* (US)
1975 *Chronicle of the Burning Years* (Alg)
1976 *Taxi Driver* (US)
1977 *Padre Padrone* (Ita)
1978 *L'Albero Degli Zoccoli* (Ita)
1979 *The Tin Drum* (Ger)
Apocalypse Now (US)
1980 *All That Jazz* (US)
Kagemusha (Jap)
1981 *Man of Iron* (Pol)
1982 *Missing* (US), *Yol* (Tur)
1983 *The Ballad of Narayama* (Jap)
1984 *Paris, Texas* (Ger)
1985 *When Father Was Away On Business* (Yug)
1986 *The Mission* (GB)
1987 *Under the Sun of Satan* (Fra)
1988 *Pelle the Conquerer* (Den)
1989 *sex, lies and videotape* (US)
1990 *Wild at Heart* (US)
1991 *Barton Fink* (US)
1992 *Best Intentions* (Swe)
1993 *Farewell My Concubine* (Chi)
The Piano (Aus)
1994 *Pulp Fiction* (US)
1995 *Underground* (Fra/Ger/Hun)
1996 *Secrets and Lies* (GB)
1997 *The Eel* (Jap)
The Taste of Cherries (Ira)

BERLIN FILM FESTIVAL

The Berlin Film Festival was established in 1951, and is held annually. From 1952 to 1955, the Best Film award was decided by the audience's vote. From 1956, the Golden Bear was introduced for the Best Picture.

1952 *She Danced for the Summer* (Swe)
1953 *The Wages of Fear* (Fra)
1954 *Hobson's Choice* (GB)
1955 *The Rats* (Ger)
1956 *Invitation to the Dance* (GB)
1957 *Twelve Angry Men* (US)
1958 *The End of the Day* (Swe)
1959 *The Cousins* (Fra)
1960 *Lazarillo de Tormes* (Spa)
1961 *La Notte* (Ita)
1962 *A Kind of Loving* (GB)
1963 *Oath of Obedience* (Ger)
The Devil (Ita)
1964 *Dry Summer* (Tur)
1965 *Alphaville* (Fra)
1966 *Cul de Sac* (GB)
1967 *Le Départ* (Bel)
1968 *Ole Dole Doff* (Swe)
1969 *Early Years* (Yug)
1970 No award
1971 *The Garden of the Finzi-Continis* (Ita)
1972 *The Canterbury Tales* (Ita)
1973 *Distant Thunder* (Ind)
1974 *The Apprenticeship of Duddy Kravitz* (Can)
1975 *Orkobefogadas* (Hun)
1976 *Buffalo Bill and the Indians* (US) – declined award
1977 *The Ascent* (USSR)
1978 *The Trouts* (Spa)
The Words of Max (Spa)
1979 *David* (Ger)
1980 *Heartland* (US)
Palermo oder Wolfsburg (Ger)
1981 *Di Presa Di Presa* (Spa)
1982 *Die Sehnsucht der Veronica Voss* (Ger)
1983 *Ascendancy* (GB)
The Beehive (Spa)
1984 *Love Streams* (US)
1985 *Wetherby* (GB)
Die Frau und der Frende (Ger)
1986 *Stammheim* (Ger)
1987 *The Theme* (USSR)
1988 *Red Sorghum* (Chi)
1989 *Rain Man* (US)
1990 *Music Box* (US)
Larks on a String (Cze)
1991 *House of Smiles* (Ita)
1992 *Grand Canyon* (US)
1993 *The Woman from the Lake of Scented Souls* (Chi)
The Wedding Banquet (Tai/US)
1994 *In the Name of the Father* (GB)
1995 *L'Appat* (Fra)
1996 *Sense and Sensibility* (US)
1997 *The People vs Larry Flynt* (US)

BAFTA AWARDS

The British Academy of Film and Television Arts (BAFTA) was founded as the Society of Film and Television Arts in 1959 (incorporating previous film-industry organizations) and reorganized as BAFTA in 1975. Each year, awards are presented in a number of categories. Winners of the award for Best Film are listed below (includes awards made by BAFTA's forerunners).

1947 *The Best Years of Our Lives* (US)
1948 *Hamlet* (GB)
1949 *Bicycle Thieves* (Ita)
1950 *All About Eve* (US)
1951 *La Ronde* (Fra)
1952 *The Sound Barrier* (GB)
1953 *Jeux Interdits* (Fra)
1954 *Le Salaire de la Peur* (Fra)
1955 *Richard III* (GB)
1956 *Gervaise* (Fra)
1957 *The Bridge on the River Kwai* (GB)
1958 *Room at the Top* (GB)
1959 *Ben Hur* (US)
1960 *The Apartment* (US)
1961 *Ballad of a Soldier* (USSR)
The Hustler (US)
1962 *Lawrence of Arabia* (GB)
1963 *Tom Jones* (GB)
1964 *Dr Strangelove* (GB)
1965 *My Fair Lady* (US)
1966 *Who's Afraid of Virginia Woolf?* (US)
1967 *A Man For All Seasons* (GB)
1968 *The Graduate* (US)
1969 *Midnight Cowboy* (US)
1970 *Butch Cassidy and the Sundance Kid* (US)
1971 *Sunday, Bloody Sunday* (GB)
1972 *Cabaret* (US)
1973 *Day For Night* (Fra)
1974 *Lacombe Lucien* (Fra)
1975 *Alice Doesn't Live Here Anymore* (US)
1976 *One Flew Over the Cuckoo's Nest* (US)
1977 *Annie Hall* (US)
1978 *Julia* (US)
1979 *Manhattan* (US)
1980 *The Elephant Man* (GB)
1981 *Chariots of Fire* (GB)
1982 *Gandhi* (GB)
1983 *Educating Rita* (GB)
1984 *The Killing Fields* (GB)
1985 *The Purple Rose of Cairo* (US)
1986 *A Room with a View* (GB)
1987 *Jean de Florette* (Fra)
1988 *The Last Emperor* (Ita/GB/Chi)
1989 *Dead Poets Society* (US)
1990 *Goodfellas* (US)
1991 *The Commitments* (US/GB)
1992 *Howards End* (GB)
1993 *Schindler's List* (US)
1994 *Four Weddings and a Funeral* (GB)
1995 *Sense and Sensibility* (US)
1996 *The English Patient* (US)

VENICE FILM FESTIVAL

Initially intended to revive the tourist trade, the Venice Film Festival was the world's first regular film festival, the first event taking place in 1932. In that year, a total of 18 films were entered, but there was no award. The Golden Lion award is now presented annually for Best Film.

1932 No award
1933 No festival
1934 *Man of Aran* (GB)
1935 *Anna Karenina* (US)
1936 *Der Kaiser von Kalifornien* (Ger)
1937 *Un Carnet de Bal* (Fra)
1938 *Olympia* (Ger)
1939 No award
1940 *Der Postmeister* (Ger)
1941 *Ohm Kruger* (Ger)
1942 *Der grosse König* (Ger)
1943 No festival
1944 No festival
1945 No festival
1946 *The Southerner* (US)
1947 *Sirena* (Cze)
1948 *Hamlet* (GB)
1949 *Manon* (Fra)
1950 *Justice Is Done* (Fra)
1951 *Rashomon* (Jap)
1952 *Jeux Interdits* (Fra)
1953 No award
1954 *Romeo and Juliet* (Ita/GB)
1955 *Ordert* (Den)
1956 No award
1957 *Aparajito* (Ind)
1958 *Muhomatsu no Issho* (Jap)
1959 *Il Generale della Rovere* (Ita)
1960 *Le Passage du Rhin* (Fra)
1961 *L'Année Dernière à Marienbad* (Fra)
1962 *Childhood of Ivan* (USSR)
1963 *Le Mani sulla città* (Ita)
1964 *Red Desert* (Ita)
1965 *Of a Thousand Delights* (Ita)
1966 *Battle of Algiers* (Ita)
1967 *Belle de Jour* (Fra)
1968 *Die Artisten in der Zirkuskuppel* (Ger)
1969–79 Discontinued
1980 *Gloria* (US)
Atlantic City (Fra/Can)
1981 *Die Bleierne Zeit* (Ger)
1982 *The State of Things* (Ger)
1983 *Prénom Carmen* (Fra/Swi)
1984 *Year of the Quiet Sun* (Pol)
1985 *Sans Toit ni Loi* aka *Vagabonde* (Fra)
1986 *Le Rayon Vert* (Fra)
1987 *Au Revoir les Enfants* (Fra)
1988 *The Legend of the Holy Drinker* (Ita)
1989 *A City of Sadness* (Tai)
1990 *Rosencrantz and Guildenstern Are Dead* (GB)
1991 *Urga* (Rus/Fra)
1992 *Qiu Ju Da Guansi* (Chi)
1993 *Short Cuts* (US)
Three Colours Blue (Fra)
1994 *Before the Rain* (Macedonia/GB/Fra)
Vive L'Amour (Tai)
1995 *Cyclo* (Fra/Vie)
1996 *Michael Collins* (US)

■ ***THE LOST WORLD: JURASSIC PARK*** **IS EXPECTED TO BECOME THE FIRST $1 BILLION**

20 TOP-GROSSING FILMS AT THE BOX OFFICE

Rising ticket prices means that most of the films are from the 1990s, although there are a few notable exceptions. George Lucas's *Star Wars* trilogy, when re-released earlier this year, has maintained the epic space saga's position as one of the most popular films ever, and it has overtaken *E.T.* to become the USA's biggest box-office smash. However, the blockbuster film market is always dynamic. With the larger studios spending upwards of $40 million on advertising and publicity alone, Hollywood cinema is truly a multibillion-dollar industry.

	US DOMESTIC GROSS (US$)	NON-US GROSS (US$)	WORLDWIDE GROSS (US$)
1 *Jurassic Park* (US 93)	357,067,947	556,000,000	913,067,947
2 *Independence Day* (US 96)	306,169,255	501,001,893	807,171,148*
3 *The Lion King* (US 94)	312,855,561	455,000,000	767,855,561†
4 *Star Wars* (US 77)	460,947,410	299,465,336	760,412,746*†
5 *E.T.* (US 82)	399,804,539	330,000,000	729,804,539†
6 *Forrest Gump* (US 94)	329,690,974	349,400,000	679,090,974†
7 *The Empire Strikes Back* (US 80)	290,178,670	239,182,829	529,361,499*†
8 *Ghost* (US 90)	217,631,306	299,968,694	517,600,000
9 *Aladdin* (US 92)	217,350,219	280,300,000	497,650,219
10 *Home Alone* (US 90)	285,016,000	212,000,000	497,016,000
11 *Terminator 2: Judgment Day* (US 91)	204,446,562	285,553,438	490,000,000
12 *Return of the Jedi* (US 83)	308,733,311	158,164,059	466,897,370*†
13 *Twister* (US 96)	241,708,908	220,741,973	462,450,881
14 *Jaws* (US 75)	260,000,000	198,000,000	458,000,000†
15 *Mission: Impossible* (US 96)	180,981,866	271,300,000	452,281,866
16 *Indiana Jones and the Last Crusade* (US 89)	197,171,806	252,628,194	449,800,000
17 *Pretty Woman* (US 90)	178,406,268	270,500,000	448,906,268
18 *Mrs Doubtfire* (US 93)	219,194,773	203,679,076	422,873,849
19 *Batman* (US 89)	251,188,924	154,000,000	411,200,000
20 *The Bodyguard* (US 92)	121,936,132	285,663,868	407,600,000

* still on general release
† including reissues

20 TOP-GROSSING FILMS OF ALL TIME

The films that took the most money at the box office are not necessarily the most popular films of all time. Many of the all-time classic films were far more popular than recent blockbusters, but grossed less due to lower ticket prices. The following table shows the top 20 films of all time adjusted for inflation. As can be seen, recent films such as *Jurassic Park* slide down the table to make way for the timeless classics of cinema.

	ADMISSIONS	ORIGINAL DOMESTIC GROSS (US$)	ADJUSTED GROSS (US$)
1 *Gone With the Wind* (US 39)	197,548,731*	193,597,756	871,189,902
2 *Star Wars* (US 77)	176,063,374*	460,947,410	774,992,216
3 *E.T.* (US 82)	135,987,938*	399,804,539	599,706,809
4 *The Ten Commandments* (US 56)	131,000,000	65,500,000	577,710,000
5 *The Sound of Music* (US 65)	130,571,429	163,214,286	575,820,001
6 *Jaws* (US 75)	128,078,818	260,000,000	564,827,586
7 *Doctor Zhivago* (US 65)	124,135,456	111,721,910	547,437,359
8 *The Jungle Book* (US 67)	111,045,538*	135,475,556	489,710,821
9 *Snow White* (US 37)	109,000,000*	184,925,486	480,690,000
10 *Ben-Hur* (US 59)	107,692,308	70,000,000	474,923,077
11 *101 Dalmatians* (US 61)	105,207,663*	152,551,111	463,965,793
12 *The Empire Strikes Back* (US 80)	98,049,707*	290,178,670	431,571,424
13 *The Exorcist* (US 73)	94,285,714	165,000,000	415,800,000
14 *Return of the Jedi* (US 83)	93,796,001*	308,733,311	412,803,112
15 *The Sting* (US 73)	91,209,330	159,616,327	402,233,144
16 *Raiders of the Lost Ark* (US 81)	87,185,055	242,374,454	384,486,094
17 *Jurassic Park* (US 93)	86,193,170	356,839,725	380,111,881
18 *The Graduate* (US 67)	85,571,393	104,397,100	377,369,845
19 *Fantasia* (US 40)	83,043,478*	76,400,000	366,221,739
20 *The Godfather* (US 72)	79,353,089	134,900,252	349,947,124

*including reissues

Note: The adjusted figures are calculated by dividing the non-adjusted gross by the average ticket price for the year of release. This gives an average number of admissions. This figure is then multiplied by the current average ticket price to get an inflation-adjusted figure. The figures relate only to the US domestic box-office, which can be used as an indicator for worldwide figures.

Jurassic Park, currently the top grossing film at the box-office, brings the world of dinosaurs to life. It tells the story of an eccentric millionaire's attempts to clone dinosaur DNA to produce genetically engineered tyrannosaurs. The film brought the latest in computer special effects to the screen and was an instant success, breaking all box-office records throughout the world. In 1997, a sequel, *Jurassic Park: The Lost World,* was released and took just five days to break the $100 million barrier in the US. The sequel unleashed even more lifelike dinosaurs, this time on an island kept secret until discovered by a research expedition.

Regarded as one of the greatest films ever, *Gone With the Wind*, the epic passionate romance between Rhett Butler and Scarlett O'Hara, set against a backdrop of the American Civil War, remains one of the blockbusters of cinema history. The film premiered in December 1939 with a cast of over 2400, a wardrobe which included 4000 costumes, and over a million props. The film went on to sweep the board at the Academy Awards. It set another record in its search for a star to fill the role of Scarlett. Producer David O. Selznick shot 162,000 ft of test film before selecting the unknown Vivien Leigh.

DANCE

▶ **The worst outbreak of tarantism (dancing mania) was in Aachen, Germany, in 1374, when hordes of people broke into frenzied dancing in the streets.**

▶ **The fastest flamenco dancer on record is Solero de Jérez, who attained 16 heel taps per second in Brisbane, Australia, in 1967.**

▶ **Fonteyn and Nureyev had a record 89 curtain calls for Swan Lake in 1964.**

DANCE

▶ Cave paintings of *c.* 15,000 BC show people who, from their postures, can only be dancing.
▶ Eastern dances make complex and subtle use of the hands, whereas hands in Western dances are often held passively.

Forms of dance vary from those that use the whole body in free and open movement, to those in which movement is restricted to certain parts of the body (just the eyes in the case of one Samoan courtship dance). Dance is usually rhythmic, often with an element of repetition, and forms a pattern in both time and space. Dancing can be a pure and simple expression of pleasure in the movement of the body or an art form involving complex patterns and significant gestures.

Some kind of musical accompaniment usually plays a part in dance, helping to maintain unison among groups of dancers. It may be instrumental, vocal, or the mere sound of clapping hands or stamping feet within the dance. Music may reinforce the rhythm of a dance or add structure and content to physical expression. Sometimes, as in some Indian forms, dancers and musicians improvise variations.

MODERN DANCE

Reaction against the formal rules of classical ballet led to freer styles of dance in the 20th century. Like the other arts, contemporary ideas have also affected dance. Modern dance can range from show dancing (such as the high-kicking *cancan* which emerged in Paris in the 1840s); tap and jazz dancing (originating in 19th-century America); free form (as expounded by the American Isadora Duncan at the beginning of the century); or popular dances (such as rock'n'roll or the twist). Recent years have seen the creation of contemporary dance, with modern dance companies drawing on existing styles and experimenting with new ideas.

■ *These two women, outside a temple at Bhubaneswar in the Orissa region of India, are performing the traditional* Bharata Natyam *dance, based on Hindu religious themes and one of the five principal classical dance styles of India*

POPULAR WESTERN DANCES

allemande: a 15th-century stately processional dance meaning 'from Germany' in French.
barn dance: traditional American form of dancing associated with celebrating the completion of a new barn.
black bottom: a type of jerky athletic foxtrot first mentioned in *The New York Times* in 1926.
bossa nova: a variation of the samba, originating in Brazil.
Boston: a slow 20th-century dance derived from the waltz.
bourée: a lively 17th-century dance starting on the upbeat.
branle: a 15th-century English clog dance with circular figures.
break dancing: a modern dance, introduced *c.* 1980, in which dancers perform acrobatic feats.
cakewalk: a graceful walking dance which takes its name from the cakes offered as prizes for competitive performances held in the southern states of the USA from *c.* 1872; it was introduced into ballrooms from *c.* 1900.
cha cha cha: a variation of the mambo in which couples dance with lightly linked hands; it was introduced in 1954.
chaconne: a graceful dance introduced into Spain from Peru *c.* 1580 which then spread through western Europe.
Charleston: one of the most popular dances of the 1920s, it is characterized by a side kick from the knee and named after a Mack and Johnson song of 1923 about the town Charleston, South Carolina.
conga: a single-file dance developed in 1935 from the rumba and African dances.
contredanse: a 17th-century dance for opposing groups which was developed in France and reintroduced into England and whose name is a mistranslation of 'country dance'.
cotillion (French 'petticoat'): a 17th-century dance for two groups of four pairs each which developed into the dance known as the quadrille in the 19th century.
courante: a stately 15th-century Italian dance including elegant bending of the knees and whose name comes from the Italian 'current', that is 'running'.
disco dancing: a flamboyant freestyle modern dance with exaggerated hand movements and popularized by the film *Saturday Night Fever* in 1977.
folk dancing: traditional dances originating from particular areas that have evolved rather than been invented. They often retain features that once had magical and ritual significance.
foxtrot: a dance in quadruple time, alternating long and short steps, introduced in 1912 in the USA and, allegedly, named after Harry Fox. There are both slow and quick variations; the slow foxtrot evolved *c.* 1927 into the 'blues dance'.
galliard: a sprightly medieval jigging dance from Italy whose name implies 'gaiety'.
gavotte: a lively 17th-century dance in which each couple had the chance to dance on their own and whose name comes from the Provençal dialect gavoto, meaning 'a native of the Alps'; it reached its greatest popularity at the court of the French king Louis XIV.
gigue: a lively 17th-century dance based on the traditional English jig.
go-go: a repetitious dance of verve, usually exhibitionist, dating from 1965.
jitterbug: a fast American dance to jazz accompaniment which gained great popularity during World War II.
jive: a jerky improvised variation of the jitterbug (see above).
the lancers: a quadrille for eight to 16 couples.
Ländler: traditional Austrian dance in which partners turn in each other's arms with a hop and a step and whose name is German for 'small country'.
mambo: an off-beat rumba of Cuban origin introduced into the USA in 1948.
matelot: a 17th-century Dutch sailor's clog dance.
mazurka: a 17th-century Polish round dance for eight couples in which the second beat is accentuated.
minuet: a delicate dance whose name comes from the French *pas menu* ('small steps') and which was often followed by the boisterous gavotte as a contrast; recorded by Lully in 1663, it was a favourite at the French court.
morisca: a Spanish dance derived from dances of Moorish Spain (it comes from the Spanish for 'Moorish') first recorded in 1446 in Burgos.
one-step: an early 20th-century dance, characterized by long quick steps, which was a precursor of the foxtrot.
pasodoble: a 20th-century Spanish-style two-step.
passacaglia: a popular Italian 17th-century dance, resembling the chaconne, but in a minor key.
Paul Jones: a 19th-century group dance in which partners are exchanged.
pavane: a stately medieval processional dance derived from instrumental music in Padua and which was possibly the first stylized dance.
pogo: a dance invented by punk rockers in 1976 in which dancers jump vertically from the ground in imitation of a pogo stick.
polka: a bouncing dance developed from a Bohemian courtship dance which was introduced to Paris in 1843.
quadrille: a 19th-century French derivation of the 17th-century contredanse comprising a series of five 'figure' dances for four couples.
quickstep: a dance in rapid quadruple time, invented in the USA in 1900, which reached its peak in the 1920s.
reggae: a dance introduced from Jamaica in 1969 and characterized by the strong accentuation of the upbeat.
rigaudon: a lively French 17th-century dance known in England as the rigadoon.
robotics: a modern style of dance in which dancers imitate clockwork dolls with rigid limb movements.
rock'n'roll: an energetic free dance introduced by Bill Haley and his Comets in 1953, characterized by a heavy beat and simple melody, partly evolved from the jive and partly improvised.
rumba: a Cuban dance popularized in 1923.
samba: a lively Latin American dance in double time which originated in Brazil *c.* 1885 and was introduced to ballrooms *c.* 1920 as the maxixe (the name 'samba' was resumed *c.* 1940).
sarabande: a slow and graceful dance, introduced to Spain probably from Morocco *c.* 1588, involving advances and retreats and couples passing between rows of dancers.
tango: a lively syncopated 20th-century Latin American dance characterized by gliding steps and dramatic pauses; it was introduced to the USA from Argentina, but its origins may have been the Cuban habañera.
turkey trot: a ragtime variation of the one-step which gained considerable popularity during World War I.
twist: a lively dance – characterized by body torsion and knee-flexing – in which partners rarely touch; it was introduced in 1961.
volta: a twirling 15th-century dance in which the woman is lifted from the floor and bounced upon the man's knees and whose name comes from the Italian for 'vault'.
waltz: an Austrian dance developed from the Ländler (see above) in the 19th century.

■ WHIRLING DERVISHES USED DANCE AS A METHOD OF ACHIEVING RELIGIOUS ECSTASY IN

BALLET

▶ Louis XIV's interest in dance led to the birth of classical ballet in the 17th century.
▶ The first ballerina to go on points (*en pointe*) was Italian Marie Taglioni in 1832.

Ballet is a theatrical form of dance based upon a set of positions, steps and expressive gestures that demand considerable skill and training. One of the most obvious ways in which ballet differs from other forms of dance is in the 90° 'turned-out' position of the feet, which permits a remarkable degree of balance in all positions. Ballet also requires arching of the foot and Achilles tendon to provide a powerful jump and to cushion landing.

THE ORIGINS OF CLASSICAL BALLET

In 1661 the French king, Louis XIV, established a group of dancing instructors, the Académie Royale de Danse, to codify court dances. Its director, Charles Louis Beauchamp (1636–1705), is credited with inventing the 'five positions', although they may have existed before he made them a recognized practice. As greater skills were demanded from the dancers, trained professionals began to replace the aristocratic amateurs, and in 1672 the Académie Royale de Musique et de Danse was formed. In 1713 the Paris Opéra founded a permanent dance company and a school in which they trained.

Dancers performing at the Opéra wore heavy court costumes and hid their faces behind masks. This was supposedly because they thought that Ancient Greek performers wore them, but also because female roles were often danced by men and court ladies preferred to disguise their faces.

Ballet involved a succession of dances with music and poetry until 1661, when dramatist/actor Molière (1622–73) used dance in his plays. Jean Georges Noverre (1727–1810) instigated even more change, creating dances in London, Stuttgart and Vienna before moving to the Paris Opéra in 1776. His aims were to get rid of heavy wigs, big padded skirts and masks and to introduce more natural gestures into dance, with a greater emphasis on dramatic action.

ROMANTIC BALLET

After 1800, women began to dance 'on point' (on the tips of their toes), stiffening the ends of their slippers for more support. As in other arts at this time, Romanticism (the expression of romantic ideals) was fashionable. Ballets began to tell stories about unrequited love and princes falling in love with nymphs, exemplified by the 1841 ballet *Giselle*, in which an abandoned country girl's spirit appears to her unfaithful princely lover. Although there were still virtuosi male dancers, men tended to be mere partners, literally supporting the women, with some male roles danced by women dressed as men.

RUSSIAN BALLET

At the end of the 19th century, ballet blossomed in Russia, with productions such as *Sleeping Beauty* and *Swan Lake* occupying whole evenings. In 1919, the impresario Serge Diaghilev (1872–1929) began a season of Russian ballet in Paris with his company the Ballets Russes. His daring dancers and stunning stage settings attracted wild enthusiasm. For the next 20 years his company toured Europe and the Americas, launching the international careers of many stars, like Anna Pavlova. Some of today's great ballet companies originated from Diaghilev's company, such as London's Sadlers Wells (now the Royal) Ballet, founded by Ninette de Valois (1898–).

MODERN BALLET

Russia has continued to produce brilliant dancers, such as Rudolph Nureyev and Mikhail Baryshnikov, but innovation and experimentation have shifted elsewhere. Many countries now have major national companies, extending the vocabulary of dance while remaining within the classical world.

■ *Ballet dancers Laura Contardi and Martin James perform in Natalia Makarova's* Swan Lake

MAJOR DANCERS AND CHOREOGRAPHERS

Baryshnikov, Mikhail (1948–): Russian dancer with Kirov Ballet who defected to the West in 1974, joining American Ballet Theatre, which he directed 1980–89. Too short to be an ideal classical partner, he dazzled his audience with his personality, aerial technique and humour, and extended his range with modern work.

Dolin, Anton, Sir (Healey-Kay, Sydney Francis Patrick Chipendall; 1904–83): First British male dancer to gain international status; member of Ballets Russes, the Vic-Wells (later Royal) Ballet, and American Ballet Theatre; later led his own companies with Alicia Markova, including Festival (now English National) Ballet.

Duncan, Isadora (1877–1927): American creator of a personal dance form, barefoot and wearing loose garments, which aimed to revive Ancient Greek dance. Equally famed for her notorious love-life and dramatic death (strangled by a scarf caught in the wheel of an open car).

Fonteyn, Margot, Dame (Hookham, Peggy; 1918–91): British ballerina of incomparable talent, overcoming technical limitations with exceptional musicality and sensitivity. Already dancing classical leads with Vic-Wells (later Royal) Ballet at only 15, she appeared in over 80 roles. Partnered with Rudolph Nureyev late in her career, she had unequalled performances in *Marguerite and Armand* (Ashton) and *Romeo and Juliet* (MacMillan).

Genee, Adeline, Dame (Jensen, Anna Kristina Margarete Petra; 1878–1970): Danish ballerina who linked the romantic and modern eras; founder of the Royal Academy of Dancing (president from 1920–54), her most famous role was Swanhilda in *Coppelia*.

Graham, Martha (1894–91): American dancer and choreographer who developed a personal dance technique which draws inward rather than stretching outward, as in ballet. Her style is exemplified in the work of the company and the school which she founded; a great influence on other modern dance styles.

Grisi, Carlotta (Caronne Adele Josephine Marie;1819–99): Leading Italian ballerina of the Romantic era, star of Paris Opera and creator of roles including Giselle and La Peri.

Guillem, Sylvie (1966–): French ballerina with Paris Opera, Royal Ballet, American Ballet Theatre, etc. Tall and technically accomplished, but criticized for lack of feeling, she mixes classical work with post-modern experimentation.

Makarova, Natalia (Romanovna; 1940–): Russian ballerina with the Kirov who defected to the West in 1970; appeared with the Royal Ballet and American Ballet Theatre. Her roles, including Giselle and Carmen, exhibit a charming defencelessness.

Markova, Alicia, Dame (Marks, Lillian Alicia; 1910–): British ballerina, engaged for the Ballets Russes at only 14 and member of the Vic-Wells (later Royal) Ballet after Diaghilev's death, she later formed companies with Dolin. Best known for traditional ballerina roles (Giselle), but modern works were also created for her.

Mitchell, Arthur (1934–): American dancer who appeared in musicals before becoming the first black to appear with an American classical company in 1955, creating many roles for Balanchine with New York City Ballet. In 1966 he founded the Dance Theatre of Harlem with Shook.

Nijinsky, Vaslav (?1888–1950): Russian dancer, choreographer and Diaghilev's charismatic protégé; creator of Petruchka, the Faun in his own *Afternoon of the Faun* and choreographer of the even more controversial *The Rite of Spring*. His meteoric career was cut short by mental illness.

Nureyev, Rudolph (1938–93): Russian dancer with the Kirov Theatre and, after defection to the West in 1961, as guest with the Royal Ballet and other companies. His sensual charisma and bravura technique in both classics and the most modern works made him an international superstar. From 1983 he became director of the Paris Opera Ballet, restoring its eminence.

Pavlova, Anna (1881–1931): Russian ballerina introduced to western Europe in 1909 by Diaghilev, who then toured with her own company. Her lyrical and ethereal talent won new audiences for ballet worldwide, her style encapsulated in the solo *The Dying Swan*.

Seymour, Lynne (1939–): Canadian ballerina for whom MacMillan and Ashton created many roles with Britain's Royal Ballet, including Juliet in the former's *Romeo and Juliet* (although not the first to appear in it).

Taglioni, Marie (1804–84): Swedish Romantic ballerina; made dancing on point part of ballet technique; original La Sylphide (choreographed by her father at the Paris Opera).

Ulanova, Galina (1910–): Russian ballerina, star of the Kirov (1930s) and the Bolshoi (from 1944); imbued performances with simplicity and sincerity in subtle characterizations that enraptured audiences, especially in *Romeo and Juliet* (Lavrovsky) and *The Fountain of Bakchisarav*.

Vestris, Marie Auguste (1760–1842): Italian dancer, trained by his father Gaetano Vestris (probably the first male dancer with modern technique) who dubbed him 'the god of the dance', he had remarkable elevation.

Villella, Edward (1936–): America's first male international ballet star. A soloist from 1957 with New York City Ballet, his physique and athleticism were ideally suited to Balanchine's choreography. Retiring due to injury, he directed several small companies.

Music

▶ **The first operas were written with Greek myths as their subject matter, so that most people had no need to hear the words as they already knew the storyline.**

▶ **Telemann was probably the most prolific composer of all time, writing a total of *c.* 2515 works, including *c.* 1270 cantatas, *c.* 400 chamber works, 135 orchestral suites, 100 concerti, *c.* 130 songs, *c.* 30 operas and *c.* 450 other works.**

▶ **The most prolific Classical composer was Mozart, who wrote *c.* 1000 operas, operettas, symphonies, divertimenti, sonatas, serenades, motets, concertos, string quartets, other chamber music, masses and litanies before dying, aged 35.**

▶ **To suggest, as some people do, that modern music lacks 'melody' is simply that the relationship between the notes and harmony are more complex and in contrast to the sounds some listeners previously associated with music.**

▶ **The horn was originally a prehistoric instrument and was, quite literally, the horn of an animal.**

THE ORIGINS OF MUSIC

▶ In its most primitive form, music tended to evoke the sounds of the elements – earth, air, fire and water – which humans imitated, along with animal sounds.
▶ Primitive humans used their voices, as well as sticks, stones, bones, bells, reed pipes or anything else available, as musical instruments.

The sophisticated evolution of music took place over a period of centuries. There was certainly a rich musical tradition in the years before Christ – for example in India, China, Egypt and Greece – and much of it was passed on orally, not written down. Even today, in Asia particularly, this tradition persists, because music is often regarded as improvisatory and contemplative, ceaselessly changing, rather than something perfected and fixed on paper. However, the history of classical Western music can be broken down into the following musical periods.

PLAINSONG AND POLYPHONY

▶ Two of the most important developments in the early history of Western music were plainsong and polyphony, both of which came about through the spread of the Christian religion, yet whose musical foundations also lay in Jewish chant.
▶ Ars Nova was the first musical style to incorporate short breaks (called 'hockets') between notes in a vocal phrase to enhance the rhythm.

Plainsong consists of a single line of vocal melody in 'free' rhythm (meaning it is not divided into metred bar lengths). It falls into the category of monophonic music (Greek for 'single sound'), implying the absence of harmonic support or other melodies performed simultaneously with the original.

Polyphony, conversely, means 'many sounds', and indicates the simultaneous sounding of two or more independent melodic lines to produce a coherent musical texture. The melodies in polyphony are described as being in counterpoint to each other, and the resulting music as contrapuntal. Polyphony originated during the early years of Christianity and reached its peak in Europe in Gregorian chant from the 12th–13th centuries. It is still used in the Roman Catholic Church today.

Antiphony, where two separate bodies of singers perform plainsong chants in response to one another, developed in Venice in the 17th century. Other parts of Europe produced their own ritual music of a similar type.

ARS ANTIQUA AND NOVA

The musical style Ars Antiqua (Latin for 'Ancient Art') flourished at the most influential centre of musical activity in the 12th and 13th centuries – the church of Notre Dame in Paris, France. Based on plainsong and organum, it was an early form of polyphony involving the addition of parts to a plainsong melody. Such music was described by writers of the early 14th century as Ars Antiqua to distinguish it from its successor Ars Nova (Latin for 'New Art').

Ars Nova thrived in France and Italy in the 14th century and introduced significant innovations in the areas of rhythm and harmony. The polyphonic setting of poetry to music began in this period in the form of the ballade, rondeau and virelai, collectively known as chansons. In France the troubadours – itinerant poet-musicians, often of aristocratic birth – were active in Provence in the 11th and 12th centuries. Their German equivalents were the Minnesinger (German for 'love singers'), whose successors, the guilds of Meistersinger ('Mastersingers'), established themselves in some German cities in the 15th and 16th centuries.

THE RENAISSANCE

▶ During the Renaissance, composers of religious music also began to write secular songs (chansons) about such everyday pastimes as love, friendship and drinking.
▶ The madrigal was significant in the development of vocal music because of its emphasis on the meaning of words.

Generally, the Renaissance in music is thought to have begun in the increasing secularization of music that took place at the court of Burgundy, France, in the early years of the 15th century. During this period, significant developments occurred in both religious and secular musical forms.

RELIGIOUS MUSIC

In the domain of religious music, composers mostly concentrated their efforts on the forms of the mass and the motet. Where the Reformation established Protestant worship, the setting and atmosphere of the mass began to change. In Germany, the Lutheran chorale (later to exercise a deep influence on the music of J.S. Bach) took root, while in England the anthem (the Protestant equivalent of the Latin motet) took its place in the liturgy of the Church of England. But as the 16th century progressed, it was Italy that emerged as the most crucially important musical centre, as the polyphonic mass reached its apogee in the work of three great composers: Palestrina, Victoria and Lassus.

THE MADRIGAL

The art of the madrigal – a secular polyphonic composition for several voices, usually based on poems of some literary merit – had its roots in 14th-century Italy, where early forms of the madrigal first appeared. Early madrigal composers were usually Flemish, resident in Italy, and their madrigals were written for three or four voices. A larger number of voices and a more consistently polyphonic style became the norm as the century progressed.

Madrigals began to appear in England in the late 16th century. A native English tradition of madrigal composition incorporated features of the secular song, as exemplified by Byrd and Gibbons, and was quickly established by composers such as Morley and Weelkes.

INSTRUMENTAL MUSIC

In the Middle Ages instruments were mainly used to double voices in vocal polyphony or to provide music for dancing. In the 16th century, a burgeoning of instrumental music took place when dance forms such as the pavane and galliard emerged (see p. 216). Non-dance forms of instrumental music included the canzona, the ricercare and the fantasia (see p. 225). Instrumental music in the 16th century was performed principally on the lute, the organ, the virginal and other stringed keyboard instruments, and by ensembles of viols and other instruments.

MUSIC OF THE BAROQUE

▶ The development of the two most popular new instrumental genres of the Baroque – the sonata and the concerto – was largely the work of Italian composers.
▶ A distinction is generally made between composers of the 'early Baroque' (such as Monteverdi, Frescobaldi and Schütz) and those of the 'late Baroque' (most notably Bach and Handel).

Most of the music performed in the concert hall or opera house falls under the categories of Baroque, Classical or Romantic. But the boundaries between them tend to be hazy. The word Baroque is particularly difficult to define as its origins are obscure in relation to music. By the 17th and 18th centuries, Baroque had become a term for the ornate, particularly ecclesiastical, architecture of the period. Other than defining a particular period between 1650 and 1750, Baroque has little meaning in application to music, though in its suggestion of ornateness of style it is obviously descriptive of certain types of 17th- and 18th-century composition.

The vocabulary and techniques of instrumental and vocal composition underwent a massive expansion in the 17th century. Revolutionary change took place also in the formal organization of music: the medieval modes that had been the basis of polyphonic composition in the 16th century gave way during the 17th century to a system involving the exclusive use of modern scales.

CONCERTATO STYLE

In addition, innovations such as the *concertato* style – in which specific instrumental or vocal parts were accompanied by a basso continuo, or 'thorough bass' (involving a low-pitched instrument such as a cello or bass viol combined with a harpsichord, organ or lute) – distinguish Baroque music from the Renaissance music that preceded it. As well as

■ GREGORIAN CHANT TOOK ITS NAME FROM POPE GREGORY THE GREAT, POPE FROM 590–604 providing the emerging vocal genres of opera, cantata and oratorio, Italy was the main source of instrumental ensemble music in the 17th century.

THE ADVENT OF THE OPERA

In France, as in England and Germany, composers were strongly influenced by Italian instrumental music. However, the greatest achievements of the French Baroque were in the realm of harpsichord music and opera. The overtures and dance movements from Lully's operas enjoyed a flourishing life outside the operatic context. So-called French overtures on the Lullian model were used by Handel in some of his operas and oratorios, and became an integral part of the Baroque orchestral suite.

The term 'opera' began to be used in 17th-century Italy for music dramas in which singers in costume enacted a story with instrumental accompaniment. The first true masterpieces in this form were by the Venetian composer Monteverdi, and many of the most prominent opera composers of the late 17th century and early 18th century came from Naples, giving rise to the term the Neapolitan School. The greatest operas of the early 18th century were written in England by Handel.

THE CLASSICAL PERIOD

▶ **If the music of J.S. Bach represents the summit of the Baroque era, then that of his sons, particularly Carl Philipp Emanuel and Johann Christian, provides a link with the period loosely known as Classical.**

▶ **The Classical era was a time of new developments in the art of the symphony and concerto, of the birth of the string quartet and piano sonata, and of the humanizing of opera.**

Vienna, the capital of the Austrian Habsburg Empire, now became the centre of musical progress, with Haydn, Mozart and, before long, Beethoven as its principal representatives. In the next generation, Schubert was to sustain Vienna's musical pre-eminence. Both Beethoven and Schubert were to extend the Classical forms and infuse them with a Romantic sensibility. All four composers collectively became known as the First Viennese School.

Classicism, in musical terms, has been defined as a style accepting certain basic conventions of form and structure (notably the sonata form; see p. 225), and using these as a natural framework for the expression of ideas. Unlike Romantic music, which developed out of Classicism, it saw no need to break the set boundaries, although in a discreet way its greatest practitioners did so more often than not.

One interesting emphasis of Classical music was the happy ending. For instance, Christoph Gluck, one of the greatest Classical opera reformers, wrote an opera based on the story of Orpheus, as did Monteverdi before him, but changed the ending to a happy one, in which the lovers were united, to fit in with the expectations of the time.

MUSIC OF THE ROMANTICS

▶ **During the Romantic period, piano music became a popular medium for personal expression, used prolifically by such composers as Beethoven, Liszt, Chopin and Schumann.**

▶ **Wind instruments also came into their own during this time and were used much more daringly and more often than ever before.**

Romanticism in music was not necessarily born in 1800. But the first year of the 19th century, when Beethoven had just produced the first of his nine symphonies, is as good a time as any by which to commemorate the establishment of composers as individual artists – rather than as servants of rich patrons, which had been the case throughout the Baroque and Classical periods.

The *Eroica* (1803–04), Beethoven's third symphony, finally shattered the bounds of Classicism. It was not only the biggest symphony ever written until that time (though Beethoven himself was to surpass it in his ninth), it was also recognized to be a personal testament in music, the first of its kind, symbolizing Beethoven's battle with the growing deafness that was to destroy his career as a public performer, but which intensified his inspiration as a composer. The crucial role played by Beethoven in the progress of symphonic form, and of the art of the string quartet and piano sonata, was something no later composer could ignore. In his last quartets in particular, Beethoven explored the most profound emotional and spiritual tensions with a musical daring not seen again for another century.

The composer as artist was attracted to representational or programme music – music that evokes pictorial scenes or finds some way to tell a story in purely musical terms. Berlioz, Mendelssohn and Liszt were notable proponents of this genre. Liszt coined the term 'symphonic poem' for his descriptive orchestral works.

In opera, Wagner expanded and transformed the art into what he preferred to describe as 'music drama'. In Italy, Verdi followed a parallel, if more cautious, path.

NATIONALISM

The rise of nationalist feeling all over Europe inspired many composers. Although Liszt's Hungarian Rhapsodies lacked Hungarian authenticity (in that Liszt mistook gypsy music for Hungarian folk music), nationalism in music was becoming a major force. Russia, which had revered the music of other European nations, particularly the French, came into its own during this time, with Glinka and Borodin writing music derived from the songs and dances of their own people. Folk rhythms, folk dances, folk songs, folk legends and folk harmonies served as important sources of inspiration to such composers as Smetana, Dvorak, Grieg, Wagner and Tchaikovsky.

MODERNISM AND NEW MUSIC

▶ **Wagner's *Tristan and Isolde* (1865) and Debussy's *Pelléas and Mélisande* (1902) were the two operas which initiated many of the major trends in 20th-century music.**

▶ **Minimalism and atonality in modernist music are the features that mark the greatest difference between 20th-century music and 19th-century Romantic music.**

The years around 1900 marked the beginnings of Modernism in music. As in the visual arts and literature, it involved a radical break with existing conventions. It also involved what often appears as a greater distancing between the composer and the audience – audiences have tended to find Modernist works 'difficult'. However, although Modernism has been in the intellectual forefront of music in the 20th century, many composers have followed more accessible paths.

Music since 1945 has evolved in many different ways. For many composers – especially in the 1950s – the once revolutionary twelve-note technique of Schoenberg became the new orthodoxy, while the avant-garde of the 1960s and 1970s enthusiastically embraced the new sound possibilities offered by the many developments in electronic music.

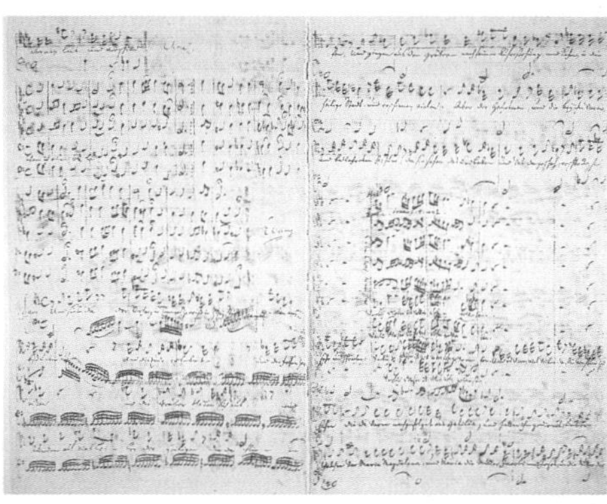

■ *An original manuscript from Johann Sebastian Bach's* St Matthew's Passion *(1727–29) shows the elaborate musical scoring that is usually a vital part of the art of composing*

MUSIC SYMBOLS

CLEFS

Clef symbols denote the register in which a work is to be performed.

𝄞 Treble (G clef). A representation of a medieval letter G, the focal point of which indicates the line G.

𝄢 Bass (F clef). A relic of the medieval letter F, centred on the F line.

INDICATIONS OF PITCH

♭ Flat. This sign flattens all the notes of the pitch indicated which follow it in the bar.

♯ Sharp. This sign sharpens all the notes of the pitch indicated which follow it in the bar.

♮ Natural. This sign indicates that a previously flattened or sharpened note is to return to its natural pitch.

REPEAT SIGNS

:‖ Repeat (or da capo). Two vertical lines preceded by a colon instruct the player(s) to return to the beginning of the movement or piece, or to the previous repeat sign.

NOTE LENGTHS

Early notation employed four note-lengths: double long, long, short ('breve'), and half-short ('semibreve'). Today, the longest note used – the breve – equals the early 'short', but it is uncommon.

NOTE	NAMES	MEANING
𝅝	semibreve (whole note)	half-short
𝅗𝅥	minim (half-note)	shortest (i.e. minimum)
♩	crotchet (quarter-note)	hook or crook (from its old appearance)
♪	quaver (eighth-note)	to trill, or quaver (quiver) in very short notes
𝅘𝅥𝅯	semiquaver (sixteenth-note)	half-quaver
𝅘𝅥𝅰	demisemiquaver (thirty-second-note)	half of half a quaver

TIME SIGNATURES

Examples of time signatures:

$\frac{4}{4}$ four quarter-notes (crotchets) to the bar

$\frac{3}{4}$ three quarter-notes (crotchets) to the bar

$\frac{3}{8}$ three eighth-notes (quavers) to the bar

COMPOSERS

Adams, John (1947–), US composer of powerful, colourful music rooted in minimalism: *Harmonium* (1981), *Short Ride in a Fast Machine* (1990) and the opera *Nixon in China* (1987).

Albéniz, Isaac (1860–1909), Spanish composer whose work is characterized by traditional Spanish rhythms: *Iberia* (1906–09).

Albinoni, Tommaso (1671–1751), Italian composer, much admired by Bach, who wrote a large amount of instrumental and vocal music, including 81 operas: *Sinfonie e Concerti a 5* (1707).

Andriessen, Louis (1939–), Dutch composer and key figure in new European music. Influenced by jazz, US minimalism and Stravinsky, he combines intense energy with strong wind and brass writing: *De Staat* (1976), *Hoketus* (1977), *Trepidus* (1983) and the opera *Rosa* (1994).

Arnold, Malcolm (1921–), English composer of melodious, often humorous, compositions including symphonies, dances, concertos and film scores: *Beckus the Dandipratt* (1946) and *Tam O'Shanter* (1955).

Bach, Carl Philipp Emanuel (1714–88), German composer of over 200 sonatas and 13 symphonies – second son of Johann Sebastian Bach.

Bach, Johann Christian ('The English Bach'; 1735–82), German composer of concertos, symphonies, sacred music and 11 operas; youngest son of Johann Sebastian Bach.

Bach, Johann Christoph Friedrich ('Bückeburg Bach'; 1732–95), German composer of oratorios, 14 symphonies and concertos – eldest son of Johann Sebastian Bach by second wife.

Bach, Johann Sebastian (1685–1750), German composer of sonatas, concertos, over 250 cantatas and keyboard music and held by many to be the greatest Baroque composer: a collection of 48 preludes and fugues, Six *Brandenburg Concertos* (1721), *The Well-Tempered Clavier* (1722–44), *St John's Passion* (1724), *St Matthew's Passion* (1729), *Mass in B Minor* (1733–38) and the *Goldberg Variations* (1742).

Balakirev, Mily (1837–1910), Russian composer who made an important contribution to the national school of Russian music: *Islamey* (1869) and *Tamara* (1867–82).

Barber, Samuel (1910–81), US composer: *Adagio for Strings* (1936), the opera *Vanessa* (1957).

Bartók, Béla (1881–1945), Hungarian composer of fiercely modernist music based on folk music: *Music for Strings, Percussion and Celesta* (1937) and *Concerto for Orchestra* (1944).

Beethoven, Ludwig van (1770–1827), German composer of chamber music, nine symphonies, five piano concertos, violin concerto, triple concertos, 32 piano sonatas, 16 string quartets and over 200 song settings: the piano sonatas *Pathétique* (1799), *Moonlight* (1800–01) and *Hammerklavier* (1817–18), the *Missa Solemnis* (1819–22), the symphonies *Eroica* (No. 3; 1803-04), *Pastoral* (No. 6; 1807–08) and *Choral* (No. 9; 1817–23), and his only opera *Fidelio* (1805).

Berg, Alban (1885–1935), Austrian composer who adopted Schoenberg's twelve-note system, particularly in his *Violin Concerto* (1935): the operas *Wozzeck* (1917–21) and *Lulu* (1929–35) and the *Lyric Suite* (1928).

Berio, Luciano (1925–), Italian composer of electronic and other modern music: *Serenade I* (1957) and the *Sequenza* series (1958–75).

Berlioz, Hector (1803–69), French composer: *Symphonie Fantastique* (1830) and *Harold in Italy* (1834) symphonies, the choral symphony *Roméo et Juliette* (1839), the cantata *La Damnation de Faust* (1846), and the operas *Benvenuto Cellini* (1834–37) and *Les Troyens* (1856–58).

Bernstein, Leonard (1918–90), American composer, pianist and conductor who successfully bridged classical and popular music: *Candide* (1956), *On the Town* (1944), *West Side Story* (1957) and *Mass* (1971).

Birtwistle, Harrison (1934–), English composer: *Tragoedia* (1965), *Panic* (1996) and the opera *Punch and Judy* (1966–67).

Edvard Grieg

Bizet, Georges (1838–75), French composer: the opera *Carmen* (1873).

Bliss, Sir Arthur (1891–1975), English composer who was originally daring and experimental, but adopted a more conservative style in the 1950s: *Colour Symphony* (1922) and *Checkmate* (1937).

Boccherini, Luigi (1743–1805), Italian composer of 20 symphonies, 102 string quartets and the opera *La Clementina* (1786).

Boulanger, Nadia (1887–79), French composer and teacher who was responsible for the education of many distinguished composers, such as Aaron Copland and Elliott Carter: *La Sirène* (1908).

Boulez, Pierre (1925–), French composer who used the twelve-note technique: *Le Marteau sans maître* (1953–55) and *Pli selon pli* (1957–62).

Brahms, Johannes (1833–97), German composer of choral works, four symphonies and a large canon of chamber music: the choral works *A German Requiem* (1868) and *Alto Rhapsody* (1869).

Britten, Benjamin (1913–76), English composer and songwriter who worked with the General Post Office film unit (1935–37). He wrote many choral works, but opera was his main passion: the operas *Peter Grimes* (1945), *Billy Budd* (1951), *The Turn of the Screw* (1954) and *Death in Venice* (1973).

Bruckner, Anton (1824–96), Austrian composer: *Te Deum* (1881–84), nine symphonies and an unfinished tenth.

Byrd, William (1543–1623), English composer of sacred music, mostly for the Roman liturgy, and of fantasias for viol consort: *Cantiones Sacrae* (1575).

Cage, John (1912–92), US composer of experimental percussion and electronic pieces: *4'33"* (1952) and *Imaginary Landscapes* (1939–52).

Carter, Elliott (1908–), US composer influenced by Charles Ives: *Symphony of Three Orchestras* (1977).

Cherubini, Luigi (1760–1842), Italian composer of masses and 30 operas: the operas *Médée* (1797) and *Les Deux Journées* (adapted in English as *The Water Carrier*; 1800).

Chopin, Frédéric (1810–49), Polish composer of nocturnes, ballades, fantasias, mazurkas, polonaises, studies, waltzes and scherzos, mostly for the piano: *Etudes* (1829–37) and *Fantasie in F Minor, Op. 49* (1841).

Cimarosa, Domenico (1749–1801), Italian composer of comic operas and harpsichord sonatas: the comic opera *Il matrimonio segreto* (*The Secret Marriage*; 1792).

Clementi, Muzio (1752–1832), Italian-born English composer and pianist who developed techniques for the piano: a series of 60 piano sonatas and *Gradus ad Parnassum* piano studies (1817).

Copland, Aaron (1900–90), US composer of works based on American folk idioms: the ballets *Billy the Kid* (1938), *Rodeo* (1942) and *Appalachian Spring* (1944).

Corelli, Arcangelo (1653–1713), Italian pioneer composer of concertos and sonatas. The 12 *Concerti Grossi* (1714) established the *concerto grosso* form.

Couperin, François ('Le Grand'; 1668–1733), French composer who composed elegant keyboard pieces, choral music and secular songs.

Cowell, Henry (1897–1965), US experimental composer who developed the use of tone clusters: 21 symphonies, chamber music, an opera, piano music and *Synchrony* (1931) for orchestra and trumpet.

Dallapiccola, Luigi (1904–75), Italian composer whose works were the first in Italy to use the twelve-note method: his opera *Volo di notte* (*Night Flight*; 1940) and his choral and orchestral piece *Canti di liberazione* (*Songs of Liberation*; 1955).

Debussy, Claude (1862–1918), French composer whose works are characterized by a 'dream-like' quality often called 'musical impressionism': many works for piano, the orchestral pieces *Prélude à l'après-midi d'un faune* (1892–94), *Nocturnes* (1897–99) and *La Mer* (1903–05), and the opera *Pelléas et Mélisande* (1902).

Delibes, Léo (1836–91), French composer: the opera *Lakmé* (1883) and the ballet *Coppélia* (1870).

Delius, Frederick (1862–1934), English composer: the orchestral piece *On Hearing the First Cuckoo in Spring* (1911–13) and the tone poem *Over the Hills and Far Away* (1895).

Denisov, Edison (1929–), Russian composer of highly original music drawing upon electronic techniques and folk music: *D-S-C-H, Guitar Concerto* and *Romantische Music.*

Des Prés, Josquin (1440–1521), Flemish composer of masses, motets and chansons.

Donizetti, Gaetano (1797–1848), Italian composer: the operas *Maria Stuarda* (1834), *Don Pasquale* (1843) and *Lucia di Lammermoor* (1835).

Dufay, Guillaume (*c.* 1400–74), Franco-Flemish composer active at the Burgundian court.

Dukas, Paul (1865–1935), Self-critical French composer, strongly influenced by Impressionism: *The Sorcerer's Apprentice* (1897) and the ballet *La Péri* (1912).

Dvorak, Antonín (1841–1904), Czech composer: *Slavonic Dances* (1878–86) and the symphony *From the New World* (No. 9; 1893).

Elgar, Edward (1857–1934), English composer: *Enigma Variations* (1898–99), the oratorio *The Dream of Gerontius* (1899–1900) and *Cello Concerto* (1919).

Falla, Manuel de (1876–1946), Spanish composer whose works echo Andalusian folk music: the ballet *The Three-Cornered Hat* (1917–19).

Fauré, Gabriel (1845–1924), French composer: the opera *Pénélope* (1913) and *Requiem* (1877–90).

Franck, César (1822–90), Belgian composer: *Symphonic Variations* (1885).

Frescobaldi, Girolamo (1583–1643), Italian organist and composer of toccatas, fugues and capriccios.

Gabrieli, Andrea (*c.* 1515–86), Venetian who composed in a flamboyant polychoral (multi-choir) style: *Primus liber missarum* (1572).

Gabrieli, Giovanni (*c.* 1557–1612), Venetian composer of motets with a rich instrumental accompaniment. He was the nephew and pupil of Andrea Gabrieli (see above): *Sonata pian'e forte* (1615).

Gershwin, George (1898–1937), US composer and pianist who successfully merged popular and classical styles: *An American in Paris* (1928), *Rhapsody in Blue* (1945) and the opera *Porgy and Bess* (1935).

Gibbons, Orlando (1583–1625), English composer of sacred and secular music, including anthems: *Madrigals and Motetts of 5 parts* (1612).

Glass, Philip (1937–), US minimalist composer of avant-garde operas whose later works included 'pop' sources: *Low Symphony* (1992).

Glazunov, Alexander (1865–1936), Russian composer: the ballet *The Seasons* (1899).

Glinka, Mikhail (1804–57), Russian composer: the operas *A Life for the Tsar* (1836) and *Ruslan and Ludmilla* (1842).

Gluck, Christoph Willibald von (1714–87), German composer who made opera more genuinely dramatic: the operas *Orpheus and Eurydice* (1762) and *Alceste* (1767).

Górecki, Henryk (1933–), Polish composer of avant-garde music until the early 1970s who now employs folk idioms and simple harmonic patterns: *Symphony No. 3* (1976).

Gounod, Charles François (1818–93), French composer: the opera *Faust* (1859).

Grainger, Percy (1882–1961), Australian-born US composer of folk songs and light works often based on traditional tunes: *Handel in the Strand* (1930) and *Harvest Hymn* (1906).

Grieg, Edvard Hagerup (1843–1907), Norwegian composer: the incidental music for the play *Peer Gynt* (1875).

Handel, George Frideric (1685–1759), German-born English composer, virtuoso keyboard player, impresario, music director and teacher. In his operas, oratorios, concertos and suites, he created a highly individual style of writing, best seen in: *Water Music* (1717), *Music for the Royal Fireworks* (1749), 42 operas, anthems including *Zadok the Priest* (1727), the *Concerti Grossi* (1734–40) and numerous oratorios, including *Israel in Egypt* (1739) and *Messiah* (1742).

Haydn, Franz Joseph (1732–1809), Austrian composer of piano sonatas and trios, concertos, operas, masses, string quartets (a form he established) and 104 symphonies: the *London Symphonies* (Nos. 92–104; 1789–95), and the oratorios *The Creation* (1798) and *The Seasons* (1801).

Henze, Hans Werner (1926–), German composer: the oratorio *The Raft of the Medusa* (1968) and the opera *We Come to the River* (1976).

Hildegard von Bingen (1098–1179), German composer, abbess, and theological and visionary writer. Much of her work came from 'visions', now understood to have been caused by violent migraine headaches: *Ordo Virtutum* (1150).

Hindemith, Paul (1895–1963), German composer who is associated with the term 'utility music': the opera *Mathis der Maler* (1933–35).

Holst, Gustav (1874–1934), English composer: the suite *The Planets* (1914–16) and *Egdon Heath* (1927).

Honegger, Arthur (1892–1955), Swiss composer: the orchestral piece *Pacific 231* (1923) and the oratorio *Jeanne d'Arc au bûcher* (1934–35).

Humperdinck, Engelbert (1854–1921), German composer: the opera *Hansel und Gretel* (1893).

Ibert, Jacques (1890–1962), French composer: the orchestral piece *Divertissement* (1930).

Ireland, John (1879–1962), English composer of piano and chamber music and songs: *The Forgotten Rite* (1913) for orchestra and *Sarnia* (1940–41) for piano.

Wolfgang Amadeus Mozart

Ives, Charles (1874–1954), US composer of highly individualistic works: the orchestral set *Three Places in New England* (1903–14).

Janácek, Leos (1854–1928), Czech composer of operas: *Jenufa* (1903), *The Cunning Little Vixen* (1924) and *The Makropoulos Case* (1926).

Khachaturian, Aram (1903–78), Armenian composer: the ballet *Spartacus* (1954).

Kodály, Zoltán (1882–1967), Hungarian composer whose works are characterized by a strong national flavour: the opera *Háry János* (1926).

Lassus, Roland de (1532–94), Flemish composer of over 2000 works.

Lehár, Franz (1870–1948), Hungarian composer of operetta: *The Merry Widow* (1905).

Leoncavallo, Ruggiero (1858–1919), Italian composer: the opera *Il Pagliacci* (1892).

Ligeti, Gyorgy (1923–), Hungarian composer: *Requiem* (1965) and the opera *Le Grand Macabre* (1975).

Liszt, (Ferencz) Franz (1811–86), Hungarian composer of a series of 13 descriptive orchestral works ('symphonic poems') and of piano pieces: the symphonies *Faust* (1854–57) and *Dante* (1856), Totentanz (1849) and the symphonic poem *Les Préludes* (1850).

Lully, Jean-Baptiste (1632–87), Italian-born French composer who established the form of the French opera, which was to reach its peak in the operas of Rameau: *Atys* (1676) and *Roland* (1685).

Lutoslawski, Witold (1913–94), Polish composer of works incorporating modern techniques: *String Quartet* (1964).

Machaut, Guillaume de (*c.* 1300–77), French composer who was a pioneer of chansons and championed isorhythms, whereby rhythm and melody followed strictly repeated patterns that were not synchronized.

Macmillan, James (1959–), Scottish composer: *Confessions of Isobel Gowdie* (1990) and *Veni, Veni Emmanuel* (1993).

Maconchy, Elizabeth (1907–88), English composer and pupil of Vaughan Williams: *Concertino* (1945) and *Little Symphony* (1981).

Mahler, Gustav (1860–1911), Austrian composer of nine large-scale symphonies: *Resurrection* (No. 2; 1884–94) and *Symphony of a Thousand* (No. 8; 1906–07).

Mascagni, Pietro (1863–1945), Italian composer: the opera *Cavalleria Rusticana* (1888).

Massenet, Jules (1842–1912), French composer: the operas *Manon* (1882–84) and *Don Quichotte* (1909).

Maxwell Davies, Peter (1934–), English composer: the opera *Taverner* (1970), and the theatre pieces *Vesalii Icones* (1969) and *Eight Songs for a Mad King* (1969).

Mendelssohn, Felix (1809–47), German composer: the overtures *A Midsummer Night's Dream* (1826) and *Hebrides* (or *Fingal's Cave*; 1830), and the oratorio *St Paul* (1836).

Messiaen, Olivier (1908–92), French composer of religious, organ and piano works: *Quartet for the End of Time* (1940), *Turangalila Symphony* (1949) and the piano work *Catalogue d'oiseaux* (1956–58).

Milhaud, Darius (1892–1974), French composer whose works are characterized by polytonality: the ballets *Le Boeuf sur le toit* (scenario by Jean Cocteau; 1919), *L'Homme et son désir* (scenario by Paul Claudel; 1918), and *La Création du monde* (scenario by Blaise Cendrars; 1923).

Monteverdi, Claudio (1567–1643), Italian composer of three innovative operas and the *Vespro della Beata Vergine* (*Vespers of the Blessed Virgin*; 1610), which runs the entire gamut of contemporary types of sacred music.

Morley, Thomas (1557–*c.* 1602), English organist and composer of madrigals: *The First Book of Ayres* (1600).

Mozart, Wolfgang Amadeus (1756–91), Austrian composer of 41 symphonies, over 40 concertos, 26 string quartets, 21 operas, seven string quintets and more: the operas *The Marriage of Figaro* (1786), *Don Giovanni* (1787), *Così fan tutte* (1789) and *The Magic Flute* (1791), the symphonies *Paris* (1778), *Prague* (1786) and *Jupiter* (1788), and the orchestral piece *Eine Kleine Nachtmusik* (1787).

Mussorgsky, Modest (1839–81), Russian composer: the opera *Boris Godunov* (1868–72) and the piano piece *Pictures at an Exhibition* (1874), later orchestrated by Ravel.

Nielsen, Carl (1865–1931), Danish composer who uses 'progressive tonality': six symphonies including *The Inextinguishable* (No. 4; 1915–16).

Nyman, Michael (1944–), English-born composer who uses simple tunes and chord progressions over an insistent pulse, often with repeated notes and loud dynamics: *The Draughtsman's Contract* (1982), *Out of the Ruins* (1989), *Propero's Books* (1990) and *The Piano* (1992).

Offenbach, Jacques (1819–80), French composer of operetta: the opera *The Tales of Hoffmann* (1881).

Orff, Carl (1895–1982), German composer: the oratorio *Carmina Burana* (1935–37).

Pachelbel, Johann (1653–1706), German composer of canons, airs and 78 choral preludes: *Canon and Gigue* (*c.* 1690).

Paganini, Niccoló (1782–1840), Italian virtuoso violinist and composer of violin concertos and caprices: *Caprice No. 24* (1820).

Palestrina, Giovanni (*c.* 1525–84), Italian composer of over 100 masses and 250 motets: *Missa Papae Marcelli* (1577).

Parry, Hubert (1848–1918), English composer of songs and choral music: *Songs of Farewell* (1916) and *Jerusalem* (1916).

Pärt, Arvo (1935–), Estonian composer: three symphonies and *St John Passion* (1982).

Penderecki, Krzysztof (1933–), Polish composer of works that use sensational effects: *Threnody for the*

Victims of Hiroshima (1960) and the opera *The Devils of Loudon* (1969).

Pérotin (*c*. 1180–1210), French choirmaster of Notre Dame in Paris: *Viderunt Omnes* (1198).

Poulenc, Francis (1899–1963), French composer: the ballet *Les Biches* (1923), four operas, piano pieces, choral works and songs.

Prokofiev, Sergey (1891–1953), Russian composer: the ballet *Romeo and Juliet* (1936), the operas *The Love for Three Oranges* (1919) and *War and Peace* (1941–52), and the piece for orchestra and narrator *Peter and the Wolf* (1936).

Puccini, Giacomo (1858–1924), Italian composer of operas: *La Bohème* (1895), *Tosca* (1899) and *Madama Butterfly* (1901–04).

Purcell, Henry (1659–95), English composer of theatre music, church music, string fantasias and sonatas: the miniature opera *Dido and Aeneas* (1683/84), the incidental music for *The Fairy Queen* (1692) and *Queen Mary's Funeral Music* (1695).

Rakhmaninov, Sergey (1873–1943), Russian composer whose works – notably for piano – are characterized by Romantic nostalgia: *Symphony No. 1 in D Minor* (1897) and *Rhapsody on a Theme of Paganini* (1934).

Rameau, Jean-Philippe (1683–1764), French composer of operas: *Hippolyte et Aricie* (1733) and *Castor et Pollux* (1737).

Ravel, Maurice (1875–1937), French composer: the orchestral pieces *Rapsodie espagnole* (1907), *Pavane pour une infante défunte* (1910), *La Valse* (1919–20), *Boléro* (1928) and the ballet *Daphnis et Chloe* (1912).

Reich, Steve (1936–), US composer and founding father of American minimalism: *Drumming* (1981), *The Cave* (1992) and a series of instrumental *Counterpoints* (1989–93).

Respighi, Ottorino (1879–1936), Italian composer: the ballet *The Fantastic Toyshop* (1919) and the orchestral suites *Fountains of Rome* (1914–16), *Ancient Airs and Dances* (1917–31) and *Pines of Rome* (1924).

Riley, Terry (1935–), US composer of minimalist music of repetition of simple melodies in changing harmonies, built up into large structures.

Rimsky-Korsakov, Nikolay (1844–1908), Russian composer: the operas *The Snow Maiden* (1880–81) and *The Golden Cockerel* (1906–07), and the orchestral piece *Scheherazade* (1888).

Rodrigo, Joaquín (1901–), Spanish composer of music for guitar and orchestra in a traditional Spanish style: *Concierto de Aranjuez* (1939).

Rossini, Gioacchino (1792–1868), Italian composer of 38 operas: *Tancredi* (1812), *The Barber of Seville* (1816), *Cinderella* (1816), *The Thieving Magpie* (1817) and *William Tell* (1829).

Saint-Saëns, Camille (1835–1921), French composer: the opera *Samson et Dalila* (1867–77) and the orchestral pieces *Danse macabre* (1874) and *Carnaval des animaux* (1886).

Salieri, Antonio (1750–1825), Italian composer of over 40 operas: the opera *Tarare* (1787).

Satie, Erik (1866–1925), French composer mainly for piano: the ballet *Parade* (1917), and the piano pieces *Trois Gymnopédies* (1888) and *Trois morceaux en forme de poire* (1903).

Scarlatti, Alessandro (1660–1725), Neapolitan composer of operas (of which 115 survive). One of Scarlatti's important innovations was the three-movement form of the Italian opera overture or sinfonia, regarded by many as being the earliest forerunner of the Classical symphony: the operas *Il Mitridate Eupatore* (1708) and *La principessa fedele* (1710).

Scarlatti, Domenico (1685–1757), Neapolitan composer – son of Alessandro (see above). His *c*. 600 single-movement sonatas for harpsichord considerably extended the technical and musical possibilities of keyboard writing.

Schoenberg, Arnold (1874–1951), Austrian composer whose later works are characterized by atonality, particularly the 12-note system which he devised: the string sextet *Verklarte Nacht* (1899), the orchestral piece for soprano and five instruments *Pierrot Lunaire* (1912) and the opera *Moses und Aron* (1932–51).

Schubert, Franz (1797–1828), Austrian composer of 9 symphonies, string quartets, piano sonatas and 600 Lieder: the symphonies *Unfinished* (No. 8; 1822) and *Great* (No. 9; 1825), the piano quintet *Die Forelle* (*The Trout*; 1819), *String Quartet in C Major* (1828), the piano sonata *Grand Duo* (1824), the song cycles *Die schöne Müllerin* (1823) and *Winterreise* (1827), and the song setting *Erlkönig* (1815).

Schumann, Robert (1810–56), German composer of songs, piano music and symphonies: the song cycles *Dichterliebe* (*Poet's Love*; 1840) and *Frauen-liebe und Leben* (1840).

Schütz, Heinrich (1585–1672), German composer of choral music whose style influenced German composers up until the time of Bach: the opera *Dafne* (1627) and the requiem *Musikalische Exequien* (1636).

Shnittke, Alfred (1934–), Russian composer whose works often include a humorous element: *Requiem* (1975), *Moz-Art* (1980) and *Viola Concerto* (1985).

Shostakovitch, Dmitri (1906–75), Russian composer of 15 symphonies, 15 string quartets and the opera *The Lady Macbeth of the Mtsensk District* (1930–32).

Sibelius, Jean (1865–1957), Finnish composer: seven symphonies, the symphonic poems *Kullervo* (1895) and *Finlandia* (1899), and *Karelia* (1893).

Skryabin, Alexander (1872–1915), Russian composer of symphonies and piano sonatas: the symphony *Prometheus* (No. 5; 1908–10).

Smetana, Bedrich (1824–84), Czech composer of operas, chamber music and symphonic poems: the opera *The Bartered Bride* (1866).

Stamitz, Karl (1745–1801), German composer of the Mannheim School – son of composer Johann Stamitz. He wrote compositions for the viola which, until then, had been mostly used as a support instrument: 70 symphonies, quartets, trios and concertos.

Stanford, Charles Villiers (1852–1924), Irish composer and teacher (Sir Arthur Bliss and Gustav Holst were his pupils): *Irish Symphony* (No. 3; 1887) and *Songs of the Sea* (1904).

Stockhausen, Karlheinz (1928–), German composer: the piece for three orchestras *Gruppen* (1957) and the seven-part opera cycle *Licht* (1984–).

Strauss, Johann the elder (1804–49), Austrian composer of waltz music and *Radetzky March* (1848).

Strauss, Johann the younger (1825–99), Austrian composer: the operetta *Die Fledermaus* (1874), and the waltzes *An der schönen blauen Donau* (*Blue Danube*; 1867) and *Kaiserwalzer* (*Emperor Waltz*; 1888).

Strauss, Richard (1864–1949), German composer of operas and symphonic poems: the operas *Salome* (1905), *Elektra* (1909) and *Der Rosenkavalier* (1911).

Stravinsky, Igor (1882–1971), Russian-born composer who used the neo-classical style from late 1915 until the 1940s when he adopted an avant-garde serial music style. His works provide a 'map' of 20th-century musical development: the ballets *The Firebird* (1910), *Petrushka* (1911) and *The Rite of Spring* (1913).

Sullivan, Sir Arthur (1842–1900), English composer of operetta and oratorios, the former to libretti by W.S. Gilbert: *H.M.S. Pinafore* (1878), *The Pirates of Penzance* (1879) and *The Mikado* (1885).

Tallis, Thomas (*c*. 1505–85), English composer who introduced the European polyphonic tradition to England: masses, two settings of the *Magnificat* and the extraordinary 40-part motet *Spem in Alium*.

Tartini, Giuseppe (1692–1770), Italian violinist and prolific composer: 135 violin concertos and *Devil's Trill sonata* (after 1745).

Taverner, John (1944–), English composer of music with a profound religious spirit: *The Protecting Veil* (1987).

Tchaikovsky, Pyotr Ilyich (1840–93), Russian composer: the symphony *Pathétique* (1893), the opera *Eugène Onegin* (1877–78), and the ballets *Swan Lake* (1875–76), *The Sleeping Beauty* (1888–89) and *Nutcracker* (1891–92).

Telemann, Georg Philipp (1681–1767), German composer of concertos and orchestral suites who, in his lifetime, enjoyed a greater reputation than his friends Bach and Handel: the comic opera *Pimpinone* (1725) and collection of compositions *Musique de Table* (1733).

Tippett, Michael (1905–), English composer: the operas *The Midsummer Marriage* (1952), *The Knot Garden* (1970) and *New Year* (1988).

Torelli, Giuseppe (1658–1709), Italian composer of concertos: *Violin concertos* (1698).

Varèse, Edgard (1883–1965), French-born US composer who made early experiments in electronic music: *Density 21.5 for solo flute* (1936).

Vaughan Williams, Ralph (1872–1958), English composer: *Sea Symphony* (1910), the opera *The Pilgrim's Progress* (1951), songs based upon folk-songs and *Fantasia on a Theme by Thomas Tallis* (1910).

Verdi, Giuseppe (1813–1901), Italian opera composer: *Nabucco* (1842), *Il Trovatore* (1853), *La Traviata* (1853), *Aida* (1871), *Otello* (1887) and *Falstaff* (1893).

Villa-Lobos, Heitor (1887–1959), Brazilian composer: the orchestral works *Bachianas Brasileiras* (1930–44).

Vivaldi, Antonio (1678–1741), Italian priest, violinist and composer: sacred music, sonatas, cantatas, 94 operas (of which 45 survive) and more than 460 concertos, including *The Four Seasons* (1725).

Wagner, Richard (1813–83), German opera composer: *The Flying Dutchman* (1841), *Tannhäuser* (1845), *Lohengrin* (1846–48), *Tristan and Isolde* (1857–59), *The Mastersingers of Nuremberg* (1862–67), *Parsifal* (1878–82) and the opera cycle *The Ring* (*Das Rheingold*, *Die Walküre*, *Siegfried* and *Götterdämmerung*; 1853–74).

Walton,William (1902–83), English composer: *Façade* (1921), the cantata *Belshazzar's Feast* (1931) and the opera *Troilus and Cressida* (1954).

Weber, Carl Maria von (1786–1826), German composer of symphonies, operas, chamber and piano music: the operas *Der Freischütz* (1821) and *Oberon* (1826).

Webern, Anton (1883–1945), Austrian composer whose work is characterized by serialism: *Six Pieces for Orchestra*, *Opus 6* (1909) and *Kinderstück* (1924).

Weelkes, Thomas (*c*. 1576–1623), English organist and composer of madrigals.

Weill, Kurt (1900–50), German composer: *Die Dreigroschenoper* (*The Threepenny Opera*; 1928).

Xenakis, Iannis (1922–), Romanian-born Greek composer of works scored for conventional instruments, but often written with the aid of a computer: *Achorripsis* (1958).

■ SALIERI'S HOSTILITY TO MOZART LED TO GROUNDLESS RUMOURS THAT HE POISONED HIM

MUSICAL FORMS, STRUCTURES AND TERMS

absolute music: music in which no extra-musical (i.e. descriptive) element is intended or should be inferred.
a cappella: vocal work without instrumental accompaniment.
aleatory music: music in which each performance is dictated by chance elements.
anthem: a short sacred vocal work.
aria: a solo sung in opera or oratorio.
arietta: a short aria.
atonal: using all 12 notes of the scale in specific rotation.
aubade or alborda: a morning song.
barcarolle: a piece suggesting the song of a Venetian gondolier.
boléro: a Spanish dance in three-time.
bourrée: an old French dance in 4/4 time.
cadence: a musical phrase used for ending phrases, sections or complete works.
cadenza: a solo virtuoso piece before the final cadence in an aria, or at appropriate places in a concerto.
canon: a work or section in which successive entries of the same melody overlap.
cantata: a vocal work – sacred or secular – for one or more voices with instruments, sometimes short and light, sometimes extensive and dramatic, but always in several movements.
capriccio or caprice: a fanciful work in free style.
cassation: a divertimento-like work, probably intended for performance in the street.
catch: a witty vocal piece for several voices in which the singers 'catch up' each other's words, often making puns with scatalogical or obscene results.
chaconne: a graceful Spanish dance in three-time, its melody varied over a repeated bass phrase. Originally it was always in a major key.
chord: a group of notes played simultaneously.
chromatic scale: a scale including semitones so that all 12 notes within the octave are sounded.
classical: strictly, a musical period *c.* 1750–*c.* 1800; loosely, 'serious' music as opposed to pop, jazz and light.
coda ('tail'): an ending piece designed to close a composition.
concertino: a small concerto; also, the soloists in a concerto grosso.
concerto: a work for one or more solo instruments with orchestra, usually in three movements.
concerto grosso: a Baroque form in which several soloists (the concertino) play against an orchestra.
concertstück ('concert piece'): piece for soloist(s) and orchestra, usually in one movement.
continuo: up to *c.* 1800. A keyboard instrument together with viol/cello. These instruments 'continued' the sound, filling in any missing harmonies not actually written down by the composer.
contrapuntal: using counterpoint.
counterpoint: two or more tunes played simultaneously without violating the rules of harmony.
development: see sonata form.
diatonic: relating to the notes of the given key.
divertimento: a multi-movement work of a diverting nature.
dodecaphony: another term for 12-note music.
dominant: keynote a fifth above the tonic.
duet: a piece for two musicians.
ecossaise: a piece in 'Scottish style'.
electronic music: music consisting entirely of electronically produced sounds.
elegy: a piece of sad or funereal music.
ensemble: a group of musicians, smaller than an orchestra.
étude or study: an exercise.
exposition: see sonata form.
fantasia: a piece whose imaginative course follows no formal rules.
finale: the last movement of a multi-movement work; also, the ending of a movement.
fugato: in fugal style (see fugue).
fugue: a polyphonic composition in which the first statement of a tune is in the tonic; the second statement overlaps the first, and is in the dominant, etc.
gavotte: a lively dance in two-time.
gigue: a jig, a sprightly dance in 6/8 or 12/8 time.
glee: an 18th-century English piece for three or more voices unaccompanied.
harmony: the art of combining notes into chords according to strict rules in a way that is 'pleasing'.
hymn: a song of praise to God.
impromptu: a form originated by Chopin, supposedly extemporized.
incidental music: music for a stage work.
intermezzo ('in the middle'): a piece lying between two sections, whether in a piece of music, a play or an opera, etc.
interval: the distance in pitch between two notes as decided by their position in the diatonic scale.
introduction: a piece which begins a work, often with material unrelated to the main work.
libretto ('little book'): the text of an oratorio or opera (the 'big book' is the musical score).
lied: a type of German Romantic song introduced in the late 18th century.
major: one of the predominant scales of the Western tonal system. Music in major keys often sounds bright.
mass: the Roman Catholic sung service of Communion.
melody: a succession of sounds which achieve a distinct musical shape.
minimalism: modern American style of composition involving much repetition of simple melodies or rhythms, sometimes over slowly changing harmonies.
minor: the other major mode of the diatonic scale. Minor scales have two forms: the harmonic minor scale where the ascending and descending scale is the same, and the melodic minor, where they differ. Music in minor keys is often dark and moody.
minuet: an 18th-century dance in three-time.
modulation: when music changes its tonal centre from one key to another.
motet: a part song, usually sacred in nature and usually unaccompanied.
movement: a division of a musical work. The term derives from the various dance movements of the original suite.
musique concrète: a French invention in which recorded sounds (usually from everyday life) are manipulated on tape into a composition.
nocturne: a night piece.
obligato or obbligato ('obligatory' meaning 'indispensable'): a vocal or instrumental part which plays an important, but not necessarily solo, role.
occasional music: music written for a specific occasion.
operetta: light opera, often with spoken dialogue.
opus ('work'): an individual work or group of works of a composer; each opus is given a number either by the composer or by a subsequent cataloguer. Opus numbers do not always reflect the chronology of composition.
oratorio: the religious equivalent of opera but without scenery, costumes or action.
ornaments: embellishments of a note or phrase, such as a trill (a rapid alternation of a written note with the one above or below), a gracenote or *appogiatura* (a subsidiary note appended to a written note), a mordent (a quick touching of the note above or below during the playing of a written note), etc.
overture: the orchestral introduction to an opera or oratorio. A concert overture has no connection with a staged work.
passacaglia ('passing along the street'): a form akin to the chaconne, but originally always in a minor key.
pentatonic scale: a scale only using five notes (such as the black notes on a piano); often used in folk music.
pitch: the precise height or depth of a note, according to its vibrations (cycles) per second.
polka: a lively dance of Bohemian or Polish origin in three-time.
polonaise: a slow or moderately-paced Polish dance in three-time.
prelude or praeludium: an introductory movement.
programme or descriptive music: music describing a place, event, person, etc. (compare to 'absolute music').
recapitulation: see sonata form.
recitative: a vocal linking passage in an opera or oratorio imitating speech patterns; often declamatory, and less florid than an aria.
register: the compass (lowest to highest notes) of a voice or instrument.
requiem: a mass for the dead.
rhapsody: a multi-sectioned piece akin to the capriccio.
rhythm: the organization of music in respect to time.
ricercare ('research'): a learned piece written in the 16th and 17th centuries to explore obscure avenues of polyphony.
romance: a vocal piece which sets a lyric tale to music; also, an instrumental work or movement in a graceful vein with a more agitated central section.
rondo: a work in which the main section alternates with different sections ('episodes').
saltarello: a quick, exciting Italian dance involving jumping steps.
sarabande: a stately Spanish dance in three-time.
scale: a progression of notes in ascending or descending order, divided into a series of tones and semitones. There are two predominant scales in Western music – major and minor.
scherzo ('joke'): usually a rapid and light-hearted piece.
semitone: half a tone; smallest inverval regularly used in Western music. In equal temperament, there are 12 equal semitones in an octave.
serenade: a work for evening performance.
serial music: music in which a sequence of notes are used equally and in strict rotation; the usual form is 12-note music (see below).
siciliano: a graceful dance in three-time, originating in Sicily.
singspiel: a play with alternating musical pieces.
solo: a work for one musician; in the 18th century, often accompanied.
sonata: a (usually) multi-movement chamber work for one to four instrumentalists.
sonata form: an 18th-century invention in which the first part ('exposition') states the musical material, modulating from tonic to dominant, the second part ('development') develops it (or other material), and the third part ('recapitulation') repeats it, often with modifications in the tonic key. There is sometimes a coda.
song: a sung melody, with or without accompaniment.
suite: a work including several separate sections, or 'movements'; each section was originally a different dance.
symphonic poem or tone poem: a 19th-century orchestral form, descriptive or evocative in character.
symphonie concertante: a showy French invention (often wrongly termed 'sinfonia concertante') in which several soloists play against an orchestra (see the earlier 'concerto grosso').
symphony: a major orchestral work, sometimes with chorus. It is usually of four movements, but there are no strict guidelines.
tempo: the pace at which a work is performed.
time signature: an indication at the start of a piece, or during a piece, of the number and type of note-values in each bar (see p. 219).
toccata: a fantasia-like piece requiring brilliant execution.
tone: the interval of a major second, i.e. C to D, E flat to F, sometimes known as a whole tone. It may be divided into two semitones.
tonic: term relating to the first degree of a minor or major scale.
trio: a piece for three musicians. Larger groupings are equally self-explanatory, i.e. quartet, quintet, sextet, septet, octet, nonet, dectet.
trio sonata: a Baroque and Classical chamber work for two melody instruments and continuo.
twelve-note music: system of musical composition devised by Arnold Schoenberg in which all 12 notes of the scale are used in sequence and in strict rotation. The 12-note melodic line can then be played inverted, backwards and, indeed, inverted and backwards (referred to as 'retrograde inversion').
variations: a work which subjects a theme to a series of variations.

 OTHER INSTRUMENTS

This list includes some instruments that are now relatively uncommon, but which play an important role in a few well-known pieces. Others, such as the hurdy-gurdy, were used to a greater extent in the past.

accordion: Invented in Germany in 1822. It is box-like, with studs and, sometimes, a keyboard for note selection. See also concertina.

bongos: Small single-headed paired drums played with the hands; popular in Latin American music.

concertina: An English invention of 1829, it resembles the accordion (see above), is hexagonal, and never boasts a keyboard.

guitar: A six-stringed development of the lute, possibly Moorish. It became the dominant instrument in Spanish music as early as the 8th century. The earliest surviving printed guitar music dates from 1546 and the first guitar concerto from 1808.

hurdy-gurdy: A European import from the East in the 9th century. Roughly violin-shaped, the strings are activated by a resined wheel turned by a crank, and a keyboard stops the strings. The first 'art' use of the instrument was in 1733.

Jew's harp: A metal frame holding a metal tongue which is plucked with the finger. The resulting vibrations are amplified by the player's mouth cavity. The first Jew's harp concerto was written *c.* 1750. Sophisticated multi-instrument versions came later.

kazoo/mirliton: A membrane-vibrating instrument popular with children. The player hums through the instrument, modifying the voice with a hand over the membrane. It was first made in the USA *c.* 1850 and was probably based on ethnic African models.

keyboards: A generic term for keyboard instruments. The tone is often extensively varied electronically. See also Keyboard, p. 225).

mouth organ/harmonica: Invented in Germany in 1821, yet the first concerto was not written for the instrument until 1951. Different notes are produced according to whether the instrument is blown or sucked; the chromatic version can reach four octaves by the use of a slide.

ocarina (Italian 'little goose'): A goose-egg-shaped wind instrument, originating in Egypt *c.* 3000 BC, originally made of clay, but now made from plastic.

synthesizer: An electronic sound-generator, created *c.* 1950 to imitate natural instruments, although it also creates its own tones. It is now common in popular music and commercialized jazz, where it is often attached to a keyboard.

tom tom: A Western imitation of African drums, used since the 1920s in dance and jazz bands. The first 'art' use of the instrument was in 1943.

ukelele (Hawaiian 'jumping flea'): Developed in Hawaii in the 1870s from the Portuguese machada. It is popular in America, and has been widely used in jazz and light music.

zither: A horizontal stringed instrument associated with central Europe, but different varieties are widespread elsewhere. The strings are plucked.

INSTRUMENTS OF THE CONCERT ORCHESTRA

The standard arrangement of a modern symphony orchestra:

1 1st violins
2 2nd violins
3 violas
4 cellos
5 double basses
6 piccolos
7 flutes
8 oboes
9 cor anglais
10 clarinets
11 bass clarinets
12 bassoons
13 double bassoons
14 harps
15 horns
16 trumpets
17 percussion
18 percussion
19 trombones
20 tubas

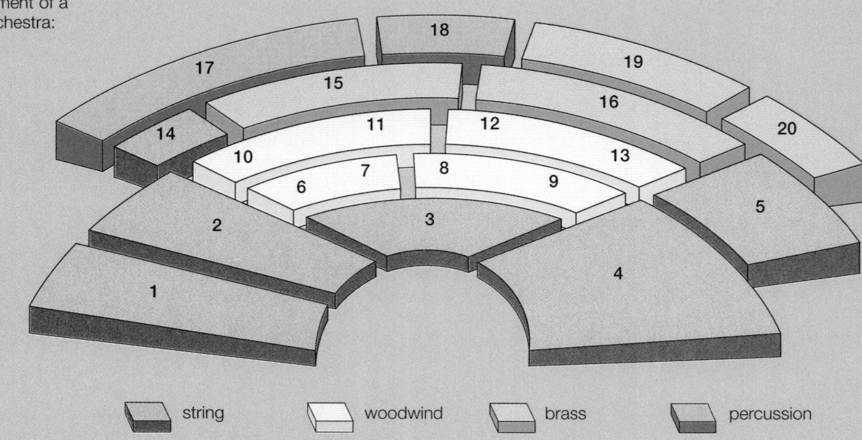

WOODWIND

The following woodwind instruments are arranged in order of octaves. The piccolo, the first listed, lies an octave above the flute.

piccolo or octave flute: *Earliest concerto*: *c.* 1735, by Vivaldi. *Earliest orchestral use*: 1717, Handel's *Water Music*. *History*: The name 'piccolo' (Italian for 'small') dates from 1856, but the instrument goes back to prehistory with the flute and sopranino recorder as its more immediate parents.

flute (transverse or cross-blown): *Earliest concerto*: 1725, A. Scarlatti. *Earliest orchestral use*: 1681, Lully. *History*: Prehistoric (*c.* 18,000 BC); the modern Boehm flute dates from 1832. Flutes are now made of metal, not wood, with a three-octave range.

oboe: *Earliest concerto*: 1708, Marcheselli. *Earliest orchestral use*: 1657, Lully's *L'amour malade*. *History*: The word 'oboe' comes from the French *hautbois*, meaning 'high wood' (1511). It originated in the Middle Ages, invented by the Schalmey family.

cor anglais: *Earliest extant concerto*: 1817, Donizetti. *Earliest orchestral use*: 1722, Volckmar cantata. *History*: Purcell wrote for 'tenor oboe' *c.* 1690; this may have become the English horn. Alternatively, the name may come from 'angled horn', referring to its crooked shape.

clarinet: *Earliest concerto: c.* 1738, Vivaldi (concerto for two clarinets); *c.* 1747, Molter (concerto for one clarinet). *Earliest orchestral use*: 1726, Faber's *Mass*. *History*: The clarinet was developed by J.C. Denner (1655–1707) from the recorder and a variation of the Schalmey family's oboe. It now has a range of three and a half octaves.

bass clarinet: *Earliest orchestral use*: 1838, Meyerbeer's *Les Huguenots*. *History*: The prototype was made in 1772 by Gilles Lot of Paris; the modern Boehm form originated in 1838.

bassoon: *Earliest concerto*: *c.* 1730, Vivaldi. *Earliest orchestral use*: *c.* 1619. *History*: The bassoon was introduced in Italy *c.* 1540 as the lowest of the double-reed group.

double bassoon: *Earliest orchestral use*: *c.* 1730, Handel. *History*: The instrument was 'borrowed' from military bands for elemental effects, particularly in opera.

saxophone: *Earliest concerto*: 1903, Debussy's *Rhapsody*. *Earliest orchestral use*: 1844, Kastner's *Last King of Judah*. *History*: The saxophone was invented by Adolphe Sax, *c.* 1840 (patented 1846).

BRASS

trumpet: *Earliest concerto*: before 1700, Torelli; 1796, Haydn (keyed trumpet). *Earliest orchestral use*: *c.* 1800, keyed; 1835, valved (three), in Halévy's *La Juive*. *History*: The natural trumpet is of prehistoric origin; it formed the basis of the earliest orchestras.

horn: *Earliest concerto*: 1717–21, Bach or Vivaldi (two horns); before 1721, Telemann (one horn). *Earliest orchestral use*: 1639, Cavalli. *History*: The earliest metallic horns were the German helical horns of the mid-16th century; the rotary valve horn was patented in 1832.

trombone: *Earliest concerto*: *c.* 1760, Wagenseil. *Earliest orchestral use*: *c.* 1600, as part of bass-line. *History*: The Roman *buccina* or slide-trumpet developed into the medieval sackbut, which became the modern trombone *c.* 1500.

tuba: *Earliest concerto:* 1954, Vaughan Williams. *Earliest orchestral use*: 1830, Berlioz's *Symphonie Fantastique*. *History*: The tuba was patented by W. Wieprecht and Moritz, in Berlin, in 1835.

PERCUSSION

anvil: *History*: The anvil, originally a blacksmith's tool, has been used for musical effects since 1528.

bass drum: *Earliest Western use*: 1680, Freschi's opera *Berenice vendicativa*. *Earliest orchestral use*: 1725, Finger's *Concerto alla Turchesa*. *History*: It is believed to have originated in the ancient Orient.

bells: *Earliest orchestral use*: *c.* 1730, a funeral cantata by G.M. Hoffman. *History*: Bells have been used since Ancient Egypt *c.* 3500 BC.

castanets: *History*: Castanets were known to the Egyptians by 730 BC. The name comes from the material from which they were made – chestnut wood (*castaña* in Spanish).

Chinese or temple blocks: *Earliest orchestral use*: 1923, Walton's *Façade*. *History*: Originating in the ancient Far East, they were used in temple ceremonials. Chinese blocks entered European music via jazz bands *c.* 1920.

cymbals: *Earliest orchestral use*: 1680, Strungk's *Esther. History*: Cymbals originated in Ottoman Turkish military bands.

gong/tam tam: *Earliest orchestral use*: 1791, Gossec's *Funeral March*. *History*: The gong originated in Indonesia by or before 300 BC.

■ The Chamber Music Trio, *a painting by Robert Tournieres (1667–1743), shows a trio, typical of his time, in rehearsal*

MUSICAL DIRECTIONS

accelerando: becoming faster.

adagietto: the diminutive of adagio, i.e. slightly quicker than adagio.

adagio ('at ease'): a slow, comfortable pace.

allegretto: the diminutive of allegro, i.e. a little slower than allegro.

allegro ('cheerful' or 'sprightly'): lively but not too fast a pace.

andante ('walking pace'): moving along unhurriedly but regularly.

andantino: the diminutive of andante. Originally this meant a little slower but today is taken to mean a little faster than andante.

arpeggio: notes of a chord played upward or downward in quick succession.

crescendo: getting louder.

diminuendo: getting quieter.

forte: loudly.

fortissimo: very loudly.

largo ('spacious'): a broad, slow tempo.

lento: slow.

mezza voce ('middle voice'): a subdued tone, between piano and forte.

mezzo: moderately.

moderato: moderate pace, often used along with allegro, andante, etc., to moderate that pace.

pianissimo: very quietly.

piano: quietly.

pizzicato: plucking the strings of a bowed instrument.

prestissimo: very fast.

presto: fast.

ralentando, ritardando, ritenuto: getting slower.

sotto voce ('under the voice' or 'secretly'): between forte and piano, but nearer the latter.

vibrato: rapid alteration of pitch or intensity of a note intended to impart 'expression'.

vivace: lively. In old music, brightly but not too fast.

marimba: *Earliest orchestral use*: Before 1914, Grainger's *In a Nutshell*. *History*: It developed as an African form of the xylophone (see below).

side (snare) drum: *Earliest orchestral use*: 1749, Handel's *Fireworks Music*. *History*: The small drums of prehistory were the direct ancestor of the medieval tabor, which developed into its modern form in the 18th century.

tambourine: *Earliest orchestral use*: 1820. *History*: The tambourine was used by the Arabs in the Middle Ages, but the prototype of the modern instrument came from either ancient Assyria or Ancient Egypt. The first known usage of the word 'tambourine' was in 1579.

tenor drum: *Earliest orchestral use*: 1842. *History*: The modern tenor drum was originally developed for military use.

timpani/kettle drum: *Earliest concerto*: *c*. 1780, J.C.C. Fischer. *Earliest orchestral use*: In an anonymous intermedia of 1565. *History*: The kettle drum originated in the ancient Orient.

triangle: *Earliest orchestral use*: 1774, Glantz's *Turkish Symphony*, but it was used in opera from about 1680. *History*: The first known use of the triangle was in Ottoman Turkish military bands.

vibraphone: A percussion instrument consisting of a set of metal bars placed over tubular metal resonators, which are caused to vibrate electronically. It is most commonly used in jazz bands. *Earliest orchestral use*: 1932. *History*: The instrument was first used in dance bands in the 1920s.

xylophone: *Earliest orchestral use*: 1852, Kastner's *Livre-Partition*. *History*: The xylophone dates back to ancient times, probably originating in Africa, and is hit with two sticks. The earliest known use in Western music was in 1511. The orchestral xylophone has a range of three octaves.

STRING

violin: *Earliest concerto*: 1698, Torelli. *Earliest orchestral use*: *c*. 1600. *History*: The violin family is descended from the lyre, although its more direct ancestors were the 6th-century Celtic crwth, French rebec and fiddle. The first modern instruments, of Lombardic (north Italian) origin, appeared *c*. 1545. The words 'violin' and 'fiddle' both derive ultimately from the Latin *vitulari* (meaning 'to skip like a calf').

viola: *Earliest concerto*: before 1721, Telemann. *Earliest orchestral use*: *c*. 1600. *History*: See the violin, above. It has a range of over four octaves.

violoncello or cello: *Earliest concerto*: 1701, Jacchini. *Earliest orchestral use*: *c*. 1600. *History*: See the violin, above. It has a range of over four octaves.

double bass: *Earliest existing concerto*: *c*. 1765, Vanhal. *Earliest orchestral use*: *c*. 1600. *History*: The modern double bass developed alongside the violin family, but is a closer relative to the bass viol or violone. It is also often used in jazz.

harp: *Earliest concerto*: 1738, Handel. *Earliest orchestral use*: *c*. 1600. *History*: The harp is possibly prehistoric in origin, but it did not attain its modern form until 1792.

KEYBOARD

celesta: Instead of strings, as in the piano (see below), the celesta's hammers strike metal plates to give a bell-like effect. See also glockenspiel (below). *Earliest orchestral use*: 1880, Widor's ballet *Der Korrigane*. *History*: Invented by Mustel, in Paris, in 1880.

clavichord: metal tangents (blades) strike upward to activate the string part-way along its length and to 'stop' (damp) the rest. Therefore, one string may serve for many notes but not simultaneously. Its exceedingly intimate voice makes it ideal for domestic use. *History*: an instrument which dates from the Middle Ages, but is little heard today.

glockenspiel (German 'bell-play'): an instrument related to the celesta (see above). The glockenspiel is sometimes equipped with a keyboard but more usually the plates are struck by hand-held hammers.

harmonium: *Earliest orchestral use*: 1858, César Franck. *History*: A portable reed-organ invented by Grenié in Paris, *c*. 1835. In modern times it is not a common instrument, and it is now most usually heard as accompaniment for hymns in church.

harpsichord: The harpsichord usually has two manuals which control sets of strings that are plucked by plectra. Mainly a domestic instrument, the harpsichord also supported the bass line in early orchestras. *Earliest concerto*: *c*. 1720. *History*: A keyboard instrument which evolved from the psaltery during the 14th century – the earliest surviving example is dated 1521. By *c*. 1800 the instrument had been eclipsed by the piano (pianoforte; see below). Since about 1903, the harpsichord has been reintroduced and has recently regained popularity with the revival of interest in ancient music. Modern composers have begun to write concertos for the instrument, particularly Górecki, and Horovitz's *Concerto for the Jazz Harpsichord*.

organ: *Earliest concerto*: *c*. 1730, Handel. *History*: A keyboard instrument which ultimately derives from the antique panpipes, but subsequent developments have made it the biggest and most powerful of all instruments. Saint-Saëns first used it in his *Organ Symphony* (1886) and Vaughan Williams used it to great effect in *Sinfonia Antarctica* (1953).

pianoforte or piano: *Earliest concerto*: 1763, J.B. Schmidt. *History*: The first piano was built by Bartolomeo Cristofori in Florence shortly before 1700, working on the dulcimer principle of hammers hitting strings, and seeking a keyboard instrument which, unlike the harpsichord (see above), could play both loud and soft (hence, its early name, 'fortepiano'). Cristofori announced his perfected model in 1709 and examples exist from the 1720s. These early pianos display most of the principles of the modern piano, although three centuries of improvements to the instrument have refined the instrument enormously. The earliest known printed music for the piano was by Giustini (1732). The instrument attained its current name about 1776 and its modern iron-framed form about 1850. The upright 'parlour piano' is usually considered to be typical of the Victorian age, but the first were made in Germany during the 1770s. The composer and pianist Muzio Clementi developed the techniques of the early piano to such a degree that he is often referred to as 'the father of the piano'. He developed both the techniques of piano playing and the instrument itself. It is now the most widely used modern keyboard instrument.

spinet: *History*: A keyboard instrument that developed early in the 15th century which is the same shape as a harpsichord (see above), but smaller. The name may come from the Latin *spina* ('spines' or 'quills' – the plucking agent).

virginals: A table harpsichord (see above), rectangular in shape. *History*: The first printed music in England for the instrument was *Parthenia*, published in London in 1611.

OPERA

▶ **The word 'opera' is short for *opera in musica* (Italian for 'musical work').**
▶ **The oldest surviving opera is Jacopo Peri's *Euridice,* written in Florence, Italy, in 1600.**

In the 17th century, opera was a narrative entertainment given by costumed singers with instrumental accompaniment. Although originating in Italy (the first public opera house opened in Venice in 1607), opera soon spread to other European countries.

The earliest operas were an attempt to recreate Ancient Greek theatre. Later, they developed into dramas with a series of songs or vocal set pieces (arias), at first linked by melodic ariosos, later by recitative, with rhythms closer to speech. As opera evolved, it became increasingly naturalistic and the music more continuous, mirroring developments in other fields of music.

■ *A scene from Wagner's* The Valkyrie *in* The Ring *cycle shows the lavish stage effects that were vital to his operas*

POPULAR OPERAS

Where translations are not normally used, operas are alphabetized under their foreign-language titles. The name of the opera is followed by the composer's name and the name of the librettist (lyricist) in brackets.

***Aida*, Verdi** (libretto – Ghislanzoni), 1871: An Egyptian general loves Aida, an enslaved Ethiopian princess, not the Pharaoh's daughter who loves him. He betrays his country and is sentenced to being entombed alive, where Aida joins him.

***La Bohème* (*Bohemian Life*), Puccini** (libretto – Giacosa and Illica after Murger), 1896: The poet Rodolfo loves tubercular Mimi in a story of impoverished Parisian artists.

***Boris Godunov*, Mussorgsky** (own libretto after Pushkin), 1874: The suffering of the Russian people under Tsar Boris.

***Carmen*, Bizet** (libretto – Melhac and Halevy after Mérimée), 1875: In Seville, soldier José falls passionately for gypsy Carmen, who drops him for bullfighter Escamillo, so he kills her. Now so popular, it was a failure when first staged in Paris.

***Cavalleria Rusticana* (*Rustic Chivalry*) Mascagni** (libretto – Targioni-Tozetti and Menasci), 1890: A Sicilian returning to his village finds his sweetheart married. He becomes engaged to another girl but clandestinely renews his old affair and is challenged and killed by the husband.

***Cosi fan Tutti* (*All Women Are the Same*), Mozart** (libretto – da Ponte), 1790: Two young men bet their fiancées will be faithful while they are away and return in disguise to test them, losing their wager.

***Don Giovanni*, Mozart** (libretto – da Ponte), 1787: The sexual adventures of Spanish seducer Don Juan who, when the statue of a nobleman he has killed comes to life, is eventually dragged down to Hell.

***Eugene Onegin* (*Evegny Onyegin*), Tchaikovsky** (libretto with Shilovsky after Pushkin), 1879: Tatiana is unrequitedly in love with guest Onegin, who kills her brother-in-law in a duel. Years later Onegin returns from abroad and their roles are reversed.

***Falstaff*, Verdi** (libretto – Boito after Shakespeare), 1893: Falstaff gets his come-uppance after simultaneously wooing two women, with a young lovers' subplot. This is Verdi's only real comedy.

***Faust*, Gounod** (libretto – Barbier and Carre after Goethe), 1859: An aging scholar promises his soul to the Devil for renewed youth and sensual pleasure, though it concentrates on the story of Maguerite whom he seduces.

***Fidelio*, Beethoven** (libretto – Sonnleithner after Bouilly), 1805: Leonora disguises herself as a youth (Fidelio) to seek and save her imprisoned husband. This is Beethoven's only opera.

***The Flying Dutchman* (*Der fliegende Hollander*), Wagner** (own libretto after Heine), 1843: A sailor condemned to sail the sea for ever until redeemed by a woman's love, which he finally finds.

***Madam Butterfly*, Puccini** (libretto – Illica and Giocasa after Belasco), 1904: A US naval lieutenant buys a geisha in mock marriage. He returns three years later with an American wife, demanding his son by the geisha, who then kills herself. It is based on a real incident.

***The Magic Flute* (*Die Zauberflote*), Mozart** (libretto – Schikaneder), 1791: A pantomime-like quest for truth and to rescue Pamino, mixing masonic symbolism with slapstick humour.

***Manon Lescaut*, Puccini** (libretto – Leoncavallo and others after Prevost), 1893: A tale of a woman who elopes with a lover, lives in luxury as a kept mistress, is deported to America and dies. Jules Massenet and Daniel Auber both wrote operas based on this story.

***The Marriage of Figaro* (*Le nozze de Figaro*), Mozart** (libretto – da Ponte after Beaumarchais), 1786: A Count neglects his wife, but is thwarted in his plans to sleep with her maid, about to marry his valet Figaro. Frothy with subplots – including young Cherubino who is enamoured of the Countess – it is a comic masterpiece.

***The Midsummer Marriage*, Tippett** (own libretto), 1955: Self-searching and symbolic tests of a young modern couple about to be married, echoing ancient rituals and drawing on classical and Hindu sources. This is the most easily accessible of Tippett's operas.

***Norma*, Bellini** (libretto – Romani), 1831: A Druid high priestess in ancient Gaul breaks her chastity vow and she and her unfaithful lover, who tries to abduct a junior priestess, are burned alive in a funeral pyre.

***Otello*, Verdi** (libretto – Boito after Shakespeare), 1887: A black general, roused to jealousy by the lies of his ensign Iago, kills his innocent Venetian wife. Rossini also used the subject for an opera, but it is not in the same class.

***I Pagliacci* (*Clowns*), Leoncavallo** (own libretto), 1892: Classic broken-hearted clown story ending in bloodshed. It is often performed as a double bill with *Cavalleria Rusticana*.

***Peter Grimes*, Britten** (libretto – Slater after Crabbe), 1945: A Suffolk fisherman first loses one boy apprentice at sea, then is responsible for the accidental death of another. Outcast by the townsfolk, he sinks his boat and drowns. Its atmospheric 'Sea Interludes' are often performed as a concert piece.

***The Rake's Progress*, Stravinsky** (libretto – Auden and Kallman), 1951: Moral but often comic tale (inspired by Hogarth's painting) of a young man's fall, squandering his inheritance to end up in a madhouse. Scored and structured like an 18th-century opera, it has a very modern vocal line.

***Rigoletto*, Verdi** (libretto – Piave after Hugo), 1851: Hunchback jester who plans to kill seducer duke discovers he has killed his own daughter instead.

***The Ring* (*Der Ring des Nibelungen*), Wagner** (own libretto): Four-part cycle of operas recounting Teutonic legends of gods as their power declines in favour of mortals – *Rhine Gold* (*Das Rheingold*) – 1869, *The Valkyrie* (*Die Walkure*) – 1870, *Siegfried* – 1876 and *Twilight of the Gods* (*Gotterdammerung*) – 1876. Wagner uses musical phrases or 'leitmotifs' to represent individuals and ideas and to suggest influences on and changes in the characters.

***Der Rosenkavalier* (*The Rose Cavalier*), R. Strauss** (libretto – Hofmannsthal), 1911: An aging beauty relinquishes her youthful lover and ensures his happy marriage. This is the most lushly romantic of Strauss's operas.

***La Traviata* (*The Lady of the Camellias*), Verdi** (libretto – Piave after Dumas), 1853: Parisian courtesan finds true love, but gives him up at the insistence of his father. But as she lies dying from tuberculosis, they are ecstatically reunited.

***The Turn of the Screw*, Britten** (libretto – Piper after James), 1954: A chilling ghost story of child corruption. Six voices and a small ensemble are used to staggering effect, with each of its 16 scenes written as a variation on the same musical theme.

***Turandot*, Puccini** (libretto – Adamai and Simoni after Gozzi), 1926: Suitors for a Chinese princess must solve three riddles or be beheaded. Prince Calaf succeeds but still offers to die if she can discover his name before dawn. It includes the aria 'Nessun Dorma', so popular with football crowds.

■ DOMINGO RECEIVED THE LONGEST OVATION FOR AN OPERA SINGER AT THE STAATSOPER IN

MUSICALS

▶ **The US show *The Brook* (1879) was probably the first to be called a musical comedy.**
▶ **The musical developed from the operetta and musical comedies of the late 19th and early 20th centuries.**

The first musicals tended to be romantic and light-hearted, with the songs a series of 'numbers', but the modern musical tends towards a much greater integration of music, song and dance, all of which help the story to unfold.

The genre of the musical was established with George Edwardes' *A Gaiety Girl* in London in 1893. *Showboat*, which opened in New York in 1927, marked an important stage in combining the book (or play) with the other elements, a trend consolidated in *Oklahoma!* and later Broadway musicals of the 1940s. *Shuffle Along* (1921) set the precedent for black musicals on Broadway and introduced jazz. In 1935, Gershwin had a hit with the black blues-oriented *Porgy and Bess*. The 1960s introduced the rock musical, such as *Hair* (1968) and, by the 1970s, it was firmly established with such hits as *Jesus Christ Superstar* and *The Rocky Horror Show* (1973). It is still thriving today with the success of The Who's *Tommy,* which was written in 1969, staged for a few months in 1979, and returned to Broadway in 1993.

Recent years have been dominated by the through-composed musical. Stephen Sondheim has stretched the genre, both musically and in content, with ascerbic and challenging material. His shows have been more of a cult success, compared with the extremely popular Andrew Lloyd Webber shows – with their lush sound and elaborate production – which enjoy long runs in many countries. The emphasis on spectacular 'production values' has made long runs essential in order to recoup costs, and a return to simpler staging has been forecast. To reflect the sound-mixes to which the modern audience is accustomed to on recordings, most shows use microphones and sound engineers to achieve a similar balance, making fewer demands on singers' voices than in the past.

POPULAR MUSICALS

Annie Get Your Gun (1946; music, lyrics – Irving Berlin; book – Herbert and Dorothy Fields): Sharp-shooter Annie Oakley's romance with Frank Butler in Buffalo Bill's Wild West Show. Full of hits, from 'Doin' What Comes Natur'lly' to 'There's No Business Like Show Business'.

Cabaret (1966; music – John Kander; lyrics – Fred Ebb; book – Joe Masterson, from John van Druten's play *I Am a Camera*, based on Christopher Isherwood's *Berlin Stories,* written during the rise of fascism in 1930s Berlin): The story of Sally Bowles, a Berlin cabaret singer and dancer, framed in the cabaret setting in which she works. Hits include the title song and 'Willkomen' ('Money, Money, Money' was written for the movie).

Carousel (1945; music – Richard Rodgers; lyrics, book – Oscar Hammerstein II, from Ferenc Molnar's play *Liliom*): Fairground barker is involved in a robbery and dies, leaving an unborn child. He is given the chance to redeem himself by returning unseen to help his daughter reach adulthood. Hits include 'You'll Never Walk Alone'.

Cats (1981; music – Andrew Lloyd Webber; lyrics, book – based on T.S. Eliot's *Old Possum's Book of Practical Cats*, but lyrics of the hit song 'Memory' were partly by the show's director Trevor Nunn): Cats in a rubbish dump compete for an extra life.

A Chorus Line (1975; music – Martin Hamlisch; lyrics – Edward Kleban; book – James Kirkwood and Nicholas Dante): Structured as an audition for dancers which investigates their individual stories.

The Fantasticks (1960; music – Harvey Schmidt; lyrics, book – Tom Jones, after a play by Edmond Rostand): A tale of young lovers whose fathers try to keep them apart until they learn the harsh realities of life. 'Try to Remember' became a hit song.

Fiddler on the Roof (1964; music – Jerry Bock; lyrics – Sheldon Harnick; book – Joseph Stein, based on stories of Sholom Aleichem): The political and domestic traumas of traditional Jewish villagers.

42nd Street (1933; music, lyrics – Harry Warren and Al Dubin; book – James Seymour and Rian James, after the novel by Bradford Ropes): A chorus girl gets a chance to become a star.

A Funny Thing Happened on the Way to the Forum (1962; music, lyrics – Stephen Sondheim; book – Burt Shevelove and Larry Gelbart, based on plays by Plautus): Hysterical carryings-on in Ancient Rome.

Grease (1972; music, lyrics, book – Jim Jacobs and Warren Casey): 1950s high-school teenagers.

Guys and Dolls (1950; music, lyrics – Frank Loesser; book – Abe Burrows and Jo Swerling, based on stories by Damon Runyon): The 'oldest established permanent floating crap game in New York' meets the holy-rollers. Hits include 'Luck Be a Lady' and 'Sit Down You're Rocking the Boat'.

Hello, Dolly! (1964; music, lyrics – Jerry Herman; book – Michael Stewart, based on Thornton Wilder's play *The Matchmaker*): A widow sets her sights on a man she has been employed to find a wife for, with a shop-clerk romance subplot.

Jesus Christ Superstar (1971; music – Andrew Lloyd Webber; lyrics – Tim Rice): Described as a 'rock opera', it is a sung-through cantata covering Christ's final days, seen through the eyes of his disciple Judas. The title song and 'I Don't Know How to Love Him' are among its hits.

Kiss Me, Kate (1948; music, lyrics – Cole Porter; book – Sam and Bella Spewack): Ex-husband and wife star in the play *The Taming of the Shrew*, feuding backstage and onstage. 'Brush Up Your Shakespeare' and 'Too Darn Hot' are among its many hit numbers.

A Little Night Music (1973; music, lyrics – Stephen Sondheim; book – Hugh Wheeler, suggested by Ingmar Bergman's movie *Smiles of a Summer Night*): An aging actress re-encounters a now married former lover, their failure in love lamented in the hit 'Send in the Clowns'.

Les Misérables (1980; music – Claude-Michel Schönberg; lyrics – Alain Boublil and Jean-Marc Natel; book – Boublil and Schönberg, from Victor Hugo's novel): A story about a good man pursued by the law and the struggles of the poor. Its success came in a greatly expanded English version by James Fenton and Herbert Kretzmer which used more of the story and added new songs.

Miss Saigon (1989; music – Claude-Michel Schönberg; lyrics – Alain Boublil and Richard Maltby Jnr; book – Boublil): The Madame Butterfly story is transferred to 1970s Vietnam.

My Fair Lady (1956; music – Frederick Loewe; lyrics, book – Alan Jay Lerner, adapted from G.B. Shaw's novel *Pygmalion*): The tale of a flower girl taught to speak 'proper'. Hits include 'Wouldn't It Be Loverly', 'I Could Have Danced All Night', 'Get Me to the Church on Time' and 'On the Street Where You Live'.

Oklahoma! (1943; music – Richard Rodgers; lyrics, book – Oscar Hammerstein II, based on Lynn Rigg's play *Green Grow the Lilacs*): Country romance and a killing. Hits include the title song, 'Oh What a Beautiful Morning' and 'People Will Say We're in Love'.

Oliver! (1960; music, lyrics, book – Lionel Bart, adapted from Charles Dickens' novel *Oliver Twist*): The heart-rending tale of an orphan who, after many mishaps, finally finds a home. Hits include 'Where is Love?', 'As Long As He Needs Me' and 'Who Will Buy?'.

Phantom of the Opera (1986; music – Andrew Lloyd Webber; lyrics – Charles Hart; book – Lloyd Webber and Richard Stilgoe from the novel by Gaston Leroux): Disfigured musical genius living in the bowels of the Opera turns a chorister into a star, but jealous of her love for her leading man, carries her off to his underground home. Hits include the title song and 'Music of the Night'.

Showboat (1927; music – Jerome Kern; lyrics, book – Oscar Hammerstein II from Edna Ferber's novel): The lives of performers on a Mississippi showboat, highlighting the stories of a handsome gambler and the ruinous effect of racist laws on a mixed-race actress. Hits include 'Ol' Man River' and 'Can't Help Lovin' that Man'.

The Sound of Music (1959; music – Richard Rodgers; lyrics – Oscar Hammerstein II; book – Howard Lindsay and Russel Crouse): Governess wins the heart of her employer and escapes the Nazis by leading her singing step-children across the Alps. Hits include the title song 'Climb Every Mountain', 'Eidelweiss' and 'My Favourite Things'.

South Pacific (1949; music – Richard Rodgers; lyrics – Oscar Hammerstein II; book – Hammerstein and Joshua Logan from James Michener's *Tales of the South Pacific*): Follows the romances between a US Navy nurse and a French planter, and an island girl and a US officer later killed in a Japanese attack. 'Bali Ha'i', 'Happy Talk', 'Some Enchanted Evening', 'I'm Gonna Wash That Man Right Out of My Hair' and 'Younger Than Springtime' are just some of its hits.

Sunset Boulevard (1993; music – Andrew Lloyd Webber; book and lyrics – Don Black and Christopher Hampton, after Billy Wilder's classic movie): An aging silent movie queen, hoping for a come-back, engages the help of a penniless writer.

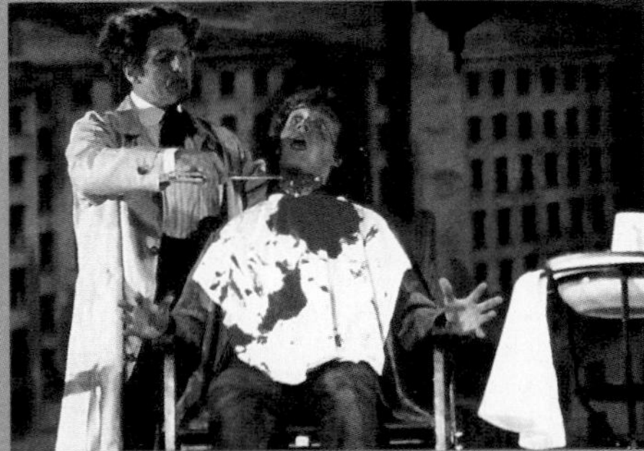

■ *The avenging barber in Sondheim's* Sweeney Todd

Sweeney Todd (1979; music, lyrics – Stephen Sondheim; book – Hugh Wheeler, based on Chris Bond's play): A thriller in which the 'demon-barber' of Fleet Street revenges his family by cutting his customers' throats before turning them into pies.

West Side Story (1957; music – Leonard Bernstein; lyrics – Stephen Sondheim; book – Arthur Laurents): Romeo and Juliet told in terms of rival New York street gangs. Hits include 'Tonight' and 'America'.

OPERA SINGERS

Allen, Thomas (1944–), Welsh baritone noted for *Eugene Onegin, Don Giovanni* and *Billy Budd* (Britten).

Baker, Janet, Dame (1933–), English mezzo-soprano noted for *Mary Stuart* (Donizetti), *Orfeo* (Gluck) and *Dido* (Purcell).

Caballé, Monserrat (Folch) (1933–), Spanish soprano notable in Donizetti and Bellini operas.

Callas, Maria (Kalogeropoulos, Cecilia Sophia Anna Maria; 1923–77), US Greek-based soprano, expressive actress and magnificent Tosca, Violetta in *La Traviata* and Norma.

Carreras, José (Josep Maria; 1946–), Spanish tenor and fine Rodolfo in *La Bohème* and José in *Carmen.*

Caruso, Enrico (1873–1921), Italian tenor, often considered the greatest ever, who sang the entire opera repertory of his time and is particularly associated with Canio in *I Pagliacci*.

De Los Angeles, Victoria (Gomez Cima; 1923–), Spanish soprano and a fine Madame Butterfly and Mimi in *La Bohème*.

Domingo, Plácido (1941–), Spanish tenor, a great José in *Carmen* and as Othello, and currently the leading dramatic tenor.

Fischer-Dieskau, (Albert) Dietrich (1925–), German baritone excellent in both traditional and modern repertoire.

Flagstad, Kirsten (Malfrid; 1895–1962), Norwegian soprano especially suited to Wagner and a famous Isolde in *Tristan and Isolde*.

Gigli, Beniamino (1890–1957), Italian tenor who was one of the greatest, his beautiful voice outweighing his lack of acting talent.

Horne, Marilyn (Bernice; 1934–), US mezzo-soprano and a favourite in the Rossini roles she loves.

Jones, Gwyneth, Dame (1936–), Welsh soprano best known for her Wagner roles and a fine Marschalin in *Der Rosenkavalier*.

Lehmann, Lotte (1888–1976), German soprano especially famed for her Marschalin in *Der Rosenkavalier*.

Lind, Jenny (Johanna Maria; 1820–87), Swedish soprano – the 'Swedish Nightingale' – for her sweet voice.

Melba, Nellie (Mitchell, Helen Porter, Dame; 1859–1931), Australian soprano and truly great singer of extraordinary range. She sang superbly until well over 60 and is the only opera singer to have had a dessert named after her.

Monaco, Mario del (1915–82), Italian tenor best known for his Othello (he was buried in the costume).

Nilsson, Birgit (Svennson, Märta Birgit; 1918–), Swedish soprano known for her roles in Wagner, Strauss and *Turandot*.

Norman, Jessye (1945–), US soprano suited to strong roles, but also encompassing the humour of *Ariadne on Naxos* (Strauss).

Pavarotti, Luciano (1935–), Italian tenor, 'King of the High Cs' and the most popular contemporary opera singer, famous for his purity of tone.

Pears, Peter (Neville Luard), Sir (1910–86), English tenor and creator of leading roles in Britten's operas.

Popp, Lucia (1939–93), Czech-born Austrian soprano admired as the Countess in *The Marriage of Figaro*.

Price, Leontyne (Mary Violet; 1927–), US soprano and first international black diva who is superb in Verdi (especially as Aida), Mozart and modern repertory.

Schwarzkopf, (Olga Maria) Elisabeth (Frederike; 1927–), German soprano great as the Countess in *The Marriage of Figaro* and Marschalin in *Der Rosenkavalier*.

Soderstrom, Elisabeth (Soderstrom-Olow, Anne Elizabeth; 1927–), Swedish soprano and a great Marschalin in *Der Rosenkavalier*.

Sutherland, Joan, Dame (1926–), Australian soprano notable as Lucia di Lammermoor (Donizetti) and other *bel canto* (Italian for 'beautiful singing') roles and in Handel's operas.

Te Kanawa, Kiri, Dame (1944–), New Zealand soprano whose Desdemona in *Otello* and the Countess in *The Marriage of Figaro* brought her fame.

Vickers, Jon (Jonathan Stewart; 1926–), Canadian tenor whose greatest roles were Othello, Peter Grimes and Tristan in *Tristan and Isolde* (Wagner).

MUSICAL COMPOSERS

Bart, Lionel (Begleiter, Lionel; English 1930–): *Lock Up Your Daughters!* (1959), *Oliver* (1960), *Blitz* (1962).

Bernstein, Leonard (US, 1918–90): *On The Town* (1944), *Wonderful Town* (1953), *Candide* (1956), *West Side Story* (1957).

Bock, Jerry (US, 1928–): *Mr Wonderful* (1956), *Fiddler on the Roof* (1964), *The Rothschilds* (1970).

Coleman, Cy (Kaufman, Seymour; US, 1929–): *Sweet Charity* (1966), *Barnum* (1980), *City of Angels* (1989).

Coward, Noel (Peirce), Sir (English, 1899–1973): Multi-talented composer, dramatist, director and actor: *Bitter Sweet* (1929), *Conversation Piece* (1934), *Ace of Clubs* (1950), *Sail Away* (1961).

Gershwin, George (US, 1898–1937): *Oh Kay!* (1926), *Funny Face* (1927), *Strike Up the Band* (1930), *Girl Crazy* (1930), *Porgy and Bess* (1935), *Crazy For You* (1992).

Hamlisch, Marvin (US, 1944–): *A Chorus Line* (1975), *They're Playing Our Song* (1979), *Smile* (1986), *The Goodbye Girl* (1993).

Herman, Jerry (US, 1933–): *Hello Dolly!* (1964), *Mame* (1966), *La Cage aux Folles* (1983).

Kander, John (US, 1927–): *From A to Z* (with Jerry Herman, 1960); then with Fred Ebb: *Cabaret* (1966), *The Happy Time* (1968), *Chicago* (1975), *Kiss of the Spider Woman* (1992).

Kern, Jerome David (US, 1885–1945): Prolific showtune writer who also wrote over 40 musicals, although *Showboat* (1927) is the only one which is regularly revived. Others include *The Girl from Utah* (1914), *Oh Boy!* (1917), *Oh Lady! Lady!!* (1918), *Sally* (1920), *Sunny* (1925), *The Cat and the Fiddle* (1931), *Music in the Air* (1932).

Lloyd Webber, Andrew, Sir (English, 1948–): *Joseph and the Amazing Technicolor Dreamcoat*, *Jesus Christ Superstar* (1971), *Evita* (1978), *Cats* (1981), *Starlight Express* (1984), *The Phantom of the Opera* (1986), *Aspects of Love* (1989), *Sunset Boulevard* (1993).

Loesser, Frank (US, 1910–69): Also wrote the lyrics for many of his shows, such as *Guys and Dolls* (1950), *The Most Happy Fella* (1956), *Greenwillow* (1960), *How to Succeed in Business Without Really Trying* (1961).

Loewe, Frederick (Austrian-born US, 1904–88): *Brigadoon* (1947), *Paint Your Wagon* (1951), *My Fair Lady* (1956), *Camelot* (1960), *Gigi* (1973).

Porter, Cole (Albert) (US, 1891–1964): Composer and lyricist of many perennial numbers and 22 shows, including *Anything Goes* (1934), *Kiss Me, Kate* (1948), *Can Can* (1953).

Rodgers, Richard (Charles) (US, 1902–79): 40 musicals, with lyricist Lorenz Hart until 1942, then with Oscar Hammerstein II, including *The Girl Friend* (1926), *Pal Joey* (1940), *Oklahoma!* (1943), *Carousel* (1945), *South Pacific* (1949), *The King and I* (1953), *The Sound of Music* (1959).

Schönberg, Claude-Michel (French, 1944–): *Les Misérables* (1980, revised English version 1985), *Miss Saigon* (1989), *Martin Guerre* (1996).

Sondheim, Stephen (Joshua; US, 1930–): Composer who writes his own lyrics and also wrote lyrics to *West Side Story* and *Gypsy*. Musicals include *A Funny Thing Happened on the Way to the Forum* (1962), *Anyone Can Whistle* (1964), *Follies* (1971), *A Little Night Music* (1973), *Sweeney Todd* (1979), *Into the Woods* (1987), *Assassins* (1991), *Passion* (1996).

Weill, Kurt (German, 1900–50): *The Threepenny Opera* (1928), *Lady in the Dark* (1941), *Street Scene* (1947), *Lost in the Stars* (1949).

JAZZ

▶ Jazz is a music of Afro-American origin characterized by syncopated rhythms (with an emphasis on the unexpected beat), solo and group improvisation, and a variety of instrumental techniques and harmonic idioms.
▶ A major jazz watershed occurred in 1945, at the end of World War II, when 'traditional' jazz, with its simple melodies, gave way to 'modern' jazz, with its complexity, tension, abrasiveness and virtuosity.

Jazz developed at the end of the 19th century with roots in the work songs, spirituals and laments of black slaves in the southern USA, especially in the bars, brothels and street parades of New Orleans.

One of the earliest forms of jazz was syncopated ragtime, especially on solo piano, and the sung blues influenced a particular twelve-bar structure for improvisation. With the movement of blacks to the northern states, jazz spread to Chicago and New York and then abroad.

The first jazz recordings were made in 1917 by the all-white *Original Dixieland Jazz Band* from New Orleans, who made a sensation in New York and in Europe, followed by *King Oliver's Creole Jass Band* in 1923. New styles such as 'Boogie-Woogie' emerged in the 1920s. Improvisation developed on the harmonic sequence of tunes rather than just on simple melodies and, by the 1940s, the original melody was left unstated in some performances and merely implied by its underlying harmonics.

Bands, black or white, tended to become larger. In the years prior to World War II, big bands, largely of white musicians, played a commercialized jazz called 'Swing', which became the most popular dance music on both sides of the Atlantic. In the 1940s a new style developed called 'bebop', followed by 'modern' jazz in the fifties, with the 'West Coast' (predominantly white musicians) and 'cool' jazz styles following the succeeding decades. 'Hard bop', a more soulful style of jazz, later developed as a reaction to the 'cool' jazz style. Modern jazz gains much of its intensity of expression from the contrast between a steady beat and a convoluted solo line.

Old New Orleans bands usually consisted of cornet or trumpet, trombone, clarinet, piano, double bass and drums. The saxophone was a latter addition. Although playing styles and size of bands have varied enormously, most jazz musicians still play one or more of these instruments, sometimes with the addition of the xylophone or violin.

■ THE LONGEST RUNNING MUSICAL IS *THE FANTASTICKS* – IT OPENED OFF-BROADWAY IN NYC IN

TOP JAZZ MUSICIANS

Armstrong, Louis 'Satchmo' (1901–71), US trumpeter, bandleader and gravelly-voiced singer who pioneered the trumpet solo, and whose 'Swing' style and talent at improvisation set a model for all.

Basie, Count (William; 1904–84), US pianist and bandleader, directing from the keyboard; famous for his bluesy jazz piano playing and 'big band' style.

Beiderbecke, Bix (Leon; 1903–31), US pianist, cornetist with a bell-like tone and composer of impressionistic piano pieces including 'In a Mist'.

Blakey, Art (1919–90), US 'hard bop' drummer and bandleader of the *Jazz Messengers*, serving as a vital talent scout for other jazz musicians.

Brubeck, Dave (1920–), US pianist and composer, influenced by classical music, who was one of the first jazz musicians to have a top 10 hit with his quartet's recording of 'Take Five' (1959), which was written by their saxophonist Paul Desmond.

Carmichael, Hoagy (Hoagland Howard; 1899–1981), US songwriter, singer, pianist and bandleader whose popular songs included 'Stardust'.

Charles, Ray (Robinson, Ray Charles; 1930–), US singer and pianist, blind since the age of seven, whose vocal style mixes gospel, jazz and blues.

Cole, Nat 'King' (Coles, Nathaniel Adam; 1919–65), US singer and pianist who was the first major black performer to have his own TV variety series. His trio format of piano, guitar and bass was much copied and his formidable and original piano style influential, although he was the most widely popular for his vocals.

Coleman, Ornette (1930–), US composer and saxophonist who later also took up trumpet and violin. He shook the foundations of jazz in the 1950s with his unique style, later called 'free jazz'.

Coltrane, John (William; 1926–67), US bandleader, composer and most widely imitated jazz tenor saxophonist after Charlie Parker.

Dankworth, Johnny (John Philip William; 1927–), English saxophonist, bandleader, composer and leading figure of British post-war jazz; often worked with his wife, singer Cleo Laine (see below).

Davis, Miles (Dewey III; 1926–91), US trumpeter and bandleader who was a leading bop player in the 1940s with Charlie Parker. He moved in the late 1950s to flamenco and 'free jazz' and then pioneered jazz-rock.

Dorsey, Jimmy (James; 1904–57), US bandleader, clarinetist and saxophonist who formed the Dorsey Brothers Orchestra which, after the departure of brother Tommy in 1935, he turned into a leading dance band.

Dorsey, Tommy (Thomas; 1905–56), US bandleader, trombonist and singer who split from his brother, forming his own band with Frank Sinatra as singer.

Louis Armstrong (1901–71)

Ellington, Duke (Edward Kennedy; 1899–74), US bandleader, pianist and leading jazz composer, estimated to have written over 2000 compositions, including 'Mood Indigo' (1930), film scores, ballet, opera and music for Shakespeare.

Fitzgerald, Ella (1918–96), US singer and supreme jazz interpreter of the popular song repertoire. After her first success with 'A-tisket, a-tasket' in 1938, she directed Chick Webb's band for three years after his death before embarking on her solo career.

Garner, Erroll (Louis; 1921–77), US mainstream pianist with an individual style. He composed the well-known song 'Misty'.

Getz, Stan (Stanley; 1927–91), US tenor saxophonist who fused jazz and bossa nova, though his style had deep roots in 'Swing'.

Gillespie, Dizzy (John Birks; 1917–93), US composer, bandleader and trumpeter who fused Afro-Cuban rhythms in the 1940s and whose later style was full of dramatic contrasts.

Goodman, Benny (Goodman, Benjamin David; 1909–86), US clarinetist and bandleader, referred to as the 'King of Swing'. He was the first white bandleader to popularize a total jazz style.

Grappelli, Stéphane (1908–), French pioneer of the jazz violin best known for his Hot Club sessions with Django Rheinhardt.

Hancock, Herbie (1940–), US pianist and composer, influenced by rock, classical and funk, who came to prominence in Miles Davis' quintet and wrote some popular tunes in the 1970s. He won an Oscar for his film score of *Round Midnight* (1986).

Handy, W(illiam) C(hristopher) (1873–1958), US composer, cornetist and bandleader, best known as a composer and collector of blues; he recorded with his Memphis Orchestra and toured with Jelly Roll Morton. He was blinded in 1943.

Hawkins, Coleman (1904–69), US tenor saxophonist who was the first to popularize the instrument.

Hines, Earl (Kenneth, also known as 'Fatha', 1903–83), US pianist and bandleader who was an innovator both in ensemble and solo breaks; he played with Louis Armstrong and featured many stars with his bands.

Billie Holiday (1915–59)

Holiday, Billie (Fagan, Eleanora; known also as 'Lady Day', 1915–59), US vocalist and one of the first black singers to feature with a white orchestra. She became famous with 'Strange Fruit', a song about a lynching. Her poignant love songs echo her own difficult life.

Jones, Elvin (1927–), US drummer and bandleader who began as a 'bop' drummer in the 1950s before coming to prominence with *John Coltrane's Quartet* in the 1960s. His drumming style brought drums into the forefront of improvisational instruments.

Laine, Dame Cleo (Campbell, Clementine Dinah; 1927–), English singer accomplished in scat and improvisation and known for her four-octave voice from contralto to falsetto.

Lewis, John (Aaron; 1920–), US pianist, composer and member of the *Milt Jackson Quartet*, which eventually became the *Modern Jazz Quartet* of which he was music director and wrote many pieces, fusing classical with jazz.

Marsalis, Wynton (1961–), US trumpeter, equally adept at jazz and classical works, from a prolific family of jazz musicians.

Miller, Glenn (1904–44), US bandleader and trombonist whose swing big-band arrangements, often doubling a melody on saxophone and higher clarinet, developed a characteristic sound, as in his famous piece 'In the Mood'.

Mingus, Charles (1922–79), US virtuoso double-bass player and composer whose passionate compositions predated and influenced 'free' jazz.

Monk, Thelonious (Sphere; 1917–82), US pianist and composer who was a formative influence on modern jazz; his works include 'Round Midnight' and 'Straight, No Chaser'.

Morton, 'Jelly Roll' (La Mothe, or Lemott or La Menthe, Ferdinand Joseph; 1890–1941), US composer and pianist whose work, though composed and well-rehearsed, exemplified the New Orleans style.

Parker, Charlie (1920–55), US saxophonist, known as 'Yardbird' or 'Bird', who was a brilliant improvisor and the most important figure in modern jazz.

Peterson, Oscar (Emmanuel; 1925–), Canadian pianist and composer who performed with his own trio in the 1950s and 60s and then increasingly as a soloist with an extraordinary technique. His compositions include the *Canadiana Suite* (1964).

Reinhardt, Django (Jean Baptiste; 1910–53), Belgian-born virtuoso (despite the handicap of a left hand mangled in a fire) on both acoustic and electric guitar with the *Hot Club de France* band, a later quintet and some big bands.

Roach, Max (1924–), US drummer known for his inventiveness and mastering of the 'bebop' style.

Rollins, Sonny (Theodore Walter; 1929–), saxophonist and bandleader considered to be the greatest living tenor saxophonist and a brilliant improvisor.

Shaw, Artie (Arschawsky, Arthur Jacob; 1910–), US clarinetist, bandleader and composer with big bands, often using unorthodox scoring (his *Gramercy Five* ensemble included harpsichord).

Shearing, George (1919–), Blind British-born pianist known for his special 'sound' using piano, vibraphone, guitar, double bass and drums. He is best known for his own composition 'Lullaby of Birdland'.

Shepp, Archie (1937–), US tenor and soprano saxophonist, clarinetist and composer known for his militant political and musical stance in the 1960s before turning to a more traditional style.

Shorter, Wayne (1933–), US tenor and soprano saxophonist and composer who formed the popular fusion band *Weather Report* and was a leading exponent of 'hard bop'.

Smith, Bessie (1894–37), US singer and the most successful black female recording artist of her time.

Tatum, Art (Arthur; 1909–56), US pianist, only partially sighted, who set new standards in technique and improvisational skills.

Taylor, Cecil (1929–), US pianist whose playing has enormous power, speed and intensity; although overshadowed by Ornette Coleman, he is hailed by many as the greatest 20th-century jazz piano virtuoso .

Vaughan, (Lois) Sarah (1924–90), US singer who used her voice more as a jazz instrument than as a vehicle for lyrics in her early career in bop.

Waller, 'Fats' (Thomas Wright; 1904–43), US pianist, singer, bandleader and composer of 'Ain't Misbehavin' (1930) and 'Honeysuckle Rose'; his wit and artistry transformed the most trite of songs.

Williams, Mary Lou (Scruggs, Mary Elfrieda; 1910–81), US pianist and composer who is often overlooked but who wrote and played impressively in many styles, from 'bebop' and 'Big Band Swing' to classical music.

Pop Music

▷ **The Beatles have scored more No.1 hits than any other act – in the UK they had 17 No.1 singles and 14 No.1 albums, and in the USA 18 of their singles and 20 of their albums reached the top spot.**

▷ **The fastest-selling single of all time is 'Do They Know It's Christmas' by Band Aid, which sold 1.6 million copies in the UK in its first six days on sale in 1984.**

▷ **The fastest-selling pop album of all time is *Spice* by the Spice Girls – in its first six months of release the album sold in excess of 14 million copies worldwide.**

▷ **The bestselling pop album is Michael Jackson's *Thriller* – released in 1982 it has now sold nearly 42 million copies worldwide.**

THE HISTORY OF POP

During World War II, big bands, fronted by such musicians as Glenn Miller and Tommy Dorsey (see p. 229), kept the people's spirits high and dance floors packed. However, soon after the last shots had been fired, their place in the public spotlight was taken by solo singers, many of whom had provided the vocal refrains on big band records.

THE 1950S

Initially, it was Tin Pan Alley's professional tunesmiths who provided these vocalists with their songs, but by the early 1950s many headliners, including crooners Bing Crosby and Frank Sinatra, were covering country and western (C&W) tunes for the mass market. Later, when it became clear that American teenagers were listening to rhythm and blues (R&B), many popular mainstream acts turned to that musical genre for their source of material.

It was only a matter of time before pop, C&W and R&B merged to form the hybrid known as rock'n'roll. Bill Haley introduced it to the world and Elvis Presley helped turn it into a force powerful enough to change the direction of music. At first, most rock'n'roll records were raw, rough and rebellious – but by the end of the 1950s rock'n'roll had lost its hard edge as the record business tried to market the music to a wider audience.

THE 1960S

Rock was given a wake-up call in the early 1960s by The Beatles who, together with other new British beat bands, revolutionized the entertainment world on both sides of the Atlantic. The sixties also heralded the arrival of innovative groups like The Rolling Stones and The Beach Boys. The cult of the singer-songwriter was also born at this time, thanks to 'folk' singers like Bob Dylan and Joni Mitchell. The era also saw the advent of various musical and dance trends including the twist, Motown, Merseybeat, bubblegum, soul and psychedelia. It was a decade when albums outsold singles and rock performers began to take themselves and their music more seriously.

THE 1970S

By the mid-1970s the majority of recording artists were, for the first time, writing their own material and professional songwriters were fast becoming an extinct breed. Myriad musical styles like heavy metal, teenybop, glam, rock, soul and disco thrived simultaneously, with acts as diverse as Led Zeppelin, Elton John and The Carpenters selling millions of albums. But by the latter half of the decade, many of these long established acts were being swept away by the punk movement, led by such New York bands as Television, Patti Smith and The Ramones in the USA and by The Sex Pistols, The Clash and The Damned in the UK.

THE 1980S

Innovations in the 1980s were largely technological rather than musical: CD appeared and began to replace vinyl and the power of MTV forced many acts to spend vast amounts of money on promotional videos. Female performers began to assert themselves in what had been a largely male-dominated industry. Madonna, Whitney Houston and Janet Jackson broke sales records globally as did the new male megastars Bruce Springsteen, U2, Prince, Michael Jackson and Dire Straits. Alongside these newer names, veteran rockers such as The Who, The Rolling Stones and Paul McCartney all experienced revivals in their fortunes, selling out lengthy stadium tours.

THE 1990S

British and American tastes diverged at the start of the 1990s. In Britain, disco was reborn as dance music, its popularity exceeding its earlier seventies heyday. Electronic synthesizer sounds, which began to be incorporated into pop as early as the 1970s, evolved swiftly through the eighties, replacing the traditional rock instruments of guitars, bass and drums. By the nineties, these electronic sounds, often digitally sampled, dominated many types of music, from ambient to 'techno' dance music, even appearing regularly in more traditional pop music. However, the sounds of the sixties were also revisited via Brit-pop and its early exponents Blur and Oasis. Americans, however, ignored certain peculiarly British trends, preferring home-grown 'grunge' acts like Pearl Jam and Nirvana. Rap became a staple of the American charts – although originating in the seventies, it finally found mass-market appeal nearly 20 years later.

POP ARTISTS

Album titles are given in italics and singles in quotes. The act's bestselling track is listed at the end of each entry.

Abba (Swe): Agnetha Faltskog, Frida Lyngstad, Bjorn Ulvaeus, Benny Andersson. Winners of the Eurovision Song Contest in 1974 with 'Waterloo' and the bestselling group of the 1970s. 'Dancing Queen'.

AC/DC (Aus/UK): Angus Young, Malcolm Young, Bon Scott (d. 19/2/80, replaced by Brian Johnson), Mark Evans, Phillip Rudd. Heavy rock act. 'You Shook Me All Night Long'.

Ace of Base (Swe): Jenny Berggren, Linn Berggren, Jonas Berggren, Ulf Ekberg. This dance pop group's debut album *Happy Nation* (titled *The Sign* in USA) sold 20 million copies worldwide. 'All That She Wants'.

Bryan Adams (Can): b. 5/11/59, Kingston, Ontario. His 1991 single '(Everything I Do) I Do It For You' spent seven weeks at No.1 in the USA and a record 16 consecutive weeks at the top in the UK.

Aerosmith (UK): Steve Tyler, Joe Perry, Brad Whitford, Tom Hamilton, Joey Kramer. Heavy rock act formed in 1970 and still recording. 'Love In An Elevator'.

Bananarama (UK): Sarah Dallin, Keren Woodward, Siobhan Fahey (left to form Shakespears Sister, replaced by Jacqui Sullivan). This vocal act have scored more UK hits than any other British female group. 'Venus'.

Shirley Bassey (UK): b. 8/1/37, Cardiff, Wales. Singer of three James Bond movie themes and the only female vocalist to score UK hits in five decades. 'As Long As He Needs Me'.

The Beach Boys (US): Brian Wilson, Mike Love, Carl Wilson (d. (drowned) 28/12/83), Al Jardine, Dennis Wilson. Surf group from Hawthorne, California. 'Good Vibrations'.

The Beatles (UK): John Lennon (shot dead 8/12/80), Paul McCartney, George Harrison, Ringo Starr. The Liverpudlian quartet are the most successful recording act of all time. After the band's demise in 1970, all four members went on to notable solo careers. 'She Loves You'.

The Beautiful South (UK): Paul Heaton, Dave Hemmingway, Briana Corrigan (replaced by Jacqueline Abbott), Dave Rotheray, Sean Welch, David Stead. Country-influenced pop group formed by vocalist/songwriter Heaton on leaving his former group The Housemartins in 1989. 'A Little Time'.

Bee Gees (UK): Barry Gibb, Robin Gibb, Maurice Gibb. As songwriters, the sibling trio spent a total of 26 weeks at No.1 in the USA in 1978. 'Night Fever'.

Chuck Berry (US): b. 18/10/26, San Jose, California. Influential rock'n'roller whose songs have been covered by artists such as The Beatles, The Rolling Stones and The Beach Boys. 'My Ding-A-Ling'.

Blondie (US): Deborah Harry, Chris Stein, Jimmy Destri, Nigel Harrison, Frank Infante, Clem Burke. Punk pop band who scored five UK No.1 hits (four in USA) from 1979–81. 'Heart Of Glass'.

Blur (UK): Damon Albarn, Graham Coxon, Alex James, Dave Rowntree. This top Britpop band won in four categories at the 1995 Brit Awards. 'Girls And Boys'.

Bon Jovi (US): Jon Bon Jovi, Richie Sambora, David Bryan, Alec John Such, Tico Torres. Heavy rock act from New Jersey. 'Livin' On A Prayer'.

Pat Boone (US): b. Charles Boone, 1/6/34, Jacksonville, Florida. First found success in the 1950s covering black R&B hits. 'Love Letters In The Sand'.

David Bowie (UK): b. David Jones, 8/1/47, Brixton, London. Theatrical rock artist, chameleon-like performer and major star since 1972. 'Let's Dance'.

Boy George (UK): b. George O'Dowd, 14/6/61, Erith, Kent. Former lead singer of Culture Club, now a successful club DJ. 'Karma Chameleon'.

Boyz II Men (US): Wanya Morris, Michael McCary, Shawn Stockman, Nathan Morris. Their singles have spent a total of 49 weeks at No.1 in the USA. 'End Of The Road'.

Garth Brooks (US): b. Troyal Brooks, 7/2/62, Tulsa, Oklahoma. Sold in excess of 35 million albums in the USA since 1990. 'The Red Strokes'.

James Brown (US): b. 3/5/33, Barnwell, South Carolina. One of the originators of soul-funk music, he has scored more hits on the US R&B chart than any other act. 'Living In America'.

Bush (UK): Gavin Rossdale, Nigel Pulsford, Dave Parsons, Robin Goodridge. Nirvana soundalikes. Their debut album, *Sixteen Stone*, sold six million copies but failed to make the UK Top 40. 'Swallowed'.

Kate Bush (UK): b. Catherine Bush 30/7/58, Bexleyheath, London. Distinctive female vocalist discovered by Dave Gilmour of Pink Floyd. 'Wuthering Heights'.

The Byrds (US): Roger (Jim) McGuinn, Gene Clark (d. 24/5/91), David Crosby, Chris Hillman, Michael Clarke. Bob Dylan-influenced electric folk band. 'Mr Tambourine Man'.

■ **THE BESTSELLING SINGLE IS CROSBY'S 'WHITE CHRISTMAS' – RELEASED IN 1942, IT HAS SOLD OVER**

Mariah Carey (US): b. 22/3/70, New York, New York. First five singles all topped the US chart. 'One Sweet Day' (a duet with Boyz II Men).

The Carpenters (US): Karen Carpenter (d. 4/2/83 of slimming disease *anorexia nervosa*), Richard Carpenter. Middle-of-the-road sibling duo from Connecticut known for Karen's perfect sweet voice. '(They Long To Be) Close To You'.

Cher (US): b. Cherilyn LaPierre 20/5/46, El Centro, California. Starting as a backing singer for Phil Spector, she married Sonny Bono in 1963 with whom she amassed 20 US hits before their divorce in 1974. Also a noteworthy actress. 'I Got You Babe' (duet with Sonny Bono).

Chicago (US): Peter Cetera (replaced by Jason Scheff in 1985), Robert Lamm, Terry Kath, Danny Seraphine, James Pankow, Lee Loughane, Walter Parazaider. Jazz-rock group formed in 1967 as Chicago Transit Authority. 'If You Leave Me Now'.

Eric Clapton (UK): b. Eric Patrick Clapp 30/3/45, Ripley, Surrey. Significant blues guitarist. A member of The Yardbirds, John Mayall's Bluesbreakers, Cream and Blind Faith in the 1960s and Derek and the Dominoes in the 1970s. 'Layla'.

The Clash (UK): Joe Strummer, Mick Jones, Paul Simonon, Nicky 'Topper' Headon. One of the first and most successful UK punk bands. 'Should I Stay Or Should I Go'.

Eddie Cochran (US): b. 3/10/38, Oklahoma City, Oklahoma (d. 17/4/60 in a motorcycle crash, Wiltshire, UK). Influential rock'n'roll performer. 'Summertime Blues'.

Phil Collins (UK): b. 31/1/51, Chiswick, London. Joined prog-rock group Genesis in 1970 as drummer and took over lead vocal duties in 1975 after the departure of Peter Gabriel. Concurrent solo career from 1981 until the demise of Genesis in 1996. 'A Groovy Kind Of Love'.

Elvis Costello (UK): b. Declan McManus 25/8/55, London. Appeared first with his band The Attractions, but later went solo. In addition to his singing career, the son of bandleader Ross McManus produced albums for The Specials, Squeeze, Dave Edmunds and The Pogues. 'Oliver's Army'.

The Cranberries (Ire): Dolores O'Riordan, Noel Hogan, Mike Hogan, Feargal Lawler. They formed as the Cranberry Saw Us in Limerick in 1990 and met with huge success in the USA. 'Linger'.

Bing Crosby (US): b. Harry Lillis Crosby 3/5/03, Tacoma, Washington (d. 14/10/77). The biggest star of the pre-rock era, he also appeared in movies. 'White Christmas'.

Crosby, Stills, Nash & Young (US/UK/Can): David Crosby (ex-The Byrds), Graham Nash (ex-The Hollies), Stephen Stills and Neil Young (both ex-Buffalo Springfield). Late 1960s supergroup whose impeccable harmonies were the hallmark of their first album *Crosby, Stills and Nash*, but Young's recruitment in 1969 added a darker element. Their second gig was Woodstock. After two studio albums, Young went solo, releasing an array of albums that has maintained his credibility through four decades. The remaining three members have scored chart success (solo and as a group) less regularly, but continue to record and tour. 'Marrakesh Express'.

Crowded House (NZ/Aus): Neil Finn, Paul Hester, Nick Seymour. Finn and Hester formed the band after the demise of Split Enz in 1985. Neil's brother, and former Split Enz vocalist, Tim, joined Crowded House temporarily in 1991. 'Don't Dream It's Over'.

The Cure (UK): Robert Smith fronts an ever-changing line-up of musicians for his goth-rock ensemble. Formed in 1976 as the Easy Cure. 'Lovesong'.

Def Leppard (UK): Joe Elliott, Phil Collen, Steve Clark (d. 8/1/91, replaced by Vivian Campbell), Rick Savage, Rick Allen. Heavy-rock outfit who were the first band to sell more than 5 million copies of two consecutive albums in the USA. 'Love Bites'.

Deep Purple (UK): Members have included Ritchie Blackmore, Jon Lord, David Coverdale, Ian Paice, Ian Gilan, Roger Glover, Nick Simper, Tommy Bolin, Glenn Hughes. Heavy-rock act which formed in 1968 and split up in 1976. Blackmore went on to form Rainbow; Coverdale, Lord and Paice formed Whitesnake; Ian Gillan formed Gillan. 'Smoke On The Water'.

Jim Morrison of The Doors

Depeche Mode (UK): Dave Gahan, Martin Gore, Andy Fletcher, Alan Wilder, Vince Clarke (later of Erasure, he was replaced by Alan Wilder in 1982, who himself quit the band in 1995). Synth band who later veered towards rock. 'Enjoy The Silence'.

Neil Diamond (US): b. Noah Kaminsky 24/1/41, Brooklyn, New York. Besides his solo success, he wrote 'Daydream Believer' for the Monkees and his 'Red Red Wine' was covered by UB40. 'Sweet Caroline'.

Celine Dion (Can): b. 30/3/69, Charlemagne, Quebec. Winner of the Eurovision Song Contest in 1988 representing Switzerland. She has since achieved international fame with both English and French language recordings. 'The Power Of Love'.

Dire Straits (UK): Mark Knopfler, John Illsey, Hal Lindes, Pick Withers (replaced by Terry Williams in 1983), Alan Clark. Dylanesque rock group whose *Brothers In Arms* was one of the bestselling albums of all time in the UK and the first album to sell a million copies on the CD format. 'Money For Nothing'.

Fats Domino (US): b. Antoine Domino 26/2/28, New Orleans, Louisiana. R&B piano playing vocalist, heavily influenced by Fats Waller. 'Blueberry Hill'.

Lonnie Donegan (UK): b. Anthony Donegan 29/4/31, Glasgow, Scotland. Originally a member of Chris Barber's Jazz Band before pioneering the 'skiffle' sound in the 1950s. 'My Old Man's A Dustman'.

Donovan (UK): b. Donovan Leitch, 10/5/46, Glasgow, Scotland. Singer/songwriter Donovan suffered comparison to Bob Dylan throughout the 1960s. 'Sunshine Superman'.

The Doors (US): Jim Morrison (d. 3/7/71), Ray Manzarek, Robbie Krieger, John Densmore. Influential rock group led by enigmatic frontman Morrison. In 1991 a movie based on their career starred Val Kilmer as Morrison. 'Light My Fire'.

Duran Duran (UK): Simon Le Bon, Nick Rhodes, John Taylor, Roger Taylor, Andy Taylor. None of the Taylors is related. Roger and Andy left in 1986, replaced by Warren Cuccurullo and Steve Ferrone in 1990. The group are named after a character in the movie *Barbarella*. 'The Reflex'.

Bob Dylan (US): b. Robert Zimmerman, 24/5/41, Duluth, Minnesota. Influential singer/songwriter and folk-rock innovator. 'Like A Rolling Stone'.

The Eagles (US): Glenn Frey, Bernie Leadon, Randy Meisner, Don Henley. Country-rock act initially recruited as Linda Ronstadt's backing band. 'Hotel California'.

East 17 (UK): Tony Mortimer, Brian Harvey, John Hendy, Terry Coldwell. Harvey was sacked in early 1997 after speaking out in favour of drugs, and Mortimer left later in the year. The vocal group was named after the postal district of its home town of Walthamstow. 'Stay Another Day'.

Enigma (Ger): This ambient dance outfit is the brainchild of producer and multi-instrumentalist Michael Cretu (b. 18/5/57, Bucharest, Romania). 'Sad(e)ness'.

Erasure (UK): Vince Clarke (ex-Depeche Mode), Andy Bell. Synth duo who scored five UK No.1 albums from 1988–94. 'Abba-Esque EP'.

Gloria Estefan (US): b. Gloria Fajardo 1/9/57, Havana, Cuba. Fronted Miami Sound Machine from 1975 until going solo in 1989. 'Don't Wanna Lose You'.

Eternal (UK): Easther Bennett, Vernie Bennett, Kelle Bryan, Louise Nurding (left 1995). Popular female R&B vocal group. 'Don't You Love Me'.

Eurythmics (UK): Annie Lennox, Dave Stewart. Prior to Eurythmics, the duo were with The Tourists from 1977–80. Since the Eurythmics split in 1990, Lennox has pursued a successful solo career and Stewart formed Spiritual Cowboys and produced Bob Dylan and others. 'Sweet Dreams (Are Made Of This)'.

The Everly Brothers (US): Don Everly, Phil Everly. Kentucky-born sibling duo were the first act on Warner Brothers Records. 'All I have To Do Is Dream'.

Everything But The Girl (UK): Tracey Thorn, Ben Watt. Formed in 1983, their name was taken from a second-hand furniture store in Hull. Their biggest hit, 'Missing', was the first single to spend a year on the US singles chart.

Fleetwood Mac (UK/US): Mick Fleetwood, John McVie, Christine McVie, Lindsey Buckingham, Stevie Nicks. Originally formed in 1967 as Peter Green's Fleetwood Mac, the group endured many line-up changes until stabilizing as the above quintet from 1975–87. *Rumours* remains one of the bestselling albums of all time and has spent more than eight years in the UK chart. 'Little Lies'.

The Four Seasons (US): Frankie Valli, Bob Gaudio, Nick Massi, Tommy DeVito. Their style evolved from barbershop harmonies in the 1950s to disco in the 1970s. 'December 1963 (Oh What A Night)'.

The Four Tops (US): Levi Stubbs, Renaldo Benson, Abdul Fakir, Lawrence Payton. This soul group has had no personnel changes since their formation in 1953 as The Four Aims, and are still recording as of 1997. 'Reach Out, I'll Be There'.

Frankie Goes To Hollywood (UK): Holly Johnson, Paul Rutherford, Brian Nash, Peter Gill, Mark O'Toole. This heavy synth dance band sold 4 million singles in the UK in 1984. 'Relax'.

Aretha Franklin (US): b. 25/3/42, Memphis, Tennessee. Nicknamed the 'Queen Of Soul', Franklin was the first woman to be inducted into the Rock and Roll Hall of Fame. 'Respect'.

The Fugees (US): Lauryn Hill, Wyclef Jean, Prakazrel Michel. Born in Haiti, Jean and Michel took the Fugees moniker (short for 'refugees') from the slang term for Haitians in New York. Their soft hip-hop cover of 'Killing Me Softly' was a worldwide hit in 1996.

Marvin Gaye (US): b. 2/4/39, Washington DC (d. 1/4/84, shot dead by his father). This unique soul singer had 56 US hits from 1962–84. 'I Heard It Through The Grapevine'.

Gary Glitter (UK): b. Paul Gadd 8/5/40. He first recorded as Paul Raven in the early 1960s, later spearheading the glam-rock craze of the 1970s. 'Rock And Roll Part 2'.

The Grateful Dead (US): Jerry Garcia (d. 9/8/95), Bob Weir, Ron McKernan (d. 8/3/73), Phil Lesh, Bill Kreutzmann, plus various musicians throughout their 25-year career. Psychedelic rock band formed in San Francisco in 1966. 'Touch Of Grey'.

Guns N' Roses (US): Axl Rose, Slash, Izzy Stradlin (replaced by Gilby Clarke in 1991), Duff Rose McKagan, Steven Adler (replaced by Matt Sorum in 1990). This heavy-rock band's first hit, 'Sweet Child O' Mine', was written about Axl Roses' wife Erin Everly, daughter of 1950s/60s singer Don Everly. 'November Rain'.

Bill Haley and His Comets (US): Bill Haley, Frank Beecher, Johnny Grande, Rudy Pompilli, Ralph Jones, Al Rex, Billy Williamson. 'Rock Around The Clock' was the first rock'n'roll record to top the charts in both Britain and America.

Hall and Oates (US): Daryl Hall, John Oates. The pair met while students at university in Philadelphia. The most successful US duo of all time. 'Maneater'.

Johnny Hallyday (France): b. Jean-Philippe Smet 15/6/43. Despite tremendous success domestically, France's most prolific rock'n'roll star has failed to make any impression on the UK and US charts. 'Let's Twist Again'.

Jimi Hendrix (US): b. 27/11/42, Seattle, Washington (d. 18/9/70). Legendary psychedelic blues guitarist discovered by Chas Chandler of The Animals. 'All Along The Watchtower'.

Herman's Hermits (UK): Peter Noone, Derek Leckenby (d. 4/6/94), Keith Hopwood, Karl Green, Barry Whitwam. Their US No.1 hits 'Mrs Brown You've Got A Lovely Daughter' and 'I'm Henry VIII I Am' were not released in the UK. 'There's A Kind Of Hush'.

The Hollies (UK): Allan Clarke, Graham Nash (left in 1968 to join Crosby, Stills and Nash), Tony Hicks, Eric Haydock (replaced by Bernie Calvert in 1966), Bobby Elliott. Formed in Manchester in 1962. 'He Ain't Heavy, He's My Brother'.

Buddy Holly and the Crickets (US): Buddy Holly (b. Charles Hardin Holley, 7/9/36, d. 3/2/59 in air crash), Sonny Curtis, Joe B. Mauldin, Jerry Allison. Holly was one of America's most influential early rock'n'roll pioneers. The group continued to record after Holly's death until 1964. 'That'll Be The Day'.

Hootie and the Blowfish (US): Darius Rucker, Mark Bryan, Dean Felber, Jim Sonefeld. Funk-rock band who were the bestselling act in the USA in 1995. 'Hold My Hand'.

Whitney Houston (US): b. 9/8/63, New Jersey, the daughter of Cissy Houston and cousin of Dionne Warwick. This gospel-influenced singer also starred in the films *The Bodyguard*, *Waiting To Exhale* and *The Preacher's Wife*. 'I Will Always Love You'.

Human League (UK): Philip Oakey, Jo Callis (left 1985), Ian Craig Marsh, Martyn Ware (both left in 1980 to form Heaven 17, replaced by Joanne Catherall, Suzanne Sulley), Ian Burden (joined 1980, left 1984). Synth-pop band formed in Sheffield in 1977. 'Don't You Want Me'.

Engelbert Humperdinck (UK): b. Arnold Dorsey 2/5/36 in Madras, India, but grew up in Leicester, UK. Took his stage name from that of a German composer. 'Release Me'.

Julio Iglesias (Spa): b. 23/9/43, Madrid. This former goalkeeper with Real Madrid represented Spain in the 1970 Eurovision Song Contest. He has sold in excess of 100 million albums worldwide. 'Begin The Beguine (Volver A Empezar)'.

INXS (Aus): Michael Hutchence, Andrew Farriss, Tim Farriss, Jon Farriss, Kirk Pengilly, Gary Beers. Formed in Sydney in 1977 as The Farriss Brothers, Hutchence still fronts this successful rock band despite continuing rumours of a solo career. 'Need You Tonight'.

Michael Jackson (US): b. 29/8/58, Gary, Indiana. Born to sing and dance, the 'King of Pop' has been in pop music since the age of eight with his brothers in The Jackson 5. His solo career, begun in 1979, is one of the most successful ever and he has been particularly influential and innovative in the fields of dancing and pop video. 'Billie Jean'.

The Jam (UK): Paul Weller, Bruce Foxton, Rick Buckler. Mod revival band formed in 1975, disbanded in 1982 when Weller went on to form The Style Council. 'Going Underground'.

Jamiroquai (UK): Jason Kaye, Simon Katz, Stuart Zender, Wallace Buchannan, Derek McKenzie. Jazz-orientated soul band. 'Virtual Insanity'.

Billy Joel (US): b. William Martin Joel, 9/5/49. A former boxer, Joel has sold more than 40 million albums in the US alone. 'Uptown Girl'.

Elton John

Elton John (UK): b. Reginald Dwight 25/3/47, Pinner, London. Formed his first group Bluesology in 1966, and took his name from the first names of Bluesology members Elton Dean and Long John Baldry. The most successful UK soloist worldwide. 'Don't Go Breaking My Heart' (a duet with Kiki Dee).

Tom Jones (UK): b. Thomas Jones Woodward 7/6/40, Pontypridd, Wales. Welsh sex symbol whose voice was mistaken in the USA for that of a black American. 'Green Green Grass Of Home' topped the chart for seven weeks in 1966.

Carole King (US): b. Carole Klein 9/2/42, Brooklyn, New York. Married lyricist Gerry Goffin in 1958 and together the pair wrote four US No.1 hits. *Tapestry* was a US No.1 album for 15 weeks. 'It's Too Late'.

The Kinks (UK): Ray Davies, Dave Davies, Peter Quaife, Mick Avory were the beginning line-up in 1964, which has changed often since then. The sibling rivalry between Ray and Dave was similar to that which now dogs Oasis, but their output of songs has been prolific and Ray is considered one of the UK's finest and most influential songwriters. The group reformed and are still recording as of 1997. 'Tired Of Waiting For You'.

KLF (UK): Bill Drummond (b. William Butterworth), Jimmy Cauty. Political trance-dance music combo famous for burning £1 million. 'Justified and Ancient' (with Tammy Wynette).

Kraftwerk (Ger): Ralf Hütter, Karl Bartos (replaced by Fritz Hilpert), Wolfgang Flur (replaced by Henning Schmitz), Florian Schneider. Pioneering synth-pop group, formed in 1970, who have had an immeasurable influence on dance music. 'The Model'.

Led Zeppelin (UK): Robert Plant, Jimmy Page, John Paul Jones, John Bonham (d. 25/9/80). One of the pioneers of heavy-metal music with psychedelic overtones. All eight albums released from 1969–79 topped the UK chart. They never released a single in their homeland. Plant and Page put out a successful album as a duo in 1996. 'Whole Lotta Love'.

Brenda Lee (US): b. Brenda Mae Tarpley 11/12/44, Lithonia, Georgia. 1950s rock'n'roll singer nicknamed 'Little Miss Dynamite'. 'Sweet Nothin's'.

M People (UK): Heather Small, Mike Pickering, Paul Heard, Shovell. Popular dance act. 'Moving On Up'.

Madness (UK): Graham McPherson (Suggs), Mike Barson, Chris Foreman, Mark Bedford, Lee Thompson, Dan Woodgate, Carl Smyth. Ska revival outfit who scored 15 UK Top 10 hits in the early 1980s. 'Our House'.

Madonna (US): b. Madonna Louise Ciccone 16/8/58, Detroit, Michigan. The artist with the most consecutive UK Top 20 hits (43 to date). Excelled in controversial and sexually explicit songs and stage shows in the 1980s, her image mellowed in the 1990s. She has acted in a number of films, with *Evita* her most successful. 'Vogue'.

Manfred Mann (UK/SA): Manfred Mann, Paul Jones (replaced by Mike D'Abo in 1966), Mike Vickers, Tom McGuinness, Mike Hugg. Formed in 1963, the band split in 1969. Mann resurfaced in 1972 with Manfred Mann's Earth Band. 'Do Wah Diddy Diddy'.

Manic Street Preachers (UK): James Dean Bradfield, Nicky Wire, Sean Moore, Richey Edwards (disappeared 1993). Welsh rock act. 'A Design For Life'.

Bob Marley and the Wailers (Jam): Bob Marley (b. 6/2/45, d. 11/5/81 of cancer), Peter Tosh (d. 11/5/87), Bunny Wailer, Carlton Barrett (d. 17/4/87), Aston Barrett. The biggest-selling reggae act of all time. 'No Woman No Cry'.

Meat Loaf (US): b. Marvin Lee Aday 27/9/47. *Bat Out Of Hell* has spent a record 472 weeks on the UK album chart. 'I'd Do Anything For Love (But I Won't Do That)'.

Metallica (US/Den): Clifford Lee Burton (d. 27/9/87 in tour bus crash, replaced by Jason Newsted), James Hetfield, David Mustaine (replaced by Kirk Hammett in 1983), Lars Ulrich. Heavy-metal band formed in Los Angeles in 1981. 'Nothing Else Matters'.

George Michael (UK): b. Georgios Kyriacou Panayiotou 25/6/63. Formed teeny-bop duo Wham! with schoolfriend Andrew Ridgeley in 1981, then went solo from 1986. *Faith* sold 8 million copies in the USA and spawned four No.1 singles. In total, he has scored ten US (11 UK) No.1's. 'Careless Whisper'.

Madonna

Kylie Minogue (Aus): b. 28/5/68, Melbourne. Former star of TV soap *Neighbours,* she made a record-breaking start with her first 11 releases, all making the UK Top 5. 'The Loco-Motion'.

Joni Mitchell (Can): b. 7/11/43, McLeod, Alberta. Influential folk singer/songwriter and guitarist known for her poignant lyrics. She developed a jazzier style through the 1970s and beyond. 'Big Yellow Taxi'.

Alanis Morissette (Can): b. 1/6/74, Ottawa. *Jagged Little Pill* is the biggest-selling debut album, as well as the biggest seller by a female artist. 'Ironic'.

Van Morrison (Ire): b. George Ivan 31/8/45, Belfast, Northern Ireland. Blues singer/songwriter and lead singer of Them in 1965–66. 'Brown-Eyed Girl'.

New Order (UK): Bernard Sumner, Peter Hook, Stephen Morris, Gillian Gilbert. Sumner, Hook and Morris were members of Joy Division before the suicide of singer Ian Curtis in 1980. Sumner has recorded with Electronic; Hook with Monaco Monaco; Gilbert and Morris as Other Two. 'Blue Monday'.

Olivia Newton-John (UK): b. 26/9/48, Cambridge. Emigrated to Australia in 1953 but returned after winning a talent contest in 1964. Starred in the 1978 film *Grease.* 'Physical' was the biggest-selling US single of the 1980s.

Nirvana (US): Kurt Cobain (b. 20/2/67, d. 8/4/94 of self-inflicted gunshot wound), Chris Novoselic, Dave Grohl. Grunge-rock trio from Washington who brought grunge out of the basement and into the forefront of pop music. After the death of Cobain, Grohl formed Foo Fighters. 'Smells Like Teen Spirit'.

Oasis (UK): Noel Gallagher, Liam Gallagher, Paul 'Bonehead' Arthurs, Paul 'Guigsy' McGuigan, Tony McCarroll (replaced by Alan White in 1995). *(What's The Story) Morning Glory?* has sold more than 4 million copies, the second-biggest selling album in the UK behind *Sergeant Pepper* by The Beatles. 'Wonderwall'.

Mike Oldfield (UK): b. 15/5/53, Reading, Berkshire. *Tubular Bells* was the first album released on Richard Branson's Virgin label. 'Moonlight Shadow'.

Roy Orbison (US): b. 23/4/36 (d. 7/12/88 of a heart attack). One of the original recording artists for Sun Records who wrote the Everly Brothers' UK No.1 'Claudette'. The silky-voiced crooner made a comeback in 1985 as a member of Traveling Wilburys. 'Oh Pretty Woman'.

Pearl Jam (US): Eddie Vedder, Stone Gossard, Jeff Ament, Mike McCreedy, Dave Abbruzzese (from 1991–94). VS sold a record 950,000 in its first week of release in the USA in 1993. 'Alive'.

Pet Shop Boys (UK): Neil Tennant, Chris Lowe. Synth-pop act. Tennant was assistant editor at pop magazine *Smash Hits* before forming the duo in 1981. They have also written hits for Dusty Springfield and Liza Minnelli. 'West End Girls'.

Pink Floyd (UK): Syd Barrett (replaced by David Gilmour in 1968), Roger Waters, Rick Wright, Nick Mason. Prog-rock pioneers who formed in 1965. Their 1972 album *Dark Side Of The Moon* has spent a record 22 years on the US album listings. 'Another Brick In The Wall (Pt 2)'.

Gene Pitney (US): b. 17/2/41, Hartford, Connecticut. Scored as a writer of 'Hello Mary Lou' (Ricky Nelson), 'Rubber Ball' (Bobby Vee) and 'He's A Rebel' (Crystals) before a successful singing career. A re-recorded 'Something's Gotten Hold Of My Heart' with Marc Almond gave him his first UK No.1 in 1989.

The Police (UK): Sting (b: Gordon Sumner), Andy Summers, Stewart Copeland. Formed in 1977, Sting has been solo since 1985. 'Every Breath You Take' spent eight weeks at No.1 in the USA and four at the top in the UK.

Elvis Presley (US): b. 8/1/35, Tupelo, Mississippi (d. 16/8/77 of heart failure). The 'King Of Rock And Roll', the most successful solo artist in history, has amassed over 100 hits in both the UK and US. 'All Shook Up'.

Prince/TAFKAP (US): b. Prince Rogers Nelson 7/6/58, Minneapolis, Minnesota. Prolific singer/songwriter who starred in the films *Graffiti Bridge*, *Sign 'O' The Times*, *Under The Cherry Moon* and *Purple Rain*; the latter's soundtrack album spent 24 weeks at No.1 in the USA in 1984. 'When Doves Cry'.

The Prodigy (UK): Liam Howlett, Keith Flint, Maxim, Leroy Thornhill. Consistently successful rave/electronic rock outfit whose album *The Fat of the Land* became an instant No.1 hit in the USA. 'Firestarter'.

Public Enemy (US): Chuck D (b. Carlton Ridenhour), Flavor Flav (b. William Drayton), Terminator X (b. Norman Lee Rogers), Professor Griff (b. Richard Griffin). Political and influential hard hip-hop rap group formed in 1982. 'Don't Believe the Hype'.

Pulp (UK): Jarvis Cocker, Russell Senior (left in 1997), Candida Doyle, Steve Mackey, Nick Banks. Formed in 1979, they eventually found chart fame in 1994. 'Common People'.

Queen (UK): Freddie Mercury (b. 5/9/46, d. 24/11/91 of AIDS-related illness), Brian May, John Deacon, Roger Taylor. 'Bohemian Rhapsody' is the only single to have topped the UK chart on two separate occasions; in total it has sold more than 2.5 million copies in Britain.

Radiohead (UK): Thom E. Yorke, Ed O'Brien, Jonny Greenwood, Colin Greenwood, Phil Selway. Formed in Oxford in 1991. Often referred to as Britpop, despite their dark and individualistic melodies. 'Creep'.

Jim Reeves (US): b. 20/8/23, Galloway, Texas (d. 31/7/64 in air crash). After his death, Reeves simultaneously charted a record eight albums in the UK Top 20. 'Distant Drums'.

REM (US): Michael Stipe, Peter Buck, Mike Mills, Bill Berry. Formed in 1980 in Athens, Georgia. The most successful American rock band of the 1990s. 'Losing My Religion'.

Cliff Richard (UK): b. Harry Rodger Webb 14/10/40, Lucknow, India. Accumulated an unprecedented 120 UK hit singles from 1958–97. 'We Don't Talk Anymore'.

Lionel Richie (US): b. 20/6/49, Tuskegee, Alabama. Former lead singer with The Commodores who wrote at least one US No.1 hit every year from 1978–86. 'Hello'.

The Rolling Stones (UK): Mick Jagger, Keith Richard, Brian Jones (d. 3/7/69, replaced by Mick Taylor in 1969, then Ron Wood in 1975), Bill Wyman (left 1993), Charlie Watts. Taking their name from a Muddy Waters song, they are the most consistent and durable rock band in history. 'Honky Tonk Women'.

Roxy Music (UK): Bryan Ferry, Andy Mackay, Phil Manzanera, Brian Eno, Paul Thompson. Celebrated art-rock act. Singer Ferry pursued a solo career alongside that of the band until it finally split in 1983, and continues to do so. Eno became an art-rock guru and ambient music pioneer. His partnership with Bowie albums such as *Heroes* and *Low* brought him fame and he has continued to work with a large number of artists, from David Byrne of Talking Heads to U2. 'Love Is The Drug'.

Prince/TAFKAP

Seal (UK): b. Sealhenry Samuel 19/2/63, Kilburn, London. First charted as the uncredited lead vocalist on Adamski's UK No.1 hit, 'Killer', he went on to achieve two No.1 albums. 'Kiss From A Rose'.

The Sex Pistols (UK): Johnny Rotten (b. John Lydon), Steve Jones, Glen Matlock (replaced by Sid Vicious (d. 2/2/79) in 1977), Paul Cook. Infamous punk group assembled by manager Malcolm McLaren. 'God Save The Queen'.

The Shadows (UK): Hank Marvin, Bruce Welch, Brian Bennett, Jet Harris, Tony Meehan. Initially called The Drifters, Cliff Richard's erstwhile backing band are the UK's most successful instrumental act of all time. 'Wonderful Land'.

Simon and Garfunkel (US): Paul Simon, Art Garfunkel. Folk-rock duo from New York City, recorded originally as Tom and Jerry (1957–60). From 1964–70 they recorded five albums, including the multimillion-selling *Bridge Over Troubled Water*. 'Bridge Over Troubled Water'.

Simple Minds (UK): Jim Kerr, Charlie Burchill, Mike McNeil, John Giblin, Mel Gaynor. Scottish rock group formed as Johnny and the Self Abusers in 1977. 'Don't You (Forget About Me)'.

Simply Red (UK): Mick Hucknall, Sylvan Richardson, Fritz McIntyre, Tony Bowers, Chris Joyce, Tim Kellett, Ian Kirkham. Their four album releases from 1989–96 all sold in excess of one million copies in the UK. 'Holding Back The Years'.

Slade (UK): Noddy Holder, Dave Hill, Jimmy Lea, Don Powell. Group notched up 12 consecutive UK Top 4 singles between 1971–74, including six No.1s. 'Merry Xmas Everybody'.

Frank Sinatra (US): b. 12/12/15, Hoboken, New Jersey. Recorded with the Tommy Dorsey Orchestra from 1940, solo from 1942 and had charted 40 US Top 10 hits by 1954. Still recording, albeit intermittently, in the 1990s. 'My Way'.

The Smiths (UK): Morrissey (b. Stephen Morrissey), Johnny Marr, Andy Rourke, Mike Joyce. Formed in Manchester in 1982, they disbanded in 1987. Marr joined Bernard Sumner, of New Order, in Electronic. Morrissey went solo. 'This Charming Man'.

Keith Flint and Maxim of The Prodigy

The Spice Girls (UK): Geri Halliwell, Melanie Brown, Melanie Chisholm, Emma Bunton, Victoria Addams. Female vocal act whose first four singles all topped the UK chart and their debut album has sold 12 million copies to date worldwide. 'Wannabe'.

Dusty Springfield (UK): b. Mary O'Brien 16/4/39, London. She started in The Springfields with her brother Tom and Tim Field. 'I Only Want To Be With You' was the first record played on BBC TV's *Top Of The Pops* in 1964. 'You Don't Have To Say You Love Me'.

Bruce Springsteen (US): b. 23/9/49, Freehold, New Jersey. Nicknamed 'the Boss', his 1984 album *Born In The USA* spent seven weeks at the top in the USA and sold more than 12 million copies. 'Dancing In The Dark'.

Status Quo (UK): Rock group based around nucleus of Francis Rossi and Rick Parfitt. First made the UK chart in 1968 and scored at least one hit every year from 1973–92. 'Rockin' All Over The World'.

Rod Stewart (UK): b. 10/1/45, Highgate, London. Joined Jeff Beck Group from 1967–69 and the Faces from 1969–75. The gravel-voiced singer has had a successful solo career since 1971. 'Maggie May'.

The Stranglers (UK): Hugh Cornwell (left 1988, replaced by John Ellis), Jean-Jacques Burnel, Dave Greenfield, Jet Black. Formed as The Guildford Stranglers in 1974, they were one of the pioneers of punk and are still recording as of 1997. 'Golden Brown'.

Barbra Streisand (US) b. 24/4/42, Brooklyn, New York. Celebrated actress, singer and film producer, Streisand has charted 45 US hit albums from 1963–94. 'Evergreen'.

Suede (UK): Brett Anderson, Bernard Butler (replaced by Richard Oakes in 1994), Neil Codling (joined 1996), Justine Frischmann (left to join Elastica in 1990), Matt Osman, Simon Gilbert. Indie band regularly compared with David Bowie. 'Trash'.

Donna Summer (US): b. LaDonna Gaines 31/12/48, Boston, Massachusetts. The 'Queen of Disco' was the first female singer to have three consecutive US No.1 albums. 'I Feel Love'.

The Supremes (US): Diana Ross (b. Diane Ernestine Ross, 26/3/44, Detroit, replaced by Jean Terrell in 1969), Mary Wilson, Florence Ballard (replaced by Cindy Birdsong in 1967). This female vocal soul group had 12 US No.1s from 1964–69. Lead singer Ross has appeared in the UK singles chart every year since 1964; her biggest solo hit was 'Upside Down'. 'Baby Love'.

SWV (US): Cheryl Gamble, Tamara Johnson, Leanne Lyons. Sisters With Voices were created by R&B producer Teddy Riley. 'Right Here'.

T Rex (UK): Marc Bolan (b. Mark Feld 30/7/47, d. 16/9/77 in car crash), Mickey Finn. Glam-rock act of the early 1970s. 'Get It On'.

Take That (UK): Gary Barlow, Robbie Williams, Mark Owen, Howard Donald, Jason Orange. The most popular 'boy band' of the 1990s with eight UK No.1s to their credit. The group disbanded in 1996 and all but Orange went on to solo success. 'Back For Good'.

Talking Heads (UK/US): David Byrne, Tina Weymouth, Jerry Harrison, Chris Frantz. New York-based, new-wave quartet led by Scottish-born Byrne. 'Once In A Lifetime'.

The Temptations (US): Eddie Kendricks, Otis Williams, Paul Williams, David Ruffin, Melvin Franklin. Soul vocal group formed from members of two groups, The Primes and The Distants; they were called The Elgins before charting in 1964. 'My Girl'.

TLC (US): T-Boz (Tionne Watkins), Left Eye (Lisa Lopes), Chilli (Rozonda Thomas). Female R&B trio based in Atlanta, Georgia. 'Creep'.

Tina Turner (US): b. Anna Mae Bullock 26/11/39, Brownsville, Tennessee. Married to Ike Turner from 1958–76, with whom she had 20 US soul hits from 1960–75. She made a comeback as a solo artist in 1984. 'What's Love Got To Do With It'.

UB40 (UK): Ali Campbell, Earl Falconer, Robin Campbell, Mickey Virtue, Brian Travers, Jim Brown, Norman Hassan, Astro. Inter-racial reggae group named after the unemployment benefit form. Consistent hitmakers from 1980–95. 'Red Red Wine'.

U2 (Ire): Bono (Paul Hewson), The Edge (David Evans), Adam Clayton, Larry Mullen, Jr. The first Irish act to top the US chart. 'I Still Haven't Found What I'm Looking For'.

Velvet Underground (US/Ger): Lou Reed, John Cale, Nico (d. 18/7/88), Sterling Morrison (d. 30/8/95), Maureen (Mo) Tucker. Innovative art-rock group, backed by Andy Warhol. Although short-lived, they influenced many subsequent bands, from Joy Division to The Jesus and Mary Chain. Singer Lou Reed went on to a successful solo career and John Cale and Nico also released solo albums. 'Venus in Furs'.

Wet Wet Wet (UK): Marti Pellow, Graeme Clark, Tom Cunningham, Neil Mitchell. Scottish pop band whose cover of the Troggs' 'Love Is All Around' topped the UK chart for 15 weeks in 1994.

The Who (UK): Roger Daltrey, Pete Townshend, John Entwhistle, Keith Moon (d. 7/9/78 of a drugs overdose, replaced by Kenney Jones). The group have had 28 UK hits, 26 in the USA, without ever topping either chart. 'I Can See For Miles'.

Stevie Wonder (US): b. Steveland Judkins 13/5/50, Saginaw, Michigan. Blind soul singer, songwriter and multi-instrumentalist who first recorded in 1962 as Little Stevie Wonder. Recipient of 17 Grammy Awards. 'I Just Called To Say I Love You'.

CLIFF RICHARD IS THE ONLY ACT TO HAVE NO.1 HITS OVER A PERIOD OF FIVE DECADES

Music Prizewinners

- *Wannabe*, by the Spice Girls, which won a Brit Award for best single, was No. 1 in 31 countries and sold in excess of 4 million copies.
- Hillary Clinton became the first First Lady to win a Grammy when she won the best spoken-word album in 1996.
- Celine Dion has won a Grammy, the Eurovision Song Contest and been nominated twice for Best International Female at the Brit Awards.
- The Irish singer Johnny Logan is the only performer to have won the Eurovision Song Contest twice.

BRIT AWARDS

The Brit Awards are the most prestigious awards in the British music industry. Sponsored by Britannia Music, they are awarded annually in a number of categories and relate to the previous year's musical achievements.

Year	BEST SINGLE BY A BRITISH ARTIST	BEST BRITISH GROUP
1982	*Tainted Love* Soft Cell	Police
1983	*Come On Eileen* Dexy's Midnight Runners	Dire Straits
1984	*Karma Chameleon* Culture Club	Culture Club
1985	*Relax* Frankie Goes to Hollywood	Wham!
1986	*Everybody Wants to Rule the World* Tears for Fears	Dire Straits
1987	*West End Girls* Pet Shop Boys	Five Star
1988	*Never Gonna Give You Up* Rick Astley	Pet Shop Boys
1989	*Perfect* Fairground Attraction	Erasure
1990	*Another Day in Paradise* Phil Collins	Fine Young Cannibals
1991	*Enjoy the Silence* Depeche Mode	The Cure
1992	*Killer* Seal	The KLF Foundation Simply Red
1993	*Stay* Shakespeare's Sister	Simply Red
1994	*Pray* Take That	Stereo MC's
1995	*Parklife* Blur	Blur
1996	*Back for Good* Take That	Oasis
1997	*Wannabe* The Spice Girls	Manic Street Preachers

GRAMMY AWARDS

The Grammy Awards are organized annually by the National Academy of Recording Arts and Sciences in America. Founded in 1957 by recording artists, composers and craftsmen to advance the arts and technology of recording, the Academy has presented Grammy awards every year since 1958. Major awards include:

Year	ALBUM OF THE YEAR	RECORD OF THE YEAR	BEST MALE POP VOCAL PERFORMANCE	BEST FEMALE POP VOCAL PERFORMANCE
1958	*The Music from Peter Gunn* Henry Mancini	*Nel Blu Dipinto Di Blu (Volare)* Domenico Modugno	*Catch a Falling Star* Perry Como	*Ella Fitzgerald Sings the Irving Berlin Song Book* Ella Fitzgerald
1959	*Come Dance with Me* Frank Sinatra	*Mack The Knife* Bobby Darin	*Come Dance with Me* Frank Sinatra	*But Not For Me* Ella Fitzgerald
1960	*Button Down Mind* Bob Newhart	*Theme From A Summer Place* Percy Faith	*Georgia on my Mind* Ray Charles	*Mack the Knife* Ella Fitzgerald
1961	*Judy at Carnegie Hall* Judy Garland	*Moon River* Henry Mancini	*Lollipops and Roses* (single) Jack Jones	*Judy at Carnegie Hall* (album) Judy Garland
1962	*The First Family* Vaughn Meader	*I Left my Heart in San Francisco* Tony Bennett	*I Left my Heart in San Francisco* (album) Tony Bennett	*Ella Swings Brightly with Nelson Riddle* (album) Ella Fitzgerald
1963	*The Barbra Streisand Album* Barbra Streisand	*The Days of Wine and Roses* Henry Mancini	*Wives and Lovers* (single) Jack Jones	*The Barbra Streisand Album* Barbra Streisand
1964	*Getz/Gilberto* Stan Getz, Joao Gilberto	*The Girl From Ipanema* Stan Getz, Astrud Gilberto	*Hello, Dolly!* (single) Louis Armstrong	*People* (single) Barbra Streisand
1965	*September of my Years* Frank Sinatra	*A Taste of Honey* Herb Alpert and the Tijuana Brass	*It Was a Very Good Year* (single) Frank Sinatra	*My Name is Barbra* (album) Barbra Streisand
1966	*Sinatra, A Man and His Music* Frank Sinatra	*Strangers in the Night* Frank Sinatra	*Strangers in the Night* Frank Sinatra	*If He Walked into my Life* (single) Eydie Gorme
1967	*Sgt Pepper's Lonely Hearts Club Band* The Beatles	*Up, Up and Away* 5th Dimension	*By the Time I Get to Phoenix* (single) Glen Campbell	*Ode to Billie Joe* (single) Bobbie Gentry
1968	*By the Time I Get To Phoenix* Glen Campbell	*Mrs Robinson* Simon and Garfunkel	*Light my Fire* (single) Jose Feliciano	*Do You Know the Way to San Jose* (single) Dionne Warwick
1969	*Blood, Sweat & Tears* Blood, Sweat & Tears	*Aquarius/Let the Sunshine In* 5th Dimension	*Everybody's Talkin'* Harry Nilsson	*Is That All There Is* (single) Peggy Lee
1970	*Bridge Over Troubled Water* Simon and Garfunkel	*Bridge Over Troubled Water* Simon and Garfunkel	*Everything is Beautiful* (single) Ray Stevens	*I'll Never Fall in Love Again* (album) Dionne Warwick
1971	*Tapestry* Carole King	*It's Too Late* Carole King	*You've Got a Friend* (single) James Taylor	*Tapestry* (album) Carole King
1972	*The Concert for Bangladesh* George Harrison, Ravi Shankar, Bob Dylan *et al.*	*The First Time Ever I Saw Your Face* Roberta Flack	*Without You* (single) Nilsson	*I Am Woman* (single) Helen Reddy
1973	*Innervisions* Stevie Wonder	*Killing Me Softly With His Song* Roberta Flack	*You Are The Sunshine of my Life* (single) Stevie Wonder	*Killing Me Softly With His Song* (single) Roberta Flack
1974	*Fulfillingness' First Finale* Stevie Wonder	*I Honestly Love You* Olivia Newton-John	*Fulfillingness' First Finale* (album) Stevie Wonder	*I Honestly Love You* (single) Olivia Newton-John
1975	*Still Crazy After All These Years* Paul Simon	*Love Will Keep Us Together* Captain & Tennille	*Still Crazy After All These Years* (album) Paul Simon	*At Seventeen* (single) Janis Ian
1976	*Songs in the Key of Life* Stevie Wonder	*This Masquerade* George Benson	*Songs in the Key of Life* (album) Stevie Wonder	*Hasten Down the Wind* (album) Linda Ronstadt
1977	*Rumours* Fleetwood Mac	*Hotel California* Eagles	*Handy Man* (single) James Taylor	*Love Song From A Star is Born (Evergreen)* (single) Barbra Streisand

EUROVISION SONG CONTEST

The Eurovision Song Contest is a European competition held annually since 1956. Each participating country submits one song, which is performed on the contest night, and then judges and votes on all entries. The event, whilst not at the cutting edge of pop music, does have a large following, and is a popular event in the television calendar. The leading country is Ireland, with a total of seven wins. France and Luxembourg and the UK have each won five times, and the Netherlands has four wins.

	SONG	PERFORMER(S)	COUNTRY
1956	*Refrain*	Lys Assia	Switzerland
1957	*Net Als Toen*	Corry Brokken	Netherlands
1958	*Dors Mon Amour*	André Claveau	France
1959	*Een Beetje*	Teddy Scholten	Netherlands
1960	*Tom Pillibi*	Jacqueline Boyer	France
1961	*Nous, Les Amoureux*	Jean-Claude Pascal	Luxembourg
1962	*Un Premier Amour*	Isabelle Aubret	France
1963	*Dansevise*	Grethe and Jorgen Ingmann	Denmark
1964	*Non Ho L'Età*	Gigliola Cinquetti	Italy
1965	*Poupée de Cire, Poupée de Son*	France Gall	Luxembourg
1966	*Merci Chérie*	Udo Jürgens	Austria
1967	*Puppet on a String*	Sandie Shaw	UK
1968	*La, La, La*	Massiel	Spain
1969	*Un Jour, Un Enfant*	Frida Boccara	France
	De Troubadour	Lennie Kuhr	Netherlands
	Vivo Cantando	Salome	Spain
	Boom Bang-a-Bang	Lulu	UK
1970	*All Kinds of Everything*	Dana	Ireland
1971	*Un Banc, Un Arbre, Une Rue*	Severine	Monaco
1972	*Apres Toi*	Vicky Leandros	Luxembourg
1973	*Tu Te Reconnaîtras*	Anne-Marie David	Luxembourg
1974	*Waterloo*	Abba	Sweden
1975	*Ding-Dinge-Dong*	Teach-In	Netherlands
1976	*Save Your Kisses For Me*	Brotherhood of Man	UK
1977	*L'Oiseau et l'Enfant*	Marie Myriam	France
1978	*A Ba Ni Bi*	Izhar Cohen and Alphabeta	Israel
1979	*Hallelujah*	Gali Atari and Milk and Honey	Israel
1980	*What's Another Year*	Johnny Logan	Ireland
1981	*Making Your Mind Up*	Bucks Fizz	UK
1982	*Ein bisschen Frieden*	Nicole	Germany
1983	*Si La Vie est Cadeau*	Corinne Hermes	Luxembourg
1984	*Diggi-Loo, Diggi-Ley*	Herreys	Sweden
1985	*La det Swinge*	Bobbysocks	Norway
1986	*J'Aime La Vie*	Sandra Kim	Belgium
1987	*Hold Me Now*	Johnny Logan	Ireland
1988	*Ne Partez pas Sans Moi*	Céline Dion	Switzerland
1989	*Rock Me*	Riva	Yugoslavia
1990	*Insieme: 1992*	Toto Cutugno	Italy
1991	*Fangad av en Stormvind*	Carola	Sweden
1992	*Why Me*	Linda Martin	Ireland
1993	*In Your Eyes*	Niamh Kavanagh	Ireland
1994	*Rock'n'Roll Kids*	Paul Harrington and Charlie McGettigan	Ireland
1995	*Nocturne*	Secret Garden	Norway
1996	*The Voice*	Eimear Quinn	Ireland
1997	*Love Shine a Light*	Katrina and the Waves	UK

	ALBUM OF THE YEAR	RECORD OF THE YEAR	BEST MALE POP VOCAL PERFORMANCE	BEST FEMALE POP VOCAL PERFORMANCE
1978	*Saturday Night Fever* Bee Gees and others	*Just the Way You Are* Billy Joel	*Copacabana (At the Copa)* (single) Barry Manilow	*You Needed Me* (single) Anne Murray
1979	*52nd Street* Billy Joel	*What a Fool Believes* The Doobie Brothers	*52nd Street* (album) Billy Joel	*I'll Never Love This Way Again* (single) Dionne Warwick
1980	*Christopher Cross* Christopher Cross	*Sailing* Christopher Cross	*This Is It* (track) Kenny Loggins	*The Rose* (single) Bette Midler
1981	*Double Fantasy* John Lennon and Yoko Ono	*Bette Davis Eyes* Kim Carnes	*Breaking Away* (album) Al Jarreau	*Lena Horne: The Lady and Her Music Live on Broadway* (album) Lena Horne
1982	*Toto IV* Toto	*Rosanna* Toto	*Truly* (single) Lionel Richie	*You Should Hear How She Talks About You* (single) Melissa Manchester
1983	*Thriller* Michael Jackson	*Beat It* Michael Jackson	*Thriller* (album) Michael Jackson	*Flashdance What A Feeling* (single) Irene Cara
1984	*Can't Slow Down* Lionel Richie	*What's Love Got To Do With It* Tina Turner	*Against All Odds (Take A Look At Me Now)* (single) Phil Collins	*What's Love Got To Do With It* (single) Tina Turner
1985	*No Jacket Required* Phil Collins	*We are the World* USA For Africa	*No Jacket Required* (album) Phil Collins	*Saving All my Love For You* (single) Whitney Houston
1986	*Graceland* Paul Simon	*Higher Love* Steve Winwood	*Higher Love* (single) Steve Winwood	*The Broadway Album* (album) Barbra Streisand
1987	*Joshua Tree* U2	*Graceland* Paul Simon	*Bring on the Night* (album) Sting	*I Wanna Dance With Somebody (Who Loves Me)* (single) Whitney Houston
1988	*Faith* George Michael	*Don't Worry Be Happy* Bobby McFerrin	*Don't Worry Be Happy* (single) Bobby McFerrin	*Fast Car* (single) Tracy Chapman
1989	*Nick of Time* Bonnie Raitt	*Wind Beneath my Wings* Bette Midler	*How Am I Supposed to Live Without You* (single) Michael Bolton	*Nick of Time* (track) Bonnie Raitt
1990	*Back on the Block* Quincy Jones	*Another Day in Paradise* Phil Collins	*Oh Pretty Woman* (single) Roy Orbison	*Vision of Love* (single) Mariah Carey
1991	*Unforgettable* Natalie Cole	*Unforgettable* Natalie Cole	*When A Man Loves a Woman* (single) Michael Bolton	*Something to Talk About* (single) Bonnie Raitt
1992	*Unplugged* Eric Clapton	*Tears in Heaven* Eric Clapton	*Tears in Heaven* (single) Eric Clapton	*Constant Craving* (single) k.d. lang
1993	*The Bodyguard* Whitney Houston	*I Will Always Love You* Whitney Houston	*If I Ever Lose my Faith In You* (single) Sting	*I Will Always Love You* (single) Whitney Houston
1994	*MTV Unplugged* Tony Bennett	*All I Wanna Do* Sheryl Crow	*Can You Feel the Love Tonight* (single) Elton John	*All I Wanna Do* (single) Sheryl Crow
1995	*Jagged Little Pill* Alanis Morissette	*Kiss From A Rose* Seal	*Kiss From a Rose* (single) Seal	*No More 'I Love You's'* (single) Annie Lennox
1996	*Falling Into you* Celine Dion	*Change the World* Eric Clapton	*Change the World* (single) Eric Clapton	*Unbreak my Heart* (single) Toni Braxton

Western Art

- The largest work of art – *Wrapped Islands* (1980–83) – was created by the conceptual artist Christo when he encircled 11 islands in Key Biscayne, Florida, with 600,000 m^2 of pink woven polypropylene.
- The Hermitage Museum in St Petersburg, Russia (containing more than 12,000 sculptures, 16,000 paintings and 600,000 drawings and works on paper), is the world's largest public collection of art.
- Leonardo da Vinci's *Mona Lisa* – assessed in 1962 at $100 million – is the most valuable painting in the world.

Altdorfer, Albrecht (*c.* 1480–1538), German painter and engraver. Developer of the landscape genre: *The Battle of Alexander and Darius on the Issus* (1529).

André, Carl (1935–), US Minimalist sculptor who caused an uproar at the Tate Gallery in 1966 with 120 bricks laid on the floor: *Equivalents VIII* (1966).

Angelico, Fra (*c.* 1400–55), early Renaissance Florentine religious painter: cycle of frescos in San Marco, Florence.

Arp, Jean (Hans) (1887–1966), French Dadaist artist celebrated for his rounded abstract sculptures.

Bacon, Francis (1909–92), English painter noted for the disturbing quality of his twisted figures: *Three Studies at the Base of a Crucifixion* (1944); *Study after Velazquez* (1499); portraits of Pope Innocent X.

Balla, Giacomo (1871–1958), Italian Futurist painter and sculptor: the painting *Dynamism of a Dog on a Leash* (1912).

Bartolomeo, Fra (*c.* 1472–*c.* 1517), Florentine High Renaissance painter: *Last Judgment* in the Santa Maria Nuova (unfinished).

Beardsley, Aubrey (1872–98), English Symbolist artist and illustrator noted for his decadent illustrations.

Beckman, Max (1884–1950), German Expressionist painter: *The Night* (1918–19).

Bellini, Giovanni (*c.* 1430–1516), early Renaissance Venetian artist: the altarpieces of the Frari (1488); San Zaccaria (*c.* 1505); other mythological scenes.

Bernini, Gian Lorenzo (1598–1680), Italian High Baroque sculptor and painter: the sculptures *Apollo and Daphne* (1625) and *Ecstasy of Saint Theresa* (1645–52).

Beuys, Joseph (1921–86), influential German artist: *Coyote* (1974), a week-long dialogue with a live coyote.

Blake, William (1757–1827), English Romantic artist, poet, engraver and visionary whose art embraced and augmented his complex poetic philosophy.

Pluto and Persephone (The Rape of Proserpina) (1621–22)
Gian Lorenzo Bernini

Boccioni, Umberto (1882–1916), Italian Futurist painter and sculptor: the sculpture *Unique Forms of Continuity in Space* (1913).

Bonnard, Pierre (1864–1947), French painter noted for his middle-class interiors and nudes.

Bosch, Hiëronymus (*c.* 1450–1516), Flemish painter celebrated for his fantastic and grotesque imagery: *Garden of Earthly Delights* (*c.* 1505–10).

Botticelli, Sandro (*c.* 1445–1510), early Renaissance Florentine painter: *Primavera* (1477–78); *Birth of Venus* (*c.* 1485).

Boucher, François (1703–70), French Rococo painter: *The Rising of the Sun, The Setting of the Sun* (1753); *Reclining Girl* (1751).

Boudin, Eugène (1824–98), French painter of seascapes and beach scenes: *Women on the Beach at Trouville* (1872).

Brancusi, Constantin (1876–1957) Romanian-born French abstract sculptor famous for his geometric concentration of form and the quality of his materials: *Endless Column* (1937).

Salvador Dali at work

Braque, Georges (1882–1963), French painter and co-founder of Cubism: *Grand Nu* (1907–08); the *Atelier* series (1948 onwards).

Bronzino, Agnolo (1503–72), Florentine Mannerist painter known for his portraits: *Venus, Cupid, Folly and Time* (*c.* 1540).

Brown, Ford Madox (1821–93), English painter stylistically similar to the Pre-Raphaelites and whose social beliefs were reflected in his famous painting *Work* (1852–65).

Bruegel, Pieter (the Elder) (*c.* 1525–69), foremost of a Flemish family of painters: *Peasant Wedding Dance* (1566); *Hunters in the Snow* (1565).

Burne-Jones, Sir Edward (1833–98), English Symbolist painter, illustrator, and designer strongly influenced by the Pre-Raphaelites and noted for his ethereal style.

Calder, Alexander (1898–1976), US Kinetic sculptor best known for his metal mobiles.

Canaletto, Antonio (1697–1768), Venetian city painter of the period noted for the topographical quality in his art.

Canova, Antonio (1757–1822), Italian Neo-Classical sculptor: *Daedalus and Icarus* (1779).

Caravaggio, Michelangelo Merisi da (1573–1610), early Italian Baroque painter noted for his dramatic use of light and shade: *The Life of St Matthew* (1599–1602).

Carrà, Carlo (1881–1966), Italian Futurist painter.

Carracci, Annibale (1560–1609), member of a family of Italian painters: decoration of the gallery ceiling in the Farnese Palace, Rome.

César (1921–), French sculptor noted for his use of plastics and used materials: *The Yellow Buick* made from crushed car bodies.

Cézanne, Paul (1839–1906), French painter who briefly painted with the Impressionist group and who had a crucial influence on the Cubists.

Chardin, Jean-Baptiste-Siméon (1699–1779), French painter of still life and everyday domestic scenes.

Chagall, Marc (1887–1985), Russian-born French painter: his work has a dreamlike atmosphere with irrational juxtapositions: *I and the Village* (*c.* 1911).

Chirico, Giorgio de (1888–1978), Italian painter and forerunner of the Surrealists notable for his haunting cityscapes: *The Great Tower* (*c.* 1913).

Christo (1935–), Bulgarian-born Belgian artist who has embarked on such projects as wrapping up sections of the Australian coastline in plastic.

Christus, Petrus (active 1444–72/3), Flemish painter noted for the use of geometric perspective: *Lamentation* (*c.* 1448); *St Eligius and Two Lovers* (1449).

Cimabue (*c.* 1240–*c.* 1302), Florentine painter who introduced more realistic painting: S. Trinità *Madonna* (*c.* 1285).

Claude Lorrain (1600–82), French Classical landscape painter notable

Early Renaissance Art

The dominant theme of this period (1400–1570) is the revival of interest in classical (ancient Greek and Roman) architecture, literature and art by artists such as Donatello, Lippi and Botticelli. Florence was the first centre of such rediscovery, followed by Padua, Venice and finally Rome. Advances were made in the realistic depiction of figures and perspective, and painting with oil was invented. After 1500, the movement spread to northern Europe.

High Renaissance and Mannerist Art

One of the most concentrated groups of artistic genius ever known was gathered in Rome in the 16th century. Artistic innovations by artists like Correggio spread to northern Europe and led to the superficial elegance of Mannerism – a display of exaggerated sophistication and virtuosity, sometimes combined with a heightened emotionalism and religiosity, as seen, for example, in the work of El Greco in Spain, Bruegel (the Elder) in the Netherlands and Holbein (the Younger) in Germany. However, the Counter-Reformation's restrictions on subject matter and treatment in religious art caused Mannerism to lose much of its vigour by the end of the 16th century.

The Dutch School

The art of painting flourished suddenly in the 17th century in the Netherlands, coinciding with the overthrow of Spanish rule and Dutch international mercantile success. Artists, such as van Dyck, Hals and Rembrandt, concentrated on the type of paintings which the Dutch had long specialized in – still life, scenes of everyday life, landscape and portraiture.

CHAGALL AND ERNST WERE RESCUED FROM NAZI GERMANY BY AMERICAN JOURNALIST

for his rendering of light and atmosphere in his paintings.

Constable, John (1776–1837), English Romantic landscape painter: *The Hay Wain* (1821).

Corot, Camille (1796–1875), French landscape and figure painter; precursor of the Impressionists: *The Studio* (1870); *Ponte de Mantes* (1870); *Sens Cathedral* (1874).

Correggio, Antonio (*c.* 1490–1534), influential Italian High Renaissance painter: *Jupiter and Io* (1531).

Cortona, Pietro da (1596–1669), Italian Baroque painter: *Allegory of Divine Providence and Barberini Power* (1633–39), a ceiling fresco.

Courbet, Gustav (1819–77), French painter and foremost Realist artist: *The Peasants of Flagey* (1850); *The Stonebreakers* (1849).

Cranach, Lucas, the Elder (1472–1553), influential German painter of the 16th century: *Rest on the Flight into Egypt* (1504).

Cuyp, Aelbert (1620–91), Dutch landscape painter noted for his views of rivers and towns in dusk and dawn: *View of Nijmegen* (*c.* 1660).

Dali, Salvador (1904–89), Spanish Surrealist artist famous for his hallucinatory paintings and films: *The Persistence of Memory* (1931).

Daubigny, Charles-François (1817–78), French landscape painter of the Barbizon School.

Daumier, Honoré (1808–79), French caricaturist whose works contain bitter satires on political and social subjects.

David, Jacques-Louis (1748–1825), French Neo-Classical painter: *Death of Marat* (1793); *View of the Luxembourg Gardens* (1794).

Degas, Edgar (1834–1917), French Impressionist painter and sculptor whose favourite subjects were dancers and race horses: *The Little Dancer of Fourteen* (1880–81); *The Rehearsal* (1882).

de Kooning, Willem (1904–97), US Abstract Expressionist: *Woman* series.

Delacroix, Eugène (1798–1863), French Romantic painter: *The Massacre at Chios* (1823); *The Death of Sardanapalus* (1827).

Delaunay, Robert (1885–1941), French painter influenced by Cubism: *Circular Forms* (from 1912).

Derain, André (1880–1954), French painter and one of the founders of Fauvism.

Donatello (*c.* 1386–1466), highly influential early-Renaissance Florentine sculptor: equestrian statue of *Gattemalata* (1443–47); high altar for the church of St Anthony.

Duccio di Buoninsegna (*c.* 1255–1319), Sienese painter influential in his introduction of two-dimensional decorative surface art.

Duchamp, Marcel (1887–1968), highly influential French Dadaist artist: *The Bride Stripped Bare by her Bachelors, Even* (1915–23).

Dufy, Raoul (1877–1953), French painter briefly connected with the Fauves: *Deauville* (1930).

Dürer, Albrecht (1471–1528), German painter, engraver and theoretician: *Knight, Death and Devil*; *Melancholia*; and *St Jerome in his Cell* (all 1513–14).

Ensor, James (1860–1949), Belgian painter who was a major influence on Expressionism and Surrealism: *Entry of Christ into Brussels* (1880).

Epstein, Jacob (1880–1959), US-born English sculptor whose early Vorticist works include *The Rock-Drill* (1913–14).

Ballet Dancers (1880)
Edgar Degas

Nude Descending a Staircase, No. 2 (1912)
Marcel Duchamp

A Cornfield, with Cypresses (1889)
Vincent van Gogh

Ernst, Max (1891–1976), German painter, sculptor and collagist, initially a Dadaist, then a Surrealist: *Here Everything is Still Floating* (1920).

Eyck, Hubert van (1366/70–1426), Flemish painter (brother of Jan).

Eyck, Jan van (*c.* 1390–1441), Flemish painter, celebrated for the realistic detail of his portraits: the Ghent altarpiece (1432; in collaboration with his brother Hubert).

Fragonard, Jean-Honoré (1732–1806), French Rococo painter: four *Progress of Love* paintings (1771–73); *The Swing* (1769).

Friedrich, Caspar David (1774–1840), German Romantic landscape painter noted for his evocative scenes of mountain peaks and moonlit shores: *The Cross in the Mountains* (*c.* 1807).

Fuseli, John Henry (1741–1825), Swiss Romantic painter living in England notable for his explorations of the darker side of human nature: *The Nightmare* (1782).

Gabo, Naum (1890–1977), Russian sculptor and co-founder of Constructivism: *Rotterdam* (1955).

Gainsborough, Thomas (1727–88), English portrait and landscape painter: *Mr and Mrs Andrews* (*c.*1750); *The Blue Boy* (*c.* 1770).

Gaudier-Brzeska, Henri (1891–1915), influential French Vorticist sculptor.

Gauguin, Paul (1848–1903), French painter, sculptor and printmaker celebrated for his brightly coloured, mystical paintings of Brittany and the South Seas: *Where Do We Come From? What Are We? Where Are We Going?* (1897).

Géricault, Théodore (1791–1824), French Romantic painter and one of the founders of Romanticism: *Derby at Epson* (1821); *The Raft of the Medusa* (1819).

Ghiberti, Lorenzo (1378–1455), early Renaissance Florentine sculptor and goldsmith: bronze doors for the Florence Baptistery (the second set, so-called 'Gates of Paradise').

Giacometti, Alberto (1901–66), Swiss sculptor well known for his elongated bronze human figures.

Giambologna (1529–1608), Flemish Mannerist sculptor: the influential sculpture *The Rape of the Sabines* (1579–83).

Gilbert and George (Gilbert Proesch, 1943–, and George Passmore, 1942–), English avant-garde artists involved in various art forms, including performance art.

Giorgione (*c.* 1476/8–1510), Venetian painter who introduced pastoral subjects to paintings.

Giotto di Bondone (1266–1337), influential Florentine painter who introduced a new naturalism: *Ognissanti Madonna* (*c.* 1310–15).

Goncharova, Natalia (1881–1962), Russian Rayonist painter.

Gorky, Arshile (1904–48), Armenian-born US painter, a Surrealist and Abstract Expressionist: *The Artist and his Mother* (*c.* 1926–29); *Garden in Sochi* (1941).

Goya y Lucientes, Francisco José de (1746–1828), Spanish Romantic painter and etcher: *Maja Nude* and *Maja Clothed* (1797–1800); *The Third of May* (1814).

Greco, El (Doménikos Theotokopoulos; 1541–1614), Greek Mannerist painter and sculptor working in Spain: *The Burial of Count Orgaz* (1586); *Christ Stripped of his Garments* (1577–79).

Gris, Juan (1887–1927), Spanish painter noted for his development of

Classicism was one of the most dominant trends in 17th-century art, particularly in Catholic countries such as Italy and France. Artists such as Lorraine and Poussin reacted against the aridity of Late Mannerism and attempted to return to the naturalism, harmonious equilibrium and compositional coherence of High Renaissance art while adding a new physical realism and emotional immediacy. Its restrained qualities of directness and precision enlivened traditional ideas of balance and decorum.

► NEO-CLASSICISM

18th-century archaeological discoveries in Italy and Greece began a re-evaluation of Europe's origins of civilization. New (Neo-) Classicism focused more on romance and sublimity than clarity and dignity. Taken up in France by painters such as David and Ingres, French intellectuals developed it into international Neo-Classicism, which spread throughout Europe to be embraced by artists such as the sculptor Canova.

► ROMANTICISM

The Romantic Movement in art emerged in the late 18th century and flourished until the middle of the 19th. Artists, such as Turner, Géricault and Goya, reacted against the aesthetic and ethical values of Classical and Neo-Classical art, as well as the materialism and ugliness of the Industrial Revolution. The influence of Romantic writers was important in providing subject matter and a philosophy for the Romantic painters and it is the content of the paintings and the attitude of the artists themselves that give the movement coherence.

the Cubist style: *Homage to Picasso* (1911–12).

Grosz, George (1893–1959), German illustrator, painter and satirical caricaturist.

Grünewald, Matthias (*c.* 1470–1528), German religious painter: crucifixion of Christ on the Isenheim altarpiece.

Guardi, Francesco (1712–93), member of a family of notable Venetian painters which included his brothers Nicolò and Giovanni Antonio, celebrated for his view paintings and architectural scenes.

Hals, Frans (1580/85–1666), Dutch genre and portrait painter: *The Merry Drinker* (*c.* 1628–30); *Laughing Cavalier* (1624).

Hamilton, Richard (1922–), English Pop artist whose work reflects his interest in marketing styles: *$he* (1958–61).

Heartfield, John (Helmut Herzfelde; 1891–1968), German artist notable for his political photomontages: *Hurrah, the Butter is Finished* (1935).

Heckel, Erich (1883–1970), German Expressionist painter, graphic artist and co-founder of *Die Brücke*.

Hepworth, Dame Barbara (1903–75), English abstract sculptress.

Hirst, Damien (1965–), provocative English installation artist noted for his explorations of mortality, particularly through the use of dead animals.

Hobbema, Meindert (1638–1709), Dutch landscape painter: *Avenue at Middelharnis* (1689).

Hockney, David (1937–), English painter, initially prominent in Pop Art but notable for his innovations in many styles: *A Bigger Splash* (1966–67).

Hogarth, William (1697–1764), English painter and engraver whose works often contained a literary element: *The Shrimp Girl* (1740); *Marriage à la Mode* (1743).

Holbein, Hans (the Younger) (1497/8–1543), German portrait and religious painter: *Dead Christ* (1521); *Erasmus* (1517).

Hooch, Pieter de (1629–84), Dutch genre painter celebrated for his use of light in garden and courtyard scenes: *Courtyard in Delft* (1658).

Hunt, William Holman (1827–1910), English painter noted for his detail and symbolism; one of the founders of the Pre-Raphaelite Brotherhood: *The Awakening Conscience* (1853–54).

Ingres, Jean Auguste Dominique (1780–1867), French Neo-Classical painter known for his Odalisque series.

Jawlensky, Alexei von (1864–1941), Russian painter loosely associated with *Der Blaue Reiter: Head of a Young Girl and Night* (1933).

Young Man Holding a Skull (*c.* 1626–28)
Frans Hals

Johns, Jasper (1930–), US painter, printmaker and sculptor, best known as the founder of Pop Art: *Field Painting* (1963–04).

Judd, Donald (1928–), US Minimalist sculptor whose work concentrates on rows of geometric units (often boxes).

Kandinsky, Wassily (1866–1944), Russian-born painter, pioneer of abstract art and member of *Der Blaue Reiter*.

Kiefer, Anselm (1945–), German Neo-Expressionist painter whose work concentrates on German history.

Kirchner, Ernest Ludwig (1880–1938), German Expressionist painter, graphic artist and co-founder of *Die Brücke*.

Klee, Paul (1879–1940), Influential Swiss painter and graphic artist whose work ranges from Symbolist to Abstract.

Klimt, Gustav (1862–1918), Austrian painter and founder of the Vienna Secession, famous for his highly decorative paintings: *The Kiss* (1908).

Kline, Franz (1910–62), US Abstract Expressionist painter.

Kokoschka, Oskar (1886–1980), Austrian Expressionist painter: *The Tempest* (1914).

La Tour, Georges de (1593–1652), French painter who worked in a style akin to Caravaggio: *The Denial of St Peter* (1650).

Madame Moitessier (1844–57)
Jean Auguste Dominique Ingres

Léger, Fernand (1881–1955), French painter famous for his distinctive semi-abstract monumental style, often depicting people and machines.

Leonardo da Vinci (1452–1519), one of the greatest Italian painters (also an engineer, architect, musician and scientist): the unfinished *Adoration of the Magi* (1481), *The Virgin of the Rocks* (1483–*c.* 1486 and 1483–1508); *The Last Supper* (*c.* 1495–97); *Mona Lisa* (*c.* 1503).

Lewis, Wyndham (1882–1957), Canadian-born British painter, writer and leader of the Vorticists: *Workshop* (1914).

LeWitt, Sol (1928–), US Minimalist sculptor.

Lucas van Leyden (1494–1533), Dutch painter and engraver of historical and domestic scenes: *Last Judgement* (1526–27).

The Water-Lily Pond (1899)
Claude Monet

Lichtenstein, Roy (1923–), US Pop artist best known for his enlarged paintings of comic strip images: *Whaam!* (1963).

Liebermann, Max (1847–1935), German painter and founder of the Berlin Secession.

Lippi, Fra Filippo (*c.* 1406–69), early Renaissance Florentine painter: fresco paintings of the lives of St Stephen and St John the Baptist, Prato Cathedral (1452–65).

Lorenzetti, Ambrogio (active *c.* 1319–48), Sienese sculptor and painter known for his early realistic landscapes.

Lorenzetti, Pietro (active *c.* 1319–48), Sienese sculptor and painter known for *The Descent from the Cross* (*c.* 1330).

Lorenzo Monaco (Lorenzo the Monk; *c.* 1370/2–1422/5), Sienese International Gothic painter and miniaturist: *Adoration* (*c.* 1424).

Macke, August (1887–1914), German painter, founder of *Der Blaue Reiter.*

Magritte, René (1898–1967), Belgian Surrealist famous for his conventional paintings made bizarre by the unexpected juxtaposition of objects: *The Key of Dreams* (1930); *Time Transfixed* (1938).

Malevich, Kasimir (1878–1935), Russian painter and founder of Suprematism: *White on White* series (*c.* 1918).

Manet, Edouard (1832–83), French painter, considered the father of modern painting: *Déjeuner sur l'herbe* ('Picnic on the grass'; 1863); *Olympia* (1863).

Mantegna, Andrea (*c.* 1431–1506), northern Italian early Renaissance painter celebrated for his perfectionist work on perspective.

Marc, Franz (1880–1916), German Expressionist painter and member of *Der Blaue Reiter: The Blue Horse* (1911); *Fighting Forms* (1913).

Marquet, Albert (1875–1947), French painter noted for his bright Fauvist colours in his early paintings.

Masaccio (1401–*c.* 1428), influential early Renaissance Florentine painter: *Trinity* fresco (1428), in Santa Maria Novella, Florence; the fresco paintings in the Brancacci Chapel, Florence (*c.* 1425–28).

▶ REALISM

Realism (1840–80) originated in France and soon spread throughout Europe to America. The Realists, such as Courbet and Millet, reacted against the subjectivity, individualism and historical obsessions of the Romantics, adopting instead a naturalistic style based on truth. Scenes of nature and everyday life were approached with detached, objective observation and their brushstrokes tended to be distinct and precise rather than the vivid, dramatic brushstrokes of the Romantics.

▶ THE BARBIZON SCHOOL

This movement takes its name from the village of Barbizon, near Fontainebleau, France, which, during the 1840s, became the centre for a group of French landscape painters. Artists such as Millet and Théodore Rousseau studied nature directly, aiming to create a realistic depiction of landscape without the restrictions of academic conventions. The Barbizon painters rejected the exaggerated idealism of Romanticism and Classicism's allegorical style. Their work helped the emergence of Impressionism.

▶ THE PRE-RAPHAELITES

The Pre-Raphaelite Brotherhood was a group of seven London artists (1848–56) formed to return to the style of Italian painting before Raphael (hence the name) as a protest against the frivolity of the prevailing English School of the day. It was started by Hunt, Millais and Rossetti who, at first, signed their paintings anonymously with the monogram PRB. Repulsed by the materialism of their time, their subject matter was often drawn from religion and legend, and their style was minutely detailed.

Masson, André (1896–1987), French Surrealist painter noted for his spontaneous drawings undertaken while in a trance.

Matisse, Henri (1869–1954), influential 20th-century artist and founder of Fauvism: *Dance* and *Music* (1909–10); series of Odalisques.

Michelangelo Buonarroti (1475–1564), foremost Italian sculptor, painter, and architect: David sculpture (1501–04); Sistine Chapel ceiling (1508–12); *Moses and the Slaves* statues (1513–16); *Last Judgement* fresco (Sistine Chapel; 1536–41).

Millais, Sir John Everett (1829–96), English painter and co-founder of the Pre-Raphaelite Brotherhood. Best known for *Bubbles* (1886).

Millet, Jean-François (1814–75), French Realist painter celebrated for his dignified depiction of French peasants: *The Gleaners* (1857); *The Angelus* (1859).

Miró, Joan (1893–1983), Spanish Surrealist painter best known for his *Still Life with an Old Shoe* and *Dog Barking at the Moon*.

Modigliani, Amedeo (1884–1920), Italian painter and sculptor famous for his elongated figures and erotic nudes: *Reclining Nude* (*c.* 1919).

Moholy-Nagy, László (1895–1946), Hungarian-born US painter and experimental artist involved with the Bauhaus and Constructivism.

Mondrian, Piet (1872–1944), Dutch painter who developed from Symbolism to the pure abstraction of De Stijl: *Composition with Red, Yellow and Blue* (1939–42).

Monet, Claude (1840–1926), French Impressionist painter, particularly of landscapes: *Women in the Garden* (1867) and the series *Waterlilies* (1899–1926).

Moore, Henry (1898–1986), English sculptor, draughtsman and graphic artist well known for his rounded forms: *Two Forms* (1934); *Reclining Figure* (1938).

Moreau, Gustav (1826–98), French painter and leading Symbolist noted for his femme fatale paintings: *The Apparition* (1876); *Sâlomé Dancing* (1876).

Morisot, Berthe (1841–95), French painter notable for her paintings of women and children: *The Artist's Sister Edma and Their Mother* (1870).

Motherwell, Robert (1915–), US Abstract Expressionist painter also notable for his collages.

Munch, Edvard (1863–1944), Norwegian painter and forerunner of Expressionism: *The Scream* (1893).

Murillo, Bartolomé Esteban (1618–82), Spanish painter best known for his sentimental paintings of the Immaculate Conception.

A Woman Bathing in a Stream (1664)
Rembrandt van Rijn

Nash, Paul (1889–1946), English painter whose visionary landscapes and war paintings show Surrealist influences.

Newman, Barnett (1905–70), US Abstract Expressionist painter noted for his large, coloured canvases broken by 'zips' (bands) of colour.

Jeune fille couchée sur l'herbe (*c.* 1895)
Auguste Renoir

Nicholson, Ben (1894–1982), English abstract painter, some of whose works involve carved relief.

Nolan, Sir Sidney (1917–92), Australian painter whose work included subjects from Australian history.

Nolde, Emil (1867–1956), German Expressionist well known for his landscapes and religious pictures and a member of *Die Brücke*.

Oldenburg, Claes (1929–), Swedish-born US sculptor and graphic artist who was one of the leaders of the Pop Art movement.

The Thinker (1880)
Auguste Rodin

Palmer, Samuel (1805–81), English Romantic painter and etcher of pastoral scenes: *Repose of the Holy Family* (1824–25).

Parmigianino (1503–40), Italian Mannerist painter and etcher: *The Vision of St Jerome* (1527); *Madonna of the Long Neck* (*c.* 1535).

Pevsner, Antoine (1886–1962), Russian-born French painter, abstract sculptor and co-founder of Constructivism.

Picabia, Francis (1879–1953), French painter of the Dada school: *I see again in memory my dear Udnie* (1914).

Picasso, Pablo (1881–1973), Spanish painter, sculptor, graphic artist, co-founder of Cubism and the most outstanding artist of the 20th century: *Les Demoiselles d'Avignon* (1907); *Guernica* (1937).

Piero della Francesca (*c.* 1420–92), early Renaissance Italian painter: *The Flagellation of Christ* (*c.* 1456); the cycle *The Legend of the True Cross* at the Church of San Francesco, Arezzo (1452–66).

Pisanello, Antonio (*c.* 1395–1455/6), Veronese painter: *St George and the Princess* (*c.* 1433–38) and *Vision of St Eustace* (1435–38).

Pisano, Giovanni (active 1265–1314), Pisan sculptor: the pulpit in S Andrea, Pistoia (1301).

Pissarro, Camille (1831–1903), French Impressionist painter who briefly flirted with Pointillism during the 1880s.

Pollock, Jackson (1912–56), US Abstract Expressionist painter, a notable exponent of Action Painting.

Pontormo, Jacopo (1494–1557), Florentine painter, and one of the creators of Mannerism: *Deposition* (*c.* 1526).

Poussin, Nicolas (1594–1665), French Classical painter notable for the mathematical precision of his landscapes: *The Finding of Moses* (1638).

Raphael (1483–1520), Italian painter: wall paintings in the Vatican, including *School of Athens* (1509–11).

Rauschenberg, Robert (1925–), US artist best known for his combination of Pop Art and Abstract Expressionism: *Combine paintings* and *Monogram* (1959).

Ray, Man (Emanuel Rabinovitch; 1890–1976), US painter, photographer and film-maker involved both with Dada and Surrealism and famous for his technical experimentation.

Redon, Odilon (1840–1916), French Symbolist painter and lithographer: *The Cyclops* (1898).

Rembrandt van Rijn (1606–69), Dutch painter, etcher and draughtsman particularly celebrated for his portraits: *The Anatomy Lesson* (1632); *The Night Watch* (1642).

Renoir, Auguste (1841–1919), French Impressionist painter: *Umbrellas* (1883); *The Bathers* (1884–87).

Reynolds, Joshua (1723–92), English portrait painter: *Mrs Siddons as the Tragic Muse* (1784).

Riley, Bridget (1931–), foremost English Op artist: *Fall* (1963).

Rodin, Auguste (1840–1917), French sculptor who produced outstanding sculptures with a high degree of realism: *Le Penseur* (1880); *Le Baiser* (1886).

Romano, Giulio (1492–1546), Italian painter, architect, decorator and one of the founders of Mannerism: the decoration of the Palazzo del Tè.

▶ IMPRESSIONISM

Impressionism was an ill-defined association of artists who joined together to mount independent group exhibitions, held from 1874 to 1886, rather than compromise their art in order to be included in the Paris Salon, the official state-sponsored exhibition. Artists such as Monet, Renoir and Sisley shared some techniques and certain subjects and their approach was naturalistic. Their two main subjects were landscape and modern (often city) life. Often painted in the open air, their paintings show a concern with capturing the fleeting moment, particularly the effects of light, which they attempted to render with a free handling of paint.

▶ THE SYMBOLISTS

The Symbolist movement emerged in the 1880s as a reaction against the naturalist movement (the idea that art was an imitation of nature) and against materialistic values and modern industrialism. Symbolists such as Moreau and Redon in France and Beardsley in England rejected the natural imagery of Impression, seeking to escape into the past or into the world of fantasy and dreams. They believed that art existed alongside, not in direct relation to, the real world, and that it had its own rules – ideas which foreshadowed Surrealism.

▶ FAUVISM

Fauvism (*c.* 1905–07) was a short-lived but highly influential French movement of artists surrounding Matisse. The name came from a critic who called them *les fauves* (wild beasts). It is summarized by the daring and spontaneous handling of paint in bold, brilliant and sometimes non-representational colour.

PICASSO CREATED ABOUT 13,500 PAINTINGS AND DESIGNS IN HIS 78-YEAR CAREER

Romney, George (1734–1802), English portrait painter.

Rossetti, Dante Gabriel (1828–82), English painter, poet and co-founder of the Pre-Raphaelite Brotherhood.

Rothko, Mark (1903–70), US Abstract Expressionist, noted for the vast expanses of colour that fill his canvases.

Rouault, Georges (1871–1958), French painter, noted for his expressionist religious work.

Rousseau, Henri (1844–1910), French naive painter, noted for his stylized jungle paintings (1900–10).

Rousseau, Théodore (1812–67), French landscape painter of the Barbizon School: *Descent of the Cattle* (1835).

Rubens, Peter Paul (1577–1640), Flemish painter celebrated for the epic grandeur of his work: *The Raising of the Cross* (1610–11); *Descent from the Cross* (1611–14).

Ruisdael, Jacob van (1628/9–82), Dutch landscape painter and etcher, distinguished by his dramatic scenes: *Jewish Cemetery* (*c.* 1660).

Sargent, John Singer (1856–1925), US painter based in England who is best known for his portraits: *Carnation, Lily, Lily, Rose* (1885–86).

Schiele, Egon (1890–1918), Austrian Expressionist draughtsman and painter famous for his explicit and angular nudes.

Schwitters, Kurt (1887–1948), German Dadaist painter and sculptor famous for his Merz pieces (haphazard combinations of materials).

Seurat, Georges (1859–91), French painter, founder and leading exponent of Neo-Impressionism: *Bathers at Asnières* (1884).

Sickert, Walter (1860–1942), English painter who concentrated on paintings of lower-class London life: *Ennui* (*c.* 1913).

Signac, Paul (1863–1935), French Neo-Impressionist painter and theoretician.

Sisley, Alfred (1839–99), French Impressionist painter born of English parents, well known for his landscapes.

Smith, David (1906–65), influential and original US sculptor: *Hudson River Landscape* (1951).

Staël, Nicolas de (1914–55), French-Russian abstract painter whose works are characterized by broad patches of paint: *The Roofs* (1952).

Steen, Jan (1626–79), prolific Dutch genre painter notable for his scenes of merry-making: *The Feast of St Nicholas* (*c.* 1660).

Stubbs, George (1724–1806), English painter best known for his portraits of horses.

Sutherland, Graham (1903–80), English painter; his early landscapes had a dream-like Surreal quality and his later works include well-known portraits.

Tàpies, Antoni (1923–), Spanish painter whose earlier work was Surrealist and who later worked in mixed media.

Tatlin, Vladimir (1885–1953), Russian painter and founder of Constructivism: *Monument to the Third International* (1920).

Tiepolo, Giambattista (1696–1770), Italian Rococo painter noted for ceiling paintings and frescos in the Labia Palace and Palacio Real, Madrid.

Tinguely, Jean (1925–91), Swiss Kinetic artist celebrated for his machines: *Homage to New York* (1960).

Samson and Delilah (*c.* 1609)
Peter Paul Rubens

Rain, Steam, and Speed – The Great Western Railway (1839–44)
J.M.W. Turner

A Lady and a Gentleman in a Carriage (1787)
George Stubbs

A Young Woman Standing at a Virginal (1670)
Jan Vermeer

Tintoretto, Jacopo (1518–94), Venetian Mannerist painter: *Last Judgment* (*c.* 1560).

Tissot, James (1836–1902), French painter and graphic artist, involved in the Paris Commune, whose illustrations of the Bible were immensely popular.

Titian (Tiziano Vecellio; *c.* 1488/90–1576), Venetian Renaissance painter known for his dream-like pastorals: *Venus and Adonis* (1554); altarpiece of the *Assumption of the Virgin* (1516–18) in the Church of Santa Maria Gloriosa dei Frari, Venice).

Toulouse-Lautrec, Henri de (1864–1901), French painter and draughtsman famous for his lithographs and posters of dance halls and cabarets: *Le Moulin Rouge* (1891).

Turner, Joseph Mallord William (1775–1851), foremost English Romantic landscape painter: *The Fighting Téméraire* (1838); *Rain, Steam and Speed* (1844).

Uccello, Paolo (*c.* 1397–1475), early Renaissance Florentine painter: the fresco *Deluge* and the panels depicting the *Rout of Romano*, which experiment with perspectives.

van Dyck, Sir Anthony (1599–1641), Flemish painter and etcher known for his elegant portraits.

Vasarély, Victor (1908–97), Hungarian-born French painter well known for his grid-like compositions and considered the pioneer of Op art.

van Gogh, Vincent (1853–90), Dutch painter and major influence on 20th-century art: *The Potato Eaters* (1885); *The Chair and the Pipe* (1888–89); *Sunflowers* (1888–89).

Velásquez, Diego (1599–1660), Spanish painter: *Las Meninas* (1656); *Pope Innocent X* (1650).

Vermeer, Jan (1632–75), Dutch genre painter noted for his domestic interiors with subtle lighting: *Allegory of the Faith* (1669–70); *Allegory of Painting* (*c.* 1665).

Veronese, Paolo (1528–88), Venetian painter: a series of religious feast scenes, including *Marriage at Cana* (1562) and *The Feast in the House of Levi* (1573).

Vlaminck, Maurice de (1876–1958), French Fauvist painter: *The Bridge at Chatou* (1906).

Vuillard, Jean-Édouard (1868–1940), French painter noted for his domestic paintings: *Mother and Sister of the Artist* (*c.* 1893).

Warhol, Andy (1928–87), US painter, sculptor and graphic designer celebrated as one of the foremost Pop artists: subjects include Campbell soup cans, Coca-Cola bottles and Marilyn Monroe.

Watteau, Antoine (1684–1721), French Rococo painter who introduced romantic figures in a park or garden setting to the Rococo style: *Embarkation for Cythera* (1717).

Weyden, Rogier van der (*c.* 1399–1464), influential Flemish painter: *The Deposition* (*c.* 1435); altarpiece of the *Last Judgement* (*c.* 1450).

Whistler, James Abbott McNeill (1834–1903), US painter and graphic artist who worked in England, briefly with the Realist school, and whose later work became abstract.

Zurbarán, Francisco de (1598–1664), Spanish painter whose religious works are characterized by a powerful but austere style.

▶ NEO-IMPRESSIONISM

Impressionism was an ill-defined association of artists who joined together to mount independent group exhibitions, held from 1874 to 1886, rather than compromise their art in order to be included in the Paris Salon. Artists such as Monet, Renoir and Sisley shared some techniques and certain subjects and their approach was naturalistic. Their two main subjects were landscape and modern (often city) life. Often painted in the open air, their paintings show a concern with capturing the fleeting moment, particularly the effects of light, which they attempted to render with a free handling of paint.

▶ CUBISM

Cubism began around 1907 when artists such as Picasso and Braque began to analyse objects, breaking them down into geometrical shapes and restructuring them in order to show each form's many facets within a single image. Cubism developed into two main forms – analytical and synthetic.

▶ EXPRESSIONISM

Expressionism attempts to emphasize – often through unnaturalistic distortion – the importance of emotion and the artist's inner vision. A group of German Expressionist artists known as *Die Brücke* ('The Bridge'), formed in 1905 to integrate art and life, with art as a means of communication. The aim of another independent German Expressionist group, *Der Blaue Reiter* ('The Blue Rider'), formed in 1911, was for each artist to achieve an individual style, but sharing a use of bold colours and a tendency towards abstraction. Ensor, Kokoschka and Rouault all painted in this style.

ARTISTS' MOST VALUABLE PAINTINGS SOLD AT AUCTION

The following are the highest prices paid at auction for works of art by the following major artists. More than one work by several of the artists listed below has reached in excess of £10 million: at least four works by van Gogh and five works by Picasso have passed this figure.

ARTIST	PRICE (£)	PAINTING	DATE OF SALE
van Gogh	44,378,696	*Portrait du Dr Gachet*	May 1990
Renoir	42,011,832	*Au Moulin de la Galette*	May 1990
Picasso	33,123,028	*Les noces de Pierrette*	Nov 1989
Pontormo	20,253,164	*Portrait of Duke Cosimo I de Medici*	May 1989
Cézanne	16,993,464	*Nature morte – les grosses pommes*	May 1993
Manet	15,483,872	*La rue Mosnier aux drapeaux*	Nov 1989
Gauguin	13,496,934	*Mata Mua, in olden times*	May 1989
Monet	13,000,000	*Dans la prairie*	Jun 1988
de Kooning	11,898,735	*Interchange*	Nov 1989
Kandinsky	11,242,604	*Fugue*	May 1990
Constable	9,800,000	*The lock*	Nov 1990
Canaletto	9,200,000	*The Old Horse Guards, London, from St James's Park, with figures parading*	Apr 1992
Guardi	8,937,960	*Vue de la Giudecca et du Zattere à Venise*	Dec 1989
Toulouse-Lautrec	8,883,700	*Seated Dancer in Pink Stockings*	May 1997
Matisse	8,741,723	*Harmonie jaune*	Nov 1992
Johns	8,611,112	*False start*	Nov 1988
Léger	8,500,000	*Contrastes de formes*	Nov 1989
Chagall	7,988,166	*Anniversaire*	May 1990
Mantegna	7,500,000	*Adoration of the Magi*	Apr 1985
Modigliani	7,197,452	*Nu assis au collier*	May 1995
Klimt	7,066,667	*Dame mit Facher*	May 1994
Degas	6,800,000	*Les Blanchisseuses, Les Repasseuses*	Nov 1987
Titian	6,800,000	*Venus and Adonis*	Dec 1991
Turner	6,700,000	*Seascape, Folkestone*	Jul 1984
Vlaminck	6,659,506	*Les Pecheurs à Nanterre*	Mar 1990
Rembrandt	6,600,000	*Portrait of a girl, wearing a gold-trimmed cloak*	Dec 1986
Pollock	6,325,302	*Number 8, 1950*	May 1989
de Vries	6,200,000	*The Dancing Faun*	Dec 1989
Sargent	6,158,537	*Cashmere*	Dec 1996
Braque	6,000,000	*Femme Lisant*	Dec 1986
Mondrian	5,645,162	*Facade in tan and grey*	Nov 1989
Derain	5,600,000	*Bateaux dans le Port*	Jun 1989
Miró	5,483,870	*L'oiseau au plumage deploye volé vers l'arbre argente*	Nov 1989
Brancusi	4,838,710	*La muse endormie III*	Nov 1989
Raphael	4,800,000	*Study for head and hand of an Apostle*	Dec 1996
Church	4,746,836	*Home by the lake, scene in the Catskill Mountains*	May 1989
Bartolomeo	4,600,000	*Argonauts in Colchis*	Dec 1989
Gentileschi	4,600,000	*The Finding of Moses*	Dec 1995
Vuillard	4,516,129	*La table de toilette, dans les fleurs*	Nov 1989
Goya	4,500,000	*Bullfight: Suerte de Varas*	Dec 1992
da Vinci	3,364,879	*Etude de draperie: personnage agenouille, tourne vers la gauche*	Dec 1989
Rubens	3,000,000	*Forest at dawn with deer hunt*	Dec 1989
Velásquez	2,310,000	*Portrait of Juan de Pareja*	Nov 1970
Warhol	2,251,656	*Marilyn X*	Nov 1992

Self Portrait (1890) by Vincent van Gogh

Picasso in his villa – 'La Californie' – in Cannes, France

Portrait of Claude Monet (1873) by Auguste Renoir

Self Portrait (1659–60) by Rembrandt van Rijn

DADA AND SURREALISM

Dada emerged in 1916 as an international movement that rejected existing social values and its art. Its exponents, such as Picabia and Duchamp, aimed to be anarchic, anti-aesthetic and anti-rational; simultaneously art and anti-art. It inspired Surrealism – a French avant-garde movement of literary origin founded in 1924. Artists such as Ernst, Magritte and Dali were greatly influenced by images evoked from dreams and by Freud's psychoanalysis theories, including irrational association, spontaneous techniques and elimination of premeditation to free the workings of the unconscious mind.

ABSTRACT EXPRESSIONISM

Abstract Expressionism emphasizes spontaneous personal expression and rejects traditional social and aesthetic values. It emerged in New York soon after World War II with a large group of artists, including Motherwell, Pollock and de Kooning. It was the first movement in the USA to develop independently of, and then actually influence, Europe, and continues to dominate American painting.

POP AND MINIMAL ART

Pop Art (late 1950s–early 1960s) was an almost simultaneous reaction in the UK and USA against Abstract Expressionism. Artists such as Warhol and Hamilton used images of mass media, advertising and pop culture, presenting the common everyday object as art. Minimal Art emerged in the mid-1960s with US sculptors such as Judd and Lewitt, who rejected the aesthetic qualities of art objects in favour of their physical reality. The material used and its placing within its setting is important.

IN 1993 A CAR BOMB DESTROYED 33 ARTWORKS IN THE UFFIZI GALLERY, FLORENCE, ITALY

ARCHITECTURE

- **The five classical orders of architecture – Doric, Ionic, Corinthian, Tuscan and Composite – were formulated by Italian architectural writers in the 16th century.**
- **The Ancient Greek concepts of proportion and harmony still have an impact on Western architectural theory.**
- **The 16th-century artist Michelangelo, known for his painting, sculpture and poetry, was also a great architect: he designed the dome of St Peter's Basilica in Rome.**
- **Art Deco took its name from the 1925 Paris *Exposition Internationale des Arts Décoratifs et Industriels Modernes*.**

WHAT IS ARCHITECTURE?

▶ Architecture is the art of designing and constructing buildings that are both attractive and useful.
▶ An architect is a person who designs buildings and supervises their construction.

In the 17th century, Henry Wotton wrote that good building should have three conditions: 'commodity, firmness and delight'. A building, in other words, should be comfortable enough to meet its users' needs, firm enough to stand up and keep out the weather and should delight the eye. Achieving these three conditions is the architect's job.

PREHISTORIC BUILDINGS

▶ Architecture is determined not by architects but by society, according to its needs.
▶ Cave dwellings from prehistoric times have provided enduring insights into the lifestyle of their inhabitants as these environments have preserved many remains, such as tools, burial sites and paintings.

It took a long time before the special skills of an architect were needed. In prehistoric times, people lived as families; they hunted their own food and they created their own dwellings. During the Ice Ages people lived in caves, or they built shelters of mammoth bones and animal skins.

Around 8300 BC, the last Ice Age ended and the climate became more temperate. Agriculture developed, the population grew, and people settled in villages. They used local materials: wood from the northern forests, stone in southern Europe, sun-dried brick in Asia Minor. When larger buildings were needed, like long-houses or granaries, specialist builders emerged.

THE RIVER VALLEY CULTURES

▶ Around 3500 BC, an 'urban revolution' took place: the first cities were founded, in Mesopotamia, Egypt, India and China.
▶ The Tower of Babel, as described in the Old Testament of the Bible, may have been a ziggurat.

Around 3500 BC, cities were established for the first time. These were located in river valleys, where the rich farmland could support a large population. Writing was invented and with it came kings and priests, politicians and poets, traders and merchants. Wealth belonged to the privileged and huge building projects were now possible, which needed the skills of special designers.

In Mesopotamia, the typical building was the ziggurat, an artificial hill surmounted by a temple, whose sun-dried bricks were protected from the weather with a layer of beautifully decorated clay tiles and intricate carving.

Brick was the most common building material, but in Egypt stone was also available, allowing the

■ *The Great Pyramid at Giza, built by Khufu (Cheops in Greek), the king of Egypt c. 2613–2494 BC, was 147 m high – the largest single building in its time*

■ *The Doric column on the left, from the Parthenon, and the Ionic column on the right, both from the Acropolis, Athens, were the two most popular styles used in Ancient Greece*

■ *The third style of column, Corinthian, invented by the Ancient Greeks, was also used in Roman architecture, as seen here supporting the dome of the Pantheon, Rome, Italy*

construction of huge structures. The Pyramids at Giza were built around 2600 BC as royal tombs. The pyramid of Khufu was 147 m (482 ft) high, with a ground area of 5.3 hectares (13 acres). It had very narrow stone joints, and its four sides were aligned on the points of the compass. This combination of size and precision was very new. The builders who made it possible were important men. Imhotep, builder to Zoser, king of Egypt at this time, is the first architect whose name has gone down in history.

The Egyptians also built temples to their gods. The temple was a sequence of rectangular open courtyards and roofed-in halls, built in 'trabeated' construction: huge, closely spaced columns of stone carrying flat stone lintels, on which the roof was supported. The temple of Amon-Re at Karnak, begun around 1500 BC, is the largest Egyptian temple, with columns 24 m (79 ft) high and ten monumental gateways, called pylons, connecting the temple's courts and halls.

THE GREEKS

▶ The ancient citadel of Mycenae reached its peak between 1600 and 1200 BC before all its palaces were destroyed by war.
▶ An acropolis is the highest part of an Ancient Greek city (usually rocky, isolated and easy to fortify against enemies) containing the administrative and religious buildings.

The use of trabeated construction crossed the Mediterranean. In Crete, the great palace of King Minos, with its hundreds of rooms, gave rise to the legend of the Labyrinth. The Cretans colonized parts of the Greek mainland, and here the Mycenaean civilization grew, centred on the warlike cities of Mycenae and Tiryns. These were citadels with defensive walls as much as 7 m (23 ft) thick, built in rough, 'Cyclopean' stonework. Mycenae was entered through the famous Lion Gate, which was surmounted by a single stone lintel, almost 5 m (16 ft) long, and by two primitive carved lions.

Around 1000 BC Greece was occupied by invaders: from the north, the Dorians brought a knowledge of timber building, and from the east the Ionians brought skills in decorative carving. New city-states were set up – Thebes, Corinth, Sparta and Athens – whose growing wealth was based on conquest and trade. During the 5th century BC, Athens became the most dominant, and there came a 'Golden Age' of science, philosophy and the arts.

THE GOLDEN AGE

It is during this time that trabeated construction (see above under *The River Valley Cultures*) reached its ultimate refinement. This is seen in the buildings on the Athenian Acropolis, especially its stone-built temple, the Parthenon. The beautiful system of mathematical proportion and the precision of the craftsmanship are amazing. The Parthenon, like other buildings on the Acropolis, displays two styles of construction. The exterior is in the Doric style which, as its name suggests, derives from the rugged timber forms brought from the north: plain, square capitals sitting on top of simple, fluted columns. Inside, for its greater height and elegance, the Ionic style is used, its richness showing its eastern origins: the capitals have spiral forms derived from rams' horns, and the fluting on the columns is more intricate.

A third and even more decorative style emerged during the 4th century BC. This was the Corinthian, whose flowery richness suited the expansive 'Hellenistic' period, following Alexander the Great's conquest of Greece.

■ **THE FIRST KNOWN ARCHITECT WAS IMHOTEP, WHO BUILT THE STEP PYRAMID AT SAQQARA.**

THE ROMANS

▶ Corinthian became the favourite style of the Romans, whose power supplanted that of the Greeks in the 2nd century BC.
▶ Rome's Colosseum was an extraordinary feat of architecture – it was 188 m (617 ft) long, 156 m (512 ft) high, seated 50,000 people, and could be flooded for mock sea battles.

Through conquest and trade, the Romans created an empire stretching from Britain to North Africa, and from Spain to Egypt. Roman builders learned new techniques from the conquered people. Using Greek styles, they applied them to more adventurous structures, such as 'arcuated' construction, based on the semi-circular arch, which could span much greater distances than the lintel. This was developed into the barrel-vault, the cross-vault and the dome. These forms, together with a variety of building materials, including an early form of concrete, resulted in an enormous range of buildings.

As Rome's wealth grew, the city was provided with temples and palaces, public baths and gymnasia, circuses and amphitheatres, blocks of workers' flats, roads, bridges, aqueducts and sewers. The Colosseum, an amphitheatre for gladiatorial displays, was built in about AD 70, and the Pantheon, a circular temple roofed with a concrete dome, in AD 120. But gradually, the empire began to decline.

Early in the 4th century, the Emperor Constantine moved the capital from Rome to Byzantium. He made Christianity his official religion and, after years of persecution, Christians were able to build churches, in Byzantium, in Rome and in the Holy Land. The model they used was that of the basilica. In imperial Rome this had been a large trading hall. Its characteristic form, with its long, central nave flanked by two lower aisles, influenced church building for many centuries to come.

THE MIDDLE AGES

▶ The Romanesque style's main inspiration was Ancient Roman architecture, but Eastern and Byzantine elements were also used.
▶ The abbey of St-Denis in Paris, rebuilt in 1140, was the first church in the Gothic style.

As the empire declined, the land was occupied by northern barbarians. They were farmers who did little trade and had no use for cities. Rome and its building techniques fell into disuse and remained that way for many centuries. But Roman cultural tradition was kept alive by the Christian monasteries.

ROMANESQUE

Wealth belonged to the big landowners, whose castles were built by peasants, pressed into service. The wealth of the Church increased too and, around the 10th century, churches began to be built that, for the first time in 500 years, rivalled the buildings of the Roman Empire. The designers were often monks, and the building forms were the half-forgotten forms of Rome itself. The use of the semi-circular arch, the barrel-vault and cross-vault has given this period the name 'Romanesque'. To the basic basilica shape, Western towers, transepts and numerous chapels were added, creating the familiar form of the medieval church building. Examples include the church of San Miniato in Florence (1018), two great churches in Caen in Normandy (1062), Durham Cathedral (1098) and the church of Ste Madeleine at Vézelay in Burgundy (1104).

GOTHIC

As trade grew, the cities grew again. Here, rich bankers, merchants and industrialists began to rival

■ *The nave of the Romanesque Cathedral of the Church of Christ and Blessed Mary the Virgin in Durham, UK. Housing St Cuthbert's remains, it was an important pilgrimage site*

■ *The Duomo of Florence Cathedral, Italy, was designed c. 1420 by Filippo Brunelleschi – the only Renaissance architect who had the technical ingenuity to build it*

■ *The semicircular Colonnade in Piazza San Pietro, Rome, Italy, is considered by many to be the pinnacle of Gian Lorenzo Bernini's many famous Baroque works*

the feudal landowners, financing the building of great cathedrals. Architects were no longer the monks of the Romanesque period, but specialist designers known as 'master-masons', with greater experience of the real, secular world.

In their desire to build longer, wider and higher, the master-masons took medieval technology as far as they could. Sometimes they went too far and the buildings collapsed. However, these failures led to the discovery of new methods to solve their architectural problems. The pointed arch allowed columns to be spaced unevenly and gave greater freedom to the plan of the building. The rib-vault allowed stresses to be concentrated on particular points, making both walls and roofs lighter, and allowing larger areas of glass. The flying buttress took the sideways thrust of the roof, allowing buildings to be built higher. These three features typify what we know as the 'Gothic' style, one of the great achievements of European architecture. It was seen first at St-Denis near Paris in 1140, then at Canterbury Cathedral in 1175. Good early examples include Notre Dame de Paris (1163), Chartres Cathedral (1195) and Westminster Abbey (13th century), but fine Gothic cathedrals can be seen in all the old cities of Europe, from Prague to Brussels, from Cologne to Seville.

THE RENAISSANCE

▶ Filippo Brunelleschi is credited with the rediscovery of linear-perspective construction practised by the Ancient Greeks and Romans.
▶ The first 'modern' work on architecture – Leon Battista Alberti's treatise *On Architecture* (1452) – influenced many other Renaissance architects.

From the 12th century, capitalism, city life, and the wealth and personal freedom they offered, had stimulated an artistic rebirth, or 'renaissance', all over Europe. The word 'Renaissance' was later applied in a narrower sense to describe the rediscovery of the culture of Ancient Rome by the artists and thinkers of 15th-century Italy.

As learning grew, architecture became more intellectua and it became important to follow the principles of Roman architectureclosely. Filippo Brunelleschi, designer of the great dome of Florence Cathedral (1420), Leon Battista Alberti, designer of the church of San Francesco in Rimini (1446), Donato Bramante, designer of the Tempietto di San Pietro in Rome (1502), and Andrea Palladio, designer of many fine country houses near Vicenza who influenced an architectural style known as Palladian, were the earliest exponents of the new style. From this time on, the names of architects are known.

Medieval architects were manual workers, not thought important enough for their names to be recorded. Renaissance architects were often gentlemen, who approached their work as much through books as through practical experience. For many, architecture was not their only occupation.

MANNERISM AND BAROQUE

▶ The term 'Mannerism' was coined by art historian, architect and painter Giorgio Vasari (1511–74) to describe the works of Leonardo da Vinci, Raphael and early Michelangelo.
▶ Bernini was the dominant figure of the Baroque style in Italy, designing churches, chapels, fountains, monuments, tombs and statues commissioned by the pope.

The term 'Renaissance Man' is used to describe those with many accomplishments. Michelangelo – painter of the Sistine Chapel ceiling, sculptor of 'David' and architect of the huge dome over St Peter's in Rome, designed in 1546 – is a perfect example. In his Medici chapel (1521) and in his Laurentian library (1524), both in Florence, he rejected the strict rules of Renaissance design, creating the inventive style we call Mannerism.

Later architects went further. In the late 16th and early 17th centuries, Vignola, Borromini, Maderna and Bernini were distorting the Renaissance rules into the flowing lines and dramatic effects of the Baroque style, as in Borromini's church of San Carlo in Rome (1638).

Meanwhile, the Renaissance style was spreading. It came to France in the 16th century where it was used for the great châteaux of the Loire Valley, first by Philibert de l'Orme at Chenonceaux (1556) and Anet (1547), and culminating in the building of the huge royal palace at Versailles. In Spain, Philip II's own royal palace, the Escorial (begun in 1559), was designed in a sober Renaissance style.

It came to England early in the 17th century when Inigo Jones, after a visit to Italy, designed the Queen's House at Greenwich (1616) and the Banqueting Hall in Whitehall (1619) in imitation of Palladio's country houses. Jones's great successor, Christopher Wren, was another Renaissance Man. Originally a mathematician and astronomer, he was given the job of rebuilding the city of London after the Great Fire of 1666. The 50 new churches he designed and the huge cathedral of St Paul, mixing Renaissance and Baroque elements, are among the greatest buildings in England. English Baroque was taken further by John Vanbrugh and Nicholas Hawksmoor. Vanbrugh's Blenheim Palace (1704) and Hawksmoor's Christ Church, Spitalfields (1723), demonstrate the dramatic power of the style.

ROCOCO AND NEO-PALLADIANISM

▶ The most extreme example of the Rococo style is probably Balthasar Neumann's church of the Vierzehnheiligen in Bavaria (1744).
▶ Variations on the classical theme, seen in Rococo and neo-Palladianism, expressed the power and dignity of the landowning aristocracy dominating Europe and the colonies at the time.

By the 18th century, the classical Roman style, in all its variations, had spread over Europe, and beyond. It was established in the Low Countries, where Jacob van Campen's Mauritshuis in the Hague (1633) was built, simply and plainly, in the local brick. It also dominated southern Germany, Austria and Bohemia, where the Baroque style was developed into an intricate form known as 'Rococo' by Balthasar Neumann (see above), Dominikus Zimmerman's Pilgrimage Church (1728) in Steinhausen and François de Cuvilliès' Residenz-Theater (1751–53) in Munich. Other examples of Rococo are Filippo Juvarra's Church of the Carmine (1732) in Turin, Italy; Pierre Lepautre's Château de Marly (1679) in Paris; Leonardo de Figuero's Church of San Luis (1699) in Seville, Spain; and Peter the Great's main architect Gaetano Chiaveri's Academy of Sciences (1725) in St Petersburg, Russia. The buildings of Peter the Great's new city of St Petersburg, like Rastrelli's Winter Palace (1754), were built in a classical style that made use of the rich colours of traditional Russian architecture.

In Britain, there was another revival of Palladio's style. Neo-Palladianism, polite and restrained, could be seen in country houses like Chiswick House (1725) by Burlington and Kent, and in the many town houses, grouped around crescents and squares, being built in London, Dublin, Edinburgh and Bath. It appeared too in British colonies, especially in America, in cities like Williamsburg, Philadelphia and Boston.

However, things were about to change. Political revolutions, in England in 1649, in America in 1776 and in France in 1789, were bringing new classes to power. The Industrial Revolution in England was about to transform the production process. The political and industrial revolutions together created the modern world and its new architecture.

■ *The elaborate interior of Balthasar Neumann's church of Vierzehnheiligen (1744), near Lichtenfels, Germany, shows Rococo's decorative extremes and penchant for pastels*

■ *Crystal Palace, designed by Joseph Paxton and constructed entirely of iron and glass, shows the shift in building materials brought about by the Industrial Revolution*

■ *C.R. Mackintosh took architecture into the 20th century with his Glasgow School of Art (1897–1909), combining a functional grid design with art nouveau details*

THE INDUSTRIAL CITY

▶ The Industrial Revolution brought about different architectural needs for society and made new building materials available.
▶ Political revolutions in America, England and France put power into the hands of the bourgeoisie, resulting in a different approach to architecture.

The Industrial Revolution created a new way of life: the production of manufactured goods for profit. The profits were shared very unevenly; factory production created great wealth for industrial entrepreneurs, but not for the people who flocked into the cities to find work and who lived in squalid, overcrowded conditions, and in cities polluted by the new mills and factories, canals, railways and gasworks. New building materials – like iron and, later, steel and reinforced concrete – changed the nature of building and transformed the city.

THE ADVENT OF THE ENGINEER

The gentlemen architects of the 18th century lacked the skills needed for the huge works of construction demanded by industrialists, so new professions emerged: engineers, contractors and quantity surveyors. Architects began to concentrate on the aesthetic aspects of architecture and big debates took place as to whether the Gothic style or the Classical was best. In this 'battle of the styles', Cuthbert Brodrick designed a Classical town hall for Leeds (1853) and Alfred Waterhouse a Gothic one for Manchester (1868). In church architecture, Gothic (best represented by A.W.N. Pugin) reigned supreme.

However, many of the most important buildings of the period were not designed by architects at all, but by engineers. Joseph Paxton's Crystal Palace in London (1851), designed for London's Great Exhibition to be 564 m (1851 ft) long, was built entirely from cast iron and glass, and was an important early example of prefabrication. The railways also needed buildings of great size; Brunel's train shed at Paddington Station (1852) was a major contribution to the science of structures.

REFORM AND REVOLUTION

▶ The Arts and Crafts movement in Britain led to the worldwide development of Art Nouveau.
▶ The Eiffel Tower, at 300 m (984 ft), was the highest building in the world until 1930.

The 19th-century gap between the rich and the poor caused social unrest, and revolution broke out in many European countries. Reformers from utopian Socialist Robert Owen to garden-city planner Ebenezer Howard tried to improve conditions by building model villages and towns. Others, like William Morris, thought that the problems created by capitalism could only be solved by a change in society itself. Through the Arts and Crafts movement, many spent their lives working for revolution and the more fulfilled society it would bring.

Meanwhile, industrialism was expanding – to France, to Germany, to the USA – and buildings began to reflect this. The engineer Gustav Eiffel built the Garabit Viaduct (1884) and his famous Tower for the Paris Exposition of 1888 as the result of careful structural analysis. In the USA, John Roebling's Brooklyn Bridge (1867) was an important contribution to suspension bridge design. In Chicago, advances in structural design and the invention of the elevator resulted in the first skyscrapers, such as those designed by architects like H.H. Richardson and Louis Sullivan's Auditorium Building in Chicago (1889) with its 17-storey tower.

Towards the end of the century, the benefits of industrialism had begun to create an affluent middle class. In England, this was reflected in the elegant houses built by architects like Norman Shaw in the so-called Queen Anne Revival style. In many European cities it was reflected in the flowering of the Art Nouveau style, seen in the work of Charles Rennie Mackintosh in Glasgow, and of Antoni Gaudí in Barcelona. The most famous Mackintosh building is the Glasgow School of Art (1897). Gaudí's masterpiece is the Church of the Sagrada Familia, begun in 1884 and still being built.

THE MODERN MOVEMENT

▶ The Nazis closed down the Bauhaus headquarters in 1933 and outlawed the movement, which they labelled as 'decadent'.
▶ The Swiss architect Le Corbusier (1887–1965) claimed that architecture should be based on geometric figures, such as cubes and cones.

By the early 20th century, many artists and writers were impatient with the conservative ideas prevailing in society. An artistic 'avant-garde' emerged; the Cubists, the Fauvists and others shocked the bourgeoisie with their progressive abstract ideas.

The Russian Revolution, in 1917, was a major turning point. The Russian Constructive architects and artists put modern architecture at the service of social revolution. Vladimir Tatlin's unbuilt Tower to the Third International (1920) was intended to be the symbol of the new society and Moisei Ginsburg's NARKOMFIN apartments in Moscow (1926) were an experiment in communal living which provided the model for all later mass housing.

Modernist ideas were taking root in western Europe too. In Germany, despite the rise of the Nazis, Walter Gropius, Hannes Meyer and Mies van der Rohe developed the Bauhaus as an avant-garde design school. The Bauhaus building at Dessau, designed by Gropius in 1925, is itself a great work of modern architecture. The Swiss-born French architect Le Corbusier, probably the most influential architect of the 20th century, was also beginning to examine new ways of living, ranging from the design of small houses to the layout of entire cities. In the USA, Frank Lloyd Wright was designing his famous 'prairie' houses and, in Finland, Alvar Aalto built his innovative Tuberculosis Sanatorium at Paimio.

The unifying feature of all these buildings was the use of modern materials, or the use of old materials in a modern way. The aim, in contrast to the dark, heavy buildings of the 19th century, was to create buildings of clarity and simplicity in which there was as much light, air and space as possible. The word 'honest' was often used about modern architecture.

THE POST-WAR BOOM

▶ The city of Brasília, Brazil's capital since 1960, was built entirely from scratch as a new modern city, designed by Lucio Costa with Oscar Niemeyer as chief architect.
▶ In Britain in the late 1960s, 400,000 new houses were being built each year.

World War II destroyed much of Europe. It also brought into being the new technologies – nuclear fission, aerospace and communications technology – on which the post-war recovery would be based.

After the war, welfare capitalism seemed to be the way forward; a strong public sector would help rebuild the shattered cities, and modern architecture would be the means of doing this. Cities from Tokyo to Rotterdam were rebuilt in the modern style. In Britain alone, a million people were rehoused in New Towns. Everywhere housing programmes were started in which factory production was used to speed up the process. High-rise housing estates, often built of prefabricated concrete, appeared in every big city. The model for these was Le Corbusier's Unite d'Habitation, a huge block of flats built in Marseille in 1949, and typical examples included the Pruitt-Igoe flats in St Louis (1953) and the Park Hill flats in Sheffield (1961).

Welfare capitalism was made possible by a post-war economic boom. Entrepreneurs were able to make big profits from property speculation; high-rise offices and luxury flats appeared in every city centre. In New York, SOM built the Lever Building in 1952 and Mies van der Rohe the Seagram Building in 1956, both of them glass-walled skyscrapers that became the model for later office blocks.

■ *Art nouveau Casa Batlló (1904–06), with its 'bird nest' balconies, shows the voluptuous organic contours and fierce individualism that were architect Antoni Gaudí's trademarks*

■ *Fallingwater (1904), a house built over a waterfall in Mill Run, Pennsylvania, USA, is one of the unique contributions architect Frank Lloyd Wright made to domestic architecture*

■ *Norman Foster's Hong Kong and Shanghai Bank (1986), in Hong Kong, China, shows the exposed skeletal girders and metallic look characteristic of High-Tech architecture*

Many kinds of buildings were being built – airports, universities, opera houses – in which all the drama and excitement of modern architecture were being exploited: Le Corbusier's pilgrimage chapel at Ronchamp in France (1950), Jorn Utzon's Sydney Opera House (1957), Wright's Guggenheim Museum in New York (1959), Saarinen's TWA air terminal at Kennedy Airport (1962) and Scharoun's Philharmonic Hall in Berlin (1963).

Despite all this, or partly because of it, there was still social unrest. The housing programme was not keeping pace with housing need. People were also concerned about the environmental effects – the pollution, the waste of resources, the use of nuclear power – and about the exploitation of the Third World, where poverty and starvation were endemic. In 1968, uprisings in Paris, Prague and other big cities reinforced the message that ordinary people wanted to be in control of their own future.

THE END OF MODERNISM?

▶ Post-Modernism is associated with a style pioneered by US architect Michael Graves, and represented by his Portland Public Building built in Portland, Oregon, USA, in 1982.
▶ The term 'Post-Modernism' was first coined by Charles Jencks in his book *Post-Modern Architecture,* published in the late 1970s.

In 1973, the Arab-Israeli War and the subsequent oil crisis marked the beginning of a worldwide economic crisis. Welfare capitalism no longer seemed possible, and governments everywhere began to withdraw from housing, hospital and school-building programmes. Politics became more conservative, and some critics, who resented the original link between modern architecture and social revolution, began to criticize modernism as being responsible for many of society's ills.

POST-MODERNISM

Around 1977 a new style of architecture emerged which became known as Post-Modernism. Its practitioners deliberately rejected modernist ideas and went back to historic forms, like classicism, which they often used in a jokey kind of way. In the USA, the architecture of Robert Venturi, Michael Graves and Philip Johnson showed this tendency, while in Britain, architects like Quinlan Terry and Robert Adam went even further, designing pastiche 18th-century buildings.

Unlike the ailing public sector, private enterprise was not starved of funds, and many commercial developments continued to be built in city centres, for which the Post-Modern style was thought appropriate. Typical of these were the Docklands development at Canary Wharf in London's East End, and the riverside Battery Park City in New York.

HIGH-TECH

One aspect of Post-Modernism is the development of so-called 'High-Tech' modernism. This uses the outward imagery of modernism – exposed structures and metallic, modern materials – but in a very complex and un-modern way. High-Tech buildings are often commercial, like Richard Rogers' office block for Lloyd's of London, or Norman Foster's Hong Kong and Shanghai Bank in Hong Kong.

ARCHITECTURE'S FUTURE

Meanwhile, the environmental problems identified during the 1960s have not been solved: people still live in poverty on the edges of Third World cities, and even in the richer countries homelessness has doubled in the last 20 years. Some architects, of course, are trying to address these problems, for example by designing housing that ordinary people can build themselves, or by finding ways of saving energy and resources. On the whole, though, the problems remain unsolved, and we are left with Morris's view that social change is needed if the environment is really to be improved.

BY THE GEOMETRIC FORMS OF SUNBURSTS AND ZIGGURATS IN AZTEC AND EGYPTIAN TEMPLES ■

LANGUAGES AND ALPHABETS

- Bikya, a language spoken in Furu-awa on the Cameroon/Nigeria border, is now used only by an 87-year-old woman.
- The ability to speak does have its drawbacks – humans have less efficient breathing and eating systems, and while monkeys cannot choke on food lodged in the larynx, humans can.
- The word 'the' is the most frequently used word, and 'e' the most frequent letter, in both written and spoken English.
- Germany's Charles V was said to have spoken French to men, Italian to women, German to horses and Spanish to God.
- The North Semitic is the earliest-known alphabet, and was developed around 1700 BC with 22 consonant letters.

LANGUAGES

▶ About 845 languages and dialects are spoken in India.
▶ Africa has more languages than any other continent – about 1300.

No one knows for sure how many living languages are spoken today, but estimates put the figure at 4000–5000. New languages continue to be discovered, while other languages die out when there are no native speakers left. Many languages classed as separate (for example, Serb and Croat) are in fact the same, but have been deemed as distinct for reasons of national identity.

THE MAIN LANGUAGE FAMILIES

Each language is unique in that it has its own system of sounds, words and structures. However, many languages are related, with much shared vocabulary and many similar terms. These similarities support the view that a few ancient languages were the ancestors of many modern ones. One example of a shared ancestor is Latin, which gave rise to Romance languages such as French, Italian and Spanish. Linguistic analysis has shown that many such groupings are related, and in this way they can be classed within families – the main ones including those that follow.

HOW DID SPEECH BEGIN

▶ It is impossible to say when the first languages arose, but the development of speech seems to have taken place between 100,000 and 20,000 years ago.
▶ Studies of the vocal tracts of Neanderthal man (70,000–35,000 BC) suggest that basic speech was possible even then.

Several theories have tried to explain why or how humans developed the power of speech. It may be that language evolved from gestural communication, with primitive sounds uttered at the same time as gestures, which then became identified with the gestures, and ultimately replaced them. Another theory suggests that speech grew out of attempts to imitate the rich sounds of nature, such as bird calls. Other theories imply a link between early speech and the instinctive sounds uttered in anger, pain and pleasure. One hypothesis even bases the origin of language on the evolution of the sounds of love and play. Perhaps speech arose from the natural rhythms of life, communal activities that were accompanied by regular grunts and which grew into song and speech. Other suggestions focus on isolated examples to suggest that language grew from reactions to the environment, such as the word mama arising from the lip movements of a baby as it approaches the mother's breast.

Exactly why early humans began to speak is still a mystery, but speech is one of the defining features of our race.

Altaic

Comprising about 40 languages, Altaic includes Azeri, Mongol, Turkish, Kazakh, Uighur and Uzbek. The family is found from the Balkan peninsula of eastern Europe to north-east Asia.

Amerind

Amerind is a large family comprising nearly 200 subgroups of languages of the native North, Central and South Americans. Many are rapidly dwindling, and some are spoken by only a few elderly people.

Austronesian

Comprising a very large group of languages (between 500 and 700), Austronesian is spoken by over 200 million people in Taiwan, Madagascar, the West Pacific, Hawaii and New Zealand. This family is also known as Malayo-Polynesian.

Dravidian

A family of over 20 languages found in southern and eastern regions of India, northern Sri Lanka and in one isolated area of Pakistan, Dravidian languages include Kannada, Malayalam, Tamil and Telugu.

Indo-European

The largest family of languages in terms of speakers. Based in Europe and southern Asia, these languages are spoken worldwide. The family contains several subgroups: Albanian, Armenian, Balto-Slavic, Celtic, Germanic, Greek, Indo-Iranian and Italic. Languages of Indo-European origin include most of the languages of Europe (including English, French, German, Italian, Portuguese and Spanish) and many languages of the Indian subcontinent (including Bengali, Hindi, Gujarati, Kashmiri, Punjabi and Sindhi). Other languages from this family include Gaelic, Greek, Polish, Romany, Russian, Welsh and Yiddish, as well as the ancient scholarly languages of Latin and Sanskrit.

Niger-Congo

The largest language family in sub-Saharan Africa, (over 1000 languages), Niger-Congo has six groups within it, each with several subgroups within it.

Sino-Tibetan

A family of languages spoken by over one billion people, the majority in China, the geographical region for this family also extends to Tibet, India, Thailand and Burma (Myanmar). Its languages include Burmese, Tibetan, and the eight varieties of Chinese (Cantonese, Hakka, Hsiang, Kan, Northern Min, Southern Min, Putonghua (Mandarin) and Wu).

Uralic

A family of languages concentrated in Estonia, northern Russia including Siberia, and Hungary. Uralic includes Estonian, Finnish, Lappish and Magyar (Hungarian).

OTHER LANGUAGE GROUPS

Minor families include Caucasian (the Caucasus region of central Asia), Paleosiberian (north-eastern Siberia), Austro-Asiatic (South-East Asia), Tai (South-East Asia), Nilo-Saharan (upper regions of the Nile and Chari rivers), Khoisan (southern Africa in the Kalahari region), Afro-Asiatic (North Africa and south-west Asia), Indo-Pacific (New Guinea) and Pama-Nyungan (Aboriginal Australia).

Some languages are called isolates – they have no historical or structural relationship to any other language. Japanese and Korean are the two best-known examples. Another is Basque, spoken in south-western France and northern Spain. Many are dying languages, such as Ainu, Nahali and Tarasca, or languages which are already extinct, such as Beothuk, Elamite and Etruscan. Sumerian, the oldest language for which there is written evidence (dating from 3100 BC), is a language isolate.

NEW LANGUAGES

▶ Several hundred artificial languages have been devised since the 17th century.
▶ Many Esperanto enthusiasts were arrested or shot in the 1930s in Germany and the Soviet Union because the authorities believed that the language was subversive.

Most languages have evolved over thousands of years. By contrast, artificial (or auxiliary) languages are created in a comparatively short period of time. Most are designed to make international communication easier.

Esperanto is the most popular artificial language. Devised by Ludwig Lazarus Zamenhof (1859–1917), it was first published in 1887 under the pseudonym 'Doktoro Esperanto' (Doctor Hopeful), and by the turn of the century the language was in use internationally. Esperanto is derived from European sources, and has 16 grammatical rules, with no irregularities permitted. It is used today mainly in eastern Europe. Over one million copies of Zamenhof's textbook have been sold.

Other artificial languages include Volapük, the first large-scale international language, schematized in 1880; and Solresol, devised by a French musician, François Sudre, in the early 19th century. Solresol is an ingenious system based upon the seven-note diatonic scale: do, re, me, fa, so, la, ti. These components form the basic syllables of the language, with compounds being formed by combinations of these words. It could be whistled or sung, as well as spoken. Other developments include simplified languages, such as Basic English, which has only 850 words.

One particular growth area for artificial languages in the past 40 years is in computer languages. Since computers can be programmed only in binary code (zeros and ones), computer languages were devised to make the art of programming more user-friendly with a system of specialized symbols and words to instruct the computer. While systems such as BASIC, C, FORTRAN and COBOL are not true spoken languages, they provide highly efficient communication systems.

THE WORLD'S MAIN LANGUAGES

Calculating the number of speakers of the main language families is made difficult by such factors as refugee movements, political activity, government manipulation of figures, and large-scale loss of life through war or natural disaster. Other problems include confusion over regional dialects and language names, and the assumption in many national surveys that because certain people are members of a particular ethnic group, they all speak that group's language. Nonetheless, general observations can be made. Chinese is spoken by more than one billion people, with Putonghua ('common speech') the most widely spoken form of Chinese. English is the most widely spoken language, and although only 335 million are native speakers, over 800 million people speak it worldwide.

		LANGUAGE FAMILY	FIRST LANGUAGE (million)	NOTES
1	GUOYO (PUTONGHUA)	Sino-Tibetan	810	The official language of China. Putonghua – also known as Mandarin – is standardized northern Chinese. Spoken in China and by Chinese communities throughout South-East Asia
2	HINDI	Indo-European (Indo-Iranian)	364	One of the official languages of India. Spoken in north and central India. An additional 60 million people speak Hindi as a second language
3	ENGLISH	Indo-European (Germanic)	335	The first language in Australia, Canada, Caribbean Commonwealth countries, Ireland, New Zealand, the UK and the USA, and widely spoken in former British colonies. An additional 185 million people speak English as a second language, and it is used in many parts of the world for communication among people of different mother tongues. English is an official language in 57 countries
4	SPANISH (CASTILIAN)	Indo-European (Romance)	308	Spoken as a first language in Spain (except in Catalonia, Galicia and the Basque Country) and in Latin America (except Brazil). An official language in 21 countries
5	ARABIC	Afro-Asiatic	210	Spoken throughout North Africa and south-western Asia. An official language in 23 countries
6	BENGALI	Indo-European (Indo-Iranian)	188	The official language of Bangladesh and the Indian state of West Bengal, and one of the official languages of India
7	PORTUGUESE	Indo-European (Romance)	164	The official language of Portugal, Brazil and former Portuguese colonies in Africa
8	RUSSIAN	Indo-European (Balto-Slavic)	156	The official language of Russia. Also spoken by a substantial minority of people in all of the former republics of the USSR
9	JAPANESE	Language isolate	126	Japanese is confined to Japan and Japanese communities abroad
10	PUNJABI	Indo-European (Indo-Iranian)	97	Spoken in the Indian state of Punjab and in adjoining areas of Pakistan. One of the official languages of India
11	WU	Sino-Tibetan	94	Spoken in east-central China
12	GERMAN	Indo-European (Germanic)	87	German is an official language in Germany, Austria, Switzerland and Liechtenstein, and is also spoken by minorities throughout central and eastern Europe
13	JAVANESE	Austronesian	77	Javanese is the first language of Java and part of Sumatra and is spoken by minorities throughout the rest of Indonesia
14	TELEGU	Dravidian	74	Spoken in Andhra Pradesh and adjoining areas of south India. One of the official languages of India
15	FRENCH	Indo-European (Romance)	73	Spoken in France, Québec, southern Belgium, western Switzerland and in French dependencies. It is widely understood in former French colonies in Africa. An official language in 34 countries
16	KOREAN	Language isolate	72	The official language of North and South Korea. Also spoken by Korean minorities in central Asia and eastern Russia
17	TAMIL	Dravidian	69	Spoken in the Indian state of Tamil Nadu and in parts of Sri Lanka and Malaysia. One of the official languages of India
18	MARATHI	Indo-European (Indo-Iranian)	68	Spoken mainly in the Indian state of Maharashtra. One of the official languages of India
19	VIETNAMESE	Austro-Asiatic	66	Spoken in Vietnam and parts of adjoining states
=20	CANTONESE	Sino-Tibetan	61	Spoken in Hong Kong and the Guangdong province of China
=20	MIN	Sino-Tibetan	61	Spoken in south-eastern China and Taiwan
=22	ITALIAN	Indo-European (Romance)	59	Spoken in Italy and the Swiss canton of Ticino and by Italian communities in the New World
=22	TURKISH	Altaic (Turkic)	59	Spoken in Turkey and in parts of neighbouring countries (particularly Bulgaria)
=22	URDU	Indo-European (Indo-Iranian)	59	Urdu is the national language of Pakistan and is one of the official languages of India
25	HSIANG	Sino-Tibetan	53	Spoken in south-central regions of China
26	GUJARATI	Indo-European (Indo-Iranian)	46	Spoken in the Indian state of Gujarat. One of the official languages of India
27	HAKKA	Sino-Tibetan	41	Spoken in south-eastern China
28	POLISH	Indo-European (Balto-Slavic)	39	Spoken in Poland and parts of Lithuania and Ukraine
29	MALAY-INDONESIAN	Austronesian	38	Spoken in Malaysia, Indonesia (where it is known as Bahasa) and parts of southern Thailand
=30	KANNADA	Dravidian	37	Spoken in southern India. One of the official languages of India
=30	UKRAINIAN	Indo-European (Balto-Slavic)	37	Spoken in Ukraine, and in parts of Russia, Belarus and other former Soviet republics
32	MALAYALAM	Dravidian	36	Spoken in Kerala in southern India
33	BURMESE	Sino-Tibetan	32	The official language of Myanmar (Burma)
=34	ORIYA	Indo-Aryan (Indo-Iranian)	31	Spoken in central and eastern India. One of the official languages of India
=34	SUNDANESE	Austronesian	31	Spoken in Sunda regions of Indonesia
=34	THAI	Tai	31	Spoken in Thailand and some adjoining areas
=37	FARSI (PERSIAN)	Indo-European (Indo-Iranian)	28	The official language of Iran
=37	PUSHTO	Indo-European (Indo-Iranian)	28	Spoken in Afghanistan and Pakistan
39	KAN	Sino-Tibetan	27	Spoken in east-central China
40	BHOJPURI	Indo-Aryan (Indo-Iranian)	26	Spoken in India, Mauritius and Nepal

ALPHABETS AND WRITING SYSTEMS

▶ Like its Phoenician parent, early Greek was written from right to left, but by 500 BC it had reversed direction, and was being written left to right.

▶ In early times, the ability to write had religious importance. Writing was believed to be a gift from a god or demigod, and early myths often equate writing with magic.

Writing systems evolved independently in several different civilizations about 5500 years ago, although symbols used to represent numbers have been found dating from the 9th millennium BC. The earliest examples of writing come from the Middle East and south-eastern Europe, and date from about 3500 BC.

Four main writing systems developed – pictographic, ideographic, logographic and alphabetic.

Pictographs (or pictograms) are symbols that look like the things they represent – a simplified drawing of a person's head, for example, comes to represent 'head'. Pictographic communication is the earliest form of systematic writing, being used in civilizations as diverse as Crete, Easter Island and Mexico. Even today pictographic symbols are used in some road signs and computer icons.

Some pictographic systems developed into what are known as ideographic systems. Ideographs (or ideograms) still look a little like the things they represent, but are more stylized – a symbol for 'head', for instance, would not be obviously head-like. Cuneiform writing and Egyptian hieroglyphics developed from this method of writing. Hieroglyphic writing is a mixture of methods, using both pictograms and ideograms, with some symbols representing certain consonants.

Logographic systems are another variation. Symbols (called graphemes) represent whole words, as in Chinese. The problem with such a system is that many graphemes have to be memorized, and up to 2000 are used in everyday writing. Logograms are also used in mathematical and scientific notation.

Alphabets are the most useful, economical and adaptable writing system. Each symbol in an alphabet corresponds to a sound (called a phoneme), rather than an object. This means that only a small number of symbols (letters) need be learnt, generally 20–30. Words are created through a combination of letters. Many writing systems used today are alphabetic, and they vary in such things as size, direction of writing and how vowels are indicated. The earliest known alphabet is the North Semitic, dating from 1700 BC, from which Hebrew, Arabic and Phoenician models were derived.

THE CODE OF SIGNALS

The International Code of Signals is a maritime communication convention devised in 1887 and adopted internationally by 1900. The system relies on a phonetic alphabet, which is used not only at sea but by air traffic control, international telegraphy, and short-wave radio users such as the police.

A Alpha
B Bravo
C Charlie
D Delta
E Echo
F Foxtrot
G Golf
H Hotel
I India
J Juliett
K Kilo
L Lima
M Mike
N November
O Oscar
P Papa
Q Quebec
R Romeo
S Sierra
T Tango
U Uniform
V Victor
W Whiskey
X X-ray
Y Yankee
Z Zulu

GREEK ALPHABET

Today's European alphabets have their roots in the Greek alphabet, which developed from the Phoenician system in the 9th century BC. The Greeks retained the order of the Phoenician symbols, but they changed the forms and names of certain characters. For example, Phoenician aleph (meaning ox), beth (house) and gimel (camel) became alpha, beta and gamma in Greek. Unlike Phoenician symbols, the Greek letters had no specific meanings.The early Greek alphabet, until about 500 BC, was like its Phoenician 'parent' written from right to left.

The Greeks had no equivalent sound for some of the Phoenician consonant symbols. They took these and used them to symbolize vowels, an important step in creating a true alphabet. Five new symbols were also added: omega, upsilon, phi, chi and psi. Another Greek innovation was the creation of separate upper case (capitals) and lower case symbols (miniscules).

Two strands of the Greek alphabet became dominant: Ionic or Ionian (also known as the eastern Greek script, or Classical Greek) and Chalcidean (western Greek script). In 403 BC, the Ionian variant was adopted as the official Athenian alphabet, and spread rapidly to replace Chalcidean.

The capital letters of the modern Greek 24-letter alphabet of seven vowels and 17 consonants have descended almost unchanged from the Ionian system.

The Greek alphabet is the oldest surviving alphabet in Europe. It is still widely understood outside the Greek-speaking world since its letters are used for scientific and mathematical purposes.

In the table below the first line gives the standard capital versions of the letters, the middle lists the name and the sound represented by each letter, and the last gives the miniscule version of each.

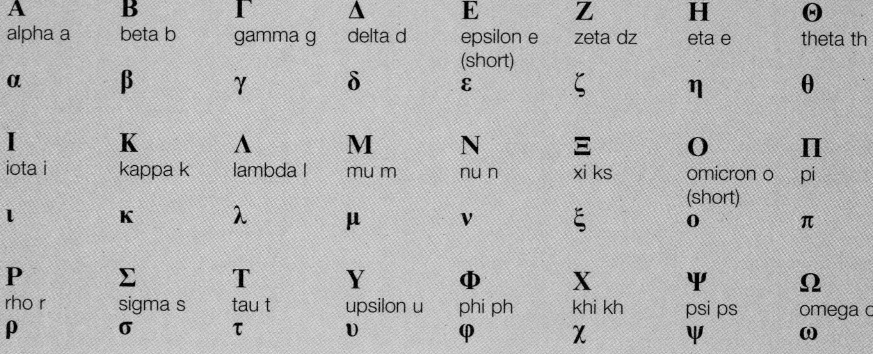

Α	Β	Γ	Δ	Ε	Ζ	Η	Θ
alpha a	beta b	gamma g	delta d	epsilon e (short)	zeta dz	eta e	theta th
α	β	γ	δ	ε	ζ	η	θ
Ι	**Κ**	**Λ**	**Μ**	**Ν**	**Ξ**	**Ο**	**Π**
iota i	kappa k	lambda l	mu m	nu n	xi ks	omicron o (short)	pi
ι	κ	λ	μ	ν	ξ	ο	π
Ρ	**Σ**	**Τ**	**Υ**	**Φ**	**Χ**	**Ψ**	**Ω**
rho r	sigma s	tau t	upsilon u	phi ph	khi kh	psi ps	omega o
ρ	σ	τ	υ	φ	χ	ψ	ω

CYRILLIC ALPHABET

The Cyrillic is the most widely used alphabet after the Roman. Its invention in the 9th century is attributed to St Cyril and his brother St Methodius, two Greek missionaries who worked in what is today Moravia, a region in the Czech Republic.

Slavonic languages are very rich in sounds – they use a great number of phonemes – and therefore require a large number of characters to represent them. Originally, Russian Cyrillic had 43 characters taken from the Greek and Hebrew system, but this was reduced to 32 (plus one variant character) after the 1917 Russian Revolution.

Cyrillic is used to write Russian, Belarusian, Bulgarian, Macedonian, Serb, Ukrainian and many other languages of Slavonic origin. However, the major languages using Cyrillic have different numbers of letters, since certain letters have been introduced in languages such as Serb and Bulgarian, while others have been dropped. Modern Russian has 32 letters, as does Belarusian; Ukrainian has 33, and Bulgarian and Serbian each have 30 letters.

Several central Asian languages such as Kazakh, Uzbek and Turkmen used to be written in Cyrillic. However, the Roman alphabet has been, or is being, introduced for most of these, although Arabic is to be used for the Tajik language.

In the table below, the standard capital versions of the letters are given on the first line, the next line lists the name of each letter and the sound represented by that letter, and the final line gives the miniscule version of the character.

А	Б	В	Г	Д	Е	Ё	Ж	З	И	Й
a	b	v	g,gh	d	e	e	j	z	i	i
а	б	в	в	д	е	ё	ж	з	и	й
К	**Я**	**М**	**Н**	**О**	**П**	**Р**	**С**	**Т**	**У**	**Ф**
k	l	m	n	o	p	r	s,ss	t	ou	f
к	я	м	н	о	п	р	с	т	у	ф
Х	**Ц**	**Ч**	**Ш**	**Щ**	**Ъ**	**Ы**	**Ь**	**Э**	**Ю**	**Я**
kh	ts	tch	ch	chtch	hard symbol	y	mute	e	iou	ia
х	ц	ч	ш	щ	ъ	ы	ь	э	ю	я

■ THE LONGEST ALPHABET IN THE WORLD IS KHMER (CAMBODIAN) WITH 74 CHARACTERS

ARABIC ALPHABET

Arabic is the third most widespread alphabet. It evolved to write the Arabic language but was adapted at various times to write Persian, Swahili, Turkish and even Spanish.

Arabic, which is written from right to left, consists of 28 consonant letters, with vowels indicated by marks. However, these vowel marks are generally omitted, except in elementary school books and the holy book, the Qur'an (Koran). An unusual feature is that each letter is written differently according to its position: whether it is at the beginning of a word (initial), in the middle (medial), or at the end (final), or even on its own (isolated).

Five main forms developed – including Kuffic and Naskhi. Kuffic dates from the 7th century, and is the form in which the Qur'an was originally written. This upright, decorative script for inscriptions on metal or stone is now rarely used. Naskhi dates from the 10th century. From this cursive form comes the numerous Arabic scripts in use today, including Persian (Farsi), Kurdish, Sindhi, Urdu, Swahili, and the languages of Indonesia and Malaysia.

Name	Trans-literation	Numerical Value	Isolated	Final	Initial	Medial
alif	'	1	ا	ـا	ا	ـا
bā	b	2	ب	ـب	بـ	ـبـ
tā	t	400	ت	ـت	تـ	ـتـ
thā	t,th	500	ث	ـث	ثـ	ـثـ
jim	j	3	ج	ـج	جـ	ـجـ
ḥā'	ḥ	8	ح	ـح	حـ	ـحـ
kha'	kh	600	خ	ـخ	خـ	ـخـ
dāl	d	4	د	ـد	د	ـد
dhāl	dh	700	ذ	ـذ	ذ	ـذ
rā'	r	200	ر	ـر	ر	ـر
zāy	z	7	ز	ـز	ز	ـز
sin	s	60	س	ـس	سـ	ـسـ
shin	sh	300	ش	ـش	شـ	ـشـ
ṣād	ṣ	90	ص	ـص	صـ	ـصـ
ḍād	ḍ	800	ض	ـض	ضـ	ـضـ
ṭā	ṭ	9	ط	ـط	طـ	ـطـ
ẓā	ẓ	900	ظ	ـظ	ظـ	ـظـ
'ayn	'	70	ع	ـع	عـ	ـعـ
ghayn	gh	1000	غ	ـغ	غـ	ـغـ
fā'	f	80	ف	ـف	فـ	ـفـ
qāf	q	100	ق	ـق	قـ	ـقـ
kāf	k	20	ك	ـك	كـ	ـكـ
lām	l	30	ل	ـل	لـ	ـلـ
mim	m	40	م	ـم	مـ	ـمـ
nūn	n	50	ن	ـن	نـ	ـنـ
hā	h	5	ه	ـه	هـ	ـهـ
wāw	w	6	و	ـو	و	ـو
yā	y	10	ي	ـي	يـ	ـيـ

LOUIS BRAILLE'S ALPHABET FOR THE BLIND

Louis Braille (1809–52) damaged his sight at the age of three when playing with an awl from the workbench of his father, a saddler. He became completely blind. As a child at a school for the blind, he learnt to read using embossed letters. He also came across a system devised by an artillery officer, Charles Barbier, for sending messages to his soldiers at night. Messages were written by punching holes in cardboard, and could be deciphered solely by touch. This crude and relatively impractical system inspired Braille. He began to experiment, and in 1824 at the age of 15 he introduced his own system: a small 'cell' consisting of two vertical rows of three embossed dots arranged and numbered 1, 2, 3, down the left hand side and 4, 5, 6, down the right.

The system gave 63 possible combinations, which Braille assigned to letters (originally excluding W, which is rarely used in French), punctuation marks, numerals, mathematical signs and a number of common words such as 'and', 'for', 'of', 'with', 'the'. Braille may seem a complicated system, but to a blind person with normal finger sensitivity, it is not so different from deciphering the graphic symbols that form our written words. To read Braille, both hands are used: the right picks up the message as the left feels for the beginning of the next line. In this way, a skilled reader can understand up to 150 words a minute, about half the speed of a sighted person.

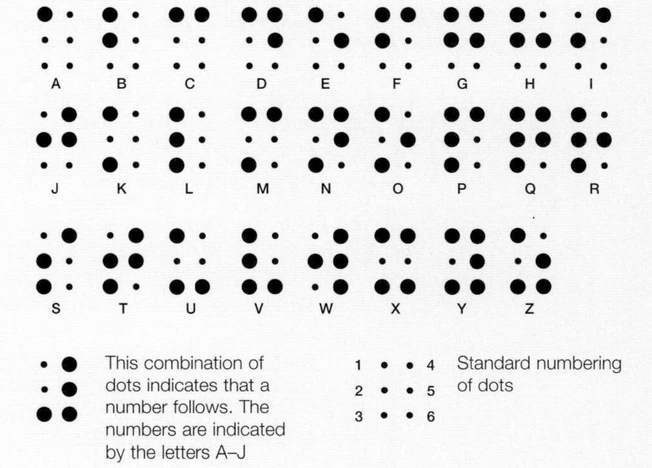

MORSE CODE

The International Morse Code was invented by an American, Samuel Finley Morse (1791–1872), in about 1835. The system was used to send messages by telegraph, and was a great improvement on previous methods, especially over long distances. Dots and dashes, or short and long beeps, form the basis of the code. Morse first exhibited his electric 'telegraph' machine in 1837, and demonstrated it with the first message in Morse at Morristown, New Jersey, USA, on 6 January 1838. The first commercial use of the Morse system was in May 1844 when a wire was strung between the US Supreme Court in Washington DC and Mount Claire Station in Baltimore. Links were soon set up between all major American cities, and between the United States and Europe. Morse code was superseded by radio in the 20th century, but is still used by a few amateur radio operators and on some shipping routes.

Code		Code		Code		Code	
•–	A	•–––	J	•••	S	•––––	1
–•••	B	–•–	K	–	T	••–––	2
–•–•	C	•–••	L	••–	U	•••––	3
–••	D	––	M	•••–	V	••••–	4
•	E	–•	N	•––	W	•••••	5
••–•	F	–––	O	–••–	X	–••••	6
––•	G	•––•	P	–•––	Y	––•••	7
••••	H	––•–	Q	––••	Z	–––••	8
••	I	•–•	R			––––•	9
						–––––	0

IN ANCIENT GREEK AND EGYPTIAN, THE WORD FOR 'WRITE' AND 'DRAW' WAS THE SAME

LITERATURE

- **Only seven of the 90-odd plays written by the Greek tragic poet and dramatist Aeschylus have survived.**
- **Some people believe the works of Shakespeare were actually written by Christopher Marlowe or Francis Bacon.**
- **William Burroughs shot his wife dead with a pistol whilst re-enacting an episode from the life of William Tell.**

Aeschylus (*c.* 525–456 BC), Greek tragic poet and dramatist: *Oresteia*, a trilogy of plays.

Albee, Edward (1928–), US dramatist: *Who's Afraid of Virginia Woolf?* (1962).

Alcaeus (7th–6th centuries BC), Greek lyric poet.

Alcott, Louisa May (1832–88), US novelist: *Little Women* (1868).

Amis, Kingsley (1922–95), English novelist and poet: *Lucky Jim* (1954).

Andersen, Hans Christian (1805–75), Danish novelist, dramatist and fairytale writer: *The Ugly Duckling*, *The Snow Queen* and *The Little Mermaid*.

Anouilh, Jean (1910–75), French dramatist: *Antigone* (1944).

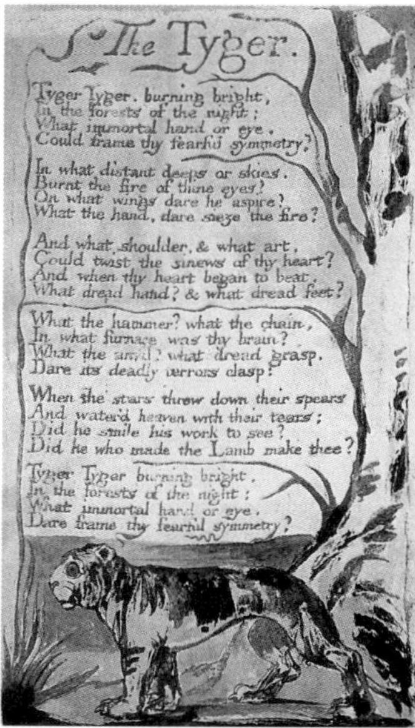

■ *William Blake's illustrated poem* The Tyger, *from his* Songs of Innocence

Apollinaire, Guillaume (1880–1918), French poet and prose writer: the collection *Alcools* (1913).

Apuleius (active AD 155), Roman philosopher and author: *The Golden Ass*, a romance.

Ariosto, Lodovico (1474–1533), Italian epic poet: *Orlando Furioso* (1516).

Aristophanes (*c.* 445–385 BC), Greek comic dramatist: *Lysistrata* (411 BC).

Aristotle (384–322 BC), Greek philosopher: treatises on logic, metaphysics, politics, biology, etc.

Arnold, Matthew (1822–88), English poet, essayist and critic: *Dover Beach* (1867) and *Essays in Criticism* (1865).

Asimov, Isaac (1920–92), US science-fiction novelist: *I, Robot* (1950) and the Foundation trilogy (1952–53).

Atwood, Margaret (1939–), Canadian novelist and poet: the novels *The Edible Woman* (1969) and *The Handmaid's Tale* (1986).

Auden, W(ystan) H(ugh) (1907–73), English-born US poet, dramatist and critic: the play *On the Frontier* (1938), the collections *The Age of Anxiety* (1948) and *About the House* (1965).

Austen, Jane (1775–1817), English novelist: *Sense and Sensibility* (1811), *Pride and Prejudice* (1813), *Emma* (1815) and *Persuasion* (1818).

Ayckbourn, Alan (1939–), English playwright: *Relatively Speaking* (1967), *Absurd Person Singular* (1973) and *The Norman Conquests* (1974).

Bacon, Francis (1561–1626), English philosopher and man of letters: *Essays* (1597) and *Novum Organum* (1620).

Baldwin, James (1924–87), US novelist and playwright: *Go Tell it on the Mountain* (1954) and the play *The Amen Corner* (1965).

Balzac, Honoré de (1799–1850), French novelist: *La Comédie Humaine*, a sequence of 94 novels, including *Old Goriot* (1835) and *Lost Illusions* (1837–43).

Barker, Pat (1943–), English novelist: *The Ghost Road* (1995).

Barrie, James (1860–1937), Scottish novelist, dramatist and children's story writer: *Peter Pan* (1904).

Baudelaire, Charles (1821–67), French poet: *Les Fleurs du mal* (1857).

Baum, L. Frank (1856–1919), US novelist and children's story writer: *The Wonderful Wizard of Oz* (1900).

Beaumarchais, Pierre-Augustin Caron de (1732–99), French comic dramatist: *Le Barbier de Seville* (1775) and *Les Noces de Figaro* (1784).

Beauvoir, Simone de (1908–86), French feminist writer: *The Second Sex* (1949).

Beckett, Samuel (1906–89), Irish dramatist and novelist: the plays *Waiting for Godot* (1952), *Endgame* (1957) and *Happy Days* (1961), and the novel *Malone Dies* (1951).

Behan, Brendan (1923–64), Irish novelist: *Borstal Boy* (1958).

Bellow, Saul (1915–), US novelist: *Henderson the Rain King* (1959), *Herzog* (1964).

Berryman, John (1914–72), US poet: *Homage to Mistress Bradstreet* (1956).

Betjeman, John (1906–84), English poet: *Collected Poems* (1968).

Blake, William (1757–1827), English poet: *Songs of Innocence* (1789) and *Songs of Experience* (1794).

Boccaccio, Giovanni (1313–75), Italian poet and storyteller: *Decameron*, a collection of 100, often earthy, tales.

Boll, Heinrich (1917–85), German novelist: *Group Portrait with Lady* (1971).

Bond, Edward (1934–), English dramatist: *Saved* (1965).

Borges, Jorge Luis (1899–1986), Argentinian poet and short-story writer: *Fictions* (1944).

Brecht, Bertolt (1898–1956), German dramatist: the musical drama *The Threepenny Opera* (1928), the plays *Mother Courage* (1941) and *The Good Woman of Setzuan* (1943).

Brontë, Anne (1820–49), English novelist: *The Tenant of Wildfell Hall* (1847).

Brontë, Charlotte (1816–55), English novelist: *Jane Eyre* (1847), *Shirley* (1849) and *Villette* (1853).

Brontë, Emily (1818–48), English novelist: *Wuthering Heights* (1847).

Brooke, Rupert (1887–1915), English war poet: *The Soldier* (1915).

Browning, Elizabeth Barrett (1806–61), English poet: *Sonnets from the Portuguese* (1847) and *Aurora Leigh* (1857).

Browning, Robert (1812–89), English poet: the play *Pippa Passes* (1841), the poem *The Pied Piper of Hamelin* (1842) and *The Ring and the Book* (1868–69), a long poem in a series of dramatic monologues.

Buchan, John (1875–1940), English adventure novelist: *The Thirty-Nine Steps* (1915).

Büchner, Georg (1813–37), German dramatist: *Danton's Death* (1835) and *Woyzeck* (1837).

Buck, Pearl (1892–1973), US novelist: *The Good Earth* (1931).

Burgess, Anthony (1917–), English novelist and critic: *Clockwork Orange* (1962) and *Earthly Powers* (1980).

Burnett, Frances Hodgson (1849–1924), Anglo-US children's story writer: *Little Lord Fauntleroy* (1885) and *The Secret Garden* (1911).

Burns, Robert (1759–96), Scottish poet notable for his use of the Scottish dialect: *'Tam o'Shanter'*.

Burroughs, William (1914–), US novelist: *Naked Lunch* (1959).

Byatt, A(ntonia) S. (1936–), English novelist: *Possession* (1990).

Byron, Lord (George Gordon Byron; 1788–1824), English poet: *Childe Harold's Pilgrimage* (1812–18) and the satirical epic *Don Juan* (1819–24).

Calderón de la Barca, Pedro (1600–81), Spanish dramatist: *El Alcalde de Zalamea* (*c.* 1640).

Camus, Albert (1913–60), French novelist, dramatist and essayist: the novels *The Outsider* (1942) and *The Plague* (1947), and the essay *The Myth of Sisyphus*.

Canetti, Elias (1905–), Bulgarian-born German writer: *Auto da fé* (1935), *Crowds and Power* (1960) and his three-volume memoirs.

Carey, Peter (1943–), Australian novelist: *Illywhacker* (1985) and *Oscar and Lucinda* (1988).

Carroll, Lewis (Charles Lutwidge Dodgson; 1832–98), English mathematician and children's story writer: *Alice's Adventures in Wonderland* (1865) and *Through the Looking-Glass* (1872).

Catullus (*c.* 84–*c.* 55 BC), Roman love poet.

Cervantes, Miguel de (1547–1616), Spanish poet and prose writer: *Don Quixote* (1615), a parody of chivalric literature; regarded by many as the first true novel.

Chandler, Raymond (1888–1969), US detective novelist: *The Big Sleep* (1939) and *The Long Goodbye* (1953).

Chateaubriand, François René de (1768–1848), French novelist and prose-writer: *Atala* (1801) and *Le Génie du Christianisme* (1802).

Chatterton, Thomas (1752–70), English poet.

Chatwin, Bruce (1940–89), English novelist: *Utz* (1988).

Chaucer, Geoffrey (?1343–1400), English poet: *Canterbury Tales* and *Troilus and Criseyde*.

Chekhov, Anton (1860–1904), Russian dramatist: *Uncle Vanya* (1899), *The Three Sisters* (1901) and *The Cherry Orchard* (1904).

Chrétien de Troyes (active 1170–90), French poet: *Erec et Enide*, *Cligès* and *Perceval*.

Christie, Agatha (1890–1976), English detective novelist; creator of the detectives Hercule Poirot and Miss Marple.

Cicero (106–43 BC), Roman orator, statesman and writer.

Clarke, Arthur C. (1917–), English science-fiction novelist: *2001: A Space Odyssey* (1968).

Cocteau, Jean (1889–1963): French poet, novelist and dramatist: the novel *Les Enfants terribles* (1929) and the play *La Machine Infernale* (1934).

Coleridge, Samuel Taylor (1772–1834), English poet: *Lyrical Ballads* (see Wordsworth), including *The Rime of the Ancient Mariner* (1798), *Kubla Khan* (1816) and his book on literary criticism *Biographia Literaria* (1817).

Collins, William Wilkie (1824–89), English novelist: the mystery novels *The Woman in White* (1860) and *The Moonstone* (1868).

Collodi, C. (Carlo Lorenzini; 1826–90), Italian novelist, journalist and writer of children's stories: *Pinocchio* (1880).

■ A.S. BYATT IS THE SISTER OF MARGARET DRABBLE ■ COLERIDGE AND DE QUINCEY WERE

Conan Doyle, Sir Arthur (1859–1930), English detective novelist: *The Memoirs of Sherlock Holmes* (1894) and *The Hound of the Baskervilles* (1902).

Congreve, William (1670–1729), English comic dramatist: *The Way of the World* (1700) and *Love for Love* (1695), Restoration comedies.

Conrad, Joseph (Teodor Jozef Konrad Korzeniowski; 1857–1924), Polish-born English writer: *Lord Jim* (1900), *Heart of Darkness* (1902), *Nostromo* (1904) and *The Secret Agent* (1907).

Cooper, James Fenimore (1789–1851), US novelist: *The Last of the Mohicans* (1826) and *The Pathfinder* (1840).

Corneille, Pierre (1606–84), French classical tragic dramatist: *Le Cid* (1637), *Horace* (1640), *Cinna* (1640) and *Le Menteur* (1643).

Coward, Noel (1899–1973), English comic dramatist: *Private Lives* (1930) and *Blithe Spirit* (1941).

Dahl, Roald (1916–91), English novelist and children's story writer: *Charlie and the Chocolate Factory* (1964).

Dante Alighieri (1265–1321), Italian poet: *The Divine Comedy*.

Daudet, Alphonse (1840–97), French novelist: *Lettres de mon moulin* (1869).

De Quincey, Thomas (1785–1859), English essayist: *Confessions of an English Opium Eater* (1821).

Defoe, Daniel (1660–1731), English novelist: *Robinson Crusoe* (1719) and *Moll Flanders* (1722).

Demosthenes (384–322 BC), Greek orator and statesman.

Dickens, Charles (1812–70), English novelist: *Oliver Twist* (1838), *Nicholas Nickleby* (1839), *The Old Curiosity Shop* (1841), *David Copperfield* (1850), *Bleak House* (1853), *Hard Times* (1854), *Little Dorrit* (1857), *A Tale of Two Cities* (1859) and *Great Expectations* (1861).

Dickinson, Emily (1830–86), US poet.

Diderot, Denis (1713–84), French philosopher and writer: editor of the *Encyclopedie*.

Disraeli, Benjamin (1804–81), English novelist and politician: the trilogy *Coningsby* (1844), *Sybil* (1845) and *Tancred* (1847).

Donne, John (1572–1631), English metaphysical poet: *Divine Sonnets*.

Dostoevski, Fyodor (1821–81), Russian novelist: *Crime and Punishment* (1866) and *The Brothers Karamazov* (1880).

Doyle, Roddy (1958–), Irish novelist: *The Commitments* (1987) and *Paddy Clarke Ha Ha Ha* (1993).

Drabble, Margaret (1939–), English novelist: *The Ice Age* (1977).

Dreiser, Theodore (1871–1945), US novelist: *An American Tragedy* (1925).

Dryden, John (1631–1700), English satirical poet and tragic dramatist: *All for Love* (1677) and the allegorical poem *Absalom and Achitophel*.

Dumas, Alexandre (1802–70), French novelist: *The Three Musketeers* (1844).

Duras, Marguerite (1914–96), French novelist: *Le Vice-Consul* (1966) and *Emily L.* (1989).

Dürrenmatt, Friedrich (1921–), Swiss dramatist: *The Physicist* (1962).

Eliot, George (Mary Ann Evans; 1819–80), English novelist: *Adam Bede* (1859), *The Mill on the Floss* (1860), *Silas Marner* (1861) and *Middlemarch* (1871–72).

Eco, Umberto (1932–), Italian semiotician and novelist: *The Name of the Rose* (1980) and *Foucault's Pendulum* (1989).

Eliot, T(homas) S(tearns) (1888–1965), English poet, dramatist and critic: the poems *The Waste Land* (1922) and *Four Quartets* (1943) and the plays *Murder in the Cathedral* (1935) and *The Cocktail Party* (1950).

Emerson, Ralph Waldo (1803–82), US poet and essayist: the poetry collection *May-Day* (1867) and the essay *The Conduct of Life* (1860).

Erasmus, Desiderius (*c.*1466–1536), Dutch humanist and scholar: *Adages* (1500) and *In Praise of Folly* (1509).

Eschenbach, Wolfram von (?1170–1220), German poet: *Parzival*.

Euripides (*c.* 485–406 BC), Greek tragic dramatist: *Medea* (431).

Faulkner, William (1897–1962), US novelist: *The Sound and the Fury* (1929).

Fichte, Johann Gottfried (1762–1814), German philosopher: *Wissenschaftslehre* (1794).

Fielding, Henry (1707–54), English novelist and dramatist: the novels *Shamela* (1741; a parody of Richardson's *Pamela*), *Jonathan Wild* (1743) and *Tom Jones* (1749).

Fitzgerald, F. Scott (1896–1940), US novelist: *The Beautiful and Damned* (1922), *The Great Gatsby* (1925) and *Tender is the Night* (1934).

Flaubert, Gustave (1821–80), French novelist: *Madame Bovary* (1857) and *Sentimental Education* (1869).

Fleming, Ian (1908–64), English suspense novelist and creator of James Bond: *Casino Royale* (1953) and *Diamonds are Forever* (1956).

Ford, John (1586–?1639), English dramatist: *'Tis Pity She's a Whore*.

Forster, E(dward) M(organ) (1879–1970), English novelist: *A Room with a View* (1908), *Howard's End* (1910) and *A Passage to India* (1924).

Forsyth, Frederick (1938–), English adventure novelist: *The Day of the Jackal* (1971) and *The Fourth Protocol* (1984).

Fowles, John (1926–), English novelist: *The Magus* (1966) and *The French Lieutenant's Woman* (1969).

France, Anatole (1844–1922), French novelist: *Les Dieux ont soif* (1912).

Frost, Robert (1874–1963), US poet: *North of Boston* (1914) and *New Hampshire* (1923).

Fry, Christopher (1907–), English dramatist: the verse drama *The Lady's Not for Burning* (1948).

Fuentes, Carlos (1928–), Mexican novelist: *When the Air is Clear* (1958).

Galsworthy, John (1867–1933), English novelist: *The Forsyte Saga* (1922–28).

García Lorca, Federico (1898–1936), Spanish dramatist and poet: the peasant tragedies *Blood Wedding* (1933), *Yerma* (1934) and *The House of Bernarda Alba* (1936), and the poems *Gypsy Ballads* (1928).

García Márquez, Gabriel (1928–), Colombian novelist: *One Hundred Years of Solitude* (1967).

Gaskel, Elizabeth (1810–65), English novelist: *Mary Barton* (1848), *Ruth* (1853) and *Cranford* (1853).

Gautier, Theophile (1811–72), French novelist, critic and poet: the poem *Albertus* (1830) and the novel *Mademoiselle de Maupin* (1835).

Genet, Jean (1910–86), French novelist and playwright: the novel *Our Lady of the Flowers* (1944) and the play *The Maids* (1964).

Geoffrey of Monmouth (d. 1155), Welsh chronicler: *History of the Kings of Britain* (1135–39) and *Vita Merlini* (1148–51).

Gide, André (1869–1951), French novelist: *The Immoralist* (1902), *Straight is the Gate* (1909) and *The Vatican Cellars* (1914).

Ginsberg, Allen (1926–97), US Beat movement poet: *Howl* (1956).

Goethe, Johann Wolfgang von (1749–1832), German poet, dramatist, and novelist: the Romantic novella *Die Leiden des jungen Werthers* (1774), the classical verse dramas *Iphigenia* (1787) and *Torquato Tasso* (1790), and his masterpiece *Faust* (1808).

Gogol, Nikolai (1809–52), Russian novelist and dramatist: the novel *Dead Souls* (1842) and the comic drama *The Government Inspector* (1836).

Golding, William (1911–93), English novelist: *Lord of the Flies* (1954).

Gordimer, Nadine (1923–), South African novelist: *The Conservationist* (1974).

Gorki, Maxim (1868–1936), Russian novelist and playwright: the novel *Mother* (1911) and the play *The Lower Depths* (1906).

Gower, John (?1330–1408), English poet: *Confessio Amantis* (*'The Lover's Confession'*).

Grahame, Kenneth (1859–1932), Scottish children's story writer: *The Wind in the Willows* (1908).

Grass, Günter (1927–), German novelist: *The Tin Drum* (1959) and *Dog Years* (1965).

Graves, Robert (1895–1985), English poet and novelist: his World War I autobiography *Goodbye to All That* (1929) and the historical novel *I, Claudius* (1934).

Gray, Thomas (1716–71), English poet: *Ode on a Distant Prospect of Eton College* (1747) and *Elegy Written in a Country Churchyard* (1751).

Greene, Graham (1904–91), English novelist: *Brighton Rock* (1938), *The Power and the Glory* (1940), *The Heart of the Matter* (1948), *Our Man in Havana* (1958) and *The Honorary Consul* (1973).

Grimm, Jakob (1785–1863) and **Wilhelm** (1786–1859), German brothers who were philologists and collectors of German folktales.

Hammett, Dashiell (1894–1961), US detective novelist: *The Maltese Falcon* (1930) and *The Thin Man* (1932).

Hardy, Thomas (1840–1928), English novelist and poet: the novels *Far from the Madding Crowd* (1874), *The Return of the Native* (1878), *The Mayor of Casterbridge* (1886), *Tess of the D'Urbervilles* (1891) and *Jude the Obscure* (1895).

Havel, Vaclav (1936–), Czech politician and dramatist: *The Garden Party* (1963) and *Largo Desolato* (1985).

Hawthorne, Nathaniel (1804–64), US novelist and short-story writer: *The Scarlet Letter* (1850) and *The Marble Faun* (1860).

■ *Coleridge's* The Rime of the Ancient Mariner, *illustrated by Gustave Doré*

Heaney, Seamus (1939–), Irish poet: *North* (1975), *Station Island* (1984) and *The Spirit Level* (1995).

Heine, Heinrich (1797–1856), German poet and essayist: *Reisebilder* (1826) and *Das Buch der Lieder* (1827).

Heller, Joseph (1922–), US novelist: *Catch 22* (1961).

Hemingway, Ernest (1899–1961), US novelist: *A Farewell to Arms* (1929) and *For Whom the Bell Tolls* (1940).

Herbert, George (1593–1633), English metaphysical poet: *The Temple*.

Herodotus (*c.* 490–*c.* 425 BC), Greek historian and prose writer, known as the 'father of history'.

Hesiod (?8th–7th centuries BC), Greek epic poet: *Theogony*.

Hesse, Herman (1877–1962), German-born Swiss novelist: *Siddhartha* (1922) and *Steppenwolf* (1927).

Hofmannsthal, Hugo von (1874–1929), Austrian poet and dramatist: *Elektra* (1903) and *Der Rosenkavalier* (1911).

Hölderlin, Friedrich (1770–1843), German novelist and poet: the novel *Hyperion* (1797–99).

Homer (?8th century BC), Greek epic poet: *Iliad* and *Odyssey*. (These may not in fact be the work of the same man.)

Hopkins, Gerard Manley (1844–89), English poet: *Pied Beauty* (1877) and *The Windhover* (1918).

Horace (65–8 BC), poet: *Odes*, *Satires* and *Epistles*.

Hughes, Ted (1930–), English poet: *The Hawk in the Rain* (1975) and *Crow* (1970).

Hughes, Thomas (1822–96), English politician, novelist and children's story writer: *Tom Brown's Schooldays* (1857).

Hugo, Victor (1802–85), French poet, dramatist and novelist: the verse collections *Autumn Leaves* (1831) and *Les Contemplations* (1856), and the

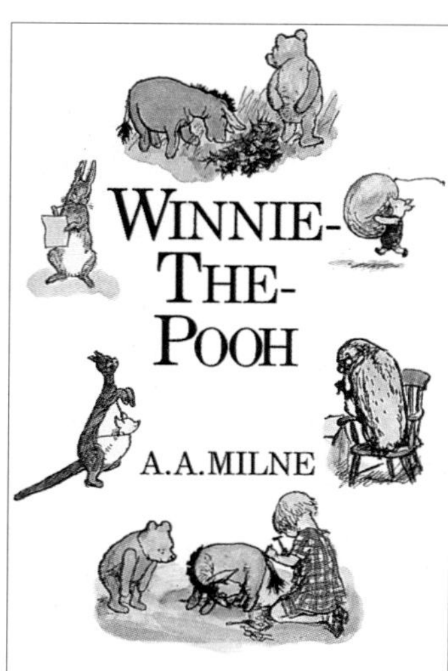

■ *A.A. Milne's endearing characters are displayed on this cover of* Winnie-the-Pooh

novels *The Hunchback of Nôtre Dame* (1831) and *Les Misérables* (1862).

Huxley, Aldous (1894–1963), English novelist: *Brave New World* (1932).

Huysmans, Joris-Karl (1848–1907), French novelist: *Against Nature* (1884).

Ibsen, Henrik (1828–1906), Norwegian dramatist: *Ghosts* (1881), *Hedda Gabler* (1890) and *The Master Builder* (1892).

Ionescu, Eugène (1912–94), Romanian-born French dramatist: the absurd dramas *The Bald Prima Donna* (1950) and *The Rhinoceros* (1959).

Irving, Washington (1783–1859), US essayist and short-story writer: *Sketch Book of Geoffrey Crayon* (1820), including the stories *Rip Van Winkle* and *The Legend of the Sleepy Hollow*.

Isherwood, Christopher (1904–87), English novelist and dramatist: *Goodbye to Berlin* (1939).

James, Henry (1843–1916), US novelist: *The Ambassadors* (1903) and *The Golden Bowl* (1904).

Johnson, Samuel (Dr Johnson; 1709–84), English lexicographer and writer: his famous *Dictionary* (1755), the poem *London* (1738) and *The Lives of the English Poets* (1779–81).

Jonson, Ben (1572–1637), English dramatist and poet: the plays *Volpone* (1606), *The Alchemist* (1610) and *Bartholomew Fair* (1614).

Joyce, James (1882–1941), Irish novelist and short-story writer: the collection of short stories *Dubliners* (1914) and the novels *Portrait of the Artist as a Young Man* (1914–15), *Ulysses* (1922) and *Finnegan's Wake* (1939).

Juvenal (?AD 60–?140), Roman satirical poet.

Kafka, Franz (1883–1924), Czech novelist writing in German: *The Trial* (1925) and *The Castle* (1926).

Kästner, Erich (1899–1974), German novelist, poet and children's story writer: *Emil and the Detectives* (1929).

Kawabata Yasunari (1899–1972), Japanese novelist: *Snow Country* (1956).

Keats, John (1795–1821), English poet: *Odes* (*To a Nightingale*, *On a Grecian Urn* and *To Autumn*).

Kerouac, Jack (1922–69), US Beat novelist: *On The Road* (1957).

Kingsley, Charles (1819–75), English novelist: *Westward Ho!* (1855) and children's story *The Water Babies* (1863).

Kipling, Rudyard (1865–1936), English novelist, poet and short-story writer: *Kim* (1902), and the children's stories *Jungle Book* (1894) and *Just So Stories* (1902).

Kleist, Heinrich von (1777–1811), German dramatist: *Prinz Heinrich von Homburg*.

Kundera, Milan (1929–), Czech novelist: *The Joke* (1967) and *The Unbearable Lightness of Being* (1984).

Kyd, Thomas (1558–94), English dramatist: the revenge tragedy *The Spanish Tragedy* (1592).

La Fayette, Madame de (Marie-Madeleine, Countess de la Fayette; 1634–93), French novelist: *The Princess of Cleves* (1678).

Laclos, Pierre Choderlos de (1741–1803), French novelist: *Dangerous Liaisons* (1782).

Lamartine, Alphonse de (1790–1869), French poet: *Méditations poétiques* (1820).

Langland, William (*c.* 1330–*c.* 1386), English alliterative poet: *Piers Plowman*.

Larkin, Philip (1922–85), English poet: *The North Ship* (1945), *The Less Deceived* (1955) and *The Whitsun Weddings* (1964).

Lawrence, D(avid) H(erbert) (1885–1930), English novelist, short-story writer and poet: the novels *Sons and Lovers* (1913), *The Rainbow* (1915), *Women in Love* (1916) and *Lady Chatterley's Lover* (1928).

Laxness, Halldor (1902–), Icelandic novelist: *Independent People* (1945).

Le Carré, John (1931–), English spy novelist: *The Spy Who Came in from the Cold* (1963) and *Tinker, Tailor, Soldier, Spy* (1974).

Lear, Edward (1812–88), English artist, poet and writer of children's verse: *The Book of Nonsense* (1846).

Lessing, Doris (1919–), English novelist: *The Golden Notebook* (1962) and *The Good Terrorist* (1985).

Lewis, C(live) S(taples) (1898–1963), English scholar, science-fiction novelist and children's story writer: *The Lion, the Witch and the Wardrobe* (1950) and *The Last Battle* (1956).

Li Bo (Li Po; 701–62), widely regarded as the greatest Chinese poet.

Livy (59 BC–AD 17), Roman historian: *History of Rome*.

Lowell, Robert (1917–77), US poet: *Lord Weary's Castle* (1946) and *For the Union Dead* (1964).

Lucretius (*c.* 98–*c.* 55 BC), Roman poet and philosopher.

Maclean, Alistair (1922–87), Scottish adventure novelist: *The Guns of Navarone* (1957) and *Where Eagles Dare* (1967).

Maeterlinck, Maurice (1862–1949), Belgian dramatist: *Pelléas and Mélisande* (1892) and *The Blue Bird* (1908).

Mailer, Norman (1923–), US novelist: *The Naked and the Dead* (1948).

Mallarmé, Stéphane (1842–98), French poet: *L'après-midi d'un faune* (1876) and *Vers et Prose* (1893).

Malory, Sir Thomas (d. 1471), English writer of Arthurian romance in prose: *Morte D'Arthur*.

Mamet, David (1947–), US dramatist: *Glengarry Glen Ross* (1984).

Mann, Thomas (1875–1955), German novelist: the short story *Death in Venice* (1912), and the novels *The Magic Mountain* (1924) and *Doctor Faustus* (1947).

Mare, Walter de la (1873–1956), English poet: *Songs for Childhood* (1902) and the collection *The Listeners and Other Poems* (1912).

Marinetti, Filippo Tommaso (1876–1944), Italian dramatist, novelist and poet.

Marivaux, Pierre (1688–1763), French comic dramatist and novelist: the play *The Game of Love and Chance* (1730), and the novels *The Life of Marianne* (1731–41) and *The Fortunate Peasant* (1735).

Marlowe, Christopher (1564–93), English dramatist and poet: *Tamburlaine the Great* (*c.* 1587), *Dr Faustus* (*c.* 1588), *The Jew of Malta* (1589) and *Edward II* (*c.* 1592).

Martial (*c.* AD 40–104), Roman epigrammatist.

Marvell, Andrew (1621–78), English poet and satirist: *Miscellaneous Poems* (published posthumously).

Matsuo Basho (1644–94), Japanese haiku poet: *The Narrow Road to the Deep North* (1694).

Maugham, W. Somerset (1874–1965), English novelist and short-story writer: *Of Human Bondage* (1915), *The Moon and Sixpence* (1919) and the play *The Circle* (1921).

Maupassant, Guy de (1850–93), French novelist and short-story writer: the short story *Boule de suif* (1881) and the novel *Bel-Ami* (1885).

Mauriac, François (1885–1970), French novelist, poet and dramatist: the novels *Le Noeud de vipères* (1932) and *Le Désert de l'amour* (1949).

Melville, Herman (1819–91), US short-story writer and novelist: *Moby Dick* (1851) and *Billy Budd* (1924).

Menander (342–292 BC), Greek comic dramatist.

Middleton, Thomas (1580–1627), English tragic dramatist: *Women Beware Women* (1621) and *The Changeling* (1622; with William Rowley).

Miller, Arthur (1915–), US dramatist: *Death of a Salesman* (1949) and *The Crucible* (1952).

Milne, A(lan) A(lexander) (1882–1956), English novelist, dramatist and children's story writer: *Winnie-the-Pooh* (1926) and *The House at Pooh Corner* (1928).

Milton, John (1608–74), English poet: the Christian epics *Paradise Lost* (1667) and *Paradise Regained* (1677).

Mishima, Yukio (1925–70), Japanese novelist: *The Temple of the Golden Pavilion* (1956) and *The Sea of Fertility* (1965–70).

Molière (Jean-Baptiste Poquelin; 1622–73), French actor and classical dramatist of comedy: *Le Bourgeois Gentilhomme* (1660), *L'Ecole des Femmes* (1662), *Tartuffe* (1664), *Don Juan* (1665), *Le Misanthrope* (1666), *L'Avare* (1668; '*The Miser*') and *Le Malade imaginaire* (1673).

Moravia, Alberto (Alberto Pincherle; 1907–90), Italian novelist: *The Time of Indifference* (1929) and *The Conformist* (1952).

More, Sir Thomas (1477–1535), English humanist: *Utopia* (1516).

Morrison, Toni (1931–), US novelist: *Song of Solomon* (1977) and *Beloved* (1987).

Muir, Edward (1887–1944), Scottish poet and novelist: *First poems* (1925).

Murasaki Shikibu (973–1014), Japanese novelist: *The Tale of Genji* (considered by some to be the greatest Japanese literary work and the first full novel).

Murdoch, Iris (1919–), English novelist: *The Bell* (1958), *A World Child* (1975) and *The Sea, the Sea* (1978).

Musset, Alfred de (1810–57), French poet and dramatist: the collection of lyric poems *Les Nuits* (1835–37) and the drama *Lorenzaccio* (1834).

Nabokov, Vladimir (1899–1977), Russian-born US writer: *Lolita* (1958), *Laughter in the Dark* (1933), *Despair* (1934) and *Pale Fire* (1962).

Naipaul, V(idiadhar) S. (1932–), Trinidadian novelist: *In a Free State* (1971).

Neruda, Pablo (1904–71), Chilean poet: *Canto general* (1945; *General Song*).

Nerval, Gérard de (1808–55), French poet: the sonnet sequence *Les Chimères* (1854).

Nesbit, E(dith) (1858–1924), English children's story writer: *Five Children and It* (1902) and *The Railway Children* (1906).

Novalis (Friedrich Leopold von Hardenberg; 1772–1801), German poet and novelist: the poem *Hymns to the Night* (1800).

Okri, Ben (1943–), Nigerian novelist: *The Famished Road* (1991).

Omar Khayyám (?1048–?1122), Iranian poet: *Rubáiyát*, well known in the West through its translation by Edward Fitzgerald.

O'Neill, Eugene (1888–1953): US dramatist: *The Iceman Cometh* (1946) and *A Long Day's Journey Into Night* (1956).

Orton, Joe (1934–67), English dramatist: *Loot* (1965) and *What the Butler Saw* (1969).

Orwell, George (1903–50), English novelist and essayist: the political allegory *Animal Farm* (1945) and the nightmarish fable of the future *Nineteen Eighty-Four* (1949).

Osborne, John (1929–94), English dramatist: *Look Back in Anger* (1956).

Ovid (43 BC–AD 17), Roman poet: *Art of Love*.

Owen, Wilfred (1893–1918), English war poet: *Anthem for Doomed Youth* and *Strange Meeting*.

Pasternak, Boris (1890–1960), Russian novelist: *Dr Zhivago* (1957).

Pater, Walter Horatio (1839–94), English critic: *Marius the Epicurean* (1885).

Paz, Octavio (1914–), Mexican poet and essayist: the essay *The Labyrinth of Solitude* (1950) and the collection of poems *The Sun Stone* (1957).

Petrarch, Francesco (1304–74), Italian sonnet writer.

Petronius (d. AD 65), Roman satirical writer: the comic novel *Satyricon*.

Pindar (*c*. 520–445 BC), Greek lyric poet: *Epinician Odes*.

Pinter, Harold (1930–), English playwright: *The Birthday Party* (1958) and *The Caretaker* (1960).

Pirandello, Luigi (1867–1936), Italian dramatist: *Six Characters in Search of an Author* (1921).

Plath, Sylvia (1932–63), US poet: the verse collections *The Colossus* (1960) and *Ariel* (1965), and the novel *The Bell Jar* (1963).

Plato (*c*. 428–347 BC), Greek philosopher: *The Republic and The Laws*.

Pliny the Younger (AD ?62–*c*.113), Roman orator and statesman, remembered for his letters.

Plutarch (*c*. AD 46–120), Greek biographer: *Parallel Lives*, a biography of 50 famous Greek and Roman lives.

Poe, Edgar Allan (1809–49), US poet, critic and short-story writer: *Tales of the Grotesque and Arabesque* (1840), including the macabre tale *The Fall of the House of Usher*.

Pope, Alexander (1688–1744), English satirical poet: *The Rape of the Lock* (1714), *The Dunciad* (1728–43), and *An Essay on Man* (1733–34).

Potter, Beatrix (1866–1943), English illustrator and children's story writer: *The Tale of Peter Rabbit* (1900).

Pound, Ezra (1885–1972), US poet: *Cantos* (1925–69).

Prévost, Antoine-François (L'Abbé Prévost; 1697–1763), French novelist: *Manon Lescaut* (1731).

Priestley, J(ohn) B(oynton) (1894–1984), English novelist and dramatist: the novel *The Good Companions* (1929) and the play *Laburnum Grove*.

Proust, Marcel (1871–1922), French novelist: the novel in seven sections *A la récherche du temps perdu* (*Remembrance of Things Past*; 1913–27).

Pushkin, Alexander (1799–1837), Russian poet and novelist: the verse novel *Eugene Onegin* (1833).

Pynchon, Thomas (1937–), US novelist: *V* (1963) and *Gravity's Rainbow* (1973).

Rabelais, François (*c*. 1494–*c*. 1553), French humanist and physician: the comic prose satire *Gargantua and Pantagruel*.

Racine, Jean (1639–99), French classical tragic dramatist: *Andromaque* (1667), *Britannicus* (1669), *Bérénice* (1670), *Bajazet* (1672) and *Phèdre* (1677).

Radcliffe, Mrs (Ann) (1764–1823), English Gothic novelist: *The Mysteries of Udolpho* (1794).

Ransome, Arthur (1884–1967), English journalist and children's story writer: *Swallows and Amazons* (1931).

Rao, Raja (1909–), Indian novelist writing in English: *Kanthapura* and *The Serpent and the Rope*.

Richardson, Samuel (1689–1761), English novelist: the epistolary novels *Pamela* (1740–41) and *Clarissa* (1747–48).

Rilke, Rainer Maria (1875–1926), Austrian poet: *Duino Elegies* (1922) and *Sonnets to Orpheus* (1923).

Rimbaud, Arthur (1854–91), French poet: the collections *Une Saison en enfer* (1873) and *Illuminations* (1886).

Robbe-Grillet, Alain (1922–), French novelist: *The Voyeur* (1955) and *Jealousy* (1957).

Robbins, Harold (1912–), US novelist: *The Carpetbaggers* (1961).

Ronsard, Pierre de (?1524–85), French poet: *Sonnets pour Hélène*.

Rosenberg, Isaac (1890–1918), English war poet: *Dead Man's Dump*.

Rousseau, Jean-Jacques (1712–78), French philosopher and novelist: *Discourses on the Origin of Inequality* (1755), the novel *Emile* (1762) and the autobiographical *Confessions* (published posthumously).

Rudaki (d. 940–41), Iranian poet.

Rushdie, Salman (1947–), Indian-born British novelist: *Midnight's Children* (1981), *Satanic Verses* (1988) and *The Moor's Last Sigh* (1995).

Sade, Marquis de (1740–1814), French sexually explicit novelist: *The Adversaries of Virtue* (1787), *Justine* (1791) and *Juliette* (1798).

Saint-Exupéry, Antoine de (1900–44), French aviator, novelist and children's story writer: *Le Petit Prince* (1943).

Salinger, J.D. (1919–), US novelist: *The Catcher in the Rye* (1951).

Sand, George (Amandine Aurore Lucie Dupin; 1804–76), French novelist: *The Haunted Pool* (1841) and *Fanchon the Cricket* (1850).

Sappho (b. mid-7th century BC), Greek lyric poetess and pioneer of the brief subjective love poem.

Sartre, Jean-Paul (1905–80), French philosopher, dramatist and novelist: the novel *Nausea* (1937), the philosophical essay *Being and Nothingness* (1943), and the trilogy *Les Chemins de la liberté* (1945–49).

Sassoon, Siegfried (1886–1967), English war poet: *Counterattack* (1918).

Schiller, Friedrich (1759–1805), German dramatist and poet: the plays *The Robbers* (1781), *Intrigue and Love* (1784), and the historical dramas *Wallenstein* (1798–99) and *Maria Stuart* (1800), *The Maid of Orleans* (1801) and *William Tell* (1803).

Scott, Sir Walter (1771–1832), Scottish novelist and poet: the ballad collection *Minstrelsy of the Scottish Border* (1802–03), and the novel *Ivanhoe* (1819).

Sei Shonagon (966/7–1013), Japanese prose writer: *The Pillow Book*.

Seneca (AD 4–65), Roman philosopher-playwright and essayist.

Shakespeare, William (1564–1616), English poet-dramatist. His 37 plays – written between 1594 and 1611 – include comedies, history plays, tragedies and tragi-comedies: the tragedies *Titus Andronicus, Romeo and Juliet, Hamlet, King Lear, Othello, Macbeth* and *Timon of Athens*; the histories *Henry VI, Richard II, Richard III, Henry IV, Henry V*, and *King John*; the comedies *The Taming of the Shrew, Love's Labour's Lost, A Midsummer Night's Dream, The Merchant of Venice, Much Ado About Nothing, Sir John Falstaff and the Merry Wives of Windsor, The Two Gentlemen of Verona, The Comedy of Errors, As You Like It* and *Twelfth Night*; the tragi-comedies *Pericles, Prince of Tyre, Troilus and Cressida, Measure for Measure, All's Well That Ends Well, Cymbelline, The Winter's Tale, The Tempest* and *Henry VIII*; the Roman plays *Julius Caesar, Antony and Cleopatra* and *Coriolanus*; the poems *The Sonnets* (1609).

Shaw, George Bernard (1856–1950), Irish dramatist and critic: *Arms and the Man* (1894), *Man and Superman* (1903), *Pygmalion* (1913) and *Saint Joan* (1923).

Shelley, Mary Wollstonecraft (1797–1851), English Gothic novelist: *Frankenstein* (1818).

Shelley, Percy Bysshe (1792–1822), English poet: *Queen Mab*, the verse dramas *Prometheus Unbound* (1820), *The Cenci* (1819) and *Hellas* (1822), and the elegy on the death of Keats *Adonais* (1821).

Sheridan, Richard (1751–1816), English dramatist: *The Rivals* (1775) and *School for Scandal* (1777).

Sidney, Sir Philip (1554–86), English pastoral poet: *Arcadia* (1590).

Simenon, Georges (1903–89), Belgian detective novelist and creator of the detective Maigret.

Sinclair, Upton (1878–1968), US novelist: *The Jungle* (1906).

Sitwell, Edith (1887–1965), English poet: *Façade* (1922).

■ *Sir John Millais's painting* Ferdinand Lured by Ariel *(1849) depicts a scene from Shakespeare's tragi-comedy* The Tempest

Solzhenitsyn, Alexander (1918–), Russian novelist: *One Day in the Life of Ivan Denisovitch* (1962), *First Circle* (1964), *Cancer Ward* (1966).

Sophocles (*c*. 497–405 BC), Greek dramatist and tragic poet: the dramas *Oedipus Rex* (*c*. 430 BC) and *Antigone* (441 BC).

Spender, Sir Stephen (1909–95), English poet and critic: *The Pylons* (1933).

Spenser, Edmund (1552–99), English poet: the moral allegory *The Faerie Queene* (1590 and 1596).

Steinbeck, John (1902–68), US novelist: *Of Mice and Men* (1937), *Grapes of Wrath* (1939) and *East of Eden* (1952).

Stendhal (Marie Henri Beyle; 1783–1842), French novelist: *Scarlet and Black* (1830) and *The Charterhouse of Parma* (1839).

Sterne, Laurence (1713–68), Irish-born English novelist: *The Life and Opinions of Tristam Shandy* (1759–68).

Stevens, Wallace (1879–1955), US poet: *Harmonium* (1923) and *The Man with the Blue Guitar* (1937).

Stevenson, Robert Louis (1850–94), Scottish novelist: *Treasure Island* (1883) and *The Strange Case of Dr Jekyll and Mr Hyde* (1886).

Stoppard, Tom (1937–), Czech-born English dramatist: *Rosencrantz and Guildenstern are Dead* (1966) and *Arcadia* (1993).

Strassburg, Gottfried von (active 1210), German poet: *Tristan and Isolde*.

Strindberg, August (1849–1912), Swedish dramatist: *Miss Julie* (1888), *The Dance of Death* (1901) and *The Ghost Sonata* (1907).

Swift, Graham (1949–), English novelist: *Waterland* (1983) and *Last Orders* (1996).

Swift, Jonathan (1667–1745), Anglo-Irish satirist: the satirical fantasy *Gulliver's Travels* (1726).

Swinburne, Algernon Charles (1837–1909), English poet: *Songs before Sunset* (1871) and *Tristram of Lyonesse* (1882).

■ *The Toilet of Salome, an illustration by Aubrey Beardsley for the English edition of Oscar Wilde's play, Salome (1894)*

Synge, J(ohn) M(illington) (1871–1909), Irish dramatist: *Playboy of the Western World* (1907).

Tacitus (*c.* AD 56–117), Roman historian.

Tagore, Rabindranath (1861–1941), poet, novelist, playwright and essayist: the collection of poems *Gitanjali* (1912).

Tennyson, Alfred, Lord (1809–92), English poet: the poems *The Lady of Shalott* (1832) and *The Lotus Eaters* (1833), the collections *In Memoriam* (1850) and *Idylls of the King* (1855).

Theroux, Paul (1941–), US novelist and travel writer: *Jungle Lovers* (1971) and *The Great Railway Bazaar* (1975).

Thackeray, William Makepeace (1811–63), English novelist: *Vanity Fair* (1846–08) and *The History of Pendennis* (1848–50).

Thomas, Dylan (1914–53), Welsh poet: *Deaths and Entrances* (1946), and the play for voices *Under Milk Wood* (1954).

Thomas, Edward (1878–1917), English poet: *Collected Poems* (1920), including the poem *Adlestrop*.

Thoreau, Henry David (1817–62), US writer and essayist: *A Life in the Woods* (1854) and the influential essay *Civil Disobedience* (1849).

Thucydides (*c.* 455–399 BC), Athenian historian.

Tolkien, J(ohn) R(onald) R(euel) (1892–1973), English novelist: *The Hobbit* (1937) and *The Lord of the Rings* (1954–55).

Tolstoy, Leo (1828–1910), Russian novelist: *War and Peace* (1869) and *Anna Karenina* (1877).

Trollope, Anthony (1815–82), English novelist: *Barsetshire Chronicles* (1857–67) – a sequence of six novels including *The Warden* (1855) and *Barchester Towers* (1857).

Turgenev, Ivan (1818–83), Russian novelist, short-story writer and dramatist: the play *A Month in the Country* (1850) and the novel *Fathers and Sons* (1861).

Twain, Mark (Samuel Langhorne Clemens; 1835–1910), US novelist and short-story writer: *The Adventures of Tom Sawyer* (1876), *Life on the Mississippi* (1883) and *The Adventures of Huckleberry Finn* (1884).

Updike, John (1932–), US novelist: *Rabbit, Run* (1960) and *Couples* (1968).

Valéry, Paul (1871–1945), French poet: *La Jeune Parque* (1917) and *Charmes* (1922).

Vanbrugh, Sir John (1664–1726), English comic dramatist: the Restoration comedies *The Relapse* (1696) and *The Provoked Wife* (1697).

Vega, Lope de Felix (1562–1635), prolific Spanish playwright and poet who claimed to have written 1500 plays, of which only 500 survive: the epic *La Dragentea* (1598).

Verlaine, Paul (1844–96), French poet: *Romances sans paroles* (1874) and *Sagesse* (1881).

Vigny, Alfred de (1797–1863), French poet: the novel *Cinq-Mars* (1826) and the play *Chatterton* (1835).

Villon, François (b. 1431), French poet: *Le Lais* and *Le Testament*.

Virgil (70–19 BC), Roman poet: *Eclogues, Georgics* and the *Aeneid* (a national epic).

Voltaire (François-Marie Arouet; 1694–1778), French philosopher, dramatist and prose-writer: the epic poem *Le Henriade* (1723), the politico-philosophical *Lettres philosophiques* (1734), and the philosophical tales *Zadig* (1747) and *Candide* (1759).

Wace (b. *c.* 1100), Anglo-Norman poet: *Roman de Brut* and *Roman de Rou*.

Walcott, Derek (1933–), St Lucian poet and playwright: *In a Green Night* (1962) and *Omeros* (1990).

Walpole, Horace (1717–97), English Gothic novelist: *The Castle of Otranto* (1765).

Waugh, Evelyn (1903–66), English novelist: *Decline and Fall* (1928), *A Handful of Dust* (1934) and *Brideshead Revisited* (1945).

Webster, John (*c.* 1578–*c.* 1632), English tragic dramatist: *The White Devil* (1612) and *The Duchess of Malfi* (1613–14).

Wedekind, Frank (1864–1918), German actor and dramatist: *The Awakening of Spring* (1909).

Wells, H(erbert) G(eorge) (1866–1946), novelist: the science-fiction stories *The Time Machine* (1895) and *War of the Worlds* (1898), the novel *The Invisible Man* (1897) and the humorous novel *Kipps* (1904).

Wheatley, Dennis (1897–1977), English horror novelist.

White, Patrick (1912–90), Australian novelist: *The Tree of Man* (1955), *Voss* (1957) and *Riders in the Chariot* (1961).

Wiess, Peter (1916–82), German dramatist and novelist: *Exile* (1962).

Wilde, Oscar (Fingal O'Flahertie Wills; 1854–1900), Irish dramatist, poet and novelist, famous for his witty epigrams: the novel *The Picture of Dorian Gray* (1891), the play *The Importance of Being Earnest* (1895) and the poem *The Ballad of Reading Gaol* (1898).

Wilder, Thornton (1897–1975), US dramatist: *The Skin of Our Teeth* (1942) and *The Match Maker* (1954).

Williams, Tennessee (1911–83), US dramatist: *The Glass Menagerie* (1944), *A Streetcar Named Desire* (1947) and *Cat On A Hot Tin Roof* (1955).

Williams, William Carlos (1883–1963), US poet: the epic *Paterson* (1946–58).

Wodehouse, P(elham) G(renville) (1881–1975), English comic novelist: the Bertie Wooster and Jeeves novels.

Woolf, Virginia (1882–1941), English novelist: *Mrs Dalloway* (1925) and *To the Lighthouse* (1927).

Wordsworth, William (1770–1850), English poet: *Lyrical Ballads* (1798; a collection of poems written with Coleridge) and *The Prelude* (1798–1805).

Wycherley, William (1641–1715), English comic dramatist: the Restoration comedy *The Country Wife* (1675).

Wyss, Johann Rudolph (1782–1830), Swiss novelist: *Swiss Family Robinson* (1827).

Yeats, W(illiam) B(utler) (1865–1939), Irish poet and dramatist: the poems *Sailing to Byzantium, Among School Children* and *Lapis Lazuli*.

Yourcenar, Marguerite (1903–88), French novelist: *Memoirs of Hadrian* (1951) and *The Abyss* (1963).

Zola, Émile (1840–1902), French novelist: *Nana* (1880), the novel cycle *The Rougon-Macquart*, including *Germinal* (1885) and *La Débâcle* (1892), and *J'accuse*, a letter criticizing the accusers of Dreyfus.

NOBEL PRIZEWINNERS

1901 Sully-Prudhomme, French poet.

1902 Theodor Mommsen, German historian.

1903 Bjornstjerne Bjornsen, Norwegian novelist, poet and dramatist.

1904 Frédéric Mistral, French poet.

1905 Henryk Sienkiewicz, Polish novelist.

1906 Giosue Carducci, Italian Classical poet.

1907 Rudyard Kipling, British novelist and poet.

1908 Rudolf Eucken, German Idealist philosopher.

1909 Selma Lagerlöf, Swedish novelist.

1910 Paul von Heyse, German poet, novelist and dramatist.

1911 Maurice Maeterlinck, Belgian Symbolist poet and dramatist.

1912 Gerhart Hauptmann, German dramatist, novelist and poet.

1913 R. Tagore, Indian playwright and poet.

1914 No award

1915 Romain Rolland, French novelist and biographer.

1916 Verner von Heidenstam, Swedish lyric poet.

1917 Karl Gjellerup, Danish novelist; and Henrik Pontoppidan, Danish novelist.

1918 No award

1919 Carl Spitteler, Swiss poet and novelist.

1920 Knut Hamsun, Norwegian novelist.

1921 Anatole France, French novelist.

1922 Jacinto Benavente y Martinez, Spanish dramatist of social satires.

1923 William Butler Yeats, Irish poet and dramatist.

1924 Wladyslaw Stanislaw Reymont, Polish novelist.

1925 George Bernard Shaw, Irish dramatist.

1926 Grazia Deledda, Italian Naturalist novelist.

1927 Henri Bergson, French dualist philosopher.

1928 Sigrid Undset, Norwegian novelist.

1929 Thomas Mann, German novelist.

1930 Sinclair Lewis, US satirical novelist.

1931 Erik Axel Karlfeldt, Swedish lyric poet.

1932 John Galsworthy, British novelist and dramatist.

1933 Ivan Bunin, Russian émigré novelist.

1934 Luigi Pirandello, Italian dramatist.

1935 No award

1936 Eugene O'Neill, US dramatist.

1937 Roger Martin du Gard, French novelist.

1938 Pearl Buck, US novelist.

1939 Frans Eemil Sillanpää, Finnish novelist.

1940 No award

■ BORGES HAS BEEN CALLED THE GREATEST WRITER NEVER TO WIN THE NOBEL PRIZE ■

1941 No award
1942 No award
1943 No award
1944 Johannes V. Jensen, Danish writer of essays and travel books.
1945 Gabriela Mistral, Chilean lyric poet.
1946 Hermann Hesse, German-born Swiss novelist and poet.
1947 André Gide, French novelist and essayist.
1948 T.S. Eliot, US-born English poet, dramatist and literary critic.
1949 William Faulkner, US novelist.
1950 Bertrand Russell, English philosopher and mathematician.
1951 Pär Lagerkvist, Swedish novelist.
1952 François Mauriac, French poet, novelist and dramatist.
1953 Sir Winston Churchill, English statesman, historian and orator.
1954 Ernest Hemingway, US novelist.
1955 Halldór Laxness, Icelandic novelist.
1956 Juan Ramón Jiménez, Spanish lyric poet.
1957 Albert Camus, French novelist and dramatist.
1958 Boris Pasternak, Russian novelist and poet; declined award.
1959 Salvatore Quasimodo, Italian poet.
1960 Saint-John Perse, French lyric poet.
1961 Ivo Andric, Yugoslav (Bosnian) novelist.
1962 John Steinbeck, US novelist.
1963 George Seferis, Greek poet and essayist.
1964 Jean-Paul Sartre, French philosopher and writer: declined award.
1965 Mikhail Sholokhov, Russian novelist.
1966 Shmuel Yosef Agnon, Israeli novelist; and Nelly Sachs, German-born Swedish Jewish poet.
1967 Miguel Angel Asturias, Guatemalan novelist and poet.
1968 Kawabata Yasunari, Japanese novelist.
1969 Samuel Beckett, Irish novelist, poet and dramatist.
1970 Aleksandr Solzhenitsyn, Russian novelist.
1971 Pablo Neruda, Chilean poet.
1972 Heinrich Böll, German novelist.
1973 Patrick White, Australian novelist.
1974 Eyvind Johnson, Swedish novelist; and Harry Martinson, Swedish novelist and poet.
1975 Eugenio Montale, Italian poet.
1976 Saul Bellow, US novelist.
1977 Vicente Aleixandre, Spanish lyric poet.
1978 Isaac Bashevis Singer, US Jewish novelist and short-story writer.
1979 Odysseus Elytis, Greek poet.
1980 Czeslaw Milosz, Polish-US poet and novelist.
1981 Elias Canetti, Bulgarian-born German novelist, playwright and essayist.
1982 Gabriel García Márquez, Colombian novelist.
1983 Sir William Golding, English novelist.
1984 Jaroslav Seifert, Czech poet.
1985 Claude Simon, French novelist and exponent of the *nouveau Roman*.
1986 Wole Soyinka, Nigerian playwright and poet.
1987 Joseph Brodsky, American (Russian émigré) poet and essayist.
1988 Naguib Mahfouz, Egyptian novelist.
1989 Camilo José Cela, Spanish novelist.
1990 Octavio Paz, Mexican poet.
1991 Nadine Gordimer, South African novelist.
1992 Derek Walcott, St Lucian poet.
1993 Toni Morrison, US novelist.
1994 Kenzaburo Oe, Japanese novelist.
1995 Seamus Heaney, Northern Irish novelist.
1996 Wislawa Szymborska, Polish poet.

OTHER PRIZEWINNERS

BOOKER PRIZE

The Booker McConnell Prize is an annual award for a novel by a citizen of the United Kingdom, the Republic of Ireland, a Commonwealth country or South Africa and first published in Britain. It was established by the trading company Booker McConnell in collaboration with the Publishers' Association in 1968.

1969 P.H. Newby: *Something to Answer For.*
1970 Bernice Rubens: *The Elected Member.*
1971 V.S. Naipaul: *In a Free State.*
1972 John Berger: *G.*
1973 J.G. Farrell: *The Siege of Krishnapur.*
1974 Nadine Gordimer: *The Conservationist*; Stanley Middleton: *Holiday.*
1975 Ruth Prawer Jhabvala: *Heat and Dust.*
1976 David Storey: *Saville.*
1977 Paul Scott: *Staying On.*
1978 Iris Murdoch: *The Sea, the Sea.*
1979 Penelope Fitzgerald: *Offshore.*
1980 William Golding: *Rites of Passage.*
1981 Salman Rushdie: *Midnight's Children.*
1982 Thomas Keneally: *Schindler's Ark.*
1983 J.M. Coetzee: *Life and Times of Michael K.*
1984 Anita Brookner: *Hôtel du Lac.*
1985 Keri Hulme: *The Bone People.*
1986 Kingsley Amis: *The Old Devils.*
1987 Penelope Lively: *Moon Tiger.*
1988 Peter Carey: *Oscar and Lucinda.*
1989 Kazuo Ishiguro: *The Remains of the Day.*
1990 A.S. Byatt: *Possession.*
1991 Ben Okri: *The Famished Road.*
1992 Michael Ondaatje: *The English Patient*; Barry Unsworth: *Sacred Hunger.*
1993 Roddy Doyle: *Paddy Clarke Ha Ha Ha.*
1994 James Kelman: *How Late It Was, How Late.*
1995 Pat Barker: *The Ghost Road.*
1996 Graham Swift: *Last Orders.*

PULITZER PRIZE

The Pulitzer prizes are annual awards endowed by the American publisher Joseph Pulitzer in 1917. They are given for achievements in American journalism and literature. Awards are made for the best reporting of national news and of international news, the most distinguished editorial, the best local reporting and the best news photograph, as well as for the best work of fiction. Winners for the best work of fiction appear below.

1918 Ernest Poole: *His Family.*
1919 Booth Tarkington: *The Magnificent Ambersons.*
1920 No award
1921 Edith Wharton: *The Age of Innocence.*
1922 Booth Tarkington: *Alice Adams.*
1923 Willa Cather: *One of Ours.*
1924 Margaret Wilson: *The Able McLaughlins.*
1925 Edna Ferber: *So Big.*
1926 Sinclair Lewis: *Arrowsmith.*
1927 Louis Bromfield: *Early Autumn.*
1928 Thornton Wilder: *The Bridge at San Luis Rey.*
1929 Julia Peterkin: *Scarlet Sister Mary.*
1930 Oliver LaFarge: *Laughing Boy.*
1931 Margaret Ayer Barnes: *Years of Grace.*
1932 Pearl S. Buck: *The Good Earth.*
1933 T.S. Stribling: *The Store.*
1934 Caroline Miller: *Lamb in His Bosom.*
1935 Josephine Winslow Johnson: *Now in November.*
1936 Harold L. Davis: *Honey in the Horn.*
1937 Margaret Mitchell: *Gone With the Wind.*
1938 John Phillips Marquand: *The Late George Apley.*
1939 Marjorie Kinnan Rawlings: *The Yearling.*
1940 John Steinbeck: *The Grapes of Wrath.*
1941 No award
1942 Ellen Glasgow: *In This Our Life.*
1943 Upton Sinclair: *Dragon's Teeth.*
1944 Martin Flavin: *Journey in the Dark.*
1945 John Hersey: *A Bell for Adano.*
1946 No award
1947 Robert Penn Warren: *All the King's Men.*
1948 James A. Michener: *Tales of the South Pacific.*
1949 James Gould Cozzens: *Guard of Honor.*
1950 A.B. Guthrie, Jr: *The Way West.*
1951 Conrad Richter: *The Town.*
1952 Herman Wouk: *The Caine Mutiny.*
1953 Ernest Hemingway: *The Old Man and the Sea.*
1954 No award
1955 William Faulkner: *A Fable.*
1956 Mackinley Kantor: *Andersonville.*
1957 No award
1958 James Agee: *A Death in the Family.*
1959 Robert Lewis Taylor: *The Travels of Jamie McPheeters.*
1960 Allen Drury: *Advise and Consent.*
1961 Harper Lee: *To Kill a Mockingbird.*
1962 Edwin O'Connor: *The Edge of Sadness.*
1963 William Faulkner: *The Reivers.*
1964 No award
1965 Shirley Ann Grau: *The Keepers of the House.*
1966 Katherine Anne Porter: *The Collected Stories of Katherine Anne Porter.*
1967 Bernard Malamud: *The Fixer.*
1968 William Styron: *The Confessions of Nat Turner.*
1969 N. Scott Momaday: *House Made of Dawn.*
1970 Jean Stafford: *Collected Stories.*
1971 No award
1972 Wallace Stegner: *Angle of Repose.*
1973 Eudora Welty: *The Optimist's Daughter.*
1974 No award
1975 Michael Shaara: *The Killer Angels.*
1976 Saul Bellow: *Humboldt's Gift.*
1977 No award
1978 James Alan McPherson: *Elbow Room.*
1979 John Cheever: *The Stories of John Cheever.*
1980 Norman Mailer: *The Executioner's Song.*
1981 John Kennedy Toole: *A Confederacy of Dunces.*
1982 John Updike: *Rabbit is Rich.*
1983 Alice Walker: *The Color Purple.*
1984 William Kennedy: *Ironweed.*
1985 Alison Lurie: *Foreign Affairs.*
1986 Larry McMurtry: *Lonesome Dove.*
1987 Peter Taylor: *A Summons to Memphis.*
1988 Toni Morrison: *Beloved.*
1989 Anne Tyler: *Breathing Lessons.*
1990 Oscar Hijuelos: *The Mambo Kings Play Songs of Love.*
1991 John Updike: *Rabbit at Rest.*
1992 Jane Simley: *A Thousand Acres.*
1993 Robert Olen Butler: *A Good Scent from a Strange Mountain.*
1994 E. Annie Proulx: *The Shipping News.*
1995 Carol Shields: *The Stone Diaries.*
1996 Richard Ford: *Independence Day.*
1997 Steven Millhauser: *Martin Dressler: The Tale of an American Dreamer.*

LITERARY FORMS AND TERMS

acrostic: a number of lines of writing, e.g. a poem, in which certain letters, especially the first letters of each line, make a word or words.

act: a major division of a dramatic work.

alexandrine: a line of verse with six iambic feet.

allegory: a poem, novel, drama, etc., in which the events and characters symbolize a deeper meaning beyond their apparent literal meaning.

alliteration: a figure of speech in which the same consonant or vowel is repeated at the beginning of each or some of the words or stressed syllables in a line of poetry (e.g. the stuttering rifle's rapid rattle).

allusion: an indirect reference, often to other literary works through an implicit mimicry of words and phrases.

anagram: a word made from another word by changing the order of the letters (e.g. god – dog).

anecdote: a short amusing story about a person or event.

antonym: a word that means the opposite of another word.

aphorism: a short statement expressing a general truth in witty fashion (e.g. necessity is the mother of invention).

assonance: the repetition of the same vowel sound in a line of verse.

autobiography: an account of a person's life written by himself or herself.

ballad: a song or poem that tells a story.

ballade: a verse form consisting of three stanzas and an envoi, each ending with the same line.

biography: an account of a person's life written by someone else.

blank verse: unrhymed verse, often in iambic pentameters.

canto: a division of a long poem.

cliché: an expression that has lost its force by being used too much (e.g. time flies).

colloquialism: a word or phrase used in everyday informal speech rather than in a formal or literary context.

couplet: two successive lines of poetry, usually rhyming and having the same metre.

dialogue: speech of the characters in a novel or play.

doggerel: comic verse of poor quality, usually with an irregular metre.

drama: a work to be performed on stage, radio or television by actors.

dramatis personae: (a list of) all the characters in a play or story.

eclogue: a short pastoral poem in the form of a conversation or soliloquy.

elegy: a serious meditative poem, especially a lament for the dead.

envoi: a brief dedicatory stanza at the end of certain forms of poetry, especially ballads.

epic: a long narrative poem recounting in an elevated style the deeds of a legendary hero.

epigram: a short witty statement in verse or prose.

epithet: a descriptive word or phrase added to or substituted for a person's name (e.g. Charles the Bold).

euphemism: an inoffensive word or phrase substituted for an unpleasant or hurtful one.

fable: a short tale in prose or verse that points to a moral.

farce: a humorous play characterized by absurd or improbable situations.

fiction: literary works invented by the imagination, such as novels and short stories.

foot: a metrical division or unit of verse, consisting of two or more syllables, one of which has a strong stress, the other or others a weak stress (e.g. for mén /may cóme/ and mén/ may gó).

free verse: unrhymed verse without a regular rhythm.

haiku: a 17-syllable verse, usually in lines of seven, five and seven syllables, which is the best known of the form of Japanese poetry.

heroic couplet: two lines of rhyming verse in iambic pentameters.

hyperbole: deliberate use of exaggeration for emphasis.

iambic pentameter: a line of verse consisting of five feet, each of which consists of an unstressed syllable followed by a stressed one.

idiom: an expression or group of words whose meaning cannot be worked out from the literal meaning of its constituent words.

idyll: a work in verse or prose describing an idealized country life.

irony: discourse that carries a latent meaning opposite to or different from the usual meaning, often for humorous, critical or satirical effect; the poignant disparity between expected and actual events.

legend: a popular story passed down from earlier times, the truth of which has not been established.

limerick: a short humorous poem five lines in length.

litotes: ironic understatement, especially the use of a negative to express the contrary (e.g. I won't be sorry when it's over = I will be extremely glad when it's over).

lyric poetry: verse expressing the personal thoughts and feelings of the writer.

maxim: a short phrase or statement expressing a general truth or principle or rule of conduct.

melodrama: a dramatic work characterized by exciting and sensational events and usually having a happy ending.

metaphor: a figure of speech in which one person or thing is described in terms of another (e.g. he is a cunning fox).

metonym: a word used as a figure of speech in which the name of an attribute or adjunct is substituted for that of the thing that is being referred to (e.g. 'crown' used to refer to 'a monarch' or 'the bottle' used for alcoholic drink).

metre: the rhythmic arrangement of syllables in poetry, according to the number and type of feet in a line.

monologue: a long speech for a single performer in a drama.

myth: a story about superhuman beings, regarded by ancient societies as being a true explanation of certain natural phenomena, how the world came into existence, etc.

novel: an extended prose narrative recounting the story of fictional characters within a recognizable social context.

novella: a short novel.

octave: group of eight lines of verse.

ode: a lyric poem in which the poet directly addresses the subject, with lines of differing lengths and a complex rhythm.

onomatopoeia: formation of words whose sound imitates the sound of the noise or action described (e.g. cuckoo, buzz, hiss).

oxymoron: a figure of speech in which apparently contradictory terms are used together to achieve an effect (e.g. darkness visible).

palindrome: a word or phrase that reads the same backward as forwards (e.g. noon, bob, level).

paradox: a statement that appears to be self-contradictory, but on closer examination can be seen to contain a truth.

parody: a literary work which imitates the style of a particular writer in a humorous or satirical way.

pastiche: a literary work composed in the style of a particular author or period.

pastoral: literature concerning an idealized rural world, often focusing on shepherd life.

plot: the story line of a novel or play.

poem: a literary work in verse, characterized by concentrated or striking language used for its suggestive power as well as its literal meaning and often making use of rhyme, metre, alliteration, etc.

prose: written language as in ordinary usage, as distinct from poetry.

prosody: the study and theory of versification, especially concerning structure and metre.

pun: the humorous use of a word to suggest different meanings, or of words of the same sound with different meanings; a play on words.

quatrain: group of four lines of verse, often with alternate rhymes.

rhetoric: the study and practice of the art of effective communication.

rhyme: identity or similarity of sound between the endings of words or lines of verse.

rhyme royal: verse form consisting of stanzas of seven lines of iambic pentameters with a complex rhyme scheme.

rondeau: verse form consisting of ten or 13 lines using only two rhymes throughout and repeating the opening words twice as a refrain.

saga: a long story recounting heroic deeds, especially a medieval tale of Scandinavian heroes; or a series of connected books about several generations of a family or other social group.

satire: a literary work using ridicule, irony or sarcasm to expose folly or vice.

scene: a subdivision of a play, smaller than an act, in which the action is continuous.

sestet: a group of six lines of verse.

short story: a prose narrative of shorter length than a novel.

simile: a figure of speech which asserts the identity of unlike things through comparison, using 'as' or 'like' (e.g. he ran like the wind).

soliloquy: a speech in a drama in which a character expresses his or her thoughts aloud without addressing a particular person.

sonnet: a poem consisting of 14 lines of iambic pentameters with rhymes arranged according to a fixed scheme, and divided into an octave and a sestet (a Petrarchan sonnet), or three quatrains and a couplet (an Elizabethan sonnet).

stanza: a group of lines in a poem, arranged in a particular metrical pattern.

synecdoche: a figure of speech in which a part is used to indicate a whole, or a whole used to indicate a part.

synonym: a word identical or similar in meaning to another one.

tercet: group of three lines of verse.

tragedy: a literary work, often dramatic in form, in which the protagonist, usually a person of outstanding personal qualities, falls from grace through an overwhelming combination of personal failing and circumstance; any literary work dealing with sad or serious events and ending in disaster.

verse: written language with a metrical structure; poetry.

villanelle: a verse form usually consisting of five stanzas of three lines (tercets) and one stanza of four lines (quatrain), using only two rhymes throughout according to a fixed scheme.

‘If winning isn’t everything, why do they keep the score?’
– Vince Lombardi

SPORTS ▷

THE OLYMPIC GAMES

- **The highest number of Olympic gold medals won in the modern Olympics is ten, achieved in track and field by Raymond Clarence Ewry (USA) from 1900–08.**
- **The XVIIIth Winter Olympics are to be held in Nagano, Japan, from 7–22 February 1998.**
- **The XXVIIth Summer Oympics will be held in Sydney, Australia, from 15 September–1 October 2000.**
- **The greatest number of gold medals achieved by a female contestant is seven, won in gymnastics by Vera Caslavska-Odlozil (Cze) in 1964 and 1968.**
- **The highest number of Olympic wins is 12, won in the ancient Olympics by Leonidas of Rhodos from 164–152 BC.**

The Olympic Games are an international sporting competition held every four years. The governing body, the International Olympic Committee (IOC), chooses a different host city for each Olympics.

THE ANCIENT OLYMPICS

The ancient Olympic Games have their historical roots in religious ceremonies held in honour of Greek gods. Ancient Greek contestants, who were all male, competed in the nude, and winners received a crown of wild olive leaves. The earliest celebrations were held in the 14th century BC, although the first Olympics for which there is an accurate record are those of 776 BC. Held in Olympia, Greece, the Games grew to become important showcases of athletic prowess, with events including charioteering, boxing, wrestling, discus and running. The Olympics lost their high reputation in the early Christian era and were finally prohibited in AD 393 by the Roman Emperor Theodosius I.

THE MODERN OLYMPICS

Based on the ideals of the ancient Greek competition, the modern Olympic Games were founded by Pierre de Fredi, Baron de Coubertin (1863–1937), who suggested a revival of the ancient Games in a lecture in 1892. In 1894, the IOC was inaugurated, and the first modern Olympics were held in 1896 in Athens, Greece. The Winter Olympics were inaugurated in 1924.

■ *A runner brings the Olympic torch to start the 1936 Games. The Berlin Olympics became a Nazi showcase*

MODERN SUMMER OLYMPIC GAMES

		Venue	Date	Participating Countries	Competitors Male	Female	Total
I	1896	Athens, Greece	6–15 Apr	14	c. 211	0	c. 211
II	1900	Paris, France	20 May–28 Oct	26	1,206	19	1,225
III	1904	St Louis, USA	1 Jul–23 Nov	13	681	6	687
	1906*	Athens, Greece	22 Apr–2 May	20	820	6	826
IV	1908	London, UK	27 Apr–31 Oct	22	1,999	36	2,035
V	1912	Stockholm, Sweden	5 May–22 Jul	28	2,490	57	2,547
VI	1916	Berlin, Germany	Not held due to war	–	–	–	–
VII	1920	Antwerp, Belgium	20 Apr–12 Sep	29	2,591	77	2,668
VIII	1924	Paris, France	4 May–27 Jul	44	2,956	136	3,092
IX	1928	Amsterdam, the Netherlands	17 May–12 Aug	46	2,724	290	3,014
X	1932	Los Angeles, USA	30 Jul–14 Aug	37	1,281	127	1,408
XI	1936	Berlin, Germany	1–16 Aug	49	3,738	328	4,066
XII	1940	Tokyo, then Helsinki	Not held due to war	–	–	–	–
XIII	1944	London, UK	Not held due to war	–	–	–	–
XIV	1948	London, UK	29 Jul–14 Aug	59	3,714	385	4,099
XV	1952	Helsinki, Finland	19 Jul–3 Aug	69	4,407	518	4,925
XVI	1956**	Melbourne, Australia	22 Nov–8 Dec	67	2,813	371	3,184
XVII	1960	Rome, Italy	25 Aug–11 Sep	83	4,736	610	5,346
XVIII	1964	Tokyo, Japan	10–24 Oct	93	4,457	683	5,140
XIX	1968	Mexico City, Mexico	12–27 Oct	112	4,749	781	5,530
XX	1972	Munich, Germany	26 Aug–10 Sep	121	6,065	1,058	7,123
XXI	1976	Montreal, Canada	17 Jul–1 Aug	92	4,781	1,247	6,028
XXII	1980	Moscow, USSR	19 Jul–3 Aug	80	4,093	1,124	5,217
XXIII	1984	Los Angeles, USA	28 Jul–12 Aug	140	5,230	1,567	6,797
XXIV	1988	Seoul, South Korea	17 Sep–2 Oct	159	6,279	2,186	8,465
XXV	1992	Barcelona, Spain	25 Jul–9 Aug	169	6,657	2,707	9,364
XXVI	1996	Atlanta, USA	20 Jul–4 Aug	197	7,060	3,684	10,744

* This celebration to mark the tenth anniversary of the modern Games is treated as an official Olympics, but is not numbered

** The equestrian events were held in Stockholm, Sweden, 10–17 June, with 158 competitors (including 13 women) from 29 countries

MODERN WINTER OLYMPIC GAMES

		Venue	Date	Participating Countries	Competitors Male	Female	Total
I*	1924	Chamonix, France	25 Jan–4 Feb	16	245	13	258
II	1928	St Moritz, Switzerland	11–19 Feb	25	438	26	464
III	1932	Lake Placid, USA	4–15 Feb	17	231	21	252
IV	1936	Garmisch-Partenkirchen, Germany	6–16 Feb	28	588	80	668
V	1948	St Moritz, Switzerland	30 Jan–8 Feb	28	592	77	669
VI	1952	Oslo, Norway	14–25 Feb	30	585	109	694
VII	1956	Cortina d'Ampezzo, Italy	26 Jan–5 Feb	32	688	132	820
VIII	1960	Squaw Valley, USA	18–28 Feb	30	522	143	665
IX	1964	Innsbruck, Austria	29 Jan–9 Feb	36	891	200	1,091
X	1968	Grenoble, France	6–18 Feb	37	947	211	1,158
XI	1972	Sapporo, Japan	3–13 Feb	35	800	206	1,006
XII	1976	Innsbruck, Austria	4–15 Feb	37	892	231	1,123
XIII	1980	Lake Placid, USA	13–24 Feb	37	839	233	1,072
XIV	1984	Sarajevo, Yugoslavia**	8–19 Feb	49	1,000	274	1,274
XV	1988	Calgary, Canada	13–28 Feb	57	1,110	313	1,423
XVI	1992	Albertville, France	8–23 Feb	64	1,313	488	1,801
XVII	1994	Lillehammer, Norway	12–27 Feb	67	1,216	521	1,737

* There were Winter Games events included in the Summer Olympics of 1908 and 1920: these attracted six countries, 14 males and seven females for the 1908 Olympics in London; and ten countries, 73 males and 12 females for the 1920 Olympics in Antwerp

** now in Bosnia-Herzegovina

■ *The opening ceremony of the 1996 Atlanta Games celebrated the centenary of the modern Olympics. A total of 10,744 competitors from 197 nations took part in 271 events in 27 sports. Seventy-nine countries shared a total of 1933 medals. The Games were remarkable for the number of nations that won medals for the first time – a total of 11: Armenia, Azerbaijan, Burundi, the Czech Republic, Ecuador, Georgia, Hong Kong, Moldova, Mozambique, Slovakia and Tonga*

SUMMER GAMES MEDAL WINNERS

		Gold	Silver	Bronze	Total
1	United States	833	634	548	2,015
2	Soviet Union[1]	485	395	354	1,234
3	Great Britain	177	233	225	635
4	France	176	181	205	562
5	Germany[2]	151	181	184	516
6	Sweden	134	152	173	459
7	Italy	166	136	142	444
8	Hungary	142	128	155	425
9	GDR[3]	153	130	127	410
10	Australia	87	85	122	294
11	Finland	99	80	113	292
12	Japan	93	89	98	280
13	Romania	63	77	99	239
14	Poland	50	67	110	227
15	Canada	49	77	91	217
16	FRG[4]	56	64	80	200
17	Netherlands	49	57	81	187
18	Bulgaria	43	76	63	182
19	Switzerland	46	68	60	174
20	China	52	63	49	164
21	Denmark	39	60	57	156
22	Czechoslovakia[5]	49	50	50	149
23	Belgium	37	50	49	136
24	South Korea	38	42	46	126
25	Norway	46	40	38	124
26	Greece	28	42	44	114
27	Cuba	45	33	31	109
28	Yugoslavia	27	31	32	90
29	Austria	19	31	34	84
30	New Zealand	30	12	29	71
31	Russia[6]	26	25	19	70
32	Spain	22	25	17	64
33	Turkey	30	16	13	59
34	South Africa	19	18	21	58
35	Brazil	12	13	29	54
36	Argentina	13	21	16	50
37	Kenya	14	17	16	47
38	Mexico	9	13	19	41
39	Iran	5	13	18	36
40	Jamaica	5	16	11	32
41	North Korea	8	6	12	26
=42	Estonia	7	6	10	23
=42	Ukraine	9	2	12	23
44	Ireland	8	5	6	19
45	Egypt	6	6	6	18
46	Ethiopia	8	1	7	16
=47	India	8	3	4	15
=47	Portugal	3	4	8	15
=47	Belarus	1	6	8	15
=50	Nigeria	2	5	7	14
=50	Mongolia	0	5	9	14
=52	Czech Republic	4	3	4	11
=52	Morocco	4	2	5	11
=52	Kazakhstan	3	4	4	11
=55	Indonesia	3	4	3	10
=55	Pakistan	3	3	4	10
=57	Uruguay	2	1	6	9
=57	Trinidad & Tobago	1	2	6	9
=57	Philippines	0	2	7	9
=60	Venezuela	1	2	5	8
=60	Chile	0	6	2	8
=62	Algeria	3	0	4	7
=62	Latvia	0	5	2	7
=64	Uganda	1	3	2	6
=64	Tunisia	1	2	3	6
=64	Thailand	1	1	4	6
=64	Colombia	0	2	4	6
=64	Puerto Rico	0	1	5	6
=69	Croatia	1	2	2	5
=69	Taiwan (Taipei)	0	3	2	5
=71	Peru	1	3	0	4
=71	Bahamas	1	1	2	4
=71	Namibia	0	4	0	4
=71	Lebanon	0	2	2	4
=71	Slovenia	0	2	2	4
=71	Ghana	0	1	3	4
=77	Slovakia	1	1	1	3
=77	Lithuania	1	0	2	3
=77	Israel	0	1	2	3
=77	Malaysia	0	1	2	3
=81	Luxembourg	1	1	0	2
=81	Tanzania	0	2	0	2
=81	Cameroon	0	1	1	2
=81	Haiti	0	1	1	2
=81	Iceland	0	1	1	2
=81	Panama	0	0	2	2
=81	Surinam	1	0	1	2
=81	Uzbekistan	0	1	1	2
=81	Costa Rica	1	1	0	2
=81	Syria	1	1	0	2
=81	Zambia	0	1	1	2
=81	Armenia	1	1	0	2
=81	Moldova	0	1	1	2
=81	Georgia	0	0	2	2
=95	Zimbabwe	1	0	0	1
=95	Ivory Coast	0	1	0	1
=95	Netherlands Antilles	0	1	0	1
=95	Senegal	0	1	0	1
=95	Singapore	0	1	0	1
=95	Sri Lanka	0	1	0	1
=95	Virgin Islands	0	1	0	1
=95	Barbados	0	0	1	1
=95	Bermuda	0	0	1	1
=95	Djibouti	0	0	1	1
=95	Dominican Republic	0	0	1	1
=95	Guyana	0	0	1	1
=95	Iraq	0	0	1	1
=95	Niger Republic	0	0	1	1
=95	Qatar	0	0	1	1
=95	Burundi	1	0	0	1
=95	Ecuador	1	0	0	1
=95	Hong Kong	1	0	0	1
=95	Azerbaijan	0	1	0	1
=95	Tonga	0	1	0	1
=95	Mozambique	0	0	1	1

[1] including the Unified Team of 1992
[2] 1896–1964, 1992–96
[3] East Germany 1968–88
[4] West Germany 1968-88
[5] until 1994
[6] pre-Soviet Union and for 1996

WINTER GAMES MEDAL WINNERS

		Gold	Silver	Bronze	Total
1	Soviet Union[1]	87	63	67	217
2	Norway	73	77	64	214
3	United States	53	56	37	146
4	Austria	36	48	44	128
5	Finland	36	45	42	123
6	GDR[2]	39	36	35	110
7	Sweden	39	26	34	99
8	Germany[3]	34	29	24	87
9	Switzerland	27	29	29	85
10	Italy	25	21	21	67
11	Canada	19	20	25	64
12	France	16	16	21	53
13	Netherlands	14	19	17	50
14	FRG[4]	11	15	13	39
15	Czechoslovakia[5]	2	8	16	26
16	Russia	12	8	4	24
17	Great Britain	7	4	12	23
18	Japan	3	8	8	19
19	South Korea	6	2	2	10
20	Liechtenstein	2	2	5	9
=21	China	0	4	2	6
=21	Hungary	0	2	4	6
=23	Belgium	1	1	2	4
=23	Poland	1	1	2	4
=23	Yugoslavia	0	3	1	4
=26	Kazakhstan	1	2	0	3
=26	Slovenia	0	0	3	3
=28	Spain	1	0	1	2
=28	Ukraine	1	0	1	2
=28	Belarus	0	2	0	2
=28	Luxembourg	0	2	0	2
=28	North Korea	0	1	1	2
=33	Uzbekistan	1	0	0	1
=33	New Zealand	0	1	0	1
=33	Australia	0	0	1	1
=33	Bulgaria	0	0	1	1
=33	Romania	0	0	1	1

[1] including the Unified Team of 1992
[2] East Germany 1968–88
[3] 1896–1964, 1992–96
[4] West Germany 1968–88
[5] until 1994

ATHLETICS

- The origins of competitive running, jumping and throwing date back to prehistory, with organized running taking place in Ancient Egypt nearly 6000 years ago.
- The word 'athlete' derives from Aethlius, King of Elis, where the Ancient Greek games at Olympia were held.
- Carl Lewis achieved a speed of 43.37 km/h during the 100 m final at the Seoul Olympics in 1988.
- When Jesse Owens took four athletics gold medals at the 1936 Olympics, Adolf Hitler refused to shake his hand because Owens was black.
- Iolanda Balas of Romania won 150 consecutive high jump events from 1956–67.

TRACK AND FIELD

Athletics is contested internationally at two major meets: the Olympics, held every four years since 1896, and the World Championships, a biennial competition instigated in 1983. The world governing body of athletics is the International Amateur Athletic Association (IAAF).

Athletic events can be categorized as: running (with a range of events, from 100 m sprints to the marathon, which is over 42 km); walking (in which walking is defined as 'progression by steps so that unbroken contact with the ground is maintained, with events up to 50 km); jumping (high jump, pole vault, long jump, triple jump); and throwing (shot, discus, hammer, javelin).

The ten-event decathlon is a track-and-field medley contested by men. Decathlon events are 100 m, long jump, shot put, high jump, 400 m, 110 m hurdles, discus, pole vault, javelin and 1500 m. For women, the heptathlon is a seven-event medley (100 m hurdles, high jump, shot put, 200 m, long jump, javelin and 800 m).

DIMENSIONS OF FIELD EQUIPMENT

Shot
Men – 7.26 kg (16 lb), 110–130 mm in diameter
Women – 4 kg, 95–110 mm in diameter

Discus
Men – 2 kg, 219–221 mm in diameter
Women – 1 kg, 180–182 mm in diameter

Hammer
Men – 7.26 kg (16 lb), 117.5–121.5 cm in length, 110–130 mm diameter of head
Women – 4 kg, 116–119.5 cm in length, 95–110 mm diameter of head

Javelin
Men – 800 g, 260–270 cm in length
Women – 600 g, 220–230 cm in length

THE MARATHON

In 490 BC, an unknown Greek courier (probably Pheidippides) ran 38.6 km (24 mi) from the Plain of Marathon to Athens with news of a military victory for the Greeks over the Persians. This legendary run has been commemorated in the marathon, which has been contested since 1896. Marathons tend to be raced through urban courses, with the oldest being in Boston. The distance is now set at 42.195 km (26 mi 385 yds), which was the distance raced at the 1908 London Olympics.

Note: women's records appear in italic in the athletics tables

1996 OLYMPIC CHAMPIONS

100 m	9.84	Donovan Bailey (Can)
	10.94	*Gail Devers (USA)*
200 m	19.32	Michael Johnson (USA)
	22.12	*Marie-José Pérec (Fra)*
400 m	43.49	Michael Johnson (USA)
	48.25	*Marie-José Pérec (Fra)*
800 m	1:42.58	Vebjoern Rodal (Nor)
	1:57.73	*Svetlana Masterkova (Rus)*
1500 m	3:35.78	Noureddine Morceli (Alg)
	4:00.83	*Svetlana Masterkova (Rus)*
5000 m	13:07.96	Venuste Niyongabo (Bur)
	14:59.88	*Wang Junxia (Chn)*
10,000 m	27:07.34	Haile Gebreselassie (Eth)
	31:01.63	*Fernanda Riberio (Por)*
Marathon	2:12:36	Josia Thugwane (SA)
	2:26:00	*Fatume Roba (Eth)*
100 m hurdles	*12.58*	*Ludmila Enquist (Swe)*
110 m hurdles	12.95	Allen Johnson (USA)
400 m hurdles	47.54	Derrick Adkins (USA)
	52.82	*Deon Hemmings (Jam)*
4 x 100 m	37.69	Canada
	41.95	*USA*
4 x 400 m	2:55.99	USA
	3:20.91	*USA*
Steeplechase	8:07.12	Joseph Keter (Ken)
10 km walk	*41:49*	*Yelena Nikolayeva (Rus)*
20 km walk	1:20:07	Jefferson Perez (Ecu)
50 km walk	3:43:30	Robert Korzeniowski (Pol)
High jump	2.39 m	Charles Austin (USA)
	2.05 m	*Stefka Kostadinova (Bul)*
Pole vault	5.92 m	Jean Galfione (Fra)
Long jump	8.50 m	Carl Lewis (USA)
	7.12 m	*Chioma Ajunwa (Nig)*
Triple jump	18.09 m	Kenny Harrison (USA)
	15.33 m	*Inessa Kravets (Ukr)*
Shot	21.62 m	Randy Barnes (USA)
	20.56 m	*Astrid Kumbernuss (Ger)*
Discus	69.40 m	Lars Riedel (Ger)
	69.66 m	*Ilke Wyludda (Ger)*
Hammer	81.24 m	Balazs Kiss (Hun)
Javelin	88.16 m	Jan Zelezny (Cze)
	67.94 m	*Heli Rantanen (Fin)*
Decathlon	8824 pts	Dan O'Brien (USA)
Heptathlon	*6780 pts*	*Ghada Shouaa (Syr)*

1994 EUROPEAN CHAMPIONS

The European Championships are held every four years. They were first staged for men in 1934 and for women in 1938. Initially held separately, men's and women's events have been combined at one venue since 1946.

100 m	10.14	Linford Christie (GB)
	11.02	*Irina Privalova (Rus)*
200 m	20.3	Geir Moen (Nor)
	22.32	*Irina Privalova (Rus)*
400 m	45.09	Du'aine Ladejo (GB)
	50.33	*Marie-José Pérec (Fra)*
800 m	1:46.12	Andrea Benvenuti (Ita)
	1:58.55	*Lyubov Gurina (Rus)*
1500 m	3:35.27	Fermin Cacho (Spa)
	4:18.93	*Lyudmila Rogachova (Rus)*
3000 m	8:31.84	Sonia O'Sullivan (Ire)
5000 m	13:36.93	Dieter Baumann (Ger)
10,000 m	28:06.03	Abel Antón (Spa)
	31:08.75	*Fernanda Ribeiro (Por)*
Marathon	2:10.31	Martin Fiz (Spa)
	2:29.54	*Manuela Machado (Por)*
Steeplechase	8:22.4	Alessandro Lambruschini (Ita)
100 m hurdles	*12.72*	*Svetla Dimitrova (Bul)*
110 m hurdles	13.08	Colin Jackson (GB)
400 m hurdles	48.06	Oleg Tverdokhleb (Ukr)
	53.33	*Sally Gunnell (GB)*
4 x 100 m relay	38.57	France
	42.9	*Germany*
4 x 400 m relay	2:59.13	Great Britain
	3:22.34	*France*
10 km walk	*42:37*	*Sari Essayah (Fin)*
20 km walk	1:18.45	Mikhail Shchennikov (Rus)
50 km walk	3:41.07	Valeriy Spitsyn (Rus)
High jump	2.35	Steinar Hoen (Nor)
	2.0	*Britta Bilac (Slo)*
Pole vault	6.0	Rodion Gataullin (Rus)
Long jump	8.09	Ivailo Mladenov (Bul)
	7.14	*Heike Drechsler (Ger)*
Triple jump	17.62	Denis Kapustin (Rus)
	14.89	*Ana Biryukova (Rus)*
Shot	20.78	Aleksandr Klimenko (Ukr)
	19.61	*Viktoriya Pavlysh (Ukr)*
Discus	64.78	Vladimir Dubrovshchik (Brs)
	68.72	*Ilke Wyludda (Ger)*
Hammer	81.1	Vasiliy Sidorenko (Rus)
Javelin	85.2	Steve Backley (GB)
	68.0	*Trine Hattestad (Nor)*
Decathlon	8453 pts	Alain Blondel (Fra)
Heptathlon	*6419 pts*	*Sabine Braun (Ger)*

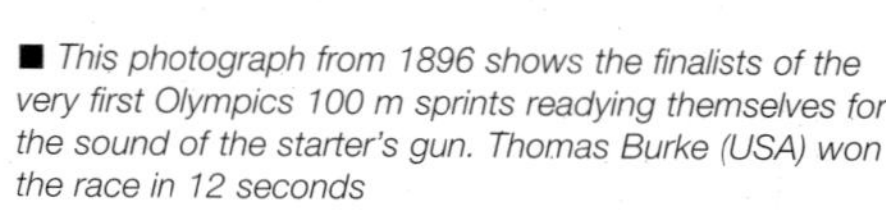

This photograph from 1896 shows the finalists of the very first Olympics 100 m sprints readying themselves for the sound of the starter's gun. Thomas Burke (USA) won the race in 12 seconds

WORLD RECORDS

World outdoor records are scheduled by the International Amateur Athletic Association. Fully automatic electronic timing is mandatory for track events up to 400 m.

Event	Record	Holder	Date	Venue
100 m	9.84	Donovan Bailey (Can)	27 Jul 1996	Atlanta, USA
	10.49	*Florence Griffith Joyner (USA)*	*16 Jul 1988*	*Indianapolis, USA*
200 m	19.32	Michael Johnson (USA)	1 Aug 1996	Atlanta, USA
	21.34	*Florence Griffith Joyner (USA)*	*29 Sep 1988*	*Seoul, South Korea*
400 m	43.29	'Butch' Reynolds Jr (USA)	17 Aug 1988	Zürich, Switzerland
	47.60	*Marita Koch (GDR)*	*6 Oct 1985*	*Canberra, Australia*
800 m	1:41.24	Wilson Kipketer (Den)	13 Aug 1997	Zürich, Switzerland
	1:53.28	*Jarmila Kratochvílová (Czs)*	*26 Jul 1983*	*Munich, Germany*
1000 m	2:12.18	Sebastian Coe (GB)	11 Jul 1981	Oslo, Norway
	2:28.98	*Svetlana Masterkova (Rus)*	*23 Aug 1996*	*Brussels, Belgium*
1500 m	3:27.37	Noureddine Morceli (Alg)	12 Jul 1995	Nice, France
	3:50.46	*Qu Yunxia (Chn)*	*11 Sep 1993*	*Beijing, China*
1 mile	3:44.39	Noureddine Morceli (Alg)	5 Sep 1993	Rieti, Italy
	4:12.56	*Svetlana Masterkova (Rus)*	*14 Aug 1996*	*Zürich, Switzerland*
2000 m	4:47.88	Noureddine Morceli (Alg)	3 Jul 1995	Paris, France
	5:25.36	*Sonia O'Sullivan (Ire)*	*8 Jul 1994*	*Edinburgh, Great Britain*
3000 m	7:20.67	Daniel Komen (Ken)	1 Sep 1996	Rieti, Italy
	8:06.11	*Wang Junxia (Chn)*	*13 Sep 1993*	*Beijing, China*
5000 m	12:41.86	Haile Gebrselassie (Eth)	13 Aug 1997	Zürich, Switzerland
	14:36.45	*Fernanda Ribeiro (Por)*	*22 Jul 1995*	*Hechtel, Belgium*
10,000 m	26:31.32	Haile Gebrselassie (Eth)	4 Jul 1997	Oslo, Norway
	29:31.78	*Wang Junxia (Chn)*	*8 Sep 1993*	*Beijing, China*
20,000 m	56:55.6	Arturo Barrios (Mex)	30 Mar 1991	La Flèche, France
	1:06:48.8	*Isumi Maki (Jap)*	*20 Sep 1993*	*Amagasaki, Japan*
25,000 m	1:13:55.8	Toshihiko Seko (Jap)	22 Mar 1981	Christchurch, NZ
	1:29:29.2	*Karolina Szabo (Hun)*	*23 Apr 1988*	*Budapest, Hungary*
30,000 m	1:29:18.8	Toshihiko Seko (Jap)	22 Mar 1981	Christchurch, NZ
	1:47:05.6	*Karolina Szabo (Hun)*	*23 Apr 1988*	*Budapest, Hungary*
1 hour	21,101 m	Arturo Barrios (Mex)	30 Mar 1991	La Flèche, France
	18,084 m	*Silvana Cruciata (Ita)*	*4 May 1981*	*Rome, Italy*
Marathon	2:06:50	Belayneh Dinsamo (Eth)	17 Apr 1985	Rotterdam, Netherlands
	2:21:06	*Ingrid Kristiansen (Nor)*	*21 Mar 1985*	*London, Great Britain*
100 m hurdles	*12.21*	*Yordanka Donkova (Bul)*	*20 Aug 1988*	*Stara Zagora, Bulgaria*
110 m hurdles	12.91	Colin Jackson (GB)	20 Aug 1993	Stuttgart, Germany
400 m hurdles	46.78	Kevin Young (USA)	6 Aug 1992	Barcelona, Spain
	52.61	*Kim Batten (USA)*	*11 Aug 1995*	*Gothenburg, Sweden*
Steeplechase	7:59.08	Wilson Boit Kipketer (Ken)	13 Aug 1997	Zürich, Switzerland
4 x 100 m	37.40	USA	8 Aug 1992	Barcelona, Spain
	37.40	USA	21 Aug 1993	Stuttgart, Germany
	41.37	*East Germany*	*6 Oct 1985*	*Canberra, Australia*
4 x 200 m	1:18.68	Santa Monica T.C. (USA)	17 Apr 1994	Walnut, California, USA
	1:28.15	*East Germany*	*9 Aug 1980*	*Jena, Germany*
4 x 400 m	2:54.29	USA	21 Aug 1993	Stuttgart, Germany
	3:15.17	*USSR*	*1 Oct 1988*	*Seoul, South Korea*
4 x 800 m	7:03.89	Great Britain	30 Aug 1982	London, Great Britain
	7:50.17	*USSR*	*5 Aug 1984*	*Moscow, USSR*
4 x 1500 m	14:38.8	West Germany	17 Aug 1977	Cologne, Germany
High Jump	2.45	Javier Sotomayor (Cub)	27 Jul 1993	Salamanca, Spain
	2.09	*Stefka Kostadinova (Bul)*	*30 Aug 1987*	*Rome, Italy*
Pole Vault	6.14	Sergey Bubka (Ukr)	31 Jul 1994	Sestriere, Italy
	4.55	*Emma George (Aus)*	*20 Feb 1997*	*Melbourne, Australia*
Long Jump	8.95	'Mike' Powell (USA)	30 Aug 1991	Tokyo, Japan
	7.52	*Galina Chistyakova (USSR)*	*11 Jun 1988*	*Leningrad, USSR*
Triple Jump	18.29	Jonathan Edwards (GB)	7 Aug 1995	Gothenburg, Sweden
	15.50	*Inessa Kravets (Ukr)*	*10 Aug 1995*	*Gothenburg, Sweden*
Shot	23.12	'Randy' Barnes (USA)	20 May 1990	Los Angeles, USA
	22.63	*Natalya Lisovskaya (USSR)*	*7 Jun 1987*	*Moscow, USSR*
Discus	74.08	Jürgen Schult (GDR)	6 Jun 1986	Neubrandenburg, GDR
	76.80	*Gabriele Reinsch (GDR)*	*9 Jul 1988*	*Neubrandenburg, GDR*
Hammer	86.74	Yuriy Sedykh (USSR)	30 Aug 1986	Stuttgart, Germany
	69.58	*Mihaela Melinte (Rom)*	*11 Mar 1997*	*Bucharest, Romania*
Javelin	98.48	Jan Zelezny (Cze)	25 May 1996	Jena, Germany
	80.00	*Petra Felke (GDR)*	*9 Sep 1988*	*Potsdam, Germany*
Decathlon	8891 pts	Dan O'Brien (USA)	4–5 Sep 1992	Talence, France
Heptathlon	*7291 pts*	*Jackie Joyner-Kersee (USA)*	*23–24 Sep 1988*	*Seoul, South Korea*

JACKIE JOYNER-KERSEE (1962–)

American Jackie Joyner-Kersee is deemed by many as the greatest woman athlete this century. At the 1987 World Championships, she won the long jump and the heptathlon, and repeated the double at the Seoul Olympics a year later. She retained the heptathlon title at the 1992 Olympics and took a silver in the long jump. Despite problems with asthma and allergies, her career has seen her win 12 successive heptathlon titles from 1985 to 1991, set four records at the seven-event discipline and become the first competitor to achieve over 7000 points. She has also held a world record in the long jump, set world indoor 55-m hurdling records and 11 US records. Her Olympic career, which began with a silver medal in the heptathlon in 1984, was completed in 1996 when she took bronze in the long jump at the age of 36.

■ *Great Britain's Linford Christie is the current men's 100 m European champion*

■ ORGANIZED RUNNING RACES WERE BEING HELD IN EGYPT AS FAR BACK AS 3800 BC ■

Swimming and Diving

- Olivier Favre (Swi) holds the world record for the highest dive from a diving board – 53.9 m on 30 August 1987.
- The largest swimming pool in the world – in Casablanca, Morocco – measures 480 m by 75 m.
- Mark Spitz's record of 11 Olympic swimming medals has been equalled by Matt Biondi, a fellow American.
- The fastest average swimming speed is 8.64 km/h, achieved by Tom Jager of the United States in 1990.
- The longest swim on record – made by Fred P. Newton in 1930 over a period of six months – covered 2938 km.

Swimming is an ancient sport, and competitive swimming existed even before the birth of Christ. In modern times, swimming has been a popularly contested sport from at least 1791 in Britain. In the middle of the 19th century, a series of national swimming associations developed, and an unofficial 100 yd championship was raced in Melbourne, Australia, in 1858.

With the possible exception of the dog paddle, the breaststroke was the first popular technique, and backstroke and butterfly developed from it. A style resembling the front crawl had been seen in various parts of the world by travellers in the mid-19th century. An event using all four strokes in turn, the medley, developed in the 1930s in the USA.

Swimming has always featured in the modern Olympics, but separate World Championships – first contested in 1973 – are now also held every four years. Synchronized swimming, a form of water ballet set to music, is a recent Olympic event, having been contested since 1984. Diving can be contested in either springboard or highboard disciplines. The world governing body is the Fédération Internationale de Natation Amateur.

■ *Australia's Kieren Perkins wins gold at the 1996 Atlanta Olympics in the men's 1500 m*

World Records

Short Course		Men				Women		
Freestyle								
50 m	21.50	Aleksandr Popov (Rus)	13 Mar 1994	Desenzano, Italy	24.23	Le Jingyi (Chn)	3 Dec 1993	Palma, Spain
100 m	46.74	Aleksandr Popov (Rus)	19 Mar 1994	Gelsenkirchen, Germany	53.01	Le Jingyi (Chn)	2 Dec 1993	Palma, Spain
200 m	1:43.64	Giorgio Lamberti (Ita)	11 Feb 1990	Bonn, Germany	1:54.17	Claudia Poll (CR)	18 Apr 1997	Gothenburg, Sweden
400 m	3:40.46	Danyon Loader (NZ)	11 Feb 1995	Sheffield, UK	4:00.03	Claudia Poll (CR)	19 Apr 1997	Gothenburg, Sweden
800 m	7:34.90	Kieren Perkins (Aus)	25 Jul 1993	Sydney, Australia	8:15.34	Astrid Strauss (GDR)	6 Feb 1987	Bonn, Germany
1500 m	14:26.52	Kieren Perkins (Aus)	15 Jul 1993	Auckland, New Zealand	15:43.31	Petra Schneider (GDR)	10 Jan 1982	Gainesville, USA
4 x 50 m	1:27.62	Sweden	2 Dec 1994	Stavanger, Norway	1:40.63	Germany	22 Nov 1992	Espoo, Finland
4 x 100 m	3:12.11	Brazil	5 Dec 1993	Palma, Spain	3:34.55	China	19 Apr 1997	Gothenburg, Sweden
4 x 200 m	7:02.74	Australia	18 Apr 1997	Gothenburg, Sweden	7:51.92	China	17 Apr 1997	Gothenburg, Sweden
Backstroke								
50 m	24.25	Chris Renaud (Can)	1 Mar 1997	St Catharine's, Canada	27.64	Bai Xiuyu (Chn)	12 Mar 1994	Desenzano, Italy
100 m	51.43	Jeff Rouse (USA)	12 Apr 1993	Sheffield, UK	58.50	Angel Martino (USA)	3 Dec 1993	Palma, Spain
200 m	1:52.51	Martin Lopez-Zubero (Spa)	11 Apr 1991	Gainesville, USA	2:06.09	He Cihong (Chn)	5 Dec 1993	Palma, Spain
Breaststroke								
50 m	26.97	Mark Warnecke (Ger)	8 Feb 1997	Paris, France	30.77	Han Xue (Chn)	2 Feb 1997	Gelsenkirchen, Germany
100 m	59.02	Frédéric Deburghgraeve (Bel)	17 Feb 1996	Bastogne, Belgium	1:05.70	Samantha Riley (Aus)	2 Dec 1995	Rio de Janeiro, Brazil
200 m	2:07.66	Ryan Mitchell (Aus)	21 Dec 1996	Melbourne, Australia	2:20.85	Samantha Riley (Aus)	1 Dec 1995	Rio de Janeiro, Brazil
Butterfly								
50 m	23.35	Denis Pankratov (Rus)	8 Feb 1997	Paris, France	26.55	Misty Hyman (USA)	19 Apr 1997	Gothenburg, Sweden
100 m	51.78	Denis Pankratov (Rus)	9 Feb 1997	Paris, France	57.79	Jenny Thompson (USA)	19 Apr 1997	Gothenburg, Sweden
200 m	1:52.64	Denis Pankratov (Rus)	1 Feb 1997	Gelsenkirchen, Germany	2:05.65	Mary Meagher (USA)	2 Jan 1981	Gainesville, USA
200 m*	1:52.34	Denis Pankratov (Rus)	3 Feb 1996	Paris, France				
Medley								
100 m	53.10	Jani Sievinen (Fin)	30 Jan 1996	Malmö, Sweden	1:01.03	Louise Karlsson (Swe)	22 Nov 1992	Espoo, Finland
200 m	1:54.65	Jani Sievinen (Fin)	21 Jan 1994	Kuopio, Finland	2:07.79	Allison Wagner (USA)	5 Dec 1993	Palma, Spain
400 m	4:05.41	Marcel Wouda (Neths)	9 Feb 1997	Paris, France	4:29.00	Dai Gouhong (Chn)	2 Dec 1993	Palma, Spain
4 x 50 m	1:36.69	Auburn Aquatics	9 Apr 1996	Auburn, USA	1:52.44	Germany	21 Nov 1992	Espoo, Finland
4 x 100 m	3:30.66	Australia	17 Apr 1997	Gothenburg, Sweden	3:57.73	China	5 Dec 1993	Palma, Spain
50 m Pool								
Freestyle								
50 m	21.81	Tom Jager (USA)	24 Mar 1990	Nashville, USA	24.51	Le Jingyi (Chn)	11 Sep 1994	Rome, Italy
100 m	48.21	Aleksandr Popov (Rus)	18 Jun 1994	Monte Carlo	54.01	Le Jingyi (Chn)	5 Sep 1994	Rome, Italy
200 m	1:46.69	Giorgio Lamberti (Ita)	15 Aug 1989	Bonn, Germany	1:56.78	Franziska van Almsick (Ger)	6 Sep 1994	Rome, Italy
400 m	3:43.80	Kieren Perkins (Aus)	9 Sep 1994	Rome, Italy	4:03.85	Janet B Evans (USA)	22 Sep 1988	Seoul, South Korea
800 m	7:46.00	Kieren Perkins (Aus)	24 Aug 1994	Victoria, Canada	8:16.22	Janet Evans (USA)	20 Aug 1989	Tokyo, Japan
1500 m	14:41.66	Kieren Perkins (Aus)	24 Aug 1994	Victoria, Canada	15:52.10	Janet Evans (USA)	26 Mar 1988	Orlando, USA
4 x 100 m	3:15.11	USA	12 Aug 1995	Atlanta, USA	3:37.91	China	7 Sep 1994	Rome, Italy
4 x 200 m	7:11.95	CIS	27 Jul 1992	Barcelona, Spain	7:55.47	GDR	18 Aug 1987	Strasbourg, France
Breaststroke								
100 m	1:00.60	Frédéric Deburghgraeve (Bel)	20 Jul 1996	Atlanta, USA	1:07.02	Penelope 'Penny' Heyns (SA)	21 Jul 1996	Atlanta, USA
200 m	2:10.16	Michael Barrowman (USA)	29 Jul 1992	Barcelona, Spain	2:24.76	Rebecca Brown (Aus)	16 Mar 1994	Brisbane, Australia
Butterfly								
100 m	52.27	Denis Pankratov (Rus)	24 Jul 1996	Atlanta, USA	57.93	Mary Meagher (USA)	16 Aug 1981	Brown Deer, USA
200 m	1:55.22	Denis Pankratov (Rus)	14 Jun 1995	Paris, France	2:05.96	Mary Meagher (USA)	13 Aug 1981	Brown Deer, USA
Backstroke								
100 m	53.86	Jeff Rouse (USA) (relay leg)	31 Jul 1992	Barcelona, Spain	1:00.16	He Cihong (Chn)	11 Sep 1994	Rome, Italy
200 m	1:56.57	Martin López-Zubero (Spa)	23 Nov 1991	Tuscaloosa, USA	2:06.62	Krisztina Egerszegi (Hun)	25 Aug 1991	Athens, Greece
Medley								
200 m	1:58.16	Jani Sievinen (Fin)	11 Sep 1994	Rome, Italy	2:11.57	Lu Bin (Chn)	7 Oct 1994	Hiroshima, Japan
400 m	4:12.30	Tom Dolan (USA)	6 Sep 1994	Rome, Italy	4:36.10	Petra Schneider (GDR)	1 Aug 1982	Guayaquil, Ecuador
4 x 100 m	3:34.84	USA	26 Jul 1996	Atlanta, USA	4:01.67	China	11 Sep 1994	Rome, Italy

* not ratified

■ SWIMMING HAS BEEN A PART OF EVERY MODERN OLYMPICS ■ BREASTSTROKE WAS

1996 OLYMPIC CHAMPIONS

		Men		Women
Freestyle				
50 m	22.13	Aleksandr Popov (Rus)	24.87	Amy van Dyken (USA)
100 m	48.74	Aleksandr Popov (Rus)	54.50	Le Jingyi (Chn)
200 m	1:47.63	Danyon Loader (NZ)	1:58.16	Claudia Poll (CR)
400 m	3:47.97	Danyon Loader (NZ)	4:07.25	Michelle Smith (Ire)
800 m			8:27.89	Brooke Bennett (USA)
1500 m	14:56.40	Kieren Perkins (Aus)		
4 x 100 m	3:15.41	USA	3:39.29	USA
4 x 200 m	7:14.84	USA	7:59.87	USA
Backstroke				
100 m	1:00.65	Frédéric Deburghgraeve (Bel)	1:7.73	Penny Heyns (SA)
200 m	2:12.57	Norbert Rozsa (Hun)	2:25.41	Penny Heyns (SA)
Breaststroke				
100 m	54.10	Jeff Rouse (USA)	1:1.19	Beth Botsford (USA)
200 m	1:58.54	Brad Bridwater (USA)	2:07.83	Krisztina Egerszegi (Hun)
Butterfly				
100 m	52.27	Denis Pankratov (Rus)	59.13	Amy van Dyken (USA)
200 m	1:56.51	Denis Pankratov (Rus)	2:07.76	Susan O'Neil (Aus)
Medley				
200 m	1:59.91	Attila Czene (Hun)	2:13.93	Michelle Smith (Ire)
400 m	4:14.90	Tom Delan (USA)	4:39.18	Michelle Smith (Ire)
4 x 100 m	3:34.84	USA	4:02.88	USA
Synchronized swimming			99.72 pts	USA
Springboard	701.46 pts	Xiong Ni (Chn)	547.68 pts	Fu Mingxia (Chn)
Platform	692.34 pts	Dmitriy Sautin (Rus)	521.58 pts	Fu Mingxia (Chn)

1994 WORLD CHAMPIONSHIPS

		Men		Women
Freestyle				
50 m	22.17	Aleksandr Popov (Rus)	24.51	Le Jingyi (Chn)
100 m	49.12	Aleksandr Popov (Rus)	54.01	Le Jingyi (Chn)
200 m	1:47.32	Antti Kasvio (Fin)	1:56.78	Franziska van Almsick (Ger)
400 m	3:43.8	Kieren Perkins (Aus)	4:09.64	Yang Aihua (Chn)
800 m			8:29.85	Janet Evans (USA)
1500 m	14:50.52	Kieren Perkins (Aus)		
4 x 100 m	3:16.9	USA	3:37.91	China
4 x 200 m	7:17.7	Sweden	7:57.96	China
Backstroke				
100 m	55.17	Martin López Zubero (Spa)	1:00.57	He Cihong (Chn)
200 m	1:57.42	Vladimir Selkov (Rus)	2:07.4	He Cihong (Chn)
Breaststroke				
100 m	1:01.24	Norbert Rózsa (Hun)	1:07.69	Samantha Riley (Aus)
200 m	2:12.81	Norbert Rózsa (Hun)	2:26.87	Samantha Riley (Aus)
Butterfly				
100 m	53.51	Rafal Szukala (Pol)	58.98	Liu Limin (Chn)
200 m	1:56.54	Denis Pankratov (Rus)	2:07.25	Liu Limin (Chn)
Medley				
200 m	1:58.16	Jani Sievinen (Fin)	2:12.34	Lu Bin (Chn)
400 m	4:12.30	Tom Dolan (USA)	4:39.14	Dai Guohong (Chn)
4 x 100 m	3:37.74	USA	4:01.67	China
25 km river/sea swim	5:35:25.56	Greg Steppel (Can)	5:48:25.04	Melissa Cunningham (Aus)
Synchronized swimming				
solo				Becky Lancer (USA)
duet				Becky Lancer & Jill Sudduth (USA)
team				USA
1 m springboard		Evan Stewart (Zim)		Chen Lixia (Chn)
3 m springboard		Yu Zhuocheng (Chn)		Tan Shuping (Chn)
Highboard		Dmitriy Sautin (Rus)		Fu Mingxia (Chn)

■ *Synchronized swimming became an Olympic event in 1984. It is one of the very few Olympic events that is women-only. Here, the Mexican team goes through its paces in Atlanta, 1996*

MARK SPITZ (1950–)

Mark Spitz, the consummate US swimmer, entered the sporting record books in 1972 with a yet-to-be-rivalled feat. At the Munich Olympic Games, he took seven gold medals, every one of which was achieved in world record time. At the Mexico Olympics four years earlier, he took only two golds, one silver and a bronze – a big disappointment which spurred him on to succeed so emphatically in 1972. Coached by three of the greatest ever swimming coaches (Sherm Cavoor, George Haines and Doc Councilman), Spitz won a total of 24 national AAU championships, eight NCAA titles, and set 35 American records and 26 world records. Disappointingly, his return to competition in 1991 did not live up to his expectations. Despite this, he is still regarded by many as the greatest swimmer who has ever lived.

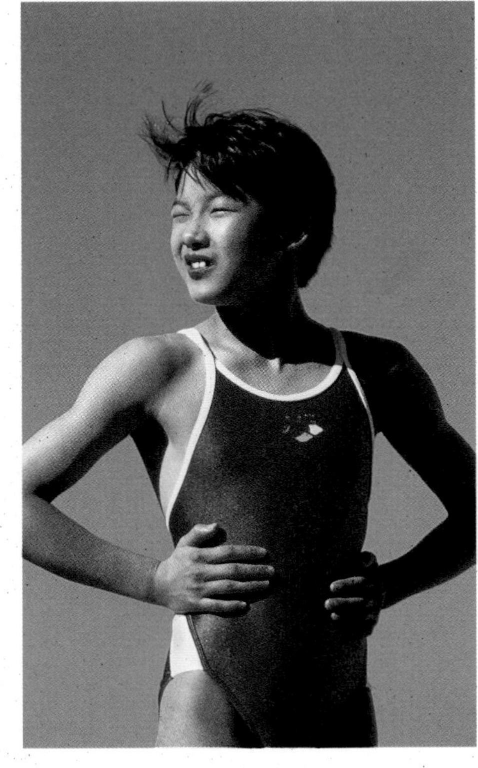

■ *China's Mingxa Fu, won the 10 m diving event at the 1991 World Championships. She was 12 years old, the youngest ever winner of an individual world title*

Rugby

- The game of rugby was born in the early 19th century at Rugby School, England.
- Rugby Union officially became a professional sport in 1996.
- The USA, minnows in rugby, are current Olympic champions, winning gold when it was last contested in 1924.

RUGBY UNION

Rugby Union has its roots in the kicking-only game that later became association football. According to tradition, during a game in November 1823 at Rugby School, England, William Webb Ellis picked up the ball and ran with it. Whatever the truth of the story, the game was definitely played at Cambridge University in 1839.

Rugby Union's world governing body, the International Rugby Football Board, was founded in 1886. It consists of the major rugby-playing nations: Australia, England, France, Ireland, New Zealand, Scotland, South Africa and Wales.

The 15-a-side game is played on a pitch with a maximum width of 68 m (75 yd) and 90 m (100 yd) between goal lines. The ball is 27.9–28.5 cm (10¾–11½ in) long and weighs 382–439 g (13½–15½ oz).

■ *Wales (red jerseys) and France compete during the 1997 Five Nations championship*

WORLD CUP

Sixteen nations contested the first Rugby Union World Cup, played in Australia and New Zealand in 1987. The second was held in Britain and France, and the third in South Africa.

1987	New Zealand
1991	Australia
1995	South Africa

INTERNATIONAL CHAMPIONSHIP (FIVE NATIONS)

England, Scotland, Wales and Ireland contested the first Rugby Union International Championship in 1884. From 1910 the competition became known as the Five Nations when France was included. The Five Nations is held annually, with each country playing each other once. A Grand Slam (GS) is when all four matches are won by a nation, and is highly prized. A Triple Crown is attained when one of the four 'home country' sides (England, Scotland, Wales or Ireland) defeats the other three.

Year	Winner	Year	Winner	Year	Winner
1884	England	1923	England (GS)	1964	Wales, Scotland
1885	Not completed	1924	England (GS)	1965	Wales
1886	England, Scotland	1925	Scotland (GS)	1966	Wales
1887	Scotland	1926	Scotland, Ireland	1967	France
1888	Not completed	1927	Scotland, Ireland	1968	France (GS)
1889	Not completed	1928	England (GS)	1969	Wales
1890	England, Scotland	1929	Scotland	1970	Wales, France
1891	Scotland	1930	England	1971	Wales (GS)
1892	England	1931	Wales	1972	Not completed
1893	Wales	1932	England, Wales, Ireland	1973	England, Wales,
1894	Ireland	1933	Scotland		Scotland, Ireland, France
1895	Scotland	1934	England	1974	Ireland
1896	Ireland	1935	Ireland	1975	Wales
1897	Not completed	1936	Wales	1976	Wales (GS)
1898	Not completed	1937	England	1977	France (GS)
1899	Ireland	1938	Scotland	1978	Wales (GS)
1900	Wales	1939	England, Wales, Ireland	1979	Wales
1901	Scotland	1940–46	No competition	1980	England (GS)
1902	Wales	1947	England, Wales	1981	France (GS)
1903	Scotland	1948	Ireland (GS)	1982	Ireland
1904	Scotland	1949	Ireland	1983	Ireland, France
1905	Wales	1950	Wales (GS)	1984	Scotland (GS)
1906	Wales, Ireland	1951	Ireland	1985	Ireland
1907	Scotland	1952	Wales (GS)	1986	Scotland, France
1908	Wales (GS)	1953	England	1987	France (GS)
1909	Wales (GS)	1954	England, Wales, France	1988	Wales, France
1910	England	1955	Wales, France	1989	France
1911	Wales (GS)	1956	Wales	1990	Scotland (GS)
1912	England, Ireland	1957	England (GS)	1991	England (GS)
1913	England (GS)	1958	England	1992	England (GS)
1914	England (GS)	1959	France	1993	France
1915–19	No competition	1960	England, France	1994	Wales
1920	Wales, Scotland	1961	France	1995	England (GS)
1921	England (GS)	1962	France	1996	England
1922	Wales	1963	England	1997	France (GS)

CURRIE CUP

First held in 1889, the Currie Cup is South Africa's Rugby Union inter-provincial tournament. Winners since 1980:

1980	Northern Transvaal
1981	Northern Transvaal
1982	Western Province
1983	Western Province
1984	Western Province
1985	Western Province
1986	Western Province
1987	Northern Transvaal
1988	Northern Transvaal
1989	Northern Transvaal and Western Province
1990	Natal
1991	Northern Transvaal
1992	Natal
1993	Transvaal
1994	Transvaal
1995	Natal
1996	Natal

FRENCH CHAMPIONSHIP

The French Championship is the country's premier Rugby Union competition. It was first contested in 1892. Winners since 1980:

1980	AS Béziers	1990	Racing Club de France
1981	AS Béziers	1991	CA Begles
1982	SU Agen	1992	RC Toulon
1983	AS Béziers	1993	Caskes Olympique
1984	AS Béziers	1994	Toulouse
1985	Toulouse	1995	Toulouse
1986	Toulouse	1996	Toulouse
1987	RC Toulon	1997	Toulouse
1988	SU Agen		
1989	Toulouse		

■ IN RUGBY UNION, HONG KONG BEAT SINGAPORE 164–13, THE HIGHEST SCORE IN AN

NEW ZEALAND LEAGUE

The New Zealand Rugby Union National League Championship was inaugurated in 1976.

1976	Bay of Plenty	1987	Auckland
1977	Canterbury	1988	Auckland
1978	Wellington	1989	Auckland
1979	Counties	1990	Auckland
1980	Manawatu	1991	Otago
1981	Wellington	1992	Waikato
1982	Auckland	1993	Auckland
1983	Canterbury	1994	Auckland
1984	Auckland	1995	Auckland
1985	Auckland	1996	Auckland
1986	Wellington		

ENGLISH LEAGUE

Most English clubs take part in the Rugby Union Courage League, a system of national, regional and divisional and county leagues.

1985/86	Gloucester	1991/92	Bath
1986/87	Bath	1992/93	Bath
1987/88	Leicester	1993/94	Bath
1988/89	Bath	1994/95	Leicester
1989/90	Wasps	1995/96	Bath
1990/91	Bath	1996/97	Wasps

SCOTTISH LEAGUE

In Scotland, the major Rugby Union competition is the McEwans League, with the first season being 1973/74. A pyramid of local competitions feeds into the league divisions.

1973/74	Hawick	1985/86	Hawick
1974/75	Hawick	1986/87	Hawick
1975/76	Hawick	1987/88	Kelso
1976/77	Hawick	1988/89	Kelso
1977/78	Hawick	1989/90	Melrose
1978/79	Heriot's Former Pupils	1990/91	Boroughmuir
1979/80	Gala	1991/92	Melrose
1980/81	Gala	1992/93	Melrose
1981/82	Hawick	1993/94	Melrose
1982/83	Gala	1994/95	Stirling County
1983/84	Hawick	1995/96	Melrose
1984/85	Hawick	1996/97	Melrose

WORLD CUP

First played in 1954 as the World Cup, Rugby League's major international competition is now known as the International Championship. Discontinued in 1977, it was revived in 1985, with the leading two nations playing off in the final in 1988.

1954	Great Britain	1975	Australia
1957	Australia	1977	Australia
1960	Great Britain	1988	Australia
1968	Australia	1992	Australia
1970	Australia	1995	Australia
1972	Great Britain		

CHALLENGE CUP

The major Rugby League trophy in England is the knockout Challenge Cup, first competed for in 1897. Winners since 1980:

1980	Hull Kingston Rovers	1989	Wigan
1981	Widnes	1990	Wigan
1982	Hull	1991	Wigan
1983	Featherstone Rovers	1992	Wigan
1984	Widnes	1993	Wigan
1985	Wigan	1994	Wigan
1986	Castleford	1995	Wigan
1987	Halifax	1996	St Helens
1988	Wigan	1997	St Helens

WELSH LEAGUE

The Welsh National League was introduced in 1990/91. Although the League only began in 1990, Cup rugby in Wales dates from 1971 – LLanelli won nine times and Cardiff seven times. Premier division winners:

1990/91	Neath
1991/92	Swansea
1992/93	Llanelli
1993/94	Swansea
1994/95	Cardiff
1995/96	Neath
1996/97	Pontypridd

■ *Gavin Hastings is Scotland's record points scorer in international Rugby Union. By the time he retired in 1995 he had scored 689 points in 62 matches for Scotland. In addition, he also scored a total of 66 points for the British Lions*

JEAN-PIERRE RIVES (1952–)

A French Rugby Union celebrity with style and verve, Jean-Pierre Rives is his nation's best-loved player. He began his international career as a flanker in 1975, and grew to be a brilliant all-rounder in support and defence. Captaining France a record 34 times, Rives won a total of 59 caps, a record for a French flanker. Although he missed out on the 1975 tour of South Africa and the 1977 home series against New Zealand, his career highlights did include taking part in the 1977 Grand Slam in the Five Nations, leading his team to victory over the All Blacks in Auckland in 1979, and a second Grand Slam in 1981. His flowing flaxen locks made him a glamorous and instantly recognizable figure both on and off the field. Rives showed his versatility after retiring by appearing in several films and making something of a name for himself as a sculptor. He told the story of his life in *A Modern Corinthian*, which was published in 1986.

■ *Australia's ace goal kicker, Michael Lynagh, carefully places the ball before attempting another conversion. He is the record points scorer in international Rugby Union*

RUGBY LEAGUE

Rugby club players in northern England in the 1890s asked to be paid for the wages they lost when playing on a Saturday. When rugby's ruling body refused to allow payments, a breakaway organization, the Northern Union, was formed in 1895. Three years later, the game became fully professional, and the title 'rugby league' was adopted in 1922.

Australia, France, Great Britain, New Zealand and Papua New Guinea are the main Rugby League-playing nations.

The Rugby League football field has a maximum length of 100 m (110 yd) and a maximum width of 68 m (75 yd). The ball is 27.3–29.2 cm (10¾–11½ in) long and at its widest point has a circumference of 584–610 mm (23–24 in). Each team has 13 players.

Scoring varies slightly from Rugby Union. A try in Rugby League is worth four points (it is five points in Union); a conversion kick for goal after a try is worth two points in both rugby codes.

■ *England's John Bentley tries to avoid two Australian tacklers in the final of the 1995 Rugby League International Championship. Australia won 16–8*

FOOTBALL

- **Geoff Hurst is the only player to have scored a hat-trick in a World Cup Final, when he helped England beat West Germany 4–2 in 1966.**
- **A form of football, called Tsu Chu (meaning 'to kick a ball of stuffed leather') was played in China *c.* 500 BC.**
- **The most goals scored in a footballing career is 1329 by Arthur Friedenreich of Brazil between 1909 and 1935.**
- **The highest transfer fee in the world was £15 million, paid by Newcastle United for Alan Shearer when he moved from Blackburn Rovers in July 1996 – Shearer was the top goal-scorer in the European Championship that year.**
- **The 1998 World Cup is to be held in France, and the 2002 finals will be held jointly in Japan and South Korea.**

Football, also referred to as soccer, developed as a sport in England in medieval times, with Edward II banning it in 1314 for excessive street noise. The first official football rules were drawn up at Cambridge University in 1846, and there were various modifications over the next few decades. The game, played with 11 players per side, was standardized in 1870.

The game of football is fiercely contested at club, national and international levels. Major international championships include the World Cup, the European Championship, the Copa América and the African Nations Cup. The major global club competition is the World Club Championship. Instituted in 1960, this is a contest between the winners of the European Cup and the Copa Libertadores de América.

The circumference of the ball must be 68–71 cm (27–28 in) and its weight 396–453 g (14–16 oz). The pitch is between 91 and 120 m (100–130 yd), and its width is 45–91 m (50–100 yd). (It is thus possible to play on a completely square pitch!) The world governing body is the Fédération Internationale de Football Association (FIFA), founded in 1904.

■ *Brazilian star Romário and Italian captain Franco Baresi tussle for possession in the closely fought 1994 World Cup final. The game was scoreless after 90 minutes' playing time and half an hour extra. Brazil won after a penalty-kick shoot-out, 3–2. Some 8,950,000 US households tuned into the match, and millions more around the world*

WORLD CUP

Held every four years since 1930 (except 1942 and 1946), the World Cup is football's premier sporting event. In 1930, 13 nations competed. By 1994, 157 nations contested the championship, with 24 qualifiers for the finals held in the USA. Although there have been 15 finals, only six teams have won the World Cup: Brazil (four times), Germany/FRG (three times), Italy (three times), Argentina (twice), Uruguay (twice) and England (once).

	Winner	Venue
1930	Uruguay	Uruguay
1934	Italy	Italy
1938	Italy	France
1950	Uruguay	Brazil
1954	Germany (W)	Switzerland
1958	Brazil	Sweden
1962	Brazil	Chile
1966	England	England
1970	Brazil	Mexico
1974	Germany (W)	Germany (W)
1978	Argentina	Argentina
1982	Italy	Spain
1986	Argentina	Mexico
1990	Germany (W)	Italy
1994	Brazil	USA

EUROPEAN CHAMPIONSHIP

The European Championship was first contested in 1960 and is held every four years.

1960	USSR	1980	Germany (W)
1964	Spain	1984	France
1968	Italy	1988	Netherlands
1972	Germany (W)	1992	Denmark
1976	Czechoslovakia	1996	Germany

5 HIGHEST TRANSFER PRICES

	£ million	Teams	
1 ALAN SHEARER	15	Blackburn Rovers to Newcastle United	Jul 1996
2 GIANLUIGI LENTINI	13	Torino to AC Milan	Jul 1992
3 GIANLUCA VIALLI	12.5	Sampdoria to Juventus	Jun 1992
4 DENNIS BERGKAMP	12	Ajax to Inter Milan	Jun 1993
5 JEAN-PIERRE PAPIN	10	Marseille to AC Milan	Jun 1992

EUROPEAN CHAMPION CLUBS' CUP

Established in 1955 as the European Cup for clubs, it is contested annually by the league champions of the member countries of the Union of European Football Associations (UEFA).

1956	Real Madrid	1970	Feyenoord (Rotterdam)	1984	Liverpool
1957	Real Madrid	1971	Ajax Amsterdam	1985	Juventus (Turin)
1958	Real Madrid	1972	Ajax Amsterdam	1986	Steaua Bucharest
1959	Real Madrid	1973	Ajax Amsterdam	1987	FC Porto
1960	Real Madrid	1974	Bayern Munich	1988	PSV Eindhoven
1961	Benfica (Lisbon)	1975	Bayern Munich	1989	AC Milan
1962	Benfica (Lisbon)	1976	Bayern Munich	1990	AC Milan
1963	AC Milan	1977	Liverpool	1991	Red Star Belgrade
1964	Internazionale Milan	1978	Liverpool	1992	Barcelona
1965	Internazionale Milan	1979	Nottingham Forest	1993	Marseille
1966	Real Madrid	1980	Nottingham Forest	1994	AC Milan
1967	Glasgow Celtic	1981	Liverpool	1995	Ajax Amsterdam
1968	Manchester United	1982	Aston Villa	1996	Juventus (Turin)
1969	AC Milan	1983	SV Hamburg	1997	Borussia Dortmund

EUROPEAN CUP WINNERS' CUP

Established in 1960, it is contested by national Cup winners (or runners-up if the winners are in the European Cup).

1961	Fiorentina (Florence)	1973	AC Milan	1986	Dynamo Kiev
1962	Atletico Madrid	1974	FC Magdeburg	1987	Ajax Amsterdam
1963	Tottenham Hotspur (London)	1975	Dynamo Kiev	1988	Mechelen
1964	Sporting Lisbon	1976	Anderlecht (Brussels)	1989	Barcelona
1965	West Ham United (London)	1977	SV Hamburg	1990	Sampdoria (Genoa)
1966	Borussia Dortmund	1978	Anderlecht (Brussels)	1991	Manchester United
1967	Bayern Munich	1979	Barcelona	1992	Werder Bremen
1968	AC Milan	1980	Valencia	1993	Parma
1969	Slovan Bratislava	1981	Dynamo Tbilisi	1994	Arsenal (London)
1970	Manchester City	1982	Barcelona	1995	Real Zaragoza
1971	Chelsea (London)	1983	Aberdeen	1996	Paris St Germain
1972	Glasgow Rangers	1984	Juventus (Turin)	1997	Barcelona
		1985	Everton (Liverpool)		

UEFA CUP

Established in 1955 as the Inter-City Fairs Cup, it has been held annually since 1960 and is open to leading European club teams not eligible to play for the two other major European trophies.

1958	Barcelona	1973	Liverpool	1985	Real Madrid
1960	Barcelona	1974	Feyenoord (Rotterdam)	1986	Real Madrid
1961	AS Roma	1975	Borussia Mönchengladbach	1987	IFK Göteborg
1962	Valencia	1976	Liverpool	1988	Bayer Leverkusen
1963	Valencia	1977	Juventus (Turin)	1989	Napoli
1964	Real Zaragoza	1978	PSV Eindhoven	1990	Juventus (Turin)
1965	Ferencvaros (Budapest)	1979	Borussia Mönchengladbach	1991	Internazionale Milan
1966	Barcelona	1980	Eintracht Frankfurt	1992	Ajax Amsterdam
1967	Dynamo Zagreb	1981	Ipswich Town	1993	Juventus (Turin)
1968	Leeds United	1982	IFK Göteborg	1994	Internazionale Milan
1969	Newcastle United	1983	Anderlecht (Brussels)	1995	Parma
1970	Arsenal (London)	1984	Tottenham Hotspur (London)	1996	Bayern Munich
1971	Leeds United			1997	Schalke 04 (Essen)
1972	Tottenham Hotspur (London)				

SOUTH AMERICAN CUP

The national league champions of the countries affiliated to the South American Confederation first contested in the South American Champion Clubs' Cup in 1960 – league runners-up were allowed to compete from 1965, from which year the championship was known as the Copa Libertadores de América.

1960	Peñarol (Uru)	1973	Independiente (Arg)	1986	River Plate (Arg)
1961	Peñarol (Uru)	1974	Independiente (Arg)	1987	Peñarol (Uru)
1962	Santos (Bra)	1975	Independiente (Arg)	1988	Nacional Montevideo (Uru)
1963	Santos (Bra)	1976	Cruzeiro (Bra)	1989	Nacional Medellin (Col)
1964	Independiente (Arg)	1977	Boca Juniors (Arg)	1990	Olimpia (Par)
1965	Independiente (Arg)	1978	Boca Juniors (Arg)	1991	Colo Colo (Chl)
1966	Peñarol (Uru)	1979	Olimpia (Par)	1992	São Paulo (Bra)
1967	Racing Club (Arg)	1980	Nacional Montevideo (Uru)	1993	São Paulo (Bra)
1968	Estudiantes (Arg)	1981	Flamengo (Bra)	1994	Vélez Sársfield (Arg)
1969	Estudiantes (Arg)	1982	Peñarol (Uru)	1995	Gremio (Bra)
1970	Estudiantes (Arg)	1983	Gremio (Bra)	1996	River Plate (Arg)
1971	Nacional Montevideo (Uru)	1984	Independiente (Arg)		
1972	Independiente (Arg)	1985	Argentinos Juniors (Arg)		

PELÉ (1940–)

Perhaps the greatest footballer in history, the Brazilian Edson Arantes do Nascimento, better known as Pelé, is recognized as a player of footballing genius. He was in the Brazilian national squad by the age of 16, and scored on his international debut. He gained international acclaim at the 1958 World Cup in Sweden, with a hat-trick in the semi-final in France and two stunning goals in the final against Sweden. His contribution to Brazil during the next two World Cup campaigns was minimal, due to injury, but he gained a third winner's medal in 1970, where he spearheaded a Brazilian team that has been hailed as one of the greatest ever. His audacious attempt to score from the halfway line in the final is typical of his flair and footballing confidence. In club football, he was a first-team regular for Santos from 1956 and helped them to win the World Club Championship in 1962 and 1963. Pelé holds the record for the most goals in a specified period (1279 in 1363 games), including 92 hat-tricks – another record. He won 111 international caps, and scored 97 international goals. Although he retired in 1977, Pelé is still one of the most revered players in football (his Brazilian nickname is 'Perola Negra', Black Pearl), and is one of the most famous sportsmen ever.

AFRICAN NATIONS CUP

Now held every two years, the African Nations Cup was first held in 1957.

1957	Egypt	1978	Ghana
1959	Egypt	1980	Nigeria
1962	Ethiopia	1982	Ghana
1963	Ghana	1984	Cameroon
1965	Ghana	1986	Egypt
1968	Zaïre	1988	Cameroon
1970	Sudan	1990	Algeria
1972	Congo	1992	Ivory Coast
1974	Zaïre	1994	Nigeria
1976	Morocco	1996	South Africa

Other Football Games

- **Australian football grew as a fusion of soccer, Gaelic football and rugby, with rules becoming codified in 1866. It was first played as a way of keeping cricketers fit in winter.**
- **Gaelic football evolved from a traditional Irish inter-parish football game in which there were no set rules, playing areas or time limits. The first recorded reference to a Gaelic football match dates back to 1712.**
- **American football evolved from soccer and rugby in US universities in the late 19th century.**

AMERICAN FOOTBALL

American football evolved in the 19th century from a game that contained elements of rugby and soccer. In 1880, Walter Camp, an official with the governing body, introduced many of the features of today's game, including the role of the quarterback.

The American Professional Football Association was formed in 1920, with 12 teams contesting the first league season. In 1922, the Association became the National Football League (NFL). The American Football League (AFL) was formed in 1960. The two leagues merged in 1970, and were reorganized into the National Football Conference (NFC) and the American Football Conference (AFC). The most prestigious prize in American football is the Super Bowl, held annually since 1967.

American Football teams consist of 11 players on each side and substitutes are freely used. The pitch dimensions (NFL) are 109.7 x 47.8 m (360 x 160 ft). The ball is 280–286 mm (11–11¼ in) long, and weighs 397–425 g (14–15 oz).

AUSTRALIAN FOOTBALL

Australian football, a kicking game with 18 players per team, is most popular in the southern states of Australia, especially in Victoria where it was first played in the 1850s.

Competition developed when the Victorian Football Association (VFA) was founded in 1877. Eight clubs broke away from the VFA to form the Victorian Football League (the Australian Football League from 1990), which became the premier competition. There are now teams from Queensland, Western Australia, South Australia and New South Wales.

The game is played on an oval pitch 110–155 m (120–170 yd) wide, 135–185 m (150–200 yd) long. The oval ball measures 749 mm (29½ in) in length, 572 mm (22½ in) in diameter and weighs 452–482 g (16–17 oz).

SUPER BOWL

The supreme American football contest held since 1967, the Super Bowl is held every January, at the end of the regular season, between the AFC and NFC champions. The Bowl is traditionally numbered by Roman numerals – the 1997 game was Super Bowl XXXI.

Year	Winner	Year	Winner	Year	Winner
1967	Green Bay Packers	1978	Dallas Cowboys	1989	San Francisco 49ers
1968	Green Bay Packers	1979	Pittsburgh Steelers	1990	San Francisco 49ers
1969	New York Jets	1980	Pittsburgh Steelers	1991	New York Giants
1970	Kansas City Chiefs	1981	Oakland Raiders	1992	Washington Redskins
1971	Baltimore Colts	1982	San Francisco 49ers	1993	Dallas Cowboys
1972	Dallas Cowboys	1983	Washington Redskins	1994	Dallas Cowboys
1973	Miami Dolphins	1984	Los Angeles Raiders	1995	San Francisco 49ers
1974	Miami Dolphins	1985	San Francisco 49ers	1996	Dallas Cowboys
1975	Pittsburgh Steelers	1986	Chicago Bears	1997	Green Bay Packers
1976	Pittsburgh Steelers	1987	New York Giants		
1977	Oakland Raiders	1988	Washington Redskins		

■ *Australian footballers launch themselves into the air to try to take a 'mark' (a ball caught on the full), which entitles a player to an unimpeded kick at goal or towards a teammate. Unlike rugby, no tackling is allowed, but even so, games can be bruising encounters. Australian football combines features of Gaelic football, soccer and rugby*

AUSTRALIAN FOOTBALL LEAGUE

The Australian Football League has been played annually since 1897. The AFL Grand Final is played at the Melbourne Cricket Ground before a capacity crowd.

Year	Winner	Year	Winner	Year	Winner	Year	Winner	Year	Winner	Year	Winner
1897	Essendon	1914	Carlton	1931	Geelong	1948	Melbourne	1965	Essendon	1982	Carlton
1898	Fitzroy	1915	Carlton	1932	Richmond	1949	Essendon	1966	St Kilda	1983	Hawthorn
1899	Fitzroy	1916	Fitzroy	1933	South Melbourne	1950	Essendon	1967	Richmond	1984	Essendon
1900	Melbourne	1917	Collingwood	1934	Richmond	1951	Geelong	1968	Carlton	1985	Essendon
1901	Essendon	1918	South Melbourne	1935	Collingwood	1952	Geelong	1969	Richmond	1986	Hawthorn
1902	Collingwood	1919	Collingwood	1936	Collingwood	1953	Collingwood	1970	Carlton	1987	Carlton
1903	Collingwood	1920	Richmond	1937	Geelong	1954	Footscray	1971	Hawthorn	1988	Hawthorn
1904	Fitzroy	1921	Richmond	1938	Carlton	1955	Melbourne	1972	Carlton	1989	Hawthorn
1905	Fitzroy	1922	Fitzroy	1939	Melbourne	1956	Melbourne	1973	Richmond	1990	Collingwood
1906	Carlton	1923	Essendon	1940	Melbourne	1957	Melbourne	1974	Richmond	1991	Hawthorn
1907	Carlton	1924	Essendon	1941	Melbourne	1958	Collingwood	1975	North Melbourne	1992	West Coast
1908	Carlton	1925	Geelong	1942	Essendon	1959	Melbourne	1976	Hawthorn	1993	Essendon
1909	South Melbourne	1926	Melbourne	1943	Richmond	1960	Melbourne	1977	North Melbourne	1994	West Coast
1910	Collingwood	1927	Collingwood	1944	Fitzroy	1961	Hawthorn	1978	Hawthorn	1995	Carlton
1911	Essendon	1928	Collingwood	1945	Carlton	1962	Essendon	1979	Carlton	1996	North Melbourne
1912	Essendon	1929	Collingwood	1946	Essendon	1963	Geelong	1980	Richmond		
1913	Fitzroy	1930	Collingwood	1947	Carlton	1964	Melbourne	1981	Carlton		

■ AUSTRALIAN FOOTBALL WAS A DEMONSTRATION SPORT AT THE 1956 OLYMPIC GAMES ■

GAELIC FOOTBALL

Gaelic football has features in common with rugby, soccer and Australian football, and has 15 players per team. One point is scored for putting the ball between the goalposts and over the crossbar and three points for putting it between the posts and under the bar into the net. The sport is played throughout Ireland, the major tournament being the All-Ireland Championship. The governing body is the Gaelic Athletic Association.

■ *Jimmy McGuinness of Meath wins the high ball in the 1996 final of the All-Ireland Championship, the high point of the Gaelic football season. Meath won 2–9 (15) to Mayo's 1–11 (14), its sixth championship win*

JOE MONTANA (1956–)

When the chips were down, quarterback Joe Montana could be relied on to work a miracle. Rising to prominence in the 1970s at Notre Dame, he established himself as an expert in getting his team out of trouble. In the 1979 Cotton Bowl, Notre Dame were 12–34 down with just seven and a half minutes to go, but Montana turned the game around, winning it 35–34. He then played for the San Francisco 49ers, helping them to win four Super Bowls, and was voted Most Valuable Player a total of three times (in 1982, 1985 and 1990). Despite a number of injuries, he repeated his trademark knife-edge rescues on more than 30 occasions. In the 1988 Super Bowl, Montana completed eight passes in less than three minutes, including the touchdown that clinched the game with 34 seconds left. Montana retired in 1995, and remains an enduring figure in American footballing history. He holds multiple career records in Super Bowl, with 11 touchdown passes, 1142 yards gained and 33 passes completed between 1982 and 1990.

ALL-IRELAND CHAMPIONSHIP

The All-Ireland Championship is the premier Gaelic football competition, held since 1887. The final is held at Croke Park, Dublin, each September.

Year	Winner	Year	Winner	Year	Winner	Year	Winner	Year	Winner	Year	Winner
1887	Limerick	1906	Dublin	1925	Galway	1944	Roscommon	1963	Dublin	1982	Offaly
1888	(Unfinished)	1907	Dublin	1926	Kerry	1945	Cork	1964	Galway	1983	Dublin
1889	Tipperary	1908	Dublin	1927	Kildare	1946	Kerry	1965	Galway	1984	Kerry
1890	Cork	1909	Kerry	1928	Kildare	1947	Cavan	1966	Galway	1985	Kerry
1891	Dublin	1910	Louth	1929	Kerry	1948	Cavan	1967	Meath	1986	Kerry
1892	Dublin	1911	Cork	1930	Kerry	1949	Meath	1968	Down	1987	Meath
1893	Wexford	1912	Louth	1931	Kerry	1950	Mayo	1969	Kerry	1988	Meath
1894	Dublin	1913	Kerry	1932	Kerry	1951	Mayo	1970	Kerry	1989	Cork
1895	Tipperary	1914	Kerry	1933	Cavan	1952	Cavan	1971	Offaly	1990	Cork
1896	Limerick	1915	Wexford	1934	Galway	1953	Kerry	1972	Offaly	1991	Down
1897	Dublin	1916	Wexford	1935	Cavan	1954	Meath	1973	Cork	1992	Donegal
1898	Dublin	1917	Wexford	1936	Mayo	1955	Kerry	1974	Dublin	1993	Derry
1899	Dublin	1918	Wexford	1937	Kerry	1956	Galway	1975	Kerry	1994	Down
1900	Tipperary	1919	Kildare	1938	Galway	1957	Louth	1976	Dublin	1995	Dublin
1901	Dublin	1920	Tipperary	1939	Kerry	1958	Dublin	1977	Dublin	1996	Meath
1902	Dublin	1921	Dublin	1940	Kerry	1959	Kerry	1978	Kerry		
1903	Kerry	1922	Dublin	1941	Kerry	1960	Down	1979	Kerry		
1904	Kerry	1923	Dublin	1942	Dublin	1961	Down	1980	Kerry		
1905	Kildare	1924	Kerry	1943	Roscommon	1962	Kerry	1981	Kerry		

■ DEATHS IN AMERICAN FOOTBALL GAMES IN 1905 LED TO DRASTIC CHANGES TO THE RULES ■

Cricket

- **Cricket has its origins in the English Middle Ages. King Edward I may have played a game called 'creag'.**
- **Early records are sketchy, but the first match for which full scoring survives took place in 1744.**
- **The first recorded women's cricket match was in Surrey, England, in 1745.**
- **A Test match was first played between England and Australia in Melbourne in 1877; Australia won by 45 runs.**

Cricket developed in England from the Middle Ages, assuming its present form during the 18th and 19th centuries. The Marylebone Cricket Club (the MCC) was formed in 1787, and codified laws of cricket followed in 1835.

The game is now played worldwide, but is most popular in the British Commonwealth.

International cricket is administered by the International Cricket Council, founded in 1909. It has nine full Test-playing members: Australia, England, India, New Zealand, Pakistan, South Africa, Sri Lanka, West Indies and Zimbabwe.

Test matches are usually decided on the best of five matches. England and Australia contest cricket's most famous trophy, the Ashes, but no matter which side wins the series, the Ashes remain in the museum of Lord's cricket ground, London.

A cricket ball's circumference is 20.79–22.8 cm ($8\tfrac{3}{16}$–9 in) and it weighs between 155 and 163 g ($5\tfrac{1}{2}$ and $5\tfrac{3}{4}$ oz). The pitch is 20.11 m (22 yd) from stump to stump.

■ *A dramatic moment at the 1996 World Cup final, held at Lahore, Pakistan. Australia's Shane Warne is stumped by Sri Lankan wicketkeeper Romesh Kaluwitharana*

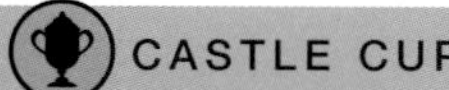

CASTLE CUP

In South Africa, the annual first-class cricket competition is the Castle Cup. It was inaugurated in 1889 and was known as the Currie Cup until 1991. Winners since 1980:

1980	Transvaal
1981	Natal
1982	Western Province
1983	Transvaal
1984	Transvaal
1985	Transvaal
1986	Western Province
1987	Transvaal
1988	Transvaal
1989	Eastern Province
1990	Eastern Province and Western Province
1991	Western Province
1992	Eastern Province
1993	Orange Free State
1994	Orange Free State
1995	Natal
1996	Western Province

RED STRIPE CUP

The Red Stripe Cup is the annual West Indian first-class competition. Barbados is the most successful team. Winners since 1980:

1980	Barbados
1981	Combined Islands
1982	Barbados
1983	Guyana
1984	Barbados
1985	Trinidad and Tobago
1986	Barbados
1987	Guyana
1988	Jamaica
1989	Jamaica
1990	Leeward Islands
1991	Barbados
1992	Jamaica
1993	Guyana
1994	Leeward Islands
1995	Barbados
1996	Leeward Islands
1997	Barbados

SHEFFIELD SHIELD

The Sheffield Shield, Australia's annual first-class inter-state competition, has been contested since 1891–92. Winners since 1980:

1980	Victoria
1981	Western Australia
1982	South Australia
1983	New South Wales
1984	Western Australia
1985	New South Wales
1986	New South Wales
1987	Western Australia
1988	Western Australia
1989	Western Australia
1990	New South Wales
1991	Victoria
1992	Western Australia
1993	New South Wales
1994	New South Wales
1995	Queensland
1996	South Australia
1997	Queensland

WORLD CUP

The World Cup, held every four to five years, is an international one-day tournament championship.

1975	West Indies	1987	Australia
1979	West Indies	1991	Pakistan
1983	India	1996	Sri Lanka

WORLD CUP (WOMEN)

The women's World Cup was first held in 1973, two years before the men's.

1973	England	1988	Australia
1978	Australia	1993	England
1982	Australia		

RANJI TROPHY

In India, the annual first-class inter-state championship is called the Ranji Trophy, and has been contested since 1934. Bombay is by far the most successful team. Winners since 1980:

1980	Delhi	1989	Delhi
1981	Bombay	1990	Bengal
1982	Delhi	1991	Haryana
1983	Karnataka	1992	Delhi
1984	Bombay	1993	Punjab
1985	Bombay	1994	Bombay
1986	Delhi	1995	Bombay
1987	Hyderabad	1996	Karnataka
1988	Tamil Nadu	1997	Bombay

SHELL TROPHY

In New Zealand, the Plunkett Shield was the annual first-class competition from 1906 to 1974–75. Since then, the competition has been sponsored by Shell, and the Shell Trophy is awarded to winners of a limited-overs competition. Winners since 1980:

1980	Northern Districts
1981	Auckland
1982	Wellington
1983	Wellington
1984	Canterbury
1985	Wellington
1986	Otago
1987	Central Districts
1988	Otago
1989	Auckland
1990	Wellington
1991	Auckland
1992	Central Districts and Northern Districts
1993	Northern Districts
1994	Canterbury
1995	Auckland
1996	Auckland
1997	Canterbury

BRIAN LARA (1969–)

Trinidad's Brian Lara is regarded by many as the greatest batsman in the current game. He gained international fame in April 1994, when he made a record-breaking Test innings of 375 for the West Indies against England in Antigua. He topped this feat seven weeks later by scoring 501 not out for Warwickshire against Durham, the highest innings of any batsman in first-class cricket. This unparalleled display of batting came in a season in which he scored centuries in his first four innings in the English county championships, seven centuries in eight innings, and equalled Sir Donald Bradman's long-standing record of 1000 runs in seven innings in England.

UK COUNTY CHAMPIONSHIP

In the UK, a county championship has been contested since 1864. There have been several changes to the way in which the championship is decided. From 1864 to 1889 it was based around the least number of matches lost. From 1890, a formal points system was introduced. Matches today are played by the 18 first-class counties over four days. Yorkshire has the most titles, with 30, followed by Surrey with 16 wins and Middlesex with 12. Winners since 1980:

1980	Middlesex
1981	Nottinghamshire
1982	Middlesex
1983	Essex
1984	Essex
1985	Middlesex
1986	Essex
1987	Nottinghamshire
1988	Worcestershire
1989	Worcestershire
1990	Middlesex
1991	Essex
1992	Essex
1993	Middlesex
1994	Warwickshire
1995	Warwickshire
1996	Leicestershire

QUAID-E-AZAM TROPHY

The Quaid-e-Azam Trophy was inaugurated in 1954. Pakistan's major national competition was named after Mohammad Ali Jinnah, known as Quaid-e-Azam ('Great Leader'). Winners since 1980:

1980	PIA
1981	United Bank
1982	National Bank
1983	United Bank
1984	National Bank
1985	United Bank
1986	Karachi
1987	National Bank
1988	PIA
1989	ADBP
1990	PIA
1991	Karachi Whites
1992	Karachi Whites
1993	Karachi Whites
1994	Lahore
1995	Karachi Blues
1996	Karachi Blues

■ All-rounder Ian Botham, playing for Worcestershire, sets off for another run in a county match. County championships, which have been played since 1864, are the bedrock of cricket in England and the proving-ground for up-and-coming Test players. Despite the popularity of one-day competitions, a championship win is still the most sought-after title in county cricket

A SINGLE BALL ■ THE HIGHEST EVER SPEED OF A BOWLED CRICKET BALL IS 160.45 KM/H ■

GOLF

- **The oldest club of which there is written evidence is the Gentlemen Golfers (now the Honourable Company of Edinburgh Golfers) formed in March 1744.**
- **The first definite mention of golf dates from 1457 when the Scottish parliament prohibited the game because it distracted men from practising archery.**
- **The first wooden golf balls were replaced by 'featheries', leather-cased balls containing compressed feathers.**

No one knows golf's origins for certain, but it was definitely being played in Scotland in the 15th century. The first club was formed there in 1744.

Golf can be played in two ways: match play and stroke play. In match play individuals or pairs compete against each other, and the contest is decided by the number of holes won. Stroke play is contested by the total number of strokes in a round.

The four major tournaments are the British Open, the US Open, the US Masters and the US Professional Golfers' Association (PGA). There are also a number of international team competitions.

The modern golf course has 18 holes of varying length, with an average total distance of between 5500 and 6400 m (about 6000 and 7000 yd). Types of club include 'irons', which are numbered 1–10 according to the angle of the face of the club, and 'woods', which are used for driving. There are also more specialized clubs: putters and sand wedges. A player may use a maximum of 14 clubs. In the UK and North America, golf balls have a minimum diameter of 42.62 mm (1 7/10 in). The Royal & Ancient Golf Club of St Andrews, Scotland, and the United States Golf Association are the game's ruling bodies.

BRITISH OPEN

First held in 1860 at the Prestwick Club, South Ayrshire, Scotland, the British Open is the world's oldest open championship. Since 1892, it has been played over 72 holes of stroke play on seaside links. The post-war winners are listed below, together with their scores.

Year	Winner	Score
1946	Sam Snead (USA)	290
1947	Fred Daly (GB)	293
1948	Henry Cotton (GB)	284
1949	Bobby Locke (SA)	283
1950	Bobby Locke (SA)	279
1951	Max Faulkner (GB)	285
1952	Bobby Locke (SA)	287
1953	Ben Hogan (USA)	282
1954	Peter Thomson (Aus)	283
1955	Peter Thomson (Aus)	281
1956	Peter Thomson (Aus)	286
1957	Bobby Locke (SA)	279
1958	Peter Thomson (Aus)	278
1959	Gary Player (SA)	284
1960	Kel Nagle (Aus)	278
1961	Arnold Palmer (USA)	284
1962	Arnold Palmer (USA)	276
1963	Bob Charles (NZ)	277
1964	Tony Lema (USA)	279
1965	Peter Thomson (Aus)	285
1966	Jack Nicklaus (USA)	282
1967	Robert de Vicenzo (Arg)	278
1968	Gary Player (SA)	299
1969	Tony Jacklin (GB)	280
1970	Jack Nicklaus (USA)	283
1971	Lee Trevino (USA)	278
1972	Lee Trevino (USA)	278
1973	Tom Weiskopf (USA)	276
1974	Gary Player (SA)	282
1975	Tom Watson (USA)	279
1976	Johnny Miller (USA)	279
1977	Tom Watson (USA)	268
1978	Jack Nicklaus (USA)	281
1979	Severiano Ballesteros (Spa)	283
1980	Tom Watson (USA)	271
1981	Bill Rogers (USA)	276
1982	Tom Watson (USA)	284
1983	Tom Watson (USA)	275
1984	Severiano Ballesteros (Spa)	276
1985	Sandy Lyle (GB)	282
1986	Greg Norman (Aus)	280
1987	Nick Faldo (GB)	279
1988	Severiano Ballesteros (Spa)	273
1989	Mark Calcavecchia (USA)	275
1990	Nick Faldo (GB)	270
1991	Ian Baker-Finch (Aus)	272
1992	Nick Faldo (GB)	272
1993	Greg Norman (Aus)	267
1994	Nick Price (Zim)	268
1995	John Daly (USA)	282
1996	Tom Lehmann (USA)	271
1997	Justin Leonard (USA)	272

US OPEN

The United States Open was first held on a nine-hole course in 1895. This annual tournament is now played over 72 holes of stroke play at a different venue each year. Listed below are the post-war winners and their scores (winners are American unless specified otherwise).

Year	Winner	Score
1946	Lloyd Mangrum	284
1947	Lew Worsham	282
1948	Ben Hogan	287
1949	Cary Middlecoff	286
1950	Ben Hogan	287
1951	Ben Hogan	287
1952	Julius Boros	281
1953	Ben Hogan	283
1954	Ed Furgol	284
1955	Jack Fleck	287
1956	Cary Middlecoff	281
1957	Dick Mayer	282
1958	Tommy Bolt	283
1959	Billy Casper	282
1960	Arnold Palmer	280
1961	Gene Littler	281
1962	Jack Nicklaus	283
1963	Julius Boros	293
1964	Ken Venturi	278
1965	Gary Player (SA)	282
1966	Billy Casper	278
1967	Jack Nicklaus	275
1968	Lee Trevino	275
1969	Orville Moody	281
1970	Tony Jacklin (GB)	281
1971	Lee Trevino	280
1972	Jack Nicklaus	290
1973	Johnny Miller	279
1974	Hale Irwin	287
1975	Lou Graham	287
1976	Jerry Pate	277
1977	Hubert Green	278
1978	Andy North	285
1979	Hale Irwin	284
1980	Jack Nicklaus	272
1981	David Graham (Aus)	273
1982	Tom Watson	282
1983	Larry Nelson	280
1984	Fuzzy Zoeller	276
1985	Andy North	279
1986	Raymond Floyd	279
1987	Scott Simpson	277
1988	Curtis Strange	278
1989	Curtis Strange	278
1990	Hale Irwin	280
1991	Payne Stewart	283
1992	Tom Kite	285
1993	Lee Janzen	272
1994	Ernie Els (SA)	279
1995	Corey Pavin	280
1996	Steve Jones	278
1997	Ernie Els (SA)	276

US MASTERS

Inaugurated in 1934, the US Masters is held annually at the Augusta National Course in Georgia. The event is invitation only, and is held over 72 holes of stroke play. Listed below are the post-war winners and their scores (winners are American unless specified otherwise).

Year	Winner	Score
1946	Herman Keiser	282
1947	Jimmy Demaret	281
1948	Claude Harmon	279
1949	Sam Snead	282
1950	Jimmy Demaret	283
1951	Ben Hogan	280
1952	Sam Snead	286
1953	Ben Hogan	274
1954	Sam Snead	289
1955	Cary Middlecoff	279
1956	Jack Burke, Jr	289
1957	Doug Ford	282
1958	Arnold Palmer	284
1959	Art Wall, Jr	284
1960	Arnold Palmer	282
1961	Gary Player (SA)	280
1962	Arnold Palmer	280
1963	Jack Nicklaus	286
1964	Arnold Palmer	276
1965	Jack Nicklaus	271
1966	Jack Nicklaus	288
1967	Gay Brewer	280
1968	Bob Goalby	277
1969	George Archer	281
1970	Billy Casper	279
1971	Charles Coody	279
1972	Jack Nicklaus	286
1973	Tommy Aaron	283
1974	Gary Player (SA)	278
1975	Jack Nicklaus	276
1976	Raymond Floyd	271
1977	Tom Watson	276
1978	Gary Player (SA)	277
1979	Fuzzy Zoeller	280
1980	Severiano Ballesteros (Spa)	275
1981	Tom Watson	280
1982	Craig Stadler	284
1983	Severiano Ballesteros (Spa)	280
1984	Ben Crenshaw	277
1985	Bernhard Langer (Ger)	282
1986	Jack Nicklaus	279
1987	Larry Mize	285
1988	Sandy Lyle (GB)	281
1989	Nick Faldo (GB)	283
1990	Nick Faldo (GB)	278
1991	Ian Woosnam (GB)	277
1992	Fred Couples	275
1993	Bernhard Langer (Ger)	277
1994	José-Maria Olazábal (Spa)	279
1995	Ben Crenshaw	274
1996	Nick Faldo (GB)	276
1997	Tiger Woods	270

US PGA

The US Professional Golfers' Association (PGA) championship used to be held on a match-play basis from 1916 until 1958; it was then contested as a stroke-play competition over 72 holes. The post-war winners are listed below, together with their scores (winners are American unless specified otherwise).

Year	Winner	Score
1946	Ben Hogan	6 & 4
1947	Jim Ferrier	2 & 1
1948	Ben Hogan	7 & 6
1949	Sam Snead	3 & 2
1950	Chandler Harper	4 & 3
1951	Sam Snead	7 & 6
1952	Jim Turnesa	1 up
1953	Walter Burkemo	2 & 1
1954	Chick Harbert	4 & 3
1955	Doug Ford	4 & 3
1956	Jack Burke	3 & 2
1957	Lionel Hebert	2 & 1
1958	Dow Finsterwald	276
1959	Bob Rosburg	277
1960	Jay Hebert	281
1961	Jerry Barber	277
1962	Gary Player (SA)	278
1963	Jack Nicklaus	279
1964	Bobby Nichols	271
1965	Dave Marr	280
1966	Al Geiberger	280
1967	Don January	281
1968	Julius Boros	281
1969	Raymond Floyd	276
1970	Dave Stockton	279
1971	Jack Nicklaus	281
1972	Gary Player (SA)	281
1973	Jack Nicklaus	277
1974	Lee Trevino	276
1975	Jack Nicklaus	276
1976	Dave Stockton	281
1977	Lanny Wadkins	282
1978	John Mahaffey	276
1979	David Graham (Aus)	272
1980	Jack Nicklaus	274
1981	Larry Nelson	273
1982	Raymond Floyd	272
1983	Hal Sutton	274
1984	Lee Trevino	273
1985	Hubert Green	278
1986	Bob Tway	276
1987	Larry Nelson	287
1988	Jeff Sluman	272
1989	Payne Stewart	276
1990	Wayne Grady (Aus)	282
1991	John Daly	276
1992	Nick Price (Zim)	278
1993	Paul Azinger	272
1994	Nick Price (Zim)	269
1995	Steve Elkington (Aus)	267
1996	Mark Brooks	277

■ Known as the home of golf, St Andrews, Scotland, is the oldest golf course in existence

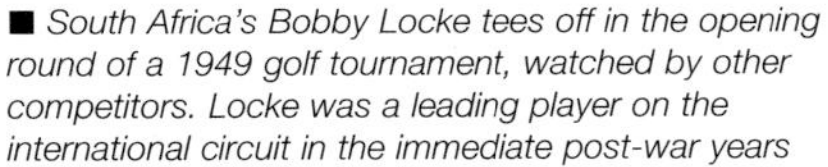

■ South Africa's Bobby Locke tees off in the opening round of a 1949 golf tournament, watched by other competitors. Locke was a leading player on the international circuit in the immediate post-war years

TEAM TOURNAMENTS

RYDER CUP

The Ryder Cup is contested between professionals every two years and was first held in 1927. The Cup has seen the United States opposed by Great Britain 1927–71, Great Britain and Ireland 1973–77 and Europe from 1979. At present, the trophy's format is to have four foursomes and four four-ball matches on each of the first two days, with 12 singles on the final day. The US dominates, with 23 wins to 6, and 2 matches drawn (1969 and 1989). Great Britain won in 1929, 1933 and 1957, Europe in 1985, 1987 and 1995.

WALKER CUP

Amateur US and British teams have contested the Walker Cup biennially since 1922. Since 1981, the United States has opposed a combined Great Britain and Ireland team. The US has 30 wins to Great Britain and Ireland's four (1938, 1971, 1989 and 1995). There has been one draw, in 1965.

CURTIS CUP

Held every two years since 1932, the Curtis Cup is played between women's teams from the United States, and Great Britain and Ireland. The US leads 20 wins to 6; Great Britain and Ireland won in 1952, 1956, 1986, 1988, 1992 and 1996. There have been three draws, in 1936, 1958 and 1994.

WORLD CUP

Inaugurated by Jay Hopkins in 1953, the World Cup is contested annually by two-man international teams over 72 holes of stroke play. It was not held in 1981 or 1986. The United States has dominated this tournament, with a total of 21 wins up to 1996 (1955–56, 1960–64, 1966–67, 1969, 1971, 1973 1975, 1978–79, 1983, 1988, 1992–95). Spain has four wins (1977–78, 1982, 1984), as does Australia (1954, 1959, 1970, 1989). Countries with three wins are South Africa (1965, 1974, 1996) and Canada (1968, 1980, 1985). Seven other nations have won the World Cup once: Argentina (1953), Japan (1957), Ireland (1958), Taiwan (1972), Wales (1987), Germany (1990) and Sweden (1991).

GARY PLAYER (1935–)

South Africa's Gary Player is one of golf's all-time greats, a golfer whose career was characterized by dedication and tenacity. Early on he identified technical faults in his game (he was a very short hitter, for example) and systematically exercised and trained to eliminate them. He went on to achieve a remarkable record of wins, becoming one of only four men to win all four major tournaments: the US Open in 1965, the Masters in 1961, 1974 and 1978, the British Open in 1959, 1968 and 1974, and the PGA in 1962 and 1972. His thirst for competition has taken him far and wide, winning tournaments in Africa, continental Europe, South America and Australia, where he has won the Australian Open seven times. His determination showed against Tony Lerna at the World Match Play Championship in 1965, which he won after being seven behind with 17 holes to play. Player is considered to be one of the Big Three of golf, along with Jack Nicklaus and Arnold Palmer.

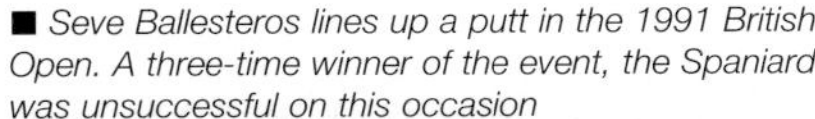

■ Seve Ballesteros lines up a putt in the 1991 British Open. A three-time winner of the event, the Spaniard was unsuccessful on this occasion

YEARS AGO ■ JAPAN HAS MORE THAN 13 MILLION GOLFERS, BUT ONLY 1200 GOLF COURSES ■

TENNIS

- **Professional tennis dates from 1926 when an American football promoter organized a tournament that featured Suzanne Lenglen, the outstanding French player.**
- **The longest tiebreak went to 26–24 in a first-round men's double match which took place at Wimbledon, 1 July 1985 – J. Gunnarsson (Swe) and M. Mortensen (Den) defeated J. Frawley (Aus) and V. Pecci (Par) 6–3, 6–4, 3–6, 7–6.**
- **The fastest timed serve was 229 km/h delivered by Mark Philippoussis (Aus) in 1997.**

Lawn tennis was patented in 1874 by Major Walter Wingfield of North Wales, who called his sport 'Sphairistikè'. It quickly gained acceptance and is now the most popular racket sport in the world.

Tennis is played on a number of surfaces, including grass, clay, concrete and carpet (for indoor matches). The court in a singles game is 23.8 m (78 ft) long and 8.2 m (27 ft) wide – in doubles the width is extended to 11 m (36 ft). The ball is 6.35–6.67 cm (2½–2⅝ in) in diameter and weighs 57–58 g (2–2$\frac{1}{16}$ oz). The net which is placed across the centre of the court is supported by a strap at a height of 0.9 m (3 ft). The lines enclosing the court are called the base-lines (end of court) and side-lines (side of court)

The four major championships are Wimbledon, and the US, French and Australian Opens. Together, they form the Grand Slam. There are also various circuits and grand prix tournaments, which are rated on a points system to produce world rankings. The International Tennis Federation, founded in 1913, is the sport's governing body.

■ Rod Laver, Wimbledon, 1962

■ Boris Becker, Australian Open, 1997

DAVIS CUP

First held in 1900, the Davis Cup is the major international team competition for men. Winners, ranked by most wins:

	Wins	
USA	31	1900, 1902, 1913, 1920–26, 1937–38, 1946–49, 1954, 1958, 1963, 1968–72, 1978–79, 1981–82, 1990, 1992, 1995
Australasia/ Australia	26	1907–09, 1911, 1914, 1919, 1939, 1950–53, 1955–57, 1959–62, 1964–67, 1973, 1977, 1983, 1986
British Isles/ Great Britain	9	1903–06, 1912, 1933–36
France	8	1927–32, 1991, 1996
Sweden	4	1975, 1984–85, 1994
FRG/Germany	3	1988–89, 1993
South Africa	1	1974
Italy	1	1976
Czechoslovakia	1	1980

FED CUP

The women's international team competition is the Fed Cup (formerly the Federation Cup), held annually since 1963. Winners, ranked by most wins:

	Wins	
USA	15	1963, 1966–67, 1969, 1976–82, 1986, 1989–90, 1996
Australia	7	1964–65, 1968, 1970–71, 1973–74
Czechoslovakia	5	1975, 1983–85, 1988
Spain	4	1991, 1993–95

1996 OLYMPIC CHAMPIONS

Lawn tennis was included in the Olympic Games from 1896 to 1924, and was a demonstration sport in 1968. It was reintroduced as a medal sport in 1988. Listed below are the 1996 gold medallists.

Men's singles: Andre Agassi (USA)

Men's doubles: Todd Woodbridge & Mark Woodforde (Aus)

Women's singles: Lindsay Davenport (USA)

Women's doubles: Gigi Fernandez & Mary Joe Fernandez (USA)

AUSTRALIAN OPEN

The Australian Open was instituted in 1905, and is now held at Flinders Park, Melbourne. There were two championships in 1977, as the event moved from early season to late season. Winners since 1970:

Men's singles

1970	Arthur Ashe (USA)
1971	Ken Rosewall (Aus)
1972	Ken Rosewall (Aus)
1973	John Newcombe (Aus)
1974	Jimmy Connors (USA)
1975	John Newcombe (Aus)
1976	Mark Edmondson (Aus)
1977	Roscoe Tanner (USA)
1977	Vitas Gerulaitis (USA)
1978	Guillermo Vilas (Arg)
1979	Guillermo Vilas (Arg)
1980	Brian Teacher (USA)
1981	Johan Kriek (SA)
1982	Johan Kriek (SA)
1983	Mats Wilander (Swe)
1984	Mats Wilander (Swe)
1985	Stefan Edberg (Swe)
1986	No championship
1987	Stefan Edberg (Swe)
1988	Mats Wilander (Swe)
1989	Ivan Lendl (Cze)
1990	Ivan Lendl (Cze)
1991	Boris Becker (Ger)
1992	Jim Courier (USA)
1993	Jim Courier (USA)
1994	Pete Sampras (USA)
1995	Andre Agassi (USA)
1996	Boris Becker (Ger)
1997	Pete Sampras (USA)

Women's singles

1970	Margaret Court (Aus)
1971	Margaret Court (Aus)
1972	Virginia Wade (GB)
1973	Margaret Court (Aus)
1974	Evonne Goolagong (Aus)
1975	Evonne Goolagong (Aus)
1976	Evonne Cawley (née Goolagong) (Aus)
1977	Kerry Reid (Aus)
1977	Evonne Cawley (Aus)
1978	Christine O'Neill (Aus)
1979	Barbara Jordan (USA)
1980	Hana Mandlikova (Cze)
1981	Martina Navratilova (Cze)
1982	Chris Evert-Lloyd (USA)
1983	Martina Navratilova (USA)
1984	Chris Evert-Lloyd (USA)
1985	Martina Navratilova (USA)
1986	No championship
1987	Hana Mandlikova (Cze)
1988	Steffi Graf (Ger)
1989	Steffi Graf (Ger)
1990	Steffi Graf (Ger)
1991	Monica Seles (Yug)
1992	Monica Seles (Yug)
1993	Monica Seles (Yug)
1994	Steffi Graf (Ger)
1995	Mary Pierce (Fra)
1996	Monica Seles (USA)
1997	Martina Hingis (Swi)

■ TENNIS HAS THE HIGHEST OFFICIAL-TO-PLAYER RATIO OF ANY SPORT ■ ROD LAVER WAS THE

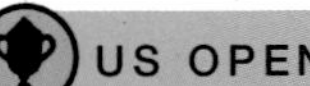

FRENCH OPEN

The French Open is held on hard courts, at the Stade Roland Garros, Paris (since 1928). Winners since 1970:

Men's singles

1970 Jan Kodes (Cze)
1971 Jan Kodes (Cze)
1972 Andrés Gimeno (Spa)
1973 Ilie Nastase (Rom)
1974 Björn Borg (Swe)
1975 Björn Borg (Swe)
1976 Adriano Panatta (Ita)
1977 Guillermo Vilas (Arg)
1978 Björn Borg (Swe)
1979 Björn Borg (Swe)
1980 Björn Borg (Swe)
1981 Björn Borg (Swe)
1982 Mats Wilander (Swe)
1983 Yannick Noah (Fra)
1984 Ivan Lendl (Cze)
1985 Mats Wilander (Swe)
1986 Ivan Lendl (Cze)
1987 Ivan Lendl (Cze)
1988 Mats Wilander (Swe)
1989 Michael Chang (USA)
1990 Andrés Gómez (Ecu)
1991 Jim Courier (USA)
1992 Jim Courier (USA)
1993 Sergi Bruguera (Spa)
1994 Sergi Bruguera (Spa)
1995 Thomas Muster (Aut)
1996 Yevgeniy Kafelnikov (Rus)
1997 Gustavo Kuerten (Bra)

Women's singles

1970 Margaret Court (Aus)
1971 Evonne Goolagong (Aus)
1972 Billie Jean King (USA)
1973 Margaret Court (Aus)
1974 Chris Evert (USA)
1975 Chris Evert (USA)
1976 Sue Barker (GB)
1977 Mimi Jausovec (Yug)
1978 Virginia Ruzici (Rom)
1979 Chris Evert-Lloyd (USA)
1980 Chris Evert-Lloyd (USA)
1981 Hana Mandlikova (Cze)
1982 Martina Navratilova (USA)
1983 Chris Evert-Lloyd (USA)
1984 Martina Navratilova (USA)
1985 Chris Evert-Lloyd (USA)
1986 Chris Evert-Lloyd (USA)
1987 Steffi Graf (Ger)
1988 Steffi Graf (Ger)
1989 Arantxa Sánchez Vicario (Spa)
1990 Monica Seles (Yug)
1991 Monica Seles (Yug)
1992 Monica Seles (Yug)
1993 Steffi Graf (Ger)
1994 Arantxa Sánchez Vicario (Spa)
1995 Steffi Graf (Ger)
1996 Steffi Graf (Ger)
1997 Iva Majoli (Cro)

US OPEN

The US Open has been contested since 1881, and is held at Flushing Meadow, New York. Winners since 1970:

Men's singles

1970 Ken Rosewall (Aus)
1971 Stan Smith (USA)
1972 Ilie Nastase (Rom)
1973 John Newcombe (Aus)
1974 Jimmy Connors (USA)
1975 Manuel Orantes (Spa)
1976 Jimmy Connors (USA)
1977 Guillermo Vilas (Arg)
1978 Jimmy Connors (USA)
1979 John McEnroe (USA)
1980 John McEnroe (USA)
1981 John McEnroe (USA)
1982 Jimmy Connors (USA)
1983 Jimmy Connors (USA)
1984 John McEnroe (USA)
1985 Ivan Lendl (Cze)
1986 Ivan Lendl (Cze)
1987 Ivan Lendl (Cze)
1988 Mats Wilander (Swe)
1989 Boris Becker (Ger)
1990 Pete Sampras (USA)
1991 Stefan Edberg (Swe)
1992 Stefan Edberg (Swe)
1993 Pete Sampras (USA)
1994 Andre Agassi (USA)
1995 Pete Sampras (USA)
1996 Pete Sampras (USA)

Women's singles

1970 Margaret Court (Aus)
1971 Billie Jean King (USA)
1972 Billie Jean King (USA)
1973 Margaret Court (Aus)
1974 Billie Jean King (USA)
1975 Chris Evert (USA)
1976 Chris Evert (USA)
1977 Chris Evert (USA)
1978 Chris Evert (USA)
1979 Tracy Austin (USA)
1980 Chris Evert-Lloyd (USA)
1981 Tracy Austin (USA)
1982 Chris Evert-Lloyd (USA)
1983 Martina Navratilova (USA)
1984 Martina Navratilova (USA)
1985 Hana Mandlikova (Cze)
1986 Martina Navratilova (USA)
1987 Martina Navratilova (USA)
1988 Steffi Graf (Ger)
1989 Steffi Graf (Ger)
1990 Gabriela Sabatini (Arg)
1991 Monica Seles (Yug)
1992 Monica Seles (Yug)
1993 Steffi Graf (Ger)
1994 Arantxa Sánchez Vicario (Spa)
1995 Steffi Graf (Ger)
1996 Steffi Graf (Ger)

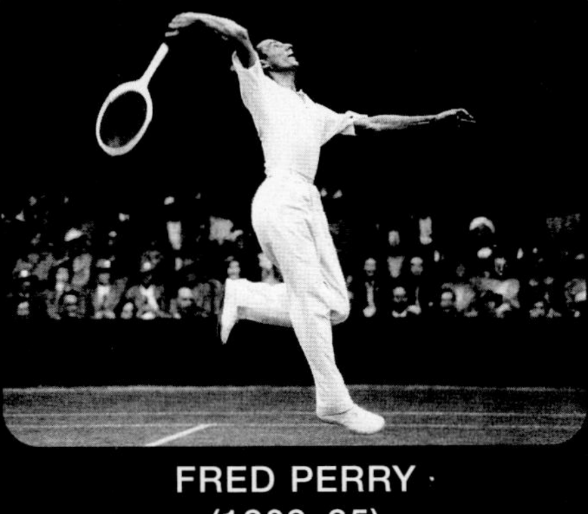

FRED PERRY (1909–95)

Britain's Fred Perry was a phenomenal tennis player. He won a total of eight Grand Slam titles: three Wimbledon (1934, 1935, 1936), three US (1933, 1934, 1936), the French (1935) and Australian (1934). He became the first player ever to win all four major singles titles, although this did not count as a Grand Slam as he did not hold them all concurrently. His record in doubles competitions was also impressive, with two men's doubles and four mixed doubles Grand Slam titles. Perry was instrumental in Britain's four consecutive Davis Cup titles, 1933–36, in which his personal record was considerable: only 7 defeats in 52 matches. He turned pro in 1936, and left for the United States, where he co-owned the Beverly Hills Tennis Club. He also began the first range of tennis clothes, successfully establishing his name as a mark of quality sportswear. The last British man to win a Grand Slam title (in 1936), he richly deserved the ultimate accolade awarded to him by the All England Club: a statue of him erected at Wimbledon, scene of so many of his greatest victories.

■ *Bjorn Borg, Wimbledon, 1973*

■ *Pete Sampras, Australian Open, 1997*

■ *Andre Agassi, Lipton Championships, USA, 1997*

■ *Chris Evert, Wimbledon, 1974*

■ *Martina Navratilova, Wimbledon, 1994*

■ *Monica Seles, Lipton Championships, USA, 1997*

WIMBLEDON

Regarded as the most prestigious tennis competition in the sporting calendar, the All-England Championships at Wimbledon, London, were first held in 1877. The competition was originally played on a challenge basis, but this system was abolished in 1922. Professionals first competed in 1968. Post-war winners:

Men's singles

1946 Yvon Petra (Fra)
1947 Jack Kramer (USA)
1948 Bob Falkenburg (USA)
1949 Ted Schroeder (USA)
1950 Budge Patty (USA)
1951 Dick Savitt (USA)
1952 Frank Sedgman (Aus)
1953 Vic Seixas (USA)
1954 Jaroslav Drobny (Cze)
1955 Tony Trabert (USA)
1956 Lew Hoad (Aus)
1957 Lew Hoad (Aus)
1958 Ashley Cooper (Aus)
1959 Alex Olmedo (USA)
1960 Neale Fraser (Aus)
1961 Rod Laver (Aus)
1962 Rod Laver (Aus)
1963 Chuck McKinley (USA)
1964 Roy Emerson (Aus)
1965 Roy Emerson (Aus)
1966 Manuel Santana (Spa)
1967 John Newcombe (Aus)
1968 Rod Laver (Aus)
1969 Rod Laver (Aus)
1970 John Newcombe (Aus)
1971 John Newcombe (Aus)
1972 Stan Smith (USA)
1973 Jan Kodes (Cze)
1974 Jimmy Connors (USA)
1975 Arthur Ashe (USA)
1976 Björn Borg (Swe)
1977 Björn Borg (Swe)
1978 Björn Borg (Swe)
1979 Björn Borg (Swe)
1980 Björn Borg (Swe)
1981 John McEnroe (USA)
1982 Jimmy Connors (USA)
1983 John McEnroe (USA)
1984 John McEnroe (USA)
1985 Boris Becker (Ger)
1986 Boris Becker (Ger)
1987 Pat Cash (Aus)
1988 Stefan Edberg (Swe)
1989 Boris Becker (Ger)
1990 Stefan Edberg (Swe)
1991 Michael Stich (Ger)
1992 Andre Agassi (USA)
1993 Pete Sampras (USA)
1994 Pete Sampras (USA)
1995 Pete Sampras (USA)
1996 Richard Krajicek (Neths)
1997 Pete Sampras (USA)

Women's singles

1946 Pauline Betz (USA)
1947 Margaret Osborne (USA)
1948 Louise Brough (USA)
1949 Louise Brough (USA)
1950 Louise Brough (USA)
1951 Doris Hart (USA)
1952 Maureen Connolly (USA)
1953 Maureen Connolly (USA)
1954 Maureen Connolly (USA)
1955 Louise Brough (USA)
1956 Shirley Fry (USA)
1957 Althea Gibson (USA)
1958 Althea Gibson (USA)
1959 Maria Bueno (Bra)
1960 Maria Bueno (Bra)
1961 Angela Mortimer (UK)
1962 Karen Susman (USA)
1963 Margaret Smith (Aus)
1964 Maria Bueno (Bra)
1965 Margaret Smith (Aus)
1966 Billie Jean King née Moffitt (USA)
1967 Billie Jean King née Moffitt (USA)
1968 Billie Jean King née Moffitt (USA)
1969 Ann Jones (UK)
1970 Margaret Smith-Court (Aus)
1971 Evonne Goolagong (Aus)
1972 Billie Jean King (USA)
1973 Billie Jean King (USA)
1974 Chris Evert (USA)
1975 Billie Jean King (USA)
1976 Chris Evert (USA)
1977 Virginia Wade (UK)
1978 Martina Navratilova (Cze)
1979 Martina Navratilova (Cze)
1980 Evonne Goolagong-Cawley (Aus)
1981 Chris Evert-Lloyd (USA)
1982 Martina Navratilova (USA)
1983 Martina Navratilova (USA)
1984 Martina Navratilova (USA)
1985 Martina Navratilova (USA)
1986 Martina Navratilova (USA)
1987 Martina Navratilova (USA)
1988 Steffi Graf (Ger)
1989 Steffi Graf (Ger)
1990 Martina Navratilova (USA)
1991 Steffi Graf (Ger)
1992 Steffi Graf (Ger)
1993 Steffi Graf (Ger)
1994 Conchita Martinez (Spa)
1995 Steffi Graf (Ger)
1996 Steffi Graf (Ger)
1997 Martina Hingis (Swi)

Men's doubles

1946 Tom Brown & Jack Kramer (USA)
1947 Bob Falkenburg & Jack Kramer (USA)
1948 John Bromwich & Frank Sedgman (Aus)
1949 Ricardo Gonzales & Frank Parker (USA)
1950 John Bromwich & Adrian Quist (Aus)
1951 Ken McGregor & Frank Sedgman (Aus)
1952 Ken McGregor & Frank Sedgman (Aus)
1953 Lew Hoad & Ken Rosewall (Aus)
1954 Rex Hartwig & Mervyn Rose (Aus)
1955 Rex Hartwig & Lew Hoad (Aus)
1956 Lew Hoad & Ken Rosewall (Aus)
1957 Budge Patty & Gardnar Mulloy (USA)
1958 Sven Davidson & Ulf Schmidt (Swe)
1959 Roy Emerson & Neale Fraser (Aus)
1960 Rafael Osuna (Mex) & Dennis Ralston (USA)
1961 Roy Emerson & Neale Fraser (Aus)
1962 Bob Hewitt & Fred Stolle (Aus)
1963 Rafael Osuna & Antonio Palafox (Mex)
1964 Bob Hewitt & Fred Stolle (Aus)
1965 John Newcombe & Tony Roche (Aus)
1966 Ken Fletcher & John Newcombe (Aus)
1967 Bob Hewitt & Frew McMillan (SA)
1968 John Newcombe & Tony Roche (Aus)
1969 John Newcombe & Tony Roche (Aus)
1970 John Newcombe & Tony Roche (Aus)
1971 Roy Emerson & Rod Laver (Aus)
1972 Bob Hewitt & Frew McMillan (SA)
1973 Jimmy Connors (USA) & Ilie Nastase (Rom)
1974 John Newcombe & Tony Roche (Aus)

1975 Vitas Gerulaitis & Sandy Mayer (USA)
1976 Brian Gottfried (USA) & Raul Ramirez (Mex)
1977 Ross Case & Geoff Masters (Aus)
1978 Bob Hewitt & Frew McMillan (SA)
1979 John McEnroe & Peter Fleming (USA)
1980 Peter McNamara & Paul McNamee (Aus)
1981 John McEnroe & Peter Fleming (USA)
1982 Peter McNamara & Paul McNamee (Aus)
1983 John McEnroe & Peter Fleming (USA)
1984 John McEnroe & Peter Fleming (USA)
1985 Balazs Taroczy (Hun) & Heinz Gunthardt (Swi)
1986 Joachim Nystrom & Mats Wilander (Swe)
1987 Ken Flach & Robert Seguso (USA)
1988 Ken Flach & Robert Seguso (USA)
1989 John Fitzgerald (Aus) & Anders Järryd (Swe)
1990 Rick Leach & Jim Pugh (USA)
1991 John Fitzgerald (Aus) & Anders Järryd (Swe)
1992 John McEnroe (USA) & Michael Stich (Ger)
1993 Todd Woodbridge & Mark Woodforde (Aus)
1994 Todd Woodbridge & Mark Woodforde (Aus)
1995 Todd Woodbridge & Mark Woodforde (Aus)
1996 Todd Woodbridge & Mark Woodforde (Aus)
1997 Todd Woodbridge & Mark Woodforde (Aus)

Women's doubles

1946 Louise Brough & Margaret Osborne (USA)
1947 Pat Todd & Doris Hart (USA)
1948 Louise Brough & Margaret Osborne-du Pont (USA)
1949 Louise Brough & Margaret Osborne-du Pont (USA)
1950 Louise Brough & Margaret Osborne-du Pont (USA)
1951 Doris Hart & Shirley Fry (USA)
1952 Doris Hart & Shirley Fry (USA)
1953 Doris Hart & Shirley Fry (USA)
1954 Louise Brough & Margaret Osborne-du Pont (USA)
1955 Angela Mortimer & Anne Shilcock (UK)
1956 Angela Buxton (UK) & Althea Gibson (USA)
1957 Althea Gibson & Darlene Hard (USA)
1958 Maria Bueno (Bra) & Althea Gibson (USA)
1959 Jean Arth & Darlene Hard (USA)
1960 Maria Bueno (Bra) & Darlene Hard (USA)
1961 Karen Hantze & Billie Jean Moffitt (USA)
1962 Karen Hantze-Susman & Billie Jean Moffitt (USA)
1963 Maria Bueno (Bra) & Darlene Hard (USA)
1964 Margaret Smith & Lesley Turner (Aus)
1965 Maria Bueno (Bra) & Billie Jean Moffitt (USA)
1966 Maria Bueno (Bra) & Nancy Richey (USA)
1967 Rosemary Casals & Billie Jean King née Moffitt (USA)
1968 Billie Jean King & Rosemary Casals (USA)
1969 Margaret Smith-Court & Judy Tegart (Aus)
1970 Billie Jean King & Rosemary Casals (USA)
1971 Billie Jean King & Rosemary Casals (USA)
1972 Billie Jean King (USA) & Betty Stove (Neths)
1973 Billie Jean King & Rosemary Casals (USA)
1974 Evonne Goolagong (Aus) & Peggy Michel (USA)
1975 Ann Kiyomura (USA) & Kazuko Sawamatsu (Jap)
1976 Chris Evert (USA) & Martina Navratilova (Cze)
1977 Helen Cawley (Aus) & Joanne Russell (USA)
1978 Kerry Reid & Wendy Turnbull (Aus)
1979 Billie Jean King (USA) & Martina Navratilova (Cze)
1980 Kathy Jordan & Anne Smith (USA)
1981 Martina Navratilova & Pam Shriver (USA)
1982 Martina Navratilova & Pam Shriver (USA)
1983 Martina Navratilova & Pam Shriver (USA)
1984 Martina Navratilova & Pam Shriver (USA)
1985 Kathy Jordan (USA) & Liz Smylie (Aus)
1986 Martina Navratilova & Pam Shriver (USA)
1987 Claudia Kohde-Kilsch (Ger) & Helena Sukova (Cze)
1988 Steffi Graf (Ger) & Gabriella Sabatini (Arg)
1989 Jana Novotna & Helena Sukova (Cze)
1990 Jana Novotna & Helena Sukova (Cze)
1991 Larisa Savchenko & Natalya Zvereva (USSR)
1992 Gigi Fernandez (USA) & Natalya Zvereva (Brs)
1993 Gigi Fernandez (USA) & Natalya Zvereva (Brs)
1994 Gigi Fernandez (USA) & Natalya Zvereva (Brs)
1995 Jana Novotna (Cze) & Aranxtia Sanchez Vicario (Spa)
1996 Martina Hingis (Swi) & Helena Sukova (Cze)
1997 Gigi Fernandez (USA) & Natalya Zvereva (Brs)

Mixed Doubles

1946 Tom Brown & Louise Brough (USA)
1947 Louise Brough (USA) & John Bromwich (Aus)
1948 Louise Brough (USA) & John Bromwich (Aus)
1949 Sheila Summers & Eric Sturgess (SA)
1950 Louise Brough (USA) & Eric Sturgess (SA)
1951 Doris Hart (USA) & Frank Sedgman (Aus)
1952 Doris Hart (USA) & Frank Sedgman (Aus)
1953 Doris Hart & Vic Seixas (USA)
1954 Doris Hart & Vic Seixas (USA)
1955 Doris Hart & Vic Seixas (USA)
1956 Shirley Fry & Vic Seixas (USA)
1957 Darlene Hard (USA) & Mervyn Rose (Aus)
1958 Lorraine Coghlan & Bob Howe (Aus)
1959 Darlene Hard (USA) & Rod Laver (Aus)
1960 Darlene Hard (USA) & Rod Laver (Aus)
1961 Lesley Turner & Fred Stolle (Aus)
1962 Margaret Osborne-du Pont (USA) & Neale Fraser (Aus)
1963 Margaret Smith & Ken Fletcher (Aus)
1964 Lesley Turner & Fred Stolle (Aus)
1965 Margaret Smith & Ken Fletcher (Aus)
1966 Margaret Smith & Ken Fletcher (Aus)
1967 Billie Jean King (USA) & Owen Davidson (Aus)
1968 Margaret Smith-Court & Ken Fletcher (Aus)
1969 Ann Jones (UK) & Fred Stolle (Aus)
1970 Rosemary Casals (USA) & Ilie Nastase (Rom)
1971 Billie Jean King (USA) & Owen Davidson (Aus)
1972 Rosemary Casals (USA) & Ilie Nastase (Rom)
1973 Billie Jean King (USA) & Owen Davidson (Aus)
1974 Billie Jean King (USA) & Owen Davidson (Aus)
1975 Margaret Smith-Court (Aus) & Marty Riessen (USA)
1976 Françoise Durr (Fra) & Tony Roche (Aus)
1977 Greer Stevens & Bob Hewitt (SA)
1978 Betty Stove (Neths) & Frew McMillan (SA)
1979 Greer Stevens & Bob Hewitt (SA)
1980 Tracey Austin & John Austin (USA)
1981 Betty Stove (Neths) & Frew McMillan (SA)
1982 Anne Smith (USA) & Kevin Curren (SA)
1983 Wendy Turnbull (Aus) & John Lloyd (UK)
1984 Wendy Turnbull (Aus) & John Lloyd (UK)
1985 Martina Navratilova (USA) & Paul McNamee (Aus)
1986 Kathy Jordan & Ken Flach (USA)
1987 Jo Durie & Jeremy Bates (UK)
1988 Zina Garrison & Sherwood Stewart (USA)
1989 Jana Novotna (Cze) & Jim Pugh (USA)
1990 Zina Garrison & Rick Leach (USA)
1991 John Fitzgerald & Elizabeth Smylie (Aus)
1992 Cyril Suk (Cze) & Larisa Savchenko (Lat)
1993 Mark Woodforde (Aus) & Martina Navratilova (USA)
1994 Todd Woodbridge (Aus) & Helena Sukova (Cze)
1995 Martina Navratilova & John Stark (USA)
1996 Cyril Suk & Helena Sukova (Cze)
1997 Cyril Suk & Helena Sukova ((Cze)

STEFFI GRAF (1969–)

The German Steffi Graf is the most successful female tennis player in the world today. Graf's success began early – she gained a Women's Tennis Association rating at the age of 13 and won the French Open in 1988 while still short of her 18th birthday. She achieved the Grand Slam in 1988, and went on to win a gold medal at the Seoul Olympics the same year, becoming the first and only tennis player to achieve the so-called 'Golden Slam'. In 1989 she narrowly missed retaining the Grand Slam title by losing only in the French final. Graf was ranked number one in the world for a record 186 weeks from 1987 to 1991, when injury and other problems resulted in her losing the top spot to Monica Seles. She regained the world number one position in 1993 following the stabbing of Seles, and she continued to dominate the tennis circuit for the next four years. Her Grand Slam career includes five US Open singles titles, five French Open titles, four Australian Open titles and seven Wimbledon singles titles. However, her position as number one in the world was lost to the young Martina Hingis in 1997.

THE GRAND SLAM

The Grand Slam is the most prestigious achievement in tennis. To win this acclaim, a player has to win all four major tournaments in the same calendar year – Wimbledon, the French, Australian and US Opens. Players who have achieved this feat in the singles game are:

Men

Donald Budge (USA) 1938
Rod Laver (Aus) 1962, 1969

Women

Maureen Connolly (USA) 1953
Margaret Court (Aus) 1970
Steffi Graf (Ger) 1988

SCORING IS SAID TO HAVE DERIVED FROM THE FOUR QUARTERS OF A CLOCK (15-30-45-60)

OTHER BALL GAMES

- Although American folklore suggests that baseball was invented by Abnet Doubleday in Cooperstown, New York, in 1839, it probably developed from English sports such as cricket and rounders.
- Games similar to basketball have been played for thousands of years, and an early ancestor may have been 'Pok-ta-Pok', played by the Olmecs in Mexico in the 10th century BC.
- Stick-and-ball games have been played for over 4000 years, with illustrations of such sports appearing in Egyptian tomb paintings *c.* 2050 BC.
- Shinty developed from the ancient game of *camanachd*, 'the sport of the curved stick'.

BASEBALL

Baseball has its roots in the British game of rounders, and was codified in 1845 by Alexander Cartwright, Jr. The first professional league, the National Association of Professional Base Ball Players, was formed in 1871.

The game is played mainly in America, Japan and the Far East. The US has two leagues, the National (NL), founded in 1876, and the American (AL), founded in 1901. Baseball was added to the Olympics in 1992, and Cuba won the gold that year and again in 1996.

The game is nine-a-side. A standard ball weighs 149 g (5¼ oz) and is 23 cm (9–9¼ in) in circumference. Bats are up to 7 cm (2¾ in) in diameter and up to 1.07 m (42 in) in length.

WORLD SERIES

The premier baseball competition is the World Series, established in 1903. It is contested by the divisional champions of the two leagues (the NL and AL) in a play-off, with the final fought as a best of seven series. Below is a list of World Series winners. The same team franchises have often played under different names at different times. Thus the Brooklyn Dodgers and the Los Angeles Dodgers are the same franchise, as are Atlanta Braves, Boston Braves and Milwaukee Braves; Minnesota Twins and Washington Senators; Oakland Athletics and Philadelphia Athletics. The World Series was not held in 1904, and in 1994 it was cancelled due to a players' strike.

Atlanta Braves (NL)	1996
Baltimore Orioles (AL)	1966, 1970, 1983
Boston Braves (NL)	1914
Boston Red Sox (AL)	1903, 1912, 1915–16, 1918
Brooklyn Dodgers (NL)	1955
Chicago Cubs (NL)	1907–08
Chicago White Sox (AL)	1906, 1917
Cincinnati Reds (NL)	1919, 1940, 1975–76, 1990
Cleveland Indians (AL)	1920, 1948,
Detroit Tigers (AL)	1935, 1945, 1968, 1984
Kansas City Royals (AL)	1985
Los Angeles Dodgers (NL)	1959, 1963, 1965, 1981, 1988
Milwaukee Braves (NL)	1957
Minnesota Twins (AL)	1987, 1991
New York Giants (NL)	1905, 1921–22, 1933, 1954
New York Mets (NL)	1969, 1986
New York Yankees (AL)	1923, 1927–28, 1932, 1936–39, 1941, 1943, 1947, 1949–53, 1956, 1958, 1961–62, 1977–78, 1996
Oakland Athletics (AL)	1972–74, 1989
Philadelphia Athletics (AL)	1910–11, 1913, 1929–30
Philadelphia Phillies (NL)	1980
Pittsburgh Pirates (NL)	1909, 1925, 1960, 1971, 1979,
St Louis Cardinals (NL)	1926, 1931, 1934, 1942, 1944, 1946, 1964, 1967, 1982
Toronto Blue Jays (AL)	1992, 1993
Washington Senators (AL)	1924

■ *The 1992 World Series was decided in a closely fought game between the Toronto Blue Jays and the Atlanta Braves. Dave Winfield, seen here, played a major role in the Jays' win by hitting a two-out, two-run double*

BASKETBALL

Basketball was invented in 1891 by Dr James Naismith, an American physical education instructor. The game has grown enormously in popularity since then, although it still has its greatest following in North America. The American professional game (governed by the National Basketball Association) attracts large amounts of money, and top players are extremely well paid.

Teams are five-a-side, with seven substitutes allowed. The rectangular court is 28 m (92 ft) in length, and 14 m (46 ft) wide, and the ball is 76 cm (30 in) in circumference and weighs 567–650 g (20–23 oz).

The governing body is the Fédération Internationale de Basketball (FIB), formed in 1932.

WORLD CHAMPIONSHIPS

The basketball World Championship was first held for men in 1950 and for women in 1953. It is now held every four years.

Men

Argentina	1950
USA	1954, 1986, 1994
Brazil	1959, 1963
USSR	1967, 1974, 1982
Yugoslavia	1970, 1978, 1990

Women

USA	1953, 1957, 1979, 1986, 1990
USSR	1959, 1964, 1967, 1971, 1975, 1983
Brazil	1994

NBA

The American professional basketball circuit is governed by the National Basketball Association (NBA), which was formed in 1949 after the merging of the Basketball Association of America and the National Basketball League. The NBA merged with the American Basketball Association in 1976. The annual NBA championship is one of the world's most prestigious team competitions.

In the United States, the same team franchises have often played under different names at different times. Thus the Golden State Warriors and the Philadelphia Warriors are the same franchise, as are Philadelphia 76ers and Syracuse Nationals; Los Angeles Lakers and Minneapolis Lakers.

Baltimore Bullets	1948
Boston Celtics	1957, 1959–66, 1968–69, 1974, 1976, 1981, 1984, 1986
Chicago Bulls	1991–93, 1996
Detroit Pistons	1989–90
Golden State Warriors	1975
Houston Rockets	1994–95
Los Angeles Lakers	1972, 1980, 1982, 1985, 1987–88
Milwaukee Bucks	1971
Minneapolis Lakers	1949–50, 1952–54
New York Knicks	1970, 1973
Philadelphia 76ers	1967, 1983
Philadelphia Warriors	1947, 1956
Portland Trail Blazers	1977
Rochester Royals	1951
Seattle Supersonics	1979
St Louis Hawks	1958
Syracuse Nationals	1955
Washington Bullets	1978

■ AT 2.31 M, GHEORGHE MURESAN OF THE WASHINGTON BULLETS IS THE TALLEST PLAYER

HANDBALL

Handball is similar to soccer, but is played with hands instead of feet, and is becoming increasingly popular. Played in the 1936 Olympics as an 11-a-side outdoor sport, its reintroduction to the Olympics in 1972 saw it as a seven-a-side indoor event. The indoor game has a court 40 x 20 m (131 x 66 ft), with goals 2 m (6 ft) high and 3 m (9 ft) wide. The sport's governing body is the International Handball Federation.

Eton Fives is a handball game first played against the buttresses of Eton College Chapel, England, and is confined to the UK. Codification of the rules came in 1877. Rugby Fives is a variation on the original sport.

1996 OLYMPIC HANDBALL

Handball was first played at the 1936 Berlin Olympics as an outdoor sport. It was reintroduced in 1972 as an indoor event. Listed below are the gold medal-winning teams.

	Men	Women
1936	Germany	–
1972	Yugoslavia	–
1976	USSR	USSR
1980	GDR	USSR
1984	Yugoslavia	Yugoslavia
1988	USSR	South Korea
1992	CIS	South Korea
1996	Croatia	Denmark

■ *A South Korean player becomes airborne in the 1996 women's Olympic handball final; Denmark won, 37– 33*

MAGIC JOHNSON (1959–)

Earvin Johnson, the US basketball legend, earned the name 'Magic' when he was 15, after he threw seemingly enchanted passes. A great all-rounder, he played guard, forward and centre, and his versatility forced the National Basketball Association to initiate a new statistic – double figures in points, rebounds and assists achieved in a single game. He helped the Los Angeles Lakers to five NBA titles in the 1980s and was voted Most Valuable Player on three occasions (1987, 1989 and 1990). He also became a multi-millionaire through playing fees and product endorsements. He announced his retirement in 1991 while still at the pinnacle of his career, after testing positive for HIV, and expressed a desire to help promote the fight against AIDS. Attempting a comeback a year later, he pulled out after opponents feared a transmission of the virus during play. Nonetheless, he formed part of the US 'Dream Team' that won gold at the 1992 Olympics, and returned to top-flight basketball in 1996 at the age of 36.

1996 OLYMPIC BASKETBALL

Basketball has been an Olympic sport for men since 1936, and for women since 1976. Listed below are the gold medal-winning teams.

	Men	Women
1936	USA	–
1948	USA	–
1952	USA	–
1956	USA	–
1960	USA	–
1964	USA	–
1968	USA	–
1972	USSR	–
1976	USA	USSR
1980	Yugoslavia	USSR
1984	USA	USA
1988	USSR	USA
1992	USA	CIS
1996	USA	USA

■ *The 1996 Olympic basketball final saw the American 'Dream Team' – comprising the cream of US professional basketball – take on and defeat the Yugoslavs. The picture shows US star Shaquille O'Neal confronting a Yugoslav opponent as the ball goes out of play*

HOCKEY

Hockey is an 11-a-side ball-and-stick game played worldwide. The modern game was established in England in the 19th century. It was included in the 1908 and 1920 Olympics, and at every Olympics since 1928. For many years the sport was dominated by India and Pakistan, although they have lost their dominance to Europe and Australasia in recent years.

Hockey is played on a pitch 91 m (100 yd) long and 50–55 m (55–60 yd) wide. The ball's circumference is 224–235 mm ($8\frac{13}{16}$–$9\frac{1}{4}$ in) and it weighs 156–163 g ($5\frac{1}{2}$–$5\frac{3}{4}$ oz).

The governing body is the Fédération Internationale de Hockey (FIH), formed in 1924

FIH WORLD CUP

The Fédération Internationale de Hockey (FIH) World Cup was first contested in 1971 for men and in 1974 for women. It is now held every four years.

Men	
Pakistan	1971, 1978, 1982, 1994
Netherlands	1973, 1990
India	1975
Australia	1986

Women	
Netherlands	1974, 1978, 1983, 1986, 1990
Germany (W)	1976, 1981
Australia	1994

HURLING

Hurling is an ancient Irish stick-and-ball game. The Gaelic Athletic Association, founded in 1884, standardized the sport.

The game is played with 15 players per side. They use a stick called a hurl, which is similar to a hockey stick but is flat on both sides, rather than one.

ALL-IRELAND CHAMPIONSHIP

The major hurling tournament, the All-Ireland Championship, was inaugurated in 1887. The final is played every September in Croke Park, Dublin. The champion teams are listed below in descending order of total wins.

	Wins	
Cork	27	1890, 1892–94, 1902–03, 1919, 1926, 1928–29, 1931, 1941–44, 1946, 1952–54, 1966, 1970, 1976–78, 1984, 1986, 1990
Kilkenny	25	1904–05, 1907, 1909, 1911–13, 1922, 1932–33, 1935, 1939, 1947, 1957, 1963, 1967, 1969, 1972, 1974–75, 1979, 1982–83, 1992–93
Tipperary	24	1887, 1895–96, 1898–1900, 1906, 1908, 1916, 1925, 1930, 1937, 1945, 1949–51, 1958, 1961–62, 1964–65, 1971, 1989, 1991
Limerick	7	1897, 1918, 1921, 1934, 1936, 1940, 1973
Dublin	6	1889, 1917, 1920, 1924, 1927, 1938
Wexford	6	1910, 1955–56, 1960, 1968, 1996
Galway	4	1923, 1980, 1987–88
Offaly	3	1981, 1985, 1994
Clare	2	1914, 1995
Waterford	2	1948, 1959
Kerry	1	1891
London Irish	1	1901
Laois	1	1915

LACROSSE

Lacrosse is a stick-and-ball game, played ten-a-side for men and principally 12-a-side for women (there are considerable differences between men's and women's lacrosse).

The lacrosse men's World Championship, begun in 1967, is held every four years (from 1974), and has been dominated by the United States. The Americans have won six of the seven times it has been contested (1967, 1974, 1982, 1986, 1990 and 1994). Canada is the only other team to have won, when they beat the US in 1978.

The women's World Championship was first held in 1969 and again in 1974 and 1978; from 1982, a World Cup has been contested. The United States has won the most times, with wins in 1974, 1982, 1989 and 1993.

The playing area measures 100 x 64 m (109 x 70 yd). The ball has different specifications in the US and England. In England, it weighs 142 g (5 oz), has a circumference of 184–203 mm ($7\frac{1}{4}$–8 in) and is yellow in colour. In the US, it weighs 142–149 g (5–$5\frac{1}{4}$ oz), has a circumference of 197–203 mm ($7\frac{3}{4}$–8 in) and is coloured orange or white.

The governing body is the International Federation of Amateur Lacrosse, founded in 1928.

NETBALL

Netball, a seven-a-side no-contact sport, was invented in the US as a development from basketball. In netball players are not allowed to run with the ball, in strong contrast to the running game of basketball. It is played mainly by women, although mixed teams are becoming popular.

The court's dimensions are 30.5 x 15.2 m (100 x 50 ft). The ball has a circumference of 68–71 cm (27–28 in) and weighs 397–454 g (14–16 oz).

The governing body is the International Federation of Women's Basketball and Netball Associations (IFWBNA), founded in 1960.

WORLD CHAMPIONSHIPS

The major international netball tournament is the World Championship, held every four years since 1963. It is dominated by Australasian countries.

1963	Australia
1967	New Zealand
1971	Australia
1975	Australia
1979	Australia
1983	Australia, New Zealand, Trinidad & Tobago
1987	New Zealand
1991	Australia
1995	Australia

PELOTA VASCA (JAÏ ALAÏ)

Pelota has its origins in Italy as *longue paume*, which was introduced to France in the 13th century. The name covers a number of fast ball games played with gloves or baskets. Different varieties of pelota are played in different countries. The game is especially popular in the US and Latin America where it is known as Jaï Alaï.

The *chistera* is the curved frame attached to a player's glove. It has made possible the high speeds involved in the sport – pelota has the fastest projectile speed of any ball game, with velocities measured at 302 km/h (188 mph).

The World Championship has been held every four years since 1952, and pelota has been a demonstration sport at the Olympics on three occasions, 1924, 1968 and 1992.

The governing body is the Federaçion Internacional de Pelota Vasca, founded in 1929.

RACKETBALL

Racketball exists in American and British forms. Racquetball, the American version, has more than 10 million followers. It was first devised by Joe Sobek in 1949, when he sawed half the handle off a tennis racquet. Racketball, the British version, was introduced in 1976 by Ian Wright in Kent, and uses softer balls and a smaller, wider court.

Unsurprisingly, the US dominates the international circuit, winning the overall team championship at all seven World Championships since 1982.

The international governing body is the International Racquetball Federation, founded in 1979.

RACKETS

Rackets is an indoor ball-and-racket game which developed from various forms of handball played in the Middle Ages in England. It is played with either two or four players.

The major events are the World Championship held on a challenge basis, the World Doubles Championship, and the British Amateur and Open Championships. Rackets was held as an Olympic sport in 1908, when both singles and doubles medals went to UK competitors.

REAL TENNIS

Real tennis, the ancestor of lawn tennis, developed from *jeue de paume* ('game of the palm'), which was played in French monasteries in the 11th century. The monastic feel of the sport is reflected in the sloping roofs of the courts.

The game became very popular in France during the Renaissance, with royalty keenly participating. This link is reflected in its name – 'real' means royal.

The sport has declined in popularity since the 18th century, and is played in only five countries: England, Scotland, USA, France and Australia. There are only 30 or so courts now in use.

The World Championship is the oldest and most established in the world and is played on a challenge basis. The first world champion, the oldest recorded for any sport, was a Frenchman named Clergé, in 1740.

SHINTY

Shinty is a 12-a-side stick-and-ball game; the stick used is curved and called the caman. Its roots are based in Celtic history and legend, and it has close links with hurling. It is played today almost exclusively in the Scottish Highlands.

The pitch has a maximum length of 155 m (170 yd) and width of 73 m (80 yd); goals are 3.0 x 3.6 m (10 x 12 ft) wide. The ball is made of cork and worsted core, with a thick leather covering, and is the size of a tennis ball.

Shinty's premier competition is the annual Camanachd Association Challenge Cup, which has been won most times by Newtonmore. The governing body is the Camanachd Association, founded in 1893.

SOFTBALL

Softball was invented as the indoor version of baseball in 1887 by George Hancock in Chicago, USA. Rules were codified in 1895.

This nine-a-side bat-and-ball game, is played in the US, Canada, Japan, the Philippines, most of Latin America, New Zealand and Australia.

In contrast to baseball, the ball is pitched underarm and is released below the hip. The pitching distance is 14 m (45 ft 11 in) for men, 11.11 m (36 ft $5\frac{1}{2}$ in) for women with a distance of 18.3 m (60 ft) between bases for both. 'Slow pitch' softball is a modern variation.

AN INMATE OF FLEET PRISON, LONDON, WON THE FIRST RACKETS WORLD TITLE IN 1820

■ *Table tennis at the 1996 Olympics – the Chinese won Gold in both the men's and women's singles and doubles*

The World Championship has been held since 1965 for women, and since 1966 for men, and is competed for every four years. Other major softball events include the US National Fast Pitch Championship and the US National Slow Pitch Championship.

The governing body is the International Softball Federation, founded in 1950.

SQUASH

Squash is a ball-and-racket sport that developed at Harrow School, England, in 1817 as a way of practising rackets using a softer ball. It spread throughout Britain's colonies, and in the 20th century has become increasingly popular in other countries since the formation of the Squash Rackets Association in 1923.

The major competition is the World Open title, first contested in 1976. The first national championship was held in 1907.

The court's dimensions are 9.75 m (31 ft 11¾ in) long and 6.4 m (21 ft) wide, with a front wall height of 4.75 m (15 ft 7 in) up to the boundary line. The ball must be hit above the 'tin', which runs along the bottom of the front wall.

The governing body is the World Squash Federation, reconstituted in 1992 from the International Squash Rackets Federation, which was founded in 1967.

TABLE TENNIS

The first evidence found of table tennis is in 1880s London, when manufacturers of sports goods were selling equipment for the game. Table tennis was originally called Ping-Pong, a trade name. The early 1920s saw the use of rubber on the wooden bats, allowing spin shots, a development which rekindled interest in the sport.

The major international competition is the World Championship, first contested in 1926. The Swaythling and Marcel Corbillon Cups are held as world team championships, inaugurated in 1927 and 1934 for men and women respectively. China dominates international table tennis, with 12 wins in the Marcel Corbillon Cup.

The ball has a diameter of 37.2–38.2 mm (1.46–1.5 in) and weighs 2.4–2.53 g (0.08–0.09 oz). The table is 2.74 m (9 ft) long and 1.52 m (5 ft) wide.

The world governing body is the International Table Tennis Federation (ITTF).

VOLLEYBALL

Volleyball was invented as 'Mintonette' in 1895 by William Morgan in Massachusetts, USA, as a less strenuous alternative to basketball. The sport soon became known as volleyball, and rapidly spread throughout the world.

The European Championship, founded in 1948, was the first international competition, with the World Championship (held every four years) following a year later. The 1994 world champions were Italy (men) and Cuba (women). Volleyball has been an Olympic sport since 1964. The 1996 Olympic titles were won by the Netherlands (men) and Cuba (women).

The court measures 18 x 9 m (59 ft ¾ in x 29 ft 6⅜ in). The ball is 65–67 cm (25½–26½ in) in circumference, 250–260 g (8⅘–9⅕ oz) in weight. The net is 2.43 m (7 ft 11¾ in) high for men and 2.24 m (7 ft 4¼ in) for women.

The governing body is the International Volleyball Federation, founded in 1947.

HEATHER McKAY (1941–)

In the hot-house world of top-class squash, one name is universally praised. Australia's Heather McKay took up the sport to improve her fitness for hockey, and within two years had become Australian champion. Taking to the international circuit, she tasted defeat at the Scottish Open in 1962. And that was the last match she ever lost. McKay remained unbeaten from 1962 until her retirement in 1979. She won the British Open 16 consecutive times, from 1962 to 1977, and took 14 consecutive Australian amateur titles from 1960 to 1973 before turning professional. McKay also won the first two World Open titles in 1976 and 1979. During her unbeaten reign, she lost only three games. Despite the rise of a number of excellent squash players, she remains a towering figure, the greatest woman squash player ever.

■ *Modern volleyball is fast and furious. Ironically, the game was invented as a less strenuous alternative to basketball*

■ SOFTBALL WAS ORIGINALLY KNOWN AS 'KITTEN BALL', 'MUSH BALL' OR 'DIAMOND BALL' ■

WINTER SPORTS

- Curling is known as the 'roaring game' because of the noise made by the stone as it slides down the ice rink.
- Archaeological evidence points to the existence of skating over 2500 years ago. The Dutch popularized skating 300 years ago on frozen canals. Steel blades, which allowed precision skating, were an American invention of 1850.
- A game similar to hockey on ice was played in 16th-century Holland.
- The first skiing races were held in the 1850s and 1860s in two widely distanced countries – Norway and Australia.

BOBSLEIGH AND LUGE

Organized bobsleighing (also called bobsledding) began in Davos, Switzerland, in 1889. The international governing body is the Fédération Internationale de Bobsleigh et de Tobogganing (FIBT), founded in 1923. Luge (a type of tobogganing) has its own governing body, the Fédération Internationale de Luge (FIL).

Bobsleigh runs are between 1100 m and 1600 m (3609 to 5249 ft), while luge runs must be no less than 1000 m (3280 ft). Women are not allowed to compete in international bobsleigh, but may contest single-seater luge races. St Moritz, Switzerland, founded in 1887, is the oldest tobogganing club. It is home to the famous Cresta Run, a course of 1212 m (3977 ft) with a 157 m (514 ft) drop. Solo tobogganists on the Cresta Run may reach speeds approaching 145 km/h (90 mph).

OLYMPIC BOBSLEIGH/LUGE

The major international competitions are the World and Olympic Championships, first held in 1924. Competition is for crews of two or four, with the driver steering and the rear man operating brakes and correcting for skidding. In four-man crews, the central two riders help cornering through weight transference. In lugeing, the rider sits up or lies back, as opposed to lying face down in tobogganing. Listed below are the 1994 gold medallists in the bobsleigh and luge.

BOBSLEIGH

Two-man
Gustav Weder and Donad Acklin (Swi)

Four-man
Germany

LUGE

Men's single-seater
Georg Hackl (Ger)

Women's single-seater
Gerda Weissensteiner (Ita)

Men's two-seater
Kurt Brugger and Wilfried Huber (Ita)

CURLING

Curling resembles lawn bowls, but played on ice. Two teams of four players slide round stones weighing about 18 kg (40 lb) towards a fixed mark (the tee or button) in a centre of a circle on an ice rink. The object is for each side to get its stones closest to the centre. One of the features of the game is the way that curlers sweep the rink with brooms to smooth the ice and remove impediments to the stone's movement.

The sport is most popular in Scotland (where it probably originated in the 15th century) and Canada (where it had been introduced by Scottish colonists). It was a demonstration sport in the 1988 and 1992 Winter Olympics. The World Championships have been held each year since 1959 for men and 1979 for women. Canada dominates the international circuit, with 24 men's titles and ten women's titles.

The sport's governing body is the Royal Caledonian Curling Club, founded in 1838.

STANLEY CUP

The National Hockey League (NHL) is the premier competition in North America. The major trophy is the Stanley Cup, contested in a play-off annually by top teams. Below are the winners of the Cup, listed from most wins to least. (Note: there was no competition in 1919, and there were two competitions in 1896 and 1907. The year given is that of the second half of the season.)

	Wins	
Montreal Canadiens	24	1916, 1924, 1930–31, 1944, 1946, 1953, 1956–60, 1965–66, 1968–69, 1971, 1973, 1976–79, 1986, 1993
Toronto Maple Leafs	13	1932, 1942, 1945, 1947–49, 1951,
also won as:		1962–64, 1967
Toronto Arenas		1918
Toronto St Patricks		1922
Detroit Red Wings	8	1936–37, 1943, 1950, 1952, 1954–55, 1997
Ottawa Senators	6	1909, 1911, 1920–21, 1923, 1927
Boston Bruins	5	1929, 1939, 1941, 1970, 1972
Edmonton Oilers	5	1984–85, 1987–88, 1990
Montreal Victorias	4	1895, 1896 (Dec), 1897–88
Montreal Wanderers	4	1906–08, 1910
New York Rangers	4	1928, 1933, 1940, 1994
New York Islanders	4	1980–83
Montreal AAA	3	1893–94, 1902
Ottawa Silver Seven	3	1903–05
Chicago Black Hawks	3	1934, 1938, 1961
Winnipeg Victorias	2	1896 (Feb), 1901
Québec Bulldogs	2	1912–13
Montreal Maroons	2	1926, 1935
Philadelphia Flyers	2	1974–75
Montreal Shamrocks	2	1899, 1900
Pittsburgh Penguins	2	1991–92
Kenora Thistles	1	1907 (Jan)
Toronto Ontarios	1	1914
Vancouver Millionaires	1	1915
Seattle Metropolitans	1	1917
Victoria Cougars	1	1925
Calgary Flames	1	1989
New Jersey Devils	1	1995
Colorado Avalanche	1	1996

OLYMPIC ICE HOCKEY

The USSR has dominated Olympic competition in the post-war years. Gold medal-winning teams:

1920	Canada	1964	USSR
1924	Canada	1968	USSR
1928	Canada	1972	USSR
1932	Canada	1976	USSR
1936	Great Britain	1980	USA
1948	Canada	1984	USSR
1952	Canada	1988	USSR
1956	USSR	1992	CIS
1960	USA	1994	Sweden

ICE HOCKEY

Modern ice hockey has its roots in mid-19th century Canada, where the puck was developed. The sport still has its biggest following in North America, and also in Russia. The World and Olympic Championships have been held since 1920.

The sport's governing body is the International Ice Hockey Federation (IIHF), founded in 1908.

ICE SKATING

There are three major disciplines in skating – figure skating, ice dancing and speed skating – and all of them are Olympic events. The first international speed skating competition was in Hamburg, Germany, in 1885; the World Championship officially dates from 1893.

The governing body is the International Skating Union, founded in 1892.

OLYMPIC CHAMPIONS

Speed skating 1994 Winter Olympics. Gold medal winners (women winners are in italics):

500 m	Aleksandr Golubev (Rus) *Bonnie Blair (USA)*
1000 m	Dan Jansen (USA) *Bonnie Blair (USA)*
1500 m	Johann Olav Koss (Nor) *Emese Hunyady (Aut)*
3000 m	*Svetlana Bazhanova (Rus)*
5000 m	Johann Olav Koss (Nor) *Claudia Pechstein (Ger)*
10,000 m	Johann Olav Koss (Nor)

■ *Germany's Katarina Witt dances the can-can in 1987, the year she became world ice figure-skating champion*

OLYMPIC ICE SKATING

Figure skating, which is contested in singles and in pairs, has been part of every Winter Olympics since their inception in 1924. Ice dancing became an Olympic sport in 1976. Speed skating for men was first included in the 1924 Olympics; women had to wait until 1960. Olympic ice skating gold medallists:

	SINGLES		PAIRS
	Men	**Women**	
1908	Ulrich Salchow (Swe) Nikolay Panin (USSR) [special figures competition]	Madge Syers (GB)	Anna Hübler & Heinrich Burger (Ger)
1920	Gillis Grafström (Swe)	Magda Julin-Mauroy (Swe)	Ludowika Jakobsson & Walter Jakobsson (Fin)
1924	Gillis Grafström (Swe)	Herma Planck-Szabó (Aut)	Helene Engelmann & Alfred Berger (Aut)
1928	Gillis Grafström (Swe)	Sonja Henie (Nor)	Andreé Joly & Pierre Brunet (Fra)
1932	Karl Schäfer (Aut)	Sonja Henie (Nor)	Andreé Bruney (née Joly) & Pierre Brunet (Fra)
1936	Karl Schäfer (Aut)	Sonja Henie (Nor)	Maxi Herber & Ernst Baier (Ger)
1948	Richard Button (USA)	Barbara Ann Scott (Can)	Micheline Lannoy & Pierre Baugniet (Bel)
1952	Richard Button (USA)	Jeanette Altwegg (GB)	Ria Falk & Paul Falk (FRG)
1956	Hayes Alan Jenkins (USA)	Tenley Albright (USA)	Elisabeth Schwarz & Kurt Oppelt (Aut)
1960	David Jenkins (USA)	Carol Heiss (USA)	Barbara Wagner & Robert Paul (Can)
1964	Manfred Schnelldorfer (FRG)	Sjoukje Dijkstra (Neths)	Lyudmila Belousova & Oleg Protopopov (USSR)
1968	Wolfgang Schwarz (Aut)	Peggy Fleming (USA)	Lyudmila Belousova & Oleg Protopopov (USSR)
1972	Ondrej Nepela (Cze)	Beatrix Schuba (Aut)	Irina Rodnina & Aleksey Ulanov (USSR)
1976	John Curry (GB)	Dorothy Hamill (USA)	Irina Rodnina & Aleksandr Zaitsev (USSR)
1980	Robin Cousins (GB)	Anett Pötzsch (GDR)	Irina Rodnina & Aleksandr Zaitsev (USSR)
1984	Scott Hamilton (USA)	Katarina Witt (GDR)	Yelena Valova & Oleg Vasilyev (USSR)
1988	Brian Boitano (USA)	Katarina Witt (GDR)	Yekaterina Gordeyeva & Sergey Grinkov (USSR)
1992	Viktor Petrenko (Ukr)	Kristi Yamaguchi (USA)	Natalya Mishkutienok & Artur Dmitriyev (CIS)
1994	Aleksey Urmanov (Rus)	Oksana Bayul (Ukr)	Yekaterina Gordeyeva & Sergey Grinkov (Rus)

ICE DANCE

1976	Lyudmila Pakhhomova & Aleksandr Gorshkov (USSR)
1980	Natalya Linichuk & Gennadiy Karponosov (USSR)
1984	Jayne Torvill & Christopher Dean (GB)
1988	Natalya Bestemianova & Andrey Bukin (USSR)
1992	Marina Klimova & Sergey Ponomarenko (CIS)
1994	Oksana Gritschuk & Yevgeniy Platov (Rus)

VRENI SCHNEIDER (1964–)

Vreni Schneider of Switzerland dominated Alpine skiing in the late 1980s and early 1990s. She holds the record for the most women's Alpine skiing Olympic gold medals: she won the giant slalom and slalom golds at Calgary in 1988, and gold at the slalom in 1994 at Lillehammer. Two other medals (a bronze and a silver) make her the most successful skier in Olympic history. As well as the Olympics, she dominated the World Cup. By the end of the 1995 season, she had accumulated a total of 55 World Cup victories, including the overall title in 1989, 1994 and 1995. In the 1988–89 season, she won a record 14 World Cup races, including all seven slalom. Schneider, who retired in 1995, will be remembered as one of the greatest Alpine skiers.

SKIING

Skiing has ancient origins – a ski dating from about 2500 BC has been found in Sweden, and there are chronicles of primitive skiing in ancient Russian and Scandinavian literature. Modern skiing developed mainly in Norway in the mid-19th century.

Skiing has developed into two main disciplines, Alpine and Nordic. Alpine is raced on prepared downhill slopes. Nordic skiing involves either cross-country or jumping. The Alpine World Championship dates from 1931, and the World Cup is held annually for the best skiers in Alpine and Nordic events.

The governing body is the International Ski Federation (FIS), founded in 1924.

Snowboarding (a form of skateboarding on snow) and freestyle skiing (acrobatic skiing) have become very popular in recent years. In freestyle skiing, there are three internationally recognised activities: aerials, ballet and moguls. The freestyle skiing World Cup has been held since 1980, and the World Championship began in 1986.

■ *Alberto Tomba of Italy, winner of the 1995 Alpine skiing World Cup, goes for broke during the 1997 Cup. Despite Tomba's best efforts, Frenchman Luc Alphand was the eventual winner*

ALPINE SKIING WORLD CUP

The World Cup has been contested annually since 1967 over a series of Alpine events. The overall winners are listed below.

	Men	Women
1967	Jean-Claude Killy (Fra)	Nancy Greene (Can)
1968	Jean-Claude Killy (Fra)	Nancy Greene (Can)
1969	Karl Schranz (Aut)	Gertrud Gabi (Aut)
1970	Karl Schranz (Aut)	Michèle Jacot (Fra)
1971	Gustavo Thoeni (Ita)	Annemarie Moser-Pröll (Aut)
1972	Gustavo Thoeni (Ita)	Annemarie Moser-Pröll (Aut)
1973	Gustavo Thoeni (Ita)	Annemarie Moser-Pröll (Aut)
1974	Piero Gros (Ita)	Annemarie Moser-Pröll (Aut)
1975	Gustavo Thoeni (Ita)	Annemarie Moser-Pröll (Aut)
1976	Ingemar Stenmark (Swe)	Rosi Mittermaier (FRG)
1977	Ingemar Stenmark (Swe)	Lise-Marie Morerod (Swi)
1978	Ingemar Stenmark (Swe)	Hanni Wenzel (Lie)
1979	Peter Lüscher (Swi)	Annemarie Moser-Pröll (Aut)
1980	Andreas Wenzel (Lie)	Hanni Wenzel (Lie)
1981	Phil Mahre (USA)	Marie-Thérèse Nadig (Swi)
1982	Phil Mahre (USA)	Erika Hess (Swi)
1983	Phil Mahre (USA)	Tamara McKinney (USA)
1984	Pirmin Zurbriggen (Swi)	Erika Hess (Swi)
1985	Marc Girardelli (Lux)	Michela Figini (Swi)
1986	Marc Girardelli (Lux)	Maria Walliser (Swi)
1987	Pirmin Zurbriggen (Swi)	Maria Walliser (Swi)
1988	Pirmin Zurbriggen (Swi)	Michela Figini (Swi)
1989	Marc Girardelli (Lux)	Vreni Schneider (Swi)
1990	Pirmin Zurbriggen (Swi)	Petra Kronberger (Aut)
1991	Marc Girardelli (Lux)	Petra Kronberger (Aut)
1992	Paul Accola (Swi)	Petra Kronberger (Aut)
1993	Marc Girardelli (Lux)	Anita Wachter (Aut)
1994	Kjetil Andre Aamodt (Nor)	Vreni Schneider (Swi)
1995	Alberto Tomba (Ita)	Vreni Schneider (Swi)
1996	Lasse Kjus (Nor)	Katja Seizinger (Ger)
1997	Luc Alphand (Fra)	Pernilla Wiberg (Swe)

WATER SPORTS

- Although steamboat races date from 1827, and petrol engine races from 1865, the first powerboat racing began at the turn of the century.
- The first recorded yacht race was for a £100 wager between King Charles II and his brother, the Duke of York, raced on the Thames in 1661.
- Canoeing as a sport is credited to James MacGregor, founder of the Royal Canoe Club in Surrey, England, in 1866.

■ *The Czech Olympic duo, Miroslav Sinek and Jiri Rohan, show that teamwork is the key to successful kayaking*

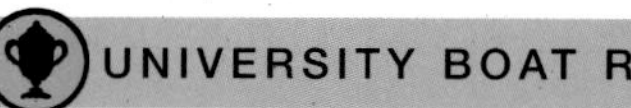

UNIVERSITY BOAT RACE

The annual Boat Race between the Universities of Oxford and Cambridge was first contested in 1829. The event arose after a challenge from the Cambridge Boat Club to its Oxford counterpart for a race of supremacy, to be held on the Thames. It was an immediate popular success, contemporary reports suggesting that there may have been more than 20,000 spectators to see Oxford triumph. The race is currently held from Putney to Mortlake on the Thames, and is 6779 m (4 miles, 374 yards) in length. To 1997, there have been 143 races, Cambridge leading the series with 74 wins to Oxford's 68. In 1849, there were two races, and in 1877 the first and only dead-heat was declared – a decision still disputed today.

Cambridge wins: 1836, 1839–41, 1845–46, 1849, 1856, 1858, 1860, 1870–74, 1876, 1879, 1884, 1886–89, 1899–1900, 1902–04, 1906–08, 1914, 1920–22, 1924–36, 1939, 1947–51, 1953, 1955–58, 1961–62, 1964, 1968–73, 1975, 1986, 1993–97

Oxford wins: 1829, 1842, 1849, 1852, 1854, 1857, 1859, 1861–69, 1875, 1878, 1880–83, 1885, 1890–98, 1901, 1905, 1909–13, 1923, 1937–38, 1946, 1952, 1954, 1959–60, 1963, 1965–67, 1974, 1976–85, 1987–92

BOARDSAILING (WINDSURFING)

Boardsailing (often called by the trade name Windsurfing) was pioneered by Henry Hoyle Schweitzer and Jim Drake in California in 1968. The sport quickly gained in popularity and the first World Championship was held in 1973. Since 1984 boardsailing has been included in the Olympics as part of the yachting events.

1996 OLYMPIC CANOEING

Canoeing has been an Olympic sport since 1936, with nine events for men at 500 m and 1000 m, and three for women over 500 m. Since 1992, there has also been a slalom competition, which has three events for men and one for women. Listed below are the 1996 Olympic gold medallists.

Men		
Slalom	K1	Oliver Fix (Ger)
Slalom	C1	Michal Martikan (Slo)
Slalom	C2	Frank Addison & Wilfrid Forgues (Fra)
500 m	K1	Antonio Rossi (Ita)
500 m	K2	Kay Bluhm & Torsten Gutsch (Ger)
500 m	C1	Martin Doktor (Cze)
500 m	C2	Csaba Horvath & Gyorgy Kolonics (Hun)
1000 m	K1	Knut Holmann (Nor)
1000 m	K2	Antonio Rossi & Daniele Scarpa (Ita)
1000 m	K4	Germany
1000 m	C1	Martin Doktor (Cze)
1000 m	C2	Andreas Dittmer & Gunar Kirchbach (Ger)
Women		
Slalom	K1	Stepana Hilgertova (Cze)
500 m	K1	Rita Koban (Hun)
500 m	K2	Agneta Andersson & Susanne Gunnarsson (Swe)
500 m	K4	Germany

CANOEING

Modern canoeing is practised in two different styles: the kayak and the Canadian canoe. In kayaking, the paddler sits in a forward-facing position; the paddle has a blade at each end. In Canadian canoes, the canoeist half-kneels in the boat, and uses single-bladed paddles.

Races are designated with a C for Canadian canoes and a K for kayaks, followed by a number signifying the number of canoeists in the vessel. Thus K1 indicates a one-person kayak, while C2 denotes a two-person Canadian canoe.

The sport's governing body is the International Canoe Federation, founded in 1924.

POWERBOAT RACING

The world's most prestigious powerboating event, the Harmsworth Trophy, was inaugurated in 1903 by the British publisher Sir Alfred Harmsworth. The American Power Boat Association (APBA) Gold Cup has been held since 1904, and is contested on an annual basis. Other competitions are held for circuits and shorter courses, and an offshore competition has been held since 1958. Speed records are also recognized for a number of different boat categories.

ROWING

Rowing dates from classical antiquity – the Roman poet Virgil referred to it in the *Aeneid*. The modern sport has its roots in the Doggett's Coat and Badge, a sculling race established in 1715 by the Irish comedian Thomas Doggett. The race was first rowed from London Bridge to Chelsea on London's River Thames, and is still contested annually.

The European Championship, the first international meeting of importance, was first held in 1893. The first World Championship was held at Lucerne, Switzerland, in 1962.

The sport's international governing body is the Fédération Internationale de Sociétés d'Aviron, founded in 1892.

1996 OLYMPIC ROWING

Rowing has been a feature of the Olympics since 1900 (1976 for women). Current events include rowing, and sculling (in which an oarsman pulls two short-handled oars). The standard Olympic course is 2000 m in length. Listed below are the 1996 Olympic gold medallists.

	Men	Women
Single sculls	Xeno Mueller (Swi)	Yekaterina Khodotvich (Brs)
Double sculls	Davide Tizzano & Agostino Abbagnale (Ita)	Marnie McBean & Kathleen Heddle (Can)
Double sculls (lightweight)	Markus Gier & Michael Gier (Swi)	Constanta Burcia & Camelia Macoviciuc (Rom)
Quad sculls	Germany	Germany
Coxless pairs	Steven Redgrave & Matthew Pinsent (GB)	Megan Still & Kate Slatter (Aus)
Coxless fours	Australia	–
Coxless fours (lightweight)	Denmark	
Eights	Netherlands	Romania

SURFING

The first reference to surfing is from Hawaii in 1779, where it was a traditional pastime. The sport spread to regions with suitable surf, notably California and Australia. Hollow boards were introduced in 1929 to replace the heavy, solid-wood planks previously used. The World Amateur Championship, now held every two years, was initiated in 1964. The World Professional Championship, first held in 1970 for men and 1977 for women, is held throughout the year at worldwide venues.

1996 OLYMPIC YACHTING

There were eight classes of boat at the 1996 Olympics, two (470 and Mistral) having separate events for men and women. Listed below are the gold medallists of 1996.

Class	Winner
Laser	Robert Scheidt (Bra)
Tornado	Jose Luis Ballester & Fernando Leon (Spa)
Soling	Germany
Star	Torben Grael & Marcelo Ferreira (Bra)
Finn	Mateusz Kusznierewicz (Pol)
Europe	Kristine Roug (Den)
470 (Men)	Yevhen Braslavets & Igor Matviyenko (Ukr)
470 (Women)	Begona Via Dufresne & Theresa Zabell (Spa)
Mistral (Men)	Nikolaos Kaklamanakis (Gre)
Mistral (Women)	Lee Lai Shan (HK)

WATER SKIING

Modern water skiing was pioneered by Ralph Samuelson on Lake Pepin, Minnesota, in 1922. In modern competition, water skiing has three disciplines: slalom, ski jumping and trick skiing (gymnastic feats executed at lower speeds). Competitions for speed records are also held. The main international championship is the World Championship, instituted in 1947 and held every two years. The US dominates the sport. Barefoot skiing is increasingly popular.

The world governing body is the International Water Ski Federation (IWSF).

YACHTING

Yachting originated in the Netherlands in the 16th and 17th centuries, and the first yacht club was founded in Ireland in 1720 as the Water Club (later the Royal Cork Yacht Club). The International Yacht Racing Union (IYRU) was founded in 1907.

Major yachting trophies include the America's Cup and the Admiral's Cup (an inter-nation challenge); yachting has been part of the Olympics since 1900.

STEVE REDGRAVE (1962–)

Steve Redgrave is a truly great rower. The British sportsman has won six World Championship titles and is the only oarsman in the world to have won Olympic gold on four occasions (in the coxed fours in 1984, and the coxless pairs in 1988, 1992 and 1996). He is also the only person to have won three rowing gold medals at a single Commonwealth Games (in 1986). His dominance of the coxless pairs category in the 1990s has been established in partnership with Matthew Pinsent, and in 1995 they became the first pair to break the seven-minute barrier for the Silver Goblets at Henley Royal Regatta. Redgrave is the most successful Henley competitor this century. A giant in the rowing world, Redgrave has also found success at bobsledding, and formed part of the four-man team that won the British championship in 1989. He was awarded the MBE in 1986.

■ *The Ukrainian boat, crewed by Yevhen Braslavets and Igor Matviyenko, cuts through the water to win the 1996 Olympic gold medal in the 470 class. The first Olympic regatta – which was to have been held on the Bay of Salamis, Greece, in 1896 – was cancelled due to bad weather, so records for Olympic yachting date from 1900*

AMERICA'S CUP

The America's Cup, one of sport's best-known trophies, was donated by the Royal Yacht Squadron in 1851 and was originally known as the Hundred Guinea Cup. In that year it was won as an outright prize by the US schooner *America* at Cowes, England, and later became known as the America's Cup. It was donated to the New York Yacht Club, which then offered it as a challenge trophy. Despite 24 attempts between 1870 and 1980, the Cup remained in American hands. The winning streak was finally broken in 1983 when *Australia II* beat *Liberty*, but the Cup was won back for the US in 1987 by Denis Conner in *Stars & Stripes* and retained in 1988 against *New Zealand*. This last victory was highly controversial, as the US Supreme Court ruled that the American's use of the catamaran against the challenger's monohull violated the Deed of Gift governing the race. Nevertheless, the legal wrangles eventually ended in Conner's favour in 1990. The United States defended the trophy again in 1992, but lost it in 1995 to New Zealand's *Black Magic*. The Cup will next be contested in the year 2000.

Combat Sports

- Boxing has ancient origins, but the first modern record of a boxing match is from England in 1681, when the Duke of Albemarle organized a match between his butler and butcher.
- Wrestling is one of the world's oldest sports, with organized matches taking place over 4500 years ago.
- Sumo wrestlers rarely weigh less than 130 kg. They maintain their massive bulk by consuming huge quantities of a high-protein stew called *chankonabe*.
- Dr Jigoro Kano developed the modern combat sport of judo in 1882.

BOXING

James Figg, generally regarded as the first boxing champion, set up his school of arms in England in 1719, and Jack Broughton formed the first ring rules for boxing in 1743. The modern rules of boxing were finally codified by the 8th Marquess of Queensberry in 1867.

The sport has several world governing bodies, with the two oldest being the World Boxing Council (WBC), founded in 1963, and the World Boxing Association (WBA), founded 1920. Fight regulations vary between bodies, and the situation has been complicated further by the creation of the International Boxing Federation (IBF) in 1983, and the World Boxing Organization (WBO) in 1988. Other boxing bodies have been created since then.

■ *George Foreman (left), one of boxing's greatest heavyweights, fights against Tommy Morrison at Las Vegas in 1993. Foreman was aged 44 at the time*

PROFESSIONAL BOXING

Professional boxing has four main controlling bodies, the World Boxing Council (WBC), the World Boxing Association (WBA), the International Boxing Federation (IBF) and the World Boxing Organization (WBO). Each has slightly differing regulations. Listed below are the weight categories for professional boxing as they apply to the four main bodies.

Limit in kg	lb	Weight category
48	105	Strawweight (WBC), mini-flyweight (WBA, IBF, WBO)
49	108	Light-flyweight (WBC), junior flyweight (WBA, IBF, WBO)
51	112	Flyweight
52	115	Super-flyweight (WBC), junior bantamweight (WBA, IBF, WBO)
54	118	Bantamweight
55	122	Super bantamweight (WBC), junior featherweight (WBA, IBF, WBO)
57	126	Featherweight
59	130	Super featherweight (WBC), junior lightweight (WBA, IBF, WBO)
61	135	Lightweight
64	140	Super lightweight (WBC), junior welterweight (WBA, IBF, WBO)
67	147	Welterweight
70	154	Super lightweight (WBC), junior middleweight (WBA, IBF, WBO)
73	160	Middleweight
76	168	Super middleweight
79	175	Light heavyweight
86	190	Junior heavyweight (WBO), cruiser-weight (WBC, WBA, IBF)
86+	190+	Heavyweight

AMATEUR BOXING

Amateur boxing is controlled by the Association Internationale de Boxe Amateur. There are 12 weight categories.

Limit in kg	lb	Weight category
48	106	Light flyweight
51	112	Flyweight
54	119	Bantamweight
57	126	Featherweight
60	132	Lightweight
63.5	140	Light welterweight
67	148	Welterweight
71	157	Light middleweight
75	165	Middleweight
81	179	Light heavyweight
91	201	Heavyweight
91+	201+	Super heavyweight

1996 OLYMPIC FENCING

One of the original Olympic sports, fencing is now contested in six categories. The 1996 gold medallists are listed below.

Foil	individual	Alessandro Puccini (Ita)
		Laura Badea (Rom)
	team	Russia
		Italy
Epée	individual	Aleksandr Beketov (Rus)
		Laura Flessel (Fra)
	team	Italy
		France
Sabre	individual	Stanislav Pozdnyakov (Rus)
	team	Russia

UNDISPUTED HEAVYWEIGHT BOXING CHAMPIONS

Professional boxing now has four main controlling bodies, each with its own heavyweight champion. Listed below are the heavyweight champions whose titles have been recognized by *all* major boxing bodies in existence at the time. Except where specified, all champions are American.

1882	John L. Sullivan
1892	James J. Corbett
1897	Bob Fitzsimmons (GB)
1899	James J. Jefferies
1905	Marvin Hart
1906	Tommy Burns (Can)
1908	Jack Johnson
1915	Jess Willard
1919	Jack Dempsey
1926	Gene Tunney
1930	Max Schmeling (Ger)
1932	Jack Sharkey
1933	Primo Carnera (Ita)
1934	Max Baer
1935	James J. Braddock
1937	Joe Louis
1949	Ezzard Charles
1951	Jersey Joe Walcott
1952	Rocky Marciano
1956	Floyd Patterson
1959	Ingemar Johansson (Swe)
1960	Floyd Paterson
1962	Sonny Liston
1964	Cassius Clay
1970	Joe Frazier
1973	George Foreman
1974	Muhammad Ali
1978	Leon Spinks
1987	Mike Tyson

■ THE WORD 'KARATE' IS JAPANESE FOR 'EMPTY HAND' ■ THE LONGEST BAR-KNUCKLE

■ *Top-class fencing requires lightning-fast reactions*

FENCING

Fencing developed from duelling in the Middle Ages. Modern fencing uses three types of sword in its disciplines: the foil, épée and sabre.

The foil (maximum weight 500 g/17.6 oz), introduced in the 17th century, is the oldest; only the trunk of the fencer's body is used as a target when the foil is used. The épée (weight 770 g/27.2 oz), introduced in the mid-19th century, allows the whole body as a target. The sabre (weight 500 g/17.6 oz) was introduced in the late 19th century and has cutting edges on both sides of the blade; the whole body from the waist upwards counts as a target and points can be scored with the blade's edge. With the sabre and the foil, the hit must follow the prescribed movements known as the 'phrase'.

Fencing has been a part of every modern Olympics, and a World Championship has been contested annually since 1921. Fencing's world governing body is the Fédération Internationale d'Escrime, founded in 1913.

JUDO

Judo developed from Japanese martial arts, especially from schools of ju-jitsu. The modern sport relies less on brute force and more on skill and speed. Throws, joint locks, immobilizations and certain pressures on the neck can score points.

Judo status is divided into student (Kyu) and master (Dan) grades. There are 12 Dan grades, although the 12th has only been awarded to Jigoro Kano, the Shihan (doctor). There are four colour grades for Dan: black for first to fifth Dan, red and white for sixth to eighth Dan, red for ninth to eleventh Dan, and white for Dan 12.

The major judo competition is the World Championship, held every two years since 1956 for men and from 1980 for women. The international regulatory body is the International Judo Federation, founded in 1951.

1996 OLYMPIC JUDO

Judo has been part of the Olympics since 1964, except for the 1968 Games. The 1996 gold medallists are listed below.

Weight division (kg)	Men
60	Tadahiro Nomura (Jap)
65	Udo Quellmalz (Ger)
71	Kenzo Nakamura (Jap)
78	Djamel Bouras (Fra)
86	Jeon Ki-young (SKo)
95	Pawel Nastula (Pol)
95+	David Douillet (Fra)
	Women
48	Kye Sun (NKo)
52	Marie-Claire Restoux (Fra)
56	Driulis Gonzalez (Cub)
61	Yuko Emoto (Jap)
66	Cho Min-sun (SKo)
72	Ulla Werbrouck (Bel)
72+	Sum Fuming (Chn)

KARATE

Funakoshi Gichin introduced the martial art of Tang Hand to Japan from Okinawa in the 1920s, and gave it the name karate, meaning 'empty hand'. Karate spread to the Western world in the 1950s, and the first World Championship was held in 1980. The championship now has combat and sequence events, the latter being a non-tactile performance of routines.

Karate, as a modern discipline, has five major styles, each placing differing importance on technique, speed and power. These are Shotokan, Wado-ryu, Gojo-ryu, Shito-ryu and Kyokushinkai.

TAEKWONDO

The Korean martial art, taekwondo, was officially recognized as part of Korean culture and tradition in 1955, and the World Taekwondo Federation governs the international sport.

Taekwondo has spread internationally, with an estimated 22 million adherents worldwide. The World Championship has been held every two years since 1973. The sport was popular enough to be a demonstration event at the 1988 and 1992 Olympic Games.

WRESTLING

There are two principal styles of wrestling – freestyle and the classical Greco-Roman. The latter, most popular in Europe, differs from freestyle in that it does not permit the use of legs or holds below the waist. The International Amateur Wrestling Association (FILA) was founded in 1912.

Other forms of wrestling include sambo and sumo. Sambo is similar to judo and played mainly in the former Soviet Union. In sumo wrestling, sheer weight and bulk are used to force the opponent out of the ring using any holds. A national sport in Japan, sumo wrestling dates back to 23 BC.

■ *On his way to a record third Olympic gold medal, the Russian freestyle wrestler, Aleksandr Karelin (left), goes head-to-head with his American opponent*

MUHAMMAD ALI (1942–)

'Float like a butterfly, sting like a bee' perfectly describes Muhammad Ali's style in the ring. The American heavyweight boxer (born Cassius Clay) is one of the most famous sportsmen ever, his fights part of sporting legend. Ali rose in the international arena by winning the light heavyweight gold medal at the Rome Olympics in 1960. Four years later, his defeat of Sonny Liston earned him the heavyweight crown. He remained unbeaten in the 1960s, but was stripped of his title after refusing US military service as a conscientious objector. He re-entered boxing in 1970, and finally regained the heavyweight title in 1974, in the famous 'Rumble in the Jungle' fight against George Foreman in Zäire (now The Congo). He again regained the title in 1978 after losing it to Leon Spinks, becoming the first boxer to hold the heavyweight crown on three separate occasions. In total, he won 22 world title fights, and lost three. His final bout was in 1982. In later years, his bravery in facing the cruelly debilitating Parkinson's disease has earned him the respect and love of many, including those who dislike boxing. Many will agree with his typically immodest declaration: 'I am the greatest'.

1996 OLYMPIC WRESTLING

Wrestling has been a part of the Olympics since the modern Games were held for the first time, in 1896. Only men compete at present, and there are ten weight divisions in both the freestyle and Greco-Roman forms. Listed below are the 1996 Olympic gold medallists.

Weight division (kg)	Freestyle	Greco-Roman
48	Kim Il (NKo)	Sim Kwon-ho (SKo)
52	Valentin Dimitrov Jordanov (Bul)	Armen Nazaryan (Arm)
57	Kendall Cross (USA)	Yuri Melnichenko (Kaz)
62	Tom Brands (USA)	Wlodzimierz Zawadski (Pol)
68	Vadim Bogiyev (Rus)	Ryszard Wolny (Pol)
74	Buvaysa Saytyev (Rus)	Feliberto Ascuy Aguilera (Cub)
82	Khadzhimurad Magomedov (Rus)	Hamza Yerlikiya (Tur)
90	Rasull Khadem Azghadi (Irn)	Vyacheslav Oleynyk (Ukr)
100	Kurt Angel (USA)	Andrzej Wronski (Pol)
130	Mahmut Demir (Tur)	Aleksandr Karelin (Rus)

Motor Sports

- Motor racing began soon after the car was invented. The first known race took place in Wisconsin, USA, in 1878.
- The first Formula One World Championship was won by Italy's Giuseppe Farina in 1950. The Manufacturers' Championship started in 1958, the first winner being Vanwall.
- The first known motorcycle race for two-wheeled vehicles took place in 1897 at Richmond, London.
- Dragsters reach extremely high speeds by the end of their runs; 506 km/h is the record, set in 1994.

MOTOR RACING

Professional motor racing embraces a range of different competitions, distinguished from each other by vehicle type or vehicle specifications, for example the engine capacity.

Competitions include Indy Car racing, the Indianapolis 500, the Le Mans 24-Hour race (a day-long race for touring cars), and Formulas One, Two and Three.

Also popular are rally-driving on public roads over several thousands of kilometres, and drag racing, a test of sheer acceleration for two cars (or bikes) over a distance of 402.3 m (0.25 mi).

The Fédération Internationale de l'Automobile is Grand Prix racing's governing body.

■ *The Formula One racing car is a highly specialized speed machine. Cars may reach speeds of more than 250 km/h (160 mph) in the straights. Despite the latest safety devices fitted to the cars, fatalities still occur*

■ *Thousands of spectators line the winding route of the Monaco Grand Prix, probably the most glamorous car race in the world. It was first held in 1929, and is now watched on television in millions of homes the world over*

FORMULA ONE

The highest level of motor racing is Formula One, held over a series of Grand Prix races at various international circuits, with each race about 322 km (200 mi) long.

Year	Winner
1950	Giuseppe Farina (Ita)
1951	Juan Manuel Fangio (Arg)
1952	Alberto Ascari (Ita)
1953	Alberto Ascari (Ita)
1954	Juan Manuel Fangio (Arg)
1955	Juan Manuel Fangio (Arg)
1956	Juan Manuel Fangio (Arg)
1957	Juan Manuel Fangio (Arg)
1958	Mike Hawthorn (GB)
1959	Jack Brabham (Aus)
1960	Jack Brabham (Aus)
1961	Phil Hill (USA)
1962	Graham Hill (GB)
1963	Jim Clark (GB)
1964	John Surtees (GB)
1965	Jim Clark (GB)
1966	Jack Brabham (Aus)
1967	Denny Hulme (NZ)
1968	Graham Hill (GB)
1969	Jackie Stewart (GB)
1970	Jochen Rindt (Aut)
1971	Jackie Stewart (GB)
1972	Emerson Fittipaldi (Bra)
1973	Jackie Stewart (GB)
1974	Emerson Fittipaldi (Bra)
1975	Niki Lauda (Aut)
1976	James Hunt (GB)
1977	Niki Lauda (Aut)
1978	Mario Andretti (USA)
1979	Jody Scheckter (SA)
1980	Alan Jones (Aus)
1981	Nelson Piquet (Bra)
1982	Keke Rosberg (Fin)
1983	Nelson Pique (Bra)
1984	Niki Lauda (Aut)
1985	Alain Prost (Fra)
1986	Alain Prost (Fra)
1987	Nelson Piquet (Bra)
1988	Ayrton Senna (Bra)
1989	Alain Prost (Fra)
1990	Ayrton Senna (Bra)
1991	Ayrton Senna (Bra)
1992	Nigel Mansell (GB)
1993	Alain Prost (Fra)
1994	Michael Schumacher (Ger)
1995	Michael Schumacher (Ger)
1996	Damon Hill (GB)

INDY CAR RACING

The Indy-car racing championship was known as the AAA National Championship from 1909–55, the United States Auto Club (USAC) National Championship from 1956–79, and the PPG IndyCar World Series from 1979.

1909	George Robertson
1910	Ray Harroun
1911	Ralph Mulford
1912	Ralph DePalma
1913	Earl Cooper
1914	Ralph DePalma
1915	Earl Cooper
1916	Dario Resta
1917	Earl Cooper
1918	Ralph Mulford
1919	Howard Wilcox
1920	Tommy Milton
1921	Tommy Milton
1922	Jimmy Murphy
1923	Eddie Hearne
1924	Jimmy Murphy
1925	Peter DePaolo
1926	Harry Hartz
1927	Peter DePaolo
1928	Louie Meyer
1929	Louie Meyer
1930	Billy Arnold
1931	Louis Schneider
1932	Bob Carey
1933	Louie Meyer
1934	Bill Cummings
1935	Kelly Petillo
1936	Mauri Rose
1937	Wilbur Shaw
1938	Floyd Roberts
1939	Wilbur Shaw
1940	Rex Mays
1941	Rex Mays
1942–45	No racing
1946	Ted Horn
1947	Ted Horn
1948	Ted Horn
1949	Johnny Parsons
1950	Henry Banks
1951	Tony Bettenhausen, Sr
1952	Chuck Stevenson
1953	Sam Hanks
1954	Jimmy Bryan
1955	Bob Swikert
1956	Jimmy Bryan
1957	Jimmy Bryan
1958	Tony Bettenhausen, Sr
1959	Rodger Ward
1960	A.J. Foyt
1961	A.J. Foyt
1962	Rodger Ward
1963	A.J. Foyt
1964	A.J. Foyt
1965	Mario Andretti
1966	Mario Andretti
1967	A.J. Foyt
1968	Bobby Unser
1969	Mario Andretti
1970	Al Unser
1971	Joe Leonard
1972	Joe Leonard
1973	Roger McCluskey
1974	Bobby Unser
1975	A.J. Foyt
1976	Gordon Johncock
1977	Tom Sneva
1978	Tom Sneva
1979*	A.J. Foyt (USAC)
	Rick Mears (CART)
1980	Johnny Rutherford
1981	Rick Mears
1982	Rick Mears
1983	Al Unser
1984	Mario Andretti
1985	Al Unser
1986	Bobby Rahal
1987	Bobby Rahal
1988	Danny Sullivan
1989	Emerson Fittipaldi
1990	Al Unser, Jr
1991	Michael Andretti
1992	Bobby Rahal
1993	Nigel Mansell
1994	Al Unser, Jr
1995	Jacques Villeneuve
1996	Jimmy Vasser

*two rival organisations each held a championship in 1979, resulting in two champions for that year

MOTORCYCLE WORLD CHAMPIONSHIP

The World Championship has been raced annually since 1949. The five classes sanctioned by the governing body for the sport, the Fédération Internationale Motocycliste, are: 50 cc, 125 cc, 250 cc, 500 cc and sidecars. The most prestigious is the 500 cc class, and the winners for this class are listed below.

1949	Leslie Graham (GB)
1950	Umberto Masetti (Ita)
1951	Geoff Duke (GB)
1952	Umberto Masetti (Ita)
1953	Geoff Duke (GB)
1954	Geoff Duke (GB)
1955	Geoff Duke (GB)
1956	John Surtees (GB)
1957	Libero Liberati (Ita)
1958	John Surtees (GB)
1959	John Surtees (GB)
1960	John Surtees (GB)
1961	Gary Hocking (Rho)
1962	Mike Hailwood (GB)
1963	Mike Hailwood (GB)
1964	Mike Hailwood (GB)
1965	Giacomo Agostini (Ita)
1966	Giacomo Agostini (Ita)
1967	Giacomo Agostini (Ita)
1968	Giacomo Agostini (Ita)
1969	Giacomo Agostini (Ita)
1970	Giacomo Agostini (Ita)
1971	Giacomo Agostini (Ita)
1972	Giacomo Agostini (Ita)
1973	Phil Read (GB)
1974	Phil Read (GB)
1975	Giacomo Agostini (Ita)
1976	Barry Sheene (GB)
1977	Barry Sheene (GB)
1978	Kenny Roberts (USA)
1979	Kenny Roberts (USA)
1980	Kenny Roberts (USA)
1981	Marco Lucchinelli (Ita)
1982	Franco Uncini (Ita)
1983	Freddie Spenser (USA)
1984	Eddie Lawson (USA)
1985	Freddie Spenser (USA)
1986	Eddie Lawson (USA)
1987	Wayne Gardner (Aus)
1988	Eddie Lawson (USA)
1989	Eddie Lawson (USA)
1990	Wayne Rainey (USA)
1991	Wayne Rainey (USA)
1992	Wayne Rainey (USA)
1993	Kevin Schwantz (USA)
1994	Michael Doohan (Aus)
1995	Michael Doohan (Aus)
1996	Michael Doohan (Aus)

MOTORCYCLE RACING

There are several different forms of motorcycle racing. Circuit racing takes place on purpose-built tracks, and the World Championship (raced in various classes) is the peak competition. Road racing is held over open roads, the most important series being the Isle of Man TT races (Auto-Cycle Union Tourist Trophy), first held in 1907 and now run on the 60.72 km (37.73 mi) mountain circuit. Motocross, or scrambling, is carried out over rough terrain, including drops, turns and climbs. Speedway is held on oval-shaped dirt tracks.

AYRTON SENNA (1960–94)

Brazilian Ayrton Senna is generally regarded as one of Formula One's greatest-ever drivers. His dominating style developed from earlier successes in the world karting championships, Formula Ford and Formula Three. He made an impressive debut in Formula One in 1984, coming second at Monaco and third in Portugal. In 1985, driving with Lotus, he won his first Grand Prix. Senna gradually moved up the championship table in 1986 and 1987, and became Formula One world champion with the McLaren team in 1988. He took motor racing's most prestigious trophy again in 1990 and 1991. His career was cut short when he was killed at the Italian Grand Prix at Imola in May 1994. His death sent shockwaves through the sporting world, and sent Brazil into national mourning. The fatality (along with Roland Ratzenberger's the day before) resulted in an overhaul of Formula One's safety guidelines. Senna, who held the world record for pole positions (65 in 161 races with 41 wins), was a strong figure, whose aggressive driving style brought him kudos as well as controversy.

SPEEDWAY

Speedway motorcycle competitions involve four riders competing in each heat over four laps of a dirt track. This type of racing has its origins in 1902 in the United States. The sport developed and by 1923 the first 'short track' races were being held in Australia.

The World Championship has been held on an annual basis since 1936. The Long Track championship was inaugurated in 1971.

Ice speedway, in which the bikes have spiked wheels, began its World Championship in 1966 with an individual competition; in 1979 a team competition was added.

■ *Australia's Michael Doohan (far left), has won the motorcycle 500 cc World Championship three times – 1994, 1995 and 1996. He has achieved his success riding for the Honda team*

Racing and Equestrian Sports

- The first recorded horseback races were staged in 648 BC by the Greeks at the 33rd Ancient Olympiad.
- The sulky, the light, two-wheeled cart used in harness racing, first appeared in 1829.
- Horsemanship schools were established in Renaissance Europe, mainly in France and Italy.

■ Olympic show-jumping champion, Ulrich Kirchhoff

■ These American pacers are part of the multimillion-dollar harness racing industries of North America and Australia

1996 OLYMPIC CHAMPIONS

Dressage, show-jumping and the three-day event have been contested at the Olympics since 1912, and horses and riders compete both individually and as national teams. Listed below are the 1996 Olympic equestrian gold medallists.

		Points
Individual		
Show jumping	Ulrich Kirchhoff (Ger) *Jus de Pommes*	1.0
Three-day event	Blyth Tait (NZ) *Ready Teddy*	56.8
Dressage	Isabell Werth (Ger) *Gigolo*	235.09
Team		
Show jumping	Germany	1.75
Three-day event	Australia	203.85
Dressage	Germany	5,553

EQUESTRIANISM

Equestrian events are held in six disciplines: dressage, show jumping, the three-day event, carriage driving, endurance riding and vaulting.

Dressage is a test of a rider's ability to control a horse through various manoeuvres within an area of 60 x 20 m (66 x 22 yd). In show jumping, riders jump a set course of fences, and faults are incurred for imperfections in the performance: four faults for knocking a fence down or landing one or more feet in the water, eight for a fall, three for a first refusal, and six then elimination for second and third refusals. The three-day event encompasses dressage, cross country and jumping. Carriage driving consists of four horses or pairs being tested for presentation and dressage, endurance marathon and obstacle driving. Endurance riding and vaulting are comparatively recent disciplines.

The World Equestrian Games are held every four years. The governing body is the Fédération Equestre Internationale, founded in 1921.

HARNESS RACING

In harness racing, a horse pulls a two-wheeled cart, the sulky. Horses may either trot, moving their legs in diagonal pairs, or pace, moving fore and hind legs on one side simultaneously. Race tracks are oval in shape, 800–1600 m (0.5–1 mi) in circumference, and have a dirt surface.

The sport is most popular in North America, where important races include the Hambletonian and the Little Brown Jug, and Australia, where the most significant race is the Inter-Dominion Championship. The North American governing body is the National Trotting Association.

HORSE RACING

Horse racing dates back thousands of years, although the first regular race meets did not take place until the 12th century, at Smithfield, London.

Races can be run either along a flat course, or as steeplechases, in which fences are jumped. Steeplechases and hurdle races (a less severe version of steeplechasing) are run over distances of 3200 m (2 mi) or more, with at least one ditch and six birch fences for every 1600 m (1 mi). Famous annual horse races include the Prix de l'Arc de Triomphe, the Derby, the Grand National, the Cheltenham Gold Cup and the Kentucky Derby.

POLO

Polo is an ancient game, originating in India over 5000 years ago. It was introduced into Britain in 1869, and the USA in 1876, and now has a strong following in Argentina and the United States.

Polo is played on the largest pitch of any sport, with a maximum length of 274 m (300 yd), and a maximum width of 182 m (200 yd) without boards, or 146 m (160 yd) with boards. There are four players per team, and each is often awarded a handicap based on goals up to a maximum of ten.

Major international polo contests include the Westchester Cup and the Cup of the Americas. The governing body is the Hurlingham Polo Association.

■ Equestrian dressage events test the horse's obedience and the rider's control

■ Two polo players in the 1995 British Open at Cowdray Park

■ *Horses breaking from the starting gate at the 1996 Kentucky Derby. The field is limited to three-year-olds*

RED RUM (1965–95)

Certain successful racehorses inspire more than just loyalty from a few punters; they come to be loved by the general public. Red Rum was such a horse, becoming one of the most famous English public personalities of his time – a racehorse with an incredible track record and an enormous following. He showed promise in his first season in 1970–71, and in 1972 was sold by Mrs Lurline Brotherton to Noel le Mare for 6000 guineas. Trained by Donald 'Ginger' McCain on the sands of Southport, north-west England, he had five successive wins before running his first Grand National. He won the National a total of three times, in 1973, 1974 and 1977, and came second in 1975 and 1976. These amazing achievements may never be equalled. Public love for him led to a life-size statue of him being unveiled at Aintree in 1988. When he died seven years later, he was given the ultimate accolade by being buried at the finishing post at the course dominated by him for so long.

PRIX DE L'ARC DE TRIOMPHE

Europe's most prestigious flat race, the Prix de l'Arc de Triomphe, has been held annually since 1920. It is run at Longchamp, Paris, over 2400 m (about 1 mi 4 furlongs). Winners since 1980:

1980	*Detroit*	Pat Eddery
1981	*Gold River*	Gary Moore
1982	*Akiyda*	Yves Saint-Martin
1983	*All Along*	Walter Swinburn
1984	*Sagace*	Yves Saint-Martin
1985	*Rainbow Quest*	Pat Eddery
1986	*Dancing Brave*	Pat Eddery
1987	*Trempolino*	Pat Eddery
1988	*Tony Bin*	John Reid
1989	*Carroll House*	Michael Kinane
1990	*Saumarez*	Gerald Mossé
1991	*Suave Dancer*	Cash Asmussen
1992	*Subotica*	Thierry Jarnet
1993	*Urban Sea*	Eric Saint-Martin
1994	*Carnegie*	Thierry Jarnet
1995	*Lammtarra*	Frankie Dettori
1996	*Helissio*	Olivier Peslier

KENTUCKY DERBY

Raced annually at Churchill Downs, Louisville, over 2012 m (1 mile 2 furlongs), the Kentucky Derby is perhaps the most famous of the American Triple Crown races. Winners since 1980:

1980	*Genuine Risk*	Jacinto Vasquez
1981	*Pleasant Colony*	Jorge Velasquez
1982	*Gato Del Sol*	Eddie Delahoussaye
1983	*Sunny's Halo*	Eddie Delahoussaye
1984	*Swale*	Laffit Pincay, Jr
1985	*Spend a Buck*	Angel Cordero, Jr
1986	*Ferdinand*	Billie Shoemaker
1987	*Alysheba*	Chris McCarron
1988	*Winning Colors*	Gary Stevens
1989	*Sunday Silence*	Pat Valenzuela
1990	*Unbridled*	Craig Perret
1991	*Strike the Gold*	Chris Antley
1992	*Lil E Tee*	Pat Day
1993	*Sea Hero*	Jerry Bailey
1994	*Go for Gin*	Chris McCarron
1995	*Thunder Gulch*	Gary Stevens
1996	*Grindastone*	Jerry Bailey

GRAND NATIONAL

The world's most famous steeplechase, the Grand National, is staged every year at Aintree, Liverpool, England. The course is 7245 m (4 mi 4 furlongs) long, over 30 fences. Winners since 1980:

1980	*Ben Nevis*	Charlie Fenwick
1981	*Aldaniti*	Bob Champion
1982	*Grittar*	Dick Saunders
1983	*Corbiere*	Ben De Haan
1984	*Hallo Dandy*	Neale Doughty
1985	*Last Suspect*	Hywel Davies
1986	*West Tip*	Richard Dunwoody
1987	*Maori Venture*	Steve Knight
1988	*Rhyme 'n' Reason*	Brendan Powell
1989	*Little Polveir*	Jimmy Frost
1990	*Mr Frisk*	Marcus Armytage
1991	*Seagram*	Nigel Hawke
1992	*Party Politics*	Carl Llewellyn
1993	Race cancelled after false start	
1994	*Miinnehoma*	Richard Dunwoody
1995	*Royal Athlete*	Jason Titley
1996	*Rough Quest*	Mick Fitzgerald
1997	*Lord Gyllene*	Tony Dobbin

CHELTENHAM GOLD CUP

One of the most prestigious races in the British National Hunt calendar, the Cheltenham Gold Cup is a 22-fence steeplechase over 5333 m (3 mi 2 furlongs 110 yds). Winners since 1980:

1980	*Master Smudge*	Richard Hoare
1981	*Little Owl*	Jim Wilson
1982	*Silver Buck*	Robert Earnshaw
1983	*Bregawn*	Graham Bradley
1984	*Burrough Hill Lad*	Phil Tuck
1985	*Forgive 'n' Forget*	Martin Dwyer
1986	*Dawn Run*	Jonjo O'Neill
1987	*The Thinker*	Ridley Lamb
1988	*Charter Party*	Richard Dunwoody
1989	*Desert Orchid*	Simon Sherwood
1990	*Norton's Coin*	Graham McCourt
1991	*Garrison Savannah*	Mark Pitman
1992	*Cool Ground*	Adrian Maguire
1993	*Jodami*	Mark Dwyer
1994	*The Fellow*	Adam Kondrat
1995	*Master Oats*	Norman Williamson
1996	*Imperial Call*	Conor O'Dwyer
1997	*Mr Mulligan*	Tony McCoy

THE DERBY

The greatest of the English Classics, this flat race takes place over 2423 m (1 mi 4 furlongs 10 yds) each June at Epsom Downs. The first Derby was in 1780. Winners since 1980:

1980	*Henbit*	Willie Carson
1981	*Shergar*	Walter Swinburn
1982	*Golden Fleece*	Pat Eddery
1983	*Teenoso*	Lester Piggott
1984	*Secreto*	Christy Roche
1985	*Slip Anchor*	Steve Cauthen
1986	*Shahrastani*	Walter Swinburn
1987	*Reference Point*	Steve Cauthen
1988	*Kahyasi*	Ray Cochrane
1989	*Nashwan*	Willie Carson
1990	*Quest for Fame*	Pat Eddery
1991	*Generous*	Alan Munro
1992	*Dr Devious*	John Reid
1993	*Commander in Chief*	Michael Kinane
1994	*Erhaab*	Willie Carson
1995	*Lammtarra*	Walter Swinburn
1996	*Shaamit*	Michael Hills
1997	*Benny the Dip*	Willie Ryan

Other Sports

- **Badminton takes its name from Badminton House in England, where the Duke of Beaufort played the sport in the 19th century.**
- **The word 'snooker' was originally used as a slang term for new recruits at the Woolwich Military Academy.**
- **The name 'chess' is derived from the Persian word Shah (king or ruler). The earliest surviving chessmen are from an ivory set found in Russia, dated *c.* AD 200.**
- **Louis XI of France is believed to be among the first to have played billiards on a table.**

ARCHERY

Archery, which developed out of hunting and warfare, is one of the oldest sports. Mesolithic cave art shows hunters with bows and arrows.

There are several different forms of modern archery – target archery being the most popular. Field archery involves targeting animal figures, and in flight shooting the aim is the greatest distance the arrow travels. Types of bow include longbows, primitive bows, standard recursive bows and compound bows.

Now held every two years, the World Championship was first contested in 1931. The sport has been an Olympic event continuously since 1972, with earlier competitions at the 1900, 1904, 1908 and 1920 Games.

BADMINTON

The shuttlecock-and-racquet sport of badminton grew out of the children's game of battledore and shuttlecock. Modern rules were codified in Poona, India, by British Army officers in 1876.

Badminton is popular in many countries throughout the world, North America and the Far East in particular. The major tournament is the World Championships, which superseded the annual All England Championships, initially held in 1899. The world governing body is the International Badminton Federation, founded in 1934.

THOMAS AND UBER CUPS

The major international badminton team competitions are the Thomas Cup for men (founded 1949) and the Uber Cup for women (first held in 1957). Both competitions were initially held every three years but are now contested every two years. Winning national teams:

Thomas Cup	Wins	
Indonesia	10	1958, 1961, 1964, 1970, 1973, 1976, 1979, 1984, 1994, 1996
Malaysia/Malaya	5	1949, 1952, 1955, 1967, 1992
China	4	1982, 1986, 1988, 1990

Uber Cup	Wins	
Japan	5	1966, 1969, 1972, 1978, 1981
China	5	1984, 1986, 1988, 1990, 1992
United States	3	1957, 1960, 1963
Indonesia	3	1975, 1994, 1996

1996 OLYMPIC BADMINTON

Badminton was a demonstration sport at the 1972 and 1988 Olympic Games, and it became a medal sport at Barcelona in 1992. Listed below are the 1996 gold medallists.

Singles

Men	Poul-Erik Hoyer-Larsen (Den)
Women	Bang Soo-hyun (SKo)

Doubles

Men	Rexy Mainaky and Ricky Subagja (Indo)
Women	Ge Fei and Gu Jun (Chn)
Mixed	Kim Dong-moon and Gil Young-ah (SKo)

1996 OLYMPIC ARCHERY

The sport has been an Olympic event continuously since 1972, with earlier competitions at the 1900, 1904, 1908 and 1920 Games. The 1996 gold medallists are listed below.

Individual

Men	Justin Huish (USA)
Women	Kim Kyung-wook (SKo)

Team

Men	USA
Women	South Korea

The court is 13.4 m (44 ft) long and 6.1 m (20 ft) wide for doubles, 5.2 m (17 ft) wide for singles. The net is 1.5 m (5 ft) high at the centre. Either two or four players take part.

BIATHLON

The biathlon is a combination of cross-country skiing and rifle shooting. Men compete individually over 10 or 20 km, and 4 x 7.5 km for the relay. For women, equivalent distances are 7.5 km, 15 km and 3 x 7.5 km relay. There are two shooting competitions at a target 50 m away over the 10 km distance and four (both prone and standing) over the 20 km distance. In the relay event each member shoots once prone and once standing. Penalties are imposed for missing the target.

The biathlon World Championship was inaugurated in 1958 for men and 1984 for women. The biathlon has been an Olympic sport since 1960 (1992 for women).

The sport's governing body is L'Union Internationale de Pentathlon Moderne et Biathlon (UIPMB), which first administered the sport in 1957.

BILLIARDS

Billiards developed in Britain in the 19th century, with rubber cushions being introduced in 1835, and slate beds in 1836. The World Professional and Amateur Championships have been held since 1870 and 1926 respectively. The sport is most popular in Britain, and it has produced the greatest number of World Professional champions. The billiard table's dimensions are 3.7 x 1.9 m (12 x 6 ft).

The world governing body is the Billiards and Snooker Control Council (formerly the Billiards Association).

BOWLS

The modern game of bowls had its rules formulated in 1848–49 in Scotland by William Mitchell, a Glasgow solicitor. There are two forms of the game – crown green and lawn bowls. Crown green bowls is played on a rink with undulations and is almost exclusively found in northern and Midland England. Lawn bowls, played on a finely grassed rink, is most popular in British Commonwealth countries.

The Men's and Women's World Championships are held every four years, with singles, pairs, triples and fours events. The World Championships for indoor bowls have been held annually since 1979. The sport's governing body is the International Bowling Board, formed in 1905.

CHESS

Chess is an ancient game thought to have originated in northern India. The game spread to Persia as Chaturanga ('four corps'), and evolved into the modern game.

Chess is played by two players on an eight-by-eight chequered board with 16 pieces per side. The pieces are: eight pawns, two knights, two bishops, two rooks (also called castles), one queen and one king. These pieces have been standard for the last 500 years.

Players are graded by the world governing body (the Fédération Internationale des Echecs, or FIDE) according to competitive results on the ELO scoring system, devised by Arpad Elo (1903–92); results are issued twice yearly. Grand Master level is 2500. The highest rating ever achieved is 2815 by the current world champion, Gary Kasparov, reached in 1993. The highest-rated woman player is Judit Polgar of Hungary at 2675. The youngest-ever International Grand Master is France's Etienne Bacrot, who qualified at 14 years 59 days in March 1997.

WORLD CHAMPIONSHIP

The World Championships have been held since 1851, although they were unofficial until 1886. The world champions are listed below. Note that in 1993, Gary Kasparov of Russia and Nigel Short of the UK were due to contest the world title, but formed the Professional Chess Association and played their championship matches outside the auspices of the governing body, FIDE. FIDE declared that a contest between Anatoliy Karpov of Russia and Jan Timman of the Netherlands, who were beaten by Short in the Challengers' Tournament, was to decide the world title. Karpov won 12.5 to 8.5.

Men

1851–58	Adolf Anderssen (Ger)
1858–62	Paul Morphy (USA)
1862–66	Adolf Anderssen (Ger)
1866–94	Wilhelm Steinitz (Aut)
1894–1921	Emanuel Lasker (Ger)
1921–27	José Capablanca (Cub)
1927–35	Alexandre Alekhine (Fra)
1935–37	Max Euwe (Neths)
1937–46	Alexandre Alekhine (Fra)
1948–57	Mikhail Botvinnik (USSR)
1957–58	Vasiliy Smyslov (USSR)
1958–60	Mikhail Botvinnik (USSR)
1960–61	Mikhail Tal (USSR)
1961–63	Mikhail Botvinnik (USSR)
1963–69	Tigran Petrosian (USSR)
1969–72	Boris Spassky (USSR)
1972–75	Bobby Fischer (USA)
1975–85	Anatoliy Karpov (USSR)
1985–	Gary Kasparov (USSR/Rus)

Women

1927–44	Vera Menchik (UK)
1950–53	Lyudmila Rudenko (USSR)
1953–56	Yelizaveta Bykova (USSR)
1956–58	Olga Rubtsova (USSR)
1958–62	Yelizaveta Bykova (USSR)
1962–78	Nona Gaprindashvili (USSR)
1978–91	Maya Chiburdanidze (USSR)
1991–	Xie Jun (Chn)

■ A PRIMITIVE HANG-GLIDER WAS ALLEGEDLY USED BY A MONK, EILMER, TO FLY OFF MALMESBURY

TOUR DE FRANCE

The most famous annual cycling race in the world is the Tour de France, which was founded in 1903. Held over 21 days on various courses, the Tour is the world's longest non-motorized sporting event, and one of the most popular, with more than 10 million people lining its course every year. The course length in recent years has been about 4000 km (nearly 2500 miles). The yellow jersey is worn during the race by the leading rider, and was introduced in 1919. Post-war winners:

Year	Winner	Year	Winner	Year	Winner
1947	Jean Robic (Fra)	1964	Jacques Anquetil (Fra)	1981	Bernard Hinault (Fra)
1948	Gino Bartali (Ita)	1965	Felice Gimondi (Ita)	1982	Bernard Hinault (Fra)
1949	Fausto Coppi (Ita)	1966	Lucien Aimar (Fra)	1983	Laurent Fignon (Fra)
1950	Ferdinand Kübler (Swi)	1967	Roger Pingeon (Fra)	1984	Laurent Fignon (Fra)
1951	Hugo Koblet (Swi)	1968	Jan Janssen (Neths)	1985	Bernard Hinault (Fra)
1952	Fausto Coppi (Ita)	1969	Eddy Merckx (Bel)	1986	Greg LeMond (USA)
1953	Louison Bobet (Fra)	1970	Eddy Merckx (Bel)	1987	Stephen Roche (Ire)
1954	Louison Bobet (Fra)	1971	Eddy Merckx (Bel)	1988	Pedro Delgado (Spa)
1955	Louison Bobet (Fra)	1972	Eddy Merckx (Bel)	1989	Greg LeMond (USA)
1956	Roger Walkowiak (Fra)	1973	Luis Ocaña (Spa)	1990	Greg LeMond (USA)
1957	Jacques Anquetil (Fra)	1974	Eddy Merckx (Bel)	1991	Miguel Induráin (Spa)
1958	Charly Gaul (Lux)	1975	Bernard Thévenet (Fra)	1992	Miguel Induráin (Spa)
1959	Federico Bahamontès (Spa)	1976	Lucien van Impe (Bel)	1993	Miguel Induráin (Spa)
1960	Gastone Nencini (Ita)	1977	Bernard Thévenet (Fra)	1994	Miguel Induráin (Spa)
1961	Jacques Anquetil (Fra)	1978	Bernard Hinault (Fra)	1995	Miguel Induráin (Spa)
1962	Jacques Anquetil (Fra)	1979	Bernard Hinault (Fra)	1996	Bjarne Riis (Neths)
1963	Jacques Anquetil (Fra)	1980	Joop Zoetemelk (Neths)	1997	Jan Ullrich (Ger)

■ *Miguel Induráin leads the way in the 1995 Tour de France. That year saw the Spaniard's fifth successive win*

1996 OLYMPIC CYCLING

Cycling has been included in every modern Olympic Games since 1896, except 1904. There are currently eight men's and six women's events on the Olympic programme, including a mountain bike event introduced in the 1996 Games. The 1996 Olympic champions are listed below.

Men

1000 m time trial: Florian Rousseau (Fra)
Sprint (200 m): Jens Fieldler (Ger)
Individual pursuit: Andrea Collinelli (Ita)
Team pursuit: France
Points race: Silvio Martinello (Ita)
Road race: Pascal Richard (Swi)
Road time trial individual: Miguel Induráin (Spa)
Mountain bike: Bart Jan Brentjens (Neths)

Women

Sprint (200 m): Felicia Ballanger (Fra)
Individual pursuit: Antonella Bellutti (Ita)
Points race: Nathalie Lancien (Fra)
Road race: Jeannie Longo-Ciprelli (Fra)
Road time trial individual: Zulfiya Zabirova (Rus)
Mountain bike: Paolo Pezzo (Ita)

CYCLING

Competitive cycling is conducted both on road and track, and is popular worldwide; the earliest cycling race took place in Paris in 1868, and was held over 2 km (1.2 mi).

A range of road and track events are contested annually. There are separate amateur and professional categories for men's road racing, but for track events the distinction was abolished in 1993, and there has never been any distinction for women's events. World Championships were first held in 1893.

The governing body is the Union Cycliste International (UCI), formed in 1900 and subdivided into amateur and professional federations in 1965.

DARTS

The modern game of darts was devised in 1896 when Brian Gamlin of Bury, England, produced the present numbering system on the dartboard. It is played mainly in the UK, where it is shown on television, and has over six million players. It is also growing in popularity in the United States and parts of continental Europe.

GLIDING

Gliding has been popular in the United States and Europe since the 1930s. Several events are contested: pure distance, distance to a declared goal, return distance to a goal, absolute height and height gain. The major competition is the World Championship, first held in 1937, and now held every two years. There are several categories for single and two-seater gliders.

Since the 1960s, there has been increased interest in hang-gliding, boosted by the invention of the flexible wing. The first official World Championship was held in 1976, and is now held every two years. Gliding, hang-gliding, paragliding and microlight records are internationally recognized.

GREYHOUND RACING

The sport of greyhound racing became popular after the perfection of the mechanical hare in 1919 by the American Owen Patrick Smith, although mechanical devices were first used in England. The first regular track was opened at Emeryville, California, in 1919, and a year later the International Greyhound Racing Association was formed.

Races are usually conducted over a range of distances between 210 m (230 yd) for the sprint and 1096 m (1200 yd) for the marathon. The major race in Britain is the Derby, first held in 1927.

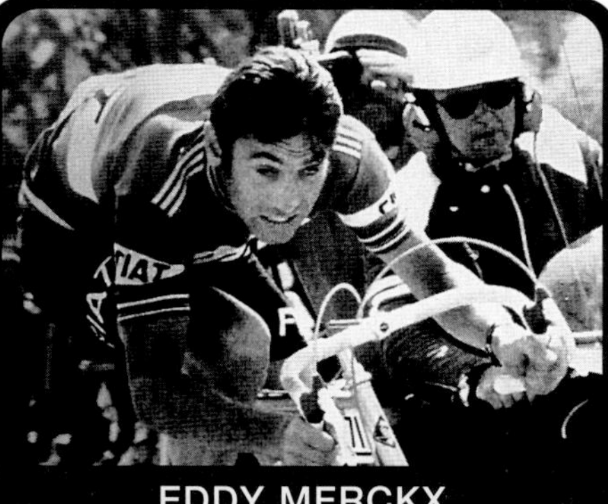

EDDY MERCKX (1945–)

Belgian Eddy Merckx is the greatest cyclist of all time. A fierce and demanding sportsman, he earned the name 'the Cannibal' for his unwavering desire for victory. He won the Tour de France five times (1969–72, 1974), and won 35 stages in seven years, wearing the yellow jersey for 96 days in total. The list of his other cycling trophies is unsurpassed: five Giro d'Italia, three world professional road race titles, seven Milan–San Remo titles and numerous others. He was the first man to win the Tour de France, Giro d'Italia and world professional road race in the same year (1974). Between 1965 and 1977 he notched up 449 victories. He retired in 1977. An uncompromising cyclist, Merckx did not believe in cautious or easy tactics.

WORLD CHAMPIONSHIP DARTS

The World Championship was first held in 1978.

Year	Winner
1978	Leighton Rees (Wal)
1979	John Lowe (Eng)
1980	Eric Bristow (Eng)
1981	Eric Bristow (Eng)
1982	Jocky Wilson (Sco)
1983	Keith Deller (Eng)
1984	Eric Bristow (Eng)
1985	Eric Bristow (Eng)
1986	Eric Bristow (Eng)
1987	John Lowe (Eng)
1988	Bob Anderson (Eng)
1989	Jocky Wilson (Sco)
1990	Phil Taylor (Eng)
1991	Dennis Priestley (Eng)
1992	Phil Taylor (Eng)
1993	John Lowe (Eng)
1994	John Part (Can)
1995	Richie Burnett (Wal)
1996	Steve Beaton (Eng)
1997	Les Wallace (Sco)

In 1992, many of the sport's top players became dissatisfied with the WBO's organization of the game, and formed the World Darts Council (WDC). The WDC introduced its own World Championship at the end of 1993.1993/94 Dennis Priestley (Eng)

Year	Winner
1994/95	Phil Taylor (Eng)
1995/96	Phil Taylor (Eng)
1996/97	Phil Taylor (Eng)

GYMNASTICS

The modern foundations of the sport were laid by the German, Johann Friedrich Simon, in 1776.

Gymnastics has several components. For men, these are horse vaults, the pommel horse, the parallel bars and the horizontal bar. For women, the components are asymmetrical bars, the beam, the horse vault and rhythmic gymnastics (handling of light objects including skipping ropes, hoops, balls, clubs and ribbons to musical accompaniment). The floor exercises discipline, conducted on a 12 m^2 (130 sq ft) square area, is common to both men's and women's gymnastics.

1996 OLYMPIC GYMNASTICS

Gymnastics has been part of all modern Olympics. Rhythmic gymnastics for women was introduced for the first time at the 1984 Los Angeles Games. Other international competitions include the World Championship, instituted in 1903 and now held every two years. The 1996 Olympic gymnastic champions are listed below.

Men
Team: Russia
Combined: Li Xiaoshuang (Chn)
Floor exercises: Ioannis Melissanidis (Gre)
Parallel bars: Rustram Sharipov (Ukr)
Pommel horse: Li Donghua (Swi)
Rings: Yuri Chechi (Ita)
Horizontal bar: Andreas Wecker (Ger)
Horse vault: Aleksey Nemov (Rus)

Women
Team: USA
Combined: Lilia Podkopayeva (Ukr)
Asymmetrical bars: Svetlana Chorkina (Rus)
Balance beam: Shannon Miller (USA)
Floor exercises: Lilia Podkopayeva (Ukr)
Horse vault: Simona Amonar (Rom)
Rhythmic gymnastics (individual): Ekaterina Serebryanskaya (Ukr)
Rhythmic gymnastics (team): Spain

MODERN PENTATHLON

The most prestigious event at the ancient Olympics was the pentathlon, which consisted of discus, javelin, running, jumping and wrestling. The modern pentathlon's governing body is L'Union Internationale de Pentathlon Moderne et Biathlon (the UIPMB), founded in 1948.

The modern pentathlon is a five-sport discipline testing a broad range of abilities. The events are cross-country riding (800 m course with 15 fences; riders do not choose their mounts); épée fencing, pistol shooting (at 25 m), swimming (300 m freestyle) and cross-country running (4000 m). Scaled points are awarded for each activity, determined against scoring tables or the performance of other competitors.

The World Championship has been held annually since 1949 for men and from 1981 for women. Modern pentathlon has been held at every Olympics since 1912. The 1996 Games did not have a team competition and focused on the individual single-day event; the winner was Aleksandr Parygin (Kaz).

ROLLER SKATING

In 1866, the first roller rink was opened at Newport, Rhode Island, USA. Initially used as practice for ice skaters, roller skating later developed into an independent discipline. Competitive events are similar to ice skating with speed, figure and dance elements. The Speed-skating World Championship has been held since 1937, and the World Figure Skating Championship was first held in 1947.

The governing body of the sport is the Fédération Internationale de Patinage à Roulettes, which was founded in 1924.

SHOOTING

The Lucerne Shooting Guild was the first recorded shooting club, and was founded around 1466. The first known shooting match took place in 1472 in Zürich, Switzerland.

There are several shooting disciplines. Skeet shooting involves attempting to hit clay pigeon targets designed to simulate a range of bird game. Pistol events, such as air rifle, have fixed targets, and are scored on accuracy.

The world governing body is the Union Internationale de Tir (UIT), founded in 1907.

1996 OLYMPIC SHOOTING

Shooting events have been held at every modern Olympics. The 1996 Games had 10 men's events and five women's events. The gold medallists are listed below.

Men
Free pistol: Boris Kokorev (Rus)
Rapid-fire pistol: Ralf Schumann (Ger)
Air pistol: Roberto Di Donna (Ita)
Air rifle: Artem Khadzhibekov (Rus)
Running game target: Yang Ling (Chn)
Small-bore rifle-prone: Christian Klees (Ger)
Small-bore rifle-three positions: Jean-Pierre Amat (Fra)
Olympic trap: Michael Diamond (Aus)
Olympic double trap: Russell Mark (Aus)
Skeet: Ennio Falco (Ita)

Women
Sport pistol: Li Duihong (Chn)
Small-bore rifle: Aleksandra Ivosev (Yug)
Air pistol: Olga Klochneva (Rus)
Air rifle: Renata Mauer (Pol)
Olympic double trap: Kim Rhode (USA)

SNOOKER

Snooker was devised by Colonel Sir Neville Chamberlain as an amalgamation of billiards, 'black pool' and 'pyramids', and was first played in Madras, India, in 1875. Snooker has been played in England since 1885, when the world billiards champion John Roberts brought it over from India. Snooker is a popular television sport, and its most successful players are British.

A full-size snooker table measures 3.66 x 1.87 m (12 x 6 ft). Ball values are: red (1), yellow (2), green (3), brown (4), blue (5), pink (6) and black (7). The world governing body is the World Professional Billiards and Snooker Association.

■ *Pyrros Dimas of Greece heads towards a gold medal in the 1996 Olympic 83 kg weightlifting event*

WORLD CHAMPIONSHIP

The World Championship has been held since 1927. The finals are held annually at the Crucible Theatre, Sheffield, England. Listed below are the world champions since 1969, when a knockout format was introduced.

1969 John Spencer (Eng)
1970 Ray Reardon (Wal)
1971 John Spencer (Eng)
1972 Alex Higgins (NI)
1973 Ray Reardon (Wal)
1974 Ray Reardon (Wal)
1975 Ray Reardon (Wal)
1976 Ray Reardon (Wal)
1977 John Spencer (Eng)
1978 Ray Reardon (Wal)
1979 Terry Griffiths (Wal)
1980 Cliff Thorburn (Can)
1981 Steve Davis (Eng)
1982 Alex Higgins (NI)
1983 Steve Davis (Eng)
1984 Steve Davis (Eng)
1985 Dennis Taylor (NI)
1986 Joe Johnson (Eng)
1987 Steve Davis (Eng)
1988 Steve Davis (Eng)
1989 Steve Davis (Eng)
1990 Stephen Hendry (Sco)
1991 John Parrott (Eng)
1992 Stephen Hendry (Sco)
1993 Stephen Hendry (Sco)
1994 Stephen Hendry (Sco)
1995 Stephen Hendry (Sco)
1996 Stephen Hendry (Sco)
1997 Ken Doherty (Ire)

WEIGHTLIFTING

While strongmen have demonstrated their feats for centuries, the amateur sport of weightlifting is relatively modern, with competitions dating from around 1850. The first World Championships took place in 1891, and the sport was included in the first modern Olympics in 1896, and then from 1920.

Weightlifting is decided on the combination of two forms of lifting, the snatch (a single movement lift from the floor to an extended arm position above the head) and the clean and jerk (a two-part movement from the floor to the shoulder and from the shoulder to the outstretched position). A third category, the press, has been dropped due to the difficulty in judging it.

The current governing body is the International Weightlifting Federation (IWF), formed in 1920.

Powerlifting is a discipline which places greater emphasis on sheer strength rather than technique. The three basic lifts are the squat (or deep knee bend), bench press and dead lift. The governing body is the International Powerlifting Federation, founded in 1972.

OLYMPIC WEIGHTLIFTING

There are currently 10 weight divisions in Olympic weightlifting, ranging from up to 54 kg (119 lb) to over 108 kg (238 lb). The sport is dominated by eastern European nations. The 1996 gold medallists are listed below.

54 kg: Halil Mutlu (Tur)
59 kg: Tang Lingsheng (Chn)
64 kg: Naim Suleymanoglü (Tur)
70 kg: Zhan Xugang (Chn)
76 kg: Pablo Lara (Chn)
83 kg: Pyrros Dimas (Gre)
91 kg: Alexey Petrov (Rus)
99 kg: Kakhi Kakhiasvilis (Gre)
108 kg: Timur Taimazov (Ukr)
+108 kg: Andrey Chemerkin (Rus)

■ RECORDS ARE SET MORE FREQUENTLY IN WEIGHTLIFTING THAN IN ANY OTHER SPORT ■

'The past is a foreign country: they do things differently there'
– L.P. Hartley

HISTORY ▷

THE ANCIENT WORLD

10,000 BC

EGYPT AND NORTH AFRICA ▶

c. 3100–2700 BC Menes conquers the Delta, unites Upper and Lower Egypt and becomes pharaoh of the first unified dynasty; foundation of Memphis.

c. 3000 Hieroglyphic and Elamite pictographic scripts in use.

c. 2575–2134 Old Kingdom. Building of Great Pyramids at Giza.

c. 2134–2040 First Intermediate Period: era of anarchy and political fragmentation.

c. 2040 Unity of Egypt is restored under Mentuhotep of Thebes; start of the Middle Kingdom; administrative reforms, co-regencies and the conquest of Nubia.

c. 1640–1550 Hyksos invade and rule Egypt; Thebans remain independent; Hebrews enter Egypt.

c. 1550 Ahmose, Prince of Thebes, expels Hyksos and reunites Egypt.

1540–1479 Tutmosis begins period of Egyptian expansion: foundation of empire in Palestine and Syria extending to the Euphrates.

ASIA ▶

2850 BC Legendary Golden Age of China begins.

c. 2300 Indus Valley civilization: development of the cities of Harappa and Mohenjo-daro.

c. 2000 Neolithic farming spread to southern India.

c. 1500 Aryan invasion of India: fall of Indus Civilization; intermingling of Aryan and indigenous Dravidian cultures produces Hinduism. Rice farming established in Indochina.

c. 1500–1050 Shang dynasty in China; Bronze Age in China; first evidence of Chinese script.

1500–400 Ganges civilization in India.

1122–256 Zhou dynasty in China.

c. 800 Hindu Iron Age culture established in the Ganges basin.

c. 800–700 Growth of Chinese cities and merchant class; iron industry develops; flourishing of literature and philosophy: Kongfuzi (Confucius), Mengzi (Mencius) and Taoism.

EUROPE ▶

c. 3000 BC Development of the Minoan civilization in Crete: foundation of Knossos and Phaestus.

c. 2500–2400 Simple henges erected in England.

c. 2200–1450 Middle Minean Age: control of the sea ensures Minean prosperity.

c. 2000 Standing stones of Carnac (Brittany) erected.

c. 1700 Bronze Age in western Europe.

c. 1600 Linear B script in use in Minoan civilization.

1500–1150 Mycenaean civilization begins its domination in mainland Greece.

c. 1500 Beginning of Urnfield cultures in Hungary and Romania.

c. 1450 Knossos falls to invaders.

c. 1300 First Celts appear in Upper Danube area.

c. 1200 Sack of Troy (possibly by Mycenaeans).

1200–1100 Dorians overthrow the Mycenaean civilization; Greek 'Dark Ages' begin.

900–500 Celtic Hallstatt culture (iron-using) supersedes Urnfield cultures.

c. 800 Emergence of polis – Greek city-states.

753 Traditional date of foundation of Rome.

750 Greeks settle southern Italy.

c. 750–600 Increase in the number of city states; the political rights of the citizen restricts the power of the aristocracy.

NEAR EAST ▶

c. 3000 BC Beginnings of the Sumerian civilization; foundation of city states Uruk, Eridu and Ur.

c. 2334–2279 Sargon the Great founds Akkad and Akkadian Empire; conquers all Mesopotamia.

c. 2200 Guti tribesmen from Iran destroy Akkadian Empire.

c. 2113 Third dynasty of Ur founded by Ur-Nammu; a period of prosperity follows.

c. 2006 Sack of Ur by Elamites.

c. 1792–1750 Hammurabi of Babylon reunites Mesopotamia.

c. 1650 Foundation of Hittite Old Kingdom by King Mursilis.

c. 1500 Migration of Phrygians into Asia Minor: establishment of Phrygia.

1380–1350 Hittite Empire reaches greatest extent under Suppiluliumas I.

1313–1283 Unsuccessful Hittite invasions of Egypt.

c. 1230 Jews occupy Israel.

c. 1200 Overthrow of Hittite Empire by Phrygians and allied tribes.

1200–1100 'Sea People' raid Syria and Palestine.

c. 1100 Assyrian Empire set up in Mesopotamia.

c. 1000 Israelite Kingdom founded by Saul and David.

THE AMERICAS ▶

10,000 BC Temporary landbridge during Ice Age connects Asia and Alaska: a few Siberian families reach North America; population spreads from Alaska over North America; their descendants become American Indian hunters.

9000 South America settled from Central America.

c. 8000 Ciboney (hunter-gatherer-fishing people) of South America reach Hispaniola.

c. 5000 First centres of population in Mexico.

5000–4000 Arrival of Inuit (Eskimo) in North America.

2500 Development of agriculture in Indian communities in Andean America.

c. 1500–400 Olmec culture in Mesoamerica (Mexico and northern Central America).

1000–200 Chavin culture flourishes on Peruvian coast; improved agriculture (maize) and metallurgy.

300 BC

1360 Amenhotep IV (Akhenaton) rejects all gods except Aton, the Sun disc; imperial neglect leads to loss of Asian empire.

***c.* 1300** Oppression of Jews under Rameses II; Jewish exodus from Egypt.

1200–1100 Attempts by the Sea People to invade Egypt thwarted by Rameses III.

1070–1000 Egypt divided: priesthood of Amun rule in Thebes, while pharaohs rule in Tanis.

850 Foundation of Carthage by Phoenicians from Tyre.

814 Traditional date associated with the foundation of Carthage.

750 Nubians conquer Egypt.

525 Egyptian attempt to regain independence fails; Persians take control.

332 Egypt conquered by Alexander the Great; on his death (305), Ptolemy (Alexander's general) founds the Hellenistic Kingdom of Egypt.

800–300 China beset by warring states.

771 Nomad attacks on China cause removal of capital to Luoyang; start of Later Zhou period; imperial power diminished.

551–479 Development of Confucian social thought in China.

***c.* 500–400** Emergence of Buddhist and Jain religions leads to a succession of Hindu and later Buddhist dynasties; Indian agriculturalists colonize Sri Lanka.

***c.* 481–221** 'Warring States' in China – a period of anarchy during which power devolved to smaller states.

***c.* 400** Rice farming reaches Japan from Korea.

326 Alexander the Great conquers the Indus Valley.

***c.* 300** Sri Lanka converted to Buddhism.

594 Solon introduces reforms in Athens.

509 Last Roman king expelled; establishment of Republic.

499–479 Greek–Persian Wars: Greek city-states revolt against Persian rule.

490 Battle of Marathon: Greeks defeat Persians.

480 Battle of Salamis: Greeks defeat Persian fleet.

479 Greek army defeats Persians at Plataca and Mycale and liberates Greece.

478 Athenian empire; Athens assumes leadership of the Delian League.

462–429 Pericles dominates Athens as the city-state's leading politician.

431 Outbreak of Peloponnesian War between Athens and Sparta.

404 Athenian surrender to Sparta: beginning of Spartan domination of Greece.

390 Rome sacked by Celts.

378–377 Athens founds the Aegean Confederacy.

371 Thebans defeat Spartans.

338 Philip II of Macedon conquers Greek city-states (at Battle of Chaeronea).

336 Philip II assassinated: accession of Alexander (the Great).

334–326 Alexander invades and conquers the Persian Empire.

326–323 Spread of Greek civilization: Alexander occupies Egypt, Syria and invades the Punjab.

323 Alexander the Great dies at Babylon.

323–301 Power-struggle between Alexander's generals for control of the empire; by 301 BC Ptolemy gains Egypt, Seleucus most of the Asiatic provinces (the Seleucid Empire).

***c.* 935** Israelite Kingdom divided into Israel and Judah.

911–824 Period of Assyrian expansion.

***c.* 850** Chaldea (now Armenia) attacked by Assyrians.

722 Palestine annexed by Assyrians; many Jews exiled to Babylon.

670 Assyrians destroy Memphis and Thebes but fail to hold Egypt.

626 Nabopolassar establishes the Chaldean dynasty of Babylon.

612 Medes, Babylonians and Scythians bring down Assyrian Empire.

605–562 Nebuchadnezzar II of Babylon extends the empire to include Syria and Palestine; extensive building programme (including the Hanging Gardens).

600 Assyrian Empire divided amongst its conquerors.

539 Cyrus the Great conquers Babylonian Empire and founds Achaemenid Persian Empire that dominates the Middle East.

536 Return of Jews from Babylon to Judah.

ROMAN AND EARLY MEDIEVAL

320 BC

MEDITERRANEAN ▶

290 BC End of Third Samnite War; Rome dominates central Italy.

275 Rome completes conquest of peninsular Italy after the defeat of Pyrrhus and southern Italian Greek cities.

264–241 First Punic War between Rome and Carthage: Sicily becomes first Roman province.

c. 240 Greece dominated by two federations of city-states: Aetolia and Achaea.

238 Foundation of kingdom of Pergamon.

218–202 Second Punic War: Hannibal initially inflicts crushing blows on Roman forces but is finally defeated at Zama.

c. 211–167 Macedonian Wars: Rome finally defeats Macedonia.

149–146 Third Punic War: Carthage destroyed and Africa becomes a Roman province.

148–146 Rome annexes Greece.

133 Attalos III of Pergamon bequeaths his kingdom to Rome.

133–96 Expansion of Roman Empire to include Asia (W. Turkey; 133), southern Gaul (121), Cilicia (101) and Cyrenaica (96).

91 Social War: Italian cities revolt against Rome. Roman franchise granted to most Italians.

73 Spartacus leads Third Servile War (suppressed 71).

64 Seleucid Empire falls to Rome.

60 First Triumvirate: Pompey, Caesar and Crassus.

49 Caesar at war with Pompey and Senate.

48 Caesar takes Rome and becomes dictator.

44 Caesar assassinated by Brutus and Cassius.

43–42 Second Triumvirate: Antony and Octavian effectively divide Roman Empire.

31 Octavian defeats Antony and Cleopatra at Actium, annexes Egypt and becomes dictator of Rome.

27 Octavian is proclaimed emperor – 'Augustus'.

NORTHERN EUROPE ▶

AD 43 Roman invasion of Britain.

122–26 Construction of Hadrian's Wall.

400–500 Saxons, Jutes and Angles (Germanic tribes) invade and settle in Britain.

407 Withdrawal of the last Roman troops from Britain.

519 Kingdom of Wessex founded.

c. 595 Kingdom of Mercia founded.

563 Foundation of Iona monastery by St Columba: Celtic Christianity established in northern Britain.

597 St Augustine of Canterbury travels to Kent to convert English to Christianity; becomes first Archbishop of Canterbury. Conversion of King Ethelbert.

654 Kingdom of Northumbria formed.

663 Synod of Whitby establishes the domination of Roman Christianity over Celtic Christianity.

757–96 Construction of Offa's Dyke separates England and Wales during the reign of Offa of Mercia.

787 Viking raids on Britain begin: pillage of Lindisfarne.

795 Norwegians settle in Ireland.

800s Viking settlements made in Ireland.

844 Kenneth MacAlpin becomes king of Picts and Scots: forms Kingdom of Alban, unifying Scotland.

866 Danes conquer Northumbria, East Anglia and Mercia.

874 Danes and Norwegians settle Iceland.

REST OF EUROPE ▶

AD 58 Caesar begins his conquest of Gaul.

202 Rome gains Carthaginian provinces in Spain.

c. 486 Clovis defeats last Roman governor in western Europe and founds the Frankish kingdom and the Merovingian dynasty.

c. 496 Franks acquire Rhineland.

c. 500 Franks conquer Visigoths and extend their empire to the Pyrenees.

638 Death of King Dagobert I: power passes to 'mayors of the palace'.

653 Lombards convert to Christianity.

711 Successful Muslim invasion of Spain.

718 Foundation of Christian kingdom of Asturias in northern Spain.

726 Beginning of the Iconoclast Movement (the abolition of the veneration of icons).

732 Battle of Poitiers: Arabs defeated by Franks under Charles Martel.

c. 750 Boniface evangelizes Germany.

751 Pepin I founds Carolingian dynasty after usurping the Merovingian throne.

754 Pope gains temporal powers in central Italy.

771–96 Charlemagne (Carolingian king) begins military campaign of conquest: Saxony (772), Lombard Kingdom (773), Bavaria (788), Avar Kingdom (795–96).

792–93 Revolts in Benevento and Saxony against Carolingian rule; attacks by Muslims; famine.

ASIA ▶

321–185 BC The Maurya dynasty becomes the first all-India Hindu empire (excluding the southern tip).

221 The State of Qin unites China: abolition of feudalism and the building of the Great Wall.

206 BC–AD 220 Han dynasty assumes power in China: conquest of Korea (107 BC), invention of paper and the introduction of Buddhism.

185 BC–AD 320 Disintegration of Maurya dynasty: India dissolves into small kingdoms with local power struggles.

2nd century AD Civil war in Japan.

220–80 North China succumbs to warlordism and invasions from non-Chinese people.

265–316 Jin dynasty in China.

320–540 Northern India is reunited by the Gupta dynasty.

c. 400–500 The Mon Kingdom in Burma is established.

c. 400 The Yamamoto clan dominate their rivals, establishing imperial rule in Japan.

589–618 Sui dynasty: reunites China and undertakes major government reforms.

594–622 In Japan, under Prince Shotoku Taishi, the study of Buddhism and Chinese writing is encouraged; the Chinese administrative system and calendar is copied.

600–50 Harsha dynasty in India: Buddhist empire in the north.

618–907 Tang dynasty in China: empire extended, invention of printing and gunpowder and increase in international trade.

THE AMERICAS ▶

c. 100 BC Development of first true city, Teotihuacán: dominates central Mexico for 600 years.

AD 200–1000 Migration of Arawak Indians from NE South America to Caribbean.

300 Rise of Maya civilization in Central America (Mexico, Guatemala and Yucatán peninsula).

500 Beginning of maize cultivation in North America.

500–1600 American Indians in the Mississippi Basin become farmers with small settlements.

AD 1100

AD **66** First Jewish revolt.

68–69 Anarchy following death of Nero; order restored by Vespasian.

70 Titus destroys Jerusalem.

98–180 Period of peace and prosperity under Antonine emperors.

193–97 Civil war in Rome.

212 All free inhabitants of Empire gain Roman citizenship.

260 Persians overrun Syria.

284–305 Diocletian reforms Roman Empire; establishes 'college' of emperors.

313 Edict of Milan: Christianity tolerated in Roman Empire.

324–37 Constantine I (the Great) reunites Roman Empire but moves the capital to Constantinople (formerly Byzantium).

395 Division of Roman Empire into East (Byzantine Empire) and West.

410 Visigoths sack Rome.

476 Fall of the Roman Empire.

***c.* 650** Byzantine Empire overrun by Persians, Slavs, Bulgars and Arabs: Constantinople besieged by Arabs in 673–77 and 718.

***c.* 750** The Byzantine Empire retains only Greece and Asia Minor.

811 Bulgars defeat Byzantines.

864–65 Bulgars and Serbs converted to Orthodox Christianity.

867–86 Revival of Byzantine Empire under Basil I.

961 Byzantines recover Crete.

965 Byzantines recover Cyprus.

1018 Byzantines finally conquer the Bulgarians under Basil II ('the Bulgar-Slayer').

1048 Seljuk Turks begin expansion into Byzantine Empire and attack Armenia.

1055 Seljuk Turks take Baghdad.

1060 Normans invade and annex Sicily.

***c.* 1070** Byzantines lose southern Italy to the Normans.

1071 Byzantine army destroyed by Seljuk Turks at Manzikert; Turks overrun Anatolia (present-day Asian Turkey).

1081 Revival of Byzantine power under Alexius I Comnenus.

1099 Godfrey of Bouillon leads First Crusade: takes Jerusalem.

937 Battle of Brunanburh: Athelstan of Wessex defeats north Welsh, Scots and Norse.

954 England united by Wessex.

965–66 Danish and Polish sovereigns accept Christianity.

991 Renewed Viking raids on England.

1013 The Dane Swegn overthrows King Aethelred and becomes King of England.

1016 Cnut, son of Swegn, becomes king of England after succession dispute with Aethelred.

1027 Cnut becomes king of Norway.

1035 Death of Cnut: division of the Danish Empire (Denmark, England and Norway).

1042 Edward the Confessor succeeds Cnut's son Harthacnut to the English throne.

1066 Harold, Earl of Wessex, succeeds Edward; William of Normandy challenges succession and defeats Harold at the Battle of Hastings.

1070 Rebellion in northern England crushed by William the Conqueror.

800 Charlemagne crowned Emperor of what became known as Holy Roman Empire.

***c.* 840** Viking raids on Carolingian Empire begin.

843 Treaty of Verdun divides Carolingian Empire.

845 Viking attack on Paris.

884–87 Temporary reunion of Carolingian Empire under Charles the Fat.

885–86 Viking siege of Paris.

955 Battle of Lechfeld: Germans halt westward expansion of Magyars; Magyars accept Christianity.

962 Coronation of Emperor Otto: Holy Roman Empire becomes largely German.

970s Christianity spreads to Bohemia.

987 Hugh Capet, King of France, founds Capetian dynasty.

988 Orthodox Christianity established in Kiev Rus.

1031 Fragmentation of Muslim Spain: northern Spain dominates Iberian Peninsula.

1053 Pope defeated and captured by the Normans at Melfi.

1054 East-West Schism: Eastern (Orthodox) Church and Western (Roman) Church finally split.

1073 Gregory VII becomes pope and enforces papal authority and Church discipline.

1092 Almoravids dominate most of Muslim Spain.

1094 Christian soldier, El Cid, takes Valencia.

***c.* 700–800** First Muslim invasion of India; Sind (southern Pakistan) is made a province of the Caliphate.

710–84 Chinese-style imperial court established at Nara in Japan.

755 Abortive rebellion of An Lushan: nomad invasions and revolts further weaken the Chinese Empire.

***c.* 800–900** Japanese imperial power is undermined by the Fujiwara family; decline in Chinese influence.

***c.* 800** Arrival of the Burmans from China; hostilities break out with indigenous people.

***c.* 800** Jayavarman II expels Javanese invaders from Khmer (Cambodia), reunites country and founds Khmer Kingdom: introduction of cult of god-king and foundation of Angkor.

***c.* 800–900** Migration of people from southern China: foundation of Lao people.

***c.* 849–1287** Burma unified by the people of Pagan; revolts by Mon and Shan people; spread of Buddhism.

***c.* 900** Tamils from southern India begin to settle in Sri Lanka.

***c.* 900–1000** People of south and western China migrate to and settle Siam (Thailand).

907 Last Tang emperor abdicates: China fragments; period of military dictators and warfare.

939 Annamese (of central Vietnam) overthrow Chinese and set up independent kingdom.

960 Sung dynasty reunites much of northern China and restores peace.

600–1000 Rise of Ayamará Indians in Bolivia.

***c.* 900** Toltecs establish a military state in Tula, northern Mexico, and by 985 control Mexico.

1000 Chimú state formed on north coast of Peru.

IT IS ESTIMATED THAT IN AD 500 THE WORLD POPULATION WAS ABOUT 100 MILLION

MEDIEVAL TO 16TH CENTURY

1000

NORTHERN EUROPE ▶

1100 William Rufus killed in New Forest.
1135 Stephen of Blois seizes English throne.
1138–46 Civil war between adherents of Stephen and Matilda.
1141 Matilda becomes 'Lady of England' for seven months.
1154 Henry Plantagenet inherits English throne and establishes Plantagenet empire in England and France.
1169 Beginning of the Anglo-Norman invasion of Ireland.
1170 Murder of Thomas Becket, Archbishop of Canterbury: later canonized by Pope.
1174 Coast of Finland settled by Swedes.
1204 King John loses Normandy to France.
1215 King John forced to concede Magna Carta.
1227 Danes defeated by Germans: cede Holstein to German Empire.
1258 Simon de Montfort forces reforms on Henry III.
1277–83 Conquest of Wales by Edward I.
1290 Scottish throne disputed by 13 claimants.
1296 Annexation of Scotland by Edward I.
1298 Robert Bruce continues struggle for Scottish independence; Scottish hero, William Wallace, defeated by Edward I.
1306 Robert Bruce crowned King Robert I of Scotland.
1314 Battle of Bannockburn: Edward II of England defeated by Robert the Bruce.
1380 Union of Norway and Denmark.
1381 Peasants' Revolt against the Poll Tax.
1384 Philip of Burgundy gains Flanders through marriage: beginning of Burgundian Empire.
1397 Norway, Sweden and Denmark come under one sovereign: Eric of Pomerania.
1399 Richard II deposed in England; the House of Lancaster usurps the throne.
1400–08 Welsh rebellion led by Owen Glendower.

WESTERN EUROPE ▶

1137 Union of Catalonia and Aragon through marriage.
1138–39 Foundation of Portugal.
1184 Creation of the Inquisition.
1209 St Francis of Assisi founds Franciscan Order.
1209–28 Simon de Montfort leads crusades against the Albigensian sect.
1229 Albigensian heretics crushed.
1248 Moors lose Seville to Ferdinand III of Castile.
1249 Moors expelled from Portugal.
1291 The Swiss cantons of Uri, Schwyz and Unterwalden declare themselves independent of the Habsburgs.
1306 Jews expelled from France.
1307–14 Destruction of the Knights Templar.
1309 Papal court moves to Avignon.
1328 Extinction of Capetian dynasty in France; Philip VI (Valois) challenged by Edward III of England.
1337 Beginning of the Hundred Years War.
1340 Battle of Sluys: English gain control of the English Channel in the Hundred Years War.
1346 English victory at Battle of Crécy.
1347 Calais is taken by Edward III.
1356 Black Prince of England captures French King John at Poitiers.
1358 Jacquerie French peasant uprising.
1360 Treaty of Brétigny temporarily halted the Hundred Years War.
1366–67 War in Castile: the Black Prince invades and restores King Pedro to the throne.
1369 Renewal of Hundred Years War.
1377 Papacy returns to Rome.
1378 The Great Schism: two Popes elected.
1396 Peace of Paris: 28-year truce in the Hundred Years War.
1417 Normandy falls to Henry V.
1429 French inspired to retake Orléans by Joan of Arc: Charles VII crowned King of France.
1431 Joan of Arc burnt at stake (1431).
1434 Cosimo di Medici begins Medici dynasty.
1442 All of southern Italy comes under Spanish rule.
1453 End of Hundred Years War.
1469 Marriage of Ferdinand II of Aragon to Isabella I of Castile leads to unification of Spain.
1475–77 War between Swiss and Charles the Bold of Burgundy.

SOUTHERN AND EASTERN EUROPE ▶

1081–1118 Revival of Byzantine power under Alexius Comnenus.
1100 Foundation of the Latin Kingdom of Jerusalem.
1109 Capture of Tripoli by Crusaders: becomes fourth Crusader state.
1138 Beginning of Hohenstaufen dynasty (Holy Roman Emperors); Poland fragments into independent principalities.
1139 Division of Russian state into independent principalities.
1147 Second Crusade: prompted by the fall of Edessa.
***c.* 1150–1200** Rise of the early Italian city-states.
1158 Imperial authority in northern Italy is restored by Frederick Barbarossa.
1176 Byzantine emperor suffers major defeat by the Seljuk Turks: end of Byzantine revival.
1189–92 Third Crusade prompted by Saladin's capture of Jerusalem.
1198 Bohemia becomes a kingdom.
1199 Foundation of the Order of Teutonic Knights by Emperor Frederick II to overcome and convert pagans in the north-east of Europe.
1202–04 Fourth Crusade: sack of Constantinople.
1217–21 Fifth Crusade: Damietta, Egypt taken.
1229 Teutonic Knights begin conversions in Prussia.
1238 Mongols conquer principality of Vladimir, the Georgians and the Cumans.
1240 Kiev falls to Mongols.
1241 Mongols invade Poland and Hungary but withdraw shortly after.
1244 Jerusalem falls to band of fugitive Turks.
1248 Seventh Crusade led by Louis IX of France.
1261 Restoration of the Byzantine Empire in Constantinople.
1266–68 Charles of Anjou takes Sicilian crown and defeats Conradin of the Hohenstaufen.
1270 Eighth Crusade.
1282 'Sicilian Vespers': rule of Charles of Anjou overthrown in successful Sicilian rebellion.
1291 Fall of Acre: end of Crusades in Holy Land.

ASIA ▶

***c.* 1000–1100** The Fujiwara effectively hold power in Japan; development of a military class – the Samurai – in the provinces.
1000–1200 Beginning of the main Muslim invasions from Afghanistan; collapse of Hindu kingdoms.
1100–92 Civil war between military rivals in Japan.
1127 Invasion of China by Jin horsemen forces the removal of the Sung dynasty to the south.
1192 Samurai Minamoto Yaritomo conquers rivals in Japan; establishes first shogunate (military government), usurping the power of the emperor.
1220–96 Overthrow of Khmer control in Siam: the kingdoms of Sukhothai and Chiangmai dominate.
1279 Mongols conquer all of China: beginning of harsh Mongol rule under Kublai Khan.
14th century Muslim conquest of northern India complete.
1339–1400 Fighting between daimyo (feudal lords) and Samurai armies leads to chaos in Japan.
1350–1400 Siamese devastate declining Khmer kingdom and unite Siam.
1368 Overthrow of the Mongols in China by the native Ming dynasty.

AFRICA AND THE AMERICAS ▶

973–1171 Fatimid dynasty in Egypt.
***c.* 1000** Rise of the Kanem Empire (northern Nigeria).
1050–1140 Almoravid Empire flourishes in Morocco.
1147–1269 Almohad Empire controls coast of North Africa.
1171–1250 Ayyubid dynasty in Egypt.
***c.* 1180** Toltec state overrun by nomadic tribes.
***c.* 1200** Christian kingdoms in the Sudan fall to Muslim invaders; foundation of Inca dynasty.
***c.* 1200–50** Migration of Aztec people into north Mexico; foundation of Aztec Empire.
***c.* 1200–1400** Great Zimbabwe Empire.
***c.* 1200–1450** Mayapán becomes a powerful city.
1250–1517 Mamelukes rule Egypt.
1400–1500 Expansion of Aztec Empire to cover most of modern Mexico.
***c.* 1400** Kanem-Borno Empire powerful in northern Nigeria and Chad; rise to power of Mossi states in modern Burkina Faso.
1441 Sack of Mayapán by rival cities; several smaller Maya states are formed.
1448 First European fort on African coast established by Portuguese at Arguin (Mauritania).
***c.* 1450** Sultanate of Agadès (in modern Niger) becomes powerful in southern Sahara.
***c.* 1450–1550** Powerful Kongo and Ndongo kingdoms in Angola and Zaïre.
1471–74 Emperor Topa Inca extends empire into southern Peru.
1476 Chimú (Ecuador) conquered by Incas.
1480 Bolivia succumbs to Inca rule.
1482 Portuguese establish trading base in Ghana.
1484 North and central Chile conquered by Incas.
1492 Columbus discovers Bahamas, Cuba and Hispaniola.

1600

1415 Henry V again claims the French throne: invades France and wins Battle of Agincourt.
1439 End of Scandinavian Union.
1455 Beginning of English War of the Roses (civil war).
1461 Yorkists defeated at Battle of St Albans; Edward IV becomes King of England.
1470 Lancastrian invasion restores Henry VI to English throne.
1471 Edward regains throne after Battles of Barnet and Tewkesbury.
1485 Henry Tudor finally defeats Richard III of England at Bosworth field; beginning of Tudor dynasty.

1494 Irish Parliament made subservient to English Parliament (Poynings' Laws).
1513 Battle of Flodden: English defeat Scots and kill James IV.
1533 Henry VIII of England divorces Catherine of Aragon and breaks with Rome.
1533–35 The English Reformation begins.
1536 Denmark becomes Lutheran; Union of England and Wales.
1536–39 Dissolution of the monasteries by Henry VIII.
1553 England becomes Catholic again under Queen Mary.

1559–63 Protestantism re-established in England.
1560s Beginning of Anglo-Spanish maritime feud.
1567 Mary Queen of Scots forced to abdicate; Protestant Dutch revolt against Spanish Habsburg rule begins.
1568 Flight of Mary Queen of Scots to England, where she is imprisoned by Elizabeth I.
1581 United Provinces – the northern Protestant Netherlands – proclaim independence from Spain.
1587 Execution of Mary Queen of Scots after implication in plot to assassinate Elizabeth I.
1588 Defeat of Spanish Armada by English fleet.

1477 Burgundy is annexed by the French crown.
1478 Establishment of the Spanish Inquisition.
1492 Granada, the last Muslim state in Spain, falls to Ferdinand and Isabella.
1494 Charles VIII invades Italy to claim the crown of Naples: start of Franco-Italian wars; Treaty of Tordesillas: Spain and Portugal agree to divide the New World.
1494–95 French invasion of Italy.
1515 Francis I invades Italy and defeats the Swiss and Milanese.
1517 Martin Luther nails his 95 Theses criticizing the Church to the Wittenberg Church door: beginning of the Reformation.

1519 Luther renounces papal supremacy; Charles I of Spain inherits Austrian Habsburg lands: elected Holy Roman Emperor as Charles V.
1522 Charles V divides his dominions between Austrian and Spanish Habsburgs.
1524–25 Peasants' War in Germany.
1525–27 Spread of Lutheranism.
1541–63 Council of Trent: the Roman Catholic Church reforms.
1550 Duke of Alba sent to restore order in rebellious Spanish Netherlands.
1555 Peace of Augsburg: every prince of the Empire allowed to choose the faith of his territory.
1556 Charles V abdicates.

1558 France gains Calais, England's last possession in France.
1559–98 French Wars of Religion between Huguenots (Protestants) and the Catholic League.
1560–74 Regency of Catherine de Medici.
1562–63 Council of Trent ends any hope of reconciliation with the Protestants.
1572 Massacre of St Bartholomew: slaughter of Huguenots.
1589 Henry, King of Navarre, becomes Henry IV of France and converts to Catholicism.
1598 Edict of Nantes recognizes the rights of Protestant Huguenots in France.

1300 Foundation of the Islamic Ottoman Empire in northern Anatolia by Osman I.
1316–41 Creation of the Lithuanian Empire
1346 The Black Death enters Europe.
1356 Ottoman Turks enter Europe.
1363 Ottomans defeat Bosnians, Serbs and Hungarians.
1386 Union of the crowns of Poland and Lithuania.
1389–93 Ottoman annexation of Serbia, the Turkish emirates in Anatolia and Bulgaria.
1395 Tamerlane defeats the Golden Horde.
1410 Battle of Tannenberg – the Teutonic Order is defeated by the Poles and Lithuanians.

1412 John Huss excommunicated for speaking out against sale of indulgences.
1414–17 Council of Constance finally ends Great Schism. John Huss burnt at stake.
1453 Constantinople falls to Ottoman Turks; end of Byzantine Empire.
1478 Hungary gains Lusatia, Moravia and Silesia through treaty with the Bohemians.
1480 Ivan III of Moscow defeats the Mongols.
1494 French forces drive the Medici out of Florence and invade Rome.
1503 Ferdinand V of Spain becomes King of Naples.
1512 France expelled from Italy.

1526 Ferdinand I gains Hungarian and Bohemian crowns through marriage.
1527 Italy falls under the control of Charles V.
1530 The Medici family return to Florence.
1531 Alessandro de Medici becomes duke of Tuscany.
1540 Milan becomes Spanish.
1547 Ivan the Terrible becomes Tsar.
1571 Battle of Lepanto between Ottoman Turks and Holy League (forces of Venice, Spain, Genoa and Papacy): Ottomans defeated.
1580 Carlo Emmanuele I begins territorial expansion of duchy of Savoy.

1403–24 Emperor Yongle extends Chinese Empire, moves capital to Beijing and encourages Confucianism.
1431 Khmer rulers abandon Angkor for Phnom Penh: decline of Khmer Empire.
1471 Annamese conquer the Champa (part of Vietnam).
1517 European traders and missionaries given limited access to the Chinese Empire.

1526 Mogul invasions; Mogul Empire established by Babur.
1539 Burma reunited under the Toungoo.
1555 Akbar, the greatest Mogul ruler, succeeds: military conquest of Rajasthan, Gujarat, Bengal, Kashmir and north Deccan.
1558 Rebellion in Annam: kingdom divides into two.

1573 The Japanese warrior, Oda Nobunaga, ousts the Shogun from Kyoto and establishes firm rule.
1582 Oda Nobunaga is assassinated; his successor, Hideyoshi, continues to unify country.
1591 Hideyoshi breaks power of daimyo and disarms peasants.
1592 Invasion of Korea by Japan; unsuccessful Japanese incursions into China.

1493 Hispaniola settled by Spanish; Columbus discovers Jamaica and Puerto Rico.
1494 Spain and Portugal agree to divide New World colonies.
1497 Cabot discovers Newfoundland.
1498 Inca territory extends to Colombia; Columbus discovers Venezuela.
c. 1500 Portuguese slaving bases established along west coast of Africa.
1500 Pedro Alvares Cabral lands in Brazil and claims territory for Portugal.

1502 Columbus explores Central American coastline.
1505 First black slaves brought to New World.
1517 Egypt comes under Ottoman rule.
1519 The Spaniard Cortés reaches the Aztec Empire.
1520 Last emperor of Aztecs surrenders to Cortés; foundation of Spanish Mexico.
c. 1520 Missionaries arrive in Spanish colonies: forced conversions begin.
1523–35 Spanish conquest of Central America.
1531 Portuguese establish trading posts in Mozambique.

1532 Portuguese begin to settle in Brazil; Spaniards, under Pizarro, reach the coast of Peru and Atahualpa is taken prisoner.
1532–33 Pizarro conquers Incas in Peru.
1535 Inca Empire completely dominated by the Spanish.
1536–1609 Beginning of French and British penetration into Spanish Caribbean.
1553 Beginning of Sharifian dynasties in Morocco.
1591 Songhay Empire (modern Mali) destroyed by Morocco.

17TH AND 18TH CENTURIES

1600

NORTHERN EUROPE ▶

1603 James VI of Scotland succeeds to English throne as James I, uniting the two crowns.

1605 Failure of Catholic Gunpowder Plot to blow up English Parliament.

1618 Protestant Bohemian revolt against future Habsburg Emperor Ferdinand II sparks off Thirty Years War.

1629 Charles I begins personal rule in England; Danes suffer a series of defeats and withdraw from war; Swedes – led by Gustavus Adolphus – declare war on Habsburg Empire.

1632 Gustavus Adolphus defeats Habsburgs at Lützen but is killed in battle.

1635 France goes to war with Habsburgs in alliance with Sweden and United Provinces.

1642 Outbreak of English Civil War between supporters of the King (Cavaliers) and Parliamentarians (Roundheads).

1645 Formation of the Roundhead New Model Army in England; Oliver Cromwell becomes second-in-command; victory in Battle of Naseby.

1648 Treaty of Westphalia settles most of the issues of the Thirty Years War except the Franco-Spanish War; full Dutch independence.

1649 Charles executed; England becomes a Commonwealth.

1649–50 Irish and Scottish rebels defeated by Cromwell.

1652–54 Anglo-Dutch sea war.

1653 Cromwell becomes Lord Protector and effective dictator of England.

1654 Abdication of Queen Christina of Sweden.

1658 Danes expelled from southern Sweden; death of Cromwell.

1660 Restoration of Charles II in England.

1665 Great Plague of London: 60,000 killed.

1665–67 Second Anglo-Dutch Naval War.

WESTERN EUROPE ▶

1607 Spanish fleet defeated by Dutch.

1609 Spain agrees to a nine-year truce in the war with the Netherlands.

1621–48 Spain wages an unsuccessful war against the United Provinces.

1627–28 La Rochelle, a Huguenot port, is attacked and besieged by Chief Minister Richelieu; Huguenots surrender and lose political power.

1635 France declares war on Spain, entering the Thirty Years War.

1640 Catalans and Portuguese rebel against Spanish rule.

1643 Louis XIV, 'The Sun King', succeeds to French throne.

1648 Fronde (a period of civil disorder) begins with riots in Paris.

1659 Treaty of Pyrenees ends Franco-Spanish War; France replaces Spain as major western European power.

1661 Louis XIV takes control of government.

1665 Colbert becomes Controller-General of Finance in France; Portugal regains independence.

1672 France declares war on Dutch who are joined by the Holy Roman Empire, Brandenburg and finally Spain and Lorraine.

1678 Treaty of Nijmegen ends war between France and the Netherlands (and Spain); Peace of Nijmegen (1679) ends war between France and the Empire.

1685 Edict of Nantes revoked: Protestantism banned; thousands of Huguenots flee France.

1688 France invades Rhineland; precipitates Nine Years War (or War of the Grand Alliance).

1689 Formation of the Grand Alliance of England, the United Provinces, Austria, Spain and Savoy against France.

1697 France finally defeated by Grand Alliance: Peace of Ryswick.

SOUTHERN AND EASTERN EUROPE ▶

1613 Beginning of Romanov dynasty in Russia.

1649 Establishment of serfdom in Russia.

1667 Truce of Andrusovo ends 13-year war between Russia and Poland; Kiev ceded to Russia.

1671 Turks declare war on Poland.

1672 Poland invaded by Turks and Cossacks; Poles surrender Podolia and Ukraine.

1673 Battle of Khorzim: Turks defeated by Poles led by Jan Sobieski.

1674 Jan Sobieski elected King of Poland.

1681 Treaty of Radzin: Russia gains most of Ukraine from Turkey.

1682 Accession of Peter the Great in Russia.

1683 Sobieski expels Turks from Vienna.

1700 Great Northern War breaks out between Sweden and Russia, Denmark and Poland over supremacy in the Baltic.

1701 Charles XII of Sweden invades Poland.

1703–12 Hungarian revolt against Austria.

1706 Sweden imposes Stanislaus on the Polish throne.

1708 Sweden invades Russia.

1709 Peter (the Great) of Russia defeats Charles XII of Sweden at Battle of Poltava.

1711 Turkey declares war on Russia.

1720 Treaty of Nystadt ends Great Northern War: Sweden loses an empire and Russia becomes a major Baltic power.

1725 Death of Peter the Great.

1733–35 War of the Polish Succession: France and Spain fight Austria and Russia.

ASIA ▶

1603 Hideyoshi dies; establishment of Tokugawa shogunate; further curbs on the freedom of daimyo.

1605–27 Encouragement of the arts in India under the rule of Jahangir.

1628–56 Reign of Shah Jahan: building of the Taj Mahal.

1630s Christianity and travel abroad is proscribed and foreigners discouraged: Japan becomes isolated from the rest of the world.

1644 Ming dynasty collapses after rebellions and attacks by the Manchus; foundation of Qing dynasty.

1650–1800 Period of economic growth in Japan: emergence of merchant class and rising educational standards.

1657 Shah Jahan falls ill; struggle for succession by his four sons; Aurangzeb kills his brothers, imprisons his father and becomes emperor.

1659–1707 Aurangzeb continues expansionist policies and by 1700 covers all of India except the far south; he ends religious tolerance which increases opposition to Mogul rule.

1674 Sivaji defeats Moguls; Maratha kingdom established in west central India.

1683 Taiwan is incorporated into China.

1692 Catholic missionaries are allowed to make conversions in China.

AFRICA AND THE AMERICAS ▶

***c.* 1600–*c.* 1800** Kingdom of Gondar flourishes in Ethiopia.

1605 French settle Nova Scotia.

1607 Jamestown, Virginia, is founded by the English.

1612 English colonize Bermuda.

1620 English Pilgrim Fathers settle Plymouth, Massachusetts.

1630–40 First English and French claims to West Indian islands.

1638 The Dutch take Mauritius; France establishes fort of Saint-Louis in Senegal.

1650s Colonization of Canada by the French.

1652 Cape settlement established by Dutch East India Company.

1655 English capture Jamaica from Spanish and begin colonization.

1664 English gain New York from the Dutch.

1670 Foundation of Hudson's Bay Company.

1697 Spain loses Haiti (half of Hispaniola) to the French.

1699–1702 French colonize Louisiana.

***c.* 1700** Rise of Asante kingdom to power in modern Ghana.

***c.* 1700–1830** Kingdom of Dahomey (modern Benin) flourishes as one of the principal slave-trading states.

1713 Britain becomes dominant in Nigerian slave trade.

1717 Spanish reorganization of South American colonies.

1800

1666 Great Fire of London.

1678 'Popish Plot': wave of anti-Catholicism in England.

1688 'Glorious Revolution': William III of Orange arrives in England to take throne (with parliamentary backing); James II flees to France.

1689 William III and Mary become joint sovereigns; Bill of Rights establishes a constitutional monarchy.

1690 Battle of the Boyne (in Ireland): William III defeats James and retains crown.

1707 Act of Union unites Scotland and England.

1714 George the Elector of Hanover becomes George I.

1715 First Jacobite uprising in Scotland defeated.

1720 South Sea Bubble: failure of South Sea Company causes financial panic.

1721 Walpole becomes first prime minister of England.

1745–46 Last Jacobite rebellion in Britain fails.

c. 1750 Development of manufacturing industry; beginning of the Industrial Revolution.

1750 Britain joins Austro-Russian alliance against Prussia.

1756 Alliance between Britain and Prussia and alliance between France and Austria; beginning of Seven Years War sparked off by British and French colonial rivalry and European struggle between Prussia and Austria.

1762 Britain declares war on Spain.

1763 End of Seven Years War.

1771 Richard Arkwright establishes first factory system for cotton spinning.

1780 Anti-Catholic riots in London.

1793 Britain joins continental powers against Revolutionary France.

1701 War of the Spanish Succession begins.

1704 British defeat French at Blenheim; British fleet captures Gibraltar from Spain.

1713 Treaty of Utrecht: end of War of Spanish Succession.

1715 Death of Louis XIV.

1719 France declares war on Spain.

1720 'Mississippi Bubble' in France. Treaty of Hague ends hostilities between Spain and Quadruple Alliance (Britain, France, Holy Roman Empire and the Netherlands).

1727–29 War between Britain, Spain and France: Spain besieges Gibraltar (until 1728).

1739 Britain and Spain at war over British trade with South American colonies; merges with War of the Austrian Succession in 1740.

1755 Lisbon destroyed by earthquake.

1761 Influenza epidemic spreads across Europe.

1763 Peace of Paris: end of Seven Years War.

1770 Smallpox epidemic in Europe.

1778 Holland and France join American colonies in War of Independence.

1779–83 Spain enters War of Independence against Britain and lays siege to Gibraltar.

1789 French Revolution: overthrow of Bourbon monarchy; abolition of feudal rights and privileges.

1792 France declares war on Austria and Prussia; beginning of Revolutionary Wars; National Convention formed to rule France; France becomes a republic.

1793 Louis XVI executed; Reign of Terror begins under Robespierre.

1794 Robespierre executed: end of Reign of Terror.

1795 Napoleon leads army into renewed Revolutionary Wars.

1799 Napoleon seizes power in France.

1734–35 War between Turkey and Persia.

1740 War of the Austrian Succession: Maria Theresa succeeds to the thrones of Austria, Bohemia and Hungary: Frederick the Great seizes Silesia for Prussia.

c. 1740s Danubian principalities (Moldavia and Walachia) increasingly independent under Greek 'princes'.

1748 End of the War of the Austrian Succession.

1756 Outbreak of the Seven Years War.

1757 Sweden joins Seven Years War against Britain and Prussia.

1762 Accession of Catherine II (the Great): Russia changes sides in Seven Years War and allies with Prussia against Austria; Russian noblemen gain economic and social rights that free them from service obligations.

1766 Catherine II grants freedom of worship in Russia.

1772 First partition of Poland between Russia, Prussia and Austria.

1773–74 The Cossack leader Pugachev leads popular revolt against rule of Catherine II: uprising crushed.

1775 Reforms of provincial government carried out by Catherine II.

1781 Joseph I of Austria introduces religious toleration and abolishes serfdom.

1784 Convention of Constantinople: Turkey accepts Russian annexation of Crimea.

1787 Russia and Turkey at war.

1793 Second partition of Poland.

1795 Third partition of Poland.

1693 Kangxi leads Chinese invasion of Mongolia.

c. 1700 British East India Company secures the important ports in India.

1701 Kingdom of Lanxang divides into two.

1707–61 Aurangzeb dies: regional dynasties assert their independence leading to a power vacuum in India.

1715 Christianity banned in China.

1735–95 Expansion of Chinese Empire into Turkistan, Annam (Vietnam), Burma and Nepal.

c. 1750 Tokyo becomes world's largest city.

1752 Toungoo dynasty falls in Burma.

1757 Foreign traders are restricted to Guangzhou; the Burmese dynasty of Konbaung is established; series of wars with Siam begins.

c. 1760s British East India Company has become the dominant force in India.

1761 Battle of Panipat: Maratha defeated in their attempt to dominate all India.

1767 Burma overthrows Ayuthia Kingdom and occupies Siam.

1777 Burmese expelled from Siam under leadership of General Taksin.

1784 Burma conquers kingdom of Arakan bringing Burmese territory to the border of British India.

1793 British delegations denied diplomatic relations in China.

1744–54 Britain and France go to war over control of North America.

1761 British dominate the West Indies.

1763 Britain gains Grenada from France; France ousted from Canada by British.

1765 British impose the Stamp Act on American colonies.

1773 Boston Tea Party.

1774 Continental Congress issues Declaration of Rights.

1775 War of American Independence breaks out at Lexington.

1776 US Declaration of Independence.

1778 France, Holland and Spain (1779) join war against Britain.

1780–81 Peruvian Indians revolt against Spanish rule.

1781 British surrender at Yorktown; American loyalists emigrate to Canada.

1787 US Constitution.

1791 Toussaint L'Ouverture leads successful Black slave revolt in Haiti.

1796 British capture Guyana.

1798 Britain occupies the Cape.

1798–1801 French invasion of Egypt.

IN THE FRENCH REVOLUTION REIGN OF TERROR (1793), *c.* 40,000 PEOPLE WERE EXECUTED

19TH CENTURY

1800

NORTHERN AND WESTERN EUROPE ▶

1801 Act of Union joins Britain and Ireland.

1802 Peace of Amiens ends war between Britain and France.

1803 Britain declares war on France in renewal of Napoleonic Wars.

1804 Napoleon becomes Emperor; Code Napoleon adopted in France.

1805 Nelson defeats the French and Spanish fleets at Trafalgar. Napoleon defeats Austro-Russian forces at Austerlitz.

1806 Napoleon abolishes Holy Roman Empire; creation of the Confederation of the Rhine.

1807 Slave trade abolished in British Empire.

1812 Assassination of British PM Spencer Perceval. Anglo-American War (until 1814).

1813 Napoleon defeated at Battle of Leipzig.

1814 Napoleon abdicates and is exiled to Elba; Congress of Vienna.

1815 Britain gains the Cape, Mauritius, Ascension Island, Heligoland, Ceylon, Trinidad, Tobago and St Lucia in postwar settlement; Napoleon's 100 Days end in defeat at Waterloo; Congress of Vienna resumes; Confederation of Germany formed.

1819 Peterloo Massacre of peaceful radical demonstrators in Manchester.

1820 Cato Street conspiracy: plot to assassinate British Cabinet uncovered.

1829 Catholic Emancipation Act: Catholics can hold office in Britain.

1830 July Revolution in France – Bourbons overthrown; Orleans monarchy established.

1830–31 Successful Belgian revolt against Dutch rule.

1832 First Reform Bill extends British vote.

1833 Slavery abolished in British Empire.

1836 Chartist Movement begins in Britain.

SOUTHERN AND EASTERN EUROPE ▶

1801 France defeats Turks at Heliopolis, Egypt; assassination of Tsar Paul of Russia: accession of Alexander I.

1804 Persia and Russia at war over Russian annexation of Georgia.

1804–13 Serbian revolt against Turkish Ottoman rule.

1805 Napoleon crowns himself king of Italy.

1807 Peninsular War sparked off by Napoleon's invasion of Portugal.

1811 French finally driven out of Portugal.

1812 Napoleon invades Russia and defeats Russian forces at Battle of Borodino, but retreats from Moscow in the severest winter conditions.

1813 Battle of Vittoria: French driven from Spain by Wellington's forces; ends Peninsular War.

1815 Kingdom of Poland re-established (under Russian rule); UK gains the Ionian Islands at Congress of Vienna.

1817 Revolt of Greeks against Turkish rule.

1820–32 Greek war of independence against Turks.

1822 End of Congress System of diplomatic alliances; civil war in Spain.

1823 Spanish Liberals defeated in civil war with help of French troops.

1825 Decembrist uprising in Russia leads to repressive rule by Tsar Nicholas I.

1826 Russia and Persia at war.

1827 Russians win war and annex Armenia.

AFRICA AND THE MIDDLE EAST ▶

1801 Third Xhosa War between the Xhosa people and colonial forces.

1805 Mehemet Ali becomes Pasha of Egypt and begins to modernize Egypt.

1806 Britain seizes Cape Colony from Dutch.

1807 Sierra Leone and Gambia become British colonies.

1809 Ecuador becomes part of Colombia.

1810 Mauritius and Seychelles annexed by Britain.

1815 UK gains the Cape at Congress of Vienna.

1818 Zulu Kingdom formed by Shaka.

1818–19 Fifth Xhosa War.

1820 Gold Coast becomes a British colony; Mehemet Ali takes northern Sudan.

1821–22 American Colonization Society establishes Liberia for freed slaves.

1824–31 First Ashanti (Asante) War in the Gold Coast.

1830 Algeria becomes a French colony.

1834–35 Sixth Xhosa War.

1835–37 The Great Trek: Boers leave the Cape to found Transvaal and Orange Free State.

1838 Massacre of Zulus at Battle of Blood River.

1841 Egypt achieves virtual independence from Ottoman Empire.

1843 Britain annexes the Gambia and Natal.

1846–53 Xhosa War: Xhosa resist expansion of colonists in Cape Colony.

1847 Liberia becomes independent.

1850 Britain ousts Danes from Ghana.

1850–68 Emperor Theodore consolidates independent Ethiopia.

1851 British occupy Lagos; end of slave trade.

1854 Livingstone begins exploration of central Africa.

1861 Britain acquires Lagos (Nigeria).

1862 France acquires Djibouti.

ASIA AND AUSTRALASIA ▶

***c.* 1800–1900** Western involvement in China increases; imperial power diminished.

***c.* 1800–50** Laos fragments into several states.

1802 Reunion of Annam under Nguyen Anh (with French assistance).

1803–05 First Maratha War in India.

1804 Castle Hill Rising of convicts in New South Wales.

1806 Sepoy mutiny against British at Vellore, India.

1808 Overthrow of Governor Bligh in Rum Rebellion, Australia.

1811 British occupy Java: restored to Dutch in 1819; Russians fail to force Japan to open trade with West.

1815 UK gains Ceylon; revolt against British rule (1817) repressed.

1819 Singapore is founded as British colony.

1824 Britain gains Assam; First Anglo-Burmese War (until 1826).

1824–51 General Chakri of Siam (later Rana I) founds new dynasty; Bangkok becomes new capital and Thai Empire extended into Laos and northern Malaya.

1825–30 Java War: Dutch defeat Javanese anti-colonial forces.

1828 Western Australia founded.

1834 South Australia founded.

1837 Colonization of New Zealand begins.

1838–42 First Anglo-Afghan War.

1839 First Opium War between Britain and China.

1840 New Zealand becomes a British colony.

1841 Britain occupies Hong Kong.

THE AMERICAS ▶

1801 Haiti becomes a republic.

1803 USA makes 'Louisiana Purchase' from France.

1804 Haiti proclaims its independence from France.

1807 Colombian independence movement begins.

1808 Uprisings in Spain's South American colonies.

1808–20 Nationalist uprisings in Spanish colonies: Simon Bolivár emerges as nationalist leader.

1811–28 Full independence in South American colonies: Paraguay and Venezuela (1811), Argentina (1816), Chile (1818), Colombia (1819), Mexico, Central America and Peru (1821), Brazil (1822), Uruguay (1828).

1812–14 Anglo-American War.

1813 USA seizes West Florida from Spain.

1817 Independent government of Venezuela formed by Bolivár.

1819 Spain cedes Florida to USA.

1820 Missouri Compromise: slave-owning states allowed to join union.

1823 Monroe Doctrine warns European powers against further New World colonization.

1830 Large-scale removal of Indians to reservations begins; Ecuador becomes independent of Colombia.

1833–80 Abolition of slavery in colonies by Britain (1833), France (1848), Holland (1863), Spain: Puerto Rico (1873) and Cuba (1880).

■ ONE MILLION PEOPLE DIED FROM STARVATION IN THE POTATO FAMINE IN IRELAND IN 1846,

1900

1838 Foundation of the Anti-Corn Law League.

1843 Agitation in Ireland for repeal of Act of Union.

1846 Potato famine in Ireland.

1848 Second French Republic established; Louis Philippe abdicates.

1851 Fall of Second Republic in France: Louis Napoleon becomes Emperor Napoleon III; Great Exhibition of London.

1862 Bismarck becomes Chancellor of Prussia; Prussia gains Schleswig Holstein after war with Denmark (1864).

1866 Austro-Prussian War: Prussia defeats Austria at Könninggrätz and ends Austrian influence in Germany; Prussia annexes Hanover, Nassau and Hesse-Cassel.

1867 Formation of North German Confederation; Austro-Hungarian 'Dual Monarchy' founded; second major Reform Act doubles the British electorate.

1871 France defeated in Franco-Prussian War: Alsace ceded to Germany; German unification under Kaiser Wilhelm I: Bismarck becomes Chancellor of Germany; Paris Commune is crushed; trade unions declared legal in Britain.

1872 Ballot Act introduces secret ballot in elections in Britain.

1882 Italy, Germany and Austria form the Triple Alliance; Phoenix Park Murders spark off Anglo-Irish Crisis.

1886 First Irish Home Rule Bill fails.

1890 Fall of Bismarck; Anglo-German agreement over colonies.

1891 Keir Hardie becomes first British Independent Labour Party MP.

1893 Second Irish Home Rule Bill fails.

1894 Dreyfus Affair begins in France; splits nation.

1897 First Zionist Congress meets in Basel, Switzerland.

1830 Polish uprising against Russia; revolution in northern Italy against Austrian occupation.

1831 Italian nationalist movement founded by Mazzini.

1832 Poland becomes a Russian province.

1841 Straits Convention closes the Dardanelles to non-Ottoman warships.

1848 Revolution against Austrian Empire in Italian states, Prague and Budapest suppressed by 1849.

1854 Crimean War starts: France, Britain, Austria and Turkey against Russia.

1856 End of Crimean War: Treaty of Paris guarantees Turkey's integrity.

1861 Italian unification led by Garibaldi and Cavour; emancipation of Russian serfs.

1863 Polish and Lithuanian revolt against Russian rule.

1868 Liberal uprising in Spain: Isabella II deposed.

1869 Carlist uprising in Spain crushed.

1870 Italy annexes Rome.

1873 First Spanish Republic.

1877 Massacre of Bulgarians by Turks: Russo-Turkish War.

1878 End of Russo-Turkish War; Romania, Serbia and Montenegro independent.

1887 Renewal of Russo-German Reinsurance Treaty and Triple Alliance.

1891 Launch of the Young Turk Movement.

1894 and 1896 Massacres of Armenians by Turks.

1867 British expedition to Ethiopia.

1869 Opening of Suez Canal.

1873 Second Ashanti War.

1875–1900 The 'Scramble for Africa' – intensifies after the 1884 Berlin Conference.

1877 Britain annexes the Transvaal.

1879 Britain and France gain control of Egypt; Zulu Wars.

1880s Brazza establishes French protectorate over the Congo.

1881 First Boer War; nationalist revolt in Egypt; France establishes a protectorate over Tunisia.

1882 Britain occupies Egypt.

1883 Kruger becomes President of the Transvaal.

1884 German protectorates of Kamerun (Cameroon) and South West Africa (Namibia) proclaimed.

1885 Congo Free State (Zaïre) becomes a personal possession of King Léopold II of the Belgians; British colonize Nigeria; Mahdists take Khartoum, kill General Gordon and create a theocratic state in the Sudan.

1889–90 French rule in Central Africa and Chad begins.

1890 Establishment of Rhodesia by Cecil Rhodes; Germany colonizes modern Rwanda, Burundi and mainland Tanzania; Zanzibar becomes a British protectorate.

1890s French take Mossi kingdom (Burkina Faso). British South Africa Company establishes control in modern Zambia and Zimbabwe.

1894 British protectorate established in Uganda.

1896 Ethiopia successfully counters attempted invasion by Italian forces; French take Madagascar.

1899 Beginning of Boer War in South Africa; joint Anglo-Egyptian rule established in Sudan; southern Somalia becomes Italian; Second Boer War starts.

1842 Massacre in Khyber Pass as British retreat from Afghanistan.

1845 Maori rising against British in New Zealand.

1845–49 Sikh Wars: British annexation of the Punjab.

1850 Taiping Rebellion starts in China.

1853–54 US commodore Perry enters two Japanese ports: US trade and technology ends Japanese isolation.

1856–60 Second Opium War.

1857–58 Indian Mutiny suppressed; Crown government of India begins.

1860 Second Maori War in New Zealand; Chinese ports forced to trade with West.

1863 Cambodia becomes a French protectorate.

1864 Qing dynasty finally crushes Taiping Rebellion in China: 20 million dead.

1867 End of transportation of convicts to Australia.

1867–69 Tokugawa shogunate toppled in Japan: Meiji reforms begin.

1877 Queen Victoria becomes Empress of India.

1878 Second Anglo-Afghan War.

1882 French capture Hanoi; Chinese assert suzerainty over Annam.

1885 Indian National Congress meets for first time; Britain and Germany annex New Guinea.

1894 War between China and Japan begins.

1895 End of war between China and Japan: Japan gains Formosa (Taiwan) and Korea.

1836 Battles of the Alamo and San Jacinto; Texas gains independence from Mexico.

1837 Papineau and Mackenzie Rebellions in Canada.

1838 Foundation of Central American republics.

1845 US–Mexican War starts.

1847 Mormons settle Salt Lake City.

1848 End of US–Mexican War; USA gains California and New Mexico; Californian gold rush.

1850 Compromise over slavery in new US states.

1850–90 Indian wars on the western US plains.

1860–61 Southern US states secede to form Confederacy.

1861 American Civil War begins.

1863 Emancipation of slaves in USA.

1865 Confederacy surrenders; Lincoln assassinated.

1866 Civil Rights Bill for US blacks passed.

1867 USA purchases Alaska from Russia.

1876 Battle of Little Big Horn: Custer's US cavalry wiped out by Sioux.

1879 War of the Pacific: Chile defeats Peru and Bolivia; Bolivia loses Pacific coast.

1889 Panama Canal Scandal; Brazil becomes a republic.

1890 Battle of Wounded Knee: final defeat of Sioux.

1893 USA overthrows Hawaiian government.

1898 Spanish–American War: Spain cedes Puerto Rico, Guam, Philippines and Cuba to USA.

FOLLOWED BY A TYPHOID EPIDEMIC WHICH KILLED A FURTHER THIRD OF A MILLION PEOPLE ■

20th Century

1900

NORTHERN AND WESTERN EUROPE ▶

1902 End of Boer War.

1904 Entente Cordiale between Britain and France established.

1905 Norway becomes independent from Sweden.

1906 British Labour Party founded after election; end of Dreyfus affair in Britain.

1907 Triple Entente of France, Britain and Russia formed.

1913 House of Lords rejects Third Irish Home Rule Bill.

1914 Britain declares war on Germany: outbreak of WWI.

1916 Easter Rising in Ireland suppressed; one million dead at Battle of the Somme.

1918 Austria–Hungary and Germany surrender; civil war in Ireland.

1919 Treaty of Versailles; Spartacist Rising in Berlin crushed.

1920 Weimar Republic established in Germany.

1921 Irish Free State established in Southern Ireland: civil war continues (until 1923).

1923–25 Franco-Belgian occupation of Ruhr when Germany defaults on reparations.

1924 First British Labour Government.

1926 General Strike in Britain.

1927 German economy collapses on Black Friday.

1930 107 Nazis are elected to Reichstag.

1931 Dominion states gain full independence.

1933 Hitler becomes Chancellor of Germany.

1935 Anti-semitism is legalized in Germany by Nuremberg laws.

1936 Germany and Japan sign Anti-Comintern Pact; Rome–Berlin Axis formed.

1937 British PM Chamberlain adopts policy of appeasement of Germany.

1938 German annexation of Austria – Anschluss – and Czech Sudetenland.

1939 Germany signs non-aggression pact with USSR; invades Czechoslovakia and Poland; Britain declares war on Germany: outbreak of WWII.

1940 Germany invades France; national government formed under Churchill following Dunkirk evacuation; Battle of Britain.

1940–41 London Blitz.

SOUTHERN AND EASTERN EUROPE ▶

1900 Assassination of Umberto I, King of Italy.

1903 Formation of Bolshevik Party in Russia.

1905 'Bloody Sunday' Revolution in Russia: Duma (Parliament) set up with limited powers.

1908 Assassination of Carlos, King of Portugal; Austria annexes Bosnia and Herzegovina.

1910 Portugal becomes a republic.

1914 Austrian heir Archduke Franz Ferdinand assassinated: Austria declares war on Serbia; Germany declares war on Russia and France: outbreak of WWI.

1915 Italy joins Allies and Bulgaria joins Central Powers.

1916 Portugal and Romania join war against Germany.

1917 October Revolution: Bolsheviks take control.

1918 Russia withdraws from war; Russian Civil War.

1919 End of Habsburg Empire: independence for Czechoslovakia, Poland, Yugoslavia and Hungary.

1921 Greece and Turkey at war; end of Russian Civil War.

1922 Fascists march on Rome: Mussolini becomes PM.

1924 Death of Lenin: Stalin emerges as successor.

1925 Mussolini establishes dictatorship.

1929 Lateran Treaties recognize sovereignty of Vatican City.

1930 Beginning of the extermination of Kulaks (wealthy peasants) in USSR.

1933 Stalinist purges begin.

1935 Soviet 'Show Trials' of ex-Party members.

1936 Outbreak of Spanish Civil War.

1937 Italy joins Anti-Comintern Pact.

1939 Nationalists win Spanish Civil War; German–Soviet pact assigns Baltic States to USSR; USSR invades Finland.

AFRICA AND THE MIDDLE EAST ▶

1900 Nigeria becomes British protectorate.

1902 End of Boer War.

1904 Massacres of Herero rebels by Germans in south-west Africa; French and Spanish rule in Morocco.

1905–06 First Moroccan Crisis: French interests in Morocco disputed by Germany.

1907 Belgian government takes over control of Congo from Léopold III following atrocities.

1910 South Africa becomes a dominion.

1914 South Africa enters the war against the Central Powers.

1917 Britain supports idea of Jewish state in Palestine in Balfour Declaration.

1919 Ottoman Empire dismantled: UK mandate over Palestine and Iraq; French mandate of Syria.

1920 Kenya becomes a British colony.

1921 Reza Khan seizes power in Iran (becomes Shah in 1925).

1922 British protectorate over Egypt ends.

1923 Turkish republic formed with Mustapha Kemal as president.

1930s Growth of Afrikaner nationalism in South Africa.

1932 Saudi Arabia established.

1935–36 Italians invade and occupy Ethiopia.

1941 War extends to North Africa.

1942 Montgomery defeats German–Italian forces at El Alamein.

1943 Germans and Italians withdraw from North Africa.

1948 State of Israel established; first Arab–Israeli War; nationalists in power in South Africa: policy of apartheid begins.

ASIA AND AUSTRALASIA ▶

1900 Anti-Western Boxer Rebellion in China ends after foreign intervention.

1901 Australian Commonwealth established.

1904 Russo-Japanese War.

1907 New Zealand becomes an independent dominion.

1911–12 Revolution in China ends imperial rule: republic established.

1914 Australia and New Zealand enter the war against the Central Powers; German territories in the Pacific occupied – Western Samoa by New Zealand, Nauru by Australia, Micronesia and the Marshall Islands by Japan.

1919 Punjab riots; Amritsar Massacre by British troops fuels Indian nationalist sentiment.

1921 Gandhi begins civil disobedience campaign in India; Chinese Communist Party formed.

1923 Sun Yat-sen establishes Nationalist Chinese government.

1927–28 Civil war in China: Nationalists defeat Communists and form government.

1931 Mukden Incident: Japan seizes Manchuria.

1932 Indian Congress is declared illegal: Gandhi is arrested.

1934–35 'Long March' by defeated Chinese Communists.

1935 Burma separated from India.

1937 Japan invades China.

1938 Japan gains effective control over China.

1940–42 Japan invades Indochina (1940), the Philippines (1941), Malaya, Singapore, East Indies and Burma (1942).

1941 Japan bombs Pearl Harbor: Britain and USA declare war on Japan.

THE AMERICAS ▶

1901 US President McKinley assassinated: T. Roosevelt succeeds him.

1902 Cuba becomes fully independent.

1903 USA gains control of Panama Canal zone; Panama secedes from Colombia.

1910 Mexican Civil War begins.

1914 Canada enters war against Central Powers.

1915 *Lusitania* sunk by German U-boat.

1916 US troops occupy Dominican Republic.

1917 USA declares war on Germany.

1919 US President Wilson instrumental in the establishment of the League of Nations.

1920 USA enters period of isolation after Senate votes against membership of the League of Nations; beginning of Prohibition in USA.

1921 US women are given the vote.

1928 Outbreak of Chaco War between Paraguay and Bolivia.

1929 Wall Street Crash precipitates Great Depression worldwide.

1930 Vargas comes to power in Brazil.

1930s Order restored in Mexico by Institutional Revolutionary Party – redistribution of land (1934–39).

1933 President F.D. Roosevelt launches New Deal policy to counter effects of Depression; end of Prohibition.

1935–39 US Neutrality Acts prevent US involvement in non-American wars.

1941 Lend Lease Act passed; USA enters war on Allied side.

■ ONE IN TEN PEOPLE WHO HAVE EVER LIVED ARE ALIVE TODAY ■ DURING THE WALL STREET

1997

1941 First extermination camps set up in Germany.
1944 D-Day Allied landings.
1945 Germany surrenders; Germany and Austria occupied; United Nations founded; Labour government comes to power in Britain: establishment of welfare state.
1945–46 Nuremburg Trials.
1948 Communists blockade Berlin: Allied Berlin Airlift.
1949 NATO is formed; Germany is divided into East and West Germany.
1952 End of Allied occupation of West Germany.
1956 Suez Crisis leads to subsequent resignation of British PM Sir Anthony Eden.
1957 Treaty of Rome establishes the European Economic Community (EEC; later EC).
1958 Fifth Republic of France established under Charles De Gaulle.
1959 EFTA founded.
1961 Berlin Wall is built.
1968 Anti-government student demonstrations and strikes in France; Britain withdraws from East of Suez.
1969 Beginning of Ostpolitik in West Germany; French president De Gaulle resigns; troops sent to Northern Ireland to restore order.
1971 Women gain the vote in Switzerland.
1972 Direct rule introduced in Northern Ireland.
1973 Britain and Ireland join EC; Denmark joins EC; East and West Germany establish diplomatic relations.
1979 Right-wing Conservative premiership of Margaret Thatcher begins in Britain.
1981 Mitterrand becomes first socialist president of French Fifth Republic.
1985 Anglo-Irish Accord on Northern Ireland.
1986 Spain and Portugal join EC.
1989 Berlin Wall opened.
1990 German reunification; Thatcher resigns and John Major becomes British PM.
1992 Single European market established.
1995 Austria, Finland and Sweden join EC/EU.

1940 Italy joins war against Allies.
1941 Germany invades Yugoslavia, Greece and USSR; Bulgaria and Romania join the Axis Powers.
1943 Invasion of Sicily by Allies; Italy surrenders.
1944 Soviet offensive in East.
1945–48 Communist takeover in eastern Europe.
1946 Civil war in Greece.
1952–57 Campaign by Greek Cypriots to end British rule.
1953 Death of Stalin; Khrushchev comes to power.
1955 Warsaw Pact formed.
1956 De-Stalinization in eastern Europe; Soviet troops crush anti-Soviet uprising in Hungary.
1964 Clashes between Greeks and Turks break out in Cyprus; Brezhnev comes to power, insists USSR has right to intervene in the affairs of Communist states.
1967 Military coup in Greece.
1968 'Prague Spring' in Czechoslovakia; reform ended when Soviet troops invade.
1970 Unrest in Poland; riots in Gdansk.
1974 Overthrow of Portuguese dictatorship; Turkish invasion of Cyprus leads to partition; democracy restored in Greece.
1975 Death of Franco: restoration of democracy in Spain.
1981 Greece joins EC.
1985 Gorbachev comes to power: begins policy of reform.
1989–90 Fall of Communist regimes in eastern Europe: free elections.
1990 German reunification.
1991 Break-up of USSR into 15 independent republics; Gorbachev resigns.
1992 Civil war leads to break-up of Yugoslavia.

1952 Moroccan uprising against French; Mau Mau rebellion starts in Kenya.
1954 Nasser takes full control of Egypt; beginning of Algerian War of Independence.
1956 Suez Crisis; independence for Morocco, Sudan and Tunisia.
1957–75 Decolonization in Black Africa.
1962 Algeria's independence after bitter struggle.
1965 White Rhodesian government unilaterally declares independence: guerrilla fighting follows.
1967 Six Day Arab–Israeli War: Israel defeats Arabs and captures Sinai, the West Bank, Gaza and Golan; PLO formed.
1970 Jordanian civil war; Palestinians expelled.
1973 Third Arab–Israeli War; Arab oil embargo on the West.
1974–75 Portuguese African colonies gain independence.
1975 Lebanese civil war begins.
1977 Crackdown on anti-apartheid activity in South Africa.
1979 Islamic Revolution in Iran.
1980 Rhodesia becomes independent; renamed Zimbabwe.
1980–88 Iran–Iraq War.
1982 Israel invades Lebanon.
1986 Palestinians intensify violent anti-Israeli campaign.
1990 South Africa begins to dismantle apartheid; Iraq invades Kuwait.
1991 Gulf War: US-led coalition defeats Iraq.
1994 Majority rule in South Africa.

1945 US atomic bombs dropped on Hiroshima and Nagasaki; Japan surrenders.
1946–49 Nationalists defeated in Chinese Civil War: Mao Zedong and Communists come to power.
1947 India gains independence; Pakistan becomes separate state.
1948 Gandhi assassinated.
1950–51 Chinese invasion of Tibet.
1950–53 Korean War.
1954 Vietnam gains independence from French; divided into Communist North and Western-backed South Vietnam.
1959 Uprising in Tibet crushed by China.
1962 A US military command is set up in South Vietnam.
1965 US marines sent to Vietnam; Chinese Cultural Revolution begins.
1968 Tet Offensive by North Vietnamese forces.
1969 USA begins talks with North Vietnamese.
1971 Bangladesh becomes an independent state.
1973 US troops leave Vietnam.
1975 South Vietnam surrenders: end of Vietnam War.
1976 Mao Zedong dies: end of era in Chinese history.
1979 Soviet forces back coup in Afghanistan: civil war breaks out; Vietnam invades Cambodia.
1988 Vietnamese forces withdraw from Cambodia.
1989 Soviet troops are gradually withdrawn from Afghanistan; peaceful pro-democracy demonstrations are violently crushed in Tiananmen Square, China.
1997 Hong Kong returned to China.

1942 US troops arrive in Europe, North Africa and the Pacific.
1946–55 Juan Perón in power in Argentina.
1947 Truman Doctrine: containment of Communism.
1948 Marshall Plan adopted to provide US aid to Europe.
1949 Escalation of Cold War between USA and USSR after explosion of first Soviet atomic bomb.
1950–54 McCarthy witch-hunt of suspected Communists in USA.
1956–58 Cuban Civil War: Fidel Castro comes to power.
1957 US Civil Rights Act passed; race riots in southern states.
1960 Bay of Pigs: attempt by US-backed exiles to invade Cuba fails.
1972 Civil war breaks out in El Salvador.
1973 Peace of Paris: US troops withdraw from Vietnam; left-wing Allende government overthrown in Chile by General Pinochet with indirect US help.
1974 Watergate scandal forces Nixon to resign.
1979 Somoza overthrown by Sandinistas in Nicaragua.
1980 Cold War heats up following Soviet invasion of Afghanistan.
1986 'Iran-gate' scandal.
1987 INF Treaty signed by USA and USSR.
1990 Chile and Brazil hold free elections: return to civilian government.

CRASH OF 1929, A TOTAL OF 12,894,650 SHARES EXCHANGED HANDS IN ONE SINGLE DAY ■

Makers and Shapers

- ‘If the nose of Cleopatra had been shorter, the whole face of the earth would have been changed’, Blaise Pascal.
- ‘Caesar was a failure. Otherwise he would not have been assassinated’, Napoleon Bonaparte.
- ‘Fifty per cent genius, fifty per cent bloody fool’, Clement Atlee on Winston Churchill.
- ‘A horrible voice, bad breath and a vulgar manner – the characteristics of a popular politician’, Aristophanes.

Abd er-Rahman I (731–88), emir of Andalus, the principal Moorish state in Spain (756).

Abdul Rahman, Tunku (1903–90), founder of Malay nationalist movement (1945), PM of Malaya (1957–63); helped form Malaysia, which he ruled (1963–70).

Abraham (*c.* 2000 BC), first of Hebrew Biblical patriarchs; commanded by God to leave Sumeria and found a new nation in Canaan.

Abu-Bakr (*c.* 570–634), companion and adviser of Muhammad; first caliph (632). Began the Arab conquest of the Middle East.

Adams, John (1735–1826), first US vice-pres. under George Washington (1789–97) and second pres. (1797–1801); a Federalist, he was influential in the American independence movement.

Adams, John Quincy (1767–1848), 6th US pres. (1825–29); son of pres. John Adams. An anti-slavery campaigner; said to be real author of the Monroe Doctrine.

Adenaeur, Konrad (1876–1967), first chancellor of W. Germany (1949–63). Dominant figure in post-war rebuilding of W. Germany.

Agrippa, Marcus Vipsanius (63–12 BC), Roman statesman and general; defeated Mark Antony at Actium (31 BC); helped Octavian become Emperor Augustus.

Akbar the Great (1542–1605), Mogul emperor of India from 1556; extended empire through conquest to most of India; initiated considerable political and cultural reform.

Akhenaton (14th century BC), name adopted by Pharaoh Amenhotep IV, king of 18th dynasty Egypt. Renounced old gods and founded monotheistic cult of Aton; moved capital to Amarna.

Alba (or Alva), 3rd Duke of, Fernando Álvarez de Toledo y Pimentel (1508–82), Spanish general under Charles V and Philip II. Re-established Spanish rule in the Netherlands (1567); conquered Portugal (1581).

Alcibiades (*c.* 450–404 BC), Athenian politician; agitated Athenians to unite against Sparta in 420 BC. Condemned to death for sacrilege, he advised Spartans in their defeat of Athens; returned to Athenian fold in 411; assassinated by Spartans.

Alexander I (1777–1825), tsar of Russia (1801–25). Helped form coalition against Napoleon in 1812; defeated retreating Napoleonic army at Dresden and Leipzig (1813). Became increasingly reactionary.

Alexander III (1845–94), tsar of Russia from 1881. Powerful autocratic ruler who promoted Russian identity by imposing Russian values and cultures on minorities.

Alexander the Great (356–323 BC), king of Macedonia from 336 BC. Began Persian expedition in 334 BC. Conquered Persian Empire, western Asia Minor, Egypt and Babylon and ventured into India in 326 BC.

Akhenaton

Alexius I Comnenus (1048–1118), Byzantine emperor from 1081. Founder of Comnenian dynasty, he helped re-establish Byzantine rule in Asia Minor.

Alfred the Great (849–99), Anglo-Saxon king of Wessex from 871. Consolidated kingdom through fortification and negotiated peace treaties with the Danes; a promoter of arts and learning.

Ali (*c.* 600–61), son-in-law of Muhammad; fourth caliph from 656. Opposition to him resulted in Islamic schism between Shia and Sunni groups, with only Shia accepting him as caliph.

Allende, Salvador (1908–73), Marxist pres. of Chile from 1970. Began nationalization before killed in military coup.

Augustus

Amin, Idi (1925–), Ugandan soldier and politician. Seized power in 1971. A brutal ruler who expelled Asians, killed many dissidents and seized foreign businesses. Deposed in 1979.

Antony, Mark (*c.* 83–30 BC), Roman general and triumvir (43–30 BC); defeated Brutus and Cassius at Philippi (42 BC) with help of Octavian. Joined Cleopatra in 37 BC and was defeated with her at Actium in 31 BC. Committed suicide.

Ashurbanipal (or Sardanapalus) (7th century BC), Assyrian king (668–*c.* 627 BC). Patron of arts and assembler of first Middle Eastern library in Nineveh.

Asoka (3rd century BC), Indian king (*c.* 262–238 BC); great promoter of Buddhism, allowing it to spread throughout India.

Bismarck

Atatürk, Kemal (1881–1938), soldier, nationalist and first pres. of Republic of Turkey from 1923. Abolished caliphate (1924); modernized and Europeanized Turkey.

Attila (*c.* 406–53), king of Huns from 434 and powerful barbarian invader who attacked and overran much of the Roman Empire.

Attlee, Clement (1883–1967), British Labour PM (1945–51). Brought in much reform, inc. formation of NHS and nationalization of much UK industry; oversaw independence of India and Burma.

Augustine of Hippo (354–430), bishop of Hippo and early Christian theologian, greatest of the Latin Church fathers. Converted to Christianity in 386, ordained in 391 and became bishop in 396. Wrote *The City of God* (412–27).

Augustus, Gaius Julius Caesar Octavianus (63 BC–AD 14), adopted son of Julius Caesar. Triumvir (43–31 BC); defeated Brutus and Cassius in 42 BC with help of Mark Antony. Defeated other triumvirs, Lepidus and Mark Antony, becoming first Roman emperor. Extended Roman rule into north and central Europe. Established *Pax Romana*; remoulded Roman society and beautified Rome.

Aurangzeb (1618–1707), last great Mogul leader. Emperor from 1658. The Mogul Empire weakened during his reign because he alienated the Hindus.

Baber (1483–1530), founder and first emperor (1526–30) of Mogul Empire in India. Defeated Lodi (1526) and Hindu Rajput confederacy (1527). He was tolerant to his non-Muslim subjects.

Baldwin I (1172–1205), count of Flanders and Hainault from 1195. A leader in the Fourth Crusade; first Latin emperor of Constantinople from 1204.

Baldwin, Stanley (1867–1947), British Conservative PM (1923–24, 1924–29, 1935–37); he outmanoeuvred the General Strike (1926), but did not recognize the rising danger of Nazi Germany.

Basil II (*c.* 958–1025), Byzantine emperor from 976; ruthlessly expanded imperial domains.

Batista y Zaldívar, Fulgencio (1901–73), Cuban dictator (1933–44, 1952–59). Strong and ruthless ruler who seized power twice in military coups; ousted by Castro in 1958.

Begin, Menachem (1913–92), Israeli PM (1977–83), hardline Zionist leader who nonetheless negotiated a peace treaty with Sadat in 1978.

Belisarius (*c.* 505–65), Byzantine general who recaptured much of western Europe from invaders for Justinian I.

Ben Bella, Mohammed Ahmed (1918–), Algerian politician. Led war of independence against France; first Algerian PM (1962–63) and first pres. (1963–65). Overthrown in 1965.

Ben-Gurion, David (1886–1973), Israeli politician and first PM (1948–53, 1955–63). Delivered Israel's declaration of independence in 1948.

Benedict of Nursia (*c.* 480–*c.* 547), originator of Western monastic tradition and founder of Benedictine Rule.

Benes, Eduard (1884–1948), Czechoslovakian statesman and pres. (1935–38). Capitulated to Hitler's demands in 1938 Czech crisis before resigning; returned to power in 1945, but refused to legitimate Communist rule in 1948 and again resigned.

Beria, Lavrenti Pavlovich (1899–1953), Soviet chief of secret police under Stalin. Enforced terror campaign on opponents; executed after unsuccessful attempt to seize power after Stalin's death.

Bhutto, Zulfikar Ali (1928–79), Pakistani politician; pres. (1971–73) and PM (1973–77). Introduced sweeping reform before being ousted and hanged.

Bismarck, Prince Otto von (1815–96), Prussian PM (1862–73, 1873–90) and founder of the German Empire. Defeated Austria in 1866 and France in 1871 to become first chancellor of the new empire (1871–90). His foreign policy was based on strategic military alliances, inc. Austro-German Treaty of Alliance (1879).

Blanc, Louis (1811–82), French socialist politician and theorist. Member of provisional government of Second Republic in 1848; proposed establishment of social workshops.

Blücher, Gebhard von (1742–1819), Prussian military leader; successful commander during Napoleonic Wars and instrumental, with Wellington, in defeat of Napoleon at Waterloo (1815).

Blum, Léon (1872–1950), French socialist politician; PM of France during Popular Front coalition (1936–37). Interned by Germany during WWII but was again PM 1946–47.

Boleslav I (966–1025), first Polish king ruling from 992; established Poland as a major European state.

■ ALEXANDER THE GREAT WAS TUTORED BY THE PHILOSOPHER ARISTOTLE ■ BENEDICT,

Bolívar, Simón (1783–1830), S. American Creole soldier and statesman; liberated much of the continent from Spanish rule. Dictator of Colombia (1821) and Peru (1824), relinquishing power in 1830.

Boniface (*c.* 675–754), Anglo-Saxon missionary who brought Christianity to much of Germany; primate in 723.

Borgia, Cesare (*c.* 1476–1507), Italian cleric and politician. Gained power in central Italy through use of terror and established the Borgia dynasty.

Botha, P.W. (1916–), S. African PM (1978–84) and first state pres. (1984–89); committed to white supremacy, he attempted to introduce token domestic reform that maintained apartheid.

Bourguiba, Habib (1903–), Tunisian politician, co-ordinator of Tunisia's independence in 1957, and first pres. (1957–87).

Brandt, Willy (1913–92), German statesman and Social Democratic chancellor of W. Germany (1969–74).

Brezhnev, Leonid (1906–82), Soviet politician; Communist Party general sec. from 1964. His Brezhnev Doctrine gave the USSR the right to intervene in Communist satellite states.

Briand, Aristide (1862–1932), French politician who served as PM 11 times. Committed to world co-operation; advocate of League of Nations.

Brown, John (1800–59), US militant abolitionist whose state execution following a raid on a federal arsenal helped to precipitate US Civil War.

Brutus, Marcus Junius (85–42 BC), Roman republican leader who joined Cassius as a leading conspirator in assassination of Julius Caesar (44 BC). Committed suicide after defeat at Philippi in 42 BC by Mark Antony and Augustus.

Buddha (Gautama Siddhartha) (*c.* 563–*c.* 483 BC), Indian founder of Buddhism. Lived in luxury until aged 29, when he realized that all is suffering and became an ascetic. After six years of extreme austerity, he sought his own path to enlightenment, which he achieved sitting under a banyan tree at Buddh Gaya. He spread his spiritual teachings for the next 40 years.

Bukharin, Nikolai (1888–1938), Soviet ideologue and Marxist thinker; key political player in pre- and post-Revolutionary Russia. Chairman of Comintern's executive committee in 1926. Executed by Stalin in 1938 for alleged counter-revolutionary activities.

Bulganin, Nikolai (1895–1975), Soviet politician and PM (1955–58); strongly identified with Khrushchev, who wielded much power through him before ousting him in 1958.

Bush, George (1924–), Republican politician and 41st US pres. (1988–92); presided over Gulf War (1991).

Cabot, John (*c.* 1425–*c.* 1500), Italian explorer and navigator; under patronage of Henry VII of England, he undertook voyages in 1497 and 1498, sighting N. America and claiming it for England.

Cabral, Pedro Álvarez (*c.* 1467–1520), Portuguese explorer and navigator, credited with discovery of Brazil (1500).

Julius Caesar

Caesar, Gaius Julius (100–44 BC), Roman general and dictator; conquered Gaul and other western territories in a nine-year campaign (58–50 BC). Defeated Pompey in Civil War and was made dictator (46–44 BC); whilst in process of social and political reforms, he was assassinated by conspirators led by Cassius and Brutus.

Caligula (AD 12–41), Roman emperor from AD 37. His reign was despotic and capricious. He suffered ill-heath and was accused of madness and incest; dissatisfaction at his rule resulted in his assassination.

Calvin, John (1509–64), French theologian and austere reformer, extremely influential in development of Protestantism. Rejecting the papacy, he wrote a manual organizing Protestant doctrine and dogma, *Institutes of the Christian Religion* (1536); became a leading authority in Reformed Protestantism in Geneva.

Catherine the Great

Cambyses II (d. 522 BC), second king of the Medes and Persians (529–522 BC) and conqueror of Egypt (525 BC).

Cárdenas, Lázaro (1895–1970), Mexican soldier, political leader and pres. of Mexican Republic (1934–40). Delivered the promise of the 1910 Mexican Revolution through widespread nationalization and land distribution.

Carol II (1893–1953), flamboyant Romanian king (1930–40); relinquished right of succession (1925) but reclaimed throne in a coup against his son (1930). Set up dictatorship (1938) to counter Fascist Iron Guard movement; deposed in favour of his son in 1940.

Carter, Jimmy (1924–), 39th US pres. (1977–81); Democrat leader who presided over Panama Treaty, Camp David Middle Eastern agreement and Iranian hostage crisis.

Cassius Longinus, Gaius (d. 42 BC), Roman general and key conspirator in assassination of Julius Caesar. Defeated by Mark Antony at Philippi (42 BC). Committed suicide.

Castlereagh, Robert (1769–1822), British politician and distinguished foreign sec. (1812–22); a key player in Congress of Vienna (1815) that led to European stability. Hugely unpopular, he committed suicide.

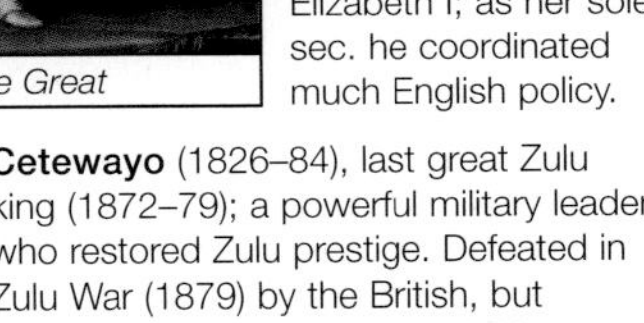
Charlemagne

Catherine de' Medici (1519–89), queen of France (1547–59) and regent (1560–74). A notable figure in Catholic-Huguenot wars (1562–69); initially a Huguenot supporter, she subsequently supported the Guises. Implicated in St Bartholomew's Day Massacre (1572).

Catherine II, the Great (1729–96), Russian empress from 1762. A harsh German-born ruler who strengthened and expanded Russia.

Cato, Marcus Porcius, 'the Elder' (234–149 BC), Roman statesman, censor and orator, noted for his conservatism, stance against Hellenic influence and enmity towards Carthage.

Cato, Marcus Porcius, 'the Younger' (95–46 BC), Roman statesman and great-grandson of Cato the Elder; a leader of the Optimates and critic of Julius Caesar. Sided with Pompey, but defeat at Thapsus (46 BC) led to suicide.

Cavour, Count Camillo (1810–61), Italian politician. Succeeded in unifying Italy (1861) under Victor Emanuel II of Sardinia through exploitation of international tensions.

Ceaucescu, Nicolae (1918–89), Romanian politician and pres. (1974–89); his Communist rule saw economic stagnation and serious human rights abuse; executed after coup.

Cecil, William, 1st Baron Burghley (1520–98), English statesman, diplomat, and chief adviser to Elizabeth I; as her sole sec. he coordinated much English policy.

Cetewayo (1826–84), last great Zulu king (1872–79); a powerful military leader who restored Zulu prestige. Defeated in Zulu War (1879) by the British, but restored by them as ruler in 1883; defeated by a rival the same year.

Chandragupta I (reigned 320–*c.* 330), Indian king and founder of imperial Gupta dynasty.

Chao K'uang-yin (T'ai Tsu) (927–76), Chinese military leader from 960 and founder of Sung dynasty; began process of Chinese unification.

Charlemagne (*c.* 742–814), king of the Franks from 768 and Lombards from 774, conqueror and uniter of much of western Europe. Emperor of Holy Roman Empire from 800. Based court at Aix-la-Chapelle, Germany, and brought about widespread revival of Christian culture – the Carolingian Renaissance.

Charles I (1600–49), king of Great Britain and Ireland from 1625. His heavy-handed reign and disagreements with Parliament resulted in Civil War (1642–46) in which he was defeated by Cromwell and Fairfax. Sentenced to death and executed.

Charles II (1630–85), king of Scotland and England from 1660. In exile during Puritan Commonwealth; restored to the throne after fall of Protectorate. His reign was plagued with much religious struggle. He was a major patron of the arts.

Charles Martel, 'the Hammer' (*c.* 688–741), mayor of palace of Austrasia (715–41); reunited and ruled Franks; repelled Moors at Poitiers (732), stemming the Arab invasion of Europe.

Charles the Bold (1433–77), duke of Burgundy from 1467; last of the great Burgundian dukes, under whom the state attained its greatest power.

Charles V, 'the Wise' (1338–80), French king from 1364; regent during John II's captivity. Regained much territory from the English; reversed Anglo-French settlement of 1360.

Charles V (1500–58), king of Spain as Charles I (1516–56), Holy Roman Emperor (1519–56). Attempted to resist growing Protestant forces in Europe; extended Spanish Empire in S. America. Abdicated after creating the largest European empire since Ancient Rome.

Charles VIII (1470–1498), king of France from 1483. Initiated a period of French excursions into Italy after an unsuccessful attempt to claim Naples (1494–96).

Charles XII (1682–1718), king of Sweden from 1697. Presided over Great Northern War in which Sweden lost its status as a great power after failed invasion of Russia (1707–09).

Charles XIV (1763–1844), French marshal (1804) and king of Sweden and Norway from 1818 (adopted by the king of Sweden). Active in Revolutionary and Napoleonic campaigns, he switched allegiance to Napoleon's enemies and helped defeat him at Leipzig (1813).

Chiang Kai-shek (1887–1975), Chinese soldier and statesman. Accomplished military unification of China (1926–28), headed its Nationalist government (1928–49), and led Chinese government-in-exile in Taiwan from 1949, following collapse of the Kuomintang government to Communism.

Chou En Lai (Zhou Enlai) (1898–1976), premier of People's Republic of China from 1949; foreign minister (1949–58); a voice of caution in Cultural Revolution; he achieved detente with the West.

Chu Teh (Zhu Teh) (1886–1976), Chinese military leader; founder of the Chinese Communist Army, which he led in the Long March (1934–35).

Churchill, Sir Winston (1874–1965), British politician, author and statesman; PM (1940–45, 1951–55), leader of Britain's Coalition war government. Formulated war strategy on global lines, forming alliances with US and Soviet leaders. Lost post-war general election, before his Conservative Party was voted back into power in 1951.

Claudius I (10 BC–AD 54), fourth Roman emperor (AD 41–54), during which time the Roman Empire expanded to include provinces of Mauretania (*c.* AD 43), Thrace (AD 46) and Britain (AD 43).

Believed poisoned by his fourth wife Agrippina to secure succession for her son, Nero.

Clausewitz, Karl von (1780–1831), Prussian general and director of the General War School of Berlin (1818–30). His treatise, *On War*, advocated total war and was influential in military strategy.

Clemenceau, Georges (1841–1929), French politician, journalist and PM (1906–09, 1917–20). A powerful influence in Allied WWI victory; presided over Paris Peace Conference of 1919.

Cleopatra VII (69–30 BC), Egyptian queen from 51 BC. Ruled alongside her brothers Ptolemy XIII (51–47 BC) and Ptolemy XIV (47–44 BC), the latter's reign a result of Caesar's victory in Alexandrine war in 47 BC. Followed Caesar to Rome in 46 BC, but left after his assassination. Linked with Mark Antony after 42 BC; jointly defeated at Actium in 31 BC by Augustus; committed suicide.

Clive, Robert (1725–74), English soldier and colonial administrator; governor of Bengal (1755–60, 1764–67), a province he added to British India; defeated French to establish British power in India.

Clovis I (*c.* 466–511), Merovingian king of the Franks from 481; founded Frankish kingdom through overthrow of Romans and subsequent expansion. A champion of Christianity after becoming first barbarian king to convert (496).

Cnut 'the Great' (d. 1035), Danish king of England from 1016, of Denmark from 1019 and of Norway from 1028. His reign in England was firm and secure, and his support of the Church earned him much respect.

Coligny, Gaspard II de (1519–72), French Huguenot leader during early years of the War of Religion.

Collins, Michael (1890–1922), Irish patriot and Sinn Fein minister; he directed guerrilla warfare during Anglo-Irish War (1919–21), but negotiated Ireland's independence from Britain. Killed in an ambush in west Cork.

Columbus, Christopher (1451–1506), Italian navigator and discoverer of New World. Gained patronage from Ferdinand and Isabella of Castile; sailed in 1492 and sighted land in the Caribbean on 12 October. Three further voyages (1493–96, 1498–1500 and 1502–04) initiated age of European exploitation of New World.

Condé, Louis II de Bourbon (1621–86), French general; a brilliant soldier who established himself in several campaigns in Thirty Years' War. Led second Fronde (uprising) but was pardoned and became an outstanding general under Louis XIV.

Confucius (or Kung Fu-tze) (551–479 BC), Chinese philosopher and political theorist whose teachings were gathered by his disciples as the *Analects*. The school of thinking named after him, Confucianism, was at the core of Chinese life until relatively recently.

Constantine I (*c.* 280–337), Roman emperor from 312 and sole emperor from 324; the first to have become a Christian (313). Rebuilt and concentrated power in Byzantium, renaming it Constantinople. Made Christianity a state religion (324).

Cook, James (1728–79), British navigator and explorer. Surveyed and charted New Zealand, the east coast of Australia and many Pacific and Atlantic islands. Killed by Polynesian natives in Hawaii.

Clovis I

Coolidge, Calvin (1872–1933), 30th US pres. (1923–29); a Republican leader who presided over a period of economic prosperity, lack of political crises and measured inaction.

Corday, Charlotte (1768–93), French revolutionary. After initial sympathy to the Revolution, she became disenchanted and resolved to kill one of the revolutionary leaders. Stabbed to death Marat; subsequently guillotined.

Cornwallis, Charles (1738–1805), British soldier, governor general of India (1786–93, 1805), and viceroy of Ireland (1798–1801). Surrendered at Yorktown to Washington in American War of Independence (1781) bringing war to a virtual end.

Cortés, Hernando (1485–1547), Spanish conquistador who defeated the Aztec Empire (1519–21) and claimed it for Spain.

Confucius

Cromwell, Oliver (1599–1658), English soldier and statesman; lord protector of England from 1653, during the Commonwealth. A leader of parliamentary forces during the Civil War, he fought at Marston Moor, Naseby, and the siege of Oxford, and reconquered Ireland. As lord protector, he helped establish Puritanism, but his political relations with parliament were strained.

Cromwell, Thomas (*c.* 1485–1540), English statesman and adviser to Henry VIII; instrumental in dissolution of monasteries, the English Reformation, and the strengthening of royal authority. Accused of treason and heresy and executed.

Cuza, Alexandru (1820–73), Romanian prince, a champion of peasant land rights and rural reform; architect of Romanian unity in 1861. Forced to abdicate by a middle-class conspiracy opposed to his policies.

Cyrus II, the Great (*c.* 590–*c.* 529 BC), founder and king of the Persian Empire. Having conquered Lydia and Babylonia, he liberated the nations held captive in Babylon.

Daladier, Édouard (1884–1970), French politician who signed Munich Pact in 1938; PM 1938–40, he was interned by the Germans until 1945.

Porfirio Díaz

Danton, Georges (1759–94), French revolutionary leader; powerful orator instrumental in overthrow of French monarchy. First pres. of Committee of Public Safety. Opposition to Reign of Terror led to his execution.

Darius I (548–486 BC), Achaemenid Persian king from 522 BC; a great administrative reformer; unsuccessful in campaigns against Greece, losing at Marathon (490 BC), although he took the Caucasus.

David (*c.* 1000 BC), first king of a united Judean Israel; slayer of Goliath, opposed by Saul after he became jealous. United Israel after death of Saul and Ishboshet; perceived as an ideal ruler and ancestor of Jesus.

Dayan, Moshe (1915–81), Israeli general and statesman, mastermind of the Six-Day War (1967) .

De Gaulle, Charles (1890–1970), French general, head of state (1944–46) and first pres. of the Fifth Republic (1958–69); led 'Free French' in exile during WWII. Recalled to power in Algerian crisis (1958). As pres. he conducted a strong foreign policy, granted independence to Algeria and other African colonies and developed nuclear capabilities.

De Valera, Eamon (1882–1975), Irish politician, PM (1932–48, 1951–54, 1957–59) and pres. (1959–73). Involved in Easter Rising (1916). Politically opposed to Collins' signing of Anglo-Irish Treaty of 1921.

De Witt, Jan (1625–72), Dutch Republican statesman, an opponent of William II, Prince of Orange. Collaborated with Cromwell to maintain the Dutch republic but was assassinated by supporters of the House of Orange.

Deng Xiaoping (1904–97), Chinese Communist politician; general sec. of Chinese Communist Party (1956–67). Remained effective leader of China until his death, although he held no official post. Encouraged modernization; responsible for Tiananmen Square massacre (1989).

Díaz de Vivar, Rodrigo, 'El Cid' (*c.* 1043–99), Castilian soldier; a warrior in the campaigns of Alfonso VI of Castile. Fell out of favour in 1081 and exiled by Alfonso, he became a mercenary serving Moors and Spaniards. Took control of Valencia in 1094, and became its ruler.

Diaz, Porfirio (1830–1915), Mexican soldier and pres. (1877–80, 1884–1911). Gained recognition for service in War of Reform (1857–60) and French Intervention (1861–67). Rebelled under Juárez's re-election of 1871, fought against government in Battle of Tecoac (1876) and was elected pres. During his presidency, he strengthened Mexico's political and industrial infrastructure.

Diocletian (Gaius Aurelius Valerius Diocletianus) (245–313), Roman emperor (285–305); restored power after various 3rd-century troubles; reorganized empire into four distinct quadrants. His reign saw the last great Christian persecution (303).

Disraeli, Benjamin (1804–81), novelist, British Conservative statesman and PM (1868, 1874–80); served as Derby's chancellor before succeeding him in 1868, but lost the election the same year. Returning to power in 1874, he consolidated Britain's imperial aims by acquiring joint ownership of the Suez Canal (1875) and making Queen Victoria empress of India (1876).

Dollfuss, Engelbert (1892–1934), Austrian statesman; chancellor from 1932. Purged Austria's government of socialist influences; established a fascist authoritarian regime before being murdered by Nazis.

Dominic, St (*c.* 1170–1221), Spanish religious missionary who, in 1215, founded the Order of Friars Preachers (Dominicans), based on scholarship and poverty. A wandering preacher, he had previously been a missionary to the Moors and Albigensian heretics.

Dönitz, Karl (1891–1980), German naval officer and U-boat advocate; created and commanded Germany's U-boat fleet from 1936. Became Führer on Hitler's death; responsible for final surrender to the Allies. Imprisoned for ten years after the war.

Drake, Sir Francis (*c.* 1540–96), English navigator and admiral who circumnavigated the globe (1577–80) in the *Golden Hind*. Instrumental in defeat of Spanish Armada (1588).

Dreyfus, Alfred (1859–1935), French soldier whose imprisonment for alleged treason sparked the political unrest known as the Dreyfus affair. Imprisoned on Devil's Island (French Guiana) in 1894, which prompted outrage. Pardoned in 1906 and awarded the Legion of Honour.

Dubcek, Alexander (1921–92), Slovak politician; led Czechoslovakian Communist Party (1968–69). His reforms provoked Soviet occupation of Czechoslovakia (1968), relegating him to an agricultural clerk. After the overthrow of the Communists (1989), he returned as chairman of the elected assembly.

Dulles, John Foster (1888–1959), US politician and Pres. Eisenhower's sec. of state (1953–59); a key strategist in early developments of Cold War US policy.

Dunant, Jean Henri (1828–1910), Swiss philanthropist and humanitarian. Founded the Red Cross (1864) after witnessing mass casualties in Battle of Solferini. Instrumental in creation of Geneva Convention (1864).

Ebert, Friedrich (1871–1925), German statesman; first pres. of Weimar Republic from 1919. Led Social Democrats in

■ OLIVER CROMWELL'S BODY WAS DISINTERRED AND HUNG AT TYBURN GALLOWS AFTER THE

Germany; played key role in bringing about Weimar constitution.

Eden, Anthony (1897–1977), British Conservative politician, foreign sec. during WWII, and again from 1951; PM (1955–57). His leadership was widely condemned during Suez Crisis of 1956, when he ordered an attack on Egypt; following this crisis, he resigned.

Edward I (1239–1307), English king from 1272; a fearful warrior who won renown for defeating Simon de Montfort (1265), as a Crusader (1270), and for subduing the Welsh. Unsuccessful in his aim to unite England and Scotland.

Edward III (1312–77), English king from 1327; his reign was characterized by ultimately unsuccessful conflicts against the French and Scots. Claiming the crown of France, he led England into the Hundred Years' War; his death resulted in power struggles culminating in the War of the Roses (1455–85).

Edward the Black Prince (1330–76), son and heir of Edward III, prince of Aquitaine from 1362; a brilliant soldier who had famed successes at Crécy and at Poitiers (1356); instrumental in English victories during Hundred Years' War. His merciless sacking of Limoges (1370) added to growing disfavour against him, and he returned to England a broken man.

Edward IV (1442–83), English king from 1461 to 1470 and 1471–83. A Yorkist, he deposed the Lancastrian Henry VI during the War of the Roses. He fostered trade and culture, leaving a solvent nation.

Eichmann, Karl Adolf (1906–62), German-born Austrian Nazi leader, member of the SS and chief architect of the Holocaust. Settled in Argentina (1950), but was hunted by Israeli agents, smuggled out of the country, tried and executed by the state of Israel.

Eisenhower, Dwight (1890–1969), American general, supreme commander of allied forces in Europe in WWII and 34th US pres. (1953–61). His Republican administration saw strong anti-Communist sentiment.

Elijah (9th century BC), Biblical Hebrew prophet who saved the Jewish faith from the cult of Baal during reign of King Ahab.

Elizabeth I (1533–1603), queen of England and Ireland from 1558. A politically-aware Protestant, her reign was a combination of realpolitik and courtly manipulation. She achieved a religious settlement and withstood the Spanish invasion (1588) and Catholic plots against her. She was fortunate to have able ministers such as Cecil.

Engels, Friedrich (1820–95), German political theorist and founder, with Marx, of scientific socialism; co-authored with Marx the *Communist Manifesto* (1848), and edited Marx's *Das Kapital* after his collaborator's death.

Erhard, Ludwig (1897–1977), German economist and politician, economics minister (1948–63), chancellor (1963–66). Engineered W. Germany's post-war recovery.

Erik the Red (10th century), Norse sailor and founder of first settlements in Greenland (*c.* 985). His son Leif Eriksson discovered America *c.* 1000.

Eugene of Savoy (1663–1736), French-born Austrian general and diplomat who had military successes against the Turks, and against Louis XIV in Italy and in the War of the Spanish Succession (1701–14).

Frederick the Great

Fairfax, Thomas (1612–71), English parliamentary soldier; leader of the New Model Army which defeated Charles I at Naseby (1645). Refused to condemn the king to death; retired to private life after declining to invade Scotland during Commonwealth. Helped organize return of Charles II after Cromwell's death.

Farnese, Alessandro (1545–92), Italian-born Spanish soldier; established himself in battles at Lepanto against the Turks (1571), Gembloux (1578) and Maastricht (1578) against the Dutch; made regent of the Netherlands (1578). Became duke of Parma and Piacenza in 1586, although he never took up his duchy in Italy.

Ferdinand I (1503–64), king of Bohemia from 1526 and Holy Roman Emperor from 1558. Achieved Peace of Augsburg (1555), which brought an end to German religious infighting; made Hungary and Bohemia integral possessions of Habsburg Empire.

Ferdinand I (*c.* 1016–65), first Castilian king and emperor of León; gained León and Navarre, and forced Toledo, Saragossa and Seville to pay tribute to him.

Ferdinand II (1578–1637), Holy Roman Emperor from 1619; instigator of the Thirty Years' War (1618–48). A leader of the Counter-Reformation and Catholic champion, he sought to impose a single absolutist rulership for the Church.

Ferdinand V, 'the Catholic' (1452–1516), king of Aragon, of Castile and of Naples; first king of all Spain. United Spain's separate kingdoms through military conquest and by marriage to Isabella of Castile. He funded Columbus's voyages.

Foch, Ferdinand (1851–1929), French WWI military leader whose strikes against the Germans in latter stages of the war contributed to Allied victory.

Fouché, Joseph, Duke of Otranto (1763–1829), French revolutionary leader and statesman; voted for execution of Louis XIV; made minister of police in 1799, a position he held intermittently until 1815.

Mahatma Gandhi

Fox, Charles James (1749–1806), English politician and first foreign sec. (1782, 1783, 1806); antagonist of George III, and rival to William Pitt. A champion of democracy and a great orator.

Fox, George (1624–91), English religious founder of the Society of Friends (Quakers); a religious experience in 1646 formed the basis of his society, 'the Friends of Truth'. He frowned upon established religious structures, but promoted concept of God-given inner light (inspiration).

Francis I (1494–1547), king of France from 1515; lost Italy in wars against Holy Roman Emperor Charles V and against Italy. A patron of Renaissance learning and erudition, with humanist leanings.

Francis II (1768–1835), last Holy Roman Emperor (1792–1806); was Francis I of Austria (1806–1835). Dissolved the Holy Roman Empire before Napoleon was able to and made himself emperor of Austria. Supported Metternich in post-Napoleonic Europe.

Francis Joseph I (1830–1916), Austrian emperor from 1848. Allowed Hungary autonomy within the Austro-Hungarian Empire; formed alliance with Germany (1879); his attack on Serbia in 1914 precipitated WWI.

Francis of Assisi, St (1181–1226), Italian religious leader. Born into a wealthy family, his spiritual conversion began with a dream in 1205. Rebuilt church of San Domiano and became a hermit; his poverty and charity gathered followers, resulting in the order of Franciscans.

Francis Xavier, St (1506–52), Spanish missionary and co-founder of the Jesuit Society (1534); helped establish Christianity in India and the Far East.

Franco, Francisco (1892–1975), Spanish dictator who spearheaded Nationalist overthrow of Spanish Republican government in Civil War (1936–39); thereafter dictator of Spain.

Franklin, Benjamin (1706–90), US statesman and scientist who supported America's struggle for independence from Great Britain; helped frame Declaration of Independence (1776) and US Constitution (1787).

Frederick I Barbarossa (*c.* 1123–90), Holy Roman Emperor (from 1152) of the Hohenstaufen clan; fierce German ruler who struggled against papal influences and Italy, taking Milan (1162).

Frederick II, the Great (1712–86), king of Prussia (1740–86). He augmented his territories with Silesia (1740–45), and held onto it in the Seven Years' War, establishing Prussia's dominance of German states.

Frederick William (1620–88), elector of Brandenburg from 1640; helped found Prussian power through his restoration of Hohenzollern territories after disruption during Thirty Years' War.

Frederick-William I (1688–1740), Prussian king from 1713; consolidated position and identity of emergent state of Prussia through strong administrative skills and a passion for soldiering.

Fujiwara Michinaga (966–1028), Japanese statesman and regent from 995. His reign saw the greatest heights of Imperial Kyoto, and saw the balance of power shift from the emperor to him.

Galbraith, John Kenneth (1908–), Canadian-born US liberal economist; professor of economics at Harvard (1949–75), US ambassador to India (1961–63). His ideas include shifting emphasis from production to public services. Writings include *The Affluent Society* (1958).

Gambetta, Léon (1838–82), French politician who helped found the Third Republic; coordinated French defence during Franco-German War (1870–71). PM (1881–82).

Gandhi, Indira (1917–84), Indian politician and PM (1966–77, 1980–84). Declared a state of emergency in 1975 after being charged with election law violation. Assassinated by her Sikh bodyguards.

Gandhi, Mohandas Karamchand, 'Mahatma' (1869–1948), Indian politician and leader of Indian independence movement. Initiated a series of non-violent civil disobedience campaigns after 1930. Instrumental in gaining eventual freedom for India, his last years were marred by internal strife between Hindus and Muslims. Assassinated by a fanatic.

Garibaldi, Giuseppe (1807–82), Italian patriot and soldier whose conquest of Sicily and Naples (1860) at the head of an army of 'Redshirts' unified Italy.

Genghis Khan (*c.* 1162–1227), Mongol leader and warrior-conqueror who extended Mongolian Empire to include China, much of Russia, and eastwards to the Black Sea. A brilliant soldier and ruler who reformed internal government structure as well as organizing the states he conquered.

George I (1660–1727), elector of Hanover from 1698, king of Great Britain and Ireland from 1714. Unpopular, he nonetheless maintained power through an alliance with Whigs.

George III (1738–1820), king of Great Britain and Ireland, elector of Hanover from 1760, king of Hanover from 1815. His reign saw the blossoming of the British Empire, the union of Britain and Ireland, and the loss of the American colonies. His reign was marked with incessant political wrangling. His later years were marred by madness. From 1811, his son acted as regent.

George IV (1762–1830), British king from 1820, having been regent from 1811. His political allegiances were Whig whilst regent, and Tory whilst king. A patron of arts and architecture, he left a wealth of art to the nation.

Gladstone, William Ewart (1809–98), British Liberal politician and PM on four occasions (1868–74, 1880–85, 1886, 1892–94); disestablished Irish church, set up a national education system and split Liberal party on issue of Irish home rule in 1886.

Glyndwr, Owen (*c.* 1350–*c.* 1416), Welsh patriot and self-proclaimed prince of Wales. Mounted an unsuccessful guerrilla campaign against the English.

Godfrey de Bouillon (*c.* 1060–1100), French crusader. Fought in First Crusade, and became first Latin ruler of Jerusalem in 1099.

Godoy, Manuel de (1767–1851), Spanish statesman and royal favourite; PM (1792–1808). His inept rule led to abdication of Charles IV and the French invasion of Spain in 1808.

Godunov, Boris (1552–1605), Russian statesman; elected tsar from 1598 upon extinction of Rurik dynasty. A strong and capable ruler, his death led to the civil disorder of the Time of Troubles.

Goebbels, Joseph (1897–1945), German Nazi leader and propagandist; a rabid anti-Semite who was instrumental in selling Nazi ideals to German populace. Effective ruler of Germany during the war, when Hitler managed the war-effort. Committed suicide shortly after Hitler had named him Führer in his will.

Goering, Hermann (1893–1946), German Nazi leader. Commanded Death Squadron (1923); president of Reichstag (1932); chief lieutenant when Hitler took power. Founded Gestapo, expanded Luftwaffe, made marshal of the Reich (1940). Fell out of favour as Germany's war effort faltered (1941). Captured by the Americans, he was main defendant at Nuremberg War Tribunal (1946), where he was condemned to hang. Committed suicide on eve of execution.

Gomulka, Wladyslaw (1905–82), Polish ruler and leader of Communist Party (1956–71). Sought to remove the more restrictive Stalinist aspects of Poland's state, although certain oppressions remained in place.

Gorbachev, Mikhail (1931–), Soviet Communist ruler (1985–91). Reformed Soviet Union with greater freedom through glasnost (openness) and perestroika (restructuring). Signed anti-nuclear treaties with Reagan (1987). Withdrew Soviet troops from Afghanistan (1989) and diminished Soviet influence in eastern Europe, allowing German reunification and end of Cold War. Briefly ousted from power in right-wing coup in 1991. Resigned after break-up of USSR in late 1991.

Gottwald, Klement (1896–1953), Czech Communist politician; PM (1946–48) and pres. from 1948 after a bloodless coup. His rule was Stalinist and dictatorial.

Gowon, Yakubu (1934–), Nigerian soldier and politician. Gained power in Nigeria after a military coup in 1966 and maintained power in civil war (1967–70); ousted by his military in 1975.

Grant, Ulysses S. (1822–85), US general and 18th pres. (1869–77). Commander of the Federal Army during Civil War. His Republican presidency saw settlement of the Alabama Claims, although his two terms were marred by corruption and scandal.

Gregory I, the Great (*c.* 540–604), Roman-born pope from 590, whose considerable Church reform and administration laid the foundations for the medieval ecclesiastical structure.

Mikhail Gorbachev

Gregory XIII (1502–85), Italian-born pope (from 1572). Leading theologian at Council of Trent (1545). Instrumental in Counter-Reformation through patronage of Jesuits. Noted for reformation of old Julian calendar in 1582.

Griffith, Arthur (1872–1922), Irish politician, journalist and founder of nationalist Sinn Fein Party (1905). Imprisoned after Easter Rising of 1916.

Gromyko, Andrei (1909–89), Soviet politician, foreign minister (1957–85), during which he represented the USSR abroad. Soviet pres. (1985–88).

Guesclin, Bertrand du (*c.* 1320–80), French soldier and constable of France from 1370. Having established his military prowess, he became highly successful in the Hundred Years' War, winning several key victories for the French against the English.

Guevara, Ernesto 'Che' (1928–67), Argentine revolutionary; instrumental in Castro's Cuban revolution (1956–59). Subsequently preached revolutionary guerrilla warfare in S. America. Executed by Bolivian troops whilst trying to create an insurrectionist group.

Guiscard, Robert (*c.* 1015–85), Norman adventurer and soldier, duke of Apulia (S. Italy) from 1059. Fought against Greeks and Saracens to maintain and extend Norman rule throughout southern Italy. Helped lay basis for Sicilian kingdom.

Gustav I (1496–1560), Swedish king from 1523, first ruler of Vasa line. Won Swedish independence by driving the Danes from Sweden. Established Lutheranism in Sweden.

Gustav II Adolphus (1594–1632), Swedish king from 1611, instrumental in Protestant involvement in Thirty Years' War (1618–48). Strengthened Sweden as a nation state by military expansion, gaining supremacy in the Baltic.

Hadrian (76–138), Roman emperor from 117. Consolidated empire and was a patron of the arts; famed for his buildings and structures, inc. the villa at Tibur and his Wall in northern England.

Haig, Douglas (1861–1928), Scottish general who commanded British troops in France in WWI. His war of attrition included costly battles at Somme (1916) and Passchendaele (1917).

Haile Selassie (originally Prince Ras Tafari Makonnen) (1891–1975), emperor of Ethiopia (1930–74). Modernized his nation, established a national assembly and made Ethiopia a leader of the Organization of African Unity. Deposed in 1974 and died in captivity. Venerated by Rastafarians.

Hammarskjöld, Dag (1905–61), Swedish economist and politician. Second sec.-general of the UN (1953–61). Involved in peace missions to the Middle East, and helped resolve Suez Crisis of 1956. Killed in a plane crash.

Hammurabi (18th century BC), Babylonian ruler (1792–50 BC), 6th of the 1st Amorite dynasty. A great administrator who extended the Babylonian Empire. Formulated the Code of Hammurabi, an advanced set of 282 laws.

Hampden, John (1594–1643), English politician and MP (1621–43). Influential opponent of Charles I's tax on coastal towns (ship money), which he refused to pay. An attempt to seize him precipitated the Civil War. He died of wounds after the battle at Chalgrove Field.

Hannibal (247–182 BC), Carthaginian general, fought the Romans in the Second Punic War (218–201 BC). Renowned for his march across Europe with his army and elephants. Committed suicide through poisoning to avoid Roman capture.

Hanno (5th century BC), Carthaginian explorer, who founded several colonies on the west coast of Africa.

Hardenberg, Karl von (1750–1822), Prussian statesman who maintained national identity in Napoleonic Wars. Key figure in treaties of Paris (1814, 1815). A great reformer in internal state structure.

Hardie, James Keir (1856–1915), British politician, and one of founders of Labour party. Independent Labour MP (1892), and a Labour MP from 1900. A key adviser to the suffragette movement.

Harding, Warren (1865–1923), 29th US pres. (1921–23). A Republican, whose administration saw the final peace negotiations after WWI, but was marred by political scandal. Died before any scandals could impeach his power.

Harold II (*c.* 1022–66), last Anglo-Saxon ruler, English king for eight months in 1066; defeated Harold Hardhraade at Stamford Bridge (1066). Lost to William the Conqueror at Hastings later that year; killed in battle.

Henry VIII

Harun-al-Rashid (766–809), fifth caliph of Abbasid dynasty (from 786), ruler of the Islamic world at the height of the Baghdad Empire. A patron of the arts, he was immortalized in *The Thousand and One Nights*.

Hastings, Warren (1732–1818), British colonist and first governor-general of India (1772–85). He made East India Company's power supreme in India and achieved widespread reforms. Impeached on return to Britain on corruption charges, but acquitted.

Henry I (1068–1135), king of England from 1100 and duke of Normandy from 1106. His reign saw great reform and the rise of government institutions.

Henry I (*c.* 876–936), German king from 919, first of the Saxon line. He consolidated the army, encouraged increased urbanization and repelled Magyar invaders.

Henry II (1133–89), king of England from 1154. Consolidated realms in England and France and increased royal authority. Argued with Thomas à Becket, resulting in the latter's murder (1170). His reign saw considerable judicial development, inc. creation of jury system at Assize of Clarendon (1166).

Henry III (1207–72), king of England from 1216. His reign saw a disastrous war with France, and was fraught with misrule, indifference and baronial struggle led by Simon de Montfort.

Henry IV (Henry Bolingbroke) (1377–1413), king of England from 1399, first of House of Lancaster. Exiled after opposition to Richard II (1398), but invaded England and usurped power in 1399. Maintained power despite a Scottish invasion and Welsh insurrection as well as uprisings by nobles.

Henry IV (1553–1610), king of Navarre from 1572 and of France from 1589, first of the Bourbon line. Brought stability to France by converting to Catholicism (1593), thus achieving unity and peace. Granted rights to Huguenots in Edict of Nantes (1598). Assassinated by a Catholic religious fanatic.

Henry V (1387–1422), king of England from 1413. Victorious over French at Agincourt (1415); regained Normandy (1418). Forced France to make peace; recognized as heir to French throne at Treaty of Troyes (1420). Noted for suppression of Lollard heretics.

Henry VI (1165–97), Holy Roman Emperor of Hohenstaufen line from 1190. Took control of kingdom of Sicily (1194), making him one of the most powerful men in Europe. Wished to make the Holy Roman Empire hereditary but failed to secure his family's position.

Henry VI (1421–71), English king (1422–61, 1470–71), last of the House of Lancaster. Early reign saw loss of English territories in France, whilst domestic affairs were dominated by wrangling between Lancastrians and Yorkists. Known for his piety, he was briefly insane (1453), and deposed by Edward of York (1461). Restored to power (1470) by Warwick the Kingmaker, but murdered on return of Edward to London (1471). His inept reign precipitated War of the Roses.

Henry VII (1457–1509), king of England from 1485, first of the Tudors. Took the crown after Richard III's death at Bosworth Field, thus ending Wars of the Roses. Conciliated Yorkists and Lancastrians by marrying Elizabeth of York. Curbed the power of the nobles.

Henry VIII (1491–1547), English king from 1509. Severed ties between England and the Roman Church; dissolved the monasteries from 1535.

■ GOEBBELS HAD A DEFORMED FOOT WHICH PREVENTED HIM FROM SERVING IN THE ARMY

Married six times: Catherine of Aragon 1509–33 (divorced); Anne Boleyn 1533–36 (executed); Jane Seymour 1536–37 (d.); Anne of Cleves 1540 (annulled); Catherine Howard 1540–42 (executed), Catherine Parr 1543–47 (outlived him).

Henry the Navigator (1394–1460), Portuguese prince whose patronage of voyages laid foundations for the great age of Portuguese maritime exploration. Whilst his interest in navigation and cartography saw forays into sub-Saharan Africa, he personally never made a voyage of discovery.

Herod I the Great (74–4 BC), king of Palestine from 31 BC. New Testament ruler in whose kingdom Jesus was born, he is portrayed as a tyrant who slew innocents at Bethlehem.

Herzl, Theodor (1860–1904), Hungarian-born Jew and founder of political Zionism. His 1896 pamphlet *The Jewish State* suggested an international council to decide upon a Jewish state. Organized first Zionist World Congress (1897); first president of the World Zionist Organization.

Hess, Rudolf (1894–1987), German Nazi leader and deputy of Nazi Party (1933–41) under Hitler. Participated in 1923 Munich uprising. Made a secret flight to Scotland in 1941 in an attempt to broker Anglo-German peace. Subsequently held as a prisoner of war. Sentenced to life imprisonment at Nuremberg (1946).

Hideyoshi Toyotomi (*c.* 1536–98), Japanese military leader and chief Imperial minister from 1585. He showed military and administrative acumen and achieved unity in Japan.

Himmler, Heinrich (1900–45), German Nazi leader; participant in 1923 Munich uprising; head of SS from 1929, and of Gestapo from 1936. Second most powerful man of the Reich after Hitler, he was one of chief architects of the Final Solution, advocating concentration camps and gas ovens. Fled office after unsuccessful plan to surrender to Allies. Captured by British, but committed suicide by cyanide poisoning.

Hirohito (1901–89), Japanese emperor from 1926. His reign saw Japanese military expansion, resulting in wars against China (1931–32, 1937–45), and against the Allies in WWII (1941–45). Renounced divine status in 1946 and, under US occupation, lost his powers and became a figurehead.

Hitler, Adolf (1889–1945), Austrian-born leader of the German Nazis. Pres. of National Socialist (Nazi) Party in 1921. Took part in 1923 Munich uprising; subsequently imprisoned. Engineered burning of the Reichstag in 1933, won the general election, becoming chancellor, and subsequently pres.; took title Führer (leader) in 1934. As dictator, he set about creating a new order through the occupation of Europe. Coordinated Rome-Berlin axis (1936) and invaded Austria (1938). Invasion of Poland precipitated WWII. His strategy of *bliztkrieg* (lightning war) saw initial successes throughout Europe, but disastrous campaigns in Russia and N. Africa saw his power diminish. Survived assassination attempt in 1944 when a bomb exploded at his feet. In dying stages of the Reich, he married his mistress Eva Braun at his underground bunker in Berlin. Shortly afterwards, it is believed that they both committed suicide.

Himmler (left) and Hitler (centre)

Ho Chi Minh (1890–1969), Vietnamese Communist leader; founder of Indochina Communist Party (1930), the Viet-Minh (1941); first pres. of N. Vietnam from 1945. He spearheaded post-WWII anticolonial effort in Asia. Final years saw the North–South Vietnamese conflict which cost the USA dearly.

Honecker, Erich (1912–94), E. German dictator (1971–89). Leader of Communist Party from 1971. Replaced in 1989 in the face of pro-democracy movement. Took refuge in Moscow after fall of E. German Communism, but deported in 1992. Deemed too ill to stand trial for corruption and abuse of power in 1993.

Hoover, Herbert (1874–1964), 31st US pres. (1929–33). Sec. of commerce (1921–28). His Republican presidency saw the Great Depression; opposed government aid to unemployed.

Thomas Jefferson

Horthy, Miklós (1868–1957), Hungarian regent (1920–44). A naval officer turned conservative politician, he ruled as a virtual dictator, quelling several revolutions. Supported Axis powers during WWII until Hitler invaded Hungary in 1944, whereupon he was imprisoned. Freed by Allies in 1945.

Hoxha, Enver (1908–85), Albanian politician and dictator. Effective ruler from 1944; deposed the king (1946). An extreme Stalinist who suppressed religion and dissidents, he practised an isolationist foreign policy.

Hsüan Tsung (685–762), Chinese emperor (712–56), sixth of T'ang dynasty. During his reign China achieved internal stability and prosperity. Abdicated after his heir-apparent declared himself emperor.

Hunyadi, János (*c.* 1387–1456), Hungarian warrior and politician; regent of Hungary (1446–52). Crusaded against the Turks throughout the 15th century, finally securing peace by breaking Turkish siege on Belgrade (1456).

Jesus Christ

Huss, Jan (*c.* 1370–1415), Czech religious reformer whose teachings anticipated Luther. Rector of Prague university (1402–11); excommunicated in 1411. His Wycliffite preachings declared Scripture as the supreme religious authority. Pronounced a heretic by Council of Constance and burned at the stake; his death precipitated the Hussite wars.

Hussein ibn Ali (1856–1931), emir of Mecca (1908–16) and king of Hejaz (1916–24). A leader of the Arab independence movement (1916); forced to abdicate after unrest and invasion by ibn-Saud.

ibn-Saud, Abdul Aziz (1880–1953), Muslim leader and founder of Saudi Arabia. An exile in Kuwait as a child, he led a daring raid on the ruling Arabian family, the Rashids, in 1902. Expanded Arabian territory, inc. the Hejaz (1924); unified all Saudi Arabia in 1932, and was declared first king. Became extremely rich through oil exploration after 1933.

Ignatius of Loyola, St (1491–1556), Spanish theologian and co-founder of the Society of Friends (Jesuits) in 1534. A leading figure in the 16th-century Catholic Reformation, he was also influential in spreading the Christian message in Asia and S. America.

Innocent III (1160–1216), Italian-born pope from 1198. Under him, the papacy secured its greatest powers over secular rulers. His reign included Fourth Crusade (1199) and Albigensian purge (1208), as well as the fourth Lateran Council (1215). Actively promoted the Franciscan and Dominican orders, both spiritual orders based upon apostolic poverty.

Innocent IV (b. end 12th century–1254), Italian-born pope from 1243. Made universal claims for the papacy, leading to antagonism with Emperor Frederick II.

Isabella I (1451–1504), queen of Spain from 1479. As ruler of Castile from 1474, and ruler of Aragon from 1479, she jointly ruled a united Spain with her husband Ferdinand II. Sponsored Columbus's voyages to the New World, thus establishing an overseas Spanish empire. She introduced the Inquisition to Spain.

Isaiah (8th century BC), Old Testament prophet who preached the holiness of God and the need for holy living.

Ismail Pasha (1830–95), khedive (viceroy) of Egypt (1863–79) under Ottoman rule. Successfully negotiated completion of Suez Canal, but the huge foreign debt he accumulated led to dual French and British control of the canal and to his deposition.

Ito Hirobumi (1841–1909), Japanese statesman, crucial in the development of modern Japan. Four-times premier (1885–88, 1892–96, 1898, 1900–01); drafted Japanese Meiji constitution (1898). After his assassination by a Korean freedom-fighter, Japan annexated Korea (1910).

Ivan III, 'the Great' (1440–1505), Russian ruler and Grand Duke of Moscow (1462–1505). He threw off the yoke of the Tartars and expanded Russia's territories.

Ivan IV, 'the Terrible' (1530–84), Grand Duke of Moscow from 1533 and tsar from 1547. Greatly diminished power of upper nobility, often through public executions. Expanded Russia eastwards with capture of Kazan (1552) and Astrakhan (1554). Centralized Russian power. He became unbalanced and killed his son.

Jackson, Andrew (1767–1845), US soldier who was victorious over the British at New Orleans (1815); 7th US pres. (1829–37). A Democrat, he centralized power against states.

Jackson, Thomas (1824–63), US Confederate general in the Civil War. Earned nickname Stonewall after strong resistance at Bull Run (1861). Killed in battle at Chancellorville.

James I (1208–76), king of Aragon from 1213. A strong leader who expanded Spanish territories in the Mediterranean.

James I (1566–1625), English king (from 1603) and king of Scotland as James VI from 1567. He became king of Great Britain, inheriting the English crown as a descendant of Henry VII. Reasserted divine right of monarch; sought European peace and New World expansion. A keen scholar, his reign was marred with parliamentary quarrels.

James II (1633–1701), king of Great Britain (1685–88), the last Roman Catholic ruler. His rule, with its many arbitrary laws curtailing institutional power, was unpopular and led to deposition by the future William III in the Glorious Revolution.

Jefferson, Thomas (1743–1826), 3rd US pres. (1801–09). A key figure in the struggle for independence, he was principal author of the Declaration of Independence (1776), and was first sec. of state (1789–94) in Washington's first government. As Republican pres. he made the Louisiana Purchase (1803), and his second term saw prohibition of the slave trade.

Jerome, St (*c.* 342–420), Dalmatian-born theologian and religious writer; a learned scholar, he was (unusually for the time) brought up as a Christian and was, for a period, a hermit. Regarded as the most learned of the Latin Fathers, he is known for his Vulgate translation of the Bible and his religious commentaries.

Jesus Christ (*c.* 4 BC–*c.* AD 30), Judean-born preacher and founder of Christianity. Born in Bethlehem; childhood spent in Nazareth. Ministry begun after baptism by John the Baptist. After 40 days in the wilderness, where he refused to succumb to various temptations, he gathered 12 disciples around him and began his mission.

The crux of his teachings were delivered at the Sermon on the Mount, where he preached love, charity and meekness. Arrived in Jerusalem *c.* AD 30, where he drove the money-changers from the Temple. Betrayed after the Last Supper by Judas Iscariot, and convicted of blasphemy. Condemned to death, a sentence confirmed by Roman procurator Pontius Pilate, and crucified. According to Christian tradition, he rose from the dead on the Sunday following, and laid the foundations for Christianity by charging Peter to build his Church.

Jinnah, Mohammad Ali (1876–1948), Pakistani politician and founder of Pakistan. Left Indian National Congress in 1931 which he thought was too Hindu-oriented. An advocate of a separate Muslim state, a position at odds with British notions and Gandhi's attempts to keep India unified. Succeeded in gaining an independent nation of Pakistan in 1947, and was its first governor-general (1947–48).

Joan of Arc, St (*c.* 1412–31), French patriot whose visions and internal 'voices' inspired her to lead the French to victory at Orléans (1429). She was captured in 1430, sold to the English, charged with heresy and burned at the stake.

John I (1357–1433), king of Portugal from 1385, and founder of the Aviz (Johannine) dynasty. Defended kingdom against Castilian invasion and stimulated maritime exploration and expansion.

John III Sobieski (1629–96), Polish king, elected to power in 1674. His reign was a continual battle against Ottoman Turks and Tartars. Victory against Turks in 1683 at Vienna made him a hero throughout Europe.

John of Austria, Don (1547–78), Spanish military general and illegitimate son of Emperor Charles V. Victorious in a famous naval battle against the Turks at Lepanto (1571). Governor-general of the Netherlands (1576–78).

John the Baptist (*c.* 9 BC–AD 28), Jewish prophet and forerunner of Jesus Christ. Preached coming of Final Judgement, and baptized people, inc. Jesus, in readiness for it. Imprisoned and executed for denouncing Herod Antipas's illegal marriage to Herodias.

Johnson, Andrew (1808–75), 17th US pres. (1865–69), taking the Republican presidency on the assassination of Lincoln. His leniency towards Southern states upset Radical Republicans and ultimately led to his impeachment (1868), which he survived by one vote.

Johnson, Lyndon B. (1908–73), vice-pres. from 1960; became 36th US pres. (1963–69) on assassination of Kennedy. His Democrat administration saw far-reaching civil rights and social welfare legislation – the 'Great Society' programme. Faced unpopularity over involvement in Vietnam.

Joseph II (1741–90), Habsburg Holy Roman Emperor from 1765; co-ruler with his mother, Maria Theresa, to 1780. Undertook widespread reform, inc. curtailing of papal power in his empire and abolition of serfdom. His later reign saw domestic unrest.

Juárez, Benito (1806–72), Mexican revolutionary leader and pres. from 1861. His radical reforms led to civil war. He deposed and executed Emperor Maximilian (1867), restoring the republic.

Joan of Arc

Jugurtha (*c.* 160–104 BC), Numidian king (118–106 BC). Gained his kingdom through murder, bribery and brute force, and attempted to secure his N. African kingdom against the Romans, who eventually captured him.

Julian the Apostate (*c.* 331–63), Roman emperor from 361. Lost faith in Christianity after the massacre of most of his family; publicly declared himself a pagan (361), and though tolerant of the Church, sought to curtail its powers. A scholar and military leader, he led a disastrous campaign into Persia (363), where he was fatally wounded.

Julius II (1443–1513), Italian-born pope from 1503. A great patron of the arts and artists. Politically, he sought to re-establish papal supremacy in Italy.

Justinian I (483–565), Roman Byzantine emperor from 527, noted for administrative reform and legislation, inc. the *Codex Justinianus* (534), which was highly influential in European law.

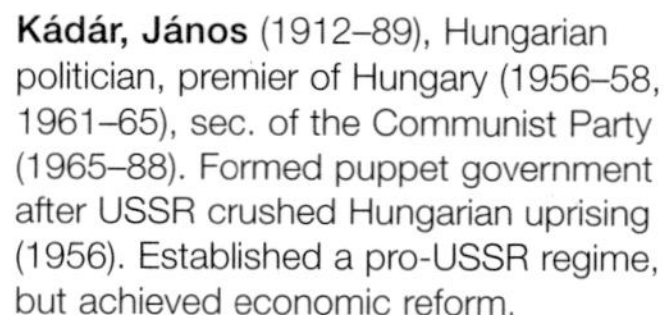
Martin Luther King and Malcolm X

K'ang-hsi (1654–1722), second Ch'ing emperor of China from 1661. Expanded China's territories into Russia and Outer Mongolia; encouraged western contact. A patron of arts and education.

Kádár, János (1912–89), Hungarian politician, premier of Hungary (1956–58, 1961–65), sec. of the Communist Party (1965–88). Formed puppet government after USSR crushed Hungarian uprising (1956). Established a pro-USSR regime, but achieved economic reform.

Kennedy, John F. (1917–63), 35th US pres. (1960–63). A Democrat, his presidency saw several near-catastrophes, inc. the failed Bay of Pigs invasion of Cuba (1961) and the Cuban missile crisis (1962). However, he also achieved a partial nuclear test ban (1963). Assassinated in Dallas, allegedly by Lee Harvey Oswald, although there is much popular support for the notion of a coordinated conspiracy against the president.

Kenneth I (d. *c.* 858), first king of a united Scotland from 843. Moved seat of Scottish Church from Iona to Dunkeld.

Kublai Khan

Kenyatta, Jomo (*c.* 1889–1978), Kenyan politician, PM (1963–64) and pres. (1964–78). Founded nationalist Kenya African Union movement (1946); imprisoned (1952–58) for alleged Mau Mau activity.

Kerensky, Alexander (1881–1970), Russian revolutionary politician, premier (1917), but ousted by the Bolsheviks in October Revolution the same year.

Kesselring, Albert (1885–1960), German field marshal under Hitler. Instrumental in early WWII successes, and who staved off Allied attack in Italy for over a year.

Khomeini, Ayatollah Ruhollah (1900–89), Iranian religious and political leader. Exiled from 1964, but returned in 1979 after collapse of the Shah's regime to lead an Islamic Revolution.

Khrushchev, Nikita (1894–1971), Soviet politician; first sec. of the Communist Party (1953–64) and Soviet premier (1958–64). Conducted a policy of destalinization, economic reform and decentralization, which led to his deposition. Involved in Cuban missile crisis of 1962.

Kim Il Sung (1912–94), N. Korean Stalinist ruler. Effective absolute ruler as premier (1948–72) and pres. (1972–94). Attempted reunification of Korea through a costly war (1950–53). Established a personality cult at home, whilst pursuing an isolationist policy in international matters.

King, Martin Luther, Jr (1929–68), US clergyman and black civil rights leader. Formed Southern Christian Leadership Conference; promoted non-violent protests, inc. the March on Washington (1963). Assassinated by sniper fire, for which James Earl Ray was convicted.

Kitchener, Horatio Herbert (1850–1916), Irish-born British field marshal; conquered the Sudan (1896–98) and was victorious in 2nd Boer War (1900–02). As war sec. (1914–16), he assembled a vast army for WWI. Lost at sea when his ship was mined.

Knox, John (*c.* 1513–72), Scottish theologian and key figure in Scottish Reformation. Founded Presbyterianism in Scotland and helped frame constitution of the Reformed Church.

Kosciuszko, Tadeusz (1746–1817), Polish soldier and patriot. He fought the colonists in US War of Independence (1775–83). In Poland, he fought Russian invaders to become a national hero. Taken by Russia (1794), he later went into exile for the rest of his life.

Kossuth, Lajos (1802–94), Hungarian revolutionary; led nationalist revolution of 1848; head of government (1849). Resigned as revolution collapsed; he went into exile for the rest of his life.

Kropotkin, Peter (1842–1921), Russian geographer, anarchist and revolutionary theorist; advocated a form of anarchist communism. Initially pleased with 1917 Russian revolution, but disenchanted after Bolshevik uprising.

Kruger, Paul (1825–1904), S. African soldier and statesman; took part in Great Trek out of British Cape Colony. Helped found Transvaal and became its pres. (1883–98). Sought to maintain Boer independence in war of 1899–1902.

Krupp, Alfred (1907–67), German industrialist who supported Hitler. Made armaments for Nazis using slave labour in concentration camps. Imprisoned and deprived of property after WWII.

Kublai Khan (1214–94), Mongolian ruler from 1260 and emperor of China from 1271. Having conquered northern China, he became its first non-Chinese ruler, and founded Yuan dynasty. His vast empire and splendid court was described by Marco Polo.

Kun, Béla (1886–*c.* 1937), Hungarian Communist dictator; coordinated failed Hungarian revolution (1919) and was forced to flee upon its collapse. Believed killed in a Stalinist purge.

Kutuzov, Mikhail (1745–1813), Russian general who successfully repelled Napoleon's advancing army (1812).

Lafayette, Marie Joseph (1757–1834), French soldier and statesman. Fought in American Revolution against the British. Commander of troops in French Revolution, in which he was initially influential. Active politically again after the fall of Napoleon (1815).

Lao-tsu (6th century BC), Chinese philosopher and prime founder of Daoism (Taoism). Little is known of his life.

Laval, Pierre (1883–1945), French politician, PM (1931–32, 1935–36), swung from the Left to the Right. Led Vichy regime; was later executed for collaboration with Germany during WWII.

Lawrence, Thomas Edward (Lawrence of Arabia) (1888–1935), British archaeologist and soldier. Joined Arab revolt against Turks. Delegate to Peace Conference (1919). Retired from public life after not achieving most of his goals for the Arab cause.

Lee, Robert E. (1807–70), US Confederate general and commander of the southern army during Civil War. Defeated at Bull Run (1861), repulsed at Gettysburg (1863); surrendered to Ulysses S. Grant at Appomattox (1865), signalling end of war.

Lenin, Vladimir Ilich (1870–1924), Russian revolutionary leader; founded the Bolsheviks, leading them in 1917 October Revolution that overthrew Kerensky. Inaugurated 'dictatorship of the proletariat', becoming first Communist Soviet leader. Planned large-scale nationalization; redistributed land; withdrew Russia from WWI. Founded Soviet Union (1922). His 'new economic policy' of limited free enterprise (1922) was abandoned by Stalin.

Leo I (*c.* 390–461), Tuscan-born pope from 440 and champion of orthodoxy. One of the Church Fathers, he suppressed Manichaean and Pelagian heretics and negotiated peace with the Huns (452) and Vandals (455).

Leo XIII (1810–1903), Italian-born pope from 1878. Ended papal quarrel with Germany (1887). Maintained a more open attitude to civil governments and adopted a modern stance with regards to scientific progress.

Leonidas I (d. 480 BC), Spartan king from 491 BC. Opposed the Persian Xerxes' advancing army at Thermopylae (480), making a celebrated last stand.

Leopold I (1790–1865), first king of Belgium from 1831. Maintained neutrality whilst strengthening the nation's infrastructure.

Li Yuan (Kao Tsu) (256–195 BC), Chinese emperor from 206 BC; first emperor of the Han Dynasty, which set Chinese political power structures for the next 2000 years.

Lin Piao (Lin Biao) (1907–71), Chinese soldier and Communist Party politician. Made Mao Tse-tung's second-in-command (and heir) after 1966 Cultural Revolution. Formulated 'Project 571', a plan to assassinate Mao in 1971 and seize power. The plot was uncovered, and he died trying to escape.

Lincoln, Abraham (1809–65), 16th US pres. (1861–65). A Republican, he led the Union to victory in the Civil War; delivered famous Gettysburg Address (1863) and proclaimed freedom of the slaves later that year. Assassinated in Ford's Theatre by John Wilkes Booth.

Livingstone, David (1813–73), Scottish missionary and explorer. His travels to Africa on missionary journeys helped fire Western imagination for Africa; influential in shaping attitudes and awareness of the continent. Rescued by Stanley after struggling in Zambia (1871).

Lloyd George, David (1863–1945), British Liberal politician and coalition PM (1916–22) during late WWI. As Chancellor of the Exchequer he introduced old age pensions (1908) and National Insurance (1911), whilst his strong wartime premiership was instrumental in British victory. A key figure in post-war peace negotiations.

Louis I (778–840), French king of Western (Carolingian) Empire from 814. Sole surviving son of Charlemagne, he attempted to divide the kingdom between his sons. Twice deprived of power by them, he recovered but left the empire in tatters.

Louis VII (*c.* 1120–80), Capetian king of France from 1137. His reign saw much rivalry and antagonism with Henry II of England.

Louis IX (St Louis) (1215–70), Capetian king of France from 1226. A model pious medieval king, he led the Seventh Crusade (1248–50), where he was defeated and briefly imprisoned. Negotiated peace with Henry III of England (1259).

Louis XIII (1601–43), Bourbon king of France from 1610. A timid ruler, he mainly led through his ministers Richelieu and Mazarin to make France a central European force.

Louis XIV

Louis XIV, 'the Sun King' (1638–1715), Bourbon king of France from 1643. Ruled in person from 1661 when Mazarin died. A symbol of absolute monarchy whose reign was one of unsurpassed brilliance. Ruling from Versailles, which he built (1676–1708), he caused the flight of Huguenots through revocation of the Edict of Nantes (1685). Appointed Colbert to restore strength of the economy and expand industry. Pushed France's borders further eastwards into Habsburg territory, and fought costly war of the Spanish Succession (1701–14) which crippled France economically.

Louis XV (1710–74), Bourbon king of France from 1715. Gained Lorraine in war of Polish Succession (1733–35), but lost much foreign French territory in Seven Years' War (1756–63). An ineffective ruler, his reign was financially costly, and saw royal power lose its strength.

Louis XVI (1754–93), king of France from 1774. He attempted reform of a bankrupt state but was met with opposition to his taxes. In a wave of rising dissatisfaction, partly brought on by the cost of involvement in American War of Independence (1776–83), he recalled the estates-general (1789). This was not enough to repel revolution in that year. The monarchy was abolished in 1792, and he was brought to trial with Marie Antoinette on charges of treason against the newly-formed Republic; found guilty, he was guillotined.

Martin Luther

Louis–Philipe (1773–1850), Orléanist king of France (1830–48); exiled 1793–1814. Reign known as July Monarchy after the July 1830 revolution which brought him to power. Liberal for most of his reign, he was forced to abdicate in the face of revolution.

Luther, Martin (1483–1546), German theologian and religious reformer; precipitated the Reformation that gave rise to Protestantism. Wrote 95 theses on abuses within the clergy, and nailed them to the church door at Wittenburg (1517). This was followed by nearly 30 years of conflict with the papacy, whilst his ideas spread throughout northern Europe.

Mao Tse-tung

Luthuli, Albert (1898–1967), S. African reformer and black resistance leader. A Zulu chief, he took part in a passive resistance campaign against apartheid. He was detained in 1960 after protesting about the Sharpeville massacre.

MacArthur, Douglas (1880–1964), US general and commander of Allied forces in the Far East in WWII. Effective authority in Japan during Allied occupation (1945–51); drafted new Japanese constitution and made sweeping reforms. UN commander-in-chief in early stages of Korean War (1950–51), but relieved of duties by Pres. Truman because of differences in opinion over possible action against Chinese involvement.

MacDonald, James Ramsay (1866–1937), first British Labour PM (1924, 1929–31) and head of the coalition government (1931–35). Caused party opposition after Great Depression of 1929 by forming a mainly Conservative coalition government.

Machiavelli, Nicolò (1469–1527), Italian statesman and political theorist. His work, *The Prince* (1532), was a masterpiece of political realism and was influential in Renaissance statecraft.

MacKenzie, William Lyon (1795–1861), Scottish-born Canadian politician. Declared independence for Toronto in 1837; when Canadian forces putting down this rebellion burnt the US steamer *Caroline*, an international incident resulted.

MacMahon, Patrice (1808–93), French soldier and politician. Made his name in the Crimean War. As commander of the army at Versailles, he suppressed the Paris Commune. President of the Third Republic (1873–79). Resigned after failing to restore the monarchy.

Macmillan, Harold (1894–1986), British Conservative politician and PM (1957–63); brought about domestic economic expansion. Heralded independence of British African colonies in his 'wind of change' speech. He antagonized De Gaulle who blocked UK's attempt to join the Common Market.

Madero, Francisco (1873–1913), Mexican revolutionary politician and pres. (1911–13). He challenged the dictator Porfirio Díaz, and took control when Díaz fell. His policies were deemed too moderate, and he was faced with Zapata's revolt. He was assassinated in a coup led by Victoriano Huerta.

Madison, James (1751–1836), 4th US pres. (1809–17). A founding father of the USA. Instrumental in crafting of the Constitution (1787). In war against Britain (1812) his Republican administration proved ineffective.

Magellan, Ferdinand (*c.* 1480–1521), Portuguese navigator and explorer who led (for Spain) the first circumnavigation of the globe (1519–22). Although he was killed in the Philippines on this voyage, the expedition was completed by the Spanish captain Juan Sebastián del Cano.

Mahavira (*c.* 599–529 BC), Indian religious teacher who founded Jainism; an austere doctrine of strict vegetarianism and non-violence.

Mahdi (Mohammad Ahmed) (1844–85), Sudanese leader and former slave trader who rebelled against Egyptian rule in Sudan. Established an Islamic state in east Sudan with El Obeid as his capital. Crushed an Egyptian army (1883). When he took control of Khartoum (1885), Gen. Gordon was killed.

Makarios III (1913–77), Cypriot religious leader and politician. Primate of the Orthodox Church of Cyprus; one of the leaders of Enosis (Union with Greece) movement; Cyprus's first pres. from 1960. He faced partition of Cyprus after Turkish invasion (1974). Briefly ousted in a coup in 1974, but reinstated in 1975.

Malcolm III (*c.* 1031–93), Scottish king from 1057. Took throne on death of Macbeth. Recognized William I's overlordship in 1072, but still invaded England on five occasions. Killed by William II on last incursion into England.

Malcolm X (Malcolm Little) (1925–65), US black Muslim leader, who followed Elijah Muhammad's Islamic sect, and believed in black-separatism. Following factional feuding, he was assassinated at a rally.

Malthus, Thomas (1766–1834), English economist and demographer, best known for theorizing that food supply will always tend to be outstripped by population growth, and so population control is necessary. He discounted humanity's ability to develop new resources. His writings were highly influential on 19th-century social policy.

Mao Tse-tung (Mao Zedong) (1893–1976), Chinese Communist theorist, revolutionary and statesman. Helped found Chinese Communist Party (CCP) in 1921. He set up a Communist people's republic in south-east China (1931–34) and when this was attacked by forces of Chiang Kai-shek was forced to retreat in the face of attack in the 'Long March' of 1934–35. Successfully repelled Japanese attack in Yanan during WWII, and subsequently achieved victory over Chiang's Nationalist government (1949). Chairman of the CCP from 1935, he became Chinese head of state (1949–58). His Cultural Revolution (1966–69), a massive purge on liberal dissidents, resulted in anarchy through the excesses of student Red Guards. He quarrelled with the USSR in 1962.

Marat, Jean Paul (1743–93), French revolutionary politician and journalist. His journal *L'ami du peuple*

(1789) was a key radical publication which incited violence. Elected to the National Convention (1792), he was responsible for the massacre of aristocrats; overthrew moderates in 1793 with the help of Danton and Robespierre. Assassinated by Charlotte Corday as he took a bath.

Marcos, Ferdinand (1917–89), Philippine politician. Elected pres. in 1965, he assumed dictatorial power in 1972 in face of rising insurgency. His repressive regime was overthrown in 1986 in a popular uprising.

Margaret I (1353–1412), Scandinavian queen; regent of Denmark (by marriage) from 1375, of Norway (by inheritance) from 1380 and of Sweden (by conquest) from 1388. She united Denmark, Norway and Sweden in Kalmar Union (1397).

Maria Theresa (1717–80), queen of Hungary and Bohemia and archduchess of Austria from 1740; with her son (Joseph II) effective ruler of Holy Roman Empire. Her accession resulted in the War of the Austrian Succession (1741–48), which saw Austria lose Silesia. Austrian power was confined in the Seven Years' War (1756–63). Gained territory in partition of Poland (1772).

Marie-Antoinette (1755–93), wife of Louis XVI and queen of France from 1774. Her extravagant lifestyle, Austrian nationality and resistance to reform contributed to the French Revolution and the overthrow of the monarchy in 1792. Guillotined.

Marlborough, John Churchill, 1st Duke of (1650–1722), English general. Crushed Monmouth's rebellion (1785); secured significant British victories in the War of the Spanish Succession (1701–14), inc. Blenheim (1704), Ramillies (1706) and Oudenaarde (1708).

Marshall, George C. (1880–1959), US soldier and statesman; directed US army during WWII as chief of staff. Subsequently US sec. of state (1947–49) and defence (1950–51). Originated European Recovery Program, the Marshall Plan, in 1947 to help reconstruct post-war Europe.

Marx, Karl (1818–83), German social and political theorist, and effective founder of 20th-century communism (his ideas became the official doctrine of the USSR). Based in London after European revolutions in 1848. A journalist, he was involved in radical political movements, notably the First International (1864–72). Author of the *Communist Manifesto* (with Friedrich Engels; 1848) and *Das Kapital* (1867).

Mary (1st century BC–1st century AD), Biblical figure. Through the Immaculate Conception, she was the virgin mother of Jesus. Present at the Crucifixion and assumed into Heaven. A key figure in Christianity, a cult of the Virgin Mary has flourished since the Middle Ages.

Mary I, Tudor (1516–58), queen of England from 1553. In an attempt to restore Catholicism to England, she violently persecuted Protestants, which earned her the name 'Bloody Mary'. Executed many political and religious opponents, inc. Ridley, Latimer, Cranmer and Lady Jane Grey.

Mary, Queen of Scots (1542–87), queen of Scotland (1542–67) and queen consort of France (1559–60). Implicated in the murder of her second husband Lord Darnley (1567), whereupon she fled to England to seek help from her cousin Elizabeth I. However, Elizabeth saw a Roman Catholic threat to the English throne and she was imprisoned for the next 18 years. Finally, after the discovery of a plot to assassinate Elizabeth, she was deemed too great a risk and was executed.

Marie-Antoinette

Masaryk, Jan (1886–1948), Czech patriot and diplomat. Son of Tomas Masaryk, he was the Czechoslovak government-in-exile's foreign minister from 1941; returned to Prague as foreign minister in 1945. Died in mysterious circumstances, falling from a window, after Communist takeover of Czechoslovakia in 1948.

Masaryk, Tomas (1850–1937), Czech philosopher and patriot. Virtual founder of Czechoslovakia and its first pres. (1918–35). He was one of the first to voice concern over the rising power of the Nazis (1933).

Karl Marx

Matthias I Corvinus (1443–90), Hungarian king from 1458. Reformed the army and the economy. He repelled the Turks, made territorial gains, at the expense of the Habsburgs, and made Hungary a great power.

Maurice, Count of Nassau (1567–1625), Dutch leader; stadholder from 1584. A great military innovator, he led the Dutch army to important victories against Spain in the 1590s. Forced Spain to recognize the Dutch republic (1608). Prince of Orange from 1618; virtual dictator of Dutch republic after 1619.

Maximilian I (1459–1519), Habsburg Holy Roman Emperor from 1493. Laid the foundations of Austria's power through marriage: his first wife was heiress to Spain, Burgundy and the Low Countries; the second brought the fortune of the Sforzas.

Maximilian, Ferdinand Joseph (1832–67), Austrian archduke; emperor of Mexico (1863–67). Supported by French arms, he accepted the crown of Mexico in 1863, but faced insurgency led by Juárez. Unwilling to desert his followers, he remained in Mexico, was deserted by France, betrayed and executed.

Cosimo de' Medici

Mazarin, Jules (1602–61), Italian-born French statesman, cardinal and chief minister of Louis XIII after death of Richelieu. Effective French ruler through early years of Louis XIV's reign. He curbed the power of the nobles but opposition to his taxes led to the Fronde uprisings, eventually subdued with the help of Condé. Deeply unpopular at home, he established French might in Europe.

Mazzini, Giuseppe (1805–72), Italian patriot. Founded Young Italy Association (1831) which sought unity. A key figure in Italian unification, he freed Milan and set up a republic in Rome, but left Italy when his revolt collapsed. He aided Garibaldi's capture of southern Italy (1860) but went into exile rather than live in a monarchy.

McCarthy, Joseph (1909–57), US senator who inaugurated a series of Communist 'witchhunts' in 1950s. Accused many fellow senators and other high-ranking officials without substance. Officially condemned for conduct contrary to Senate traditions in 1954.

McKinley, William (1843–1901), 25th US pres. (1897–1901). His Republican administration saw acquisition of Cuba and the Philippines after Spanish-American War (1898) and the annexation of Hawaii (1900). Assassinated by anarchist Leon Czolgosz in New York.

Medici, Cosimo de' (1389–1464), Italian financier and statesman; founder of princely line of the Medici family that ruled Tuscany until 1737. Seizing power in Florence in 1434, he secured peace for the city and made it a cultural centre, building magnificent buildings and sponsoring art and learning.

Medici, Lorenzo de' (1449–92), Italian ruler of Florence from 1469. Co-ruling with his brother Giuliano, he survived the Pazzi papal coup attempt (1478) in which Giuliano was assassinated; subsequent sole ruler of Florence, elevating it to a powerful European state. A major patron of the arts, whose library of classical literature helped accelerate the Renaissance, he was hailed as the most brilliant of the Medici family.

Mehemet (Muhammad) 'Ali (1769–1849), Egyptian ruler; viceroy and pasha (1805–48) and founder of the dynasty that ruled Egypt until 1832. He allied with Turkey in the Greek War of Independence, and briefly annexed Crete, Sudan and Syria. Incapacitated by insanity from 1848.

Meir, Golda (1898–1978), Israeli politician, one of the founders of the state of Israel and its PM (1969–74).

Melbourne, William Lamb, 2nd Viscount (1779–1848), English Whig politician and PM (1834, 1835–41). A key advisor to Queen Victoria in her early reign.

Menzies, Sir Robert (1894–1978), Australian politician and PM (1939–41, 1949–66), whose administration saw Australian industrial expansion and creation of formal ties with USA.

Metternich, Klemens, Prince (1773–1859), Austrian statesman; foreign minister (1809–48) and chancellor from 1821. An influential figure on the European political stage, he helped form the alliance against Napoleon I and hosted Congress of Vienna (1814–15). He strove to maintain peace and the status quo. Reactionary, his belief in autocratic rule built up tensions which led to the European Revolutions of 1848, when he was driven into exile.

Michael Romanov (1596–1645), Russian tsar from 1613; founder of Romanov dynasty that ruled Russia for 300 years. His election to tsar ended the Time of Troubles; he made peace with Sweden (1617) and Poland (1618).

Minamoto Yorimoto (1147–99), Japanese founder of the feudal shogunate; supreme shogun from 1192.

Mirabeau, Honoré Gabriel Riqueti (1749–91), French revolutionary leader and orator, elected deputy for the Third Estate (1789) and pres. of the National Assembly (1791). A moderate, he believed in constitutional monarchy but was mistrusted by the royal court and the revolutionary extremists.

Miranda, Francisco de (1750–1816), Venezuelan revolutionary politician. Led Venezuelan independence movement to initial success (1811), but surrendered in the face of superior Spanish forces in 1812.

Mitterrand, François (1916–96), French Socialist statesman and pres. (1982–95). He opposed, but later used, the strong powers of the Fifth French Republic. Reformed and realigned the Left in France, refounding the Socialist Party (1971). His presidency saw closer French and German cooperation.

Molotov, Vyacheslav (1890–1986), Russian politician; member of Bolsheviks from 1906, and active in 1917 October Revolution. Soviet PM (1930–41) and foreign minister (1939–49, 1953–56). A key player in post-war European affairs, he prolonged the Cold War. Removed from power after disagreements with Khrushchev.

Monck, George (1608–70), English general who fought as a royalist in the Civil War (1642–51), and for Cromwell's Commonwealth in Ireland and Scotland. Helped to restore Charles II to the throne in 1660.

Monroe, James (1758–1831), 5th US pres. (1817–25). Negotiated the Louisiana Purchase (1803). As pres., he

■ MEHEMET 'ALI, WHO FOUNDED THE ROYAL FAMILY OF EGYPT, WAS AN ALBANIAN, FROM

promulgated the Monroe Doctrine (1823), which warned Europe not to interfere in the American continent.

Montezuma II (1466–1520), last Aztec emperor from 1502. He initially tried to propitiate Cortés, mistaking the Spaniards for gods. Killed by his own subjects.

Montfort, Simon de (*c.* 1208–65), French-born English statesman and soldier. Led barons' revolt against Henry III; virtual ruler of England (1264–65).

Montgomery, Bernard (1887–1976), British general and Allied commander during WWII. Victorious at El Alamein (1942) and at Normandy landings (1944).

Montrose, James Graham (1612–50), Scottish patriot who fought as a royalist in the English Civil War; gained royalist supremacy in Scotland until 1645. Hanged after returning from exile.

Moses (*c.* 14th–13th century BC), Old Testament prophet and lawgiver. Brought up in Egyptian court. Led people of Israel from Egypt to the Promised Land. Received Ten Commandments on Mt Sinai. Denied entrance into Canaan.

Muhammad (*c.* 570–632), Arab Prophet and founder of Islam. Born in Mecca, he began life as a trader. About 610 he received revelations from Allah, which formed the Qur'an. Tensions in Mecca led to his flight (the Hegira) to Medina in 622; the founding date of the Muslim era. Managed to gain control over Mecca in 629 after a series of conflicts, during which he was wounded (625). Welded together the warring tribes of Arabia into an Islamic empire by 630.

Murat, Joachim (1767–1815), French soldier and one of Napoleon's finest marshals. King of Sicily from 1808, when he inspired a nationalist spirit in Italy. Court-martialled and shot on the fall of Napoleon Bonaparte.

Mussolini, Benito, 'Il Duce' (1883–1945), Italian politician, PM (1922–43) and Fascist dictator. Gained power after march on Rome (1922). Recognized independence of Vatican City (1929), formed Rome–Berlin Axis (1936), and annexed Abyssinia (1936) and Albania (1939). Entered WWII in 1940, with disastrous consequences, forcing his resignation in 1943. Executed by partisans in dying stages of the war.

Mutsuhito (Meiji) (1852–1912), emperor of Japan from 1867. Assumed total imperial control by removing the shogun. Modernized Japan, set up Western-style government, ended Japan's isolation and led the nation in victories against China (1894, 1895).

Nagy, Imre (1895–1958), Hungarian politician and Communist PM (1953–55, 1956). His reformist views led to his deposition, but he returned, promising free elections, in unsuccessful 1956 uprising. Displaced by Soviet intervention, he was tried and executed.

Nanak (Guru Nanak) (1469–1539), Indian religious founder of Sikhism. Based in Kartarpur, Punjab, he attracted many followers, earning the title Guru.

Napoleon I (Napoleon Bonaparte) (1769–1821), Corsican-born French general and emperor. Established military reputation in north Italian campaign (1796–97) which saw France gain much territory. Assumed supreme power in 1799 coup against the Directory; named first consul (1799–1804). Made considerable reforms in France, inc. the civil code (the Napoleonic Code). Maintained military supremacy, inc. victories over Austria (1800). Made himself emperor in 1804. His navy lost at Trafalgar (1805), but he won significant battles against Austria and Russia, inc. Austerlitz (1805) and Jena (1806). By 1810, most of Europe was part of his empire. Attempted to cripple Britain financially through a Europe-wide boycott of British goods. The invasion of Russia (1812) overstretched his resources. After the retreat from Moscow, the allies gradually advanced, until he was forced to abdicate (1814) and retire to Elba. Returned to France to rule for the 'Hundred Days' in 1815. Abdicated after defeat at Waterloo (1815); banished to St Helena for life.

Mussolini and von Ribbentrop

Napoleon III (1808–73), French statesman and ruler, nephew of Napoleon Bonaparte; pres. of Second Republic (1850–52) and, following a coup, emperor of France (1852–71). His authoritarian rule had ambitious foreign aims, cut short by defeat in Franco-German War (1870–71).

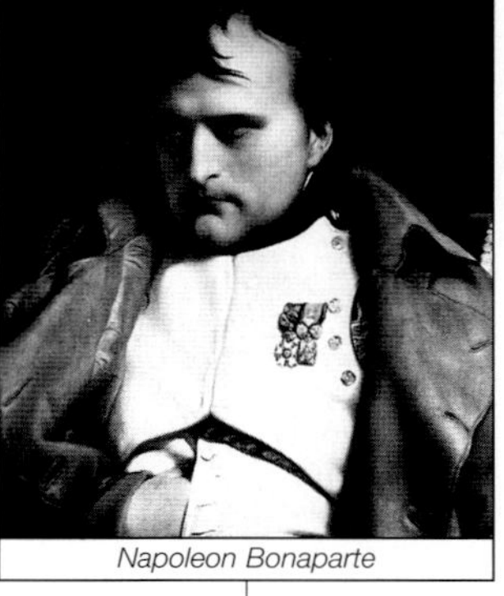
Napoleon Bonaparte

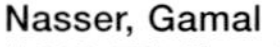

Nasser, Gamal (1918–70), Egyptian soldier and statesman; PM (1954–56), and pres. from 1956. Effective leader of coup against King Farouk (1952). Nationalized Suez Canal (1956), provoking Franco-British intervention. Became radical leader of Arab nationalism; created United Arab Republic (1958–61); lost two wars against Israel (1956, 1967).

Nebuchadnezzar II (or Nebuchadrezzar) (*c.* 630–562 BC), king of Babylon from 605 BC; restored and rebuilt Babylon, making it a great power again. Took Jerusalem (597).

Nehru, Jawaharlal (1889–1964), Indian nationalist and politician. Joined Gandhi's struggle for independence, becoming first PM of India (1947–64). Became a world leader of great moral stature.

Nelson, Horatio (1758–1805), British naval commander. Fought against Revolutionary and Napoleonic France, inc. battle of the Nile (1798); fatally wounded at battle of Trafalgar (1805).

Nero (AD 37–68), Roman emperor from AD 54. An extravagant and debauched ruler, he persecuted the Christians after the burning of Rome (AD 64). He was ousted in a coup. Committed suicide to avoid execution.

Nero

Nesselrode, Karl (1780–1862), Russian diplomat. Foreign minister (1822–56), who was instrumental in crushing the revolution in Hungary (1848). Played major role in Peace of Paris, which set the frontiers of post-Napoleonic Europe.

Neville, Richard, earl of Warwick (1428–71), English nobleman, known as the 'kingmaker' for making Henry VI his puppet (1460) and for then switching allegiance to help place Edward IV on the throne (1461) in the Wars of the Roses. Exiled for being too powerful. Warwick returned to restore Henry VI to power (1470–71). Killed in battle by Edward IV's forces in battle of Barnet as they returned to power.

Ney, Michel (1769–1815), French marshal. He distinguished himself at the battles of Ulm (1805) and Borodino (1812). Supported the restored Bourbon monarchy on Napoleon's abdication in 1814, but when his old ruler returned in 1815, he sided with him and commanded Old Guard at Waterloo (1815). Tried and executed for treason despite Louis XVIII's attempts to save him.

Nicholas I (1796–1855), Russian tsar from 1825. An autocratic heavy-handed ruler who crushed a revolt in Poland (1830–31) and revolution in Hungary (1849). He attempted the Russification of all the peoples in his empire. His scheme to partition the Ottoman Empire led to the Crimean War.

Nicholas II (1868–1918), Russian tsar (1895–1917); he was ill-suited to rule. Forced to abdicate after Russian revolution (1917); shot with his entire family in 1918.

Nixon, Richard (1913–94), 37th US pres. (1969–74). A Republican, he served as vice-pres. under Eisenhower. Involved in Watergate scandal (1972–73) in which the Democratic National Committee HQ were bugged. Facing almost certain impeachment, he resigned.

North, Frederick (1732–92), British Tory PM (1770–82); his uncompromising stance over American rebels won the favour of George III, but he was largely responsible for the loss of America.

Nurhachi (1559–1626), Manchurian tribal chieftain who helped found Manchu (Ch'ing) dynasty of China. Invaded China (1616), a move which led to eventual conquest of all China by his son in 1644.

Nyerere, Julius (1922–), Tanzanian politician; first pres. of independent Tanganyika from 1962. Coordinated merger of Tanganyika and Zanzibar (1964) to form Tanzania. His attempts to implement his African brand of Socialism and his intervention in Uganda (1978–79) brought major economic problems.

O'Connell, Daniel (1775–1847), Irish nationalist, known as the 'Liberator'. Leader of the agitation for rights for Catholics in Ireland. Subsequently sought to repeal Anglo-Irish union. He gradually lost his political judgement and was briefly jailed for sedition (1847).

Obote, Milton (1924–), Ugandan politician, PM (1962–66) and, following a coup, pres. (1966–71). Ousted from presidency in 1971 by Idi Amin, he was restored to power in 1980 with the help of Nyerere, but again ousted in 1985.

Obregón, Álvaro (1880–1928), Mexican soldier and statesman. A liberal, he joined Carranza in the counter-revolution (1913–15), then helped overthrow him (1920) for breaching the constitution. As pres., he achieved important land reforms but was assassinated.

Odoacer (*c.* 433–493), German barbarian king of Italy from 476, the date of his accession is seen as the end of the Western Roman Empire. Defeated by the Ostrogoth leader, Theodoric.

Olaf II Haraldsson (*c.* 995–1030), king of Norway (1014–28). After a celebrated raid on London (1013), he seized the Norwegian throne (1014). He strove to convert Norway to Christianity. Forced to flee (1028), he was killed in battle attempting to retake his throne.

Oleg (d. *c.* 912), Viking leader. Founded a Russian state based on Kiev (882).

Otto I (912–73), king of Germany from 936 and Holy Roman Emperor from 962. Brought the tribal duchies under central control; gained a decisive victory over the Hungarians in 955.

Ottokar II (1230–78), king of Bohemia from 1253. Made Bohemia the leading Germanic state, expanding his kingdom at the expense of Austria and Hungary, but eventually lost most of his gains before being killed in battle by Rudolf I.

Owen, Robert (1771–1858), Welsh industrialist Socialist pioneer. Set up a model community at New Lanark mills, Scotland, and other Utopian communities elsewhere, inc. one at New Harmony, Indiana (1825–28).

Oxenstierna, Axel (1583–1654), Swedish statesman and chancellor from 1612 under Gustav II Adolphus and later regent for Queen Christina until 1644. Noted for administrative and diplomatic acumen. Steered nation through Thirty Years' War (1618–48).

Pahlavi, Mohammad Reza (1919–80), last Iranian shah (1941–79). He achieved real reforms, but social inequality increased and his attempts at westernization were increasingly met with scorn by fundamentalists. Lost control in 1979, and fled as Khomeini seized control. Died in exile in Egypt.

Pahlavi, Reza Shah (1878–1944), Iranian soldier and shah (1925–41). Took part in 1921 coup; PM (1923-25); elected shah in 1925. Began a process of regeneration in his country. Abdicated as British and Soviet troops occupied Iran in WWII.

Paine, Thomas (1737–1809), English social and political reformer. Moved to America in 1774. His pamphlet *Common Sense* (1776) advocated the colonists' cause. Returned to England in 1787, but his republicanism led to charges of treason, and he fled to France, where he became a moderate member of the Convention. Arrested in 1793, he was released and returned to America (1794).

Palme, Olof (1927–86), Swedish politician and PM (1969–76, 1982–86). Achieved major constitutional reform. Campaigned against US war policy in Vietnam. His assassination remains a mystery.

Palmerston, Henry John, 3rd Viscount (1784–1865), British Whig politician; foreign minister (1830–34, 1835–41, 1846–51) and PM (1855–58, 1859–65). He initially espoused the cause of small nations (e.g. supporting Belgian independence) but by 1846 had adopted a (popular) bellicose imperialist stance.

Papandreou, Andreas (1919–96), Greek politician and first Socialist PM of Greece (1981–89, 1993–96). Exiled after 1967 Colonels' coup, but returned in 1974 to found the PASOK party. In later years a controversial figure.

Papandreou, Georgios (1888–1968), Greek politician. Led government in exile during WWII; PM (1944, 1963, 1964–65). A republican, he was forced out of power after disagreements with Constantine II. Arrested in 1967 after the military coup.

Parnell, Charles Stewart (1846–91), Protestant Irish nationalist politician. Leader of the Irish Home Rule movement and pres. of Irish Land League (1879), he encouraged peasants to boycott their landlords, leading to his brief imprisonment (1881–82). Supported Gladstone over Home Rule Bill of 1886. A divorce scandal ended his political career in 1889.

Patton, George Smith (1885–1945), US soldier; in WWII, he led US troops into North Africa (1942), Italy (1943) and France and Germany (1944–45).

Paul III (1468–1549), Italian-born pope from 1534. Excommunicated Henry VIII (1538), instituted Jesuit order (1540) and called the Council of Trent (1542).

Paul, St (1st century AD), apostle responsible for much of the growth of the early Church. Initially a persecutor of the Christians, he converted after seeing a vision of Christ en route to Damascus. Becoming Apostle of the Gentiles, he began an extensive missionary programme. Captured in Rome in AD 62, and probably executed under Nero (64).

Pearson, Lester Bowles (1897–1972), Canadian PM (1963–68). An international mediator in the Suez Crisis.

Pedro II (1825–91), the last Brazilian emperor (1831–89), whose reign saw progress and stability and final abolition of slavery (1888). Forced to abdicate after a military coup in 1889.

Peel, Robert (1788–1850), British Conservative politician and PM (1834–35, 1841–46). Founder of Conservative Party, he repealed the Corn Laws (1846). As home sec. he founded the Metropolitan Police force.

Pericles

Penn, William (1644–1718), English Quaker leader. Founded Pennsylvania (1682) as a refuge for Quakers.

Pepin III, the Short (c. 715–68), Carolingian king of the Franks from 751, father of Charlemagne. Helped Pope Stephen III against the Longobards (754), laying foundation of papal states.

Pericles (c. 490–429 BC), Athenian statesman and naval commander who created an Athenian empire. Undisputed leader of Athens by 444, which he built up into a magnificent architectural, social and cultural centre. Eventual war with Sparta erupted in the Peloponnesian War (431).

Perón, Juan (1895–1974), Argentinian soldier and pres. (1946–55, 1973–74). Elected pres. after a populist uprising, he undertook nationalization and social reforms but greatly increased state spending with dire economic consequences. His wife Eva (Evita) (1919–52) became a cult figure after her death. Deposed in 1955, he returned triumphant in 1973.

Pershing, John Joseph (1860–1948), US army general; commander-in-chief of American Expeditionary Force in WWI.

Pétain, Henri Philippe (1856–1951), French soldier and statesman; a national hero in WWI for defence of Verdun (1916). In WWII he collaborated with Germany to form Vichy government (1940–44), of which he was chief of state. Condemned to death for treason (1945), his sentence was commuted to life imprisonment.

Peter I, the Great (1672–1725), tsar of Russia from 1682. Co-ruler with his half-brother Ivan V until 1696, and thereafter sole ruler. Modernized and Europeanized Russia after incognito 'study visits' to western Europe; moved the capital from Moscow to St Petersburg, which he founded. Fought Great Northern War (1700–21) with Sweden, over which he gained a major victory at Poltava (1709).

Peter the Great

Peter, St (1st century AD), disciple of Jesus and one of the Apostles. A fisherman by trade, he became a disciple early on in Christ's ministry. Denied knowledge of Christ three times before the Crucifixion. Regarded as leader of the Apostles, he was called the rock on which the Church was to be built, and is regarded as the first pope. Martyred in Rome.

Philip II (1527–98), king of Spain from 1556, and of Portugal from 1580. A key figure in the Counter-Reformation, he extended the empire of Spain, although involved in financially disastrous campaigns against the Netherlands (from 1567). Lost Spanish Armada in 1588 in unsuccessful invasion attempt on England.

Philip II (382–336 BC), king of Macedonia from 359 BC. Led Macedonians in conquest of Greece. Set up League of Corinth (337), a federal union of Greek states. Assassinated.

Philip II Augustus (1165–1223), first great Capetian king of France from 1180. Gained many territories from England, thus strengthening France. Involved in Third Crusade (1191).

Philip III, the Good (1396–1467), duke of Burgundy from 1419. Made Burgundy a prosperous and powerful European state.

Philip IV (1605–65), king of Spain from 1621. Preferring art to politics, he ruled through his minister Olivares. His reign saw the decline of Spain as a major power; lost Portugal in 1640 and Holland in the Treaty of Westphalia (1648).

Philip IV, the Fair (1268–1314), king of France from 1285. Involved in a lengthy dispute with the papacy, resulting in seizure of Boniface VIII (1303). Set up the papacy at Avignon, the Babylonian Captivity (1305). Forced the pope to dissolve order of the Knights Templar (1314), whose wealth he coveted.

Philip VI (1293–1350), first Valois king of France from 1328. The Hundred Years' War began (1337) when Edward III of England claimed the French crown. Made concessions to nobles to help fund the war.

Pierce, Franklin (1804–69), 14th US pres. (1853–57). A Democrat who defended slavery, his Kansas-Nebraska act of 1854 led to violence from abolitionists, and contributed to the causes of the Civil War.

Pilate, Pontius (d. c. AD 36), Roman prefect of Judaea (AD 26–36). Legitimized the death sentence on Jesus Christ.

Pilsudski, Józef (1867–1935), Polish soldier who fought to free Poland from Russian rule in WWI. Pres. (1918–22) and PM (1926–28) but remained virtual dictator of Poland as minister of war until his death.

Pinochet, Augusto (1915–), Chilean soldier and pres. (1973–90). Led a military coup against the Marxist Allende to become dictator. His harsh regime saw many human rights abuses.

Pitt, William, 'the Elder', 1st Earl of Chatham (1708–78), British Whig PM (1766–68). Virtual leader as sec. of state under Newcastle from 1756–61, during which time he established Britain as an imperial power and ensured France's defeat in the Seven Years' War. Bad health made his own premiership weak.

Pitt, William, 'the Younger' (1759–1806), British Tory PM (1783–1801, 1804–06). Became Chancellor of the Exchequer at the age of 23 and PM at 24. Increased the power of the PM and Cabinet. His main concerns were financial, e.g. he introduced income tax (1798). Established UK by union of Britain and Ireland (1800). Organized three European coalitions against revolutionary France (1793, 1799, 1805).

Pius IX (1792–1878), Italian-born pope from 1846. Hailed as a liberal by Italian patriots on election, he became increasingly reactionary. When Rome fell to the new united Italy (1870) he lost temporal power and declared himself a prisoner in the Vatican. Promulgated dogma of Papal Infallibility (1870).

Pizarro, Francisco (c. 1478–1541), Spanish conquistador. Conquered Incan Empire in Peru (1531–33). Founded Lima (1535). Killed by followers of his rival, Almagro.

Pol Pot (1926–), Cambodian Communist politician. Leader of Khmer Rouge (1962–85), PM (1976–79). His brutal regime led to death of at least one million Cambodians in the 'killing fields'. Overthrown by Vietnamese in 1978. Tried by Khmer Rouge in 1997.

Polk, James (1795–1849), 11th US pres. (1845–49). A Democrat, he admitted Texas to the Union and presided over Mexican War (1846–47), which saw large US accessions inc. California and New Mexico.

Polo, Marco (c. 1254–1324), Venetian merchant and explorer. Travelled overland to China (1271–75); entered the service of Kublai Khan (1275–92). The account of his travels was a revelation to Europe.

Pombal, Sebastião José de Carvalho, Marquis of (1699–1782), Portuguese PM (1756–77). As a minister he rebuilt after Lisbon earthquake (1755). As PM, he established primary education, reorganized the army, curbed the powers of nobles and the Church and expelled the Jesuits.

Pompey the Great (106–48 BC), Roman general and statesman who gained south-west Asia for Rome. A triumvir (61–54) with Caesar and Crassus, his rivalry with Caesar grew, culminating in defeat at Pharsalus (48), shortly after which he was killed.

Proudhon, Pierre-Joseph (1809–65), French socialist political theorist. A journalist, his writings anticipated Marx, and were the basis for later anarcho-radical theories. Imprisoned several times for his views, which included assertion that property is theft.

Ptolemy I, Soter (c. 365–c. 283 BC), ruler of Egypt, and founder of Ptolemic

Egyptian dynasty. One of Alexander the Great's generals, he took control of Egypt in 323 BC, and assumed kingship in 305. Made Alexandria a cultural and commercial centre.

Pym, John (1584–1643), English statesman who led parliamentary opposition to James I and Charles I. He initiated impeachment of royal favourites and Charles I's attempt to arrest him advanced the outbreak of the Civil War.

Ramses II (13th century BC), Egyptian pharaoh (1304–1237 BC) whose reign saw Egypt at a peak of imperial might. Many of the great buildings bearing his name are earlier monuments reworked to his glory.

Ramses III (d. 1166 BC), Egyptian pharaoh from 1198 BC. The last great pharaoh, he defended Egypt against the Libyans and Sea Peoples.

Rasputin, Grigori (*c.* 1871–1916), Russian mystic. His apparent power to heal the haemophiliac Russian crown prince made him an influential figure and royal favourite. Assassinated by noblemen who sought to curb his power.

Rathenau, Walther (1867–1922), German Jewish industrialist and statesman. Structured war industry and economy during WWI; after the war he was minister in charge of reparation as dictated by the Treaty of Versailles. Assassinated by nationalists shortly after becoming foreign minister.

Reagan, Ronald (1911–), 40th US pres. (1981–89). Film actor turned Republican politician, he deregulated the economy, and cut federal spending and taxes ('Reaganonomics'). He increased defence spending but signed anti-nuclear treaties with Russia (1987). His last years in administration saw the Iran–Contragate scandal in which arms were allegedly exchanged for hostages in Iran and anti-Marxist guerrillas in Nicaragua illegally supplied with arms.

Reynauld, Paul (1878–1966), conservative French statesman and PM (1940). An opponent of appeasement he led France's war effort and resigned rather than surrender. Held captive by the Germans until 1945.

Rhee, Syngman (1875–1965), Korean politician and pres. (1948–60). Led opposition to Japanese rule in exile (1919–45). Led South Korea during Korean War but his patriotism was bellicose. Resigned after riots.

Rhodes, Cecil (1853–1902), British businessman and colonist in southern Africa. Founded British S. Africa Company (1889), and added Rhodesia (modern Zimbabwe) and Bechuanaland (Botswana) to British possessions. PM of Cape Colony (1890–96). Resigned after the failure of his Jamestown Raid (1895) to overthrow Boer Transvaal.

Ribbentrop, Joachim von (1893–1946), German Nazi leader; foreign minister (1938–45) under Hitler. Negotiated several pre-war treaties, inc. those with Japan and Soviet Union, which paved the way for German aggression in Europe. Tried at Nuremberg and executed.

Richard I, the Lionheart (1157–99), king of England from 1189. Involved in Third Crusade (1189–92) where he fought against Saladin. Captured by Leopold V of Austria on his return and imprisoned by Emperor Henry VI, until a ransom was paid (1194).

Richard III (1452–85), king of England from 1483. The last Yorkist king, he usurped power by imprisoning and possibly murdering the young Edward V and his brother. Quashed Buckingham's rebellion (1483). Defeated and killed by Henry (VII) Tudor at Bosworth.

Rasputin

Richelieu, Armand-Jean du Plessis, Duc de (1585–1642), French cardinal and chief minister to Louis XIII from 1624. Established absolute monarchical power through curbing power of nobles. Destroyed Huguenot power at La Rochelle (1628). He made France supreme in Europe over the Habsburgs of Spain and the Holy Roman Empire.

Rivera, Miguel Primo de (1878–1930), Spanish soldier and dictator. Established the Directory governing Spain under Alfonso XIII (1923–30).

Robert I (Robert the Bruce) (1274–1329), king of Scotland from 1306. Fought a guerrilla war against the English occupation of Scotland (1306–14) and won struggle for Scottish independence through victory at Bannockburn (1314).

Robespierre, Maximilien-François Marie Isadore de (1758–94), French revolutionary leader. Achieved great popular appeal and, at the Convention, headed the Jacobin faction. Elected to National Convention (1792), and called for the king's execution and routed out the moderate Girondins (1793). A leader of the Committee of Public Safety, he gained absolute control of France, inaugurating the Terror. After introducing the Cult of the Supreme Being he was deposed by moderates and guillotined.

Churchill, Roosevelt and Stalin

Roger II (1095–1154), Norman king of Sicily from 1130. United south Italy and Sicily in a single strong kingdom. His court, with Eastern and Western scholars, was a centre for learning.

Rommel, Erwin (1891–1944), German general who led Afrika Korps to initial success in N. Africa. Lost at El Alamein (1942). Committed suicide after involvement in failed 1944 attempt on Hitler's life.

Roosevelt, Franklin Delano (1882–1945), 32nd US pres. (1933–45). A Democrat, he introduced a series of government economic interventions (the New Deal) to counter the Great Depression. Tried to keep USA neutral, but favoured the Allies on the outbreak of war, inc. passing Lend-Lease Act with Great Britain (1941). After Japan's attack on Pearl Harbor forced USA into WWII (1941) he cooperated closely with Churchill.

Roosevelt, Theodore (1858–1919), soldier, explorer, hunter, author and Republican politician; 26th US pres. (1901–09). Gained fame as leader of 'Rough Riders' in Spanish-American War (1898) in Cuba. Intervened high-handedly in the internal affairs of several Latin American countries (e.g. Colombia).

Rudolph I (1218–91), first Habsburg Holy Roman Emperor from 1273 and founder of Habsburg dynasty. Defeated Ottokar II of Bohemia (1278) to gain Austria and Styria.

Rundstedt, Gerd von (1875–1953), German general under Hitler. Orchestrated the blitzkrieg in France and Poland, playing a key role in conquest of the former (1940). Given role of counter-opposing Allies after their 1944 offensive, culminating in Battle of the Bulge (1944). Captured in 1945, he did not face trial on grounds of ill health.

Russell, John, 1st Earl Russell (1792–1878), British Whig politician and PM (1846–52, 1865–66). Responsible for drafting parliamentary Reform Bill (1832).

Ruyter, Michiel de (1607–76), Dutch admiral, involved in campaigns against England in Second and Third Anglo-Dutch Wars (1665–67, 1672–78), securing key victories which prevented English invasion.

Sadat, Anwar (1918–81), Egyptian president from 1970. In 1978 he negotiated Israeli-Egypt peace treaty, which was unpopular in the Arab world. He was murdered by extremists.

Saladin (1137–93), Kurdish sultan of Egypt and Syria from 1174; founded Ayyubid dynasty in Egypt. Captured Jerusalem (1187), fought against Christians in Third Crusade (1189–92). Known for his generous treatment of prisoners.

Saladin

Salazar, António de (1889–1970), Portuguese dictator; PM (1932–68). He revived the economy but fought costly colonial wars in Africa.

Salisbury, Robert Cecil, 3rd Marquis of (1830–1903), British Conservative politician; foreign minister (1878, 1885–86, 1886–92, 1895–1900) and PM (1885–86, 1886–92, 1895–1902). Opposed Gladstone on issue of Irish home rule. Exercised an imperialist policy, resulting in colonial wars, inc. Boer War (1899–1902), but avoided European alliances and conflicts.

San Martín, José de (1778–1850), Argentine revolutionary soldier. Played major role in liberating S. America from Spanish rule, inc. Argentina (1814–16), Chile (1817–18) and Peru (1821). Ruler of Peru (1821–22), he went into exile after differences of Bolivar.

Santa Ana, Antonio López de (1797–1876), Mexican leader; pres. (1833–36, 1839, 1841–44. 1846, 1846–47, 1853–55). A hero of Mexico's War of independence. His reactionary policies lost Texas for Mexico (1836). Defeated in war by the USA (1846).

Savonarola, Girolamo (1452–98), Italian preacher and Dominican religious leader. Outspoken against Pope Alexander VI. He became ruler of Florence in 1494 on expulsion of the Medicis; tried to set up a Christian state purged of worldly enjoyment. Excommunicated (1497), hanged and burned for heresy.

Schmidt, Helmut (1918–), German Social Democrat politician and chancellor of W. Germany (1974–82). Instrumental in founding what is now G7.

Schuman, Robert (1886–1963), French politician and PM (1947–48, 1948). His Schuman Plan (1950), for pooling European coal and steel resources, eventually led to foundation of the EC.

Schweitzer, Albert (1875–1965), German Lutheran theologian and missionary. Dedicated to philanthropy, he became a mission doctor, setting up medical centres in Gabon.

Scipio, Publius Cornelius, Africanus Major (237–183 BC), Roman general. Defeated Hannibal at Zama (202 BC), ending Carthaginian threat to Rome.

Seleucus I Nicator (*c.* 358–281 BC), Macedonian general under Alexander the Great. When Alexander died (323), he founded an empire including Babylon, (312), Persia and Syria. The Seleucid Empire lasted 250 years.

Selim I (1470–1520), Ottoman sultan from 1512; greatly expanded Ottoman Empire, adding Kurdistan, Egypt, Syria, and the Hejaz. Became leader of the Muslim world.

Seneca, Lucius (*c.* 4 BC–AD 65), Roman philosopher, statesman and orator. A considerable influence in the politics of Rome, he rose to power in 54 on the death of Claudius. Retired from public life in 62 in face of increasing despotism from Nero. Ordered to commit suicide after being implicated in Piso conspiracy.

Sennacherib (d. 681 BC), king of Assyria from 705 BC; known for making Nineveh a splendid capital. Sacked Babylon (689 BC). His attack on Jerusalem (701 BC) made him a prominent figure in the Old Testament.

Sforza, Francesco (1401–66), Milanese mercenary and statesman; duke of Milan from 1450. The son-in-law and heir to the Visconti duke of Milan, he gained high office through military skill and founded the Sforza dynasty which ruled Milan until 1535.

Sforza, Lodovico (1452–1508), duke of Milan from 1494. A ruthless statesman; regent of Milan (1480–94) before usurping power. He frustrated France's attempts to take Naples, but was deposed by Louis XII in 1499. He was a patron of the arts, and made Milan a splendid cultural centre.

Shaftsbury, Anthony Ashley Cooper, 7th earl of (1801–85), English social and industrial reformer and evangelist. Improved working conditions in industrial Britain, inc. the factory acts (1847, 1850, 1859) and Coal Mines Act (1842).

Shah Jahan (1592–1666), Mogul emperor of India (1628–58). Lost territory to the Persians, but extended his empire in the Deccan. Deposed by his son Aurangzeb in 1658. Famed for the beautiful buildings he commissioned, inc. the Taj Mahal.

Sherman, William Tecumseh (1820–91), US general in Civil War. Led Union forces into Georgia and Carolina. After burning of Atlanta (1864), he forced Lee to surrender in 1865. He was US Army Commander-in-Chief until 1874.

Shih Huang-ti (*c.* 259–210 BC), Chinese Ch'in dynasty emperor from 246 BC. Created first unified Chinese Empire (221). Ordered burning of all historical documents (212). Started work on Great Wall of China.

Shivaji (1627–80), Indian king from 1674, founder of Maratha Empire. Made use of Mogul Empire's weakness to establish independent kingdom which would endure for nearly 150 years.

Sieyès, Emmanuel Joseph (1748–1836), French priest and revolutionary leader. Wrote a series of pamphlets (1788–89) which fomented much enthusiasm for the Revolution. Helped form National Assembly (1789), and voted for execution of the king, but withdrew support as the Terror grew. Instrumental in organizing 1799 coup that overthrew the Directory and established Napoleon Bonaparte.

Smith, Adam (1723–90), Scottish economist and philosopher. Famous for his work *Inquiry into the Nature and Causes of the Wealth of Nations* (1776), a major study of the free economy and laissez-faire policy.

Smuts, Jan Christian (1870–1950), S. African soldier and statesman; PM (1919–24, 1939–48). Served in Transvaal government before Boer War (1899–1902) when he fought the British. A key WWI military commander, he became mistrusted by Afrikaners. His influence did much to transform the British Empire into a Commonwealth of dominions.

Solomon (*c.* 1015–977 BC), Old Testament king of Israel, traditionally regarded as one of its greatest and wisest rulers. Built Temple at Jerusalem.

Solon (*c.* 640–560 BC), Athenian statesman and lawgiver. Reformed Athenian state and lawcode. Laid foundations for Athenian democracy.

Spaak, Paul Henri (1899–1972), Belgian statesman. Foreign minister (1936–38, 1939–45, 1945–47, 1954–57,1961–66), PM (1938–39, 1947–50). Helped form United Nations in 1945. Instrumental in formation of EEC, helping negotiate Treaty of Rome (1957). Sec.-general of NATO (1957–61).

Lenin and Stalin

Spartacus (d. 71 BC), Thracian leader of a slave revolt (73 BC), which overran much of southern Italy before he was defeated and killed by Marcus Licinius Crassus (71 BC).

Stalin, Joseph (1879–1953), Soviet totalitarian dictator. Sec.-general of Communist Party from 1922 and leader of Soviet Union from 1924 on death of Lenin. Completely reorganized the country with his Five Year Plans; his attempts at collectivization led to widespread famine and execution. Coordinated purges within Communist Party, expelling rivals, and conducted show trials of old Bolshevik elements in the 1930s. Signed non-aggression pact with Hitler (1939) but entered WWII on German invasion (1941). Repulsed Germans in a long, hard struggle. Russia occupied the countries of eastern Europe as WWII ended (1945), beginning the Cold War and rise of the USSR as a global power.

Stanley, Henry (1841–1904), Welsh-born US explorer of central Africa. Rescued Livingstone (1871).

Stauffenberg, Claus von (1907–44), German soldier. Conspired with other German officers in 1944 in the attempted assassination of Hitler, but the bomb he placed at Hitler's headquarters failed to kill him. Immediately executed.

Stefan Dusan (1308–55), Serbian king from 1331 and emperor from 1346. Expanded Serbian territories to include Bosnia, Albania and Macedonia. His empire proved short-lived.

Stephen Báthory (1533–86), prince of Transylvania (1571–76); king of Poland from 1575. Successfully defended eastern Poland from Ivan IV's invasion.

Stephen I (977–1038), first king of Hungary from 1000, having unified several Magyar states. Converted Hungary to Christianity.

Strafford, Thomas Wentworth, 1st earl of (1593–1641), English royalist statesman and chief adviser to Charles I from 1639. Impeached and executed by Pym's government.

Stresemann, Gustav (1878–1929), German politician; chancellor of Weimar Republic (1923) and foreign minister (1923–29). Conducted a conciliatory policy which enabled Germany to regain an international footing following WWI.

Sukarno, Achmed (1902–70), Indonesian statesman and pres. (1949–66). He led a war against Dutch rule (1945–49). Deposed in 1967, after implication in Communist takeover plot (1965).

Leon Trotsky

Süleyman I, the Magnificent (1494–1566), Turkish Ottoman sultan from 1520. Extended empire to its greatest extent taking Hungary, Georgia and Baghdad; he was unsuccessful in taking Vienna. His fleet gained control of the Mediterranean.

Sulla, Lucius Cornelius (138–78 BC), Roman general; victorious in civil war of 88–82 BC against Marius, and subsequently dictator (82–79 BC).

Sully, Maximilien de Béthume, duc de (1560–1641), French statesman and minister to Henri IV. Helped rebuild French economy after decimation of Wars of Religion (1562–98).

Sun Yat-sen (1866–1925), Chinese revolutionary leader. Successful in 1911 revolution against Manchu dynasty as leader of Kuomintang movement. Provisional Chinese pres. (1911–12) and ruler of southern China (1923–25). Regarded as father of modern China.

Taft, William (1857–1930), 27th US pres. (1909–13). A Republican, his presidency saw the split in his party over his conservative line. Chief justice of the USA (1921–30), during which he undertook many judicial reforms.

T'ai Tsung (600–49), Chinese ruler and emperor from 626. Expelled Turks to reunite China. He secured the T'ang dynasty, founded by his father.

Talleyrand-Périgord, Charles-Maurice de (1754–1838), French politician (and former bishop) who held office for successive French regimes during a period of European upheaval; involved in French Revolution. Foreign minister (1797–99); helped Napoleon overthrow Directory (1799); foreign minister (1799–1807). Organized Confederation of the Rhine (1806) with Napoleon. French delegate to Congress of Vienna (1815); helped Louis-Philippe become king in 1830.

Tamerlane (Timur) (1336–1405), Turkic conqueror. Led his army into Russia, central Asia, Persia and India, creating an empire which died with him.

Thatcher, Margaret (1925–), British Conservative politician and PM (1979–90). Successful in Falklands Conflict (1982). She moved the Conservatives to the right, privatizing state enterprises and placing emphasis on the market economy.

Themistocles (*c.* 523–*c.* 460 BC), Athenian statesman whose naval strategy was chiefly responsible for the victory over Xerxes at Salamis (480 BC).

Theodoric the Great (454–526), Ostrogoth king from 471 and king of Italy from 493 after invading and conquering most of the peninsula from Odoacer.

Thiers, Louis Adolphe (1797–1877), French statesman. French PM (1836, 1840, 1848); a founder and pres. (1871–73) of the Third Republic. As head of provisional government (1870) he negotiated peace with Bismarck and put down revolt by Paris Commune (1871).

Thutmose III (d. 1450 BC), Egyptian pharaoh from 1504 BC. Conquered Syria, Palestine and the Aegean, bringing Egypt to its greatest extent. Regarded as one of the most brilliant of pharaohs.

Tiberius (42 BC–AD 37), Roman emperor from AD 14. Adopted son of Augustus. His reign brought peace and prosperity but after his friend and adviser Sejanus attempted a coup, he retired to Capri.

Tito, Josip Broz (1892–1980), (Croat) Yugoslav Communist politician, whose partisans fought Nazi occupation during WWII; effective ruler from 1943; PM (1945–53), pres. from 1953. Broke with USSR in 1948 and refounded Yugoslavia as a decentralized non-aligned state.

Titus (AD 39–81), Roman emperor from AD 79. Seized Jerusalem in AD 70. Tolerant to opposition; generous to victims of Mt Vesuvius' eruption (AD 79) and the fire of Rome (AD 80).

Tojo, Hideki (1884–1948), Japanese soldier and statesman; PM and dictator (1941–44) when he led Japanese involvement in WWII. Tried and executed by Allies for war crimes.

Tokugawa, Ieyasu (1543–1616), Japanese shogun (1603–05) and founder of Edo shogunate which ruled Japan for over 250 years.

Torquemada, Tomás de (1420–98), Spanish monk and first grand inquisitor of the Spanish Inquisition. Responsible for expulsion of Jews from Spain (1492).

Touré, Ahmed Sékou (1922–84), Guinean politician and first pres. (1958–84). Led independence campaign; established a dictatorship when pres.

Tromp, Maarten (1597–1653), Dutch naval commander who established the Dutch Republic as a sea power. Defeated Spanish fleet (1639), eclipsing Spain as a great naval power.

Trotsky, Leon (1879–1940), Russian revolutionary leader. Played leading role in 1917 Bolshevik revolution; commissar of foreign affairs and war (1917–24). An internationalist (believing in permanent world revolution), he was exiled by Stalin (1929). He was killed with an ice-pick by a Soviet agent in Mexico.

Truman, Harry S. (1884–1972), 33rd US pres. (1945–53). Became pres. on Franklin Roosevelt's death in 1945. His eventful presidency inc. first nuclear bombs on Japan (1945), Berlin airlift (1948–49), UN war with Korea (1950–53) and dismissal of MacArthur (1951).

Tshombe, Moise (1919–69), Congolese politician. Led secession of Katanga (1960), and became its pres. until 1963. Premier of The Congo (1964–65).

Turenne, Henri de la Tour d'Auvergne, Vicomte de (1611–75), French soldier and marshal of France from 1643. A brilliant commander, he made his reputation in the Thirty Years' War; played a major role in Louis XIV's scheme to make France the leading military power in Europe, and conquered much of Spanish Netherlands.

Tz'u Hsi (1835–1908), Chinese empress dowager and regent (1861–89), who began her career as concubine to Emperor Hsien Feng. She opposed modernization, and when her nephew Kuang-hsu assumed power in 1889, she confined him to his palace after he attempted reform. Responsible for xenophobic Boxer rebellion (1900). Had Kuang-hsu killed a day before she died.

U Nu (1907–95), Burmese politician and first PM of independent Burma (1948–56, 1957–58, 1960–62). Overthrown in coup in 1962 and imprisoned until 1966.

Ulbricht, Walter (1893–1973), E. German Communist dictator; PM (1949), party leader (1950–71) and head of state from 1960; installed as leader of puppet state set up by USSR in E. Germany. Erected Berlin Wall (1961) to stop E. Germans escaping his harsh regime.

Valdemar IV (1320–75), Danish king from 1340. Took advantage of Sweden's weakness to make Denmark the leading Scandinavian power.

Valerian, Publius Licinius (*c.* 193–260), Roman emperor from 253. Persecuted Christians; died in captivity after a disastrous war against the Persians.

Vargas, Getúlio (1883–1954), Brazilian politician and pres. (1930–45, 1951–54). Seizing power in 1930, he established a corporatist dictatorship, but achieved social reforms. Deposed in 1945, he was re-elected in 1951 but killed himself in the face of mounting opposition.

Vauban, Sébastien Le Prestre de (1633–1707), French military engineer under Louis XIV who revolutionized fortifications, mines and artillery.

Venizélos, Eleuthérios (1864–1936), Greek politician and PM (1910–15, 1917, 1924, 1928–30, 1933). He led Greece into wars against Turkey (1912) and Bulgaria (1913), gaining much territory. A republican and rival of King Constantine I whom he forced to abdicate in 1917, when Venizélos took Greece into WWI against Germany. His efforts to seize power in 1935 led to civil war.

Verwoerd, Hendrik (1901–66), Dutch-born S. African politician; PM (1958–66). Implemented harsh apartheid policy despite domestic and international objections. Assassinated.

Vespasian, Titus Flavius (AD 9–79), Roman emperor from AD 69. Brought element of stability following uncertainty of Nero's rule; extended Roman rule to much of Germany and Wales.

Vespucci, Amerigo (1454–1512), Italian explorer who served Spain. In voyages to the New World (1499–1500, 1501–02) he reached Brazil. America is named after him.

Victor Emmanuel II (1820–78), king of Sardinia-Piedmont from 1849; first king of a united Italy from 1861. Unified the country with the help of Garibaldi.

Victoria (1819–1901), British queen from 1837. Married her cousin Albert in 1840, but his early death in 1861 led to a 40-year mourning period out of the public eye. Crowned empress of India in 1876 by Disraeli. She restored the image of the monarchy; later years saw her re-emerge onto public stage and as a respected matriarch.

Villa, Pancho (Francisco Villa) (1878–1923), Mexican revolutionary leader and bandit. Joined uprisings against Díaz (1909) and Huerta (1914). Seized Mexico City with Carranza (1914), but fell out with him and fled. Conducted civil war against pres. Carranza (1914–20). Assassinated.

Queen Victoria and Prince Albert

Visconti, Gian Galeazzo (1351–1402), duke of Milan from 1378. Fought and bought his way to control of much of north and central Italy.

Vladimir I (*c.* 956–1015), prince of Novogrod from 970 and of Kiev from 980 after seizing power. Converted the infant Russian state to Christianity.

Voroshilov, Kliment (1881–1969), Soviet general and pres. (1953–60). A long-time friend of Stalin, he modernized the Red Army in the 1930s.

Vorster, Balthazar Johannes (1915–83), S. African politician; premier (1966–78) and pres. (1978–79). Maintained apartheid policy. Resigned presidency following a political scandal.

Walesa, Lech (1943–), Polish politician and pres. (1990–95). As an underground trade union organizer, he helped create free trade union Solidarity. Imprisoned (1981–83) when martial law was declared; awarded Nobel Peace Prize (1983). After leading crippling strikes (1988), he negotiated the agreement that ended Communist rule in Poland (1989).

Wallace, William (*c.* 1274–1305), Scottish patriot who fought against English army of occupation. Defeated English at Stirling Bridge (1297), but lost to Edward I at Falkirk (1298). Led a guerrilla war until arrested in 1305, charged with treason and executed.

Wallenstein, Albrecht von (1583–1634), Austrian general who fought Denmark and Sweden in the Thirty Years' War (1618–48). Intrigues aimed at establishing himself as supreme ruler in Germany led to his assassination.

Walpole, Robert (1676–1745), British statesman and first PM (1721–42). Consolidated ministerial power through the inability of German-speaking George I to chair ministerial meetings. He developed Cabinet government.

Washington, George (1732–99), American general and first US pres. (1789–97). Commander of American army at Boston (1775) in War of Independence. Defeated Cornwallis at Yorktown in 1781, which brought the war to an effective end. Presided over delegates at Constitutional Convention (1787) and was unanimously elected pres. in 1789, and re-elected in 1792. Moved towards Federalist party whilst his sec. of state, Jefferson, assumed leadership of Jeffersonians (Republicans). Retired from presidency in 1797.

George Washington

Weber, Max (1864–1920), German political economist and a founder of modern sociology. Famous for the 'Protestant Ethic', relating Protestantism to capitalism.

Weizmann, Chaim (1874–1952), Jewish Zionist leader and Israel's first pres. (1949–52). Instrumental in rise of 20th-century Zionism; helped secure Balfour Declaration (1917).

Wellington, Arthur Wellesley, 1st duke of (1769–1852), British military commander and Tory politician; PM (1828–30). Defeated Napoleon's armies in Peninsular War (1809–14); shared victory with Blücher at Waterloo (1815). As PM his opposition to parliamentary reform made him unpopular.

Wesley, John (1703–91), English founder of Methodism. In half a century he travelled Britain, preaching 40,000 sermons. He always regarded himself and Methodism as part of Anglicanism.

Wilberforce, William (1759–1833), English philanthropist and anti-slavery campaigner. His Bill to ban the slave trade became law in 1807.

Wilkes, John (1727–97), English politician and champion of free speech. His attack on George III led to expulsion from parliament and brief imprisonment, but he was released on grounds of parliamentary privilege.

William I (1797–1888), king of Prussia from 1861 and first German emperor from 1871. A conservative, he appointed Bismarck as PM of Prussia (1862) and Germany (1871), and came to rely on him, refusing his resignation in 1877.

William I, the Conqueror (1027–87), duke of Normandy from 1035 and king of England from 1066, after defeating Harold at Hastings. Brought feudal system to England, whose government he centralized. Ordered Domesday Book to be compiled (1086).

William I, the Silent (Prince of Orange) (1533–84), Dutch patriot and first stadholder (chief magistrate/ruler) from 1572. Governor of three Dutch provinces for Spain, he became leader of Protestant Dutch nationalism. When Spain sent Duke of Alba to reimpose Catholicism, he led the resistance and became stadholder of northern Netherlands (1579), which became the Dutch Republic. Assassinated.

William II (1859–1941), German emperor and king of Prussia (1888–1918). Remembered as a militarist, he dismissed Bismarck (1890). Little more than a figurehead during WWI, he was forced to abdicate in 1918.

William III (William of Orange) (1650–1702), Dutch stadholder from 1672 and king of England from 1689. Took English throne in Glorious Revolution that forced James II to abdicate; co-ruled with his wife Mary II (James's daughter) until her death (1694). Defeated James II at Battle of the Boyne (1690). Spearheaded European opposition to Louis XIV; championed Protestant cause.

Wilson, Harold (1916–95), British Labour PM (1964–70, 1974–76). He faced a balance of payments crisis, the Rhodesia problem and French opposition to UK membership of EC.

Wilson, Thomas Woodrow (1856–1924), 28th US pres. (1913–21). A Democrat, he led USA into WWI and was the principal founder of the League of Nations. His health collapsed when he failed to prevent USA retreating into isolationism.

Wolsey, Thomas, Cardinal (*c.* 1475–1530), English prelate and statesman. An efficient but vain chief minister to Henry VIII (1515–29), his fall resulted from failing to gain an annulment for Henry VIII in his marriage to Catherine of Aragon.

Wycliffe, John (*c.* 1329–84), English theologian and religious reformer, a forerunner of the Protestant movement. Attacked the practices of the Church and began an English translation of the Bible. The heretical Lollards adopted his controversial views.

Xerxes I (*c.* 519–465 BC), Persian king from 486 BC. Invaded Greece (480 BC); fought at Thermopylae (480 BC) and Salamis (480 BC) before being finally beaten at Plataea (479 BC).

Yamamoto, Isoroku (1884–1943), Japanese admiral. Planned and executed attack on Pearl Harbor (1941), although personally against Japanese involvement in WWII.

Yamashita, Tomoyuki (1885–1946), Japanese general who successfully attacked Singapore (1942). Tried and hanged for war crimes.

Yoshida, Shigeru (1878–1967), Japanese politician and premier (1946–47, 1948–55). Maintained cordial relations with US occupation authorities and masterminded Japan's economic recovery and transition to a democracy.

Zhivkov, Todor (1911–), Bulgarian dictator. General sec. of Communist Party (1954–89), premier (1962–71) and pres. (1971–89). His dictatorship was characterized by loyalty to the Soviets. Ousted by Communist reformers (1989).

Zog (1895–1951), Albanian dictator, PM (1925–28) and king (1928–39). Real founder of modern Albania, he fled when Mussolini invaded the country (1939).

Zoroaster (*c.* 630–*c.* 553 BC), Median founder of Zoroastrianism (Parsiism). His system is based on the struggle between Good and Evil personified. His teachings were influential for over 1500 years, but waned in favour of Islam.

Zwingli, Huldrych (1484–1531), Swiss theologian and Protestant reformer. His teachings were based on the principle of supreme authority in Scripture.

MAJOR BATTLES

- **Although outnumbered three to one, Henry V of England defeated the French in 1415 at the Battle of Agincourt during the Hundred Years War, thereby gaining control of much of France.**
- **The greatest death toll in a battle was estimated at 1,109,000 during the Battle of Stalingrad, Russia, in 1943.**
- **The largest armed force is the People's Liberation Army in China which, in 1996, had an estimated personnel of 2,930,000 in land, sea and air forces.**
- **The Germany Army Group Centre lost 350,000 men on the Eastern Front in a period of 17 days in 1944.**

490 BC Marathon Greco-Persian Wars: under Miltiades and Callimachus, the Athenians defeated a Persian sea-borne invasion of Attica (Greece). By tradition, Pheidippides ran to bring news of the victory to Athens, giving the name 'marathon' to the long-distance race.

480 BC Thermopylae Greco-Persian Wars: the Greek advance guard – 300 Spartans under Leonidas, Helots (semi-slaves) and others – defended the pass against Xerxes' army. Even when surrounded, cut off and facing certain death, the Greeks fought on with epic heroism.

480 BC Salamis Greco-Persian Wars: following Themistocles' strategy, the Greeks were able to outmanoeuvre and defeat the Persian fleet, force the Persians out of the Peloponnese and check their conquest of Greece.

479 BC Plataea Greco-Persian Wars: victory of the Greek infantry forces led by Pausanias the Spartan over the Persian forces of Xerxes I, at Plataea. The battle forced the Persians to abort their attempt to conquer Greece and ended the Greco-Persian Wars.

405 BC Aegosopotami Peloponnesian War (Athens against Sparta): the Athenian fleet was taken by surprise and destroyed by the Spartans under Lysander. The siege and surrender of Athens followed and Sparta became dominant in Greece.

371 BC Leuctra Epaminondas led the Thebans to victory over the Spartans, making Thebes the main power in Greece.

338 BC Chaeronea Philip II of Macedon defeated the Thebans and Athenians to ensure Macedonian domination of Greece.

333 BC Issus Conquests of Alexander the Great: Alexander led the Macedonian army to victory against the Persians under King Darius which added Syria and Egypt to his sphere of domination.

331 BC Gaugamela Conquests of Alexander the Great: despite being outnumbered, Alexander led the Macedonian army to victory against the Persians under King Darius. He conquered Mesopotamia (modern Iraq) and Persia (modern Iran), ending the Persian Empire.

326 BC Hydaspes Conquests of Alexander the Great: Alexander and the Macedonian army defeated the forces of King Porus, but the troops demanded a return home.

216 BC Cannae Second Punic War (Rome against Carthage): at Cannae in southern Italy, Rome suffered its worst military defeat when Hannibal's Carthaginian army surrounded and annihilated the Roman forces, with estimates of *c.* 50,000 to 70,000 Roman losses. However, Hannibal was unable to follow up his victory.

207 BC Metaurus Second Punic War: Hasdrubal led a Carthaginian force to bring reinforcements to his brother Hannibal, but was defeated and destroyed by the Romans at Metaurus in northern Italy, forcing Hannibal to withdraw from Italy.

202 BC Zama Second Punic War: Hannibal was defeated at Zama (in modern Tunisia) by Scipio Africanus in northern Africa, forcing Carthage to surrender and ending the Second Punic War. Rome became the main power in the western Mediterranean.

168 BC Pydna Rome against Macedonia: the Romans showed the superiority of their tactics when they defeated the Macedonian phalanx led by King Perseus. The victory at Pydna (central Greece) gave Rome effective control of Greece.

53 BC Carrhae Crassus's expedition against the Parthians: Crassus's Roman army was defeated by the Parthian horse-archers and heavy cavalry when they attempted to capture Ctesiphon, the capital of the Parthian Empire. The defeat checked Roman eastward expansion.

31 BC Actium Mark Antony and Cleopatra's Egyptian fleet was defeated by Octavian, the nephew of Julius Caesar, at Actium (western Greece). It brought to an end the civil wars that had plagued the Roman world for the last 50 years.

AD 9 Teutoburger Wald In their attempt to conquer Germany, three Roman legions led by Quintilius Varus were defeated and killed by the Germans under Arminius. The defeat fixed the Roman frontier at the Rhine.

AD 312 Milvian Bridge In the power struggle to run the Roman Empire, Constantine defeated his rival Maxentius. Having had a dream in which he saw the 'Chi-rho' symbol and words *In hoc signo vinces* ('in this sign you will conquer'), Constantine became the first Christian emperor.

AD 378 Adrianople In an attempt to escape the Huns, the Goths settled in the Roman Empire. However, they were treated so badly that they rebelled, defeating the Romans and killing the Emperor Valens. They went on to sack Rome in AD 410, eventually establishing a kingdom in Spain.

AD 451 Catalaunian Fields Attila and the Huns were defeated by a combined force of Romans and Visigoths under Aetius and Theodoric. Attila retreated into central Europe.

AD 636 Yarmuk Arab conquests: at Yarmuk in Palestine the Arabs defeated the forces of the Byzantine emperor and conquered Syria and Palestine (including the Holy Places). It allowed them to go on to conquer Egypt and North Africa.

AD 636 Quadisiya Arab conquests: the Arabs defeated the Persians and conquered Iraq, enabling them to conquer Persia the following year.

AD 732 Poitiers Arab conquests: the Franks, led by Charles Martel, defeated an Arab invasion of France, limiting the Arab conquests in Europe to Spain and Portugal.

AD 878 Ethandune Viking battles: Alfred of Wessex defeated the 'Great Army' of Danish Vikings, and forced them to make peace at Wedmore. The defeat prevented the total conquest of England by Vikings, and allowed Alfred's successors to reconquer and unite the country.

AD 955 Lechfeld Magyar conquests: at Lechfeld, southern Germany, the Emperor Otto I inflicted a crushing defeat on the Hungarians, who became Christian and settled down as a bulwark against attacks on Europe from the East during the rest of the Middle Ages.

1066 Hastings Norman Conquest: an army of Norman and French soldiers led by Duke William of Normandy defeated the Saxon army of King Harold (who died in battle). William was subsequently crowned king of England.

1071 Manzikert At Manzikert (in modern Turkey), the Seljuk Turks, under their sultan Alp Arslan, defeated a large Byzantine army led by Emperor Romanus Diogenes. The Byzantine Empire was severely weakened by the permanent loss of control of the interior of Asia Minor.

1187 Hattin The Crusades: Saladin led the Arab forces in victory against the army of the Latin (Christian) kingdom of Jerusalem at Hattin, conquering almost all of Palestine.

1212 Las Navas de Tolosa La Reconquista: the Christian Spaniards defeated the Muslim Almoravids of North Africa, recovering the impetus in their reconquest of Spain from the Muslims. The success of the Reconquista was now assured.

1213 Muret Albigensian Crusade: northern French forces under Simon de Montfort defeated the forces of Count Raymond of Toulouse and King Peter of Aragon. Most of Languedoc fell under de Montfort's control, marking the beginning of the end of the Cathar heresy.

■ *The Battle of Salamis, 480 BC – 310 ships defeat 2000* ■ *The Battle of Cannae, 216 BC – Hannibal and his army march on Rome* ■ *The Battle of Actium, 31 BC – The defeat of Antony and Cleopatra*

1260 Ain Jalut Mongol conquests: at Ain Jalut in Palestine, the Egyptian Mamluks, led by Sultan Qutuz, defeated the Mongols and repelled their invasion of Syria. The Mamluks became the chief power in the eastern Mediterranean.

1302 Courtrai The communal militias of Flanders showed that infantry, if determined, could repel armoured knights. They defeated the army of the king of France when the French knights embarked on a rash charge.

1314 Bannockburn Anglo-Scottish Wars: Robert the Bruce's Scottish forces defeated the English under Edward II who had employed poor tactics. The victory helped secure Scottish independence.

1315 Morgarten Swiss Wars of Independence: the Swiss combined missile and halberd attacks with an ambush to defeat a superior Austrian army, ensuring the independence, in time, of the Swiss Confederation.

1346 Crécy Hundred Years War: a small English army, led by Edward III, used its archers to shoot up the ill-coordinated and poorly led French.

1356 Poitiers Hundred Years War: the French led by John II dismounted most of their fully armoured men to avoid a repetition of Crécy, but were outmanoeuvred and defeated by the Black Prince (son of Edward III of England). King John was captured.

1389 Kosovo Ottoman conquests: Turkish forces destroyed the Serbian army, gaining control over much of the western Balkans, as the Serbian Empire collapsed.

1396 Nicopolis Ottoman conquests: a Crusading force, intending to bring help to Byzantium, was outmanoeuvred at Nicopolis (in modern Bulgaria) and forced to surrender by the Turks under Sultan Bayezit. Subsequent Turkish conquests continued unchecked.

1415 Agincourt Hundred Years War: Henry V of England invaded France and, although outnumbered three to one, defeated the over-confident French. Much of France then fell under English control.

1429 Orléans Hundred Years War: inspired by Joan of Arc, the French defeated the English and raised the siege of Orléans.

1454 Castillon Hundred Years War: the English attempt to recover lost territory in France came to an end with their defeat at the hands of a reorganized French army. Cannon played a part in the French victory.

1477 Nancy Swiss-Burgundian War: Swiss pikemen defeated the army of Charles the Bold, Duke of Burgundy, whose dreams of creating a powerful state between France and Germany died with him on the battlefield. Swiss mercenaries became the most sought-after troops in Europe.

1485 Bosworth Wars of the Roses: Henry Tudor's Lancastrian army defeated the army of King Richard III (the Yorkist claimant). Richard was killed, and Henry became King Henry VII, founding the Tudor dynasty.

1515 Marignano Italian Wars: French and Venetian forces under King Francis I defeated forces of the Holy Roman Empire (Swiss mercenaries), shattering the myth of their invincibility.

1525 Pavia Italian Wars: Francis I of France was defeated and captured by forces of the Holy Roman Empire which recaptured control of Italy.

1526 Panipat An Indian (Hindu) army was defeated and destroyed by the Muslim forces of Zahir-ud-din (Babur) at Panipat in northern India. He went on to found the Mogul Empire, which later dominated most of India.

1526 Mohács Turkish forces led by Suleiman 'the Magnificent' defeated the Hungarians and Hungary was incorporated into the Ottoman Empire. The Turks went on to besiege Vienna (1529), but failed to take it.

1565 Malta Turkish forces led by Dragut and Piali attacked Malta, which was defended by the Knights of St John under Grand Master La Valette. The Turks' failure to capture Malta put a limit on their expansion.

1571 Lepanto In a major sea battle off the coast of central Greece, the Ottoman fleet was destroyed by the fleet of the Holy League organized by Pope Pius V and led by Don John of Austria. It was the first major Turkish defeat by the Christian powers.

1588 Gravelines The Spanish Armada fleet sent by Philip II of Spain to conquer England was attacked at anchor and defeated by the English fleet led by Lord Howard of Effingham. Invasion plans were abandoned and the fleet suffered severe losses on the way home round the north and west of the British Isles.

1590 Ivry French Wars of Religion: Huguenot (French Protestant) forces under Henry of Navarre (later Henry IV of France) defeated the forces of the Catholic League. The wars ended when Henry became a Catholic and introduced religious toleration.

1620 White Mountain Thirty Years War: the army of the Catholic League, commanded by Tilly, defeated the Bohemian rebels near Prague, and the authority of the Habsburgs was restored in Bohemia. However, the campaign against Frederick of the Palatinate, named as king by the rebels, led to the spread of war in central Europe.

1631 Breitenfeld Thirty Years War: the Swedes under King Gustavus Adolphus defeated the army of the Catholic League, commanded by Tilly, in southern Germany. This checked Habsburg attempts to increase their control over the Holy Roman Empire and strengthen Catholicism.

1632 Lützen Thirty Years War: the Swedes again defeated the Habsburg forces under Wallenstein and achieved a dominant position in Germany. However, Gustavus Adolphus was killed in this southern German battle.

1634 Nordlingen Thirty Years War: the combined forces of the Austrian and Spanish Habsburgs inflicted a severe defeat on the Swedes at Nordlingen in Bavaria. This led France (Sweden's ally) to take a direct part in the war, which prevented the Peace of Prague (1635) from taking effect.

1643 Rocroi Thirty Years War: the French, under Prince de Condé, defeated the Spanish, shattering the myth of Spanish invincibility and beginning an era of French military superiority.

1644 Marston Moor English Civil War: Parliamentary forces under the command of Sir Thomas Fairfax, David Leslie and Oliver Cromwell, defeated Royalist forces led by Prince Rupert of the Rhine, nephew of King Charles I. The king lost control of virtually all of the north of England.

1645 Naseby English Civil War: the reorganized forces of Parliament – the New Model Army under Oliver Cromwell – inflicted a crushing defeat on King Charles I's army, deciding the outcome of the war. The king surrendered to the Scots in 1646.

1690 Boyne War of the English Succession: north of Dublin, the army of William of Orange (King William III) defeated the Irish and French forces of King James II, who abandoned the struggle to regain his throne and returned to France.

1697 Zenta War of the Holy League: the Turks had been in retreat since the failure of the siege of Vienna, and this defeat by the Austrians forced them to make peace at Carlowitz, and cede the whole of Hungary to Austria.

1704 Blenheim War of the Spanish Succession: English and Dutch troops under John Churchill, later Duke of Marlborough, marched across Germany to defeat a Franco-Bavarian force at Blenheim in Bavaria and save Vienna. This prevented France from gaining an advantage in the first years of the war, and marked England's re-emergence as a military power.

1706 Ramillies War of the Spanish Succession: the Anglo-Dutch army under Marlborough defeated the French. However, they were unable to break through the French ring of fortresses that defended the north-eastern frontier.

1708 Oudenarde War of the Spanish Succession: Marlborough's army again defeated the French, but without any conclusive result.

1709 Poltava Great Northern War: Charles XII of Sweden turned his forces on his Russian enemy, Peter 'the Great'. However, his invasion failed when he was surrounded during an extremely hard winter and defeated at Poltava (in modern Ukraine). Although the war continued until 1721, Sweden never really recovered and her days of empire were over.

1716 Peterwardein Austro-Turkish War: Eugene of Savoy, the colleague of Marlborough, led the Austrian forces to its greatest victory over the Turks. By the Peace of Passarowitz the Turks handed Serbia to Austria.

1744 Dettingen War of the Austrian Succession: Allied forces – British, Dutch and German – under George II of England defeated the French. This was the last time a British sovereign commanded his troops in battle.

1746 Culloden Jacobite Rebellions: the British army under the Duke of Cumberland defeated the Scottish Highland clans – led by Prince Charles Edward (Bonnie Prince Charlie) – who were supporting the Stuart claim to the throne. It marked the end of Jacobite Rebellions.

■ *The Battle of Poitiers, 1346 – The Black Prince defeats King John II of France* ■ *The Battle of Malta, 1565 – Knights defend Malta under siege* ■ *The Battle of Blenheim, 1704 – The rescue of Vienna*

1757 Plassey Seven Years War: the forces of the British East India Company under Robert Clive defeated a larger army under the Rajah of Bengal, partly by bribing an ally of the Rajah. The victory allowed the company (and therefore Britain) to begin its control over India.

1759 Heights of Abraham Seven Years War: British forces led by General Wolfe captured Québec, defeated the French under Montcalm and put Canada under British control.

1760 Wandewash Seven Years War: British forces, led by Sir Eyre Coote, defeated the French under Lally Tollendal at Wandewash, south of Madras. This ended any interference to British dominance in India.

1775 Bunker Hill American War of Independence: the British redcoats defeated the American rebels, despite their stiff resistance, in the first major battle of the war, but at the cost of 1000 British casualties.

1777 Saratoga American War of Independence: a British attack, led by 'Gentleman Johnny' Burgoyne, on New England through the Hudson Valley failed when he was surrounded and forced to surrender at Saratoga.

1781 Yorktown American War of Independence: the British under Cornwallis were penned into a corner by the Americans, led by George Washington, and the French fleet. The British were forced to surrender and accept American independence.

1792 Valmy French Revolutionary Wars: an Austro-Prussian army under the Duke of Brunswick, which had invaded France to restore the monarchy, was defeated by the French, safeguarding the Revolution.

1805 Trafalgar Napoleonic Wars: after a failed attempt to invade England, the combined fleets of France and Spain were defeated by the British fleet under Horatio Nelson. The victory – off the southern coast of Spain – heralded the era of total British command of the sea, despite Nelson's death.

1805 Austerlitz Napoleonic Wars: abandoning his invasion of England, Napoleon turned on his continental enemies and, at Austerlitz, near Brno, defeated the Austrians and Russians, who both soon made peace.

1806 Jena Napoleonic Wars: the Prussians challenged Napoleon and were routed at Jena in five weeks. It left Napoleon supreme in Europe, and led to massive reforms in Prussia which enabled her to become dominant in Germany later.

1813 Leipzig Napoleonic Wars: following his disastrous Russian campaign, Napoleon was attacked by a large coalition of Austrian, Prussian, Russian and Swedish forces under Schwarzenberg and Blücher. Napoleon was defeated, abandoning Germany to his enemies, contributing to the collapse of the Napoleonic empire (Napoleon abdicated in 1814).

1815 Waterloo Napoleonic Wars: escaping from exile in Elba, Napoleon returned to France, only to be defeated by the army of Arthur Wellesley, Duke of Wellington. When he returned to exile in St Helena, Europe had a long period of peace.

1863 Gettysburg American Civil War: the Confederate (Southern) invasion of the North under Lee failed with heavy losses. The repeating rifles of the Union army inflicted massive casualties on the attackers.

1866 Königgratz (Sadowa) Austro-Prussian War: Moltke's Prussian forces defeated the Austro-Hungarian army under Benedek at Sadowa (in the modern Czech Republic). Austria was forced to accept Prussian dominance in Germany.

1870 Sedan Franco-Prussian War: the French forces under Marshal MacMahon and Emperor Napoleon III were defeated by the Prussians under General Helmuth von Moltke and forced to surrender. It led ultimately to the overthrow of the Second Empire and the unification of Germany.

1898 Ondurman Second Sudanese Campaign: the British and Egyptian forces under Kitchener defeated the Sudanese thanks to their repeating rifles. It was the first battle in which a fully automatic machine-gun (the Maxim gun) was used.

1905 Tsushima Russo-Japanese War: the Russian Baltic fleet was sent to Korea, but was completely defeated by the Japanese, who went on to win the war and emerge as a major power while Russia experienced an unsuccessful revolution.

1914 Marne World War I: the German invasion of France via Belgium was stopped by French counter-attacks on the line of the River Marne. The Germans fell back to the River Aisne and 'dug in', setting the pattern of trench warfare.

1914 Tannenberg World War I: two Russian armies in Königsberg (modern Kaliningrad) in Russia were respectively defeated and forced to retreat by Generals von Hindenburg and Ludendorff. Russia never again entered Germany during the war.

1916 Verdun World War I: in an attempt to inflict massive casualties on the French, German commander Falkenhayn attacked the symbolic fortress of Verdun with massive firepower. The French, commanded by Pétain, held the fort, but at a cost of 700,000 lives on each side.

1916 Somme World War I: the British Army under Haig attacked in their first major offensive of the war. Allied casualties were high (600,000 men) and the gains, a few kilometres of mud, very limited.

1916 Jutland World War I: in the war's only major sea battle, the Germans inflicted more damage to the British fleet than they suffered, but the Germans retired into harbour for the rest of the war, leaving Britain's vital control of the sea secure.

1917 Passchendaele World War I: a British offensive under Haig to relieve the pressure on the mutinous French army and capture German submarine bases on the Belgian coast failed as a result of atrocious conditions. The sea of mud made advance impossible, and 300,000 British casualties were suffered by German frontal assaults.

1917 Cambrai World War I: the first use of tanks on a large scale (381 British tanks) made a serious gap in the German defences. Unfortunately, the initial success was not exploited.

1918 Meggido World War I: in the Battle of Meggido, fought on the traditional site of Armageddon (Palestine), the British under Allenby defeated the Turks to occupy Damascus and the rest of Syria, thereby ending the Ottoman Empire.

1940 Battle of Britain World War II: in the first air battle the German Air Force (Luftwaffe) attempted to gain air control to neutralize the British Navy and allow an invasion of Britain. After early successes, the switch to attacking London gave the RAF time to recover as German losses mounted. The Germans abandoned day bombing attacks and postponed invasion plans.

1942 El Alamein World War II: the British 8th Army under Montgomery defeated the German and Italian forces under Rommel, removing the threat to Egypt and the Suez Canal and beginning a continuous advance that cleared North Africa by 1943. It is often seen as the turning point in British fortunes in the war.

1942 Stalingrad World War II: following a successful offensive in the second year of the Russian campaign, the German Sixth Army was surrounded and cut off by the Russians in Stalingrad (now Volgograd). Hitler refused to allow them to retreat, and 100,000 German troops were captured.

1942 Coral Sea World War II: Japanese and American carrier-borne aircraft clashed and, although losses were about even, Japanese plans for an attack on New Guinea were halted.

1942 Midway World War II: in a naval battle dominated by carrier-borne aircraft, the Japanese attack on the Hawaiian Islands was defeated. This marked the end of the Japanese advance in the Pacific.

1944 Philippine Sea World War II: the biggest carrier battle of all time was a crushing American victory. Japanese losses of carriers and planes were so heavy that the Japanese Navy lost its capability to launch airborne operations.

1944 Leyte Gulf World War II: in the last major naval battle of the war, the Japanese fleet lost three battleships, four carriers, ten cruisers and eleven destroyers in clashes with American forces at Leyte Gulf in the Philippines.

1944 Imphal/Kohima World War II: after the Japanese conquest of Malaya and Burma, their attempted invasion of India was checked by General Slim's 14th Army at Imphal and Kohima. Supported by the American-led Chinese in the north-east, the British and Commonwealth forces began an offensive that liberated all of Burma (Myanmar) by summer 1945.

1954 Dien Bien Phu The French attempt to keep control of their former colony Vietnam ended when their fortified base at Dien Bien Phu was overrun by the Vietminh guerrillas led by General Giap. It led to the establishment of the Communist state of North Vietnam and the non-Communist state of South Vietnam.

■ *The Battle of Waterloo, 1815 – Napoleon is defeated for the very last time* ■ *The Battle of the Somme, 1916 – A battle remembered as a bitter victory for its major loss of life and minor gain*

■ RADAR WAS USED FOR THE VERY FIRST TIME IN THE BATTLE OF BRITAIN IN 1940 ■

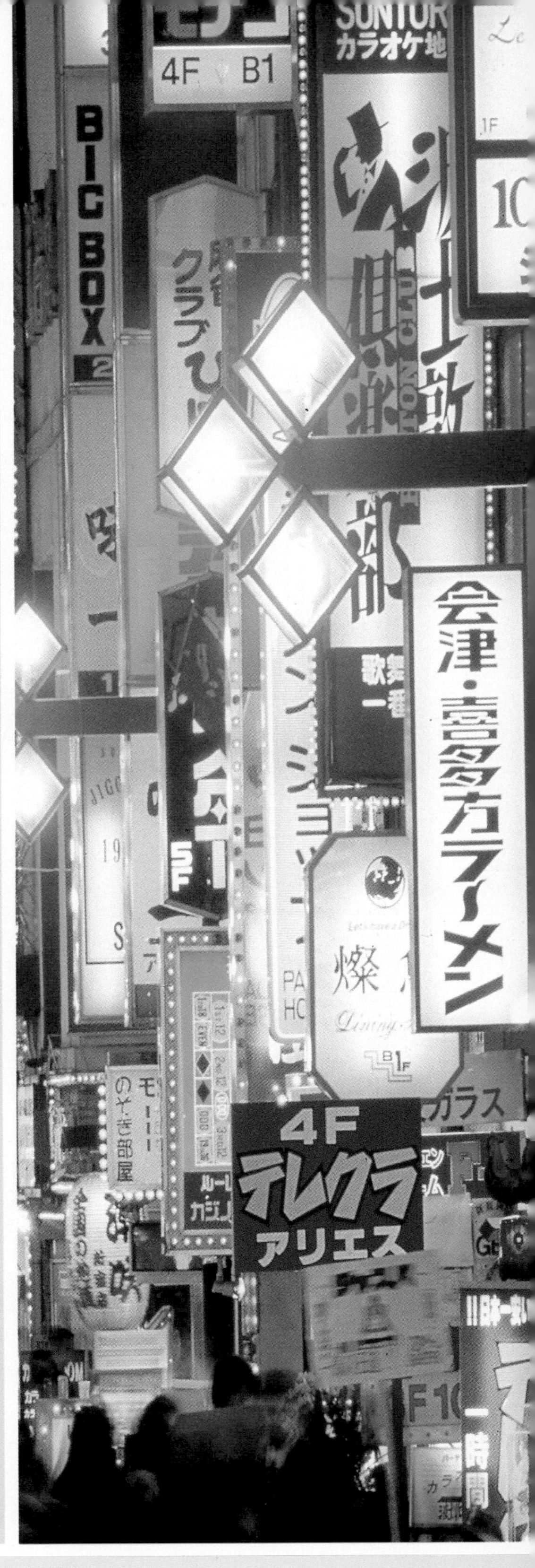

'History is
past politics,
and politics
present history'
– J.R. Seeley

THE WORLD TODAY ▷

STANDARDS OF LIVING

- You are nearly five times as likely to get assaulted in Gibraltar as in the UK.
- Taiwan's citizens spend more of their own private money on recreation than any other nation.
- Only 0.7% of an average Indian's diet is derived from meat, whilst for a US citizen it is 21 times this, at 14.7%.
- The average length of a hospital stay in Barbados is 32 days, over twice as long as the average stay in the UK.
- Nearly half of US citizens over the age of 25 have had some form of higher education.
- A car is stolen in the UK every minute, while one is stolen every 20 seconds in the USA.

Tokyo has the highest city population in the world, yet one of the smallest crime rates

HIGHEST SOCIAL SECURITY EXPENDITURE

	% OF TOTAL GOVERNMENT SPENDING
Uruguay	55.7
Switzerland	49.9
Finland	49.2
Germany	48.5
Luxembourg	46.5
Sweden	46.4
Austria	44.6
Belgium	41.3
Denmark	38.5
Norway	38.0
Spain	36.7
New Zealand	36.2
Argentina	35.3
Malta	34.7
France	34.2
Lithuania	33.6
The Netherlands	33.6
Estonia	33.5
Bulgaria	32.3
Canada	32.1

Note: The UK's social security expenditure is 29.6% of total government spending, and the USA's is 22.2%.

20 MAJOR CITY POPULATIONS

Almost one half of the world's population lives in cities. At the end of the 19th century, only one-tenth were city dwellers. By the year 2025, over three-quarters of all humans will live in cities. This change represents one of the greatest revolutions in social history. There are over 300 cities in the world with a population of over 1,000,000. Of these, nearly half are in Asia.

The population figures given below relate to the urban area of each major city: that is the city, its immediate suburbs and the surrounding built-up area, rather than to local government districts. By using this definition for the urban area of every city listed below, a more accurate comparison of size has been possible. Some very large cities, for example Tokyo and Bombay, have satellite 'millionaire' cities within their urban areas.

	CITY (000s)	URBAN AREA (000s)
1 Tokyo, Japan	11,610	25,000
2 New York, USA	7,323	19,670
3 São Paulo, Brazil	9,646	16,567
4 Mexico City, Mexico	8,276	15,048
5 Los Angeles, USA	3,486	15,048
6 Cairo, Egypt	6,955	14,525
7 Bombay, India	9,926	12,596
8 Buenos Aires, Argentina	2,961	12,582
9 Calcutta, India	4,399	11,022
10 Karachi, Pakistan	11,000	11,000
11 Seoul, South Korea	10,628	11,000
12 Rio de Janeiro, Brazil	5,481	10,390
13 Paris, France	2,152	9,319
14 Djakarta, Indonesia	9,161	9,161
15 Moscow, Russia	8,957	8,957
16 Shanghai, China	8,930	8,930
17 Osaka, Japan	2,495	8,735
18 Delhi, India	7,207	8,419
19 Chicago, USA	2,784	8,410
20 London, UK	4 (City of London)	7,651

By contrast, it is interesting to note that in 1900, only 16 cities (including suburbs) had over 1,000,000 inhabitants. In time, the term 'millionaire city' came to be used for a city with over 1,000,000 inhabitants.

London, UK	6,400,000
New York, USA	4,200,000
Paris, France	3,900,000
Berlin, Germany	2,400,000
Chicago, USA	1,700,000
Vienna, Austria	1,600,000
Tokyo, Japan	1,400,000
St Petersburg, Russia	1,400,000
Philadelphia, USA	1,400,000
Manchester, UK	1,200,000
Birmingham, UK	1,200,000
Moscow, Russia	1,200,000
Peking (now known as Beijing), China	1,100,000
Calcutta, India	1,000,000
Boston, USA	1,000,000
Glasgow, UK	1,000,000

HEALTH CARE

HOSPITAL BEDS

	MOST (per 10,000 pop.)
Monaco	168
Japan	136
North Korea	135
Kazakhstan	134
Ukraine	130

	FEWEST (per 10,000 pop.)
Afghanistan	3
Bangladesh	3
Ethiopia	3
Nepal	3
Mali	4

Note: The number of beds per 10,000 in the UK is 54, and in the USA 46.

HEALTH CARE EXPENDITURE

	Per person per year (US$)
USA	2,765
Switzerland	2,520
Sweden	2,343
Finland	2,046
Canada	1,945
Iceland	1,884
France	1,869
Norway	1,835
Austria	1,711
Luxembourg	1,662

Note: The UK spends US$1039 per person per year on health care.

PATIENTS PER DOCTOR

	HIGHEST
Niger	54,472
Eritrea	49,200
Malawi	49,118
Mozambique	36,428
Chad	27,765
Burkina Faso	27,158
Rwanda	24,697
Liberia	24,600
Ghana	22,452
Uganda	20,720

	LOWEST
Georgia	183
Italy	193
Israel	214
Cuba	231
Belarus	233
Moldova	241
Russia	241
Spain	246
Hungary	248
Lithuania	255

Note: In the UK, there are 667 patients per doctor, and in the USA 385.

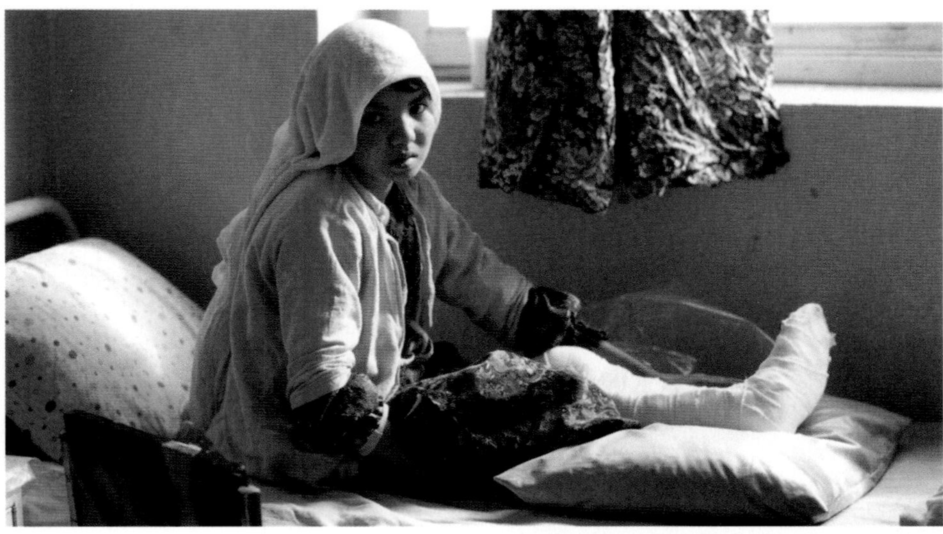

■ *A young woman, a victim of a land mine, sits in bed at a Red Cross hospital in Kabul, Afghanistan*

CRIME

LARGEST NUMBER OF REPORTED BURGLARIES

	Per 100,000 pop.
The Netherlands	3,803
New Zealand	2,942
UK	2,404
Denmark	2,381
Germany	2,039
Australia	1,963
Bermuda	1,949
Finland	1,922
Sweden	1,802
Malta	1,669

Note: The USA has 1099 reported burglaries per 100,000 population.

MOST MURDERS

	Per 100,000 pop.
Colombia	81.9
Swaziland	71.6
Aruba	38.5
Belize	34.6
Lesotho	33.9
Philippines	30.1
Botswana	29.2
French Guiana	27.2
Guatemala	27.2
Puerto Rico	26.2

Note: The murder rate in the UK is 2.5 per 100,000, and in the USA 9.5.

TOTAL REPORTED OFFENCES

	Per 100,000 people (annually)
Suriname	17,819
St Kitts and Nevis	15,468
New Zealand	14,496
Sweden	13,750
Canada	13,297

Note: The UK reported 10,403 offences per 100,000 people and the USA 5482.

EDUCATION

MOST STUDENTS

	SECONDARY SCHOOL (millions)
India	60.82
China	47.39
USA	13.17
Russia	12.42
Japan	9.54
Indonesia	9.43
Iran	5.99
France	5.74
Germany	5.53
Pakistan	5.20

Note: The UK has 3.951 million secondary school students.

	HIGHER EDUCATION Per 100,000 pop.
Canada	6,980
USA	5,611
South Korea	4,756
New Zealand	4,675
Peru	4,188
Norway	4,111
Finland	3,902
Armenia	3,711
France	3,607
Spain	3,474

Note: There are 2646 higher education students per 100,000 population in the UK.

SMALLEST PRIMARY CLASS SIZES

	PUPILS PER TEACHER
San Marino	5.2
Monaco	7.5
Georgia	9.0
Qatar	9.2
Bahamas	9.9
Sweden	9.9
Denmark	10.4
Greenland	10.4
Latvia	10.5
Armenia	11.0

Note: There are 22.2 primary school pupils per teacher in the UK and 18.7 in the USA.

National Economies

- The gross national product (GNP) is the money value of the total amount of goods and services produced by a national economy over a one-year period, plus net property income, such as profits, interest and dividends.
- GDP (gross domestic product) is GNP minus net property income.
- The poorest country in Europe is Albania, with a GNP per head of US$320, while the poorest state in the New World is Haiti with a GNP per head of only US$220.
- Azerbaijan's economy has contracted by 10% a year over the last decade.

Gross National Product

HIGHEST Country	US$ million	LOWEST Country	US$ million
USA	7,051,000	Tuvalu	9
Japan	4,638,000	São Tomé and Principe	31
Germany	2,176,000	Kiribati	56
France	1,415,000	Marshall Islands	88
Italy	1,144,000	Palau	90
UK	1,106,000	Nauru	103
China (including Hong Kong)	881,000	Tonga	160
Canada	590,000	Samoa	163
Brazil	560,000	Equatorial Guinea	172
Spain	557,000	Vanuatu	189
South Korea	434,000	Micronesia	202
Russia	393,000	St Kitts-Nevis	216
Mexico	390,000	Dominica	218
Netherlands	356,000	Comoros	249
Australia	338,000	Maldives	251
India	307,000	St Vincent	255
Argentina	294,000	Grenada	260
Taiwan	285,000	Guinea-Bissau	263
Switzerland	273,000	Bhutan	297
Belgium	243,000	Solomon Islands	302

Minerals

The economies of many countries depend upon the extraction of ores and other valuable minerals. Countries such as Canada, Russia, Australia, the USA and Brazil are major producers of a number of important minerals, which are not only used in their industries, but are also exported. Other countries, such as Guinea and Jamaica, are dependent upon the export of a single major mineral and their economies are, as a result, vulnerable to fluctuations in the world price for that product. For example, many mineral prices fell in 1995–96, giving rise to countries that depend upon exporting ores.

For fuels (coal, oil and natural gas) see p. 166.

ALUMINIUM (BAUXITE ORE)	Million tonnes (per year)
Australia	42.31
Guinea	14.40
Brazil	9.41
Russia	7.60
Jamaica	6.56

DIAMONDS	Million carats (per year)
Australia	43.59
Congo (ex-Zaïre)	17.30
Botswana	16.80
Russia	11.80
South Africa	9.80

GOLD	Tonnes (per year)
South Africa	600
USA	320
Australia	295
Canada	180
Russia	180

IRON ORE	Million tonnes (per year)
China	235
Brazil	150
Australia	135
India	60
Ukraine	50

PHOSPHATES (FOR FERTILIZER)	Million tonnes (per year)
USA	46
Russia	21
China	21
Morocco	19
Kazakhstan	6.50

URANIUM	Million tonnes (per year)
Canada	10.10
Kazakhstan	2.70
Uzbekistan	2.60
Russia	2.40
Niger	2.20

Industrial Products

The growth of industry (which both creates and consumes industrial products) has slowed considerably during the mid-1990s in western Europe, Japan and North America. The fall in production in eastern Europe and the former Soviet Union since 1992 has been reversed in Poland, Estonia, Slovenia, the Czech Republic and (almost) in Hungary, and stabilized in many other former Communist states. However, in Ukraine and, particularly, Belarus, industrial production is still in decline.

By contrast, high growth rates have been experienced in less-industrialized states in Latin America (for example Chile) and the Pacific Rim of Asia, where Thailand, Malaysia and Indonesia have all experienced considerable growth. Major industrial products include the following:

CEMENT	Millions of tonnes (per year)
China	450.00
Japan	91.60
USA	76.10
India	62.40
South Korea	52.10

FERTILIZERS	Millions of tonnes (per year)
USA	25.40
China	20.80
Canada	10.70
India	9.80
Russia	9.20

IRON (PIG IRON)	Millions of tonnes (per year)
China	102
Japan	75
USA	51
Russia	40
Germany	30

PAPER	Millions of tonnes (per year)
USA	76.70
Japan	28.30
China	24.00
Canada	22.10
Germany	12.30

CARS	Millions of units (per year)
Japan	6.70
USA	5.96
Germany	4.25
France	3.20
South Korea	1.75

SHIPPING	Millions of tonnes (per year)
Japan	7.90
South Korea	4.00
Taiwan	1.00
Germany	0.88
Denmark	0.40

STEEL	Millions of tonnes (per year)
Japan	102.70
USA	95.00
China	93.00
Russia	52.00
Germany	42.00

■ CYPRUS IS EUROPE'S FASTEST GROWING ECONOMY ■ THAILAND'S ECONOMY HAS MORE THAN

FARMING AND FISHING

Food production is rising sharply almost throughout the world, matching the demand from growing populations. As incomes rise in much of the world, especially in the rapidly expanding countries of the Pacific Rim, there is a greater demand for more food and for different varieties of food. For example, rising standards of living in China have resulted in a huge increase in the demand for meat in that country; this, in turn, has led to a worldwide rise in demand for cattle feed as other states rush to cater for the Chinese meat market. Grain production, in particular, is increasing in less-developed countries. However, there remain low-income food-deficit countries where shortages persist, often exacerbated by civil strife (for example, Rwanda and Somalia) or by natural disasters (as in Bangladesh). Major producers of agricultural and fisheries products are:

BEEF	Million tonnes (per year)	MAIZE (CORN)	Million tonnes (per year)	TEA	Million tonnes (per year)
USA	11.80	USA	161.20	India	0.74
Brazil	5.00	China	104.00	China	0.60
China	4.40	Brazil	30.00	Kenya	0.25
Argentina	2.60	Mexico	16.20	Sri Lanka	0.24
Russia	2.60	France	12.80	Indonesia	0.17
BEER	**Million hectolitres (per year)**	**POTATOES**	**Million tonnes (per year)**	**TOBACCO**	**Million tonnes (per year)**
USA	240	China	40.04	China	2.26
Germany	115	Russia	39.90	USA	0.73
China	105	Poland	36.27	India	0.58
United Kingdom	75	USA	19.24	Brazil	0.46
Japan	75	Ukraine	14.28	Turkey	0.21
COCOA BEANS	**Million tonnes (per year)**	**RICE**	**Million tonnes (per year)**	**WHEAT**	**Million tonnes (per year)**
Ivory Coast/Côte d'Ivoire	1.20	China	178.25	China	101.20
Ghana	0.42	India	81.25	India	65.25
Indonesia	0.28	Indonesia	49.90	USA	65.00
Brazil	0.23	Bangladesh	26.50	France	30.90
Nigeria	0.14	Vietnam	25.00	Russia	30.10
COFFEE	**Million tonnes (per year)**	**SHEEP MEAT**	**Million tonnes (per year)**	**WOOD, CONIFEROUS**	**Million m³ (per year)**
Brazil	1.01	China	0.70	USA	303
Colombia	0.75	Australia	0.64	Canada	188
Indonesia	0.35	New Zealand	0.50	China	145
Mexico	0.27	United Kingdom	0.33	Russia	115
Ethiopia	0.23	Turkey	0.30	Sweden	57
COTTON LINT	**Million bales (per year)**	**SUGAR BEET**	**Million tonnes (per year)**	**WOOD, DECIDUOUS**	**Millions m³ (per year)**
China	21.90	France	30.36	India	280
USA	17.90	Ukraine	29.65	Brazil	235
India	12.30	Germany	28.60	USA	190
Pakistan	8.20	USA	23.94	Indonesia	186
Uzbekistan	5.70	Russia	19.10	China	155
FISHING CATCHES	**Million tonnes (per year)**	**SUGAR CANE**	**Million tonnes (per year)**	**WOOL**	**Million tonnes (per year)**
China	20.72	Brazil	300.59	Australia	0.45
Peru	11.59	India	271.20	New Zealand	0.20
Japan	7.81	China	65.66	China	0.13
USA	7.36	Pakistan	45.66	Russia	0.11
India	5.94	Mexico	42.56	Kazakhstan	0.05

25 WEALTHIEST NATIONS

Country	GNP per head US$	Country	GNP per head US$
(1) Luxembourg	40,280	(14) Sweden	23,540
(2) Switzerland	38,520	(15) Netherlands	22,830
(3) Japan	36,920	(16) United Arab Emirates	22,710
(4) Liechtenstein	33,550	(17) Monaco	21,210
(5) Denmark	28,510	(18) Italy	19,890
(6) Norway	27,040	(19) Canada	19,790
(7) Germany	26,580	(20) Kuwait	19,040
(8) USA	26,560	(21) United Kingdom	18,750
(9) Austria	25,760	(22) Finland	18,710
(10) Singapore	25,220	(23) Australia	18,500
(11) Iceland	24,920	(24) San Marino	16,580
(12) France	24,240	(25) Israel	15,770
(13) Belgium	23,830		

Note: The people of Rwanda and Mozambique are the poorest people on Earth with a GNP per head of US$80.

NOBEL ECONOMICS PRIZE

1969 Ragnar Frisch, Norwegian, and Jan Tinbergen, Dutch: for work in econometrics.

1970 Paul A. Samuelson, US: for scientific analysis of economic theory.

1971 Simon Kuznets, Russian-born US: for research on the economic growth of nations.

1972 Sir John Hicks, English, and Kenneth J. Arrow, US: for general economic equilibrium theory.

1973 Wassily Leontief, Russian-born US: for work on input analysis.

1974 Gunnar Myrdal, Swedish, and Friedrich von Hayek, Austrian-born British: for analysis of the interdependence of economic, social and institutional phenomena.

1975 Leonid V. Kantorovich, Russian, and Tjalling C. Koopmans, Dutch-born US: for contributions to the theory of optimum allocation of resources.

1976 Milton Friedman, US: for consumption analysis, monetary theory and economic stabilization.

1977 Bertil Ohlin, Swedish, and James Meade, English: for contributions to theory of international trade.

1978 Herbert A. Simon, US: for decision-making processes in economic organization.

1979 W. Arthur Lewis, St. Lucian-born British, and Theodore W. Schultz, US: for economic processes in developing nations.

1980 Lawrence R. Klein, US: for development and analysis of empirical models of business fluctuations.

1981 James Tobin, US: for empirical macroeconomic theories.

1982 George Stigler, US: for work on the economic effects of governmental regulation.

1983 Gerard Debreu, French-born US: for mathematical proof of supply and demand theory.

1984 Sir Richard Stone, English: for the development of a national income accounting system.

1985 Franco Modigliani, Italian-born US: for analysis of household savings and financial markets.

1986 James McGill Buchanan, US: for political theories advocating limited government role in the economy.

1987 Robert M. Solow, US: for contributions to the theory of economic growth.

1988 Maurice Allais, French: for contributions to the theory of markets and efficient use of resources.

1989 Trygve Haavelmo, Norwegian: for testing fundamental econometric theories.

1990 Harry Markowitz, Merton Miller and William Sharpe, US: for pioneering theories on managing investment portfolios and corporate finances.

1991 Ronald H. Coase, British-born US: for work on the value and social problems of companies.

1992 Gary S. Becker, US: for work linking economic theory to aspects of human behaviour, drawing on other social sciences.

1993 Robert W. Fogel, and Douglas C. North, US: for economic history research.

1994 John F. Nash, US, John C. Harsanyi, Hungarian-born US, and Reinhard Selten, German: for game theory.

1995 Robert Emerson Lucas Jr, US: for development and application of the hypothesis of rational expectations.

1996 James A. Mirrlees, Scottish, and William Vickrey, Canadian: for fundamental contributions to the economic theory of incentives under asymetric information.

World Business

- The 100 largest companies account for more than one-fifth of the world's productive assets and around one-quarter of world trade.
- The top 75 companies in the world have assets of more than US$4.5 trillion, equivalent to the GNP of France, Germany and the UK combined.
- Europe's oldest business is Stora Kopparbergs Bergslags (timber and metal production), founded in *c.* 1000.

World business is reflected in the international nature of the world's largest companies. Many multinationals originated or are based in the USA, Japan or northern Europe, but increasing numbers are from east Asia, notably South Korea and Taiwan.

The giant automotive and electric companies dominate the ranks of the very largest firms by assets. The assets of a firm measure all the money, equipment, land and buildings at the company's disposal. Almost inevitably, banks and financial institutions have the greatest assets.

Giants from the Emerging Economies

COMPANY, Country	TURNOVER (US$ million)
SAMSUNG, South Korea	51,345
DAEWOO, South Korea	30,839
SAUDI ARABIAN OIL, Saudi Arabia	26,621
PEMEX, Mexico	26,572
PDVSA, Venezuela	21,275
SUNKYONG, South Korea	15,912
PETROBRAS, Brazil	15,029
SSANGYONG, South Korea	14,479
KOC HOLDINGS, Turkey	14,409
HYUNDAI, South Korea	13,738
SINOCHEM, South Korea	13,241
SONATRACH, Algeria	12,300
BARLOW RAND, South Africa	11,467

10 Top Insurance Companies

	COMPANY, Country	SPECIALIZATION	ASSETS (US$ million)
1	NIPPON LIFE INSURANCE COMPANY, Japan	Life & health (mutual)	364,763
2	FEDERAL NATIONAL MORTGAGE ASSOCIATION, USA	Diversified financials	316,550
3	THE DAI-ICHI MUTUAL LIFE INSURANCE, Japan	Life & health (mutual)	256,010
4	COINTERNATIONALE NEDERLANDEN GROUP, The Netherlands	Life & health (stock)	247,124
5	PRUDENTIAL INSURANCE COMPANY OF AMERICA, USA	Life & health (mutual)	219,380
6	SUMITOMO LIFE INSURANCE COMPANY, Japan	Life & health (mutual)	218,593
7	AXA S.A., France	Prop. & casualty (stock)	192,656
8	UNION DES ASSURANCES DE PARIS, France	Prop. & casualty (stock)	183,862
9	GAN, France	Prop. & casualty (stock)	169,402
10	ALLIANZ HOLDING, Germany	Prop. & casualty (stock)	164,655

Note: American International Group Inc., USA, is the world's leading insurance company by profits (US$2510 million); Nippon Life Insurance Company, Japan, is the top insurance company by revenues (US$83,207).

50 Top Companies

	COMPANY, Country	INDUSTRY	ASSETS (US$ million)
1	FORD MOTOR COMPANY, USA	Motor vehicles and parts	243,283
2	GENERAL ELECTRIC COMPANY, USA	Electronics, electrical equipment	228,035
3	GENERAL MOTORS CORPORATION, USA	Motor vehicles and parts	217,123
4	THE TOKYO ELECTRIC POWER CO., INC., Japan	Electric and gas utilities	131,485
5	NIPPON TELEGRAPH & TELEPHONE CORPORATION, Japan	Telecommunications	127,077
6	ROYAL DUTCH/SHELL GROUP, UK/Netherlands	Petroleum refining	118,012
7	TOYOTA MOTOR CORPORATION, Japan	Motor vehicles and parts	106,004
8	MITSUBISHI CORPORATION, Japan	Trading	91,921
9	HITACHI, LTD., Japan	Electronics, electrical equipment	91,621
10	EXXON CORPORATION, USA	Petroleum refining	91,296
11	AT&T CORP., USA	Telecommunications	88,884
12	INTERNATIONAL BUSINESS MACHINES CORPORATION, USA	Computers, office equipment	80,292
13	MATSUSHITA ELECTRIC INDUSTRIAL CO., LTD., Japan	Electronics, electrical equipment	74,877
14	MARUBENI CORPORATION, Japan	Trading	71,439
15	B.A.T. INDUSTRIES PLC, UK	Tobacco	70,254
16	MITSUI & CO., LTD., Japan	Trading	68,771
17	EAST JAPAN RAILWAY COMPANY, Japan	Railroads	68,652
18	NISSAN MOTOR CO., LTD., Japan	Motor vehicles and parts	66,277
19	ITOCHU CORPORATION, Japan	Trading	65,709
20	FIAT, Italy	Motor vehicles and parts	64,300
21	DAIMLER-BENZ AG, Germany	Motor vehicles and parts	63,813
22	THE KANSAI ELECTRIC POWER CO., INC., Japan	Electric and gas utilities	63,748
23	DAEWOO GROUP, South Korea	Electronics, electrical equipment	63,598
24	ENEL S.P.A., Italy	Electric and gas utilities	59,493
25	VOLKSWAGEN, Germany	Motor vehicles and parts	58,611

20 TOP COMMERCIAL BANKS

	BANK, Country	ASSETS (US$ million)
1	THE SUMITOMO BANK LTD., Japan	524,668
2	THE SANWA BANK LTD., Japan	520,118
3	THE DAI-ICHI KANGYO BANK LTD., Japan	515,705
4	THE FUJI BANK LTD., Japan	508,424
5	DEUTSCHE BANK*, Germany	503,078
6	THE MITSUBISHI BANK LTD., Japan	497,395
7	THE SAKURA BANK LTD., Japan	494,687
8	THE NORINCHUKIN BANK, Japan	431,641
9	CREDIT AGRICOLE GROUP, France	386,585
10	THE INDUSTRIAL BANK OF JAPANESE LTD., Japan	380,727
11	CS HOLDING, Switzerland	357,646
12	HSBC HOLDINGS, UK	352,362
13	ABN-AMRO HOLDING N.V., The Netherlands	340,833
14	CREDIT LYONNAIS, France	339,567
15	DRESDNER BANK AG, Germany	337,736
16	UNION BANK OF SWISS, Switzerland	335,168
17	BANQUE NATIONALE DE PARIS, France	325,416
18	FEDERAL NATIONAL MORTGAGE ASSOCIATION**, USA	316,550
19	THE TOKAI BANK LTD., Japan	309,672
20	THE LONG-TERM CREDIT BANK OF JAPANESE LTD., Japan	304,128

* The world's top bank for profit is HSBC Holdings, UK (US$3885.5 million); Germany's Deutsche Bank is the top bank for revenues (US$38,420 million).

** The Federation National Mortgage Association is not a commercial bank, but deals in diversified financials.

15 WEALTHIEST PEOPLE

		US$ billion (est.)	SOURCE OF WEALTH
1	HASSANAL BOLKIAH, Sultan of Brunei	38,000	Oil, gas
2	WILLIAM H. GATES III, USA	36,400	Microsoft Corporation
3	WALTON FAMILY, USA	27,600	Inheritance, Wal-Mart Stores
4	WARREN E. BUFFET, USA	23,200	Stock market
5	King FAUD BIN ABDUL AZIZ ALSUD, Saudi Arabia	20,000	Oil, investments, real estate
6	President T. SUHARTO, Indonesia	16,000	Investments
7	PAUL GARDNER ALLEN, USA	15,314	Microsoft Corporation
8	Sheikh JABER AL-AHMED AL-JABER AL-SABAH, Emir of Kuwait	15,000	Oil, investments, real estate
9	SHAU KEE LEE, China/Hong Kong	14,700	Real estate
10	OERI, HOFFMAN AND SACHER FAMILIES, Switzerland	14,300	Pharmaceuticals: Roche
11	WALTER AND THOMAS KWOK, China/Hong Kong	12,300	Real estate
12	HAAS FAMILY, USA	12,300	Inheritance (Levi Strauss)
13	FOREST EDWARD MARS SR. AND FAMILY, USA	12,000	Inheritance (Confectionary)
14	ALBRECHT, THEO AND KARL QUANDT AND FAMILY, Germany	11,700	BMW
15	WAN-LIN TSAI AND FAMILY, Taiwan	11,300	Insurance, financial services

Source: *Forbes Magazine*

	COMPANY, Country	INDUSTRY	ASSETS (US$ million)
26	FRANCE TÉLÉCOM SA, France	Telecommunications	57,921
27	SIEMENS AG, Germany	Electronics, electrical equipment	57,347
28	CHUBU ELECTRIC POWER CO., INC., Japan	Electric and gas utilities	56,990
29	PHILIP MORRIS COMPANIES, USA	Tobacco	53,811
30	CHRYSLER CORPORATION, USA	Motor vehicles and parts	53,756
31	RWE GROUP, Germany	Electric and gas utilities	52,948
32	ALCATEL ALSTHOM, France	Electronics, electrical equipment	52,205
33	TOSHIBA CORPORATION, Japan	Electronics, electrical equipment	51,967
34	SUMITOMO CORPORATION, Japan	Trading	50,269
35	THE BRITISH PETROLEUM PLC, UK	Petroleum refining	50,259
36	ELF AQUITAINE, France	Petroleum refining	49,454
37	COMPAGNIE GÉNÉRALE DES EAUX, France	Engineering, construction	47,333
38	VEBA AG, Germany	Trading	47,230
39	SONY CORPORATION, Japan	Electronics, electrical equipment	47,156
40	NISSHO IWAI CORPORATION, Japan	Trading	46,754
41	BRITISH GAS PLC, UK	Electric and gas utilities	44,840
42	NEC CORPORATION, Japan	Electronics, electrical equipment	43,768
43	NIPPON STEEL CORPORATION, Japan	Metals	42,311
44	MOBIL CORPORATION, USA	Petroleum refining	42,138
45	FUJITSU LIMITED, Japan	Computers, office equipment	40,416
46	TELEFÓNICA DE ESPAÑA, S.A., Spain	Telecommunications	39,689
47	MITSUBISHI HEAVY INDUSTRIES, LTD., Japan	Industrial and farm equipment	38,999
48	KYUSHU ELECTRIC POWER CO., INC., Japan	Electric and gas utilities	38,594
49	NESTLÉ S.A., Switzerland	Food	38,354
50	WAL-MART STORES, INC., USA	General merchandisers	37,871

World Political Leaders

- Since becoming a republic in 1946, Italy has had a total of 35 different prime ministers.
- Cuba's Fidel Castro does not have an official residence; it is thought that he moves from house to house to foil any assassination attempt.
- Tony Blair's Labour Party swept into power in the UK in 1997 with the largest ever Labour majority
- In 1952, Albert Einstein was offered the presidency of Israel, but politely declined the position.

Abacha, Sani (1943–), Nigerian soldier and pres. 1993–. A general, Abacha took power in 1993 after ousting an interim civilian government. His regime has attracted international criticism for a perceived lack of human rights: the execution of nine members of the Ogoni minority gained widespread adverse publicity, leading to a suspension of Nigeria from full Commonwealth membership. Abacha has pledged an eventual return to democracy and allowed the registration of five political parties in 1996.

Ahern, Bertie (1951–), Irish Fianna Fail politician and PM (Taoiseach) 1997–. A former accountant, Ahern entered national politics in 1977. He held ministerial office (1987–94) and became leader of the opposition in 1994 when Fianna Fail was defeated at the polls.

Albright, Madeline (1936–), US Democrat politician and Secretary of State 1997–. The highest ranking woman ever in the US government, her advocacy of US military participation in foreign interventions has sometimes been controversial. Albright was US ambassador at the UN (1993–97).

Annan, Kofi (1938–), Ghanaian UN administrator and UN Secretary General 1996–. Except for two years working for Ghana's tourist development, Annan has worked with the UN since 1959 (mainly for WHO). Known as an eloquent speaker.

Arafat, Yasser (1937–), Palestinian politician and pres. of the Palestinian Authority 1996–. A former engineer, Arafat was leader of the Palestinian Students Union at Cairo University (1952–56), where he founded the terrorist movement El Fatah. When the Palestine Liberation Organization (PLO) was founded (1964) from disparate factions, El Fatah soon gained control and Arafat became Chairman (1969). Arafat gained UN recognition of the PLO as the Palestinians' official representative (1974), but he was forced out of Lebanon (1983), taking the PLO to Tunisia. He modified his outright opposition to the State of Israel and signed the Oslo Peace Agreement with Israel (1993), reaching an agreement for limited Palestinian self-rule in Gaza and Jericho and Israeli military withdrawal from these territories. Further territorial gains in the West Bank were agreed in 1996–97, but the peace process has been stalled on the issue of the continuing development of Israeli settlements on the West Bank and in east Jerusalem. Under Arafat's presidency of the Palestinian Authority, anti-Israeli terrorism by Hamas has continued.

Tony Blair

Assad, Hafez al- (1930–), Syrian Ba'ath Party politician and pres. 1971–. Assad rose through the Syrian air force to become commander-in-chief in 1965. He led the 1970 coup which ended a long period of extreme political instability. Curbing opposition, he allied himself closely with the USSR, but the Soviet collapse forced a rethink and participation in the US-led coalition against Saddam Hussein's Iraq (1991). Assad intervened in Lebanon (1976–), ending that country's civil war (1990) and securing for Syria a leading role in Lebanon's affairs. He has consistently opposed Israel, while seeking the return of the occupied Golan Heights to Syria.

Aznar, José Maria (1953–), Spanish Popular Party politician and PM 1996–. A former tax inspector, Aznar entered politics in 1984, becoming pres. of Castile-León region in 1987 and, in 1989, leader of the (conservative) Popular Party, which he has modernized. Perceived as unassuming, Aznar's calmness in the face of an assassination attempt by the Basque terrorists ETA increased his popularity (1995).

Blair, Tony (1953–), British Labour politician and PM 1997–. A former lawyer, Blair entered parliament in 1983 and served in the Shadow Cabinet from 1988. Elected leader of the Labour Party (1994), he reformed the party, rejecting nationalization and advocating low taxes and limited social spending. Blair led 'New Labour' to a crushing electoral victory in 1997 after the party had been in opposition for 18 years.

Fidel Castro

Caldera, Rafael (1916–), Venezuelan politician and pres. 1969–74 and 1994–. Caldera's long political career includes two presidential terms: in 1969 he came to office at the head of a Christian Social (COPEI) government, the first occasion on which an incumbent Venezuelan government peacefully handed over power to the opposition. He returned to power in 1994 as an independent.

Cardoso, Fernando Enrique (1931–), Brazilian politician and pres. 1994–. A professor of sociology and one of the leaders of the leftist opposition to the Brazilian generals' regime (1964–85), Cardoso was elected to parliament in 1986 and co-founded the Social Democratic Party (1988). He served as a minister (1992–94) and the success of his anti-inflation programme secured his election to the presidency in 1994.

Castro, Fidel (1927–), Cuban Communist politician and pres. 1976–. A former student political activist, Castro led a revolt against Cuban dictator Batista (1953), but was captured and jailed. Released, he went into exile to return with a small force (1956) and eventually forced Batista to flee (1959). Taking control, he became PM (1959–76) and merged his revolutionary movement with the Communist Party to remodel Cuba on Soviet lines. He faced an unsuccessful US-backed invasion of Cuban exiles (1961) and the installation of Soviet missiles in Cuba (1962) almost led to world war. Castro backed revolutionary movements throughout Latin America and sent troops to bolster Marxist regimes in Africa. The fall of the USSR (1991) left him increasingly isolated and facing severe economic problems. The aging revolutionary, famous for his beard and army fatigues, has since been forced into more pragmatic policies.

Chernomyrdin, Viktor (1938–), Russian politician and PM 1992–. A former engineer in the oil and gas industry, he became Soviet deputy gas minister (1982), then minister (1985), before presiding over the conversion of the gas ministry into a state corporation. He joined the Russian government in 1992, becoming PM the same year. He was regarded as an able bureaucrat without political ambition, but has since founded his own moderate reformist political party, Our Home is Russia. He gained respect for his handling of the Chechnya crisis.

Chirac, Jacques (1932–), French Gaullist politician and pres. 1995–. He held ministerial offices (1972–74), and was PM from 1974–76, after which he reformed the Gaullist Party, and 1986–88, when his right-wing majority formed a government under the Socialist President Mitterrand. Chirac, who had been Mayor of Paris, won the presidency at the third attempt, but the return of a left-wing majority in 1997 meant that for the remainder of his term of office he would have to share power with a Socialist government.

Chrétien, Jean (1934–), Canadian Liberal Party politician and PM 1993–. Chrétien, a French Canadian lawyer, entered parliament in 1963, served as a minister (1968–79 and 1980–84), but left parliament after failing to win the party leadership (1986). Returning to parliament as party leader (1990), Chrétien became PM (1993) on a platform of Canadian unity, although seeking to delegate more powers to provinces.

Chubais, Anatoly (1955–), Russian politician. A former lecturer, Chubais came to prominence as advisor to the governor of St Petersburg (1990–91) and was appointed to the Russian government and placed in charge of privatization of state industry (1991–94). He became deeply unpopular with ordinary Russians, who blamed him for their country's economic ills. He lost his post in 1994, but in 1997 was reappointed to the government as 1st deputy PM and minister of the economy, effectively in charge of Russia's reforms.

Clinton, Bill (1946–), US Democrat politician and pres. 1993–. Born William Jefferson Blythe, Clinton took his stepfather's name. A lawyer, Clinton served as Governor of Arkansas (1979–81 and 1983–93) before winning the US presidential election in 1992. Elected on a policy of reform, Clinton has faced a Republican majority in the House of Representatives since 1994. The presidency has been clouded by allegations of wrongdoing: the Whitewater financial scandal and allegations of sexual impropriety.

BILL CLINTON IS THE FIRST POST-WAR DEMOCRAT PRESIDENT TO BE ELECTED FOR TWO TERMS

D'Alema, Massimo (1949–), Italian former Communist politician. A former journalist, D'Alema became leader of the (ex-Communist) Democratic Party of the Left (PDS) in 1994. As leader of the largest party in Italy, and leader of the biggest party in the Olive Tree coalition government, D'Alema is a very influential figure, although he holds no ministerial office.

Fahd (1923–), King of Saudi Arabia 1982. Fahd served as a minister under his father, King ibn-Saud, and his half-brothers, kings Saud, Faisal and Khalid. He was a leading member of the US-led coalition against Saddam Hussein's Iraq in the Gulf War (1991). An absolute monarch, he has taken a less visible role in the late 1990s owing to ill health.

Gadaffi, Moamar al- (1942–), Libyan military leader and head of state 1969–. Gadaffi led the junior officers' coup that overthrew the monarchy (1969). He expelled foreigners, closed foreign bases, nationalized the oil industry and replaced the government with a new system based on local committees. As autocratic head of state (without the formal title of president), he has sponsored Islamic fundamentalism at home and radical Arab nationalism abroad. His regime has been accused of supporting terrorism and has faced UN sanctions.

Gore, Al (1948–), US Democrat politician and vice pres. 1993–. Born into a political family, Gore entered state politics in Tennessee (1976) and was elected to the US Senate (1984), where he concentrated on health and environmental issues. After an unsuccessful attempt to secure the Democratic presidential nomination in 1988, he was picked to run as vice-pres. with Bill Clinton (1992).

Gujral, Inder Kumar (1919–), Indian politician and PM 1997–. He was arrested at the age of 11 for organizing children to protest about British rule in India and jailed in 1942 for Quit India Activities. He became a member of the national parliament in 1964 and has held various ministerial posts since 1967, and from 1976–80 was India's ambassador in Moscow. After serving as foreign minister (1996–97), Gujral successfully formed a coalition government in 1997 when the previous administration collapsed.

Hashimoto, Ryutaro (1937–), Japanese Liberal Democrat Party politician and PM 1996–. Hashimoto entered politics winning his late father's parliamentary seat in 1963. He held various ministerial posts (1978–91), but resigned when his private secretary was involved in a financial scandal. Perceived as a 'loner' and a skilful negotiator, Hashimoto became Liberal Democrat leader and PM in 1996.

Havel, Vaclav (1936–), Czech playwright, politician and pres. of the Czech Republic 1993–. Havel began work as a stagehand and became resident writer at a Prague theatre. He was arrested as a subversive and jailed (1979–84 and 1989). He founded the pro-democracy Civic Forum movement (1989), leading anti-Communist demonstrations in the 'Velvet Revolution' and was elected pres. of Czechoslovakia after the fall of Communism (1989). When Czechoslovakia split (1993), he was confirmed in office as pres. of the Czech Republic.

Helmut Kohl

Howard, John (1939–), Australian Liberal politician and PM (1996–). A solicitor, he entered national politics in 1974, holding several ministerial posts after 1975. In 1985–89 and 1995–96 he led the Liberal-National opposition, which was returned to power in 1996, in part owing to Howard's personal popularity.

Jiang Zemin (1926–), Chinese Communist Party politician; pres. 1993– and general sec. of the Chinese Communist Party 1989–. In the 1950s Jiang held various administrative posts in government ministries, served in China's embassy in Moscow and spent a year at a Moscow car factory. After holding junior ministerial posts he became a minister in 1983. As mayor of Shanghai (1985–89) he came to prominence supporting Deng Xiaoping's economic reforms and was rewarded by promotion to the national leadership of the party (Deng, who held no official post, was still effective leader until his death in 1997). His elevation to the presidency strengthened his hand and Jiang emerged as undisputed leader when Deng died. Jiang is committed to Deng's reforms but remains opposed to ideological changes.

Jospin, Lionel (1937–), French Socialist politician and PM 1997–. A former civil servant and university lecturer, Jospin entered national politics in 1977, became 1st secretary of the Socialist Party (1981–88) and served as a minister (1988–92). Perceived as cerebral, he was defeated in presidential elections (1995), but led the Socialists to victory in parliamentary elections in 1997.

Khamenei, Ayatollah Mohammed Ali Hoseni (1940–), Iranian politician and Muslim cleric; pres. 1981–89 and Religious Leader 1989–. A Muslim cleric, Khamenei was imprisoned six times for opposition to the Shah before being exiled (1978). He returned to play a role in Ayatollah Khomeini's Islamic revolution, becoming leader of the hardline Revolutionary Guards (1980). Perceived as an Islamic militant, he succeeded Khomeini as Religious Leader, exercising supreme authority over the government, judiciary and military.

Nelson Mandela

Khatemi, Mohammed (1943–), Iranian Islamic cleric and pres. 1997–. Active in opposition to the Shah in the 1970s and 1980s, Khatemi served as minister of culture and Islamic guidance in the Islamic regime (1982–92), but was dismissed when hardliners accused him of being too liberal. His campaign for a more tolerant society won him election to the presidency in 1997.

Kim Jong Il (1942–), North Korean Communist Party leader 1994–. Son of dictator Kim Il Sung, Kim became a member of the party Politburo in 1976. Kim, known in North Korea as 'Dear Leader', took over the day-to-day running of the country upon his father's death, although he has not formally adopted either the presidency or party leadership. Although reclusive, he is the object of a personality cult almost as lavish as that of his father.

Kim Young Sam (1927–), South Korean Democratic Liberal Party politician and pres. 1993–. Kim entered national politics aged 25 (1954), but was briefly imprisoned in 1961 when he opposed the military coup. He became a focus of opposition when he was expelled from parliament after the assassination of President Park (1979), and was placed under house arrest and banned from politics until 1985. Unsuccessful in the 1987 presidential election, he merged his Reunification Democratic Party with President Roh's ruling Democratic Justice Party to found the Democratic Liberal Party. As pres. he has brought former presidents Roh and Chun to justice for their part in the 1979 coup.

Kohl, Helmut (1930–), German Christian Democrat politician and chancellor (PM) 1982–. Kohl entered state politics direct from university (1959), and served as state PM of Rhineland-Palatinate (1969–76) before entering the national arena as leader of the opposition (1976–82). Since becoming chancellor (1982), Kohl has presided over German reunification (1990) and been an enthusiast for European unity and the single European currency. He has, however, faced growing economic problems, including record unemployment and an increasing opposition to monetary union from the German public and within his own coalition.

Kuchma, Leonid (1938–), Ukrainian politician and pres. 1994-. A native Russian speaker, Kuchma was an engineer, industrial manager and Communist Party official during the Soviet era. In independent Ukraine he was non-party PM (1992–93) before being elected pres. on a platform of economic reform, personal management skills and reassurance to Ukraine's large ethnic Russian population.

Li Peng (1928–), Chinese Communist Party politician; acting PM 1987–88 and PM 1988–. A long-serving Communist Party official, Li first held ministerial office in 1979 and became a vice-PM in 1983 and a member of the Politburo in 1989. Li was appointed at a time of economic difficulty to counter inflation, corruption and inefficiency. His measured approach gained acceptance over the radical proposals of Zhao Ziyang, who lost leadership of the party to Jiang Zemin.

Mahathir bin Mohammad (1925–), Malaysian United Malays National Organization (UMNO) politician and PM 1981. Mahathir held various ministerial offices (1974–81) before becoming PM. An outspoken leader, he has been a critic of the West. Mahathir has modernized the country (with the aim of making Malaysia an industrial state) and has fostered the interests of ethnic Malays.

Mandela, Nelson (1918–), South African ANC politician and pres. (1994–). A member of the Tembu royal family, he became a lawyer, co-founding South Africa's first black legal firm. Arrested in 1956 for nationalist activities, he was acquitted of treason (1960), went underground, was arrested again (1962) and sentenced to life (1964) on charges of sabotage and treason. After 18 years jailed on Robben Island, he was transferred to less harsh conditions. During his captivity Mandela gained almost legendary status among the black community. He was released in 1990 after secret negotiations with the white apartheid government. Elected pres. in 1994, he has overseen South Africa's transformation to a multi-racial democracy and won international admiration for his perseverance and spirit of reconciliation.

Menem, Carlos (1930–), Argentinian Peronist politician and pres. 1989–. A former trade union lawyer from a Syrian immigrant family, Menem became involved in Peronist politics in the mid-1950s and was briefly imprisoned for his part in a Peronist revolt (1956). He was a provincial governor (1973–76) during Peron's second presidency, but was imprisoned by the military regime that deposed Peron's widow. Menem returned to provincial politics in 1981 and was elected pres. in 1988. A populist, his government has been careful in economic matters.

Milosevic, Slobodan (1941–), Yugoslav (Serbian) former Communist politician and pres. 1997–. A former banker, Milosevic was active in the Serbian Communist Party, becoming its leader in 1987. As pres. of Serbia, within federal Yugoslavia (1989–97), he fostered the idea of Greater Serbia, uniting all ethnic Serbs in one state. This led to war between Serbia and Croatia (1992) as the old Yugoslavia collapsed and to encouragement of the Bosnian Serbs in their resistance to the independence of Bosnia-Herzegovina. Milosevic's Serbia was widely blamed for the continuing Bosnian conflict and was subjected to UN sanctions. As Serbian pres., Milosevic often seemed to act as head of state of a sovereign country rather than of a state within a state. The limitations to his powers became apparent as he was unable to get Bosnian Serbs to accept various international peace plans (1992–96), until the Dayton Agreement was reached (1996). Opposition to his rule in Serbia has been curbed, though demonstrators (1996–97) forced him to accept opposition gains in municipal elections. In 1997 he became Yugoslav pres. and sought to increase the powers of a hitherto low-profile post.

Mubarak, Mohammad Hosni (1928–), Egyptian politician and pres. 1981–. A former pilot, Mubarak rose to become commander of the Egyptian air force. Appointed vice-pres. (1975), he succeeded to the presidency after the assassination of President Sadat (1981). He has continued the peace process with Israel and re-established Egypt as leader of the Arab world.

Mugabe, Robert (1924–), Zimbabwean ZANU politician and PM 1980–87 and pres. 1987–. A self-educated former teacher, Mugabe became involved in nationalist politics in what was then Southern Rhodesia and co-founded the Zimbabwe African National Union (ZANU). After detention (1964–74), he was exiled in Mozambique where he continued his fight against the white government of Rhodesia. After independence (as Zimbabwe), Mugabe fell out with Joshua Nkomo, leader of the rival nationalist movement ZAPU, but the two parties merged in 1988 to create a virtual one-party state.

Netanyahu, Benjamin (1949–), Israeli Likud Party politician and PM 1996–. Having spent much of his youth in the USA, Netanyahu was elected to the Knesset in 1988, having gained international media publicity as an Israeli spokesman during the Gulf War. He became leader of the opposition in 1993. Elected PM on a hard-line security platform, the peace process with the Palestinians has virtually collapsed under his government.

Moamar al-Gadaffi

Prodi, Romano (1939–), Italian independent politician and PM 1996–. After a period as economics professor at Bologna University, Prodi was appointed to head the large state holding company IRI (1982–89). He returned to Bologna (1990–93), but was reappointed to head IRI again (1993–94). Prodi's original ideas concerning Italy's economic problems and his independent approach attracted a wide public hearing and he was chosen to head the centre-left Olive Tree coalition government which came to power in 1996.

Rawlings, Jerry (1947–), Ghanaian air force officer and politician; head of state, then pres. 1981–. The son of a Scottish father and a Ghanaian mother, Rawlings was one of the leaders of the peaceful coup in 1979, when he and his fellow officers handed power back to a civilian government within months. After he was forcibly retired from the air force, Rawlings retained his public popularity and led another successful coup (1981). Having restored a multi-party system (1992), he led his National Democratic Convention to victory in elections.

Saddam Hussein (1937–), Iraqi politician and pres. 1979– and PM 1994–. Active in Ba'ath Party politics since 1957, Saddam went into exile after involvement in a failed coup (1959). One of the leaders of the 1968 coup, Saddam became pres. in 1979 and immediately had 500 possible Ba'ath opponents executed. He embroiled Iraq in two disastrous and very costly wars: the Iran-Iraq war (1980–88) and the Gulf War (1991), when he was defeated by a US-led international coalition following his invasion and attempted annexation of Kuwait. After the Gulf War, Saddam suppressed revolts by Shiites in the south and Kurds in the north. He has defied international efforts to create 'safe zones' for these oppressed minorities but was forced to accept international inspection of Iraq's biological and chemical weapons and nuclear capacity. Surrounding himself with his family and members of his Takriti clan, Saddam has created a one-man dictatorship which has withstood many assassination plots. He has built many palaces despite Iraq's dire economic plight. Opposition has been ruthlessly exterminated (two of his sons-in-law have been executed).

Jacques Chirac and Boris Yeltsin

Santer, Jacques (1937–), Luxembourgeois Christian Social People's Party politician and pres. of the European Commission 1995–. A lawyer, he served as a minister (1972–84) and then PM of Luxembourg (1984–95) before being chosen as compromise candidate for the EU Commission presidency.

Sharif, Nawaz (1949–), Pakistani politician and PM 1990–93, 1993, and 1997–. Sharif entered local politics in the Punjab (Pakistan's largest province) in 1977, rising to become chief minister in 1988. In 1990 he led the Islamic Democratic Alliance to power nationally, but was dismissed by the pres. and lost the subsequent election to Benazir Bhutto. After she, in turn, was dismissed by the pres., Sharif won elections in 1997 at the head of the Pakistan Muslim League coalition.

Suharto, Thojib N.I. (1921–), Indonesian soldier and politician; pres. 1967/68–. Suharto served in the Japanese-sponsored Indonesian army in WW II, becoming its commander in 1943. His service career continued in independent Indonesia, and in 1965 he was made chief of the army staff. When President Sukarno's policies threatened instability (and there seemed to be the danger of a Communist coup), Suharto took over (1967), assuming presidential authority, although he did not become pres. in name until 1968. His rule has witnessed great economic advances, but opposition is limited. There have been allegations of corruption in the regime, which earned international criticism when the former Portuguese colony of East Timor was invaded (1975) and annexed (1976).

Tudjman, Franjo (1922–), Croat politician and pres. of independent Croatia 1992–. A Communist partisan under Tito in WWII, Tudjman became the youngest general in the Yugoslav army. An advocate of sovereignty for Croatia, he became disillusioned and went into the academic world, becoming a professor of history, but was twice jailed (1972 and 1981) for anti-Communist Croat nationalist sentiments. As Communist regimes collapsed around eastern Europe, he founded the Croat Democratic Union (1989), leading it to victory in 1990, when he became pres. of Croatia. As pres. he led Croatia into secession from Yugoslavia (1991) and war against Serbia (1992), and obtained international recognition of Croat independence (1992). In 1995 a swift campaign removed the Serbs from the one-third of Croatia that they had taken during the 1992 war. There has been criticism of perceived limitations of his commitment to democracy.

Yeltsin, Boris (1931–), Russian politician and pres. (1990–). A construction engineer, he worked full-time for the Soviet Communist Party after 1968 and gained popularity as the approachable Moscow party boss after 1985. He was sacked for criticism of hardliners (1987), but returned to public life in 1989 when he was elected to the new Soviet parliament. Elected pres. of Russia (1990), he led resistance to the coup by Communist hard-liners (1991), mounting a tank in front of the parliament to denounce the plotters. Yeltsin seized power from Gorbachev as the USSR disintegrated and was first pres. of independent Russia (1991). Economic reforms were hampered by opposition and in 1993 he put down a revolt by hardliners in the parliament complex. The problem of the breakaway Caucasian republic of Chechnya has proved difficult and has cost him popularity, but Yeltsin was re-elected (1996) despite ill health. Young economic reformers have played a leading role in his second term.

Zedillo, Ernesto (1951–), Mexican Institutional Revolutionary Party politician and pres. 1994–. A former banker, Zedillo served under President Salinas (1988–94), where he was instrumental in reducing runaway inflation and producing Mexico's first balanced budget. Elected on a platform of his proven financial record, Zedillo has liberalized the political system.

NOBEL PEACE PRIZE

The Nobel Peace Prize is awarded annually by the Norwegian Nobel Committee, which is appointed by the Norwegian Parliament, the Storting.

1901 Jean Henri Dunant, Swiss philanthropist: for founding the Red Cross; Frédéric Passy, French economist: for advocating international arbitration and peace.

1902 Elie Ducommun, Swiss writer, and Charles Albert Gobat, Swiss: for work for peace within the International Peace Bureau.

AUNG SAN SUU KYI COULD NOT COLLECT HER NOBEL PRIZE AS SHE WAS UNDER HOUSE ARREST

1903 Sir William Cremer, English trade unionist: for advocating international arbitration.

1904 Institute of International Law (founded 1873): for helping the world move towards the rule of law.

1905 Bertha von Suttner, Austrian novelist: for her influential peace novels.

1906 Theodore Roosevelt, US pres.: for mediation at the end of Russo-Japanese War (1904).

1907 Ernesto Teodoro Moneta, Italian journalist: for founding the International League for Peace, and presidency of the International Peace Conference (1906); Louis Renault, French jurist: for his international arbitration.

1908 Klas Pontus Arnoldson, Swedish politician: for mediating the dissolution of the Norwegian-Swedish Union; Fredrik Bajer, Danish politician: for his work for female emancipation and the peace movement.

1909 Baron d'Estournelles de Constant, French diplomat: for founding a parliamentary group for voluntary arbitration; Auguste Beernaert, Belgian politician: for work at the Hague Peace Conferences.

1910 International Peace Bureau (founded 1891): for promoting the use of arbitration in disputes.

1911 Tobias Asser, Dutch jurist: for his part in forming the Permanent Court of Justice; Alfred Fried, Austrian pacifist: for co-founding the German peace movement.

1912 Elihu Root, US politician: for his international arbitration.

1913 Henri Lafontaine, Belgian lawyer: for presidency of the International Peace Bureau.

1914–16 No awards

1917 International Red Cross Committee: for work with prisoners of war during WWI.

1918 No award

1919 Woodrow Wilson, US pres.: for his role in the post-World War I international settlement.

1920 Léon Bourgeois, French politician: for advocating the League of Nations and international cooperation.

1921 Karl Branting, Swedish politician: for his conciliatory international diplomacy; Christian Lous Lange, Norwegian peace advocate: for his work as secretary general of the Inter-Parliamentary Union.

1922 Fridtjof Nansen, Norwegian explorer and statesman: for relief work after World War I.

1923–24 No awards

1925 Sir Austen Chamberlain, English politician: for work on the Locarno Pact (1925); Charles G. Dawes, US politician: for reorganization of German reparation payments.

1926 Aristide Briand, French politician: for contributions to the Locarno Pact and Kellogg-Briand Pact; Gustav Stresemann, German politician: for work for European reconciliation.

1927 Ferdinand Buisson, French educationalist: for co-founding League of Human Rights (1898); Ludwig Quidde, German historian and politician: for his work for peace in Germany.

1928 No award

1929 Frank B. Kellogg, US politician: for the Kellogg-Briand Pact (1928).

1930 Nathan Söderblom, Swedish Lutheran archbishop: for his efforts for peace through church unity.

1931 Jane Addams, US social reformer and pacifist: for her social work and support of women's suffrage and peace; Nicholas Murray Butler, US educationalist: for his work in forming the Carnegie Endowment for International Peace.

1932 No award

1933 Sir Norman Angell, English economist: for his work on the economic futility of war.

1934 Arthur Henderson, English politician: for his work on disarmament.

1935 Carl von Ossietzky, German journalist: for speaking out against Nazi rearmament.

1936 Carlos Saavedra Lamas, Argentinian jurist: for his efforts to end the Chaco War (1932–35).

1937 Viscount Cecil of Chelwood, English politician: for drafting the League of Nations Covenant 1919.

1938 Nansen International Office for Refugees: for work with refugees.

1939–43 No awards

1944 International Red Cross Committee: for work during WWII.

1945 Cordell Hull, US politician: for his part in organizing the United Nations.

1946 Emily Greene Balch, US sociologist and political scientist: for leading the women's movement for peace; John R. Mott, US Methodist evangelist: for work in international missionary movements.

1947 American Friends Service Committee, a US Quaker organization, and the Friends Service Council, its British counterpart: for promoting peace through programmes of social service.

1948 No award

1949 Lord Boyd-Orr, Scottish scientist: for his work on nutritional requirements.

1950 Ralph Bunche, US diplomat: for negotiating the Arab-Israeli truce in 1949.

1951 Léon Jouhaux, French trade unionist: for co-founding the International Confederation of Free Trade Unions.

1952 Albert Schweitzer, German missionary, doctor and philosopher: for his medical and other work in Africa.

1953 George C. Marshall, US politician: for the Marshall Plan for European recovery.

1954 Office of the United Nations High Commissioner for Refugees: for work in war relief and reconstruction.

1955–56 No award

1957 Lester B. Pearson, Canadian politician: for his efforts to solve the Suez Crisis (1956).

1958 Dominique Georges Pire, Belgian cleric and educationalist: for his aid to displaced Europeans after WW II.

1959 Philip Noel-Baker, English politician: for advocating world disarmament.

1960 Albert Lutuli, South African: for his non-violent struggle against apartheid.

1961 Dag Hammarskjöld, Swedish Secretary General of the UN (posthumously awarded): for his work in resolving world conflicts.

1962 Linus Pauling, US chemist: for campaigns for the control of nuclear weapons and nuclear testing.

1963 International Red Cross Committee, and League of Red Cross Societies: for their relief work after natural disasters.

1964 Martin Luther King, Jr, US black leader: for his civil rights work.

1965 United Nations Children's Fund: for its promotion of brotherhood among the nations.

1966–67 No award

1968 René Cassin, French jurist: for work as principal author of the UN Declaration of Human Rights.

1969 International Labour Organization: for promoting economic development in the Third World.

1970 Norman E. Borlaug, US agricultural scientist: for agricultural technology.

1971 Willy Brandt, German politician: for reconciliation between West and East Germany.

1972 No award

1973 Henry Kissinger, US politician, and Le Duc Tho, North Vietnamese politician (declined award): for the peace settlement of the Vietnam War.

1974 Eisaku Sato, PM of Japan: for his anti-nuclear policies; Sean MacBride, Irish statesman: for his campaign for human rights.

1975 Andrei D. Sakharov, Russian nuclear physicist: for his advocacy of human rights and disarmament.

1976 Mairead Corrigan, Northern Irish, and Betty Williams, Northern Irish: for campaigning to end sectarian strife in Northern Ireland.

1977 Amnesty International: for work to secure the release of political prisoners.

1978 Menachem Begin, Israeli PM, and Anwar el-Sadat, pres. of Egypt: for Israel-Egypt peace treaty (1979).

1979 Mother Teresa of Calcutta, (ethnic Albanian) Macedonian-born Indian charity worker: for her charity for the destitute in India.

1980 Adolfo Pérez Esquivel, Argentinian sculptor and architect: for work for human rights in Latin America.

1981 UN High Commissioner for Refugees: for work in war relief and reconstruction.

1982 Alva Myrdal, Swedish diplomat, and Alfonso García Robles, Mexican diplomat: for advocacy of nuclear disarmament.

1983 Lech Walesa, Polish politician and trade unionist: for the Solidarity free trade union movement.

1984 Desmond Tutu, South African Anglican Archbishop of Johannesburg: for peaceful anti-apartheid campaigns.

1985 International Physicians for the Prevention of Nuclear War.

1986 Elie Wiesel, French writer and humanitarian: for human rights work.

1987 Oscar Arias Sánchez, pres. of Costa Rica: for promoting peace in Central America.

1988 UN Peacekeeping Forces: for work that contributed to reducing tensions and initiating peace negotiations.

1989 The Dalai Lama, spiritual and exiled temporal leader of Tibet: for advocating peaceful solutions based upon tolerance and mutual respect.

1990 Mikhail Gorbachev, Soviet pres.: for promoting greater openness in the Soviet Union, and helping to end the Cold War.

1991 Aung San Suu Kyi, Burmese politician: for her non-violent campaign for democracy in Myanmar (Burma).

1992 Rigoberta Menchu, Guatemalan Indian activist: for her campaign for the rights of indigenous people.

1993 Nelson Mandela, South African leader of the African National Congress (ANC), and F.W. de Klerk, South African pres.: for their work to bring about an end to apartheid.

1994 Yasser Arafat, chairman of the Palestine Liberation Organization (PLO), Yitzhak Rabin, PM of Israel, and Shimon Peres, foreign secretary of Israel: for bringing about an accord on Palestinian self-rule.

1995 Joseph Rotblat, Polish-born British physicist: for his campaigning against nuclear weapons.

1996 Carlos Filepe Ximenes Belo, East Timorese bishop, and José Ramos-Horta, East Timorese former guerrilla and academic: for their efforts to end abuses by Indonesian forces in East Timor.

THE UNITED NATIONS

- **The largest UN peacekeeping effort of the 1990s was in the former Yugoslavia, where more than 40,000 troops from 27 different countries were serving in 1995.**
- **Although Fiji has armed forces of less than 4000 personnel, it contributes to no less than five peacekeeping operations – in Angola, Sinai, Iraq/Kuwait, Lebanon and Rwanda.**
- **US millionaire John D. Rockefeller, Jr, gave the UN land in New York City, USA, on which to build its headquarters.**

■ *A British Spartan CVR (T) tank with part of the British contingent to the United Nations peacekeeping forces on a snowy road in Bosnia in 1996*

THE BIRTH OF THE UN

▶ **United Nations Day is 24 October, the anniversary of the day that the UN came into being in 1945.**
▶ **Only seven sovereign states are not UN members.**

During World War II, the Allies agreed to create a new international organization to replace the League of Nations, which had never fulfilled its promise as a global peacemaker. At the United Nations Conference in San Francisco, USA, in April 1945, 50 countries signed the United Nations Charter, which came into effect on 24 October 1945.

The United Nations Organization (UNO), or simply the United Nations (UN), was founded as 'a general organization...for the maintenance of international peace and security'. The UN was also aimed at achieving 'international cooperation in solving international problems of an economic, social, cultural or humanitarian character'. However, the UN cannot intervene in the essentially domestic affairs of states.

UNITED NATIONS MEMBERS

Today, almost all the world's sovereign states are UN members. Only Kiribati, Nauru, Switzerland, Taiwan, Tonga, Tuvalu and Vatican City are not members, although Switzerland and Vatican City have observer status. The Palestine Liberation Organization (PLO) and the Sovereign Military Order of Malta have special observer status.

UN ORGANS AND AGENCIES

▶ **The first secretary-general was Norway's Trygve Lie.**
▶ **Japan, Germany and three other states (probably including Brazil and India) have been proposed as additional permanent members of the Security Council.**

The UN has five principal organs, the most important of which are the General Assembly and the Security Council. All are based in New York City, USA, except for the World Court which has its headquarters at The Hague, Netherlands. In addition to these five, there are also a number of other important specialized agencies which are situated in various parts of the world.

SPECIALIZED AGENCIES AND SUBSIDIARY ORGANS

A number of intergovernmental agencies are related to the UN and attached to it in some way. Some, such as the International Labour Organization (ILO), were 'inherited' by the UN from its predecessor, the League of Nations.

FAO (Food and Agriculture Organization of the United Nations. *HQ*: Rome, Italy): aims to improve levels of nutrition and standards of living and the production and distribution of food and all agricultural products, and, in so doing, to eliminate hunger.

IAEA (International Atomic Energy Agency. *HQ*: Vienna, Austria): aims to encourage the use of atomic energy for peaceful purposes.

ICAO (International Civil Aviation Organization. *HQ*: Montreal, Canada): encourages safety measures and coordinates facilities for international flight.

IDA (International Development Association): assists less developed countries by providing credits on special terms. It is an affiliate of the World Bank (see below).

IFAD (International Fund for Agricultural Development. *HQ*: Rome, Italy): generates grants or loans to increase food production in developing countries.

IFC (International Finance Corporation): promotes the flow of private capital internationally and stimulates the capital markets. The IFC is an affiliate of the World Bank (see below).

ILO (International Labour Organization. *HQ*: Geneva, Switzerland): aims to establish international labour standards and to improve social and economic well-being.

IMF (International Monetary Fund. *HQ*: Washington DC, USA): promotes international monetary cooperation.

IMO (International Maritime Organization. *HQ*: London, UK): coordinates safety at sea.

ITU (International Telecommunications Union. *HQ*: Geneva, Switzerland): allocates telecommunications frequencies and standardizes telecommunications practices.

UNESCO (United Nations Educational, Scientific and Cultural Organization. *HQ*: Paris, France): stimulates popular education and the spread of culture.

UNIDO (United Nations Industrial Development Organization. *HQ*: Vienna, Austria): promotes industrialization in developing countries.

UPU (Universal Postal Union. *HQ*: Berne, Switzerland): aims to unite members in a single postal territory.

WHO (World Health Organization. *HQ*: Geneva, Switzerland): promotes the attainment by all peoples of the highest possible standards of health.

WIPO (World Intellectual Property Organization. *HQ*: Geneva, Switzerland): promotes protection of intellectual property such as inventions and copyright.

WMO (World Meteorological Organization. *HQ*: Geneva, Switzerland): standardizes meteorological observations and applies the information to the greatest international benefit of all users, such as those involved in shipping and agriculture.

The World Bank (*HQ*: Washington DC, USA): encourages development through capital investment, in particular, investment in poorer nations. It is formally known as the International Bank for Reconstruction and Development.

WTO (World Trade Organization. *HQ*: Geneva, Switzerland): lays down a common code of practice in international trade and encourages tariff cuts and other measures to achieve world free trade. It replaced GATT (the General Agreement on Tariffs and Trade) in 1995. It is based in Geneva, Switzerland.

The subsidiary organs of the UN are programmes or funds that are devoted to achieving economic and social progress in developing countries. They include:

UNDP (United Nations Development Programme. *HQ*: New York City, USA): the funding source of the technical assistance provided through the UN system.

UNFPA (United Nations Population Fund. *HQ*: New York City, USA): responds to needs in population and family planning.

UNHCR (United Nations High Commissioner for Refugees. *HQ*: Geneva, Switzerland): provides international protection for refugees.

UNICEF (United Nations International Children's Emergency Fund. *HQ*: New York City, USA): aims to meet the needs of children, particularly those in developing countries.

UNRWA (United Nations Relief and Works Agency. *HQ*: Vienna, Austria): provides relief and welfare services for Palestinian refugees.

■ THE NAME 'UNITED NATIONS' WAS FIRST USED IN THE WASHINGTON DECLARATION OF

THE GENERAL ASSEMBLY

The General Assembly, composed of all the member states, can discuss anything within the scope of the Charter. Each member state has up to five delegates but only one vote.

A president is elected by the Assembly in September for a term of one year. Decisions of the Assembly are made by a qualified majority (two-thirds) of those present on 'important' questions, and by a simple majority on other issues.

THE SECURITY COUNCIL

The main organ for maintaining world peace and security, the Security Council has five permanent members: China, France, Russia (this seat was held by the USSR from 1945 to 1991), UK and USA.

Ten other members are elected by the General Assembly for a term of two years, giving a total of 15 members. Chile, Egypt, Guinea-Bissau, Poland and South Korea end their terms on the Council in 1997; Costa Rica, Japan, Kenya, Portugal and Sweden's terms end in 1998.

Decisions of the Security Council are reached by a majority vote of at least nine members, although any of the five existing permanent members can exercise its right of veto.

THE ECONOMIC AND SOCIAL COUNCIL

The Council acts as a coordinating body for the numerous specialized agencies created by the UN, and aims to promote international cooperation in economic, social and related fields. It has 54 members elected for a term of three years.

THE WORLD COURT

Formally known as the International Court of Justice, the World Court offers legal rulings on any case brought before it by UN members. If a party fails to adhere to a judgment of the Court, the other party may have recourse to the Security Council.

The World Court comprises 15 judges elected by the Security Council and the General Assembly for a term of nine years.

THE SECRETARIAT

The Secretariat performs the role of a civil service for the UN. Its head is the Secretary-General, who combines the task of administrative officer of the organization with that of international mediator.

THE TRUSTEESHIP COUNCIL

The Council was established to oversee the progress to independence of former German, Japanese and Italian colonies. As its work has been completed, it has ceased to exist.

WHO PAYS FOR THE UN

	% of budget
USA	25.00
Japan	12.45
Germany	8.93
Russia	6.91
France	6.00
UK	5.02
Italy	4.29
Canada	3.11
Spain	1.98
Australia	1.51
Others	24.80

SECRETARIES-GENERAL

Trygve Lie Norway	1946–53
Dag Hammarskjöld Sweden	1953–61
U Thant Burma	1961–72
Kurt Waldheim Austria	1972–81
Javier Perez de Cuellar Peru	1982–92
Boutros Boutros Ghali Egypt	1992–96
Kofi Annan Ghana	1997–

UN PEACEKEEPING MISSIONS

- **Peacekeeping forces, composed of contingents provided by UN members, have been established by the UN Security Council to act as observers, to provide assistance, maintain cease-fires and prevent or contain conflicts.**
- **Currently, over 55,000 personnel are deployed.**

The majority of UN troops have traditionally come from nations that are not aligned with the major powers. The following missions were in existence in May 1995 or have been created since.

1948 UNMOGIP (United Nations Military Observer Group in India and Pakistan): supervises the cease-fire line established between India and Pakistan in Kashmir in 1948. A total of 40 personnel.

1948 UNTSO (United Nations Truce Supervision Organization): created in June 1948 to observe a truce in Palestine organized by the Security Council. Military observers are stationed in Beirut, South Lebanon, Sinai, Jordan, Israel and Syria. A total of 220 personnel.

1964 UNFICYP (United Nations Peacekeeping Force in Cyprus): created in 1964 to prevent a recurrence of fighting between Greeks and Turks in Cyprus; since the Turkish invasion and occupation of northern Cyprus in 1974, the mission has been expanded to include supervision of the cease-fire line and maintenance of a buffer zone. A total of 1173 personnel.

1974 UNDOF (United Nations Disengagement Observer Force): supervises a cease-fire line between Israel and Syria on the Golan Heights, established on 31 May 1974. A total of 1036 personnel.

1978 UNIFIL (United Nations Interim Force in Lebanon): created in 1978 to confirm the withdrawal of Israeli forces from southern Lebanon and to restore peace and security in the area. A total of 4963 personnel.

1991 MINURSO (United Nations Mission for the Referendum in Western Sahara): created in April 1991 to supervise a referendum to choose between independence and integration with Morocco. This proved difficult, chiefly because Morocco obstructed the identification of eligible voters. A total of 398 personnel.

1991 UNIKOM (United Nations Iraq/Kuwait Observer Mission): created in April 1991 in the aftermath of the Gulf War to monitor a demilitarized zone along the Iraq–Kuwait border, deter violations and observe potentially hostile acts. A total of 1111 personnel.

1991 UNSCOM (United Nations Special Commission): established in 1991 to oversee the destruction of Iraq's nuclear, chemical and biological weapons stockpiles and ballistic missiles and to ensure continued compliance with UN demands. Inspection of facilities continues. Personnel numbers vary.

1993 UNAMIR (United Nations Assistance Mission for Rwanda): created in October 1993 to monitor an agreement between the then Rwandan government and the Rwanda Patriotic Front (RPF). Civil violence forced most of the mission to withdraw, but in June 1994 a new mandate established a force to negotiate and supervise a fresh cease-fire. A total of 6019 personnel.

1993 UNOMIG (United Nations Observer Mission in Georgia): created in August 1993 to verify compliance with a cease-fire between the Republic of Georgia and forces in Abkhazia; extended in July 1994 to include observing the operation of a Commonwealth of Independent States peacekeeping force and monitoring the withdrawal of Georgian troops to beyond the borders of Abkhazia. A total of 135 personnel.

1993 UNOMIL (United Nations Observer Mission in Liberia): created in September 1993 to investigate violations of a cease-fire agreement, supervise elections, provide humanitarian assistance and train a Military Observer Group from the Economic Community of West African States in mine clearance. A total of 70 personnel.

1994 UNMOT (United Nations Mission of Observers in Tajikistan): created in December 1994 to monitor a cease-fire between Tajikistan government forces and Islamic opponents, and to cooperate with a Commonwealth of Independent States peacekeeping force. A total of 39 personnel.

1995 UNAVEM III (United Nations Angola Verification Mission III): created in February 1995 to replace an earlier mission (UNAVEM II), the primary tasks are to assist in the disengagement of forces in Angola, set up verification procedures and coordinate communications between the government, UNITA (National Union for the Total Independence of Angola) and UNAVEM. A total of 1969 personnel.

UN MISSIONS IN THE FORMER YUGOSLAVIA

The following UN missions were largely replaced in December 1995 by a NATO-run Implementation Force (IFOR), renamed Stabilization Force (SFOR) in December 1996. Its mission is to supervise the implementation of the Dayton Peace Accords.

United Nations Peace Force HQ: coordinates all UN forces and missions in former Yugoslavia; based at Zagreb, Croatia. A total of 7613 personnel.

1992 UNPROFOR (United Nations Protection Force: Bosnia-Herzegovina): originally known as UNPROFOR II, this was set up in September 1992 in an attempt to keep Sarajevo international airport open for humanitarian-aid flights. In May 1993, the mandate was extended to include the protection of 'safe havens' throughout Bosnia-Herzegovina, backed by NATO air power. A total of 19,071 personnel.

1992 UNREDEP (United Nations Preventative Deployment Force: Former Yugoslav Republic of Macedonia): created in December 1992 to monitor the Former Yugoslav Republic of Macedonia's borders with Albania and the Federal Republic of Yugoslavia. A total of 1150 personnel.

1995 UNCRO (United Nations Confidence Restoration Operations in Croatia): created in March 1995 to replace the original UNPROFOR (United Nations Protection Force), its mandate was to ensure the demilitarization of UN Protected Areas (UNPAs) in Croatia and verify the withdrawal of all Yugoslav Army and Serbian forces from the country. Following the Croat recapture of western Slavonia and Krajina in August 1995, the UN began to withdraw some of its contingents. A total of 12,564 personnel.

Korea

In June 1950, the UN launched their biggest ever single operation: a UN army was sent to Korea after the UN Security Council passed a resolution calling for all members to aid the South Koreans in their struggle against the North Korean invasion. The USA was the main protagonist in the UN sanctioned 'police action', and this war set a precedent for US involvement in defeating the Communist threat.

THE EUROPEAN UNION

▶ The European Union now embraces the largest and richest market in the Western world.

▶ By special arrangement Andorra, Monaco and San Marino are included in the EU.

▶ More than 300 individual pieces of legislation were necessary to complete the process of economic union.

▶ Poland, the Czech Republic, Hungary, Estonia, Slovenia and Cyprus will open negotiations for membership during 1997–98.

▶ The majority leader in the European Parliament is Pauline Green (UK).

■ *The European flag and those of other member nations*

THE QUEST TO UNITE EUROPE

▶ The drive to create a more unified Europe grew out of a desire to avoid the mistrust and divisiveness that had led to World War II.
▶ Europe Day is 9 May, the anniversary of the first step towards a unified Europe.

On 9 May 1950, French Foreign Minister Robert Schuman called on France, Germany and other European countries to pool together their coal and steel production as 'the first concrete foundation of a European federation'. The fruit of this declaration was the 1951 Treaty of Paris, which brought the European Coal and Steel Community (ECSC) into being. Six countries signed: Belgium, France, the Federal Republic of Germany (West Germany), Italy, Luxembourg and the Netherlands.

In 1957, the 'six' signed the Treaty of Rome, establishing the European Economic Community (EEC) and the European Atomic Energy Commission (Euratom). The EEC aimed to abolish import and export duties on goods in general, while Euratom's purpose was to promote a common effort in the development of nuclear energy for peaceful purposes.

The three bodies were distinct entities until 1967 when, for all practical purposes, they merged into a single European Community (EC), popularly known as the Common Market.

The European Union (EU) came into being on 1 November 1993 following the ratification of the Maastricht Treaty, and expressed a desire for 'an ever closer union among the people of Europe'.

THE EU AND ITS INSTITUTIONS

▶ The European Investment Bank is the world's largest international financing institution.
▶ There are 370 million citizens of the European Union.

The formation of the EU was a decisive step from a 'common market' to a much closer and deeper unification of the economic, political and social systems of EU countries. The governments of the member countries agreed to a series of objectives, including a single currency and a commitment that the EU should 'assert its identity on the international scene'.

The EU is made up of a number of institutions and consultative bodies, the most important being the European Commission, the Council of Ministers and the European Parliament.

THE EUROPEAN COMMISSION

The Commission consists of 20 members, known as commissioners, who are appointed by their national governments for a term of four years. The commissioners appoint from their number a president and six vice-presidents. Acting separately from national governments, the Commission makes proposals to the Council of Ministers and executes the decisions of the Council. The Commission has its headquarters in Brussels, Belgium.

THE COUNCIL OF MINISTERS

The Council, formally known as the Council of the European Union, consists of the foreign ministers of each of the 15 members. It is the main decision-making body of the EU – it adopts regulations, sets directives and makes decisions at ministerial sessions. Specialist councils, for example the 15 ministers of agriculture, also meet, while heads of government meet three times a year as the European Council. Ministers represent national interests. The decisions of Council are normally unanimous, though in certain areas a majority vote is taken.

Council meetings are normally held in the country that currently holds the presidency, but are also held in Brussels.

THE EUROPEAN PARLIAMENT

The Parliament's 626 members are directly elected for five-year terms by universal adult suffrage according to local practice in each member state (all members except the UK use proportional representation). Members of the European Parliament, who are called MEPs, have the right to be consulted on legislative proposals submitted by the Council of Ministers or the Commission and have the power to reject or amend the budget of the EC. The Parliament also has authority to dismiss the European Commission in a vote of censure.

There are 19 parliamentary standing committees specializing in matters ranging from foreign affairs and security to women's rights. Parliament is run by a bureau consisting of a president and 14 vice-presidents, elected by MEPs from their number.

MEPs sit in multinational political groupings, similar to parties. A grouping with members from one country only must have at least 26 MEPs to gain recognition; a grouping from two countries requires 21 MEPs; a grouping from three requires 16 MEPs; and a grouping from four or more requires only 13 MEPs.

The largest political groupings are the Party of European Socialists, the (conservative) European People's Party, the European Liberal Democratic and Reformist Group, the (largely former Communist) Confederal Group of the European United Left, and the Green Group.

The Parliament meets in Strasbourg, France, although there is also a parliamentary building which is used for meetings in Brussels, where committees of the European Parliament also meet. The Secretariat of the Parliament is based in Luxembourg City.

THE EUROPEAN COURT

Known formally as the Court of Justice of the European Communities, it is made up of 13 judges and six advocates appointed for six years by the member states' governments acting in concert, with at least one representative from each country. The Court is responsible for deciding upon the legality of the decisions of the Council of Ministers and the Commission, and for adjudicating in disputes. Its headquarters are in Luxembourg City.

THE COURT OF AUDITORS OF THE EUROPEAN COMMISSION

Established in 1977, the Court of Auditors is responsible for the external audit of the resources managed by the EU/EC. It consists of 15 members (one from each country) elected for six years by the Council of Ministers. The Court has its headquarters in Luxembourg City.

THE EUROPEAN INVESTMENT BANK

Based in Luxembourg City, the bank makes or guarantees loans for investment projects in member states. It works on a non-profit basis, and priority is given to regional development.

CONSULTATIVE BODIES

Besides the EU's principal institutions, there are a number of advisory and consultative bodies.

The Economic and Social Committee: an advisory body consulted by the Commission and the Council of Ministers on issues such as the free movement of workers, agriculture and transport.

The European Coal and Steel Community Consultative Committee: an advisory body consulted by the Commission. It is appointed by the Council of Ministers for two years from coal and steel producers, consumers and dealers.

The Agricultural Advisory Committees: four committees that deal with the organization of the market, structures, and social matters in agriculture.

The Committee of the Regions: an advisory body set up under the terms of the Maastricht Treaty. It comprises representatives from local and regional authorities within member states.

THE SINGLE MARKET

▶ A key objective of the European Union is to secure the economic benefits of free trade through the creation of a market without national barriers. This would allow the unrestricted movement of goods, services, capital and labour through EU countries, and bring consumers a wider choice of goods and services, as well as lower prices owing to increased competition.
▶ EU citizens would also benefit by being able to live and work anywhere in the Union.

The 1957 Treaty of Rome laid the groundwork for the single market by doing away with such restrictions on interstate trade as tariffs, quotas and cartels. But trade was still obstructed and costs and prices raised by such factors as different national bureaucratic requirements and technical standards, different national tax structures, and restrictive government procurement practices and subsidies given to local firms. The Single European Act (SEA), passed in 1986, committed members to remove these impediments. The aim was to create a 'level playing field' so that businesses could produce and sell their products throughout the Union in a single market.

Introduced at a time when trade within the EU already accounted for over 50% of members' total external trade, the SEA has helped boost that figure to well over 60%. Norway, Iceland and Liechtenstein – all non-members of the EU – have also applied the provisions of the single market, expanding the free-trade area beyond the EU into the European Economic Area.

WHO ARE THE COMMISSIONERS

The European Commission is made up of 20 commissioners, two each from France, Germany, Italy, Spain and the UK, and one each from the other member countries.

President of the Commission: Jacques Santer (Lux)

Africa, Caribbean, Pacific: Joâo de Deus Pinheiro (Por)

Agriculture: Franz Fischler (Aut)

Budget: Erkki Liikanen (Fin)

Competition policy: Karel Van Miert (Bel)

Economic and monetary matters: Yves-Thibaut de Silguy (Fra)

Energy: Christos Papoutsis (Gre)

Environment: Rita Bjørregaard (Den)

Fishing and consumer policy, humanitarian office: Emma Bonino (Ita)

Foreign policy, Eastern Europe: Hans van den Broek (Neths)

Immigration and interior policy: Anita Gradin (Swe)

Industrial policy: Martin Bangemann (Ger)

Institutional affairs: Marcelino Oreja (Spa)

Internal market: Mario Monti (Ita)

Mediterranean, Latin America: Manuel Marin (Spa)

Regional policy: Monika Wulf-Mathies (Ger)

Research, training: Edith Cresson (Fra)

Social policy: Padraig Flynn (Ire)

Trade, Asia, North America: Sir Leon Brittan (UK)

Transport: Neil Kinnock (UK)

PRESIDENTS OF THE COMMISSION

Walter Hallstein Germany	1958–67
Jean Rey Belgium	1967–70
Franco Maria Malfatti Italy	1970–72
Sicco L. Mansholt Netherlands	1972
François-Xavier Ortoli France	1973–76
Roy Jenkins United Kingdom	1977–80
Gaston E. Thorn Luxembourg	1981–84
Jacques Delors France	1985–94
Jacques Santer Luxembourg	1995–

THE 'PILLARS' OF THE EU

Under the Maastricht Treaty (1991), cooperation in certain fields is to be channelled through new intergovernmental bodies rather than through the existing bodies of the European Community. The first pillar is the existing EC, which is scheduled to assume additional monetary responsibilities. The second pillar, concerning foreign and security matters, and the third pillar, concerning cooperation in a wide variety of areas such as immigration, political asylum and law enforcement, were defined as intergovernmental bodies representing the member states. With the probable postponement of monetary union, Maastricht implies a considerable widening of cooperation between members at governmental level, without adding substantially to the powers of the European Commission.

EU MEMBERS

	Date joined	Votes in Council of Ministers	Seats in European Parliament	Council Presidency
Germany	1957	10	99	Jan–Jun 1999
France	1957	10	87	Jul–Dec 2000
Italy	1957	10	87	–
UK	1973	10	87	Jan–Jun 1998
Spain	1986	8	64	Jan–Jun 2002
Belgium	1957	5	25	Jul–Dec 2001
Greece	1981	5	25	–
The Netherlands	1957	5	31	–
Portugal	1986	5	25	Jan–Jun 2000
Austria	1995	4	21	Jul–Dec 1998
Sweden	1995	4	22	Jan–Jun 2001
Ireland	1973	3	15	–
Denmark	1973	3	16	Jul–Dec 2002
Finland	1995	3	16	Jul–Dec 1999
Luxembourg	1957	2	6	Jul–Dec 1997

Note: At the beginning of 2003 the 'rota' may be changed by the addition of six new members.

MONETARY UNION

Monetary Union is the change to a single currency, the European Currency Unit, now known as the euro. The first stage of achieving union was to obtain the participation of all member countries in the European Exchange Rate Mechanism (ERM). ERM requires members to keep the exchange value of their currencies to a 'fixed' rate against other members' currencies, but in 1992 speculative pressures on the British pound and the Italian lira forced the withdrawal of these currencies from the system, and further pressure on other currencies in 1993 forced governments effectively to suspend the ERM by allowing member currencies to move by 15% on either side of their central rates. This enabled members to pursue their own exchange policies but at the cost of at least postponing monetary union. Monetary union has been earmarked for 1999, but many member countries doubt that this target will be met.

UNIT OF CURRENCY WITHIN THE EUROPEAN UNION WAS CHRISTENED THE 'EURO' IN 1995 ■

World Organizations

- The International Olympic Committee has more member nations, over 200 in 1997, than G7, NATO, the OECD, the Council of Europe and the Commonwealth put together.
- Mozambique is the first country to join the Commonwealth that has no former ties to the UK or any other Commonwealth state and where English is not an official language.
- The International Red Cross and Red Crescent has won the Nobel Peace Prize more times than any other organization or official body – in 1917, 1944 and 1963.
- Belarus was suspended from the Council of Europe in 1997 due to its poor human rights record.
- NATO's communist equivalent during the Cold War was known as the Warsaw Pact. It ceased to exist in 1991.

G7, NATO, AND OECD

▶ Invitations for full NATO membership were issued to three of NATO's former foes – the Czech Republic, Hungary and Poland – in 1977.
▶ The OECD superseded a post-war body that helped to rebuild Europe after World War II.

World organizations serve a wide variety of purposes. Many are formed to advance the economic, political and social interests of a particular region, while others are based on a single issue, for example religion, and are truly international in membership. Countries may also group together around a common defence policy or on the basis of a shared political outlook. A few international organizations are entirely apolitical and have sporting cohesion or humanitarian causes as their purpose. G7, NATO and the OECD are three organizations with particularly far-reaching global power and influence.

THE GROUP OF SEVEN (G7)/SUMMIT OF EIGHT

An informal grouping of the world's leading economic powers. Since 1975, the heads of government of these states have met for annual summits concerning major economic, monetary and political problems. The inclusion of Russia in several summits has created the Summit of Eight. G7 has neither a constitution nor a Secretariat. *Membership*: Canada, France, Germany, Italy, Japan, UK, USA. (Russia participates in nearly all G7 meetings; the EU has observer status.)

NORTH ATLANTIC TREATY ORGANIZATION (NATO)

A collective defence organization, founded in 1949, whose members agree to treat an attack on any one of them as an attack against all.

The North Atlantic Council, the highest authority of the alliance, comprises 16 permanent representatives (one from each member), plus observers from the signatories of NATO's Partnership for Peace. The Council is chaired by a Secretary-General. The foreign ministers of NATO countries meet at least twice a year. The defence of the NATO area is the responsibility of the Defence Planning Committee (DPC). NATO's Partnership for Peace (PFP), adopted in 1994, aims to provide former Warsaw Pact countries, Commonwealth of Independent States members and neutral states with an agreement that will bring them closer to NATO without formal membership, although it is expected that some PFP members are moving to full NATO membership. PFP is flexible, offering each partner a different relationship with NATO. Partners open up their defence plans to NATO scrutiny and advice, and share training with NATO. *Secretary-General*: Javier Solona (Spa). *Headquarters*: Brussels, Belgium. *Membership*: Belgium, Canada, Denmark, France, Germany, Greece, Iceland, Italy, Luxembourg, Netherlands, Norway, Portugal, Spain, Turkey, UK, USA. *Partners for Peace*: Albania, Armenia, Austria, Azerbaijan, Belarus, Bulgaria, Czech Republic, Finland, Georgia, Hungary, Kazakhstan, Kyrgyzstan, Latvia, Lithuania, Macedonia, Moldova, Poland, Romania, Slovakia, Slovenia, Sweden, Turkmenistan, Ukraine, Uzbekistan. (Russia agreed to sign a long-delayed partnership agreement – separate to Partners for Peace – in 1995.)

ORGANIZATION OF ECONOMIC COOPERATION AND DEVELOPMENT (OECD)

Aims to encourage and develop economic and social welfare in member nations and to stimulate aid to developing countries. The OECD was founded in 1961 to replace the Organization for European Economic Cooperation, which had been established in connection with the Marshall Aid Plan in 1948. *Secretary-general*: Daniel Johnson (Can). *Headquarters*: Paris, France. *Membership* (by invitation rather than application): Australia, Austria, Belgium, Canada, Czech Republic, Denmark, Finland, France, Germany, Greece, Hungary, Iceland, Ireland, Italy, Japan, Luxembourg, Mexico, Netherlands, Norway, Poland, Portugal, Spain, Sweden, Switzerland, Turkey, UK, USA.

OTHER MAJOR WORLD ORGANIZATIONS

Asia-Pacific Economic Cooperation (Apec): Apec was founded in 1993 to encourage trade between the countries bordering the Pacific Ocean. Its 18 members have 38% of the world's population, are responsible for 50% of the world's economic production, and 41% of the world's trade. Trade barriers are to be removed between industrial members by 2010 and developing nations by 2020. *Members*: Australia, Brunei, Canada, Chile, China, Indonesia, Japan, Malaysia, Mexico, New Zealand, Papua New Guinea, Philippines, Singapore, South Korea, Taiwan, Thailand, USA.

Association of South-East Asian Nations (ASEAN): founded in 1967 to accelerate the economic, social and cultural development of members, to maintain stability in the region and to encourage cooperation between members. *Secretary-general*: Dato' Ajit Singh (Mal). *Headquarters*: Jakarta, Indonesia. *Members*: Brunei, Indonesia, Laos, Malaysia, Myanmar (Burma), Philippines, Singapore, Thailand, Vietnam.

The Commonwealth: has its foundations in the 1926 Imperial Conference, which defined the position of the dominions as 'freely associated...members of the British Commonwealth of Nations'. The modern Commonwealth dates from 1949 when India became a republic but remained a member of the Commonwealth, recognizing the British sovereign as 'the symbol of the free association of...independent member states'. The majority of members are republics and some have their own sovereign, but all recognize the British sovereign as Head of the Commonwealth. The Commonwealth is an informal grouping of the UK and the majority of its former dependencies, and has recently received applications from countries with no colonial ties to Britain (for example Mozambique). It has no written constitution. It aims to encourage international, scientific and technical, educational and economic cooperation between members. *Secretary-general*: Chief Emeka Anyaoku (Nig). *Headquarters*: London, UK. *Membership*: Antigua and Barbuda, Australia (founder member), Bahamas, Bangladesh, Barbados, Belize, Botswana, Brunei, Cameroon, Canada (founder member), Cyprus, Dominica, Gambia, Ghana, Grenada, Guyana, India (founder member), Jamaica, Kenya, Kiribati, Lesotho, Malawi, Malaysia, Maldives, Malta, Mauritius, Mozambique, Namibia, Nauru (special member), New Zealand (founder member), Nigeria (suspended from certain Commonwealth activities 1996), Pakistan (founder member; withdrew 1972, readmitted 1989), Papua New Guinea, St Christopher and Nevis, St Lucia, St Vincent and the Grenadines, Seychelles, Sierra Leone, Singapore, Solomon Islands, South Africa (founder member; withdrew 1960; readmitted 1994), Sri Lanka (founder member as Ceylon), Swaziland, Tanzania (joined as Tanganyika), Tonga, Trinidad and Tobago, Tuvalu (special member), Uganda, UK (founder member), Vanuatu, Western Samoa, Zambia, Zimbabwe. (Special members do not participate in Commonwealth ministerial meetings.)

Commonwealth of Independent States (CIS): following the dissolution of the USSR in December 1991, Belarus, Russia and Ukraine concluded an agreement to found an organization that is, in some limited respects, the successor to the USSR in economic, military and political cooperation. All former Soviet states, except the three Baltic republics, have now joined. The principal objective of the CIS is to provide unitary control of strategic armed forces (including nuclear weapons) that formerly belonged to the USSR. The aim to create a 'single economic space' has largely been abandoned as individual members have adopted their own economic policies and agreements as well their own currencies. CIS peacekeeping forces have been in operation in Moldova, Azerbaijan and Tajikistan. In 1993, some members established a defence alliance, an economic coordination committee and a Commonwealth bank. The affairs of the CIS are largely dealt with on a direct interstate basis rather than by central institutions. The chairmanship rotates between member states. *Headquarters*: Minsk, Belarus. *Members*: Armenia, Azerbaijan, Belarus, Georgia, Kazakhstan, Kyrgyzstan, Moldova, Russia, Tajikistan, Turkmenistan, Ukraine, Uzbekistan.

THE INTERNATIONAL RED CROSS ORGANIZATION IS KNOWN AS THE RED CRESCENT IN ISLAMIC

Communauté Financière Africaine (CFA): a monetary union founded to supply a common currency for former French African possessions. The CFA franc is pegged to the French franc. *Headquarters*: Paris, France. *Members*: Benin, Burkina Faso, Cameroon, Central African Republic, Chad, Congo-Brazzaville, Côte d'Ivoire, Equatorial Guinea, Gabon, Mali, Niger, Senegal, Togo.

The Council of Europe: founded in 1949 to achieve greater European unity, to safeguard members' common European heritage and to facilitate economic and social progress. Membership is restricted to European democracies. The Council of Ministers (foreign ministers of members) meets twice a year. Agreements are formalized as European Conventions or recommendations to governments. The Parliamentary Assembly of the Council (which meets three times a year) comprises delegations from member states. Delegations range in size from 18 members (Italy, France, Germany, UK) to two (San Marino, Liechtenstein). The Council has concluded over 140 conventions and agreements including the European Convention of Human Rights (1950). *Secretary-general*: Daniel Tarschys (Swe). *Headquarters*: Strasbourg, France. *Members*: Albania, Andorra, Austria, Belgium, Bulgaria, Croatia, Cyprus, Czech Republic, Denmark, Estonia, Finland, France, Germany, Greece, Hungary, Iceland, Ireland, Italy, Latvia, Liechtenstein, Lithuania, Luxembourg, Macedonia, Malta, Moldova, Netherlands, Norway, Poland, Portugal, Romania, Russia, San Marino, Slovakia, Slovenia, Spain, Sweden, Switzerland, Turkey, Ukraine, UK. *Guest members*: Belarus (suspended 1997), Bosnia-Herzegovina.

International Olympic Committee (IOC): formed in 1894. The first Olympic Games of the modern era took place in Athens, Greece, in 1896. *Headquarters*: Lausanne, Switzerland. *Membership*: a record 197 countries took part in the 1996 summer Olympic Games.

The International Red Cross and Red Crescent: a neutral organization founded to negotiate between warring parties, to protect casualties of armed conflict, to develop the activities of individual societies, to protect prisoners of war (under the terms of the Geneva Convention), and to coordinate relief for the victims of natural and other disasters. The Conference of the International Red Cross and Red Crescent meets every four years. *Headquarters*: Geneva, Switzerland. *Membership*: over 165 countries.

Latin American Integration Association (ALADI): founded in 1980 as a replacement for the Latin American Free Trade Area (founded 1961). It aims to encourage trade and to remove tariffs between members. ALADI maintains a small Secretariat. *Secretary-general*: Antonio Antunes (Uru). *Headquarters*: Montevideo, Uruguay. *Members*: Argentina, Bolivia, Brazil, Chile, Colombia, Ecuador, Mexico, Paraguay, Peru, Uruguay, Venezuela. *Observers*: Costa Rica, Cuba, Dominican Republic, El Salvador, Guatemala, Honduras, Italy, Nicaragua, Panama, Portugal, Spain.

League of Arab States (Arab League): founded in 1945 to protect the independence and sovereignty of members, to strengthen ties between them, and to encourage coordination of their social, economic, political, cultural and legal policies. The League comprises a Council (on which each state has one vote), special committees, over 20 specialized agencies and a Secretariat. *Secretary-general*: Dr Ahmad al-Meguid (Egy). *Headquarters*: Cairo, Egypt. *Members*: Algeria, Bahrain, Comoros, Djibouti, Egypt, Iraq, Jordan, Kuwait, Lebanon, Libya, Mauritania, Morocco, Oman, Qatar, Saudi Arabia, Somalia, Sudan, Syria, Tunisia, United Arab Emirates, Yemen. (The Palestine Liberation Organization is also in membership.)

■ *Flags of the Red Cross and the Red Half Moon hang at the Red Cross Museum, Geneva, Switzerland*

Mercosur (Mercado del Sur): the Market of the South originated in a free-trade agreement between Argentina and Brazil in 1988, and is scheduled to become a free market in goods, services and labour. The first tariff reductions were made at the beginning of 1995. *Headquarters*: Montevideo, Uruguay. *Members*: Argentina, Brazil, Paraguay, Uruguay. *Associate members*: Bolivia, Chile.

North American Free Trade Agreement (NAFTA): origins lie in the free-trade agreement signed by the USA and Canada in 1989. It was extended in 1994 to include Mexico. NAFTA aims to eliminate tariffs, quotas and import licences between states of the North American continent. NAFTA may eventually include Central and South American countries in the future. There is no formal Secretariat. *Members*: Canada, Mexico, USA. (Chile is a candidate for membership.)

Organization of African Unity (OAU): founded in 1963 to promote African unity and collaboration in economic, social, cultural, political, defence, scientific, health and other matters, and to eliminate colonialism from Africa. The OAU Assembly of heads of state/government meets annually and is presided over by a chairman, who is elected annually by the Assembly. The main administrative body of the OAU is the Secretariat. *Secretary-general*: Salim Ahmed Salim (Tan). *Headquarters*: Addis Ababa, Ethiopia. *Members*: Algeria, Angola, Benin, Botswana, Burkina Faso, Burundi, Cameroon, Cape Verde, Central African Republic, Chad, Comoros, Congo-Brazzaville, Congo (ex-Zaïre), Côte d'Ivoire, Djibouti, Egypt, Equatorial Guinea, Eritrea, Ethiopia, Gabon, Gambia, Ghana, Guinea, Guinea-Bissau, Kenya, Lesotho, Liberia, Libya, Madagascar, Malawi, Mali, Mauritania, Mauritius, Mozambique, Namibia, Niger, Nigeria, Rwanda, São Tomé and Principe, Senegal, Seychelles, Sierra Leone, Somalia, South Africa, Sudan, Swaziland, Tanzania, Togo, Tunisia, Uganda, Zambia, Zimbabwe. (In 1982, the Sahrawi Democratic Republic (Western Sahara) was admitted to membership; Morocco, which claims Western Sahara, withdrew in protest.)

Organization of American States (OAS): founded in 1948 as the successor to the Pan American Union; aims to maintain the independence and territorial integrity of members, to achieve peace and justice on the continent, and to encourage collaboration and inter-American solidarity. *Secretary-general*: Dr Cesar Gaviria (Col). *Headquarters*: Washington DC, USA. *Members*: Antigua and Barbuda, Argentina, Bahamas, Barbados, Belize, Bolivia, Brazil, Canada, Chile, Colombia, Costa Rica, Cuba (suspended 1962), Dominica, Dominican Republic, Ecuador, El Salvador, Grenada, Guatemala, Guyana, Haiti, Honduras, Jamaica, Mexico, Nicaragua, Panama, Paraguay, Peru, St Christopher and Nevis, St Lucia, St Vincent and the Grenadines, Suriname, Trinidad and Tobago, USA, Uruguay, Venezuela.

Organization of Petroleum Exporting Countries (OPEC): aims to coordinate the petroleum-producing and petroleum-exporting policies of members. Founded in Baghdad, Iraq, in 1960. *Secretary-general*: Dr Subroto (Indo). *Headquarters*: Vienna, Austria. *Membership*: Algeria, Gabon, Indonesia, Iran, Iraq, Kuwait, Libya, Nigeria, Qatar, Saudi Arabia, United Arab Emirates, Venezuela.

Organization of Security and Cooperation in Europe (OSCE): founded as the Conference on Security and Cooperation in Europe (CSCE), which grew out of a security conference held in Helsinki, Finland, in 1975. The aims of the OSCE were formulated by the Charter of Paris (1990), which has been described as the formal end of the Cold War. Members affirm an adherence to democracy and human rights, and a commitment to settle disputes by peaceful means. OSCE foreign ministers meet at least once a year. *Secretary-general*: Wilhelm Hoynck (Ger). *Headquarters of the Secretariat* (and Forum for Security Cooperation): Vienna, Austria. *Office for Democratic Institutions and Human Rights*: Warsaw, Poland. *Office of the High Commission on National Minorities*: The Hague, Netherlands. *Members*: Albania, Armenia, Austria, Azerbaijan, Belarus, Belgium, Bulgaria, Canada, Croatia, Cyprus, Czech Republic, Denmark, Estonia, Finland, France, Georgia, Germany, Greece, Hungary, Iceland, Ireland, Italy, Kazakhstan, Kyrgyzstan, Latvia, Liechtenstein, Lithuania, Luxembourg, Malta, Moldova, Monaco, Netherlands, Norway, Poland, Portugal, Romania, Russia, San Marino, Slovakia, Slovenia, Spain, Sweden, Switzerland, Tajikistan, Turkey, Turkmenistan, Ukraine, Uzbekistan, UK, USA, Vatican City. *Observer*: Former Yugoslav Republic of Macedonia. (Yugoslavia has been suspended from membership.)

The West European Union (WEU): founded in 1955, seeks to harmonize the security and defence of the countries of western Europe. The WEU was reactivated in 1984 to strengthen NATO and has virtually taken on the role of the EU/EC's putative defence arm. A Council of Ministers (the foreign and defence ministers of members) meets twice a year under a rotating presidency (each member holds the presidency for six months). The Permanent Council of the WEU (the members' ambassadors in Brussels) meets on a regular basis; representatives of the associate and observer members also participate. The Assembly of the WEU, which meets twice a year, comprises 108 members of the national parliaments of full members. *Secretary-general*: José Cutileiro (Por). *Headquarters*: Brussels, Belgium. *Parliamentary headquarters*: Paris, France. *Members*: Belgium, France, Germany, Greece, Italy, Luxembourg, Netherlands, Portugal, Spain, UK. *Associate members*: Iceland, Norway, Turkey. *Associated partners*: Bulgaria, Czech Republic, Estonia, Hungary, Latvia, Lithuania, Poland, Romania, Slovakia. *Observers*: Austria, Denmark, Finland, Ireland, Sweden.

Armed Forces

- In 1996, Iraq was bombed by US B-52s that flew to and from Guam in the central Pacific, refuelling in mid-air – a round-trip of *c*. 20,000 km.
- The shortest war of the 1990s to date was that between Peru and Ecuador in 1995 – it lasted less than a week.
- Europe's smallest army is Luxembourg's 800-men light infantry battalion.

Armed forces of the world are most commonly compared in terms of nuclear capability or total manpower. Other important factors include the numbers of combat aircraft, warships and tanks, as well as the proportion of GDP (gross domestic product) devoted to defence. Six countries are known to possess the ultimate threat to world peace – nuclear weapons. Paradoxically, the menace of nuclear war has acted as a deterrent, helping to prevent direct conflict between the major powers since the end of World War II. The collapse of communism in eastern Europe has brought another change in effectively ending the confrontation between East and West. The signature of the Charter of Paris in November 1990 formally ended the Cold War, although large nuclear stockpiles remain. However, fear of superpower imbalance has been replaced by fear of 'proliferation' – the spread of nuclear capability to powers outside the major blocs.

 Most Nuclear Warheads

Six countries are known to possess nuclear weapons. The USA and Russia together hold over 85% of this total. Russian and US stockpiles are in the process of being reduced in accordance with the Strategic Arms Reduction Treaty (START). Other countries are suspected of having nuclear weapons; these include Israel, India and North Korea. In 1993 South Africa admitted that it formerly had a nuclear capability but had destroyed its weapons.

USA	9,800
Russia	6,100
France	390
China	310
UK	120
Belarus*	18

* At independence in 1991, 1592 former Soviet warheads were based in Ukraine and 690 in Kazakhstan. Under a CIS agreement these were moved to Russia to be dismantled. The last of these missiles left Ukraine in 1996. A similar agreement exists to remove warheads from Belarus, but that country has retained 18 warheads.

 Wars in the 1990s

1947–49; since 1965 Kashmir Kashmir has been the main area of conflict between India and Pakistan since the partition of the subcontinent in 1947. Tension over the state has twice led to war and the problem of Kashmir – part of which (Azad Kashmir) is occupied by Pakistan – remains unresolved. Fighting between Indian and Pakistani forces continues intermittently along the far northern end of the cease-fire line and, since 1989, Kashmiri separatist guerrillas have been active in different areas of the state.

1961–91 Ethiopia/Eritrea Rebel forces in Eritrea and Tigray fought Ethiopian government forces for independence. Eritrea effectively seceded in 1991 and assumed full sovereignty in May 1993; spasmodic fighting continues in Ethiopia, especially in the Tigray and Oromo districts.

Since 1965 Chad The country has seen civil wars between the Muslim Arab north and the Christian and animist black African south. Idriss Déby successfully led rebel forces against the government in 1989. Unrest, and Libyan interference, continues in the north.

Since 1969 Northern Ireland Sectarian conflict continues between Loyalist extremists intent on remaining part of the UK and Republican (or Nationalist) extremists intent on reuniting Ireland. British troops – initially deployed in a peacekeeping role – are opposed by paramilitary groups, such as the (loyalist) Ulster Defence Association (UDA) and the (nationalist) Provisional Irish Republican Army (PIRA). A cease-fire was declared by PIRA in 1994 and by the loyalists soon afterwards. Peace talks began, but the PIRA ceasefire ended in 1996 and violence continues.

1972–91 Western Sahara The Polisario liberation movement began its fight against Spanish rule in the territory in 1972. Spain withdrew, dividing the Western Sahara between Morocco and Mauritania in 1976. Morocco absorbed the Mauritanian sector when Mauritania withdrew in 1979. In 1976, the Polisario declared independence and conducted a guerrilla campaign against Moroccan rule until 1991, when a UN-brokered cease-fire was agreed. Sporadic fighting continues.

1975–91 Lebanon Civil war between Christian and Muslim forces reduced Lebanon to chaos. Syria and Israel intervened and a Syrian-backed government imposed a semblance of order in 1991, but spasmodic fighting in the south between Hizbollah fundamentalists and Israeli-backed forces continues.

1975–94 Mozambique Mozambique virtually disintegrated in civil war between the Front for the Liberation of Mozambique (FRELIMO) government and the Mozambique National Resistance Organization (RENAMO). Peace moves were made in 1993–94 and the civil war officially ended in 1994.

Since 1975 East Timor Indonesia seized the former Portuguese colony of East Timor in 1975, despite the territory's declaration of independence and the opposition of the UN. Rebel Timorese activity and Indonesian repression continue.

Since 1975 Sri Lanka Indian intervention (1987–90) led to a bitter counter-insurgency operation in support of the ruling Sinhalese against the ethnic-Indian Tamils (particularly the Tamil Tigers), who are fighting for an independent Tamil state. After a brief cease-fire in 1995, fighting resumed.

1976–97 Angola UNITA (National Union for the Total Independence of Angola) forces – initially aided by South Africa – fought the left-wing MPLA (People's Movement for the Liberation of Angola) movement. The MPLA won the civil war of 1975–76, but continued to be opposed by UNITA rebels. A UN-supervised cease-fire in 1991 was breached and the civil war resumed in 1992 when UNITA refused to accept the results of multiparty elections. A further cease-fire in 1995 followed heavy UNITA losses in 1994–95, but spasmodic fighting continued to 1997 when a power-sharing agreement was reached.

1979–91; 1997 Cambodia The 1991 cease-fire ended civil war between the Vietnamese-backed government and Pol Pot's Khmer Rouge. Free elections were held under UN supervision and the monarchy restored, but intermittent fighting continued as the Khmer Rouge withdrew from the peace process. Recent reports suggest that Pol Pot has been captured by dissident Khmer Rouge. There was fighting in 1997 between royalists and former Communists.

Since 1979 Afghanistan Civil war was triggered by the Soviet invasion of Afghanistan in 1979. Mujahaddin guerrillas (Muslim fundamentalists) fought government forces even after the Soviet withdrawal in 1989. In 1992 fundamentalists took Kabul, the capital, and formed a provisional government. However, factional – largely ethnic – fighting continues.

1980–91 El Salvador A UN-supervised peace agreement ended civil war between the government and the left-wing Farabundo Marti National Liberation Front (FMLN) guerrillas.

Since 1982 Peru Revolutionary activities of the Maoist Sendero Luminoso ('Shining Path') group triggered a counter-insurgency campaign by the government. Guerrilla activity has decreased since the capture of the Sendero Luminoso leader, although in late 1996 another left-wing group, the Tupac Amaru, caught the headlines by seizing the Japanese embassy in Lima and holding diplomats hostage until they were rescued by Peruvian commandos.

Since 1982 Philippines Communist insurgency increased in 1982 but, by the early 1990s, the problem had been largely contained, although spasmodic fighting continues.

Since 1983 Sudan Civil war continues between Islamic government forces and the Christian and animist guerrillas of the Sudan People's Liberation Army (SPLA). The SPLA is subject to violent internal fighting. Western humanitarian aid has been disrupted. By 1995, government forces had gained an advantage, but fighting continues.

Since 1987 Palestinian *intifada* The *intifada*, the Palestinian uprising in the West Bank and Gaza Strip against Israeli occupying forces, has been characterized by riots and shootings. Unrest continues despite a peace agreement between the Israelis and the Palestinian Liberation Organization (PLO) which granted limited Palestinian autonomy in Gaza and West Bank towns.

Since 1988 Myanmar/Burma Military rule since 1988 has been opposed by a variety of political and nationalist groups. Non-Burman minorities have joined forces to fight against the military. However, by 1995 government forces had contained most of the minorities.

Since 1988 Somalia An Ethiopian-backed uprising in northern Somalia in 1988 began armed opposition to President Barre, who fled in 1991 after guerrillas attacked the capital, Mogadishu. The rebels have since fought among themselves and Somalia has descended into chaos. The US, with UN backing, intervened with force in 1992 to deliver humanitarian aid, but to little lasting effect, and after a US withdrawal in 1994, the UN quickly also withdrew its forces. Factional fighting continues and Somalia has effectively

■ SWITZERLAND'S ARMY OF 3500 PERSONNEL CAN BE EXPANDED TO 363,000 IN THE EVENT

BIGGEST DEFENCE BUDGETS

Countries that spend the greatest percentage of their gross domestic product (GDP) on defence are:

	%
Ukraine	49.57
Saudi Arabia	33.75
Kuwait	33.20
North Korea	26.70
Croatia	25.00
Belarus	23.74
Ethiopia	21.62
Iraq	21.10
Moldova	18.42
Angola	17.21
Oman	15.92
Georgia	15.70
United Arab Emirates	14.55
Israel	13.20
Syria	13.02

LARGEST ARMED FORCES

Armed forces' total manpower (the combined number of army, navy and air force personnel), excluding reserves.

China	2,930,000
USA	1,547,300
Russia	1,520,000
India	1,145,000
North Korea	1,128,000
South Korea	633,000
Pakistan	587,000
Vietnam	572,000
Iran	513,000
Turkey	507,800
Ukraine	452,500
Egypt	436,000
Syria	423,000
France	409,000
Iraq	382,500

■ *The Chinese army is the largest in the world*

descended into chaos with the north in (unrecognized) secession.

Since 1989 Papua New Guinea Secessionist guerrillas were active on the mineral-rich island of Bougainville until 1991, when government forces contained the situation. Unrest on the island continues, although a peace conference began in 1997.

Since 1989 Liberia West African states deployed an ECOWAS (Economic Community of West African States) peacekeeping force in 1990 to end a civil war initially between the National Patriotic Front of Liberia (NLFL) and government forces, but fighting flared up between NLFL and rival rebel groups in 1992 and is still continuing on a small scale.

1990–91 Kuwait Iraqi troops invaded Kuwait in August 1990. A US-led multinational force – under the auspices of the UN – used air attacks on Iraq and a 100-hour ground campaign to liberate Kuwait in early 1991. Since then, the UN has monitored the border and the US has initiated air strikes to deter Iraqi aggression.

Since 1990 Rwanda In 1990, the Front Patriotique Rwandais (FPR), an army of Tutsi refugees, invaded Rwanda, occupying much of the north. After a plane carrying President Habyarimana was shot down in 1994, government (Hutu) forces went on the rampage. In the ensuing ethnic violence, between 500,000 and one million Tutsis were massacred by Hutus and over two million refugees fled the country, spreading unrest into neighbouring states (see The Congo (ex-Zaïre) below).

1991–92 Georgia A civil war between supporters and opponents of President Gamsakhurdia was followed by continuing secessionist wars (see Georgia–Abkhazia and Georgia–South Ossetia, below).

1991–96 Bosnia-Herzegovina After Bosnia-Herzegovina received international recognition as a sovereign state in 1992, Bosnian Serbs fought against Croats and Muslims (although the latter two groups also fought each other) for control of what used to be central Yugoslavia. The Serbs occupied about 70% of Bosnia, killing or expelling Muslims and Croats in a campaign of 'ethnic cleansing'. A UN force was deployed in 1992 to supervise the delivery of humanitarian aid. The Serbs set up an internationally unrecognized republic based at Pale. Peace negotiations (and UN use of air power) led to the Dayton Peace Accords in late 1995, monitored by a NATO-led Implementation Force (IFOR), replaced in late 1996 by a Stabilization Force (SFOR).

1991–96 Croatia War between Croats and ethnic Serbs in Krajina and parts of Slavonia followed the break-up of Yugoslavia. A cease-fire was negotiated in early 1992 and a UN force deployed, but fighting resumed in 1993. Further uneasy cease-fires followed but, in 1995, Croat forces retook Serb-occupied Krajina and most of Slavonia.

Since 1991 Iraq After the Gulf War (see Kuwait, above), the Iraqi leader Saddam Hussein faced uprisings by Shi'ite Muslims in the south and Kurds in the north. Allied 'no-fly' zones in these areas (and threats of armed intervention) have restrained Iraq, but small-scale attacks by Saddam on his enemies continue. The Kurds also come under sporadic cross-border attack from both the Turks and Iranians.

1991–96; since 1997 Sierra Leone The rebel Revolutionary United Front (RUF), a product of the civil war in Liberia, began activities against the central government in 1991. By 1995, the RUF controlled the greater part of the country, but violence continued until 1996. A military coup in 1997 overthrew civilian rule, and Nigerian intervention was unsuccessful.

1992 Georgia–South Ossetia Muslim secessionists in the South Ossetia region of Georgia fought an intermittent campaign to unite with their North Ossetian co-nationalists in Russia. A peace force established a buffer zone in June 1992.

1992 Moldova Civil war broke out in 1992 when Russian and Ukrainian minorities, fearing a reunion of Moldova with Romania, proclaimed the republic of Transdniestria. The intervention of mainly Russian forces of the Commonwealth of Independent States (CIS) brought an uneasy peace, but the Moldovan authorities have little control in Transdniestria.

1992–93 Georgia–Abkhazia Muslim secessionist forces in the Abkhazia region of Georgia were aided by Russians in 1993. By September 1993, Abkhazian forces had gained control of almost the entire region. A Russian-brokered cease-fire came into force in December 1993, but unrest continues and the Georgian authorities have lost control of the area.

Since 1992 Armenia–Azerbaijan (Nagorno-Karabakh region) Armenian and Azeri forces are fighting for control of Nagorno-Karabakh, an enclave of Orthodox Christian Armenians surrounded by Shi'ite Muslim Azeris. A Russian-initiated cease-fire has been brokered, but sporadic fighting continues.

Since 1992 Tajikistan The ex-Communist rulers of this former Soviet republic have effectively defeated Islamic fundamentalists in the north, but fighting continues intermittently in the south along the Afghan border.

1992–97 The Congo (ex-Zaïre) Spasmodic fighting occurred in the two Kasai provinces and in Shaba (the former Katanga) as secessionists took advantage of the collapse of law and order in much of the country. In 1996–97, this escalated when armed refugees from Rwanda allied themselves with eastern rebels. They overthrew the government of President Mobutu in 1997.

1994 Haiti US forces intervened to replace a repressive military regime and to ensure that the results of a presidential election were enforced. A small UN monitoring force remains in Haiti, but the US has withdrawn.

1994 Yemen The uneasy union between former (traditionalist) North Yemen and former (Communist) South Yemen, negotiated in 1990, proved more apparent than real in many respects. Regional stresses, and resentment in the South, resulted in civil war in 1994. The South declared independence but was defeated by the North within a month.

Since 1994 Algeria Elections that seemed to give power to Muslim fundamentalists were overturned by the government, leading to continuing widespread terrorist attacks.

Since 1994 Chechnya Intervention by Russian forces to prevent the secession of Chechnya from the Russian Federation led to heavy fighting, particularly in the Chechen capital, Grozny. Russian military victory was proclaimed in 1995, but spasmodic fighting continues in the mountains.

Since 1994 Mexico An uprising by Zapatista guerrillas in Chiapas province (southern Mexico) has led to a counter-insurgency campaign which still continues.

1995 Peru–Ecuador Border disputes between Peru and Ecuador led to some fighting early in 1995. A cease-fire was quickly negotiated.

1997 Albania Civil unrest spread in early 1997, fuelled by popular anger at failed financial schemes. Rebel forces briefly took over the southern region, but the government held the capital, Tirana. A mainly Italian peacekeeping force was deployed in March 1997. Sporadic violence continues.

OF AN EMERGENCY ■ ICELAND IS THE ONLY MEMBER OF NATO TO HAVE NO ARMED FORCES ■

■ *The US Navy has, by far, the largest number of naval personnel in the world*

NAVIES

PERSONNEL*		WARSHIPS	
USA	613,700**	Russia	1,396
China	260,000	China	1,311
Russia	200,000	USA	536
Taiwan	68,000	North Korea	503
Thailand	66,000	South Korea	206
France	64,200	Taiwan	196
South Korea	60,000	Germany	175
India	55,000	Japan	159
Turkey	51,000	UK	159
UK	50,500	France	152
Brazil	50,000	Turkey	139
North Korea	46,000	Mexico	134
Italy	44,000	Romania	133
Japan	43,700	India	133
Vietnam	42,000	Italy	115

* excludes reserves
** includes US Marine Corps

■ *American A-10 Thunderbolts II combat aircraft – the US air force has the most planes*

AIR FORCES

PERSONNEL*		COMBAT AIRCRAFT	
China	470,000	USA	5,973
USA	408,700	China	5,825
Ukraine	151,000	Russia	3,243
Russia	130,000	Ukraine	1,476
India	110,000	India	912
France	89,200	France	766
North Korea	82,000	Israel	699
Germany	75,300	Japan	660
Poland	72,600	UK	639
UK	70,400	Syria	579
Taiwan	68,000	Egypt	564
Italy	67,800	Germany	542
Turkey	56,800	North Korea	509
Romania	54,000	South Korea	484
South Korea	53,000	Taiwan	462

* excludes reserves

■ *Russia has 19,000 tanks, compared with the USSR's staggering total of 54,000 in 1991*

ARMIES

PERSONNEL*		TANKS	
China	2,200,000	Russia	19,000
North Korea	1,000,000	USA	12,516
India	980,000	China	7,500–8,000
Russia	670,000	Ukraine	4,775
USA	524,900	Syria	4,600
Pakistan	520,000	Israel	4,095
South Korea	520,000	Egypt	3,500
Vietnam	500,000	North Korea	3,400
Iran	465,000**	Iraq	2,700
Turkey	400,000	Germany	2,695
Iraq	350,000	India	2,400
Syria	315,000	Belarus	2,348
Egypt	310,000	Greece	2,268
Myanmar (Burma)	265,000	Libya	2,210
France	241,400	Pakistan	2,050
		South Korea	2,050

* excludes reserves
** includes Revolutionary Guard

■ THE SOVIET-DESIGNED T-34 TANK WAS FIRST DEPLOYED IN 1941, AND IS STILL IN USE ■

'I am not an Athenian or a Greek, but a citizen of the world'
– Socrates

THE WORLD ▷

COUNTRY LOCATOR

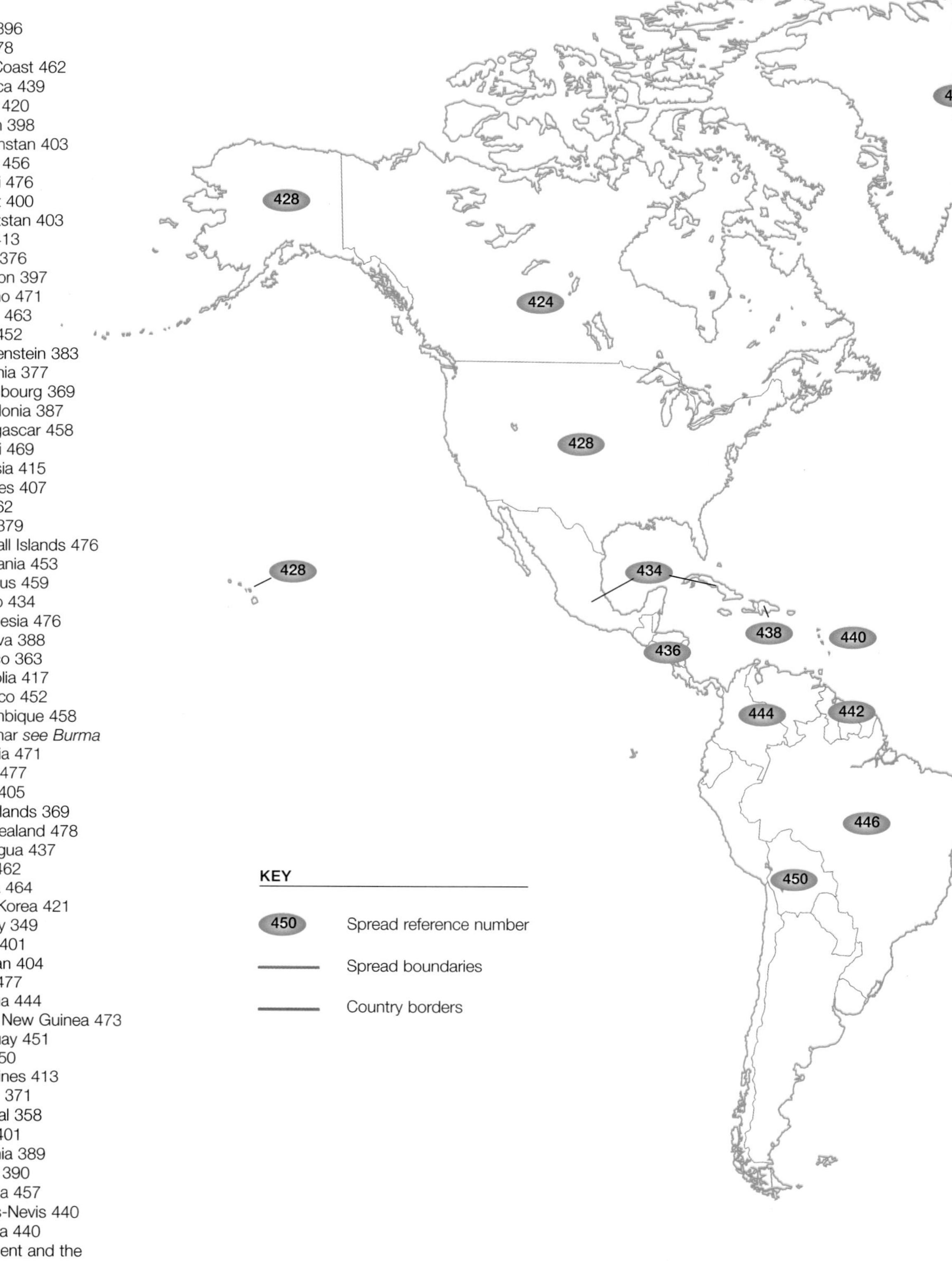

COUNTRIES

OTHER TERRITORIES

IT IS ESTIMATED THAT THE WORLD POPULATION AT THE TURN OF THE MILLENNIUM WILL BE

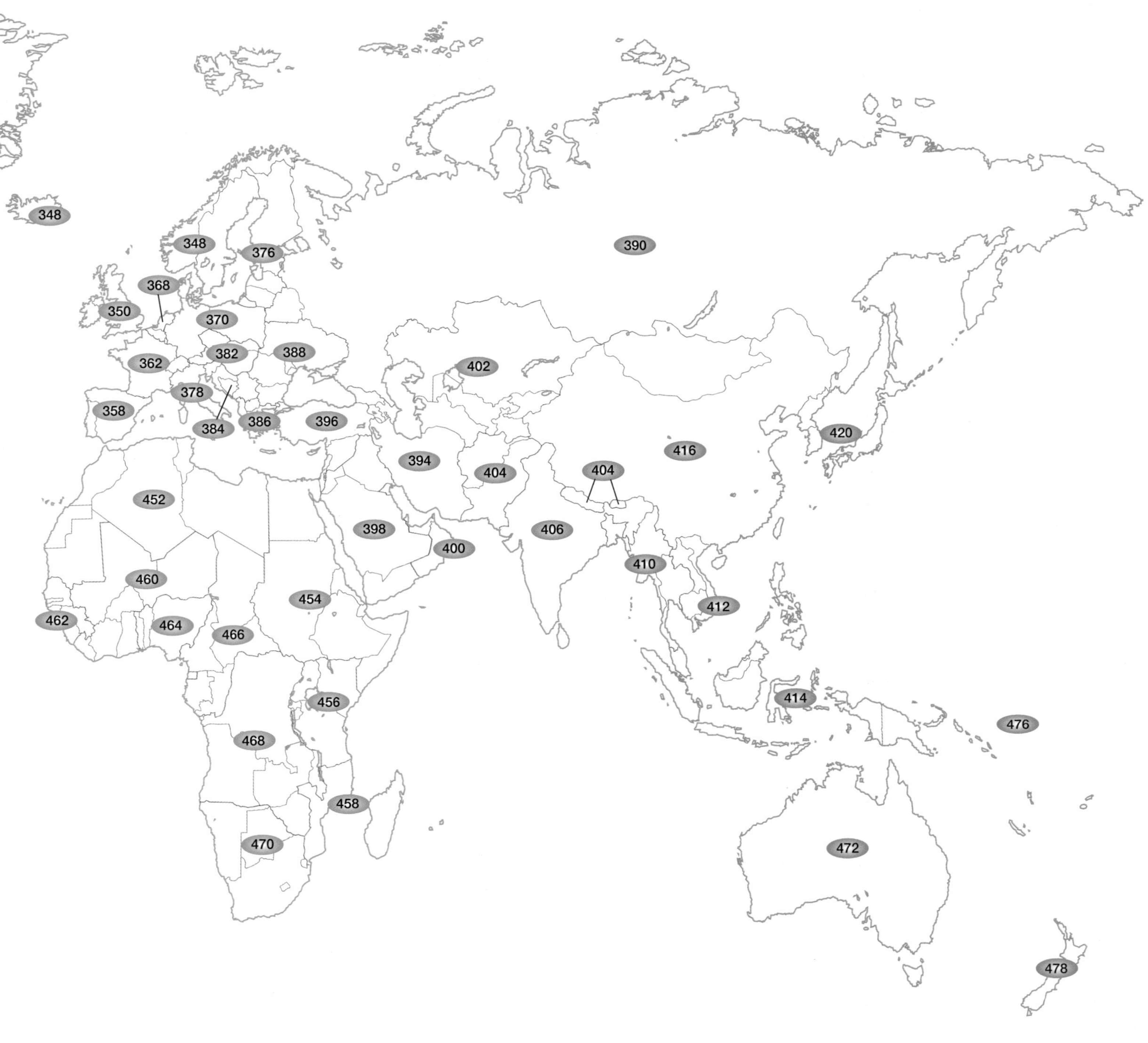
348
348
376
390
368
350
370
382
388
362
402
378
358
384
386
396
420
416
394
404
404
452
398
406
400
410
460
454
412
462
464
466
414
456
476
468
458
470
472
478

SCANDINAVIA

ICELAND

Iceland is an island-republic just south of the Arctic Circle in the North Atlantic. The greater part of Iceland has a volcanic landscape with hot springs, geysers and volcanoes, some active. Much of the country is tundra and treeless. The south and centre are covered by glacial icefields, the largest of which contains the country's highest peak.
Highest point: Hvannadalshnúkur 2119 m (6950 ft).
Climate: The cool temperate climate is warmed by the Gulf Stream, which keeps Iceland milder than most places at the same latitude.

The 63-member Parliament (Althing) is elected under a system of proportional representation by universal adult suffrage for a four-year term and meets as a 20-member Upper House and a 43-member Lower House. The President, who is also directly elected for four years, appoints a Prime Minister who commands a majority in the Althing. The PM, in turn, appoints a Cabinet.
Largest parties: (1995 election) (conservative) Independence Party (IP) 25 seats, (centre) Progressive Party (PP) 42, (socialist) People's Alliance (PA) 9, Social Democratic Party (SDP) 7, (centre-left) People's Movement (PM) 4, Women's Alliance (WA) 3.
President: (since 1996) Olafur Grimsson (PA).
Prime Minister: (since 1993) David Oddsson (IP; IP-PP government).

Official name: Lydhveldidh Island (The Republic of Iceland).
Area: 102,819 km² (39,699 sq mi).
Population: 269,000 (1995 est.).
Doubling time: 68 years. **Adult life expectancy:** male 76.8 years, female 80.7 years. **Birth rate:** 0.67 times world average. **Death rate:** 0.7 times world average. **Urban population:** 91%. **Capital:** Reykjavik 154,000 urban area (city 103,000; Kópavogur 17,000; Hafnarfjördhur 17,000; 1994 est.). **Other main centres:** Akureyri 15,000, Keflavik 8000 (1994 est.; inc. suburbs).
Language: Icelandic 99% (official).
Adult literacy: almost 100%.
Religion: Evangelical Lutheran 88%, other Protestant Churches 7%, non-religious 2%.

The fishing industry provides the majority of Iceland's exports. Hydroelectric power is used to smelt aluminium, while geothermal power warms domestic buildings and extensive greenhouses. Ample grazing land makes Iceland self-sufficient in meat and dairy products.
Currency: Icelandic Krona.

1918 Iceland gained independence although still linked to Denmark by a shared monarchy. **1944** Declaration of a republic. **1945** Icelandic independence recognized by Denmark. **1950s and 1976** 'Cod War' fishing dispute with the UK.

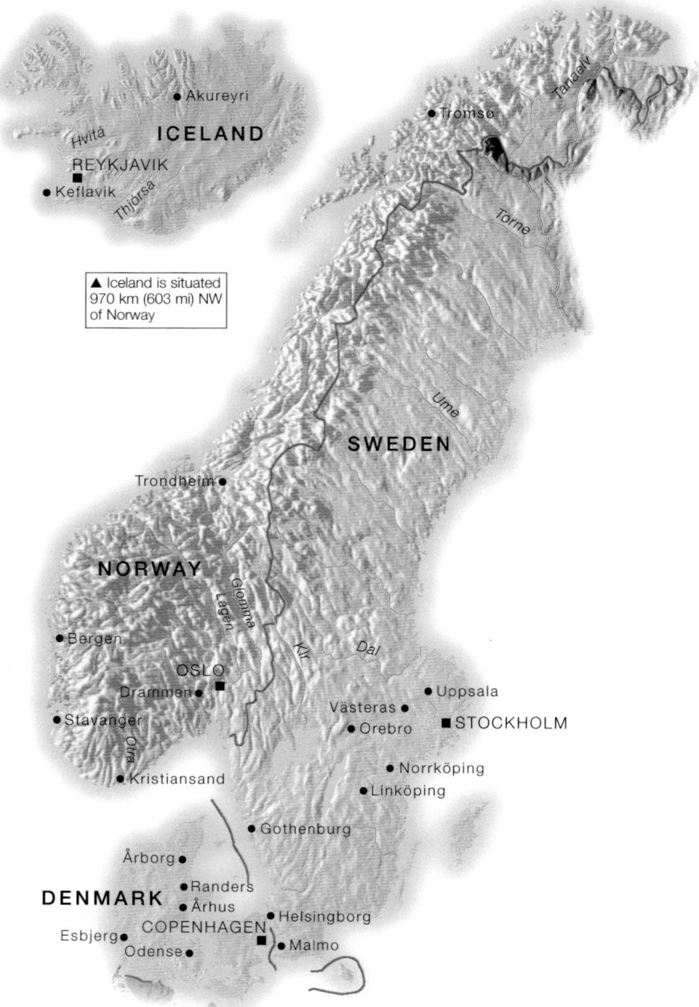

▲ Iceland is situated 970 km (603 mi) NW of Norway

DENMARK

The smallest of the Scandinavian countries, Denmark is a kingdom consisting of a peninsula (Jutland) to the north of Germany and an archipelago of over 400 islands, of which 97 are inhabited, lying to the east of Jutland. The country is a lowland of glacial moraine; only Bornholm, in the Baltic, has ancient hard surface rocks. The highest point is on the Jutland peninsula, which occupies about two-thirds of Denmark. The largest islands are Zealand (Sjaelland), Fyn and Lolland.
Highest point: Yding Skovhøj 173 m (568 ft).
Climate: The climate is temperate and moist, with mild summers and cold winters. Bornholm, in the east, is more extreme.

Denmark is a constitutional monarchy. The 179-member Parliament (Folketing) is elected under a system of proportional representation by universal adult suffrage for a four-year term. Two members are elected from both of the autonomous dependencies (Greenland and the Faeroe Islands). The monarch appoints a Prime Minister who commands a majority in the Folketing. The PM, in turn, appoints a State Council (Cabinet), which is responsible to the Storting.
Largest parties: (1994 election) Social Democratic Party (SDP) 62 seats, Liberal Party (Venstre) 42, (right-wing) Conservative People's Party (KF) 27, Socialist People's Party (SFP) 13, (anti-tax, extreme-right) Progress Party (FP) 11, Social Liberal Party (SV) 8, (extreme-left) Unity List 6, Centre Democrats (CD) 5, others 5.
Queen: (since 1972) Margrethe II.
Prime Minister: (since 1993) Poul Nyrup Rasmussen (SDP; SDP-SV government).

Denmark has a high standard of living, but few natural resources. Agriculture is organized on a co-operative basis, and produces cheese and other dairy products, bacon and beef (all mainly for export to Germany and the UK). Over one-sixth of the labour force is involved in manufacturing, with iron and metal working, food processing, brewing, engineering and chemicals as the major industries. Petroleum and natural gas from the North Sea have reduced the costly burden of fuel imports. **Currency:** Danish Krone.

1914–18 Neutral during World War I. **1917** Danish West Indies sold to the USA. **1918** Iceland gained independence although still linked to Denmark. **1940** Invaded by Nazi Germany. **1940–45** Under German occupation. **1945** Icelandic independence recognized. **1948** Home rule granted to the Faeroes. **1973** Denmark joined the EC/EU. **1989** Home rule granted to Greenland.

Dependent Territories
Faeroe Islands (see this page) and Greenland (see p. 425).

Official name: Kongeriget Danmark (Kingdom of Denmark).
Area: 43,094 km² (16,639 sq mi) – 'metropolitan' Denmark, excluding dependencies.
Population: 5,220,000 (1995 est.).
Doubling time: pop. almost stable.
Adult life expectancy: male 72.5 years, female 77.8 years.
Birth rate: 0.54 times world average.
Death rate: 1.27 times world average. **Urban population:** 85%.
Capital: Copenhagen (København) 1,353,000 urban area (city 471,000; Frederiksberg 88,000; 1995 est.).
Other main centres: Århus 277,000 urban area (city 204,000), Odense 183,000 (city 141,000), Ålborg 159,000 (city 115,000), Frederiksberg *see Copenhagen*, Esbjerg 83,000, Randers 61,000, Kolding 60,000 (1995 est.; inc. suburbs).
Language: Danish 97% (official).
Adult literacy: almost 100%.
Religion: Evangelical Lutheran 88%, other Christian Churches 2%, non-religious 9%.

FAEROE ISLANDS

Official names and status: Færøerne (in Danish) or Føroyar (in Faeroese) (Faeroe Islands); a Danish dependency with internal self-government.
Area: 1399 km² (540 sq mi).
Population: 43,400 (1995 est.).
Capital: Tórshavn 15,300 (1995 est.).
Geography: Lying between Scotland and Iceland, the Faeroes comprise 17 inhabited islands, one uninhabited island and many rocky islets, all with high cliffs.
Economy: Farming is dominated by sheep-rearing. Fishing, the main industry, has diminished owing to declining stocks. The Faeroese economy is in crisis and depends heavily upon considerable subsidies from Denmark. The islands, although part of Denmark for many purposes, actually remain outside the EU.

■ ICELAND'S LOW POPULATION MEANS THAT MANY PEOPLE HAVE A SECOND PART-TIME JOB ■

NORWAY

Norway is a kingdom occupying the western half of the Scandinavian peninsula. Norway's coastline is characterized by fjords, a series of long narrow inlets formed by glacial action. The greater part of Norway comprises highlands of hard rock. The principal lowlands are along the Skagerrak coast and around Olsofjord and Trondheimfjord. Svalbard is a bleak archipelago in the Arctic. Jan Mayen is an active volcano between Norway and Greenland.
Highest point: Galdhopiggen 2469 m (8098 ft).
Climate: Norway's temperate climate is the result of the warming Gulf Stream. Summers are remarkably mild for the latitude, while winters are long and very cold. Precipitation is heavy: over 2000 mm (80 in) in the west, with marked rain shadows inland.

Norway is a constitutional monarchy. The 165-member Parliament (Storting) is elected under a system of proportional representation by universal adult suffrage for a four-year term. In order to legislate, the Storting divides itself into two houses: the Lagting (containing one-quarter of the members) and the Odelsting (containing the remaining three-quarters of the members). The King appoints a Prime Minister who commands a majority in the Storting. The PM, in turn, appoints a Council of Ministers who are responsible to the Storting.
Largest parties: (1993 election) (social democratic) Labour Party (DnA) 63 seats, (centre-right) Centre Party (SP) 32, (right-wing) Conservative Party (H) 28, (liberal) Christian People's Party (KrF) 13, Socialist Left Party (SVP) 13, (conservative) Progress Party (FP) 10, others 2.
King: (since 1991) Harald V.
Prime Minister: (since 1996) Thorbjoern Jagland (DnA; minority government).

Official name: Kongeriket Norge (Kingdom of Norway).
Area: 323,878 km² (125,050 sq mi) or 386,958 km² (149,469 sq mi) if the Arctic island territories of Svalbard (formerly Spitsbergen) and Jan Mayen are included.
Population: 4,360,000 (1995 est.).
Doubling time: pop. almost stable.
Adult life expectancy: male 74.2 years, female 80.3 years.
Birth rate: 0.55 times world average.
Death rate: 1.17 times world average. **Urban population:** 75%.
Capital: Oslo 578,000 urban area (city 483,000; Baerum 96,000; 1995 est.). **Other main centres:** Bergen 222,000, Trondheim 143,000, Stavanger 103,000, Baerum *see Oslo*, Kristiansand 66,000, Drammen 52,000, Tromsø 51,000 (1995 est.; inc. suburbs).
Language: Norwegian 98% (official). There are two official forms of Norwegian: Bokmaal (78%) and Nynorsk (or Landsmaal; 20%), Lappish under 2%.
Adult literacy: almost 100%.
Religion: Evangelical Lutheran (Church of Norway) 88%, other Protestant Churches 5%, small Roman Catholic minority, non-religious 3%.

Norway enjoys a high standard of living. Farming is heavily subsidized: only a small proportion of the land can be cultivated, chiefly for fodder crops for dairying cattle. Timber is a major export and over 50% of the country is forested. Fishing is an important foreign-currency earner; fish farming (which has been encouraged by government schemes) is taking the place of whaling and deep-sea fishing. Manufacturing has traditionally been concerned with processing fish, timber and iron ore, but is now dominated by petrochemicals and allied industries, based upon large reserves of petroleum and natural gas in Norway's sector of the North Sea. Petroleum and natural gas supply over 45% of Norway's export earnings. The growth of industries such as electrical engineering has been helped by cheap hydroelectric power. **Currency:** Norwegian Krone.

1900 Norway had been under the rule of the kings of Sweden (although allowed a considerable degree of independence) since 1815. **1905** Nationalist pressure in Norway led to the end of the union with Sweden; Prince Carl of Denmark elected King of Norway. **1914–18** Neutral during World War I. **1940** Invaded by Nazi Germany; a puppet government set up under Vidkun Quisling. **1940–45** Under German occupation. **1972** In a referendum, Norway rejected membership of the Common Market. **1994** Norway again rejected EU membership.

Dependent Territories

Bouvet Island (see p. 480), Peter I Island (see p. 480) and Queen Maud Land (see p. 480).

■ *The waterfront at Bergen – an historic fishing port which is now a centre for Norway's booming North Sea oil industry*

SWEDEN

Sweden is a kingdom occupying the eastern half of the Scandinavian peninsula. The mountains of Norrland, in the north of Sweden along the border with Norway, cover two-thirds of the country. A plain adjoins the Gulf of Bothnia. Svealand, in the centre, is characterized by many lakes, including the three 'Great Lakes' (Vänern, Vättern and Mälaren). In the south are the low Smaland highlands and the fertile lowland of Skane. The islands of Öland and Gotland lie in the Baltic Sea.
Highest point: Kebnekaise 2111 m (6926 ft).
Climate: Sweden experiences long, cold winters and warm summers, although winters in the north (where snow remains on the ground for up to eight months) are more severe than in the south, where Skane has a relatively mild winter.

Sweden is a constitutional monarchy in which the sovereign is a ceremonial head of state without any executive power. The 349-member Parliament (Riksdag) is elected under a system of proportional representation by universal adult suffrage for a three-year term. The Speaker of the Riksdag appoints a Prime Minister who commands a majority in the Riksdag. The PM, in turn, appoints a Cabinet of Ministers who are responsible to the Riksdag.
Largest parties: (1994 election) (social democratic) Labour Party (SDP) 161 seats, (conservative) Moderate Coalition Party (MS) 80, (centre-right) Centre Party (CP) 27, Liberal People's Party (FP) 26, (former Communist) Left Party (VP) 22, Greens 18, (right-wing) Christian Democratic Party (KdS) 15.
King: (since 1973) Carl XVI Gustaf.
Prime Minister: (since 1996) Goran Persson (SDP).

Sweden's high standard of living is based upon its neutrality in the two World Wars, its cheap and plentiful hydroelectric power and its mineral riches. The country has about 15% of the world's uranium deposits and large reserves of iron ore that provide the basis of domestic heavy industry and important exports to other western European countries. Agriculture is concentrated in the south, along with the bulk of the population. Principal products include dairy produce, meat, barley, sugar beet and potatoes. Vast coniferous forests supply the paper, board and furniture industries, and produce large timber exports. Heavy industries include motor vehicles (Saab and Volvo), aerospace and engineering (although the once large shipbuilding industry has now ceased to exist). Rising labour costs, inflation and labour unrest have added to growing economic problems and Sweden was badly hit by recession in the 1990s. As a result, the state has reduced its activities and implemented a privatization programme.
Currency: Krona.

Official name: Konungariket Sverige (Kingdom of Sweden).
Area: 449,964 km² (173,732 sq mi).
Population: 8,830,000 (1995 est.).
Doubling time: pop. almost stable.
Adult life expectancy: male 75.1 years, female 80.6 years.
Birth rate: 0.51 times world average.
Death rate: 1.13 times world average. **Urban population:** 83%.
Capital: Stockholm 1,539,000 urban area (city 704,000; Södertälje 82,000; 1994 est.). **Other main centres:** Gothenburg (Göteborg) 783,000 urban area (city 445,000), Malmö 489,000 (city 243,000; Lund 96,000), Uppsala 181,000, Linköping 130,000, Norrköping 123,000; Västerås 123,000, Örebro 119,000, Jönköping 115,000, Helsingborg 113,000, Borås 102,000, Umeå 99,000, Lund *see Malmö*, Sundsvall 95,000 (1994 est.; inc. suburbs).
Language: Swedish 90% (official), Finnish 2%, Lappish, various groups of recent immigrants. **Adult literacy:** almost 100%.
Religion: Lutheran (Church of Sweden) 87% nominal (practising, including occasional attendance, 56%), Roman Catholic 2%, non-religious over 5%.

1905 Nationalist pressure in Norway led to the end of union with Sweden. **1914–18** Neutral during World War I. **1932–76** Comprehensive welfare state established under successive SDP governments. **1939–45** Neutral during World War II, although German troops passed through Swedish territory. **After 1945** Neutral Sweden assumed a moral leadership on many world issues during the Cold War. **1986** Unclaimed assassination of PM Olof Palme. **1990s** Sweden dismantled many aspects of the comprehensive welfare state due to economic necessity. **1995** EU membership.

UNITED KINGDOM AND IRELAND

IRELAND

The Republic of Ireland consists of all but the north-east corner of the island of Ireland. Central Ireland is a lowland crossed by slight ridges and broad valleys, bogs and large lakes, including Loughs Derg and Ree. Except on the east coast north of Dublin, the lowland is surrounded by coastal hills and mountains, including the Wicklow Mountains, the Ox Mountains and the hills of Connemara and Donegal. The highest uplands are the Macgillicuddy's Reeks in Kerry (the south-west). The rugged Atlantic coast is highly indented.
Highest point: Carrauntuohill 1041 m (3414 ft).
Climate: Ireland has a mild temperate climate. Rainfall is high ranging from over 2500 mm (100 in) in the west and south-west to 750 mm (30 in) in the east.

The Seanad (Senate) comprises 60 members: 11 nominated by the Taoiseach (Prime Minister), the remainder indirectly elected for a five-year term to represent vocational and special interests. The Dáil (House) comprises 166 members elected for five years by universal adult suffrage under a system of proportional representation. The President (whose role is largely ceremonial) is directly elected for a seven-year term. The Taoiseach and a Cabinet of Ministers are appointed by the President upon the nomination of Dáil, to which they are responsible.
Largest parties: (1997 election) (centre-right) Fianna Fáil (FF) 77 seats, (centre) Fine Gael (FG) 54, (social democratic) Labour Party (Lab) 17, (conservative) Progressive Democrats (PD) 4, (Socialist) Democratic Left (DL) 4, Greens 2, others 8.
President: (since 1990) Mary Robinson (non-party).
Taoiseach/Prime Minister: (since 1997) Bertie Ahern (FF; FF-PD minority coalition government).

Manufactured goods (in particular machinery, metals and engineering, electronic and chemical products) now account for over one-half of Ireland's exports. Agriculture, the traditional mainstay of the economy, concentrates upon the production of livestock, meat and dairy products. Food processing and brewing are major industries. Natural resources include lead-zinc, offshore petroleum and natural gas, and HEP sites. Ireland has suffered high rates of unemployment and emigration, but in the 1990s the economy has boomed and many 'high tech' industries have been established.
Currency: Punt.

1916 Unsuccessful Easter Rising in Dublin against British rule. **1918** Irish nationalist MPs formed a provisional government in Dublin. **1919–21** British administration crumbled (except in the north-east, now Northern Ireland); Ireland collapsed into violence. **1921** Signing of Anglo-Irish Treaty which allowed for an (independent) Irish Free State in the south and Northern Ireland (still part of the UK) in the north-east. **1922** Proclamation of Irish Free State was not accepted by Eamon de Valera and his republicans; civil war broke out between the provisional government (led by Arthur Griffith and Michael Collins) and the republicans. **1923** Collins assassinated; end of civil war. **1937** Free State became the Republic of Ireland. **1939–45** Neutral during World War II. **1949** Ireland left the Commonwealth. **1968–94** The 'Troubles' in Northern Ireland: relations with the UK often tense. **1973** Joined the EC (now EU). **1985** Anglo-Irish Agreement provided for participation in some Northern Irish matters. **1996** Northern Irish peace process stumbled as terrorist cease-fire ended.

Official name: Poblacht na h'Éireann (The Republic of Ireland).
Area: 70,285 km² (27,137 sq mi).
Population: 3,590,000 (1995 est.).
Doubling time: not applicable; slow pop. growth. **Adult life expectancy:** male 71 years, female 76.7 years.
Birth rate: 0.56 times world average.
Death rate: 0.96 times world average. **Urban population:** 57%.
Capital: Dublin 1,025,000 urban area (city 478,000; Dun Laoghaire-Rathdown 185,000; 1991 census).
Other main centres: Cork 175,000 urban area (city 127,000), Limerick 77,000 (city 52,000), Galway 51,000, Waterford 40,000, Dundalk 31,000 (town 27,000), Bray 26,000, Drogheda 25,000, Sligo 18,000 (1991 census; inc. suburbs).
Language: Irish 5% as a first language (official), English 95% as a first language. **Adult literacy:** almost 100%.
Religion: Roman Catholic 92%, Church of Ireland (Anglican) 2%, non-religious 5%.

Shetland
Orkney
Outer Hebrides
SCOTLAND
Aberdeen
Dundee
Tay
Forth
Glasgow
Edinburgh
NORTHERN IRELAND
Belfast
Isle of Man
Newcastle-upon-Tyne
Sunderland
Middlesbrough
ENGLAND
Dundalk
REPUBLIC OF IRELAND
Galway
DUBLIN
Limerick
Waterford
Cork
Blackpool
Bradford
Leeds
Hull
Humber
Preston
Barnsley
Liverpool
Birkenhead
Manchester
Sheffield
Trent
Stoke-on-Trent
Derby
Nottingham
Wolverhampton
Birmingham
Leicester
Coventry
Ouse
Norwich
Northampton
Wye
Severn
Luton
WALES
Thames
LONDON
Southend
Swansea
Cardiff
Bristol
Reading
Rochester
Aldershot
Southampton
Brighton
Bournemouth
Portsmouth
Plymouth
Isle of Wight
Alderney
Guernsey
Jersey

■ *Shrimp traps and fishing nets at Roundstone Harbour. Ireland has a small but important fishing industry, with the main ports on the west coast*

UNITED KINGDOM

The UK comprises the island of Great Britain and the north-east part of Ireland plus over 4000 other islands. Lowland Britain occupies the south, east and centre of England. Clay valleys and river basins, including those of the Thames and the Trent, separate relatively low ridges of hills including the limestone Cotswolds and Cleveland Hills, and the chalk North and South Downs and the Yorkshire and Lincolnshire Wolds. In the east, low-lying Fenland is largely reclaimed marshland. The flat landscape of East Anglia is covered by glacial soils. The north-west coastal plain of Lancashire and Cheshire is the only other major lowland in England. A peninsula in the south-west (Devon and Cornwall) contains granitic uplands including Dartmoor and Exmoor. The limestone Pennines form a moorland backbone running through northern England. The Lake District (Cumbria) is a mountainous dome containing England's highest point, Scafell Pike.

Wales is a highland block, formed by a series of plateaux above which rise the Brecon Beacons in the south, Cader Idris and Berwyn range in the centre and Snowdonia in the north.

In Scotland, the Highlands in the north and the Southern Uplands are separated by the rift valley of the Central Lowlands, where the majority of Scotland's population, agriculture and industry are to be found. The Highlands are divided by the Great Glen in which lies Loch Ness. Although Ben Nevis is the highest point, the most prominent range of the Highlands is the Cairngorm Mountains. The Southern Uplands lie below about 850 m (2800 ft). Scottish lowlands include Buchan in the north-east, Caithness in the north and a coastal plain around the Moray Firth. To the west of Scotland are the many islands of the Inner and Outer Hebrides (the latter also being known as the Western Isles), while to the north are the Orkney and Shetland islands.

Uplands in Northern Ireland include the Sperrin Mountains in the north-west, the uplands of County Antrim and the Mourne Mountains, rising to Slieve Donard, in the south-east. Lough Neagh, at the centre of Northern Ireland, is the UK's largest lake.

Highest point: Ben Nevis 1343 m (4406 ft).
Climate: The temperate climate of the UK is warmed by the North Atlantic Drift. There is considerable local variety, particularly in rainfall totals, which range from just over 500 mm (20 in) in the south-east of England to 5000 mm (200 in) in north-west Scotland.

The UK is a constitutional monarchy without a written constitution. The House of Lords (the upper non-elected House of Parliament) comprises over 750 hereditary peers and peeresses, over 20 Lords of Appeal (non-hereditary peers), nearly 400 life peers, and two archbishops and 24 bishops of the Church of England. The House of Commons (the lower house of Parliament) comprises 659 members elected for five years. The sovereign appoints a Prime Minister who commands a majority in the Commons. The PM, in turn, selects a Cabinet and other Ministers.

Largest parties: (Commons 1997 election) (social democratic) Labour Party (Lab) 418 seats, (centre-right) Conservative Party (Con) 165, (centre-left) Liberal Democratic Party (LDP) 46, (right-wing Northern Irish) Ulster Unionists 13 including Ulster Unionist Party (UU) 10 and (ultra-Protestant) Democratic Unionist Party (DUP) 2, (separatist) Scottish National Party (SNP) 6, (Welsh Nationalist) Plaid Cymru 4, (Northern Irish republican) Social Democratic and Labour Party (SDLP) 3, (ultra-republican Northern Irish separatist) Sinn Fein 2, others 2.
Queen: (since 1952) Elizabeth II.
Prime Minister: (since 1997) Tony Blair (Lab).

Nearly one-fifth of the British labour force is involved in manufacturing. The principal industries include iron and steel, motor vehicles, electronics and electrical engineering, textiles and clothing, and consumer goods. British industry relies heavily upon imports of raw materials. The UK is self-sufficient in petroleum (from the North Sea) and has major reserves of natural gas. The coal industry declined as seams became uneconomic. As Britain is a major trading nation, London is one of the world's leading banking, financial and insurance centres, and the 'invisible earnings' from these services make an important contribution to exports. Tourism is another major foreign-currency earner. Agriculture involves about 1% of the labour force and is principally concerned with raising sheep and cattle. Arable farming is widespread in the east, where the main crops are barley, wheat, potatoes and sugar beet. Since 1980 most nationalized industries have been privatized.

Currency: Pound sterling.

1908–16 Reforming Liberal government of Herbert Asquith. **1914–18** World War I. **1916** Easter rising against British rule in Ireland. **1922** Partition of Ireland: Northern Ireland remained part of the UK. **1926** The General Strike. **1930s** Mass unemployment during the Depression. **1931** Statute of Westminster confirmed the independence of Canada, Australia, New Zealand, South Africa and Ireland. **1939–45** World War II. **1940–41** Battle of Britain: Britain, led by Winston Churchill, stood alone against an apparently invincible Nazi Germany. **1945–51** Labour government under Clement Atlee established the 'welfare state'. **1947** Independence of India and Pakistan: the beginning of the end of the British Empire. **1956** Suez Crisis: Anglo-French intervention in Egypt. **1960–70s** Independence granted to most British Asian, African and Caribbean colonies. **1968–94** Conflict in Northern Ireland: terrorist violence of the (republican nationalist) IRA and Loyalist illegal organizations; British troops stationed in Ulster to keep the peace. **1973** Membership of the EEC (now EU). **1979–90** Major restructuring of the economy and welfare state under the Conservative premiership of Margaret Thatcher. **1982** Falklands War. **1991** Participation in the US-led coalition against Iraq in the Gulf War. **1996** End of IRA truce.

Dependencies
See following UK section.

Official name: The United Kingdom of Great Britain and Northern Ireland.
Area: 244,088 km^2 (94,242 sq mi).
Population: 58,590,000 (1995 est.).
Doubling time: not applicable; slow pop. growth. **Adult life expectancy:** male 74.4 years, female 79.7 years.
Birth rate: 0.52 times world average.
Death rate: 1.22 times world average.
Urban population: 89%.
Capital: London 7,651,000 urban area (City of London 4000; former county of Greater London 6,935,000; Watford 113,000; 1991 census).
Other main centres: Birmingham 2,296,000 urban area (Birmingham subdivision 966,000; Wolverhampton 258,000; Walsall 175,000; West Bromwich 146,000; Smethwick-Oldbury 145,000; Sutton Coldfield 106,000), Manchester 2,277,000 (Manchester subdiv. 403,000; Bolton 139,000; Stockport 133,000; Oldham 104,000), Leeds 1,446,000 (Leeds subdiv. 424,000; Bradford 289,000; Huddersfield 144,000), Glasgow 940,000 (Glasgow locality 663,000), Newcastle 886,000 (Newcastle subdiv. 189,000), Liverpool 838,000 (Liverpool subdiv. 482,000; St Helens 106,000), Sheffield 633,000 (Sheffield subdiv. 432,000; Rotherham 121,000), Nottingham 614,000 (Nottingham subdiv. 270,000), Bristol 523,000 (Bristol subdiv. 408,000), Brighton 438,000 (Brighton subdiv. 123,000), Belfast 434,000 (Belfast city 279,000), Edinburgh 422,000 (Edinburgh locality 402,000), Leicester 417,000 (Leicester subdiv. 319,000), Portsmouth 409,000 (Portsmouth subdiv. 175,000), Middlesbrough 370,000 (Middlesbrough subdiv. 147,000), Stoke-on-Trent 368,000 (Stoke-on-Trent subdiv. 267,000), Bournemouth 358,000 (Bournemouth subdiv. 156,000; Poole 139,000), Reading 336,000 (Reading subdiv. 214,000), Coventry 331,000 (Coventry subdiv. 299,000), Hull 311,000 (Kingston-upon-Hull 311,000), Cardiff 308,000 (Cardiff subdiv. 272,000), Bradford *see Leeds*, Southampton 277,000 (Southampton subdiv. 210,000), Swansea 273,000 (Swansea subdiv. 171,000), Birkenhead 270,000 (Birkenhead subdiv. 93,000), Southend 267,000 (Southend subdiv. 156,000), Blackpool 261,000 (Blackpool subdiv. 146,000), Wolverhampton *see Birmingham*, Preston 256,000 (Preston subdiv. 178,000), Plymouth 245,000, Aldershot 231,000 (Aldershot subdiv. 51,000), Derby 224,000, Rochester 222,000 (Rochester subdiv. 24,000), Luton 221,000 (Luton subdiv. 172,000), Barnsley 221,000 (Barnsley subdiv. 72,000), Aberdeen 201,000 (Aberdeen locality 190,000), Sunderland 189,000 (Sunderland subdiv. 183,000), Norwich 185,000 (Norwich subdiv. 171,000), Northampton 183,000 (Northampton subdiv. 179,000), Walsall *see Birmingham*, (Wigan 174,000 (Wigan subdiv. 86,000), Dundee 159,000, Milton Keynes 156,000 (Milton Keynes subdiv. 44,000), Mansfield 155,000 (Mansfield subdiv. 72,000), Warrington 153,000 (Warrington subdiv. 83,000), Burnley 150,000 (Burnley subdiv. 75,000) (1991 census; inc. suburbs).
Language: English 97% (official), various languages of the Indian subcontinent nearly 2%, Welsh 1%.
Adult literacy: almost 100%.
Religion: Church of England 57% nominal or 3% practising, Roman Catholic 13%, Methodist 2%, Sunni and Shia Islam 2%, Sikhs 1%, Baptists 1%, non-religious and atheist 10%; only 15% of the population participates in any religion.

■ *Architect Richard Rogers' 1986 Lloyds of London building is one of the new hi-tech buildings to grace London's skyline*

PLACES OF INTEREST

Tourism makes a large contribution to Britain's invisible earnings, but the majority of foreign visitors (nearly 25 million a year) tread a well-worn route that includes London, Canterbury, Oxford and Stratford-upon-Avon. Large numbers of foreign-language students learning English boost the revenue earned from tourism. American, French and German visitors account for over one-third of those visiting the UK. Other popular tourist destinations include Alton Towers; Blackpool Tower and Pleasure Beach; Brighton Pavilion and the Lanes; The British Museum, Madame Tussaud's, The National Gallery, The Natural History Museum and the Science Museum in London; Chessington World of Adventures; Exmoor; the Lake District; Legoland; Windsor Castle and York Minster.

World Heritage sites include: Blenheim Palace; Canterbury Cathedral; St Augustine's Abbey and St Martin's Church; City of Bath; Durham Cathedral and Castle; the castles and town walls of King Edward in Gwynedd; Hadrian's Wall; Ironbridge Gorge; the Giant's Causeway and Causeway coast; old and new towns of Edinburgh; Palace of Westminster, Westminster Abbey and St Margaret's Church, London; Stonehenge; Avebury and associated sites; Studley Royal Park, including the ruins of Fountains Abbey; The Tower of London.

COUNTRIES OF THE UNITED KINGDOM

	Area km²	Area sq mi	% of area of UK*	Population (mid-1995 est.)	% of UK pop.	Capital City
England	130,439	50,363	53.4	48,903,000	83.4	London
Northern Ireland	14,122	5,453	5.8	1,649,000	2.8	Belfast
Scotland	78,759	30,409	32.3	5,137,000	8.8	Edinburgh
Wales (Cymru)	20,768	8,019	8.5	2,917,000	5.0	Cardiff (Caerdydd)

*does not add up to 100% due to rounding

Edinburgh, the Scottish capital, attracts most of its visitors during the annual International Festival in August and September.

The Giant's Causeway, on Antrim's Atlantic coast, is Northern Ireland's most popular tourist attraction.

! The narrowest house is at 50 Stuart Street, Millport on the island of Great Cumbrae in North Ayrshire. The house frontage is 119 cm (47 in).

Ben Nevis

! The Humber Estuary Bridge, linking E. Yorkshire and Lincolnshire, is the world's second-longest cable-suspension bridge with a length of 1410 m (4626 ft).

Manchester's Metrolink tram is a symbol of the city's urban regeneration. The city is to host the 2002 Commonwealth Games.

Snowdonia is the highest area in Wales, attracting scores of climbers, hill-walkers and sightseers.

! The smallest commercial brewery is at the Tynllidiart Arms, Capel Bangor in Ceredigion, Wales. Its capacity is 41 litres (9 gal) per brew.

! The fountain at Whitley Court in Worcestershire is the largest in Europe.

! The Ashmolean Museum in Oxford, founded 1679–83, is the world's oldest museum.

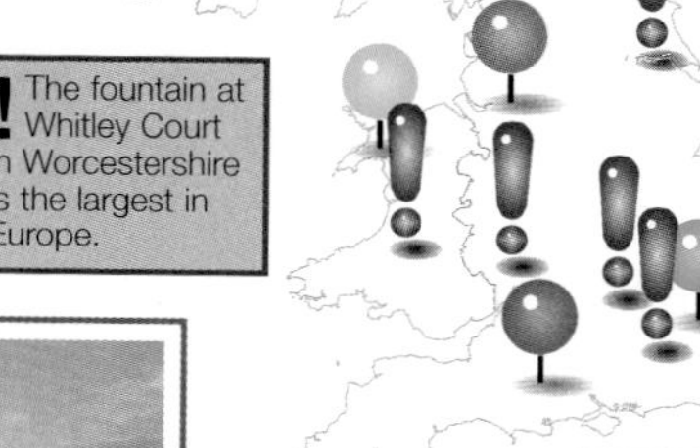

Stonehenge, on Salisbury Plain, is one of the most important ancient sites in Europe. It has been beset with controversy concerning the possible rerouting of nearby major roads.

! Windsor Castle in Windsor is the world's largest inhabited castle, measuring 576 x 164 m (1890 x 540 ft).

The National Gallery and Trafalgar Square, with its famous fountain, in the centre of London.

KINGS AND QUEENS OF ENGLAND, GREAT BRITAIN (AFTER 1707) AND UNITED KINGDOM (AFTER 1801)

1066–87	William I
1087–1100	William II
1100–35	Henry I
1135–41	Stephen
1141	Matilda
1141–54	Stephen (restored)
1154–89	Henry II
1189–99	Richard I
1199–1216	John
1216–72	Henry III
1272–1307	Edward I
1307–27	Edward II
1327–77	Edward III
1377–99	Richard II
1399–1413	Henry IV
1413–22	Henry V
1422–61	Henry VI
1461–70	Edward IV
1470–71	Henry VI (restored)
1471–83	Edward IV (restored)
1483	Edward V
1483–85	Richard III
1485–1509	Henry VII
1509–47	Henry VIII
1547–53	Edward VI
1553	Jane
1553–58	Mary I
1558–1603	Elizabeth I
1603–25	James I (VI of Scotland)
1625–49	Charles I
1649–58	Lord Protector Oliver Cromwell
1658–59	Lord Protector Richard Cromwell
1660–85	Charles II
1685–88	James II (VII of Scotland)
1688–89	Interregnum
1689–1702	William III co-ruled with
1689–94	Mary II
1702–14	Anne
1714–27	George I
1727–60	George II
1760–1820	George III
1820–30	George IV
1830–37	William IV
1837–1901	Victoria
1901–10	Edward VII
1910–36	George V
1936	Edward VIII
1936–52	George VI
1952–	Elizabeth II

SCOTLAND'S MONARCHS (FROM 1306)

1306–29	Robert I
1329–32	David II
1332–38	Edward
1338–71	David II (restored)
1371–90	Robert II
1390–1406	Robert III
1406–37	James I
1437–60	James II
1460–88	James III
1488–1513	James IV
1513–42	James V
1542–67	Mary
1567–1625	James VI

TELEVISION AND RADIO

No. of TVs: 20,000,000 (2.9 persons per TV)
No. of radio receivers: 65,400,000 (0.9 persons per radio)

The BBC (British Broadcasting Corporation) is a public corporation. It runs five national radio services, national regional services in Wales, Scotland and Northern Ireland, and over 35 local BBC radio stations. In addition, there are four national and 80 local independent radio stations.

There are five national terrestrial television channels – BBC1, BBC2, ITV (Channel 3; an independent commercial station made up of regional programme contractors), Channel 4 (which is replaced by S4C in Wales) and Channel 5, which began broadcasting in 1997. In addition, British Sky Broadcasting and other satellite channels offer sport, film, music and news. Television is one of the United Kingdom's most popular pastimes; on average the British spend more than three hours every day watching television.

The structure of British televisual media has changed radically in the past few years. With the birth of satellite TV in the late 1980s, a whole new range of channels have become available. Cable TV, which has grown enormously in the 1990s, has also increased the viewer's choice, with a greater emphasis on regional and speciality channels. Many of these cable and satellite channels are subscription-based, and their content includes a variety of US imports and major UK and international sporting events. Digital TV channels are set to expand the horizon of television in the coming years.

CINEMA

No. of cinemas: 1780

British cinema is undergoing a global renaissance. Recent international successes, such as *Four Weddings and a Funeral* and *Secrets and Lies*, have demonstrated a new regard for British films, whilst the wealth of talent behind and in front of the camera is shown in such hits as the multi-Oscar-winning *The English Patient*, US-funded, but with British film expertise behind it. Further confirmation of the UK's new film industry status came when George Lucas announced that one of the largest film projects in history, his three prequels to the *Star Wars* trilogy, would be filmed in the UK. British film funding has also increased, with the BBC, Channel 4 and the National Lottery (via the Arts Council) amongst the biggest benefactors.

MAGAZINES

Around 7500 periodicals are published in the UK. The top six weekly titles are:

*Reader's Digest**	general interest	1,673,000
Radio Times	TV listings	1,464,000
Bella	women's magazine	1,197,000
TV Times	TV listings	1,015,141
Woman	women's magazine	800,000
Woman's Own	women's magazine	795,000

* denotes monthly publication

NEWSPAPERS

The UK has the highest circulation of newspapers in the EU. The tabloids, in particular, enjoy a very large readership. The UK has 28 national papers (daily, Sunday and weekly), plus over 2000 regional daily and weekly papers; Sunday newspapers have a wider readership. The national press is centred in London, but the Scottish, Welsh and Northern Irish daily titles may be regarded as national within their own countries. Those with the highest circulations are:

				Sunday papers	
The Sun, London	4,064,000	*The Times*, London	614,000	*News of the World*, London	4,307,000
Daily Mirror, London	2,477,000	*Evening Standard,* London	440.000	*Sunday Mirror*, London	2,652,000
Daily Mail, London	1,761,000	*The Guardian*, London and Manchester	405,000	*The People*, London	2,038,000
Daily Express, London	1,293,000	*Financial Times*, London	305,000	*Sunday Express*, London	1,281,000
The Daily Telegraph, London	1,043,000	*The Independent*, London	287,000	*The Sunday Times*, London	1,273,000
Daily Star, London	782,000	*Daily Sport*, London	230,000	*The Mail on Sunday*, London	887,000
Daily Record , Glasgow	756,000	*Birmingham Evening Mail,* Birmingham	192,000	*The Observer*, London	459,000

UK DEVOLUTION

The return of a Labour government to power in 1997 began moves towards devolution for Wales and Scotland. Devolution involves handing over much of the power that is currently concentrated at Westminster to Scotland and Wales. Scotland would have a 129-member Parliament with wide-ranging powers over areas such as health, transport, education, local government, agriculture, culture and sport. The majority in the Scottish Parliament would be headed by a First Minister, leading what would effectively be a government. Wales is being offered far less: a smaller Assembly which, unlike its Scottish equivalent, would not have the power to make laws nor would it have the power to raise taxes. Devolution would not affect such key areas as defence, foreign affairs, social security and the national budget.

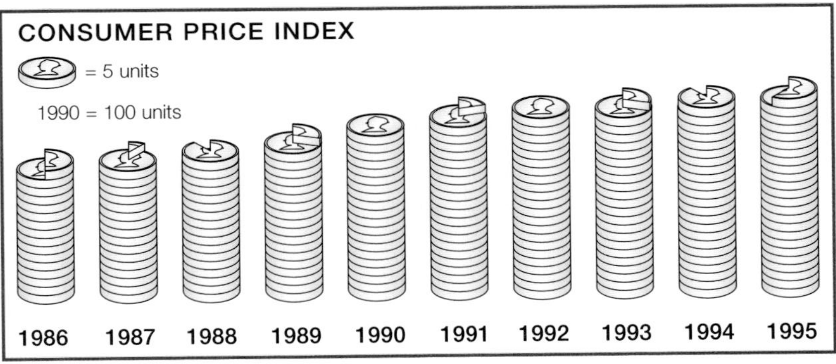

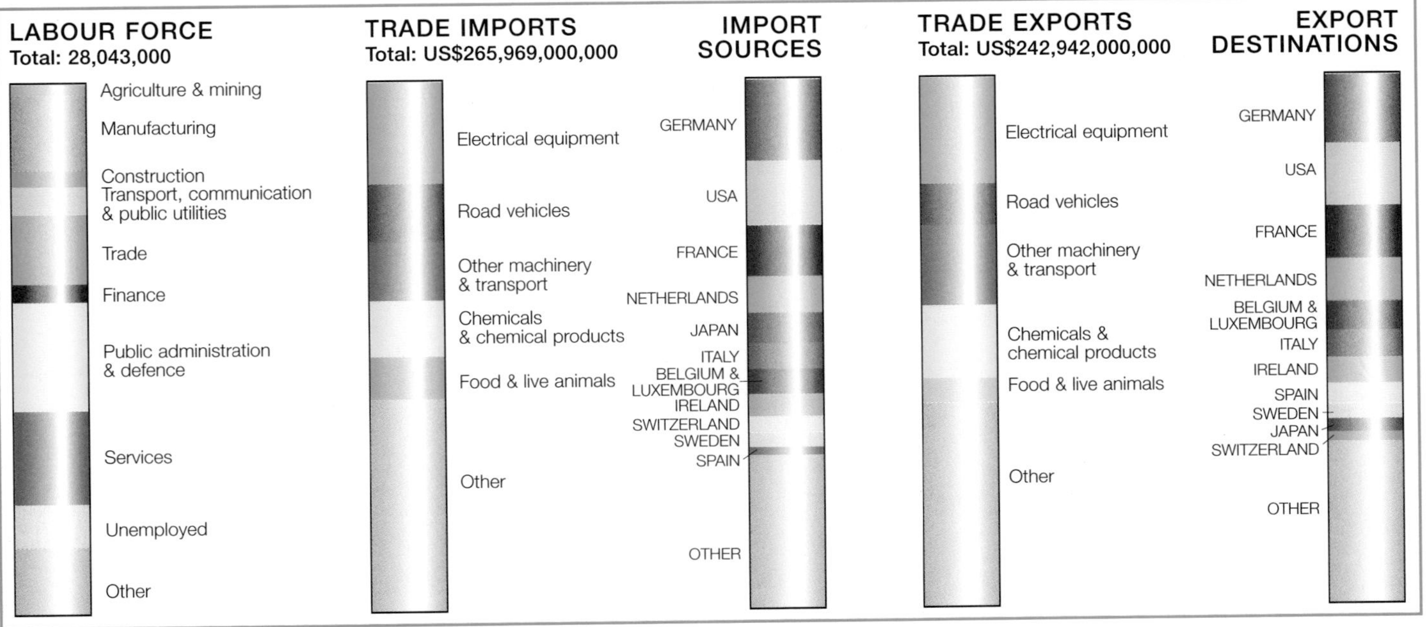

ENGLAND

England is now divided into 149 counties, unitary authorities (some of them counties), and metropolitan boroughs, all of equal status. The numbers in brackets refer to the geographical counties shown in the map, and (AC) is Administrative County and (UA) Unitary Authorities.

County	Admin. HQ	Area km²	Area sq mi	Population 1994 est.
BEDFORDSHIRE (1)		1,236	477	543,000
Bedfordshire (AC)	Bedford	1,192	460	362,000
Luton (UA)	Luton	43	17	181,000
BERKSHIRE (2)		1,259	486	768,000
Bracknell Forest (UA)	Bracknell	109	42	105,000
Newbury (UA)	Newbury	704	272	142,000
Reading (UA)	Reading	40	16	139,000
Slough (UA)	Slough	27	11	105,000
Windsor and Maidenhead (UA)	Maidenhead	198	77	137,000
Wokingham (UA)	Wokingham	179	69	142,000
BUCKINGHAMSHIRE (3)		1,877	725	658,000
Buckinghamshire (AC)	Aylesbury	1,568	605	470,000
Milton Keynes (UA)	Milton Keynes	309	119	188,000
CAMBRIDGESHIRE (4)		3,400	1,313	688,000
Cambridgeshire (AC)	Cambridge	3,067	1,184	529,000
Peterborough (UA)	Peterborough	333	129	159,000
CHESHIRE (5)		2,331	900	976,000
Cheshire (AC)	Chester	2,081	804	665,000
Halton (UA)	Widnes	74	29	124,000
Warrington (UA)	Warrington	176	68	187,000
CORNWALL (6)	Truro	3,530	1,363	479,000
CUMBRIA (7)	Carlisle	6,817	2,632	490,000
DERBYSHIRE (8)		2,629	1,015	954,000
Derby (UA)	Derby	78	30	231,000
Derbyshire (AC)	Matlock	2,551	985	724,000
DEVON (9)		6,698	2,586	1,051,000
Devon (AC)	Exeter	6,561	2,533	674,000
Plymouth (UA)	Plymouth	74	29	254,000
Torbay (UA)	Torquay	63	24	123,000
DORSET (10)		2,653	1,024	672,000
Bournemouth (UA)	Bournemouth	46	18	160,000
Dorset (AC)	Dorchester	2,542	981	374,000
Poole (UA)	Poole	65	25	138,000
DURHAM (11)		2,726	1,053	878,000
County Durham (AC)	Durham	2,231	901	507,000
Darlington (UA)	Darlington	197	76	101,000
Hartlepool (UA)	Hartlepool	94	36	92,000
Stockton-on-Tees (UA)	Stockton-on-Tees	204	79	178,000
EAST SUSSEX (12)		1,794	693	726,000
Brighton and Hove (UA)	Brighton	81	31	246,000
East Sussex (AC)	Lewes	1,713	661	480,000
EAST YORKSHIRE (13)		2,530	977	584,000
East Riding of Yorkshire (UA)	Beverley	2,459	949	315,000
Kingston upon Hull (UA)	Hull	71	28	269,000
ESSEX (14)		3,662	1,414	1,569,000
Essex (AC)	Chelmsford	3,456	1,334	1,227,000
Southend (UA)	Southend-on-Sea	42	16	170,000
Thurrock (UA)	Grays	164	63	131,000
GLOUCESTERSHIRE (15)		3,260	1,259	1,181,000
Bristol (UA)	Bristol	110	42	399,000
Gloucestershire (AC)	Gloucester	2,653	1,024	550,000
South Gloucestershire (UA)	Thornbury	497	192	233,000
GREATER LONDON (16)		1,578	609	6,967,000
Barking and Dagenham (a)	Dagenham	34	13	155,000
Barnet (b)	Hendon	89	35	308,000
Bexley (c)	Bexleyheath	61	23	220,000
Brent (d)	Wembley	44	17	245,000
Bromley (e)	Bromley	152	59	293,000
Camden (f)	St Pancras	22	8	183,000
City of London (g)	City of London	2.7	1	5,000
Croydon (h)	Croydon	87	33	327,000
Ealing (i)	Ealing	55	21	290,000
Enfield (j)	Enfield	81	31	260,000
Greenwich (k)	Woolwich	48	18	212,000
Hackney (l)	Hackney	20	8	193,000
Hammersmith and Fulham (m)	Hammersmith	16	6	157,000
Haringey (n)	Wood Green	30	12	212,000
Harrow (o)	Harrow	51	20	210,000
Havering (p)	Romford	117	45	232,000
Hillingdon (q)	Uxbridge	110	43	243,000
Hounslow (r)	Hounslow	58	22	203,000
Islington (s)	Islington	15	6	175,000
Kensington and Chelsea (t)	Kensington	12	5	152,000
Kingston upon Thames (u)	Kingston upon Thames	38	15	139,000
Lambeth (v)	Brixton	27	11	261,000
Lewisham (w)	Catford	35	13	242,000
Merton (x)	Morden	38	15	177,000
Newham (y)	East Ham	36	14	227,000
Redbridge (z)	Ilford	56	22	225,000
Richmond upon Thames (aa)	Twickenham	55	21	172,000
Southwark (bb)	Camberwell	29	11	229,000
Sutton (cc)	Sutton	43	17	173,000
Tower Hamlets (dd)	Bethnal Green	20	8	171,000
Waltham Forest (ee)	Walthamstow	40	15	222,000
Wandsworth (ff)	Wandsworth	35	13	267,000
Westminster (gg)	Westminster	22	8	190,000
GREATER MANCHESTER (17)		1,289	496	2,578,000
Bolton (a)	Bolton	140	54	265,000
Bury (b)	Bury	99	38	182,000
Manchester (c)	Manchester	116	45	431,000
Oldham (d)	Oldham	141	54	220,000
Rochdale (e)	Rochdale	160	62	207,000
Salford (f)	Salford	97	37	231,000
Stockport (g)	Stockport	126	49	291,000
Tameside (h)	Ashton-under-Lyne	103	40	222,000
Trafford (i)	Stretford	106	41	218,000
Wigan (j)	Wigan	199	77	310,000
HAMPSHIRE (18)		3,777	1,458	1,606,000
Hampshire (AC)	Winchester	3,685	1,423	1,203,000
Portsmouth (UA)	Portsmouth	42	16	192,000
Southampton (UA)	Southampton	50	19	212,000
HEREFORDSHIRE (19)	Hereford	2,182	842	165,000
HERTFORDSHIRE (20)	Hertford	1,639	633	1,005,000
ISLE OF WIGHT (21)	Newport	380	147	125,000
KENT (22)		3,728	1,440	1,546,000
Kent (AC)	Maidstone	3,537	1,366	1,304,000
The Medway Towns* (UA)	Strood	191	74	242,000
LANCASHIRE (23)		3,070	1,185	1,424,000
Blackburn and Darwen (UA)	Blackburn	137	53	140,000
Blackpool (UA)	Blackpool	35	13	154,000
Lancashire (AC)	Preston	2,898	1,119	1,130,000
LEICESTERSHIRE (24)		2,157	833	883,000
Leicester (UA)	Leicester	73	25	293,000
Leicestershire (AC)	Glenfield, Leicester	2,084	805	590,000
LINCOLNSHIRE (25)		6,899	2,664	917,000
Lincolnshire (AC)	Lincoln	5,921	2,286	611,000
North Lincolnshire (UA)	Scunthorpe	786	303	155,000
North East Lincolnshire (UA)	Grimsby	192	74	161,000
MERSEYSIDE (26)		655	253	1,434,000
Knowsley	Kirkby	97	38	154,000
Liverpool	Liverpool	113	44	474,000
St Helens	St Helens	133	51	181,000
Sefton	Bootle	153	59	292,000
Wirral	Wallasey	159	61	333,000
NORFOLK (27)	Norwich	5,385	2,079	769,000
NORTHAMPTONSHIRE (28)	Northampton	2,367	915	595,000
NORTHUMBERLAND (29)	Morpeth	5,026	1,941	308,000
NORTH YORKSHIRE (30)		8,608	3,324	1,017,000
Middlesbrough	Middlesbrough	54	21	147,000
North Yorkshire (AC)	Northallerton	8,007	3,092	552,000
Redcar and Cleveland (UA)	Eston	245	95	143,000
York (UA)	York	273	105	175,000
NOTTINGHAMSHIRE (31)		2,160	834	1,031,000
Nottingham (UA)	Nottingham	75	29	283,000
Nottinghamshire (AC)	West Bridgford, Nottingham	2,085	805	748,000
OXFORDSHIRE (32)	Oxford	2,583	997	590,000
RUTLAND (33)	Oakham	394	152	34,000
SHROPSHIRE (34)		3,488	1,347	416,000
Shropshire (AC)	Shrewsbury	3,197	1,235	273,000
The Wrekin (UA)	Telford	290	112	143,000
SOMERSET (35)		4,178	1,613	824,000
Bath & North East Somerset (UA)	Bath	351	136	164,000
North West Somerset (UA)	Weston-super-Mare	375	145	183,000
Somerset (AC)	Taunton	3,452	1,333	478,000
SOUTH YORKSHIRE (36)		1,559	602	1,305,000
Barnsley	Barnsley	328	127	227,000
Doncaster	Doncaster	581	224	293,000
Rotherham	Rotherham	283	109	256,000
Sheffield	Sheffield	367	142	530,000
STAFFORDSHIRE (37)		2,715	1,048	1,055,000
Staffordshire (AC)	Stafford	2,623	1,023	800,000
Stoke-on-Trent (UA)	Stoke-on-Trent	93	36	254,000
SUFFOLK (38)	Ipswich	3,798	1,466	649,000
SURREY (39)	Kingston upon Thames**	1,677	648	1,044,000
TYNE AND WEAR (40)		537	207	1,134,000
Gateshead	Gateshead	143	55	202,000
Newcastle upon Tyne	Newcastle upon Tyne	112	43	284,000
North Tyneside	North Shields	84	32	194,000
South Tyneside	South Shields	63	24	157,000
Sunderland	Sunderland	135	52	297,000
WARWICKSHIRE (41)	Warwick	1,979	764	496,000
WEST MIDLANDS (42)		899	347	2,628,000
Birmingham	Birmingham	265	102	1,008,000
Coventry	Coventry	97	37	303,000
Dudley	Dudley	98	38	312,000
Sandwell	Oldbury	86	33	294,000
Solihull	Solihull	179	69	202,000
Walsall	Walsall	106	41	264,000
Wolverhampton	Wolverhampton	69	27	245,000
WEST SUSSEX (43)	Chichester	1,969	760	722,000
WEST YORKSHIRE (44)		2,034	785	2,104,000
Bradford	Bradford	366	141	482,000
Calderdale	Halifax	363	140	194,000
Kirklees	Huddersfield	410	158	387,000
Leeds	Leeds	562	217	724,000
Wakefield	Wakefield	333	129	317,000
WILTSHIRE (45)		3,476	1,342	588,000
Swindon (UA)	Swindon	230	88	174,000
Wiltshire (AC)	Trowbridge	3,246	1,253	414,000
WORCESTERSHIRE (46)	Worcester	1,742	672	535,000

* official name not finally decided
** outside the county

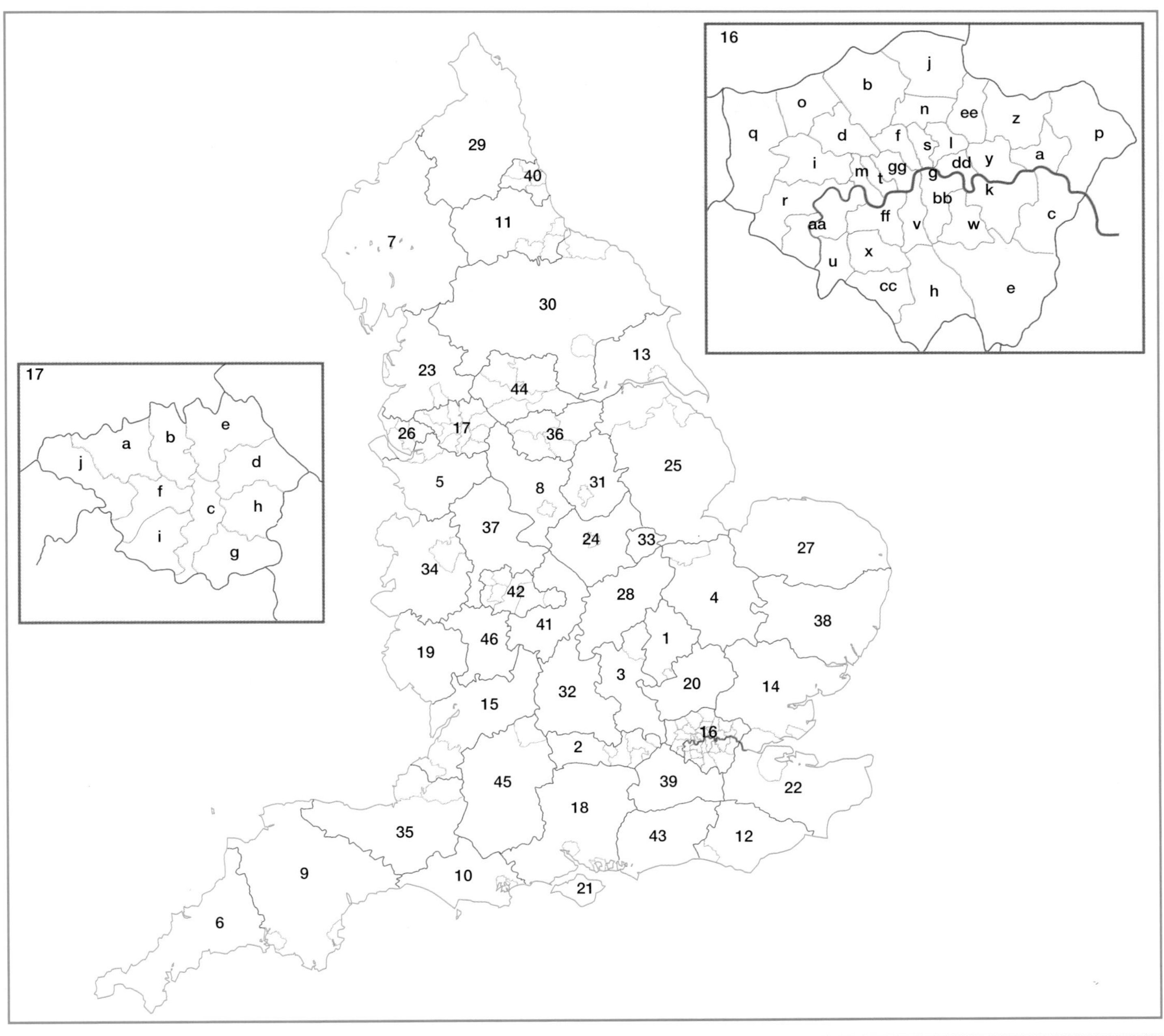

PRIME MINISTERS

Years	Prime Minister
1721–42	Sir Robert Walpole
1742–43	Sir Spencer Compton, Earl of Wilmington
1743–46	Henry Pelham
1746	Sir William Pulteney, Earl of Bath
1746–54	Henry Pelham
1754–56	Sir Thomas Pelham-Holles, Duke of Newcastle upon Tyne
1756–57	Sir William Cavendish, Duke of Devonshire
1757	James Waldegrave, Earl of Waldegrave
1757–62	Sir Thomas Pelham-Holles, Duke of Newcastle upon Tyne
1762–63	Sir John Stuart, Earl of Bute
1763–65	George Grenville
1765–66	Lord Charles Watson-Wentworth, Marquess of Rockingham
1766–68	William Pitt, Earl of Chatham
1768–70	Sir Augustus Henry FitzRoy, Duke of Grafton
1770–82	Lord North
1782	Lord Charles Watson-Wentworth, Marquess of Rockingham
1782–83	Sir William Petty, Earl of Shelburne
1783	Sir William Henry Cavendish Bentinck, Duke of Portland
1783–1801	William Pitt
1801–04	Henry Addington
1804–06	William Pitt
1806–07	William Wyndham Grenville, Baron Grenville
1807–09	Sir William Henry Cavendish Bentinck, Duke of Portland
1809–12	Spencer Perceval
1812–27	Sir Robert Banks Jenkinson, Earl of Liverpool
1827	George Canning
1827–28	Frederick John Robinson, Viscount Goderich
1828–30	Sir Arthur Wellesley, Duke of Wellington
1830–34	Sir Charles Grey, Earl Grey
1834	Sir William Lamb, Viscount Melbourne
1834	Sir Arthur Wellesley, Duke of Wellington
1834–35	Sir Robert Peel
1835–41	Sir William Lamb, Viscount Melbourne
1841–46	Sir Robert Peel
1846–52	Lord John Russell
1852	Sir Edward Geoffrey Smith-Stanley, Earl of Derby
1852–55	Sir George Hamilton Gordon, Earl of Aberdeen
1855–58	Sir Henry John Temple, Viscount Palmerston
1858–59	Sir Edward Geoffrey Smith-Stanley, Earl of Derby
1859–65	Sir Henry John Temple, Viscount Palmerston
1865–66	Lord John Russell
1866–68	Sir Edward Geoffrey Smith-Stanley, Earl of Derby
1868	Benjamin Disraeli
1868–74	William Ewart Gladstone
1874–80	Benjamin Disraeli
1880–85	William Ewart Gladstone
1885–86	Robert Arthur Talbot Gascoyne-Cecil, Marquess of Salisbury
1886	William Ewart Gladstone
1886–92	Robert Arthur Talbot Gascoyne-Cecil, Marquess of Salisbury
1892–94	William Ewart Gladstone
1894–95	Sir Archibald Philip Primrose, Earl of Rosebery
1895–1902	Robert Arthur Talbot Gascoyne-Cecil, Marquess of Salisbury
1902–05	Arthur James Balfour
1905–08	Sir Henry Campbell-Bannerman
1908–16	Herbert Henry Asquith
1916–22	David Lloyd George
1922–23	Andrew Bonar Law
1923–24	Stanley Baldwin
1924	Ramsay Macdonald
1924–29	Stanley Baldwin
1929–35	Ramsay Macdonald
1935–37	Stanley Baldwin
1937–40	Neville Chamberlain
1940–45	Sir Winston Churchill
1945–51	Clement Atlee
1951–55	Sir Winston Churchill
1955–57	Anthony Eden
1957–63	Harold Macmillan
1963–64	Sir Alexander Douglas-Home
1964–70	Sir Harold Wilson
1970–74	Sir Edward Heath
1974–76	Sir Harold Wilson
1976–79	Sir James Callaghan
1979–90	Margaret Thatcher
1990–97	John Major
1997–	Tony Blair

WALES (CYMRU)

This table records the new map of Wales, divided into counties (Co.) and county boroughs (Co. Boro.).

COUNTIES AND COUNTY BOROUGHS OF WALES

(Welsh names are given in brackets)

UNITARY AUTHORITY	ADMINISTRATIVE HQ	AREA km²	AREA sq mi	POPULATION (1994 est.)
Anglesey (Co.) (1) (Ynys Môn)	Llangefni	719	278	69,000
Blaenau Gwent (Co. Boro.) (2)	Ebbw Vale (Glyn Ebwy)	109	42	73,000
Bridgend (Co. Boro.) (3) (Penybont ar Ogwr)	Bridgend (Penybont ar Ogwr)	246	95	130,000
Caerphilly (Co. Boro.) (4) (Caerffili)	Ystrad Mynach	279	108	171,000
Cardiff, City of (Co. Boro.) (5) (Caerdydd)	Cardiff (Caerdydd)	139	54	302,000
Carmarthenshire (Co.) (6) (Sir Caerfyrddin)	Carmarthen (Caerfyrddin)	2,398	926	169,000
Ceredigion (Co.) (7)	Aberaeron	1,797	694	68,000
Conwy (Co. Boro.) (8)	Conwy	1,130	436	109,000
Denbighshire (Co.) (9) (Sir Dinbych)	Ruthin (Rhuthun)	844	436	91,000
Flintshire (Co.) (10) (Sir y Fflint)	Mold (Yr Wyddgrug)	437	169	144,000
Gwynedd (Co.) (11)	Caernarfon	2,548	984	116,000
Merthyr Tydfil (Co. Boro.) (12) (Merthyr Tudful)	Merthyr Tydfil (Merthyr Tudful)	111	43	60,000
Monmouthshire (Co.) (13) (Sir Fynwy)	Cwmbran*	851	329	81,000
Neath Port Talbot (Co. Boro.) (14) (Castellnedd Port Talbot)	Port Talbot	442	171	140,000
Newport (Co. Boro) (15) (Casnewydd)	Newport (Casnewydd)	191	74	137,000
Pembrokeshire (Co.) (16) (Sir Benfro)	Haverfordwest (Hwlffordd)	1,590	614	114,000
Powys (Co.) (17)	Llandrindod Wells (Llandrindod)	5,204	2,009	121,000
Rhondda, Cynon, Taff (18) (Co. Boro.)	Clydach Vale** (Glyn Clydach)	424	164	238,000
Swansea, City of (Co. Boro.) (19) (Abertawe)	Swansea (Abertawe)	378	146	232,000
Torfaen (Co. Boro.) (20)	Pontypool (Pontypwl)	126	49	91,000
Vale of Glamorgan, The (21) (Cyngor Bro Morgannwg) (Co. Boro.)	Barry (Y Barri)	337	130	119,000
Wrexham (Co. Boro) (22) (Wrecsam)	Wrexham (Wrecsam)	499	193	123,000

* outside the county
** moving to Pontypridd in 1999

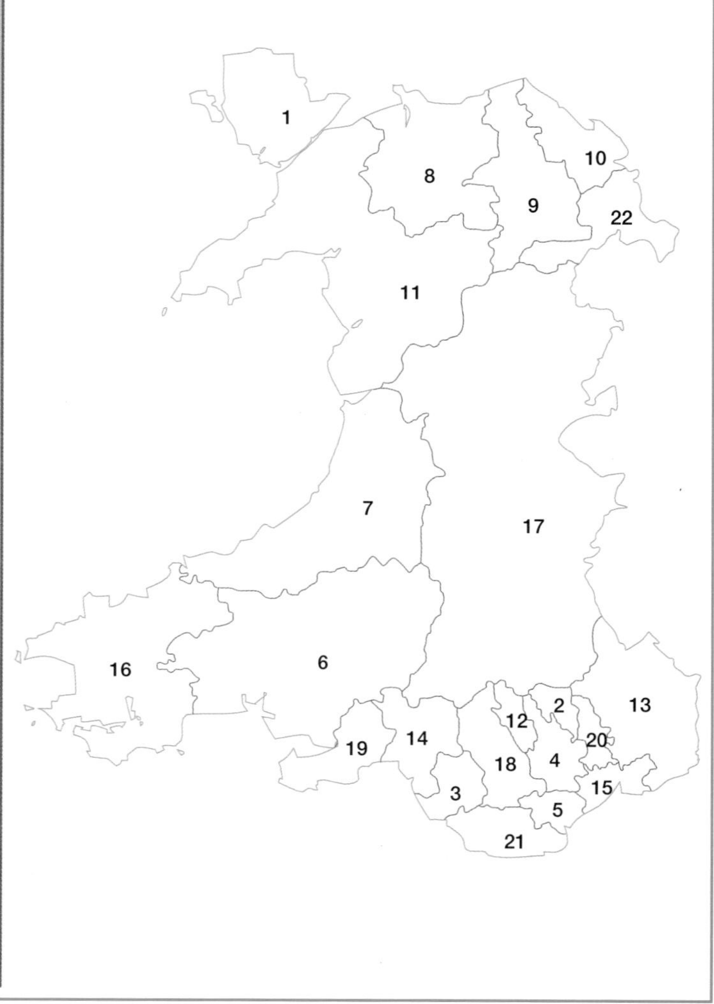

NORTHERN IRELAND

The six traditional counties of Northern Ireland have been reorganized into a system of 22 all-purpose unitary authorities.The traditional counties are Antrim, Armagh, Down, Londonderry/Derry, Fermanagh and Tyrone. Although they no longer have any administrative significance (except for Fermanagh), the traditional counties are still in popular usage. This records the new map of Northern Ireland, divided into districts.

UNITARY AUTHORITY	ADMINISTRATIVE HQ	AREA km²	AREA sq mi	POPULATION (1994 est.)
Antrim (1)	Antrim	578	223	48,000
Ards (2)	Newtownards	381	147	67,000
Armagh (3)	Armagh	671	259	53,000
Ballymena (4)	Ballymena	632	244	57,000
Ballymoney (5)	Ballymoney	419	162	25,000
Banbridge (6)	Banbridge	446	172	37,000
Belfast, City of (7)	Belfast	115	44	297,000
Carrickfergus (8)	Carrickfergus	82	32	35,000
Castlereagh (9)	Cregagh	85	33	63,000
Coleraine (10)	Coleraine	486	187	54,000
Cookstown (11)	Cookstown	622	240	31,000
Craigavon (12)	Portadown	379	146	78,000
Derry (13)	Londonderry/Derry	387	150	102,000
Down (14)	Downpatrick	650	251	60,000
Dungannon (15)	Dungannon	783	302	47,000
Fermanagh (16)	Enniskillen	1,877	725	55,000
Larne (17)	Larne	336	130	30,000
Limavady (18)	Limavady	586	226	31,000
Lisburn (19)	Lisburn	446	172	105,000
Magherafelt (20)	Magherafelt	572	221	37,000
Moyle (21)	Ballycastle	494	191	15,000
Newry and Mourne (22)	Newry	909	351	83,000
Newtownabbey (23)	Ballyclare	151	58	78,000
North Down (24)	Bangor	82	31	74,000
Omagh (25)	Omagh	1,130	436	47,000
Strabane (26)	Strabane	862	333	36,000

THE NATIONAL SYMBOL OF WALES IS THE LEEK ■ NORTHERN IRELAND'S NEWEST CITY IS ARMAGH

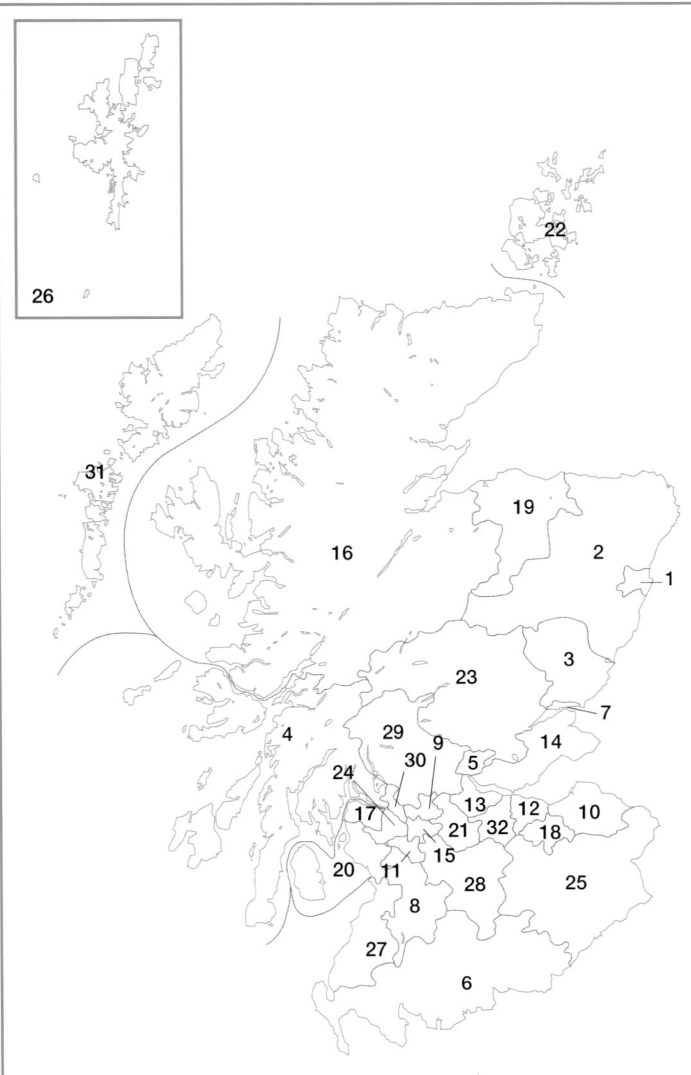

SCOTLAND

This table records the new map of Scotland, divided into what are officially known as council areas.

COUNCIL AREAS OF SCOTLAND

UNITARY AUTHORITY	ADMINISTRATIVE HQ	AREA km²	sq mi	POPULATION (1994 est.)
Aberdeen, City of (1)	Aberdeen	182	70	218,000
Aberdeenshire (2)	Aberdeen*	6,317	2,439	224,000
Angus (3)	Forfar	2,184	843	112,000
Argyll & Bute (4)	Lochgilphead	7,023	2,712	90,000
Clackmannanshire (5)	Alloa	158	61	49,000
Dumfries & Galloway (6)	Dumfries	6,446	2,489	148,000
Dundee, City of (7)	Dundee	55	21	153,000
East Ayrshire (8)	Kilmarnock	1,275	492	124,000
East Dunbartonshire (9)	Kirkintilloch	176	68	110,000
East Lothian (10)	Haddington	666	257	86,000
East Renfrewshire (11)	Giffnock	168	65	84,000
Edinburgh, City of (12)	Edinburgh	260	100	442,000
Falkirk (13)	Falkirk	293	113	143,000
Fife (14)	Glenrothes	1,340	518	351,000
Glasgow, City of (15)	Glasgow	175	67	524,000
Highland (16)	Inverness**	26,119	10,085	207,000
Inverclyde (17)	Greenock	167	65	90,000
Midlothian (18)	Dalkeith	350	135	80,000
Moray (19)	Elgin	2,237	864	86,000
North Ayrshire (20)	Irvine	888	343	139,000
North Lanarkshire (21)	Motherwell	476	184	327,000
Orkney (22)	Kirkwall	1,025	396	20,000
Perth & Kinross (23)	Perth	5,395	2,083	131,000
Renfrewshire (24)	Paisley	262	101	178,000
Scottish Borders, The (25)	Newtown St Boswells	4,727	1,825	105,000
Shetland (26)	Lerwick	1,471	568	23,000
South Ayrshire (27)	Ayr	1,230	475	114,000
South Lanarkshire (28)	Hamilton	1,778	686	308,000
Stirling (29)	Stirling	2,243	866	82,000
West Dunbartonshire (30)	Dumbarton	176	68	98,000
Western Isles (31)	Stornoway	3,070	1,185	29,000
West Lothian (32)	Livingston	427	165	147,000

* outside the council area
** although the council meets at Dingwall

THE UNITED KINGDOM

Area: 244,088 km² (94,242 sq mi).
The UK comprises the island of Great Britain – England, Wales and Scotland – and Northern Ireland, as well as over 4000 other islands. There are differing definitions for the islands geographically known as the British Isles, depending on whether the usage is legal, geographical, or political.

THE BRITISH ISLES

Area: 314,798 km² (121,544 sq mi).
The British Isles is a convenient but purely geographical term to describe the group of islands lying off the north-west coast of Europe comprising the UK, the Republic of Ireland and the Crown dependencies of the Isle of Man and the Channel Islands.

GREAT BRITAIN

Area of the island of Great Britain: 218,041 km² (84,186 sq mi).
Area of the union of England and Wales with Scotland: 229,966 km² (88,791 sq mi).
Great Britain is the geographical and political name of the main or principal island of the British Isles group. In a strict geographical sense, offshore islands such as the Isle of Wight, Anglesey and Shetland, are not part of Great Britain.

The name Great Britain for the union of England and Wales with Scotland came into popular (but unofficial) use when James VI of Scotland succeeded Queen Elizabeth I of England in 1603. With the Union of the parliaments of England and Scotland, on 1 May 1707, the style 'Great Britain' was formally adopted.

CROWN DEPENDENCIES OF JERSEY, GUERNSEY AND THE ISLE OF MAN

The Crown dependencies are territories associated with the UK, but not part of it.

DEPENDENCIES

Guernsey and its dependencies, Jersey and the Isle of Man (see this spread), and Anguilla (p. 441), Bermuda (p. 425), British Antarctic Territory (p. 480), British Indian Ocean Territory (p. 459), British Virgin Islands (p. 439), Cayman Islands (p. 435), Falkland Islands (p. 447), Gibraltar (p. 359), Montserrat (p. 441), Pitcairn Islands (p. 477), St Helena and its dependencies (p. 470), South Georgia and South Sandwich Islands (p. 480), and Turks and Caicos Islands (p. 439).

GUERNSEY AND DEPENDENCIES

Official name and status: The States of Guernsey; a British Crown Dependency (an internally self-governing state associated with, but not part of, the UK).
Area: 78.5 km² (30 sq mi); Guernsey 65 km² (25 sq mi), Alderney 8 km² (3 sq mi), Sark 0.5 km² (0.2 sq mi).
Population: 61,300 (1994 est.); Guernsey 58,400, Alderney 2300, Sark 600.
Capital: St Peter Port 21,000 (1996 est.).
Other major centre: St Anne's (capital of Alderney) 1800 (1996 est.). (Sark has no capital: settlement on the island is dispersed.)
Geography: Guernsey, a plateau surrounded by coastal cliffs, is 48 km (30 mi) west of Normandy. Its smaller dependencies of Alderney and Sark are respectively north and east of Guernsey.
Economy: Dominated by tourism and market gardening, Guernsey is also an 'offshore' banking centre (not yet rivalling Jersey).

JERSEY

Official name and status: States of Jersey; a British Crown Dependency (an internally self-governing state associated with, but not part of, the UK).
Area: 116 km² (45 sq mi).
Population: 84,000 (1996 est.).
Capital: St Helier 35,000 urban area (1996 est.).
Geography: The island of Jersey, which is 19 km (12 mi) west of the French Cotentin peninsula, is surrounded by cliffs and is deeply incised by valleys.
Economy: Jersey depends upon tourism, farming (which concentrates upon dairying, the breeding of Jersey cattle for export, tomatoes and early potatoes) and, increasingly, upon 'offshore' banking.

ISLE OF MAN

Official name and status: Isle of Man; a British Crown Dependency (an internally self-governing state associated with, but not part of, the UK).
Area: 572 km² (221 sq mi).
Population: 71,000 (1994 est.).
Capital: Douglas 31,000 urban area (town 22,000; Onchan 8500; 1991 census).
Geography: The island, which has a rocky indented coast, lies in the Irish Sea between the north-west coast of England and Northern Ireland.
Economy: Man largely depends upon tourism, 'offshore' banking and other financial interests.

IBERIA

PORTUGAL

Portugal is a republic on the Atlantic coast of the Iberian peninsula. Behind a coastal plain, Portugal north of the River Tagus is a highland region at the centre of which is the mainland's principal mountain range, the Serra da Estrela. A wide plateau in the north-east is a continuation of the Spanish Meseta. Portugal south of the Tagus is mainly an undulating lowland. The mountainous Atlantic island groups of the Azores and Madeira are respectively 1200 km (745 mi) and 1000 km (620 mi) south-west of the mainland. The Azores are volcanic.
Highest point: (mainland) Estrela 1993 m (6539 ft); at 2351 m (7713 ft) Pico in the Azores is Portugal's highest peak.
Climate: Portugal has a mild and temperate climate which is wetter and more Atlantic in the north, and drier, hotter and more Mediterranean in the south.

An executive President is elected for a maximum of two consecutive five-year terms by universal adult suffrage. The 230-member Assembly is directly elected for four years under a system of proportional representation. The President appoints a Prime Minister who commands a majority in the Assembly. The PM, in turn, nominates a Council of Ministers. The autonomous governments of the Azores and Madeira have considerable powers.
Largest parties: (1995 election) (centre-left) Socialist Party (PS) 112 seats, (centre-right) Social Democratic Party (PSD) 88, (Communist-led) United Democratic Coalition (CDU) 15, (right-wing) Popular Party (PP) 15.
President: (since 1996) Jorge Sampaio (PS).
Prime Minister: (since 1995) Antônio Guterres (PS).

Agriculture involves over 10% of the labour force, but has suffered a lack of investment following land reforms in the 1970s, and production has fallen. Major crops include wheat and maize, grapes (for wines such as port and Madeira), tomatoes, potatoes and cork trees. Portugal lacks natural resources. Manufacturing industry includes textiles and clothing (both major exports), footwear, food processing, transport equipment, cork products and, increasingly, electrical appliances and petrochemicals. Tourism (particularly in the Algarve) and money sent back by Portuguese working abroad are major foreign-currency earners. The eastern districts suffer large-scale emigration to Lisbon and Oporto and to many parts of western Europe. Despite impressive recent economic growth, Portugal remains western Europe's poorest country.
Currency: Escudo.

1908 Assassination of King Carlos I and his heir. **1910** Overthrow of the monarchy; republic established. **1916–18** Portuguese participation in World War I: troops sent to France and Belgium against German forces. **1921** Wide-scale political instability and assassinations. **1926** The military seized power. **1932–68** Dictatorship of Antônio Salazar: stability achieved at great cost; Portugal became a one-party state. **1939–45** Neutrality during World War II. **1960** India invaded Portugal's colonies on the Indian coast. **1961–64** Beginning of expensive colonial wars as Portugal tried to check independence movements in Guinea-Bissau, Mozambique and Angola. **1970** Death of Salazar. **1974** Left-wing military coup whose leaders initially attempted to impose Marxism on Portugal. **1974–75** Independence granted to Portuguese colonies, except Macau. **1976** Democratic civilian rule restored; Portugal joined the EU. **1980** The Azores and Madeira received autonomy.

Dependencies
Macau (see p. 417)

Official name: República Portuguesa (Portuguese Republic).
Area: 92,135 km² (35,573 sq mi).
Population: 9,910,000 (1995 est.).
Doubling time: pop. is stable.
Adult life expectancy: male 70.8 years, female 78 years. **Birth rate:** 0.46 times world average.
Death rate: 1.15 times world average. **Urban population:** 35%.
Capital: Lisbon (Lisboa) 1,832,000 urban area (city 663,000; Loures 322,000; Sintra 261,000; Amadora 177,000; Cascais 153,000; Oeiras 151,000; 1991 census). **Other main centres:** Oporto (Porto) 1,168,000 urban area (city 302,000; Vila Nova de Gaia 249,000; Matosinhos 152,000; Gondomar 143,000), Loures *see Lisbon*, Sintra *see Lisbon*, Vila Nova de Gaia *see Oporto*, Amadora *see Lisbon*, Guimarães 158,000, Cascais *see Lisbon*, Matosinhos *see Oporto*, Almada 152,000, Oeiras *see Lisbon*, Setubal 144,000 (city 103,000), Gondomar *see Oporto*, Braga 141,000, Coimbra 139,000, Seixal 117,000, Funchal 115,000 (1991 census; inc. suburbs).
Language: Portuguese virtually 100% (official). **Adult literacy:** 87%.
Religion: Roman Catholic 94%, non-religious 4%.

PORTUGUESE AUTONOMOUS REGIONS

Azores (Açores)
Area: 2247 km² (868 sq mi).
Pop.: 234,000 (1993 est.).
Capital: Ponta Delgada.
Madeira
Area: 794 km² (306 sq mi).
Pop.: 254,000 (1993 est.).
Capital: Funchal.

ANDORRA

Andorra is a small principality in the eastern Pyrenees between France and Spain. The country is surrounded by mountains almost 3000 m (9840 ft) in height.
Highest point: Coma Pedrosa 2949 m (9675 ft) is the highest peak entirely within Andorra.
Climate: Andorra is mild in spring and summer, but cold in winter with snow for up to five months.

Andorra is a constitutional monarchy without a royal family. It has joint heads-of-state (co-Princes): the President of France and the Spanish Bishop of Urgel who delegate their powers to permanent representatives. The 28-member General Council, which is elected for four years by universal adult suffrage, comprises 14 members elected nationally and two members elected by each of the seven parishes. The co-Princes appoint a Prime Minister who commands a majority in the General Council; the PM, in turn, appoints an Executive Council (government).
Largest parties: (1997 election): (centrist) Liberal Union (UL) 16 seats, (centre-right) National Democratic Grouping (AND) 6, (centre) New Democracy (ND) 2, (centrist) Independent New Democracy (IDN) 2.
Prime Minister: (since 1994) Marc Forné (LU-CNA minority coalition).

Over 15 million tourists a year have been encouraged by the development of ski resorts, by the duty-free status of consumer goods and an airport for tourists is being developed just over the border. Over three-quarters of the rapidly growing population are foreign settlers. Andorra is included in the EU by special arrangement. **Currency:** French franc and Spanish peseta.

1981–82 Beginning of constitutional changes: first PM appointed. **1993** New democratic constitution; legalization of trade unions and political parties; independent diplomatic representation and UN membership.

Official name: Principat d'Andorra (The Principality of Andorra).
Area: 468 km² (181 sq mi).
Population: 63,000 (1995 est.).
Doubling time: 82 years. **Adult life expectancy:** male 76 years, female 82 years. **Birth rate:** 0.44 times world average. **Death rate:** 0.3 times world average. **Urban population:** 63%. **Capital:** Andorra la Vella 35,600 urban area (town 22,400; Les Escaldes-Engordany 13,200; 1993 est.). **Other main centre:** Encamp 9700 (1993 est.).
Language: Catalan (Andorran) 29% (official), Spanish (Castilian) 46%, Portuguese 11%, French 8%.
Adult literacy: almost 100%.
Religion: Roman Catholic 92%, Protestant and Jewish minorities.

SPAIN

Spain is a kingdom separated from the rest of south-west Europe by the high barrier of the Pyrenees Mountains; the country includes 80% of the Iberian peninsula plus the island groups of the Canaries and Balearics. In the north of Spain a mountainous region stretches from the Pyrenees through the Cantabrian mountains to Galicia on the Atlantic coast. Much of the country is occupied by the central plateau, the Meseta. This is around 600 m (2000 ft) high, but rises to the higher Sisterna Central in Castile, and ends in the south at the Sierra Morena. The Sierra Nevada range in Andalusia in the south contains Mulhacén, mainland Spain's highest peak. The principal lowlands include the Ebro valley in the north-east, a coastal plain around Valencia in the east and the valley of the Guadalquivir in the south. The Balearic Islands in the Mediterranean comprise four main islands (Mallorca, Minorca, Ibiza and Formentera) with seven much smaller islands. The Canary Islands, off the coast of Morocco and Western Sahara, comprise five large islands (Tenerife, Fuerteventura, Gran Canaria, Lanzarote and La Palma) plus two smaller islands and six islets. The cities of Ceuta and Melilla are enclaves on the north coast of Morocco.
Highest point: (mainland) Mulhacén 3478 m (11,411 ft); at 3718 m (12,198 ft) Pico de Tiede in the Canaries is Spain's highest peak.
Climate: The south-east has a Mediterranean climate with hot summers and mild winters. The dry interior is more continental with warm summers and cold winters. The high Pyrenees have a cold Alpine climate, while the north-west (Galicia) has a wet Atlantic climate with cool summers. The Canaries are both hotter and drier than the mainland.

Official name: Reino de España (The Kingdom of Spain).
Area: 505,990 km² (195,364 sq mi).
Population: 39,190,000 (1995 est.).
Doubling time: pop. is stable.
Adult life expectancy: male 73.2 years, female 81.1 years.
Birth rate: 0.39 times world average.
Death rate: 0.92 times world average. **Urban population:** 78%.
Capital: Madrid 5,035,000 urban area (city 3,041,000; Móstoles 199,000; Leganés 178,000; Alcalá de Henares 166,000; Fuenlabrada 158,000; Getafe 144,000; Alcorcón 142,000; 1994 est.). **Other main centres:** Barcelona 2,862,000 urban area (city 1,631,000; Hospitalet 266,000; Badalona 219,000; Sabadell 189,000; Tarrasa 161,000; Santa Coloma de Gramanet 132,000), Seville (Sevilla) 791,000 (city 714,000), Valencia 764,000, Zaragoza 607,000, Málaga 531,000, Bilbao 476,000 (city 372,000), Las Palmas de Gran Canaria 372,000, Murcia 342,000, Valladolid 337,000, Palma de Mallorca 322,000, Córdoba 316,000, Vigo 289,000, Alicante 275,000, Granada 271,000, Gijón 270,000, Hospitalet *see Barcelona*, La Coruña 255,000, Cádiz 240,000 (city 155,000), Badalona *see Barcelona*, Vitoria (Gasteiz) 214,000, Santa Cruz de Tenerife 204,000, Oviedo 202,000, Móstoles *see Madrid*, Santander 195,000, Elche 191,000, Jérez de la Frontera 190,000, Sabadell *see Barcelona*, Pamplona 182,000, Cartagena 180,000, Donostia-San Sebastián 178,000, Leganés *see Madrid* (1994 est.; inc. suburbs).
Language: Spanish 80% (official), Catalan 13%, Galician (Gallego) 4%, Basque 2%. **Adult literacy:** 85%.
Religion: Roman Catholic 95%, Sunni Islam 1%.

Spain is a constitutional monarchy. The Cortes (Parliament) comprises a Senate (Upper House) and a Congress of Deputies (Lower House). The Senate consists of 252 senators: four from each province, five from the Balearic Islands, six from the Canary Islands and two each from Ceuta and Melilla (all elected by universal adult suffrage for four years), plus 47 senators elected by the parliaments of the autonomous communities (regions) into which the provinces are grouped. The Congress of Deputies has 350 members directly elected for four years under a system of proportional representation. The King appoints a Prime Minister (President of the Council) who commands a majority in the Congress. The PM, in turn, appoints a Cabinet (Council of Ministers). The autonomous communities have their own governments with varying degrees of self-government.
Largest parties: (1996 election) (right-wing) Popular Party (PP) 156 seats, (socialist) Spanish Workers' Socialist Party (PSOE) 141, (Communist-led) United Left Coalition (IU) 21, (Catalan nationalist) Convergence and Union (CiU) 16, Basque Nationalist Party (PNV) 5, Canarian Coalition (CC) 4, Galician Nationalist Bloc 2, (Basque separatists) Herri Batasuna 2, others 3.
King: (since 1975) Juan Carlos I.
Prime Minister: (since 1996) Josë María Aznar (PP).

Agriculture involves nearly 10% of the labour force. The principal crops include barley, wheat, sugar beet, citrus fruit and grapes (for wine). Pastures for livestock occupy nearly one-fifth of the land but increasing drought is a problem. Manufacturing developed rapidly from the 1960s and there are now major motor-vehicle, textile, plastics, metallurgical, shipbuilding, chemical and engineering industries. Foreign investors have been encouraged to promote new industry, but unemployment remains high (over 20% of the labour force since 1993). Banking and commerce are important, and tourism is a major foreign-currency earner. Over 63 million foreign tourists a year visit Spain, mainly staying at beach resorts on the Mediterranean, in the Balearic Islands and in the Canaries.
Currency: Peseta.

SPANISH AUTONOMOUS COMMUNITIES (REGIONS)

Andalusia (Andalucía)
Area: 87,599 km² (33,822 sq mi).
Pop.: 7,053,000 (1994 est.).
Capital: Seville.
Ceuta and Melilla – see below (Ceuta and Melilla are, for some purposes, part of Andalusia.)
Aragón
Area: 47,720 km² (18,425 sq mi).
Pop.: 1,184,000 (1994 est.).
Capital: Zaragoza.
Asturias
Area: 10,604 km² (4094 sq mi).
Pop.: 1,083,000 (1994 est.).
Capital: Oviedo.
Balearic Islands (Baleares)
Area: 4992 km² (1927 sq mi).
Pop.: 737,000 (1994 est.).
Capital: Palma de Mallorca.
Basque Country (País Vasco or Euskadi)
Area: 7234 km² (2793 sq mi).
Pop.: 2,076,000 (1994 est.).
Capital: Vitoria (Gasteiz).
Canary Islands (Islas Canarias)
Area: 7447 km² (2875 sq mi).
Pop.: 1,535,000 (1994 est.).
Joint capitals: Santa Cruz de Tenerife and Las Palmas.
Cantabria
Area: 5321 km² (2054 sq mi).
Pop.: 526,000 (1994 est.).
Capital: Santander.
Castile-La Mancha (Castilla-La Mancha)
Area: 79,461 km² (30,680 sq mi).
Pop.: 1,656,000 (1994 est.).
Capital: Toledo.
Castile and León (Castilla y León)
Area: 94,224 km² (36,380 sq mi).
Pop.: 2,504,000 (1994 est.).
Capital: Valladolid.
Catalonia (Cataluña or Catalunya)
Area: 32,112 km² (12,399 sq mi).
Pop.: 6,090,000 (1994 est.).
Capital: Barcelona.
Ceuta
Area: 20 km² (8 sq mi).
Pop.: 69,000 (1994 est.).
Capital: Ceuta.
Extremadura
Area: 41,634 km² (16,075 sq mi).
Pop.: 1,051,000 (1994 est.).
Capital: Mérida.
Galicia (Galiza)
Area: 29,575 km² (11,419 sq mi).
Pop.: 2,721,000 (1994 est.).
Capital: Santiago de Compostela.
La Rioja
Area: 5045 km² (1948 sq mi).
Pop.: 263,000 (1994 est.).
Capital: Logroño.
Madrid
Area: 8028 km² (3100 sq mi).
Pop.: 5,035,000 (1994 est.).
Capital: Madrid.
Melilla
Area: 12 km² (5 sq mi).
Pop.: 58,000 (1994 est.).
Capital: Melilla.
Murcia
Area: 11,314 km² (4368 sq mi).
Pop.: 1,070,000 (1994 est.).
Capital: Murcia.
Navarre (Navarra)
Area: 10,391 km² (4012 sq mi).
Pop.: 524,000 (1994 est.).
Capital: Pamplona.
Valencia
Area: 23,255 km² (8979 sq mi).
Pop.: 3,909,000 (1994 est.).
Capital: Valencia.

1898 Defeat in the Spanish-American War: last significant colonial possessions (Guam, Philippines, Cuba and Puerto Rico) lost. **1923** Military coup led by General Miguel Primo de Rivera. **1930** King Alfonso XIII withdrew support from Rivera. **1931** Threat of civil war; Alfonso XIII abdicated; Second Spanish Republic founded. **1936** Army generals rose against the republican government: Spanish Civil War began with Nationalist forces led by General Francisco Franco and supported by Nazi Germany and Fascist Italy confronting the republicans (who were aided by socialist and liberal volunteers, the Brigades). **1937** Mass bombardment of Guernica by Nationalists caused outrage abroad. **1939** Franco triumphed in the civil war and became leader (Caudillo) of the neo-Fascist Spanish State. **1939–67** Dictatorship of Franco: the Cortes was not directly elected; political expression restricted. **1969** Juan Carlos, grandson of Alfonso XIII, named heir to Franco. **1973** Assassination of PM Luis Carrero Blanco by terrorists belonging to the Basque separatist movement ETA. **1975** Death of Franco; monarchy restored. **1978** Democracy fully restored under a liberal constitution. **Since 1978** Granting of regional autonomy but Spain continues to be troubled by ETA violence. **1981** King Juan Carlos played an important role in putting down an attempted military coup. **1986** Spain joined the EU.

GIBRALTAR

Official name and status: City of Gibraltar; a British Crown Colony with internal self-government.
Area: 6.5 km² (2.5 sq mi).
Population: 28,000 (1995 est.).
Capital: Gibraltar 28,000 (1995 est.).
Geography: A small rocky peninsula connected to the south coast of Spain and commanding the north side of the Atlantic entrance to the Mediterranean.
Economy: Gibraltar depends upon tourism, the re-export trade, ship repair and, particularly, banking and finance.

PLACES OF INTEREST

Tourism transformed Spain from the 1950s when cheap package deals became available to foreign holidaymakers. After France and the USA, Spain is the world's most visited state, with 45 million visitors a year, three-quarters of whom are from France, the UK, Germany and the Low Countries. Popular destinations include Andalusia, the Balearic and Canary Islands, Costa Blanca, Costa del Sol, the Dali Museum, Figueras, Madrid and the Prado Museum, Ronda, Barcelona and the Sagrada Familia, and historic Seville.

World Heritage sites include: the Alcazar, Seville; the Alhambra and Generalife, Granada; Altamira Cave; Ávila old town; Burgos Cathedral; Cáceres old town; Doñana National Park; historic Córdoba; historic Toledo; El Escorial, Madrid; Parque y Palacio Güell and Casa Mila, Barcelona; route of Santiago de Compostela; Salamanca old city; Segovia and its aqueduct; Seville Cathedral; the walled town of Cuenca.

REGIONS

1	Andalusia	8	Castile-Leon	15	La Palma
2	Aragón	9	Catalonia	16	La Rioja
3	Asturias	10	Extremadura	17	Madrid
4	Balearic Islands	11	Fuerteventura	18	Murcia
5	Basque Country	12	Galicia	19	Navarre
6	Cantabria	13	Gran Canaria	20	Tenerife
7	Castile-La Mancha	14	Lanzarote	21	Valencia

For further information on regions, see p. 359.

! The Casa Botín in Madrid is the world's oldest restaurant. It opened in 1725.

! The crypt of the underground Civil War Memorial Church in the Guadarrama Mountains is the longest in the world at 260 m (853 ft) in length.

The Dali Museum, Figueras, houses one of the largest collections of works by the Surrealist painter Salvador Dali (see pp. 236–237), who was born in the town.

! Dragon Khan at Port Aventura, Salou, is the rollercoaster with the greatest number of loops or inversions. Riders are turned upside-down eight times along the steel track.

The Great Mosque in Córdoba, a big tourist destination, dates from the 10th–11th centuries when the city was the capital of a Moorish caliphate.

! The highest motorable road in Europe is the Pico de Veleta in the Sierra Nevada, with a highest point of 3469 m (11,384 ft) above sea level.

The Pilgrimage of the Dew in Andalucia, held during Pentecost (see p.18), is a festival (one of hundreds held in the region throughout the year) when locals wear traditional dress and take part in processions.

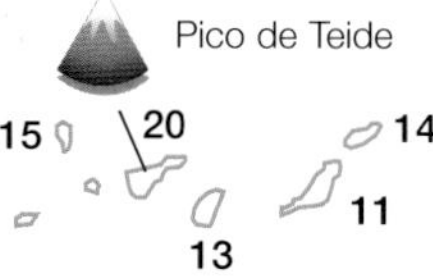

Cadiz beach, hugely popular in the summer months, adjoins the walled city which was a Phoenician and Carthaginian city in ancient times and headquarters of Spain's New World treasure fleet from the 15th century.

Costa del Sol, the rocky coast of Andalusia, was developed as a major tourist region with the birth of the package tour in the 1950s.

HEADS OF STATE

Kings and Queens*

1474–1516 Fernando V (Ferdinand V)
1474–1504 Isabel I (Isabella I)
1504–55 Juana
1504–06 Felipe I (Philip I)
1515–56 Carlos I (Emperor Charles V)
1556–98 Felipe II (Philip II)
1598–1621 Felipe III (Philip III)
1621–65 Felipe IV (Philip IV)
1665–1700 Carlos II (Charles II)
1700–24 Felipe V (Philip V)
1724 Luis
1724–46 Felipe V (restored)
1746–59 Fernando VI (Ferdinand VI)
1759–88 Carlos III (Charles III)
1788–1808 Carlos IV (Charles IV)
1808 Fernando VII (Ferdinand VII)
1808 Carlos IV (restored)
1808–13 José (Joseph Bonaparte)
1813–33 Fernando VII (restored)
1833–68 Isabel II (Isabella II)
1868–70 Regency
1870–73 Amadeo

Presidents of the First Republic

1873 Estanislao Figueras y Moragas
1873 Francisco José Pi y Margall
1873 Nicolás Salmerón
1873–74 Emilio Castelar y Ripoli
1874 Marshal Francisco Serrano y Domínguez

Kings and Queens

1874–85 Alfonso XII
1885–86 Maria Cristina
1886–1931 Alfonso XIII

Presidents of the Second Republic

1931–36 Niceto Alcalá Zamora y Torres
1936 Manuel Azaña y Diaz

Leader (Caudillo) of the Spanish State

1936–75 Francisco Franco y Bahamonde

King

1975– Juan Carlos I

* including joint sovereigns

TELEVISION AND RADIO

No. of TVs: 17,000,000 (2.3 persons per TV)
No. of radio receivers: 12,000,000 (3.3 persons per radio)

RTVE is a public corporation that controls and coordinates TV and radio. Seven regional television companies include those broadcasting in Basque, Catalan and Galician. RNE runs 17 regional radio channels; three regional stations broadcast in Basque, Catalan and Galician. There are over 300 other local radio stations.

NEWSPAPERS

Strong historic regional identities, and the existence of three major linguistic minorities (Catalan, Basque and Galician) have prevented the emergence of a national press in Spain. Only *ABC*, *Ya* and *El País* circulate thoughout most of the country. *El País* is the nearest thing to a national newspaper. Circulation figures for Spain's 120 daily papers are low. The top six newspapers are:

	Circulation	Sunday circulation
El País, Madrid, Barcelona, Valencia and Seville	575,000 (combined)	1,122,000
Marca, Madrid	474,000	
ABC, Madrid and Seville	335,000 (combined)	766,000
El Periódico de Catalunya, Barcelona	210,000	380,000
La Vanguardia, Barcelona	208,000	316,000
Diario 16, Madrid	179,000	209,000

CINEMA

No. of cinemas: 1810

The modern Spanish film industry, which has a large audience in Central and South America as well as in Spain itself, is thriving. A large amount of money is being invested from both Spanish and foreign sources. A recent blossoming of creative talent and increasing international links are allowing the industry to become more competitive and internationally accessible. Film-makers such as Pedro Almodóvar and the Basque Julio Medem are producing distinctly innovative films which have been received with great acclaim throughout western Europe and Latin America, as well as in Spain. Madrid and Barcelona are the major film-making centres.

MAGAZINES

Current affairs, women's and general interest magazines and TV listings guides outsell newspapers in Spain. The weekly periodicals with the largest sales are:

TP Teleprogramma	TV listings	1,000,000
Pronto	general interest	925,000
Tele Indiscreta	TV listings	700,000
Hola!	general interest	580,000
Interviú	general interest	494,000
Lecturas	women's magazine	342,000
Semana	general interest	341,000

DEVOLUTION IN SPAIN

The 1978 constitution of Spain saw the establishment of 19 autonomous communities (regions). The regions enjoy varying degrees of power according to the strength of local demand and tradition. Some regions, such as Catalonia and the Basque Country, have been given a high level of self-government by Madrid; in the case of Catalonia, the government of the autonomous community receives a percentage of taxes raised locally. Catalonia and the Basque Country both have a long history of local freedom but lost their autonomy under General Franco.

It is significant that the regions that enjoy the greatest powers are those in which local nationalist and separatist movements are strongest, such as the Catalan and Basque regions. Catalan nationalists form a sizeable parliamentary group in Madrid, a situation which they have been able to use to advantage; Basque nationalists include the terrorist movement ETA, whose activities in 1997 attracted widespread revulsion throughout Spain. Galicia has slightly less autonomy, while the Canary and Balearic islands come next on the 'sliding scale' of Spanish devolution.

PRIME MINISTERS (SINCE 1936)

1936	Augusto Barcia
1936	Santiago Casares Quiroga
1936	José Giral
1936–73	premiership in abeyance
1973	Luis Carrero Blanco
1973–75	Carlos Arias Navarro
1975–81	Adolfo Suárez González
1981–82	Leopoldo Calvo Sotelo
1982–96	Felipe González Márquez
1996–	José María Aznar

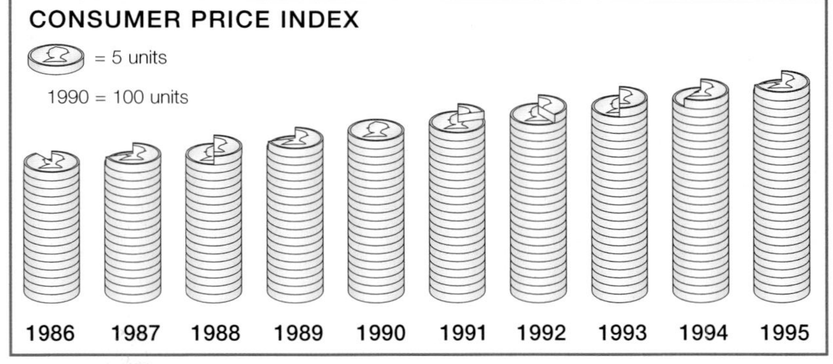

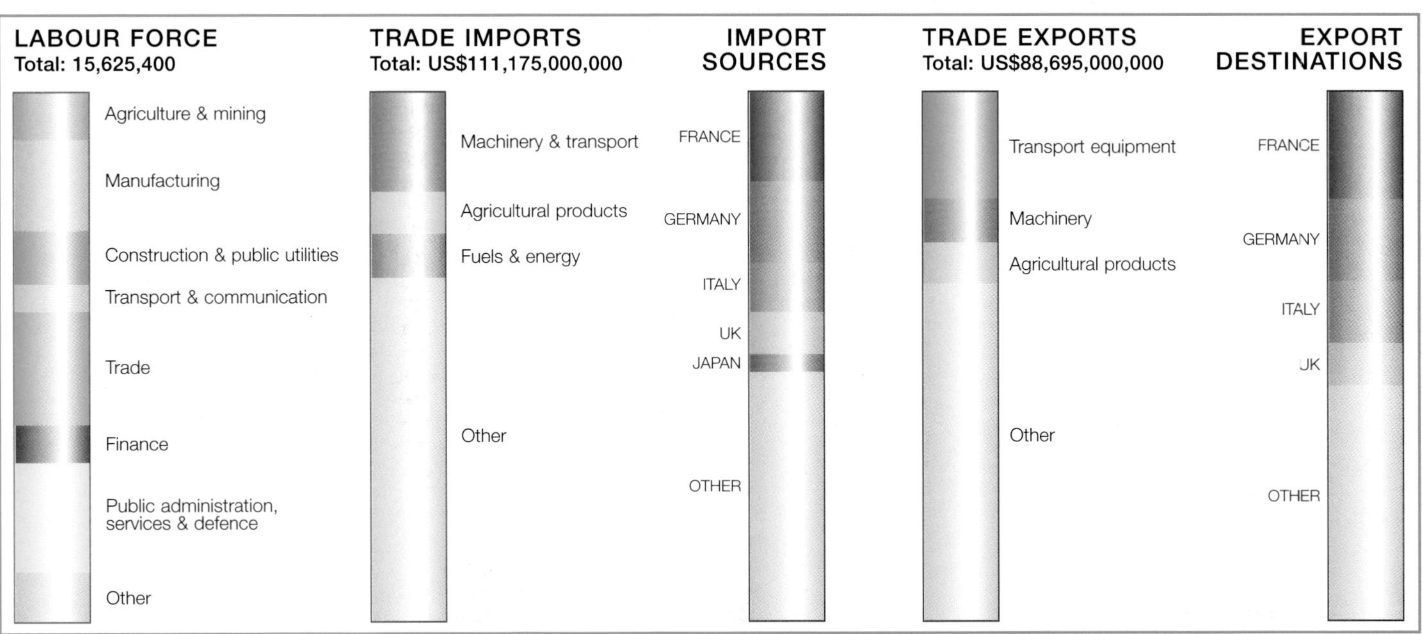

FRANCE AND SWITZERLAND

FRANCE

France is a west European republic with coastlines on the Atlantic, the Mediterranean and the English Channel. The Massif Central, a plateau of old hard rocks rising to almost 2000 m (6500 ft), occupies the middle of France. The Massif is surrounded by four major lowlands which together make up over 60% of the total area of France. The Paris Basin, the largest of these lowlands, is divided by low ridges and fertile plains and plateaux, but is united by the river system of the Seine and its tributaries. To the east of the Massif Central is the narrow Rhône-Saône Valley, while to the west the Loire Valley stretches to the Atlantic. South-west of the Massif Central lies the Aquitaine Basin, a large fertile region drained by the River Garonne and its tributaries. A discontinuous ring of uplands surrounds France. In the north-west the Armorican Massif (Brittany) rises to 411 m (1350 ft). In the south-west the Pyrenees form a high natural boundary with Spain. The Alps in the south-east divide France from Italy and contain Europe's highest peak, Mont Blanc. The lower Jura, in the east, lie on the Swiss border, while the Vosges Mountains separate the Paris basin from the Rhine Valley. In the north-east the Ardennes uplands extend into Belgium. The Mediterranean island of Corsica is an ancient massif rising to 2710 m (8891 ft).
Highest point: Mont Blanc 4807 m (15,771 ft).
Climate: The Mediterranean south has warm summers and mild winters. The rest of France has a temperate climate, although the more continental east experiences warmer summers and colder winters. Rainfall is moderate, with highest falls in the mountains and lowest falls around Paris.

Executive power is invested in the President, who is elected for a seven-year term by universal adult suffrage. The President appoints a Prime Minister and a Council of Ministers (both responsible to Parliament) but it is the President, rather than the PM, who presides over the Council of Ministers. The Senate (the upper house) comprises 321 members (296 of whom represent individual départements and 13 represent overseas départements and territories), all elected by members of municipal, local and regional councils. The remaining 12 senators are elected by French citizens abroad. Senators serve for nine years, with one third of the Senate retiring every three years. The National Assembly (the lower house) comprises 577 deputies elected for a five-year term by universal adult suffrage from single member constituencies, with a second round if no candidate obtains an absolute majority in the first round. The départements are grouped into regions which have become the most powerful local government unit.
Largest parties: (Assembly 1997 election) Socialist Party (PS) 253 seats, (conservative) Rally for the French Republic (RPR) 134, (centre-right coalition) Union for French Democracy (UDF) 108, Communist Party (PC) 38, other left-wing parties 21, other right-wing parties 15, Greens (Verts) 7, (extreme right-wing) National Front (FN) 1, others 1.
President: (since 1995) Jacques Chirac (RPR).
Prime Minister: (since 1997) Lionel Jospin (PS; PS-Verts-PC coalition government).

French regions
See following section on France.

Nearly two-thirds of France is farmed. The principal products include cereals (wheat, maize, barley), meat and dairy products, sugar beet and grapes for wine. France is remarkably self-sufficient in agriculture, with tropical fruit and animal feeds being the only major imports. However, the small size of land holdings remains a problem despite consolidation and the efforts of co-operatives. Reafforestation is helping to safeguard the future of the important timber industry. Natural resources include coal, iron ore, copper, bauxite and tungsten, as well as petroleum and natural gas and plentiful sites for hydroelectric power plants. Major French industries include textiles, chemicals, steel, food processing, motor vehicles, aircraft, and mechanical and electrical engineering. Traditionally French firms have been small but mergers have resulted in larger corporations able to compete internationally. France is the world's fourth industrial power after the USA, Japan and Germany. Since the late 1980s many state-owned corporations have been privatized. Over one half of the labour force is now involved in service industries including administration, banking, finance and tourism. **Currency:** French franc.

1914–18 World War I: much of north-east France under German occupation; trench warfare and major battles in the north. **1918** Restoration to France of Alsace and Lorraine (which had been annexed by Germany in 1870). **1940** Invasion of France by Nazi Germany. General Charles de Gaulle led the Free French in exile from London. **1942–45** All of France under German occupation, although the south and west was under a collaborationist regime headed by Marshal Philippe Pétain in Vichy. **1945** Liberation from Nazi occupation. **1946–58** Fourth French Republic which was marked by instability. **1954** Beginning of the bitter revolt against French rule in Algeria. France expelled from Indochina with the French surrender to the North Vietnamese at Dien Bien Phu. **1956** Suez Crisis: Anglo-French forces intervened in Egypt. **1957** Founder-member of the EEC (now EU). **1958–59** Rising of French settlers in Algeria (and then terrorist activities of their illegal organization, the OAS) led to a constitutional crisis in France, the end of the Fourth Republic and the accession of de Gaulle, who founded the Fifth Republic in 1959. **1960** Most French African colonies gained independence. **1962** Algeria granted independence. **1968** Student revolt in Paris against Gaullist rule. **1969** De Gaulle resigned. **1981–95** Governments of François Mitterrand, France's first Socialist President.

Dependencies
French Guiana (Guyane; see p. 443), Guadeloupe (p. 441), Martinique (p. 441), Réunion (p. 459), Mayotte (p. 459), St Pierre and Miquelon (p. 425), Clipperton Island (p. 435), French Polynesia (p. 479), French Southern and Antarctic Territories (p. 480), New Caledonia (p. 473), Wallis and Futuna Islands (p. 479).

Official name: République Française (French Republic).
Area: 543,965 km² (210,026 sq mi), metropolitan France, excluding overseas départements and territories.
Population: 58,172,000 (1995 est.).
Doubling time: not applicable; slow pop. growth. **Adult life expectancy:** male 73.1 years, female 81.3 years.
Birth rate: 0.49 times world average.
Death rate: 0.97 times world average. **Urban population:** 73%.
Capital: Paris 9,319,000 urban area (city 2,152,000; 1990 census).
Other main centres: Lyon 1,262,000 urban area (city 415,000; Villeurbanne 117,000), Marseille 1,230,000 (city 801,000; Aix-en-Provence 124,000), Lille 959,000 (city 172,000; Roubaix 98,000), Bordeaux 696,000 (city 210,000), Toulouse 650,000 (city 359,000), Nice 517,000 (city 342,000), Nantes 496,000 (city 245,000), Toulon 438,000 (city 168,000), Grenoble 405,000 (city 151,000), Strasbourg 388,000 (city 252,000), Rouen 380,000 (city 103,000), Valenciennes 339,000 (town 39,000), Cannes 336,000 (city 69,000), Nancy 329,000 (city 99,000), Lens 323,000 (town 35,000), Saint-Étienne 313,000 (city 198,000), Tours 282,000 (city 130,000), Béthune 262,000 (town 25,000), Clermont-Ferrand 254,000 (city 136,000), Le Havre 254,000 (city 196,000), Montpellier 248,000 (city 208,000), Rennes 245,000 (city 199,000), Orléans 243,000 (city 105,000), Dijon 230,000 (city 147,000), Mulhouse 224,000 (city 108,000), Angers 208,000 (city 141,000), Reims 206,000 (city 181,000), Brest 201,000 (city 148,000), Douai 200,000 (city 44,000), Metz 193,000 (city 120,000), Caen 191,000 (city 113,000), Dunkerque 191,000 (town 70,000), Le Mans 189,000 (city 145,000), Mantes-la-Jolie 189,000 (town 45,000), Avignon 181,000 (city 87,000), Limoges 170,000 (city 133,000), Bayonne 164,000 (city 42,000), Perpignan 158,000 (city 106,000), Amiens 156,000 (city 132,000), Pau 145,000 (city 82,000) (1990 census; inc. suburbs).
Language: French 94% as a first language but universally understood (official), Arabic nearly 3%, German under 3%, with Occitan, Breton and other minorities. **Adult literacy:** 99%.
Religion: Roman Catholic 73%, non-religious 16%, Sunni Islam over 5%, various Protestant Churches 2%.

SWITZERLAND

Switzerland is a landlocked mountainous federal republic in western Europe; it has been neutral for almost 200 years. The parallel ridges of the Jura Mountains lie in the north-west on the French border. The south of the country is occupied by the Alps. Between these two mountain ranges is a central plateau that contains the greater part of Switzerland's population, agriculture and industry.
Highest point: Dufourspitze (Monte Rosa) 4634 m (15,203 ft).
Climate: Altitude and aspect modify Switzerland's temperate climate. Considerable differences in temperature and rainfall are experienced over relatively short distances: for instance, the cold Alpine climate around the St Gotthard Pass is only 50 km (just over 30 mi) from the Mediterranean climate of Lugano.

Switzerland is a federal republic in which each of the 20 cantons and six half-cantons has its own government with very considerable powers. The Federal Assembly comprises the 46-member Council of States and the 200-member National Council. The Council of States is directly elected for three or four years (depending upon the canton) with two members from each canton and one from each half-canton. The National Council is elected for four years by universal adult suffrage under a system of proportional representation. The Federal Assembly elects a seven-member Federal Council (the equivalent of a Cabinet) for four years. The Federal Council appoints one of its members to be President for one year. All constitutional amendments must be approved by referendum.
Largest parties: (National Council 1995 election) (social democratic) Swiss Socialist Party (PSS) 54 seats, (centre) Radical Democratic Party (PRD) 45, (centre-right) Christian Democrat Party (PDC) 34, (right-wing) Swiss People's Party-Democratic Centre Union (UDC) 29, Greens 9, Swiss Liberal Party (PLS) 7, (nationalist) Freedom Party 7, others 15.
President: (for 1997) Arnold Koller (PDC; PDC-PSS-UDC-PRD coalition government).
President: (for 1998) Flavio Cotti (PDC).

Nearly two centuries of neutrality have allowed Switzerland to build a reputation as a secure financial centre. Zürich is one of the world's leading banking and commercial cities. The country enjoys one of the highest standards of living in the world. Industry, in part based upon cheap hydroelectric power, includes engineering (from turbines to watches), textiles, food processing (including cheese and chocolate), pharmaceuticals and chemicals. Dairying, grapes (for wine), and fodder crops are important in agriculture, and there is a significant timber industry. Tourism and the international organizations based in Switzerland are major foreign-currency earners. Foreign workers, particularly Italians and Croats, help alleviate the country's labour shortage.
Currency: Swiss franc.

1920 As a neutral country, Switzerland became the base for the ill-fated League of Nations. **1971** First female suffrage in federal elections. **1986** National vote against joining UN. **1992** National vote against joining EEA (the trade agreement linking EU and other west European states).

SWISS CANTONS

Aargau
Area: 1404 km² (542 sq mi).
Pop.: 519,000 (1994 est.).
Capital: Aarau.
Appenzell Ausser-Rhoden (half-canton)
Area: 243 km² (94 sq mi).
Pop.: 54,000 (1994 est.).
Capital: Herisau.
Appenzell Inner-Rhoden (half-canton)
Area: 173 km² (87 sq mi).
Pop.: 15,000 (1994 est.).
Capital: Appenzell.
Basel-Landschaft (half-canton)
Area: 517 km² (200 sq mi).
Pop.: 235,000 (1994 est.).
Capital: Liestal.
Basel-Stadt (half-canton)
Area: 37 km² (14 sq mi).
Pop.: 197,000 (1994 est.).
Capital: Basel.
Bern (Berne)
Area: 5961 km² (2302 sq mi).
Pop.: 957,000 (1994 est.).
Capital: Bern.
Fribourg
Area: 1671 km² (645 sq mi).
Pop.: 219,000 (1994 est.).
Capital: Fribourg.
Geneva (Genève)
Area: 282 km² (109 sq mi).
Pop.: 388,000 (1994 est.).
Capital: Geneva.
Glarus
Area: 685 km² (264 sq mi).
Pop.: 39,000 (1994 est.).
Capital: Glarus.
Graubünden (Grisons)
Area: 7105 km² (2743 sq mi).
Pop.: 182,000 (1994 est.).
Capital: Chur.
Jura
Area: 836 km² (323 sq mi).
Pop.: 69,000 (1994 est.).
Capital: Delémont.
Lucerne (Luzern)
Area: 1493 km² (576 sq mi).
Pop.: 335,000 (1994 est.).
Capital: Lucerne.
Neuchâtel
Area: 803 km² (310 sq mi).
Pop.: 2,183,000 (1994 est.).
Capital: Neuchâtel.
Nidwalden (half-canton)
Area: 276 km² (107 sq mi).
Pop: 35,000 (1994 est.).
Capital: Stans.
Obwalden (half-canton)
Area: 490 km² (189 sq mi).
Pop.: 31,000 (1994 est.).
Capital: Sarnen.
St Gallen (Sankt Gallen)
Area: 2026 km² (782 sq mi).
Pop.: 437,000 (1994 est.).
Capital: St Gallen.
Schaffhausen
Area: 299 km² (115 sq mi).
Pop.: 74,000 (1994 est.).
Capital: Schaffhausen.
Schwyz
Area: 908 km² (351 sq mi).
Pop.: 119,000 (1994 est.).
Capital: Schwyz.
Solothurn
Area: 791 km² (305 sq mi).
Pop.: 237,000 (1994 est.).
Capital: Solothurn.
Thurgau
Area: 991 km² (383 sq mi).
Pop.: 217,000 (1994 est.).
Capital: Frauenfeld.
Ticino
Area: 2812 km² (1086 sq mi).
Pop.: 298,000 (1994 est.).
Capital: Bellinzona.
Uri
Area: 1077 km² (416 sq mi).
Pop.: 36,000 (1994 est.).
Capital: Altdorf.
Valais
Area: 5225 km² (2017 sq mi).
Pop.: 267,000 (1994 est.).
Capital: Sion.
Vaud
Area: 3212 km² (1240 sq mi).
Pop.: 597,000 (1994 est.).
Capital: Lausanne.
Zug
Area: 239 km² (92 sq mi).
Pop.: 89,000 (1994 est.).
Capital: Zug.
Zürich
Area: 1729 km² (668 sq mi).
Pop.: 1,162,000 (1994 est.).
Capital: Zürich.

Official name: Confédération Suisse (in French), Schweizerische Eidgenossenschaft (German), Confederazione Svizzera (Italian) and Confederaziun Helvetica (Romansch) (Swiss Confederation).
Area: 41,285 km² (15,940 sq mi).
Population: 7,040,000 (1995 est.).
Doubling time: not applicable; slow pop. growth. **Adult life expectancy:** male 74.7 years, female 81.4 years.
Birth rate: 0.48 times world average.
Death rate: 0.95 times world average.
Urban population: 68%.
Capital: Berne (Bern) 332,000 urban area (city 129,000; 1994 est.).
Other main centres: Zürich 940,000 urban area (city 343,000), Geneva (Genève) 424,000 (city 172,000), Basel 406,000 (city 176,000), Lausanne 264,000 (city 123,000), Lucerne (Luzern) 162,000 (city 62,000), St Gallen (Sankt Gallen) 128,000 (city 76,000), Winterthur 111,000 (city 88,000), Biel/Bienne 83,000 (city 52,000), Thun 78,000 (city 39,000), Lugano 69,000 (city 25,000), Neuchâtel 66,000 (city 32,000), Fribourg 57,000 (city 33,000) (1994 est.; inc. suburbs).
Language: German 64% as a first language (official), French 19% as a first language (off.), Italian 8% as a first language (off.), Romansch 0.5% (off.).
Adult literacy: virtually 100%.
Religion: Roman Catholic 46%, various Protestant Churches 40%, non-religious 10%.

MONACO

Monaco is a tiny principality surrounded by French territory on three sides. It comprises a rocky peninsula and a narrow stretch of Mediterranean coast. Since 1964 Monaco's area has increased by over 20% as a result of reclamation of land from the sea. Monaco stretches only 300 m (985 ft) inland.
Highest point: an unnamed point 162 m (533 ft).
Climate: Monaco has a Mediterranean climate.

Monaco is a constitutional monarchy. Legislative power is held jointly by the Prince and the 8-member National Council, which is elected or five years by universal adult suffrage. Executive power remains in the hands of the Prince who appoints a four-member Council of Government and a French civil servant (the Minister of State) to head it.
Largest parties: (1993 election) National and Democratic Union 15 seats, others 3.
Prince: (since 1949) Rainier III.
Minister of State: (since 1994) Paul Dijoud.

The principality depends upon real estate, banking, insurance, light industry and tourism.
Currency: French franc.

1911 First constitution granted. **1942–44** Occupied by Italy, and later by Germany, during World War II. **1962** Rainier III granted a liberal constitution.

Official name: Principauté de Monaco (Principality of Monaco).
Area: 2 km² (0.75 sq mi).
Population: 30,400 (1995 est.).
Doubling time: pop. almost stable.
Adult life expectancy: male 72 years, female 80 years. **Birth rate:** 0.56 times world average **Death rate:** 1.97 times world average. **Urban population:** 100%. **Capital:** Monaco-ville 30,400 urban area (town 1200; Monte Carlo 14,700, La Condamine 12,200; Fontvieille 2000; 1990 census).
Language: French 39% as a first language but universally understood (official), Italian 17%, Monegasque 16%, English 7%. **Adult literacy:** almost 100%.
Religion: Roman Catholic 92%.

PLACES OF INTEREST

France receives more foreign visitors than any other country (60,000,000), with one-quarter being German and one-sixth British. The French also tend to take their vacations in France rather than outside the country. Some of the most popular places are the Alps, the Ardèche, Bayeux, Carnac, EuroDisney, the French Riviera, Futuroscope, Les Landes, the Normandy beaches, Nice, Paris, Poitiers and St Malo.

World Heritage sites include: Amiens Cathedral; Arles Roman monuments; historic centre of Avignon; Bourges Cathedral; Cape Girolata, Cape Porto, Scandola Natural Reserve and Piano Calanches, Corsica; Cathedral of Notre-Dame, former Abbey of Saint-Remi and Tau Palace, Reims; Chambord Chateau and estate; Chartres Cathedral; Chateau and park of Versailles; Cistercian Abbey of Fontenay; Fontainebleau Palace and park; Grande Isle, Strasbourg; grottoes of the Vézere Valley, including grotto of Lascaux; Le Canal du Midi; Mont-St Michel, including the abbey and the bay; Pont du Gard Roman aqueduct; Roman theatre and triumphal arch of Orange; Vézelay, church and hill.

The Eiffel Tower in Paris, an object of scepticism and controversy when it was built in 1889, is now one of the world's top tourist attractions (see p. 177).

Notre Dame Cathedral, on the Ile de Cité on the River Seine in Paris, is one of the most famous Gothic cathedrals from the Middle Ages (see p. 243).

Chartres Cathedral is famous for its stained glass, as shown in this ambulatory of *Charlemagne Departing for Spanish Crusade.* The medieval cathedrals of Chartres, Reims and Beauvais are among the most visited in France.

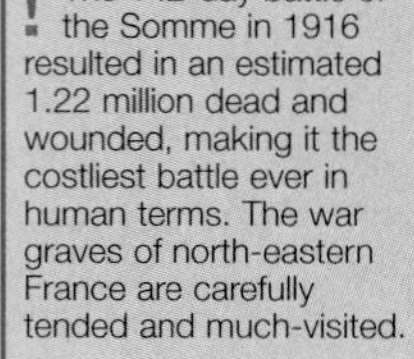

! The 142-day battle of the Somme in 1916 resulted in an estimated 1.22 million dead and wounded, making it the costliest battle ever in human terms. The war graves of north-eastern France are carefully tended and much-visited.

! Le Havre has the longest cable-stayed bridge in the world – Pont de Normandie – at 856 m (2808 ft), and the world's longest deep-water jetty, which is 1520 m (5000 ft) long.

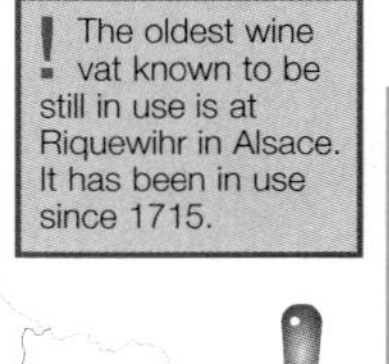

! The oldest wine vat known to be still in use is at Riquewihr in Alsace. It has been in use since 1715.

16 18 22 14 10 7 13 1 4 17 6 5 9 Mont Blanc 19 12 3 21 2 15 20 11 8

Mont Blanc, the highest mountain in the French Alps (see p. 37), attracts visitors all year round: skiers in winter and climbers and sightseers in spring and summer.

! Futuroscope, near Poitiers, has the world's first circular cinema and the largest image wall in the world, with 850 video screens, covering a surface area of 162 m^2 (1744 sq ft).

! The largest spa in terms of available accommodation is Vichy, with 14,000 hotel rooms.

! The largest sunken garden in the world, created for Béatrice de Rothschild at Villa Ephrussi de Rothschild, is at St Jean-Cap Ferrat, Most of the 17-ha (42-acre) garden is sunken.

! The largest naturist site is Domaine de Lambeyran, near Lodève, covering 340 ha (840 acres).

The Kermario standing stones near Carnac were carved from local granite in prehistoric times. The 3000 or more stones have served as a religious site for ancient pagan Bretons, Romans and Christians.

REGIONS

For further information, see p. 366.

Cannes on the Côte d'Azur, one of Europe's main tourist regions during the 19th century, still draws a stylish clientele with attractions such as the Cannes Film Festival.

PRESIDENTS OF THE THIRD, FOURTH AND FIFTH REPUBLICS

Third Republic

1871–73	Adolphe Thiers
1873–79	Patrice Mac-Mahon, duc de Magenta
1879–87	Jules Grévy
1887–94	Sadi Carnot
1894–95	Jean Casimir-Périer
1895–99	Félix Faure
1899–1906	Emile Loubet
1906–13	Armand Fallières
1913–20	Raymond Poincaré
1920	Paul Deschanel
1920–24	Alexandre Millerand
1924–31	Gaston Doumergue
1931–32	Paul Doumer
1932–40	Albert Lebrun

Vichy State

1940–44	Marshal Philippe Pétain

Heads of Provisional Government

1944–46	Gen. Charles de Gaulle
1946	Félix Gouin
1946	Georges Bidault
1946	Vincent Auriol
1946–47	Léon Blum

Fourth Republic

1947–54	Vincent Auriol
1954–58	René Coty

Fifth Republic

1959–69	Gen. Charles de Gaulle
1969–74	Georges Pompidou
1974–81	Valéry Giscard d'Estaing
1981–95	François Mitterrand
1995–	Jacques Chirac

TELEVISION AND RADIO

No. of TVs: 29,300,000 (2.0 persons per TV)
No. of radio receivers: 50,000,000 (1.2 persons per radio)

Radio France broadcasts seven main channels through 49 local radio stations. There are over 2730 local commercial radio stations and seven national commercial stations. There are three state-run TV channels (France2, France3 and La Cinquième) and four independent TV channels. Over 1,000,000 households subscribe to cable television.

NEWSPAPERS

Although 23 daily newspapers are published in Paris, France has a regional rather than a national press. The 68 provincial daily papers dominate sales outside Paris. There are only two Sunday papers in Paris – instead, weekly news magazines are characteristic of the French press. There are seven large newspaper groups. The leading daily newspaper titles are:

Ouest-France, Rennes	789,000
*France-Dimanche**, Paris	640,000
Le Parisien, Paris	431,000
Le Figaro, Paris	380,000
La Voix du Nord, Lille	369,000
L'Humanité-Dimanche, Paris*	360,000
Sud-Ouest, Bordeaux	359,000
L'Équipe (sports), Paris	337,000
Le Monde, Paris	307,000
France-Soir, Paris	200,000

* denotes Sunday publication

CINEMA

No. of cinemas: 4535

France, the birthplace of cinema and home to the Cannes Film Festival, has a thriving modern film industry based in and around Paris. Half of the films are international co-productions (French companies are also major backers for foreign films), mostly with Italy, followed by other European countries such as the UK, Germany, Spain, Portugal, Belgium and Switzerland. However, finance also comes from (in order of amount of investment) French TV channels, French producers, foreign producers and the *fonds de soutien,* which are fed by a tax levied on tickets sold at the box office. The increasing tendency is for the majority of productions to be either big commercial films or art-house features. Period films, comedies and films on contemporary life are popular, with French comedies becoming the largest French box-office hits internationally. In France, Hollywood nets 54% of the market, the lowest share of any other European country.

MAGAZINES

The periodicals with the largest circulations are:

Télé 7 Jours	weekly, TV listings	2,800,000
Télé-Poche	weekly, TV listings	1,800,000
Modes et travaux	monthly, fashion	1,500,000
Sélection du Reader's Digest	monthly, general interest	1,072,000
Nous Deux	monthly, women's illustrated stories	823,000
Paris-Match	weekly, news	690,000
Marie-Claire	monthly, women's magazine	600,000
L'Express	weekly, news	545,000

PRIME MINISTERS OF THE FIFTH REPUBLIC

1959–62	Michel Debré
1962–68	Georges Pompidou
1968–69	Maurice Couve de Murville
1969–72	Jacques Chaban-Delmas
1972–74	Pierre Messmer
1974–76	Jacques Chirac
1976–81	Raymond Barre
1981–84	Pierre Mauroy
1984–86	Laurent Fabius
1986–88	Jacques Chirac
1988–91	Michel Rocard
1991–92	Edith Cresson
1992–93	Pierre Bérégovoy
1993–95	Edouard Balladur
1995–97	Alain Juppé
1997–	Lionel Jospin

Pompidou Centre (Beaubourg), Paris is an art museum designed by Renzo Piano and Richard Rogers. Built in 1977 in the Hi-Tech style, it is one of the many stunning new buildings of the past 20 years in which the French have invested huge government funds in a campaign to modernize the Paris skyline. Others include the Pyramid, designed by I.M. Pei, outside the Louvre; the new Bibliothèque Nationale on the Left Bank; and the Arc de la Défense. As host of the 1998 World Cup, France is redeveloping its major soccer stadia with stunning effect.

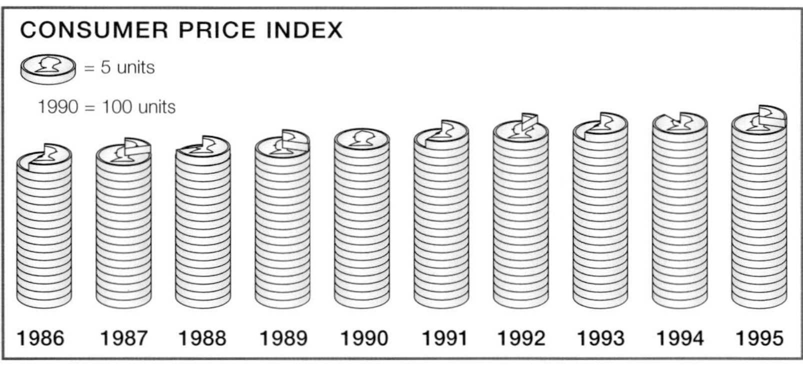

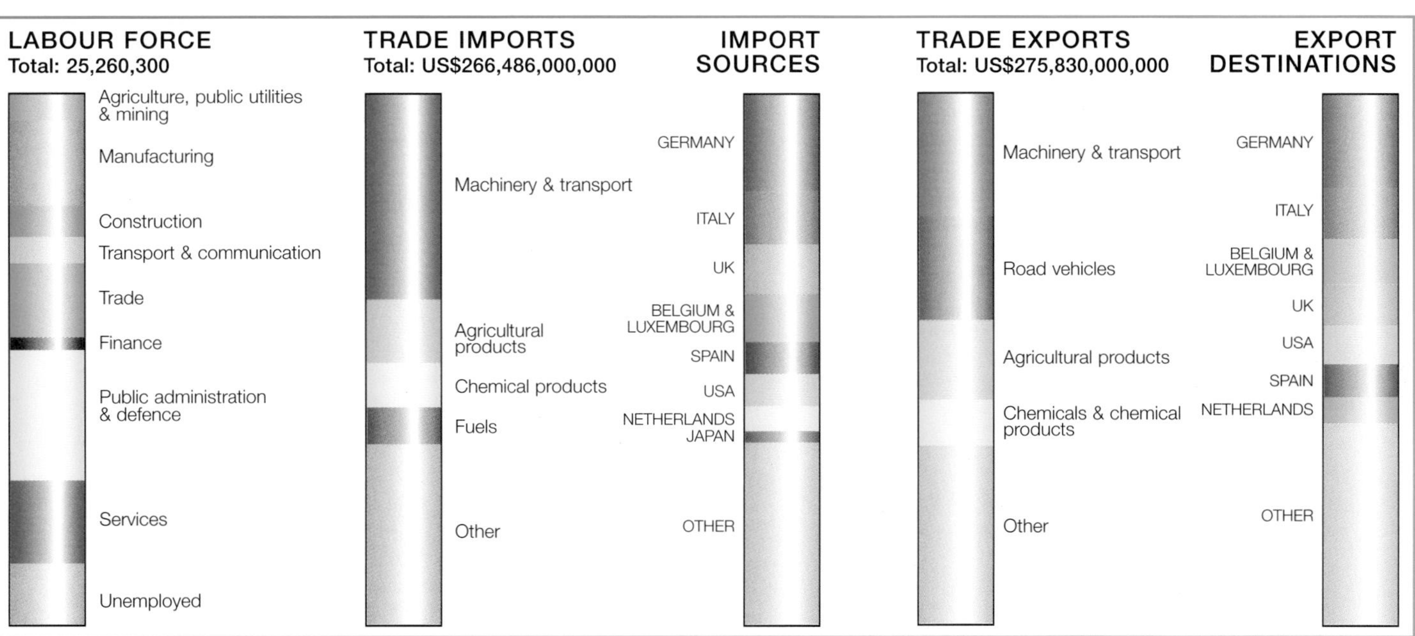

REGIONS

The regions are formed from groups of départements, which (with their capitals) are listed below.

Alsace (1)
Area: 8280 km² (3197 sq mi).
Pop.: 1,649,000 (1993 est.).
Capital: Strasbourg.
Départements: Bas-Rhin (Strasbourg), Haut-Rhin (Colmar).

Aquitaine (2)
Area: 41,309 km² (15,950 sq mi).
Pop.: 2,841,000 (1993 est.).
Capital: Bordeaux.
Départements: Dordogne (Périgueux), Gironde (Bordeaux), Landes (Mont-de-Marsan), Lot-et-Garonne (Agen), Pyrénées-Atlantiques (Pau).

Auvergne (3)
Area: 26,013 km² (10,044 sq mi).
Pop.: 1,315,000 (1993 est.).
Capital: Clermont-Ferrand.
Départements: Allier (Moulins), Cantal (Aurillac), Haute-Loire (Le Puy), Puy-de-Dôme (Clermont-Ferrand).

Brittany (Bretagne) (4)
Area: 27,209 km² (10,506 sq mi).
Pop.: 2,828,000 (1993 est.).
Capital: Rennes.
Départements: Côtes-d'Armor (Saint-Brieuc), Finistère (Quimper), Ille-et-Vilaine (Rennes), Morbihan (Vannes).

Burgundy (Bourgogne) (5)
Area: 31,582 km² (12,195 sq mi).
Pop.: 1,614,000 (1993 est.).
Capital: Dijon.
Départements: Côtes-d'Or (Dijon), Nièvre (Nevers), Saône-et-Loire (Tours), Yonne (Auxerre).

Centre-Val de Loire (6)
Area: 39,151 km² (15,116 sq mi).
Pop.: 2,404,000 (1993 est.).
Capital: Orléans.
Départements: Cher (Bourges), Eure-et-Loir (Chartres), Indre (Châteauroux), Indre-et-Loire (Tours), Loiret (Orléans), Loir-et-Cher (Blois).

Champagne-Ardenne (7)
Area: 25,606 km² (9886 sq mi).
Pop.: 1,351,000 (1993 est.).
Capital: Reims.
Départements: Ardennes (Charleville-Mézières), Aube (Troyes), Haute-Marne (Chaumont), Marne (Châlons-sur-Marne).

Corsica (Corse) (8)
Area: 8681 km² (3352 sq mi).
Pop.: 253,000 (1993 est.).
Capital: Ajaccio.
Départements: Corse-du-Sud (Ajaccio), Haute-Corse (Bastia).

Franche-Comté (9)
Area: 16,202 km² (6256 sq mi).
Pop.: 1,107,000 (1993 est.).
Capital: Besançon.
Départements: Doubs (Besançon), Haute-Saône (Vesoul), Jura (Lons-le-Saunier), Territoire de Belfort (Belfort).

Ile de France (10)
Area: 12,011 km² (4637 sq mi).
Pop.: 10,908,000 (1993 est.).
Capital: Paris.
Départements: Essonne (Évry), Hauts-de-Seine (Nanterre), Paris (Paris), Seine-et-Marne (Melun), Seine-Saint-Denis (Bobigny), Val-de-Marne (Créteil), Val-d'Oise (Pontoise), Yvelines (Versailles).

Languedoc-Roussillon (11)
Area: 27,376 km² (10,570 sq mi).
Pop.: 2,183,000 (1993 est.).
Capital: Montpellier.
Départements: Aude (Carcassonne), Gard (Nîmes), Hérault (Montpellier), Lozère (Mende), Pyrénées-Orientales (Perpignan).

Limousin (12)
Area: 16,942 km² (6541 sq mi).
Pop.: 718,000 (1993 est.).
Capital: Limoges.
Départements: Corrèze (Tulle), Creuse (Guéret), Haute-Vienne (Limoges).

Lorraine (13)
Area: 23,547 km² (9092 sq mi).
Pop.: 2,296,000 (1993 est.).
Capital: Nancy.
Départements: Meurthe-et-Moselle (Nancy), Meuse (Bar-le-Duc), Moselle (Metz), Vosges (Épinal).

Lower Normandy (Basse-Normandie) (14)
Area: 17,589 km² (6791 sq mi).
Pop.: 1,405,000 (1993 est.).
Capital: Caen.
Départements: Calvados (Caen), Manche (Saint-Lô), Orne (Alençon).

Midi-Pyrénées (15)
Area: 45,349 km² (17,509 sq mi).
Pop.: 2,492,000 (1993 est.).
Capital: Toulouse.
Départements: Ariège (Foix), Aveyron (Rodez), Gers (Auch), Haute-Garonne (Toulouse), Haute-Pyrénées (Tarbes), Lot (Cahors), Tarn (Albi), Tarn-et-Garonne (Montauban).

Nord-Pas-de-Calais (16)
Area: 12,413 km² (4793 sq mi).
Pop.: 3,983,000 (1993 est.).
Capital: Lille.
Départements: Nord (Lille), Pas-de-Calais (Arras).

Pays de la Loire (17)
Area: 32,082 km² (12,387 sq mi).
Pop.: 3,113,000 (1993 est.).
Capital: Nantes.
Départements: Loire-Atlantique (Nantes), Maine-et-Loire (Angers), Mayenne (Laval), Sarthe (Le Mans), Vendée (La Roche-sur-Yon).

Picardy (Picardie) (18)
Area: 19,399 km² (7490 sq mi).
Pop.: 1,848,000 (1993 est.).
Capital: Amiens.
Départements: Aisne (Laon), Oise (Beauvais), Somme (Amiens).

Poitou-Charentes (19)
Area: 25,809 km² (9965 sq mi).
Pop.: 1,617,000 (1993 est.).
Capital: Poitiers.
Départements: Charente (Angoulême), Charente-Maritime (La Rochelle), Deux-Sèvres (Niort), Vienne (Poitiers).

Provence-Alpes-Côte-d'Azur (20)
Area: 31,400 km² (12,123 sq mi).
Pop.: 4,375,000 (1993 est.).
Capital: Marseille.
Départements: Alpes-de-Haute-Provence (Digne), Alpes-Maritimes (Nice), Bouches-du-Rhône (Marseille), Hautes-Alpes (Gap), Var (Toulon), Vaucluse (Avignon).

Rhône-Alpes (21)
Area: 43,698 km² (16,871 sq mi).
Pop.: 5,489,000 (1993 est.).
Capital: Lyon.
Départements: Ain (Bourg-en-Bresse), Ardèche (Privas), Drôme (Valence), Haute-Savoie (Annecy), Isère (Grenoble), Loire (Saint-Étienne), Rhône (Lyon), Savoie (Chambéry).

Upper Normandy (Haute Normandie) (22)
Area: 12,318 km² (4756 sq mi).
Pop.: 1,760,000 (1993 est.).
Capital: Rouen.
Départements: Eure (Évreux), Seine-Maritime (Rouen).

THE TRICOLOUR

In 1789 the French statesman Marie Joseph Lafayette (see p. 314) created a new revolutionary cockade (a ribbon worn on military headwear) for the revolutionary National Guard of Paris. It comprised three stripes: the traditional white of the French monarchy plus the Guards' existing blue and red. These colours were adopted by the Paris Commune in 1789 as their official symbol. Flags using these colours, but not in the tricolour form, were adopted in 1790.

In 1794 the painter Jacques Louis David (see p. 237) was consulted by the French National Convention to recommend a design for the flag: he proposed three equal vertical stripes (blue, white and red). This flag was replaced by the white banner under the restored Bourbon monarchy, but the tricolour was reinstated in 1830. However, in 1836 the flag was modified to its present form: although the three stripes appear to be equal, the blue, white and red are actually in the ratio 30:33:37 to give the appearance of being the same size when the flag is seen from a distance.

The refusal of the exiled Henri V to accept the tricolour flag cost him the chance of restoration to the throne in the 1870s.

MARIANNE

Marianne, a young woman wearing a Revolutionary bonnet, symbolizes the triumph of the republic. The first reference to Marianne, the official symbol of the French Republic, was in a patriotic song of 1792. However, the name did not stick until 1797 when the republican leader Barras, at a reception at the home of Mme. Reubell, recounted his wish to give the republic a suitable 'nickname'. He asked his hostess her first name. On hearing her reply 'Marianne', he declared 'Perfect'; the French Republic has had the nickname Marianne since that time.

Since 1877 a head and shoulders statue of Marianne has held pride of place in every French town hall. The model for the statue, whose appearance changes from time to time, has usually been a well-known Frenchwoman of the period. In 1985, for example, the actress Catherine Deneuve replaced Brigitte Bardot as the official model for Marianne. The current model is the actress Emmanuelle Béart.

LA MARSEILLAISE

The words of the French national anthem, 'La Marseillaise', were written by Claude-Joseph Rouget de Lisle, a captain at the garrison of Strasbourg, in 1792 during the French Revolution. Rouget de Lisle co-wrote the music with the Austrian musician Ignatius Pleyel, who was in charge of music at Strasbourg Cathedral at the time.

The tune was originally called the 'War Song of the Army of the Rhine'. It was heard for the first time in Paris when sung by troops from Marseille as they marched into the capital in July 1792. The Parisians immediately rechristened the song 'La Marseillaise'. It became the French national anthem in 1795, but ceased to hold that status from 1804. 'La Marseillaise' was not restored as the anthem until 1879 under the Third Republic. There are seven verses (the seventh by Louis-François Dubois), but only verses one, six and seven are ever heard today.

ACADÉMIE FRANÇAISE

The most prestigious literary academy in the world, the Académie Française was established in 1634 by King Louis XIII at the suggestion of Cardinal Richelieu. The Academy was created to maintain standards in literature and to develop and protect the French language. At times it has been perceived as conservative if not actually reactionary.

Membership is limited to 40 academicians. Past members (the 'immortals') include most of the greatest names of French literature. Members fill any vacancies by election, though the French head of state (as Protector of the Academy) may veto a candidate, as de Gaulle did on two occasions. Unanimous election is almost unheard of, but no opposing vote was cast against Voltaire in 1746. Sixteen votes were taken to fill a vacancy in 1921–24.

'The 41st chair' is a list of those great figures of French literature who, for one reason or another, were not elected to a seat in the Academy: the list includes Descartes, Diderot, Beaumarchais, Balzac, Molière, Zola, Flaubert, Proust, Gide, Verlaine and George Sand.

LA FRANCOPHONIE

The status and international importance of the French language is a matter vital to French national pride. In the 20th century, English has been increasingly used as the global lingua franca. Chinese, Hindi, Spanish, Arabic, Bengali, Russian, Portuguese, Japanese, Urdu, German, Punjabi and Korean are all spoken by more people than French. The French government has therefore intervened to help maintain the language's position, and to ensure that it continues to have influence and prestige worldwide in the next millennium.

One of the threats to French is the current trend towards globalization in the media and technology industries. As enterprise and industry enter the global sphere, there is a every likelihood that English will become the lingua franca of international trade.

The development of new digital technology, such as the Internet, has predominantly been a US initiative, thus the role of English in international communications has been enhanced. Currently, less than one in twenty websites are French-based, with many of these being developed in Quebec province, Canada. To exacerbate the situation further, many of those French-language sites have an option to display information in English, to ensure that the websites attract as many international surfers as possible.

An important factor in maintaining the use of French is to ensure that the culture and arts of France itself are preserved. Many speakers of French believe that there is a threatening move towards uniformity of language and culture worldwide, partly precipitated by the spread of English in many cultural products.

Hollywood films, computer games, blockbuster novels – all seem, covertly at least, to promote the global use of English. There have been efforts to ensure that such cultural products are not considered in major international trade agreements, as this would allow American imports to considerably upset the potential of French-subsidized arts and crafts.

The French Ministry for Culture is far more active than many other EU governments in promoting home-grown arts. Its effectiveness in promoting French-language cinema is illustrated by the fact that French films account for more than one-third of all cinema ticket receipts in France.

Attempts by other high-profile authorities, such as the Académie Française, have also been influential in suggesting how French can be promoted as a global language. Some ideas include setting up a worldwide French press to counteract the very high circulation enjoyed by English-language journals, and restoring French as the first language of the Olympic Games.

Whilst the urge to promote French is very much grounded in the celebration of French identity and culture, another major reason for promoting French as a global language is to help secure jobs in the realms of information technology, science and economics. At present, these fields have specialized terminologies dominated with English-language constructions. There is no real dedicated vocabulary available in French, and so there is a real threat that the future jobs market in these important areas will be biased against French-speakers. To help combat this danger, a Terminology Commission has been set up to counterbalance the influx of English and American neologisms (newly coined words or phrases) by creating French equivalents.

There are other examples in France of direct government intervention to help protect the national language. In 1994, the Culture and Francophone Affairs Minister, Jacques Toubon, formulated a law named after him.

The Toubon Law sought to protect French against invasion and corruption by other languages, especially English. The law, which was considered controversial by the international community, but was welcomed wholeheartedly by many French-speakers themselves, legislates against businesses and enterprises which wilfully use English (or other languages) in preference over French. Thus commercial signs, broadcasts, advertisements, meetings and congresses, and company regulations must use French. For example, products must be named in French. Imported goods, such as electrical products, must be labelled in French. If signs displayed in public are not in French, then they must be accompanied with a translation (with letters of at least the same size). Failure to adhere to the law could result in fines of up to 5000 francs for an individual, or up to 25,000 francs for companies, and watchdogs have been set up to help enforce the law.

The law does have its critics, but the majority of French people consider it a necessary measure to combat the anxiety and fear of cultural marginalization, and the unwelcome 'mongrelization' of French by the inclusion of more and more English words ('*Franglais*'), for example, *le shopping*, *les leaders*, *le weekend*, *le building*, *le bulldozer*, etc.

French language and culture have been exported worldwide, resulting in the rise of *La Francophonie* – a global union of countries and territories united by their common usage of the French language, which they wish to promote. This worldwide group was set up in 1986 to rival the Commonwealth and the Hispanidad – two international organizations founded on, amongst other things, common linguistic grounds. Francophone nations meet in a summit every two years; these summits are funded by the French government. Although a celebration of the French language is at the heart of such meetings, there are also political motives.

Many countries in post-colonial Africa have affiliations to the French language, even though in several cases there has been no direct political ties with France. By providing communications and media through satellite channels and radio broadcasts, France can both encourage a reciprocal relationship with poorer countries, and can offer a political voice for those countries that are voiceless. However, that voice must be French.

Currently, *La Francophonie* represents 250 million French-language speakers in 49 countries. The political power of French-language speakers worldwide is on the increase. Organizations such as *La Francophonie* are helping to promote the francophone world, by providing a cohesive and integral identity.

This emerging political voice was heard throughout the world in October 1995, when the province of Quebec, Canada, held a referendum on whether to seek independence from the rest of Canada. Many people in Quebec, which is a largely French-speaking region, felt that French cultural and linguistic identity could be better fostered through independence. In the event, the referendum was lost by the francophones by the narrowest of margins – about 1%. However, the closeness of the final result graphically showed that, in an area where four-fifths of the populace speak French, the views of the francophones cannot be ignored.

The status of French as a world language is not to be doubted. It has a long history, and with many classics of world literature and philosophy penned in French, it is certainly never going to die out. The pro-active attitude adopted by the French government to help preserve its tongue has been matched by powerful authorities such as the Académie Française to maintain the purity of the language and eradicate hybrid compromises such as '*Franglais*', as well as providing a strong focal point for the celebration of French culture and identity worldwide.

HEADS OF STATE 987–1870

987–996	Hugues
996–1031	Robert II
1031–60	Henri I
1060–1108	Philippe I
1108–37	Louis VI
1137–80	Louis VII
1180–1223	Philippe II
1223–26	Louis VIII
1226–70	Louis IX (St Louis)
1270–85	Philippe III
1285–1314	Philippe IV
1314–16	Louis X
1316	Jean I
1316–22	Philippe V
1322–28	Charles IV
1328–50	Philippe VI
1350–64	Jean II
1364–80	Charles V
1380–1422	Charles VI
1422–61	Charles VII
1461–83	Louis XI
1483–98	Charles VIII
1498–1515	Louis XII
1515–47	François I
1547–59	Henri II
1559–60	François II
1560–74	Charles IX
1574–89	Henri III
1589–1610	Henri IV
1610–43	Louis XIII
1643–1715	Louis XIV
1715–74	Louis XV
1774–92	Louis XVI
1793–95	(Louis XVII nominally)
First Republic	
1792–95	The Convention
1795–99	Directorate
1799–1804	Consulate (three consuls)
Emperor (First Empire)	
1804–14	Napoleon I (Bonaparte)
King	
1814–15	Louis XVIII
Emperors (First Empire)	
1815	Napoleon I (restored)
1815	Napoleon II (nominally, for 16 days)
Kings	
1815–24	Louis XVIII (restored)
1824–30	Charles X
1830	Louis XIX (nominally, for 1 day)
1830	Henri V (nominally, for 8 days)
1830–48	Louis-Philippe
President of the Second Republic	
1848–52	Louis-Napoleon Bonaparte
Emperor (Second Empire)	
1852–70	Napoleon III (Louis-Napoleon Bonaparte)

The Low Countries

BELGIUM

Belgium is a small, densely populated kingdom beside the North Sea in north-east Europe.The forested Ardennes plateau occupies the south-east. The plains of central Belgium, an important agricultural region, are covered in fertile loess. The flat, low-lying north contains the sandy Kempenland plateau in the north-east and the plain of Flanders in the west. Enclosed by dykes behind coastal sand dunes are polders, former marshes reclaimed from the sea.
Highest point: Botrange 694 m (2277 ft).
Climate: Belgium experiences relatively cool summers and mild winters, with ample rainfall throughout the year. Summers are hotter and winters colder inland.

Belgium is a federal constitutional monarchy. The Chamber of Deputies (the lower house of Parliament) comprises 150 members elected by compulsory universal adult suffrage for four years under a system of proportional representation. The Senate (upper house) has 71 members (40 indirectly elected, 21 chosen by community councils, 10 co-opted), plus certain members of the Royal Family including the heir to the throne. The King appoints a Prime Minister who commands a majority in the Chamber, and, upon the PM's advice, other members of the Cabinet. The directly elected councils of Flanders, Wallonia and Brussels have very considerable powers. There are also powerful linguistic-cultural councils for the French-, Flemish- and German-speaking regions.
Largest parties: (Chamber of Deputies 1995 election) (centre) Flemish Christian Social Party (CVP) 29 seats, (centre-right) Flemish Liberal and Democratic Party (VLD) 21, (social democratic) Francophone Socialist Party (PS) 21, (social democratic) Flemish Socialist Party (SP) 20, (centre-right) Francophone Liberal Reform Party-Democratic Front of Francophones (PRL-FDF) 18, (centre) Francophone Christian Social Party (PSC) 12, (right-wing Flemish nationalist) Vlaams Blok 11, Francophone Ecology Party (ECOLO) 6, (right-wing Flemish nationalist) Volksunie 5, Flemish Ecology Party (AGALEV) 5, (conservative Francophone nationalist) National Front (FN) 2.
King: (since 1993) Albert II.
Prime Minister: (since 1992) Jean-Luc Dehaene (CVP; CVP-PS-SP-PSC coalition government).

Despite severe recent contraction, particularly in Wallonia, Belgium remains an industrial country. In the centre and the north soils are generally fertile and the climate encourages high yields of wheat, sugar beet, grass and fodder crops. Metalworking, originally based on small mineral deposits in the Ardennes, and manufacturing are major industries. Chemicals, textiles, ceramics, glass and rubber are important although most raw materials now have to be imported (coal mining ceased in 1992). Economic problems since the 1970s have mirrored Belgium's linguistic divide with high unemployment largely confined to the Francophone (Walloon) south, while industry in the Flemish-speaking north has prospered. Banking, commerce and administration employ increasing numbers, and Belgium has benefited from its role as the unofficial 'capital' of the EU. **Currency:** Belgian franc.

1914 Belgium's neutrality broken by the German invasion. **1914–18** World War I: most of Belgium under German occupation; trench warfare and major battles in western Flanders. **1940** Belgium invaded by Nazi Germany; capitulation by King Leopold III. **1940–45** All of Belgium under German occupation. **1948** Formed Benelux customs union with Luxembourg and the Netherlands. **1950–51** Unrest between Flemish and Francophone communities largely concerning controversy over the wartime role of Leopold III (who abdicated in 1951). **1957** Founder-member of the EEC (now EU). **1960** Belgian Congo relinquished amidst scenes of chaos. **1962** Rwanda and Burundi granted independence. **1980** Increase in rivalry between French- and Flemish-speaking Belgians; violent incidents occurred. **1993** New federal constitution.

■ *The rooftops of Bruges, one of Flanders' historic cities. The Flemish region, the most prosperous region in Europe in the Middle Ages, has recently become one of the boom regions of the EU*

BELGIAN FEDERAL REGIONS

Brussels (Bruxelles or Brussel)
Area: 161 km² (62 sq mi).
Pop.: 952,000 (1995 est.).
Capital: Brussels.
Flanders (Vlaanderen)
Area: 13,522 km² (5221 sq mi).
Pop.: 5,866,000 (1995 est.).
Capitals: Brussels and Ghent.
Wallonia (Wallonie)
Area: 16,844 km² (6504 sq mi).
Pop.: 3,313,000 (1995 est.).
Capital: Namur.

Official name: Koninkrijk België and Royaume de Belgique (Kingdom of Belgium).
Area: 30,528 km² (11,787 sq mi).
Population: 10,064,000 (1995 est.).
Doubling time: pop. almost stable.
Adult life expectancy: male 72.4 years, female 79.1 years.
Birth rate: 0.48 times world average.
Death rate: 1.14 times world average. **Urban population:** 97%.
Capital: Brussels (Bruxelles or Brussel) 952,000 (1995 est.; inc. suburbs). **Other main centres:** Antwerp (Antwerpen or Anvers) 668,000 urban area (city 459,000), Liège (Luik) 485,000 (city 192,000), Charleroi 295,000 (city 206,000), Ghent (Gent or Gand) 251,000 (city 228,000), Bruges (Brugge) 116,000, Namur (Namen) 105,000, Mons (Bergen) 93,000, Leuven (Louvain) 87,000, La Louvière 77,000, Aalst (Alost) 76,000, Kortrijk (Courtrai) 76,000, Mechelen (Malines) 76,000, Ostend (Oostende or Ostende) 69,000 (1991 census; inc. suburbs).
Language: Dutch (Flemish) 59% (official), French 33% (off.), German under 1% (off.), Italian 2%.
Adult literacy: almost 100%.
Religion: Roman Catholic 86%, Sunni Islam 1%, others and non-religious 13%.

■ THE TULIP, THE NETHERLANDS' NATIONAL SYMBOL, WAS INTRODUCED FROM THE MIDDLE EAST ■

NETHERLANDS

The Netherlands, one of the world's most densely populated countries, is a kingdom of north-west Europe beside the North Sea. Over one-third of the population is in the two provinces of North Holland (Noord-Holland) and South Holland (Zuid-Holland) where the urban areas of Rotterdam, Amsterdam and The Hague have almost merged. Over one-quarter of the Netherlands lies below sea level. A network of canals and canalized rivers cross the west of the country where sand dunes and man-made dykes protect low-lying areas and polders (land reclaimed from the sea). The coast has been straightened by sea walls protecting Zeeland in the south and enclosing a freshwater lake, IJsselmeer, in the north. The province of Flevoland consists entirely of polders reclaimed from IJsselmeer. The east of the country contains low sandy plains.
Highest point: Vaalserberg 321 m (1050 ft).
Climate: The country has a maritime temperate climate with cool summers, mild winters and ample rainfall.

The Netherlands is a constitutional monarchy whose head of state is King or (since 1890) a Queen. The 75-member First Chamber of the States-General is elected for six years by the 12 provincial councils, with one-half of the members retiring every three years. The 150-member Second Chamber of the States-General is elected for four years by universal adult suffrage under a system of proportional representation. The sovereign appoints a Prime Minister who commands a majority in the Second Chamber. The PM, in turn, appoints a Council of Ministers who are responsible to the Second Chamber. (Representatives of Aruba and the Netherlands Antilles are included in the Dutch government.)
Largest parties: (Second Chamber 1994 election) (social democratic) Labour Party (PvdA) 37 seats, (centre-right) Christian Democratic Appeal (CDA) 34, (liberal) People's Party for Freedom and Democracy (VVD) 31, (centre-left) Democrats 66 (D66) 24, (pensioners' rights) General Union of the Elderly (AOV) 18, Green Left 5, (right-wing) Centre Democrats 3, others 3.
Queen: (since 1980) Beatrix.
Prime Minister: (since 1994) Wim Kok (PvdA; PvdA-VVD-D66 coalition government).

Despite having few natural resources, except natural gas, the country has a high standard of living. Agriculture and horticulture are highly mechanized and concentrate on dairying and glasshouse crops, particularly flowers. Pig farming is a major interest. Food processing is a major industry and the country is a leading exporter of cheese and other dairy produce. Manufacturing includes chemical, machinery, petroleum refining, metallurgical and electrical engineering. Raw materials are imported through Rotterdam, the largest port in the world, which serves much of western Europe, particularly Germany, eastern France and Switzerland. Banking and finance are well developed, and there is an important trade in precious stones.
Currency: Guilder (or florin).

1914–18 Neutral during World War I. **1932** Completion of the major dyke which turned the Zuider Zee sea inlet into the freshwater IJsselmeer. **1940** Invaded by Nazi Germany. **1940–45** Under German occupation. **1948** Formed Benelux customs union with Belgium and Luxembourg. **1945–49** Bitter colonial war in Dutch East Indies, whose independence, as Indonesia, was recognized by the Dutch in 1949. **1953** Major flooding and loss of life (2000 drowned), when dykes burst during storms in Zeeland. **1957** Founder-member of the EEC (now EU). **1986** Completion of the southern Delta Project, which straightened the coast of Zeeland.

Dependencies
Aruba (see p. 443) and the Netherlands Antilles (see p. 443).

Official name: Koninkrijk der Nederlanden (Kingdom of the Netherlands).
Area: 41,526 km² (16,033 sq mi).
Population: 15,490,000 (1995 est.).
Doubling time: pop. almost stable.
Adult life expectancy: male 74 years, female 80 years.
Birth rate: 0.51 times world average.
Death rate: 0.94 times world average. **Urban population:** 90%.
Capital: Amsterdam 1,101,000 urban area (city 724,000; 1995 est.) is capital in name only; The Hague ('s Gravenhage or Den Haag) 694,000 (city 445,000) is the seat of government. **Other main centres:** Rotterdam 1,079,000 urban area (city 599,000), Utrecht 547,000 (city 234,000), Eindhoven 396,000 (city 196,000), Arnhem 314,000 (city 134,000), Heerlen-Kerkrade 271,000 (Heerlen town 96,000), Enschede-Hengelo 255,000 (Enschede town 148,000), Nijmegen 250,000 (city 147,000), Tilburg 238,000 (city 163,000), Dordrecht 214,000 (city 113,000), Haarlem 213,000 (city 150,000), Groningen 211,000 (city 171,000), 's-Hertogenbosch 199,000 (town 95,000), Leiden 195,000 (city 115,000) (1995 est.).
Language: Dutch 95% (official) of whom over 3% also speak Frisian, Turkish 1%, Arabic 1%. Adult literacy: almost 100%.
Religion: Roman Catholic 33%, Dutch Reformed 15%, Calvinist 8%, Sunni and Shia Islam 3%, non-religious 39%.

■ *A field of red fluted tulips in the 'Bollenstreek' or bulb-region of south Holland (Zuid-Holland), Netherlands*

LUXEMBOURG

Luxembourg, the last remaining grand duchy, is a small country bordered by France, Germany and Belgium. The Oesling, in the north, is a wooded plateau. The Gutland, in the south, is a lowland of valleys and ridges.
Highest point: Huldange 559 m (1835 ft).
Climate: Luxembourg has relatively cool summers and mild winters.

A constitutional monarchy, the 60-member Chamber of Deputies is elected by universal adult suffrage for five years under a system of proportional representation. The sovereign (a Grand Duke or Duchess) appoints a Prime Minister who commands a majority in the Chamber, and, upon the PM's advice, other members of the Cabinet.
Largest parties: (1994 election) (centre-right) Christian Social People's Party (CS) 21 seats, Socialist Workers' Party (S) 12, (centre) Democratic Party (PD) 12, Green Alternative (GLEI-GAP) 5, (pensioners' rights) Action Committee for Democracy 5.
Grand Duke: (since 1964) Jean I.
Prime Minister: (since 1995) Jean-Claude Juncker (CS; CS-S coalition government).

The iron and steel industry, originally based upon local iron ore, is important. Other industries include pharmaceuticals and synthetic textiles. Luxembourg has become a major banking centre. The north grows potatoes and fodder crops; the more densely populated south produces wheat and fruit, including grapes for wine. **Currency:** Luxembourg franc.

1914 Belgium's neutrality broken by the German invasion. **1914–18** World War I: under German occupation. **1922** Economic union with Belgium. **1940** Luxembourg invaded by Nazi Germany. **1940–45** Under German occupation. **1948** Formed Benelux customs union with Belgium and the Netherlands. **1957** Founder-member of the EEC (now EU); Luxembourg City has become one of the three centres of administration of the EU.

Official name: Groussherzogtum Letzeburg (in Letzeburgish), Grande-Duché de Luxembourg (in French) and Grossherzogtum Luxemburg (in German) (Grand Duchy of Luxembourg).
Area: 2586 km² (999 sq mi).
Population: 409,000 (1995 est.).
Doubling time: pop. almost stable.
Adult life expectancy: male 72.6 years, female 79.1 years.
Birth rate: 0.54 times world average.
Death rate: 1.05 times world average. **Urban population:** 88%.
Capital: Luxembourg 124,000 (city 76,000; 1995 est.).
Other main centres: Esch-sur-Alzette 24,000, Differdange 16,000, Dudelange 16,000, Pétange 13,000, Sanem 12,000 (1995 est.).
Language: Letzeburg 70% as a first language (national), German 10% as a first language but universally understood (official), Portuguese 10%, French 6% as a first language but universally understood (cff.).
Adult literacy: almost 100%.
Religion: Roman Catholic 95%.

Germany and Poland

GERMANY

Germany is a republic stretching from the North and Baltic Seas to the Alps and occupying a strategic position at the centre of Europe. The North German Plain, a region of fertile farmlands and sandy heaths, is drained by the rivers Elbe, Weser and Oder. In the west, the plain merges with the North Rhine lowlands which contain the Ruhr coalfield and over 20% of the country's population. A belt of plateaux, formed of old hard rocks, crosses the country from east to west and includes the Hunsrück and Eifel highlands in the Rhineland and the Taunus and Westerwald uplands in Hesse, and extends into the Harz and Erz Mountains in Thuringia. The Rhine cuts through these central highlands in a deep gorge. In southern Germany, the Black Forest (Schwarzwald) separates the Rhine Valley from the fertile valleys and scarplands of Swabia. The forested edge of the Bohemian uplands marks the Czech border, while the Bavarian Alps form the frontier with Austria.
Highest point: Zugspitze 2962 m (9718 ft).
Climate: Temperate, but there are considerable variations between the generally mild north coastal plain and the Bavarian Alps in the south, which have cool summers and cold winters. Eastern regions have warm summers and cold winters.

Germany is a federal republic in which the 16 states (Länder) have considerable powers. The Federal Council or Bundesrat (upper house) consists of 79 members, with three, four or six members appointed for a limited period by each state government (with the number of members being in proportion to the state's population). The Federal Assembly or Bundestag (lower house) has 662 members elected for four years by universal adult suffrage under a mixed system of single-member constituencies and proportional representation. Executive power rests with the Federal Government, led by the federal Chancellor, who is elected by the Bundestag. The Chancellor appoints a Cabinet. The President, whose role is largely ceremonial, is elected for a maximum of two five-year terms by the Bundestag and an equal number of representatives of the states.
Largest parties: (1994 election) (conservative) Christian Democratic Union (CDU) and (Bavarian conservative) Christian Social Union (CSU) 294 seats, Social Democratic Party (SPD) 252, the Greens 49, (Liberal) Free Democratic Party (FDP) 47, (former East German Communist Party) Party for Democratic Socialism (PDS) 30.
President: (since 1994) Roman Herzog (CDU).
Federal Chancellor: (since 1982) Helmut Kohl (CDU; CDU–CSU–FDP government).

Germany is the world's third economic power after the USA and Japan. The country's recovery after World War II has been called the German 'economic miracle'. The principal industries include mechanical and electrical engineering, chemicals, textiles, food processing, and vehicles, with heavy industry and engineering concentrated in the Ruhr, chemicals on the Rhine and motor vehicles in large provincial cities such as Stuttgart. From the 1980s, there has been a spectacular growth in high-tech industries. Apart from coal and brown coal, Germany has relatively few natural resources, and the country relies heavily upon imports. Labour has also been in short supply and large numbers of 'guest workers' (*Gastarbeiter*), particularly from Turkey and the former Yugoslavia, have been recruited. Since reunification in 1990 the labour shortage in the west has been met by migration from the former East Germany (GDR). Service industries employ almost twice as many people as manufacturing industry. Banking and finance are major currency earners and Frankfurt is one of the world's leading financial and business centres. Reunification presented many problems and its costs led to considerable economic downturn. The GDR's economy had been the most successful in the Communist bloc, but since reunification many firms in the east have been unable to compete with their more efficient western counterparts. A trust (the *Treuhandanstalt*) was set up to oversee the privatization of over 8000 state-run firms in the east, but many have gone bankrupt and nearly one-quarter of the workforce in the eastern states is unemployed. The main German agricultural products are hops (for beer), grapes (for wine), sugar beet, wheat, barley, and dairy products. The collectivized farms of the former East Germany were privatized in 1991. Forests cover one-third of Germany and support a flourishing timber industry.
Currency: Deutsche Mark.

1871–1914 Expansionist unified Germany attempted to extend influence in Europe and build colonial empire. **1914–18** World War I: defeat for Germany led to much loss of territory in Europe and the colonies overseas, and the end of the German monarchies. **1918–30** Occupation of the Rhineland by allied forces; Germany paid reparations. **Early 1930s** Nazi Party gained popularity through advocacy of strong centralized government, aggressive foreign policy and overturn of post-war settlement. **1933** Adolf Hitler came to power. **1938** Third Reich annexed Austria. **1939** Czechoslovakia dismembered; invasion of Poland; beginning of World War II. **1939–45** Nazi Germany and its allies occupied much of Europe and North Africa. **1940** German invasion of France. **1941** German invasion of

■ *The Rhineland is characterized by ruined castles and famous vineyards on sunny south-facing slopes*

Official name: Bundesrepublik Deutschland (The Federal Republic of Germany).
Area: 356,973 km^2 (137,828 sq mi).
Population: 81,910,000 (1995 est.).
Doubling time: population relatively stable; slight increase only. **Adult life expectancy:** male 73.2 years, female 79.8 years. **Birth rate:** 0.39 times world average. **Death rate:** 1.19 times world average. **Urban population:** 85%. **Capitals:** Berlin (capital in name only; Parliament will be transferred to Berlin by 2000) 3,590,000 urban area (city 3,475,000; 1992 est.). Bonn (legislative and administrative capital) 542,000 urban area (city 296,000) (1992 est.; inc. suburbs). **Other main centres:** Essen 4,700,000 Essen-Ruhr urban area (Essen city 627,000; Dortmund 601,000; Duisburg 537,000; Bochum 399,000; Gelsenkirchen 294,000; Oberhausen 225,000; Herne 179,000; Mülheim 177,000), Hamburg 1,924,000 (city 1,703,000), Munich (München) 1,465,000 (city 1,229,000), Cologne (Köln) 1,419,000 (city 960,000; Leverkusen 161,000), Frankfurt 1,268,000 (city 654,000), Stuttgart 1,091,000 (city 592,000), Düsseldorf 913,000 (city 578,000), Hannover 680,000 (city 518,000), Bremen 622,000 (city 553,000), Nuremberg (Nürnberg) 617,000 (city 498,000), Dortmund *see Essen-Ruhr*, Dresden 580,000 (city 481,000), Mannheim 539,000 (city 315,000; Ludwigshafen 165,000), Duisburg *see Essen-Ruhr*, Leipzig 532,000 (city 494,000), Wuppertal 485,000 (city 386,000), Bochum *see Essen-Ruhr*, Solingen 357,000 (city 166,000), Hagen 342,000 (city 216,000), Mönchengladbach 341,000 (city 263,000), Bielefeld 322,000, Chemnitz 306,000 (city 282,000), Halle 298,000, Gelsenkirchen *see Essen-Ruhr*, Augsburg 281,000 (city 260,000), Karlsruhe 279,000, Magdeburg 272,000, Münster 264,000, Wiesbaden 264,000, Brunswick (Braunschweig) 259,000, Kiel 259,000 (city 247,000), Krefeld 246,000, Aachen 244,000, Rostock 240,000, Saarbrücken 236,000 (city 192,000), Lübeck 230,000 (city 216,000), Oberhausen *see Essen-Ruhr*, Erfurt 202,000, Kassel 197,000, Freiburg 194,000, Mainz 183,000, Hamm 180,000 (1992 est.; inc. suburbs).
Language: German over 94% (official), Turkish over 2%, Serb and Croat 1%, with Kurdish, Italian, Greek, Polish and other minorities.
Adult literacy: virtually 100%.
Religion: Protestant (mainly Evangelical Lutheran) 44%, Roman Catholic 37%, non-religious over 16%, Sunni Islam 2%.

GERMAN STATES (LÄNDER)
Baden-Württemberg
Area: 35,751 km^2 (13,804 sq mi).
Pop.: 10,234,000 (1993 est.).
Capital: Stuttgart.
Bavaria (Bayern)
Area: 70,548 km^2 (27,239 sq mi).
Pop.: 11,863,000 (1993 est.).
Capital: Munich (München).
Berlin
Area: 889 km^2 (343 sq mi).
Pop.: 3,475,000 (1993 est.).
Capital: Berlin.
Brandenburg
Area: 29,481 km^2 (11,383 sq mi).
Pop.: 2,538,000 (1993 est.).
Capital: Potsdam.
Bremen
Area: 404 km^2 (156 sq mi).
Pop.: 683,000 (1993 est.).
Capital: Bremen.
Hamburg
Area: 755 km^2 (292 sq mi).
Pop.: 1,703,000 (1993 est.).
Capital: Hamburg.
Hesse (Hessen)
Area: 21,114 km^2 (8,152 sq mi).
Pop.: 5,967,000 (1993 est.).
Capital: Wiesbaden.
Lower Saxony (Niedersachsen)
Area: 47,606 km^2 (18,381 sq mi).
Pop.: 7,648,000 (1993 est.).
Capital: Hannover.
Mecklenburg-West Pomerania (Mecklenburg-Vorpommern)
Area: 23,169 km^2 (8946 sq mi).
Pop.: 1,844,000 (1993 est.).
Capital: Schwerin.
North Rhine-Westphalia (Nordrhein-Westfalen)
Area: 34,072 km^2 (12,155 sq mi).
Pop.: 17,759,000 (1993 est.).
Capital: Düsseldorf.
Rheinland-Palatinate (Rheinland-Pfalz)
Area: 19,845 km^2 (7662 sq mi).
Pop.: 3,926,000 (1993 est.).
Capital: Mainz.
Saarland
Area: 2570 km^2 (992 sq mi).
Pop.: 1,085,000 (1993 est.).
Capital: Saarbrücken.
Saxony (Sachsen)
Area: 18,409 km^2 (7108 sq mi).
Pop.: 4,608,000 (1993 est.).
Capital: Dresden.
Saxony-Anhalt (Sachsen-Anhalt)
Area: 20,446 km^2 (7894 sq mi).
Pop.: 2,778,000 (1993 est.).
Capital: Magdeburg.
Schleswig-Holstein
Area: 15,739 km^2 (6077 sq mi).
Pop.: 2,695,000 (1993 est.).
Capital: Kiel.
Thuringia (Thüringen)
Area: 16,175 km^2 (6245 sq mi).
Pop.: 2,533,000 (1993 est.).
Capital: Erfurt.

USSR, Yugoslavia and Greece; extermination camps set up in Germany. **1945** Defeat, occupation and division of Germany: four zones of occupation (US, Soviet, British and French). **1948–49** Soviet blockade of West Berlin. **1949** Federal Republic formed in the west; Soviet zone became the (Communist) German Democratic Republic (East Germany). **1949–63** Reconstruction of West Germany under Konrad Adenauer. **1950–71** Dictatorship of Walter Ulbricht in East Germany; Berlin Wall constructed (1961) to stem outflow of East Germans. **1953** Abortive rising against repressive Communist rule in East Germany. **1955** West Germany regained sovereignty. **Early 1970s** West Germany signed treaties with USSR and Poland recognizing new frontiers; relations normalized with GDR. **1989** Floods of East Germans fled through Czechoslovakia and Hungary; Berlin Wall opened; collapse of Communist regime in GDR. **1990** German reunification. **1994** Soviet troops withdrew from the east.

POLAND

Poland is a republic occupying part of the great plains of northern central Europe. In the north are the Baltic lowlands and the Pomeranian and Mazurian lake districts. Central Poland is a region of plains and low sandy hills running in parallel ridges from east to west. In the south are the hills of Little Poland and the Tatra Mountains.
Highest point: Rysys 2499 m (8199 ft).
Climate: Tends towards continental with short warm summers and long, quite severe, winters.

The 100-member Senate (upper house) and 460-member Sejm or Diet (lower house) are elected for four years by universal adult suffrage. In the Sejm 391 seats are contested in constituencies and the remainder are elected according to a system of proportional representation. The President is elected by universal adult suffrage for five years. The Prime Minister, who chooses a Council of Ministers, is elected by the Diet to which he is responsible.
Largest parties: (1993 election) (former Communist) Democratic Left Alliance (SLD) 171 seats, (centre-left) Polish Peasant Party (PSL) 132, (centre) Democratic Union (UD) 74, (former Solidarity) Union of Labour (UP) 71, (conservative) Federation for an Independent Poland (KPN) 22, (independent) Non-Party Bloc to Support Reform (BBWR) 16, others 4.
President: (since 1995) Aleksander Kwasniewski (SLD).
Prime Minister: (since 1996) Wlodzimierz Cimoszewiez (SLD; SLD–PSL government).

The agriculture in Poland is predominantly small-scale and privately owned. About one-fifth of the workforce is still involved in farming, growing potatoes, wheat, barley, sugar beet, and fodder crops. The industrial sector is large scale. Poland has major deposits of coal, as well as reserves of natural gas, copper and silver. Engineering, food processing and the chemical, metallurgical and paper industries are important. Privatization in the 1990s has transformed the economy which is one of the success stories of eastern Europe (with high growth rates), although inequality has increased and, for many, living standards have decreased. Poland is a candidate for EU membership. **Currency:** Zloty.

1914–18 Poland was fought over by Germany, Russia and Austro-Hungary which had partitioned the country in the late 18th century. **1919** An independent Polish republic emerged. **1926** Coup by Marshal Jozef Pilsudski who became virtual dictator until his death in 1935. **1939** German invasion of Poland at beginning of World War II. **1939–45** Occupation by Nazi Germany: Poland lost nearly one-sixth of its population. **1944** Ill-fated Warsaw Rising against the Germans. **1945** Poland liberated by Soviet Red Army; Communist state established. **1956** Political crisis led to rule by popular Communist strongman Wladyslaw Gomulka. **1980** Increasing unrest led to birth of independent trade union Solidarity, led by Lech Walesa. **1981** Martial law under Marshal Jaruzelski; Solidarity banned. **1989** Solidarity legalized; Communist system collapsed. **1990** Walesa became President. **1990** Free elections to the Sejm.

■ *Katowice is the largest industrial region in Poland*

Official name: Rzeczpospolita Polska (The Republic of Poland).
Area: 312,685 km^2 (120,727 sq mi).
Population: 38,640,000 (1995 est.).
Doubling time: population stable; slight increase only. **Adult life expectancy:** male 67.4 years, female 76 years. **Birth rate:** 0.51 times world average. **Death rate:** 1.1 times world average. **Urban population:** 62%. **Capital:** Warsaw (Warszawa) 1,643,000 (1994 est.). **Other main centres:** Katowice 2,200,000 urban area (city 367,000; Sosnowiec 260,000; Bytom 230,000; Gliwice 222,000; Zabrze 202,000; Tychy 190,000; Chorzów 132,000), Lodz 848,000, Gdansk 768,000 (city 465,000; Gydnia 252,000), Kraków 751,000, Wroclaw 643,000, Poznan 590,000, Szczecin 413,000, Bydgoszcz 382,000, Lublin 351,000, Bialystok 271,000, Sosnowiec *see Katowice*, Czestochowa 258,000, Bytom *see Katowice*, Radom 226,000, Gliwice *see Katowice*, Kielce 213,000, Zabrze *see Katowice* (1992 est.; inc.suburbs).
Language: Polish nearly 98% (official), German 1%, with Ukrainian and Belarusian minorities.
Adult literacy: 99%.
Religion: Roman Catholic 92%, non-religious over 5%, Polish Orthodox 1%.

PLACES OF INTEREST

Despite the many tourist attractions of Germany, the country attracts fewer tourists than any other major west European country (only about 15 million visitors a year). One-sixth of visitors to Germany are Dutch, while Britons and Americans together account for one-fifth. Southern Germany is a popular spot for motoring holidaymakers. Some of the most popular destinations are Aachen, the castles of Bavaria, Berlin, the Black Forest, Dresden, Hamburg, the Mittelrhein wine-growing area, Munich, Neuschwanstein Castle, Quedlinburg and the Rhine river valley.

World Heritage sites include: Aachen Cathedral; Bamberg town; The Bauhaus and its sites in Weimar and Dessau; Cologne Cathedral; Hanseatic city of Lübeck; the pilgrimage church of Wies; palaces and parks of Potsdam and Berlin; Quedlinburg's collegiate church, castle and old town; Rammelsberg mines and historic town of Goslar; Speyer Cathedral; St Mary's Cathedral and St Michael's Church, Hildesheim; Trier's Roman monuments, cathedral and Liebfrauen Church; Würzburg Residence, including court gardens and Residence Square.

LÄNDER

For further information, see p. 370 and pp. 374–375.

The New Palace at Sans Souci Park in Potsdam, the former summer palace of the Hohenzollern imperial family, is one of many palaces that have become more accessible to visitors since German reunification in 1990.

The New Synagogue in Berlin, with its ornate gold and glass cupola, is one of the many rebuilt structures in central Berlin.

Quedlinburg, with its tall, timber-framed buildings overlooking a square. Such 'typical' German townscapes are great tourist attractions, yet many were reconstructed after World War II damage.

! Ohlsdorf Cemetery in Hamburg is the world's largest cemetery, covering 400 ha (990 acres).

! The Hannover Exhibition complex is the largest in the world, with a covered space of 26 halls.

The School of Bauhaus building in Dessau, designed by Gropius. The Bauhaus movement left its imprint on many German cities with a range of distinguished buildings dating from the 1920s and 1930s.

! Mathäser in Munich is the largest beer-selling establishment in the world, selling 48,000 litres (10,559 gal) a day.

Charlemagne's Throne at Aachen, made from Roman stone. German kings were crowned at Aachen until the 16th century. Unlike much of Aachen, the Cathedral was untouched in World War II.

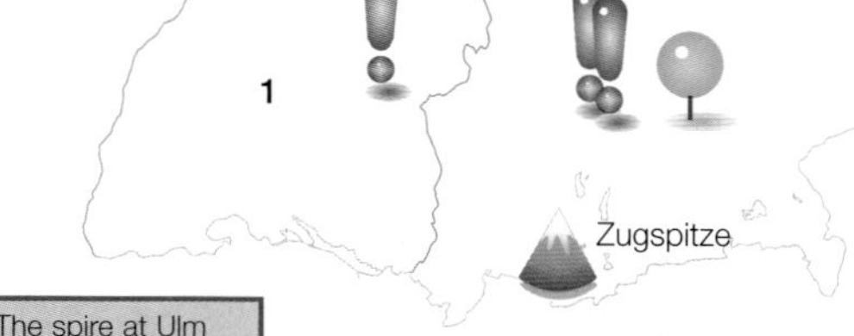

! The spire at Ulm Cathedral is almost 161 m (528 ft) high, making it the tallest in the world.

! The largest roof in the world is the acrylic 'tent' roof over the Munich Olympic Stadium, with an area of 85,000 m^2 (915,000 sq ft).

A schloss (castle) in Bavaria. The *schlösser* of Bavaria range from small, elegant hunting lodges and summer palaces to extraordinary late 19th-century excesses, such as the many-turreted Neuschwanstein Castle in the Bavarian Alps.

CHANCELLORS

1871–90	Otto, Prince von Bismarck-Schönhausen
1890–94	George Leo, Count von Caprivi
1894–1900	Chlodwig, Prince von Hohenlohe-Schillingsfürst
1900–09	Prince Bernhardt von Bülow
1909–17	Theobald von Bethmann-Hollweg
1917–18	Dr Georg Michaelis
1918	Count Georg von Hertling
1918	Prince Maximilian von Baden
1918–19	Friedrich Ebert
1919	Philipp Scheidemann
1919–20	Gustav Adolf Bauer
1920	Hermann Müller
1920–21	Konstantin Fehrenbach
1921–22	Dr Joseph Wirth
1922–23	Dr Wilhelm Carl Josef Cuno
1923	Dr Gustav Stresemann
1923–25	Dr Wilhelm Marx
1925–26	Dr Hans Luther
1926–28	Wilhelm Marx
1928–30	Hermann Müller
1930–32	Dr Heinrich Brüning
1932	Franz von Papen
1932–33	Gen. Curt von Schleider
1933–34	Adolf Hitler (Führer 1934–45)
1934–45	Third Reich (Führer Adolf Hitler 1934–45; Admiral Karl Dönitz 1945)
1945–49	Occupied
1949–63	Konrad Adenauer
1963–66	Prof. Ludwig Erhard
1966–69	Dr Kurt Georg Kiesinger
1969–74	Dr Willy Brandt
1974	Walter Scheel
1974–82	Helmut Schmidt
1982–90	Helmut Kohl

TELEVISION AND RADIO

No. of TVs: 32,314,000 (2.5 persons per TV)
No. of radio receivers: 36,186,000 (2.3 persons per radio)

ARD is the coordinating body for radio and TV networks in Germany. Five radio channels operate throughout the country. There are 15 regional broadcasting organizations. There are three television channels – one produced by ARD, one controlled by a public corporation and a third educational channel, and nearly 80 private regional stations throughout the country. Cable and satellite television are also very popular.

NEWSPAPERS

Nearly 360 daily newspapers are published in Germany, most of them confined to small regional circulations. For historic reasons there is no national press, although *Frankfurter Allgemeine Zeitung, Berliner Zeitung* and *Süddeutsche Zeitung* enjoy national circulations and prestige. 'Tabloid' papers such as *Bild-Zeitung* have increased in popularity. There are six major newspaper groups – three of which are based in Hamburg. The leading daily papers and their circulation figures are:

Bild-Zeitung, Hamburg (and printed in 15 regional centres)	4,892,000 (combined)
Bild am Sonntag, Hamburg*	2,400,000
Der Tagesspiegel, Berlin	910,000
Westdeutsche Allgemeine Zeitung, Essen	650,000
Freie Presse, Chemnitz	560,000
Mitteldeutsche Zeitung, Halle	510,000
Die Zeit, Hamburg**	491,000
Sächsische Zeitung, Dresden	450,000
Welt am Sonntag, Hamburg*	430,000
Süddeutsche Zeitung, Munich	405,000
Frankfurter Allgemeine Zeitung, Frankfurt	391,000
Rheinische Post, Düsseldorf	390,000

* denotes Sunday publication
** denotes weekly publication

CINEMA

No. of cinemas: 3685

Since the 1960s, a new wave of German film-makers has emerged who are intent on leaving the old school (known as 'Grandpa's Cinema') behind. Instead, they aim to provide a real home-based alternative to Hollywood and, rather than a cinema of *auteurs* in the vein of Werner Herzog and Wim Wenders, modern film-makers are focusing on creating entertainment. They are responsible for German film-making regaining some of the international esteem that the German cinema industry earned during the 1920s and 1930s. However, in Germany, the real Hollywood still dominates and a knock-on effect has been an 'Americanization' of German films, and an exodus of directors, mostly to the USA. Back in Germany, the largest film subsidy boards are, unsurprisingly, unwilling to fund anything other than real commercial possibilities. Munich, Hamburg and Berlin are the main centres for modern German film production.

MAGAZINES

Periodicals are mainly national rather than regional. Most of those with large circulations are based in Hamburg or Berlin. Weekly magazines with the largest circulations are:

Hörzu	TV listings	3,857,000
TV Hören + Sehen	TV listings	2,937,000
*Burda Moden**	fashion and cookery	2,300,000
Funk Uhr	TV listings	2,013,000
Neue Post	general interest	1,729,000
*Das Beste aus Readers Digest**	general interest	1,500,000
Stern	current affairs, general interest	1,479,000
Bravo	youth magazine	1,354,000
*Brigitte***	women's magazine	1,300,000
Neue Revue	general interest	1,121,000
Der Spiegel	current affairs	1,100,000

* denotes monthly publication
** denotes fortnightly publication

PRESIDENTS OF THE FEDERAL REPUBLIC

1919–25	Friedrich Ebert
1925–34	Marshal Paul von Hindenberg
1934–45	Adolf Hitler (Führer of the Third German Reich)
1949–59	Prof. Theodor Heuss
1959–69	Dr Heinrich Lübke
1969–74	Dr Gustav Heinemann
1974–79	Walter Scheel
1979–84	Karl Carstens
1984–94	Richard von Weizsacker
1994–	Roman Herzog

CONSUMER PRICE INDEX

= 5 units

1990 = 100 units

1986 1987 1988 1989 1990 1991 1992 1993 1994 1995

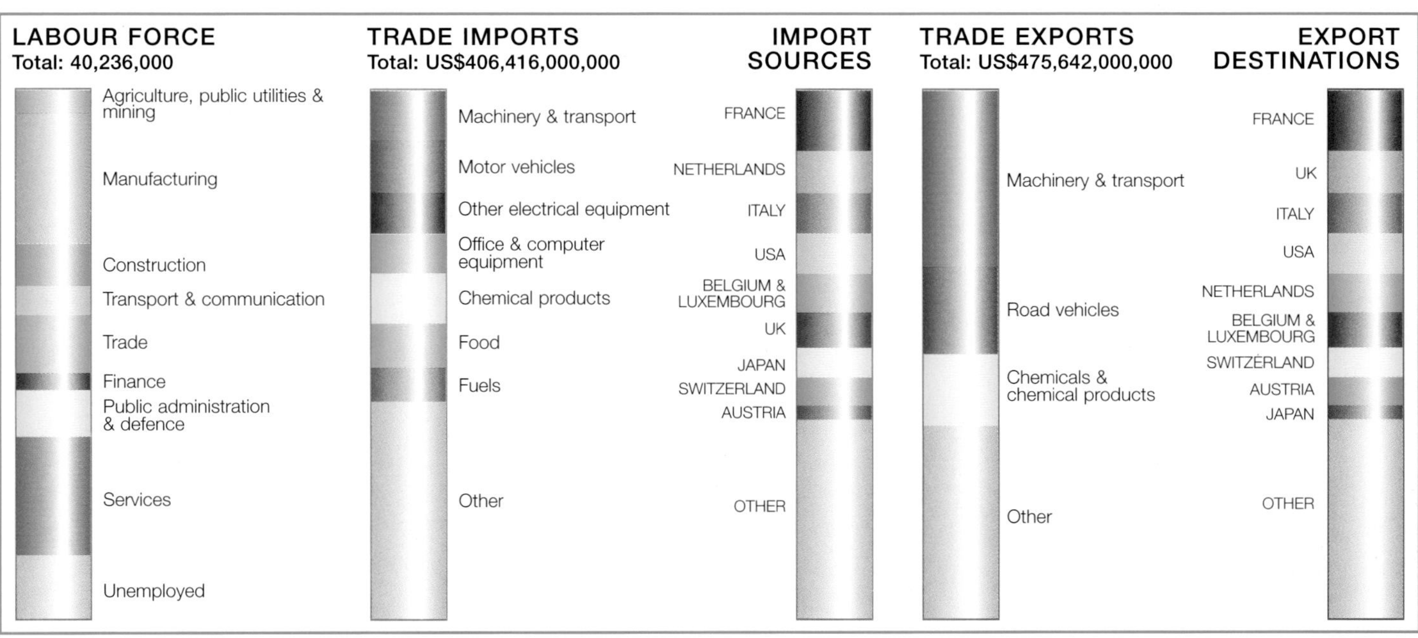

LÄNDER

BADEN-WÜRTTEMBERG (1)
Formed by the union in 1952 of the historic states of Baden, Württemberg and Hohenzollern.

Minister-president: Erwin Teufel (since 1991).

Baden-Württemberg is a state with a varied character. With its stunning landscapes, including the Black Forest and the valleys of the Rhine and Danube, it is very popular with tourists. Yet the Land is also strong on industry – several global automobile manufacturers have their base here (for example, Mercedes-Benz at Stuttgart), and digital technologies and research bases are well-established. The Land is also a key area in culture: many of Germany's literary and philosophical legends (including Schiller, Hegel, Schelling and Heidegger) are from the region. The country's oldest university is based at Heidelberg, whilst the state boasts a large output in media and publishing, with two-fifths of all German books published in the region.

BAVARIA (2)
Bavaria dates from the 9th century, becoming a duchy in 911 and a kingdom in 1805. It joined the German empire in 1871.

Minister-president: Edmund Stoiber (1993–).

Bavaria has a long history, and is a state which has cultivated strong traditions. This has, in turn, helped establish the Land as a haven for tourists who wish to experience an 'authentic' Germany. The state is one which has seen a shift in economic focus from forestry and farming to industry and services. Whilst forestry and agriculture are still highly active components of the state economy, emergent service sectors and new technologies are helping Bavaria keep abreast of current concerns. Yet the state is one which is proud of its cultural heritage, and it has actively encouraged arts festivals and a host of museums and galleries.

BERLIN (3)
West Berlin gained special status within West Germany in 1950. It was reunited with East Berlin in 1990, when the City of Berlin became a fully-fledged Land of the Federal Republic.

Governing mayor: Eberhard Diepgen (1991–).

Founded in the 13th century (and becoming the capital of Brandenburg-Prussia in the 15th century and of Germany in 1871), Berlin is steeped in history – not all of it pleasant. The 20th century saw the construction of many monumental imperial and Nazi-era buildings, and the rise of the city as a major industrial centre, only to have it decimated at the close of World War II. The war-torn city was the focus for the 1948 airlift, which saved thousands of lives when the Allies supplied West Berlin during the Soviet blockade of the city, but raised international tensions. And in 1961 the infamous Wall was erected – a graphic and deadly symbol of a country divided. However, Berlin has been home to more optimistic scenes, such as the 1989 mass protest that led to the destruction of the Wall. In 1990, the city was reunited, and, soon after, was once more declared the capital of Germany. Whilst Berlin is at present capital in name only, the Chancellery, most ministries, embassies and at least the lower house of Parliament will be located in Berlin by the year 2000.

Berlin's centre is being redesigned. A massive programme of federal investment is creating a showcase new capital, and there is a real sense that the city is experiencing a rebirth. One symbol of this urban euphoria of regeneration was the 1995 wrapping of the Reichstag by the artist Christo. The city of Berlin has begun to attain the levels of cultural and industrial splendour it had prior to World War II. Whilst industry is re-shifting its focus to more high-tech sectors, educational and artistic endeavours are on the increase. One particular annual festival of international importance is the Berlin Film Festival.

■ *Reunification celebrations in front of the Brandenburg Gate in central Berlin, 1990*

BRANDENBURG (4)
Brandenburg dates from the 12th century, and from the 15th century it came under Hohenzollern rule. The Land of Brandenburg was carved out of Prussia in 1946, but it was dissolved in 1952. It was reconstituted in 1990.

Minister-president: Manfred Stolpe (1990–).

Brandenburg is a state rich in natural reserves; mining and forestry, along with agriculture, are particularly productive areas. There are also many nature reserves and parks. However, more industrial enterprises are springing up. Since reunification, this Land has also become a major thoroughfare for travel to and from Poland. Potsdam, the capital of Brandenburg, was the site of the famous 1945 meeting between Churchill, Stalin and Truman which decided the post-war fate of Germany.

BREMEN (5)
Bremen was an imperial free city from the 14th century and became a state of the German empire in 1871.

Mayor: Henning Scherf (1995–).

Bremen is a state steeped in history and tradition which has nonetheless made the transitions necessary down the years to maintain itself as a major state. Its past stretches back over 1200 years, and it has maintained its status as a free city since the 14th century. The core industries of shipbuilding and international trade are facilitated by the River Weser, which connects the two cities that form the Land – Bremen and Bremerhaven. Bremen is one of the largest container ports in Europe, and acts as a central hub for much of the continent. Its position as an international port has also paved the way for trade in exotic commodities, such as luxury foodstuffs.

HAMBURG (6)
Hamburg dates as a free city from 1188–89. It joined the German empire in 1871.

First Mayor: Henning Voscherau (1988–).

The Free and Hanseatic City of Hamburg has maintained its position as a key international centre of trade for more than 800 years. Today a large industrial city with a vast port, it is well-situated for global shipping roots and has good internal rail connections. The city also has rich cultural aspirations. As well as being home to the more established arts, such as opera and theatre, and publishing (Hamburg is the principal centre of the German press), the city is embracing newer forms of artistic media, such as television and radio.

HESSE (7)
Hesse was founded in the 13th century and later divided between several branches of the ruling family. All of Hesse, except Hesse-Darmstadt, was annexed by Prussia in 1866. It was reunited in 1949 as a Land.

Minister-president: Hans Eichel (1991–).

Hesse is a state with rich and lucrative service industries. Its largest city, Frankfurt, is home to the central German finance banks, such as the Bundesbank, and one of Europe's major stock exchanges. This, along with the strong base in the engineering, vehicle and electrical industries, has made Hesse a rich state. The position of Hesse on key transport links has helped establish it as a centre for international trade fairs, such as the Frankfurt Book Fair. The concept of staging the world's largest annual book fair in Hesse is unsurprising considering the artistic and literary connections of the Land – Frankfurt is home to the national German Library.

LOWER SAXONY (8)
Lower Saxony was formed as a Land in 1949 from Hannover, and the historic states of Brunswick and Oldenburg.

Minister-president: Gerhard Schröder (1990–).

In part dominated by central heathland and coastal marshes, Lower Saxony is a state dominated by farming and agriculture. Nevertheless, it is also home to a successful motor industry (Volkswagen at Wolfsburg) and a successful shipbuilding base. Alongside these traditional concerns, the new digital technology industry has begun to thrive in the region. Hannover, the capital, is home to large international trade and industry fairs, and will be the site of the Expo in the year 2000. Natural gas is produced in the north-west of the state.

MECKLENBURG-WEST POMERANIA (9)
Mecklenburg dates from 1229: the duchy (later grand duchy) was divided in the 14th century and was only reunited as a single state in 1934. West Pomerania was added when the Land was formed in 1946. Dissolved in 1952, it was reconstituted in 1990.

Minister-president: Berndt Seite (1992–).

Mecklenburg-West Pomerania is a state which is famed for its natural beauty. Its lakes and hills, nature reserves and parks, and sandy coastline make tourism a key part of its economy. It is also the Land with the lowest population density. The tourist trade has been helped by reunification, and by excellent road and rail links to neighbouring regions. Much of the land is farmed, an important concern for the state. Industry, in cities such as Rostock and Schwerin, is still important, though restructuring is taking place.

NORTH RHINE-WESTPHALIA (10)
The state was formed as a Land in 1949, mainly from areas that had been part of Prussia.

Minister-president: Johannes Rau (1978–).

By far the most populous state, North Rhine-Westphalia has seen a shift in emphasis from its traditional industrial base. It has a history of steel and coal mining in what is today the Ruhr valley industrial zone. Yet while these are still very important sectors for the state, the Land also has major interests in services and commerce – today over half of its workers are employed in the services sector. The state is characterized by its industrial past, although it has made considerable headway in cleaning up its environment. North Rhine-Westphalia is also home to a growing media industry and has a strong higher education sector. For 40 years, the state was home to the West German government at Bonn; the functions of national capital are now being transferred to Berlin.

RHINELAND-PALATINATE (11)
The Land was formed in 1949 from areas of the Rhineland and of Nassau (both of which had been part of Prussia) plus the Palatinate.

Minister-president: Kurt Beck (1994–).

The Rhine dominates this state, its valley providing stunning landscapes that attract millions of tourists each year; the river has also been a key factor in the rise of its economic and industrial base. The state has a cosmopolitan feel, since it borders three countries, and has a wide range of industries from gemstones to wine production. Tourism is lucrative, with a host of architectural and cultural sites dating back hundreds of years to complement its natural beauty.

SAARLAND (12)
Saarland was removed from Germany by the Allies after World War I, and its coal mines were given to France as compensation for war losses. It rejoined Germany in 1935, but after World War II, the French again occupied the region. Following a referendum in 1955, the people of this small state decided to rejoin (West) Germany.

Minister-president: Oskar Lafontaine (1985–).

The Land's economy has traditionally been based on industry and mining, especially the coal and steel sectors. However, the changing face of industry throughout Germany has seen Saarland embrace the new information technologies. The state's geographical location and historical relation to France has seen a fusion of French and German lifestyle in many cultural aspects, such as its cuisine.

SAXONY (13)
Saxony's history as a duchy and then a kingdom stretches back over 1000 years. The Land of Saxony consists of the heart of the former kingdom of Saxony, after the rest of it was annexed to Prussia in 1815. It was reconstituted as a Land in 1990.

Minister-president: Kurt Biedenkopf (1990–).

The Free State of Saxony is an industrial state with a rich cultural past. During the years prior to the reintegration of East Germany, it reaffirmed its position as a major industrial region. Following the turnaround of 1989 and 1990, with key events taking place in the Saxon city of Leipzig, much of the industrial base collapsed. Whilst there was inevitable unemployment, the Land had the opportunity to be reborn as a player in the economic and service sectors. It is now beginning to re-establish its financial footing. The state has a rich heritage of culture and arts, and both Leipzig and Dresden attract many tourists.

SAXONY-ANHALT (14)
Saxony-Anhalt comprises those parts of Saxony annexed by Prussia in 1815 plus the ancient former duchy of Anhalt. The state was reconstituted in 1990.

Minister-president: Reinhard Höppner (1994–).

Saxony-Anhalt is a somewhat sparsely populated state with areas of outstanding scenery (there are several important nature reserves). To these sites of natural beauty, the centuries have added a wealth of architectural works of art in cities such as Magdeburg, Halle and Dessau. The area was at the heart of East Germany's chemical industries and whilst this has led to the creation of several ground-breaking products, such as colour film, it has also seen much of the landscape affected by the byproducts of such industries. Following reunification, efforts are being made to clean up the area and encourage more environmentally friendly industries.

SCHLESWIG-HOLSTEIN (15)
Schleswig and Holstein were for centuries linked with the Danish crown. They were annexed to Prussia in the 1860s and became a Land in 1949.

Minister-president: Heide Simonis (1993–).

Schleswig-Holstein is a state with a strong cosmopolitan and international feel. Located in the north of the country, it is home to diverse ethnic groups, including Frisians and Danes. Its strong natural features also help to make the area one which thrives on tourism. Whilst the natural resources have also made agriculture the traditional strongest sector, emergent technologies are utilizing the region. One example is the use of wind-turbines to create cleaner, greener energy; Schleswig-Holstein is the top producer of wind-power in the country. The southern part of the state shares in the thriving economy of Hamburg.

THURINGIA (16)
Thuringia was formed in 1920 when seven small former princely states were merged. Thuringia was reconstituted as a Land in 1990.

Minister-president: Bernhard Vogel (1992–).

Thuringia is a mountainous and forested state whose many castles (the legacy of centuries of division into tiny principalities) continually attract tourists. Places associated with Schiller, Liszt, Goethe and the Bach family also attract visitors. The Bauhaus school of design was founded in Weimar (the capital of Thuringia from 1920–48) in 1919. Centrally located, Thuringia is well situated for internal trade and commerce, and is near the commercial crossroads of Germany. The state still has an important cultural role – Weimar has been selected as European City of Culture in 1999.

THE REINTEGRATION OF EASTERN GERMANY

The reunification of West and East Germany was a process of economic, social and political upheaval that transformed the lives and landscapes of millions of people. In the late 1980s, unrest and mass uprisings throughout eastern Europe heralded the beginning of the end for the Iron Curtain. For Germans, 1990 was a landmark year, which saw the reintegration of the eastern Länder of Brandenburg, Mecklenburg-West Pomerania, Saxony, Saxony-Anhalt and Thuringia into the Federal Republic of Germany. At the same time, Berlin was once again reunited. Since then, whilst the country has experienced a unity that it had previously only known from 1871 to 1945, the process and price of unity has not been cheap.

It was in 1989 that Communism collapsed in East Germany (the GDR). The events in the country came at a time when the entire political landscape of eastern Europe was undergoing a radical shift from hardline Communism to a free-market economy. Throughout the year, East Germany's citizens had been showing increasing unrest at the harsh and inflexible state regime. In June of that year, a steady stream of citizens fled daily from the GDR by way of Czechoslovakia and Hungary, where liberalization had been much more rapid. Those that remained demonstrated a mounting resilience to the Communist state. Mass protests in Leipzig in early October precipitated the resignation of Erich Honecker, the head of state. This was followed on 4 November by the biggest protest in East Germany in living memory – a congregation of over one million people gathered in Berlin. Then, on 9 November, restrictions on East Germans entering the West were finally lifted, and the Berlin Wall collapsed. This relatively violence-free revolution became known as the *Wende* (turnaround). Eventual unification came in 1990. Following agreements between the Soviet Union and the West, Germany was allowed to reunify on 3 October 1990, and elections followed shortly afterwards.

The years following the reintegration of the East have seen an economic and social transformation. Beyond the initial celebrations and optimism, Germany has had to merge two republics that have lived separate lives for over 40 years. The five eastern states, at the time of reunion, were considerably poorer than their western counterparts. Industry and trade, once regulated by the ever-present state, needed to be entirely overhauled. As the eastern states lost their major trading partners in eastern Europe and the USSR following the collapse of Communism, thousands of businesses went bankrupt. Unemployment rose sharply as a result. Those enterprises that remained were steadily privatized by a trust, the *Treuhandanstalt*.

Monetary union also came into effect in 1990. The exchange rate, of one West German Mark for two East German ones, was more of a political gesture than an economically viable one. It allowed people in the eastern Länder to purchase a whole new selection of goods from their modern western counterparts. As a result, East German goods were not being bought, and this eroded further the industry of the ex-Communist region. The consumption rates of the eastern Länder far outstripped their productivity levels. The consequence was that, ever since reunification, the more affluent western states have been making financial transfers to the eastern Länder in the region of 150–200 billion DM (US$100–130 billion) per year, with up to one-quarter of this being unemployment benefit.

One of the reasons for the failure of a smooth economic transition to materialize was the commitment to equal standards of living throughout Germany – the West German constitution which has been extended to the East demands 'uniformity of living standards' throughout the country. The East Germans have gained in social terms – better health and pension coverage, for example. Nonetheless, faced with the more obvious and immediate uncertainties of unemployment and financial insecurity, there is an element of unease in the German populace. Whilst many Germans from the western Länder do not feel openly hostile at having to bear the load for reunification, there is a small degree of resentment present.

The unification of Germany has seen dissatisfaction as well as benefit. Whilst the country now boasts an integral identity, there are still differences. Two cultural clichés have emerged – the (western) *Besserwessi* and the (eastern) *Jammer-Ossi*. A sign that nearly half a century of differing recent histories and lifestyles cannot be readily erased through geopolitical union overnight, these stereotypes do indeed exist. The *Besserwessi* is the informed, knowledgeable, market-oriented and opinionated Western German, whilst the *Jammer-Ossi* is the complaining, community-oriented Eastern German. In years to come, it may well be that these symbols of the not-quite-seamless integration of Germany will fall away, as economic and social differences are finally eliminated.

Baltic Countries

ESTONIA

Estonia, the smallest and most northerly of the three Baltic States, is separated from Finland, with which it has much in common culturally and linguistically, by the Gulf of Finland. Estonia is gently undulating and low-lying.
Highest point: Munamägi 318 m (1042 ft). **Climate:** Moist with mild summers and cold snowy winters.

The 101-member Parliament (Riifikogu) is elected under a system of proportional representation by universal adult suffrage for four years. The President, whose role is largely ceremonial, is elected for five years by Parliament. The President appoints a Prime Minister and a Council of Ministers.
Largest parties: (1995 election) (centre-left) Coalition and Rural People's Union (K-M) 41 seats, (centre-right) Estonian Reform Party (R) 19, (centre-left) Estonian Centre Party 16, (centre-right) Fatherland Alliance/Pro Patria (PP) 8, (social democratic) Moderate Party 6, (ethnic-Russian) Our Home is Estonia 6, (right-wing) Republican and Conservative People's Party 5.
President: (since 1992) Lennart Meri (PP).
Prime Minister: (since 1997) Mart Siiman (non-party; K-M and non-party minority government).

Major industries include engineering and food processing. Gas is extracted from bitumen shale. Farming is dominated by dairying. After 1991 the disruption of trade with Russia led to severe economic difficulties but the adoption of a new stable currency, wide-reaching privatization and foreign investment has brought economic recovery, making Estonia the most successful of the Baltic States.
Currency: Kroon.

Official name: Eesti Vabariik (Republic of Estonia).
Area: 45,227 km² (17,462 sq mi).
Population: 1,490,000 (1995 est.).
Doubling time: population declining.
Adult life expectancy: male 65 years, female 75 years.
Birth rate: 0.38 times world average.
Death rate: 1.58 times world average. **Urban population:** 70%.
Capital: Tallinn 443,000 (1994 est.).
Other main centres: Tartu 106,000, Narva 79,000, Kohtla-Järve 73,000 (1994 est.).
Language: Estonian 62% (official), Russian 34%, with Ukrainian and Belarusian minorities.
Adult literacy: almost 100%.
Religion: Lutheran nearly 30%, Russian Orthodox about 5%, Estonian Orthodox, Baptist and Methodist minorities; non-religious nearly 50%.

1918 Estonia (Russian since 1712) attempted secession; German and Russian invasions. **1919** Independence secured. **1939** Non-Aggression Pact, between Hitler and Stalin, assigned Estonia to the USSR. **1940** USSR invaded and annexed Estonia. **1941–44** Occupied by Nazi Germany. **1945** Re-annexed by USSR; large-scale Russian settlement replaced over 120,000 Estonians who had been killed or deported to Siberia. **After 1988** USSR reforms allowed Estonian nationalists to operate more openly. **1990** Nationalists won majority in Estonian Parliament. **1991** Declared Independence (later recognized by USSR). **1991–93** Russia concerned over Estonia's ethnic Russian minority, many of whom were denied citizenship.

LATVIA

Latvia is the central of the three Baltic States, lying between Estonia and Lithuania on the eastern side of the Baltic Sea. The large Gulf of Riga is the major physical feature of Latvia, which is an undulating plain, lower in the west (Courland) than in the east (Livonia).
Highest point: Osveyskoye 311 m (1020 ft).
Climate: Moist and continental with cold snowy winters, although summers are relatively mild.

The 100-member Parliament (Saeima) is elected under a system of proportional representation by universal adult suffrage for three years. The President, whose role is largely ceremonial, is elected for three years by Parliament. The President appoints a Prime Minister and a Council of Ministers, who command a majority in Parliament.
Largest parties: (1995 election) (centre-left) Democratic Saimnieks (In-Charge) Party (DPS) 18 seats, (centrist) Latvia's Way (LC) 17, (far-right) (Zigerist) People's Movement for Latvia (TKL) 16, (far-right) Fatherland and Freedom Party (TB) 14, (Communist) Unity Party (LVP) 8, (centre-right) Farmer's Union and allies (LZS) 8, Greens 8, (pro-Russian) National Harmony Party (TPS) 6, others 5.
President: (since 1993) Guntis Ulmanis (LZS).
Prime Minister: (since 1995) Andris Skele (non-party; DPS–LC–LZS–TB–Green and non-party government).

Engineering dominates a heavily industrialized economy. Latvia, which previously relied upon trade with Russia, now faces severe economic problems as it adapts to a free-market economy. Foreign investment is increasing and the country benefits from Riga's position as the leading city of the Baltic States. Agriculture specializations include dairy farming and raising cattle.
Currency: Lat.

1917 Latvia (Russian since the 18th century) attempted secession; German invasion. **1918** Attempt by German forces to re-establish an independent Courland; Latvian nationalists declared independence. **1919** Allied intervention removed German forces and secured Latvian independence. **1939** Non-Aggression Pact, between Hitler and Stalin, assigned Latvia to the USSR. **1940** USSR invaded and annexed Latvia. **1941–44** Occupied by Nazi Germany during World War II. **1945** Re-annexed by USSR; large-scale Russian settlement replaced over 200,000 Latvians who had been killed or deported to Siberia. **After 1990** Reforms in USSR allowed Latvian nationalists to operate more openly. **1991** Independence declared but initially opposed by dispatch of Soviet forces. **Since 1991** Tensions remain concerning the large ethnic Russian minority in Latvia (in Riga, Russians are almost the majority).

Official name: Latvija Republika (Republic of Latvia).
Area: 64,610 km² (24,945 sq mi).
Population: 2,515,000 (1995 est.).
Doubling time: population declining.
Adult life expectancy: male 64.2 years, female 74.6 years.
Birth rate: 0.41 times world average.
Death rate: 1.63 times world average. **Urban population:** 69%.
Capital: Riga 804,000 (1993 est.).
Other main centres: Daugavpils 121,000, Liepaja 95,000, Jelgava 69,000 (1993 est.).
Language: Latvian (also known as Lettish) 52% (official), Russian 42%, with Belarusian, Ukrainian, Polish and Lithuanian minorities.
Adult literacy: almost 100%.
Religion: Lutheran 24%, Roman Catholic 21%, Russian Orthodox about 5%, non-religious nearly 50%.

FINLAND

Finland is a north European republic immediately east of Scandinavia (with which it is often grouped). Situated on the Baltic Sea, Finland is larger than its three small neighbours (the Baltic States) put together. Nearly one-third of Finland lies within the Arctic Circle, and one-tenth of the country is covered by lakes, some 50,000 in all. Saimaa (the largest lake) has an area of over 4400 km^2 (1700 sq mi). During the winter months the Gulfs of Bothnia (to the west) and Finland (to the south) freeze. The land is glaciated and except for mountains in the north-west most of Finland is low-lying.

Official names: Suomen Tasavalta (in Finnish) and Republiken Finland (Swedish) (The Republic of Finland). **Area:** 338,145 km^2 (130,559 sq mi). **Population:** 5,100,000 (1995 est.). **Doubling time:** population stable. **Adult life expectancy:** male 71.7 years, female 79.4 years. **Birth rate:** 0.52 times world average. **Death rate:** 1.01 times world average. **Urban population:** 64%. **Capital:** Helsinki (Helsingfors) 875,000 urban area (city 516,000; Espoo (Esbo) 187,000; Vantaa (Vanda) 164,000; 1994 est.). **Other main centres:** Espoo *see Helsinki*, Tampere (Tammerfors) 179,000, Vantaa *see Helsinki*, Turku (Abo) 162,000, Oulu (Uleåborg) 109,000, Lahti (Lahtis) 95,000, Kuopio 85,000 (1994 est.). **Language:** Finnish 93% (official), Swedish 6% (off.). **Adult literacy:** almost 100%. **Religion:** Evangelical Lutheran 86%, non-religious 12%, Finnish (Greek) Orthodox 1%.

Highest point: Haltiatunturi 1328 m (4357 ft).
Climate: Warm summers and long, extremely cold, winters. Conditions become harder in the winter further away from the coast.

The 200-member Diet is elected under a system of proportional representation by universal adult suffrage for four years. The President, who shares executive power with the Prime Minister, is directly elected for a maximum of two six-year terms. The President appoints a Prime Minister and a Council of Ministers, who command a majority in Parliament. The Åland Islands enjoy considerable autonomy.
Largest parties: (1995 election) Social Democratic Party (SDP) 63 seats, Centre Party (Kesk) 44, (centre-right) National Coalition Party (Kok) 39, Left-Wing Alliance (V) 22, Greens (VL) 9, (ethnic) Swedish People's Party (SFP) 12, (right-wing) Finnish Christian Union (SKL) 7, others 4.
President: (since 1994) Martti Ahtisaari (SDP).
Prime Minister: (since 1995) Paavo Lipponen (SDP; SDP–Kok–SFP–V–VL and non-party government).

Forests cover about two-thirds of the country and form the basis of the important paper and paper products industry which accounts for over one-quarter of Finnish exports. Metalworking and engineering (in particular shipbuilding) are among the main Finnish industries which have a high reputation for quality and good design. Forests, copper and plentiful sites for hydroelectric power stations are the only significant natural resources. However, Finland enjoys a high standard of living although the collapse of trade with Russia (traditionally a major trading partner) after 1991 led to economic difficulties. The fishing industry is large and the agricultural sector produces enough dairy products for export.
Currency: Markka.

■ *The exterior of the Finlandia Concert Hall. The Finnish architect Alvar Aalto (1898–1976) was a major world figure in the Modern Movement*

1906 Finland (Russian since 1809) was given autonomy within Tsarist Russia. **1917** Civil war in Finland during the Russian Revolution; pro-Russian party defeated the Whites (led by Gen. Carl Gustaf Mannerheim). **1919** Independent Finnish republic established. **1939** USSR invaded Finland which lost one-tenth of its territory to the USSR. **1941–44** Alliance with Nazi Germany led to defeat and further loss of territory to the USSR. **After 1945** Strict neutrality. **1995** Membership of EC/EU.

FINNISH AUTONOMOUS PROVINCE

Åland (Ahvenanmaa)
Area: 1527 km^2 (590 sq mi).
Pop.: 25,000 (1995 est.).
Capital: Mariehamn (Maarianhamina).

LITHUANIA

Lithuania is the largest and most southerly of the three Baltic States, and, unlike its two northern neighbours, has only a short coastline. Lithuania consists of a low-lying plain dotted with small lakes and crossed by ridges of glacial moraine that rise to their greatest height in the south-east.
Highest point: Juozapine 294 m (964 ft).
Climate: Transitional between the milder temperate type, experienced on the coast, and the more severe continental climate experienced inland. Winters are long, cold and snowy.

The 141-member Parliament (Seimas) is elected by universal adult suffrage for four years, with 71 members elected from constituencies and 70 members elected under a system of proportional representation. The President, whose role is largely ceremonial, is directly elected for five years. The President appoints a Prime Minister and a Council of Ministers, who command a majority in Parliament.
Largest parties: (1996 election) (centre-right) Homeland Union (Homeland) 70 seats, (centrist) Lithuanian Centre Union (LCU) 17, (right-wing) Christian Democratic Party (PDC) 16, Social Democratic Party (SD) 12, (former Communist) Democratic Labour Party (LDDP) 12, others 14.
President: (since 1993) Algirdas Brazauskas (LDDP).
Prime Minister: (since 1996) Gediminas Vagnorius (Homeland; Homeland–PDC government).

Over one-fifth of the labour force is still engaged in agriculture (mainly cattle rearing and dairying) and in forestry. Much of the country is heavily forested. The engineering, timber, cement and food-processing industries are important, but Lithuania has faced many economic problems as it has gradually dismantled state control (over one-half of the economy was privatized by 1996) and broken away from the former Soviet trade system. However, living standards and both industrial and agricultural production have decreased. **Currency:** Litas.

1915 Invasion of Lithuania (Russian since 1795) by German forces during World War I. **1917** Germany attempted to establish a puppet Lithuanian kingdom. **1918** Independent Lithuanian republic declared. **1919** Invasion by Russian Red Army and by Polish forces. **1923** Internationally recognized boundaries established. **1926–40** Dictatorships of Augustinas Voldemaras (1926–29) and Antonas Smetona (1926–40). **1939** Non-Aggression Pact, between Hitler and Stalin, assigned Lithuania to the USSR. **1940** USSR invaded and annexed Lithuania. **1941–44** Occupied by Nazi Germany during World War II. **1945** Re-annexed by USSR; large-scale Russian settlement replaced over 250,000 Lithuanians who had been killed or deported to Siberia. **After 1988** Reforms in USSR allowed Lithuanian nationalists to operate more openly. **1990** Nationalists gained a majority in the Lithuanian Parliament; independence declared. **1991** Soviet forces confronted Lithuanian nationalists, but USSR eventually recognized the country's independence.

Official name: Lietuvos Respublika (Republic of Lithuania). **Area:** 65,301 km^2 (25,213 sq mi). **Population:** 3,700,000 (1995 est.). **Doubling time:** population declining. **Adult life expectancy:** male 63.3 years, female 75 years. **Birth rate:** 0.46 times world average. **Death rate:** 1.34 times world average. **Urban population:** 68%. **Capital:** Vilnius 584,000 (1994 est.). **Other main centres:** Kaunas 424,000, Klaipeda 205,000, Siauliai 145,000, Panevezys 130,000 (1994 est.). **Language:** Lithuanian 80% (official), Russian 12%, Polish 6%, with Belarusian and Ukrainian minorities. **Adult literacy:** 98%. **Religion:** Roman Catholic 80%, with Russian Orthodox, Lutheran and other minorities; non-religious over 5%.

ITALY AND ITS NEIGHBOURS

ITALY

Italy is a republic occupying a long peninsula stretching south into the central Mediterranean, plus two large and several dozen smaller adjoining islands. The Alps form a natural boundary between Italy and its western and northern neighbours. A string of lakes where the mountains meet the foothills include Maggiore, Como and Lugano. The fertile Po valley (the great lowland of northern Italy) lies between the Alpine foothills in the north, the Alps in the west, the Apennine Mountains in the south and the Adriatic Sea in the east. The narrow ridge of the Ligurian Alps joins the Maritime Alps to the Apennines, which form a backbone down the entire length of the Italian peninsula. The Italian coastal lowlands are few and relatively restricted, but include the Arno Basin in Tuscany, the Tiber Basin around Rome, the Campania lowlands around Naples, and plains beside the Gulf of Taranto and in Puglia. The islands of Sardinia and Sicily are both largely mountainous. Much of Italy is liable to earthquakes. Italy has four active volcanoes including Etna on Sicily and Vesuvius, near Naples.
Highest point: 4760 m (15,616 ft) just below the summit of Mont Blanc (Monte Bianco).
Climate: Italy enjoys a Mediterranean climate with warm dry summers and mild winters. Sicily and Sardinia tend to be warmer and drier than the mainland. The Alps and the Po Valley have colder wetter climates.

Official name: Repubblica Italiana (The Republic of Italy).
Area: 301,277 km² (116,324 sq mi).
Population: 57,390,000 (1995 est.).
Doubling time: population stable; slight increase only. **Adult life expectancy:** male 73.6 years, female 80.2 years. **Birth rate:** 0.37 times world average. **Death rate:** 1.02 times world average. **Urban population:** 67%. **Capital:** Rome (Roma) 2,985,000 urban area (city 2,791,000; 1990 census; inc. suburbs). **Other main centres:** Milan (Milano) 3,670,000 urban area (city 1,432,000), Naples (Napoli) 2,905,000 (city 1,206,000), Turin (Torino) 1,114,000 (city 992,000), Genoa (Genova) 786,000 (city 701,000), Palermo 755,000 (city 734,000), Florence (Firenze) 433,000 (city 408,000), Bologna 412,000, Catania 384,000 (city 364,000), Bari 373,000 (city 353,000), Venice (Venezia) 321,000, Messina 275,000, Verona 257,000, Trieste 252,000 (city 230,000), Taranto 244,000, Padua (Padova) 218,000, Cagliari 212,000, Salerno 206,000 (city 151,000), Brescia 202,000 (city 196,000), Reggio di Calabria 179,000, Modena 178,000, Parma 178,000, Livorno 171,000, Prato 166,000, Foggia 159,000, Perugia 151,000 (1990 census; inc. suburbs).
Language: Italian over 94% (official), Italian-Sardinian over 2%, Rhaetian (Friulian and Ladin) 1%, with German, French, Albanian, Slovene and other minorities. **Adult literacy:** 97%.
Religion: Roman Catholic 83%, non-religious over 15%, Sunni Islam 1%.

The two houses of parliament are elected by universal adult suffrage for five years. The Senate (upper house) has 315 members elected by citizens aged 25 and over to represent the regions, plus 11 life senators chosen by the President. The Chamber of Deputies has 630 members elected by citizens aged 18 and over. Three-quarters of the members of both houses are elected by the first-past-the-post system; the remainder are elected by a system of proportional representation. The President, whose role is largely ceremonial, is elected for a seven-year term by a joint session of Parliament and 58 regional representatives. The President appoints a Prime Minister, who enjoys a majority in the Chamber; the PM, in turn, appoints a Council of Ministers responsible to the Chamber.
Largest parties: (1996 election) (centre-left) Olive Tree Coalition comprising (former Communist) Democratic Party of the Left (PDS) with the Greens plus the (centrist) Popular Party (PPI) and (centrist) Italian Renewal Party and smaller parties 284 seats, (right-wing) Freedom Alliance comprising (conservative) Forza Italia (FI) with (right-wing) National Alliance (AN; including the former neo-Fascists) and (centre-right) Christian Democrats (CDU) 246, (northern regional separatist) Northern League (Lega) 59, Communist Party Refoundation (RC) 35, others 6.
President: (since 1992) Oscar Luigi Scalfaro (independent).
Prime Minister: (since 1996) Romano Prodi (independent; Olive Tree government).

Northern Italy, with its easy access to the rest of Europe, is the main centre of Italian industry and has a much higher average standard of living than the south (the Mezzogiorno). The south, in contrast, remains mainly agricultural, producing grapes, sugar beet, wheat, maize and tomatoes. Southern farms tend to be small and under-mechanized. Farming in the north is more mechanized and major crops include wheat, maize, rice, grapes (for the important wine industry), fruit and fodder crops for dairy herds. Industrialization in the south is actively promoted. Industries of the north are well developed and include electrical and electronic engineering, motor vehicles and bicycles, textiles, clothing, leather goods, cement, glass and china. The north is also an important financial and banking centre: Milan is the financial capital of Italy. Apart from marble and Alpine rivers harnessed for HEP, Italy has few natural resources. Tourism and money sent back by Italians abroad are important sources of foreign currency. Crippling public debt has added to Italy's financial problems. **Currency:** Lira.

1900 Assassination of King Umberto I. **1914–18** World War I: Italy participated on allied side with action against Austro-Hungary.

ITALIAN REGIONS

Abruzzi
Area: 10,794 km² (4168 sq mi).
Pop.: 1,256,000 (1993 est.).
Capital: L'Aquila (although Pescara shares with L'Aquila some of the functions of capital.)
Basilicata
Area: 9992 km² (3858 sq mi).
Pop.: 611,000 (1993 est.).
Capital: Potenza.
Calabria
Area: 15,080 km² (5823 sq mi).
Pop.: 2,075,000 (1993 est.).
Capital: Catanzaro.
Campania
Area: 13,595 km² (5249 sq mi).
Pop.: 5,669,000 (1993 est.).
Capital: Naples (Napoli).
Emilia-Romagna
Area: 22,123 km² (8542 sq mi).
Pop.: 3,920,000 (1993 est.).
Capital: Bologna.
Friuli-Venezia Giulia
Area: 7845 km2 (3029 sq mi).
Pop.: 1,195,000 (1993 est.).
Capital: Trieste.
Lazio
Area: 17,203 km² (6642 sq mi).
Pop.: 5,162,000 (1993 est.).
Capital: Rome (Roma).
Liguria
Area: 5418 km² (2092 sq mi).
Pop.: 1,669,000 (1993 est.).
Capital: Genoa (Genova).
Lombardy (Lombardia)
Area: 23,857 km² (9211 sq mi).
Pop.: 8,882,000 (1993 est.).
Capital: Milan (Milano).
Marche
Area: 9693 km² (3743 sq mi).
Pop.: 1,434,000 (1993 est.).
Capital: Ancona.
Molise
Area: 4438 km² (1713 sq mi).
Pop.: 240,000 (1993 est.).
Capital: Campobasso.
Piemonte (Piedmont)
Area: 25,399 km² (9807 sq mi).
Pop.: 4,304,000 (1993 est.).
Capital: Turin (Torino).
Puglia
Area: 19,348 km² (7470 sq mi).
Pop.: 4,050,000 (1993 est.).
Capital: Bari.
Sardinia (Sardegna)
Area: 24,090 km² (9301 sq mi).
Pop.: 1,652,000 (1993 est.).
Capital: Cagliari.
Sicily (Sicilia)
Area: 25,709 km² (9926 sq mi).
Pop.: 4,998,000 (1993 est.).
Capital: Palermo.
Tuscany (Toscana)
Area: 22,992 km² (8877 sq mi).
Pop.: 3,529,000 (1993 est.).
Capital: Florence (Firenze).
Trentino-Alto Adige
Area: 13,618 km² (5258 sq mi).
Pop.: 897,000 (1993 est.).
Capitals: Bolzano-Bozen and Trento, which shares some of the functions of capital.
Umbria
Area: 8456 km² (3265 sq mi).
Pop.: 815,000 (1993 est.).
Capital: Perugia.
Valle d'Aosta
Area: 3262 km² (1259 sq mi).
Pop.: 117,000 (1993 est.).
Capital: Aosta.
Venetia (Veneto)
Area: 18,364 km² (7060 sq mi).
Pop.: 4,395,000 (1993 est.).
Capital: Venice (Venezia).

1922 Fascist leader Benito Mussolini became PM with programme of extensive domestic modernization and aggressive foreign policy. **1936** Italy allied to Nazi Germany in Rome-Berlin Axis; Italian invasion of Ethiopia. **1939** Italian invasion of Albania. **1940** Italy entered World War II as an ally of Nazi Germany. **1943** Allied forces invaded Italy: Mussolini dismissed by king; Italy joined the allies. **1946** Monarchy replaced by a republic. **1946–93** Political instability: many short-lived coalition governments. **1956** Became founder member of EC (now EU). **1970s** Terrorist movements of right and left active; former PM Aldo Moro abducted (1978) and murdered by terrorists. **1992–93** The public became disillusioned with state institutions; major corruption scandals; old political parties collapsed; new political movements emerged; a new constitution was formed.

SOVEREIGN MILITARY ORDER OF MALTA

Official name and status: Sovereign Military Order of Malta; a sovereign Roman Catholic order that has extra-territorial rights accorded to its buildings by the Italian state and whose ruler is recognized as sovereign by 73 countries (excluding the UK and USA) and which has a permanent observer at the UN. It is sometimes called 'the smallest country in the world'. The Order is a monarchy headed by a Prince and Grand Master, elected for life by the Knights. Prince and Grand Master: (since 1988) Fra Andrew Bartie.
Area: 1.2 ha (3 acres).
Population: 30 (1994 est.).
Geography: The territory of the Order (which formerly ruled Rhodes and then Malta) has been confined since 1831 to the Villa del Priorato di Malta (on the Aventine Hill) and No. 38 Via Condotti, both in Rome.

MALTA

Malta is a republic comprising three islands in the central Mediterranean south of Italy. Malta, Gozo and Comino consist of low limestone plateaux with little surface water.
Highest point: an unnamed point 249 m (816 ft).
Climate: Mediterranean with hot dry summers and cooler wetter winters.

The 65-member House of Representatives is elected by universal adult suffrage under a system of proportional representation for five years. The President, whose role is largely ceremonial, is elected for five years by the House. The President appoints a Prime Minister and a Cabinet who command a majority in the House.
Largest parties: (1996 election) (left-wing) Labour Party (Lab) 33 seats, (right-wing) Nationalist Party (NP) 32.
President: (since 1994) Ugo Mifsud Bonnici (non-party).
Prime Minister: (since 1996) Alfred Sant (Lab).

The main industries are footwear and clothing, food processing and ship repairing. Tourism is the principal foreign-currency earner. Malta is virtually self-sufficient in agricultural products.
Currency: Maltese lira.

1939–45 Allied naval base during World War II; suffered massive bombing (the island received the George Cross for its valour). **1964** Independence after 150 years of British rule. **1974** Became a republic.

Official name: Malta
Area: 316 km² (122 sq mi).
Population: 370,000 (1995 est.).
Doubling time: 93 years. **Adult life expectancy:** male 73 years, female 77.8 years. **Birth rate:** 0.59 times world average. **Death rate:** 0.78 times world average. **Urban population:** 89%. **Capital:** Valletta 209,000 urban area (city 9000; Birkirkara 22,000; Qormi 20,000; Hamrun 14,000; Sliema 14,000; Zabbar 13,000; 1994 est.).
Language: Maltese nearly 96% as a first language (official), English 2% as a first language (official).
Adult literacy: 96%.
Religion: Roman Catholic over 98%.

SAN MARINO

San Marino is a tiny republic completely surrounded by Italian territory. The country is dominated by the triple limestone peaks of Monte Titano.
Highest point: Monte Titano 739 m (2424 ft).
Climate: Mild Mediterranean climate.

The 60-member Great and General Council is elected by universal adult suffrage for five years. The Council elects two of its members to be Captains-Regent, who jointly hold office as heads of both state and government for a non-renewable term of six months. The Captains-Regent preside over a ten-member Congress of State (the equivalent of a Cabinet), which is elected by the Council for five years.
Largest parties: (1993 election) (centre-right) Christian Democratic Party (PDCS) 26 seats, Socialist Party (PSS) 14, (former Communist) Progressive Democratic Party (PDP) 11, Popular Democratic Alliance 4, others 5. (A PDCS–PSS government was formed.)

Manufacturing and tourism (in particular visitors on excursions) are the mainstays of the economy.
Currency: Italian lira.

1957 A bloodless 'revolution' replaced the Communist-Socialist administration (in power since 1945).

Official name: Serenessima Repubblica di San Marino (The Most Serene Republic of San Marino)
Area: 61 km² (24 sq mi).
Population: 25,000 (1995 est.).
Doubling time: not applicable; no population growth. **Adult life expectancy:** male 77.2 years, female 85.3 years. **Birth rate:** 0.43 times world average. **Death rate:** 0.75 times world average. **Urban population:** 90%. **Capital:** San Marino 4600 urban area (city 2300; Borgo Maggiore 2300; 1995 est.).
Other main centre: Serravalle 4700 (1995 est.).
Language: Italian 100% (official).
Adult literacy: over 98%.
Religion: Roman Catholic 96%.

VATICAN CITY

The Vatican City is a sovereign state consisting of a walled enclave around St Peter's near the west bank of the Tiber in Rome, plus a number of churches in Rome (including the cathedral of St John Lateran), the papal villa at Castelgandolfo and the Vatican radio station at Santa Maria di Galeria, all surrounded by Italian territory.

The Pope is elected Bishop of Rome and head of the Roman Catholic Church for life by the Sacred College of Cardinals. The Vatican City is administered by a Pontifical Commission appointed by the Pope.
Pope: (since 1978) John Paul II (Karol Wojtyla)
Head of Pontifical Commission: (since 1992) Cardinal Angelo Sodano

1929 Lateran Treaty with Italy: Italy recognized the Vatican as a sovereign state. (The Pope had remained a voluntary 'prisoner' in the Vatican since the annexation of Lazio by Italy in 1870.) **Since 1960s** The Pope has played an important role in international diplomacy again. **1984** New Concordat with Italy, replacing Lateran Treaty.

Official name: Stato della Cittá del Vaticano (The State of the Vatican City); also known as the Holy See.
Area: 0.44 km² (0.17 sq mi).
Population: 740 (1995 est.).
Language: Italian and Latin (both official).
Religion: The Vatican is the headquarters of the Roman Catholic Church.

PLACES OF INTEREST

Italy draws 30 million visitors a year. Except for people on 'city tours' to, for example, Rome, Florence and Venice, Italy tends to attract the independent traveller rather than the package holidaymaker. Two-thirds of foreign visitors to Italy are from Germany, France and Switzerland. Rome is the centre of Italian tourism, with visitors drawn by the Ancient Roman remains and Vatican pilgrimage sites. Some other popular destinations are Campania, Elba, Emilia Romagna, the Italian Lake District, Lazio, Liguria, Lombardy, Milan Cathedral, Palermo, Sicily, Piedmont, Portofino and the Riviera di Levante, Trentino-Alto Adige, Tuscany, Mt Vesuvius and Pompeii.

World Heritage sites include: Castel del Monte; church and Dominican convent of Santa Maria delle Grazie; Ferrara, city of the Renaissance; city of Vicenza and Palladian villas of the Veneto; historic centre of Florence; historic centre of Naples; historic centre of Pienza; historic centre of San Gimignano; historic centre of Siena; Piazza del Duomo, Pisa; early Christian monuments and mosaics of Ravenna; rock drawings of Valcamonica (near Bresica); Venice and its lagoon.

REGIONS

1	Abruzzi	11	Molise
2	Basilicata	12	Piemonte (Piedmont)
3	Calabria	13	Puglia
4	Campania	14	Sardinia (Sardegna)
5	Emilia-Romagna	15	Sicily (Sicilia)
6	Friuli-Venezia Giulia	16	Tuscany (Toscana)
7	Lazio	17	Trentino-Alto Adige
8	Liguria	18	Umbria
9	Lombardy (Lombardia)	19	Valle d'Aosta
10	Marche	20	Venetia (Veneto)

For further information, see p. 379.

The Duomo (Cathedral) in Florence is the best-known element (see p. 243) of Florence's incomparable skyline.

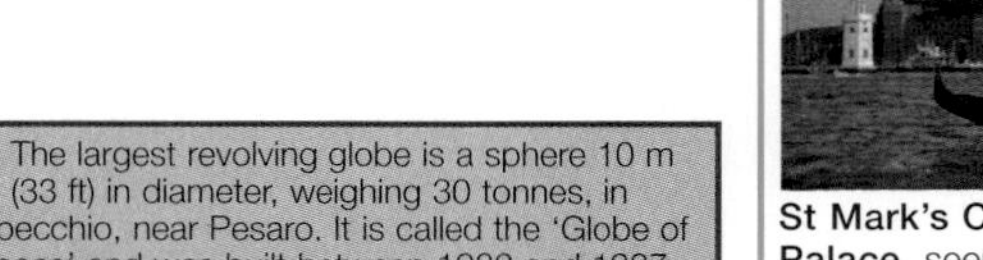

! The largest revolving globe is a sphere 10 m (33 ft) in diameter, weighing 30 tonnes, in Apecchio, near Pesaro. It is called the 'Globe of Peace' and was built between 1982 and 1987.

St Mark's Cathedral and the Doge's Palace, seen from the Canale di San Marco in Venice. The city has become almost too popular as a tourist attraction – visitors are encouraged to park on the mainland and use public transport to cross the causeway.

! The world's narrowest street is Vicolo della Virilita at Ripatransone, Marche – it is, on average, 43 cm (17 in) wide.

The Colosseum in Rome could seat 50,000 spectators to watch gladiatorial contests. It has become a symbol for Rome and is the most famous of the classical monuments that attract millions of tourists to the city each year.

! The world's largest rose garden, with 7500 varieties, is at Cavriglia.

! The Vatican, entirely surrounded by Rome, is the world's smallest sovereign state.

The Leaning Tower of Pisa, a campanile (bell tower), is the most famous building (see p. 176) of a spectacular group of structures which also includes the cathedral and the baptistry.

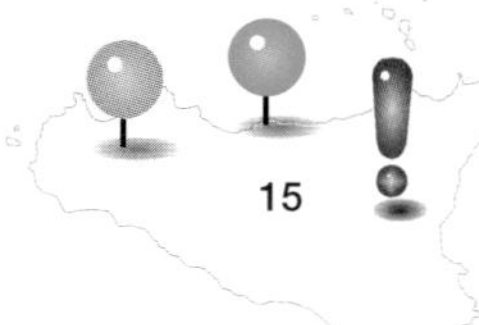

Segesta temple is one of the best preserved Greek monuments in Sicily. The ancient town of Segesta, a Carthaginian ally in the Punic Wars, is one of many major archaeological sites in Sicily.

! The tree with the greatest recorded girth ever was the 'Tree of the Hundred Horses' on Mt Etna, with a record circumference of 57.9 m (190 ft).

The Duomo (Cathedral) of Cefalu, an historic city situated on a promontory overlooking the Tyrrhenian Sea. The city, like many Sicilian hilltop towns, dates back to Ancient Greek times.

TELEVISION AND RADIO

No. of TVs: 17,000,500 (3.4 persons per TV)
No. of radio receivers: 45,350,000 (1.3 persons per radio)

Italy has about 900 local commercial TV stations, seven of which are broadcast nationwide, as well as RAI (Radiotelevisione Italiana) – the national network which runs three channels – and a Catholic network. RAI also broadcasts national radio channels; there are over 1000 local commercial radio stations.

CINEMA

No. of cinemas: 3100

Italy has a long tradition of film-making. Studios such as Cinecittà, the biggest studio in Europe when it opened in 1937, have produced everything from neo-realist masterpieces to spaghetti western films, which have elicited a cult following. Today the major studios are all based in Rome and are producing a healthy output of romantic comedies, literary adaptations and neo-realist tributes. However, the bulk of Italy's top-grossing films at the box office are from Hollywood.

NEWSPAPERS

The Italian press is characterized by the small number of daily papers published – only 79 – and by their low circulations compared with other G7 countries. The press is concentrated in Milan and Rome. There is no national press, but *Corriere della Sera, La Repubblica* and *La Stampa* enjoy national circulations and prestige. Principal daily newspaper titles and their circulation figures are:

Corriere della Sera, Milan	790,000
La Repubblica, Rome	662,000
La Gazetta dello Sport, Milan	455,000
Il Sole/24 Ore (financial), Milan	435,000
La Stampa,Turin	421,000
Corriere dello Sport, Rome with 13 regional editions	267,000
Il Messaggero, Rome	260,000

MAGAZINES

Italy has about 10,000 periodicals – most with small circulations. However, a few motoring, women's and general interest magazines attract circulations that compare with the top magazines in major Western countries. The weekly periodicals with the largest circulations are:

*L'Automobile**	motoring	1,083,000
Famiglia Cristiana	Catholic illustrated	1,071,000
Gente	political and current affairs	790,000
Oggi	topical and literary	748,000
*Quattroruote**	motoring	700,000
Panorama	current affairs	541,000
Intimità	women's magazine	468,000

* denotes monthly publication

PRIME MINISTERS OF THE REPUBLIC

1946–53	Alcide de Gasperi
1953–54	Giuseppe Pella
1954	Amintore Fanfani
1954–55	Mario Scelba
1955–57	Antonio Segni
1957–58	Adone Zoli
1958–59	Amintore Fanfani
1959–60	Antonio Segni
1960	Fernando Tambroni
1960–63	Amintore Fanfani
1963	Giovanni Leone
1963–68	Aldo Moro
1968	Giovanni Leone
1968–70	Mariano Rumor
1970–72	Emilio Colombo
1972–73	Giulio Andreotti
1973–74	Mariano Rumor
1974–76	Aldo Moro
1976–79	Giulio Andreotti
1979	Ugo La Malfa
1979	Giulio Andreotti
1979–80	Francesco Cossiga
1980–81	Arnaldo Forlani
1981–82	Giovanni Spaldolini
1982–83	Amintore Fanfani
1983–87	Bettino Craxi
1987	Amintore Fanfani
1987–88	Giovanni Goria
1988–89	Ciriaco De Mita
1989–92	Giulio Andreotti
1992	Giovanni Spadolini
1992–93	Giuliano Amato
1993–94	Carlo Azeglio Ciampi
1994–95	Silvio Berlusconi
1995–96	Lamberto Dini
1996–	Romano Prodi

PRESIDENTS

1946–48	Enrico de Nicola
1948–55	Luigi Einaudi
1955–62	Giovanni Gronchi
1962–64	Antonio Segni
1964–71	Giuseppe Saragat
1971–78	Giovanni Leone
1978	Amintore Fanfani (acting)
1978–85	Alessandro Pertini
1985–92	Francesco Cossiga
1992–	Oscar Luigi Scalfaro

NATIONAL ANTHEM

'Inno di Mameli' is the most famous of the patriotic songs of the Italian Risorgimento (unity movement) of the mid-19th century. It was written in Genoa in 1847 by Goffredo Mameli (words) and Michele Novaro (music).

CONSUMER PRICE INDEX

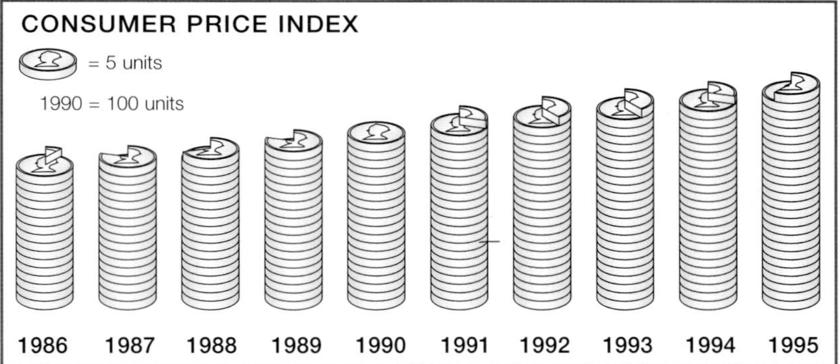

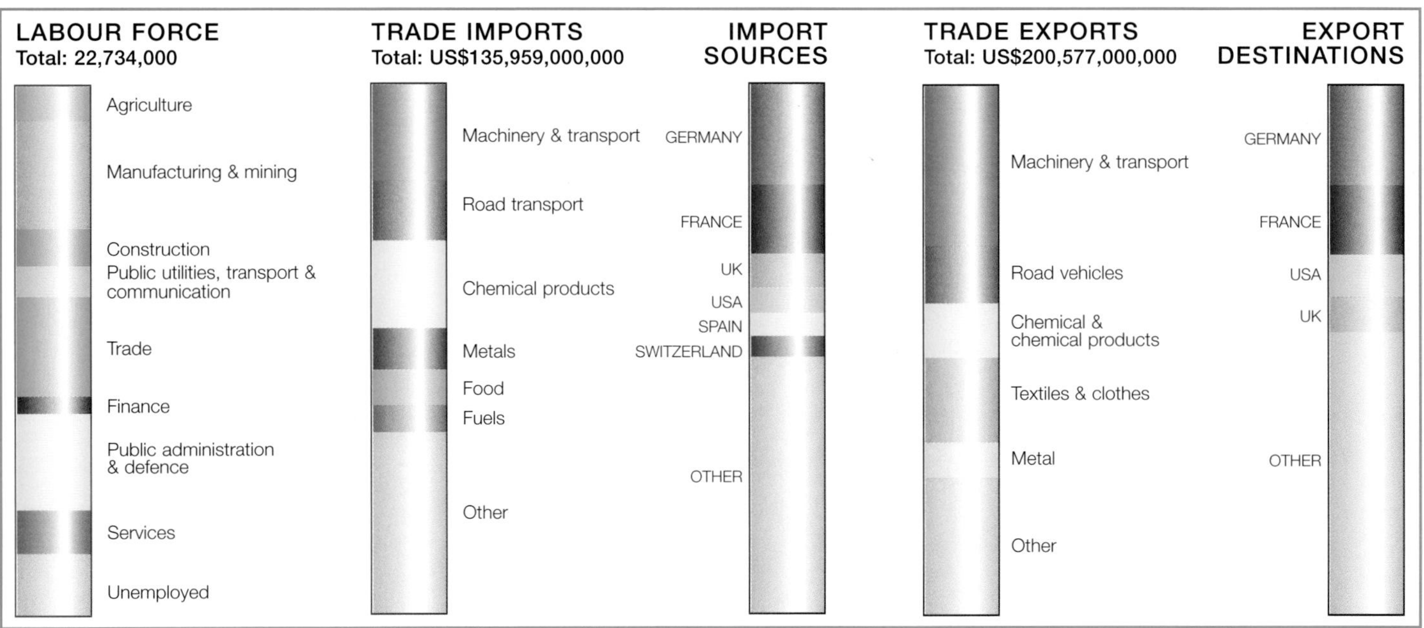

Central Europe

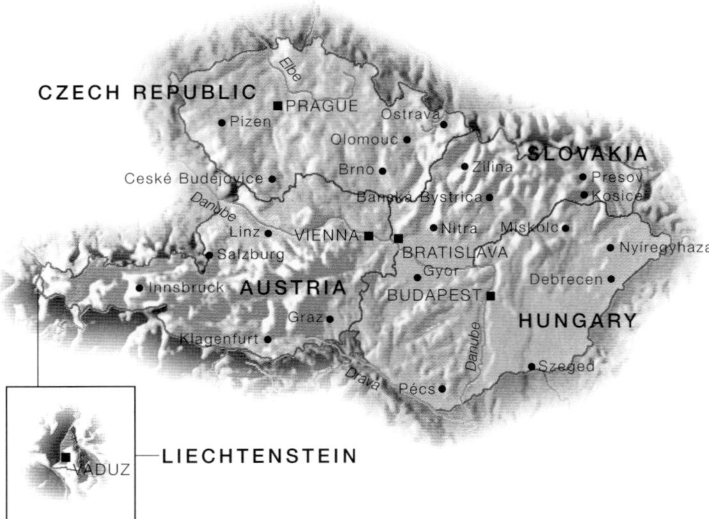

HUNGARY

Hungary is a land-locked central European republic occupying most of a basin through the middle of which flows the Danube. West of the Danube is an undulating lowland; east of the river is a large expanse of flat plain (the Great Alfold). The north-east contains a range of thickly wooded uplands.
Highest point: Kékes 1015 m (3330 ft). **Climate:** The climate is continental with long, hot, dry summers and cold winters.

The 394-member Assembly is elected by universal adult suffrage for four years, with 176 deputies elected from single-member constituencies and the remainder under two systems of proportional representation (one-quarter by national list; three-quarters by county). The Assembly elects a President for a five-year term. The President appoints a Prime Minister and a Council of Ministers, who command a majority in the Assembly.
Largest parties: (1994 election) (former Communist) Hungarian Socialist Party (MSzP) 61 seats, (centre-left) Alliance of Free Democrats (SzDSz) 70, (centre-right) Hungarian Democratic Forum (MDF) 37, (right-wing) Independent Smallholders (FKgP) 26, (centrist) Christian Democratic People's Party (KDNP) 22, (left-wing) federation of Young Democrats (FIDESz) 20, others 2.
President: (since 1990) Arpad Goncz (SzDSz).
Prime Minister: (since 1994) Gyula Horn (MSzP; MSzP-SzDSz government).

Despite large reserves of coal, Hungary imports over 50% of its energy needs. The steel, chemical fertilizer, pharmaceutical, machinery and vehicle industries are important. Since the early 1980s private enterprise and foreign investment have been encouraged and most state enterprises have been privatized. Western investment has underpinned sustained growth. Farming still occupies 12% of the labour force; major crops include cereals (maize, wheat and barley), sugar beet, fruit and grapes for wine. **Currency:** Forint.

1914–18 Habsburg Austro-Hungary fought in World War I allied to Germany. **1918** Collapse of Habsburg Empire; Hungary became a separate state. **1919** Communist revolution in Hungary, followed by occupation by Romania. **1920** Trianon Treaty reduced area of Hungary by two-thirds. **1941** German troops entered Hungary, which, under Regent Admiral Miklás Horthy, co-operated with the Axis powers in an attempt to regain lost territory. **1944** Hungary became an ally of Nazi Germany. **1945** Occupied by Soviet Red Army. **1949** Communist republic declared. **1956** Hungarian Uprising, an heroic attempt (led by Imre Nagy) to overthrow Communist rule, was suppressed by Soviet forces. **1980s** Gradual reforms. **1989–90** Democracy restored; Russian troops left Hungary.

Official name: Magyar Köztársaság (Republic of Hungary).
Area: 93,030 km^2 (35,919 sq mi).
Population: 10,230,000 (1995 est.).
Doubling time: pop. declining.
Adult life expectancy: male 64.5 years, female 73.8 years. **Birth rate:** 0.45 times world average. **Death rate:** 1.54 times world average.
Urban population: 63%. **Capital:** Budapest 1,996,000 (1994 est.; inc. suburbs). **Other main centres:** Debrecen 218,000, Miskolc 190,000, Szeged 179,000, Pécs 172,000, Györ 131,000 (1994 est.; inc. suburbs).
Language: Hungarian nearly 99% (official), Romany and German minorities. **Adult literacy:** almost 100%.
Religion: Roman Catholic 68%, Slovak Evangelical 6%, other Protestant Churches 25%, non-religious 5%.

AUSTRIA

Austria is a land-locked central European republic stretching from the upper Rhine to the Danube valley. The Alps (much of which are covered by pastures and forests) occupy nearly two-thirds of Austria. Lowland Austria, in the east, consists of low hills, the Vienna Basin and a flat marshy area beside the Neusiedler See on the Hungarian border. Along the Czech border is a forested massif rising to 1200 m (4000 ft).
Highest point: Grossglockner 3797 m (12,457 ft).
Climate: There are many local variations in climate owing to altitude and aspect. The east is drier than the west, and is, in general, colder than the Alpine region in winter and hotter, but more humid, in the summer.

Executive power is shared by the Federal President (who is elected by universal adult suffrage for a six-year term) and the Council of Ministers, led by the Federal Chancellor. The President appoints the Chancellor, who commands a majority in the Federal Assembly's lower house, the Nationalrat, whose 183 members are elected for four years under a system of proportional representation. The 64-member upper chamber, the Bundesrat, is elected by provincial assemblies.
Largest parties: (1995 election) Austrian Social Democratic Party (SPO) 72 seats, (centrist) Austrian People's Party (OVP) 53, (right-wing) Austrian Freedom Party (FPO) 41, Liberal Forum (LF) 9, Greens 8.
Federal President: (since 1992) Thomas Klestil (OVP).
Federal Chancellor: (since 1997) Viktor Klima (SPO; SPO-OVP government).

Although Austria produces 90% of its own food, farming employs only 7% of the labour force. The arable land in the east has fertile soils producing good yields of cereals and grapes for wine. Dairy produce is an important export from pasturelands in the east and the Alps. The mainstay of the economy is manufacturing, including machinery and transport equipment, iron and steel, refined petroleum products, cement and paper. Natural resources include hydroelectric power potential and extensive forests. The Alps attract winter and summer visitors, making tourism a major foreign-currency earner. Since the fold of Communist Eastern Europe Austria has increased trade with Hungary, Slovenia and the Czech Republic. **Currency:** Schilling.

By 1900 The (Habsburg) Austro-Hungarian Empire was increasingly unstable. **1914** Assassination of the heir to the throne by a Serb in Sarajevo brought Austro-Hungary to war with Serbia and precipitated World War I. **1918** Defeat in World War I led to end of Habsburg Empire: what are now Hungary, the Czech Republic, Slovakia, Slovenia, Croatia, Bosnia-Herzegovina, south Poland and west Ukraine broke away. Austrian republic declared. **1920s–30s** Period of great instability; Chancellor Dollfuss assassinated in 1934. **1938** Austria annexed by Germany (the Anschluss). **1945** Occupied by the Allied powers, which divided Austria into zones, Russia occupying the east. **1955** Allied forces withdrew: Austrian independence (as a neutral state) regained. **1995** Joined EU/EC.

Official name: Republik Österreich (Republic of Austria).
Area: 83,858 km^2 (32,378 sq mi).
Population: 8,063,000 (1995 est.).
Doubling time: pop. stable. **Adult life expectancy:** male 72.9 years, female 79.4 years. **Birth rate:** 0.46 times world average. **Death rate:** 1.09 times world average. **Urban population:** 65%. **Capital:** Vienna (Wien) 2,045,000 urban area (city 1,540,000; Mödling 101,000; 1991 census). **Other main centres:** Linz 434,000 urban area (city 203,000), Graz 395,000 (city 238,000), Salzburg 267,000 (city 144,000), Innsbruck 235,000 (city 118,000), Klagenfurt 89,000, Villach 55,000, Wels 53,000, Sankt Pölten 50,000 (1991 census).
Language: German over 92% (official), Croat 2%, Turkish 2%, Hungarian and Slovene minorities.
Adult literacy: almost 100%.
Religion: Roman Catholic 78%, non-religious 9%, Lutheran 5%, Sunni Islam 2%.

AUSTRIAN PROVINCES

Burgenland
Area: 3965 km^2 (1531 sq mi).
Pop.: 274,000 (1994 est.).
Capital: Eisenstadt.

Carinthia (Kärnten)
Area: 9533 km^2 (3681 sq mi).
Pop.: 560,000 (1994 est.).
Capital: Klagenfurt.

Lower Austria (Niederösterreich)
Area: 19,174 km^2 (7403 sq mi).
Pop.: 1,512,000 (1994 est.).
Capital: Sankt Pölten.

Salzburg
Area: 7154 km^2 (2762 sq mi).
Pop.: 504,000 (1994 est.).
Capital: Salzburg.

Styria (Steiermark)
Area: 16,388 km^2 (6327 sq mi).
Pop.: 1,204,000 (1994 est.).
Capital: Graz.

Tirol
Area: 12,648 km^2 (4883 sq mi).
Pop.: 655,000 (1994 est.).
Capital: Innsbruck.

Upper Austria (Oberösterreich)
Area: 11,980 km^2 (4626 sq mi).
Pop.: 1,384,000 (1994 est.).
Capital: Linz.

Vienna (Wien)
Area: 415 km^2 (160 sq mi).
Pop.: 1,596,000 (1994 est.).
Capital: Vienna.

Vorarlberg
Area: 2601 km^2 (1004 sq mi).
Pop.: 342,000 (1994 est.).
Capital: Bregenz.

BUDAPEST, HUNGARY'S CAPITAL, WAS FORMED FROM TWO TOWNS, BUDA AND PEST, ON EITHER

CZECH REPUBLIC

The Czech Republic is a land-locked central European republic. In the west (Bohemia), the Elbe basin is ringed by uplands: the Bohemian Forest in the south and west, the Ore Mountains and the Giant Mountains in the north and the Bohemian-Moravian uplands in the east. The Moravian plain lies east of Bohemia.
Highest point: Snezka 1602 m (5256 ft). **Climate:** The republic is continental with warm to hot summers and cold (snowy) winters.

The 200-member House of Representatives (lower house) is elected under a system of proportional representation by universal adult suffrage for four years; the 81-member Senate (upper house) is elected from single-member districts, with one-third of the members retiring every two years. The President is elected by a joint session of Parliament for a five-year term. The President appoints a Prime Minister and a Council of Ministers, who command a majority in the House.
Largest parties: (1996 election) (centre-right) Civic Democratic Party (ODS) 67 seats, Czech Social Democratic Party (CSSD) 61 seats, Communist Party (KSCM) 22, (centre-right) Christian Democrats (KD) 18, (right-wing) Republican Party (SPR-RSC) 18, (centre-right) Civic Democratic Alliance (ODA) 14.
President: (since republic founded) Václav Havel (non-party).
Prime Minister: (since republic founded) Václav Klaus (ODS; ODS-KD-ODA government).

Official name: Ceská Republika (Czech Republic).
Area: 78,864 km² (30,450 sq mi).
Population: 10,325,000 (1995 est.).
Doubling time: pop. stable.
Adult life expectancy: male 68.9 years, female 76.6 years.
Birth rate: 0.47 times world average.
Death rate: 1.23 times world average. **Urban population:** 65%.
Capital: Prague (Praha) 1,217,000 (1994 est.; inc. suburbs).
Other main centres: Brno 390,000, Ostrava 326,000, Plzen 172,000, Olomouc 106,000, Hradec Králové 100,000 (1994 est.; inc. suburbs).
Language: Czech 81% (official), Moravian 13%, Slovak 3%, with Polish, German and other minorities.
Adult literacy: almost 100%.
Religion: Roman Catholic 39%, various Protestant Churches 20%, non-religious 40%.

The Czech Republic, the first former-Communist state to join the OECD (the 'rich nations' club'), is the success story of eastern Europe. Apart from coal, there are few natural resources but the country is heavily industrialized. Manufactures include industrial machinery, motor vehicles and consumer goods. Most industry has been privatized. The Czech Republic has attracted considerable foreign investment (over 80% German) and its economy is increasingly linked to that of Germany. The timber industry is important. Farming interests include wheat, maize, potatoes, barley and sugar beet. Tourism to Prague is a major foreign-currency earner. **Currency:** Koruna.

1918 Bohemia and Moravia, the Czech lands (which had been part of Austria within the Habsburg Empire), joined Slovakia to form Czechoslovakia. **1938** Czechoslovakia dismembered by Nazi Germany; Germany annexed the Sudetenland, while Bohemia and Moravia became German protectorates. **1938–45** German occupation, including massacre of the inhabitants of Lidice (1942). **1945–93** Part of Czechoslovakia (after 1948 a Communist state). **1968** Russian invasion of Czechoslovakia to suppress the reforms of Alexander Dubcek. **1989** Collapse of Communist rule. **1993** Division of Czechoslovakia when Slovakia seceded.

Prague, untouched by modern architecture, is now one of Europe's major tourist centres

SLOVAKIA

Slovakia is a land-locked mountainous central European republic. The highest mountains are the Tatra range on the Polish border. The only significant lowlands are in the south adjoining the River Danube.
Highest point: Gerlachovka 2655 m (8711 ft). **Climate:** The climate is continental with warm, relatively dry, summers and cold winters.

The 150-member Assembly is elected under a system of proportional representation by universal adult suffrage for four years. The Assembly elects a President for a five-year term who appoints a Prime Minister and Council of Ministers, responsible to the Assembly.
Largest parties: (1994 election) (centre-right) Movement for a Democratic Slovakia (HZDS) 61 seats, (former Communist) Democratic Left Party (SDL) 18, (centre-left) Christian Democratic Movement (KDH) 17, (ethnic Hungarian coalition) MKDH-ESWS 17, (centrist) Democratic Union (DU) 15, (left-wing) Slovak Workers Association (ZRS) 13, (extreme right-wing) Slovak National Party (SNS) 9.
President: (since independence) Michal Kovac (non-party).
Prime Minister: (since 1994) Vladimir Meciar (HZDS; HZDS-ZRS-SNS government).

Slovakia had a predominantly agricultural economy into which heavy industry (particularly steel and chemicals) was introduced when part of Communist Czechoslovakia. Wheat, maize, potatoes, barley and sheep are important. Mineral resources include iron ore and brown coal. By 1993, 60% of industry was privatized. Since then the economy has declined, in part owing to the uncompetitive out-of-date nature of its factories. **Currency:** Koruna.

1918 The Slovak lands (which had been part of Hungary) joined the Czech lands to form Czechoslovakia. **1938** Czechoslovakia dismembered by Nazi Germany; Slovakia became an Axis puppet state. **1944** Slovak uprising against German rule. **1945–93** Part of Czechoslovakia (after 1948 a Communist state). **1968** Russian invasion to suppress the reforms of Alexander Dubcek (a Slovak). **1989** Collapse of Communist rule. **1993** Division of Czechoslovakia when Slovakia, which was ill-equipped to face dramatic market reforms, seceded. **Since 1993** Sporadic tension (regarding a large Hungarian minority) and political instability (focused upon rivalry between the President and Prime Minister).

Official name: Slovenská Republika (Slovak Republic).
Area: 49,036 km² (18,933 sq mi).
Population: 5,355,000 (1995 est.).
Doubling time: pop. stable.
Adult life expectancy: male 66.6 years, female 75.4 years.
Birth rate: 0.56 times world average.
Death rate: 1.09 times world average. **Urban population:** 57%.
Capital: Bratislava 449,000 (1994 est.; inc. suburbs). **Other main centres:** Kosice 239,000, Presov 91,000, Nitra 87,000, Zilina 86,000, Banská Bystrica 85,000 (1994 est.; inc. suburbs).
Language: Slovak 86% (official), Hungarian 11%, Romany 2%.
Adult literacy: almost 100%.
Religion: Roman Catholic 60%, Slovak Evangelical 6%, other Protestant Churches 23%, non-religious 10%.

LIECHTENSTEIN

Liechtenstein is a principality in the upper Rhine valley between Switzerland and Austria. The east of the country is occupied by the Alps; the west is the Rhine floodplain.
Highest point: Grauspitze 2599 m (8326 ft). **Climate:** The country has a mild Alpine climate.

Liechtenstein is a monarchy ruled by the Prince. The 25-member Landstag is elected by proportional representation by universal adult suffrage for four years. The Landstag elects a five-member Cabinet, including a Prime Minister.
Largest parties: (1993 election) (centre) Fatherland Union (VU) 13 seats, (centre-right) Progressive Citizens Party (FBP) 11, (Green) Free List 1.
Prince: (since 1989) Hans Adam II.
Prime Minister: (since 1993) Dr Mario Frick (VU).

The principality has one of the highest standards of living in the world. Banking, tourism and precision goods are all important. **Currency:** Swiss francs.

1924 Monetary and customs union with Switzerland. **Since 1989** More active international role, e.g. joining UN and EEA.

Official name: Fürstentum Liechtenstein (Principality of Liechtenstein).
Area: 160 km² (62 sq mi).
Population: 30,900 (1995 est.).
Doubling time: pop. almost stable.
Adult life expectancy: male 66.5 years, female 79.5 years.
Birth rate: 0.47 times world average.
Death rate: 0.72 times world average. **Urban population:** 21%.
Capital: Vaduz 5100 (1995 est.).
Other main centre: Schaan 5200 (1995 est.).
Language: German 88% (official), Italian 3%, Turkish 3%.
Adult literacy: almost 100%.
Religion: Roman Catholic 80%, Lutheran 7%.

South-east Europe I

YUGOSLAVIA (SERBIA AND MONTENEGRO)

Yugoslavia is a federal republic in the Balkans which now comprises two equal republics: Serbia and Montenegro. Ridges of mountains occupy the greater part of the country. The north (Vojvodina, where there is a Hungarian minority) is occupied by plains and drained by the rivers Danube and Tisa. The Yugoslav Adriatic coastline is now confined to a short stretch in Montenegro. East of Montenegro is the mountainous region of Kosovo, populated mainly by ethnic Albanians.
Highest point: Deravica 2656 m (8714 ft).
Climate: Coastal Montenegro has a Mediterranean climate; inland Serbia is more continental with cold winters and warm summers.

The Federal Assembly consists of the Chamber of Republics (upper house) with 40 members (20 chosen from each of the two republican assemblies) and the 138-member Chamber of Citizens (lower house), which is elected by universal adult suffrage for four years. A Federal President, who appoints a Federal Prime Minister and other Ministers, is elected by the Federal Assembly for four years. In practice, the governments and assemblies of the two republics (Serbia and Montenegro) exercise very considerable powers and the Serb authorities, in particular, have assumed virtually sovereign powers.
Largest parties: (Chamber of Citizens 1996 election) coalition of (former Communist) Socialist Party of Serbia (SPS) with (extreme left-wing Serbian) Yugoslav United Left and (left-wing Serbian) New Democracy Party 64 seats, (former Communist Montenegrin) Democratic Socialist Party (DSP) 23, (Serbian opposition coalition) Zajedno (Together) 22, (extreme right-wing) Serbian Radical Party 16, others 13.
Federal President: (since 1997) Slobodan Milosevic (SPS).
Federal Prime Minister: (since 1993) Radoje Kontic (SPS).
President of Montenegro: (since 1990) Momir Bulatovic (DSP).
President of Serbia: (since 1997) Zoran Lilac (SPS).

The country's economy was severely damaged by the war that lasted from 1991 to 1995, by hyper-inflation and by the international embargo on trade with Serbia and Montenegro that existed from 1991 to 1995 as a result of Serbia's involvement in Bosnia-Herzegovina. Mining and manufacturing involve over one-quarter of the labour force, with food processing, textiles, motor vehicles, metallurgy and consumer goods as the most important industries. Major crops include maize, wheat, sugar beet, potatoes, citrus fruit and fodder crops for sheep.
Currency: Yugoslav Dinar.

1900 Both Serbia and Montenegro had been recognized as independent monarchies since 1878. **1914** The assassination of Archduke Franz Ferdinand, heir to the Austro-Hungarian Habsburg throne, by a Serb in Sarajevo led to Austria's ultimatum to Serbia and precipitated World War I. **1918** Serbia and Montenegro were joined by South Slavs formerly in the Habsburg Empire to form what became Yugoslavia. **1934** Assassination of King Alexander by Croat nationalists. **1941** German invasion during World War II: Serbia and Montenegro occupied. **1945** Serbia and Montenegro became constituent republics of Communist Yugoslavia. **1990** Free elections held all over Yugoslavia. **1991** Croatia, Slovenia and Macedonia declared independence. Yugoslav (Serbian-Montenegrin) forces occupied one-third of Croatia. Unrest increased among ethnic Albanian in Serbian Kosovo. Condemnation of the role played by Serbia, in trying to create a 'Greater Serbia', led to international trade sanctions. **1992** Bosnian Serbs, encouraged by Serbia, seized 70% of Bosnia-Herzegovina, killing or expelling Muslims and Croats in a campaign of ethnic cleansing. UN peace-keeping involvement began. **1995** Cease-fire came into effect in Bosnia. Trade blockade on Serbia lifted. **1996–97** Daily demonstrations followed flawed municipal elections in Serbia; President Milosevic eventually conceded defeat.

Official name: Savezna Republika Jugoslavija (Federal Republic of Yugoslavia).
Area: 102,173 km² (39,449 sq mi).
Population: 10,555,000 (1995 est.).
Doubling time: pop. stable.
Adult life expectancy: male 68.6 years, female 74.4 years.
Birth rate: 0.54 times world average.
Death rate: 1.1 times world average.
Urban population: 52%.
Capital: Belgrade (Beograd) 1,169,000 (1994 est.; inc. suburbs).
Other main centres: Novi Sad 180,000, Nis 175,000, Kragujevac 147,000, Subotica 100,000 (1994 est.; inc. suburbs).
Language: Serbian 77% (official), Albanian 14%, Hungarian 4%, Vlach 1%, Romany 1%.
Adult literacy: 89%.
Religion: Serbian Orthodox 65%, Sunni Islam 19%, non-religious 10%, Roman Catholic 4%.

YUGOSLAV REPUBLICS

Montenegro (Crnagora)
Area: 13,812 km² (5333 sq mi).
Pop.: 630,000 (1994 est.).
Capital: Podgorica.
Serbia (Srbija)
Area: 88,361 km² (34,116 sq mi).
Pop.: 9,925,000 (1994 est.).
Capital: Belgrade.

SLOVENIA

Slovenia is a small mountainous central European republic. The Julian and Karawanken Alps occupy the north-west and the Dinaric Alps occupy the west. In the east, hills characterize the Drava valley; in the south-west Slovenia has a 30-km (19-mi) Adriatic coastline.
Highest point: Triglav 2864 m (9396 ft).
Climate: The south and west are Mediterranean; the north and east are more continental. Rainfall is heavy in the mountains.

The 90-member National Assembly (lower house) is elected under a system of proportional representation by universal adult suffrage for four years. The 40-member State Council (upper house) is elected for five years by social, economic, local and other councils. The President is directly elected for a maximum of two five-year terms. The President appoints a Prime Minister and a Council of Ministers, who command a majority in the Assembly.
Largest parties: (1996 election) (centre-left) Liberal Democratic Party (LDS) 25 seats, Slovenian Spring, a coalition of (right-wing) Slovenian People's Party (SP) 19 with Social Democratic Party 16 (SDSS) and (centre-right) Christian Democratic Party (SKD) 10, (left-wing) United List (ZLSD) 9, Democratic Party of Pensioners 5 (DPP), (right-wing) Slovenian National Party 4, others 2.
President: (since independence) Milan Kucan (non-party).
Prime Minister: (since 1992) Dr Janos Drnovsek (LDS; LDS minority government, with DPP and ZLSD support).

With the highest standard of living in eastern Europe, Slovenia was the most industrialized and commercially developed part of Yugoslavia. Privatization of agriculture and industry was completed by 1995. Industries include iron and steel, textiles and coal mining. The farming industry specializes in livestock and fodder crops. Slovenia has not suffered the severe economic decline typical of the other former Yugoslav republics and is seen as a candidate for EU membership. Slovenia's tourist industry is now improving and making strong progress in its recovery.
Currency: Tolar.

1918 The Slovenes (who had been under Austro-Hungarian rule) joined the Serbs and Croats to form what became Yugoslavia. **1941–45** The country was divided between Germany, Italy and Hungary during World War II. **1945** Slovenia created as constituent republic of Communist Yugoslavia. **1991** Slovenia declared independence; unsuccessful attempt was made by Yugoslav forces to retake Slovenia. **1992** Slovenian independence received international recognition.

Official name: Republika Slovenija (Republic of Slovenia).
Area: 20,256 km² (7821 sq mi).
Population: 1,970,000 (1995 est.).
Doubling time: pop. stable.
Adult life expectancy: male 69.4 years, female 77.3 years.
Birth rate: 0.4 times world average.
Death rate: 1.08 times world average. **Urban population:** 49%.
Capital: Ljublana 323,000 urban area (city 28,000; 1991 census).
Other main centres: Maribor 153,000 urban area (city 108,000), Celje 41,000, Kranj 37,000 (1991 census; inc. suburbs).
Language: Slovene 88% (official), Croat 8%, Hungarian and Italian minorities. **Adult literacy:** almost 100%.
Religion: Roman Catholic 94%.

BOSNIA-HERZEGOVINA

Bosnia-Herzegovina is a mountainous Balkan republic which, but for a 20-km (13-mi) coastline, is landlocked. Ridges of the Dinaric Alps, rising to over 1800 m (6000 ft), occupy the greater part of the country and, in places, form arid limestone karst plateaux. There are restricted lowlands in the north in the Sava valley.
Highest point: Maglic 2387 m (7831 ft).
Climate: Bosnia (the north) has cold winters and warm summers; Herzegovina (the south) enjoys milder winters and warmer summers.

A 42-member House of Representatives is directly elected for four years. The 15-member House of the Peoples (upper house) consists of 10 members chosen by the Bosnian-Muslim-Croat parliament and five by the Bosnian Serb parliament. A three-person collective Presidency is directly elected with one representative from each community. The Presidency appoints a federal Cabinet, which has limited powers. The country is divided into two entities: the (Muslim-Croat) Federation of Bosnia-Herzegovina and the (Bosnian Serb) Republika Srpska, each of which is virtually self-governing.
Largest parties: (1996 election) (Muslim) Party of Democratic Action (SDA) 16 seats, Democratic Serb Party (SDS) 9, Croatian Democratic Union (HDZ) 8, (Serb) Party for Democratic Action 3, (moderate multi-ethnic) United List, (moderate Bosnian Muslim) Party for Bosnia-Herzegovina (SBiH) 2, (Serb) People's Union for Peace 2.
President of Collective Presidency: (since 1996) Alija Izetbegovic (SDA).
Prime Minister: (since 1996) Hasan Muratovic (SDA).

The economy was devastated by war from 1992 to 1995 and both industrial and agricultural production are a fraction of their former totals. Much of the country's infrastructure has been destroyed and large-scale population movement has disrupted economic activity. Central and east Bosnia is forested. Agriculture is the major employer and sheep, maize, olives, grapes and citrus fruit are important. Little industry remains and over one-third of the labour force is unemployed.
Currency: Dinar and Kuna; agreement was reached to establish a common currency in 1997.

1908 The (Habsburg) Austro-Hungarian Empire, which had controlled Bosnia since 1878, officially absorbed the region. **1914** The assassination of Archduke Franz Ferdinand, heir to the Habsburg throne, by a Serb in Sarajevo precipitated World War I. **1918** Bosnia was joined to what became Yugoslavia. **1941** German invasion during World War II: Bosnia annexed by 'independent' Croatia. **1945** Bosnia-Herzegovina became a constituent republic of Communist Yugoslavia. **1992** Referendum, boycotted by Bosnian Serbs, gave majority in favour of Bosnian independence. Bosnian Serbs, encouraged by Serbia, seized 70% of the country, killing or expelling Muslims and Croats in a campaign of ethnic cleansing. UN peace-keeping involvement began. **1994** Muslims and Croats agreed to federate. **1995** Cease-fire came into effect. NATO troops took over from UN forces. **1996** After many international peace attempts both sides agreed the virtual partition of Bosnia-Herzegovina into a very loose federation.

Official name: Republika Bosna i Hercegovina (Republic of Bosnia and Herzegovina).
Area: 51,129 km² (19,741 sq mi).
Population: 3,230,000 (1997 est.).
Doubling time: pop. stable after declining 1991–95. **Adult life expectancy:** male 72.1 years, female 77.7 years. **Birth rate:** 0.54 times world average. **Death rate:** 0.69 times world average.
Urban population: 36%.
Capital: Sarajevo 300,000 (1993 est.). **Other main centres:** Tuzla 230,000, Banja Luka 150,000 (1993 est.).
Language: Serbo-Croat almost 100% (official). **Adult literacy:** 86%.
Religion: Sunni Islam 40%, Serbian Orthodox 31%, Roman Catholic 15%, Protestant minority.

BOSNIAN STATES

Federation of Bosnia-Herzegovina (Muslim-Croat)
Area: 26,076 km² (10,068 sq mi).
Pop.: 2,075,000 (1995 est.).
Capital: Sarajevo.
Republika Srpska
Area: 25,053 km² (9673 sq mi).
Pop.: 1,385,000 (1995 est.).
Capital: Pale.

CROATIA

Croatia is a Balkan republic which stretches in a crescent from the Danube to the Adriatic Sea. The north and east (Slavonia) form plains; the centre of the region, situated around Zagreb, is hill country. Barren limestone ridges in Krajina run parallel to the Dalmatian coast. This coast is lined with many islands running parallel to it. The area around Dubrovnik is detached from the rest of Croatia.
Highest point: Dinara 1831 m (6007 ft).
Climate: The climate of the interior is colder and drier than along the Mediterranean coast.

The 127-member House of Representatives (Sabor; lower house) is elected partly by single-member constituencies and partly under a system of proportional representation by universal adult suffrage for four years. Twelve seats are reserved for Croats abroad and three are reserved for the Serb minority. The 68-member Chamber of Counties (upper house) comprises 63 members elected by local councils and five chosen by the President, all for four years. The executive President, who is elected by the Sabor for five years, appoints a Prime Minister and a Council of Ministers, who command a majority in the Sabor.
Largest parties: (1995 election) (right-wing) Croatian Democratic Union (HDZ) 75 seats, (centre) Peasant Party (HSS) 16 plus its allies 4, (centre-left) Croatian Social-Liberal party (HSLS) 11, (former Communist) Social Democratic Party (SDP) 9, (right-wing) Croatian Party of Rights (HSP) 4, others 8.
President: (since independence) Franjo Tudjman (HDZ).
Prime Minister: (since 1995) Zlatko Matesa (HDZ).

■ *The island of Sveti Stefan, linked to the Dalmatian coast, was formerly a fishing village. It has now been redeveloped as an up-market international tourist resort*

Manufacturing (aluminium, textiles and chemicals), mining (mainly for bauxite) and oil dominate the economy. Slavonia grows cereals, potatoes and sugar beet. The economy was badly damaged by the Yugoslav wars (1991–95) and the formerly lucrative Dalmatian tourist industry collapsed, but made a tentative recovery after 1996. Large areas of the Krajina hill country were depopulated by the exodus of Serbs.
Currency: Kuna.

By 1900 Croat nationalism within the Habsburg Austro-Hungarian Empire was growing. **1918** The Croats joined the Serbs and Slovenes to form what became known as Yugoslavia. **1920s–30s** The Croats became increasingly resentful of the Serb-dominated centralized Yugoslavia. **1941** German invasion during World War II: an 'independent' Croat puppet state was established, which adopted harsh anti-Serb policies. **1945** Croatia became a constituent republic of Communist Yugoslavia. **1990** Separatists came to power in the Croatian elections. **1991** Croatia declared independence; Serb insurgents backed by Yugoslav forces seized 30% of Croatia (Krajina and east Slavonia). **1992** Serbo-Croat war halted; the independence of Croatia received international recognition. **1995** Croatia retook Krajina and most of Slavonia and expelled the resident Serbs; east Slavonia was drawn temporarily under UN control but was subsequently returned to Croatia in 1997.

Official name: Republika Hrvatska (Republic of Croatia).
Area: 56,691 km² (21,889 sq mi).
Population: 4,490,000 (1995 est.).
Doubling time: pop. stable.
Adult life expectancy: male 65.6 years, female 75 years.
Birth rate: 0.43 times world average.
Death rate: 1.23 times world average. **Urban population:** 51%.
Capital: Zagreb 931,000 urban area (city 708,000; 1991 census).
Other main centres: Split 207,000 urban area (city 189,000), Rijeka 206,000 (city 168,000), Osijek 165,000 (city 104,000), Zadar 76,000 (1991 census).
Language: Croat 94% (official), **Adult literacy:** 97%. Serbian and Slovene minorities.
Religion: Roman Catholic 87%, Old Catholic, Protestant and Serbian Orthodox minorities.

South–East Europe II

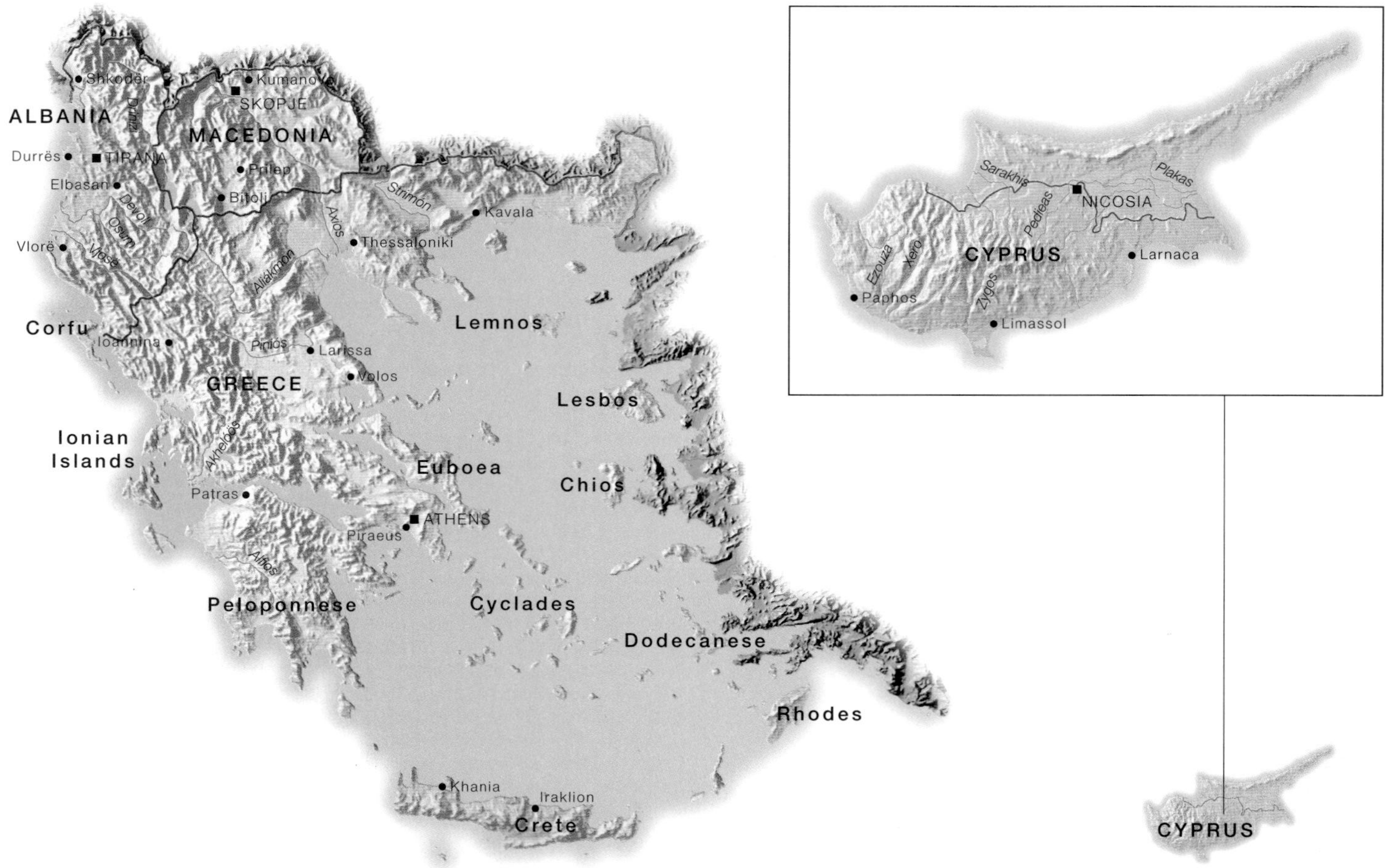

GREECE

Greece is a Balkan republic bounded by the Ionian, Mediterranean and Aegean seas in south-east Europe. Over 80% of Greece is mountainous. The mainland is dominated by the Pindus Mountains, which extend from the Albanian border south into the Peloponnese Peninsula. The Rhodope Mountains lie along the Bulgarian border. Greece has some 2000 islands, of which only 154 are inhabited.
Highest point: Olympus (Olimbos) 2917 m (9570 ft).
Climate: Mediterranean climate with hot dry summers and mild wet winters. The north and the mountains are cooler, with winter snow in the mountains.

The 300-member Chamber of Deputies comprises 288 members elected by universal adult suffrage under a system of proportional representation for four years and 12 extra members chosen by the principal parties. The President, whose role is largely ceremonial, is elected by the Chamber for five years. The President appoints a Prime Minister and other Ministers who enjoy a majority in the Chamber. Mount Athos is an autonomous monastic republic.
Largest parties: (1996 election) Panhellenic Socialist Movement (Pasok) 162, (centre-right) New Democracy Party (NDP) 108, Communist Party (KKE) 11, Coalition of the Left and Progress 10, (left-wing) Democratic Social Movement (Dikki) 9.
President: (since 1995) Costis Stefanopoulos (non-party).
Prime Minister: (since 1996) Costas Simitis (Pasok).

Agriculture still involves nearly one-fifth of the labour force. Much of the land is marginal, in particular the extensive sheep pasture. Greece is largely self-sufficient in wheat, barley, maize, sugar beet, fruit, vegetables and cheese, and produces enough wine, olives (and olive oil) and tobacco for export. The industrial sector is expanding rapidly and includes clothing and textiles, and processing local petroleum, natural gas, bauxite and lignite. Tourism (especially to the Greek islands), a large merchant fleet and money sent back by Greeks working abroad are all important sources of foreign currency. Greece receives special economic aid from the EC/EU. **Currency:** Drachma.

1912–13 Balkan Wars against Turkey and then Bulgaria. **1913** Greece received Crete, many Aegean islands, Epirus and Greek Macedonia; King George I assassinated. **1915–18** Involvement in World War I: rivalry between King Constantine I, who favoured Germany, and his PM Eleutherios Venizelos resulted in Greek alliance with the Allies and the king's abdication. **1919** Greece received Thrace from Bulgaria and part of Asia Minor from Turkey. **1921–22** Unsuccessful Greek attempt to seize much of Asia Minor from Turkey; military defeat – expulsion of Greece from Asia Minor. **1924** Monarchy overthrown. **1924–35** Greek republic. **1935** Monarchy restored with Gen. Ioannis Metaxas as virtual dictator. **1941–45** German occupation during World War II; rival royalist and Communist resistance groups. **1945–49** Civil war between royalists and Communists; US and British aid secured victory for the monarchists. **1967** Military coup; King Constantine II went into exile. **1967–74** Dictatorship of the 'Colonels' Junta'. **1974** Military regime overthrown when their encouragement of a Greek Cypriot coup almost brought Greece to war with Turkey. **1975** New republican democratic constitution. **1981** Membership of the EC (now EU). **1994** Greece, which denies there is a Macedonian people and language, blockaded the former Yugoslav Republic of Macedonia.

GREEK AUTONOMOUS MONKS' REPUBLIC

Mount Athos (Ayion Oros)
Area: 336 km^2 (130 sq mi).
Pop.: 1400 (1991 est.).
Capital: Karyai.

Official name: Ellinikí Dhimokratía (The Hellenic Republic).
Area: 131,957 km^2 (50,949 sq mi).
Population: 10,490,000 (1995 est.).
Doubling time: population relatively stable. **Adult life expectancy:** male 74.6 years, female 79.8 years.
Birth rate: 0.39 times world average.
Death rate: the world average.
Urban population: 72%.
Capital: Athens (Athínai) 3,100,000 urban area (city 772,000; Piraieus (Piraiévs) 183,000; Peristerion 137,000; Kallithea 111,000; 1991 census). **Other main centres:** Thessaloníki (formerly Salonika) 706,000 urban area (city 384,000), Piraeus *see Athens*, Patras (Pátrai) 153,000, Peristerion *see Athens*, Iráklion (Heraklion) 117,000, Lárissa 113,000, Kallithea *see Athens*, Ioannina 90,000, Volos 76,000, Khania 65,000, Kavala 58,000 (1991 census; inc. suburbs).
Language: Greek 96% (official), Macedonian nearly 2% (Greece denies the existence of a Macedonian language, classing it as a dialect of Bulgarian), with Turkish and Albanian minorities. **Adult literacy:** 95%.
Religion: Greek Orthodox 98%, Sunni Islam 1%.

■ BOTH THE PRESENCE OF FEMALE ANIMALS AND WOMEN ARE FORBIDDEN ON MOUNT ATHOS IN

CYPRUS

Cyprus is an island-republic in the eastern Mediterranean 65 km (40 mi) south of the Turkish coast. The south of the island is covered by the Troodos Mountains. Running east to west across the centre of Cyprus is a fertile plain, north of which are the Kyrenian Mountains and Karpas Peninsula.
Highest point: Olympus (Olimbos) 1951 m (6401 ft).
Climate: Mediterranean climate with hot dry summers and mild variable winters. Rainfall is low.

A 56-member House of Representatives is elected by compulsory universal adult suffrage, using a system of proportional representation, in the Greek Cypriot community for five years. An additional 24 seats reserved for the Turkish Cypriot community remain unfilled. An executive President is directly elected by the Greek Cypriot electorate for five years; there is constitutional provision for a Vice-President to be elected in a similar manner by the Turkish Cypriot community. The President appoints a Cabinet of Ministers. Turkish Cypriots unilaterally established the 'Turkish Republic of Northern Cyprus', which, except for Turkey, has no international recognition.
Largest parties: (1996 election): (conservative) Democratic Rally (DISY) 20, (reformed Communist) Progressive Party of the Working People (AKEL) 19, (centre-right) Democratic Party (DIKO) 10, (centre-left) Socialist Party (EDEK) 5, Free Democrats (KED) 2.
President: (since 1993) Glafcos Clerides (DISY).

Potatoes, fruit, wine, clothing and textiles are exported from the Greek Cypriot area, in which ports, resorts and international airports have been constructed to replace facilities lost since partition. The Turkish Cypriot area (which exports potatoes, fruit and tobacco) relies heavily upon aid from Turkey and has a much lower standard of living than the south. Tourism is important throughout Cyprus.
Currency: Cyprus pound; Turkish currency is used in the north.

1878 Cyprus passed from Turkish to British rule. **1950s** Greek Cypriots, led by Archbishop Makarios III, campaigned for Enosis (union with Greece); increasing activity by Greek Cypriot terrorist movement EOKA. **1960** Independence: power shared by two communities. **1960–77** Makarios President. **1963** UN intervention to stop communal fighting. **1974** Pro-Enosis coup by Greek Cypriots: Turkish forces invaded the north and over 200,000 Greek Cypriots were displaced into the south; Cyprus effectively partitioned; Makarios eventually restored. **1975** Turkish administration in the north declared independence.

Official names: Kypriaki Dhimokratía (in Greek) and Kibris Cumhuriyeti (Turkish) (The Republic of Cyprus).
Area: 9251 km² (3572 sq mi), of which 3355 km² (1295 sq mi) are in the Turkish-controlled zone.
Population: 805,000 (1995 est.), including Turkish 'settlers' in the north. The population of the Turkish-controlled zone was 175,000 in 1995.
Doubling time: population relatively stable. **Adult life expectancy:** male 74.6 years, female 79 years.
Birth rate: 0.67 times world average.
Death rate: 0.83 times world average. **Urban population:** 68%.
Capital: Nicosia (Lefkosia or Lefkosa) 220,000 urban area (Lefkosia/Greek Cypriot area 178,000; Lefkosa/Turkish Cypriot area 42,000; 1994 est.).
Other main centres: Limassol (Lemesos) 137,000, Larnaca (Larnax) 61,000, Paphos (Pafos) 31,000 (1994 est.; inc. suburbs).
Language: Greek 78% (official), Turkish 19% (official), English minority.
Adult literacy: 95%.
Religion: Greek Orthodox 76%, Sunni Islam 19%.

ALBANIA

Albania is a Balkan republic on the eastern shores of the Adriatic Sea, where it joins the main body of the Mediterranean. Coastal lowlands support most of the country's agriculture and the greater part of the population. Mountains occupy most of Albania.
Highest point: Korab 2751 m (9025 ft).
Climate: The Mediterranean coastal areas experience hot, dry summers and mild, wet winters. The mountainous interior has equally hot summers but very cold winters.

The 155-member People's Assembly is elected under a system of proportional representation by universal adult suffrage for four years. The President, who shares executive power with the Prime Minister, is elected by the Assembly for five years. The President appoints a Prime Minister and other Ministers who are responsible to the Assembly.
Largest parties: (1997 election) (former Communist) Socialist Party (PS) 100 seats, (centre right) Democratic Party (PDA) 27, (ethnic-Greek) Party for the Defence of Human Rights and others 28.
President: Vacant following the resignation of Sali Berisha (PDA). A SP president will be installed.
Prime Minster: (since 1997) Fatos Nano (PS).

Albania is the poorest state in Europe. The economy relies upon agriculture and the export of chromium and copper. In 1990 Albania ended its self-imposed economic isolation and sought international assistance. Nevertheless, the country has experienced continuing emigration and a sharp decline in industrial output. The collapse of several pyramid savings schemes in 1996–97 devastated an already enfeebled economy. Most state-owned farms have been redistributed into private hands and the majority of the outdated industrial sector is no longer nationalized.
Currency: Lek.

1912 Independence declared after nearly 500 years of Turkish Ottoman rule. **1913** Occupied by Greece, Serbia and Montenegro. **1914–16** Independent principality. **1916** Republic declared. **1928** President Ahmed Bey Zogu declared himself king (Zog I) and began modernization of Albania. **1939** Albania invaded by Italy; Zog fled. **1943–44** German occupation during World War II. **1944** Communist-led partisans took power upon German retreat. **1946** Communist republic established. **1946–85** Dictatorship of Enver Hoxha; Communist regime pursued rapid modernization in alliance with, in turn, Yugoslavia, the USSR and China, before adopting isolation in 1978; all practice of religion banned. **1990** Liberal wing of Communist Party won internal party power struggle. **1991** Economic, social and political reforms; free elections. **1997** Southern Albania in revolt after large numbers were ruined by collapse of pyramid savings schemes; Italian-led multinational force brought humanitarian aid.

Official name: Republika e Shqipërisë (The Republic of Albania).
Area: 28,748 km² (11,100 sq mi).
Population: 3,410,000 (1995 est.).
Doubling time: 37 years. **Adult life expectancy:** male 70 years, female 76.2 years. **Birth rate:** 0.95 times world average. **Death rate:** 0.59 times world average. **Urban population:** 36%. **Capital:** Tirana (Tiranë) 251,000 (1991 est.).
Other main centres: Durrës 86,000, Elbasan 83,000, Shkodër 82,000, Vlorë 74,000 (1990 est.).
Language: Albanian (Gheg and Tosk dialects) 98% (Tosk official), Greek 2%. **Adult literacy:** 92%.
Religion: Sunni Islam 70% (the majority non-practising), Albanian Orthodox 20%, Roman Catholic 9%.

MACEDONIA

A small landlocked south Balkan republic, Macedonia is mostly plateau, about 760 m (2500 ft) high, bordered by mountains including the north-west Sar range. The central Vardar valley is the only lowland.
Highest point: Rudoka 2748 m (9016 ft). **Climate:** Tends towards continental, with cold, snowy winters and warm summers. The Vardar valley is more Mediterranean.

The 120-member National Assembly (Sobranie) is elected by universal adult suffrage for four years. The President, who is directly elected for five years, appoints a Prime Minister and a Council of Ministers, who command a majority in the Assembly.
Largest parties: (1994 election) (former Communist) Alliance for Macedonia (ASDM) 58 seats, Liberal Party (PLM) 29, (ethnic Albanian) Democratic Prosperity Party (DPPM) 8, Socialist Party (PSM) 8, others 17.
President: (since independence) Kiro Gligorov (ASDM).
Prime Minister: (since 1992) Branko Crvenkovski (ASDM).

The republic is still largely agricultural, raising sheep and cattle and growing cereals and tobacco. Steel, chemical and textile industries rely, in part, upon local resources that include iron ore, lead and zinc. The economy was damaged by the 1994-95 Greek trade blockade and by disruption of trade with Serbia. One-quarter of the labour force is unemployed. **Currency:** Denar.

1912 After Second Balkan War, Turkish-ruled Macedonia was divided between Greece, Bulgaria and Serbia, the latter receiving the present republic. **1918** Serbian Macedonia incorporated in what became Yugoslavia. **1941–44** Occupied by Bulgaria during World War II. **1945** Became a constituent republic of Communist Yugoslavia. **1991** After outbreak of Yugoslav civil wars, Macedonia declared independence. **1992** Despite opposition from Greece (which denies a Macedonian people or language), Macedonia received international recognition. **1994–95** Greek blockade **1995** Tensions grew among Macedonia's Albanian minority; assassination attempt on President Gligorov.

Official name: Republika Makedonija (Republic of Macedonia). At the UN the country is known as The Former Yugoslav Republic of Macedonia (abbreviated to FYROM).
Area: 25,713 km² (9928 sq mi).
Population: 2,105,000 (1995 est.).
Doubling time: pop. stable. **Adult life expectancy:** male 70.1 years, female 74.4 years. **Birth rate:** 0.63 times world average. Death rate: 0.81 times world average. **Urban population:** 59%. **Capital:** Skopje 441,000 (1994 census; inc. suburbs).
Other main centres: Bitolj (Bitola) 75,000, Prilep 67,000, Kumanovo 66,000 (1994 census; inc. suburbs).
Language: Macedonian 69% (official), Albanian 21%, Serbian 6%, Turkish 3%. **Adult literacy:** 89%.
Religion: Macedonian Orthodox 67%, Sunni Islam 30%.

Black Sea States

BULGARIA

Bulgaria is a Balkan republic on the western shore of the Black Sea. The Balkan Mountains run from east to west across central Bulgaria. To the north, low-lying hills slope down to the River Danube. To the south, a belt of lowland (including the Maritsa valley) separates the Balkan Mountains from a high rugged massif on the Greek border.
Highest point: Musala 2925 m (9596 ft).
Climate: The continental north has warm summers and cold winters; the south-east and east have a more Mediterranean climate with drier summers and milder winters.

The 240-member National Assembly is elected by universal adult suffrage for five years by a system of proportional representation. The President, who is directly elected for a maximum of two five-year terms, appoints a Prime Minister and other Ministers who enjoy a majority in the Assembly.
Largest parties: (1997 election) (centrist-liberal) Union of Democratic Forces (UDF) 137 seats, (former Communist) Bulgarian Socialist Party (BSP) 57, (monarchist/ethnic Turkish coalition) Union for National Salvation 20, others 26.
President: (since 1997) Petar Stoyanov (UDF).
Prime Minister: (since 1997) Ivan Kostov (UDF)

Official name: Republika Bulgarija (Republic of Bulgaria).
Area: 110,994 km^2 (42,855 sq mi).
Population: 8,350,000 (1995 est.).
Doubling time: population declining.
Adult life expectancy: male 68.9 years, female 75.3 years. **Birth rate:** 0.38 times world average. **Death rate:** 1.42 world average. **Urban population:** 68%. **Capital:** Sofia (Sofiya) 1,114,000 (1993 est.; inc. suburbs). **Other main centres:** Plovdiv 345,000, Varna 307,000, Burgas 198,000, Ruse 170,000, Stara Zagora 165,000, Pleven 138,000 (1993 est.; inc. suburbs).
Language: Bulgarian 80% (official), Turkish 9%, Romany 4%, Macedonian 3%. **Adult literacy:** 96%.
Religion: Bulgarian Orthodox over 80%, Sunni Islam 13%, non-religious minority.

With fertile soils and few other natural resources, Bulgaria's economy has a strong agricultural base specializing in cereals (maize, wheat and barley), fruit (particularly grapes), and, increasingly, tobacco. For nearly half a century, production was centred on large-scale mechanized co-operatives, but privatization of land, begun in 1990, is virtually complete. Agricultural products are the basis of the food processing, wine and tobacco industries. Other major industries include engineering, fertilizers and chemicals, and most of the industrial sector has been privatized. Tourism is increasingly important. The disruption of the trading links of the former Communist bloc in the early 1990s disrupted Bulgaria's economy: industrial output fell and unemployment soared. Between 1994 and 1997 hyper-inflation wrecked the economy, hardship intensified and the banking sector virtually collapsed.

Currency: Lev.

1878 Autonomous Bulgarian principality established within the Turkish Ottoman Empire. **1908** Bulgaria became an independent kingdom. **1912** Bulgaria was one of the victorious allies against Turkey in the second Balkan War. **1913** Bulgaria defeated by neighbours quarrelling over the spoils from the Balkan Wars. **1915–18** Defeated after alliance with Germany, Turkey and Austro-Hungary in World War I. **1919** Bulgaria lost one-tenth of its territory in the post-World War I peace. **1941–44** Defeated after alliance with Germany in World War II. **1944** Invaded by Soviet Red Army; Communist regime established. **1946** King forced into exile; republic declared. **1989** Popular demonstrations led to removal of Communist dictator Todor Zhivkov. **1990** Free elections held. **1990–97** Short-lived governments failed to conquer Bulgaria's severe economic problems.

MOLDOVA

Moldova is a Balkan republic between Romania and Ukraine, and does not quite reach the Black Sea coast. Most of Moldova consists of a plain between the River Prut and the Dnestr valley. In the centre, the Kodry hills form the only high ground in the republic.
Highest point: Balaneshty 430 m (1409 ft).
Climate: Generally mild climate with some continental features including snow in the winter, warm summers and moderate rainfall.

The executive President is elected by universal adult suffrage for four years. The 104-member Assembly is directly elected under a system of proportional representation for four years. The President appoints a Prime Minister and other Ministers who enjoy a majority in the Assembly. Transdniestria and Gagauzia are autonomous republics (the former is largely self-governing).
Largest parties: (1994 election) (centrist former Communist) Agrarian Democratic Party (PAD) 56 seats, (pro-Russian former Communist) Socialist/Unity Bloc (PS/Yedinstvo) 28, (centrist) Peasant Party and Congress of Intellectuals 11, (right-wing) Popular Front Alliance 9.
President: (since 1996) Petru Lucinshi (PAD).
Prime Minister: (since 1992) Andrei Sangheli (PAD).

Moldova is one of the poorest countries in Europe but, since independence in 1991, reforms have brought the beginnings of privatization and the lowest rate of inflation in the former Soviet Union. The economy is still largely agricultural, with two-fifths of the workforce on the land. Moldova grows fruit (particularly grapes for wine), vegetables, wheat, maize and tobacco. The country's industry includes engineering and food processing. The collapse of the Soviet trade system and the war in Transdniestria damaged the economy. Moldova has virtually no energy resources of its own and relies upon Russia, to whom it owes a very considerable trading debt.
Currency: Moldovan leu.

1917 Russian Bessarabia (modern Moldova) briefly became independent. **1918** Invasion by Russian Bolshevik forces, followed by an invasion by Romania and incorporation into that country. **1940** USSR retook Bessarabia. **1944** Bessarabia reorganized as the Moldavian Soviet Socialist Republic within the USSR. **1991** Independence as Moldova upon the collapse of the Soviet Union. **1992** Brief civil war as the (mainly Russian and Ukrainian) Transdniestria region (fearing eventual reunion of Moldova with Romania) attempted secession; intervention of CIS forces brought uneasy peace; Russian troops remain in Transdniestria. **1994** National referendum overwhelmingly against union with Romania.

AUTONOMOUS MOLDOVAN REPUBLICS

Gagauzia
Area: 1800 km^2 (695 sq mi).
Pop.: 200,000 (1992 est).
Capital: Komrat.
Transdniestria (Transnistria)
Area: 5000 km^2 (1930 sq mi).
Pop.: 800,000 (1992 est).
Capital: Tighina.

Official name: Republica Moldova (Republic of Moldova).
Area: 33,700 km^2 (13,010 sq mi).
Population: 4,350,000 (1995 est.).
Doubling time: population declining.
Adult life expectancy: male 67.9 years, female 71.5 years. **Birth rate:** 0.57 times world average. **Death rate:** 1.28 times world average.
Urban population: 47%. **Capital:** Chisinau (formerly Kishinev) 754,000 (1991 est.; inc. suburbs). **Other main centres:** Tiraspol 186,000, Balti 165,000, Tighina (formerly Bendery) 142,000 (1991 est.; inc. suburbs).
Language: Romanian (Moldovan) 62% (official), Russian 23%, Ukrainian 9%, Gagauz 3%.
Adult literacy: 96%.
Religion: Russian (Moldovan) Orthodox over 97%.

■ BULGARIA'S ETHNIC TURKS WERE FORCED TO ADOPT BULGARIAN NAMES IN THE 1970S ■ UNDER

ROMANIA

Romania is a Balkan republic at the mouth of the River Danube on the western shore of the Black Sea. The Carpathian Mountains run through the north, east and centre of Romania. Moldavia is the plateau east of the Carpathians; Wallachia is the plain to the south of those mountains. To the west of the Carpathians is the basin of Transylvania and the Banat lowland. In the south the Danube Plain ends in a delta on the Black Sea.
Highest point: Moldoveanu 2544 m (8346 ft).
Climate: Cold, snowy winters and hot summers. Rainfall is moderate in the lowlands but heavier in the mountains.

The executive President is elected by universal adult suffrage for five years. The 343-member National Assembly (lower house) and 143-member Senate (upper house) are elected under a modified system of proportional representation for four years. The President appoints a Prime Minister and other Ministers who enjoy a majority in the Assembly.
Largest parties: (1996 election) (centre-right coalition) Democratic Convention (CD) (including the Christian Democratic Peasants' Party 88 seats and National Liberal Party 25) 122 seats, (socialist) Party of Social Democracy of Romania (PSDR) 91, (coalition centrist) Social Democratic Union (USD) 53, Hungarian Democratic Federation of Romania 25, (right-wing ultra-nationalist) Greater Romanian Party (RM) 19, Party of Romania National Unity (PUNR) 18, others 15.
President: (since 1996) Emil Constantinescu (CD).
Prime Minister: (since 1996) Victor Ciorbea (CD; CD-USD coalition government).

Natural resources include coal, petroleum and natural gas, which have encouraged the growth of chemical, metallurgical, and mechanical engineering industries. Privatization of industry has been slow and economic problems include high rates of inflation, unemployment, low investment and obsolete industrial plant. The economy has yet to recover from mismanagement under Ceausescu when already low living standards decreased. About one-third of the labour force is still involved in agriculture, growing maize, sugar beet, wheat, potatoes, grapes (for wine) and fodder crops. Farming was neglected under Ceausescu but recent progress has been made and most of the land has been privatized.
Currency: Leu.

1914–18 Involvement in World War I against Germany and Austro-Hungary. **1918–19** Romania won much extra territory upon the collapse of the Russian and Austro-Hungarian empires. **1930s** Rise of Fascist Iron Guard. **1937** King Carol II suppressed the constitution and imposed his own dictatorship. **1940** USSR took Bessarabia (modern Moldova) from Romania; Hungary regained much of Transylvania and the Banat. **1941** Carol II fled; Romania, under dictatorship of Gen. Ion Antonescu, entered alliance with Germany in World War II. **1944** Invaded by Soviet Red Army; King Michael dismissed Antonescu. **1945** Communist government installed; Transylvania and the Banat regained. **1947** King forced into exile; republic declared. **1952–65** Dictatorship of Gheorghe Gheorghiu-Dej. **1965–89** Increasingly despotic dictatorship of Nicolae and Elena Ceausescu, who impoverished Romania. **1989** Popular demonstrations in Timisoara; leaders of an anti-Ceausescu conspiracy in the army took power; the Ceausescus executed on charges of genocide and corruption. **1990–96** Government remained largely in the hands of former Communists. **1996** Centre-right reforming government formed.

Official name: România (Romania).
Area: 237,500 km² (91,699 sq mi).
Population: 22,690,000 (1995 est.).
Doubling time: population declining.
Adult life expectancy: male 69.3 years, female 75.4 years. **Birth rate:** 0.44 times world average. **Death rate:** 1.25 times world average.
Urban population: 55%. **Capital:** Bucharest (Bucuresti) 2,067,000 (1993 est.; inc. suburbs). **Other main centres:** Constanta 349,000, Iasi 338,000, Timisoara 325,000, Galati 324,000, Brasov 324,000, Cluj-Napoca 322,000, Ploiesti 254,000, Braila 236,000, Oradea 222,000, Bacau 207,000 (1993 est.; inc. suburbs).
Language: Romanian 91% (official), Hungarian 7%, with Romany, German, Ukrainian and other minorities. **Adult literacy:** 97%.
Religion: Romanian Orthodox 86%, Roman Catholic 5%, Greek Orthodox 3%.

UKRAINE

Ukraine, after Russia the largest country in Europe, is a republic to the north of the Black Sea. Most of Ukraine consists of plains (steppes) interrupted by low plateaux and basins. The north includes part of the Pripet Marshes, the south is a coastal lowland beside the Black Sea and the Sea of Azov. Central Ukraine comprises the Dnepr Lowland and the Dnepr Plateau, the most extensive area of upland in the republic. Eastern Ukraine consists of the Don Valley and part of the Central Russian Upland. The most diverse scenery is in the west, where the Carpathian Mountains form a barrier before a lowland which stretches into Hungary. The Crimean Peninsula consists of parallel mountain ridges and fertile valleys.
Highest point: Hoverla 2061 m (6762 ft).
Climate: Crimea has a Mediterranean climate. Western Ukraine is generally temperate with milder winters and cooler summers than the more continental east. Snowfall is heaviest in the north and in the Carpathians. Rainfall is moderate everywhere with a summer maximum.

Ukraine has a 450-member single-chamber Parliament (Rada) elected by universal adult suffrage for four years. Under the 1996 constitution, an executive President, who will be directly elected, will appoint a Prime Minister and other Ministers, responsible to the Rada. Crimea is an autonomous republic.
Largest parties: (1994 election) Communist Party 91 seats, (pro-Russian Communist) Agrarian Party 53, (democratic nationalist) Democratic Movement for Ukraine (Rukh) 20, Centre Party 17, various centrists 15, other democratic nationalists 48, extreme right-wing nationalists 5, independent left-wing members 201.
President: (since 1994) Leonid Kuchma (non-party).
Prime Minister: (since 1997) Valery Pustovoitenko (non-party).

Ukraine was known as the bread basket of the Soviet Union. Large collective farms on the steppes grow cereals, fodder crops and vegetables. Potatoes and flax are important in the north; fruit farming (including grapes and market gardening) is widespread, particularly in Crimea. Natural resources include iron ore, oil, manganese, and rock salt, but the vast (old-fashioned) Donets coalfield is the principal base of Ukraine's industry. The iron and steel industry was diminished since the break-up of the USSR but ferrous metals are Ukraine's principal export. Other major industries include food processing, consumer goods, heavy engineering (railway locomotives and generators as well as a declining shipbuilding industry), chemicals and chemical equipment. Since independence the economy has declined with the end of the Soviet trade system: production has fallen and the country faces a huge energy deficit, rampant inflation and declining standards of living. Privatization and other economic reforms have been slow and only partially successful.
Currency: Hryvnia.

1917 Ukraine took advantage of Russia's involvement in World War I, and the chaos of the Russian Revolutions, to declare independence after centuries of rule from Moscow. **1918** Independent Ukraine joined by former Austro-Hungarian Galicia (present-day western Ukraine); a rival Soviet government established in the east; Polish invasion. **1919** Red Army took most of Ukraine. **1922** Ukraine became a Union Republic of the USSR. **1928–1930s** Stalin's purges in Ukraine: 'Russification' of Ukraine. **1933–34** Widespread famine: 6,000,000 people died. **1941** Invasion by Nazi Germany; Ukraine occupied until 1943. **After 1945** Ukraine enlarged by addition of Lvov (now Lviv) from Poland, Bukovina from Romania, Ruthenia from Czechoslovakia and, finally in 1954, Crimea from Russia. **1986** Ukrainian nationalism received a strong boost by perceived Russian indifference to the results of the nuclear accident at Chernobyl in northern Ukraine. **1991** Ukraine declared independence after the abortive coup by Communist hardliners in Moscow; Ukraine's actions hastened the demise of the USSR. **Since 1991** Tensions remain with Moscow over the future status of ethnic Russians in the east and Crimea (which is largely ethnic Russian and is the base of the former Soviet Black Sea fleet, which was disputed until 1997). Reforms retarded by a large left-wing group in the Ukrainian parliament.

Official name: Ukrayina (Ukraine).
Area: 603,700 km² (233,100 sq mi).
Population: 52,000,000 (1995 est.).
Doubling time: population relatively stable. **Adult life expectancy:** male 65.3 years, female 74.7 years. **Birth rate:** 0.43 times world average.
Death rate: 1.53 times world average. **Urban population:** 68%.
Capital: Kiev (Kyyiv) 2,645,000 (1994 est.; inc. suburbs). **Other main centres:** Kharkov (Kharkiv) 1,599,000, Dnepropetrovsk 1,176,000, Donetsk 1,114,000, Odessa 1,073,000, Zaporizhzhya 898,000, Lviv (formerly Lvov) 807,000, Kryvyy Rih (formerly Krivoyrog) 729,000, Mariupol 523,000, Mykolayiv 515,000, Luhansk 505,000 (1994 est.; inc. suburbs).
Language: Ukrainian 65% (official), Russian 33%, with Romanian, Hungarian, Belarusian and Bulgarian minorities. **Adult literacy:** over 98%.
Religion: Ukrainian Orthodox over 25%, Russian Orthodox about 20%, Ukrainian Catholic (Uniat) 10%; non-religious over 40%.

AUTONOMOUS UKRAINIAN REPUBLIC

Crimea (Krim)
Area: 27,000 km² (10,400 sq mi).
Pop.: 2,652,000 (1994 est.).
Capital: Simferopol.

Russia and Belarus

RUSSIA

Russia is the largest country in the world and covers over 10% of the total land area of the globe. It occupies the extreme eastern part of Europe plus much of western, central and eastern north Asia. Most of the land between the Baltic and the Ural Mountains is covered by the North European Plain, south of which the relatively low-lying Central Russian Uplands stretch from the Ukrainian border to north of Moscow. To the east of the Ural Mountains is the vast West Siberian Lowland, the greater part of which is occupied by the basin of the River Ob and its tributaries. The Central Siberian Plateau (between the rivers Yenisey and Lena) rises to around 1700 m (5500 ft). Beyond the River Lena are the mountains of east Siberia, including the Chersky Mountains and the Kamchatka Peninsula. Much of the south of Siberia is mountainous. The Yablonovy and Stanovoy mountains rise inland from the Amur Basin, which drains to the Pacific coast. The Altai Mountains lie south of Lake Baikal and along the border with Mongolia. Between the Black and Caspian seas are the high Caucasus Mountains on the Georgian border. The Kaliningrad enclave between Poland and Lithuania on the Baltic is a detached part of Russia.
Highest point: Elbrus 5642 m (18,510 ft).
Climate: Russia has a wide range of climates but most of the country is continental and experiences extremes of temperature. The Arctic north is a severe tundra region in which the subsoil is nearly always frozen. The forested taiga zone, to the south, has long, hard winters and short summers. The steppes and the Central Russian Uplands have cold winters, but hot, dry summers. Between the Black and Caspian seas conditions are almost Mediterranean. The Kaliningrad enclave has a temperate climate.

Russia is a federation of republics and other regions, which exercise varying degrees of autonomy. An executive President, who appoints a Council of Ministers including a Prime Minister, is elected by universal adult suffrage for a maximum of two five-year terms. The Federal Assembly comprises two chambers directly elected for four years. The lower house (State Duma) has 450 members: 225 elected by single-member constituencies and 225 elected from party lists under a system of proportional representation. The upper house (Federal Council) has two members elected from each of the 89 republics, regions and other territories of the Russian Federation.
Largest parties: (Duma 1995 election) Communist Party 157 seats, (centrist) Our Home is Russia 55, (extreme right-wing) Liberal Democratic Party 51, (reformist centre-left) Yabloko 45, (left-wing) Agrarian Party 20, (regional left-wing) Power to the People 9, (centrist) Russia's Democratic Choice 9, (centre-right) Congress of Russian Communities 5, independents 17, others 22.
President: (since 1991) Boris Yeltsin (non-party).
Prime Minister: (since 1992) Viktor Chernomyrdin (Our Home is Russia).

Russia is one of the largest producers of coal, iron ore, steel, petroleum and cement. However, its economy has declined during the 1990s and is only slowly emerging from crisis, although living standards have declined. Since 1991 reform has accelerated through the dismantling of the Soviet centrally planned economy, the introduction of free-market prices and the strong encouragement of private enterprise. Over 7000 companies have been privatized. Lack of motivation in the labour force remains a problem and poor distribution has resulted in shortages of some basic items. Inflation was rampant in the early 1990s but has now been brought under control. Manufacturing still employs over one-quarter of the labour force and includes the steel, textile, chemical and heavy engineering industries. The production of consumer goods has increased dramatically since 1991. Agriculture is large-scale and still largely organized into state-owned and collective farms, and although the right to own and farm land privately has been introduced, under 5% of agricultural production comes from the private sector. Despite mechanization and the world's largest fertilizer industry, Russia cannot produce enough grain for its needs, in part because of poor harvests and inadequate storage and transport facilities. Major Russian crops include wheat, barley, oats, sugar beet, potatoes and fruit. Natural resources include the world's largest reserves of coal, nearly one-third of the world's forests, and major deposits of manganese, gold, potash, bauxite, nickel, lead, zinc and copper, as well as plentiful sites for hydroelectric power installations. Machinery, petroleum and petroleum products are Russia's major exports and the country is self-sufficient in energy, although poor distribution and out-of-date infrastructure have hindered supplies. Russia has a large trade surplus with the other former Soviet republics, but trade has been increasing with the West and Japan.
Currency: Rouble.

1905 Abortive rebellion against Tsarist system; defeat in a short war against Japan. **After 1906** Some constitutional reform. **1914** German invasion of Russia at beginning of World War I. **1917** Russian Revolution: Tsar forced to abdicate; republic declared. A second revolution in November brought Vladimir Lenin and the Bolsheviks (Communists) to power; Russia withdrew from the war; Finland, the Baltic states, Ukraine and the states of Central Asia and Transcaucasia declared their independence. **1917–22** Civil war between the Bolsheviks and the Whites (former Tsarists); Tsar and Imperial family murdered at Yekaterinburg. **1922** Soviet Union (USSR) formed; Central Asia, Ukraine and Transcaucasia were reconquered. **1924** Death of Lenin; power struggle between supporters of Joseph Stalin and Leon Trotsky. **From 1929–30** Increasing repression under Stalin; show trials of Stalin's opponents; millions died as a result of starvation or political execution. **1939** Russian pact with Hitler; Russia invaded

Finland, the Baltic states and Poland. **1941** German invasion of Russia. **1941–45** Russia participated in World War II, in which up to 20 million Soviet citizens died. **After 1945** USSR established a cordon of Communist satellite states in Eastern Europe; beginning of the Cold War between USSR and the West. 1953 Death of Stalin; brief period of reform under Nikita Khrushchev. **1956** Russia put down the Hungarian uprising against Soviet rule. **1964–82** The economy stagnated and the USSR was impoverished through attempting to hold down an overstretched empire under Leonid Brezhnev. **1968** The Soviet invasion of Czechoslovakia crushed reforms. **After 1985** Far-reaching reforms begun by Mikhail Gorbachev. **1989** Reformers beat many hard-line Communists in Soviet elections; growing nationalism in the USSR's republics. **1989–91** Collapse of the satellite Communist regimes in Eastern Europe. **1991** Attempted coup by Communist hard-liners against Gorbachev; secession of the Baltic states (Estonia, Latvia and Lithuania); Yeltsin came to power in Russia; Gorbachev resigned; collapse and dissolution of the Soviet Union; Russia and the remaining 11 other republics became independent states. Russia took over the international responsibilities of the former USSR. **1993** Constitutional crisis: Communist and nationalist hard-liners staged an uprising in Moscow's parliament building. **1995** Russia invaded the rebellious secessionist republic of Chechnya. **1996** Russian troops brought to a standstill in Chechnya; cease-fire agreed; Russian troops withdrew; Chechnya effectively independent (although its final status will not be decided for five years).

Official name: Rossiyskaya Federatsiya (Russian Federation).
Area: 17,074,400 km^2 (6,592,800 sq mi).
Population: 147,170,000 (1995 est.).
Doubling time: pop. declining.
Adult life expectancy: male 57.7 years, female 71.1 years.
Birth rate: 0.38 times world average.
Death rate: 1.56 times world average. **Urban population:** 73%.
Capital: Moscow (Moskva) 8,957,000 (1992 est.; inc. suburbs).
Other main centres: Saint Petersburg (Sankt Peterburg; formerly Leningrad) 5,004,000, Novosibirsk 1,472,000, Nizhny Novgorod (formerly Gorki) 1,451,000, Yekaterinburg (formerly Sverdlovsk) 1,413,000, Samara (formerly Kuybyshev) 1,271, Omsk 1,193,000, Chelyabinsk 1,170,000, Perm 1,108,000, Kazan 1,107,000, Ufa 1,100,000, Volgograd 1,031,000, Rostov-on-Don (Rostov-na-Donu) 1,027,000, Voronezh 958,000, Krasnoyarsk 925,000, Saratov 916,000, Krasnodar 751,000, Togliattigrad (formerly Togliatti) 677,000, Vladivostok 675,000, Barnaul 665,000, Izhevsk 651,000, Irkutsk 644,000, Simbirsk (formerly Ulyanovsk) 638,000, Yaroslav 637,000, Khabarovsk 626,000, Novokuznetsk 614,000 (1992 est.; inc. suburbs).
Language: Russian over 86% as a first language (official) but understood almost universally, Tatar 3%, Ukrainian 1%, Chuvash 1%; Bashkir, Chechen and Mordovinian are each spoken by over 0.5%; over 100 other languages.
Adult literacy: no recent figures available.
Religion: Orthodox *c.* 27% practising, with Sunni Islam, Baptist, Jewish and other minorities; non-religious over 50%.

RUSSIAN REPUBLICS

Adygea
Area: 7600 km^2 (2900 sq mi).
Pop.: 450,000 (1995 est.).
Capital: Maykop.
Bashkortostan
Area: 143,600 km^2 (55,400 sq mi).
Pop.: 4,080,000 (1995 est.).
Capital: Ufa.
Buryatia
Area: 351,300 km^2 (135,600 sq mi).
Pop.: 1,050,000 (1995 est.).
Capital: Ulan-Ude.
Chechnya
Area: 14,300 km^2 (5500 sq mi).
Pop.: 900,000 (1995 est.).
Capital: Dzhokhar-Ghala (formerly Grozny).
Chuvashia
Area: 18,300 km^2 (7100 sq mi).
Pop.: 1,360,000 (1995 est.).
Capital: Cheboksary.
Dagestan
Area: 50,300 km^2 (19,400 sq mi).
Pop.: 2,010,000 (1995 est.).
Capital: Makhachkala.
Gorno-Altay
Area: 92,600 km^2 (35,700 sq mi).
Pop.: 200,000 (1995 est.).
Capital: Gorno-Altaisk.
Ingushetia
Area: 5000 km^2 (2000 sq mi).
Pop.: 410,000 (1995 est.).
Capital: Nazran.
Kabardino-Balkaria
Area: 12,500 km^2 (4800 sq mi).
Pop.: 790,000 (1995 est.).
Capital: Nalchik.
Kalmykia (Khalmg Tangch)
Area: 76,100 km^2 (29,400 sq mi).
Pop.: 320,000 (1995 est.).
Capital: Elista.
Karachay-Cherkessia
Area: 14,100 km^2 (5400 sq mi).
Pop.: 435,000 (1995 est.).
Capital: Cherkessk.
Karelia
Area: 172,400 km^2 (66,600 sq mi).
Pop.: 790,000 (1995 est.).
Capital: Petrozavodsk.
Khakassia
Area: 61,900 km^2 (23,900 sq mi).
Pop.: 580,000 (1995 est.).
Capital: Abakan.
Komi
Area: 415,900 km^2 (160,600 sq mi).
Pop.: 1,200,000 (1995 est.).
Capital: Syktyvkar.
Mari El
Area: 23,200 km^2 (9000 sq mi).
Pop.: 770,000 (1995 est.).
Capital: Yoshkar-Ola.
Mordvinia
Area: 26,200 km^2 (10,100 sq mi).
Pop.: 960,000 (1995 est.).
Capital: Saransk.
North Ossetia (Severo-Ossetiya)
Area: 8000 km^2 (3100 sq mi).
Pop.: 665,000 (1995 est.).
Capital: Vladikavkaz.
Russia (Rossiya)
Area: 12,198,300 km^2 (4,709,800 sq mi).
Pop.: 124,530,000 (1995 est.).
Capital: Moscow (Moskva). Unlike the other republics, Russia has no government but is divided into autonomous regions, districts, territories and cities, each with its own administration.
Sakha (formerly Yakutia)
Area: 3,103,200 km^2 (1,198,200 sq mi).
Pop.: 1,035,000 (1995 est.).
Capital: Yakutsk.
Tatarstan
Area: 68,000 km^2 (26,300 sq mi).
Pop.: 3,755,000 (1995 est.).
Capital: Kazan.
Tyva (formerly Tuva)
Area: 170,500 km^2 (65,800 sq mi).
Pop.: 310,000 (1995 est.).
Capital: Kyzyl-Orda.
Udmurtia
Area: 42,100 km^2 (16,300 sq mi).
Pop.: 1,640,000 (1995 est.).
Capital: Izhevsk.

Note: Chechnya is largely outside the control of the Russian authorities. Tatarstan exercises greater autonomy than the other republics.

BELARUS

Belarus is a former Soviet republic lying between Russia and Poland. It comprises lowlands covered with glacial debris in the north, fertile well-drained tablelands in the centre and the low-lying Pripet Marshes in the south and east. Much of the country is flat.
Highest point: Dzyarzhynskaya 346 m (1135 ft). **Climate:** The continental climate is moderated by the proximity of the Baltic Sea. Winters are milder than those in European Russia to the east.

The constitution provides for elections by universal adult suffrage for five years for a president and four a 110-member House of Representatives. The president, who may override Parliament and rule by decree, appoints a prime minister and ministers who are responsible to him. A 63-member Senate has 21 members appointed by the president and 42 from local authorities. The current legislature is formed by Government supporters who withdrew from the Assembly, elected in 1995. Activities of parties outside the Communist-Agrarian bloc restricted.
President: (since 1994) Aleksandr Lukashenko (non-party).
Prime Minister: (since 1994) Mikhail Chigir (non-party).

Although Belarus has few resources its economy is overwhelmingly industrial. Major heavy engineering, chemical, fertilizer, petroleum refining and synthetic fibre industries were established as part of the centrally planned Soviet economy before independence. However, output has declined drastically since 1991 and almost no progress has been made towards establishing a market economy. The country depends heavily upon trade with other former Soviet republics. Major economic problems include high inflation, unemployment, old industrial plant, and contamination from Chernobyl which affected about 20% of Belarus. Farming is dominated by raising fodder crops for pigs, beef cattle and poultry. Flax is grown for export and the local linen industry. Extensive forests supply important woodworking and paper industries.
Currency: Belarusian rouble.

1900 Belarus had been part of the Russian empire since the late 18th century. **1919** Following the Russian Revolution, an independent (Communist) Republic of Byelorussia was proclaimed. **1921** Belarus invaded by Poland and subsequently divided between Poland and Russia. **1922** As Byelorussia the region became a republic of the USSR. **1941–45** Invaded by Nazi Germany; Belarusian towns and industries devastated. **1945** All mainly Belarusian regions reunited within the USSR. **1986** Large areas evacuated after Chernobyl nuclear power station accident just over the border in Ukraine. A perceived lack of Soviet concern strengthened a reawakening national spirit. **1991** Dissolution of the USSR; Byelorussia, as Belarus, became independent . **Since 1994** Restrictions in civil rights; power in the hands of President Lukashenko; steps taken towards eventual reunion with Russia begun. **1996** Constitutional crisis; a rump parliament of government supporters formed; opposition curtailed.

Official name: Respublika Belarus (Republic of Belarus).
Area: 207,546 km^2 (80,134 sq mi).
Population: 10,332,000 (1995 est.).
Doubling time: pop. almost stable.
Adult life expectancy: male 66 years, female 75.7 years.
Birth rate: 0.45 times world average.
Death rate: 1.33 times world average. **Urban population:** 68%.
Capital: Minsk (Mensk) 1,671,000 (1992 est.; inc. suburbs). **Other main centres:** Homel (formerly Gomel) 517,000, Vitebsk 373,000, Mahilyou (formerly Mogilev) 364,000, Hrodno (formerly Grodno) 291,000, Brest 277,000, Bobruisk (formerly Babruysk) 223,000 (1992 est.; inc. suburbs).
Language: Belarusian 66% (official), Russian 32% (off.) but understood by almost 100%, Ukrainian and Polish minorities. **Adult literacy:** 98%.
Religion: Belarusian Orthodox about 70%, Roman Catholic under 5%, others and non-religious 25%.

PLACES OF INTEREST

Tourism in Russia is still in its infancy. Russia has not shared the east European tourist boom that has pushed Hungary, Poland and the Czech Republic into the top ten tourist destinations. A popular way to visit Russia is to join a tour of the historic sites of European Russia, but independent travel is also increasing. Over one-fifth of the visitors to Russia are from Finland. Ethnic Russians from other countries of the former Soviet Union are another important element. Popular destinations include Moscow (the Golden Ring, Red Square and St Basil's Cathedral), St Petersburg (Hermitage Museum, the Russian Museum and the Summer Palace), Irkutsk, Sochi (Black Sea) and the Trans-Siberian railway.

World Heritage sites include: Church of the Ascension, Kolomenskoye; Kremlin and Red Square; historic monuments of Novgorod and its surroundings; historic centre of St Petersburg and related groups of monuments; Kamchatka volcanoes; Lake Baikal; Virgin Komi forests; white monuments of Vladimir and Suzdal.

REPUBLICS

1 Adygea
2 Bashkortostan
3 Buryatia
4 Chechnya
5 Chuvashia
6 Dagestan
7 Gorno-Altay
8 Ingushetia
9 Kabardino-Balkaria
10 Kalmykia (Khalmg Tangch)
11 Karachay-Cherkessia
12 Karelia
13 Khakassia
14 Komi
15 Mari El
16 Mordvinia
17 North Ossetia (Severo-Ossetiya)
18 Russia (Rossiya)
19 Sakha (formerly Yakutia)
20 Tatarstan
21 Tyva (formerly Tuva)
22 Udmurtia

For further information, see p. 391.

The Catherine Palace in Pushkin near St Petersburg is built in an ornate baroque style. Pushkin (formerly Tsarskoye Selo) grew up around the summer palaces of Russia's royal family.

St Petersburg is Russia's second city, whose splendid architecture, palaces and museums are major tourist attractions.

The Taz river region, Siberia, is part of a vast plain varying little in relief, and containing huge swamps. Like most of northern Siberia it is underdeveloped.

! Verkhoyansk in Siberia has the world's greatest temperature range, fluctuating between –68°C and 37°C (–90°F and 99°F).

! The River Ob has the longest estuary in the world at 885 km (550 mi).

! The Tatar Strait between Sakhalin Island and Russia is 800 km (500 mi) long, making it the world's longest strait.

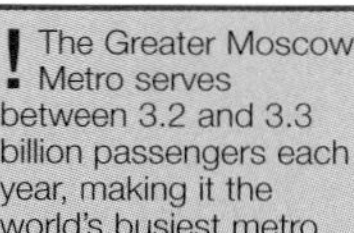

! The Greater Moscow Metro serves between 3.2 and 3.3 billion passengers each year, making it the world's busiest metro.

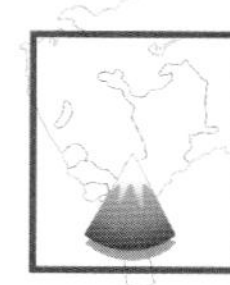

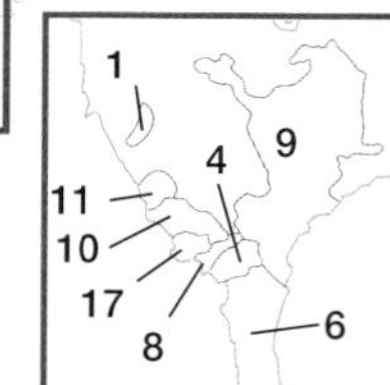

! The Sayano-Shushenskaya dam on the River Yenisey is designed to bear a load of 18 million tonnes, making it the world's strongest dam.

! Lake Baikal is the freshwater lake with the greatest volume in the world. It is also the world's deepest lake.

! The longest rail journey possible without changing trains is 9297 km (5777 mi) on the Trans-Siberian line from Moscow to Vladivostok.

St. Basil's Cathedral, with its colourful onion domes, stands at the south end of Red Square, Moscow. It was commissioned by Ivan IV, the Terrible.

The Moscow River passes through the Russian capital in sweeping bends, in places cutting steep cliffs from which magnificent panoramas of the city can be obtained.

The Trans-Siberian railway was built between 1891 and 1905. The development of Siberia this century has been concentrated along the railway line, which is a vital communications link.

TELEVISION AND RADIO

No. of TVs: 54,200,000 (2.7 persons per TV)
No. of radio receivers: 48,800,000 (3.0 persons per radio)

Despite the 1991 coup and the growth of privitization, very few Russian media outlets are entirely financed independently. Even the independent NTV station depends on state-controlled satellites and transmitters. ORT (often known as the First Channel), which reaches 200 million viewers in Russia and the former USSR, and RTR (Channel 2), which reaches 140 million viewers in Russia, are the main companies which broadcast radio and TV programmes.

CINEMA

No. of cinemas: 1810

Russia's film industry has declined since the Soviet Union's collapse in 1991. Economic instability has resulted in a reluctance by private individuals and companies to fund films. There are two main film companies – Mosfilm and Lenfilm – based in Moscow and St Petersburg respectively. Roskomkino, the State Ministry of Film, is now the principal source of funding for the Russian Film Industry. Films (full or partially funded by the state) have included those dealing with contemporary themes, comedies, adaptations of literary classics and historical pictures.

NEWSPAPERS

The new 'freedom of the press' still has restrictions. By 1993, there were 200 national papers. High-circulation papers of Communist days – *Izvestia* ('News'), *Pravda* ('Truth') and *Trud* ('Labour') – shrank, as new, innovative papers such as *Argumenty y Fakty* appeared. Shortages of materials, increasing taxes and high costs cause some 'dailies' to be published intermittently. Major daily titles (all published in Moscow) and their circulation figures are:

*Argumenty y Fakty**	3,600,000
Trud	1,400,000
Izvestia	1,000,000
Pravda	630,000
Selskaya Zhizn	180,000

* denotes weekly publication

MAGAZINES

Periodicals used to be published by various Communist Party bodies. The vast majority were of an educational and 'improving' nature, and carried propaganda. Some of these titles are still published – in much smaller numbers – by successor bodies, although they have changed greatly in style. A number of new magazines have appeared whose emphasis is on sensationalism and mysticism. The principal monthly magazines and their circulation figures are:

Rabotmitsa	working women's interests	20,500,000
Zdorovye	health and hygiene	16,800,000
Yunost	literature and writing	3,300,000
*Krokodil**	satire	2,200,000

* three issues per month

PRIME MINISTERS

Russia	
1917	Prince Georgy Lvov
1917	Aleksandr Kerensky
1917–22	Vladimir Ilich Lenin
The USSR	
1922–24	Vladimir Ilich Lenin
1924–30	Aleksey Rykov
1930–31	Genrikh Yagoda
1931–41	Vyacheslav Molotov
1941–53	Joseph Stalin
1953–55	Georgy Malenkov
1955–58	Nikolai Bulganin
1958–64	Nikita Khruschev
1964–80	Alexei Kosygin
1980–85	Nikolai Tikhonov
1985–90	Nikolai Ryzhkov
1990–91	Valentin Pavlov
Russia	
1992	Ygor Gaidar (acting)
1992–	Victor Chernomyrdin

PRESIDENTS

Presidents of Russia	
1917–19	Yakov Sverdlov
1919–22	Mikhail Kalinin
Presidents of the USSR	
1922–46	Mikhail Kalinin
1946–53	Nikolai Shvernik
1953–60	Kliment Voroshilov
1960–64	Leonid Ilich Brezhnev
1964–65	Anastas Mikoyan
1965–77	Nikolai Podgorny
1977–82	Leonid Ilich Brezhnev
1982–83	Vassili Kuznetsov (acting)
1983–84	Yuri Andropov
1984–85	Konstantin Chernenko
1985–88	Andrei Gromyko
1988–91	Mikhail Gorbachev
Presidents of Russia	
1991–	Boris Yeltsin

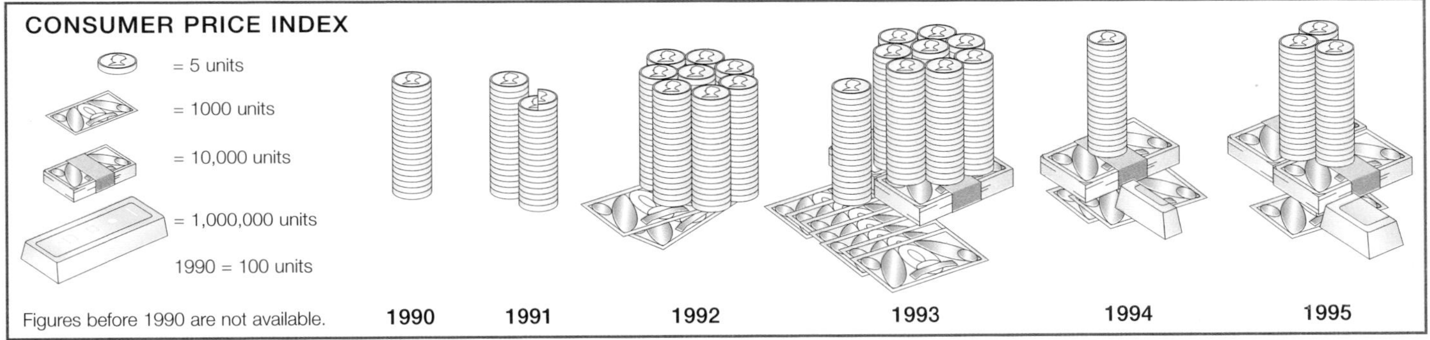

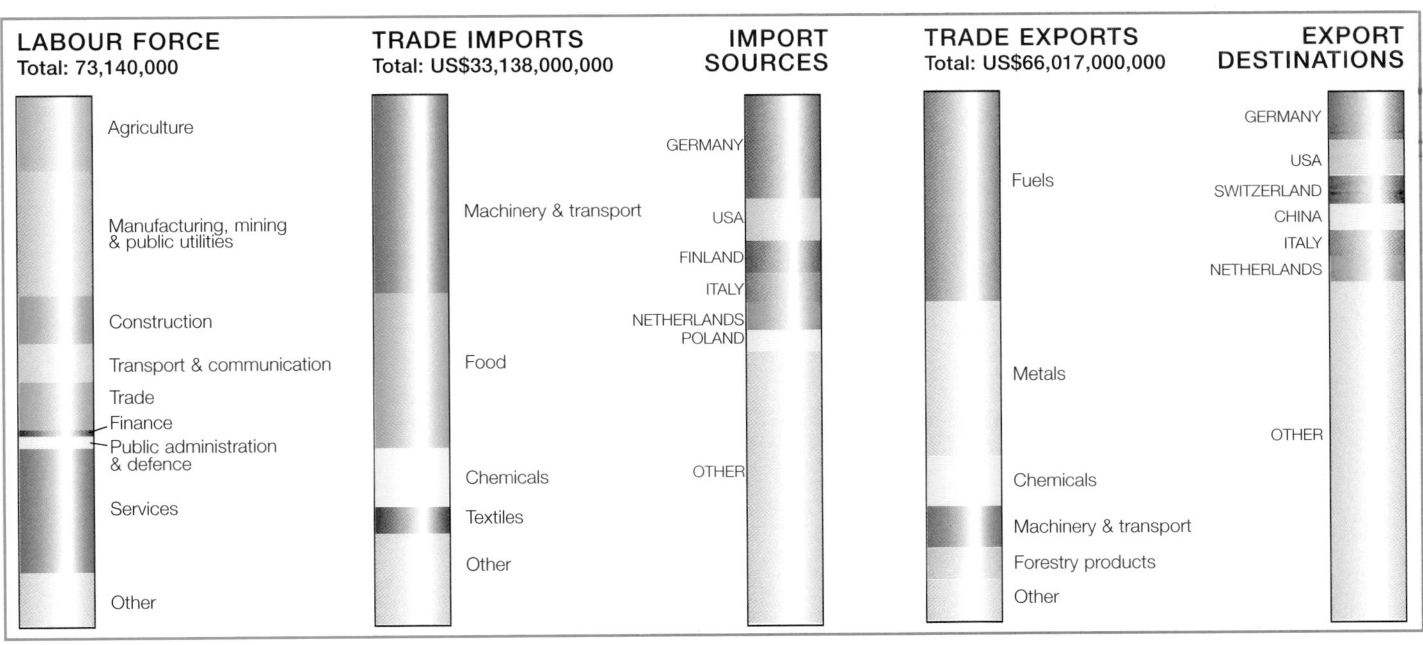

The Caucasus and Iran

IRAN

Iran is an ancient nation forming a bridge between the Middle East and south Asia. Apart from restricted lowlands along the Gulf, the Caspian Sea and the Iraqi border, Iran is a high plateau, surrounded by mountains. The Zagros Mountains form a barrier running parallel to the Gulf. In the east, lower areas of the plateau are covered by salt deserts including the Kevir Desert. **Highest point:** Demavend 5604 m (18,386 ft). **Climate:** Iran has an extreme climate ranging from very hot on the Gulf to sub-zero temperatures in winter in the north-west. The Caspian Sea coast has a subtropical climate with adequate rainfall. Most of Iran, however, is arid.

An 83-member Assembly of Experts (Shiite clerics) is elected for eight years by universal adult suffrage to appoint the Wali Faqih (Leader), who exercises supreme authority over the executive, legislature, judiciary and military. The 270-member Islamic Consultative Assembly (Majlis) and an executive President are directly elected for four years. The President appoints a Cabinet, which is responsible to the Majlis.
Largest groups: (there are no parties) (1996 election) (extreme right-wing fundamentalist) Society of Combatant Clergy 110 seats, (right-wing fundamentalist) Servant's of Iran's Construction 80, others 80.
Leader: (Wali Faqih) (since 1989) Ayatollah Seyed Ali Khamenei.
President: (since 1997) Mohammed Khatemi.

Petroleum is Iran's main source of foreign currency. The principal industries are petrochemicals, carpet-weaving, textiles, vehicles and cement. The war with Iraq in the 1980s and the country's international isolation have severely interrupted trade, and Iran suffers a lack of investment. High inflation, unemployment and deteriorating living standards are major problems. Over one-quarter of the labour force is involved in agriculture, mainly producing cereals (wheat, maize and barley) and keeping livestock, but lack of water, land ownership problems and manpower shortages in the countryside have restricted yields.
Currency: Rial.

1921 Reza Khan Pahlavi seized power. **1925** Overthrow of the Qajar dynasty: Pahlavi made himself Shah (emperor) as Reza I. **1925–89** Modernization of the country under the Pahlavi dynasty. **1935** Persia renamed Iran. **1941** Reza I forced to abdicate by the UK and USSR because of his pro-German sympathies; succeeded by Mohammed Reza. **1953** Radical nationalist PM Mohammed Mussadiq briefly toppled the monarchy. **1953–79** Mohammed Reza tightened his grip through oppression and sought popularity through land reform. **1979** Overthrow of the Shah. A fundamentalist Islamic republic was established inspired by Ayatollah Ruhollah Khomeini. Western-educated classes fled Iran. **1979–81** Radical anti-Western students invaded US embassy and held 66 American hostages. **1980** Iraq invaded Iran. **1988** End of Iran-Iraq war. **After 1989** Economic need brought a less militant phase of the Islamic revolution after the death of Khomeini. **1990** Iraq returned occupied Iranian territory.

■ *The Shah Mosque in Isfahan, built in 1612–37, is regarded to be an outstanding example of Persian architecture*

Official name: Jomhuri-ye Eslami-ye Iran (The Islamic Republic of Iran).
Area: 1,638,057 km² (632,457 sq mi).
Population: 61,270,000 (1995 est.).
Doubling time: 21 years. **Adult life expectancy:** male 65 years, female 67 years. **Birth rate:** 1.68 times world average. **Death rate:** 0.86 times world average.
Urban population: 57%.
Capital: Tehran 6,475,000 (1991 census; inc. suburbs). **Other main centres:** Mashhad 1,759,000, Esfahan 1,127,000, Tabriz 1,089,000, Shiraz 965,000, Ahvaz 725,000, Qom 681,000 (1991 census; inc. suburbs).
Language: Farsi (Persian) 83% (47% as a first language; official), Azeri 17%, Kurdish 9%, Gilaki 5%, Luri 4%, Mazandarani 4%, Baluchi 2%, Bakhtyari 2%. **Adult literacy:** 54%.
Religion: Shia Islam 94%, Sunni Islam nearly 6%.

ARMENIA

Armenia is a small landlocked former Soviet republic in the Caucasus Mountains between Europe and Asia. All of Armenia is mountainous – only 10% of the country is below 1000 m (3300 ft). The Araks valley along the Turkish border is the main lowland. Forests are widespread.
Highest point: Aragats 4090 m (13,418 ft). **Climate:** Armenia has a dry continental climate with considerable local variations owing to aspect, altitude and rainshadows.

Official name: Hayastani Hanrapetutyun (The Republic of Armenia).
Area: 29,800 km² (11,506 sq mi).
Population: 3,548,000 (1995 est.).
Doubling time: 87 years. **Adult life expectancy:** male 68.4 years, female 75.4 years. **Birth rate:** 0.54 times world average. **Death rate:** 0.7 times world average. **Urban population:** 68%. **Capital:** Yerevan 1,283,000 (1991 est.; inc. suburbs). **Other main centres:** Gyumri (or Kumayri; formerly Leninakan) 206,000, Vanadzor (or Karaklis; formerly Kirovakan) 170,000 (1991 est.).
Language: Armenian 94% (official), Azeri 3%, Russian minority.
Adult literacy: no figures available.
Religion: Armenian Apostolic (Orthodox) 94%, Shia Islam 3%, Roman Catholic and Russian Orthodox minorities.

A President is elected for a five-year term by universal adult suffrage. The National Assembly has 190 members elected by universal adult suffrage for four years, with 150 members elected from single-member constituencies and 40 members elected nationally under a system of proportional representation. The President nominates a Prime Minister.
Largest parties: (National Assembly 1995 election) (reformist) Republican Bloc (including the Pan-Armenian National Movement – HHSh) 119 seats, Shamiram (women's movement) 8, (former Communist) Democratic Party 7, National Democratic Union 5, others 51.
President: (since independence) Levon Ter-Petrosyan (HHSh).
Prime Minister: (since 1997) Robert Kocharyan (HHSh).

Industries include chemicals, precision goods, metallurgy and mining (copper) and food processing but Armenian industry has declined in the 1990s. Major projects have provided hydroelectric power and irrigation water for farming (particularly cotton and cereals). Privatization has begun, but the war against Azerbaijan, and a severe earthquake in 1988, have devastated the economy and led to a severe energy shortage. **Currency:** Dram.

1900 Armenia had been under Tsarist Russian rule since 1813–28. **1918** Revolt against Russian rule. **1918–22** Armenia independent. **1922** Annexation by the Soviet Union. **1936** Armenia became a separate Union republic of the USSR. **1989–94** Armenian and Azeri forces involved in a violent dispute over Nagorno-Karabakh, an enclave of Orthodox Christian Armenians surrounded by Shiite Muslim Azeris. **1990** Nationalists gained power in Armenia; independence declared. **1991** Dissolution of the USSR; Armenian independence recognized. **1994** Russian-brokered ceasefire left Armenian forces in control of 20% of Azerbaijan including Nagorno-Karabakh.

■ IRAN'S OIL RESERVES ARE IN EXCESS OF 14 TRILLION LITRES ■ THE CASPIAN SEA,

AZERBAIJAN

Azerbaijan is a former Soviet republic on the western shores of the Caspian Sea. The country comprises lowlands beside the Caspian Sea, part of the Caucasus Mountains in the north and the Little Caucasus Mountains in the south-west. The republic includes the Naxçivan enclave to the west of Armenia.
Highest point: Bazar-Dyuzi 4466 m (14,652 ft).

Climate: A wide climatic range includes dry and humid subtropical conditions beside the Caspian Sea and continental conditions in the mountains.

An executive President and a 125-member Assembly (Melli Majlis) are elected by universal adult suffrage for four years. The President appoints a Prime Minister and a Cabinet.
Largest parties: (1995 election) (nationalist) New Azerbaijan Party and allies 88; the Musavat Party, the Communist Party, and the Islamic Party were banned from taking part in the election.
President: (since 1993) Geidar Aliyev (NAP).
Prime Minister: (since 1996) Artur Rasizade (NAP).

Reserves of oil and natural gas are the mainstays of the economy and the basis of heavy industries. Although industry dominates the Azeri economy, agriculture contributes a variety of exports including cotton and tobacco. Sturgeon, for caviar, are caught in the Caspian Sea. War with Armenia has damaged the economy and there is high inflation. Privatization has begun and the West has invested in the oil industry. **Currency:** Manat.

■ *Azeri's oil production makes it one of the richest former Soviet republics*

1900 Under Tsarist Russian rule since 1813–28. **1918** Revolt against Russian rule; an Azeri republic, allied to Turkey, was proclaimed. **1918–20** Azerbaijan independent. **1920** Invasion by the Soviet Red Army. **1922** Became part of the USSR. **1936** Became a separate Union republic of the USSR. **1989–94** Armenian and Azeri forces involved in violent dispute over Nagorno-Karabakh, an enclave of Orthodox Christian Armenians surrounded by Shiite Muslim Azeris. **1990** Soviet troops sent to restore order after the nationalist Popular Front declared independence. **1991** Dissolution of the USSR; Azeri independence recognized. **1993** Following rebellion and defeat by Armenian forces the government of President Abulfaz Elchibey toppled in coup. Former Communist Geidar Aliyev came to power. **1994** Russian-brokered ceasefire in Nagorno-Karabakh left Armenian forces in control of 20% of Azerbaijan including Nagorno-Karabakh. **1994–95** Unsuccessful coup attempts.

Official name: Azärbayjan Respublikasi (The Republic of Azerbaijan).
Area: 86,600 km² (33,400 sq mi).
Population: 7,525,000 (1995 est.).
Doubling time: 50 years. **Adult life expectancy:** male 66.7 years, female 74.6 years. **Birth rate:** 0.86 times world average. **Death rate:** 0.8 times world average. **Urban population:** 53%. **Capital:** Baku 1,713,000 (1991 est.; inc. suburbs). **Other main centres:** Gäncä (or Gyandzha; formerly Kirovabad) 282,000, Sumqayit (formerly Sumgait) 236,000, Mingacevir (formerly Mingechaur) 91,000 (1991 est.).
Language: Azeri 82% (official), Russian 8%, Armenian 5%, Lezgian 2%. **Adult literacy:** 97%.
Religion: Shia Islam 65%, Sunni Islam 28%, Russian Orthodox 3%, Armenian Apostolic (Orthodox) 2%.

AUTONOMOUS AZERI REPUBLIC

Naxçivan (formerly Nakhichevan)
Area: 5500 km² (2100 sq mi).
Pop.: 306,000 (1991 est.).
Capital: Naxçivan.

GEORGIA

Georgia is a former Soviet republic on the eastern shores of the Black Sea.The spine of the Caucasus Mountains forms the northern border of Georgia. A lower range, called the Little Caucasus, occupies southern Georgia. Central Georgia comprises the Kolkhida lowlands.
Highest point: the lower slopes of Elbrus at 5642 m (18,510 ft) are in Georgia but the peak is across the Russian border; the highest peak entirely within Georgia is Kasbek at 5047 m (16,558 ft). **Climate:** Coastal and central Georgia have a moist Mediterranean climate. The rest of the country is drier. Climate varies considerably dependent on both altitude and aspect.

A President and a 235-member Parliament are elected by universal adult suffrage for a total of five years and four years respectively. Seventy-five members of parliament are elected to represent single-member constituencies; the remainder of the members are elected under a system of proportional representation. The President is responsible for appointing a Council of Ministers.
Largest parties: (1995 election) (nationalist) Citizens' Union (CUP) 91, (centre-right coalition) All-Georgian Union of Revival and the National Democratic Party 59, others (including government supporters) and independents 78.
President: (since 1992) Eduard Shevardnadze (CUP).

■ *Much of Georgia is fertile, and farming occupies 25% of the working population*

Despite a shortage of cultivable land Georgia has a diversified agricultural sector including tea, citrus fruit, tobacco, cereals, vines, livestock and vegetables. Natural resources include coal, manganese and plentiful hydroelectric power. Machine building, food processing and chemicals are the principal industries. The economy was damaged by civil war, rampant crime, high inflation and power shortages from 1991 to 1994 when increased stability brought a moderate recovery. **Currency:** Lari.

1900 Georgia had been under Tsarist Russian rule since 1801–78. **1918** Revolt against Russian rule; a Georgian republic, allied to Germany, was proclaimed. **1918–20** British occupation of Georgia in favour of the White Russians. **1921** Invasion by the Soviet Red Army; Georgia became part of the USSR. **1936** Armenia became a separate Union republic of the USSR. **1989–94** Armenian and Azeri forces involved in a violent dispute over Nagorno-Karabakh, an enclave of Orthodox Christian Armenians surrounded by Shiite Muslim Azeris. **1991** Independence declared; dissolution of the USSR; Georgian independence recognized. **1991–92** Civil war. **1992–94** Attempted secession by Muslim Abhazians. **1994** Russian-brokered ceasefire in Nagorno-Karabakh left Armenian forces in control of 20% of Azerbaijan and in Abkhazia left the latter largely in the hands of secessionists.

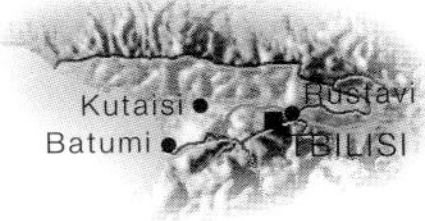

Official name: Sakartvelos Respublika (The Republic of Georgia).
Area: 69,492 km² (26,831 sq mi).
Population: 5,510,000 (1995 est.).
Doubling time: 77 years. **Adult life expectancy:** male 68.9 years, female 76.5 years. **Birth rate:** 0.5 times world average. **Death rate:** 1.1 times world average. **Urban population:** 56%. **Capital:** Tbilisi 1,270,000 (1993 est.; inc. suburbs). **Other main centres:** Kutaisi 240,000, Rustavi 158,000, Batumi 137,000, Sukhumi 112,000 (1993 est.).
Language: Georgian 72% (official), Russian 9%, Armenian 7%, Azeri 6%, Ossetian 2%. **Adult literacy:** 99%.
Religion: Georgian Orthodox 65%, Sunni and Shia Islam 11%, Russian Orthodox 10%, Armenian Apostolic (Orthodox) 8%.

AUTONOMOUS GEORGIAN REPUBLICS

Abkhazia
Area: 8660 km² (3343 sq mi).
Pop.: 517,000 (1993 est.).
Capital: Sukhumi.
Ajaria (formerly Adzharia)
Area: 2900 km² (1120 sq. mi).
Pop.: 387,000 (1993 est.).
Capital: Batumi.

MIDDLE EAST I

SYRIA

Syria is a republic of the Middle East stretching from the Mediterranean to the upper basin of the Tigris and Euphrates. Behind a well-watered coastal plain, mountains run from north to south. Further east is the Syrian Desert.
Highest point: Mt Hermon (Jabal ash Shaikh) 2814 m (9232 ft).
Climate: The coastal lowlands have a Mediterranean climate; the mountains are cooler. The arid interior has hot summers and cool winters.

An executive President, who is nominated by the 250-member People's Council, is confirmed for a seven-year term by universal adult suffrage. The People's Council is directly elected for four years; only parties compatible with the aims of the Ba'ath party are allowed to stand for election. The President appoints a Prime Minister and other Ministers.
Largest parties: (1994 election) (socialist, virtual monopoly) National Progressive Front (including Ba'ath Party) 167 seats, independents 83.
President: (since 1971) Hafez al-Assad (Ba'ath).
Prime Minister: (since 1987) Mahmoud Zubi (Ba'ath).

Petroleum is the main export, although Syrian reserves are small by Middle Eastern standards. Agriculture involves one-quarter of the labour force, with farming concentrated in coastal areas and irrigated land in the Euphrates valley. Until the mid-1990s Syria's economy was largely state-run but privatization has begun. **Currency:** Syrian pound.

1917 Four hundred years of Turkish rule was ended by a joint Franco-British force during World War I. **1920** Independence as a kingdom was declared, but France received a League of Nations mandate over Syria. **1946** Independence. **1948–49** War against Israel. **1949–70** Period of great political instability, coups and assassinations. **1958–61** Brief unsuccessful union with Egypt. **1967** War against Israel: Golan Heights seized from Syria. **1970** Hafez al-Assad's socialist Ba'ath Party came to power. **Since 1976** Syria has intervened in Lebanon during the latter's civil war; in 1990 Syria crushed Lebanese Christian militias and now has an unofficial 'leading role' in that country. **1989–90** Economic necessity lessened Syria's dependence upon the USSR; collapse of Soviet Union brought a more pragmatic phase in Syria's foreign relations. **1990–91** Syria participated in the US-led coalition against Iraq in the Gulf War.

Official name: al-Jumhuriyah al-'Arabiyah al-Suriyah (The Arab Republic of Syria).
Area: 185,180 km² (71,498 sq mi), including areas of the Golan Heights occupied by Israel.
Population: 14,310,000 (1995 est.). **Doubling time:** 28 years. **Adult life expectancy:** male 65.2 years, female 69.2 years. **Birth rate:** 1.15 times world average. **Death rate:** 0.36 times world average. **Urban population:** 52%. **Capital:** Damascus (Dimashq) 1,550,000 (1994 est.; inc. suburbs). **Other main centres:** Aleppo (Halab) 1,591,000, Homs (Hims) 644,000, Latakia (al-Ladhiqiyah) 307,000, Hamah 229,000 (1994 est.; inc. suburbs).
Language: Arabic 89% (official), Kurdish 6%, Armenian 3%.
Adult literacy: 71%.
Religion: Sunni Islam 74%, Shia Islam 15%, various Uniat Christian Churches 9%, Druze 3%.

ISRAEL

Israel is a Middle Eastern republic on the eastern Mediterranean coast and extends south to a short coastline on the Gulf of Aqaba of the Red Sea. It consists of a fertile thin coastal plain beside the Mediterranean, parts of the arid mountains of Judaea in the centre, the Negev desert in the south and part of the Jordan valley in the east.
Highest point: Meron (or Jebel Jarmaq) 1208 m (3963 ft).
Climate: Mediterranean with hot, dry summers and mild, wetter winters. The south is more arid than the north and most of Israel receives less than 200 mm (8 in) of rain a year.

The 120-member Parliament or Knesset is elected under a system of proportional representation by universal adult suffrage for four years. The Prime Minister, who is also directly elected to office, appoints other Ministers. The President, whose role is largely ceremonial, is also directly elected.
Largest parties: (1996 election) (left-wing) Labour Party 34 seats, (right-wing) Likud 32, non-religious parties 13, (oriental religious) Shas (Guardians of the Torah) 10, (left-wing) Meretz 9, (non-aligned) Yisra'el Bar Elia 7, (Communist) Hadash 5, Third Way 4, United Arab List 4 (right-wing) Moledet 2.
President: (since 1993) Ezer Weizman (non-party).
Prime Minister: (since 1996) Benjamin Netanyahu (Likud; Likud-Moledet-religious parties coalition).

Economic problems stem, in part, from Israel's large defence budget and from the fact that until recent years it has been unable to trade with any of its neighbours. Israel is a major producer and exporter of citrus fruit. Much land is irrigated and about 75% of Israel's arable land is farmed by co-operatives. Mineral resources are few but processing imported diamonds is a major source of foreign currency. Tourism, to biblical sites, is important. Unemployment is high and many recent migrants (particularly from the former USSR) have been unable to find employment suited to their qualifications.
Currency: New sheqel.

1917 400 years of Turkish rule was ended when British forces occupied Palestine during World War I; Zionists hoped for establishment of a Jewish homeland after the favourable Balfour Declaration (by the UK foreign secretary). **1920** UK received League of Nations mandate over Palestine. **1946** Independence. **1948–49** Establishment of Israel after murder of six million Jews in concentration camps in Europe in World War II. The Arabs rejected partition of Palestine; 1st Arab-Israeli War. **1956** During Suez Crisis, Israel attacked Egyptian Gaza and Sinai but later withdrew. **1967** 2nd Arab-Israeli War: Israel took West Bank from Jordan, Gaza from Egypt and Golan Heights from Syria. **1973** Egypt attacked Israel, cease-fire arranged in three days. **1979** Egypt and Israel made peace: Israeli withdrawal from Sinai began. **1982** Israel invaded and occupied southern Lebanon intent on destroying bases of the Palestine Liberation Organization (PLO). **1987** Palestinian uprising (intifada) began in Israeli-occupied West Bank and Gaza. **After 1990** Large-scale influx of Jews from former USSR. **1993** Oslo Peace Accord with PLO: limited autonomy in Gaza for Palestinians and parts of West Bank. **Since 1996** Peace process stalled over Israel's expansion of settlements in disputed areas.

Official name: Medinat Yisra'el (The State of Israel).
Area: 20,400 km² (7876 sq mi), excluding areas annexed by Israel (east Jerusalem and the Golan Heights); 21,620 km² (8347 sq mi), including east Jerusalem and the Golan Heights (whose annexation by Israel is not recognized by the international community).
Population: 5,390,000 (1995 est.), including Golan Heights and east Jerusalem, but excluding Israeli settlements in the West Bank and Gaza. **Doubling time:** 44 years.
Adult life expectancy: male 75.1 years, female 78.5 years.
Birth rate: 0.85 times world average.
Death rate: 0.67 times world average. **Urban population:** 91%.
Capital: Jerusalem (Yerushalayim) 576,000 (1994 est.; inc. suburbs and east Jerusalem). Jerusalem is not recognized as the capital of Israel by the international community.
Other main centres: Tel Aviv-Jaffa (Tel Aviv-Yafo) 1,141,000 urban area (city 357,000; Holon 163,000; Rishon le Zion 154,000; Petah Tiqwa 151,000; Bat Yam 143,000; Bene Beraq 125,000; Ramat Gan 123,000), Haifa (Hefa) 247,000, Holon, Rishon le Zion, Petah Tiqwa and Bat Yam *see Tel Aviv*, Netanya 143,000, Beersheba (Be'er Sheva) 141,000, Bene Beraq and Ramat Gan *see Tel Aviv*, Ashdod 95,000 (1994 est.; inc. suburbs).
Language: Hebrew 69% as a first language but understood by 85% (official), Arabic 18% (official), with Yiddish, Russian and other minorities.
Adult literacy: 95%.
Religion: Judaism 82%, Sunni Islam 14%, various Uniat Christian Churches 2%.

GOLAN HEIGHTS

Official name and status: Golan; Syrian territory under Israeli military administration; annexed to Israel in 1981.
Area: 1150 km² (444 sq mi).
Population: 29,000 (1995 est.).
Geography: The mountainous Golan Heights, fertile in the south, form a barrier between Syria and Israel.
Economy: Golan has been settled by Israelis who have established kibbutzim and large vineyards.

■ ISRAEL IS THE ONLY COUNTRY IN THE WORLD TO DIRECTLY ELECT ITS PRIME MINISTER TO OFFICE ■

TURKEY

Turkey is a republic straddling the border between south-east Europe and Asia Minor. Turkey, west of the Dardanelles (the straits between Europe and Asia), accounts for 5% of the country's area. Asiatic Turkey to the east of the straits consists of the Anatolian Plateau and its basins, bordered to the north by the Pontic Mountains, to the south by the Taurus Mountains and to the east by high ranges bordering Iraq and Armenia. **Highest point:** Agridagi (Mt Ararat) 5137 m (16,853 ft). **Climate:** The coastal regions have a Mediterranean climate with warm to hot dry summers and mild wet winters. The interior is continental with hotter summers and cold, snowy winters.

The 450-member National Assembly of Deputies is elected by universal adult suffrage for five years. The President, who is elected by the Assembly for seven years, appoints a Prime Minister, who, in turn, appoints other Ministers. **Largest parties:** (1995 election) (right-wing Islamic) Welfare Party (Refah) 158, (centre-right) True Path Party (DYP) 135, (conservative) Motherland Party (ANAP) 132, (centre-left) Democratic Left Party (DSP) 75, (social democratic) Republican People's Party (CHP) 50. **President:** (since 1993) Suleyman Demirel (DYP).
Prime Minister: (since 1997) Mesut Yilmaz (ANAP; ANAP–DSP government).

Farming involves 40% of the labour force. Crops include wheat, rice, tobacco, barley, fruit and cotton. Cotton and tobacco have given rise to major processing industries; textiles are Turkey's main export. Manufacturing, in particular chemicals and steel, has grown rapidly. Natural resources include copper and coal. Unemployment is high. Money sent back by many Turks working in western Europe, Germany in particular, is a major source of foreign currency, but tourism is now the greatest foreign-currency earner. **Currency:** Turkish Lira.

1908 Young Turks revolt in an attempt to halt the long decline of the Turkish Ottoman Empire. **1912–13** Balkan Wars virtually expelled Turkey from Europe. **1915–18** Alliance with Germany and Austro-Hungary in World War I ended in defeat and loss of all non-Turkish areas including much of the Middle East. **1921–22** Unsuccessful Greek attempt to seize much of Asia Minor from Turkey; Gen. Mustafa Kemal (later known as Ataturk) led forces of resistance and went on to defeat Greece. **1922** Sultanate abolished; Turkey became a secular republic. **1923** Boundaries of Turkey fixed at Treaty of Lausanne. **1923–38** Reformist presidency of Kemal Ataturk, who westernized Turkey, disestablished Islam, introduced the Latin script, abolished veils for women. **1945** Turkey joined western alliance (joining NATO in 1952). **1960** Military coup; PM Adnan Menderes tried on charges of corruption and hanged. **1961** Constitutional civilian rule restored. **1974** Following a Greek Cypriot coup Turkey invaded northern Cyprus and set up a Turkish administration (1975). **1980** Military coup after period of violence and ineffective government. **1983** Constitutional civilian rule restored. **Since 1980s** Increase in Islamic fundamentalism has raised doubts about Turkey's European identity. **Since 1991** Increase in unrest among Turkey's ethnic Kurds in the south-east; Kurdish terrorist attacks. **1995** Turkey intervened in northern Iraq to attack Kurdish bases.

Official name: Türkiye Cumhuriyeti (The Republic of Turkey).
Area: 779,452 km² (300,948 sq mi).
Population: 62,530,000 (1995 est.).
Doubling time: 35 years. **Adult life expectancy:** male 69 years, female 73 years. **Birth rate:** 1.04 times world average. **Death rate:** 0.65 times world average. **Urban population:** 66%. **Capital:** Ankara 3,022,000 urban area (city 2,559,000; 1990 census; inc. suburbs). **Other main centres:** Istanbul 7,332,000 urban area (city 6,620,000), Izmir 2,665,000 (city 1,727,000), Adana 1,430,000 (city 916,000), Bursa 1,031,000 (city 835,000), Konya 1,015,000 (city 513,000), Gaziantep 760,00 (city 603,000), İçel (or Mersin) 701,000 (city 422,000), Kayseri 588,000 (city 421,000), Diyarbakir 560,000 (city 381,000), Manisa 557,000 (city 159,000) (1990 census; inc. suburbs).
Language: Turkish 88% (official), Kurdish 11% (some unofficial estimates are much higher).
Adult literacy: 82%.
Religion: Sunni Islam 99%.

LEBANON

Lebanon is a mountainous republic of the Middle East on the Mediterranean. Behind a narrow coastal plain are the Lebanon Mountains. Further east, beyond the fertile Beka'a Valley, are the Anti-Lebanese Mountains and the Hermon Mountains.
Highest point: Qurnat as-Sawda 3088 m (10,131 ft). **Climate:** The lowlands have a Mediterranean climate; the highlands are cooler and the highest mountains have heavy snowfall in winter.

The President (who must be a Maronite) is elected for a single nine-year term by the 128-member National Assembly. The Assembly, which is elected by universal adult suffrage for four years, comprises 64 members representing the Muslim communities and 64 members representing the Christian communities. The President appoints a Prime Minister, who must be Sunni Muslim, and a Speaker of the Assembly, who must belong to the Shia Muslim community, as well as other Ministers, with a strict balance between communities in the Cabinet overall. There are cultural-religious groupings rather than political parties. **Political parties/groups:** (1996 election) 64 Christian members comprising 34 Maronites, 14 Greek Orthodox, 8 Greek Catholic, 6 Armenians and 2 other Christians, including the Phalange Party (Al-Kataëb), National Liberal Party (PNL), the Lebanese National Bloc (BNL) and ad-Destour, 64 Muslim members, comprising 27 Shia Muslims (including 8 members of the Islamic fundamentalist Hizbollah movement), 27 Sunni Muslims, 8 Druze members (from the Progressive Socialist Party; PSP) and 2 other Muslims.
President: (since 1989) Elias Hrawi (Maronite).
Prime Minister: (since 1992) Rafik al-Hariri (Sunni Islam).

Economic reconstruction (following the 1975–91 civil war) is progressing and Beirut itself is being rebuilt. The textile and food processing and electrical equipment industries are important and the once-major financial sector has recovered significantly. Major farming interests include citrus fruit (grown mainly for export), wheat, barley and olives. The illegal cultivation of opium poppies is economically important. **Currency:** Lebanese pound.

1916 French intervention in Lebanon (which had been Turkish since 1320) during World War I. **1920** France received a League of Nations mandate over Syria, including Lebanon, and created a separate Lebanese entity to protect Christian interests. **1943** Independence, with a constitution designed to balance Christian and Muslim interests. **Late 1950s** Gradual breakdown of relations between communities as Muslims became the majority but failed to gain constitutional dominance. **1958** Short civil war between radical Muslims, seeking union with Syria, and Western Maronites; US intervention to restore order. **Mid 1970s** Presence of large Palestinian refugee community destabilized Lebanon. **1975–91** Civil war between various sectarian militias, provoking intervention by Syria and Israel; Israel occupied (and continues to occupy) far south of the country; Lebanon fell into ungovernable chaos; and Islamic fundamentalist Hizbollah guerrillas took Western hostages; in 1990 Syrian troops defeated Christian militia allowing the Lebanese government to regain authority. **Since 1991** Sectarian militias disarmed; new constitution; Syria now has unofficial 'leading role'.

Official name: al-Jumhuriyah al-Lubnaniyah (The Republic of Lebanon).
Area: 10,230 km² (3950 sq mi).
Population: 3,010,000 (1995 est.). pop. relatively stable. **Adult life expectancy:** male 72.5 years, female 77.9 years. **Birth rate:** 1.11 times world average. **Death rate:** 0.69 times world average. **Urban population:** 87%. **Capital:** Beirut (Bayrut) 1,100,000 (1991 est.; inc. suburbs). **Other main centres:** Tripoli (Tarabulus) 240,000, Juniyah (formerly Jounjé) 100,000, Zahlah (formerly Zahlé) 45,000 (1991 est.; inc. suburbs).
Language: Arabic 93% (official), Armenian 4%. **Adult literacy:** 92%.
Religion: Shia Islam *c.* 40%, Sunni Islam *c.* 26%, Maronite (Uniat) Christian *c.* 17%, Druze *c.* 7%, Greek Orthodox *c.* 5%, Greek Catholic 3%, Armenian Orthodox 4%. (There has been no official census of religious affiliation since 1932.)

PALESTINIAN ENTITY/WEST BANK AND GAZA

Official name and status: no official name – those areas controlled by Palestinian Authority are known as the 'Palestinian entity'. Territory partly under Israeli military administration and partly (since 1994 and 1996) under the control of the autonomous Palestinian Authority.
Area: 6257 km² (2416 sq mi), comprising West Bank 5879 km² (2270 sq mi) and Gaza 378 km² (146 sq mi). Palestinian Authority has civil control over 2142 km² (827 sq mi); Israel continues to occupy 4115 km² (1589 sq mi). Palestinian Authority has complete control, civil and military, over only 545 km² (214 sq mi).
Population: 1,984,000 (1995 est.), of whom 1,084,000 are in the West Bank and 900,000 in Gaza. Of this, 1,854,000 live in areas under control of Palestinian Authority. 'Capital': Gaza 735,000 urban area (city 60,000; 1992 est.). 'President of Palestinian Authority': (since 1994) Yasser Arafat (PLO).
Geography: Gaza is an arid low-lying strip beside the Mediterranean. West Bank is an arid, mountainous region between Israel and Jordan Valley.
Economy: Unemployment is high. The Jordan Valley supports farming under irrigation, mainly for citrus fruit and vegetables; Gaza also grows citrus fruit. Textiles and clothing industries are important in Gaza; trade is affected by intermittent closure of Israeli border. Many Palestinians live in refugee camps, relying upon international aid schemes. Many residents formerly worked in Israel, but continuing terrorist activities by the Palestinian Hamas movement has led Israel to end commuting by Arabs from the West Bank and Gaza, thus adding to the Palestinian territory's economic distress.

MIDDLE EAST II

SAUDI ARABIA

Saudi Arabia is a desert kingdom occupying 80% of the Arabian peninsula. Over 95% of the country is desert, including the Rub 'al-Khali ('The Empty Quarter'), the world's largest expanse of sand. The Arabian plateau ends in the west in a steep escarpment overlooking a coastal plain beside the Red Sea.
Highest point: Jebel Razikh 3658 m (12,002 ft).
Climate: The country is very hot with temperatures up to 54°C (129°F). The average rainfall is 100 mm (4 in), but many areas have far less and may not get any precipitation for years.

Saudi Arabia is an absolute monarchy. The King appoints and heads a Council of Ministers and a 60-member consultative Council, which holds office for four years. There are no political parties.
King: (since 1982) Fahd ibn Abdul Aziz.

Saudi Arabia's spectacular development and prosperity are based almost entirely upon exploiting vast reserves of petroleum and natural gas. Industries include petroleum refining, petrochemicals and fertilizers. There are major banking and commercial interests. Less than 1% of the land can be cultivated.
Currency: Riyal.

Official name: al-Mamlakah al-'Arabiyah as-Sa'udiyah (The Kingdom of Saudi Arabia).
Area: 2,240,000 km² (865,000 sq mi).
Population: 17,880,000 (1995 est.).
Doubling time: 24 years. **Adult life expectancy:** male 66.8 years, female 70.3 years. **Birth rate:** 1.55 times world average. **Death rate:** 0.59 times world average.
Urban population: 80%.
Capital: Riyadh (ar-Riyad) 1,800,000 (1991 est.; inc. suburbs).
Other main centres: Jeddah (Jiddah) 1,800,000, Mecca (Makkah) 650,000, Medina (al-Madinah) 500,000, Taif (at-Ta'if) 400,000, Damman (ad-Damman) 350,000 (1995 est.; inc. suburbs).
Language: Arabic 95% (official).
Adult literacy: 63%.
Religion: Sunni Islam 95%, Shia Islam 3%.

1902 Ibn Saud, from Najd (central Arabia), conquered 80% of the Arabian peninsula. **1932** Kingdom of Saudi Arabia proclaimed with Ibn Saud as king.

■ *Lines of sand dunes seen from the space shuttle* Atlantis. *This part of eastern Saudi Arabia gets very little rain*

After 1973 Saudi Arabia cut oil production to pressurize the USA to encourage Israel to withdraw from West Bank. **1975** Assassination of King Faisal. **1991** Saudi Arabia played a major role in the coalition against Iraq in the Gulf War. **1990s** Growth of fundamentalist and liberal opposition to the absolute Saudi rule.

JORDAN

Jordan is a Middle Eastern kingdom occupying the eastern bank of the River Jordan. The greater part of the country's population and agriculture are in and adjoining the Jordan valley. Beyond a sharp escarpment overlooking the valley are hills and plateaux, deeply incised by gorges. Further east, deserts make up 80% of Jordan.
Highest point: Jabal Ramm 1754 m (5754 ft).
Climate: Summers are hot and dry; winters are cooler and wetter, although most of Jordan experiences very low rainfall.

Jordan is a constitutional monarchy in which the King appoints the 40-member Senate (the upper house of the National Assembly) and a Prime Minister and other Ministers, who are responsible to the House of Deputies (the lower house of the National Assembly). The 80-member House is elected by universal adult suffrage every four years.
Largest parties: (1993 election) Centrist independents 44 seats, Islamic parties 20, left-wing independents 6, Al-Ahd 2, Democratic Arab Party of Jordan 2, others 6.
King: (since 1952) Hussein I.
Prime Minister: (since 1997) Abdul-Salam al-Majali (independent).

Apart from potash (the main export) Jordan has few resources. The fertilizer and phosphate industries are important, and there has been significant recent growth of other industries and finance. Arable land accounts for only 5% of the area and produces enough fruit and vegetables for export. Money sent home by Jordanians working abroad is an important source of foreign currency. **Currency:** Jordanian dinar.

1916 Arab uprising in the Ottoman Turkish provinces that now form Jordan during World War I. **By 1918** Modern Jordan was under British control. **1920** Palestine (modern Israel, Jordan and the West Bank) became a British mandated trust territory under the League of Nations. **1923** Transjordan became an emirate with Abdullah I (a prince from Hejaz) as monarch. **1946** Independence: the emirate of Transjordan became the kingdom of Jordan. **1948** Arab–Israeli War: Jordan occupied the West Bank. **1951** King Abdullah I assassinated. **1967** Arab–Israeli War: Jordan lost the West Bank to Israel. **1970s** The large number of Palestinian refugees in Jordan and the power of Palestinian guerrillas threatened the existence of Jordan; short civil war in 1979 after which the Palestinian leadership fled Jordan. **1988** Jordan renounced all responsibility for the West Bank. **1991** Party politics restored. **1994** Jordan signed a peace treaty with Israel.

Official name: al-Mamlakah al-Urdunniyah al-Hashimiyah (The Hashemite Kingdom of Jordan).
Area: 88,946 km² (34,342 sq mi).
Population: 4,190,000 (1995 est.).
Doubling time: 20 years. **Adult life expectancy:** male 70 years, female 73 years. **Birth rate:** 1.55 times world average. **Death rate:** 0.33 times world average. **Urban population:** 72%. **Capital:** Amman 1,095,000 urban area (city 964,000; al-Rusayfah 131,000; 1994 census; inc. suburbs).
Other main centres: az-Zarqa 345,000, Irbid 208,000, as-Salt 178,000, al-Rusayfah *see Amman*, al-Mafraq 110,000 (1994 census; inc. suburbs).
Language: Arabic 99% (official).
Adult literacy: 83%.
Religion: Sunni Islam 92%, various Uniat Christian denominations 5%.

IRAQ

Iraq is a Middle Eastern republic in the basin of the rivers Tigris and Euphrates, which contains most of the country's arable land and the greater part of its population. Desert in the south and west occupies nearly one-half of Iraq. The north-east is occupied by the hills and mountains of Kurdistan. Iraq has a very short coastline on the Gulf. **Highest point:** Rawanduz 3658 m (12,001 ft). **Climate:** Summers are hot and dry with temperatures over 40°C (104°F). Most of the rainfall, ranging from 100 mm (4 in) in the desert to 1000 mm (40 in) in the mountains, comes in winter.

Iraq is a republic whose constitution provides for multi-party elections to a 250-member National Assembly by universal adult suffrage every four years. The non-elected Revolutionary Command Council appoints a President who appoints a Council of Ministers. The Kurdish northern provinces, in theory, enjoy autonomy. **Largest parties:** (1989 election) National Progressive Front (including the ruling Arab Socialist Renaissance Ba'ath Party, allied Kurdish parties and others) 250 seats. **President:** (since 1979) Saddam Hussein al-Takriti (Ba'ath). **Prime Minister:** (since 1994) Saddam Hussein al-Takriti (Ba'ath).

Irrigated land in the Tigris-Euphrates basin produces cereals, fruit and vegetables for domestic consumption and dates for export. Substantial reserves of petroleum were the mainstay of Iraq's economy but UN sanctions after 1991 curbed exports and only limited trade through a UN 'oil-for-food deal' is permitted. The effects of the Gulf War (1991) and subsequent sanctions have devastated the economy; inflation is rampant and there are shortages of many basic items. However, some improvements began in 1996. **Currency:** Iraqi dinar.

1914–18 Conquest of the Ottoman Turkish provinces of Mesopotamia during World War I. **1920** Mesopotamia became the British mandated trust territory of Iraq under the League of Nations. **1921** British-protected Kingdom of Iraq proclaimed with Faisal I (a prince from Hejaz) as king. **1932** Independence. **1941** Military coup brought pro-German officers to power and a British invasion during World War II. **1941–45**. British occupation. **1958** Royal family massacred during the 'Free Officers' coup. **1963** Reign of terror against the left following a coup. **1968** Coup by pan-Arab nationalist Ba'ath officers; Iraq became a Soviet ally. **1979** Saddam Hussein came to power. **1980–88** Costly and inconclusive war against Iran. **1990** Iraq invaded and annexed Kuwait. **1991** Gulf War: US-led coalition liberated Kuwait; Saddam suppressed revolts by Kurds in the north and Shiites in the south; international efforts created 'safe zone' for the Kurds who were able to throw off Saddam's authority; UN sanctions against Iraq. **1994** Civil war in the north between Kurdish factions. **1996** Iraqi forces entered the Kurdish region in favour of one of the rival factions.

AUTONOMOUS KURDISH REGION

Area: 38,650 km² (14,923 sq mi).
Pop.: 2,360,000 (1991 est.).
Capital: Irbil.

Official name: al-Jumhuriyah al-'Iraqiyah (The Republic of Iraq). **Area:** 435,052 km² (167,975 sq mi); this figure reflects the cession of territory to Kuwait in 1993 under the terms of a UN resolution. **Population:** 20,400,000 (1995 est.). **Doubling time:** 19 years. **Adult life expectancy:** male 46 years, female 57 years. **Birth rate:** 1.76 times world average. **Death rate:** 0.75 times world average. **Urban population:** 70%. **Capital:** Baghdad 5,790,000 urban area (city 3,841,000; Diyala 961,000, Kadhimain 521,000; Adhamiyah 464,000; 1987 census; inc. suburbs). **Other main centres:** Diyala *see Baghdad*, as-Sulaymaniyah 952,000, Mosul (al-Mawsil) 664,000, Kadhimain *see Baghdad*, Irbil 486,000, Adhamiyah *see Baghdad*, Kirkuk 419,000, Basra 406,000 (1987 census; inc. suburbs). **Language:** Arabic 77% (official), Kurdish 19%, Azeri 2%. **Adult literacy:** 60%. **Religion:** Shia Islam 63%, Sunni Islam 35%, various Uniat Christian denominations nearly 2%.

YEMEN

A republic in south-west Arabia, the Yemen Highlands rise from a narrow coastal plain beside the Red Sea. An arid plateau in the east extends into the Arabian Desert. Includes the island of Socotra. **Highest point:** Hadur Shu'ayb 3760 m (12,336 ft). **Climate:** Most of the highlands have a temperate climate; the rest of Yemen is hot and dry.

A 301-member House of Representatives and a President are elected for four years by universal adult suffrage. The President appoints a Prime Minister and a Council of Ministers. **Largest parties:** (1997 election) (nationalist) General People's Congress (GPC) 187 seats, (conservative Islamic) Yemeni Alliance for Reform (Islah) 53, (Communist) independents 54, others 7. Yemeni Socialist Party refused to participate. **President:** (since 1978) Ali Abdullah Saleh (GPC). **Prime Minister:** (since 1994) Abd al-Aziz Abd al-Ghani (GPC; GPC-Islah-independent government).

Cereal crops, coffee and citrus fruit are grown under irrigation in the fertile highlands. On the coasts, subsistence farming and fishing are important. Money sent back by Yemenis working abroad is an important source of revenue. **Currency:** Rial.

1911 The Turks were expelled from north Yemen; The UK controlled the south from the important naval base situated at Aden. **1962** Republican revolution in north: the monarchy was overthrown. **1963** Armed rebellion against British rule in the south; FLOSY guerrilla movement controlled much of the interior. **1963–70** Civil war in the north between the republicans (supported by Egypt) and the royalists (supported by Saudi Arabia). **1967** South Yemen gained independence from the UK; the country became a Marxist state. **1990** Merger of North and South Yemen following collapse of the South's economy when aid from the Communist bloc ended. **1994** Short civil war as south attempted to secede from what was perceived as an unequal partnership.

Official name: al-Jumhuriyah al-Yamaniyah (The Republic of Yemen). **Area:** 472,099 km² (182,278 sq mi). **Population:** 13,060,000 (1995 est.). **Doubling time:** 19 years. **Adult life expectancy:** male 61.6 years, female 63.5 years. **Birth rate:** 1.8 times world average. **Death rate:** 0.86 times world average. **Urban population:** 25%. **Capital:** Sana'a (San'a) 972,000 (1995 est.; inc. suburbs). **Other main centres:** Aden ('Adan) 562,000, Ta'iz 178,000, Hodeida 155,000 (1995 est.; inc. suburbs). **Language:** Arabic 98% (official). **Adult literacy:** 43%. **Religion:** Sunni Islam virtually 100%.

■ *A decorative building at the Old City sector of San'a, South Yemen*

THE GULF

KUWAIT

Kuwait is a relatively flat and low-lying desert emirate beside the Gulf.
Highest point: Ash Shaqaya 289 m (951 ft).
Climate: The country experiences extremes of heat during the summer. Almost all of the annual rainfall of 100 mm (4 in) comes during the cooler winter.

Kuwait is a monarchy ruled by an Emir, who appoints a Prime Minister and a Council of Ministers. A 50-member National Assembly is elected for four years by literate male Kuwaiti citizens whose families fulfil stringent residence requirements. There are no formal political parties but members sit in unofficial groups.
Emir: (since 1977) Shaikh Jabir III (bin Ahmad as-Sabah).
Prime Minister: (since 1978) Shaikh Saad al-Abdullah as-Sabah, the Crown Prince.

The economy was devastated by the Iraqi invasion and the Gulf War (1991), but reconstruction followed rapidly. Large reserves of petroleum and natural gas are the mainstay of the economy. Little agriculture is possible, owing to the lack of water. Since 1991, most of the non-Kuwaiti Arab workers have fled or been deported, to be replaced by migrants from the Indian subcontinent on short-term contracts.
Currency: Kuwaiti Dinar.

Official name: Dawlat al-Kuwayt (State of Kuwait).
Area: 17,818 km² (6,880 sq mi).
Population: 1,690,000 (1995 est.).
Doubling time: 30 years. **Adult life expectancy:** male 73 years, female 77 years. **Birth rate:** 1.02 times world average. **Death rate:** 0.26 times world average.
Urban population: 97%.
Capital: Kuwait City (al-Kuwayt) 420,000 (city 31,000; al-Jahra 140,000; as-Salimiya 116,000; Hawalli 85,000; al-Farwaniyah 47,000; 1993 est.).
Language: Arabic 98% (official).
Adult literacy: 80%.
Religion: Sunni Islam 38%, Shia Islam 26%, other Islam 9%.

1899 British protectorate established. **1968** Constitution suspended. **1971** Independence. **1990** Iraq invaded and annexed Kuwait. **1991** A US-led coalition liberated Kuwait in the short Gulf War; Iraqi forces damaged much of the country's infrastructure; expulsion of the large Palestinian population, which was accused of favouring the Iraqi invaders. **1992** Constitution restored. **1994** Iraq recognized Kuwaiti independence.

UNITED ARAB EMIRATES

The UAE is a federation of seven small low-lying desert states beside the Gulf. Major features include the Hajar Mountains in the east and the Buraymi oasis on the Omani border.
Highest point: al-Hajar 1189 m (3901 ft).
Climate: Summer temperatures exceed 40°C (104°F); winter temperatures are milder. Rainfall is very low.

The hereditary absolute monarchs of the seven emirates form the Supreme Council of Rulers. The Council appoints one of its members as President for five years and a 40-member advisory Federal National Council for two years. The President appoints a Prime Minister and Council of Ministers. There are no political parties. Each emirate has its own government.
President: (since 1971) Shaikh Zayid bin Sultan Al Nihayyan.
Prime Minister: (since 1979) Shaikh Maktoum bin Rashid al-Maktoum.

Based upon the export of its petroleum and natural gas, the federation has a high standard of living. Dry docks, fertilizer factories, commercial banking interests, and international airports have been developed. Immigrants from the Indian subcontinent form the majority of the labour force. Farming is confined to oases and a few coastal sites irrigated by desalinated water. **Currency:** Dirham.

1971 Britain withdrew from the Gulf: the UAE was formed. **1991** Member of the coalition against Iraq in the Gulf War.

■ *Dubai harbour showing the development of skyscrapers and modern buildings which reflects the UAE's high standard of living*

Official name: al-Imarat al-Arabiyah al-Muttahidah (United Arab Emirates).
Area: 83,600 km² (32,280 sq mi).
Population: 2,200,000 (1995 est.).
Doubling time: 24 years. **Adult life expectancy:** male 70.4 years, female 74.7 years. **Birth rate:** 1.08 times world average. **Death rate:** 0.32 times world average.
Urban population: 84%.
Capital: Abu Dhabi (Abu Zaby) 363,000 (1989 est.; inc. suburbs).
Other main centres: Dubai (Dubayy) 585,000, al-'Ayn 176,000, Sharjah (ash-Shariqah) 125,000 (1989 est.; inc. suburbs).
Language: Arabic 42% (official), languages of the Indian subcontinent 58%. **Adult literacy:** 79%.
Religion: Sunni Islam 80%, Shia Islam 16%.

EMIRATES

Abu Dhabi (Abu Zaby)
Area: 73,060 km² (28,210 sq mi).
Pop.: 798,000 (1991).
Capital: Abu Dhabi.
Ajman
Area: 260 km² (100 sq mi).
Pop.: 76,000 (1991 est.).
Capital: Ajman.
Dubai (Dubbay)
Area: 3900 km² (1510 sq mi).
Pop.: 501,000 (1991 est.).
Capital: Dubai.
Fujairah (al-Fujayrah)
Area: 1300 km² (500 sq mi).
Pop.: 63,000 (1991 est.).
Capital: Fujairah.
Ras al-Khaimah (R'as al-Khaymah)
Area: 1700 km² (660 sq mi).
Pop.: 130,000 (1991 est.).
Capital: Ras al-Khaimah.
Sharjah (ash-Shariqah)
Area: 2600 km² (1000 sq mi).
Pop.: 314,000 (1991 est.).
Capital: Sharjah.
Umm al-Qaiwan (Umm al-Qaywayn)
Area: 789 km² (300 sq mi).
Pop.: 274,000 (1991 est.).
Capital: Umm al-Qaiwan.

■ IRAQ'S INVASION OF KUWAIT IN 1990 TOOK ONLY A FEW HOURS ■ THE UAE ONLY HAS

BAHRAIN

Bahrain is an archipelago of 35 small islands in the Gulf. Bahrain Island, the largest, consists of sandy plains and salt marshes, and is linked to Saudi Arabia by road causeway.
Highest point: Jabal al-Dukhan 134 m (440 ft).
Climate: The country is very hot. The annual average rainfall is only 75 mm (3 in).

Bahrain is ruled directly by an Emir (an hereditary monarch), who appoints a Council of Ministers and a 30-member Consultative Council. There are no political parties.
Emir: (since 1961) Shaikh Isa II (bin Salman al-Khalifa).
Prime Minister: (since 1970) Shaikh Khalifa bin Salman al-Khalifa.

The wealth of Bahrain is due to its petroleum and natural gas resources, and the oil-refining industry. As reserves waned in the 1970s, the government encouraged diversification and Bahrain is now one of the Gulf's major banking and communication centres. Migrants from the Indian sub-continent make up a considerable proportion of the labour force. **Currency:** Bahraini Dinar.

1900 Bahrain had been a British protectorate since 1861. **1932** Bahrain became the first Gulf state to produce oil. **1971** Independence. **1975** Civil unrest with tension between the country's majority Shia community and minority, but ruling, Sunni community; suspension of the constitution; absolute monarchy reinstated. **1991** Became a member of the coalition against Iraq in the Gulf War. **Since 1994** Increase in unrest among the Shia population; some riots and bombing attempts.

■ *The extensive causeway which links the island-state of Bahrain to its large neighbour Saudi Arabia*

Official name: Dawlat al-Bahrayn (State of Bahrain).
Area: 694 km² (268 sq mi).
Population: 579,000 (1995 est.).
Doubling time: 29 years. Adult life expectancy: male 71 years, female 76 years. **Birth rate:** 1.08 times world average. **Death rate:** 0.43 times world average. **Urban population:** 90%.
Capital: Manama (al-Manamah) 142,000 (1992 est.; incl. suburbs).
Other main centres: ar-Rifa 46,000, al-Muharraq 45,000 (1991 census; inc. suburbs).
Language: Arabic 73% (official), languages of the Indian subcontinent 27%. **Adult literacy:** 70%.
Religion: Shia Islam 57%, Sunni Islam 24%, religions of the Indian subcontinent 18%.

OMAN

Oman is a sparsely populated sultanate in the south-east of the Arabian peninsula. A barren range of hills rises sharply behind a narrow coastal plain. Desert extends inland into the Rub'al Khali ('The Empty Quarter'). A small detached portion of Oman lies north of the United Arab Emirates.
Highest point: Jabal al-Akhdar 3107 m (10,194 ft).
Climate: Oman is very hot in the summer, but milder in winter and in the mountains. The state is extremely arid with an average annual rainfall of only 50–100 mm (2–4 in).

Oman is a monarchy ruled by a Sultan, who appoints and heads a Cabinet. An 80-member advisory Majlis comprises 40 members who are elected by a limited electorate for three years and 40 members who are chosen by the Sultan from nominees from the provinces. Women are eligible for election and some women are also able to vote. There are no political parties.
Sultan: (since 1970) Qaboos bin Said.

Oman depends almost entirely upon exports of petroleum and natural gas. Less than 1% of Oman is cultivated. The oil industry and much of the commercial infrastructure depends upon foreign workers.
Currency: Rial.

1890 The British protectorate of Muscat and Oman became established; the country had formerly ruled a trading empire which included Zanzibar and ports situated on the coast of modern Pakistan. **1951** The restoration of independence. **1963–64** Rebellion in the south; British troops aided Oman against a left-wing uprising in the southern region of Dhofar where rebels were aided by Marxist South Yemen. **1970** Ultra-conservative Sultan Said deposed in family coup: the development and modernization of Oman (which previously had virtually no schools or hospitals) began. **1991** Oman became a member of the coalition against Iraq in the Gulf War.

Official name: Saltanat 'Uman (Sultanate of Oman).
Area: 306,000 km² (118,150 sq mi).
Population: 2,160,000 (1995 est.).
Doubling time: 21 years. **Adult life expectancy:** male 68.3 years, female 72.3 years. **Birth rate:** 1.52 times world average. **Death rate:** 0.54 times world average.
Urban population: 13%.
Capital: Muscat (Masqat) 215,000 urban area (city 41,000; Matrah 174,000; 1993 census). **Other main centres:** Salalah 132,000, Sohar 92,000 (1993 census; inc. suburbs).
Language: Arabic 74% (official), Baluchi 19%. **Adult literacy:** 41%.
Religion: Ibadiyah Islam 56%, Hindu 23%, Sunni Islam 19%.

QATAR

Qatar is a low, barren peninsula projecting into the Gulf.
Highest point: Dukhan 73 m (240 ft).
Climate: Qatar is very hot in summer, but milder in winter. Rainfall averages 50–75 mm (2–3 in).

Qatar is an absolute monarchy. The Emir, who is head of state and government, appoints a Council of Ministers and a 35-member Advisory Council. There are no political parties.
Emir: (since 1995) Shaikh Hamad (bin Khalifah al-Thani).

The export of petroleum and natural gas gives a high standard of living. The steel and cement industries have been developed in an attempt to diversify.
Currency: Riyal.

1860s The intervention of the British established the present dynasty. **1872–1915** Turkish (Ottoman) rule. **1915** British rule confirmed. **1971** Independence. **1972** Shaikh Ahmad deposed in a family coup by Shaikh Khalifah. **1991** Qatar becomes a member of the coalition against Iraq in the Gulf War. **1995** Shaikh Khalifah deposed in a family coup.

Official name: Dawlat Qatar (State of Qatar).
Area: 11,427 km² (4412 sq mi).
Population: 579,000 (1995 est.).
Doubling time: 39 years. Adult life expectancy: male 70.5 years, female 75.5 years. **Birth rate:** 0.78 times world average. **Death rate:** 0.17 times world average. **Urban population:** 90%. **Capital:** Doha (ad-Dawhah) 514,000 urban area (city 339,000; ar-Rayyan 143,000; al-Wakrah 31,000; 1993 est.). **Other main centre:** Umm Sa'id 17,000 (1993 est.).
Language: Arabic 40% (official), languages of the Indian subcontinent 35%, Iranian and other minorities.
Adult literacy: 76%.
Religion: Sunni Islam 95%, Christian and Hindu minorities.

CENTRAL ASIA

TURKMENISTAN

Turkmenistan is a sparsely populated former Soviet republic in the south of Central Asia. The sandy Kara-Kum Desert occupies the centre of the republic, over 90% of which is desert. The Kopet Dag mountains form the boundary with Iran.
Highest point: Firyuza 2942 m (9652 ft).
Climate: Turkmenistan has a continental climate characterized by hot summers, freezing winters and very low precipitation.

An executive President (Turkmenbashi – Leader of Turkmens) and a 50-member legislature (Majlis) are elected for five years by universal adult suffrage. (President Niyazov's term in office has been extended to 2002.) The President appoints a Council of Ministers.
Largest party: (1995 election) (former Communist) Democratic Party (DP) 50 seats.
President: (since independence) Saparmurad Niyazov (DP).

Turkmenistan is rich in oil and natural gas. Industries include engineering, metal processing and textiles. Collective farms grow cotton under irrigation and keep sheep, camels and horses. The economy remains largely state-owned and centrally planned although there is Western investment in the oil and natural gas industries.
Currency: Manat.

1900 Turkmenistan had been under Tsarist Russian rule since 1881. **1916** Revolt against Russian rule; Transcaspian Republic declared. **1919** Invasion by the Soviet Red Army. **1925** Turkmenistan became a separate Union republic of the USSR. **1991** Dissolution of the USSR; Turkmen independence recognized. **Since 1992** Increasing curtailment of civil and political rights; opposition parties banned; growing personality cult of President Niyazov.

Official name: Türkmenistan Jumhuriyäti (The Republic of Turkmenistan).
Area: 488,100 km² (188,500 sq mi).
Population: 4,080,000 (1995 est.).
Doubling time: 27 years. **Adult life expectancy:** male 61.4 years, female 68.6 years. **Birth rate:** 1.32 times world average. **Death rate:** 0.85 times world average. **Urban population:** 45%. **Capital:** Ashgabat (formerly Ashkabad) 416,000 (1991 est.; inc. suburbs). **Other main centres:** Chardzhou 166,000, Dashovuse (formerly Tashauz) 117,000, Mariy 95,000 (1991 est.).
Language: Turkmen 72% (official), Russian 12%, Uzbek 9%.
Adult literacy: 98%.
Religion: Sunni Islam 87%, Russian Orthodox 10%.

UZBEKISTAN

Uzbekistan is a former Soviet republic of Central Asia. Western Uzbekistan is flat and mainly desert. The mountainous east includes ridges of the Tien Shan and the fertile Fergana valley.
Highest point: Bannovka 4488 m (14,724 ft).
Climate: Uzbekistan has a warm continental climate characterized by hot summers and low rainfall. Only the mountains receive over 500 mm (20 in) of rain a year.

A President and a 250-member Supreme Assembly (Olii Majlis) are elected for five years by universal adult suffrage. (In 1995 President Karimov's term was extended until 2000.) The President appoints a Prime Minister and a Council of Ministers.
Largest parties: (1994–95 election) (former Communist) People's Democratic Party (DP) 213 seats, (allied) Fatherland Progress Party 12, independents and others 25. (Birlik and Erk, two nationalist parties, were not permitted to stand.)
President: (since independence) Islam Karimov (DP).
Prime Minister: (since 1996) Otkir Sultonov (DP).

Uzbekistan is one of the world's leading producers of cotton, but the extraction of irrigation water from the Amu Darya and its tributaries has contributed to the gradual shrinkage of the Aral Sea. The republic has important reserves of natural gas and major machine and heavy engineering industries. Much of the economy is still state-owned and centrally planned and, although Western investment is beginning, the pace of market reform has been slow.
Currency: Sum.

1900 Uzbek khanates had been under Russian rule since 1868–73. **1918–22** Basmachi revolt against Russian rule. **1920** Uzbek khans deposed. **1924** Uzbekistan became a separate Union republic of the USSR. **1991** Dissolution of the USSR; Uzbek independence recognized. **Since 1992** Increasing curtailment of human rights.

Official name: Ozbekistan Jumhuriyäti (The Republic of Uzbekistan).
Area: 447,400 km² (172,700 sq mi).
Population: 22,890,000 (1995 est.).
Doubling time: 28 years. **Adult life expectancy:** male 65.1 years, female 71.8 years. **Birth rate:** 1.26 times world average. **Death rate:** 0.71 times world average. **Urban population:** 39%. **Capital:** Tashkent (Toshkent) 2,120,000 (1992 est.; inc. suburbs). **Other main centres:** Samarkand (Samarqand) 372,000, Namangan 333,000, Andijon 302,000, Bukhara (Bukhoro) 235,000 (1992 est.).
Language: Uzbek 71% (official), Russian 11%, Tajik 4%, Kazakh 4%, Karakalpak 2%, Tatar 2%.
Adult literacy: 97%.
Religion: Sunni Islam 88%, Russian Orthodox 9%.

■ *This ship is a remnant of the Aral Sea's once thriving fishing fleet, depleted by steadily decreasing water levels since 1960*

■ ERRATICALLY MEANDERING BOUNDARIES DIVIDE THE FERTILE FERGANA VALLEY BETWEEN THREE

KAZAKHSTAN

Kazakhstan, the ninth largest country in the world, is a former Soviet republic stretching across Central Asia from the Caspian Sea to China. It comprises a vast expanse of low tablelands (steppes). In the west, plains descend below sea level beside the Caspian Sea. Uplands include ranges of hills in the north and mountain chains, including the Tien Shan, in the south and east. Kazakhstan has several salt lakes, including the Aral Sea, which is shrinking because of excessive extraction of irrigation water from its tributaries. Deserts include the Kyzylkum in the south, the Kara Kum in the centre and the Barsuki in the north.

Highest point: Khan Tengri 6995 m (22,949 ft).

Climate: The Kazakh climate is characterized by bitterly cold winters and hot summers. Rainfall is low, ranging from 200 mm (8 in) in the north to 500 mm (20 in) or more in the south-east, and negligible in the deserts.

An executive President and a 67-member lower house (Kenges) are elected by universal adult suffrage for five years and four years respectively. The 47-member upper house (Senate) comprises seven senators chosen by the President and 40 senators elected by members of local authorities. The President appoints a Prime Minister and a Council of Ministers.

Largest parties: (Kenges 1995 election) (nationalist) Congress of People's Unity of Kazakhstan (SNEK), allies and independents 67 seats.

President: (since independence) Nursultan Nazarbayev (SNEK), whose term of office has been extended by referendum to the year 2000.

Prime Minister: (since 1994) Akezhan Kazhegeldin (SNEK).

Kazakhstan is a major supplier of food and raw materials for industry to other former Soviet republics, particularly Russia. The transition to a market economy was begun in earnest in 1994. Agriculture employs one-quarter of the workforce. Large collective farms on the steppes in the north produce over 16 million tonnes of grain a year. Other major farming interests include sheep, fodder crops, fruit, vegetables and rice. Kazakhstan is rich in natural resources, including coal, tin, copper, lead, zinc, gold, chromite, oil and natural gas. The country is attracting Western investment to exploit its mineral wealth. Industry is represented by iron and steel (in the Qaraghandy coalfield), pharmaceuticals, food processing and cement.

Currency: Tenge.

1917 Revolt against Tsarist Russian rule (which dated from the 18th century); Kazakh nationalists formed a government and demanded autonomy. **1920** Kazakhstan invaded by Soviet Red Army. **1936** Kazakhstan became a separate Union republic of the USSR. **1954–56** Widespread immigration from other parts of the USSR as the 'Virgin Lands' of north Kazakhstan were opened up for farming. **1991** Independence declared following the abortive coup by Communist hard-liners in Moscow; dissolution of the USSR; Kazakh independence recognized. **1995** President Nursultan Nazarbayev dissolved parliament to rule by decree. **Since 1995** Development of new capital to strengthen allegience of ethnic-Russian north to Kazakhstan.

Official name: Qazaqstan Respublikasï (Republic of Kazakhstan).
Area: 2,717,300 km^2 (1,049,200 sq mi).
Population: 16,670,000 (1995 est.).
Doubling time: 58 years.
Adult life expectancy: male 63.2 years, female 72.7 years.
Birth rate: 0.74 times world average.
Death rate: world average.
Urban population: 57%.
Capital: Almaty (formerly Alma-Ata) 1,164,000 (1994 est.; inc. suburbs). Aqmola (formerly Tselinograd) 281,000 (1991 census) will become capital by 2000. **Other main centres:** Qaraghandy (formerly Karaganda) 609,000, Shymkent (formerly Chimkent) 439,000, Semey (formerly Semipalatinsk) 345,000, Pavlodar 343,000 (1991 census; inc. suburbs).
Language: Kazakh 41% (official), Russian 37%, German 3%, Ukrainian 2%, Uzbek 2%, Tatar, Uighur and other minorities. **Adult literacy:** 99%.
Religion: Sunni Islam 47%, with significant Russian Orthodox and Baptist minorities.

TAJIKISTAN

Tajikistan is a mountainous former Soviet republic in Central Asia. The country lies within the Tien Shan range and part of the Pamirs. The most important lowland, and most populous area, is the Fergana valley.

Highest point: Garmo 7495 m (24,590 ft), formerly known as Pik Kommunizma (when it was the highest peak in the USSR).

Climate: High altitude and the country's position deep in the interior of Asia combine to give most of Tajikistan a harsh continental climate. The Fergana valley has a subtropical climate.

A President and a 181-member National Assembly are elected for five-year terms by universal adult suffrage. The President appoints a Prime Minister and Cabinet.

Largest parties: (1995 election) (Communist) Popular Front (CP) 60 seats, independents and others 121. (Islamic and pro-Western parties were banned.)

President: (since 1992) Imamali Rakhmanov (non-party).

Prime Minister: (since 1996) Yakhyo Azimov (non-party).

Cotton is the mainstay of a centrally planned (and largely still state-owned) economy, which has been totally devastated by civil war. Other farming interests include fruit, vegetables and raising cattle. Textiles and carpet-making are the principal industries. Natural resources include coal, natural gas, oil, iron ore, lead and zinc. **Currency:** Tajik rouble.

1900 Tajikistan had been under Tsarist Russian rule since 1860–68. **1917** Tajik revolt against Russian rule. **1920** Soviet Red Army re-annexed Tajikistan. **1922–31** Simmering Tajik revolts against Soviet rule. **1929** Tajikistan became a separate Union republic of the USSR. **1990** Ethnic riots in Dushanbe. **1991** Dissolution of the USSR; the independence of Tajikistan was recognized. **1992–93** Civil war: former Communists defeated Islamic fundamentalist forces and pro-Western factions. **Since 1993** Sporadic fighting between Islamic fundamentalists and government forces; CIS (mainly Russian) peace-keeping forces have been based in Tajikistan; on-going UN-sponsored peace talks taking place. **1996** Islamic faction seized part of the east.

Official name: Jumhurii Tojikistan (The Republic of Tajikistan).
Area: 143,100 km^2 (55,300 sq mi).
Population: 5,830,000 (1995 est.).
Doubling time: 35 years. **Adult life expectancy:** male 65.7 years, female 71.5 years. **Birth rate:** 1.09 times world average. **Death rate:** 0.78 times world average. **Urban population:** 30%. **Capital:** Dushanbe 592,000 (1991 est.; inc. suburbs).
Other main centres: Khujand (formerly Leninabad) 165,000, Kulob (formerly Kulyab) 79,000 (1991 est.).
Language: Tajik 62% (official), Uzbek 33%, Russian 10%. **Adult literacy:** 98%.
Religion: Sunni Islam 84%, Shia Islam 4%, non-religious over 10%, Russian Orthodox minority.

KYRGYZSTAN

Kyrgyzstan is a mountainous former Soviet republic in Central Asia. Most of the country lies within the Tien Shan mountains. Restricted lowlands, including the Chüy (formerly Chu) valley and part of the Fergana valley, contain most of the population.

Highest point: Pik Pobedy 7439 m (24,406 ft).

Climate: The country's altitude and position deep within Central Asia combine to produce an extreme continental climate with low precipitation.

A President is elected for a five-year term by universal adult suffrage. Parliament comprises a 35-member Legislative Assembly (Zogorkhu Kenesh) elected by universal adult suffrage for five years, and a 70-member Assembly of People's Representatives (upper house) elected regionally. The President nominates a Council of Ministers and a Prime Minister who commands a majority in the lower house.

Largest parties: (lower house 1995–96 election) reformists, nationalists and independents 30 seats, Communist Party 5.

President: (since independence) Askar Akayev (non-party).

Prime Minister: (since 1994) Apas Djumagulov (non-party).

Agriculture, which employs nearly 40% of the labour force, specializes in growing cereals, fodder crops (for sheep and goats) and cotton under irrigation. Natural resources include coal, lead, zinc, oil and great HEP potential. Food processing and light industry are expanding and privatization is more advanced than in any other Asian former Soviet republic. Kyrgyzstan is attracting Western investment.

Currency: Som.

1900 Kyrgyzstan had been under Tsarist Russian rule since 1850. **1916** Revolt against Russian rule. **1916–20** Guerrilla activity against Russian rule. **1926** An autonomous Kyrgyz Soviet republic was founded. **1936** Kirghizia became a separate Union republic of the USSR. **1990** Ethnic clashes. **1991** Dissolution of the USSR; Kirghizia was internationally recognized as the independent state of Kyrgyzstan.

Official name: Kyrgyz Republikasy (The Republic of Kyrgyzstan).
Area: 198,500 km^2 (76,600 sq mi).
Population: 4,485,000 (1995 est.).
Doubling time: 39 years. **Adult life expectancy:** male 63.9 years, female 72.6 years. **Birth rate:** 0.98 times world average. **Death rate:** 0.89 times world average.
Urban population: 37%.
Capital: Bishkek 634,000 (1993 est.; inc. suburbs). **Other main centres:** Osh 219,000, Jalal-Abad 74,000, Tokmak 71,000 (1991 est.).
Language: Kyrgyz 53% (official), Russian 26%, Uzbek 13%.
Adult literacy: 97%.
Religion: Sunni Islam nearly 70%, non-religious over 25%, Russian Orthodox minority.

South Asia I

PAKISTAN

Pakistan is a republic of the Indian subcontinent, stretching from the Hindu Kush to the Arabian Sea. The Indus Valley divides Pakistan into a highland region in the west and a lowland region in the east. In Baluchistan (the south-west) the highlands consist of ridges of hills and low mountains running north-east to south-west. In the North-West Frontier Province and the disputed territories the mountain chains rise to over 7000 m (21,300 ft) and include the Karakorum, and parts of the Hindu Kush and Himalaya. The valley of the Indus and its tributaries form a major agricultural region and contain the majority of Pakistan's population. A continuation of India's Thar Desert occupies the south-east.
Highest point: Tirich Mir 7700 m (25,263 ft). (K2 or Mount Godwin Austen, the world's second highest mountain, at 8607 m (28,238 ft), lies in the disputed territories.)
Climate: The north and west of Pakistan are arid; the south and much of the east experience a form of the tropical monsoon. Temperatures vary dramatically by season and with altitude from the hot tropical coast to the cold mountains of the far north.

The 87-member Senate (upper house) has 19 senators elected for six years by each of the four provinces, plus eight senators elected from the federally administered Tribal Areas and three from the federal capital. The 217-member National Assembly (lower house) is elected by universal adult suffrage for five years. A President (who is chosen by an electoral college consisting of the Senate, National Assembly and the provincial assemblies) serves for five years and appoints a Prime Minister who commands a majority in the Assembly. The PM, in turn, appoints a Cabinet of Ministers. The four provinces have their own legislatures.
Largest parties: (1997 election) (centre-right religious) Muslim League (PML) 134 seats, (centre-left) Pakistan People's Party (PPP) 17, (ethnic regional) Mohajir Qaumi Movement (MQM) 12, Awami National Party (ANP) 9, independents 29, others 16.
President: (since 1993) Farooq Leghari (PPP).
Prime Minister: (since 1997) Nawaz Sharif (PML).

About 45% of the labour force is involved in subsistence farming, with wheat and rice as the main crops. Cotton is a major foreign-currency earner. The government is encouraging irrigation schemes but over one-half of the cultivated land is subject to either waterlogging or salinity. Although there is a wide range of minerals (including coal, gold and copper) these resources have not been extensively developed. The main manufacturing industries are food processing, textiles and consumer goods. The country is in economic crisis with inadequate government revenue, high unemployment and considerable underemployment. Pakistan relies upon foreign aid and money sent back by Pakistanis working abroad.

Currency: Pakistan rupee.

1930 First proposals for a Muslim state independent from British India. **1940** Muslim League, led by Muhammad Ali Jinnah, demanded a Muslim state. **1947** Partition of British India into India and Pakistan, the latter with two 'wings', West Pakistan (the present state) and East Pakistan (now Bangladesh), separated by 1600 km (1000 mi) of Indian territory. **1947–49** Indo-Pakistani clashes over Kashmir, which was disputed by both countries; Kashmir was effectively partitioned. **1956** Republican constitution adopted. **1958–69** Military rule under Gen. Muhammad Ayub Khan. **1965** War with India over Kashmir. **1969–71** Military rule under Gen. Muhammad Yahya Khan. **1971** East Pakistan broke away as Bangladesh; Pakistani army sent from the West but India intervened forcing Pakistan to surrender. **1977** PM Zulfiqar Ali Bhutto (PPP) deposed in military coup; executed in 1979. **1977–88** Military rule under Army Chief of Staff Muhammad Zia al-Haq. **Since 1988** Constitutional rule restored; prolonged instability with three governments ended by presidential dismissal of the PM.

■ *The minarets and rooftops of the Faisal mosque, Islamabad, Pakistan*

PAKISTANI PROVINCES

Baluchistan (Balochistan)
Area: 347,190 km^2 (134,051 sq mi).
Pop.: 6,200,000 (1992 est.).
Capital: Quetta.

North-West Frontier
Area: 74,521 km^2 (28,773 sq mi).
Pop.: 15,800,000 (1992 est.).
Capital: Peshawar.

Punjab
Area: 205,344 km^2 (79,284 sq mi).
Pop.: 68,600,000 (1992 est.).
Capital: Lahore.

Sind (Sindh)
Area: 140,914 km^2 (54,407 sq mi).
Pop.: 27,600,000 (1992 est.).
Capital: Karachi.

Tribal Areas
Area: 27,220 km^2 (10,509 sq mi).
Pop.: 3,100,000 (1992 est.).
Capital: administered from Islamabad.

Federal Capital Territory
Area: 906 km^2 (350 sq mi).
Pop.: 430,000 (1996 est.).
Capital: Islamabad.

Official name: Islam-i Jamhuriya-e Pakistan (The Islamic Republic of Pakistan).
Area: 796,095 km^2 (307,374 sq mi) excluding Pakistani-held areas of Kashmir (known as Azad Kashmir) and the disputed Northern Areas (Gilgit, Baltistan and Diamir) – these Pakistani-occupied territories have an area of 83,716 km^2 (33,323 sq mi).
Population: 140,500,000 (1995 est.) excluding Pakistani-held areas of Kashmir and the disputed Northern Areas which had an estimated pop. of 3,500,000 in 1995. **Doubling time:** 24 years. **Adult life expectancy:** male 62 years, female 64 years.
Birth rate: 1.56 times world average.
Death rate: 0.97 times world average. **Urban population:** 32%.
Capital: Islamabad 2,130,000 Rawalpindi-Islamabad urban area (Islamabad city 430,000; Rawalpindi 1,700,000, 1996 est.). **Other main centres:** Karachi 11,000,000, Lahore 5,600,000, Faisalabad 2,300,000, Rawalpindi *see Islamabad*, Hyderabad 1,600,000, Multan 1,500,000, Gujranwala 1,400,000, Peshawar 1,100,000, Sialkot 600,000 (1996 est.).
Language: Urdu 8% (official), Punjabi 48%, Pashto 13%, Sindhi 12%, Siraiki 10%, Baluchi 3%. **Adult literacy:** 35%.
Religion: Sunni Islam nearly 92%, Shia and Ismaili Islam 5%, various Christian denominations over 1%, Hindu over 1%.

■ 'PAKISTAN' DERIVES FROM AN ACRONYM OF PARTS OF THE NAMES OF ITS PROVINCES ■

AFGHANISTAN

Afghanistan is a landlocked mountainous republic between Central Asia and the Indian subcontinent. The central highlands, dominated by the Hindu Kush, cover over 75% of the country and contain several peaks over 6400 m (21,000 ft). North of the highlands are plains, an important agricultural region, while the south-west of the country is desert and semidesert.
Highest point: Noshaq 7499 m (24,581 ft).
Climate: The highlands have very cold winters and short cool summers, while the desert regions have cold winters and hot summers. Except in some mountainous regions, it is dry.

Afghanistan has an interim non-elected 250-member Assembly. The President was named by the previous supreme state body (the Loya Jirgha). Conventional central government no longer exists owing to multifactional warfare.
Largest parties: There are various regional and religious factions rather than conventional political parties.
President: (since 1994) Prof. Burahanuddin Rabbani.
Chief of Muslims: (effective head of government and leader of the Taliban movement) Mohammad Omar Akhund.

Afghanistan has been devastated by the multifactional civil war that has raged since 1993. Little industry remains; much of the infrastructure has been damaged and Kabul lies in ruins. Most of the usable land is pasture, mainly for sheep, but cereal crops (particularly wheat and maize) are important. Principal exports are fresh and dried fruit, wool, cotton, and natural gas. **Currency:** Afghani.

1919 3rd Afghan War: Afghanistan regained independence from British intervention. **1933** Period of anarchy ended when a strong ruler, Mohammad Zahir Shah, came to the throne. **1973** Coup overthrew monarchy. **1978** Saur Revolution: close relationship with USSR developed. **1979** Soviet invasion; beginning of civil war. **1989** Soviet troops withdrew. **1992** Islamic fundamentalists took Kabul. **1993** Government collapsed as multifactional war dismantled the infrastructure of the state. **1996** Radical Islamic fundamentalist Taliban movement took Kabul and controlled most of the south and west. Rival factions continued in control of the north and north-west.

Official name: Dowlat-e Eslami-ye Afghanestan (The Islamic State of Afghanistan).
Area: 652,225 km² (251,824 sq mi).
Population: 18,130,000 (1993 est. excluding some 2,500,000 Afghan refugees in Iran and Pakistan).
Doubling time: 25 years. **Adult life expectancy:** male 46 years, female 44.7 years. **Birth rate:** 1.71 times world average. **Death rate:** 1.99 times world average.
Urban population: 20%.
Capital: Kabul 700,000 (1993 est.).
Other main centres: Kandahar (Qandahar) 226,000, Herat 177,000, Mazar-e Sharif 131,000 (1988 est.).
Language: Pashto 52% (official), Dari (Persian) 32% (off.), Uzbek 8%, Turkmen 2%. **Adult literacy:** 29.4%.
Religion: Sunni Islam 84%, Shia Islam 15%.

BHUTAN

Bhutan is a small landlocked mountainous kingdom between India and China. Most of the country lies in the Himalaya. The valleys of central Bhutan are wide and fertile. The Duars Plain, a subtropical jungle, lies along the Indian border.
Highest point: Khula Kangri 7554 m (24,784 ft).
Climate: The Duars Plain is tropical and very wet. Temperatures get progressively lower with altitude, resulting in permanent snow cover in the north. Precipitation is heavy.

Bhutan is an hereditary monarchy in which the King shares power with a Council of Ministers, the Buddhist Head Abbot and a 152-member National Assembly. Two-thirds of the Assembly members are elected for three years by universal adult suffrage; the remainder are appointed.
Largest parties: There are no political parties.
King: (since 1972) Jigme Singhye Wangchuk.
Prime Minister: The King.

Bhutan is one of the poorest and least developed countries in the world. Nearly 90% of the labour force is involved in farming. Electricity (from hydroelectric power stations) and wood are the main exports.
Currency: Ngultrum.

1907 Governor of Tongsa became the first king of Bhutan. **1949** India returned the Duars region (annexed by British India in 1865). **1990s** Discrimination against the Nepali minority.

Official name: Druk-Yul (The Kingdom of Bhutan).
Area: 46,500 km² (17,954 sq mi).
Population: 820,000 (1995 est.); some estimates state a population as high as 1,600,000.
Doubling time: about 30 years.
Adult life expectancy: male 51 years, female 50 years.
Birth rate: 1.6 times world average.
Death rate: 1.7 times world average.
Urban population: about 13%.
Capital: Thimphu 30,000 (1993 est.).
Other main centres: Phuntsholing 10,000 (1993 est.).
Language: Dzongkha (Bhutanese) about 50% (official), Nepali about 35%, Assamese about 15%.
Adult literacy: under 20%.
Religion: Buddhist about 75%, Hindu about 25%.

■ *Takstang Monastery, Tiger's Nest*

NEPAL

Nepal is a landlocked mountainous kingdom between India and China. In the south are densely populated subtropical lowlands. A hilly central belt is divided by fertile valleys. The Himalaya dominate the north and include Mt Everest on the Chinese border.
Highest point: Mt Everest 8863 m (29,078 ft).
Climate: The climate varies between the subtropical south and the glacial Himalayan peaks. All of Nepal experiences the monsoon.

Nepal is a constitutional monarchy. The 205-member House of Representatives (lower house) is elected by universal suffrage for five years. The 60-member Chamber of Estates is indirectly elected and appointed, with ten members appointed by the King. The House elects a Prime Minister and other Ministers.
Largest parties: (1994 election) Communist Party of Nepal-United Marxist-Leninist Party (CPN-UML) 88 seats, (centre) Nepali Congress (NCP) 75, (right-wing) National Democratic Party (NDP) 20, others 22.
King: (since 1972) Birendra.
Prime Minister: (since 1997) Lokendra Bahadur Chand (NDP; CPN-UML-NDP coalition government).

Nepal is one of the least developed countries in the world. Over 80% of the labour force is involved in subsistence farming, mainly growing rice, barley and maize. Pressure on the land has led to deforestation and serious soil erosion. Tourism is a major foreign-currency earner. **Currency:** Nepalese rupee.

1923 Nepalese independence recognized by British India. **1950** Overthrow of the isolationist Rana family, who were hereditary prime ministers of Nepal. **1959–60** Brief experiment with democracy. **1990** Violent pro-democracy demonstrations. **1991** Multi-party democracy reintroduced.

Official name: Nepal Adhirajya (The Kingdom of Nepal).
Area: 147,181 km² (56,827 sq mi).
Population: 20,090,000 (1995 est.).
Doubling time: 29 years. **Adult life expectancy:** male 52.4 years, female 52.7 years. **Birth rate:** 1.5 times world average. **Death rate:** 1.4 times world average. **Urban population:** 10%. **Capital:** Kathmandu 419,000 (1991 census). **Other main centres:** Biratnagar 130,000, Lalitpur 117,000 (1991 census).
Language: Nepali 53% (official), Maithili 12%, Bhojpuri 7%, Tamang 5%, various Indian and Tibeto-Burman languages.
Adult literacy: 38%.
Religion: Hindu 86%, Buddhist 8%, Sunni Islam 4%.

■ *Everest was known in the Tibetan language as Chomolungma, 'Goddess Mother of the World'. It was established as the world's highest mountain in 1852. In 1865 the mountain (previously referred to as Peak XV) was renamed after Sir George Everest (1790–1866), who was Surveyor-General of India from 1830–43*

■ 'BHUTAN' MEANS COUNTRY OF DRAGONS ■ NEPAL IS THE WORLD'S ONLY HINDU STATE ■

South Asia II

INDIA

India is a republic occupying the greater part of the Indian subcontinent, stretching from the Himalaya to within 8° of the Equator. The Himalaya, which cut the Indian subcontinent off from the rest of Asia, contain several peaks over 7000 m (23,000 ft) within India and the disputed territories under Pakistani and Chinese occupation. South of the Himalaya, the basins of the rivers Ganges and Brahmaputra and their tributaries are intensely farmed and densely populated. The Thar Desert lies along the border with Pakistan. In south India, the Deccan (a large plateau of hard rocks) is bordered in the east and west by the Ghats, a discontinuous range of hills descending to coastal plains. Natural vegetation ranges from tropical rain forest on the west coast and monsoon forest in the north-east and far south, through dry tropical scrub and thorn forest in the Deccan, to Alpine and temperate vegetation in the Himalaya.
Highest point: (in Indian controlled territory) Kangchenjunga 8598 m (28,208 ft). (K2 or Mt Godwin Austen, the world's second highest mountain, at 8607 m (28,238 ft), lies in the disputed territories.)
Climate: India has three distinct seasons: a hot season from March to June; a wet season (when the south-west monsoon brings heavy rainfall) from June to October; and a cooler drier season from November to March. Temperatures range from the cool of the Himalaya to tropical heat in the south.

The upper house of the Federal Parliament is the 245-member Council of States (Rajya Sabha) which consists of 12 members nominated by the President and 233 members elected by state assemblies for six years. One-third of the council retires every two years. The lower house is the 545-member House of the People (Lok Sabha) which consists of 543 members elected by universal adult suffrage for five years plus two nominated members. The President, whose duties are largely ceremonial, is elected for five years by the Federal Parliament and state assemblies. The President appoints a Prime Minister who has a majority in the House. The PM, in turn, appoints a Council of Ministers, who are responsible to the House. The states have their own governments and legislatures.
Largest parties: (1996 election) (right-wing religious) Bharatiya Janata Party (BJP) and allies 194 seats, (centre-left coalition of 13 parties) United Front-Left Front (UF-LF) including the Janata Dal Party (JDP) and Communist Party of India (Marxist) 187, (centre) Congress (I) Party (CongI) and allies 149, others 15.
President: (since 1997) K.R. Narayanan (non-party).
Prime Minister: (since 1997) Inder Kumar Gujral; (UF-LF government supported by CongI).

Nearly two-thirds of the labour force are involved in subsistence farming, with rice and wheat as the principal crops. Cash crops, which tend to come from large plantations, include tea, cotton, jute and sugar cane, all of which are grown for export. The monsoon rains and irrigation make cultivation possible in many areas, but drought and floods are common. India is a major industrial power. Major coal reserves provide the power base for industry, and other mineral deposits include diamonds, bauxite, titanium, copper and iron ore as well as substantial reserves of natural gas and petroleum. The textile, iron and steel, vehicle, pharmaceutical and electrical industries make important contributions to the economy, but India has balance-of-payments difficulties and relies upon foreign aid for development. A high rate of population increase, high unemployment (including inadequate opportunities for qualified labour) and poor infrastructure add to India's economic problems, the chief of which is poverty, with over one-third of the population living below the official poverty line. The privatization of state enterprises that began in the early 1990s is slowly continuing.
Currency: Indian rupee.

■ *A pair of rickshaw drivers wait for customers on a low, flooded street during a monsoon in Calcutta, West Bengal, India*

Official name: Bharat (Republic of India).
Area: 3,287,263 km^2 (1,269,219 sq mi) inc. 121,667 km^2 (44,976 sq mi) of Jammu and Kashmir claimed by India but occupied by Pakistan and China.
Population: 935,740,000 (1995 est.).
Doubling time: 37 years.
Adult life expectancy: male 60.4 years, female 61.2 years.
Birth rate: 1.16 times world average.
Death rate: 1.08 times world average.
Urban population: 27%.
Capital: Delhi 8,419,000 urban area (city 7,207,000; 1991 census; inc. suburbs).
Other main centres: Bombay (Mumbai) 12,596,000 urban area (city 9,926,000; Kalyan 1,014,000; Thane 797,000), Calcutta 11,022,000 (city 4,399,000; Hoara 946,000), Madras (Chennai) 5,422,000 (city 3,841,000), Hyderabad 4,254,000 (city 3,146,000), Bangalore 4,130,000 (city 3,303,000), Ahmadabad 3,298,000 (city 2,873,000), Poona (Pune) 2,485,000 (city 1,560,000), Kanpur 2,111,000 (city 1,958,000), Nagpur 1,661,000 (city 1,622,000), Lucknow 1,642,000 (city 1,592,000), Surat 1,517,000 (city 1,497,000), Jaipur 1,514,000 (city 1,455,000), Kochi (formerly Cochin) 1,140,000 (city 564,000), Coimbatore 1,136,000 (city 853,000), Vadodara (formerly Baroda) 1,115,000 (city 1,021,000), Indore 1,104,000 (city 1,087,000), Patna 1,099,000 (city 917,000), Madurai 1,094,000 (city 952,000), Bhopal 1,064,000, Vishakhapatam 1,052,000 (city 750,000), Varanasi (formerly Benares) 1,026,000, Kalyan *see Bombay*, Ludhiana 1,012,000, Agra 956,000 (city 899,000), Hoara *see Calcutta*, Jabalpur 887,000 (city 740,000), Allahabad 858,000 (city 806,000), Meerut 847,000 (city 752,000), Vijayawada 845,000 (city 701,000), Jamshedpur 835,000 (city 461,000), Thiruvananthapuram (formerly Trivandrum) 826,000 (city 524,000), Dhanbad 818,000, Kozhikode (formerly Calicut) 801,000 (city 420,000) (1991 census; inc. suburbs).
Language: Hindi 39% (official) but understood by 45%, English 3% (official), Telegu 8%, Bengali 8%, Marathi 7%, Tamil 7%, Urdu 5%, Gujarati 5%, Kannada 4%, Malayam 4%, Oriya 3%, Punjabi nearly 3%, Assamese nearly 2%, plus over 1600 other languages. **Adult literacy:** 53%.
Religion: Hindu 80%, Sunni Islam 8%, Shia Islam nearly 3%, Sikh nearly 2%, Roman Catholic over 1%, other Christian denominations 1%, Buddhist nearly 1%, Jain nearly 1%.

1919 Amritsar Massacre: British troops fired without warning on a nationalist demonstration. **1920** Congress Party, led by Mohandas (Mahatma) Gandhi, began campaign of non-violence and non-cooperation with British authorities. **1930s** Relations between (largely Hindu) Congress and the Muslim League deteriorated. **1940** Muslim League demanded a Muslim state. **1947** Partition of British India into India and Pakistan. Over 70 million Hindus and Muslims became

■ AT SOME POINT IN THE NEXT CENTURY, INDIA WILL OVERTAKE CHINA TO BECOME THE WORLD'S

INDIAN STATES AND TERRITORIES

Andhra Pradesh
Area: 275,068 km^2 (106,204 sq mi).
Pop.: 66,508,000 (1991 census).
Capital: Hyderabad.
Arunachal Pradesh
Area: 83,743 km^2 (32,333 sq mi).
Pop.: 865,000 (1991 census).
Capital: Itanagar.
Assam
Area: 78,438 km^2 (30,285 sq mi).
Pop.: 22,414,000 (1991 census).
Capital: Dispur.
Bihar
Area: 173,877 km^2 (67,134 sq mi).
Pop.: 86,374,000 (1992 est.).
Capital: Patna.
Goa
Area: 3702 km^2 (1429 sq mi).
Pop.: 1,170,000 (1991 census).
Capital: Panaji.
Gujarat
Area: 196,024 km^2 (75,685 sq mi).
Pop.: 41,310,000 (1991 census).
Capital: Gandhinagar.
Haryana
Area: 44,212 km^2 (17,070 sq mi).
Pop.: 16,464,000 (1991 census).
Capital: Chandigarh (see below).
Himachal Pradesh
Area: 55,673 km^2 (21,495 sq mi).
Pop.: 5,171,000 (1991 census).
Capital: Shimla.
Jammu and Kashmir
Area: 222,236 km^2 (85,806 sq mi), of which 121,667 km^2 (46,976 sq mi) are occupied by China and Pakistan.
Pop.: 7,719,000 (1991 census) in Indian-administered areas.
Capital: Srinagar.
Karnataka
Area: 191,791 km^2 (74,051 sq mi).
Pop.: 44,977,000 (1991 census).
Capital: Bangalore.
Kerala
Area: 38,863 km^2 (15,005 sq mi).
Pop.: 29,099,000 (1991 census).
Capital: Thiruvananthapuram (Trivandrum).
Madhya Pradesh
Area: 443,446 km^2 (171,215 sq mi).
Pop.: 66,181,000 (1991 census).
Capital: Bhopal.
Maharashtra
Area: 307,690 km^2 (118,800 sq mi).
Pop.: 78,937,000 (1991 census).
Capital: Bombay (Mumbai).
Manipur
Area: 22,327 km^2 (8621 sq mi).
Pop.: 1,837,000 (1991 census).
Capital: Imphal.
Meghalaya
Area: 22,429 km^2 (8660 sq mi).
Pop.: 1,775,000 (1991 census).
Capital: Shillong.
Mizoram
Area: 21,081 km^2 (8140 sq mi).
Pop.: 690,000 (1991 census).
Capital: Aizawl.
Nagaland
Area: 16,579 km^2 (6401 sq mi).
Pop.: 1,210,000 (1991 census).
Capital: Kohima.
Orissa
Area: 155,707 km^2 (60,119 sq mi).
Pop.: 3,660,000 (1991 census).
Capital: Bhubaneshwar.
Punjab
Area: 50,362 km^2 (19,445 sq mi).
Pop.: 20,282,000 (1991 census).
Capital: Chandigarh (see below).
Rajasthan
Area: 342,239 km^2 (132,140 sq mi).
Pop.: 44,006,000 (1991 census).
Capital: Jaipur.
Sikkim
Area: 7096 km^2 (2740 sq mi).
Pop.: 406,000 (1991 census).
Capital: Gangtok.
Tamil Nadu
Area: 130,058 km^2 (50,216 sq mi).
Pop.: 55,859,000 (1991 census).
Capital: Madras (Chennai).
Tripura
Area: 10,486 km^2 (4049 sq mi).
Pop.: 2,757,000 (1992 est.).
Capital: Agartala.
Uttar Pradesh
Area: 294,411 km^2 (113,673 sq mi).
Pop.: 139,112,000 (1991 census).
Capital: Lucknow.
West Bengal
Area: 88,752 km^2 (34,267 sq mi).
Pop.: 68,078,000 (1991 census).
Capital: Calcutta.
Andaman and Nicobar Islands Union Territory
Area: 8249 km^2 (3185 sq mi).
Pop.: 281,000 (1991 census).
Capital: Port Blair.
Chandigarh Union Territory
Area: 114 km^2 (44 sq mi).
Pop.: 642,000 (1991 census).
Capital: Chandigarh.
Dadra and Nagar Haveli Union Territory
Area: 491 km^2 (190 sq mi).
Pop.: 138,000 (1991 census).
Capital: Silvassa.
Daman and Diu Union Territory
Area: 112 km^2 (43 sq mi).
Pop.: 102,000 (1991 census).
Capital: Daman.
Delhi Union Territory
Area: 1483 km^2 (572 sq mi).
Pop.: 9,421,000 (1991 census).
Capital: Delhi.
Lakshadweep Union Territory
Area: 32 km^2 (12 sq mi).
Pop.: 52,000 (1991 census).
Capital: Kavaratti.
Pondicherry Union Territory
Area: 492 km^2 (190 sq mi).
Pop.: 808,000 (1991 census).
Capital: Pondicherry.

refugees and crossed the new boundaries; thousands killed in communal violence. **1947–49** Indo-Pakistani clashes over Kashmir, which was disputed by both countries; Kashmir was effectively partitioned. **1947–64** Premiership of Jawaharlal Nehru. **1948** Gandhi assassinated. **1962** Border clashes with China. **1965** War with Pakistan over Kashmir. **1971** India intervened to aid the secessionists in East Pakistan (now Bangladesh), forcing Pakistan to surrender. **1975–77** State of emergency during premiership of Indhira Gandhi. **1984** Rise of violent Sikh nationalism; PM Indhira Gandhi ordered storming of the Sikh Golden Temple of Amritsar (which extremists had turned into an arsenal); Mrs Gandhi assassinated by Sikh bodyguard. **1990** Rise in communal tension following campaign to build a Hindu temple on site of a Muslim mosque at Ayodhya. **1991** PM Rajiv Gandhi assassinated.

SRI LANKA

Sri Lanka is an island-republic south of India. The relief of the island is dominated by a massif in the south and centre. Most of the rest of the island consists of forested lowlands, which in the north are fertile. **Highest point:** Pidurutalagala 2524 m (8281 ft). **Climate:** The island has a tropical climate modified by the monsoon. Rainfall is heaviest in the south-west but the south-east and north-west are relatively dry.

Sri Lanka is a republic in which an executive President is elected by universal adult suffrage for a maximum of two six-year terms. The 225-member Parliament is directly elected under a system of proportional representation for six years. The President appoints a Prime Minister and other Ministers who are responsible to Parliament.
Largest parties: (1994 election) (centre-left coalition) People's Alliance (PA) including Sri Lanka Freedom Party (SLFP) 105 seats, (centre-right) United National Party 94, the Tamil Party (EPDP) 9, Sri Lanka Muslim Congress 7, Tamil United Liberation Front 5, others 3.
President: (since 1994) Chandrika Kumaratunga (Bandaranaike) (SLFP). Prime Minister: (since 1994) Sirima Bandaranaike (SLFP).

About two-fifths of the labour force are involved in agriculture, growing rice for domestic consumption and tea, rubber and coconuts for export. Development has been encouraged by major hydroelectric power projects on the Mahaweli River. Industries include food processing and textiles, but the economy, particularly the lucrative tourist industry, has been damaged by separatist guerrilla activity.
Currency: Sri Lankan rupee.

1948 Independence after 150 years of British rule. **1958** Major disorders arising from Singhalese–Tamil rivalry. **1961** Further ethnic violence. **1971** Marxist rebellion crushed after heavy fighting. **1972** Name of country changed from Ceylon to Sri Lanka. **Since 1977** Tamil separatist guerrillas have been active, at times controlling Jaffna and much of the east and north. **1987–90** Indian intervention to aid Singhalese forces in the near civil war in the north-east. **1993** President Premadasa assassinated by Tamils.

Official names: Sri Lanka Prajathanthrika Samajavadi Janarajaya (in Sinhala) and Ilangai Jananayaka Socialisa Kudiarasu (in Tamil) (The Democratic Socialist Republic of Sri Lanka).
Area: 65,610 km^2 (25,332 sq mi).
Population: 18,090,000 (1995 est.).
Doubling time: 50 years. **Adult life expectancy:** male 70 years, female 75 years. **Birth rate:** 0.8 times world average. **Death rate:** 0.65 times world average. **Urban population:** 22%. **Capitals:** Colombo, the administrative capital, and Sri Jawardenepura Kotte (usually known as Kotte), the legislative capital. Colombo 2,026,000 urban area (city 615,000; Dehiwala-Mount Lavinia 196,000; Moratuwa 170,000; Sri Jawardenepura Kotte 109,000; 1990 est.; inc. suburbs). **Other main centres:** Jaffna 129,000, Kandy 104,000 (1990 est.).
Language: Sinhala 69% (official), Tamil 21% as a first language (official), English (understood by 10%).
Adult literacy: 87%.
Religion: Buddhist 69%, Hindu 16%, Sunni Islam 8%, Roman Catholic 7%.

THE MALDIVES

A republic lying south-west of Sri Lanka, consisting of 1196 small low-lying coral islands, 203 of which are inhabited. During tropical storms tidal waves inundate the islands, and the country is judged to be one of the most vulnerable from the effects of global warming.
Highest point: an unnamed point 4 m (13 ft). **Climate:** The islands have a tropical climate with heavy rainfall brought by the monsoon between May and August.

The Maldives is a republic in which an executive President (who appoints a Council of Ministers) is elected by the People's Council (Majlis) for four years. The 48-member Majlis comprises 40 members elected by universal adult suffrage and eight appointed by the President, all for five years.
Largest parties: There are no political parties.
President: (since 1978) Maumoon Abdul Gayoom.

Official name: Dihevi Jumhuriyya (The Republic of Maldives).
Area: 298 km^2 (115 sq mi).
Population: 253,000 (1995 est.).
Doubling time: 26 years. **Adult life expectancy:** male 65 years, female 62 years. **Birth rate:** 1.3 times world average. **Death rate:** 0.59 times world average. **Urban population:** 30%. **Capital:** Male 55,000 (1990 census; inc. suburbs).
Language: Dihevi (Maldivian) virtually 100% (official). Adult literacy: 91%.
Religion: Sunni Islam virtually 100%.

One-quarter of the labour force is involved in fishing, but tourism is now the mainstay of the economy. Tinned and frozen fish, and clothing, are the only significant exports. **Currency:** Rufiyaa.

1965 Independence after 80 years of British rule. **1968** The 600-year-old sultanate abolished: republic formed. **1988** Attempted coup by Sri Lankan Tamils.

PLACES OF INTEREST

India has a wide range of tourist attractions and regions, but the beaches of Goa, the palaces of the north-west and the scenery of the Himalaya are among the most popular, attracting package tourists, independent travellers and young backpackers. Britain's abiding fascination with the Raj is reflected in its role as the major source of visitors to India: one in nine foreign tourists are British, while one in ten are American. Other popular destinations include Bombay, the Golden Temple, Amritsar, historic Madras, the holy town of Varanasi (Benares), the holy town of Mathura, Kashmir and New Delhi.

World Heritage sites include: Agra Fort; Brihadisvara Temple, Thanjavur; Fatehpur Sikri; group of monuments at Hampi; Humayun's Tomb; Kaziranga National Park; Keoladeo National Park; group of monuments at Mahabalipuram; Nanda Devi National Park; Qutb Minar and monuments, Delhi; Sun Temple, Konarak; Sundarbans National Park; Taj Mahal; Agra.

STATES AND TERRITORIES

1 Andhra Pradesh
2 Arunachal Pradesh
3 Assam
4 Bihar
5 Goa
6 Gujarat
7 Haryana
8 Himachal Pradesh
9 Jammu and Kashmir
10 Karnataka
11 Kerala
12 Madhya Pradesh
13 Maharashtra
14 Manipur
15 Meghalaya
16 Mizoram
17 Nagaland
18 Orissa
19 Punjab
20 Rajasthan
21 Sikkim
22 Tamil Nadu
23 Tripura
24 Uttar Pradesh
25 West Bengal
26 Andaman and Nicobar Islands Union Territory
27 Chandigarh Union Territory
28 Dadra and Nagar Haveli Union Territory
29 Daman and Diu Union Territory
30 Delhi Union Territory
31 Lakshadweep Union Territory
32 Pondicherry Union Territory

For further information, see p. 407.

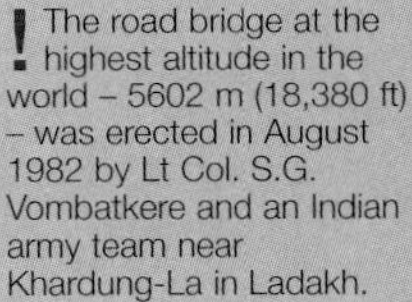

! The road bridge at the highest altitude in the world – 5602 m (18,380 ft) – was erected in August 1982 by Lt Col. S.G. Vombatkere and an Indian army team near Khardung-La in Ladakh.

The Taj Mahal outside Agra is a mausoleum that was built by Shah Jahan (see p.177). It is also known as Mumtaz Mahal (meaning Chosen One of the Palace), being named after his beloved wife, Mumtaz.

Camels, a common sight in northern India, are sold at an important market, held each year at Pushkar in Rajasthan. The town is also an important pilgrimage centre.

Varanasi, Uttar Pradesh, is situated on the banks of the sacred River Ganges. The waterfront of this holy city is the finest in India, being lined with miles of steps (*ghats*) for religious bathing.

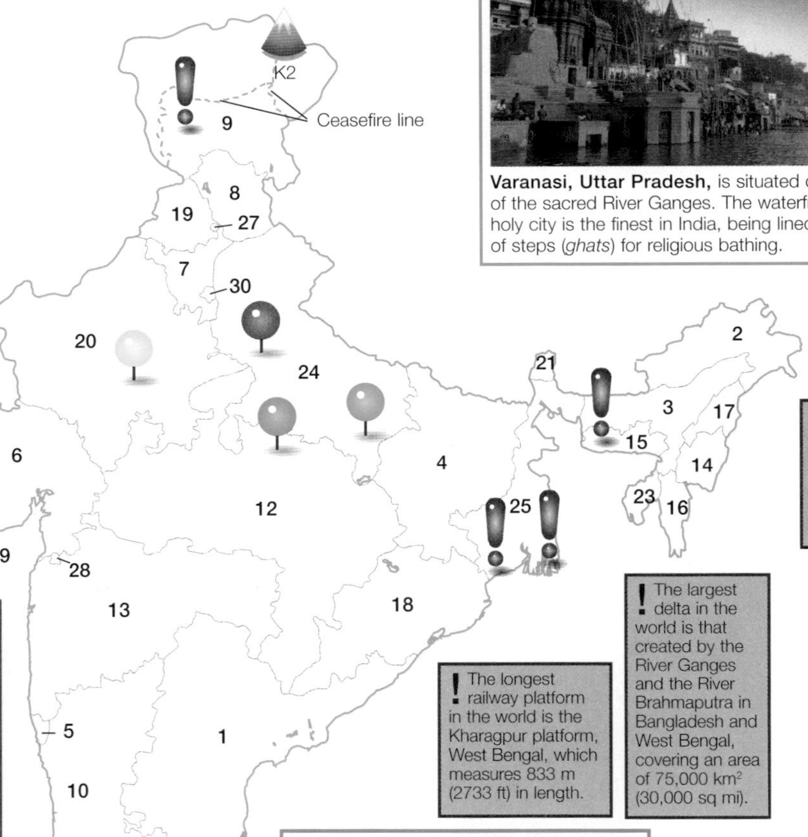

! The wettest place in the world by average annual rainfall is Mawsynram in Meghalaya State, with 11,873 mm (467½ in) per year.

! The largest delta in the world is that created by the River Ganges and the River Brahmaputra in Bangladesh and West Bengal, covering an area of 75,000 km² (30,000 sq mi).

! The longest railway platform in the world is the Kharagpur platform, West Bengal, which measures 833 m (2733 ft) in length.

Madurai's Meenakshi Temple is covered with brightly painted figures of Hindu gods.

The Vishvanath Temple in Khajuraho, Madhya Pradesh is one of the town's many Hindu temples. The temple dates from around AD 1002.

TELEVISION AND RADIO

No. of TVs: 20,000,000 (47 persons per TV)
No. of radio receivers: 65,000,000 (14 persons per radio)

All India Radio (AIR) runs 148 radio stations, operating in 72 languages, and Doordarshan India (Television India) runs 14. Both organizations are government-financed and controlled. Satellite TV has recently become popular and influential.

NEWSPAPERS

India's size and its many social, religious and linguistic barriers have prevented the development of a national press. However, a small number of English-language newspapers – *The Times of India*, *The Indian Express*, *The Statesman* and *The Hindu* – enjoy nationwide circulations. These papers have largely metropolitan readerships and cover international issues as well as Indian events. Newspapers published in Indian languages have mainly rural readerships and tend to be more parochial. The daily papers with the largest circulations are:

	Language	
Malayala Manorama Kottayam and four other centres	Malayalam	800,000
The Times of India Delhi, Bombay, Bangalore, etc.	English	736,000
Punjab Kesari Jalandhar, Delhi, and Ambala	Punjabi	614,000 (892,000 Sunday edition)
Gujarat Samachar Ahmedabad and three other centres	Gujarati	577,000
Indian Express Delhi, Vijayawada Madras, Bombay, etc.	English	544,000
Aj Varanasi and 10 other centres	Hindi	542,000
Dainik Jagran Kanpur and eight other centres	Hindi	540,000

CINEMA

No. of cinemas: 13,030

Popular Indian cinema, affectionately termed 'Bollywood', has a massive following and India is the world's largest film-producer. The top grossing films are all Indian, with foreign films (mostly British and American) making up just 20% of the total films released. However, it is common practice for Indian studios (based mostly in Bombay) to make their own versions of Hollywood hits. Indian films are made in a number of Indian languages, but the majority are made in Telugu, followed by Tamil, Hindi, Kannada and Malayalam. Due to the influence of films (and television) from abroad, there is also a growing trend of making action films rather than the more traditional films about family values and romance. Art films have received a boost, with Plus Channel funding 15 art films a year along with guaranteed distribution. Indians living abroad are choosing to make films on Indian themes, which are often filmed in India, but with unconventional and challenging story lines.

MAGAZINES

The magazines with the largest circulations are:

	Language		
India Today	English, Tamil, Hindi, Telugu, Malayalam	fortnightly, general interest	970,000 *
Grih Shobha	Hindi, Marathi, Gujarati, Kannada	monthly, women's magazine	551,000 *
Employment News	English, Hindi, Urdu	weekly, official publication	507,000*
Competition Success Review	English	monthly, general interest	248,000

* denotes totals for all language editions

PRESIDENTS

1949–62	Rajendra Prasad
1962–67	Sarvapalli Radhakrishnan
1967–69	Zahir Hussain
1969–74	Varahgiri Venkata Giri
1974–77	Fakhruddin Ali Ahmed
1977	Basappa Danappa Jatti
1977–82	Neelam Sanjiva Reddy
1982–87	Giani Zail Singh
1987–92	Ramaswamy Venkataraman
1992–97	Shankar Dayal Sharma
1997–	K.R. Narayanan

PRIME MINISTERS

1949–64	Jawaharlal Nehru
1964	Gulzarilal Nanda
1964–66	Lal Bahadur Shashtri
1966	Gulzarilal Nanda
1966–77	Indira Gandhi
1977–79	Moraji Desai
1979–80	Charan Singh
1980–84	Indira Gandhi
1984–89	Rajiv Gandhi
1989–90	Vishwanath Pratap Singh
1990–91	Chandra Shekhar
1991–96	P.V. Narasimha Rao
1996	Atal Bihari Vajpayee
1996–97	H.D. Deve Gowda
1997–	Inder Kumar Gujral

CONSUMER PRICE INDEX

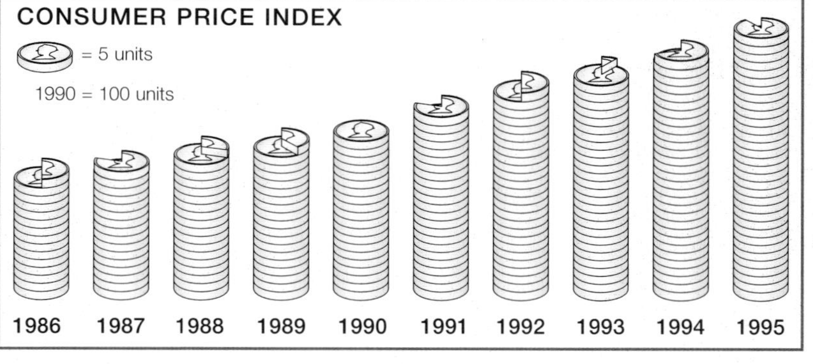

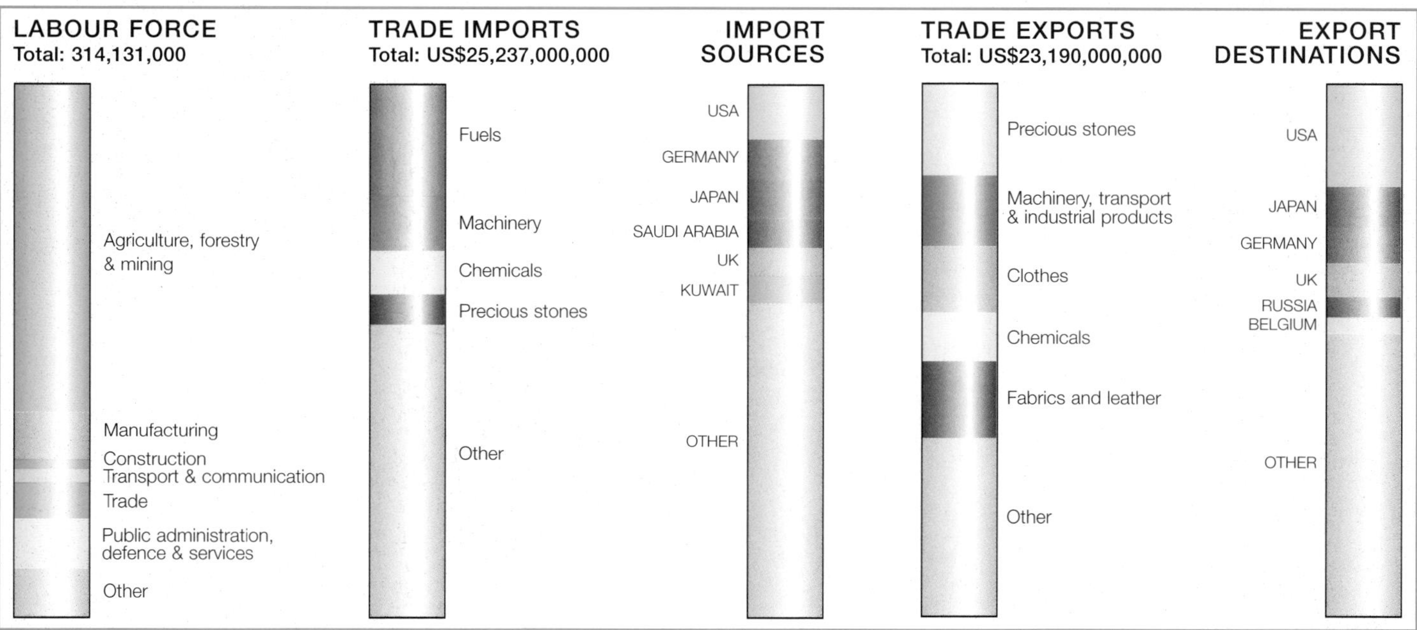

South Asia III

BANGLADESH

Bangladesh is a low-lying republic at the head of the Bay of Bengal in south Asia. Most of Bangladesh is alluvial plains in the deltas of the rivers Ganges and Brahmaputra, which combine as the Padma. The swampy plains, generally less than 9 m (30 ft) above sea level, are dissected by rivers dividing into numerous distributaries with raised banks. The south and south-east coastal regions contain mangrove forests (the Sundarbans). The only uplands are the Sylhet Hills in the north-east and the Chittagong hill country in the east.
Highest point: Keokradong 1230 m (4034 ft).
Climate: Tropical with highest temperatures between April and September. Most of the country's heavy rainfall is during the annual monsoon (June to October) when intense storms accompanied by high winds bring serious flooding. Rainfall totals range from 1000 mm (40 in) in the west to 5000 mm (200 in) in the Sylhet Hills.

The 330-member Parliament (Jatiya Sangsad) comprises 300 members elected by universal adult suffrage for five years plus 30 seats reserved for women (who are chosen by the 300 elected members). Parliament elects a President (whose duties are largely ceremonial). The President appoints a Prime Minister who enjoys a majority in Parliament; the PM, in turn, appoints a Cabinet of Ministers.
Largest parties: (1996 election) (social democratic) Awami League (Awami) 176 seats, (centre-right) Bangladesh Nationalist Party (BNP) 113, (left-wing) Jatiya Party (JP) 33, (Islamic) Jamit e-Islami 3, others 4.
President: (since 1991) Abdul Rahman Biswas (BNP).
Prime Minister: (since 1996) Sheik Wazed Hasina (Awami).

With a rapidly increasing population, Bangladesh is one of the world's poorest countries and is heavily dependent upon foreign aid. Money sent home by Bangladeshis working abroad is important. About two-thirds of the labour force are involved in agriculture. Rice is produced on over 75% of the cultivated land, but, although the land is fertile, crops are subject to floods and cyclones. A major Flood Action Plan, started in 1992, is altering the courses of rivers and raising embankments. The main cash crops are jute and tea. Industries include those processing agricultural products – jute milling, sugar refining and cotton textile manufacturing. There are reserves of natural gas.
Currency: Taka.

BANGLADESH
Rajshahi
Brahmaputra
Ganges
DHAKA
Khulna
Chittagong
BURMA/MYANMAR
Mandalay
Irrawaddy
Salween
Chiang Mai
Mekong
Pegu
Bassein
RANGOON
Moulmein
Khon Kaen
THAILAND
Nakhon Ratchasima
BANGKOK
Songkhla

Official name: Gana Prajatantri Bangladesh (People's Republic of Bangladesh).
Area: 147,570 km² (56,977 sq mi).
Population: 120,090,000 (1995 est.).
Doubling time: 30 years. **Adult life expectancy:** male 57 years, female 57 years. **Birth rate:** 1.36 times world average. **Death rate:** 1.18 times world average.
Urban population: 20%.
Capital: Dhaka 6,105,000 urban area (city 3,397,000; Narayanganj 269,000; 1991 census; inc. suburbs).
Other main centres: Chittagong 2,041,000 urban area (city 1,364,000), Khulna 877,000 (city 546,000), Rajshahi 517,000 (city 300,000), Narayanganj *see Dhaka*, Rangpur 204,000, Mymensingh 186,000, Barisal 163,000 (1991 census; inc. suburbs).
Language: Bengali 98% (official), Chakma, Magh and other minorities.
Adult literacy: 35%.
Religion: Sunni Islam 88%, Hindu 11%.

■ *Homes built above the flood plain near Dhaka. Regular flooding, following tropical cyclones, causes loss of life and economic hardship*

1947 Partition of British India into India and Pakistan, the latter with two 'wings', West Pakistan (the present Pakistan) and East Pakistan (now Bangladesh), separated by 1600 km (1000 miles) of Indian territory. **1970** Great loss of life in flooding. **1971** East Pakistan broke away as Bangladesh under Sheik Mujib-ur Rahman; Pakistani army sent from the West but India intervened forcing Pakistan to surrender. **1975** Mujib-ur Rahman assassinated. **1975–81** Military (1975–77) and then civilian (1978–81) rule under General Zia-ur-Rahman, who was assassinated in 1981. **1982–90** Military (1982–86) and then civilian (1986–90) rule under General Hussain Ershad, who was deposed in 1990. **Since 1990** Democratic parliamentary system restored.

■ OVER 80% OF BANGLADESH COULD BE UNDER WATER IF THE ICE-CAPS MELT

BURMA/MYANMAR

Burma is a republic to the east of the Bay of Bengal in south Asia. The north and west of Burma are mountainous. In the east is the Shan Plateau along the border with Thailand. South Burma consists of tropical lowlands; central Burma is the Irrawaddy basin.
Highest point: Hkakado Razi 5881 m (19,296 ft). **Climate:** Tropical with monsoon rains up to 5000 mm (200 in) between May and October.

There is constitutional provision for a 489-member Assembly elected by universal adult suffrage, a Council of Ministers and a Council of State, whose chair is President. However, power is held by the State Law and Order Restoration Council (SLORC), which has stated its intention to restore civilian rule under a constitution it will itself approve. There is a 706-member Constitutional Convention in which the largest party (the opposition National League for Democracy) was awarded 107 seats; however, the NLD withdrew in 1995.
Head of State (Chair of the SLORC) **and Prime Minister:** (since 1992) General Than Shwe.

Burma is rich in agriculture, timber and minerals but, because of poor communications, self-imposed isolation, lack of development and rebellions by a number of ethnic minorities, the country has been unable to realize its potential. Subsistence farming (mainly for rice) involves nearly 70% of the labour force. **Currency:** Kyat.

Official name: Pyidaungzu Myanma Naingngandaw (Union of Myanmar). The name Burma was officially dropped in 1989 but is still in widespread use internationally and by the opposition within the country.
Area: 676,577 km² (261,228 sq mi).
Population: 46,530,000 (1995 est.).
Doubling time: 33 years.
Adult life expectancy: male 57 years, female 61 years.
Birth rate: 1.24 times world average.
Death rate: 1.08 times world average. **Urban population:** 26%.
Capital: Rangoon (Yangon) 4,000,000 (1993 est.; inc. suburbs).
Other main centres: Mandalay 533,000, Moulmein (Mawlamyine) 230,000, Pegu (Bago) 151,000, Bassein (Pathein) 144,000 (1983 census; inc. suburbs).
Language: Burmese 69% (official), Shan 8%, Karen 6%, Arakanese (Rakhine) 4%, Mon 2%, Chin 2%, Kachin 1%. **Adult literacy:** 79%.
Religion: Buddhist 89%, various Christian Churches 5%, Sunni Islam 4%, traditional beliefs 1%

■ *The head of the colossal Shwethalyaung Buddha in Pegu, Burma*

BURMESE STATES
(in theory, autonomous areas)

Chin
Area: 36,019 km² (13,907 sq mi).
Pop.: 369,000 (1983 census).
Capital: Hakha.
Kachin
Area: 89,041 km² (34,379 sq mi).
Pop.: 905,000 (1983 census).
Capital: Myitkyina.
Karen
Area: 30,383 km² (11,731 sq mi).
Pop.: 1,055,000 (1983 census).
Capital: Pa-an (Hpa-an).
Kayah
Area: 11,733 km² (4530 sq mi).
Pop.: 168,000 (1983 census).
Capital: Loi-kaw.
Mon
Area: 12,297 km² (4748 sq mi).
Pop.: 1,680,000 (1983 census).
Capital: Moulmein (Mawlamyine).
Rakhine (Arakan)
Area: 36,778 km² (14,200 sq mi).
Pop.: 2,046,000 (1983 census).
Capital: Sittwe (Akyab).
Shan
Area: 155,801 km² (60,155 sq mi).
Pop.: 3,717,000 (1983 census).
Capital: Taunggyi.

1937 Burma separated from British India. **1939** Aung San founded Burmese independence movement. **1941–45** Burma became a battleground between British and Japanese forces during World War II. **1948** Independence. **1962** Military coup: General U Ne Win came to power; Burma became isolationist; continuing rebellions by various ethnic minorities. **1990** Multi-party elections (won by the National League for Democracy led by Aung San Suu Kyi, daughter of Aung San) were not accepted by the military who retained power; Aung San Suu Kyi detained (awarded the 1991 Nobel Peace Prize). **1995** Aung San Suu Kyi released from detention. **Since 1995** Most of the long-running rebellions have been either put down or contained.

THAILAND

Thailand is a kingdom lying between south Asia and South-East Asia. Central Thailand is a densely populated fertile plain. The north comprises rugged ranges of fold mountains. The infertile Khorat plateau occupies the north-east, while the mountainous isthmus of Kra joins Thailand to Malaysia.
Highest point: Doi Inthanon 2595 m (8514 ft).
Climate: Thailand has a subtropical climate with monsoon rains from June to October, a cool season from October to March and a hot season from March to June.

Thailand is a constitutional monarchy. The National Assembly comprises a non-political Senate (upper house), whose 270 members are appointed by the King, and a 393-member House of Representatives (lower house), which is elected by universal adult suffrage for four years.
Largest parties: (1996 election) (reformist) New Aspiration Party (NAP) 125 seats, (liberal) Democrat Party (DP) 123, Chart Patana 51, (conservative) Thai Nation/Chart Thai (CT) 38, Social Action Party (SAP) 21, Prakachorn Thai (Citizens' Party; PT) 17, Seritham Party (SP) 6, Muon Chon (MC) 2, Palang Dharma Party (PDP) 1, others 9.
King: (since 1946) Bhumipol Adulyadej (Rama IX).
Prime Minister: (since 1996) General Chavalit Yongchaiyudh (NAP; NAP–SAP–PT–SP–MC coalition government).

High economic growth rates in the 1980s and 1990s has made Thailand one of the boom economies of the Pacific Rim region. Trade and manufacturing now employ nearly one-quarter of the labour force, while agriculture (once the mainstay of the economy) now employs about one-half of the workforce. Manufacturing, based on cheap labour (although living standards are rising appreciably), is expanding rapidly and includes clothing, textiles, plastic goods, and electrical and electronic engineering. The downside to rapid development has been overcrowding and daily traffic gridlock in Bangkok. Tin and natural gas are the main natural resources. Tourism has become a major foreign-currency earner. Agriculture produces rice (in part, for export), tapioca and rubber.
Currency: Baht.

1932 Bloodless coup removed the king's powers; Pibul Songgram and Pridi Phanomyang, the westernized coup leaders, struggled for power for the next quarter century. **1939** Siam changed its name to Thailand. **1941** Japanese invasion: Thailand forced into an alliance with Japan. **Since 1945** Thailand has been a staunch US ally, bringing major benefits in military and technical aid. **1949–51** Military rule. **Since 1961** Regular military interventions in politics (including coups in 1975, 1977 and 1991).

Official name: Muang Thai (or Prathet Thai) (Kingdom of Thailand).
Area: 513,115 km² (198,115 sq mi).
Population: 58,790,000 (1995 est.).
Doubling time: 58 years. **Adult life expectancy:** male 66 years, female 71 years. **Birth rate:** 0.76 times world average. **Death rate:** 0.75 times world average. **Urban population:** 18%. **Capital:** Bangkok 5,884,000 (city 5,621,000; Nonthaburi 264,000; 1993 est.; inc. suburbs). The site for an eventual new capital, near Chachoengsao, 120 km (75 mi) east of Bangkok, has been approved.
Other main centres: Nakhon Ratchasima 278,000, Nonthaburi *see Bangkok*, Songkhla 243,000, Khon Kaen 206,000, Chiang Mai 167,000 (1990 census; inc. suburbs).
Language: Thai 51% (official), Lao 27%, Chinese 12%, Malay 4%, Khmer 1%. **Adult literacy:** 89%.
Religion: Buddhist 94%, Sunni Islam 4%, traditional beliefs.

■ *Small boat traffic crowds through the Damnern Saduak floating market in Ratchaburi Province*

HAS THE HIGHEST SUSTAINED ECONOMIC GROWTH RATES OF ANY COUNTRY IN THE 1990S ■

SOUTH-EAST ASIA I

VIETNAM

Vietnam is a republic stretching along the western side of the South China Sea in South-East Asia. Central Vietnam (Annam) comprises plateaux, hill country and chains of mountains. The rest of the country is relatively low-lying. The fertile Red River delta in the north forms the ancient region of Tonkin, while the Mekong delta in the south was formerly known as Cochinchina. **Highest point:** Fan si Pan 3142 m (10,308 ft). **Climate:** In the south and centre the climate is tropical and humid throughout the year; Tonkin, however, is cool in winter. Heavy rainfall comes during the monsoon season (April to October).

The 395-member National Assembly is elected for five years by universal adult suffrage from candidates offered by the Communist Party and by allies as part of the Fatherland Front. The Assembly elects a President and appoints a Prime Minister and other Ministers. Effective power rests with the 17-member Politburo of the Communist Party. **Only permitted parties:** (1992 election) Communist Party (PC) and other members of the Fatherland Front 395 seats. **President:** (since 1992) Le Duc Anh (PC). **Prime Minister:** (since 1991) Vo Van Kiet (PC). **Secretary General of the Communist Party:** (since 1991) Do Muoi (PC).

Official name: Cong Hoa Xa Hoi Chu Nghia Viet Nam (The Socialist Republic of Vietnam). **Area:** 331,041 km^2 (127,816 sq mi). **Population:** 74,550,000 (1995 est.). **Doubling time:** 69 years. **Adult life expectancy:** male 63.7 years, female 67.9 years. **Birth rate:** 1.05 times world average. **Death rate:** 0.82 times world average. **Urban population:** 21%. **Capital:** Hanoi 2,154,000 (1993 est.; inc. suburbs). **Other main centres:** Ho Chi Minh (formerly Saigon) 4,322,000, Haiphong 1,584,000, Da-Nang 371,000, Hue 270,000 (1993 est.; inc. suburbs). **Language:** Vietnamese 87% (official), Tho 2%, Tai 2%, Khmer 2%, Chinese 2%, Muong 2%. **Adult literacy:** 88%. **Religion:** Buddhist 67%, non-religious 19%, Roman Catholic 8%, Cao Dai 4%.

Nearly three-quarters of the labour force are involved in agriculture, mainly cultivating rice. Other crops include cassava, maize and sweet potatoes for domestic consumption and rubber, tea and coffee for export. Natural resources include petroleum (the main export), coal, phosphates and tin, which are the basis of industries in the north. The wars in Vietnam, involvement in Cambodia and the emigration of skilled labour have all had a serious effect on the economy. Attempts have been made to encourage western investment since 1989–90 and reforms have brought substantial recent development, allowing Vietnam to join the ASEAN trade bloc. **Currency:** Dong.

1930s Revolts against French colonial rule (which began in the 1880s). **1940–45** Japanese occupation during World War II; puppet regime set up under (Annamese) Emperor Bao Dai. **1945** The Viet Minh movement, headed by Ho Chi Minh, established a republic in Hanoi, with US support. **1946** French rule restored; Bao Dai recognized as emperor. **1946–54** Ho Chi Minh led a guerrilla war against the French and Bao Dai culminating in the French surrender at Dien Bien Phu. **1954** Vietnam partitioned between a Communist republic in the north and a monarchy in the south. **1955** Coup in South Vietnam; republic established under Ngo Dinh Diem. **Late 1950s** Diem's oppressive rule encouraged Communist guerrilla activity (the Viet Cong). **1961** US military advisers sent to aid South Vietnam. **1964** Full-scale US military involvement in South Vietnam and US bombardments of the north. **1968** Major Communist Tet offensive against the south. **1973** Peace treaty: US troops withdrew. **1975** Communist takeover of the south. **After 1975** The 'Boat people' (large numbers of refugees fleeing the south in small craft). **1979** Border war with China. **1979–89** Vietnamese involvement in Cambodia to overthrow the Khmer Rouge. **Since 1989–90** More pragmatic economic policies adopted but no political reforms.

CAMBODIA

Cambodia is a kingdom lying on the eastern side of the Gulf of Thailand in South-East Asia. Central Cambodia consists of fertile plains, mostly in the Mekong River valley and surrounding the Tonle Sap (Great Lake). North and east of the lowlands are plateaux covered by forests and grasslands. In the south, a range of mountains runs parallel to the coast. **Highest point:** Phnum Aural 1813 m (5947 ft). **Climate:** Cambodia is humid and tropical. The monsoon season (June to November) brings heavy rain with totals as high as 5000 mm (200 in) in the southern mountains.

Cambodia is a kingdom in which the King is elected from princes of the Royal Family by the Throne Council. The 120-member Assembly is elected for five years by universal adult suffrage. The Assembly elects co-Prime Ministers and other Ministers for a transitional period. **Largest parties:** (1993 election) (royalist) United National Front for an Independent, Neutral Peaceful and Co-operative Cambodia (Funcinpec) 58 seats, (former Communist) Cambodian People's Party (PPC) 51, (social democratic) Democratic Liberal Party (PDL) 10, others 1. **King:** (from 1941–55 and since 1993) (Norodom) Sihanouk. **Prime Ministers:** (since 1997) Ung Huot (Funcinpec), 1st PM; (since 1993) Hun Sen (PPC) 2nd PM, who declared former 1st PM Prince Norodom Ranariddh deposed.

Invasion, civil wars, massacres of the civilian population and the complete evacuation of towns (during 1976–79) all but destroyed Cambodia's economy. During the (virtual) restoration of peace (1993–97) Cambodia had to rebuild its agriculture, industry, towns and infrastructure, but the country remains one of the poorest in the world. Although 70% of the workforce is involved in subsistence farming, rice, formerly an export, has to be imported. Timber and rubber are the mainstays of a diminished economy. **Currency:** Riel.

1907 Thailand restored territories it had previously taken from the French protectorate of Cambodia. **1941** Thai invasion. **1945** Japanese occupation. **1946** French rule restored. **1953** Independent kingdom of Cambodia. **1955** King Sihanouk abdicated to lead a broad-based government but could not prevent Cambodia being dragged into the Vietnam War. **1969** USA bombed Vietnamese positions in eastern Cambodia. **1970** Pro-US coup overthrew Sihanouk; republic declared but opposed by both royalists and Communist Khmer Rouge guerrillas. **1975** Khmer Rouge took over, under the dictatorship of Pol Pot, and massacred over one million of their compatriots, returning 'Kampuchea' to the 'year zero'. **1978** Vietnamese invasion overthrew Pol Pot and instituted pro-Russian Communist regime of a different nature. **1989** Vietnamese forces withdrew; Chinese-sponsored Khmer Rouge forces invaded. **1991** UN sponsored peace plan; UN supervision and participation in administration. **1993** Free elections held; monarchy restored. **1997** Khmer Rouge activity virtually ended; Pol Pot reported to be detained; Funcinpec and PPC forces clashed and 1st PM Prince Norodom Ranariddh left the country as civil war threatened.

Official name: Preah Reach Ana Pak Kampuchea (The Kingdom of Cambodia). **Area:** 181,916 km^2 (70,238 sq mi). **Population:** 9,610,000 (1995 est.). **Doubling time:** 25 years. **Adult life expectancy:** male 51 years, female 54 years. **Birth rate:** 1.6 times world average. **Death rate:** 1.4 times world average. **Urban population:** 21%. **Capital:** Phnom Penh 920,000 (1994 est.; inc. suburbs). **Other main centres:** Battambang (Batdâmbâng) 45,000, Kâmpóng Cham 33,000 (1985 est.; inc. suburbs). **Language:** Khmer 89% (official), Vietnamese 6%, Chinese 3%, Cham 2%. **Adult literacy:** almost 75%. **Religion:** Buddhist 93%, Sunni Islam 2%, Roman Catholic and other minorities.

■ 1.75 MILLION LIVES WERE LOST IN THE VIETNAM WARS ■ LAOS' NATIONAL TREASURES,

THE PHILIPPINES

The Philippines form an island-republic on the Pacific Rim of South-East Asia. Some 2770 of the 7000 islands that make up the country are inhabited. The two largest islands, Luzon and Mindanao, make up over two-thirds of the republic's area. Most of the archipelago is mountainous with restricted coastal plains, although Luzon has a large, densely populated central plain.
Highest point: Mt Apo (in Mindanao) 2954 m (9692 ft).
Climate: Tropical maritime climate with high humidity, high temperatures and heavy rainfall. Typhoons are frequent.

The executive President and the 24-member Senate (the upper house of Congress) are elected for six years by universal adult suffrage, with one-half of the senators retiring every three years. The House of Representatives (lower house) comprises 204 directly elected members and no more than 50 members appointed by the President to represent minority groups.
Largest parties: (1995 election) (coalition) National Union of Christian Democrats (Lakas-NUCD) 141 seats, National Popular Coalition 23, Filipino Democrats (LDP) 21, others 19.
President: (since 1992) Fidel Ramos (Lakas-NUCD supported).

About two-fifths of the labour force are involved in agriculture. Rice and maize are the principal crops, while coconuts, sugar cane, pineapples and bananas are grown for export. Deforestation is a problem as land is cleared for cultivation. Relying on inexpensive labour, the country has become one of the rapidly expanding economies of the Pacific Rim region and has experienced high rates of growth. Major industries include textiles, food processing, chemicals, machinery and transport equipment, and electrical engineering. Mineral resources include copper, gold, petroleum, and nickel. Money sent home by Filipinos working abroad is an important source of foreign currency. **Currency:** Philippine peso.

1896 Unsuccessful revolt against Spanish colonial rule. **1898** Islands ceded to USA after Spanish-American War but US rule had to be imposed by force. **1906** End of Filipino resistance to US rule. **1935** Semi-independent Commonwealth formed under presidency of Manuel Quezon. **1941–45** Japanese occupation during World War II. **1946** Independence. **1953–57** Hukbalahap Communist guerrillas crushed. **1965–86** Presidency of Ferdinand Marcos who became increasingly dictatorial and was overthrown in a popular revolution in favour of Corazon Aquino in 1986. **Since 1986** Democratic constitutional rule restored; Communist and Islamic nationalist guerrillas remained a problem until 1996.

Official names: Republika ng Pilipinas (in Filipino) and Republic of the Philippines.
Area: 300,076 km^2 (115,860 sq mi).
Population: 70,010,000 (1995 est.).
Doubling time: 30 years. **Adult life expectancy:** male 66 years, female 69 years. **Birth rate:** 1.16 times world average. **Death rate:** 0.65 times world average. **Urban population:** 54%. **Capital:** Manila 6,720,000 urban area (city 1,895,000; Quezon City 1,667,000; Caloocan City 629,000; Makati 452,000; Pasig 395,000; Pasay City 382,000; 1991 census; inc. suburbs).
Other main centres: Quezon City *see Manila*, Davao City 868,000, Cebu City 641,000, Caloocan City *see Manila*, Zamboanga City 453,000, Makati, Pasig and Pasay City *see Manila* (1991 census; inc. suburbs).
Language: Pilipino (Filipino or Tagalog) 28% (official), English spoken as a first language by under 1% of the population and used by 52% (official), Cebuano 24%, Ilocano 10%, Hiligaynon 9%, Bicol 6%, Waray-Waray 4%, with Pampango, Pangasinan and other minorities.
Adult literacy: 94%.
Religion: Roman Catholic 83%, various Protestant Churches 5%, Sunni Islam 5%, Aglipayan 3%.

FILIPINO AUTONOMOUS REGION

Muslim Mindanao
Area: 11,638 km^2 (4,493 sq mi).
Pop.: 2,103,000 (1995 est.).
Capital: Cotabato City.
(There is also provision for Cordillera region to attain autonomy.)

SPRATLY ISLANDS

Official name and status: Nansha (Chinese) or Spratly Islands; a territory disputed between China, Taiwan, Malaysia, the Philippines, Brunei and Vietnam.
Area: not defined.
Population: no permanent population; forces from all claimants (except Brunei) are stationed in the islands.
Geography: The islands comprise a large number of very small rocky islets in the South China Sea.

PARACEL ISLANDS

Official name and status: Penghu (in Chinese; the Paracel Islands); a territory disputed between China and Vietnam and occupied by China since 1950.
Area: 160 km^2 (62 sq mi).
Population: no permanent population; Chinese forces are stationed in the islands.
Geography: The islands comprise over 130 small low-lying arid coral reefs which are situated in the South China Sea.

LAOS

Laos is a landlocked republic in South-East Asia, lying almost entirely to the east of the River Mekong, which forms the frontier with Thailand for much of its course. Most of the country is mountainous except for the Plain of Jars in the north, the Mekong valley and some low plateaux in the south.
Highest point: Phou Bia 2819 m (9248 ft). **Climate:** Tropical climate with high temperatures and heavy rainfall, peaking during the monsoon from May to October.

The 85-member National Assembly is elected for five years by universal adult suffrage from candidates offered by the (Communist) Lao People's Revolutionary Party (PPRL). The Assembly elects a President. The Prime Minister and other Ministers are effectively responsible to the 11-member Politburo of the PPRL.
Only permitted party: (1992 election) (Communist) Lao People's Revolutionary Party (PPRL) 85 seats.
President: (since 1992) Nouhak Phoumsavanh (PPRL).
Prime Minister: (since 1991) Khamtay Siphandone (PPRL).

Laos is one of the poorest countries in the world. Nearly three-quarters of the labour force work on collective farms, mainly growing rice. The main exports are timber, electricity and coffee. Western investment, particularly Thai, has been encouraged since 1990.
Currency: Kip.

1893 French protectorate established. **1945** Japanese occupation. **1946** French rule restored. **1953** Independent kingdom of Laos. **1959–60** Several coups; armed struggle between Communist Pathet Lao movement and the royalists intensified. **1960s** Intermittent civil war. **1970** North Vietnamese intervention in Plain of Jars; US bombed North Vietnamese in Laos. **1970–75** Infrastructure collapsed in civil war. **1975** Communist takeover; King imprisoned. **Since 1990** Gradual reform but no suggestion of multi-party politics.

Official name: Sathalanalat Paxathipatai Paxaxôn Lao (Lao People's Democratic Republic).
Area: 236,800 km^2 (91,429 sq mi).
Population: 4,880,000 (1995 est.).
Doubling time: 24 years. **Adult life expectancy:** male 51 years, female 54 years. **Birth rate:** 1.72 times world average. **Death rate:** 1.5 times world average. **Urban population:** 22%. **Capital:** Vientiane (Viangchan) 449,000 (1992 est.; inc. suburbs).
Other main centres: Savannakhet 97,000, Luang Prabang (Louangphrabang) 68,000 (1985 est.; inc. suburbs).
Language: Lao 67% (official), Khmer 17%, with Thai and other minorities. Adult literacy: 84%.
Religion: Buddhist 58%, traditional beliefs 34%, non-religious 8%.

INCLUDING ITS CROWN JEWELS, WERE ACCIDENTALLY DROWNED IN THE MEKONG RIVER IN 1910

SOUTH-EAST ASIA II

INDONESIA

Indonesia is a republic consisting of over 3700 South-East Asian islands (some 3000 of which are inhabited). The southern chain of mountainous volcanic islands includes Sumatra, Java with Madura, Bali and the Lesser Sunda Islands. Java and Madura are fertile and densely populated, containing 65% of the country's population. The northern chain of islands includes Kalimantan (Borneo), the irregular mountainous island of Sulawesi (Celebes), the Moluccas group and Irian Jaya (western New Guinea). Over one-half of Indonesia is still covered by tropical rain forest.
Highest point: Ngga Pulu (in Irian Jaya) 5030 m (16,503 ft).
Climate: Tropical climate with heavy rainfall and high temperatures throughout the year.

The 500-member House of Representatives comprises 425 members elected for five years by universal adult suffrage, plus 75 army members appointed by the President. The People's Consultative Assembly has 1000 members (comprising the House of Representatives, plus 500 representatives of provincial governments, occupational and special interests) and meets every five years to oversee principles of state policy and to elect an executive President, who appoints a Cabinet.
Largest parties: (1997 election) (government alliance) Golkar 325 seats plus 75 appointees, (officially sanctioned Islamic) United Development Party (PPP) 89, (officially sanctioned mainly Christian and nationalist) Indonesian Democratic Party (PDI) 11.
President: (since 1967) Gen. Mohammed Suharto (Golkar).

Indonesia has great mineral wealth (petroleum, natural gas, tin, nickel and bauxite) but is relatively poor because of its great population. Nearly 50% of Indonesians are subsistence farmers with rice being the major crop, but both estate and peasant farmers produce important quantities of rubber, tea, coffee and spices for export. Industry, formerly concerned mainly with processing mineral and agricultural products, is expanding and textiles and clothing, and electrical and transport equipment are significant. Indonesia has achieved very high growth rates since the 1980s and is one of the booming economies of the Pacific Rim region. Standards of living are increasing sharply but only in urban areas. An ambitious programme of resettlement has been attempted to relieve overcrowded Java, but Javanese settlers have been resented in the outlying, underdeveloped islands. **Currency:** Indonesian Rupiah.

1908 Completion of conquest of outer islands by the Dutch; Dutch East Indies had been the major part of the Dutch colonial empire since 1602. **1942** Present-day Indonesia overrun by the Japanese, who were largely welcomed as liberators from colonial rule. **1945** Japanese surrender; Achmed Sukarno declared Dutch East Indies to be the independent republic of Indonesia. **1945–49** Dutch attempted to reimpose colonial rule in an intermittent but often brutal struggle. **1949** Indonesian independence recognized by Dutch. **1962** Indonesia gained control of Dutch New Guinea, which was annexed in 1969. **1965–66** Indonesian 'confrontation' against Malaysia in Borneo; the Communist uprising in Indonesia suppressed with great loss of life by General Suharto, who took over from the increasingly dictatorial Sukarno in 1967. **1976** Indonesia annexed the former Portuguese colony of East Timor; guerrilla action by local nationalist groups continues; up to 200,000 people have died in Indonesia's conquest and subsequent occupation of the territory. **Since mid-1990s** Increasing unrest owing to the perceived corruption and restriction of democracy. **1997** Serious violence against Madurese settlers in Borneo.

Official name: Republik Indonesia (Republic of Indonesia).
Area: 1,919,317 km² (741,052 sq mi) including East Timor (Indonesian administration of East Timor is not recognized by the UN) or 1,904,413 km² (735,309 sq mi) excluding East Timor.
Population: 195,280,000 (1995 est.) inc. East Timor or 194,440,000 exc. East Timor. **Doubling time:** 47 years.
Adult life expectancy: male 62 years, female 65 years. **Birth rate:** 0.92 times world average. **Death rate:** 0.86 times world average. Urban population: 35%. **Capital:** Djakarta 9,161,000 (1995 est.; inc. suburbs). **Other main centres:** Surabaya 2,421,000, Bandung 2,027,000, Medan 1,686,000, Palembang 1,084,000, Semarang 1,005,000, Ujung Pandang 913,000, Malang 650,000, Surakarta 504,000 (1990 census; inc. suburbs).
Language: Bahasa Indonesia (Indonesian Malay) 12% (official), Javanese 40%, Sundanese 16%, Madurese 4%, Minang 2%, Batak 2%, Buginese 2%, with Banjarese, Balinese and other minorities.
Adult literacy: 77%.
Religion: Sunni Islam 88%, Protestant Churches 6%, Roman Catholic 3%, Hindu 2%, Buddhist 1%.

INDONESIAN AUTONOMOUS PROVINCES

Aceh
Area: 55,392 km² (21,387 sq mi).
Pop.: 3,860,000 (1995 est.).
Capital: Banda Aceh.

Yogyakarta
Area: 3169 km² (1224 sq mi).
Pop.: 2,917,000 (1995 est.).
Capital: Yogyakarta.

SINGAPORE

Singapore is a republican city-state at the southern tip of the Malay peninsula in South-East Asia. The state consists of one main low-lying island (and 56 other islets) joined to the mainland by a causeway.
Highest point: Bukit Timah 177 m (581 ft). **Climate:** Tropical with heavy monsoon rainfall from December to March.

The 83-member Parliament comprises 81 members elected by universal adult suffrage for five years from single-member and group representation constituencies plus additional appointed members. The President, directly elected for six years, is largely ceremonial but appoints a Prime Minister and other Ministers.
Largest parties: (1997 election) (centre-right) People's Action Party (PAP) 81, (left-wing) Worker's Party 1, (left-wing) Singapore People's Party 1.
President: (since 1993) Ong Teng Cheong (PAP).
Prime Minister: (since 1990) Goh Chok Tong (PAP).

Singapore relies upon imports for its flourishing manufacturing industries (electronics, petroleum refining, rubber processing) and re-export trade. Singapore is one of the world's major ports. Finance and tourism are important. The city-state's standard of living (the second highest in Asia) is higher than that of many west European states. High-tech industries are being encouraged.
Currency: Singaporean dollar.

1819 Acquired by Britain and became the major port for Malaya's tin and rubber trade. **1942** Overrun by the Japanese. **1945** Liberated after World War II. **1963** Became part of Malaysia. **1965** Seceded from Malaysia. **1965–91** Strong premiership of Lee Kuan Yew; increasing international criticism of perceived limitations to democracy.

Official names: Hsin-chia-p'o Kung-ho-kuo (Chinese), Republik Singapura (Malay), Singapore Kudiyarasu (Tamil) and Republic of Singapore
Area: 641 km² (248 sq mi).
Population: 2,990,000 (1995 est.).
Doubling time: 60 years. **Adult life expectancy:** male 74.4 years, female 78.5 years. **Birth rate:** 0.66 times world average. **Death rate:** 0.51 times world average. **Urban population:** 100%.
Capital: Singapore (Hsin-chia-p'o or Singapura) 2,990,000 (1995 est.).
Language: Chinese 77% (official), Malay 14% (official), English is a first language to less than 1% of the population but is understood by 37% (official), Tamil 7% (official).
Adult literacy: over 91%.
Religion: Buddhist and Chinese folk religions (including Daoism) 54%, Sunni Islam 15%, non-religious 14%, various Protestant denominations over 7%, Roman Catholic 5%, Hindu over 3%.

MALAYSIA

Malaysia is a federation of 13 states: 11 states (western Malaysia) occupying a peninsula at the south-east tip of Asia and two larger states (eastern Malaysia) occupying the northern part of the island of Borneo. Western Malaysia consists of mountain ranges (including the Trengganu and Cameron Highlands) running north to south and bordered by densely populated coastal lowlands. Tropical rain forests cover much of Sabah and Sarawak (eastern Malaysia), but there has been very considerable deforestation. **Highest point:** Kinabalu (in Sabah) 4101 m (13,455 ft).

MALAYSIAN STATES AND TERRITORIES

Johore (Johor)
Area: 18,986 km² (7331 sq mi).
Pop.: 2,074,000 (1991 census).
Capital: Johore Bahru (Johor Baharu).
Kedah
Area: 9426 km² (3639 sq mi).
Pop.: 1,305,000 (1991 census).
Capital: Alor Star (Alor Setar).
Kelantan
Area: 14,943 km² (5769 sq mi).
Pop.: 1,182,000 (1991 census).
Capital: Kota Bahru (Kota Baharu).
Malacca (Melaka)
Area: 1650 km² (637 sq mi).
Pop.: 505,000 (1991 census).
Capital: Malacca (Melaka).
Negeri Sembilan
Area: 6643 km² (2565 sq mi).
Pop.: 691,000 (1991 census).
Capital: Seremban.
Pahang
Area: 35,965 km² (13,886 sq mi).
Pop.: 1,037,000 (1991 census).
Capital: Kuantan.
Perak
Area: 21,005 km² (8110 sq mi).
Pop.: 1,880,000 (1991 census).
Capital: Ipoh.
Perlis
Area: 795 km² (307 sq mi).
Pop.: 184,000 (1991 census).
Capital: Kangar.
Pulau Penang (Pulau Pinang)
Area: 1031 km² (398 sq mi).
Pop.: 1,065,000 (1991 census).
Capital: Penang (Pinang; formerly Georgetown).
Sabah
Area: 73,620 km² (28,425 sq mi).
Pop.: 1,737,000 (1991 census).
Capital: Kota Kinabalu.
Sarawak
Area: 124,449 km² (48,050 sq mi).
Pop.: 1,648,000 (1991 census).
Capital: Kuching.
Selangor
Area: 7956 km² (3072 sq mi).
Pop.: 2,290,000 (1991 census).
Capital: Shah Alam.
Trengganu (Terengganu)
Area: 12,955 km² (5002 sq mi).
Pop.: 771,000 (1991 census).
Capital: Trengganu Bahru (Terengganu Baharu).
Federal Capital Territory
Area: 243 km² (94 sq mi).
Pop.: 1,145,000 (1991 census).
Capital: Kuala Lumpur.
Labuan Territory
Area: 91 km² (35 sq mi).
Pop.: 54,000 (1991 census).
Capital: Victoria.

Climate: Tropical climate with heavy rainfall (up to 2500 mm (98 in) in the west). There is more seasonal variation in precipitation than in temperature, with the north-east monsoon (from October to February) and the south-west monsoon (from May to September) bringing increased rainfall, particularly to western Malaysia.

The 69-member Senate (Dewan Negara) comprises two senators elected for three years by each of the 13 states, plus 43 senators appointed by the Supreme Head of State. The 192-member House of Representatives (Dewan Rakyat) is elected by universal adult suffrage for five years. The Yang di-Pertuan Agong (Supreme Head of State, popularly called the King) serves for a five-year term; he is chosen, from their own number, by the hereditary sultans who reign in nine of the 13 states. The King appoints a Prime Minister and a Cabinet enjoying a majority in the House. The states have their own legislatures.
Largest parties: (1995 election) (coalition) Barisan Nasional (National Front, which includes the predominant United Malays National Organization) (BN) 162 seats, (social democrat) Democratic Action Party (DAP) 9, various Islamic parties 13, others 8.
Supreme Head of State: (popularly referred to as King) (since 1994) Tuanku Ja'afar ibni Al-Marhum, Sultan of Negeri Sembilan.
Prime Minister: (since 1981) Dr Mahathir Mohamad (BN).

Petroleum, rubber and tin are the three traditional mainstays of the economy, but all three suffered drops in price on the world market in the 1980s. Pepper (from Sarawak), cocoa and timber are also important. About one-fifth of the labour force is still involved in agriculture, with many Malays growing rice as a subsistence crop. However, manufacturing industry is now the largest exporter. Major industries include rubber and tyres, tin, textiles, machinery, cement, motor vehicles, radios and other electrical equipment. The country has experienced high growth rates since the 1980s and Malaysia is one of the booming economies of the Pacific Rim region. The government has greatly encouraged industrialization, investment (much of it Japanese) and a more active role for the ethnic Malay population in industry, which (with commerce and finance) had been largely the preserve of Malaysia's Chinese population. Tourism is a major growth area. **Currency:** Ringgit.

1888 Sabah became British North Borneo (Penang and Malacca were already British). **1895** Four Malay sultanates formed a British-protected federation. **1914** The remaining Malay sultanates became British protectorates. **1941** Present-day Malaysia overrun by the Japanese. **1945** Area liberated after World War II. **1946** Sarawak, ruled by the Brooke family (the 'white rajahs') since 1841, became a British colony. **1948** Federation of Malaya (western Malaysia) was formed. **1948–60** Communist insurgency in Malaya. **1957** Malaya became independent. **1963** Malaya joined by Singapore, Sabah and Sarawak to form Malaysia. **1965** Singapore seceded. **1965–66** British armed support in the face of Indonesian 'confrontation' in Borneo. **1969–71** Suspension of constitutional government amid Malay–Chinese tension. **Since 1980s** Rise of Islamic fundamentalism; rapid economic growth.

Official name: Malaysia (Melaysiu). **Area:** 330,442 km² (127,584 sq mi). **Population:** 19,950,000 (1995 est.). **Doubling time:** 30 years. **Adult life expectancy:** male 69 years, female 73 years. **Birth rate:** 1.12 times world average. **Death rate:** 0.54 times world average. **Urban population:** 54%. **Capital:** Kuala Lumpur 1,145,000 (1991 census; inc. suburbs). A new 'high-tech' capital, Putrajaya, is under construction nearby. **Other main centres:** Ipoh 383,000, Johore Bahru (Johor Baharu) 329,000, Malacca (Melaka) 296,000, Petaling Jaya 255,000, Kelang 244,000, Kuala Trengganu (Kuala Terengganu) 229,000, Kota Bahru (Kota Baharu) 220,000, Penang (Pinang; formerly Georgetown) 219,000, Kota Kinabalu 208,000 (1991 census; inc. suburbs). **Language:** Malay 58% (official), English is a first language to less than 1% of the population but is understood by 31%, Chinese 9%, Tamil 4%, Iban 3%. **Adult literacy:** 84%. **Religion:** Sunni Islam 53%, Buddhist 17%, Chinese folk religions (including Daoism) 12%, Hindu 9%, various Christian denominations over 6%.

EAST TIMOR

Official name and status: Timor Timur (East Timor); administered as a province of Indonesia, a status not recognized by the UN. **Area:** 14,874 km² (5743 sq mi). **Population:** 843,000 (1995 est.). **Capital:** Dili 60,000 (1990 est.). **Geography:** The mountainous eastern half of the tropical South-East Asian island of Timor, plus a small enclave in the west of the island. **Economy:** The economy depended upon coffee when the territory was a Portuguese colony (before 1974). Since annexation by Indonesia (in 1975) the economy has been devastated, much of the population has been uprooted or killed and many villages destroyed.

CHRISTMAS ISLAND

Official name and status: Territory of Christmas Island; an Australian external territory. **Area:** 135 km² (52 sq mi). **Population:** 2400 (1994 est.). **Capital:** Flying Fish Cove. **Geography:** An isolated mountainous tropical island, south of Java (Indonesia). **Economy:** The island depends upon phosphate workings staffed by Chinese and Malay migrants.

COCOS (KEELING) ISLANDS

Official name and status: Territory of Cocos (Keeling) Islands; an Australian external territory. **Area:** 14 km² (6 sq mi). **Population:** 600 (1993 est.). **Capital:** Bantam Village. **Geography:** Two atolls of small coral islands, south-west of Sri Lanka. **Economy:** The islands are dependent upon coconut plantations worked by Malay migrants.

BRUNEI

Brunei is a small sultanate in two enclaves on the north coast of the South-East Asian island of Borneo. The larger (western) part is hilly; the eastern enclave is more mountainous and forested. **Highest point:** Bukit Pagon 1850 m (6070 ft). **Climate:** The climate is tropical with heavy monsoon rainfall in excess of 2500 mm (100 in).

Brunei is an absolute monarchy in which the hereditary Sultan is head of state and of government. He appoints a Council of Ministers and a 21-member advisory body. There are no political parties.
Sultan: (since 1967) Hassanal Bolkiah.

Exploitation of substantial deposits of petroleum and natural gas has given Brunei one of the world's highest per capita incomes (while the Sultan is described as the world's richest man). Most of the country's food has to be imported. **Currency:** Brunei dollar.

1888 British protectorate over Brunei established. **1962** Attempted popularist coup. **1984** Independence.

Official name: Negara Brunei Darussalam (State of Brunei). **Area:** 5765 km² (2226 sq mi). **Population:** 291,000 (1995 est.). **Doubling time:** 29 years. **Adult life expectancy:** male 69.5 years, female 72.8 years. **Birth rate:** 1.05 times world average. **Death rate:** 0.54 times world average. **Urban population:** 90%. **Capital:** Bandar Seri Begawan 46,000 (1991 est.). **Other main centres:** Kuala Belait 21,000, Seria 21,000 (1991 est.). **Language:** Malay 78% (official), Chinese 9%, English as a first language 6%. **Adult literacy:** 88%. **Religion:** Sunni Islam 67%, Buddhist 13%, various Christian denominations 10%.

China and its Neighbours

CHINA

China is the third largest country in the world in area and the largest in population. Almost one-half of China comprises mountain chains, mainly in the west, including the Altaï and Tien Shan Mountains in Xinjiang Uygur, and the Kun Lun Mountains to the north of Tibet. The Tibetan Plateau, 3000 m (10,000 ft) high, is arid. In the south of Tibet is the Himalaya, containing 40 peaks over 7000 m (23,000 ft). In the far south, the Yunnan Plateau rises to nearly 3700 m (12,000 ft), while in the far north-east ranges of hills and mountains almost enclose the Northeast Plain. The Nan Ling Range of hills and mountains crosses central China separating the basins of the Yellow (Huang He) and Yangtze (Chang Jiang) rivers. In east and central China, three great lowlands support intensive agriculture and dense populations: the plains of central China, the Sichuan Basin and the North China Plain. A vast loess plateau, deeply dissected by ravines, lies between the Mongolian Plateau (which contains the Gobi desert) and the deserts of the Tarim and Dzungarian Basins in the north-west.
Highest point: Mt Everest 8863 m (29,078 ft).
Climate: In general, temperatures increase from north to south, and rainfall increases from north-west to south-east. North-east China has a continental climate with warm and humid summers, long cold winters and rainfall under 750 mm (30 in). The central lowlands contain the hottest areas of China, and have 750–1100 mm (30–40 in) of rainfall. The south is wetter, while the extreme subtropical south experiences the monsoon. The continental loess plateau is cold in the winter, warm in summer and has under 500 mm (20 in) of rain. The north-west is arid, continental and experiences cold winters. The west (Tibet, Xinjiang Ugyur, Gansu and Nei Monggol) experiences an extreme climate owing to its altitude and distance from the sea: rainfall is low and most of Tibet has ten months of frost.

Amur
Harbin
Darhan
Erdenet
ULAN BATOR
Changchun
Shenyang
MONGOLIA
BEIJING
Dalian
Tianjin
Zibo
Jinan
Qingdao
Huang He
CHINA
Xian
Nanjing
Shanghai
Wuhan
Mekong
Chengdu
Chongqing
Xigase
Yangtze
TAIPEI
Tainan
TAIWAN
Kaohsiung
Kunming
Guangzhou
Hong Kong
Macau

The 2962 deputies of the National People's Congress are elected for a five-year term by the People's Congresses of the provinces and the army. The Congress elects a Standing Committee, President (for a five-year term), Prime Minister and State Council (Cabinet), all responsible to the Congress. Hong Kong, not represented in the Congress, has its own administration and legislature.
Political party: The only legal party, the Chinese Communist Party, holds a Congress every five years. The Party Congress elects a Central Committee. This Committee, in turn, elects a Politburo: these last two bodies hold effective power.
President: (since 1989) Jiang Zemin.
Prime Minister: (since 1987) Li Peng.
General Secretary of the Communist Party: (since 1989) Jiang Zemin.

■ *The sterile machine-like interior of the Shenzhen Stock Exchange. Shenzhen was the first of China's Special Economic Zones*

Agriculture occupies over one-half of the labour force. All large-scale production is on collective farms, but traditional and inefficient practices remain. Almost one-half of the arable land is irrigated and China is the world's largest producer of rice. Other crops include wheat, maize, sweet potatoes, sugar cane and soybeans. Livestock, fruit, vegetables and fishing are also important. Mineral and fuel resources are considerable, and underdeveloped for the most part. They include coal, petroleum, natural gas, iron ore, bauxite, tin and antimony in major reserves, as well as huge hydroelectric power potential. The economy is centrally planned but all businesses are no longer owned by the state. Petrochemical products account for nearly one-quarter of China's exports. Other major industries include iron and steel, cement, vehicles, fertilizers, food processing, clothing and textiles. Reforms since the late 1980s have promoted ventures with other countries and foreign loans and small-scale private enterprise have been encouraged. Special Economic Zones were designated on the south and central coasts to encourage industrial links with the West. Economic progress has been sustained, in Shanghai and Guangdong particularly, and the economy has achieved very high growth rates. The return of Hong Kong has increased China's GDP by one-fifth. **Currency:** Yuan. The Hong Kong dollar remains in Hong Kong.

1911 A revolution, led by the Guomintang (Kuomintang or Nationalists) under Sun Zhong Shan (Sun Yat-sen), overthrew the last of the Manchu emperors. **1916** Sun established a republic in the south; warlords controlled the north. Tibet gained independence. **After 1928** Sun's successor, Jiang Jie Shi (Chiang Kai-shek), made inroads into the north. **1930s** Increase in Communist activity; after disastrous urban risings. Communist activity was concentrated in rural areas. **1931** The Japanese seized Manchuria and established a puppet regime. **1934** Communist leader Mao Zedong (Mao Tse-tung) was forced to retreat from Jiangsi and began the 9000 km (5600 mi) 12-month 'Long March' to the remote province of Shaanxi. **1937** Japan seized Beijing and most of coastal China; Mao and Jiang combined against the invaders. **1937–45** Much of north-east, eastern and southern China occupied by Japanese forces. **1946** Mao marched into Manchuria, beginning the Chinese civil war. **1949** Communists won civil war: Mao declared the People's Republic in Beijing; Jiang and his forces fled to Taiwan, where a Nationalist government was set up. **1950** Chinese forces invaded Tibet. **1950–53** Chinese 'volunteers' active in the Korean War supporting Communist N. Korea. **1950s** 'Great Leap Forward', an ambitious programme of radicalization, largely failed. Border clashes with USSR – relations deteriorated rapidly. **1960s** Mao tried to spread more revolutionary ideas in the Cultural Revolution: militant students formed the Red Guards to attack existing hierarchy; thousands died as the students went out of control; army

■ ONE IN FIVE PEOPLE ALIVE TODAY IS CHINESE ■ MACAU HAS THE WORLD'S HIGHEST POPULATION

Official name: Zhonghua Renmin Gongheguo (The People's Republic of China).
Area: 9,573,980 km² (3,696,520 sq mi), excluding Taiwan.
Population: 1,212,800,000 (1995 est.; inc. Hong Kong).
Doubling time: 63 years. **Adult life expectancy:** male 69.1 years, female 72.4 years. **Birth rate:** 0.71 times world average. **Death rate:** 0.7 times world average. **Urban population:** 28%. **Capital:** Beijing (formerly Peking) 6,690,000 (1993 est.). **Other main centres:** Shanghai 8,930,000, Hong Kong 6,200,000, Tianjin (formerly Tientsin) 5,000,000, Shenyang 4,050,000, Wuhan 3,870,000, Chongqing 3,870,000, Guangzhou (formerly Canton) 3,750,000, Harbin 3,120,000, Chengdu 2,760,000, Nanjing (formerly Nanking) 2,490,000, Changchun 2,470,000, Xian 2,410,000, Zibo 2,400,000, Dalian (formerly Darien) 2,400,000, Qingdao 2,300,000, Jinan 2,150,000, Hangzhou 1,790,000, Taiyuan 1,720,000, Zhengzhou 1,690,000, Shijiazhuang 1,610,000, Changsha 1,510,000, Kunming 1,500,000, Nanchang 1,440,000, Fuzhou 1,380,000, Lanzhou 1,340,000, Anshan 1,210,000, Fushan 1,200,000, Ürümqi 1,130,000, Hefei 1,110,000, Ningbo 1,100,000, Guiyang 1,080,000, Qiqihar 1,070,000, Tangshan 1,050,000, Jilin 1,040,000, Linhe 1,020,000, Macheng 1,010,000, Shenzhen 1,000,000 (1993 est. of the urban pop. of municipalities).
Language: Chinese (Guoyo or 'Mandarin') 66% as a first language but almost universally understood (official), Wu 8%, Cantonese (Yüeh) 5%, Xiang 5%, Min 4%, Hakka 3%, Kan 2%, Manchu 1%, Hui 1%. English is an official language alongside Chinese in Hong Kong. **Adult literacy:** 78%.
Religion: Non-religious over 60%, Chinese folk religions (inc. Daoism) under 20%, atheist 12%, Buddhist 6%, Sunni Islam 2%.

had to restore order. **1962** Border clashes with India. **1964** First atomic weapon tested. **1970s** Gradual rapprochement with USA. **1976** Death of Mao. **1977–97** Deng Xiaoping, effective leader, instituted economic reforms. **1989** Rapprochement with the USSR. Increase in pressures for political reform: large pro-democracy workers and students demonstrations brutally repressed in massacre of students in Tiananmen Square. **1997** Return of Hong Kong to Chinese rule.

MACAU

Official name and status: Macao (Macau); a Chinese territory under Portuguese administration; Macau will be returned to China in 1999.
Area: 18 km² (7 sq mi).
Population: 428,000 (1995 est.).
Capital: Macau 428,000 (1995 est.).
The territory comprises the peninsula of Macau on the Guangdong coast of China and two small adjoining islands. Nearly one-half of the labour force is involved in the manufacturing industry; tourism, attracted by casinos, is a major industry.

TAIWAN

Taiwan is an island 160 km (100 mi) off the south-east coast of China. Its mountainous interior rises in the south to Yu Shan. Most inhabitants live on the coastal plain in the west.
Highest point: Yu Shan 3997 m (13,113 ft).
Climate: Subtropical in the north and tropical in the south, with rainy summers and mild winters. Tropical cyclones (typhoons) may occur between July and September.

The 161-member Parliament (Legislative Yuan) comprises 128 members elected by universal adult suffrage for six years and additional members chosen according to the share of the vote received by the principal parties. The 325-member National Assembly, directly elected for four years, has no legislative powers other than to amend the constitution. The President, who is directly elected for six years, appoints a Prime Minister and a Council of Ministers.
Largest parties: (1995 election) Kuomintang (Nationalist) Party (KMT) 85 seats, (Taiwanese independence) Democratic Progressive Party (DPP) 54, (pro-unification) New Party 21, others and independents 4.
President: (since 1988) Lee Teng-hui (KMT).
Prime Minister: (since 1993) Lien Chan (KMT).

Despite its diplomatic isolation, Taiwan is a major international trading nation, exporting machinery, textiles and electronics. Mineral resources include coal, gold, marble, petroleum and natural gas. Taiwan has achieved a GDP one-third that of its giant neighbour, mainland China. Agriculture has declined in relative importance, despite the fertile soil.
Currency: Taiwan dollar.

1895 Taiwan was annexed by the Japanese who began its modernization. **1949** Defeated in the Chinese civil war, Kuomintang forces fled to Taiwan, where a Nationalist government was set up. Under US protection, the resulting authoritarian regime on Taiwan declared itself to be the legitimate government of China. **1971** US rapprochement with mainland China; Taiwan lost its seat in the UN to the People's Republic of China. **1978** USA withdrew recognition. **1980s** Moves towards democracy. **1988** A native Taiwanese elected President. **1991** Taiwan effectively recognized Communist China. New liberal constitution marked the transition to a more Taiwanese, less Chinese, identity. **By 1997** No major countries retained recognition of Taiwan.

Official name: Chung-hua Min-kuo (Republic of China).
Area: 36,179 km² (13,969 sq mi), including Quemoy and Matsu islands.
Population: 21,270,000 (1995 est.).
Doubling time: 67 years. **Adult life expectancy:** male 71.6 years, female 77.6 years. **Birth rate:** 0.61 times world average. **Death rate:** 0.58 times world average.
Urban population: 75%.
Capital: Taipei 3,501,000 urban area (city 2,653,000; Pan-ch'iao 544,000, Sanchung 304,000; 1993 est.). **Other main centres:** Kaohsiung 1,405,000, T'aichung 817,000, Tainan 700,000, Pan-ch'iao *see Taipei*, Chungho 387,000, Chilung (Keelung) 363,000, Hsinchu 335,000, Sanchung *see Taipei* (1993 est.; inc. suburbs).
Language: Chinese ('Mandarin') 13% as a first language but almost universally understood (official), Min 75%, Hakka 10%, Ami 1%.
Adult literacy: 93%.
Religion: Chinese folk religions (inc. Daoism) 48%, Buddhist 43%, various Christian denominations 7%.

MONGOLIA

Mongolia is a large sparsely populated Central Asian republic that forms a buffer between Russia and China. It comprises mountains in the north, a series of basins covered by grasslands (steppes) in the centre and the Gobi Desert and Altai Mountains in the south.
Highest point: Nayramdal Uul (Hüyten Orgil) 4362 m (14,350 ft).
Climate: Mongolia has a dry climate with generally mild summers and severely cold winters.

A President and a 76-member Great Hural are elected for four years by universal adult suffrage. The President nominates a Prime Minister and a Council of Ministers.
Largest parties: (1995 election) (reformist) Democratic Union (DU; comprising the National Democratic Party and the Social Democratic Party) 50 seats, (former Communist) Mongolian People's Revolutionary Party (BDY) 25, Mongolian Traditional Conservative Party 1.
President: (since 1997) Natsagiyn Bagabandi (BDY).
Prime Minister: (since 1996) M. Enkhsaikhan (DU).

Mongolia depends upon the (formerly collectivized) herding of cattle, sheep, goats and camels. Cereals, including cereal crops, are grown on a large scale. The industrial sector is dominated by food processing, hides and wool. Copper is a major export. The former Soviet Union was Mongolia's principal trading partner and Soviet grants represented one-third of Mongolia's GNP. The end of aid from Russia and the disruption of trade since 1991, combined with expensive recent market reforms, have brought severe economic difficulties. **Currency:** Tugrik.

■ *A herder's yurt in the northern Gobi Desert – many agricultural workers are still nomadic*

1911 Mongolia threw off Chinese rule. **1911–18** An autonomous Mongol state under Russian protection. **1921** With Russian assistance, Mongolia finally rejected Chinese overlordship. **1924** A Communist People's Republic of Mongolia was founded. **1946** China recognized Mongolia's independence. **1952–84** Rule by Marshal Tsedenbal, first as PM and after 1974 as President. **1990** Pro-democracy demonstrations; the Communist Party renounced its leading role. **1992** Communist regime dismantled; market reforms began; first multi-party elections.

Official name: Mongol Uls (Mongolia).
Area: 1,566,500 km² (604,800 sq mi).
Population: 2,310,000 (1995 est.).
Doubling time: 44 years. **Adult life expectancy:** male 60 years, female 63.5 years. **Birth rate:** 0.96 times world average. **Death rate:** 0.91 times world average.
Urban population: 59%.
Capital: Ulan Bator (Ulaanbaatar) 680,000 (1994 est.; inc. suburbs).
Other main centres: Darhan 86,000, Erdenet 63,000 (1994 est.).
Language: Khalka Mongolian 79% (official), Kazakh 6%, Dorbed 3%, with Bayad, Buryat and other minorities.
Religion: Tantric Buddhist majority, Sunni Islam minority.

PLACES OF INTEREST

China is now the world's fifth most visited tourist destination. Hong Kong is the main tourist centre of China, attracting one-third of the foreign visitors, one-quarter of whom are Japanese and one-fifth American, mainly independent travellers. In mainland China, however (where over one-third of visitors are Japanese), the independent traveller is in a small minority; most tourists are on organized package tours. Places of interest include Anjang, Beijing (The Forbidden City, 13 Ming Tombs and Imperial Gardens of the Summer Palace), Nanjing, Xian and the River Yangtze.

World Heritage sites include: The Great Wall; Huanglong Scenic and Historic Interest Area; Imperial Palace of the Ming and Qing Dynasties, Beijing; Jiuzhaigou Valley Scenic and Historic Interest Area; Lushan National Park; mausoleum of the first Qin Emperor (terracotta army), Xian; Mt Emei and Leshan giant Buddha; the mountain resort and its outlying temples, Chengde; Peking Man site, Zhoukoudian; the Potala Palace, Lhasa; temple of Confucius, cemetery of Confucius, and Kong Family Mansion, Qufu; Wulingyuan Scenic and Historic Interest Area.

Tiananmen Square, Beijing, is the world's largest square. On its northern side, behind the wall, lies the Forbidden City, once the residence of the emperor.

Shanghai is China's most populous city. Its bustling downtown district is a major commercial centre.

The Great Wall of China, Mutianyu, Hebei Province (see p. 177).

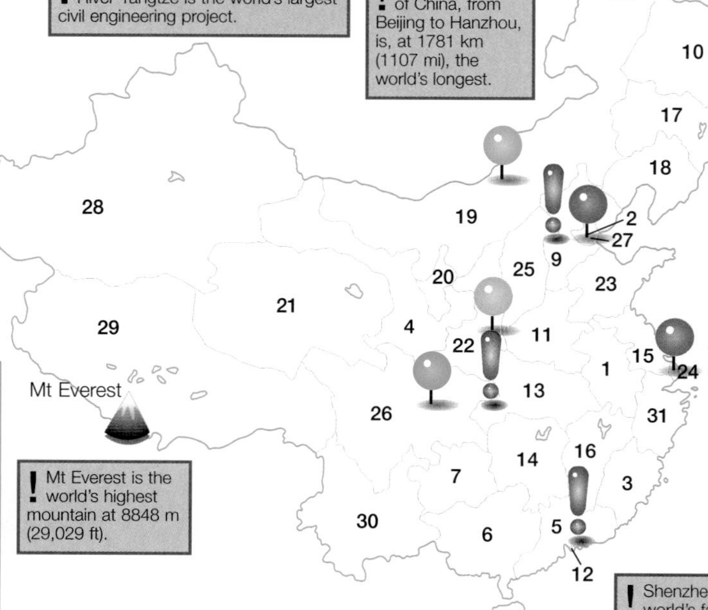

! The Three Gorges Project on the River Yangtze is the world's largest civil engineering project.

! The Grand Canal of China, from Beijing to Hanzhou, is, at 1781 km (1107 mi), the world's longest.

! Mt Everest is the world's highest mountain at 8848 m (29,029 ft).

! Shenzhen is the world's fastest-growing city.

The terracotta army of around 8000 figures, including soldiers and horses, was entombed with emperor Qin Shi Huangdi at Xian when he died in 210 BC. It was discovered in 1974.

The endangered giant panda is only found in central China's mountainous forests (see p. 105).

CHINESE PROVINCES

Anhui (1)
Area: 139,900 km² (54,000 sq mi).
Pop.: 58,970,000 (1994 est.).
Capital: Hefei.

Beijing (Peking) (2)
(municipal province)
Area: 16,800 km² (6500 sq mi).
Pop.: 11,120,000 (1994 est.).
Capital: Beijing.

Fujian (3)
Area: 123,100 km² (47,500 sq mi).
Pop.: 31,500,000 (1994 est.).
Capital: Fuzhou.

Gansu (4)
Area: 366,500 km² (141,500 sq mi).
Pop.: 23,450,000 (1994 est.).
Capital: Lanzhou.

Guangdong (5)
Area: 197,100 km² (76,100 sq mi).
Pop.: 66,070,000 (1994 est.).
Capital: Guangzhou (Canton).

Guangxi Zhuang (6)
(autonomous region)
Area: 220,400 km² (85,100 sq mi).
Pop.: 44,380,000 (1994 est.).
Capital: Nanning.

Guizhou (7)
Area: 174,000 km² (67,200 sq mi).
Pop.: 34,090,000 (1994 est.).
Capital: Guiyang.

Hainan (8)
Area: 34,300 km² (13,200 sq mi).
Pop.: 7,010,000 (1994 est.).
Capital: Haikou.

Hebei (9)
Area: 202,700 km² (78,200 sq mi).
Pop.: 63,340,000 (1994 est.).
Capital: Shijiazhuang.

Heilongjiang (10)
Area: 463,600 km² (179,000 sq mi).
Pop.: 36,400,000 (1994 est.).
Capital: Harbin.

Henan (11)
Area: 167,000 km² (64,500 sq mi).
Pop.: 89,490,000 (1994 est.).
Capital: Zhengzhou.

Hong Kong (12)
(autonomous special administrative region)
Area: 1076 km² (415 sq mi).
Pop.: 6,200,000 (1994 est.).
Capital: Hong Kong.

Hubei (13)
Area: 187,500 km² (72,400 sq mi).
Pop.: 56,530,000 (1994 est.).
Capital: Wuhan.

Hunan (14)
Area: 210,500 km² (81,300 sq mi).
Pop.: 63,110,000 (1994 est.).
Capital: Changsha.

Jiangsu (15)
Area: 102,600 km² (39,600 sq mi).
Pop.: 69,670,000 (1994 est.).
Capital: Nanjing.

Jiangxi (16)
Area: 164,800 km² (63,600 sq mi).
Pop.: 39,660,000 (1994 est.).
Capital: Nanchang.

Jilin (17)
Area: 187,000 km² (72,200 sq mi).
Pop.: 25,550,000 (1994 est.).
Capital: Changchun.

Liaoning (18)
Area: 151,000 km² (58,300 sq mi).
Pop.: 40,420,000 (1994 est.).
Capital: Shenyang.

Nei Monggol (Inner Mongolia) (19)
(autonomous region)
Area: 1,177,500 km² (454,600 sq mi).
Pop.: 22,320,000 (1994 est.).
Capital: Hohhot.

Ningxia Hui (20)
(autonomous region)
Area: 66,400 km² (25,600 sq mi).
Pop.: 4,950,000 (1994 est.).
Capital: Yinchuan.

Qinghai (21)
Area: 721,000 km² (278,400 sq mi).
Pop.: 4,670,000 (1994 est.).
Capital: Xining.

Shaanxi (22)
Area: 195,800 km² (75,600 sq mi).
Pop.: 34,430,000 (1994 est.).
Capital: Xian.

Shandong (23)
Area: 153,300 km² (59,200 sq mi).
Pop.: 86,420,000 (1994 est.).
Capital: Jinan.

Shanghai (24)
(municipal province)
Area: 6200 km² (2400 sq mi).
Pop.: 13,490,000 (1994 est.).
Capital: Shanghai.

Shanxi (25)
Area: 157,100 km² (60,700 sq mi).
Pop.: 30,120,000 (1994 est.).
Capital: Taiyuan.

Sichuan (26)
Area: 569,000 km² (219,700 sq mi).
Pop.: 111,040,000 (1994 est.).
Capital: Chengdu.

Tianjin (Tientsin) (27)
(municipal province)
Area: 11,300 km² (4400 sq mi).
Pop.: 9,280,000 (1994 est.).
Capital: Tianjin.

Xinjiang Uygur (Sinkiang) (28)
(autonomous region)
Area: 1,646,900 km² (635,900 sq mi).
Pop.: 16,050,000 (1994 est.).
Capital: Ürümqi .

Xizang (Tibet) (29)
(autonomous region)
Area: 1,221,600 km² (471,700 sq mi).
Pop.: 2,320,000 (1994 est.).
Capital: Lhasa.

Yunnan (30)
Area: 436,200 km² (168,400 sq mi).
Pop.: 38,850,000 (1994 est.).
Capital: Kunming.

Zhejiang (31)
Area: 101,800 km² (39,300 sq mi).
Pop.: 42,660,000 (1994 est.).
Capital: Hangzhou.

TELEVISION AND RADIO

No. of TVs: 227,880,000 (1.5 persons per TV)
No. of radio receivers: 215,950,000 (5.5 persons per radio)

The Ministry for Radio, TV and Films censors all broadcasts. There are 764 local television stations and the China Central Television Station operates three channels nationwide. A cable network covers some 30,000,000 households. The government has tried to restrict access to foreign satellite broadcasting and cable operators. There are two national radio stations and over 1100 local stations, some broadcasting in local languages. Hong Kong, which has a tradition of free speech, has four TV networks.

CINEMA

No. of cinemas: 3100

Chinese cinema is highly censored, with the Film Bureau (the industry's regulator and chief censor) itself being overseen by the Ministry of Radio, Film and TV, and the propaganda committee of the Chinese Communist Party. In the last couple of years, the first 'big foreign movies' (i.e. Hollywood and Hong Kong block-busters) have been shown in mainland China, practically doubling box-office takings. The profits of revenue-sharing deals with foreign producers are fed into China's own film industry. However, it is not uncommon for Chinese producers to finish their films only to see them rejected by the censors.

NEWSPAPERS

The large circulation figures of the daily press reflect the enormous population of mainland China. There are about 1750 newspapers. Each province publishes its own daily paper. The press is entirely state-controlled. The principal daily titles are:

Sichuan Ribao, Chengdu	8,000,000
Gongren Ribao (trade union paper), Beijing	2,500,000
Renmin Ribao (official organ of the Communist Party of China), Beijing	2,150,000
Wenhui Bao, Shanghai	1,700,000

MAGAZINES

The periodicals with the largest circulations are:

Ban Yue Tan	fortnightly, review	6,000,000
Nongmin Wenzhai ('Peasants Digest')	weekly, rural interest	3,540,000
Jiating ('Family')	weekly, family interest	1,890,000
Qiushi ('Seeking Truth')	bi-monthly, theoretical journal	1,830,000
China TV	weekly, TV listings	1,700,000
Shichang Zhoubao ('Market Weekly')	weekly, economic and financial	1,000,000

HEADS OF STATE (SINCE 1949)

Chairmen of the People's Republic of China

1949–58 Mao Tse-tung (Mao Zedong)
1958–59 Marshal Zhu De
1959–68 Liu Shaoqui
1968–75 Dung Pi Wu

Chairmen of the Permanent Standing Committee of the National People's Congress

1975–76 Zhu De
1976–78 Song Qingling (acting Chairwoman)
1978–83 Ye Jianying

Presidents

1983–88 Li Xiannian
1988–93 Yang Shangkun
1993– Jiang Zemin

LEADERS OF THE COMMUNIST PARTY

1949–76 Mao Tse-tung (Mao Zedong)
1976–81 Hua Guofeng
1981–87 Hu Yaobang
1987–89 Zhao Ziyang
1989– Jiang Zemin

PRIME MINISTERS

1949–76 Zhou Enlai
1976–80 Hua Guofeng
1980–87 Zhao Ziyang
1987– Li Peng

Note: From 1977 to 1997, Deng Xiaoping was the effective ruler of China although he did not hold any of the three major offices of state.

HONG KONG HANDOVER

On 1 July 1997, Hong Kong was handed back to China. The event, which was beamed across the globe, saw the end of 155 years of British involvement in the colony. The process of the handover began in 1984, when the then British PM, Margaret Thatcher, and Zhao Ziyang issued a declaration on Hong Kong's status as a special administrative region under a 'One Country, Two Systems' rule. Social and economic conditions in Hong Kong will remain unchanged for 50 years, under an agreement which grants the region very considerable autonomy. The general mood at handover was one of cautious optimism. Economic investment in the region expanded heavily prior to the reversion, whilst China itself staged a host of celebrations. It is possible that capitalist Hong Kong will change attitudes in Communist China more than China will be able to alter Hong Kong.

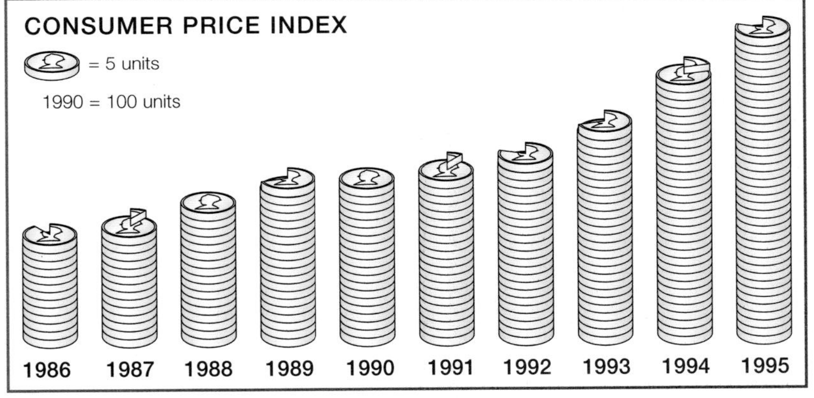

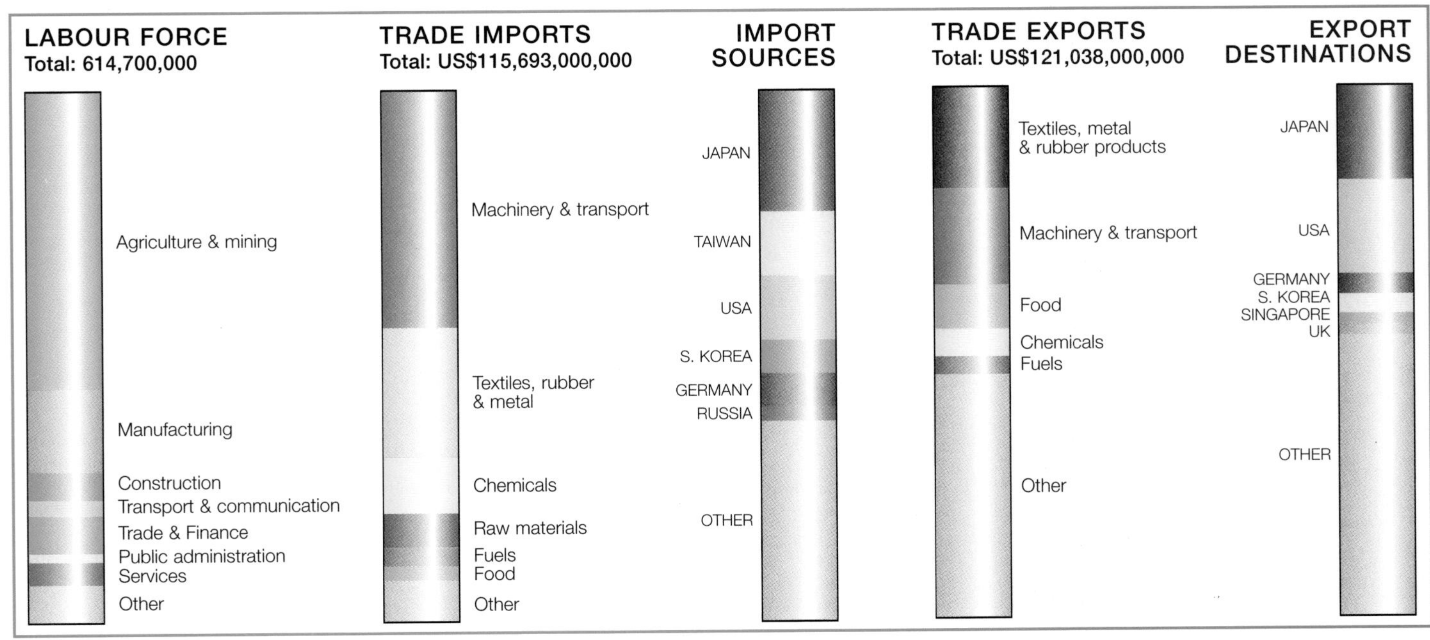

FAR EAST

JAPAN

Japan is an Empire consisting of four main islands and over 3900 smaller islands in the north-east Pacific region of the Far East. Mountainous Hokkaido, in the north, occupies 22% of the total land area, while Shikoku and Kyushu in the south respectively occupy 5% and 11% of the area. The central island of Honshu, down whose spine runs mountain chains, occupies 61% of the area and contains 80% of the population. To the south of the main islands the Ryukyu Islands (including Okinawa) stretch almost to Taiwan. Nearly 75% of the country is mountainous. The population is concentrated into small coastal plains. The principal lowlands are Kanto (around Tokyo), Nobi (around Nagoya) and the Sendai Plain of north Honshu. There are over 60 active volcanoes and Japan is prone to severe earthquakes.
Highest point: Fujiyama 3776 m (12,388 ft). **Climate:** Japan experiences great variations in climate. Although the whole country is temperate, the north has long cold winters, while the south has hot summers and mild winters. Rainfall totals are high, with heavy rain and typhoons common in summer months.

Japan is a constitutional monarchy in which the Emperor has a symbolic role and no executive power. The National Diet comprises the 252-member House of Councillors (upper house) and the 511-member House of Representatives (lower house). The upper house is elected for six years by universal adult suffrage, with one-half of the councillors retiring every three years; 100 of the councillors are elected under a system of proportional representation. The lower house is directly elected for four years.
Largest parties: (House of Representatives 1996 election) (conservative) Liberal Democratic Party (LDP) 239 seats, (centre-right) New Frontier Party (NFP) 156, (anti-bureaucratic) Democracy Party of Japan (Dem) 52, Communist Party (JPC) 26, Social Democratic Party of Japan (SDPJ) 15, New Harbinger Party (Sakigake) 2, others 10.
Emperor: (since 1989) the Heisei Emperor (known outside Japan as Emperor Akihito).
Prime Minister: (since 1996) Ryutaro Hashimoto (LDP; LDP–SDPJ–Sakigake coalition).

Despite the generally crowded living conditions in the cities, the Japanese enjoy one of the highest standards of living in the world. The country has the second largest industrial economy in the world, despite having very few natural resources. Japanese industry is heavily dependent on imported raw material; about 90% of Japan's energy requirements are imported and petroleum is the single largest import. Japan's economic success is based upon manufacturing industry, which, with construction, employs nearly one-third of the labour force. Japan is the world's leading manufacturer of motor vehicles, and one of the major producers of ships, steel, synthetic fibres, chemicals, cement, electrical goods and electronic equipment. Rapid advances in Japanese research and technology have helped the expanding export-led economy, although growth slowed in the 1990s. Japanese industry has established components factories throughout South-East Asia. The banking and financial sectors have prospered and Tokyo is one of the world's main stock exchanges and commercial centres. Agriculture is labour intensive and although Japan is self-sufficient in rice, agriculture is not a priority and a high percentage of food requirements (particularly cereals and fodder crops) have to be imported. The traditional Japanese diet is sea-based and the fishing industry is one the world's largest. **Currency:** Yen.

■ *The Shinjuku district of central Tokyo. With 25 million inhabitants in the urban area, which stretches round Tokyo Bay, the Japanese capital is the world's largest city*

1904–05 Japan startled Europe by beating Russia in war by land and sea. **1912** End of the Meiji era. (The Meiji Emperor had overthrown the last shogun and restored power to the throne. He encouraged Western institutions and a Western-style economy.) **1914–18** Japan involved in World War I against Germany but became disillusioned after the war when not treated as an equal by the Great Powers. **1920s–1930s** Rise of militarism. **1931–32 and 1937–45** War with China: Japan occupied much of coastal China and set up a puppet regime in Manchuria. **1941** Allied to Nazi Germany, Japan entered World War II with a sudden attack on the US base at Pearl Harbor, Hawaii; initial rapid Japanese military expansion across South-East Asia and the Pacific. **1945** USA dropped atomic weapons on Japan; disastrous defeat in the war.
1945–52 Allied occupation of Japan; politics were democratized and rapid economic recovery began.
1946 Emperor renounced divinity.
1955–93 Liberal Democrats held power continuously despite a number of financial scandals.

Official name: Nihon (Japan).
Area: 377,835 km² (145,883 sq mi).
Population: 125,360,000 (1995 est.).
Doubling time: population relatively stable; slight increase only. **Adult life expectancy:** male 76.6 years, female 83 years. **Birth rate:** 0.4 times world average. **Death rate:** 0.76 times world average.
Urban population: 77%.
Capital: Tokyo 25,000,000 urban area (city 11,610,000; Yokohama 3,251,000; Kawasaki 1,168,000; Chiba 834,000; Sagamihara 545,000; Funabashi 529,000; 1992 est.).
Other main centres: Osaka 8,735,000 urban area (city 2,495,000; Kobe 1,468,000; Sakai 799,000; Higashiosaka 496,000), Yokohama *see Tokyo*, Kyoto 2,606,000 (city 1,345,000), Nagoya 2,095,000, Sapporo 1,704,000, Kobe *see Osaka*, Fukuoka 1,214,000, Kawasaki *see Tokyo*, Hiroshima 1,072,000, Kitakyushu 1,015,000, Sendai 920,000, Chiba *see Tokyo*, Sakai *see Osaka*, Kumamoto 625,000, Okayama 595,000, Hamamatsu 548,000, Kagoshima 532,000, Funabashi *see Tokyo* (1992 est.; inc. suburbs).
Language: Japanese over 99% (official), with Korean, Chinese and Ainu minorities.
Adult literacy: virtually 100%.
Religion: Buddhist as a first religion or tradition over 70%, Shinto as a first or sole religion 3–5%, Shinto tradition over 88%, various Christian Churches 1%; up to 50% of the population follow one or more religious tradition rather than practice and could be described as non-religious.

■ JAPAN'S GNP IS 200 TIMES GREATER THAN THAT OF NORTH KOREA ■ THE POPULATION OF

NORTH KOREA

North Korea is a Communist republic occupying the northern (larger) sector of the Korean peninsula in the Far East of Asia. Over three-quarters of the country consists of mountains, which rise in the north-east to the volcanic peak Paek-tu. There is a wide coastal plain in the west.
Highest point: Paek-tu 2744 m (9003 ft).
Climate: Long cold dry winters and hot wet summers.

The Party Congress of the (Communist) Korean Worker's Party elects a Central Committee, which, in turn, elects a Politburo, the seat of effective power. Unopposed elections by universal adult suffrage are held every five years to the 687-member Supreme People's Assembly. The Assembly elects a President (who serves for four years), a Prime Minister and Central People's Committee, which nominates other Ministers.
Only permitted party: Korean Worker's Party (Comm) 687 seats. (The puppet Chongu Party and Korean Social Democratic Party also function.)
President: Vacant, but Kim Jong Il (Comm) has been President in all but name since his father's death in 1994.
Prime Minister: (since 1997) Hong Song-nam (Comm).

Over 40% of the labour force work on co-operative farms, mainly growing rice but in insufficient amounts to feed the isolationist state's population. Natural resources include coal, zinc, magnetite and iron ore. Great emphasis has been placed on industrial development, notably metallurgy and machine-building. The end of barter deals with the former USSR (1990–91) brought a sharp decline in the economy and food, energy and other shortages are increasing. Money sent home by North Koreans working in Japan and Russia is the main foreign-currency earner. **Currency:** Won.

Official name: Choson Minjujuui In'min Konghwaguk (Democratic People's Republic of Korea).
Area: 122,762 km² (47,399 sq mi).
Population: 23,490,000 (1995 est.).
Doubling time: 39 years. **Adult life expectancy:** male 67 years, female 73.7 years. **Birth rate:** 0.93 times world average. **Death rate:** 0.59 times world average.
Urban population: 61%.
Capital: Pyongyang 2,355,000 (1987 est.). **Other main centres:** Hamhung 701,000, Ch'ongjin 520,000, Namp'o 370,000, Sunch'on 356,000 (1987 est.).
Language: Korean almost 100% (official). **Adult literacy:** 95%.
Religion: Non-religious 68%, traditional beliefs 16%, Chondogyo 14%.

1948 The Communist republic founded by the USSR in its zone of occupation of formerly Japanese Korea. **1948–92** Dictatorship of Kim Il-Sung, renowned for his almost religious personality cult. **1950–53** Korean War – see S. Korea. **1990–91** Following the demise of the Communist bloc N. Korea became more isolated. **1994** Tension following N. Korea's refusal to allow international inspection of suspected nuclear weapons. **1997** Famine.

■ *A mourning poster for North Korean dictator Kim Il-Sung, whose personality cult surpassed even those of Hitler and Stalin*

SOUTH KOREA

South Korea is a republic occupying the southern (smaller) sector of the Korean peninsula in the Far East of Asia. Apart from restricted coastal lowlands and the Han and Naktong basins, most of the country is mountainous.

Official name: Taehan Min'guk (The Republic of Korea).
Area: 99,392 km² (38,375 sq mi).
Population: 44,840,000 (1995 est.).
Doubling time: 70 years. **Adult life expectancy:** male 68 years, female 76 years. **Birth rate:** 0.64 times world average. **Death rate:** 0.65 times world average.
Urban population: 81%.
Capital: Seoul (Soul) 10,628,000 (1990 census; inc. suburbs).
Other main centres: Pusan 3,798,000, Taegu 2,229,000, Inchon 1,818,000, Kwangju 1,145,000, Taejon 1,062,000, Ulsan 683,000 (1987 est.).
Language: Korean almost 100% (official). **Adult literacy:** 96%.
Religion: Non-religious 50%, Buddhist 24%, various Protestant Churches 18%, Roman Catholic 6%, Confucian, Chondogyo and other minorities.

Highest point: Halla-san (an extinct volcano on Cheju island) 1950 m (6398 ft). **Climate:** Dry cold winters and hot summers during which the monsoon brings heavy rainfall.

The 299-member National Assembly is elected by universal adult suffrage for four years: 237 members are elected to represent single-member constituencies; 62 members are elected under a system of proportional representation. The executive President (who appoints a State Council headed by a Prime Minister) is directly elected for a maximum of two four-year terms.
Largest parties: (1996 election) (centre-right) New Korea Party (NKP) 139 seats, (centre) National Congress for New Politics 79, (centre-right) United Liberal Democratic Party (ULDP) 51, (centre-left) Democratic Party 15, others 15.
President: (since 1993) Kim Yung Sam (NKP).
Prime Minister: (since 1995) Lee Soo-Sung (NKP).

South Korea is a major industrial power whose industry is dominated by a small number of large family conglomerates. The important textile industry was the original manufacturing base. South Korea is now the world's largest shipbuilder, the major manufacturer of footwear and a major producer of electronic equipment, electrical goods, motor vehicles, steel and petrochemicals. Banking and finance are expanding. South Korea achieved high economic growth rates in the 1980s and 1990s. About 15% of the labour force is involved in farming, with rice and barley as the main crops. **Currency:** Won.

1910 Korea fell victim to harsh Japanese colonial rule; Yi dynasty (which had reigned since 1392) deposed. **1945** Korea divided into US and Soviet zones of occupation after World War II. **1948** The US-supported westernized Republic of Korea was founded in the US zone of occupation. **1950–53** Korean War caused by surprise invasion of the South by the Communist North; much of South Korea overrun before UN forces turned the tide of the war which cost a million lives and confirmed the partition of the peninsula. **1961** Military coup: General Park came to power. **1979** President Park assassinated. **1980** Military coup. **1987** Large-scale student demonstrations in favour of democracy; new constitution adopted. **Since 1987** More open government; increasing democracy.

■ *An array of neon advertisements light up the centre of Seoul, a city which has been largely rebuilt since the devastating effects of the Korean War*

PLACES OF INTEREST

Despite its many scenic and historic attractions, and the modern facilities offered by its major cities and seaside resorts, Japan attracts few (under 3 million) foreign visitors – possibly due to its high cost of living. One-quarter of foreign visitors are from the USA and Canada and a further one-fifth are from Taiwan. The majority of foreign tourists take in Tokyo (including Disneyland), Mt Fuji and the ancient imperial capital of Kyoto. Other popular places include Fukuoka, Kanazawa Shirakawago Snow Country, Kiso Valley, Kobe, Nagoya, Nara, Osaka and Yokahama.

World Heritage sites include: Historic monuments of ancient Kyoto; Buddhist monuments in the Horyuji area; historic villages of Gokayama and Shirakawa-go; Hiroshima Peace Memorial; Shirakami-Sanchi.

! The world's longest rail tunnel is the Seikan tunnel, which is 53.85 km (33 mi 809 yd) long, lying below the seabed between the islands of Honshu and Hokkaido.

Itsuku-shima-jinja is an important Shinto shrine located on an island in the inland sea of Seto. Built in the 6th century, the shrine looks as if it is floating on water at high tide.

! The Nikko Cryptomeria Avenue is the longest avenue of trees in the world. Its three sections converge on Imaichi (Tochigi) and have a total length of 35.41 km (22 mi).

Cherry blossom in Tokyo, a popular spring festival where Japanese celebrate the end of winter by flocking to the parks during cherry blossom time.

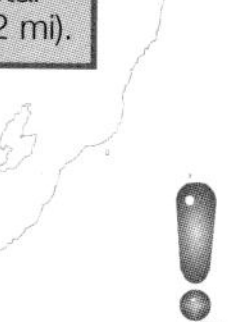

! The world's narrowest navigable strait is the Strait of Dofuchi between Shodoshima island and Mae island. It is 9.93 m (32 ft 7 in) at its narrowest point.

Fujiyama

Mt Fuji (*Fujiyama*), a dormant volcano, is Japan's tallest mountain with a height of 3776 m (12,388 ft). It last erupted in 1707, and its symmetrical and usually snow-capped peak is a popular motif in Japanese arts and crafts.

! The world's largest Ferris wheel is the Cosmoclock 21 at Yokohama. It is 105 m (344 ft 6 in) high.

! The world's longest cable-suspension bridge is the 1991-m (6532-ft) Akashi-Kaikyo bridge, linking Awaji island to Honshu. Opening to traffic in 1998, it is also the world's tallest bridge.

! The world's largest indoor waterpark is Ocean Dome at Miyazaki. It is 300 m (984 ft) long. Miyazaki is traditionally a resort popular with honeymooners.

The Shinto shrine in Ise, established in the 12th century, where priests perform a ceremony. Shinto sites attract millions of Japanese visitors who, today, are more likely to be interested in Shinto as a tradition than a religion.

The Shinkansen, or bullet train, first started operation in 1964, on a route which passes the spectacular Mt Fuji. Eventually, all the major cities of Japan will be linked by this high-speed service.

RECENT EMPERORS

1183–98	Gotoba
1198–1210	Tsuchimikado
1210–21	Juntoku
1221	Chukyo
1221–32	Gonorikawa
1232–42	Shijo
1242–46	Gosaga
1246–59	Gofukakusa
1259–74	Kameyama
1274–87	Go-Uda
1288–98	Fushimi
1301–08	Gonijo
1308–18	Hanazono
1318–39	Godaigo
1339–68	Gomurakami
1368–83	Chokei
1383–92	Gokameyama
1392–1412	Godomatsu
1412–28	Shoko
1428–64	Gohanazono
1465–1500	Gotsuchamikado
1500–26	Gokashiwabara
1526–57	Gonara
1557–86	Ogimachi
1586–1611	Goyozei
1611–29	Gomizuno-o
1629–43	Meisho (Empress)
1643–54	Gokomyo
1654–63	Gosai
1663–87	Reigen
1687–1709	Higashiyama
1709–35	Nakamikado
1735–47	Sakuramachi
1747–62	Momozono
1763–71	Gosakuramachi
1771–79	Gomomozono
1779–1817	Kokaku
1817–46	Ninko
1846–66	Komei (personal name Osahito)
1867–1912	Meiji (personal name Mutsuhito)
1912–26	Taisho (personal name Yoshihito)
1926–89	Showa (personal name Hirohito)
1989–	Heisei (personal name Akihito)

Note: Emperors and empresses can be verified back to Sujin in 30 BC.

TELEVISION AND RADIO

No. of TVs: 100,000,000 (1.2 persons per TV)
No. of radio receivers: 97,000,000 (1.3 persons per radio)

NHK – a non-commercial public corporation – runs two TV and three radio stations. There are 463 commercial radio stations and over 7500 commercial television stations.

CINEMA

No. of cinemas: 1805

Over the last couple of years, Japanese cinema has experienced an increase of film imports from the USA, indeed foreign films as a whole account for some two-thirds of the films distributed. Coupled with the highest average admission price in the world ($12) and a decline in box-office takings, the industry is in the process of a nationwide overhaul – including improving the film theatre infrastructure. However, there is an increased interest in Japanese films around the world, especially Japanese animated films which, like strip cartoon comic books, are hugely popular in Japan.

NEWSPAPERS

Japanese papers enjoy some of the highest circulations in the world. There are over 120 principal daily newspapers in Japan, where 580 copies of papers are printed for every 1000 people. The press is concentrated in Tokyo, whose papers form a national press. There are also important regional papers in Osaka, Nagoya and other major cities. Most Japanese newspapers publish both morning and evening editions. The principal daily titles and their circulation figures are:

Yomiuri Shimbun, Tokyo, Osaka, Seibu and Nagoya	10,000,000	(morning)
	4,500,000	(evening)
Asahi Shimbun, Tokyo, Osaka, Seibu and Chubu	8,300,000	(morning)
	4,400,000	(evening)
Mainichi Shimbun, Tokyo	4,000,000	(morning)
	1,900,000	(evening)
Nihon Keizai Shimbun, Tokyo	2,900,000	(morning)
	1,700,000	(evening)
Chunichi Shimbun, Nagoya	2,900,000	(morning)
	796,000	(evening)

MAGAZINES

In contrast with newspapers, Japanese periodicals have low circulations and, because of the great number of TV stations, TV listings guides are largely absent. The periodicals with the highest circulations are fortnightly magazines (except where indicated):

Title	Type	Circulation
*Ie-no-Hikari**	countryside magazine	1,112,000
Lettuce Club	cookery	800,000
*Bungei-Shunju**	general interest	656,000
Hot-Dog Press	men's magazine	650,000
Croissant	women's and domestic magazine	600,000
Popeye	teenage magazine	600,000

* denotes monthly publication

PRIME MINISTERS (SINCE 1945)

1945–46	Kijuro Shidehara
1946	Ichiro Hatayma
1946–47	Shigeru Yoshida
1947–48	Tetsu Katayama
1948	Hitoshi Ashida
1948–55	Shigeru Yoshida
1955–56	Ichiro Hatoyama
1956–57	Tanzan Ishibashi
1957–60	Nobusuke Kishi
1960–64	Hayeto Ikeda
1964–72	Eisaku Sato
1972–74	Kakeui Tanaka
1974–76	Takeo Miki
1976–78	Takeo Fukuda
1978–80	Masayoshi Ohira
1980–82	Zenko Suzuki
1982–87	Yasuhiro Nakasone
1987–89	Noboru Takeshita
1989	Sosuke Uno
1989–91	Toshiki Kaifu
1991–93	Kiichi Miyazawa
1993–94	Morihiro Hosoakawa
1994	Tsutomu Hata
1994–96	Tomiichi Murayama
1996–	Ryutaro Hashimoto

THE EMPEROR OF JAPAN

The Emperor of Japan is a symbol and head of state, but has no powers. In 1946 the Emperor of a defeated Japan formally renounced his divinity. However, the title by which the head of state is still known in everyday parlance reflects the tradition that he is descended from the Sun Goddess: the emperor is referred to as *Tenno Heika* (meaning 'Heavenly Monarch') and never by his personal name. After death, the emperor is referred to by his reign name (or *nengo*), the title he selects upon accession. Thus, the present monarch is known as *Tenno Heika* or the Heisei Emperor, but his personal name may only be used abroad (where he is called the Emperor Akihito). He will be known to history as the Heisei Emperor.

CONSUMER PRICE INDEX

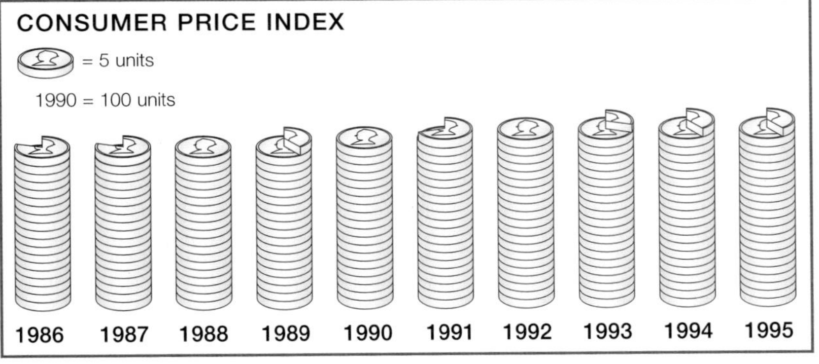

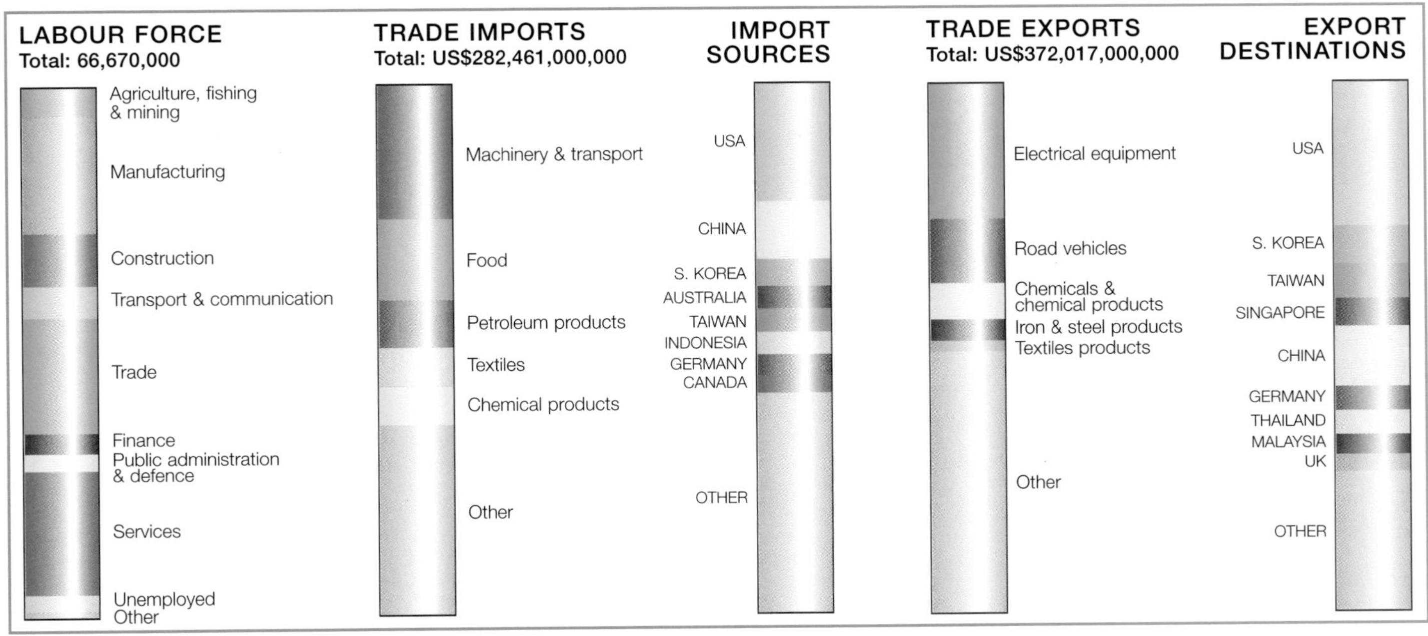

CANADA AND ITS NEIGHBOURS

Greenland
Sisimiut
NUUK
Mackenzie
Pelly
Yukon
Back
Dubawnt
Leaf
Peace
Athabasca
CANADA
Nelson
Grande Rivière
Severn
Saskatchewan
Edmonton
Calgary
Vancouver
Victoria
Regina
Winnipeg
Albany
St John's
St Pierre and Miquelon
Québec
Halifax
Montréal
OTTAWA
Toronto
London
Hamilton

CANADA

Canada, the second largest country in the world, consists of most of the northern half of North America. It is one of the most sparsely populated nations – the overwhelming majority of the population live in the narrow band adjoining the border with the USA. Only about one-half of the country is developed – much of the north is still an untouched wilderness.

Nearly one-half of Canada is covered by the Laurentian (or Canadian) Shield, a relatively flat region of hard rocks stretching round Hudson's Bay. Inland, the Shield ends in an escarpment that is pronounced in the east, beside the St Lawrence River and the Great Lakes. To the west, a line of major lakes (including Lake Winnipeg) marks the boundary with the interior plains, the Prairies. A broad belt of mountains, over 800 km (500 mi) wide, lies west of the plains. The western cordillera comprises the Rocky, Mackenzie, Coast and St Elias mountains, which include Canada's highest peak, Mt Logan. A lower, discontinuous, chain of highlands borders the east of Canada, running from Baffin Island to Nova Scotia.

Highest point: Mt Logan 5951 m (19,524 ft).

Climate: Much of Canada experiences extreme temperatures, with mild summers and long, cold winters. The climate in the far north is polar. Average winter temperatures only remain above freezing point on the Pacific coast. Precipitation is heavy in the west. In the rest of the country rainfall totals are moderate or light. Most of Canada experiences heavy winter snowfalls.

■ Paper mill near Dawson Creek, in the north-eastern part of British Columbia

The Canadian Federal Parliament has two houses: a Senate of 112 members, appointed by the Governor General (the representative of the British monarch as Queen of Canada) to represent the provinces, and the House of Commons, whose 295 members are elected by universal adult suffrage for a five-year term. A Prime Minister, who commands a majority in the House, is appointed by the Governor General. The PM, in turn, appoints a Cabinet of Ministers which is responsible to the House. Each of the provinces has its own legislature with considerable powers.

Largest parties: (House of Commons 1997 election) (centre) Liberal Party (Lib) 155, (right-wing) Reform Party (Reform) 60, (Québec nationalist) Bloc Québecois (BQ) 44, (social democratic) New Democratic Party (NDP) 21, (centre-right) Progressive Conservative Party 20, others 1.

Prime Minister: (since 1993) Jean Chrétien (Lib).

Canada enjoys one of the highest standards of living in the world due, in part, to great mineral resources. There are substantial deposits of zinc, nickel, gold, silver, iron ore, uranium, copper, cobalt and lead, as well as major reserves of petroleum and natural gas and enormous hydroelectric-power potential. These resources are the basis of such industries as petroleum refining, motor vehicles, metal refining, chemicals and iron and steel. Canada

■ IN 1995, QUÉBEC REJECTED SUCESSION BY ONLY 53,498 VOTES ■ DURING PROHIBITION

■ *Bugaboo Glacier in the Bugaboo Mountains, British Columbia, Canada*

is one of the world's leading exporters of cereals, in particular wheat from the Prairie provinces. Other agricultural interests include fruit (mainly apples), beef cattle and potatoes. Vast coniferous forests have given rise to large lumber, wood-pulp and paper industries. Rich Atlantic and Pacific fishing grounds made Canada one of the world's leading exporters of fish and seafood, but depleted stocks have meant that the east coast fishing industry is now in crisis. The country has an important banking and insurance sector. The economy is closely linked with that of the USA within NAFTA and some Canadian industries have been unable to compete with their American counterparts which benefit from a larger home market. **Currency:** Canadian dollar.

1880–1900 Important mineral finds in the north; rapid development of the Prairie provinces. **1914–18** Canadian participation in World War I: Canadian forces distinguished themselves at Vimy Ridge. **1930s** The Depression had a severe impact on Canada. **1931** Canadian independence recognized internationally by the terms of the Statute of Westminster. **1939–45** Canadian participation in World War II, mainly on the West European front. **1949** Bankrupt Newfoundland joined Canada as the tenth province. **Since 1970s** Growing friction over the use and status of the French language. **1990** Constitutional amendments recognizing Québec's special status were rejected. **1995** Québec narrowly rejected cession from Canada in a referendum.

Official name: Canada. **Area:** 9,970,610 km^2 (3,849,674 sq mi). **Population:** 29,460,000 (1995 est.). **Doubling time:** pop. relatively stable. **Adult life expectancy:** male 74.7 years, female 81.7 years. **Birth rate:** 0.52 times world average. **Death rate:** 0.77 times world average. **Urban population:** 77%. **Capital:** Ottawa 921,000 urban area (city 314,000; 1991 census). **Other main centres:** Toronto 3,893,000 urban area (city 636,000), Montréal 3,127,000 (city 1,018,000), Vancouver 1,603,000 (city 472,000), Edmonton 840,000 (city 617,000), Calgary 754,000 (city 711,000), Winnipeg 652,000 (city 617,000), Québec 646,000 (city 168,000), Hamilton 600,000 (city 318,000), London 381,000 (city 303,000), St Catharines-Niagara 365,000 (St Catharines city 129,000), Kitchener 356,000 (city 168,000), Halifax 321,000 (city 114,000), Victoria 288,000 (city 71,000), Windsor 262,000 (city 191,000), Oshawa 240,000 (city 129,000), Saskatoon 210,000 (city 186,000), Regina 192,000 (city 179,000), St John's 172,000 (city 96,000), Chicoutimi-Jonquière 161,000 (Chicoutimi 63,000; Jonquière 58,000), Sudbury 158,000 (city 93,000), Sherbrooke 139,000 (city 76,000), Trois Rivières 136,000 (city 49,000), Saint John 125,000 (city 75,000), Thunder Bay 124,000 (city 114,000) (1991 census). **Language:** English 61% as a first language (official), French 24% as a first language (official), English-French bilingual 3% (first language not specified), German 2%, Chinese 1%, Ukrainian 1%. **Adult literacy:** 97%. **Religion:** Roman Catholic 45%, various Protestant Churches 28%, Anglicans 8%, Orthodox Churches 1%, Jewish 1%, non-religious 12%.

GREENLAND

Official names and status: Grønland (in Danish) or Kalaallit Nunaat (in Greenland Inuit) (Greenland); a Danish dependency with internal self-government.
Area: 2,175,600 km^2 (839,800 sq mi).
Population: 55,700 (1995 est.).
Capital: Nuuk (formerly Godthab) 13,200 (1995 est.).
Other major centre: Sisimiut (formerly Holsteinborg) 5200 (1995 est.).
Geography: Arctic Greenland, the largest non-continental island in the world, has a highly indented fjord coastline. Over four-fifths of the island is covered by a permanent ice-cap. The ice-free land is largely mountainous with a tundra vegetation.
Economy: Greenland relies on fishing and fish-processing. The harsh environment restricts agriculture to 1% of the island in the south-west where hay and vegetables are grown and sheep are kept.

ST PIERRE AND MIQUELON

Official name and status: St-Pierre-et-Miquelon (St Pierre and Miquelon); a French territorial collectivity, a status between that of an overseas département and an overseas territory, and an integral part of the French Republic.
Area: 242 km^2 (93 sq mi).
Population: 6600 (1995 est.).
Capital: St Pierre 5700 (1995 est.).
Geography: The territory comprises three main islands: Miquelon (the largest), Langlade and St Pierre (the smallest), plus three islets, lying 25 km (16 mi) off the south coast of Newfoundland. Miquelon and Langlade are connected by a low isthmus.
Economy: Fishing, fish-freezing and tourism are, apart from government service, the only significant sources of employment.

BERMUDA

Official name and status: Bermuda; a British Crown colony with internal self-government.
Area: 54 km^2 (21 sq mi).
Population: 60,000 (1994 est.).
Capital: Hamilton 6000 urban area (1991 est.).
Geography: Bermuda comprises over 100 small islands in the north-western Atlantic. Seven islands are linked by causeway.
Economy: Tourism dominates the economy, supplying over 60% of foreign-currency earnings and accounting for 65% of employment, both directly and indirectly. There has been an important recent growth of 'offshore' financial services.

CANADIAN PROVINCES AND TERRITORIES

Alberta
Area: 661,190 km^2 (255,287 sq mi).
Pop.: 2,727,000 (1995 est.).
Capital: Edmonton.
British Columbia
Area: 947,800 km^2 (365,948 sq mi).
Pop.: 3,719,000 (1995 est.).
Capital: Victoria.
Manitoba
Area: 649,950 km^2 (250,947 sq mi).
Pop.: 1,133,000 (1995 est.).
Capital: Winnipeg.
New Brunswick
Area: 73,440 km^2 (28,355 sq mi).
Pop.: 761,000 (1995 est.).
Capital: Fredericton.
Newfoundland
Area: 405,720 km^2 (156,649 sq mi).
Pop.: 580,000 (1995 est.).
Capital: St John's.
Nova Scotia
Area: 55,490 km^2 (21,425 sq mi).
Pop.: 938,000 (1995 est.).
Capital: Halifax.
Ontario
Area: 1,068,580 km^2 (412,581 sq mi).
Pop.: 11,005,000 (1993 est.).
Capital: Toronto.
Prince Edward Island
Area: 5660 km^2 (2185 sq mi).
Pop.: 136,000 (1993 est.).
Capital: Charlottetown.
Québec
Area: 1,540,680 km^2 (594,860 sq mi).
Pop.: 7,334,000 (1993 est.).
Capital: Québec.
Saskatchewan
Area: 652,330 km^2 (251,866 sq mi).
Pop.: 1,017,000 (1993 est.).
Capital: Regina.
Northwest Territories
Area: 3,426,320 km^2 (1,322,910 sq mi).
Pop.: 65,000 (1993 est.).
Capital: Yellowknife. In 1999, Northwest Territories will be divided by the creation of Nunavut Territory. Northwest Territory will have an area of 1,224,920 km^2 (477,950 sq mi), a pop. of 41,000 (1993 est.) and its capital will remain Yellowknife. Nunavut Territory will have an area of 2,201,400 km^2 (844,960 sq mi), a pop. of 22,000 (1993 est.) and its capital will be Iqaluit (formerly Frobisher Bay).
Yukon Territory
Area: 483,450 km^2 (186,661 sq mi).
Pop.: 31,000 (1995 est.).
Capital: Whitehorse.

ST PIERRE AND MIQUELON WERE INVOLVED IN SUPPLYING ILLICIT ALCOHOL INTO THE USA

PLACES OF INTEREST

Tourism in Canada is dominated by visitors from the USA, who outnumber other tourists by 11 to 1. Canada offers a mostly unspoilt natural landscape, wide-open spaces and interesting wildlife. The most popular places to visit are almost all within a short distance of the US border, including Banff and Whistler winter ski resorts, Calgary, the Canadian Pacific Railway, Montreal, Niagara Falls, Nova Scotia/Halifax, Ontario, Toronto, Vancouver, the west coast and Vancouver Island.

World Heritage sites include: Canadian Rocky Mountain Parks, including Burgess Shale Site; Head-Smashed-In Buffalo Jump Complex; historic area of Québec; L'Anse aux Meadows National Historic Park; Lunenberg Old Town; Nahanni National Park; Wood Buffalo National Park.

PROVINCES

AB	Alberta	ON	Ontario
BC	British Columbia	PE	Prince Edward Island
MB	Manitoba	PQ	Quebec
NB	New Brunswick	SK	Saskatchewan
NF	Newfoundland	NT	Northwest Territories
NS	Nova Scotia	YT	Yukon Territory

For further information, see p. 425.

Moraine Lake in Banff National Park, Canada's oldest national park, was established in 1885 (see p. 106).

Lake à l'Eau Claire (Clearwater Lake) in northern Quebec. The north of Canada, the Canadian Shield, is an area of ancient hard rocks.

! The Davis Strait, between Baffin Island in Canada and Greenland, is the world's broadest strait, 338 km (210 mi) wide.

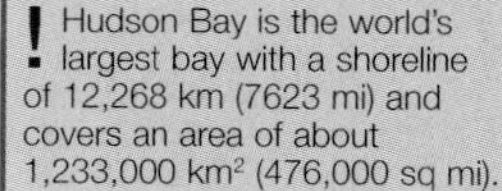

! Hudson Bay is the world's largest bay with a shoreline of 12,268 km (7623 mi) and covers an area of about 1,233,000 km^2 (476,000 sq mi).

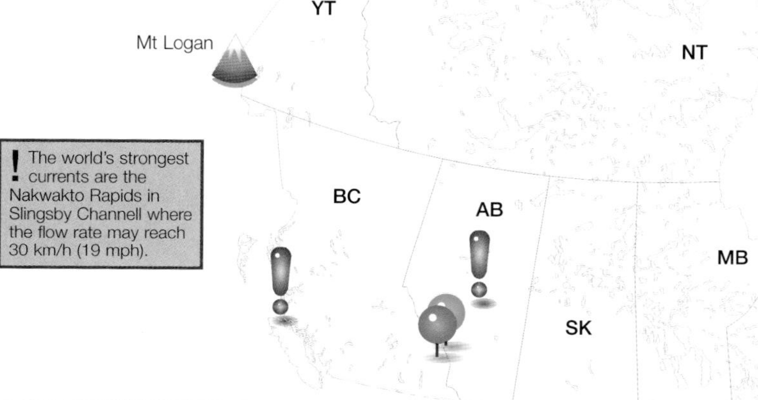

! The world's strongest currents are the Nakwakto Rapids in Slingsby Channell where the flow rate may reach 30 km/h (19 mph).

Kootenay National Park with snow-clad pines on a mountain slope. The lakes, waterfalls, forest and fauna (including caribou, elk, moose and bears) attract many visitors.

! The world's largest shopping mall is the US$1.1-billion West Edmonton Mall, which opened on 15 September 1981 and was completed four years later. It covers 483,000 m^2 (5.2 million sq ft) on a 49-ha (121-acre) site and includes 800 stores and 11 major department stores.

The CN Tower in Toronto is the world's tallest free-standing tower, dominating the city skyline (see p. 177).

Confederation Bridge, joining Prince Edward Island to the Canadian mainland, is 12.9 km (8 mi) long. It is the world's longest bridge continuing over sea (see p. 176).

TELEVISION AND RADIO

No. of TVs: 19,400,000 (1.5 persons per TV).
No. of radio receivers: 26,878,000 (1.1 persons per radio).

The Canadian Broadcasting Corporation (CBC), established in 1968, is a public corporation, operating both TV and radio channels. CBC broadcasts in English and French, and (in the north) in the local languages of Dene and Inuktitut. There are many privately owned TV and radio stations, most of which have affiliations with CBC. The four main private networks are CTV, TVA (serving Ontario), Quatre Saisons (serving Quebec) and Global (serving Ontario). Satellite and cable TV are received by over 75% of households. US channels are also popular.

CINEMA

No. of cinemas: 775

In recent years, American production companies have flocked to Canada, largely because of a beneficial exchange rate and consequent cheaper productions, which has led to Canada becoming known as 'Hollywood North'. This is encouraged by the Canadian government, which sees it as a more profitable alternative to investing in and subsidizing Canada's own film-making industry. The province of Quebec has been able to maintain a much healthier indigenous film and TV industry than the nation as a whole, due to its strong regional identity.

NEWSPAPERS

Satellite transmission has enabled the Toronto-based *Globe and Mail* and *The Financial Post* to achieve national circulations, but the Canadian press remains regional. There are 106 daily newspapers, with those in Quebec province published mainly in French. The principal daily titles are:

Toronto Star	503,000 (Saturday edition 743,000)
Globe and Mail	318,000
Le Journal de Montréal	288,000 (weekend edition 332,000)
Toronto Sun	245,000 (Sunday edition 415,000)
The Vancouver Sun	194,000 (Sunday edition 256,000)
The Financial Post	101,000 (Saturday edition 203,000)

MAGAZINES

Some of the large circulation Canadian magazines are published in both English and French. Many magazines have suffered due to competition from the US market. The principal magazines and their circulation figures are:

Chatelaine	monthly, women's magazine	1,074,000 (English & French editions)
WestWorld Magazine	quarterly, regional	853,000
TV Guide	weekly, TV listings	815,000
Leisure Ways	six times a year, general interest	614,000
Canadian Living	monthly, general interest	593,000
Maclean's Canada's Weekly News magazine	weekly, general interest	539,000

PRIME MINISTERS

1867–73	Sir John Alexander MacDonald
1873–78	Alexander MacKenzie
1878–91	Sir John Alexander MacDonald
1891–92	Sir John Joseph Caldwell Abbott
1892–94	Sir John Sparrow David Thompson
1894–96	Sir MacKenzie Bowell
1896	Sir Charles Tupper
1896–1911	Sir Wilfred Laurier
1911–20	Sir Robert Laird Borden
1920–21	Arthur Meighen
1921–26	William Lyon MacKenzie King
1926	Arthur Meighen
1926–30	William Lyon MacKenzie King
1930–35	Richard Bedford Bennett
1935–48	William Lyon MacKenzie King
1948–57	Louis Stephen St Laurent
1957–63	John George Diefenbaker
1963–68	Lester Bowles Pearson
1968–79	Pierre Elliott Trudeau
1979–80	Charles Joseph Clark
1980–84	Pierre Elliott Trudeau
1984	John Napier Turner
1984–93	Brian Mulroney
1993	Kim Campbell
1993–	Jean Chrétien

The Mounties (Royal Canadian Mounted Police) are Canada's federal police force and an internationally recognized symbol of Canada. They also serve as the provincial and criminal police in all provinces except Québec and Ontario. Founded in 1873, they were originally set up to sort out problems caused by US traders selling cheap whiskey to Amer-Indians in exchange for buffalo hides. They were so successful at this task that they soon became a vital institution.

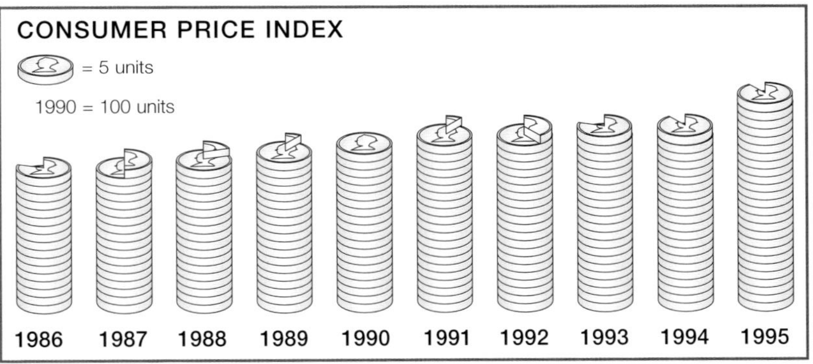

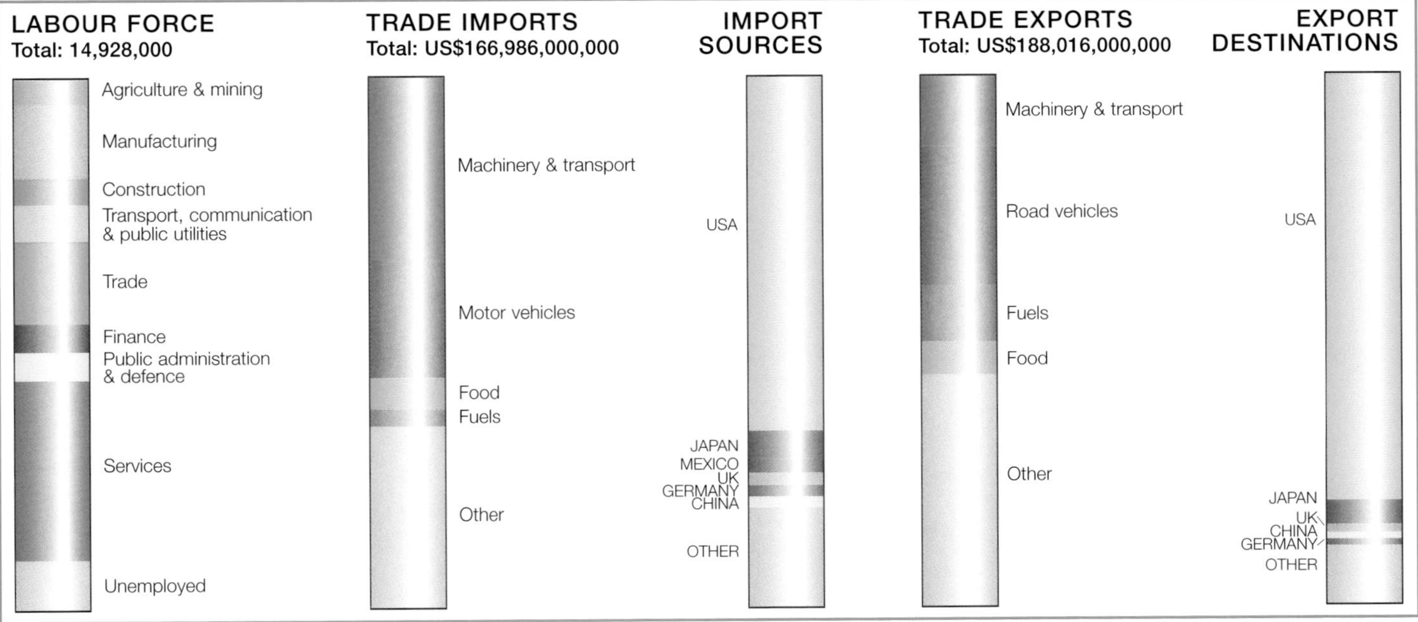

United States of America

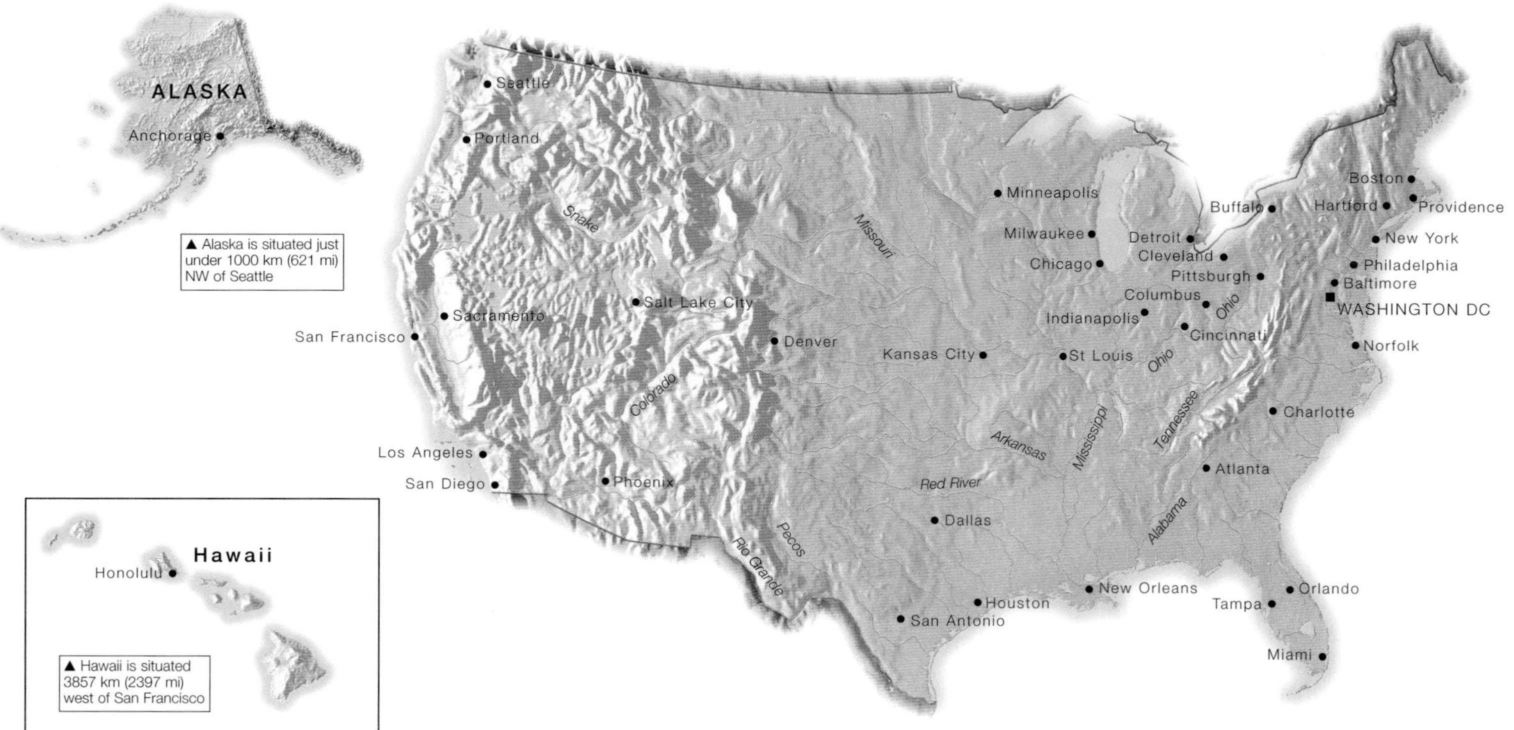

The USA is a republic of 50 states stretching from the North Atlantic to the Pacific Ocean and including Alaska (to the north-west of Canada) and the islands of Hawaii in the middle of the Pacific. The Atlantic coastal plain stretches along the entire east coast, including the lowland peninsula of Florida, and along the coast of the Gulf of Mexico, where it reaches 800 km (500 mi) inland. The Blue Ridge escarpment rises sharply to the west of the plain. This is the most easterly part of the forested Appalachian Mountains, which stretch for some 2400 km (1500 mi) and reach 2037 m (6684 ft) at Mt Mitchell. The largest physical region of the USA is the vast interior plain, drained by the Mississippi and major tributaries including the Missouri, Arkansas, Nebraska, Ohio and Red rivers. This lowland extends from the Great Lakes in the north to the coastal plain in the south, and from the Rocky Mountains in the west to the Appalachians in the east. The Central Lowlands (the eastern part of this lowland) comprise the cotton belt in the south and the corn (maize) belt in the north. The Great Plains (the drier western part of this great lowland) begin some 480 km (300 mi) west of the Mississippi. The west of the USA is the country's highest region and includes the Rocky Mountains in the east and the Cascades, the Sierra Nevada and the Coastal Ranges in the west. The mountains continue north into Alaska. The western mountain belt is prone to earthquakes, in particular along the line of the San Andreas Fault in California. Within the mountains are deserts, including the Mojave and the Arizona deserts, and the large Intermontane Plateau containing the Great Basin, an area of internal drainage to the Great Salt Lake. The 20 islands of Hawaii are volcanic in origin and contain active volcanoes. The USA's natural vegetation ranges from tundra in Alaska to tropical vegetation in Hawaii.

Highest point: Mt McKinley 6194 m (20,320 ft).

Climate: The mountains behind the Pacific north-west coast are the wettest region of the USA. Coastal California has a Mediterranean climate. Desert or semidesert conditions prevail in mountain basins. The continental Great Plains receive 250–750 mm (10–30 in) of rain a year, while the Central Lowlands to the east are generally wetter. Extremes of temperature are experienced in the north of the continental interior. The east is generally temperate. The Appalachians and the east coastal plain are humid, with temperatures rising in the south where Florida is subtropical. Coastal Alaska has a cold maritime climate while the north and interior are polar. Hawaii has a Pacific climate with high temperatures and little seasonal variation.

Congress comprises the Senate (the Upper House) and the House of Representatives (the Lower House). The Senate has 100 members (two from each state) elected by universal adult suffrage for six years, with one-third of the senators retiring every two years. The 435-member House of Representatives is directly elected for a two-year term from single-member constituencies. (Additional non-voting members of the House are returned by the District of Columbia, Guam, Puerto Rico and the US Virgin Islands.) Executive power is vested in the President, who serves a maximum of two four-year terms. The President and Vice-President are elected by an electoral college of delegates pledged to support individual presidential candidates (the college itself is elected by universal adult suffrage). Upon the approval of the Senate, the President appoints a Cabinet of Secretaries. Each of the 50 states has its own constitution and legislature with wide-ranging powers. Executive power in each state is exercised by a directly elected Governor.

Largest parties: (House 1996 election) (centre-right) Republican Party (Rep) 227 seats, (centre) Democratic Party (Dem) 207, independent 1.

Largest parties: (Senate 1996 election) Republican Party 55 seats, (centre) Democratic Party 45.

Official name: United States of America.
Area: 9,529,063 km^2 (3,679,460 sq mi).
Population: 263,060,000 (1995 est.).
Doubling time: over 100 years.
Adult life expectancy: male 71.6 years, female 78.5 years.
Birth rate: 0.56 times world average.
Death rate: 0.91 times world average.
Urban population: 76%.
Capital: Washington DC 4,360,000 urban area (city 570,000; 1992 est.).
Other main centres: New York 19,670,000 urban area (city 7,323,000; Newark 275,000), Los Angeles 15,048,000 (city 3,486,000; Long Beach 439,000; Anaheim 274,000), Chicago 8,410,000 (city 2,784,000), San Francisco 6,410,000 (city 724,000; San José 782,000; Oakland 372,000), Philadelphia 5,939,000 (city 1,586,000), Boston 5,439,000 (city 574,000), Detroit 5,246,000 (city 1,028,000), Dallas 4,215,000 (city 1,008,000; Fort Worth 448,000), Houston 3,962,000 (city 1,630,000), Miami 3,309,000 (city 359,000), Atlanta 3,143,000 (city 394,000), Seattle 3,131,000 (city 516,000), Cleveland 2,890,000 (city 506,000), Minneapolis-St Paul 2,618,000 (Minneapolis 368,000; St Paul 272,000), San Diego 2,601,000 (city 1,111,000), St Louis 2,519,000 (city 397,000), Baltimore 2,434,000 (city 736,000), Pittsburgh 2,406,000 (city 370,000), Phoenix 2,330,000 (city 983,000), Tampa 2,107,000 (city 280,000; St Petersburg 242,000), Denver 2,089,000 (city 468,000), Portland 1,897,000 (city 439,000), Cincinnati 1,865,000 (city 364,000), Milwaukee 1,629,000 (city 628,000), Kansas City 1,617,000 (city 435,000), Sacramento 1,563,000 (city 369,000), Norfolk 1,497,000 (city 261,000), Indianapolis 1,424,000 (city 731,000), Columbus 1,394,000 (city 633,000), San Antonio 1,379,000 (city 936,000), Orlando 1,359,000 (city 174,000), New Orleans 1,303,000 (city 497,000), Charlotte 1,212,000 (city 396,000), Buffalo 1,194,000 (city 328,000), Hartford 1,156,000 (city 140,000), Providence 1,131,000 (city 155,000), Salt Lake City 1,128,000 (city 160,000), Rochester 1,081,000 (city 232,000), Greensboro 1,078,000 (city 184,000), Memphis 1,034,000 (city 610,000), Nashville 1,023,000 (city 517,000), Las Vegas 971,000 (city 258,000) (1992 est.).
Language: English 86% as a first language (official), Spanish 8%, French 1%.
Adult literacy: 95%.
Religion: Various Protestant Churches 40%, Roman Catholic 21%, Christians not belonging to any Church 17%, Orthodox 2%, Anglicans 1%, Scientologists 3%, Jewish 2%, Sunni and Shia Islam 2%, non-religious 9%.

■ THE USA GENERATES OVER 7 TONNES OF HAZARDOUS WASTE EVERY SECOND ■ THERE ARE

President: (since 1993) Bill (William Jefferson) Clinton (Dem).

The position of the USA as the world's leading economic power is threatened in some fields by Japan. The USA is self-sufficient in most products apart from petroleum, chemicals, certain metals and manufactured machinery, and newsprint. Agriculture is heavily mechanized and produces considerable surpluses for export. The main crops include maize (corn), wheat, soyabeans, sugar cane, barley, cotton, potatoes, and a wide variety of fruit (including citrus fruit in California and Florida). More than one-quarter of the USA is pastureland, and cattle and sheep are important in the Great Plains. Forests cover about one-third of the country and are the basis of one the world's largest timber industries. The USA has great natural resources, including coal (mainly in the Appalachians), iron ore, petroleum and natural gas (mainly in Texas, Alaska and California), copper, bauxite, lead and silver, and major rivers that have proved suitable for hydroelectric power plants. The industrial base of the USA is diverse. Principal industries include iron and steel, motor vehicles, electrical and electronic engineering, food processing, chemicals, cement, aluminium, aerospace industries, telecommunications, textiles and clothing, and consumer goods. Tourism is a major foreign-currency earner. Service industries involve about three-quarters of the labour force. Finance, insurance and banking are important, and Wall Street (New York) is one of the world's three major stock exchanges. US economic policy exerts a powerful influence throughout the world. **Currency:** US dollar.

1880–1900 Emergence of the USA as an industrial giant. **1898** War with Spain led to cession of the Philippines, Puerto Rico and Guam to the USA. Hawaii annexed. **1917–18** US participation in World War I. **After 1919–21** President Wilson's idealistic 14 Points led to foundation of League of Nations but USA retreated into isolationism and protectionism. **1919–34** Prohibition: increased smuggling and rise of gangsterism. **1929** Wall Street Crash: beginning of the Depression. **1933** Start of President Roosevelt's New Deal, a programme of federal investment and intervention to bring relief to those hit by the Depression. **1941** Japanese attack on Pearl Harbor (Hawaii). **1941–45** US involvement in World War II was decisive, committing the USA to a world role. **Late 1940s–late 1980s** USA confronted the USSR's perceived global threat in the Cold War. **1950–53** US involvement in Korean War against Chinese and N. Korean forces. **1954** US military involvement in Guatemala. **After 1954** The civil rights movement, led by Martin Luther King, campaigned for full political rights for Blacks and for desegregation of schools, hospitals, buses, etc. **1958** US military involvement in Lebanon. **Early 1960s** Racial discrimination became illegal. **1961** US-backed unsuccessful invasion of Cuba by right-wing exiles. **1963** Assassination of President Kennedy. **1964–73** Involvement in Vietnam where US forces attempted to hold back a Communist takeover of Indochina. **1965** US military involvement in the Dominican Republic. **1968** Assassination of Martin Luther King; US military involvement in Panama. **1970s** Growing economic problems. **1973–74** Watergate scandal: resignation of President Nixon. **1979–80** US hostages held in Iran. **1983** US military involvement in Grenada. **1983–85** US military involvement in Lebanon. **1989** US military involvement in Panama. **1990–91** USA led the coalition against Iraq in the Gulf War. **After 1990** Some overseas bases closed following the end of the Cold War. **1992** USA led international relief efforts in Somalia. **1994** US military involvement in Haiti. **1995** US-brokered Bosnian peace deal; US forces involved in peace-keeping in the former Yugoslavia.

Dependencies

American Samoa (see p. 479), Guam (p. 477), Howland, Baker and Jarvis Islands (p. 477), Johnston Atoll (p. 477), Kingman Reef (p. 477), Midway Islands (p. 477), Northern Mariana Islands (p. 477), Puerto Rico (p. 439), Virgin Islands of the United States (p. 439), and Wake Island (p. 477).

US STATES

Alabama
Area: 133,915 km² (51,705 sq mi).
Pop.: 4,274,000 (1995 est.).
Capital: Montgomery.

Alaska
Area: 1,530,693 km² (591,004 sq mi).
Pop.: 634,000 (1995 est.).
Capital: Juneau.

Arizona
Area: 295,259 km² (114,000 sq mi).
Pop.: 4,072,000 (1995 est.).
Capital: Phoenix.

Arkansas
Area: 137,754 km² (53,187 sq mi).
Pop.: 2,468,000 (1995 est.).
Capital: Little Rock.

California
Area: 411,407 km² (158,860 sq mi).
Pop.: 32,398,000 (1995 est.).
Capital: Sacramento.

Colorado
Area: 269,594 km² (104,091 sq mi).
Pop.: 3,710,000 (1995 est.).
Capital: Denver.

Connecticut
Area: 12,997 km² (5018 sq mi).
Pop.: 3,274,000 (1995 est.).
Capital: Hartford.

Delaware
Area: 5294 km² (2045 sq mi).
Pop.: 718,000 (1995 est.).
Capital: Dover.

Florida
Area: 151,939 km² (58,664 sq mi).
Pop.: 14,210,000 (1995 est.).
Capital: Tallahassee.

Georgia
Area: 152,576 km² (58,910 sq mi).
Pop.: 7,102,000 (1995 est.).
Capital: Atlanta.

Hawaii
Area: 16,760 km² (6471 sq mi).
Pop.: 1,221,000 (1995 est.).
Capital: Honolulu.

Idaho
Area: 216,430 km² (83,564 sq mi).
Pop.: 1,156,000 (1995 est.).
Capital: Boise.

Illinois
Area: 149,885 km² (57,871 sq mi).
Pop.: 11,853,000 (1995 est.).
Capital: Springfield.

Indiana
Area: 94,309 km² (36,413 sq mi).
Pop.: 5,820,000 (1995 est.).
Capital: Indianapolis.

Iowa
Area: 145,752 km² (56,275 sq mi).
Pop.: 2,861,000 (1995 est.).
Capital: Des Moines.

Kansas
Area: 213,096 km² (82,277 sq mi).
Pop.: 2,601,000 (1995 est.).
Capital: Topeka.

Kentucky
Area: 104,659 km² (40,410 sq mi).
Pop.: 3,851,000 (1995 est.).
Capital: Frankfort.

Louisiana
Area: 123,677 km² (47,752 sq mi).
Pop.: 4,359,000 (1995 est.).
Capital: Baton Rouge.

Maine
Area: 86,156 km² (33,265 sq mi).
Pop.: 1,236,000 (1995 est.).
Capital: Augusta.

Maryland
Area: 27,091 km² (10,460 sq mi).
Pop.: 5,078,000 (1995 est.).
Capital: Annapolis.

Massachusetts
Area: 21,455 km² (8284 sq mi).
Pop.: 5,976,000 (1995 est.).
Capital: Boston.

Michigan
Area: 251,493 km² (97,102 sq mi).
Pop.: 9,575,000 (1995 est.).
Capital: Lansing.

Minnesota
Area: 224,329 km² (86,614 sq mi).
Pop.: 4,619,000 (1995 est.).
Capital: St Paul.

Mississippi
Area: 123,514 km² (47,689 sq mi).
Pop.: 2,666,000 (1995 est.).
Capital: Jackson.

Missouri
Area: 180,514 km² (69,697 sq mi).
Pop.: 5,286,000 (1995 est.).
Capital: Jefferson City.

Montana
Area: 380,847 km² (147,046 sq mi).
Pop.: 862,000 (1995 est.).
Capital: Helena.

Nebraska
Area: 200,349 km² (77,355 sq mi).
Pop.: 1,644,000 (1995 est.).
Capital: Lincoln.

Nevada
Area: 286,352 km² (110,561 sq mi).
Pop.: 1,477,000 (1995 est.).
Capital: Carson City.

New Hampshire
Area: 24,032 km² (9279 sq mi).
Pop.: ,1,132,000 (1995 est.).
Capital: Concord.

New Jersey
Area: 20,168 km² (7787 sq mi).
Pop.: 7,931,000 (1995 est.).
Capital: Trenton.

New Mexico
Area: 314,924 km² (121,593 sq mi).
Pop.: 1,676,000 (1995 est.).
Capital: Santa Fe.

New York
Area: 136,583 km² (52,735 sq mi).
Pop.: 18,178,000 (1995 est.).
Capital: Albany.

North Carolina
Area: 136,412 km² (52,669 sq mi).
Pop.: 7,150,000 (1995 est.).
Capital: Raleigh.

North Dakota
Area: 183,117 km² (70,702 sq mi).
Pop.: 637,000 (1995 est.).
Capital: Bismarck.

Ohio
Area: 115,998 km² (44,787 sq mi).
Pop.: 11,203,000 (1995 est.).
Capital: Columbus.

Oklahoma
Area: 181,185 km² (69,956 sq mi).
Pop.: 3,271,000 (1995 est.).
Capital: Oklahoma City.

Oregon
Area: 251,418 km² (97,073 sq mi).
Pop.: 3,141,000 (1995 est.).
Capital: Salem.

Pennsylvania
Area: 119,251 km² (46,043 sq mi).
Pop.: 12,134,000 (1995 est.).
Capital: Harrisburg.

Rhode Island
Area: 3139 km² (1212 sq mi).
Pop.: 1,001,000 (1995 est.).
Capital: Providence.

South Carolina
Area: 80,582 km² (31,113 sq mi).
Pop.: 3,732,000 (1995 est.).
Capital: Columbia.

South Dakota
Area: 199,730 km² (77,116 sq mi).
Pop.: 735,000 (1995 est.).
Capital: Pierre.

Tennessee
Area: 109,152 km² (42,144 sq mi).
Pop.: 5,228,000 (1995 est.).
Capital: Nashville.

Texas
Area: 691,027 km² (266,807 sq mi).
Pop.: 18,592,000 (1995 est.).
Capital: Austin.

Utah
Area: 219,887 km² (84,899 sq mi).
Pop.: 1,944,000 (1995 est.).
Capital: Salt Lake City.

Vermont
Area: 24,900 km² (9614 sq mi).
Pop.: 579,000 (1995 est.).
Capital: Montpelier.

Virginia
Area: 105,586 km² (40,767 sq mi).
Pop.: 6,646,000 (1995 est.).
Capital: Richmond.

Washington
Area: 176,479 km² (68,139 sq mi).
Pop.: 5,497,000 (1995 est.).
Capital: Olympia.

West Virginia
Area: 62,758 km² (24,232 sq mi).
Pop.: 1,824,000 (1995 est.).
Capital: Charleston.

Wisconsin
Area: 171,496 km² (66,215 sq mi).
Pop.: 5,159,000 (1995 est.).
Capital: Madison.

Wyoming
Area: 253,324 km² (97,809 sq mi).
Pop.: 487,000 (1995 est.).
Capital: Cheyenne.

District of Columbia
Area: 179 km² (69 sq mi).
Pop.: 559,000 (1995 est.).
Capital: Washington DC.

PLACES OF INTEREST

Tourism has become a major source of revenue for the USA, which has 45,000,000 visitors a year. In terms of numbers of visitors, California (particularly Disneyland, Golden Gate Recreational Area, Hollywood, Beverly Hills and Sunset Boulevard and the south-east), Florida (particularly Disney World, The Epcot Center, Universal Studios and NASA Space Center) and New York City (particularly Central Park and the Empire State Building) are the most popular destinations. Other places popular with visitors include Cape Cod National Sea Shore, Chicago, Death Valley, Delaware Water Gap National Recreational Area, George Washington Memorial National Park, The Rockies and The White House in Washington, DC.

World Heritage sites include: Carlsbad Cavern National Park; Chaco Culture National Historic Park; Everglades National Park; Grand Canyon; Great Smokey Mountains National Park; Hawaii Volcanoes National Park; Independence Hall; Mammoth Cave National Park; Mesa Verde National Park; Monticello and University of Virginia, Charlottesville; Olympic National Park; Pueblo de Taos; Redwood National Park; San Juan National Historic Site and La Fortaleza; Statue of Liberty; Yellowstone National Park; Yosemite National Park.

Niagara Falls in New York State (see p. 142) receives millions of visitors a year, and is an extremely popular honeymoon destination.

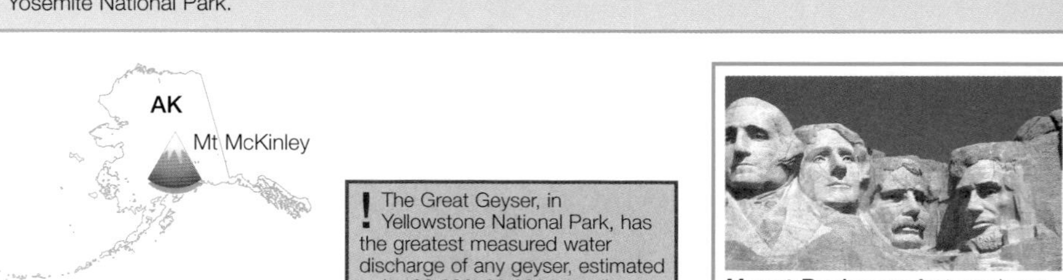

Mount Rushmore features huge sculptures (see p. 177) of presidents (left to right) Washington, Jefferson, T. Roosevelt and Lincoln.

! The Great Geyser, in Yellowstone National Park, has the greatest measured water discharge of any geyser, estimated to be 28,000–38,000 hectolitres (616,000–836,000 gal).

! The Metropolitan Opera House, New York City, is the world's largest, with room for an audience of 4065.

The Golden Gate Bridge, the symbol of San Francisco, is now the second-tallest bridge in the world.

The White House is the official residence of the US president. Tours of the building are the most popular tourist attraction in the US capital.

! Yuma, Arizona, is the sunniest place in the world, with an average of 4055 out of 4456 possible hours of sun.

! Galveston has the longest breakwater in the world at 10.9 km (6.75 mi).

Niihau, with the small island of Lehau to the north, is the westernmost of the eight islands forming the state of Hawaii. The island of Oahu, and particularly the capital city, Honolulu, is the main Hawaiian tourist destination.

Downtown LA. Tours of the Hollywood studios and other sites associated with the film industry are among Los Angeles's many attractions.

STATES

For further information, see p. 429, pp. 432–433.

Paria Plateau, just north-east of the Grand Canyon, has similar layers of sandstone, which can be seen throughout the Grand Canyon area.

The Epcot Center, a cross between a science museum and a theme park, is part of Disney World, Florida's greatest tourist attraction.

PRESIDENTS

Years	President
1789–97	George Washington
1797–1801	John Adams
1801–09	Thomas Jefferson
1809–17	James Madison
1817–25	James Monroe
1825–29	John Quincy Adams
1829–37	Andrew Jackson
1837–41	Martin Van Buren
1841	William H. Harrison
1841–45	John Tyler
1845–49	James K. Polk
1849–50	Zachary Taylor
1850–53	Millard Fillmore
1853–57	Franklin Pierce
1857–61	James Buchanan
1861–65	Abraham Lincoln
1865–69	Andrew Johnson
1869–77	Ulysses Simpson Grant
1877–81	Rutherford B. Hayes
1881	James A. Garfield
1881–85	Chester A. Arthur
1885–89	Grover Cleveland
1889–93	Benjamin Harrison
1893–97	Grover Cleveland
1897–1901	William McKinley
1901–09	Theodore Roosevelt
1909–13	William H. Taft
1913–21	Woodrow Wilson
1921–23	Warren Gamaliel Harding
1923–29	Calvin Coolidge
1929–33	Herbert C. Hoover
1933–45	Franklin Delano Roosevelt
1945–53	Harry S. Truman
1953–61	Dwight D. Eisenhower
1961–63	John Fitzgerald Kennedy
1963–69	Lyndon B. Johnson
1969–74	Richard M. Nixon
1974–77	Gerald R. Ford
1977–81	James Earl (Jimmy) Carter
1981–89	Ronald Reagan
1989–93	George Bush
1993–	William J. (Bill) Clinton

TELEVISION AND RADIO

No. of TVs: 211,000,000 (1.2 persons per TV)
No. of radio receivers: 538,000,000 (0.5 persons per radio)

Broadcast media is big business in the USA. There are nearly 1600 commercial TV stations and 325 educational TV stations. About 10,100 commercial and educational radio stations exist. Cable television is widespread, with over 11,000 systems operating to over 60 million households.

NEWSPAPERS

In the USA there are almost 1550 daily newspapers – 44 of which have a circulation of over 250,000 – with a combined circulation of nearly 60 million. American daily papers place great emphasis on local news because of the strong interest in state, as opposed to national, news. The size of the USA has prevented the emergence of a national press, although the *Wall Street Journal* and the *New York Times* (both of which are printed at several locations) and the *Washington Post*, the *Los Angeles Times* and the Boston-based *Christian Science Monitor* enjoy national readerships. There are nine major newspaper groups. Newspaper circulations have fallen significantly, particularly among young people who tend to rely upon television for news. The daily papers with the biggest circulations are:

Wall Street Journal (New York)	1,841,000	
USA Today (New York)	1,524,000	
New York Times	1,082,000	(1,721,000 Sunday edition)
Los Angeles Times	1,062,000	(1,502,000 Sunday edition)
Washington Post	794,000	(1,163,000 Sunday edition)
New York Daily News	753,000	(931,000 Sunday edition)
Newsday (New York)	694,000	(827,000 Sunday edition)
Chicago Tribune	685,000	(1,083,000 Sunday edition)
Detroit Free Press	550,000	(1,173,000 Sunday edition)
San Francisco Chronicle	510,000	(704,000 Sunday edition)
Chicago Sun-Times	501,000	(469,000 Sunday edition)
Boston Globe	507,000	(798,000 Sunday edition)
Philadelphia Inquirer	475,000	(925,000 Sunday edition)
Atlanta Journal-Constitution	310,000	(723,000 Sunday edition)

CINEMA

No. of cinemas: 24,640

The American film industry, which is largely synonymous with Hollywood, generates billions of dollars every year. Many of the major block-busters also earn vast amounts through secondary merchandizing. Each year, the Academy of Motion Picture Arts and Sciences awards trophies to commemorate the efforts of film-makers, actors and cinema technicians. These 'Oscars' are guaranteed to boost box-office takings of the films concerned. However, the USA is also well-known for its somewhat less lucrative independent and documentary films, which are often received with more critical acclaim than Hollywood's offerings. Indeed, in recent years, several big box-office hits, which have also scooped many Oscars, have been films that were funded by large independent production companies.

MAGAZINES

The periodicals with highest circulations in the USA are:

Reader's Digest	monthly, general interest	16,262,000
TV Guide	weekly, TV listings	14,123,000
National Geographic Magazine	monthly, geography, travel, natural history and culture	9,177,000
Better Homes and Gardens	monthly, lifestyle	7,600,000
Good Housekeeping	monthly, lifestyle	5,163,000
Family Circle	every three weeks, general interest	5,114,000
Consumer Reports	monthly	4,600,000
Ladies' Home Journal	monthly, women's magazine	4,500,000
National Enquirer	weekly, general interest	4,381,000
McCall's Magazine	monthly, women's magazine	4,200,000
Time	weekly, current affairs	4,104,000
People	weekly, general interest	3,447,000
Playboy	monthly, men's magazine	3,403,000
Sports Illustrated	weekly, sports	3,357,000
Redbook Magazine	monthly, women's magazine	3,345,000
Newsweek	weekly, current affairs	3,156,000

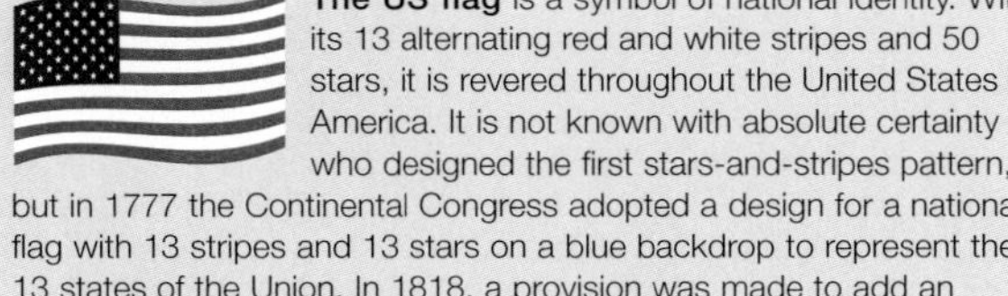

The US flag is a symbol of national identity. With its 13 alternating red and white stripes and 50 stars, it is revered throughout the United States of America. It is not known with absolute certainty who designed the first stars-and-stripes pattern, but in 1777 the Continental Congress adopted a design for a national flag with 13 stripes and 13 stars on a blue backdrop to represent the 13 states of the Union. In 1818, a provision was made to add an additional star to the flag on the 4th of July, following the entry of each new state into the Union; the number of stripes stayed the same. In 1892, the Pledge of Allegiance to the flag was first published, in which citizens swear allegiance to the United States and its embodiment in the flag. The flag was last changed in 1960, with the addition of the 50th state, Hawaii.

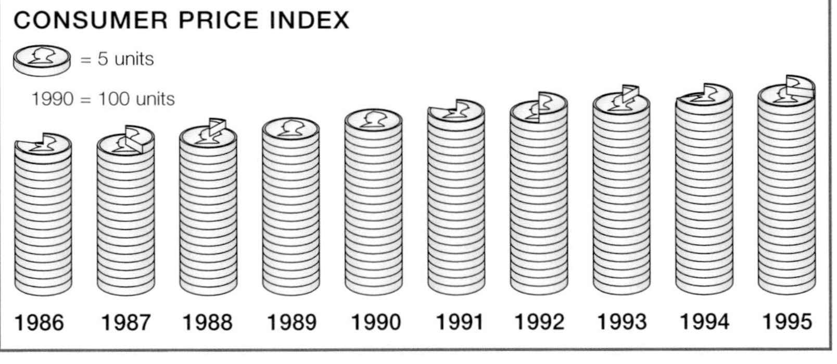

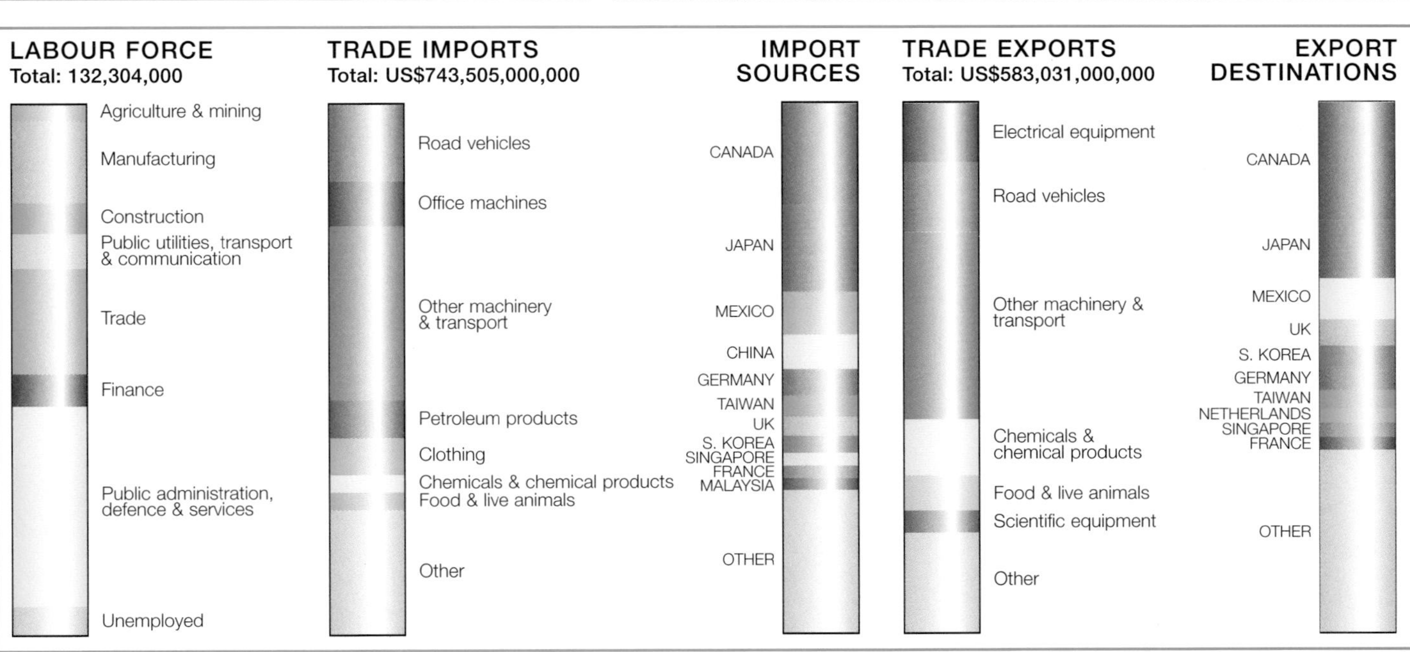

STATE INFORMATION

State	Postal abbrev.	Entry into Union	State nickname(s)	State motto	State bird	State tree	State flower	State governor
Alabama	AL	Dec 14 1819 (22nd State)	Heart of Dixie, Cotton State	*Audemus Jura Nostra Defendere*, We Dare Defend Our Rights	yellowhammer	southern pine	camellia	Forrest H. James, Jr, Republican, 1995–
Alaska	AK	Jan 3 1959 (49th State)	The Last Frontier, Land of the Midnight Sun, The Great Land	North to the Future	willow ptarmigan	Sitka spruce	forget-me-not	Tony Knowles, Democrat, 1994–
Arizona	AZ	Feb 14 1912 (48th State)	Grand Canyon State	*Ditat Deus*, God Enriches	cactus wren	paloverde	saguaro cactus blossom	Fife Symington, Republican, 1991–
Arkansas	AR	Jun 15 1836 (25th State)	Land of Opportunity, The Natural State, Wonder State	*Regnat Populus*, The People Rule	mockingbird	pine	apple blossom	Mike Huckabee, Republican, 1996–
California	CA	Sep 9 1850 (31st State)	Golden State	*Eureka*, I Have Found It	California valley quail	California redwood	golden poppy	Pete Wilson, Republican, 1991–
Colorado	CO	Aug 1 1876 (38th State)	Centennial State	*Nil Sine Numine*, Nothing Without Providence	Prairie lark-finch	Colorado blue spruce	Rocky Mountain columbine	Roy Romer, Democrat, 1987–
Connecticut	CT	Jan 9 1788 (5th State)	Constitution State, Nutmeg State	*Qui Transtulit Sustinet*, He Who Transplanted Still Sustains	robin	white oak	mountain laurel	John Rowland, Republican, 1995–
Delaware	DE	Dec 7 1787 (1st State)	Diamond State, First State	Liberty and Independence	blue hen chicken	American holly	peach blossom	Tom Carper, Democrat, 1993–
District of Columbia	DC	(not a State)		*Justitia Omnibus*, Justice For All	woodthrush	scarlet oak	American Beauty rose	
Florida	FL	Mar 3 1845 (27th State)	Sunshine State, Peninsula State	In God We Trust	mockingbird	Sabal palm	Orange blossom	Lawton Chils, Democrat, 1991–
Georgia	GA	Jan 2 1788 (4th State)	Peach State, Empire of the South	Wisdom, Justice and Moderation	brown thrasher	live oak	Cherokee rose	Zell Miller, Democrat, 1991–
Hawaii	HI	Aug 21 1959 (50th State)	Aloha state, Paradise of the Pacific	*Ua Mau Ke Ea O Ka Aina I Ka Pono*, The Life of the Land is Perpetuated in Righteousness	nene (Hawaiian goose)	kukui (candlenut)	red hibiscus	Ben Cayetano, Democrat, 1994–
Idaho	ID	Jul 3 1890 (43rd State)	Gem State	*Esto Perpetua*, It is Forever	mountain bluebird	white pine	Syringa	Phil Batt, Republican, 1995–
Illinois	IL	Dec 3 1818 (21st State)	Land of Lincoln, Prairie State	State Sovereignty – National Union	cardinal	white oak	violet	Jim Edgar, Republican, 1991–
Indiana	IN	Dec 11 1816 (19th State)	Hoosier State	The Crossroads of America	cardinal	tulip tree	peony	Frank O'Bannon, Democrat, 1997–
Iowa	IA	Dec 28 1846 (29th State)	Hawkeye State, Corn State	Our Liberties We Prize and Our Rights We Will Maintain	eastern goldfinch	oak	wild rose	Terry E. Branstad, Republican, 1983–
Kansas	KS	Jan 29 1861 (34th State)	Sunflower State, Jayhawker State	*As Astra Per Aspera*, To The Stars Through Difficulties	western meadowlark	cottonwood	sunflower	Bill Graves, Republican, 1995–
Kentucky	KY	June 1 1792 (15th State)	Bluegrass State	United We Stand, Divided We Fall	cardinal	Kentucky coffeetree	goldenrod	Paul Patton, Democrat, 1995–
Louisiana	LA	Apr 30 1812 (30th State)	Pelican State, Creole State, Sugar State	Union, Justice, and Confidence	eastern brown pelican	bald cypress	magnolia	Mike Foster, Republican, 1996–
Maine	ME	Mar 15 1820 (23rd State)	Pine Tree State	*Dirigo*, I Direct	chickadee	eastern white pine	white pine cone and tassel	Angus S. King, Jr, Independent, 1995–
Maryland	MD	Apr 28 1788 (7th State)	Old Line State, Free State	*Fatti Maschii, Parole Femine*, Manly Deeds, Womanly Words	Baltimore oriole	white oak	black-eyed Susan	Parris N. Glendening, Democrat, 1995–
Massa-chusetts	MA	Feb 6 1788 (6th State)	Bay State, Old Colony State	*Ense Petit Placidam Sub Libertate Quietem*, By the Sword We Seek Peace, But Peace Only Under Liberty	chickadee	American elm	mayflower	Paul Cellucci, Republican, 1997–
Michigan	MI	Jan 26 1837 (26th State)	Wolverine State, Water Wonderland, Great Lakes State	*Si Quaeris Peninsulam Amoenam Circumspice*, If You Seek a Pleasant Peninsula, Look About You	robin	white pine	apple blossom	John Engler, Republican, 1991–
Minnesota	MN	May 11 1858 (32nd State)	North Star State, Gopher State, Land of 10,000 Lakes	*L'Étoile du Nord*, The North Star	loon	red pine	pink and white lady's slipper	Arne Carlson, Republican, 1991–
Mississippi	MS	Dec 10 1817 (20th State)	Magnolia State	*Virtue et Armis*, By Valour and Arms	mockingbird	magnolia	magnolia	Kirk Fordice, Republican, 1992–
Missouri	MO	Aug 10 1821 (24th State)	Show Me State	*Salus Populi Suprema Lex Esto*, The Welfare of the People Shall Be the Supreme Law	bluebird	flowering dogwood	hawthorn	Mel Carnahan, Democrat, 1993–
Montana	MT	Nov 8 1889 (41st State)	Treasure State, Big Sky Country	*Oro y Plata*, Gold and Silver	western meadowlark	ponderosa pine	bitterroot	Marc Racicot, Republican, 1993–
Nebraska	NB	Mar 1 1867 (37th State)	Cornhusker State, Beef State	Equality Before the Law	western meadowlark	cottonwood	goldenrod	E. Benjamin Nelson, Democrat, 1991–

State	Postal abbrev.	Entry into Union	State nickname(s)	State motto	State bird	State tree	State flower	State governor
Nevada	NV	Oct 31 1864 (36th State)	Silver State, Sagebrush State, Battle Born State	All For Our Country	mountain bluebird	single leaf pinon and bristlecone pine	sagebrush	Bob Miller, Democrat, 1989–
New Hampshire	NH	Jun 21 1788 (9th State)	Granite State	Live Free or Die	purple finch	white birch	purple lilac	Jeanne Shaheen, Democrat, 1997–
New Jersey	NJ	Dec 18 1787 (3rd State)	Garden State	Liberty and Prosperity	eastern goldfinch	red oak	purple violet	Christine Todd Whitman, Republican, 1994–
New Mexico	NM	Jan 6 1912 (47th State)	Land of Enchantment, Sunshine State	*Crescit Eundo*, It Grows as it Goes	roadrunner	pinon	yucca flower	Gary E. Johnson, Republican, 1995–
New York	NY	Jul 26 1788 (11th State)	Empire State, Excelsior State	Excelsior, Ever Upward	bluebird	sugar maple	rose	George E. Pataki, Republican, 1995–
North Carolina	NC	Nov 21 1789 (12th State)	Tar Heel State, Old North State	*Esse Quam Videri*, To Be Rather Than To Seem	cardinal	longleaf pine	dogwood	James B. Hunt, Jr, Democrat, 1993–
North Dakota	ND	Nov 2 1889 (39th State)	Flickertail State, Sioux State, Peace Garden State	Liberty and Union, Now and Forever, One and Inseparable	western meadowlark	American elm	prairie rose	Edward T. Schafer, Republican, 1993–
Ohio	OH	Mar 1 1803 (17th State)	Buckeye State	With God, All Things Are Possible	cardinal	buckeye	scarlet carnation	George V. Voinovich, Republican, 1991–
Oklahoma	OK	Nov 16 1907 (46th State)	Sooner State	*Labor Omnia Vincit*, Labour Conquers All Things	scissor-tailed flycatcher	redbud	mistletoe	Frank Keating, Republican, 1995–
Oregon	OR	Feb 14 1859 (33rd State)	Beaver State	The Union	western meadowlark	Douglas fir	Oregon grape	John A. Kitzhaber, Democrat, 1995–
Pennsylvania	PA	Dec 12 1787 (2nd State)	Keystone State	Virtue, Liberty and Independence	ruffed grouse	hemlock	mountain laurel	Tom Ridge, Republican, 1995–
Rhode Island	RI	May 29 1790 (13th State)	Little Rhody, The Ocean State, Plantation State	Hope	Rhode Island red	red maple	violet	Lincoln C. Almond, Republican, 1995–
South Carolina	SC	May 23 1788 (8th State)	Palmetto State	*Animus Opibusque Parati*, Prepared in Mind and Resources	Great Carolina wren	palmetto	yellow jessamine	David M. Beasley, Republican, 1995–
South Dakota	SD	Nov 2 1889 (40th State)	Mt Rushmore State, Coyote State, Sunshine State	Under God the People Rule	ring-necked pheasant	Black Hills spruce	pasque flower	William J. Janklow, Republican, 1995–
Tennessee	TN	Jun 1 1796 (16th State)	Volunteer State	Agriculture and Commerce	mockingbird	tulip poplar	iris	Don Sundquist, Republican, 1995–
Texas	TX	Dec 29 1845 (28th State)	Lone Star State	Friendship	mockingbird	pecan	bluebonnet	George W. Bush, Republican, 1995–
Utah	UT	Jan 4 1896 (45th State)	Beehive State	Industry	American seagull	blue spruce	sego lily	Mike Leavitt, Republican, 1993–
Vermont	VT	Mar 4 1791 (14th State)	Green Mountain State	Freedom and Unity	hermit thrush	sugar maple	red clover	Howard Dean, Democrat, 1991–
Virginia	VA	Jun 25 1788 (10th State)	The Old Dominion State, Mother of Presidents	*Sic Semper Tyrannis*, Thus Always to Tyrants	cardinal	dogwood	dogwood	George F. Allen, Republican, 1994–
Washington	WA	Nov 11 1889 (42nd State)	Evergreen State	*Alki*, Bye and Bye	willow goldfinch	western hemlock	coast rhododendron	Gary Locke, Democrat, 1997–
West Virginia	WV	Jun 20 1863 (35th State)	Mountain State	*Montani Semper Liberi*, Mountaineers Are Always Free	cardinal	sugar maple	rhododendron	Cecil H. Underwood, Republican, 1997–
Wisconsin	WI	May 29 1848 (30th State)	Badger State, America's Dairyland	Forward	robin	sugar maple	wood violet	Tommy G. Thompson, Republican, 1987–
Wyoming	WY	Jul 10 1890 (44th State)	Equality State, Cowboy State	Equal Rights	western meadowlark	cottonwood	Indian paintbrush	Jim Geringer, Republican, 1995–

THE USA AS A GLOBAL SUPERPOWER

Since World War II, the USA has established itself as a world superpower. Since the fall of Communism in the USSR and eastern Europe, this status has been unchallenged, providing the USA with a host of global roles. It continues to act as world policeman. This has been achieved through a combination of direct action, such as in Haiti in 1994, and through the role of international mediator. This latter role was exercised in the Israeli-PLO treaty of 1993 and in the Dayton Accord of 1995 that brought the troubles in former Yugoslavia to a precarious end. In Northern Ireland, too, the USA has attempted to broker a peace. However, despite the USA's position as a mediator and peace negotiator, its efforts at arbitration have not always been successful – the USA failed to secure peace in Somalia, where UN-sponsored US troops were ignominiously forced to withdraw.

From an economic perspective, the USA has only just begun to relinquish its dominance. Since World War II, the USA has been the major player in world economics. Recently, however, its position has become less secure. Japan and the Pacific Rim (including China) have both emerged as economic strongholds; the European Union is also a potential threat. The USA has counteracted this with its own trade treaties, such as NAFTA (with Canada and Mexico), but with a US$4.9 trillion national debt and over-valued stock markets, its economic stability and status as the global economic superpower is challenged.

The USA continues to promote itself abroad, both culturally and politically. Hollywood cinema and American TV programmes are exported worldwide. The USA has made headway in establishing itself in the new digital landscape by investing heavily in the media infrastructure. The emergent information world is one which the USA is pioneering. Meanwhile, American brand-names continue to permeate throughout the Western world, as well as in Asia and the Far East. Politically, the USA still reigns supreme. It continues to seek further expansion of NATO into eastern Europe, and is highly influential within the UN. Although not likely to remain entirely uncontested, the USA shall, in all probability, remain the sole world superpower.

MEXICO AND CUBA

MEXICO

Mexico is a republic between the Pacific and the Gulf of Mexico and bordered by the USA in the north and Central America in the south. Between the Sierra Madre Oriental in the east and the Sierra Madre Occidental in the west is a large high central plateau, which has several volcanoes including Volcán Citlaltepetl (Pico de Orizaba). The coastal plains are generally narrower in the west, but wider in the east. The Yucatán Peninsula in the south-east is a broad limestone lowland; Baja California in the north-west is a long narrow mountainous peninsula. **Highest point:** Volcán Citlaltepetl (Pico de Orizaba) 5610 m (18,405 ft). **Climate:** There is considerable climatic variation in part reflecting the complexity of the relief. In general the south and the coastal lowlands are tropical; the central plateau and the mountains are cooler and drier.

The Federal Parliament comprises two chambers elected by universal adult suffrage. The lower house (Chamber of Deputies) has 500 members elected for three years: 200 elected under a system of proportional representation, 300 from single-member constituencies. The upper house (the Senate) has 128 members elected for six years, with four senators representing each state and four representing the Federal District. One half of the senators retire every three years. An executive President, who appoints a Cabinet, is directly elected for a single six-year term. Each state has its own government. **Largest parties:** (Chamber 1994 election) (centre) Institutional Revolutionary Party (PRI) 239 seats, (centre-left) Democratic Revolutionary Party (PRD) 125, (centre-right) National Action Party (PAN) 122, Greens 8, (left-wing) Labour Party 6. **President:** (since 1994) Ernesto Zedillo (PRI).

Over one-quarter of the labour force is involved in agriculture and many Mexicans are still subsistence farmers growing maize, wheat, kidney beans and rice. Coffee, cotton, fruit and vegetables are major export crops. Mexico is the world's leading producer of silver. The exploitation of large reserves of natural gas and oil enabled Mexico's spectacular economic growth since the 1970s, but social and economic reforms did not keep up with this growth. An expanding industrial base includes important petrochemical, textile, motor-vehicle and food-processing industries. In the 1990s low labour costs and the new NAFTA trade agreement encouraged major US companies to set up plants in Mexico. However, economic problems remain and high unemployment has stimulated immigration (often illegal) to the USA. Since 1995 a major crisis of confidence has sent the peso into steep decline and Mexico required a US rescue package. **Currency:** Mexican peso.

1910 End of the authoritarian rule of President General Porfirio Díaz (in power 1876–80 and 1888–1910). **1910** Revolution against the power of the landowners broke out; reformist policies of President Madero were supported by the outlaw Pancho Villa. **1916–17** US expeditionary force sent against Villa. **After 1924** The revolution became anticlerical and the Church was persecuted. **1929** PRI came to power: order restored. Opposition tolerated but PRI was virtually guaranteed perpetual power. **1930s** Large estates were divided and much of the economy was nationalized. **1985** Major earthquake hit Mexico City. **1990s** Emergence of a more liberal economic and political climate: Mexico's 'coming-of-age' marked by membership of NAFTA and OECD. **1994** Political assassinations. **Since 1994** Peasant uprisings in Chiapas and, later, Guerrero states. **1995** Major economic crisis.

■ *Acapulco, Mexico's premier resort, has grown up around one of the finest natural harbours on the Pacific coast*

MEXICAN STATES AND TERRITORIES

Aguascalientes
Area: 5471 km^2 (2112 sq mi).
Pop.: 771,000 (1992 est.).
Capital: Aguascalientes.
Baja California Norte
Area: 69,921 km^2 (26,997 sq mi).
Pop.: 1,908,000 (1992 est.).
Capital: Mexicali.
Baja California Sur
Area: 73,475 km^2 (28,369 sq mi).
Pop.: 352,000 (1992 est.).
Capital: La Paz.
Campeche
Area: 50,812 km^2 (19,619 sq mi).
Pop.: 569,000 (1992 est.).
Capital: Campeche.
Chiapas
Area: 74,211 km^2 (28,653 sq mi).
Pop.: 3,437,000 (1992 est.).
Capital: Tuxtla Gutiérrez.
Chihuahua
Area: 244,938 km^2 (94,571 sq mi).
Pop.: 2,504,000 (1992 est.).
Capital: Chihuahua.
Coahuila
Area: 149,982 km^2 (57,908 sq mi).
Pop.: 2,040,000 (1992 est.).
Capital: Saltillo.
Colima
Area: 5191 km^2 (2004 sq mi).
Pop.: 459,000 (1992 est.).
Capital: Colima.
Durango
Area: 123,181 km^2 (47,560 sq mi).
Pop.: 1,395,000 (1992 est.).
Capital: Durango.
Guanajuato
Area: 30,491 km^2 (11,773 sq mi).
Pop.: 4,171,000 (1992 est.).
Capital: Guanajuato.
Guerrero
Area: 64,281 km^2 (24,819 sq mi).
Pop.: 2,733,000 (1992 est.).
Capital: Chilpancingo.
Hidalgo
Area: 20,813 km^2 (8036 sq mi).
Pop.: 1,946,000 (1992 est.).
Capital: Pachuca.
Jalisco
Area: 80,836 km^2 (31,211 sq mi).
Pop.: 5,693,000 (1992 est.).
Capital: Guadalajara.
México
Area: 21,355 km^2 (8245 sq mi).
Pop.: 10,706,000 (1992 est.).
Capital: Toluca.
Michoacán
Area: 59,928 km^2 (23,138 sq mi).
Pop.: 3,724,000 (1992 est.).
Capital: Morelia.
Morelos
Area: 4950 km^2 (1911 sq mi).
Pop.: 1,259,000 (1992 est.).
Capital: Cuernavaca.
Nayarit
Area: 26,979 km^2 (10,417 sq mi).
Pop.: 872,000 (1992 est.).
Capital: Tepic.
Nuevo León
Area: 64,924 km^2 (25,067 sq mi).
Pop.: 3,336,000 (1992 est.).
Capital: Monterrey.
Oaxaca
Area: 93,952 km^2 (36,275 sq mi).
Pop.: 3,207,000 (1992 est.).
Capital: Oaxaca.
Puebla
Area: 33,902 km^2 (13,090 sq mi).
Pop.: 4,407,000 (1992 est.).
Capital: Puebla.
Querétaro
Area: 11,449 km^2 (4420 sq mi).
Pop.: 1,126,000 (1992 est.).
Capital: Querétaro.
Quintana Roo
Area: 50,212 km^2 (19,387 sq mi).
Pop.: 577,000 (1992 est.).
Capital: Chetumal.
San Luis Potosí
Area: 63,068 km^2 (24,351 sq mi).
Pop.: 2,089,000 (1992 est.).
Capital: San Luis Potosí.
Sinaloa
Area: 58,328 km^2 (22,521 sq mi).
Pop.: 2,341,000 (1992 est.).
Capital: Culiacán.
Sonora
Area: 182,052 km^2 (70,291 sq mi).
Pop.: 1,867,000 (1992 est.).
Capital: Hermosillo.
Tabasco
Area: 25,267 km^2 (9756 sq mi).
Pop.: 1,595,000 (1992 est.).
Capital: Villahermosa.
Tamaulipas
Area: 79,384 km^2 (30,650 sq mi).
Pop.: 2,352,000 (1992 est.).
Capital: Ciudad Victoria.
Tlaxcala
Area: 4016 km^2 (1551 sq mi).
Pop.: 813,000 (1992 est.).
Capital: Tlaxcala.
Veracruz
Area: 71,699 km^2 (27,683 sq mi).
Pop.: 6,405,000 (1992 est.).
Capital: Jalapa.
Yucatán
Area: 38,402 km^2 (14,827 sq mi).
Pop.: 1,390,000 (1992 est.).
Capital: Mérida.
Zacatecas
Area: 73,252 km^2 (28,283 sq mi).
Pop.: 1,309,000 (1992 est.).
Capital: Zacatecas.
Federal District (Distrito Federal)
Area: 1479 km^2 (571 sq mi).
Pop.: 8,276,000 (1992 est.).
Capital: Mexico City.

Official name: Estados Unidos Mexicanos (United States of Mexico). **Area:** 1,958,201 km^2 (756,066 sq mi). **Population:** 91,145,000 (1995 est.). **Doubling time:** 26 years. **Adult life expectancy:** male 66.5 years, female 73.1 years. **Birth rate:** 1.26 times world average. **Death rate:** 0.51 times world average. **Urban population:** 71%. **Capital:** Mexico City 15,048,000 urban area (city 8,276,000; Ciudad Netzahualcóyotl 1,255,000; 1990 census). **Other main centres:** Guadalajara 2,847,000 urban area (city 1,650,000), Monterrey 2,522,000 (city 1,069,000), Ciudad Netzahualcóyotl *see Mexico City*, Puebla 1,057,000 (city 1,007,000), León 868,000 (city 758,000), Ciudad Juárez 798,000 (city 789,000), Tijuana 747,000 (city 699,000), Mexicali 602,000 (urban area), Culiacán 602,000 (city 415,000), Acapulco 593,000 (city 515,000), Mérida 557,000 (city 523,000), Chihuahua 531,000 (city 516,000), San Luis Potosí 526,000 (city 489,000), Aguascalientes 506,000 (city 480,000) (1990 census). **Language:** Spanish 92% as a first language (official), Amerindian languages including Aztec, Yucatec (Mayan), Zapotec and Mixtec 8%. **Adult literacy:** 86%. **Religion:** Roman Catholic 90%, various Evangelical Protestant Churches 5%.

CUBA

Cuba is a republic occupying the largest island in the Caribbean. Three ranges of hills and mountains (including the Sierra Maestra in the south-east) run east to west across Cuba. The Island of Youth (Isla de la Juventud) lies south-west of Cuba.
Highest point: Pico Turquino 1974 m (6476 ft).
Climate: The climate is semitropical. Temperatures average 26°C (38°F) and rainfall is heavy. the island is subject to hurricanes.

The 589-member National Assembly is directly elected for five years by citizens aged 16 and over. The Assembly elects 31 of its members to form the Council of State, whose President, as head of state and of government, appoints a Council of Ministers.
Only permitted party: (1993 election) Communist Party (PC) 589 seats.
President: (since 1976) Fidel Castro (PC).

Sugar (the leading export), tobacco and coffee are the leading crops. State-controlled farms occupy most of the land but are unable to meet Cuba's food needs. Nickel is Cuba's second most important export. The end of the Communist trade bloc and of Soviet subsidies brought the Cuban economy to the verge of collapse: the value of the currency plummeted in real terms and severe fuel shortages hit both industry and transport. A modest upturn in the economy began after 1995. **Currency:** Cuban peso.

1898 Independence from Spain. **1899–1901** Period of US administration. **1901** Independence restored. **1906–09** Further period of US administration. **1933–44** First dictatorship of Fulgencio Batista. **1952–59** Second dictatorship of Fulgencio Batista. **1959** Batista overthrown by Fidel Castro. **1960** US businesses in Cuba expropriated without compensation. **1961** US-sponsored Cuban exiles attempted to invade Cuba at the Bay of Pigs. **1962** Soviet missiles installed in Cuba but subsequently withdrawn owing to US pressure. **1965–76** Communist system established. **1976–88** Cuban forces supported Soviet client regimes in Africa. **1988** Cuban troops withdrawn from Angola. **1991** Last Soviet forces removed from Cuba: collapse of Communism elsewhere left Cuba increasingly isolated as a hardline Marxist state. **1994** Flood of refugees from Cuba to the USA. **Since 1994** Rising discontent with the Castro regime.

Official name: República de Cuba (The Republic of Cuba). **Area:** 110,861 km^2 (42,804 sq mi). **Population:** 11,070,000 (1995 est.). **Doubling time:** 100 years. **Adult life expectancy:** male 73.9 years, female 77.6 years. **Birth rate:** 0.56 times world average. **Death rate:** 0.78 times world average. **Urban population:** 73%. **Capital:** Havana (La Habana) 2,176,000 (1993 census; inc. suburbs). **Other main centres:** Santiago de Cuba 440,000, Camagüey 294,000, Holguín 242,000, Guantánamo 208,000, Santa Clara 200,000 (1993 census). **Language:** Spanish 100% (official). **Adult literacy:** 96%. **Religion:** Roman Catholic 40%, non-religious 55%, various Protestant Churches nearly 5%.

■ *Cuba has not been able to trade with the USA for 40 years and, therefore, many of the cars seen in Cuba's capital city of Havana date from the 1950s*

CAYMAN ISLANDS

Official name and status: Cayman Islands; a British colony with internal self-government.
Area: 259 km^2 (100 sq mi).
Population: 32,000 (1994 est.).
Capital: George Town 13,000 (1989 census).
Geography: The three low-lying Cayman Islands are 290 km (180 mi) west of Jamaica.
Economy: The economy relies upon tourism which employs about one-third of the labour force, and upon financial services: owing to its stability, nearness to the USA and banking secrecy laws, the colony is one of the world's major offshore financial centres.

CLIPPERTON ISLAND

Official name and status: Ile Clipperton (Clipperton Island); a French dependency, administered by French Polynesia although not legally part of that territory.
Area: 7 km^2 (3 sq mi).
Population: uninhabited. A Pacific atoll some 1300 km (810 mi) west of Mexico.

Central America

BELIZE

Belize is a small Central American state on the Caribbean coast between Mexico and Guatemala and the smallest country on the American mainland. Tropical jungle covers most of the country. The south contains the Maya Mountains; the north is swampy lowlands.
Highest point: Victoria Peak 1122 m (3681 ft).
Climate: The subtropical climate is tempered by trade winds. Rainfall is heavy, but there is a dry season from February to May.

The eight-member Senate is appointed by the Governor General, the representative of the British Queen as sovereign of Belize. The 29-member House of Representatives is elected by universal adult suffrage for five years. The Governor General appoints a Prime Minister, who enjoys a majority in the House; the PM, in turn, appoints a Cabinet.
Largest parties: (1993 election) (conservative) United Democratic Party (UDP) 16 seats, (centre) People's United Party (PUP) 13.
Prime Minister: (since 1993) Manuel Esquivel (UDP).

The production of sugar cane, bananas and citrus fruit (particularly oranges) for export dominates the economy. The clothing industry is expanding. **Currency:** Belize dollar.

1981 Independence after 129 years of British rule as the colony of British Honduras. **1991** Guatemala abandoned its claim to Belize.

Official name: Belize.
Area: 22,965 km² (8867 sq mi).
Population: 216,000 (1995 est.).
Doubling time: 23 years. **Adult life expectancy:** male 66 years, female 70 years. **Birth rate:** 1.43 times world average. **Death rate:** 0.66 times world average.
Urban population: 48%.
Capital: Belmopan 3900 (1993 est.).
Other main centres: Belize City 48,000, Orange Walk 12,000, San Ignacio 10,000 (1993 est.).
Language: English 50% (official), English Creole spoken by 78%, Spanish 31%, Mayan languages.
Adult literacy: 93%.
Religion: Roman Catholic 57%, various Protestant Churches 27% (mainly Anglican and Pentecostal).

EL SALVADOR

El Salvador is the smallest of the Central American republics and the only one to have only a Pacific coast. It is mountainous with ranges along the border with Honduras and a higher volcanic chain in the south. Of 20 major volcanoes, several are still active.
Highest point: Volcán de Santa Ana 2381 m (7812 ft).
Climate: The tropical coast is humid and hot; the interior is temperate.

An executive President (who appoints Ministers) is elected by universal adult suffrage for a non-renewable five-year term. The 84-member Legislative Assembly is directly elected for three years.
Largest parties: (1997 election) (right-wing) Nationalist Republican Alliance (ARENA) 28 seats, (centre and left-wing coalition) Farabundo Marti Liberation Front (FLMN) 27, (conservative) Christian Democratic Party (PCD) 2, others 27.
President: (since 1994) Armando Calderón Sol (ARENA).

Agricultural products, in particular coffee and sugar cane, account for almost two-thirds of the country's exports. The country is overpopulated and there is pressure on land. The economy declined from the 1970s to 1992 owing to the state of near civil war. **Currency:** Colon.

1932 Major peasant uprising harshly suppressed. **1969** War broke out with Honduras after a soccer match (the real cause was illegal migration of Salvadoreans to Honduras). **1970s–1992** Virtual civil war (in which over 125,000 people were killed and 8000 disappeared) with US-backed military assisted by extreme right-wing death squads combating left-wing guerrillas; in 1980 Archbishop Oscar Romero assassinated by right-wing extremist in his own cathedral. **1992** Peace agreement between government and guerrillas.

Official name: La República de El Salvador (The Republic of El Salvador).
Area: 21,041 km² (8124 sq mi).
Population: 5,770,000 (1995 est.).
Doubling time: 26 years. **Adult life expectancy:** male 64 years, female 70 years. **Birth rate:** 1.32 times world average. **Death rate:** 0.65 times world average.
Urban population: 45%.
Capital: San Salvador 1,522,000 urban area (city 423,000; Soya Pango 252,000; Mejicanos 145,000; Nueva San Salvador 117,000; Delgado 105,000; Apopa 101,000; 1992 census; inc. suburbs). **Other main centres:** Soya Pango *see San Salvador*, Santa Ana 202,000, San Miguel 183,000 (1992 census; inc. suburbs).
Language: Spanish 100% (official).
Adult literacy: 75%.
Religion: Roman Catholic 75%, various Protestant Evangelical Churches over 20%.

GUATEMALA

Guatemala is the largest and most northerly of the Central American republics. A mountain chain, containing over 30 volcanoes, separates Pacific and Atlantic coastal lowlands.
Highest point: Tajumulco 4220 m (13,845 ft).
Climate: The coastal plains have a tropical climate; the mountains are more temperate.

An executive President (who appoints Ministers) is elected by universal adult suffrage for a four-year term and is not immediately eligible for re-election. The 80-member Congress, directly elected for four years, comprises 64 members elected from single-member constituencies and 16 members elected nationally under a system of proportional representation.
Largest parties: (1995 election) (conservative) Party of National Advancement (PAN) 42 seats, (right-wing) Guatemalan Republic Front (FRG) 21, (centre) New Democratic Front of Guatemala (FNDG) 5.
President: (since 1996) Alvaro Arzu (PAN).

More than one-half of the labour force is engaged in farming. Coffee is the main export; other crops include sugar cane and bananas. **Currency:** Quetzal.

1951 After a history of dictators allied to landowners, a reformist President, Jacobo Arbenz, came to power and expropriated estates, dividing them among the peasantry. **1954** US-backed army coup deposed Arbenz. **After 1970** The Left was suppressed, leading to emergence of guerrilla armies; up to 100,000 dissidents were killed and many disappeared during 35 years near civil war. **1986** Civilian government restored. **1996** Accord between government and guerrillas; peace restored.

Official name: República de Guatemala (The Republic of Guatemala).
Area: 108,889 km² (42,042 sq mi).
Population: 10,620,000 (1995 est.).
Doubling time: 24 years. **Adult life expectancy:** male 61.9 years, female 67.1 years. **Birth rate:** 1.42 times world average. **Death rate:** 0.81 times world average.
Urban population: 39%.
Capital: Guatemala City (Ciudad de Guatemala) 2,074,000 (city 1,133,000; Mixco 437,000; Villa Nueva 166,000; 1995 est.; inc. suburbs). **Other main centres:** Mixco *see Guatemala City*, Puerto Barrios 338,000, Quezaltenango 246,000, Villa Nueva *see Guatemala City*, Cobán 120,000 (1992 est.; inc. suburbs).
Language: Spanish 65% as a first language (official), Mayan languages 35%. **Adult literacy:** 60%.
Religion: Roman Catholic 75%, various Protestant Evangelical Churches 25%.

■ EL SALVADOR HAS HAD A CHANGE OF GOVERNMENT, ON AVERAGE, EVERY 18 MONTHS

HONDURAS

Honduras is the second largest of the Central American republics. Over three-quarters of Honduras is mountainous. There are small coastal plains. The majority of Hondurans live in somewhat isolated valleys in the mountains. (This fact is sometimes cited to explain Honduras' traditional isolationism in Central America.)
Highest point: Cerro Selaque 2849 m (9347 ft).
Climate: The tropical lowlands in Honduras experience high rainfall, 1500–2000 mm (60–80 in). The country's more temperate highlands are drier.

An executive President (who appoints Ministers) and the 128-member Congress are elected by universal adult suffrage for four years. Congress is elected by proportional representation.
Largest parties: (1993 election) (centre-right) Liberal Party (PLH) 71 seats, (right-wing) National Party (PNH) 55, Unity Party 2.
President: (since 1994) Carlos Roberto Meina (PLH).

Over 40% of Hondurans work in farming, but, despite agrarian reforms, living standards are low. Bananas and coffee are the main exports, while maize for domestic consumption is the main crop. Low labour costs have attracted industry, particularly clothing manufacture which is the biggest growth area of the economy. The northern city of San Pedro Sula is the scene of most of this expansion, and the city is the fastest growing in Central America. There are few natural resources. High inflation is a constantly recurring problem.
Currency: Lempira.

1925 Short-lived civil war. **1925–80** A succession of military dictators. **Since 1980** There have been democratically elected centre-right civilian governments.

Official name: República de Honduras (The Republic of Honduras).
Area: 112,088 km² (43,277 sq mi).
Population: 5,510,000 (1995 est.).
Doubling time: 24 years. **Adult life expectancy:** male 64.8 years, female 69.2 years. **Birth rate:** 1.43 times world average. **Death rate:** 0.69 times world average.
Urban population: 42%.
Capital: Tegucigalpa 739,000 (1993 est.; inc. suburbs). **Other main centres:** San Pedro Sula 354,000, La Ceiba 83,000, El Progreso 77,000 (1993 est.; inc. suburbs).
Language: Spanish 98% (official), Black Carib and Miskito minorities.
Adult literacy: 88%.
Religion: Roman Catholic 85%, various Protestant Evangelical Churches 10%.

NICARAGUA

Nicaragua is a Central American republic between Honduras and Costa Rica. Most Nicaraguans live on the fertile Pacific coast plain. Tropical jungle occurs on the Atlantic coast, while mountain ranges line the west. Lake Nicaragua occupies a large central basin.
Highest point: Pico Mogotón 2107 m (6913 ft).
Climate: Tropical and humid with a rainy season from May to October.

An executive President (who appoints Ministers) is elected by universal adult suffrage for a non-renewable five-year term. The 92 members of the National Assembly are directly elected by proportional representation for five years; the losing presidential candidate automatically qualifies for membership.
Largest parties: (1996 election) (right-wing) Liberal Alliance (AL) 42 seats, (centre and left-wing coalition) Sandinista National Liberation Front (FSLN) 21, others 14.
President: (since 1997) José Arnoldo Aleman (AL).

The largely agricultural economy was damaged in the 1980s by guerrilla warfare, a US trade embargo and natural disasters. Austerity measures are in force. Coffee, beef and sugar cane are the main exports. **Currency:** Cordoba.

1912–25 US military intervention. **1927–33** US military intervention. **1937–79** Dictatorship of members of the Somoza family and their supporters. **1972** Massive earthquake destroyed much of the capital; 9000 fatalities. **1979** Coup following popular uprising by the left-wing Sandinista guerrilla movement, resulting in 40,000 fatalities. **1979–90** USA, which accused Sandinistas of Communism, imposed trade embargo on Nicaragua; US-sponsored right-wing Contra guerrillas active until 1989. **1990** Free elections held.

Official name: República de Nicaragua (The Republic of Nicaragua).
Area: 131,670 km² (50,838 sq mi).
Population: 4,340,000 (1995 est.).
Doubling time: 25 years. **Adult life expectancy:** male 60.7 years, female 66.4 years. **Birth rate:** 1.4 times world average. **Death rate:** 0.75 times world average.
Urban population: 62%.
Capital: Managua 974,000 (1992 est.; inc. suburbs). **Other main centres:** León 172,000, Masaya 102,000, Chinandega 102,000 (1992 est.; inc. suburbs).
Language: Spanish 95% (official), Miskito 4%. **Adult literacy:** 74%.
Religion: Roman Catholic 89%, various Protestant Evangelical Churches over 10%.

COSTA RICA

Costa Rica is the most southerly republic of Central America (if neighbouring Panama is regarded as a link between South and Central America). It is also unique in the region in having a population almost entirely of European extraction. Between a narrow plain on the Pacific coast and wider plain on the Caribbean rise a central plateau and mountain ranges.
Highest point: Chirripó Grande 3819 m (12,529 ft).
Climate: Rainfall is heavy along the Caribbean coast but the Pacific coast is drier. Temperatures are warm in the lowlands, cooler in the highlands.

An executive President (who appoints Ministers) and a 57-member Legislative Assembly are elected by universal adult suffrage for four years.
Largest parties: (1994 election) (centre-left) National Liberation Party (PLN) 28 seats, (conservative) Social Christian Unity Party (PUSC), others 4.
President: (since 1994) José-Maria Figueres (PLN).

Coffee is Costa Rica's main export. Bananas, sugar cane, beef cattle, cocoa and timber are also important. The country has benefited from half a century of stable government. Tourism is now the country's major foreign-currency earner. **Currency:** Costa Rica colon.

Official name: República de Costa Rica (The Republic of Costa Rica).
Area: 51,100 km² (19,730 sq mi).
Population: 3,345,000 (1995 est.).
Doubling time: 32 years. **Adult life expectancy:** male 71.9 years, female 77.5 years. **Birth rate:** 1.03 times world average. **Death rate:** 0.45 times world average.
Urban population: 44%.
Capital: San José 922,000 urban area (city 281,000; Desamparados 55,000; 1992 est.; inc. suburbs).
Other main centres: Desamparados *see San José*, Limón 51,000, Alajuela 45,000 (1992 est.; inc. suburbs).
Language: Spanish over 97% (official), English Creole and Chibchan minorities. **Adult literacy:** 93%.
Religion: Roman Catholic 81%, various Protestant Evangelical Churches 18%.

1948 Brief civil war after which army was disbanded. **Since 1948** Stable democracy; Costa Rica has acted as a regional peacemaker.

■ *Plantation workers harvest bananas at Chiquita Banana Plantation, Costa Rica. They work in teams of three and tie inner tubes around themselves to protect the bananas from bruising*

NORTHERN CARIBBEAN

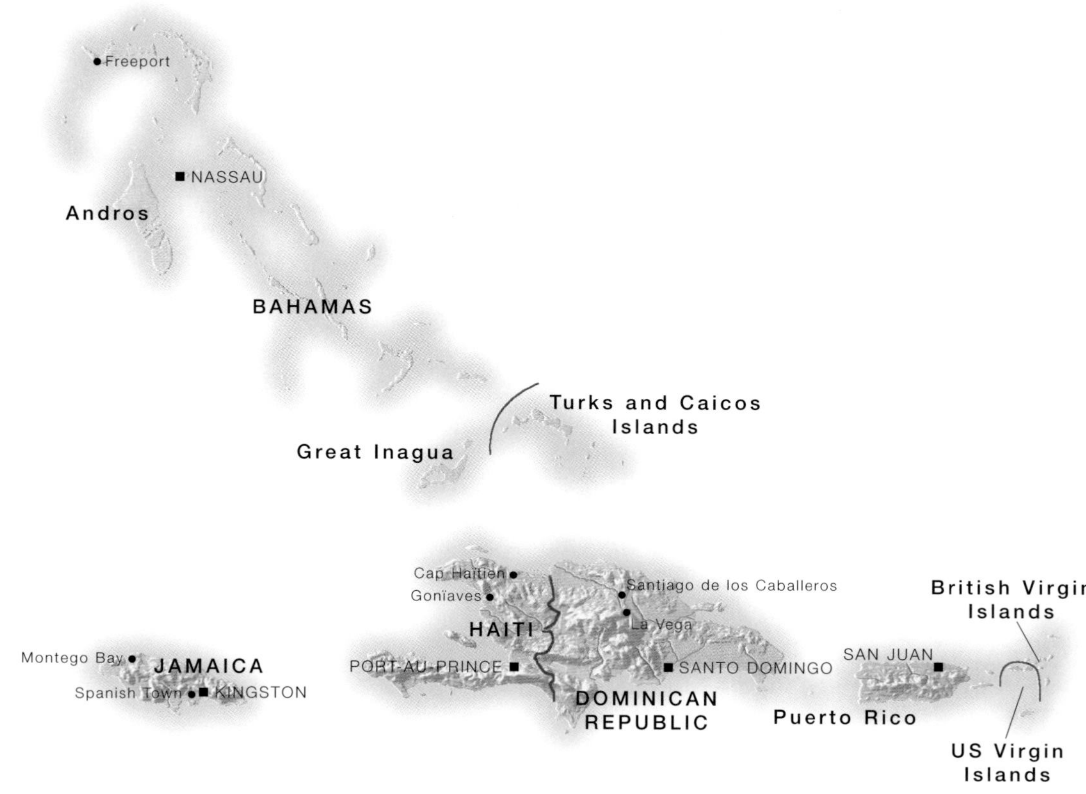

HAITI

Haiti is a republic forming the (smaller) western part of the West Indian island of Hispaniola. Mountains run from east to west separated by densely populated valleys and coastal plains.
Highest point: Pic La Selle 2674 m (8772 ft).
Climate: Tropical climate is moderated by altitude and by the sea.

The executive President (who appoints a Prime Minister and a Council of Ministers) is elected by universal adult suffrage for a maximum of two non-consecutive five-year terms. The 83-member National Assembly is directly elected for five years.
Largest parties: (1995 election) (reformist left-wing) Lavalas Movement (ML) 68, others 15.
President: (since 1995) Réné Préval (supported by ML).
Prime Minister: (since 1996) Rosny Smarth (non-party).

With few resources, overpopulated Haiti is the poorest state in the Western Hemisphere. Over one-half of the labour force is involved in farming, mainly growing crops for local consumption. Coffee is the main cash crop. Exports include textiles and clothing and processed food. The country suffers from the emigration of skilled young people. **Currency:** Gourde.

1915 US military intervention ended a period of coups, instability and tension between blacks and mulattos. **1934–35** End of US intervention. **1957–86** Dictatorship of François Duvalier (d. 1971) and his son Jean-Claude; Haiti cowed into submission through the activities of their infamous private militia, the Tontons. **1986** Violent end of the Duvalier era. **1986–91** Period of instability: several coups. **1991** First free multi-party elections, but constitutional rule suspended within months when military deposed reformist President Aristide. **1994** International sanctions and US involvement restored constitutional rule and Aristide to power.

Official name: La République d'Haïti (The Republic of Haiti).
Area: 27,750 km² (10,714 sq mi).
Population: 6,590,000 (1995 est.).
Doubling time: 33 years. **Adult life expectancy:** male 43 years, female 47 years. **Birth rate:** 1.6 times world average. **Death rate:** 2.04 times world average. **Urban population:** 31%. **Capital:** Port-au-Prince 1,255,000 urban area (city 753,000; Carrefour 241,000; Delmas 200,000; 1992 est.; inc. suburbs). **Other main centres:** Carrefour and Delmas *see Port-au-Prince*; Cap Haïtien 92,000, Gonïaves 63,000 (1992 est.).
Language: French 1% (official), French-Haitian Creole 99% (official).
Adult literacy: 53%.
Religion: Roman Catholic 80%, various Evangelical Protestant Churches 8%, Baptist minority. Voodoo is practised by the majority (at least 75%) of the population while also owing allegiance to a Christian denomination.

■ *Slums, which house about 50% of the city's people, surround Port-au-Prince*

DOMINICAN REPUBLIC

The Dominican Republic occupies the (larger) eastern half of the West Indian island of Hispaniola. The fertile Cibao valley in the north is the most important agricultural region. Most of the rest of the country is mountainous.
Highest point: Pico Duarte 3175 m (10,417 ft).
Climate: Largely subtropical, but it is cooler in the mountains. Rainfall is heavy in the east and north, but the west and south-west are arid. Hurricanes are a hazard.

An executive President, 30-member Senate (upper house) and 120-member Chamber of Deputies (lower house) are elected by universal adult suffrage for four years. The President appoints a Cabinet of Secretaries of State.
Largest parties: (1994 election) (left-wing) Dominican Revolutionary Party and allies (PRD) 57 seats, (centre-right) Social Christian Reformist Party (PRSC) 50, (left-wing) Dominican Liberation Party (PLD) 13.
President: (since 1996) Leonel Fernandez (PLD; PLD-PRSC government).

Ferronickel is the major export. About 30% of Dominicans work in farming, with sugar (once the mainstay of the economy), coffee, cocoa and tobacco as the principal crops. Tourism is now a major foreign-currency earner. **Currency:** Dominican peso.

1900 The republic was bankrupt and in chaos following rule by a succession of dictators. **1916–24** US military intervention. **1930** Rafael Trujillo became president and ruthlessly suppressed opposition. **1971** Trujillo assassinated. **1965** Short civil war ended by US military intervention. **Since 1965** An infant democracy has faced severe economic problems; presidencies of Joaquín Balaguer 1966–78 and 1986–96.

Official name: República Dominicana (The Dominican Republic).
Area: 48,443 km² (18,704 sq mi).
Population: 7,825,000 (1995 est.).
Doubling time: 32 years. **Adult life expectancy:** male 60 years, female 64 years. **Birth rate:** 1.2 times world average. **Death rate:** 0.86 times world average. **Urban population:** 65%. **Capital:** Santo Domingo 2,100,000 (1993 est.; inc. suburbs).
Other main centres: Santiago de los Caballeros 690,000, La Vega 190,000, San Francisco de Macorís 165,000, San Pedro de Macorís 140,000, La Romana 140,000 (1993 est.; inc. suburbs).
Language: Spanish 98% (official), French Haitian Creole minority.
Adult literacy: 82%.
Religion: Roman Catholic 93%, various Protestant Evangelical Churches 6%.

JAMAICA

Jamaica is an independent island-state south of Cuba in the Caribbean. Coastal lowlands surround interior limestone plateaux (the 'Cockpit Country') and mountains, including the Blue Mountains.
Highest point: Blue Mountain Peak 2256 m (7402 ft).
Climate: The lowlands are tropical and rainy; the highlands are cooler and wetter.

The 21 members of the Senate are appointed (13 on the advice of the Prime Minister and eight on the advice of the leader of the opposition) by the Governor General, who is the representative of the British Queen as sovereign of Jamaica. The 100-member House of Representatives (lower house) is elected by universal adult suffrage for five years. The Governor General appoints a Prime Minister who commands a majority in the Assembly. The PM, in turn, appoints other Ministers.
Largest parties: (1993 election) (leftist) People's National Party (PNP) 61 seats, (centre-left) Jamaica Labour Party (Lab) 39.
Prime Minister: (since 1992) Percival J. Patterson (PNP).

The export of alumina and bauxite is the mainstay of the economy, accounting for one-half of Jamaica's exports. About 20% of the labour force is involved in farming, producing sugar cane and bananas for export. Tourism is a major foreign-currency earner. **Currency:** Jamaican dollar.

1930s Severe social and economic conditions led to riots by Black Jamaicans. **1962** Independence after over 300 years of British rule. **1972–80 and 1989–92** Premierships of radical PNP leader Michael Manley.

Official name: Jamaica.
Area: 10,991 km² (4244 sq mi).
Population: 2,520,000 (1995 est.).
Doubling time: 38 years. **Adult life expectancy:** male 71.4 years, female 75.8 years. **Birth rate:** 0.95 times world average. **Death rate:** 0.58 times world average. **Urban population:** 50%. **Capital:** Kingston 588,000 urban area (city 104,000; Portmore 90,000; 1991 census).
Other main centres: Spanish Town 92,000, Portmore *see Kingston*, Montego Bay 83,000 (1990 census).
Language: English (including Creole) 95% (official), Hindi and other minorities. **Adult literacy:** 98%.
Religion: Church of God 17%, Baptist 10%, Anglican 7%, Seventh-day Adventist 6%, Pentecostal 5%, Roman Catholic 5%, Rastafarian 5%, non-religious 20%.

■ *Montego Bay market, in the north of Jamaica, showing fruits vital to Jamaica's economy*

BAHAMAS

The Bahamas are an independent state east of the coast of Florida. The group comprises some 700 long, flat, narrow islands and over 2000 barren rocky islets.
Highest point: Mt Alvernia 63 m (206 ft).
Climate: The climate is mild and subtropical, with no great seasonal variation in temperature. Rainfall averages just over 1000 mm (40 in). The islands are liable to hurricanes.

The Senate (upper house) has 19 appointed members. The 40-member House of Assembly (lower house) is elected by universal adult suffrage for five years. A Prime Minister, who commands a majority in the House, is appointed by the Governor General, the representative of the British Queen as sovereign of the Bahamas. The PM, in turn, appoints other Ministers.
Largest parties: (1997 election) (centre) Free National Movement (FNMP) 34 seats, (centre-right) Progressive Liberal Party (PLP) 6.
Prime Minister: (since 1992) Herbert Ingraham (FNMP).

Tourism, mainly from the USA and Canada, is the main source of income and, with related industries, it employs the majority of the labour force. The islands have become a tax haven and financial centre. **Currency:** Bahamian dollar.

1973 Independence after over 250 years of British rule.

Official name: The Commonwealth of The Bahamas.
Area: 13,939 km² (5382 sq mi).
Population: 276,000 (1995 est.).
Doubling time: 52 years. **Adult life expectancy:** male 67.7 years, female 75.5 years. **Birth rate:** 0.76 times world average. **Death rate:** 0.58 times world average. **Urban population:** 86%. **Capital:** Nassau 172,000 (1990 census; inc. suburbs).
Other main centre: Freeport 26,600 (1990 census; inc. suburbs).
Language: English (inc. English Creole) 82% (official), French (Haitian) Creole 12%. **Adult literacy:** no recent figures available.
Religion: Anglican 32%, Roman Catholic 19%, various Protestant Churches 29%, non-religious 20%.

TURKS AND CAICOS ISLANDS

Official name and status: Turks and Caicos Islands; a British Crown colony with internal self-government.
Area: 430 km² (166 sq mi).
Population: 12,400 (1990 census).
Capital: Cockburn Town 2500 (on Grand Turk; 1990 census).
Geography: The 30 Turks and Caicos Islands form two groups of low-lying islands to the south-east of the Bahamas.
Economy: The colony depends upon tourism, 'offshore banking' and finance.

PUERTO RICO

Official names and status: Estado Libre Asociado de Puerto Rico and The Commonwealth of Puerto Rico; a US Commonwealth territory.
Area: 9104 km² (3515 sq mi).
Population: 3,725,000 (1995 est.).
Capital: San Juan 1,230,000 urban area (city 427,000; 1990 census).
Geography: Puerto Rico, the easternmost of the Greater Antilles, is crossed from east to west by a mountain chain. The islands of Vieques and Culebra are included in the Commonwealth.
Economy: Although Puerto Rico has no natural resources, manufacturing dominates, with pharmaceuticals, petrochemicals, food processing, electrical and electronic engineering and textiles as the major industries. The island is densely populated and there has been large-scale migration to the USA. US federal funds have developed the infrastructure and encouraged the service sector.

BRITISH VIRGIN ISLANDS

Official name and status: British Virgin Islands; a British Crown colony with internal self-government.
Area: 153 km² (59 sq mi).
Population: 16,700 (1991 census).
Capital: Road Town 2500 (1991 census).
Geography: The colony consists of three main mountainous islands (Tortola, Virgin Gorda and Jost van Dyke), a flat coralline island (Anegada) and more than 60 small cays. They form the eastern part of the Virgin Islands in the north-east Caribbean.
Economy: The British Virgin Islands are completely overshadowed by their larger neighbour, the US Virgin Islands, and use US currency. Tourism and 'offshore' financial services dominate the economy and money sent home by the many islanders working in the US Virgin Islands is of great importance.

VIRGIN ISLANDS OF THE UNITED STATES

Official name and status: Virgin Islands of the United States; an unincorporated US external territory.
Area: 352 km² (136 sq mi).
Population: 98,000 (1995 est.).
Capital: Charlotte Amalie 12,300 (1990 census).
Geography: The territory (which was the Danish West Indies before being sold to the USA in 1917) includes three main islands (St Croix, St John and St Thomas) and about 50 small cays, 65 km (40 mi) east of Puerto Rico in the north-east Caribbean. The strategically important islands command the Anegada Passage, one of the principal shipping routes from the Atlantic to the Caribbean.
Economy: The islands have no natural resources. Tourism, encouraged by the climate and the free port status of the entire territory, dominates the economy. St Croix has one of the world's largest oil refineries.

CHRISTOPHER COLUMBUS, DISCOVERER OF THE NEW WORLD, ARE BURIED IN SANTO DOMINGO ■

Central Caribbean

ST LUCIA

St Lucia is an independent island state in the east Caribbean. The island is well-watered and forested, with many streams flowing through fertile valleys.
Highest point: Mt Gimie 959 m (3145 ft).
Climate: Moist and tropical although there is a dry season from January to April. The island is subject to hurricanes.

The 11-member Senate is appointed: six members by the Prime Minister, three by the opposition and two by the Governor General, who is the representative of the British Queen as sovereign of St Lucia. The 17-member House of Assembly (lower house) is elected by universal adult suffrage for five years. The Governor General appoints a Prime Minister who commands a majority in the Assembly. The PM, in turn, appoints other Ministers.
Largest parties: (1997 election) (centrist) United Workers' Party (UWP) 11 seats, (centre-left) St Lucia Labour Party (SLP) 6.
Prime Minister: (since 1997) Vaughn Lewis (UWP).

The economy depends upon tourism, which is the largest single employer, and upon farming, with bananas and coconuts as the main crops. The once-important sugar industry ended in 1964. Industries include food processing, rum, soap and electrical components.
Currency: East Caribbean dollar.

1979 Independence after British rule since 1814.

Official name: St Lucia.
Area: 617 km² (238 sq mi).
Population: 143,000 (1995 est.).
Doubling time: 41 years. **Adult life expectancy:** male 67 years, female 72 years. **Birth rate:** 0.92 times world average. **Death rate:** 0.65 times world average. **Urban population:** 48%. **Capital:** Castries 14,000 urban area (city 2100; 1992 est.).
Language: English nearly 100% (official), French Creole understood by 80%. **Adult literacy:** 80%.
Religion: Roman Catholic 79%, Seventh-day Adventist 7%, Pentecostal 3%, with Anglican, Baptist and other minorities.

GRENADA

Grenada is an independent island-state in the south-east Caribbean. A forested mountain ridge covers much of this well-watered island which has many fast-flowing streams in steep valleys. The island of Carriacou forms part of Grenada.
Highest point: Mt St Catherine 840 m (2757 ft).
Climate: A tropical climate with a dry season from January to May.

The 13 members of the Senate are appointed by the Prime Minister, the opposition and the Governor General, who is the representative of the British Queen as sovereign of Grenada. The 15-member House of Representatives (lower house) is elected by universal adult suffrage for five years. The Governor General appoints a Prime Minister who commands a majority in the Assembly. The PM, in turn, appoints other Ministers.
Largest parties: (1995 election) (centre) New National Party (NNP) 8 seats, (centrist) National Democratic Congress (NDC) 5, (right-wing) United Labour Party 2.
Prime Minister: (since 1995) George Brizan (NNP).

The production of spices, in particular nutmeg, is the mainstay of a largely agricultural economy. Cocoa beans, fish and bananas are also exported. Tourism is increasing in importance and the island is regularly visited by cruise ships. **Currency:** East Caribbean dollar.

1974 Independence after 190 years of British rule. **1979** Left-wing New Jewel Movement seized power in a coup. **1983** PM Maurice Bishop was killed in a further coup by more extreme members of the government; US and East Caribbean military intervention; coup leaders detained; interim government was formed. **1984** Constitutional rule was restored.

Official name: Grenada.
Area: 344 km² (133 sq mi).
Population: 92,000 (1995 est.).
Doubling time: 29 years. **Adult life expectancy:** male 68 years, female 73 years. **Birth rate:** 1.2 times world average. **Death rate:** 0.65 times world average. **Urban population:** 32%. **Capital:** St George's 36,000 urban area (city 4400; 1991 census).
Language: English (including English Creole) 100% (official).
Adult literacy: 85%.
Religion: Roman Catholic 53%, Anglican 14%, Seventh-day Adventist 9%, Pentecostal 7%, others and non-religious 17%.

ST KITTS NEVIS (OR ST CHRISTOPHER AND NEVIS)

St Kitts-Nevis is a two-island independent state in the north-east Caribbean. The islands, which are well-watered and mountainous, are 3 km (2 mi) apart.
Highest point: Mt Misery 1156 m (3792 ft).
Climate: The moist tropical climate is cooled by sea breezes. The islands are subject to hurricanes.

The 14-member Parliament comprises eight members elected by universal adult suffrage for five years in St Kitts, three directly elected members from Nevis and three appointed senators. The Governor General, who is the representative of the British Queen as sovereign of St Kitts-Nevis, appoints a Prime Minister who commands a majority in the Assembly. The PM, in turn, appoints other Ministers. Nevis is an autonomous island which has the right of secession.
Largest parties: (1995 election) (social democratic) Labour Party (Lab) 7 seats, (Nevis-based) Concerned Citizens Movement (CCM) 2, (centre-left) People's Action Movement (PAM) 1, (Nevis-based centre-left) Nevis Reformation Party 1.
Prime Minister: (since 1995) Dr Denzil Douglas (Lab).

The economies of both islands are based upon agriculture (mainly sugar cane but also yams, bananas, and coconuts) and tourism.
Currency: East Caribbean dollar.

1882 The British colonies of St Kitts, Nevis and Anguilla were united as a single dependency. **1967** Anguilla, a reluctant partner, declared independence (and was returned to British rule after intervention by British troops and police in 1969). **1983** Independence. **Mid-1990s** Increasing support in Nevis for secession. **1996** Nevis's parliament voted in favour of independence, but as yet no referendum has been held to decide its future status.

AUTONOMOUS ISLAND

Nevis
Area: 93 km² (36 sq mi).
Pop.: 9100 (1991 census).
Capital: Charlestown.

Official names: The Federation of St Kitts and Nevis and The Federation of St Christopher and Nevis.
Area: 269 km² (104 sq mi).
Population: 39,400 (1995 est.).
Doubling time: population almost stable. **Adult life expectancy:** male 63 years, female 69 years. **Birth rate:** 0.96 times world average. **Death rate:** 1.08 times world average.
Urban population: 43%.
Capital: Basseterre 18,000 (1995 est.). **Language:** English (inc. English Creole) 100% (official).
Adult literacy: 90%.
Religion: Anglican 33%, Methodist 28%, Roman Catholic 7%, Pentecostal 6%, Baptist 4%, Church of God 4%, others and non-religious 24%.

■ THE FRENCH ISLAND OF ST-BARTHÉLEMY IN GUADELOUPE WAS FORMERLY SWEDEN'S ONLY

ANTIGUA AND BARBUDA

Antigua and Barbuda is a two-island independent state in the north-east Caribbean. Antigua is a low-lying limestone island; Barbuda, which is 45 km (25 mi) north, is a flat wooded coral island. The state also includes the uninhabited rocky outcrop of Redonda.
Highest point: Boggy Peak 402 m (1319 ft).
Climate: The tropical climate is moderated by sea breezes. Rainfall is low for the West Indies and Antigua suffers drought. The islands are subject to hurricanes.

The 17-member Senate is appointed by the Prime Minister, Leader of the Opposition and the Governor General, who is the representative of the British Queen as sovereign of Antigua and Barbuda. The 17-member House of Representatives is elected by universal adult suffrage for five years. The Governor General appoints a Prime Minister who enjoys a majority in the House. The PM, in turn, appoints other Ministers.
Largest parties: (1994 election) (centrist) Antigua Labour Party (ALP) 11 seats, (centrist) United Progressive Party (UPP) 5, Barbuda People's Movement (BPM) 1.

■ *English Harbour, Antigua, a port of call for a number of Caribbean cruise liners*

Prime Minister: (since 1994) Lester Bryant Bird (ALP).

Tourism is the mainstay of the economy. In an attempt to diversify, the government has encouraged agriculture, but lack of water on Antigua is a problem.
Currency: East Caribbean dollar.

1981 Independence after nearly 350 years of British rule.

Official name: Antigua and Barbuda. **Area:** 442 km² (170.5 sq mi). **Population:** 63,900 (1995 est.). **Doubling time:** 58 years. **Adult life expectancy:** male 71.1 years, female 75.3 years. **Birth rate:** 0.69 times world average. **Death rate:** 0.58 times world average. **Urban population:** 36%. **Capital:** St John's 36,000 urban area (city 21,500; 1991 census).
Other main centre: Codrington (capital of Barbuda) 1400 (1991 census).
Language: English (including English Creole) almost 100% (official).
Adult literacy: 90%.
Religion: Anglican 33%, Roman Catholic 11%, various Protestant Churches 28%, others and non-religious 28%.

DOMINICA

Dominica is a republic in the eastern Caribbean. The island is surrounded by steep cliffs and has a mountainous interior.
Highest point: Morne Diablotin 1447 m (4747 ft).
Climate: A tropical climate with heavy rainfall and very little seasonal variation. The island is subject to hurricanes.

The 30-member House of Assembly comprises 21 members elected for five years by universal adult suffrage plus nine or ten members chosen by the President. The President, whose role is largely ceremonial, is nominated by the Prime Minister and Leader of the Opposition and elected by the Assembly for a maximum of two five-year terms. The President appoints a Prime Minister who commands a majority in the Assembly. The PM, in turn, appoints other Ministers.
Largest parties: (1995 election) (social democratic) United Workers' Party (DUWP) 11 seats, (centre-right) Dominica Freedom Party (DFP) 5, (left-wing) Labour Party 5, others 10.
Prime Minister: (since 1995) Edison James (DUWP).

Dominica is a poor island which produces bananas, timber and coconuts, and exports water to its drier neighbours. Limes are also grown commercially and exported as lime juice. Tourism is increasing in importance. **Currency:** East Caribbean dollar.

1978 Independence after 195 years of British rule.

Official name: Commonwealth of Dominica.
Area: 739 km² (285 sq mi).
Population: 72,000 (1995 est.).
Doubling time: 45 years. **Adult life expectancy:** male 74.1 years, female 79.9 years. **Birth rate:** 0.82 times world average. **Death rate:** 0.54 times world average. **Urban population:** 41%. **Capital:** Roseau 16,000 (1991 census).
Other main centre: Portsmouth 4000 (1991 census).
Language: English 4% as a first language but almost universally understood (official), French Creole 96%. **Adult literacy:** 90%.
Religion: Roman Catholic 55%, Seventh-day Adventist 5%, Pentecostal 4%, Methodist 4%, other Protestant Churches 9%, Anglican minority.

■ *Cruise ship moored in Roseau Harbor on the south-western coast of Dominica*

ANGUILLA

Official name and status: Anguilla; a British dependent territory with internal self-government (Anguilla formally returned to colonial rule in 1971, after a unilateral declaration of independence.)
Area: 96 km² (37 sq mi), including Sombrero (a rocky islet to the north).
Population: 9000 (1993 est.).
Capital: The Valley 500 (1993 est.).
Geography: Anguilla is a low-lying coral island in the eastern Caribbean.
Economy: Tourism is the main industry.

GUADELOUPE

Official name and status: Le Département de la Guadeloupe (The département of Guadeloupe); a French overseas département and an integral part of the French Republic.
Area: 1780 km² (687 sq mi): Basse-Terre 848 km² (327 sq mi), Grande-Terre 590 km² (228 sq mi), Marie-Galante 158 km² (61 sq mi), St Martin 54 km² (21 sq mi), St Barthélemy 21 km² (8 sq mi), La Désirade 20 km² (8 sq mi), Iles des Saintes 13 km² (5 sq mi).
Population: 434,000 (1995 est.).
Capital: Basse-Terre (also capital of Basse-Terre island) 53,000 urban area (city 14,000; 1990 census). The capitals of the other islands are: Pointe-à-Pitre (Grande-Terre), Grand-Bourg (Marie-Galante), Marigot (St Martin), Gustavia (St Barthélemy), Grande Anse (La Désirade), Terre-de-Bas (Iles des Saintes).
Other main centre: Pointe-à-Pitre 141,000 urban area (city 26,000; Les Abymes 63,000; 1990 census).
Geography: Guadeloupe comprises a group of Caribbean islands: Grande-Terre, Basse-Terre and their neighbours, lying between Antigua and Dominica. St Martin is the northern half of a north Caribbean island whose southern half is Dutch. St Barthélemy (which was once Swedish) lies south of St Martin.
Economy: Bananas and sugar cane are the main exports. Tourism is the main employer and the smaller islands have specialized in upmarket tourism.

MARTINIQUE

Official name and status: Le Département de la Martinique (The département of Martinique); a French overseas département and an integral part of the French Republic.
Area: 1128 km² (436 sq mi).
Population: 388,000 (1995 est.).
Capital: Fort-de-France 100,000 (1990 census).
Geography: Martinique lies between St Lucia and Dominica. A tropical Caribbean island, it rises steeply to a mountainous interior.
Economy: Bananas and sugar cane (for rum) are the main exports. Tourism is increasingly important.

MONTSERRAT

Official name and status: Montserrat; a British Crown Colony with internal self-government.
Area: 98 km² (38 sq mi).
Population: 12,000 (1991 census); 3000 (1997 est.) after the majority had left the island owing to a volcanic eruption.
Capital: The former capital, Plymouth, was abandoned to the volcanic eruption in 1997.
Geography: Montserrat is a small mountainous island in the north-eastern Caribbean.
Economy: The economy was dominated by tourism before the volcanic eruptions of 1995–97 devastated the island. In mid-1997 a complete evacuation was a possibility.

SOUTHERN CARIBBEAN

GUYANA

Guyana, a republic on the Atlantic coast in the north of South America, is by history and culture part of the Caribbean world. A coastal plain is protected by dykes. Tropical rain forest and high, steep-sided plateaux cover much of the interior. The Pakaraima range rises on the western border.
Highest point: Mt Roraima 2770 m (9094 ft).
Climate: The interior is tropical with high temperatures and heavy rainfall. The coastal regions are more moderate with drier spells between February and April and September to December.

The 65-member National Assembly is elected for five years: 53 members are elected by universal adult suffrage under a system of proportional representation; 12 members are chosen by the regional authorities. An executive President, who is directly elected for a five-year term, appoints a Prime Minister and other Ministers, who are responsible to the Assembly.
Largest parties: (1992 election) (left-wing) People's Progressive Party (PPP) 32 seats, (left-wing) People's National Congress (PNC) 31, (left-wing) Working People's Alliance 1, (centre-right) United Force 1.
President: (since 1997) Sam Hinds (PPP).
Prime Minister: (since 1997) Janet Jago (PPP).

Guyana depends upon mining bauxite and gold (which together make up almost one-third of the country's exports) and growing sugar cane and rice (which account for nearly one-half of the exports). The demands of a large state sector (including nationalized industries) and the problems caused by large-scale emigration have hampered economic development. **Currency:** Guyana dollar.

Mid 19th century Large-scale migration of Indians and Chinese into British Guiana to work on plantations. **1964** Violence between the Black majority and the Indian and Chinese minority. **1966** Independence as Guyana after 170 years of British rule. **1970** Republic declared. **1978** Further ethnic unrest.

Official name: Co-operative Republic of Guyana.
Area: 215,083 km² (83,044 sq mi).
Population: 770,000 (1995 est.).
Doubling time: 54 years. **Adult life expectancy:** male 62 years, female 68 years. **Birth rate:** 0.8 times world average. **Death rate:** 0.75 times world average. **Urban population:** 31%. **Capital:** Georgetown 249,000 (1992 est.; inc. suburbs). **Other main centre:** Linden 27,000 (1992 est.; inc. suburbs).
Language: English spoken as a first language by under 1% (official), English Creole 97%, Cariban 1%, Arawak 1%. **Adult literacy:** 98%.
Religion: Hindu 34%, Roman Catholic 18%, various Protestant Churches 17%, Anglican 16%, Sunni Islam 9%.

TRINIDAD AND TOBAGO

Trinidad and Tobago is a two-island republic in the south-eastern Caribbean. Trinidad, which lies off the coast of Venezuela, is low-lying and undulating, rising to hills in the Northern Range. Tobago, 35 km (22 mi) to the north-east, is more mountainous.
Highest point: Cerro del Aripo 940 m (3085 ft).
Climate: The islands have a humid tropical climate with a dry season from January to May.

The 31-member Senate is nominated: nine members by the President, 16 by the Prime Minister and six by the opposition. The 36-member lower house (Assembly) is elected by universal adult suffrage for five years. A President, whose role is largely ceremonial and who is elected for five years by a joint session of the Senate and Assembly, appoints a Prime Minister who commands a majority in the Assembly. The PM, in turn, appoints other Ministers. Tobago enjoys considerable autonomy.
Largest parties: (1995 election) (centrist-left) United National Congress (UNC) 17 seats, (centre) People's National Movement (PMP) 17, (Tobago-based) National Alliance for Reconstruction (NAR) 2.
President: (since 1987) Noor Mohammed Hassanali (non-party).
Prime Minister: (since 1995) Basdeo Panday (UNC).

Petroleum and petroleum products (mainly refined Venezuelan oil) are the mainstays of the economy. Trinidad has important reserves of asphalt and natural gas. Tourism (particularly to the island of Tobago) is a major foreign-currency earner. **Currency:** Trinidad and Tobago dollar.

1899 The two British colonies of Trinidad and Tobago became a single dependency. **1962** Independence. **1976** Republic proclaimed. **1990** Attempted coup by Muslim fundamentalists.

Official name: Republic of Trinidad and Tobago.
Area: 5128 km² (1980 sq mi).
Population: 1,265,000 (1995 est.).
Doubling time: 64 years. **Adult life expectancy:** male 68 years, female 73.2 years. **Birth rate:** 0.7 times world average. **Death rate:** 0.7 times world average. **Urban population:** 71%. **Capital:** Port of Spain 60,000 (1992 est.). **Other main centres:** Chaguanas 57,000, San Fernando 30,000, Arima 30,000 (1990 census).
Language: English (including Trinidad English Creole) 95%, Hindi 3%.
Adult literacy: 97%.
Religion: Roman Catholic 29%, Hindu 24%, various Protestant Churches 19%, Anglican 11%, Sunni Islam 6%.

AUTONOMOUS ISLAND

Tobago
Area: 300 km² (116 sq mi).
Pop.: 50,300 (1990 census).
Capital: Scarborough.

■ 923 PEOPLE DIED IN THE SUICIDE OF THE TEMPLE OF THE PEOPLE CULT IN GUYANA IN 1978 ■

ST VINCENT AND THE GRENADINES

St Vincent and the Grenadines is an independent state comprising the main island of St Vincent and a chain of seven smaller islands (the Grenadines) in the east Caribbean. St Vincent is a mountainous wooded island rising to an active volcano. Bequia and Mustique are the largest Grenadines.
Highest point: Mt Soufrière 1234 m (4048 ft).
Climate: Moist and tropical with heavy rainfall in the mountains. The islands are subject to hurricanes.

The 21-member House of Assembly comprises 15 members elected by universal adult suffrage for five years, plus six senators (four appointed by the Prime Minister and two by the opposition). The Governor General, who is the representative of the British Queen as sovereign of St Vincent, appoints a Prime Minister who commands a majority in the Assembly. The PM, in turn, appoints other Ministers.
Largest parties: (1994 election) (centrist) New Democratic Party (NDP) 12 seats, (social democratic) Unity Labour Party (ULP) 3, others 6.
Prime Minister: (since 1984) James Mitchell (NDP).

Official name: St Vincent and the Grenadines.
Area: 389 km² (150 sq mi).
Population: 112,000 (1995 est.).
Doubling time: 39 years. **Adult life expectancy:** male 71 years, female 74 years. **Birth rate:** 0.99 times world average. **Death rate:** 0.71 times world average. **Urban population:** 25%.
Capital: Kingstown 27,000 urban area (city 15,800; 1993 est.).
Language: English (including English Creole) nearly 100% (official).
Adult literacy: 80%.
Religion: Anglican 42%, Methodist 21%, Roman Catholic 12%, other Protestant Churches and non-religious 35%.

Bananas and arrowroot are the main crops of a mainly agricultural economy. Upmarket tourism is being promoted in the Grenadines. St Vincent has traditionally had high rates of emigration. **Currency:** East Caribbean dollar.

1979 Independence after British rule since 1763.

BARBADOS

Barbados is an independent island-state in the south-east of the Caribbean. The island is generally flat and low, except in the north.
Highest point: Mt Hillaby 340 m (1115 ft).
Climate: A tropical climate. Rainfall is heavy, with totals everywhere above 1000 mm (40 in). The island is subject to hurricanes.

The 21 members of the Senate are appointed: 12 by the Prime Minister, two by the opposition and seven by the Governor General, who is the representative of the British Queen as sovereign of Barbados. The 28-member Assembly (lower house) is elected by universal adult suffrage for five years. The Governor General appoints a Prime Minister who commands a majority in the Assembly. The PM, in turn, appoints other Ministers.
Largest parties: (1994 election) (social democratic) Barbados Labour Party (BLP) 19 seats, (centrist) Democratic Labour Party (DLP) 8, National Democratic Party 1.
Prime Minister: (since 1994) Owen S. Arthur (BLP).

Tourism (the main source of income) employs over one-third of the workforce. The government has encouraged diversification and there has been growth in banking, insurance and data processing. Sugar, once the mainstay of the economy, remains the major crop. **Currency:** Barbados dollar.

1937 Riots by Black Barbadians, whose economic and social conditions were poor, led to reform. **1966** Independence after 340 years of British rule.

Official name: Barbados.
Area: 430 km² (166 sq mi).
Population: 265,000 (1995 est.).
Doubling time: population almost stable. **Adult life expectancy:** male 72.9 years, female 77.4 years. **Birth rate:** 0.54 times world average.
Death rate: 0.94 times world average. **Urban population:** 38%.
Capital: Bridgetown 85,000 urban area (city 6100; 1990 census). **Other main centre:** Speightstown 4000 (1990 census).
Language: English (including Bajan/English Creole) 100% (official).
Adult literacy: 98%.
Religion: Anglican 33%, Pentecostal 10%, Methodist 9%, other Protestant Churches 11%, Roman Catholic 5%, others and non-religious 32%.

SURINAME

Suriname is a republic on the Atlantic coast in the north-east of South America. It has a swampy coastal plain, a forested central plateau and mountains in the south.
Highest point: Juliana Top 1230 m (4035 ft).
Climate: A tropical climate with heavy rainfall except during the drier seasons between February and April and September to December.

The 51-member National Assembly, which is elected by universal adult suffrage for five years, chooses a President, who serves for a five-year term. The President shares executive power with a Prime Minister, whom he appoints. The PM, in turn, appoints other Ministers, who are responsible to the Assembly.
Largest parties: (1996 election) (centre-right coalition) New Front for Democracy and Development (NF) 24 seats, (right-wing) Democratic National Party (NDP) 16, others (mainly Democratic Alternative) 11.
President: (since 1996) Jules Wijdenbosch (NDP).
Prime Minister: (since 1996) Pretaapnarian Radhakishun (NDP minority government).

The extraction and mining of bauxite is the mainstay of the economy, contributing over one-half of the exports. Other exports include shrimps, fish and rice. The economy has been hampered by political instability and by large-scale emigration (mainly to the Netherlands). **Currency:** Suriname guilder.

1870s–90s Plantation workers came to Suriname from India and Java. **1975** Independence; 130,000 Surinamese emigrated before independence. **1980–86** Six coups (others were attempted); periods of military rule; ethnic unrest.

Official name: Republiek Suriname (The Republic of Suriname).
Area: 163,820 km² (63,251 sq mi).
Population: 430,000 (1995 est.).
Doubling time: 29 years. **Adult life expectancy:** male 66.6 years, female 71.8 years. **Birth rate:** 1.24 times world average. **Death rate:** 0.7 times world average. **Urban population:** 49%. **Capital:** Paramaribo 201,000 (1993 est.; inc. suburbs). **Other main centre:** Nieuw Nickerie 6000 (1993 est.; inc. suburbs).
Language: Dutch spoken as a first language by under 1% (official), Sranantonga (Surinamese Creole) 79%, with Hindi, Javanese, and Saramacca minorities; it is intended that Spanish should eventually become an official language.
Adult literacy: 95%.
Religion: Hindu 27%, Roman Catholic 23%, Sunni Islam 20%, various Protestant Reformed Churches 19%.

FRENCH GUIANA

Official name and status: Le Département de la Guyane (The département of Guyane); a French overseas département and an integral part of the French Republic.
Area: 86,504 km² (33,399 sq mi).
Population: 145,000 (1995 est.).
Capital: Cayenne 42,000 (1990 census).
Geography: French Guiana is a tropical lowland lying between Brazil and Suriname. Much of its area is still covered by rain forest.
Economy: The economy depends upon timber and upon government subsidies from metropolitan France. Very little land is cultivated and mineral ores, including bauxite, are not as yet widely exploited.

ARUBA

Official name and status: Aruba; an autonomous part of the Kingdom of the Netherlands. (Aruba is scheduled to gain independence before 2000.)
Area: 193 km² (75 sq mi).
Population: 73,000 (1995 est.).
Capital: Oranjestad 20,000 (1991 est.).
Geography: Aruba is a relatively flat Caribbean island 24 km (15 mi) north of the Venezuelan coast.
Economy: Tourism is a major foreign-currency earner, and financial services and data processing are of growing importance. Lack of water restricts farming and means that most foodstuffs are imported.

NETHERLANDS ANTILLES (also known as THE ANTILLES OF THE FIVE)

Official name and status: De Nederlandse Antillen (The Netherlands Antilles); an autonomous part of the Kingdom of the Netherlands.
Area: 800 km² (309 sq mi): Curaçao 444 km² (171 sq mi), Bonaire 288 km² (111 sq mi), Sint Maarten 34 km² (13 sq mi), St Eustatius (or Statia) 21 km² (8 sq mi), Saba 13 km² (5 sq mi).
Population: 202,000 (1995 est.): Curaçao 149,000, Bonaire 13,000, Sint Maarten 37,000, St Eustatius (or Statia) 1100, Saba 1800.
Capital: Willemstad 50,000 (1991 est.). The capitals of the islands are: Willemstad (Curaçao), Kralendijk (Bonaire), Philipsburg (Sint Maarten), Oranjestad (St Eustatius/Statia), The Bottom (Saba).
Geography: Curaçao and Bonaire are relatively arid Caribbean islands off the coast of Venezuela; Sint Maarten is the southern half of an island shared with France in the Leeward group in the northern Caribbean; Statia and Saba are two very small islands north of St Kitts in the north Caribbean.
Economy: Curaçao depends upon refining Venezuelan oil and upon ship repairing. Bonaire produces textiles and salt. Tourism is important in all the islands.

IN 1667 ENGLAND CEDED SURINAME TO THE DUTCH IN EXCHANGE FOR WHAT IS NOW NEW YORK

SOUTH AMERICA I

COLOMBIA

Colombia is a republic occupying the north-west corner of South America and with two coastlines, one Pacific, the other Caribbean. The Andes run north to south through Colombia. The greater part of the country lies east of the Andes in the mainly treeless grassland plains of the Llanos and the tropical Amazon rain forest. A coastal plain lies to the west of the mountains.
Highest point: Pico Cristóbal Colón 5775 m (18,947 ft).
Climate: The lower Andes are temperate; the mountains over 4000 m (13,100 ft) experience permanent snow. The rest of Colombia is tropical: the coasts and the Amazon basin are hot and humid with heavy rainfall, while the Llanos have a savannah climate.

An executive President (who appoints a Cabinet of Ministers) is elected by universal adult suffrage for a four-year term and is not immediately eligible for reelection. The 102-member Senate and the 161-member House of Representatives are also directly elected for four years.
Largest parties: (1994 election House) Liberal Party (PL) 89 seats, Social Conservative Party (PCS) 56, (left-wing) Democratic Alliance-18 April Movement (ADM19) 2, others 14.
President: (since 1994) Ernesto Samper (PL).

Colombian coffee, forestry and fisheries products and petroleum are the main exports. Other important agriculture products include bananas, sugar cane, tobacco and flowers, but the illegal cultivation and export of marijuana and cocaine probably produce the greatest revenue. Mineral resources include iron ore, silver, coal and natural gas as well as petroleum. The principal industries are food processing, petroleum refining, fertilizers, cement, textiles, clothing and iron and steel,
Currency: Colombian peso.

Official name: República de Colombia (The Republic of Colombia).
Area: 1,141,568 km² (440,762 sq mi).
Population: 35,100,000 (1995 est.).
Doubling time: 39 years. **Adult life expectancy:** male 69.3 years, female 72.3 years. **Birth rate:** 0.96 times world average. **Death rate:** 0.65 times world average. **Urban population:** 70%. **Capital:** (Santafé) de Bogota 5,238,000 (1995 est.; inc. suburbs). **Other main centres:** Cali 1,719,000, Medellín 1,621,000, Barranquilla 1,064,000, Cartagena 746,000, Cúcuta 450,000 (1995 est.; inc. suburbs).
Language: Spanish 99% (official), Amerindian languages 1%.
Adult literacy: 87%.
Religion: Roman Catholic 93%, various Protestant Churches over 5%.

1899–1902 Civil war between centralizing, pro-clerical Conservatives and federalist Liberals. **1948–57** Second Conservative-Liberal civil war: cost up to 400,000 lives. **1957–74** Power sharing between Conservatives and Liberals; fragile democracy. **Since 1970s** Rise of left-wing guerrilla movements and right-wing death squads. **1980s–early 1990s** Powerful drug-dealing cartels threatened the stability of the state. **Early 1990s** Some left-wing guerrillas abandoned violence in favour of legitimate political activity; infamous Medellin drugs cartel curbed, but new Cali drugs barons took their place.

■ *Coffee plants grow in a plantation, near Armenia, Colombia*

PANAMA

Panama is a republic occupying the isthmus, between the Caribbean and the Pacific, which joins Central America to South America. Much of the country is heavily forested and mountainous and the Darien Gap on the Colombian border is impassable to traffic.
Highest point: Baru 3475 m (11,401 ft), an extinct volcano.
Climate: Humid tropical climate with little seasonal change in temperature.

An executive President (who appoints a Council of Ministers) and a 72-member Legislative Assembly are elected by universal adult suffrage for five years.
Largest parties: (1994 election) (nationalist) Democratic Revolutionary Party (PDR) and allies 33 seats, (right-wing) Arnulfist Party (PA) and allies including the Authentic Liberal Party (PLA) 21, Liberal Republican Nationalist Movement (MORILENA) and allies 9, (centre-right) Papa Egoro Movement (MPE) 6, others 3.
President: (since 1994) Ernesto Pérez Balladares (PDR).

Income from the Panama Canal is a major foreign-currency earner. Panama, which has a higher living standard than many of its neighbours, has become an important 'offshore' banking centre. Major exports include bananas and shrimps.
Currency: Balboa.

1903 Panama, formerly part of Colombia, became independent with US encouragement after Colombia rejected US proposals for completing a ship canal through the isthmus. **1903–79** US controlled a separate Canal Zone 8 km (5 mi) either side of the canal. **1914** Panama Canal opened. **1983–89** Effective power in hands of Gen. Manuel Noriega who was deposed by US invasion and taken for trial in USA, where he was found guilty of criminal activities. **1994** First completely free elections in Panamanian history.

Official name: República de Panama (Republic of Panama).
Area: 75,517 km² (29,157 sq mi).
Population: 2,630,000 (1995 est.).
Doubling time: 35 years. **Adult life expectancy:** male 70.8 years, female 75 years. **Birth rate:** almost the world average. **Death rate:** 0.54 times world average. **Urban population:** 53%. **Capital:** Panama 828,000 urban area (city 585,000; San Miguelito 133,000; 1990 census; inc. suburbs). **Other main centres:** Colón 141,000, David 103,000 (1990 census; inc. suburbs).
Language: Spanish 77% as a first language (official), English Creole 14%, Chibchan 7%.
Adult literacy: 52%.
Religion: Roman Catholic 80%, various Protestant Churches 10%, Sunni Islam 5%.

VENEZUELA

Venezuela is a republic on the Caribbean coast of South America. Mountains, which include part of the Andes, rise sharply behind coastal plains in the north and north-east. In the north-west the Maracaibo basin contains a large freshwater lake. Central Venezuela comprises low-lying grassland plains (Llanos). The Guiana Highlands in the south-east contain many high steep-sided plateaux. Venezuela includes a number of Caribbean islands.
Highest point: Pico Bolívar 5007 m (16,423 ft).
Climate: The tropical coast is arid. The cooler mountains and the tropical Llanos are wet, although the latter has a dry season from December to March.

An executive President (who appoints a Council of Ministers) and both Houses of the National Congress are elected by compulsory universal adult suffrage for five years. The 50-member Senate (upper house) comprises senators elected from the states and the federal district, plus former presidents who are life members. The 204-member Chamber of Deputies (lower house) is elected from constituencies. Individual states have their own legislatures.
Largest parties: (1993 election Chamber of Deputies) (centre-left) Democratic Action (AD) 55 seats, (centre-right) Social Christian Party (Copei) 54, National Convergence Movement to Socialism including Socialist Movement (MAS) 50, (extreme left) Radical Cause (CR) 40, others 5.
President: (since 1994) Rafael Caldera Rodriguez (supported by Copei–MAS alliance).

As petroleum and petroleum products account for nearly 80% of Venezuelan exports the fall in oil prices in the 1980s damaged the economy but the oil sector recovered by the mid-1990s and export earnings increased strongly. Other exports include timber, aluminium and iron ore. Agriculture is mainly concerned with raising beef cattle (nearly 20% of the country is permanent pasture) and growing sugar cane and coffee for foreign markets; bananas, maize and rice are grown as subsistence crops.
Currency: Bolivar.

1909–35 Dictatorship of Juan Vicente Gómez. **1948–58** Military dictatorships. **Since 1958** Civilian democracy, although there have been two unsuccessful coup attempts in the 1990s with periods of social unrest. **1980** Expulsion of 300,000 illegal Colombian immigrants.

Official name: República de Venezuela (The Republic of Venezuela). **Area:** 912,050 km² (352,144 sq mi). **Population:** 21,845,000 (1995 est.). **Doubling time:** 33 years. **Adult life expectancy:** male 70.1 years, female 76 years. **Birth rate:** 1.03 times world average. **Death rate:** 0.5 times world average. **Urban population:** 85%. **Capital:** Caracas 2,270,000 (1995 est.; inc. suburbs). **Other main centres:** Maracaibo 1,364,000, Valencia 1,032,000, Maracay 800,000, Barquisimeto 745,000, Ciudad Guayana 524,000 (1992 est.; inc. suburbs). **Language:** Spanish 97% (official), Amerindian languages nearly 1%. **Adult literacy:** 92%. **Religion:** Roman Catholic 92%, various Protestant Churches 5%.

VENEZUELAN STATES AND TERRITORIES

Amazonas
Area: 175,750 km² (67,900 sq mi).
Pop.: 67,000 (1995 est.).
Capital: Puerto Ayacucho.
Anzoátegui
Area: 43,300 km² (16,700 sq mi).
Pop.: 1,029,000 (1995 est.).
Capital: Barcelona.
Apure
Area: 76,500 km² (29,500 sq mi).
Pop.: 376,000 (1995 est.).
Capital: San Fernando de Apure.
Aragua
Area: 7,014 km² (2,700 sq mi).
Pop.: 1,335,000 (1995 est.).
Capital: Maracay.
Barinas
Area: 35,200 km² (13,600 sq mi).
Pop.: 517,000 (1995 est.).
Capital: Barinas.
Bolívar
Area: 238,000 km² (91,900 sq mi).
Pop.: 1,123,000 (1995 est.).
Capital: Ciudad Bolívar.
Carabobo
Area: 4560 km² (1795 sq mi).
Pop.: 1,808,000 (1995 est.).
Capital: Valencia.
Cojedes
Area: 14,800 km² (5700 sq mi).
Pop.: 226,000 (1995 est.).
Capital: San Carlos.
Delta Amacuro
Area: 40,200 km² (15,500 sq mi).
Pop.: 111,000 (1995 est.).
Capital: Tucupita.
Falcón
Area: 24,800 km² (9600 sq mi).
Pop.: 684,000 (1995 est.).
Capital: Coro.
Guárico
Area: 64,986 km² (25,091 sq mi).
Pop.: 585,000 (1991 census).
Capital: San Juan de Los Morros.
Lara
Area: 19,800 km² (7600 sq mi).
Pop.: 1,424,000 (1995 est.).
Capital: Barquisimeto.
Mérida
Area: 11,300 km² (4400 sq mi).
Pop.: 687,000 (1995 est.).
Capital: Mérida.
Miranda
Area: 7950 km² (3070 sq mi).
Pop.: 2,326,000 (1995 est.).
Capital: Los Teques.
Monagas
Area: 28,900 km² (11,200 sq mi).
Pop.: 551,000 (1995 est.).
Capital: Maturín.
Nueva Esparta
Area: 1150 km² (440 sq mi).
Pop.: 326,000 (1995 est.).
Capital: La Asunción.
Portuguesa
Area: 15,200 km² (5900 sq mi).
Pop.: 719,000 (1995 est.).
Capital: Guanare.
Sucre Area: 11,800 km² (4600 sq mi).
Pop.: 772,000 (1995 est.).
Capital: Cumaná.
Táchira Area: 11,100 km² (4300 sq mi). Pop.: 944,000 (1995 est.).
Capital: San Cristóbal.
Trujillo
Area: 7400 km² (2900 sq mi).
Pop.: 550,000 (1995 est.).
Capital: Trujillo.
Yaracuy
Area: 7100 km² (2700 sq mi).
Pop.: 464,000 (1995 est.).
Capital: San Felipe.
Zulia
Area: 63,100 km² (24,400 sq mi).
Pop.: 2,752,000 (1995 est.).
Capital: Maracaibo.

Federal Dependencies (Dependencias Federales)
Area: 120 km² (50 sq mi).
Uninhabited Caribbean islands administered from Caracas.
Federal District (Distrito Federal)
Area: 1930 km² (745 sq mi).
Pop.: 2,269,000 (1995 est.).
Capital: Caracas.

ECUADOR

Ecuador is a republic on the Equator (hence its name) on the Pacific coast of South America. The Andes divide the Pacific coast plain in the west from the Amazon rain forest in the east. Much of the country is mountainous. Ecuador includes the Galapagos Islands, comprising 16 main islands and associated islets about 1000 km (600 mi) offshore.
Highest point: Chimborazo 6266 m (20,556 ft).
Climate: The Amazon basin has a wet tropical climate. The tropical coastal plain is humid in the north and arid in the south. The highland valleys are mild and 'Spring-like'; the highest peaks have permanent snow.

An executive President (who appoints a Cabinet of Ministers) is elected by compulsory universal adult suffrage for a non-renewable four-year term. The 77-member National Congress comprises 65 members directly elected for two years on a provisional basis and 12 members elected for four years on a national basis.
Largest parties: (1996 mid-term election) (centre-right) Social Christian Party (PSC) 28 seats, (right-wing) Roldosist Party (PRE) 11, (conservative coalition) United Republican Party (PUR) 10, Democratic Party of the Left 7, Conservative Party (PC) 7, Popular Democratic Party (DP) 6, others 8.
President: (since 1997) Fabian Alarcon (independent provisional president; multi-party provisional government).

Agriculture is the single biggest employer and major exports include cocoa, coffee and, in particular, bananas. Other important exports include shrimps and petroleum (the largest single foreign-currency earner). Problems include high inflation and foreign debt.
Currency: Sucre.

1895–78 Long periods of military rule and short periods of civilian government. **1941** Border war with Peru in the Amazon basin: Ecuador lost much territory. **Since 1978** Democratically elected governments have been in power. **1991 and 1995** Border skirmishes with Peru. **1997** President Bucaram voted out of office on grounds of incompetence.

Official name: República del Ecuador (Republic of Ecuador). **Area:** 272,045 km² (105,037 sq mi). **Population:** 11,460,000 (1995 est.). **Doubling time:** 34 years. **Adult life expectancy:** male 67.5 years, female 72.6 years. **Birth rate:** 1.06 times world average. **Death rate:** 0.62 times world average. **Urban population:** 60%. **Capital:** Quito 1,401,000 urban area (city 1,101,000; 1995 est.; inc. suburbs). **Other main centres:** Guayaquil 1,877,000 urban area (city 1,508,000), Cuenca 272,000 (city 240,000), Amabato 151,000, Machala 144,000, Portoviejo 133,000 (1995 est.; inc. suburbs). **Language:** Spanish 93% as a first language (official), Quechua and other Amerindian languages nearly 7%. **Adult literacy:** 88%. **Religion:** Roman Catholic 88%, various Protestant Churches over 5%.

■ *One of a small number of giant tortoises indigenous to the Galapagos Islands*

SOUTH AMERICA II

URUGUAY

Uruguay is a republic on the northern banks of the Plate estuary between Brazil and Argentina. It consists mainly of low-lying plains and plateaux. The coastline is fringed by tidal lakes.
Highest point: Sierra Carapé 514 m (1685 ft).
Climate: Temperate (but windy) with warm summers and mild winters. Rainfall averages around 900 mm (35 in).

An executive President, who appoints a Council of Ministers, is elected by universal adult suffrage for five years. The 31-member Senate (consisting of 30 senators and the Vice-President) and the 99 Chamber of Deputies are also directly elected for five years under a system of proportional representation.
Largest parties: (1994 election) (centrist) Colorado Party (PC) 32 seats, (centre-right) National Party (Blanco) 31, (left-wing) Progressive Encounter (PC) 31, (centre-left) New Space (NE) 5.
President: (since 1995) Julio Sanguinetti (PC).

Pastureland (for sheep and beef cattle) covers about 80% of the land. Meat, wool and hides are the leading exports. Despite a lack of natural resources, Uruguay has a high standard of living, but the demands of a welfare state have placed a burden on the economy. **Currency:** Peso.

1903 End of a long period of civil war and rule by dictators. **1903–07 and 1911–15** Reformist presidencies of José Battle who turned Uruguay into a democracy and advanced welfare state. In the first half of the 20th century Uruguay had a reputation for political stability unique in Latin America. **1958** Increased economic difficulties; left-wing Tupamaros urban guerrillas became active. **1973** Armed forces took power; abuses of human rights widespread. **1985** Constitutional rule restored.

Official name: República Oriental del Uruguay (The Oriental Republic of Uruguay).
Area: 176,215 km² (68,037 sq mi).
Population: 3,190,000 (1995 est.).
Doubling time: 90 years. **Adult life expectancy:** male 70.9 years, female 77.5 years. **Birth rate:** 0.71 times world average. **Death rate:** 1.01 times world average.
Urban population: 90%.
Capital: Montevideo 1,442,000 urban area (city 1,384,000; Las Piedras 58,000; 1992 est.; inc. suburbs).
Other main centres: Salto 81,000, Paysandú 78,000, Las Piedras *see Montevideo*, Rivera 57,000 (1989 est.).
Language: Spanish 97% (official).
Adult literacy: 95%.
Religion: Roman Catholic 66%, non-religious 31%, various Protestant Churches 2%.

ARGENTINA

Argentina is a republic, which extends along over 4700 km (nearly 3000 mi) of the south-eastern coastline of the South American continent. The Andes form a rugged barrier along the border with Chile. South of the Colorado River is Patagonia, an important pastureland, although large areas are semidesert. Over 80% of the population live in the pampas whose prairies form one of the world's most productive agricultural regions. The subtropical plains of north-east Argentina contain part of the Gran Chaco prairie and rain forests.
Highest point: Cerro Aconcagua 6960 m (22,834 ft).
Climate: Most of Argentina has a mild temperate climate, although the south is cooler and the north-east is subtropical. The higher parts of the Andes have a subpolar climate. Rainfall is heavy in the Andes and the far north-east, but generally decreases towards the south and south-west, which are dry.

A President is elected for a maximum of two four-year terms by universal adult suffrage. The lower house of Congress (the Chamber of Deputies) has 259 members elected by universal adult suffrage for four years, with one-half of its members retiring every two years. The upper house (the Senate) has 72 members (three chosen by each provincial legislature for nine years), with 16 members retiring every three years.
Largest parties: (Chamber of Deputies 1995 election) (centre Peronist) Justicialist Party (PJ) 136 seats, (centre-right) Radical Civic Union 69, (centre-left) Frepaso coalition 26, others 26.
President: (since 1989) Carlos Saúl Menem (PJ).

Argentina is one of the world's leading producers of beef, wool, mutton, wheat and wine. The pampas produce cereals while fruit and vines are important in the north-west. Pasturelands cover over 50% of Argentina – for beef cattle in the pampas and for sheep in Patagonia. However, manufacturing (including chemicals, paper, steel, cement and machinery) now makes a greater contribution to the economy. Inflation and political instability affected Argentina between the 1930s and 1980s, and the country's status as an economic power declined, but reforms have improved prospects in the 1990s and trade with Mercosur and Brazil has increased substantially. **Currency:** Peso.

After 1880 Large-scale European (particularly Italian) immigration and British investment. **1890** Major financial and political crisis which brought about economic collapse. **1916–30** Reforms under Radical Front presidents. **1929** Start of the Depression: major economic slump. **1930–46** Military rule. **1946** Constitutional rule restored under populist leader Gen. Juan Perón, whose wife Eva (Evita) became a cult figure after her death. The huge increase in state spending under Perón began a period of high inflation that lasted until the 1990s. **1955** Perón deposed. **1966–73** Military rule; thousands of government opponents arrested and up to 8000 disappeared. **Early 1970s** Rise of urban terrorism (the montoneros). **1973** Civilian rule restored; Perón served as President again from 1973–74. **1976–83** Military rule. **1982** Argentine invasion of the (British) Falkland Islands ordered by President Gen. Leopoldo Galtieri. British forces retook the Falklands after an Argentine occupation which lasted for a period of just over two months. **1983** Constitutional rule was restored.

Official name: República Argentina (The Argentine Republic).
Area: 2,766,889 km² (1,068,302 sq mi) excluding territories claimed by Argentina (the Falkland Islands or Islas Malvinas, South Georgia, South Sandwich Islands and parts of Antarctica).
Population: 34,587,000 (1995 est.).
Doubling time: 63 years. **Adult life expectancy:** male 68.2 years, female 71.5 years. **Birth rate:** 0.78 times world average. **Death rate:** 0.92 times world average.
Urban population: 87%.
Capital: Buenos Aires 12,582,000 urban area (city 2,961,000; 1991 census). **Other main centres:** Córdoba 1,198,000, Rosario 1,096,000, Mendoza 775,000, La Plata 640,000, (San Miguel de) Tucumán 622,000, Mar del Plata 520,000, Santa Fé 395,000 (1991 census; inc. suburbs).
Language: Spanish 97% (official), Italian 2%, Amerindian languages.
Adult literacy: 90%.
Religion: Roman Catholic 92%, various Protestant Churches 7%, Jewish 1%.

Argentine Dependency
Argentine Antarctic Territory see p. 480.

BRAZIL

Brazil, the fifth largest country in the world, is a republic on the Atlantic coast of South America. Nearly one-half of Brazil is drained by the world's largest river system, the Amazon, whose low-lying basin is still largely covered by tropical rain forest, although pressure on land has encouraged deforestation. North of the Amazon Basin, the Guiana Highlands contain Brazil's highest peak. A central plateau of savannah grasslands lies south of the Basin. In the east and south, a densely populated coastal plain adjoins the Brazilian Highlands, a vast plateau divided by fertile valleys and mountain ranges.
Highest point: Pico da Neblina 3014 m (9888 ft).
Climate: The Amazon Basin and the south-east coast are tropical with heavy rainfall. Most of the rest of Brazil is subtropical while the savannah grassland is temperate. Only the north-east has inadequate rainfall.

An executive President, who appoints a Council of Ministers, is elected for a four-year term by universal adult suffrage. The Congress consists of an 81-member Senate (upper house) and a 513-member Chamber of Deputies (lower house). The Senate comprises three senators from each state with 54 members elected by universal adult suffrage for eight years and 27 members (one per state) indirectly elected. The Chamber is directly elected for four years. Each state has its own legislature.
Largest parties: (1995 election) (centrist) Social Democratic Party (PDS) and allies 175 seats, (centre-left) Democratic Movement (PMDB) and allies 105, (right-wing coalition) National Reconstruction Party (PRN) and allies 90, (left-wing) Workers' Party (PTB) and allies 77, others 66.
President: (since 1995) Henrique Cardoso (PDS).

Agriculture involves just under one-quarter of the labour force. The principal export crops include sugar cane, soyabeans, oranges, beef cattle and cocoa, and while coffee is still significant the crop has lost its former dominance. Timber is important but environmental concerns are restricting its trade. Rapid industrialization since 1945 has made Brazil a major manufacturing country, the most important industrial power after the G7 states and China. While textiles, clothing and food processing are still the biggest industries, the iron and steel, chemical, cement, petroleum-refining, electrical, motor-vehicle and fertilizer industries have all attained international stature. Brazil has enormous (and, in part, unexploited) natural resources including iron ore, phosphates, uranium, copper, manganese, bauxite, and coal as well as hydroelectric power potential. Economic problems over the past two decades include high rates of inflation and unemployment. **Currency:** Real.

1889 Overthrow of the liberal monarchy by the military. **1930–45** Dictatorship of Getulio Vargas. **1950–54** Vargas's second presidency; ended by his suicide. **1964–85** Military rule. **1985** Restoration of constitutional rule.

Official name: República Federativa do Brasil (Federative Republic of Brazil).
Area: 8,547,404 km² (3,300,171 sq mi).
Population: 155,820,000 (1995 est.).
Doubling time: 58 years. **Adult life expectancy:** male 57 years, female 67 years. **Birth rate:** 0.84 times world average. **Death rate:** 0.97 times world average. **Urban population:** 71%. **Capital:** Brasilia 1,601,000 urban area (city 1,493,000; 1991 census). **Other main centres:** São Paulo 16,567,000 urban area (city 9,646,000; Guarulhos 788,000; São André 617,000; São Bernardo do Campo 567,000), Rio de Janeiro 10,390,000 (city 5,481,000; Nova Iguaçu 1,298,000; São Gonçalo 780,000; Duque de Caxias 668,000; Niteroi 436,000), Belo Horizonte 4,621,000 (city 2,020,000), Pôrto Alegre 3,758,000 (city 1,263,000), Salvador 3,135,000 (city 2,075,000), Recife 2,922,000 (city 1,298,000; Jaboatão 487,000), Curitiba 2,320,000 (city 1,315,000), Belém 1,621,000 (city 1,245,000), Nova Iguaçu *see Rio de Janeiro*, Goiânia 1,268,000 (city 922,000), Manaus 1,164,000 (city 1,012,000), Campinas 848,000, Guarulhos *see São Paulo* (1991 census; inc. suburbs).
Language: Portuguese over 97% (official), with Japanese, German, Italian and Amerindian minorities.
Adult literacy: 83%.
Religion: Roman Catholic 64%, various Protestant Evangelical Churches 19%, Candomblé, spiritist and other minorities.

BRAZILIAN STATES

Acre
Area: 153,150 km² (59,132 sq mi).
Pop.: 455,000 (1995 est.).
Capital: Rio Branco.
Alagoas
Area: 27,933 km² (10,785 sq mi).
Pop.: 2,685,000 (1995 est.).
Capital: Maceió.
Amapá
Area: 143,454 km² (55,388 sq mi).
Pop.: 326,000 (1995 est.).
Capital: Macapá.
Amazonas
Area: 1,577,820 km² (609,200 sq mi).
Pop. 2,320,000 (1995 est.).
Capital: Manaus.
Bahia
Area: 567,295 km² (219,034 sq mi).
Pop.: 12,646,000 (1995 est.).
Capital: Salvador
Ceará
Area: 146,348 km² (56,505 sq mi).
Pop.: 6,714,000 (1995 est.).
Capital: Fortaleza.
Espírito Santo
Area: 46,194 km² (17,836 sq mi).
Pop.: 2,787,000 (1995 est.).
Capital: Vitória.
Goiás
Area: 341,289 km² (131,772 sq mi).
Pop.: 4,308,000 (1995 est.).
Capital: Goiânia.
Maranhão
Area: 333,366 km² (128,713 sq mi).
Pop.: 5,231,000 (1995 est.).
Capital: São Luís.
Mato Grosso
Area: 906,807 km² (350,120 sq mi).
Pop.: 2,314,000 (1995 est.).
Capital: Cuiabá.
Mato Grosso do Sul
Area: 358,159 km² (138,286 sq mi).
Pop.: 1,913,000 (1995 est.).
Capital: Campo Grande.
Minas Gerais
Area: 588,384 km² (227,176 sq mi).
Pop.: 16,505,000 (1995 est.).
Capital: Belo Horizonte.
Pará
Area: 1,253,165 km² (483,850 sq mi).
Pop.: 5,449,000 (1995 est.).
Capital: Belém.
Paraíba
Area: 56,585 km² (21,848 sq mi).
Pop.: 3,340,000 (1995 est.).
Capital: João Pessoa.
Paraná
Area: 199,709 km² (77,108 sq mi).
Pop.: 8,713,000 (1995 est.).
Capital: Curitiba.
Pernambuco
Area: 98,938 km² (38,200 sq mi).
Pop.: 7,445,000 (1995 est.).
Capital: Recife.
Piauí
Area: 252,379 km² (97,444 sq mi).
Pop.: 2,725,000 (1995 est.).
Capital: Teresina.
Rio de Janeiro
Area: 43,910 km² (16,954 sq mi).
Pop.: 13,296,000 (1995 est.).
Capital: Rio de Janeiro.
Rio Grande do Norte
Area: 53,307 km² (20,582 sq mi).
Pop.: 2,582,000 (1995 est.).
Capital: Natal.
Rio Grande do Sul
Area: 282,062 km² (108,905 sq mi).
Pop.: 9,579,000 (1995 est.).
Capital: Pôrto Alegre.
Rondônia
Area: 238,513 km² (92,090 sq mi).
Pop.: 1,340,000 (1995 est.).
Capital: Pôrto Velho.
Roraima
Area: 225,116 km² (86,918 sq mi).
Pop.: 262,000 (1995 est.).
Capital: Boa Vista.
Santa Catarina
Area: 95,443 km² (36,851 sq mi).
Pop.: 4,837,000 (1995 est.).
Capital: Florianópolis.
São Paulo
Area: 248,809 km² (96,066 sq mi).
Pop.: 33,700,000 (1995 est.).
Capital: São Paulo.
Sergipe
Area: 22,050 km² (8514 sq mi).
Pop.: 1,605,000 (1995 est.).
Capital: Aracaju.
Tocantins
Area: 278,421 km² (107,499 sq mi).
Pop.: 1,007,000 (1995 est.).
Capital: Palmas.
Federal District (Distrito Federal)
Area: 5822 km² (2248 sq mi).
Pop.: 1,738,000 (1995 est.).
Capital: Brasilia.
Fernando de Noronha
Area: 26 km² (10 sq mi).
Pop.: 1300 (1995 est.).
Capital: no capital; administered from the mainland.

■ *Like many Brazilian cities, Rio de Janeiro is surrounded by shanty towns*

FALKLAND ISLANDS

Official name and status: The Falkland Islands; a British Crown Colony.
Area: 12,170 km² (4698 sq mi).
Population: 2100 (1995 est., excluding the British garrison).
Capital: Stanley 1560 (1995 est.).
Geography: The Falklands consist of two main bleak islands and over 100 small islets in the southern Atlantic, about 700 km (435 mi) north-east of Cape Horn.
Economy: The barren interior is used as pasture for sheep and wool, which is the only significant export. Licences to fish in Falkland waters (and associated activities) are now the main source of revenue. Offshore exploration for petroleum is growing in importance.

PLACES OF INTEREST

The growth of tourism from Europe and North America to the Caribbean has not yet extended as far south as Brazil. There are many sites with great tourist potential, but Rio de Janeiro is currently the principal tourist centre. Currently, foreign visitors are largely restricted to those with considerable means. Argentines account for one-third of visitors, while Americans (the next largest group) account for only one-tenth. Some of the most popular destinations are the Amazon, Curitiba, Fortaleza, Florianópolis, Maceio, Manaus, Natal, Recife, Rio de Janeiro, Salvador, São Paulo and the Pantanal.

World Heritage sites include: Brasília; historic centre of the town of Olinda; historic centre of Salvador de Bahia; historic town of Ouro Prêto; Iguazú National Park; Serra da Capivara National Park.

STATES

1 Acre
2 Alagoas
3 Amapá
4 Amazonas
5 Bahia
6 Ceará
7 Espírito Santo
8 Goiás
9 Maranhão
10 Mato Grosso
11 Mato Grosso do Sul
12 Minas Gerais
13 Pará
14 Paraíba
15 Paraná
16 Pernambuco
17 Piauí
18 Rio de Janeiro
19 Rio Grande do Norte
20 Rio Grande do Sul
21 Rondônia
22 Roraima
23 Santa Catarina
24 São Paulo
25 Sergipe
26 Tocantins
27 Federal District (Distrito Federal)
28 Fernando de Noronha

For further information, see p. 447.

The Amazon rain forest occupies the drainage basin of the River Amazon and its tributaries. The forest once covered over 40% of Brazil's land area, but deforestation (see p.58) is rapidly reducing its size.

! The largest island mostly surrounded by freshwater is Marajó at the mouth of the Amazon. It is 48,000 km² (18,500 sq mi).

Sugar Loaf Mountain (Pão de Açúcar) is one of Rio de Janeiro's best known landmarks. Its summit can be reached by cable car.

! The Amazon, at 6750 km (4195 mi), is the world's longest river.

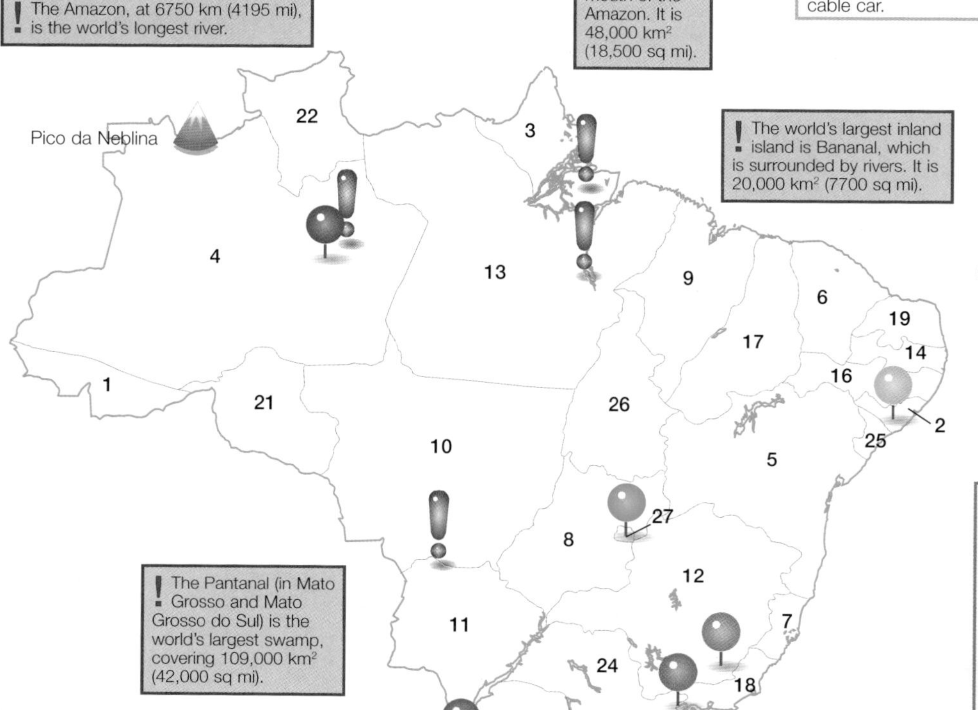

! The world's largest inland island is Bananal, which is surrounded by rivers. It is 20,000 km² (7700 sq mi).

The Cathedral Metropolitana, Brasília, designed by the Brazilian architect Oscar Niemeyer, is built partially underground. The Square of the Three Powers in the foreground was dedicated in 1960. Brasília was chosen as the site of Brazil's capital in 1956 (see p. 245).

! The Pantanal (in Mato Grosso and Mato Grosso do Sul) is the world's largest swamp, covering 109,000 km² (42,000 sq mi).

Ouro Prêto was established as a mining settlement in 1698. A national monument, the colonial town remains largely untouched and is one of Brazil's major tourist attractions.

Iguazú Falls, on the border of Brazil and Argentina (see p. 42), are 82 m (269 ft) high. During the winter rainy season, the rate of flow can exceed 12,750 m³ (450,000 cu ft).

! Lagoa dos Patos (Rio Grande do Sul) is the world's largest lagoon. It is 280 km (174 mi) long and extends over 9850 km² (3803 sq mi).

São Paulo is Brazil's largest city and Latin America's leading industrial centre.

TELEVISION AND RADIO

No. of TVs: 30,000,000 (5.2 persons per TV)
No. of radio receivers: 55,000,000 (2.8 persons per radio)

There are six main TV networks which operate 256 television stations. Most are under governmental control, although privatization has begun. Soap operas ('novelas') are by far the most popular programmes, commanding a dedicated and passionate following, not only in Brazil, but in many other countries in which they have been sold. There are nearly 3000 radio stations, mainly under state control.

CINEMA

No. of cinemas: 1570

A recent boost to the Brazilian film industry has been the implementation of laws to increase state support. The Secretariat of Culture is the main benefactor, paying 80% of costs of approved projects. Rio and São Paulo are the principal production centres and have the highest audience attendances (70% of Brazil's total box-office takings). Due to its huge population, Brazil is the top Latin-American market and the eighth-best market in the world for American films.

NEWSPAPERS

The size of Brazil, and the rivalry between São Paulo and Rio de Janeiro, has prevented the emergence of a national press. There are about 373 daily newspapers, most with Sunday editions. Most people rely upon radio and television for news. The top daily newspapers and their circulation figures are:

	Daily	Sunday Editions
Fôlha de São Paulo, São Paulo	558,000	1,401,000
O Globo, Rio de Janeiro	350,000	600,000
O Dia, Rio de Janeiro	250,000	500,000
O Estado de São Paulo, São Paulo	242,000	460,000
Jornal do Brasil, Rio de Janeiro	200,000	325,000

MAGAZINES

Despite Brazil's large population, few magazines have more than a small circulation. Perhaps most surprising is the lack of a mass circulation sports magazine in a country which is sports-mad (particularly with regards to soccer). The top monthly periodicals and their circulation figures are:

*Veja**	general interest	800,000
Claudia	women's magazine	460,000
Nova	women's magazine	300,000
Manequim	fashion	300,000
Quatro Rodas	motoring	250,000

* denotes weekly publication

PRESIDENTS

1889–91	Marshal Manuel Deodoro da Fonseca
1891–94	Marshal Floriano Peixoto
1894–98	Dr Prudente de Morais Barros
1898–1900	Dr Manuel Ferraz de Campos Salles
1900–02	Francisco Rosa e Silva
1902–06	Dr Francisco Rodrigues Alva
1906–09	Dr Affonso Moreira Pena
1909–10	Dr Nilo Pecanha
1910–14	Marshal Hermes da Fonseca
1914–17	Dr Venceslau Pereira Gomes
1917	Urbano Santos da Costa Araújo
1918	Dr Francisco Rodrigues Alva
1918–19	Dr Delifim da Costa Ribeiro
1919–22	Dr Epitácio da Silva Pessoa
1922–26	Dr Artur da Silva Bernardes
1926–30	Dr Washington Pereira de Souza
1930–45	Dr Getúlio Dornelles Vargas
1945–46	Dr José Linhares
1946–51	Gen. Eurico Gaspar Dutra
1951–54	Dr Getúlio Dornelles Vargas
1954–55	Dr João Café Filho
1955	Carlos Coimbra de Luz
1955–56	Nereu de Oliveira Ramos
1956–61	Juscelino Kubitschek de Oliveira
1961	Jãnio de Silva Quadros
1961	Pascoal Ranieri Mazzilli
1961–64	João Belchior Goulart
1964	Pascoal Ranieri Mazzilli
1964–67	Marshal Humberto Castelo Branco
1967–69	Marshal Artur da Costa e Silva
1969–74	Gen. Emilio Garrastazu
1974–79	Gen. Ernesto Geisel
1979–85	João Baptista de Oliveira Figueiredo
1985	Tancredo Neves
1985–90	José Sarney
1990–92	Fernando Collor de Mellor
1992–95	Itamar Franco
1995–	Fernando Henrique Cardoso

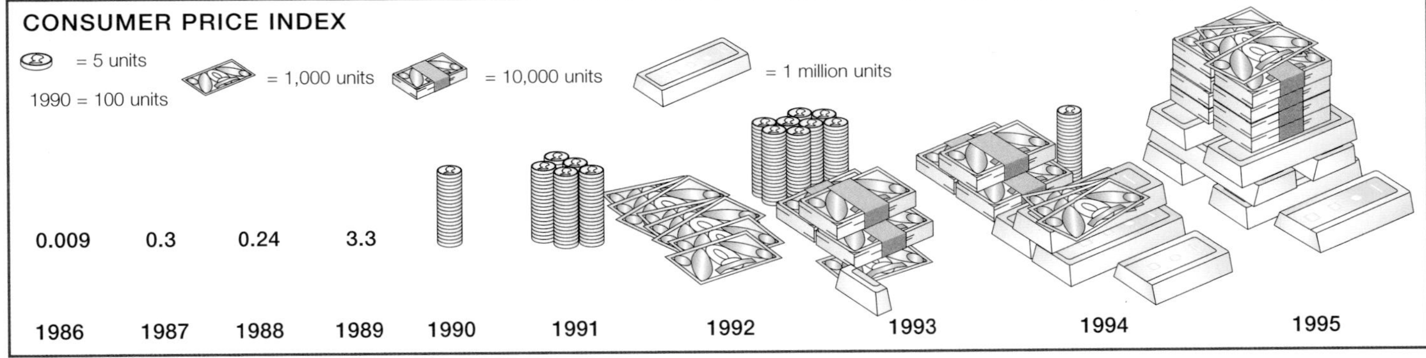

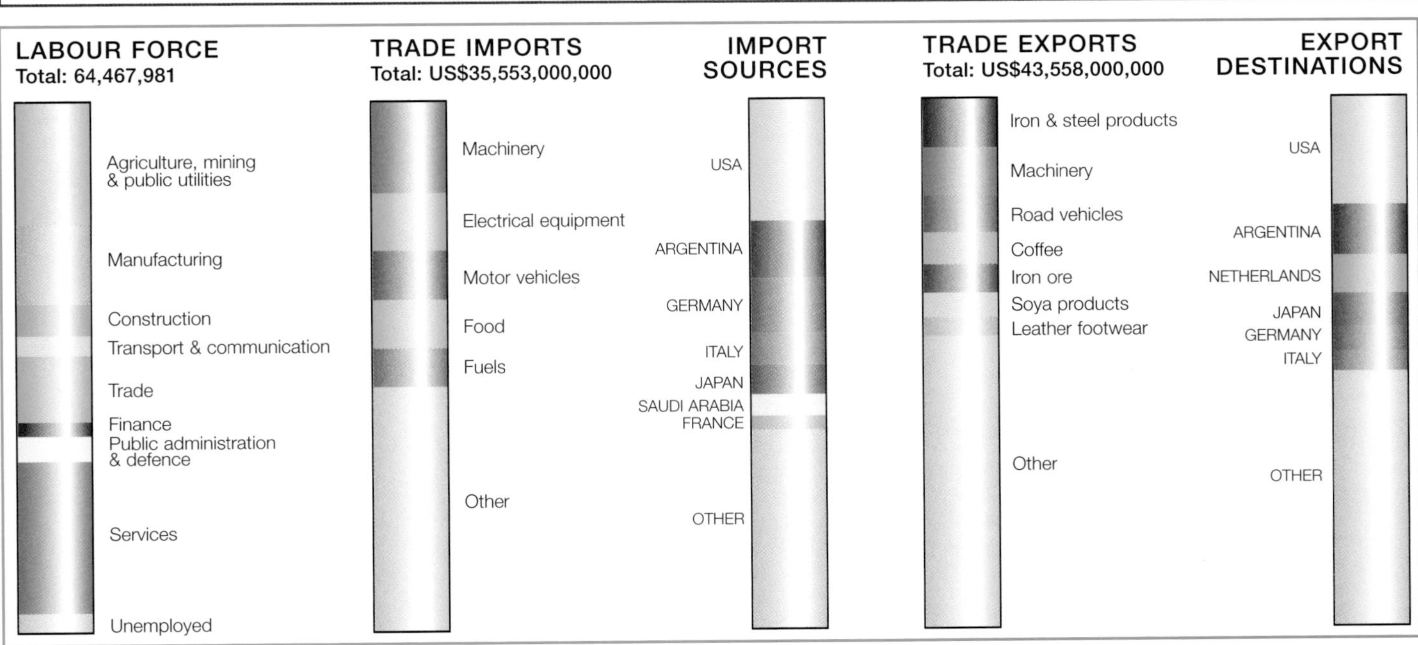

SOUTH AMERICA III

PERU

Peru is a mountainous republic on the Pacific coast of South America. The coastal plain is narrow and arid. The Andes, which are prone to earthquakes, run in three high parallel ridges from north to south. Nearly two-thirds of Peru in the east is tropical forest (the Selva) in the Amazon Basin. Every few years El Niño ocean current in the Pacific brings torrential rain and also drastically reduces stocks for Peru's important fishing industry.
Highest point: Huascarán 6786 m (22,263 ft).
Climate: A wide climatic range includes semitropical desert (cooled by the Humboldt Current in the Pacific Ocean) on the coast, the very cold High Andes and the wet tropical climate of the Selva in the east.

An executive President and a 120-member National Congress are elected by universal adult suffrage for four years. The President appoints a Cabinet headed by a Prime Minister (the only surviving example of this office in Latin America).
Largest parties: (1995) (coalition of independents and government supporters) Change 90-New Majority (Cambio 90) 67 seats, (centrist) Union for Peru (UP) 17, (left-wing) American Popular Revolutionary Alliance (APRA) 8, Independent Moral Front 6, (centre-right) Popular Action (AP) 4, (right-wing) Popular Christian Party 3, others 15.
President: (since 1990) Alberto Fujimori (Cambio 90).
Prime Minister: (since 1996) Alberto Pandolfi (Cambio 90).

About one-third of the labour force is involved in agriculture: subsistence farming dominates the interior while crops for export are more important nearer the coast. Major crops include coffee, sugar cane, cotton and potatoes, as well as coca for cocaine. Sheep, vicuñas and alpacas are kept for wool; llamas are kept as beasts of burden. Natural resources include silver, copper, coal, gold, iron ore, phosphates and petroleum. The fishing industry (once the world's largest) has declined since 1971. A combination of natural disasters, a high birth rate, guerrilla warfare and the declining value of exports have severely damaged the economy. **Currency:** New Sol.

1941 Border clashes with Ecuador. **1968–75** Reformist military government of President Juan Velasco Alvarado instituted land reforms, but faced mounting economic problems. **1975–80** Coup: right-wing military rule. **1980** Free elections held, but stability threatened by growth of extreme left-wing Sendero Luminoso (Shining Path) guerrilla movement. **1992** President Alberto Fujimori effected a coup, suspending the constitution; subsequent elections boycotted by some opposition groups. **After 1992** Sendero Luminoso activity declined after its leader was captured. **1995** Brief border war with Ecuador. **After 1996** Increased activity by Tupac Amaru left-wing guerrillas, including seizure of Japanese Embassy.

Official name: República del Perú (Republic of Peru).
Area: 1,285,216 km^2 (496,225 sq mi).
Population: 23,490,000 (1995 est.).
Doubling time: 28 years. **Adult life expectancy:** male 62.7 years, female 66.6 years. **Birth rate:** 1.16 times world average. **Death rate:** 0.82 times world average. **Urban population:** 72%. **Capitals:** Lima 6,601,000 urban area (city 5,706,000; Callao 615,000; 1993 census; inc. suburbs). **Other main centres:** Arequipa 620,000, Callao *see Lima,* Trujillo 509,000, Chiclayo 410,000, Chimbote 297,000 (1993 census; inc. suburbs).
Language: Spanish 80% as a first language (official), Quechua 16% (official), Aymara over 1%, other Amerindian languages.
Adult literacy: 87%.
Religion: Roman Catholic 86%, various Evangelical Protestant Churches 7%, traditional and other beliefs 4%.

BOLIVIA

Bolivia is a landlocked republic high in the Andes Mountains of South America. The Bolivian Andes divide into two parallel chains between which is an extensive undulating depression (the Altiplano), containing Lake Titicaca, the highest navigable lake in the world. The lowlands in the east and north-east include tropical rain forest (the Llanos), subtropical plains and semiarid grasslands (the Chaco).
Highest point: Sajama 6542 m (21,463 ft).
Climate: Temperature varies with altitude from the cold Andean summits and cool, windy Altiplano to the tropical north-east. Rainfall is negligible in the south-west and heavy in the north-east.

An executive President (who appoints a Cabinet), a 27-member senate (upper house) and a 130-member Chamber of Deputies (lower house) are elected by universal adult suffrage for four years.
Largest parties: (1993 election Chamber of Deputies) (centre-right) Nationalist Revolutionary Movement (MNR) 52 seats, (centrist coalition) Patriotic Accord (AP) 35, (right-wing) Civic Solidarity Union (UCS) 20, (centre-left) Conscience of the Fatherland (Condepa) 13, (left-wing) Free Bolivia Movement (MBL) 7, others 3.
President: (since 1993) Gonzalo Sánchez de Lozada (MNR; MNR-UCS-MBL government).

Bolivia is relatively poor, despite being rich in natural resources such as petroleum, natural gas, zinc (the major export) and tin. Lack of investment, past political instability and high mining costs have retarded development. Farming is labour intensive, producing domestic foodstuffs (potatoes and maize) and export crops (sugar cane and cotton). The illegal cultivation of coca for cocaine is causing concern. Large-scale privatization (1990s) provoked unrest. **Currency:** Boliviano.

1928–29 Border clashes with Paraguay. **1932–35** Bolivia sustained substantial loss of life and territory in the Chaco War against Paraguay. **1935–82** Instability: a succession of military regimes and weak civilian governments including brief civil war in 1952. **Since 1982** Democracy restored.

Official name: República de Bolivia (Republic of Bolivia).
Area: 1,098,581 km^2 (424,164 sq mi).
Population: 7,410,000 (1995 est.).
Doubling time: 29 years. **Adult life expectancy:** male 60.9 years, female 65.9 years. **Birth rate:** 1.29 times world average. **Death rate:** 0.9 times world average. **Urban population:** 58%. **Capitals:** La Paz (administrative and legislative capital) 1,115,000 urban area (city 711,000; El Alto 404,000; 1992 census; inc. suburbs). Sucre (legal capital) 131,000 (1992 census; inc. suburbs). **Other main centres:** Santa Cruz 695,000, El Alto *see La Paz*, Cochabamba 404,000, Oruro 183,000 (1992 census; inc. suburbs).
Language: Spanish 42% as a first language but widely used by 88% (official), Quechua 34% (official), Aymara 23% (official), Guaraní minority.
Adult literacy: 80%.
Religion: Roman Catholic 79%, various Evangelical Protestant Churches 10%.

■ BOLIVIA HAS HAD 191 ATTEMPTED COUPS – 23 HAVE BEEN SUCCESSFUL ■ CHILE'S FASTER

CHILE

Chile is a republic stretching along the southern Pacific coast of South America. For almost 4000 km (2500 mi) the Andes form the eastern boundary of Chile. Parallel to the Andes is a depression in which lies the Atacama Desert in the north and fertile plains in the centre. A mountain chain runs between the depression and the sea, and, in the south, where the depression is flooded, forms a long string of islands.
Highest point: Ojos del Solado 6895 m (22,621 ft).
Climate: The temperate climate is influenced by the cool Humboldt Current in the Pacific Ocean. The High Andes are cold. Rainfall ranges from being negligible in the Atacama Desert in the north to heavy, over 2300 mm (90 in), in the south.

■ *An aerial view shows Chuquicamata, the world's largest opencast copper mine. The pit, measuring 3 km across, employs approximately 7500 people*

An executive President (who appoints a Cabinet) is elected by universal adult suffrage for a non-renewable six-year term. The 120-member Chamber of Deputies (lower house) is directly elected for four years; the 47-member Senate (upper house) comprises 39 directly elected members and eight nominated members.
Largest parties: (1993 election Chamber of Deputies) (conservative) Christian Democrat Party (PDC) 37 seats, Socialist Party (PAIS) 33, (right-wing) National Renovation Party and allies (RN) 31, (extreme right) Independent Democratic Union (UDD) 15, others 4.
President: (since 1994) Eduardo Frei (PDC; PDC-PS government).

Chile has achieved high economic growth rates in the 1990s and has developed important trading links with other Pacific Rim countries. By Latin American standards, Chile has a high standard of living. There are considerable mineral riches and great hydroelectric power potential. Industrial and mineral products account for over 90% of exports. Chile is a leading exporter of copper, and has major reserves of iron ore, coal, petroleum and natural gas. Industry includes food processing, timber industries (cellulose and newsprint), manufactures (motor tyres and vehicles), cement and textiles. The main agricultural region is the central plains, where cereals (mainly wheat and maize) and fruit (notably grapes for wine) are important. Major fishing grounds yield one of the world's largest catches of fish.
Currency: Peso.

1920s–40s Rule by liberal and radical regimes, but social and economic change was slow. **1970** Election of Marxist government of Salvador Allende; major changes including land reforms; Chile became polarized between right and left. **1973** US-backed military coup brought General Augusto Pinochet to power; Allende killed in coup. **1973–90** Right-wing military dictatorship of Gen. Pinochet: tens of thousands of leftists imprisoned, killed or exiled; Allende's reforms undone but startling economic growth. **1990** Constitutional government restored; free elections.

Official name: República de Chile (Republic of Chile).
Area: 756,626 km² (292,135 sq mi).
Population: 14,210,000 (1995 est.).
Doubling time: 44 years. **Adult life expectancy:** male 70.4 years, female 76 years. **Birth rate:** 0.86 times world average. **Death rate:** 0.58 times world average. **Urban population:** 86%. **Capital:** Santiago 5,681,000 urban area (city 4,628,000; Puente Alto 255,000; San Bernardo 189,000; 1994 est.; inc. suburbs). The legislature meets in Valparaiso (which is not, however, officially the legislative capital), see below.
Other main centres: Valparaiso-Viña del Mar 621,000 urban area (Valparaiso city 302,000; Viña del Mar 319,000), Concepción 577,000 (city 318,000; Talcahuano 247,000), Viña del Mar *see Valparaiso*, Temuco 263,000, Puente Alto *see Santiago*, Talcahuano *see Concepción*, Antofagasta 227,000, San Bernardo *see Santiago*, Rancagua 187,000, Talca 172,000, Arica 169,000 (1994 est.; inc. suburbs).
Language: Spanish 90% (official), Araucanian 10%.
Adult literacy: 81%.
Religion: Roman Catholic 77%, various Evangelical Protestant Churches 12%, non-religious 6%.

Chilean Dependency
Chilean Antarctic Territory see p. 480.

PARAGUAY

Paraguay is a landlocked republic between Brazil and Argentina. The country west of the Paraguay River (the Chaco) is a flat semi-arid plain. The region east of the river is a partly forested undulating plateau.
Highest point: Cerro San Rafael 850 m (2789 ft).
Climate: Subtropical with considerable variation in rainfall between the wet south-east and the dry Chaco in the west.

An executive President (who appoints a Council of Ministers) is elected by universal adult suffrage for a non-renewable five-year term. The 80-member Chamber of Deputies (lower house) is elected from constituencies and the 45-member Senate (upper house) is elected nationally, also for five years.
Largest parties: (1993 election Chamber of Deputies) (conservative) Colorado Party (PC) 38 seats, (centre-left) Authentic Radical Liberal Party (PLRA) 33, (coalition) National Encounter 9.
President: (since 1993) Juan Carlos Wasmosy (PC).

■ *The 19th-century presidential palace in Asunción. Only since 1992 has it been occupied by a leader who has been elected in totally free elections*

Agriculture, the main economic activity, is dominated by cattle ranching, cotton and soyabeans. Cheap hydroelectric power, from installations on the Paraná, particularly the Yacyreta-Agipe dam (the world's largest), has stimulated industry. From 1945 to 1971 Paraguay's population declined owing to emigration.
Currency: Guarani.

1928–29 Border clashes with Bolivia. **1932–35** Paraguay weakened by Chaco War with Bolivia but recovered part of the Chaco. **1954** Military coup led by General Alfredo Stroessner. **1954–89** Stroessner in power; increasing disregard for human rights. **1989** Stroessner overthrown. **1992** Free elections held; democracy restored.

Official names: República del Paraguay (in Spanish) and Tetä Paraguáype (in Guaraní) (The Republic of Paraguay).
Area: 406,752 km² (157,048 sq mi).
Population: 4,830,000 (1995 est.).
Doubling time: 26 years. **Adult life expectancy:** male 65 years, female 69.4 years. **Birth rate:** 1.34 times world average. **Death rate:** 0.69 times world average. **Urban population:** 51%. **Capital:** Asunción 831,000 urban area (city 502,000; San Lorenzo 133,000; Lambaré 100,000; San Fernando de la Mora 95,000; 1992 census; inc. suburbs).
Other main centres: Ciudad del Este 134,000, San Lorenzo, Lambaré and San Fernando de la Mora *see Asunción*, San Pedro Caballero 80,000, Encarnación 69,000 (1992 census; inc. suburbs).
Language: Spanish 7% as a first language but widely used by 67% (official), Guaraní 91% (official).
Adult literacy: 92%.
Religion: Roman Catholic 93%, various Protestant Churches over 5%.

North Africa

MOROCCO

Morocco is a kingdom occupying the north-west corner of North Africa, with coasts on both the Mediterranean and the Atlantic. Over one-third of the country is mountainous. The principal uplands are the Grand, Middle and Anti Atlas Mountains in the west and north, and a plateau in the east. Much of Morocco is desert.
Highest point: Jebel Toubkal 4165 m (13,665 ft). **Climate:** The north has a Mediterranean climate with hot dry summers and warm wetter winters. The south and much of the interior have semi-arid and tropical desert climates.

Morocco is a constitutional monarchy in which the King appoints a Prime Minister and other Ministers. The 333-member House of Representatives comprises 222 members elected by universal adult suffrage for five years and 111 members elected by local councils, trades bodies and professional organizations.
Largest parties: (1993 election) (centre-right and right-wing) Party of National Unity (PEN) 154 seats inc. Constitutional Union 54 and (ethnic Berber) Popular Movement (MP) 51 with National Popular Movement (MNP) 25 and National Democracy Party (PND) 24, (left) Democratic Bloc (BD) 115 including Socialist Union of Popular Forces 52 and Independence Party/Istiqlal 50, (centrist) National Rally for Independents (RNI) 41, Democratic Independence Party (PDI) 9, others 12,
King: (since 1961) Hassan II.
Prime Minister: (since 1994) Abdellatif Filali (PEN; PEN–RNI government).

Nearly 40% of the labour force is involved in farming, producing citrus fruit, grapes (for wine) and vegetables mainly for export, and wheat and barley for local consumption. Morocco is the world's leading exporter of phosphates. Other resources include iron ore, lead and zinc. Many important industries and services are in state ownership. Tourism is a major foreign-currency earner. **Currency:** Dirham.

1905–06 and 1911 French interests disputed by Germany in the 'Moroccan Crises'. **1912** French protectorate established over Morocco; Spain retained long-established coastal enclaves. **1925** Rif rising against French rule. **1956** Independence as a kingdom. **1956 and 1969** Spanish territories returned to Morocco. **1975** Moroccan 'Green March' into former Spanish Western Sahara. Morocco still holds Western Sahara despite international pressure and the activities of Polisario guerrillas fighting for the territory's independence. **1991** Cease-fire in Western Sahara.

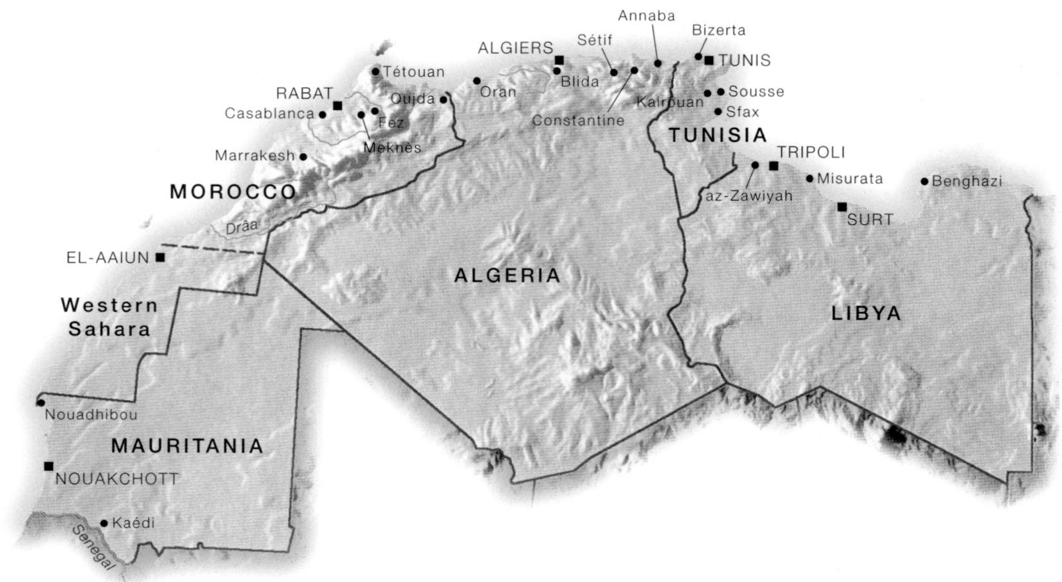

Official name: al-Mamlakah al-Maghribiyah (The Kingdom of Morocco).
Area: 458,730 km² (177,116 sq mi) excluding the disputed Western Sahara.
Population: 26,980,000 (1995 est.).
Doubling time: 32 years. **Adult life expectancy:** male 67 years, female 71 years. **Birth rate:** 1.12 times world average. **Death rate:** 0.65 times world average. **Urban population:** 48%. **Capital:** Rabat 1,220,000 (city 707,000; Salé 692,000; 1993 est.; inc. suburbs). **Other main centres:** Casablanca (Dar el Beida) 3,406,000 urban area (city 1,081,000), Fez (Fès) 775,000, Marrakesh (Marrakech) 746,000, Oujda 679,000, Tétouan-Larache 367,000, Meknès 530,000 (1993 est.; inc. suburbs).
Language: Arabic 65% (official), Berber 33%. **Adult literacy:** 50%.
Religion: Sunni Islam over 99%, Roman Catholic minority.

WESTERN SAHARA

Official names and status: al-Jumhuriyah al-'Arabiyah al-Sahrawiyah ad-Dimuqratiyah (The Democratic Sahrawi Arab Republic), the name given to the territory by the Polisario movement; however, most of the area is under Moroccan administration and divided into four Moroccan provinces. The territory is disputed between Morocco and the Polisario guerrilla movement, which has sought independence since Spain withdrew in 1976.
Area: 252,120 km² (97,344 sq mi).
Population: 218,000 (1995 est.).
Capital: El-Aaiun 97,000 (1982 est.).
Geography: The Western Sahara, on the Atlantic coast of North Africa is a low flat desert region with no permanent streams.
Economy: Dominated by the production of phosphate at Ben Cruu, the largest phosphate deposit in the world.

LIBYA

Libya is a North African republic most of whose area is covered by the Sahara Desert. In the north-west (Tripolitania), coastal oases and a low plain support farming and the majority of the country's population. The other main centre of settlement is in the north-east (Cyrenaica) where a coastal plain and mountains support Mediterranean vegetation. The south-west (Fezzan) is sparsely populated. The Tibesti Mountains lie along the border with Chad.
Highest point: Bette 2286 m (7500 ft).
Climate: Libya is hot and dry, with lower temperatures and higher (though still sparse) rainfall near the coast.

The 750-member General People's Congress comprises the heads of the local people's congresses, which are elected. The Congress elects a Revolutionary Leader (the equivalent of a head of state) and a General People's Committee (the equivalent of a Cabinet), headed by a Secretary (the head of government). There are no political parties.
Head of state: (Revolutionary Leader) (since 1969) Moamar al-Gaddafi.
Head of government: (since 1990) Abd al-Majid al-Qa'ud.

Libya is one of the world's largest producers of petroleum. Liquefied natural gas is also exported. Coastal oases produce wheat, barley, nuts, dates and grapes. Libya is overdependent upon a single commodity and the imposition of UN sanctions (since 1992) has damaged the economy. **Currency:** Libyan dinar.

1911 Italy took Libya from the Turkish Ottoman Empire. **1942** British Eighth Army defeated the Italians and Germans at El Alamein in the Libyan Desert; Libya passed under British control. **1945–51** Libya divided between British and French administrations (with the latter controlling Fezzan). **1951** Reunification as an independent kingdom ruled by Idris I, head of the Sanusi Islamic order in Cyrenaica. **1969** Junior officers' coup, led by Col. Gaddafi, overthrew the monarchy; oil industry nationalized. **1970s** Gaddafi dismantled the formal government system, instituted a cultural revolution, collectivized economic activity and suppressed opposition. **1970s–80s** Attempts to federate with other Arab states proved abortive. **1985** 100,000 foreigners expelled. **1986** US air raids on Libya provoked by Libya's alleged support of international terrorism. **1992** UN sanctions against Libya because of Libya's alleged support of terrorism.

Official name: al-Jumhuriyah al-Arabiyah al-Libiyah ash-Sha'biyah al-Ishtirakiyah (The Socialist People's Libyan Arab Jumhuriya).
Area: 1,757,000 km² (678,400 sq mi).
Population: 5,410,000 (1995 est.).
Doubling time: 21 years. **Adult life expectancy:** male 62.1 years, female 66.6 years. **Birth rate:** 1.8 times world average. **Death rate:** 0.85 times world average.
Urban population: 86%.
Capitals: Tripoli (Tarabulus) 591,000; the legislative capital is Surt 75,000 (some ministries are at Al Jofrah and Benghazi) (1988 est.; inc. suburbs).
Other main centres: Benghazi (Banghazi) 446,000, Misurata (Misratah) 122,000, az-Zawiyah 89,000 (1988 est.; inc. suburbs).
Language: Arabic 96% (official), Berber 3%. **Adult literacy:** 64%.
Religion: Sunni Islam 97%, Roman Catholic minority.

TUNISIA

Tunisia is a North African republic with a 1300-km (810-mi) coastline on the central Mediterranean. The Northern Tell and High Tell Mountains occupy the north and north-west. Wide plateaux cover central Tunisia. The Sahara Desert lies south of a zone of salt lakes.
Highest point: Jabal ash-Shanabi 1544 m (5066 ft). **Climate:** The north has a Mediterranean climate with hot summers, mild winters and adequate rainfall. The desert south has a hot, dry climate.

The executive President and a 163-member Assembly are elected by universal adult suffrage for five years. Nineteen seats are reserved for opposition parties if these parties fail to win single-member constituencies. The President appoints a Prime Minister and other Ministers.
Largest parties: (1994 election) (centre-left) Constitutional Democratic Rally (RCD) 144 seats, Democratic Socialist Movement (MDS) 10, (former Communist) Ettajdid/Renovation 4, Democratic United Union (DUU) 3, Party of Popular Unity (PUP) 2.
President: (since 1987) Gen. Zine El-Abidine Ben Ali (RCD).
Prime Minister: (since 1989) Hamid Karaoui (RCD).

Phosphates and petroleum are the mainstays of the economy. The main crops are wheat, barley and vegetables, plus olives and citrus fruit for export. Tourism is a major foreign-currency earner. Unemployment is high and many Tunisians seek work in Europe. **Currency:** Tunisian dinar.

1881 French established a protectorate; the bey (monarch) remained nominal ruler. **1942–43** German occupation during World War II. **1956** Independence. **1957** Monarchy abolished. **1957–88** Presidency of Habib Bourguiba, who became increasingly intolerant of opposition. **1988** Bourguiba removed by his PM; multi-party politics permitted.

Official name: al-Jumhuriyah at-Tunisiyah (The Republic of Tunisia).
Area: 164,150 km² (63,378 sq mi).
Population: 8,900,000 (1995 est.).
Doubling time: 39 years. **Adult life expectancy:** male 66.9 years, female 68.7 years. **Birth rate:** 0.96 times world average. **Death rate:** 0.68 times world average.
Urban population: 53%.
Capital: Tunis 1,700,000 urban area (city 674,000; Aryanah 153,000; Ettadhamen 149,000; 1994 census; inc. suburbs). **Other main centres:** Sfax (Safaqis) 231,000, Aryanah *see Tunis*, Ettadhamen *see Tunis*, Sousse (Susah) 125,000, Kairouan (al-Qayrawan) 102,000, Bizerta (Banzart) 99,000, Gabès (Qabis) 99,000 (1994 census; inc. suburbs).
Language: Arabic 99% (official), French is understood by 29%.
Adult literacy: 67%.
Religion: Sunni Islam 99%, Roman Catholic minority.

MAURITANIA

Mauritania is a desert-republic on the Atlantic coast of North Africa. Isolated peaks rise above the plateaux of the Sahara Desert that cover most of Mauritania, which is remarkably flat.
Highest point: Kediet Ijill 915 m (3002 ft).
Climate: Hot and dry with adequate (though seasonal) rainfall only in the south.

The executive President and the 56-member Senate (the upper house of Parliament) are elected by universal adult suffrage for six years; the 79-member National Assembly (lower house) is directly elected for five years. The President appoints a Prime Minister and other Ministers.
Largest parties: (1996 election) (former monopoly right-wing) Democratic and Social Republican Party (PRDS) 70 seats, others 9. (The election was boycotted by some opposition parties.)
President: (since 1992) Maaouya Ould Sid'Ahmed Taya (PRDS).
Prime Minister: (since 1996) Sheikh El Afia Ould Mohammed Khouna (PRDS).

Persistent drought has greatly reduced the nomads' herds of cattle and sheep although over one-third of the workforce remains in farming. Fish from the Atlantic and iron ore from the north-west are virtually the only exports.
Currency: Ouguiya (the world's only non-decimal currency).

1903 France annexed the interior, having claimed the coast in the 17th century. **1960** Independence. **1976** Mauritania received southern part of Western Sahara when Spain withdrew from that territory. **1979** Mauritania could not defeat Polisario guerrillas fighting for Western Sahara's independence and withdrew (south Western Sahara then annexed by Morocco). **1979–92** Period of military rule.

Official name: al-Jumhuriyah al-Muritaniyah (The Republic of Mauritania).
Area: 1,030,700 km² (398,000 sq mi).
Population: 2,275,000 (1995 est.).
Doubling time: 22 years. **Adult life expectancy:** male 45 years, female 51 years. **Birth rate:** 1.92 times world average. **Death rate:** 1.72 times world average. **Urban population:** 54%. **Capital:** Nouakchott 480,000 (1992 est.; inc. suburbs). **Other main centres:** Nouadhibou 72,000, Kaédi 35,000 (1992 est.; inc. suburbs).
Language: Arabic 81% (official), Wolof 7%, Tukulor 5%.
Adult literacy: 38%.
Religion: Sunni Islam nearly 100%.

ALGERIA

Algeria is a North African republic stretching from the Mediterranean Sea southwards deep into the Sahara Desert. Over 85% of Algeria is desert. In the north of the country lie the Atlas Mountains, which enclose a dry plateau, and in the south-east are the Hoggar Mountains. Plains and low mountain ranges line the Mediterranean coast region, which contains the overwhelming majority of the population.
Highest point: Tahat 3003 m (9852 ft).
Climate: Algeria's Mediterranean climate along the coast is characterized by hot summers, mild winters and adequate, though seasonal, rainfall. The interior is hot and arid.

The constitution of Algeria provides for an executive President and a 380-member Assembly which is elected by universal adult suffrage for five years. Since 1992 the (military-dominated) High Council of Security, chaired by the head of state, has been the effective centre of power. Elections under a revised constitution (which bans religious-based parties) were held for 1997.
Largest parties: (1997 election) (pro-military) National Democratic Rally (RND) 155 seats, (Islamist) Movement for a Peaceful Society (ex-Hamas) 69, (socialist) National Liberation Movement/National Democratic Rally (FLN) 64, (Islamist) Al Nahda 34, (ethnic Berber) Front for Socialist Forces (FFS) 19, Rally for Democracy and Culture (RCD) 19, others 30.
President: (since 1994) Gen. Liamine Zeroual.
Prime Minister: (since 1995) Ahmed Ouyahia.

Petroleum and natural gas are the main exports and important industries are based on oil and gas. However, the economy has been devastated by near civil war and terrorism since 1992. Foreign investment in the country has slumped. High unemployment adds to the economic problems. Farmers and farm workers account for about one-sixth of the labour force, but lack of rain and suitable land mean that Algeria has to import two-thirds of its food supply. The small amount of arable land mainly produces wheat, barley, fruit and vegetables, while arid pasturelands support sheep, goats and cattle. **Currency:** Algerian dinar.

1942 The French possession of Algeria (French since 1830–60) became the seat of the French government in exile during World War II. **1945** Nationalist riots ruthlessly suppressed in Sétif. **1954** National Liberation Movement (FLN) began its violent campaign against French rule. **1958** Rising by French settlers (and the activities of the colonists' terrorist organization, the OAS) led to crisis in France returning de Gaulle to power. **1962** De Gaulle granted Algeria independence. **1965** President Ahmed Ben Bella was overthrown. **1965–78** One-party socialist state under President Houari Boumédienne. **1990** Multi-party system restored. **1992** Elections were cancelled when Islamic fundamentalists gained a large majority in the first round of the voting; military took control. **Since 1994** Near civil war between military and fundamentalists (in particular the GIA terrorist movement); thousands killed in unrest in which intellectuals and foreigners working in Algeria have been targeted and the inhabitants of isolated villages have been massacred by fundamentalists.

Official name: al-Jumhuriyah al-Jaza'iriyah ad-Dimuqratiyah ash-Sha'biyah (The Democratic and Popular Republic of Algeria).
Area: 2,381,741 km² (919,595 sq mi).
Population: 27,940,000 (1995 est.).
Doubling time: 31 years. **Adult life expectancy:** male 67 years, female 69 years. **Birth rate:** 1.16 times world average. **Death rate:** 0.67 times world average.
Urban population: 56%.
Capital: Algiers (al-Jaza'ir or Alger) 2,168,000 (1995 est.; inc. suburbs).
Other main centres: Oran (Ouahran) 664,000, Constantine (Qacentina) 449,000, Annaba 348,000, Blida (al-Boulaida) 191,000, Sétif 187,000, Sidi-bel-Abbès 186,000, Tlemcen 146,000 (1989 est.; inc. suburbs).
Language: Arabic 83% (official), Berber 17%, French minority.
Adult literacy: 57%.
Religion: Sunni Islam 99%, Ibadiyah Islamic and Roman Catholic minorities.

NORTH-EAST AFRICA

ETHIOPIA

Ethiopia is a landlocked republic in north-eastern Africa. The Western Highlands, including the Tigray Plateau and Semien Mountains, which rise to over 4000 m (13,000 ft), are separated from the lower Eastern Highlands by a wide rift valley. The east is semidesert.
Highest point: Ras Dashen 4620 m (15,157 ft). **Climate:** Very hot and dry in the north and east. The highlands have a more temperate climate.

Ethiopia is a republic in transition to a federal system of nine regions which are based on linguistic groups and which will have the right to secede. The 117-member Federal Council comprises delegates appointed by the regional authorities; the 548-member Council of People's Representatives is elected by universal adult suffrage for five years. The President, whose role is largely ceremonial, is elected by the Council. The President appoints a Prime Minister and other Ministers, who are responsible to the Council.
Largest party: (1995 election) (coalition) Ethiopian People's Revolutionary Democratic Front (EPRDF) 540 seats, others 8.
President: (since 1995) Negasso Guidada (EPRDF).
Prime Minister: (since 1995) Meles Zenawi (EPRDF).

Secessionist wars have damaged an impoverished underdeveloped economy. Three-quarters of Ethiopians are involved in subsistence farming, but drought and overgrazing have led to desertification. Coffee is the main foreign-currency earner. Aid from international relief agencies is important. **Currency:** Birr.

1896 Unsuccessful Italian invasion which, apart from Liberia, left Ethiopia as the only independent African state. **1936–41** Ethiopia overrun by Italian forces. **1952** Eritrea became part of Ethiopia. **1962–91** Secessionist movement active in Eritrea. **1974** Emperor Haile Selassie, who had played a major role in African affairs, but who had failed to modernize his country, was overthrown. **1977** Border war with Somalia. **1977–91** Rule by a repressive Communist government. **1980s–90s** Drought, soil erosion and civil war brought severe famine. **1991** Eritrean and Tigrayan secessionists instrumental in toppling Ethiopia's Communist government. **1993** Eritrea's independence recognized. **1995** New federal constitution agreed.

Official name: Itiopiya (Federal Democratic Republic of Ethiopia). **Area:** 1,133,882 km² (437,794 sq mi). **Population:** 55,050,000 (1995 est.). **Doubling time:** 25 years. **Adult life expectancy:** male 45.9 years, female 49.1 years. **Birth rate:** 1.94 times world average. **Death rate:** 1.94 times world average. **Urban population:** 12%. **Capital:** Addis Ababa 2,213,000 (1992 est.; inc. suburbs). **Other main centres:** Dire Dawa 184,000, Gondar 156,000, Nazerit 139,000, Harrar 116,000 (1992 est.). **Language:** Amharic 30% (official), Oromo 31%, Tigrinya 7%, with Gurage, Somali and Sidamo minorities. **Adult literacy:** 36%. **Religion:** Ethiopian Orthodox 54%, Sunni Islam 30%, traditional beliefs 12%.

EGYPT

Egypt is a Middle Eastern republic in north-east Africa. Desert covers more than 90% of the country. The Western Desert, which stretches into Libya and Sudan, is low-lying. The Eastern Desert is divided by wadis and ends in the south-east in mountains beside the Red Sea. Most Egyptians live in the Nile Valley and delta, intensively cultivated lands that rely upon irrigation by the annual flood of the Nile. East of the Suez Canal is the Sinai Peninsula.
Highest point: Mt Catherine (Jabal Katrina) 2642 m (8668 ft).
Climate: Winters are mild and summers are hot and arid. Alexandria has the highest rainfall total (200 mm or 8 in); the area beside the Red Sea receives virtually no rain at all.

The 454-member People's Assembly (Majlis) consists of 44 members elected for five years by universal adult suffrage and ten members appointed by the President. The executive President, who is nominated by the Assembly, and confirmed by referendum for a six-year term, appoints a Prime Minister and other Ministers.
Largest parties: (1995 election) (centrist) National Democratic Party (NDP) 317 seats, independents 113, (right-wing traditionalist) Wafd 6, (left-wing) National Progressive Unionist Party (NPU) 5, others 3.
President: (since 1981) Mohammed Hosni Mubarak (NDP).
Prime Minister: (since 1996) Kamal al-Ganzouri (NDP).

Over one-third of the labour force is involved in agriculture, producing maize, wheat, rice and vegetables for the domestic market and cotton and dates mainly for export. Petroleum reserves (small by Middle Eastern standards), Suez Canal tolls and tourism are important foreign-currency earners. However, tourism has suffered owing to the activities of militant Islamic fundamentalists. Cement and fertilizers are major industries.

Official name: Jumhuriyah Misr al-Arabiyah (Arab Republic of Egypt). **Area:** 997,739 km² (385,229 sq mi). **Population:** 59,700,000 (1995 est.). **Doubling time:** 29 years. **Adult life expectancy:** male 65 years, female 69.3 years. **Birth rate:** 1.13 times world average. **Death rate:** 0.74 times world average. **Urban population:** 45%. **Capital:** Cairo (al-Qahirah) 14,525,000 urban area (city 6,955,000; Giza (al-Giza) 4,525,000; Qalyub 3,045,000; Shubra al-Kheima 834,000; 1992 est.; includes suburbs). **Other main centres:** Giza (al-Giza) *see Cairo*, Alexandria (al-Iskandariyah) 3,430,000, Qalyub *see Cairo*, Shubra al-Kheima *see Cairo*, Port Said (Bur Sa'id) 461,000, al-Mahalla al Kubra 408, Suez (al-Suweis) 388,000, Tanta 380,000, al-Mansura 371,000, Helwan 328,000, Asyut 321,000 (1992 est.; inc. suburbs). **Language:** Arabic almost 100% (official). **Adult literacy:** 48%. **Religion:** Sunni Islam 90%, various Christian Churches (mainly Coptic) almost 10%.

The economy is held back by rapid population growth and by the demands of a large public sector and food subsidies. **Currency:** Egyptian pound.

1914–22 British protectorate over Egypt. **1952** Corrupt regime of King Farouk overthrown. **1953** Republic established. **1954–70** Radical presidency of Gamal Abdel Nasser who made Egypt the leader of Arab nationalism. **1956** Egypt attacked by UK, France and Israel after nationalization of Suez Canal. **1958** Short-lived merger with Syria. **1967** Six Day War with Israel; Israel occupied Gaza and Sinai. **1973** Egypt lost third war against Israel. **1978–79** President Anwar Sadat made peace with Israel, recovered Sinai but was ostracized by Arab world. **1981** Sadat assassinated. **After 1983** Egypt regained its place in the Arab fold. **1990s** Rise of violence accompanying growth of militant Islamic fundamentalism. **1991** Egypt played major role in coalition against Iraq in Gulf War.

■ *The Nile, Egypt's source of irrigation water and hydroelectric power*

SUDAN

Sudan, the largest country in Africa, extends from the deserts of the north-east of the continent into central tropical Africa. The Sahara Desert covers much of the north and west, but is crossed by the fertile Nile valley. Highlands are confined to hills beside the Red Sea and mountains on the Ugandan border.
Highest point: Kinyeti 3187 m (10,456 ft).
Climate: The south is equatorial with high temperatures and rainfall; the north is dry with some areas receiving negligible rainfall.

The 400-member National Assembly comprises 225 members elected for four years by universal adult suffrage and 175 members appointed by the National Congress, a meeting of women, students, trade union officials and others. Future Presidents will be appointed by the Assembly. A federal system of 27 states is being instituted but local autonomy is not yet effective.
Largest parties: (1996 election) National Islamic Front (NIF) and allies 400 seats.
President: (since 1993) Gen. Omar Hassan Ahmed al-Bashir (NIF).

Over 60% of the workforce are engaged in subsistence farming, growing millet and sorghum for domestic consumption. Cotton is grown for export. Since the early 1980s Sudan has been severely affected by drought, civil war and famine. **Currency:** Sudanese dinar.

1899 Sudan came under joint Anglo–Egyptian rule. **1956** Sudan gained independence. **Since late 1950s** Intermittent civil war between Muslim north and the animist-Christian south, where rival groups have also fought against one another. Political instability. **1989** Military coup: establishment of an Islamic fundamentalist regime which has been resented in the south. Sudan has become internationally isolated owing to its support of Iraq and Libya. **1997** Animist and Christian forces in the south suffered major reverses; Islamic north on the verge of victory in civil war.

Official names: Jumhuriyat as-Sudan (Republic of the Sudan).
Area: 2,503,890 km² (966,757 sq mi).
Population: 28,100,000 (1995 est.).
Doubling time: 23 years. **Adult life expectancy:** male 53.4 years, female 55.2 years. **Birth rate:** 1.68 times world average. **Death rate:** 1.29 times world average. **Urban population:** 22%. **Capital:** Khartoum 2,300,000 urban area (1993 est.) (city 476,000; Omdurman, the legislative capital, 526,000; Khartoum North 341,000; 1983 census). **Other main centres:** Port Sudan (Bur Sudan) 207,000, Wadi Medani 145,000, Al-Obeid 138,000 (1983 census).
Language: Arabic 49% (official), Dinka 12%, Nubian languages 8%, Beja 6%, Nuer 5%.
Adult literacy: 46%.
Religion: Sunni Islam 72%, traditional beliefs 17%, various Christian Churches 9%.

ERITREA

Eritrea is an African republic beside the Red Sea. Most of the country is physically an extension of the Ethiopian high plateau, although there are low coastal plains. Eritrea includes the Dahlak Islands.
Highest point: Ramlo 2130 m (6986 ft).
Climate: Eritrea has a dry tropical climate with high temperatures.

The transitional 130-member National Assembly consists of 70 members of the Central Committee of the ruling People's Front for Democracy (PFDJ; former EPLF) plus provision for 60 deputies elected by universal adult suffrage (with 11 seats reserved for women). The Assembly elects the executive President, who serves for four years and who appoints the State Council of Ministers.
Largest party: (nationalist) PFDJ (see above) is the only party in the transitional Assembly.
President: (since independence) Issaias Afewerki (PFDJ).

The 30-year war of secession shattered the economy and substantial foreign aid will be needed for reconstruction. However, a resilient nationalism is being harnessed to rebuild the infrastructure and many skilled Eritreans, who had taken refuge abroad, have returned home. Most Eritreans are involved in subsistence farming, growing sorghum or keeping livestock for hides (the main export), but aridity is a problem. Eritrea has traditionally had more industry than many African states and the footwear and textile industries are being revived. Priority is being given to the reconstruction of the Asmara–Massawa railway.
Currency: Ethiopian currency still in use.

1890 Eritrea became an Italian colony. **1935–36** Became a base for Italian conquest of Ethiopia. **1941–52** Eritrea came under British rule. **1952** Became part of Ethiopia. **1962–91** EPLF movement led secessionist war against Ethiopia after Eritrea's autonomy was suppressed by Ethiopia. **1991** EPLF was instrumental in toppling Ethiopia's Communist government. **1993** Independence after internationally recognized referendum.

Official name: Eritrea.
Area: 117,400 km² (45,300 sq mi).
Population: 3,530,000 (1995 est.).
Doubling time: 24 years. **Adult life expectancy:** male 46 years, female 46 years. **Birth rate:** 1.88 times world average. **Death rate:** 1.94 times world average. **Urban population:** 15%. **Capital:** Asmara (Asmera) 367,000 (1992 est.).
Other main centres: Assab (Asseb) 50,000, Keren 40,000, Massawa (Mitsiwa) 40,000 (1992 est.).
Language: Tigrinya 49% (official), Arabic spoken as first language by less than 1% (official), Afar 4%, with Hadareb, Bilin, Kunama and other minorities. **Adult literacy:** about 20%.
Religion: Sunni Islam 50%, Ethiopian Orthodox 50%.

DJIBOUTI

Djibouti is a small African republic at the entrance to the Red Sea. Most of the state is low-lying desert and dips below sea level in two basins, but rises to hills in the north.
Highest point: Musa Ali Terara 2062 m (6768 ft).
Climate: Extremely hot and dry, with rainfall under 125 mm (5 in) on the coast.

The 65-member Chamber of Deputies and an executive President (who appoints a Council of Ministers headed by a Prime Minister) are elected by universal adult suffrage for five years and six years respectively.
Largest parties: (1992 election) (former monopoly) Popular Rally for Progress (RPP) 65 seats. Other parties have been unsuccessful in contesting elections.
President: (since 1977) Hassan Gouled Aptidon (RPP).
Prime Minister: (since 1978) Barkhat Gourat Hamadou (RPP).

Lack of water largely restricts agriculture to grazing sheep and goats. The economy depends upon the expanding seaport and the railway line which serves landlocked Ethiopia. There has been some recent expansion in financial services, encouraged by political stability.
Currency: Djibouti franc.

1888 Colony of French Somaliland established. **1977** Independence as Djibouti. **1981–92** Single-party state. **1992** Multi-party politics restored.

Official names: Jumhuriyah Jibuti (in Arabic) and République de Djibouti (French) (The Republic of Djibouti).
Area: 23,200 km² (8950 sq mi).
Population: 590,000 (1995 est.), excluding about 45,000 refugees from Somalia and Ethiopia. **Doubling time:** 32 years. **Adult life expectancy:** male 46.7 years, female 50 years. **Birth rate:** 1.52 times world average. **Death rate:** 1.73 times world average. **Urban population:** 81%. **Capital:** Djibouti 383,000 (1995 est.). **Other main centre:** Ali Sabih 4000 (1995 est.).
Language: French understood by 9% (official), Arabic 7% (official), Somali 61%, Afar 20%. **Adult literacy:** 46%.
Religion: Sunni Islam 94%.

SOMALIA

Somalia is a republic occupying the 'Horn of Africa'. Low-lying plains occupy most of the south, while semi-arid mountains occupy the north.
Highest point: Surud Ad 2408 m (7900 ft).
Climate: Hot and largely dry with rainfall totals in the north under 330 mm (13 in).

The most recent constitution provides for a 171-member Assembly and a President to be elected by universal adult suffrage. Since 1991 there has been no effective government.

Nearly two-thirds of the labour force are nomadic herdsmen or subsistence farmers. Bananas are grown for export in the south, but much of the country suffers from drought. As a result of civil wars since 1991 much of the economic infrastructure has been destroyed and famine has been widespread.
Currency: Somali shilling.

1886 Britain established a protectorate in the north while Italy took the south. **1960** Both Somaliland colonies united as an independent republic. **1969** Military coup led by Gen. Muhammad Siad Barre who established a Socialist Islamic state allied to the USSR. **1977** Border war with Ethiopia. **1991** Barre overthrown in a coup. **Since 1991** Bitter civil wars between several factions; infrastructure of the state has collapsed; the former British north has attempted secession. **1992–95** Unsuccessful US-led UN intervention.

Official name: Soomaaliya (Somalia).
Area: 637,000 km² (246,000 sq mi).
Population: 6,730,000 (1995 est.).
Doubling time: 22 years. **Adult life expectancy:** male 45.4 years, female 48.6 years. **Birth rate:** 2.01 times world average. **Death rate:** 1.99 times world average.
Urban population: 37%.
Capital: Mogadishu (Muqdishu) 900,000 (1990 est.). **Other main centres:** Kismaayo 90,000, Hargeysa 90,000, Berbera 80,000 (1990 est.).
Language: Arabic spoken as a first language by under 1% (official), Somali almost 100%.
Adult literacy: 24%.
Religion: Sunni Islam almost 100%.

EAST AFRICA

UGANDA

Uganda is a landlocked republic in East Africa, with many substantial lakes. Most of Uganda is a plateau, which ends in the west at the steep-sided Great Rift Valley and the Ruwenzori Mountains. Lake Victoria covers south-east Uganda.
Highest point: Ngaliema (formerly Margherita Peak) 5118 m (16,791 ft).
Climate: Hot and humid equatorial climate, which is moderated by altitude in the milder uplands.

An executive President (who appoints a Prime Minister and a Cabinet of Ministers) and a non-party 214-member Constituent Assembly are elected by universal adult suffrage for five years.
Largest parties: (1996 election) (non-party) National Resistance Movement (NRM) 214 seats.
President: (since 1986) Yoweri Museveni (NRM).

The turnaround of the Ugandan economy in the 1990s is cited as the economic success story of the continent. Instability, including coups and civil wars, had previously destroyed much of the country's infrastructure. Many problems continue including AIDS, which has devastated the population in some rural areas. Over three-quarters of the labour force are involved in farming, growing plantains, cassava and sweet potatoes as subsistence crops. Coffee is the major export and tea and cotton are also grown.
Currency: Uganda shilling.

Official name: The Republic of Uganda.
Area: 241,040 km² (93,070 sq mi).
Population: 18,660,000 (1995 est.).
Doubling time: 19 years. **Adult life expectancy:** male 51.4 years, female 54.7 years. **Birth rate:** 2.06 times world average. **Death rate:** 1.52 times world average.
Urban population: 12%.
Capital: Kampala 773,000 (1991 census; inc. suburbs). **Other main centres:** Jinja 61,000, Mbale 54,000 (1991 census).
Language: Swahili spoken as a first language by under 1% but understood by 35% (official), English understood by 1% (official), Ganda 18%, Teso 9%, Soga 8%, Nkole 8%, Gisu 7%, Kiga 7%, Lango 6%, Rwanda 6%, with Acholi, Lugbara, Nyoro, Toro and other minorities.
Adult literacy: 48%.
Religion: Roman Catholic 50%, Anglican 26%, traditional beliefs 13%, Sunni Islam 7%, various Protestant Churches 4%.

1894 British protectorate established. **1962** Independence. **1962–71** Presidency of Milton Obote, who suppressed the traditional monarchies (Buganda kingdom had been a destabilizing influence). **1971** Gen. Idi Amin came to power in a coup; political and civil rights curtailed; political opponents murdered; Asian population expelled. **1979** Military coup aided by Tanzanian forces; Obote restored. **1985** Obote overturned in a coup. **1996** New constitution introduced, but political parties still restricted.

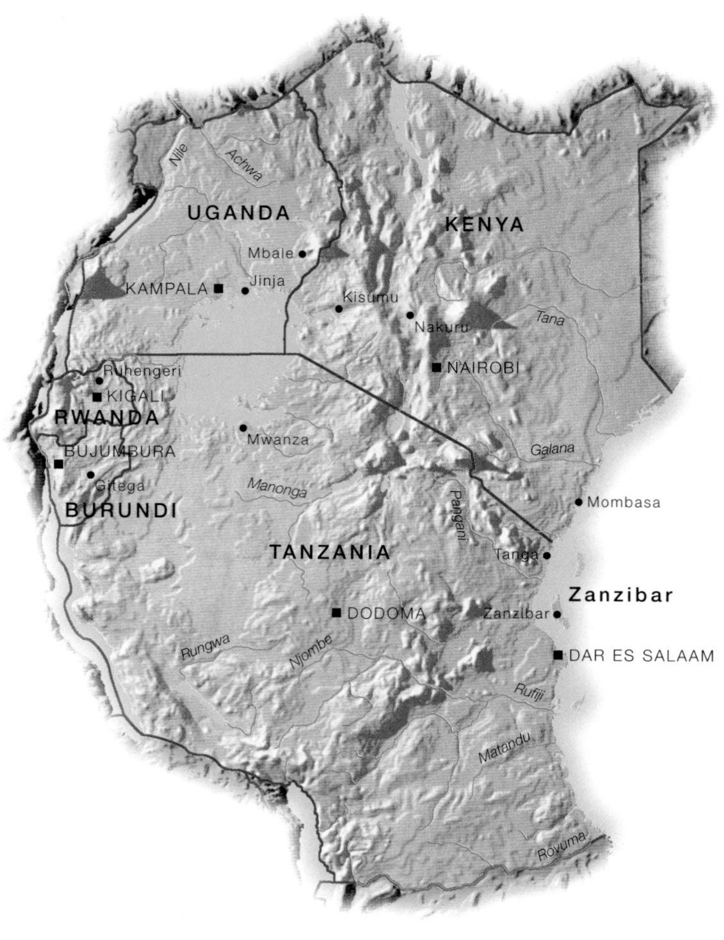

KENYA

Kenya is a republic on the Indian Ocean coast of Africa. Central Kenya, a region of highlands, is divided by the steep-sided Rift valley which runs from north to south through the country. Plateaux extend from the central highlands west towards Lake Victoria and east towards the coastal lowlands.
Highest point: Mt Kenya 5199 m (17,058 ft). **Climate:** The coastal areas have a hot and humid equatorial climate. The highlands, which are cooler, experience high rainfall. The north is very hot and arid.

The executive President, who appoints a Cabinet of Ministers, is elected by universal adult suffrage for five years. The 202-member Assembly comprises 188 members directly elected for five years plus 12 members chosen by the President and two ex officio members.
Largest parties: (1992 election) (former monopoly) Kenya African National Union (KANU) 100, (centrist) Forum for the Restoration of Democracy–Kenya (FORD–Kenya) 31, (centrist) Forum for the Restoration of Democracy–Asili (FORD–Asili) 31, Democratic Party 26, independents and others 14.
President: (since 1978) Daniel arap Moi (KANU).

Nearly one-quarter of the labour force is involved in farming. Major crops include wheat and maize for domestic consumption, and coffee, tea, sisal and sugar cane for export. Large numbers of beef cattle are reared and Kenya is one of the few states in Africa to have a substantial dairy industry. Tourism is a major foreign-currency earner. Economic difficulties include high unemployment, overmanning of the public services and administration and major public health problems (including AIDS). **Currency:** Kenya shilling.

1895 British East African Protectorate (modern Kenya) established. **1952–56** Mau Mau uprising against British rule. **1963** Independence. **1963–78** Presidency of Jomo Kenyatta. **1969–91** One-party state. **1991** Multi-party system restored. **1997** Increased opposition causes unrest.

■ *Herd of buffalo, Tsavo East National Park, Kenya*

Official names: Jamhuri ya Kenya (in Swahili) and The Republic of Kenya.
Area: 582,646 km² (224,961 sq mi).
Population: 28,630,000 (1995 est.).
Doubling time: 21 years. **Adult life expectancy:** male 54.2 years, female 57.3 years. **Birth rate:** 1.78 times world average. **Death rate:** 1.26 times world average. **Urban population:** 20%. **Capital:** Nairobi 1,678,000 (1993 est.; inc. suburbs).
Other main centres: Mombasa 465,000, Kisumu 185,000, Nakuru 163,000 (1989 est.).
Language: Swahili spoken as a first language by under 1% but understood by 66% (official), English understood by 8%, Kikuyu 21%, Luhya 14%, Luo 13%, Kamba 11%, Kalenjin 11%, Gusii 6%, Meru 5%, Nyika 5%, with Masai, Turkana, Embu and other minorities.
Adult literacy: 69%.
Religion: Roman Catholic 26%, traditional beliefs 19%, various Protestant Churches 19%, African Christian Churches 18%, Anglican 7%, Sunni Islam 6%.

■ THE RUWENZORI MOUNTAIN RANGE IN UGANDA IS KNOWN AS 'THE MOUNTAINS OF THE

BURUNDI

Burundi is a small landlocked heavily populated republic in the Great Lakes region of Central Africa. Most of the country is a high plateau rising from Lake Tanganyika in the west.
Highest point: Mont Hela 2685 m (8809 ft).
Climate: The tropical lowlands are hot and humid. Temperatures are cooler in the mountains.

The executive President, who appoints a Prime Minister and a Cabinet of Ministers, is elected by universal adult suffrage for five years. The 81-member Assembly is also directly elected for five years.
Largest parties: (1993 election) Burundi Democratic Front (Frodebu) 65 seats, (former monopoly) Union for National Progress (UPRONA) 16.
President: (since 1996) Maj. Pierre Buyoya (military).
Prime Minister: (since 1996) Pascal Ndimira (non-party).

Over 90% of the labour force is involved in farming, mainly producing subsistence crops but also coffee and tea for export; coffee now accounts for over 80% of Burundi's exports. The economy has been badly damaged by recurring tribal conflicts and near civil war. **Currency:** Burundi franc.

1890 Burundi, a kingdom in which the minority Tutsi people dominated the Hutu majority, was colonized by Germany. **1919** Came under Belgian rule as part of the trust territory of Ruanda-Urundi. **1962** Independence as a kingdom, after much ethnic conflict between the dominant Tutsi people and the Hutu majority. **1966** Military coup: republic declared. **1972** Killing of deposed king led to a massacre of the Hutu. **Since 1972** Repeated coups and ethnic unrest, including a wave of ethnic murders following the assassination of the first democratically elected (Hutu) president by Tutsi military in 1993. **1995** Influx of Hutu refugees from Rwanda. **1996** Military coup and further ethnic killings, with Hutus largely driven out of the towns into the countryside.

Official names: Republika y'u Burundi (in Rundi) and La République de Burundi (The Republic of Burundi).
Area: 27,816 km² (10,740 sq mi).
Population: 5,900,000 (1995 est.).
Doubling time: 22 years. **Adult life expectancy:** male 50 years, female 54 years. **Birth rate:** 1.88 times world average. **Death rate:** 1.6 times world average. **Urban population:** 6%. **Capital:** Bujumbura 236,000 (1990 census; inc. suburbs).
Other main centre: Gitega 21,000 (1990 census).
Language: Rundi 98% (official), French is understood by 9% (official).
Adult literacy: 35%.
Religion: Roman Catholic 65%, non-religious 19%, traditional beliefs 19%, various Protestant Churches 16%.

RWANDA

Rwanda is a small landlocked heavily populated republic in the Great Lakes region of Central Africa. Over one-half of the country is mountainous; the remainder is hill country.
Highest point: Mont Karisimbi 4507 m (14,787 ft).
Climate: Tropical with heavy rainfall. The wet highlands are cooler.

There is a temporary Assembly of 74 members, but since 1994 the constitution has been effectively suspended and political parties have not operated. Power is held by the Rwanda Patriotic Front (FPR) which appoints a President, Prime Minister and government.
President: (since 1994) Pasteur Bizimungu (FPR). (However, effective power rests with the Vice-President Paul Kagame.)
Prime Minister: (since 1996) Pierre Celestin Rwigema (FPR).

The economy was devastated by civil war and genocide in 1994 and Rwanda is now unable to support the large number of refugees returning from The Congo (ex-Zaïre). International aid supports a high percentage of the population. The majority of Rwandans are subsistence farmers. There are major (unexploited) reserves of natural gas under Lake Kivu. **Currency:** Rwanda franc.

1890 Rwanda, a kingdom in which the minority Tutsi people dominated the Hutu majority, colonized by Germany. **1919** Came under Belgian rule as part of the trust territory of Ruanda-Urundi. **1961** The Tutsi monarchy overthrown and many Tutsis were driven into exile by the majority Hutus. **1962** Independence as a republic. **1978–91** One-party state. **1990–91** An army of largely Anglophone Tutsi exiles (the FPR) invaded northern Rwanda from Uganda. **1994** After the assassination of the president, government forces went on the rampage. In ensuing ethnic violence Hutu militias massacred over 500,000 Tutsis and over two million Hutus were then driven into exile as the FDR took power; international force attempted peace-keeping. **1996–97** Hundreds of thousands of Hutus returned from Zaire, driven out of that country by civil war.

Official names: Repubulika y'u Rwanda (in Rwanda) and La République de Rwanda (The Republic of Rwanda).
Area: 26,338 km² (10,169 sq mi).
Population: 6,700,000 (1995 est.).
Doubling time: 21 years. **Adult life expectancy:** male 45.8 years, female 48.9 years. **Birth rate:** 1.76 times world average. **Death rate:** 1.8 times world average. **Urban population:** 5%. **Capital:** Kigali 120,000 (1994 est.). **Other main centre:** Ruhengeri 25,000 (1994 est.).
Language: Rwanda almost 100% (official), French is understood by 8% (official). **Adult literacy:** 60%.
Religion: Roman Catholic 44%, traditional beliefs 28%, various Protestant Churches 10%, Sunni Muslim minority.

TANZANIA

Tanzania is an East African republic stretching from the Indian Ocean coast and the island-group of Zanzibar to the Great Lakes of Central Africa. The mainland, formerly Tanganyika, consists of savannah-covered plateaux divided by rift valleys and a north–south ridge of mountains which culminates in Kilimanjaro, the highest peak in Africa. Zanzibar comprises Zanzibar and Pemba islands plus several small islets.
Highest point: Kilimanjaro 5894 m (19,340 ft).
Climate: A hot moist tropical climate, although the mountains are cooler and Kilimanjaro has a small ice-cap.

The executive President, who appoints a Cabinet of Ministers, is elected by universal adult suffrage for five years. The 244-member National Assembly comprises 169 members directly elected for five years (119 from the mainland and 50 from Zanzibar), plus 15 members elected by the Assembly, 15 women members elected by the Assembly, 5 chosen by the local government in Zanzibar, 25 ex officio members (local authority commissioners) and 15 chosen by the President. Zanzibar is autonomous; its President is automatically Vice-President of Tanzania.
Largest parties: (1995 election) (former monopoly left-wing) Revolutionary Party of Tanzania (CCM) 182 seats, others (including Zanzibari parties, appointed and ex officio members) 62.
President: (since 1995) Benjamin Mkapa (CCM).
Prime Minister: (since 1995) Frederick Sumaye (CCM).

Over 80% of the labour force is involved in farming. Cash crops include coffee and cotton (which together account for over 40% of exports), plus cashew nuts and tea. Mineral resources include diamonds and gold. Economic difficulties include high unemployment and a high rate of population increase, plus an overlarge state sector. Although President Nyerere's policies of self-reliance and egalitarian socialism have now been largely abandoned, Tanzania still lags behind Kenya and Uganda.
Currency: Tanzania shilling.

1884 The mainland became a German colony. **1890** Zanzibar came under British rule. **1919** The mainland became the British trust territory of Tanganyika. **1961** Tanganyika independent. **1961–85** Presidency of Julius Nyerere who (after 1965) created a one-party socialist state. **1963** Zanzibar becomes independent. **1964** Tanganyika and Zanzibar united to form Tanzania. **1992** Multi-party system restored.

TANZANIAN AUTONOMOUS STATE

Zanzibar
Area: 1554 km² (601 sq mi).
Pop.: 376,000 (1988 census).
Capital: Zanzibar.

Official names: Jamhuri ya Muungano wa Tanzania (in Swahili) and The United Republic of Tanzania.
Area: 942,799 km² (364,017 sq mi).
Population: 28,070,000 (1995 est.).
Doubling time: 27 years. **Adult life expectancy:** male 41.5 years, female 45 years. **Birth rate:** 1.82 times world average. **Death rate:** 2.09 times world average. **Urban population:** 24%.
Capitals: Dodoma (legislative capital and capital designate) 204,000; Dar es Salaam (administrative capital) 1,361,000 (1988 census; inc. suburbs).
Other main centres: Mwanza 223,000, Tanga 188,000, Zanzibar 158,000 (1989 est.).
Language: Swahili spoken as a first language by 9% but understood by 89% (official), English understood by 3% (official), Nyamwezi 21%, Hehet 7%, Makonde 6%, Haya 6%, Nyakyusa 5%, Luguru 5%, Shambala 4%, Gogo 4%, with Ha, Iramba, Yao and other minorities.
Adult literacy: 69%.
Religion: Traditional beliefs 35%, Sunni Islam 35%, various Christian Churches (mainly Roman Catholics, Anglicans and Lutherans) 30%.

INDIAN OCEAN

MOZAMBIQUE

Mozambique is a republic stretching for nearly 2500 km (1600 mi) along the Indian Ocean coast of south-eastern Africa. The Zambezi River separates high plateaux in north Mozambique from lowlands in the south. Much of the country comprises the largest coastal plain in southern Africa.
Highest point: Bingo 2436 m (7992 ft).
Climate: Tropical climate with maximum rainfall and temperatures from November to March.

An executive President and a 250-member Assembly are elected by universal adult suffrage for five years. The President appoints a Council of Ministers, headed by a Prime Minister.
Largest political parties: (1995 election) (former-Marxist former-monopoly) Mozambique Liberation Front (Frelimo) 129 seats, (rightist former-guerrilla movement) Mozambique National Resistance (Renamo) 112, Democratic Union (UD) 9.
President: (since 1986) Joaquim Chissano (Frelimo).
Prime Minister: (since 1994) Pascoal Mocumbi (Frelimo).

Over 80% of the labour force is involved in subsistence farming, mainly growing cassava and maize. Cotton is grown commercially. Fishing is a major interest – shrimps and prawns make up nearly one-half of Mozambique's exports. The economy and much of the infrastructure was devastated by prolonged civil war and drought, and famine still occurs. Mozambique is usually stated to be the poorest country in the world. **Currency:** Metical.

1964 Frelimo (see above) launched a guerrilla war against Portuguese rule. **1975** Independence after nearly 450 years as a Portuguese possession; a Marxist–Leninist state established. **1976–92** Civil war as influence of Renamo guerrilla movement (supported by white-ruled South Africa) spread. **1989** Frelimo abandoned Marxism in favour of a free market. **1992** Ceasefire in civil war. **1995** First free multi-party elections.

Official name: República de Moçambique (Republic of Mozambique).
Area: 812,379 km^2 (313,661 sq mi).
Population: 17,890,000 (1995 est.).
Doubling time: 26 years. **Adult life expectancy:** male 44.9 years, female 48 years. **Birth rate:** 1.82 times world average. **Death rate:** 1.97 times world average. **Urban population:** 28%. **Capital:** Maputo 932,000 (1991 est.). **Other main centres:** Beira 299,000, Nampula 250,000, Nacala 104,000 (1991 est.).
Language: Portuguese 1% as a first language but widely understood (official), Makua 28%, Tsonga 12%, Sena 9%, Lomwe 8%, Shona 7%, Tswa 6%, Chuaba 6%, Ronga 4%.
Adult literacy: 40%.
Religion: Traditional beliefs 48%, Roman Catholic 31%, Sunni Islam 13%, various Protestant Churches.

■ *Decaying boats in Mozambique, whose transport structure was destroyed (1976–92)*

MADAGASCAR

Madagascar is an Indian Ocean republic comprising the fourth largest island in the world plus several small islets. Massifs form a spine running north to south through the island. To the east is a narrow coastal plain; to the west are fertile plains and low plateaux.
Highest point: Tsaratanana 2876 m (9436 ft).
Climate: Tropical, although the highlands are cooler. The north receives monsoon rain but the south is prone to drought.

The executive President (who appoints a Council of Ministers headed by a Prime Minister) is elected by universal adult suffrage for seven years. The 138-member National Assembly is directly elected for five years.
Largest parties: (1993 election) (nationalist) Raslama Active Forces Cartel (Cartel HVR) 46 seats, Movement for the Progress of Madagascar (MPM) 15, Leader-Farito 13, FAMIMA 11, Fihaonana 8, Rally for Socialism and Democracy (RPSD) 8, AKFM 5, UNDD-Raslama 5, others 27.
President: (since 1997) Didier Ratsiraka (FAMIMA; FAMIMA-led multi-party coalition).
Prime Minister: (since 1995) Emmanuel Rakotovahiny (UDD-Raslama).

Over four-fifths of the labour force are involved in farming although soil erosion is a major problem. The main crops are coffee and vanilla for export and rice and cassava for domestic consumption. The island is an important producer of chromite. **Currency:** CFA franc.

1895–97 Madagascar annexed by France; monarchy abolished. **1896–1904** Continued resistance to French rule. **1947–48** Major uprising against French rule suppressed heavy loss of life. **1960** Independence. **1972** Military coup. **1972–91** Left-wing single-party state. **1976** Intercommunal violence between Madagascans and Comoran migrants; many fatalities. **Mid-1980s** Under Soviet influence. **1992** Multi-party rule restored.

Official names: Repoblikan'i Madagasikara (in Malagasy) and République de Madagascar (French) (The Republic of Madagascar).
Area: 587,041 km^2 (226,658 sq mi).
Population: 14,760,000 (1995 est.).
Doubling time: 22 years. **Adult life expectancy:** male 55 years, female 58 years. **Birth rate:** 1.76 times world average. **Death rate:** 1.27 times world average. **Urban population:** 24%. **Capital:** Antananarivo 1,053,000 (1993 census; inc. suburbs). **Other main centres:** Toamasina 127,000, Antsirabe 120,000, Mahajanga 101,000 (1993 census).
Language: Malagasy 99% (official), French understood by over 10% (official). **Adult literacy:** 80%.
Religion: Traditional beliefs 55%, Roman Catholic 20%, Protestant Church of Madagascar 20%, Sunni Islam minority.

■ AVERAGE ANNUAL INCOME IN MOZAMBIQUE IS UNDER $80 A YEAR ■ MAURITIUS WAS HOME

MAURITIUS

Mauritius is an island-republic east of Madagascar in the Indian Ocean. The central plateau is surrounded by mountains. (Mauritius was uninhabited when discovered by the Portuguese in the 16th century.) The republic includes Rodrigues island and the Agalega Islands.
Highest point: Piton de la Rivière Noire 826 m (2711 ft).
Climate: Subtropical, although it can be very hot from December to April. Rainfall is high in the uplands.

The 70-member Legislative Assembly comprises 62 members elected by universal adult suffrage for five years and eight members appointed to ensure representation of all the island's ethnic communities. A President, whose role is largely ceremonial, is elected by the Assembly for five years. The President appoints a Prime Minister, who enjoys a majority in the Assembly; the PM, in turn, appoints a Council of Ministers.
Largest political parties: (1995 election) (centre-left coalition) Mauritius Labour Party (PTM) and Mauritian Militant Movement (MMM) 62 seats, Organization of the People of Rodrigues (OPR) 2, others 4.
President: (since 1992) Cassam Uteem (PTM–MMM).
Prime Minister: (since 1995) Dr Navinchandra Ramgoolam (PTM; PTM–MMM government).

Tourism (the main foreign-currency earner) and the export of sugar cane dominate the economy. Tea, fruit, maize and tobacco are also grown. Diversification is being encouraged and the clothing industry is of increasing importance.
Currency: Mauritius rupee.

1965 Diego Garcia detached from Mauritius to form British Indian Ocean Territory. **1968** Independence after over 150 years British rule. **1992** Republic proclaimed.

Official name: Republic of Mauritius
Area: 2040 km² (788 sq mi).
Population: 1,130,000 (1995 est.).
Doubling time: 52 years. **Adult life expectancy:** male 65.6 years, female 73.4 years. **Birth rate:** 0.81 times world average. **Death rate:** 0.73 times world average. **Urban population:** 41%. **Capital:** Port Louis 143,000 (1992 est.). **Other main centres:** Vacoas-Phoenix 167,000 urban area (Vacoas and Phoenix 92,000; Curepipe 75,000), Beau Bassin-Rose Hill 166,000 (Beau Bassin and Rose Hill 94,000; Quatre Bornes 72,000) (1992 est.).
Language: English under 1% as a first language but almost universally understood (official), French Creole 70%, Bhojpuri 21%, with Hindi, Tamil, Marathi and other minorities.
Adult literacy: 80%.
Religion: Hindu 50%, Roman Catholic 27%, Sunni Islam 16%, various Protestant Churches.

SEYCHELLES

The Seychelles form a republic in the Indian Ocean, consisting of 40 mountainous granitic islands and over 70 smaller coral islands.
Highest point: Morne Seychellois 906 m (2972 ft).
Climate: Pleasant maritime tropical climate with heavy rainfall.

The 33-member National Assembly comprises 22 members elected by universal adult suffrage for five years and 11 members appointed from party lists under a system of proportional representation. An executive President, who is also directly elected for five years, appoints a Council of Ministers.
Largest political parties: (1993 election) (left-wing former monopoly) People's Progressive Front (SPPF) 28, (conservative) Democratic Party (DP) 4, (coalition) United Opposition 1.
President: (since 1977) Albert René (SPPF).

The economy depends heavily upon tourism which employs over one-third of the labour force. Fishing has expanded – canned tuna is a major export. The islands have a large balance of payments deficit.
Currency: Seychelles rupee.

1976 Independence after over 180 years of British rule. **1977** Left-wing coup; one-party state established. **1981** Attempted coup by white South African mercenaries. **1991** Multi-party constitution was restored.

Official names: Repiblik Sesel (in Creole), République des Seychelles (French) and Republic of Seychelles.
Area: 455 km² (176 sq mi).
Population: 75,000 (1995 est.).
Doubling time: 45 years. **Adult life expectancy:** male 66 years, female 73 years. **Birth rate:** 0.92 times world average. **Death rate:** 0.82 times world average. **Urban population:** 59%. **Capital:** Victoria 30,000 (1992 est.).
Language: Creole 92% (official), English 3% as a first language but universally understood (official), French 1% as a first language (official).
Adult literacy: 84%.
Religion: Roman Catholic 88%, Anglican 6%, various Protestant Churches.

BRITISH INDIAN OCEAN TERRITORY

Official name and status: British Indian Ocean Territory; a British dependency.
Area: 60 km² (23 sq mi).
Population: no permanent settlement; 2900 (mainly US) military personnel on the island of Diego Garcia.
Geography: The territory comprises five coral atolls in the Chagos Archipelago in the Indian Ocean.

COMOROS

The Comoros form a three-island federal republic between Madagascar and Mozambique. Ngazidja, the main island, is dry and rocky, rising to an active volcano (Mt Kartala). Ndzouani is a heavily-eroded volcanic massif. Moili (sometimes spelt Mwali) is a forested plateau with fertile valleys.
Highest point: Mt Kartala 2361 m (7746 ft).
Climate: The tropical climate of the islands is dry from May to October, but with heavy rain during the rest of the year.

The executive president (who appoints a Council of Ministers headed by a Prime Minister) is elected by universal adult suffrage for five years. The 15-member Senate (upper house) consists of five members chosen by the regional government of each island to serve for six years. The 42-member Assembly (lower house) is directly elected for five years. The 1996 constitution increased local autonomy on the three islands.
Largest parties: (1996 election) (nationalist) Democratic Rally for Renewal (RDR) 36 seats, (Islamic fundamentalist) National Front for Justice (FNJ) 3, independents 4. The opposition National Union for Democracy in the Comoros (UNDC) and (former monopoly) Comorian Union for Progress (Udzima) boycotted the election.
President: (since 1996) Mohammed Taki Abdoulharim (UNDC).
Prime Minister: (since 1994) Said Ali Mohammed (independent).

Poor and eroded soils, overpopulation and few resources combine to make these underdeveloped islands one of the world's poorest countries. Service industries employ less than 5% of the population. Subsistence farming occupies over 50% of the workforce growing bananas, coconuts and cassava, but vanilla, ylang-ylang and cloves are exported.
Currency: Comorian franc.

1912 The four Comorian islands became a French colony. **1974** Three islands (the present republic) voted to become independent, which they declared unilaterally; Mayotte (the fourth island) remained French but is claimed by The Comoros. **1978–90** Single-party Islamic state. **1990** Multi-party politics restored. **1995** Attempted coup by mercenaries put down by French troops: President Djohar held hostage.

Official names: Jumhuriyat al-Qumur al-Ittihadiyah al-Islamiyah (in Arabic) and République Fédérale Islamique des Comores (French) (The Federal Islamic Republic of the Comoros).
Area: 1862 km² (719 sq mi) excluding Mayotte.
Population: 545,000 (1995 est.).
Doubling time: 20 years. **Adult life expectancy:** male 56 years, female 60 years. **Birth rate:** 1.84 times world average. **Death rate:** 1.18 times world average. **Urban population:** 29%. **Capital:** Moroni 24,000 (1991 census). **Other main centre:** Mutsamudu 15,000 (1991 census).
Language: Comorian 99% (official), French understood by 18% (official), Arabic understood by 2% (official).
Adult literacy: 53%.
Religion: Sunni Islam 99%, Roman Catholic 1%.

COMORIAN ISLANDS

Moili or Mwali (formerly Mohéli)
Area: 290 km² (112 sq mi).
Pop.: 24,000 (1991 census).
Capital: Fomboni.
Ndzouani or Ndzuwani (formerly Anjouan)
Area: 424 km² (164 sq mi).
Pop.: 189,000 (1991 census).
Capital: Mutsamudu.
Ngazidja (formerly Grande Comore)
Area: 1148 km² (443 sq mi).
Pop.: 234,000 (1991 census).
Capital: Moroni.

REUNION

Official name and status: Le Département de la Réunion (The département of Réunion); a French overseas département and an integral part of the French Republic.
Area: 2542 km² (982 sq mi), including the tiny Indian Ocean islets of Iles Glorieuses, Ile Juan de Nova, Ile Tromelin, Bassas de India and Ile Europa.
Population: 660,000 (1995 est.).
Capital: Saint-Denis 122,000 (1990 census).
Geography: Réunion is a rugged and forested, tropical volcanic island nearly 800 km (500 mi) east of Madagascar in the Indian Ocean.
Economy: The economy is dominated by sugar cane, which accounts for over 70% of exports. Tobacco and vanilla are also grown.

MAYOTTE

Official name and status: Mayotte; a French territorial collectivity, a status between that of an overseas département and an overseas territory, and an integral part of the French Republic. (The Comoros continue to claim Mayotte as an integral part of their territory.)
Area: 376 km² (145 sq mi).
Population: 120,000 (1995 est.).
Capital: Mamoudzou 20,500 (1994 est.).
Geography: Mayotte is the most south-easterly island of the Comoros group (of which it formed a part politically until 1975 when the other Comorian islands unilaterally declared independence).
Economy: Mayotte depends upon French aid and investment, and upon the export of vanilla and ylang-ylang.

West Africa I

THE GAMBIA

The Gambia is a narrow republic, no more than 50 km (31 mi) wide, on the coast of West Africa. It extends through tropical jungle and grassland, on either bank of the Gambia River, 350 km (219 mi) inland.
Highest point: an unnamed point on the Senegalese border 43 m (141 ft).
Climate: Tropical with a dry season between November and May.

The constitution provides for the election, by universal adult suffrage for five years, of an executive President, who appoints a Vice President to lead the government of Ministers in the House of Representatives. There is provision for a 50-member House of Representatives comprising 36 members directly elected for five years, plus five members chosen by the traditional assembly of chiefs, one ex-officio member and eight members nominated by the President. The constitution was suspended in 1994.
President: (since 1996, and head of state and of government since 1994) Col. Yahya Jammeh.

Over 60% of the workforce is involved in agriculture, growing ground nuts, millet, rice and maize. However, the economy depends upon tourism, which accounts for over 50% of the national income.
Currency: Dalasi.

Official name: The Republic of The Gambia.
Area: 10,689 km² (4127 sq mi).
Population: 1,120,000 (1995 est.).
Doubling time: 28 years. **Adult life expectancy:** male 43.4 years, female 46.6 years. **Birth rate:** 1.76 times world average. **Death rate:** 2.09 times world average. **Urban population:** 37%. **Capital:** Banjul 271,000 urban area (city 42,000; Serekunda 103,000, Bakau 24,000; 1986 est.; inc. suburbs). **Other main centres:** Serekunda *see Banjul*, Brikama 24,000, Bakau *see Banjul* (1986 est.; inc. suburbs).
Language: English is understood by about 5% (official), Malinke 34%, Fulani 16%, Wolof 13%, Dyola 9%, with Soninke and other minorities.
Adult literacy: 27%.
Religion: Sunni Islam 95%, traditional beliefs 2%, with small Protestant and Roman Catholic minorities.

1965 Independence after over 120 years of British colonial rule. **1965–94** The Gambia was unique in West Africa as the only multi-party state during this period. **1980–89** Unsuccessful confederation with Senegal. **1994** Military coup: Armed Forces Ruling Council formed.

GUINEA-BISSAU

Guinea-Bissau is a small republic on the coast of West Africa. Most of the country is low-lying with swampy coastal lowlands and offshore islands, and a flat forested inland plain. The north-east is occupied by a plateau.
Highest point: an unnamed point on the Fouta Djallon plateau 180 m (591 ft).
Climate: Tropical with heavy rainfall, but there is a dry season from December to May.

An executive President (who appoints a Prime Minister and a Council of Ministers) and a 100-member National Assembly are elected by universal adult suffrage for five years.
Largest parties: (1994 election) (left-wing former monopoly) African Party for the Independence of Guinea and Cape Verde (PAIGC) 62 seats, (regional) Bafatá Movement 19, Guinea-Bissau Resistance (PRS) and allied parties (including the Union for Change) 19.
President: (since 1980) João Bernardo (Nino) Vieira (PAIGC).
Prime Minister: (since 1994) Manuel Saturnino (PAIGC).

The country has one of the lowest standards of living in the world. Its subsistence economy is based upon rice. Cashew nuts (named for Cacheu in Guinea-Bissau), peanuts and frozen fish are exported.
Currency: Guinea-Bissau peso.

1879 Establishment of the colony of Portuguese Guinea. **1961–74** Failing to achieve independence by peaceful means, the PAIGC movement (see above) mounted a liberation war. **1973** Independence proclaimed. **1974** Independence recognized by Portugal. **1974–91** One-party state. **1991** Multi-party system permitted.

Official name: Républica da Guiné-Bissau (The Republic of Guinea-Bissau).
Area: 36,125 km² (13,948 sq mi).
Population: 1,075,000 (1995 est.).
Doubling time: 33 years. **Adult life expectancy:** male 41.9 years, female 45.1 years. **Birth rate:** 1.71 times world average. **Death rate:** 2.29 times world average. **Urban population:** 20%. **Capital:** Bissau 145,000 (1992 est.; inc. suburbs).
Other main centres: Bafatá 15,000, Cacheu 14,000 (1992 est.).
Language: Portuguese spoken as a first language 8% (official) but understood by 44%, Crioulo (Portuguese Creole) 36%, Fulani 16%, Balante 15%, with Malinke, Mandyako and other minorities.
Adult literacy: 55%.
Religion: Traditional beliefs 65%, Sunni Islam 30%, Roman Catholic minority.

SENEGAL

Senegal is a republic on the coast of West Africa. Its territory is almost cut in two by the long narrow republic of The Gambia, which occupies the Gambia River valley in the south. Most of Senegal is low-lying and covered by tropical grassland. The Fouta Djallon Mountains occupy the extreme south.
Highest point: Fouta Djallon 581 m (1906 ft).
Climate: Wet tropical climate with a pronounced dry season between October and June.

An executive President, who appoints a Prime Minister and other Ministers, is elected by universal adult suffrage for seven years. The National Assembly is elected by proportional representation for five years.
Largest parties: (1993 election) (former monopoly) Socialist Party (PS) 103 seats, (liberal) Social Democratic Party (PDS) 27.
President: (since 1981) Abdou Diouf (PS).
Prime Minister: (since 1991) Habib Thiam (PS).

Agriculture involves 65% of the labour force. Groundnuts and cotton are grown as exports, while rice, maize, millet, sorghum and vegetables are grown for domestic consumption. Fishing is a major industry, and canned and fresh fish and shellfish now account for one-quarter of the country's exports. The manufacturing sector is one of the largest in West Africa, but high unemployment is a problem.
Currency: CFA franc.

Early 20th century Development of a political awareness which contributed substantially to the growth of nationalism in French Africa. **1959–60** Attempted federation with Mali. **1960** Independence after over 300 years of French colonial rule. **1960–80** Presidency of the francophile poet Léopold Senghor. **1966–74** One-party state. **1974** Re-establishment of multi-party system. **1980–89** Unsuccessful confederation with The Gambia.

Official name: La République du Sénégal (The Republic of Senegal).
Area: 196,712 km² (75,951 sq mi).
Population: 8,310,000 (1995 est.).
Doubling time: 26 years. **Adult life expectancy:** male 48.3 years, female 50.39 years. **Birth rate:** 1.72 times world average. **Death rate:** 1.72 times world average. **Urban population:** 41%. **Capital:** Dakar 1,730,000 (1992 est.; inc. suburbs).
Other main centres: Thiès 201,000, Kaolack 180,000, Ziguinchor 149,000, St-Louis 126,000 (1992 est.; inc. suburbs).
Language: French is understood by 5% (official), Wolof is spoken by 48% as a first language but understood by 79%, Fulani 22%, Serer 13%, Diola 5%, with Malinke and other minorities.
Adult literacy: 27%.
Religion: Sunni Islam 94%, Roman Catholic 5%.

SIERRA LEONE

Sierra Leone is a republic on the coast of West Africa. The savannah interior comprises plateaux and mountain ranges rising to Bintimani Peak. The swampy coastal plain is still relatively forested.
Highest point: Bintimani Peak 1948 m (6390 ft).
Climate: Wet and tropical with a pronounced dry season between November and June and a particularly rainy season from June to September.

The constitution provides for the election, by universal adult suffrage for five years, of an executive President, who appoints a Council of Ministers. There is provision for an 80-member Parliament comprising 68 members directly elected from constituencies for five years, plus 12 traditional tribal chiefs. The constitution was suspended in 1997 following a military coup.
President: (since 1997) Maj. Johnny Koroma.

Sierra Leone is one of the poorest countries in the world. Subsistence farming occupies over 60% of the workforce, growing rice, cassava, pulses, plantains and millet. Coffee and cocoa are grown for export. The principal exports are titanium ores, diamonds and bauxite but civil war and continuing unrest have devastated the economy and destroyed much of the infrastructure. Much of the diamond production is now smuggled out of the country rather than traded. There is a sharp division between Freetown and the countryside: the former, which has a considerable Creole population (the descendants of freed slaves) has a much higher standard of living than the rural areas.
Currency: Leone.

Official name: The Republic of Sierra Leone.
Area: 71,740 km² (27,699 sq mi).
Population: 4,510,000 (1995 est.).
Doubling time: 26 years. **Adult life expectancy:** male 41.4 years, female 44.6 years. **Birth rate:** 1.92 times world average. **Death rate:** 2.32 times world average. **Urban population:** 35%. **Capital:** Freetown 600,000 urban area (city 505,000; Koidu 80,000; 1992 est.; inc. suburbs).
Other main centres: Koidu *see Freetown*, Bo 50,000 (1992 est.; inc. suburbs).
Language: English is understood by 16% (official), Krio (English Creole lingua franca) understood by 95%, Mende 35%, Temne 32%, Limba 8%, Kono 5%, with Fulani, Bullom-Sherbro and other minorities.
Adult literacy: 21%.
Religion: Sunni Islam 60%, traditional beliefs 30%, with Protestant and Roman Catholic minorities.

1896 The interior was added to the coastal British colony founded in 1808. **1961** Independence. **1967** Military coup following a disputed election. **1968–85** One-party rule under Siaka Stevens. **1985** Multi-party system restored in theory. **1991** Guerrillas took most of the east. **1992** Military coup led by Valentine Strasser. **1992–96** Civil war: country slowly descended into anarchy. **1996** Military coup in Freetown; the countryside remained in rebel hands; Strasser exiled; multi-party civilian rule restored. **1997** Military coup; regional West African forces under Nigeria intervened unsuccessfully. Guerrilla movement again became active in east.

CAPE VERDE

Cape Verde, an island-republic in the North Atlantic, is the most European state of West Africa. (Three-quarters of the people are of mixed Portuguese and Black African ancestry.) The country consists of ten volcanic semi-arid islands 455 km (285 mi) west of Senegal. The islands were uninhabited when they were discovered in the 15th century.
Highest point: Canon/Monte Fogo (an active volcano) 2829 m (9281 ft).
Climate: Cooled by north-east winds, temperatures seldom exceed 27°C (80°F). Precipitation is very low and as much moisture comes from cooled sea mists as from rain. Average rainfall is only about 60 mm (2½ in). This is the result of predominating north-easterly dry winds blowing from the Sahara Desert for most of the year.

An executive President (who appoints a Prime Minister and a Council of Ministers) and an 82-member National Assembly are elected by universal adult suffrage for five years. The Assembly includes three seats for Cape Verdeans living abroad.
Largest parties: (1995 election) (centrist) Movement for Democracy (MPD) 50 seats, (socialist former monopoly) African Party for the Independence of Cape Verde (PAICV) 20 seats, Party of Democratic Convergence (PCD) 1, representatives of overseas Cape Verdeans 3, others 8.
President: (since 1991) Antonio Mascarenhas Monteiro (MPD).
Prime Minister: (since 1991) Carlos Veiga (MPD).

Since 1968 Cape Verde has experienced very dry conditions. Lack of water hinders agriculture and 90% of Cape Verde's food has to be imported, but bananas are grown for export. The government has used substantial overseas aid and investment to embark on soil and water conservation schemes in an attempt to reverse the gradual desertification of the islands. Fishing is the principal industry and accounts for two-thirds of exports. Money sent back by over 700,000 Cape Verdeans living abroad, mainly in North America, is vital to the economy. The republic has a standard of living that is considerably higher than that of any of the other countries of the region.
Currency: Cape Verde escudo.

Official name: Républica da Cabo Verde (The Republic of Cape Verde).
Area: 4033 km² (1557 sq mi).
Population: 392,000 (1995 est.).
Doubling time: 19 years. **Adult life expectancy:** male 60.7 years, female 64.6 years. **Birth rate:** 1.85 times world average. **Death rate:** 0.97 times world average. **Urban population:** 30%. **Capital:** Praia 62,000 (1990 census; inc. suburbs). **Other main centre:** Mindelo 47,000 (1990 census).
Language: Portuguese universally understood (official), Crioulo (Portuguese Creole) as a first language virtually 100%.
Adult literacy: 65%.
Religion: Roman Catholic 93%, various Protestant Churches 6%.

1975 Independence after 520 years as a colony of Portugal. **1975–90** Single-party Marxist-Leninist state. **1980** End of plans for a merger with the former Portuguese colony of Guinea-Bissau. **1990** A free market economy and a multi-party system were introduced. **1991** Free elections: centrists were returned to power.

GUINEA

Guinea is a republic on the coast of West Africa. Tropical rain forest covers much of the coastal plain. The interior highlands and plains are covered by grass and scrubland. The irregular coast is lined by many small islands.
Highest point: Mont Nimba 1752 m (5747 ft).
Climate: Tropical with heavy rainfall, although there is a drier season in the winter. Temperatures are cooler in the uplands.

An executive President (who appoints a Prime Minister and a Council of Ministers) and a 114-member National Assembly are elected by universal adult suffrage for seven years and five years respectively. The Assembly comprises 38 members elected by first-pass-the-post in single-member constituencies and 76 elected by proportional representation from a national list.
Largest parties: (1995 election) Party of Unity and Progress (PUP) 71 seats, Popular Guinean Rally 19, Renewal and Progress Party (PRP) 9, Union for a New Republic (UNR) 9.
President: (since 1983) Lanasa Conté.
Prime Minister: (since 1996) Sidia Touré (PUP).

Bauxite accounts for 70%, and diamonds for over 10%, of Guinea's exports. However, nearly 80% of the labour force is involved in agriculture, producing bananas and pineapples for export and yams, plantains, maize, rice and cassava as subsistence crops. Despite mineral wealth, Guinea is one of the world's poorest countries and suffered economic collapse under President Touré. **Currency:** Guinean franc.

Official name: La République du Guinea (The Republic of Guinea).
Area: 245,857 km² (94,926 sq mi).
Population: 6,700,000 (1995 est.).
Doubling time: 27 years. **Adult life expectancy:** male 44 years, female 45 years. **Birth rate:** 1.89 times world average. **Death rate:** 2.26 times world average. **Urban population:** 26%.
Capital: Conakry 810,000 (1992 est.; inc. suburbs). **Other main centres:** Kankan 90,000, Kindia 56,000 (1992 est.).
Language: French is understood by 10% (official), Fulani 39%, Malinke 23%, Susu 11%, Kissi 6%, Kpelle 5%, with Yalunka, Loma and other minorities. **Adult literacy:** 36%.
Religion: Sunni Islam 85%, Roman Catholic 8%, traditional beliefs 6%.

1890 Colony of French Guinea was established. **1958** Independence, but unlike the rest of French Africa, Guinea voted for complete separation from the French sphere of influence and suffered severe economic reprisals as a result. **1958–84** Authoritarian rule of President Sékou Touré; one-party state; regime became less repressive after 1971 and by 1975–77 was reconciled with France. **1984** Touré died; military coup shortly afterwards. **1992** Multi-party system permitted. **1995** First multi-party elections. **1996** Attempted coup and military mutiny.

GUINEA'S SECOND CITY KANKAN IS A CLUSTER OF VILLAGES RATHER THAN AN URBAN AREA

West Africa II

IVORY COAST

The Ivory Coast is a republic on the coast of West Africa and the most populous, and most prosperous, French-speaking country in the region. The north is a grassland plateau. In the south, tropical rain forest, increasingly cleared for farming, ends at the narrow coastal plain.
Highest point: A point just below the summit of Mont Nimba (on the Guinean border) 1752 m (5748 ft).
Climate: The south is equatorial with high temperatures and heavy rainfall (except in two short dry seasons in December to March and July to September); the north has similar temperatures but is drier, while the far north has little rain from December to June.

The executive President (who appoints a Council of Ministers headed by a Prime Minister) and a 175-member National Assembly are elected by universal adult suffrage for five years.
Largest parties: (1995 election) (nationalist former monopoly) Democratic Party of Côte d'Ivoire-African Democratic Rally (PDCI-RDA) 148 seats, (centrist) Republican Rally (RDR) 13, (social democratic) Ivorian People's Front (FPI) 11, others 3.
President: (since 1993) Henri Konan-Bédié (PDCI-RDA).
Prime Minister: (since 1993) Daniel Kaplan-Duncan (PDCI-RDA).

The country depends upon exports of cocoa (which accounts for over one-third of exports), coffee and timber, and suffered after the decline in price of cocoa and coffee in the 1980s. Natural resources include petroleum, natural gas and iron ore. Political stability has helped economic development and attracted labour from neighbouring states (over one-quarter of the population is non-Ivorian). **Currency:** CFA franc.

1889 French protectorate established. **1960** Independence. **1960–90** One-party state. **1960–94** Dictatorial presidency of Félix Houphouët-Boigny, who kept close links with France. **1990** Multi-party rule restored.

Official name: La République de Côte d'Ivoire (The Republic of Côte d'Ivoire; since 1986 Côte d'Ivoire has been the official version of the name in all languages but the state is still popularly referred to in English as Ivory Coast).
Area: 320,763 km^2 (123,847 sq mi).
Population: 14,250,000 (1995 est.).
Doubling time: 21 years. **Adult life expectancy:** male 53.6 years, female 57.2 years. **Birth rate:** 2 times world average. **Death rate:** 1.62 times world average. **Urban population:** 42%. **Capitals:** Yamoussoukro (administrative capital and capital designate) 126,000 (1988 est.); Abidjan (legislative and joint capital) 2,500,000 (city 1,929,000; 1988 est.; inc. suburbs). **Other main centres:** Bouaké 362,000, Daloa 128,000, Korhogo 113,000 (1988 est.; inc. suburbs).
Language: French understood by 35% (official), Akan 30%, Malinke 12%, Kru 12%, Voltaic-Gur 12%, Mande 8%, with other minorities.
Adult literacy: 40%.
Religion: Sunni Islam 39%, Roman Catholic 21%, traditional beliefs 17%, non-religious 13%, various Protestant Churches 7%.

MALI

Mali is a large land-locked arid republic in West Africa. The low-lying flat plateaux and plains of Mali rise towards the Adrar des Iforas in the north-east. The south is grassland; the north is part of the Sahara Desert.
Highest point: Hombori Tondo 1155 m (3789 ft).
Climate: Hot and largely dry although the south has a wet season from June to October. The north has very little rain.

The executive President (who appoints a Council of Ministers headed by a Prime Minister) and the 129-member National Assembly are elected by universal adult suffrage for five years.
Largest parties: (1992 election) (nationalist) Alliance for Democracy in Mali (Adema) 76 seats, others (including Party for Democracy and Progress, National Congress for Democratic Initiative and Sudanese Union-Democratic African Rally) 40.
President: (since 1992) Alpha Oumar Konaré (Adema).
Prime Minister: (since 1994) Ibrahim Boubakar Keita (Adema).

Drought between 1969 and 1985 devastated Mali's livestock herds (goats, sheep and cattle). Only one-fifth of the country (mainly the Niger Valley and the south) can be cultivated, producing mainly rice, sorghum and millet for domestic consumption. Cotton accounts for over 40% of Mali's exports. Other exports include gold and live animals.
Currency: CFA franc.

1880–95 France conquered the region, naming it French Sudan. **1959–60** Abortive federation with Senegal. **1960** Independence. **1968** Military coup; multi-party system abandoned; military governments. **1992** Constitutional multi-party system restored.

Official name: La République du Mali (The Republic of Mali).
Area: 1,248,574 km^2 (482,077 sq mi).
Population: 9,010,000 (1995 est.).
Doubling time: 22 years. **Adult life expectancy:** male 44.7 years, female 48.1 years. **Birth rate:** 2.08 times world average. **Death rate:** 2.14 times world average. **Urban population:** 26%. **Capital:** Bamako 810,000 (1996 est.; inc. suburbs).
Other main centres: Ségou 107,000, Sikasso 90,000, Mopti 86,000 (1996 est.; inc. suburbs).
Language: French understood by 8% (official), Bambara 32% as a first language and 60% as a lingua franca, Fulani-Tukulor 14%, Senufo 12%, Soninke 9%, Tuareg 7%, Songhai 7%, Malinke 7%, with Dogon, Dyula and other minorities. **Adult literacy:** 19%.
Religion: Sunni Islam 90%, traditional beliefs 9%, Roman Catholic under 1%.

NIGER

Niger is a large landlocked republic in West Africa. Most of the country lies in the Sahara Desert; the south and the Niger Valley is tropical grassland. The central Aïr Mountains run from north to south in a series of 'islands' rising out of the desert.
Highest point: Mont Gréboun 1944 m (6379 ft). **Climate:** Hot and dry although the south has a rainy season from June to October.

The executive President (who appoints a Council of Ministers headed by a Prime Minister) is elected by universal adult suffrage for seven years. The 83-member National Assembly is directly elected for five years.
Largest parties: (1996 election) National Union of Independents for Democratic Renewal (UNIRD) 69 seats, others 14.
President: (since 1996) Gen. Ibrahim Mainassara Bare (UNIRD).
Prime Minister: (since 1996) Amadou Boubacar Cisse (UNIRD).

Livestock herds (goats, sheep and cattle) and harvests of subsistence crops (mainly millet, sorghum and vegetables) have been reduced by drought and desertification. Uranium provides almost one-half of Niger's exports but the country remains one of the poorest in the world, with one of the highest birth rates and the lowest standard of literacy on Earth.
Currency: CFA franc.

1901 French territory of Niger was established. **1920** Pacification of Niger completed by the French. **1960** Independence. **1969–mid 1970s** Severe drought. **1974** Military coup: multi-party system ended. **1983** Civilian rule restored under one-party state. **1992** Multi-party system restored: power changed hands peacefully in 1993 and 1995. **1996** Military coup: new constitution; multi-party system restored.

Official name: La République du Niger (The Republic of Niger).
Area: 1,186,408 km^2 (458,075 sq mi).
Population: 9,150,000 (1995 est.).
Doubling time: 22 years. **Adult life expectancy:** male 44.9 years, female 48.1 years. **Birth rate:** 2.1 times world average. **Death rate:** 2.03 times world average. **Urban population:** 20%. **Capital:** Niamey 398,000 (1988 census; inc. suburbs).
Other main centres: Zinder 120,000, Maradi 104,000 (1988 census; inc. suburbs).
Language: French understood by 15% (official), Hausa 53% as a first language and 70% as a lingua franca, Songhai 21%, Tuareg 10%, Fulani 10%, with Kanuri and other minorities.
Adult literacy: 14%.
Religion: Sunni Islam 99%, Roman Catholic minority.

PRESIDENT HOUPHOUËT-BOIGNY DEVELOPED HIS HOME VILLAGE, YAMOUSSOUKRO, AS IVORY

BURKINA FASO

Burkina Faso is a landlocked republic in the dry Sahel region of West Africa. The country consists of plateaux, relatively well-watered grassland in the south where the headwaters of the Volta flow, but extending to arid scrub country in the north.
Highest point: Mont Tema 747 m (2451 ft). **Climate:** Hot and dry with adequate rainfall (1000 mm (40 in) in the savannah south. The north is semi-desert.

The executive President (who appoints a Council of Ministers headed by a Prime Minister) is elected by universal adult suffrage for seven years. The 107-member National Assembly is directly elected for five years. The 120-member Chamber of Representatives is a consultative upper house, composed of delegates from social, religious and professional bodies and also from political parties and organizations.
Largest parties: (1992 election) (left-wing former Marxist) Organization for Popular Democracy-Labour Movement (ODP-MT) 78 seats, National Convention of Progressive Patriots-Social Democratic Party (CNPP-PSD) 12, others 17.
President: (since 1991) Capt. Blaise Compoaré (ODP-MT).
Prime Minister: (since 1995) Kadré Desiré Ouédraogo (ODP-MT).

Burkina Faso, one of the world's poorest states, was severely stricken by drought in the 1970s and 1980s when desertification of the north intensified. Nomadic herdsmen (keeping goats, sheep and cattle) and subsistence farmers (producing sorghum, millet, maize and rice) account for nearly 85% of the labour force. Cotton, the main commercial crop, accounts for almost one-quarter of exports. Other exports include gold, live animals and animal hides. Over 2 million Burkinans work in Ivory Coast and Ghana, and money they send back to their families is an important source of foreign currency.
Currency: CFA franc.

1890s France conquered the Mossi kingdoms in the region. **1919** A separate French colony of Upper Volta (modern Burkina Faso) was established. **1919–60** In colonial times the area was a labour reservoir for more developed French colonies to the south. **1960** Independence. **1966–87** Period of instability: military coups in 1966, 1974, 1980, 1983, 1987. **1984** Name changed to Burkina Faso. **1987** Capt. Blaise Compoaré seized power. **1991** Constitutional multi-party system restored.

Official name: Burkina Faso (sometimes referred to as Burkina).
Area: 274,400 km² (105,946 sq mi).
Population: 10,320,000 (1995 est.).
Doubling time: 24 years.
Adult life expectancy: male 45.8 years, female 49 years. **Birth rate:** 1.87 times world average. **Death rate:** 1.97 times world average.
Urban population: 14%.
Capital: Ouagadougou 634,000 (1991 est.; inc. suburbs).
Other main centres: Bobo-Dioulasso 269,000, Koudougou 60,000 (1991 est.).
Language: French understood by 6% (official), Mossi 50%, Fulani 10%, Gurma 6%, Bisa 4%, with Dagara, Gyula, Lyele and other minorities.
Adult literacy: 18%.
Religion: Traditional beliefs 59%, Sunni Islam 31%, Roman Catholic about 10%.

GHANA

Ghana, a republic on the coast of West Africa, is, after Nigeria, the most populous and important state in the region. Most of the country is low-lying plains and plateaux. The central Volta Basin (which ends in steep escarpments) contains the large reservoir Lake Volta.
Highest point: Afadjato 885 m (2903 ft).
Climate: Tropical with heavy rainfall, decreasing markedly inland. The north is subject to the hot, dry Harmattan wind from the Sahara and is dry from November to June.

The executive President, who appoints a Cabinet of Ministers, and the 200-member Parliament are elected by universal adult suffrage for four years.
Largest parties: (1996 election) National Democratic Congress (NDC) 133 seats, (centre-right) New Patriotic Party (NPP) 60, others 7.
President: (since 1981) Jerry Rawlings (NDC).

Political instability and mismanagement damaged a promising economy in the 1970s and 1980s, but a recovery has occurred. Nearly 60% of the workforce is involved in farming. Cocoa is the main cash crop (accounting for one-quarter of exports). Gold accounts for 45% of exports. Timber and mining for diamonds are also important. Electricity from the Volta Dam stimulated industry and some electricity is exported. **Currency:** Cedi.

1850 Britain bought Danish settlements in Gold Coast. **1872** The Dutch withdrew from their coastal forts. **1874** British Gold Coast colony (modern Ghana) was established. **1875–1901** Ashanti (Asante) wars gradually added the interior to the British coastal colony. **1945–57** Prosperity from cocoa exports, increasing literacy and the dynamism of Dr Kwame Nkrumah helped Gold Coast to set the pace for decolonization of Black Africa. **1957** Independence as Ghana. **1960** Republic was declared. **1960–66** Presidency of Nkrumah, whose dictatorial rule and increasingly grandiose projects ruined Ghana; one-party state. **1966** Coup: Nkrumah deposed. **1966–81** Period of great political instability: with coups in 1972, 1979 and 1981, and brief periods of civilian government. **1981** Military coup led by Jerry Rawlings. **1992** Multi-party system restored.

Official name: The Republic of Ghana.
Area: 238,533 km² (92,098 sq mi).
Population: 16,470,000 (1995 est.).
Doubling time: 23 years. **Adult life expectancy:** male 53.2 years, female 57.2 years. **Birth rate:** 1.67 times world average. **Death rate:** 1.26 times world average. **Urban population:** 35%. **Capital:** Accra 1,696,000 urban area (city 949,000; Tema 110,000; 1991 est.; inc. suburbs). **Other main centres:** Kumasi 385,000, Tamale 153,000, Tema *see Accra*, Sekondi-Takoradi 104,000 (1989 est.).
Language: English understood by over 5% (official), Hausa (used as a lingua franca) understood by 60%, Akan 52%, Mossi 16%, Ewe 12%, Ga-Adangme 8%, with Gurma and other minorities.
Adult literacy: 60%.
Religion: Traditional beliefs 38%, Sunni Islam 30%, Roman Catholic 12%, various Protestant Churches 5%, African Christian Churches 5%, Anglican 2%.

LIBERIA

Liberia, the only African state never to have been a colony, is a republic on the coast of West Africa. A low swampy coastal belt borders a higher zone of tropical forest. Further inland, plateaux rise to a mountainous region on the Guinean frontier.
Highest point: Mt Wuteve 1381 m (4531 ft).
Climate: Tropical with a wet season from May to October and a dry season between November and June.

The constitution provides for the election of an executive President, a 26-member Senate and a 64-member House of Representatives by universal adult suffrage for six years.
Largest parties: (1997 election House of Representatives) National Patriotic Party (NPP) and allies 50 seats, Unity Party 6, others 8.
President: (since 1997) Charles Taylor (NPP).

Civil war from 1989–94 devastated the economy of an already poor nation. Over two-thirds of the labour force are involved in subsistence farming, growing cassava, sweet potatoes, pulses and plantains. Coffee is grown for export. Iron ore and rubber made up over 80% of exports before the civil war, but trade has decreased. **Currency:** Liberian dollar (the US dollar is also in circulation as legal tender).

1821–22 Founded as a settlement for freed slaves by the American Colonization Society. **1847** Became a republic. **1878–1980** Rule by True Whig Party (including President William Tubman 1944-71); black American settlers and their descendants dominated local Africans. **1980** Military coup by Samuel Doe, the first Liberian of local ancestry to rule. **1989–94** Civil war between three main factions; regional West African force (led by Nigeria) intervened. **1994** Cease-fire: transitional Council of State formed by warringfactions.**1997** Free elections.

Official name: The Republic of Liberia.
Area: 99,067 km² (38,250 sq mi).
Population: 2,400,000 (1995 est.), including up to 500,000 Liberian refugees in surrounding states.
Doubling time: 23 years. **Adult life expectancy:** male 54 years, female 57 years. **Birth rate:** 1.72 times world average. **Death rate:** 1.29 times world average. **Urban population:** 45%.
Capital: Monrovia 1,000,000 (1995 est.; inc. suburbs). **Other main centres:** Harbel 60,000, Gbarnga 30,000 (1986 est.; inc. suburbs).
Language: English is understood by 20% (official), Krio (English Creole lingua franca) understood by 88%, Kpelle 19%, Bassa 14%, Grebo 9%, Gio 8%, Kru 7%, Mano 7%, with Loma, Malinke and other minorities.
Adult literacy: 38%.
Religion: Various Protestant Churches under 50% (mainly African Churches, Methodist, Baptist, Lutheran and Anglican), Sunni Islam 35%, Roman Catholic 5%, traditional beliefs.

WEST AFRICA III

NIGERIA

Nigeria is the leading country of West Africa and has the largest population of any state on the continent. Inland from the swampy forest and (rapidly diminishing) tropical jungle of the coastal plains, Nigeria comprises a series of plateaux covered, for the most part, with open woodland and savannah. The far north is semi-desert. Isolated ranges of hills rise above the plateaux, the highest of which are the central Jos Plateau and the Biu Plateau in the north-east.
Highest point: Vogel Peak (Dimlang) 2042 m (6700 ft).
Climate: The coastal areas are very humid and hot, with an average temperature of 32°C (90°F). Rainfall is heavy on the coast but decreases gradually inland, although there is a rainy season from April to October. The dry far north experiences the Harmattan, a hot wind blowing out of the Sahara.

The constitution and political activity were suspended in 1993 by the military regime. There is currently a President, who heads the 11-member Provisional Ruling Council and who appoints a Cabinet of Ministers. The current President has an open-ended term of office. Under the constitution which will come into effect after the military regime cedes power, there will be an executive Presidency, which will alternate between the north and south of the country, and a directly-elected Assembly. Five new political parties have been allowed to form. Nigeria is divided into 36 states (plus the Federal Capital), which will have limited autonomy under the new constitution.
President: (since 1993) Gen. Sani Abacha.

Nigeria is the major economic power of West Africa. The country depends upon revenue from petroleum exports (petroleum accounts for 98% of Nigeria's exports by value). However, in the 1990s, falling petroleum prices resulted in major economic problems. Corruption has also hindered development. Other exports include cocoa, fertilizer, textiles and cashew nuts. Industries include petrochemicals, food processing and textiles. Over 40% of the labour force is involved in subsistence farming, growing maize, sorghum, cassava, yams, rice and millet. Cocoa is the main commercial crop. **Currency:** Naira.

Official name: The Federal Republic of Nigeria
Area: 923,768 km² (356,669 sq mi).
Population: 95,450,000 (1995 est.).
Doubling time: 22 years. **Adult life expectancy:** male 53.5 years, female 55.9 years. **Birth rate:** 1.86 times world average. **Death rate:** 1.51 times world average. **Urban population:** 38%. **Capital:** Abuja 375,000 (1991 census; inc. suburbs).
Other main centres: Lagos 5,686,000, Ibadan 1,295,000, Kano 700,000, Ogbomosho 661,000, Oshogbo 442,000, Ilorin 431,000, Abeokuta 387,000, Port Harcourt 371,000, Zaria 345,000, Ilesha 342,000, Onitsha 337,000, Iwo 335,000, Ado-Ekiti 325,000, Kaduna 310,000 (1989 est.).
Language: English understood by 14% (official), English Creole understood by 35%, Hausa 21% but understood by 50%, Yoruba 21%, Ibo 18%, Fulani 11%, Ibibio 6%, Kanuri 4%, Edo 3%, Tiv 2%, with Ijo, Bura, Nupe and other minorities.
Adult literacy: 52%.
Religion: Sunni Islam 50%, various Protestant Churches (particularly Anglican, Methodist and Baptist) 21%, Roman Catholic 10%, traditional beliefs 10%, African Churches 9%.

1885 British protectorate was established on the coast, where Lagos had been British since 1861. **1900** Northern Nigeria became British. **1914** The interior and the coast merged to form the region's largest colony. **1954** Unwieldy federal system introduced with three states (since when the number of states has gradually increased by division to 36). **1960** Independence. **1966** PM and other prominent politicians assassinated in military coup. **1966–75** Military government of Gen. Yakubu Gowon. **1967–70** Bitter civil war when the Eastern Region (Biafra) attempted to secede. **1975** Military coup. **1979–83** Restoration of civilian rule. **1983** Military coup. **1985** Military coup brought Gen. Ibrahim Babangida to power. **1993** Limited civilian rule restored; further military coup; constitution suspended after elections annulled. **Since 1993** The military regime of Gen. Sani Abacha has attracted international criticism for perceived human rights infringements.

NIGERIAN STATES

Abia
Area: 6320 km² (2440 sq mi).
Pop.: 2,367,000 (1992 est.).
Capital: Umuahia. (Area and population include Ebonyi.)
Adamawa
Area: 36,917 km² (14,254 sq mi).
Pop.: 2,188,000 (1992 est.).
Capital: Yola.
Akwa Ibom
Area: 7081 km² (2734 sq mi).
Pop.: 2,431,000 (1992 est.).
Capital: Uyo.
Anambra
Area: 4844 km² (1870 sq mi).
Pop.: 2,851,000 (1992 est.).
Capital: Akwa.
Bauchi
Area: 64,605 km² (24,944 sq mi).
Pop.: 4,432,000 (1992 est.).
Capital: Bauchi. (Area and population include Gombe.)
Bayelsa
(created out of Rivers in 1996–97)
Capital: Yenagoa.
Benue
Area: 34,059 km² (13,150 sq mi).
Pop.: 2,864,000 (1992 est.).
Capital: Makurdi.
Borno
Area: 70,898 km² (27,374 sq mi).
Pop.: 2,674,000 (1992 est.).
Capital: Maiduguri.
Cross River
Area: 20,156 km² (7782 sq mi).
Pop.: 1,912,000 (1992 est.).
Capital: Calabar.
Delta
Area: 17,698 km² (6833 sq mi).
Pop.: 2,647,000 (1992 est.).
Capital: Asaba.
Ebonyi
(created out of Abia and Enugu in 1996–97)
Capital: Abakaliki.
Edo
Area: 17,802 km² (6873 sq mi).
Pop.: 2,225,000 (1992 est.).
Capital: Benin City.
Ekiti
(created out of Ondo in 1996–97)
Capital: Ado-Ekiti.
Enugu
Area: 12,831 km² (4954 sq mi).
Pop.: 3,256,000 (1992 est.).
Capital: Enugu. (Area and population include Ebonyi.)
Gombe
(created out of Bauchi in 1996–97)
Capital: Gombe.
Imo
Area: 5530 km² (2135 sq mi).
Pop.: 2,560,000 (1992 est.).
Capital: Owerri.
Jigawa
Area: 23,154 km² (8940 sq mi).
Pop.: 2,915,000 (1992 est.).
Capital: Dutse.
Kaduna
Area: 46,053 km² (17,891 sq mi).
Pop.: 4,088,000 (1992 est.).
Capital: Kaduna.
Kano
Area: 20,131 km² (7773 sq mi).
Pop.: 5,801,000 (1992 est.).
Capital: Kano.
Katsina
Area: 24,192 km² (9341 sq mi).
Pop.: 3,995,000 (1992 est.).
Capital: Katsina.
Kebbi
Area: 35,800 km² (14,209 sq mi).
Pop.: 2,125,000 (1992 est.).
Capital: Birnin Kebbi.
Kogi
Area: 29,833 km² (11,519 sq mi).
Pop.: 2,162,000 (1992 est.).
Capital: Lokoja.
Kwara
Area: 36,825 km² (14,218 sq mi).
Pop.: 1,614,000 (1992 est.).
Capital: Ilorin.
Lagos
Area: 3345 km² (1292 sq mi).
Pop.: 5,847,000 (1992 est.).
Capital: Ikeja.
Nassarawa
(created out of Plateau in 1996–97)
Capital: Lafia.
Niger
Area: 76,363 km² (29,484 sq mi).
Pop.: 2,557,000 (1992 est.).
Capital: Minna.
Ogun
Area: 16,762 km² (6472 sq mi).
Pop.: 2,409,000 (1992 est.).
Capital: Abeokuta.
Ondo
Area: 20,960 km² (8092 sq mi).
Pop.: 4,001,000 (1992 est.).
Capital: Akure. (Area and population include Ekiti.)
Osun
Area: 9251 km² (3572 sq mi).
Pop.: 2,269,000 (1992 est.).
Capital: Oshogbo.
Oyo
Area: 28,454 km² (10,986 sq mi).
Pop.: 3,593,000 (1992 est.).
Capital: Ibadan.
Plateau
Area: 58,030 km² (22,406 sq mi).
Pop.: 3,382,000 (1992 est.).
Capital: Jos. (Area and population include Nassarawa.)
Rivers
Area: 21,850 km² (8436 sq mi).
Pop.: 4,103,000 (1992 est.).
Capital: Port Harcourt. (Area and population include Bayelsa.)
Sokoto
Area: 65,735 km² (25,380 sq mi).
Pop.: 4,524,000 (1992 est.).
Capital: Sokoto.
Taraba
Area: 54,473 km² (21,032 sq mi).
Pop.: 1,524,000 (1992 est.).
Capital: Jalingo.
Yobe
Area: 45,502 km² (17,568 sq mi).
Pop.: 1,454,000 (1992 est.).
Capital: Damaturu.
Zamfara
(created out of Sokoto in 1996–97)
Capital: Gusau.
Federal Capital Territory
Area: 7315 km² (2824 sq mi).
Pop.: 390,000 (1992 est.).
Capital: Abuja.

■ A 1997 SURVEY FOUND NIGERIA TO BE THE WORLD'S MOST CORRUPT COUNTRY ■ THE WORLD'S

BENIN

Benin is a West African republic stretching in a narrow strip from the Atlantic coast to the River Niger. The Atacora Massif occupies the north-west; in the north-east plains slope down to the Niger Valley. The plateaux of central Benin fall in the south to a low fertile region. A narrow coastal plain is lined by lagoons.
Highest point: Atacora Massif 641 m (2103 ft).
Climate: The south is equatorial with high temperatures and heavy rainfall all year; the north is tropical with high temperatures but drier and more seasonal rainfall.

An executive President is elected by universal adult suffrage for five years; the 82-member National Assembly is directly elected under a system of proportional representation for four years. The President appoints a Prime Minister and other Ministers.
Largest parties: (1995 election) (centrist) Party for the Renaissance of Benin (PRB) 20 seats, Party for Democratic Renewal (PRD) 19, FARD-Alafia 10, Social Democratic Party (PSD) 8, Union for Democracy and National Solidarity (UDS) 5, others (including supporters of the (former monopoly) Union for the Triumph of the Return of Democracy (URTD) 21.
President: (since 1996) Matthieu Kérékou (URTD).
Prime Minister: (since 1996) Adrien Houngbedji (PRD; PRD-led coalition).

The economy is based on agriculture which involves over 60% of the workforce. Cotton is the major export. Cassava, maize and manioc are grown as subsistence crops. Over one-half of the population lives in the coastal region. In the late 1980s, the centrally planned economy was dismantled and a free market economy encouraged. **Currency:** CFA franc.

Official name: La République du Bénin (The Republic of Benin).
Area: 112,680 km² (43,500 sq mi).
Population: 5,410,000 (1995 est.).
Doubling time: 24 years. **Adult life expectancy:** male 49 years, female 52 years. **Birth rate:** 1.76 times world average. **Death rate:** 1.61 times world average. **Urban population:** 40%.
Capitals: Porto-Novo (official and legislative capital) 178,000; Cotonou (administrative capital) 533,000 (1992 census; inc. suburbs). **Other main centres:** Djougou 132,000, Abomey 126,000, Parakou 107,000 (1992 census).
Language: French understood by 16% (official), Fon 39%, Yoruba 12%, Adja 11%, Bariba 9%, Houéda 9%, with Somba, Fulani and other minorities.
Adult literacy: 37%.
Religion: Traditional beliefs 62%, Roman Catholic 21%, Sunni Islam 12%, various Protestant Churches 4%.

1890s Region was conquered by the French and organized as the colony of Dahomey. **1960** Independence. **1963–72** Political instability; five coups. **1972–91** One-party Marxist state. **1975** Dahomey renamed Benin. **Since 1991** Multi-party system restored.

EQUATORIAL GUINEA

Equatorial Guinea is a West African republic comprising the fertile island of Bioko (formerly Fernando Póo) off the coast of Nigeria, the much smaller island of Pagalu (formerly Annobón) nearly 600 km (375 mi) to the south, plus the district of Mbini (formerly Río Muni) on the African mainland and the small adjoining Corisco and Elobey islands.
Highest point: Pico de Basilé 3008 m (9868 ft).
Climate: Temperatures are high and rainfall is heavy all year. Mbini has a lower rainfall and is less hot and humid than Bioko and Pagalu.

An executive President, who appoints a Prime Minister and other Ministers, is elected by universal adult suffrage for seven years; the 80-member National Assembly is directly elected for five years.
Largest parties: (1993 election) (former monopoly) Democratic Party of Equatorial Guinea (PDGE) 68 seats, Democratic Social Union (UDS) 5, Social Democratic Popular Convergence (CSDP) 6, others 1. The international community withheld recognition of the 1994 elections, judging them to be flawed.
President: (since 1979) Gen. Teodoro Obiang (Nguema Mbasogo) (PDGE).
Prime Minister: (since 1992) Silvestre Siale Bileka (PDGE).

Nearly 60% of the workforce is involved in subsistence farming. Mbini exports coffee and timber; Bioko exports cocoa. Living standards declined drastically during dictatorships in the 1970s and 1980s and the country relies heavily upon foreign aid. The considerable distances between the different components of the republic make the development of Equatorial Guinea problematic. **Currency:** CFA franc.

1843–56 Spain acquired the four components that now make up the state, organizing them as Spanish Guinea. **Early 20th century** Harsh colonial rule attracted much criticism. **1968** Independence as Equatorial Guinea. **1969–93** Dictatorships of Francisco Nguema and Teodoro Obiang. **1993** Gradual transition from single-party rule.

Official name: República de Guinea Ecuatorial (The Republic of Equatorial Guinea).
Area: 28,051 km² (10,831 sq mi).
Population: 396,000 (1995 est.).
Doubling time: 27 years. **Adult life expectancy:** male 50 years, female 54.3 years. **Birth rate:** 1.63 times world average. **Death rate:** 1.58 times world average. **Urban population:** 29%. **Capital:** Malabo 48,000 (1995 est.; inc. suburbs).
Other main centre: Bata 37,000 (1995 est.).
Language: Spanish spoken by less than 1% as a first language but widely understood (official), Fang 83%, Bubi 10%, English Creole.
Adult literacy: 62%.
Religion: Roman Catholic 98%.

TOGO

Togo is a West African republic stretching in a narrow strip along the eastern border of Ghana. Inland from a restricted coastal plain is a series of plateaux rising in the north to the Chaine du Togo highlands.
Highest point: Mont Agou 986 m (3235 ft).
Climate: A hot and humid tropical climate, although the north is drier.

An executive President is elected by universal adult suffrage for seven years; the 81-member National Assembly is directly elected for five years. The President appoints a Prime Minister and other Ministers.
Largest parties: (1994 election) (centrist) Action Committee for Renewal (CAR) 36 seats, (former monopoly) Rally for Togolese People (RPT) 35, Togolese Union for Democracy (UTD) 7, Union for Justice and Democracy 2, others 1.
President: (since 1967) Gen. Gnassingbe Eyadema (RPT).
Prime Minister: (since 1996) Klutse Kwassi (RPT).

Nearly 70% of the workforce is involved in subsistence farming, mainly growing yams and millet. Coffee and cotton are grown for export. Phosphates are the major export. **Currency:** CFA franc.

1884 German colony of Togoland established. **1914** Togoland occupied by Franco-British forces during World War I. **1919** Colony divided between France and UK, the latter merging its share with what is now Ghana. **1960** Independence. **1969–91** One-party state under Gen. Eyadema. **1991–93** Gradual transition to democracy.

Togolese village houses are grouped in family units

Official name: La République Togolaise (The Republic of Togo).
Area: 56,785 km² (21,925 sq mi).
Population: 4,140,000 (1995 est.).
Doubling time: 22 years. **Adult life expectancy:** male 53.2 years, female 56.8 years. **Birth rate:** 1.78 times world average. **Death rate:** 1.38 times world average. **Urban population:** 26%. **Capital:** Lomé 375,000 (1989 est.; inc. suburbs). **Other main centres:** Sokodé 50,000, Kara 30,000 (1989 est.).
Language: French understood by 17% (official), Ewe 23%, Kabre 14%, Watyi (or Ouatchi) 10%, Kotokoli 6%, Ane 6%, Moba 6%, with Losso, Adja and other minorities.
Adult literacy: 52%.
Religion: Traditional beliefs 59%, Roman Catholic 21%, Sunni Islam 12%, various Protestant Churches 7%.

Central Africa I

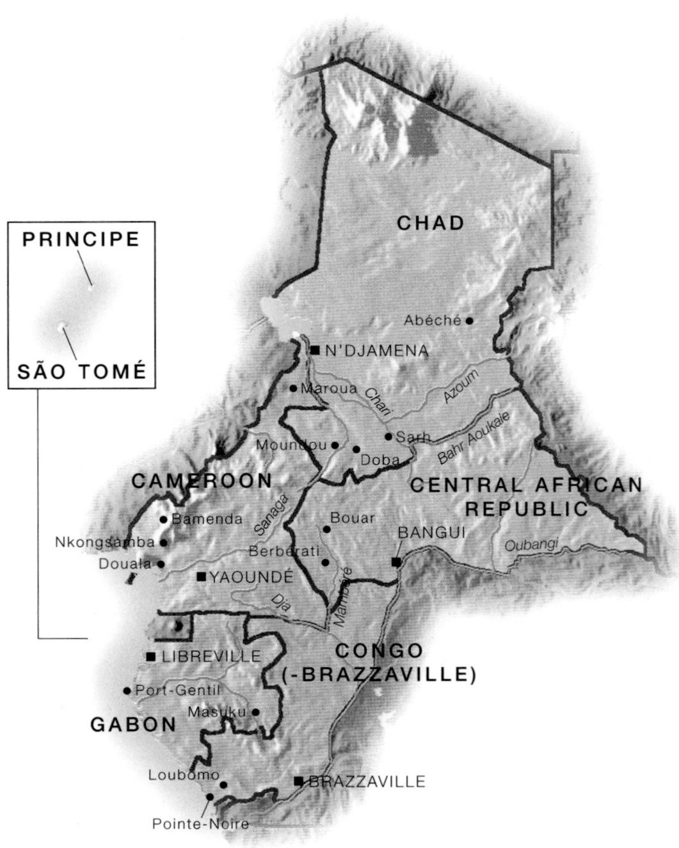

SAO TOME AND PRINCIPE

São Tomé and Príncipe form a two-island republic in the Atlantic Ocean off the west coast of Central Africa. The mountainous islands are 144 km (90 mi) apart and have an Afro-European population.
Highest point: Pico de São Tomé 2024 m (6640 ft).
Climate: Tropical. Rainfall occurs all year but there is a marked wet season from October to May.

The executive President (who appoints a Prime Minister and other Ministers) and the 55-member Assembly are elected by universal adult suffrage for five years and four years respectively.
Largest parties: (1994 election) (left-wing former monopoly) Movement for the Liberation of São Tomé and Príncipe (MLSTP) 27 seats, (centrist) Party of Democratic Convergence (PCD) 14, Independent Democratic Action (ADI) 14.
President: (since 1991) Miguel Trovoada (ADI).
Prime Minister: (since 1996) Raul Bragança (ADI-PCD-MLSTP coalition).

Cocoa is the mainstay of a largely agricultural economy and accounts for over 75% of exports. Privatization of a formerly centrally planned economy has begun. **Currency:** Dobra.

1975 Independence after over 450 years of Portuguese colonial rule. **1975–90** Single-party Marxist state. **Since 1990** Multi-party constitutional rule but instability remains (with attempted coups in 1978, 1979, 1988 and 1995).

Official name: República democrática de São Tomé e Príncipe (The Democratic Republic of São Tomé and Príncipe).
Area: 1001 km² (386 sq mi).
Population: 131,000 (1995 est.).
Doubling time: 23 years. **Adult life expectancy:** male 61.5 years, female 65.2 years. **Birth rate:** 1.41 times world average. **Death rate:** 0.96 times world average. **Urban population:** 44%. **Capital:** São Tomé 43,000 (1991 census). **Other major centre:** Trinidade 11,000 (1991 census).
Language: Portuguese (including Portuguese Creole/Crioulo) 86% (official), Spanish minority.
Adult literacy: 63%.
Religion: Roman Catholic 84%, various Protestant Pentecostal Churches 15%.

AUTONOMOUS ISLAND
Príncipe
Area: 142 km² (55 sq mi).
Pop.: 5600 (1991 census).
Capital: Santo António.

GABON

Gabon is a sparsely populated republic on the Atlantic coast of Central Africa. Apart from the narrow coastal plain, low plateaux make up much of the country. The centre is occupied by the low Massif du Chaillu mountains.
Highest point: Mt Iboundji 981 m (3219 ft).
Climate: A hot wet equatorial climate with very little seasonal variation.

The executive President (who appoints a Council of Ministers headed by a Prime Minister) is elected by universal adult suffrage for seven years. The 120-member National Assembly comprises 111 members directly elected for five years and nine members chosen by the President.
Largest parties: (1997 election) (nationalist) Gabonese Democratic Party (PDG) 76 seats, (rural/ethnic) National Rally of Woodcutters (RNB) 12, Gabonese Progress Party (PPG) 6, others 18.
President: (since 1967) Omar Bongo (PDG).
Prime Minister: (since 1994) Paulin Obame (PDG).

Petroleum, natural gas, manganese, uranium, iron ore and a relatively low population make Gabon one of the richest Black African countries, although nearly 40% of the labour force are subsistence farmers or employed in forestry. Petroleum and petroleum products account for 80% of exports. **Currency:** CFA franc.

1883 Gabon became a French colony, although the Libreville area had been French since 1862. **1960** Independence. **1964** President Léon M'Ba restored by French troops after a coup. **1968–90** Single-party state closely allied to France. **1990** Multi-party constitutional rule restored.

Official name: République du Gabon (The Republic of Gabon).
Area: 267,667 km² (103,347 sq mi).
Population: 1,155,000 (1995 est.).
Doubling time: 32 years. **Adult life expectancy:** male 51.9 years, female 55.2 years. **Birth rate:** 1.49 times world average. **Death rate:** 1.67 times world average. **Urban population:** 73%. **Capital:** Libreville 420,000 (1993 census; inc. suburbs).
Other main centres: Port-Gentil 164,000, Masuku (formerly Franceville) 78,000 (1993 census; inc. suburbs).
Language: French understood by 34% (official), Fang 35%, Punu-Sira 16%, Mpongwe 15%, Mbete 14%, with Kota and other minorities.
Adult literacy: 63%.
Religion: Roman Catholic 53%, traditional beliefs 35%, African Churches 10%.

CONGO (-BRAZZAVILLE)

Congo-Brazzaville is a Central African republic bordered on the west by the Atlantic Ocean and on the south by the Congo River. Behind the narrow Atlantic plain, the plateaux of the interior are covered by tropical rain forests.
Highest point: Mont de la Lékéti 1040 m (3412 ft).
Climate: Hot and humid. Rainfall exceeds 1200 mm (47 in) a year.

An executive President, the 125-member National Assembly and 60-member Senate are elected by universal adult suffrage for five years. The President appoints a Prime Minister and a Council of Ministers.
Largest parties: (1995 election) Panafrican Union for Social Democracy (UPADS) and allies 66, (former Communist former monopoly) Congolese Workers' Party (PTC) and allies 57, others 2.
President: (since 1992) Pascal Lissouba (UPADS).
Prime Minister: (since 1997) David Charles Ganao (UPADS).

Petroleum (which accounts for 85% of exports) and timber are the mainstays of the economy, which was centrally planned until 1991. The country is crippled with foreign debt. Subsistence farming, chiefly for cassava, occupies over 55% of the workforce. **Currency:** CFA franc.

1905 The region became the French colony of Moyen-Congo. **1960** Independence as Congo. **1963** A one-party Marxist-Leninist regime was established. **1991** Multi-party rule restored. **1993–94 and 1997** Severe unrest and virtual civil war between political rivals in Brazzaville.

Official name: La République du Congo (The Republic of the Congo). Popularly known as Congo-Brazzaville to avoid confusion with its neighbour The Congo (ex-Zaïre).
Area: 342,000 km² (132,047 sq mi).
Population: 2,590,000 (1995 est.).
Doubling time: 23 years. **Adult life expectancy:** male 48.9 years, female 53.8 years. **Birth rate:** 1.79 times world average. **Death rate:** 1.6 times world average. **Urban population:** 41%. **Capital:** Brazzaville 938,000 (1992 est.; inc. suburbs).
Other main centres: Pointe-Noire 576,000, Loubomo 84,000 (1992 est.; inc. suburbs).
Language: French understood by 29% (official), Monokutuba understood by 62% (the lingua franca of much of the country), Kongo 51%, Teke 17%, Mboshi 12%, with Mbete and other minorities.
Adult literacy: 75%.
Religion: Traditional beliefs 48%, Roman Catholic 39%, various Protestant Churches 11%.

■ FROM 1913 UNTIL 1964 ALBERT SCHWEITZER RAN A HOSPITAL IN GABON ■ IN 1986,

CENTRAL AFRICAN REPUBLIC

The Central African Republic is a landlocked republic in the middle of the African continent. The country is a low plateau, rising on the border with Sudan to the Bongos Mountains and in the west to the Monts Karre.
Highest point: Mont Gaou 1420 m (4659 ft).
Climate: The north is savannah with little rain between November and March. The south is equatorial with high temperatures and heavy rainfall.

The executive President (who appoints a Prime Minister and a Council of Ministers) is elected by universal adult suffrage for a maximum of two seven-year terms. The 85-member National Assembly is directly elected for five years.
Largest parties: (1993 election) Central African People's Liberation Movement (MPLC) 34, Democratic Central African Rally (RDC) 13, Patriotic Front for Progress (FPP) 7, Liberal Democratic Party (PLD) 7, David Dacko Movement (MDD) 6, others 18.
President: (since 1993) Ange Patassé (MLPC).
Prime Minister: (since 1996) Paul Ngoupandé (MLPC-led government of national unity).

Subsistence farming dominates (growing cassava, yams, bananas, sorghum and ground nuts), although cotton and coffee are also grown for export. Diamonds contribute over one-half of the state's foreign earnings, and timber products a further one-quarter. The country is poor and, largely owing to mismanagement under Bokassa, its economy has declined severely since independence. **Currency:** CFA franc.

1903 The region became the French colony of Oubangui-Chari. **1960** Independence as the Central African Republic. **1965** Jean-Bédel Bokassa seized power in a coup and (in 1976) made himself Emperor in an extravagantly expensive ceremony. **1979** Revolts by students and schoolchildren helped end Bokassa's murderous rule. **1996** Worsening economic crisis led to unrest and army mutiny.

Official name: La République Centrafricaine (The Central African Republic).
Area: 622,436 km² (240,324 sq mi).
Population: 3,140,000 (1995 est.).
Doubling time: 32 years. **Adult life expectancy:** male 44.7 years, female 49.4 years. **Birth rate:** 1.69 times world average. **Death rate:** 2.23 times world average. **Urban population:** 48%. **Capital:** Bangui 524,000 (1994 est.; inc. suburbs). **Other main centres:** Berberati 47,000, Bouar 43,000 (1994 est.).
Language: French understood by 11% (official), Sango understood by 89% (the lingua franca of most of the country), Baya 24%, Banda 24%, Manjia 15%, with Ngbaka, Mbum, Sara and other minorities.
Adult literacy: 60%.
Religion: Roman Catholic 25%, various Protestant Churches 25%, traditional beliefs 24%, Sunni Islam 15%.

CHAD

Chad is a large landlocked republic of Central Africa stretching from the Sahara Desert to the equatorial rain forests. Deserts in the north include the Tibesti Mountains. Savannah grasslands and semi-desert in the centre slope to Lake Chad, which varies considerably in size seasonally. The Oubangui Plateau in the south is covered by tropical forest.
Highest point: Emi Koussi 3415 m (11,204 ft).
Climate: Hot and very dry in the north; rains are seasonal in the centre, while the south has a wet tropical climate.

The executive President (who appoints a Council of Ministers headed by a Prime Minister) and a 125-member National Assembly are elected for five years by universal adult suffrage.
Largest parties: (1997 election) (nationalist, mainly northern) Patriotic Salvation Movement (MPS) 55 seats, (nationalist mainly southern) Union for Democracy and Renewal (URD) 31, National Union for Development and Renewal (UNDR) 15, others 22; 2 seats vacant.
President: (since 1990) Idriss Deby (MPS).
Prime Minister: (since 1997) Djimasta Koibla (MPS-UNDR coalition).

Chad, one of the poorest countries in the world, has been wracked by civil wars and drought. With few natural resources (except in the disputed Aozou strip), the country relies upon subsistence farming, exports of cotton and foreign aid. Live cattle are also exported. Over 80% of the labour force are subsistence farmers and herders.
Currency: CFA franc.

1916 France completed the conquest of the north of Chad, having established a protectorate in the south in 1897. **1960** Chad gained independence. **1960–87** Intermittent civil wars between the Muslim Arab north and the Christian and animist south; both Libya and France forcefully intervened on some occasions. **1973** Libya invaded and occupied the mineral-rich northern Aozou strip of the country. **1987** Uneasy cease-fire. **1990 and 1991** Military coups. **1996** The central government signed peace agreements with separatist/guerrilla movements in the north and south of the country. For the first time since 1960 Chad was at peace. **1996–97** Multi-party constitutional rule restored.

Official names: République du Tchad (French) and Jumhuriyah Tshad (Arabic) (The Republic of Chad).
Area: 1,284,000 km² (495,755 sq mi).
Population: 6,360,000 (1995 est.).
Doubling time: 27 years. **Adult life expectancy:** male 45.9 years, female 49.1 years. **Birth rate:** 1.75 times world average. **Death rate:** 1.94 times world average. **Urban population:** 21%. **Capital:** N'Djamena 530,000 (1993 census; inc. suburbs). **Other main centres:** Moundou 282,000, Sarh 198,000, Abéché 188,000, Doba 185,000 (1993 census; inc. suburbs).
Language: French understood by 13% (official), Arabic 26% (official), Sara and allied languages 31%, Teda 7%, Mbum 6%, Masalit 6%, Tama 6%, with Mubi and other minorities. **Adult literacy:** 30%.
Religion: Sunni Islam 54%, Roman Catholic 20%, various Protestant Churches 14%, traditional beliefs 7%.

CAMEROON

Cameroon is a republic on the Atlantic coast of Central Africa. In the west of the country a chain of highlands rises to the volcanic Mt Cameroon. In the north, savannah plains dip towards Lake Chad. The coastal plains and plateaux in the south and centre are covered with tropical forest but deforestation is rapid.
Highest point: Mt Cameroon 4069 m (13,353 ft).
Climate: Cameroon has a tropical climate, with hot rainy conditions on the coast, although the interior is drier, with parts of the north prone to drought.

The executive President (who appoints a Council of Ministers headed by a Prime Minister) and the 180-member National Assembly are elected by universal adult suffrage for five years.
Largest parties: (1997 election) (nationalist) People's Democratic Movement (MDP) 109 seats, (centre-left) Social Democratic Front (FSD) 43, National Union for Democracy and Progress (UNDP) 13, others 8; 7 seats vacant.
President: (since 1982) Paul Biya (MDP).
Prime Minister: (since 1997) Peter Mafany Musonge (MDP).

Cameroon is a major producer of coffee and timber; other export crops include cocoa, bananas, cotton, rubber and palm oil. Other crops include sugar cane and cassava. The diversity of Cameroon's agriculture and the rapid development of the petroleum industry (making oil the largest export) have given the country one of the higher standards of living in Central Africa.
Currency: CFA franc.

1884 Germany declared a protectorate over the area, naming it Kamerun. **1916** Conquered by Franco-British forces during World War I. **1919** Divided into British and French territories; Cameroon halved by cession of territory to French Moyen-Congo colony. **1960** French Cameroons became independent as Cameroon. **1961** Plebiscite in British Cameroons: the south joined Cameroon, the north became part of Nigeria. **1961-72** Cameroon was a federal republic, comprising a (large) former French state and a (much smaller) former British state. **1966–92** Single-party state. **1992** Multi-party rule restored.

Official names: République du Cameroun (French) and The Republic of Cameroon.
Area: 475,442 km² (183,569 sq mi).
Population: 13,230,000 (1995 est.).
Doubling time: 25 years. **Adult life expectancy:** male 54.5 years, female 57.5 years. **Birth rate:** 1.63 times world average. **Death rate:** 1.31 times world average. **Urban population:** 41%. **Capital:** Yaoundé 750,000 (1991 est.; inc. suburbs). **Other main centres:** Douala 884,000, Maroua 143,000, Bamenda 138,000, Nkongsamba 112,000 (1991 est.; inc. suburbs).
Language: French understood by over 15% (official), English understood by under 3% of the population (official), Fang 20%, Bamileke-Widikum and Murri 18%, Fulani 10%, Tikar 7%, Mandara 6%, with Maka, Masana and other minorities.
Adult literacy: 54%.
Religion: Roman Catholic 35%, traditional beliefs 26%, Sunni Islam 22%, various Protestant Churches 17%.

CENTRAL AFRICA II

CONGO (EX-ZAÏRE)

The Congo is a huge almost landlocked republic occupying 'the heart of Africa'. Over 60% of the country comprises a basin of tropical rain forest drained by the River Congo and its tributaries including the Oubangui, Lomani, Lualaba and Kasai. Plateaux and mountain ranges surround the basin, including the Ruwenzori Mountains on the Rwandan border. The Congo has a 40 km (25 mi) coastline.
Highest point: Mont Ngaliema (formerly Margherita Peak) 5109 m (16,763 ft).
Climate: A hot and humid tropical climate, with very little seasonal variation, although the north is drier from December to February.

The constitution was suspended in 1997 following the take-over by the Alliance of Democratic Forces for the Liberation of Congo-Zaïre whose leader assumed the executive Presidency. A new constitution is promised for 1998. There are over 200 small political parties.
President: (since 1997) Laurent Kabila. (President Kabila has not appointed a PM but has assumed sweeping powers.)

The economy was devastated by corruption under the regime of President Mobutu. Much of the country's infrastructure has broken down and there are now fewer roads than in colonial days. The Congo is one of the poorest countries in the world although rich in minerals, whose profits were not used for development in the period 1965–97. Minerals include copper and diamonds (which together account for 60% of the exports), plus cobalt and zinc. Over 65% of the workforce is involved in subsistence farming, although coffee, tea and palm oil are exported.
Currency: A new Congolese franc is to be introduced.

1885 The region became the personal possession of King Leopold II of the Belgians. **1908** International outrage at the brutality of the regime forced the king to cede the region to Belgium. **1908–60** Belgian Congo: provision of primary education and other services was advanced but little African political activity allowed. **1960** Independence: within days the army mutinied and Katanga, the richest province, attempted secession under Moïse Tshombe; UN intervention. **1965** Gen. Mobutu took power and restored central authority. **1967–91** One-party state; large-scale corruption. **1971** Country renamed Zaïre. **1991** Pressure for reform; constitutional conference called. **1990s** Infrastructure of the state had largely decayed; Kasai and Katanga (called Shaba from 1971–97) virtually independent. **1996–97** Eastern rebels under Laurent Kabila gradually took over the country, forcing Mobutu to flee in 1997; Kabila became President; Zaïre renamed The Congo.

Official name: La République Démocratique du Congo (The Democratic Republic of the Congo). **Area:** 2,344,856 km² (905,354 sq mi). **Population:** 43,900,000 (1995 est.). **Doubling time:** 22 years. **Adult life expectancy:** male 50.4 years, female 53.7 years. **Birth rate:** 1.9 times world average. **Death rate:** 1.56 times world average. **Urban population:** 40%. **Capital:** Kinshasa 4,655,000 (1994 est.; inc. suburbs). **Other main centres:** Lubumbashi 851,000, Mbuji-Mayi 807,000, Kisangani 418,000, Kananga 393,000, Likasi 280,000, Boma 246,000, Bukavu 210,000, Matadi 179,000 (1989 est.). **Language:** French understood by 8% (official), Lingala understood by 68% (the lingua franca of the west), Swahili understood by 50% (the lingua franca of the east), Kongo spoken as first language by 16% but understood by 30%, Luba 18%, Mongo 13%, Rwanda 10%, Azande 6%, with Ngala, Bangi, Rundi, Teke and other minorities. **Adult literacy:** 77%. **Religion:** Roman Catholic 48%, various Protestant Churches (inc. Anglicans) 29%, African Churches (mainly Zimbanguists) 17%, traditional beliefs 3%, Sunni Islam minority.

■ *A group of hippos wallow in a Central African river*

ANGOLA

Angola is a republic on the Atlantic coast of southern Central Africa. Plateaux over 1000 m (3300 ft) cover 90% of the country. There is a narrow coastal plain and the coastal region in the south-west is desert. The enclave of Cabinda, north of the Congo estuary, is part of Angola.
Highest point: Serra Mòco 2620 m (8596 ft).
Climate: Tropical with slightly lower temperatures in the uplands. There is a dry season from October to May but the south-west is dry all year.

The 220-member National Assembly and the executive President are elected by universal adult suffrage for five years. The President appoints a Prime Minister and other Ministers.
Largest parties: (1992 election) (former Communist former monopoly) People's Liberation Movement of Angola (MPLA) 129 seats, (former guerrilla movement) National Union for the Total Independence of Angola (UNITA) 70. UNITA initially refused to accept the results of this election.
President: (since 1979) José Eduardo dos Santos (MPLA).
Prime Minister: (since 1996) Fernando Franca Van-Dunem (MPLA).

Angola is potentially rich but the economy has been wrecked by civil war since independence. Major mineral deposits include diamonds, petroleum and iron ore. Although less than 5% of the land is cultivated, nearly 70% of the labour force is engaged in agriculture. The main export crop is coffee. Large areas of the country were laid with mines during the war. **Currency:** New Kwanza.

Early 20th century Forced labour, heavy taxation and discrimination by the Portuguese settlers stimulated nationalism. **1961** Guerrilla activity against Portuguese rule began. **1975** Independence but several guerrilla movements fought for control: MPLA (see above), a Marxist-Leninist movement, gained the upper hand with Soviet and Cuban support. UNITA, backed by South Africa, was repulsed. **1980s** Continuing Cuban backing for MPLA against UNITA. **1990–91** Foreign involvement ended the civil war. **1992** First multi-party elections: UNITA refused to accept the result and the civil war recommenced. **1994** New cease-fire and (ineffectual) power-sharing agreement. **1997** Power-sharing between MPLA and UNITA agreed.

Official name: A República de Angola (The Republic of Angola). **Area:** 1,246,700 km² (481,354 sq mi). **Population:** 11,560,000 (1995 est.). **Doubling time:** 22 years. **Adult life expectancy:** male 44.9 years, female 48.1 years. **Birth rate:** 2.05 times world average. **Death rate:** 2.06 times world average. **Urban population:** 28%. **Capital:** Luanda 2,250,000 (1995 est.; inc. suburbs). **Other main centres:** Huambo 400,000 (1995 est.), Benguela 155,000 (1983 est.), Lobito 150,000 (1983 est.), Lubango 105,000 (1990 est.). **Language:** Portuguese understood by 35% (official), Umbundu (or Ovimbundu) 37%, Kimbundu (or Mbundu) 22%, Kongo (or Kikongo) 13%, Luimbe-Nganguela 5%, Nyaneke-Humbe 5%. **Adult literacy:** 42%. **Religion:** Roman Catholic 62%, various Protestant Churches 18%, primal religions 10%.

■ KINSHASA WAS ONCE CALLED LÉOPOLDVILLE ■ IN 1997 THERE WERE OVER 200,000

ZIMBABWE

Zimbabwe is a landlocked republic in Central Africa, lying between the Zambezi River and South Africa. Central Zimbabwe is a ridge of (tropical grassland) High Veld rising to between 1200 and 1500 m (4000 and 5000 ft). The High Veld is bounded on the south-west and north-east by the Middle Veld and Low Veld plateaux. Plateaux cover the north and centre of the country.
Highest point: Mt Inyangani 2592 m (8503 ft).
Climate: Tropical in the lowland and subtropical in the higher plateaux. There is a pronounced dry season from June to September.

The 150-member House of Assembly comprises 120 members elected by universal adult suffrage for six years plus 12 members nominated by the President, 10 traditional chiefs and eight provincial governors. The executive President, who appoints a Cabinet of Ministers, is also directly elected for six years.
Largest parties: (1995 election) (near monopoly) Zimbabwe African National Union-Patriotic Front (ZANU-PF) 148 seats, others 2.
President: (since 1987) Robert Mugabe (ZANU-PF).

Agriculture involves over one-quarter of the labour force. Tobacco, sugar cane, cotton, wheat and maize are exported as well as being the basis of processing industries. Natural resources include coal, gold, asbestos and nickel. Industry includes food processing, basic manufactures, clothing and textiles, chemicals, and paper.
Currency: Zimbabwe dollar.

■ *Mist rises from Victoria Falls on the border between Zimbabwe and Zambia*

1890s Area occupied by the British South Africa Company of Cecil Rhodes. **1923** British government took over the administration and granted self-government to the new Southern Rhodesia. **1920s–30s** White settlement increased. **1953–63** Federation with British Northern Rhodesia and Malawi, which was dominated by white-ruled Southern Rhodesia. **1965** White government of Ian Smith declared independence unilaterally. **1970s** Black guerrilla movements became increasingly effective against the illegal government of Rhodesia. **1979** Smith forced to accept majority rule; brief reimposition of British rule. **1980** Independence under Robert Mugabe's ZANU. **1987** Merger of the rival ZANU and ZAPU, the two former guerrilla movements against white rule, created a virtual one-party state.

Official name: The Republic of Zimbabwe.
Area: 390,757 km² (150,872 sq mi).
Population: 11,260,000 (1995 est.).
Doubling time: 28 years. **Adult life expectancy:** male 58 years, female 62 years. **Birth rate:** 1.38 times world average. **Death rate:** 1.02 times world average. **Urban population:** 26%. **Capital:** Harare 1,184,000 (1992 est.; inc. suburbs).
Other main centres: Bulawayo 621,000, Chitungwiza 274,000, Mutare 131,000, Gweru 125,000 (1992 est.; inc. suburbs).
Language: English 2% as a first language but widely understood (official), Shona 72%, Ndebele 16%, Nyanga 2%. **Adult literacy:** 85%.
Religion: Various Protestant Churches including Anglicans 32%, traditional beliefs 23%, African Churches 16%, Roman Catholic 12%.

ZAMBIA

Zambia, a landlocked republic in Central Africa, comprises plateaux 1000–1500 m (3300–5000 ft) high. Above the plateaux rise the Muchinga Mountains and the Mufinga Hills. A seasonal marsh occupies parts of the low-lying west.
Highest point: An unnamed peak in the Muchinga escarpment 2164 m (7100 ft). **Climate:** High rainfall and high temperatures, with most rainfall from November to April.

The 150-member National Assembly and the executive President are elected by universal adult suffrage for five years. The President, who may add up to eight additional members of the Assembly, appoints a Cabinet of Ministers.
Largest parties: (1996 election) (centrist) Movement for Multiparty Democracy (MMD) 131 seats, Zambia Democratic Congress (ZDC) 19. The (former monopoly) United Nationalist Independence Party (UNIP) boycotted the poll.
President: (since 1991) Frederick Chiluba (MMD).

Zambia depends upon the mining and processing of copper, lead, zinc and cobalt. Although almost 70% of the workforce is engaged in subsistence farming, agriculture is underdeveloped and many basic foodstuffs have to be imported. Zambia faces many problems including widespread AIDS.
Currency: Zambian Kwacha.

1890s Area brought under the control of the British South Africa Company of Cecil Rhodes. **1924** British government took over the region from the company: it became Northern Rhodesia. **1920s–50s** Slow development, with most skilled mining jobs reserved for white settlers. **1953–63** Federation with British Southern Rhodesia and Nyasaland (now Malawi) was much resented. **1964** Independence as Zambia. **1973–90** One-party state under President Kenneth Kaunda. **1990** Multi-party system restored.

Official name: The Republic of Zambia.
Area: 752,614 km² (290,586 sq mi).
Population: 9,460,000 (1995 est.).
Doubling time: 19 years. **Adult life expectancy:** male 45 years, female 46.2 years. **Birth rate:** 2.01 times world average. **Death rate:** 1.33 times world average. **Urban population:** 42%. **Capital:** Lusaka 982,000 (1990 census; inc. suburbs).
Other main centres: Ndola 376,000, Kitwe 348,000, Mufulira 175,000, Kabwe 167,000 (1990 census; inc. suburbs).
Language: English understood by 8% (official), Bemba 25%, Tonga 11%, Lozi 6%, Chewa 5%, with Nyanja, Nsenga, Tumbuka and other minorities. **Adult literacy:** 73%.
Religion: Various Protestant Churches 34%, traditional African beliefs 27%, Roman Catholic 26%, African Churches over 9%.

MALAWI

Malawi is a landlocked republic in Central Africa, lying on the western shore of Lake Malawi. Plateaux cover the north and centre of the country. The Great Rift Valley contains Lake Malawi (Lake Nyasa) and the Shire valley. The Shire Highlands lie along the Mozambican border.
Highest point: Mt Sapitawa 3002 m (9849 ft).
Climate: An equatorial climate with high temperatures and heavy rainfall, greatest from November to April.

The 177-member National Assembly and the executive President are elected by universal adult suffrage for five years. The President appoints a Cabinet of Ministers.
Largest parties: (1994 election) (centrist) United Democratic Front (UDF) 84 seats, (former monopoly) Malawi Congress Party (Congress) 55, Alliance for Democracy (AFORD) 36, others 2.
President: (since 1994) Bakili Muluzi (UDF).

Agriculture is the mainstay of Malawi's economy, providing the majority of the exports (these consist of tobacco, tea, sugar and cotton). The greatest proportion of the workforce in Malawi, namely 80%, make their living as subsistence farmers. Malawi is one of the poorest nations in the world. **Currency:** Malawi Kwacha.

1891 British protectorate of Nyasaland established. **1915** Violent revolt led by Rev. John Chilembwe against white settlers in the south, where Africans had been deprived of much land. **1953–63** Federation with British Northern and Southern Rhodesia was much resented. **1964** Independence as Malawi (a republic after 1996). **1964–94** Increasingly authoritarian rule of Hastings Banda (the first President); single-party state. Banda maintained close relations with South Africa. **1992–93** Pressure for political reforms. **1993** Multi-party system restored. **1994** Banda defeated in elections by United Democratic Front.

Official name: The Republic of Malawi.
Area: 118,484 km² (45,747 sq mi).
Population: 9,940,000 (1995 est.).
Doubling time: 23 years. Adult life expectancy: male 45 years, female 46.2 years. **Birth rate:** 2.02 times world average. **Death rate:** 2.15 times world average. **Urban population:** 11%. **Capital:** Lilongwe 396,000 (1994 est.; inc. suburbs).
Other main centres: Blantyre-Limbe 447,000, Mzuzu 62,000 (1994 est.; inc. suburbs).
Language: English understood by 5% (official), Chewa 58% (official), Lomwe 18%, Yao 13%, Ngoni 7%.
Adult literacy: 56%.
Religion: Presbyterian 33%, Roman Catholic 20%, Sunni Islam 20%, primal religions 10%.

SOUTHERN AFRICA

SOUTH AFRICA

South Africa is a republic occupying the southern tip of Africa; it is the continent's leading power, politically and economically. The Great Escarpment rises behind a discontinuous coastal plain and includes the Drakensberg Mountains. A vast plateau occupies the interior, undulating in the west and rising to over 2400 m (about 8000 ft) in the east. Much of the west is semi-desert, while the east is predominantly savannah grassland (veldt).
Highest point: Injasuti 3408 m (11,182 ft).
Climate: South Africa has a subtropical climate with considerable regional variations. The hottest period is between December and February. Rainfall is highest on the east coast, but much of the country is dry.

The 90-member Senate has ten senators appointed from each province in proportion to the vote received by major parties; the 400-member National Assembly is elected by universal adult suffrage. From 1999 there will be a 90-member Council of Provinces (with 10 members elected by provincial legislatures) and a 400-member National Assembly elected by universal adult suffrage for five years. An executive President will be elected for a five-year term by the largest party in the Assembly. The President will appoint a Cabinet.
Largest parties: (Assembly 1994 election) (centre-left) African National Congress (ANC) 252 seats, (centre-right) National Party (NP) 82, (mainly Zulu) Inkatha Freedom Party (Inkatha) 43, (white right-wing) Freedom Front 9, (centre) Democratic Party 7, (left-wing) Pan African Congress 5, others 2.
President: (since 1994) Nelson Mandela (ANC).

Official name: Republic of South Africa.
Area: 1,219,080 km² (470,723 sq mi).
Population: 41,465,000 (1995 est.).
Doubling time: 27 years.
Adult life expectancy: male 63 years, female 68 years.
Birth rate: 1.36 times world average.
Death rate: 0.86 times world average. **Urban population:** 49%.
Capitals: Pretoria (administrative capital) 1,080,000 and Cape Town (legislative capital) 1,912,000 (1991 census; inc. suburbs). **Other main centres:** Johannesburg 4,165,000 urban area (city 1,196,000; East Rand district 1,379,000; West Rand district 870,000; inc. Soweto 597,000; Tembisa 209,000; Springs 170,000; Roodepoort 163,000; Germiston 134,000; Boksburg 120,000; Benoni 114,000; Kempton Park 107,000), Durban 1,137,000, Port Elizabeth 853,000, Vereeniging-Vanderbijlpark 774,000, Soweto *see Johannesburg*, Sasolburg 540,000, Bloemfontein 300,000, East London 270,000 (1991 census; inc. suburbs).
Language: English 9% as a first language (official) but almost universally understood, Afrikaans 16% as a first language (official), Zulu 22% (official), Xhosa 17% (official), South Sotho 9% (official), Tswana 9% (official), North Sotho 7% (official), Tsonga 3% (official), Swazi 2% (official), Ndebele 2% (official), Venda 2% (official). **Adult literacy:** *c.* 60%.
Religion: Traditional beliefs about 29%, African Christian Churches 22%, Afrikaans (Dutch) Reformed Church 12%, Roman Catholic 8%, Methodist 6%, Anglicans 4%, various Protestant Churches 15%.

■ *Blyde River canyon, part of the Great Escarpment, in Mpumalanga, South Africa*

The country is the world's leading exporter of gold (which normally forms about 40% of exports) and a major producer of uranium, diamonds, chromite, antimony, platinum and coal (which meets about 75% of energy needs). Industry includes chemicals, food processing, textiles, motor vehicles and electrical engineering. Agriculture supplies about one-third of exports, including fruit, wine, wool and maize. The highest standard of living in Africa is very unevenly distributed between Whites and Blacks. A fall in foreign investment in the 1970s and 1980s encouraged self-sufficiency. The new South Africa has staged a partial economic recovery. **Currency:** Rand.

1899–1902 Boer War: Britain, which controlled Natal and the Cape, overran the Boer republics of Transvaal and the Orange Free State. **1910** Union of South Africa was founded with power exercised by the White minority. **1914–18** South Africa took part in World War I; German South West Africa (Namibia) was conquered in 1915. **1920s** Black industrial protest increased. **1931** Independence of South Africa was recognized internationally by the terms of the Statute of Westminster. **1939–45** South African participation in World War II, mainly on the west European front. **1948** The National Party came to power, implementing its policy of apartheid (that of separate development from Whites), depriving Blacks of civil rights and establishing separate facilities for them. **1960** ANC banned. **1960s and 1970s** Increase in Black opposition to apartheid. **1966** The assassination of PM Hendrik Verwoerd. **1961** South Africa left the Commonwealth, becoming a republic. **1976** Soweto uprising. **1981** South African intervention in Angola against Marxist government. **1986** State of emergency: further crackdown on opposition. **1990** Reform: ANC legalized and its imprisoned leader, Nelson Mandela, was released. **1990s** Ethnic violence erupts in KwaZulu/Natal between the Zulus and Xhosas. **1994** Multiracial elections; Mandela became President with the ANC victory.

SOUTH AFRICAN PROVINCES

Eastern
Area: 169,600 km² (65,487 sq mi).
Pop.: 6,437,000 (1994 est.).
Capital: Bisho.
Free State (formerly Orange Free State)
Area: 129,480 km² (49,996 sq mi).
Pop.: 2,727,000 (1994 est.).
Capital: Bloemfontein.
Gauteng
Area: 18,810 km² (7262 sq mi).
Pop.: 6,870,000 (1994 est.).
Capital: Johannesburg.
KwaZulu/Natal
Area: 92,180 km² (35,593 sq mi).
Pop.: 8,505,000 (1994 est.).
Capital: Ulundi.
Mpumalanga (formerly Eastern Transvaal)
Area: 78,370 km² (30,261 sq mi).
Pop.: 2,922,000 (1994 est.).
Capital: Nelspruit.
Northern
Area: 123,280 km² (47,602 sq mi).
Pop.: 5,202,000 (1994 est.).
Capital: Pietersburg.
Northern Cape
Area: 361,800 km² (139,702 sq mi).
Pop.: 737,000 (1994 est.).
Capital: Kimberley.
North-West
Area: 116,190 km² (44,864 sq mi).
Pop.: 3,253,000 (1994 est.).
Capital: Mafikeng (administration in Mmabatho).
Western Cape
Area: 129,370 km² (49,953 sq mi).
Pop.: 3,633,000 (1994 est.).
Capital: Cape Town.

ST HELENA AND DEPENDENCIES

Official name and status: St Helena; a British Crown Colony.
Area: 411 km² (159 sq mi): St Helena 122 km² (47 sq mi), Ascension 88 km² (34 sq mi), Tristan da Cunha group 201 km² (78 sq mi).
Population: 7100 (1992 est.): St Helena 5700, Ascension 1100 (excluding service personnel), Tristan da Cunha 300.
Capital: Jamestown (on St Helena) 1500 (1992 est.). (The capital of Ascension is Georgetown; the capital of Tristan da Cunha is Edinburgh.)
Geography: St Helena is a mountainous island in the south Atlantic. Ascension is a barren rocky island 1130 km (700 mi) north-west of St Helena. The Tristan da Cunha group of six bleak, mountainous islands lies 2120 km (1320 mi) south-west of St Helena.
Economy: St Helena relies upon UK subsidies and fishing. Ascension is a communications base.

NAMIBIA

Namibia is a sparsely populated republic on the Atlantic coast of southern Africa. The forbidding coastal Namib desert stretches up to 160 km (100 mi) inland and contains the highest point, the Brandberg. Beyond the Central Plateau the Kalahari desert occupies the eastern half of the country.
Highest point: Brandberg 2579 m (8461 ft).
Climate: Namibia has a hot dry tropical climate. Average coastal rainfall is under 100 mm (4 in).

A 72-member National Assembly is elected for five years by universal adult suffrage. A President, who appoints a Prime Minister and a Cabinet of Ministers, is directly elected for a maximum of two five-year terms.
Largest parties: (1994 election) (left-wing) South West African People's Organization (SWAPO) 53 seats, (centre) Democratic Turnhalle Alliance (DTA) 15, United Democratic Front 2, others 2.
President: (since independence) Sam Nujoma (SWAPO).
Prime Minister: (since 1990) Hage Geingob (SWAPO).

Nearly 40% of the labour force is involved in farming, raising sheep and cattle, but Namibia is prone to prolonged drought. The economy depends upon exports of diamonds and uranium and is closely tied to that of South Africa.
Currency: South African rand.

1884 German protectorate of South West Africa declared; Walvis Bay had been British since 1878. **1903–04** German massacre of the Herero people. **1915** South West Africa taken by South Africa during World War I. **1919** South African mandate internationally established. **1960** SWAPO (see *Largest parties*) began a guerrilla campaign to free the area from South African rule. **1966** UN's cancellation of South Africa's mandate was ignored. **1989** Ceasefire agreed. **1990** Independence as Namibia. **1994** South Africa ceded Walvis Bay to Namibia.

Official name: The Republic of Namibia.
Area: 825,118 km^2 (318,602 sq mi).
Population: 1,650,000 (1995 est.).
Doubling time: 23 years. **Adult life expectancy:** male 57.5 years, female 60 years. **Birth rate:** 1.66 times world average. **Death rate:** 1.14 times world average.
Urban population: 35%.
Capital: Windhoek 126,000 (1992 est.; inc. suburbs). **Other main centres:** Walvis Bay 25,000, Swakopmund 16,000 (1992 est.).
Language: English as a first language 2% (official) but understood by 16%, Ovambo 51%, Nama 12%, Kavango 10%, Afrikaans 9%, Herero 8%.
Adult literacy: 76%.
Religion: Lutheran 51%, Roman Catholic 20%, Dutch Reformed Church 6%, Anglican 5%.

LESOTHO

Lesotho is a kingdom entirely surrounded by South Africa. Most of Lesotho is mountainous, with the highest peaks in the Drakensberg Mountains in the east and north-east of the country.
Highest point: Thabana Ntlenyana 3482 m (11,425 ft).
Climate: Lesotho has a mild subtropical climate with lower temperatures in the mountains. The Maloti Mountains are snow-capped in winter.

Lesotho is a constitutional monarchy in which the King is ceremonial head of state. A 65-member National Assembly is elected by universal adult suffrage for five years. A Prime Minister and a Cabinet of Ministers are responsible to the Assembly. The 33-member Senate comprises 22 chiefs and 11 nominated members.
Largest parties: (1993 election) Basotho Congress Party 65 seats. (The opposition Basotho National Party failed to win a seat.)
King: (since 1996 and from 1990–95) Letsie III.
Prime Minister: (since 1994) Ntsu Mokhehle (BCP).

Livestock (cattle, sheep and goats for mohair) are the mainstay of the economy. The monarch nominally owns all the land; local chiefs allocate plots to families. Natural resources include diamonds. Abundant water is exported to South Africa and Lesotho's rivers (especially the Orange and the Tugela) have considerable hydroelectric power potential. About one-third of Lesotho's adult male labour force is employed in South Africa. **Currency:** Maluti.

1900 The kingdom had been under British rule since 1868. **1966** Independence. **1986** Constitutional crisis: PM Chief Jonathan deposed. **1990–95** King Moshoeshoe II deposed by the military. **1993** Constitutional rule restored. **1994** Constitutional crisis: King Letsie III attempted to dismiss the elected government; riots and attempted coup.

Official names: Lesotho and The Kingdom of Lesotho.
Area: 30,355 km^2 (11,720 sq mi).
Population: 2,060,000 (1995 est.).
Doubling time: 28 years. **Adult life expectancy:** male 58 years, female 63 years. **Birth rate:** 1.48 times world average. **Death rate:** 1.08 times world average.
Urban population: 21%.
Capital: Maseru 130,000 (1992 est.; inc. suburbs). **Other main centres:** Teyateyaneng 15,000, Mafeteng 13,000 (1986 census).
Language: English understood by the majority (official), Setho 85% (off.), Zulu 15%. **Adult literacy:** 38%.
Religion: Roman Catholic 40%, Lesotho Evangelical Church 27%, other Christian Churches 20%, traditional beliefs 7%.

BOTSWANA

Botswana is a sparsely populated landlocked republic in southern Africa. A central plateau divides a flat near-desert in the east of Botswana from the Kalahari desert and Okavango Swamps in the west.
Highest point: Mount Otse 1489 m (4885 ft).
Climate: The climate is subtropical with extremes of heat and occasionally temperatures below freezing. Much of Botswana suffers drought.

Forty of the 47 members of the National Assembly are elected for five years by universal adult suffrage; the remaining members are elected by the Assembly. There is also an advisory 17-member House of Chiefs. The President, who chairs and appoints a Cabinet, is elected for five years by the Assembly.
Largest parties: (1994 election) (centre) Botswana Democratic Party (BDP) 27, (centre-left) Botswana National Front (BNF) 13, independents 7.
President: (since 1980) Quett Ketumile Masire (BDP).

Nomadic cattle herding and the cultivation of subsistence crops occupies the majority of the labour force. The mainstay of the economy is mining for diamonds, copper-nickel and coal. **Currency:** Pula.

1885 British protectorate of Bechuanaland declared. **1900–1950s** Development of Bechuanaland was slow: many Africans had to seek work in South Africa. **1966** Independence as Botswana. **Since 1966** The country has remained a democracy.

Official name: The Republic of Botswana.
Area: 581,730 km^2 (224,624 sq mi).
Population: 1,550,000 (1995 est.).
Doubling time: 23 years. **Adult life expectancy:** male 59.5 years, female 65.6 years. **Birth rate:** 1.48 times world average. **Death rate:** 0.71 times world average.
Urban population: 26%.
Capital: Gaborone 134,000 (1991 est.; inc. suburbs). **Other main centres:** Francistown 65,000, Selebi-Pikwe 40,000 (1991 est.).
Language: English understood by 40% (official), Tswana 76%, Shona 12%, San 3%. **Adult literacy:** 74%.
Religion: Traditional beliefs 49%, various Protestant Churches 29%, African Christian Churches 12%, Roman Catholic 9%.

SWAZILAND

Swaziland is a small landlocked kingdom in southern Africa. From the mountains of the west, which rise to 1870 m (6135 ft), Swaziland descends in steps of savannah (veld) towards hill country in the east.
Highest point: Emlembe 1863 m (6113 ft).
Climate: The veld is subtropical while the highlands are temperate.

Swaziland is a monarchy in which the King appoints a Prime Minister and a Cabinet. The King is advised by a 30-member Senate (to which he appoints 20 members) and by a 65-member House of Assembly (to which he appoints 10 members). The 55 other members of the House are elected by universal adult suffrage; the 10 remaining members of the Senate are chosen by the House. The Queen Mother traditionally shares power with the King.
Political parties: There are no political parties.
King: (since 1986) Mswati III.
Queen Mother or Queen Regent: (known in Swaziland as the Indlovukazi) (since 1983) Ntombi.
Prime Minister: (since 1989) Prince Jameson Mbilini Dlamini.

The majority of Swazis are subsistence farmers. Cash crops include sugar cane (the main export) and fruit. **Currency:** Lilangeni.

1904 The kingdom came under British rule. **1968** Independence. **1973** King Sobhuza II suspended constitutional rule. **1996–97** Increasing pressure for political rights.

Official names: Umbuso weSwatini and The Kingdom of Swaziland.
Area: 17,363 km^2 (6704 sq mi).
Population: 915,000 (1995 est.).
Doubling time: 25 years. **Adult life expectancy:** male 55.2 years, female 59.8 years. **Birth rate:** 1.54 times world average. **Death rate:** 1.15 times world average. **Urban population:** 34%. **Capitals:** Mbabane (administrative capital) 42,000 (1992 est.; inc. suburbs) and Lobamba (royal and legislative capital) 2000 (1986 census). **Other main centre:** Manzini 53,000 (1988 est.).
Language: English understood by the majority (official), Swazi 90% (off.), Zulu 2%. **Adult literacy:** 77%.
Religion: Various Protestant Churches 29%, African Christian Churches 22%, traditional beliefs 21%, Roman Catholic 8%.

SECOND-HIGHEST MURDER RATE IN THE WORLD, WHILST LESOTHO HAS THE FIFTH-HIGHEST ■

Australia and its Neighbours

AUSTRALIA

The island of Australia is not only an independent nation but also (with its attendant islands) a continent (Australasia) in its own right. Vast areas of desert cover most of central and western Australia, a region of plateaux between 400 and 600 m (1300 and 2000 ft) with occasional higher regions such as the Kimberley Plateau. In contrast to this scarcely populated area, which covers over 50% of the country, are the narrow coastal plains of the fertile, well-watered east coast, where the majority of Australians live. Behind the plains (which range from temperate forest in the south, through subtropical woodland to tropical rain forest in the north) rise the Eastern Uplands or Great Divide, a line of ridges and plateaux stretching from Cape York Peninsula in the north to the Australian Alps and the island-state of Tasmania in the south. The Great Artesian Basin extends from the Gulf of Carpentaria in the north to the Murray River and Eyre basins. Landforms in the basin include rolling plains, plateaux, salt lakes and river valleys, while to the south rise the Flinders and Mt Lofty ranges. Many of Australia's rivers flow intermittently.

Highest point: Mt Kosciuszko 2230 m (7316 ft). (Note: the spelling of Mt Koscuiuszko was officially changed in 1997.)

Climate: Australia's climate is tropical in the north with wet summers (January to March) and dry winters. The Timor Sea coast is subject to summer monsoons. The Queensland coast experiences tropical cyclones and has the highest rainfall – over 2500 mm (100 in) near Cairns. The interior is extremely hot and dry and over 30% of Australia has less than 255 mm (10 in) of rain a year. The coastal fringes of the south are either temperate or subtropical, with winter rainfall, hot or warm summers and mild winters. Winter snowfall occurs in Australia in the south-eastern mountains of New South Wales and the Tasmanian uplands.

The Federal Parliament comprises two chambers elected by compulsory universal adult suffrage. The lower house (House of Representatives) has 148 members elected for three years. A Prime Minister, who commands a majority in the House, chairs the Federal Executive Council (Cabinet). The upper house (the Senate) has 76 members elected by proportional representation for six years. Twelve senators represent each state and two represent the Northern Territory and the Australian Capital Territory. The British sovereign is represented as head of state of Australia by a Governor General. Each state has its own government, while the Northern Territory and the Australian Capital Territory have limited autonomy.

Largest parties: (House of Representatives 1996 election) National-Liberal coalition 94 seats, comprising (conservative) National Party 18 and (centre) Liberal Party (Lib) 75, (left-wing) Australian Labor Party 48, independents 5, others 1.

Prime Minister: John Howard (Lib).

Since World War II, Australia's economy has been dominated by mining. Minerals and mineral products (including fuels) now account for over 30% of exports. Australia has major reserves of coal, petroleum, natural gas, uranium, iron ore, copper, nickel, bauxite, gold and diamonds. Manufacturing and processing based upon these resources include iron and steel, construction, oil refining and petrochemicals, vehicle manufacturing and engineering. Food-processing and textile industries are also prominent. Australia's reliance upon agriculture has decreased, although the country is still the world's leading

■ *Sydney Harbour Bridge is one of the largest steel-arch bridges in the world, spanning 503 m. Completed in 1932, it joins Sydney's south shore to its northern suburbs*

■ *The Olga Rocks, named* Katajura *by the Aborigines, are 30 red domes which occupy 28 km² of the arid desert in Uluru National Park in Northern Territory, Australia*

■ SHEEP OUTNUMBER HUMANS EIGHT TO ONE IN AUSTRALIA ■ 72% OF AUSTRALIANS LIVE

producer of wool. Major farming interests include sheep, cattle, cereals (particularly wheat), sugar (in Queensland) and fruit. Severe drought affected large areas in the early 1990s. A strong commercial sector, with banks and finance houses, adds to the diversity of an economy which is vulnerable to fluctuations in commodity prices. Asia, particularly Japan, dominates Australia's trade. **Currency:** Australian dollar.

1901 Commonwealth of Australia formed through a federation of British colonies. **1914–18** World War I: Australia lost one-fifth of its servicemen in action (including Gallipoli, 1915). **1926** British recognition of the independence of Australia (confirmed by the Statute of Westminster). **1929** Start of the Depression: major economic slump. **1939–45** Australian participation in World War II: the north threatened by Japanese invasion; increased ties with the USA. **After 1945** Migrants from all over Europe (and later from Asia) gained assisted passage to Australia; British connection diluted. **1960s–1970s** Greater interest in Asia, including participation in the Vietnam War as a military ally of the USA. **1967** Aborigines get full citizenship. **1975** Constitutional crisis: Governor General dismissed Labor PM Gough Whitlam after the Senate blocked the government's financial legislation. **1990s** Rise of republicanism. Increased recognition of aboriginal land rights.

AUSTRALIAN STATES AND TERRITORIES

New South Wales
Area: 801,600 km² (309,500 sq mi).
Pop.: 6,241,000 (1996 est.).
Capital: Sydney.

Queensland
Area: 1,727,200 km² (666,900 sq mi).
Pop.: 3,374,000 (1996 est.).
Capital: Brisbane.

South Australia
Area: 984,000 km² (379,900 sq mi).
Pop.: 1,477,000 (1996 est.).
Capital: Adelaide.

Tasmania
Area: 67,800 km² (26,200 sq mi).
Pop.: 474,000 (1996 est.).
Capital: Hobart.

Victoria
Area: 227,600 km² (87,900 sq mi).
Pop.: 4,582,000 (1996 est.).
Capital: Melbourne.

Western Australia
Area: 2,525,500 km² (975,100 sq mi).
Pop.: 1,783,000 (1996 est.).
Capital: Perth.

Australian Capital Territory
Area: 2,330 km² (900 sq mi).
Pop.: 309,000 (1996 est.).
Capital: Canberra.

Jervis Bay Territory
Area: 70 km² (27 sq mi).
Pop.: 800 (1996 est.).
Capital: administered from Canberra.

Northern Territory
Area: 1,346,200 km² (519,800 sq mi).
Pop.: 185,000 (1996 est.).
Capital: Darwin.

Official name: Commonwealth of Australia.
Area: 7,682,300 km² (2,966,136 sq mi).
Population: 18,427,000 (1996 est.).
Doubling time: 99 years.
Adult life expectancy: male 74.5 years, female 80.8 years.
Birth rate: 0.58 times world average.
Death rate: 0.76 times world average. **Urban population:** 85%.
Capital: Canberra 345,000 urban area (city 309,000; 1996 census).
Other main centres: Sydney 3,821,000, Melbourne 3,249,000, Brisbane 1,526,000, Perth 1,283,000, Adelaide 1,087,000, Newcastle 471,000, Gold Coast 345,000, Wollongong 256,000, Hobart 195,000, Sunshine Coast 157,000, Geelong 154,000, Townsville 127,000, Cairns 104,000, Launceston 98,000, Albury 94,000, Darwin 81,000, Burnie-Devonport 80,000, Ballarat 78,000, Bendigo 76,000, Bathurst 74,000 (1996 census).
Language: English almost 100% (official). **Adult literacy:** over 99%.
Religion: Roman Catholic 26%, Anglican 24%, non-religious 13%, Uniting Church 8%, Presbyterian 4%, other Protestant Churches 6%, Orthodox 3%.

Dependencies
Ashmore and Cartier Islands (see below), Australian Antarctic Territory (p. 480), Christmas Island (p. 415), Cocos (Keeling) Islands (p. 415), Coral Sea Islands Territory (see below), Heard and McDonald Islands (p. 480), and Norfolk Island (see below).

ASHMORE AND CARTIER ISLANDS

Official names and status: Territory of Ashmore and Cartier Islands; an Australian external territory.
Area: 5 km² (2 sq mi).
Population: uninhabited.
Geography: A group of sandy tropical islands in the Timor Sea.

CORAL SEA ISLANDS TERRITORY

Official names and status: Territory of Coral Sea Islands; an Australian external territory.
Area: 8 km² (3 sq mi) in a sea area of 1,000,000 km² (386,000 sq mi).
Population: no permanent settlement; a weather station on Willis Island is manned by three people.
Geography: Many tiny widely scattered outcrops of sand and coral east of the Queensland coast.

NORFOLK ISLAND

Official names and status: Territory of Norfolk Island; an internally self-governing Australian external territory.
Area: 35 km² (13 sq mi).
Population: 2700 (1993 est.).
Capital: Kingston.
Geography: A fertile, hilly island east of Queensland. Economy: The island relies upon tourism and revenue from postage stamps and company registration.

PAPUA NEW GUINEA

Papua New Guinea is an independent dominion consisting of the eastern half of the large island of New Guinea in the south-west Pacific. Over 15% of the total land area comprises outlying islands, of which the largest are New Britain, Bougainville and New Ireland. Broad swampy tropical plains surround the mountainous interior of Papua New Guinea.
Highest point: Mt Wilhelm 4509 m (14,493 ft).
Climate: The hot tropical climate is characterized by high temperatures and heavy monsoonal rainfall.

A 109-member National Parliament is elected for five years by universal adult suffrage. The Governor General, the representative of the British Queen as sovereign of Papua New Guinea, appoints a Prime Minister and a Cabinet of Ministers, who command a majority in Parliament.
Largest parties: (1992 election) (centrist) Pangu Pati (PP) 22 seats, People's Democratic Movement (PDM) 15, People's Action Party (PAP) 13, People's Progress Party (PPP) 10, Melanesian Alliance 9, League for National Advancement 5, others 3.
Prime Minister: (since 1994) Sir Julius Chan (PP; PP-led minority government).

Over three-quarters of the labour force are involved in agriculture, mainly subsistence farming, although agricultural and related exports include coffee, cocoa, coconuts and timber. The mainstay of the economy is minerals, including important reserves of copper, gold and petroleum. Copper revenue has fallen due to unrest in Bougainville.
Currency: Kina.

1906 British protectorate in the south transferred to Australia. **1914** Australian forces took German New Guinea (the north). **1942–45** Occupied by Japanese forces in World War II. **1949** The two territories unified under Australian rule as Papua New Guinea. **1975** The Independence of Papua New Guinea. **Since 1990** Bougainville, a major source of copper, has attempted secession; the island continues to be a centre of unrest and guerrilla activity. **1997** Constitutional crisis over use of mercenaries in Bougainville.

■ *Abundant coconut palms, seen shading this coastal village, have made coconuts Papua New Guinea's second largest export*

Official name: The Independent State of Papua New Guinea.
Area: 462,840 km² (178,704 sq mi).
Population: 4,300,000 (1995 est.).
Doubling time: 30 years. **Adult life expectancy:** male 56 years, female 58 years. **Birth rate:** 1.32 times world average. **Death rate:** 1.08 times world average.
Urban population: 16%.
Capital: Port Moresby 193,000 (1990 census; incl. suburbs).
Other main centres: Lae 81,000, Madang 25,000, Wewak 23,000 (1990 census; inc. suburbs).
Language: English over 1% (official), Tok Pisin (Pidgin English) is understood by 66%, nearly 700 Papuan languages 78%, various Melanesian languages 20%.
Adult literacy: 52%.
Religion: various Protestant Churches 58%, Roman Catholic 3%, traditional beliefs.

NEW CALEDONIA

Official name and status: Nouvelle Calédonie (New Caledonia); a French overseas territory.
Area: 18,576 km² (7172 sq mi) including dependencies.
Population: 187,000 (1995 est.).
Capital: Nouméa. 98,000 urban area (city 65,000; 1989 census).
Geography: New Caledonia island is a long, narrow, mountainous semi-tropical island 1500 km (90 mi) east of Queensland. The Loyalty Islands, Isle of Pines and Chesterfield and Beleep Islands are part of the territory, which is to hold an independence referendum in 1998.
Economy: Tourism and the production of nickel, the main foreign-currency earners, have been affected by political unrest since the 1980s.

PLACES OF INTEREST

Despite a remote global position, Australia has a growing tourist industry. The principal destinations are the major cities of the south-east (Adelaide, Brisbane, Canberra, Sydney and Melbourne), and the major beach resorts of the Gold Coast and Sunshine Coast in Queensland. Visitors from New Zealand make up one-quarter of foreign tourists, but holidaymakers from Japan are an increasing element in the booming Queensland tourist industry. Other places of interest include Alice Springs, Australian Outback, Barossa River Valley, Blue Mountains, Byron Bay, Coober Pedy, the Great Ocean Road between Melbourne and Adelaide, Kangaroo Island, Perth, Port Arthur, Tasmania and the Snowy Mountains.

World Heritage sites include: Central Eastern Australian Rainforest; Fraser Island; Great Barrier Reef; Kakadu National Park; Shark Bay, Western Australia; Uluru-Kata Tjuta National Park (including Ayers Rock and the Olgas); Tasmanian Wilderness; Wet Tropics of Queensland; Willandra Lakes Region.

STATES

NSW	New South Wales
NT	Northern Territory
Qld	Queensland
SA	South Australia
Tas	Tasmania
Vic	Victoria
WA	Western Australia

Uluru (Ayers Rock) in Australia's 'red heart' is one of the most sacred aboriginal sites. The monolith changes colour according to the Sun's position in the sky. Some parts of the rock are severely weathered; one area is called 'The Brain' because of the pattern of weathering on the rock.

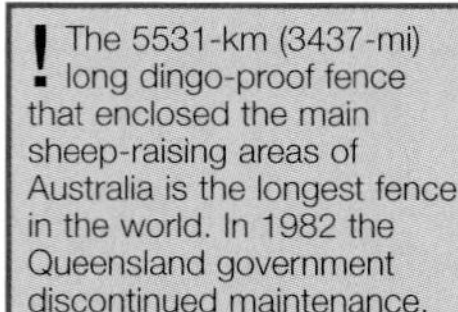

! The 5531-km (3437-mi) long dingo-proof fence that enclosed the main sheep-raising areas of Australia is the longest fence in the world. In 1982 the Queensland government discontinued maintenance.

The Great Barrier Reef, which lies off the coast of Queensland, is a coral reef and the largest living structure ever created. It is dotted with coral islands, most of which are uninhabited (see p.106).

! A record 160 consecutive days with maximum temperatures of 37.8°C (100°F) or higher were recorded at Marble Bar, WA, between 31 October 1923 and 7 April 1924.

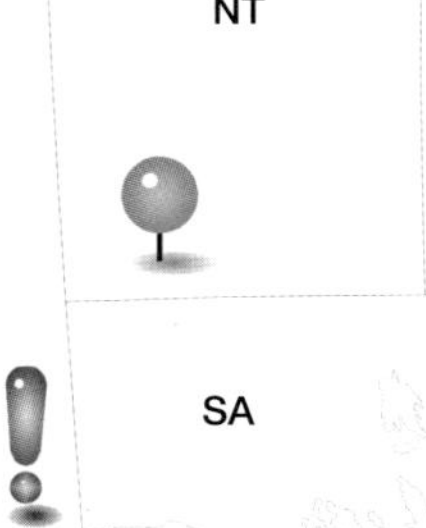

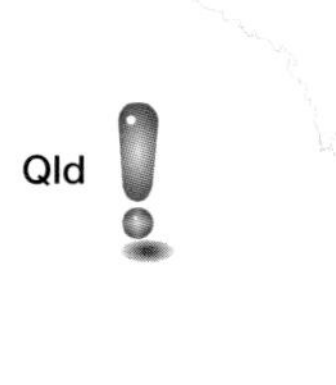

! The largest sand island in the world is Fraser Island, Queensland, with a sand dune 120 km (75 mi) long.

! The world's steepest railway is the Katoomba Scenic Railway in the Blue Mountains of NSW. It is 311 m (1020 ft) long with a gradient of 1 in 0.82.

Nambung National Park, near Cervantes, is famous for its Pinnacle Desert. The hardened limestone columns stand up to 3 m (9 ft 6 in) high in the sandy desert.

! The longest dead straight railway is part of the Trans-Australian line over the Nullarbor Plain, from near Loongana, WA, to between Ooleda and Watson, SA. Although not level, it stretches for a record 478 km (297 mi).

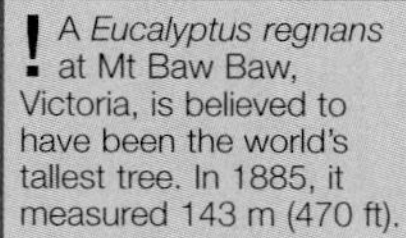

! A *Eucalyptus regnans* at Mt Baw Baw, Victoria, is believed to have been the world's tallest tree. In 1885, it measured 143 m (470 ft).

Surfers Paradise on Australia's Gold Coast is one of the country's most popular holiday centres. The coastline is heavily developed and is flanked by hotels and condominiums.

The Sydney Opera House, one of Australia's best-loved symbols (see p.177), is especially impressive viewed from the Sydney Harbour Bridge.

Perth, in Western Australia, lies on the banks of the River Swan, at the mouth of which lies the major port of Fremantle.

TELEVISION AND RADIO

No. of TVs: 8,000,000 (2.3 persons per TV)
No. of radio receivers: 21,000,000 (0.9 persons per radio)

The government-funded Australian Broadcasting Corporation (ABC) operates nationally, providing one television network and five radio networks. Commercial TV and radio operate under licences granted by the Australian Broadcasting Tribunal. There are 44 television and 163 radio stations. Many productions (particularly 'soap operas') are exported overseas, particularly to Europe.

NEWSPAPERS

Due to the great distances between Australia's five major cities, Australian newspapers are mainly regional. There are only two major national dailies: *The Australian* (149,000 copies) and *The Australian Financial Review*. There are five leading newspaper groups. The top titles and their circulation figures are:

Sunday Telegraph	Sydney, Sunday	705,000
Sunday Mail	Brisbane, Sunday	582,000
Herald-Sun News Pictorial	Melbourne, daily	575,000
Sun-Herald	Sydney, weekly	568,000
Sunday Mail	Adelaide, Sunday	352,000
Sunday Times	Perth, Sunday	335,000
The West Australian	Perth, daily	263,000
The Sydney Morning Herald	Sydney, daily	228,000 (400,000 Saturday edition)
Courier-Mail	Brisbane, daily	220,000 (330,000 Saturday edition)

CINEMA

No. of cinemas: 855

Australian cinema has achieved international recognition since the 1970s. After a lull in the early 1990s, the industry has picked up again; film and television together provide around 2% of the nation's gross domestic product. Government support and funding is especially impressive, although some of the most recent hits, such as *Babe, The Piano* and *Muriel's Wedding,* were made with funding from overseas. Consequently, the profits from these films ended up outside Australia. The greatest threat to the industry is the lack of non-government funding – if government funding is cut due to economic rationalization, home-grown Australian cinema will be hard hit.

MAGAZINES

The majority of periodicals are published in Melbourne or Sydney and distributed nationally. The periodicals with the largest circulations are:

The Open Road	six a year, motoring	1,500,000
Woman's Day	weekly, women's magazine	1,119,000 (including New Zealand)
Australian Women's Weekly	monthly, women's magazine	1,017,000
New Idea	weekly, women's magazine	873,000
Reader's Digest	monthly, general interest	480,000
TV Week	weekly, TV listings	470,000
Cleo	monthly, women's magazine	363,000
Family Circle	14 a year, general interest	331,000

PRIME MINISTERS

1901–03	Sir Edmund Barton
1903–04	Alfred Deakin
1904	John Christian Watson
1904–05	Sir George Houston Reid
1905–08	Alfred Deakin
1908–09	Andrew Fisher
1909–10	Alfred Deakin
1910–13	Andrew Fisher
1913–14	Sir Joseph Cook
1914–15	Andrew Fisher
1915–23	William Morris Hughes
1923–29	Stanley Melbourne Bruce
1929–32	James Henry Scullin
1932–39	Joseph Aloysius Lyons
1939	Sir Earle Christmas Grafton Page
1939–41	Sir Robert Gordon Menzies
1941	Sir Arthur William Fadden
1941–45	John Joseph Curtin
1945	Francis Michael Forde
1945–49	Joseph Benedict Chifley
1949–66	Sir Robert Gordon Menzies
1966–67	Harold Edward Holt
1967–68	Sir John McEwen
1968–71	John Grey Gorton
1971–72	William McMahon
1972–75	Edward Gough Whitlam
1975–83	John Malcolm Fraser
1983–91	Robert (Bob) James Lee Hawke
1991–96	Paul Keating
1996–	John Howard

THE RISE OF REPUBLICANISM

One of the concerns of the people of Australia is whether or not to become a republic. Presently, the country is a federal parliamentary state; the British sovereign Elizabeth II is titular head of state, with an Australian governor-general resident in Canberra as her representative. Under Paul Keating's rule, the republican movement gained momentum. There has been a growth in national identity, reflected in the wish to phase out the post of governor-general, to be replaced by the post of Australian president. There is a growing feeling that the 2000 Sydney Olympics should be opened by an Australian, not by the British monarch. To convert to a republic will require not only a majority of voters but also a majority in each state (which may not be easy to obtain).

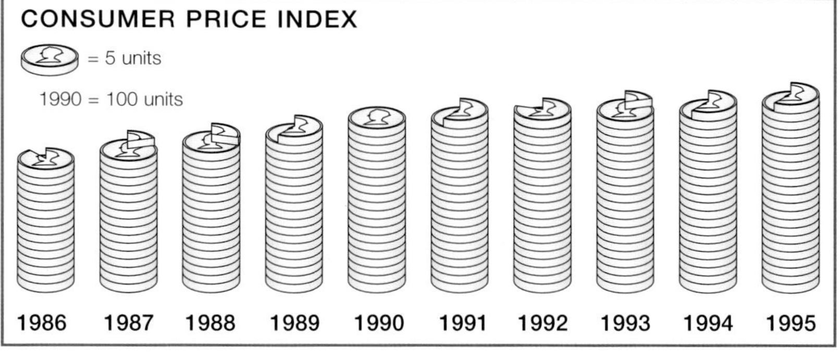

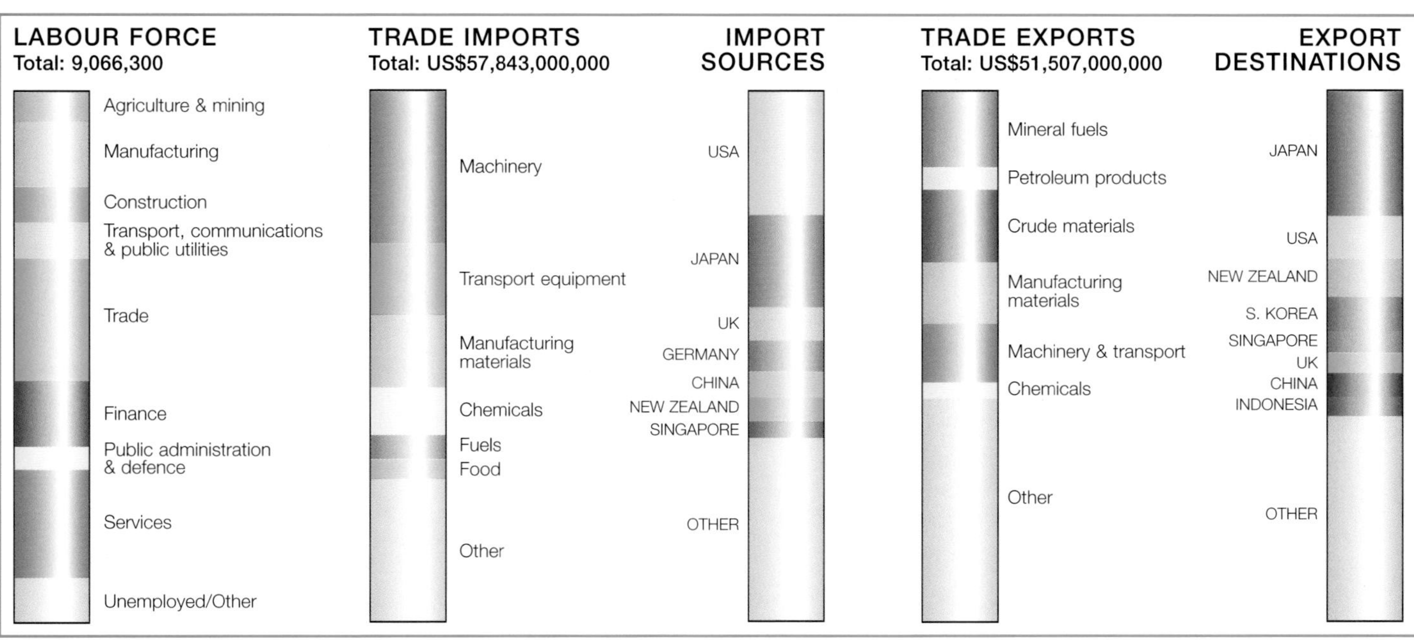

PACIFIC I

MICRONESIA

Micronesia is a federal republic comprising 607 islands in two main groups north of Papua New Guinea in the West Pacific. The majority of islands are small, low coral atolls but Kosrae and Pohnpei are larger and mountainous.
Highest point: Mt Totolom 791 m (2595 ft). **Climate:** The tropical climate is characterized by heavy rainfall and no seasons.

An executive President (who appoints a government) is elected for four years by Congress. The 14-member Congress, which is elected by universal adult suffrage, comprises ten members elected for four years plus one senator elected from each of the four states for two years. The states have their own governments.
Largest parties: (1995 election) Independents 14; there are no political parties.
President: (since independence) Bailey Olter.

Apart from phosphate, the islands have virtually no natural resources. Fishing is the major industry and fish and fish products account for over 80% of exports. The islands depend upon subsistence farming, tourism and grants from the USA (which account for over 60% of the national budget). **Currency:** Micronesia uses US currency.

Official name: Federated States of Micronesia.
Area: 701 km² (271 sq mi).
Population: 105,000 (1995 est.).
Doubling time: 24 years. **Adult life expectancy:** male 70.6 years, female 77.3 years. **Birth rate:** 1.47 times world average. **Death rate:** 0.84 times world average. **Urban population:** 26%. **Capital:** Palikir (on Pohnpei) 2000 (1994 census).
Other main centres: Weno (formerly Moen) 15,300, Tofol 7000, Kolonia 6200 (1994 census).
Language: English is spoken as a first language by under 1% but is almost universally understood (official), Chuukese 42%, Pohnpeian 24%, Mortlockese 8%, Kosraean 8%, Yapese 6%. **Adult literacy:** 77%.
Religion: Roman Catholic 45%, Congregational over 40%, other Protestant Churches over 10%.

1899 The Caroline Islands (modern Micronesia) were sold to Germany after over 300 years of Spanish rule. **1914** Japanese forces invaded during World War I. **1914–44** Administered by Japan. **1944** Taken by US forces during World War II. **1947** Became part of the UN Pacific Trust Territory under US administration. **1979** Palau and the Marshall Islands refused to join the Caroline Islands in the new Federated States of Micronesia. **1986** Virtual self-government. **1990** Independence recognized internationally.

SOLOMON ISLANDS

The Solomon Islands are an independent state of 992 islands and islets in the south-west Pacific. The principal islands form a parallel double chain of mountainous volcanic islands. The smaller islands are coral atolls. Over three-quarters of the Solomon Islands is still heavily forested.
Highest point: Mt Makarakomburu 2447 m (8028 ft).
Climate: Tropical with high temperatures and heavy rainfall, with maxima of both experienced between November and April.

The 47-member Parliament is elected by universal adult suffrage for four years. The Governor General, the representative of the British Queen as sovereign of the Solomon Islands, appoints a Prime Minister and other Ministers who are responsible to Parliament. There are plans to adopt a republican constitution.
Largest parties: (1993 election) People's Alliance Party (PAP) with United Party (UP) and National Front for Progress (NFP) and Liberation Party (Lib) 24 seats; Group for National Unity (GNUR) with National Action Party (NAP) and Labour Party (Lab) and Christian Fellowship Group 23 seats.
Prime Minister: (since 1994) Solomon Mamaloni (PAP–UP–NFP–Lib).

Over one-quarter of the labour force is involved in subsistence farming and fishing. Timber accounts for over one-half of exports and fish over 20%. Copra and cocoa beans are also exported. **Currency:** Solomon Islands dollar.

1893 The islands became a British protectorate and were used as a reserve of labour for plantations on other Pacific islands. **1942–45** Occupied by Japan during World War II: major battle at Guadalcanal (1942). **1945** British rule restored. **1978** Independence.

Official name: Solomon Islands.
Area: 28,370 km² (10,954 sq mi).
Population: 382,000 (1995 est.).
Doubling time: 21 years. **Adult life expectancy:** male 69 years, female 73 years. **Birth rate:** 1.48 times world average. **Death rate:** 0.43 times world average. **Urban population:** 17%. **Capital:** Honiara 37,000 (1992 est.). **Other main centre:** Gizo 4000 (1992 est.).
Language: English spoken as a first language by under 1% but widely understood (official), various Melanesian languages 86%, various Papuan languages 10%.
Adult literacy: 54%.
Religion: Anglican 34%, Roman Catholic 19%, Protestant Evangelical 18%, other Protestant Churches 24%, traditional beliefs.

MARSHALL ISLANDS

The Marshall Islands form a republic north of Papua New Guinea in the West Pacific. The two groups (Patak and Palik) comprise over 1150 small coral islands below 6 m (20 ft) high, which would be at risk if global warming raised the sea level.
Highest point: an unnamed point 6 m (20 ft). **Climate:** The islands have a tropical climate with heavy rainfall and no seasons.

An executive President (who appoints a government) is elected for four years by universal adult suffrage. The 33-member Assembly (Nitijela) is directly elected for four years; the 12-member Council of Chiefs is an advisory body.
Largest parties: (1995 election) Independents 33; there are no political parties.
President: (since independence) Amata Kabua.

Fishing is the major industry and fish account for over 65% of exports. With practically no resources, the islands depend upon subsistence farming, tourism and US assistance (grants from Washington account for over one-half of the national budget). **Currency:** The Marshall Islands use US currency.

Official names: Majol (in Marshallese) and The Republic of the Marshall Islands.
Area: 181 km² (70 sq mi).
Population: 56,000 (1995 est.).
Doubling time: 18 years. **Adult life expectancy:** male 61.9 years, female 65 years. **Birth rate:** 1.86 times world average. **Death rate:** 0.85 times world average. **Urban population:** 65%.
Capital: Dalap-Uliga-Darrit (on Majuro) 14,600 (1988 est.; inc. suburbs).
Other main centre: Ebeye 8300 (1988 est.).
Language: Marshallese 97% (official), English is almost universally understood (official).
Adult literacy: 91%.
Religion: Congregational over 65%, other Protestant Churches over 10%, Roman Catholic under 10%, Baha'i minority.

1899 The islands were sold to Germany after over 300 years of Spanish rule. **1914** Japanese forces invaded during World War I. **1914–44** Administered by Japan. **1944** Taken by US forces during World War II. **1946–58** US atomic tests on Bikini and Eniwetok islands. **1947** Became part of the UN Pacific Trust Territory under US administration. **1986** Virtual self-government. **1990** Independence recognized internationally.

KIRIBATI

Kiribati (pronounced Kiri-bass) is a republic in the West Pacific comprising three groups of small coral islands plus the island of Banaba, which is composed of phosphate rock. There are 33 islands in all spread over 3,500,000 km² of ocean.
Highest point: an unnamed point on Banaba 81 m (266 ft).
Climate: The southern islands have an equatorial maritime climate with heavy rainfall and no seasons; the northern islands do not have such high temperatures.

An executive President (who appoints a government) is elected for four years by universal adult suffrage. The 40-member Assembly comprises 39 members elected by universal adult suffrage for four years plus one member chosen by the Assembly to represent Banaba.
Largest parties: (1994 election) Independents 19, Christian Democratic Party (CDP) 13, Gilbertese National Progressive Party (GNPP) 7.
President: (since 1994) Teburoro Tito (non-party).

Over 70% of the workforce are involved in subsistence farming and fishing. Copra accounts for two-thirds of exports. Between 1988 and 1993, 5% of the population of overcrowded Tarawa island was resettled in the Line Islands.
Currency: Kiribati uses Australian currency.

1892 The islands (then known as the Gilbert Islands) became British and united with the Ellis Islands (now Tuvalu). **1942–43** Japanese occupation during World War II. **1957–64** British nuclear weapons were tested on Christmas Island. **1975** Ellis Islands became a separate colony. **1979** Independence as Kiribati.

Official name: Republic of Kiribati.
Area: 811 km² (313 sq mi).
Population: 81,000 (1995 est.).
Doubling time: 36 years. **Adult life expectancy:** male 52.6 years, female 55.8 years. **Birth rate:** 1.26 times world average. **Death rate:** 1.32 times world average. **Urban population:** 36%. **Capital:** Bairiki (on Tarawa) 25,000 (1990 census; inc. suburbs).
Language: English spoken as a first language by under 1% but universally understood (official), Kiribati 99%, Tuvaluan minority.
Adult literacy: 90%.
Religion: Roman Catholic 53%, Congregational 39%, various Protestant Churches 5%.

PALAU

Palau is a republic in the West Pacific comprising eight major islands and 252 islets. The volcanic hilly island of Babelthuap accounts for 75% of the country's area. The other smaller islands are hilly; the islets are atolls.
Highest point: Makelulu 218 m (715 ft). **Climate:** Tropical maritime climate with heavy rainfall and little seasonal variation.

An executive President (who appoints a government) is elected for four years by universal adult suffrage. The 18-member House of Delegates (lower house) is directly elected for four years; the 16-member Senate (composed of traditional chiefs) is elected for four years with one senator from each island-state.
Largest parties: (1996 election) Independents 16; there are no political parties.
President: (since independence) Kuniwo Nakamura.

Fruit and vegetables are the main crops, and processed food is the principal export. However, tourism and the sale of fishing rights to foreign fleets are the main sources of foreign currency. Grants from the USA provide over one-third of the budget. **Currency:** Palau uses US currency.

1899 The islands were sold to Germany after over 350 years of Spanish rule. **1914** Japanese forces invaded during World War I. **1914–44** Administered by Japan. **1944** Taken by US forces during World War II. **1947** Became part of the UN Pacific Trust Territory under US administration. **1983–94** Palauans repeatedly voted against independence because the proposed Compact with the USA would have entitled America to base nuclear weapons in the islands. **1994** Independence.

Official names: Belu'u era Belau (in Palauan) and The Republic of Palau. **Area:** 488 km² (188 sq mi). **Population:** 17,000 (1995 est.). **Doubling time:** 35 years. **Adult life expectancy:** male 69.1 years, female 73 years. **Birth rate:** 0.88 times world average. **Death rate:** 0.71 times world average. **Urban population:** 60%. **Capital:** Koror 10,500 (1992 est.; inc. suburbs). A new capital (Melekeok) is under construction on Babelthuap island. **Language:** Palauan 82% (official), English under 2% as a first language but understood by 99% (official), Filipino 9%. **Adult literacy:** 98%. **Religion:** Roman Catholic 41%, traditional beliefs 30%, various Protestant Churches 24%.

GUAM

Official name and status: Guam; an unincorporated territory of the United States.
Area: 541 km² (209 sq mi).
Population: 149,000 (1995 est.).
Capital: Agaña 5000 urban area (city 1100; 1990 census). **Other main centre:** Dededo 32,000 (1990 census). **Geography:** Guam is a tropical island in the western Pacific. The north is a limestone plateau; the south has volcanic hills. **Economy:** Guam, a duty-free port, attracts large numbers of Japanese tourists. US military bases are the main employer.

NORTHERN MARIANA ISLANDS

Official name and status: Commonwealth of the Northern Mariana Islands; a United States Commonwealth territory, an internally-self-governing territory in free association with the USA.
Area: 477 km² (184 sq mi).
Population: 58,000 (1995 est.).
Capital: Saipan 39,000 (1990 census). **Geography:** The 16 mountainous tropical islands form a chain in the western Pacific.
Economy: Farming, mainly in smallholdings, produces subsistence crops as well as vegetables for export. Tourism dominates the economy.

HOWLAND, BAKER AND JARVIS ISLANDS

Official name and status: Howland, Baker and Jarvis Islands; an unincorporated territory of the United States.
Area: 5 km² (2 sq mi). **Population:** Uninhabited. **Geography:** Three arid tropical islands situated in the South Pacific.

MIDWAY ISLANDS

Official name and status: Midway Islands; an unincorporated territory of the United States.
Area: 5 km² (2 sq mi). **Population:** No permanent population; there is a US service establishment.
Geography: The subtropical Midway Islands form a circular atoll, north-west of Hawaii.

WAKE ISLAND

Official name and status: Wake Island; an unincorporated territory of the United States.
Area: 8 km² (3 sq mi). **Population:** No permanent population; about 300 US service personnel in 1990.
Geography: Wake comprises three small tropical islands around a lagoon, west of Hawaii.

PITCAIRN

Official name and status: Pitcairn Island; a British dependency.
Area: 14 km² (5 sq mi). **Population:** 30 (1997 est.). **Capital:** Adamstown 30 (1994 est.). **Geography:** The three Pacific islands of the Pitcairn group (Pitcairn, Ducie and Oeno) are midway between New Zealand and Panama.
Economy: Pitcairn relies upon subsistence farming, fishing and the production of postage stamps.

JOHNSTON ATOLL

Official name and status: Johnston Atoll; an unincorporated territory of the United States.
Area: 1.3 km² (0.5 sq mi).
Population: No permanent population. **Geography:** Johnston Atoll, a semi-circular reef, comprises four small tropical Pacific islands.

KINGMAN REEF

Official name and status: Kingman Reef; an unincorporated territory of the United States.
Area: 0.03 km² (0.5 sq mi).
Population: Uninhabited.
Geography: Only parts of Kingman Reef, a coral atoll in the Pacific, are permanently above sea level.

VANUATU

Vanuatu is a republic of 80 islands and islets in the south-west Pacific. Many of the islands are mountainous and/or volcanic, while others contain low plateaux and undulating hill country. All the islands are still heavily forested and 67 are inhabited.
Highest point: Mont Tabwémasana 1879 m (6165 ft).
Climate: Tropical climate is moderated by cooling south-east trade winds from May to October.

The 46-member Parliament is elected by universal adult suffrage for four years. Parliament elects a Prime Minister who appoints other Ministers, who are responsible to Parliament. The President, whose role is largely ceremonial, is elected for five years by an electoral college comprising Parliament, the leaders of regional councils and Church leaders.
Largest parties: (1995 election) Unity Front (UF) 20 seats, Union of Moderate Parties (UPM) 17, National United Party (NUP) 9, others 4.
President: (since 1994) Jean-Marie Leyé (UPM).
Prime Minister: (since 1996) Maxime Carlot Korman (UPM; UPM-NUP coalition).

Subsistence farming (based on coconuts, roots, tubers, pigs, cattle and vegetables) occupies nearly three-quarters of the workforce. Copra (from coconuts), beef and timber are the only significant exports. **Currency:** Vatu.

Late 19th century Franco-British rivalry in the islands, then known as New Hebrides.
1906 UK and France established a condominium over the islands.
1980 Independence as Vanuatu.
Since 1980 Political instability: attempted secession of Santo (1980).

Official names: Ripablik blong Vanuatu (in Bislama), La République de Vanuatu (French) and The Republic of Vanuatu.
Area: 12,190 km² (4707 sq mi).
Population: 168,000 (1995 est.).
Doubling time: 26 years. **Adult life expectancy:** male 65 years, female 68 years. **Birth rate:** 1.36 times world average. **Death rate:** 0.75 times world average. **Urban population:** 19%. **Capital:** Vila (Port-Vila) 19,400 (1989 census). **Other main centre:** Luganville 6900 (1989 census).
Language: Bislama (English Creole) understood by 65% (official), English understood by 30% (official), French understood by 18% (official), plus over 100 Melanesian and Polynesian languages. **Adult literacy:** 53%.
Religion: Presbyterian 36%, Roman Catholic 14%, Anglican 14%, with various Protestant minorities and traditional beliefs, including cargo cult (John Frum cult).

NAURU

Nauru, a low-lying coral atoll, is a republic in the West Pacific.
Highest point: an unnamed point 68 m (225 ft). **Climate:** Tropical climate with heavy rainfall particularly between November and February.

An 18-member Parliament is elected for three years by universal adult suffrage. Parliament elects an executive President, who appoints Ministers.
Largest parties: (1995 election) Independents 18; there are no political parties.
President: (since 1995) Lagumot Harris.

Nauru used to depend entirely upon the mining and export of phosphate rocks, stocks of which will run out by 2010. Shipping, air services and tax haven facilities are being developed to provide revenue when phosphate runs out. All drinking water has to be imported. **Currency:** Nauru uses Australian currency.

1888 Nauru became a German colony. **1914** Australian forces invaded during World War I. **1914–42** Administered by Australia. **1942–44** Japanese occupation during World War II.
1944–68 Administered by Australia.
1968 Independence (as the world's smallest republic).

Official name: The Republic of Nauru.
Area: 21 km² (8 sq mi).
Population: 10,400 (1995 est.).
Doubling time: 20 years. **Adult life expectancy:** male 64 years, female 69 years. **Birth rate:** 0.92 times world average. **Death rate:** 0.54 times world average. **Urban population:** n/a. **Capital:** Yaren 600 (1990 est.).
Language: Nauruan 58% (official), English is spoken by 8% as a first language but understood by 99%, Kiribati 17%, with Tuvaluan and Chinese minorities.
Adult literacy: 95%.
Religion: Congregational 55%, Roman Catholic over 30%, various Protestant Churches.

PACIFIC II

FIJI

Fiji is a republic of 332 islands (106 inhabited) in the South Pacific. The mountainous larger islands are volcanic in origin. The smaller islands are mainly coral reefs.
Highest point: Tomaniivi (formerly Mt Victoria) 1424 m (4672 ft).
Climate: High temperatures and heavy rainfall with local variations caused by aspect.

The 34-member Senate (upper house) is appointed for four years; the 70-member House of Representatives (lower house) is elected by universal adult suffrage for five years with 37 members elected by indigenous Fijians, 27 by Fijians of Indian descent, five by Fijians of other races and one by the island of Rotuma. The President, who must be an indigenous Fijian and whose role is largely ceremonial, is elected for five years by the Fijian Great Council of Chiefs. The President appoints a Prime Minister and other Ministers who are responsible to the House.
Largest parties: (1994 election) (ethnic Fijian) Alliance Party or Soqosoqo ni Vakavulewa ni Taukei (SVT) 31 seats, (ethnic Indian) National Federation Party (NFP) 20, (social democratic) Fiji Labour Party (Lab) 13, (non-ethnic) General Voters' Party (GVP) 5, others 1.
President: (since 1994) Kamisese Mara (SVT).
Prime Minister: (since 1992) Sitiveni Rabuka (SVT).

Fiji's economy depends upon agriculture, with sugar cane as the main cash crop. Copra, ginger, fish and timber are also exported. Tourism is growing in importance.
Currency: Fiji dollar.

1874 Fiji became British. **1879–1916** Indian labourers arrived to work on sugar plantations, eventually outnumbering the ethnic Fijians. **1970** Independence. **1987** Military takeover overthrew an Indian-led government, following racial tension between Indians and ethnic Fijians. **Since 1987** New constitution guaranteeing power to the ethnic Fijians; some emigration of ethnic Indians has restored indigenous Fijians to the majority.

Official name: Sovereign Democratic Republic of Fiji.
Area: 18,272 km² (7055 sq mi).
Population: 790,000 (1995 est.).
Doubling time: 32 years. **Adult life expectancy:** male 70 years, female 74 years. **Birth rate:** the world average. **Death rate:** 0.58 times world average. **Urban population:** 39%. **Capital:** Suva 144,000 urban area (city 75,000; 1992 est.; inc. suburbs). **Other main centre:** Lautoka 29,000 (1986 census).
Language: English understood by 20% (official), Fijian 50%, Hindi 44%.
Adult literacy: 87%.
Religion: Christian (mainly Methodist and Roman Catholic) 53%, Hindu 38%, Sunni Islam 8%, Sikh 1%.

NEW ZEALAND

New Zealand, an independent state in the South Pacific, comprises two main islands and many smaller islands. Mountains run from north to south through South Island, and in the south-west reach the sea in the deeply indented coast of Fjordland. The Canterbury Plains lie east of the mountains. North Island is mainly hilly with isolated mountains, including volcanoes (two of which are active). Lowlands in North island are largely restricted to coastal areas and the Waikato valley. New Zealand's isolated position has had a considerable effect upon the country's society and culture and an even greater effect upon the development of its economy.
Highest point: Mt Cook, which, since a major rock fall in 1991, rises to 3754 m (12,315 ft).
Climate: Temperate, although the north is warmer. Rainfall is abundant almost everywhere, but totals vary considerably with altitude and aspect, rising to over 6350 mm (250 in) on the west coast of South Island.

The 120-member House of Representatives is elected by universal adult suffrage under a system of proportional representation for three years. The Governor General, the representative of the British Queen as sovereign of New Zealand, appoints a Prime Minister, who commands a majority in the House. The PM, in turn, appoints other Ministers, who are responsible to the House.
Largest parties: (1996 election) (centre-right) National Party (Nat) 44 seats, (social democratic) Labour Party (Lab) 37, (nationalist) New Zealand First (NZ 1st) 17, (left-wing) Alliance Party 13, (liberal) ACT New Zealand (ACT) 8, United Front 1.
Prime Minister: James Bolger (Nat; Nat-NZ 1st government).

The majority of New Zealand's export earnings come from agriculture, in particular meat, wool and dairy products. New Zealand's fine wools, mainly from Merino sheep, come from the Canterbury Plains. Forestry is expanding and supports an important pulp and paper industry. (Nearly 75% of New Zealand was covered by forests last century; intensive felling reduced this percentage to 25% in the 1980s, since when reafforestation projects have been undertaken.) Apart from coal, lignite, natural gas and gold, the country has few natural resources, although its considerable hydroelectric power potential has been exploited to produce plentiful cheap electricity (an important basis for New Zealand's manufacturing industries). Natural gas (from the Kapuni Field on North Island and from the Maui field off the Taranaki coast) is converted to liquid fuel. Despite its small domestic market and being remote from the world's major powers, New Zealand developed a high standard of living. After losing much of the British market for agricultural produce in the 1970s, New Zealand now depends upon trade with Asia, particularly Japan, and the economic rise of the Pacific Rim (of which New Zealand is a part) has greatly benefited the country.
Currency: New Zealand dollar.

1891–1912 Liberal governments pioneered many social reforms including votes for women (1893) and the world's first old-age pensions (1898). **1907** New Zealand became a dominion after over 100 years as a British colony. **1914–18** Participation in World War I: many New Zealand servicemen lost at Gallipoli in 1915. **1926** British recognition of New Zealand's independence (although the country did not formally acknowledge its independent status until 1947). **1939–45** World War II: New Zealand threatened by Japanese invasion. **1990s** Restrictions to welfare state; settlement of Maori land rights.

Official names: New Zealand and Aotearoa (in Maori).
Area: 270,534 km² (104,454 sq mi).
Population: 3,570,000 (1995 est.).
Doubling time: 81 years.
Adult life expectancy: male 73.4 years, female 79.1 years. **Birth rate:** 0.66 times world average. **Death rate:** 0.83 times world average.
Urban population: 69%.
Capital: Wellington 329,000 urban area (city 154,000; 1994 est.; inc. suburbs). **Other main centres:** Auckland 929,000 urban area (city 337,000; Manukau 243,000; North Shore 164,000), Christchurch 318,000 (city 309,000), Hamilton 153,000 (city 101,000), Napier-Hastings 112,000 (Napier city 52,000), Dunedin 112,000, Tauranga 76,000 (city 67,000), Palmerston North 75,000 (city 71,000), Rotorua 55,000, Invercargill 52,000, Nelson 50,000 (1994 est.; inc. suburbs).
Language: English 95% as a first language (official), Maori over 1% as a first language but spoken by 6%.
Adult literacy: almost 100%.
Religion: Anglican 22%, non-religious 20%, Presbyterian 16%, Roman Catholic 15%, Methodist 4%, with Baptist, Ratana, Mormon and other minorities.

New Zealand Dependencies

Cook Islands (see p. 479), Niue (p. 479), Ross Dependency (p. 480). Note that Tokelau is not a dependency but part of New Zealand.

NEW ZEALAND AUTONOMOUS ISLAND TERRITORY

Tokelau
Area: 13 km² (5 sq mi).
Pop.: 1700 (1994 est.).
Capital: There is no capital; each of the three atolls has its own administration.

BEFORE EUROPEAN SETTLERS ARRIVED, NEW ZEALAND HAD NO WILD MAMMALS, EXCEPT BATS

SAMOA

Samoa is a state in the South Pacific comprising two large high volcanic islands (Savaii and Upolu) and seven much smaller islands. (Before 1997 the country was known as Western Samoa.)
Highest point: Silisili 1858 m (6096 ft).
Climate: The islands of Samoa have a tropical climate with very heavy rainfall and high temperatures.

Samoa has a system which is akin to a constitutional monarchy until the death of the present head of state, when a republican system, with a ceremonial President elected for five years by the Assembly (Fono), will be established. The 49-member Assembly comprises 47 members elected by universal adult suffrage for five years (only members of the Matai, the elected clan leaders, are allowed to stand for election) and two members elected by non-Samoans. The head of state appoints a Prime Minister and other Ministers who are responsible to the Assembly.
Largest parties: (1996 election) Human Rights Protection Party (HRPP) 24 seats, National Development Party (NDP) 11, others 14.
Head of state: (since independence) Malietoa Tanumafili II.
Prime Minister: (since 1982) Tofilau Eti Alesana (HRPP).

Nearly two-thirds of Samoans are involved in subsistence agriculture. Taro and coconut cream are the main exports. Food processing, brewing and cigarettes are the main industries. Tourism is developing. A large proportion of the economically active population has emigrated to New Zealand. **Currency:** Tala.

1899 The islands became German. **1914** Occupied by New Zealand during World War I. **1914–62** Administered by New Zealand as Western Samoa. **1962** Independence. **1997** The country was renamed Samoa.

Official names: Malo Sa'oloto Tuto'atasi (in Samoan) and The Independent State of Samoa. (In 1997 the name of the state in English was officially changed from Western Samoa to Samoa.)
Area: 2831 km^2 (1093 sq mi).
Population: 166,000 (1995 est.).
Doubling time: 23 years. **Adult life expectancy:** male 63.8 years, female 70 years. **Birth rate:** 1.44 times world average. **Death rate:** 0.65 times world average. **Urban population:** 21%. **Capital:** Apia 34,000 (1991 est.; inc. suburbs).
Language: Samoan over 99% (official), English under 1% as a first language but understood by 52% (official). **Adult literacy:** almost 100%.
Religion: Congregational 48%, Roman Catholic 22%, Methodist 15%, Mormon 9%, Anglican and other minorities.

TONGA

Tonga is a kingdom of 172 islands (36 inhabited) in the South Pacific. The eastern islands form a low limestone chain; the higher western islands are volcanic.
Highest point: Kao 1030 m (3380 ft).
Climate: Warm with heavy rain throughout the year.

Tonga is a monarchy in which the King appoints a Prime Minister and other Ministers who are responsible to the Legislative Assembly. The 30-member Assembly comprises 12 members appointed by the King, nine members elected by universal adult suffrage for five years and nine members chosen by the 33 hereditary nobles from their number.
Largest parties: (1993 election) (reformist) Pro-Democracy Movement 6, others and non-party 24.

Official names: Pule'anga Fakatu'i 'o Tonga (in Tongan) and Kingdom of Tonga.
Area: 750 km^2 (290 sq mi).
Population: 100,000 (1995 est.).
Doubling time: 39 years. **Adult life expectancy:** male 65.6 years, female 70.4 years. **Birth rate:** 0.99 times world average. **Death rate:** 0.73 times world average. **Urban population:** 39%. **Capital:** Nuku'alofa 21,400 (1986 census; inc. suburbs). **Other main centre:** Neiafu 4000 (1986 census).
Language: Tongan 98% (official), English is widely understood (official).
Adult literacy: 93%.
Religion: Free Wesleyan Methodist 43%, Roman Catholic 16%, Mormon 12%, Free Church 11%, other Protestant Churches over 7%.

King: (since 1965) Taufa'Ahau Tupou IV.
Prime Minister: (since 1991) baron Vaea (non-party).

Agriculture involves over one-third of the labour force. Yams, cassava and taro are grown as subsistence crops. Squash, fish and vanilla are the main export, with sugar cane as the main cash crop. Tourism is growing in importance. **Currency:** Pa'anga.

1900 Tonga became a British protectorate. **1970** Independence. **Since 1987** Pressure for constitutional reform has grown; pro-democracy activists jailed.

TUVALU

Tuvalu is an independent state of nine small low-lying atolls in the South Pacific. The country would be threatened by any rise in sea level owing to global warming.
Highest point: an unnamed point 6 m (20 ft).
Climate: High temperatures and heavy rainfall.

The 12-member Parliament is elected by universal adult suffrage for four years. The Governor General, the representative of the British Queen as sovereign of Tuvalu, appoints a Prime Minister and other Ministers who are responsible to Parliament. There are no political parties.
Prime Minister: (since 1997) Bikenibeu Paeniu.

Subsistence farming (based on coconuts, pigs and poultry) occupies over two-thirds of the workforce. Clothing, footwear and copra (from coconuts) are the only significant exports. The country has a very large balance of payments deficit. **Currency:** Tuvalu dollar.

Official name: Tuvalu.
Area: 24 km^2 (9 sq mi).
Population: 9400 (1995 est.).
Doubling time: 43 years. **Adult life expectancy:** male 67.2 years, female 64 years. **Birth rate:** 1.02 times world average. **Death rate:** 0.98 times world average. **Urban population:** 46%. **Capital:** Fongafale (on Funafuti atoll) 3400 (1990 est.).
Language: English spoken as a first language by under 1% but understood by 43% (official), Tuvaluan 93%, Kiribati (formerly known as Gilbertese) 7%. **Adult literacy:** 95%.
Religion: Congregational 97%, with Seventh-day Adventist and Baha'i minorities.

1892 The islands became the British colony of the Ellice Islands and were linked administratively with the Gilbert islands (now Kiribati). **1974** The Polynesian Ellice Islands were separated from the Micronesian Gilbert Islands. **1978** Independence. **1996–97** First major political crisis with dispute between those favouring a monarchy and those advocating the adoption of a republican system.

FRENCH POLYNESIA

Official name and status: Polynésie française (French Polynesia); an overseas French territory.
Area: 4000 km^2 (1544 sq mi).
Population: 220,000 (1995 est.).
Capital: Papeete 61,000 urban area (city 24,000; 1988 census).
Geography: The territory has over 130 mainly mountainous tropical islands and coral atolls in five groups in the south-east Pacific: the Windward Islands (including Tahiti), the Leeward Islands and the Tuamotu, Austral and Marquesas islands.
Economy: Tourism is the main foreign-currency earner. Coconut oil and pearls are exported.

NIUE

Official name and status: Niue; a self-governing territory of New Zealand, empowered to declare independence unilaterally at any time.
Area: 259 km^2 (100 sq mi).
Population: 2300 (1994 est.).
Capital: Alofi 1000 (1991 est.).
Geography: Subtropical Niue, which is 2700 km (1700 mi) north of New Zealand, is a coral plateau ending in very steep cliffs.
Economy: The island lacks natural resources and has little water. Tourism is being developed. Over 12,000 Niueans have emigrated to New Zealand to work.

AMERICAN SAMOA

Official name and status: American Samoa; an unincorporated territory of the United States.
Area: 199 km^2 (77 sq mi).
Population: 57,000 (1995 est.).
Capital: Fagatogo (in Pago Pago urban area) 4000 urban area (1990 census).
Geography: The territory, in the western Pacific, comprises six main rocky tropical islands (of which Tutuila is the largest) plus Swain's Island to the north.
Economy: The main employers are tuna-canning and tourism. Lack of resources and a rapidly increasing population have forced many islanders to migrate to the USA and a high percentage of the population is on welfare.

COOK ISLANDS

Official name and status: The Cook Islands. A self-governing territory of New Zealand, the islands are empowered to declare independence unilaterally at any time.
Area: 237 km^2 (92 sq mi).
Population: 18,500 (1994 est.).
Capital: Avarua 3000 (1991 est.).
Geography: The 15 tropical Cook Islands comprise a northern group of volcanic mountainous islands and a southern group of coral atolls some 3000 km (1900 mi) north of New Zealand.
Economy: Papayas are the main export. Other sources of income include offshore banking, postage stamps and money sent home by over 20,000 Cook Islanders working in New Zealand.

WALLIS AND FUTUNA ISLANDS

Official name and status: Iles Wallis-et-Futuna (Wallis and Futuna Islands); an overseas French territory.
Area: 274 km^2 (106 sq mi).
Population: 13,700 (1990 est.).
Capital: Mata-Utu 1100 (1990 est.).
Geography: The territory comprises two tropical South Pacific island groups: Wallis (or the kingdom of Uvea), a volcanic island, and Futuna, two mountainous islands divided between the kingdoms of Sigave and Alo.
Economy: Large numbers of islanders have left, owing to unemployment. The economy relies upon government employment and money sent back by over 15,000 islanders working in New Caledonia. Copra is the only significant export.

ANTARCTIC

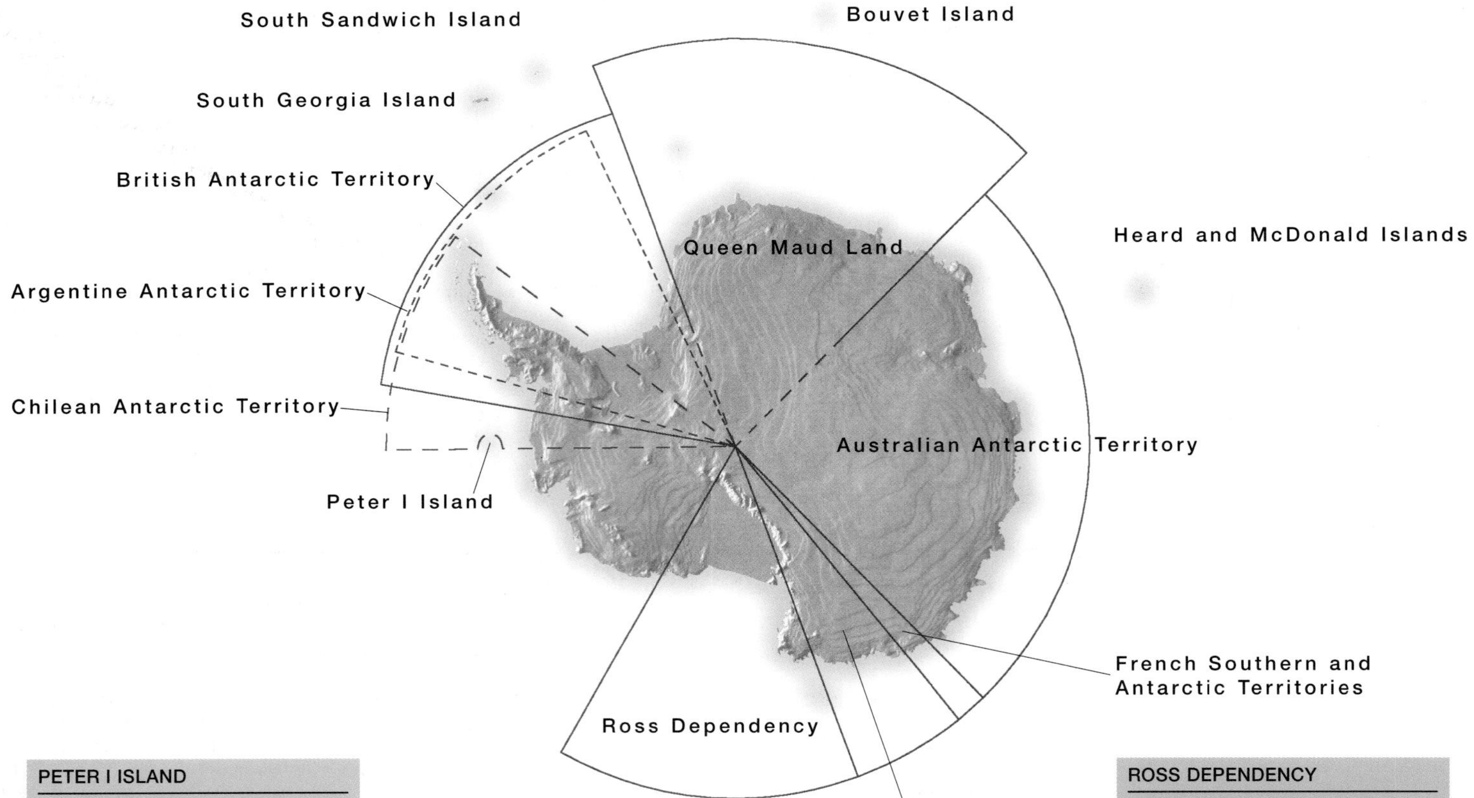

PETER I ISLAND

Official name and status: Peter I Øy (Peter I Island); a Norwegian territorial claim in Antarctica; all territorial claims in Antarctica are in abeyance under the terms of the Antarctic Treaty (1959).
Area: 180 km² (69 sq mi).
Population: no permanent settlement.
Geography: An ice-covered island 450 km (280 mi) north of Antarctica.

FRENCH SOUTHERN AND ANTARCTIC TERRITORIES

Official name and status: Terres Australes et Antarctiques Françaises (known as TAAF; French Southern and Antarctic Territories); French dependencies (Kerguelen and other islands) plus the French territorial claim in Antarctica (Adélie Land); all territorial claims in Antarctica are in abeyance under the terms of the Antarctic Treaty (1959).
Area: 439,797 km² (169,806 sq mi): Adélie Land 432,000 km² (166,800 sq mi); Kerguelen archipelago 7215 km² (2786 sq mi); Crozet archipelago 515 km² (199 sq mi); Amsterdam Island 60 km² (23 sq mi); St Paul Island 7 km² (3 sq mi).
Population: no permanent settlement, although there is a permanently staffed long-established base at Port-aux-Français (on Kerguelen), the 'capital' of the territory.
Geography: The territory comprises that part of Antarctica claimed by France (Adélie Land) between 142°E and 136°E, plus two bleak archipelagos (Kerguelen and Crozet) and two small islands (Amsterdam and St Paul) in the extreme south of the Indian Ocean.

HEARD AND McDONALD ISLANDS

Official name and status: Territory of Heard and McDonald Islands; an Australian external territory.
Area: 417 km² (161 sq mi).
Population: no permanent settlement.
Geography: Ice-covered islands 4000 km (2500 mi) south-west of Australia.

BRITISH ANTARCTIC TERRITORY

Official name and status: British Antarctic Territory: a British territorial claim in Antarctica; all territorial claims in Antarctica are in abeyance under the terms of the Antarctic Treaty (1959).
Area: 1,800,000 km² (700,000 sq mi).
Population: no permanent settlement.
Geography: Britain claims that part of Antarctica between 20°W and 80°W, a claim that overlaps with Chilean and Argentine claims.

AUSTRALIAN ANTARCTIC TERRITORY

Official name and status: Australian Antarctic Territory: an Australian external territory; all territorial claims in Antarctica are in abeyance under the terms of the Antarctic Treaty (1959).
Area: 6,043,700 km² (2,333,500 sq mi).
Population: no permanent settlement.
Geography: Australia claims that part of Antarctica between 160°E and 142°E and between 136°E and 45°E.

CHILEAN ANTARCTIC TERRITORY

Official name and status: Chilean Antarctic Territory; a Chilean territorial claim – all claims south of 60°S are in abeyance under the terms of the Antarctic Treaty (1959).
Geography: Chile claims that part of Antarctica between 90°W and 53°W, a claim that overlaps with the British and Argentine territorial claims.

ARGENTINE ANTARCTIC TERRITORY

Official name and status: Argentine Antarctic Territory; an Argentine territorial claim – all claims south of 60°S are in abeyance under the terms of the Antarctic Treaty (1959).
Geography: Argentina claims that part of Antarctica between 74°W and 25°W, a claim that overlaps with the British territorial claim.

QUEEN MAUD LAND

Official name and status: Dronning Maud Land (Queen Maud Land); a Norwegian territorial claim in Antarctica; all territorial claims in Antarctica are in abeyance under the terms of the Antarctic Treaty (1959).
Area: as no inland limit to the claim has been made, no estimate of the area can be given.
Population: no permanent settlement.
Geography: Norway claims that part of Antarctica between 20°W and 45°E.

ROSS DEPENDENCY

Official name and status: Ross Dependency: a New Zealand dependency; all territorial claims in Antarctica are in abeyance under the terms of the Antarctic Treaty (1959).
Area: 730,000 km² (282,000 sq mi).
Population: no permanent settlement.
Geography: New Zealand claims that part of Antarctica between 160°E and 150°E.

BOUVET ISLAND

Official name and status: Bouvet Øy; a Norwegian dependency.
Area: 59 km² (23 sq mi).
Population: no permanent settlement.
Geography: Bouvet is a bleak volcanic island 1600 km (1000 mi) north of the Antarctic mainland.

SOUTH GEORGIA AND SOUTH SANDWICH ISLANDS

Official name and status: South Georgia and South Sandwich Islands; a British dependency.
Area: 4091 km² (1580 sq mi): South Georgia 3755 km² (1450 sq mi); South Sandwich Islands 336 km² (130 sq mi).
Population: no permanent settlement, although there is a permanently staffed long-established base at Grytviken (on South Georgia), the 'capital' of the territory.
Geography: South Georgia is a bleak, mountainous island 1290 km (800 mi) east of the Falklands. Much of the island is under permanent snow cover. The South Sandwich Islands, which are 760 km (470 mi) south-east of South Georgia, are active volcanoes which are covered by glaciers.

‘Knowledge
advances by steps,
and not by leaps’
– T.B. Macaulay

A

B

C

D

E

F

G

H

M

N

O

P

Q

R

S

ACKNOWLEDGEMENTS

Guinness Publishing would like to thank the following: Fred Gill for proofreading; Kathy Gill for compiling the index; Stewart Newport for assisting with the Sports section and for invaluable help throughout the production of the book; and the following consultants:

John Arblaster, Richard Balkwill, Tony Brown, Mark Bennett, Tom Cannon, Dr Owen Cole, Sarah Dunworth, Barbara Edwards, Exhibitor Relations Co. Inc., Tim Furniss, Max Glaskin, Dr Martin Godfrey, Duncan Hislop, Della Howes, Dr Gareth Jones, Philip Littlemore, Howard Loxton, Dr David Nash, John Pimlott, Will Pratt, Jonathan Ree, Bill Risebero, David Roberts, Ian Sinclair, Dr Noel Smith, Dr Peter Smithson, Sheik Gamal Sulaiman, Dr Iris Turner, Dr J.R. Walton, Dr Richard Weston.

PICTURE/ARTWORK CREDITS

Mountain High Maps® Copyright © 1993 Digital Wisdom, Inc.

t=top; c=centre; b=bottom; l=left; r=right

7 Jerry Lodriguss/Science Photo Library; 8 Space Telescope Science Institute/NASA/Science Photo Library; 10 Science Photo Library; 13 NASA/Science Photo Library; 14 NASA/Science Photo Library; 16 NASA/Science Photo Library; 17 NASA/Science Photo Library; 18 Charles and Josette Lenar/Corbis; 19t Dave Bartruff/Corbis; 19b Maury/Sipa-Press/Rex Features; 20t Heoner Heine/AKG London; 20c Science Museum London/Bridgeman Art Library; 20b Bridgeman Art Library; 25 Ric Ergenbrigh/Corbis; 27l Tom Van Sant/Science Photo Library; 27cl Tom Van Sant/Science Photo Library; 27cr Tom Van Sant/Science Photo Library; 27r Tom Van Sant/Science Photo Library; 28–29t David Muench/Corbis; 28–29c Paul Souders/Corbis; 28–29b John Shaw/NHPA; 30t Earth Satellite Corporation/Science Photo Library; 30b NASA/Corbis; 31 Pat O'Hara/Corbis; 32 Paul Souders/Corbis; 34 G.A. Rossi/The Image Bank; 35 Nik Wheeler/Corbis; 37tl Galen Rowell/Corbis; 37tc Colin Monteath/Mountain Camera; 37bc Cees Van Leeuwen/Corbis; 37cl Daryl Balfour/ABPL/Corbis; 37c David Hamilton/The Image Bank; 37cr Alisa Crandal/Corbis; 37b Colin Monteath/Mountain Camera; 37r John Warburton-Lee/Mountain Camera; 38t USGS-Hawaii Volcano Observatory/Corbis; 38c Vittoriano Rastelli/Corbis; 38b David Muench/Corbis; 39 Gary Braasch/Corbis; 40t Massonnet Et Al/Science Photo Library; 40b US GeologicalSurvey/Science Photo Library; 42 Charles Lenars/Corbis; 44 Kevin R. Morris/Corbis; 45 Tom Bean/Corbis; 48l Christine Osborne/Corbis; 48r David Muench/Corbis; 49 Galen Rowell/Corbis; 50 Roger Ressmeyer/Corbis; 51t NASA/Corbis; 51c Scott T. Smit /Corbis; 51b Gary Braasch/Corbis; 52tr Richard Hamilton Smith/Corbis; 52c Adrian Carroll/Eye Ubiquitous/Corbis; 52l Perry Conway/Corbis; 53tl Jim Corwin/Corbis; 53tc Johnathon Smith/Sylvia Cordaiy Photo Library/Corbis; 53tr Galen Rowell/Corbis; 53b Nasa/Science Photo Library; 54tl Michael Yamashita/Corbis; 54tc Paul Souders/Corbis; 54tr Winfried Wisniewski/Frank Lane Picture Agency/Corbis; 54bl Andrey Zvoznikov/Planet Earth Pictures; 54bc Wolfgang Kaehler/Corbis; 56 Nik Wheeler/Corbis; 57t Perry Conway/Corbis; 57b Michael S. Yamashita/Corbis; 58 Herbert Giradet/AGDE Agriculture/Environmental Images; 59 Dan Guravic/Corbis; 62 Michael Boys/Corbis; 63t Robert Pickett/Corbis; 63tc Kevin Schafer/Corbis; 63bc Robert Gill/Papilio/Corbis; 63b Kennan Ward/KW Photography/Corbis; 64t Micheal Pogden/Bruce Coleman Ltd; 64bl Sinclair Stammers/Science Photo Libary; 64br Harvey Pincis/Science Photo Libary; 65t Morton Beebe/Corbis; 65bl Ed Young/Agstock/Science Photo Libary; 65br Claude Nuridsany & Marie Perennou/Science Photo Library; 66 Amos Nachoum/Corbis; 67 Jeffery L. Rothman/Corbis; 68l Felix Labhardt/Bruce Coleman Ltd; 68r Haroldo Palo Jr/NHPA; 69t Wolfgang Kaehler/Corbis; 69c Lawson Wood/Corbis; 69b G.I. Bernard/NHPA; 70t Erik Bjurstrom/Bruce Coleman Ltd; 70b Charles & Sandra Hood/Bruce Coleman Ltd; 70br Erik Bjurstrom/Bruce Coleman Ltd; 70–71 Charles & Sandra Hood/Bruce Coleman Ltd; 71t Erik Bjurstrom/Bruce Coleman Ltd; 71b Brandon Cole/Corbis; 72t Robert Picket/Corbis; 72b Perry Conway/Corbis; 73t Joe McDonald/Corbis; 73b Daniel Heuclin/NHPA; 74tr George McCarthy/Bruce Coleman Ltd; 74l George McCarthy/Bruce Coleman Ltd; 75t James L. Amos/Corbis; 75b Galen Rowell/Corbis; 77t John Paul Ferrero/Ardea; 77c NHPA; 77b Michael Philip Maconachie/Papilio/Corbis; 78l Clem Haagner/ ABPL/Corbis; 78r Morten Strange/NHPA; 80l Kevin Schafer/Corbis; 80r Kenan Ward/KW Photography/Corbis; 81l Ron Austing/Frank Lane Picture Agency/Corbis; 81r Brandon Cole/Corbis; 82t Brandon Cole/Corbis; 82b Alissa Crandall/Corbis; 83t Stuart Westmorland/Corbis; 83b Mark Carwardine/Bruce Coleman Limited; 84l Kevin Schafer/Corbis; 84c John Visser/Bruce Coleman Limited; 84r Lorri Franz/Corbis; 85l John Canalosi/Bruce Coleman Ltd; 85c Daryl Balfour/NHPA; 85r Kevin Schafer/Corbis; 86l K. Ghani/NHPA; 86c Rod Williams/Bruce Coleman Ltd; 86r Jorg & Petra Wegner/Bruce Coleman Ltd; 87l Christer Frederiksson/Bruce Coleman Ltd; 87c Nigel J. Dennis/NHPA; 87r Planet Earth Pictures; 90t Bsip Vem/Science Photo Library; 90bl Francis Leroy/Science Photo Library; 90br Alfred Pasieka/Science Photo Library; 91t John Bavosi/Science Photo Library; 91c Mehau Kulyk/Science Photo Library; 91b Clinical Radiology Dept Salisbury District Hospital/Science Photo Library; 92 A.B. Dowsett/Science Photo Library; 93t Science Photo Library; 93b Eye Of Science/Science Photo Library; 94l Eddy Gray/Science Photo Library; 94r Clinical Radiology Dept Salisbury District Hospital/Science Photo Library; 95l Moredun Animal Health Ltd/Science Photo Library; 95r Dept of Clinical Radiology, Salisbury Hospital/Science Photo Library; 96t Nadar/Hulton Deutsch Collection/Corbis; 96c Alfred Pasieka/Science Photo Library; 96b AKG London; 97l John Mead/Science Photo Library; 97cl David Scharf/Science Photo Library; 97cr Perry Conway/Corbis; 97r Nik Wheeler/Corbis; 98t Pictor International; 98b Mabel Step/Mary Evans Picture Libray; 99 Bob Thomason/Tony Stone Images; 100t A. Boulat/Sipa Press/Rex Features; 100b Paul Souders/Corbis; 101 Chris Butler/Science Photo Library; 102 Jonathan Blair/Corbis; 103 David Gifford/Science Photo Library; 104tl Adrian Warren/Ardea London Ltd; 104tr R. De La Harpe/Planet Earth Pictures; 104bl Planet Earth Pictures; 104br Rod Williams/Bruce Coleman Ltd; 105tc Steve Kaufman/Corbis; 105tl Keren Su/Corbis; 105tr Orion Press/NHPA; 105c Planet Earth Pictures; 105bl J.A.L. Cooke/Oxford Scientific Films; 105bc Martin Harvey/NHPA; 105br François Gohier/Ardea London Ltd; 106 Gerald Kubitt/Bruce Coleman Collection; 107l David Muench/Corbis; 107r Perry Conway/Corbis; 109 E.O. Hopp/Corbis; 111 Alfred Pasieka/Science Photo Library; 114 Stephen Dalton/Science Photo Library; 118 Walter Dickenham/ Sandia National Laborator/Corbis; 121 Harry S. Truman Library/Corbis; 122 Library of Congress/Corbis; 123 Library of Congress/Corbis; 124 Bettmann/Corbis; 125 Philippe Plailly/Science Photo Library; 129 David Taylor/Science Photo Library; 132 Hulton Deutsch Collection/Corbis; 134 Hulton Deutsch Collection/Corbis; 135 Ken Eward/Science Photo Library; 143 Lee Snyder/Science Photo Library; 164 Bettmann/Corbis; 165l Hulton Deutsch Collection/Corbis; 165r Hulton Deutsch Collection/Corbis; 166 Martin Bond/Science Photo Library; 167t Richard Hamilton Smith/Corbi; 167b Roger Ressmeyer/Corbis; 168t Anthony Bannister/ABPl/Corbis; 168c Rex Features; 168b John Edward Linden/Arcaid; 169 Kevin Fleming/Corbis; 170 Kevin Fleming/Corbis; 171t Julie Meech/Ecoscene/Corbis; 171b Charles O'Rear/Corbis; 172t Gil Moti/Still Pictures; 172b Craig Lovell/Corbis; 173 Nathalie Tepper/Arcaid; 174t Ric Ergenbright/Corbis; 174b Kevin R. Morris/Corbis; 175t Carnival Cruise Lines; 175b U.S. Department Of Defence/Corbis; 176 Morten Bebe/S.F./Corbis; 177 F. Stuart Westmorland/Corbis; 178 The Science Museum/Science & Society Picture Library; 179 Everett/Corbis ; 182 Frances Evelegh/Science Photo Library; 183 Charles Lenars/Corbis; 186t Roger Wood/Corbis; 186b Roger Wood/Corbis; 187 Roger Wood/Corbis; 188 Wolfgang Kaehler/Corbis; 190 Vittoriano Rastelli/Corbis; 192 Paul Souders/Corbis; 194 Abbas/Magnum Photos; 195l Arthur Thevanart/Corbis; 195r Abbas/Magnum Photos; 196 Robert Holmes/Corbis; 197l Sheldan Collins/Corbis; 197r Nazima Kowall/Corbis; 198 Frank Leather/Eye Ubiquitous/Corbis; 199t Charles and Josette Lenar/Corbis; 199b DeWitt Jones/Corbis; 200t Annie Griffiths Belt/Corbis; 200b Nik Wheeler/Corbis; 201 Brian Rasic/Rex Features; 202l Michael Nicholson/Corbis; 202r Everett/Corbis; 203b Everett/Corbis; 203t Everett/Corbis; 205 A The Kobal Collection; 205 B Bettmann/Corbis; 205 C Everett/Corbis ; 205 D Columbia Pictures/The Roland Grant Archive; 205 E The Roland Grant Archive; 205 F Everett/Corbis ; 207t Everett/Corbis ; 207tc Everett/Corbis; 207c Roland Grant Archive; 207bc Everett/Corbis; 207b Everett/Corbis; 209 A Everett/Corbis; 209 B Everett/Corbis; 209 C The Ronald Grant Archive ; 209 D Everett/Corbis; 209 E The Ronald Grant Archive; 209 F Everett/Corbis ; 215t Fotos International/Rex Features; 215b Ronald Grant Archive; 218 Barnabas Bosshart/Corbis; 219 AKG London; 219 Richard Faley/English National Ballet; 220 Lebrecht Collection; 221 AKG London; 225 AKG London; 226 Catherine Ashmore; 227 Zoe Dominic; 229t David Redfern/Redferns; 229b Michael Ochs /Redferns; 231 Baron Wolman/Retna; 232t Ross Marino/Retna; 232b Neal Preston/Retna; 233t Van Iperen/Retna; 233b Mick Hutson/Redferns; 236t Gianni Dagli Orti/Corbis; 236b Bradley Smith/Corbis; 237t Corbis; 237c © ADAGP, Paris and DACS, London 1997/Corbis; 237b The National Gallery, London/Corbis; 238t The National Gallery, London/Corbis; 238c The National Gallery, London/Corbis; 238b The National Gallery, London/Corbis; 239t The National Gallery, London/Corbis; 239c AKG London; 239b Hubert Stadler/Corbis; 240t The National Gallery, London/Corbis; 240tc The National Gallery, London/Corbis; 240bc The National Gallery, London/Corbis; 240b The National Gallery, London/Corbis; 241t Gianni Dagli Orti/Corbis; 241tc Hulton Deutsch Collection/Corbis; 241bc Gianni Dagli Orti/Corbis; 241b Gianni Dagli Orti/Corbis; 242t Richard T. Nowitz/Corbis; 242cl Dave Bartuff/Corbis; 242cr Dave Bartuff/Corbis; 242b Hubert Stadler/Corbis; 243t Angelo Hornack/Corbis; 243c Stephanie Colasanti/Corbis; 243b Dennis Marsico/Corbis; 244t Erich Lessing/AKG London; 244c AKG London; 244b Mark Fiennes/Arcaid; 245t David S. Robbins/Corbis; 245c Richard A. Cooke III/Corbis; 245b Martin Jones/Ecoscene/Corbis; 250 Bridgeman Art Library; 251 Mary Evans Picture Library; 252 Copyright E.H. Shepard under the Berne Convention, and in the United States © 1926 by E.P. Dutton. Renewal © 1954 by A.A. Milne; Colouring © 1973 by E.H. Shepard and Methuen Children's Books Limited; 253 Bridgeman Art Library; 254 Bridgeman Art Library; 257 David Cannon/Allsport; 258 Allsport; 259 Simon Bruty/Allsport; 260 Allsport; 261t Tony Duffy/Allsport; 261b Gray Mortimore/Allsport; 262 Simon Bruty/Allsport; 263t Tony Duffy/Allsport; 263bl Simon Bruty/Allsport; 263br David Leah/Allsport; 264 Colorsport; 265t Mike Powell/Allsport; 265tc Allsport; 265bc Simon Bruty/Allsport; 265b Clive Brunskill/Allsport; 266 Simon Bruty/Allsport; 267 Bettman/UPI/Corbis; 268 Bob Martin/Allsport; 269l Billy Stickland/Allsport; 269r Mike Powell/Allsport; 270 Ross Kinnaird/Allsport; 271t Shaun Botterill/Allsport; 271b Adrian Murrell/Allsport; 273tl David Cannon/Allsport; 273tr David Cannon/Allsport; 273bl Bettmann/UPI/Corbis; 273br David Cannon/Allsport; 274t Hulton Deutsch/Allsport; 274b Clive Brunskill/Allsport; 275t Hulton Deutsch/Allsport; 275bl Tony Duffy/Allsport; 275bc Clive Brunskill/Allsport; 275br Clive Brunskill/Allsport; 276t Allsport; 276c Clive Brunskill/Allsport; 276b Clive Brunskill/Allsport; 277 Gary Prior/Allsport; 278 Rick Stewart/Allsport; 279t Allsport; 279c Doug Pensinger/Allsport; 279b Rick Stewart/Allsport; 281tl Pascal Rondeau/Allsport; 281tr Coloursport; 281b Gary M. Prior/Allsport; 282 Yahn Cuichadua/Allsport; 283t Chris Cole/Allsport; 283b Agence Vandystadt/Allsport; 284 Simon Bruty/Allsport; 285t Simon Bruty/Allsport; 285b Allsport; 286 Mark Morrison/Allsport; 287tl Simon Bruty/Allsport; 287tr Hulton Deutsch/Allsport; 287b Pascal Rondeau/Allsport; 288t Agence Vandystadt/Allsport; 288b Pascal Rondeau/Allsport; 289t Pascal Rondeau/Allsport; 289b Mike Cooper/Allsport; 290tl Kit Houghton Photography; 290tr Bob Langrish; 290bl Bob Langrish; 290br Colorsport; 291l Simon Bruty/Allsport; 291r Allsport; 293l Mike Powell/Allsport; 293r Hulton Deutsch Collection/Allsport; 294 Shaun Botterill/Allsport; 295 E.T. Archive; 308t Richard T. Nowitz/Corbis; 308c Roger Wood/Corbis; 308b Gianni Dagli Orti/Corbis; 309t Bettmann/Corbis; 309c Vladamir Dovokhov, Dmitry Grigorevic Levicky/The State Russian Museum/Corbis; 309b The National Gallery, London/Corbis; 310t Gianni Dagli Orti/Corbis; 310c Jack Fields/Corbis; 310b Library Of Congress/Corbis; 311t Bettmann/Corbis; 311b Hulton Deutsch Collection/Corbis; 312t Joe Marquette/ UPI/ Bettmann/Corbis; 312b Gianni Dagli Orti/Corbis; 313t Hulton Deutsch Collection/Corbis; 313c Bettmann/Corbis; 313b Kimbell Art Museum/Corbis; 314t Dagli Orti/Corbis; 314c UPI/Bettmann/Corbis; 314b M. Gauci, C. Hullmande/Library Of Congress/Corbis; 315t Library Of Congress/Corbis; 315c Hulton Deutsch Collection/Corbis; 315b Hulton Deutsch Collection/Corbis; 316t Philip De Bay/ Historical Picture Archive/Corbis; 316c Bettmann/Corbis; 316b Christel Gerstenberg/Corbis; 317t The National Archives/Corbis; 317c Library Of Congress/Corbis; 317b Library Of Congress/Corbis; 318t Bettmann/Corbis; 318b Library Of Congress/Corbis; 319t Hulton Deutsch Collection/Corbis; 319c UPI/Bettmann/Corbis; 319b Bettmann/Corbis; 320t Hulton Deutsch Collection/Corbis; 320b The National Archive/Corbis; 321t Bettmann/Corbis; 321b Philadelphia Museum Of Art/Corbis; 322l H. Leutemann/Mary Evans Picture Library; 322c Gianni Dagli Orti/Corbis; 322r Neroccio di Bartolommeo/Corbis; 323l Erich Lessing/AKG London; 323c ET Archive; 323r AKG London; 324l AKG London; 324r Hulton Deutsch Collection/Corbis; 325 Colour Library Images; 326 Images Colour Library; 327 Peter Turnley/Corbis; 332t Simon Walker/Rex Features; 332b Raphael Gaillarde/Frank Spooner Pictures; 333t Patrick Piel/Gamma/Frank Spooner Pictures; 333b Bettmann/AFP/Corbis; 334t A. Denize/Frank Spooner Pictures; 334b Bettmann/ AFP/Corbis; 336 Yves Debay/The Military Picture Library/Corbis; 338 Wim Van Cappellen/Katz Pictures; 339 Piel Patrick/Frank Spooner Pictures; 341 Barnabus Rosshart/Corbis; 343 Gamma/Frank Spooner Pictures; 344t Robert Y. Kaufman/Yogi Inc/Corbis; 344c George Hall/Corbis; 344b Ardenis/ Sipa Press/Rex Features; 345 Galen Rowell/Corbis; 349 Dave G. Houser/Corbis; 350 McDuff Everton/Corbis; 351 Nick Wheeler/Corbis; 352tl David Woodfall/NHPA; 352tc Heather Angel/Biofotos; 352tr Ric Ergenbright/Corbis; 352bl John Heseletine/Corbis; 352bc David Batterbury/Eye Ubiquitous/Corbis; 352br The Image Bank; 360tl McDuff Everton/Corbis; 360tr Nik Wheeler/Corbis; 360bl Owen Franken/Corbis; 360bc Adam Woolfitt/Corbis; 360br Nik Wheeler/Corbis; 364tl Dean Conger /Corbis; 364tc Dave G. Houser/Corbis; 364tr Richard List/Corbis; 364c Richard Nowitz/Corbis; 364bl Robert Estall/Corbis; 364br Ric Ergenbright/Corbis; 365 Selby McCreey/Corbis; 368 Dave Bartruff/Corbis; 369 Michael John Kielty/Corbis; 370 Patrick War/Corbis; 371 Bruno Barbey/Magnum Photos; 372tl Carmen Redono/Corbis; 372tc Hugh Rooney/Eye Ubiquitous/Corbis; 372tr Andrew Cohen/Travel Ink/Corbis; 372bl Adam Woolfitt/Corbis; 372bc Erich Lessing/AKG London; 372br Dennis Gilbert/Arcaid; 374 Action Press/Rex Features; 377 Adam Woolfit/Corbis; 380tl Dennis Marsico/Corbis; 380tc Carl Purcell/ The Purcell Team/Corbis; 380tr John Heseletine/Corbis; 380bl John Heseletine/Corbis; 380bc Johnathon Blair/Corbis; 380br Vanni Ruggero/Corbis; 383 Ellen Rooney/Robert Harding Picture Library; 385 Don Klumpp/The Image Bank; 392tl Wolfgang Kaehler/Corbis; 392tc Steve Raymer/Corbis; 392tr Andrey Zvoznikov/Planet Earth Pictures; 392bl Nik Wheeler/Corbis; 392bc Enzo Raggazzini/Corbis; 392br Wolfgang Kaehler/Corbis; 394 Corbis; 395t Michael S. Yamashita/Corbis; 395b John Egan/IOUR/Hutchinson Library; 398 NASA/Corbis; 399 Ecoscene/Corbis; 400 Kevin Schafer/Corbis; 401 Adam Woolfit/Corbis; 402 Rex Features; 404 David Cumming; Eye Ubiquitous/Corbis; 405t Tom Owen Edmunds/The Image Bank; 405b Craig Lovell/Corbis; 406 Earl Kowa/Corbis; 408tl Brian Vikander/Corbis; 408tc Galen Rowell/Corbis; 408tr Brian Vikander/Corbis; 408bl Arvind Garg/Corbis; 408br Arvind Garg/Corbis; 410 Peter Barker/Panos Pictures; 411t Owen Franken/Corbis; 411b Brian Vikander/Corbis; 416 Joseph Sohm/Corbis; 417 Hutchinson Library; 418tl Joseph Sohm/ChromoSohm Inc/Corbis; 418tc Carl Purcell/The Purcell Team/Corbis; 418tr Karen Su/Corbis; 418bl Jean Paul Ferrero/Ardea; 418br Wolfgang Kaehler/Corbis; 420 Charles Gupton/Tony Stone Images; 421 Wolfgang Kaehler/Corbis; 421 Frank Spooner Pictures; 422tl Michael Freeman/Corbis; 422tr Images Colour Library; 422bl Michael Freeman/Corbis; 422bc Richard Nowitz/Corbis; 422br Michael Yamashita/Corbis; 424 Patrick Bennett/Corbis; 425 Galen Rowell/Corbis; 426tl Michael T. Sedam/Corbis; 426tr Richard A. Cooke III/Corbis; 426bl Gunter Marx/Corbis; 426bc Richard T. Nowitz/Corbis; 426br Rex Features; 427 Paul Souder/Corbis; 430tl Galen Rowell/Corbis; 430tc Dave G. Houser/Corbis; 430tr David Muench/Corbis; 430cl Joseph Sohm/ChromoSohm Inc/Corbis; 430cr Tom Bean/Corbis; 430c Adam Woolfitt/Corbis; 430bl James L. Amos/Corbis; 430r Douglas Peebles/Corbis; 434 Nik Wheeler/Corbis; 435 Richard Bickel/Corbis; 437 Martin Rodgers/Corbis; 438 Owen Franken/Corbis; 439 David Cumming/Eye Ubiquitous/Corbis; 441t Dave G. Houser/Corbis; 441b Earl Kowall/Corbis; 444 Paolo Ragazzini/Corbis; 445 Craig Lovell/Corbis; 447 A. Berg/Frank Spooner Pictures; 448tl Owen Franken/Corbis; 448tc Robert Holmes/Corbis; 448tr Jeremy Horner/Corbis; 448bl Joel Creed/Ecoscene/Corbis; 448bc Stephanie Maze/Corbis; 448br Jack Fields/Corbis; 451t Charles O'Rear/Corbis; 451b Hugo Fernandez/Andes Press Agency; 454 Abbie Enock/Travel Ink/Corbis; 456 Ann Purcell/The Purcell Team/Corbis; 458 Frank Spooner Pictures; 465 Micheal Friedel/Rex Features; 468 Craig Lovell/Corbis; 469 Nik Wheeler/Corbis; 470 Rob Nunnington/Oxford Scientific Films; 472l Corbis; 472r Patrick Ward/Corbis; 473 Wolfgang Kaehler/Corbis; 474tl John Noble/Corbis; 474tr Dave G. Houser/Corbis; 474c Paul Souder/Corbis; 474bl Paul Souder/Corbis; 474bc Paul Souder/Corbis; 474br Dave G. Houser/Corbis